lonely planet

South America on a shoestring

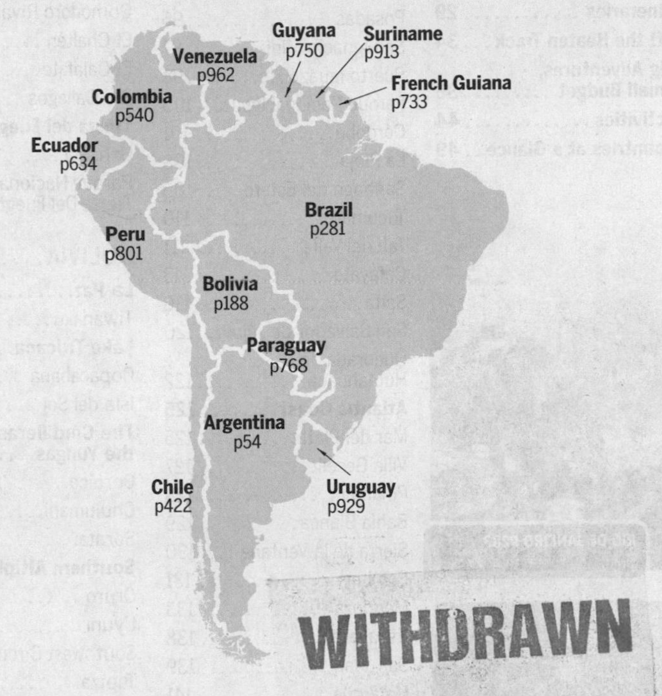

THIS EDITION WRITTEN AND RESEARCHED BY

Regis St Louis, Sandra Bao, Celeste Brash, Gregor Clark, Alex Egerton, Brian Kluepfel, Tom Masters, Carolyn McCarthy, Kevin Raub, Paul Smith, Phillip Tang, Lucas Vidgen

PLAN YOUR TRIP

RIO DE JANEIRO P283

MICHAEL HEFFERNAN/LONELY PLANET ©

IGLESIA DE SAN FRANCICSO P639, QUITO

PHILIP LEE HARVEY/LONELY PLANET ©

ON THE ROAD

Contents

ON THE ROAD

Contents

UNDERSTAND

SURVIVAL GUIDE

Welcome to South America

Andean peaks, Amazonian rainforest, Patagonian glaciers, Inca ruins, colonial towns, white-sand beaches and vertiginous nightlife: the wonders of South America set the stage for incredible adventures.

Captivating Landscapes

From the snow-capped peaks of the Andes to the undulating waterways of the Amazon, South America spreads a dazzling array of natural wonders. This is a continent of lush rainforests, towering volcanoes, misty cloud forests, bone-dry deserts, red-rock canyons, ice-blue glaciers and sun-kissed beaches. As landscapes go, there aren't many other places on earth that offer so much variety.

Big Adventures

You can hike past ancient temples first laid down by the Inca, contemplate the awe-inspiring power of Iguazú Falls, or spend the day watching wildlife from a dugout canoe on one of the Amazon's countless *igarapés* (narrow waterways). You can barrel down Andean roads by mountain bike, go white-water rafting on Class V rivers and surf amazing breaks off both coasts. And once you think you've experienced it all, head to the dramatic landscapes in Tierra del Fuego, go eye-to-eye with extraordinary creatures in the Galápagos, and scramble up tableland mountains in the Gran Sabana for a panorama that seems straight out of the Mesozoic era.

Cultural Treasures

South America's diversity doesn't end with geography. You'll find colonial towns where cobblestone streets lead past gilded churches and stately plazas little changed since the 18th century. You can haggle over colorful textiles at indigenous markets, share meals with traditional dwellers of the rainforest and follow the pounding rhythms of Afro-Brazilian drums corps. South America is home to an astounding variety of living and ancient cultures, and experiencing it first-hand is as easy as showing up.

La Vida Musical

Nothing compares with hearing the rhythms of Colombian salsa, Brazilian samba, Argentine tango and Andean folk music in the place where they were born. Buenos Aires' sultry *milongas* (tango clubs), Rio's simmering *garrafeiras* (dance halls), Quito's *salsotecas* (salsa clubs) – all great places to chase the heart of Saturday night. Yet this is only the beginning of a great musical odyssey that encompasses Peruvian *trovas*, soulful Ecuadorian *passillos*, fast-stepping Brazilian *forró*, whirling Venezuelan merengue, steel-pan Guyanese drumming, Paraguayan harp music and more. Simply plunge in – though you might want to take a dance class along the way!

Why I love South America

By Regis St Louis, Writer

Be mindful of what you're getting into: South America can be a lifetime addiction. I didn't realize this when I first hiked Andean trails and visited pre-Columbian sites more than 15 years ago. Like other travelers who shared the journey, I was hooked. I fell hard for the incredible wonders of this continent: its mist-covered peaks, thundering falls and vast rainforests. Add to this the human-made treasures: buzzing indigenous markets, picturesque colonial towns and vibrant cityscapes. This is just the beginning, and in South America there really is no end. It's the reason I've returned so many times, but I know there is still much more to discover.

For more about our writers, see p1104

Above: Handicrafts market between Cuzco (p844) and Machu Picchu (p860), Peru

South America

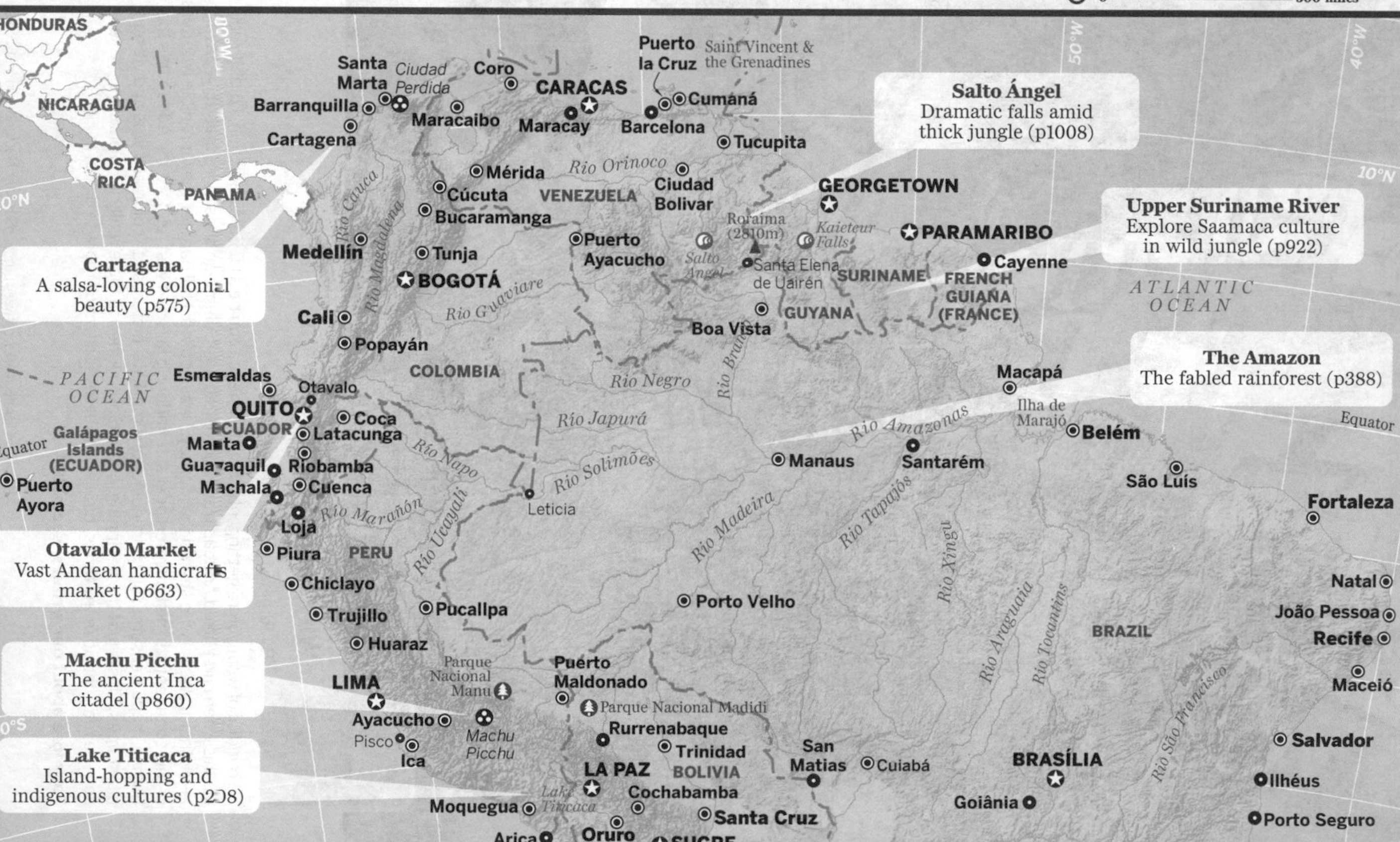

Salar de Uyuni
Otherworldly salt flats (p230)
Buenos Aires
Blazing nightlife and colorful neighborhoods (p57)
Rio de Janeiro
Beaches, caipirinhas and samba (p283)
Iguazú Falls
One of earth's mightiest falls (p100)
Encarnación
Paraguay's most captivating city (p779)
Colonia del Sacramento
Photogenic 18th-century charmer (p940)
Glaciar Perito Moreno
Massive, dramatically set glacier (p168)
Torres del Paine
Granite peaks soaring over Patagonia (p522)
Iquique
Uyuni
Potosí
Tupiza
Tarija
Villazón
Calama
San Pedro de Atacama
Antofagasta
San Salvador de Jujuy
Salta
Tucumán
PARAGUAY
Campo Grande
Ciudad del Este
Foz do Iguaçu
Puerto Iguazú
ASUNCIÓN
Corrientes
Encarnación
Posadas
Belo Horizonte
Ouro Prêto
São Paolo
Rio de Janeiro
Curitiba
Florianópolis
Caxias do Sul
Porto Alegre
Pelotas
Río Paraná
Río Uruguay
La Serena
Córdoba
Santa Fe
Rosario
URUGUAY
Punta del Diablo
Punta del Este
MONTEVIDEO
BUENOS AIRES
Mendoza
Viña del Mar
Valparaíso
SANTIAGO
ARGENTINA
Archipiélago Juan Fernández (CHILE)
PACIFIC OCEAN
Concepción
Chillan
Mar del Plata
Temuco
Pucón
Valdivia
Osorno
Bariloche
Puerto Montt
El Bolsón
Ilha Grande de Chiloé
Puerto Madryn
ATLANTIC OCEAN
Coyhaique
CHILE
Parque Nacional Los Glaciares
El Calafate
Parque Nacional Torres del Paine
Puerto Natales
Río Gallegos
Falkland Islands (Islas Malvinas)
Stanley
Punta Arenas
Ushuaia
Tropic of Capricorn
Rapa Nui (CHILE)
Rapa Nui (Easter Island)
20°S
30°S
40°S
50°S
100°W
90°W
80°W
60°W
50°W
40°W
30°W

South America's Top 15

1

Machu Picchu

1 A fantastic Inca citadel lost to the world until its early-20th-century rediscovery, Peru's Machu Picchu (p860) stands as a ruin among ruins. With its emerald terraces and steep peaks that echo on the horizon, the sight simply surpasses the imagination. This marvel of engineering has withstood half a dozen centuries of earthquakes, foreign invasion and howling weather. Discover it for yourself, wander through its stone temples and scale the dizzying heights of Wayna Picchu.

The Amazon

2 Home to the greatest collection of plant and animal life on earth, the awe-inspiring Amazon encompasses more than 7 million sq kilometers. There are countless ways to experience its astounding biodiversity: trekking through dense jungle, visiting indigenous villages, flying over the vast green expanse of undulating waterways, slow-boating between river towns or lounging in a jungle lodge after a day spent wildlife-watching. Nine countries share a bit of the famous rain-forest, all of which have excellent bases to experience it firsthand. Below: Scarlet Macaw

PHILIP LEE HARVEY / LONELY PLANET ©

2

CZEKMA13 / GETTY IMAGES ©

Rio de Janeiro

3 Few cities in the world enjoy more seductive charm than Brazil's *Cidade Maravilhosa* (marvelous city), but calling Rio (p283) merely marvelous doesn't quite cut it. Flanked by striking Atlantic-blue waters, sugary-white sands and a mountainous backdrop of Crayola-green rainforest, Rio's cinematic cityscape has few rivals. And once its soundtrack kicks in – a high-on-life siren's song of bossa nova and samba – Rio's raw energy seizes you with the come-hither allure of a tropical fantasy. You'll have no choice but to follow. Below: Ipanema Beach (p287)

Buenos Aires

4 Buenos Aires (p57), Argentina, is a beautiful metropolis with gourmet cuisine, awesome shopping, frenzied nightlife and gorgeous locals. It's a European-like, cosmopolitan city encompassing both slick neighborhoods and downtrodden ghettos, but that's the appeal. You can experience classic cafes, amazing steaks, surprising architecture, energizing *fútbol* games and, of course, that sultry tango. It's elegant, seductive, emotional, confounding, frustrating and full of attitude – and there's absolutely no other place like it in the world.

PHILIPPE COHAT / GETTY IMAGES ©

MICHELE FALZONE / GETTY IMAGES ©

PETER ADAMS / GETTY IMAGES ©

HAGENMULLER JEAN-FRANCOIS / HEMIS.FR / GETTY IMAGES ©

Lake Titicaca

5 Less a lake than a highland ocean, Lake Titicaca (p208) in Bolivia is the highest navigable body of water in the world. In Andean tradition it's the birthplace of the sun. Here, banner blue skies turn to bitterly cold nights. Among its fantastical sights are the surreal floating islands crafted entirely of tightly woven *totora* reeds. Enthralling and in many ways singular, the shimmering deep-blue Lake Titicaca is the longtime home of highland cultures steeped in the old ways.

Salar de Uyuni

6 Who knew feeling this cold could feel so good? While the three- to four-day jeep tour through the world's largest salt flat (p230) will leave your bones chattering, it quite possibly could be the singular experience that defines your Bolivian adventure. The salt flat in its vastness, austerity and crystalline perfection will inspire you, while your early morning exploration of rock gardens, geyser fields and piping hot springs along with the camaraderie of three days on the road with your fellow 'Salterians' will create a kinship not likely to fade anytime soon.

Glaciar Perito Moreno

7 Possibly the world's most dynamic glacier, the Perito Moreno (p168) in Argentina advances up to 2m per day, which means plenty of exciting, spine-tingling calving. It's supremely accessible, too – you can get very close to the action via a complex network of steel boardwalks, perfectly situated near (but not too near!) the glacier's face. Everyone stands there, watching in suspense, for the next building-size chunk to sheer off and slowly tip into the water below, creating thunderous crashes and huge waves. Trust us, it's awesome.

Iguazú Falls

8 The thunderous roar, the dramatic cascades, the refreshing sprays, the absolute miraculous work of Mother Nature – nothing prepares you for that flooring first moment you set eyes upon Iguazú Falls (p100). On the Brazilian side, the wide-eyed view of the whole astounding scene stretches out before you in all its panoramic wonder. In Argentina, get up close and personal with the deafening Devil's Throat, which provides the fall's single most mind-blowing moment. In all, some 275 falls deliver one of the world's best wows in unforgettable fashion.

Otavalo Market, Ecuador

9 Every Saturday the world seems to converge on the bustling town of Otavalo in the Andes, where a huge market (p663) spreads from the Plaza de Ponchos throughout the town. While the crowds can be a drag and the quality is immensely changeable, the choice is enormous and you'll find some incredible bargains here among the brightly colored rugs, traditional crafts, clothing, Tigua folk art and quality straw hats. Nearby, the squawks and squeals of livestock drown out the chatter of Kichwa-speaking farmers at Otavalo's equally famous animal market.

8

LUCOP / GETTY IMAGES ©

MICHELE FALZONE / GETTY IMAGES ©

Colonia del Sacramento, Uruguay

10 Take a step back in time as you explore the gracious 18th-century cobbled streets and fascinating history of former smugglers' haven, Colonia del Sacramento (p940). Then check out the great bar and restaurant scene and the gorgeous position on a peninsula of the Río de la Plata. All this and its super-accessible location a short hop away from both Montevideo and Buenos Aires make 'Colonia' a classic tourist town, but even on weekends it's worth dodging the crowds and letting yourself get seduced by the town's eternal charms.

Torres del Paine

11 The wind is whipping and dark clouds form overhead as the hiking trail suddenly opens to reveal a stunning vista of rugged granite spires soaring high over the Patagonian steppe. These are the Torres del Paine (p522), the proud centerpiece of Chile's famous national park. Trekking through this Unesco Biosphere Reserve isn't for the faint of heart – guides say the park sees all four seasons in a single day – but hiking the 'W' remains a rite of passage for generations of adventurous travelers.

Cartagena

12 Stroll through the preserved streets of Cartagena's old town (p575) and be swept away by the grace, romance and legend of one of the continent's finest colonial settlements. Inside its imposing walls, much of the Colombian city still looks as it did during Spanish rule – pastel-hued mansions boast elegant wooden balconies, which open onto majestic plazas shaded by magnificent churches. Throw away the map, get lost in the maze of narrow cobblestone streets and discover why this magical place has seduced travelers for centuries.

Encarnación

13 With its new beach, sparkling coastal promenade and wildly energetic Carnaval, Paraguay's 'Pearl of the South' (p779) is billing itself as the local answer to Rio de Janeiro. Though that might be a bit ambitious, there is no doubt that Encarnacion's unique take on Carnaval is a whole lot of fun, where the crowd dances as much as the participants, spray snow fills the hot summer air and the party goes on well into the early hours of the morning.

The Upper Suriname River

14 Cascading rapids rush past smooth boulders and forested islands lined with white-sand beaches. The sun-dappled jungle is hot and muggy, but the beauty of the foliage, birdsong and musky scents outweigh the discomforts. In Central Suriname Nature Reserve (p923), one of Suriname's largest reserves, you can trek to plateaus with views over pristine forest, then cool off in a waterfall at the end of the day. At night dance to African drums before gazing at shooting stars in the deep black sky, in near-mosquito-free bliss. Top: Squirrel monkeys

Angel Falls

15 Fly over a surreal landscape of *tepuis* (flat-topped mesa) to Venezuela's Parque Nacional Canaima, and touch down alongside the pink-tinted cascades of Canaima lagoon. Your next step is a five-hour river journey through lush jungle. From the Mirador Laime lookout, witness the cascade of Salto Ángel (p1008), the world's tallest waterfall, as it thunders 979m from the plateau of Auyantepui. Swim while gazing up at the water flow, and then sleep in a hammock camp, serenaded by the evening jungle.

Need to Know

For more information, see Survival Guide (p1047)

Planes

Flying between countries can be expensive; pre-purchased air passes provide decent value. Domestic flights are generally more affordable.

Buses

Amazonia aside, buses – from slow local options to comfy internationals – go everywhere and connect major towns of neighboring countries.

Cars

Handy for exploring remote areas and national parks. Car hire can be pricey and crossing borders is a hassle.

Trains

Few trains, although scenic lines operate in Argentina, Bolivia, Brazil, Ecuador and Peru.

Boat

The prime mode of travel in the Amazon; slow, crowded boats make multiday journeys between towns.

Bicycle

Daunting yet highly rewarding. Beware poor roads, reckless drivers and high altitudes.

When to Go

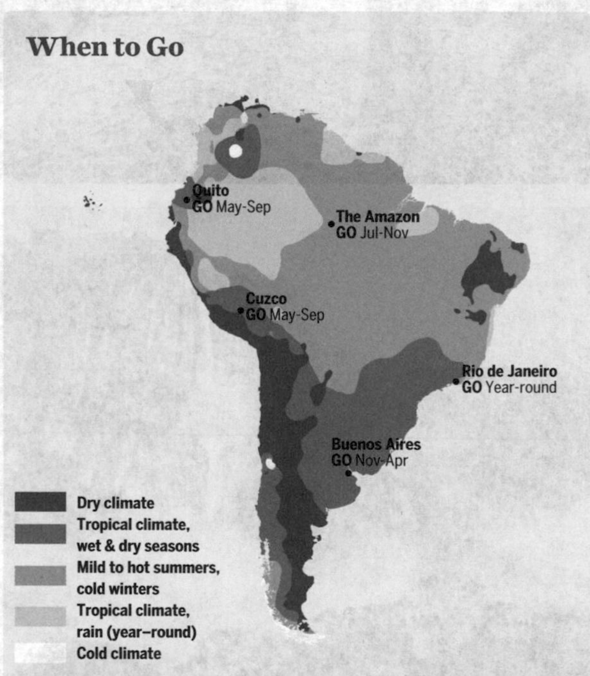

High Season
(Dec–Mar)

➡ It's high season in Brazil and the Atlantic coast; beaches and festivals (such as Carnaval) are big draws.

➡ The best time to visit Patagonia, though expect higher prices.

Shoulder
(Oct–Nov)

➡ It's dry season in the Amazon, making for fine wildlife-watching.

➡ Fewer crowds and lower prices make this a good time to visit Buenos Aires, Rio and other coastal destinations.

Low Season
(Jul–Aug)

➡ In Chile and Argentina, many services close at beach resorts, and mountain passes can be blocked by snow.

Daily Costs

Budget: less than $US30

- ➡ Cheapest in Bolivia, Paraguay, Ecuador, Colombia and Venezuela
- ➡ Dorm beds from $US7, double rooms from $US20
- ➡ Shopping at markets, eating inexpensive set meals: from $US2.50

Midrange: $US30–90

- ➡ Budget jungle lodge in the Amazon: $US50 to $US80 per day
- ➡ Excursions: hiking and cycling tours, from $US50 per day
- ➡ 3½-day boat trip from Manaus to Belem: from $US100 (hammock fare)

Top end: more than $US90

- ➡ Hiking the Inca Trail (four-day trek): $US500 per person
- ➡ Multiday Galápagos cruise: around $US200 per day

Websites

Lonely Planet (www.lonelyplanet.com/south-america) Thorn Tree forum, destination information and hotel bookings.

Latin American Network Information Center (www.lanic.utexas.edu) Links to all things Latin American.

UK Foreign & Commonwealth Office (www.fco.gov.uk) Travel advisories.

US State Department (www.state.gov) Travel advice and warnings.

Money

ATMs Available in major towns and cities, and are generally the best way of getting cash. Stock up on funds before visiting remote areas.

Hostels and budget hotels Most accept cash only.

Bargaining Hone your bargaining skills before visiting markets.

Cash Keep an emergency stash of US dollars (the easiest currency to exchange).

Exchange Rates Be careful changing money at borders; read up on exchange rates and scams before you arrive.

Visas

Visitors from the US and some other countries require visas (best arranged in advance) when visiting Brazil, Bolivia, Paraguay, Suriname and Venezuela. (For Argentina, a reciprocity fee must be paid in advance before arriving.) Make sure you have enough blank pages in your passport, and that it will be valid for six months beyond your proposed entry date to each country.

Arriving in South America

Buenos Aires: Aeropuerto Internacional de Ezeiza

Shuttle Bus: Frequent to downtown (AR$145)

Taxi: AR$450

Lima: Aeropuerto Internacional Jorge Chávez

Combi: Take 'La S' (S2-3); find it southbound along Av Elmer Faucett

Taxi: S60

Bogotá: Aeropuerto El Dorado

Shuttle: shuttle bus to Portal El Dorado and transfer to TransMilenio bus (COP$1700)

Taxi: COP$30,000

Get Inspired

Literature

- ➡ **Gabriel Garcia Marquez & Mario Vargas Llosa** Marquez *(Love in the Time of Cholera)* and Llosa *(War of the End of the World)* – Nobel Prize winners and sometime rivals – are considered the continent's best writers.
- ➡ **Jorge Luis Borges** Giant of modern literature best known for his labyrinthine tales, and playful melding of myth and truth, such as in *Ficciones*.
- ➡ **Jorge Amado** Colorful, ribald stories set in Bahia such as the classic *Dona Flor and Her Two Husbands*.
- ➡ **Ernesto 'Che' Guevara** Breezy travelogue *The Motorcycle Diaries* was written by this Argentine-born revolutionary.
- ➡ **Bruce Chatwin** Poignant and beautifully written travel narrative, *In Patagonia*, blends fact and fable.

Music

- ➡ **África Brasil** (Jorge Ben Jor) Celebratory album from the 1970s that blends funk, samba and blues.
- ➡ **Amanecer** (Bomba Estéreo) A blend of African, indigenous and vibrant dance beats by an inventive Colombian band.
- ➡ **Lunático** (Gotan Project) Brilliant fusing of tango with electronic grooves.
- ➡ **Roots of Chicha** (various artists) Wild Peruvian cumbias that channel psychedelic, rock and melodic sounds.
- ➡ **Tropicália ou Panis et Circencis** A famed Brazilian collaboration between Gilberto Gil, Caetano Veloso, Gal Costa and Tom Zé.

For much more on **getting around**, see p1058

First Time South America

For more information, see Survival Guide (p1047)

Checklist

➡ Ensure your passport is valid for six months past your arrival date.

➡ Apply for visas well in advance.

➡ Organize travel insurance.

➡ Medical check-up and vaccinations.

➡ Stock up on contact lenses and prescription medicines.

➡ Inform bank of travel plans.

➡ Scan key documents (passports, visas, credit cards) and email them to yourself in case of loss.

What to Pack

➡ A week's worth of clothes

➡ Rain gear (jacket, dry pack for electronics)

➡ Hat (for sun and rain)

➡ Good walking shoes

➡ Flip-flops (for beaches and dodgy showers)

➡ Earplugs

➡ Medicine/first-aid kit

➡ USB drive

➡ GSM mobile phone

➡ Refillable water bottle

➡ Sunscreen

➡ Tissues (for public toilets)

Top Tips for Your Trip

➡ Don't be shy. Talk to locals, who are often happy to share their culture.

➡ Be prepared. Read up on destinations before you arrive; know the exchange rate. Have a map handy when arriving in a new town.

➡ Slow down. Don't be in such a hurry to tick off sites that you miss the beauty in front of you.

➡ Learn some Spanish and Portuguese. A little effort goes a long way.

➡ Prepare for crazy driving. Pedestrians have no rights.

➡ Carry valuables in a hidden money belt to prevent theft.

➡ Don't overpack. You can wash clothes and purchase things you need on the road.

➡ Don't cram the whole continent into a month. Pick a country or two, and get to know it.

➡ Prepare for huge contrasts in weather and terrain.

What to Wear

In general, lightweight, loose-fitting clothes will be the most comfortable options. Bring a jacket for cool highland temperatures and over-air-conditioned buses. Pants and long-sleeve shirts are handy insect protection for jungle hikes.

Sleeping

➡ **Hostels** Dorm rooms provide cheap and social lodging for solo travelers.

➡ **Hotels** A wide range of options, from boxy cells to flashy boutiques.

➡ **Guesthouses** Often family-owned, guesthouses run the gamut from bare bones to lavish.

➡ **Homestays** Live like a local in a family home.

Safety

The dangers of traveling in South America are greatly exaggerated, often by people who've never been here. While there are threats, traveling sensibly will reduce your risk of becoming a victim.

➡ Dress down. Leave flashy looking jewelry and designer sunglasses at home.

➡ Don't use iPhones and other expensive-looking electronic devices in public.

➡ Credit- and debit-card fraud is rife in Brazil. To avoid card cloning, use only high-traffic ATMs inside banks during regular opening hours.

➡ In urban areas, take a taxi after dark.

➡ Be mindful of walking in deserted areas.

➡ Don't take valuables to the beach or leave them lying around your guestroom.

➡ Don't accept food and drink from strangers. Druggings can occur.

Bargaining

Bargaining is common practice at markets and when arranging long-term accommodations.

Tipping

➡ At many restaurants, the service charge (and tax) is already included in the bill.

➡ Bartenders are rarely tipped.

➡ Taxi drivers aren't commonly tipped, though it is polite to round up the bill.

➡ If you take a guided tour (to the Amazon, the Galápagos etc), it's common to tip the guide.

Buenos Aires (p57)

Etiquette

➡ Greetings are important. In Spanish-speaking countries, greet people you encounter with *buenos días* (good morning), *buenas tardes* (good afternoon) or *buenas noches* (good evening). Use *bom dia, boa tarde* and *boa noite* in Brazil.

➡ Always greet people when entering and exiting a shop.

➡ When meeting people socially, give *besos* (kisses) on the cheek (both cheeks for Brazilians). Men shake hands.

➡ Dress for the occasion; for example, only tourists and athletes wear shorts in Buenos Aires.

➡ Ask before photographing people, particularly in indigenous communities – payment may be requested.

Language

English is not widely spoken in South America, and learning a few phrases of Spanish will be be helpful in your travels. You can also plan your trip around language study: many countries offer inexpensive language-immersion classes, particularly in Ecuador. Spanish won't be much help in Brazil, where Portuguese is the official language. If you speak some Spanish, however, you'll be able to read a fair bit of Portuguese. Learn some basic phrases and pronunciation to take your skills to the next level. Many locals are quite patient with language learners, and appreciate your efforts, however rudimentary.

If You Like...

Colonial Splendor

South America has a stunning array of architectural wonders, where cobblestone streets lead past magnificent cathedrals, photogenic plazas and brightly painted town houses, some of which date to the 16th century.

Quito Wandering the buzzing streets of the *centro histórico* (old town) presents dramatic scenery at every turn. (p638)

Colonia del Sacramento Uruguay's delightfully picturesque riverfront town, just a short ferry ride from Buenos Aires. (p940)

Ouro Prêto One of Brazil's most alluring colonial towns, hilly Ouro Prêto is packed with 18th-century treasures. (p322)

Cartagena Colombia's comeliest coastal town has a beautifully preserved center scenically set on the Caribbean. (p575)

Arequipa A Peruvian charmer with striking colonial *sillar* (volcanic stone) architecture and salt-of-the-earth eateries. (p829)

Paramaribo A strange and exotic blend of colonial Dutch buildings and grassy squares in oft-overlooked Suriname. (p916)

Big Cities

South America's cities are home to first-rate museums, foodie-loving restaurants and rocking nightlife. You can shop at atmospheric markets, cozy up at an art-filled cafe or spend the day exploring the charming neighborhoods.

Rio de Janeiro The *Cidade Maravilhosa* (Marvelous City) lives up to its name with lovely beaches, samba-fueled nightlife and jaw-dropping scenery. (p283)

Buenos Aires A place that's hard to leave with colorful neighborhoods, late-night dining, old-world cafes, sultry tango clubs, and French and Italianate architecture. (p57)

Lima Great for seafood feasts and late-night bar-hopping in bohemian Barranco. Its museums house Peru's best pre-Columbian collections. (p803)

Bogotá Colombia's capital has salsa-fueled nightclubs and an intriguing colonial center – plus fascinating nearby sights such as the surreal underground salt cathedral at Zipaquirá. (p544)

Valparaíso A bohemian city and Unesco World Heritage Site that's often considered Chile's cultural capital. (p441)

Ancient Ruins

Pre-Columbian peoples left behind a wide-ranging legacy: the awe-inspiring monuments and artfully crafted works in ceramic, gold and stone comprise but a fraction of the great works in existence before the Europeans arrived.

Machu Picchu The godfather of great ruins, this mountaintop Inca citadel is best enjoyed as the finale of a multiday trek. (p860)

Cuzco The continent's oldest continuously inhabited city, with flawless Inca-built walls lining cobblestone streets. (p844)

Kuélap Perched atop a limestone mountain, this monumental stone-fortified city is a relic of a fierce cloud-forest-dwelling civilization. (p890)

San Agustín In southwest Colombia, the mysterious San Agustín culture left behind hundreds of statues carved from volcanic rock. (p612)

Rapa Nui Better known as Easter Island, this Polynesian outpost is home to utterly mystifying *moai* statues. (p526)

Nazca Lines Mysterious carvings in the sand spread across hundreds of square kilometers; scenic flights are the best way to see it. (p825)

Beaches

Shimmering beaches wedged between tropical rainforest and deep blue sea: South America has many enticements, includ-

Top: Blue-footed booby, Galápagos Islands (p710), Ecuador

Bottom: The World's Most Dangerous Road (p197), Bolivia

ing remote island getaways, party-loving surf towns and glittering sands amid big-city allure.

Archipiélago Los Roques Due north of Caracas, 300 pristine islands make a magnificent setting for beach-combing, snorkeling and diving. (p982)

Arraial d'Ajuda Brazil is spoiled for choice when it comes to world-class beaches; this peaceful town in the northeast is gateway to some of Bahia's prettiest coastline. (p365)

Punta del Diablo Forget the overhyped mayhem of Punta del Este; Uruguay's more tranquil summertime getaway is this coastal beauty just south of the Brazilian border. (p954)

Parque Nacional Natural Tayrona Fronting the Caribbean Sea, this pristine national park in Colombia has gorgeous beaches and does a fine imitation of paradise lost. (p570)

Baia de Sancho On Fernando de Noronha, easily one of Brazil's most gorgeous beaches. (p370)

Outdoor Adventures

Adrenaline junkies can get their fix negotiating snow-capped peaks, rushing rivers and pounding surf. Rafting, rock climbing, mountain biking, hang-gliding, sand-boarding and ziplining: there are hundreds of ways to get your heart racing.

White-water rafting Head to the heart-thumping rivers – from turquoise to crystalline – that draw rafters and kayakers to the Chilean south. (p47)

Mountain biking The World's Most Dangerous Road: the name says it all. This 64km mountain-bike trip outside La Paz takes in perilous descents. Make sure your brakes (and travel insurance!) are top notch. (p197)

Hang-gliding Sail high above the forest-covered hills of Rio to a beachside landing on a fantastic tandem flight. (p291)

Sandboarding Take a wild ride down 150m-high sand dunes just outside a desert oasis town in northern Chile. (p462)

Mountain climbing Strap on your crampons and make your way up 5897m Volcan Cotopaxi, one of Ecuador's most popular climbs. (p667)

Dramatic Scenery

Thundering waterfalls, cone-shaped volcanoes and red-rock canyons – the only things missing are the pterodactyls. You might feel like you've stepped back a few million years.

Parque Nacional da Chapada Diamantina Head to Brazil's northeast to hike across dramatic plateaus and swim in refreshing waterfalls. (p360)

Iguazú Falls Spread between Argentina and Brazil, these are some of the most spectacular waterfalls on earth. (p100)

Cañón del Cotahuasi Hard to reach but immensely rewarding is this Central Andean icon, the world's deepest canyon. (p835)

Salar de Uyuni The world's largest salt flats are a dazzling remnant of a vast prehistoric lake. (p230)

Roraima In southeastern Venezuela, you'll find otherwordly landscapes of tableland mountains, wind-carved gorges, ribbon waterfalls and carnivorous plants. (p1011)

Parque Nacional Torres del Paine In southern Patagonia, sparkling glaciers, topaz lakes and sheer granite cliff-faces defy the imagination. (p522)

Festivals & Events

Whether you prefer the pageantry of Semana Santa or the revelry of Carnaval, the continent has you covered. From traditional to surreal, here are a few events worth planning a trip around.

Carnaval Many towns in Brazil throw a wild pre-Lenten bash, but Salvador and Rio are the best places to celebrate a few sleepless nights. Paraguay's Encarnación also stages a legendary party. (p25)

Mamá Negra This Ecuadorian fest features processions, witches, whole roast pigs, a bit of cross-dressing and plenty of alcohol. (p27)

Festival y Mundial de Baile Learn some new moves at this massive tango festival in Buenos Aires in August. (p65)

Virgen de la Candelaria In Puno, Peru gives a thunderous street party for its patron saint. (p839)

Fiesta del Santo Patrono de Moxos One of Bolivia's biggest bashes with fireworks, dancing, feasts and wild costumes. (p27)

Hiking & Trekking

Against a backdrop of Andean peaks, misty cloud forests and Amazonian jungle, trekking here is world class, whether you're out for a short day hike or a multiday journey.

Quilotoa Avid walkers shouldn't miss this scenic multiday Ecuadorian journey, overnighting at simple village guesthouses along the way. (p669)

Choro Traversing Bolivia's Parque Nacional Cotopata, the four-day Choro Trek begins amid alpine scenery before descending into the lush, subtropical Yungas region. (p219)

Cordillera Huayhuash Circuit Rivaling the big Himalayan treks, this 10-day Peruvian odyssey takes you among alpine lakes with condors circling the surrounding 6000m peaks. (p881)

El Chaltén In Argentine Patagonia, El Chaltén offers unparalleled trekking amid glaciers, alpine lakes and craggy mountains. (p162)

Ciudad Perdida Like a scene torn from an *Indiana Jones* film, the trek to Colombia's 'Lost City' is a challenging four-day (return) journey to the overgrown ruins of a large pre-Columbian town. (p572)

Wildlife

South America is home to more plant and animal species than any other place on earth and there are countless settings to watch wildlife.

The Amazon Manaus is still one of the top gateways for a journey into the mother of all rainforests. (p396)

The Pantanal At these wildlife-rich wetlands, you're likely to see even more animal species than in the Amazon. Cuiabá is one of the top spots to plan a trip. (p346)

The Galápagos Needing little introduction, these volcanic islands are home to creatures so tame, you'll practically be tripping over all the sea lions. (p710)

Parque Nacional San Rafael Paraguay's verdant strand of Atlantic Forest has refreshing lakes, forest paths and superb bird-watching. (p784)

North Rupununi Lodges in Guyana make a fine base for exploring the amazingly rich wildlife found here. (p761)

Month by Month

TOP EVENTS

Carnaval February

Fiesta de la Virgen de la Candelaria February

Semana Santa March/April

Inti Raymi June

Festival Mundial de Tango August

January

It's peak season in Brazil and Argentina. Expect high prices, big crowds and sweltering temperatures as city dwellers head to the coast. This is also the most popular time to travel to Patagonia.

Santiago a Mil

This long-running theater and dance fest features dozens of shows and events around the Chilean capital, staged by international and local companies. The 17-day event begins in early January (www.santiagoamil.cl) and is held throughout the city, including in free outdoor venues.

Festival Nacional del Folklore

Near the city of Córdoba, the town of Cosquín hosts Argentina's National Festival of Folk Music (www.aquicosquin.org) during the last week of January. It's the country's largest and best known folk festival.

February

The sizzling summer is still in full swing in the southern half of the continent, with exorbitant prices and sparse accommodations during Brazilian Carnaval. It's fairly wet in the Andes and the Amazon region.

Carnaval

The famous bacchanalian event happens across South America, though the pre-Lenten revelry is most famous in Brazil. Rio and Salvador throw the liveliest bashes, with street parades, costume parties and round-the-clock merriment. Carnaval runs from Friday to Tuesday before Ash Wednesday in February or early March.

Carnaval Encarnaceno

Although its northern neighbor hogs all the attention, Paraguay is also a great place to celebrate Carnaval – especially in Encarnación, which throws a riotous fest on every weekend in February. Come for the costumed parades, pounding rhythms and partying through the late hours (www.carnaval.com.py).

Fiesta de la Virgen de la Candelaria

Celebrated across the highlands in Bolivia and Peru, this festival features music, drinking, eating, dancing, processions, water balloons (in Bolivia) and fireworks. The biggest celebrations take place in Copacabana (Bolivia) and Puno (Peru). The big day is February 2.

March

While the weather is still warm in the south, the crowds thin and prices fall a bit at beach destinations. It's still rainy in the Andes.

Semana Santa

Throughout Latin America, Holy Week is celebrated with fervor. In Quito (Ecuador), purple-robed penitents parade through the streets on Good Friday, while Ouro Prêto (Brazil) features streets 'painted' with flowers. Ayacucho hosts Peru's most colorful Semana Santa culminating in an all-night street party before Easter.

Fiesta Nacional de la Vendimia

In Argentina's wine country, Mendoza hosts a renowned five-day harvest festival (www.vendimia.mendoza.gov.ar) with parades, folkloric events, fireworks, the blessing of the fruit and a royal coronation – all in honor of Mendoza's intoxicating produce.

Pujillay

Celebrated in Tarabuco (Bolivia) on the second Sunday in March, hordes of indigenous folks gather to celebrate the 1816 victory of local armies over Spanish troops with ritual dancing, song, music and *chicha* (corn beer) drinking.

Rupununi Rodeo

In Lethem (Guyana), Easter weekend means good fun at the rodeo. Some 10,000 visitors come to watch the blend of Wild West meets Amerindian traditions. There's roping, saddle- and bareback riding (broncos, bulls) and a beauty pageant.

Lollapalooza Chile

Chile's biggest rock fest (www.lollapaloozacl.com) kicks off in Santiago in late March or early April, and features an impressive line-up of homegrown and international groups on par with the North American version of Lollapalooza. Buy tickets early for the best deals.

Semana Criolla

After Carnaval, this is Montevideo's liveliest fest, and is essentially a celebration of gaucho culture – those tough-looking, leather-boot-wearing cowboys from Uruguay's interior who manage to make oversized belt buckles look cool. Come for rodeo events, concerts, open-air barbecues and craft fairs.

May

Buenos Aires and Rio head into low season, with cooler weather and lower prices; the rain begins to taper off in the Andes, making it a fine time to go trekking.

Diablos Danzantes

In Caracas, Diablos Danzantes (Dancing Devils), features hundreds of diabolically clothed dancers parading through the streets to the sounds of pounding drums. The Venezuelan fest, which blends Spanish and African traditions, takes place on Corpus Christi, 60 days after Easter (May or June).

Q'oyoriti

A fascinating indigenous pilgrimage to the holy mountain of Ausangate, outside Cuzco, takes place around Corpus Christi (May or June). Though relatively unknown outside Peru, it's well worth checking out.

June

High season in the Andean nations corresponds with the North American summer (June to August), when the weather is also sunniest and driest. Book major tours (such as hiking the Inca Trail) well in advance.

Inti Raymi

This millennia-old indigenous celebration of the summer solstice and harvest is celebrated in many Andean towns. In Cuzco it's the event of year, attracting thousands of visitors for street fairs, open-air concerts and historical reenactments. In Ecuador, Otavalo is the place to be.

Bumba Meu Boi

This traditional fest, celebrated across Brazil's Maranhão region in late June, blends African, indigenous and Portuguese traditions. Hundreds of troupes take to the streets in São Luís, dancing, singing and reenacting one of the region's great creation myths.

São Paulo Pride

It's official: São Paulo throws the largest gay-pride parade on the planet, attracting some four million people. There are street fairs, concerts, film screenings and exhibitions in the days leading up to the big parade – which usually happens on Sunday in mid-June.

July

July is one of the coldest months in the far south (not a good time to visit Patagonia or Buenos Aires). It is, however, a great time to plan a wildlife-watching trip in the Pantanal.

Fiesta del Santo Patrono de Moxos

Running from July 22 to the end of the month, this spirited festival transforms sleepy San Ignacio de Moxos into a hard-partying town. Expect processions, outrageous costumes (including locals dressed as Amazon warriors), fireworks and plenty of drinking.

Founding of Guayaquil

Street dancing, fireworks and processions are all part of the celebration on the nights leading up to the anniversary of Guayaquil's founding (July 25). Along with the national holiday on July 24 (Simón Bolívar's birthday), Ecuador's largest city closes down and celebrates with abandon.

August

It's dry in many parts of the continent, making August a fine time to visit the Amazon, the Pantanal or the Andes. It's chilly to freezing south of the Tropic of Capricorn.

Festival Mundial de Tango

World-class tango dancers perform throughout Buenos Aires during this two-week festival (www.tangobuenosaires.gob.ar). Competition is fierce for the title of 'world's best tango dancer.' You can also hone your own moves at classes and workshops.

Festival de Música del Pacífico Petronio Álvarez

In Cali, one of Colombia's best fests celebrates Afro-Colombian music and culture over five days in mid-August (www.festivalpetronioalvarez.com), when more than 100 groups light up the city. You'll find infectious rhythms and welcoming, dance-happy crowds.

La Virgen del Cisne

In Ecuador's southern highlands, thousands of colorfully garbed pilgrims take to the roads each year around August 15 in the extraordinary 70km procession to Loja, carrying the Virgen del Cisne (Virgin of the Swan).

Feria de las Flores

The Flower Festival (www.feriadelasfloresmedellin.gov.co) brings sweet smells to the Colombian city of Medellín. Highlights include concerts, a gastronomy fair, a horse parade, orchid exhibits and the Desfile de Silleteros when farmers parade through the streets laden with enormous baskets of flowers.

September

The weather remains dry and sunny (but chilly) in the Andes, though you'll find fewer crowds. September is also a good (less rainy) time to visit the Amazon.

Bienal de São Paulo

One of the world's most important arts events showcases some 3000 works by more than 100 artists from across the globe. It runs from September to December in even-numbered years, and is mainly based in Parque do Ibirapuera (www.bienal.org.br).

Fiesta de la Mamá Negra

Latacunga (Ecuador) hosts one of the highlands' most famous celebrations, in honor of La Virgen de las Mercedes. La Mamá Negra, played by a man dressed as a black woman, pays tribute to the 19th-century liberation of African slaves.

October

Heavy rains make for tough traveling in Colombia, while the Andes generally have milder weather. In Bolivia, Brazil, Chile and Argentina, temperatures are mild, making it a pleasant time to visit.

Oktoberfest

Celebrating the historical legacy of Brazil's substantial German immigrants, Oktoberfest features 17 days of folk music, dancing and beer drinking. It's considered the largest German fest in the Americas and goes down in mid-October in Blumenau (www.oktoberfestblumenau.com.br).

Círio de Nazaré

Belém's enormous annual event brings one million people to the streets to take part in the procession of one of Brazil's most important icons. Fireworks, hymns and one massive flower-bedecked carriage creaking through the throngs are all part of this wild spiritual gathering.

November

Rainier days are on the horizon in the Amazon. Generally November nets better prices, good weather and fewer crowds than December in most parts of South America.

Puno Day

The traditional city of Puno in Peru hosts dozens of colorful fiestas throughout the year. One of the best is Puno Day, where costumed dancers, military parades and folk bands celebrate the legendary emergence of the first Inca, Manco Cápac, from Lake Titicaca.

Festival Internacional de Cine de Mar del Plata

Launched in 1950, this cinematic event is one of the most important film festivals in Latin America (www.mardelplatafilmfest.com). Running for nine days in mid-November, the fest screens an international lineup of features, shorts, documentaries and experimental works.

Hmong New Year

For something completely different, head to the small village of Cacao (French Guiana) to celebrate the Hmong New Year with a thriving community of Laotians. Traditional singing and dancing, Laotian cuisine and beautifully embroidered costumes are all part of the experience. Held in November or December.

December

December marks the beginning of summer, with beach days (and higher prices) on both the Atlantic and Pacific coasts. It's fairly rainy in the Andes.

Buenos Aires Jazz Festival Internacional

BA's big jazz festival (www.buenosairesjazz.gob.ar) showcases the talents of more than 200 musicians to play in 70 different concerts around town. Jazz musicians of all kinds are featured – emerging and established, avant-garde and mainstream, national and international.

Fiestas de Quito

Quito's biggest bash is a much anticipated event, with parades and street dances throughout the first week of December. Open-air stages all across town fill the Ecuadorian capital with music, while colorful *chivas* (open-sided buses) full of revelers maneuver through the streets.

Carnatal

Brazil's biggest 'off-season Carnaval' is this Salvador-style festival held in Natal in December. It features raucous street parties and thumping *trios elétricos* (amplified bands playing atop mobile-speaker trucks). You can get in on the fun by joining one of the *blocos* (drumming and dancing processions).

Réveillon

There are many great spots in South America to celebrate New Year's Eve, but Rio is a perennial favorite. Some two million revelers, dressed in white to bring good luck, pack the sands of Copacabana Beach, to watch fireworks light up the night sky.

Itineraries

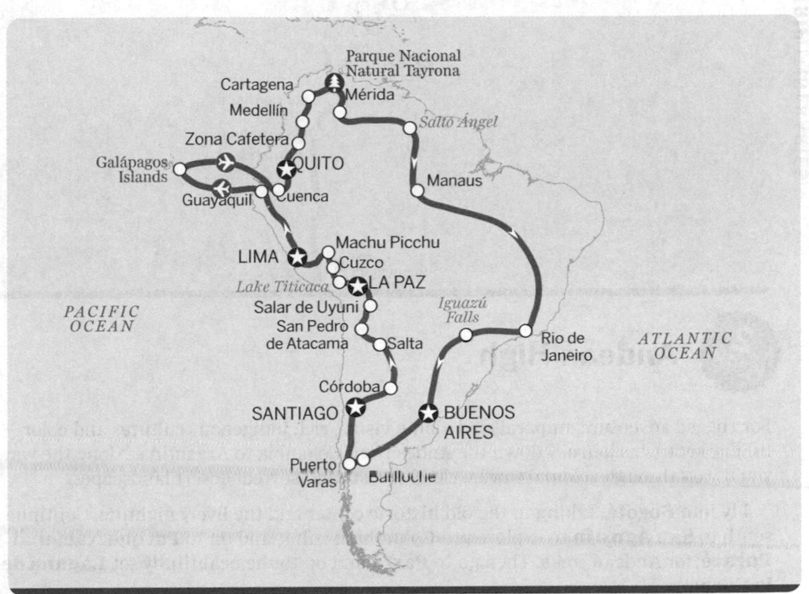

The Big Loop

This classic South American journey takes in some of the continent's most famous sites, including Andean peaks, Amazonian rainforest, Machu Picchu, Iguazú Falls and the Galápagos Islands.

Start off in **Buenos Aires**. Spend several days exploring the mesmerizing Argentine capital. Go west to **Bariloche** for spectacular scenery then head to Chile's verdant Lakes District at **Puerto Varas**. Continue north to **Santiago**, then cross back into Argentina to **Córdoba** and gorgeous **Salta** before re-entering Chile at the desert oasis of **San Pedro de Atacama**. Head into Bolivia to experience the surreal **Salar de Uyuni**. Continue to **La Paz** and on to Peru via **Lake Titicaca**. Linger at ancient **Cuzco** and **Machu Picchu** before going to **Lima** and on to Ecuador.

From **Guayaquil**, fly to the **Galápagos Islands**. Back on the mainland, visit colonial **Cuenca** and historic **Quito**. Pass into Colombia to the lush **Zona Cafetera** and bustling **Medellín**, then go to **Cartagena** for Caribbean allure. See beautiful **Parque Nacional Natural Tayrona** and relax in **Mérida**, Venezuela, before visiting **Salto Ángel**. Cross into Brazil and onto **Manaus** for a jungle trip. Afterwards fly down to **Rio de Janeiro** for beaches and nightlife. Visit thundering **Iguazú Falls** and return to Buenos Aires.

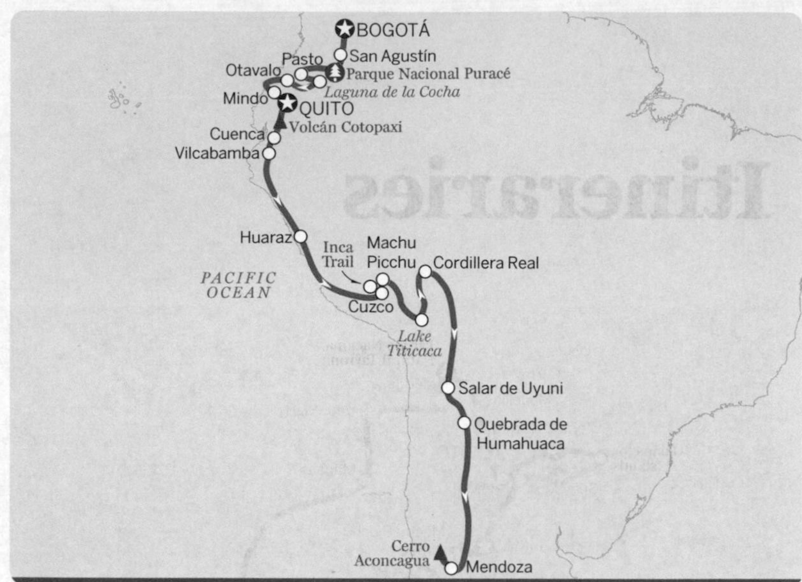

Andean High

For rugged adventure, unparalleled alpine vistas, rich indigenous cultures and colorful market towns journey down the Andes from Colombia to Argentina. Along the way, you'll pass through colonial towns, cloud forests and surreal desert landscapes.

Fly into **Bogotá**, taking in the old historic center and the lively nightlife. Continue south to **San Agustín** to explore pre-Columbian ruins, and on to **Parque Nacional Puracé**, for Andean treks. Then go to **Pasto** and on to the beautifully set **Laguna de la Cocha**.

Cross into Ecuador and visit **Otavalo**, for markets and day trips to alpine lakes. Head west to **Mindo** for misty cloud-forest adventures. Continue south through **Quito** and on to **Volcán Cotopaxi**, for hikes and majestic scenery.

Visit colonial **Cuenca**, relax in laid-back **Vilcabamba**, then continue into Peru and down to **Huaraz** for trekking in the Cordillera Blanca.

Spend a few days in **Cuzco**, then hike the **Inca Trail** to **Machu Picchu**. Head across shimmering **Lake Titicaca** into Bolivia for more hiking in the **Cordillera Real**. Continue south to the **Salar de Uyuni**, before crossing to Argentina by way of the spectacular **Quebrada de Humahuaca**.

Continue into Argentina toward enchanting **Mendoza**, near massive **Cerro Aconcagua**, the western hemisphere's highest peak.

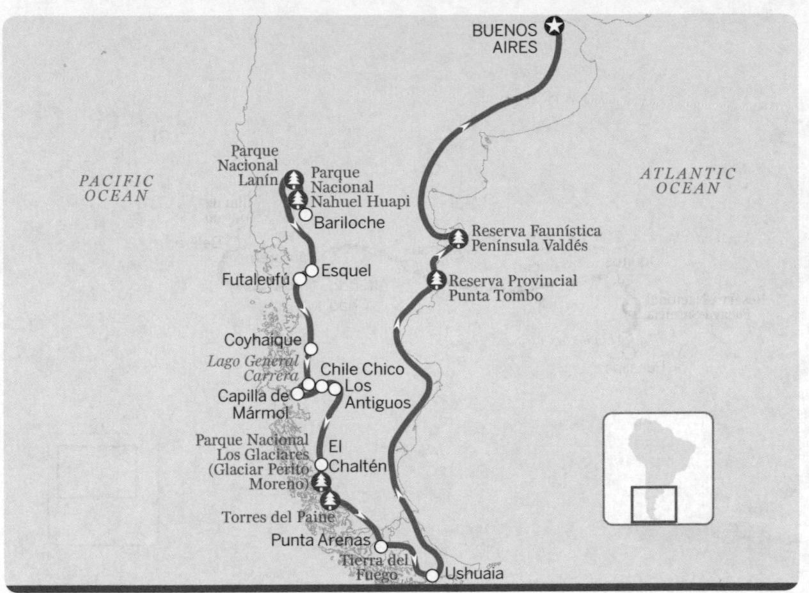

Deep South

Mysterious, windswept, glacier-riddled Patagonia is one of South America's most magical destinations. Patagonia – and the archipelago of Tierra del Fuego – is best visited November through March, and you can see more for cheaper if you camp.

Start in the outdoors-loving town of **Bariloche**. Take in the stunning **Parque Nacional Nahuel Huapi** and **Parque Nacional Lanín**. Head south to **Esquel**, for a taste of the Old Patagonian Express.

Travel west into Chile to the Andean hamlet of **Futaleufú** for outstanding rafting. Take the scenic Carretera Austral to **Coyhaique** and on to **Lago General Carrera**, and visit the caves of **Capilla de Mármol**. Head to windswept **Chile Chico**, then cross into Argentina to **Los Antiguos**.

Bounce down to **El Chaltén** in spectacular **Parque Nacional Los Glaciares**, and on to the wondrous **Glaciar Perito Moreno** near El Calafate.

Cross back into Chile at Puerto Natales to hike beneath the granite spires of **Torres del Paine**. Head to **Punta Arenas**, then south into Argentina's **Tierra del Fuego** and bottom out at edge-of-the-earth **Ushuaia**.

Travel north along the Atlantic, stopping for penguins in **Reserva Provincial Punta Tombo** and whales in **Reserva Faunística Península Valdés**. End the trip in **Buenos Aires**.

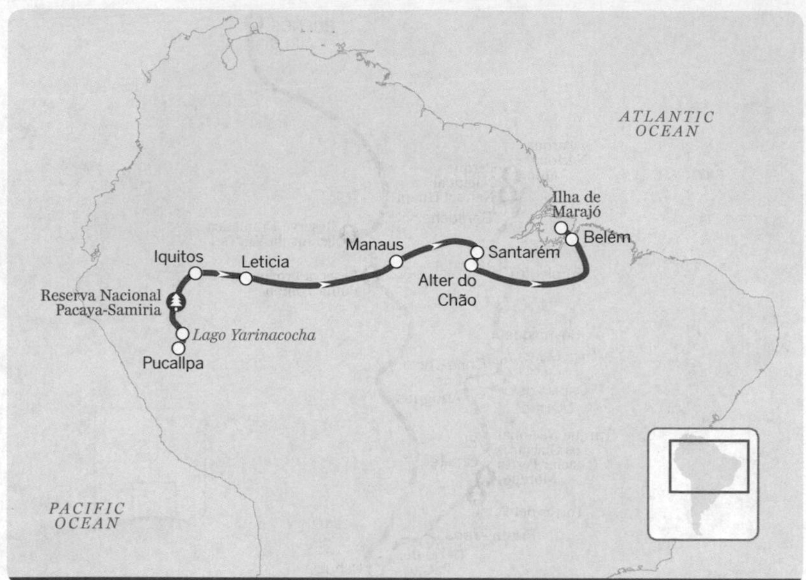

Sailing the Mighty Amazon

This tough but rewarding journey travels the length of the fabled Amazon, taking in wildlife-watching, historic cities and beautiful river beaches.

Start in **Pucallpa**, Peru (a flight or bus ride from Lima). Before hitting the river, visit nearby **Lago Yarinacocha**, a lovely oxbow lake ringed by tribal villages. From Pucallpa, begin the classic slow riverboat journey north along the Río Ucayali to Lagunas, where you can continue on to reach the wildlife-rich **Reserva Nacional Pacaya-Samiria**.

Afterwards, spend a day exploring the bustling city of **Iquitos**. From here, get a boat to the triborder region of Peru, Colombia and Brazil, and take a break in Colombia's **Leticia**.

From Leticia, it's three more arduous days to the bustling city of **Manaus**, which is famed for its 19th-century opera house and buzzing markets. This is also a great base for jungle excursions.

Chug east to **Santarém**, where you can visit the white-sand beaches of **Alter do Chão**. Another 3½ days further, and you'll reach culturally rich Belém, a good spot for sampling traditional Amazonian cuisine.

From here, cross over to **Ilha de Marajó**, a massive river island dotted with friendly towns, wandering buffaloes and pleasant beaches.

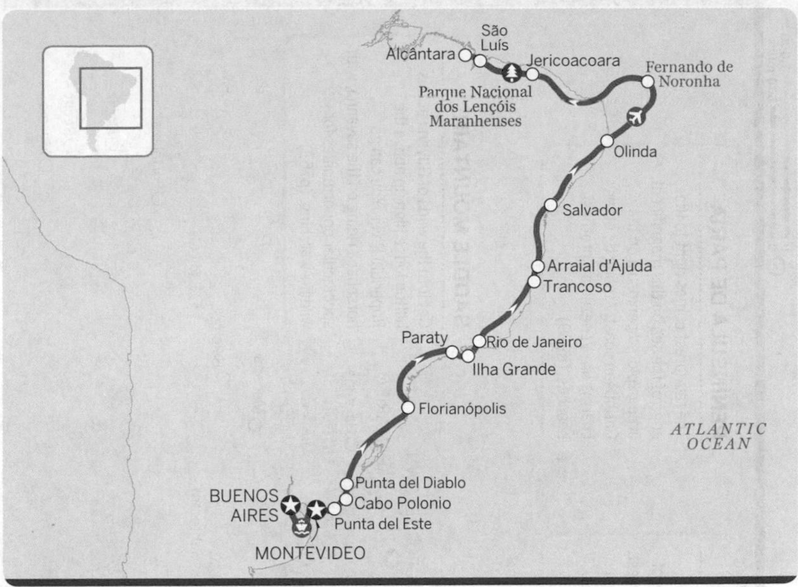

Atlantic Coast

Colonial towns, Afro-Brazilian culture, gorgeous beaches and buzzing nightlife set the stage for an epic 7400km ramble up the Atlantic coast. Surfing, snorkeling, forest treks and urban exploring are all essential experiences along the way.

Start off in Argentina, spending a few days taking in the charms of **Buenos Aires** before ferrying over to historic **Montevideo**. Follow Uruguay's coastline north through glitzy **Punta del Este**, dune-fringed **Cabo Polonio** and the laid-back beach town of **Punta del Diablo**.

Make your way to **Florianópolis**, gateway to secluded beaches and stunning scenery, then head up to the scenic colonial town of **Paraty**, and rainforest-covered **Ilha Grande**.

Continue to **Rio de Janeiro** for pretty beaches, lush scenery and samba-fueled nightlife. Fly to Porto Seguro and continue to **Trancoso** and **Arraial d'Ajuda** – both enticing, laid-back towns near cliff-backed beaches.

Spend a few days in **Salvador**, Brazil's mesmerizing Afro-Brazilian gem. Further up the coast, visit pretty **Olinda**, then catch a flight from Recife to the spectacular **Fernando de Noronha**.

Back on the mainland, travel north, stopping at the backpackers' paradise of **Jericoacoara** and the surreal dunes of **Parque Nacional dos Lençóis Maranhenses**. The final stops are reggae-charged **São Luís** and colonial **Alcântara**.

South America: Off the Beaten Track

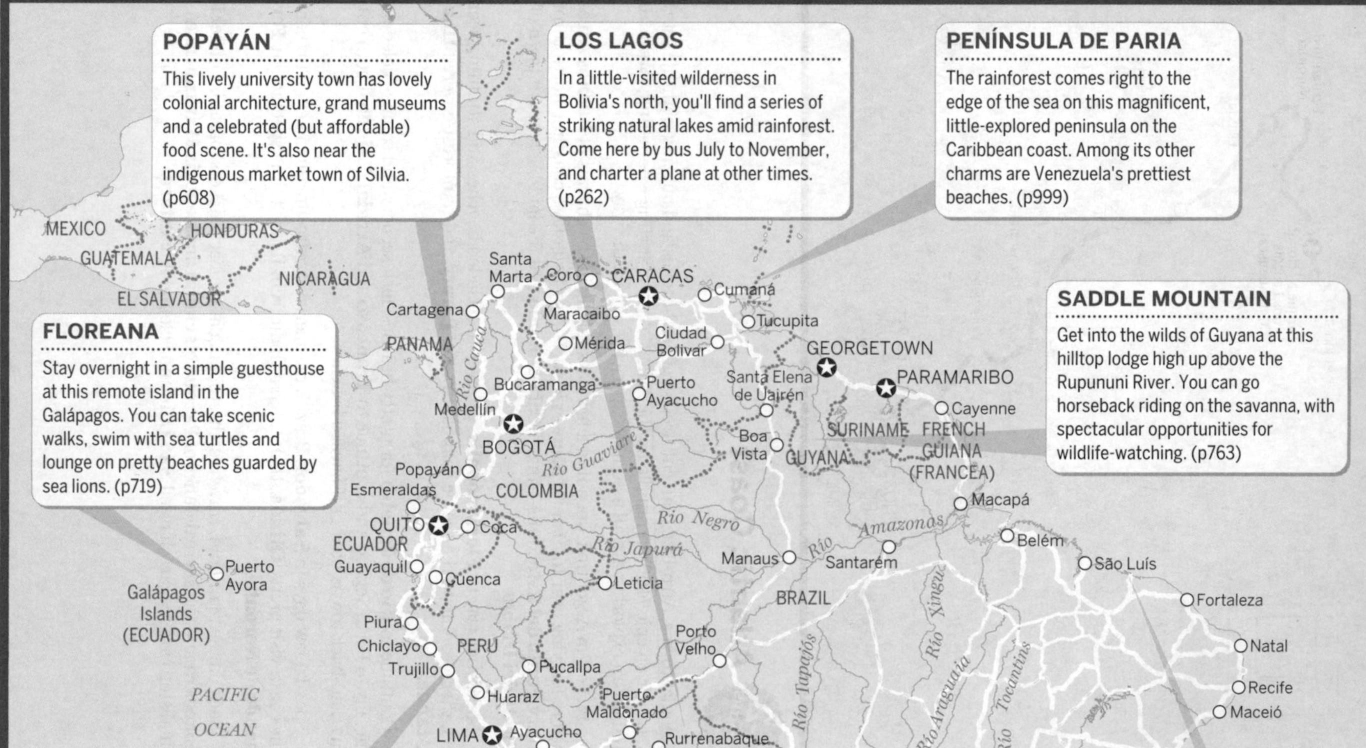

KUÉLAP

Escape the Machu Picchu crowds at this stunning pre-Columbian citadel in the north of Peru. You can make the most of the experience by overnighting at one of the basic guesthouses here. (p890)

THE CHACO

Paraguay's wild, dusty west teems with animal life. You can camp out under star-filled skies and spend your days spying macaws, otters, tapirs and countless other creatures. (p789)

PATAGONIA NATIONAL PARK

This gem of restored grasslands, rushing rivers and snowbound peaks is home to guanacos, flamingos, foxes and pumas, and has great infrastructure for camping and hiking. (p512)

PARQUE NACIONAL DOS LENÇÓIS MARANHENSES

Come between March and September to see this landscape at its most dramatic, when crystal-clear freshwater lagoons fill the hollows between high, undulating dunes. (p386)

Carnaval (p293), Rio de Janeiro, Brazil

Plan Your Trip

Big Adventures, Small Budget

In South America there are plenty of memorable experiences to be had even if you're traveling on a tiny budget. Frolicking on beaches, wildlife-watching and exploring captivating towns are some of the myriad ways to enjoy the continent on a shoestring. While deep pockets aren't a necessity, a bit of planning can help you make the most of the grand journey.

Planning & Costs

Planning Timeline

Twelve months before Calculate a trip budget and start saving.

Six months Pick which countries to visit, when and for how long.

Eight weeks Book flights. Renew your passport if it's expired or about to soon.

Six to four weeks Get vaccinations and travel insurance.

Four weeks Make visa and passport arrangements. Book specialty tours/accommodation (Amazon jungle lodges, Galápagos cruises).

Two weeks Reserve high-season accommodation for popular destinations.

One week Book accommodation for international arrival city; start packing.

Average Costs

Bottle of beer US$2–4

Fixed-price market lunch special US$3–6

Dorm bed US$10–20

Guesthouse bedroom for two from US$20

Long-distance bus ticket around US$1–2 per hour of travel

One-hour domestic flight from US$100

Cable-car ride up Pão de Açúcar US$18

White-water rafting on the Upper Napo River around US$65

When to Go

Before penciling in dates for your trip, take into consideration the regions you want to visit, and what you want to see when you're there. Rainy months in the Amazon and Pantanal should be avoided when planning a wildlife-watching expedition for instance. And once you get below the tropic line, you'll see much more dramatic seasonal fluctuations, with a very cold winter in Chile and Argentina (and even southern Brazil) and very hot summers.

Festivals & Holidays

Even if you're not planning a trip around a major festival, these events can affect your travel plans, so keep them in mind when designing your itinerary. The big one is Carnaval, which happens on the four days preceding Ash Wednesday. The biggest celebrations happen in Brazil, and you should pick where you want to be for a few days when it all goes down. Flights are expensive then, bus services crowded (with fewer runs), and banks and many other businesses will close. You'll also pay a premium for accommodations, with some places requiring minimum stays (four days is common). Brazil aside, Carnaval is celebrated in pretty much every other part of South America.

Another big event in the South American calendar is Semana Santa (Holy Week – the week leading up to Easter Sunday), when many people go on holiday. Students also have a two-week break in July, and many families travel at this time.

Beaches

It can be a challenge figuring out the perfect time to plan a beach getaway: getting warm weather (but not stiflingly hot) while still avoiding the worst of the crowds. Try to visit during shoulder seasons, which bookend (before and after) the hot, busy summer season. November and March (after Carnaval) can be great times to enjoy the beach with fewer crowds and lower prices.

In Brazil, the beaches in the far south (in the states of Santa Catarina and Rio Grande do Sul) have chilly weather, not conducive to swimming. Elsewhere, you'll find beach weather throughout the year. Rio has a handful of cooler, wintery days, but is mostly sunny and warm even in July (winter). The northeast has no winter (it's too hot!).

Jungle Trips

If you're heading into the Amazon, be mindful of the wet and dry seasons. Although it rains year-round (it's not called a 'rainforest' for nothing), the heaviest, longest downfalls happen from January to May. The dry season (and best time to visit) is from July to October. The Pantanal, which also has spectacular wildlife-watching opportunities, has nearly identical seasons, with the winter dry season from July to October and the heaviest rains from January to March. The Orinoco Basin of Venezuela has different wet and dry periods. The drier months from January to May are best for seeing wildlife.

Mountain Treks

In the Andes, the wettest months are from November to March. February can be the worst (and the Inca Trail is closed in this month). May through August are considered the best months for hikes in the Andes, with June and July being particularly pleasant – that said, they're also the busiest months, so consider coming in April, May, September or October.

Surfing

In Brazil you can surf all year round, though you'll have to chase the waves. In the north, you'll catch northern swells and the best conditions from November to March, particularly in Fernando de Noronha. In the south, April to November brings the best waves, when offshore winds and South Atlantic storms drive the swell to fine conditions all along the coast. In Argentina, the best waves are from April to June. Uruguay gets decent waves year-round, with waves the biggest in winter from June to August (although you'll need a good wetsuit then!).

On the Pacific side, things are a little different. All along Chile's coast you'll find excellent breaks, which are consistent all year long. Peru, meanwhile, gets its best waves in the winter months, with sizable swells from March through November.

Surfing at Ipanema Beach (p283), Brazil

TOURIST SEASONS

High season The busiest travel time for South Americans is during their summer, roughly from mid-December through late February. You should expect higher accommodation prices, bustling beach resorts and generally heavy crowds, especially at popular holiday destinations (all along the coast).

Shoulder season The pre-winter (April to May) and pre-summer months (October to November) can be great times to visit. You'll find lower prices and thinner crowds than during high season, but the weather can still be quite lovely for beach days and outdoor activities.

Low season From June through August, the southern half of the continent is quite cold. Resorts are closed and prices are lower in cities such as Buenos Aires, Santiago and Rio de Janeiro (apart from July, which is when locals have a winter break).

Skiing

To take advantage of the great powdery runs of the southern Andes, plan to visit Chile and Argentina during the ski season running from mid-June to mid-October. If you have to pick just one month, come in August, when the skiing is at its finest.

Skiing at Cerro Chapelco (p145), Argentina

The Galápagos

The islands have two distinct seasons, though the tourism high season is generally December to April, and July and August.

The warm and wet season runs from January to May, and is characterized by sunny days with strong but short periods of rain. The cool and dry season runs June to December. It's often known as the *garúa* for the misty precipitation that affects the highlands. While the air temperature is pleasant (averaging 22°C), the water is colder.

Budget Guide

Western currencies enjoy a favorable exchange rate in South America, giving you greater purchasing power. The cost of living is noticeably cheaper in most parts of the continent, and shoestringers can skimp their way to a budget of about US$40 a day. In the Andean countries, you can get by on as little as US$30 a day, but in pricier Chile and French Guiana, you may struggle to keep the daily budget below US$50. This covers the basics: food, shelter, local transportation and a few beers. This budget will vary not only by country but even regionally within a country (eg southeast Brazil versus cheaper northeast Brazil), the popularity of the destination and the time of year (high versus low season).

In addition to this base rate, factor in the costs of long-distance travel – by bus, boat or air. Add any special activities, such as diving, mountain biking, jungle trekking or a sightseeing tour. Then allow for unexpected expenses, such as increased costs for transportation or accommodations due to holidays or having to pay for a pricier room if the budget accommodations are booked up.

Accommodation costs occupy the largest portion of your budget. Generally, the continent has ample lodging options that charge simple prices. The more creature comforts (air-con, hot water, en suite) you can forsake, the more money you'll save. Bus and river transportation within each

DANIEL AGUILERA / GETTY IMAGES ©

Valparaíso (p441), Chile

country is generally affordable. Costs rise with air travel and wherever road conditions are rough, or require unique forms of transportation (dune buggies in parts of northeast Brazil, for instance).

Budget Tips

There are many ways to rack up some great memories in South America without putting a big ding in the budget. This country-by-country list gives a few places for you to start:

➡ **Argentina** With its fascinating blend of old and new, Córdoba makes for some worthwhile exploring. Grand architecture, free churches and galleries, affordable lodging options and cheap market dining all add to the appeal.

➡ **Bolivia** There are many great DIY adventures to be had in this enchanting country. A great base is Copacabana, where you can take boat trips out across Lake Titicaca to the Isla del Sol for some scenic hiking. By night you can feast on rainbow trout and lodge for under US$10 per night. For a fun, cheap experience in La Paz, the Botanical Garden is an oasis of quiet and costs B$2, and the *teleférico* (aerial cable car) is B$3. People-watching in Plaza Murillo or Plaza Avaroa is of course free. You can also talk to a shoeshine kid and arrange a cheap tour around the community.

➡ **Brazil** Rio de Janeiro doesn't have to be an expensive destination. There are hostels aplenty (from US$15 per night), cheap caipirinhas served right on the beach, and plenty of free amusements (forest walks up Morro da Urca, free exhibitions at Centro Cultural Banco do Brasil and great people-watching at the outdoor street party in Lapa on weekends).

➡ **Chile** It's easy to fall for the bohemian charms of Valparaíso. There are fascinating cobblestone neighborhoods to explore, with great bay views lurking around every corner. This student-loving town also has great eating and drinking spots that are quite budget friendly.

➡ **Colombia** It's hard to beat the beauty of the Caribbean coast, especially around Parque Nacional Natural Tayrona. You can sleep in a hammock near Arrecifes and spend the day scouting gorgeous coves and sparkling beaches.

➡ **Ecuador** In Baños, you can take a scenic DIY bike ride from highland to jungle, stopping at waterfalls along the way. In the evening, recover with a soak in the hot springs followed by dinner and microbrews at one of the town's enticing eateries.

➡ **French Guiana** Spend time exploring the culturally rich town of Cayenne. Don't miss the buzzing central market with its mishmash of African, Amerindian and European elements. Vietnamese vendors serve up the best *pho* (noodle soup) on the continent.

➡ **Guyana** Base yourself in the Africa-like savanna of North Rupununi. You can stay in a rustic hut on a jungle island and visit indigenous villages, and go forest trekking, fishing and caiman-spotting.

➡ **Paraguay** A city on the make, Encarnación has a lovely waterfront promenade, an enticing river beach, and cheap and tasty *lomito Arabe* – a kind of Paraguayan-style kebab.

➡ **Peru** If you've been traveling hard for a few weeks, Cuzco is a great place for some R&R. Walking the ancient streets past stunning Inca architecture and taking in its grand plazas and picturesque views won't cost a penny. It's also an excellent town for meeting other travelers.

➡ **Suriname** Take in Paramaribo's wooden Dutch colonial architecture then feast on

Above: Cabo San Juan de la Guía (p571), Parque Nacional Natural Tayrona, Colombia

Right: Escalera del Inca (p213), Isla del Sol, Bolivia

delicacies from the East (thanks to Suriname's immigrants): try Javanese rice dishes, Chinese dumplings and Indian roti – plus hearty, rich Creole cooking.

➡ **Uruguay** One of the prettiest beach towns on the Atlantic Coast, the Punta del Diablo has an easy-going vibe and laid-back guesthouses, beachfront bars and fireside parties on the sands.

➡ **Venezuela** Your dollars go far in the Ciudad Bolívar, a riverside town with a charming colonial center. This is also the launch pad for treks to the jaw-dropping Salto Ángel, the highest waterfall on earth. Mérida has the continent's cheapest activities and extreme sports, including paragliding and mountain climbing. Multiday tours are also great value, whether you're heading to Los Llanos or the Orinoco Delta.

Sticking to a Budget

➡ Slow down: stick around and enjoy a place rather than rushing off to the next destination. The further and faster you go, the more you'll pay.

➡ Eat like a local at street stalls or markets.

➡ Opt for dorm rooms or share a room with a buddy.

➡ Stay in fan (non-air-con) rooms with shared bathroom.

➡ Travel overland instead of flying.

➡ Book flights online (and bus tickets where possible) rather than paying a travel agent's commission.

➡ Snorkel instead of dive.

➡ Stick to small towns instead of big cities.

➡ Be discriminating about which sites and national parks to visit.

➡ Factor in more free days: on the beach and exploring neighborhoods.

➡ Avoid package deals (transportation, lodging, touring).

➡ Know how much local transportation should cost and bargain accordingly.

➡ Avoid surprises by negotiating taxi fares before getting inside.

➡ Don't forget to factor in the costs of visas.

➡ Do souvenir shopping at the end of your trip with surplus funds.

➡ Track all of your daily expenses so you know your average costs.

Accommodation Tips

Lodging will be one of your biggest expenses. Here are some tips for keeping sleeping costs down:

➡ If the price is too high, ask if the hotel or guesthouse has anything cheaper.

➡ Unless it is the low season, most rates are non-negotiable – though it never hurts to ask for a discounted price.

➡ Once you've paid for a room, there is little chance of a refund, regardless of the size of the cockroach that scurried across the floor.

➡ Pay for the first day rather than for multiple days all at once. This gives you the option of changing hotels if the conditions are unsuitable.

➡ However, if you do decide you are going to stay for a few days, ask for a discount. Some hotels will give better rates if you're staying more than a couple of nights.

➡ Advance reservations (especially with advance deposits) are generally not necessary.

➡ If you do make a booking, don't rely on an agent, who will charge a commission.

Packing

Take as little as possible because you're going to have to carry it everywhere. Pack your bag once and then repack it with a third less stuff. Repeat until your pack is small enough to fit into the aircraft's overhead locker. The smaller your pack the easier it will be to climb on and off public transportation (which doesn't always come to a complete stop), the easier it will be to walk if taxi drivers are asking too much money, and you'll look like less of a target for touts and hustlers.

Going with Gadgets

More and more travelers are taking multiple gadgets – phones, tablets, laptops, cameras – with them on their trips, but the risk of theft or damage is high. South America poses a mix of hot and icy temperatures, bags get dropped or tossed, thieves and pickpockets want what you

Paragliding near Mérida (p990), Venezuela

have, and you or your stuff could easily get caught in a rainstorm long enough for a short-circuit.

However, it is wise to travel with at least some form of wi-fi-enabled device so you communicate with people back home (via email, Skype etc). Don't rely on internet cafes, which have largely disappeared from most South American towns.

Here are some tips for traveling smart with technology:

- Limit yourself to one or two versatile devices: a tablet or iPad that can read books and check emails or a smartphone that can do it all
- Store your electronics in dry packs and separate the batteries in case of rain.
- Get a travel-insurance policy that covers theft or damage to your equipment.
- Sign up for WhatsApp or another messaging service so you can communicate with locals and travelers you meet on the road.

Plan Your Trip
Activities

There's a whole range of adventures awaiting in South America. You can go hiking amid the soaring peaks of the Andes, go rafting along rushing jungle-lined rivers and overnight in a rainforest lodge with the sounds of the Amazon all around you. And you'll find many more astounding options in every country on the continent.

Best Outdoors

Exploring the Atacama, Chile

Scale massive dunes, admire petroglyphs and question the shimmering visions of oases.

Climbing a volcano, Ecuador

Volcán Cotopaxi (5897m) provides a fantastic view for those fit enough to make the summit.

Hiking Cañón del Colca, Peru

Andean condors glide over this rugged canyon in Peru, the second deepest in the world.

Wildlife-watching in the Amazon

Seeing monkeys, macaws, capybara, caimans, toucans and dozens of other species while based in a jungle lodge (such as Brazil's Mamirauá Reserve).

Trekking to the Lost City, Colombia

This fabulous four- to six-day journey will earn you bragging rights. After a challenging 44km-long walk through jungle you'll arive at the remarkably preserved ruins of the lost city of Tayrona.

Mountain biking the World's Most Dangerous Road, Bolivia

The name says it all in this dramatic Andean descent. Check your brakes before departing!

White-water rafting, Chile

Rushing down thundering rapids in Patagonia's Futaleufú Rio.

Hiking

The opportunities for hiking are practically limitless. Stunning scenery is a guarantee wherever you go, with snow-covered peaks, cloud forests and verdant lowland jungle setting the stage for hiking and wildlife-watching.

The Andean countries are famous for their old Inca roads, which are ready-made for scenic excursions. The overtrodden, four-day tramp along the Inca Trail to Machu Picchu is, of course, the classic, but alternative routes are more highly recommended because they are cheaper, less traveled, more scenic and less destructive. Other possibilities around Cuzco include the spectacular six-day trek around the venerated Ausangate (6372m), which will take you over 5000m passes, through huge herds of alpacas and past tiny hamlets unchanged in centuries.

There are other treks along Inca trails as well, including Ecuador's lesser-known Inca trail to Ingapirca, and numerous trails along ancient Inca routes through Bolivia's Cordilleras to the Yungas.

There are lots of great places to hike in Brazil, both in the national and state parks and along the coastline. In Bahia, the Parque Nacional da Chapada Diamantina has spectacular day hikes and multiday treks; Lençóis is a good base. Other highlights are the parks around Cambara do Sul, and the Chapada Guimarães and Chapada Veaderos.

Colombia has some outstanding trekking opportunities. The casual hiker looking for good one-day walks also has many options to choose from – most of which, such as Laguna Verde and Valle de Cocora, can be done independently without a guide.

The national parks of southern South America, including Chile's Torres del Paine, those within the Argentine Lake District, and even Argentina's storm-pounded but spectacular Fitz Roy range, are superb and blessed with excellent trail infrastructure and accessibility. And for getting well off the beaten path, northern Patagonia in Chile has some excellent treks.

Lesser-known mountain ranges, such as Colombia's Sierra Nevada de Santa Marta (for the Ciudad Perdida) and Venezuela's Sierra Nevada de Mérida, also have great potential. The two- to three-day hike to the top of Venezuela's Roraima is one of the continent's most unforgettable experiences. Colombia's Parque Nacional El Cocuy is also a great site for nontechnical trekking among glaciers.

BE PREPARED

Many trails in South America are poorly marked or not marked at all. Trekkers should always inquire ahead, as navigation may be a major component of hiking and many travelers come unprepared. When it comes to packing, quality mountain gear is a must. Even in summer the Andes can have extreme temperatures—summer sleeping bags and nonwaterproof gear will not work!

Top Destinations

Peru The main trekking centers are Cuzco and Arequipa in the southern Andes, and Huaraz in the north. Hikers will find many easily accessible trails around Peru's archaeological ruins, which are also the final destinations for more challenging trekking routes. From Arequipa, you can get down in some of the world's deepest canyons – the world-famous Cañón del Colca and the Cañón del Cotahuasi. Outside Huaraz, the Cordillera Blanca can't be beat for vistas of rocky, snowcapped mountaintops, while the remote and rugged Cordillera Huayhuash is similarly stunning. The classic and favorite trekking route is the four-day journey from Llanganuco to Santa Cruz, where hardy mountaineers climb the 4760m Punta Union pass, surrounded by ice-clad peaks.

Argentina The Lakes District offers outstanding day and multiday hikes in several national parks, including Nahuel Huapi and Lanín. For Patagonia, El Bolsón is an excellent base for hiking both in the forests outside of town and in nearby Parque Nacional Lago Puelo. Parque Nacional Los Glaciares offers wonderful hiking in and around the Fitz Roy range; base yourself in El Chaltén and wait out the storms.

Chile Head to Parque Nacional Torres del Paine in Patagonia for epic hiking. For awe-inspiring isolation, Tierra del Fuego's Dientes de Navarino hiking circuit is also stunning but harder to access.

Colombia On the Caribbean coast, the long trek to the Ciudad Perdida (Lost City) involves a sweaty, multiday hike through the jungle and across waist-high rivers. In PNN El Cocuy, you'll find a dozen 5000m-high peaks and phenomenal high-altitude landscapes. Parque Nacional Natural (PNN) Tayrona offers accessible short hikes through tropical dry forest with the opportunity to eat, drink and swim along the way.

Ecuador Near the dramatic topaz crater lake of Quilotoa there are some excellent hikes including village-to-village trips and a few shortcuts through high-altitude canyons. One excellent DIY route goes from Quilotoa to Isinliví, overnighting in Chugchilán along the way.

Venezuela Aside from the spectacular journey to Roraima, Venezuela has some great Andean treks near Mérida. There's also good hiking near Caracas Parque Nacional El Ávila, just north of the city.

Wildlife-Watching

The number of creatures great and small reaches epic proportions in the land of cloud forests, Andean mountains and Amazon rainforest. Whether you're an avid bird-watcher or just want to see monkeys in the wild, South America is hard to top. Its biodiversity is staggering.

Brazil has superb places for seeing wildlife. You can look for toucans, sloths, river dolphins and various monkey species at a jungle lodge in the Amazon. Odds are higher that you'll see even more species in the Pantanal, an extensive wetlands area that can also be accessed from Bolivia or Paraguay.

Speaking of Bolivia, Parque Nacional Madidi harbors over 1000 bird species as well as wildlife endemic to the majority of Bolivia's ecosystems, from tropical rainforest and savanna to cloud forest and alpine tundra. Agencies, often run by scientists or environmentalists, run nature trips out of Santa Cruz, Cochabamba and Samaipata and, to a lesser extent, La Paz.

Peru boasts a spectacular variety of plant and animal life. In the expansive Parque Nacional Manu, jaguars, tapirs and monkeys inhabit one of the continent's wildest rainforest reserves. On the Islas Ballestas, colonies of honking sea lions and penguins claim these rocky Pacific outcrops off Peru's south coast.

Clocking in at over 1900 bird species, Colombia is the world's number-one country in bird diversity and easily holds its own against Peru and Brazil in endemic species. The Andean mountains are full of hummingbirds (more than 160 species); the Amazonian jungle is full of toucans, parrots and macaws; and PNN Puracé, near Popayán, is home to condors. The single-best bird-watching spot in the country is Montezuma Peak, located inside PNN Tatamá in the Cordillera Occidental.

Despite its small size, Ecuador has amazingly diverse wildlife. Birdwatchers should head to the cloud forests around Mindo. The lower Río Napo region of the Amazon has even more biological diversity. And of course, the Galápagos are simply extraordinary in every way.

Mountain Biking

From a leisurely ride around enchanting lowland scenery to bombing down smouldering volcanoes, South America has some exciting destinations for mountain bikers. The Andes are blessed with some of the most dramatic mountain-biking terrain in the world, and offer relatively easy access to mountain ranges, magnificent lakes, precolonial ruins and trails, and myriad eco-zones connected by an extensive network of footpaths and jeep roads. Mountain bikes are widely available for hire, though quality varies considerably. Make a thorough inspection of key components (brakes, tires, gears) before committing. For longer multiday trips, it's better to bring your own bike.

Peru There is no shortage of incredible terrain. Single-track trails ranging from easy to expert

ALTERNATIVE ADVENTURES

If you can dream it up, you can probably make it happen in South America. Whether you want to hang glide over rainforest or board down towering sand dunes, the continent has you covered.

Sandboarding Be prepared to get sand in places you never imagined possible. Try it in Argentina at San Pedro de Atacama or Iquique, or in Peru around Nazca.

Whale-watching With an annual population of around 400 humpback whales, Puerto López (Ecuador) is considered the epicenter of whale breeding grounds. Numerous boat operators ply the waters from June to September.

Hang-gliding The 10-minute descent from Pedra Bonita to a beachside landing in Rio de Janeiro is pure magic (or terror, depending on your fear threshold).

Horse riding In San Agustín (Colombia) you can travel between remote pre-Columbian monuments in stunning natural settings.

Dog sledding You can't say you've done it all until you've tried dog sledding. Argentina's a great place to start, with operators near Caviahue, San Martín de los Andes and Ushuaia.

Land sailing Near Barreal (Argentina) you can zip across a dry lake bed beneath Andean peaks in so-called sail cars.

Lightning-watching In Venezuela, you can gaze at an amazing permanent lighting storm where the Río Catatumbo flows into the Lago de Maracaibo.

await mountain bikers outside Huaraz, Arequipa and even Lima. If you're experienced, there are incredible mountain-biking possibilities around the Sacred Valley and downhill trips to the Amazon jungle, all accessible from Cuzco. Easier cycling routes include the wine country around Lunahuaná and in the Cañón del Colca, starting from Chivay.

Colombia Mountain biking is most popular in San Gil and Villa de Leyva, where several adventure companies and bike-rental shops can facilitate your adrenaline fix.

Bolivia One of the world's longest downhill rides will take you from Parque Nacional Sajama down to the Chilean coast at Arica. More famous is the thrilling 3600m trip down the World's Most Dangerous Road from La Cumbre to Coroico. Another popular route near La Paz is the lush Zongo Valley ride, which can be started from Chacaltaya (5395m).

Chile A favorite mountain-biking destination in the north is San Pedro de Atacama. Fabulous trips in the Lakes District access pristine areas with limited public transportation. The new bike lane around Lago Llanquihue is very popular, as is the Ojos de Caburgua loop near Pucón.

Argentina At outdoor hot spots you can rent a mountain bike for a day of independent pedaling or for guided mountain-bike rides. Good bases include San Martín de los Andes, Villa la Angostura, Bariloche and El Bolsón in the Lake District; Esquel in Patagonia; Mendoza and Uspallata in Mendoza province; Barreal in San Juan province; Tilcara in the Andean Northwest and Tandil in La Pampa province.

Ecuador It's hard to beat the adrenaline-charged downhills on the flanks of Cotopaxi and Chimborazo. From Baños, you can travel 'La Ruta de las Cascadas' (Highway of the Waterfalls), a 61km (mostly) downhill ride to Puyo, with some refreshing dips in waterfalls along the way.

Mountaineering

On a continent with one of the world's greatest mountain ranges, climbing opportunities are almost unlimited. Ecuador's volcanoes, the high peaks of Peru's Cordillera Blanca and Cordillera Huayhuash, Bolivia's Cordillera Real and Argentina's Aconcagua (6960m; the Western Hemisphere's highest peak) all offer outstanding mountaineering opportunities. Despite its relatively low elevation, Argentina's Fitz Roy range – home to Cerro Torre, one of the world's most challenging peaks – chalks in as a major climbing destination. The Venezuelan Andes are no less appealing: Pico Bolívar is the most popular destination, but there are many other peaks you can summit around Mérida.

The Andes are a mountaineer's dream, especially in the San Juan and Mendoza provinces, where some of the highest peaks in the Western Hemisphere are found. While the most famous climb is Aconcagua, there are plenty of others that are more interesting and far more technical. Near Barreal, the Cordón de la Ramada boasts five peaks over 6000m, including the mammoth Cerro Mercedario, which tops out at 6770m. The region is less congested than Aconcagua, offers more technical climbs and is preferred by many climbers. Also near here is the majestic Cordillera de Ansilta, with seven peaks scraping the sky at between 5130m and 5885m.

The magnificent and challenging Fitz Roy range, in southern Patagonia near El Chaltén, is one of the world's top mountaineering destinations, while the mountains of Parque Nacional Nahuel Huapi offer fun for all levels.

River Rafting

You'll find churning white water all over the continent. The settings are spectacular: splashing through deep canyons or pounding down the forest-lined banks of a Class IV rapid.

Ecuador boasts world-class river rafting and kayaking. Some of the rivers offer up to 100km of continuous Class III to Class IV white water before flattening out to flow toward the Pacific on one side of the Andes and into the Amazon Basin on the other. Tena is Ecuador's de facto white-water capital, with the nearby upper Río Napo (Class III+) and the Río Misahuallí (Class IV+) among the country's best-known rivers.

The wealth of scenic rivers, lakes, fjords and inlets in southern Chile make it a dream destination. Chile's rivers, raging through narrow canyons from the Andes, are world class. Northern Patagonia's

Futaleufú River offers memorable Class IV and V runs. Less technical runs include those outside Pucón and the beautiful Petrohué, near Puerto Varas, as well as Aisén's Río Simpson and Río Baker. Near Santiago, the Cajón del Maipo offers a gentle but enjoyable run.

In Peru, Cuzco is the launch point for the greatest variety of river-running options. Choices range from a few hours of mild rafting on the Urubamba to adrenaline-pumping rides on the Santa Teresa to several days on the Apurímac, technically the source of the Amazon. A river-running trip on the Tambopata, available from June through October, tumbles down the eastern slopes of the Andes, culminating in a couple of days of floating in unspoiled rainforest. River running is also possible on the Río Cañete south of Lima, and in the canyon country around Arequipa, in Peru.

In Argentina, several rivers around Bariloche and Mendoza are worth getting wet in. In Colombia, the Río Suárez near San Gil has decent runs.

Surfing

Brazil is South America's best-known surfing destination, with great breaks near Rio and in the southeast, and sprinkled all along the coast from Santa Catarina to São Luís. If you've got the cash, the surfing in Fernando de Noronha is spectacular.

In Peru, national championships are held at Punta Rocas as well as Pico Alto, an experts-only 'kamikaze' reef break with some of the largest waves in Peru. Peru's north coast has a string of excellent breaks. The most famous is Puerto Chicama, where rides of more than 2km are possible on what's considered the longest left-hand break in the world.

With breaks lining the long Pacific Coast, Chile nurtures some serious surf culture, most active in middle and northern Chile; you'll need a wetsuit. With big breaks and long left-handers, surf capital Pichilemu hosts the national surfing championship. Pilgrims crowd the perfect left break at Pichilemu's Punta de Lobos, but beginners can also have a go nearby at La Puntilla. The coastal Ruta 1 is lined with waves.

Ecuador's best breaks are off Isla San Cristóbal in the Galápagos. On the mainland, Montañita, has a fast, powerful reef-break that can cough up some of the mainland's best barrels.

You'll also find good waves in Mar del Plata (Argentina) and Uruguay. In Venezuela, there's great kitesurfing in Adicora and Margarita.

Skiing & Snowboarding

Powder junkies rejoice. From June to September world-class resorts in the Chilean and Argentine Andes offer myriad possibilities for skiing, snowboarding and even heliskiing. Don't expect too many bargains; resorts are priced to match their quality. 'First descents' of Chilean Patagonia's numerous mountains is a growing (but limited) trend.

Most resorts are within an hour's drive of Santiago, including a wide variety of runs at family-oriented La Parva, all-levels El Colorado, and Valle Nevado, with a lot of terrain and renowned heliskiing. Legendary Portillo, the site of several downhill speed records and the summer training base for many of the Northern Hemisphere's top skiers, is northeast of Santiago near the Argentine border crossing to Mendoza.

Termas de Chillán, just east of Chillán, is a more laid-back spot with several beginners' slopes, while Parque Nacional Villarrica, near the resort town of Pucón, has the added thrill of skiing on a smoking volcano. On Volcán Lonquimay, Corralco has great novice and expert terrain, as well as excellent backcountry access. Volcanoes Osorno and Antillanca, east of Osorno, have open terrain with incredible views and a family atmosphere.

In Argentina, there are three main snow-sport areas: Mendoza, the Lake District and Ushuaia. Mendoza is near Argentina's premier resort, Las Leñas, which has the best snow and longest runs; the resort Los Penitentes is also nearby. The Lake District is home to several low-key resorts, including Cerro Catedral, near Bariloche, and Cerro Chapelco, near San Martín de los Andes.

Countries at a Glance

Thirteen countries strong, South America is home to astounding natural and cultural wonders. The challenge is deciding where to begin. Peru, Bolivia, Ecuador and Colombia offer affordable adventures: climbing Andean peaks, trekking through cloud forests and visiting remote indigenous villages. Brazil is the land of magnificent beaches, outstanding nightlife and unforgettable journeys, from slow-boating down the Amazon to dune buggy rides across the northeast. Chile and Argentina harbor fantastic alpine adventures, picturesque coastlines and the rugged wilderness of Patagonia. For off-the-beaten-path travel, explore the jungle-lined interior of French Guiana and Guyana. All over the continent you'll find colonial towns and laid-back seaside villages – just the antidote after a few days (or weeks) of taking in South America's jaw-dropping sights.

Argentina

Big Cities
Scenery
Outdoors

Urban Allure

Buenos Aires is a scintillating metropolis of steamy tango halls, old-world cafes and hip boutiques. Córdoba boasts a flourishing arts scene, while Mendoza draws adventure seekers.

Natural Wonders

The Moreno glacier is awe-inspiring. The Peninsula Valdes is home to whales, penguins and other wildlife. Witness spectacular rock formations in Quebrada de Humahuaca and nature's raw power at Iguazú Falls.

Outdoor Adventure

You'll find magnificent hiking in Patagonia, the Mendoza area and the Lake District, white-water rafting near Bariloche and Mendoza, and skiing at Las Leñas and Cerro Catedral.

p54

Bolivia

Scenery
Trekking
Wildlife

Stunning Vistas

As you travel across this remarkable remote wilderness, you'll marvel at the world's largest salt flat, whimsical rock formations, cacti-encrusted valleys straight out of the Old West, volcanic peaks, Technicolor lakes and a sky that seems to stretch forever.

Inca Trails

For long hauls and shorter day trips along ancient Inca paving, down cloud-encased valleys and through vast swaths of wilderness, you can't beat Bolivia's treks.

Wild Explorer

Nature is everywhere, making Bolivia a hands-down favorite for nature lovers. A series of large national parks and nature preserves protect (to a certain degree) the country's endemic and at-risk species.

p188

Brazil

Beaches
Wildlife
Culture

Captivating Coastlines

Synonymous with paradise, Brazil boasts nearly 7500km of perfect-palmed coastline to prove it. For idyllic sands, start with Fernando de Noronha, Bahia and Ceará.

Unrivaled Biodiversity

The world's most biodiverse country is home to a lifetime's worth of wildlife, most famously found in the Amazon and the Pantanal, but from Bonito to Belém, you'll be floored.

The Melting Pot

Portuguese colonists; Japanese, African, Arab and European immigrants; and a healthy indigenous population shaped the Brazil melting pot. From food to film, *isso é Brasil* (this is Brazil)!

p281

Chile

Outdoors
Landscapes
Wine & Pisco

Trekking in Chilean Patagonia

Strong winds, sudden rain, rustic *refugios* (shelters) and striking landscapes – hiking the classic 'W' is an unforgettable adventure in Torres del Paine.

Dreamy Desertscapes

The driest desert in the world, the Atacama is an otherworldly place of salt caves, eerie moonlike surfaces and powerful geysers circled by snow-tipped volcanoes.

House of Spirits (and Wine)

Chile is still battling Peru over the ownership of *pisco;* here, the potent grape brandy is produced in Valle Elqui. But no one can contest Chile's mastery of Carmenere, a full-bodied red wine – it's the toast of the nation.

p422

Colombia

Landscapes
Outdoors
Coffee

Nature's Bounty

From the towering sand dunes near Punta Gallinas to the glaciers of Parque Nacional El Cocuy and flooded forests of the Amazon, Colombia's phenomenal landscapes make for your very own nature documentary.

Endless Excitement

The small city of San Gil is a one-stop adventure playground with rafting, climbing, paragliding and more – just a fraction of the adventures on offer around the country to keep your adrenaline pumping.

Black Gold

Learn to pick and grade coffee beans (and sample the final product) at award-winning plantations around Manizales and Armenia in the Zona Cafetera.

p540

Ecuador

Architecture
Landscapes
Ecotourism

Cultural Exploration

The picturesque colonial centers of Quito and Cuenca are packed with architectural treasures. Quito and Guayaquil have outstanding collections of pre-Columbian art and modern works by Oswaldo Guayasamín.

Dramatic Vistas

Get a taste of the Amazon in jungle lodges, and stunning Andean scenery in Quilotoa. If money allows, take a cruise around the other-worldly Galápagos.

Ecotourism

Top ways to experience the great outdoors include climbing Andean peaks (Cotopaxi is popular), mountain biking down them (try Chimborazo), ecotourism in the cloud forests of Mindo and white-water rafting near Tena.

p634

French Guiana

History
Cuisine
Wildlife

Haunted Prisons

Between 1852 and 1938 around 70,000 prisoners were sent to French Guiana from France. Today, the old structures are eerily crumbling into the jungles; the most interesting are offshore on the relaxing Îles du Salut.

Spicy Mix

African, Hmong, French, Javanese and Brazilian culinary traditions plus local spices and fresh jungle produce equals the most interesting food in the region.

Turtles, Birds & Caimans

Look for caimans and the brilliant scarlet ibis on a wildlife-watching tour in the Kaw Nature Reserve. Or take a trip to the coast in turtle season to watch crowds of turtles laying eggs in the sand.

p733

Guyana

Wildlife
Culture
Architecture

Amazonian Monsters

You want big? Track the world's largest scaled freshwater fish (arapaima), anteaters, caimans and more. The best part: they're all relatively easy to find.

Amerindian Eco-Trail

Hop from one village-run Amerindian lodge to the next through the Rupununi Savannahs. Birdwatch and learn to shoot a bow and arrow while supporting sustainable businesses.

Dilapidated Gems

Nothing is shined up in colonial Georgetown, but that's part of its charm. Marvel at the ingenious natural cooling system even as the paint seems to chip off before your eyes.

p750

Paraguay

History
Culture
Wildlife

Colonial Relics

The Jesuit revolution began and ended in the jungles of eastern Paraguay, and though the social experiment is gone, the wonderful churches the Jesuits left behind stand in silent testament.

Indigenous Influences

Paraguayan culture has been shaped by a history of corrupt dictatorships and a strong indigenous influence, a cultural cocktail that makes it a strange and fascinating country to explore.

Biodiversity in the Chaco

Paraguay's arid Chaco positively teems with wildlife, and though the dusty surroundings look inhospitable, it's arguably the best place to see big animals such as tapir, puma and the endangered Chaco peccary.

p768

Peru

Culture
Ruins
Landscapes

Indigenous Lore

In Peru, culture isn't something you enter a dusty museum to find. It's all around you. The strong traditions of indigenous cultures are easily witnessed in many religious or seasonal festivals.

Civilization of the Incas

From the heights of Machu Picchu to the cloud forest of Kuélap, Peru's ruins garner due fame, but that doesn't always mean crowds. Many are reached by gorgeous hikes, attractions in their own right.

The Andes to the Amazon

From the ample sands of the coast to verdant Amazonian rainforest, lost canyon villages and the majestic peaks of the Cordillera Blanca, Peru features stark and stunning scenery.

p801

Suriname

Culture
Wildlife
Architecture

Maroon Adventures

Boat down the Upper Suriname River to find myriad lodges run by Maroon tribes who have retained a distinctive African-Amazonian culture. Lodging ranges from luxurious bungalows to simple hammock shelters.

Vast Jungles

Deep in the Central Suriname Nature Reserve you'll see troupes of monkeys, tons of birds, caimans and maybe even a jaguar or harpy eagle.

Unesco City

Paramaribo's heritage district is unlike anywhere else in the world. Imagine colonial Dutch lines in a Wild West setting doused in all the colors and culture of the Caribbean.

p913

Uruguay

Beaches
Architecture
Landscapes

Sun, Sand & Surf

With over 300km of quality coastline, Uruguay pretty much guarantees you'll find a spot to lay your towel.

Colonial Riches

Colonia del Sacramento's the superstar, of course, and Montevideo's Old Town has its fans, too. But visit pretty much any plaza in the country for gorgeous Spanish-influenced streetscapes.

Inland Adventures

While everyone's chuckling it up beachside, those in the know head for Uruguay's interior – a beautiful rolling hillscape that's the epitome of getting off the gringo trail.

p929

Venezuela

Beaches
Outdoors
Wildlife

Caribbean Beauty

Venezuela has some mighty enticing beaches. A few seaside getaways include the pristine island of Los Roques, colonial Puerto Colombia and the lush Península de Paria.

Adrenaline Rush

Take your pick from surfing the sand dunes near Coro, kitesurfing along the Caribbean or paragliding in Mérida. Or grab your pack and summit the mysterious Roraima *tepui* (plateau).

All Creatures Great & Small

From bird-watching in Parque Nacional Henri Pittier, the anacondas, anteaters and capybaras around Los Llanos, and howler monkeys, caimans and piranhas in the Orinoco Delta, the landscape invites discovery.

p962

On the Road

Guyana
p750
Suriname
p913
Venezuela
p962
French Guiana
p733
Colombia
p540
Ecuador
p634
Brazil
p281
Peru
p801
Bolivia
p188
Paraguay
p768
Argentina
p54
Chile
p422
Uruguay
p929

Argentina

Includes ➡

Best Places to Eat

- Sarkis (p71)
- Chan Chan (p70)
- La Nieta 'e la Pancha (p105)
- Kalma Resto (p171)

Best Places to Stay

- Chill House Hostel (p69)
- Hostel Rupestre (p103)
- La Casona de Odile (p152)
- Nothofagus B&B (p163)

Why Go?

With its gorgeous landscapes, cosmopolitan cities and lively culture, Argentina is a traveler's paradise. It stretches almost 3500km from Bolivia to the tip of South America, encompassing a wide array of geography and climates. Nature lovers can traverse the Patagonian steppe, climb South America's highest peak, walk among thousands of penguins and witness the world's most amazing waterfalls. Hikers can sample the stunning scenery of the lush Lake District – with its glorious lakes and white-tipped mountains – and revel in Patagonia's glacier-carved landscapes and painted Andean deserts. City slickers will adore fabulous Buenos Aires, where they can dance the sexy tango, shop for designer clothes, sample a wide range of ethnic cuisine and party at nightclubs till dawn.

Argentina is a safe, friendly and spirited destination to explore. Now is a great time to visit, so get your spirit in gear and prepare for an unforgettable adventure!

When to Go

Buenos Aires

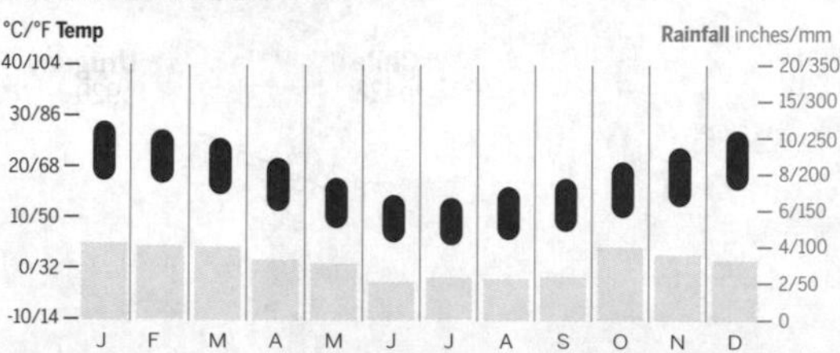

Dec–Feb Best for Patagonia and beaches. Buenos Aires and the north are hot.

Mar–May & Sep–Nov Great months for Buenos Aires, the Lake District and Mendoza.

Jun–Aug Peak ski season. A good time to visit the north. Beaches shut down.

Connections

Buenos Aires is linked by air to most other country capitals in South America. Overland, Argentina has a few border crossings each with Bolivia, Paraguay, Brazil and Uruguay, and many, many border crossings with Chile. Generally, border formalities are staightforward if your documents are in order. When crossing into Chile by air or land, don't take fresh fruits or vegetables (even in sandwiches), dairy products or meat; fines are steep.

ITINERARIES

Two Weeks

Spend your first few days taking in Buenos Aires, then head to Mendoza (for wine tasting and outdoor adventures) and Bariloche (for hiking in summer and skiing in winter). If you love summertime hiking, however, make the Patagonian hamlet of El Chaltén your priority instead; once here you can't miss the nearby destination of El Calafate for its amazing Perito Moreno glacier.

One Month

Seeing all of Argentina in one month will likely require a few key airplane flights. Or, depending on the season you'll be there, concentrate on the north or south. First, take a few days to explore the wonders of Buenos Aires. Spectacular Iguazú Falls is worth a couple of days any time of year. Colonial Salta is best April to November, while Córdoba, Mendoza and the Lake District can be visited year-round. Some Patagonian destinations, such as El Chaltén and Ushuaia, have limited services from June to August (except for skiing).

Essential Food & Drink

- **Beef** Argentines have perfected grilling beef, instilling a smoky, salty outer layer to their delectable steaks.
- **Wine** Exploring Argentina by the glass will take you from the malbecs of Mendoza to the torrontés of Cafayate to the syrahs of San Juan.
- **Maté** Although most first-time maté drinkers can barely choke the stuff down, this bitter, grassy tea is an important social bonding experience.
- **Ice cream** Argentina makes some of the world's best *helado*, swirled into a miniature peaked mountain with a spoon stuck in the side.
- **Italian food** You'll find pizza and pasta at so many restaurants, it's a wonder the locals can consume it all.
- **Dulce de leche** Argentina has turned milk and sugar into the world's best caramel sauce; find it in most of the country's sweetest concoctions.

AT A GLANCE

- **Currency** Argentine Peso (AR$)
- **Language** Spanish
- **Money** ATMs widespread; credit cards accepted at higher-end places
- **Visa** Generally not required; some nationalities pay a reciprocity fee
- **Time** GMT minus three hours

Fast Facts

- **Area** 2.8 million sq km
- **Population** 43 million
- **Capital** Buenos Aires
- **Emergency** ☎101
- **Country code** ☎54

Exchange Rates

Australia	A$1	AR$11.43
Canada	C$1	AR$11.54
Euro zone	€1	AR$16.81
New Zealand	NZ$1	AR$10.16
UK	UK£1	AR$21.73
USA	US$1	AR$15.30

Set Your Budget

- **Dorm bed** US$15-19, **doubles** US$75-150
- **Two-course evening meal** AR$150
- **Beer in a bar** AR$30
- **Four-hour bus ticket** AR$350

Resources

- **The Argentina Independent** (www.argentinaindependent.com)
- **Landing pad BA** (www.landingpadba.com)

Argentina Highlights

1. Eat, shop, tango and party all night long in Argentina's sophisticated capital, **Buenos Aires** (p57).
2. Take in **Iguazú Falls** (p100), the world's most amazing waterfall, stretching almost 3km long.
3. Explore **Córdoba** (p101), Argentina's second-largest city, an attractive destination with alternative culture.
4. Hike, trek and camp to your heart's content in **El Chaltén** (p162), where the scenery's not bad either.
5. Fish, ski, hike and go white-water rafting among gorgeous mountains and lakes at **Bariloche** (p147).
6. Sip world-class wines and partake in outdoor adventures at **Mendoza** (p133).
7. Check out the amazing and constantly calving Perito Moreno glacier in the **Parque Nacional Los Glaciares** (p168).
8. Ogle whales, elephant seals and penguins at the wildlife mecca of the **Reserva Faunística Península Valdés** (p159).
9. Set your sights on lovely, vivid and harsh cacti-dotted mountainscapes at **Quebrada de Humahuaca** (p122).

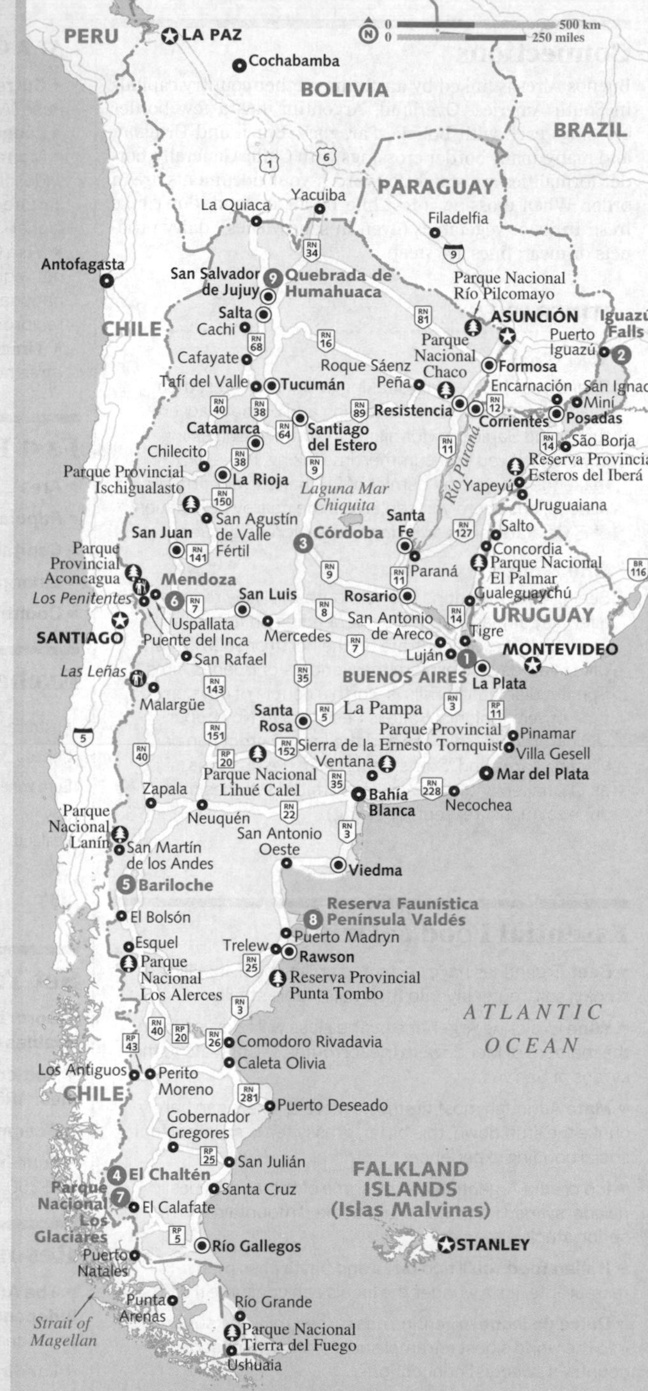

BUENOS AIRES

☎011 / POP 13 MILLION (GREATER BA)

Believe everything you've heard – Buenos Aires is one of South America's most electrifying cities, graced with European architecture, atmospheric neighborhoods and bustling nightlife. BA's passionate residents are proud and even haughty, but once you get to know them they'll bend over backward to help.

After Argentina's economic collapse in 2002, BA bounced back and created a renaissance that's still keeping the city aglow today. Argentines found the 'outside' world prohibitively expensive, so turned their energy inward, with impressive results. New restaurants, boutiques and businesses keep popping up, not only to serve the locals and their pesos, but also to cater to the influx of foreign tourists bringing hard currency.

Yet every great metropolis has a poor side. Cracked sidewalks, ubiquitous graffiti and rough edges – even in the wealthiest neighborhoods – speak volumes about this city. Poverty and beggars exist, and there's a deep melancholy here: an acknowledgement of Argentina's riches coupled with the despair of not realizing its full potential. The undeniable reality is that BA comes with a darker side.

So throw yourself into this heady mix and hold on tight, 'cause you're going for a wild ride. Don't be surprised if you fall in love with this amazing and sexy city – you won't be the first, or the last.

Sights

At Buenos Aires' heart is its *microcentro*, which holds many of the city's historical buildings and museums. To the north lies upper-crust Recoleta, with its famous cemetery, and park-filled Palermo, home to many great restaurants and bars. Down south is where the blue-collar class hangs: this includes tango mecca San Telmo and colorful, roughhousing La Boca. There's enough bustle in this city to keep you trotting around all day and all night.

City Center

Buenos Aires' *microcentro* holds many 19th-century European buildings, which surprises many travelers expecting a more Latin American feel. The liveliest street here is pedestrian street Florida, packed with masses of harried businesspeople, curious tourists, angling leather salespeople and shady money changers. Make sure to stop at Galerías Pacífico, one of BA's most gorgeous shopping malls and home to some amazing ceiling paintings.

Florida intersects busy Av Corrientes, and if you head west on this thoroughfare you'll cross superbroad Av 9 de Julio (run!). It's decisively punctuated by the famously phallic Obelisco, a major symbol of Buenos Aires. Just beyond is the city's traditional theater district, also full of many cheap bookstores.

East of the city center is BA's newest *barrio*, Puerto Madero. This renovated docklands area is lined with pleasant pedestrian walkways, expensive lofts, trendy restaurants and bars and some of the city's priciest hotels.

★Plaza de Mayo PLAZA

(Map p60; cnr Av de Mayo & San Martín) Planted between the Casa Rosada, the Cabildo and the city's main cathedral, grassy Plaza de Mayo is BA's ground zero for the city's most vehement protests. In the plaza's center is the **Pirámide de Mayo**, a white obelisk built to mark the first anniversary of BA's independence from Spain. If you happen to be here on Thursday at 3:30pm, you'll see the Madres de la Plaza de Mayo gather; these 'mothers of the disappeared' continue to march for social justice causes.

Casa Rosada BUILDING

(Pink House; Map p60; ☎011-4344-3600; ⏲free half-hour tours 10am-6pm Sat & Sun) On the eastern side of Plaza de Mayo stands the stately Casa Rosada. It's from the balconies here that Eva Perón famously preached to throngs of impassioned Argentines.

The building's color could have come from President Sarmiento's attempt at making peace during his 1868–74 term (by blending the red of the Federalists with the white of the Unitarists). Another theory, however, is that the color comes from painting the palace with bovine blood, a common practice in the late 19th century.

Museo del Bicentenario MUSEUM

(Map p60; ☎011 4344-3802; www.museobicentenario.gob.ar; cnr Av Paseo Colón & Hipólito Yrigoyen; ⏲10am-6pm Wed-Sun) FREE Behind the Casa Rosada you'll notice a glassy wedge marking this airy and sparkling underground museum, housed within the brick vaults of the old *aduana* (customs house). Head down into the open space, which has over a dozen side rooms – each dedicated

Greater Buenos Aires

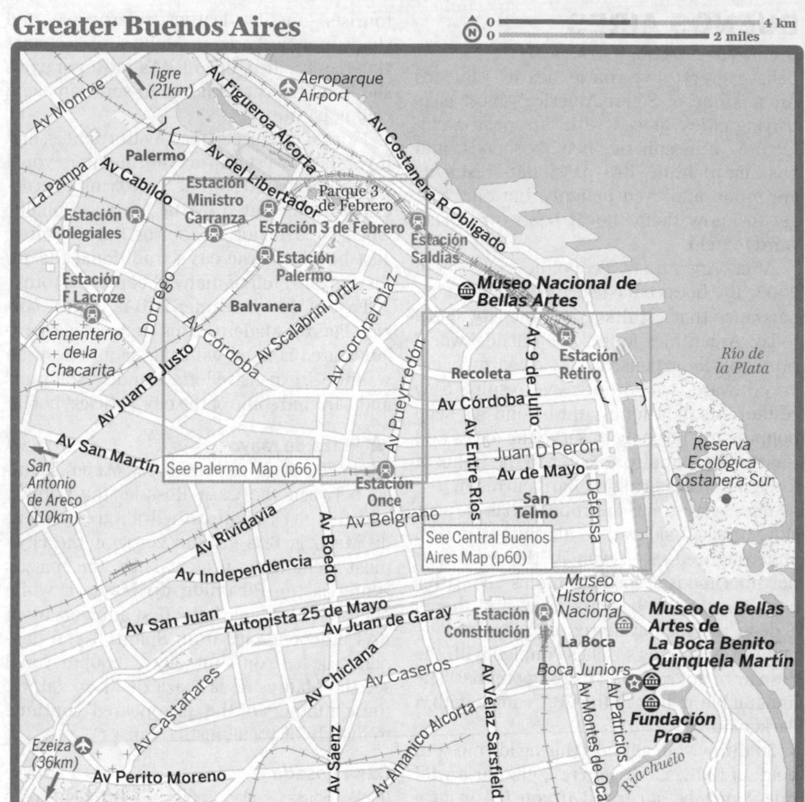

to a different era of Argentina's tumultuous political history. There are mostly videos (in Spanish) and a few artifacts to see, along with temporary art exhibitions and an impressive restored mural by Mexican artist David Alfaro Siqueiros. Also check out Evita's gown.

Catedral Metropolitana CATHEDRAL
(Map p60; museum admission AR$40; ⏲7:30am-6:30pm Mon-Fri, 9am-7pm Sat & Sun, museum 10am-12:30pm Mon-Fri) This solemn cathedral was built on the site of the original colonial church and not finished until 1827. It's a significant religious and architectural landmark, and carved above its triangular facade and neoclassical columns are bas-reliefs of Jacob and Joseph. The spacious interior is equally impressive, with baroque details and an elegant rococo altar. There's a small museum dedicated to the cathedral's history inside. For Pope Francis souvenirs, visit the small gift shop near the entrance.

Cabildo MUSEUM
(Map p60; ☎011 4342-6729; www.cabildonacional.com.ar; Bolívar 65; admission AR$15; ⏲10:30am-5pm Tue-Wed & Fri, to 8pm Thu, to 6pm Sat & Sun) This mid-18th-century town-hall building is now a museum. It used to have colonnades that spanned Plaza de Mayo, but the building of surrounding avenues unfortunately destroyed them. Inside you'll find a few mementos of the early-19th-century British invasions, some paintings in colonial and early independence-style, and the occasional temporary exhibit. There are good views of Plaza de Mayo from the 2nd-floor balcony.

Teatro Colón BUILDING
(Map p60; ☎011 4378-7127; www.teatrocolon.org.ar; Tucumán 1171; tours AR$180; ⏲tours 9am-5pm) This gorgeous and impressive seven-story building is one of BA's most prominent landmarks. The city's main performing-arts venue, it's the only facility of its kind in

the country, a world-class forum for opera, ballet and classical music with astounding acoustics. Occupying an entire city block, the Colón can seat 2500 spectators and provide standing room for another 500. The theater's opening night was a presentation of Verdi's *Aïda,* and visitors have been wowed ever since. Worthwhile backstage tours run frequently.

★Centro Cultural Kirchner CULTURAL CENTER
(Map p60; ☎800-333-9300; www.culturalkirchner.gob.ar; Sarmiento 151; ⏲5-9pm Thu & Fri, 2-9pm Sat & Sun, limited hours outside summer) Néstor Kirchner just *had* to leave a physical legacy, and this breathtaking cultural center is possibly his best. It's located in Buenos Aires' former main post office, a massive beaux arts structure eight stories tall and filling an entire city block. Dozens of rooms hold art galleries, theaters, event halls, auditoriums and even an Eva Perón room; there's also a rooftop terrace. The highlight, however, is La Ballena Azul, giant concert hall that seats 1800 and is home to Argentina's national symphony orchestra.

Colección de Arte Amalia Lacroze de Fortabat MUSEUM
(Museo Fortabat; Map p60; ☎011 4310-6600; www.coleccionfortabat.org.ar; Olga Cossettini 141; admission AR$60; ⏲noon-8pm Tue-Sun, tours in Spanish 3pm & 5pm Tue-Sun) Rivaling Palermo's Malba for cutting-edge looks is this stunning art museum, prominently located at the northern end of Puerto Madero. It shows off the collection of billionaire, philanthropist and socialite Amalia Lacroze de Fortabat, Argentina's wealthiest woman. There are galleries devoted to Antonio Berni and Raúl Soldi (both famous Argentine painters) and works by international stars like Dalí, Klimt, Rodin and Chagall; look for Warhol's colorful take on Fortabat herself in the family portrait gallery. Call ahead for group tours in English.

Reserva Ecológica Costanera Sur NATURE RESERVE
(☎011 4893-1588; Av Tristán Achaval Rodríguez 1550; ⏲8am-7pm Tue-Sun Nov-Mar, to 6pm Apr-Oct) FREE The beautifully marshy land of this 350-hectare nature reserve has become a popular site for weekend picnics and walks. Bring binoculars if you're a birder – over 300 bird species can be spotted, along with river turtles, iguanas and nutria. Further in at the eastern shoreline of the reserve you can get a close-up view of the Río de la Plata's muddy waters. On warm weekends and holidays you can rent bikes just outside either the northern (Map p60) or southern entrances.

Manzana de las Luces BUILDING
(Block of Enlightenment; Map p60; ☎011-4342-6973; www.manazadelasluces.org; Perú 272; tours AR$35; ⏲tours 3pm Mon-Fri, 3pm, 4:30pm & 6pm Sat & Sun) In colonial times, the Manzana de las Luces was Buenos Aires' most important center of culture and learning. Even today, this collection of buildings still symbolizes high culture in the capital. On the northern side of the block are two of the five original buildings; Jesuit defensive tunnels were discovered in 1912. Tours (in Spanish) are available, and a cultural center on the premises offers classes, workshops and theater.

Palacio del Congreso BUILDING
(Congress Building; Map p60; Hipólito Yrigoyen 1849) Colossal and topped with a green dome, the Palacio del Congreso cost more than twice its projected budget and set a precedent for contemporary Argentine public-works projects. It was modeled on the Capitol Building in Washington, DC, and was completed in 1906. Across the way, the **Monumento a los Dos Congresos** honors the congresses of 1810 in BA and 1816 in Tucumán, both of which led to Argentine independence.

San Telmo

Six blocks south of Plaza de Mayo, San Telmo – home of BA's main tango culture – is full of cobbled streets, aging mansions and antique shops. Historically, its low rents have attracted artists, but these days you'll see more boutiques than studios. The neighborhood was a fashionable place until 1870,

DON'T MISS

- Shopping and eating in Palermo Viejo.
- Looking for finds at San Telmo's bustling Sunday antiques fair.
- Wandering through Recoleta's amazing cemetery.
- Experiencing a *fútbol* game's passion.
- Taking in the high kicks at a tango show.
- Soaking up Buenos Aires' second-to-none nightlife.

Central Buenos Aires

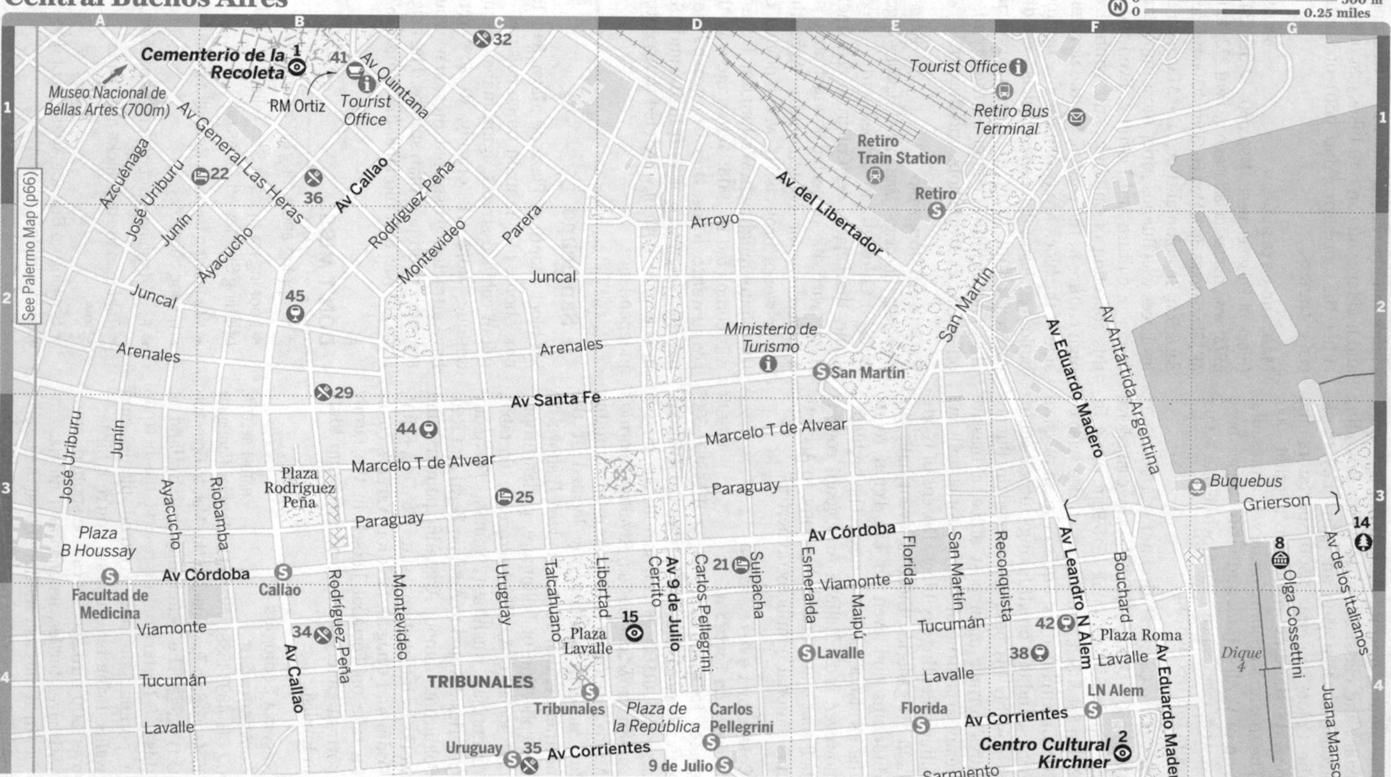

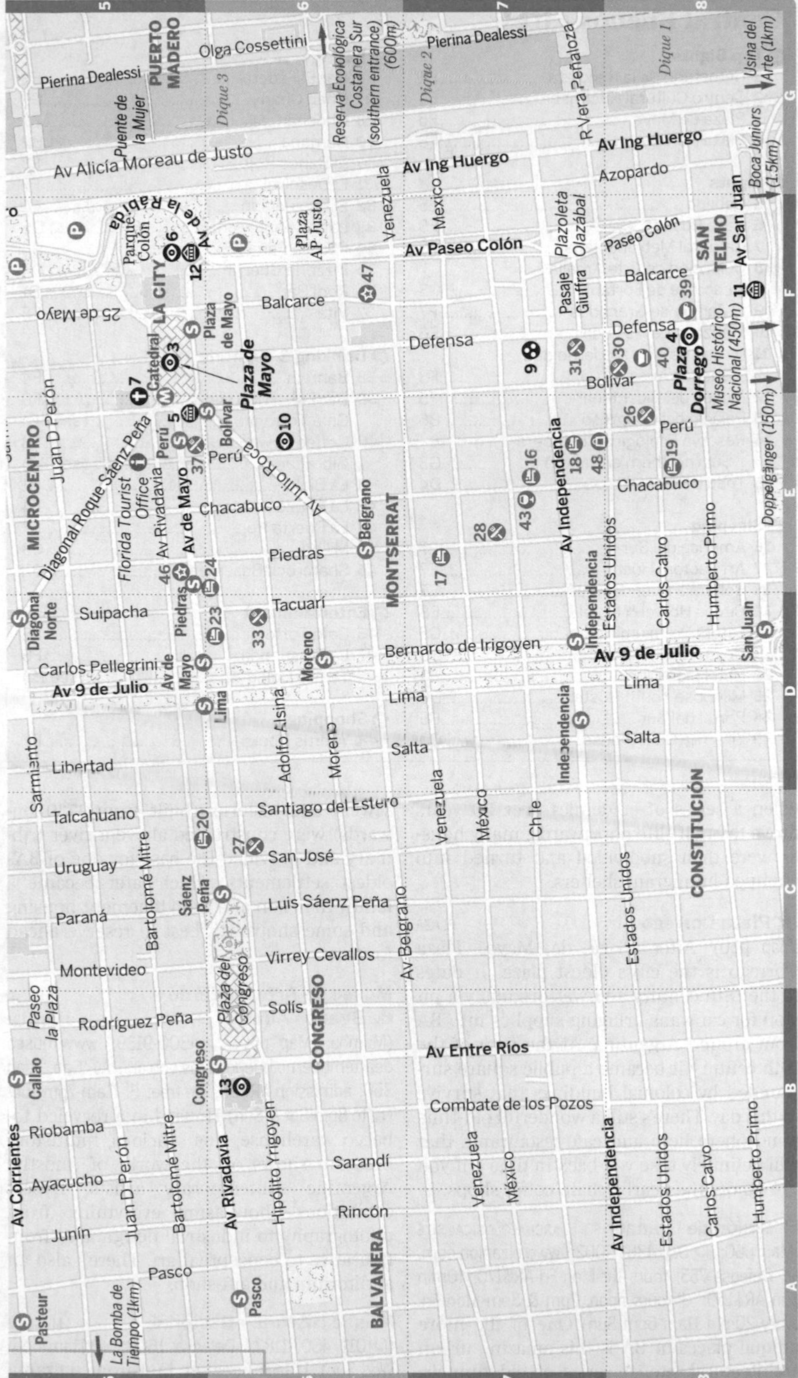
PUERTO MADERO
Pierina Dealessi
Olga Cossettini
Puente de la Mujer
Dique 3
Dique 2
Dique 1
Reserva Ecológica Costanera Sur (southern entrance) (600m)
R Vera Peñaloza
Usina del Arte (1km)
Av Alicía Moreau de Justo
Av Ing Huergo
Azopardo
Boca Juniors (1.5km)
Av de la Rábida
Parque Colón
LA CITY
Plaza AP Justo
Venezuela
Mexico
Av Paseo Colón
Paseo Colón
Plazoleta Olazábal
SAN TELMO
Av San Juan
Balcarce
25 de Mayo
Catedral
Plaza de Mayo
Pasaje Giuffra
Defensa
Plaza Dorrego
Museo Histórico Nacional (450m)
Bolívar
Perú
Av Independencia
MICROCENTRO
Juan D Perón
Diagonal Roque Sáenz Peña
Florida Tourist Office
Av Rivadavia
Av de Mayo
Av Julio Roca
Chacabuco
Belgrano
MONTSERRAT
Doppelgänger (150m)
Humberto Primo
Piedras
Tacuarí
Carlos Calvo
Estados Unidos
Independencia
Diagonal Norte
Suipacha
Carlos Pellegrini
Av 9 de Julio
Moreno
Bernardo de Irigoyen
San Juan
Lima
Salta
Adolfo Alsina
Libertad
Sarmiento
Talcahuano
Santiago del Estero
Chile
CONSTITUCIÓN
Uruguay
Bartolomé Mitre
Sáenz Peña
San José
Paraná
Luis Sáenz Peña
Av Belgrano
Montevideo
Plaza del Congreso
Virrey Cevallos
Paseo la Plaza
Rodríguez Peña
Solís
CONGRESO
Av Entre Ríos
Callao
Congreso
Combate de los Pozos
Av Corrientes
Riobamba
Ayacucho
Av Rivadavia
Hipólito Yrigoyen
Sarandí
Rincón
Junín
Pasco
BALVANERA
Pasteur
La Bomba de Tiempo (1km)
A
B
C
D
E
F
G
5
6
7
8

Central Buenos Aires

Top Sights

1 Cemeterio de la Recoleta ... B1
2 Centro Cultural Kirchner ... F4
3 Plaza de Mayo ... F5
4 Plaza Dorrego ... F8

Sights

5 Cabildo ... E5
6 Casa Rosada ... F5
7 Catedral Metropolitana ... F5
8 Colección de Arte Amalia Lacroze de Fortabat ... G3
9 El Zanjón de Granados ... F7
10 Manzana de las Luces ... E6
11 Museo de Arte Moderno de Buenos Aires ... F8
12 Museo del Bicentenario ... F5
13 Palacio del Congreso ... B6
14 Reserva Ecológica Costanera Sur (northern entrance) ... G3
15 Teatro Colón ... D4

Sleeping

16 América del Sur ... E7
17 Art Factory Hostel ... E7
18 Bohemia Buenos Aires ... E7
19 Circus Hostel & Hotel ... E8
20 Estoril Premium Hostel ... C5
21 Goya Hotel ... D3
22 Hotel Lion D'or ... B1
23 Milhouse Youth Hostel ... D6
24 Portal del Sur ... E6
25 Yira Yira Guesthouse ... C3

Eating

26 Bar El Federal ... E8
27 Chan Chan ... C6
28 Chochán ... E7
29 Cumaná ... B2
30 El Banco Rojo ... F8
31 El Desnivel ... F7
32 El Sanjuanino ... C1
33 Latino Sandwich ... D6
34 Parrilla Peña ... B4
35 Pizzería Güerrín ... C4
36 Rodi Bar ... B1
37 Vita ... E5

Drinking & Nightlife

38 Bahrein ... F4
39 Bar Plaza Dorrego ... F8
Café Tortoni ... (see 46)
40 Coffee Town ... F8
Gibraltar ... (see 48)
41 La Biela ... B1
42 La Cigale ... F4
43 La Puerta Roja ... E7
44 Milión ... C3
45 Shamrock Basement ... B2

Entertainment

46 Café Tortoni ... E5
47 La Trastienda ... F6
Teatro Colón ... (see 15)

Shopping

48 Walrus Books ... E7

when a series of epidemics over 20 years drove the rich elite northwards; many houses were then subdivided and turned into cramped immigrant shelters.

★ Plaza Dorrego — PLAZA

(Map p60) After Plaza de Mayo, Plaza Dorrego is the city's oldest plaza. It dates to the 18th century and was originally a pit stop for caravans bringing supplies into BA from around Argentina. At the turn of the 19th century it became a public square surrounded by colonial buildings that survive to this day. There's still a wonderful old-time atmosphere here and cafe-restaurants that will definitely take you back in time – if you can ignore the nearby chain coffee shops.

El Zanjón de Granados — ARCHAEOLOGICAL SITE

(Map p60; ☎011 4361-3002; www.elzanjon.com.ar; Defensa 755; tours 1hr Mon-Fri AR$170, 40min Sun AR$150; ⊙tours noon, 2pm & 3pm Mon-Fri, every 20min 11am-6pm Sun) One of the more unique places in BA is this amazing urban architectural site. A series of old tunnels, sewers and cisterns (built from 1730 onwards) were constructed above a river tributary and provided the base for one of BA's oldest settlements, which later became a family mansion and then tenement housing and some shops. It's best to reserve ahead for tours.

Museo de Arte Moderno de Buenos Aires — MUSEUM

(Mamba; Map p60; ☎4300-9139; www.museodeartemoderno.buenosaires.gob.ar; Av San Juan 350; admission AR$20, Tue free; ⊙11am-7pm Tue-Fri, to 8pm Sat & Sun) Housed in a recycled tobacco warehouse, this spacious, multistory museum shows off the works of (mostly) Argentine contemporary artists. Expect exhibitions showcasing everything from photography to industrial design, and from figurative to conceptual art. There's also an auditorium and gift shop.

Museo Histórico Nacional — MUSEUM

(☎011 4307-1182; Defensa 1600; ⊙11am-6pm Wed-Sun) FREE Located in Parque Lezama is the city's national historical museum. It's dedicated to Argentina's revolution on May 25, 1810, though it covers a bit of precolonial times too. There are several portraits of presidents and other major figures of the time, along with a beautifully lit generals' room. Peek into the re-created version of José de San Martín's bedroom – he was a military hero and liberator of Argentina (along with other South American countries).

La Boca

Vivid, working-class La Boca, situated along the old port and at the *boca* (mouth) of the Río Riachuelo, was built by Italian immigrants from Genoa. Its main attraction is colorful Caminito, a short pedestrian walk lined with corrugated-metal buildings. Local artists display their brightly colored paintings, adding to the vibrant ambience. The neighborhood is also home to the Boca Juniors soccer team.

Be aware that this is one of the poorer *barrios* (neighborhoods) of Buenos Aires and you shouldn't wander from the beaten path of tourist hangouts, day or night. Buses 29, 130 and 152 run to La Boca.

★Fundación Proa — MUSEUM

(☎4104-1000; www.proa.org; Av Don Pedro de Mendoza 1929; admission AR$40; ⏲11am-7pm Tue-Sun) Only the most cutting-edge national and international artists are invited to show at this elegant art museum, which features high ceilings, white walls and large display halls. Stunning contemporary installations utilize a wide variety of media and themes, while the rooftop terrace is the stylish place in La Boca for relaxing with a drink or snack – it boasts a view of the Riachuelo. Plenty of cultural offerings include talks, lectures, workshops, music concerts and cinema screenings.

★Museo de Bellas Artes de La Boca Benito Quinquela Martín — MUSEUM

(☎011 4301-1080; www.museoquinquela.gov.ar; Av Don Pedro de Mendoza 1835; suggested donation AR$20; ⏲10am-6pm Tue-Fri, 11:15am-6pm Sat & Sun) Once the home and studio of surrealist painter Benito Quinquela Martín (1890–1977), this fine-arts museum exhibits his works and those of other classic Argentine artists. Martín used silhouettes of laboring men, smokestacks and water reflections as recurring themes, and painted with broad, rough brush strokes and dark colors. There are outdoor sculptures on the rooftop terraces, and the top tier has awesome views of the port.

Recoleta

The plushest of Buenos Aires' neighborhoods is ritzy Recoleta, filled with gorgeous European-style buildings and international boutiques. It also holds some pleasant green spaces, like Plaza Intendente Alvear, where a crafts fair takes place on weekends. Sit at a cafe nearby, note the giant ombú trees and if you're lucky you'll spot a *paseaperros* (professional dog-walker) strolling with 15 or so leashed canines of all shapes and tails.

★Cementerio de la Recoleta — CEMETERY

(Map p60; ☎0800-444-2363; cnr Junín & Guido; AR$100; ⏲7am-5:30pm) This cemetery is arguably BA's number-one attraction, and a must on every tourist's list. You can wander for hours in this amazing city of the dead, where countless 'streets' are lined with impressive statues and marble mausoleums. Peek into the crypts and check out the dusty coffins and try to decipher the history of its inhabitants. Past presidents, military heroes, influential politicians and the just plain rich and famous have made it past the gates here.

★Museo Nacional de Bellas Artes — MUSEUM

(☎011-5288-9900; www.mnba.gob.ar; Av del Libertador 1473; ⏲12:30-8:30pm Tue-Fri, 9:30am-8:30pm Sat & Sun) FREE This is Argentina's most important national arts museum and contains many key works by Benito Quinquela Martín, Xul Solar, Edwardo Sívori and other Argentine artists of the 19th and 20th centuries. There are also impressive international works by European masters such as Cézanne, Degas, Picasso, Rembrandt, Toulouse-Lautrec and Van Gogh. Everything is well displayed, and there's also a cinema, concerts and classes.

Palermo

Full of grassy parks, imposing statues and elegant embassies, Palermo on a sunny weekend afternoon is a *porteño* (people from Buenos Aires) yuppie dream. On weekends a ring road around Parque 3 de Febrero is closed to motor vehicles, and you can rent bikes or in-line skates (among other things) and do some serious people-watching while on wheels. Palermo also contains the Campo de Polo (Polo Grounds), Hipódromo (Racetrack) and Planetario (Planetarium).

Make sure to stroll through the subneighborhood of Palermo Viejo, just south of the parks. It's further divided into Palermo Soho and Palermo Hollywood. Here you'll find BA's hippest restaurants, trendiest boutiques and liveliest nightlife. Its beautiful old buildings make for some great wanderings too.

★ Museo de Arte Latinoamericano de Buenos Aires MUSEUM
(Malba; Map p66; ☎011 4808-6500; www.malba.org.ar; Av Figueroa Alcorta 3415; admission AR$75, Wed AR$36; ⏲noon-8pm Thu-Mon, to 9pm Wed) Sparkling inside its glass walls, this airy modern arts museum is one of BA's fanciest. Millionaire and philanthropist Eduardo Costantini displays his fine collection of Latin American art, which includes work by Argentines Xul Solar and Antonio Berni, plus some pieces by Mexicans Diego Rivera and Frida Kahlo. A cinema screens art-house films, and there's a gift shop and upscale cafe as well.

Jardín Zoológico ZOO
(Map p66; ☎011 4011-9900; www.zoobuenosaires.com.ar; cnr Avs General Las Heras & Sarmiento; adult/child AR$180/free; ⏲10am-6pm Tue-Sun Oct-Mar, to 5pm Apr-Sep) Set on 18 hectares, Buenos Aires' Jardín Zoológico is a decent zoo, housing over 350 species – many in 'natural' and good-sized animal enclosures. On sunny weekends it's packed with families enjoying the large green spaces and artificial lakes. Some of the buildings housing the animals are impressive; check out the elephant house. An aquarium, a monkey island, reptile house and large aviary are other highlights; a few special exhibits (like the sea-lion show or carousel) cost extra.

Jardín Japonés GARDENS
(Map p66; ☎011 4804-4922; www.jardinjapones.org.ar; cnr Avs Casares & Berro; adult/child AR$50/free; ⏲10am-6pm) First opened in 1967 and then donated to the city of Buenos Aires in 1979 (on the centenary of the arrival of Argentina's first Japanese immigrants), Jardín Japonés makes a peaceful rest stop. Inside there's a Japanese restaurant along with lovely ponds filled with koi and spanned by pretty bridges. Japanese culture can be experienced through occasional exhibitions and workshops on ikebana, haiku, origami, *taiko* (Japanese drumming) and other events.

Museo Evita MUSEUM
(Map p66; ☎011 4807-0306; www.museoevita.org; Lafinur 2988; admission AR$40; ⏲11am-7pm Tue-Sun) Everybody who's anybody in Argentina has their own museum, and Eva Perón (1919–52) is no exception. Museo Evita immortalizes the Argentine heroine with plenty of videos, historical photos, books, old posters and newspaper headlines. However, the prize memorabilia has to be her wardrobe: dresses, shoes, handbags, hats and blouses lie proudly behind glass, forever pressed and pristine. Even Evita's old wallets and perfumes are on display. Our favorite is a picture of her kicking a soccer ball – in heels.

Activities

Porteños' main activities are walking, shopping and dancing tango. Those searching for greener pastures, however, head to Palermo's parks, where joggers run past strolling families and young men playing *fútbol.*

Safe cycling is possible in BA, and protected bike lanes have popped up on certain streets. Good places to pedal are Palermo's parks (weekend rentals on Av de la Infanta Isabel near Av Pedro Montt), along with Puerto Madero and its nearby Reserva Ecológica Costanera Sur (weekend rentals outside the main entrance). Bike-tour companies rent bikes and also do guided tours.

Unless you stay at a fancy hotel or join a gym, swimming pools are hard to come by; to cool off, try **Parque Norte** (☎011-4787-1382; www.parquenorte.com; Avs Cantilo & Guiraldes; Mon-Fri AR$80, Sat AR$100, Sun AR$110; ⏲pool 8:30am-8pm Mon-Fri, to 10pm Sat & Sun), a fun water park. Soccer players should check out Buenos Aires Fútbol Amigos (www.fcbafa.com), while yoga aficionados can try Buena Onda Yoga (www.buenaondayoga.net).

Some companies like Tangol (p77) offer activities such as tango, kayaking, fishing and *estancia* (ranch) visits, which often include horse riding. For something totally different, learn to play polo with Argentina Polo Day (www.argentinapoloday.com.ar).

Courses

Language

Buenos Aires is a popular destination for Spanish-language students. There are plenty of schools and even more private teachers, so ask around for recommendations. All schools offer social excursions and can help with accommodations; some have volunteer opportunities. For something fun and different, join www.spanglishexchange.com – sort of a speed-dating concept, but with language.

Tango

Tango classes are available everywhere – your own hostel may offer them. Many inexpensive classes are available at *milongas* (dance halls), which can put you in touch with private teachers, some of whom speak English. Cultural centers and dance academies often have affordable classes as well.

La Catedral COURSE
(Map p66; ☎15-5325-1630; www.lacatedralclub.com; Sarmiento 4006, 1st fl) If tango can be trendy and hip, this is where you'll find it. The grungy warehouse space is very casual, with funky art on the walls and jeans on the dancers. A great place to come to learn tango, especially if you're young. Located 1.5 blocks south of the Medrano Subte stop.

Tours

If you want to take a tour, plenty of creative choices exist. Tangol (p77) is a travel agency that brokers many kinds of city tours, while www.LandingPadBA.com has some interesting options as well.

BA Free Tour WALKING TOUR
(☎15-6395-3000; www.bafreetour.com; donation recommended) Free (actually, donation) walking tours given by enthusiastic young guides who love their city. Even if you can't give anything you're welcome to join.

Biking Buenos Aires BICYCLE TOUR
(☎011 4300-5373; www.bikingbuenosaires.com) Friendly American and Argentine guides take you on various tours of Buenos Aires; tour themes include graffiti and architecture.

Foto Ruta PHOTOGRAPHY
(☎011-6030-8881; www.foto-ruta.com) This workshop is run by two expat women who send folks out into neighborhoods with a few 'themes' to photograph – then everyone watches the slide show.

Graffitimundo TOUR
(☎15-3683-3219; www.graffitimundo.com) Excellent tours of some of BA's best graffiti. Learn artists' history and the local graffiti culture. Several tours available; stencil workshops too.

Festivals & Events

The following are a few of Buenos Aires' biggest celebrations.

Festival y Mundial de Baile DANCE
(www.tangobuenosaires.gob.ar) Late February to early March.

Festival Internacional de Cine Independiente FILM
(http://festivales.buenosaires.gob.ar) Highlights national and international independent films at venues all around Buenos Aires in mid-April.

Arte BA ART
(www.arteba.org) Popular event in May highlighting contemporary art, introducing exciting new young artists, and showing off top gallery works.

Vinos y Bodegas WINE
(www.expovinosybodegas.com.ar) A can't-miss event for wine aficionados, offering vintages from over 100 Argentine *bodegas* (wineries) in September.

Sleeping

Buenos Aires' *microcentro* is close to many sights and services, though it's busy and noisy during the day. San Telmo is about 15 minutes' walk south and good for those seeking old colonial atmosphere, cobbled streets, proximity to some tango venues and a blue-collar flavor around the edges. Palermo Viejo is northwest of the center and about a 10-minute taxi ride. It's a pretty area full of wonderful old buildings and dotted with the city's best ethnic restaurants, trendiest boutiques and liveliest bars.

Private rooms in some hostels don't always come with private bathroom, though they can cost more than rooms in a cheap hotel. All hostels listed here include kitchen access, light breakfast and free internet; most have free wi-fi and lockers (bring your own lock). The bigger ones offer more services and activities, and many take credit cards. Hostelling International cards are available at any HI hostel or BA's Hostelling International office (p181).

BA has some good budget hotel choices. Most offer a simple breakfast and cable TV; some take credit cards (which might incur a fee of up to 10% – ask beforehand). Most listings also have internet and/or wi-fi available for guests.

Palermo

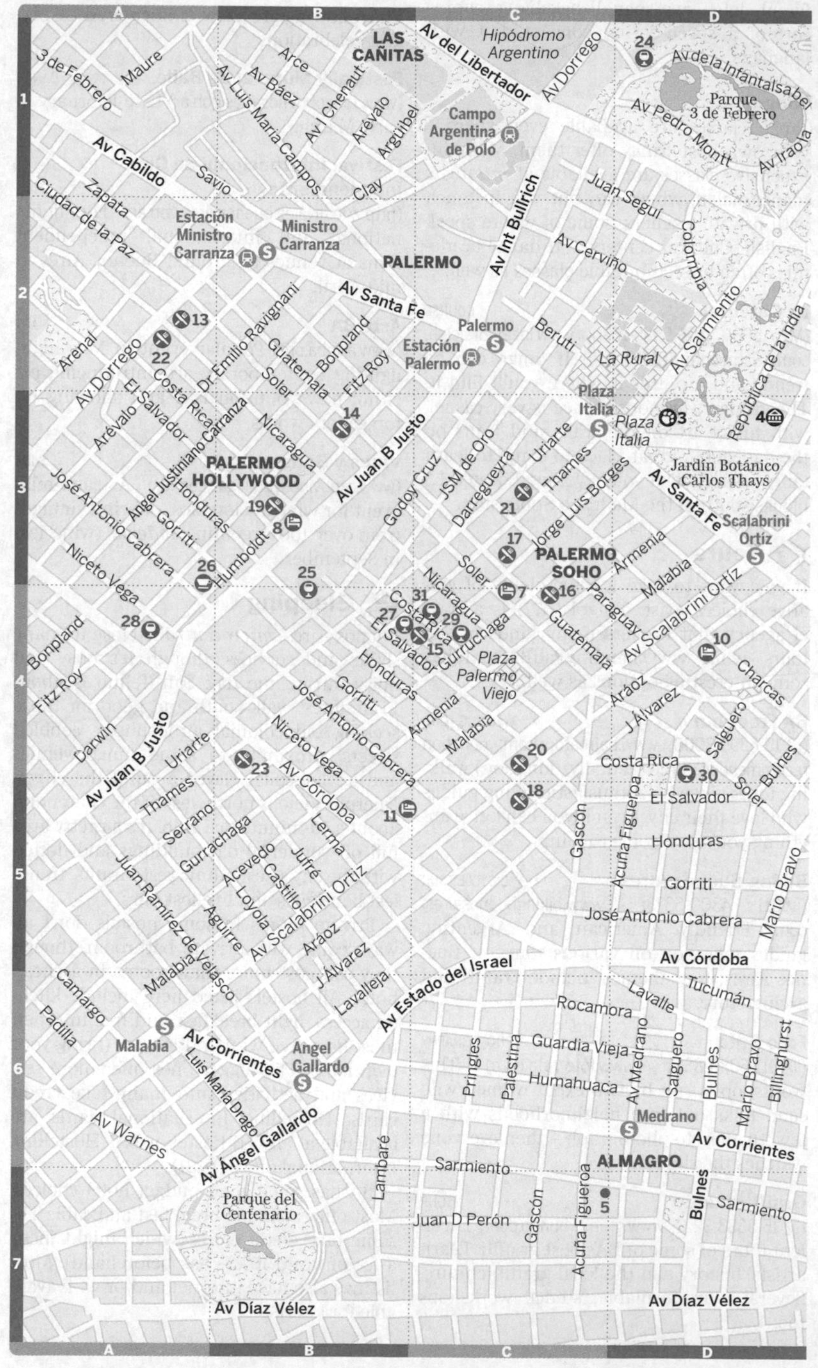

LAS CAÑITAS
Hipódromo Argentino
Campo Argentina de Polo
Parque 3 de Febrero
Estación Ministro Carranza
Ministro Carranza
PALERMO
Palermo
Estación Palermo
La Rural
Plaza Italia
PALERMO HOLLYWOOD
PALERMO SOHO
Jardín Botánico Carlos Thays
Scalabrini Ortíz
Plaza Palermo Viejo
Malabia
Angel Gallardo
Medrano
ALMAGRO
Parque del Centenario
Av del Libertador
Av Dorrego
Av de la Infanta Isabel
Av Pedro Montt
Av Iraola
Av Cabildo
Av Santa Fe
Av Int Bullrich
Av Cerviño
Av Sarmiento
Av Juan B Justo
Av Scalabrini Ortíz
Av Córdoba
Av Estado del Israel
Av Corrientes
Av Warnes
Av Ángel Gallardo
Av Díaz Vélez
Av Medrano

City Center

Milhouse Youth Hostel HOSTEL $
(Map p60; ☎011 4345-9604; www.milhousehostel.com; Hipólito Yrigoyen 959; dm/s/d from US$16/55/60; ; Línea A Av de Mayo) BA's premiere party hostel, this popular HI spot offers a plethora of activities and services. Dorms are good and private rooms can be very pleasant; most surround an appealing open patio. Common spaces include a bar-cafe (with pool table) on the ground floor, a TV lounge on the mezzanine and a rooftop terrace. A gorgeous annex building nearby offers similar services.

Yira Yira Guesthouse GUESTHOUSE $
(Map p60; ☎011 4812-4077; www.yirayiraba.com; Uruguay 911, No 1b; s/d/tr US$40/55/85; ; Línea D Callao) This casual, intimate apartment-home is run by the helpful Paz, who lives on-site. The floors are wooden and the ceilings high, and there are just four large rooms (all with shared bathrooms) facing the central living area with tiny patio. It's a good place to meet other travelers and is centrally located near downtown. Reserve ahead.

Portal del Sur HOSTEL $
(Map p60; ☎011 4342-8788; www.portaldelsurba.com.ar; Hipólito Yrigoyen 855; dm/s/d from US$16/40/50; ; Línea A Piedras) Located in a charming old building, this is one of the city's best hostels. Beautiful dorms and sumptuous, hotel-quality private rooms surround a central common area, which is rather dark but open. The highlight is the lovely rooftop deck with views and attached bar and lounge. Free tango and Spanish lessons, plus a walking tour; plenty of other activities available.

Estoril Premium Hostel HOSTEL $
(Map p60; ☎011 4382-9073; www.hostelestoril.com.ar; Av de Mayo 1385, 1st & 6th fl; dm/s/d from US$19/45/60;) A great hostel located across two floors in an old building. It's stylish and clean, with pleasant, good-sized dorms and hotel-quality doubles. There's a nice kitchen and internal patio, and the awesome rooftop terrace has amazing views of Av de Mayo. The same family also runs a cheaper hostel on the 3rd floor.

Hotel Lion D'or HOTEL $
(Map p60; ☎011 4803-8992; www.hotel-liondor.com.ar; Pacheco de Melo 2019; s/d/tr from

Palermo

Top Sights
1 Museo de Arte Latinoamericano de Buenos Aires ... F2

Sights
2 Jardín Japonés ... E2
3 Jardín Zoológico ... D3
4 Museo Evita ... D3

Activities, Courses & Tours
5 La Catedral ... C7

Sleeping
6 Chill House Hostel ... E6
7 Eco Pampa Hostel ... C4
8 Hotel Clasico ... B3
9 Infinito Hotel ... E3
10 Mansilla 3935 B&B ... D4
11 Palermo Viejo B&B ... B5
12 Reina Madre Hostel ... E5

Eating
13 Almacén Oui Oui ... A2
14 Bio ... B3
15 Burger Joint ... C4
16 Don Julio ... C4
17 El Preferido de Palermo ... C3
18 El Tejano ... C5
19 Fukuro Noodle Bar ... B3
20 Gran Dabbang ... C4
21 Las Pizarras ... C3
22 Oui Oui ... A2
23 Sarkis ... B4

Drinking & Nightlife
24 Crobar ... D1
25 Kika ... B4
26 LAB Training Center & Coffee Shop ... A3
27 Magdalena's Party ... B4
28 Niceto Club ... A4
29 Sugar ... C4
30 Verne ... D4
31 Victoria Brown ... C4

Entertainment
32 La Bomba de Tiempo ... E7

US$32/43/59; ❄ 📶; Ⓢ Línea D Pueyrredón) These digs have their charm (it's an old embassy), but rooms vary widely – some are small, basic and dark, while others are grand. Despite some rough edges, all are good value and most have been modernized for comfort. The old marble staircase and elevator are fabulous, and there's a nice rooftop area. The cheapest rooms share bathrooms; air-con costs extra.

Goya Hotel HOTEL $$
(Map p60; ☎ 011 4322-9269; www.goyahotel.com.ar; Suipacha 748; s US$60-70, d US$85-95; ❄ @ 📶) A good midrange choice with 42 modern, comfortable and carpeted rooms. Located on a pedestrian street, so little traffic noise. 'Classic' rooms are older and have open showers; 'superior' rooms are slicker and come with bathtubs. Pleasant breakfast room with patio; good breakfast too.

San Telmo

★**América del Sur** HOSTEL $
(Map p60; ☎ 011 4300-5525; www.americahostel.com.ar; Chacabuco 718; dm/d from US$18/70; ❄ @ 📶; Ⓢ Línea C Independencia) This gorgeous boutique-like hostel is the fanciest of its kind in BA, and built especially to be a hostel. Beyond reception is a fine bar-bistro area with large, elegant wooden patio. Clean dorms with four beds all have amazingly well-designed bathrooms, while private rooms are tastefully decorated and better than those at many midrange hotels. A multitude of services are on offer.

Art Factory Hostel HOSTEL $
(Map p60; ☎ 011 4343-1463; www.artfactoryba.com.ar; Piedras 545; dm/d from US$17/47; ❄ @ 📶) Friendly and uniquely art-themed, this fine hostel offers more private rooms than most – and all feature huge murals, painted and decorated by different international artists. Even the hallways and water tanks have colorful cartoonish themes, and the 1850s rambling mansion adds some elegant atmosphere. There's a large rooftop terrace with hammocks and separate bar-lounge area with pool table.

Circus Hostel & Hotel HOSTEL $
(Map p60; ☎ 011 4300-4983; www.hostelcircus.com; Chacabuco 1020; dm/d from US$15/50; ❄ @ 📶 🏊; Ⓢ Línea C Independencia) From the trendy lounge in front to the wooden-deck-surrounded wading pool in back, this hotel-hostel exudes hipness. Both dorms and private rooms, all small and simple, have basic furniture and their own bathrooms. There's a pool table and slick TV area too, but no kitchen.

Bohemia Buenos Aires HOTEL $
(Map p60; ☎011 4115-2561; www.bohemiabuenosaires.com.ar; Perú 845; r from US$60; ❄@☎; Ⓢ Línea C Independencia) With its slightly upscale-motel feel, this good-value San Telmo hotel offers 22 simple and neat rooms, most good-sized, if a bit antiseptic with their white-tiled floors. None of the rooms has a bathtub, so instead of taking a soak enjoy the peaceful grassy backyard and small interior patios. The breakfast buffet is a plus, and there's a restaurant. Cash discount.

Palermo

★**Chill House Hostel** HOSTEL $
(Map p66; ☎011 4861-6175; www.chillhouse.com.ar; Agüero 781; dm US$17, d US$49-67; @☎; Ⓢ Línea B Carlos Gardel) One of the coolest-vibe hostels in BA is at this remodeled old house boasting high ceilings and a rustic artsy style. There are two dorms and eight private rooms with bathroom (No 6 is especially nice). There's also an awesome rooftop terrace where weekly *asados* (barbecues) take place, occasional live music and free bike rentals.

Reina Madre Hostel HOSTEL $
(Map p66; ☎011 4962-5553; www.rmhostel.com; Av Anchorena 1118; dm/s/d from US$16/40/44; ❄@☎; Ⓢ Línea D Pueyrredón) This wonderful hostel is clean, safe and well run. It's in an old building that has plenty of personality, with high ceilings and original tiles, and all rooms are comfortable and modern (and share bathrooms). There's a cozy living room with balcony and small kitchen plus lots of dining tables, but the highlight is the wooden-deck rooftop with *asado*. Pet cat on premises.

Eco Pampa Hostel HOSTEL $
(Map p66; ☎011 4831-2435; www.hostelpampa.com.ar; Guatemala 4778; dm/s/d US$20/70/85; @☎; Ⓢ Línea D Plaza Italia) Buenos Aires' first 'green' hostel is this casual spot sporting vintage furniture, low-energy lightbulbs and a recycling system. The rooftop is home to a small veggie garden, compost pile and solar panels. Dorms are a good size and each of the eight private rooms comes with bathroom and flat-screen TV (most have air-con). There's another branch in Belgrano.

Mansilla 3935 B&B B&B $
(Map p66; ☎011 4833-3821; www.mansilla3935.com; Mansilla 3935; s/d US$40/60; ❄@☎) Family-run B&B in a homey, darkish house, offering a great deal. Each of the six simple but lovely rooms comes with its own bathroom. Ceilings are high, and a few tiny patios add charm.

Hotel Clasico HOTEL $$
(Map p66; ☎011 4773-2353; www.hotelclasico.com; Costa Rica 5480; r US$120-170; ❄☎) Attractive hotel with 33 tastefully 'classic' rooms, some with tiny balconies but all with wood floors, modern conveniences and earthy color schemes. Go for the penthouse with terrace for something special. Creative elevator with one glass wall facing an artsy mural. Great breakfast served in the downstairs, rustic-hip restaurant.

Infinito Hotel BOUTIQUE HOTEL $$
(Map p66; ☎011 2070-2626; www.infinitohotel.com; Arenales 3689; r from US$105; ❄@☎; Ⓢ Línea D Scalabrini Ortíz) Starting at its small lobby cafe-reception, this hotel exudes a certain trendiness. Rooms are small but good, boasting flat-screen TVs, fridges and a purple color scheme, and there's a sauna and Jacuzzi. It tries to be ecologically conscious, mostly by recycling. Located near some parks but still within walking distance of Palermo's nightlife. Buffet breakfast is included.

Palermo Viejo B&B GUESTHOUSE $$
(Map p66; ☎011 4773-6012; www.palermoviejobb.com; Niceto Vega 4629; s/d US$70/80; ❄@☎; 🚌140) This small and intimate B&B is located in a remodeled casa chorizo – a long, narrow house. The six rooms all front a leafy outdoor patio hallway and are simple but quite comfortable; two have lofts. All come with fridge and a good breakfast. RSVP or call them ahead of time – they often leave on errands in the afternoon.

The nearest Subte stop – Línea B, Malabia – is nine blocks away.

Eating

Buenos Aires is overflowing with excellent food, and you'll dine well at all budget levels. Typical restaurants serve a standard fare of *parrilla* (grilled meats), pasta, pizza and *minutas* (short orders), but for something different head to Palermo, home to a large number of ethnic eateries. Another food-oriented neighborhood is Puerto Madero, but most of the restaurants here cater to the business set and are consequently very fancy and relatively expensive, and lean more toward steaks than stir-fries.

Vegetarians rejoice: unlike in the rest of Argentina, there is a good range of meat-free restaurants in BA – you just have to know where to look. Most nonvegetarian restaurants offer a few pasta dishes, salads and pizzas, but not much else is meat-free.

City Center

★Chan Chan PERUVIAN $

(Map p60; ☎011 4382-8492; Hipólito Yrigoyen 1390; mains AR$60-90; ⏰noon-4pm & 8pm-12.30am Tue-Sat, to 11.30pm Sun) Thanks to fair prices and relatively quick service, this colorful Peruvian eatery is jam-packed at lunchtime with office workers devouring plates of *ceviche* (seafood cured in citrus) and *ajiaco de conejo* (rabbit and potato stew). There are also plenty of *arroz chaufa* (Peruvian-style fried rice) dishes, easily downed with a tangy pisco sour or a pitcher of *chicha morada* (a sweet fruity drink).

Latino Sandwich SANDWICHES $

(Map p60; ☎011-4331-0859; www.latinosandwich.com; Tacuari 185; sandwiches AR$40-56; ⏰8am-5pm Mon-Fri) Some of the best eateries in BA are holes-in-the-wall – and here's a case in point. This is the downtown place to grab sandwiches like an Argentine *milanesa* (breaded steaks but with arugula and guacamole!), BBQ pork with cheddar cheese, or grilled zucchini and eggplant. There's only one communal table, as it caters to mostly to-go business clientele.

Pizzería Güerrín PIZZA $

(Map p60; ☎011 4371-8141; Av Corrientes 1368; pizza slice AR$16; ⏰11am-1am Sun-Thu, to 2am Fri & Sat) A quick pit stop on Av Corrientes is this cheap but classic old pizza joint. Just pay, then point at a prebaked slice behind the glass counter and eat standing up with the rest of the crowd. Or sit down and order one freshly baked – this way you can also choose from a greater variety of toppings for your pizza.

Vita HEALTH FOOD $

(Map p60; ☎011 4342-0788; www.vitamarket.com.ar; Hipólito Yrigoyen 583; mains AR$60-65; ⏰8am-8pm Mon-Wed, to 1am Thu & Fri, 10:30am-1am Sat, 11am-7pm Sun; 🌿) Here's a hippie-ish, casual and health-oriented eatery offering tasty vegetarian dishes like organic seitan pizzas, lentil burgers and vegetable calzones. Various freshly mixed juices and *licuados* (fruit shakes) are available (with the option of adding a wheatgrass shot) and there are plenty of gourmet salads. Organic coffee is also served. Another branch is in Palermo.

A few shelves are lined with health-oriented products for sale.

Parrilla Peña PARRILLA $$

(Map p60; ☎011 4371-5643; Rodríguez Peña 682; mains AR$80-160; ⏰noon-4pm & 8pm-midnight Mon-Sat, noon-4pm Sun) This simple, traditional and long-running *parrilla* (grill-house) is well known for its excellent-quality meats and generous portions. The service is fast and efficient and it's great value. Don't expect many tourists – this is a local's sort of place. Also on offer are homemade pastas, salads and *milanesas*, along with several tasty desserts and a good wine list.

San Telmo

El Banco Rojo INTERNATIONAL $

(Map p60; ☎011 4362-3177; Bolivar 914; mains AR$50-60; ⏰noon-12:30am Tue-Sat, to 11:30pm Sun) A San Telmo youth magnet, this small and trendy joint serves up sandwiches (Tandoori pork, lamb *kofta*), falafels, burgers, tacos and salads. Try the *empanada de cordero* (lamb turnover) if it's available. Very casual, with blasting rock music and counter seating only.

Bar El Federal ARGENTINE $

(Map p60; ☎011 4361-7328; Carlos Calvo 599; mains AR$65-160; ⏰8am-2am Sun-Thu, to 4am Fri & Sat; 📶) Dating from 1864, this historic bar has a classic, somewhat rustic atmosphere accented with original wood, tiles and an eye-catching antique bar. The specialties here are sandwiches (especially turkey) and *picadas* (shared appetizer plates), but there are also lots of pastas, salads, desserts and tall mugs of icy beer.

El Desnivel PARRILLA $$

(Map p60; ☎011 4300-9081; Defensa 855; mains AR$100-180; ⏰noon-midnight Tue-Sun, 7pm-midnight Mon) This famous, long-running *parrilla* joint packs in both locals and tourists, serving them treats like chorizo sandwiches and *bife de lomo* (tenderloin steak). The sizzling grill out front is torturous while you wait for a table (which could be in the large back room) – get here early, especially on weekends.

Chochán ARGENTINE $$

(Map p60; ☎011 4307-3661; Piedras 672; mains AR$125-175; ⏰8pm-midnight Mon-Fri, noon-4pm & 8pm-midnight Sat & Sun) This eatery is for pork-lovers only – ribs, braised shoulder, elbows and ravioli – everything is made from pork, or *chanchos* in Spanish (Chochán being a play on words). Grab a sandwich: pork belly, pulled pork, pork tongue. Or white corn and smoked pork soup. Or a small plate like pork blood sausage. No guilt – pigging out here is totally allowed.

Recoleta

Cumaná ARGENTINE $
(Map p60; 011 4813-9207; Rodriguez Peña 1149; mains AR$75-125; noon-4pm & 8pm-1am) To sample Argentina's regional cuisine, check out this colorful, budget-friendly eatery with huge picture windows and an old-fashioned adobe oven. Cumaná specializes in delicious *cazuela* (stick-to-your-ribs stews filled with squash, corn, eggplant, potatoes and meat). Also popular are the empanadas, *locro* (corn and meat stew) and *humitas* (corn, cheese and onion tamales). Come early to avoid a wait.

El Sanjuanino ARGENTINE $
(Map p60; 011 4805-2683; Posadas 1515; empanadas AR$19, mains AR$80-150; noon-4pm & 7pm-1am) This long-running, cozy little joint probably has the cheapest food in Recoleta, attracting both penny-pinching locals and thrifty tourists. Sit either upstairs or downstairs (in the basement) and order spicy empanadas, tamales or *locro*. The curved brick ceiling adds to the atmosphere, but many take their food to go – Recoleta's lovely parks are just a couple of blocks away.

Rodi Bar ARGENTINE $$
(Map p60; 011 4801-5230; Vicente López 1900; mains AR$100-200; 7am-1am Mon-Sat) A great option for well-priced, unpretentious food in upscale Recoleta. This traditional corner restaurant with fine old-world atmosphere and extensive menu offers something for everyone, from inexpensive combo plates to relatively unusual dishes such as marinated beef tongue.

Palermo

★**Sarkis** MIDDLE EASTERN $
(Map p66; 011 4772-4911; Thames 1101; mains AR$65-160; noon-3pm & 8pm-1am) The food is fabulous and well priced at this longstanding Middle Eastern restaurant – come with a group to sample many exotic dishes. Start with the roasted eggplant hummus, *boquerones* (marinated sardines), *keppe crudo* (raw meat) or *parras rellenas* (stuffed grape leaves), then follow up with kebabs or lamb in yogurt sauce. Less busy at lunchtime; expect a long wait for dinner.

Fukuro Noodle Bar JAPANESE $
(Map p66; 15-3290-0912; www.fukuronoodlebar.com; Costa Rica 5514; noodle soup AR$110; 8pm-midnight Tue-Thu, to 1am Fri & Sat) For a welcome change from all that meat consumption, check into this comfort-food eatery. Four kinds of ramen are on offer, along with a good selection of *bao* (steamed buns) and *gyoza* (potstickers). Gluten-free noodles available, plus sake and microbrew draft beer. Popular, with counter seating only.

Oui Oui INTERNATIONAL $
(Map p66; 011 4778-9614; www.ouioui.com.ar; Nicaragua 6068; mains AR$70-90; 8am-8pm Mon-Sat;) *Pain au chocolat* and shabby chic? *Oui*. This charming and popular French-style cafe produces the goods – dark coffee, buttery croissants and jars of tangy lemonade – and boasts a small and cozy interior. Choose also from creative salads, gourmet sandwiches and luscious pastries. Its annex, **Almacén Oui Oui** (Map p66; cnr Dorrego & Nicaragua; 8am-9pm Tue-Sun), is on the same block.

Burger Joint AMERICAN $
(Map p66; 011 4833-5151; Jorge Louis Borges 1766; burgers AR$60; noon-midnight) For some of the juiciest burgers in BA, head to this popular, graffiti-covered spot. NYC-trained chef Pierre Chacra offers just four kinds to choose from, but they're all stellar. Try the Mexican (jalapeños, guacamole and hot sauce) or Jamaican (pineapple, cheddar and bacon) with a side of hand-cut fries.

El Preferido de Palermo ARGENTINE $
(Map p66; 011 4774-6585; Jorge Louis Borges 2108; mains AR$100-120; 9am-11:30pm Mon-Sat) You can't get much more traditional than this atmospheric, family-run joint. Order tapas, meat platters, homemade pastas and seafood soups, or try one of its specialties – the tortillas, *milanesas* and Cuban rice with veal and polenta. Hanging hams, jars of olives and high tables with blocky wood stools add to the charm.

★**Don Julio** PARRILLA $$
(Map p66; 011 4832-6058; Guatemala 4699; mains AR$115-230; noon-4pm & 7:30pm-1am) Classy service and a great wine list add an

upscale bent to this traditional, and very popular, corner steakhouse. The *bife de chorizo* (thick sirloin) is the main attraction here, but the baked goat-cheese provolone, *bondiola de cerdo* (pork shoulder) and gourmet salads are a treat as well, and portions are large. Come early to avoid a wait.

Gran Dabbang INTERNATIONAL, FUSION **$$**
(Map p66; ☎011 4832-1186; Scalabrini Ortiz 1543; small plates AR$80-95; ⏰8pm-midnight Mon-Sat) Unique and creative would be the minimal words to describe the stunning cuisine at this unassuming restaurant on a busy avenue. About eight small plates are offered, a wild-eyed fusion of Indian, Thai and Paraguayan influences (among many), drawn from chef Mariano Ramón's world travels. Come early or late to avoid the inevitable wait.

Las Pizarras INTERNATIONAL **$$**
(Map p66; ☎011 4775-0625; www.laspizarrasbistro.com; Thames 2296; mains AR$140-215; ⏰8pm-midnight Tue-Sun) At this simple and unpretentious yet excellent restaurant, Chef Rodrigo Castilla cooks up a changing rainbow of eclectic dishes such as grilled venison or rabbit stuffed with cherries and pistachios. Those with meeker stomachs can choose the asparagus and mushroom risotto or any of the homemade pastas. The chalkboard menu on the wall adds to the casual atmosphere.

Bio VEGETARIAN **$$**
(Map p66; ☎011 4774-3880; www.biorestaurant.com.ar; Humboldt 2192; mains AR$120-150; ⏰11am-midnight Sun-Thu, to 1am Fri & Sat; ✎) Tired of meat? Then make a beeline for this casual, family-run restaurant, which specializes in healthy, organic and vegetarian fare. Try the quinoa risotto, curry seitan, Mediterranean couscous or mushrooms a la Bahiana (Brazilian-style). Don't miss the refreshing ginger lemonade. Also caters to celiacs, vegans and raw foodists. Cooking class available.

El Tejano BARBECUE **$$**
(Map p66; www.facebook.com/ElTejanoBA; Honduras 4416; mains AR$105-145; ⏰12:30-4:30pm & 9pm-midnight Tue-Sat) Missing Texas barbecue from back home? Here's the place to scratch that itch. Authentic Texan Larry Rogers grills up the city's best beef and pork ribs, along with smoked brisket, pulled pork and chicken wings. The offerings may change by the day but you can always expect amazingly tender and delicious meats; the empanadas and fries are also amazing.

Drinking

Buenos Aires is all about the night, and there are plenty of cafes, bars and nightclubs in which to drink the dark away. Cafes are commonplace and usually open early morning until late, offering a long list of food and drinks. Bars open late and stay open even later; on weekends they'll often be hopping until 6am. And at nightclubs, the action often doesn't start until 2am.

For a night of rowdy drinking, join the expat-run **Pub Crawl** (☎15-5464-1886; www.pubcrawlba.com).

City Center

Café Tortoni CAFE
(Map p60; ☎011 4342-4328; www.cafetortoni.com.ar; Av de Mayo 829) BA's oldest and most famous cafe, the classic Tortoni has become so popular with foreigners that it's turned into a tourist trap. Still, it's practically an obligatory stop for any visitor to town: order a couple of churros (fried pastry dough) with your hot chocolate and forget about the inflated prices. There are also tango shows (p75) nightly – reserve ahead.

Milión COCKTAIL BAR
(Map p60; ☎011 4815-9925; www.milion.com.ar; Paraná 1048; ⏰6pm-2am Sun-Wed, to 3am Thu, to 4am Fri & Sat) One of BA's most gorgeous and elegant bars, this sexy spot takes up three floors of a renovated old mansion. The garden out back is a leafy paradise, overlooked by a solid balcony that holds the best seats in the house. Nearby marble steps are also an appealing place to lounge with a frozen mojito or basil daiquiri, the tastiest cocktails on the menu. The downstairs restaurant serves international dishes.

La Cigale COCKTAIL BAR
(Map p60; ☎011 4893-2332; www.facebook.com/lacigalebar; 25 de Mayo 597; ⏰noon-4pm & 6pm-close) This sensuous upstairs bar-restaurant is popular with both office workers (during the day) and music-industry folks (later in the evening). There's either live music or DJs most nights, but it's best known for its 'Minelek' night on Tuesday, when electronica and exotic cocktails draw heavy crowds. Fusion foods are served for both lunch and dinner.

Bahrein CLUB
(Map p60; ☎011 6225-2731; www.bahreinba.com; Lavalle 345; ⏰Thu-Sun) Attracting a good share of BA's tattooed youth, Bahrein is a

hugely popular downtown club housed in an old bank (check out the 'vault' in the basement). On the ground floor is the lounge-like Funky Room where resident DJs spin house music and electronica. Downstairs is the happening Xss discotheque, an impressive sound system and a dance floor for hundreds.

San Telmo

★Bar Plaza Dorrego CAFE

(Map p60; ☎011 4361-0141; Defensa 1098; ⏰8am-midnight Sun-Thu, to 3:30am Fri & Sat) You can't beat the atmosphere at this traditional joint; sip your *submarino* (hot milk with chocolate) by a picturesque window and watch the world pass by, or grab a table on the busy plaza. Meanwhile, traditionally suited waiters, piped-in tango music, antique bottles and scribbled graffiti on walls and counters might take you back in time.

Coffee Town COFFEE

(Map p60; ☎011 4361-0019; www.coffeetownargentina.com; Bolivar 976, Mercado de San Telmo; ⏰10am-8pm) For some of BA's best coffee, drop into this very casual kiosk inside the Mercado de San Telmo (enter via Carlos Calvo). Experienced baristas serve up organic, fair-trade coffee derived from beans from all over the world – think Colombia, Kenya, Sumatra and Yemen. A few pastries help the java go down easy.

La Puerta Roja BAR

(Map p60; ☎011 4362-5649; Chacabuco 733; ⏰5pm-late) There's no sign at this upstairs bar – just look for the red door. It has a cool, relaxed atmosphere with low lounge furniture in the main room and a pool table tucked behind. This is a traditional place, so you won't find fruity cocktails on the menu – but there is good international food like curries, tacos and chicken wings.

Doppelgänger COCKTAIL BAR

(☎011 4300-0201; www.doppelganger.com.ar; Av Juan de Garay 500; ⏰7pm-2:30am Tue-Thu, to 4am Fri, 8pm-4am Sat) This cool, emerald-hued corner bar is one of the only places in BA where you can count on a perfectly mixed martini. That's because Doppelgänger specializes in vermouth cocktails. The atmosphere is calm and the lengthy menu is fascinating: start with the journalist, a martini with a bitter orange twist, or channel Don Draper and go for the bar's bestseller – an old-fashioned.

Gibraltar PUB

(Map p60; ☎011 4362-5310; Perú 895; ⏰noon-4am) One of BA's classic pubs, the Gibraltar has a cozy atmosphere and good bar counter for those traveling alone. It's also a great place for fairly authentic foreign cuisine – try the Thai, Indian or English dishes. For a little friendly competition, head to the pool table in the back. There are sports on TV, and happy hour runs from noon to 8pm every day.

Recoleta

La Biela CAFE

(Map p60; ☎011 4804-0449; www.labiela.com; Av Quintana 600; ⏰7am-2am Sun-Thu, to 3am Fri & Sat) A Recoleta institution, this classic landmark has been serving the *porteño* elite since the 1950s – when race-car champions used to frequent the place. The outdoor front terrace is unbeatable on a sunny afternoon, especially when the nearby weekend *feria* (street market) is in full swing. Just know that this privilege will cost 20% more.

Shamrock Basement CLUB

(Map p60; ☎011 4812-3584; Rodríguez Peña 1220; ⏰Thu-Sat) This cool but unpretentious subterranean club is known for first-rate DJ lineups, pounding house music and a diverse young crowd. Thanks to the Shamrock, the ever-popular Irish pub upstairs, the place sees plenty of traffic throughout the night. Come at 3am to see the club in full swing, or just descend the stairs after enjoying a few pints at ground level.

Palermo

★LAB Training Center & Coffee Shop CAFE, COFFEE

(Map p66; ☎011 4843-1790; www.labcafe.com.ar; Humbolt 1542; ⏰8am-8pm Mon-Sat) High ceilings and industrial chic are hallmarks of this excellent coffee shop. Choose your house-roasted beans and have them run through a Chemex, AeroPress, V60, Kalita, siphon or clever dripper. It mostly has counter seating, though upstairs there's a communal table for those serious about work. Brewing and espresso classes also on offer.

★Verne COCKTAIL BAR

(Map p66; ☎011 4822-0980; Av Medrano 1475; ⏰8pm-3am Tue-Thu, to 4am Fri, 9pm-4am Sat, to 3am Sun) Upscale yet casual bar with slight Jules Verne theme. Cocktails are the specialties here, whipped up by one of BA's best bartenders, Fede Cuco. A few tables, some cushy sofas and an airy outdoor patio offer a variety of seating options, but plant yourself at the bar to see drinks being made; check out the French absinthe server. House-made Negroni available.

Magdalena's Party BAR
(Map p66; ☎011 4833-9127; www.magdalenasparty.com; Thames 1795; ⏰8pm-2am Mon, 11am-3am Thu, to 4am Fri & Sat, to 5pm Sun) Popular bar-restaurant with laid-back atmosphere and *buena onda* (good vibes). DJs spin from Thursday to Saturday nights, and with cheap drinks this is a good pre-club spot; try the vodka lemonade by the pitcher. Happy hour runs from noon to midnight daily, and tasty expat-friendly food is served, such as freshly ground hamburgers, California-style burritos and organic coffee. Popular weekend brunch too.

Sugar SPORTS BAR
(Map p66; ☎011 4831-3276; www.sugarbuenosaires.com; Costa Rica 4619; ⏰7pm-5:30am Tue-Fri, 11am-5:30am Sat, 11am-3am Sun) This lively expat watering hole brings in a youthful nightly crowd with well-priced drink specials and comfort food like chicken fingers and buffalo wings. Watch sports on the five large TV screens or come on Thursdays – also known as ladies' night – when things can get a little rowdy. On weekends, you can roll out of bed and arrive in time for eggs and mimosas.

Niceto Club CLUB
(Map p66; ☎011 4779-9396; www.nicetoclub.com; Niceto Vega 5510; ⏰Thu-Sat) One of the city's biggest crowd-pullers, the can't-miss event at Niceto Club is Thursday night's Club 69, a subversive DJ extravaganza featuring gorgeously attired showgirls, dancing drag queens, futuristic video installations and off-the-wall performance art. On weekend nights, national and international spin masters take the booth to entertain lively crowds with blends of hip-hop, electronic beats, cumbia and reggae.

Crobar CLUB
(Map p66; ☎011 4778-1500; www.crobar.com.ar; cnr Av de la Infanta Isabell & Freyre; ⏰Fri & Sat) Stylish and spacious Crobar remains one of BA's most popular nightlife spots. Friday usually features international DJs mashing up the latest techno selections, while Saturday is popular with the LGBTIQ crowd and tends to feature electro-pop and Latin beats. The main levels are strewn with mezzanines and catwalks that allow views from above; bring a hefty wallet as this is a top-end spot.

Kika CLUB
(Map p66; www.kikaclub.com.ar; Honduras 5339; ⏰Tue-Sun) Being supremely well located near the heart of Palermo Viejo's bar scene makes Kika's popular Tuesday-night 'Hype' party easily accessible for the trendy crowds. It's a mix of electro, rock, hip-hop, drum and bass, and dubstep, all spun by both local and international DJs. Other nights see electronica, reggaeton, Latin beats and live bands ruling the roost.

Victoria Brown COCKTAIL BAR
(Map p66; ☎011 4831-0831; www.victoriabrownbar.com; Costa Rica 4827; ⏰9pm-4am Tue-Sat) Secreted behind a large draped door inside a cute coffee shop, this speakeasy lounge serves up excellent food and tasty, high-quality cocktails. It's a very popular place so dress up and come early to snag a sofa or curvy table-booth. Boasts a beautiful and sophisticated industrial-decor atmosphere; even the bathrooms fittings are creative. Reserve ahead for dinner.

☆ Entertainment

Buenos Aires never sleeps, so you'll find something to do every night of the week. There are continuous theater and musical performances, and tango shows are everywhere.

Every modern shopping center has its multiscreen cinema complex; most movies are shown in their original language, with subtitles. Check local newspapers on Friday for screening times; the Buenos Aires Herald (www.buenosairesherald.com) is in English and available at most newspaper kiosks.

Discount ticket vendors (selling tickets for select theater, tango and movie performances) include **Cartelera Vea Más** (☎011 6320-5319; www.veamasdigital.com.ar; Av Corrientes 1660, Local 2), **Cartelera Baires** (☎011-4372-5058; www.cartelerabaires.com; Av Corrientes 1382, Galería Apolo) and **Cartelera Espectáculos** (☎011 4322-1559; www.123info.com.ar; Lavalle 742)

Ticketek (☎011 5237-7200; www.ticketek.com.ar) has outlets throughout the city and sells tickets for large venues.

Tango Shows

Most travelers will want to take in a tango show in BA, but it's a bit futile to look for 'nontouristy' shows – tango is a participatory dance and so shows are geared toward voyeurs. Less expensive shows tend to be more traditional. *Milongas* are where dancers strut their stuff, but spectators don't really belong there (though some *milonga* venues put on occasional spectator shows).

There are many dinner-tango shows oriented to wealthier tourists. Some have a Las Vegas–like feel and often involve costume changes, dry ice and plenty of high kicks. The physical dancing feats can be spectacular. Reserve ahead.

There are 'free' (donation) street tango shows on Sunday at San Telmo's antiques fair and on El Caminito in La Boca, and sometimes on Calle Florida near Lavalle. Cultural centers are also good places for affordable shows, especially Centro Cultural Borges (www.ccborges.org.ar).

You can also take tango classes at Confitería Ideal.

Café Tortoni TANGO

(Map p60; ☎011 4342-4328; www.cafetortoni.com.ar; Av de Mayo 829) Nightly tango shows (reserve ahead) take place at this historic yet very touristy place. If you come earlier for the cafe, you may have to line up outside beforehand. Despite these downfalls, the Tortoni is BA's most famous cafe and still offers a beautiful atmosphere.

Get your ticket the day of or one day beforehand at the cafe between 11am and 5pm (cash only).

Live Music

Some bars have live music too.

★La Bomba de Tiempo LIVE MUSIC

(Map p66; www.labombadetiempo.com; Sarmiento 3131; ⊙Mon 7pm) For one of BA's biggest and most unique parties, check out La Bomba de Tiempo; it's at 7pm every Monday at Ciudad Cultural Konex.

Teatro Colón CLASSICAL MUSIC

(Map p60; ☎011 4378-7100; www.teatrocolon.org.ar; Cerrito 628) BA's premier venue for the arts, with ballet, opera and classical music.

La Trastienda LIVE MUSIC

(Map p60; ☎011 5254-9100; www.latrastienda.com; Balcarce 460) This large, atmospheric theater in San Telmo welcomes over 700, features a well-stocked bar, and showcases national and international live-music acts almost nightly. Look for headers such as Charlie García, Divididos, José González, Damien Rice and Conor Oberst. Check its website for the latest.

Usina del Arte CONCERT VENUE

(www.usinadelarte.org; Agustín Caffarena 1) This restored old electricity factory is a valiant attempt to breathe new life into an edgy section of La Boca. It's a gorgeous red-brick building complete with scenic clock tower, and its concert hall – boasting top-notch acoustics – can seat 1200 spectators. Offers free or inexpensive art exhibitions, along with music, theater and dance performances. Check the website for current happenings.

Spectator Sports

If you're lucky enough to witness a *fútbol* match, you'll encounter a passion unrivaled in any other sport. The most popular teams are **Boca Juniors** (☎011 4309-4700; www.bocajuniors.com.ar; Brandsen 805) in La Boca and **River Plate** (☎011 4789-1200; www.cariverplate.com; Alcorta 7597) in Belgrano, northwest of Aeroparque Jorge Newberry.

Ticket prices ultimately depend on the teams playing and the demand. In general, however, *entradas populares* (bleachers) are the cheapest seats and attract the more emotional fans of the game; don't show any signs of wealth in this section, including watches, necklaces or fancy cameras. *Plateas* (fixed seats) are a safer bet. There are also tour companies that take you to games, like Tangol (p77).

Polo in Buenos Aires is most popular from October to December, and games take place at Campo de Polo in Palermo. Rugby, horse racing and *pato* (a traditional Argentine game played on horseback) are some other spectator possibilities.

Shopping

Buenos Aires has its share of modern shopping malls, along with flashy store-lined streets like Calle Florida and Av Santa Fe. You'll find decent-quality clothes, shoes, leather, accessories, electronics, music and homewares, but anything imported (like electronics) will be very expensive.

Palermo Viejo is the best neighborhood for boutiques and creative fashions. Avenida Alvear, toward the Recoleta cemetery, means designer labels. Defensa in San Telmo is full of pricey antique shops. There are several weekend crafts markets, such as the hippy *feria artesanal* in front of Recoleta's cemetery. The famous San Telmo antiques fair takes place on Sunday. Leather jackets and bags are sold in stores on Calle Murillo (599 to 600 blocks) in the neighborhood of Villa Crespo. For cheap third-world imports, head to Av Pueyrredón near Estación Once (Once train station); you can find just about anything there.

Walrus Books (Map p60; ☎011 4300-7135; Estados Unidos 617; ⏲noon-8pm Tue-Sun) is run by an American-Argentine couple, and carries new and used books in English (including Lonely Planet titles).

ℹ Information

DANGERS & ANNOYANCES

Like in any big city, petty crime exists in Buenos Aires. In general, however, BA is pretty safe. You can walk around at all hours of the night in many places, even as a lone woman (people stay out late, and there are often other pedestrians on the streets). Most tourists leave unscathed – they tend to be travel-smart and don't wear fancy jewelry or go around with their wallets hanging out or purses left carelessly on a chair. They're cautious of pickpockets in crowded places, aware of their surroundings and at least *pretend* to know where they're going.

If anything, BA is besieged more by minor nuisances. When buying anything, count your change and keep an eye out for fake bills, especially in dark places like taxis and nightclubs (search for clear lines and a good watermark). Watch carefully for traffic when crossing streets, and look out for the piles of dog droppings underfoot. Note that fresh air is often lacking – air pollution and smoking are big issues.

Every city has its edgy neighborhoods, and in BA these include Constitución Estación (train station), the eastern border of San Telmo and La Boca (where, outside tourist streets, you should

GETTING INTO TOWN

If you fly into Buenos Aires from outside Argentina, you'll probably land at Ezeiza Airport, 35km south of the city center (about a 40-minute ride from downtown). Ezeiza is clean and modern and has food services, shops, internet access, luggage storage and an **information counter** (☎011-5480-6111; ⏲24hr).

To enter Argentina, some nationalities are charged a 'reciprocity fee' equivalent to what Argentines pay to visit those countries. This fee applies to Americans (US$160, valid for 10 years), Australians (US$100, valid for one year) and Canadians (US$92, valid until a month before your passport expires). You must pay this fee online before arriving in Argentina; see www.migraciones.gov.ar/accesibleingles. Print the receipt and bring it with you.

One way into town is the frequent, comfortable shuttle service (AR$145) by **Manuel Tienda León** (MTL; ☎011 4315-5115; www.tiendaleon.com; Av Eduardo Madero 1299, Ezeiza Airport); its booth is just outside customs. Another option is **Hostel Shuttle** (☎011 4511-8723; www.hostelshuttle.com.ar).

For taxis, avoid the drivers holding signs; head instead to the city taxi booth, which charges AR$450.

Penny-pinchers can take public bus 8 (AR$8, two hours). Catch it outside Terminal B, or outside Terminal A (turn to the right and walk a couple minutes to the bus stop across from the Petrobras gas station). You'll need a SUBE card (p78) to pay for the bus; buy one at the *kiosko* across from check-in stand 25 (the sign says 'open 25 hours!').

Avoid the *cambios* (exchange houses) as their rates are generally bad. Instead, head to the nearby Banco de la Nación, which has fair rates and is open 24 hours. There are several ATMS in Ezeiza.

Most domestic flights land at **Aeroparque Jorge Newbery** (☎011 5480-6111; www.aa2000.com.ar), only a few kilometers north of the city center. Manuel Tienda León shuttles to the city center take 15 minutes and cost AR$60. Bus 45 also goes to the center; take it going south (to the right as you leave the airport). Taxis to downtown cost about AR$130.

Shuttle transfers from Ezeiza to Aeroparque cost AR$155.

Retiro bus station is about 1km north of the city center; it has shops, cafes, telephone and internet services and luggage storage. Dozens of BA's local bus lines converge here; outside, it's a seething mass and not to be figured out after a 10-hour bus ride. You can take the Subte (subway) if your destination is near a stop, or head to one of the *remise* (a type of taxi) booths near the bus slots. There's a tourist office.

be careful even during the day). Avenida Florida can be edgy only very, very late at night.

IMMIGRATION OFFICES

Immigration (011 4317-0234; www.migraciones.gov.ar; Av Antártida Argentina 1355; 7:30am-2pm Mon-Fri)

INTERNET ACCESS

Internet access is everywhere and connections are generally fast and affordable.

MONEY

Banks and *cambios* (exchange houses) are the safest places to change money, and US dollars are the best foreign currency to exchange. In December 2015 currency controls were abolished, decreasing demand for US dollars on Argentina's 'blue' (ie black) market, but you'll still hear people on pedestrian Av Florida call out '*cambio, cambio, cambio*.' These folks are best avoided.

Most transactions require ID, and lines can be long at banks. *Cambios* have slightly poorer exchange rates, but are quicker and have fewer limitations. You can get a pretty fair rate for US dollars at many retail establishments.

Traveler's checks are very hard to cash and incur bad exchange rates; one exception is **American Express** (011 4310-3000; Arenales 707). ATMs are commonplace, though there are withdrawal limits that depend on your banking system. Visa and MasterCard holders can get cash advances, but check with your bank before traveling.

POST

National post branches are all over the city.

Correo Internacional (Map p60; 011 4891-9191; www.correoargentino.com.ar; Av Antártida Argentina; 9am-3:30pm Mon-Fri) For international parcels weighing 2kg to 20kg. Bring an open box or parcel as contents will be checked; boxes are also sold here. Look for the building with the yellow facade.

TELEPHONE

The easiest way to make a call is from a *locutorio* (small telephone office), where you enter a booth and make calls in a safe, quiet environment. Costs are comparable to street telephones and you don't need change. Most *locutorios* offer reasonably priced fax and internet services as well.

Public phones are numerous; use coins, or buy a magnetic phone card from any kiosk. For more on using telephones in Argentina, see p184.

TOURIST INFORMATION

Buenos Aires' small tourist offices are spread out in key tourist locations throughout the city. Hours vary throughout the year.

Ministerio de Turismo (Map p60; 011 4312-2232; www.turismo.gov.ar; Av Santa Fe 883, Retiro; 9am-7pm Mon-Fri) Mostly info on Argentina but helps with BA.

Tourist offices (www.bue.gov.ar) Florida (tourist kiosk; Map p60; cnr Avs Florida & Diagonal Roque Sáenz Peña); Recoleta (tourist kiosk; Map p60; cnr Av Quintana & Ortiz); Retiro bus station (Map p60; 7:30am-2:30pm Mon-Fri, to 4:30pm Sat & Sun).

Tourist Police (Comisaría del Turista; 011 4346-5748, 0800-999-5000; Av Corrientes 436; 24hr) Provides interpreters for travel-insurance reports.

TRAVEL AGENCIES

Say Hueque (011 5258-8740; www.sayhueque.com; Thames 2062, Palermo) This independent travel agency specializes in customized adventure trips all around Argentina, and will also make air, bus and hotel reservations. It offers various BA tours as well. Also has a branch in San Telmo (011 4307-2614; Chile 557).

Tangol (011 4363-6000; www.tangol.com; Florida 971, Suite 31) Do-all agency that offers city tours, tango shows, guides to *fútbol* games, hotel reservations, Spanish classes, air tickets and countrywide packages. Also offers unusual activities including helicopter tours and skydiving. Has another branch in San Telmo (Defensa 831).

Getting There & Away

AIR

Most international flights leave from **Ezeiza Airport** (www.aa2000.com.ar).

BOAT

Buquebus (Map p60; 011 4316-6500; www.buquebus.com; cnr Avs Antártida Argentina & Córdoba), which has several offices around town, has several daily ferries to Colonia via fast boat (one hour) or slow boat (three hours). At least one boat daily also goes directly to Montevideo (three hours), though boat-bus combinations via Colonia are cheaper. There are also seasonally available boat-bus services to Punta del Este, Uruguay's top beach resort.

There are more services in the summer season, when it's a good idea to buy your ticket in advance. Ticket prices vary throughout the year.

BUS

Retiro (Map p60; www.tebasa.com.ar; Av Antártida Argentina) is a huge three-story bus terminal with slots for 75 buses. Inside are cafeterias, shops, bathrooms, luggage storage, telephone offices with internet, ATMs, and a 24-hour information kiosk to help you navigate the terminal. There's also a **tourist**

office (p77); look for it across from bus slot 36.

The following lists are a small sample of very extensive services. Prices will vary widely depending on the season, the company and the economy. During holidays, prices rise; buy your ticket in advance. For current prices check www.omnilineas.com.

Domestic

DESTINATION	COST (AR$)	DURATION (HR)
Bariloche	1900	24
Comodoro Rivadavia	1900	24
Córdoba	775	10
Mar del Plata	600	5½
Mendoza	1300	15
Puerto Iguazú	1700	18
Puerto Madryn	1500	19
Rosario	350	4
Salta	1600	21
Tucumán	1400	15

International

DESTINATION	COST (AR$)	DURATION (HR)
Asunción, Paraguay	1400	18
Foz do Iguazú, Brazil	1500	19
Montevideo, Uruguay	600	8
Rio de Janeiro, Brazil	3000	42
Santiago, Chile	1500	20
São Paulo, Brazil	2700	34

TRAIN

With a few exceptions, rail travel in Argentina is limited to Buenos Aires' suburbs and provincial cities. It's cheaper but not nearly as fast, frequent or comfortable as hopping on a bus.

Getting Around

BICYCLE

BA is not the best city to cycle around, but things are getting better – a bike-lane system exists and there's a free bike-share program, though it's geared more toward residents than travelers (one-hour rental limits; copy of passport and entry stamp page required).

The city's best places for two-wheeled exploration are Palermo's parks and the Reserva Ecológica Costanera Sur – on sunny weekends you can rent bikes at these places. Companies like Biking Buenos Aires (p65) offer bike tours and bike rentals. And if you're around on the first Sunday of each month, check out BA's version of Critical Mass.

> **SUBE CARD**
>
> SUBE (www.sube.gob.ar) is an inexpensive rechargeable card that you use for the Subte (subway), local buses and trains. Get it at some kioskos, lottery offices, post offices or any other business that diplays the SUBE logo. Ezeiza Airport and Retiro bus terminal also have SUBE kiosks where you can buy this card. Charging the card itself is easy, and can be done at many kiosks or Subte stations.

BUS

Sold at many kiosks, the Guía T (get the pocket version) details some 200 bus routes. Fares depend on the distance, but are cheap; you'll need a SUBE card to pay. Offer front seats to elderly passengers or those with kids.

Check out www.omnilineas.com to figure out the system.

CAR & MOTORCYCLE

We don't recommend you rent a car to drive around Buenos Aires. *Porteño* drivers turn crazy behind the wheel and you shouldn't try to compete with them. In any case, public transport is excellent. Cars are good to explore the countryside, however. Try **Avis** (☎ 011 4326-5542; www.avis.com.ar; Cerrito 1535), **New Way** (☎ 011 4515-0331; www.new-wayrentacar.com; Marcelo T de Alvear 773) or **Hertz** (☎ 011 4816-0899; www.hertz.com.ar; Paraguay 1138).

For motorcycle rentals contact **Motocare** (☎ 011-4761-2696; www.motocare.com.ar/rental; Echeverria 738, Vicente Lopez) in the *barrio* of Vicente Lopez.

SUBWAY

Buenos Aires' Subte is fast, efficient and cheap. The most useful lines for travelers are Líneas A, B, D and E (which run from the *microcentro* to the capital's western and northern outskirts) and Línea C (which links Estación Retiro and Constitución).

Trains operate from approximately 5am to 10:30pm except Sunday and holidays (when hours are 8am to 10pm); they run frequently on weekdays, less so on weekends.

TAXI & REMISE

Black-and-yellow cabs are ubiquitous on BA's streets and relatively inexpensive. Tips are unnecessary, but rounding up to the nearest peso is common.

It's generally safe to hail a street taxi, though some drivers take advantage of tourists. Make sure the driver uses the meter: it's good to have an idea of where you're going, and make sure the meter doesn't run fast (it should change every 200m, or about every three blocks). Know your money: fake bills feel fake and either don't have watermarks or have a bad one. Finally, watch your money as some drivers deftly replace high bills with low ones, or switch your real bill for a fake one.

Remises (unmarked call taxis) are considered safer than street taxis, since an established company sends them out. Any business can phone a *remise* for you. And remember that most taxi and *remise* drivers are honest people just making a living.

AROUND BUENOS AIRES

Day trips to charming, cobbled Colonia del Sacramento (p940) in Uruguay are popular, and it's also easy to reach Montevideo (p932); Uruguay's capital), and the beach resort of Punta del Este (p949), only a few hours away from Buenos Aires.

Tigre

About an hour north of Buenos Aires is this favorite *porteño* weekend destination. You can check out the popular **riverfront**, take a relaxing boat ride in the **Delta del Paraná** and shop at **Mercado de Frutos** (a daily crafts market that's best on weekends).

Tigre's **tourist office** (☎011-4512-4497; www.vivitigre.gov.ar; Mitre 305; ⌚9am-6pm Mon-Fri) is behind McDonald's. Nearby are ticket counters for commuter boats that cruise the waterways; the tourist office is good and can recommend a destination.

The quickest, cheapest way to get to Tigre is by taking the train 'Mitre-Ramal Tigre' from Retiro train station all the way to Tigre (50 minutes, frequent). The most scenic way, however, is to take this same train to the suburb of Olivos, then transfer to the Tren de la Costa, a pleasant electric train that also ends up in Tigre. Buses 59, 60 and 152 also stop at the Tren de la Costa's Olivos station.

San Antonio De Areco

☎02326 / POP 23,000

Dating from the early 18th century, this serene village northwest of Buenos Aires is the symbolic center of Argentina's diminishing *gaucho* (cowboy) culture. It's also host to the country's biggest *gaucho* celebration, **Día de la Tradición**, on November 10. There's a cute plaza surrounded by historic buildings, while local artisans are known for producing maté paraphernalia, *rastras* (silver-studded belts) and *facones* (long-bladed knives). Buses run regularly from BA's Retiro bus terminal (AR$105, two hours).

NORTHEAST ARGENTINA

From the spectacular natural wilderness of Iguazú Falls in the north to the chic sophistication of Rosario in the south, the northeast is one of Argentina's most diverse regions. Wedged between the Ríos Paraná and Uruguay (thus earning it the nickname Mesopotamia), the region relies heavily on these rivers for fun and its livelihood. In contrast, the neighboring Chaco is sparsely populated, and often called Argentina's 'empty quarter.'

The northeast was one of the Jesuits' Argentinean power bases until their expulsion from the Americas in 1767, the legacy of which can be seen in the remains of the many missions in the region's northeast.

Rosario

☎0341 / POP 1,190,000

So, you dig the vibe of Buenos Aires, but its sheer size is sending you a little loco in the coco? Rosario may be the place for you.

Located just a few hours north, this is in many ways Argentina's second city – not in terms of population, but culturally, financially and aesthetically. Its roaring port trade and growing population even made it a candidate for national capital status for a while.

These days the city's backpacker scene is growing slowly, and the huge university and corresponding population of students, artists and musicians give it a solid foundation.

Nighttime, the streets come alive and the bars and clubs pack out. In the day, once everybody wakes up, they shuffle down to the river beaches for more music, drinks and lounging about.

It's not all fun and games, though. Culture vultures will enjoy the choice of museums and galleries, and Che Guevara fans will want to check out his birthplace.

Northeast Argentina

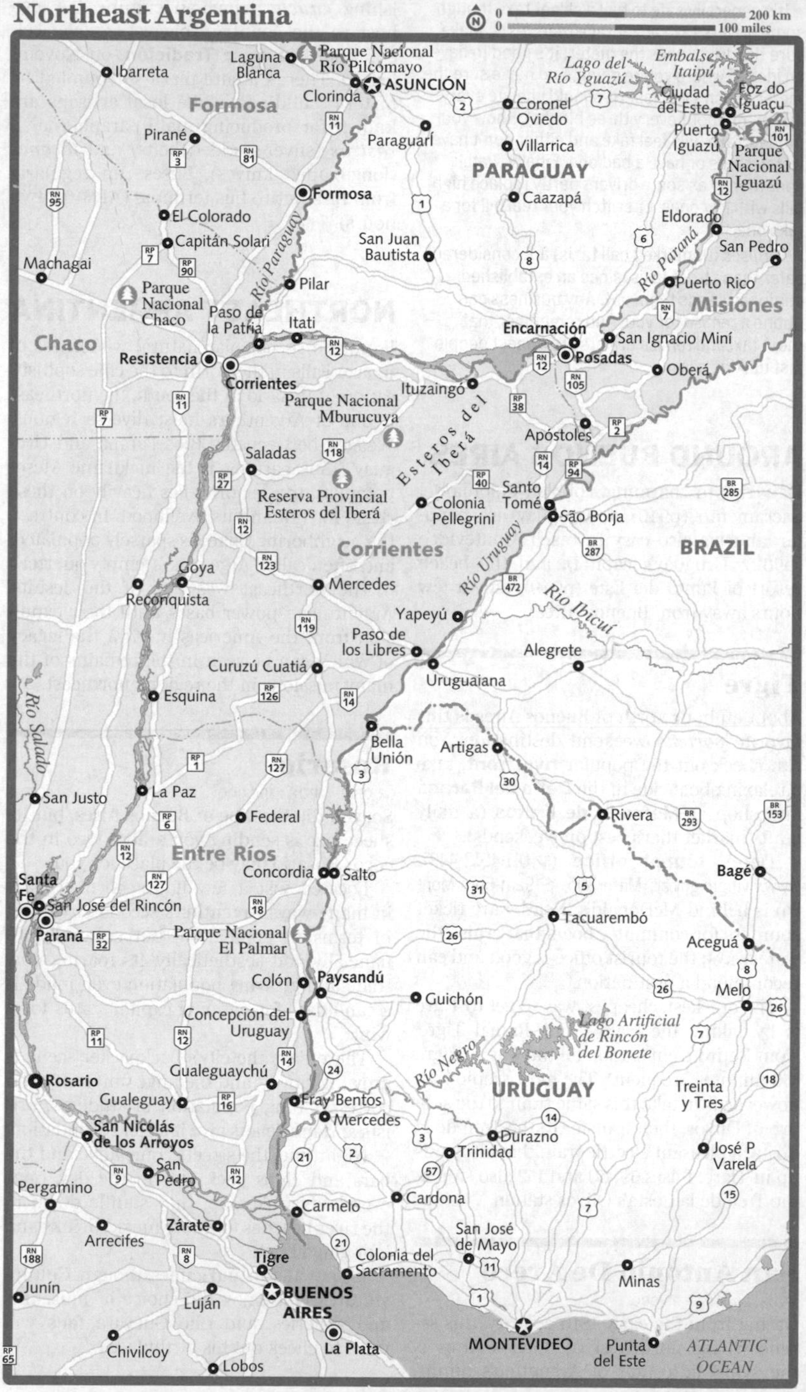

0 200 km
0 100 miles

Laguna Blanca
Parque Nacional Río Pilcomayo
Ibarreta
ASUNCIÓN
Clorinda
Formosa
Lago del Río Yguazú
Embalse Itaipú
Coronel Oviedo
Ciudad del Este
Foz do Iguaçu
RN 11
Paraguarí
Pirané
RP 3
RN 81
Villarrica
Puerto Iguazú
RN 101
Parque Nacional Iguazú
PARAGUAY
RN 95
Formosa
1
Caazapá
RN 12
El Colorado
Eldorado
Capitán Solari
Río Paraguay
San Juan Bautista
6
San Pedro
Machagai
RP 7
RP 90
8
Río Paraná
Parque Nacional Chaco
Pilar
Puerto Rico
RN 7
Misiones
Paso de la Patria
Itati
Chaco
Encarnación
San Ignacio Miní
RN 12
Resistencia
Corrientes
RN 12
Posadas
RN 105
Oberá
Ituzaingó
RN 11
Parque Nacional Mburucuyá
RP 7
Esteros del Iberá
RP 38
RP 2
Apóstoles
Saladas
RN 118
RN 14
RP 94
RP 27
RP 40
Santo Tomé
BR 285
Reserva Provincial Esteros del Iberá
Colonia Pellegrini
São Borja
RN 12
Río Uruguay
BR 287
Corrientes
BRAZIL
RN 123
Goya
Mercedes
BR 472
Reconquista
Río Ibicuí
Yapeyú
RN 119
Paso de los Libres
Alegrete
Curuzú Cuatiá
Uruguaiana
RP 126
RN 14
Esquina
Río Salado
Bella Unión
Artigas
RP 1
RN 127
3
30
La Paz
San Justo
Rivera
Federal
RP 6
BR 293
BR 153
RN 12
Entre Ríos
Concordia
Salto
Bagé
Santa Fe
RN 127
31
5
San José del Rincón
RN 18
Tacuarembó
Paraná
RP 32
Parque Nacional El Palmar
26
Aceguá
8
Colón
Paysandú
26
Melo
26
Guichón
Concepción del Uruguay
Lago Artificial de Rincón del Bonete
RP 11
RN 12
7
RN 14
Río Negro
24
18
Rosario
Gualeguaychú
URUGUAY
Treinta y Tres
Gualeguay
RP 16
Fray Bentos
Mercedes
14
San Nicolás de los Arroyos
3
Durazno
2
Trinidad
José P Varela
21
San Pedro
RN 9
RN 12
57
Pergamino
Carmelo
Cardona
15
7
Zárate
Arrecifes
San José de Mayo
21
RN 188
RN 8
Tigre
Colonia del Sacramento
11
Minas
Junín
BUENOS AIRES
Luján
1
9
La Plata
MONTEVIDEO
Punta del Este
ATLANTIC OCEAN
Chivilcoy
RP 65
Lobos

Sights & Activities

Central Rosario

Museo de Arte Contemporáneo de Rosario GALLERY

(MACRO; www.macromuseo.org.ar; Av de la Costa at Blvd Oroño; admission AR$10; ⏲2-8pm Thu-Tue) Housed in a brightly painted grain silo on the waterfront, this is part of Rosario's impressive riverbank renewal. It features temporary exhibitions, mostly by young local artists, of varying quality, housed in small galleries spread over eight floors. There's a good view of river islands from the *mirador* (viewpoint) at the top and an attractive cafe-bar by the river.

Museo de la Memoria MUSEUM

(www.museodelamemoria.gob.ar; Córdoba 2019; AR$10; ⏲10am-6pm Tue-Fri, 4-7pm Sat & Sun) A former army HQ not far from where police held, tortured and killed people during the Dirty War (Argentina's military dictatorships of 1976–83), this museum seeks to remember the violence and victims. If you can read Spanish, it's a small but very moving display, with witness descriptions, photos of the 'disappeared' and an attempt to look at the wider history of man's inhumanity to man. Temporary exhibitions upstairs.

Monumento Nacional a La Bandera MONUMENT

(www.monumentoalabandera.gob.ar; Santa Fe 581; elevator AR$10; ⏲9am-6pm Tue-Sun, 2-6pm Mon) Manuel Belgrano, who designed the Argentine flag, rests in a crypt beneath this colossal stone obelisk built where the blue-and-white stripes were first raised. If rampant nationalism isn't your thing, it's nevertheless worth taking the elevator to the top for great views over the waterfront, Paraná and islands. The attractive colonnade houses an eternal flame commemorating those who died for the fatherland.

★**Museo Municipal de Bellas Artes** GALLERY

(www.museocastagnino.org.ar; cnr Av Carlos Pellegrini & Blvd Oroño; admission AR$10; ⏲2-8pm Wed-Mon) This gallery is worth a visit for its inventive displays of contemporary and 20th-century artworks from the MACRO collection, and its small collection of European works, which contains a couple of very fine pieces.

Museo Histórico Provincial MUSEUM

(www.museomarc.gob.ar; Av del Museo, Parque Independencia; admission AR$10; ⏲9am-6pm Tue-Fri, 2-7pm Sat & Sun, 3-8pm Sat & Sun Dec-Mar) The well-presented collection features plenty of postindependence exhibits plus excellent displays on indigenous cultures from all over Latin America. Particularly interesting is the collection of baroque religious art from the southern Andes. Information in Spanish only. Closed when Newell's Old Boys are playing at home in the adjacent stadium.

Casa Natal de 'Che' Guevara BUILDING

(Entre Ríos 480) The apartment building at Entre Ríos 480 was where Ernesto Guevara Lynch and Celia de la Serna lived in 1928 after the birth of their son, Ernesto Guevara de la Serna, popularly known as 'Che.' According to biographer Jon Anderson, young Ernesto's birth certificate was falsified (he was born more than a month before the official date of June 14), but this was certainly Che's first home, although briefly. It's now a private flat, so you can't go inside.

Costanera

Rosario's most attractive feature is its waterfront, where what was once derelict warehouses and train tracks has been reclaimed for the fun of the people. It stretches some 15km from its southern end at Parque Urquiza to the city's northern edge, just short of the suspension bridge crossing into Entre Ríos province. It's an appealing place to wander and watch what's going on, from the plentiful birdlife and impromptu *fútbol* games to massive cargo ships surging past on the river.

Costanera Norte WATERFRONT, BEACH

In summer this strip beginning 5km north of downtown attracts crowds for its beaches. The mediocre public beach of Rambla Catalunya is backed by a promenade and bar-restaurants; beyond, the best beach is **Balneario La Florida** (admission AR$25; ⏲9am-8pm Oct-Apr), with services and a safe bathing area. Picturesque stalls behind it sell river fish. The summer-only 'Linea de la Costa' bus heads here from Rioja/Roca. Otherwise take bus 102N/103N/143N and walk a few blocks east from Blvd Rondeau.

Costanera Sur WATERFRONT

The grassy zone below downtown includes plenty of space for jogging and courting, as well as the **Estación Fluvial** (La Fluvial; ☎0341-447-3838; www.estacionfluvial.com; ⊙noon-5pm Mar-Oct, 10am-6pm Nov-Feb) building, offering boat trips and eating and drinking options. Heading further north, you pass various cultural venues before reaching **Parque de España** (Paraná riverbank) and its mausoleum-like edifice. Beyond here is a zone of bars and restaurants that gets lively at weekends, and then the city's contemporaryart museum.

Courses

Spanish in Rosario LANGUAGE COURSE
(☎15-560-3789; www.spanishinrosario.com; Catamarca 3095) Rosario is a great base for learning Spanish; this place offers enjoyable language programs and can arrange family stays and volunteer work placements.

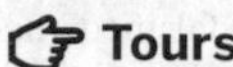

Tours

★**Rosario Kayak & Motor Boat Tours** TOUR
(Paseos en Lancha y Kayak; ☎15-571-3812; www.boattours.com.ar; Estación Fluvial) A friendly, professional, recommended multilingual set-up with great boat trips around the Paraná delta (AR$180 to AR$250, one to 1½ hours) with an optional lunch stop on a delta island. You can also explore the islands by kayak (AR$350, three hours). It also offers water-taxi service to the delta islands (from AR$70 return) and rents bikes for AR$150 per day. Book by phone, email or at the Estación Fluvial.

Rosario Free Tour WALKING TOUR
(☎0341-560-3789; www.rosariofreetour.com; Maipú & Urquiza; ⊙11:30am Sat) Two-hour walking tours in Spanish/English. Meet on the steps of the old customs building at the end of Maipú. Though it's technically free, a donation/tip is appropriate.

Festivals & Events

Rosario packs out for the long weekend on October 12. Many hotels and hostels double their prices and fill up well ahead of time.

Semana de la Bandera FIESTA
Climaxing in ceremonies on June 20, the anniversary of the death of Belgrano, Flag Week is Rosario's major fiesta.

Sleeping

There are dozens of hostels, but they're often booked up by groups of police or other government workers. There's also a group of average midrange hotels. Prices generally drop midweek.

Rosario

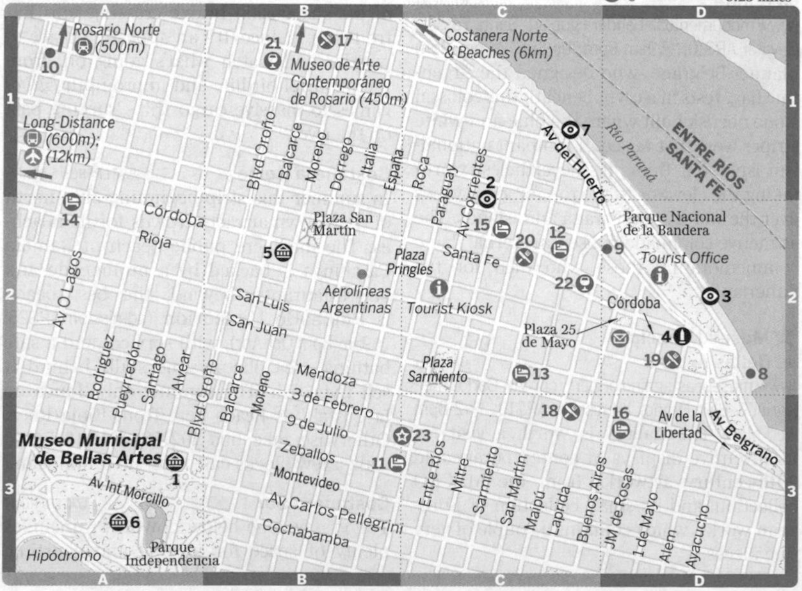

0 — 500 m
0 — 0.25 miles

Rosario Norte (500m)
Museo de Arte Contemporáneo de Rosario (450m)
Costanera Norte & Beaches (6km)
Long-Distance (600m); (12km)
Río Paraná
ENTRE RÍOS
SANTA FE
Av del Huerto
Parque Nacional de la Bandera
Tourist Office
Plaza San Martín
Plaza Pringles
Aerolíneas Argentinas
Tourist Kiosk
Córdoba
Plaza 25 de Mayo
Plaza Sarmiento
Av de la Libertad
Av Belgrano
Museo Municipal de Bellas Artes
Av Int Morcillo
Parque Independencia
Hipódromo
Av O Lagos
Av Carlos Pellegrini
Cochabamba

Residence Boutique Hostel HOTEL, HOSTEL $

(☎0341-421-8148; www.residenceboutique.com.ar; Buenos Aires 1145; dm/d/tr US$23/60/80; ❄@📶) Rather a special place, this lovely early-20th-century building houses a serene, beautiful hotel/hostel. Public spaces are full of art nouveau flourishes, and the compact, stylish private rooms offer great value for this level of comfort. Dorms are similarly upmarket, and the little garden patio and breakfast area are lovely places to relax. Original and striking.

La Casa de Arriba HOSTEL $

(☎0341-430-0012; www.lacasadearriba.com.ar; Córdoba 2889; dm weekend/weekday US$19/15; @📶) A designer's flair has made a fabulous hostel from this old house. Exposed brick, creative use of space, modern shelf-style bunks and a welcoming attitude makes this a comfortable, stylish Rosario base. Its distance from the center is offset by its relative proximity to bars and nightlife.

Hotel La Paz HOTEL $

(☎0341-421-0905; www.hotellapazrosario.com.ar; Barón de Maua 36; s/d US$35/42; ❄@📶) Well positioned on Plaza Montenegro, and still looking good after 70 years in operation, this welcoming budget hotel offers value for money. Family rooms at the front have balconies overlooking Plaza Montenegro.

La Casa de Pandora HOSTEL $

(☎0341-679-0314; www.lacasadepandora.com.ar; Entre Ríos 583; dm US$14-15; @📶) Small, arty and welcoming, this is one of many Rosario hostels but it does some basics – cleaning, for example – better than many competitors. It's a cute spot with attractive dorms, kitchen and a petite courtyard. Various workshops – yoga, dance, folk music – are held, and it hires bikes.

Esplendor Savoy Rosario HOTEL $$

(☎0341-429-6000; www.esplendorsavoyrosario.com; San Lorenzo 1022; r standard/superior/ste US$110/120/180; P❄@📶🏊) Even among Rosario's many elegant early-20th-century buildings, this art nouveau gem is a standout. It's a flawless contemporary conversion; rooms feature modern conveniences that blend well with the centenarian features. An indoor pool, elegant cafe-bar and roof garden are among the attractions. It's popular for events, so don't expect a peaceful stay.

1412 HOTEL $$

(☎0341-448-7755; www.1412.com.ar; Zeballos 1412; r US$84; ❄📶) Comfortably stylish, this decent-value modern hotel is perfectly located for sorties to the busy restaurant strip on Avenida Carlos Pellegrini. The handsome lobby offers free tea, coffee and cakes all day, while rooms are pleasingly, flawlessly modern.

Eating

If you feel like exploring, take a wander along Av Carlos Pelligrini between Maipú and Moreno. This is Rosario's restaurant strip: 10 blocks dedicated to the pillars of Argentine cuisine: pizza, *parrilla*, pasta, *tenedores libres* (all-you-can-eat restaurants) and ice cream, sometimes all gloriously

Rosario

Top Sights
1 Museo Municipal de Bellas Artes A3

Sights
2 Casa Natal de 'Che' Guevara C1
3 Costanera Sur D2
4 Monumento Nacional a La Bandera D2
5 Museo de la Memoria B2
6 Museo Histórico Provincial A3
7 Parque de España C1

Activities, Courses & Tours
8 Estación Fluvial D2
9 Rosario Free Tour D2
Rosario Kayak & Motor Boat Tours .... (see 8)
10 Spanish in Rosario A1

Sleeping
11 1412 .... B3
12 Esplendor Savoy Rosario C2
13 Hotel La Paz C2
14 La Casa de Arriba A2
15 La Casa de Pandora C2
16 Residence Boutique Hostel D3

Eating
17 Comedor Balcarce B1
18 El Ancla C3
19 La Marina D2
20 Lo Mejor del Centro C2

Drinking & Nightlife
21 Bound B1
22 El Diablito C2

Entertainment
23 La Chamuyera C3

LOCAL KNOWLEDGE

PICHINCHA

Between Oroño and Francia, and north of Urquiza, the *barrio* (neighborhood) of Pichincha is the city's most interesting for nightlife. The leafy streets and wide pavements make it seem a sleepy suburb by day, but at night every corner seems to have a quirky bar or hipster restaurant. The city's best *boliches* (nightclubs) are also found here.

available in the one location. Otherwise, there's a *confitería* (cafe/snack bar) on just about every street corner.

★La Marina SPANISH, SEAFOOD $

(1 de Mayo 890; mains AR$40-95; ⏲noon-4pm & 8pm-midnight Mon-Sat) Just above the flag monument, this basement place decorated with faded Spanish tourism posters is a top spot for inexpensive and really delicious seafood, like *rabas* (calamari) or succulent river fish on the grill. No bookings, so be prepared to wait, as it's deservedly popular. Don't confuse with the restaurant above.

Lo Mejor del Centro PARRILLA $

(Santa Fe 1166; mains AR$65-160; ⏲noon-3pm & 8pm-midnight; 📶) When this *parrilla* went bust, the staff managed to reopen it as a cooperative, and what a great job they've done. The meat's as good as you'll taste in Rosario, but you can also enjoy homemade pasta, paella, creative salads and a warm, convivial buzz at the tightly packed, ageing tables. There are various midweek set menus that are great value.

El Ancla ARGENTINE $

(Maipú 1101; mains AR$50-100; ⏲7am-1am Mon-Fri, 8am-4pm & 7pm-1am Sat, 10am-4pm & 7pm-1am Sun) One of Rosario's many beloved corner restaurants, this well frequented local has an appealingly venerable interior and an authentic feel. The food – with lots of inexpensive single-plate meals – is reliably good and you always seem to get a friendly welcome. A good budget choice.

Comedor Balcarce ARGENTINE $

(cnr Balcarce & Brown; mains AR$50-120; ⏲noon-3pm & 8:15pm-midnight Mon-Sat) In business for decades, this typical corner *bodegón* (traditional diner) is one of a fast-disappearing breed. Home-style Argentine cooking comes in big portions. Quality is average to good, prices are great and it's an authentic, friendly experience. Its affectionate nickname, El Vómito (the Vomit), shouldn't put you off.

Escauriza SEAFOOD $$

(☎0341-454-1777; cnr Bajada Escauriza & Paseo Ribereño; mains AR$110-195; ⏲noon-3:30pm & 8pm-midnight) Backing Florida beach, this legendary place is one of Rosario's best spots for fish. The enormous indoor-outdoor dining area is redolent with the aromas of chargrilling river catch like surubí; start with some delicious seafood empanadas. Service, quality and quantity are all highly impressive. Book, get there at noon, or wait and wait at summer weekend lunchtimes. No credit cards. Awful coffee.

🍷 Drinking & Entertainment

Rosario has a great number of *restobares*, which function as hybrid cafes and bars and generally serve a fairly standard selection of snacks and plates. Many are good for a morning coffee, an evening glass of wine – or anything in between.

There are lots of tango places in Rosario; grab the monthly listings booklet from the tourist office and check www.rosarioturismo.com.

El Diablito PUB

(Maipú 622; ⏲9pm-3:30am Tue-Sat) With a red-lit interior true to its origins as a brothel, this place has an atmosphere all of its own. The soundtrack is '70s and '80s rock, and the decor is sumptuous with stained-glass panels and age-spotted mirrors. A classic place to drink.

Bound CLUB

(Blvd Oroño 198; ⏲9pm-late Fri & Sat) Rosario's best *boliche* (nightclub) at the time of research, this stylish spot is in the heart of the liveliest nightlife zone. It operates a pretty fascist door policy, so think twice if the queue's long.

La Chamuyera TANGO

(Av Corrientes 1380; ⏲Mon-Sun) With an underground feel reminiscent of its semi-illegal past, this atmospheric venue is one of Rosario's best tango spots. The Thursday *milonga* kicks off at 10:30pm and there's a practice session on Monday nights. Other events include language nights, poetry readings and a variety of concerts: it's always worth stopping by for a beer and a look.

Information

The informative **tourist office** (☎0341-480-2230; www.rosarioturismo.com; Av del Huerto; ⏲8am-7pm Mon-Fri, 9am-7pm Sat, 9am-6pm Sun) is on the waterfront. There's a more central **branch** (Córdoba, near Av Corrientes; ⏲8am-7pm Mon-Fri, 9am-7pm Sat, 10am-6pm Sun) downtown.

Cambios along San Martín and Córdoba change traveler's checks; there are many banks and ATMs on Santa Fe between Mitre and Entre Ríos.

The **post office** (www.correoargentino.com.ar; Córdoba 721; ⏲8am-8pm Mon-Fri) is near Plaza Sarmiento.

Getting There & Around

AIR

Aerolíneas Argentinas (☎0810-22286 527; www.aerolineas.com.ar; España 840; ⏲10am-6pm Mon-Fri, 9am-noon Sat) flies four times weekly to Buenos Aires. **Sol** (☎0810-444-4765; www.sol.com.ar) flies daily to Buenos Aires and also services Córdoba and, seasonally, Punta del Este. A *remise* to/from the airport (8km from town) should cost around AR$130.

BUS

The **long-distance bus terminal** (☎0341-437-3030; www.terminalrosario.gob.ar; Cafferata & Santa Fe) is 4km west of the center. To get there, any bus along Santa Fe will do the trick. Going into town, take a bus marked 'Centro' or 'Plaza Sarmiento.' It's about AR$40 to AR$70 in a taxi.

Buses from Rosario

DESTINATION	COST (AR$)	DURATION (HR)
Buenos Aires	250-285	4
Córdoba	360	5½-7
Mendoza	750-820	12-15
Montevideo, Uruguay	1162	8½

TRAIN

From **Rosario Sur train station** (www.trenesargentinos.gob.ar; cnr San Martín & Battle y Ordóñez; ⏲ticket office 6pm-1am), 7.5km south of the center down Avenida San Martín, new trains run an improved service daily to Buenos Aires (2nd/1st class AR$175/225, 6½ hours), leaving Rosario at 12:26am and leaving Retiro at 4:07pm.

The **Rosario Norte train station** (www.trenesargentinos.gob.ar; Av del Valle 2750), 3km northwest of the center, has services to Buenos Aires, Tucumán and Córdoba. Due to the poor condition of tracks and carriages and frequent delays, you'd have to be a true train buff to appreciate these services; trains are slow, downmarket and cheap, and they book out well in advance.

REMOTE NATIONAL PARKS IN NORTHEAST ARGENTINA

Northeast Argentina is home to some incredible parks that take some getting to, but are well worthwhile. Here are a few. For more information, log on to www.parquesnacionales.gov.ar.

Parque Nacional El Palmar (☎03447-493049; www.parquesnacionales.gob.ar; RN 14, Km199; admission Argentines/Mercosur/foreigners AR$70/100/120) Home to capybara, *ñandú* (rhea; a large flightless bird resembling the ostrich) and poisonous pit vipers, this 8500-hectare park protects the endangered yatay palm. The park also has cheap camping, good walking trails and swimming holes. It lies between Colón and Concordia, on the Uruguayan border; both are easily accessible from Gualeguaychú.

Parque Nacional Chaco (☎03725-499161; www.parquesnacionales.gob.ar) FREE This park protects 150 sq km of marshes, palm savannas and strands of the disappearing *quebracho colorado* tree. Birds far outnumber mammals – there are plenty of rhea, jabiru, roseate spoonbills, cormorants and common caracaras – but mosquitoes outnumber them all. Bring repellent. Camping is free, but facilities are basic. Capitán Solari (5km from the park entrance) is the nearest town, and is easily accessed from Resistencia.

Parque Nacional Río Pilcomayo (☎03718-470045; www.parquesnacionales.gob.ar; RN 86; ⏲8am-6pm) This 600-sq-km park is home to caiman, tapirs, anteaters, maned wolves and an abundance of birdlife, particularly around the centerpiece, Laguna Blanca (where piranhas make swimming a bad idea). Access is via the small town of Laguna Blanca (9km east of the actual lagoon), which can be reached from Formosa.

Bus 140 runs south down Sarmiento to the Rosario Sur station. Take bus 134 north up Mitre to a block from the Rosario Norte train station.

Santa Fe

☎0342 / POP 526,100

Santa Fe would be a fairly dull town if not for the university population. Thanks to this, there's a healthy bar and club scene, and plenty of fun to be had during the day.

Relocated during the mid-17th century because of hostile indigenous groups, floods and isolation, the city duplicates the original plan of Santa Fe La Vieja (Old Santa Fe). But a 19th-century neo-Parisian building boom and more recent construction have left only isolated colonial buildings, mostly near Plaza 25 de Mayo.

Sights & Activities

★Convento y Museo de San Francisco MONASTERY
(Amenábar 2257; admission AR$15; ⏲8am-12:30pm & 3:30-7pm Tue-Fri, 8am-noon & 4-7pm Sat) Santa Fe's principal historical landmark is this Franciscan monastery and museum, built in 1680. While the museum is mediocre, the church is beautiful, with an exquisite wooden ceiling. The lovely cloister has a real colonial feel and is full of birdsong and the perfume of flowers. The monastery is still home to a handful of monks.

Museo Etnográfico y Colonial Provincial MUSEUM
(www.museojuandegaray.gob.ar; 25 de Mayo 1470; donation AR$4; ⏲8:30am-12:30pm & 3-7pm Tue-Fri, 8:30am-12:30pm & 4-7pm Sat & Sun) Run with heartwarming enthusiasm by local teachers, this museum has a chronological display of stone tools, Guaraní ceramics, jewelry, carved bricks and colonial objects. Highlights include a set of *tablas* – a colonial game similar to backgammon – and a scale model of both original Santa Fe settlements. Afternoon opening hours vary.

Cervecería Santa Fe BREWERY
(☎0342-450-2237; www.cervezasantafe.com.ar; Calchines 1401) This brewery produces Santa Fe lager as well as brewing Budweiser and Heineken under license. Free tours run at 5pm Tuesday to Saturday; you'll need to wear sturdy footwear and long pants for safety reasons. Numbers are limited: you can reserve online.

Costa Litoral BOAT TOUR
(☎0342-456-4381; www.costalitoral.info; Dique 1) From the redeveloped harbor area, a large catamaran runs weekend trips around the river islands (adult/child AR$160/100, two hours, 11am Saturday and Sunday) or to Paraná (adult/child AR$260/160, 5½ hours, 2pm Saturday and Sunday) with a couple of hours to explore the city. Book tickets in the cafe opposite the dock.

Sleeping

The surprisingly seedy area around the bus terminal is the budget-hotel zone. It's not dangerous – just the town center for various unsavory transactions.

Hotel Constituyentes HOTEL $
(☎0342-452-1586; www.hotelconstituyentes.com.ar; San Luis 2862; s/d US$35/45, without bathroom US$25/35; ❄@📶) Spacious rooms, low prices and proximity to the bus terminal are the main drawcards of this relaxed place. It's not luxury, but the owners are always looking to improve things and it makes a pleasant budget base. Rooms at the front suffer from street noise. Breakfast is extra.

Hotel Galeón HOTEL $
(☎0342-454-1788; www.hotelgaleon.com.ar; Belgrano 2759; s/d US$52/64; ❄@📶) Handy for the bus, this unusual hotel is all curved surfaces and weird angles. There's a variety of room types, none of which is a conventional shape; the place is in need of a refit but the beds are comfortable enough and wi-fi is decent. Substantial discounts offered for cash.

Hostal Santa Fe de la Veracruz HOTEL $
(☎0342-455-1740; www.hostalsf.com; Av San Martín 2954; s/d standard US$46/63, superior US$66/80; P❄@📶) Decorated with indigenous motifs, this retro hotel on the pedestrian street offers polite service, spacious superior rooms and slightly downbeat standards. It's time for repainting though – those dozen shades of beige are looking very dated. Siesta fans will love the 6pm checkout.

★Ámbit Boulevard BOUTIQUE HOTEL $$
(☎0342-455-7179; www.ambithotel.com.ar; Blvd Gálvez 1408; r superior/premium US$100/112; ❄📶🏊) An early-20th-century flour magnate's mansion has been converted into this compact, rather lovely hotel. Exquisitely decorated rooms were each designed as a

Santa Fe

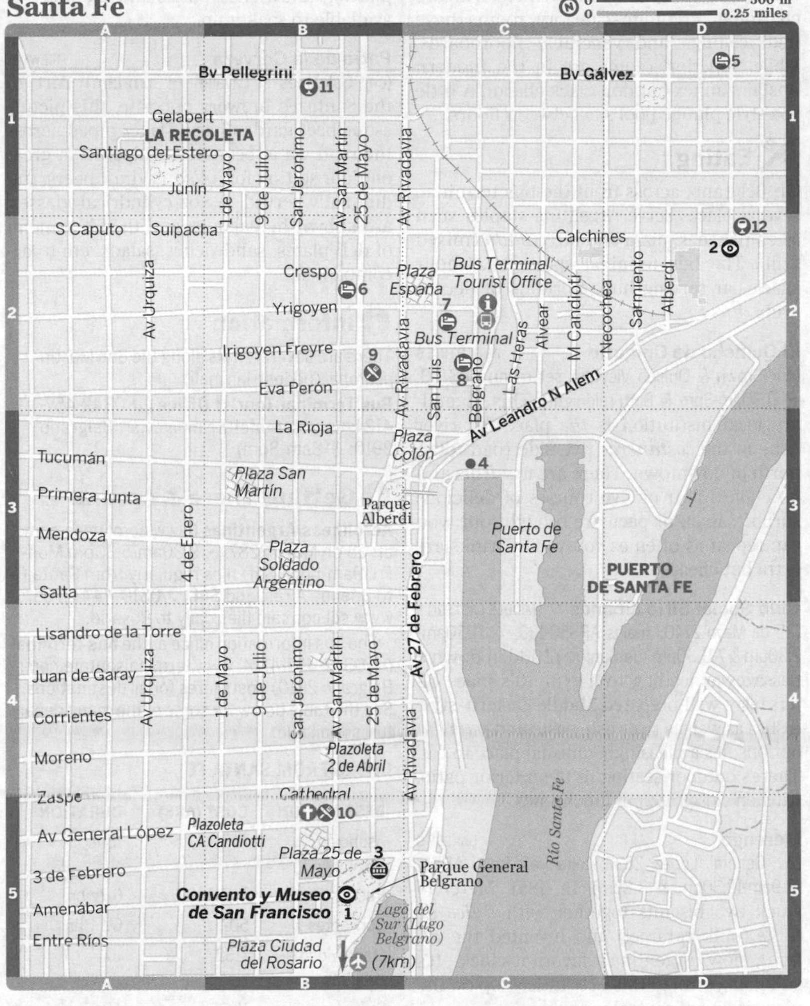

Santa Fe

Top Sights
1 Convento y Museo de San Francisco B5

Sights
2 Cervecería Santa Fe D2
3 Museo Etnográfico y Colonial Provincial B5

Activities, Courses & Tours
4 Costa Litoral C3

Sleeping
5 Ámbit Boulevard D1
6 Hostal Santa Fe de la Veracruz B2
7 Hotel Constituyentes C2
8 Hotel Galeón C2

Eating
9 Club Social Sirio Libanés B2
10 Merengo B5

Drinking & Nightlife
11 Chopería Santa Fe B1
12 Patio de la Cerveza D2

charity project by different architects; all are charming. Premium category rooms have high ceilings and venerable floorboards, while 'superior' rooms are in the modern upstairs annex but don't lack charm. A little spa-style plunge pool sits between floors.

Eating

On Belgrano, across from the bus terminal, several places serve Argentine staples such as empanadas, pizza and *parrillada* (mixed grill). The bus terminal sports a 24-hour snack bar serving huge portions of decent grub.

El Quincho de Chiquito ARGENTINE $
(cnr Brown & Obispo Vieytes; set menu AR$150; 11:30am-3pm & 8pm-midnight) This legendary local institution is *the* place for river fish, on the *costanera* (riverside road) 6km north of downtown. There are few frills and no choice: four or five courses of delicious surubí, sábalo or pacú are brought out; you can repeat as often as you want. Drinks are extra but cheap.

Club Social Sirio Libanés MIDDLE EASTERN $
(25 de Mayo 2740; mains AR$50-130; 11:30am-2:30pm & 7-11:30pm Tue-Sun;) Hidden down a passageway leading to a gym, this place offers tasty, well-prepared Middle Eastern–style dishes as well as river fish, pasta and *parrilla* options; it's a pleasingly unusual place to eat. There's outdoor seating in the interior patio. Kitchen closes at 2pm lunchtimes.

Merengo BAKERY $
(Av General López 2632; alfajores from AR$5; 9am-12:30pm & 3-8pm) In 1851 Merengo stuck two biscuits together with *dulce de leche* (milk caramel) and invented the *alfajor*, now Argentina's favorite snack. It's still going strong: this cute little shop on the plaza is one of several branches.

Drinking

Santa Fe's rock-steady nightlife once centered on the intersection of Av San Martín and Santiago del Estero, an area known as La Recoleta, but is now starting to spread through town.

Chopería Santa Fe BAR
(San Jerónimo 3498; 8am-2am;) A great place to try the local lager is this historic corner pub. It's a huge affair, with streetside tables, a cypress-shaded terrace and an immense interior. A wide range of Argentine bar food – *picadas* (shared appetizer plates), sandwiches, pizzas and the like – is available to soak it up.

Patio de la Cerveza BREWERY
(cnr Calchines & Lavalle; 2pm-1am) Part of the Santa Fe brewery opposite, this picturesque beer garden has its lager piped across the road via a 'beerduct' bridge. It's a great outdoor setting for a *liso*, as draft beers, traditionally served in 8oz cylindrical glasses, are known hereabouts, and there's a menu of deli plates, sandwiches, salads, etc to accompany it.

Information

There are several ATMs along the San Martín *peatonal* (pedestrian mall).

Bus Terminal Tourist Office (0342-457-4124; www.santafeturismo.gov.ar; Belgrano 2910; 8am-8pm)

Getting There & Around

Aerolíneas Argentinas (www.aerolineas.com.ar; 25 de Mayo 2287; 9:30am-5:30pm Mon-Fri, 9am-noon Sat) flies regularly from Santa Fe to Buenos Aires, and **Sol** (0810-444-4765; www.sol.com.ar) flies daily to Rosario.

The bus information office at the **bus terminal** (0342-457-4124; www.terminalsantafe.com; Belgrano 2910) posts fares for all destinations. See the table below for some of the many departures available.

BUSES FROM SANTA FE

DESTINATION	COST (AR$)	DURATION
Asunción, Paraguay	746	13hr
Buenos Aires	410-440	6-7½hr
Corrientes	507	6½-8hr
Montevideo, Uruguay	1162	10
Paraná	16.25	40min
Posadas	750	12hr
Rosario	128	2hr

Paraná

0343 / POP 247,700

Although less famous than Santa Fe, Paraná is, in many ways, a more attractive place.

Built on the hilly banks of its namesake river, the historical center is largely intact, and the city boasts a couple of majestic plazas. As is the rule in this part of the world, fun seekers hit the riverbanks at night to choose from an array of restaurants, clubs and bars.

Sights & Activities

From Plaza Primero de Mayo, the town center, San Martín is a *peatonal* for six blocks. Plaza Primero de Mayo has had an **Iglesia Catedral** since 1730, but the current building dates from 1885. When Paraná was capital of the confederation, the Senate deliberated at the **Colegio del Huerto**, at the corner of 9 de Julio and 25 de Mayo.

★Museo Histórico de Entre Ríos MUSEUM
(cnr Buenos Aires & Laprida; donation AR$5; 8am-12:30pm & 3-8pm Tue-Fri, 9am-noon & 4-7pm Sat, 9am-noon Sun) Flaunting local pride, this modern museum on Plaza Alvear contains information on the short-lived Republic of Entre Ríos and the battle of Monte Camperos, as well as maté paraphernalia and numerous solid wooden desks and portraits of Urquiza. Much of it was the collection of a local poet.

★Museo y Mercado Provincial de Artesanías MUSEUM
(Av Urquiza 1239; 7am-1pm & 4-8pm Mon-Fri, 9am-noon Sat) FREE Promoting handicrafts from throughout the province, this is a likable little place. Ask the curator to explain things to you; you'll be amazed at the intricacy of some of the work, like the hats made from tightly woven palm fibers.

Costanera WATERFRONT
From the northern edge of downtown, Parque Urquiza slopes steeply downward to the banks of the Río Paraná. During summer, the waterfront fills with people strolling, fishing and swimming. There's a public beach, **Playa El Parque**, west of the Paraná Rowing Club's private strand, but a better strip of sand, **Playas de Thompson**, is 1km further east, beyond the port.

Costa Litoral BOAT TOUR
(0343-423-4385; www.costalitoral.info; Buenos Aires 212) This outfit runs weekend afternoon one-way trips to Santa Fe (adult/child AR$160/100) and one-hour cruises on the river (adult/child AR$100/60) in a large catamaran. Trips leave from near the tourist office on the *costanera*.

Paraná en Kayak KAYAKING
(0343-422-7143; www.paranaenkayak.com.ar) Easy kayak trips on the river as well as longer routes.

Sleeping

★Las Mañanitas HOTEL $
(0343-407-4753; www.lasmanianitas.com.ar; Carbó 62; s/d US$40/65;) There's a summer-house feel about this delightfully relaxed little budget place, which has nine rooms alongside a courtyard and garden with pool. The rooms are colorful and comfortable; they differ widely from darkish duplexes to simpler, lighter chambers – but it's the grace and friendliness of the whole ensemble that makes this a winner.

Entre Ríos Apart Hotel APARTMENT $
(0343-484-0906; www.aparthotel-entrerios.com; Montevideo 55; s/d US$44/68;) Spotless, spacious apartments here have stove, microwave and fridge, as well as a fold-out sofa, decent bathroom and attractive bedroom. In a clean-lined modernized building, rates include breakfast and parking, making this a great deal.

Eating

Giovani ARGENTINE $
(Av Urquiza 1045; mains AR$60-110; noon-3pm & 8pm-midnight Mon-Fri, to 1am Sat, to 11pm Sun;) With as-it-should-be service and thoughtful touches such as free coffee, this stylish restaurant in the center of town serves excellent meats from the *parrilla* and delectable pasta. There's a good line in river fish and a rather refined, romantic atmosphere.

GUALEGUAYCHÚ CARNAVAL

A mellow riverside town, Gualeguaychú is quiet out of season but kicks off in summer with the country's longest and flashiest **Carnaval celebration** (www.carnavaldelpais.com.ar). Any weekend from mid-January to late February you'll find things in full swing. The main venue is the Corsódromo, where admission is AR$150 to AR$220 most nights.

There's a string of decent budget hotels along Bolívar between Bartolomé Mitre and Monseñor Chalup, and several hostels in town.

Gualeguaychú is easily reached by bus from Buenos Aires (3½ hours), Paraná and other Río Uruguay towns. Gualeguaychú is also a crossing point to Uruguay: Fray Bentos lies just across the bridge.

Lola Valentina ARGENTINE $$
(0343-423-5234; Mitre 310; mains AR$80-150; noon-4pm & 8pm-midnight;) Blending the cheerful vibe of a favorite corner eatery with formal service, this place offers great value for a long menu of Argentine classics, delicious homemade pastas, *parrilla* options and plenty of river fish choice. It fills fast, so get there early or book.

Drinking & Entertainment

Paraná is quiet midweek, but gets busy at weekends. Most of the action is at the eastern end of the riverfront around Liniers Lineal.

Information

There are several ATMs along the San Martín *peatonal*.

Tourist Office (0343-423-0183; www.turismoparana.gov.ar; Plaza 1 de Mayo s/n; 8am-8pm) Helpful, with good brochures. There's another branch by the Río Paraná (0343-420-1837; Laurencena & San Martín; 8am-8pm), and in the bus terminal (0343-420-1862; 8am-8pm).

Getting There & Around

The **bus terminal** (0343-422-1282) is on Ramírez between Posadas and Moreno. Buses 1, 4, 5 and 9 run downtown. Buses leave every 30 minutes for Santa Fe (AR$16.25, 40 minutes); you may have to queue as commuter-card holders have priority. Other services and fares closely resemble those to and from Santa Fe.

Reserva Provincial Esteros del Iberá

Esteros del Iberá is a wildlife cornucopia comparable to Brazil's Pantanal in Mato Grosso. Aquatic plants and grasses, including 'floating islands,' dominate this wetlands wilderness covering 13,000 sq km. The most notable wildlife species are reptiles such as the caiman and anaconda, mammals such as the maned wolf, howler monkey, neotropical otter, capybara, and pampas and swamp deer, as well as more than 350 bird species.

Bird-watchers and nature nuts from all over the world converge on the village of Colonia Pellegrini, 120km northeast of Mercedes, to take advantage of the ease of access to the park (Colonia Pellegrini lies within the park's boundaries). It's a charming enough place in its own right: dirt roads, little traffic and plenty of trees. There's a visitors center across the causeway from Colonia Pellegrini with information on the reserve and a couple of short self-guided **walking trails**. The **tourist office** (www.ibera.gov.ar; RP40; 8am-noon and 2-7pm) at the entrance to the village is helpful. Two-hour **launch tours** (per person AR$150-180), available everywhere, are good value. Horse tours (AR$200) are pleasant, but you'll see more wildlife from the boat.

Many hotel operators in Mercedes (the gateway town) will try to railroad you into buying a package tour with tales of over-

GETTING TO BRAZIL

The small, largely uninteresting town of **Paso de los Libres** is the gateway to the Brazilian town of Uruguaiana. The border crossing is marked by a bridge about 10 blocks southwest of central Plaza Independencia. Buses to Uruguaiana (AR$15) leave frequently, stopping on Av San Martín at Colónand opposite the bus terminal. The border is open 24 hours. Once in Brazil, the nearest town to the border we recommend is **Porto Alegre**.

Between Paso's bus terminal and the center are some very dodgy neighborhoods – it's well worth investing in the AR$2.25/20 bus/taxi fare to get you through.

Hotels include the basic, well-kept **Hotel Las Vegas** (03772-423490; hotellasvegas2000@hotmail.com; Sarmiento 554; s/d US$30/50;) and the vastly more comfortable **Hotel Alejandro Primero** (03772-424100; www.alejandroprimero.com.ar; Coronel López 502; s/d US$50/70;). There are resto-bars all along Colón between Mitre and Sitja Nia. The best restaurant in town is **El Nuevo Mesón** (Colón 587; mains AR$65-110; 11:30am-3pm & 8pm-midnight;).

Moving on from Paso de los Libres, there are regular buses to Mercedes (AR$71, two hours), Buenos Aires (AR$570, nine hours), Corrientes (AR$220, five hours) and many other destinations.

OFF THE BEATEN TRACK

YAPEYÚ

This delightfully peaceful place is no one-horse town: there are many horses, and the sound of their hooves thumping the reddish earth in the evening is one of the nicest things about it. Yapeyú is a great spot to relax; the sort of place where locals will greet you on the street.

An hour north of Paso de los Libres by bus, Yapeyú was founded in 1626 as the southernmost of the Jesuit missions. It's also famous for being the birthplace of the great Argentine 'Liberator,' José de San Martín.

You can examine the Jesuit ruins – the **museum** (Sargento Cabral s/n; 8am-noon & 3-6pm Tue-Sun) FREE here has a comprehensive overview of all the missions – and admire the ornate **Casa de San Martín** (8am-noon & 2-6pm) FREE, a pavilion that now shelters the ruins of the house where San Martín was born in 1778.

On the plaza between these, **Hotel San Martín** (03772-493120; Sargento Cabral 712; s/d US$25/40;) is a simple, welcoming place set around an echoey inner courtyard. Up a notch, **El Paraíso Yapeyú** (03772-493056; www.paraisoyapeyu.com.ar; cnr Paso de los Patos & San Martín; bungalow for 2/4 people US$60/95;) is a faded complex of bungalows with a nice riverside position. More upmarket options are on the highway west of town. **Comedor del Paraíso** (Matorras s/n; mains AR$40-60; 7am-3pm & 8-10:30pm) is a likably simple central spot to eat with no menu, just a limited choice of what's available that day.

Four daily buses (AR$36, one hour) run to/from Paso de los Libres and to Posadas (AR$181, 4½ hours) in the other direction. More buses stop on the highway at the edge of the town.

booking, closed hotels and so on. If you want to book ahead and go all-inclusive, fine, but there's really no need to panic – there are way more beds available than there will ever be tourists and it's easy (and much cheaper) to organize your room, food and tours on the spot. The tourist office in Colonia Pellegrini has a complete list of accommodations and eateries in town.

Camping is possible at the **municipal campground** (15-629656; www.ibera.gov.ar; Mbiguá s/n; per person 1st/subsequent days AR$70/50, per vehicle 1st day only AR$40) in Colonia Pellegrini, which has excellent, grassy waterfront sites.

A number of *hospedajes* (basic hotels) offer rooms with private bathroom, the best of which is probably **Posada Rancho Jabirú** (15-443569; www.posadaranchojabiru.com.ar; Yaguareté s/n; s/d/tr US$30/44/66;). **Hospedaje Los Amigos** (15-493753; hospedajelosamigos@gmail.com; cnr Guazú Virá & Aguapé; r per person US$15;) is the budget-watchers' current favorite.

If you've got the budget and are loloking for more comfort, **Rancho de los Esteros** (15-493041; www.ranchodelosesteros.com.ar; cnr Ñangapiry & Capivára; s US$318, d standard/superior US$407/424, incl full-board & activities;) has pretty much everything you could hope for.

Transport options alter regularly: check tourist information at the Mercedes bus terminal. The road from Mercedes to Colonia Pellegrini (120km) is drivable in a normal car except after rain.

At time of research, there were no buses. The cheapest way to get here were two scheduled minibus/4WD services. Chartered transfers (from those listed here) or other operators) cost AR$1400 from Mercedes for up to four people. If it hasn't been raining, you could also get a *remise*.

Daniel Ortiz TRANSFERS

(15-431469; AR$250-300) Runs daily from Mercedes at 7:30am to 8:30am, stopping outside the bus terminal but also doing hotel pick-ups. Returns from Pellegrini at around 4pm to 5pm. Price a little variable.

Iberá Bus TRANSFERS

(Mario Azcona; 15-462836; AR$200) Leaves from the market on Pujol between Gómez and Alvear in Mercedes at midday to 12:30pm Monday to Friday and 9:30am Saturdays. Returns from Pellegrini 4am Monday to Saturday.

Corrientes

0379 / POP 368,400

It's hard to love Corrientes, but you're welcome to try. It's a big, serious city with a couple of decent museums and a reputation for being very budget-unfriendly. Once the sun starts setting, a walk along the riverfront might make you feel a bit happier about being here. The once-moribund **Carnaval Correntino** is now one of the country's showiest, running over four consecutive weekends starting nine weeks before Easter.

Sights & Activities

Various operators run boat trips on the Paraná; the tourist office has a list.

★Museo de Artesanías Tradicionales Folclóricas MUSEUM
(Quintana 905; 8am-noon & 3-7pm Mon-Fri, 9am-noon & 4-7pm Sat) FREE This intriguing museum in a converted colonial house has small displays of fine traditional *artesanía* (handicrafts) plus a good shop, but the highlight is watching students being taught to work leather, silver, bone and wood by master craftspeople. Other rooms around the courtyard are occupied by working artisans who will sell to you directly. Museum guides are enthusiastic, knowledgeable and friendly.

Turistas Con Ruedas CYCLING
(Costanera at 9 de Julio; 8am-noon & 3-7pm) FREE Head down to the riverside tourist office with your passport, and grab a free bike to explore the city for a couple of hours.

Sleeping

Corrientes is finally catching on to the hosteling scene, and actually features one of the best in the country. The hotel scene is still rather dispiriting – what there is isn't cheap, and what's relatively cheap isn't very good. Cheaper, better hotels are on offer across the river in Resistencia. The tourist office maintains a list of *casas de familia* (modest family accommodations) offering rooms.

Bienvenida Golondrina HOSTEL $
(0379-443-5316; www.hostelbienvenidagolondrina.com; La Rioja 455; dm US$21-23, s/d US$41/57;) Occupying a marvelous centenarian building, all high ceilings, stained glass and artistic flourishes, this hostel makes a great base a few steps from the *costanera*. Comfortable wide-berthed dorm beds have headroom, facilities (including free bikes) are great, and the warmly welcoming management couldn't be more helpful. Prices drop midweek.

Orly Hotel HOTEL $
(0379-442-0280; www.hotelorlycorrientes.com.ar; San Juan 867; s/d US$50/60, superior r US$130;) This professional, central three-star hotel is divided in two; older standard rooms are fine but smallish. They're gradually being renovated, so ask for a newer one. Superior 'suites', however, are much better, with huge beds, modish couches and good bathrooms, though we'd change the carpet. A sunlit breakfast room overlooks the pool deck. A sauna, Jacuzzi and gym add value.

La Rozada BOUTIQUE HOTEL $$
(0379-443-3001; www.larozada.com; Plácido Martínez 1223; s/d US$78/88;) An excellent option near the riverfront, this hotel has commodious apartments and suites unusually set in a tower in the courtyard of an appealing 19th-century, battleship-gray historic building. Fine views are on offer from most rooms. A balcony room is slightly more expensive. There's an attractive bar area; guests can use the pool at the nearby rowing club.

Eating & Drinking

Be on the lookout for *chipas* (crunchy, cheesy scones) and *sopa paraguaya* (a flour-based, quiche-like pie). They occasionally turn up on restaurant menus, but your best bet are the street vendors around the bus terminal.

The main nightlife area is around the intersection of Junín and Buenos Aires, where several bars and clubs get going on weekends. The *costanera* west of the bridge also sees some action.

El Quincho PARRILLA $
(cnr Av Juan Pujol & Calle Roca; parrillada for 2 AR$200-260; 11:30am-3pm & 9pm-2am Mon-Sat, 11:30am-3pm Sun) Rustic and welcoming, this Corrientes classic sits on a roundabout a short walk from the center. It's more about Argentine grill staples such as chorizo and *morcilla* (blood sausage) than fancy cuts of steak; there's always a great-value *parrilla* deal on, plus regular regional specials and live *chamamé* music at weekends. Quality good; quantity enormous

Entertainment

Parrilla Puente Pexoa TRADITIONAL MUSIC
(0379-445-1687; RN 12 at Virgen de Itatí roundabout; from 8:30pm Fri & Sat) This relaxed restaurant features *chamamé* dances every weekend and is outrageous fun when the dancing starts. Men and women show up in full *gaucho* regalia, and up to four *conjuntos* (bands) may play each night, starting around 11pm.

It's around AR$60 in a taxi; make sure you specify it's the *parrilla* you're going to, as Puente Pexoa itself is a place further away.

Information

Municipal tourist kiosk (Plaza JB Cabral; 7am-8pm) This helpful little kiosk on the plaza is theoretically open daily.

Municipal tourist office (0379-447-4733; www.ciudaddecorrientes.gov.ar; cnr Av Costanera & 9 de Julio; 7am-8pm) The main municipal tourist office, though opening can be patchy.

Provincial Tourist Office (0379-442-7200; http://turismo.corrientes.gob.ar; 25 de Mayo 1330; 7:30am-2pm & 3:30-8:30pm Mon-Fri) Helpful for information about the province.

Getting There & Around

Aerolíneas Argentinas (0379-442-3918; www.aerolineas.com.ar; Junín 1301; 8am-12:30pm & 4:30-8pm Mon-Fri, 9am-noon Sat) flies daily to Buenos Aires from Corrientes. Local bus 105 (AR$5.50) goes to the **airport** (RN 12), about 15km east of town.

Frequent buses (AR$7.40) and shared taxis (AR$25) to Resistencia leave from the **local bus terminal** (cnr Av Costanera General San Martín & La Rioja). Shared taxis also leave from the corner of Santa Fe and 3 de Abril. Listed here are some departures from the **long-distance bus terminal** (0379-447-7600; Av Maipú 2400).

Bus 106 runs between San Lorenzo downtown and the bus terminal.

BUSES FROM CORRIENTES

DESTINATION	COST (AR$)	DURATION (HR)
Asunción, Paraguay	226	6-7
Buenos Aires	864	12-14
Mercedes	146	3-4
Paso de los Libres	220	5
Posadas	270	4-4½
Puerto Iguazú	527	9-10

Resistencia

0362 / POP 385,700

Sculpture lovers wallow like pigs in the mud in Resistencia. A joint project between the local council and various arts organizations has led to the placement of more than 500 sculptures in the city streets and parks, free for everyone to see. Delightful Plaza 25 de Mayo, a riot of tall palms and comical *palo borracho* trees, marks the city center.

Sights

There's insufficient space to detail the number of **sculptures** in city parks and on the sidewalks, but the tourist office distributes a map with their locations that makes a good introduction to the city. The best starting point is the **MusEUM** (www.bienaldelchaco.com; Av de los Inmigrantes 1001; 9:30am-1:30pm & 4-8pm Mon-Sat) FREE, an open-air workshop on the north side of Parque 2 de Febrero. Several of the most impressive pieces are on display here, and this is where, during the **Bienal de Escultura** (www.bienaldelchaco.com), held on the third week of July in even years, you can catch sculptors at work.

★ **Museo del Hombre Chaqueño** MUSEUM
(http://museohombrechaco.blogspot.com; JB Justo 280; 8am-1pm & 3-8:30pm Mon-Fri) FREE This small but excellent museum is run by enthusiastic staff (some English spoken) who talk you through displays covering the three main pillars of Chaco population: indigenous inhabitants (there are some excellent ceramics and Toba musical instruments here); *criollos* who resulted from interbreeding between the European arrivals and the local populations; and 'gringos', the wave of mostly European immigration from the late 19th century onwards. Best is the mythology room upstairs, where you'll get to meet various quirky characters from Chaco popular religion.

El Fogón de los Arrieros CULTURAL CENTER
(www.fogondelosarrieros.com.ar; Brown 350; admission AR$10; 8am-noon & 4-7pm Mon-Fri) Founded in 1943, this is a cultural center and gallery that for decades has been the driving force behind Resistencia's artistic commitment. It's famous for its eclectic collection of objets d'art from around the Chaco and Argentina. The museum also features the wood carvings of local artist and cultural activist Juan de Dios Mena. Check out the irreverent epitaphs to dead patrons

in the memorial garden; it's called Colonia Sálsipuedes'(Leave if You Can).

Sleeping

Hotel Colón HOTEL $

(☎0362-442-2861; www.colonhotelyapart.com; Santa María de Oro 143; s/d/apt US$44/60/68; ❄@☎) Art deco fans mustn't miss this 1920s classic, just south of the plaza. It's an amazingly large and characterful building with enticingly curious period features. Refurbished rooms are great; make sure you get one, as there are some far sketchier chambers with foam mattresses and dilapidated bathrooms. Good-value apartments available.

Hotel Alfil HOTEL $

(☎0362-442-0882; Santa María de Oro 495; s/d US$25/35; ❄☎) A few blocks south of Plaza 25 de Mayo, the old-fashioned Alfil is a reasonable budget choice. Interior rooms are dark but worthwhile if the significant street noise in the exterior rooms (with their strangely inaccessible balconies) will bother you. Air-con is US$2 extra, but it's a decent deal despite the lack of breakfast.

★**Amerian Hotel Casino Gala** HOTEL $$

(☎0362-445-2400; www.hotelcasinogala.com.ar; Perón 330; s/d US$113/125; ❄@☎≋) The city's smartest choice, with various grades of room and slick service. Rooms are excellent for these rates: very spacious, attractively stepped and with a dark, elegant, vaguely Asian feel to the decor. As well as slot machines, there's a sauna, gym and self-contained spa complex. The huge outdoor pool with bar is a highlight.

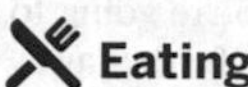

Eating

Several attractive *confiterías* and ice-cream parlors have rejuvenated the area north and northwest of Plaza 25 de Mayo.

Juan Segundo ARGENTINE $$

(Av Paraguay 24; mains AR$105-180; ⊙noon-2pm daily, plus 9pm-12:30am Tue-Sat; ☎) With a casually elegant chessboard-tiled interior and appealing outdoor tables in an upmarket zone of the city, Juan Segundo offers decent *parrilla* choices and salads, and even better fish and meat dishes with well-prepared

OFF THE BEATEN TRACK

NORTH TOWARD PARAGUAY

Buses run from Resistencia to Asunción, Paraguay's capital, crossing in Argentina's far north at **Clorinda**, a chaotic border town with little of interest beyond bustling markets.

A better stop is baking-hot **Formosa**, a medium-sized provincial capital two hours' bus ride north of Resistencia. Hotels, restaurants and services can be found along Av 25 de Mayo, which links the sleepy plaza with the Río Paraguay waterfront – the best place to stroll once the temperatures drop.

Laguna Oca offers good bird-watching 6km from town, but the rest of Formosa province has even more.

One good spot is Parque Nacional Río Pilcomayo (p85), 126km northwest of Formosa and 55km west of Clorinda. Daily buses connect these with **Laguna Blanca**, an easy-paced citrus town where you'll find inexpensive lodgings – **Residencial Guaraní** (☎03718-470024; cnr San Martín & Sargento Cabral; r per person US$18; ❄) is the standout – and *remises* (unmarked call taxis) to the national park. The park's main feature is also called **Laguna Blanca**, where rangers can take you out in boats to spot caiman.

Formosa province's standout attraction is **Bañado la Estrella** (www.banadolaestrella.org.ar). This stunning wetland area, a floodplain of the Río Pilcomayo, harbors an astonishing range of birdlife, as well as alligators, capybaras, sizable serpents and beautiful water plants. From the roads that cross this 200km-long finger-shaped area, it's easy to spot a huge variety of wildlife: pack binoculars.

The handiest town is **Las Lomitas**, 300 km west of Formosa on RN 81 with regular bus service (AR$197, 5½ to 6 hours). From here, paved RP28 heads north, cutting across the wetlands via causeway, starting 37km north of Las Lomitas and extending for some 15km. Las Lomitas has accommodations, including **Hotel Eva** (☎03715-432092; hotel_eva@hotmail.com; Av San Martín 250; r US$28-43; ❄@☎), a friendly place whose dark rooms don't live up to the elegant stone-faced exterior. Upgrade to an intermediate room for a better bed.

sauces. There's a play area for kids but not many cheap choices on the short wine list.

No Me Olvides ARGENTINE $$
(Laprida 198; mains AR$90-175; 6am-3am;) Huge windows and a high-ceilinged interior make this popular corner spot feel much larger than it is. Verve and color are added by vibrant paintings, paper lampshades and arty touches. As the heroic opening hours suggest, it does everything from breakfasts to late-night cocktails. The menu is a touch overpriced but the pasta, ciabattas and *lomitos* are really excellent.

Coco's Resto ARGENTINE $$
(Av Sarmiento 266; mains AR$110-160; noon-2:30pm & 8:30pm-midnight Mon-Sat, noon-2:30pm Sun;) In two front rooms of a house, this intimate, well-decorated restaurant is popular with suited diners from the nearby state parliament. A wide-ranging menu of pastas, meats in various sauces, river fish and a long wine list make this a pleasant Chaco choice.

Drinking & Nightlife

El Viejo Café CAFE
(Pellegrini 109; 6am-3am;) In an elegant old edifice, with an eclectically decorated interior, this is a fine choice any time of day. Its terrace is sweet for a sundowner, and it gets lively later on weekends, when there's usually live music. Solid if unspectacular meals (mains AR$65 to AR$110) are also available

Information

There are ATMs near Plaza 25 de Mayo.

Provincial tourist office (0362-445-3098; www.chaco.travel; López y Planes 185; 7:30am-8pm) This regional tourist office has reasonably up-to-date information on the further-flung parts of the Chaco.

Terminal tourist office (www.chaco.travel; 7am-8pm Mon-Fri Sat, 7am-9:30am & 6-8:30pm Sat & Sun) In the bus terminal. There's a municipal office opposite it.

Tourist office (0362-445-8289; Roca 20; 7am-noon & 2:30-8pm) On the southern side of Plaza 25 de Mayo.

Getting There & Around

AIR

Aerolíneas Argentinas (0362-444-5551; www.aerolineas.com.ar; Justo 184; 8am-12:30pm & 4:30-8pm Mon-Fri, 8am-noon Sat) has daily flights from Resistencia to Buenos Aires. Aeropuerto San Martín is 6km south of town on RN 11; a *remise* costs around AR$80.

BUS

The **bus terminal** (0362-446-1098; cnr MacLean & Islas Malvinas) is a AR$80 taxi from the center, or you can take bus 3, 9 or 110 from Santa María de Oro near Perón. Don't walk it: travelers have reported muggings. A two-ride city bus ticket costs AR$15 from the main shop in the terminal, or at Roca 35 on the plaza.

There's an urban service (marked 'Chaco-Corrientes') between Resistencia and Corrientes for AR$7. You can catch it in front of the post office on Plaza 25 de Mayo.

La Estrella buses service Capitán Solari, near Parque Nacional Chaco, four times daily (AR$57, 2½ hours). Other destinations include the following.

DESTINATION	COST (AR$)	DURATION (HR)
Asunción, Paraguay	203	6
Buenos Aires	864	13-14
Córdoba	833	10-14
Posadas	287	4½-5
Puerto Iguazú	542	10-11
Salta	719	12-13
Santiago del Estero	586	8½-9½
Tucumán	675-735	11-12

Posadas

0362 / POP 324,800

If you're heading north, now's about the time that things start to feel very tropical, and the jungle begins to creep into the edges of the picture. Posadas is mainly interesting as an access point, both to Paraguay and the Jesuit mission sites north of here, but it's a cool little city in its own right, with some sweet plazas and a well-developed eating, drinking and partying scene down on the waterfront.

Sights & Activities

The Jesuit missions are the area's big attraction.

Costanera WATERFRONT
In the afternoon, the *costanera* comes alive with joggers, cyclists, dog walkers, maté sippers, hot-dog vendors and young couples staring at Paraguay across the water. Pride of place goes to 'Andresito,' a huge stainless-steel **sculpture** of Guaraní provincial strongman Andrés Guacaruri (Guazurary), looking like the Tin Man in search of a heart.

Fundación Artesanías Misioneras GALLERY (www.famercosur.com.ar; cnr Alvarez & Arrechea; 8:30am-12:30pm & 5-8:30pm Mon-Fri, 9:30am-12:30pm & 5-8pm Sat) FREE Guaraní culture is strong in this part of Argentina; particularly fine pieces are displayed and sold here. There's another branch on the *costanera*.

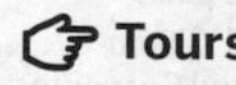

Tours

Yacaré Tours TOUR (0376-442-1829; www.yacaretours.com.ar; Bolívar 1419) Offers half-day trips to Argentine (two people AR$1650) and Paraguayan (two people AR$1250) missions. Also has trips to maté plantations, the Saltos del Moconá, Esteros del Iberá and more.

Sleeping

Posadeña Linda HOSTEL $ (0376-443-9238; www.hostelposadasmisiones.com; Bolívar 1439; dm US$13-15, d US$32;) Run with a caring attitude, this narrow hostel a short walk from the plaza offers a genuine welcome, comfortable bunkrooms with bathroom and a patio with a tiny plunge pool. Ensuite private rooms are a little musty but a decent deal. It's colorful and relaxing with a compact but OK kitchen. Despite the address, it's between 1411 and 1419.

Le Petit Hotel HOTEL $ (0376-443-6031; www.hotellepetit.com.ar; Santiago del Estero 1630; s/d US$50/60;) Not so petit after a recent expansion, but peaceful and simple, this hotel is run by kindly people. It features dark, adequate rooms that are spotlessly clean and surround a leafy patio or central atrium. It feels a little overpriced but has a nice location in a quiet, safe residential zone seven blocks from the heart of things. Cards 20% extra.

> **GETTING TO PARAGUAY**
>
> Buses to Encarnación (AR$18), Paraguay, leave every 20 minutes, stopping at the corner of San Lorenzo and Entre Ríos. With queues and border formalities, the trip can take more than an hour.
>
> Everyone gets out to clear Argentine emigration. If the bus leaves without you, keep your ticket and catch the next one. The same happens on the Paraguayan side. There's a tourist office by Paraguayan immigration, and official money changers hanging around. Get small bills: a 100,000 guaraní note is hell to change.

★ **Hotel Posadas Urbano** HOTEL $$ (0376-444-3800; www.hahoteles.com; Bolívar 2176; s/d/ste US$96/111/157;) This smartly renovated hotel has rapidly become top dog, with its wide array of facilities and great central location. Bright, large carpeted chambers all have gleaming bathrooms, balconies and big windows with views over town. Suites add space but little else. The atrium pool area, art exhibitions, gym and spa facilities, and appealing lounge add points.

Eating & Drinking

For cheap eats with few surprises, head for the semipedestrian intersection of Bolívar and San Lorenzo, where there's a range of pizza and pasta joints with sidewalk seating.

★ **La Tradicional Rueda** PARRILLA $$ (La Ruedita; Arrechea & Av Costanera; mains AR$85-150; 11am-3:30pm & 7:30pm-midnight or later;) Stylish and traditional in feel, with uniformed waiters and sturdy wooden seats, this two-level grillhouse has a prime riverside position: look for the wooden wheel outside. Quality meats and nice lines in salads and river fish put this a class above most *parrilla* places. Service is excellent.

La Querencia PARRILLA $$ (Bolívar 1867; mains AR$90-130; noon-2:30pm & 8pm-12:30am Mon-Sat, noon-2:30pm Sun;) On the plaza, this upmarket *parrilla* specializes in delicious *galeto*. Also memorable are the brochettes (giant spikes with various delicious meats impaled upon them). Salads are also unusually well prepared. Service is great and the atmosphere a highlight.

Astillero ARGENTINE $$ (Av Costanera s/n; mains AR$110-170; noon-3pm & 8pm-midnight;) Tucked away behind foliage on the riverbank strip, place this has a treehouse feel with three levels and a balcony with limited Paraná vistas. The food was a bit up and down when we visited, but the setting is romantic and the menu has potential. The wine list is full of good things, but lacks budget options.

Information

There are several downtown ATMs.

Misiones tourist office (0376-444-7539; www.misiones.tur.ar; Colón 1985; 7am-8pm)

There are other tourist kiosks around town, but this is the most reliably open.

Getting There & Away

AIR

Aerolíneas Argentinas (0810-222-86527; Sarmiento 2280; 8am-noon & 4-8pm Mon-Fri, 8am-noon Sat) flies daily to Buenos Aires.

TRAIN

A shiny new rail service connects Posadas and Encarnación in Paraguay, leaving Posadas every 30 minutes from 7:15am to 6:15pm (AR$18, six minutes). You clear both Argentine and Paraguayan authorities at the Apeadero Posadas station (www.sofse.gob.ar).

BUS

DESTINATION	COST (AR$)	DURATION (HR)
Buenos Aires	957	12-14
Corrientes	270	4-4½
Puerto Iguazú	258	4½-5½
Resistencia	287	4½-5
San Ignacio	46	1

Getting Around

Posadas' bus terminal can be reached from downtown by bus 8, 15 (from Junín), 21 or 24 (AR$8). It's around AR$90 in a taxi. From the terminal, catch buses from the adjacent local terminal.

Bus 28 (AR$8) goes to the airport from San Lorenzo (between La Rioja and Entre Ríos). A *remise* costs around AR$100.

Buses 7 and 12 (AR$8) go to the Apeadero Posadas station.

San Ignacio Miní

0376 / POP 6800

A mellow little town between Posadas and Puerto Iguazú, San Ignacio attracts most visitors for the large, well-preserved ruins of the Jesuit mission that gives the town its name. If you're staying here and have some time to kill, it's also well worth checking out the Casa de Quiroga. If you're just passing through, you can leave your bags in the ticket office at the bus terminal while you check out the ruins.

Sights & Activities

Mission of San Ignacio Miní RUIN
(admission AR$60; 7am-6pm) These mission ruins are the most complete of those in Argentina and impress for the quantity of carved ornamentation still visible and for the amount of restoration done. No roofs remain, but many of the living quarters and workshops have been reerected.

Casa de Horacio Quiroga MUSEUM
(Av Quiroga s/n; admission AR$50; 7am-5:30pm) Uruguayan writer Horacio Quiroga was a get-back-to-nature type who found his muse in the rough-and-ready Misiones backwoods lifestyle. His simple stone house at the southern end of town (a 30-minute walk) was built by himself. An adjacent wooden house is a reconstruction made for a biopic. To reach them, a trail through sugarcane lets you learn via panels and audioguide about Quiroga's deeply tragic life, so full of shotgun accidents and doses of cyanide it's almost funny.

Sleeping & Eating

Rivadavia, between the bus stop and the ruins, is lined with small restaurants serving *milanesas* (breaded cutlets), pizza and so on.

Adventure Hostel HOSTEL $
(0376-447-0955; www.sihostel.com.ar; Independencia 469; campsite per person US$10, dm US$12-16, d US$50;) This well-run, motivated place has comfortable dorms with either three beds or four bunk-berths, decent private rooms with renovated bathrooms, and excellent facilities. There's everything from a climbing wall to pool (both kinds), ping-pong and seesaws in the spacious grounds. Tasty homemade breakfasts are included. The restaurant does decent pasta-pizza-type meals; there's also bike hire (per day AR$120) and powered campsites. HI discount.

Hotel La Toscana HOTEL $
(0376-447-0777; www.hotellatoscana.com.ar; cnr H Irigoyen & Uruguay; s/d/tr/q US$30/40/45/50;) In a peaceful part of town half a block from the highway, this simple, welcoming Italian-run place is a relaxing retreat indeed. Cool, spacious basic rooms surround a great pool, deck and garden area. It's a top spot to unwind and offers top value.

La Misionerita ARGENTINE $
(RN 12; mains AR$65-110; 4am-midnight;) On the highway opposite the town entrance, this place has impressive opening hours, friendly service and a decent range of burgers, *milanesas* and the like, along with grill options and river fish. One of few evening options.

Getting There & Away

The new bus terminal is out on the highway, about a 1km walk from the ruins. There are regular services between Posadas (AR$45, one hour) and Puerto Iguazú (AR$140 to AR$180, four to six hours).

Puerto Iguazú

03757 / POP 42,000

With a world-class attraction just down the road, Puerto Iguazú should feel overrun by tourists, but it absorbs the crowds well and manages to retain some of its relaxed, small-town atmosphere. The falls are definitely the drawcard here: you'll meet your share of people who have come straight from Buenos Aires, and are heading straight back again. There's a steady backpacker population and a lively hostel and restaurant scene.

Sights

Güirá Oga ZOO
(www.guiraoga.com.ar; RN 12, Km 5; admission AR$100; 9am-6pm, last entry 5pm) On the way to the falls, this is an animal hospital and center for rehabilitation of injured wildlife. It also carries out valuable research into the Iguazú forest environment and has a breeding program for endangered species. You get walked around the jungly park by one of the staff, who explains about the birds and animals and the sad stories of how they got there. The visit takes about 80 minutes.

Casa Ecológica de Botellas ARCHITECTURE
(http://lacasadebotellas.googlepages.com; RN 12, Km5; adult/child AR$70/40; 9am-6:30pm) About 300m off the falls road, this fascinating place is well worth a visit. The owners have used packaging materials – plastic bottles, juice cartons and the like – to build not only an impressive house, but furnishings and a bunch of original handicrafts that make unusual gifts. The guided visit talks you through their techniques.

Sleeping

Garden Stone HOSTEL $
(03757-420425; www.gardenstonehostel.com; Av Córdoba 441; dm US$14, d with/without bathroom US$55/45;) The best feature about this amiably-run hostel is its perfectly relaxing garden area, where there's a pool, common area and simple kitchen. Other good things include handiness for the bus terminal, the tasty breakfast (included), darkish but OK dorms, and its general peaceful vibe. Private en-suite rooms are attractive and good value.

Porämbá Hostel HOSTEL $
(03757-423041; www.porambahostel.com; El Urú 120; dm US$13-14, r US$38-68;) In a peaceful location but an easy walk from the bus terminal, this is a welcoming family-run hostel with a variety of uncrowded dorms, private rooms with or without bathroom, and a small pool. It's a chilled place with a kitchen and a calming atmosphere.

Hospedaje Lola GUESTHOUSE $
(03757-423954; residenciallola@hotmail.com; Av Córdoba 255; r US$25-30;) Plenty of price gouging goes on in Puerto Iguazú, but it stops at Lola's front door. This cheap, cheerily run spot is very close to the bus terminal and features compact, clean rooms with bathroom for a great price. Wi-fi is good if you're close to the family part of the house.

Hotel Lilian HOTEL $
(03757-420968; hotellilian@yahoo.com.ar; Beltrán 183; s/d/superior d/q US$42/55/65/79;) Run by a hospitable family that isn't out to rip tourists off, this friendly place offers plenty of value, with bright and cheerful rooms around a plant-filled patio. Most superiors – worth the small extra outlay – have a balcony and heaps of natural light. All bathrooms are spacious and spotless. Things get done the way they should here.

Irupé Mini GUESTHOUSE $
(Hostel Irupe; 03757-423618; Av Misiones 82; s/d US$10/20, d with air-con US$25;) This place is very basic but offers friendliness, location and decent value for cheap private rooms, which are tight, with tiny bathrooms. Go for rooms at the back, which have more light. Sometimes offers dorm rates.

Jasy Hotel HOTEL $$
(03757-424337; www.jasyhotel.com; San Lorenzo 154; d/q US$110/136;) Original and peaceful, these 10 two-level rooms, with a great design for family sleeping, climb a hill like a forest staircase and are all equipped with a balcony gazing over plentiful greenery. Artful use of wood is the signature; you'll fall in love with the bar and deck area. Prepare to stay longer than planned. There's a decent restaurant open evenings.

Eating

Feria MARKET $

(Feirinha; cnr Av Brasil & Félix de Azara; picadas for 2 AR$100-150; ⏰8am-midnight) A really nice place to eat or have a beer is this market in the north of town. It's full of stalls selling Argentine wines, sausages, olives and cheese to visiting Brazilians, and several of them put out *picadas*, grilled meats, other simple regional dishes and cold beer. There's folk music some nights and a good evening atmosphere.

La Misionera EMPANADAS $

(P Moreno 210; empanadas AR$12; ⏰11am-midnight Mon-Sat) Excellent empanadas with a big variety of fillings, as well as delivery option.

Lemongrass CAFE $

(Bompland 231; snacks AR$30-75; ⏰8:30am-2:30pm & 5-9:30pm Mon-Sat;) One of few decent cafes in Puerto Iguazú, this place offers good fresh juices, decent coffee, delicious sweet temptations, sandwiches, burgers and tasty savory tarts. Beers, mint-dependent mojitos and *caipirinhas* (cocktails) are also available.

★ **María Preta** ARGENTINE $$

(Av Brasil 39; mains AR$85-165; ⏰7pm-12:30am;) The indoor-outdoor eating area and live music make this a popular dinner choice, whether it's for steaks that are actually cooked the way you want them, for a wide range of typical Argentine-Spanish dishes, or for something a little snappier: caiman fillet. It stays open as a bar and venue until 2am or later.

Puerto Iguazú

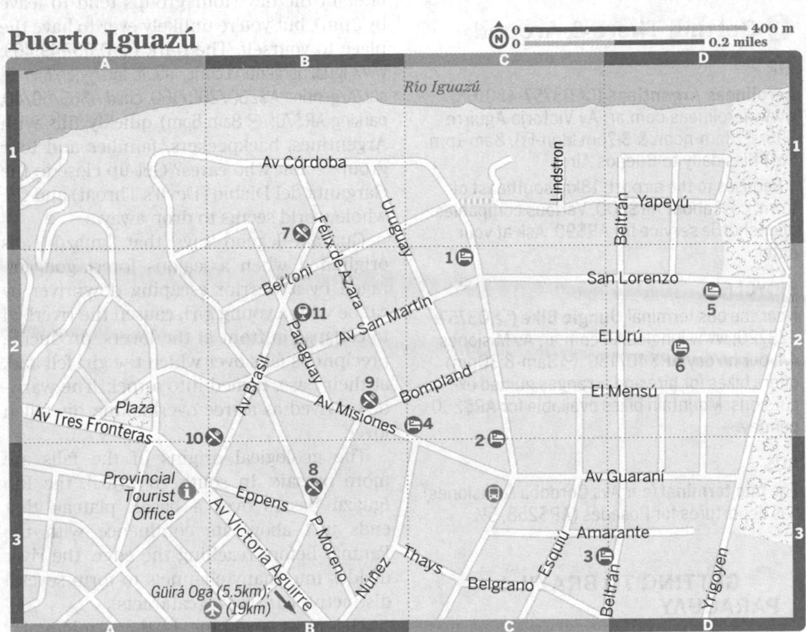

Puerto Iguazú

Sleeping

1 Garden Stone C2
2 Hospedaje Lola C3
3 Hotel Lilian C3
4 Irupé Mini C2
5 Jasy Hotel D2
6 Porämbá Hostel D2

Eating

7 Feria B1
8 La Misionera B3
9 Lemongrass B2
10 María Preta B2

Drinking & Nightlife

11 Cuba Libre B2

Drinking

Going out in Puerto Iguazú is so much fun that even Brazilians come here to dance. Imagine that. Most of the action revolves around the six-way intersection of Avs Brazil and San Martín. The perrenial favorite is **Cuba Libre** (www.facebook.com/cuba.mega disco; cnr Av Brasil & Paraguay; ⏲11pm-late Wed-Sun), which has long happy hours and occasional live music.

Information

The Brazilian Consulate (p182) here arranges visas in half a day, much better than the week it takes their Buenos Aires counterparts to do the same job.

Provincial tourist office (☎03757-420800; www.turismo.misiones.gov.ar; Av Victoria Aguirre 311; ⏲8am-9pm) The most helpful office.

Getting There & Around

AIR

Aerolíneas Argentinas (☎03757-420168; www.aerolineas.com.ar; Av Victoria Aguirre 295; ⏲8am-noon & 3-7pm Mon-Fri, 8am-1pm Sat) flies daily to Buenos Aires.

Remises to the airport, 18km southeast of town, cost about AR$200. Various companies offer shuttle service for AR$90. Ask at your hotel.

BICYCLE

Near the bus terminal, **Jungle Bike** (☎03757-423720; www.junglebike.com.ar; Av Misiones 44; per hr/day AR$40/150; ⏲8am-8:30pm) offers bikes for hire and arranges guided excursions. Mountain bikes available for AR$250 per day.

BUS

The **bus terminal** (cnr Avs Córdoba & Misiones) has departures for Posadas (AR$258, 5½ hours), Buenos Aires (AR$1212, 20 hours) and intermediate points. Frequent buses also leave for Parque Nacional Iguazú (AR$50, 30 minutes).

GETTING TO BRAZIL & PARAGUAY

Buses to Foz do Iguaçu, Brazil (AR$20, one hour), leave regularly from Puerto Iguazú's bus terminal. The bus will wait as you complete immigration procedures. The border is open 24 hours, but buses only run in daylight hours.

Frequent buses go from Puerto Iguazú's bus terminal to Ciudad del Este, Paraguay (AR$30, one hour), and wait at the border as you complete customs formalities.

Parque Nacional Iguazú

People who doubt the theory that the negative ions generated by waterfalls make people happier might have to reconsider after visiting the **Iguazú Falls**. Moods just seem to improve the closer you get to the falls, until eventually people degenerate into a giggling, shrieking mess. And these are grown adults we're talking about.

But sheer giddiness isn't the only reason to come here. The power, size and sheer noise of the falls have to be experienced to be believed. You could try coming early, or later in the day (tour groups tend to leave by 3pm), but you're unlikely ever to have the place to yourself. The **park** (☎03757-491469; www.iguazuargentina.com; adult foreigner/Mercosur/Argentine A$260/200/160, child A$65/50/40, parking AR$70; ⏲8am-6pm) quickly fills with Argentines, backpackers, families and tour groups – but who cares? Get up close to the Garganta del Diablo (Devil's Throat) and the whole world seems to drop away.

Guaraní legend says that Iguazú Falls originated when a jealous forest god, enraged by a warrior escaping downriver by canoe with a young girl, caused the riverbed to collapse in front of the lovers, producing precipitous falls over which the girl fell and, at their base, turned into a rock. The warrior survived as a tree overlooking his fallen lover.

The geological origins of the falls are more prosaic. In southern Brazil, the Río Iguazú passes over a basalt plateau that ends just above its confluence with the Paraná. Before reaching the edge, the river divides into many channels to form several distinctive *cataratas* (cataracts).

The most awesome is the semicircular Garganta del Diablo, a deafening and dampening part of the experience, approached by launch and via a system of *pasarelas* (catwalks). There's no doubt that it's spectacular – there's only one question: where's the bungee jump?

Despite development pressures, the 550-sq-km park is a natural wonderland of subtropical rainforest, with more than 2000 identified plant species, countless insects,

400 bird species, and many mammals and reptiles.

If you've got the time (and the money for a visa), it's worth checking out the Brazilian side of the falls too, for a few different angles, plus the grand overview.

Dangers & Annoyances

The Río Iguazú's currents are strong and swift; more than one tourist has been swept downriver and drowned near Isla San Martín.

The wildlife is also potentially dangerous: in 1997 a jaguar killed a park ranger's infant son. Visitors should respect the big cats; in case you encounter one, it's important not to panic. Speak calmly but loudly, do not run or turn your back, and try to appear bigger than you are by waving your arms or clothing.

Sights

Before seeing Iguazú Falls themselves, grab a map, look around the **museum**, and climb the nearby **tower** for a good overall view. Plan hikes before the midmorning tour-bus invasion. Descending from the visitors center, you can cross by free launch to **Isla Grande San Martín**, which offers unique views and a refuge from the masses on the mainland.

Several *pasarelas* (footbridges) give good views of smaller falls and, in the distance, the **Garganta del Diablo**. A train from the visitors center operates regularly to shuttle visitors from site to site. At the last stop, follow the trail to the lookout perched right on the edge of the mighty falls.

Activities

Best in the early morning, the Sendero Macuco nature trail leads through dense forest, where a steep sidet rack goes to the base of a hidden waterfall. Another trail goes to the *bañado,* a marsh abounding in birdlife. Allow about 2½ hours return (6km) for the entire Sendero Macuco trail.

To get elsewhere in the forest, you can hitchhike or hire a car to take you out along RN 101 toward the village of Bernardo de Irigoyen. Few visitors explore this part of the park, and it is still nearly pristine forest.

Iguazú Jungle Explorer BOAT TOUR
(☎03757-421696; www.iguazujungle.com) Offers three combinable tours: most popular is the short boat trip leaving from the Paseo Inferior that takes you right under one of the waterfalls for a high-adrenaline soaking (AR$350). The Gran Aventura combines this with a jungle drive (AR$650), while the Paseo Ecológico (AR$200) is a wildlife-oriented tour in inflatable boats upstream from the falls.

Full Moon Walks WALKING TOUR
(☎03757-491469; www.iguazuargentina.com/en/luna-llena) For five consecutive nights per month, these guided walks visit the Garganta del Diablo. There are three departures nightly. The first, at 8pm, offers the spectacle of the inflated rising moon; the last, at 9:30pm, sees the falls better illuminated. Don't expect wildlife. The price (AR$500) includes admission and a drink; dinner is extra (AR$200). Book in advance as numbers are limited. Extra buses from Puerto Iguazú cater for moon walkers.

Information

Buses from Puerto Iguazú drop passengers at the Centro de Informes, where there's a small natural-history museum.

Getting There & Away

Regular buses run to Puerto Iguazú (AR$50, 30 minutes).

NORTHWEST ARGENTINA

With a very tangible sense of history, the northwest is Argentina's most indigenous region, and the sights and people here show much closer links with the country's Andean neighbors than the European character of its urban centers.

Córdoba

☎0351 / POP 1,317,000

Argentina's second city is everything it should be – vibrant, fun, manageable in size and (in places) gorgeous to look at. Culture vultures beware: you may get stuck here. Music, theater, film, dance: whatever you want, you can be pretty sure it's going on somewhere in town. The city also rocks out with seven universities, and has a buzz that some say is unmatched in the entire country.

Northwest Argentina

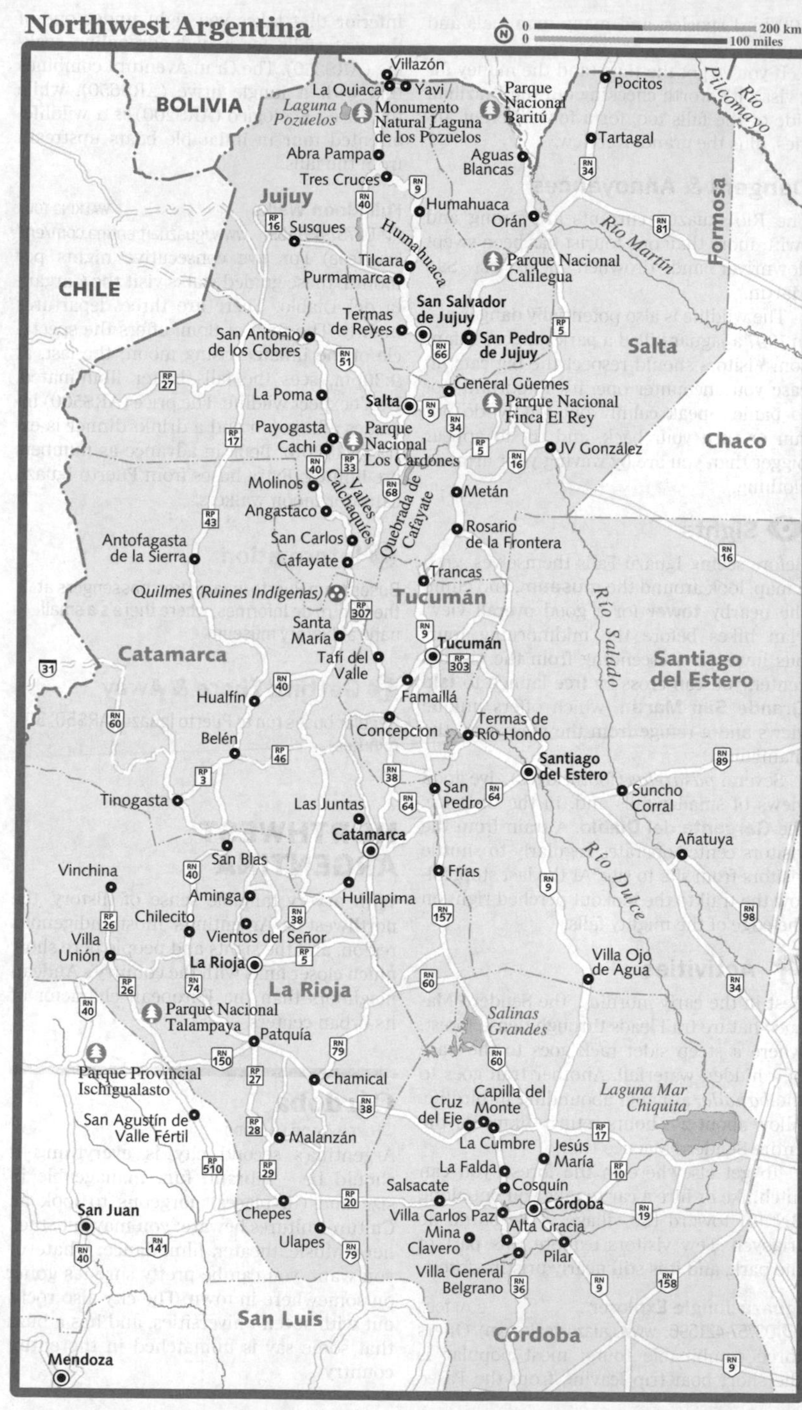

Sights

To see Córdoba's colonial buildings and monuments, start at the **cabildo**, on Plaza San Martín. At the plaza's southwest corner, crowned by a Romanesque dome, the **Iglesia Catedral** (cnr Independencia & 27 de Abril; 8am-8pm Mon-Fri, 8am-noon & 5-8pm Sat & Sun), begun in 1577, mixes a variety of styles.

South of the center is Córdoba's **Milla Cultural** (Cultural Mile) – 1.6km of theaters, art galleries and art schools. The highlights here are the **Paseo del Buen Pastor** (Av H Yrigoyen 325; 10am-9pm) FREE, which showcases work by Córdoba's young and emerging artists; the **Museo Superior de Bellas Artes Evita** (Av H Yrigoyen 551; admission AR$15, Wed free; 10am-8pm Tue-Sun), housing 400 works of fine art; and the **Museo Provincial de Bellas Artes Emilio Caraffa** (www.museocaraffa.org; Av H Yrigoyen 651; admission AR$15; 10am-8pm Tue-Sun), which features a rotating collection of top-shelf contemporary art.

Museo Histórico de la Universidad Nacional de Córdoba MUSEUM
(Obispo Trejo 242; guided visits per person AR$15; tours Mon-Sat 10am & 5pm in English, 11am & 3pm in Spanish) In 1613 Fray Fernando de Trejo y Sanabria founded the Seminario Convictorio de San Javier, which, after being elevated to university status in 1622, became the Universidad Nacional de Córdoba. The university is the country's oldest and contains, among other national treasures, part of the Jesuits' Grand Library and the Museo Histórico de la Universidad Nacional de Córdoba.

Guided visits are the only way to see the inside and are well worth taking. The guides let you wander through the Colegio and peek into the classrooms while students run around.

Museo de la Memoria MUSEUM
(www.apm.gov.ar; San Jerónimo s/n; 10am-5pm Tue-Fri) FREE A chilling testament to the excesses of Argentina's military dictatorship, this museum occupies a space formerly used as a clandestine center for detention and torture. It was operated by the dreaded Department of Intelligence (D2), a special division created in Córdoba dedicated to the kidnap and torture of suspected political agitators and the 'reassignment' of their children to less politically suspect families.

Courses

Able Spanish School LANGUAGE COURSE
(0351-422-4692; www.ablespanish.com; Tucumán 76; 9am-8pm Mon-Sat) Offers accommodations and afternoon activities at extra cost and discounts for extended study.

Tsunami Tango DANCE
(Laprida 453) Tango classes and *milongas* (from Tuesday to Sunday. Check www.tangoencordoba.com.ar for the schedule and other tango-related information for Córdoba in general.

Sleeping

★ **Hostel Rupestre** HOSTEL $
(15-226-7412; www.rupestrehostel.com.ar; Obispo Oro 242; dm US$11-14, s/d without bathroom US$24/30;) A very well-appointed, stylish hostel just on the edge of Nueva Córdoba's party zone. The location's great and the whole setup is very well thought out, with a small wading pool on the rooftop, an indoor climbing gym, spacious dorms and friendly, enthusiastic staff.

Hostel Alvear HOSTEL $
(0351-421-6502; www.alvearhostel.com.ar; Alvear 158; dm/d from US$11/38;) An excellent location and spacious dorms set in an atmospheric old building make this one of the better hostels in the downtown area.

Gaiadhon Hostel HOSTEL $
(15-800-5923; www.gaiadhonhostel.com.ar; Buenos Aires 768; dm US$11-13, s/d without bathroom US$26/39;) A cozy little hostel tucked away in a good location. If it ever fills up there wouldn't be much elbow room, but it's got a good atmosphere, and spotless if slightly cramped dorms and private rooms.

Hotel Quetzal HOTEL $
(0351-426-5117; www.hotelquetzal.com.ar; San Jerónimo 579; s/d US$43/64;) Spacious, minimalistic, modern rooms are on offer here. A surprisingly tranquil option in a busy neighborhood.

Sacha Mistol HOTEL $$
(0351-424-2646; www.sachamistol.com; Rivera Indarte 237; r from US$98;) Another of Córdoba's new breed of stylish and original hotels. Rooms are spacious and comfortable, decorated with eclectic art and well-chosen furnishings. It's set in a carefully renovated classic house and features art exhibitions

Córdoba

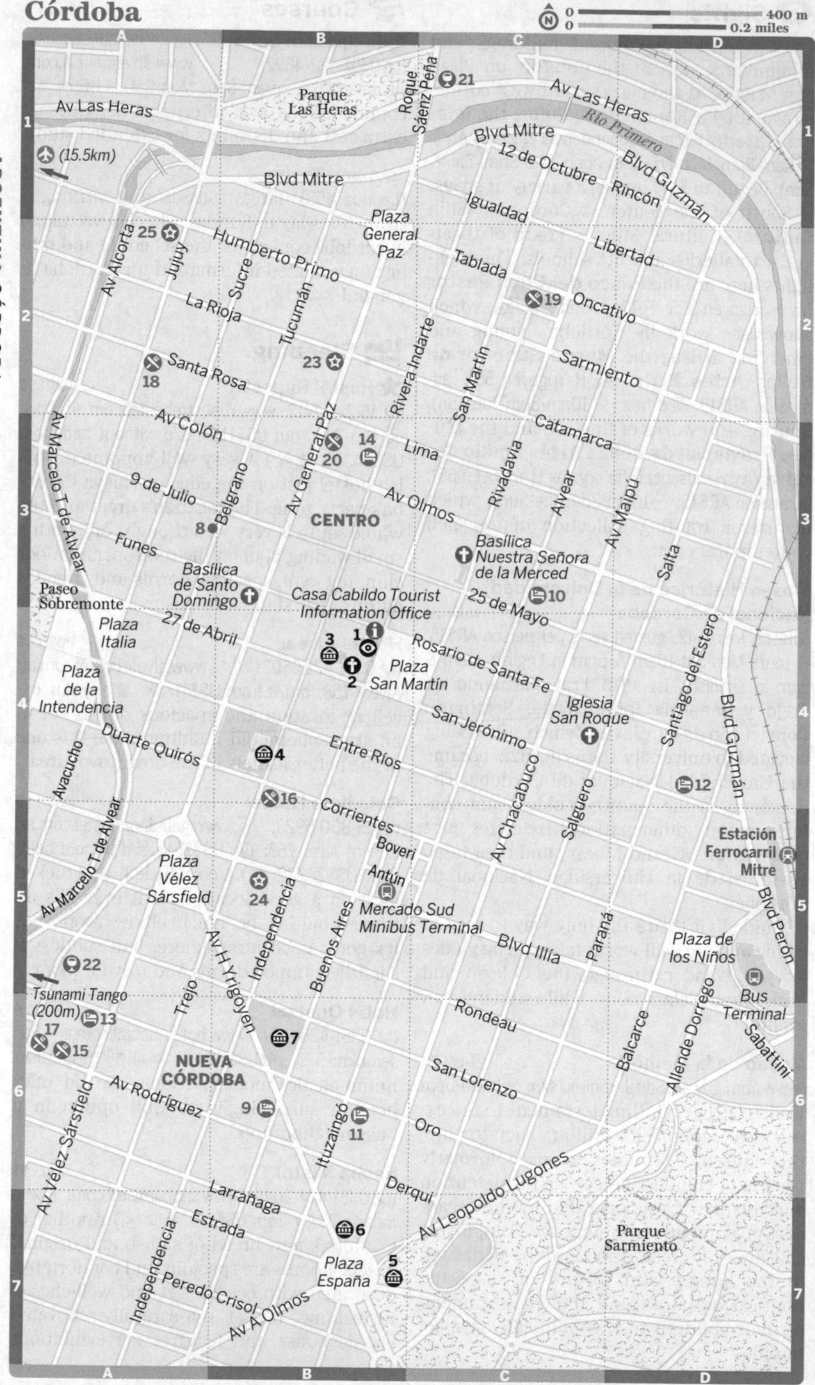
0 400 m
0 0.2 miles
Av Las Heras
Parque Las Heras
Roque Sáenz Peña
21
Río Primero
Blvd Mitre
12 de Octubre
Rincón
Blvd Guzmán
(15.5km)
Igualdad
Plaza General Paz
25
Av Alcorta
Jujuy
Humberto Primo
Sucre
Tablada
Libertad
La Rioja
Tucumán
19
Oncativo
23
Rivera Indarte
San Martín
Sarmiento
18
Santa Rosa
Av Colón
Av General Paz
14
20
Lima
Catamarca
Av Marcelo T de Alvear
9 de Julio
Belgrano
Av Olmos
Rivadavia
Alvear
Av Maipú
8
CENTRO
Funes
Basílica Nuestra Señora de la Merced
Salta
Paseo Sobremonte
Basílica de Santo Domingo
Casa Cabildo Tourist Information Office
25 de Mayo
10
Plaza Italia
27 de Abril
1
3
2
Plaza San Martín
Rosario de Santa Fe
Santiago del Estero
Plaza de la Intendencia
Iglesia San Roque
Blvd Guzmán
San Jerónimo
Duarte Quirós
4
Entre Ríos
Av Chacabuco
Salguero
12
Avacucho
16
Corrientes
Boveri
Estación Ferrocarril Mitre
Plaza Vélez Sársfield
Antún
24
Independencia
Buenos Aires
Mercado Sud Minibus Terminal
Blvd Illía
Paraná
Blvd Perón
Plaza de los Niños
22
Tsunami Tango (200m)
13
Trejo
Av H Yrigoyen
Bus Terminal
17
15
7
Rondeau
Balcarce
Allende Dorrego
Sabattini
NUEVA CÓRDOBA
San Lorenzo
Av Rodríguez
9
11
Oro
Av Vélez Sársfield
Ituzaingó
Derqui
Larrañaga
Av Leopoldo Lugones
Estrada
6
Parque Sarmiento
Plaza España
5
Independencia
Peredo Crisol
Av A Olmos

and a small lap pool, all in a quiet, central location on the pedestrian mall.

Hotel Viena HOTEL $$
(0351-460-0909; www.hotelviena.com.ar; Laprida 235; s/d US$59/75;) This modern hotel in the heart of Nueva Córdoba offers bright, clean rooms and an excellent breakfast buffet. There are lots of nooks for sitting in the lobby area, and there's a restaurant on the premises. Good choice.

Eating

La Candela ARGENTINE $
(Duarte Quirós 67; empanadas AR$10, locro AR$45; 11am-1am) Rustic and wonderfully atmospheric, run by three cranky but adorable señoras.

Mercado Norte MARKET $
(cnr Rivadavia & Oncativo; set meals from AR$60; 8am-3pm Mon-Sat) Córdoba's indoor market has delicious and inexpensive food, such as pizza, empanadas and seafood. Browsing the clean stalls selling every imaginable cut of meat, including whole *chivitos* (goat) and pigs, is a must.

Bruncheria CAFE $
(Rodriguez 244; mains AR$60-100; 9.30am-1.30am Mon-Thu, 10am-3am Fri-Sun;) Down in the hipster sector of Güemes, the Bruncheria offers a great mix of fresh decor, yummy food and cool music. It's a good spot for that second breakfast (in case the coffee and croissant didn't fill you up), but the sandwiches are winners too.

Sol y Luna VEGETARIAN $
(General Paz 278; mains from AR$45; noon-3:30pm Mon-Sat;) A fantastic selection of vegetarian offerings. Pay by the kilo or choose from the limited selection of set meals.

La Parrilla de Raul PARRILLA $
(cnr Jujuy & Santa Rosa; mains from AR$60; noon-3pm & 8.30pm-12.30am;) Of Córdoba's *parrillas*, this is probably one of the most famous. *Parrillada* for two costs only AR$120, not including extras such as drinks or salad.

★ **La Nieta 'e la Pancha** FUSION $$
(Belgrano 783; mains AR$120-170; 7pm-12:30am Mon-Fri, 11:30am-1am Sat & Sun;) The wonderful staff prepares and serves a changing menu of delectable regional specialties, creative pastas and house recipes. Be sure to save room for dessert. Check out the lovely upstairs terrace, which catches breezes and gives ample people-watching ops on the street below.

Drinking

Córdoba's drink of choice is fernet (a strong, medicinal-tasting herbal liqueur from Italy), almost always mixed with Coke.

For barhopping, head straight to Calle Rondeau, between Independencia and Ituzaingo. These two blocks are packed with bars. The other area to check out is in the neighborhood of Güemes, alongside the Cañada. **Los Infernales** (Belgrano 631;

Córdoba

Sights
1 Cabildo ... B4
2 Iglesia Catedral ... B4
3 Museo de la Memoria ... B4
4 Museo Histórico de la Universidad Nacional de Córdoba ... B4
5 Museo Provincial de Bellas Artes Emilio Caraffa ... B7
6 Museo Superior de Bellas Artes Evita ... B7
7 Paseo del Buen Pastor ... B6

Activities, Courses & Tours
8 Able Spanish School ... A3

Sleeping
9 Gaiadhon Hostel ... B6
10 Hostel Alvear ... C3
11 Hostel Rupestre ... B6
12 Hotel Quetzal ... D4
13 Hotel Viena ... A6
14 Sacha Mistol ... B3

Eating
15 Bruncheria ... A6
16 La Candela ... B4
17 La Nieta 'e la Pancha ... A6
18 La Parrilla de Raul ... A2
19 Mercado Norte ... C2
20 Sol y Luna ... B3

Drinking & Nightlife
21 Captain Blue ... C1
22 Los Infernales ... A5

Entertainment
23 Centro Cultural Casona Municipal ... B2
24 Cineclub Municipal Hugo del Carril ... B5
25 La Sala del Rey ... A2

⏲8pm-5am Tue-Sun) is the stand-by here, but go for a wander – you're sure to find plenty of others.

Discos are mostly north of the center, along Av Las Heras. Music styles vary – listen for something you like and look for people handing out free passes. **Captain Blue** (Las Heras 124; ⏲8pm-late Wed-Sat) gets seriously crowded, especially when bands play; there are plenty of others in this area.

☆ Entertainment

Cuarteto music (Argentina's original pop, a Córdoba invention) is predictably big here and played live in many venues, though it tends to attract undesirable crowds. **La Sala del Rey** (Humberto Primero 439; ⏲9pm-late Thu-Sat) is a respectable venue and the best place to catch a *cuarteto* show.

Cineclub Municipal Hugo del Carril CINEMA (☎0351-433-2463; www.cineclubmunicipal.org.ar; Blvd San Juan 49; admission Mon-Wed AR$2.50, Thu-Sun AR$4; ⏲box office 9am-late) For a great night (or day) at the movies, pop into this municipal film house, which screens everything from art flicks to Latin American award winners and local films. Stop by for a program. There's also live music and theatrical performances here.

Centro Cultural Casona Municipal CONCERT VENUE (www.casonamunicipal.com.ar; cnr Av General Paz & La Rioja; ⏲9am-9pm Mon-Fri) Shows contemporary and avant-garde art, hosts concerts and offers month-long art and music courses.

ℹ Information

There are ATMs near Plaza San Martín.

Casa Cabildo Tourist Information Office (☎0351-434-1200; Independencia 30; ⏲8am-8pm) The provincial and municipal tourist boards occupy the same office in the historic Casa Cabildo. There are also branches located at the airport and the bus terminal.

ℹ Getting There & Around

AIR

Aerolíneas Argentinas/Austral (☎0351-410-7600; Av Colón 520) flies to Buenos Aires, Salta and Puerto Iguazú. **Sol** (☎0810-122-7765; www.sol.com.ar) flies to Rosario and Neuquén.

The **airport** (☎0351-475-0877) is about 15km north of town. Bus A5 (marked 'Aeropuerto') leaves from Plaza San Martín. You'll either need a magnetic card or *cospel* (token), both available from kiosks. Taxis to the airport cost about AR$140.

BUS

Local buses don't serve the bus terminal, but it's an easy eight-block walk to the center; just keep moving toward the big steeple. A taxi shouldn't cost more than AR$40.

Frequent minibuses leave from the **Mercado Sud Minibus Terminal** (Blvd Illía), near Buenos Aires, for Cosquín, Jesús María and Alta Gracia.

Long-distance buses depart from Córdoba's **bus terminal** (Netoc; ☎0351-434-1692; Blvd Perón 300).

WORTH A TRIP

COSQUÍN

Up in the hills, 55km outside Córdoba, this sleepy little town springs to life once a year for the world-famous nine-day **Festival Nacional del Folklore** (www.aquicosquin.org), held every January since 1961. Aside from that, there's not a whole lot going on, but the **aerosilla** (chairlift; return AR$85; ⏲9am-6pm) up Cerro Pan de Azúcar (1260m), 15km out of town, gives some great views over the valley. A taxi there costs AR$65, including waiting time.

Hotels in town include the basic **Hospedaje Petit** (☎0351-451311; petitcosquin@hotmail.com; A Sabattini 739; s/d US$45/60) and the more comfortable **Hospedaje Siempreverde** (☎0351-450093; www.hosteriasiempreverde.com; Santa Fe 525; s/d US$60/80; 📶). Accommodations can get tricky during festival time – book early or consider commuting from Córdoba.

San Martín between the plaza and the stadium is lined with cafes, restaurants and *parrillas* (grillhouses). **La Casona** (cnr San Martín & Corrientes; mains AR$80-120; ⏲11:30am-11pm) has good homemade pastas plus the standard *parrilla* offerings.

Frequent buses run to Córdoba (AR$34, 1½ hours).

QUIRKY TOWNS IN CÓRDOBA'S SIERRAS

For some reason, Córdoba's Sierras region is one of the quirkiest in Argentina. The great thing about traveling here is that every once in a while you stumble upon something truly wonderful and unexpected. Here are a few of our favorites:

Capilla del Monte This otherwise sleepy little hill town is world famous among UFO watchers, who come here in the hope of communing with the extraterrestrials from on top of the mystical Cerro Uritorco.

Villa General Belgrano The town's strong German heritage gives it a very European flavor, which really takes off when the beer starts flowing in Oktoberfest (www.elsitiodelavilla.com/oktoberfest).

Villa Carlos Paz (www.villacarlospaz.gov.ar/turismo) Like a mix between Vegas and Disneyland, this lakeside getaway is dotted with theme hotels (the Great Pyramids, the Kremlin) and centered around a massive cuckoo clock.

Museo Rocsen (www.museorocsen.org) Near the tiny town of Nono, outside of Mina Clavero, the 11,000-plus pieces on display at this museum form probably the most eclectic collection of trash/treasure you're ever likely to see.

Buses from Córdoba

DESTINATION	COST (AR$)	DURATION (HR)
Buenos Aires	810	10
Mendoza	725	10
Montevideo, Uruguay	1230	15
Salta	1181	12
Tucumán	670	8

TRAIN

Córdoba's **Estación Ferrocarril Mitre** (☎0351-426-3565; Blvd Perón s/n) has departures for Buenos Aires (AR$50 to AR$300, 15 hours) via Rosario. Book tickets well in advance.

Trains to Cosquín (AR$6.50, two hours) leave from **Estación Rodriguez del Busto** (☎0351-477-6195; Cardeñosa 3500) on the northwest outskirts of town daily at 10:25am and 4:25pm. Buses A4 and A7 from the central plaza go to the station or it's an AR$55 taxi ride.

Around Córdoba

Jesús María

☎03525 / POP 53,100

After losing their operating funds to pirates off the coast of Brazil, the Jesuits produced and sold wine from Jesús María to support their university in colonial Córdoba. The town is located 51km north of Córdoba via RN 9.

If you're only planning on seeing one Jesuit mission, **Museo Jesuítico Nacional de Jesús María** (☎03525-420126; admission AR$20; ⌚8am-7pm Tue-Fri, 10am-noon & 3-7pm Sat & Sun) should probably be it. Easily accessed, but in a peaceful rural setting, it's been wonderfully preserved and restored, and is crammed full of artifacts.

Buses run between Córdoba and Jesús María (AR$19, one hour).

Alta Gracia

☎03547 / POP 48,300

Only 35km southwest of Córdoba, the colonial mountain town of Alta Gracia is steeped in history. Its illustrious residents have ranged from Jesuit pioneers to Viceroy Santiago Liniers, Spanish composer Manuel de Falla and revolutionary Ernesto 'Che' Guevara. The tourist office, located in the clock tower opposite the museum Virrey Liniers, has a good town map.

Sights

From 1643 to 1762 Jesuit fathers built the **Iglesia Parroquial Nuestra Señora de la Merced** on the west side of the central Plaza Manuel Solares; the nearby Jesuit workshops of **El Obraje** (1643) are now a public school. Liniers, one of the last officials to occupy the post of viceroy of the Río de la Plata, resided in what is now the **Museo Histórico Nacional del Virrey Liniers** (☎03547-421303; www.museoliniers.org.ar; admission AR$20, Wed free; ⌚9am-7pm Tue-Fri, 9:30am-6:30pm Sat, Sun & holidays), alongside the church.

Though the Guevaras lived in several houses in the 1930s, their primary residence was Villa Beatriz, which has now been converted into the **Museo Casa de Ernesto Che Guevara** (Avellaneda 501; admission AR$75; ⌚2-7pm Mon, 9am-7pm Tue-Sun). The museum focuses heavily on the legend's early life, and, judging by the photographs, Che was already a pretty intense guy by the time he was 16, and definitely had his cool look down by his early 20s. Particularly touching are some of Che's letters that he wrote to his parents and children toward the end of his life.

Sleeping & Eating

The **Alta Gracia Hostel** (☎03547-428810; www.altagraciahostel.com.ar; Paraguay 218; dm/r US$12/35) offers spacious, clean dorms a few blocks downhill from the clock tower.

The most comfortable digs in town can be found at **279 Boutique B&B** (☎03547-424177; www.279altagracia.com; Giorello 279; r US$65;) , run by a vivacious New Yorker who is full of local info.

Parrillas and sidewalk cafes line Av Belgrano in the few blocks downhill from the *estancia*. The best restaurant in town by a long, long shot is **El Bistro del Alquimista** (Castellanos 351; meals AR$130-250; ⌚4pm-midnight Mon-Sat;), with a rotating menu of excellent local and international dishes and a great wine list.

Getting There & Away

From the **bus terminal** (Tacuarí at Perón), buses run every 15 minutes to and from Córdoba (AR$17, one hour). You can flag them down as they pass through town.

La Rioja

☎0380 / POP 181,000

This is siesta country, folks. Between noon and 5pm, pretty much *everything* shuts down (except, for some reason, bookstores). Once the sun starts dipping behind the surrounding mountains, people emerge from their homes and the plazas take on a lively, refreshed feel. Most travelers use the town as a break on the long haul beween Mendoza and Salta, detouring to the remote Parque Nacional Talampaya if they have time.

Sights

★Museo Folklórico MUSEUM

(Pelagio Luna 811; admission by donation; ⌚9am-1pm & 5-9pm Tue-Fri, 9am-1pm Sat & Sun) This hugely worthwhile museum is set in a wonderful early-17th-century adobe building, and has fine displays on various aspects of the region's culture. Themes include *chaya* (local La Rioja music), the Tinkunaco festival, weaving and winemaking. The informative guided tour is excellent if your Spanish is up to it.

Convento de San Francisco CHURCH

(cnr 25 de Mayo & Bazán y Bustos; ⌚7am-1pm & 5-9pm) The order of Saint Francis was on the scene very early and began building here in the late 16th century. Bad luck with construction and then an earthquake mean the current church is an early-20th-century neo-Gothic affair. It houses the image of the Niño Alcalde, a Christ-child icon symbolically recognized as the city's mayor, and dressed in robes of office.

Festivals & Events

El Tinkunaco HISTORICAL

(⌚noon 31 Dec) The December 31 ceremony El Tinkunako re-enacts San Francisco Solano's mediation between the Diaguitas and the Spaniards in 1593. When accepting peace, the Diaguitas imposed two conditions: resignation of the Spanish mayor and his replacement by the Niño Alcalde.

Sleeping

Accommodations in La Rioja suffer from two problems: they're overpriced and often booked out. The tourist office keeps a list of homestays.

Wayra Hostel HOSTEL $

(☎15-435-4140; www.wayrahostel.com.ar; Escalada 1008; dm US$11-15, d US$25-35;) Pleasant, clean and friendly, this is a well-run place with a peaceful feel despite some main-road noise. Pay the extra pesos for the downstairs dorm, which has plenty of space and is a little quieter. Private rooms are neat and decent value. The hostel picks you up for free from the bus terminal, rents out bikes and can organize paragliding and tours.

Hostel Apacheta HOSTEL $

(☎15-444-5445; www.facebook.com/apachetahostel; San Nicolás de Bari 669; dm/d US$15/45;) This central hostel is a simple but likable place in a great location; dorms feature a variety of beds and bunks, with air-con and room to move. It's clean, but a bit like when you told your parents you'd cleaned your room. Rental bikes and an inflatable paddling pool are on hand. Knock US$3 off if you don't want breakfast.

★ Hotel Pucara HOTEL $$
(0380-443-7789; www.hotelpucaralarioja.com.ar; República de Siria 79; s/d US$50/77;) Cool and tranquil, this modern hotel has attractive, comfortable lodgings in a quiet *barrio*. The friendly young owners have made it a welcoming place, with stonework and traditional art decorating public areas and the five clean, dark rooms, which have decent mattresses. Though not a luxury establishment, in many ways it's La Rioja's best hotel.

Eating

Rivadavia east of Plaza 9 de Julio is lined with cafes, restaurants and *parrillas*.

Café del Paseo CAFE $
(cnr Pelagio Luna & 25 de Mayo; light meals AR$60-100; 7:30am-3pm & 5:30pm-1am;) This is your spot on the corner of the plaza to observe local life. Executives with i-gadgets mingle with families, and tables of older men chew the fat over another slow-paced La Rioja day.

El Marqués ARGENTINE $
(Av San Nicolás de Bari 484; meals AR$50-80; 8am-1am Mon-Sat) This simple local eatery just off the plaza puts many pricier restaurants to shame. Sandwiches, traditional local dishes, pasta, pizza, omelets and grilled meats are well prepared and fairly priced. It's something of a bargain and the fruit *licuados* are delicious too.

La Stanza ITALIAN $$
(Dorrego 164; mains AR$100-180; 12:30-3pm & 8:30pm-midnight Tue-Sat, 12:30-3pm Sun) One of the best places in town, this stylish, attractive restaurant has an upbeat, surprisingly urban vibe and serves imaginative pasta dishes that are a cut above most places. Better still are the main dishes, which feature delicious and inventive portions of meat, accompanied by tasty medleys of baked vegetables. Service is helpful and there's an appealingly cheery ambience.

Information

La Rioja's handiest information source is the **tourist kiosk** (Plaza 25 de Mayo; 8am-1pm & 4-9pm Mon-Fri, 8am-9pm Sat & Sun) on the plaza. It has a decent city map, good accommodations information and many kilos worth of brochures covering other provincial destinations.

Getting There & Away

Aerolíneas Argentinas (0380-442-6307; www.aerolineas.com.ar; Belgrano 63; 8am-1pm & 5:30-8:30pm Mon-Fri, 8:30am-12:30pm Sat) flies Monday to Saturday to Buenos Aires.

La Rioja's new **bus terminal** (Av Circunvalación s/n) is 5km from the center. Buses 2, 6, 7 and 8 (AR$6) runs between the two. A taxi costs around AR$50.

BUSES FROM LA RIOJA

DESTINATION	COST (AR$)	DURATION (HR)
Buenos Aires	985	14-17
Chilecito	120	3
Córdoba	400	6
Mendoza	563	8-9½
Salta	616	10
Tucumán	343	5½-6½

Santiago del Estero

0385 / POP 360,900

Placid, hot Santiago enjoys the distinction 'Madre de Ciudades' (Mother of Cities). Founded in 1553, this was the first Spanish urban settlement in what is now Argentina. Sadly, it boasts no architectural heritage from that period, but still makes a pleasant stop.

Sleeping & Eating

Hotel Avenida HOTEL $
(0385-421-5887; www.havenida.com.ar; Pedro León Gallo 403; s/d US$27/50;) You have to feel for these people: they set up a welcoming little hotel, beautifully decorated with indigenous art and right opposite the bus terminal. Then the city moved the bus terminal to the other side of town. Nevertheless, it's well worth the short walk from the center. Spotless, renovated, friendly and always improving: a great little place.

★ Altos del Estero HOTEL $$
(0385-422-7718; www.hotelaltosdelestero.com; Salta 40; s/d US$60/80;) Converted from a car park, ensuring plenty of space in a central location, this modern offering is cool and pleasant, with helpful service. Its inviting rooms offer significant value; many have streetside or poolside balconies, decked out in soft contemporary beiges and browns.

The pool is decent, and the price includes parking.

Mía Mamma ARGENTINE $$
(24 de Septiembre 15; mains AR$75-130; ⌚noon-3pm & 9pm-12:15am;) Tucked away but on the plaza, this is a discreet and reliable restaurant with well-dressed waiters who see to your every need. There's a salad bar with plenty of vegetables and a wide choice of food that includes enormous *parrilla* options as well as tasty *arroz a la valenciana* (paella).

Information

The provincial **tourist office** (☎0385-421-3253; www.turismosantiago.gob.ar; Libertad 417; ⌚7am-9pm Mon-Fri, 10am-1pm & 5-8pm Sat, 10am-1pm Sun) is on the plaza.

Several banks have ATMs. The post office is at the corner of Buenos Aires and Urquiza.

Getting There & Away

Aerolíneas Argentinas (☎0385-422-4333; www.aerolineas.com.ar; 24 de Septiembre 547; ⌚8:30am-noon & 5-8pm Mon-Fri, 9am-noon Sat) flies daily to Buenos Aires.

The **bus terminal** (☎0385-422-7091; www.tosde.com.ar; Chacabuco 550) has frequent departures to Tucumán (AR$125, two hours) and Buenos Aires (AR$960, 12 hours).

Santiago del Estero's twin town La Banda is on the line between Tucumán (four hours) and Buenos Aires' Retiro station (23 hours). Bus 117 does a circuit of Santiago's center before heading across the river to the station.

Tucumán

☎0381 / POP 864,700

A big city with a small-town feel, Tucumán is definitely improving in terms of the backpacking scene. There are some good hostels, a pumping nightlife and some excellent adventures to be had in the surrounding hills. Independence Day (July 9) celebrations are especially vigorous in Tucumán, which hosted the congress that declared Argentine independence in 1816.

Sights & Activities

Casa de la Independencia MUSEUM
(Casa Histórica; Congreso 151; adult/child AR$30/free; ⌚10am-6pm) Unitarist lawyers and clerics declared Argentina's independence from Spain on July 9, 1816, in this late-colonial mansion. Portraits of the signatories line the walls of the original room. There's plenty of information in Spanish on the lead-up to this seismic event, and English guided tours (free) are available. There's a sound-and-light show nightly except Thursdays; entry is AR$10/5 per adult/child. Get tickets at the tourist office.

Alongside the building are areas with handicrafts stalls and stands selling traditional foods.

Museo Folclórico Manuel Belgrano MUSEUM
(Av 24 de Septiembre 565; ⌚9am-1pm & 5-9pm Tue-Fri, 5-9pm Sat & Sun) FREE In a colonial house, this pleasant museum features a good collection of traditional gaucho gear, indigenous musical instruments (check out the armadillo *charangos*; Andean stringed instruments) and weavings, as well as some pottery.

Sleeping

A La Gurda HOSTEL $
(☎0381-497-6275; www.lagurdahostel.com.ar; Maipú 490; dm/s/d US$12/25/36, tw without bathroom US$32;) Upstairs in a lovely old house, this very pleasant hostel does lots right. It offers eight-bed dorms with lockers and OK-value private bunk rooms with air-con. There's a pool table and excellent bathroom facilities, bar service and a kitchen; everything's spotless. Management is helpful and friendly.

Casa Calchaquí GUESTHOUSE $
(☎0381-425-6974; www.casacalchaqui.com; Lola Mora 92, Yerba Buena; d/q US$53/80, s/d without bathroom US$35/40; ⌚Mar-Jan;) Eight kilometers west of the center in upmarket Yerba Buena *barrio*, this is a welcome retreat. Comfortably rustic rooms surround a relaxing garden space with hammocks, bar service and a mini-pool. Yerba Buena has good restaurants and nightlife. Grab a taxi (AR$75) or bus 102 or 118 from opposite the bus terminal.

Hotel Colonial HOTEL $
(☎0381-422-2738; www.hotelcolonialweb.com.ar; San Martín 36; s/d US$35/56;) If you can handle a few dated color schemes – the milk-chocolate-brown toilets aren't looking as slick as they no doubt used to – this is a reliable and comfortable budget base. There is a touch of colonial to the decor of the public areas, and service is taken seriously. There's a pool in an annex across the street.

★**Tucumán Center** HOTEL $$
(☎0381-452-5555; www.tucumancenterhotel.com.ar; 25 de Mayo 230; s/d US$109/125;)

It's hard to fault this upmarket business-class hotel that's bang in the center. Service and facilities – including an outdoor pool and access to a proper gym just down the road – are first-rate, and the huge beds are mighty comfortable. Suites come with space to spare and a bathtub with bubbles. Excellent value.

Eating & Drinking

From Thursday to Saturday nights, the action is in the Abasto region, on Calle Lillo. Follow San Lorenzo west from the town center, and you'll hit the middle of the zone. There are dozens of bars and nightclubs – take your pick. Other *boliches* can be found in Yerba Buena, 6km west of the town center.

★Mi Nueva Estancia PARRILLA $
(Córdoba 401; mains AR$70-110; 11am-3pm & 8pm-12:30am Mon-Thu, 11am-4pm & 8pm-1:30am Fri-Sun;) Delicious! That's the verdict on the cuts of meat at this popular grill restaurant, but the salad bar and other menu choices also win points. Value is great here for both quality and quantity, and service is friendly and efficient.

El Portal ARGENTINE $
(Av 24 de Septiembre 351; empanadas AR$9, mains AR$60-90; noon-4pm & 8pm-midnight) Half a block east of Plaza Independencia, this rustic indoor-outdoor eatery has a tiny but perfectly formed menu, based around empanadas, *locro* and the like, supplemented by some *milanesas* and pizzas. Delicious and authentic.

Shitake VEGETARIAN $
(9 de Julio 94; all you can eat AR$70; 11:30am-3:30pm & 7:30pm-1am Mon-Sat;) With a tasty array of vegetarian dishes in its buffet, this small, well-run spot gives value for money. Pizzas, empanadas, soy *milanesas* and much more are on offer. Drinks are extra. You can also take out, paying by weight.

★Setimio ARGENTINE $$
(Santa Fe 512; mains AR$120-210, tapas AR$60-100; food 10am-4pm & 7:30pm-1:30am;) Wall-to-wall bottles decorate this smart wine shop and restaurant, where the menu features Spanish-style tapas, fine salads and well-prepared fish dishes among other toothsome gourmet delights. Several wines are available by the glass, and you can pick any of the hundreds of bottles from the shelves for a small corkage fee. Several wines are available by the glass too.

Information

Tourist office (0381-430-3644; www.tucumanturismo.gob.ar; Av 24 de Septiembre 484; 8am-9pm Mon-Fri, 9am-9pm Sat & Sun) On the plaza; very helpful and knowledgeable. There's another office in the shopping center at the bus terminal, open the same hours.

Getting There & Around

AIR

Tucumán's **Aeropuerto Benjamín Matienzo** (TUC; 0381-426-5072) is 8km east of downtown. To get there, catch bus 121, which passes the center and the bus terminal (AR$4), or take a taxi (AR$100). **Aerolíneas Argentinas** (0381-431-1030; www.aerolineas.com.ar; 9 de Julio 110; 8:30am-1pm & 5-8pm Mon-Fri, 9am-12:30pm Sat) and **LAN** (0381-422-0606; www.lan.com; San Juan 426; 9am-1pm & 5-8pm Mon-Fri) fly several times daily to Buenos Aires. Aerolíneas also flies to Córdoba.

BUS

Tucumán's **bus terminal** (0381-430-0352; Brígido Terán 350;) is a few blocks from the center, a decent walk if you don't want to stump for a cab. It has a post office, *locutorios*, a supermarket, bars and restaurants – all blissfully air-conditioned.

Aconquija services Tafí del Valle (AR$80, 2½ hours) and Cafayate (AR$240 to AR$ 270, six hours).

Long-distance destinations include Santiago del Estero (AR$125, two hours), Córdoba (AR$561, 11 hours), Salta (AR$290, four hours) and Buenos Aires (AR$1107, 15 hours).

TRAIN

Trains run from **Estación Ferrocarril Mitre** (0381-430-9220; www.sofse.gob.ar; Plaza Alberdi s/n) to Buenos Aires Wednesdays at 4:16pm and Saturdays at 9:01pm (AR$70 to AR$400, 25 hours).

Tafí del Valle

03867 / POP 3400

Set in a pretty valley overlooking a lake, Tafí is where folks from Tucumán come to escape the heat in summer months. In the low season it's much mellower (which isn't to imply that there's any sort of frenzy here in summertime), but still gorgeous, and makes a good base for exploring the surrounding countryside and nearby ruins at Quilmes.

Sights & Activities

Parque de los Menhires MUSEUM
(Plaza s/n, El Mollar; admission AR$15; 9am-7pm Tue-Fri, 2-7pm Sat & Sun) At pretty El Mollar,

at the other end of the valley from Tafí, you can visit the Parque de los Menhires on the plaza, a collection of more than 100 carved standing stones found in the surrounding area. They were produced by the Tafí culture some 2000 years ago.

Festivals & Events

At 2000m, Tafí, a temperate island in a subtropical sea, produces some exceedingly good handmade cheese. The **cheese festival**, held during the second week in February, is well worth a look (and, possibly, a nibble).

Sleeping & Eating

Numerous *parrillas*, specializing in *lechón* (suckling pig) and *chivito* (goat), line Av Perón.

Nomade Hostel HOSTEL $
(☎0381-307-5922; www.nomadehostel.com.ar; Los Castaños s/n; dm US$18, d with/without bathroom US$48/60; @ 📶) Relaxed, colorful, enthusiastic and welcoming, this hostel is an easy 10-minute walk from the bus terminal (turn right, go round the bend, veer right). It's got a lovely location with great views from the spacious garden. Rates include breakfast and tasty home-cooked dinners; the atmosphere here is excellent. It's best to book ahead in summer. Prices drop substantially off-season. HI discount.

IT'S ALL DOWNHILL FROM HERE

One of the best day trips you can do from Tafí del Valle needs no guide at all. Rent a bike, and coast downhill past the lake and out onto the road to Tucumán. It's a 40km (mostly) downhill cruise, following the course of the Río Los Sosa, with literally hundreds of gorgeous swimming holes and picnic spots right by the roadside.

Once you lose sight of the river and houses start appearing, you know the best part of the ride is over. You can hail any Tafí-bound bus (make sure you choose a safe place for them to pull over), stash your bike underneath and ride home in style.

There's no food or water anywhere along this route, so come prepared. And check your brakes before leaving too – you'll definitely be using them.

Hotel Virgen del Valle HOTEL $
(☎03867-421016; virgendelvalle@tafidelvalle.com; Los Menhires s/n; d US$48; ❄ @ 📶) Just off the main drag in the heart of town, this place features spacious, comfortable but darkish rooms around a small courtyard. It's not luxury, and there are a few inconveniences, but it's a good deal for two at this price.

Hospedaje Celia GUESTHOUSE $
(☎03867-421170; Belgrano 443; r per person US$15) Set back from the road 100m uphill from the church, Celia offers bright, white and comfortable rooms in a tranquil, friendly setting, with heating and private bathrooms. There are inconveniences – no in-room sockets, for example – but staff will give you an extension lead and the price is right.

★ **Estancia Los Cuartos** ESTANCIA $$
(☎15-587-4230; www.estancialoscuartos.com; Critto s/n; d US$65-90; P @ 📶) Oozing with character, this lovely spot with grazing llamas lies between the bus terminal and the center. Two centuries old, it feels like a museum, with venerable books lining antique shelves, and authentic rooms redolent with aged wood and woollen blankets but with great modern bathrooms. Newer rooms offer less history but remain true to the feel of the place.

Restaurante El Museo ARGENTINE $
(Av José Silva s/n; dishes AR$30-90; ⏲noon-4pm) Set in the venerable adobe Jesuit chapel a kilometer from the center, this makes a very atmospheric venue to lunch on traditional home-cooked local specialties, such as *humitas*, tamales and empanadas. Just turn up and see what's cooking that day.

Rancho de Félix ARGENTINE $
(cnr Belgrano & Perón; mains AR$75-130; ⏲11:30am-3pm & 8pm-midnight; 📶) This big, warm thatched barn of a place is incredibly popular for lunch. Regional specialties such as *locro* and *humitas* feature heavily on the menu, but *parrilla* and pasta are also on offer. Quality is reasonably good, and prices are fair. It sometimes doesn't open evenings if things are quiet.

Information

Casa del Turista (☎15-594-1039; www.tafidelvalle.gob.ar; Los Faroles s/n; ⏲8am-10pm) On the pedestrian street.

Getting There & Around

Tafí's **bus terminal** (☎03867-421025; Av Critto) is an easy walk from the center. Departures include Cafayate (AR$140, four hours) and Tucumán (AR$80, 2½ hours). Mountain bikes can be rented from Hostel Nomade.

Cafayate

☎03868 / POP 13,700

Set at the entrance to the **Quebrada de Cafayate**, 1600m above sea level and surrounded by some of the country's best vineyards, Cafayate provides the opportunity to indulge in two of life's great pleasures: drinking wine and exploring nature. If you're pressed for time, you can combine the two and take a bottle out into the *quebrada* (gorge) with you, in which case we would recommend a local torrontés, provided you can keep it chilled.

February's **La Serenata** (www.serenata.todowebsalta.com.ar; admission Thu AR$150, Sat & Sun AR$300) music festival draws big crowds.

Sights & Activities

From 25 de Mayo, two blocks south of Colón, a 5km walk southwest leads you to the **Río Colorado**. Follow the river upstream for about two hours to get to a 10m **waterfall**, where you can swim. Look out for hidden **rock paintings** on the way (for a couple of pesos, local children will guide you).

Several operators around the plaza offer tours of the *Quebrada* for AR$200 per person. **Majo Viajes** (☎03868-422038; majoviajes@gmail.com; Nuestra Señora del Rosario 77) is straight-talking and reliable. Try to go in the late afternoon, when it's cooler and the colors and photo opportunities are better.

Museo de la Vid y El Vino MUSEUM
(www.museodelavidyelvino.gov.ar; Av General Güemes; foreigner/Argentine AR$30/10; ⏲9am-7pm Tue-Sun) This impressive museum gives a good introduction to the area's wine industry. The atmospheric first section, which deals with the viticultural side – the life of the vines – through a series of poems and images, is particularly appealing. The second part covers the winemaking side, and there's a cafe where you can try and buy. English translations are good throughout.

Sleeping

★Rusty-K Hostal HOSTEL $
(☎03868-422031; rustykhostal@hotmail.com; Rivadavia 281; dm US$18, d with/without bathroom US$50/45; @ 📶) The peace of the vine-filled patio garden here is a real highlight, as is the spotlessness of the rooms and dorms, and the friendliness. Cute doubles and an excellent attitude make this Cafayate's budget gem. These prices are for high summer and drop substantially out of season. Book ahead.

Casa Árbol GUESTHOUSE, HOSTEL $
(☎03868-422238; www.facebook.com/casaarbolcafayate; Calchaquí 84; dm/d US$12/35; 📶) 🌿 There's something really pleasant about this casual spot which has airy, beautiful decor and a really genuine welcome. Pretty, spotless rooms and a four-bed dorm share two bathrooms. There's lounging room to spare in the patio, breakfast area and garden.

El Hospedaje GUESTHOUSE $
(☎03868-421680; elhospedaje@gmail.com; Salta 13; d US$70; ❄ 📶 🏊) On a corner just a block from the plaza, this easygoing guesthouse dotted with antique cash registers is nonetheless peaceful. Rooms vary in layout but are mostly on the compact side. They surround a pretty patio fragrant with the smell of lavender.

Portal del Santo HOTEL $$
(☎03868-422400; www.portaldelsanto.com.ar; Chavarría 250; d downstairs/upstairs US$135/154; P ❄ @ 📶 🏊) Cool white elegance is the stock-in-trade of this hospitable family-run hotel that resembles a colonial palace with arched arcades. Lower rooms open onto both the front porch and the inviting garden-pool-Jacuzzi area; top-floor chambers have mountain views and even more space. All have fridge and microwave; suites sleep four. The owners are helpful and put on a great homemade breakfast.

Eating

★Casa de las Empanadas EMPANADAS $
(Mitre 24; 12 empanadas AR$90; ⏲11am-3pm & 8pm-midnight Tue-Sun) Decorated with the scrawls of contented customers, this no-frills place has a wide selection of empanadas that are all absolutely delicious. Local wine in ceramic jugs, and *humitas* and tamales can round out the meal. If it's closed, head

to its other **branch** (Nuestra Señora del Rosario 156; 12 empanadas AR$90; ⏲11am-3pm & 7-11pm).

Parrilla Restaurants PARRILLA **$**
(Rivadavia, btwn San Lorenzo & 12 de Octubre; steaks AR$60-110; ⏲7pm-midnight Mon-Sat, 11am-3pm Sun) A long way from the slightly mannered tourist scene around the plaza, this string of no-frills grillhouses makes a worthwhile dinner escape. The Gallito is locally renowned, but adjacent Parrilla Santos – just a concrete floor, a barbecue and a corrugated-metal roof – has equally tasty meat. Uncomplicated and great value.

Heladería Miranda ICE CREAM **$**
(Av General Güemes N s/n; cones AR$25-40; ⏲1:30pm-midnight) A frequent dilemma in Argentina is whether to go for a rich red cabernet or a dry white torrontés, but it doesn't usually occur in ice-cream parlors. It does here: the Miranda's wine sorbets are Cafayate's pride and joy, but other fresh fruit flavors, including *tuna* (cactus-fruit), are also delicious.

Piattelli ARGENTINE **$$**
(☎15-405491; RP 2; mains AR$110-190; ⏲12:30-4pm; 📶) A lovely indoor-outdoor setting overlooking picture-perfect vineyards at this upmarket winery 5km from Cafayate makes a fine lunch stop; the sophisticated food doesn't disappoint. A range of international influences spice up the menu, and at weekends (when booking is advisable) the staff fire up the outdoor grill with some of the finest parrilla offerings in this part of the nation.

El Terruño ARGENTINE **$$**
(☎03868-422460; www.terruno.todowebsalta.com.ar; Av General Güemes N 30; mains AR$110-200; ⏲noon-3:30pm & 7:30pm-midnight; 📶) This place with plaza-side seating and polite if scatty service presents, strangely, two

Cafayate

THE BACK ROAD BETWEEN CACHI & CAFAYATE

If you're in Cachi and heading toward Cafayate (or vice versa), buses reach Molinos and start again in Angastaco, leaving a 42km stretch of gorgeous, lonely road unserviced. Hitching is common in these parts, but traffic is rare and even the towns that have bus service have infrequent departures.

It's hard, but not impossible. The last thing you want to do is stand on the roadside with your thumb out. The best thing to do? When you hit town, start asking around literally everywhere – the police station, hospital, *kioskos* – to see if anybody knows anyone who is going your way. Somebody will and you won't be stuck for long. If you do get stuck, there are decent, cheap places to stay and eat in Molinos, Angastaco and San Carlos.

You may end up in the back of a pickup truck with the wind in your hair and the mountains in your face. But really, this is possibly the sort of adventure you had in mind when you booked your airfare.

Sound like too much? You can always ask at the *remisería* (*remise* office) in front of Cachi's bus terminal if there's a group going that you can join. *Remises* seat four passengers and cost AR$1100 from Cafayate to Cachi. The stretch from Molinos to Angastaco should cost about AR$200.

menus. One is less traditional, with dishes such as inventive seafood-based salads, and well-prepared mains, including plenty of fish dishes. Overpriced but friendly and reliable enough.

Information

The **tourist information kiosk** (☎03868-422442; Av General Güemes s/n; ⏲9am-7pm Tue-Sun) is at the northeast corner of Plaza San Martín.

Getting There & Around

The new **bus terminal** (RN 40) is at the northern entrance to town. Getting between Cafayate and Cachi can mean a tough but rewarding back-road trip, up the Valles Calchaquíes.

Cafayate

Sights

1 Museo de la Vid y El Vino C4

Activities, Courses & Tours

2 Majo Viajes B3

Sleeping

3 Casa Árbol B3
4 El Hospedaje C2
5 Portal del Santo C4
6 Rusty-K Hostal B2

Eating

7 Casa de las Empanadas B2
8 Casa de las Empanadas II B3
9 El Terruño C3
10 Heladería Miranda C2

Flechabus (www.flechabus.com.ar) has buses to Salta (AR$159, four hours) and up the Valle Calchaquíes to Angastaco (AR$60, two hours) via San Carlos.

El Aconquija (☎03868-421052; http://transportesaconquija.com.ar) has departures to Tucumán (AR$240-270, six hours), passing through Tafí del Valle (AR$140-170, five hours). There are various departures for Santa María to visit the ruins at Quilmes, in Tucumán province (AR$45, one hour).

Around Cafayate

Quebrada de Cafayate

From Cafayate, RN 68 slices through the Martian-like landscape of the Quebrada de Cafayate on its way to Salta. About 50km north of Cafayate, the eastern Sierra de Carahuasi is the backdrop for distinctive sandstone landforms such as the Garganta del Diablo (Devil's Throat), El Anfiteatro (Amphitheater), El Sapo (Toad), El Fraile (Friar), El Obelisco (Obelisk) and Los Castillos (Castles).

Other than car rental or organized tours, the best way to see the *quebrada* is by bike or on foot. Bring plenty of water and go in the morning, as unpleasant, strong winds kick up in the afternoon. At Cafayate, cyclists can load their bikes onto any bus heading to Salta and disembark at the impressive box canyon of Garganta del Diablo. From here, the 50-odd kilometers back to Cafayate can be biked in about four hours, but it's too far on foot. When you've had enough, walkers should simply hail down another bus on its way back to Cafayate.

Valles Calchaquíes

In this valley north and south of Cafayate, once a principal route across the Andes, the Calchaquí people resisted Spanish attempts to impose forced labor obligations. Tired of having to protect their pack trains, the Spaniards relocated many Calchaquí to Buenos Aires, and the land fell to Spaniards, who formed large rural estates.

CACHI

03868 / POP 2600

Cachi is a spectacularly beautiful town and by far the most visually impressive of those along the Valles Calchaquíes. There's not a whole lot to do here, but that's all part of the charm.

While you're here, definitely stop in at the **Museo Arqueológico** (admission by donation; 9am-6pm Tue-Sun), a slickly presented collection of area finds, including an impressive array of petroglyphs.

Various companies offer excursions and activities in the surrounding hills. **Urkupiña** (03868-491317; www.urkupinatur.wix.com/cachi; Zorrilla s/n) offers cycling trips, quad-bike excursions and reasonably priced transportation to Cafayate along the RN 40.

For budget accommodations, check out the **municipal campground & hostel** (03868-491902; oficinadeturismo.cachi@gmail.com; campsites per 2 people plus tent US$5, with power US$8, cabins US$32;) or **Nevado de Cachi** (03868-491912; Ruiz de los Llanos s/n; s/d US$20/35;). One of the better hotels in town is **El Cortijo** (03868-491034; www.elcortijohotel.com; Av ACA s/n; s US$100, d standard/superior US$125/145;), a reasonably priced boutique hotel on the edge of town.

Some cheap restaurants surround the plaza. The most interesting restaurant in town is **Ashpamanta** (Bustamante s/n; dishes AR$60-105; noon-3pm & 7-10pm;), just off the plaza, where all ingredients are locally grown.

The **tourist office** (03868-491902; oficinadeturismo.cachi@gmail.com; Güemes s/n; 9am-9pm) is in the municipal building on the plaza. It has an atrocious city map but good info on hotels and attractions.

It's difficult but not impossible to get directly from Cachi to Cafayate. It's easier to take a bus back to Salta (AR$45, 4½ hours), via the scenic Cuesta del Obispo route past Parque Nacional Los Cardones.

Quilmes

This pre-Hispanic **pucará** (walled city; adult/child AR$30/free; 8am-6pm), in Tucumán province, 50km south of Cafayate, is Argentina's most extensive preserved ruin. Dating from about AD 1000, this complex urban settlement covered about 30 hectares and housed perhaps 5000 people. The Quilmes people abided contact with the Incas but could not outlast the Spaniards, who, in 1667, deported the last 2000 to Buenos Aires.

Quilmes' thick walls underscore its defensive functions, but evidence of dense occupation sprawls north and south of the nucleus.

Buses from Cafayate to Santa María pass the Quilmes junction; from there, it's 5km to the ruins.

Salta

0387 / POP 655,500

Salta has experienced a huge surge in popularity as a backpacking destination over the last few years, and rightly so – the setting's gorgeous, the hostels are attractive, the nightlife pumps and there's plenty to do in and around town.

Sights

Salta owes much of its reputation for beauty to the various churches scattered around the downtown area. The 19th-century **Iglesia Catedral** (España 590; 6:30am-12:15pm & 4:30-8:15pm Mon-Fri, 7:30am-12:15pm & 4:30-8:15pm Sat, 7:30am-1pm & 5-9pm Sun) guards the ashes of General Martín Miguel de Güemes, a hero of the wars of independence. So ornate it's almost gaudy, the **Iglesia San Francisco** (www.conventosanfranciscosalta.com; cnr Caseros & Córdoba; 8am-1pm & 2-9pm Mon-Sat, 8am-1pm & 5-9pm Sun) is a Salta landmark. Only Carmelite nuns can enter the 16th-century adobe **Convento de San Bernardo** (Caseros s/n; pastries 9am-noon & 4-6pm Mon-Sat), but anyone can admire its carved *algarrobo* (carob wood) door or peek inside the chapel during Mass, held at 8am daily.

★Museo de Arqueología de Alta Montaña MUSEUM

(MAAM; www.maam.gob.ar; Mitre 77; foreigner/Argentine AR$70/50; 11am-7:30pm Tue-Sun) One of northern Argentina's premier museums, this has a serious and informative exhibition focusing on Inca culture and, in particular, the child sacrifices left on some of the Andes' most imposing peaks.

The centerpiece is the mummified body of one of three children (rotated every six months) discovered at the peak of Llullaillaco in 1999. It was a controversial decision to display the bodies and it is a powerful experience to come face to face with them.

★Pajcha – Museo de Arte Étnico Americano MUSEUM
(www.museopajchasalta.com.ar; 20 de Febrero 831; foreigner/Argentine AR$40/20; ⏲10am-1pm & 4-8pm Mon-Sat) This eye-opening private museum is a must-see if you're interested in indigenous art and culture. Juxtaposing archaeological finds with contemporary and recent artisanal work from all over Latin America in a series of sumptuously realized displays, it takes an encouragingly broad view of Andean culture and beyond. It's an exquisite dose of color and beauty run with great enthusiasm by the English-speaking management.

Cerro San Bernardo HILL
For outstanding views of Salta, take the **teleférico** (☎0387-431-0641; 1 way/round trip AR$55/110; ⏲10am-7pm) from Parque San Martín to the top of this hill, a kilometer's ride that takes eight minutes. Alternatively, take the trail starting at the **Güemes monument**. Atop is a cafe (its terrace has the best views), a watercourse and *artesanía* (handicraft) shops.

Activities

Whitewater rafting outside of town is available with various companies along Buenos Aires, near the Plaza 9 de Julio. **Salta Rafting** (☎0387-421-3216; www.saltarafting.com; Caseros 177) can take care of all your rafting, ziplining, mountain biking, trekking and horse-riding requirements.

Tren a las Nubes TOUR
(www.trenalasnubes.com.ar; cnr Ameghino & Balcarce; round trip US$182; ⏲Sat Apr–mid-Dec) The 'Train to the Clouds', Argentina's most famous rail trip, heads from Salta down the Lerma Valley before ascending multicolored Quebrada del Toro, continuing past Tastil ruins and San Antonio de los Cobres, before reaching a stunning viaduct spanning a desert canyon at La Polvorilla (altitude 4220m).

Sleeping

★Espacio Mundano B&B $
(☎0387-572-2244; www.espaciomundano.com.ar; Guemes 780; r US$58-82; ❄📶) There's absolutely nothing mundane about this artistic oasis in the heart of Salta. The place is a riot of color, lovely ceramic beasts and all manner of craft creations. It's highly original, friendly and likably chaotic. The three rooms are individually decorated and appealing, with either en suite or exterior bathroom.

Posada de las Farolas HOTEL $
(☎0387-421-3463; www.posadalasfarolas.com.ar; Córdoba 246; s/d US$45/65; ❄📶) Good value for neat, clean air-conditioned rooms in the center, some of which look onto tiny garden patios. It's run by kindly, courteous people, is spotless and is a pleasingly reliable choice. A few extras such as big fluffy towels and hairdryers put it above most in its price band.

Residencial El Hogar GUESTHOUSE $
(☎0387-431-6158; www.residencialelhogar.com.ar; Saravia 239; d US$51; ❄📶) Run with genuine warmth, this pleasing little place is on a quiet residential street with the San Bernardo hill looming over the end of it. It's still an easy stroll into the center, though. Attractive rooms with nice little touches, helpful owners and a tasty breakfast make this a recommendable base at a fair price.

Coloria Hostel HOSTEL $
(☎0387-431-3058; www.coloriahostel.com; Güemes 333; dm US$10-12, d US$35; ❄📶🏊) Upbeat, engaged staff and a glorious open-plan common area that looks over the garden and small pool are the major highlights of this enjoyable central hostel. It's colorful and quite upmarket by Salta standards; cleanliness is good; and dorms, though there's not a huge amount of space, are comfortable. Private rooms are very tight.

La Posta GUESTHOUSE, HOSTEL $
(☎0387-422-1985; hostallaposta@gmail.com; Córdoba 368; dm/s/d US$15/28/45; 📶) This simple but enchanting guesthouse makes a great budget choice for those looking for a quiet, peaceful central stay. Caring owners keep it spotless, and the en suite rooms are excellent. Dorms have breathing room and lockers, and breakfast is tasty with decent coffee. An appealingly relaxing place.

★**Carpe Diem** B&B $$
(☎0387-421-8736; www.carpediemsalta.com.ar; Urquiza 329; s/d US$100/110; @📶) There's a real home-from-home feel about this B&B that's full of thoughtful touches, such as home-baked bread at breakfast, enticing places to sit about with a book, and a computer with internet connection in the attractive rooms, which are stocked with noble antique furniture. Single rooms with shared bathroom in the appealing grassy garden are small but are a good deal at US$56.

Eating & Drinking

The west side of Plaza 9 de Julio is lined with cafes and bars that have tables out on the plaza; there are some great spots for coffee, snacks or a few drinks.

★**Chirimoya** VEGETARIAN $
(España 211; mains AR$50-90; ⏲9am-4pm & 8:30pm-12:30am Mon-Sat; 📶🖉) Colorful and upbeat, this vegan (some honey is used) cafe-restaurant makes an enticing stop. Delicious blended juices and organic wines wash down daily changing specials served

Salta

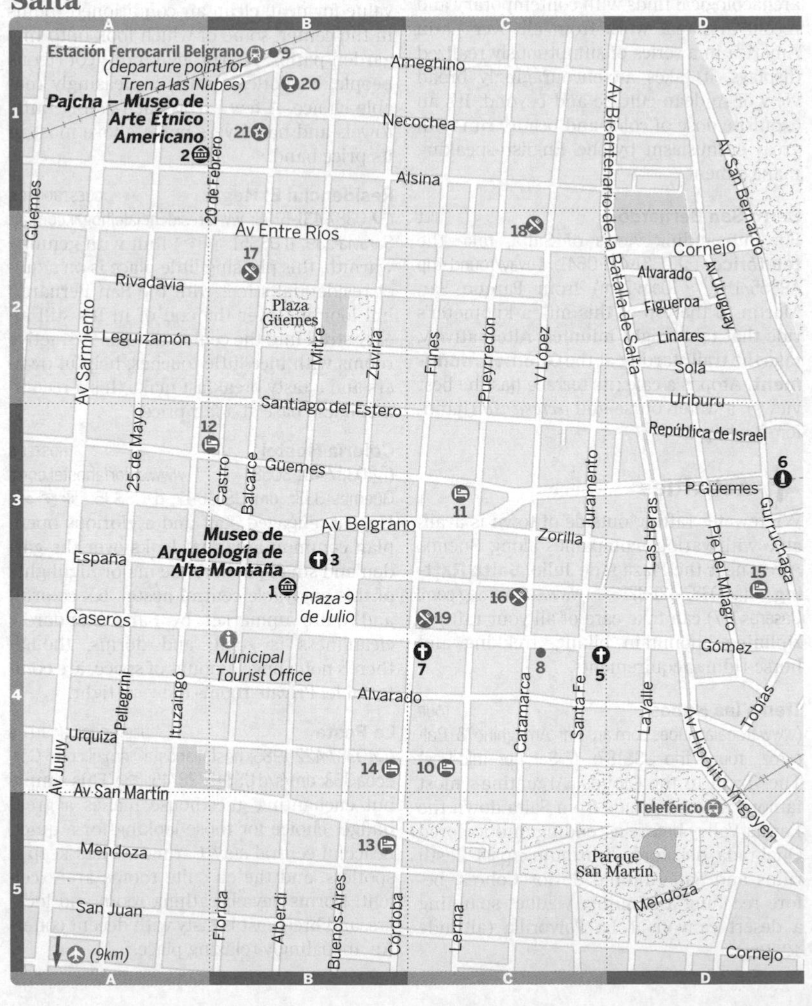

in generous portions. It's all delicious. Does deliveries, too.

Jovi II ARGENTINE $

(Balcarce 601; mains AR$70-110; ⏲noon-4pm & 8pm-1am) A long terrace overlooking the palms of Plaza Güemes is just one reason to like this popular local restaurant. It does a huge range of dishes well, without frills and in generous portions.

Several rabbit dishes, tasty fish and a succulent plate of the day are backed up by excellent service.

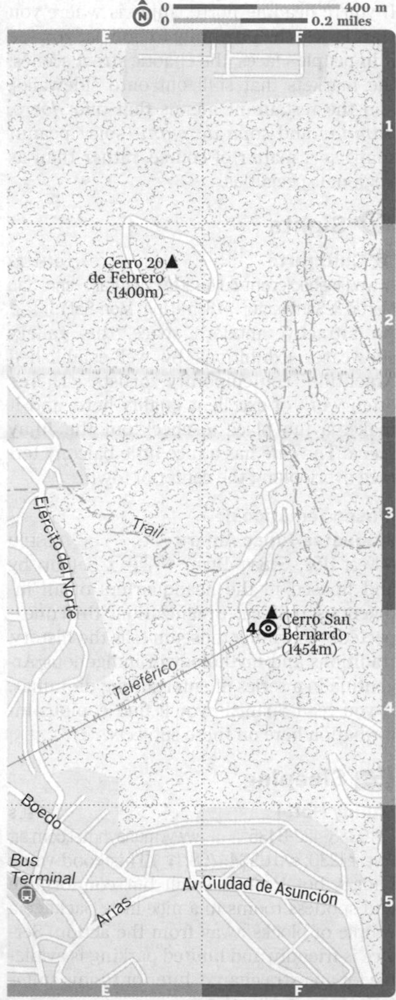

La Tacita EMPANADAS $

(Caseros 396; empanadas AR$8; ⏲8am-11pm Mon-Sat, 10am-11pm Sun) This very basic little eatery offers some of the city's best empanadas in a welcoming no-frills setting. Great for a quick stop while sightseeing.

La Monumental PARRILLA $

(Entre Ríos 202; mains AR$105-155; ⏲noon-3pm & 8pm-1am) The fluorescent lighting and phalanx of fans mark this out as a classic neighborhood grill. Generous quantities, including an impressive array of free nibbles, cheap house wine and decent meat seal the deal. Half-portions (70% of the full-portion price) are more than enough for one. Don't confuse it with the more upmarket restaurant with the same name diagonally opposite.

 Drinking & Nightlife

The Balcarce area south of the train station is well known for its nightlife and there's

Salta

plenty of dance-club action to choose from here. **Macondo** (www.facebook.com/macondo.barensalta; Balcarce 980; ⌚8pm-late Wed-Sun; 📶) is the place for a few quiet drinks (midweek, anyway). As well as bars and discos, the northern end of Balcarce has a good little string of *peñas* (folk music clubs). It's as much about the crowd as it is about the music in these places, so it's worth having a wander around, but **La Vieja Estación** (☎0387-421-7727; www.la-viejaestacion.com.ar; Balcarce 885; cover charge AR$20; ⌚7pm-3am) is the perennial favorite.

Information

ATMs are downtown.

Municipal tourist office (☎0387-437-3340; www.saltalalinda.gov.ar; Caseros 711; ⌚8am-9pm Mon-Fri, 9am-9pm Sat & Sun) Gives out maps. Also runs desks in the bus terminal and at the airport, open roughly 9am to 9pm, depending on staffing.

Getting There & Around

AIR

Aerolíneas Argentinas (☎0810-2228 6527; www.aerolineas.com; Caseros 475; ⌚8am-12:45pm & 4-6:45pm Mon-Fri, 9am-12:45pm Sat) flies several times daily to Buenos Aires; it also serves Córdoba, Mendoza and Puerto Iguazú. **LAN** (☎0810-999-9526; www.lan.com; Caseros 476; ⌚9am-1pm & 5-8pm Mon-Fri) flies regularly to Buenos Aires and Santiago, Chile. **Andes** (☎0810-7772 6337; www.andesonline.com; Caseros 459; ⌚8am-1pm & 4:30-7pm Mon-Fri, 9:30am-1pm Sat) has flights to Buenos Aires with connection to Puerto Madryn. **BoA** (☎0387-471-1558; www.boa.bo; Mitre 37, shop 24), in a shopping arcade off the plaza, flies to Santa Cruz in Bolivia.

Bus 8A runs to Salta's **airport** (SLA; ☎0387-424-3115), 9km southwest of town on RP 51, from San Martín by Córdoba. Otherwise it's a AR$100 taxi.

BUS

Salta's **bus terminal** (☎0387-431-5022; Av Hipólito Yrigoyen; ⌚information 6am-10pm) is southeast of downtown, an easy walk from most central hotels. Bus 5 runs between the bus terminal, downtown area and train station.

Buses from Salta

Three companies run to San Pedro de Atacama, Chile (nine to 10 hours, AR$810), with daily departures at 7am via Jujuy and Purmamarca. They continue to Calama, Antofagasta, Iquique and Arica (AR$1283).

Other destinations include the following:

DESTINATION	COST (AR$)	DURATION (HR)
Buenos Aires	1300-1500	18-22
Cachi	120	4½
Cafayate	159	4
Jujuy	75	2
La Quiaca	240	7½
Mendoza	1275-1350	18-20
Resistencia	719	10-12
Tucumán	290	4¼

San Salvador de Jujuy

☎0388 / POP 265,300

If you're heading north, Jujuy is where you start to feel the proximity to Bolivia; you see it in people's faces, the chaotic street scenes, the markets that spill out onto sidewalks, and the restaurant menus that offer *locro, humitas* and *sopa de maní* (spicy peanut soup) as a matter of course, rather than as 'regional specialties.'

Sights

★Culturarte GALLERY

(www.facebook.com/culturarte.ccultural; cnr San Martín & Sarmiento; ⌚8am-11pm Mon-Sat) FREE An attractive modern space, this gallery showcases exhibitions by well-established Argentine contemporary artists. There's often work of excellent quality here, and it makes a fun place to check out the Jujuy scene. The cafe has a nice little balcony terrace overlooking the center of town.

Museo Temático de Maquetas Tupac Amaru MUSEUM

(Alvear 1152; ⌚8am-11pm) FREE Set up by and housed in the headquarters of an indigenous political organization, this unexpectedly charming museum tells the history, traditions and mythology of indigenous Argentina in a series of entertaining dioramas. If you read Spanish, you'll find copious information here on these subjects.

Sleeping

Munay Hotel HOTEL $

(☎0388-422-8435; www.munayhotel.com.ar; Alvear 1230; s/d US$44/68; 📶) This good-value budget hotel offers small but comfortable and spotless rooms in a nice little package a couple of blocks away from the action. Service is friendly, and limited parking is available for an extra charge. Interior rooms suffer from some ambient noise.

D-Gira Hostel HOSTEL $

(☎15-408-0386; www.facebook.com/dgira.hostel jujuy; JM Gorriti 427; dm US$10-11, d US$33; @ 📶) Located in an unfashionable but relatively central zone of the city, this place beats the downtown hostels on several points. Number one is the genuine welcome, then you can add the purple walls and seriously comfortable blond-timber bunks with their plump mattresses and decent bedding. Dorms all have en suite bathrooms and plenty of room. Ongoing improvements and a can-do attitude make this a worthwhile stop.

★**Posada El Arribo** BOUTIQUE HOTEL $$

(☎0388-422-2539; www.elarribo.com; Belgrano 1263; s/d US$70/109; ❄ @ 📶 🏊) An oasis in the heart of Jujuy, this highly impressive family-run place is a real visual feast. The renovated 19th-century mansion is wonderful, with original floor tiles, high ceilings and wooden floors; there's patio space galore and a huge garden. The modern annex behind doesn't lose much by comparison, but go for an older room if you can.

Eating

Jujuy's lively Mercado del Sur is a genuine trading post where indigenous Argentines swig *mazamorra* (cold maize soup) and peddle coca leaves. Simple eateries around here serve hearty regional specialties; try *chicharrón con mote* (stir-fried pork with boiled maize) or spicy *sopa de maní*.

Manos Jujeñas ARGENTINE $

(Av Pérez 381; mains AR$60-110; ⏱11am-3pm & 7-11pm Tue-Sun) One of Jujuy's best addresses for no-frills traditional slow-food cooking, this place fills up with a contented buzz on weekend evenings. There are several classic northeastern dishes to choose

San Salvador de Jujuy

Top Sights
1 Culturarte ... C2

Sights
2 Museo Temático de Maquetas Tupac Amaru ... A1

Sleeping
3 D-Gira Hostel ... D3
4 Munay Hotel ... A1
5 Posada El Arribo ... A1

Eating
6 Krysys ... B2
7 Madre Tierra ... C1
8 Manos Jujeñas ... B1
9 Mercado del Sur ... C3

San Salvador de Jujuy

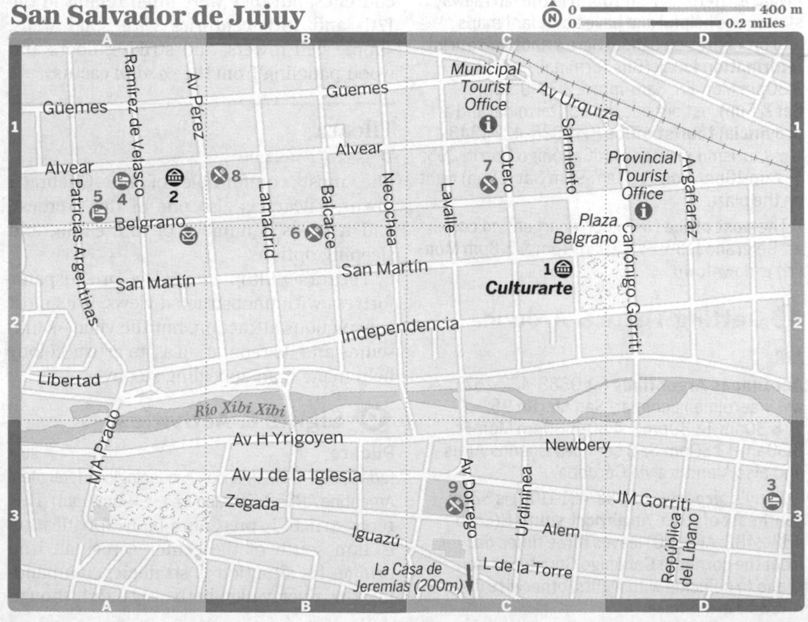

from, but it's the *picante* – marinated chicken or tongue (or both) with onion, tomato, rice and Andean potatoes – that's the pride of the house. Take-out also available.

Madre Tierra BAKERY, CAFE $

(Belgrano 619; mains AR$50; 6:30am-3pm & 4-10:30pm Mon-Sat;) This place is a standout. The vegetarian food (there's a daily set menu) is excellent and the sandwiches and pizzas can be washed down with fresh juice or organic beer. There's lovely garden-patio seating and the bakery out the front does wholesome breads.

★Krysys ARGENTINE $$

(Balcarce 272; mains AR$80-140; 12:30-3pm & 8:30pm-12:30am Mon-Sat, 12:30-3:30pm Sun;) The best *parrilla* option is this central, upscale place offering all your barbecued favorites in a relaxed atmosphere. But there's plenty more on the menu, with a range of tasty sauces to go with the chicken, pork or beef, and various appetizing starters. Prices are fair, and you'll get the meat the way you want it cooked.

Information

ATMs are common on Belgrano, and banks should be able to change traveler's checks.

Staff at the **municipal tourist office** (0388-402-0246; www.sansalvadordejujuy.gob.ar; cnr Alvear & Otero; 7am-10pm) in the old railway station are helpful and have abundant maps and brochures on hand. There's another **tourist information kiosk** (Bus Terminal; 7:30am-9:30pm Mon-Fri, 8am-1pm & 3:30-9:30pm Sat & Sun) just outside the bus terminal and a **provincial tourist office** (0388-422-1343; www.turismo.jujuy.gov.ar; Canónigo Gorriti 295; 7am-10pm Mon-Fri, 8am-9pm Sat & Sun) right on the plaza.

The **post office** (www.correoargentino.com.ar; Belgrano 1136; 8:30am-1pm & 5-8pm Mon-Fri) is downtown.

Getting There & Around

AIR

Aerolíneas Argentinas (0388-422-2575; www.aerolineas.com.ar; San Martín 96; 8:30am-12:30pm & 4:30-8:30pm Mon-Fri, 8:30am-12:30pm Sat) services Buenos Aires and also Mendoza via Córdoba.

Jujuy's **airport** (0388-491-1102) is 32km southeast of town. An **airport shuttle** (15-432-2482; AR$100) leaves three times daily from the corner of Canónigo Gorriti and Belgrano to coincide with flights; otherwise it's AR$340 in a remise.

BUS

The new bus terminal is 6km southeast of the center. It's got great facilities, including showers and a tourist office.

Daily buses going from Salta to Chile stop here.

DESTINATION	COST (AR$)	DURATION (HR)
Buenos Aires	1400	20-23
Córdoba	835	12-16
Humahuaca	66	2
La Quiaca	115	4-5
Mendoza	1207	21
Purmamarca	42	1¼
Salta	75	2
Tilcara	45	1¾
Tucumán	325	5

Quebrada de Humahuaca

North of Jujuy, RN 9 snakes its way through the Quebrada de Humahuaca, a painter's palette of color on barren hillsides, dwarfing hamlets where Quechua peasants scratch a living growing maize and raising scrawny livestock. On this colonial post route to Potosí, the architecture and other cultural features mirror Peru and Bolivia.

Earthquakes leveled many of the adobe churches, but they were often rebuilt in the 17th and 18th centuries with solid walls, simple bell towers, and striking doors and wood paneling from the *cardón* cactus.

Tilcara

0388 / POP 4400

The most comfortable of the Quebrada towns, Tilcara is also one of the prettiest, and it hosts a number of fine eating and sleeping options.

Tilcara's hilltop *pucará,* a pre-Hispanic fortress with unobstructed views, is its most conspicuous attraction, but the village's museums and its reputation as an artists colony help make it an appealing stopover.

Sights & Activities

Pucará RUIN

(admission incl Museo Arqueológico foreigner/Argentine AR$50/25, Mon free; 9am-6pm) This reconstructed pre-Columbian fortification is 1km south of the center across an iron bridge. Its situation is strategic, commanding the river valley both ways and, though the site was undoubtedly used earlier, the ruins date from the 11th to 15th centuries. There are great views and, seemingly, a cardón cactus for every soul that lived and died here. For further succulent stimulation, there's a botanic garden by the entrance.

Museo Arqueológico MUSEUM
(Belgrano 445; admission incl Pucará foreigner/Argentine AR$50/25, Mon free; ⏲9am-6pm) This well-presented collection of regional artifacts in a striking colonial house has some pieces from the *pucará* fortification just south of the center, and exhibits give an insight into the life of people living around that time (from the 11th to 15th centuries). The room dedicated to ceremonial masks is particularly impressive.

Bicicletería Carlitos BICYCLE RENTAL
(Tilcara Mountain Bike; ☎15-500-8570; tilcarabikes@hotmail.com; Belgrano s/n; per hr/day US$3.50/15; ⏲9am-7pm) A friendly setup about 100m past the bus terminal that hires out well-maintained mountain bikes and provides a helpful map of trips in the area.

Sleeping & Eating

Cheap places to eat line Belgrano and Lavalle between the bus terminal and Plaza Prado.

★ **La Casa del Indio** GUESTHOUSE $
(☎15-862526; www.argentinaturismo.com.ar/casadelindio; Ambrosetti s/n; d/tr US$50/65;) It would be difficult to find more charming hosts than the young couple that run this appealing place, which consists of two rooms off a sweet little courtyard beside the family home. Simple and traditional in style, with some attractive stonework, it offers tranquillity, independence and comfort, as well as a relaxingly wild garden.

Albahaca Hostel HOSTEL $
(☎15-585-5994; www.albahacahostel.com.ar; Padilla s/n; dm/d US$9/25;) Simple but well priced and very friendly, with decent dorms, comfortable private rooms and a sociable roof terrace. A place to make friends.

★ **Posada de Luz** LODGE $$
(☎0388-495-5017; www.posadadeluz.com.ar; Ambrosetti 661; r US$105-143;) With a nouveau-rustic charm, this little place is a fantastic spot to unwind for a few days. The pricier rooms have sitting areas, but all feature adobe walls, cane ceilings, pot-bellied stoves and individual terraces with deck chairs and views out over the valley. Pretty grounds include a barbecue area and children's playground; excellent personal service is a real highlight.

Ma'koka CAFE $
(Belgrano s/n; sandwiches AR$45-65; ⏲8:30am-9pm;) With a gloriously eclectic music mix and interesting texts on the area and the Andes in general, this excellent bookstore-cafe has the best coffee in town, tasty cakes and top sandwiches on bread made from coca or local corn varieties. Great choices for celiacs too, with manioc bread and other treats. The owner is knowledgeable about indigenous Argentina.

★ **El Nuevo Progreso** ARGENTINE $$
(☎0388-495-5237; Lavalle 351; mains AR$105-160; ⏲6-11:30pm Mon-Sat;) An engaging atmosphere and delicious tourist-oriented cuisine features imaginatively prepared llama dishes, excellent meat plates, interesting veggie options and great salads. Service can be a bit standoffish but it's well worthwhile. Book at weekends.

Entertainment

Nightlife is limited in Tilcara, but there are plenty of *peñas* around, hosting live folk music every night. **La Peña de Carlitos** (Lavalle 397; ⏲10am-midnight;) is probably the most consistent.

Information

The **tourist office** (Belgrano 366; ⏲8am-9pm Mon-Fri, 9am-1pm & 2-9pm Sat, 9am-1pm Sun), in the municipal offices, distributes a useful map.

Banco Macro, on Plaza Prado, has an ATM.

Getting There & Around

Both northbound and southbound buses leave from the bus terminal on Exodo, three blocks west of Plaza Prado. Sample destinations include Jujuy (AR$45, 1½ hours), Humahuaca (AR$20, 40 minutes) and La Quiaca (AR$90, four hours).

Humahuaca

☎03887 / POP 8000

A popular stopover on the Salta–Bolivia route, Humahuaca is a mostly Quechuan village of narrow cobbled streets lined with adobe houses. There's plenty to do in the surrounding countryside, and the town provides some great photo opportunities.

Sights & Activities

Built in 1641, Humahuaca's **Iglesia de la Candelaria** (Buenos Aires) faces Plaza Gómez. Nearby, the lovably knobbly **cabildo** is famous for its clock tower, where a life-size figure of San Francisco Solano emerges at noon to deliver a benediction. From the plaza, a staircase climbs to rather vulgar **Monumento a la Independencia**.

Festivals & Events

Carnaval celebrations are particularly boisterous here.

On 2 February, the village holds a **festival** in honor of the town's patron saint, the Virgen de la Candelaria.

Sleeping & Eating

Many restaurants around town feature live folk music most nights.

★ La Humahuacasa HOSTEL $
(☎15-412-0868; www.humahuacasa.com.ar; Buenos Aires 740; dm/d US$15/50; 📶) Artistic, superwelcoming and personable, this place is central and offers appealingly cozy dorms around a small patio. It's an involved, social place with a decent kitchen and a good vibe. Everything is very clean and well run. There's one private room – an en suite double.

Hostal La Soñada GUESTHOUSE $
(☎03887-421228; www.hostallasoniada.com; San Martín s/n; d/q US$50/70; @📶) Just across the tracks from the center, this place is run by a kindly local couple and features eight spotless rooms with colorful bedspreads and good bathrooms. Rooms surround a pretty courtyard. Breakfast is served in the attractive common area, and guests are made to feel very welcome.

Hostal El Coquena HOTEL $
(☎15-480-0384; hostalelcoquena@hotmail.com; Tres Sargentos s/n; r US$60; 📶) Just across the bridge from the center, this place is quiet and cordially run by a welcoming couple. It's attractively spacious, with plenty of room to move in the common area, wide covered gallery, sizeable rooms and very ample bathrooms. Breakfast is tasty, and there's a kitchen guests can use. A good deal and, though not luxurious, Humahuaca's best hotel.

Aisito ARGENTINE $
(Buenos Aires 435; mains AR$50-90; ⏲11am-3pm & 7-11pm) Warmly decorated and blessed with caring service, this is a pleasing option for well-priced local cuisine. Tasty baked empanadas take their place alongside well-blended stir-fries and succulent llama. There's excellent live music at weekends, and nightly in summer.

Mikunayoc ARGENTINE $
(cnr Corrientes & Tucumán; mains AR$50-110; ⏲11am-3:30pm) The wide-ranging menu here includes several interesting llama dishes, and a range of empanadas with intriguing fillings. The salads are also a good bet. It's a pleasant, colorful place with cordial service so you can forgive the odd lapses.

Information

The **tourist office** (Plaza Gómez s/n; ⏲7am-9pm Mon-Fri, 9am-9pm Sat & Sun) underneath

GETTING TO BOLIVIA

Cold, windy **La Quiaca** is a major crossing point to Bolivia. It has decent places to stay and eat, but little to detain the traveler. If you arrive late at night, however, it's best to stay here as services are much better than across the border in Villazón.

La Quiaca has no tourist office, but the ACA station on RN 9 has maps. **Hostel El Apolillo** (☎03885-422388; http://elapolillohostel.blogspot.com; Árabe Siria 146; dm/d US$15/45; @📶) is one of the finer hostels in the country, and is full of information on what to do in the area and how to move on. In terms of hotels, **Hostería Munay** (☎0388-5423924; Belgrano 51; s/d from US$30/40) is about as good as it gets. The **Hotel de Turismo** (☎0388-423390; laquiacahotel@gmail.com; cnr Árabe Siria & San Martín; s/d US$35/50; @📶) serves decent meals (mains AR$90 to AR$130).

From the **bus terminal** (cnr Belgrano & España), there are frequent connections to Jujuy (AR$110, five hours), Salta (AR$240, seven hours) and intermediate points, plus long-distance services.

The border is a 1km walk from the bus terminal. There is no public transportation, but there may be a taxi around. The border is generally open 24 hours, but this is subject to change – don't arrive at 2am without a plan B.

the clock tower keeps irregular hours but has excellent information on accommodations and local attractions.

Getting There & Away

From the **bus terminal** (cnr Belgrano & Entre Ríos) there are several departures to Salta (AR$148, five hours) and Jujuy (AR$66, two hours), and northbound buses to La Quiaca (AR$60, two hours).

ATLANTIC COAST

The beaches along the Atlantic coast form Buenos Aires' backyard, and summer sees millions of *porteños* pouring into towns such as Mar del Plata and Pinamar for sun and fun. The rest of the year, and in smaller towns, the pace of life rarely approaches anything resembling hectic.

Mar del Plata

0223 / POP 614,000

On summer weekends, the beach in Mardel (as it's commonly known) gets really, seriously, comically crowded. We're talking people standing shoulder to shoulder, knee-deep in water. During the week, and in the nonsummer months, the crowds disperse, hotel prices drop and the place takes on a much more relaxed feel.

Founded in 1874, this most popular of Argentine beach destinations was first a commercial and industrial center, then a resort for upper-class *porteño* families. Mardel now caters mostly to middle-class vacationers.

Sights & Activities

★Puerto Mar del Plata PORT
(www.puertomardelplata.net) Mar del Plata is one of Argentina's most important fishing centers. Its port area, 8km south of the city center, is worth a visit, though public access to the jetty – and its graveyard of ruined ships, half-sunken and rusting in the sun – is now restricted. You can still watch the fishing boats come and go from the **Banquina de Pescadores**, the port's scenic and slightly touristy wharf. Grab some calamari and a beer here while you're at it.

Torreón del Monje HISTORIC BUILDING
(0223-486-4000; www.torreondelmonje.com.ar; cnr Viamonte & Paseo Jesús de Galindez) Grand and castle-like, positioned on a cliff over the ocean, Torreón del Monje is hard to miss – look for the red domes and the stone footbridge straddling the oceanfront road. This classic landmark is a throwback to Mar del Plata's glamorous heyday. The Argentine businessman Ernestro Tornquist, intent on beautifying the area around his own summer getaway, had the medieval-style lookout tower built in 1904. Stop for the view, and perhaps a coffee break on the terrace.

Bicicletería Madrid BICYCLE RENTAL
(0223-494-1932; Yrigoyen 2249; per hr from AR$45; 9am-7pm Mon-Fri, 10am-7pm Sat & Sun) Bicycles can be rented from Bicicletería Madrid.

Kikiwai Surf School SURFING
(0223-485-0669; www.clubdesurfkikiwai.wix.com/kikiwaisurfclub; Av Martínez de Hoz 4100, Playa Kikiwai; 1-day class per person AR$450) This long-running surf school offers board rental and surf classes at Waikiki Beach, an 11km drive south of town.

Acción Directa OUTDOORS
(0223-474-4520; www.acciondirecta.com.ar; Av Libertad 3902; 10am-1pm & 5-9pm Mon-Fri, 10am-1pm Sat) The rocky cliffs by the sea and the hills of Sierra de los Padres make for excellent climbing and rappelling. Acción Directa runs a school – it also offers mountain biking, canoeing and overnight active camping trips.

Festivals & Events

International Film Festival FILM
(www.mardelplatafilmfest.com) Mar del Plata's elaborate tourist infrastructure guarantees a wide variety of special events throughout the year. It's worth being in town for the city's International Film Festival, which takes place in November. Launched in 1950, though interrupted for decades by Argentina's political and economic woes, it is South America's most important film festival, attracting participants from all over the world.

Sleeping

Prices are about 30% higher in January and February, so it's worth making reservations.

Rates at Mardel's crowded campgrounds, mostly south of town, are around AR$30 per person; the tourist office has information about their facilities.

Che Lagarto Hostel HOSTEL $
(☎0223-451-3704; www.chelagarto.com; Alberti 1565; dm/d from US$19/65; @ wi-fi) This popular branch of the Che Lagarto chain pretty much has it all: friendly staff, a central location close to Mardel's best nightlife and shopping, and squeaky clean (fan-cooled) private rooms and dorms. There's also a guest kitchen and a pleasant living area and cocktail bar. There's free wi-fi in the public areas.

★**Villa Nuccia** GUESTHOUSE $$
(☎0223-451-6593; www.villanuccia.com.ar; Almirante Brown 1134; d from US$134; air-con @ wi-fi pool) This beautiful guesthouse offers a small range of elegant and spacious rooms. Some are in a renovated house, others are in a modern annex; all are individually decorated. There's a rear garden with a swimming pool and Jacuzzi, and guests rave about the breakfast and afternoon tea, both featuring homemade cakes.

Hotel 15 de Mayo HOTEL $$
(☎0223-495-1388; www.hotel15demayo.com; Mitre 1457; s/d from US$68/98; air-con wi-fi) Conveniently located between Plaza San Martín and La Perla beach, this modern hotel is great value for its guest rooms (on the small side, but spotless, with flat-screen TVs), professional service, breakfast buffet and fast wi-fi.

Hotel Sirenuse HOTEL $$
(☎0223-451-9580; www.hotelsirenuse.com.ar; Mendoza 2240; d from US$82; air-con @ wi-fi) Friendly, family-run and wonderfully cozy, this small hotel on Stella Maris hill, just a few blocks from Playa Varese, is one of Mardel's best-value choices. With dark wood furnishings and a hearty breakfast, the place feels more like a mountain lodge than a beach getaway. Travelers rave about the kind owners; you'll need to book well ahead.

Eating

There are many *tenedores libres* in the center of town. The quality isn't exactly top shelf, but they're a great deal if you're a big eater.

La Fonte D'Oro CAFE $
(cnr Córdoba & San Martín; snacks AR$15-45; ⌚8am-late) This stylish cafe has several locations in town; one of the nicest is on the pedestrian promenade of San Martín, near the cathedral. Have a quick *cortado* (espresson with a little milk) at the curving coffee bar, or grab an outdoor table and order a freshly baked pastry or a slice of chocolate cake while you watch the world go by.

Montecatini ARGENTINE $
(cnr La Rioja & 25 de Mayo; mains AR$52-120; ⌚noon-3pm & 8pm-midnight; air-con family) For solid, good-value dishes, make like the locals and head to this large, modern and popular restaurant, one of four branches in town. There's something for everyone on the menu – meat, fish, pasta, *milanesas,* sandwiches – and portions are generous. The weekday lunch special (AR$110, including dessert and a drink) is a steal. Good for families and large groups.

El Bodegón ARGENTINE $
(La Rioja 2068; mains AR$75-150) Thanks to a recent change in ownership, there's a youthful crowd and free-flowing *cerveza* (beer) at this stylish pub and *parrilla.* On weekdays, there are great-value set menus at both lunch and dinner (AR$120 to AR$150). It's conveniently located in the center, a quick walk from either Plaza Mitre or Plaza San Martín.

★**Sur** SEAFOOD $$
(☎0223-493-6260; Alvarado 2763; mains AR$95-250; ⌚8pm-midnight) The hype around Sur creates high expectations: many locals consider it the best seafood restaurant in town. Brick walls hung with nautical-themed prints form a cozy backdrop; specials all revolve around fresh fish and shellfish. There's also an extensive wine list and famously delicious desserts.

Drinking

The following venues are located in chic Barrio Los Troncos and the area along Irigoyen and LN Alem, between Almafuerte and Rodríguez Peña, which is thick with cocktail bars and nightlife. It's a small area – the best thing to do is wander around the neighborhood for yourself and see what appeals.

★**Almacén Estación Central** BAR
(cnr Alsina & Garay; ⌚7pm-late) This hip corner bar in a quaint and thoughtfully restored antique building – an old corner store where the former president of Argentina, Marcelo Torcuato de Alvear, reportedly did his shopping – gets packed with locals every night. Gourmet pub food and frequent happy-hour deals, even on weekends, only add to the appeal.

La Deguita del Medio BAR
(Castelli 1252; ⌚6pm-4am) Come for the famously delicious mojitos, the Cuban-inspired food and the live music at this atmospheric and art-filled cocktail bar, named after one of Hemingway's favorite haunts in Havana.

Antares BAR
(Olavarría 2724; ⌚7pm-4am) The cool microbrewery mini-chain has several locations in Mar del Plata; this one, in Barrio Los Troncos is arguably the most popular. Come for a variety of craft beers on tap, plus excellent pub food and a lively local crowd. Come early if you want to actually have a conversation with someone – Antares gets louder as the night rolls on.

Information

The **tourist office** (☎495-1777; www.turismomardelplata.gov.ar; Blvd Marítimo 2270; ⌚10am-8pm Mar-Dec, to 10pm Jan & Feb) is near Plaza Colón.

Most *cambios*, banks and ATMs are near the intersections of San Martín and Córdoba, and Avs Independencia and Luro.

Getting There & Away

AIR

Aerolíneas Argentinas (☎0223-496-0101; www.aerolineas.com.ar; Moreno 2442; ⌚10am-6pm Mon-Fri) and **Sol** (www.sol.com.ar) have frequent flights to Buenos Aires.

BUS

Mardel's new bus terminal is adjacent to the train station. There are departures to Buenos Aires (AR$520, 5½ hours), Pinamar (AR$152, 2½ hours) and Villa Gesell (AR$138, two hours).

TRAIN

The **train station** (☎0223-475-6076; www.sofse.gob.ar; Av Luro 4700 at Italia; ⌚6am-midnight) is adjacent to the bus terminal. In summer there are daily departures to Buenos Aires for AR$200 in *primera* and AR$240 in Pullman. The trip takes about six hours. Visit www.ferrobaires.gba.gov.ar for more information, and be sure to reserve tickets well ahead in summer.

Getting Around

The **airport** (☎0223-478-0744) is 9km northwest of town (take bus 542 marked 'aeropuerto'); taxis there cost around AR$100. To reach the center from the bus terminal, cross Av Luro in front of the terminal and take local bus 511, 512 or 513 heading southeast; taxis to downtown cost around AR$35.

Villa Gesell

☎02255 / POP 30,000

This laid-back dune community sleeps in the low season, but in summer it's a favorite for young *porteños*, who stream in to party the warm nights away. It's one of the prettiest coastal towns: small, with windy, sandy roads sporting charming summer cottages (and also grander retreats).

Sights & Activities

Gesell's long **beach** and boardwalk draw swimmers, sunbathers and horse riders. There's year-round **fishing** from the pier.

Feria Artesanal MARKET
(Crafts Fair; Av 3 btwn Paseos 112 & 113) There's a nightly handicrafts fair held from mid-December to mid-March. Expect lots of handmade jewelry, carved wood, paintings and souvenirs. The rest of the year it's a weekend-only event.

Windy Playa Bar SURFING
(www.windyplayabar.com.ar; cnr Paseo 104 & beach; ⌚8am-dusk summer) You can't miss it: just look for the faux pirate ship parked on the sand. At Windy, you can rent surf gear or sign up for lessons; the beach bar is also one-stop shopping for renting beach equipment or just grabbing some cold drinks and sandwiches with a view.

Casa Macca BICYCLE RENTAL
(Av Buenos Aires 449; per hr AR$50) For bicycle rentals, try Casa Macca. It's located between Paseo 101 & Av 5.

Sleeping

The most affordable *hospedajes* are north of Av 3. It's important to book ahead in summer, especially in the second half of January, when prices rise even more.

★**La Deseada Hostel** HOSTEL $
(☎02255-473276; www.ladeseadahostel.com.ar; cnr Av 6 & Paseo 119; dm/d from US$35/75; @📶) Teeming with young Argentines in January but tranquil in the off-season, this ultrahomey hostel sits atop a sloping, evergreen-fringed lawn in a residential area between the bus terminal and the center, six blocks from the beach. Eight-bed dorms, plus private rooms (only available outside high season), are complemented by spacious common areas and a nice guest kitchen. Breakfast is served till 1pm.

Medamar Playa Hotel HOTEL $$

(☎02255-463106; www.medamarplaya.com; cnr Costanera & Paseo 111; s/d from US$79/92;) This boxy green-and-white beachfront hotel is dated, but service is friendly and the location can't be beat. Outside of busy summertime it's worth trying for one of the rooms with a private balcony facing the ocean and the tiny swimming pool.

Hotel de la Plaza HOTEL $$

(☎02255-468793; www.delaplazahotel.com; Av 2, No 375; d/tr from US$100/140) Centrally located between the beach and Villa Gesell's commercial center, this tidy hotel is professionally run and open 365 days of the year – a great pick if you happen to be passing through out of season. Several restaurants are located less than a block away.

Eating

Av 3 is the place to go for pizza, sandwiches, ice cream and *parrilla*.

The biggest concentration of bars is on Paseo 105, between Avs 2 and 3. The beachside restaurants are great places to have a few drinks and a snack at sunset, or have a meal if your wallet is up to the challenge.

Rancho Hambre EMPANADAS $

(Av 3, No 871; empanadas AR$15, pizzas AR$90-180; noon-3pm & 7:30pm-late, closed Sun lunch & all day Wed) This main street hot spot features 36 varieties of empanadas, from the humble (minced beef) to the more elaborate (arugula, parmesan and walnuts, or bacon with mozzarella and muscat-infused prunes). Pick up a dozen to go, or stick around and order a pizza. There's a second location on the corner of Av 3 and Paseo 125.

El Viejo Hobbit PUB FOOD $$

(Av 8 btwn Paseos 11 & 12; snacks AR$60-110, fondue AR$200-340; 6pm-late Fri & Sat Apr-Nov, daily Dec-Mar) An obligatory stop for beer lovers and Tolkien fans, this whimsical backstreet bar plunges you straight into Hobbit-land from the minute you pass through the round front door. Several beers brewed on-site complement a menu focused on fondue. There's a cozy 2nd floor, plus a backyard with a miniature Hobbit house for kids to play in.

La Delfina PARRILLA $$

(cnr Paseo 104 & Av 2; mains AR$80-125; noon-3pm & 8pm-midnight) A huge menu means there's something for everyone at this popular *parrilla,* from steaks, pastas, and salads to desserts and a lengthy wine list. Right on the main drag, it's easy to find.

Information

Banks and ATMs are on Av 3. There's a central **tourist office** (☎02255-478042; www.turismo.gesell.gob.ar; Paseo 107 btwn Avs 2 & 3; 8am-8pm Mar-Dec, to midnight Jan & Feb) just off the main street.

Getting There & Around

The main **bus terminal** (cnr Av 3 & Paseo 140) is south of town; bus 504 (AR$6) will get you to the center. Bus destinations include Buenos Aires (AR$424, five hours), Mar del Plata (AR$125, two hours) and Pinamar (AR$45, one hour).

Pinamar

☎02254 / POP 25,000

Rivaling Uruguay's Punta del Este in the fashion stakes, Pinamar and the surrounding towns are where wealthy Argentine families come to play in summertime.

Sights & Activities

Many places are only open on weekends and in summer, but at other times you can stroll peacefully in bordering pine forests and along the wide, attractive **beach** without being trampled by vacationers.

Bike hire is available from **Leo** (☎02254-488855; Av Bunge 1111; bike rental per hr AR$50; 9am-9pm). There are many more activities on offer, especially in the summer months – look for brochures in the tourist office.

Festivals & Events

The **Pinamar Film Festival** (www.pantallapinamar.gov.ar) draws crowds in early March.

Sleeping

Reservations are a must in January, when some places have a one-week minimum stay. Best options for the budget-minded are near the southern beaches of Ostende and Valeria, though you'll also find some cheaper hotels and *hospedajes* (family homes) along Calle del Cangrejo, north of the tourist office.

Cabañas Pinaforet CABAÑAS $$

(☎02254-409277; www.pinaforet.com.ar; cnr Apolo & Jason; per week Jan & Feb from US$1290;) This sweet cluster of five spacious log cabins set among piney grounds is only a few paces from the bus terminal, within a few minutes' walk of the town center and beach. Each sleeps up to four people, making this a great budget option in low season (despite the high weekly prices quoted in summer). Contact them for the low-season rates.

Hotel Mojomar HOTEL **$$**
(02254-407300; www.hotelmojomar.com.ar; De las Burriquetas 247; d from US$107;) The Mojomar is upscale, if not luxurious, with a great location three blocks off Av Bunge, and only a block from the beach. The look is modern but warm; guest rooms are small but comfortable, and some have sea views.

Eating & Drinking

Av Bunge is lined with restaurants, snack bars and ice-cream parlors. During summer, the restaurants along the beachfront turn into bars and discos (don't worry – you'll hear 'em) and generally go until the break of dawn. In the low season, check the area bounded by Avs Bunge, Libertador and de las Artes.

★**Tante** INTERNATIONAL **$$**
(De las Artes 35; mains AR$55-175; noon-midnight) This elegant tearoom, restaurant and bar – a few blocks in from the beach, just off Av Bunge – was once the home of a well-known 1950s soprano. Nowadays it serves up German, French and alpine specialties such as fondue, crepes, goulash, wurst and sauerkraut. Afternoon teas are a delight. There's a second location in Cariló.

Los Troncos ARGENTINE **$$**
(cnr Eneas & Lenguado; mains AR$45-130; noon-3pm & 8pm-midnight Thu-Tue) In business for four decades, this beloved backstreet eatery is often packed with locals even in low season. There's a casual but convivial old-school ambience, and the menu includes everything from roast meats to seafood stews to homemade pastas, all done to perfection.

Information

Libertador, roughly paralleling the beach, and perpendicular Av Bunge are the main drags; streets on each side of Bunge form large fans. The **municipal tourist office** (491680; www.pinamar.tur.ar; cnr Av Bunge & Shaw; 8am-8pm Mon-Fri, 10am-8pm Sat, 10am-5pm Sun) has a good map.

Getting There & Away

The **bus terminal** (02254-403500; Jason 2250) is 12 blocks from the beach and seven from the center. Bus destinations include Buenos Aires (AR$350, 4½ hours), Mar del Plata (AR$152, 2½ hours) and Villa Gesell (AR$45, one hour).

Bahía Blanca

0291 / POP 291,000

Mostly a stopover point for people headed elsewhere, Bahía Blanca is surprisingly cosmopolitan for its size, and boasts Argentina's worst-signposted museum.

Sights

On weekends there's a **feria artesanal** (crafts fair) on Plaza Rivadavia.

Museo del Puerto MUSEUM
(0291-457-3006; www.museodelpuerto.blogspot.com; cnr Guillermo Torres & Cárrega; voluntary donation requested; 9am-noon Mon-Fri, 4-8pm Sat & Sun) Housed in a colorfully painted former customs building, this small but engaging museum is a tribute to the region's immigrants. The rooms include archives and photographs, and mock-ups of an old *peluquería* (barber shop) and bar. The historical collection starts in the yard outside, where a wooden fishing boat and other antique artifacts hearken back to the port's intriguing past.

Sleeping & Eating

★**Hotel Muñiz** HOTEL **$$**
(0291-456-0060; www.hotelmuniz.com.ar; O'Higgins 23; s/d from US$48/73;) A downtown landmark, the Muñiz is located in a beautiful old building. Note the vintage charm on the lobby level: black-and-white tiled floors, polished woodwork, an antique phone booth. Upstairs, four levels of guest rooms are linked by long hallways. It's a great (and affordable) choice only steps away from the central plaza.

Apart Hotel Patagonia Sur HOTEL **$$**
(0291-455-2110; www.apartpatagoniasur.com.ar; Italia 64; s/d from US$72/85;) A popular pick for families and budget travelers, this friendly aparthotel has dated but perfectly functional apartment-style rooms with kitchenettes. An added bonus: the included continental breakfast features fresh fruits and a surprising variety of homemade cakes and pastries. It's a short walk south of the

plaza near the intersection of O'Higgins and Italia.

★ **El Mundo de la Parrilla** PARRILLA $$
(Av Colón 379; mains AR$60-150; ⏲8pm-late Mon, noon-3pm & 8pm-late Tue-Sun) Locals agree that this busy and casually elegant *parrilla* is one of the best dining options in town. In addition to gourmet empanadas, succulent *lechón* and practically every cut of steak imaginable, the restaurant offers 20 varieties of salads and a range of excellent and traditionally Argentine desserts.

Bamboo BUFFET $$
(Chiclana 298; buffet lunch/dinner AR$150/165, half-price for children; ⏲noon-3pm & 8:30pm-midnight) This *tenedor libre*, efficiently run by a Chinese family, is a good choice if you're famished after a marathon bus ride. Choose from a range of Asian-inspired dishes and Argentine classics, including a wide array of grilled meats.

Information

For the lowdown on music, art and theater happenings around town, pick up a copy of the *Agenda Cultural*, available in the tourist office, restaurants and bars.

Tourist kiosk (☎0291-459-4000; www.turismo.bahiablanca.gov.ar; Alsina 65, Municipalidad de Bahía Blanca; ⏲9am-6pm Mon-Fri, 9:30am-1pm & 2:30-6pm Sat) The bus terminal also has a tourist office.

Getting There & Around

The airport is 15km east of town. **Aerolíneas Argentinas** (☎0291-456-0561; www.aerolineas.com.ar; San Martín 298; ⏲10am-6pm Mon-Fri) has flights to Buenos Aires.

The **bus terminal** (Brown 1700) is about 2km east of Plaza Rivadavia; there are many local buses heading into town (buy magnetic cards from kiosks). A taxi costs around AR$50. To avoid the trek out to the terminal you can buy bus tickets at the kiosks around the south end of Plaza Rivadavia. Destinations include Buenos Aires (AR$750, nine hours), Mar del Plata (AR$505, seven hours) and Neuquén (AR$630, seven hours).

Travelers to Sierra de la Ventana have two options: Condor Estrella runs two daily buses (AR$110, 2½ hours) and Norte Bus operates a door-to-door shuttle (AR$120, one hour) with two to three departures per day. Call ahead to reserve a spot.

The **train station** (☎0291-452-9196; Cerri 750) has services to Buenos Aires several days of the week. Fares cost AR$115/205 in *turista*/Pullman class.

Sierra de la Ventana

☎0291 / POP 5000

Sierra de la Ventana is where *porteños* come to escape the summer heat, hike around a bit and cool off in swimming holes. The nearby mountain range of the same name in Parque Provincial Ernesto Tornquist attracts hikers and climbers to its jagged peaks, which rise over 1300m.

Activities

For a nice walk, go to the end of Calle Tornquist and cross the small dam (which makes a local **swimming hole**). On the other side you'll see **Cerro del Amor**; hike to the top for good views of town and pampas.

Rodados El Montañes (☎0291-648-0142; cnr Fortín Mercedes & Iguazú ; ⏲9am-1pm & 5-8:30pm Mon-Sat) rents quality mountain bikes.

Sleeping & Eating

There are several free campsites along the river, with bathroom facilities nearby at the pleasant and grassy municipal swimming pool. Some restaurants close one or more days per week outside the December to March summer months. Self-caterers will find several supermarkets and artisanal food shops on the main street.

Alihuen Hotel HOTEL $$
(☎0291-491-5074; www.lasierradelaventana.com.ar/alihuen; cnr Tornquist & Frontini; d/tr from US$81/108;) About four blocks from the main drag and strategically positioned on the banks of the river is this charmingly antique hotel. It's not exactly luxurious, with creaky wood floors and simple furnishings, but there's plenty of atmosphere – and plenty of outdoor space for relaxing, including a swimming pool when the weather's warm.

Cabañas Bodensee CABAÑAS $$
(☎0291-491-5356; www.sierrasdelaventana.com.ar/bodensee; Rayces 455, Villa La Arcadia; cabaña for 2/4 people from US$78/97;) This peaceful complex of cabins, situated around an appealing swimming pool, is a lovely respite within easy walking distance of the town center. Each cabin features a small kitchen and a porch with a large *parrilla*. It's located in the neighborhood of Villa La Arcadia, just across the river from most of Sierra de la Ventana's attractions.

Hotel Provincial HOTEL **$$**
(☎0291-491-5024; www.hotelprovincialsierra.com; Drago 130; d/tr from US$139/157;) A grand old place that's been recently remodeled. Guest rooms feel fresh and relatively luxurious, but the real draw are the public spaces: two swimming pools, a living room with a soaring fireplace and views of the mountains, a modern restaurant, and a spa. It's a favorite pick for families and couples alike.

Information

You'll find the **tourist office** (☎0291-491-5303; www.sierradelaventana.org.ar; Av del Golf s/n; ⏲8am-8pm) near the train station.

Getting There & Away

Sierra de la Ventana has no bus terminal; buses leave from the respective companies' offices. **Condor Estrella** (☎0291-491-5091; www.condorestrella.com.ar) has buses to Buenos Aires (AR$550,nine hours, six times weekly) and Bahía Blanca (AR$110, 2½ hours, twice daily). If times don't suit, there are various *combi* companies, including **Norte Bus** (☎0291-15-468-5101), that run slightly quicker minibuses to Bahía Blanca for around AR$120.

Ferrobaires (www.ferrobaires.gba.gov.ar) operates twice-weekly train service to Sierra de la Ventana on the train line that runs between Bahía Blanca and Buenos Aires (AR$115 to AR$205).

Around Sierra de la Ventana

Popular for ranger-guided walks and independent hiking, the 6700-hectare **Parque Provincial Ernesto Tornquist** (☎0291-491-0039; www.tornquist.gov.ar; adult/child AR$10/4; ⏲8am-5pm Dec-Mar, 9am-5pm Apr-Nov) is the starting point for the 1136m summit of **Cerro de la Ventana**. It's about two hours' routine hiking for anyone except the wheezing *porteño* tobacco addicts who struggle to the crest of what is probably the country's most climbed peak. Leave early: you can't climb after 11am in winter, noon in summer.

Buses traveling between Bahía Blanca and Sierra de la Ventana can drop you at the park entrance; there are also buses directly to the park from the village (AR$40, one hour).

CENTRAL ARGENTINA

Containing the wine-producing centers of Mendoza, San Luis and San Juan (which themselves comprise an area known as Cuyo), there's no doubt what Central Argentina's main attraction is. But once you've polished off a few bottles, you won't be left twiddling your thumbs – this is also Argentina's adventure playground, and the opportunities for rafting, trekking, skiing and climbing are almost endless.

San Luis

☎0266 / POP 170,000

San Luis is coming up as a backpacking destination, but it still has a long way to go. Most people come here to visit the nearby Parque Nacional Sierra de las Quijadas. The commercial center is along the parallel

REMOTE NATIONAL PARKS IN CENTRAL ARGENTINA

Central Argentina has an amazing range of landscapes, which is reflected in its national parks. For more information, log on to www.parquesnacionales.gov.ar. A couple of hard-to-reach but extremely worthwhile examples:

Parque Nacional Lihué Calel (☎436595; www.parquesnacionales.gob.ar; ⏲8am-7pm) FREE In a desert-like landscape in the middle of the pampa, this 320-sq-km park is surprisingly biodiverse, playing host to puma, jaguarondi, armadillos and many birds of prey, such as the *carancho* (crested caracara), alongside flowering cacti and petroglyphs. Santa Rosa is the nearest town of any size – there are cheap hotels near the bus terminal and restaurants on the plaza, but it's still 226km away and access is complicated – hiring a car is the best way to see the park.

Parque Nacional Sierra de las Quijadas (☎02652-490182; usopublicoquijadas@apn.gov.ar; admission AR$80) Covering 150,000 hectares, this park features spectacular, surreal rock formations and dinosaur tracks and fossils. Hiking is excellent and camping is free, but be careful of flash flooding. The nearest town is San Luis; its park office can help with transportation and logistics.

Central Argentina

0 200 km
0 100 miles

RN 40
Parque Nacional Talampaya
RP 38
RN 79
Angualasto
La Ciénaga
Huaco
Patquía
La Rioja
Rodeo
Parque Provincial Ischigualasto
RN 150
Salinas Grandes
RN 150
San José de Jáchal
RP 27
Chamical
Iglesia
Tama
RN 38
Cruz del Eje
RP 412
San Agustín de Valle Fértil
RP 27
Olta
Malanzán
San Juan
Villa Santa Rita
RP 510
RP 15
Talacasto
Salsacate
Calingasta
RP 12
Chepes
RP 20
Tamberías
San Juan
Río Blanco
RN 141
Ulapes
RN 79
Barreal
RN 40
Vallecito
Villa Dolores
Mina Clavero
RP 412
Cerro Mercedario (6770m)
Río San Juan
Quines
Parque Provincial Aconcagua
RP 39
Parque Nacional Sierra de las Quijadas
Santa Rosa
Merlo
RN 20
Uspallata
Puente del Inca
Los Penitentes
Mendoza
RN 146
Tilisarao
RP 1
Las Cuevas
Potrerillos
San Martín
La Toma
Parque Provincial Volcán Tupungato
Cacheuta
Rivadavia
RN 147
Tupungato
Santa Rosa
RP 20
La Paz
RN 7
San Luis
SANTIAGO
Volcán Tupungatito (5682m)
Tunuyán
Río Tunuyán
RN 8
San Carlos
Mercedes
Zanjitas
Mendoza
RN 7
To Buenos Aires
San Luis
RN 143
RN 146
RP 3
RN 148
San Rafael
RN 40
Buena Esperanza
Villa Huidobro
General Alvear
El Nihuil
Unión
RN 188
RP 222
RN 143
Nueva Galia
Las Leñas
Malargüe
Río Atuel
Río Salado
RP 224
Bardas Blancas
Santa Isabel
Victoria
RP 102
RN 40
RP 10
Algarrobo del Aguila
RP 105
Santa Rosa
La Pampa
Barrancas
RP 13
Buta Ranquil
Salina Grandes o Salitral
RN 143
Chacharramendi
Río Colorado
Salitral de la Perra
Chos-Malal
General Acha
RP 20
Parque Nacional Lihué Calel
Neuquén
25 de Mayo
Río Neuquén
RP 28
Puelches
RP 28
RN 151
RN 152

streets of San Martín and Rivadavia, between Plaza Pringles in the north and Plaza Independencia to the south.

The large, multibed dorms at **San Luis Hostel** (0266-442-4188; www.sanluishostel.com.ar; Falucho 646; dm/tw US$12/28;) are a bit of a turnoff, but the rest of the hostel is beautiful. Staff can arrange trips to Sierra de las Quijadas and tours of local gold mines.

Av Illia, which runs northwest from the delightful Plaza Pringles, is the center of San Luis' moderately hopping bar scene. There are plenty of fast-food options along this street. **Aranjuez** (cnr Pringles & Rivadavia; mains AR$60-100; 8am-11:30pm;) is a fairly standard plazaside cafe/bar/restaurant that gets a mention for its sidewalk tables, a great place to take a breather.

Several banks, mostly around Plaza Pringles, have ATMs. The **tourist office** (0266-442-3957; www.turismo.sanluis.gov.ar; cnr Av Illia & Junín; 9am-9pm) has an almost overwhelming amount of information on San Luis' surrounding areas.

Aerolineas Argentinas (0266-442-5671; Av Illia 472; 9am-6pm Mon-Fri, to 1pm Sat) flies daily to Buenos Aires. The bus terminal has departures to Mendoza (AR$335, 3½ hours), San Juan (AR$425, five hours), Rosario (AR$725, 11 hours) and Buenos Aires (AR$1150, 12 hours).

Mendoza

0261 / POP 1,100,000

In 1861 an earthquake leveled the city of Mendoza. This was a tragedy for the *mendocinos* (people from Mendoza), but rebuilding efforts created some of the cities most loved aspects: the authorities anticipated (somewhat pessimistically) the *next* earthquake by rebuilding the city with wide avenues (for the rubble to fall into) and spacious plazas (to use as evacuation points). The result is one of Argentina's most seductive cities – stunningly picturesque and a joy to walk around.

Add to this the fact that it's smack in the middle of many of the country's best vineyards (the region produces 70% of the country's wine) and that it's the base for any number of outdoor activities, and you know you'll be spending more than a couple of days here.

Early March's **Fiesta Nacional de la Vendimia** (wine harvest festival) attracts big crowds; book accommodation well ahead. The surrounding countryside offers wine tasting, mountaineering, cycling and whitewater rafting. Many different tours of the area are available.

Sights

Plaza Independencia has a **crafts fair** Thursday through Sunday night, while Plaza Pellegrini holds its own weekend **antiques market** with music and dancing.

★ Museo Fundacional MUSEUM

(cnr Alberdi & Videla Castillo; admission AR$27; 8am-8pm Tue-Sat, from 2pm Sun) Mendoza's Museo Fundacional protects excavations of the colonial *cabildo* (town council), destroyed by an earthquake in 1861. At that time, the city's geographical focus shifted west and south to its present location. A series of small dioramas depicts Mendoza's history, working through all of human evolution as if the city of Mendoza were the climax (maybe it was).

Museo Municipal de Arte Moderno GALLERY

(Plaza Independencia; admission AR$23; 9am-8pm Tue-Fri, from 2pm Sat & Sun) This is a relatively small but well-organized facility with modern and contemporary art exhibits. Free concerts and theatrical performances are usually held here on Sunday night at 8pm; stop by for the weekly program. It's underground at the Plaza Independencia.

Parque General San Martín PARK

Walking along the lakeshore and snoozing in the shade of the rose garden in this beautiful 420-hectare park is a great way to enjoy one of the city's highlights. Walk along Sarmiento/Civit out to the park and admire some of Mendoza's finest houses on the way. Pick up a park map at the **Centro de Información** (0261-420-5052; cnr Avs Los Platanos & Libertador; 9am-5pm), just inside the impressive entry gates, shipped over from England and originally forged for the Turkish Sultan Hamid II.

Bodega la Rural WINERY

(0261-497-2013; www.bodegalarural.com.ar; Montecaseros 2625; tours AR$90; 9am-1pm & 2-5pm Mon-Fri) Winery tours here are fairly standard but the museum is fascinating – there's a huge range of winemaking equipment from over the years on display, including a grape press made from an entire cowskin. Tours in Spanish leave on the

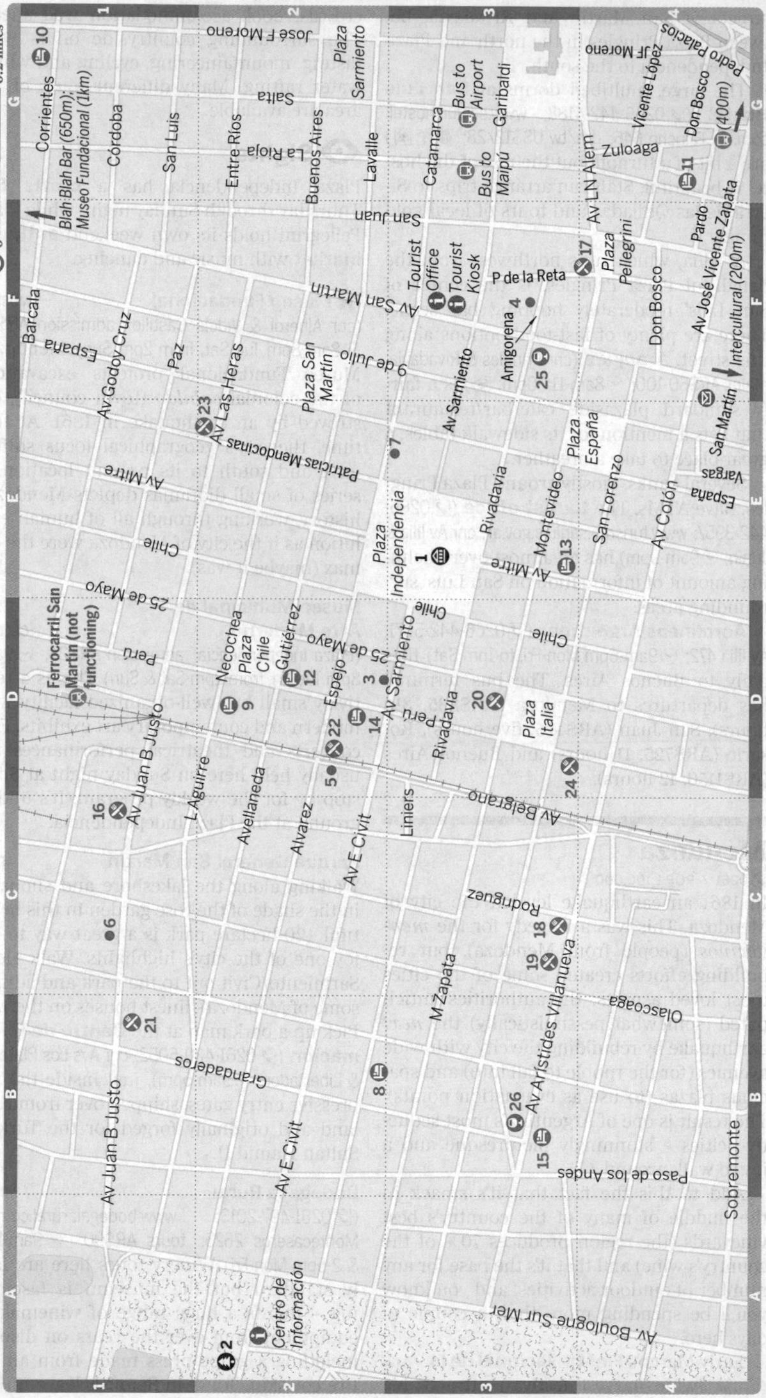

Mendoza

0 400 m
0 0.2 miles
Barcala
Corrientes
10
Blah Blah Bar (650m); Museo Fundacional (1km)
Córdoba
San Luis
Entre Ríos
La Rioja
Salta
José F Moreno
Buenos Aires
Plaza Sarmiento
Lavalle
San Juan
Catamarca
Bus to Airport
Bus to Maipú
Garibaldi
Ferrocarril San Martín (not functioning)
16
6
21
Av Juan B Justo
Av Juan B Justo
Perú
25 de Mayo
Chile
Av Mitre
España
Av Godoy Cruz
Paz
23
Av Las Heras
L Aguirre
Grandaderos
2
Centro de Información
Av E Civit
Avellaneda
Necochea
Plaza Chile
9
Gutiérrez
12
Alvarez
5
22
Espejo
25 de Mayo
Patricias Mendocinas
Plaza San Martín
Av E Civit
14
3
8
Av Sarmiento
Plaza Independencia
7
9 de Julio
Av San Martín
Tourist Office
Tourist Kiosk
Liniers
Perú
Chile
1
M Zapata
Rivadavia
Av Sarmiento
20
Rivadavia
Amigorena
4
P de la Reta
Rodriguez
Av Belgrano
Plaza Italia
Av Mitre
Montevideo
25
26
15
Av Arístides Villanueva
19
18
24
Chile
13
Plaza España
17
Av LN Alem
Plaza Pellegrini
San Lorenzo
Av. Boulogne Sur Mer
Paso de los Andes
Olascoaga
Av Colón
Don Bosco
Zuloaga
Vicente López
JF Moreno
11
Pardo
Don Bosco
Pedro Palacios
Av José Vicente Zapata
(400m)
España
Vargas
San Martín
Intercultural (200m)
Sobremonte

hour. If you want one in English, call ahead, or you can simply walk around on your own for free.

Di Tomasso WINERY
(0261-587-8900; www.familiaditommaso.com; Urquiza 8136; tours AR$40; 10am-6pm Mon-Sat) Di Tomasso is a beautiful, historical vineyard dating back to the 1830s. The tour includes a quick pass through the original cellar section.

Activities

Scaling nearby Aconcagua is one of the most popular activities here, but there are also plenty of operators offering rafting, climbing, mountain biking and trekking, among other things. Most hostels can organize these.

Ski rental places operate along Av Las Heras during winter.

Inka Expediciones HIKING
(0261-425-0871; www.inka.com.ar; Av Juan B Justo 345, Mendoza; 9am-6pm Mon-Fri, to 1pm Sat) Fixed and tailor-made expeditions.

Argentina Ski Tours TOUR
(0261-423-6958; www.argentinaskitours.com; Av Belgrano 1194B; 11am-8:30pm Mon-Fri, from 5:30pm Sat) Full-service ski tours and lessons in Spanish or English. Best quality ski-equipment rental in town. Also brokers a range of on-mountain accommodations.

Argentina Rafting ADVENTURE TOUR
(0261-429-6325; www.argentinarafting.com; Amigorena 86; 9am-6pm Mon-Sat) Rafting, mountain biking, kayaking, paragliding and rock climbing, among other activities.

Courses

Intercultural LANGUAGE COURSE
(0261-429-0269; www.spanishcourses.com.ar; República de Siria 241; 9am-8pm Mon-Sat) Offers group and private Spanish classes and internationally recognized exams. Can also help find longer-term accommodations in Mendoza.

Sleeping

Note that hotel prices rise from January to March, most notably during the wine festival in early March. Some hostels in Mendoza will only rent you a bed if you buy one of their tours. Needless to say, none of these are recommended here.

★**Hostel Alamo** HOSTEL $
(0261-429-5565; www.hostelalamo.com.ar; Necochea 740; dm US$14-17, d US$37-58;) An impeccable hostel in a great location, the Alamo offers roomy four-bed dorms, great hangout areas and a wonderful backyard with a small swimming pool.

Hostel Lagares HOTEL $
(0261-423-4727; www.hostellagares.com.ar; Corrientes 213; dm/d US$17/65;) This 'deluxe' hostel may charge a bit more than some of the competition, but you get a whole lot in return – it's spotlessly clean, the dorms are spacious and the breakfast generous. Some charming indoor and outdoor common areas add to the appeal.

Hostel Lao HOSTEL $
(0261-438-0454; www.laohostel.com.ar; Rioja 771; dm US$20, r US$58-65, r without bathroom US$40;) More like a cool B&B than a hostel, there are only four dorm beds here.

Mendoza

Sights
1 Museo Municipal de Arte Moderno E3
2 Parque General San Martín A2

Activities, Courses & Tours
3 Ampora Wine Tours D2
4 Argentina Rafting F3
5 Argentina Ski Tours D2
6 Inka Expediciones C1
7 Trout & Wine E3

Sleeping
8 Banana Hostel B2
9 Hostel Alamo D2
10 Hostel Lagares G1
11 Hostel Lao G4
12 Hotel Casino D2
13 Hotel Nutibara E3
14 Hotel Zamora D2
15 Mendoza Inn B3

Eating
16 Anna Bistro C1
17 Arrope F4
18 Cocina Poblana C3
19 El Palenque C3
20 Fuente y Fonda D3
21 La Flor de la Canela B1
22 La Mira D2
23 Mercado Central E2
24 Patancha D3

Drinking & Nightlife
25 La Reserva F3
26 Por Acá B3

The rest of the accommodations are in spacious private rooms set in a converted family home. More expensive rooms front straight onto the pretty backyard area.

Mendoza Inn HOSTEL $
(0261-438-0818; www.mendozahostel.com; Av Arístides Villanueva 470; dm US$12-15, d with/without bathroom US$45/39;) With a great location and friendly, bilingual staff, this is one of the city's better hostels. Common areas are spacious and the big shady backyard and pool are definite pluses.

Hotel Casino HOTEL $
(0261-425-6666; www.nuevohotelcasino.com.ar; Gutiérrez 668; s/d US$40/56;) Facing on to Plaza Chile, the Hotel Casino offers some good, spacious rooms and some smallish, ordinary ones. They're all clean and comfortable, but have a look at a few before deciding.

Banana Hostel HOSTEL $
(0261-423-3354; www.bananahostel.com.ar; Julio A Roca 344; dm US$16-30, d with/without bathroom US$76/65;) A spacious hostel set in the quiet residential neighborhood known as La Quinta. The common areas are great, as is the big backyard and huge swimming pool.

Hotel Zamora HOTEL $
(0261-425-7537; Perú 1156; s/d US$37/48;) With a lot more style than most in this price range, this sweet little family-run hotel offers comfortable rooms, a buffet breakfast and a charming courtyard with tinkling fountain and Spanish tilework.

Hotel Nutibara HOTEL $$
(0261-429-5428; www.nutibara.com.ar; Mitre 867; s/d US$94/113;) A short hop from the main plaza, the Nutibara offers a good deal in this price range. Rooms vary in size (and some singles are quite cramped) and there's some serious beige-and-cream color scheming going on, but the pool area is fantastic and the whole setup is very well run and maintained.

Eating

Sidewalk restaurants on pedestrian Av Sarmiento are fine places to people-watch. The restaurants along Avs Las Heras and San Martín offer good-value set meals; see signboards for details.

Mercado Central MARKET $
(cnr Av Las Heras & Patricias Mendocinas; mains from AR$70; 8:30am-11pm) The renovat-

THE GRAPE ESCAPE

It would be a crime to come to Mendoza and not visit at least one vineyard. A crime, people. Argentina's wines are constantly improving and, consequently, attracting international attention. Wine tasting is a popular activity at the many wineries in the area.

Depending on your budget and time frame, there are a few options:

- Bussing around Maipú and Luján.
- Bussing to Maipú, then renting a bike (AR$80) for a self-guided tour. Cyclists can consider biking a 40km circuit that would cover Di Tomasso (p135), Bodega la Rural (p133) and more. Call first to confirm opening hours. Established operators in Maipú include **Coco Bikes** (0261-481-0862; Urquiza 1781; bike hire AR$70; 9am-6pm Mon-Sat) and **Mr Hugo** (0261-497-4067; www.mrhugobikes.com; Urquiza 2228; bikes per day AR$80; 9am-7pm Mon-Sat). They provide basic maps and reasonable rides, but check your wheels (brakes, seat etc) before heading out. Tourist information offices in Mendoza also have area maps.
- A low-cost (around AR$360) tour, available through any hostel or tour operator. These are fine for your average Joe, but they can get crowded and rushed, and tastings certainly won't include any of the good stuff.
- A high-end wine tour with outfits such as **Trout & Wine** (0261-425-5613; www.troutandwine.com; Espejo 266; 9am-1pm & 3-8pm Mon-Sat) or **Ampora Wine Tours** (0261-429-2931; www.mendozawinetours.com; Av Sarmiento 647; 9am-9pm Mon-Sat, from 5pm Sun). These start at around AR$1950, but you'll be visiting some exclusive wineries in small groups and be getting samples of some of the finest wines that the region has to offer.

ed Mercado Central is a good hunting ground for cheap pizza, empanadas and sandwiches.

El Palenque ARGENTINE **$**
(Av Arístides Villanueva 287; mains AR$80-140; noon-2am Mon-Sat;) Don't miss this superb, extremely popular restaurant styled after an old-time *pulpería* (tavern), where the house wine is served in traditional *pinguinos* (white ceramic penguin-shaped pitchers). The food and appetizers are outstanding, and the outside tables are always full and fun.

La Flor de la Canela PERUVIAN **$**
(Av Juan B Justo 426; mains AR$65-100; noon-3pm & 9pm-1am, closed Wed) Need something spicy? Check out this authentic, bare-bones Peruvian eatery a few blocks from the center. What it lacks in atmosphere it makes up for in flavor.

Cocina Poblana MIDDLE EASTERN **$**
(Av Arístides Villanueva 217; dishes from AR$70; noon-3pm & 7pm-1am Mon-Sat) The very tasty, inexpensive Middle Eastern food here (hummus, falafel, dolmas) comes as a welcome break from all that steak. The shish kebab served with tabouleh salad is a definite winner.

Arrope VEGETARIAN **$**
(Primitiva de la Reta 927; per 100g AR$18; 8am-3pm;) Feeling a little meat-heavy? Slip into this cozy vegetarian cafe-restaurant and choose from a wide range of animal-free goodies on the buffet table.

La Mira FUSION **$**
(Av Belgrano 1191; mains AR$85-140; 9am-midnight) Delicious, innovative dishes in a relaxed environment. Each dish comes as a full meal (some with side orders of vegetables) and there's a small but respectable wine list.

★ **Anna Bistro** FUSION **$$**
(Av Juan B Justo 161; mains from AR$120; noon-2am;) One of Mendoza's best-looking restaurants offers a wonderful garden area, cool music and carefully prepared dishes.

Fuente y Fonda ARGENTINE **$$**
(Montevideo 675; mains AR$150; noon-3pm & 8pm-midnight) Good, honest home-style cooking. The concept is traditional family dining, so expect big portions of hearty food in the middle of the table for everyone to share. A decent wine list and yummy free desserts round out the picture.

Patancha INTERNATIONAL **$$**
(Perú 778; mains AR$90-150; 10am-2am Mon-Sat) A cute little place serving up some great tapas alongside traditional favorites such as *humitas* and the occasional surprise such as seafood stir-fry. The AR$55 set lunch is a bargain.

Drinking

Av Arístides Villanueva, west of the center, is ground zero in terms of Mendoza's happening bar scene. Going for a wander is your best bet, but here are a few places to get you started.

Por Acá BAR
(Av Arístides Villanueva 557; 8pm-late Wed-Sat) Purple and yellow outside and polka-dotted upstairs, this bar-lounge gets packed after 2am, and by the end of the night, dancing on the tables is not uncommon. Good retro dance music.

Blah Blah Bar BAR
(Escalada 2307; from 6pm) A Tajamar favorite, Mendoza's version of a dive bar is hip but restrained, with a casual atmosphere and plenty of outdoor seating.

La Reserva GAY
(Rivadavia 34; admission free-AR$75; from 9pm Tue-Sat) This small, nominally gay bar packs in a mixed crowd and has outrageous drag shows at midnight every night, with hardcore techno later.

Information

Wine snobs and the wine-curious should pick up a free copy of the **Wine Republic** (www.wine-republic.com), an English-language magazine devoted to Mendoza's wining and dining scene.

Information office (0261-431-5000; 8am-8pm) In the bus terminal. Another kiosk is at the corner of Avs Las Heras and Mitre.

Post office (cnr Av San Martín & Colón; 8am-6pm Mon-Fri, 9am-1pm Sat)

Tourist kiosk (0261-420-1333; Garibaldi; 8am-6pm) This helpful kiosk near Av San Martín is the most convenient information source.

Tourist office (0261-420-2800; www.turismo.mendoza.gov.ar; Av San Martín 1143; 8am-10pm Mon-Fri) Good maps; plenty of brochures.

Getting There & Away

AIR

Aerolíneas Argentinas/Austral (☎0261-420-4185; Av Sarmiento 82; ⏲10am-6pm Mon-Fri, to 1pm Sat) These airlines share offices; Aerolíneas flies several times daily to Buenos Aires.

LANChile (☎0261-425-7900; Rivadavia 256; ⏲10am-7pm Mon-Fri) LANChile flies twice daily to Santiago de Chile.

BUS

The **bus terminal** (☎0261-431-3001; cnr Avs de Acceso Este & Costanera) is about 10 blocks east of the town center.

DESTINATION	COST (AR$)	DURATION (HR)
Aconcagua	90	3½
Buenos Aires	1375	14
Córdoba	805	9
Las Leñas	200	7
Los Penitentes	82	4
Malargüe	201	6
Neuquén	1025	12
San Juan	224	2
San Luis	335	3½
Tucumán	1127	14
Uspallata	68	2
Valparaíso, Chile	500	8

Getting Around

Mendoza's airport is 6km north of the city. **Bus 60 (Aeropuerto)** (Salta, btw Garibald & Catamarca) goes from Calle Salta straight there. The bus terminal is about 15 minutes' walk from the center; catch the Villa Nueva trolley if you don't feel like walking.

Local buses cost AR$3.50 – more for longer distances – and require a magnetic Redbus card, which can be bought at most kiosks in denominations of AR$5 and AR$10.

Uspallata

☎02624 / POP 3800

In an exceptionally beautiful valley surrounded by polychrome mountains, 105km west of Mendoza at an altitude of 1751m, this crossroads village along RN 7 is a good base for exploring the surrounding area, which served as a location for the Brad Pitt epic *Seven Years in Tibet*.

Sights

One kilometer north of the highway junction toward Villavicencio, a signed side road leads to ruins and a museum at the **Bóvedas Históricas Uspallata**, a metallurgical site since pre-Columbian times. About 4km north of Uspallata, in a volcanic outcrop near a small monument to San Ceferino Namuncurá, is a faded but still visible set of **petroglyphs.**

Sleeping & Eating

Hostel International Uspallata HOSTEL $
(☎15-466-7240; www.hosteluspallata.com.ar; RN 7 s/n; dm/d US$11/45, cabin US$60-80) Friendly hostel 7km east of town with plain but comfortable rooms and a couple of sweet little cabins. Dinner (AR$85 to AR$120) is available. There's good hiking from the hostel and you can rent bikes and horses here. Ask the bus driver to drop you at the front before you hit Uspallata.

Hotel Portico del Valle HOTEL $$
(☎02624-420103; Las Heras s/n; dm/s/d US$18/54/64) A recently constructed, vaguely modern hotel right on the crossroads. It's nothing fancy, but fine for a few days. The hostel is in a separate building a few blocks away. Enquire at reception.

★**Café Tibet** CAFE $
(cnr RN 7 & Las Heras; mains AR$65-100; ⏲8am-11pm) No visit to Uspallata would be complete without at least a coffee in this little oddity. The food is nothing spectacular, but the decor, comprising leftover props from *Seven Years in Tibet*, is a must for fans of the surreal.

El Rancho PARRILLA $$
(cnr RN 7 & Cerro Chacay; mains AR$100-150; ⏲noon-3pm & 7pm-1am Tue-Sun) This is the coziest and most reliable *parrilla* in town, serving all the usual, plus a good roasted *chivo* (goat).

Information

The **tourist information** (☎02624-420009; RN 7 s/n; ⏲8am-9pm) office is opposite the YPF station.

Getting There & Away

The bus terminal is tucked behind the new, rampantly ugly casino on the main drag. There are departures for Mendoza (AR$68, 2½ hours) and Puente del Inca (AR$60, one hour) and points in between. Santiago-bound buses will carry passengers to and across the border but are often full; in winter, the pass can close to all traffic for weeks at a time.

Around Uspallata

Los Penitentes

Both the terrain and snow cover can be excellent for downhill and Nordic skiing at **Los Penitentes** (☎0261-429-9953; www.lospenitentes.com; lifts per day AR$360-490), two hours southwest of Uspallata at an altitude of 2580m. Lifts and accommodations are very modern; the maximum vertical drop on its 21 runs exceeds 700m. A day ski pass costs AR$360 to AR$490, depending on the time of year. The season runs from June to September.

The cozy converted cabin of **Hostel Los Penitentes** (☎in Mendoza 0261-425-5511; www.penitentes.com.ar; dm US$24-31) accommodates 38 in very close quarters, and has a kitchen, wood-burning stove and three shared bathrooms. Meals are available from AR$70, and dorm rates are halved in summer. The hostel offers Nordic- and downhill-skiing trips in winter and Aconcagua treks and expeditions in summer. If you're looking for a bit more comfort, the **Hotel Ayelén** (☎in Mendoza 0261-428-4343; s/d from US$129/193) is open year-round; it has an excellent setup and offers good meals in its on-site restaurant.

From Mendoza, several buses pass daily through Uspallata to Los Penitentes (AR$82, four hours).

Puente del Inca

About 8km west of Los Penitentes, on the way to the Chilean border and near the turnoff to Aconcagua, is one of Argentina's most striking wonders. Situated 2720m above sea level, Puente del Inca is a natural stone bridge spanning the Río Mendoza. Underneath it, rock walls and the ruins of an old spa are stained yellow by warm, sulfurous thermal springs. You can hike into Parque Provincial Aconcagua from here.

The little, no-frills **Hostel El Nico** (☎0261-592-0736; elnicohostel@gmail.com; dm/d US$22/44) offers mountain climbing, glacier trekking and snowshoeing. There's a cheap restaurant and bar on the premises. Other restaurants are scattered around the car park.

Daily buses to Mendoza take about four hours (AR$93).

Parque Provincial Aconcagua

On the Chilean border, Parque Provincial Aconcagua protects 710 sq km of high country surrounding the western hemisphere's highest summit: 6962m **Cerro Aconcagua**. There are trekking possibilities to base camps and refuges beneath the permanent snow line.

Reaching Aconcagua's summit requires at least 13 to 15 days, including some time for acclimatization. Potential climbers should get RJ Secor's *Aconcagua Climbing Guide*, and check www.aconcagua.mendoza.gov.ar for more information.

Mid-November to mid-March, permits are mandatory for trekking and climbing. Fees vary according to the complex park-use seasons – check www.aconcagua.mendoza.gov.ar for the latest information. Mid-December to late January is high season. Purchase permits in Mendoza from the main tourist office (p137).

Many adventure-travel agencies in and around Mendoza arrange excursions into the high mountains.

San Juan

☎0264 / POP 109,000

Smelling kerosene? Don't panic – that's just the proud folks of San Juan *polishing the sidewalks*. Uh-huh. An attractive enough place, San Juan's big claim to fame are the nearby wineries and access to Parque Provincial Ischigualasto.

Rather than changing names as they intersect the central plaza (which is what happens in most Argentine towns), streets in San Juan keep their names but are designated by compass points, with street numbers starting at zero at the plaza and rising from there. Thus there will be two Laprida 150s – one Laprida 150 Este and one Laprida 150 Oeste.

Sights & Activities

Museo de Vino Santiago Graffigna MUSEUM
(☎0264-421-4227; www.graffignawines.com; Colón 1342 Norte; ⏰10am-7pm Mon-Sat, to 4pm Sun) **FREE** Museo de Vino Santiago Graffigna is a wine museum well worth a visit. It also has a wine bar where you can taste many of San Juan's best wines. Take bus

12A from in front of the tourist office on Sarmiento (AR$3, 15 minutes) and ask the driver to tell you when to get off.

Triasico Turismo TOUR
(0264-422-8566; www.triasico.com.ar; Sarmiento 42 Sur; 9am-1pm & 4-8pm Mon-Sat) Specializes in Ischigualasto tours (AR$640, minimum two people) – come here if you're struggling to get a group together.

Sleeping

San Juan Hostel HOSTEL $
(0264-420-1835; www.sanjuanhostel.com; Av Córdoba 317 Este; dm US$11-12, s/d US$25/32, without bathroom US$16/21;) An excellent little hostel with a variety of rooms placed conveniently between the bus terminal and downtown. Good info on tours and local attractions, and a rooftop Jacuzzi rounds out the picture.

Hotel Alhambra HOTEL $
(0264-421-4780; www.alhambrahotel.com.ar; General Acha 180 Sur; s/d US$30/40;) Smallish, carpeted rooms with splashes of dark-wood paneling, giving them a classy edge. Little touches such as leather chairs and gold ashtray stands in the hallways give it a kitschy appeal and the central location seals the deal.

Hotel Selby HOTEL $
(0264-422-4766; www.hotelselby.com.ar; Rioja 183 Sur; s/d US$45/50) There's nothing really flash going on here, but the rooms are a decent size and the downtown location can't be beat. Good value for the price.

Hotel del Bono Suite HOTEL $$
(0264-421-7600; www.hoteldelbono.com.ar; Mitre 75 Oeste; d/ste US$96/110;) With some slick design features taking the edge off the corporate blandness, this is a good deal for the price, and the well-stocked kitchenettes and rooftop pool are added bonuses.

Eating

The pedestrian section of Rivadavia is crammed with sidewalk cafes and fast-food joints.

Baró INTERNATIONAL $
(Rivadavia 55 Oeste; mains AR$80-120; 8am-11:30pm) This popular, main-street cafe-restaurant has the best variety of pasta dishes in town and a relaxed atmosphere that makes it a good stop for coffee or drinks at any time.

Soychú VEGETARIAN $
(Av José Ignacio de la Roza 223 Oeste; buffet AR$60; noon-9pm Mon-Sat, 11am-3pm Sun;) Excellent vegetarian buffet attached to a health-food store selling all sorts of groceries and a range of teas. Arrive early for the best selection.

★ **de Sánchez** FUSION $$
(Rivadavia 61 Oeste; mains AR$130-200; noon-3pm & 8pm-midnight Tue-Sun) San Juan's snootiest downtown restaurant is actually pretty good. It has a creative menu with a smattering of seafood dishes, an adequate wine list (featuring all the San Juan heavy hitters) and a hushed, tranquil atmosphere.

Information

Tourist office (0264-422-2431; www.turismo.sanjuan.gov.ar; Sarmiento 24 Sur; 8am-7pm) Has a good map of the city and its surroundings plus useful information on the rest of the province, particularly Parque Provincial Ischigualasto.

Getting There & Away

Aerolíneas Argentinas (0264-421-4158; Av San Martín 215 Oeste; 10am-6pm Mon-Fri, to 1pm Sat) flies daily to Buenos Aires.

The **bus terminal** (0264-422-1604; Estados Unidos 492 Sur) has buses to Mendoza (AR$225, three hours), Córdoba (AR$675, nine hours), San Agustín de Valle Fértil (AR$130, four hours), La Rioja (AR$506, six hours) and Buenos Aires (AR$1460, 15 hours).

For car rental, try **Classic** (0264-422-4622; Av San Martín 163 Oeste; 9am-7pm). If you're heading to Ischigualasto, one of the cheapest ways to do it is to get a group together in your hostel and hire a car for the day.

Around San Juan

San Agustín de Valle Fértil

This relaxed, green little village is 250km northeast of San Juan and set amid colorful hills and rivers. It relies on farming, animal husbandry, mining and tourism. Visitors to Parques Ischigualasto and Talampaya use San Agustín as a base, and there are also nearby **petroglyphs** and the Río Seco to explore.

The **tourist office** (General Acha; 7am-1pm & 5-10pm Mon-Fri, 8am-1pm Sat), on the plaza, can help set you up with tours of the area. There's camping and cheap accommodations, and a couple of good *parrillas*. Change money before you get here.

Buses roll daily to and from San Juan (AR$130, four hours).

Parque Provincial Ischigualasto

At every meander in the canyon of Parque Provincial Ischigualasto, a desert valley between sedimentary mountain ranges, the intermittent waters of the Río Ischigualasto have exposed a wealth of Triassic fossils and dinosaur bones – up to 180 million years old – and carved distinctive shapes in the monochrome clays, red sandstone and volcanic ash. The desert flora of algarrobo trees, shrubs and cacti complement the eerie moonscape, and common fauna include guanacos, condors, Patagonian hares and foxes.

Camping is (unofficially) permitted at the visitors center near the entrance, which also has a *confitería* with simple meals and cold drinks. There are toilets and showers, but water shortages are frequent and there's no shade.

Ischigualasto is about 80km north of San Agustín. Given its size and isolation, the only practical way to visit the park is by vehicle. After you pay the entrance fee, a ranger will accompany your vehicle on a two- or three-hour circuit over the park's unpaved roads, which may be impassable after rain.

If you have no transportation, ask the San Agustín tourist office about tours or hiring a car and driver, or contact the **park** (Valle de la Luna, Valley of the Moon; admission AR$160; 8am-6pm). Tour operators in San Juan do tours here, but it's way cheaper to make your own way to San Agustín and line something up there. Some tours can be combined with **Parque Nacional Talampaya**, almost 100km northeast of Ischigualasto.

Malargüe

0260 / POP 21,600

From precolonial times, the Pehuenche people hunted and gathered in the valley of Malargüe, but the advance of European agricultural colonists dispossessed the original inhabitants of their land. Today petroleum is a principal industry, but Malargüe, 400km south of Mendoza, is also a year-round outdoor activity center: Las Leñas offers Argentina's best **skiing**, and there are archaeological sites and fauna reserves nearby, plus organized **caving** possibilities.

Sleeping & Eating

Restaurants line the five blocks of San Martín south of the plaza.

Eco Hostel Malargüe HOSTEL $
(0260-447-0391; www.hostelmalargue.com; Finca 65, Colonia Pehuenche; dm US$13, d with/without bathroom US$72/56;) Six kilometers south of town, this hostel/B&B is set on an organic farm and built using sustainable practices. Rooms are simple but comfortable, the surrounds are beautiful and breakfast (featuring farm produce) is a winner too.

Hosteria Keoken HOTEL $
(0260-447-2468; Puebla 252; s/d US$45/55;) A cute little no-frills option right off the main street. Rooms are cozy and comfortable enough for the price and the place is run by a doting señora.

El Nevado APARTMENT $$
(15-440-0712; www.aparthotelnevado.com.ar; Puebla 343; apt from US$65;) Excellent-value apartments available by the day or for longer stays. They come with fully equipped kitchens, separate sleeping areas and a cute little garden out back.

★ **El Quincho de María** ARGENTINE $
(Av San Martín 440; mains AR$80-130; noon-11pm) The finest dining in the center is at this cozy little *parrilla* where everything from the gnocchi to the empanadas is handmade. Don't miss the mouth-watering shish kebabs for AR$60.

Los Olivos ARGENTINE $$
(San Martín 409; mains AR$110-170; noon-11:30pm) There's a good range of well-prepared food here; the menu's split into 'gourmet' (offering regional faves like goat and trout) and 'classic,' with inventive twists on Argentine standards.

Information

Tourist office (0260-447-1659; www.malargue.gov.ar; RN 40, Parque del Ayer; 8am-8pm) Helpful tourist office with facilities at the northern end of town, on the highway. A small kiosk (9am-9pm) operates out of the bus terminal.

Getting There & Away

The **bus terminal** (cnr Av General Roca & Aldao) has regular services to Mendoza (AR$201, six hours) and Las Leñas (AR$45, 1½ hours). There is a weekly summer service across the 2500m Paso Pehuenche and down the awesome canyon of the Río Maule to Talca, Chile.

If you're heading south, there is a daily bus to Buta Ranquil (AR$271, five hours) in Neuquén province, with connections further south from there. Book at least a day in advance at **Transportes Leader** (☎0260-447-0519; San Martín 775), which operates out of the Club los Amigos pool hall.

Las Leñas

Wealthy Argentines and foreigners alike come to Las Leñas, the country's most prestigious ski resort, to look dazzling zooming down the slopes and then spend nights partying until the sun peeks over the snowy mountains. Summer activities include hiking, horse riding and mountain biking. Despite the fancy glitter, it's not completely out of reach for budget travelers.

Open from approximately July to October, Las Leñas is only 70km from Malargüe. Its 33 runs reach a peak of 3430m, with a maximum drop of 1230m. Lift tickets cost roughly from AR$495 to AR$795 (depending on the season) for a full day of skiing.

Budget travelers will find regular transportation from Malargüe, where accommodation is cheaper. Buses from Mendoza (AR$150) take seven hours.

THE LAKE DISTRICT

Extending from Neuquén down through Esquel, Argentina's Lake District is a gorgeous destination with lots of opportunities for adventure. There are lofty mountains to climb and ski down, rushing rivers to raft, clear lakes to boat or fish and beautiful national parks to explore. From big-city Bariloche to hippie El Bolsón, the Lake District's towns and cities each have their own distinct geography, architecture and cultural offerings. There's something fun to do every month of the year, so don't miss visiting this multifaceted region.

The Lake District's original inhabitants were the Puelches and Pehuenches, so named for their dependence on pine nuts from the *pehuén* (monkey puzzle tree). Though Spaniards explored the area in the late 16th century, it was the Mapuche who dominated the region until the 19th century, when European settlers arrived. Today you can still see Mapuche living around here, especially on national park lands.

Neuquén

☎0299 / POP 231,200

Palindromic (forgiving the accent) Neuquén is a provincial capital nestled in the confluence of two rivers, the Limay and the Neuquén. It's the gateway to Patagonia and the Andean Lake District, as well as an important commercial and agricultural center. Neuquén isn't a major tourist magnet, but it isn't unpleasant either – and if you're interested in old bones, those belonging to the largest dinosaurs ever have been found in the surrounding countryside.

Sights

Museo Nacional de Bellas Artes MUSEUM
(cnr Bartolomé Mitre & Santa Cruz; ⏰10am-8pm Mon-Sat, 4-8pm Sun) FREE Showcases fine arts from the region and often features traveling exhibitions.

Sleeping & Eating

Punto Patagonico Hostel HOSTEL $
(☎0299-447-9940; www.puntopatagonico.com; Periodistas Neuquinas 94; dm US$25, d with/without bathroom US$70/50; @📶) Neuquén's best hostel is a good deal – it's well set up with comfy dorms, a spacious lounge and a good garden area.

Parque Hotel HOTEL $
(☎0299-442-5806; www.parquehotelnqn.com.ar; Av Olascoaga 271; s/d US$40/56; 📶) There are a few charming touches in the spacious, tile-floored rooms here. Some are showing their age these days, but most have good views out over the busy street below.

Hotel Neu HOTEL $$$
(☎0299-443-0084; www.hotelneu354.com; Rivadavia 354; s/d US$135/178; ❄📶) One of the better business-class hotels in town, the Neu keeps it simple with fresh, modern decor in medium-sized but uncramped rooms. The location is super-central and there's an on-site gym.

La Nonna Francesa INTERNATIONAL $
(☎0299-430-0930; 9 de Julio 56; mains AR$90-150; ⏰11am-3pm & 8pm-midnight Mon-Sat) Some of Neuquén's finest dining can be found at this French-Italian trattoria – the pastas are all extremely good, but the trout dishes are the absolute standouts.

Tres Catorce INTERNATIONAL **$$**
(9 de Julio 63; mains AR$100-160; ⊙8pm-2am Tue-Sun; 📶) The dining scene in Neuquén has improved considerably over the past few years, with this casually stylish eatery at the forefront. On offer here are carefully prepared dishes, thoughtful garnishes and a small but well-selected range of boutique wines.

ℹ Information

There are several banks with ATMs.

Provincial tourist office (☎0299-442-4089; www.neuquentur.gov.ar; Félix San Martín

The Lake District

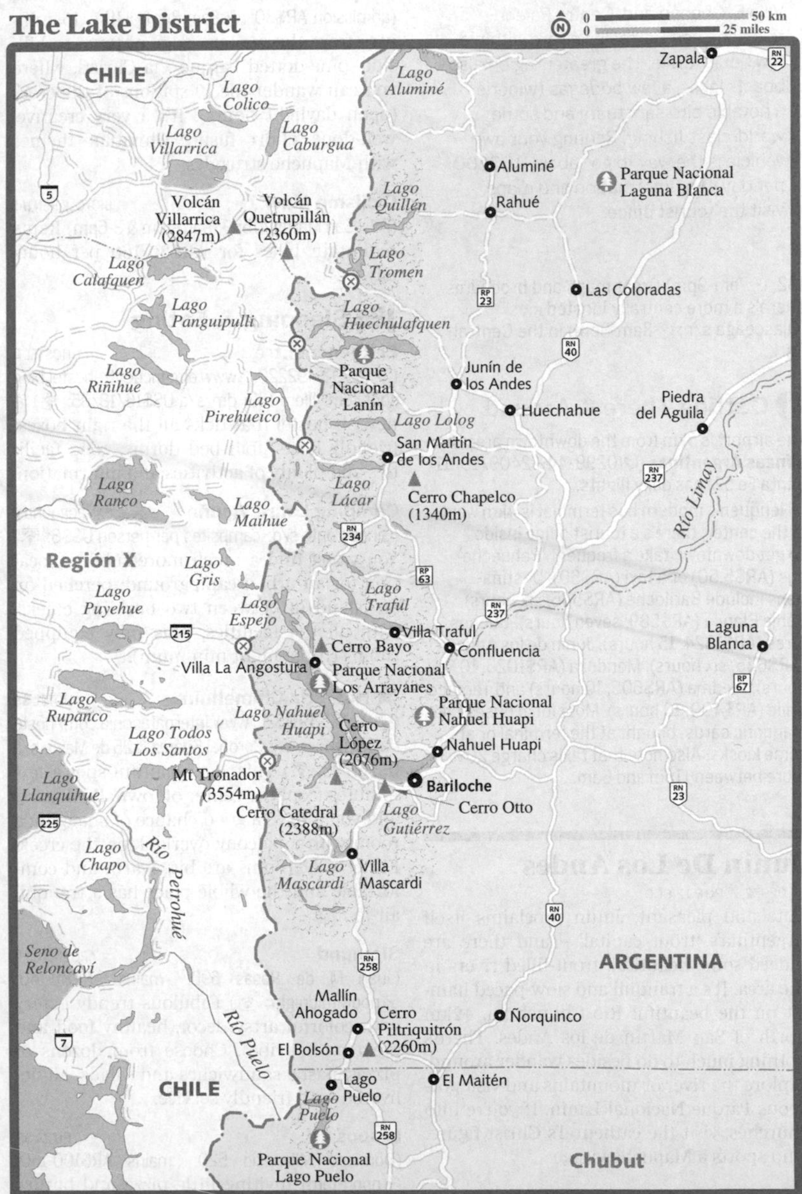

DINOSAURS

Neuquén province has one of the world's richest concentrations of dinosaur bones, along with a couple of dinosaur museums highlighting gigantic specimens. A few hints: Plaza Huincul, Villa El Chocón and Centro Paleontológico Lago Barreales all are within a few hours' drive. The greater region also boasts lakes, a few *bodegas* (wineries), a notable bird sanctuary and some world-class fishing. Renting your own vehicle is the way to go (about AR$600 per day). For information and maps, visit the tourist office.

182; ⏲7am-9pm) Great maps and brochures. There's a more centrally located kiosk (Olascoaga s/n; ⏲8am-8pm) in the Central Park.

Getting There & Around

The airport is 5km from the downtown area. **Aerolíneas Argentinas** (☎0299-442-2409/10/11; Santa Fe 52) has daily flights.

Neuquén's modern bus terminal is 4km west of the center; there's a tourist office inside. To get downtown take a frequent 'Pehueche' bus (AR$5.50) or a taxi (AR$50). Destinations include Bariloche (AR$546, six hours), Bahía Blanca (AR$589, seven hours), Buenos Aires (AR$1324, 15 hours), Junín de los Andes (AR$645, six hours), Mendoza (AR$1025, 10 hours), Viedma (AR$605, 10 hours) and Temuco, Chile (AR$400, 10 hours). Most local buses take magnetic cards, bought at the terminal or at some kiosks. Also note that taxis charge 20% more between 11pm and 6am.

Junín De Los Andes

☎02972 / POP 12,600

Cute and pleasant, Junín proclaims itself Argentina's 'trout capital' – and there are indeed some beautiful, trout-filled rivers in the area. It's a tranquil and slow-paced hamlet on the beautiful Río Chimehuín, 42km north of San Martín de los Andes. There's nothing much to do besides wander around, explore the river or mountains and visit gorgeous Parque Nacional Lanín. If you're into churches, visit the cathedral's Christ figure, who sports a Mapuche visage.

Sights & Activities

Museo Mapuche MUSEUM

(Padre Milanesio 751; entry by donation; ⏲9am-12:30pm & 2-7pm Mon-Fri, 9am-12:30pm Sat) The collection here includes Mapuche weavings and archaeological pieces.

Parque Vía Christi PARK

(admission AR$30; ⏲8am-8pm) Hike 15 minutes from the western edge of town to hillside, pine-dotted Parque Vía Christi, where you can wander the 19 stations of the cross (open daylight hours). It's a very creative, well-done effort fusing Christian themes with Mapuche struggles.

Ciclismo Mavi BICYCLE RENTAL

(Felix San Martín 415; ⏲9am-1pm & 3-6pm) Rents mountain bikes for AR$30/160 per hour/day.

Sleeping & Eating

El Reencuentro HOSTEL $

(☎02792-492220; www.elreencuentrohostel.blogspot.com; Illera 189; dm/s/d US$16/18/35; 📶) A newish hostel that ticks all the right boxes: friendly hosts, four-bed dorms, good facilities and plenty of activities and information.

Camping Laura Vicuña CAMPGROUND $

(Ginés Ponte s/n; campsites per person US$6; 📶) You won't find a much more sublime location for an urban campground: perched on an island in between two burbling creeks, with all the facilities, plus fully equipped cabins (three-night minimum).

★**Hostería Chimehuín** HOTEL $$

(☎02972-491132; www.interpatagonia.com/hosteriachimehuin; cnr Coronel Suárez & 25 de Mayo; s/d US$67/95; 📶) This is a beautiful spot a few minutes from the center of town. Book early and you'll have a good chance of snagging a room with a balcony overlooking the creek. Either way, rooms are big, warm and comfortable and the whole place has a tranquil air to it.

Sigmund ARGENTINE $

(Juan M de Rosas 690; mains AR$80-140; ⏲noon-midnight; 📶) Fabulous trendy eatery with colorful artsy decor, healthy food and great *onda* (vibe). Choose from dozens of pizzas, pasta, sandwiches and salads, all delivered with friendly service.

Lespos PIZZA $$

(Domingo Milanesio 520; mains AR$100-150; ⏲noon-1am) Inviting little pizza and burger bar, with a better atmosphere than most. There's a wide range of pizzas on offer and a good music selection seals the deal.

Information

There's a bank (ATM) on the plaza.

Tourist Office (02792-491160; www.junindelosandes.gov.ar; cnr Domingo Milanesio & Coronel Suárez; 8am-9pm) Enthusiastically helpful staff. Fishing permits and a list of licensed fishing guides available.

Getting There & Away

The airport is 19km south, toward San Martín de los Andes.

The bus station is three blocks west of the plaza. Destinations include San Martín de los Andes (AR$55, 45 minutes), Bariloche (AR$145, three hours) and Neuquén (AR$645, six hours).

Parque Nacional Lanín

At 3776m, snowcapped Volcán Lanín is the dominating centerpiece of this tranquil **national park** (www.parquenacionallanin.gov.ar; admission AR$80), where extensive stands of *lenga* (southern beech) and the curious monkey puzzle tree flourish. Pleistocene glaciers left behind blue finger-shaped lakes, excellent for fishing and camping. For more information and maps, contact the National Park Office in Junín or San Martín.

In summer (January and February) **Lago Huechulafquen** is easily accessible from Junín; there are outstanding views of Volcán Lanín and several worthwhile hikes. Mapuche-run campgrounds include **Raquithue** (per person US$5) and **Bahía Cañicul** (0297-249-0211; per person US$5). Free campsites around the park are also available; bring supplies from town. The forested **Lago Tromen** area also offers good hiking and camping.

From San Martín you can boat west on **Lago Lácar** to Paso Hua Hum and cross by road to Puerto Pirehueico (Chile); there's also bus service. Hua Hum has camping and hiking trails. Fifteen kilometers north of San Martín, serene **Lago Lolog** has good camping and fishing.

In summer, vans from Junín's bus station go all along Lago Huechulafquen to Puerto Canoa and beyond (AR$55, two to three times daily). There are also services to Lagos Tromen and Curruhué. Buses to Chile over the Hua Hum and Tromen passes can also stop at intermediate points, but in summer are often full.

San Martín De Los Andes

02972 / POP 28,000

Attractive San Martín is a small, fashionable destination crowded with rowdy Argentines in summer. Nestled between two verdant mountains on the shores of Lago Lácar, the town boasts many wood and stone chalet-style buildings, many of them chocolate shops, ice-cream stores and souvenir boutiques. But behind the touristy streets lie pleasant residential neighborhoods with pretty rose-filled gardens, and the surrounding area has wonderful forested trails perfect for hiking and biking.

Sights & Activities

Che Guevara fans can check out **La Pastera**, a small museum dedicated to this icon.

The 2.5km steep, dusty hike to **Mirador Bandurrias** (admission AR$10) ends with awesome views of Lago Lácar; be sure to take a snack or lunch. Tough cyclists can rent bikes at several shops in town and reach the *mirador* in about an hour via dirt roads. **Playa la Islita** is a pleasant little beach located 2.5km further from the mirador.

In winter you can ski at **Cerro Chapelco**, a ski center 20km away.

From the pier there are seven-hour boat tours to Paso Hua Hum (round-trip AR$750) to access walks and a waterfall. There's also boat transport to Quila Quina (round trip AR$250) for beaches and water sports.

Sleeping & Eating

Reserve ahead during the high seasons (late December to March, Easter, and July to August).

El Oso Andaluz Hostel HOSTEL $
(02972-427232; www.elosoandaluz.com.ar; Elordi 569; dm/d from US$11/35;) San Martín's coziest little downtown hostel has a good bed-to-bathroom ratio, atmospheric common areas and good-value private rooms.

Camping ACA CAMPGROUND $
(02972-427332; Av Koessler 2175; campsites per person US$9) This is a spacious campground on the eastern outskirts of town. However, you should try to avoid sites near the highway. There's a two-person minimum per site.

Hostería Hueney Ruca HOTEL $

(☎02972-421499; www.hosteriahueneyruca.com.ar; cnr Obeid & Coronel Pérez; s/d US$63/74; 📶) The big terracotta-tiled rooms here look onto a cute, well-kept little backyard. Beds are big and firm and bathrooms spacious, with glass-walled shower stalls.

★**Hostería La Masía** HOTEL $$

(☎02972-427688; www.hosterialamasia.com.ar; Obeid 811; s/d AR$560/890; 📶) Taking the whole Edelweiss thing to the next level, La Masía offers plenty of dark-wood paneling, arched doorways and cast-iron light fittings. Rooms are big and comfortable and most have mountain views. Fireplaces warm the lobby, and the owners are usually around to make sure everyone feels at home. Superb.

Rotui HOTEL $$

(☎02972-429539; www.rotui.com.ar; Perito Moreno 1378; s/d from US$60/120; ❄📶) A lovely wood-and-stone lodge set on immaculately manicured grounds overlooking the Arroyo Pochulla creek. Rooms are sumptuously appointed, with king-sized beds, polished floorboards and duck-down quilts. The apartments and cabins on offer are a good deal for groups.

★**Corazón Contento** CAFE $

(Av San Martín 467; mains AR$85; ⏰9am-11pm; 📶) A cute little bakery-cafe serving up an excellent range of fresh and healthy snacks and meals. The salads are great and the freshly baked scones and muffins hit the spot.

Pizza Cala PIZZA $

(Av San Martín 1129; mains AR$60-130; ⏰noon-1am; 📶) The local's choice for pizza is this ever-expanding place near the plaza. All the classics are here, plus some 'gourmet' options such as smoked trout, spinach and eggplant.

Bamboo PARRILLA $$

(cnr Belgrano & Villegas; mains from AR$140; ⏰noon-4pm & 9pm-1am; 📶) One reader claims this upmarket *parrilla* serves 'the best meat in all of Argentina.' We haven't tried all the meat in Argentina (yet), so you be the judge.

Information

There are several ATMs near Plaza San Martín.

Lanín National Park Office (Intendencia del Parque Nacional Lanín; ☎02972-427233; www.parquenacionallanin.gov.ar; cnr Elordi & Perito Moreno; ⏰8am-2pm Mon-Fri) The office provides limited maps as well as brochures and information on road conditions on the Ruta de los Siete Lagos.

Tourist office (☎02972-427347; www.sanmartindelosandes.gov.ar; cnr Av San Martín & M Rosas; ⏰8am-9pm) Provides surprisingly candid information on hotels and restaurants, plus excellent brochures and maps.

Getting There & Away

The airport is 23km north of town. **Aerolíneas Argentinas** (☎02972-410588; Mariano Moreno 859; ⏰8am-10pm Mon-Sat, 9am-9pm Sun) has daily flights.

The bus station is five blocks west of Plaza San Martín. Destinations include Junín de los Andes (AR$7, 55 minutes), Villa La Angostura (AR$121, 2½ hours) and Bariloche (AR$177, four hours). There are departures to Chilean destinations such as Temuco (AR$720, six hours) from December to February, book these trips at least two days in advance.

Villa La Angostura

☎0294 / POP 11,100

Tiny Villa La Angostura is a darling chocolate-box town that takes its name from the *angosta* (narrow) 91m neck of land connecting it to the striking Península Quetrihué. There's no doubt that Villa is touristy, but it's also charming; wood-and-stone alpine buildings line the three-block-long main street. There's skiing at nearby Cerro Bayo in winter.

El Cruce is the main part of town and contains the bus terminal and most hotels and businesses; the main street is Arrayanes. Woodsy La Villa, with a few restaurants, hotels and a nice beach, is 3km southwest and on the shores of Lago Nahuel Huapi.

Sights & Activities

The cinnamon-barked *arrayán,* a myrtle relative, is protected in the small but beautiful **Parque Nacional Los Arrayanes** (admission AR$120) on the Península Quetrihué. The main *bosque* (forest) of *arrayanes* is situated at the southern tip of the peninsula; it's reachable by a 40- to 60-minute boat ride (one way/round trip AR$95/170) or via hike on a relatively easy 12km trail from La Villa.

Experienced mountain-bike riders (there are stairs and hills) should rent a bike to reach the *arrayán* forest. It's possible to boat either there or back, hiking or biking the other way (buy your return boat ticket in advance). Take food and water; there's an ideal picnic spot next to a lake near the end of the trail.

At the start of the Arrayanes trail, near the beach, a steep 30- to 45-minute hike leads to a panoramic viewpoints over Lago Nahuel Huapi.

From the El Cruce part of town, a 3km walk north takes you to the **Mirador Belvedere** trailhead; hike another 30 minutes for good views. Nearby is **Cascada Inayacal**, a 50m waterfall, and a few hours' hike further on is **Cajón Negro**, a pretty valley (but get a map and directions beforehand from the tourist office, as trails and shortcuts around here can be confusing).

Sleeping & Eating

The following are all in or near El Cruce. Reserve ahead in January and February.

★Hostel Bajo Cero HOSTEL **$**
(☎0294-449-5454; www.bajocerohostel.com; Río Caleufu 88; dm/d US$25/63; @ 📶) A little over a kilometer west of the bus terminal is this gorgeous hostel with large, well-designed dorms and lovely doubles. It has a nice garden and kitchen, plus airy common spaces.

Residencial Río Bonito GUESTHOUSE **$**
(☎0294-449-4110; www.riobonitopatagonia.com.ar; Topa Topa 260; d/tr US$50/65; @ 📶) Bright and cheery rooms in a converted family home a few blocks from the bus terminal. The big, comfortable dining-lounge area is a bonus, as are the friendly hosts and kitchen use for guests.

Camping Cullumche CAMPGROUND **$**
(☎0294-449-4160; moyano@uncu.edu.ar; Blvd Quetrihué s/n; campsites per person US$8) Well signed from Blvd Nahuel Huapi, this secluded but large lakeside campground can get very busy in summer, but when it's quiet, it's lovely.

La Roca de la Patagonia HOTEL **$$**
(☎0294-449-4497; www.larocadelapatagonia.com.ar; Pascotto 155; s/d US$82/94; ❄ 📶) A cute little place just off the main drag, with just six rooms. It's set in a large converted house, so there are some great dimensions here. Decor is very Patagonia – lots of wood and stone – and there are fantastic mountain views from the deck.

Gran Nevada ARGENTINE **$**
(Av Arrayanes 106; mains AR$90-130; ⏰noon-11:30pm) With its big-screen TV (quite possibly showing a football game) and big, cheap set meals, this is a local favorite. Come hungry, leave happy.

Nicoletto ITALIAN **$$**
(Pascotto 165; mains AR$100-180; ⏰noon-3pm & 8-11:30pm) The best pasta for miles around is to be found at this unassuming family-run joint just off the main street. It's all good – freshly made and with a fine selection of sauces – but the trout *sorrentino* with leek sauce come highly recommended.

La Encantada ARGENTINE **$$**
(☎0294-449-5515; Cerro Belvedere 69, El Cruce; mains AR$120-170; ⏰noon-midnight; 📶) A cute little cottage offering all of your Patagonian and Argentine favorites. The food is carefully prepared and beautifully presented, and the atmosphere is warm and inviting. The pizza is some of the best in town and there's a good selection of local beers and wines.

Information

ATMs are readily available.

Post office (Las Fuschias 121; ⏰8am-6pm Mon-Fri, 9am-1pm Sat) In a shopping gallery behind the bus terminal

Tourist office (☎0294-449-4124; Av Arrayanes 9; ⏰8am-9pm)

Getting There & Around

From the bus terminal, buses depart for Bariloche (AR$60, 1¼ hours) and San Martín de los Andes (AR$121, 2½ hours, sit on left). If heading into Chile, reserve ahead for buses passing through. Buses to La Villa (where the boat docks and park entrance are located) leave every two hours. There are several bike-rental places in town.

Bariloche

☎0294 / POP 109,300

The Argentine Lake District's largest city, San Carlos de Bariloche attracts scores of travelers in both summer and winter. It's finely located on the shores of beautiful Lago Nahuel Huapi, and lofty mountain peaks are visible from all around. While Bariloche's center bustles with tourists shopping at myriad chocolate shops, souvenir stores and trendy boutiques, the real attractions lie outside the city. Parque Nacional Nahuel Huapi offers spectacular hiking, and there's also great camping, trekking, rafting, fishing and skiing in the area. Despite the heavy touristy feel, Bariloche is a good place to stop, hang out, get errands done and, of course, have some fun.

Bariloche

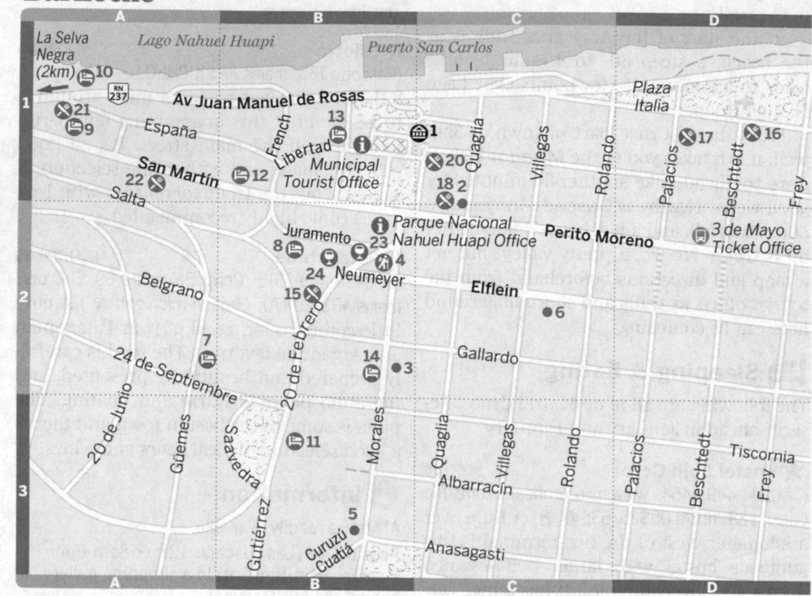

Sights & Activities

The heart of town is the Centro Cívico, a group of well-kept public buildings built of log and stone (architect Ezequiel Bustillo originally adapted Middle European styles into this form of architecture, now associated with the Lake District area). The **Museo de la Patagonia** (☎0294-442-2309; Centro Cívico; entry by donation; ⊙10am-12:30pm & 2-5pm Tue-Fri, 10am-5pm Sat), located here, offers a history of the area, along with good displays of stuffed critters and archaeological artifacts.

Rafting trips on the Río Limay (easy class II) or Río Manso (class III to IV) are very popular. **Extremo Sur** (☎0294-442-7301; www.extremosur.com; Morales 765; ⊙9am-6pm) and **Aguas Blancas** (☎0294-443-2799; www.aguasblancas.com.ar; Morales 564; ⊙9am-1pm & 3-7pm) have good tours.

For kayaking, **Pura Vida Patagonia** (☎0294-15-441-4053; www.puravidapatagonia.com.ar) gets consistently good reviews. Other activities include hiking, rock climbing, biking, paragliding, horse riding, fishing and skiing.

Many agencies and hostels offer tours. One backpacker-oriented agency is **Adventure Center** (☎0294-442-8368; www.adventurecenter.com.ar; Perito Moreno 30; ⊙9am-6pm), with several interesting area offerings.

Courses

La Montaña LANGUAGE COURSE
(☎0294-452-4212; www.lamontana.com; Elflein 251, 2nd fl; ⊙9am-4pm Mon-Fri) This is a recommended Spanish school.

Sleeping

Make reservations from late December to February, July and August and during holidays (especially Easter).

Hostel Los Troncos HOSTEL $
(☎0294-443-1188; www.hostellostroncos.com.ar; San Martín 571; dm/d from US$26/63; 📶) A step above most other hostels in town, the Troncos offers modern rooms with private bathrooms and cozy touches such as private reading lamps. There's also a range of supercomfy hangout areas, an industrial-sized kitchen and a cute little courtyard garden.

Hostel 41 Below HOSTEL $
(☎0294-443-6433; www.hostel41below.com; Juramento 94; dm US$16-19, d without bathroom US$50; @📶) An intimate hostel with clean dorms, fine doubles (with good views) and

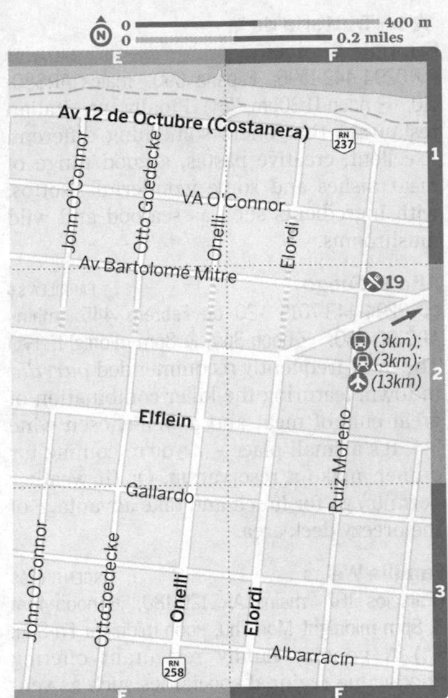

Bariloche

Sights

1 Museo de la Patagonia C1

Activities, Courses & Tours

2 Adventure Center C1
3 Aguas Blancas B2
4 Club Andino Bariloche B2
5 EXtremo Sur B3
6 La Montaña C2

Sleeping

7 Hospedaje Wikter A2
8 Hostel 41 Below B2
9 Hostel Los Troncos A1
10 Hostel Patanuk A1
11 Hostería La Paleta del Pintor B3
12 Hotel Aconcagua B1
13 Hotel Tirol B1
14 Periko's B2

Eating

15 Alto El Fuego B2
16 Covita D1
17 Familia Weiss D1
18 Helados Jauja C1
19 La Fonda del Tio F2
20 La Marca C1
21 La Trattoria de la Famiglia Bianchi A1
22 Rock Chicken A1

Drinking & Nightlife

23 Los Vikingos B2
24 South Bar B2

a mellow vibe. The kitchen and common room are excellent.

Periko's HOSTEL $
(☎0294-452-2326; www.perikos.com; Morales 555; dm US$180, d with/without bathroom US$54/45; @☎) An atmospheric little hostel set up on the hill overlooking town. There's a good variety of rooms on offer, excellent common areas and kitchen and you can get some good-quality info from the on-site travel agency.

Hospedaje Wikter HOTEL $
(☎0294-442-3248; www.hospedajewikter.com.ar; Güemes 566; s/d US$35/60; ☎) Up the hill away from the center, this friendly little *hospedaje* offers spacious rooms in a bright, modern building. Bathrooms are bigger than most in this price range and some rooms have good views.

La Selva Negra CAMPGROUND $
(☎0294-444-1013; www.campingselvanegra.com.ar; Av Bustillo, Km 2.950; campsites per person US$12) Located 3km west of town on the road to Llao Llao, this is the nearest organized camping area. It has good facilities and, in the fall, you can step outside your tent to pick apples.

Hostel Patanuk HOSTEL $
(☎0294-443-4991; www.patanuk.com; Av Juan Manuel de Rosas 585; dm/d AR$90/260; ☎) Bariloche's only lakefront hostel is a definite winner. Big picture windows put you right in front of the water and mountains. Hardwood floors, a spacious kitchen and comfy lounge round out the picture.

Hotel Tirol HOTEL $$
(☎0294-442-6152; www.hosteriatirol.com.ar; Libertad 175; r with city/lake view US$128/148; @☎) Right in the middle of town, this charming little lodge offers comfortable, spacious rooms. Those out the back have spectacular views out over the lake and to the mountain range beyond, as does the bright sitting/breakfast area.

Hostería La Paleta del Pintor HOTEL $$
(☎0294-442-2220; www.lapaletadelpintor.com.ar; 20 de Febrero 630; s/d US$73/90; ☎) Everything about this place screams 'cute,'

but the rooms are big and airy, with small but spotless bathrooms and big-screen TVs.

Hotel Aconcagua HOTEL $$
(0294-442-4718; www.hotelaconcaguabariloche.com; San Martín 289; s/d US$67/79;) You can't beat the central location here, right on the main drag, and the lake/mountain views out the back windows are pretty stunning as well. The rooms themselves are aging a bit, but the whole place is neat as a pin and very well run.

Eating

Regional specialties include *jabalí* (wild boar), *ciervo* (venison), and *trucha* (trout). Most bars serve food too.

Covita VEGETARIAN $
(0294-442-1708; VA O'Connor 511; mains AR$30-60; noon-3pm Mon-Sat, 8-11pm Fri & Sat;) Wonderfully healthy cafe that caters to macrobiotic, vegan and even raw-food diets. Choose from salads, stir-fries, curries and sushi, among others. Fresh organic juices too.

La Fonda del Tio ARGENTINE $
(Av Bartolomé Mitre 1130; mains AR$60-120; noon-3:30 & 8pm-midnight) No tourist nonsense here – just big servings of straight-up Argentine classics. It's a short menu which changes daily, so it's always worth popping in to see what's on offer.

La Marca INTERNATIONAL $
(Urquiza 240; mains AR$100-160; noon-midnight;) Upscale *parrilla* with reasonable (for Bariloche) prices. Choose from the impressive range of *brochettes* – beef, chicken, venison, lamb and salmon. On a sunny day, grab a garden table at the side.

Helados Jauja ICE CREAM $
(Perito Moreno 48; ice cream from AR$35; 9am-11:30pm) Ask anyone in town who serves the best ice cream in Bariloche and they'll reply with one word: 'Jauja.' Many say it's the best in the country.

Rock Chicken FAST FOOD $
(San Martín 234; mains AR$75-120; 10am-late) Late-night munchies? Midday junk-food cravings? The beef, burgers and fried chicken here won't be winning any culinary awards, but they get the job done.

★ **La Trattoria de la Famiglia Bianchi** ITALIAN $$
(0294-442-1596; España 590; mains AR$80-110; noon-11:30pm;) Finally, an Italian restaurant that offers something different. Excellent, creative pastas, a good range of meat dishes and some wonderful risottos, with ingredients such as seafood and wild mushrooms.

Alto El Fuego PARRILLA $$
(0294-443-7015; 20 de Febrero 445; mains AR$130-250; noon-3pm & 8pm-midnight;) The most frequently recommended *parrilla* in town, featuring the killer combination of great cuts of meat and a well-chosen wine list. It's a small place – if you're coming for dinner, make a reservation. Or (if weather permits) go for lunch and take advantage of the breezy deck area.

Familia Weiss ARGENTINE $$
(Palacios 167; mains AR$120-180; noon-4pm & 8pm-midnight Mon-Thu, noon-midnight Fri-Sun;) A popular family restaurant offering good-value regional specialties such as venison, trout and goulash. The picture menu is handy for the Spanish-challenged, there's a good atmosphere and nightly live music.

Drinking

There are four small but popular bars on Juramento, just off San Martín. Most bars serve some food too.

Los Vikingos BAR
(cnr Juramento & 20 de Febrero; 7pm-3am Mon-Sat) A laid-back little corner bar serving a good range of local microbrewery beers at excellent prices. The music's cool and the decor eclectic. DJs play on weekends.

South Bar BAR
(Juramento s/n; 8pm-4am) Mellow local pub where you can actually have a conversation while you drink your beer. Darts, too.

Information

Internet cafes and ATMs are common.

Club Andino Bariloche (0294-442-2266; www.clubandino.org; 20 de Febrero 30; 9am-1:30pm & 3-7pm) Provides loads of information (including on camping), and issues obligatory permits for trekking in Parque Nacional Nahuel Huapi. It also sells trekking maps, all of which include mountain-bike trails. Gives information on hikers' refuges in the park.

Municipal tourist office (☎0294-442-3022; Centro Cívico; ⊙8am-9pm) It has many giveaways, including useful maps and the blatantly commercial but still useful *Guía Busch*, updated biannually and loaded with basic tourist information about Bariloche and the Lake District.

Parque Nacional Nahuel Huapi office (☎0294-442-3111; San Martín 24; ⊙8am-4pm Mon-Fri, 9am-3pm Sat & Sun) Office for the nearby national park.

Getting There & Around

AIR

The airport is 15km east of town; take bus 72 (AR$15) from the town center or a taxi (AR$140).

Aerolíneas Argentinas (☎0294-443-3304; Av Bartolomé Mitre 185; ⊙9am-7pm Mon-Fri, to 1pm Sat), **LAN** (☎0810-999-9526; www.lan.com; Av Bartolomé Mitre 534; ⊙9am-2pm & 3-6pm Mon-Sat) and **LADE** (☎0294-442-3562; www.lade.com.ar; John O'Connor 214; ⊙9am-3pm Mon-Sat) provide services.

BICYCLE

Bikeway (☎0294-461-7686; www.bikeway.com.ar; Av Bustillo Km 12.5) rents bicycles and does area bike excursions.

BUS

The bus terminal is 2.5km east of the center. To bus to the center, you'll need to buy an AR$9 ticket at the 3 de Mayo bus counter, then go outside and wait at the bus-stop shelter (it's nearby, toward the train station). If you arrive outside the 9am to 7pm hours, however, you'll have to taxi (AR$50) as the bus counter will be closed.

Some long-distance bus companies have a ticket office downtown, so you might be able to buy an advance bus ticket without going to the bus terminal.

Chaltén Travel (☎0294-442-3809; www.chaltentravel.com; Quaglia 262) has a two-night transport package to El Calafate.

Buses from Bariloche

DESTINATION	COST (AR$)	DURATION (HR)
Buenos Aires	1784	20-21
El Bolsón	123	2¼
Osorno, Chile	350	5
Puerto Montt, Chile	375	6
San Martín de los Andes	177	4
Villa La Angostura	60	1¼

BARILOCHE'S LOCAL BUSES

Bariloche's local buses work with magnetic cards that can be purchased at the **3 de Mayo ticket office** (☎0294-442-5648; Perito Moreno 480), downtown or at the bus terminal. You can also pick up handy *horarios* (schedules) for all destinations from these offices. Cards cost AR$20 (recharged with however much credit you want). For most routes a ride will cost AR$9, with AR$15 being the highest fare. Some hostels loan cards to guests on payment of a deposit.

CAR

There are plenty of car-rental agencies in town; try **Andes** (☎0294-443-1648; www.andesrentacar.com.ar; San Martín 162; ⊙9am-6pm). Car-rental rates are around AR$550 (with 200km) per day.

TRAIN

The **train station** (☎02944-423172) is next to the bus terminal. The **Tren Patagonico** (☎02944-423172; www.trenpatagonico-sa.com.ar) may be doing its 16-hour run to Viedma, but then again it may not. Check with the tourist office or on the website.

Parque Nacional Nahuel Huapi

Lago Nahuel Huapi, a glacial relic over 100km long, is the centerpiece of this gorgeous national park. To the west, 3554m Monte Tronador marks the Andean crest and Chilean border. Humid Valdivian forest covers its lower slopes, while summer wildflowers blanket alpine meadows.

The 60km **Circuito Chico** loop is a popular excursion. Every 20 minutes, bus 20 (from San Martín and Morales in Bariloche) heads along Lago Nahuel Huapi to end at Puerto Pañuelos, where boat trips leave a few times daily for beautiful **Puerto Blest**, touristy **Isla Victoria** and pretty **Península Quetrihué**. Bus 10 goes the other way, inland via **Colonia Suiza** (a small, woodsy Swiss community), and ends at Bahía López, where you can hike a short way to the tip of the peninsula Brazo de la Tristeza. In summer bus 11 does the whole Circuito, connecting Puerto Pañuelos with Bahía López, but in winter you can walk the 8km stretch along the sleepy highway, with much of that being on a woodsy nature trail. There's a beautiful two-hour side hike to Villa Tacul, on the shores of Lago Nahuel Huapi. It's best to walk from Bahía López to Puerto Pañuelos rather than the other way around, since many more buses head back to Bariloche from Pañuelos. Be sure to confirm bus schedules in Bariloche's tourist office, as schedules vary from season to season.

Tough cyclists can hop a bus to Km 18.600 and rent a bike at **Bike Cordillera** (☎0294-452-4828; www.cordillerabike.com; per day AR$300; ⏲9am-6pm). This way you'll bike less, avoid busy Av Bustillo and take advantage of the loop's more scenic sections. Be aware this is a hilly, 25km ride, but you can extend it to visit area attractions. Call ahead to reserve a bicycle.

Skiing is a popular winter activity from mid-June to October. **Cerro Catedral** (☎0294-440-9000; www.catedralaltapatagonia.com; ⏲mid-Jun–mid-Oct), some 20km west of town, is one of the biggest ski centers in South America. It boasts dozens of runs, a cable car, gondola and plenty of services (including rentals). The best part, however, is the view: peaks surrounding the lakes are gloriously visible.

Area hikes include climbing up **Cerros Otto**, **Catedral** and **Campanario**; all have chairlifts as well. The six-hour hike up Monte Tronador flanks to Refugio Meiling usually involves an overnight stay as it's a 2½-hour drive to the trailhead (Pampa Linda) from Bariloche. Summiting Tronador requires technical expertise.

If trekking, check with Club Andino (p150) or Parque Nacional Nahuel Huapi office (p151), in Bariloche, for trail conditions; snow can block trails, even in summer.

El Bolsón

☎0294 / POP 17,000

Hippies rejoice: there's a must-see destination for you in Argentina, and it's called El Bolsoń. Within its liberal and artsy borders live alternate-lifestyle folks who've made their town a 'nonnuclear zone' and 'ecological municipality.' Located about 120km south of Bariloche, nondescript El Bolsón is surrounded by dramatically jagged mountain peaks. Its economic prosperity comes from a warm microclimate and fertile soil, both of which support a cadre of organic farms devoted to hops, cheese, soft fruits such as raspberries, and orchards. This, and El Bolsón's true personality, can be seen at its famous **feria artesanal** (craft market), where creative crafts and healthy food are sold; catch it during the day on Plaza Pagano on Tuesdays, Thursdays and weekends (best on Saturdays).

For summer activities like rafting on Río Azul, paragliding and horse riding, contact **Grado 42** (☎0294-449-3124; www.grado42.com; Av Belgrano 406; ⏲8:30am-8:30pm Mon-Sat, 10:30am-1pm & 5-7pm Sun).

Sleeping

Surrounding mountains offer plenty of camping opportunities, plus *refugios* (shelters; bunks AR$50 to AR$60).

★La Casona de Odile Hostel HOSTEL $
(☎0294-449-2753; www.odile.com.ar; dm/d US$18/55; @📶) 🍃 Five kilometers north of the center is one of the best hostels in the country. Set on two hectares of park-like riverside land, this is one of those places you come for a couple of days and find yourself there two weeks later.

La Casa del Arbol HOSTEL $
(☎0294-472-0176; www.hostelelbolson.com; Perito Moreno 3038; dm from US$16, d with/without bathroom from US$47/40; @📶) A great little hostel, with a couple of good private rooms, spacious dorms, and excellent kitchen, living and outdoor areas.

Hostería Luz de Luna HOTEL $
(☎0294-449-1908; www.luzdeluna.guiapatagonia.net; Dorrego 150; s/d US$55/75; 📶) Although spacious, the rooms here manage to retain a pleasant, homelike feel. Individual decoration and spotless bathrooms add to the appeal. Go for one upstairs for better light and views.

Camping Refugio Patagónico CAMPGROUND $
(☎0294-448-3888; www.refugiopatagonico.com.ar; Islas Malvinas s/n; campsites per person US$7, dm/d US$14/100; 📶) Not bad as far as campgrounds go – basically a bare field, but a pleasant stream burbles alongside it. Services are good, including *asados* and a modern toilet block. If you're looking for a room, there are much better deals elsewhere.

La Posada de Hamelin GUESTHOUSE $$
(☎0294-449-2030; www.posadadehamelin.com.ar; Granollers 2179; s/d US$70/90; 📶) A beautiful little rustic getaway. There are only four rooms, but they're all gorgeous, with

exposed beams and rough-hewn walls. The sunny upstairs dining area is a great place to munch on an empanada.

Hostería La Escampada HOTEL $$
(☎0294-448-3905; www.laescampada.com.ar; Azcuénaga 561; s/d US$60/100; 📶) A refreshing break from El Bolsón's stale accommodations scene, the Escampada is all modern design with light, airy rooms and a relaxed atmosphere.

Hostería San Jorge HOSTEL $$
(☎0294-449-1313; www.sanjorgepatagonico.com; Perito Moreno & Azcuénaga; s/d US$65/90; 📶) Big, spotless rooms set around a cute little garden in a great central location. The breakfast buffet featuring home-made yummies adds to the appeal.

Eating & Drinking

Food at the **feria artesanal** (Plaza Pagano; ⏲10am-4pm Tue, Thu, Sat & Sun) is tasty, healthy and good value.

La Salteñita FAST FOOD $
(Av Belgrano 515; empanadas AR$10; ⏲10am-9pm) For spicy northern empanadas, try this cheap rotisserie.

Jauja ICE CREAM $
(Av San Martin 2867; cones from AR$35; ⏲8am-11pm; 📶) The most dependable *confiteria* (cafe offering light meals) in town serves up all your faves with some El Bolsón touches (such as homemade bread and strawberry juice) thrown in. The daily specials are always worth checking out – the risotto with lamb and wild mushrooms is divine. The attached ice-creamery is legendary – make sure you leave room for a kilo or two.

★**La Gorda** INTERNATIONAL $$
(☎0294-472-0559; 25 de Mayo 2709; mains AR$130-190; ⏲7-11:30pm Tue-Sun; ✍) This is El Bolsón's don't-miss eating spot. It offers huge portions of delicious, well-prepared food in relaxed, stylish surrounds. There are good vegetarian options, a couple of Asian dishes, fine cuts of meat and some interesting sides. If it's a warm night, try for a garden table. Bookings highly recommended either way.

Otto Tipp ARGENTINE $$
(☎0294-449-3700; cnr Roca & Islas Malvinas; mains AR$120-200; ⏲noon-1am Dec-Feb, from 8pm Wed-Sat Mar-Jan; 📶) After a hard day of doing anything (or nothing) there are few better ways to unwind than by working your way through Mr Tipp's selection of microbrews. Guests are invited to a free sampling of the six varieties and there's a good selection of regional specialties, such as smoked trout and Patagonian lamb cooked in black beer.

Information

The competent **tourist office** (☎0294-449-2604; www.elbolson.gov.ar) is next to Plaza Pagano, and it has good info on area hikes and bus schedules. There are no exchange houses and just two ATMs (where lines can get long). The post office is opposite the tourist office.

Getting There & Around

There's no central bus terminal; several bus companies are spread around town, with Via Bariloche having the most departures to and from Bariloche. See the tourist office for schedules. Destinations include Bariloche (AR$115, 2½ hours), Esquel (AR$170, 2½ hours) and Buenos Aires (from AR$2042, 23 hours).

Rent bikes at **El Tabano** (☎0294-449-3093; Perito Moreno 2871; ⏲9am-6pm Mon-Sat).

Around El Bolsón

The spectacular granite ridge of 2260m **Cerro Piltriquitrón** looms to the east like the back of some prehistoric beast. From the 1100m level (*'plataforma'*), reached by *remise*, a further 40-minute hike leads to **Bosque Tallado** (admission AR$20, charged Jan, Feb & Easter), a shady grove of about 50 figures carved from logs. Another 20-minute walk uphill is **Refugio Piltriquitrón** (dm US$8, camping free), where you can have a drink or even sack down (bring your sleeping bag). From here it's 2½ hours to the summit. The weather is very changeable, so bring layers.

On a ridge 7km west of town is **Cabeza del Indio** (admission AR$4), a rock outcrop resembling a man's profile; the trail has great views of the Río Azul and Lago Puelo. There are also a couple of **waterfalls** (admission each AR$4) about 10km north of town. These are all most accessible by bus in January and February.

A good three-hour hike reaches the narrow canyon of pretty **Cajón del Azul**. At the end is a friendly *refugio* where you can eat or stay for the night. From where the town buses (AR$15) drop you off, it's a 15-minute steep, dusty walk to the Cajón del Azul trailhead.

About 18km south of El Bolsón is windy **Parque Nacional Lago Puelo**. You can camp, swim, fish, hike or take a boat tour to the Chilean border. In summer regular buses run from El Bolsón.

Esquel

02945 / POP 32,400

If you tire of the gnome-in-the-chocolate-shop ambience of Bariloche and other cutesy Lakes District destinations, regular old Esquel will feel like a breath of fresh air. Set in western Chubut's dramatic, hikeable foothills, Esquel is a hub for Parque Nacional Los Alerces and an easygoing, friendly base camp for abundant adventure activities – the perfect place to chill after hard travel on RN 40.

Sights & Activities

Check the tourist office for current train schedules.

La Trochita TRAIN
(02945-451403; fare AR$400) Argentina's famous narrow-gauge steam train averages less than 30km/h on its meandering weekly journey between Esquel and El Maitén – if it runs at speed. In its current incarnation, *La Trochita*, which Paul Theroux facetiously called *The Old Patagonian Express*, provides both a tourist attraction and a service for local citizens.

EPA ADVENTURE TOUR
(Expediciones Patagonia Aventura; 02945-457015; www.epaexpediciones.com; Av Fontana 484) Offers rafting, canyoning, horse riding and trekking. Those whitewater rafting (half-day AR$1550 with transport) on Río Corcovado (90km away) can overnight at the recommended riverside hostel. Canopy tours, horse riding and trekking use the mountain center, an attractive wooden lodge in Parque Nacional Los Alerces. Guests have access to kayaks, and camping is also available.

Coyote Bikes BICYCLE RENTAL
(02945-455505; www.coyotebikes.com.ar; Rivadavia 887; all-day rental AR$120; 9am-1pm & 3:30-8pm Mon-Fri, 9am-1pm Sat) For mountain-bike rentals and trail details in summer.

Sleeping

★Sol Azul HOSTEL $
(02945-455193; www.hostelsolazul.com.ar; Rivadavia 2869; dm US$15; @) With the good looks of a mountain lodge, this welcoming hostel ups the ante with a sauna and a fully decked-out kitchen with industrial stoves. There are also dinners serving local products. Dorms are in a house at the back, with small but tidy bathrooms. It's a taxi ride to the center, on the northern edge of town. Breakfast is not included.

Planeta Hostel HOSTEL $
(02945-456846; www.planetahostel.com; Av Alvear 1021; dm/d US$25/70;) This old but boldly painted downtown house features friendly service but cramped rooms. Down comforters, a spotless communal kitchen and a TV lounge are a cut above the usual.

Sur Sur HOTEL $$
(www.hotelsursur.com; Av Fontana 282; d/tr US$75/90;) A popular option, this family enterprise delivers warmth and comfort. Small tiled rooms feature TV, fan and hair dryers, and the hallways are decked with regional photos taken by former guests. Breakfast is served buffet-style.

Eating & Drinking

Dimitri Coffeehouse CAFE $
(Rivadavia 805; mains AR$45-80; 9am-8pm Mon-Sat) Overboard adorable, this pastel cafe serves big salads, baked goods and sandwiches on mismatched china. There's both beer and barista drinks in a cheerful, casual atmosphere.

★Don Chiquino ITALIAN $$
(Av Ameghino 1641; mains AR$160; noon-3:30pm & 8pm-midnight) Of course, pasta is no novelty in Argentina, but the owner-magician performing tricks while you wait for your meal is. There's a happy-cluttered ambience, and dishes such as *sorrentinos* with arugula prove satisfying.

Quillen VEGETARIAN $$
(02945-400212; Av Fontana 769; mains AR$90-180; 9am-3pm Tue, 9am-3pm & 8pm-1am Thu-Sat;) Serving organic pizza, pastas, fresh lemonade and artisan beer, Quillen might be more at home in Palermo, Buenos Aires than the Andean foothills, but here it is. The light vegan and vegetarian options are a godsend for those fresh from the Ruta 40.

El Bodegón BAR
(☎15-428117; Rivadavia 905; ⏰11am-3pm & 7pm-late) A comfortable brick restobar with sidewalk tables and big cold beers made for splitting. With live performances daily in summer and weekly off-season, ranging from Argentine rock to blues and alt music.

Hotel Argentino BAR
(25 de Mayo 862; ⏰4pm-5am) This lanky and lowbrow Wild West saloon is much better suited to drinking than sleeping, but by all means stop by: the owner is friendly, the 1916 construction is stuffed with relics and sculptures, and the place gets more than a little lively on weekends.

Information

Banks with ATMs are located on Alvear and on 25 de Mayo near Alvear.

Tourist office (☎02945-451927; www.esquel.gov.ar; cnr Av Alvear & Sarmiento; ⏰8am-8pm Mon-Fri, 9am-8pm Sat & Sun) Well organized, helpful and multilingual, with an impressive variety of detailed maps and brochures.

Getting There & Around

The airport is 24km east of town (taxi AR$80). **Aerolíneas Argentinas** (☎02945-453614; Av Fontana 406) flies to Buenos Aires (one way from AR$2890) several times a week.

Esquel's modern bus terminal is eight blocks north of the center, at the corner of Av Alvear and Brun. Destinations include El Bolsón (AR$180, 2½ hours), Bariloche (AR$280, 4½ hours), Puerto Madryn (AR$644, 10 hours) and Comodoro Rivadavia (AR$530, nine hours). Buses go to Trevelin (AR$19, 25 minutes) from the terminal, stopping along Av Alvear on their way south.

WORTH A TRIP

TEATIME IN TREVELIN

Historic Trevelin (treh-veh-lehn), from the Welsh for town (*tre*) and mill (*velin*), is the only community in interior Chubut with a notable Welsh character. Easygoing and postcard pretty, it makes a tranquil day trip for afternoon tea (from 3pm to 8pm). Conquer a platter of pastries at **Nain Maggie** (☎02945-480232; www.nainmaggie.com; Perito Moreno 179; ⏰3:30-8:30pm) or **La Mutisia** (☎02945-480165; Av San Martín 170; ⏰3:30-8:30pm), while keeping your ears pricked for locals speaking Welsh.

Half-hourly buses run from Esquel to Trevelin (AR$19, 30 minutes).

Parque Nacional Los Alerces

Just 33km west of Esquel, this collection of spry creeks, verdant mountains and mirror lakes resonates as unadulterated Andes. The real attraction of the **park** (admission AR$120), however, is the alerce tree (*Fitzroya cupressoides*), one of the longest-living species on the planet, with specimens that have survived up to 4000 years. Lured by the acclaim of well-known parks to the north and south, most hikers miss this gem, which makes your visit here all the more enjoyable.

The receding glaciers of Los Alerces' peaks, which barely reach 2300m, have left nearly pristine lakes and streams with charming vistas and excellent fishing. Westerly storms drop nearly 3000mm of rain annually, but summers are mild and the park's eastern zone is much drier. **Intendencia** (Park Office; ☎02945-471015; ⏰8am-9pm summer, 9am-4pm rest of year) can help you plan excursions.

A popular five-hour boat tour sails from Puerto Chucao (on Lago Menéndez) and heads to **El Alerzal**, an accessible stand of rare alerces (AR$560). A two-hour stopover permits a walk around a loop trail that passes Lago Cisne and an attractive waterfall to end up at **El Abuelo** (Grandfather), a 57m-tall, 2600-year-old alerce.

In the park there are organized **campgrounds** (campsites per person US$13), along with some free sites. Lago Krüger, reached by foot (17km, 12 hours) or taxi boat from near Villa Futalaufquen, has a campground, restaurant and expensive *hosterías*. See Esquel's tourist office for a complete list of accommodations options.

From January to mid-March there are twice-daily buses from Esquel (AR$50, 1¼ hours); outside summer there are four buses per week.

PATAGONIA

Few places in the world inspire the imagination like mystical Patagonia. You can cruise bleak RN 40 (South America's Route 66), watch an active glacier calve house-size icebergs and hike among some of the most fantastic mountain scenery in the world. There are Welsh teahouses, petrified forests,

Patagonia

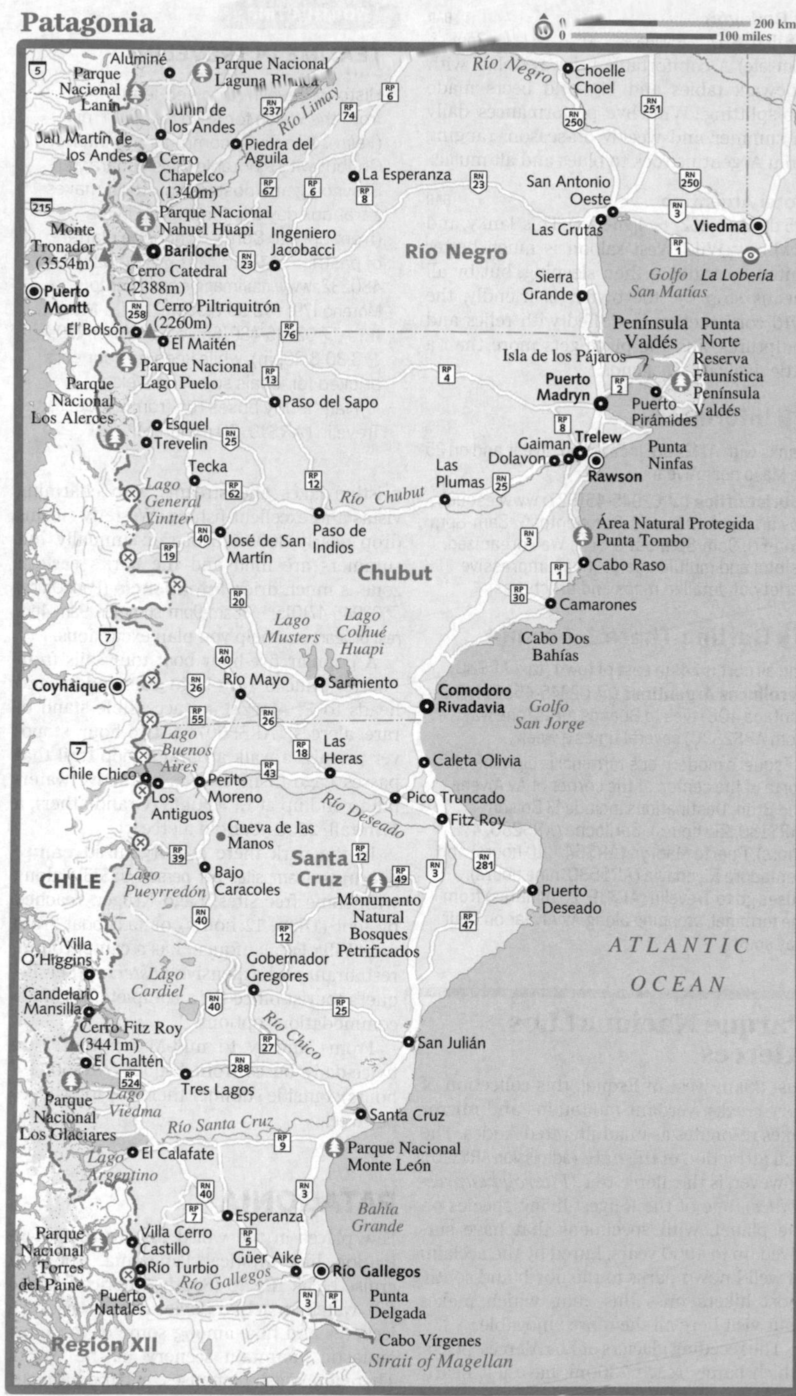

0 200 km
0 100 miles
Aluminé
Parque Nacional Laguna Blanca
Parque Nacional Lanín
Junín de los Andes
San Martín de los Andes
Cerro Chapelco (1340m)
Piedra del Aguila
Río Limay
Río Negro
Choelle Choel
La Esperanza
San Antonio Oeste
Las Grutas
Viedma
La Lobería
Parque Nacional Nahuel Huapi
Monte Tronador (3554m)
Bariloche
Ingeniero Jacobacci
Cerro Catedral (2388m)
Puerto Montt
Cerro Piltriquitrón (2260m)
El Bolsón
El Maitén
Sierra Grande
Golfo San Matías
Península Valdés
Punta Norte
Isla de los Pájaros
Reserva Faunística Península Valdés
Puerto Madryn
Puerto Pirámides
Parque Nacional Lago Puelo
Parque Nacional Los Alerces
Paso del Sapo
Esquel
Trevelin
Gaiman
Trelew
Dolavon
Rawson
Punta Ninfas
Tecka
Las Plumas
Río Chubut
Lago General Vintter
José de San Martín
Paso de Indios
Área Natural Protegida Punta Tombo
Cabo Raso
Chubut
Camarones
Lago Musters
Lago Colhué Huapi
Cabo Dos Bahías
Coyhaique
Río Mayo
Sarmiento
Comodoro Rivadavia
Golfo San Jorge
Lago Buenos Aires
Las Heras
Caleta Olivia
Chile Chico
Perito Moreno
Los Antiguos
Pico Truncado
Río Deseado
Fitz Roy
Cueva de las Manos
Santa Cruz
CHILE
Lago Pueyrredón
Bajo Caracoles
Monumento Natural Bosques Petrificados
Puerto Deseado
ATLANTIC OCEAN
Villa O'Higgins
Lago Cardiel
Gobernador Gregores
Candelario Mansilla
Cerro Fitz Roy (3441m)
El Chaltén
Río Chico
San Julián
Tres Lagos
Lago Viedma
Parque Nacional Los Glaciares
Río Santa Cruz
Santa Cruz
El Calafate
Lago Argentino
Parque Nacional Monte León
Esperanza
Bahía Grande
Parque Nacional Torres del Paine
Villa Cerro Castillo
Río Turbio
Güer Aike
Río Gallegos
Puerto Natales
Punta Delgada
Región XII
Cabo Vírgenes
Strait of Magellan
ARGENTINA

quirky outpost towns, penguin colonies, huge sheep *estancias* and some of the world's largest trout. The sky is wide and the late sunsets nearly spiritual.

Patagonia is thought to be named after the Tehuelche people's moccasins, which made their feet appear huge – in Spanish, *pata* means foot. Geographically, the region is mostly a windy, barren expanse of flat nothingness that offers rich wildlife only on its eastern coast, and rises into the spectacular Andes way into its western edge. It's attracted an interesting range of famous personalities, however, from Charles Darwin to Bruce Chatwin to Butch Cassidy and the Sundance Kid. Despite the big names, however, Patagonia maintains one of the lowest population densities in the world.

Puerto Madryn

☎0280 / POP 73,600

The gateway to Península Valdés bustles with tourism and industry. It retains a few small-town touches: the radio announces lost dogs, and locals are welcoming and unhurried. With summer temperatures matching those of Buenos Aires, Madryn holds its own as a modest beach destination, but from June to mid-December the visiting right whales take center stage.

Sights & Activities

★EcoCentro MUSEUM

(☎0280-445-7470; www.ecocentro.org.ar; J Verne 3784; AR$125; ⊙5-9pm Wed-Mon, cruise-ship days 10am-1pm) Celebrating the area's unique marine ecosystem, this masterpiece brings an artistic sensitivity to extensive scientific research. There are exhibits on the breeding habits of right whales, dolphin sounds and southern elephant-seal harems, a touch-friendly tide pool and more. The building includes a three-story tower and library; the top features glass walls and comfy couches for reading.

Observatorio Punta Flecha WILDLIFE RESERVE

(⊙high tide) FREE Run by Fundación Patagonia Natural, this whale-watching observatory sits 17km north of Puerto Madryn on Playa el Doradillo. It offers tourist information and opens at high tide, when there are more whales and visitors to the beach.

Napra Club WATER SPORTS

(☎0280-445-5633; www.napraclub.com; Blvr Brown 860; ⊙9am-8pm) This rental shack offers bicycles (per day ARG$210), stand-up paddle boards (per hour AR$200) and guided sea kayaking (per two hours AR$250) in sit-on-tops. If need be you can also rent a wet suit. Located next to Bistro de Mar Nautico.

Tours

Countless agencies and nearly all hotels and hostels sell land tours to Península Valdés and Punta Tombo (both AR$350). Take water (and lunch, to save costs), as it's a very long drive to both reserves.

Regina Australe CRUISE

(☎0280-445-6447; www.reginaaustrale.com.ar; Muelle Piedra Buena; adult/4-12yr AR$350/250; ⊙ticket office 10am-1pm & 2-7pm) This 300-passenger ship cruises the Golfo Nuevo to Punta Lobo, departing conveniently from the town pier, where tickets are sold. The three-hour tour leaves at 1pm on Saturday, Sunday, Wednesday and holidays. The ship has three decks, a bar and fast food.

Flamenco Tour TOUR

(☎0280-445-5505; www.flamencotour.com; Belgrano 25) Offerings range from the standard whale-watching and snorkeling trips to stargazing 4WD journeys along the coast (telescopes and bilingual instruction included).

Sleeping

Prices listed are for the high season, approximately October to March. In January it's a good idea to reserve ahead.

★La Tosca HOSTEL $

(☎0280-445-6133; www.latoscahostel.com; Sarmiento 437; dm US$26, d/tr/q US$104/117/130, s/d/tr without bathroom US$65/78/98; @ 📶) A cozy guesthouse where the owners and staff greet you by name. The creation of a well-traveled couple, La Tosca is modern and comfy, with a grassy courtyard, good mattresses, and varied breakfasts with homemade cakes, yogurt and fruit. Double suites and a post-checkout bathroom with showers are wonderful additions. There's also bike rental.

La Casa de Tounens HOSTEL $

(☎0280-447-2681; www.lacasadetounens.com; Passaje 1 de Marzo 432; dm US$18, s/d US$45/55, without bathroom US$40/45; @ 📶) A congenial nook near the bus station, run by a friendly Parisian-Argentine couple. With few rooms, personal attention is assured. There's a cozy stone patio strewn with hammocks, a barbecue grill for guests and homemade bread for breakfast.

Chepatagonia Hostel HOSTEL $
(☎0280-445-5783; www.chepatagoniahostel.com.ar; Storni 16; dm/d US$19/60; @) This stylish and cheerful hostel is owned by a friendly couple who book tours for guests and fire up the grill for barbecues twice a week. Adding to the appeal are comfortable beds and the possibility of glimpsing whales from the hostel balcony. Guests can wash clothes and cook. Bikes are available for rent (AR$150 per day).

El Gualicho HOSTEL $
(☎0280-445-4163; www.elgualicho.com.ar; Marcos A Zar 480; dm/d/tr US$15/55/63; @) This sleek, contempo hostel provides very stylish digs, though mattresses are mysteriously cheap quality. We love its ample common spaces, with billiards and hammocks, but being truly massive (with 120 beds) makes it somewhat impersonal. Doubles have TVs. Bikes are for rent and a massive activity board keeps you posted.

Camping ACA CAMPGROUND $
(☎0280-445-2952; info@acamadryn.com.ar; Camino al Indio; s/d campsites US$9/12; closed May-Aug) These 800 gravel campsites are sheltered by trees to break the incessant wind. Although there are no cooking facilities, some snacks (and sometimes prepared meals) are available. From downtown, city bus 2 goes within 500m of the campground; get off at the last stop (La Universidad).

★ El Patio B&B B&B $$
(☎15-440-8887, 0280-447-5224; www.elpatiohostalpatagonia.com; Mitre 46; d with/without bathroom US$90/75; @) Guests get a warm welcome at this rustic B&B located in an old-fashioned building with quotes from songs adorning the walls. There are seven whitewashed rooms around a pleasant sunny courtyard. Breakfast includes wholewheat bread, yogurt, fruit and cereal. The owner Carla has also worked as a naturalist guide and has helpful tips.

Eating & Drinking

La Taska CAFE $
(☎15-499-4870, 0280-445-7200; 9 de Julio 461; mains AR$80-150; noon-11:45pm) Locals laud the abundant portions and affordable prices at this small neighborhood eatery run by an effervescent chef.

Puerto Madryn

0 — 200 m
0 — 0.1 miles

Puerto Madryn

Activities, Courses & Tours
1 Flamenco Tour B2
Napra Club .... (see 8)
2 Regina Australe B1

Sleeping
3 Chepatagonia Hostel B3
4 El Gualicho A3
5 El Patio B&B A3
6 La Casa de Tounens A2
7 La Tosca A3

Eating
8 Bistro de Mar Nautico B4
9 La Taska A2
10 Lupita A3
11 Olinda B2

Drinking & Nightlife
12 Margarita Bar B2

Lupita MEXICAN $

(☎15-472-2454; Av Gales 195; mains AR$80-120; 8pm-1am) This tiny, colorful eatery serves up nachos and fajitas to travelers yearning for something spicy. While it's not straight out of Guadalajara, a valiant effort is made with homemade whole-wheat tortillas and house salsas.

Olinda ARGENTINE $$

(☎0280-447-0304; Av Roca 385; mains AR$70-235; noon-4pm & 7:30pm-1am) With deck seating and a cool candlelit atmosphere, this contemporary cafe serves a range of tasty blackboard specials that go down easy with pitchers of lemonade or gin and tonic. Dishes like Patagonian lamb, local shrimp grilled with sea salt and homemade bread come fresh. Set menus are a good deal and the elaborate desserts easily serve two.

Bistro de Mar Nautico SEAFOOD $$

(☎0280-447-4289; Blvr Brown 860; mains AR$75-280; 8am-midnight) With unbeatable beachfront atmosphere and bustling old-school waiters, this busy cafe does the job. Seafood lovers can get grilled fish or crisp calamari. There are also burgers, pizzas and even breakfast with gorgeous water views that few Madryn restaurants can boast. After 8pm there's a limited menu.

Margarita Bar PUB

(Roque Sáenz Peña; 11am-4am) With a trendy edge, this low-lit brick haunt has a laundry list of cocktails, friendly bar staff and decent food (mains AR$60 to AR$175). On weekends there's dancing after 1:30am.

Information

There's a **tourist office** (☎0280-445-3504; www.madryn.gov.ar/turismo; Av Roca 223; 8am-9pm Dec-Feb, limited hours Apr-Nov) in the center and at the bus terminal. ATMs abound.

Getting There & Around

Madryn has an airport, but most flights arrive 65km south at Trelew (door-to-door shuttle per person AR$50, taxi AR$200; buses between Puerto Madryn and Trelew can stop at the airport). **Aerolíneas Argentinas** (☎0280-445-1998; Av Roca 427), **LADE** (☎0280-445-1256; Av Roca 119) and **Andes** (☎0280-445-2355; www.andesonline.com; Belgrano 41) have services. The departure tax is AR$32.

From the **bus terminal** (www.terminalmadryn.com; cnr Ciudad de Nefyn & Dr Ávila), destinations include Puerto Pirámides (AR$75, 1½ hours), Trelew (AR$47, one hour), Comodoro Rivadavia (AR$438, six hours), Río Gallegos (AR$1312, 18 hours), Esquel (AR$650, 10 hours), Bariloche (AR$814, 15 hours) and Buenos Aires (from AR$1350, 18 hours).

Rental cars are available through **Hi Patagonia Rent-a-Car** (☎0280-445-0155; www.hipatagonia.com; Rawson 419); rates run about AR$1350 per day with 200km.

Reserva Faunística Península Valdés

☎0280

Home to sea lions, elephant seals, guanacos, rheas, Magellanic penguins and numerous seabirds, Unesco World Heritage Site **Reserva Faunística Península Valdés** (admission adult/5-12yr AR$260/130; 8am-8pm) is one of South America's finest wildlife reserves. More than 80,000 visitors per year visit this sanctuary with a total area of 3600 sq km and more than 400km of coastline. The wildlife-viewing is truly exceptional, though the undisputed main attraction is the endangered *ballena franca austral* (southern right whale). The warmer, more enclosed waters along the gulf become prime breeding zones for right whales between June and mid-December.

As you enter the reserve you'll pass the thin 5km neck of the peninsula. Squint northwards for a glimpse of **Isla de los Pájaros**. This small island inspired Antoine de Saint-Exupéry's description of a hat, or 'boa swallowing an elephant,' in his book *The Little Prince*. From 1929 to 1931, Saint-Exupéry flew the mail here. Watch for salt flats **Salina Grande** and **Salina Chico** (42m below sea level) – South America's lowest spots.

Caleta Valdés is a bay sheltered by a long gravel spit and favored by elephant seals. Just north of here lives a substantial colony of burrowing Magellanic penguins. At **Punta Norte** a mixed group of sea lions and elephant seals snoozes, with the occasional orca pod patrolling.

The hub is **Puerto Pirámides**, a sandy, shrubby, one-street kinda town that's home to 500 souls. You can stay here to be closer to wildlife attractions. Services are minimal: there's only one ATM (that may not work) and no car rentals. Scuba diving, horse riding and mountain-biking tours are available. Boat tours outside whale-watching season aren't really worth it unless you adore shorebirds and sea lions, though there's a chance of seeing dolphins. For information visit the **Tourist Office** (☎0280-449-5048; www.puertopiramides.gov.ar; 1era Bajada; 8am-8pm).

Sleeping & Eating

Hostel Bahía Ballenas HOSTEL $
(☎15-456-7104; www.bahiaballenas.com.ar; Av de las Ballenas s/n; dm US$20; ❄@📶) A welcoming brick hostel with two enormous dorms; the 'Backpackers' sign will catch your eye. Guests get discounts on area tours. Rates include kitchen use; breakfast is extra (AR$40).

Camping Municipal CAMPGROUND $
(☎15-420-2760; per person US$12) Convenient, sheltered gravel campsites with clean toilets, a store and hot pay showers, down the road behind the gas station. Come early in summer to stake your spot. Avoid camping on the beach: high tide is very high.

La Casa de la Tía Alicia GUESTHOUSE $$
(☎0280-449-5046; Av de las Ballenas s/n; d US$83; 📶) A cozy spot for couples, this petal-pink house has just three cabin-style rooms in bright crayon-box colors around a cute garden area. There's in-room tea service, and the management has a conscientious approach to recycling water and composting.

★**Guanaco** PUB FOOD $$
(☎0280-449-5046; Av de las Ballenas s/n; mains AR$142-180; ⏲7-11:30pm Mon, Tue, Thu & Fri, noon-3:30pm & 7-11:30pm Sat & Sun) Art installations on a covered porch announce this funky *cervecería* serving Hernan's artisan brews and other regional brews. Dishes like lamb ravioli, fish with butter and herbs and huge salads are satisfying. Service might be slow; it's a small operation. A sure sign things are going well is that it has been known to close for lack of inventory.

Getting There & Away

Buses from Puerto Madryn leave for Puerto Pirámides two to three times daily in summer (AR$75, 1½ hours). Schedules are less frequent on weekends and in the off season.

Trelew

☎0280 / POP 98,600

Though steeped in Welsh heritage, Trelew isn't a postcard city. In fact, this uneventful midsized hub may be convenient to many attractions, but it's home to few. The region's commercial center, it's a good base for visiting the Welsh villages of Gaiman and Dolavon. Also worthwhile is the top-notch dinosaur museum.

Late October's **Eisteddfod de Chubut** celebrates Welsh traditions.

Sights

★**Museo Paleontológico Egidio Feruglio** MUSEUM
(☎0280-442-0012; www.mef.org.ar; Av Fontana 140; adult/child AR$95/65; ⏲9am-6pm Mon-Fri, 10am-7pm Sat & Sun) Showcasing the most important fossil finds in Patagonia, this natural-history museum offers outstanding life-sized dinosaur exhibits and more than 1700 fossil remains of plant and marine life. Nature sounds and a video accent the informative plaques, and tours are available in a number of languages. The collection includes local dinosaurs, such as the tehuelchesaurus, patagosaurus and titanosaurus.

Tours

Nievemar TOUR
(☎0280-443-4114; www.nievemartours.com.ar; Italia 20) Offers trips to Punta Tombo and conventional tours.

Sleeping

Hostel El Agora HOSTEL $
(☎0280-442-6899; www.hostelagora.com.ar; Edwin Roberts 33; dm US$19; ❄@📶) A backpacker haven, this cute brick house is sparkling and shipshape. Features include a tiny patio, book exchange and laundry. It also does guided bicycle tours. It's two blocks from Plaza Centenario and four blocks from the bus terminal.

★**La Casa de Paula** B&B $$
(☎15-435-2240; www.casadepaula.com.ar; Marconi 573; s/d/tr/q US$100/120/130/140; ❄📶) A haven after a day of sun and wind, artist Paula's house beckons with huge king beds covered in down duvets and woven throws. An eclectic and warm decor fills this modern home, with jazz on the radio and cozy living areas stacked with fashion mags. There's also a lush garden and an outstanding breakfast with homemade jam.

The new suites with balcony or patio are ideal for families.

Eating & Drinking

Sugar MODERN ARGENTINE $$
(25 de Mayo 247; mains AR$90-190; ⏲7am-1am; 🖉) Facing Plaza Independencia, this modern restaurant spices up a basic menu of classic Argentine fare with options like quinoa *milanesas*, stir-fried beef, grilled vegetables and herbed fish. There are salads

and fresh juice on offer too. While it isn't gourmet, it's still a welcome change from Argentine same-old, same-old.

★ **Touring Club** CAFE
(Av Fontana 240; ⏲6:30am-2am) This historic *confitería* (snacks AR$60) exudes old lore, from the Butch Cassidy 'Wanted' poster to the embossed tile ceiling and antique bar back. Even the tuxedoed waitstaff appear to be plucked from another era. Service is weak and the sandwiches are only so-so, but the ambience is one of a kind.

Information

There's a helpful **tourist office** (☎0280-442-0139; www.trelewtourismo.wordpress.com; cnr San Martín & Mitre; ⏲8am-8pm Mon-Fri, 9am-9pm Sat & Sun) on the plaza, where many banks with ATMs can be found, along with the **post office** (cnr 25 de Mayo & Mitre).

Getting There & Around

The airport is 6km north of town (take Puerto Madryn bus and walk 300m; taxi AR$30). **Aerolíneas Argentinas** (☎0280-442-0222; Rivadavia 548) flies to Buenos Aires.

Trelew's bus station is six blocks northeast of downtown. Destinations include Puerto Madryn (AR$45, one hour), Gaiman (AR$15, 30 minutes), Comodoro Rivadavia (AR$294, five hours), Bariloche (AR$577, 12 hours) and Buenos Aires (AR$935, 18 hours).

Car-rental stands are at the airport and in town.

Around Trelew

Gaiman

☎0280 / POP 9600

For a taste of Wales in Patagonia, head 17km west of Trelew to Gaiman. The streets are calm and wide and the buildings are nondescript and low; on hot days the local boys swim in the nearby river. The real reason travelers visit Gaiman, however, is to down pastries and cakes at one of several good **Welsh teahouses**. Most open around 2pm and offer unlimited tea and homemade sweets for AR$150 to AR$200.

The small **Museo Histórico Regional Gales** (cnr Sarmiento & 28 de Julio; admission AR$10; ⏲3-8pm daily Dec-Mar, 3-7pm Tue-Sun Apr-Nov) details Welsh colonization with old pioneer photographs and household items.

Gaiman is an easy day trip from Trelew, but if you want to stay, try homey **Dyffryn Gwirdd** (☎0280-449-1777; patagongales@yahoo.com.ar; Av Eugenio Tello 103; s/d US$30/45; 📶), with seven simple but good rooms (breakfast extra). Some teahouses also let rooms.

To get oriented visit the **tourist office** (☎0280-449-1571; www.gaiman.gov.ar; cnr Rivadavia & Belgrano; ⏲9am-8pm Dec-Mar, to 6pm Apr-Nov). Frequent buses go to/from Trelew (AR$15, 30 minutes).

Área Natural Protegida Punta Tombo

Continental South America's largest penguin nesting ground, **Área Natural Protegida Punta Tombo** (admission AR$180; ⏲8am-6pm Sep-Apr) has a colony of more than half a million Magellanic penguins and attracts king and rock cormorants, giant petrels, kelp gulls, flightless steamer ducks and black oystercatchers. Rangers accompany visitors on rookery visits.

Centro Tombo (⏲8am-6pm) is an interpretive visitor center; there's also a *confitería* on site. To visit, arrange a tour in Trelew or Puerto Madryn or rent a car, a good option for groups.

Comodoro Rivadavia

☎0297 / POP 177,000

Tourism in the dusty port of Comodoro – surrounded by dry hills of drilling rigs, oil tanks and wind-energy farms – usually means little more than a bus transfer. What this modern, hardworking city does provide is a gateway to nearby attractions with decent services (cue the Walmart). Hotels are expensive.

Sleeping & Eating

Belgrano Nuevo Hotel HOTEL $
(☎0297-406-9615; Belgrano 738; s/d US$38/50; 📶) Wood-beamed ceilings and arched doorways add flair to this centrally located guesthouse – at least in the entryway. Once inside, the place feels more institutional, with small and often dark rooms. The best options have outside windows, like rooms 18, 19 and 20.

Puerto Mitre PIZZA $
(☎0297-446-1201; Ameghino 620; mains AR$90; ⏲noon-3pm & 8-11pm) The place for pizza and classic Argentine empanadas – staple traveler fare.

Information

Tourist office (☎0297-444-0664; www.comodoroturismo.gob.ar; Av Rivadavia 430; ⊙8am-8pm Mon-Fri, 9am-3pm Sat & Sun) Friendly, well stocked and well organized.

Getting There & Around

The airport is 8km east of the center (bus AR$1.75, taxi AR$63). **Aerolíneas Argentinas** (☎0297-444-0050; Av Rivadavia 156), **Lan Argentina** (☎0297-454-8160; Airport) and **LADE** (☎0297-447-0585; Av Rivadavia 360) operate flights here.

The bus terminal is in the center of town. Destinations include Puerto Madryn (AR$533, six hours), Los Antiguos (AR$410, five hours), Esquel (AR$610, 10 hours), Bariloche (AR$860, 12 hours), Río Gallegos (AR$815, 11 hours) and Buenos Aires (AR$1825, 24 hours).

Los Antiguos

☎02963 / POP 3360

On the windy shores of Lago Buenos Aires, the agricultural oasis of Los Antiguos is home to *chacras* (small independent farms) of cherries, strawberries, apples, apricots and peaches. It makes an attractive crossing to Chile, and getting here via RN 40 can be an adventure in itself.

With rodeos and live music, the **Fiesta de la Cereza** (Cherry Festival) occurs the second weekend in January. **Chelenco Tours** (☎02963-491198; www.chelencotours.tur.ar; Av 11 de Julio Este 584; ⊙10am-1pm & 4:30-9:30pm) leads trips to Cueva de las Manos, with incredible rock art from 7370 BC, and Monte Zeballos, for trekking and mountain biking.

A 20-minute walk east of the center is the cypress-sheltered **Camping Municipal** (☎02963-491265; Av 11 de Julio s/n; campsite tent US$10 plus per person AR$20, dm/cabin US$40/50), which also has cabins. **Hotel Los Antiguos Cerezos** (☎02963-491132; hotel_losantiguoscerezos@hotmail.com; Av 11 de Julio 850; s/d/tr US$50/78/90; 📶) offers sterile rooms, or upgrade to plush **Hotel Mora** (☎15-420-7472; www.hotelmorapatagonia.com; Av Costanera 1064; s/d with lake view US$96/122, s/d/tr without view US$72/102/128; 📶) on the lakeshore. Good cafe fare is served at **Viva El Viento** (☎02963-491109; www.vivaelviento.com; Av 11 de Julio 447; mains AR$40-220; ⊙9am-9pm Oct-Apr; 📶).

The **Tourist Information Office** (☎0297-491261; info@losantiguos.tur.ar; Av 11 de Julio 446; ⊙8am-8pm) has information on activities, including fishing and windsurfing. There's one bank with an ATM.

Buses cross the border to Chile Chico, 12km away, on weekdays at noon (AR$100). From November through March, **Chaltén Travel** (www.chaltentravel.com) goes to El Chaltén and El Calafate on even-numbered days (AR$1290, 12 hours). Other bus destinations include Perito Moreno (AR$43, 45 minutes), Bariloche (AR$1290, 12 hours) and Comodoro Rivadavia (AR$518, seven hours). The tourist office has current bus schedules.

El Chaltén

☎02962 / POP 1630

This colorful village overlooks the stunning northern sector of Parque Nacional Los Glaciares. Every summer thousands of trekkers come to explore the world-class trails under the toothy spires of the **Fitz Roy range**. Climbers from around the world make their bid to summit the premier peak **Cerro Fitz Roy** (3441m), among others. Pack for wind, rain and cold temperatures even in summer, when views of the peaks can be obscured. If the sun is out, however, El Chaltén is an outdoor-lover's paradise.

Note that El Chaltén is within national park boundaries. Rules regarding fires and washing distances from rivers must be followed. The area's river waters are potable without filtration – please help keep them clean. El Chaltén mostly shuts down from April to October.

Activities

Laguna Torre HIKING

Views of the stunning rock needle of Cerro Torre are the highlight here. If you have good weather – ie little wind – and clear skies, make this hike (9km, three hours one way) a priority, since the toothy Cerro Torre is the most difficult local peak to see on normal blustery days.

Laguna de Los Tres HIKING

This hike to a high alpine tarn is a bit more strenuous (10km and four hours one way) than the hike to Laguna Torre. It's also one of the most photogenic spots in the park. Exercise extra caution in foul weather as trails are very steep.

Lago del Desierto & Chile HIKING

Some 37km north of El Chaltén (a one-hour drive on a gravel road), Lago del Desierto sits near the Chilean border. At the lake a 500m trail leads to an overlook with fine lake and glacier views. A lake trail along the eastern side extends to Candelario Mansilla in Chile.

An increasingly popular way to get to Chile is crossing the border here with a one- to three-day trekking/ferry combination to Villa O'Higgins, the last stop on the Carretera Austral. The route is also popular with cyclists, though much of their time is spent shouldering bike and gear through steep sections too narrow for panniers. Plans have started to put a road in here, but it may take decades.

Spa Yaten HEALTH & FITNESS
(☎02962-493394; spayaten@gmail.com; San Martín 36; 1hr massage AR$650; ⊙10am-9pm) Spa Yaten has showers, robes and slippers, so sore hikers can come straight here off the trail. There are various therapies, massage, Jacuzzi tubs in a communal room and dry sauna. Reserve massages ahead.

Tours

Patagonia Aventura ADVENTURE TOUR
(☎02962-493110; www.patagonia-aventura.com; Av San Martín 56) Offers ice trekking (AR$1700, two hours) and ice climbing (AR$3000, all day) on Glaciar Viedma with cruise-ship access. Tours do not include transportation to Puerto Bahía Túnel (AR$170), where excursions depart.

Casa de Guias MOUNTAINEERING
(☎02962-493118; www.casadeguias.com.ar; Lago del Desierto s/n) Friendly and professional, with English-speaking guides certified by the Argentine Association of Mountain Guides (AAGM). It specializes in small groups. Offerings include mountain traverses, ascents for the very fit and rock-climbing classes.

Sleeping

Prices listed are for late December through February, when you should arrive with reservations. Some places include breakfast.

Albergue Patagonia HOSTEL $
(☎02962-493019; www.patagoniahostel.com.ar; Av San Martín 392; dm US$17, s/d/tr US$65/77/88, s/d without bathroom US$40/45; ⊙Sep-May; @📶) A gorgeous and welcoming wooden farmhouse with helpful staff. Dorms in a separate building are spacious and modern, with good service and a humming atmosphere. The B&B features rooms with private bathrooms, kitchen use and a sumptuous buffet breakfast at Fuegia Bistro.

Also rents bikes and offers a unique bike tour to Lago del Desierto with shuttle options.

Lo de Trivi HOSTEL $
(☎02962-493255; www.lodetrivi.com; Av San Martín 675; dm US$22, d with/without bathroom US$84/62; 📶) A good budget option, this converted house has added shipping containers and decks with antique beds as porch seating. It's a bit hodgepodge but works. There are various tidy shared spaces with and without TV; the best is the huge industrial kitchen for guests. Doubles in snug containers can barely fit a bed.

Rancho Grande Hostel HOSTEL $
(☎02962-493092; www.ranchograndehostel.com; Av San Martín 724; dm/d/tr/q US$25/98/120/140; @📶) Serving as Chaltén's Grand Central Station (Chaltén Travel buses stop here), this bustling backpacker factory has something for everyone, from bus reservations to internet (extra) and cafe service. Clean four-bed rooms are stacked with blankets, and bathrooms sport rows of shower stalls. Private rooms have their own bathroom and free breakfast.

Condor de Los Andes HOSTEL $
(☎02962-493101; www.condordelosandes.com; cnr Río de las Vueltas & Halvor Halvorsen; dm/d/tr US$18/66/79; @📶) This homey hostel has the feel of a ski lodge, with worn bunks, warm rooms and a roaring fire. The guest kitchen is immaculate and there are comfortable lounge spaces.

Camping El Relincho CAMPGROUND $
(☎02962-493007; www.elrelinchopatagonia.com.ar; Av San Martín 545; campsite per person/vehicle US$10/5, 4-person cabin US$100) A private campground with wind-whipped and exposed sites.

★ **Nothofagus B&B** B&B $$
(☎02962-493087; www.nothofagusbb.com.ar; cnr Hensen & Riquelme; s/d/tr US$84/92/110, without bathroom US$68/76/95; ⊙Oct-Apr; @📶) 🍃 Attentive and adorable, this chalet-style inn offers a toasty retreat with hearty breakfast options. Practices that earn it the Sello Verde (Green Seal) include separating organic waste and replacing towels only when asked. Wooden-beam rooms have carpet and some views. Those with hallway bathrooms share with one other room.

Posada La Base GUESTHOUSE $
(☎02962-493031; www.elchaltenpatagonia.com.ar; Calle 10, No 16; d/tr US$70/90) A smart, sprawling house with spacious rooms that all face outside and have access to an immaculate kitchen. Large groups should book rooms 5 and 6, which share an inside kitchen with dining area. The reception area has a popular video loft with a multilingual collection. The rates we have indicated don't include the discount for two or more nights.

Eating & Drinking

Packed lunches are available at most hostels and hotels and at some restaurants.

★**La Cervecería** PUB FOOD $$
(☎02962-493109; Av San Martín 320; mains AR$80-160; ⏲noon-midnight) That après-hike pint usually evolves into a night out in this humming pub with simpatico staff and a feisty female beer master. Savor a stein of unfiltered blond pilsner or turbid bock with pasta or *locro*.

Techado Negro CAFE $$
(☎02962-493268; Av Antonio Rojo; mains AR$60-145; ⏲noon-midnight; ✎) With local paintings on the wall, bright colors and a raucous, unkempt atmosphere in keeping with El Chaltén, this homespun cafe serves up abundant, good-value and sometimes healthy Argentine fare. Think homemade empanadas, squash stuffed with humita, brown rice vegetarian dishes, soups and pastas. It also offers box lunches.

Patagonia Rebelde ARGENTINE $$
(☎02962-493208; San Martín 430; mains AR$130-240; ⏲12:30-4pm & 6pm-midnight) With left-leaning murals and a rustic finish, this no-frills eatery serves huge, tasty portions *al disco*, cooked in enormous iron platters. One portion of orange chicken or lamb with mushrooms and bacon could easily serve two famished hikers, veggies and fries included. The fried *provoleta* cheese is nice too. Service is friendly but no one is rushing.

La Vinería WINE BAR
(☎02962-493301; Av Lago del Desierto 265; ⏲4pm-3am) Transplanted from Alaska, this tiny wine bar offers a long Argentine wine list as well as craft-beer options and standout appetizers.

Information

On the left just before the bridge into town, the **Park Ranger Office** (☎02962-493004, 493024; pnlgzonanorte@apn.gov.ar; donations welcome; ⏲9am-8pm Dec-Feb, 10am-5pm Mar-Nov) has maps and hiking information (and videos for rainy days); day buses automatically stop here. The helpful **municipal tourist office** (☎02962-493370; Terminal de Omnibus; ⏲9am-10pm) is at the bus terminal.

Bring extra Argentine pesos, since there are only two ATMs (one in the bus station). Few places take traveler's checks or credit cards and exchange rates are poor.

A decent selection of camping food and supplies is available at the small supermarkets in town. Gear like stoves, fuel, sleeping bags, tents and warm clothes can be bought or rented from several businesses on San Martín (the main drag). Bike rentals and mountain guide services are also available.

Getting There & Away

The following schedules are for December through February; off-season services are less frequent or nonexistent. There are several daily buses to El Calafate (AR$350, 3½ hours). Las Lengas goes a few times daily to Lago del Desierto (AR$250, one hour) and Hostería El Pilar (AR$100, 20 minutes).

Chaltén Travel (☎02962-493092; www.chaltentravel.com; cnr Av MM De Güemes & Lago del Desierto) provides transport to Los Antiguos (AR$1290, 12 hours) and Bariloche (AR$2190, two days, overnight accommodations not included) from mid-November to mid-April on odd-numbered days.

Growing numbers of travelers are making the one- to two-day crossing to Villa O'Higgins, Chile (the end of the Carretera Austral) that's done via a hiking and ferry combination between November and March; see Argentina via the Back Door (p513) for details.

El Calafate

☎02902 / POP 21,300

Named for the berry that, once eaten, guarantees your return to Patagonia, El Calafate hooks you with another irresistible attraction: Glaciar Perito Moreno, 80km away in Parque Nacional Los Glaciares. The glacier is a magnificent must-see, but its massive popularity has encouraged tumorous growth and rapid upscaling in once-quaint El Calafate. However, it's still a fun place to be with a range of traveler services. The strategic location between El Chaltén and Torres del Paine (Chile) makes it an inevitable stop for those in transit.

Sights

★Glaciarium MUSEUM

(☎02902-497912; www.glaciarium.com; adult/child AR$230/100; ⏰9am-8pm Sep-May, 11am-8pm Jun-Aug) Unique and exciting, this gorgeous museum illuminates the world of ice. Displays and bilingual films show how glaciers form, along with documentaries on continental ice expeditions and stark meditations on climate change. Adults suit up in furry capes for the *bar de hielo* (AR$140 including drink), a blue-lit below-zero club serving vodka or fernet and Coke in ice

El Calafate

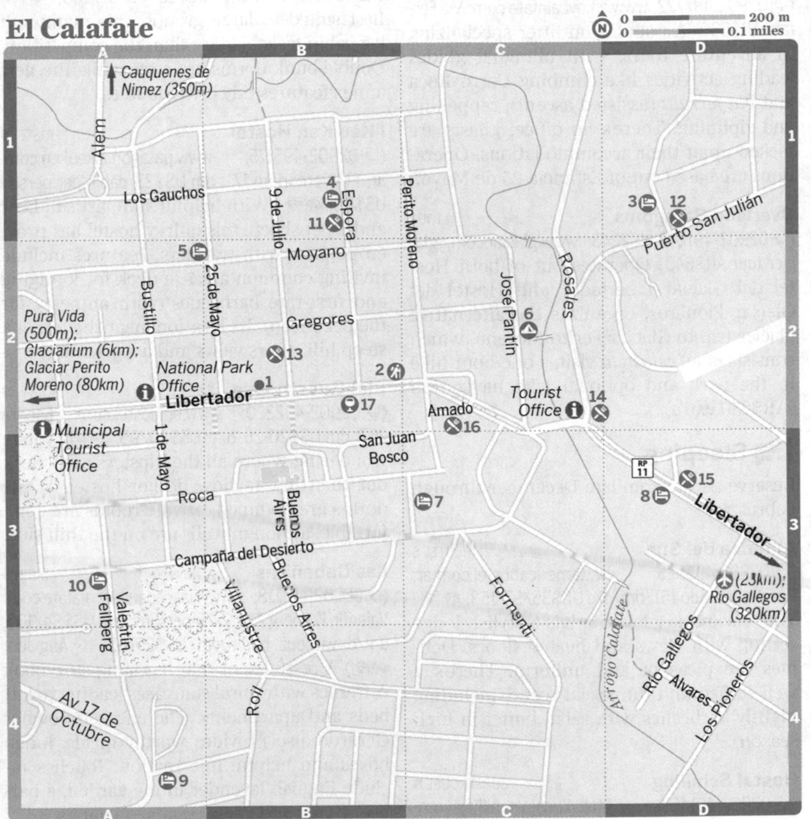

El Calafate

Activities, Courses & Tours

1 Chaltén Travel B2
2 Hielo y Aventura B2

Sleeping

3 America del Sur D1
4 Bla! Guesthouse B1
5 Calafate Hostel A2
6 Camping El Ovejero C2
7 Hostal Schilling C3
8 Hostel del Glaciar Libertador D3
9 I Keu Ken Hostel A4
10 Las Cabañitas A3

Eating

11 Buenos Cruces B1
12 Esquina Varela D1
13 La Fonda del Parillero B2
14 La Tablita C2
15 María Brownies D3
16 Viva la Pepa C2

Drinking & Nightlife

17 Librobar B2

glasses. The Glaciarium is 6km from Calafate toward the national park. To get there, take the free hourly transfer from 1 de Mayo between Av Libertador and Roca. Transfers stop one hour before closing time.

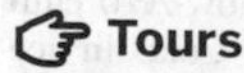

Enjoy! ADVENTURE TOUR

(☎02902-497722; www.enjoycalafate.com; Via Ferrata AR$580) A popular outfitter specializing in adventure tours, with bilingual guides leading activities like climbing Cerro Roca and *via ferrata* (assisted ascent), rappelling and ziplining. There's no office; guests are picked up at their accommodations. Operations are based out of Estancia 25 de Mayo.

Overland Patagonia TOUR

(☎02902-491243, 492243; www.glaciar.com; glacier tour AR$640) Operates out of both Hostel del Glaciar Libertador and Hostel del Glaciar Pioneros; organizes the alternative glacier trip to Glaciar Perito Moreno, which consists of an *estancia* visit, a one-hour hike in the park and optional lake navigation (AR$250 extra).

Sleeping

Reserve ahead from late December through February.

America del Sur HOSTEL $

(☎02902-493525; www.americahostel.com.ar; Puerto Deseado 151; dm/d/q US$35/97/153; @📶) This backpacker favorite has a stylish lodge setting with views and heated floors. Doubles are pleasant and uniform. There's a well-staffed and fun social scene, including nightly barbecues with salad buffet in high season.

Hostal Schilling GUESTHOUSE $

(☎02902-491453; http://hostalschilling.com; Paradelo 141; dm/s/d/tr US$25/63/75/95, d without bathroom US$60; 📶) Good value and centrally located, this friendly guesthouse is a good choice for travelers. Much is due to the family owners, Cecilia, Marcelo and Raimiro, who look after guests with a cup of tea or help with logistical planning. It also has multiple living rooms and cafe service, with hearty lentil stew, if you don't feel like eating out.

Hostel del Glaciar Libertador HOSTEL $

(☎02902-492492; www.glaciar.com; Libertador 587; dm/d/tr/q US$22/92/109/123; @📶) The best deals here are dorm bunks with thick covers. Behind a Victorian facade, modern facilities include a top-floor kitchen, radiant floor heating, computers and a spacious common area with a plasma TV glued to sports channels. Breakfast is extra for dorm users (AR$84).

Calafate Hostel HOSTEL $

(☎02902-492450; www.calafatehostels.com; Moyano 1226; dm/s/d/tr US$20/60/80/100; @📶) Best suited to large groups, this mammoth log cabin feels blander than the competition. Double-bunk dorms are cozy, while the new annex features tidy brick doubles.

I Keu Ken Hostel HOSTEL $

(☎02902-495175; www.patagoniaikeuken.com.ar; FM Pontoriero 171; dm US$23, cabin per person US$80; @📶) With helpful staff, artisan beer and a pet sheep, this quirky hostel has proven popular with travelers. Features include inviting common areas, a deck for lounging and first-rate barbecues (with amnesty for the pet sheep). Its location, near the top of a steep hill, offers views and a workout.

Bla! Guesthouse HOSTEL $

(☎02902-492220; www.blahostel.com; Espora 257; dm US$20-25, d/tr US$80/95; 📶) If you're wondering where all the hipsters are, check out this tiny, mellow design hostel. While dorms are cramped, private rooms are comfortable, although walls are on the thin side.

Las Cabañitas CABIN $

(☎02902-491118; www.lascabanitascalafate.com; Valentín Feilberg 218; 2-/3-person cabin US$84/105, dm/d without bathroom US$25/65; ⊙Aug-Jun; @📶) A restful spot that has snug storybook A-frames with spiral staircases leading to loft beds and apartments. The energetic owner Gerardo also provides worthy meals, lunch boxes and helpful information. Touches include English lavender in the garden, a barbecue area and guest cooking facilities.

Camping El Ovejero CAMPGROUND $

(☎02902-493422; www.campingelovejero.com.ar; José Pantín 64; campsite per person US$9; @📶) Woodsy, well-kept (and slightly noisy) campsites with spotless showers that have 24-hour hot water. Locals boast that the on-site restaurant is one of the best deals in town for grill food. Extras include private tables, electricity and grills. It's located by the creek just north of the bridge into town.

Cauquenes de Nimez B&B $$

(☎02902-492306; www.cauquenesdenimez.com.ar; Calle 303, No 79; d/tr US$98/120; ❄📶) 🍃 Both modern and rustic, Gabriel's welcoming two-story lodge offers views of flamingos on the lake (from November through summer). Smart rooms decorated with corduroy duvets and nature photography also feature lock boxes and TVs. Personalized attention is a plus, as is the complimentary tea time with lavender muffins, and free bikes (donations support the nature reserve).

Eating & Drinking

Some cafes provide box lunches. Bring bags to the supermarkets as plastic bags have been banned in El Calafate.

Viva la Pepa
CAFE $

(☎02902-491880; Amado 833; mains AR$60-120; ⏲noon-9pm Mon-Sat) Decked out in children's drawings, this cheerful cafe specializes in crepes, but also offers great sandwiches with homemade bread (try the chicken with apple and blue cheese), fresh juice and gourds of maté.

María Brownies
DESSERTS $

(☎02902-496817; Libertador 524; snacks AR$60; ⏲3:30-8:30pm Wed-Mon) This adorable teahouse is your go-to spot for homemade brownies, tart lemon pie and scones.

Esquina Varela
ARGENTINE $

(☎02902-490666; Puerto Deseado 22; mains AR$85-110; ⏲7pm-late) Marrying good and cheap, this corrugated-tin eatery is a find in expensive Calafate. Start with some fried calamari and beer. Filling lamb stew, steak and *locro* grace a short menu with vegetarian options. There's also live music.

La Fonda del Parillero
PARRILLA $

(9 de Julio 29; mains AR$45-180; ⏲10am-11pm) Skip the pretension and dine at this busy grill with a few sidewalk tables and takeout, a boon for late-night snacking. In addition to lamb steaks, it also offers homemade pastas, pies and a variety of empanadas.

★Buenos Cruces
ARGENTINE $$

(☎02902-492698; Espora 237; mains AR$130-220; ⏲7-11pm Mon-Sat) The new sensation in town is this tiny family-run enterprise bringing a twist to Argentine classics. Start with a warm beet salad with balsamic reduction. The nut-crusted trout is both enormous and satisfying, served on a bed of risotto, as are baked ravioli crisped at the edge and bubbling with Roquefort cheese. Service is good.

Pura Vida
ARGENTINE $$

(☎02902-493356; Libertador 1876; mains AR$90-185; ⏲7:30-11:30pm Thu-Tue; 🌿) Featuring the rare treat of Argentine home cooking, this offbeat, low-lit eatery is a must. Its longtime owners are found cooking up buttery spiced chicken pot pies and filling wine glasses. For vegetarians, brown rice and wok veggies or various salads are satisfying. Don't skip the decadent chocolate brownie with ice cream, steeped in warm berry sauce. Reserve ahead.

La Tablita
PARRILLA $$

(☎02902-491065; www.la-tablita.com.ar; Rosales 24; mains AR$100-150; ⏲noon-3:30pm & 7pm-midnight) Steak and spit-roasted lamb are the stars at this satisfying *parrilla*, popular beyond measure for good reason. For average appetites a half-steak will do, rounded out with a good malbec, fresh salad or garlic fries.

Librobar
PUB

(Libertador 1015; ⏲10am-3am; 📶) Upstairs in the gnome village, this hip bookstore-bar serves coffee, pricey cocktails and bottled beers. Peruse the oversized photography books on Patagonian wildlife or bring your laptop and take advantage of the free wi-fi.

Information

There are several banks with ATMs in town, though money can run out on busy weekends. If you're planning on visiting El Chaltén, withdraw enough money here.

Municipal tourist office (☎02902-491090, 491466; www.elcalafate.tur.ar; Av Libertador 1411; ⏲8am-8pm) Has town maps and general information. There's also a kiosk at the bus terminal (☎02902-491090; www.elcalafate.gov.ar; cnr Libertador & Rosales; ⏲8am-8pm); both have some English-speaking staff.

National park office (☎02902-491545; Libertador 1302; ⏲8am-8pm Dec-Apr, to 6pm May-Nov) Offers brochures and a decent map of Parque Nacional Los Glaciares. It's best to get information here before reaching the park.

Getting There & Around

Ves Patagonia (☎02902-494355; www.vespatagonia.com) has door-to-door shuttle services for AR$120. **Aerolíneas Argentinas** (☎02902-492816, 492814; Libertador 1361), **LADE** (☎02902-491262; Jean Mermoz 168) and **Lan** (☎02902-495548; 9 de Julio 57) operate flights here. Book your flight into and out of El Calafate well ahead of time.

Calafate's bus terminal is a couple blocks above the main drag. Bus destinations include Río Gallegos (AR$360, four hours), El Chaltén

(AR$350, 3½ hours) and Puerto Natales, Chile (AR$475, five hours).

In summer, **Chaltén Travel** (☎02902-492212; www.chaltentravel.com; Libertador 1174; ⏰9am-9pm) does the two-day trip from El Calafate to Bariloche via adventurous Ruta 40 (AR$2190). For car rentals try **Servi Car** (☎02902-492541; www.servi4x4.com.ar; Libertador 695; ⏰9:30am-noon & 4-8pm Mon-Sat).

Parque Nacional Los Glaciares

Few glaciers can match the suspense and excitement of the blue-hued **Glaciar Perito Moreno**. Its 60m jagged ice peaks shear off and crash with huge splashes and thunderous rifle-cracks, birthing small tidal waves and large bobbing icebergs – all while your neck hairs rise a-tingling. The highlight of **Parque Nacional Los Glaciares** (admission AR$260, collected after 8am), it measures 35km long, 5km wide and 60m high, constantly dropping chunks of ice off its face. While most of the world's glaciers are receding, the Glaciar Perito Moreno is considered 'stable.' And every once in a while, part of its facade advances far enough to reach the Península de Magallanes to dam the Brazo Rico arm of Lago Argentino. This causes tremendous pressure to build up, and after a few years a river cuts through the dam and eventually collapses it – with spectacular results.

The Glaciar Perito Moreno was born to be a tourist attraction. The Península de Magallanes is close enough to the glacier to provide glorious panoramas, but far enough away to be safe. A long series of catwalks and platforms gives everyone a great view. It's worth spending several hours just looking at the glacier (or condors above) and waiting for the next great calving.

Most tours from El Calafate charge AR$450 and up for transport (sit on the left), guide and a few hours at the glacier. If you don't want a tour, negotiate a taxi trip or head to El Calafate's bus station; round-trip transport costs AR$130 and gives you several hours at the glacier. Also consider visiting later in the afternoon, when crowds disperse and more ice falls after the heat of the day.

There are no hiking trails. A cafeteria sells sandwiches and snacks on site, but for best selection bring a lunch. The weather is very changeable and can be windy, so bring layers.

Boat tours to other glaciers are also available; the most adventurous option is to take a tour with **Hielo y Aventura** (☎02902-492205, 02902-492094; www.hieloyaventura.com; Libertador 935, El Calafate) for optional glacier hiking or introductory ice climbing.

Río Gallegos

☎02966 / POP 95,800

Hardly a tourist destination, this coal shipping, oil-refining and wool-raising hub is a busy port with few merits for travelers, though some of the continent's best fly-fishing is nearby. Traveler services are good here, but most visitors zip through en route to El Calafate, Puerto Natales or Ushuaia.

Sleeping

El Viejo Miramar HOTEL $

(☎02966-430401; hotelviejomiramar@yahoo.com.ar; Av Kirchner 1630; d US$58) Snug carpeted rooms and spotless bathrooms make this a good choice. At the time of research it was changing ownership. Rates include breakfast.

Hostel Elcira HOSTEL $

(☎02966-429856; Zuccarino 431; dm/d US$17/40; 📶) An impeccable yet kitschy family home with friendly hosts. It's far from the town center but just a 10-minute walk from the bus terminal.

★**La Lechuza** ARGENTINE $$

(☎02966-425421; Sarmiento 134; mains AR$115-168; ⏰11:30am-4pm & 8pm-midnight) The most ambient eatery in Río Gallegos is this chic pizzeria and restaurant that first found success in El Calafate. The room is low-lit, with walls sheathed in old newspapers and wine crates. There's a long list of pizzas, including spinach, caprese and Patagonian lamb and mushroom. Also offers wines and liquor.

Information

Centro de Informes Turistico (Av San Martín s/n; ⏰9am-8pm Oct-Apr) Useful info kiosk on median strip.

Getting There & Around

The airport is 7km from the center (taxi AR$60). **Aerolíneas Argentinas** (☎0810-2228-6527; Av San Martín 545), **LADE** (☎02966-422316; Fagnano 53) and LAN operate services.

The bus terminal is about 2km from the center, on RN 3 (bus B or C AR$3). Destinations include El Calafate (AR$360, four hours), Ushuaia (AR$628, 12 hours), Comodoro Rivadavia (AR$715, 11 hours), Río Grande (AR$488, eight hours) and Buenos Aires (AR$2680, 36 hours). Buses to Punta Arenas, Chile (AR$300, six hours) run only twice weekly; try buying your ticket in advance.

TIERRA DEL FUEGO

The southernmost extreme of the Americas, this windswept archipelago is as alluring as it is moody – at turns beautiful, ancient and strange. Travelers who first came for the ends-of-the-earth novelty discovered a destination that's far more complex than these bragging rights. Intrigue still remains in a past storied with shipwrecks, native peoples and failed missions. In Tierra del Fuego, nature is writ bold and reckless, from the scoured plains, rusted peat bogs and mossy lenga forests to the snowy ranges above the Beagle Channel. Shared with Chile, this archipelago features one large island, Isla Grande, Chile's Isla Navarino and many smaller uninhabited ones.

In 1520 Magellan paid a visit while seeking passage to the Asian spice islands. Passing ships named Tierra del Fuego for the distant shoreline campfires that they spotted. Native inhabitants were Ona (or Selknam) and Haush, who hunted land animals, and fishing tribes Yámana and Alacalufe. The early 1800s, however, brought on European settlement – and the untimely demise of these indigenous peoples.

Ushuaia

☎02901 / POP 57,000

A busy port and adventure hub, Ushuaia is a sliver of steep streets and jumbled buildings below the snowcapped Martial Range. Here the Andes meet the Southern Ocean in a sharp skid, making way for the city before reaching a sea of lapping currents.

It's a location matched by few, and chest-beating Ushuaia takes full advantage of its end-of-the-world status as an increasing number of Antarctica-bound vessels call in to port. Its endless mercantile hustle knows no irony: the souvenir shop named for Jimmy Button (a native kidnapped for show in England), the ski center named for a destructive invasive species...you get the idea. That said, with a pint of the world's southernmost microbrew in hand, you can happily plot the dazzling outdoor options: hiking, sailing, skiing, kayaking and even scuba diving are just minutes from town.

Sights & Activities

The small but good **Museo del Fin del Mundo** (☎02901-421863; www.museodelfindelmundo.org.ar; cnr Av Maipú & Rivadavia; admission AR$130; ⏰10am-7pm) explains Ushuaia's indigenous and natural histories; check out the bone implements and bird taxidermy room. It has a nearby annex in a historical building at Av Maipú 465. The excellent **Museo Marítimo & Museo del Presidio** (☎02901-437481; www.museomaritimo.com; cnr Yaganes & Gobernador Paz; admission AR$200; ⏰9am-8pm) is located in an old prison that held up to 700 inmates in 380 small jail cells. There are interesting exhibits on expeditions to Antarctica, plus stuffed penguins and an art gallery. Tiny **Museo Yámana** (☎02901-422874; Rivadavia 56; admission AR$75; ⏰10am-7pm) has some history on the area's indigenous people.

After seeing the Glaciar Perito Moreno in El Calafate, the **Glaciar Martial** here will seem like a piddly ice cube – but at least it's located in a beautiful valley with great views of Ushuaia and the Beagle Channel. Walk or shuttle (AR$120) to the base 7km northwest of town; from here it's about two hours' walk up to the glacier. There's a teahouse serving snacks, and **canopy tours** (www.canopyushuaia.com.ar; Refugio de Montaña, Cerro Martial; adult/child incl transfer US$32/28; ⏰10am-5:15pm Oct-Jun).

Hop on a **boat tour** to *estancias,* a lighthouse, Puerto Williams, bird island and sea-lion or penguin colonies. Ask about the size of the boat and its covered shelter area, whether there are bilingual guides and if there are any landings (only Pira Tour actually lands at the penguin colony, which is active October through March). Tours run around AR$750; tickets are available at the pier, travel agencies and hotels.

Founded by missionary Thomas Bridges and located 85km east of Ushuaia, **Estancia Harberton** (☎Skype estanciaharberton.turismo; www.estanciaharberton.com; ⏰10am-7pm Oct 15-Apr 15) was Tierra del Fuego's first *estancia*. This 200-sq-km ranch boasts splendid scenery and alluring history. There's a good museum, and you can take an optional boat trip to the area's penguin colony. Get here by taxi, rental car or boat tour. Overnight stays (dorm US$50, single/double with full board and activities US$325/580) are possible.

Hiking and trekking opportunities aren't limited to the national park: the entire range behind Ushuaia, with its lakes and rivers, is a natural wonderland. Trails are poorly marked; you can hire a guide from **Compañía de Guías** (☎02901-437753; www.

Tierra del Fuego

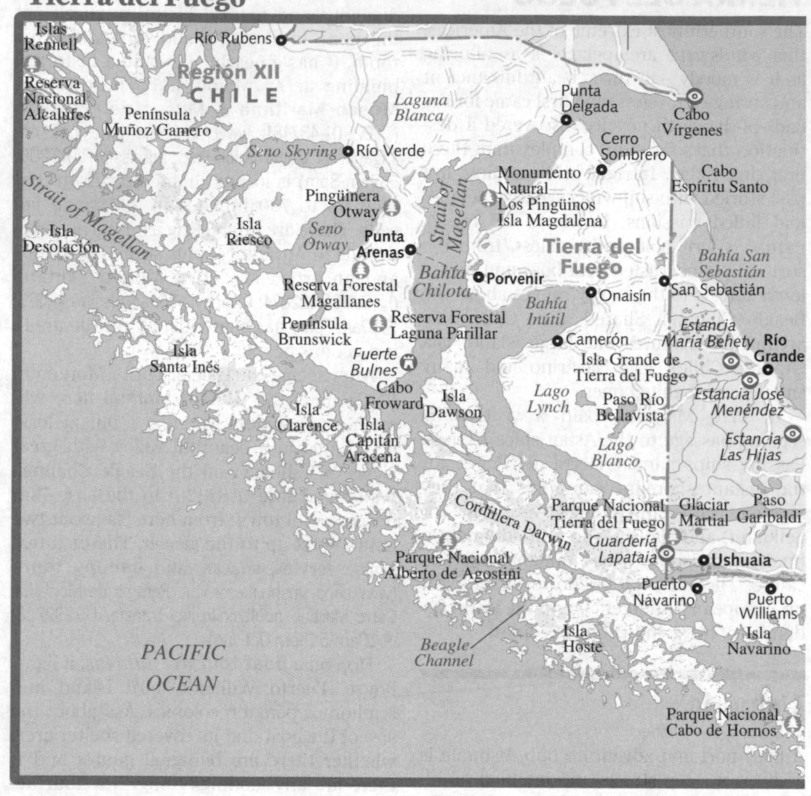

companiadeguias.com.ar; full-day hike US$105) for trekking or mountaineering.

Winter offers both downhill and cross-country skiing options. The main resort is **Cerro Castor** (☎02901-499301; www.cerrocastor.com; full-day lift ticket adult/child AR$730/500; ⊙mid-Jun–mid-Oct), about 27km from Ushuaia, with almost 20 slopes. The ski season runs from June to October.

Tours

Many travel agencies sell regional tours. You can go horse riding, canoeing or mountain biking, visit nearby lakes, spy on birds and beavers, and even ride dogsleds during winter. Some of the better adventure-tour operators include **Tierra** (☎02901-433800, 15-486886; www.tierraturismo.com; Onas 235, office 4C), **Canal Fun** (☎02901-435777; www.canalfun.com; Roca 136) and **Rayen Aventura** (☎02901-437005; www.rayenaventura.com; Av San Martín 611).

Sleeping

Reservations are a good idea in December and January.

★Antarctica Hostel HOSTEL $
(☎02901-435774; www.antarcticahostel.com; Antártida Argentina 270; dm/d US$26/85; @☎) This friendly backpacker hub delivers with a warm atmosphere and helpful staff. The open-floor plan and beer on tap are plainly conducive to making friends. Guests lounge and play cards in the common room and cook in a cool balcony kitchen. Cement rooms are clean and ample, with radiant floor heating.

Hostel Cruz del Sur HOSTEL $
(☎02901-434099; www.xdelsur.com.ar; Deloquí 242; dm US$25; @☎) This easygoing, organized hostel comprises two renovated houses (1920 and 1926), painted tangerine and joined by a passageway. Dorm prices are based on room capacity, the only disad-

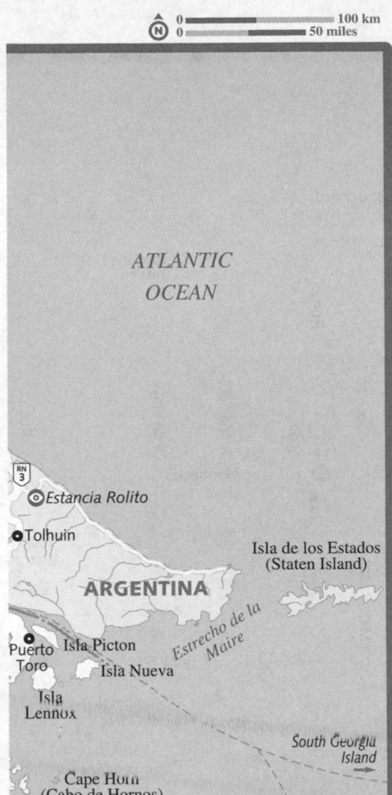

vantage being your bathroom might be on another floor. There's a fine backyard patio, though indoor shared spaces are scant.

Torre al Sur HOSTEL $
(☎02901-430745; www.torrealsur.com.ar; Gobernador Paz 855; dm/d US$20/35; 📶) The sister hostel to Cruz del Sur may seem like not much on the outside but inside there's a welcoming, organized ambience with colorful rooms, renovated bathrooms and a well-stocked kitchen. Marisa is the warm host.

Los Cormoranes HOSTEL $
(☎02901-423459; www.loscormoranes.com; Kamshen 788; dm US$31-40, d/tr/q US$107/132/155; @📶) This friendly, mellow HI hostel is a 10-minute (uphill) walk north of downtown. Six-bed dorms with radiant floors face outdoor plank hallways, some with private bathrooms. Doubles have polished cement floors and down duvets – the best is room 10, with bay views. Linens could use an update and common spaces are so-so. Breakfast includes DIY eggs and fresh orange juice.

Yakush HOSTEL $
(☎02901-435807; www.hostelyakush.com; Piedrabuena 118; dm US$28-30, d with/without bathroom US$105/95; ⏰mid-Oct–mid-Apr; @📶) A colorful hostel that seems expensive for what you get, particularly for the dark doubles.

★**Galeazzi-Basily B&B** B&B $$
(☎02901-423213; www.avesdelsur.com.ar; Valdéz 323; s/d without bathroom US$45/65, 2-/4-person cabin US$110/140; @📶) The best feature of this elegant wooded residence is its warm and hospitable family who will make you feel right at home. Rooms are small but offer a personal touch. Since beds are twin-sized, couples may prefer a modern cabin out back. It's a peaceful spot, and where else can you practice your English, French, Italian and Portuguese?

Mysten Kepen GUESTHOUSE $$
(☎02901-430156, 15-497391; http://mystenkepen.blogspot.com; Rivadavia 826; d/tr/q US$94/144/175; 📶) If you want an authentic Argentine family experience, this is it. Hosts Roberto and Rosario still recount stories of favorite guests from years past, and their immaculate two-kid home feels busy and lived in – in a good way. Rooms have newish installations, bright corduroy duvets and handy shelving for nighttime reading. Airport transfers and winter discounts available.

Eating & Drinking

Almacen Ramos Generales CAFE $
(☎02901-4247317; Av Maipú 749; mains AR$73-175; ⏰9am-midnight) With quirky memorabilia and postings of the local environmental

DON'T MISS

KALMA RESTO

Creating quite a stir, tiny **Kalma Resto** (☎02901-425786; www.kalmaresto.com.ar; Antártida Argentina 57; mains AR$180-390; ⏰4-11pm Mon-Sat) presents Fuegian staples, like crab and octopus, in a giddy new context. Black sea bass contrasts with a tart tomato sauce and the roast lamb stew revels in earthy pine mushrooms. Service is stellar, with young chef Jorge Monopoli making the rounds of the few black linen tables.

Ushuaia

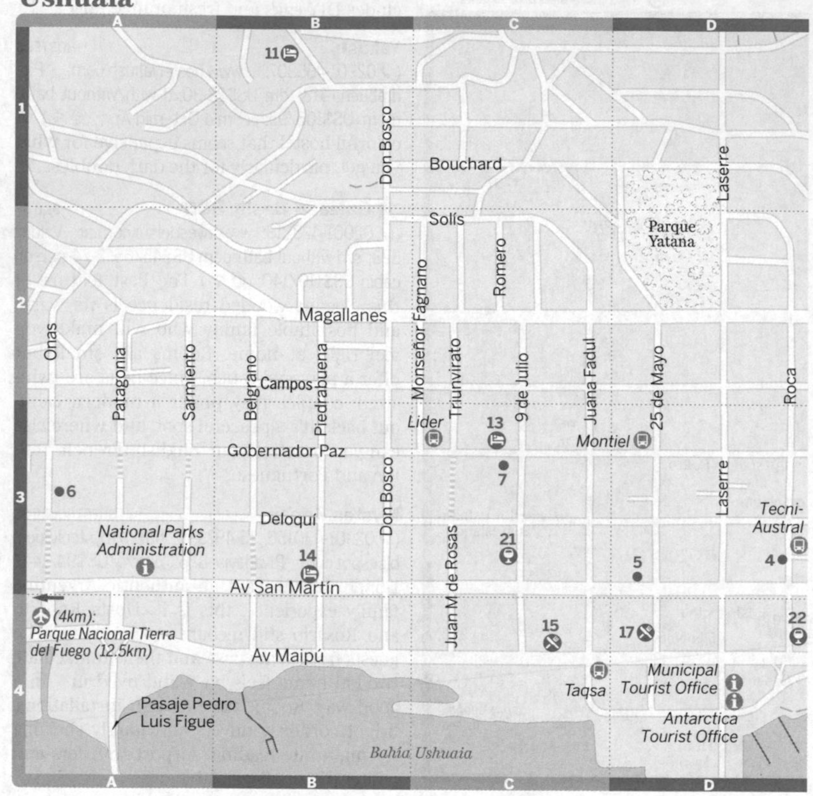

issues you've never heard of, this former general store is a peek inside the real Ushuaia. Locals hold their pow-wows here. Croissants and crusty baguettes are baked by the French pastry chef. There's also local beer on tap, a wine list, and light fare such as sandwiches, soups and quiche.

Freddo ICE CREAM $

(Av San Martín 209; cones AR$50; ⌚9:30am-12:30am) One of Argentina's best gelato shops has opened its doors to snowbound Ushuaia – and suddenly it's summer.

Cafe Bar Banana CAFE $

(☎02901-424021; Av San Martín 273; mains AR$60-130; ⌚8am-1am Mon-Fri, to 2am Sat, 9am-1am Sun) Serving homemade burgers and fries, sandwiches and steak and eggs, this is a local favorite for high-octane, low-cost dining with friends.

Paso Garibaldi ARGENTINE $$

(☎02901-432380; Deloquí 133; mains AR$150-250; ⌚noon-3pm & 7-11:30pm Tue-Sat, 7-11:30pm Sun) Serving hearty local fare including black-bean stew, flavorful salads and roasted hake, this new addition is refreshingly without pretension. The recycled decor looks a little too improvised, but service couldn't be more attentive and dishes are well priced.

Chiko SEAFOOD $$

(☎02901-431736; 25 de Mayo 62; mains AR$110-260; ⌚noon-3pm & 7:30-11:30pm Mon-Sat) A boon to seafood lovers. Crisp oversize calamari rings, *paila marina* (shellfish stew) and fish dishes like *abadejo a pil pil* (pollock in garlic sauce) are done so right that you might not mind the slow service. An odd assemblage of Chilean memorabilia spells homesickness for the owners from Chile.

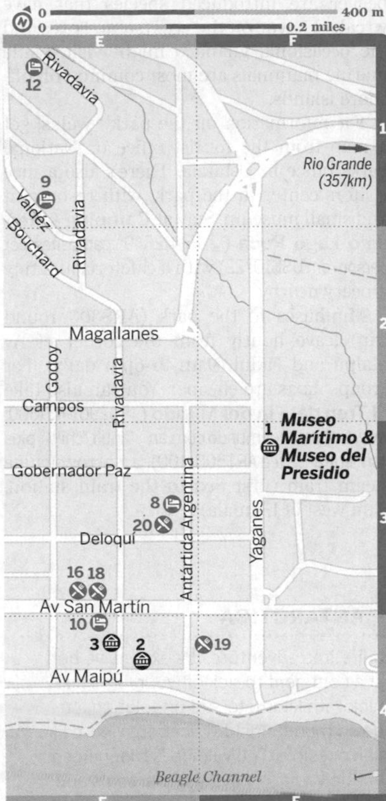

Ushuaia

Top Sights

1 Museo Marítimo & Museo del Presidio F3

Sights

2 Museo del Fin del Mundo E4
3 Museo Yamaná E4

Activities, Courses & Tours

4 Canal Fun D3
5 Rayen Aventura D3
6 Tierra A3
7 Ushuaia Turismo C3

Sleeping

8 Antarctica Hostel E3
9 Galeazzi-Basily B&B E1
10 Hostel Cruz del Sur E4
11 Los Cormoranes B1
12 Mysten Kepen E1
13 Torre al Sur C3
14 Yakush B3

Eating

15 Almacen Ramos Generales C4
16 Cafe Bar Banana E3
17 Chiko D4
18 Freddo E3
19 Kalma Resto F4
20 Paso Garibaldi E3

Drinking & Nightlife

21 Dublin Irish Pub C3
22 Viagro D4

Dublin Irish Pub PUB
(☎ 02901-430744; 9 de Julio 168; ⏲ 7pm-4am) Dublin doesn't feel so far away with the lively banter and free-flowing drinks at this dimly lit foreigners' favorite. Look for occasional live music and be sure to try at least one of its three local Beagle beers.

Viagro BAR
(☎ 02901-421617; Roca 55; ⏲ 8pm-4am) If you can get past the unfortunate name, this cocktail nook is the perfect low-lit rendezvous spot, with exotic concoctions and appetizing tapas to fuel your night out. There's dancing on Saturday nights.

Information

ATMs are common.

Municipal tourist office (☎ 02901-437666; Prefectura Naval 470; ⏲ 8am-9pm) Very helpful, with English- and French-speaking staff, a message board and multilingual brochures, as well as good lodging, activities and transport info. Also at the airport (☎ 02901-423970; ⏲ during flight arrivals).

National Parks Administration (☎ 02901-421315; Av San Martín 1395; ⏲ 9am-5pm Mon-Fri) Offers information on Parque Nacional Tierra del Fuego.

Getting There & Around

In January and February book your passage in and out of Ushuaia in advance.

Ushuaia's airport is 4km south of the center (taxi AR$120). **Aerolíneas Argentinas** (☎ 0810-2228-6527; cnr Av Maipú & 9 de Julio) and **LADE** (☎ 02901-421123; Av San Martín 542) have offices, LAN sells tickets through travel agencies.

Ushuaia does not have a bus terminal, but the tourist office can help with transport options. **Taqsa** (☎ 02901-435453; Fadul 126) and **Tecni-Austral** (☎ 02901-431408; Roca 157) have daily services to Río Grande (AR$250, three hours) and Río Gallegos (AR$750, 12 hours); both also go to Punta Arenas (AR$920, 12 hours) a few times weekly. **Lider** (☎ 02901-

442264; Gobernador Paz 921) and **Montiel** (☎02901-421366; Gobernador Paz 605) head to Río Grande up to eight times daily. You can connect to Puerto Natales via Río Gallegos or Punta Arenas.

Taxis around town are available. Rental cars cost around AR$800 per day with 200km free.

Parque Nacional Tierra Del Fuego

Twelve kilometres west of Ushuaia lies beautiful **Parque Nacional Tierra del Fuego** (admission AR$170, collected 8am-8pm), which extends from the Beagle Channel in the south to beyond Lago Fagnano in the north. Only a small part of the park is accessible to the public, and despite a tiny system of short trails, the views along the bays, rivers and forests are wonderfully scenic. Keep your eyes peeled for *cauquén* (upland geese), cormorants and grebes. Commonly seen European rabbit and North American beaver are introduced species that have wreaked havoc on the ecosystem. Foxes and the occasional guanaco might visit, while marine mammals are most common on offshore islands.

For information on the park's walks, get a map from the tourist office or National Parks office in Ushuaia. There's also a nice visitors center in the park, with restaurant and small museum. Stay at **Camping & Refugio Lago Roca** (☎15-412649; campsites per person/dm US$10/22) with a cafeteria and tiny grocery nearby.

Minibuses to the park (AR$300 round trip) leave hourly from the corner of Av Maipú and Fadul (9am to 6pm daily). For groups, taxis are cheaper. You can also take **El Tren del Fin del Mundo** (☎02901-431600; www.trendelfindemundo.com.ar; adult/child plus park entrance fee AR$500/100), a narrow-gauge steam train (first taxi to the train station, 8km west of Ushuaia).

BEYOND THE EDGE OF THE WORLD – ANTARCTICA

A trip to awe-inspiring Antarctica is a once-in-a-lifetime adventure. It's expensive but worth every penny, and so much more than just a continent to tick off your list. The land and ice shelves pile hundreds of meters thick with kilometers of undulating, untouched snow, while countless glaciers drape down mountainsides. Icebergs loom like tall buildings and come in shapes you didn't think possible. The wildlife is magnificent; you'll see thousands of curious penguins and a wide variety of flying birds, seals and whales.

For the average person, cruising is the easiest and best way to visit the White Continent. The season runs from November through March; peak-season voyages often get sold out. Last-minute tickets might be available later in the season, but sailings on reasonably small ships (fewer than 100 passengers) will still cost at least US$5000. Regular tickets start from around US$7000. Ask how many days you will actually spend in Antarctica – crossing the Southern Ocean takes up to two days each way – and how many landings will be included. The smaller the ship, the more landings per passenger (always depending on the weather).

Thanks to its proximity to the Antarctic peninsula (1000km), most cruises leave from Ushuaia. Last-minute bookings can be made through **Freestyle Adventure Travel** (☎2901-609792; www.freestyleadventuretravel.com; Gobernador Paz 866), a 1% for the Planet member that also offers discount Cape Horn trips, and **Ushuaia Turismo** (☎02901-436003; www.ushuaiaturismoevt.com.ar; Gobernador Paz 865). Other agencies offering packages include **Rumbo Sur** (☎02901-421139; www.rumbosur.com.ar; Av San Martín 350; ⏲9am-7pm Mon-Fri), **All Patagonia** (☎02901-433622; www.allpatagonia.com; Juana Fadul 48; ⏲10am-7pm Mon-Fri, to 1pm Sat) and Canal Fun (p170).

Check that your company is a member of IAATO (www.iaato.org), which has strict guidelines for responsible travel to Antarctica. For basic info in Ushuaia, visit the very helpful **Antarctica Tourist Office** (☎02901-430015; www.tierradelfuego.org.ar/antartida; Av Maipú 505; ⏲9am-5pm with ship in port) at the pier.

Lonely Planet's *Antarctica* guidebook is an indispensable guide to the region's history and wildlife.

UNDERSTAND ARGENTINA

Argentina Today

In December 2015 Mauricio Macri, Buenos Aires' mayor since 2007, took over Argentina's presidency. In a surprising run-off election he beat Cristina Kirchner's preferred candidate, Daniel Scioli, ending 12 years of Peronist-run government. Macri promised drastic economic changes, and he immediately started implementing them: currency controls over foreign currencies were abolished (essentially ending the 'blue market' for US dollars), export taxes were lowered to boost agricultural trade and thousands of redundant public sector jobs were eliminated.

His idea is to encourage economic growth and foreign investment (again) while reducing Argentina's immense deficit and, eventually, its unsustainable inflation rate. It's quite a difference from Cristina Kirchner's practices, which implemented heavy state intervention and used the country's central bank reserves to artificially prop up the peso. Macri's reign is young: only time will tell if his changes will improve Argentina's economy, which could very well continue to sputter or even worsen. However, there is a new optimism in the air – after all, many people believe that after hitting rock bottom, things can only go up. And considering the country has been through these cycles many times before, they have no choice but to take a ride on Argentina's economic roller coaster once again.

History

The Good Old Days

Before the Spanish hit the scene, nomadic hunter-gatherers roamed the wilds of ancient Argentina. The Yámana (or Yahgan) gathered shellfish in Patagonia, while on the pampas the Querandí used *boleadoras* (weights on cords) to snag rhea (ostrich-like birds) and guanaco (the llama's cousin). Up in the subtropical northeast, the Guaraní settled down long enough to cultivate maize, while in the arid northwest the Diaguita developed an irrigation system for crops.

In 1536 the Querandí were unfortunate enough to meet pushy Spaniards in search of silver. They eventually drove the explorers away to more welcoming Paraguay. (Left behind were cattle and horses, which multiplied and gave rise to the legendary *gaucho*). The Spanish were persistent, however, and in 1580 they returned and managed to establish Buenos Aires, though trade restrictions from Spain limited the new settlement's growth. The northern colonies of Tucumán, Córdoba and Salta, however, thrived by providing mules, cloth and foodstuffs for the booming silver mines of Bolivia. Meanwhile, Spaniards from Chile moved into the Andean Cuyo region, which produced wine and grain.

Cutting the Purse Strings

In 1776 Spain designated the bootlegger township of Buenos Aires as 'capital of the new viceroyalty of the Río de la Plata,' a nod to its strategic port location. A rogue British force, hoping to snag a piece of the trade pie, invaded in 1806 but was given the boot soon after by the rallied settlers. With newfound power, the confident colonists revolted against Spain; complete independence was their reward six years later in 1816.

Despite this unity, the provinces resisted Buenos Aires' authority. Argentina split allegiances between the inhabitants of Buenos Aires (Unitarists) and the country folk (Federalists). A civil war ensued, and the two parties' bloody, vindictive conflicts nearly exhausted the country.

In 1829 Juan Manuel de Rosas came into power as a Federalist, but applied his own brand of Unitarist principles to centralize control in Buenos Aires. He built a large army, created the *mazorca* (a ruthless secret police) and forced overseas trade through the port city. Finally, in 1852, Justo José de Urquiza led a Unitarist army that forced the dictator from power. Urquiza drew up a constitution and became Argentina's first president.

The Fleeting Golden Age

Argentina's new laws opened up the country to foreign investment, trade and immigration. In the following decades, sheep, cattle and cereal products were freely exported, while Spanish, Italian, French and other European immigrants came in search of a better life. Prosperity arrived at last, and Argentina became one of the richest countries in the world in the early 20th century.

The prosperity was tenuous, however, as global economic fluctuations brought about new foreign trade restrictions. After the 1880s poor immigrants continued flooding into the city, nearly doubling Buenos Aires' population to one million residents. The industrial sector couldn't absorb all the immigrants and their needs, however, and the gap between rich and poor widened. In 1929 the military took power from an ineffectual civilian government, but an obscure colonel – Juan Domingo Perón – was the first leader to really confront the looming social crisis.

The Peróns: Love 'em or Hate 'em

Today, the Peróns have become Argentina's most revered – as well as most despised – political figures. Many people believe that Argentina never recovered, either economically or spiritually, following Perón's first presidency.

From a minor post in the labor ministry, and with the help of his charismatic soon-to-be wife, Eva Duarte (Evita), Juan Perón won the presidency in 1946. His social-welfare and new economic order programs helped the working class, but his heavy control over the country was tinged with fascism: he abused his presidential powers by using excessive intimidation and squelching free press. Dynamic Evita, meanwhile, had her own sometimes vindictive political ends, though she was mostly championed for her charitable work and women's-rights campaigns.

Rising inflation and economic difficulties undermined Perón's second presidency in 1952; Evita's death the same year was another blow. After a coup against him in 1955, Perón retreated to Spain to plot his return. The opportunity came almost two decades later when Héctor Cámpora resigned the presidency in 1973. Perón won the elections easily, but his death in mid-1974 sucked the country back into the governmental coups and chaos that had plagued it since his exile. In 1976 military rule prevailed once again, and Argentina entered its darkest hour.

Dirty War (1976–83)

In the late 1960s, when antigovernment sentiment was rife, a left-wing, highly organized Peronist guerrilla group called the Montoneros was formed. The mostly educated, middle-class youths bombed foreign businesses, kidnapped executives for ransom and robbed banks to finance their armed struggle and spread their social messages. On March 24, 1976, a bloodless military coup led by General Jorge Videla took control of the Argentine government and ushered in a period of terror and brutality. Euphemistically called the Process of National Reorganization (aka El Proceso), this movement begat a period of state-sponsored violence and anarchy, and the primary target was the Montoneros.

Some estimate that up to 30,000 people died in the infamous Guerra Sucia (Dirty War). Zero tolerance was the theme: the dictatorship did not distinguish between the revolutionary guerrillas or those who simply expressed reservations about the dictatorship's indiscriminate brutality. To 'disappear' meant to be detained, tortured and probably killed, without legal process. Ironically, the Dirty War ended only when the Argentine military attempted a real military operation, the repossession of the Falkland Islands (Islas Malvinas).

Falklands War

Argentina's economy continued to decline during military rule and eventually collapsed into chaos. El Proceso was coming undone.

In late 1981 General Leopoldo Galtieri took the presidential hot seat. To stay in power amid a faltering economy, a desperate Galtieri played the nationalist card and launched an invasion in April 1982 to dislodge the British from the Falkland Islands (Islas Malvinas).

The brief occupation of the islands, claimed by Argentina for 150 years, unleashed a wave of nationalist euphoria that lasted about a week. Then the Argentines realized that iron-clad British prime minister Margaret Thatcher was not a wallflower, especially when she had political troubles of her own. Britain fought back, sending a naval contingent to set things straight, and Argentina's ill-trained forces surrendered after 74 days. The military, stripped of its reputation, finally withdrew from government. In 1983 Argentina handed Raúl Alfonsín the presidency.

Crisis...

Alfonsín brought democracy back to Argentina and solved some territorial disputes with Chile. He also managed to curb inflation a bit, but couldn't pull the long-struggling country back onto its feet.

Carlos Menem, president from 1989 to 1999, brought brief prosperity to Argentina by selling off many private industries and borrowing heavily. He also practically stopped inflation in its tracks by pegging the peso with the US dollar, but this was only a quick fix. After a few years the peso became so overvalued that Argentine goods weren't competitive on the global market. Toward the end of Menem's rule unemployment spiraled steadily upward.

In 1999 Fernando de la Rúa was sworn into office. He inherited an almost bankrupt government, which witnessed yet another economic downturn, even higher unemployment and a widespread lack of public confidence. By 2001 the economy teetered on the brink of collapse, and in December Fernando de la Rúa resigned. The country went through three more presidents within two weeks before finally putting Eduardo Duhalde in charge. Duhalde devalued the peso in January 2002, defaulting on AR$140 billion in debt.

...And Comeback

After some instability, the peso settled to around three to the US dollar, which, due to Argentina's suddenly cheap exports, created a booming economy. In 2003 the left-leaning Néstor Kirchner was handed the presidential reins and became an immensely popular leader. He kept the economy growing strong, paid some of Argentina's debts to the International Monetary Fund (IMF) and curbed corruption to a degree. Argentina was living high and there was optimism in the air.

In 2007 Kirchner's term was up, but he wasn't through with politics. His wife, Cristina Fernández de Kirchner, ran for and won the nation's highest office, becoming Argentina's first elected woman president. And despite a rocky first tenure that included the occasional corruption scandal and a major tax-hike conflict, Cristina easily won re-election in 2011 – probably helped by the the sympathy she gained after her husband passed away from a sudden heart attack in 2010.

Cristina administered generous social programs and liberal same-sex marriage laws, and addressed abuses of the military dictatorship (1976–1983). But her presidencies were also plagued by high inflation, economic instability and mass protests. Her eventual unpopularity cut short lofty ambitions to repeal the two-tenure presidential limit.

Culture

Lifestyle

Nearly a third of Argentines are considered to be living in poverty. To save resources and maintain family ties, several generations often live under one roof.

Families are pretty close, and Sundays are often reserved for the family *asado* (barbecue). Friends are also highly valued and Argentines love to go out in large groups. They'll give each other kisses on the cheek every time they meet – even introduced strangers, men and women alike, will get a kiss.

Argentines like to stay out *late;* dinner is often at 10pm, and finishing dessert around midnight on a weekend is the norm. Bars and discos often stay open until 6am or so, even in smaller cities.

The important culture of maté is very visible in Argentina; you'll see folks sipping this bitter herb drink at home, work and play. They carry their gourds and hot-water thermoses while traveling and on picnics. Consider yourself honored if you're invited to partake in a maté-drinking ritual.

Population

About 90% of the country's population lives in urban areas. Argentina's literacy rate is over 97%.

Nineteenth-century immigration created a large population of Italians and Spanish, though many other European nationalities are represented. Newer mixes include Japanese, Koreans and Chinese (rarer outside the capital), and other South American nationalities, such as Peruvians, Bolivians, Paraguayans and Uruguayans.

Indigenous peoples make up less than 1% of Argentina's population, with the Mapuche of Patagonia being the largest group. Smaller groups of Guaraní, Tobas, Wichi and Tehuelche, among others, inhabit other northern pockets. Up to 15% of the country's population is *mestizo* (of mixed indigenous and Spanish descent); most *mestizo* reside up north.

Religion

Most of Argentina's population is Roman Catholic (the official state religion), with Protestants making up the second most popular group. Buenos Aires is home to one of the largest Jewish populations outside Israel, and also claims what is likely Latin America's largest mosque.

Spiritualism and veneration of the dead are widespread: visitors to Recoleta and Chacarita cemeteries will see pilgrims communing with icons like Juan and Evita Perón and Carlos Gardel. Cult beliefs like the Difunta Correa of San Juan province also attract hundreds of thousands of fans.

Arts

Literature

Argentina's biggest literary name is Jorge Luis Borges, famous for his short stories and poetry. Borges created alternative-reality worlds and elaborate time circles with vivid and imaginative style; check out his surreal compendiums *Labyrinths* or *Ficciones*. Internationally acclaimed Julio Cortázar wrote about seemingly normal people while using strange metaphors and whimsical descriptions of people's unseen realities. His big novel is *Hopscotch*, which requires more than one reading.

Ernesto Sábato is known for his intellectual novels and essays, many of which explore the chasm between good and evil. Sábato's notable works include *Sobre héroes y tumbas* (On Heroes and Tombs), popular with Argentine youth in the '60s, and the startling essay *Nunca más,* which describes Dirty War atrocities. Other famous Argentine writers include Manuel Puig *(Kiss of the Spider Woman),* Adolfo Bioy Casares *(The Invention of Morel),* Osvaldo Soriano *(Shadows),* Roberto Arlt *(The Seven Madmen)* and Silvina Ocampo (poetry and children's stories).

Contemporary writers include Juan José Saer, who penned short stories and complex crime novels, and novelist and journalist Rodrigo Fresán, who wrote the best-selling *The History of Argentina* and the psychedelic *Kensington Gardens*. Ricardo Piglia and Tomás Eloy Martínez are other distinguished Argentine writers who, in addition to their important works, have taught at prominent American universities.

Cinema

In the past, Argentine cinema has achieved international stature through such directors as Luis Puenzo (*The Official Story;* 1984) and Héctor Babenco (*Kiss of the Spider Woman;* 1985).

More recent notable works by Argentine directors include Fabián Bielinsky's witty *Nueve reinas* (Nine Queens; 2000), Juan José Campanella's *El hijo de la novia* (The Son of the Bride; 2001) – which got an Oscar nomination for Best Foreign Language Film – and Lucrecia Martel's sexual-awakening film *La niña santa* (The Holy Girl; 2004). Carlos Sorín's *Bombón el perro* (Bombón, the Dog; 2004) is a captivating tale of man's best friend and changing fortunes.

Pablo Trapero is one of Argentina's foremost filmmakers. Among his works are the comedy-drama *Familia rodante* (Rolling Family; 2004) and *The Clan,* which won the 2015 Silver Lion award at the Venice international Film Festival. Daniel Burman is another bright directoral star whose most recent effort is *El Misterio de la felicidad* (The Mystery of Happiness; 2015), a warm comedy. Burman also co-produced Walter Salles' Che Guevara–inspired *The Motorcycle Diaries*.

Other noteworthy films include Damián Szifron's hilarious *Tiempo de valientes* (On Probation; 2005) and Lucía Puenzo's *XXY* (2007), the tale of a teenage hermaphrodite. Mariano Cohn and Gastón Duprat's *El hombre de al lado* (The Man Next Door; 2009) is an award-winning moral drama that screened at Sundance Film Festival. Argentina's most recent Oscar-winning film is Campanella's crime thriller *El secreto de sus ojos* (The Secret in Their Eyes; 2009).

In 2013 Puenzo directed *Wakolda* (The German Doctor), a true story about the family who unknowingly lived with Josef Mengele during his exile in South America. Finally, Damián Szifron's black comedy *Relatos salvajes* (Wild Tales; 2014) was Oscar-nominated for Best Foreign Language Film.

Music

Legendary figures like Carlos Gardel and Astor Piazzolla popularized tango music, and contemporaries such as Susana Rinaldi, Adriana Varela and Osvaldo Pugliese carry on the tradition. Recent tango 'fusion' groups include Gotan Project, BajoFondo Tango Club and Tanghetto.

Folk musicians Mercedes Sosa, Leon Gieco, Horacio Guarany, Atahualpa Yupanqui and Los Chalchaleros have been very influential in the evolution of Argentine *folklórica* (folk music), as have Mariana Baraj and Soledad Pastorutti.

Rock stars Charly García, Gustavo Cerati, Andrés Calamaro, Luis Alberto Spinetta and Fito Páez are some of Argentina's best-known musicians, while popular groups have included Soda Stereo, Sumo, Los Pericos, Babasónicos, Divididos, Sui Generis and Los Fabulosos Cadillacs.

Contemporary Argentine musical artists include wacky Bersuit Vergarabat, alternative Catupecu Machu, versatile Gazpacho and the multitalented Kevin Johansen.

Heavyweights in the DJ-based club-music scene include Aldo Haydar (progressive house), Bad Boy Orange (drum 'n' bass), Diego Ro-K ('the Maradona of Argentine DJs') and Gustavo Lamas (blending ambient pop and electro house). Award-winning Hernan Cattáneo has played with Paul Oakenfold and at Burning Man.

Córdoba's edgy *cuarteto* is Argentina's original pop music, while coarse *cumbia villera* was born in shantytowns and fuses cumbia with gangsta rap, reggae and punk. Finally, *murga* is a form of athletic musical theater composed of actors and percussionists; they often perform at Carnaval.

TANGO

Tango is Argentina's sultry dance, thought to have started in Buenos Aires' bordellos in the 1880s (though Montevideo in Uruguay also stakes a claim to the dance's origin). It wasn't mainstream until it was filtered through Europe, finally hitting high popularity in Argentina around 1913. Carlos Gardel is tango's most famous songbird.

Cuisine

Food

As a whole, Argentina does not have a widely varied cuisine – most folks here seem to survive on meat, pasta and pizza – but the country's famous beef is often sublime. At a *parrilla* (grillhouse) or *asado* (barbecue) you should try *bife de chorizo* (thick sirloin), *bife de lomo* (tenderloin) or a *parrillada* (mixed grill). Ask for *chimichurri*, a tasty sauce of garlic, parsley and olive oil. Steaks tend to come medium *(a punto)*, so if you want it rare, say *jugoso*.

The Italian influence is apparent in dishes like pizza, spaghetti, ravioli and chewy *ñoquis* (gnocchi). Vegetarian fare is available in Buenos Aires and other large cities. *Tenedores libres* (all-you-can-eat buffets) are popular and good value. Middle Eastern food is common in the north, while the northwest has spicy dishes like those of Bolivia or Peru. In Patagonia lamb is king, while specialties such as trout, boar and venison are served around the Lake District.

Confiterías (cafes) usually grill sandwiches like *lomito* (steak), *milanesa* (a thin breaded steak) and hamburgers. *Restaurantes* have larger menus and professional waiters. Cafes usually serve alcohol and simple meals.

Large supermarkets often have a counter with good, cheap takeout. Western fast-food chains exist in larger cities.

Breakfast is usually a simple affair of coffee or tea with *tostadas* (toast), *manteca* (butter) and *mermelada* (jam). *Medialunas* (croissants) come either sweet or plain.

Empanadas are baked or fried turnovers with vegetables, beef, cheese or other fillings. *Sandwichitos de miga* (thin, crust-free sandwiches layered with ham and cheese) are great at teatime. Commonly sold at kiosks, *alfajores* are cookie sandwiches filled with *dulce de leche* (a thick milky caramel sauce) or *mermelada* and covered in chocolate.

Postres (desserts) include *ensalada de fruta* (fruit salad), pies and cakes, *facturas* (pastries) and flan, which can be topped with *crema* (whipped cream) or *dulce de leche*. Argentina's Italian-derived *helados* (ice cream) are South America's best.

The usual *propina* (tip) at restaurants is 10%. At fancier restaurants, a *cubierto* (a service charge separate from the tip) of a few pesos is often included in the bill to cover bread and 'use of utensils.'

Drinks

ALCOHOLIC DRINKS

Argentines like to drink (but not to excess), and you'll find lists of beer, wine, whiskey and gin at many cafes, restaurants and bars. Both Quilmes and Isenbeck are popular beers; ask for *chopp* (draft or lager). Microbrews are widely available in the Lake District.

Some Argentine wines are world-class; both reds (*tintos*) and whites (*blancos*) are excellent, but malbecs are especially well known. The major wine-producing areas are near Mendoza, San Juan, La Rioja and Salta.

Argentina's legal drinking age is 18.

NONALCOHOLIC DRINKS

Soft drinks are everywhere. For water, there's *con gas* (carbonated) or *sin gas* (noncarbonated) mineral water. Or ask for Argentina's usually drinkable *agua de canilla* (tap water). *Licuados* are water- or milk-blended fruit drinks.

Argentines love their coffee, and you can order several versions. A *café con leche* is half coffee and half milk, while a *cortado* is an espresso with a little milk. A *café chico* is an espresso.

Tea is commonplace. You shouldn't decline an invitation for grass-like maté, although it's definitely an acquired taste.

Sports

Rugby, tennis, basketball, polo, golf, motor racing, skiing and cycling are popular sports, but soccer is an obsession. The national team has twice won the World Cup, once in 1978 and again in 1986. Today, Lionel Messi is Argentina's biggest *fútbol* star.

The game between River Plate and Boca Juniors is a classic match not to be missed, as the rivalry between the two teams is intense.

Environment

The Land

Argentina is huge – it's the world's eighth-largest country. It stretches some 3500km north to south and encompasses a wide range of environments and terrain.

The glorious Andes line the edge of northwest Argentina, where only hardy cactus and scrubby vegetation survive. Here, soaring peaks and salt lakes give way to the subtropical lowland provinces of Salta and Santiago del Estero. To the south, the hot and scenic Tucumán, Catamarca and La Rioja provinces harbor agriculture and viticulture.

Drier thornlands of the western Andean foothills give way to the forked river valleys and hot lowlands of Formosa and Chaco provinces. Rainfall is heaviest to the northeast, where swampy forests and subtropical savannas thrive. Densely forested Misiones province contains the awe-inspiring Iguazú Falls. Rivers streaming off these immense cataracts lead to the alluvial grasslands of Corrientes and Entre Ríos provinces. Summers here are very hot and humid.

The west-central Cuyo region (Mendoza, San Juan and San Luis provinces) pumps out most of Argentina's world-class wine vintages. Central Argentina has the mountainous Córdoba and richly agricultural Santa Fe provinces. The Pampas is a flat, rich plain full of agriculture and livestock. Along the Atlantic Coast are many popular and attractive beaches.

Patagonia spans the lower third of Argentina. Most of this region is flat and arid, but toward the Andes rainfall is abundant and supports the lush Lake District. The southern Andes boasts huge glaciers, while down on the flats cool steppes pasture large flocks of sheep.

The Tierra del Fuego archipelago mostly belongs to Chile. Its northern half resembles the Patagonian steppe, while dense forests and glaciers cover the mountainous southern half. The climate can be relatively mild, even in winter (though temperatures can also drop below freezing). The weather in this region is very changeable year-round.

Like several other countries, Argentina lays claim to a section of Antarctica.

Wildlife

The famous Pampas are mostly sprawling grasslands and home to many birds of prey and introduced plant species. The northern swamplands are home to the odd-looking capybara (the world's largest rodent), swamp deer, the alligator-like caiman and many large migratory birds.

The main forested areas of Argentina are in subtropical Misiones province and on the eastward-sloping Andes from Neuquén province south, where southern beech species and coniferous woodlands predominate; look for the strange monkey-puzzle tree (*Araucaria araucana* or *pehuén*) around the Lake District. In the higher altitudes of the Andes and in much of Patagonia, pasture grasses are sparse. Northern Andean saline lakes harbor pink flamingos, and on the Patagonian steppe you're likely to see guanacos, rheas, Patagonian hares, armadillos, crested caracaras and gray foxes. Pumas and condors live in the southern Andean foothills, but sightings are rare.

Coastal Patagonia, especially around Península Valdés, has dense and viewable concentrations of marine fauna, including southern right whales, sea lions, southern elephant seals, Magellanic penguins and orcas.

National Parks

Argentina has a good range of national and provincial parks. A wide variety of climates is represented, including swamps, deserts and rainforest. Highlights include giant trees, waterfalls and glaciers.

Some of Argentina's best parks include the following:

Parque Nacional Iguazú (p100) World-renowned for its waterfalls.

Parque Nacional Los Alerces (p155) Site of ancient *alerce* (false larch) forests.

Parque Nacional Los Glaciares (p168) Awesome for its glaciers and alpine towers.

Parque Nacional Nahuel Huapi (p151) Offers vivid alpine scenery.

Parque Nacional Tierra del Fuego (p174) Exceptional beech forests and fauna.

Parque Provincial Aconcagua (p139) Boasts the continent's highest peak.

Reserva Faunística Península Valdés (p159) Famous for coastal fauna.

Reserva Provincial Esteros del Iberá (p90) Home to swamp-dwelling wildlife.

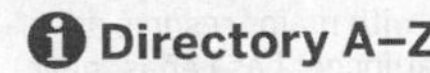

SURVIVAL GUIDE

Directory A–Z

ACCOMMODATIONS

There's an excellent range of affordable hostels throughout Argentina. Most hostels are friendly and offer tours and services. All include kitchen access and sheets; most have towel rental, internet access, free wi-fi, luggage storage, light breakfast and double rooms (book these ahead). Hostel organizations include **Hostelling International** (011 4511-8723; www.hostels.org.ar; Av Florida 835, Buenos Aires) and **HoLa** (www.holahostels.com); membership is not required to stay at any hostel, but members get around a 10% discount.

Residenciales are small hotels, while *hospedajes* or *casas de familia* are usually family homes with extra bedrooms and shared bathrooms. Hotels can range from one to five stars, and rooms usually come with private bathroom and a light breakfast (coffee, tea and bread or croissants). In Buenos Aires, apartment rentals are popular and can be a money-saver if you're staying a long time.

Camping is cheap and popular in Argentina, though sites aren't always near the center of town. National parks usually have organized sites, and some offer distant *refugios* (basic shelters for trekkers).

Peak tourist months in Buenos Aires are November to January, when accommodations prices are at their highest. Patagonia is busiest during the summer (November to February), though ski resort towns fill up fast in July and August. Northern destinations and the Atlantic beach towns attract the most travelers in December and January (the latter are practically ghost towns the rest of the year). In peak season it's wise to make reservations ahead of time.

ACTIVITIES

- Argentina has plenty for adventure-seeking travelers. A multitude of beautiful national parks offer awesome summer hiking and trekking, especially around Bariloche and Patagonia's Fitz Roy range. For the highest

SLEEPING PRICE RANGES

The following price ranges refer to a double room with bathroom in the high season. Accommodation prices are in US$ and include taxes.

$ less than US$75; US$15 to US$19 for a dorm bed

$$ US$75 to US$150

$$$ more than US$150

peak outside Asia there's lofty Aconcagua, at 6962m.

- Skiing is world-class, with major resorts at Cerro Catedral, near Bariloche; Las Leñas, near Malargüe; Los Penitentes; and Chapelco, near San Martín de los Andes. The ski season runs from about mid-June to mid-October. In summer, these mountains turn into activity centers for mountain biking.
- Cycling is a popular activity in Mendoza, the Andean northwest, the Lake District and Patagonia (where winds are fierce!). Mountain bikes are best for pedaling the sometimes remote and bad roads, many of which are gravel. Many tourist cities have bike rentals, though the quality is not up to Western standards.
- The Lake District and Patagonia have some of the world's best fly-fishing, with introduced trout and landlocked Atlantic salmon reaching epic proportions. The season in these areas runs from November to mid-April. It's almost always catch-and-release.
- Whitewater rafting can be enjoyed near Mendoza (as well as in the Lake District) and horse riding and paragliding are popular in many tourist areas.

ELECTRICITY

Argentina's electric current operates on 220V, 50Hz. Most plugs are either two rounded prongs (as in Europe) or three angled flat prongs (as in Australia).

EMBASSIES & CONSULATES

Embassies listed here are in Buenos Aires. Regional consulates are also provided.

Australian Embassy (☎011-4779-3500; www.argentina.embassy.gov.au; Villanueva 1400)

Bolivian Embassy (☎011-4394-1463; www.embajadadebolivia.com.ar; Av Corrientes 545); La Quiaca Consulate (☎03885-422283; www.consuladoboliviano.com.ar; 9 de Julio 100; ⏰7am-6:30pm Mon-Fri)

Brazilian Embassy (☎011-4515-6500; www.conbrasil.org.ar; Carlos Pellegrini 1363, 5th fl); Paso de Los Libres Consulate (☎03772-425444; Mitre 894); Puerto Iguazú Consulate (☎03757-420192; Córdoba 278; visa fee Australia/Canada/Japan/USA/other R$35/65/25/160/20; ⏰visas 8am-1:30pm Mon-Fri)

Canadian Embassy (☎011-4808-1000; www.embassy-canada.com; Tagle 2828)

Chilean Embassy (☎011-4808-8601; www.chile.gob.cl/argentina; Tagle 2762); Bariloche Consulate (☎02944-523050; España 275); Esquel Consulate (☎02945-451189; Molinari 754); Mendoza Consulate (☎0261-425-5024; Belgrano 1080); Neuquén Consulate (☎0299-442-2447; La Rioja 241); Río Gallegos Consulate (☎02966-422364; Moreno 148); Salta Consulate (☎0387-431-1857; http://chileabroad.gov.cl; Santiago del Estero 965; ⏰9am-1pm Mon-Fri); Ushuaia Consulate (☎02901-430909; Jainén 50)

Dutch Embassy (☎011-4338-0050; http://argentina.nlembajada.org; Olga Cossettini 831, 3rd fl)

French Embassy (☎011-4515-7030; www.embafrancia-argentina.org; Cerrito 1399)

German Embassy (☎011-4778-2500; www.buenosaires.diplo.de; Villanueva 1055)

New Zealand Embassy (☎011-5070-0700; www.nzembassy.com/argentina; Carlos Pellegrini 1427, 5th fl)

UK Embassy (☎011-4808-2200; www.ukinargentina.fco.gov.uk; Dr Luis Agote 2412)

US Embassy (☎011-5777-4533; http://argentina.usembassy.gov; Colombia 4300)

GAY & LESBIAN TRAVELERS

Argentina is a strongly Catholic country, but enclaves of tolerance toward gays and lesbians do exist. This is especially true in Buenos Aires, which is a top gay tourist destination. In fact, BA was the first city in Latin America to accept civil unions between same-sex couples (in 2002).

Argentine men are more physically demonstrative than you may be used to, so behaviors such as cheek kisses or a vigorous embrace are commonplace. Lesbians walking hand in hand should attract little attention, as heterosexual Argentine women sometimes do this, but this would be suspicious behavior for males. In general, do your thing – but be discreet.

HEALTH

Argentina requires no vaccinations. In 2009 there was a dengue outbreak in some parts of northern Argentina. In the high Andes, watch for signs of altitude sickness and use more sunscreen. For more information see http://wwwnc.cdc.gov/travel/destinations/argentina.htm.

Urban water supplies are usually potable, making salads and ice safe to consume. Many prescription drugs are available over the counter. Seek out an embassy recommendation if you need serious Western-type medical services.

INTERNET ACCESS

- Wi-fi is available at many (if not most) hotels and cafes, restaurants and airports, and it's

EATING PRICE RANGES

The following price ranges indicate the cost of a main course.

$ less than AR$110

$$ AR$110 to AR$180

$$$ more than AR$180

generally good and free. Internet cafes and *locutorios* (telephone centers) with affordable internet access can be found in practically all Argentine towns and cities.

➡ To type the @ (*arroba*) symbol, hold down the Alt key and type 64, or type AltGr-2. Or ask the attendant *'¿Cómo se hace la arroba?'*

LANGUAGE

Besides flamboyance, the unique pronunciation of *castellano* – Argentina's Italian-accented version of the Spanish language – readily identifies an Argentine elsewhere in Latin America or abroad. If you're in Buenos Aires you'll also hear *lunfardo*, the capital's colorful slang.

Quechua speakers, numerous in the northwest, tend to be bilingual in Spanish. Many Mapuche speakers live in the southern Andes, while most Guaraní speakers live in northeastern Argentina.

Argentina is a good destination in which to learn Spanish, and there are dozens of schools (and private instructors) to choose from in Buenos Aires. Other large cities, such as Bariloche, Mendoza and Córdoba, also have Spanish schools.

LEGAL MATTERS

Many drugs that are illegal in the US and most European countries are also illegal here. Constitutionally, a person is innocent until proven guilty, although people are regularly held for years without trial. If arrested, you have the constitutional right to a lawyer, a telephone call and to remain silent.

If you behave, it's unlikely you'll run into trouble with the police. Politely mention contacting your consulate if you do have a run-in. Drivers sometimes take care of matters on the spot by saying *'¿Cómo podemos arreglar esto más rapido?'* (How can we sort this out faster?). In all events, it's a good idea to carry identification (or copies) and always be courteous and cooperative when dealing with police or government officials.

MONEY

Carrying a combination of US dollars, Argentine pesos and ATM or credit cards is best.

ATMs

➡ *Cajeros automáticos* (ATMs) are found in nearly every city and town in Argentina and can also be used for cash advances on major credit cards. They're the best way to get money and often have instructions in English.

➡ Depending on your home bank there are varying upper limits per withdrawal, and a small fee is charged on ATM transactions by the local bank (not including charges by your home bank). You can withdraw several times per day, but beware the fees, which are per transaction.

> **ELECTRONICS WARNING**
>
> Note that buying certain electronic products is now practically impossible in Argentina due to severe import restrictions. If you bring your smartphone, don't flash it around unnecessarily or leave it unprotected. The same goes for tablet and laptop computers.

➡ When getting cash out, consider withdrawing an odd number like AR$990, instead of AR$1000; this will guarantee you some small bills for change. ATMs in Argentina do not give out US dollars.

Bargaining

➡ Bargaining might be possible in the northwest and in craft fairs countrywide, especially if you buy several items, but it's not the sport that it is in some other countries in Latin America, and certainly not something you do in most stores in Argentina.

➡ If you stay several days at a hotel, you can often negotiate a better rate. Many higher-range hotels will give discounts for cash payments.

Cash

➡ Bills come in denominations of two, five, 10, 20, 50 and 100 pesos (though new 200 and 500 peso notes are due to be printed in 2016, with a possible 1000 peso note to be introduced in 2017). One peso equals 100 centavos. Coins come in five, 10, 25 and 50 centavos as well as one and two pesos. US dollars are accepted by many tourist-oriented businesses, but always carry some pesos.

➡ US dollars are the easiest currency to exchange, though euros are also widely accepted at *cambios* (exchange houses). In Buenos Aires especially, beware fake bills; see www.landingpadba.com/ba-basics-counterfeit-money.

Credit Cards

➡ The larger a hotel is, the greater the chance it will accept credit cards. Ditto for stores and other services like bus tickets. Some businesses add a *recargo* (surcharge) of up to 10% to credit-card purchases; ask beforehand. Note that restaurant tips (10%) can't be added to the bill and must be paid in cash.

➡ MasterCard and Visa are the main honchos, but American Express is also commonly accepted. Limited cash advances are possible (try Banco de la Nación) but are difficult, involving paperwork and fees.

Moneychangers

➡ US dollars and certain other currencies can be converted to Argentine pesos at most

TWO-TIER COSTS IN ARGENTINA

A few upscale hotels, some museums and tango shows, most national parks and one major airline have adopted a two-tier price system. Rates for foreigners can be double (or more) the local prices.

banks or *cambios*. *Cambios* offer slightly poorer rates but have fewer restrictions, and often shorter lines. Bring your passport for identification.

➡ In Buenos Aires, you might encounter shady figures calling out '*cambio, cambio, cambio*' to passing pedestrians on Av Florida. It's best to ignore these illegal moneychangers.

➡ Traveler's checks are generally not accepted at stores, are very difficult to cash (even at banks) and suffer poor exchange rates.

➡ Check the exchange rate before you travel, as Argentina's peso is highly volatile.

OPENING HOURS

➡ Traditionally, businesses open by 9am, break at 1pm for lunch and then reopen at 4pm until 8pm or 9pm. This pattern is still common in the provinces, but government offices and many businesses in Buenos Aires have adopted the 9am to 6pm schedule.

➡ Restaurants generally open noon to 3pm for lunch and 8pm to midnight for dinner. On weekends hours can be longer.

➡ Cafes are open all day long; most bars tend to open their doors late, around 9pm or 10pm.

POST

Letters and postcards (up to 20g) can be sent to the US, Europe and Australia; even small towns usually have a post office. You can send packages under 2kg from any post office, but anything heavier needs to go through the *aduana* (customs office). Don't send anything too valuable.

The privatized postal service, Correo Argentino (www.correoargentino.com.ar), has become more dependable over the years, but send essential mail *certificado* (registered). Private couriers, such as OCA and FedEx, are available in some larger cities, but are much more expensive.

PUBLIC HOLIDAYS

Government offices and businesses close on most national holidays, which are often moved to the nearest Monday or Friday to extend weekends. Provincial holidays are not listed here.

Año Nuevo (New Year's Day) January 1

Carnaval February/March (floating Monday and Tuesday)

Día de la Memoria (Memorial Day; anniversary of 1976's military coup) March 24

Semana Santa (Easter) March/April

Día de las Malvinas (Malvinas Day) April 2

Día del Trabajador (Labor Day) May 1

Revolución de Mayo (May Revolution of 1810) May 25

Día de la Bandera (Flag Day) June 20

Día de la Independencia (Independence Day) July 9

Día del Libertador San Martín (Anniversary of San Martín's death) Third Monday in August

Día del Respeto a la Diversidad Cultural (Cultural Diversity Day) October 12 (observed second Monday in October)

Día de la Soberanía Nacional (National Sovereignty Day) November 20 (observed fourth Monday in November)

Día de la Concepción Inmaculada (Immaculate Conception Day) December 8

Navidad (Christmas Day; businesses close starting midday December 24) December 25

SAFE TRAVEL

Despite occasional crime waves, Argentina remains one of the safest countries in Latin America. Most alert tourists who visit Buenos Aires leave happy and unscathed. Outside the big cities, serious crime is not common. Lock your valuables up in hostels, where, sadly enough, your own fellow travellers are occasionally to blame for thefts.

In general, the biggest dangers in Argentina are speeding cars and buses: *never* assume you have the right of way as a pedestrian. If you're sensitive to cigarette smoke, be aware that Argentines are addicted to nicotine and tobacco rules are looser here than in some other countries.

TELEPHONE & TEXTING

➡ *Locutorios* are common in any city; you enter private booths, make calls, then pay at the front counter. These are a better choice than street phones (which are relatively rare) as they offer privacy and quiet, and you won't run out of coins.

➡ Calling the US, Europe and Australia from *locutorios* is best on evenings and weekends, when rates are lower. Least expensive is buying credit phone cards at kiosks or calling over the internet via Skype or another system.

➡ Cell-phone numbers in Argentina always start with ☎15. If you're calling a cell-phone number from a landline, you'll have to dial 15 first. But if you're calling a cell phone from another cell phone, you don't need to dial 15.

➡ To call someone in Argentina from outside Argentina, dial your country's international access code, then Argentina's country code (☎54), then the city's area code (leaving out the first 0), then the number itself.

➡ When dialing an Argentine cell phone from outside Argentina, dial your country's international access code, then ☎54, then ☎9, then the area code without the 0, then the number – leaving out the 15.

➡ Argentina operates mainly on the GSM 850/1900 network. If you have an unlocked, tri- or quad-band GSM cell phone, you can buy a prepaid SIM chip in Argentina and insert it into your phone, adding credits as needed. You can also buy or rent cell phones in Argentina. This is a fast-changing field, so research ahead of time.

➡ You don't need to dial ☎15 to send text messages. Whatsapp is a popular way of sending free texts in Argentina, providing both parties have it installed.

TOILETS

Argentina's public toilets are better than most other South American countries, but not quite as good as those in the West. Head to restaurants, fast-food outlets, shopping malls and even large hotels to scout out a seat. Carry toilet paper and don't expect hot water, soap or paper towels to be available. In smaller towns, some public toilets charge a small fee for entry.

TOURIST INFORMATION

All tourist-oriented cities in Argentina have a conveniently located tourist office, and many of them have English-speaking staff.

In Buenos Aires, each Argentine province has a tourist office. Also in BA is the excellent Ministerio de Turismo (p77), which dispenses information on all of Argentina.

VISAS

➡ Residents of Canada, the US, Australia, and many western European countries do not need visas to enter Argentina; they receive an automatic 90-day stamp on arrival. Citizens from the US, Canada and Australia will, however, be charged a significant 'reciprocity fee' when they arrive in an airport in Buenos Aires.

➡ For visa extensions (90 days, AR$600), visit *migraciones* (immigration offices) in the provincial capitals. There's also an immigration office (p77) in Buenos Aires.

VOLUNTEERING

Volunteer opportunities in Argentina include the following:

Anda Responsible Travel (www.andatravel.com.ar/en/volunteering) Buenos Aires travel agency supporting local communities.

Conservación Patagonica (www.conservacionpatagonica.org/) Help to create a national park.

Fundación Banco de Alimentos (www.bancodealimentos.org.ar) Short-term work at a food bank.

Patagonia Volunteer (www.patagoniavolunteer.org) Opportunities in Patagonia.

Volunteer South America (www.volunteersouthamerica.net) List of NGOs offering volunteer opportunities in South America.

WWOOF Argentina (www.wwoofargentina.com) Organic farming in Argentina.

WOMEN TRAVELERS

Being a woman traveler in Argentina is not difficult, even if you're alone. In some ways Argentina is a safer place for a woman than Europe, the USA and most other Latin American countries. Argentina is a machismo culture, however, and some men will feel the need to comment on a woman's attractiveness. They'll try to get your attention by hissing, whistling, or making *piropos* (flirtatious comments). Much as you may want to kick them where it counts, the best thing to do is completely ignore them – like Argentine women do. After all, most men don't mean to be rude, and many local women even consider *piropos* to be compliments.

On the plus side of machismo, expect men to hold a door open for you and let you enter first, including getting on buses; this gives you a better chance at grabbing an empty seat, so get in there quick.

WORK

In Argentina, casual jobs are limited for foreigners. Teaching English is your best bet, especially in Buenos Aires and other major cities. However, most teachers make just enough to get by. A TESOL or TESL certificate will be an advantage in acquiring work. Foreigners also find work in traveler-oriented bars and hostels.

Many expats work illegally on tourist visas, which they must renew every three months (in BA this usually means hopping to Uruguay a few times per year). Work schedules drop off during the holiday months of January and February.

For job postings, check out http://buenosaires.en.craigslist.org or the classifieds in www.baexpats.org.

PESKY INFLATION

While accurate at research time, prices in this book are likely to rise rapidly due to Argentina's unofficial inflation of around 25% (officially it's 10%). Check before booking to avoid surprises.

Getting There & Away

AIR

Cosmopolitan Buenos Aires is linked to most of the capitals in South America. Argentina's main international airport is Buenos Aires' Aeropuerto Internacional Ministro Pistarini (known as Ezeiza). Aeroparque Jorge Newbery (known as Aeroparque) is the capital's domestic airport. A few other Argentine cities have 'international' airports, but they mostly serve domestic destinations. The national airline is Aerolíneas Argentinas.

BOAT

Ferries link Buenos Aires to several points in Uruguay.

BUS

It's possible to cross into Argentina from Bolivia, Paraguay, Brazil, Uruguay and Chile.

Getting Around

AIR

- The airline situation in Argentina is in constant flux; minor airlines go in and out of business regularly. Ticket prices are unpredictable, though they are always highest during holiday times (July and late December to February). Certain flights in extensive Patagonia are comparable to bus fares when you consider time saved.
- The major airlines in Argentina are **Aerolíneas Argentinas** (www.aerolineas.com.ar) and **LAN** (www.lan.com). Each airline has a principal office, as well as regional offices in various cities.
- There may be special air-pass deals available; check with a travel agency specializing in Latin America, since deals come and go regularly. These passes may need to be purchased outside Argentina (sometimes in conjunction with an international ticket); you need to be a foreign resident to use them, and they're often limited to travel within a certain time period.

GETTING TO CHILE

For most travelers, crossing the border from Argentina into Chile is a relatively quick, easy procedure. Usually the same bus takes you right through and there are no fees. Border outposts are open daylight hours; Dorotea (near Puerto Natales) is open 24 hours in summer. Just have your papers in order, don't take anything illegal (including fresh food) and you should be golden. And try to get your ticket as soon as possible, as Chile-bound buses often fill up quickly.

BICYCLE

- Cycling around the country has become popular among travelers. Beautiful routes in the north include the highway from Tucumán to Tafí del Valle and the Quebrada de Cafayate. Around Mendoza, there's touring that includes stops at wineries. The Lake District also has scenic roads, like the Siete Lagos route.
- Drawbacks include the wind (which can slow progress to a crawl in Patagonia) and reckless motorists. Less-traveled secondary roads with little traffic are good alternatives.
- Rental bikes are common in tourist areas and a great way to get around.

BUS

- Long-distance buses are modern, fast, comfortable and usually the best budget way to get around Argentina. Journeys of more than six hours or so will either have pit stops for refreshments or serve drinks, sweet snacks and sometimes simple meals. All have bathrooms, though they're often grungy, lack water (bring toilet paper/wet wipes) and are sometimes for 'liquids only.'
- The most luxurious companies offer more expensive *coche-cama*, *ejecutivo* or *suite* seats, most of which can lay flat. But even regular buses are usually comfortable enough, even on long trips.
- Bus terminals usually have kiosks, restrooms, cheap eats and luggage storage. In small towns you'll want to be aware of the timetable for your next bus out (and possibly buy a ticket), since some routes run infrequently.
- In summer there are many more departures. During holiday periods like January, February or July, buy advance tickets. If you know your exact traveling dates, you can often buy a ticket from any departure point to any destination, but this depends on the bus company.
- To get an idea of bus ticket prices from Buenos Aires, check www.omnilineas.com.

CAR

- Renting a car in Argentina is not cheap, but can get you away from the beaten path and start you on some adventures. The minimum driving age in Argentina is 18.
- Forget driving in Buenos Aires; traffic is unforgiving and parking is a headache, while public transport is great.
- The **Automobile Club Argentina** (ACA; Map p66; www.aca.org.ar) has offices, service stations and garages in major cities. If you're a member of an overseas affiliate (like AAA in the United States) you may be able to obtain vehicular services and discounts on maps –

bring your card. The ACA's main headquarters is in Buenos Aires.

➡ To rent a car in Argentina you must be 21 years old and have a credit card and valid driver's license from your country. An International Driving Permit is not necessary.

HITCHHIKING

➡ Hitchhiking is never entirely safe, and we don't recommend it. Travelers who hitch should understand they are taking a small but potentially serious risk.

➡ Good places for a pickup are gas stations on the outskirts of large cities, where truckers refuel their vehicles. In Patagonia, distances are great and vehicles few, so expect long waits and carry snack foods and warm, windproof clothing. Carry extra water as well, especially in the desert north.

➡ *Haciendo dedo* (hitchhiking) is fairly safe for women in Argentina; however, don't do it alone, don't get in a car with two men and don't do it at night. There is nothing especially unsafe about hitchhiking in rural Argentina, but don't hitchhike in Buenos Aires.

➡ Having a sign will improve your chances for a pickup, especially if it says something like *visitando Argentina de Canadá* (visiting Argentina from Canada), rather than just a destination. Argentines are fascinated by foreigners.

LOCAL TRANSPORTATION

➡ Even small towns have good bus systems. A few cities, including Buenos Aires, use magnetic fare cards, which can be bought at kiosks and small stores.

➡ Taxis have digital readout meters. Tipping isn't expected, but you can leave extra change. *Remises* are taxis that you book over the phone, or regular cars without meters; any hotel or restaurant can call one for you. They're considered more secure than taxis since an established company sends them out. Ask the fare in advance.

➡ Buenos Aires is the only city with a subway system, which is known as Subte.

TOURS

➡ Most of Argentina can be seen independently, but in certain destinations it can be more informative and cost-effective to take a tour. Visiting Perito Moreno outside El Calafate is one place; Peninsula Valdés and Punta Tombo, both near Puerto Madryn, are two others.

➡ Whitewater rafting, whale-watching and other adventures often require signing up for tours. Buenos Aires is full of interesting tours that give you deeper insight into that great city – these include biking tours, graffiti tours and even food tours.

TRAIN

➡ Bus travel is faster, more flexible and more reliable. However, there are long-distance services from Buenos Aires to Rosario, Córdoba, Tucumán, Bahía Blanca and some Atlantic beach towns. There's also service from Viedma to Bariloche.

➡ The very scenic and famous Tren a las Nubes (p117) chugs from Salta toward Chile. It's notoriously undependable, however, so double-check services beforehand.

➡ In Patagonia there are a couple of short touristy train rides (both narrow gauge) such as La Trochita (p154), which originates in Esquel or El Maitén, and El Tren del Fin del Mundo (p174), in Ushuaia.

Bolivia

Includes ➡

Best Adventures

- ➡ El Choro Trek (p219)
- ➡ Amazon tour (p257)
- ➡ Trekking from tip-to-tail on Isla del Sol (p213)
- ➡ Climbing in the Cordilleras (p197)

Best Places to Stay

- ➡ Las Olas (p211)
- ➡ Hostal Sol y Luna (p216)
- ➡ Casa Verde (p244)
- ➡ La Posada del Sol (p256)
- ➡ Chalalán Ecolodge (p261)

Why Go?

Bolivia is not for the faint of heart: whether your tools are crampons and an ice-axe for scaling 6000m Andean peaks, a helmet and bravado for biking the World's Most Dangerous Road or jumping into the abyss on a glider, or a rod and reel to do battle with 3m fish, Bolivia's rocks, rivers and ravines will challenge – nay, provoke – you into pushing your own personal limits.

On the wild side, you can tiptoe into caves of the tube-lipped nectar bat or tread lightly on the terrain of the poisonous annellated coral snake. Listen for the cackling call-and-response of a dozen different macaw species including the world's rarest, the bluebeard. Multihued, brilliant butterflies and moths flit at your feet in the jungle; lithe alpacas and vicuñas stand out in the stark Altiplano.

When to Go

La Paz

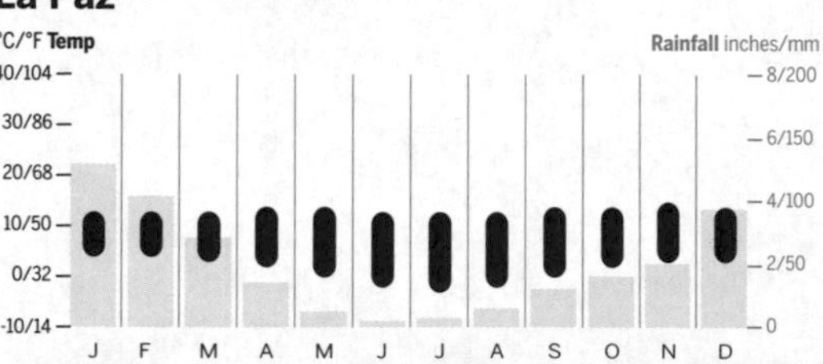

May–Oct Winter is high season; expect sunny days and good hiking, biking and climbing conditions.

Nov–Apr Rainy season makes for tough travel; the lowlands can be miserable, but city life is still fun.

Feb–Apr Festivals across the nation put a smiley face on the rainy season.

Connections

Bolivia's border crossings include Guajará-Mirim and Corumbá (Brazil), La Quiaca and Pocitos (Argentina), Tambo Quemado and Hito Cajón near San Pedro de Atacama (Chile), Yunguyo and Desaguadero (Peru) and Fortín Infante Rivarola (Paraguay). Getting in and out of Bolivia is fairly straightforward, though at some off-the-beaten-track border crossings you may be charged a small fee. Depending on the border crossing, you may also be asked to provide proof of yellow fever vaccination. The border crossing to San Pedro de Atacama is best done with a tour outfit from Uyuni.

ITINERARIES

Two Weeks

Start out with a day of acclimatization in La Paz, visiting the markets. From there, head to Lake Titicaca, then circle down the Altiplano to the Salar de Uyuni for a bone-chatteringly-cold three-day 4WD tour. Swing up to Potosí, a starkly beautiful Unesco World Heritage city, then head to the white city of Sucre to hang out with students in grand plazas. Return to La Paz via Cochabamba, taking in the good views along the way. On your last day in La Paz, consider a mountain bike down to Coroico.

One Month

Start from where the two-week itinerary leaves off. From there, the adventurous can take on the Takesi or Choro treks, then puddle-jump their way to Rurrenabaque and Parque Nacional Madidi. City explorers could simply head over to Santa Cruz, where you can kick off a multi-day road trip through the Jesuit Mission Circuit, curling back around to the unique ruins and spectacular Parque Nacional e Área de Uso Múltiple Amboró near the tranquil village of Samaipata.

Essential Food & Drink

- **Salteñas, tucumanas or empanadas** Pastry shells stuffed with vegetable and meat goodness.
- **Sopa (soup)** Starts every meal. For those with nut allergies, note that *maní* means peanut.
- **Pollo (chicken)** It's either *frito* (fried), *a la broaster* (cooked on a spit), *asado* (barbecued) or *dorado* (broiled).
- **Carne (beef)** Typically *asado* or *parrillada* (grilled).
- **Api** A yummy drink made from a ground purple corn.
- **Mate de coca** An infusion of water and dried coca leaves.
- **Singani** Grape brandy.
- **Sonso** Santa Cruz fried yucca-and-cheese pancake.

AT A GLANCE

- **Currency** Boliviano (B$)
- **Languages** Spanish, Quechua, Aymará
- **Money** ATMs can be tough to find; US dollars are best to exchange
- **Visas** US travelers have to pay
- **Time** GMT minus four hours

Fast Facts

- **Area** 1,098,580 sq km
- **Population** 11 million
- **Capital** Sucre (constitutional), La Paz (de facto)
- **Emergency** ☎ 119
- **Country code** ☎ 591

Exchange Rates

Australia	A$1	B$5
Canada	C$1	B$5
Euro zone	€1	B$7.6
New Zealand	NZ$1	B$4.1
UK	£1	B$10
USA	US$1	B$7

Set Your Budget

- **Hostel bed** B$30–50
- **Dinner** B$20–35
- **Bus** B$35
- **Beer** B$7

Resources

- **Bolivia Express** (www.bolivianexpress.org)
- **Bolivia Online** (www.bolivia-online.net)
- **Bolivia Web** (www.boliviaweb.com)

Bolivia Highlights

1. Explore **Potosí** (p246), the silver city of contrasts.
2. Make your way through **Parque Nacional e Área de Uso Múltiple Amboró** (p256) for spectacular biodiversity and landscapes.
3. Dive into history with a walking tour of **Sucre** (p241), where architecture and culture come to light.
4. Discover the living history of Chiquitania along the **Jesuit Mission Circuit** (p256).
5. Kick back in **Samaipata** (p255) before exploring the nearby El Fuerte ruins.
6. Jungle trek through **Parque Nacional Madidi** (p261) for ecotourism, howlers, birds and bugs at their best.
7. Enjoy hiking, biking, climbing, rafting... The world is your playground in the **Cordillera Real** (p197).
8. Worship the sun and sand with visits to the ruins and lost coves and mini-treks around **Lake Titicaca** (p208).
9. Create your own requiem for a dream at the surreal **Salar de Uyuni** (p230).
10. Challenge yourself to extreme hammocking in **Coroico** (p216).

0 200 km
0 100 miles

Río Guaporé (Iténez)
Costa Marques
San Joaquín
Magdalena
BRAZIL
Parque Nacional Noel Kempff Mercado
Serranía Huanchaca
Perseverancia
TRINIDAD
9
Concepción
San Javier
San Ignacio de Velasco
Jesuit Mission Circuit
4
Santa Ana de Velasco
San Miguel de Velasco
San Rafael de Velasco
4
Río Ichilo
Puerto Villarroel
Buena Vista
Parque Nacional e Área de Uso Múltiple Amboró
2
SANTA CRUZ
Puerto Pailas
San José de Chiquitos
Pantanal
5
Samaipata
Llanos de Chiquitos
Serranía de San José
Serranía de Santiago
Roboré
Río Grande o Guapay
Bañados del Izozog
Puerto Suárez
Corumbá
Quijarro
Tarabuco
Gran Chaco
Camiri
Boyuibe
6
Fortín General Eugenio A Garay
Río Paraguay
Villamontes
PARAGUAY
TARIJA
Río Pilcomayo
Yacuiba
Pocitos
Filadelfia
Aguas Blancas
Tartagal

LA PAZ

☎02 / POP 1.6 MILLION

A mad carnival of jostling pedestrians, cavalcades of street vendors, honking, diesel-spewing minivans, street marches and dances, La Paz seems to reinvent itself at every turn. A jaw-dropping subway in the sky brings you from the heights of El Alto to the depths of Zona Sur in the blink of an eye, and new boutique hotels are springing up like rows of Altiplano corn.

If arriving from the Bolivian countryside, you'll be struck by the gritty city reality. It's the urban jungle, baby: diesel, dust and detritus, as well as blinding Altiplano sun and cold cavernous corners of Dickensian darkness.

A maze of contradictions, where cobblestones hit concrete, and Gothic spires vie with glassine hotels, La Paz amazes and appalls all who enter.

Sights

The metropolitan area of La Paz is divided into three very distinct zones. North of the city center is the separate municipality of El Alto (where the airport is). This fast-growing commercial and industrial city is the center for Aymará culture, has fascinating markets and few tourist attractions. Down from here in the valley is the city of La Paz, where most travelers spend their time. On the west side of the valley are the notable commercial districts of Rosario, Belen, San Pedro and Sopocachi. To the east, the action centers on the Plaza Murillo, Santa Bárbara and Miraflores neighborhoods. If you get lost in La Paz, head downhill. You'll soon enough find yourself somewhere along the main thoroughfare or El Prado. Further down the valley to the south is the wealthy Zona Sur, with a good collection of upscale restaurants and hotels.

La Paz

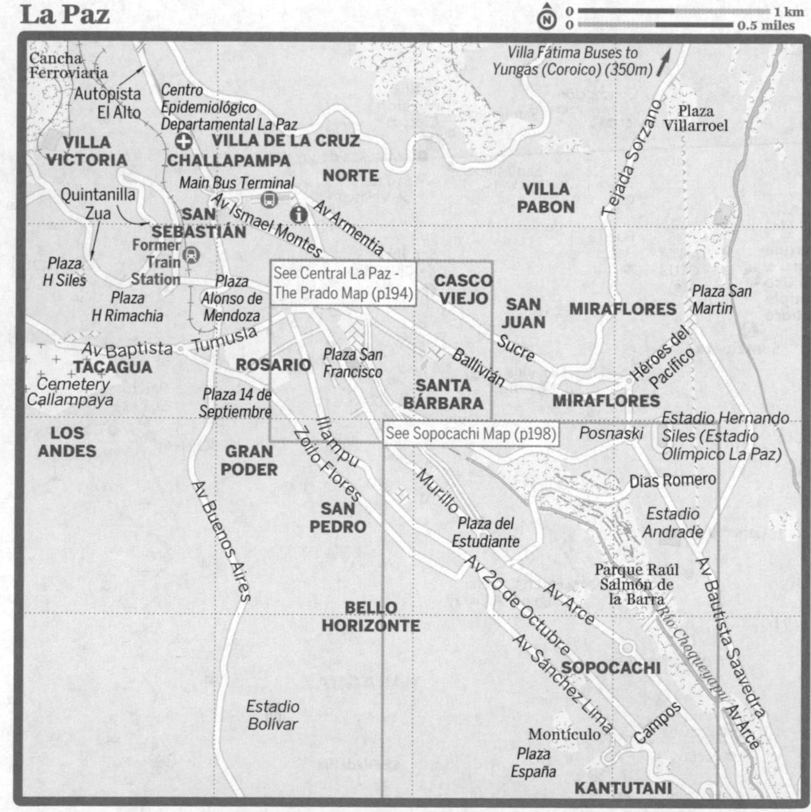

STAYING SAFE IN LA PAZ & OTHER BIG CITIES

Travelers should exercise caution while in La Paz and the rest of the country, especially at night. A little common sense goes a long way.

- Travel in groups, take a radio taxi after 8pm (these have a radio in the car and a promo bubble on the roof; do not take cabs that merely have a 'taxi' sticker), carry small amounts of cash, and leave the fancy jewelry and electronics in the hotel. Don't try to score cocaine anywhere; the dealers can be dangerous characters and the penalties for getting caught are harsh.
- Fake police officers and bogus tourist officials exist. Authentic police officers will always be uniformed (undercover police are under strict orders not to hassle foreigners) and will never insist that you show them your passport, get in a taxi with them or allow them to search you in public. If confronted by an imposter, refuse to show them your valuables (wallet, passport, money etc), or insist on going to the nearest police station on foot. If physically threatened, it is always best to hand over valuables immediately.
- At night, ask the restaurant or hotel to call a cab – the cab's details are recorded at a central base. Don't share cabs with strangers and beware of accepting lifts from drivers who approach you (especially around dodgy bus areas).
- Petty theft and pickpocketing is not uncommon in restaurants, bus terminals, markets and internet cafes. Keep a close eye on your stuff.
- One popular scam involves someone spilling a substance on you or spitting a phlegm ball at you. While you or they are wiping it off, another lifts your wallet or slashes your pack. Similarly, make sure that you don't bend over to pick up a valuable item that has been 'dropped.' You risk being accused of theft, or of being pickpocketed.

West of El Prado

The areas west of the Prado include the fascinating markets around Rosario, Belen and San Pedro, the cemetery and the sophisticated Sopocachi neighborhood.

Iglesia de San Francisco CHURCH

(Map p194; Plaza San Francisco) The hewed stone basilica of San Francisco was founded in 1548 by Fray Francisco de los Ángeles. The original structure collapsed under heavy snowfall around 1610, but it was rebuilt between 1744 and 1753. The second building is made of stone quarried at nearby Viacha. The facade is decorated with carvings of natural themes such as *chirimoyas* (custard apples), pine cones and tropical birds.

Mercado de Hechicería MARKET

(Witches' Market; Map p194) The city's most unusual market lies along Calles Jiménez and Linares between Sagárnaga and Santa Cruz, amid lively tourist *artesanías* (stores selling locally handcrafted items). What is on sale isn't witchcraft as depicted in horror films; the merchandise is herbal and folk remedies, plus a few more unorthodox ingredients intended to supplicate the various spirits of the Aymará world.

★ **Fundación Solón** GALLERY

(Walter Solón Romero Art Gallery; Map p198; ☎241-7507; www.funsolon.org; 2519 Av Ecuador, Sopocachi; B$10; 9am-12:30pm, 3-7pm Mon-Fri) This building was once home to Walter Solón Romero, one of the nation's most important and politically active artists. Known for his elaborate murals and fascination with Don Quijote, Solón paid the ultimate price when his son died in prison during the repressive 1970s. A sense of humor only slightly shades the visceral cry for justice in the maestro's works.

Museo de Instrumentos Musicales MUSEUM

(Museum of Musical Instruments; Map p194; Jaén 711, Casco Viejo; admission B$5; 9:30am-1pm & 2-6:30pm) A must for musicians. The brainchild of *charango* master Ernesto Cavour Aramayo displays all possible incarnations of the *charango* (a traditional Bolivian ukulele-type instrument) and other Bolivian folk instruments. You can also arrange *charango* and wind instrument lessons here for around B$50 per hour.

Museo de Arte Contemporáneo Plaza MUSEUM

(MAC, Contemporary Art Museum; Map p198; ☎231-3036; Av 16 de Julio 1698, Prado; admission B$15; 9am-9pm) This private museum wins the gold star for the most interesting building: a restored 19th-century mansion (one of four left on the Prado) with stained-glass panels designed by Gustave Eiffel. The eclectic collection is a mix of reasonable – but not mind-blowing – Bolivian and international work. An entire Che Guevara room includes one piece made entirely of dominoes.

La Paz Cemetery CEMETERY

(cementerio.lapaz.bo; Av Baptista) As in most Latin American cemeteries, bodies are first buried in the traditional Western way or are placed in a crypt. Then, within 10 years, they are disinterred and cremated. After cremation, families purchase or rent glass-fronted spaces in the cemetery walls for the ashes, affix plaques and mementos of the deceased, and place flowers behind the glass door.

Sopocachi NEIGHBORHOOD

Sopocachi has some of La Paz's best restaurants and nightspots. You can spend a few hours people watching on **Plaza Eduardo Avaroa**, before hoofing up to the wonderful views from **Monticulo Park**.

Be aware of your surroundings, especially at night near Plaza Avaroa and Plaza España. Take a radio taxi.

Central La Paz - The Prado

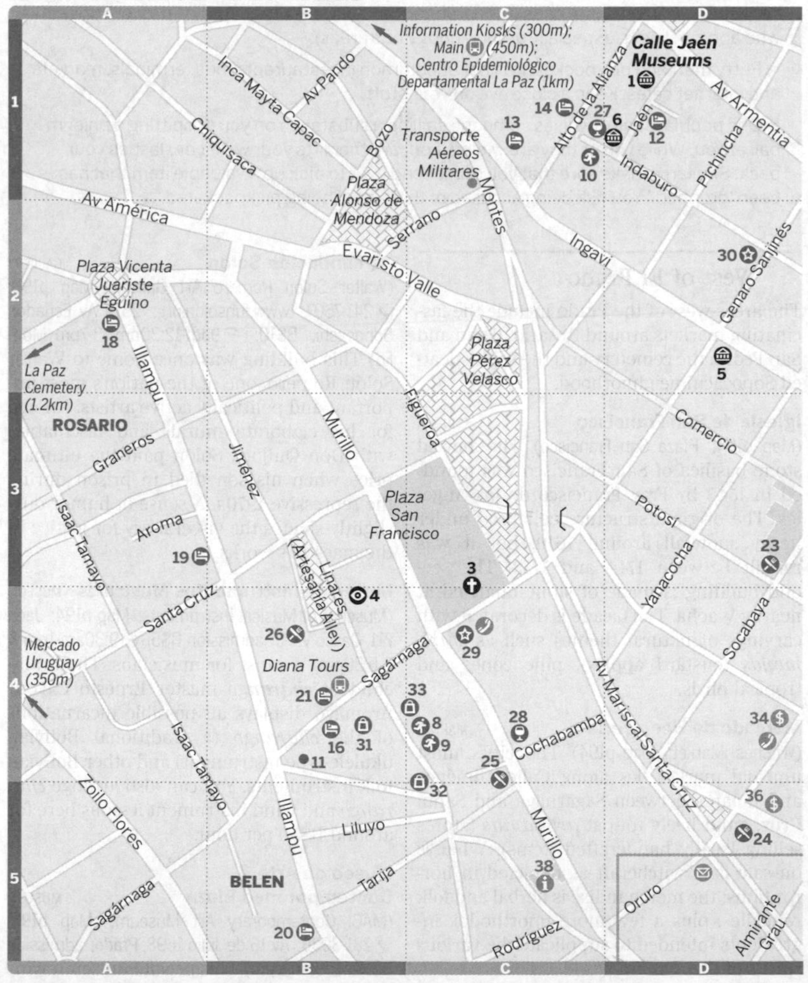

★Mi Teleférico CABLE CAR

(Aerial Cable Car System; Map p198; www.miteleferico.bo/teleferico/maps; ticket B$3; ⏲6am-11pm) Designed by Austrian company Doppelmayr, the *teleférico* has been an apple in the eye of Bolivian politicians for decades. Opposition to the project faded under Morales presidency, and the red, green and yellow lines – the colors of the national flag – debuted in May 2014.

A convenient boarding point is the Supu Kachi (Sopacachi) station, 2 blocks above Plaza España.

At 10km combined it is the world's longest aerial cable-car system. Riders can combine trips from the yellow to green lines to get to the Zona Sur from El Alto, but you must pay the fare twice – there are no free transfers. Ambitiously, six more lines are slated to be implemented in the coming two years, but political opponents in late 2015 pointed out that the first three lines were operating at only 30 percent capacity – each car having the potential for 10 riders.

The thrill of riding above La Paz's swirling traffic and deep canyons is undeniably cool. You'll feel the car gently shudder as it passes through each concrete stanchion, and probably giggle a bit as the enthusiastic teens in their bright vests help you onto the car, ensuring a balanced load. There's more than enough time to cruise down to the Zona Sur for lunch or dinner, and back. Not for the faint of heart – but then again, what in Bolivia is?

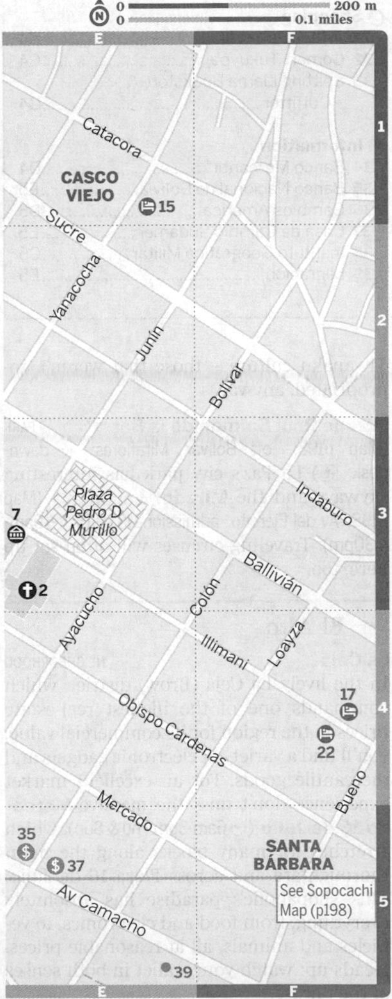

East of El Prado

Cathedral CHURCH

(Map p194; Plaza Murillo) Although it's a relatively recent addition to La Paz's religious structures, the 1835 cathedral is impressive – mostly because it is built on a steep hillside. The main entrance is 12m higher than its base on Calle Potosí. The cathedral's sheer immensity, with its high dome, hulking columns, thick stone walls and high ceilings, is overpowering, but the altar is relatively simple.

Museo Nacional del Arte MUSEUM

(National Art Museum; Map p194; www.mna.org.bo; cnr Comercio & Socabaya, Casco Viejo; admission B$15; ⏲9:30am-12:30pm & 3-7pm Tue-Fri, 10am-5:30pm Sat, 10am-1:30pm Sun) This stunning building was constructed in 1775 of pink Viacha granite and has been restored to its original grandeur, in mestizo (mixed) baroque and Andino baroque styles. In the center of a huge courtyard, surrounded by three stories of pillared corridors, is a lovely alabaster fountain. The various levels are dedicated to different eras, with an emphasis on religious themes.

Museo de Etnografía y Folklore MUSEUM

(Ethnography & Folklore Museum; Map p194; ☎240-8640; www.musef.org.bo; cnr Ingavi & Sanjinés, Casco Viejo; admission B$20; ⏲9am-12:30pm & 3-7pm Mon-Fri, 9am-4:30 Sat, 9am-12:30pm Sun) Anthropology buffs should check out this museum. The building, itself a real treasure, was constructed between 1776 and 1790, and was once the home of

Central La Paz - The Prado

Top Sights

1 Calle Jaén Museums D1

Sights

2 Cathedral E3
3 Iglesia de San Francisco C3
4 Mercado de Hechicería B4
5 Museo de Etnografía y Folklore D2
6 Museo de Instrumentos Musicales D1
Museo de Metales Preciosos .... (see 1)
7 Museo Nacional del Arte E3

Activities, Courses & Tours

8 B-Side C4
9 Gravity Assisted Mountain Biking C4
10 La Paz on Foot C1
11 Pico Verde Languages B4

Sleeping

12 Ananay Hostal D1
13 Arthy's Guesthouse C1
14 Bacoo Hostel C1
15 Hospedaje Milenio E1
16 Hostal Maya Inn B4
17 Hostal República F4
18 Hotel Continental A2
19 Hotel Las Brisas A3
20 Hotel Milton B5
21 Hotel Sagárnaga B4
22 Wild Rover F4

Eating

23 Alexander Coffee & Pub D3
24 Confitería Club de La Paz D5
25 Irupana C4
26 Pepe's Coffee Bar B4

Drinking & Nightlife

27 Bocaisapo C1
28 Café Sol y Luna C4

Entertainment

Peña Huari .... (see 16)
29 Peña Parnaso C4
30 Teatro Municipal Alberto Saavedra Pérez D2

Shopping

31 Artesanía Sorata B4
32 Comart Tukuypaj C4
33 Spitting Llama Bookstore & Outfitter C4

Information

34 Banco Mercantil D4
35 Banco Nacional de Bolivia E5
36 Cambios América D5
37 Casa de Cambio Sudamer E5
38 Instituto Geográfico Militar C5
39 Migración E5

the Marqués de Villaverde. The highlight is the Tres Milenios de Tejidos exhibition of stunning weavings from around the country – ask a guide for a look inside the drawers beneath the wall hangings.

★ Calle Jaén Museums MUSEUM
(Map p194; Calle Jaén, Casco Viejo; combination admission B$4; ⏲9am-12:30pm & 2:30-7pm Tue-Fri, 9am-1pm Sat & Sun) These four small museums are clustered together along La Paz's finest colonial street, and can generally be bundled into one visit. Buy tickets at the Museo Costumbrista. Also known as Museo del Oro (Gold Museum), the **Museo de Metales Preciosos** (Museum of Precious Metals; Jaén 777) houses four impressively presented salons of pre-Columbian silver, gold and copper works and pieces from Tiwanaku.

Museo Nacional de Arqueología Tiwanaku MUSEUM
(National Archaeology Museum; Map p198; ☎231-1621; Tiawanacu 93, Casco Viejo; admission B$10; ⏲9am-12:30pm & 3-7pm Mon-Fri, 9am-noon Sat) Two blocks east of the Prado, this small but well-sorted collection of artifacts illustrates the most interesting aspects of Tiwanaku culture – those that weren't appropriated, anyway.

Parque Raúl Salmón de la Barra PARK
(Map p198; off Bolívar, Miraflores; ⏲dawn-dusk; 👪) La Paz's city park has interesting skyways and the **Mirador Laikakota** (Map p198; Av del Ejército; admission US$0.15; ⏲9am-5:30pm). Traveling circuses will often set up here, too.

El Alto

La Ceja NEIGHBORHOOD
In the lively La Ceja (Brow) district, which commands one of the highest real-estate prices in the region for its commercial value, you'll find a variety of electronic gadgets and mercantile goods. For an excellent market experience don't miss the massive **Mercado 16 de Julio** (⏲6am-3pm Thu & Sun), which stretches for many blocks along the main thoroughfare and across Plaza 16 de Julio. This shopaholic's paradise has absolutely everything, from food and electronics, to vehicles and animals, all at reasonable prices. Heads up: watch your wallet in both senses of the phrase.

Activities

Mountain Biking

There are tons of mountain-biking options just outside of La Paz. Intermediate riders can take on a thrilling downhill ride on the **World's Most Dangerous Road**, while advanced riders may wish to go for the less traveled **Chacaltaya to Zongo Route**, the rides near **Sorata**, or include a bit of single track on the top of the **Dangerous Road Route** for an extra B$100. Beginners should check out the **Balcón Andino** descent near the Zona Sur.

Gravity Assisted Mountain Biking MOUNTAIN BIKING
(Map p194; ☎231-3849; www.gravitybolivia.com; Linares 940, La Paz) This knowledgeable, highly regarded and professional outfit has an excellent reputation among travelers and tip-top Kona downhill bikes. Their Dangerous Road Trip (B$750 per person) ends with hot showers, an all-you-can-eat buffet and a tour of the Senda Verde animal refuge.

B-Side MOUNTAIN BIKING
(Map p194; ☎211-4225; bside-adventures.blogspot.com; Linares 943, Rosario) B-Side is recommended for the Coroico trip (B$310 to B$690 per person). It receives positive reports from travelers and hooks you up with a bike operator based on the type of bike you want, the size of the group and your experience level.

Trekking & Climbing

La Paz is the staging ground for most of the climbs in the Cordilleras. From here novice climbers can arrange trips to Huayna Potosí (two to three days, B$900 to B$1100), while more experienced climbers may look to climb Illimani (four to five days, US$485), Sajama (five days, US$650), Parinacota (four days, US$530) and beyond.

Except for the altitude, La Paz and its environs are made for hiking. Many La Paz tour agencies offer daily 'hiking' tours to Chacaltaya, a rough 35km drive north of La Paz, and an easy way to bag a high peak. Head to Valle de la Luna, Valle de las Animas or Muela del Diablo for do-it-yourself day-hikes from La Paz. Other longer day trips or guided tours take you to the Hampaturi Valley and Cotopata National Park.

Andean Expeditions/ Dirninger CLIMBING, HIKING
(☎7755-0226, 241-4235; www.andean-expeditions.com; Sagárnaga 271, Galeria Las Brujas) An Austrian-founded company which offers mountain treks in Bolivia and neighboring countries, and uses UIAGM-certified guides.

DEADLY TREADLIES & THE WORLD'S MOST DANGEROUS ROAD

Many agencies offering the La Cumbre-to-Coroico mountain-bike plunge give travelers T-shirts boasting about surviving the road. Keep in mind that the gravel road is narrow (just over 3.2m wide) and has precipitous cliffs with up to 600m drops and few safety barriers.

In March 2007 a new replacement road opened. Prior to this, the road between La Paz and Coroico was identified as the World's Most Dangerous Road (WMDR) by an Inter-American Development Bank (IDB) report, citing an average of 26 vehicles per year that disappeared over the edge into the great abyss.

With the new road up and running, the old road – the WMDR – is now used almost exclusively by cyclists, support vehicles and the odd tourist bus.

Around 15 cyclists have died doing the 64km trip (with a 3600m vertical descent) and readers have reported close encounters and nasty accidents. Be careful when selecting your agency – talk with the guide, look at the bike, inspect brake pads and gears, and ask what they do to prevent accidents. Cheaper isn't always necessarily better.

Nuts & Bolts

The trip begins around 7am in La Paz. Your agency will arrange a hotel pickup. From there, you bus it up to the *cumbre* (summit), about 45 minutes outside La Paz. Trips cost anywhere from B$310 to B$750, but you get what you pay for. Advanced riders can include a fun section of single track up top for an extra B$100. Most operations provide a solid buffet lunch in Coroico, and some even have arrangements with hotels for showers/swimming pool rights. There is a B$25 surcharge to use the old road. Bring sunscreen, a swimsuit and dust-rag (if they don't provide one), and ask about water allotments. The bus takes you back up in the early evening. Expect to arrive back in La Paz at around 9pm.

Sopocachi

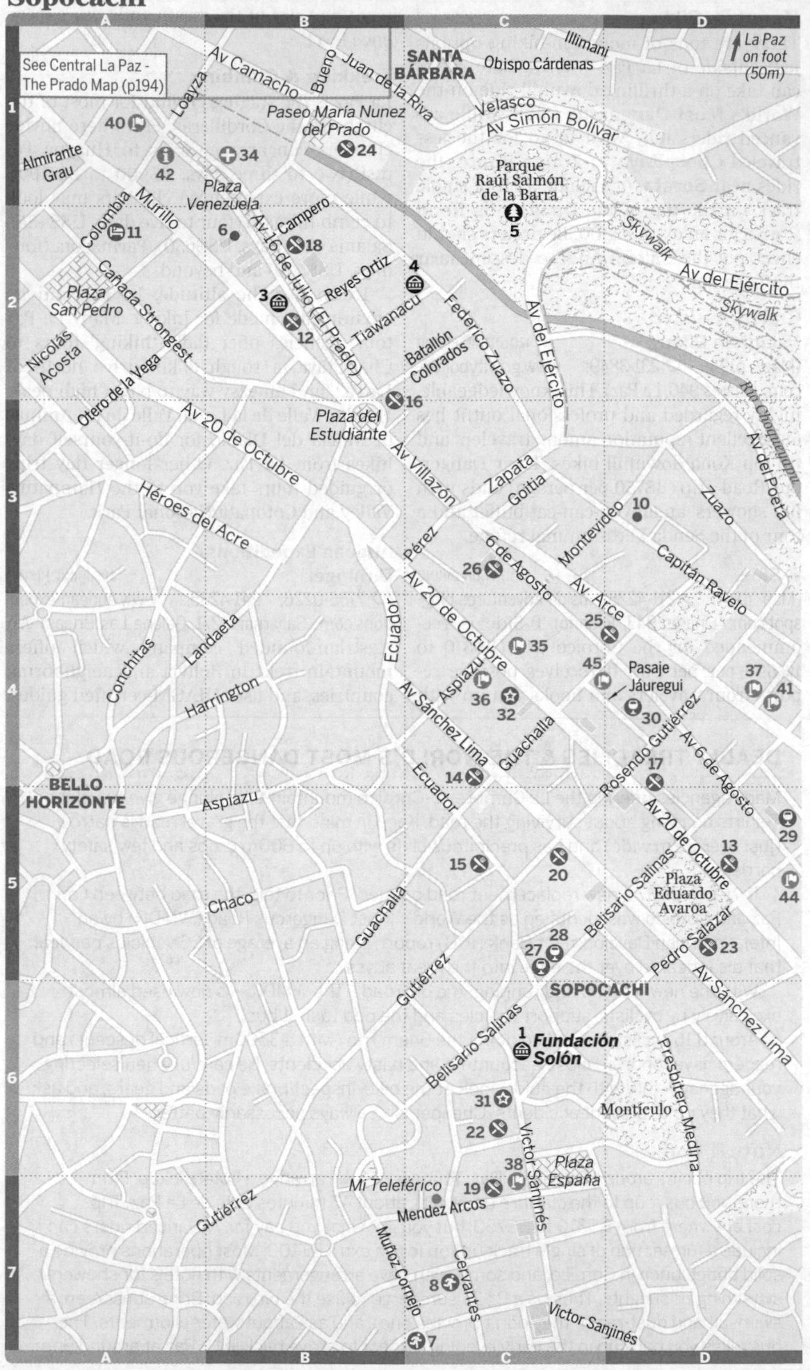

See Central La Paz - The Prado Map (p194)
La Paz on foot (50m)
SANTA BÁRBARA
Illimani
Obispo Cárdenas
Av Camacho
Bueno
Juan de la Riva
Loayza
Paseo María Nunez del Prado
Velasco
Av Simón Bolívar
Almirante Grau
Plaza Venezuela
Parque Raúl Salmón de la Barra
Colombia
Murillo
Campero
Av 16 de Julio (El Prado)
Reyes Ortiz
Skywalk
Av del Ejército
Plaza San Pedro
Cañada Strongest
Tiwanacu
Federico Zuazo
Nicolás Acosta
Batallón Colorados
Otero de la Vega
Plaza del Estudiante
Río Choqueyapu
Av 20 de Octubre
Av Villazón
Zapata
Goitia
Av del Poeta
Héroes del Acre
Pérez
Montevideo
Zuazo
6 de Agosto
Capitán Ravelo
Av Arce
Landaeta
Conchitas
Ecuador
Aspiazu
Pasaje Jáuregui
Harrington
Av Sánchez Lima
Guachalla
Rosendo Gutiérrez
Av 6 de Agosto
BELLO HORIZONTE
Belisario Salinas
Plaza Eduardo Avaroa
Chaco
Pedro Salazar
Gutiérrez
SOPOCACHI
Fundación Solón
Presbitero Medina
Montículo
Victor Sanjinés
Plaza España
Mi Teleférico
Mendez Arcos
Muñoz Cornejo
Cervantes

More than 10 years in Bolivia, and not the same old run-of-the-mill tours.

Andean Summits CLIMBING

(Map p198; ☎242-2106; www.andeansummits.com; Muñoz Cornejo 1009, Sopocachi) Offers a variety of outdoor activities from mountaineering and trekking to 4WD tours in Bolivia and beyond. The owners are professional UIAGM/IFMGA mountain guides.

La Paz on Foot ECOTOUR

(Map p194; ☎7154-3327, 240-6238; www.lapazonfoot.com; 710 Indaburo, near Jaén) This tip-top operation run by the passionate English-speaking ecologist Stephen Taranto offers a range of activities, including walks in and around La Paz, Apolobamba, the Yungas, Chulumani, Madidi and Titicaca. The interactive La Paz urban trek (half-day tours and day tours, fee depending on group size) heads from the heights of El Alto to the depths of Zona Sur. Other tours include art and architecture, living history, stimulants (think coca, cocoa and coffee) and a mural explorer tour. Multilingual guides are available.

Paragliding

★ AndesXtremo PARAGLIDING

(☎7358-3349; www.andresextremo.com; B$450) If the *teleférico* wasn't enough for you, then take a ride with three brothers who will get you higher than you've ever been in La Paz. Soaring high above the craggy crevices near the village of Yanari, you can look an eagle practically in the eye during your 20- to 30-minute descent. They'll even let you drive/fly (for a minute). Also offered in Cochabamba.

Courses

Pico Verde Languages LANGUAGE

(Map p194; ☎231-8328; www.pico-verde.com; Sagárnaga 363, 2nd fl, Rosario) Offers flexible schedules and homestays.

Tours

Many of Bolivia's tour agencies are based in La Paz. Most agencies run day tours (B$70 to B$500 per person) in and around La Paz, to Lake Titicaca, Tiwanaku, Zongo Valley, Chacaltaya, Valle de la Luna and other sites.

America Tours GUIDED TOUR

(Map p198; ☎237-4204; www.america-ecotours.com; Av 16 de Julio 1490 Oficina No 9, El Prado, La Paz) This warmly recommended agency

Sopocachi

Top Sights
1 Fundación Solón C6

Sights
2 Mirador Laikakota E2
3 Museo de Arte Contemporáneo Plaza B2
4 Museo Nacional de Arqueología Tiwanaku C2
5 Parque Raúl Salmón de la Barra C2

Activities, Courses & Tours
6 America Tours B2
7 Andean Summits C7
8 Animales SOS C7
9 Centro Boliviano-Americano E5
10 Magri Turismo D3

Sleeping
11 Onkel Inn A2

Eating
12 Alexander Coffee & Pub B2
13 Alexander Coffee & Pub D5
14 Arco Iris C4
15 Armonía C5
16 Café Ciudad B2
17 Cafe La Terraza D4
18 Cafe La Terraza B2
19 Horno Camba C7
20 Irupana C5
21 Ketal Hipermercado E5
22 La Espinita C6
23 La Guinguette D5
24 Mercado Camacho B1
25 Paceña La Salteña D4
26 Sergiu's Pizza C3

Drinking & Nightlife
27 Abbey Road C5
28 Green Bar C5
29 Mongo's D5
30 Reineke Fuchs D4

Entertainment
31 Centro Arte y Culturas Bolivianos C6
32 Thelonious Jazz Bar C4
33 Traffic Dance E5

Information
34 24-hour Pharmacy B1
35 Argentinian Embassy C4
36 Australian Embassy C4
37 Brazilian Embassy D4
38 Canadian Embassy C7
39 Clínica Alemana F6
40 Ecuadorian Embassy A1
41 German Embassy D4
42 InfoTur A1
43 Italian Embassy E5
44 Paraguayan Embassy D5
45 Peruvian Embassy C4
46 Spanish Embassy F6
47 Tourist Police E1
48 UK Embassy F6
49 US Embassy F6

offers a wide range of community-based ecotourism projects and tours around La Paz and Bolivia. English spoken.

Magri Turismo GUIDED TOUR
(Map p198; 244-2727; www.magriturismo.com; Capitán Ravelo 2101, La Paz) A range of tours organized around Bolivia.

Turisbus GUIDED TOUR
(245-1341; www.gruporosario.com/turisbus-tours; La Paz) A large range of day and multi-day tours organized for groups and individuals around Bolivia.

Festivals & Events

Of the major festivals and holidays during the year, Alasitas (January 24), the festival of abundance, and El Gran Poder (late May to early June) are the most interesting to visitors. The Fiestas Universitarias take place during the first week in December, accompanied by riotous merrymaking and plenty of water-balloon bombs.

Sleeping

Most backpackers beeline for central La Paz to find a bed. The area around Mercado de Hechicería (Witches' Market; between Illampu, Santa Cruz and Sagárnaga) is about as close as Bolivia gets to a travelers ghetto. If you want to be closer to movie theaters, a wider array of restaurants and a bar or two, consider staying closer to Sopocachi.

West of El Prado

Hotel Continental HOTEL $
(Map p194; 245-1176; www.hotelcontinentalbolivia.com; Illampu 626, Rosario; s/d/tr B$100/150/200, with shared bathroom B$80/120/190;) This dark and slightly dreary downtown option is popular among thrift-sters. The detergent smell can be overpowering, but at least you know somebody was cleaning the place.

Hostal Maya Inn HOTEL $
(Map p194; 231-1970; www.hostalmaya.com; Sagárnaga 339, Rosario; s/d/tr incl break-

fast B$100/180/240, with shared bathroom B$80/140/180; @📶) This is a friendly, if basic, place. The most appealing rooms have windows (note: a few don't), although rooms at the front can be a little noisy. Non-smokers may be bothered by the smokiness, and the electric showers can be rough for hot-water lovers.

Hotel Sagárnaga HOTEL $
(Map p194; ☎235-0252; www.hotel-sagarnaga.com; Sagárnaga 326, Rosario; s/d incl breakfast B$180/270; @📶) The knight in shining armor at the front desk (and no, we're not talking about the receptionist, although he *is* friendly) and the mirrors are the brightest things in this otherwise slightly tarnished and smoky, yet wholly adequate, '80s-style place. East-facing rooms are the best, 1st-floor 'A' rooms have newer beds (and cost more), and decent solar showers should keep you warm come bath-time.

Onkel Inn HOSTEL $$
(Map p198; ☎249-0456; www.onkelinn.com; Colombia 257, Sopocachi; dm/s/d/tr incl breakfast B$75/130/200/300; @📶) A bright, HI-affiliated place in a fabulous spot between San Pedro and El Prado. It's less of a scene than the hostels up by the terminal, good for *tranquilo* travelers. The dorms are the nicest in town with crispy-cream orange bedcovers and a bright modern feel. Some bunks will leave you with vertigo; nice common areas include a pool table.

Hotel Milton HOTEL $$
(Map p194; ☎236-8003, 235-3511; www.hotelmiltonbolivia.com; Illampu 1126-1130, Rosario; s/d/tr incl breakfast B$120/230/330; @📶) Tune in and drop out! This '70s pad truly is a paradise lost with red vinyl-studded walls, painted murals and funky wallpaper. Darker rooms at the back are a bit dingy, but the higher and lighter front rooms afford stupendous views over La Paz, making this a solid budget bet.

Hotel Las Brisas HOTEL $$
(Map p194; ☎246-3691; www.hotelbrisas.net; Illampu 742, Rosario; s/d/tr incl breakfast B$196/280/406; @📶) This is a solid budget bet with a 'Bolivia moderna' style – think stark but neat rooms (some with internal windows), funky murals and crispy sheets coupled with a few shabby bits and external glassy walls. The rooms at the front have excellent views and the staff are friendly, with a nice courtyard and sunny top-floor restaurant.

East of El Prado

Wild Rover HOSTEL $
(Map p194; ☎211-6903; www.wildroverhostel.com; Illimani s/n, Miraflores; dm B$45-65, s with shared bathroom B$65; @📶) Your best bet to meet fellow travelers, the Wild Rover has a high-octane take-no-prisoners vibe that 20-somethings will love and 30-somethings will loathe. The rooms at some other hostels are better, and the dorm rooms are too tightly packed, but you'll be spending most of your day at the boisterous Irish pub anyway.

Arthy's Guesthouse GUESTHOUSE $
(Map p194; ☎228-1439; arthyshouse.tripod.com; Ismael Montes 693; r per person with shared bathroom B$100; @) This clean and cozy place hidden behind a bright orange door deservedly receives rave reviews as a 'tranquil oasis,' despite its location on one of La Paz's busiest roads. The friendly, English-speaking owners will do all they can do to help you. Kitchen facilities are available. Note, though, that there is a midnight curfew.

Ananay Hostal HOSTEL $
(Map p194; ☎290-6507; www.hostal.ananay.com; Jaén 710; per person incl breakfast B$140, with shared bath B$105; @📶) A brightly painted courtyard centers this historic home, a former *peña* (folk-music venue), in the heart of Jaen's museum district. This new addition includes rooftop city views, several comfortable common areas, including a bean-bag-chair lounge with TV. The name, which fits, means 'how nice' in Quechua.

Bacoo Hostel HOSTEL $
(Map p194; ☎228-0679; www.bacoohostel.com; Alto de la Alianza 693; dm B$45-70, d B$190; @📶) This sprawling party-focused hostel has a bar and Jacuzzi (ooh-la-la), and plenty of travelers looking to hook up (in more ways than one). Welcomed touches include down comforters and thick mattresses. Dorm rooms hold four to 18 people, so book ahead or bring ear plugs. There's a rather unkempt feel to the place, but you're close to the bus station and Calle Jaén.

Hospedaje Milenio HOTEL $
(Map p194; ☎228-1263; hospedajemilenio.blogspot.com; Yanacocha 860, Casco Viejo; r per person with shared bathroom B$40; 📶) It's a long walk uphill to this simple, laid-back joint, run by friendly staff, with fun common areas, a book exchange and truly dirt-cheap

rooms: a solid budget bet. The best rooms are upstairs and outward facing (most single rooms have internal windows). The mushy beds may leave you limping, though. Architectural enhancements were coming as of late 2015.

Hostal República HOSTEL **$$**
(Map p194; ☎220-2742; www.hostalrepublica.com; Illimani s/n, Miraflores; d/apt B$240/550, dm/s with shared bathroom B$66/180; @📶) Three blocks from the historic heart of the city, this hostel occupies a lovely historic building that was home to one of Bolivia's first presidents. Its two large courtyards make for a quiet oasis. All the rooms are fairly basic, but will make for a pleasant stay--in stark contrast to its raucous Irish neighbors! Two apartments sleep five each.

Eating

For local fare, your cheapest bets are the *almuerzos* (set lunches) in the countless hole-in-the-wall restaurants; look for the chalkboard menus out front. Street stalls and markets offer tasty morsels, and there are vegetarian restaurants around.

If you don't mind the hectic settings and questionable hygiene, your most interesting (and cheapest) food options are found in the markets. The *comedor* (dining hall) at **Mercado Uruguay** off Max Paredes sells set meals (of varying standards and in basic surrounds), including tripe and *ispi* (similar to sardines), for less than B$8. Other areas to look for cheap and informal meals include the street markets around Av Buenos Aires, and the **Mercado Camacho** (Map p198; cnr Av Simon Bolivar & Bueno), known for its juice stands, fresh breads and puffy *llauchas* (cheese pastries).

West of El Prado

Horno Camba SOUTH AMERICAN **$**
(Map p198; Mendez Arcos 732; B$10-20) If you're missing yummy Santa Cruz breakfast and lunch treats like *sonsos* and *cuñapes,* here's your recompense. Some nice set lunches, as well. There's a separate location around the corner from Plaza de Estudiante on Landaete.

Paceña La Salteña FAST FOOD **$**
(Map p198; Av 20 de Octubre 2379, Sopocachi; salteña B$5-10; ⏲8:30am-2pm) Eating a *salteña* (a baked pastry stuffed with out-of-this-world meat and vegetable goodness) is a not-to-be-missed local experience. The peach walls, chintz curtains and gold trimmings give the fare a gilded edge at this award-winning *salteñería*. Vegetarian *salteñas* are available, too. How many triangular napkins will *you* need?

Armonía VEGETARIAN **$**
(Map p198; Ecuador 2284, Sopocachi; buffet B$32; ⏲lunch Mon-Sat; 🖉) A recommended all-you-can-eat vegetarian lunch is found above Librería Armonía in Sopocachi. Organic products are served when possible.

Sergiu's Pizza PIZZA **$**
(Map p198; 6 de Agosto 2040, Prado; slices from B$12; ⏲noon-10pm) Popular among students, this hole-in-the-wall near the Aspiazu steps serves up a reasonable New York–style pizza and fast food.

La Espinita SEAFOOD **$**
(Map p198; 712 Quintin Barrios; mains B$15-25; ⏲noon-2:30pm & 6:30-9pm Mon-Fri, 2-3pm Sat & Sun) Get down to 'the bones' with a hearty Andean lunch of four favorite fried fish in

EASY EATS

While they are a bit saccharine, these chain restaurants are good spots if your stomach is easily upset.

Alexander Coffee & Pub Branches in **Prado** (Map p198; www.alexandercoffee.com; Av 16 de Julio 1832, Prado; mains B$16-40; ⏲6am-11pm), **Socabaya** (Map p194; www.alexandercoffee.com; Calle Potosí 1091, Socabaya ; mains B$16-40; ⏲6am-11pm) and **Sopocachi** (Map p198; www.alexandercoffee.com; 20 de Octubre 2463, Sopocachi; mains B$16-40; ⏲6am-11pm).

La Terraza Café Branches in **Prado** (Map p198; 16 de Julio 1615, Prado; mains B$10-40; ⏲until late) and **Sopocachi** (Map p198; 20 de Octubre 2331, Montenegro Bloque; mains B$10-40; ⏲until late).

Api Happy Serves variations on the piping-hot purple *paceña* wonder drink and accompanying snacks. Branches at Plaza Murillo, Plaza Estudiante and Zona Sur.

a delicious home-made batter, all served with crisy *ispi* (little sardine-sized fish) on top, and sides of potato and *mote* (big corn). Delicious desserts include a homespun ice-cream and it's no wonder locals are flocking to this pint-sized eatery. Don't mind the eyes!

Pepe's Coffee Bar CAFE $
(Map p194; Jiménez 894, Rosario; snacks B$10-25) This cheery, inviting, artsy cafe is tucked away on a sunny bend in the Witches' Market. It's a cozy place for coffee or cocktails. Big breakfasts and veggie lunch options go down easily while browsing the library of guidebooks and English-language periodicals.

Irupana SUPERMARKET
(Map p194; cnr Murillo 1014 & Tarija, Rosario) Locally made organic produce is sold at this health-food chain. There is another branch in **Sopocachi** (Map p198; cnr Fernando Guachalla & Av Sanchez Lima, Sopocachi).

Arco Iris SUPERMARKET
(Map p198; Guachalla 554, Sopocachi; ⏲8am-8pm Mon-Sat) Arco Iris has an extensive *pastelería* (cake shop) and deli featuring fine specialty regional meat and dairy treats like smoked llama salami, plus products such as fresh palm hearts and dried Beni fruits.

Ketal Hipermercado SUPERMARKET
(Map p198; cnr Av Aniceto Arce & Pinilla, Sopocachi) If you're heading off for a picnic, load up here on everything from olives to cheese, crackers and beer.

La Guinguette FRENCH $$
(Map p198; Pedro Salazar 497, Sopocachi; mains B$45-70; ⏲9am-11pm Mon-Sat) Polyglot cool cats abide at this chic eatery on the top corner of Plaza Avaroa. The cozy bistro serves an excellent soup, sandwich and dessert combo at lunch for B$45. Try an anise-laced Ricard or a quinoa beer and retire to the smoking side of the bar for some continental conviviality. Live music when it feels right (weekends).

East of El Prado

Café Ciudad INTERNATIONAL $
(Map p198; Plaza del Estudiante, Prado; B$15-40; ⏲24hr; 📶) This La Paz institution serves up warm coffee, surly service, yummy pizzas, hamburgers and other international favorites (plus one of the best *pique machos,* a Bolivian dish with sausages and french fries in sauce, in town) 24 hours a day, seven days a week.

Confitería Club de La Paz CAFE $
(Map p194; cnr Avs Camacho & Mariscal Santa Cruz, Prado; mains B$10-30) For a quick coffee or empanada, join the well-dressed elderly patrons in their daily rituals. The cafe was formerly renowned as a literary cafe and haunt of politicians (and, formerly, of Nazi war criminals); today, it's better known for its strong espresso and cakes.

Drinking & Nightlife

Bocaisapo PUB
(Map p194; Jaén, Casco Viejo; ⏲7pm-late Thu-Sat) This bohemian favorite has live music, a maddening elixir de coca drink, plenty of affected La Paz artsters and a candlelit ambience.

Mongo's PUB
(Map p198; Hermanos Manchego 2444, Sopocachi; ⏲6pm-3am) The easiest spot to pull in La Paz – that's hook up to you Americanos – Mongo's is a perennial favorite, with dancing on the tables, excellent pub grub and a good mix of locals and tourists.

Café Sol y Luna PUB
(Map p194; www.solyluna-lapaz.com; cnr Murillo & Cochabamba, Rosario; ⏲9am-1am) This is a low-key, Dutch-run hang-out offering cocktails, good coffee and tasty international meals. It has three cozy levels with a book exchange and an extensive guidebook reference library (many current Lonely Planet titles), talks, salsa nights, live music and other activities. Try the *chala* (white) Bolivian beer.

Green Bar PUB
(Map p198; Belisario Salinas 596, Sopocachi) For a cloistered pub setting with intellectual types, girls straight out of a Modigliani painting, weirdos, rockers and other ne'er-do-wells, check out this beloved hole in the wall.

Reineke Fuchs BEER HALL
(Map p198; Jáuregui 2241, Sopocachi; ⏲from 6pm Mon-Sat) This Sopocachi *brewhaus* features imported German beers, *schnappsladen* and hearty sausage-based fare. They also make their own beer, based on centuries-old *Deutschland* traditions – a heady concoction, indeed. Also in Zona Sur.

Abbey Road PUB

(Map p198; Belisario Salinas, Sopocachi; ⊙evening Wed-Sat) Ask for a blonde from Cochabamba anywhere else and you might get slapped. But here owner Jaime knows you mean one of that city's fine artesanal beers, one of a handful of national craft brews served under the watchful eye of many Beatles posters. Liberate yourself from the tyranny of Paceña and Huari! It's two doors up from Green Bar.

☆ Entertainment

Most *peñas* (folk-music venues) present traditional Andean music rendered on *zampoña* (pan flute), *quena* (simple reed flute) and *charango* (ukulele-type instrument), but also often include guitar shows and song recitals. Many advertise nightly shows, but in reality most only have shows on Friday and Saturday nights, starting at 9pm or 10pm and lasting until 1am or 2am. Admission ranges from B$30 to B$80 and usually includes the first drink; meals cost extra.

Pick up a copy of the free monthly booklet *Kaos* (available in bars and cafes) for a day-by-day rundown of what's on in La Paz.

Soccer matches are played at Estadio Hernando Siles (Estadio Olímpico La Paz; Miraflores). Sunday (year-round) is the big game day, and Wednesday and Saturday also have games. Prices vary according to seats and whether it's a local or international game (B$20 to B$100).

Peña Huari TRADITIONAL MUSIC

(Map p194; ☎231-6225; Sagárnaga 339, Rosario; cover charge B$105; ⊙show 8pm) The city's best-known *peña* is aimed at tourists and Bolivian business people. The attached restaurant specializes in Bolivian cuisine, including llama steak, Lake Titicaca trout, *charquekan* (jerky) and salads. The show starts at 8pm.

Peña Parnaso TRADITIONAL MUSIC

(Map p194; ☎231-6827; Sagárnaga 189, Rosario; cover B$80; ⊙show 8:30pm) Also open for lunch (B$35) with no show.

Centro Arte y Culturas Bolivianos LIVE MUSIC

(Map p198; Ecuador 2582, Sopocachi) This arts complex has rotating exhibits, live music (Thursday through Saturday), a decent restaurant and terrace cafe. They call it the Luna Llena rock bar come 8pm.

Thelonious Jazz Bar JAZZ

(Map p198; Av 20 de Octubre 2172, Sopocachi; cover around B$25; ⊙7pm-3am Mon-Sat) Bebop fans love this charmingly low-key bar for its live and often impromptu performances and great atmosphere. The marquee promotes upcoming sessions.

Traffic Dance DANCE

(Map p198; Av Aniceto Arce 2549, Prado) Popular for cocktails, live music – from world beats to disco – and all the attitude and dancing – including salsa lessons – you can muster.

Teatro Municipal Alberto Saavedra Pérez THEATER

(Map p194; cnr Sanjinés & Indaburo, Casco Viejo; tickets B$20-50) The Teatro Municipal Alberto Saavedra Pérez has an ambitious program of folklore shows, folk-music concerts and foreign theatrical presentations. It's a great old restored building with a round auditorium, elaborate balconies and a vast ceiling mural.

Shopping

La Paz is a shopper's paradise: not only are prices very reasonable, but the quality of what's offered can be astounding.

The main tourist shopping area lies along the very steep and literally breathtaking Calle Sagárnaga between Santa Cruz and Tamayo, and spreads out along adjoining streets. Here, you'll also find Calle Linares, an alley chockablock with artisans' stores.

To trade books, the best library is Oliver's Travels bar. Also try Gravity Assisted Mountain Biking or Café Sol y Luna.

Artesanía Sorata ARTS & CRAFTS

(Map p194; www.artesaniasorata.com; Sagárnaga 303, Rosario) A community-focused project that specializes in export-quality handmade dolls, original alpaca products and other beautiful items.

Comart Tukuypaj ARTS & CRAFTS

(Map p194; www.comart-tukuypaj.com; Linares 958, Rosario) Offers export-quality, fair-trade llama, alpaca and *artesanías* from around the country. Upstairs the Inca Pallay women's weaving cooperative has a gallery with justly famous Jal'qa and Candelaria weavings.

Spitting Llama Bookstore & Outfitter OUTDOOR EQUIPMENT
(Map p194; www.thespittingllama.com; Linares 947) Inside Posada de la Abuela, this friendly one-stop shop stocks everything from maps to gear, including tents, backpacks and hiking boots.

Information

DANGERS & ANNOYANCES

La Paz is a great city to explore on foot, but take the local advice '*camina lento, toma poco... y duerme solo*' (walk slowly, drink little... and sleep by your lonesome) to avoid feeling the effects of *soroche* (altitude sickness). *Soroche* pills are said to be ineffective, and can even increase altitude sickness. Acetaminophen (also known as Tylenol or paracetemol) does work, and drinking lots of water helps too.

Take care when crossing roads and avoid walking in busy streets at peak hours when fumes can be overwhelming.

Protests are not uncommon in La Paz (and they do sometimes turn violent). These center around Plazas San Francisco and Murillo.

EMERGENCY

Fire & Ambulance (☎118)

Police (☎110)

Tourist Police (Policía Turística; Map p198; ☎800-140-081, 800-140-071; Puerta 22, Plaza del Estadio, Miraflores) Next to Disco Love City. English-speaking. Report thefts to obtain a *denuncia* (affidavit) for insurance purposes – they won't recover any stolen goods. There is also a kiosk in front of the bus terminal. Insist on getting the paperwork!

IMMIGRATION OFFICES

Migración (Map p194; ☎211-0960; www.migracion.gob.bo; Camacho 1468; ⊗8:30am-4pm Mon-Fri) Some call this place 'Migraine-ation' but this is where you must obtain your visa extensions.

INTERNET ACCESS

Charges range from B$2 to B$4 an hour. Many of the smarter cafes and most hotels now have wi-fi access.

MEDIA

La Razón (www.la-razon.com), *El Diario* (www.eldiario.net) and *La Prensa* (www.laprensa.com.bo) are La Paz's major daily newspapers. National media chains **ATB** (www.bolivia.com) and **Grupo Fides** (www.radiofides.com) host the most up-to-date online news sites. See *Bolivian Express* (www.bolivianexpress.org) for Bolivian cultural events and articles in English.

MEDICAL SERVICES

For serious medical emergency conditions, contact your embassy for doctor recommendations.

24-hour Pharmacy (Farmacia 24 Horas; Map p198; Av 16 de Julio; ⊗24hr) A good pharmacy on the Prado.

Centro Epidemiológico Departamental La Paz (Centro Pilote; ☎245-0166; Vásquez, near Perú; ⊗8:30-11:30am Mon-Fri) Anyone heading for malarial areas can pick up antimalarials, and rabies and yellow fever vaccinations, for the cost of a sterile needle – bring one from a pharmacy.

Clínica Alemana (Map p198; ☎243-2521; Av 6 de Agosto; ⊗24hr) Offers German efficiency.

High Altitude Pathology Institute (☎224-5394, 7325-8026; www.altitudeclinic.com; Saavedra 2302, Miraflores) Bolivian member of the International Association for Medical Assistance to Travelers (IAMAT). Offers computerized medical checkups and can help with high altitude problems. English spoken.

MONEY

Cash withdrawals of bolivianos and US dollars are possible at numerous ATMs at major intersections around the city. For cash advances (bolivianos only; amount according to your limit in your home country) with no commission and little hassle, try the listings below.

Go to **Western Union/DHL**, which has outlets scattered all around town, for urgent international money transfers.

Casas de cambio (exchange bureaus) in the city center can be quicker and more convenient than banks.

Be wary of counterfeit US dollars and bolivianos, especially with *cambistas* (street money changers) who loiter around the intersections of Colón, Camacho and Santa Cruz. Traveler's checks can be virtually impossible to change, except at money changers and banks.

Banco Mercantil (Map p194; cnr Mercado & Ayacucho)

Banco Nacional de Bolivia (Map p194; cnr Colón & Camacho)

Cambios América (Map p194; Camacho 1223, Casco Viejo) Money changing bureau.

Casa de Cambio Sudamer (Map p194; Colón 206, near Camacho, Casco Viejo; ⊗8:30am-6:30pm Mon-Fri, 9:30am-12:30pm Sat) Also has MoneyGram service for money transfers.

POST

Central Post Office (Ecobol; Map p194; cnr Mariscal Santa Cruz & Oruro, Prado; ⊗8am-8pm Mon-Fri, 8:30am-6pm Sat, 9am-noon Sun) *Lista de correos* (poste restante) mail is held for two months for free here – bring your passport. A downstairs customs desk facilitates international parcel posting.

TELEPHONE

Convenient *puntos* (privately run phone offices) of various carriers – Entel, Cotel, Tigo, Viva etc – are scattered throughout the city, and some cell services now have wandering salespeople who will allow you to make a call from their cell phone. Street kiosks, which are on nearly every corner, also sell phone cards, and offer brief local calls for around B$1 per minute. You can buy cell phone sim cards (known as *chips*) for around B$10 from Entel or any carrier outlet.

Entel (Map p194; Ayacucho 267, Casco Viejo; ⏲8:30am-9pm Mon-Fri, to 8:30pm Sat, 9am-4pm Sun) The main Entel office is the best place to receive incoming calls and faxes.

International Call Center (Map p194; Galería Chuquiago, cnr Sagárnaga & Murillo; ⏲8:30am-8pm) International calls can be made at low prices from the international call center.

TOURIST INFORMATION

Free city maps are available at the tourist offices and inside the central post office.

Information Kiosks (Main bus terminal; ⏲vary) The kiosks have maps and may help you find a hotel.

InfoTur (Map p198; ☎265-1778; www.visitbolivia.org; cnr Av Mariscal Santa Cruz & Colombia, Prado; ⏲8:30am-7pm Mon-Fri, 9:30am-1pm Sat & Sun) Stop by to grab some maps and get detailed information. English is spoken by some staff.

ℹ Getting There & Away

Most travelers will arrive at either El Alto International Airport or the main bus terminal. Buses from within Bolivia may also drop you in Villa Fátima or the Plaza 1 de Mayo area.

AIR

El Alto International Airport (LPB) is 10km via toll road from the city center on the Altiplano. The domestic departure tax is B$15, while the international departure tax is US$25 (payable by cash only in the airport lobby).

Minibus 212 runs frequently between Plaza Isabel la Católica and the airport between 7am and 8pm approximately. Heading into town from the airport, this service will drop you anywhere along the Prado.

Radio taxis (around B$70 for up to four passengers) will pick you up at your door; confirm the price with the dispatcher when booking, or ask the driver to verify it when you climb in. For a fifth person there is an additional B$10 charge. Transportes Aéreos Militares (TAM) flights leave from the military airport in El Alto. Catch a Río Seco *micro* from the upper Prado. Taxi fares should be about the same as for the main El Alto airport.

Times and schedules change often. Check online and call ahead.

BUS

La Paz has three bus terminals/bus areas. You can use the main bus terminal for most national and international destinations. If you are going to the Yungas or the Amazon, you'll need to go to Villa Fátima. For Sorata, Titicaca and Tiwanaku, head to the Cemetery area. Most national destinations are serviced hourly for major cities and daily for less visited spots. International departures generally leave once weekly; check ahead as schedules change. You can get to all the bus areas by *micro*, but radio taxis are recommended for your safety.

Tourist bus services to Copacabana, Puno (book with La Paz tour agencies), Tiwanaku, Uyuni and Valle de la Luna cut down on risk and up your comfort.

Diana Tours (Map p194; www.diana-tours.com; Main Bus Terminal; trips B$60) Round-trip guided trips to Valle de la Luna, leaving at 8:30am.

Nuevo Continente (Main Bus Terminal; B$60) Round-trip guided trips to Tiwanaku, leaving at 9am and returning at 4pm.

Todo Turismo (www.todoturismo.bo; Main Bus Terminal; B$230) Overnight direct buses to Uyuni leaving at 9pm (10 hours).

Main Terminal

The **main bus terminal** (Terminal de Buses; Plaza Antofagasta) services all national destinations south and east of La Paz, as well as international destinations. It is a 15-minute uphill walk north of the city center. Fares are relatively uniform among companies. The station was designed by Gustave Eiffel.

DESTINATION	COST (B$)	DURATION (HR)
Arequipa	117-220	14
Arica	150-200	10
Buenos Aires	650-730	48-50
Camargo	100	16
Cochabamba	43-106	8
Copacabana	30	3-4
Cuzco	160-180	14
Iquique	120-180	11-13
Juliaca	110	9
Lima	450-500	28
Oruro	20-25	3½
Potosí	120	9
Puno	70-150	8
Santa Cruz (new road)	220	17
Sucre	180	12

Tarija	80-120	18
Tupiza	120-180	18
Uyuni	120-200	11-12
Villazón	140-250	18

Cemetery Area

Buses leaving the Cemetery (Baptista La Paz) offer cheap service to Tiwanaku, Titicaca and Sorata (via Desaguadero). This area is especially hairy at night, and you should watch your bags while boarding.

DESTINATION	COST (B$)	DURATION (HR)
Copacabana	15	3
Desaguadero	15	2
Huarina (for Cordillera Apolobamba)	10	3
Sorata	17	5
Tiwanaku	6-15	1½

Villa Fátima

Villa Fátima (Tejada Sorzano) services Coroico, and other Yungas and Amazon destinations, mostly via *micros*. It's about 1km uphill from Plaza Gualberto Villarroel. There's no central station, so ask around to find the buses servicing your particular destination. Buses service Coroico (office on Yanacachi, by an old gas station); the Amazon Basin (office on Las Americas, also by a gas station); and Chulumani (office on San Jorge). There are more operations clustered along Virgen del Carmen, just west of Av Las Américas.

DESTINATION	COST (B$)	DURATION (HR)
Caranavi	15-25	8
Chulumani	30	4
Coroico	20-30	3
Cumbre	20	1
Rurrenabaque	120	18-20
Yolosa	20	3

ℹ Getting Around

MICRO & MINIBUS

Sputtering and smoke-spewing *micros* (small buses or minibuses) charge around B$2 per trip. Minibuses service most places as well, for a slightly higher cost. In addition to a route number or letter, *micros* plainly display their destination and route on a signboard in the front window. Minibuses usually have a young tout screaming the stops. Wave to catch the bus. They stop at signed *paradas* (official stops), or if the cops aren't watching, whenever you wave them down.

RADIO TAXI

Radio taxis (with roof bubbles advertising their telephone numbers) are recommended. They charge about B$10 around the center, B$12 to B$14 (more in peak hours) from Sagárnaga to Sopocachi or Sopocachi to the Cemetery district, and B$15 to B$20 to Zona Sur. Charges are a little higher after 11pm. Normal taxi services (with just a taxi sign, no phone number and no bubble) work as collective cabs, charging each passenger around B$6, but these are known for express kidnappings.

Ask your hotel or restaurant to ring for a taxi if possible. Otherwise, taxis can be waved down anywhere, except near intersections or in areas cordoned off by the police. Always confirm the fare before you leave.

SHARED CARS & MINIBUSES

Trufis are shared cars or minibuses that ply set routes. Destinations are identified on placards on the roof or the windscreen. They charge approximately B$3 around town and B$4 to Zona Sur.

AROUND LA PAZ

Tiwanaku

While it's no Machu Picchu or Tikal, the ruins of Tiwanaku (sometimes spelled Tiahuanaco or Tihuanaco) make for a good day trip from La Paz. The site itself is less than outstanding, with a few carved monoliths, archways and arcades, and a decent museum, but history buffs will love diving into the myths and mysteries of this lost civilization. In the eponymous village there are a number of hotels, restaurants, a fun little plaza with excellent sculptures inspired by Tiwanaku styles, and a 16th-century church, built, no doubt, with stones from the Tiwanaku site.

Little is actually known about the people who constructed the ceremonial center on the southern shore of Lake Titicaca more than a thousand years ago. Archaeologists generally agree that the civilization that spawned Tiwanaku rose around 600 BC. Construction on the ceremonial site was underway by about AD 700, but by around 1200 the group had melted into obscurity, becoming another 'lost' civilization. Evidence of its influence, particularly its religion, has been found throughout the vast area that later became the Inca empire.

Visiting the Ruins

Entrance to the **site and museum** (site & museum B$80; ⏲tickets 9am-4pm, site 9am-5pm) is paid opposite the visitors center. If you go on your own, start your visit in the museum to get a basic understanding of the history, then head to the ruins. Guided **tours** (☎7524-3141; tiwanakuguias_turismo@hotmail.com; up to 6 people B$80) are available in English and Spanish, and are highly recommended.

The star of the show at the on-site museum is the massive 7.3m Monolito Bennett Pachamama, rescued in 2002 from its former smoggy home at the outdoor Templete Semisubterráneo in La Paz.

Just 100m west of the site, **Hotel Akapana** (☎289-5104; www.hotelakapana; Ferrocarril; s/d incl breakfast B$80/150) has three levels, simple rooms with good views, hot water 24 hours a day, and a top-floor *mirador* with amazing views of the neighboring site.

ℹ Getting There & Away

Many La Paz agencies offer reasonably priced, guided, full- and half-day Tiwanaku tours (B$70 to B$140 per person), including transportation and a bilingual guide.

Nuevo Continente (Main Bus Terminal; tickets B$60) has round-trip guided trips to Tiwanaku, leaving from La Paz's main bus terminal at 9am and returning at 4pm.

For those who prefer to go it alone, buses from La Paz's Cemetery leave every hour, and cost between B$6 and B$15.

Minibuses, which are often crowded, pass the museum near the entrance to the complex. To return to La Paz, catch a minibus from the village's main plaza. Make sure it says Cementario, otherwise, you'll get dropped off in El Alto's Ceja. **Empresa Ferroviaria Andina** (FCA; ☎241-6545; www.fca.com.bo; tickets B$10-40) has started a pilot program to run occasional return train trips from La Paz' El Alto to Tiwanaku (with a 1½-hour stop), and to Guaqui on Lake Titicaca (with a two-hour stop). The train departs La Paz the second Sunday of each month at 8am (B$10 to B$40). Check the website or call ahead.

LAKE TITICACA

Everything – and everyone – that sits beside this impressive body of water, from the traditional Aymará villages to the glacier-capped peaks of the Cordillera Real, seems to fall into the background – the singularity, power and sheer gravity of the lake pulling all eyes, energy and power to its massive depths.

Set between Peru and Bolivia at 3808m, the 8400-sq-km lake offers trips to the many islands that speckle the shoreline, hikes to lost coves and floating islands, parties in the tourist hub of Copacabana, and chance encounters with locals that will provide new insight into the culture and traditions of Bolivia's top attraction.

Copacabana

☎02 / POP 14,900

Nestled between two hills on the southern shore of Lake Titicaca, Copacabana is a small, bright and enchanting town. Long a religious mecca, local and international pilgrims still flock to its fiestas.

A true Gringo Trail crossroads, you may feel like there are more Argentinians and Dutch than locals here. But lakeside strolls and meanderings up El Calvario get you far from the madding crowd. Copa is the launching pad for visiting Isla del Sol and Isla de la Luna and makes a pleasant stopover between La Paz and Puno or Cuzco.

👁 Sights & Activities

Much of the action in Copa centers on Plaza 2 de Febrero and 6 de Agosto, the main commercial drag, which runs east to west. The transportation hub is at Plaza Sucre. At its western end is the lake and a walkway (Costañera), which traces the lakeshore.

The sparkling Moorish-style **cathedral** (6 de Agosto) dominates town with its domes and colorful *azulejos* (blue Portuguese-style ceramic tiles). The famous black Virgin de Candelaria statue is housed upstairs in the Camarín de la Virgen de Candelaria (open all day but hours are unreliable). The colorful Bendiciones de Movilidades (*cha'lla*; blessing of automobiles) occurs daily (though more reliably on weekends) during the festival season at 10am in front of the cathedral.

The hill north of town is **Cerro Calvario** – it can be reached in 30 minutes and is well worth the climb, particularly at sunset. (A more scenic, dusty trail ascends from the intersection of 6 de Agosto and Costañera.) The trail to the summit begins near the church at the end of Destacamento 211 and climbs past the 14 stations of the cross.

Other sights around town (all with sporadic opening hours) include the pre-Inca astronomical observatory at **Horca del Inca** (Inti Watana; admission B$10); the neglected **Tribunal del Inca** (Intikala; admission B$5) north

Lake Titicaca

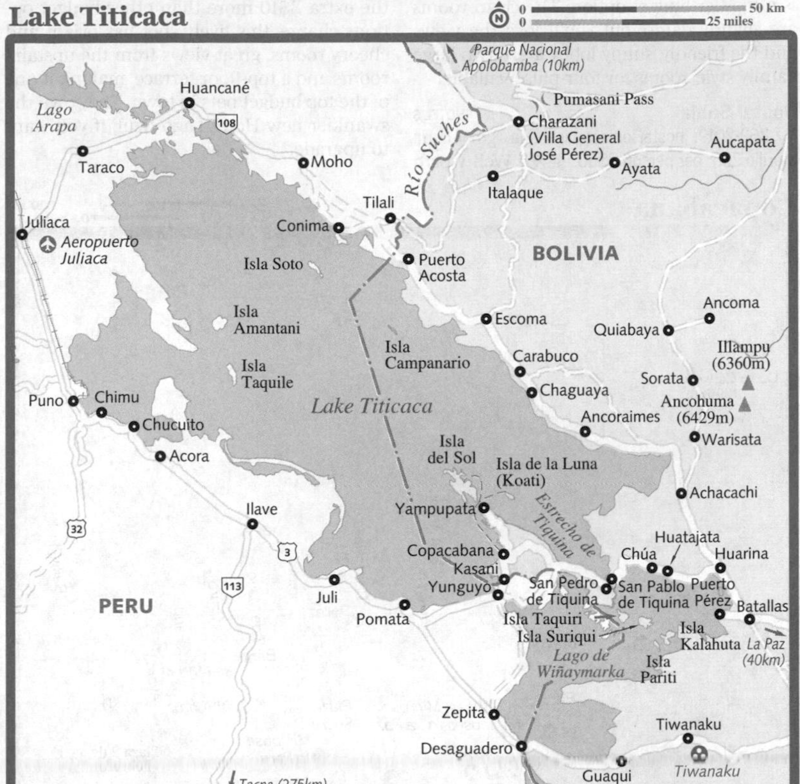

of the cemetery; and the community-run colonial manor known as **Kusijata**, with a small archaeological display, 3km northeast of town; the **Baño del Inca** is nearby.

Head to the lakeshore to rent all manner of boating craft, bicycles (B$70 per day) and motorbikes (B$50 per hour).

Hiking, biking or simply busing along the road from Copacabana to Yampupata, a small hamlet about 17km north of town, are fun little adventures.

Festivals & Events

Alasitas Festival RELIGIOUS
A local tradition is the blessing of miniature objects, such as cars or houses. Supplicants pray that the real thing will be obtained in the coming year. Held January 24.

Fiesta de la Virgen de Candelaria RELIGIOUS
Honors the patron saint of Copacabana and all Bolivia. Copacabana holds an especially big bash, and pilgrims and dancers come from Peru and around Bolivia. There's much music, traditional Aymará dancing, drinking and feasting. On the third day celebrations culminate with the gathering of 100 bulls in a stone corral along the Yampupata road – braver and drunker locals join the bulls. Held February 2 to 5.

Good Friday RELIGIOUS
The town fills with pilgrims, who join a solemn candlelit procession at dusk.

Sleeping

A host of budget options abound, charging around B$30 per person (significantly more in high season and festivals), especially along Calle Jáuregui. Water is scarce here, so watch your shower time, and expect some cold water.

Hostal Flores del Lago HOTEL $
(☎862-2117; www.hostalfloresdellago.com; Jáuregui; s/d/tr B$100/140/210; 📶) This large four-story hotel on the north of the harbor

is a top-tier budget option. The clean rooms are slightly damp, but you'll love the views and the friendly, sunny lobby area. Two large 'family style' rooms for four-plus available.

Hostal Sonia HOTEL $
(☎ 862-2019; hostalsoniacopacabana@gmail.com; Murillo 256; per person B$50; @ 📶) Well worth the extra B$10 more than other budget options charge, this lively spot has bright and cheery rooms, great views from the upstairs rooms and a top-floor terrace, making it one of the top budget bets in town. They own the swankier new Hotel Lago Azul, if you want to upgrade.

Copacabana

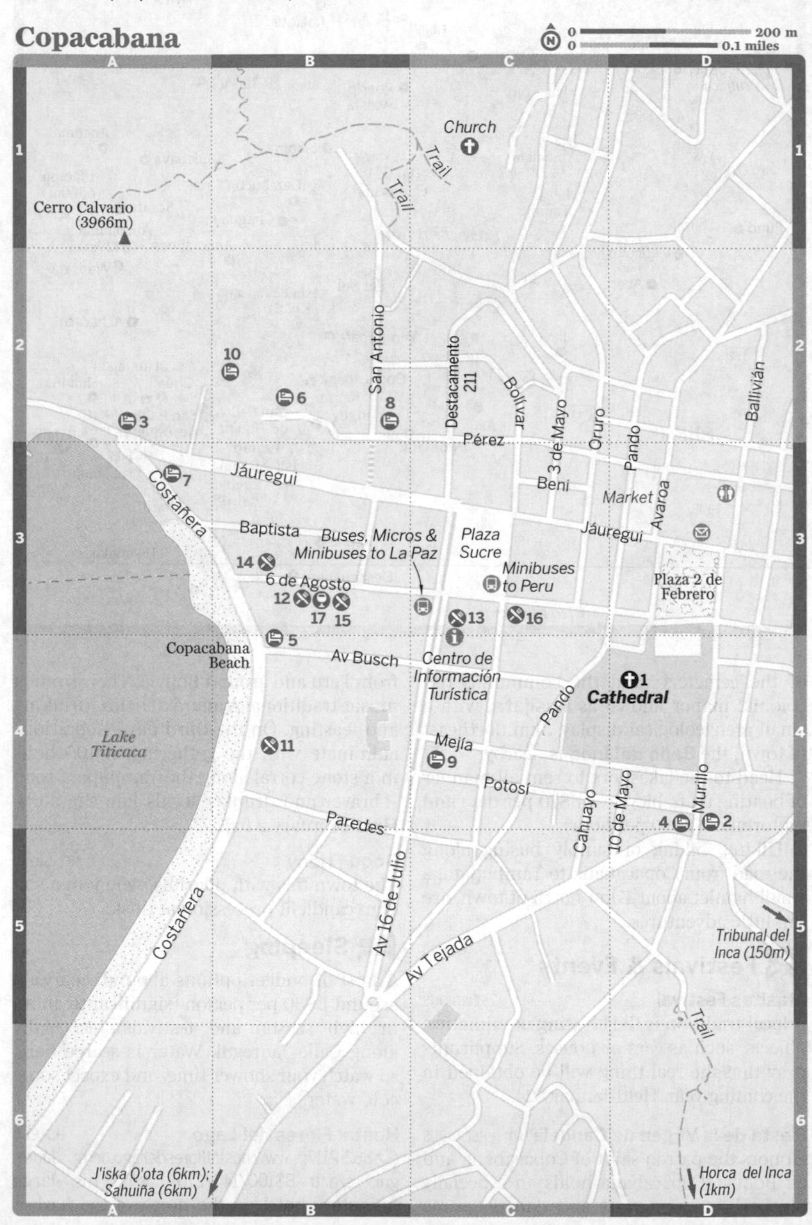

Hostal Emperador HOTEL $

(☎862-2083; Murillo 235; r per person B$35, without bathroom B$25) This budget travelers' favorite is a basic, albeit lively and colorful, joint with hot showers, a laundry service, a small shared kitchen and luggage storage. A newer wing at the back has brighter rooms with bathrooms and a sunny terrace, ideal for lounging and views.

★**Las Olas** BOUTIQUE HOTEL $$

(☎862-2112, 7250-8668; www.hostallasolas.com; Pérez 1-3; s/d/tr US$39/49/64, ste US$74; @📶) To say too much about this place is to spoil the surprise, so we'll give you a taste: quirky, creative, stylish, ecofriendly, million-dollar vistas. Plus there are kitchens, private terraces with hammocks and a solar-powered Jacuzzi. A once-in-a-lifetime experience and well worth the splurge.

Hotel La Cúpula HOTEL $$

(☎862-2029; www.hotelcupula.com; Pérez 1-3; s/d/tr US$19/39/52, s/d/tr ste US$30/55/66; 📶) International travelers rave about this inviting oasis, marked by two gleaming white domes on the slopes of Cerro Calvario, with stupendous lake views. The rooms are pretty basic but we love the gardens, hammocks, shared kitchen and friendly atmosphere. The helpful staff speak several languages, and you can even buy the artwork hanging in your room. Best to reserve ahead.

Hostel Leyenda HOSTEL $$

(☎7067-4097; hostel.leyenda@gmail.com; cnr Av Busch & Constañera; s/d incl breakfast B$100/200, ste B$250; 📶) A solid bet for budgeteers, with views of the water, a lush garden and 'Bolivian Boutique' rooms. The corner rooms have lots of space for the same price while the top-floor suite is a bit pricier and nicier – it even has a *totora*-reed raft and its own terrace.

Hotel Lago Azul HOTEL $$

(☎862-2581; cnr Costañera 13 & Jáuregui; s & d B$120) The new kid in town, right on the lake, has nicely painted rooms, heaters, small balconies and nice new mattresses. A bit austere, but you can hardly get a better location.

Hotel Wendy Mar HOTEL $$

(☎7882-4240, 862-2124; www.hotelwendymar.com; Av 16 de Julio; s/d/tr incl breakfast B$150/260/360; 📶) Everything about this excellent budget option is neat and orderly, from the hospital corner sheets to the spotless floors. Ask for a lake view.

Hotel Utama HOTEL $$

(☎862-2013; www.utamahotel.com; cnr Peréz & San Antonio; s/d incl breakfast B$140/250; P@📶) Set on the hill overlooking town, this clean reliable option has firm beds, a fun central terrace and improved gas showers. Try to get a room with a view. Free bag storage, a nice garden and a book exchange add to the mix.

Eating

The local specialty is *trucha criolla* (rainbow trout) and *pejerrey* (king fish) from Lake Titicaca. These are served along the beachfront stalls for as little as B$20. The bargain basement is the market *comedor*, where you can have an 'insulin shock' breakfast or afternoon tea of hot *api morado* (hot corn drink; B$2) and syrupy *buñuelos* (doughnuts or fritters; B$1).

Restaurant Aransaya BOLIVIAN $

(Av 6 de Agosto 121; lunch menú B$15, mains B$30-45; ⏲lunch) Super-friendly local favorite for a tall, cold beer and trout heaped with all the trimmings. It's neat, clean, very traditional and popular with the locals.

Copacabana

Top Sights

1 Cathedral D4

Sleeping

2 Hostal Emperador D4
3 Hostal Flores del Lago A2
4 Hostal Sonia D4
5 Hostel Leyenda B4
6 Hotel La Cúpula B2
7 Hotel Lago Azul A3
8 Hotel Utama B2
9 Hotel Wendy Mar C4
10 Las Olas B2

Eating

11 Beachfront Stalls B4
12 Huanchaco B3
13 La Choza C3
La Cúpula Restaurant .... (see 6)
14 La Orilla B3
15 Puerto Viejo B3
16 Restaurant Aransaya C3

Drinking & Nightlife

17 KM/0 .... B3

Shopping

Hotel La Cúpula .... (see 6)

La Choza CAFE $

(Av 16 de Julio, btwn Busch & 6 de Agosto; snacks & sandwiches B$10-25; ⏲10am-8pm) Where the rasta-fied Argies abide. Breezy cafe open all day; nice place to have a sandwich while waiting for a bus and stare at the holy trinity of Jimi Hendrix, Bob Marley and Marilyn Monroe posters.

La Orilla INTERNATIONAL $$

(☎862-2267; Av 6 de Agosto s/n; mains B$45-52; ⏲4-9:30pm Mon-Sat; ✍) Some say this cozy maritime-themed restaurant is the best restaurant in town, with fresh, crunchy-from-the-vine vegetables and interesting trout creations that incorporate spinach and bacon (mmm, bacon). They might just be right. Even the high-altitude falafels are pretty good.

Huanchaco PERUVIAN $$

(Restaurant Peruana; 6 de Agosto s/n; mains B$40-110) Why eat Peruvian food once you've crossed the border? Because this place kicks ass. Forget Copa's *ad nauseam* pizzas and go for a *Papa a la Huancaino* (potato in spicy yellow sauce) or a *chupe de camarones,* and be transported. The kicker, *suspira a la limeña,* is a heady concoction of pisco, egg whites, and condensed milk.

La Cúpula Restaurant INTERNATIONAL $$

(www.hotelcupula.com; Pérez 1-3; mains B$24-59; ⏲7:30am-3pm & 6-9pm, closed lunch Tue; ✍) Inventive use of local ingredients make up an extensive international and local menu. The vegetarian range includes a tasty lasagna and there's plenty for meat lovers, too. Dip your way through the cheese fondue with authentic Gruyère cheese – it's to die for... which leaves the Bolivian chocolate fondue with fruit platter beyond description.

Puerto Viejo INTERNATIONAL $$

(puertoviejocafecopacabana.blogspot.com; Av 6 de Agosto 684; mains B$35-50) Readers love this rustic, cozy and chilled cafe-bar, with its ethnic decor and laid-back atmosphere. It serves up a good burger and pizza, and is open until late. Service can be a bit slow. Sister location on Costañera next to Trout Stand #1.

Drinking & Nightlife

KM/0 BAR

(KM Zero; Av 6 de Agosto) Sixties rock stars adorn the walls, dreadlocked Argies rock the acoustic guitars, and there are drink specials along with basic, tasty bar food. Just 50m up the road from the big anchor. Friendly service makes all the difference.

Shopping

The best book exchange is at **Hotel La Cúpula** (www.hotelcupula.com; Michel Pérez 1-3).

Information

There are continuing reports of nasty incidents involving travelers on illegal minibuses and taxis that offer service between Copacabana and La Paz, especially on those who arrive in La Paz at night. The smaller minibuses tend to be packed with people and are prone to speed. Travelers are encouraged to take the formal tourist buses (or the larger buses), and schedule your trip to arrive by day.

The thin air, characteristically brilliant sunshine and reflection off the water combine for scorching levels of ultraviolet radiation. Wear a hat and sunscreen in this region, and drink lots of water to avoid dehydration.

A trio of ATMs dots the Plaza Sucre. Av 6 de Agosto is the Wall Street of Copacabana and nearly every shop will exchange foreign currency (US dollars are preferred over euros and must be clean – not ripped – bills. You can buy Peruvian nuevos soles at most *artesanías,* but you'll normally find better rates in Kasani, or Yunguyo, just beyond the Peruvian border.

Centro de Información Turística (☎6717-9612, 7251-6220; www.visitacopacabana.com; cnr Avs 16 de Julio & 6 de Agosto; ⏲9am-1pm & 2-6pm Wed-Sun) The official Copa community tourism website offers a breadth of info on local events and festivals, and a link to community-based tourism projects, as well as an interesting and free museum. There is a helpful English-speaking attendant, although only rudimentary information is available.

Post Office (Plaza 2 de Febrero; ⏲10am-8pm Mon-Fri, 9am-noon Sat) The post office opens on the same days as the banks in Copacabana.

Getting There & Away

BUS

Most buses leave from near Plazas 2 de Febrero or Sucre. The more comfortable nonstop tour buses from La Paz to Copacabana – including Milton Tours and Combi Tours – cost from around B$40 and are well worth the investment. They depart from La Paz at around 8am and leave Copacabana at 1:30pm (B$30, 3½ hours). Tickets can be purchased from tour agencies. You will need to exit your bus at the Estrecho de Tiquina (Straits of Tiquina), to cross via ferry (B$1.50 per person, 5am to 9pm) between the towns of San Pedro de Tiquina (tourist information office on the main plaza) to San Pablo de Tiquina.

Buses to Peru, including to Arequipa (B$120, 8½ hours), Cuzco (B$110, 15 hours) and Puno (B$30, three to four hours), depart and arrive

GETTING TO PERU

Most travelers enter/exit Peru via Copacabana (and the Straits of Tiquina) or the scruffy town of Desaguadero (avoiding Copacabana altogether). Note that Peruvian time is one hour behind Bolivian time. Always keep your backpack with you when crossing the border.

Micros (small bus or minibus) to the Kasani–Yunguyo border leave Copacabana's Plaza Sucre regularly, usually when full (B$3, 15 minutes). At Kasani you obtain your exit stamp at passport control and head on foot across the border. Sometimes the border agent will charge you a nominal fee for the crossing (around B$30). On the Peruvian side, *micros* and taxis will ferry you to Yunguyo (around 6 Peruvian nuevos soles, 15 minutes). From here, you can catch a bus heading to Puno. An efficient alternative is to catch a tourist bus from La Paz to Puno via Copacabana (from B$60); some allow you a couple of days' stay in Copacabana. Note: even if you've bought a ticket to Cuzco or elsewhere in Peru, you'll change buses in Puno at the international terminal; this is located about three blocks from the local terminal.

A quicker, if less interesting, route is via Desaguadero, on the southern side of the lake. Several bus companies head to/from this border from/to Peru. The crossing should be hassle-free: you obtain your exit stamp from **Bolivian Passport Control** (possible fee B$30; ⏲8:30am-8:30pm), walk across a bridge and get an entry stamp at *migración* in Peru. Frequent buses head to Puno hourly (around 3½ hours).

For details on making this crossing on the opposite direction, see p842.

in Copacabana from Av 6 de Agosto. You can also get to Puno by catching a public minibus from Plaza Sucre to the border at Kasani (B$3, 15 minutes). Across the border there's frequent, if crowded, onward transportation to Yunguyo (five minutes) and Puno (2½ hours).

BOAT

Buy your tickets for boat tours to Isla de la Luna and Isla del Sol from agencies on Av 6 de Agosto or from beachfront kiosks. Traveling in a big group? Consider renting a private boat through these operators for B$600 to B$800 per day. Separate return service is available from both islands.

Isla del Sol

☎02 / POP 2500

Easily the highlight of any Lake Titicaca excursion (and perhaps your entire Bolivia romp), Isla del Sol (elevation 3808m) is a large island with several traditional communities, decent tourist infrastructure, a few worthwhile pre-Columbian ruins, amazing views, great hikes and, well, lots of sun.

The large 70-sq-km island definitely merits a night or two – you can then devote a day each to the northern and southern ends. While you can do a walking circuit of the main sights in a long day, whirlwind half-day tours are strictly for the been-there-done-that crowd.

The island's permanent residents are distributed between the main settlements of **Cha'llapampa**, near the island's northern end; **Cha'lla**, which backs up to a lovely sandy beach on the central east coast; and the biggest town, **Yumani**, which straddles the ridge above the Escalera del Inca on the south.

There are no vehicles on Isla del Sol, so visitors are limited to hiking along rocky trails (some are now paved in Inca style) or traveling by boat. The main ports are at **Pilko Kaina**, the **Escalera del Inca** in Yumani and near the **Templo del Inca** and **Chincana ruins** at Cha'llapampa. There's also a small port at **Japapi** on the southwest coast.

Sights

Each site attracts its own admission fee.

Escalera del Inca GARDENS

(admission B$5) Just uphill from the ferry dock at the village of Yumani, along the beautifully reconstructed Escalera del Inca (Inca stairway), you'll pass plenty of terraced gardens, small shops and hotels. It's a lung-buster that gains almost 200m in elevation over less than 1km, so take your time – or hire donkeys (B$30 to B$50) to carry your pack.

Pilko Kaina RUINS

(admission B$5) This prominent ruins complex near the southern tip of the island about 30 minutes (2km) south by foot from Yumani sits well camouflaged against a steep terraced slope. The best-known site is the two-level **Palacio del Inca**, thought to have been constructed by the Incan Emperor Tupac-Yupanq.

Cha'lla VILLAGE

(admission B$15) This agreeable little village stretches along a magnificent sandy beach that could be straight out of a holiday brochure for the Greek islands. The village is spread out – it extends over the hill to the south. There's a small kiosk and a newish hostal on the beach, and one on the hill, **Hostal Qhumphuri** (☎7152-1188, La Paz 02-284-3534; hostalqhumphuri@hotmail.com; s/d B$20/40). You have to pay an admission fee to pass along the trail into town.

Cha'llapampa VILLAGE

Most tours visiting the northern ruins land at Cha'llapampa, a small village straddling a slender isthmus. The small **Cha'llapampa Museum** (Cha'llapampa; admission incl Chicana Ruins B$10) contains artifacts excavated in 1992 from Marka Pampa, referred to by locals as La Ciudad Submergida (Sunken City). Among the dusty exhibits are anthropomorphic figurines, Tiwanaku-era artifacts, animal bones, puma-shaped ceramic *koa* censers and cups resembling Monty Python's Holy Grail.

Chincana Ruins RUINS

(admission B$10) The island's most spectacular ruins lie near the island's northern tip. Its main feature is the **Palacio del Inca**, a maze of stone walls and tiny doorways, also known as El Laberinto (the Labyrinth). Within the labyrinth there is a small well, believed by pilgrims to contain sacred purifying water.

Sleeping

The most scenic place to stay is Yumani. Ch'allapampa and Ch'alla have basic options. In high season (June to August and during festivals) prices listed here may double.

Hotel Imperio del Sol HOTEL $

(☎7196-1863, 7373-4303; r per person with/without bathroom B$100/50) This peachy and central place on the hillside running into town is a good bet, with clean rooms and friendly, reliable service.

Inti Wasi Lodge HOSTEL $

(☎7196-0223; museo_templodelsol@yahoo.es; dm per person B$30, cabins per person incl breakfast B$80) Four basic but cozy cabins with en suites, smashing views and a recommended restaurant, Palacio de la Trucha, attached. To get here, turn right just before Hostal Illampu as you head up the hill.

Palla Khasa CABIN $$

(☎7321-1585; es-la.facebook.com/palla.khasa; s/d incl breakfast B$260/310, s/d bungalows B$510/710) About 300m north of Yumani proper, this top choice has lovely grounds, simple (but workable) rooms below – we like numero 3 the best – funky carved-wood bedstands and remarkably low ceilings. The half-dozen circular stone bungalows above are an amazing touch of class, and include gas-heated showers, lovingly tiled bathrooms, and better views. The restaurant is highly recommended.

Las Cabañas CABIN $$

(s/d incl breakfast B$80/160) Perched on the hill leading into town from the dock, these simple adobe bungalows afford great views and have 24-hour hot water. The beds are nice and soft.

Hostal Puerta del Sol HOTEL $$

(s without/with bathroom B$40/150, cabin per person B$150, d B$200) On the promontory on top of the hill, this friendly option has good views from most rooms (number 14 is awesome), clean sheets and a nice terrace. The rooms with bathrooms are much better, and the Andean textiles add a nice touch. Passive solar heating in the cabins helps keep you warm at night.

Eating

There are more pizzerias in Yumani than Titicaca has *trucha*. Nearly all menus are identical; *almuerzos* and set dinners cost between B$25 and B$30.

Getting There & Away

Launches embark from Copacabana beach around 8:30am and 1:30pm daily. Depending on the season and the company, they may drop you off at a choice of the island's north or south (check with the agency). Return trips leave Yampupata at 10:30am and 4pm (B$20 one way) and Cha'llapampa at 1pm (B$20).

Most full-day trips go directly north to Cha'llapampa (two to 2½ hours). Boats anchor for 1½ hours only – you'll have just enough time to hike up to the Chincana ruins, and return again to catch the boat at 1pm to the Escalera del Inca and Pilko Kaina in the island's south. Here, you'll spend around two hours before departing for Copa.

Half-day trips generally go to the south of Isla del Sol only.

Those who wish to hike the length of the island can get off at Cha'llapampa in the morning and

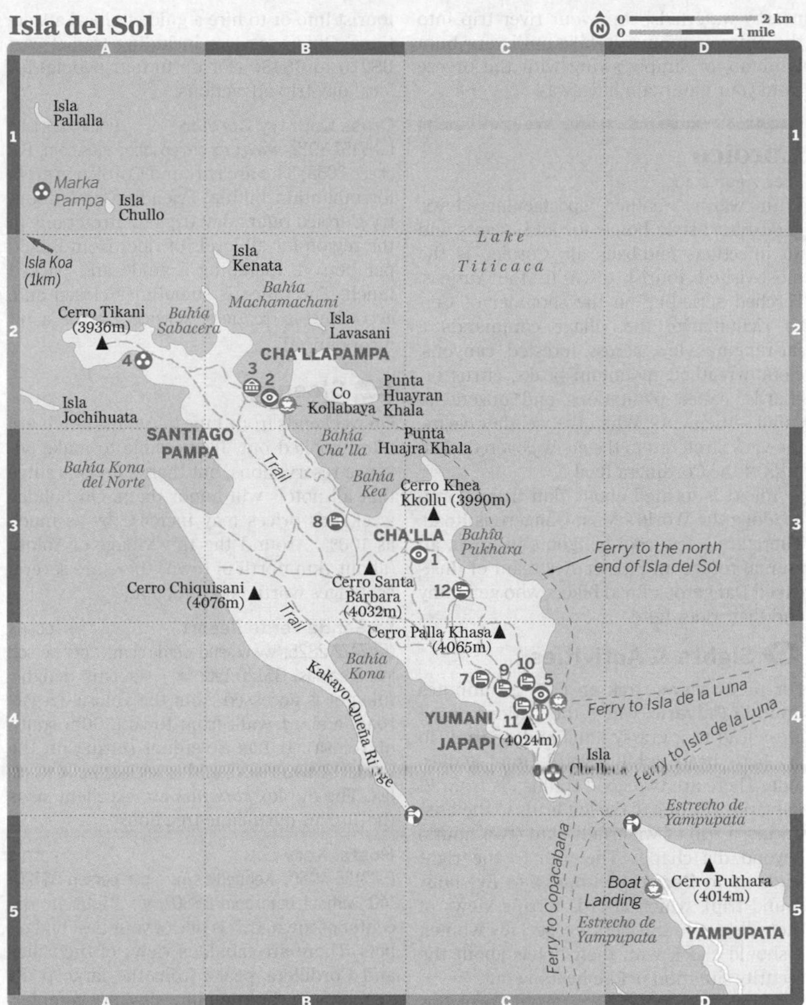

walk south to the Escalera del Inca (Yumani) for the return boat in the afternoon.

Asociación Unión Marines (Costañera, Copacabana; one way B$20, round trip B$25; ⏲ departs Copacabana 8:30am & 1:30pm) Right by the big anchor at the end of 6 de Agosto, this ferry service goes to the north and south of Isla del Sol, with a stop on the return at a floating island.

Titicaca Tours (Costañera, Copacabana; round-trip B$35 ; ⏲ departs Copacabana 8:30am) Offers a round-trip boat tour that stops in Isla de la Luna for an hour, continuing to the southern end of Isla del Sol for a two-hour stop before heading back to Copacabana.

THE CORDILLERAS & THE YUNGAS

Caught between the Andes and the Amazon, this rugged transition zone has just about everything you could ask for from your Bolivia adventure.

For the vertically inspired, there are glacier-capped 6000m peaks and adrenaline-charged mountain-bike descents. Nature lovers and the culturally curious will dig the cloud forests and hillside semi-tropical Yungas towns of Chulumani, Coroico and Sorata. Here, you can kick off hikes to nearby waterfalls, start your river trip into the Amazon, mountain-bike until your bum is numb, or simply swing with the breeze from your mountain hideaway.

Coroico

☎02 / POP 19,400

With warm weather, spectacular views, good resort-style hotels for all budgets and an infectious laid-back air, Coroico is the most-visited tourist town in the Yungas. Perched aerie-like on the shoulder of Cerro Uchumachi, the village commands a far-ranging view across forested canyons, cloud-wreathed mountain peaks, citrus orchards, coffee plantations and dozens of small settlements. When the weather clears, the view stretches to the snow-covered summits of the Cordillera Real.

Yolosa is located about 7km from Coroico along the World's Most Dangerous Road. There are a few cool hangouts in town, an animal refuge and a steady stream of dust-caked Dangerous Road bikers who generally end their rides here.

Sights & Activities

For pretty views, trek an easy 20 minutes up to **El Calvario**, where the stations of the cross lead to a grassy knoll and **chapel**. To get here, head uphill toward Hotel Esmeralda. There are two good trailheads from El Calvario. The one to the left leads to the **cascadas**, a trio of waterfalls 5km (two hours) beyond the chapel. The trail to the right leads up to **Cerro Uchumachi** (a five-hour round trip), which affords terrific views of the valley. Solo travelers – especially women – should check with their hotels about the security situation before heading out.

About three hours north from Coroico is the **Río Coroico**, which flows through the Nor Yungas. This is the country's most popular commercially rafted river, and is the most convenient to La Paz.

La Paz agencies can take you down the World's Most Dangerous Road to Coroico but the Coroico Star cafe on the plaza arranges this trip well, say many travelers. From town, you can rent bikes from most hotels to take you to some of the nearby attractions.

Asociación de Guias Turismo Local de Coroico GUIDED TOUR
(☎7306-9888, 7207-8732; Plaza García Lanza; ⏰8am-noon & 2:30-7:30pm) Stop here for good tourist info or to hire a guide to local attractions. Guide services including transit cost B$250 to B$450 (for up to four people) for local day-trip attractions.

Cross Country Coroico MOUNTAIN BIKING
(☎7157-3015; www.cxccoroico.lobopages.com; Pacheco 2058) The area around Coroico is great for mountain biking. Friendly Cross Country Coroico offers day trips to attractions in the region for all levels of rider from B$280 per person, including a guide and packed lunch. The office is sometimes closed and, according to readers, service can be a bit disorganized.

Sleeping

On weekends from June to August hotels are often booked out. It's possible to make advance reservations, but there's no guarantee that all hotels will honor them. On holiday weekends prices may increase by as much as 100%. Around the tiny village of Yolosa (about 7km north of town) there are several ecolodges worth checking out.

La Senda Verde Resort LODGE $
(☎7472-2825; www.sendaverde.com; r per person incl breakfast B$120-150;) This delightful spot is accessed from the Yolosa–La Paz road, a short walk from town (500m south of Yolosa). It has a verdant setting on the banks of two rivers and is a great spot to relax. The duplex *cabañas* are excellent, as is the Tarzan-meet-Jane tree house.

Hostal Kory HOTEL $
(☎7156-4050; Kennedy s/n; r per person B$120-140, without bathroom B$80;) Right in the center of town, this is one of your best budget bets. There are fabulous views of the valley and Cordillera peaks from the large pools or rooms in the rambling six-story complex. The rooms have older sheets, but are clean. The pool is open to nonguests for B$25.

Hostal Tunqui Eye HOTEL $
(☎7350-0081; miranda_gui@hotmail.com; Iturralde 4043; r per person B$80, without bathroom B$40;) In the ultra-budget spectrum, this recent entrant has newer beds, clean(ish) sheets and good views from the terrace. An outdoor kitchen is handy for prepping your own grub though we lament the loss of the Tiki bar.

Hostal Sol y Luna RESORT $$
(☎7156-1626; www.solyluna-bolivia.com; campsite B$40, s B$145-220, d B$240-360, s/d with shared bathroom B$85/120;) Set on a jungle-covered hill, this inspiring spot offers appeal-

ingly rustic accommodations in a variety of *cabañas* (cabins), simple rooms and camping spots (dry season only). The rambling 6-hectare grounds includes two pools, a small hot tub, yoga classes, secluded bungalows and enchanted forests. A 20-minute uphill walk from town, or a B$20 taxi, provides some seclusion for the non-party set.

Hotel Esmeralda HOTEL **$$**

(☎213-6017; www.hotelesmeralda.com; Julio Suazo s/n; s/d B$250/440, dm/s/d without bathroom B$90/160/280; @ 📶 🏊) A top pick for the party set, this resort-style hotel on the hillside has amazing grounds, tremendous views and a swimming pool. There's a room for all tastes, from cheap dorms to larger digs with balconies and private bathrooms. The rooms with shared bathrooms can be a bit dark. A book exchange and onsite restaurant mean you may never leave the hotel.

Eating

The plaza is ringed by a number of inexpensive local cafes and pizzerias.

Cafe Tafaddalu MIDDLE EASTERN **$**

(☎7728-9130; Heroes del Chaco; mains B$20-40; ⏰8am-9pm Thu-Sun) Piped-in Arabic music and shisha pipes, combined with the falafel, kefta and kibbeh on the menu bring a whiff of Arabia to the Yungas. There are also specialty coffees, American breakfasts (if you must) and Bolivian empanadas on offer. The name means 'please, sit down' in Arabic, and the family will make you feel welcome. One block off the plaza.

Bamboo's Café MEXICAN **$**

(Iturralde 1047; mains B$20-40) This friendly candlelit Mexican restaurant has pretty authentic guacamole, tacos, burritos and refried beans. It's a fun spot for a drink or two later on.

Cafe Almendra VEGETARIAN **$**

(Héroes del Chaco s/n; mains B$10-20) One block uphill from Hotel Bella Vista, a lovely young couple makes wholesome meals and snacks including delish *sonsos* and *patacones*. A selection of books and local fruit jams is on sale. A bit hippy but not over-the-top.

Carla's Garden Pub GERMAN **$$**

(Back-Stübe Konditorei; ☎7207-5620; Pasaje Linares; mains B$30-50; ⏰9:30am-2:30pm & 6:30-10pm Wed-Fri, 9:30am-10pm Sat & Sun) A Dutch pub owner has combined her thatched-roof beer hall with the established German restaurant and moved it to the bottom of the plaza's steep stairs (check for the 'Open' sign.) They've maintained the same tasty breakfasts, tempting cakes and pastries as well as pasta and memorable *sauerbraten* (marinated pot-roast beef) with *spätzle* (German noodles). Occasional bands liven things up.

El Cafetal INTERNATIONAL **$$**

(elcafetal.coroico.info; Miranda s/n; mains B$30-50; ⏰Wed-Mon) This secluded hotel restaurant has unbeatable views, cane chairs and slate-topped tables where you can enjoy a range of dishes prepared with a French touch. The menu includes sweet and savory crepes, soufflés, curries, vegetarian lasagna and specials that include llama goulash. They also run Bon Apetit Cafe downtown.

WORTH A TRIP

GREAT DAY TRIPS FROM COROICO

Coroico is a good launching point for day trips or longer excursions into the neighboring countryside.

Poza Esmeralda y Turquesa Book a trip with a Coroico agency for an afternoon swim in this 'secret' spot.

La Senda Verde Refugio Natural (☎7472-2825; www.sendaverde.com; Yolosa; admission B$69; ⏰10am-12:30pm) This 12-hectare animal refuge is located just 500m north of Yolosa (B$40 taxi or B$10 minibus). You can volunteer here (two-week minimum) for B$1370 per week, including three meals, stay overnight, or simply head over for an hour-long tour. The refuge provides a sanctuary for animals that have been rescued from illegal traffickers. Reservations are required, children under 10 are not admitted.

Zzip the Flying Fox (☎2231-3849; www.ziplinebolivia.com; Yolosa; 1 trip B$255; ⏰9-11am & 1-5pm) Three zipline sections take you flying through the forest canopy near Yolosa at speeds of up to 85km per hour. The 1500m zipline can be combined with trips down the World's Most Dangerous Road. Book your ticket at a La Paz or Coroico agency.

Entertainment

Oasis Diskoteka DANCE
(Murcielaguitos; Pacheco s/n; B$5; ⏲Fri-Sun) After midnight, when the restaurant bars shut, it's time for Oasis and a pitcher of Huari with the locals because, let's face it, you didn't get enough of Bolivia's non-stop *cumbia* party on the bus ride to town, did you?

Information

There's a basic regional hospital near Hostal El Cafetal, on the upper road out of town, but for serious medical treatment you'll be better off in La Paz. There are no foreign-card-accepting ATMs in Coroico, and not all hotels accept credit cards. For tourist information online, try www.coroico-info.com.

Prodem (☎213-6009; Plaza García Lanza; ⏲8:30am-12:30pm & 2:30-6pm Wed-Fri) Changes dollars at a fair rate and does cash advances for 5% commission.

Tourist Office (Bus Terminal; ⏲8am-8pm) There's also a small information kiosk at the bus terminal.

Getting There & Away

The La Paz–Coroico road is now open, replacing the World's Most Dangerous Road as the town's access route. It's asphalted along its whole length, but in the short time it's been open several landslides have cut up some sections. Buses and *micros* from La Paz arrive at the bus terminal on Av Manning. It's a steep walk uphill to the plaza, or you can hop in a taxi (B$5). **Turbus Totaí** (☎289-5573) run comfortable taxi services to La Paz from the terminal, leaving when full (B$25, two hours).

From the Villa Fátima area in La Paz, buses and *micros* leave for Coroico (B$25, 3½ hours) at least hourly from 7:30am to 8:30pm, with extra runs on weekends and holidays. En route they stop in Yolosita, a dusty crossroads where you can connect with buses and *camiones* (flatbed trucks) north to Rurrenabaque (B$100, 15 to 18 hours) and further into Bolivian Amazonia.

For Chulumani, the quickest route is to backtrack to La Paz. Although the junction for the Chulumani road is at Unduavi, few passing *micros* have spare seats at this point.

The road to Caranavi was only open from 3pm to 6am at the time of research. Buses from the Coroico terminal will take you there (and on to other Amazonian destinations) for B$30.

Chulumani

☎02 / POP 17,700

Perched scenically on the side of a hill, this peaceful little town is the capital of the Sud Yungas. It's a lot like Coroico, with a friendly town square, bustling market and tropical attitude, but receives next to no international visitors.

Chulumani has its ghosts – Nazi war criminal Klaus Barbie lived in the saw mill above town after WWII, and it's said that the spirit of José Luis Tejada Sorzano, president of Bolivia during the Chaco War, haunts a local castle.

Sights & Activities

There are several lovely walks in the Chulumani area. A butterfly-clouded, five-hour (one-way) downhill hike will take you from Chulumani down to the Río Solacama; you can easily get a bus or *micro* back. In three to four hours you can also walk to Ocabaya, while other walks take you from the higher village of Villa Remedios to the lower one, or from Chicaloma down to Ocabaya. Another beautiful hike is the four-hour walk from Chulumani to Chirca, where there's the church of a revered local virgin.

Sleeping & Eating

For cheap and cheerful fried chicken, Restaurant Rinconcito Chulameño on Plaza Libertad is friendly. Snack San Bartolomé is another decent option on the plaza.

Country House HOTEL $
(☎7528-2212; Tolopata 13; r per person incl breakfast B$100;) Probably your best bet in town, this welcoming home is 10 minutes west of the plaza by the basketball court. The rustic, spotless rooms have hot-water showers and fresh flowers. Great breakfasts, abundant bird life, and delicious home-cooked dinners (killer quinoa pie!). Owner Javier can organize many local excursions, including inner-tubing.

Hostal Dion HOTEL $
(☎289-6034; hostaldion@hotmail.com; Bolívar s/n; r per person with/without bathroom incl breakfast B$80/60) Half a block south of Plaza Libertad, this is the best of the central options. The homey setting includes extremely clean rooms, cable TV, electric showers and sparkling tile floors. Enjoy the courtyard garden, but be sure to ask about the curfew.

Information

Chulumani's tourist office is in a kiosk on the main plaza. There's no ATM in Chulumani; Banco Fie on the main plaza and Prodem (two blocks west of the Plaza on Pando) give cash advances.

Getting There & Away

Since the closure of the original La Paz–Coroico road to traffic, the nail-biting route from La Paz to Chulumani has claimed the title of the 'World's Most Dangerous Road.' If you can keep your nerves in check, it is actually an exceptionally beautiful route.

Yunga Cruz trekkers finish in Chulumani, and the town is readily accessed from Yanacachi at the end of the Takesi trek. From Yanacachi, walk down to the main road and wait for transportation headed downhill; it's about 1½ hours to Chulumani.

From Villa Fátima in La Paz, around the corner of Calles San Borja and 15 de Abril, different companies depart when full for Chulumani (B$20, four hours) from 8am to 4pm. From Chulumani, La Paz–bound buses wait around the *tranca* (police post). If you're coming from Coroico, get off at Unduavi and wait for another vehicle. It will likely be standing-room only; if a seat is a priority, you'll have to go all the way back to La Paz.

Sorata

02 / POP 23,000

Knocked back a peg in the early 2000s, Sorata is making a slow recovery, and in fact is a bit of a hidden gem in Los Yungas. The road's paved, and the locals are getting friendlier. While it doesn't have the shiny digs of its arch-nemesis Coroico, this semi-tropical village sitting high above a verdant agricultural valley does offer great weather, access to some of Bolivia's best treks and kick-ass downhill mountain biking.

It's worth your while to pick up a guide in La Paz – or better yet, hire a local one in Sorata – and explore this under-appreciated treasure.

Activities

Hiking & Walking

Peak hiking season is May to September. Ambitious adventurers can do the seven-day **El Camino del Oro trek**, an ancient trading route between the Altiplano and the Río Tipuani gold fields. Note that this is a rough part of Bolivia, and not many people are taking on this trek these days. With wildcat miners, it can be quite dangerous, plus, without regular traffic, you'll need to clear some trail with machetes. If you go here, it's highly recommended you travel with a local guide.

Alternatively, there's the steep climb up to **Laguna Chillata**, a long day trek with multiple trails (it's best to take a guide; you can't see the lake until you get there); **Laguna Glacial** (5100m), a two- to three-day high-altitude trek; the challenging five-day **Mapiri Trail**; or the seven-day **Illampu circuit**.

With Sorata's economy turning from tourism to mining and farming (coca, marijuana, you name it), there are fewer guides offering services here, and fewer pack animals for hire. Scattered reports indicate this could be a dangerous area for trekking and many agencies are no longer offering treks in the region. Check with locals before you depart.

Asociación de Guías y Portaedores de Sorata GUIDED TOURS
(Sorata Guides & Porters Association; 213-6672; guiasorata.com; Sucre 302) Rents equipment of varying quality, and arranges many different treks. Cooking equipment is included in the price, but food is extra. Clients are expected to pay for the guide's food. The cooperative benefits workers and community-based projects. Spanish-speaking guides.

Gruta de San Pedro CAVE
(San Pedro Cave; admission B$15; 8am-5pm) A popular excursion. The cave, known in the Aymará tongue as Chussek Uta (House of Owls), is approximately 500m deep with an enclosed lagoon which can be crossed in pedal boats (B$20). Guides with the necessary lamps will help you find your way around. PCMB, the Bolivian program to conserve bats, has identified three nectar- and insect-eating *murciélagos* in the pitch-black surroundings.

TREKKING IN THE CORDILLERAS

Several worthwhile treks run between the Altiplano and the Yungas. Most popular are the **Choro** (La Cumbre to Coroico; 70km), **Takesi** (Taquesi; 45km) and **Yunga Cruz** (114km). These two- to four-day treks all begin with a brief ascent, then head down from spectacular high-mountain landscapes into the riotous vegetation of the Yungas. This area is also home to **Huayna Potosí** (6088m), the most popular major peak to climb; many agencies in La Paz can organize the ascent.

The best time for these treks is during the May to September dry season. Security is a concern, so it's best to check the situation ahead of time and avoid solo hiking.

Mountain Biking

Gravity Tours MOUNTAIN BIKING
(Andean Epics; ☎7127-6685; www.gravitybolivia.com) This La Paz–based operator is your best bet for rides near Sorata. A remarkable six-day trip can take you from La Paz to Rurrenabaque, including a night in Sorata (B$3350 to B$3850 per person, all inclusive). Shorter, thriftier one- to three-day options for just Sorata are offered, as well as a day trip down the 'ghost road' to the haunted castle.

Sleeping

Hotel Santa Lucia HOTEL $
(☎7151-3812; r per person with/without bathroom B$55/45) Located near the soccer field, this is the cleanest, neatest option in town. The bright yellow hotel does have a slightly institutional feel, but in return you get excellent mattresses (by Sorata standards), crisp linens and tidy shared facilities. The owner, Seracín, is as friendly as they come.

Hostal Las Piedras HOTEL $
(☎7191-6341; www.laspiedrashostal.lobopages.com; Ascarrunz s/n; s/d/tr B$120/160/195, s/d without bathroom B$70/110) This German-owned joint has amazing views from most rooms, a cool vibe, shared kitchen and fun common area. The sheets are clean, but the mattresses and pillows are paper thin. The optional breakfast (B$30 to B$46) includes homemade wholegrain German bread and yogurt.

Hotel Paraíso HOTEL $
(Villavicencio s/n; r per person B$40) This central spot has a bright, flowery patio, a series of roof terraces with nice views, new beds and old carpets, and decent rooms with private bathrooms and circumspect electrical wiring on the showers.

★ **Altai Oasis** LODGE $$
(☎7151-9856; www.altaioasis.lobopages.com; Av Samuel Tejerin; camp site B$30, s/d B$245/315, cabin B$700, dm/s/d without bathroom B$84/125/250; 📶🏊) This really does feel like an oasis, with a lush garden, hammocks, and a pretty balcony cafe. The riverside retreat offers grassy campsites, comfortable rooms, and romantically rustic *cabañas*, intricately and fancifully painted. We only wish they'd update their slumping mattresses.

Eating

Small, inexpensive restaurants around the market and the plaza sell cheap and filling *almuerzos*.

★ **Café Illampu** BAKERY $
(snacks B$20-35; ⏰9am-6:30pm Wed-Mon) A 15-minute down-and-up walk from town, this lovely relaxing spot is en route to the Gruta de San Pedro. Stop in on the return journey – if you stop on the way to the cave, you might not make it there as Café Illampu is exceedingly tranquil with views, a garden and llamas.

Mercado MARKET $
(Muñecas s/n; mains B$5-20) Head to the market to grab the goods for a picnic lunch. There's some food stands here, too.

Altai Oasis INTERNATIONAL $$
(mains B$20-50; 🌿) The peaceful balcony restaurant at this lovely retreat, 20 minutes' walk from town, serves coffee, drinks and a range of vegetarian dishes. There are also T-bone steaks and, for an Eastern European touch, Polish borscht and tasty goulash. It's a great place to just sit with a drink too, with views over the valley and the tinkle of wind chimes.

Information

Sunday is market day, and Tuesday, when many businesses are closed, is considered *domingo sorateño* (Sorata's Sunday). There's no tourist information center or ATM.

Getting There & Away

From near La Paz's cemetery, buses leave hourly between 4am and 5:30pm (B$17, three hours). From the plaza in Sorata, La Paz–bound *micros* depart when full and *flotas* (long-distance buses) leave on the hour between 4am and 5pm.

Sindicato de Transportes Unificada Sorata (Plaza Enrique Peñaranda s/n) has daily service to Copacabana (B$40, 9am), Coroico via La Paz (B$36, 9am), Achacachi (B$12, no set time) and Huarina (B$15, hourly). For Copacabana you can also get off at the junction town of Huarina and wait for another, probably packed, bus. They also service the town on the rough 4WD track to the gold mining settlement of Mapiri.

SOUTHERN ALTIPLANO

The harsh, at times almost primeval, geography of the Southern Altiplano will tug at the heartstrings of those with a deep love of bleak and solitary places. Stretching southwards from La Paz, this high-plains wilderness is framed by majestic volcanic peaks, swathes of treeless wilderness and the white

Southwest Bolivia

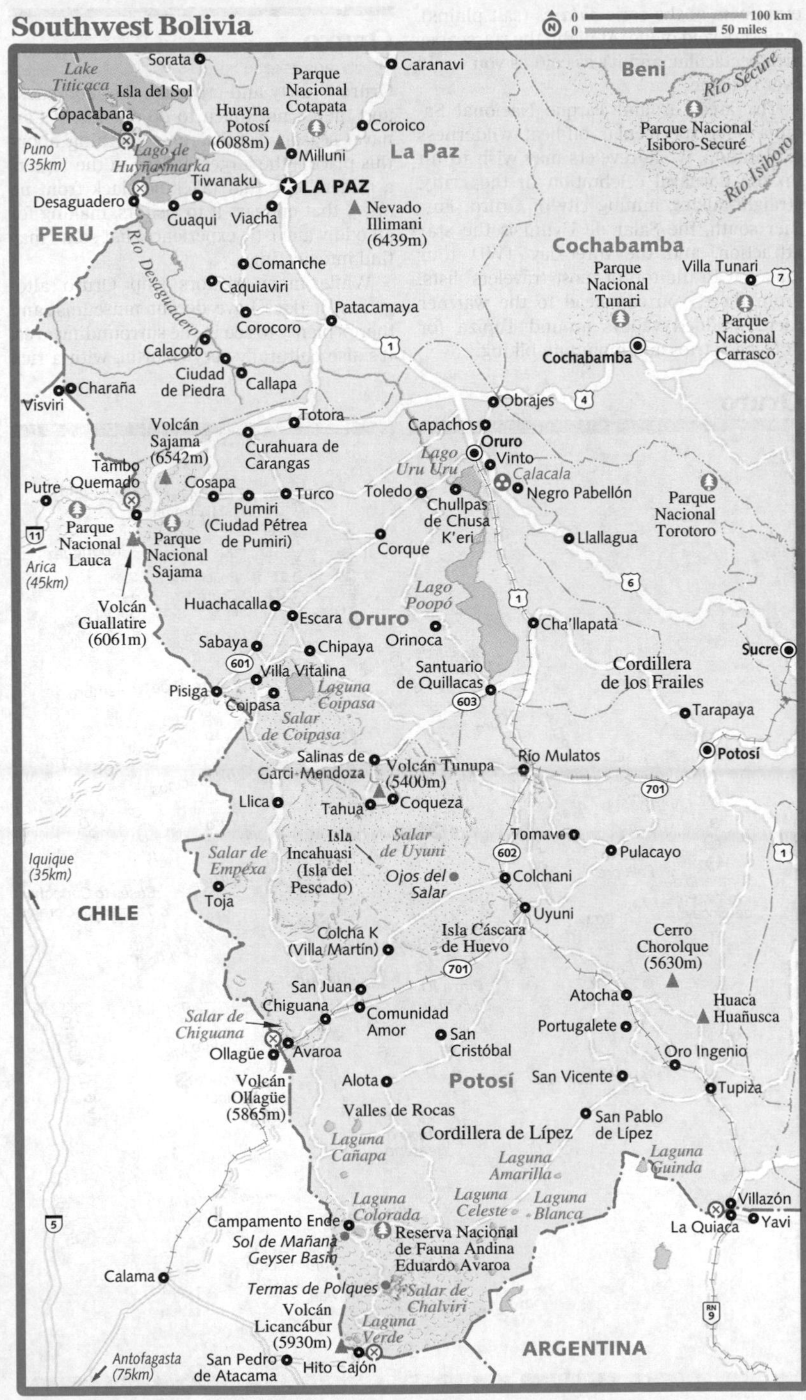

emptiness of the eerie *salares* (salt plains), almost devoid of life. At night, the starscapes are spectacular, and it's as cold as you could ever imagine.

The areas around Parque Nacional Sajama offer spectacular off-beat wilderness exploration, while revelers may wish to hit up the Carnaval celebration in the gritty, straight-talking mining city of Oruro. Further south, the Salar de Uyuni is the star attraction, and the three-day 4WD tour makes it to the top of most travelers' lists. From there, you can head to the warmer cactus-studded valleys around Tupiza for horseback trips and mountain biking.

Oruro

☎02 / POP 264,700

Oruro is dirty and crowded, the food sucks and there's not much to do outside of Carnaval season. Yet, there's something about this place – the largest village in the region, a miners' city that takes no slack from no one – that endears it to visitors, making for an oddly atavistic experience that some may find intoxicating.

While many visitors skip Oruro altogether, it does have decent museums, and there's plenty to see in the surrounding area. It's also culturally very colorful, with a rich

Oruro

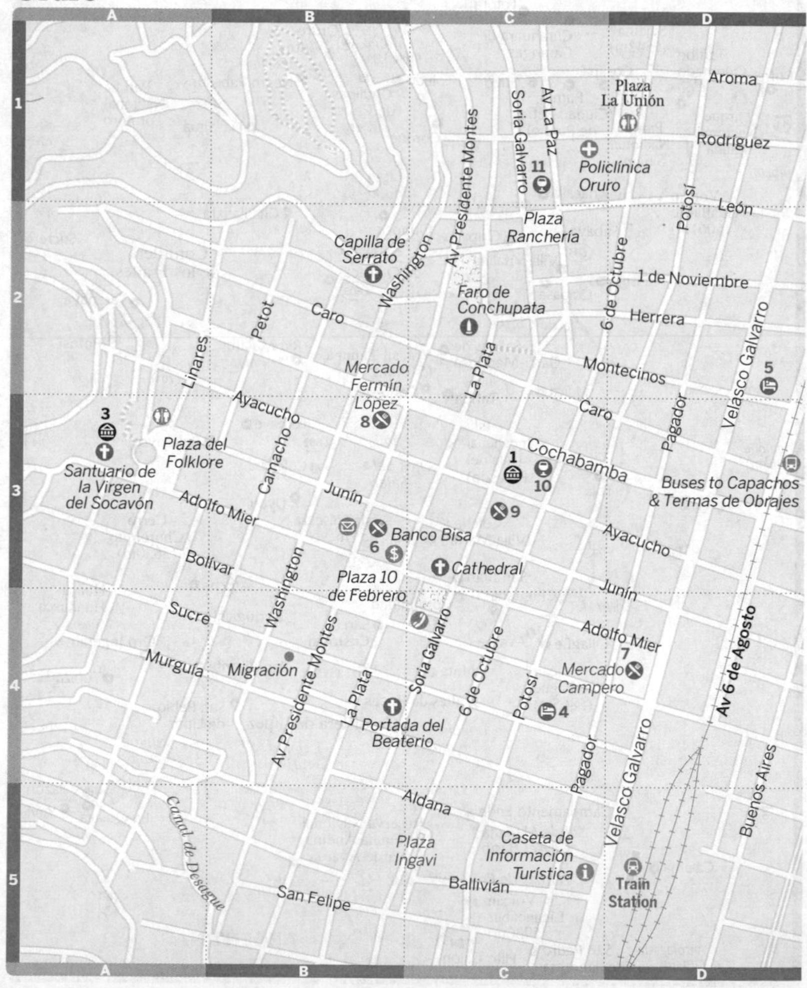

dance and musical heritage that culminates in the riotous Carnaval celebrations.

Sights & Activities

The action around town tends to center around the Plaza 10 de Febrero and Plaza del Folklore. Bolívar is the main commercial drag and a fun evening people-watching walk.

Museo Sacro, Folklórico, Arqueológico y Minero MUSEUM
(Plaza del Folklore s/n; admission B$10, camera/video use B$3/20; ⏲9-11:45am & 1:45-5:30pm) An excellent double museum attached to the Santuario de la Virgen del Socavón. The tour descends from the church down an old mining tunnel lined with mining tools and representations of the devilish El Tío, spirit of the underground. Upstairs are a variety of archaeological and folklore exhibits, from Wankarani-period stone llama heads to Carnaval costumes.

Access is by guided tour only, leaving every 45 minutes. Guides are knowledgeable but often don't speak English – some exhibits have bilingual explanations.

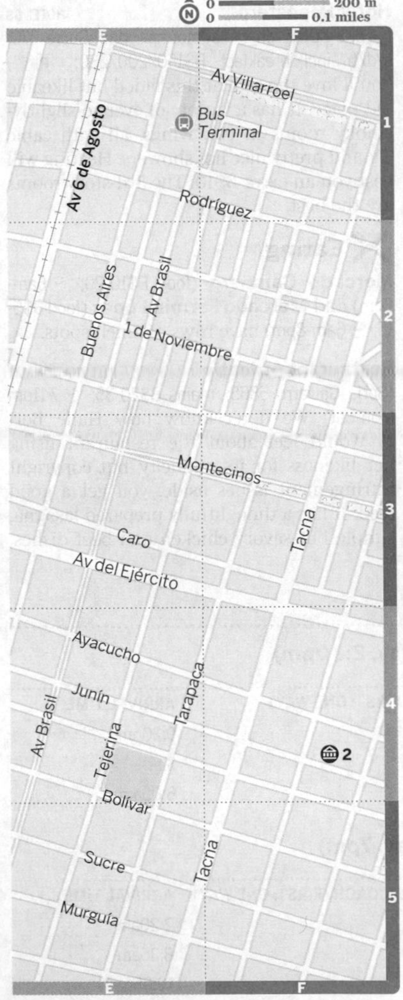

Casa de la Cultura Simón Patiño MUSEUM
(Soria Galvarro 5755; admission B$8; ⏲8:30-11:30am & 3-6pm Mon-Fri, 9am-2pm Sat) The former residence of tin baron Simón Patiño includes his furniture, personal bric-a-brac, fine toys (you're not allowed to play with them though) and an ornate art-nouveau stairway. Visiting exhibitions are featured in the downstairs lobby; the permanent collection is on the upper level. Entry is by guided tour only.

Museo Casa Arte Taller Cardozo Velasquez MUSEUM
(☎527-5245; juegueoruro@hotmail.com; Junín 738; admission B$8; ⏲hours vary) A family of seven artists – Gonzalo (sculptor), his wife María (potter) and their five daughters – open their whimsical house and art studio to visitors. Take a peek into the nooks and crannies of their workshop, overflowing with artsy bric-a-brac and the leafy patio with Gonzalo's fascinating sculptures – the one in the middle is devoted to Pachamama (Mother Earth).

Oruro

Mina San José MINE TOUR
(English tour per person B$400) There are numerous mines in the Oruro area, many operated by *cooperativos* (small groups of miners who purchase temporary rights). One of the most important is Mina San José, which has been in operation for over 450 years, and has part of the mine open to tourists. Half-day English tours are available through Charlie Tours.

Termas de Obrajes HOT SPRINGS
(admission B$15) These hot springs, 25km northeast of town, are a popular weekend destination. It's a well-run complex, with a pool and private bathrooms with tubs which you can reserve for half an hour and gradually fill up with the magnesium-rich water.

Charlie Tours GUIDED TOUR
(524-0666; charlietours@yahoo.com) Run by the knowledgeable Juan Carlos Vargas, Charlie Tours is a real specialist in the region. In addition to city tours, mine visits and excursions to nearby attractions such as Calacala and Termas de Obrajes, it offers trips to places further afield, including the Chipaya, Salar de Coipasa and Sajama. The offices are outside of town, so call or email.

Festivals & Events

Carnaval FESTIVAL
During the spectacular Carnaval, from the Saturday before Ash Wednesday, the city turns into a parade of party animals. Revelers – including proud locals, 90% of whom call themselves *quirquinchos* (armadillos) – pitch water at each other (which, frankly, can be downright tiresome). Several parades (including the **Entrada** and **La Diablada**) feature dancers in garish masks and costumes.

Sleeping

There are quite a few handy, if not classy, *alojamientos* (basic accommodations) near the train station on Velasco Galvarro.

Residencial 3 de Diciembre HOSTEL $
(527-9205; Montecinos 198; r per person B$60, with shared bathroom B$50; P) A fair budget bet that at least has large airy rooms. They won't win any prizes for decor (especially with the bright-pink shared bathrooms) but if you are watching your pennies then you can do a lot worse for this price.

Hotel Repostero HOTEL $$
(525-8001; ph_tania@hotmail.com; Sucre 370; s/d/tr incl breakfast B$150/200/230; P) You'll love the sign at this faded but likeable old place. It has a variety of ever-so-slightly-smoky rooms in two wings, all with cable TV and pretty nice hot showers. Heating will cost you an extra B$10. The 3rd-story rooms are the best.

Eating

Mercado Campero (food B$10-20; 6am-8pm) and **Mercado Fermín López** (food B$5-15; 6am-8pm) have rows of lunch spots.

Restaurant Ardentia INTERNATIONAL $
(Soria Galvarro 5865; mains B$20-35; 7-11pm Mon-Sat) We don't know how Halle Berry would feel about the restaurant using her likeness for its publicity, but copyright infringement issues aside, you get a good feed. It has a thoughtfully prepared lasagna, simple but savory chicken and beef dishes,

TRAINS DEPARTING ORURO

Expreso del Sur Train (Tuesday & Friday, 2:30pm)

DESTINATION	COST (B$ COACH/FIRST; ONE WAY)	ARRIVAL TIME
Uyuni	60/120	9:20pm
Tupiza	107/239	3am
Villazón	126/279	6:05am

Wara Wara Train (Wednesday & Sunday, 7pm)

DESTINATION	COST (B$ NORMAL/COACH/FIRST; ONE WAY)	ARRIVAL TIME
Uyuni	32/47/102	2:20am
Tupiza	56/80/181	8:35am
Villazón	67/100/220	12:05pm

and familiar standards such as hamburgers. Surely Halle would approve.

La Casona ITALIAN $$

(Montes 5969; pizzas from B$55) Straight-out-of-the-oven *salteñas* for lunch, and pizza for dinner keep this little place buzzing, especially at night when it gets really busy and warm.

Drinking & Nightlife

Pub the Alpaca BAR

(527-5715; La Paz 690; 8pm-1am Thu-Sat) A worthwhile option, this Swedish- and Bolivian-run pub is an intimate, recently renovated spot set up in a front room. The good-mood feel is helped with good mixed drinks. If the door is locked, just knock or ring the bell.

Dali PUB

(cnr 6 de Octubre & Cochabamba, 2nd fl; 10am-2am) About as hoity-toity as you can get in Oruro, this pub-style cafe-bar with wooden floors caters to Oruro's young set. Come for the drinks – not the food – its a perfect launch pad for a night out on the town.

Information

There are several banks with ATMs in town, particularly around Plaza 10 de Febrero. Exchange kiosks at the bus and train stations will change several currencies, including euros (at a pretty poor rate).

Banco Bisa (Plaza 10 de Febrero) ATM.

Caseta de Información Turística (Tourist Information Office; 24hr) These booths give out city maps and leaflets – tourist police are usually on hand and sometimes the only staff in attendance!

Migración (527-0239; www.migracion.gob.bo; Sucre, btwn Washington & Av Montes; 8:30am-12:30pm & 2:30-6:30pm Mon-Fri) Extend your stay here.

Getting There & Away

BUS

All long-distance buses use the **bus terminal** (527-9535; Brasil s/n; terminal fee B$1.50), a 15-minute walk or short cab ride northeast of Oruro's center. To get here, head north along 6 de Agosto until you hit Aroma, then turn right one block. There's a luggage storage office (B$5 to B$8) on the ground floor.

Buses to La Paz depart every half-hour, and there are several departures for Cochabamba, Potosí and Sucre. For Santa Cruz, you must make a connection in Cochabamba. There are daily evening services to Arica, Calama and Iquique in Chile.

Night buses to Uyuni leave between 7pm and 9pm – they are freezing cold, so bring a sleeping bag – or head to Potosí and catch a more comfortable and frequent connection there. Most Uyuni buses arrive before dawn and they will let you sleep on the bus until the sun comes up. The exception is a luxury Cruz del Norte (B$120) service from La Paz which passes through Oruro around midnight and arrives at a more reasonable hour, but you'll need to book this in advance.

DESTINATION	COST (B$)	DURATION (HR)
Arica (Chile)	140	8
Calama (Chile)	120-250	15
Cochabamba	30	5
Iquique (Chile)	70-100	8
La Paz	35	3-5
Potosí	30	5
Sucre	50-80	8
Tarija	60-80	12
Tupiza	60	10-12
Uyuni	30–35	7-8
Villazón	70–120	12

TRAIN

Trains run from Oruro south to Villazón on the Argentina border, passing through Uyuni, Atocha and Tupiza along the way. The Expreso del Sur is slightly more luxurious, departing Oruro on Tuesday and Friday at 2:30pm. Cheaper service is had on the Wara Wara line, leaving Oruro Wednesday and Sunday at 7pm. There is return service from Villazón on Monday, Wednesday, Thursday and Saturday. From Uyuni, you can get slow trains to Calama (Chile). Buy tickets at least a day ahead from the **train station** (527-4605; www.fca.com.bo; 8:15-11:30am & 2:30-6pm Sun-Fri, hours vary); don't forget your passport. On train days, there's a left-luggage kiosk here. Watch your belongings on the train, and bring a sleeping bag.

Uyuni

02 / POP 29,500

Seemingly built in defiance of the desert-like landscape, Uyuni stands desolate yet undaunted in Bolivia's southwestern corner. Mention Uyuni to a Bolivian and they will whistle and emphasize *'harto frío'* – extreme cold. Yet, despite the icy conditions, Uyuni has a cheerful buzz about it with hundreds of travelers passing through every week to kick off their tour of the Salar de Uyuni along the Southwest Circuit.

Sights

You can take day trips to the Salar de Uyuni from town, but most choose to head out on a three- or four-day tour.

Cementerio de Trenes HISTORIC SITE

(Train Cemetery) FREE The only real attraction in Uyuni itself, the Cementerio de Trenes is a rusty collection of historic steam locomotives and rail cars dating back to the 19th century, when there was a rail-car factory in Uyuni. Today they sit decaying in the yards about 3km southwest of the modern-day station along Av Ferroviaria.

Museo Arqueología y Antropológico de los Andes Meridionales MUSEUM

(Av Arce, near Colón; admission B$5; ⌚8:30am-12:30pm & 2:30-6:30pm Mon-Fri) A small museum featuring mummies, long skulls, fossils, ceramics and textiles. There are Spanish descriptions of the practices of cranial deformation.

Tours

While you can theoretically visit the Salar de Uyuni and the attractions of the Southwest Circuit independently, it is extremely challenging due to unreliable transport and the remoteness of the area. So the vast majority of people take an organized tour from either Uyuni or Tupiza. From the end of December to the end of March, the salt flat floods. During this time, many agencies shut down, and you can travel just 10km into the salt flat, but not beyond.

Costs

Tours cost B$700 to B$800 for three days at a standard agency, and B$800 to B$1000 at a high-end operation. Four-day and custom trips will run B$800 and up. Tours include a driver (who also serves as your guide, mechanic and cook, but probably doesn't speak English), two nights accommodation (quality varies depending on the agency), three meals a day and transit. You'll also need to pay a B$30 entrance fee to Isla Incahuasi and a B$150 fee to enter the nature reserve. Those traveling on to Chile will need B$21 to B$50 for the border. Many agencies don't accept credit cards.

Don't choose an agency solely on price: the cheaper operators can be unsafe.

What to Bring

You'll want to bring a couple of liters of water, snacks, headlamp, sunscreen, sunglasses, sunhat and warm clothes, including gloves and a decent jacket. A sleeping bag is highly recommended. Ask your operator to include free sleeping bag rental in your fee. Otherwise, they cost about B$50 to rent and are really worth it.

CHOOSING A TOUR AGENCY

Generally, it doesn't matter which agency you book with (other than the high-end ones), as most agencies run the same routes, share drivers and sort travelers into groups of five or six people (don't accept more!). This means that while you may book with Agency A, you may end up traveling with Agency Z.

This said, you do have some power here. Talk to returning travelers and multiple agencies, and use your judgment to pick a good operator. If you are custom-building an itinerary, have the agency put it in writing. If you can make your own group (try the pub), you'll be better off. The high-end agencies have better hotels, can customize tours, and have more reliable cars.

Though things are improving, a number of travelers have died on this trip, mostly in drunk-driving accidents. Ask to see the car you will be traveling in and to meet the driver ahead of time. If the agency tries to switch drivers or cars on you, call them on it. Along the way, make sure your driver is not drinking alcohol (and demand to switch cars if he is).

Cordillera Tours (☎693-3304; www.cordilleratraveller.com; Av Ferroviaria 314) Good choice for transfers to Chile.

Esmeralda Tours (☎693-2130; www.esmeraldatoursuyuni.com; Av Ferroviaria) Friendly and honest standard tour operator that is getting excellent reviews.

Toñito Tours (☎693-2094; www.bolivianexpeditions.com; Av Ferroviaria 152) Upmarket, quality tours.

Uyuni

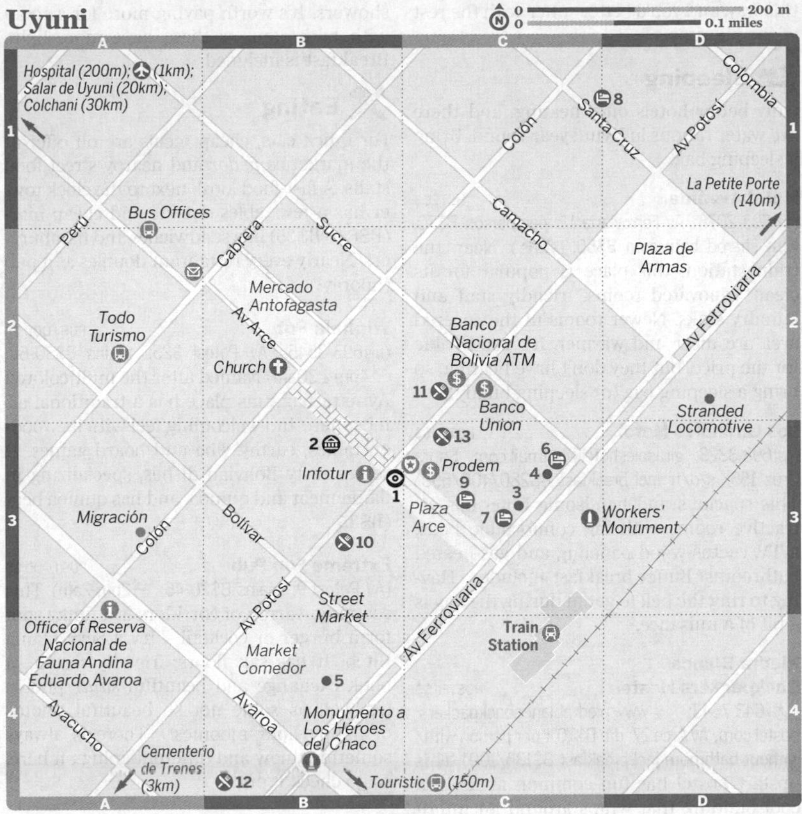

Uyuni

Sights

1 Clock Tower....B3
2 Museo Arqueología y Antropológico de los Andes Meridionales....B3

Activities, Courses & Tours

3 Cordillera Tours....C3
4 Esmeralda Tours....C3
5 Toñito Tours....B4

Sleeping

6 Hotel Avenida....C3
7 Hotel Julia....C3
8 Los Girasoles Hotel....D1
9 Piedra Blanca Backpackers Hostel....C3

Eating

10 Extreme Fun Pub....B3
11 Lithium Club....C2
12 Minuteman Revolutionary Pizza....B4
13 Wiphala Pub....C3

Sleeping & Eating

On a standard tour, you will stay in a hotel made of salt the first night (just on the edge of the salt flat). The next night, you'll stay in a basic lodge. None have heaters, some have hot showers (for B$10 extra), and you will be cold. They generally put your whole group in one room. If you are doing it yourself, these basic hotels cost about B$30 per night.

Your driver is generally your cook, and the quality of food varies. Vegetarians should make arrangements with the operator ahead of time.

Standard Tours

The most popular tour is the three-day circuit taking in the Salar de Uyuni, Laguna Colorada, Sol de Mañana, Laguna Verde and points in between. There are probably 20 to 50 people a day doing this trip.

You can also book a day trip for B$200 to Isla Incahuasi, but really, you've come all this way, and you'd better suffer with the rest of the pilgrims.

Sleeping

Only better hotels offer heating, and there are water rations in Uyuni year-round. Bring a sleeping bag.

Hotel Avenida HOTEL $
(☎693-2078; Av Ferroviaria 11; per person B$70, with shared bathroom B$50; @ 📶) Near the train station, this place is popular for its clean, renovated rooms, friendly staff and laundry sinks. Newer rooms in the covered area are nicer and warmer. It's good value for the price, but they don't have heating, so bring a sleeping bag (or sleeping buddy).

Los Girasoles Hotel HOTEL $$
(☎693-3323; girasoleshotel@hotmail.com; Santa Cruz 155; s/d/tr incl breakfast B$280/400/550) This spacious and handsome hotel has attractive rooms with big comfortable beds, a TV, cactus-wood paneling and gas-heated bathrooms. Buffet breakfast included. Having to ring the bell to get in during the day is a bit of a nuisance.

Piedra Blanca Backpackers Hostel HOSTEL $$
(☎7643-7643; www.piedrablancabackpackers.hostel.com; Av Arce 27; dm B$70, r per person with/without bathroom incl breakfast B$135/100) This upstart hostel has fun common areas in a cool building that wraps around an interior courtyard. There are three dorm rooms that sleep six to eight people, plus a handful of private rooms with or without attached bathrooms. The dorms are worth it, with large pine bunks, heat (yes!), comfy mattresses and thick comforters.

Hotel Julia HOTEL $$
(☎693-2134; www.juliahoteluyuni.com; cnr Avs Ferroviaria & Arce; s/d/tr/q B$200/300/420/500, s/d with shared bathroom B$120/200; @ 📶) This neat and tidy option right in the center of town has heated rooms and piping-hot showers. It's worth paying more for a room with bathroom, as these have more light. Breakfast is included.

Eating

For quick eats, cheap meals are on offer at the market *comedor* and nearby street food stalls. A fast-food kiosk next to the clock tower has a few tables outside and cheap bites (B$8 to B$35) like sandwiches and hamburgers. Nearly every restaurant doubles as a pub (hooray!).

Wiphala Pub PUB FOOD $$
(☎693-3545; Av Potosí 325; mains B$30-60; ⏲4pm-1:30am) Named after the multicolored Aymará flag, this place has a traditional atmosphere and welcoming feel with its wooden tables, earthy vibe and board games. It serves tasty Bolivian dishes, specializing in llama meat and quinoa, and has quinoa beer (B$35).

Extreme Fun Pub PUB FOOD $$
(Av Potosí 9; mains B$20-45; ⏲2pm-2am) This roaming warren of corridors is a funky spot for a burger or cocktail – try a Sexy Llama Bitch. It has salt floors, friendly service, a book exchange and beautiful *salar* photos (as well as some not so beautiful photos of happy hour moonies!). There is always something new and different going on here, so go check it out.

★ Minuteman Revolutionary Pizza PIZZA $$$
(☎693-3186; Av Ferroviaria 60; breakfast B$30-40, pizzas B$60-110; ⏲breakfast & dinner) This convivial spot, inside the Toñito Hotel, run by Chris from Boston and his Bolivian wife Sussy, is a deserved travelers' favorite. Sample the best pizzas in Bolivia, each served with a gourmet salad. It's also a cozy spot for a beer, glass of Tarija wine, or a hearty breakfast with all-you-can-drink coffee or tea. Reserve ahead!

GETTING TO CHILE

Most agencies now offer cross-border connections to San Pedro de Atacama by arrangement with Chilean operators. You'll make the connection not long after passing Laguna Verde. Arrange this ahead of time with your operator. It may be wise to stop by the Migración office in Uyuni before doing this. The Hito Cajón border post is much more reliable than it used to be. They charge an exit tax of B$15 to B$30 (B$21 is the standard), and supposedly operate 24 hours a day. Try to be there before 6pm just to be on the safe side.

TRAINS DEPARTING UYUNI

Expreso del Sur Train

DESTINATION	COST (B$ COACH/FIRST; ONE WAY)	DEPARTURE TIME	ARRIVAL TIME
Oruro	60/120	Thu & Sun 12:05am	6:55am
Tupiza	47/120	Tue & Fri 9:40pm	3am
Villazón	72/180	Tue & Fri 9:40pm	6:05am

Wara Wara Train

DESTINATION	COST (B$ NORMAL/FIRST CLASS/ EXECUTIVE; ONE WAY)	DEPARTURE TIME	ARRIVAL TIME
Oruro	32/47/102	Tue & Fri 1:45am	9:05am
Tupiza	25/38/76	Mon & Thu 2.50am	8:35am
Villazón	38/56/118	Mon & Thu 2.50am	12:05pm

Lithium Club BOLIVIAN **$$$**
(693-3399; Av Potosí 24; mains B$80-120; 4pm-midnight) This upper-end choice has international takes on traditional Bolivian dishes like *charque de llama* (llama jerky) and *pailita de llama* (llama stew), bringing together authentic flavor combinations with a smidge of European styling. The high-roofed colonial dining room is only made better by the '80s rock anthems that play in the background.

Information

Watch your cash stash, especially around the train and bus stations. Drunken Carnaval time is pickpocket season; beware helpful young men who want to 'help' you buy a bus ticket or with your luggage.

There are cash machines in town, but they don't always work.

Banco Nacional de Bolivia ATM (Av Potosí)

Banco Union (cnr Sucre & Av Potosí) Handy location for ATM.

Hospital Obrero (693-2025) Along Arce on the edge of town; does good work and accepts most travel insurance.

Infotur (693-3666; cnr Avs Potosí & Arce; 8am-noon & 2:30-6:30pm Mon-Fri) Well-stocked with leaflets on Uyuni and the rest of Bolivia.

Migración (7307-9328; Colón; 8:30am-noon & 2:30-6:30pm Mon-Fri) Visa extensions only. Get your visas and exit/entry stamps at the border or face a fine.

Office of Reserva Nacional de Fauna Andina Eduardo Avaroa (REA; 693-2225; www.boliviarea.com; cnr Colón & Avaroa; 9am-6pm Mon-Fri) Somewhat helpful administrative office for the park in Uyuni. You can buy your park entry (B$150) here if going under your own steam.

Post Office (693-2405; Av Arce Esquina Cabrera)

Prodem (Plaza Arce) Changes dollars and gives cash advances.

Getting There & Away

You can get to Uyuni by bus, plane or train. Buy your bus ticket the day before and your train ticket as far in advance as you can.

AIR

The quickest way to get to town is by flying direct from La Paz to Uyuni International Airport, 1km north of Uyuni.

BUS

A brand new touristic bus terminal was nearing completion at the time of research, and no doubt bus companies will migrate there as soon as it is finished. Until then buses leave from the west end of Av Arce, a couple of minutes' walk from Plaza Arce. There's a choice of companies to most destinations, so ask around to get the best price, time and service. Potosí buses leave hourly; for Sucre it's easiest to head to Potosí and change there.

The safest and most comfortable terrestrial transport to La Paz is with **Todo Turismo** (693-3337; www.todoturismo.bo; Cabrera 158; one way B$270), which runs a heated-bus service with friendly staff and an onboard meal, departing daily at 8pm. The service from La Paz departs at 9pm, from Edificio Paola on Uruguay, a block from the main terminal. Other regular destinations from Uyuni include:

Oruro & La Paz Omar buses generally leave around 7pm or 8pm. Alternatively, heading to Potosí avoids the unpaved stretch to Oruro and means you don't have to wait round until evening for the connection.

Tupiza & Villazón Predilecto buses leave at 6am and 8pm, but it's easier by train.

Calama (Chile) Cruz del Norte buses depart at 4am (B$120, nine hours). The return from Calama is at 6am.

DESTINATION	COST (B$)	DURATION (HR)
Cochabamba	72-155	12
La Paz	71-270	10-12
Oruro	35-117	7-8
Potosí	35-40	3½
Sucre	60-70	8
Tupiza	50	7-8
Villazón	60	10

TRAIN

Uyuni has a modern, well-organized **train station** (☎693-2153; www.fca.com.bo; Ferroviaria s/n). Trains take you north to Oruro, south to Villazón and east to Calama (Chile). Seats often sell out so buy your ticket several days in advance or get an agency to do it for you. There are numerous reports of slow or cancelled trains and large gaps in service – but that's all part of the adventure.

Depending on size, you may have to check your backpack/case into the luggage compartment. Look out for snatch thieves on the train just before it pulls out.

A train for Avaroa on the Chilean border departs on Monday and Friday at 3am (B$31, five hours). From here you cross to Ollagüe and may have to wait a few hours to clear Chilean customs. Another train then continues to Calama (B$91 from Uyuni, six hours from Ollagüe). The whole trip can take up to 24 hours but it's a spectacular, if uncomfortable, journey. Taking a bus to Calama is more reliable.

Expreso del Sur is the slightly more luxurious line, departing Uyuni for Oruro on Thursday and Sunday at 12:05am and heading south for Atocha, Tupiza and Villazón on Tuesday and Friday at 9:40pm.

Wara Wara offers a cheaper service that leaves Uyuni Tuesday and Friday at 1:45am for Oruro and heads south to Atocha, Tupiza and Villazón on Thursday and Monday at 2:50am.

Southwest Circuit

Bolivia's southwestern corner is an awe-inspiring collection of harsh, diverse landscapes ranging from the blinding white Salar de Uyuni salt flat to the geothermal hotbed of Los Lípez, one of the world's harshest wilderness regions and an important refuge for many Andean wildlife species.

Much of the region is nominally protected in the **Reserva Nacional de Fauna Andina Eduardo Avaroa** (REA; www.bolivia-rea.com; admission B$150), which was created in 1973, covers an area of 7150 sq km and receives in excess of 50,000 visitors annually.

Salar de Uyuni

One of the globe's most evocative and eerie sights, the world's largest salt flat (12,106 sq km) sits at 3653m. When the surface is dry, the *salar* is a pure white expanse of the greatest nothingness imaginable – just the blue sky, the white ground and you. When there's a little water, the surface perfectly reflects the clouds and the blue Altiplano sky, and the horizon disappears.

STANDARD CIRCUIT

After stopping in the **Cementerio de Trenes**, **Cochani salt extraction areas**, and a now-closed **Salt Hotel** (admission B$25), your tour will continue on to the spectacular **Isla Incahuasi** (admission B$30), better known as Isla del Pescado, in the heart of the *salar* 80km west of Colchani. This hilly outpost is covered in Trichoreus cactus and surrounded by a flat white sea of hexagonal salt tiles. At the base of the island, the **Museo Ritual** has some interesting Spanish-language displays on Aymará rituals, beliefs and cultures.

Most groups have their lunch here. There's also a **cafe-restaurant** (nyc0079@hotmail.com; mains B$14-48, set lunch B$40; ⏲lunch Jul-Oct) run by La Paz–based Mongo's; email to make a reservation.

Many tours stay the first night in the handful of salt hotels around the village of Chuvica, which sits on the eastern edge of the salt flat. A signed 1km **trail** just south of the village takes you up the hillside to a small cavern (make sure you get down before sunset). There's a basic store here. The **salt hotels** (☎7441-7357; per person B$50, full board B$150) in town are nearly identical, with no heat, salt floors, furniture and walls, and common dining rooms where you can eat dinner and shiver. An extra B$10 gets you a hot shower.

Far Southwest

Several startlingly beautiful sights are hidden away in this remote corner, normally visited on your second and third day. The surreal landscape is nearly treeless, punctuated by gentle hills and volcanoes near the Chilean border. Wildlife in the area includes three types of flamingos (most notably the rare James species), plus plenty of llamas, vicuñas and owls.

The following sites comprise the major stops on most tours. **Laguna Colorada** is a bright adobe-red lake fringed with cake-white minerals, 25km east of the Chilean border. The 4950m-high **Sol de Mañana geyser basin** has boiling mud pots and sulfurous fumaroles. Tread carefully when approaching the site; any damp or cracked earth is potentially dangerous. The nearby **Termas de Polques** hot springs spout comfortable 30°C (86°F) sulfurous water and provide a relaxing morning dip at 4200m.

Laguna Verde, a splendid aquamarine lake, is tucked into Bolivia's southwestern corner at 5000m. Behind the lake rises the dramatic 5960m cone of **Volcán Licancábur**, which can be climbed; take a local guide.

If you have a few more days in Uyuni, consider heading out to explore some of the forgotten towns and sites around the area.

The semi-ghost town of **Pulacayo**, 22km northeast of Uyuni, has some interesting architecture – including the mansion of Bolivia's 22nd president, Aniceto Arce Ruíz. There are decaying locomotives from the area's 18th-century heyday, cooperative mines, cool rock formations, and the potential to do lo-fi mine tours with a local guide. A bus (B$5) leaves for Pulacayo from in front of Uyuni's post office.

Sometimes included on the *salar* tours, the town of **Colchani** has a small **museum** (B$5) dedicated to the salt trade, plenty of salty arts and crafts and a few interesting salt-extraction cooperatives that might let you look around. If you are doing the salt flat on your own, this is the kick-off spot.

Getting There & Around

The easiest way to visit the far southwest is with a group from Uyuni; the above attractions are all visited on the standard three-day trip. Alternatively, you can set out from Tupiza and end up in Uyuni, a very worthwhile option.

Tupiza

02 / POP 44,700

The pace of things in tranquil Tupiza seems a few beats slower than in other Bolivian towns, making this a great place to peace out for a few days, head off for a rip-romping cowboy adventure like Butch Cassidy and Sundance did 100 years ago, or trundle out on the back road to the Salar de Uyuni.

Set in a spectacular 'Wild West' countryside, the capital of Sud Chichas corners itself into the Río Tupiza Valley, and is surrounded by rugged scenery – weird eroded rainbow-colored rocks cut by tortuous, gravelly *quebradas* (ravines, usually dry) and cactus-studded slopes.

Sights & Activities

Tupiza's main attraction is the spectacular surrounding countryside, best seen on foot or horseback. Recommended destinations in the vicinity, all less than 32km away, include the canyons and rock formations of **Quebrada de Palala**, **Quebrada de Palmira**, **El Cañon del Duende**, **Quebrada Seca** and **El Sillar**.

A short trek up **Cerro Corazón de Jesús** reveals lovely views over the town, especially at sunset. Lively **street markets** convene on Thursday and Saturday morning near the train station.

Tours

There's an ever-increasing number of operators in Tupiza offering trips through the Southwest Circuit ending in Uyuni or back in Tupiza (or, in some cases, San Pedro de Atacama in Chile). Expect to pay between B$1300 and B$1600 per person for the standard four-day trip.

All agencies offer horseback riding (B$200/350/490 for three/five/seven hours). Longer rides include a sleepover in basic accommodations in the villages of Espicaya or Quiriza. Also on offer by all the agencies is the triathlon (B$300 to B$380 per person, including lunch, based on four people), an active full-day tour of the surrounding area by jeep, horseback and mountain bike. You can also arrange a jeep tour (B$480 to B$600 per day) or a guided trek (B$150 to B$240 per half-day).

La Torre Tours TOUR
(694-2633; www.latorretours-tupiza.com; Chichas 220, Hotel La Torre) Run by a friendly couple, this agency offers personalized tours of Tupiza's surroundings and into the *salar*. It rents bikes for B$80 per three hours.

Tupiza Tours TOUR
(☎694-3003; www.tupizatours.com; Chichas 187, Hotel Mitru) This outfit pioneered many of the Tupiza-area routes now also offered by competitors. Their two-day Butch and Sundance tour (B$1500, based on two people) is popular, with an overnight stay in the hamlet of San Vicente and a visit to the abandoned mining village of **Portugalete**.

Sleeping

The cheapest options are basic *residenciales* (budget accommodations) opposite the train station.

Hotel La Torre HOTEL $
(☎694-2633; www.latorretours-tupiza.com; Chichas 220; s/d incl breakfast B$100/160, r per person with shared bathroom B$60) This sound, central choice run by a retired nurse and doctor offers clean rooms with good beds and smart bathrooms. Rooms at the front of the rambling colonial-era home are much lighter but chillier, and the beds can be a bit lumpy. Guests have use of a kitchen, roof terrace and TV lounge – a good place to meet other travelers.

Hostal Valle Hermoso HOSTEL $
(☎694-4344; www.vallehermosotours.com; Arraya 478; s/d B$70/120, dm/r per person with shared bathroom B$30/50; 📶) An old-school hostel with a book exchange, roof terrace and plenty of social space. It's HI-affiliated (members get a 10% discount), clean and convenient.

Tupiza Hostal HOTEL $
(☎694-5240; Florida 10; r per person with shared bathroom B$40) Budget seekers should check out this hostel. The rooms are a bit dark, some beds are pretty poor quality and the staircase is deadly, but the sheets are clean and the courtyard is a great spot to hang out with fellow travelers. It offers use of a communal shower and a shared kitchen.

★**Hotel Mitru** HOTEL $$
(☎694-3001; www.hotelmitru.com; Chichas 187; s B$260, d B$350-450, s/d with shared bathroom B$90/160; @📶🏊) The best and most reliable hotel in town, the busy Mitru has been run by the same family for generations and is a relaxing choice, built around a swimming pool that's just the ticket after a dusty day out on horseback. It has a variety of rooms in two sections: the older 'garden' part and the newer 'cactus' area.

Eating

Affordable street meals are served outside the train station and at the *comedores* (cheap restaurants) around the market.

Alamo MEXICAN $
(cnr Chichas & Avaroa; almuerzo B$15, snacks B$8-15, mains B$20-40; ⊙Mon-Sat) A saloon-style spot where locals and tourists mingle in the funky two-story space with a Mexican vibe and lots of knickknacks. The menu features mainly meat dishes, like *pique macho* (beef chunks and sausages over french fries with lettuce, tomatoes, onions and spicy *locote* peppers), and they come in huge tasty portions.

★**Milan Center** PIZZA $$
(cnr Chichas & Chuquisaca; mains B$25-55, pizza B$33-111; ⊙Mon-Sat) For the best pizza in town, head over to Milan Center, which serves up crispy thin-crust pizzas with a fine variety of

TRAINS DEPARTING TUPIZA

Expreso del Sur Train

DESTINATION	COST (B$ COACH/FIRST; ONE WAY)	DEPARTURE TIME	ARRIVAL TIME
Villazón	25/60	3am Wed & Sat	6:15am
Uyuni	47/120	5.30pm Wed & Sat	11:50pm
Oruro	107/239	5.30pm Wed & Sat	7:10am

Wara Wara Train

DESTINATION	COST (B$ NORMAL/COACH/FIRST; ONE WAY	DEPARTURE TIME	ARRIVAL TIME
Villazón	14/20/45	8:45am Thu & Mon	12:05pm
Uyuni	25/38/76	11am Wed & Sat	1:15am
Oruro	56/80/181	11am Wed & Sat	10:05am

GETTING TO ARGENTINA

The Bolivian side of the main border crossing to Argentina in the town of **Villazón** is a sprawling, dusty, chaotic sort of place. The frontier and bus station are always busy as numerous Bolivians work in Argentina. Watch out for the usual scammers who tend to congregate at borders; dodgy banknotes and petty theft are not unknown.

The **Argentine consulate** (7386-2411; Plaza 6 de Agosto 123; 8am-1pm Mon-Fri) is on the main square. Numerous *casas de cambio* near the bridge along Av República Argentina offer reasonable rates of exchange for US dollars and Argentine pesos, less for bolivianos. **Banco Mercantil** (JM Deheza 423) changes cash and has an ATM dispensing US dollars and bolivianos.

All northbound buses depart from the **Villazón bus terminal** (fee B$2). All except those bound for Tarija pass through Tupiza (B$15 to B$22, 2½ hours); it's a beautiful trip, so try to go in the daylight and grab a window seat – at night, it can be a very scary ride. Regular bus services also head to La Paz (B$140 to B$170, 21 hours) via Potosí (B$80 to B$120, 11 hours) and Oruro (B$140 to B$160, 17 hours). Daily evening buses along the rough but amazing route to Tarija (B$40, seven to eight hours) continue to Bermejo (there are four onward departures per day). Argentine bus companies have ticket offices opposite Villazón's terminal, but all Argentine buses leave from the La Quiaca bus terminal, across the border. You'll be hassled by ticket sellers for both Argentine and Bolivian bus services; don't be rushed into buying a ticket, as there may be a service leaving sooner. You can easily bargain down the price on longer routes; conversely, the sellers may try and overcharge you on shorter journeys.

The Villazón train station is 1.5km north of the border crossing – a taxi costs B$5. Note that the ticket window at the station is closeday on Sunday.

To just visit La Quiaca briefly, there's no need to visit immigration; just walk straight across the bridge. Crossing the border is usually no problem, but avoid the line of traders getting their goods searched; otherwise it may take you hours to clear customs.

On the north side of the international bridge, **Bolivian customs & immigration** (24hr) issues exit and entry stamps (the latter normally only for 30 days) – there is no official charge for these services, but a B$21 to B$50 'service fee' is sometimes leveraged. Argentine immigration and customs are open from 7am to 11pm. Formalities are minimal but the wait and exhaustive customs searches can be very long. In addition, those entering Argentina may be held up at several control points further south of the border by more searches.

topping options. The covered back patio is a nice break from the streets of Tupiza.

Rinconcito Quilmes ARGENTINIAN **$$**
(Suipacha 14; almuerzo B$13, mains B$20-50) You'll see few other tourists in this little spot known for cheap, filling lunches served in a spacious dining room and a couple of outside tables. It's popular on weekends for its *asados* (barbecues) with quality meat from Argentina.

Information

Most accommodations can do a load of washing for you and most agencies distribute small maps of the town and the surroundings.

Banco Union (7 de Noviembre, cnr Sucre) ATM that accepts foreign cards.

Latin America Cambio (Avaroa 160) Changes several currencies but not always at the best rates.

Getting There & Away

BUS

The bus station (Arraya) has buses to most major destinations or hubs in the region, though most leave in the evening. For Villazón and the crossing to Argentina take a *rapidito*; they leave when full from in front of the terminal (B$20). *Rapiditos* also run to Potosí (B$80, 3½ hours) and get there faster than the bus. For Uyuni it's often quicker to go to Potosí and catch a connection there.

DESTINATION	COST (B$)	DURATION (HR)
Cochabamba	80	16-18
La Paz	50-70	13-15
Oruro	50-60	10-11
Potosí	25-50	5
Tarija	50-80	7
Uyuni	40-50	7
Villazón	15-22	2

TRAIN

Unfortunately, if you travel by train you'll miss most of the brilliant scenery on the route to Uyuni, so you might consider the less comfortable bus service. The ticket window at the **train station** (☎ 694-2529; www.fca.com.bo) opens irregularly on days when there's a train, so it can be easier to have an agency buy your tickets for a small surcharge.

Tarija

☎ 04 / POP 205,300

With its pleasantly mild climate and easily walkable colonial center, Tarija is a place you may find yourself lingering in longer than expected, despite the fact that many Bolivians from bigger cities regard South Central Bolivia as a half-civilized backwater. Tarija's palm-lined squares, tight streets, laid-back feel and lively restaurants seem like just the right amount of cosmopolitan and sophistication. After an afternoon with a glass of local *vino* on the central plaza you might consider relocating.

Sights & Activities

Casa Dorada MUSEUM

(Ingavi O-370; guided tour B$5; ⏲ by guided tour 9-11am & 3-5pm Mon-Fri, 9-11am Sat) With a freshly painted coat of gold and silver, the appropriately named Gilded House, whose roof is topped with a row of liberating angels, looks impressive from afar but less so upon closer inspection. Entry is by guided visits only, which leave on the hour.

Museo de Arqueología y Paleontología MUSEUM

(cnr Lema & Trigo; ⏲ 8am-noon & 3-6pm Mon-Sat) FREE The university-run Archaeology & Paleontology Museum provides a glimpse of the prehistoric creatures and lives of the early peoples that once inhabited the Tarija area. Downstairs you'll see well-preserved animal remains and upstairs the focus is on history, geology and anthropology, with displays of old household implements, weapons, ceramics and various prehistoric hunting tools, including a formidable cudgel known as a *rompecabezas* (head-breaker).

Viva Tours TOUR

(☎ 663-8325; Bolívar 251, 2nd fl) For wine tours and adventurous ecotrips to Tarija's hinterlands – including four nearby national reserves – it's tough to beat Viva Tours.

VTB Tours TOUR

(☎ 664-4341; www.vtbtourtarija.com; Ingavi O-784) One of the city's longest established agencies, with a reliable reputation and English-speaking guides, is located inside Hostal Carmen. With advance notice and a minimum of three people, they're a good bet for the Inca Trail or Tajzara lagoons in the Reserva Biológico Cordillera de Sama (B$1600 per person).

Sleeping

Casa Blanca HOSTEL $

(☎ 664-2909; luiszilvetiali@gmail.com; Ingavi 645; dm B$60; @ 📶) The whitewashed colonial-era facade and shady courtyard make Casa Blanca easily the most attractive of the city's budget accommodations. Three dorm rooms have two bunk beds each and the bathrooms are kept clean and have reliably hot showers. It's on a quiet block a short walk to the central plaza, however the soundness of your sleep depends on other guests.

Hostal Zeballos HOSTAL $

(☎ 664-2068; Sucre N-966; s/d B$120/160, without bathroom B$60/120; 📶) Superficially attractive, with dozens of potted plants and climbers giving the place a fresh, spring feel. However, make sure you see the room before you commit: they've all seen better days and the basement ones are grim and dark.

Hostal del Sol HOTEL $$

(☎ 666-5259; www.hoteldelsol.com.bo; Sucre 782; s/d incl breakfast B$250/350; ❄ @) Good value and conveniently located only two blocks from the central plaza, Hostal del Sol is a reliable choice for its sunny street-facing rooms with mini balconies and breakfasts served in a similarly light-filled 2nd-floor dining room. Interior rooms are darker, less preferred but all have flat-screen TVs and sparkling-clean marble floors.

Hostal Carmen HOTEL $$

(☎ 664-3372; www.hostalcarmentarija.com; Ingavi O-0784; s/d from B$190/280; @ 📶) On a quiet block west of the center, this professionally run place offers standard rooms in a large three-story building. The less expensive, top-floor rooms are more basic, though you have quick access to the rooftop's fabulous city views. VTB the onsite tour company, is recommended and staff are accustomed to helping foreign tourists.

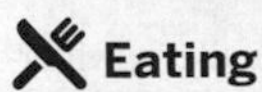

Eating

You'll need to be brave to try *ranga ranga* (tripe with onion, tomato and chilli) and *chan faina* (lamb guts with greens), but even delicate stomachs will enjoy *sopa de maní* (peanut soup) or *saice* (diced meat and vegetables). Don't forget to sample the desserts too; *dulce de lacayote* (fig-leaf gourd marmalade mixed with cinnamon), *pepitas de leche* (cinnamon fudge) and *tojori* (pancakes with cloves and aniseed) are all favorites. Get a hold of the *Guía Gastronomica* from the tourist office for more mouthwatering ideas.

Hot Wings: The Unique Flavor AMERICAN $

(Calle 15 de Abril 147; mains B$30) Tasty and messy like hot wings should be, though certainly not unique, this Coca-Cola–themed fast-food joint on Plaza Sucre makes for a quick and cheap meal if you don't mind the bright, fluorescent lighting and videos of U2 and other pop concerts on the large screen TV.

★Guten GERMAN $$

(cnr Calle 15 de Abril & Colón; mains B$55; 9am-midnight Mon-Thu, to 3am Fri & Sat, 10am-3pm Sun) Local families and groups of friends and tourists, mainly Bolivian, frequent Guten where you can chow down on juicy cuts of steak, schnitzel and fish. You'll likely want to linger and lounge with drinks as it has a sophisticated and warm vibe, with classic American blues playing, large, candlelit wood tables and colorful paintings on brick walls.

Taberna Gattopardo INTERNATIONAL $$

(Plaza Luis de Fuentes y Vargas; mains B$20-55; 8am-midnight;) Worthy of repeat visits, if only for people watching while sipping an espresso, this European-run tavern and cafe occupies one of the central plaza's choicest corners. The menu is large and eclectic, the food merely mediocre – choose from salads, burgers, pizzas, a few Bolivian specialties, steaks and fondue bourguignonne. Inside, the high-ceilinged dining room is cavernous.

La Floresta Don Ñato BUFFET $$

(Carretera a San Jacintom, Barrio Germán Busch; buffet B$45-60; Fri-Sun;) A great place for pitchers of fresh lemonade and all-you-can-eat buffets of pork, chicken and salads served in a huge and lovely, leafy garden with a swimming pool. It's a bit out of town, so get a taxi here – the staff will call you one for the return journey.

★Pizza Pazza PIZZA $$$

(Carlos Lazcano, cnr Belgrano y Pino; pizza B$40-110) Exuberant hostess Edith Paz Zamora has put together a really unique blend of art and, you guessed it, pizza. The walls are splashed with colorful paintings and those with a creative ilk take over on Thursdays (art night) and Fridays (Bohemian night), when folklore, music and dancing are added to the tasty menu. Ring the bell to get in!

Drinking & Entertainment

Keep an eye out for flyers advertising *peñas*, usually held at restaurants on weekends.

Xoxo BAR

(Calle 15 de Abril; 8am-midnight) Adorned with pop art and drinks cans from across the globe, this bar-cafe with outdoor seating on the main plaza generally attracts a young crowd at night.

Information

There are numerous ATMs around the plaza.

Casas de cambio (Bolívar) change US dollars and Argentine pesos.

Infotur (667-2633; www.turismo.tarija.gob.bo; cnr 15 de Abril & Sucre; 8am-noon & 2:30-6:30pm Mon-Fri, 9am-noon & 4-7pm Sat & Sun) Distributes basic town maps and is reasonably helpful with queries regarding sites in and around town – Spanish speaking only.

Migración (664-3450; cnr La Paz & Oruro) Head to this office in front of Parque Bolívar for entry/exit stamps or to extend your stay.

Getting There & Around

AIR

The **Oriel Lea Plaza Airport** (664-2195) is 3km east of town off Av Victor Paz Estenssoro. **TAM** (664-2734; www.tam.bo; La Madrid O-470), **BOA** (611-2787; www.boa.bo; Trigo, btwn Alejandro del Carpio & Lema), **Ecojet** (611-3427; www.ecojet.bo; cnr Colón & Madrid) and Amaszonas service La Paz, Santa Cruz, Sucre and Cochabamba (tickets for these destinations range from B$220 to B$450; for La Paz and Sucre it usually involves a stop in Cochabamba). TAM and Amaszonas also make the short hop to Yacuiba (B$300 to B$500) one to two days a week.

BUS

A new, modern bus terminal is being built 7km south of town. However, at the time of research, the cramped, though much more conveniently located old **bus terminal** (663-6508) was still operating. There's a **tourist kiosk** here of very limited helpfulness. Most long-haul services leave in the afternoon between 4:30pm and 8:30pm. Services to Santa Cruz pass through Villamontes from where there are connections to Yacuiba and Asunción in Paraguay, though frustratingly the latter pass through in the early hours of the morning, meaning you'll have to wait a long time for your onward ride. The bus company Juarez has Tuesday, Thursday and Sunday departures direct to Salta in Argentina (B$220, eight hours).

DESTINATION	COST (B$)	DURATION (HR)
Cochabamba	90-115	26
Oruro	90	20
Potosí	60-70	12-15
Santa Cruz	90-115	24
Sucre	70-90	18
Villamontes	40-50	9

Around Tarija

San Lorenzo, 15km north of Tarija along the Tupiza road, is a quaint colonial village with cobbled streets and carved balconies. *Micros* and *trufis* (B$3, 30 minutes) leave from the corner of Av Domingo Paz and Saracho in Tarija approximately every 20 minutes during the day.

Tomatitas, with its natural swimming holes, three lovely rivers (the Sella, Guadalquivir and Erquis) and happy little eateries, is popular with day-trippers from Tarija. From here you can walk or hitchhike the 9km to **Coimata**, where there's more swimming and a walking track 40 minutes upstream to the base of the two-tiered **Coimata Falls**, which has a total drop of about 60m.

The **Sama Biological Reserve** protects representative samples of both the Altiplano and the inter-Andean valley ecosystems. Entry to the reserve costs US$15 and the fee is not included in the prices offered by tour companies.

To get to the reserve and Comaita, *micros* A and B to Tomatitas leave every 20 minutes from the corner of Av Domingo Paz and Saracho in Tarija (B$1.50), some continuing on to Jurina (B$5) via San Lorenzo. Get off near the school and then walk the rest of the way. For Coimata, similarly frequent departures leave from the corner of Campesino and Comercio (B$3) in Tarija.

El Valle de la Concepción, or simply 'El Valle,' is the heart of Bolivian wine and *singani* production.

For a guided visit to the valley's wineries, contact Viva Tours (p234) in Tarija. If you prefer to visit under your own steam, El Valle lies off the route toward Bermejo; take the right fork at the *tranca* east of Tarija. Taxis and *micro V* leave when full (B$5, 30 minutes) from the corner of Corrado and Trigo.

CENTRAL HIGHLANDS

Cochabamba

☎04 / POP 630,600

Busy, buzzy Cochabamba is one of Bolivia's boom cities, and it has a distinct, almost Mediterranean vitality that perhaps owes something to its clement climate. While much of the city's population is typically poor, parts of town have a notably prosperous feel.

The spacious new-town avenues have a wide choice of restaurants, eagerly grazed by the food-crazy *cochabambinos*, and the bar life is lively, driven by students and young professionals. Cochabamba is famous for its *chicha*, a fermented corn drink that is the locals' favorite tipple.

You could easily find yourself staying a lot longer than you planned.

Sights & Activities

★Palacio Portales PALACE
(c.pedagogicocultral@fundacionpatino.org; Potosí 1450; admission incl guide B$15; ⏲gardens 3-6:30pm Tue-Fri, 9am-noon Sat & Sun, English tours 4pm & 5pm Mon-Fri, 10:30am & 11:30am Sat, 12:30pm Sun) Nothing symbolizes Bolivia's gilded mineral age like tin baron Simón Patiño's European-style Palacio Portales. Though he never actually inhabited this opulent mansion completed in 1927, it was stocked with some of the finest imported materials available at the time – Carrara marble, French wood, Italian tapestries and delicate silks. The gardens and exterior were inspired by the palace at Versailles, the games room is an imitation of Granada's Alhambra and the main hall takes its design inspiration from Vatican City.

Convento de Santa Teresa CONVENT
(cnr Baptista & Ecuador; admission B$20; ⏲tours hourly 9-11am & 2:30-4:30pm Mon-Fri, 2:30-4:30pm Sat) Straight out of a Gabriel García Márquez novel is the noble, timeworn

Convento de Santa Teresa. Guided tours (around 45 minutes) of this gracefully decaying complex allow you to see the peaceful cloister, fine altarpieces and sculptures (from Spanish and Potosí schools) and the convent church. However, it's not so much the quality of the architecture or art that's noteworthy, but rather the challenge to your imagination in picturing and conceiving what life was like for the cloistered nuns here.

Museo Arqueológico MUSEUM
(cnr Jordán E-199 & Aguirre; admission B$25; 8am-6pm Mon-Fri, to 12:30pm Sat) The Museo Arqueológico provides an excellent overview of Bolivia's various indigenous cultures. The collection is split into three sections: the archaeological collection, the ethnographic collection and the paleontological collection. There's good information in Spanish and an English-speaking guide is sometimes around in the afternoons.

Cristo de la Concordia LANDMARK
(Innominada, Zona la Chimba; 10am-6pm Tue-Sat, 9am-6pm Sun) This immense Christ statue standing atop Cerro de San Pedro (2800m) behind Cochabamba is the second largest of its kind in the world. It's 44cm higher than the famous *Cristo Redentor* in Rio de Janeiro, which stands 33m high, or 1m for each year of Christ's life. *Cochabambinos* justify the one-upmanship by claiming that Christ actually lived *'33 años y un poquito'* (33 years and a bit). Fantastic 360-degree panoramic views of the city and valley are worth the trip.

Tourist Bus BUS TOUR
(450-8920; per person B$25) This bus leaves from Plaza Colón at 10am and 3pm and visits all the city sights.

Courses

Cochabamba is a popular place to hole up for a few weeks of Spanish or Quechua lessons. Cultural centers offer courses for around B$50 per hour.

Centro Boliviano Americano LANGUAGE COURSE
(422-1288; www.cbacoch.org; Calle 25 de Mayo N-0365) Can recommend private language teachers.

Escuela Runawasí LANGUAGE COURSE
(424-8923; www.runawasi.org; Maurice Lefebvre N-0470, Villa Juan XXIII) Offers a recommended program that involves linguistic and cultural immersion from B$1340 per week. It also offers excursions to Tunari, Torotoro and a relaxing Chapare rainforest hideout.

Tours

Bolivia Cultura ADVENTURE TOUR
(452-7272; www.boliviacultura.com; Ecuador E-0342) Professional trips to Parque Nacional Torotoro and other regional attractions. Friendly and accustomed to dealing with foreign travelers; some English is spoken. Highly recommended.

Fremen Tours ADVENTURE TOUR
(425-9392; www.frementours.com.bo; Tumusla N-245) Organizes local excursions and high-quality trips to the Chapare, Amazon and Salar de Uyuni.

Sleeping

Don't be tempted by the rock-bottom prices for accommodations in the market areas and around the bus station. It's cheap for a reason – the area is positively dangerous after dark.

COCA-LAND

About 1.2 million kilos of coca leaf are consumed monthly in Bolivia, leading President Evo Morales to declare it an intrinsic part of Bolivia's heritage in his 2009 constitution.

But not all the coca grown in the country is for traditional use. Bolivia is the world's second- or third-biggest cocaine producer, depending on whom you ask, producing up to 290 tons of the white stuff each year. Between 240 sq km and 300 sq km of coca are cultivated nationally (varying with eradication efforts). Legal production of coca is capped at 120 sq km.

If you get caught with the illegal stuff, your embassy will not help you, so don't buy it. It's also illegal to carry coca leaves into most countries, so if you have some chew them all before you leave the country.

Cochabamba

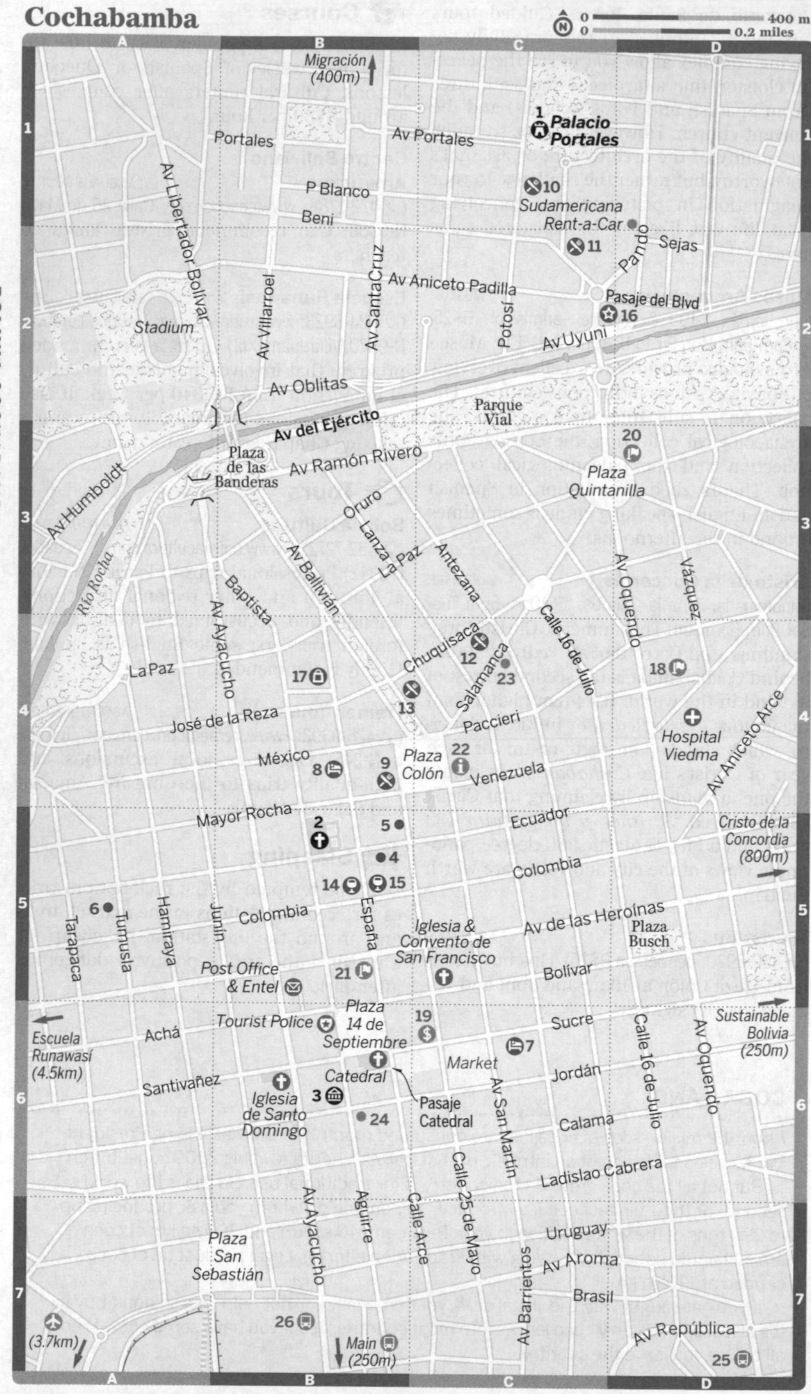
0 400 m
0 0.2 miles
Migración (400m)
1 Palacio Portales
Portales
Av Portales
Av Libertador Bolívar
P Blanco
Beni
10
Sudamericana Rent-a-Car
11
Pando
Sejas
Av Aniceto Padilla
Av Villarroel
Av SantaCruz
Potosí
Pasaje del Blvd
16
Stadium
Av Uyuni
Av Oblitas
Parque Vial
Av del Ejército
20
Plaza de las Banderas
Av Ramón Rivero
Plaza Quintanilla
Av Humboldt
Oruro
Lanza
La Paz
Antezana
Av Oquendo
Vázquez
Río Rocha
Av Ballivián
Baptista
Av Ayacucho
Calle 16 de Julio
Chuquisaca
12
Salamanca
23
18
La Paz
17
13
Paccieri
José de la Reza
Hospital Viedma
Av Aniceto Arce
22
México
Plaza Colón
8
9
Venezuela
Mayor Rocha
2
5
Ecuador
Cristo de la Concordia (800m)
4
Colombia
14
15
6
Tarapaca
Tumusla
Hamiraya
Junín
Colombia
España
Iglesia & Convento de San Francisco
Av de las Heroínas
Plaza Busch
Post Office & Entel
21
Bolívar
Plaza 14 de Septiembre
19
Escuela Runawasí (4.5km)
Achá
Tourist Police
Sucre
Calle 16 de Julio
Av Oquendo
Sustainable Bolivia (250m)
7
Market
Catedral
Santivañez
Jordán
Iglesia de Santo Domingo
3
Pasaje Catedral
Av San Martín
24
Calama
Calle 25 de Mayo
Ladislao Cabrera
Av Ayacucho
Aguirre
Calle Arce
Plaza San Sebastián
Uruguay
Av Aroma
Av Barrientos
Brasil
26
(3.7km)
Main (250m)
Av República
25

★ Running Chaski Hostal HOSTEL $

(☎425-0559; www.runningchaski.com.bo; España 449; dm B$75, s/d B$130/195; @📶) Opened in 2014, the Running Chaski is easily the best choice for budget-minded travelers. With exceptional service, the hostel is justifiably busy – reserve in advance, especially for weekends. The handsome colonial-style entryway leads to a small grassy back garden. Wood-floored rooms have modern furnishings and staff can help with travel plans.

Cochabamba

Top Sights

1 Palacio Portales C1

Sights

2 Convento de Santa Teresa B5
3 Museo Arqueológico B6

Activities, Courses & Tours

4 Bolivia Cultura B5
5 Centro Boliviano Americano B5
6 Fremen Tours A5

Sleeping

7 Residencial Familiar C6
8 Running Chaski Hostal B4

Eating

9 Gopal B1
10 Kabbab C1
11 María Bonita C2
12 Páprika C4
13 Sucremanta B4

Drinking & Nightlife

14 Cerebritos B5
15 Simón Bolívar B5

Entertainment

16 Levoa C2

Shopping

17 Spitting Llama B4

Information

18 Argentinian Consulate D4
19 Banco Unión C6
20 Brazilian Consulate D3
21 German Consulate B5
22 Infotur C4
23 Lavaya C4

Transport

24 BoA B6
25 Micros & Buses to Chapare D7
26 Micros to Quillacollo, Pahirumani & Sipe Sipe B7

Residencial Familiar PENSION $

(☎422-7988; Sucre E-554; s/d B$100/130, without bathroom B$50/80; @📶) Set in a lovely, if crumbling, old building, this budget flophouse is built around a patio courtyard with a nude sculpture in the non-functioning fountain. Unfortunately, the basic rooms, with concrete floors and ratty furniture, hold little appeal. It's not signposted; look for it across the street from the blue-walled Colegio Nacional Bolívar.

Eating

Cochabambinos pride themselves on being the most food-loving of Bolivians, and there is a dazzling array of local specialties for foodies to try including *lomo borracho* (beef with egg in a beer soup) and *picante de pollo* (chicken in spicy sauce). Ask at the tourist office for its *Cochabamba Gastronòmica* leaflet.

There's tasty street food and snacks all over Cochabamba, with the *papas rellenas* (potatoes filled with meat or cheese) at the corner of Achá and Villazón particularly delicious. Great *salteñas* (filled pastry shells) and empanadas are ubiquitous. Locals swear by the *anticuchos* (beef-heart shish kebabs) that sizzle all night at the corner of Avs Villaroel and América.

Sucremanta LATIN AMERICAN $

(Av Ballivián 510; mains from B$18; ⏰10am-2pm) This Av Ballivián branch of a chain of traditional restaurants offers dependable local dishes, including *mondongo* (pork ribs) and *menudito* (pork, chicken and beef stew).

María Bonita MEXICAN $

(Bení 0539, near Potosí; mains B$15-25; ⏰6-11pm Mon-Sat, 11am-9pm Sun) This charming spot decorated with bright pastel colors and Mexican signifiers such as Frida Kahlo posters and football team jerseys is run by the son of a Mexico City–Bolivian couple. Tasty burritos, enchiladas and chimichangas are nicely presented, and the weekend brunch of ceviche and *sopa de frijol* (black bean soup) is a good deal. The vibe is friendly – a sign encourages talking.

Kabbab MIDDLE EASTERN $$

(Potosí N-1392; mains B$30-60; ⏰5pm-midnight) Sharing an entryway with the Muele del Diablo bar and adjacent to the Palacio Portales, Kabbab offers a thousand-and-one variations on Persian kebabs. Highlights include clay-oven flatbread, Turkish coffee and decent baklava.

Gopal VEGETARIAN **$$**
(Mayor Rocha 3577; buffet B$18, mains B$20-40; 11am-2pm Mon-Sat;) Half-decent vegetarian dishes, including soy-based versions of Bolivian dishes and a few curries.

Páprika INTERNATIONAL **$$$**
(www.paprika.com.bo; Chuquisaca; mains B$30-95; 11:30am-midnight;) Classy and fashionable, this popular restaurant-bar has an eclectic menu, both Bolivian and international, including tasty baked potatoes and fondues, and more unusual plates such as ostrich and llama. After dark it becomes a trendy spot for a late drink and is also a good place to meet up with young bolivianos.

Drinking & Entertainment

There's plenty of drinking action along El Prado (Av Ballivián), and Calle España is also fertile territory, the latter with an ever-changing parade of appealing, bohemian cafe-bars.

Many of the bars along El Prado and España turn into mini-discos after midnight throughout the week, but at weekends the in-crowd head to the Recoleta and Av Pando.

Simón Bolívar BAR
(España E-250; 6:30pm-1am Mon-Sat;) Girls in glasses reading Pablo Neruda while sipping artisanal beer. Young guys barbecuing meat on a portable grill just outside the entrance. Live performances by 'new reggae' bands. Warhol-style paintings of Evo Morales. This snapshot of a single night should give you an idea of the vibe of this hip, casual spot above the entrance to the Hostal Nawpa.

Cerebritos BAR
(España N-251; 6pm-late) A grungy, likable bar with cable drums for tables and loud rock and hip-hop music. The house special is a mixed platter of colorful shooters; local students down them as *cacho* (dice) forfeits.

Levoa CLUB
(Paseo del Blvd, La Recoleta) At weekends the in-crowd head to La Recoleta to the trendy dancing place Levoa.

Shopping

Spitting Llama BOOKS, OUTDOOR EQUIPMENT
(www.thespittinglama.com; España 615; 9am-8pm Mon-Fri, to 1pm Sat) Camping equipment and foreign-language books, including Lonely Planet guidebooks.

Information

According to locals the streets south of Ave Aroma are best avoided and are positively dangerous at night – don't be tempted by the cheaper accommodation in this area. The bus station is around here, so don't be surprised if, when arriving in the early hours of the morning, you are not allowed off the bus until sunrise. Pickpocketing and petty thefts are common in the markets. The Colina San Sebastián and Coronilla Hill near the bus station are both extremely dangerous throughout the day. Avoid them.

Money changers gather along Av de la Heroínas and near the market at 25 de Mayo. Their rates are competitive but some only accept US cash. There are numerous ATMs (a handy cluster of them is at the corner of Heroínas and Ayacucho), and cash advances are available at major banks. A **Banco Unión** (25 de Mayo cnr Sucre) has one of several Western Union offices.

Hospital Viedma (453-3240; Venezuela; 24hr) Full-service public hospital.

Infotur (466-2277; www.cochabambaturistica.com.bo; Plaza Colón; 8am-noon & 2:30-6:30pm Mon-Fri) Hands out good city material, but of limited use in answering questions and providing up-to-date advice. There are several information kiosks, including at the bus station and airport, which also open Saturday mornings.

Lavaya (cnr Salamanca & Antezana; closed Sun) Most hotels offer laundry services, but for a commercial laundry, try Lavaya.

Migración (452-4625; Av Rodríguez Morales, btwn Santa Cruz & Potosí; 8.30am-12:30pm & 2:30-6:30pm Mon-Fri) For visa and length-of-stay extensions.

Post Office & Entel (cnr Ayacucho & Av de las Heroínas; 6:30am-10pm) The main post and Entel offices are together in a large complex. The postal service from Cochabamba is reliable and the facilities are among the country's finest. Downstairs from the main lobby is an express post office.

Tourist Police (450-3880, emergency 120; Plaza 14 de Septiembre; 24hr)

Getting There & Around

AIR

The flight between La Paz and Cochabamba's **Jorge Wilstermann Airport** (domestic/international departure tax B$14/170) is amazing. Sit on the left coming from La Paz.

TAM (441-1545), **BOA** (414-0873; www.boa.bo; cnr Jordan & Aguirre), **Ecojet** (www.ecojet.bo; Plazuela Constitución 0879, cnr 16 de Julio) and Amaszonas combined run a bunch of daily flights between Santa Cruz and La Paz via Cochabamba and a couple of daily flights to Sucre. There are also daily flights to Trinidad and Tarija, the latter continuing on to Yacuiba a couple of days a week (the schedule changes).

BUS

Cochabamba's **main bus terminal** (☎422-0550; Ayacucho; terminal fee B$4), just south of the center, has an information kiosk, a branch of the tourist police, ATMs, luggage storage and a *casa de cambio*. The traffic around the terminal is a mess; if it's daytime and your bags are small and light it might be worth walking a few blocks to hail a taxi.

Trufis and *micros* to eastern Cochabamba Valley villages leave from along Av República at the corners of Barrientos or 6 de Agosto. Torotoro *micros* (B$25) depart daily at 6pm except Thursday, with an additional 6am service on Thursday and Sunday. Services to the western part of the valley leave from the corner of Ayacucho and Aroma. For Villa Tunari, *micros* leave from the corner of Av República and Oquendo.

Departures to La Paz and Santa Cruz leave frequently throughout the day. Oruro and Potosí are mostly nighttime trips.

DESTINATION	COST (B$)	DURATION (HR)
Buenos Aires	750	54
La Paz	30-100	7
Oruro	25	4½
Potosi	65-85	15
Santa Cruz	40-110	10
Sucre	40-100	11
Villa Tunari	bus 15, *trufi* 35	bus 4, *trufi* 3

Around Cochabamba

Parque Nacional Tunari, an easily accessible 3090-sq-km park, was created in 1962 to protect the forested slopes above Cochabamba. It encompasses a wide diversity of habitats from dry inter-Andean valleys to the more humid and highly endangered Polylepis forests of the Cordillera Tunari.

The ruins of **Inka-Rakay** are a 2½-hour cross-country (but well-signed) walk from the village of **Sipe Sipe**, 27km southwest of Cochabamba. It makes a good side trip, but note that there have been several serious reports of campers being assaulted here. Sunday is market day in Sipe Sipe. Direct *micros* run on Wednesday and Saturday; otherwise go via **Quillacollo**, which is reached by *micro* from Cochabamba.

About 160km northeast of Cochabamba is the steamy, relaxed Chapare town of **Villa Tunari**, and **Inti Wara Yassi** (Parque Machía; www.intiwarayassi.org; B$2-6; ⏲9:30am-4:30pm Tue-Sun), a wildlife refuge and mellow place to warm up after the Altiplano.

Parque Nacional Torotoro is 135km southeast of Cochabamba in Potosí department. Here you'll find dinosaur tracks, cool geological formations, hikes, caves and ruins. The road has been improved in recent years, but can be tricky from November to February.

Sucre

☎04 / POP 259,400

Proud, genteel Sucre is Bolivia's most beautiful city, and the symbolic heart of the nation. It was here that independence was proclaimed, and while La Paz is now the seat of government and treasury, Sucre is recognized in the constitution as the nation's capital.

A glorious ensemble of whitewashed buildings sheltering pretty patios, it's a spruce place that preserves a wealth of colonial architecture. Strict controls on development have kept Sucre as a real showpiece: it was declared a Unesco World Heritage Site in 1991.

Set in a valley surrounded by low mountains, Sucre enjoys a mild and comfortable climate. It's still a center of learning, and both the city and its university enjoy reputations as focal points of progressive thought within the country.

Sights

For the best view in town, inquire about climbing the cupola at the national police office inside the **Prefectura de Chuquisaca** (State Government Building; cnr Estudiantes & Arce), next to the cathedral.

★Casa de la Libertad MUSEUM

(www.casadelalibertad.org.bo; Plaza 25 de Mayo 11; admission incl optional guided tour B$15; ⏲9am-noon & 2:30-6:30pm Tue-Sat, 9am-noon Sun) For a dose of Bolivian history, it's hard to beat this museum where the Bolivian declaration of independence was signed on August 6, 1825. It has been designated a national memorial and is considered the birthplace of the nation. Spanish-speaking guides are top flight – you'll likely applaud at the end of your guided tour.

Museo de Arte Indígena MUSEUM
(www.asur.org.bo; Pasaje Iturricha 314; admission B$22; ⌚9am-12:30pm & 2:30-6pm Mon-Sat) This superb museum of indigenous arts is a must for anyone interested in the indigenous groups of the Sucre area, focusing particularly on the woven textiles of the Jal'qa and Candelaria (Tarabuco) cultures. It's a fascinating display and has an interesting subtext: the rediscovery of forgotten ancestral weaving practices has contributed to increased community pride and revitalization. Information in English is available and you can observe the weavers patiently at work.

Museo Nacional de Etnografía y Folklore MUSEUM
(Musef; www.musef.org.bo; España 74; ⌚9:30am-12:30pm & 2:30-6:30pm Mon-Fri, 9:30am-12:30pm Sat) FREE Known locally as Musef and housed in the impressive former Banco Nacional building, this museum brings together a series of fascinating displays that vividly illustrate the great diversity of Bolivia's ethnic cultures. On the ground floor are two rows of dramatically lit masks, most of which you wouldn't want to bump into in a dark alleyway, and flamboyant festival costumes and apparel. The other permanent display deals with the Uru-Chipaya culture,

Sucre

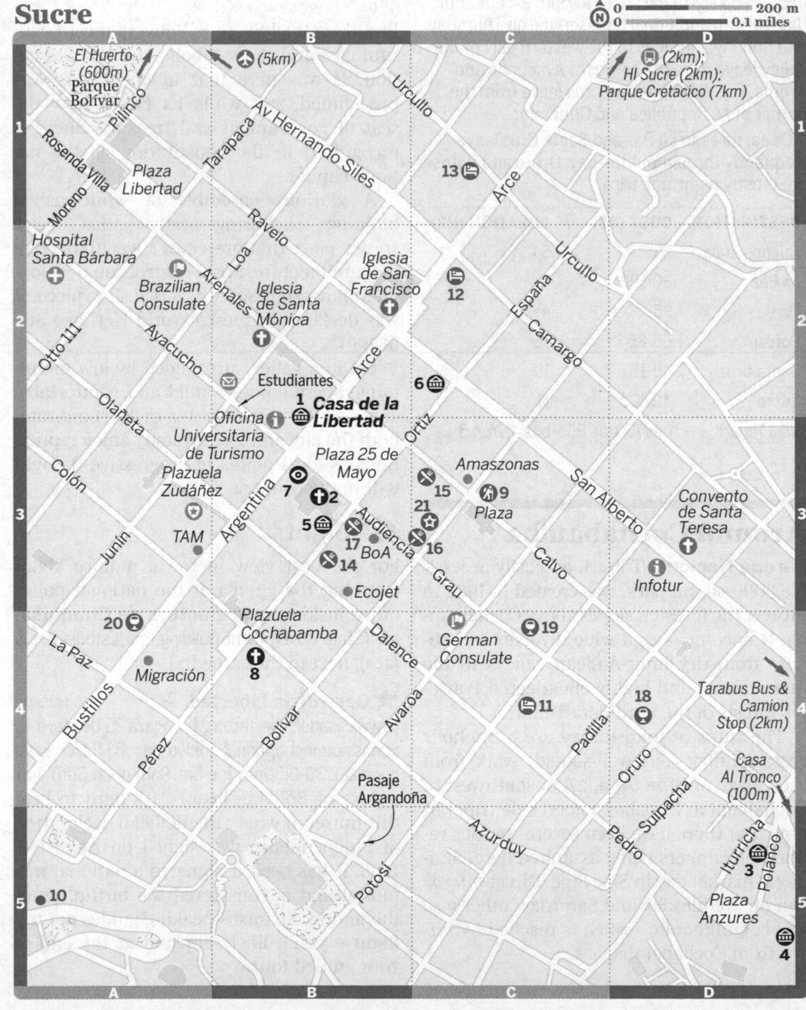

with reconstructions of village life and exhibitions of everyday artifacts.

Parque Cretácico (Cal Orck'o) ARCHAEOLOGICAL SITE
(Cretaceous Park; www.parquecretacicosucre.com; admission B$30; ⌚9am-5pm Mon-Fri, 10am-8pm Sat, to 5pm Sun) It seems that 65 million years ago the site of Sucre's Fabrica Nacional de Cemento SA (Fancesa) cement quarry, 5km north of the center, was the place to be for large, scaly types. When the grounds were being cleared in 1994, plant employees uncovered a nearly vertical mudstone face bearing about 5000 tracks of at least eight different species of dinosaur – the largest collection of dinosaur footprints in the world.

Templo Nuestra Señora de la Merced CHURCH
(Pérez 1; admission B$10; ⌚10am-noon & 3-5pm Mon-Fri) Following the current restoration work (completion date unknown at the time of writing), this church's interior will no doubt once again be one of the most beautiful of any church in Sucre. Much of it was bare when visited, however the views from the bell tower are splendid. Because the order of La Merced left Sucre for Cuzco in 1826, taking its records with it, the church's founding date is uncertain, but it's believed to be sometime in the 1540s.

Catedral CHURCH
(Plaza 25 de Mayo; ⌚mass 8-9am Mon-Sat, 9-11:30am Sun) Sucre's cathedral dates from the middle of the 16th century and is a harmonious blend of Renaissance architecture with later baroque additions. It's a noble structure, with a bell tower that is a local landmark. Inside, the white single-naved space has a series of oil paintings of the apostles, as well as an ornate altarpiece and pulpit. If you are not attending mass, you can enter as part of a visit to the Museo Eclesiàstico de Sucre next door.

Museo Eclesiàstico de Sucre MUSEUM
(Ortiz 31; admission B$20; ⌚10am-noon & 3-5pm Mon-Fri) Next door to Sucre's cathedral, this museum holds one of Bolivia's best collections of religious relics. There are four sections, ritually unlocked as your guided tour progresses.

Museo de la Recoleta MUSEUM
(Plaza Anzures; admission B$10; ⌚9-11:30am & 2:30-4:30pm Mon-Fri, 3-5pm Sat) Overlooking the city of Sucre from the top of Calle Polanco, La Recoleta was established by the Franciscan Order in 1601. It has served not only as a convent and museum, but also as a barracks and prison. The highlight is the church choir and its magnificent wooden carvings dating back to the 1870s, each one intricate and unique, representing the martyrs who were crucified in 1595 in Nagasaki.

Activities

There are numerous agencies in town, and nearly all offer trips to Tarabuco (around B$40 per person) for the Sunday market; many hotels and *hostales* can also arrange this trip. Many also offer day trips to the

Sucre

Top Sights
1 Casa de la Libertad B2

Sights
2 Catedral B3
3 Museo de Arte Indígena D5
4 Museo de la Recoleta D5
5 Museo Eclesiàstico de Sucre B3
6 Museo Nacional de Etnografía y Folklore C2
7 Prefectura de Chuquisaca B3
8 Templo Nuestra Señora de la Merced B4

Activities, Courses & Tours
Bolivia Specialist .... (see 17)
9 Condor Trekkers C3
10 Fox Language Academy A5
Joy Ride Turismo SRL .... (see 17)

Sleeping
11 Casa Verde C4
12 Hostal San Francisco C2
13 La Dolce Vita C1

Eating
14 Bibliocafé B3
15 Doña Lía C3
16 Florín C3
17 Joy Ride Café B3

Drinking & Nightlife
18 Goblin Brew Pub D4
19 La Quimba C4
20 Salfari A4

Entertainment
21 Centro Cultural los Masis C3

Cordillera de los Frailes, but you will contribute more to the local communities by going for longer.

Bolivia Specialist GUIDED TOUR
(☎4643-7389; www.boliviaspecialist.com; Ortiz 30, Sucre) Tours organized all over Bolivia as well as in the region around Sucre. If the office in Sucre is closed, ask at the bar/restaurant Florín.

Condor Trekkers HIKING
(☎7289-1740; www.condortrekkers.org; cnr Calvo & Bolivar; ⌚8:30am-6:30pm Mon-Sat) Popular and recommended tour agency that organizes a variety of multiday hikes in the surrounding region. Housed in the popular cafe of the same name, you can put your name up on the whiteboard and hope to find other takers to share the cost. A portion of earnings are said to go towards social-development projects.

Joy Ride Turismo SRL OUTDOORS
(☎645-7603; www.joyridebol.com; Ortiz 26) Popular hikes, bikes and horseback-riding trips, with groups leaving almost daily. Also offers paragliding – both tandem jumps and courses. Bookings and inquiries can be made at the cafe of the same name.

Courses

Fox Language Academy LANGUAGE COURSE
(☎644-0688; www.foxacademysucre.com; Av Chuquisaca 134) Fox Language Academy runs volunteer schemes, and learning Spanish or Quechua with the academy subsidizes English classes for underprivileged local kids. The academy is inside the Instituto Médico building.

Festivals & Events

Sucre loves an excuse for a celebration. It's worth checking out the list of many religious festivals at the tourist office.

Fiesta de la Virgen de Guadalupe RELIGIOUS
On the weekend closest to September 8, people from all over the country flock to join local *campesinos* in a celebration of the Fiesta de la Virgen de Guadalupe with songs, traditional dances and poetry recitations. The following day, they dress in colorful costumes and parade around Plaza 25 de Mayo carrying religious images and silver arches.

Sleeping

Accommodations in Sucre are among the country's most expensive. The cheapest places cluster near the market and along Calles Ravelo and San Alberto.

La Dolce Vita GUESTHOUSE $
(☎691-2014; www.dolcevitasucre.com; Urcullo 342; s/d/tr B$90/140/195; s/d without bathroom B$55/100; @📶) A traveler-friendly guesthouse, offering basic rooms for a variety of budgets. The kitchen is somewhat ratty, but the terrace is a good spot to catch some sun. Discounts offered for long-term stays.

Casa Al Tronco GUESTHOUSE $
(☎642-3195; www.casaaltronco.com; Topater 57; s/d B$80/150; 📶) This charming guesthouse in the Recoleta district has just three rooms, so book in advance. Glorious views of the city from two terraces, use of a kitchen and a welcoming reception might make you stay longer than planned. Stay more than five nights and there is a price reduction.

HI Sucre HOSTEL $
(☎644-0471; www.hostellingbolivia.org; Loayza 119; dm/s/d B$40/140/200, s/d without bathroom B$50/100; @📶) The main reason to stay here is for its convenience to the bus station two blocks away. True, it's housed in an architecturally idiosyncratic building with surprising features such as wood floors and even fireplaces in the dorm rooms, as well as pleasant backyard garden. Some of the private rooms have spa baths and cable TV.

Hostal San Francisco PENSION $
(☎645-2117; Arce 191; s/d B$80/140; 📶) With a stunning entry hall and eye-catchingly ornamental staircase, this place looks as though it belongs in a higher price bracket. While the rooms don't quite live up to the initial impression, you won't feel like you've wasted your bolivianos.

★**Casa Verde** B&B $$
(☎645-8291; www.casaverdesucre.com; Potosí 374; s/d/ste incl breakfast B$140/250/360; @📶🏊) The immaculate Casa Verde is a real home away from home. It's deservedly popular and frankly underpriced for the quality of service; Belgian owner Rene almost bends over backwards to be helpful to his guests. Rooms are named after Rene's children and grandchildren and are arranged around a small courtyard with a pool. If you visit in winter you'll be thankful for the thick comforters.

Doña Lía

FAST FOOD $

(Calvo 75; mains B$24; 6-11pm) Strictly a fried chicken and french fries joint, with unadorned concrete floors and walls. Nevertheless, and despite the fact that the chicken is dry, a quick helping can satisfy. Wings go fast, so go early if that's your thing.

Florín

INTERNATIONAL $$

(Bolívar 567; mains B$35-45; 10am-2am Mon-Fri, 8:30am-late Sat & Sun) This atmospheric bar-restaurant serves a mixture of typical Bolivian food and international dishes (the latter, such as chicken tandoori, pad thai or moussaka, are generally pale imitations), including a 'full English' breakfast. Popular with locals and gringos alike, who line up along the enormous 13m-long bar at night to swill down the beers.

Joy Ride Café

INTERNATIONAL $$

(www.joyridebol.com; Ortiz 14; mains B$35-70; 7:30am-2am Mon-Fri, 9am-2am Sat & Sun;) This wildly popular gringo-tastic cafe, restaurant and bar has everything from dawn espressos to midnight vodkas and nightly movies to weekend table-dancing. It's spacious, friendly and you'll need an hour just to read through the menu. Service can be slow on busy nights.

Bibliocafé

LATIN AMERICAN $$

(Ortiz 42 & 50; mains B$20-40; 11am-3am) With two adjacent locations, this has something for everyone: one side is dark and cozy, the other a little smarter. There's good service and a menu of pasta and Mexican-Bolivian food and drinks served until late in a cheerful and unpretentious atmosphere, plus regular live music.

★El Huerto

INTERNATIONAL $$$

(645-1538; www.elhuertorestaurante.net; Cabrera 86; mains B$65-80; noon-4pm Tue & Sun, noon-4pm & 7-10pm Wed-Sat) Set in a lovely secluded garden, El Huerto has the atmosphere of a classy lawn party, with sunshades and grass underfoot; there's great service and stylishly presented traditional plates (especially the chorizo) that don't come much better anywhere in the country.

Drinking & Entertainment

For *discotecas* (weekends only) you'll need to head north of the center; it's easiest by taxi.

There's a monthly brochure detailing Sucre's cultural events; look for it at tourist offices or in bars and restaurants.

Goblin Brew Pub

BAR

(Grau 246; 8pm-late Fri & Sat) This high-ceilinged place resembles a Spanish taverna and offers a good selection of craft beers.

Salfari

PUB

(Bustillos 237; 8pm-12.30am) This little gem of a pub has a loyal local crowd and lively games of poker and *cacho* (dice) usually going on. Try their tasty but potent homemade fruit shots.

La Quimba

BAR

(Grau 238; 7:30pm-late Tue-Sat) Somehow, in this postage-stamp-sized spot, there's space made for musicians (of the jazz and world-music variety) to perform most Friday nights. There are drinks, of course, a laid-back bohemian vibe, and a menu of vegetarian dishes such as a lentil and quinoa burger (B$20).

Centro Cultural los Masis

PERFORMING ARTS

(645-3403; Bolívar 561; 10am-noon & 3:30-9pm Mon-Fri) This venue hosts concerts and other cultural events. It also has a small museum of local musical instruments and offers Quechua classes.

Information

ATMs are located all around the city center, but not at the bus station.

Head online to www.sucreturistico.gob.bo for good info.

Hospital Santa Bárbara (646-0133; cnr Ayacucho & René Moreno; 24hr) Good hospital.

Infotur (645-5983; San Alberto 413; 8am-noon & 4-6pm Mon-Sat, 9am-noon & 2:30-6pm Sun) Can help with information about the Chuquisaca region.

Main Post Office (cnr Estudiantes & Junín; 8am-8pm Mon-Fri) This tranquil office has an *aduana* (customs) office downstairs for *encomiendas* (parcels).

Migración (645-3647; www.migracion.gob.bo; Bustillos 284; 8:30am-4:30pm Mon-Fri) A no-fuss place to extend visas and lengths of stay.

Oficina Universitaria de Turismo (644-7644; Estudiantes 49; 4-7pm Mon-Sat, 2-7pm Sun) Information office run by university students; sometimes offer guides for city tours.

Tourist Police (648-0467; Plazuela Zudáñez)

Getting There & Away

AIR

TAM (☎646-0944; Bustillos 143), **BOA** (☎691-2360; www.boa.bo; Audiencia 21), **Ecojet** (☎691-4711; www.ecojet.bo; Dalence 138) and **Amaszonas** (☎643-7000; www.amaszonas.com; Calvo 90) offer several flights a day to Cochabamba, La Paz and Santa Cruz. At the time of research, **Juana Azurduy de Padilla Airport** (☎645-4445), 5km northwest of the city, was still operating but a new airport named Alcantarí International Airport was being built 25km south of Sucre and was scheduled to open by March 2016. The domestic departure tax is B$11.

BUS & SHARED TAXI

The **bus terminal** (☎644-1292; Av Ostria Gutiérrez) is a 3km uphill walk from the center along Av Guiterrez and most easily accessed by *micros A* or *3* (B$1.50) from along Ravelo, or by taxi (as the *micros* are too crowded for lots of luggage). Unless you're headed for Potosí, it's wise to book long-distance buses a day in advance in order to reserve a seat. There's a terminal tax of B$2.50; services include an information kiosk but no ATM. You can save a trip to the bus station to get tickets as many central travel agents also sell tickets on selected services for a small commission.

Buses to La Paz generally leave in the afternoon between 4pm and 6:30pm.

If you are headed to Tarija, Villazón or Uyuni, you'll have more luck going to Potosí; the quickest and comfiest (if not the cheapest) way to get there is in a shared taxi (B$50, two hours), which can be arranged through your hotel or by calling direct – try **Turismo Global** (☎642-5125) or **Cielito Lindo** (☎644-1014).

DESTINATION	COST (B$)	DURATION (HR)
Camiri	100	14
Cochabamba	40-70	10-12
La Paz	70-180	12-14
Oruro	40-60	8-10
Potosí	15-30	3
Santa Cruz	94-105	15-20

Getting Around

Local *micros* (B$2) take circuitous routes around Sucre's one-way streets. Most seem to congregate at or near the market; they can be waved down virtually anywhere. You can reach the bus terminal on *micro A* or the airport on *micros F* or *1* (allow an hour) or by taxi (B$25).

Around Sucre

The small, predominantly indigenous village of **Tarabuco**, 65km southeast of Sucre, is known for its beautiful weavings, the colorful, sprawling **Sunday market** and the festival of Pujllay on the third Sunday in March, when hundreds of indigenous people from the surrounding countryside descend on the town in local costumes.

The easiest way to get to Tarabuco is by charter bus (B$40 round-trip, two hours each way) from Sucre, which leaves from outside Hostal Charcas on Ravelo around 8:30am. Tickets must be bought in advance from bigger hotels or any travel agent. From Tarabuco, the buses return to Sucre anytime between 11 am and 3pm.

Alternatively, *micros* (B$10, two hours) leave when full from Av de las Américas in Sucre on Sunday between 6:30am and 9:30am. Return trips to Sucre leave between 11am and 3:30pm.

For scenic trekking opportunities, head to **Cordillera de los Frailes**, a spectacular mountain range that runs through much of the western Chuquisaca and northern Potosí departments. Home to the Quechua-speaking Jalq'a people, it has a string of sites worth visiting, including the rock paintings of **Pumamachay** and **Incamachay**, the weaving village of **Potolo**, the dramatic **Maragua Crater** and the **Talula hot springs**. There are plenty of hiking routes but they traverse little-visited areas; to minimize cultural impact and avoid getting hopelessly lost, hire a registered guide (around B$200 per day plus costs) in Sucre.

Potosí

☎02 / POP 189,700

The conquistadors never found El Dorado, the legendary city of gold, but they did get their hands on Potosí and its Cerro Rico, a 'Rich Hill' full of silver. The city was founded in 1545 as soon as the ore was discovered, and pretty soon the silver extracted here was bankrolling the Spanish empire. Even today, something very lucrative is said to *vale un Potosí* (be worth a Potosí).

During the boom years, it became the largest and wealthiest city of the Americas. The ore is still being extracted in some of the most abysmal conditions imaginable – a visit to see today's miners at work invokes disbelief. But the rest of Potosí – its grand churches, ornate colonial architecture and down-to-earth, friendly inhabitants – is a real delight.

Sights

Potosí's central area contains a wealth of colonial architecture.

★Casa Nacional de la Moneda MUSEUM
(www.casanacionaldemoneda.org.bo; Ayacucho near Bustillos; admission by guided tour B$40, photo permit B$20; ⏲tours 9am, 10:30am, 2:30pm & 4:30pm Tue-Sat, 9am & 10:30am Sun) The National Mint is Potosí's star attraction and one of South America's finest museums. Potosí's first mint was constructed on the present site of the Casa de Justicia in 1572 under orders from the Viceroy of Toledo. This, its replacement, is a vast and strikingly beautiful building that takes up a whole city block. You don't have to be a numismatist to find the history of the first global currency fascinating.

Los Ingenios HISTORIC BUILDING
On the banks of the Río Huana Mayu, in the upper Potosí barrios of Cantumarca and San Antonio, are some fine ruined examples of the *ingenios* (smelters) formerly used to extract silver from the ore hauled out of Cerro Rico. Some remaining ones – there were originally 82 along a 15km stretch – date back to the 1570s and were in use until the mid-1800s. Most Cerro Rico mine tours include a stop at a working *ingenio.*

Museo & Convento de San Francisco MUSEUM
(☎622-2539; cnr Tarija & Nogales; admission by guided tour B$15; ⏲tours 9:30am, 11am, 3pm & 4pm Mon-Fri, 9am & noon Sat) This convent, founded in 1547 by Fray Gaspar de Valverde, is the oldest monastery in Bolivia. Owing to its inadequate size, it was demolished in 1707 and reconstructed over the following 19 years. The museum has a fine collection of religious art, including paintings from the Potosí school, such as *The Erection of the Cross* by Melchor Pérez de Holguín, various mid-19th-century works by Juan de la Cruz Tapia and 25 scenes from the life of St Francis of Assisi.

Torre de la Compañía de Jesús CHURCH
(Ayacucho near Bustillos; mirador admission B$10; ⏲8-11:30am & 2-5:30pm Mon-Fri, 8am-noon Sat) The ornate and beautiful bell tower, on what remains of the former Jesuit church, was completed in 1707 after the collapse of the original church. Both the tower and the doorway are adorned with examples of mestizo baroque ornamentation. Also the location of the Sucre tourist office.

Catedral CHURCH
(Plaza 10 de Noviembre) Construction of Potosí's cathedral began in 1564 and finally completed around 1600. The original building lasted until the early 19th century, when it mostly collapsed. Most of what is now visible is the neoclassical reconstruction – the building's elegant lines represent one of Bolivia's best exemplars of that style, and the interior decor is some of the finest in Potosí. You can visit the **bell tower** (admission B$10; ⏲8am-noon & 2-6pm Mon-Fri) for nice views of the city. Large-scale restoration work was ongoing at the time of writing.

La Capilla de Nuestra Señora de Jerusalén CHURCH
(Plaza del Estudiante; ⏲9am-7pm Sun) This church is a little-known Potosí gem. Originally built as a humble chapel in honor of the Virgen de Candelaria, it was rebuilt more lavishly in the 18th century. There's

WARNING: MINE TOURS

The cooperatives are not museums, but working mines and fairly nightmarish places. Anyone undertaking a tour needs to realize that there are risks involved. Anyone with doubts or medical problems – especially claustrophobes, asthmatics and others with respiratory conditions – should avoid these tours. Medical experts note that limited exposure from a few hours on a tour is extremely unlikely to cause any lasting health impacts, although if you have any concerns whatsoever about exposure to asbestos or silica dust, you should not enter the mines. Accidents can also happen – explosions, falling rocks, runaway trolleys etc. Tour companies that are careful to document the dangers of the mine, and spell it out with paperwork that visitors must sign, are considered more reliable that tour operators that do not, because they are letting visitors know the true risk of what lies ahead.

a fine gilt baroque *retablo* (portable box with depictions of religious and historical events) – the Virgin has pride of place – and a magnificent series of paintings of Biblical scenes by anonymous Potosí school artists. The impressive pulpit has small paintings by Melchor Pérez de Holguín.

Tours

In addition to mine tours, there are a variety of guided tours offered by the huge number of local agencies, including a three-hour city tour (B$70 to B$100, not including entry fees) of the museums and monuments. Other popular options include Tarapaya (B$50 to B$100); guided trekking trips around the Lagunas de Kari Kari (B$160 to B$280); and tours of colonial haciendas around Potosí (B$150).

Cooperative Mines MINE TOUR
A visit to the cooperative mines will almost certainly be one of the most memorable experiences you'll have in Bolivia, providing an opportunity to witness working conditions that are among the most grueling imaginable. We urge you not to underestimate the dangers involved in going into the mines and to consider the voyeuristic factor involved in seeing other people's suffering. You may be left stunned and/or ill.

Altiplano Tours MINE TOUR
(622-5353; Ayacucho 19) At the end of Altiplano's mine tours, you can try some of the work yourself. This company also offers *tinku* (ritual fighting) excursions.

Big Deal Tours MINE TOUR
(623-0478; www.bigdealtours.blogspot.com; Bustillos 1092) The specialty of this outfit, run by current and ex-miners, is of course mine tours. Guides are informative, passionate, and have a good sense of humor, plus clearly have a good relationship with the mine workers encountered along the way.

Potosí

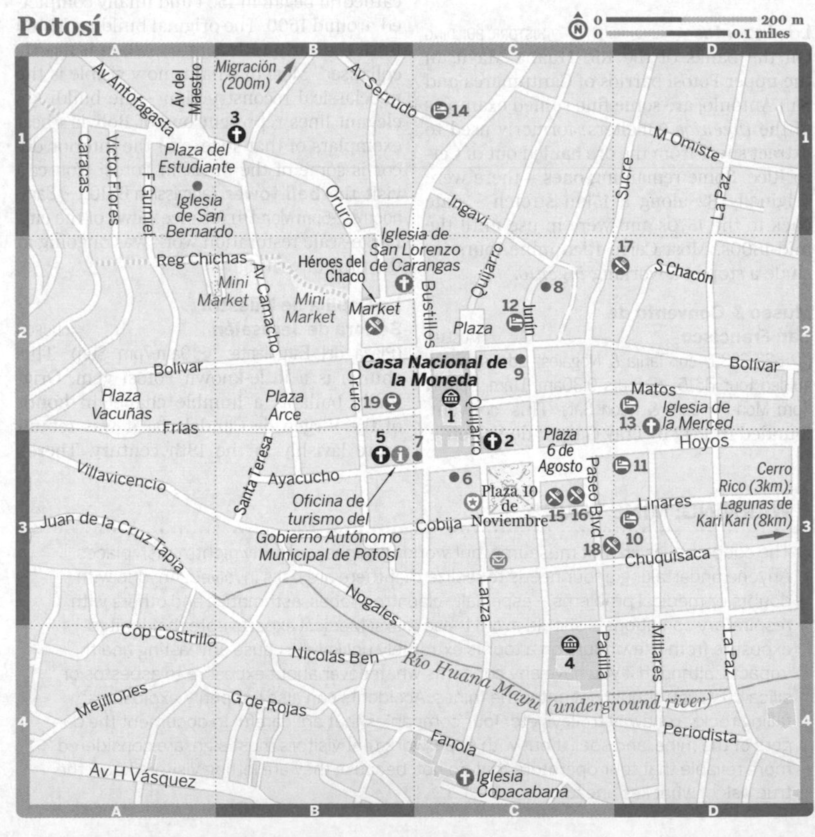

Greengo Tours MINE TOUR
(☎623-1362; Junín 17) This agency has been getting good reader reviews for its responsible mine tours and has a small cafe in its office. The passionate owner, ex-miner Julio Zambrana, is actively fighting to improve conditions for miners.

Hidalgo Tours TOUR
(☎622-9512; www.salardeuyuni.net; cnr Bolívar & Junín) One of the better upmarket options.

Sleeping

Options here are a bit disappointing overall – only top-end hotels have heating, and there may be blanket shortages in the cheapies, so you'll want a sleeping bag. Hard-core budget places may charge extra for hot showers.

Hostal Felimar HOTEL $
(☎622-4357; Junín 14; s/d/tr B$100/140/170, s/d without bathroom B$60/90) This pleasant and centrally located hostel has some low-ceilinged rooms and some nicer upstairs rooms with balconies affording views over the colonial street below. A small breakfast is included and there's a great suite on the top floor.

Residencial Felcar PENSION $
(☎622-4966; Av Serrudo 345; s/d B$70/140, without bathroom B$30/60) This is a sound choice with simple rooms (you'll want a sleeping bag in the cheaper ones), reliably hot showers and a nice terrace; some rooms have TVs and heaters. On Sunday it offers a traditional lunch of barbecued llama for B$25.

Hostal Carlos V Imperial HOTEL $$
(☎623-1010; frontdesk@hostalcarlosv.com; Linares 42; s/d incl breakfast B$180/240, without bathroom B$80/160, ste B$280; 📶) Not bad value for Potosí, however the rooms with shared bathroom are a little cramped and dark. The en-suite rooms are worth the extra bolivianos and the spacious and light-filled suite is a bargain, the equal of any room in a higher priced hotel.

Hostal Patrimonio HOTEL $$
(☎622-2659; www.hostalpatrimonio.com; Matos 62; r from B$380; 📶) Fairly standard hotel with rooms opening onto a central atrium. That said, the friendly service and reliable hot water make up for the lack of character, and it is better than most options in this price range in Potosí. Avoid the rooms at the front, especially on weekends, as it is opposite a nightclub.

Hostal Colonial HOTEL $$
(☎622-4265; www.hostalcolonialpotosi.com; Hoyos 8; s/d/tr B$320/420/510; @📶) In a well-kept colonial building near the main plaza, this warm whitewashed retreat has smallish rooms with windows onto a central courtyard; all rooms have minibars and cable TV, and some have bathtubs. It's a longstanding favorite with midrange travelers and boasts very helpful English-speaking staff and a great location.

Eating & Drinking

Stalls in the market *comedores* serve inexpensive breakfasts of bread, pastries and coffee. Downstairs there are some excellent juice stands. Cheese or meat empanadas are

BOLIVIA POTOSÍ

Potosí

Top Sights
1 Casa Nacional de la Moneda....C2

Sights
2 Catedral....C3
3 La Capilla de Nuestra Señora de Jerusalén....B1
4 Museo & Convento de San Francisco....C4
5 Torre de la Compañía de Jesús....B3

Activities, Courses & Tours
6 Altiplano Tours....C3
7 Big Deal Tours....C3
8 Greengo Tours....C2
9 Hidalgo Tours....C2

Sleeping
10 Hostal Carlos V Imperial....D3
11 Hostal Colonial....D3
12 Hostal Felimar....C2
13 Hostal Patrimonio....D2
14 Residencial Felcar....C1

Eating
15 Café la Plata....C3
16 La Salteña....C3
17 Phishqa Warmis....D2
18 Pizzeria Lobo's Cafe-Pub....C3

Drinking & Nightlife
19 La Casona Pub....B2

sold around the market until early afternoon, and in the evening, street vendors sell cornmeal and cheese *humitas*.

★Café la Plata CAFE $
(Plaza 10 de Noviembre; mains B$14-35; ⏲1:30-11pm Mon, 10am-11pm Tue-Sat) The city's most sophisticated cafe by far, this handsome, high-ceilinged place is comfortable and chic in a restored sort of way, and a good place to hang out, especially at one of the window seats with views of the plaza. There are rich espressos, magazines to read, and wine served by the glass. Pastas, cakes, salads, sandwiches – it's all done well.

La Salteña LATIN AMERICAN $
(Padilla 6; salteña B$3.50) Most Bolivians acknowledge, when pushed, that Potosí does the best *salteñas* – juicy, spicy and oh-so-tasty. Go no further than La Salteña, where one of these delicious items goes for B$3.50.

Pizzeria Lobo's Cafe-Pub INTERNATIONAL $$
(Padilla; mains B$35-70; ⏲10am-11pm) This dim and chilly place overlooks a narrow cobblestone street. It has a large menu of the usual beef and chicken standards, plus burgers and sandwiches, though the two dozen varieties of pizzas are, of course, the specialty. The decor is a hodgepodge of football posters and hanging musical instruments and there's a billiards table.

Phishqa Warmis INTERNATIONAL $$
(Sucre 56; meals B$20-50, almuerzo B$25; ⏲8am-midnight) A pleasingly cozy little restaurant lounge with colored walls and a vaulted ceiling. The pub-style à la carte food gets mixed reviews, but the buffet *almuerzo* is better. Attentive service and a refined but friendly atmosphere make it worth a try.

La Casona Pub PUB
(Frías 41; ⏲6pm-midnight Mon-Sat) This atmospheric pub is tucked away in the historic 1775 home of the royal envoy sent to administer the mint. It's a friendly watering hole with pub grub. On Friday it stages live music performances.

ℹ Information

ATMs are common in the center of town.

Oficina de turismo del Gobierno Autónomo Municipal de Potosí (☎622-7404; www.potosy.com.bo; Ayacucho near Bustillos; ⏲8am-noon & 2-6pm Mon-Fri, 8am-noon Sat) Quite helpful and making a big effort to improve the standard of Potosí's services.

Migración (☎622-5989; Calama 188) For visa extensions.

Post Office (cnr Lanza & Chuquisaca; ⏲8am-8pm Mon-Fri, to 5:30pm Sat, 9am-11:30pm Sun) Close to the main square.

Tourist Police (Plaza 10 de Noviembre; ⏲8am-noon & 2-6pm) Helpful; on the ground floor of the Gobernación building.

ℹ Getting There & Away

Timetables and contact details for all transportation operators can be found online at www.potosy.com.bo.

Micros and minibuses (B$1.30) shuttle between the center and the Cerro Rico mines, as well to the bus terminal. Taxis charge B$4 per person around the center – slightly more at night – and B$10 to the bus terminal.

BUS & SHARED TAXI

All road routes into Potosí are quite scenic and arriving by day will always provide a dramatic introduction to the city. The bus terminal is about 2km north of the center on Av Las Banderas and nearly all *flotas* (except for those for Uyuni) depart from here. *Micros I* or *A* run between the bus terminal and the cathedral.

There are direct *flotas* to La Paz but in many cases it can be quicker to look for a connection in Oruro. Similarly for Sucre, shared taxis (B$50, 2¼ hours) are pricier than the *flotas*, but are faster and more comfortable and can pick you up at your hotel. Try **Cielito Express** (☎624-6040) or **Correcaminos** (☎624-3383); if solo, sometimes it's quicker to go to their offices behind the bus terminal since they won't depart without a full car.

For Uyuni (B$40, five hours) buses depart from the old terminal, 15 minutes downhill on foot from the center on Av Universitaria, roughly every half hour from 7am to noon, with several more in the early evening. The rugged 210km route to Uyuni is quite breathtaking.

Autobuses Quirquincho and two other companies service Buenos Aires, Argentina.

DESTINATION	COST (B$)	DURATION (HR)
Cochabamba	52-120	10-12
La Paz	52-135	8-9
Oruro	30-40	5-6
Sucre	15-30	3
Tarija	60-70	10-12
Tupiza	60-100	7
Villazón	60-80	9

Around Potosí

The **Lagunas de Kari Kari** are artificial lakes constructed in the late 16th and early 17th centuries by 20,000 indigenous slaves to provide water for the city and for hydropower to run the city's 82 *ingenios*. The easiest way to visit Lagunas de Kari Kari is with a Potosí tour agency – they charge around B$180 per person per day based on a group of three.

Belief in the curative powers of **Tarapaya** (3600m), the most frequently visited hot-springs area around Potosí, dates back to Inca times. *Camiones* leave for Tarapaya (B$4, 30 minutes) from Plaza Chuquimia near the old bus terminal in Potosí roughly every half hour from 7am to 7pm. Taxis cost about B$70 one way. The last *micro* from Tarapaya back to Potosí leaves between 5pm and 6pm.

For a peaceful retreat or some comfortable hill walking, visit **Hacienda Cayara** (☎622-6380; www.hotelmuseocayara.com.bo; r per person B$180), which lies 25km down the valley northwest of Potosí.

THE SOUTHEAST

The Bolivian Oriente is not what you generally see in Bolivian tourist brochures. This tropical region, the country's most prosperous, has a palpable desire to differentiate itself from Bolivia's traditional highland image.

Though Santa Cruz is Bolivia's most populous city, it manages to retain a small-town atmosphere despite its cosmopolitan population. From here you can visit the charming mission towns, which contain the country's loveliest and most fascinating examples of Jesuit architecture. Pre-Inca ruins hide near the small town of Samaipata; revolutionaries can make a pilgrimage to where Che Guevara met his maker around Vallegrande; and there are miles of trekking and tons of wildlife at the little-disturbed Parque Nacional e Área de Uso Múltiple Amboró.

Santa Cruz

☎03 / POP 1.45 MILLION

Santa Cruz may surprise you with its small-town feel, lack of high-rise blocks and a lightly buzzing, relaxed tropical atmosphere. The city center is vibrant and thriving, its narrow streets crowded with suited businessmen sipping *chicha* (fermented corn drink) at street stalls, while taxis jostle with horses and carts for pole position at traffic lights. Locals still lounge on the main square listening to *camba* (Eastern Lowlands) music, restaurants close for siesta and little stores line the porch-fronted houses selling cheap local products.

It's worth spending a few days here, wandering the streets, eating at the many international restaurants and checking out the rich kids' play area, Equipetrol, where nightlife is rife with naughtiness. Alternatively, join the locals and chill out on the town square.

Sights & Activities

There are few attractions in Santa Cruz proper, but the shady **Plaza 24 de Septiembre** with its **cathedral** is an attractive place to relax by day or night. There are good city views from the **bell tower** (admission B$3; ⏲10am-noon & 4-6pm Tue, Thu, Sat & Sun).

Parque El Arenal PARK

Locals relax around the lagoon at Parque El Arenal, but it's best not to dawdle here at night. On an island in the lagoon, a bas-relief mural by renowned Bolivian artist Lorgio Vaca depicts historic and modern-day aspects of Santa Cruz.

Jardín Zoológico ZOO

(adult/child B$10/5; ⏲9am-6:30pm) Santa Cruz's zoo has a collection of native birds, mammals and reptiles kept in pleasingly humane conditions, although the llamas are a bit overdressed for the climate. Keep your eyes open for free-ranging sloths and squirrel monkeys in the trees.

Museo Guaraní MUSEUM

(3er anillo; admission B$5; ⏲8am- noon & 2-6pm Mon-Fri) A small but fascinating and

WORTH A TRIP

BIOCENTRO GÜEMBE

A great place for a day out of Santa Cruz, **Biocentro Güembe** (☎370-0700; www.biocentroguembe.com; Km 5, Camino Porongo, Zona Urubó; adult/child B$90/50; ⏲8:30am-6pm) has a butterfly farm, orchid exhibitions and 15 natural pools. The best way to get out here is by taxi (B$40).

professionally presented exhibition of Guaraní culture in front of the zoo. Look for the animal masks and *tinajas* (huge clay pots) used for making *chicha*.

Aqualand SWIMMING
(half day B$35-50, full day B$50-70; ⊙10am-6pm Thu-Sun) For a real splash, dive into this water park near Viru-Viru airport, north of the city center. It can provide a welcome relief from the stifling muggy heat in the city. The best way to get here is by taxi (around B$40).

Tours

Amboró Tours TOUR
(☎339-0600; www.amborotours.com; Libertad 417, 2nd fl) Trips to Amboró national park and the Pantanal. Ask about possibilities for visiting Kaa-Iya and Noel Kempff Mercado national parks.

Bird Bolivia BIRDWATCHING
(☎3-356-3636; www.birdbolivia.com) Professional birding and wildlife tours with expert guides for those with a special interest in nature.

Misional Tours TOUR
(☎4-360-1985; www.misionaltours.com; Los Motojobobos 2515, Santa Cruz) One of Santa Cruz's most well-organized and reliable operators, specializing in the Mission Circuit, but just as good for other attractions across Bolivia.

Sleeping

★**Los Aventureros** HOSTEL $$
(☎343-4793; www.losaventureros.net; Rivera Méndez, btwn Beni & Alemania; dm B$70, s/d incl breakfast B$175/245; ❄@📶🏊) Run by a couple of ex-*mochilleros* (backpackers) from Sucre, who have combined the experience of their own world wanderings to create the ultimate hostel for the adventurous independent traveler. A cool place to stay, this is a new breed of hostel offering great value rooms and little quirks such as Arabian tents for those who like to sleep under the stars.

Residencial Ikandire HOTEL $$
(☎339-3975; www.residencialikandire.com; Sucre 51; s/d/tr B$180/270/340, s/d without bathroom B$110/190; ❄) A converted 18th-century colonial house that retains a number of quaint original features. This place isn't bad value compared to other central options, being located just half a block from the main plaza.

Jodanga Backpackers Hostel HOSTEL $$
(☎339-6542; www.jodanga.com; El Fuerte 1380, Zona Parque Urbano; dm B$85-100, d/tr B$300/340, d without bathroom B$210; ❄@🏊) The 'in' place for Santa Cruz backpackers, this superbly equipped HI-affiliated hostel has a pool, Jacuzzi, pool table and seriously groovy, air-conditioned rooms, as well as a party atmosphere inspired by its own bar. It also organizes great-value Spanish classes from B$60 per hour.

Hostal Rio Magdalena HOTEL $$
(☎339-3011; www.hostalriomagdalena.com; Arenales 653; s/d/tr B$140/200/270; ❄📶🏊) A former Peace Corps hangout, this is an atmospheric midrange option with comfortable rooms, an inviting pool and a roof terrace with glorious views of the city.

Eating

Av Monseñor Rivero is lined with snazzy cafes.

Naturalia ORGANIC, GROCERY
(Independencia 452) An organic grocery store with a wide selection of locally produced healthy goodies and a small cafe to try them in.

Vegetarian Center Cuerpomonte VEGETARIAN $
(Aroma 64; buffet per kg B$35; ⊙11:30am-6pm Mon-Sat; 🌿) This place has a buffet selection of basic and simple food including quinoa cake, mashed sweet potato, salad-bar goodies, veggie soups and lots of other wholesome, healthy treats.

Naïs INTERNATIONAL $$
(Av Alemania; mains B$40-89) This Chilean-owned place serves a bit of everything, from juicy grills with notable racks of ribs, to saucy chicken and fine fish dishes. The food is reasonably priced and tasty, but what really sets this place apart is the superbly attentive service, effective without ever being overbearing.

★**Taj Mahal** INDIAN $$$
(Bumberque 365; mains B$55-130; ⊙dinner) Hallelujah! It's pretty hard to find an Indian restaurant in South America, and even harder to find a good one, but this upmarket curry house is a cut above the rest. Bangladeshi-owned (despite the Taj Mahal images on the wall), it has mouthwateringly good shrimp, chicken and lamb dishes, and

portions are generous. It's on a side street behind Cinecenter.

Drinking & Nightlife

The hippest nightspots are along Av San Martin, between the second and third *anillos* (rings) in Barrio Equipetrol, a B$10 to $B15 taxi ride from the center. Cover charges run from B$20 to B$70 and drinks are expensive.

A young beach crowd gathers on weekends at Río Pira'i. The area is potentially unsafe at other times though. Near the university, Av Busch is lined with places catering to serious drinkers.

Irish Pub IRISH PUB
(Plaza 24 de Septiembre) On the east side of the plaza this place is something of a second home to travelers in Santa Cruz, and has pricey beers, delicious soups and comfort food plus tasty local specialties. It serves breakfast, lunch and dinner, though most people while the hours away drinking beer, relaxing and watching the goings-on in the plaza below.

Lorca BAR
(Moreno 20; ⏲8am-late) A meeting point for the city's arty crowd and those loving diversity, Lorca is one of the most innovative and happening places in town. It's perfect for a chilled *caipirinha* or *mojito* while you enjoy the live music (B$30 cover). Before the music starts, short films are screened.

Tapekuá LOUNGE
(www.tapekua.com; cnr La Paz & Ballivián; ⏲from 7:30pm Wed-Sat) This casual yet upscale Swiss- and Bolivian-owned place serves good, earthy food and has live music most nights (B$20 to B$30 cover).

Kiwi's BAR
(Bolívar 208; ⏲Mon-Sat) A laid-back place where you can sip on *bebidas extremas* served in 2L receptacles, or puff away on *shisha* (Arabic flavored-tobacco pipes). Great snacks and sandwiches, too, all served with trademark *papas kiwi* (kiwi potatoes).

Liberty Resto Bar PUB
(Libertad 321) With the walls adorned with sweating images of rock legends, this is one of those places that metamorphoses from a chilled restaurant serving pub grub by day into a wild rock club by night. Live music at weekends.

☆ Entertainment

Eleguá PERFORMING ARTS
(24 de Septiembre 651) During the week this is a Cuban cultural-center-cum-bar-cum-dance-school (it depends which day you visit!). At weekends it morphs into a groovy Latino disco where you can swing your thing to the latest samba sounds.

El Rincón Salteño TRADITIONAL MUSIC
(cnr 26 de Febrero & Charagua; ⏲from 10pm Fri-Sun) Traditional *peñas* (folk-music programs) are scarce in modern Santa Cruz, but this is an excellent choice. Positioned on the

GETTING TO BRAZIL

The main border crossing to Brazil is at Quijarro at the end of the train line, with a second, minor crossing at San Matías, the access point to the northern Brazilian Pantanal.

You'll more than likely arrive in Quijarro by train between 7am and 9am to be greeted by a line of taxi drivers offering to take you the 3km to the border (B$10). **Customs offices** (⏲8am-11am & 2-5pm Mon-Fri, 9am-1pm Sat & Sun) are on opposing sides of the bridge. Bolivian officials have been known to unofficially charge for the exit stamp, but stand your ground politely. Crossing this border you are generally asked to show a yellow-fever vaccination certificate. No exceptions are granted and you will be whisked off to a vaccination clinic if you fail to produce it. On the Brazilian side of the border yellow *canarinho* (city buses) will take you into Corumbá (R$2.50). Brazilian entry stamps are given at the border. Get your stamp as soon as possible to avoid later problems and make sure you have the necessary visas if you require them.

For a slightly more adventurous border crossing try San Matías. In the dry season, a Trans-Bolivia bus leaves at 7:45pm from Santa Cruz to Cáceres in Brazil (30 hours), via San Matías (B$150, 26 hours). Brazilian entry or exit stamps should be picked up from the Polícia Federal office at Rua Antônio João 160 in Cáceres; get your exit and entry stamps for Bolivia in Santa Cruz.

second *anillo* (ring), there's a great variety of musical styles, from Argentine guitarists to Cuban village drummers, local singers and dancers in costume.

Information

Roughly oval in shape, Santa Cruz is laid out in *anillos* (rings), which form concentric circles around the city center, and *radiales* (spokes) that connect the rings. Radial 1, the road to Viru-Viru airport, runs roughly north–south; the *radiales* progress clockwise up to Radial 27.

Within the *primer anillo*, Junín is the street with the most banks, ATMs and internet cafes, and Av René Moreno is lined with souvenir stores and bars. To the northwest of the center, Av San Martin, otherwise known as Barrio Equipetrol, is the main area for the party crowd, being full of bars and clubs.

Beware of bogus immigration officials and carefully check the credentials of anyone who demands to see your passport or other ID. No real police officer will ever ask to see your documents in the street; be especially wary of 'civilian' police who will most certainly turn out to be fraudsters.

Clínica Foianini (☎336-2211; Av Irala 468) Hospital used by embassies, but be aware that some travelers have reported unnecessary tests and being required to stay for longer than is strictly necessary in order to push up their bill.

Clínica Japonesa (☎346-2038; Av Japón 3er anillo interno) On the third *anillo*, east side; recommended for inexpensive and professional medical treatment.

Entel Office (Warnes 82) Best rates are found at phone centers in the main Entel office.

Fundación Amigos de la Naturaleza (FAN; ☎355-6800; www.fan-bo.org; Carretera a Samaipata, Km 7.5; ⊙8am-4:30pm Mon-Thu, to 2pm Fri) Though no longer in charge of the parks, FAN is still the best contact for national parks information. It's west of town (*micro* 44) off the old Cochabamba road.

Infotur (☎336-9581; www.gmsantacruz.gob/turismo; Sucre; ⊙8am-noon & 3-7pm) Within the free Museo de Arte Contemporáneo, this office provides information for the whole region and the rest of the country.

Migración (☎333-2136; Av Omar Chávez; ⊙8:30am-4:30pm Mon-Fri) *Migración* is south of the center, near the football stadium. Visa extensions are available here and at Viru-Viru airport.

Tourist Police (☎800-14-0099; Plaza 24 de Septiembre) On the north side of the plaza.

Getting There & Around

AIR

Viru-Viru International Airport (VVI; ☎338-5000), 15km north of the center, handles some domestic and most international flights. The smaller **Aeropuerto El Trompillo** (☎351-1010), in the southeast of the city, receives the majority of the domestic flights.

Flights to national destinations leave frequently and it's easy enough to find a seat to anywhere, or at least a suitable connection via Cochabamba. Tickets can be bought online, via travel agents or by paying on arrival at the airport.

BUS, MICRO & SHARED TAXI

The full-service **bimodal terminal** (☎348-8482; terminal fee B$3), the combined long-distance bus and train station, is 1.5km east of the center, just before the third *anillo* at the end of Av Brasil. For departmental destinations turn right on entering, for national and international destinations turn left.

TRAINS DEPARTING SANTA CRUZ

Expreso Oriental (Monday, Wednesday & Friday 1:20pm)

DESTINATION	COST (B$)	ARRIVAL TIME
San José	35	7:30pm
Roboré	50	11:42pm
Quijarro	70	6:02am

Ferrobus (Tuesday, Thursday & Sunday 6pm)

DESTINATION	COST (B$)	ARRIVAL TIME
San José	100	11:08pm
Roboré	100	2:12am
Quijarro	235	7am

The main part of the terminal is for *flotas* (long-distance buses) and the train; on the other side of the tunnel is the *micro* (minibus) terminal for regional services. Most *flotas* leave in the morning before 10am and in the evening after 6pm. Taking a series of connecting *micros* or taxis can be a faster, if more complicated, way of reaching regional destinations, rather than waiting all day for an evening *flota*.

For the Jesuit missions and Chiquitania, *flotas* leave in the morning and early evening (after 8pm). *Micros* run throughout the day, every two hours or so, but only go as far as Concepción. Buses to San Rafael, San Miguel and San Ignacio (B$60 to B$70, eight hours) run via San José de Chiquitos and depart between 6:30am and 8pm.

Smaller *micros* and *trufis* to regional destinations in Santa Cruz department leave regularly from outside the old bus terminal and less regularly from the *micro* platforms at the bimodal terminal. Trufis to Buena Vista (Izozog) (B$23, two hours), wait on Izozog (Isoso), near the old bus terminal. **Trufis to Samaipata** (☎333-5067; cnr Av Chavez Ortíz & Solis de Olguin, Santa Cruz) (B$30, three hours), leave on the opposite side of Av Cañoto, about two blocks from the old bus terminal. Trufis to Vallegrande (B$60, six hours) depart from the Plazuela Oruro on the third *anillo*.

DESTINATION	COST (B$)	DURATION (HR)
Camiri	30	5
Cochabamba	old road 54-110; new road 50-131	8-10
Concepción	35-50	5
La Paz	old road 91-228; new road 81-220	8-10
Quijarro	70-150	9
San Javier	30-40	4
San José de Chiquitos	50	4
San Matías	120-150	16-18
Sucre	70-170	13-23
Tarija	80-254	14
Trinidad	49-134	8-10
Yacuiba	47-126	15

TRAIN

Trains depart from the bimodal terminal bound for Yacuiba on the Argentine border and Quijarro on the Brazil border. For access to the platform you need to buy a platform ticket and show your passport to the platform guard.

With the recent completion of the road paving all the way from Santa Cruz to Quijarro the relevance of the Trans-Chiquitano train has declined sharply. No longer the harrowing journey that once earned this line the nickname 'Death Train,' these days it's a nice lazy route, and is more comfortable than the bus if you have time on your hands.

Two types of train run this line via San José de Chiquitos and Roboré (for Santiago de Chiquitos). The slowest and cheapest service is the Expreso Oriental, which operates a comfortable Super Pullman class. The fastest, comfiest and priciest is the Ferrobus.

WORTH A TRIP

PARQUE NACIONAL NOEL KEMPFF MERCADO

The wonderfully remote and globally important Parque Nacional Noel Kempff Mercado is home to a broad spectrum of Amazonian flora and fauna.

An attempt to generate a tourist trail to the park appears to have failed. The park still remains an exciting off-the-beaten-track option for adventurous independent travelers – check with a Santa Cruz agency about visits to the park.

Around Santa Cruz

Samaipata

Samaipata has developed into one of the top Gringo Trail spots in eastern Bolivia over the last few years. This sleepy village in the foothills of the Cordillera Oriental is brimming with foreign-run hostels and restaurants. Visitors flock to see the pre-Inca site of **El Fuerte**, some in search of a dose of the ancient site's supposed mystical energy. Increasingly it's the main jumping-off point for forays to Parque Nacional Amboró.

Samaipata is a popular weekend destination for *cruceños*, too. The Quechua name, meaning 'Rest in the Highlands,' could hardly be more appropriate.

Trufis run throughout the day when full between Santa Cruz and Samaipata (B$30, three hours). From Santa Cruz, services leave from the corner of Av Omar Chavez Ortíz and Solis de Olguin, a few blocks from the old terminal, and in Sampaipata from the main plaza.

Tours

Jukumari Tours TOUR
(☎7262-7202; Av del Estudiante) An excellent locally run agency; in addition to the local attractions it offers packages to the Che Trail and the Jesuit Mission Circuit.

Michael Blendinger Tours ECOTOUR
(☎944-6227; www.discoveringbolivia.com; Bolívar) Biologist-run orchid, birding and full-moon tours, in English and German.

Sleeping

Finca La Víspera CABINS $
(☎944-6082; www.lavispera.org; campsite B$50, d B$420, cabins for 7 people B$850-1100) This relaxing organic farm and retreat is a lovely place on the outskirts of Samaipata. The attractive rooms with communal kitchens, and four self-contained guesthouses (for two to seven people), enjoy commanding views across the valley. The camp site includes hot showers and kitchen facilities. It's an easy 15-minute walk southwest of the plaza.

La Posada del Sol HOTEL $$
(☎7211-0628; www.laposadadelsol.net; Zona Barrio Nuevo; s/d B$240/340;) Modern, tastefully furnished en suite rooms have high-quality Egyptian cotton sheets on every bed. Rooms are set around an attractive garden and have spectacular views. One free meal at the excellent Luna Verde restaurant and bar is included in the price of lodging. Three blocks uphill north of the plaza.

Parque Nacional e Área de Uso Múltiple Amboró

This extraordinary park crosses two 'divides': the warmer northern Amazonian-type section, and the southern Yungas-type section, with cooler temperatures (and fewer mosquitoes). The village of Buena Vista, 100km (two hours) northwest of Santa Cruz, is a staging point for trips into the spectacular forested lowland section of Parque Nacional e Área de Uso Múltiple Amboró.

By far the easiest and safest way to visit the park is by guided tour with one of the recommended tour agencies in Santa Cruz.

Jesuit Mission Circuit

From the late 17th century, Jesuits established settlements called *reducciones* in Bolivia's eastern lowlands, building churches, establishing farms and instructing the indigenous in religion, agriculture, music and crafts in return for conversion and manual labor. A circuit north and east of Santa Cruz takes in some mission sites, with buildings in various stages of decay; food and lodging are found in most of the towns.

Check out the Unesco website: http://whc.unesco.org/en/list/529.

San Xavier The oldest mission (1691) and popular getaway for wealthy cruceños.

Concepción An attractive town with a gaudy 1709 church and restoration studios.

San Ignacio de Velasco The commercial heart of the Jesuit mission district.

San Miguel de Velasco A sleepy town with a beautiful, painstakingly restored church (1721).

Santa Ana de Velasco A tiny village with a rustic 1755 church.

San Rafael de Velasco The 1740s church here is noted for its fine interior.

San José de Chiquitos Frontier town with the area's only stone church (restoration was nearing completion at the time of research).

To travel the mission circuit on public transport, the bus schedules synchronize better going counterclockwise, starting at San José de Chiquitos. Traveling the opposite way, unsynchronized and irregular bus schedules make for a frustrating journey. A much less time-consuming way of doing it is by taking a guided tour from Santa Cruz, which costs around US$500 per person for a four-day package taking in all the major towns. Misional Tours (p252) is a recommended operator.

THE AMAZON BASIN

The Amazon Basin is one of Bolivia's largest and most mesmerizing regions. The rainforest is raucous with wildlife and spending a few days roaming the sweaty jungle is an experience you're unlikely to forget. But it's not only the forests that are enchanting: it's also the richness of the indigenous cultures, traditions and languages that exist throughout the region.

Mossy hills peak around the town of Rurrenabaque, most people's first point of entry into the region and the main base camp for visits to the fascinating Parque Nacional Madidi. This is home to a growing ethno-ecotourism industry that looks to help local communities. The village of San Ignacio de Moxos is famous for its wild July fiesta. Trinidad, the region's biggest settlement and an active cattle-ranching center, is the transit point toward Santa Cruz. North of here the frontier towns of Riberalta and Cobija are in remote regions where few travelers dare to tread.

Rurrenabaque

☎03 / POP 19,200

The gentle whisking of brooms on the plaza serves as a wake-up call in sleepy Rurre, a gringo crossroads sliced by the deep Río Beni and surrounded by mossy green hills. Mesmerizing sunsets turn the sky a burnt orange, and a dense fog sneaks down the river among the lush, moist trees. Once darkness falls, the surrounding rainforest comes alive with croaks, barks, buzzes and roars. This is civilization's last stand.

Backpackers fill the streets, and restaurants, cafes and hotels cater mainly to Western tastes. Some travelers spend their days relaxing in the ubiquitous hammocks, but at some stage the majority go off on riverboat adventures into the rainforest or pampas.

The area's original people are responsible for the curious name, which is derived from 'Arroyo Inambaque,' the Hispanicized version of the Tacana name 'Suse-Inambaque,' the 'Ravine of Ducks.'

Sights & Activities

El Chorro SWIMMING

El Chorro, an idyllic waterfall and pool 1km upstream, makes for a pleasant excursion. On a rock roughly opposite El Chorro is an ancient **serpentine engraving**, which was intended as a warning to travelers: whenever the water reached serpent level, the Beni was considered unnavigable. You can only reach it by boat so inquire at the harbor and strike a deal.

Canopy Zipline Villa Alcira ADVENTURE SPORTS

(☎892-2875; www.ziplinecanopy.amawebs.com; per person B$250) If you need more adrenaline, then try the unambiguously named Biggest Canopy in Bolivia, a community-run forest canopy zipline in nearby Villa Alcira. It's only for those with a head for heights and a strong stomach.

Tours

Bala Tours TOUR

(☎892-2527; www.balatours.com; cnr Santa Cruz & Comercio) Has its own jungle camp, Caracoles, a comfortable pampas lodge on Río Yacumo and a forest lodge in Tacuaral.

Fluvial Tours/Amazonia Adventures TOUR

(☎892-2372; www.fluvialtoursbolivia.com; Avaroa) This is Rurrenabaque's longest-running agency.

CHOOSING A JUNGLE & PAMPAS TOUR

Jungle and pampas tours are Rurrenabaque's bread and butter, but the quality of service provided by the numerous tour agencies varies considerably, and in the name of competition some operators are much less responsible than they ought to be.

Not all companies provide the same level of service, and cheaper most definitely does not mean better. Local authorities have set minimum prices at B$900 for a three-day, two-night excursion.

Use only SERNAP-authorized operators as these are the only ones allowed to legally enter Parque Nacional Madidi.

Foreigners must be accompanied by a local guide, but not all speak good English.

Jungle Tours

Most trips are by canoe upstream along the Río Beni, and some continue up the Río Tuichi, camping and taking shore and jungle walks along the way, with plenty of swimming opportunities and hammock time. Accommodations are generally at agencies' private camps.

Pampas Tours

It's easier to see wildlife in the wetland savannas northeast of town, but the sun is more oppressive, and the bugs can be worse.

The Amazon Basin

Sleeping

If you're willing to pay more, consider staying in an ecolodge in Madidi.

Hotel Oriental HOTEL $

(☎892-2401; Plaza 2 de Febrero; s/d/tr B$100/150/210) If you meet people who are staying at the Oriental, right on the plaza, they'll invariably be raving about what an excellent place it is – and it really is. Comfy rooms, great showers, garden hammocks for snoozing, and big breakfasts, are included in the price.

Hostal Pahuichi HOSTEL $

(☎892-2558; Comercio; s/d/tr B$100/130/170; 📶) It's amazing what a good facelift can do to an ageing hotel. The newly renovated suites here are tasteful, colorful and – dare we say it – stylish (almost!), with sleek wooden furniture and sparkling tiled private bathrooms.

Hotel Los Tucanes de Rurre HOTEL $

(☎892-2039; cnr Bolívar & Aniceto Arce; s/d B$80/100, with shared bathroom B$70/80) This big, thatched-roof house offers a sprawling garden, a roof terrace and sweeping views over the river. There are hammocks swing-

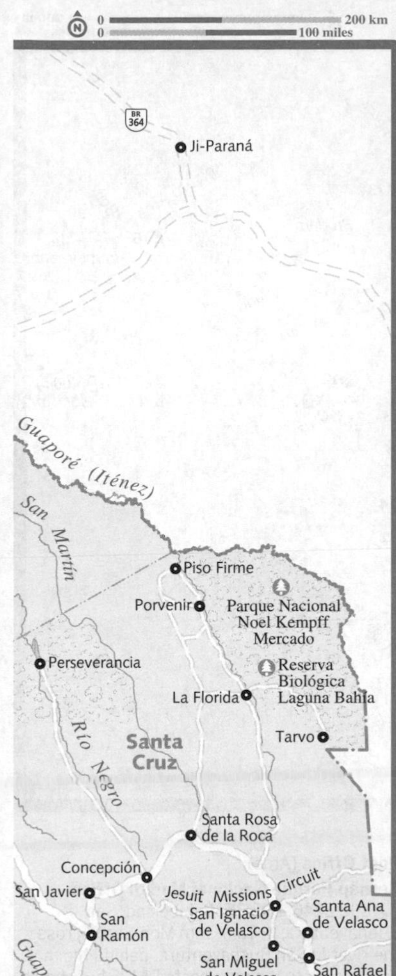

ing on the patio, a pool table and the clean and simple rooms are painted in gentle colors. Breakfast is included.

Hostal El Lobo HOSTEL **$**
(☎7012-5362; hostalellobo@gmail.com; Comercio; dm per person B$50, s B$120;) Two hundred meters from the main plaza, this former mutt is a real contender. A complete makeover includes crafty *tacuara* (bamboo) doors, a kidney-shaped swimming pool overlooking the Beni, and a sweet hammock-filled terrace. Rooms have no screened windows, but are equipped with *mosquiteros* (nets). Cool budget option.

Eating & Drinking

Several fish restaurants line the riverfront: candlelit La Cabaña and Playa Azul grill or fry up the catch of the day for around B$40. In addition to the Beni standard, *masaco* (mashed yucca or plantains, served with dried meat, rice, noodles, thin soup and bananas), try the excellent *pescado hecho en taquara* (fish baked in a special local pan) or *pescado en dunucuabi* (fish wrapped in a rainforest leaf and baked over a wood fire).

★ **La Perla de Rurre** SOUTH AMERICAN **$$**
(cnr Bolívar & Vaca Diez; mains B$40-50) Many in Rurre will tell you that this is their favorite restaurant and 'the Pearl' does indeed serve up some mean fresh fish and chicken dishes. The surroundings are simple but the service is excellent.

★ **Juliano's** EUROPEAN **$$**
(Santa Cruz, btwn Avaroa & Bolívar; mains B$45-70; ⏱5-11pm) Fusion in the jungle! This Tunisian emigre to Bolivia – via Paris – makes some awesome fish dishes (*pescado* Juliano is tasty) and has the only imported Peruvian shellfish in town. Save some room for the crème brûlée.

Restaurant Tacuaral INTERNATIONAL **$$**
(cnr Santa Cruz & Avaroa; mains B$15-40, sandwiches B$18) This open-air eatery with shaded sidewalk seating has an ambitious menu, covering breakfast to dinner. It's friendly and popular, especially for its lasagna. The Mexican dishes won't have you tossing your *sombrero* into the air, but the sandwiches are huge.

Casa de Campo HEALTH FOOD **$$$**
(☎7199-3336; Comercio; breakfast B$25-75; ⏱8am-2pm & 6-10pm) Healthy food is the name of the game here, with all-day breakfasts, homemade pastries, vegetarian dishes, soups and salads, on a breezy terrace across from El Lobo. Hospitable Adele is keen to make her guests happy (and give local hiking advice), but her breakfast is the priciest in town.

Jungle Bar Moskkito BAR
(www.moskkito.com; Vaca Diez) Peruvian-run, but English is spoken here. There's a positive vibe, cheery service and the foliage that hangs from the roof makes you feel like you are in the jungle, whether there are 'moskkitos' or not. Throw some darts, shoot some pool and choose your own music – the extensive menu of CDs is played by request.

Rurrenabaque

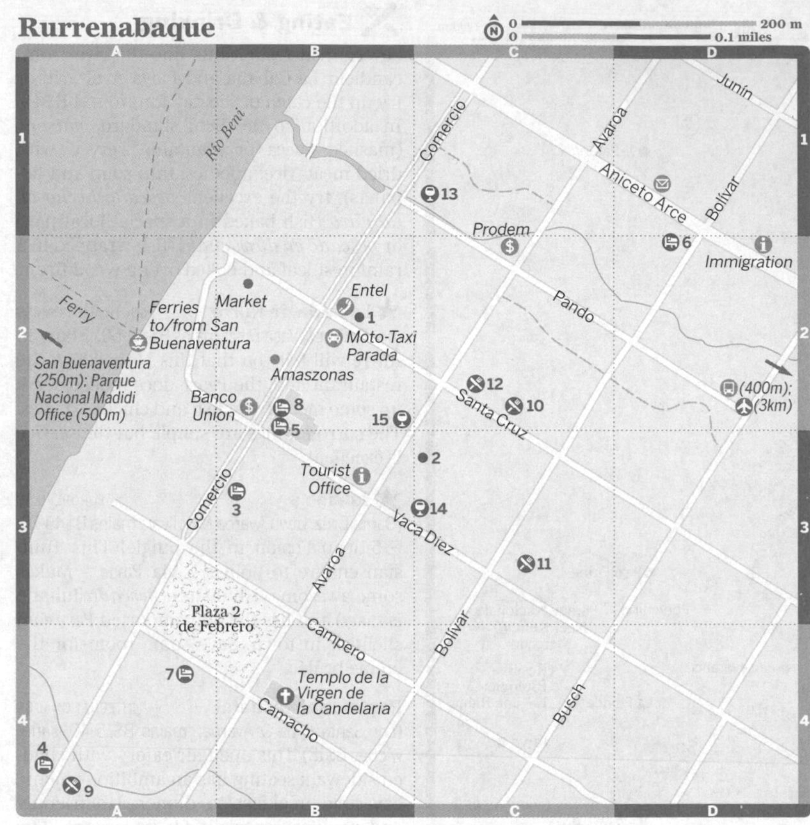

Luna Lounge BAR
(Avaroa, near Santa Cruz) One of Rurre's longest standing bars with a bouncing atmosphere, good pizza and great cocktails.

Banana Pub Disco CLUB
(Comercio; admission incl 1 drink B$15) If you want to try salsa dancing or Bolivian-style grooving, this slightly sleazy club has Cuban doctors shaking their booties, locals getting drunk and gringos joining in.

Information

There are two ATMs here, the most convenient a block north of the plaza at **Banco Union** (Comercio). For emergencies you can get cash advances at **Prodem** (Avaroa; 8am-6pm Mon-Fri, to 2pm Sat), but only with Visa and Mastercard (including Visa debit cards). Tours can usually be paid for with credit cards.

Immigration (892-2241; Arce btwn Busch & Bolívar; 8:30am-12:30pm & 2:30-6:30pm Mon-Fri) For visa extensions.

Post Office (Arce)

Sernap Parque Nacional Madidi Office (892-2246, 892-2540; Libertad, San Buenaventura; 7am-3pm Mon-Sun) Across the river in San Buenaventura, behind the market. Access to the park costs B$125 but should be included in tour quotes.

Tourist Office (7138-3684; cnr Vaca Diez & Avaroa; 8am-noon & 2:30-6pm Mon-Fri) Happy to answer questions and keen to advise on responsible tourism, but short on material.

Getting There & Around

AIR

Rurre's airport is a few kilometers north of town. The brief flight to La Paz is an affordable way of avoiding the arduous 24-hour bus journey. Flights sell out fast but are frequently cancelled during bad weather.

Amaszonas (892-2472; Comercio, near Santa Cruz) has daily flights to La Paz (B$480 and up) but at the time of research only one plane – you're screwed if it's 'in maintenance.'

Rurrenabaque

Activities, Courses & Tours
1 Bala Tours ... B2
2 Fluvial Tours/Amazonia Adventures ... C3

Sleeping
3 Chalalán Ecolodge Booking Office ... B3
4 Hostal El Lobo ... A4
5 Hostal Pahuichi ... B2
6 Hotel Los Tucanes de Rurre ... D2
7 Hotel Oriental ... A4
8 San Miguel del Bala Office ... B2

Eating
9 Casa de Campo ... A4
10 Juliano's ... C2
11 La Perla de Rurre ... C3
12 Restaurant Tacuaral ... C2

Drinking & Nightlife
13 Banana Pub Disco ... C1
14 Jungle Bar Moskkito ... C3
15 Luna Lounge ... B2

BOAT

Thanks to the Guayaramerín road, there's little cargo transportation down the Río Beni to Riberalta these days and there's no traffic at all during periods of low water. You'll need a dose of luck to find something and will have to negotiate what you consider a fair price for the trip, which may take as long as 10 days.

BUS

The bus terminal is across from the airport and a B$5 *mototaxi* (motorbike rickshaw) ride from town. Prices do not vary between companies.

Several daily services make the daunting trip from Rurrenabaque to La Paz (B$80, 18 to 24 hours), via Yolosa (B$65, 14 to 20 hours), the hop-off point for Coroico. If you find the narrow, twisting Andean roads and sheer drops a harrowing experience on a bus, another option is to bus it as far as Caranavi (B$70) and take a shared taxi from there, the rest of the trip being the most scary, or picturesque, depending on your point of view.

The road to Trinidad (B$130, 17 to 30 hours) via San Borja (taxi/bus B$80/60, nine to 18 hours) and San Ignacio de Moxos (B$100, 12 hours) remains one of the worst in the country and is typically closed during the rainy season. A new road was begun in 2015 between here and Trinidad, scheduled for completion in two years' time – this may ease a lot of passengers' minds and behinds.

Buses now run year-round to Riberalta (B$120, 17 to 40 hours) and Guayaramerín (B$120, 18 hours to three days), but you need a healthy dose of stamina, insect repellent and food if you're going to attempt it in the wet season.

Parque Nacional Madidi

The Río Madidi watershed is one of South America's most intact ecosystems. Most of it is protected by the 18,000-sq-km Parque Nacional Madidi, which takes in a range of habitats, from steaming lowland rainforests to 5500m Andean peaks. This little-trodden utopia is home to an astonishing variety of Amazonian wildlife: 44% of all New World mammal species, 38% of neotropical amphibian species, around 1000 species of bird and more threatened species than any park in the world.

The populated portions of the park along the Río Tuichi have been accorded a special Unesco designation permitting indigenous inhabitants to utilize traditional forest resources, but the park has also been considered for oil exploration and as a site for a major hydroelectric scheme in the past.

It is difficult to visit the park independently, but if you wish to do so the B$125 admission fee is payable at the Sernap office in San Buenaventura – you must be accompanied by an authorized guide. By far the easiest and most responsible way to arrange access is by visiting one of the community projects.

Sleeping

★Chalalán Ecolodge LODGE $$$
(☎892-2419; www.chalalan.com; 3 nights & 4 days all inclusive per person US$490, per day US$145) Bolivia's oldest and most successful community-based ecotourism project. Chalalán provides the opportunity to amble through relatively untouched rainforest and appreciate the diversity of the native wildlife. The lodge's simple and elegant huts surround the idyllic oxbow lake, Laguna Chalalán. There is a booking office in **Rurrenabaque** (☎892-2419; www.chalalan.com; Comercio, near Campero) and also in **La Paz** (☎02-231-1451; www.chalalan.com; Sagárnaga St, La Paz).

WORTH A TRIP

EXPLORING MORE OF THE AMAZON

San Ignacio de Moxos is a friendly, tranquil indigenous Moxos village, 92km west of Trinidad, that dedicates itself to agriculture and oozes an ambience quite distinct from any other Bolivian town. The best time to visit San Ignacio is during the annual festival on July 30 and 31. The easiest access is from Trinidad, with *camionetas* (open-backed 4WDs) running when full from the *parada* at 1 de Mayo near Velarde (B$70, four hours).

North of Santa Ana de Yacuma is a cluster of 11 wonderful natural lakes flanked by wild rainforest and linked together by a network of weed-choked streams, which are known collectively as **Los Lagos**. This unique and enchanting region has hardly been explored by foreign tourists because of its remoteness. Chartering a plane from Trinidad or Santa Cruz is your safest bet if you want to get here as painlessly as possible. From July to November land transport can be arranged in Santa Ana de Yacuma. It's a spectacular six-hour drive.

★Sadiri LODGE $$$

(☎in Santa Cruz 7162-2567; www.sadirilodge.com; all-inclusive per person per day US$150) The newest kid on the community-project block is wonderful Sadiri: six luxury cabins in dense foothill rainforest in the Serranía Sadiri. Community members staff the lodge and it has the best-trained wildlife guides in the Rurrenabaque area. Email bookings are preferred at sadirilodge@gmail.com. Rates include full board and return transfer to Rurrenabaque.

San Miguel del Bala LODGE $$$

(☎892-2394; www.sanmigueldelbala.com; per person per day B$450) A glorious community ecolodge in its own patch of paradise right on Madidi's doorstep, 40 minutes upstream by boat from Rurre. This Tacana community will be happy to show you their traditional agricultural methods, weaving and wood-carving. Accommodations are in cabins with mahogany wood floors, separate bathrooms and beds covered by silky mosquito nets. The **booking office** (☎892-2394; www.sanmigueldelbala.com; Comercio) is in Rurrenabaque.

Trinidad

☎03 / POP 106,400

Trinidad is the place you'll come to if you're after a trip down the long and deep Río Mamoré, or on your way between Santa Cruz and Rurrenabaque. Despite its colonial architecture and colonnaded streets, it's a modern town that is growing rapidly. Its most notable feature is the massive, green, tropical main square (Trinidad is only 14 degrees south of the equator), once home to a population of friendly sloths.

The city of La Santísima Trinidad (the Most Holy Trinity) was founded in 1686 by Padre Cipriano Barace as the second Jesuit mission in the flatlands of the southern Beni. It was originally constructed on the banks of the Río Mamoré, 14km from its present location, but floods and pestilence along the riverbanks necessitated relocation. In 1769 it was moved to the Arroyo de San Juan, which now divides the city in two.

Sights & Activities

Plaza Gral José Ballivián PLAZA

Trinidad's loveliest feature is Plaza Gral José Ballivián, with its tall, tropical trees, lush gardens and community atmosphere. You can spend a pleasant evening eating ice cream and listening to the rhythmic drone of hundreds of motorcycles orbiting around the square. In the past, the traffic was refereed by a police officer who sat in a big wooden chair and conjured up red, yellow and green traffic lights by touching an electric wire against one of three nails.

Kenneth Lee Ethno-Archaeological Museum MUSEUM

(Av Ganadera; admission B$5; ⌚8am-noon & 3-6pm) Named for the *gringo querido del Beni*, the beloved white man of the Amazon, this museum north of the center is considered the city's top cultural attraction. It exhibits artifacts from the Trinidad region, including traditional instruments and tribal costumes.

Parque Pantanal PARK
(Av Laureano Villar; 8am-6pm) FREE On the road to the airport, this wooded park no longer serves as a wildlife rehab center – the inmates got a bit feisty – but it's still a nice place to wander the pathways and check out bird life, like the yellow-winged jacanas hopping on and off the lily pads. Skip the B$1 zoo at the end of the park – it only houses a very depressed anaconda in about 2ft of water.

Turismo Moxos TOUR
(462-1141; turmoxos@entelnet.bo; Av 6 de Agosto 114) Turismo Moxos organizes three-day dolphin cruises on the Río Ibare, visits to Sirionó villages, four-day canoe safaris into the jungle and one-day horseback trips into remote areas.

Sleeping

Hostal El Tajibo HOTEL $
(462-2324; Av Santa Cruz 423; s/d B$100/160, with air-con B$200/260;) One of Trinidad's better-value budget options, this hotel has attractive, almost stylish rooms and comfortable beds. Some rooms have balconies overlooking the street and breakfast is included with air-con rooms. New mattresses are a bonus, but the joint could use a coat of paint. Hotel Colonial, a couple of blocks away, is run by the same owners and is almost identical.

Hotel Colonial HOTEL $
(462-2864; Vaca Diez 306; s/d B$100/160, with air-con B$200/260;) Run by the owners of Hostal El Tajibo, Hotel Colonial is a few blocks from the plaza.

Hostal Santa Cruz PENSION $
(462-0711; Av Santa Cruz 537; s/d B$80/150, s without bathroom B$60) A budget place that's a bit beat up, but makes a real effort to cheer up its rooms with colorful decor, hand-painted wall hangings and bright bedclothes. Rooms on the top floor are airier (and slightly pricier). All rooms have cable TV. Nice old couple also offers a shared kitchen (but won't help you cook!).

★**Hostal Sirari** HOSTEL $$
(462-4472; Av Santa Cruz 538; s/d/tr B$100/170/200, with air-con B$170/200/250;) Has a bit more pinache than the other Trini hotels, at about the same price.

Eating & Drinking

Trinidad is cattle country, so beef is bountiful here. If budget is the priority, hit the Mercado Municipal, where for a pittance you can try the local specialty, *arroz con queso* (rice with cheese), plus shish kebabs, *yuca* (cassava), plantains and salad. There are several decent places to eat around the plaza.

GETTING TO BRAZIL

Crossing to Brazil from the northern Bolivian towns of Cobija and Guayaramerín involves crossings of the Ríos Acre and Mamoré respectively.

Popping into the Brazilian town of Guajará-Mirim for the day from Bolivian Guayaramerín is really easy. Day visits are encouraged, and you don't even need a visa. *Lanchas* (B$10) across the river leave from the port every half an hour from 6am to 6pm, and sporadically through the night. To travel further into Brazil or to enter Bolivia, you'll have to complete border formalities. The immigration offices in **Guajará-Mirim** (Av Quintina Bocaiúva; 8am-noon & 2-6pm Mon-Fri) and **Guayaramerín** (Av Costanera) are in the respective port areas.

It's a long, hot slog across the bridge from Cobija to Brasiléia. Entry/exit stamps are available at immigration in Cobija at the Bolivian end of the bridge and from **Brasiléia's Polícia Federal** (Av Prefeito Moreira; 8am-noon & 2-5pm). With some negotiation, taxis will take you to the Polícia Federal in Brasiléia, wait while you clear immigration, then take you on to the center or to the bus terminal. Alternatively, take the *lancha* (B$5) across the Río Acre; from there it's another 1.5km to the Polícia Federal.

Although officials don't always check, technically everyone needs to have a yellow-fever vaccination certificate to enter Brazil. If you don't have one, head for the convenient and relatively sanitary clinic at the port on the Brazilian side.

Pescaderia Don Pedrito FISH & CHIPS **$$**
(☎346-22545; Manuel Maraza, Zona German Busch; mains B$60) There's six things on the menu, and they all cost B$60: fried, grilled, ceviche, whatever. Got it? Good. The local *mototaxi* drivers will tell you this is the place to go. Chill with a beer while taking in a football match on the telly. The friendly cats will patiently await your table scraps beneath the mango trees.

El Tabano SEAFOOD **$$**
(Villavicencio, near Mamoré; mains B$20-55) With cool beers and cocktails served in the courtyard, this grass-roofed resto-pub is a popular place with Trinidad's young crowd on account of its lively atmosphere and excellent food. The menu consists of a number of inventive variations on fish and caiman dishes.

★**Churrasquería La Estancia** BARBECUE **$$$**
(Ibare, near Velarde; mains B$40-120) Ask anybody in Trinidad where to get a good bit of beef and you will be sent here. With its palm roof and coal-fire barbecue hamming up the ranch-house setting, the succulent and juicy cuts will make you wonder how other restaurants even dare to call themselves *churrasquerías* (grilled meat restaurants).

Los Faroles INTERNATIONAL **$$$**
(Av 6 de Agosta, near Av 18 de Noviembre; almuerzo B$25, mains B$40-130) Don't fall out of your chair! They serve (two) salads here! In fact this upmarket (by Trinidad standards) restaurant serves a bit of everything, from pizza and steak to chicken and fish. It's the restaurant of the swish Hotel Campanario, but that doesn't stop them from offering a well-cooked and excellent-value *almuerzo* (set lunch) as well.

ℹ Information

Use bottled water for everything in Trinidad except your shower – the town water supply is contaminated.

Several Enlace ATMs near the main plaza accept international cards; this is a good spot to get some cash before heading out to the Amazon proper. Money changers gather on Av 6 de Agosto between Suárez and Av 18 de Noviembre.

Immigration Office (☎462-1449; Av Los Tajibos, near Ibañez Carranza) Top floor of the white building a block from the bus terminal.

Tourist Office (☎462-1322; Vaca Diez, btwn 18 Noviembre & Suarez; ⊙8am-12:30pm & 2:30-6:30pm Mon-Fri)

ℹ Getting There & Around

AIR

Departing air travelers must pay B$7 for use of the Jorge Henrich Arauz Airport, which is just outside the northwest corner of town along Av Laureano Villar (*mototaxi* B$7).

BOA (Boliviana de Aviación; ☎901-105010; www.boa.bo; Sucre, btwn Ballivian & Cochabamba) has six flights weekly to La Paz, Santa Cruz, Cobija, Tarija, Sucre and Cochabamba. **EcoJet** (☎901-105055, 465-2617; www.ecojet.bo; cnr Av 6 de Agosto & Santa Cruz) has daily flights to Cochabamba, and regular flights to La Paz, Santa Cruz, Guayaramerín, Riberalta, Cobija, Sucre and Tarija. **TAM** (☎462-2363; cnr Avs Bolívar & Santa Cruz) has daily flights to La Paz (B$650) via Cochabamba (B$400) or Santa Cruz (B$550), and daily flights to Guayaramerín and Riberalta (B$630).

Taxis to and from the airport charge around B$25, but if you don't have much luggage, *mototaxis* are cheaper (B$10) – you'll be surprised how much luggage they can accommodate with a bit of creativity.

BUS & CAMIONETA

The rambling bus terminal is a 10-minute walk or B$20 taxi east of the center. Several *flotas* depart nightly between 6pm and 10pm for Santa Cruz (normal/*bus cama* B$50 to B$80, eight to 10 hours). A number of companies theoretically serve Rurrenabaque (B$130, 17 to 30 hours) daily via San Borja (B$70, eight to 12 hours), though from November to May these services are typically suspended. There are also daily dry-season departures to Riberalta (B$200, 17 to 30 hours) and Guayaramerín (B$200, 22 to 35 hours).

Camionetas (pickup trucks) run to San Ignacio de Moxos (B$70, four hours) when full from the *parada* at 1 de Mayo near Velarde. Buses (B$50, six hours) occasionally run from the terminal around 9am.

Across from the terminal there are a few van and car services that depart when full: to San Ignacio (B$50) and San Borja (B$70; change in San Borja for Yucumo for an additional B$20, or an extra B$70 for Rurrenabaque).

UNDERSTAND BOLIVIA

Bolivia Today

In Bolivia, crisis is the status quo. Protests, poverty, inequality and slow economic progress are part of everyday life – as are movements toward greater social inclusion. At the center of it all is president Evo Morales and his constitution, institutional reforms, and broad policies that have marked the nation's revolutionary movement toward socialism.

Economically, the nationalization of energy and mining interests was applauded by Bolivia's poor, but has soured relations with foreign investors and some foreign governments. And despite sky-high commodity prices, Bolivia's economy hasn't grown as fast as it should. The export of raw materials remains the nation's bread and butter. And with the world's largest lithium deposits, plenty of natural gas and mineral wealth, Bolivia could very well continue to see moderate economic progress for the foreseeable future. The stumbling blocks will include environmental conditions (deforestation, desertification and climate change), depressed foreign markets, and the reluctance of foreign companies to invest their money and know-how in a country with a growing track record of nationalizations.

Despite modest economic growth, over half of Bolivians still live in poverty, and the social programs of the Evo Morales administration outlined under the new constitution have only made minimal progress in remedying the nation's poverty traps.

These new measures have succeeded, however, in re-framing Bolivia's social structure. Despite having practically no escape from poverty (even today), there seems to be a sparkle of self-awareness and hope that's never been more evident among the nation's indigenous majority, who are playing a significant role in politics and policy.

On the political front, conflict is on the rise. People protest poor working conditions, mining operations that contaminate rivers, and roads that displace communities and affect ecosystems. These protests regularly shut down the nation's roads and are having a detrimental effect on the economy. In addition, violence stemming from the ever-evolving drug trade is building throughout the region.

Morales' moves to redistribute lands and redistribute wealth have met with strong opposition from Bolivia's gas- and resource-rich eastern region (where autonomy movements are ongoing). But despite this opposition – and growing discontent over what many perceive as weak rule of law and widespread corruption – many expect that the numerous social entitlement programs sponsored by the Morales administration, and paid for with the growing incomes from mining, agriculture and gas exports, will keep Morales' revolution moving forward.

History

Bolivia's living history is evident in every corner of daily life. And the significant events that shaped the past – from the rise of Tiwanaku and the Pax Incaica to the Spanish Conquest, independence movement, discovery of vast mineral wealth, loss of territories to neighbors on all sides, economic twists, flips and flops, and coup after coup after coup – have piled on top of each other to create the Bolivia you see today.

You can connect with the artistic threads of history in the country's Pre-Hispanic ruins, Colonial-era churches and in the museums, galleries and chaotic markets of the city centers. The cultural imprint that dates back more than 6000 years is seen in the language, dress, customs and traditions of native peoples, and in the unique dual society that is only now being challenged with the rise of the country's first self-declared indigenous president.

The economic wake from this dual society is viscerally palpable in the underclasses and indigenous majority, and in the sky-scraping edifices of La Paz and the broad haciendas around Santa Cruz.

From a purely economic standpoint, Bolivia is a country that never should have been. The country has vast natural resources, but a small, sparse population, meaning it primarily produces raw goods. Politically, it has been pushed and pulled and bent out of shape by the stronger spheres of influence centering in Cuzco, Madrid, Lima, Buenos Aires and Washington, DC. And while much of Bolivia's history follows the macro-trends of the rest of South America, the country's spirit, character and context have come together to form a complex and intricate story unique unto itself.

Pre-Colonial Times

Advanced civilizations first developed along the Peruvian coast and in the valleys in the early AD period. Highland civilizations developed a little later on. Some archaeologists define the prehistory of the Central Andes in terms of 'horizons' – Early, Middle and Late – each of which was characterized by distinct architectural and artistic trends.

The so-called Early Horizon (1400–400 BC) was an era of architectural innovation and activity, most evident in the ruins of Chavín de Huantar, on the eastern slopes of the Andes in Peru. Chavín influences resounded far and wide, even after the decline of Chavín society, and spilled over into the Early Middle Horizon (400 BC–AD 500).

The Middle Horizon (AD 500–900) was marked by the imperial expansion of the Tiwanaku and Huari (of the Ayacucho Valley of present-day Peru) cultures. The Tiwanakans produced technically advanced work, most notably the city itself. They created impressive ceramics, gilded ornamentation, engraved pillars and slabs with calendar markings, and designs representing their bearded white leader and deity, Viracocha.

The period between AD 900 and 1475 is known as the Late Intermediate Horizon. After the fall of Tiwanaku, regionalized city-states like Chan-Chan in Peru and the Aymará Kingdoms around the southern shores of Lake Titicaca came to power. But it was the rise and fall of the Inca empire that would truly define the pre-Columbian period.

Around 1440 the Inca started to expand their political boundaries. The eighth Inca king, Viracocha (not to be confused with the Tiwanaku deity of the same name), believed the mandate from their Sun God was not just to conquer, plunder and enslave, but to organize defeated tribes and absorb them into the realm of the benevolent Sun God.

Between 1476 and 1534 the Inca civilization was able to extend its influence over the Aymará Kingdoms around Lake Titicaca.

By the late 1520s internal rivalries began to take their toll on the empire with the sons of Inca Huayna Capac – Atahualpa and Huáscar – fighting a bloody civil war after the death of their father. Atahualpa (who controlled the northern reaches of the empire) won the war.

Conquistadors

The Spanish conquest of South America was remarkably quick. The power vacuum left by the Inca Civil War helped, as did the epidemics caused by European diseases.

Alto Perú (the area we now know as Bolivia) was aligned with Huáscar during the Inca Civil War, making its conquest rather easy for Diego de Almagro.

In 1544, Diego Huallpa revealed his discovery of silver at Cerro Rico in Potosí. By this time, Spanish conquerors had already firmly implanted their customs on the remnants of the Inca empire.

Potosí was officially founded in 1545, and in 1558 Alto Perú gained its autonomy from Lima with the placement of an Audiencia (Royal Court) in Sucre. Spider-webbing out from Potosí, transportation hubs, farming communities and other support centers sprung up. Due to the world's most prolific mine, Potosí's silver underwrote Spain's international ambitions – enabling the country to fight the Counter-Reformation in Europe – and also supported the extravagance of its monarchy for at least two centuries.

Independence

The early part of the 19th century was a time of revolution and independence in Bolivia (and much of the world for that matter). Harvest failures and epidemics severely affected the Bolivian economy between 1803 and 1805. And when the economy is bad, the conditions are good for revolution. To top it off, with the French Revolution, Napoleon's wars in Europe and British support for Latin America independence movements, the colonists of the Americas were finally able to perceive what the world without royalty would look like.

By May 1809, Spanish America's first independence movement had gained momentum, and was well underway in Chuquisaca (later renamed Sucre), with other cities quick to follow suit.

By the early 1820s General Simón Bolívar had succeeded in liberating both Venezuela and Colombia from Spanish domination. In 1822 he dispatched Mariscal (Field Marshall) Antonio José de Sucre to Ecuador to defeat the Royalists at the battle of Pichincha. In 1824, after years of guerrilla action against the Spanish and the victories of Bolívar and Sucre in the battles of Junín (August 6) and Ayacucho (December 9), Peru won its independence.

With both Argentina and Peru eyeing the prize of the Potosí mines, Sucre incited a declaration of independence from Perú and, in 1825, the new Republic of Bolivia was born. Bolívar (yep, the country was named after him) and Sucre served as Bolivia's first and second presidents, but after a brief attempt by the third president, Andrés Santa Cruz, to form a confederation with Peru, things began to go awry. Chilean opposition eventually broke up this potentially powerful nation, and thereafter Bolivia was relegated to a more secondary role in regional affairs with a period of *caudillo* rule dominating national politics until the 1880s. Thereafter Bolivia was ruled by a civilian oligarchy divided into liberal and conservative groups until the 1930s, when the traditional political system again fell apart, leading to constant military intervention until the 1952 Revolution.

Shrinking Territory

At the time of independence Bolivia's boundaries encompassed well over 2 million sq km. But its neighbors soon moved to acquire its territory, removing coastal access and much of the area covered by its ancient Amazonian rubber trees.

The coastal loss occurred during the War of the Pacific, fought against Chile between 1879 and 1884. Many Bolivians believe that Chile stole the Atacama Desert's copper- and nitrate-rich sands and 850km of coastline from Peru and Bolivia by invading during Carnaval. Chile did attempt to compensate for the loss by building a railroad from La Paz to the ocean and allowing Bolivia free port privileges in Antofagasta, but Bolivians have never forgotten this devastating *enclaustramiento* (landlocked status).

The next major loss was in 1903 during the rubber boom when Brazil hacked away at Bolivia's inland expanse. Brazil and Bolivia had both been ransacking the forests of the Acre territory – it was so rich in rubber trees that Brazil engineered a dispute over sovereignty and sent in its army. Brazil then convinced the Acre region to secede from the Bolivian republic, and promptly annexed it.

There were two separate territory losses to Argentina. First, Argentina annexed a large slice of the Chaco in 1862. Then, in 1883, the territory of Puna de Atacama also went to Argentina. It had been offered to both Chile and Argentina, the former in exchange for return of the Litoral, the latter in exchange for clarification over Bolivia's ownership of Tarija.

After losing the War of the Pacific, Bolivia was desperate to have the Chaco, an inhospitable region beneath which rich oilfields were mooted to lie, as an outlet to the Atlantic via the Río Paraguay. Between 1932 and 1935, a particularly brutal war was waged between Bolivia and Paraguay over the disputed territory (more than 80,000 lives were lost). Though no decisive victory was reached, both nations had grown weary of fighting, and peace negotiations in 1938 awarded most of the disputed territory to Paraguay.

Continuing Political Strife

During the 20th century wealthy tin barons and landowners controlled Bolivian farming and mining interests, while the peasantry was relegated to a feudal system of peonage known as *pongueaje*. The beating Bolivia took in the Chaco War made way for reformist associations, civil unrest among the *cholos* (indigenous people who dress traditionally but live in cities – now referred to as mestizos, with the term *cholo* deemed pejorative), and a series of coups by reform-minded military leaders.

The most significant development was the emergence of the Movimiento Nacionalista Revolucionario (MNR) political party. They united the masses behind the common cause of popular reform, sparking friction between peasant miners and absentee tin bosses. Under the leadership of Víctor Paz Estenssoro, the MNR prevailed in the 1951 elections, but a last-minute military coup prevented it from actually taking power. What ensued was a period of serious combat, which ended with the defeat of the military and Paz Estenssoro's rise to power in what has been called the National Revolution of 1952. He immediately nationalized mines, evicted the tin barons, put an end to *pongueaje* and set up Comibol (Corporación Minera de Bolivia), the state entity in charge of mining interests.

The MNR remained in power for 12 years under various leaders. But even with US support, its effectiveness and popularity ground to a halt and Víctor Paz Estenssoro became increasingly autocratic; in 1964 his government was overthrown by a military junta headed by General René Barrientos Ortuño. Five years later Barrientos died in a helicopter accident, and a series of coups, military dictators and juntas followed.

It was in this context that right-wing coalition leader General Hugo Banzer Suárez eventually took over in 1971 and served a turbulent term through 1978, punctuated by reactionary extremism and human rights abuses.

The next three years were filled with failed elections, appointed presidents, military coups and brutal regimes, a rash of tortures, arrests and disappearances, as well as a marked increase in cocaine production and trafficking.

In 1982 Congress elected Hernán Siles Zuazo, the civilian left-wing leader of the Communist-supported Movimiento de la Izquierda Revolucionaria (MIR), which began one of the longest democratic periods in Bolivian history to date. His term was beleaguered with labor disputes, ruthless government overspending and huge monetary devaluation, resulting in a truly staggering inflation rate that at one point reached 35,000% annually.

When Siles Zuazo gave up after three years and called general elections, Víctor Paz Estenssoro returned to politics to become president for the fourth time. He immediately enacted harsh measures to revive the shattered economy: he ousted labor unions, removed government restrictions on internal trade, slashed the government deficit, imposed a wage freeze, eliminated price subsidies, laid off workers at inefficient government-owned companies, allowed the peso to float against the US dollar and deployed armed forces to keep the peace.

Inflation was curtailed within weeks, but spiraling unemployment threatened the government's stability.

Chaos Prevails

The early '90s were characterized by political apathy, party politics, and the struggle between *capitalization* (the opening of state companies to international investment) and populist models. The free market won with the election of Gonzolo 'Goni' Sanchéz de Lozada, the MNR leader who had played a key role in the curtailing of inflation through 'shock therapy' during the Estenssoro government.

Overseas investors in formerly state-owned companies received 49% equity, total voting control, license to operate in Bolivia and up to 49% of the profits. The remaining 51% of the shares were distributed to Bolivians as pensions and through Participación Popular, a program meant to channel spending away from cities and into rural schools, clinics and other local infrastructure.

In late 1995, reform issues were overshadowed by violence and unrest surrounding US-directed coca eradication in the Chapare. In 1997 voters upset by the reforms cast 22.5% of the ballot in favor of comeback king and former dictator General Hugo Banzer Suárez. In the late 1990s Banzer faced swelling public discontent with his coca eradication measures and widespread corruption, and unrest in response to increasing gas prices, a serious water shortage and economic downturn in the department of Cochabamba.

Following a successful campaign advised by a team of US political consultants that he hired, 'Goni' was appointed president in August 2002. His economic policies were met

BOLIVIA'S INDIGENOUS GROUPS

Highlands

Aymará The Aymará culture emerged on the southern shores of Titicaca after the fall of Tiwanaku. Today, Aymará live in the areas surrounding the lake and in the Yungas, calling La Paz' El Alto the capital of Aymará culture.

Quechua Descended from the Inca, there are some 9 to 14 million Quechua speakers in Bolivia, Peru, Ecuador, Chile, Colombia and Argentina today.

Chipaya Perhaps the direct descendants of Tiwanaku.

Kallawaya A remote tribe with a dying language.

Lowlands

Chiquitano Living primarily in the Chiquitania tropical savanna outside Santa Cruz, but also in Beni and into Brazil. There are about 180,000 Chiquitanos in Bolivia. About a quarter of them speak Chiquitano.

Guaraní This tribe shares a common language and lives in Paraguay, Brazil and parts of Uruguay and Bolivia.

Mojeńo From the Beni department, this significant ethnic group was quite large before the 17th century, with over 350,000 people.

with widespread demonstrations and the loss of 67 lives during a police lock-down in La Paz the following year. In October 2003, Goni resigned amid massive popular protests and fled to the US. Bolivia has unsuccessfully been seeking his extradition to stand a political trial for the events of 2003. Victims' representatives have pursued compensatory damages for extrajudicial killings in a suit against him in the US. In 2014 the US District Court in Florida ruled the case could proceed under the Torture Victim Protection Act; both sides filed appeals on this ruling in 2015.

Protests, rising fuel prices and continued unrest pushed Goni's successor, Carlos Mesa, to resign in 2005.

The Morales Era

In December 2005 Bolivians elected their country's first indigenous president. A former *cocalero* (coca grower) and representative from Cochabamba, Evo Morales of Movimiento al Socialismo (MAS) won nearly 54% of the vote, having promised to alter the traditional political class and to empower the nation's poor (mainly indigenous) majority. After the election, Morales quickly grabbed the lefty spotlight, touring the world and meeting with Venezuela's Hugo Chávez, Cuba's Fidel Castro, Brazil's Lula da Silva and members of South Africa's African National Congress. Symbolically, on May Day 2006, he nationalized Bolivia's natural gas reserves and raised taxes on energy investors in a move that would consolidate Bolivian resources in Bolivian hands.

In July 2006, Morales formed a National Constituent Assembly to set about rewriting the country's constitution: in 2009, the new socially focused document was approved by 67% of voters in a nationwide referendum. The first constitution in Bolivia approved by popular vote, it gave greater power to the country's indigenous majority and allowed Morales to seek and win a second five-year term. It also limited the size of landholdings in order to redistribute Bolivia's land from large ranchers and landowners to poor indigenous farmers.

In 2014 Evo was elected again with a similar majority of 60% (more than twice that of his nearest rival), giving him power until 2020 and providing him with a strong platform to continue his social development and empowerment policies.

Culture

The National Psyche

Bolivia is a remarkably stratified society. And while the archetypes defined by 500 years of Spanish-descendent rule are starting to slowly fade, who you are – where you fit in society and what opportunities you will have throughout life – is still largely defined by the color of your skin, the language you speak, the clothes you wear and the money you have.

Attitude depends on climate and altitude. *Cambas* (lowlanders) and *kollas* (highlanders) enjoy expounding on what makes them different (ie better) than the other. Lowlanders are said to be warmer, more casual and more generous to strangers; highlanders are supposedly harder working but less open-minded. While the jesting used to be good-natured, regional tensions have increased over the past few years, with Santa Cruz' threats of succession constantly in the news.

Life's not easy – it's actually really tough for most Bolivians – so many try to take joy from the little things: soccer, the rising of the sun, good rains and harvests, birthdays, religious festivals, coca, *cerveza* (beer), births and christenings.

Lifestyle

Life in this fiercely self-reliant nation begins with the family. No matter what tribe or class you come from, it's likely that you have close ties to your extended family. In the highlands, the concept of *ayllu* (the traditional peasant system of communal land ownership, management and decision making) that dates back to the Inca times is still important today.

Day-to-day life varies: many *campesinos* (subsistence farmers) live without running water, heat or electricity, and some wear clothing that has hardly changed in style since the Spanish arrived. But in the Bolivian cities, thousands of people enjoy the comforts of contemporary conveniences and live very modern lifestyles.

Homosexuality is legal in Bolivia but isn't openly flaunted in this society of machismo. Despite a growing number of gay bars in some larger cities, gay culture remains fairly subdued.

Religion

Roughly 95% of Bolivia's population professes Roman Catholicism and practices it to varying degree. The remaining 5% are Protestant, agnostic and belonging to other religions. Strong evangelical movements are rapidly gaining followers with their fire-and-brimstone messages of the world's imminent end. Despite the political and economic strength of Western religions, it's clear that most religious activities have mixed Inca and Aymará belief systems with Christianity.

Population

Bolivia is a multi-ethnic society with a remarkable diversity of linguistic, cultural and artistic traditions. In fact, the country has the largest population of indigenous peoples in South America, with most sociologists and anthropologists stating that over 60% of the population is of indigenous descent.

Bolivia has 36 identified indigenous groups. The vast majority of those who identify themselves as indigenous are Aymará (about 25%) and Quechua (about 30%), many of whom live in the highlands. The remaining groups (including Guaraní and Chiquitano) are located almost entirely in the lowlands.

Mestizos (a person of mixed indigenous and Spanish descent), make up a substantial portion of the population. Mestizos sometimes fall into 'white society', while others retain their roots within the indigenous societal makeup.

Cuisine

Meat invariably dominates Bolivian cuisine and it is usually accompanied by rice, a starchy tuber (usually potato) and shredded lettuce. Often, the whole affair is drowned by *llajhua* (a fiery tomato-based salsa). The soups are a specialty.

Desayuno (breakfast) consists of little more than coffee and a bread roll, and is often followed by a mid-morning street snack such as a *salteña* (meat and vegetable pasty), *tucumana* (an empanada-like pastry) or empanada.

Almuerzo (lunch) is the main meal of the day. The best-value meals are found in and around markets (often under B$10) and at no-frills restaurants offering set lunches (usually between B$15 and B$40). *La cena,* the evening meal, is mostly served à la carte.

Vegetarian options are on the rise, but you'll be stuck with lots of over-cooked vegetables, rice, potatoes, pizza and pasta. Quinoa is a super grain, perfect for vegetarians.

Arts

Music & Dance

While all Andean musical traditions have evolved from a series of pre-Inca, Inca, Spanish, Amazonian and even African influences, each region of Bolivia has developed distinctive musical traditions, dances and instruments.

The instrument Bolivia is most known for, and understandably proud of, is the *charango,* considered the king of all stringed instruments. Modeled after the Spanish *vihuela* and mandolin, it gained initial popularity in Potosí during the city's mining heyday. Another instrument commonplace in the gringo markets is the *quena,* a small flute made of cane, bone or ceramic. The instrument predates Europeans by many centuries and the earliest examples, made of stone, were found near Potosí. A curious instrument known as a jaguar-caller comes from the Amazon region. This hollowed-out calabash, with a small hole into which the player inserts his hand, seems to do the trick in calling the big cats to the hunt.

Traditional Altiplano dances celebrate war, fertility, hunting prowess, marriage and work. After the Spanish arrived, European dances and those of the African slaves were introduced, resulting in the hybrid dances that now characterize many Bolivian celebrations.

Oruro's Carnaval draws huge local and international crowds. Potosí is famed for *tinku,* a traditional festival that features ritual fighting, while La Paz is renowned for La Morenada, which re-enacts the dance of African slaves brought to the courts of Viceroy Felipe III.

Weaving

Bolivian textiles come in diverse patterns. The majority display a degree of skill that results from millennia of artistry and tradition. The most common piece is a *manta* or *aguayo,* a square shawl made of two handwoven strips joined edge to edge. Also common are the *chuspa* (coca pouch), *chullo* (knitted hat), the *falda* (skirt), woven belts and touristy items such as camera bags made from remnants.

Regional differences are manifested in weaving style, motif and use. Weavings from Tarabuco often feature intricate zoomorphic patterns, while distinctive red-and-black designs come from Potolo, northwest of Sucre. Zoomorphic patterns are also prominent in the wild Charazani country north of Lake Titicaca and in several Altiplano areas outside La Paz, including Lique and Calamarka.

Some extremely fine weavings originate in Sica Sica, one of the many dusty and nondescript villages between La Paz and Oruro, while in Calcha, southeast of Potosí, expert spinning and an extremely tight weave – more than 150 threads per inch – produce Bolivia's finest textiles.

Vicuña fibers, the finest and most expensive in the world, are produced in Apolobamba and in Parque Nacional Sajama.

Sports

As with many of its Latin American neighbors, Bolivia's national sport is *fútbol* (soccer). La Paz's Bolívar and The Strongest usually participate (albeit weakly) in the Copa Libertadores, the annual showdown of Latin America's top clubs. Professional *fútbol* matches are held every weekend in big cities, and impromptu street games are always happening. While small towns lack many basic services, you can be sure to find a well-tended *cancha* (football field) almost everywhere you go – and you'll be welcome to join in. Some communities still bar women from the field, but in the Altiplano women's teams have started popping up, where they play clad in *polleras* (skirts) and jerseys.

In rural communities volleyball is a sunset affair, with mostly adults playing a couple of times a week. Racquetball, billiards, chess and *cacho* (dice) are also popular. The unofficial national sport, however, has to be feasting and feting – the competition between dancers and drinkers knows no bounds.

Environment

When people think of Bolivia it generally conjures up images of somewhere high (La Paz), dry (Altiplano) and salty (Uyuni salt plains). While this may be true for large areas of the country, there's much more to the Bolivian landscape than just mountains. The range of altitude – from 130m above sea level in the jungles of the Amazon Basin to 6542m on the peaks of the rugged Andes – has resulted in a huge variety of ecological and geological niches supporting a bewildering variety of nature. Environmentally it is one of the most diverse countries on the continent.

The country's 1415 bird species and 5000 described plant species rank among the highest numbers in the world. It's also among the neotropical countries with the highest level of endemism (species which exist only in Bolivia), with 21 birds, 28 reptiles, 72 amphibians and 25 mammals found nowhere else on earth.

But while it may seem obvious that Bolivia's natural resources are one of its greatest assets, not everybody values assets that don't have a direct monetary value. From the lush tropical forests of Parque Nacional e Área de Uso Múltiple Amboró to the wetlands of the Pantanal, the scrub that obscures the Chaco gas fields and the Polylepis woodlands of the Andes, the Bolivian environment is under constant threat from destruction for economic exploitation.

The Land

Two Andean mountain chains define the west of the country, with many peaks above 6000m. The western Cordillera Occidental stands between Bolivia and the Pacific coast. The eastern Cordillera Real runs southeast, then turns south across central Bolivia, joining the other chain to form the southern Cordillera Central.

The haunting Altiplano (altitude 3500m to 4000m), is boxed in by these two great cordilleras. It's an immense, nearly treeless plain punctuated by mountains and solitary volcanic peaks. At the Altiplano's northern end, straddling the Peruvian border, Lake Titicaca is one of the world's highest navigable lakes. In the far southwestern corner, the land is drier and less populated. The salty remnants of two vast ancient lakes, the Salar de Uyuni and the Salar de Coipasa, are there as well.

East of the Cordillera Central are the Central Highlands, a region of scrubby hills, valleys and fertile basins with a

Mediterranean-like climate. North of the Cordillera Real, the rainy Yungas form a transition zone between arid highlands and humid lowlands.

More than half of Bolivia's total area is in the Amazon Basin, with sweaty tropical rainforest in the western section, and flat *cerrado* and extensions of the Pantanal wetland in the east. In the country's southeastern corner is the nearly impenetrable scrubland of the Gran Chaco, an arid, thorny forest that experiences the highest temperatures in the country.

Wildlife

The distribution of wildlife is dictated by the country's geography and varies considerably from region to region. The Altiplano is home to vicuñas, flamingos and condors; the Chaco to secretive jaguars, pumas and peccaries; the Pantanal provides refuge for giant otters, marsh deer and waterbirds; while the Amazon Basin contains the richest density of species on earth, featuring an incredible variety of reptiles, parrots, monkeys, hummingbirds, butterflies, fish and bugs (by the zillions!).

Of course the animals that steal the show are the regional giants. The majestic jaguar, the continent's top predator; the elephant-nosed tapir (*anta*); and the walking vacuum cleaner that is the giant anteater. The continent's biggest bird is here too, the ostrich-like rhea or *ñandú,* and it can be surprisingly common in some areas. You may even be lucky enough to spot the breathtaking Andean condor, unsurprisingly revered by the Inca, soaring on mountain thermals.

River travelers are almost certain to spot capybaras (like giant aquatic guinea pigs) and caiman (alligators). It's not unusual to see anacondas in the rivers of the department of Beni and a spot of piranha fishing is virtually an obligation for anybody spending time in the Amazon.

Overland travelers frequently see armadillos, foxes, *jochis* (agoutis) and the grey-faced, llama-like guanaco. Similar, but more delicately proportioned, is the fuzzy vicuña, once mercilessly hunted for its woolly coat but now recovering well. You won't have to work quite as hard to spot their domesticated relatives, the llama and the alpaca.

Many nonprofit groups are working on countrywide environmental conservation efforts. Besides the international conservation organizations, the following local groups are having a positive impact.

Asociación Armonía (www.armonia-bo.org) Everything you need to know about birding and bird conservation.

Fundación Amigos de la Naturaleza (www.fan-bo.org) One of the most active of the local conservation groups, working at the national level.

Protección del Medio Ambiente Tarija (http://prometa.org.bo) Works in the Gran Chaco region on a series of social and conservation initiatives.

National Parks

Our favorite national parks and protected areas (there are 22 in total) and what you'll see.

Parque Nacional e Área de Uso Múltiple Amboró (p256) Near Santa Cruz, home to rare spectacled bears, jaguars and an astonishing variety of birdlife.

Parque Nacional Apolobamba Excellent hiking in this remote mountain range abutting the Peruvian border, with Bolivia's densest condor population.

Parque Nacional Cotapata Most of the Choro trek passes through here, midway between La Paz and Coroico in the Yungas.

Parque Nacional Madidi (p261) Protects a wide range of wildlife habitats; more than 1000 species of birds have been identified in Madidi.

Parque Nacional Noel Kempff Mercado Remote park on the Brazilian border; contains a variety of wildlife and some of Bolivia's most inspiring scenery.

Reserva Nacional de Fauna Andina Eduardo Avaroa (p230) A highlight of the Southwest Circuit tour, including wildlife-rich lagoons.

Parque Nacional Sajama (p222) Adjoining Chile's magnificent Parque Nacional Lauca; contains Volcán Sajama (6542m), Bolivia's highest peak.

Parque Nacional Torotoro (p241) Enormous rock formations with dinosaur tracks from the Cretaceous period, plus caves and ancient ruins.

Parque Nacional Tunari (p241) Within hiking distance of Cochabamba; features lovely nature trails through mountain scenery.

SURVIVAL GUIDE

Directory A–Z

ACCOMMODATIONS

Bolivian accommodations are among South America's cheapest, though price and value are hardly uniform.

The Bolivian hotel-rating system divides accommodations into *posadas* (inns), *alojamientos, residenciales, casas de huéspedes, hostales* (hostels) and *hoteles* (hotels). Rock-bottom places are usually found around the bus and train stations, though this area is often the most dangerous in town. Room availability is only a problem at popular weekend getaways like Coroico and during fiestas (especially Carnaval in Oruro and festivals in Copacabana), when prices double.

In the Altiplano, heat and hot water often makes the difference in price, while in lowland areas, air-con and fans are common delimiters.

Warning: several readers have alerted us to improper use of propane heaters in Bolivia. These are sometimes offered in cheaper accommodations but are not meant to be used in enclosed spaces so refrain from using them if supplied.

Bolivia offers excellent camping, especially along trekking routes and in remote mountain areas. Gear (of varying quality) is easily rented in La Paz and at popular trekking base camps like Sorata. It's always a good idea to ask for permission if somebody is around. Theft and assaults have been reported in some areas – always inquire locally about security before heading off to set up camp.

ACTIVITIES

Bolivia is like a theme park for grown-up adventurers. There are multiday treks, 'easy' day hikes, mountain-bike rides that'll leave your teeth chattering, climbs to lost Andean peaks, rivers for rafting and romping, rugged 4X4 journeys to the lost corners of the old Inca empire, and just about anything you could ask for in between. While do-it-yourself expeditions add an element of adventure, bringing a local guide lowers your risk of incident (getting robbed, lost or just plain lonely), plus you're contributing to the local economy.

Hiking and trekking are arguably the most rewarding Andean activities – add a porter, llama train and experienced guide and you have all the makings for a grand adventure. Some of the most popular hikes and treks in Bolivia begin near La Paz, traverse the Cordillera Real along ancient Inca routes and end in the Yungas.

Trekking in Bolivia by Yossi Brain and Lonely Planet's *Trekking in the Central Andes* are good resources.

> **SLEEPING PRICE RANGES**
>
> The following price ranges refer to a double room with bathroom in high season, including all taxes and fees.
>
> **La Paz**
>
> **$** less than B$180
>
> **$$** B$180 to B$560
>
> **$$$** more than B$560
>
> **The Rest of the Country**
>
> **$** less than B$160
>
> **$$** B$160 to B$400
>
> **$$$** more than B$400

Climbing in Bolivia is an exercise in extremes – like the country itself. In the dry southern winter (May to October) temperatures may fluctuate by as much as 40°C in a single day. Once you're acclimatized to the Altiplano's relatively thin air (you'll need at least a week), there is still 2500m of even thinner air lurking above.

A plus for climbers is the access to mountains; although public transportation may not always be available, roads pass within easy striking distance of many fine peaks.

The **Asociación de Guias de Montaña** (☎214-7951; www.agmtb.org) in La Paz certifies climbing guides in Bolivia.

Bolivia is blessed with some of the most dramatic mountain-biking terrain in the world: there's seven months every year of near-perfect weather and relatively easy access to mountain ranges, magnificent lakes, pre-Hispanic ruins and trails, and myriad ecozones connected by an extensive network of footpaths and jeep roads.

One of Bolivia's greatest secrets is the number of whitewater rivers that drain the eastern slopes of the Andes between the Cordillera Apolobamba and the Chapare.

Some La Paz tour agencies can organize day trips on the Río Coroico. Other options include the Río Unduavi and numerous wild Chapare rivers.

Amazon canoe tours along the Río Beni are unforgettable, as are the trips along the Río Mamoré from Trinidad.

ELECTRICITY

Most electricity currents are 220V AC, at 50Hz. Most plugs and sockets are the two-pin, round-prong variety, but a few anomalous American-style two-pin, parallel flat-pronged sockets exist.

EMBASSIES & CONSULATES

For a full list of foreign diplomatic representations in Bolivia, see www.embassiesabroad.com/embassies-in/bolivia.

Argentinian Embassy (Map p198; ☎02-241-7737; www.ebolv.cancilleria.gov.ar; Aspiazu 475, La Paz) Consulates in Cochabamba (☎04-425-5859; www.ccoch.cancilleria.gov.ar; Federico Blanco 929), Santa Cruz (☎03-332-4153; www.cscrs.cancilleria.gov.ar; Junín 22, 3rd fl) and Tarija (☎04-7298-9168; www.ctari.cancilleria.gov.ar; Ballivian 699).

Australian Embassy (Map p198; ☎2-211-5655, 7061-0626; australiaconsbolivia@mac.com; Aspiazu 416, La Paz)

Brazilian Embassy (Map p198; ☎02-244-0202; Av Arce, Edificio Multicentro, La Paz) There are consulates in Cochabamba (☎04-425-5860; Av Oquendo N-1080), Guayaramerín (☎855-3766; cnr Avs Beni & 24 de Septiembre; ⏱9am-5pm Mon-Sat), Santa Cruz (☎03-333-7368; Av Busch 330) and Sucre (☎04-645-2661; Arenales 212).

Canadian Embassy (Map p198; ☎02-241-5141; www.international.gc.ca; Victor Sanjinés 2678, 2nd fl, La Paz)

Chilean Consulate (☎02-279-7331; www.chileabroad.gov.cl; Calle 14 No 8024, Calacoto, La Paz) There's a consulate in Santa Cruz (☎03-335-8989; René Moreno 551, 1st fl).

Ecuadorian Embassy (Map p198; ☎02-278-4422; Calle 10 No 8054, Calacoto, La Paz) There's a consulate in Sucre (☎04-646-0622; Los Ceibos 2, Barrio Tucsupaya).

French Embassy (☎02-214-9900; www.ambafrance-bo.org; Siles 5390, Obrajes , La Paz)

German Embassy (Map p198; ☎02-244-0066; www.la-paz.diplo.de; Av Arce 2395, La Paz) There are consulate in Cochabamba (☎04-425-4024; cnr España & Av de las Heroínas, Edificio La Promontora, 6th fl) and Sucre (☎04-645-2091; Avaroa 326).

Italian Embassy (Map p198; ☎02-278-8001; www.amblapaz.esteri.it; Jordan Cuellar 458, Obrajes, La Paz)

Paraguayan Embassy (Map p198; ☎02-243-2201; Pedro Salazar 351, Edificio Illimani, La Paz)

EATING PRICE RANGES

The following price ranges refer to the cost of a main meal.

$ less than B$30

$$ B$30 to B$60

$$$ more than B$60

Peruvian Embassy (Map p198; ☎02-244-1250; www.embaperubolivia.com; Fernando Guachalla 300, Sopocachi, La Paz)

Spanish Embassy (Map p198; ☎02-243-3518; www.maec.es; Av 6 de Agosto 2827, La Paz) There's a consulate in Santa Cruz (☎03-312-1349; cnr Av Cañoto & Perú).

UK Embassy (Map p198; ☎02-243-3424; www.ukinbolivia.fco.gov.uk; Arce 2732, La Paz)

US Embassy (Map p198; ☎02-216-8000; www.bolivia.usembassy.gov; Av Arce 2780, La Paz; ⏱8-11:30 am Mon-Wed, 8:15-11:45am & 1:45-3pm Thu, closed US & Bolivian holidays)

GAY & LESBIAN TRAVELERS

Homosexuality is legal in Bolivia but still not widely accepted. In 2004 parliament attempted (unsuccessfully) to introduce Law 810, which would allow homosexual couples to marry and foster children.

Gay bars and venues are limited to the larger cities, especially Santa Cruz and La Paz, but these are still somewhat clandestine affairs. As for hotels, sharing a room is no problem – but discretion is still in order.

Gay rights lobby groups are active in La Paz (MGLP Libertad), Cochabamba (Dignidad) and most visibly in progressive Santa Cruz, which held Bolivia's first Gay Pride in 2001. La Paz is known for La Familia Galan, the capital's most fabulous group of cross-dressing queens, who aim to educate Bolivians around issues of sexuality and gender through theater performances. The feminist activist group **Mujeres Creando** (www.mujerescreando.org) is based in La Paz and promotes the rights of oppressed groups.

HEALTH

Sanitation and hygiene are not Bolivia's strong suits, so pay attention to what you eat. Most tap water isn't safe to drink; stick to bottled water if your budget allows (your bowels will thank you). Carry iodine if you'll be trekking.

The Altiplano lies between 3000m and 4000m, and many visitors to La Paz, Copacabana and Potosí will have problems with altitude sickness. Complications like cerebral edema have been the cause of death in otherwise fit, healthy travelers. Diabetics should note that only the Touch II blood glucose meter gives accurate readings at altitudes over 2000m.

Bolivia is officially in a yellow-fever zone, so a vaccination is recommended; it is in fact obligatory for US citizens requesting visas and for onward travel (such as to Brazil, which requires the certificate). Anyone coming from a yellow-fever-infected area needs a vaccination certificate to enter Bolivia. Take precautions against malaria in the lowlands.

While medical facilities might not be exactly what you're used to back home, there are decent hospitals in the biggest cities and passable clinics in most towns (but *not* in remote parts of the country).

INTERNET ACCESS

Nearly every corner of Bolivia has a cybercafe and wi-fi is now standard in most midrange and top-end hotels (and many cafes). Rates run from B$2 to B$5 per hour. In smaller towns, expect to pay more – check the local Entel offices and be ready for slow satellite connections.

LEGAL MATTERS

Regardless of its reputation as the major coca provider, drugs – including cocaine – are highly illegal in Bolivia, and possession and use brings a jail sentence. Foreign embassies are normally powerless to help (or won't want to know!). In short, don't even think about it.

MAPS

Maps are available in La Paz, Cochabamba and Santa Cruz through Los Amigos del Libro and some bookstores. Government 1:50,000 topographical and specialty sheets are available from the **Instituto Geográfico Militar** (IGM; Map p194; Juan Pablo 23, Edificio Murillo, San Pedro; ⏲8:30am-12:30pm & 2:30-6:30pm Mon-Fri), with offices in La Paz and most other major cities.

International sources for hard-to-find maps include the US-based **Maplink** (www.maplink.com) and **Omnimap** (www.omnimap.com), and the UK-based **Stanfords** (www.stanfords.co.uk). In Germany, try **Deutscher Alpenverein** (www.alpenverein.de), which publishes its own series of climbing maps.

MONEY

Bolivia uses the boliviano (B$). Most prices are pegged to the US dollar. Only crisp US dollar bills are accepted (they are the currency for savings).

The boliviano is divided into 100 centavos. Bolivianos come in 10, 20, 50, 100 and 200 denomination notes, with coins worth 1, 2 and 5 bolivianos as well as 10, 20 and 50 centavos. Often called pesos (the currency was changed from pesos to bolivianos in 1987), bolivianos are extremely difficult to unload outside the country.

Counterfeit bolivianos and US dollars are less common than they used to be, but they can still be encountered often than you'd like.

ATMs

Sizable towns have *cajeros automáticos* (ATMs) – usually Banco Nacional de Bolivia, Banco Bisa, Banco Mercantil Santa Cruz and Banco Unión. They dispense bolivianos in 50 and 100 notes (sometimes US dollars as well) with Visa, Mastercard, Plus and Cirrus cards; note that in the past, many Europeans have reported trouble using their cards.

In smaller towns, the local bank Prodem is a good option for cash advances with Visa and Mastercard (3% to 6% commission charged) and many branches are meant to be open on Saturday mornings; the hours and machines are unreliable. Don't rely on ATMs in general; always carry some cash with you, especially if venturing into rural areas.

Cash

Finding change for bills larger than B$10 is a national pastime, as change for larger notes is scarce outside big cities. When exchanging money or making big purchases, request the *cambio* (change) in small denominations. If you can stand the queues, most banks will break large bills. Also, check any larger bills for damage as you may not be able to change them if they're torn or taped together.

Credit Cards

Brand-name plastic, such as Visa, Mastercard and (less often) American Express, may be used in larger cities at the better hotels, restaurants and tour agencies.

Money Changers

Visitors fare best with US dollars (travelers have reported that it's difficult to change euros). Currency may be exchanged at *casas de cambio* (exchange bureaus) and at some banks in larger cities. You can often change money in travel agencies, hotels and sometimes in stores selling touristy items. *Cambistas* (street money changers) operate in most cities but only change cash dollars, paying roughly the same as *casas de cambio*. They're convenient after hours, but guard against rip-offs and counterfeit notes.

The rate for cash doesn't vary much from place to place, and there is no black-market rate. Currencies of neighboring countries may be exchanged in border areas and at *casas de cambio* in La Paz. Beware, too, mangled notes: unless both halves of a repaired banknote bear identical serial numbers, the note is worthless. Also note that US$100 bills of the CB-B2 series are not accepted anywhere, neither are US$50 bills of the AB-B2 series.

International Transfers

The fastest way to have money transferred from abroad is with **Western Union** (www.westernunion.com). A newer, alternative option is through **MoneyGram** (www.moneygram.com), which has offices in all major cities – watch the hefty fees, though. Your bank can also wire money to a cooperating Bolivian bank; it may take a couple of business days.

PayPal is increasingly used to make bank transfers to pay for hotels.

Tipping

Formal tipping is haphazard except in the nicer restaurants. Elsewhere, locals leave coins amounting to a maximum of 10% of the total in recognition of good service.

OPENING HOURS

Most businesses are closed on Sundays, save for restaurants, so take care of business on weekdays.

Banks 9am to 4pm or 6pm Monday to Friday; 9am or 10am to noon or 5pm Saturday

Markets Stir as early as 6am and some are open on Sunday mornings

Restaurants Hours vary but generally run from breakfast (8am to 10am), lunch (noon to 3pm) and dinner (6pm to 10pm or 11pm)

Shops 9:30am to noon and 2pm to 6pm Monday to Friday; 10am to noon or 5pm on Saturdays

PHOTOGRAPHY

While some Bolivians are willing photo subjects, others may be superstitious about your camera, suspicious of your motives or interested in payment. Many children will ask for payment, often after you've taken their photo. It's best to not take such shots in the first place – be sensitive to the wishes of locals.

POST

Even the smallest towns have post offices – some are signposted 'Ecobol' (Empresa Correos de Bolivia). From major towns, the post is generally reliable (although often involving long delays), but when posting anything important, it's better to pay extra to have it registered or send it by courier. **DHL** (www.dhl.com) is the most reliable courier company with international service.

Airmail *postales* (postcards) or letters weighing up to 20g cost around B$7.50 to the USA, B$9 to Europe and B$10.50 to the rest of the world. Relatively reliable express-mail service is available for rates similar to those charged by private international couriers.

PUBLIC HOLIDAYS

On major holidays, banks, offices and other services are closed and public transport is often bursting at the seams; book ahead if possible.

New Year's Day January 1

Semana Santa (Easter Week) March/April

Día del Trabajo (Labor Day) May 1

Día de la Independencia (Independence Day) August 6

Día de Colón (Columbus Day) October 12

Día de los Muertos (All Souls' Day) November 2

Navidad (Christmas) December 25

Not about to be outdone by their neighbors, each Bolivian department (region) has its own holiday: February 10 in Oruro, April 15 in Tarija, May 25 in Chuquisaca, July 16 in La Paz, September 14 in Cochabamba, September 24 in Santa Cruz and Pando, November 10 in Potosí and November 18 in Beni.

SAFE TRAVEL

Crime against tourists is on the increase in Bolivia, especially in La Paz and, to a lesser extent, Cochabamba, Copacabana and Oruro. Scams are commonplace and fake police, false tourist police and 'helpful tourists' are on the rise.

There is a strong tradition of social protest in Bolivia, and with over 1000 ongoing conflicts, demonstrations are a regular occurrence and this can affect travelers. While generally peaceful, they can turn threatening in nature at times: agitated protestors throw stones and rocks and police occasionally use force and tear gas to disperse crowds. *Bloqueos* (roadblocks) and strikes by transportation workers often lead to long delays. Be careful using taxis during transportation strikes – you may end up at the receiving end of a rock, which people pelt at those who are not in sympathy with them.

The rainy season means flooding, landslides and road washouts, which in turn means more delays. Getting stuck overnight behind a landslide can happen; you'll be a happier camper with ample food, drink and warm clothes on hand.

Note that the mine tours in Potosí, bike trips outside La Paz and the 4WD excursions around Salar de Uyuni have become so hugely popular that agencies are willing to forgo safety. Make sure you do your research before signing up for the tour.

As always when traveling, safety is in numbers; solo travelers should remain alert when traveling, especially at night.

TELEPHONE

Bolivia's country code is ☎591. The international direct-dialing access code is ☎00. Calls from telephone offices are getting cheaper all the time, especially now that there's competition between the carriers – they can vary between B$1.50 and B$8 per minute. In La Paz the cheapest of cheap calls can be made from international calling centers around Calle Sagárnaga for around B$2 per minute.

Cell phones are everywhere and easy (as is internet calling).

Even Bolivians struggle with their own telephone network. Here's a quick kit to get you dialing.

Numbers

Numbers for *líneas fijas* (landlines) have seven digits; cellular numbers have eight digits. Numerous telecommunications carriers include, among others, Entel, Cotel, Tigo, Boliviatel and Viva. Each carrier has an individual code between ☎010 and ☎021.

Area Codes

Each department (region) has its own single-digit area code that must be used when dialing from another region or to another city, regardless of whether it's the same area code as the one you're in. The department codes are: (☎2) La Paz, Oruro, Potosí; (☎3) Santa Cruz, Beni, Pando; and (☎4) Cochabamba, Chuquisaca, Tarija.

Public Phones

Dialing landlines from public phone booths is easy; ask the cashier for advice.

Placing Calls

To make a call to another landline within the same city, simply dial the seven-digit number. If you're calling another region, dial ☎0 plus the single-digit area code followed by the seven-digit number, eg ☎02-123-4567. If calling a cell phone, ask the cashier for instructions; most *puntos* have different phones for calls to cellulars and landlines, so you may have to swap cabins if calling both.

Cellular Phones

Cellular-to-cellular calls within the same city are simple – just dial the eight-digit number. A recorded message (in Spanish) may prompt you for a carrier number, indicating that the person is either not within the same city or region (or has a SIM card from another region), in which case you must then redial using a '0' plus the 2-digit carrier number plus the eight-digit cellular number. For cellular-to-landline calls within the same city, in most cases, you must dial the single-digit area code, and then the seven-digit number. For cellular-to-landline calls to another region, in most cases, you must dial a '0' plus the 2-digit carrier code, followed by the single-digit area code, and then the seven-digit number, eg if dialing Sucre from La Paz, dial ☎0 + 10 (or any one of the carrier codes – 10 is Entel's network carrier) + 4 (Sucre's area code) + the seven-digit number.

International Calls

For international calls, you must first dial ☎00 followed by a country code, area code (without the first '0') and the telephone number.

TOILETS

- Poorly maintained *baños públicos* (public toilets) abound and charge around B$1 in populated areas and B$5 in the wilderness, eg around the Salar de Uyuni.
- Carry toilet paper with you wherever you go, at all times.
- Toilet paper isn't flushed down any Bolivian toilet – use the wastebaskets provided.

TOURIST INFORMATION

There are often offices covering the *prefectura* (department) and *alcaldía* (local municipality) of a particular city. The major cities, such as Santa Cruz and La Paz, have offices for both, although the different tourism bodies range from helpful to useless, often flying under the new InfoTur banner. Servicio Nacional de Áreas Protegidas (Sernap) is the best source of information about Bolivia's national parks.

VISAS

Passports must be valid for six months beyond the date of entry. Entry or exit stamps are supposed to be free. In remote border areas, you will often be charged anywhere from B$15 to B$30 for an exit stamp. Personal documents – passports and visas – must be carried at all times, especially in lowland regions. It's safest to carry photocopies rather than originals.

Bolivian visa requirements can be arbitrarily changed and interpreted. Regulations, including entry stays, are likely to change. Each Bolivian consulate and border crossing may have its own entry procedures and idiosyncrasies.

In 2007, as an act of reciprocity, the Morales government introduced visas for US citizens visiting Bolivia (a 90-day visa valid for five years costs US$135). At the time of research, it was possible to obtain the visa upon arrival in Bolivia; check with the **Bolivian Embassy** (☎202-483-4410; www.bolivia-usa.org) before traveling.

Citizens of most South American and Western European countries can get a tourist card on entry for stays up to 90 days (depending on the nationality). Citizens of Canada, Australia, New Zealand and Japan are granted 30 days, while citizens of Israel are granted 90 days. This is subject to change; always check with your consulate prior to entry. If you want to stay longer, you have to extend your tourist card. This is accomplished at the immigration office in any major city with a letter requesting the extension; it's free for some nationalities – for others, it costs B$198 per 30-day extension. The maximum time travelers are permitted to stay in the country is 180 days in one year. Alternatively, you can apply for a visa. Visas are issued by Bolivian consular representatives, including those in neighboring South American countries. Bolivian visas can be complicated, so check ahead. Costs vary according to the consulate and the nationality of the applicant but hover around B$2500.

Overstayers can be fined B$14 per day (or more, depending on the nationality) – payable at the immigration office or airport – and may face ribbons of red tape at the border or airport when leaving the country.

In addition to a valid passport and visa, citizens of many communist, African, Middle Eastern and Asian countries require 'official permission' from the Bolivian Ministry of Foreign Affairs before a visa will be issued.

VOLUNTEERING

Animales SOS (Map p198; ☎02-230-8080; www.animalessos.org; Illampú 665, La Paz) An animal-welfare group caring for mistreated or abused stray animals.

Senda Verde (☎7472-2825; www.sendaverde.com; Yolosa) Just outside Coroico, this wildlife refuge has a two-week volunteer program.

Sustainable Bolivia (☎04-423-3783; www.sustainablebolivia.org; Julio Arauco Prado 230, Cochabamba) Cochabamba-based nonprofit organization with a variety of volunteering programs, both short- and long-term, through 22 local organizations.

WOMEN TRAVELERS

Despite the importance of women in Bolivian society and the elevation of females in public life (including a female president and women mayors), the machismo mindset still pervades in Bolivia. In the home, women rule, while external affairs are largely managed by men. As a female traveling alone, the mere fact that you appear to be unmarried and far from your home and family may cause you to appear suspiciously disreputable.

Bear in mind that modesty is expected of women in much of Spanish-speaking Latin America.

As a safety measure for a woman traveler, try to avoid arriving at a place at night. If you need to take a taxi at night, it's preferable to call for a radio taxi than to flag one down in the street. Note that during the period leading up to Carnaval and during the festivities, a woman traveling solo can be a popular target for water bombs, which can feel like quite a harassment or at least an annoyance.

Women should avoid hiking alone, and never walk alone at night.

WORK

For paid work, qualified English teachers can try the professionally run **Centro Boliviano-Americano** (CBA; Map p198; ☎02-243-0107; www.cba.edu.bo; Parque Zenón Iturralde 121, La Paz) in La Paz; there are also offices in other cities. New, unqualified teachers must forfeit two months' salary in return for their training. Better paying are private school positions teaching math, science or social studies. Accredited teachers can expect to earn up to US$500 per month for a full-time position.

Other travelers find work in gringo bars, tour operators or hostels. Keep in mind, however, that you are likely taking the job from a Bolivian by doing this.

Getting There & Away

A landlocked country, Bolivia has numerous entry/exit points, and you can get here by boat, bus, train, plane, foot and bike. Some options are easier and more accessible than others.

Flights, tours and rail tickets can be booked online at www.lonelyplanet.com/bookings.

ENTERING THE COUNTRY

If you have your documents in order and you are willing to answer a few questions about the aim of your visit, entry into Bolivia should be a breeze. If crossing at a smaller border post, you might well be asked to pay an 'exit fee.' Unless otherwise noted in the text, these fees are strictly unofficial. Note that Bolivian border times can be unreliable at best; always check with a *migración* (immigration) office in the nearest major town. Also, if you plan to cross the border outside the stated hours, or at a point where there is no border post, you can usually do so by obtaining an exit/entry stamp from the nearest *migración* office on departure/arrival.

AIR

There are only a few US and European airlines offering direct flights to Bolivia, so airfares are high. There are direct services to most major South American cities; the flights to/from Chile and Peru are the cheapest. Santa Cruz is an increasingly popular entry point from Western European hubs. Due to altitude-related costs, flying into La Paz is more expensive than into Santa Cruz. High season for most fares is from early June to late August, and mid-December to mid-February.

Bolivia's principal international airports are La Paz' El Alto International Airport (LPB), formerly known as John F Kennedy Memorial, and Santa Cruz's Viru-Viru International Airport (VVI).

Aerolíneas Argentinas (☎800-100-242; www.aerolineas.com.ar)

American Airlines (☎800-100-541; www.aa.com)

Avianca (☎1-866-998-3357; www.avianca.com)

BOA (☎901-105-010; www.boa.bo)

LAN Airlines (☎800-100-521; www.lan.com)

TAM (☎2-244-3442; www.tam.com.br)

LAND

Bus

Daily *flotas* (long-distance buses) link La Paz with Buenos Aires (Argentina) via Bermejo or

Yacuiba; Salta (Argentina) via Tupiza/Villazón; Corumbá (Brazil) via Quijarro; and Arica and Iquique (Chile) via Tambo Quemado. Increasingly popular is the crossing to San Pedro de Atacama (Chile) as a detour from Salar de Uyuni tours. The most popular overland route to and from Puno and Cuzco (Peru) is via Copacabana, but traveling via Desaguadero is quicker. Several bus services from Santa Cruz via Villamontes run the route to Asunción (Paraguay) on a daily basis.

Car & Motorcycle

Motoring in Bolivia is certain to try your patience (and mechanical skills!), but will be a trip of a lifetime. Most rental agencies accept national driver's licenses, but if you plan on doing a lot of motoring bring an International Driving Permit. For motorcycle and moped rentals, a passport is all that is normally required.

Train

Bolivia's only remaining international train route detours west from the Villazón–Oruro line at Uyuni. It passes through the Andes to the Chilean frontier at Avaroa/Ollagüe then descends precipitously to Calama, Chile. Other adventurous routes dead end at the Argentine frontier at Villazón/La Quiaca and Yacuiba/Pocitos and in the Brazilian Pantanal at Quijarro/Corumbá.

RIVER

The Brazilian and Peruvian Amazon frontiers are accessible via irregular riverboats.

Getting Around

Bolivian roads are getting better, with several new paved routes popping up in the last few years. Air transit is also easier, slightly more cost effective and more prevalent, especially in the lowlands. Most of Bolivia is covered by small bus, boat, train and airline companies. It still takes a while to get from place to place, and roadblocks (by protesters) and closed roads due to construction or landslides are not uncommon, nor are flooded roads and rivers with too little water to traverse.

AIR

Air travel in Bolivia is inexpensive and it's the quickest and most reliable means of reaching out-of-the-way places. It's also the only means of transportation that isn't washed out during the wet season. Although weather-related disruptions definitely occur, planes eventually get through even during summer flooding in northern Bolivia. Schedules tend to change frequently and cancellations are frequent, so plan ahead of time.

Amaszonas (☎901-105-500; www.amaszonas.com) Small planes fly from La Paz to Uyuni, Rurrenabaque, Trinidad, Santa Cruz and other lowland destinations. There are also services to Cuzco, Peru and Asunción, Paraguay.

Transporte Aéreos Militares (Map p194; ☎02-268-1111; www.tam.bo; Montes 738, Prado) Flights to Cobija, Cochabamba, Guayaramerín, Puerto Suárez, Riberalta, Rurrenabaque, Santa Cruz, Sucre, Tarija, Trinidad, Yacuiba, Ixiamas and Uyuni.

DEPARTURE TAX

Departure taxes vary on your airport and destination. All are payable at the airport (either at the counter or a separate window), and are not included in ticket prices. Domestic departure taxes range from B$11 to B$15. The international departure tax is US$25. Some airports also levy a municipal tax of up to B$7.

BOAT

There's no scheduled passenger service on the Amazon, so travelers almost invariably wind up on some sort of cargo vessel. The most popular routes are from Puerto Villarroel to Trinidad and Trinidad to Guayaramerín. There are also much less frequented routes from Rurrenabaque or Puerto Heath to Riberalta. Journeys are harder and harder to arrange these days.

BUS

Buses and their various iterations are the most popular form of Bolivian transportation. It's cheap and relatively safe but also quite uncomfortable and nerve-wracking at times. Long-distance bus lines in Bolivia are called *flotas*, large buses are known as *buses*, three-quarter (usually older) ones are called *micros*, and minibuses are just that. If looking for a bus terminal, ask for *la terminal terrestre* or *la terminal de buses*. Each terminal charges a small fee of a couple of bolivianos, which you pay to an agent upon boarding or when purchasing the ticket at the counter.

The only choices you'll have to make are on major, long-haul routes, where the better companies offer *coche* (or '*bus*'), *semi-cama* (half-sleepers with seats that recline a long way and have footrests) and *cama* (sleeper) services. The price can double for the sleeper service, but can be worth it. Tourist buses to major destinations like Copacabana and Uyuni cost double, but are safer and more comfortable.

Keep your valuables with you on the bus (not in the overhead bin). You should padlock your bag if it's going on top. Take warm clothes and even a sleeping bag for anything in the Altiplano, and expect transit times to vary up to three hours. Getting stranded overnight is not uncommon.

HITCHHIKING

Thanks to relatively easy access to *camiones* and a profusion of buses, hitchhiking isn't really necessary or popular in Bolivia. Still, it's not unknown and drivers of *movilidades* – cars, *camionetas* (pickup trucks), NGO vehicles, gas trucks and other vehicles – are usually happy to pick up passengers when they have room. Always ask the price, if any, before climbing aboard, even for short distances; if they do charge, it should amount to about half the bus fare for the equivalent distance.

LOCAL TRANSPORTATION

Micro, Minibus & Trufi

Micros (small buses or minibuses) are used in larger cities and serve as Bolivia's least expensive form of public transportation. They follow set routes, and the route numbers or letters are usually marked on a placard behind the windshield. This is often backed by a description of the route, including the streets that are followed to reach the end of the line. They can be hailed anywhere along their routes, though bus stops in some bigger cities are starting to pop up. When you want to disembark, move toward the front and tell the driver or assistant where you want them to stop.

Minibuses and *trufis* (which may be cars, vans or minibuses), also known as *colectivos*, are prevalent in the larger towns and cities, and follow set routes that are numbered and described on placards. They are always cheaper than taxis and nearly as convenient. As with *micros*, you can board or alight anywhere along their route.

Taxi

Urban taxis are relatively inexpensive. Few are equipped with meters but in most cities and towns there are standard per-person fares for short hauls. In some places taxis are collective and operate more like *trufis*, charging a set rate per person.

Radio taxis, on the other hand, always charge a set rate for up to four people; if you squeeze in five people, the fare increases by a small margin. When using taxis, try to have enough change to cover the fare; drivers often like to plead a lack of change in the hope that you'll give them the benefit of the difference. As a general rule, taxi drivers aren't tipped.

In larger cities, especially at night if traveling solo, it's advisable to go for a radio taxi instead of hailing one in the street; have your hotel or restaurant call for one.

TOURS

Tours are a convenient way to visit a site when you're short on time or motivation, and are frequently the easiest way to visit remote areas. They're also relatively cheap, but the cost will depend on the number of people in your group. Popular organized tours include those to Tiwanaku, Uyuni, and excursions to remote attractions such as the Cordillera Apolobamba. Arrange organized tours in La Paz or the town closest to the attraction you wish to visit.

There are scores of outfits offering trekking, mountain climbing and rainforest adventure packages. For climbing in the Cordilleras, operators offer customized expeditions including guides, transport, porters, cooks and equipment. Some also rent trekking equipment.

TRAIN

Since privatization in the mid-1990s, passenger rail services have been cut back. The western network operated by **Empresa Ferroviaria Andina** (FCA; www.fca.com.bo) runs from Oruro to Villazón on the Argentine border; a branch line runs southwest from Uyuni to Avaroa (on the Chilean border).

The east is operated by **Ferroviaria Oriental** (www.ferroviariaoriental.com), which has a line from Santa Cruz to the Brazilian frontier at Quijarro, where you cross to the Pantanal. An infrequently used service goes south from Santa Cruz to Yacuiba on the Argentine border, and there's a pilot project running tourist trains from La Paz to Tiwanaku.

Brazil

Includes ➡

Best Places to Eat

- ➡ Peixe Brasileiro (p383)
- ➡ Espírito Santa (p300)
- ➡ Aconchego Carioca (p315)
- ➡ Xapuri (p321)
- ➡ Estação das Docas (p392)

Best Beaches

- ➡ Baía de Sancho (p370)
- ➡ Praia do Espelho (p366)
- ➡ Praia Lopes Mendes (p308)
- ➡ Praia de Jericoacoara (p381)
- ➡ Baía dos Golfinhos (p374)

Why Go?

Brazil. The mere whisper of its name awakens the senses with promises of paradise: cerulean waters giving way to 7500km of sun-kissed sands; music-filled metropolises and idyllic tropical islands; enchanting colonial towns and rugged red-rock canyons; majestic waterfalls and crystal-clear rivers; lush rainforests and dense jungles; gorgeous people and the Beautiful Game. It's all here in spectacular cinematic overload.

The country has enthralled for centuries for good reason: every bit of the hyperbole is unequivocally true. It all climaxes in Brazil's most famous celebration, Carnaval, which storms through the country's cities and towns like a host of blitz of hip-shaking samba, dazzling costumes and carefree lust for life, but Brazilians hardly check their passion for revelry at Lent. The Brazilian Way – *O Jeito Brasileiro* – embodies the country's lust for life, and will seize you in its sensational clutches every day of the year.

When to Go

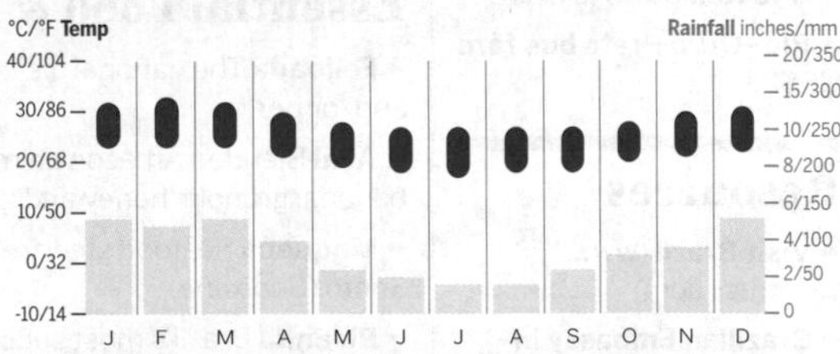

Dec–Feb Summer sizzles in the lead-up to Carnaval. Rainy season in the Amazon.

Sep–Nov Crowds dispel as spring brings serenity and pleasant temperatures.

Mar–Jun Low season offers good-value travel, moderate temperatures and a sunny Northeast.

AT A GLANCE

- **Currency** Real (R$)
- **Languages** Portuguese and 180 indigenous languages
- **Money** ATMs widespread, credit cards widely accepted
- **Visas** Required for Americans, Australians and various others

Fast Facts

- **Area** 8,456,510 sq km
- **Capital** Brasília
- **Country code** 55
- **Emergency** 192

Exchange Rates

Australia	A$1	R$2.76
Canada	C$1	R$2.87
Euro	€1	R$4.06
New Zealand	NZ$1	R$2.52
UK	£1	R$5.77
US	US$1	R$3.84

Set Your Budget

- **Rio budget sleeps** US$15 (dorm) to US$45 (double)
- **Pay-by-weight lunch** US$5 to US$9
- **Cocktail** US$3 to US$8
- **Rio–Ouro Prêto bus fare** US$28

Resources

- **Visit Brazil** (www.visitbrasil.com)
- **Brazilian Embassy in London** (www.brazil.org.uk)
- **Rio Times** (www.riotimesonline.com)
- **Gringoes** (www.gringoes.com)

Connections

Brazil shares land borders with every country on the continent except Chile and Ecuador. The most common land crossings for travelers include the epic Amazon river crossing from Belém or Manaus to Leticia (Colombia) or Iquitos (Peru); a trek through the Pantanal, the world's largest wetlands, and out through Corumbá into Bolivia via the daily train link with Santa Cruz; and the waterlogged triborder linking Iguaçu Falls with Ciudad del Este, Paraguay and Puerto Iguazú, Argentina. By air, you can reach most South American capitals directly, including Asunción, Buenos Aires, Caracas, Lima, Montevideo and Santiago (as well as Santa Cruz, Bolivia); and common overland bus routes reach Asunción, Buenos Aires, Montevideo, Santiago and Santa Cruz, Bolivia.

ITINERARIES

Two Weeks

Get into the thick of it in the Cidade Maravilhosa (Marvelous City), as Rio de Janeiro is nicknamed, taking in the sights, sounds, seductions and samba of South America's most stunning city. Spend a view days dazzled by nature in two of the world's most important ecological hot spots, the Amazon and the Pantanal; get up close to the world's most stupendous waterfall, Iguaçu Falls.

One Month

Follow the two-week itinerary, but supplement Brazil's greatest hits with visits to some of the most cinematic destinations: beautifully preserved colonial towns in Rio (Paraty) and Minas Gerais (Ouro Prêto and Tiradentes); postcard-perfect beaches in Fernando de Noronha, Bahia, or Florianópolis; miraculous dune desertscapes in Parque Nacional dos Lençóis Maranhenses; and the unique aquatic wonderland of Bonito.

Essential Food & Drink

- **Feijoada** The national dish: a savory stew of beans, beef and/or pork
- **Açaí** Blended Amazon palm berries, usually mixed with banana, granola, honey and guaraná syrup
- **Moqueca** Seafood stew from Bahia (*Bahiana*) or Espírito Santo (*Capixaba*)
- **Picanha** Brazil's most succulent meat cut, roughly translated as 'rump cap'
- **Pão de Queijo** Ubiquitous cheese bread made with *manioc* flour, milk, eggs and cheese
- **Cachaça** Rum-like liquor made from fermented sugarcane juice
- **Caipirinha** The national cocktail: *cachaça*, limes & sugar

RIO DE JANEIRO

0XX21 / POP 6.4 MILLION

Flanked by gorgeous mountains, white-sand beaches and verdant rainforests fronting deep-blue sea, Rio de Janeiro occupies one of the most spectacular settings of any metropolis in the world. Tack on one of the sexiest populations on the planet and you have an intoxicating tropical cocktail that leaves visitors punch-drunk on paradise.

Rio's residents, known as *cariocas*, have perfected the art of living well. From the world-famous beaches of Copacabana and Ipanema to the tops of scenic outlooks of Corcovado and Pão de Açúcar to the dance halls, bars and open-air cafes that proliferate the city, *cariocas* live for the moment without a care in the world. This idea of paradise has enchanted visitors for centuries, and there are dozens of ways to be seduced. You can surf great breaks off Prainha, hike through Tijuca's rainforests, sail across Guanabára, dance the night away in Lapa or just people-watch on Ipanema Beach.

While Rio has its share of serious problems, there are plenty of residents (expats included) who wouldn't dream of relocating. It's no coincidence that Christo himself stands, arms outstretched across the city.

History

The city earned its name from early Portuguese explorers, who entered the huge bay, Baía de Guanabara (Guanabara Bay), in January 1502, and believing it a river, named it Rio de Janeiro (January River). The French were actually the first settlers along the bay, establishing the colony of Antarctic France in 1555. The Portuguese, fearing that the French would take over, gave them the boot in 1567 and remained from then on. Thanks to sugar plantations and the slave trade, their new colony developed into an important settlement and grew substantially during the Minas Gerais gold rush of the 18th century. In 1763, with a population of 50,000, Rio replaced Salvador as the colonial capital. By 1900, after a coffee boom, heavy immigration from Europe and internal migration by ex-slaves, Rio had 800,000 inhabitants.

The 1920s to 1950s were Rio's golden age, when it became an exotic destination for international high society. But by the time the capital was moved to Brasília in 1960, Rio was already grappling with problems that continue to this day. Immigrants poured into favelas (slums; informal communities) from poverty-stricken areas of the country, swelling the number of urban poor and increasing the chasm between the haves and have-nots.

Despite its problems though, the city has enjoyed a near-unbelievable cornucopia of good fortune of late, being chosen as the championship host city for the 2014 FIFA World Cup, the host of the 2016 Summer Olympic Games – the first South American city to ever host the most important event in sports – *and* it earned Unesco World Heritage status in 2012.

While violence and poverty still remain worrying problems in Rio, things have improved in the past decade. The favela pacification program has brought down the level of violence, while improving sanitation and transport in some favelas. In the build-up to the 2014 World Cup and 2016 Summer Olympics, large investments have been used to revitalize Rio's waterfront port, vastly expand its metro system and create new museums and cultural spaces around town.

Sights

In addition to sand, sky and sea, Rio has dozens of attractions: historic neighborhoods, colorful museums, colonial churches, picturesque gardens and spectacular overlooks.

Ipanema, Leblon & Gávea

Boasting magnificent beaches and pleasant tree-lined streets, Ipanema and Leblon are Rio's loveliest destinations and the favored residence for young, beautiful (and wealthy) *cariocas*. Microcultures dominate the beach, often centering around *postos* (elevated stands where lifeguards sit). **Posto 9**, off Vinícius de Moraes, is the gathering spot for the beauty crowd; nearby, in front of Farme de Amoedo, is the **gay section** (Map p296); **Posto 11** in Leblon attracts families.

Gávea is an affluent residential neighborhood known for its bohemian tendencies.

Copacabana & Leme

The gorgeous curving **beach** (Map p292; Av Atlântica) of Copacabana stretches 4.5km from end to end, and pulses with an energy unknown elsewhere. Dozens of restaurants and bars line Av Atlântica, facing the sea, with tourists, prostitutes and favela kids all a part of the wild people-parade.

Museu do Imagem e Som MUSEUM
(Map p292; www.mis.rj.gov.br; Av Atlântica, near Miguel Lemos) Copacabana finally has an outstanding rainy-day attraction, thanks to the

Brazil Highlights

❶ Fall under the seductive spell of **Rio de Janeiro** (p283) amid the whirlwind of wild samba clubs, sizzling sands, soaring peaks and sexy sundowns.

❷ Feel the breath of Mother Nature's ferocious roar at the jaw-dropping waterfalls of **Iguaçu Falls** (p336).

❸ Dig into some of the world's most pristine sands in **Fernando de Noronha** (p370).

❹ Spying pointy-toothed piranhas and glowing caiman eyes while cruising the mighty **Amazon** (p400).

❺ Meander along cobblestones in cinematic colonial towns such as **Ouro Prêto** (p322), **Paraty** (p309) and **Tiradentes** (p325).

❻ Follow delirious drumbeats through the colonial center during regular evening street parties in **Salvador** (p352).

❼ Shutter-stalk spectacular animals in the **Pantanal** (p343) followed by a dip into the nearby aquatic wonderland of **Bonito** (p350).

❽ Hike surreal landscapes in dramatic national parks like **Lençóis Maranhenses** (p386) and **Chapada Diamantina** (p360).

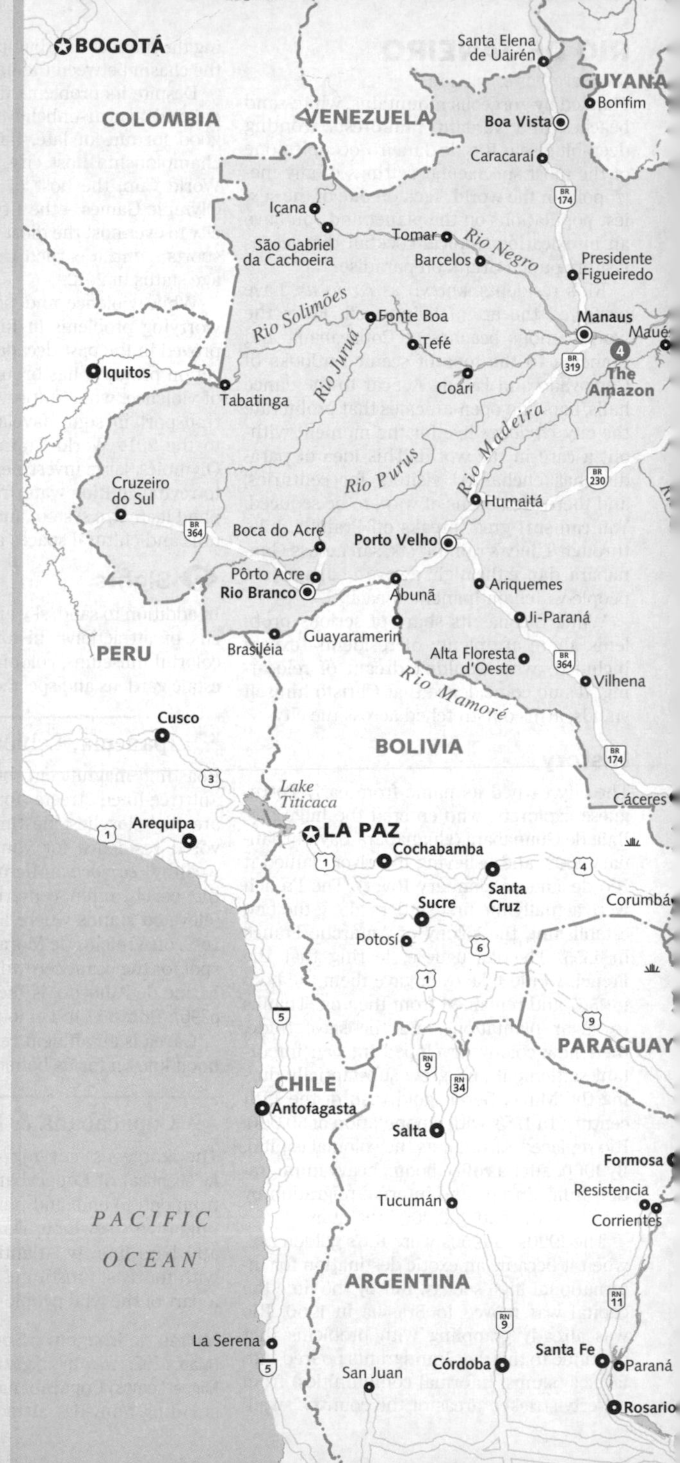

ATLANTIC OCEAN
0 500 km
0 300 miles
SURINAME
FRENCH GUIANA (France)
Cayenne
Oiapoque
Vila Velha
Amapá
Porto Grande
Macapá
Ilha Caviana
Salinópolis
Ilha de Marajó
Belém
Abaetetuba
Rio Amazonas
Santarém
Altamira
Itaituba
Miritituba
Carioca
Tucuruí
São Luís
Parque Nacional dos Lençóis Maranhenses
8
Parnaíba
Jericoacoara
Camocim
Sobral
Fortaleza
Santa Luzia
Canoa Quebrada
Mossoró
Fernando de Noronha
3
Caxias
Teresina
Imperatriz
Marabá
Carajás
Tocantinópolis
Araguaína
Carolina
Natal
Sousa
Picos
Campina Grande
João Pessoa
Olinda
Caruaru
Recife
Maceió
Juazeiro
Conceição do Araguaia
Rio Xingu
Rio Tocantins
Teles Pires
Alta Floresta
Palmas
Santa Teresinha
São Felix do Araguaia
Xique-Xique
Rio São Francisco
Aracaju
Parque Nacional da Chapada Diamintina
8
Feira de Santana
6
Salvador
Valença
Bom Jesus da Lapa
Porangatu
Rio Araguaia
Vitória da Conquista
Ilhéus
Cuiabá
Barra do Garças
BRASÍLIA
Rodonópolis
Goiânia
Montes Claros
Porto Seguro
Itamaraju
Pôrto Joffre
Jataí
Patos de Minas
Teófilo Otoni
Coxim
Uberlândia
Governador Valadares
Belo Horizonte
Três Lagoas
Ouro Prêto
5
Vitória
Pantanal
7
Campo Grande
São José do Rio Preto
Tiradentes
5
Barbacena
7
Bonito
Presidente Prudente
Bauru
Limeira
Campos dos Goitacazes
Ponta Porã
Paraty
5
1
Rio de Janeiro
Maringá
Londrina
São Paulo
Registro
ASUNCIÓN
Cascavel
Curitiba
Paranaguá
Foz do Iguaçu
2
Iguaçu Falls
Joinville
Rio Pelotas
Posadas
Florianópolis
Lages
Cruz Alta
Caxias do Sul
Uruguaiana
Porto Alegre
Rivera
Salto
Pelotas
Río Grande
Paysandú
URUGUAY
Chuí
BR 156
BR 316
BR 010
BR 230
BR 222
BR 020
BR 116
BR 304
BR 316
BR 343
BR 232
BR 163
BR 080
BR 153
BR 135
BR 407
BR 101
BR 324
BR 242
BR 020
BR 158
BR 116
BR 365
BR 116
BR 364
BR 060
BR 050
BR 040
BR 163
BR 262
BR 153
BR 267
BR 101
BR 369
BR 376
BR 277
BR 116
BR 285
BR 290
BR 392

stunning Museum of Image and Sound, due to open in September 2016. The building, designed by celebrated New York firm Diller Scofidio + Renfro (who also designed NYC's High Line), will feature high-tech interactive galleries devoted to the great Brazilian music and film that has played such a pivotal role in the nation's culture. Performance halls and an open-air rooftop amphitheater (for outdoor films) are other highlights.

Santa Teresa & Lapa

Set on a hill overlooking the city, Santa Teresa, with its cobbled streets and aging mansions, retains the charm of days past and is Rio's most atmospheric neighborhood. Currently the residence of a new generation of artists and bohemians, Santa Teresa has colorful restaurants and bars, and a lively weekend scene around Largo do Guimarães and Largo das Neves.

★Escadaria Selarón LANDMARK
(Map p298; stairway btwn Joaquim Silva in Lapa & Pinto Martins in Santa Teresa) One of Rio's best loved attractions, the steps leading up from Rua Joaquim Silva became a work of art when Chilean-born artist Jorge Selarón decided to cover the steps with colorful

Rio de Janeiro

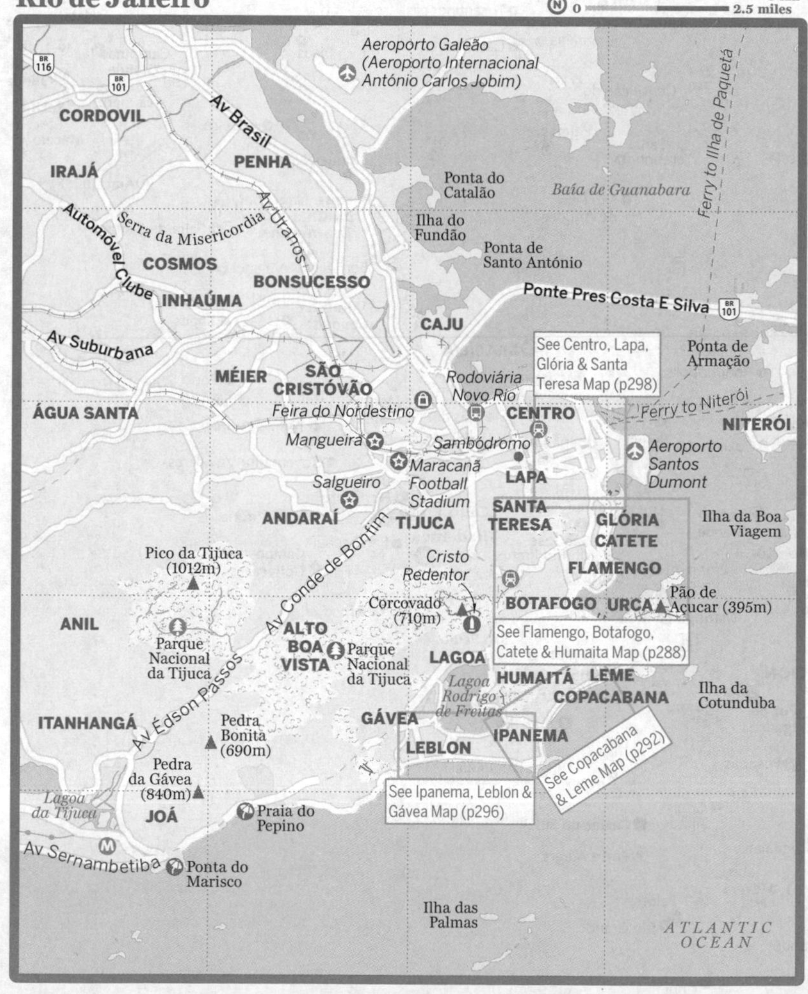

WHAT'S NEW IN RIO

Praça Mauá

Rio's once derelict port has seen a dramatic makeover. The Praça Mauá is now home to several stunning new museums, including the beautiful **Museu do Amanhã** (Map p298; www.museudoamanha.org.br; Rodrigues Alves 1) designed by Santiago Calatrava.

Botafogo & Humaitá

All eyes are on these twin neighborhoods north of Copacabana. Some of the city's best new restaurants have opened here, along with atmospheric gastropubs, creative art spaces and buzzing nightspots such as **Cabaret Lounge** (Map p288; ☎2226-4126; www.cabaretlounge.com.br; Voluntários da Pátria 449, Humaitá; cover R$15-40; ⊙7pm-3am Tue-Thu, 9pm-5am Fri & Sat).

Metro Expansion

In preparation for the 2016 Summer Olympics, six new metro stations are opening at long last. The new *linha* 4 connects Ipanema with Jardim Oceânico in Barra via Leblon, Gávea and São Conrado.

Light Rail

A new light rail called the **VLT** (www.vltcarioca.com.br) provides efficient, speedy transport around downtown. This is a great way to reach Praça Mauá and to travel east–west between Praça Tiradentes and Praça XV (Quinze) de Novembro.

Favela Chic

There's a lot happening in Rio's favelas (slums, informal communities). You can find great hostels, lively bars and first-rate restaurants in the informal communities near the Zona Sul – all of which make fine use of those fantastic hilltop views.

Microbrews

The craft-beer scene has exploded in Rio, and there's now a wide range of brewpubs across the city, such as **As Melhores Cervejas do Mundo** (Map p292; Ronald de Carvalho 154, Copacabana; ⊙3-11pm Mon-Sat). You can sample locally made beers as well as unique brews from across Brazil, including from brewers who use fruits and spices from the Amazon.

Copacabana on the Rise

A renaissance is under way in this seaside neighborhood, with the arrival of creative new restaurants, microbrew-loving bars and a fantastic music and film museum, **Museu do Imagem e Som** (p283).

The Bonde Returns

The quaint yellow **Bonde streetcar** (p290) has returned to the rails after a tragic accident in 2011, meaning you can once again make the scenic journey from Centro to Santa Teresa across the Arcos da Lapa.

Bikes

New bike lanes have been added to the city, with another 33km on the way. Rio also has a bike-share program – **Bike Rio** (☎4003-6054; www.mobilicidade.com.br/bikerio.asp) – though you'll need a local number to use it.

Foodie City

An infusion of globally minded new restaurants are helping to reshape the dining scene. New arrivals include authentic Mexican, Peruvian and Spanish eateries, along with places that showcase Brazilian recipes in inventive new ways.

Flamengo, Botafogo, Catete & Humaitá

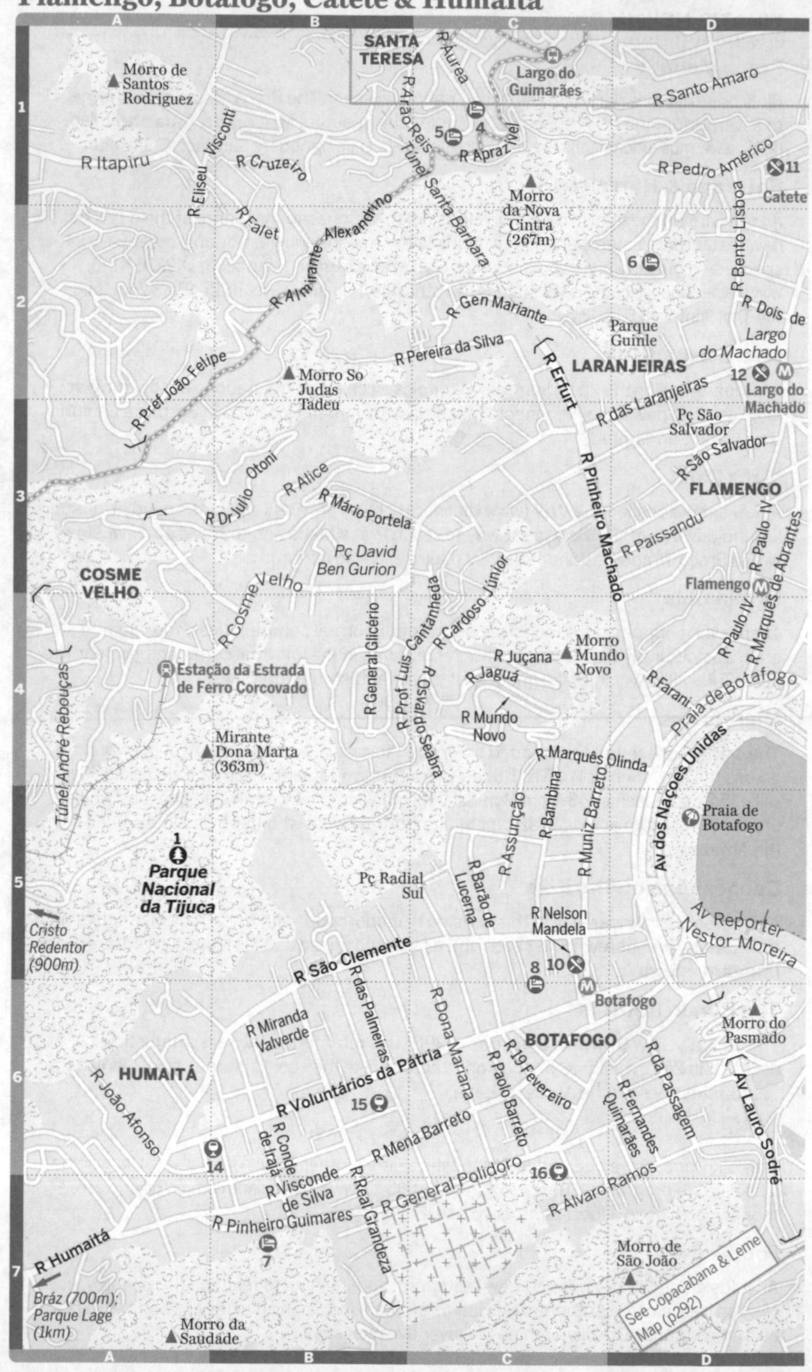

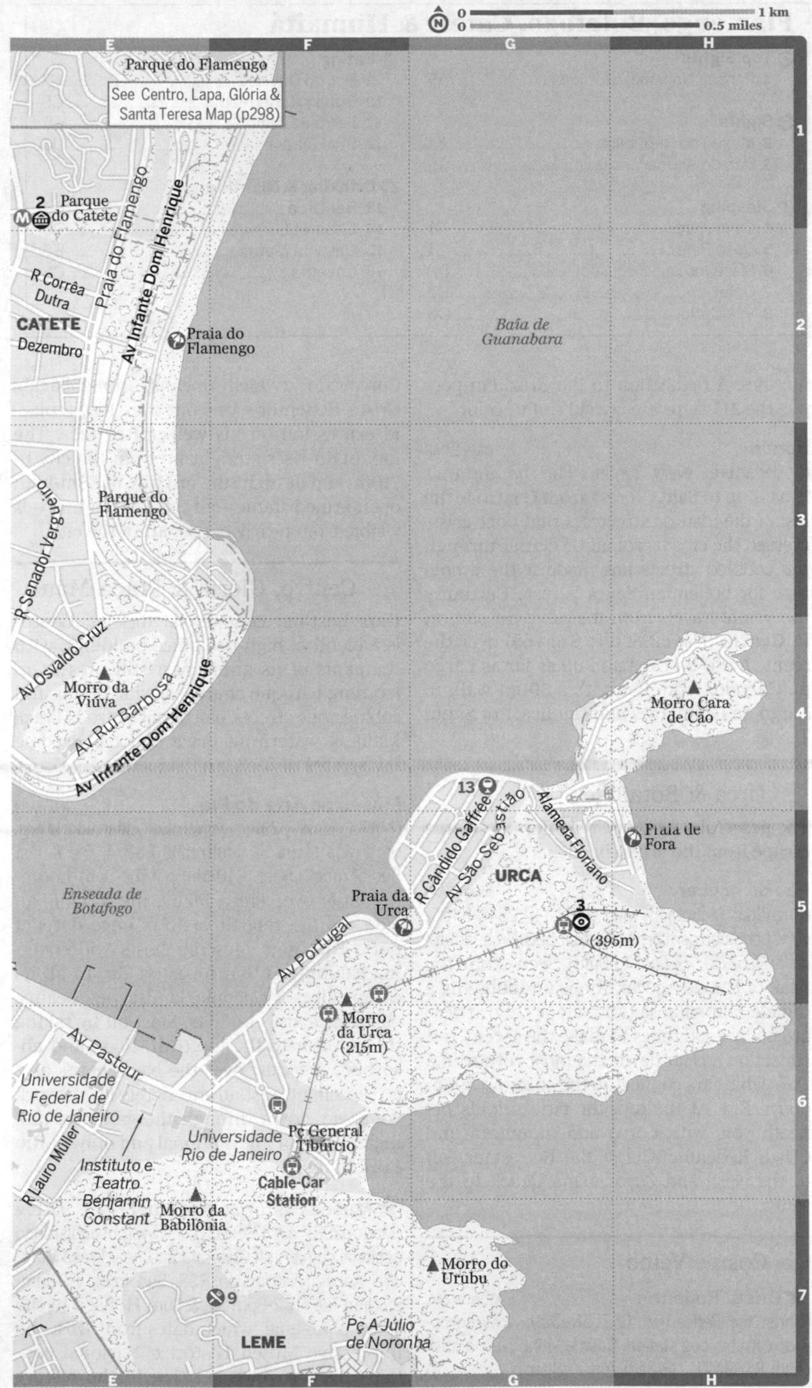
0 1 km
0 0.5 miles
Parque do Flamengo
See Centro, Lapa, Glória & Santa Teresa Map (p298)
2 Parque do Catete
Praia do Flamengo
Av Infante Dom Henrique
R Corrêa Dutra
CATETE
Dezembro
Praia do Flamengo
Baía de Guanabara
Parque do Flamengo
R Senador Vergueiro
Av Osvaldo Cruz
Morro da Viúva
Av Rui Barbosa
Av Infante Dom Henrique
Morro Cara de Cão
13
R Cândido Gaffrée
Av São Sebastião
Alameda Floriano
Praia de Fora
URCA
Enseada de Botafogo
Praia da Urca
3
(395m)
Av Portugal
Morro da Urca (215m)
Av Pasteur
Universidade Federal de Rio de Janeiro
Universidade Rio de Janeiro
Pç General Tibúrcio
R Lauro Müller
Instituto e Teatro Benjamin Constant
Morro da Babilônia
Cable-Car Station
Morro do Urubu
9
LEME
Pç A Júlio de Noronha

Flamengo, Botafogo, Catete & Humaitá

Top Sights
1 Parque Nacional da Tijuca A5

Sights
2 Museu da República E1
3 Pão de Açúcar G5

Sleeping
4 Casa Áurea C1
5 Casa Beleza C1
6 Maze Inn D2
7 Oztel B7
8 Vila Carioca C6

Eating
9 Bar do David F7
10 Boua Kitchen & Bar C5
11 Ferro e Farinha..D1
12 Sírio Libaneza D2

Drinking & Nightlife
13 Bar Urca...G4
14 Cabaret Lounge B6
15 Casa da Matriz B6
16 Caverna.. C6

mosaics. A dedication to the Brazilian people, the 215 steps are a vivid riot of color.

Bonde CABLE CAR
(departures every 30min) The *bonde* that travels up to Santa Teresa from Centro is the last of the historic streetcars that once crisscrossed the city. Its romantic clatter through the cobbled streets has made it the archetype for bohemian Santa Teresa. Currently the *bonde* travels from the cable-car station in **Centro** (Map p298; Lélio Gama 65) over the scenic Arcos da Lapa and up as far as Largo do Curvelo. From there it's a 500m walk to Largo do Guimarães and the heart of Santa Teresa.

Urca & Botafogo

The peaceful streets of Urca offer a welcome escape from the urban bustle.

Pão de Açúcar MOUNTAIN
(Sugarloaf Mountain; Map p288; 2546-8400; www.bondinho.com.br; Av Pasteur 520, Urca; adult/child R$62/31; 8am-7:50pm) Seen from the peak of Pão de Açúcar, Rio is undoubtedly a Cidade Maravilhosa (Marvelous City). There are many good times to make the ascent, but sunset on a clear day is the most rewarding. Two cable cars connect to the summit, 396m above Rio. At the top, the city unfolds beneath you, with Corcovado mountain and Cristo Redentor (Christ the Redeemer) off to the west, and Copacabana Beach to the south.

Cosme Velho

★**Cristo Redentor** MONUMENT
(Christ the Redeemer; 2558-1329; www.corcovado.com.br; cog station, Cosme Velho 513; adult/child R$62/40; 8am-7pm) Standing atop Corcovado (which means 'hunchback'), Cristo Redentor gazes out over Rio, a placid expression on his well-crafted face. The mountain rises straight up from the city to 710m, and at night the brightly lit 38m-high open-armed statue – all 1145 tons of him – is visible from nearly every part of the city.

Centro, Glória & Praça Mauá

Rio's bustling commercial district, Centro is a blend of high-rise office buildings, with remnants of its grand past still present in looming baroque churches, wide plazas and cobblestone streets. North of Centro is Praça Mauá, a waterfront plaza that has become the symbol of Rio's renaissance.

Museu de Arte do Rio MUSEUM
(MAR; Map p298; www.museudeartedorio.org.br; Praça Mauá 5; adult/child R$8/4, Tue & last Sun of month free; 10am-6pm Tue-Sun) Looming large over Praça Mauá, the MAR is an icon for the rebirth of Rio's once derelict port. The huge museum hosts wide-ranging exhibitions that focus on Rio in all its complexity – its people, landscapes, beauty, challenges and conflicts. Start off by taking the elevator to the top (6th) floor, and absorbing the view over the bay. There's also an excellent restaurant here. Then work your way down through the galleries, taking in a mix of international and only-in-Rio exhibitions.

★**Museu Histórico Nacional** MUSEUM
(Map p298; 3299-0311; www.museuhistoriconacional.com.br; off General Justo, near Praça Marechal Âncora; admission R$8, Sun free; 10am-5:30pm Tue-Fri, 2-6pm Sat & Sun) Housed in the colonial arsenal, which dates from 1764, the impressive Museu Histórico Nacional contains historic relics relating to the history

of Brazil from its founding to its early days as a republic. Highlights include gilded imperial coaches, the throne of Dom Pedro II, massive oil paintings depicting the horrific war with Paraguay and a full-sized model of a colonial pharmacy.

Catete & Flamengo

Museu da República MUSEUM

(Map p288; ☎2127-0324; museudarepublica.museus.gov.br; Rua do Catete 153; admission R$6, Wed & Sun free; ⊙10am-5pm Tue-Fri, 2-6pm Sat & Sun) The Museu da República, located in the **Palácio do Catete**, has been wonderfully restored. Built between 1858 and 1866 and easily distinguished by the bronze condors on its eaves, the palace was home to the president of Brazil from 1896 until 1954, when President Getúlio Vargas committed suicide here. The museum has a good collection of art and artifacts from the Republican period, and also houses a good lunch restaurant, an art-house cinema and a bookstore.

Jardim Botânico & Lagoa

Jardim Botânico GARDENS

(☎3874-1808; www.jbrj.gov.br; Jardim Botânico 920; admission R$9; ⊙9am-5pm) This exotic 137-hectare garden, with more than 8000 plant species, was designed by order of the Prince Regent Dom João (later to become Dom João VI) in 1808. The garden is quiet and serene on weekdays and blossoms with families on weekends. Highlights of a visit here include the row of palms (planted when the garden first opened), the Amazonas section, the lake containing the huge Vitória Régia water lilies and the enclosed **orquidário**, home to 600 species of orchids.

★**Lagoa Rodrigo de Freitas** LAKE

(Map p296) One of the city's most picturesque spots, Lagoa Rodrigo de Freitas is encircled by a 7.2km walking and cycling path. Bikes are available for hire from stands along the east side of the lake, as are paddle boats. For those who prefer *caipirinhas* (cocktail made from limes, sugar, ice and high-proof sugarcane alcohol) to plastic swan boats, the **lakeside kiosks** on either side of the lake offer alfresco food and drinks, sometimes accompanied by live music on warm nights.

Parque Lage PARK

(☎3257-1800, guided visits 3257-18721; www.eavparquelage.rj.gov.br; Jardim Botânico 414; ⊙9am-7pm) This beautiful park lies at the base of Floresta da Tijuca, about 1km from Jardim Botânico. It has English-style gardens, little lakes, and a mansion that houses the **Escola de Artes Visuais** (School of Visual Arts), which hosts free art exhibitions and occasional performances. The park is a tranquil place and the cafe here offers a fine setting for a coffee or a meal.

Parque Nacional da Tijuca

Lush trails through tropical rainforest lie just 15 minutes from concrete Copacabana. The 120-sq-km refuge of the **Parque Nacional da Tijuca** (Map p288; www.parquedatijuca.com.br; ⊙8am-5pm), a remnant of the Atlantic rainforest, has excellently marked trails over small peaks and past waterfalls.

It's best to go by taxi or organized tour.

Activities

The fantastic hang glide off 510m Pedra Bonita, one of the giant granite slabs towering over the city, is a highlight of any trip to Brazil.

Delta Flight in Rio HANG GLIDING

(☎3322-5750, 99693-8800; www.riobyjeep.com/deltaflight) With more than 20 years' experience, Ricardo Hamond has earned a solid reputation as a safety-conscious and extremely professional pilot; he has flown more than 12,000 tandem flights.

Cook in Rio COOKING COURSE

(Map p292; ☎8761-3653; www.cookinrio.com; 2nd fl, Belfort Roxo 161; per person US$75) Run by Simone Almeida, Cook in Rio is a hands-on one-day course that shows you how to prepare either *moqueca* (seafood stew) or *feijoada* (black bean and pork stew). You'll also learn how to make other sides and drinks including *aipim frito* (fried cassava slices), a perfect pot of rice, dessert and a masterful *caipirinha* (the secret is in the slicing of the lime).

Tours

Brazil Expedition TOUR

(☎99998-2907; www.brazilexpedition.com; city tour R$120) The friendly English-speaking guides run a variety of traditional tours around Rio, including trips to Cristo Redentor, nightlife outings to samba schools, game-day trips to Maracanã football stadium, street-art tours and *favela* tours.

Copacabana & Leme

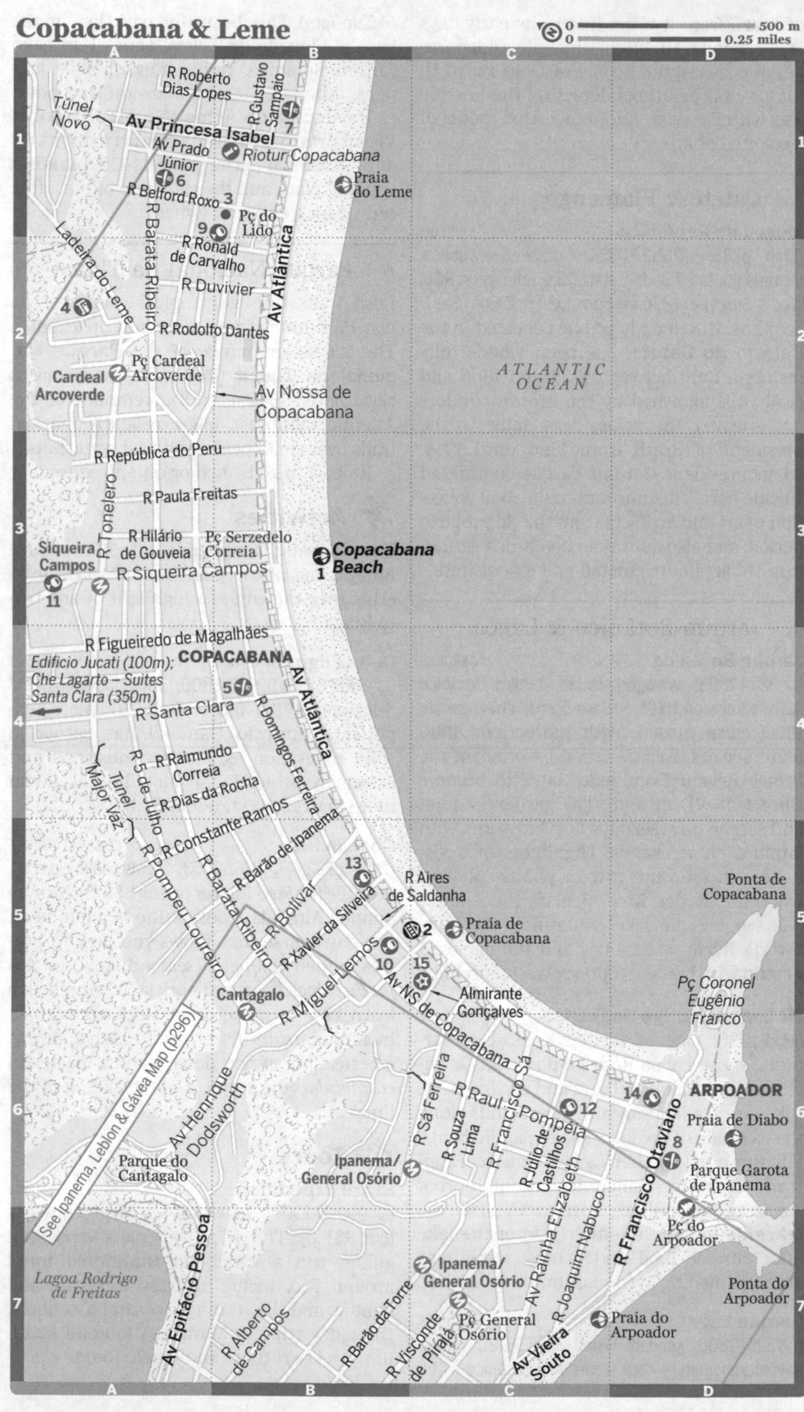

Jungle Me HIKING, GUIDED TOUR

(☎4105-7533; www.jungleme.com.br; tours from R$150) This top-notch outfit offers excellent hiking tours through Parque Nacional da Tijuca, led by knowledgeable guides. The Peaks & Waterfalls tour offers challenging walks up several escarpments that offer stunning views of Rio, followed by a refreshing dip in a waterfall. The Wild Beaches of Rio tour takes you on a hike between scenic beaches in Rio's little-visited western suburbs.

Rio by Bike BICYCLE TOUR

(☎96871-8933; www.riobybike.com; tours R$100-125) Two Dutch journalists operate this biking outfit, and their excellent pedaling tours combine a mix of scenery and cultural insight. It's a great way to get an overview of the city, with guides pointing out key landmarks and describing key events that have shaped Rio. Tours last three to four hours and travel mostly along bike lanes separated from traffic.

Eat Rio Food Tours WALKING TOUR

(www.eatrio.net; per person US$90) On these highly recommended small-group tours, you'll visit markets, snack bars and other foodie hot spots to taste a wide range of exotic fruits, juices and street food little known outside of Brazil. The English-speaking guides are excellent and provide culinary as well as cultural insight. The cost of the tour includes all foods and snacks, including a big meal at the end.

Paulo Amendoim CULTURAL TOUR

(☎99747-6860; http://favelatourrio.com; tour R$75) Recommended guide Paulo Amendoim is the former president of Rocinha's residents association. He seems to know everyone in the favela, and leads a warm and personalized tour that helps visitors see beyond the gross stereotypes.

Free Walker Tours WALKING TOUR

(☎97101-3352; www.freewalkertours.com) This well-organized outfit runs a free walking tour that takes in a bit of history and culture in downtown Rio. You'll visit the Travessa do Comércio, Praça XV, Cinelândia, the Arcos da Lapa and the Selarón steps, among other places. Although it's free, the guide asks for tips at the end: by our reckoning, R$50 seems fair for the insightful three-hour walk.

Festivals & Events

One of the world's biggest and wildest parties, **Carnaval** in all its colorful, hedonistic bacchanalia is virtually synonymous with Rio. Although Carnaval is ostensibly just five days of revelry (Friday to Tuesday preceding Ash Wednesday), *cariocas* begin partying months in advance. The parade through the Sambódromo (samba parade ground), featuring elaborate floats flanked by thousands of pounding drummers and twirling dancers, is the culmination of the festivities, though the real action is at the parties about town.

Nightclubs and bars throw special costumed events. There are also free live concerts throughout the city (Largo do Machado, Arcos do Lapa, Praça General Osório), while those seeking a bit of decadence can head to various balls about town. *Bandas,* also called *blocos,* are one of the best ways to celebrate *carioca*-style. These consist of a procession of drummers and vocalists followed by anyone who wants to dance through the streets of Rio. Check Riotur (p304) for times and locations. *Blocos* in Santa Teresa and Ipanema are highly recommended.

Copacabana & Leme

Top Sights
1 Copacabana Beach ... B3

Sights
2 Museu do Imagem e Som ... C5

Activities, Courses & Tours
3 Cook in Rio ... B1

Sleeping
4 Cabana Copa ... A2

Eating
5 Bibi Sucos ... B4
6 Galeto Sat's ... A1
7 Joaquina ... B1
8 TT Burger ... D6

Drinking & Nightlife
9 As Melhores Cervejas do Mundo ... B1
10 Escondido ... B5
11 Fosfobox ... A3
12 Le Boy ... C6
13 Mais Que Nada ... B5
14 TV Bar ... D6

Entertainment
15 Bip Bip ... C5

The spectacular main parade takes place in the **Sambódromo** (www.sambadrome.com; Marques do Sapuçai) near Praça Onze metro station. Before an exuberant crowd of some 30,000, each of 12 samba schools has its hour to dazzle the audience. Top schools compete on Carnaval Sunday and Monday (February 26 and 27 in 2017, February 11 and 12 in 2018). The safest way of reaching the Sambódromo is by taxi or metro, which runs round the clock during Carnaval.

Liesa (Map p298; ☎3213-5151; http://liesa.globo.com; Av Rio Branco 4, Centro; ⏰10am-4pm Mon-Fri Sep-Carnaval), the official samba-school league, begins selling tickets in December or January, most of which get immediately snatched up by travel agencies then later resold at higher prices. Check with Riotur about where you can get them, as the official outlet can vary from year to year. At face value, tickets run R$140 to R$500. By Carnaval weekend, most tickets are sold out, but there are lots of scalpers. If you buy a ticket from a scalper (no need to worry about looking for them – they'll find you!), make sure you get both the plastic ticket with the magnetic strip and the ticket showing the seat number. The tickets for different days are color-coded, so double-check the date as well.

If you haven't purchased a ticket but still want to go, during Carnaval you can show up at the Sambódromo at around midnight. This is when you can get grandstand tickets for about R$50 from scalpers outside the gate. Make sure you check which sector your ticket is for. Most ticket sellers will try to pawn off their worst seats.

Sleeping

Zona Sul is the chic Rio zone where all the tourist action happens. Ipanema and Leblon are the most appealing Zona Sul neighborhoods to base yourself. The historic hillside bohemian quarter of Santa Teresa is Rio's most charming *bairro* (suburb of Brazil). Other northern neighborhoods along the metro line (Botafogo, Flamengo and Catete) generally have cheaper options than the beachside southern neighborhoods.

Ipanema, Leblon & Gávea

Rio Hostel – Ipanema HOSTEL $

(Map p296; ☎2287-2928; www.riohostelipanema.com; Casa 1, Canning 18, Ipanema; dm/d from R$60/180; @📶) This friendly hostel is in a small villa on a peaceful stretch of Ipanema. A mix of travelers stay here, enjoying the clean rooms, the airy top-floor deck with hammocks and the small front veranda. The location is fantastic: it's less than 10 minutes' walk to either Ipanema or Copacabana Beach. The entrance is unsigned, behind a gate, so make sure the hostel knows you're coming.

Lemon Spirit Hostel HOSTEL $

(Map p296; ☎2294-1853; www.lemonspirit.com; Cupertino Durão 56, Leblon; dm R$70-90; ❄@📶) One of Leblon's only hostels, Lemon Spirit boasts an excellent location one block from the beach. The dorm rooms (four to six beds in each) are clean and simple without much decor. There's a tiny courtyard in front, and the attractive lobby bar is a good place to meet other travelers over *caipirinhas*.

FAVELA CHIC

Favela (slum, informal community) sleeps are nothing new – intrepid travelers have been venturing into Rio's urban mazes for nearly a decade – but as more and more of Rio's *favelas* are pacified, hostels and *pousadas* (guesthouses) are popping up faster than the rudimentary constructions which make up the *favelas* themselves.

Maze Inn (Map p288; ☎2558-5547; www.jazzrio.com; Casa 66, Tavares Bastos 414, Catete; dm R$90, s/d from R$175/225) Owned by English renaissance man Bob Nadkarni, this *pousada* and jazz house in Tavares Bastos *favela* is almost legendary. Jazz nights are the 1st and 3rd Friday of every month (R$30).

Vidigalbergue (☎3114-8025; www.vidigalbergue.com.br; Casa 2, Av Niemeyer 314, Vidigal; dm R$45-60; ❄@📶) Stunning sea views are the coup at this friendly hostel at the bottom of Vidigal *favela*.

Mirante do Arvrão (☎3114-1868; mirantedoarvrao.com.br; Armando de Almeida Lima 8, Vidigal; dm/s/d from R$58/158/400; ❄📶) A surprising find in Vidigal offering beautiful rooms and stunning views; and built from sustainable materials to boot.

Leblon Spot Design Hostel HOSTEL $$
(Map p296; ☎2137-4310; www.leblonspot.com; Dias Ferreira 636, Leblon; dm weekday/weekend R$62/110, d R$260-350;) The location is outstanding: you're within a short stroll to some of Rio's best restaurants and liveliest drinking spots. The setting is a former house, with bright but rather cramped rooms with wood floors, a small lounge and a tiny veranda. Unlike other Rio hostels, there isn't much socializing here, and the staff isn't the friendliest.

Margarida's Pousada POUSADA $$
(Map p296; ☎2239-1840; www.margaridaspousada.com; Barão da Torre 600, Ipanema; d from R$300;) Those seeking something smaller and cozier than a high-rise hotel should try this superbly located Ipanema *pousada* (guesthouse). You'll find 11 pleasant, simply furnished rooms scattered about the low-rise building. Margarida also rents out several private, fully equipped apartments nearby.

Bonita HOSTEL $$
(☎2227-1703; www.bonitaipanema.com; Barão da Torre 107, Ipanema; dm R$60, d with/without bathroom R$270/220;) This peacefully set converted house has history: it's where bossa nova legend Tom Jobim lived from 1962 to 1965 and wrote some of his most famous songs. Rooms are clean but simply furnished, and most open onto a shared deck overlooking a small pool and patio.

Copacabana & Leme

Cabana Copa HOSTEL $
(Map p292; ☎3988-9912; www.cabanacopa.com.br; Travessa Guimarães Natal 12, Copacabana; dm R$40-80, d R$180-250;) Top hostel honors go to this Greek-Brazilian-run gem in a colonial-style '50s house tucked away in a Copacabana cranny. Four- to 10-bed dorms prevail throughout the home, which is chock-full of original architectural details and a hodgepodge of funky floorings. There's a lively bar and common areas.

Che Lagarto – Suites Santa Clara BOUTIQUE HOSTEL $$
(☎3495-3133; www.chelagarto.com; Santa Clara 304, Copacabana; r with/without bathroom from R$220/170;) On a tree-lined street in Copacabana's Bairro Peixoto neighborhood, this converted house has clean, simple and well-maintained rooms (all private rooms, no dorms), and a small downstairs lounge where you can meet other travelers. The friendly staff gives out helpful advice, and can direct you to loads of activities.

Edificio Jucati HOSTEL, APARTMENT $$
(☎2547-5422; www.edificiojucati.com.br; Tenente Marones de Gusmão 85, Copacabana; d/q from R$230/290;) Near a small park and on a tranquil street, Jucati has large, simply furnished serviced apartments with slate floors and small but serviceable kitchens. Have a look at the layout before committing. Most apartments have just one bedroom with a double bed and a living room with a bunk bed. The small covered courtyard is a fine spot to unwind.

Santa Teresa & Lapa

Rio Hostel HOSTEL $
(Map p298; ☎3852-0827; www.riohostel.com; Joaquim Murtinho 361, Santa Teresa; dm/s/d from R$35/80/120;) This Santa favorite provides travelers with a home away from home. The backyard patio with its pool is a great place to meet other travelers, and there's also a kitchen for guests. Rooms are clean, and there are attractive doubles, including private suites with fine views behind the pool.

Casa da Gente GUESTHOUSE $
(Map p298; ☎2232-2634; www.casadagente.com; Gonçalves Fontes 33, Santa Teresa; s/d from R$125/185;) A short stroll from the top of the Escadaria Selarón, the Casa da Gente is a welcoming French-Brazilian-run guesthouse with a strong interest in sustainability. Rainwater catchment, solar panels, composting and a green roof are all part of the ethos. The rooms themselves are bright, clean and simply furnished.

★**Casa Beleza** POUSADA $$
(Map p288; ☎98288-6764; www.casabeleza.net; Laurinda Santos Lobo 311, Santa Teresa; r R$260-450;) This lovely property dates back to the 1930s and was once a governor's mansion. Tropical gardens overlook the picturesque pool, and you can sometimes spot toucans and monkeys in the surrounding foliage. It's a small and peaceful operation, with just four guestrooms and one peacefully set villa (complete with a rooftop deck offering panoramic views).

Ipanema, Leblon & Gávea

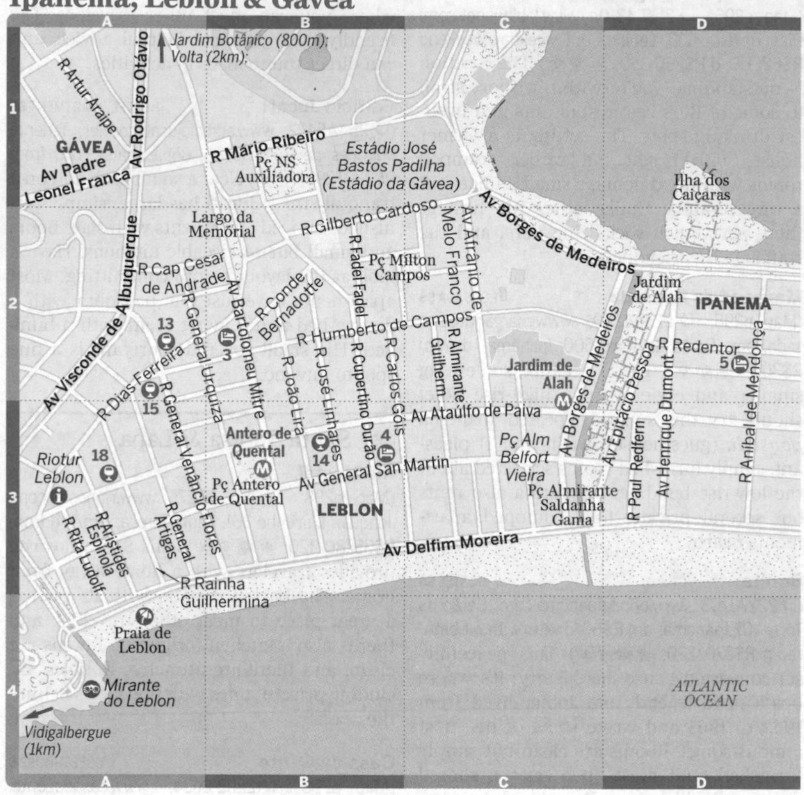

Ipanema, Leblon & Gávea

Top Sights
1 Lagoa Rodrigo de Freitas ... E1

Sights
2 Gay Section of Beach ... F3

Sleeping
3 Leblon Spot Design Hostel ... B2
4 Lemon Spirit Hostel ... B3
5 Margarida's Pousada ... D2
6 Rio Hostel – Ipanema ... H3

Eating
7 Brasileirinho ... G3
8 Cafeína ... F3
9 Delírio Tropical ... E3
10 Frontera ... G3
11 Vero ... F3
12 Zazá Bistrô Tropical ... F3

Drinking & Nightlife
13 Belmonte ... A2
14 Bibi Sucos ... B3
15 Brewteco ... A2
16 Canastra ... G3
17 Garota de Ipanema ... F3
18 Jobi ... A3
19 Palaphita Kitch ... G1
20 Tô Nem Aí ... F3

Entertainment
21 Vinícius Show Bar ... F3

Shopping
22 Hippie Fair ... G3
23 Toca do Vinícius ... F3

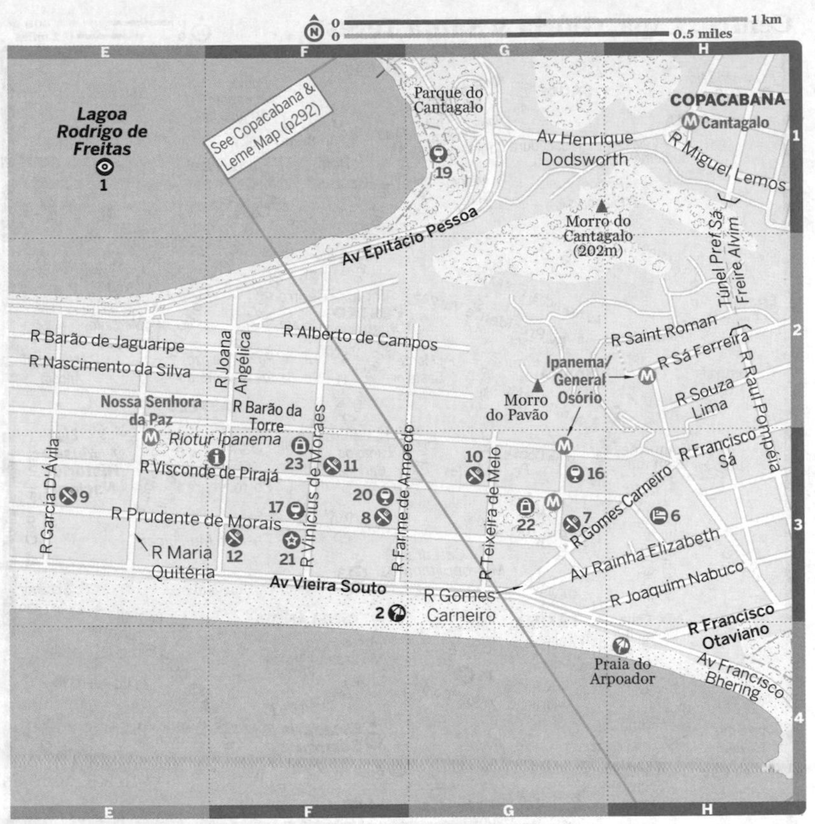

Casa Áurea GUESTHOUSE $$
(Map p288; ☎2242-5830; www.casaaurea.com.br; Áurea 80, Santa Teresa; d R$300-340, s/d without bathroom R$170/220; ❄📶) Set in one of Santa Teresa's oldest homes (1871), the two-story Casa Áurea has rustic charm, simple but cozy rooms and a large covered garden where you can lounge on hammocks, fire up the barbecue or whip up a meal in the open-air kitchen. Very welcoming and kindhearted hosts.

Cama e Café HOMESTAY $$
(Map p298; ☎2225-4366; www.camaecafe.com; Progresso 67, Santa Teresa; r R$196-300) A fine alternative to hotels and guesthouses, Cama e Café is a B&B network that allow travelers to book a room from local residents. There are several dozen options to choose from, with the majority of listings in Santa Teresa, and a few scattered options in Laranjeiras, the Zona Sul and Barra.

Botafogo & Urca

Vila Carioca HOSTEL $
(Map p288; ☎2535-3224; www.vilacarioca.com.br; Estácio Coimbra 84, Botafogo; dm R$35-60, d R$130-320; ❄@📶) On a peaceful tree-lined street, this low-key and welcoming hostel has four- to 15-bed dorms in an attractively decorated house. The common areas are a fine spot to mingle with other travelers.

Oztel HOSTEL $$
(Map p288; ☎3042-1853; www.oztel.com.br; Pinheiro Guimarães 91, Botafogo; dm R$45-75, d R$240-300; ❄@📶) Evoking a Warholian aesthetic, Rio's coolest and most colorful hostel is like sleeping in an art gallery. The artsy front deck and bar is an inviting hangout lounge but the real coup are the private rooms: with a garden patio under the nose of Cristo Redentor, you'll be hard-pressed to find a groovier room in Rio.

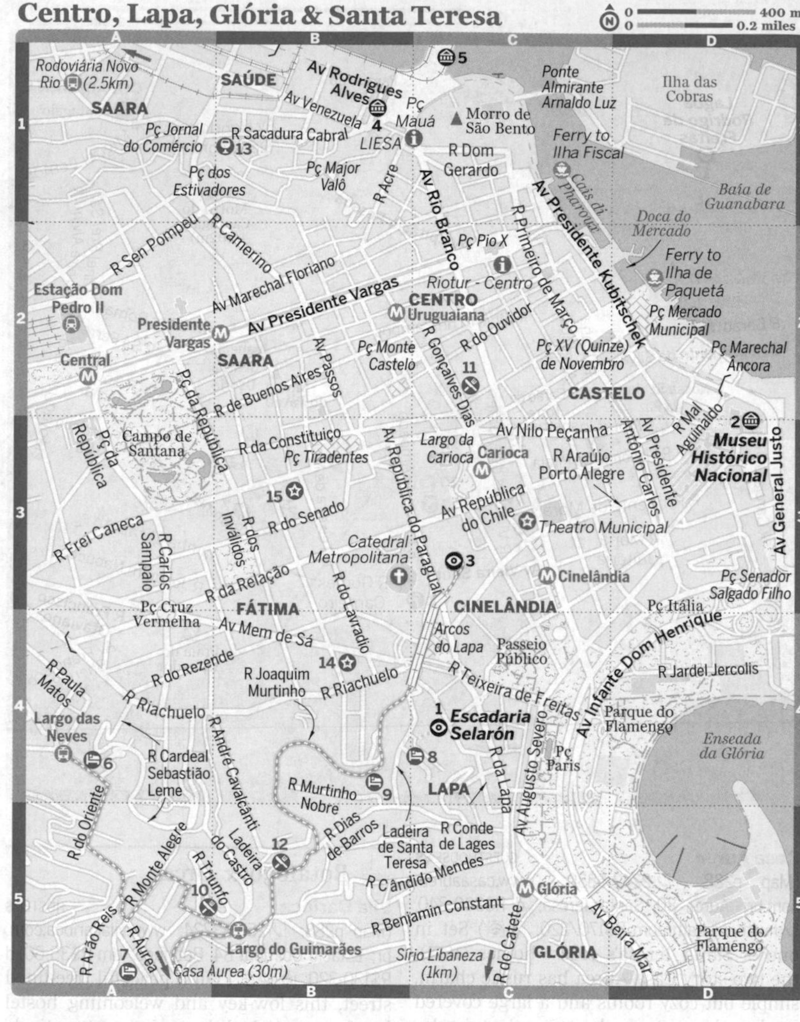

Centro, Lapa, Glória & Santa Teresa

Top Sights
1 Escadaria Selarón C4
2 Museu Histórico Nacional D3

Sights
3 Bonde Station C3
4 Museu de Arte do Rio B1
5 Museu do Amanhã C1

Sleeping
6 Cama e Café A4
7 Casa Cool Beans A5
8 Casa da Gente C4
9 Rio Hostel B4

Eating
10 Bar do Mineiro A5
Cafecito .... (see 10)
11 Confeitaria Colombo C2
Cristóvão .... (see 11)
12 Espírito Santa B5

Drinking & Nightlife
13 Week B1

Entertainment
14 Carioca da Gema B4
15 Rio Scenarium B3

Eating

The best places for cheap dining are self-serve lunch buffets and juice bars. Another atmospheric choice is along Joaquim Murtinho in Santa Teresa, and the corner of Mem de Sá and Lavrádio in Lapa is full of pre-party *botecos* (neighborhood bars). Self-caterers should look out for the ubiquitous Rio grocery chain, Zona Sul – named after the city's most coveted zone.

Ipanema, Leblon & Gávea

Vero ICE CREAM $
(Map p296; 3497-8754; Visconde de Pirajá 260; ice creams R$11-16; 11am-midnight) This artisanal Italian-run *gelateria* whips up Rio's best ice cream. You'll find more than two dozen rich and creamy temptations, including *gianduia* (chocolate with hazelnut), *caramelo com flor de sal* (caramel with sea salt), *figo com amêndoas* (fig with almond) and classic flavors such as *morango* (strawberry). The selection changes daily.

Cafeína CAFE $
(Map p296; 2521-2194; www.cafeina.com.br; Farme de Amoedo 43; quiches R$10, sandwiches R$20-40; 8am-11:30pm;) In the heart of Ipanema, this inviting cafe with sidewalk tables is a fine spot for an espresso while watching the city stroll by. You'll also find freshly made sandwiches, salads, quiches and some very rich desserts.

Delírio Tropical BRAZILIAN $
(Map p296; 3624-8164; www.delirio.com.br; Garcia d'Ávila 48; salads R$15-22; 11am-9pm Mon-Sat;) Delírio Tropical serves a tempting array of salads, which you can enhance by adding grilled trout, salmon carpaccio, filet mignon and other items. The open layout has a pleasant, casual ambience, but you'll need to go early to beat the lunchtime crowds.

Frontera BUFFET $$
(Map p296; 3289-2350; Visconde de Pirajá 128; per kg R$60; 11:30am-11pm) Run by a Dutch chef, Frontera offers more than 60 plates at its delectable lunch buffet, which features a mouthwatering assortment of grilled meats, baked casseroles and seafood pastas, plus salads, fresh fruits, grilled vegetables and desserts. Sushi and the dessert counter costs extra. Dark woods and vintage travel posters give it a cozier feel than most per-kilo places.

Brasileirinho BRAZILIAN $$
(Map p296; 2523-5184; Jangadeiros 10; mains R$38-59; noon-11pm) Facing Praça General Osório, this rustically decorated restaurant serves good, traditional Mineiro cuisine. Favorites include *tutu a mineira* (mashed black beans with manioc), *carne seca* (dried beef) and *picanha* (rump steak). The *feijoada* here is tops – unsurprising given that Brasileirinho is run by the same owner as Ipanema's top-notch *feijoada* eatery Casa da Feijoada.

★ **Zazá Bistrô Tropical** FUSION $$$
(Map p296; 2247-9101; www.zazabistro.com.br; Joana Angélica 40; mains R$60-86; 7:30pm-midnight Mon & Tue, noon-midnight Wed-Fri, from 1pm Sat & Sun) Inside an art-filled and whimsically decorated converted house, Zazá serves beautifully prepared dishes with Asian accents, and uses organic ingredients when possible. Favorites include chicken curry with jasmine rice, flambéed prawns with risotto, and grilled fish served with caramelized plantain. Don't miss the cocktails.

Copacabana & Leme

Bibi Sucos BRAZILIAN $
(Map p292; 2255-5000; Santa Clara 36; mains R$18-36; 8am-1am Sun-Thu, to 2am Fri & Sat) Offering much the same recipe for success as its **Leblon branch** (Map p296; 2259-4298; www.bibisucos.com.br; Av Ataúlfo de Paiva 591A; juices R$6-15; 8am-1am), Bibi serves dozens of juices, along with savory and sweet crepes, sandwiches, burgers, pastas, quiches and build-your-own salads. It has outdoor tables and a bustling vibe. Go early or late to beat the lunchtime crowds.

Galeto Sat's BRAZILIAN $
(Map p292; 2275-6197; Barata Ribeiro 7; mains R$18-26; noon-5am) One of Rio's best roast-chicken spots, laid-back Galeto Sat's has earned many fans since its opening back in 1962. Grab a seat along the mirrored and tiled wall, order a *chope* (draft beer) and enjoy the scent of grilled spit-roasted birds before tucking into a filling meal. Price-wise you can't beat the R$50 feast for two.

Joaquina BRAZILIAN $$
(Map p292; 2275-8569; Av Atlântica 974; mains R$34-46; 11:30am-midnight;) Joaquina has much to recommend it: a great ocean-facing location with outdoor seating; excellent *caipirinhas* that don't stint on the fresh

fruit; and tasty Brazilian fare served up at fair prices. On Sundays Joaquina serves *feijoada* (R$34); on Saturdays it's oxtail rice (also R$34). Arrive early before it runs out. Other hits: *moqueca* for one, shrimp risotto and vegetarian stroganoff.

Bar do David BRAZILIAN **$$**
(Map p288; Ladeira Ary Barroso 66; appetizers R$20-30, mains around R$35; ⏲8am-10pm Tue-Sun) Located in Chapéu Mangueira favela, this simple open-sided eatery serves excellent snacks. The chef and owner David Vieira Bispo was formerly a fisherman, and his seafood *feijoada* (stew with rice) is outstanding – but available weekends only. At other times, you can nibble on seafood *croquetes,* garlic shrimp, sausage with manioc, and other hits that go nicely with a *caipirinha* or two.

TT Burger BURGERS **$$**
(Map p292; Francisco Otaviano 67; mains around R$30; ⏲noon-midnight Sun-Wed, to 4am Thu-Sat) The son of famed local chef Claude Troisgros runs this high-end Brooklyn-style burger outpost, and has gained a strong following for his delicious burgers (the guava ketchup is outstanding), crispy fries and milkshakes. It's a charming spot, with subway tiles, framed photos, wood floors and a small front deck. There's a second location on Leblon's main drag (Av Ataúlfo de Paiva).

Centro

Confeitaria Colombo BRAZILIAN **$**
(Map p298; ☎2505-1500; www.confeitariacolombo.com.br; Gonçalves Dias 34; pastries around R$9, sandwiches R$18-40; ⏲9am-7pm Mon-Fri, to 5pm Sat) Stained-glass windows, brocaded mirrors and marble countertops create a lavish setting for coffee or a meal. Dating from the late 1800s, the Confeitaria Colombo serves desserts – including a good *pastel de nata* (custard tart) – befitting its elegant decor. The restaurant overhead, **Cristóvão** (Map p298; Gonçalves Dias 34; buffet per person R$87; ⏲noon-4pm), spreads an extensive buffet of Brazilian dishes for those wanting to further soak up the splendor.

Lapa & Santa Teresa

Cafecito CAFE **$**
(Map p298; ☎2221-9439; www.cafecito.com.br; Paschoal Carlos Magno 121; sandwiches R$14-26; ⏲9am-10pm Thu-Tue; 📶) A few steps above street level, this open-air cafe attracts a mix of foreigners and neighborhood regulars; the Argentine owner is a longtime Santa Teresa resident. You'll find imported beers, desserts, cocktails (*caipirinhas* and mojitos), tapas plates and tasty ciabatta sandwiches with ingredients such as artichoke hearts, Gorgonzola and prosciutto.

Bar do Mineiro BRAZILIAN **$$**
(Map p298; ☎2221-9227; Paschoal Carlos Magno 99; mains R$51-75; ⏲noon-2am Tue-Sat, to midnight Sun) Black-and-white photographs of legendary singers cover the walls of this old-school *boteco* (small open-air bar) in the heart of Santa Teresa. Lively crowds have been filling this spot for years to enjoy traditional Minas Gerais dishes. The *feijoada* (bean-and-meat stew served with rice) is tops, and served every day, along with appetizers, including *pasteis* (savory pastries). Strong *caipirinhas* will help get you in the mood.

★**Espírito Santa** AMAZONIAN **$$$**
(Map p298; ☎2507-4840; Almirante Alexandrino 264; mains R$50-88; ⏲noon-midnight Wed-Mon) Espírito Santa is set in a beautifully restored mansion in Santa Teresa. Take a seat on the back terrace with its sweeping views or inside the charming, airy dining room, and feast on rich, expertly prepared meat and seafood dishes from the Amazon and the northeast.

Jardim Botânico & Lagoa

★**Volta** BRAZILIAN **$$**
(☎3204-5406; www.restaurantevolta.com.br; Visconde de Carandaí 5; mains R$40-60; ⏲noon-midnight Mon-Sat, to 6pm Sun) Set in a classy old villa with an outdoor patio on a peaceful corner of Jardim Botânico, Volta serves up playful, contemporary fare inspired by Brazilian comfort food. Start off with creative appetizers such as the sardine-topped tapioca crisp or the *coxinha* (cornmeal balls filled with chicken) with creamy Minas cheese, before moving on to sweet-potato gnocchi with pumpkin cream or a perfectly tender filet mignon.

Botafogo & Urca

Boua Kitchen & Bar BISTRO **$**
(Map p288; www.theboua.com.br; Nelson Mandela 102, Botafogo; burgers R$26-38) Behind the Botafogo metro station, this lively gastropub is one of more than a dozen eating

and drinking spots along this lane. The microbrew selection is outstanding (with a rotating lineup of Belgian, German, American and Brazilian beers). You can sit outside and nosh on thick burgers, appetizers or steak and Gorgonzola risotto while watching the passing people parade.

Glória, Catete & Flamengo

Sírio Libaneza MIDDLE EASTERN **$**
(Map p288; www.rotisseriasl.com.br; Largo do Machado 29, Loja 16-19; snacks R$8-24; 8am-11pm Mon-Sat;) This bustling place is always packed, and serves up tasty and cheap Syrian-Lebanese cuisine and great juices. Try the hearty *kibe de forno* (oven-baked ground beef dish with spices), a hummus platter or *kafta* (spiced meat patty), followed by baklava and other sweets. It's inside the Galleria Condor on Largo do Machado.

★Ferro e Farinha PIZZERIA **$$**
(Map p288; Andrade Pertence 42; pizzas R$30-40; 7-11:30pm Wed-Sat, from 6:30pm Sun) Sei Shiroma, an expat from NYC, and a dexterous team of dough handlers serve up Rio's best pizza at this atmospheric and delightfully ramshackle spot in Catete. Seats are few, with just a handful of bar stools crowding around the pizza makers and oven at center stage, plus a few outdoor tables, so go early to try to beat the crowds.

Drinking

Ipanema, Leblon and Copacabana offer flashy nightspots as well as old-school watering holes. A youthful bar scene draws revelers to Gávea, while scenic Lagoa draws mostly couples. The narrow pedestrian streets of Centro near Praça XV attract drinkers during weekday cocktail hours, while Santa Teresa is a laid-back spot for cocktails. Lapa, with its samba clubs and frenetic outdoor bars, becomes a late-night street party on weekends.

Rio's numerous juice bars are a must. For coffee culture and people-watching, head to the sidewalk cafes scattered about Ipanema and Leblon.

Ipanema, Leblon & Gávea

★Canastra WINE BAR
(Map p296; Jangadeiros 42; 6:30pm-1am Tue-Sat) At first glance, Canastra looks like any other casual *boteco* on the back streets of Rio: sidewalk tables with a crowd milling about with drinks and snacks. But the food here is also outstanding, and the drink of choice is wine: perhaps unsurprising given that it's run by a trio of Frenchmen.

Belmonte BAR
(Map p296; Dias Ferreira 521; 11am-3am) An icon in Leblon, Belmonte always draws huge crowds: it's pretty much a massive street party every night, with beer-drinking revelers

GAY RIO

On the beaches, you'll find gay-friendly drink stands across from the Copacabana Palace Hotel in Copacabana and opposite Farme de Amoedo (Rio's gayest street) in Ipanema. On Ipanema Beach, the gay-friendly spot is between Posto 8 and 9. For sleeps, **Casa Cool Beans** (Map p298; 2262-0552; www.casacoolbeans.com; Laurinda Santos Lobo 136, Santa Teresa; d R$250-400;) is a fantastic gay-owned and operated B&B. For more info, check out www.riogayguide.com.

Le Boy (Map p292; 2513-4993; www.leboy.com.br; Raul Pompéia 102, Copacabana; cover R$10-30; 11pm-5am Tue-Sun) Open since 1992, Le Boy is Rio's gay temple. There are theme nights with drag shows and go-go boys.

Tô Nem Aí (Map p296; 2247-8403; cnr Farme de Amoedo & Visconde de Pirajá; noon-3am) Slang for 'I couldn't care less,' this relaxed hangout on Ipanema's gayest street is a great after-beach spot.

TV Bar (Map p292; www.bartvbar.com.br; Shopping Cassino Atlântico, Av NS de Copacabana 1417, Copacabana; cover R$15-50; 10pm-5am Thu-Sat, to 3am Sun) The trendy favorite in town, with DJs spinning amid an audiovisual assault in the space of a former TV station.

Week (Map p298; 2253-1020; www.theweek.com.br; Sacadura Cabral 135, Centro; 10pm-5am Sat) The 2007 importation of this massive São Paulo institution was a smash hit from go. Saturdays are the biggest, with international DJs and the lot. It's inside a historical *carioca* mansion near the port.

spilling onto the sidewalk from 8pm onward. If you can score a table, don't miss the delicious well-priced *pasteis* (dough that's filled then deep-fried) stuffed with crab, jerked beef with cheese, shrimp, heart of palm and other tasty ingredients.

Brewteco BAR
(Map p296; Dias Ferreira 420; ⏱11am-1am) A clear sign that the microbrew scene has arrived in Rio, Brewteco has scores of unique craft beers by the bottle from around the globe. California IPAs from Ballast Point, German hits such as Weihenstephaner, Belgian ales and unique Brazilian options including Fraga Weiss, a wheat beer from Rio, draw the crowds.

★**Palaphita Kitch** LOUNGE
(Map p292; ☎2227-0837; www.palaphitakitch.com.br; Av Epitácio Pessoa s/n; ⏱6pm-1am) A great spot for a sundowner, Palaphita Kitch is an open-air, thatched-roof wonderland with rustic bamboo furniture, flickering tiki torches and a peaceful setting on the edge of the lake. This is a popular spot with couples, who come for the view and the creative (but pricey) cocktails: the *caipirinhas*, made from unusual fruits from the Northeast and Amazonia, are a hit.

Garota de Ipanema BAR
(Map p296; ☎2522-0340; Vinícius de Moraes 49; ⏱noon-2am) During its first incarnation, this small, open-sided bar was called the Bar Veloso. Its name and anonymity disappeared once two scruffy young regulars – Tom Jobim and Vinícius de Moraes – penned the famous song, 'The Girl from Ipanema'. It changed history, and the name of the street, too.

Jobi BOTECO
(Map p296; ☎2274-0547; Av Ataúlfo de Paiva 1166; ⏱9am-5am) A favorite since 1956, Jobi has served a lot of beer in its day, and its popularity hasn't waned. The unadorned *botequim* (bar with table service) still serves plenty; grab a seat by the sidewalk and let the night unfold. If hunger beckons, try the tasty appetizers; the *carne seca* (jerked beef) and the *bolinhos de bacalhau* (codfish croquettes) are tops.

Copacabana & Leme

Escondido BAR
(Map p292; Aires de Saldanha 98, Copacabana; ⏱6pm-1am Tue-Sun) One of the top beer bars in Copacabana, Escondido has a rotating selection of microbrews such as American Pale Ales (IPAs), stouts and ciders, including about two dozen on draft at any one time. It's a laid-back spot to head to with friends to sample a few brews and nibble on pub grub (including huge burgers).

Botafogo & Urca

Caverna BAR
(Map p288; ☎3507-5600; www.espacocaverna.com; Assis Bueno 26; ⏱6pm-1am Mon-Fri, 7pm-2am Sat) Yet another reason why Botafogo may be surpassing Ipanema in the cool factor these days, this always-buzzing rock-and-roll loving bar and bistro serves up microbrews and juicy burgers amid a fun and festive atmosphere (though the music rocks a little loud some nights).

Bar Urca BAR
(Map p288; ☎2295-8744; Cândido Gaffrée 205, Urca; ⏱8am-11pm) This much-loved neighborhood bar and restaurant has a marvelous setting near Urca's bayside waterfront. At night, young and old crowd along the seaside wall to enjoy cold drinks, appetizers and fine views.

☆ Entertainment

Live Music

★**Bip Bip** LIVE MUSIC
(Map p292; ☎2267-9696; Almirante Gonçalves 50, Copacabana; ⏱6pm-midnight Sun-Fri) For years Bip Bip has been one of the city's favorite spots to catch a live *roda de samba* (informal samba played around a table), despite it being just a storefront with a few battered tables. As the evening progresses the tree-lined neighborhood becomes the backdrop to serious jam sessions, with music and revelers spilling into the street.

Rio Scenarium SAMBA
(Map p298; www.rioscenarium.com.br; Rua do Lavradio 20, Lapa; cover R$25-50; ⏱7pm-4am Tue-Sat) One of the city's most photogenic nightspots, Rio Scenarium has three floors, each lavishly decorated with antiques. Balconies overlook the stage on the 1st floor, where dancers keep time to the jazz-infused samba, *choro* or *pagode* (popular samba music) filling the air. Rio Scenarium receives much press outside of Brazil, and attracts at least as many foreigners as locals.

Carioca da Gema SAMBA
(Map p298; www.barcariocadagema.com.br; Av Mem de Sá 79, Lapa; cover R$25-40; ⏱7pm-2am

Mon-Fri, from 9pm Sat & Sun) Although it's now surrounded by clubs, Carioca da Gema was one of Lapa's pioneers when it opened in 2000. This small, warmly lit club still attracts some of the city's best samba bands, and you'll find a festive, mixed crowd filling the dance floor most nights.

★ Vinícius Show Bar LIVE MUSIC
(Map p296; ☎2523-4757; www.viniciusbar.com.br; 2nd fl, Prudente de Morais 34, Ipanema; admission R$35-50) Billing itself as the 'temple of bossa nova,' this place has been an icon in the neighborhood since 1989. The intimate space makes a fine setting to listen to first-rate bossa nova, and occasional Música Popular Brasileira (MPB) and samba. Shows typically start between 9:30pm and 11pm.

Nightclubs

Fosfobox CLUB
(Map p292; ☎2548-7498; www.fosfobox.com.br; Siqueira Campos 143, Copacabana; admission R$15-60; ⊙11pm-4am Wed-Sat) This subterranean club is hidden under a shopping center near the metro station. Good DJs spin everything from funk to glam rock, and the crowd here is one of the more eclectic in the club scene.

Mais Que Nada CLUB
(Map p292; www.maisquenada-rio.com.br; Xavier da Silveira 34, Copacabana; ⊙7pm-2am Wed-Sun) This small, festive club draws an equal mix of *cariocas* and gringos who come for a dance-loving lineup of samba, salsa and rock. Cover charge varies from R$10 to upwards of R$25. Wednesday nights (samba) are free.

Casa da Matriz CLUB
(Map p288; ☎2266-1014; www.facebook.com/casadamatriz; Henrique de Novaes 107, Botafogo; admission R$20-40; ⊙11pm-5am Wed-Sat) Artwork lines this space in Botafogo. With numerous rooms to explore (lounge, screening room, dance floors), this old mansion embodies the creative side of the *carioca* spirit. It usually attracts a student crowd. Check out its Facebook page for party listings.

Dance

Starting in September, the big Carnaval schools open their rehearsals to the public. These are lively but informal affairs where you can dance, drink and join the party. The schools are in dodgy neighborhoods, so don't go alone, but by all means go.

> **ℹ BEACH BLANKET BURY IT!**
>
> Rio's beaches are targets for thieves and there has been an alarming rise in *arrastãos* of late – waves of bandits robbing everyone in their path across broad swaths of sand. Don't take anything valuable to the beach. *Ever!* But if you must, locals in the know bury their valuables in a plastic bag in the sand and cover it with their beach towel. Out of sight, out of mind!

Mangueira SAMBA
(☎2567-3419; www.mangueira.com.br; Visconde de Niterói 1072, Mangueira; ⊙10pm Sat) Samba school.

Salgueiro SAMBA
(☎2238-9226; www.salgueiro.com.br; Silva Teles 104, Andaraí; ⊙10pm Sat) Samba school.

Sports

Maracanã Football Stadium STADIUM
(☎8871-3950; www.suderj.rj.gov.br/maracana.asp; Av Maracanã, São Cristóvão; R$40-80; ⊙9am-7pm; Ⓢ Maracanã) For a quasi-psychedelic experience, go to a *futebol* match at Maracanã, Brazil's temple to football (soccer). Matches here rate among the most exciting in the world, particularly during a championship game or when local rivals Flamengo, Vasco da Gama, Fluminense or Botafogo go head-to-head. Games take place year-round and generally happen on a Wednesday, Thursday, Saturday or Sunday.

Shopping

★ Hippie Fair MARKET
(Map p296; Praça General Osório; ⊙9am-6pm Sun) The Zona Sul's most famous market, the Hippie Fair (aka Feira de Arte de Ipanema) has artwork, jewelry, handicrafts, clothing and souvenirs for sale. Stalls in the four corners of the plaza sell tasty plates of *acarajé* (croquettes made from mashed black-eyed peas, with a sauce of *vatapá* – manioc paste, coconut and *dendê* oil – and shrimp; R$9), plus excellent desserts (R$4). Don't miss it.

Toca do Vinícius MUSIC
(Map p296; ☎2247-5227; www.tocadovinicius.com.br; Vinícius de Moraes 129; ⊙11am-7pm Mon-Fri, 10am-6pm Sat, 3-6pm Sun) Bossa nova fans shouldn't miss this store. In addition to its ample CD and vinyl selection (starting at R$40) of contemporary and old performers,

GETTING TO RIO

Premium Auto Ônibus (www.premiumautoonibus.com.br; one way R$15) operates safe air-con buses from the international airport along several different itineraries. For the Zona Sul, take No 2018, which heads southward through the *bairros* (districts) of Glória, Flamengo and Botafogo, and along the beaches of Copacabana, Ipanema and Leblon to Barra da Tijuca (and vice versa) every 30 minutes from 5:30am to 11pm and will stop wherever you ask. It takes 75 minutes to two hours depending on traffic. If you're going straight to Barra, it's faster to take bus No 2918 instead. There's also a bus that links to Santos Dumont Airport (No 2101) and a line to the bus station (No 2145). You can also transfer to the metro at Carioca metro station in Centro.

If you arrive in Rio by bus, it's a good idea to take a taxi to your hotel, as the bus station is in a seedy area. To arrange a cab, go to the small booth near the Riotur desk, on the 1st floor of the bus station. Average fares are R$50 to the international airport and R$40 to Copacabana or Ipanema.

it also sells music scores and composition books. Around the store you'll find memorabilia from great songwriters including Vinícius de Moraes and Chico Buarque.

 Information

DANGERS & ANNOYANCES

In preparation for the 2014 World Cup and 2016 Summer Olympics, the city made great strides in cleaning up its none-too-stellar criminal record, though a recent economic downturn has seen some of the progress erased. Much of the city's headline-grabbing ferocity traditionally rose from an ongoing urban war between police and drug traffickers, who historically controlled many *favelas* around the city. But the continuing implementation of the Unidade de Polícia Pacificadoras (UPPs; Police Pacification Units) has dramatically reduced the areas in which traffickers freely operate. There is a visibly heavier police presence around high-traffic tourism areas in the Zona Sul which, together with installations of more CCTV cameras clustered around hotels in Copacabana and Ipanema, has contributed to less tourist crime.

Buses are well-known targets for thieves. Avoid taking them after dark, and keep an eye out while aboard. Take taxis at night to avoid walking along empty streets and beaches. That holds especially true for Centro, which you should avoid on weekends when it's deserted and dangerous.

Maracanã football stadium is worth a visit, but take only spending money for the day and avoid the crowded sections.

Despite the UPPs, it's still a bad idea to wander into the *favelas* unless with a knowledgeable guide.

If you have the misfortune of being robbed, hand over the goods. Thieves are only too willing to use their weapons if provoked. It's sensible to carry a fat wad of singles to hand over in case of a robbery.

EMERGENCY

Tourist Police (☎2332-2924; cnr Afrânio de Melo Franco & Humberto de Campos, Leblon; ⏰24hr) Report robberies to the tourist police; no major investigation is going to occur, but you will get a police form to give to your insurance company.

MEDICAL SERVICES

Clinica Galdino Campos (☎2548-9966; www.galdinocampos.com.br; Av NS de Copacabana 492, Copacabana; ⏰24hr) The best hospital for foreigners, with high-quality care and multilingual doctors (who even make outpatient calls). The clinic works with most international health plans and travel insurance policies.

MONEY

ATMs for most card networks are widely available but often fussy. The best options are Bradesco and Banco do Brasil, which are foreigner-friendly and don't charge fees (and then Citibank, though it charges fees). Regardless, there will be a relatively frustrating trial-and-error period finding the best fit for your foreign ATM card.

Banco do Brasil Centro (Senador Dantas 105, Centro); Copacabana (Av NS de Copacabana 1292, Copacabana); Galeão international airport (1st fl, Terminal 1, Galeão international airport)

Citibank Centro (Rua da Assembléia 100, Centro); Ipanema (Visconde de Pirajá 260, Ipanema)

TOURIST INFORMATION

Riotur (Map p298; ☎2271-7000; www.rioguiaoficial.com.br; 9th fl, Praça Pio X; ⏰9am-6pm Mon-Fri) has offices and kiosks for getting maps, transport info and tips on attractions and events. Its multilingual website is a good source of information. All the Riotur offices distribute maps and the bimonthly *Rio Guide*, which is packed with information and major seasonal events. As well as branches at Galeão international airport's **Terminal 1** (☎3398-4077; Terminal 1, Domestic Arrival Hall, Galeão International Airport; ⏰6am-11pm) and **Terminal 2** (☎3367-6213; Terminal 2, International Arrival Hall, Galeão International Airport; ⏰6am-11pm), you'll also find information kiosks at the following locations:

Riotur Copacabana (Map p292; ☎2541-7522; Av Princesa Isabel 183; ⏰9am-6pm Mon-Fri, to 3pm Sat) Good for information on events during Carnaval.

Riotur Ipanema (Map p296; Visconde de Pirajá & Joana Angélica; ⏰8am-9pm) Useful info kiosk in the heart of Ipanema.

Riotur Leblon (Map p296; Ataulfo de de Paiva & Dias Ferreira; ⏰8am-6pm) Tourist info at the entrance to Leblon's best eat street.

Getting There & Away

AIR

Most flights depart from Aeroporto Galeão (GIG; also called Aeroporto António Carlos Jobim), 15km north of the center on Ilha do Governador. Shuttle flights (*ponte aérea*) to/from São Paulo, and some flights for other nearby cities, use Aeroporto Santos Dumont (SDU) in the city center, 1km east of Cinelândia metro station.

BUS

Buses leave from the sleek **Rodoviária Novo Rio** (☎3213-1800; Av Francisco Bicalho 1), about 2km northwest of Centro. Several buses depart daily from here to most major destinations, but it's best to buy tickets in advance. **ClickBus** (www.clickbus.com.br) accepts international cards and Paypal for payments. After purchasing, you'll receive the booking reference and ticket number.

Getting Around

BIKE

Rio has many kilometers of bike paths along the beach, around Lagoa and along Parque do Flamengo. In addition to a public bike-sharing scheme, you can rent bikes from stands along the east side of Lagoa Rodrigo de Freitas for around R$15 per hour, and at various bike shops along the bike path between Copacabana and Ipanema.

For an excellent guided bike tour, contact Rio by Bike (p293).

BUS

Rio's new BRS (Bus Rapid System) features dedicated public-transportation corridors in Copacabana, Ipanema, Leblon and Barra. Fares on most buses are around R$3.40. Every bus has its key destination displayed on the illuminated signboard in front. If you see the bus for you, hail it by sticking your arm straight out (drivers won't stop unless flagged down).

BUSES FROM RIO

DESTINATION	STARTING FARE (R$)	DURATION (HR)	COMPANY
Belém	600	54-60	Expresso Brasileiro (www.expressobrasileiro.com.br)
Belo Horizonte	95	7	Util (www.util.com.br)
Brasília	150	18	Util (www.util.com.br)
Buenos Aires (AR)	450	46	Pluma (www.pluma.com.br), Crucero del Norte (www.crucerodelnorte.com.ar)
Búzios	66	3	Viação 1001 (www.autoviacao.com.br)
Curitiba	170	13	Penha (http://vendas.nspenha.com.br)
Florianópolis	230	18	Kaissara (www.kaissara.com.br)
Iguaçu Falls	245	23	Pluma (www.pluma.com.br), Kaiowa
Ouro Prêto	80	7	Util (www.util.com.br)
Paraty	70	4½	Costa Verde (www.costaverdetransportes.com.br)
Porto Alegre	321	1½	Penha (http://vendas.nspenha.com.br)
Recife	445	28	São Geraldo (www.saogeraldo.com.br)
Salvador	300	38	Aguia Branca (www.aguiabranca.com.br)
Santiago (CH)	486	62	Pluma (www.pluma.com.br), Crucero del Norte (www.crucerodelnorte.com.ar)
Vitória	110	8	Aguia Branca (www.aguiabranca.com.br)

METRO

Rio's **metro system** (www.metrorio.com.br; ⌚5am-midnight Mon-Sat, 7am-11pm Sun) is an excellent way to get around. The main line goes from Ipanema-General Osório to Saens Peña, connecting with the secondary line to Estácio (which provides service to São Cristóvão, Maracanã and beyond). The main stops in Centro are Cinelândia and Carioca. An ambitious R$2.5 billion expansion was due to be completed by June 2016. A single ride costs R$3.70.

TAXI

Rio's taxis are useful late at night and when you're carrying valuables. The flat rate is R$5.20, plus R$2.05 per kilometer – slightly more at night and on Sunday.

THE SOUTHEAST

Those who manage to tear themselves away from Rio's charming clutches will find some of Brazil's most endearing attractions right in its backyard. Coastal highlights include the Costa do Sol (Sun Coast) north of Rio, home to the upscale beach resort of Búzios – a weekend city escape for hot-to-trot *cariocas*; and the spectacular Costa Verde (Green Coast), stretching south from Rio to São Paulo, boasting rainforest-smothered islands (Ilha Grande), beautifully preserved colonial villages (Paraty) and postcard-perfect beaches (the whole stretch).

Or head inland to the convivial state of Minas Gerais, famous throughout Brazil for its hearty cuisine and friendly population. Here time has frozen colonial-era gold-mining towns such as Ouro Prêto or sleepy villages like Tiradentes, where magical historical delights beckon around every corner.

It all culminates in South America's intimidating cultural capital, São Paulo, where you'll find some of the best museums, nightclubs and restaurants in South America.

Southeast Brazil

Getting There & Around

Rio de Janeiro is the major gateway to the coastal regions, though if coming from the south or west you can reach the Costa Verde via São Paulo. Belo Horizonte, Brazil's third-largest city, is the gateway to the old gold-mining towns in Minas Gerais.

Numerous flights connect the three major cities of the Southeast – Belo Horizonte, Rio and São Paulo – with plenty of bus links covering southeastern destinations. Ilha Grande is reached by ferry from Angra dos Reis, Mangaratiba or Conceição de Jacareí.

Búzios

0XX22 / POP 27,000

Before Búzios was to Rio de Janeiro what the Hamptons are to New York City – a summer playground for the blessed and beautiful – it was a simple fishing village and sun-soaked hideaway for French starlet Brigitte Bardot, who frolicked among the town's 17 fabled beaches way back in the '60s, when nobody cared but the fishermen. Located 167km east of Rio, wonderful and wild Búzios is today playfully referred to as *Búzios Aires* due to the increasing numbers of Argentines that live and vacation here (payback for *Brasiloche*, we reckon).

Activities

The biggest draws in Búzios are the natural setting plus its endless array of opportunities for relaxation, nightlife, shopping and ocean sports.

Tour Shop Búzios BUS TOUR, BOAT TOUR
(2623-4733; www.tourshop.com.br; Orla Bardot 550; tours from R$50) This agency runs the Búzios Trolley, an open-sided bus that visits 12 of the peninsula's beaches daily. Additional offerings include snorkeling, diving and rafting tours, along with excursions by schooner and glass-bottomed catamaran.

Sleeping

Búzios caters to couples, so things can get pricey for solo travelers. Rates quoted here are for the high season: December through March, plus July.

★**Local Friend Hostel** HOSTEL $$
(2623-0614; www.localfriendbuzios.com; Av Geribá 585; dm R$60-65, d/tr/q R$180/235/290) The name says it all at this brilliant new hostel one block from Geribá beach. After an eight-year round-the-world trip (New Zealand, Europe, United States) Rio-Grande-do-Sul-born chef Eduardo Ghilardi has brought his infectious *gaucho* hospitality to Búzios, inviting guests to disconnect from technology and enjoy human interaction: surfing, kayaking, playing board games or joining one of his regular cooking class/dinners.

★**Nomad Búzios** HOSTEL $$
(2620-8085; www.nomadbuzios.com.br; Rua das Pedras 25; dm R$57-75, d R$200-325;) Búzios' best-positioned hostel boasts a seaside perch in the thick of the Rua das Pedras nightlife zone. The seven private doubles (four with terraces) enjoy gorgeous full-on ocean views. Meanwhile, the deck chairs and lounging bed on the waterfront terrace, coupled with R$7 *caipirinhas* in the bar downstairs, make life in the four- to 13-bed dorms pretty cushy as well.

L'Escale POUSADA $$
(2623-2816; www.pousadalescale.com; Travessa Santana 14, Ossos; r from R$280, with sea view R$340; closed May-Sep;) Book ahead for one of the three ocean-facing rooms with terraces and hammocks at this sweet, petite French-run *pousada* with a divine beachfront location in relaxed Ossos. Owners Sylvia and Francis also operate the eponymous restaurant downstairs serving fish soup, seafood and French specialties including beef bourguignon, sweet and savory crepes, and profiteroles.

Eating & Drinking

Chez Michou Crêperie CREPERIE $
(2623-2169; www.chezmichou.com.br; Rua das Pedras 90; crepes R$15-28; noon-late Thu-Tue, from 5pm Wed) Crowds flock here not only for the sweet and savory crepes, but also for mixed drinks at the outdoor bar, sports events on the big screen TVs and the weekend DJ mixes (from 9pm).

★**Nami Gastrobar** JAPANESE, FUSION $$
(2623-6637; www.facebook.com/namigastrobar; cnr Rua dos Namorados & Gerbert Perissé; mains R$33-89; 6:30-11pm Wed-Fri, 12:30-11pm Sat, 12:30-5pm Sun) Near Geribá beach, this restaurant fuses traditional Japanese cuisine with Peruvian, Mexican and other influences to create a spectacularly eclectic international dining experience. Fresh seafood takes center stage in citrusy ceviche, crunchy wasabi-salmon tacos, tempura shrimp and miso-marinated black cod, but meatier delights also abound, including

delicate slices of grilled beef with sesame seeds or spare ribs with roasted corn.

Restaurante do David SEAFOOD $$
(2623-2981; Manoel Turíbio de Farias 260; mains R$21-75; noon-midnight) Still going strong after 40 years, David's serves high-quality seafood at little wooden tables with red tablecloths in the heart of town.

Information

Bradesco (Av José Bento Ribeiro Dantas 254) One of several downtown ATMs.

Secretaria de Turismo (www.buzios.rj.gov.br/informacoes_turisticas.aspx) Two well-staffed offices distribute city maps and hotel information, at the town entrance portal (2623-4254; Av José Bento Ribeiro Dantas; 8am-9pm) and just off the main square in Armação (2623-2099; Travessia dos Pescadores 110, Armação; 8am-9pm).

Getting There & Away

The Búzios **bus station** (Estrada da Usina 444) is a simple covered bus stop with no building attached, five blocks south of the Armação waterfront. **Viação 1001** (2623-2050; www.autoviacao1001.com.br) runs buses from Búzios to Rio's Novo Rio bus station (R$48 to R$61, 2¾ hours) at least 10 times daily between 6am and 8pm; the same company offers direct transfers four times daily to Rio's Galeão airport (R$80) and once daily to Copacabana and other Zona Sul beaches (R$90).

Getting Around

Municipal buses between Búzios and Cabo Frio (R$4.50; 45 minutes) travel along Av José Bento Ribeiro Dantas and Estrada da Usina; there's a convenient **bus stop** (Estrada da Usina) directly opposite the Rio-bound bus stop.

Ilha Grande

0XX24 / POP 3600

Located 150km southwest of Rio de Janeiro, Ilha Grande was once a tranquil hideaway that saw more bait and tackle than paparazzi, but these days it's a full-blown party. Most of the international partiers jet set on private yachts and islands around Baía de Angra, while backpackers, middle-class Brazilians and international nomads collect in and around Vila do Abraão, Ilha Grande's main settlement.

The increase in popularity of Brazil's third-largest island is a no-brainer: gorgeous beaches flank hillsides covered in lush forests, important remnants of the rapidly disappearing Mata Atlântica ecosystem. Sixty percent of the island is devoted to the 12,052-hectare Parque Estadual da Ilha Grande, Brazil's largest island park.

There are no banks or private cars on Ilha Grande, so get cash before you relax.

Sights & Activities

The outdoor-adventure options on Ilha Grande are endless. Posted around town are maps showing 16 different signposted trails leading through the lush forest to several of the island's 102 beaches. When visiting some beaches, it's possible to hike one way and take a boat the other.

Before hitting the trail, let people at your *pousada* know where you're going and when you'll be back, stock up on water and bug repellent, and bring a flashlight, as darkness comes swiftly under the jungle canopy. Guides are advisable for exploring beyond the most heavily traveled routes; poorly marked trails and poisonous snakes can make things challenging.

★Praia Lopes Mendes BEACH
Facing the open Atlantic, this seemingly endless beach with good surfing waves (shortboard/longboard rentals available on-site) is considered by some the most beautiful in Brazil. It's accessible by Ilha Grande's most popular walking trail, a three-hour, 6.1km trek that starts at the eastern end of Abraão's town beach, crosses the hills to **Praia de Palmas**, then follows the coast to **Praia do Pouso**. Alternatively, take a boat from Abraão to Pouso. From Pouso, it's a 15-minute walk to Lopes Mendes.

Sleeping & Eating

Vila do Abraão is swarming with *pousadas*. Note that we quote prices for high season (December to March). Prices drop by as much as 50% between April and November. Restaurants abound along Rua da Praia, Rua Getúlio Vargas and the small pedestrian street Travessa Buganville.

Che Lagarto HOSTEL $
(3361-9669; www.chelagarto.com; Praia do Canto; dm R$39-75, d R$175-235; @) Unbeatable location at the far eastern end of Abraão's main beach, a panoramic waterfront deck and a bar with free-flowing *caipirinhas* are the prime attractions at this hostel, part of South America's largest chain. Some boats from Conceição de Jacareí will drop you at

the Aquário hostel next door; otherwise, it's a 10-minute walk from Abraão's town center.

Jungle Lodge GUESTHOUSE **$**
(☎99977-2405; www.ilhagrandeexpeditions.com; Caminho de Palmas 4; d R$140-160; @) Tucked away above town in the rainforest, this rustic, five-room guesthouse and open-air chalet is run by a wild-haired Pantanal guide and his German wife. It's an entirely different experience than sleeping in Abraão, a 1.5km hike away. The view from the outdoor shower is miraculous.

★**Pousada Manacá** POUSADA **$$**
(☎3361-5404; www.ilhagrandemanaca.com.br; Praia do Abraão 333; d R$280-320, tr R$360-400; ❄📶) It's worth reserving ahead and paying the small surcharge for a front room with balcony and hammock at this French-run beachfront *pousada*. The ample breakfast is accompanied by sea views from the pleasant front terrace; other nice touches include in-room fridges, dependable solar hot water and a central patio for lounging. Septuagenarian owner Gerard speaks five languages.

Las Sorrentinas ARGENTINE, ITALIAN **$**
(www.facebook.com/Sorrentinas; Getúlio Vargas 638; mains R$24-27; ⏲6:30-10:30pm Mon-Sat) Superb homemade *sorrentinos* (ravioli-like stuffed pasta pockets) are the specialty at this breezy Argentine-run upstairs restaurant. Fillings range from Gorgonzola, walnuts and mozzarella to ham, cheese and basil, accompanied by your choice of sauces. The place wins extra points for its friendly service and potent *caipirinhas*.

Lua e Mar SEAFOOD **$$**
(Praia do Canto; mains for 2 R$80-155; ⏲11am-11pm Thu-Tue) Candlelit tables on the sand make a tranquil place to watch the crashing waves and scurrying crabs while you enjoy tasty *moqueca* (fish stew) and other seafood dishes for two.

ℹ Getting There & Away

The quickest and most hassle-free way to reach the island from Rio is via door-to-door shuttle services such as **Easy Transfer** (☎99386-3919; www.easytransferbrazil.com) – these will pick you up at any hostel, hotel or *pousada* in Rio and deliver you to the island (R$85, 3½ to 4½ hours), with a synchronized transfer from van to speedboat in the coastal town of Conceição de Jacareí. Easy Transfer also offers a similar service from Paraty (R$75, 3½ hours).

Reaching the island via public transport is slightly cheaper but more complicated, as you have to choose from multiple routes and buy two separate tickets (one for the bus, one for the boat).

Costa Verde (www.costaverdetransportes.com.br) runs buses from Rio to the three ports where boats for Ilha Grande depart: Conceição de Jacareí (R$49, 2½ hours, five buses daily), Mangaratiba (R$30, 2½ hours, four daily) and Angra dos Reis (R$49, three hours, hourly).

The most frequent boat crossings are from Conceição de Jacareí, where speedboats (R$30 to R$35, 20 minutes) and schooners (R$15 to R$20, 50 minutes) leave every hour or two between 8:30am and 6pm, returning from Abraão between 8am and 5:30pm. From Angra dos Reis, a similar service is available by speedboat (R$40, 30 minutes) and schooner (R$25, 80 minutes). Boat companies operating along one or both routes include **Objetiva** (☎3361-5963; www.objetivatour.com), **Cambeba Flex** (☎3361-5662; www.cambebailhagrande.com), **Angra Flex** (☎3365-2125, 3365-4180; www.facebook.com/angraflex) and **Acquaflex** (☎3361-5156; www.aguavivatour.com.br).

More affordable but less frequent are the daily ferries to Ilha Grande operated by **CCR Barcas** (www.grupoccr.com.br/barcas), leaving from Angra dos Reis and Mangaratiba (R$14, 80 minutes from either port). Ferries depart Angra at 3:30pm weekdays and 1:30pm weekends, returning from Abraão at 10am daily. From Mangaratiba, ferries leave at 8am daily and 10pm Friday, returning from Abraão at 5:30pm daily. Extra ferries are sometimes added during high season; confirm locally before departure.

Angra is the most useful port for those traveling west from Ilha Grande. Colitur buses for Paraty (R$11.30, two hours) leave Angra's bus station, 1.5km east of the boat docks, at least hourly from 6am to 11pm daily.

Paraty

☎0XX24 / POP 37,533

You know a place is authentic when the cobblestones are so uneven, it's actually painful to walk the streets. That's Paraty. One of Brazil's most cinematic destinations, this staunchly preserved colonial village can be overly touristy at times, but a sleepy dream of cobblestones and whitewash at others, only upset by the kaleidoscopic hues that pepper its historic walls.

👁 Sights

Hours and opening times at Paraty's historic churches seem to be in constant flux; check with the tourist office for up-to-the-minute details.

Casa da Cultura MUSEUM
(☎3371-2325; www.casadaculturaparaty.org.br; Dona Geralda 177; ⊙10am-10pm Tue-Sun) FREE In a beautiful colonial mansion, Paraty's Casa da Cultura hosts rotating exhibitions and events, with a focus on local culture. There are nice views of town from the main gallery upstairs.

Activities

★**Paraty Adventure** OUTDOORS
(☎3371-6135; www.paratyadventure.com; Marechal Deodoro 12) Friendly Brazilians Alessandra and Edsom run this great little agency offering off-the-beaten-track opportunities for adventure and cultural immersion. Highlights include their all-day mountain biking and hiking trip to Pedra da Macela, the region's highest peak (R$180), and a three-day trek to Ponta da Juatinga, the remote fishing village where Alessandra grew up (R$840, including food and accommodation in local homes).

★**Paraty Explorer** OUTDOORS
(☎99952-4496; www.paratyexplorer.com; Praia do Jabaquara) This agency on Jabaquara beach, run by friendly outdoors enthusiasts Paddy (from Ireland) and Rodrigo (from Brazil), specializes in sea kayaking, stand-up paddle boarding (SUP) and hiking adventures around Paraty Bay. Hiking destinations include dramatic Pão de Açúcar do Mamanguá, the historic Trilha do Ouro (Gold Trail) in Serra da Bocaina national park, and remote beaches of the Costa Verde.

Sleeping

Book ahead if you're coming from December to February. Once you hit the cobblestones, prices rise substantially. Budget-minded travelers will find several campgrounds and hostels along the Pontal and Jabaquara beachfronts (just north of town, across the pedestrian bridge).

★**Happy Hammock** HOSTEL $
(☎99994-9527; www.facebook.com/happyhammockparaty; Ponta Grossa; dm/d R$55/150) This Swiss-run waterfront hostel sits on isolated Ponta Grossa, 15 minutes by boat from Paraty. With no road access, limited generator-fueled electricity and gorgeous sea views, it's a dreamy end-of-the-line getaway where guests can lounge in hammocks, swim in phosphorescent waters or hike to nearby beaches before the tour boats arrive. Book dinners (R$15) and boat transfers (R$30) in advance.

Che Lagarto HOSTEL $
(☎3361-9669; www.chelagarto.com; Benina Toledo do Prado 22; dm R$39-56, r R$153-180;) Tucked down a back street between the bus station and the historic center, this good-time hostel is a social oasis, with a welcoming bar, BBQ, small pool area, zillions of organized activities and direct transfers to Rio, Ilha Grande and São Paulo; solitude seekers should ask for a room in the annex, which faces away from the commotion.

Hotel Solar dos Gerânios INN $$
(☎3371-1550; www.paraty.com.br/geranio; Praça da Matriz; s/d/tr R$120/180/240;) Run by the same family for decades, this rustic place on lively Praça da Matriz is the most affordable hotel in Paraty's colonial center. Wood and ceramic sculptures, stone walls and floors, columns and beamed ceilings, and a courtyard full of plants, cats and dogs all add character. Several rooms have balconies overlooking the square.

Eating & Drinking

Don't miss the sweet carts rolling around town as well as the *caipirinhas* – Paraty is second only to Minas Gerais in *cachaça* (a high-proof sugarcane spirit) fame.

Manuê SANDWICHES, JUICE BAR $
(www.facebook.com/manueparaty; Rua João do Prado 1; sandwiches R$6-13, juices R$6-8; ⊙10am-11pm Wed-Mon;) With good coffee, free wi-fi, two dozen varieties of juice and a delicious array of budget-friendly omelettes and *dobrados* (toasted flatbread sandwiches), this little eatery draws a mixed crowd of locals and tourists.

Quiosque Dito e Feito SEAFOOD $$
(Praia do Pontal; mains for 2 R$50-90; ⊙10am-6pm) Ask locals where to find reasonably priced fresh seafood and they'll send you to this simple beachfront kiosk on Praia do Pontal. From straightforward fried fish to *moqueca* to the *caldeirada do mar* (a seafood stew for three), dishes are huge, but half-portions are available upon request.

Casa do Fogo BISTRO $$
(☎3371-3163; www.casadofogo.com.br; Comendador Jose Luiz 390; mains R$38-79; ⊙6pm-1am) The name says it all here – everything's on fire! The menu focuses on seafood set ablaze with the local *cachaça,* and desserts don't escape a fiery death either.

☆ Entertainment

Van Gogh Pub LIVE MUSIC
(Samuel Costa 22; ⌚9pm-late Thu-Mon) Paraty's new kid on the block keeps the old town hopping with five nights of live music per week, including reggae, samba, rock, jazz, blues and *forró*.

Paraty 33 LIVE MUSIC
(www.paraty33.com.br; Rua da Lapa 357; ⌚noon-1am Sun-Thu, to 4am Fri & Sat) With an early evening happy hour featuring MPB and bossa nova, and a late-night weekend mix of DJs and live acts, Paraty 33 is the historic center's liveliest nightspot.

ℹ Information

Bradesco (Av Roberto Silveira) Multiple ATMs two blocks north of the bus station; more at Banco do Brasil next door.

CIT (☎3371-1222; Dr Samuel Costa 29; ⌚8am-8pm) Recently relocated to the historic center, Paraty's tourist office also has a second branch (☎3371-1897; Av Roberto da Silveira s/n; ⌚8am-8pm) just off highway BR-101.

ℹ Getting There & Away

The **bus station** (Rua Jango Pádua) is 500m west of the old town. **Costa Verde** (www.costaverdetransportes.com.br) offers frequent services to Rio de Janeiro (R$66, 4¾ hours, 12 daily). Colitur has buses to Angra dos Reis (R$11.30, two hours, hourly from 5am to 8pm) and **Reunidas** (www.reunidaspaulista.com.br) buses head to São Paulo (R$58, 5¾ hours, six daily).

São Paulo

☎0XX11 / POP 11.3 MILLION

São Paulo is a monster. The gastronomic, fashion, finance and culture capital of Latin America is a true megalopolis in every sense of the word, home to 21 million people (metropolitan) and more skyscrapers than could ever possibly be counted. Calling it the New York of South America wouldn't be inaccurate. Besides a dizzying avalanche of first-rate museums, cultural centers, experimental theaters and cinemas, Sampa's nightclubs and bars are among the best on the continent and its restaurants are among the world's best. Trendsetting *paulistanos* (inhabitants of the city) believe in working hard and playing harder, and despite constantly complaining about street violence, clogged roads and pollution, most wouldn't dare consider moving from the largest city in the southern hemisphere.

👁 Sights

The atmospheric old center of São Paulo lies between Praça da Sé, Luz metro station and Praça da República. Cleverly titled Centro Velho, it's a pedestrianized maze offering a fascinating cornucopia of architectural styles (always look above the ground floors, which have all lost their charm to everyday shops). Other interesting neighborhood strolls are found in Liberdade, Sampa's Japan town (also home to other Asian communities); and Vila Madalena, the artistic quarter. Both host lively weekend street markets, the former at Praçada Liberdade, the latter at Praça Benedito Calixto (Saturday only).

★**Mercado Municipal** MARKET
(Mercadão; Map p312; www.oportaldomercadao.com.br; Rua da Cantareira 306; ⌚6am-6pm Mon-Sat, to 4pm Sun) This covered market is a belle époque confection of stained glass and a series of vast domes. Inside, a fabulous urban market specializes in all things edible. It's also a great place to sample a couple of classic Sampa delights: mortadella sandwiches at Bar do Mané and *pasteis* (pockets of dough stuffed with meat, cheese or fish and then fried).

Museu do Futebol MUSEUM
(www.museudofutebol.org.br; Praça Charles Miller s/n, Pacaembu; adult/student R$6/3, Thu free; ⌚9am-5pm Tue-Sun; 👪) Tucked under the bleachers of colorfully art deco Pacaembu Stadium, this fantastic museum is devoted to Brazil's greatest passion – football (soccer). Its multimedia displays over two floors manage to evoke the thrill of watching a championship game, even for nonfans.

★**Pinacoteca do Estado** MUSEUM
(Map p312; www.pinacoteca.org.br; Praça da Luz 2; adult/student R$6/3, Sat free; ⌚10am-6pm Tue-Sun) This elegant neoclassical museum houses an excellent collection of Brazilian – and especially Paulista – art from the 19th century to the present, including works by big names such as Portinari and Di Cavalcanti. There is a lovely cafe that faces adjacent Parque da Luz.

★**Theatro Municipal** THEATER
(Map p312; ☎3397-0300; www.theatromunicipal.org.br; Praça Ramos de Azevedo) São Paulo's most splendid construction, this theater was

Central São Paulo

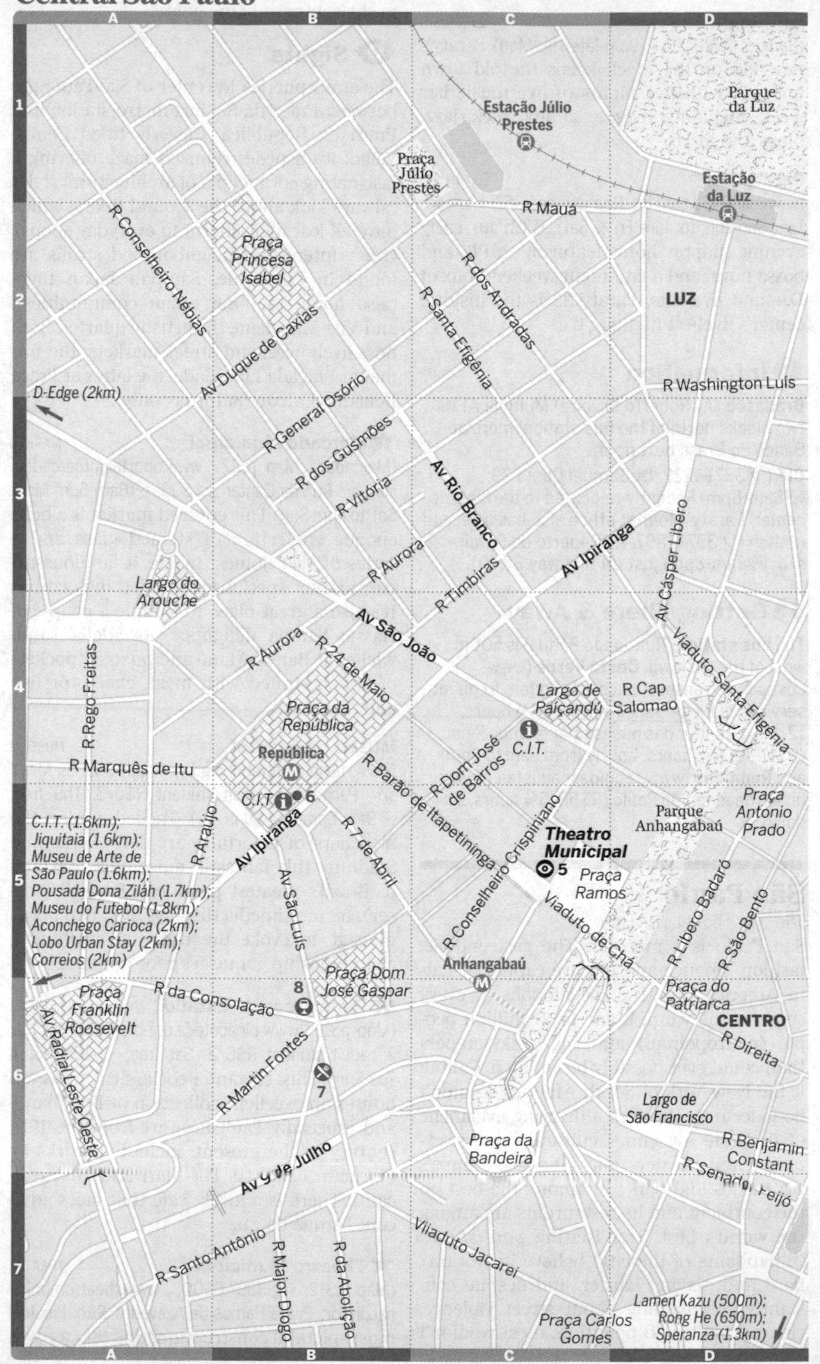

begun in 1903 in the style of Paris' Palais Garnier. Its heavily ornamented facade seems to combine every architectural style imaginable, from baroque to art nouveau, and its interior is clad in gold and marble. Free English tours run twice daily Tuesday to Friday at 11am and 5pm, and Saturday at noon.

★Museu de Arte de São Paulo MUSEUM
(MASP; www.masp.art.br; Av Paulista 1578, Bela Vista; adult/student R$25/12, Tue all day & Thu after 5pm free; ⌚10am-6pm Tue & Thu-Sun, to 8pm Wed) Sampa's pride, this museum possesses Latin America's most comprehensive collection of Western art. Hovering above a concrete plaza that turns into an antiques fair on Sunday, the museum, designed by architect Lina Bo Bardi and completed in 1968, is considered a classic of modernism by many and an abomination by a vocal few.

★Museu Afro-Brasil MUSEUM
(www.museuafrobrasil.com.br; Av. Pedro Alvares Cabral s/n, Parque Ibirapuera, Gate 10; adult/student R$6/3, Thu & Sat free; ⌚10am-5pm Tue-Sun) This hugely important, absolutely fascinating Parque do Ibirapuera museum features a permanent 3rd-floor collection chronicling five centuries of African immigration (and a nod to the 10 million African lives lost in the construction of Brazil) and hosts a rotating array of contemporary Afro-centric exhibitions on its bottom two floors.

Sleeping

The best spots for travelers include the bohemian *bairro* of Vila Madalena, 6km west of Praça da Sé, which now boasts a bona fide hip hostel scene in addition to being the city's longstanding cradle of artsy boutiques,

Central São Paulo

Top Sights
1 Banespa E5
2 Mercado Municipal F4
3 Mosteiro São Bento E4
4 Pinacoteca do Estado E1
5 Theatro Municipal C5

Activities, Courses & Tours
6 SP Free Walking Tour B5

Eating
7 Estadão B6

Drinking & Nightlife
8 Alberta #3 .... B6

cutting-edge galleries and boisterous nightlife; and the leafy, upscale district of Jardim Paulista, 5km southwest of Centro.

★We Hostel Design HOSTEL $
(☎2615-2262; www.wehostel.com.br; Morgado de Mateus 567, Vila Mariana; dm R$57-73, d without bathroom R$160-210; ❄@📶) Simply gorgeous, São Paulo's best hostel sits inside a beautiful 100-year-old historic white mansion on a quiet Vila Mariana residential corner. From the guest kitchen to the hammock-strewn, quasi-wraparound porch to the kitschy living room, everything here has been designed with expert connoisseurship of retro furniture and coveted antiques.

Ô de Casa HOSTEL $
(Map p314; ☎3063-5216; www.odecasahostel.com; Inácio Pereira da Rocha 385 , Vila Madalena; dm R$50-60, r R$150, r without bathroom R$130; ❄📶) This artsy and colorful hostel is one of the neighborhoods oldest and nicest, with a sociable bar and rooftop terrace that gives way to shotgun-style in four-, six- and eight-bed mixed dorm configurations and well-kept bathrooms. An annex across the street houses quieter private rooms, which attract couples looking for privacy and shorter bathroom waits, without sacrificing the hostel atmosphere.

LimeTime Hostel HOSTEL $
(Map p314; ☎3798-0051; www.limetimehostels.com; Mourato Coelho 973, Vila Madalena; dm from R$35, d R$110; @📶) Vila Madalena's most sociable hostel and the better of LimeTime's two in the city, thanks to the courtyard bar that is open to the general public and superb location within the neighborhood's nightlife and arts scenes. Digs are dorm-only, but each has its own private bath, and there's a dilapidated rooftop patio that oozes potential. No breakfast, no free towels.

Vila Madalena

★Guest Urban BOUTIQUE HOTEL $$
(Map p314; ☎3081-5030; www.guesturbansp.com.br; Lisboa 493, Pinheiros; s/d from R$253/273; ❄@📶) This 1930s mansion, opened in late 2015, holds 14 suites reeking of industrial chic (exposed brick and beams, unfinished steel and concrete) offset by a sunny open patio and cutting-edge art (reprints for sale in lobby). It's one block from Praca Benedito Calixto in the heart of hip Pinheiros.

Lobo Urban Stay GUESTHOUSE $$
(☎3569-7198; www.lobourbanstay.com; Haddock Lobo 839, Jardins; dm/s/d/tr R$60/150/200/250; @📶) This quiet, design-forward newcomer easily offers the best location for money in the city, located smack dab in the middle of São Paulo's toniest environs. Run by two young journalists, there's one eight-bed dorm with its own private bath and two spacious privates (especially good-value for solo travelers).

Pousada Dona Ziláh POUSADA $$
(☎3062-1444; www.zilah.com; Minas Gerais 112, Higienópolis; r/tr R$315/390; @📶) After 30 years in Jardins, a move to this Paulista-adjacent 1932 mansion in Higienópolis spells the end of an era, but not the end of the charm. These six new rooms offer upgraded comforts, especially where the bathrooms are concerned, and extensive gardens that are watered with filtered shower and sink water.

Eating

Eating is Sampa's Godsend, boasting quality unrivaled in South America.

Vila Madalena

Sleeping
1 Guest Urban D2
2 LimeTime Hostel B2
3 Ô de Casa B3

Eating
4 Bráz Pizzaria A3
5 Feijoada da Lana B2

Drinking & Nightlife
6 Boca de Ouro C3
7 Empório Alto de Pinheiros A3
8 São Cristóvão B2
9 Superloft A4

Entertainment
10 Ó do Borogodó C3

Butantan Food Park FOOD TRUCK $
(www.butantanfoodpark.com.br; Agostinho Cantu 47, Butantã; mains R$15-25; ⏲11am-4pm Mon-Wed, to 10pm Thu-Sat, noon-7pm Sun) The best spot to dive into the city's exploding food truck scene is this permanent parking lot, which hosts a daily revolving door of 15 to 35 vendors (food trucks, carts, bikes and craft brewer tents) – no two visits are the same. On weekends, it's a full-on foodie fest. It's 650m from Metrô Butantã on the yellow line.

Rong He CHINESE $
(www.ronghe.com.br; Rua da Glória 622, Liberdade; mains for 2 R$14-45; ⏲11:30-3pm & 6-10:30pm Mon-Fri, 11:30am-10:30pm Sat & Sun) A Liberdade institution and the city's best Chinese. First and foremost, expect surly service; second to that, the *gyoza* (pan-fried Japanese dumplings) and the house-made Chinese noodle dishes, are served in great-value portions *yakisoba*-style or in soupy, piping hot caldrons *(ensopada)* to out-the-door lines of devoted patrons. You can watch the dough masters at work through the show kitchen window.

Estadão FAST FOOD $
(Map p312; www.estadaolanches.com.br; Viaduto 9 de Julho 193, Centro; specialty sandwiches R$14-29; ⏲24hr) This classic Centro *lanchonete* (snack bar) serves working folk's meals at all hours, but its signature *pernil* (pork loin) sandwich, smothered in the cheese of your choice (provolone!) and sautéed onions, is one of Sampa's gastronomic musts.

★Aconchego Carioca BRAZILIAN $$
(☎3062-8262; Alameda Jaú 1372, Jardins; mains for 2 R$56-86; ⏲6-11pm Mon, noon-midnight Tue-Sat, noon-6pm Sun; 📶) A *boteco* (small open-air bar) import from Rio that quickly gained an avid following in Sampa due to its undivided attention to specialty Brazilian microbrews, creative *bolinhos* (fried finger foods - try *virado à paulista*, with beans, kale, sausage, beef and egg; or the *feijoada* version) and fabulous, well-portioned takes on traditional dishes like *bobó de camarão* (shrimp in manioc puree; feeds three!).

★Jiquitaia BRAZILIAN $$
(☎3262-2366; www.jiquitaia.com.br; Antônio Carlos 268, Consolação; mains R$43-68; ⏲noon-3pm Mon, 7-11:30pm Tue-Fri, noon-11:30pm Sat) Accolades abound for upstart Brazilian chef Marcelo Bastos and his affordable entry level into contemporary Brazilian cuisine – pick any three courses at this cute and cozy bistro-style restaurant to create your own

set menu (R$69), including – drum roll, please! – the elusive *moqueca* (Bahian fish stew) for one person. Sister Nina admirably handles the excellent fresh fruit *caipirinhas*.

★Feijoada da Lana BRAZILIAN $$
(Map p314; Aspicuelta 421, Vila Madalena; feijoada weekday/weekend R$42/74; ⊙noon-3:30pm Tue-Fri, 12:30-5pm Sat & Sun) Lana, a journalist by trade, offers her hugely popular version of *feijoada*, Brazil's national dish, inside a smallish Vila Madalena house. Production here isn't as elaborate as at more expensive options or fancy hotels, but it's long on smiling service, hearty goodness and (included on weekends!) *batidinhas de limão*, a sort of shaken *caipirinha*.

★Lamen Kazu JAPANESE $$
(www.lamenkazu.com.br; Tomás Gonzaga 51, Liberdade; mains $22-48; ⊙11am-3pm & 6-10:30pm Mon-Sat, 11am-3pm & 6-9pm Sun;) It's not as famous (or cheap) as its nearby rival Aska, but take the hint: the 99% Japanese clientele should tell you something. The fiery Kara Misso Lamen (spicy broth and spiced pork in addition to the usual condiments; R$35), doused with the house-made chili sauce, is a revelation, as is everything on the menu.

Drinking

Traditional bar neighborhoods are Vila Madalena (witness the corner of Aspicuelta and Mourato Coelho on weekends!), along Mario Ferraz in Itaim Bibi; and Baixo Augusta, where the GLS scene (Portuguese slang for Gay, Lesbian and Sympathetics) mingles with artsy, alterna-hipsters in the city's edgiest/coolest nightlife district. Paulista is also very lively at happy hour along the sidewalk bars near Joaquim Eugênio de Lima.

Bars

★Veloso BOTECO
(www.velosobar.com.br; Conceição Veloso 56, Vila Mariana; ⊙5:30pm-12:30am Tue-Fri, from 12:45pm

DON'T MISS

PIZZA PAULISTANA

Forget New York and Chicago (or even Naples, for that matter): one of the world's best-kept secrets is São Paulo's excellent *pizza paulistana*. Locals say the city's pizza is so good, even the Italians are jealous! It shouldn't be a surprise, though, as swarms of Italian immigrants settled here in the late 19th century, giving the city one of the largest Italian populations in the world outside Italy. Today, nearly 6000 or so pizzerias pepper the sprawling cityscape, with more than one million pies engulfed per day. Do not depart without trying one of the following.

Bráz (Map p314; www.brazpizzaria.com.br; Vupabussu 271, Pinheiros; pizza R$49-75; ⊙6:30pm-12:30am Sun-Thu, to 1:30am Fri & Sat;) Start to finish, the experience here will leave you forgetting pizza ever originated in Italy. Do as Brazilians do and order a Brahma draft beer *(chope)* followed by an appetizer of warm sausage bread *(pão de calabresa)* dipped in spiced olive oil, then let the feast commence. *Fosca* (smoked ham,-Catupiry cheese, mozzarella and tomato sauce) is a current favorite. You can duplicate this unforgettable experience in **Rio** (2535-0687; Maria Angélica 129; pizzas R$50-80; ⊙6pm-midnight) if São Paulo is not in your itinerary; and at additional Sampa locations in Moema and Higienópolis.

Speranza (3288-3512; www.pizzaria.com.br; Treze de Maio 1004, Bixiga; pizza R$44-86; ⊙6pm-1am Sun-Thu, to 1:30am Fri & Sat;) One of São Paulo's oldest and most traditional pizzerias in the Italian neighborhood of Bixiga, where the Famiglia Tarallo has been serving serious pizza since 1958. Perfect meal: the life-changing bruschetta appetizer followed by an excellent, fiercely traditional pizza margherita. It's an easy walk from Paulista/Brigadeiro Metrô.

Leggera Pizza Napoletana (3862-2581; www.pizzerialeggera.com.br; Diana 80; pizza R$30-38; ⊙7-11pm Sun & Tue-Thu, to 11:30pm Fri & Sat;) Brazilian-Italian-American *pizzaiolo* Andre Guidon imports everything humanly possible from Italy – and this small, family-run affair epitomizes the Brazilian-Italian diaspora. The individual-sized, uncut pies here (plus a few calzones) are easily Sampa's best, and they emerge from one of just 500 or so Neapolitan pizzeria ovens in the world certified by the *Associação Verace Pizza Napoletana*. Reservations are prudent.

FREE SP!

There's no sugarcoating it: Brazil is expensive and São Paulo is the beast of the bunch. But that doesn't mean you can't have fun on a shoestring budget. Our favorite freebies:

Banespa (Edifício Altino Arantes; Map p312; João Brícola 24; ⌚10am-3pm Mon-Fri) For one of Sampa's best panoramas, head to the top of this 161m-high skyscraper, Brazil's version of the Empire State Building, completed in 1939. Ride free to the observation deck on the top floor for views of the city.

Note: you will need some form of ID to sign in. You'll need to hurry up and wait: first to sign in, then for an elevator to the 26th floor, then a second elevator and finally for the spiral staircase to the top. The five-minute maximum visit is enforced heavy-handedly, but the view will floor you.

Mosteiro São Bento (Map p312; ☎2440-7837; www.mosteiro.org.br; Largo de São Bento s/n; ⌚6am-6pm Mon-Wed & Fri, 6am-8am Thu, 6am-noon & 4-6pm Sat & Sun) Among the city's oldest and most important churches, São Bento dates to 1598, though its neo-Gothic facade dates only to the early 20th century. Step inside the church to view its impressive stained glass. Masses (7am weekdays, 6am on Saturday and 10am Sunday) include Gregorian chanting.

SP Free Walking Tour (Map p312; www.spfreewalkingtour.com; ⌚11:30am Mon, Wed & Sat) Culls over 450 years of Sampa history into a long but fascinating 'Old Downtown' walk three times a week at 11:30am. The tour meets next to the CIT at Praça da República and ends 3½ hours later at Largo São Bento; and there's walk-exclusive discounts to be had along the way.

A Paulista Ave tour covers the modern city every Thursday and Sunday at 3:30pm, leaving from Banco do Brasil at the corner of Paulista and Rua Augusta on the Jardins side and ending 3¼ hours later at Praça Oswaldo Cruz. An artsy, graffiti-heavy tour in Vila Madalena leaves from just outside Fradique Countinho metro station on Tuesdays and Sundays at 11am.

Sat, 4-10:30pm Sun) Arrive early to this outstanding *boteco* a quick walk from Vila Mariana's metro station – crowds fight over tables for some of the city's best *caipirinhas*, in exotic flavors (*jabuticaba*, starfruit with basil, tangerine with *dedo-de-moça* pepper; R$18-30), and shockingly good *coxinhas* (battered and fried shredded chicken, *catupiry* cheese and spices; R$27.60).

Alberta #3 BAR

(Map p312; www.alberta3.com.br; Av São Luís 272, Centro; cover R$15-35; ⌚7pm-late Tue-Sat) This three-story hipster hideout off Praça da República draws inspiration from '50s-era hotel bars and lobbies, and rides a soundtrack steeped mostly in classic rock, jazz and soul (DJs often spin vinyl on the small dance floor).

Empório Alto de Pinheiros BAR

(Map p314; www.altodospinheiros.com.br; Vupabussu 305, Alto de Pinheiros ; ⌚noon-midnight Sun-Wed, to 1am Thu-Sat; 📶) This neighborhood beer emporium evolved into a full-on gourmet craft beer bar as the brew scene in Brazil exploded. *Cerveza* geeks fret nervously over more than 400 bottled or 33 choices on draft, including rarer Brazilian microbrews. You'll need a few drinks to tolerate the service.

Boca de Ouro COCKTAIL BAR

(Map p314; www.bocadeouro.com.br; Cônego Eugênio Leite 1121 , Pinheiros; cocktails R$8-24; ⌚6pm-midnight Mon-Thu, to 2am Fri & Sat; 📶) Classic cocktails mixed with the methodicalness of art restoration and a distinctly un-Brazilian setup (an actual belly-up-to bar behind a Brownstone-like facade that could easily pass for Brooklyn with a little imagination), Boca de Ouro feels novel and attracts an artistic crowd.

São Cristóvão BOTECO

(Map p314; www.facebook.com/barsaocristovao; Aspicuelta 533, Vila Madalena; mains R$32-84) This wildy atmospheric *boteco* is spilling over with football memorabilia from the owner's collection, more than 3500 pieces in all.

GETTING TO SÃO PAULO

Passaro Marroon (www.passaromarron.com.br) operates two airport buses. The **Airport Bus Service** (www.airportbusservice.com.br; one way from R$42) is the most efficient way to/from Guarulhos international airport, making stops at Aeroporto Congonhas, Barra Funda, Tiête, Praça da República and various hotels around Paulista and Augusta.

The *cheapest* way is to catch suburban Airport Service line 257 (or line 299, but this takes a lot longer and is best avoided) to/from Metrô Tatuapé (R$5.15, 30 to 45 minutes), which departs every 15 minutes between 5am and 12:10am. (Airport Service is easily confused with the flashier aforementioned Airport Bus Service – they depart right next to each other outside Terminal 2.)

Guarucoop (☎2440-7070; www.guarucoop.com.br) is the only taxi service allowed to operate from the international airport and charges vacation-spoiling prices to the city (R$135.64 to Av Paulista, R$161.04 to Vila Madalena).

Uber was cleared to operate out of GRU Airport in early 2015 and is generally R$30 to R$40 cheaper than Guarucoop, especially if you can snag an UberX. They cannot pick you up on the near curve, however; you must meet the driver on the far curve.

From Congonhas, catch bus 875A-10 'Perdizes-Aeroporto' from Metrô São Judas or catch a regular taxi (R$40 to R$60 to/from most neighborhoods of interest).

Both Terminal Tietê and Barra Funda, the two main bus stations, are connected to metro stations of the same name.

Suco Begaço JUICE BAR
(www.sucobagaco.com.br; Haddock Lobo 1483, Jardins; juice R$8-15; ⏲9am-9pm Mon-Sat, noon-8pm Sun; 👪) The flagship of this rapidly expanding juice chain burns through 600 glasses daily, mixed with water, orange juice, tea or coconut water. Also offers awesome-value, build-your-own salads and sandwiches.

☆ Entertainment

Clubbing here rivals the excitement of New York and the prices of Moscow. The hottest districts are Vila Olímpia (flashy, expensive, electronica) and Barra Funda/Baixo Augusta (rock, alternative, down-to-earth). Some clubs offer a choice between a cover charge or pricier *consumação* option, recoupable in drinks. Most clubs offer a discount for emailing or calling ahead to be on the list.

São Paulo's three biggest football teams are **São Paulo FC** (www.saopaulofc.net), who play at the 67,428-capacity Estádio do Morumbi (also a 2016 Olympic Games venue); **Palmeiras** (www.palmeiras.com.br), who play in the new 43,600-capacity Allianz Parque near Barra Funda; and **Corinthians** (www.corinthians.com.br), who play at the new Arena Corinthians, 24km east of Centro.

D-Edge CLUB
(☎3665-9500; www.d-edge.com.br; Auro Soares de Moura Andrade 141, Barra Funda; cover R$30-140; ⏲11pm-late Mon & Wed-Sat) With one of the city's most remarkable sound systems and a roster of world-famous DJs, this mixed gay-straight club is an elder statesmen of the club scene, but remains a 'don't miss' for fans of electronica.

Ó do Borogodó SAMBA
(Map p314; ☎3814-4087; Horácio Lane 21, Vila Madelena; cover R$25; ⏲9pm-3am Mon-Fri, from 1pm Sat, 7pm-midnight Sun) Probably the best spot in town for live samba, *chorinho* and *pagode* (popular samba music), uneven floors and cramped space notwithstanding, especially when you combine the serious muscianship on display here with cheap *caipirinhas* and the rump-shaking, sweat-soaked crowd of sexy revelers.

Superloft CLUB
(Map p314; www.superloft.com.br; Cardeal Arcoverde 2926, Pinheiros) Constructed with 34 shipping containers, this multi-cultural space hosts a smorgasbord of art and music/club events. Free entry before 12:30am.

ℹ Information

You are never far from an ATM – every bank imaginable lines Paulista (though they are pretty scarce in Vila Madalena).

DANGERS & ANNOYANCES

Crime is an issue in São Paulo, though tourists aren't often targeted unless you're an unlucky victim of an *arrastão*, when armed *banditos* rob an entire restaurant of patrons. Be especially careful in the center at night and on weekends (when fewer people are about). Watch out for pickpockets on buses and at Praça da Sé.

EMERGENCY

Deatur Tourist Police (☎3120-4417; Rua da Cantareira 390; ⊙8am-7pm) A special police force just for tourists, with English-speaking officers, located at Mercado Municipal.

MEDICAL SERVICES

Einstein Hospital (☎2151-1233; www.einstein.com.br; Albert Einstein 627, Morumbi) Located on a southwestern corner of Morumbi, Einstein is one of Latin America's best hospitals.

MONEY

Bradesco ATM (www.bradesco.com.br; Wisard 308, Vila Madalena) Best international-friendly ATM in Vila Madalena.

POST

Correios (www.correios.com.br; Haddock Lobo 566, Jardins; ⊙9am-5pm) A particularly convenient location; one of Sampa's many post offices.

TOURIST INFORMATION

CIT (Map p312; ☎3331-7786; www.cidadedesaopaulo.com; Praça da República; ⊙9am-6pm); GRU Airport (Terminals 1 & 2; ⊙8am-8pm); Mercado Municipal (Map p312; Rua da Cantareira 306, Rua E, Portão 4; ⊙8am-5pm Mon-Sat, 7am-4pm Sun); Paulista (Av Paulista 1853; ⊙9am-6pm); Olido (Map p312; São João 473; ⊙9am-6pm); Tietê Bus Station (Av Cruzeiro do Sul 1800, Rodoviário Tietê, Santana; ⊙6am-10pm); Congonhas Airport (Av Washington Luis s/n, Congonhas Airport, Vila Congonhas; ⊙7am-10pm) São Paulo's tourist-information booths all have good city maps, as well as helpful walking maps for individual neighborhoods.

Getting There & Away

AIR

GRU Airport (☎2445-2945; www.gru.com.br; Rod Hélio Smidt s/n), the international airport, is 25km east of the center. Most domestic flights depart from Terminals 1 and 2 in the main building, but Azul and Passaredo operate out of the newer Terminal 4, 2km to the southwest. Most international flights now operate out of the new Terminal 3, connected to the main building, an impressive world-class terminal that opened in 2014. Exceptions include midhaul flights from Central and South America and the Caribbean (Aerolíneas Argentinas/Austral, Aeromexico, Avianca/Taca, Boliviana de Aviacion, Copa,Tame, etc) and a few stragglers from Africa (Ethiopian, Royal Air Maroc, TAAG) and Europe (Air Europa) – but check ahead, as the migration to T3 will continue. Frequent free shuttles connect the terminals 24/7.

BUSES FROM SÃO PAULO

DESTINATION	STARTING FARE (R$)	DURATION (HR)	BUS COMPANY
Angra dos Reis	70	7½	Reunidas Paulista (www.reunidaspaulista.com.br)
Asunción (PY)	184.50	20	Pluma (www.pluma.com.br)
Belo Horizonte	102	8	Cometa (www.viacaocometa.com.br)
Brasília	171	15	Real Expresso (www.realexpresso.com.br)
Buenos Aires (AR)	370.50	36	Pluma (www.pluma.com.br)
Curitiba	75	6	Cometa (www.viacaocometa.com.br)
Florianópolis	126	11	Catatrinense (www.catarinense.net)
Iguaçu Falls	114.50	15	Pluma (www.pluma.com.br)
Montevideo (UY)	390	32	TTL (www.ttl.com.br)
Paraty	54	6	Reunidas Paulista (www.reunidaspaulista.com.br)
Pantanal (Cuiabá)	247	26	Andorinha (www.andorinha.com)
Pantanal (Campo Grande)	193	13½	Andorinha (www.andorinha.com)
Recife	436	45	Itapemirim (www.itapemirim.com.br)
Rio de Janeiro	78	6	1001 (www.autoviacao1001.com.br)
Salvador	326	32	São Geraldo (www.saogeraldo.com.br)
Santos	22	1¼	Cometa (www.viacaocometa.com.br)
Santiago (CH)	405	54	Pluma (www.pluma.com.br)

The domestic-only airport, Aeroporto Congonhas, 14km south of the center, services many destinations, including the majority of flights to Rio (Santos Dumont Airport), which depart every half-hour (or less).

BUS

South America's largest bus terminal, Terminal Tietê, 4.5km north of Centro, offers buses to destinations throughout the continent. Avoid bus arrivals during early morning or late afternoon – traffic jams are enormous.

Buses to the Pantanal leave from Terminal Barra Funda, 5.3km northwest of Centro.

Getting Around

São Paulo's immense public transport system is the world's most complex, boasting 15,000 buses and 1333 lines. Buses (R$3.50) are crowded during rush hours and confusingly thorough, with many lines covering every patch of the city. You can reach many places on the excellent **Metrô São Paulo** (www.metro.sp.gov.br), the city's subway system. The metro is cheap, safe, fast and runs from 4:40am to midnight. A single ride costs R$3.50.

Belo Horizonte

0XX31 / POP 2.5 MILLION

Belo Horizonte is Brazil's third-largest city and the sprawling capital of Minas Gerais. Though it hides a wealth of cultural attractions and architectural jewels peppered amid a concrete jungle, it is most famous as a place to eat, drink and be merry. Fueling the city's backbone as a rapidly growing industrial giant are hundreds of *botecos*, each with its own distinct personality and character. Its plethora of drinking dens has earned Beagá (the city's nickname, named for the pronunciation of its initials, BH) the title of the Bar Capital of Brazil.

Sights

Fans of modernist architect Oscar Niemeyer won't want to miss his creations dotted around a huge artificial lake in the Pampulha district, north of downtown. For information on all of Praça da Liberdade's new museums, visit the website www.circuitoculturalliberdade.com.br.

★**Centro Cultural Banco do Brasil** ARTS CENTER
(www.bb.com.br/cultura; Praça da Liberdade 450; 9am-9pm Wed-Mon) FREE Inaugurated in late 2013, this magnificent palace on Praça da Liberdade is one of Belo Horizonte's cultural gems. The vast 3rd-floor gallery hosts special exhibitions that rotate every couple of months, while the downstairs is dedicated to free or low-cost arts events including film, theatre and dance; pick up a schedule onsite. The interior courtyard makes for a pleasant break anytime of day with its cafes, stained glass windows and retractable roof.

★**Memorial Minas Gerais – Vale** MUSEUM
(www.memorialvale.com.br; Praca da Liberdade s/n; 10am-5:30pm Tue, Wed, Fri & Sat, to 9:30pm Thu, to 3:30pm Sun) FREE The best element of Praça da Liberdade's 2010 makeover, this

WORTH A TRIP

THE WORLD-CLASS MUSEUM IN BELO'S BACK YARD

The world's largest open-air contemporary-art museum, and greater Belo Horizonte's standout attraction, **Instituto de Arte Contemporânea Inhotim** (3571-97000; www.inhotim.org.br; Rua B, Inhotim, Brumadinho; adult/student R$25/12.50 Tue & Thu, R$40/20 Fri-Sun, Free Wed; 9:30am-4:30pm Tue-Fri, to 5:30pm Sat & Sun) is a sprawling complex of gardens dotted with 21 world-class modern-art galleries and numerous outdoor sculptures that lies 50km west of the city, near the town of Brumadinho. Much of the international artwork on view is monumental in size, with galleries custom-built to display it. The constantly expanding gardens, opened to the public in 2006, boast more than 4000 different species of plants (including one of the world's most extensive collections of palm trees) and lakes with swans.

You can wander at will, or attend daily scheduled programs led by guides trained in visual arts and natural science. Ten on-site eateries serve everything from hot dogs to gourmet international fare. Wednesday is a great day to visit, as the museum is free; weekends can get crowded, but offer a wider range of guided tours.

From Tuesday through Sunday, **Saritur** (3479-4300; www.saritur.com.br) runs direct buses (R$53.40 round-trip, 1½ hours each way) from Belo Horizonte to Inhotim at 8:15am, returning at 4:30pm weekdays, 5:30pm Saturday and Sunday.

supremely cool contemporary museum chronicles Minas culture from the 17th to 21st centuries via three floors of cutting-edge interactive galleries and audiovisual installations.

★ **Mineirão & Museu Brasileiro de Futebol** STADIUM, MUSEUM
(☎3499-4300; www.minasarena.com.br/mineirao; Av Antônio Abrahão Caram 1001; adult/child stadium tour R$8/4, incl football museum R$14/7; ⏲9am-5pm Tue-Fri, to 1pm Sat & Sun) FREE An obligatory stop for football fans, Belo Horizonte's legendary 65,000-seat stadium was completely renovated for the 2014 World Cup, incorporating a brand-new football museum, esplanade and LEED-certified energy conservation enhancements. One-hour guided tours take in the locker rooms, showers, press room, stands and revamped playing field, with occasional wistful comments about Brazil's heartbreaking 7–1 World Cup loss to Germany here. Combined tickets include a self-guided museum visit, with exhibits covering the stadium's construction, famous games and players, and football history.

Sleeping

Belo Horizonte lacks a centralized traveler neighborhood – most budget accommodations are scattered around residential areas.

★ **Hostel Savassi** HOSTEL $
(☎3243-4771; hostelsavassi.com.br; Antônio de Albuquerque 626; dm R$45-50; 📶) Opened for the World Cup in 2014, this hostel enjoys a dream location on a pedestrianized street in the heart of Savassi. The trio of six- to 12-person dorms offers individual reading lights and power outlets for every bed, while the bright upstairs guest kitchen and artistically decorated lounge/TV area invite travelers to stick around and mingle.

Samba Rooms Hostel HOSTEL $
(☎3267-0740; www.sambaroomshostel.com.br; Av Bias Fortes 368; dm R$35-55, s/d R$100/150, s/d without bathroom R$90/140; @📶) Within easy walking distance of Praça da Liberdade, Mercado Central and the airport bus stop, this friendly hostel in a historic building has five- to nine-bed dorms and pleasant common spaces including a spacious parquet-floored living room, a well-equipped guest kitchen and a cluster of open-air terraces. Downsides are the street noise and the rather musty private rooms out back.

Hotel Ibis HOTEL $$
(☎2111-1500; www.ibis.com.br; João Pinheiro 602; r R$145-215; ❄@📶) Midway between downtown and Savassi, and just steps from leafy Praça da Liberdade, this ultra-convenient chain hotel has comfortable if predictable rooms in an ugly high-rise behind a pretty 1930s townhouse. Breakfast (R$17) and parking (R$17) cost extra.

Eating & Drinking

The area between Praça Sete and Praça da Liberdade is best for cheap eats, with countless *lanchonetes* (snack bars) and self-serve *por kilo* restaurants. The neighborhood of Savassi has many top restaurants, including the lion's share of *botecos* that Beagá is famous for.

Casa Cheia MINEIRA $
(☎3274-9585; www.restaurantecasacheia.com.br; Shop 167, Mercado Central; daily specials R$25-29; ⏲11am-11:30pm Mon-Sat, to 5pm Sun) People line up by the dozen for a table at this long-established Mercado Central eatery, the name of which means 'full house'. A bevy of women prepare traditional favorites on a giant stove, including *pratos do dia* (low-priced daily specials) such as the not-to-be-missed Saturday *feijoada*. A new branch in **Savassi** (☎3234-6921; Cláudio Manoel 784; daily specials R$25-29; ⏲11am-11:30pm Mon-Sat, to 5pm Sun) offers the same menu and prices.

San Ro ASIAN, VEGETARIAN $
(☎3264-9236; Professor Moraes 651; per kg R$53.90; ⏲11:30am-3pm Mon-Fri, to 3:30pm Sat & Sun; 🖉) If you're not a meat eater, or just need a break from Minas' meat-heavy repertoire, make a beeline for the buffet at this popular Asian-vegetarian, per-kilo place.

★ **Xapuri** MINEIRA $$
(☎3496-6198; www.restaurantexapuri.com.br; Mandacarú 260; mains per person R$49-70; ⏲noon-11pm Tue-Sat, to 6pm Sun) Dona Nelsa's local institution features fabulous *mineira* food served at picnic tables under a thatched roof, with hammocks close at hand for pre-meal children's entertainment or post-meal relaxation. The traditional wood stove blazes up front, while colorful desserts are attractively displayed in two long cases.

★ **Café com Letras** CAFE
(☎3225-9973; www.cafecomletras.com.br; Antônio de Albuquerque 781; ⏲noon-midnight Mon-Thu,

BUSES FROM BELO HORIZONTE

DESTINATION	COST (R$)	DURATION (HR)	BUS COMPANY
Brasília	145	11-12	União (www.expressouniao.com.br), Kaissara (www.kaissara.com.br)
Diamantina	88	5	Pássaro Verde (www.passaroverde.com.br)
Ouro Prêto	30	2	Pássaro Verde (www.passaroverde.com.br)
Rio de Janeiro	93	7	Util (www.util.com.br), Cometa (www.viacaocometa.com.br)
Salvador	259	23	Gontijo (www.gontijo.com.br)
São João del Rei	55	3½	Sandra (www.viacaosandra.com.br)
São Paulo	116	8¼	Cometa (www.viacaocometa.com.br)
Vitória	103	8¾	São Geraldo (www.saogeraldo.com.br), Kaissara (www.kaissara.com.br)

to 1am Fri & Sat, 5-11pm Sun;) With live jazz on Sundays, DJs Thursday through Saturday, and a bohemian buzz between sets, this bookstore-cafe is a fun place to kick back over light meals (R$22 to R$60) and drinks, browse the shelves and enjoy the free wi-fi. Check out their new branch in the **Centro Cultural Banco do Brasil** (Centro Cultural Banco do Brasil, lower level; 10am-9pm). They also sponsor jazz performances at the annual **Savassi Festival** (www.savassifestival.com.br; mid-Sep).

Arcangelo BAR
(2nd fl, Ed Maletta, Rua da Bahia 1148; 6pm-midnight Tue-Sat) The best bar of many inside the indie-intellectual Maletta building in Centro, with great views from its consistently packed 2nd-floor open-air balcony. Voted Beagá's best happy hour.

Information

Belotur Confins Airport (3689-2557; 8am-10pm Mon-Fri, to 5pm Sat & Sun) At the main airport exit, outside baggage claim.

Belotur Mercado Central (3277-4691; 9am-5:20pm Mon, 8am-4:20pm Tue, 8am-5:20pm Wed-Sat, 8am-1pm Sun) On the ground floor of Belo's famous indoor market.

Belotur Mercado das Flores (3277-7666; Av Afonso Pena 1055; 9am-6pm Mon-Fri, 8am-3pm Sat & Sun) At the flower market on the western edge of Parque Municipal.

Belotur Pampulha Airport (3246-8015; 8am-5pm Mon-Fri, 8am-4pm Sat, 1-5pm Sun)

Belotur Pampulha Lakeshore (3277-9987; Av Otacílio Negrão de Lima 855; 8am-5pm Tue-Sun) On the lakeshore in the northern suburb of Pampulha.

Belotur Rodoviária (3277-6907; Praça Rio Branco; 8am-6pm Mon-Fri, to 5pm Sat & Sun) Inside the bus station.

Getting There & Away

Belo Horizonte has two airports. International flights use the recently renovated and expanded **Aeroporto Confins** (CNF), 40km north of the city. The **Aeroporto da Pampulha** (PLU), 10km north of the city center, is more conveniently located but only has domestic flights. Flights from the two airports serve most locations in Brazil.

Expresso Unir (3689-2415; www.conexaoaeroporto.com.br) runs frequent, comfortable Conexão Aeroporto buses between downtown and both airports. The *convencional* bus (R$10.70 to either airport) leaves Belo's bus station every 15 to 45 minutes between 3:45am and 10:45pm (slightly less frequently on weekends). Travel time is approximately 30 minutes to Pampulha airport and 70 minutes to Confins. Buses return from Confins between 5:15am and 12:15am.

Belo's **long-distance bus station** (3271-3000; Praça Rio Branco 100) is near the northern end of downtown.

Ouro Prêto

0XX31 / POP 70,281

Nestled among gorgeous mountain scenery 114km southeast of Belo Horizonte, Ouro Prêto rises from the lush landscape like a bygone living museum unyielding in its grip on the 18th century. Here the Unesco World Heritage–recognized historical center features numerous stunning baroque churches perched high on surrounding hillsides, standing sentinel over picturesque plazas and winding cobbled streets that were once the gilded paths of the crown jewel of the Minas Gerais gold-mining towns.

Sights & Activities

There are virtually no 20th-century buildings to defile this stunning colonial town. Avoid visiting on Mondays when most sites are closed.

★ Igreja de São Francisco de Assis CHURCH
(www.museualeijadinho.com.br; Largo de Coimbra s/n; adult/reduced R$10/5; ⌚8:30-11:50am & 1:30-5pm Tue-Sun) This exquisite church is Brazil's most important piece of colonial art, after Aleijadinho's masterpiece *The Prophets* in Congonhas. Its entire exterior was carved by Aleijadinho himself, from the soapstone medallion to the cannon waterspouts to the Franciscan two-bar cross. The interior was painted by Aleijadinho's long-term partner, Manuel da Costa Ataíde.

Ouro Prêto

Top Sights
1 Igreja de São Francisco de Assis ... C2

Sights
2 Igreja NS do Carmo ... C2
3 Matriz NS da Conceição de Antônio Dias ... D2
4 Matriz NS do Pilar ... A2
5 Museu da Inconfidência ... C2
Museu do Aleijadinho ... (see 3)
Museu do Oratório ... (see 2)

Sleeping
6 Pousada Nello Nuno ... C1
7 Pouso do Chico Rei ... C2
8 Trilhas de Minas Hostel ... D2

Eating
9 Adega Ouro Preto ... A1
10 Chafariz ... A2
11 O Passo ... B1

Ouro Prêto

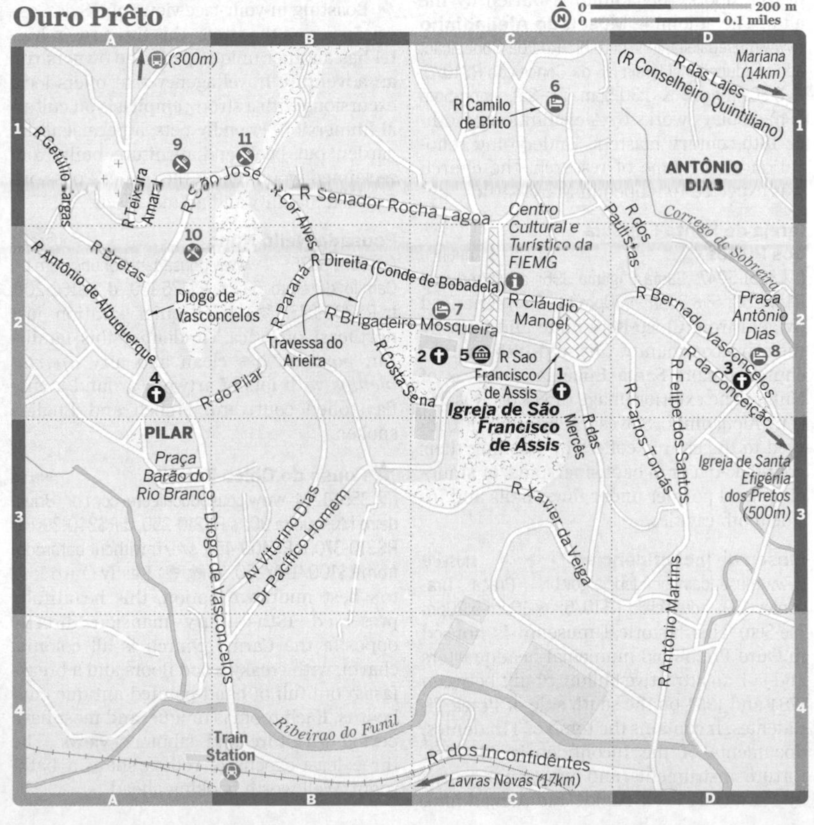

Matriz NS do Pilar CHURCH

(Praça Monsenhor Castilho Barbosa; adult/reduced R$10/5; ⌚9-10:45am & noon-4:45pm Tue-Sun) On the southwest side of town, this is Brazil's second-most-opulent church (after Salvador's São Francisco). It has 434kg of gold and silver and is one of the country's finest showcases of artwork. Note the wild-bird chandelier holders, the scrolled church doors and the hair on Jesus (the real stuff, donated by a penitent worshipper).

Matriz NS da Conceição de Antônio Dias CHURCH

(www.museualeijadinho.com.br; Praça Antônio Dias; adult/reduced incl Museu do Aleijadinho R$10/5; ⌚8:30am-noon & 1:30-5pm Tue-Sat, noon-5pm Sun) Designed by Aleijadinho's father, Manuel Francisco Lisboa, this church was built between 1727 and 1770. The eagle with downturned head and the Virgin Mary surrounded by cherubs both stand atop images of the moon, Portuguese iconographic elements that symbolize the Christians' domination of the Moors. Aleijadinho is buried by the altar. The adjoining **Museu do Aleijadinho** (www.museualeijadinho.com.br; Rua da Conceição; adult/reduced incl Igreja NS da Conceição R$10/5; ⌚8:30am-noon & 1:30-5pm Tue-Sat, noon-5pm Sun) displays works by Aleijadinho and other 18th-century masters. Undergoing renovation at the time of research, the church was expected to reopen in March 2016.

Igreja de Santa Efigênia dos Pretos CHURCH

(☎3551-5047; Santa Efigênia 396; adult/reduced R$5/2.50; ⌚8:30am-4:30pm Tue-Sun) Financed by gold from Chico-Rei's mine and built by the slave community, this mid-18th-century church honors Santa Efigênia, princess of Nubia. The exterior image of NS do Rosário is by Aleijadinho. Slaves legendarily contributed to the church coffers by washing their gold-flaked hair in baptismal fonts, or smuggling gold powder under fingernails and inside tooth cavities.

Museu da Inconfidência MUSEUM

(www.museudainconfidencia.gov.br; Praça Tiradentes 139; adult/child R$10/5; ⌚10am-5:20pm Tue-Sun) This historical museum is housed in Ouro Preto's old municipal headquarters and jail, an attractive building built between 1784 and 1854 on the south side of Praça Tiradentes. It contains the tomb of Tiradentes, documents of the Inconfidência Mineira, torture instruments and important works by Manuel da Costa Ataíde and Aleijadinho.

Museu do Oratório MUSEUM

(www.museudooratorio.org.br; Adro da Igreja do Carmo 28; adult/reduced R$5/2.50; ⌚9:30am-5:30pm) This museum features a fabulous collection of hand-carved *oratórios* – miniature home altars and portable devotional shrines dating back to the 17th century. It's housed in the Casa do Noviciado, a triple-level colonial building where Aleijadinho is said to have lived while working on the adjacent Igreja NS do Carmo.

Igreja NS do Carmo CHURCH

(Brigadeiro Mosqueira; admission R$3; ⌚8:30-11:10am & 1-5pm Tue-Sat, 10am-3pm Sun) Built between 1766 and 1772, this lovely church was a group effort by the area's most important artists. It features a facade and two side altars by Aleijadinho.

Sleeping

Trilhas de Minas Hostel HOSTEL $

(☎3551-6367; www.trilhasdeminashostel.com; Praça Antônio Dias 21; dm R$45-50, d R$120; 📶) 🍃 Boasting in-your-face views of NS de Conceição across the street, this three-room hostel has another unique perk: the owners run an adventure travel agency that offers local excursions with a strong emphasis on cultural immersion. Friendly pets, a permaculture garden out back and furniture built from reclaimed wood reflect the owner's passions for sustainability and animal rescue.

Pousada Nello Nuno POUSADA $

(☎3551-3375; www.pousadanellonuno.com.br; Camilo de Brito 59; s R$125-130, d R$160-200, tr R$200-273; 📶) In a quiet location just northeast of Praça Tiradentes, this family-run *pousada* has clean and airy *apartamentos* with lots of artwork around a cute flagstoned courtyard. French and English spoken.

★**Pouso do Chico Rei** INN $$

(☎3551-1274; www.pousodochicorei.com.br; Brigadeiro Musqueira 90; s R$210-250, d R$240-290, tr R$310-370, q R$400-450; s/d/tr without bathroom from R$100/175/260; ❄@📶) Easily Ouro Preto's best midrange option, this beautifully preserved 18th-century mansion directly opposite the Carmo church is all colonial charm, with creaky wood floors and a breakfast room full of hand-painted antique cupboards. Each room is unique, and most have period furniture and fabulous views. The three least-expensive rooms share a bathroom. Well worth booking ahead.

Eating

Plenty of budget eateries are clustered along lively Direita, São José and Praça Tiradentes. Typical Minas dishes include *tutu*, a puréed black-bean side dish; and *feijão tropeiro*, a mix of brown beans, kale, onions, eggs, manioc flour and sometimes bacon.

Adega Ouro Preto SELF-SERVE $
(Teixeira Amaral 24; all-you-can-eat R$30, per kg R$42; 11am-4pm) The cavelike Adega is a great deal at lunchtime, when *mineira* specialties are sold by the kilo or on an all-you-can-eat basis.

Chafariz BUFFET $$
(3551-2828; São José 167; all-you-can-eat R$52; noon-4pm Tue-Sun) Eclectically decorated with old photos, religious art, Brazilian flags and antiques, this local institution serves one of Minas' tastiest (if priciest) buffets. The menu showcases traditional local favorites such as *lombo* (roasted pork loin) and *feijão tropeiro*, followed by Minas cheese and *goiabada* (guava paste) for dessert. Post-meal shots of *cachaça*, coffee and *jabuticaba* liqueur are included in the price.

★**O Passo** ITALIAN $$
(www.opassopizzajazz.com; São José 56; pizzas R$32-69, mains R$39-79; noon-midnight Sun-Thu, to 1am Fri & Sat) In a lovely 18th-century building with intimate candlelit interior, this local favorite specializes in pizza, pasta and salads complemented by a good wine list. Outside, the relaxed creekside terrace is ideal for an after-dinner drink. On Tuesday nights, don't miss the *rodizio de pizzas* (all-you-can-eat pizza, R$35.90). There's live jazz on Thursdays and Friday evenings, and during Sunday lunch.

Information

Banco do Brasil (São José 189)

Centro Cultural e Turístico da FIEMG (3559-3269; turismo@ouropreto.mg.gov.br; Praça Tiradentes 4; 9am-6pm) Offers information in English, Spanish and French, including a leaflet listing museum and church hours and a rough town map.

Getting There & Away

Long-distance buses leave from Ouro Prêto's main **bus station** (3559-3252; Padre Rolim 661), a 10-minute uphill walk from Praça Tiradentes at the northwest end of town. **Pássaro Verde** (www.gabrasil.com.br) provides service to Belo Horizonte (R$29, two hours, hourly from 6am to 8pm). **Util** (3551-3166; www.util.com.br) goes to Rio (R$115, 7¾ hours, 8am and 10pm daily) and São Paulo (R$140, 11 hours, 9am and 7pm daily); the São Paulo bus stops en route at São João del Rei (R$60, 4½ hours).

Tiradentes

032 / POP 6900

Sleepy Tiradentes is full of camera-ready charm, from its colorful, cobbled streets to its mountain vistas, with a wandering river trickling through town. Gastronomy and shopping rule here – it's home to the highest concentration per capita of starred restaurants in the country and is famous throughout Brazil for its artisan furniture and high-quality homewares, arts and crafts. But there is plenty of wonderful countryside hiking on offer to turn back the caloric onslaught.

Sights

★**Igreja Matriz de Santo Antônio** CHURCH
(Padre Toledo s/n; admission R$5; 9am-5pm) Named for Tiradentes' patron saint, this gorgeous church is one of Aleijadinho's last designs. The dazzling gold interior is rich in Old Testament symbolism. Noteworthy elements include the polychrome organ, built in Portugal and brought here by donkey in 1798, and the seven golden phoenixes suspending candleholders from long braided chains. The famous sundial out front dates back to 1785.

Igreja NS Rosário dos Pretos CHURCH
(Praça Padre Lourival; admission R$3; 9am-5pm) This beautiful stone church, with its many images of black saints, was built in 1708, by and for slaves. Since they had no free time during daylight hours, construction took place at night – note the nocturnal iconography in the ceiling paintings of an eight-pointed black star and a half-moon.

Museu de Sant'Ana MUSEUM
(museudesantana.org.br; Cadeia; adult/reduced R$5/2.50; 10am-7pm Wed-Mon) Opened in 2014 in Tiradentes' former town jail, this is the latest innovative museum project conceived by Belo Horizonte–based Angela Gutierrez, creator of Ouro Preto's Museu do Oratório (p324) and Belo Horizonte's **Museu de Artes e Ofícios** (3248-8600; www.mao.com.br; Praça Rui Barbosa 600; adult/child R$5/2.50, free Sat & 5-9pm Wed & Thu; noon-7pm Tue & Fri, noon-9pm Wed & Thu, 11am-5pm Sat

& Sun). The simple but beautifully presented collection features 270 images of St Ann in wood, stone and terracotta, from the 17th century to the present. Bilingual exhibits trace the importance of St Anne imagery throughout Brazil and its evolution through the baroque and rococo periods.

Museu do Padre Toledo MUSEUM

(Padre Toledo 190; adult/reduced R$10/5; ⏲10am-5pm Tue-Fri, to 4.30pm Sat, 9am-3pm Sun) Dedicated to 18th-century Brazilian priest and revolutionary hero Padre Toledo, this recently renovated museum occupies the 18-room house where Padre Toledo himself once lived and where the Inconfidentes first met. The collection features regional antiques and documents from the 18th century, along with some fine ceiling paintings artistically reflected in floor-mounted mirrors.

Sleeping & Eating

Pousada da Bia POUSADA $$

(☎3355-1173; www.pousadadabia.com.br; Ozanan 330; s/d midweek R$180/240, weekend R$200/260; 📶🏊) Just outside the historical center, French- and English-speaking owner Bia runs this pleasant *pousada* with a sunny breakfast house, fragrant herb garden and relaxing pool area. Rooms to the right of the garden offer nicer views but less privacy than those on the left. There are also two spacious new deluxe rooms (R$180 to R$200 per couple, plus 30% per extra person).

Pousada da Sirlei INN $$

(☎3355-1440; www.facebook.com/PousadadaSirlei; Antonio de Carvalho 113; s/d R$100/200; P@📶🏊) Five minutes' walk from the cobblestones and bus station but kitty-corner to a pleasant plaza, this quaint inn is long on mismatched flooring and doting grandmotherly charm.

Divino Sabor SELF-SERVE $

(Gabriel Passos 300; per kg R$41.90; ⏲11:30am-2:30pm Tue-Sun) Very popular with locals for its self-serve offerings, including grilled meats and the normal range of *mineira* specialties.

Bar do Celso MINEIRA $

(Largo das Forras 80a; mains R$20-36; ⏲noon-8pm Wed-Mon) On the main square, this locally run restaurant specializes in down-to-earth *mineira* fare at reasonable prices. Folks with less voracious appetites will appreciate the R$18 *prato mini*, a smaller plate designed for one person.

Getting There & Around

Tiradentes' bus station is just north of the main square, across the stream. Two companies, Presidente (R$3.35, 20 minutes) and Vale do Ouro (R$3.80, 30 minutes), run regular buses between Tiradentes and São João del Rei.

The best approach to Tiradentes is the wonderful train trip from São João del Rei. The *Maria-Fumaça* ('Smoking Mary'), operated by **Trilhos de Minas** (☎3355-2789; trilhosdeminas.com; R$40/56 one way/round trip, half price 6-12yr and over 60yr), is pulled by 19th-century steam locomotives and chugs along a picturesque 13km track from São João. Trains run twice daily in each direction on Friday, Saturday, Sunday and holidays. When leaving São João the best views are on the left side.

THE SOUTH

Spectacular white-sand beaches, pristine subtropical islands and the thunderous roar of Iguaçu Falls are a few of the attractions of Brazil's affluent South. While often given short shrift by first-time visitors, the states of Paraná, Santa Catarina and Rio Grande do Sul offer a radically different version of what it means to be Brazilian. Here *gaúchos* still cling to the cowboy lifestyle on the wide plains bordering Argentina and Uruguay, while old-world architecture, European-style beer, blond hair and blue eyes reveal the influence of millions of German, Italian, Swiss and Eastern European immigrants.

Getting There & Away

The major air gateways are Curitiba, Florianópolis, Porto Alegre, and Iguaçu Falls, which borders both Argentina and Paraguay. All these cities have good bus connections to São Paulo.

Getting Around

Short flights and longer bus journeys connect the four major cities of the South. If you're heading to Ilha do Mel, don't miss the scenic train ride from Curitiba through the Serra do Mar to Morretes.

Curitiba

☎0XX41 / POP 1.7 MILLION

Known as Brazil's eco-evolved capital and famous for its efficient urban planning, Curitiba is one of Brazil's metropolitan success stories, with pleasant parks, well-preserved historic buildings, little traffic congestion and a large university population.

Sights & Activities

★Museu Oscar Niemeyer MUSEUM

(MON; ☎3350-4400; www.museuoscarniemeyer.org.br; Marechal Hermes 999; adult/child R$9/4.50; ⊙10am-6pm Tue-Sun) Designed by and named for the architect responsible for much of Brasília, this exotic, eye-shaped museum is painted with whimsical dancing figures in bold colors. Rotating exhibits highlight Brazilian and international artists of the 20th and 21st centuries; and there's an excellent permanent exhibit on Niemeyer himself.

South Brazil

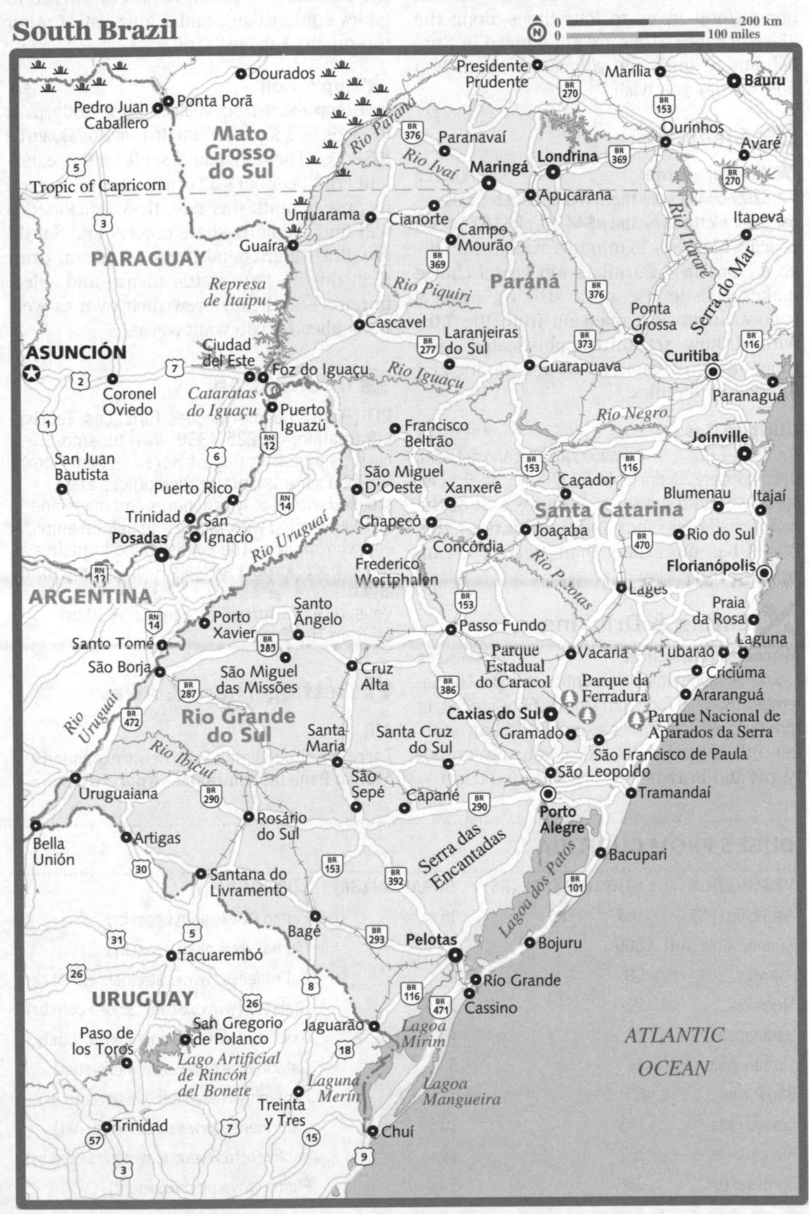

Linha Turismo CITY TOUR
(www.urbs.curitiba.pr.gov.br/transporte/linha-turismo; tours R$35; ⏲every 30min 9am-5:30pm Tue-Sun Mar-Oct, every 15min 8:45am-6pm Nov-Carnival) This double-decker city tour bus is a convenient way to see the sights both inside and outside Curitiba's downtown. It starts at Praça Tiradentes and you can hop-off/hop-on up to four times along the 25-sight route. Stops are announced in English and Spanish and you can use your hop offs any day you wish.

Sleeping

★ **Motter Home** HOSTEL $
(☎3209-5649; www.motterhome.com.br; Desembargador Motta 3574; dm R$44-48, r R$140; @📶) In leafy Mercês – 15 minutes' walk from Largo da Ordem – Curitiba's top hostel choice makes artistic use of a striking canary-yellow, turret-style mansion from the '50s, with striking art, retro-sophisticated common areas, original hardwood floors and funky door handles.

Curitiba Casa HOSTEL $
(☎3044-7313; www.curitibacasahostel.com; Brasílio Itiberê 73; dm R$44-52, r R$145; @📶) Despite its odd location 15 minutes east of the *rodoferroviária* (bus and train station), this hostel has more fans than *futebol*. Clean, colorful and classy.

Eating & Drinking

Mercado Municipal MARKET $
(www.mercadomunicipaldecuritiba.com.br; 7 de Setembro 1865; ⏲7am-2pm Mon, to 6pm Tue-Sat, to 1pm Sun) Curitiba's excellent urban market, full of food stalls, cafes, gourmet emporiums and Brazil's first organic food court.

Yü ASIAN $$
(www.yurestaurante.com.br; Praça General Osório 485; per kg R$72.90; ⏲11:30am-3pm Mon-Fri, noon-3:30pm Sat & Sun; 📶) Reflecting Curitiba's significant Asian immigration, this pricier *por-kilo* does outstanding Korean, Chinese and Japanese dishes, including sushi, sashimi and fantastic *lula apimentada* (spicy squid salad), and a long list of other top-quality Far East fare.

★ **Hop'N Roll** BAR
(www.hopnroll.com.br; Mateus Leme 950; pints R$13-29; ⏲5:30pm-1:30am Mon-Thu, to 2:30am Fri & Sat; 📶) The hophead assault on this excellent craft beer bar's 32 draft options – served in proper pints – is relentless. Aficionados will find the lion's share of local and Southern Brazil's artisanal beers (if not on draft then on the 130+ bottle menu) and select imports – and they brew their own as well. Book ahead if you want a seat.

Information

PIT (Postos de Informações Turísticas, Tourist Information; ☎3225-4336; www.turismo.curitiba.pr.gov.br; Rua 24 Horas; ⏲9am-6pm) Curitiba's tourist information offices are stocked with glossy brochures and maps and are well staffed with willing and helpful employees who speak a little English. Find branches at the airport (Airport Arrivals Hall; ⏲7am-11pm) and Oi Torre Panorâmica (☎3339-7613; Castro Vellozo 19 , Oi Torre Panorâmica; ⏲10am-6:30pm Tue-Sun).

Getting There & Away

AIR

There are direct flights from newly expanded **Afonso Pena International Airport** (CWB;

BUSES FROM CURITIBA

DESTINATION	STARTING FARE (R$)	DURATION (HR)	BUS COMPANY
Asunción (PY)	163	15	Pluma (www.pluma.com.br)
Buenos Aires (AR)	366	32	Pluma (www.pluma.com.br)
Joinville	28	2	Catarinense (www.catarinense.net)
Morretes	22	1½	Graciosa (www.viacaograciosa.com.br)
Paranaguá	27	1¾	Graciosa (www.viacaograciosa.com.br)
Florianopólis	74	5	Catarinense (www.catarinense.net)
São Paulo	80	7	Itapemirim (www.itapemirim.com.br)
Iguaçu Falls	155	10	Catarinense (www.catarinense.net)
Rio de Janeiro	162	13	Penha (http://vendas.nspenha.com.br)
Santiago (CL)	396	54	Pluma (www.pluma.com.br)

(☎3381-1515; Av Rocha Pombo s/n, São José dos Pinhais), 18km southeast of Centro, to cities throughout Brazil.

BUS

Curitiba's long-distance bus and train stations form a single three-block complex called the *rodoferroviária*, which sits 2km southeast of downtown and received a World Cup 2014 makeover. Access to the departures area is now restricted to ticket holders. Ticket counters for interstate bus travel *(interestadual)* sit on the 2nd floor of the first block; bus companies for destinations within Paraná *(estadual)* are located on the 2nd floor of the second block. The train station block sits behind the two bus-station blocks.

TRAIN

The marvelous **Serra Verde Express** (☎3888-3488; www.serraverdeexpress.com.br; Estação Ferroviária) leaves Curitiba at 8:15am daily, descending 900m through the lush Serra do Mar to the historic town of Morretes, arriving at noon and returning at 3pm, arriving back in Curitiba at 6:30pm. There are three classes of service. One-way economy/tourist/executive class tickets cost R$79/99/149. Executive class includes a bilingual guide (and beer!).

Getting Around

URBS (www.urbs.curitiba.pr.gov.br) runs Curitiba's space-age bus system, made up of integrated station pods, known as *tubos*. City buses, several of which are electric/biodiesel buses called Hibribuses, cost R$3.30 (R$1.50 on Sunday).

Bus 208 (Ligeirinho/Aeroporto) serves Centro every 30 minutes (R$3.30, 30 minutes). Catch it heading east from Av 7 de Setembro. The classier, wi-fi-enabled **Aeroporto Executivo** (☎3381-1326; www.aeroportoexecutivo.com.br; one way R$13) goes direct every 15 minutes between 5:15am (starting from *rodoferroviária*; from 6am Sunday) to 12:30am (last bus from airport) along selected, well-marked Centro stops.

Paranaguá

Paranaguá is the embarkation point for ferries to idyllic Ilha do Mel. Colorful but now faded buildings along the colonial waterfront create a feeling of languid tropical decadence.

Sleeping

Hostel Continente HOSTEL $

(☎3423-3224; www.hostelcontinente.com.br; General Carneiro 300; dm R$50, s/d/tr R$80/140/165; ❄📶) This HI hostel has clean if cramped dorms and doubles in an enviable location across from the ferry dock. Facilities include laundry and a communal kitchen.

Getting There & Away

Abaline-PR (☎3455-2616; www.abaline.com.br; General Carneiro 258) runs boats to Ilha do Mel throughout the day; see p330.

From the **bus station** (☎3420-2925; Ponta do Caju) on the waterfront, **Viação Graciosa** (☎3462-1115; www.viacaograciosa.com.br) has 15 buses per day to Curitiba (R$25, 1½ hours) and one to Morretes (R$11.50, one hour, 5pm).

Ilha do Mel

☎0XX41 / POP 1200

Ilha do Mel (Honey Island) is Paraná state's most enchanting getaway. This oddly shaped island at the mouth of the Baía da Paranaguá offers mostly wild beaches, good surfing waves and scenic coastal walks. There are no cars, so traffic jams throughout the island's scenic sandy lanes consist of surfboard-toting Brazilians on bicycles and bedazzled foreigners in their new Havaiana sandals.

Sights & Activities

Ilha do Mel consists of two parts joined by the beach at Nova Brasília. The larger, northern part is mostly an ecological station, little visited except for Praia da Fortaleza, where a well-preserved 18th-century **fort** still stands.

For fine views, visit **Farol das Conchas** (Conchas Lighthouse), east of Nova Brasília. The best **beaches** are east-facing Praia Grande, Praia do Miguel and Praia de Fora. It's a 1½-hour walk along the coast from Nova Brasília to Encantadas or an R$10 boat ride.

Sleeping & Eating

Pousadinha Ilha do Mel POUSADA $

(☎3426-8026; www.pousadinha.com.br; Caminho do Farol s/n, Nova Brasília; r from R$140, r without bathroom from R$80; ❄📶) A newer annex of chic rooms built from local hardwoods and outfitted with hammocks and solar-heated water are the best bet, though the cheaper rooms are the most comfortable and best-value for money for *centavo* pinchers. The Pousadinha has a popular **restaurant** serving pastas and seafood (mains R$56 to R$96 for two people) open to nonguests.

Hostel Encantadas Ecologic HOSTEL $
(☎9678-6428; www.facebook.com/hostelcantadasecologic; Encantadas; camping per person R$20, dm R$35, with bathroom R$45, d with/without bathroom R$110/80; 📶) The island's cheapest hostel is a colorful though extremely rustic choice, with rickety dorms and private rooms. Breakfast is R$10.

Recanto Francês POUSADA $$
(☎3426-9105; www.recantodofrances.com.br; s/d with fan R$120/200; 📶) Though the French have now departed, the charming Luciane has taken over this *pousada* steps from Mar do Fora beach and is ensuring the rustic but colorful clapboard rooms surrounding a pleasant garden remain good hospitality for money. Her *crepiocas* (a mix between a crepe and tapioca) at breakfast are a nice touch.

★**Mar e Sol** SEAFOOD $$
(Praça Felipe Valentim, Farol dos Conchas; meals R$18-30; ⏰11am-10pm; 📶) En route to the lighthouse, Mar e Sol serves up spectacular fish, shrimp or crab *moquecas* (R$87 to R$125 for two), seafood risottos and cheaper daily specials in individual portions. Junior, the local pet parrot, offers recommendations.

ℹ Information

CIT (Centro de Informaçãos Turística; www.fumtur.com.br; Arrival Dock, Nova Brasília; ⏰8am-7pm, to 8pm Nov-Mar) Encantadas (⏰8am-noon & 2-6pm, closed Mon & Tue) Helpful tourist information booths.

ℹ Getting There & Away

Abaline-PR (p329) runs boats (R$40 return) at 8:30am, 9:30am, 11am, 1pm, 3pm, 4:30pm and 6pm in summer (these dwindle down to 9:30am and 3:30pm in low season from the jetty opposite Paranaguá's tourist office, stopping first in Nova Brasília (1½ hours), and afterwards in Encantadas (two hours). Back to the mainland, boats depart Nova Brasília for Paranaguá in summer at 7:30am, 10am, 1:30pm, 3:30pm, 4:30pm, 6:30pm and 7pm. In low season, departures are at 8am and 5pm during the week and 10am and 5pm on weekends. All boats leave a half-hour earlier from Encantadas.

Alternatively, **Viação Graciosa** (p329) runs six daily buses from Curitiba to Pontal do Sul (R$34.50, 2½ hours), on the mainland opposite Encantadas, where you can embark for the 30-minute crossing to Nova Brasília or Encantadas (R$30 return). In high season, boats leave every half hour from 8am to 8pm from Pontal and 7am to 8pm from Ilha do Mel; in low season, every hour.

Ilha de Santa Catarina

☎0XX48

For years, gorgeous Ilha de Santa Catarina has been luring surfers and sun worshippers from all over Brazil, Argentina and Uruguay. Beaches are the island's main attraction, from long sweeps of unbroken sand to secluded little coves tucked into the wild, verdant shoreline.

Activities

Surfing, **kitesurfing** and **diving** outfits line the beach at Barra da Lagoa, on the island's eastern shore. A few kilometers south, try your hand at **sand boarding** on the dunes at Praia da Joaquina or **stand-up paddling** at Lagoa da Conceição.

The island's southern tip offers excellent **hiking**, including the one-hour trek through lush forest from Pântano do Sul to pristine Lagoinha do Leste beach, and whale-watching from June to November.

Sleeping & Eating

Our favorite places are around the rowdy and social Lagoa da Conceição and the more tranquil south island, but the island has many more nooks and crannies of surf and sand spread throughout its 42 beaches. Prices drop between 15% and 40% outside high season. Check out the **Food Truck Parking Lot** (www.foodtruckparkinglot.com.br; Henrique Veras do Nascimento 190; ⏰6pm-midnight Wed-Fri, 4pm-midnight Sat & Sun) for cheap eats.

★**Tucano House** HOSTEL $
(☎3207-8287; www.tucanohouse.com; Rua das Araras 229; dm R$55-70, r with/without bathroom R$220/$200; ⏰closed Mar 15-Nov; ❄@📶🏊) 🍃 Siblings Lila and Caio are your easy-on-the-eyes hosts at this eco-forward hostel in the heart of the Lagoa action. Their childhood home now features solar-heated showers, recycled rainwater cistern and amenities like free use of bikes and surfboards, and island adventures in a decked-out VW van.

Backpackers Share House HOSTEL $$
(☎3232-7606; www.backpackersfloripa.com; Servidão da Prainha 29; dm R$55, d/tr without bathroom R$180/210; @📶) Across the pedestrian

Ilha de Santa Catarina

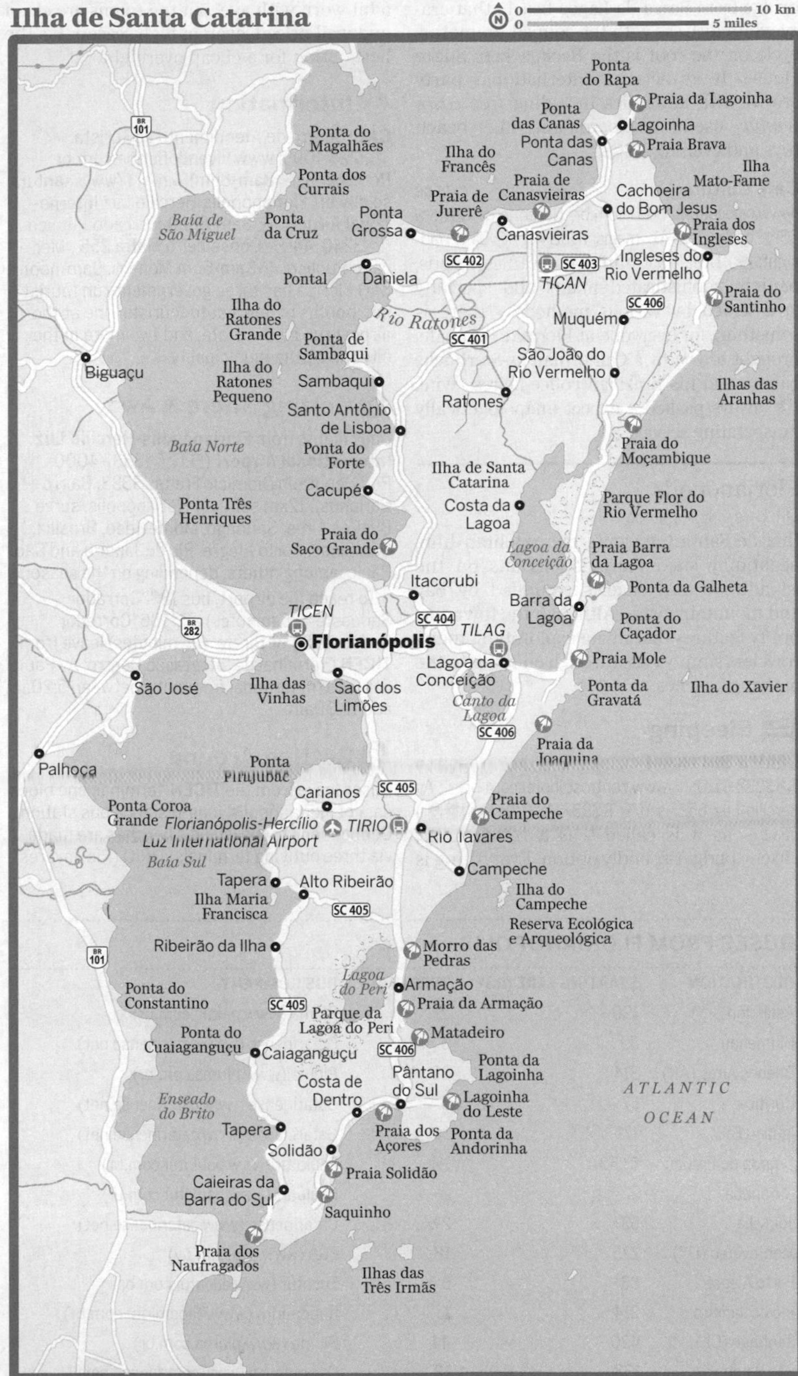

bridge from Barra da Lagoa beach, that crazy white fortress with the souped-up motorcycle on the roof is the Backpackers Share House. It attracts an international party crowd with amenities including free *caipirinhas*, use of surfboards and other beach toys and evening BBQs.

Café Cultura CAFE **$$**
(www.cafeculturafloripa.com.br; Severino de Oliveira 669; coffee R$4-11, mains R$18-43; 9am-midnight;) Breakfast until 1pm, waffles, salads, paninis, sophisticated mains and specialty java served by various methods – there is something for everyone at Floripa's best cafe, brought to you by a Californian ex-Starbucks barista and his Brazilian coffee-heiress wife. It's always packed – expect unapologetically exasperating service.

Florianópolis

0XX48 / POP 421,000

Ilha de Santa Catarina's metropolitan hub, beautifully sited Florianópolis sits on the island's western edge, surrounded by bay and mountain vistas. Although the town has pretty features that invite exploration, many travelers simply pass through en route to the outlying beaches.

Sleeping

Centro Sul Hotel HOTEL **$**
(3222-9110; www.centrosulhotel.com.br; Av Hercílio Luz 652; s/d/tr R$98/148/188;) CSH – as it is called – is a comfortable, kitschy budget-friendly option. Everything is a bit worn with age, but the rooms are clean and well priced, even in high season. It's the best option for a cheap overnight.

Information

CAT (Centro de Atendimento ao Turista; 3228-1095; www.vivendofloripa.com.br; Rodoviária; 8am-6pm) Airport (www.santur.sc.gov.br; Florianópolis-Hercílio Luz International Airport; 8am-8pm) Mercado Público (3240-4407; Conselheiro Mafra 255 , Mercado Público; 8am-6pm Mon-Fri, 9am-noon Sat) Floripa has three government-run tourist info booths of interest to tourists, one at the airport run by the state; and two more in the city run by the municipality.

Getting There & Away

Daily flights from **Florianópolis-Hercílio Luz International Airport** (FLN; 3331-4000; Rod Deputado Diomício Freitas 3393, Bairro Carianos), 12km south of Florianópolis, serve Buenos Aires, Santiago, Montevideo, Brasília, Campinas, Porto Alegre, Rio de Janeiro and São Paulo, among others, depending on the season.

To reach the airport, bus 183 'Corredor Sudoeste' (35 minutes) and 186 'Corredor Sudoeste Semi-Direto' (25 minutes) leave from **TICEN** (Terminal de Integração Centro; Av Paulo Fontes s/n) terminal frequently between 5:20am and 12:30am.

Getting Around

Buses leave from the **TICEN** terminal, one block east of Florianópolis' long-distance bus station. Connections to the island's beaches are made via three outlying terminals: TIRIO (Rio Tavares

BUSES FROM FLORIANÓPOLIS

DESTINATION	STARTING FARE (R$)	TIME (HR)	BUS COMPANY
Asunción (PY)	190	21	Pluma (www.pluma.com.br)
Blumenau	39	3	Catarinense (www.catarinense.net)
Buenos Aires (AR)	314	25	Pluma (www.pluma.com.br)
Curitiba	57	5	Catarinense (www.catarinense.net)
Iguaçu Falls	179	14	Catarinense (www.catarinense.net)
Guarda do Embaú	13.50	1½	Paulotur (www.paulotur.com.br)
Garopaba	22	2	Paulotur (www.paulotur.com.br)
Joinville	53	2½	Catarinense (www.catarinense.net)
Montevideo (UY)	275	18	EGA (www.ega.com.uy)
Porto Alegre	83	6	Eucatur (www.eucatur.com.br)
Rio de Janeiro	214	17	Itapemirim (www.itapemirim.com.br)
Santiago (CL)	420	44	Pluma (www.pluma.com.br)
São Paulo	133	12	Catarinense (www.catarinense.net)

WORTH A TRIP

PARQUE NACIONAL DE APARADOS DA SERRA

This magnificent **national park** (☎3251-1227; admission R$7; ⊙8am-5pm Tue-Sun) is 18km from the town of Cambará do Sul, approximately 200km northeast of Porto Alegre. The most famous attraction is the **Cânion do Itaimbezinho**, a fantastic narrow canyon with dramatic waterfalls and sheer escarpments of 600m to 720m.

Two easy self-guided trails, **Trilha do Vértice** (2km return) and **Trilha Cotovelo** (6km return), lead from the park's visitor center to waterfalls and canyon vistas; the more challenging **Trilha do Rio do Boi** follows the base of the canyon for 7km; it also requires a guide and is closed during rainy season. For guided trips, try the excellent eco-agency **Cânion Turismo** (☎3251-1027; www.canionturismo.com.br; Getúlio Vargas 876; ⊙8am-7pm).

Citral (www.citral.tur.br) offers one bus from Porto Alegre for Cambará do Sul (R$36, 5½ hours) at 6am Monday to Saturday. Returning, you must catch a 6:30am or 1:30pm bus to São Francisco de Paula (R$14.80, one hour) and switch there for Porto Alegre (from R$21.60, three hours), Canela (from R$7.90, one hour) or Gramado (from R$9.15, one hour). A taxi to the national park costs R$100 round trip.

Terminal), TILAG (Lagoa Terminal) and TICAN (Canasvieiras Terminal).

For southern beaches, including Armação, Pântano do Sul and Costa de Dentro, catch bus 410 'Rio Tavares' (Platform B) then transfer at TIRIO to bus 563.

For eastern beaches, catch bus 330 'Lagoa da Conceição' (Platform A), then transfer at TILAG for a second bus to your final destination, for example bus 360 to Barra da Lagoa.

For Canasvieiras and northern beaches, catch bus 210 'Canasvieiras Direito' (Platform B) from TICEN to TICAN.

A single fare of R$3.10 (paid at the TICEN ticket booth) covers your initial ride plus one transfer.

Porto Alegre

☎0XX51 / POP 1.4 MILLION

Porto Alegre is a good introduction to progressive Rio Grande do Sul. Built on the banks of the Rio Guaíba, this lively, modern port has a well-preserved neoclassical downtown, with handsome plazas, good museums, and a vibrant arts and music scene.

Sights

Museu de Arte do Rio Grande do Sul MUSEUM
(www.margs.rs.gov.br; Praça da Alfândega; ⊙10am-7pm Tue-Sun) FREE A pedestrian promenade runs into Praça da Alfândega, the leafy square that is home to the Museu de Arte do Rio Grande do Sul. The neoclassical building is an impressive venue for regional artists. On the ground floor, the inviting Bistrot de MARGS takes advantage of the leafy setting, which is a lovely spot for lunch.

Museu Histórico Júlio de Castilhos MUSEUM
(www.museujuliodecastilhos.blogspot.com; Duque de Caxias 1205; ⊙10am-5pm Tue-Sat) FREE Near the Praça da Matriz is Museu Histórico Júlio de Castilhos, displaying *gaúcho* artifacts in a typical 19th-century home.

Sleeping

Most travelers stay in Cidade Baixa, the first neighborhood southeast of the historic center. In addition to being Porto Alegre's nightlife enclave, a healthy hostel scene has popped up.

★**Porto Alegre Eco Hostel** HOSTEL $
(☎3019-2449; www.portoalegreecohostel.com.br; Luiz Afonso 276; dm R$49, s/d from R$70/120; @☜≋) Down a quiet residential street in the heart of Cidade Baixa, this excellent hostel, chock-full of demolition wood furniture and eco-awareness, offers a lovely backyard garden in a pristine '30s-era home. English spoken.

Brick Hostel HOSTEL $
(☎3028-3333; www.brickhostel.com; Cabral 217; dm R$39-45, r R$140; ❄☜) This Rio Branco hostel is walkable to Parque Farroupilha, Moinhos dos Ventos and Centro but offers a quiet respite from both the latter and the more rambunctious Cidade Baixa. Dripping in retro funk, there's an artsy common area (hipster local art for sale) and dorms with individual lockers, reading lights and electrical outlets, and a few minimalist privates.

Porto Alegre

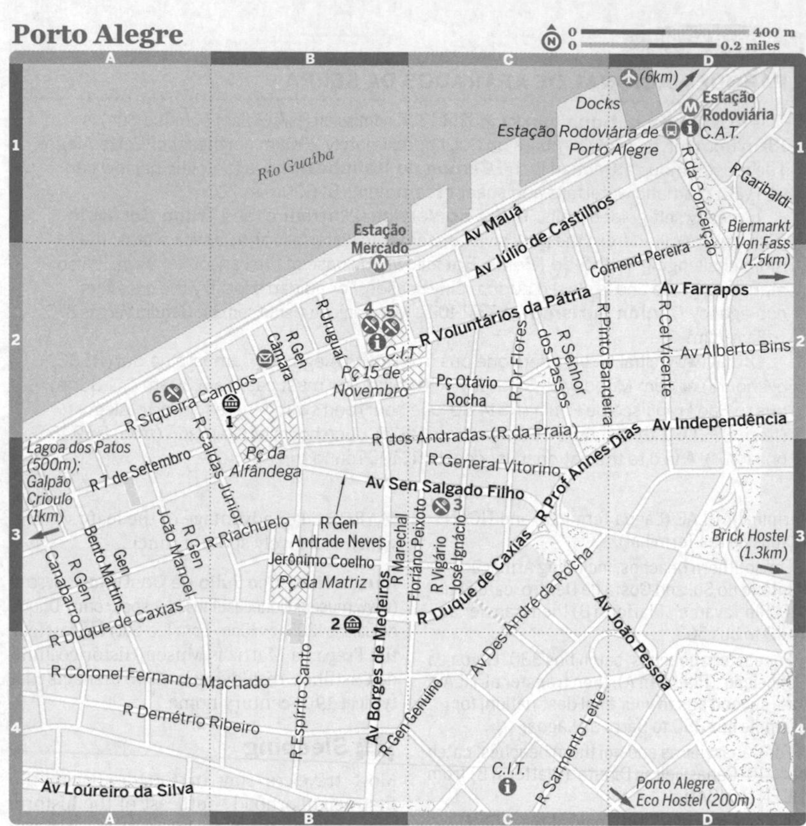

Eating & Drinking

Sabor Natural BUFFET $
(Siqueira Campos 890; buffet R$20; 11am-3pm Mon-Fri;) Vegetarians will delight at this all-organic, beef-free, all-you-can-eat buffet that caters to the downtown lunch crowd. Enjoy limitless soups, salads and other mostly herbivore-leaning fare.

★ **Atelier das Massas** ITALIAN $$
(3255-8888; www.atelierdemassas.com.br; Riachuelo 1482; pasta R$30-54; 11am-2:30pm & 7-11:30pm Mon-Sat;) Crammed with atmosphere as much as artisanal pastas, put this dive-like pasta bar on your immediate to-do list and never mind the curmudgeon old-school servers. There's an irresistible antipasti buffet and a very long list of delectable homemade pastas.

Mercado Público MARKET $$
(www2.portoalegre.rs.gov.br/mercadopublico; 7:30am-7:30pm Mon-Fri, to 6:30pm Sat) Porto Alegre's bustling public market offers a wealth of eats. Recommended options include **Banco 40** (www.banca40.com.br; Mercado Público; 8am-7:30pm Mon-Fri, to 6:30pm Sat), home of the incomparable *super bomba royal* (a showy ice cream and fruit salad concoction; R$14.90); **Gambrinus** (www.gambrinus.com.br; Mercado Público; mains R$36-85; 11:30am-8:30pm Mon-Fri, to 4pm Sat), an old-world seafood restaurant; and **Café Do Mercado** (www.cafedomercado.com.br; Mercado Público; coffee R$4-13.50; 8am-7:30pm Mon-Fri, 9:30am-5pm Sat), one of the city's best cafes.

★ **Biermarkt Von Fass** BAR
(www.biermarkt.com.br; Barão de Santo Ângelo 497; beers R$9-48; 6-11:30pm Mon-Sat;) With its 38 taps, this Moinhos dos Ventos drinking den is said to offer the most beers on draft in all of Latin America. We're not sure about that, but it is the stomping

Porto Alegre

Sights

1 Museu de Arte do Rio Grande do Sul B2
2 Museu Histórico Júlio de Castilhos B3

Eating

3 Atelier das Massas C3
Banco 40 .... (see 4)
Bar Gambrinus .... (see 4)
4 Café do Mercado B2
5 Mercado Público B2
6 Sabor Natural A2

grounds of craft beer fiends with a strong emphasis on local breweries, including co-brews by Seasons (with San Diego's Green Flash) and Tupiniquim (with Copenhagen's Evil Twin).

Information

CAT (Centro de Atencão ao Turista; ☎3225-0677; www.turismo.rs.gov.br; Rodoviária; ⏰8am-4pm Mon-Fri, to 1pm Sat & Sun) Airport (Arrivals Hall, Terminal 1; ⏰7:30am-10pm) Rio Grande do Sul state tourism board runs two helpful tourist information centers.

CIT (Centro de Informações Turísticas; ☎3211-5705; www.portoalegre.travel; Mercado Público; ⏰9am-6pm Mon-Sat) Cidade Baixa/Linha Turismo (☎3289-6765; Travessa do Carmo 84; ⏰8am-6pm) Airport (☎3358-2048; Arrivals Hall, Terminal 1; ⏰8am-10pm) Three of the most convenient and well-organized municipality tourist information booths.

Correios (www.correios.com.br; Siqueira Campos 1100; ⏰9am-6pm Mon-Fri, to noon Sat) Postal services.

Getting There & Away

Terminals 1 and 2 of Porto Alegre's **Salgado Filho International Airport** (POA; ☎3210-0101; Av Severo Dulius), 6km from downtown, are connected by a free shuttle. In addition to major destinations throughout Brazil, international destinations include Buenos Aires, Lima, Lisbon, Miami, Montevideo, Panama City and Santiago. Take a taxi (R$25 to R$30, 15 minutes) or ride the metro (R$1.70, 30 minutes), connecting to the terminals on the free **Aeromóvel** (Brazil's first air-powered people mover).

The busy **long-distance bus station** (☎3210-0101; www.rodoviaria-poa.com.br; Largo Vespasiano Julioveppo 70), 1.5km northeast of Centro, is accessible by metro; alternatively, a taxi downtown costs R$10 or so from the prepaid **Ponte do Taxi** (☎3221-9371; Rodovíaria). If your baggage is considered large, they will tack on an additional R$6.55.

Two day buses and two overnight buses go to Chuí on the Uruguayan border during the week (two less on weekends); otherwise you can connect in Pelotas.

Getting Around

Porto Alegre's metro, **Trensurb** (www.trensurb.gov.br; one way R$1.70; ⏰5am-11:20pm), has convenient stations at Estação Mercado (by the port), Estação Rodoviária (the next stop) and the

WORTH A TRIP

JESUIT MISSIONS

In the early 17th century, Jesuit missionaries established a series of Indian missions in a region straddling northeast Argentina, southeast Paraguay and neighboring parts of Brazil. Between 1631 and 1638, after devastating attacks by Paulista slaving expeditions and hostile indigenous people, activity was concentrated in 30 more easily defensible missions. These places became centers of culture as well as religion – in effect a nation within the colonies, considered by some scholars an island of utopian progress and socialism, which at its height in the 1720s had more than 150,000 Guarani indigenous inhabitants.

Seven of the now-ruined missions lie in the northwest of Brazil's Rio Grande do Sul state, eight are in Paraguay and 15 in Argentina.

The town of **Santo Ângelo** is the main jumping-off point for the Brazilian missions; the most interesting and intact site is **Sítio Arqueológico São Miguel Arcanjo** (adult/child R$5/2.50; ⏰9am-noon & 2-6pm, closed Mon), 53km southwest of Santo Ângelo in São Miguel das Missões. Several buses daily run from Porto Alegre to Sânto Angelo, where you can make onward connections to São Miguel das Missões (R$10.20, one hour, four daily).

BUSES FROM PORTO ALEGRE

DESTINATION	STARTING FARE (R$)	TIME (HR)	BUS COMPANY
Buenos Aires (AR)	249.50	21	Pluma (www.pluma.com.br)
Cambará do Sul	36	6	Citral (www.citral.tur.br)
Canela	29	3	Citral (www.citral.tur.br)
Chuí	101.50	7	Planalto (www.planalto.com.br)
Curitiba	126	13	Penha (http://vendas.nspenha.com.br)
Florianópolis	86	6	Santo Anjo (www.santoanjo.com.br)
Gramado	27	3	Citral (www.citral.tur.br)
Montevideo (UY)	205.50	12	TTL (www.ttl.com.br)
Pelotas	50	3½	Embaixador (www.expressoembaixador.com.br)
Rio de Janeiro	295	26	Penha (http://vendas.nspenha.com.br)
Rio Grande	73	5	Planalto (www.planalto.com.br)
Sânto Angelo	110	7	Ouro e Prata (www.ouroeprata.com)
São Francisco de Paula	22	3	Citral (www.citral.tur.br)
São Paulo	213	19	Penha (http://vendas.nspenha.com.br)
Torres	36	3	Unesul (www.unesul.com.br)

airport (three stops beyond). For Cidade Baixa, catch bus T5 from the airport or 282, 2821, 244 or 255 from the bus station (R$3.25).

Foz do Iguaçu

☎0XX45 / POP 251,000

The stupendous roar of 275 waterfalls crashing 80m into the Rio Iguaçu seems to create a low-level buzz of excitement throughout the city of Foz, even though the famed Cataratas (falls) are 20km southeast of town. Apart from the waterfalls, you can dip into the forests of Paraguay or check out Itaipu Dam, one of the world's largest hydroelectric power plants.

Sights & Activities

To see the falls properly, you must visit both sides. Brazil gives the grand overview and Argentina the closer look. Most hostels offer full day trips to the Argentine side (p100) of the falls for R$150.

Parque Nacional do Iguaçu WATERFALL
(☎3521-4400; www.cataratasdoiguacu.com.br; adult foreigners/Mercosul/Brazilians R$52.30/41.30/31.30, child R$8; ⏲9am-5pm) To visit the falls, take the bus to the third stop, site of Hotel das Cataratas. Here you can pick up the Trilha das Cataratas, or 'Waterfall Trail', a 1200m trail following the shore of the Iguaçu river, terminating at the Garganta do Diablo. From here, take the panoramic elevator to get a view of the falls from above.

Itaipu DAM
(☎0800-645-4645; www.turismoitaipu.com.br; Tancredo Neves 6702; panoramic/special tour R$27/68; ⏲regular tour hourly 8am-4pm) With a capacity of 14 million kilowatts, this binational dam is the world's second largest hydroelectric power station, and the one that produces the most electricity per year. The impressive structure, at some 8km long and 200m high, is a memorable sight, especially when the river is high and a vast torrent of overflow water cascades down the spillway.

Parque das Aves BIRD PARK
(Bird Park; www.parquedasaves.com.br; Av das Cataratas, Km 17.1; admission foreigners/Brazilians R$34/24; ⏲8:30am-5:30pm) This 5-hectare bird park, located 300m from the entrance to Parque Nacional do Iguaçu, is home to 800-plus species of birds, including red ibis, bare-throated bellbird, and flamingos galore. They live in 8m-high aviaries that are constructed right in the forest, some of which you can walk through. Well worth it.

Macuco Ecoaventura/Safari BOAT TOUR, HIKING
(☎3574-4244; www.macucosafari.com.br; Brazil) For boat tours and hiking on the Brazilian side.

Sleeping

★Tetris Container Hostel HOSTEL $
(045-3132-0019; www.tetrishostel.com.br; Av das Cataratas 639; dm R$35-40, d from R$160;) Brazil's coolest hostel is crafted from 15 shipping containers – even the pool is a water-filled shipping container! – and makes full use of other industrial byproducts as well, like sinks made from oil drums. Colorful bathrooms brighten the dorms (a four-bed female plus 10- and 12-bed mixed) and the patio/bar area is tops. Adorable staff to boot.

★Hostel Natura HOSTEL $
(3529-6949; www.hostelnatura.com; Av das Cataratas Km 12.5; camping/dm per person R$28/50, d/tr R$140/150, s/d/tr without bathroom R$105/130/154;) This hostel is set on a gorgeous piece of land, amid two small lakes and lush scenery. The rooms themselves are pleasant and tidy, and there's ample outdoor lounge space, a restaurant and a fun bar. The hostel is 12km from town on the way to the falls. Cash only.

Pousada Sonho Meu GUESTHOUSE $
(045-3573-5764; www.pousadasonhomeufoz.com.br; Mem de Sá 267; s/d R$160/210;) What from the outside looks like an administrative building becomes a delightful oasis barely 50m from the local bus terminal. Rooms are newly upgraded and simply decorated with bamboo; there's a standout pool (complete with a mini waterfall!), breakfast area and outdoor guest kitchen and a warm welcome throughout.

Eating

Tropicana CHURRASCARIA $
(www.pizzariareopicana.com.br; Av Juscelino Kubitschek 228; buffet R$26; 11am-3:30pm & 6:30-11:30pm ;) This all-you-can-eat shoestring savior offers absolutely ridiculous taste for money. Expect a madhouse.

Foz do Iguaçu

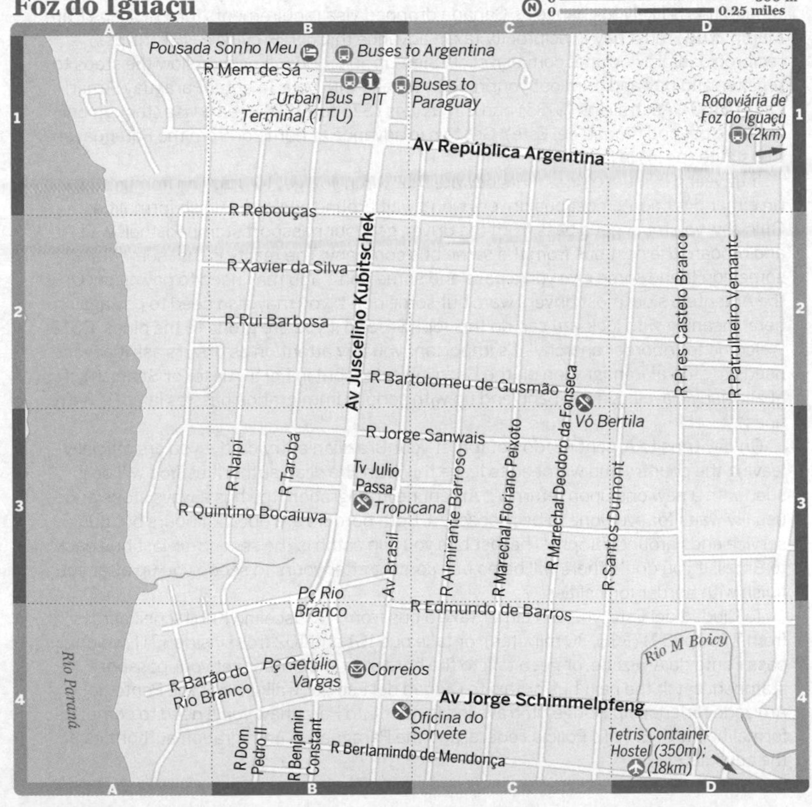

Oficina do Sorvete CAFE $
(www.oficinadosorvete.com.br; Av Jorge Schimmelpfeng 244; per kg sandwiches/ice cream R$44.50/44.90; ⌚1pm-12:30am; 📶👪) Take a dive into nearly 50 colorful, beat-the-heat ice cream flavors on hand, from decadent *(doce de leite, caramelo, coco quemado)* to exotic fruits *(jabuticaba)* to inebriating *(caipirinha)*.

★**Vó Bertila** PIZZA $$
(www.vobertilla.com.br; Bartolomeu de Gusmão 1116; pizza R$22-68, pasta for 2 R$48-82; ⌚6:30pm-12:30am, closed Mon) This informal, family-run cantina churns out wood-fired pizza – even in personal sizes! – and authentic pastas in heaping portions. All homey and hardwoods, it's the kind of down-home Italian spot Brazil does so very well. Expect it to be packed.

ℹ Information

PIT (☎0800-45-1516; www.pmfi.pr.gov.br/turismo; Av das Cataratas 2330, Vila Yolanda; ⌚7am-11pm) Provides maps and detailed info about the area. The main office is in Vila Yolanda, out of town on Av das Cataratas towards the falls, reachable on bus 120.There are other branches at the airport (☎0800-45-1516; Aeroporto Internacional de Foz do Iguaçu/Cataratas; ⌚8am-10pm), long-distance bus station (☎0800-45-1516; Av Costa e Silva 1601; ⌚7am-6pm) and local bus station (☎0800-45-1516; Kubitschek 1310; ⌚7:30am-6pm).

ℹ GETTING TO ARGENTINA & PARAGUAY

Many nationalities can enter Argentina without a visa, but double-check before you arrive or at the Argentine Consulate (p413). Overland-traveling citizens of the US (10 years $160), Australia (single entry $100) and Canada (single entry/five years $75/150; though this is likely to change as Canada dropped visa requirements for Brazilians from March 2016) must pay a reciprocity tax in advance through Provincia NET (https://reciprocidad.provincianet.com.ar); click 'Sign Up' just under 'Log In,' follow the steps to register, and pay and print out your receipt to take with you. To enter Paraguay, Americans ($160), Australians ($135) and Canadians ($75 to $150) need a visa (though only if you go beyond Ciudad del Este). Get this in advance at home or from the Paraguayan Consulate (p414) in Foz.

If traveling by bus to Argentina, beware that when you get to Brazilian immigration (in either direction), most bus drivers won't wait around while you finish formalities. Officially, you must get a pass from the driver, get your passport stamped, then wait and reboard the next bus from the same bus company. The reality is that some wait, some don't; and some give you a pass and some don't. You may need to pay again. On the Argentine side, most drivers wait, but some don't; you may also need to pay again here, meaning with luck you can do this for R$4, and if you are prone to the blues, R$12. Welcome to triborder anarchy! It's important you pay attention as drivers ask if anyone needs to stop at immigration on the Brazilian side – but in Portuguese (or Spanish), if at all. Many travelers miss it and end up with serious immigration hassles later (ie hefty fines).

On day trips to Argentina, do not forget your Brazilian entry card – you are officially leaving the country and will need to leave this with Brazilian authorities. You will be issued with a new one upon return. At Argentine immigration, the bus always stops and usually waits for everyone to be processed. Both borders are open 24 hours but bus service ends around 7:15pm. The last bus you can catch is the second-to-last bus back to Brazil. If you don't, there will be no bus coming after yours to scoop you up after you finish with border formalities.

To Ciudad del Este, you can either take a bus from Av Juscelino Kubitschek across from TTU (p339) (R$5, 30 minutes), or take bus 101 and 102 from inside TTU, which pass Ponte da Amizade, or get a taxi to the border. At the border get your passport stamped, catch the next bus or taxi to Ciudad del Este, or walk across the Ponte da Amizade (Friendship Bridge). If traveling further into Paraguay, you'll need to complete formalities with Brazil's Polícia Federal and the Paraguayan immigration authorities at the consulate.

BUSES FROM FOZ

The **long-distance bus station** (☎045-3522-3336; Av Costa e Silva 1601) is 3km northeast of the town center.

DESTINATION	STARTING FARE (R$)	TIME (HR)	BUS COMPANY
Asunción	55	6½	Sol del Paraguay (www.soldelparaguay.com.py)
Buenos Aires	290	18	Crucero del Norte (www.crucerodelnorte.com.ar)
Campo Grande	140	13	Eucatur (www.eucatur.com.br)
Curitiba	153.50	10	Catarinense (www.catarinense.net)
Florianópolis	185	16	Catarinense (www.catarinense.net)
São Paulo	195.95	16	Kalowa (www.expressokaiowa. com.br)
Rio de Janeiro	273.53	24	Kalowa (www. expressokaiowa.com.br)

Correios (www.correios.com.br; Praça Getúlio Vargas 72 ; ⊙9am-5pm Mon-Fri) Postal sevices.

Polícia Federal (☎3576-5500; www.dpf.gov.br; Av Paraná 3471) For immigration procedures.

ℹ Getting There & Away

Daily flights link **Foz do Iguaçu/Cataratas International Airport** (IGU; ☎3523-4244) to Lima and several major Brazilian cities. Sit on the left hand side of the plane on arrival for good views of the falls.

ℹ Getting Around

The local transport terminal is known as **TTU** (Terminal Turístico Urbano; ☎2105-1385; Av Juscelino Kubitschek 1385; ⊙5am-midnight). Bus 120 'Aeroporto/Parque Nacional' runs to the airport (R$2.90, 30 minutes) and the Brazilian side of the waterfalls (40 minutes) every 22 to 30 minutes from 5:25am to midnight. Bus 120 'Centro/TTU' goes from the airport to Centro (exit to the far left end and look for blue 'Ônibus' sign). City buses 105 and 115 cover the 6km between the long-distance bus station and TTU.

To get to the Argentine side, catch a Puerto Iguazú bus (R$4, one hour) on Mem de Sá across from the local bus terminal or along Av das Cataratas closer to most hostels. They pass every 30 minutes or so between 6:15am and 7:15pm (less on Sunday). At Puerto Iguazú bus station, **Río Uruguay** (www.riouruguaybus.com.ar) services the falls (A$100 return, 30 minutes) frequently between 7:20am and 8:50pm.

THE CENTRAL WEST

A land of breathtaking panoramas and exceptional wildlife, Brazil's Central West is a must-see for nature lovers and outdoor enthusiasts. The Pantanal, one of the planet's most important wetland systems, is the region's star attraction. Its meandering rivers, savannas and forests harbor one of the densest concentrations of plant and animal life in the New World. Other regional attractions include dramatic *chapadas* (tablelands), which rise like brilliant red giants from the dark-green cerrado (savanna), punctuated by spectacular waterfalls and picturesque swimming holes; Bonito, where crystal-clear rivers teeming with fish highlight one of the world's most unique natural destinations; and Brazil's surreal, master-planned capital, Brasília.

Brasília

☎0XX61 / POP 2.6 MILLION

Well into its middle age, Brazil's once futuristic capital remains an impressive monument to national initiative. Built from nothing in about three years, Brasília replaced Rio de Janeiro as Brazil's center of government in 1960 under the visionary leadership of President Juscelino Kubitschek, architect Oscar Niemeyer, urban planner Lucio Costa and landscape architect Burle Marx.

Sights

Brasília's major edifices are spread along a 5km stretch of the Eixo Monumental and are listed in northwest–southeast order. Further south, in the 'cockpit' of the airplane ground plan, are the most interesting government buildings: **Palácio do Itamaraty** (Palace of Arches; ☎3411-8051; www.itamaraty.gov.br; Esplanada dos Ministérios, Bloco H; ⊙9am-11am & 2-6pm Mon-Fri, 9-11am & 1-6pm Sat & Sun) FREE, **Palácio da Justiça** (☎3216-3216; Esplanada dos Ministérios; ⊙2-4pm Mon-Fri, 10am-3pm Sat & Sun) FREE and **Congresso Nacional** (Parliament; ☎3216-1771; www.congressonacional.leg.br; Praça dos Três Poderes; ⊙9am-5pm) FREE. To

Central West Brazil

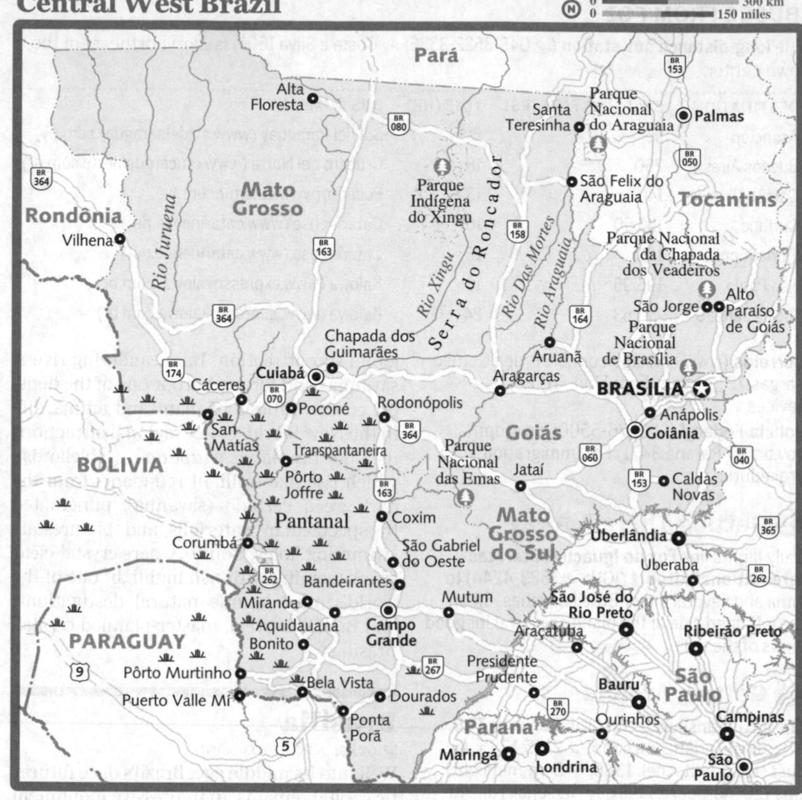

visit them, you can combine local buses 104 and 108 with some long walks or, most conveniently, take a city tour.

Memorial JK MUSEUM

(☎3226-7860; www.memorialjk.com.br; Praça do Cruzeiro; adult/child R$10/5; ⊙9am-6pm Tue-Sun) The tomb of JK (President Juscelino Kubitschek) lies underneath eerily beautiful stained glass by French artist Marianne Peretti inside the Memorial JK. The museum houses JK's 3000-book-strong personal library as well as a pictorial history of Brasília. Don't miss JK's 1973 Ford Galaxie!

★TV Tower TOWER

(Eixo Monumental; ⊙9am-7:45pm Tue-Sun) FREE The 75m-high observation deck of the TV Tower gives a decent overview of the city, but it's still not quite tall enough to really get a sense of the city's airplane design. The mezzanine houses a charming cafe run by a farming cooperative.

★Santuário Dom Bosco CHURCH

(☎3223-6542; www.santuariodombosco.org.br; W3 Sul, Quadra 702; ⊙7am-8pm) FREE Santuário Dom Bosco is made of 80 concrete columns that support 7400 pieces of illuminated Murano glass, symbolizing a starry sky, which cast a blue submarine glow over the pews. The central chandelier weighs 2.5 tonnes and adds an amazing 435 light bulbs' worth of energy to the monthly electricity bill.

★Museu Nacional MUSEUM

(☎3325-5220; Esplanada dos Ministérios; ⊙9am-6:30pm Tue-Sun) FREE A spherical half-dome by architect Oscar Niemeyer, the inside features a discreet mezzanine mostly held up by columns suspended from the roof. A signature curved ramp juts out from its base and runs around the outside like a ring of Saturn.

★Catedral Metropolitana CHURCH

(☎3224-4073; www.facebook.com/catedraldebrasilia; Esplanada dos Ministérios; ⏲8am-5pm Mon, Wed & Thu, 10:30am-5pm Tue & Sat, 8am-6pm Sun) FREE With its 16 curved columns and wavy stained-glass interior, the Catedral Metropolitana is heavenly viewing. At the entrance are the haunting *Four Disciples* statues carved by Ceschiatti, who also made the aluminum angels hanging inside.

Sleeping

Brasília suffers from a severe dearth of budget accommodations, though many downtown hotels slash prices on weekends. In Brasília, the fewer stories a hotel has, the cheaper it is.

Hostel 7 HOSTEL $

(☎3033-7707; www.hostel7.com.br; SCLRN 708, Bloco I, Loja 20; dm R$80-90; ❄@🛜) Brasília's best hostel is an all-dorm affair, coming in three mixed variations of eight- or 12-beds and one female-only. The rooms are basic, but have lockers, air-con and bathrooms, while the common spaces are tight. There's a nice covered courtyard/bar area in the back. Local art and historic photos of the city add a nice local touch.

Econotel HOTEL $$

(☎3204-7337; www.hoteleconotel.com.br; SHS, Quadra 3, Bloco B; s/d/tr from R$139/239/309; ❄🛜) The closest thing to a budget hotel in the SHS, though the rooms are newer, fresher and better equipped and the hall ways a tad brighter than many of the other stagnant options in a higher range. Pricier 'luxury' rooms are spacious and more modern, and the front desk steps up the professionalism compared with similar SHN options.

Central Brasília

Top Sights

1 Catedral Metropolitana	A5
2 Congresso Nacional	A6
3 Museu Nacional	A4
4 Palácio do Itamaraty	A6
5 TV Tower	B2

Sights

6 Palácio da Justiça	B6

Sleeping

7 Econotel	A2
8 Hotel Diplomat	B2

Eating

9 Conjunto Nacional	B3
10 Marietta	B2
11 Shopping Brasília	B2

Shopping

12 Pátio Brasil	A2

WORTH A TRIP

NATURE CALLS!

You're in cerrado country, the South American savanna. Nature lovers approaching urban overdose in Brasília should seek refuge in the surrounding grasslands.

A Brazilian National Heritage site backed by lovely mountains, **Pirenópolis** attracts weekend escapees from Brasília (165km east) for some of the country's most picturesque 18th-century architecture and abundant waterfalls. Within 20km of town, **Parque Estadual da Serra dos Pireneus** (☎3265-1320; www.semarh.goias.gov.br/site/conteudo/parque-estadual-dos-pirineus-pep; ⊙8am-5pm, 9am-8pm summer) and **Reserva Ecológica Vargem Grande** (☎3331-3071; www.vargemgrande.pirenopolis.tur.br; Rua do Frota 888; admission R$25; ⊙9am-5pm) both have beautiful waterfalls and swimming holes; while **Santuário de Vida Silvestre Vagafogo** (☎3335-8515; www.vagafogo.com.br; ⊙9am-5pm) offers a self-guided forest walk (R$20) and a delicious weekend brunch (R$45). **Goianésia** (☎3331-2763; www.viacaogoianesia.com.br) offers four daily buses from Brasília (R$24.50, three hours).

The spectacular **Parque Nacional da Chapada dos Veadeiros**, 220km north of Brasília, showcases the high-altitude cerrado, a sublime landscape where maned wolves, giant anteaters and 7ft-tall rheas roam amid big skies, canyons, waterfalls and oasis-like stands of wine palms. The closest towns to the park are the new-age **Alto Paraíso de Goias** (40km east) and tranquil **São Jorge** (2km south), both offering an abundance of comfy and charming accommodations. **Real Expresso** (☎2106-7144; www.realexpresso.com.br) has three daily buses from Brasília to Alto Paraíso (R$43.10, 4½ hours, 10am, 7pm and 9pm).

Hotel Diplomat HOTEL $$
(☎3204-2010; www.diplomathotelbrasilia.com; SHN, Quadra 2, Bloco L; s/d/tr from R$199/239/279; ❄📶) Near the TV Tower, this updated cheapie wins votes for its ample breakfast, free wi-fi and substantial weekend discounts (basement rooms are the cheapest). There's also train compartment-sized cabins for solo travelers.

✕ Eating & Drinking

For walkable cheap eats from the SHS and SHN areas, you're stuck with food courts in the air-conditioned downtown malls: **Shopping Brasília** (www.brasiliashopping.com.br; Quadra 5, Asa Norte SCN; ⊙10am-10pm Mon-Sat, 2-8pm Sun), **Pátio Brasil** (www.patiobrasil.com.br; Asa Sul, W3 SCS; ⊙10am-10pm Mon-Sat, noon-8pm Sun) and **Conjunto Nacional** (www.conjuntonacional.com.br; SDN CNB, Conjunto A; ⊙10am-10pm Mon-Sat, noon-8pm Sun).

Students congregate over cheap suds at **Quadrado de Cerveja** (SCLN 408 Norte).

Naturetto BRAZILIAN $
(www.naturetto.com.br; CLN 405, Block C; per kg R$46.90; ⊙11:30am-3pm & 6:30-9:30pm Mon-Fri, 11:30am-4pm Sun; 📶🥗) This excellent, near-vegetarian (there's fish) only *por-kilo* restaurant is worth seeking out for creative dishes and the rustic, inner-city environment in which to enjoy it all. Nutritionists are on hand, overseeing the food and answering questions; it's packed at lunchtime.

Marietta SANDWICHES $
(www.marietta.com.br; 2nd fl, Shopping Brasília; sandwiches R$14.50-28; ⊙10am-10pm Mon-Sat, 2-8pm Sun) This sandwich shop turns out the capital's best: a triangular triple-decker of arugula, buffalo mozzarella and sun-dried tomatoes. It has prizewinning juices and killer salads as well.

Nossa Cozinha Bistrô FUSION $$
(☎3326-5207; www.nossacozinhabsb.blogspot.com.br; SCLN 402, Bloco C; mains R$32-56.40; ⊙11.30am-3pm & 7.30pm-midnight Mon-Sat; 📶) At this near-makeshift bistro tucked away on Bloco C's backside, superb value awaits. The US-trained chef excels at gourmet treats like the signature pork ribs (velvety! chocolaty! tasty!). For Brazil, the check is a pleasant shock.

Bar Beirute BOTECO
(www.facebook.com/barbeirute; SCLS 109, Bloco A; ⊙11am-1am Sun-Wed, to 2am Thu-Sat) This Brasília institution has a massive outdoor patio packed with an edgier crowd than most. It's a GLS point – the clever Brazilian

acronym for gays, lesbians and sympathetics – but it's really a free-for-all, the most classic drinking experience in the city and no better spot for a mug of teeth-numbing cold Beira – Beirute's own brand of beer!

Information

Banks are spread around various sectors, but ATMs are most easily accessed in the shopping malls and transport stations, as well as along Via W3.

CAT (www.vemviverbrasilia.df.gov.br; Presidente Juscelino Kubitschek International Airport; 8am-6pm) Tres Poderes (Centro Atendimento ao Turista; 8693-2542; Praça dos Três Poderes ; 8am-6pm) The city's two most helpful tourist information booths.

Correios (www.correios.com.br; SHS, Quadra 2, Bloco B; 9am-5pm Mon-Fri) There are also branches in the arrivals hall of the airport and at the main malls.

Getting There & Away

Brasília's shiny new **Aeroporto Presidente Juscelino Kubitschek** (BSB; 3364-9037; www.aeroportobrasilia.net) is 12km south of the center. The easiest way to or from the airport is **Ônibus Executivo Aeroporto** (Bus 113; 3344-2769; www.tcb.df.gov.br; fare R$8; 6:30am-11pm). It does a loop from the airport to the Rodoviária Plano Piloto (local bus station), the entirety of the Esplanada dos Ministérios, and both SHS (15 minutes) and SHN (30 minutes), every 30 minutes between 6:30am and midnight (11pm on weekends). Cheaper still is local bus 0.102/102.1 (R$2, 40 minutes).

From the new long-distance bus station **Nova Rodoviária Interestadual** (3234-2185; SMAS, Trecho 4, Conjunto 5/6), 3km southwest off the edge of Asa Sul, buses go almost everywhere.

TAXI TALK

Always carry a taxi phone number with you in Brasília. They are as scarce as snow in the Superquadras. With **Unitaxi** (3325-3030) or **Rádio Táxi Alvorada** (3321-3030; www.radiotaxi33213030.com.br) (you can also download their apps), you are entitled to a 20% to 30% discount off the meter if you call (not always announced to foreigners). Remind both the dispatcher *and* the driver: *'Com o desconto, por favor.'*

Getting Around

Estação Shopping of the **Metrô DF** (www.metro.df.gov.br; weekends/weekdays R$2/3; 6am-11:30pm Mon-Fri, 7am-7pm Sat & Sun) connects the Rodoviária Interestadual with the local Rodoviária Plano Piloto bus station (Estacão Central) in the city center, as does local bus 108.8 (R$2, 20 minutes)

The Pantanal

This vast natural paradise, covering an estimated 210,000 sq km (81,081 sq miles) and stretching into Paraguay and Bolivia, is Brazil's major ecological attraction and offers a density of exotic wildlife found nowhere else in South America. During the rainy season (December to April), the Rio Paraguai and lesser rivers of the Pantanal inundate much of this low-lying region, creating *cordilheiras* (vegetation islands above the high water level). The waters here in the world's largest freshwater wetlands rise as much as 3m above low-water levels around March in the northern Pantanal and as late as June

BUSES FROM BRASÍLIA

DESTINATION	STARTING FARE (R$)	DURATION (HR)	BUS COMPANY
Belém	358	35	Transbrasiliana (www.transbrasiliana.com.br)
Campo Grande	255	19	Motta (www.motta.com.br)
Cuiabá	178	20	Expresso São Luiz (www.expressosaoluiz.com.br)
Goiânia	28	3	Araguarina (www.araguarina.com.br)
Porto Velho	332	42	Andorinha (www.andorinha.com)
Rio de Janeiro	195	17	Itapemirim (www.itapemirim.com.br)
Salvador	150	22	Real Expresso (www.realexpresso.com.br)
São Paulo	189	14	Real Expresso (www.realexpresso.com.br)

The Pantanal

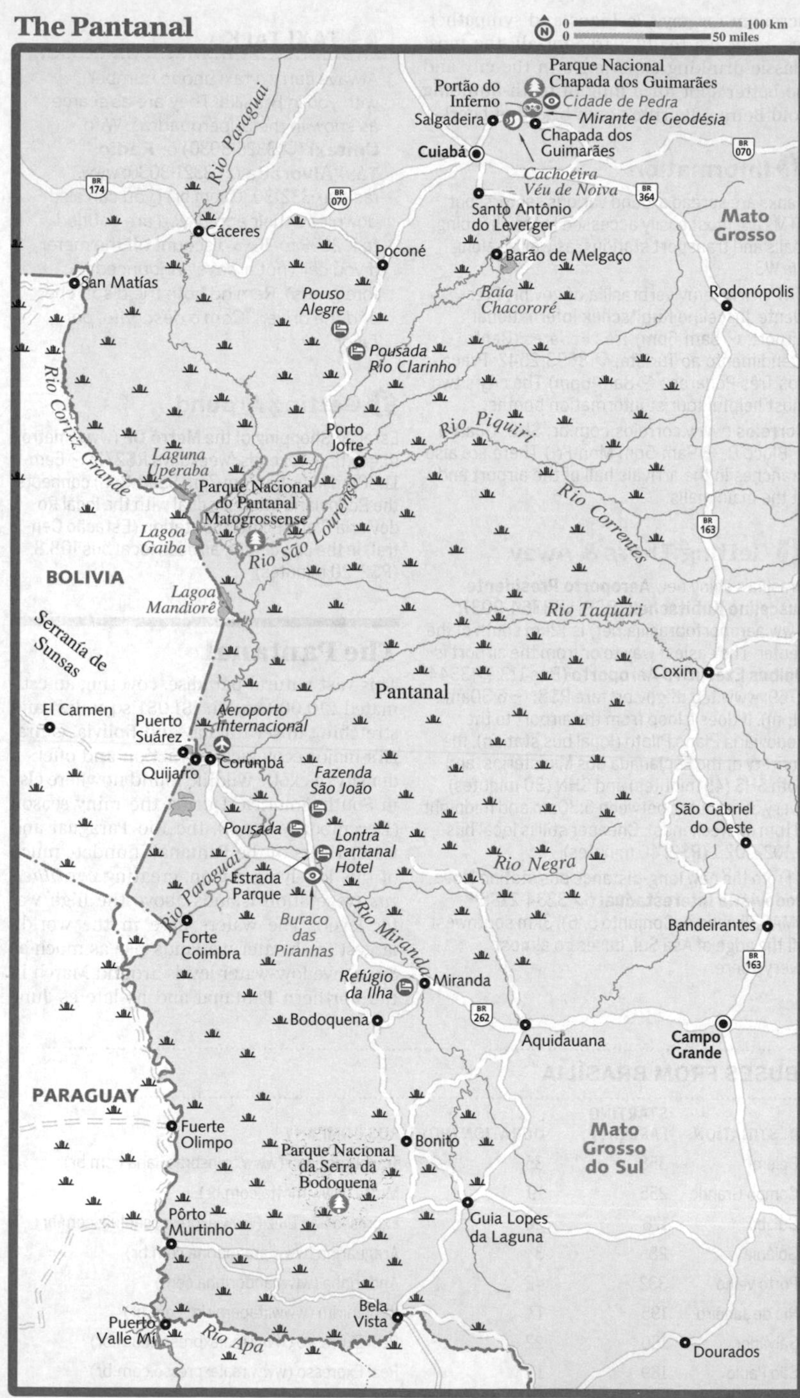

further south. This seasonal flooding, while severely limiting human occupation of the area, provides an enormously rich feeding ground for wildlife, including 650 bird species and 80 mammal species, including jaguars, ocelots, pumas, maned wolf, deer, anteaters, armadillos, howler and capuchin monkeys, and tapirs. The waters teem with fish; birds fly in flocks of thousands and gather in enormous rookeries. In dry season (July to November), when animals concentrate around limited water sources, the wildlife spotting is nothing short of spectacular. For nature and animal lovers, the Pantanal is Brazil's Eden.

Tours

Tours generally include transportation, accommodations, meals, hikes, horse-riding excursions and boat rides.

The principal access towns where you can arrange tours are Cuiabá in the north (for the Transpantaneira) and Campo Grande in the south (for the Estrada Parque), with Corumbá on the Bolivian border more of a sideshow these days. Tours from Cuiabá tend to be slightly more expensive, but also more professional with smaller groups and better-trained guides than those from either Campo Grande or Corumbá. They also go deeper into the Pantanal.

Northern Pantanal

★Pantanal Nature NATURE TOUR

(☎0xx65-9994-2265, 0xx65-3322-0203; www.pantanalnature.com.br; Professor Francisco Torres 48; per day high/low season R$700/450) Superb agency run by Ailton Lara that has quickly built up a sterling reputation for its professional tours and expert guides. It also runs the Panatal Jaguar Camp near Porto Jofre, with excellent success rates in seeing the animal in the dry season.

Ecoverde Tours NATURE TOUR

(☎0xx65-9638-1614, 0xx65-3624-1386; www.ecoverdetours.com.br; Pedro Celestino 391; per day R$500-700) Top-notch company with 25 years of service and experienced guides. Working with local *pousadas* toward an ecofriendly approach, Joel Souza can guide you in English, German, French, Portuguese or Spanish. You can find him at Hostel Pousada Ecoverde.

Southern Pantanal

Pantanal Viagens & Turismo NATURE TOUR

(☎0xx67-3321-3143; www.pantanalviagens.com.br; room 09, old bus terminal, Joaquim Nabuco 200) A nice agency working with Pousada Passo do Lontra and other Pantanal lodgings that

CHOOSING A TOUR OPERATOR

Pantanal tourism is big business and in the past some companies have been guilty of employing underhand tactics in the race to hook clients. Measures have finally been taken to clamp down on the worst offenders, but these few suggestions will help you have a safe and enjoyable trip:

- Resist making a snap decision, especially if you've just climbed off an overnight bus.
- Do not make your decision based on cost. Cheaper very rarely means better, but even expensive tours can be a letdown.
- Go on forums. Read online reviews. Speak to other travelers. What was their experience like? In Campo Grande some of the tour companies are quick to badmouth others. Get your advice straight from the horse's mouth.
- Compare your options, but remember that the owner or salesperson is not always your guide, and it's the guide you're going to be with in the wilderness for several days. Ask to meet your guide if possible. Ascertain your guide's linguistic abilities.
- Don't hand over your cash to a go-between. Don't buy bus tickets that somebody other than the person you give your money to is going to give you.
- If you are even remotely concerned about sustainable tourism, do not use operators and lodges that harm this fragile environment (that means no picking up the animals for selfies or touching them whatsoever!).
- Group budget tours focus squarely on the spectacular and easy-to-see species. Serious wildlife-watchers should be prepared to pay more for a private guide.

has worked hard to maintain its excellent reputation. Caters to mid- to high-range budgets, but offers professional and reliable packages.

Pantanal Discovery NATURE TOUR
(☎0xx67-9163-3518; www.gilspantanaldiscovery.com.br; Hotel Nacional, Dom Aquino 610; per 3 days dm/r R$900/1000) A perennial operator with a polished sales pitch; owner Gil is assertive and helpful and is the pick of budget operators in town.

Sleeping & Eating

Northern Pantanal

There are numerous accommodations on and off the Transpantaneira. Prices quoted include meals and daily excursions.

Pantanal Jaguar Camp LODGE $$$
(www.pantanaljaguarcamp.com.br; s/d R$300/670;) Intimate, solar-powered wilderness lodge with private bathrooms, comfortable beds and an onsite restaurant. This is a great Porto Jofre base for jaguar-seeking boat trips that is affiliated with Pantanal Nature (p345). Other activities include night safaris on the Transpantaneira and bird-watching.

Pousada Rio Clarinho POUSADA $$$
(☎0xx65-9977-8966; www.pousadarioclarinho.com.br; Transpantaneira Km 40; s/d/tr incl meals & excursions R$250/420/600;) An avian symphony is your wake-up call at this rustic *fazenda* right on the Rio Clarinho (there's a river platform for swimming). With an extensive area of forested trails, there are more than 260 species of birds on the property, as well as capybaras and giant otters. The food is authentic *pantaneiro* and the owners' warmth transcends the language barrier.

Southern Pantanal

Pantanal Jungle Lodge LODGE $$$
(☎0xx67-3325-8080; www.pantanaljunglelodge.com.br; 3-day, 2-night package per person in dm/d R$900/1100;) This brand-new lodge is set to become another backpacker favorite, thanks to its enviable riverside location and well-organised activities – from canoeing and piranha fishing to night safaris on the river and wildlife-spotting treks. Lodge either in one of the breezy dorms or in a private room with air-conditioning.

Pousada Santa Clara POUSADA $$
(☎0xx67-3384-0583; www.pantanalsantaclara.com.br; Office 12, Campo Grande bus station; 3-day package per person camping R$440, dm R$660, d R$770;) This is one of the most popular budget lodges in the southern Pantanal. A host of activities (hikes, piranha fishing, night safaris, horseback riding), accommodations to suit all budgets and hearty *pantaneiro* cooking have clinched its popularity with the backpacker market. Expect large groups.

Cuiabá

☎0XX65 / POP 530,300

Mato Grosso's state capital is a sprawling frontier boomtown near the edge of three distinct ecosystems: the northern Pantanal, the cerrado of nearby Chapada dos Guimarães and the southern Amazon.

Sleeping

★Hostel Pousada Ecoverde POUSADA $
(☎3624-1386; www.ecoverdetours.com.br; Celestino 391; s/d without bathroom R$50/80;) A rustic *pousada* in a 100-year-old colonial house with a tranquil, hammock-hung mini-jungle out back, filled with cats, chickens and guinea fowl. Friendly owner and local wildlife expert Joel Souza of Ecoverde Tours is one of the founders of ecotourism in the area and his *pousada* consists of five fan-cooled rooms that share four external bathrooms.

Pantanal Backpacker HOSTEL $
(☎9939-6152; www.pantanalbackpacker.com; Av Mal Deodoro 2301; dm/tw R$40-60/150;) Positively luxurious budget crash pad, a 10-minute walk from the main nightlife area, complete with waterfall and pool. A lot of thought has gone into what backpackers need – a kitchen, bathrooms and lockers in every room, comfy bunks, attentive staff – and it's all present and correct. Organised tours to Nobres and beyond get good feedback.

Hotel Mato Grosso HOTEL $$
(☎3614-7777; www.hotelmt.com.br; Costa 643; s/d/tr R$148/194/228;) For basic comfort in a central location, the simple but clean rooms here are good value.

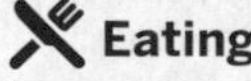

Eating

Mistura Cuiabana SELF-SERVE $
(☎3624-1127; cnr Pedro Celestino & Cândido Mariano; per kg R$28; ⏱11am-2:30pm Mon-Fri) An

excellent buffet of regional selections for lunch (the fried bananas are divine). It's inside the blue-and-white colonial building on the corner.

Choppão BOTECO $$
(www.choppao.com.br; Praça 8 de Abril; mains for 2 R$58-90; daily 11.30am-midnight;) Occupying an entire junction and hugely popular with locals, this Cuiabá institution offers huge portions of meat and fish for two, all chased with frigid *chope* (draft beer) in specially iced tankards.

Getúlio INTERNATIONAL $$
(3624-9992; www.getuliogrill.com.br; Av Getúlio Vargas 1147; mains R$39-65; 11am-2:30pm & 5pm-2am Tue-Sun) At this sports-bar-meets-refined-restaurant, popular with the young and the trendy, you can sample from the respectable wine list, eat your fill at the lunchtime buffet or take your date for a romantic Italian/Brazilian/Japanese dinner. The desserts are worth lingering over and DJs feature on the outdoor patio every night.

Entertainment

There are two main nightlife clusters in town: the buzzy sports bars with ample outdoor seating around the lovely Praça Popular (aka Praça Eurico Gaspar Dutra) and more establishments along Av Getúlio Vargas. For something a bit more 'local', head for the tiny Praça da Mandioca, where you'll find locals getting drunk on Skols at three virtually identical bars, with live bands on weekends.

Information

Sedtur (3613-9300; www.sedtur.mt.gov.br; Voluntários da Pátria 118; 9am-6pm Mon-Fri) Has some helpful maps and brochures in Portuguese.

Getting There & Away

Multiple airlines connect Cuiabá's Marechal Rondon International Airport (CGB) with cities throughout Brazil. The bus station is 3km north of the center.

Car-rental agencies outside the airport tend to be cheaper than those inside. The best vehicles for the Transpantaneira are a VW Gol or Fiat Uno; beware treacherous road conditions in wet weather, especially south of the Rio Pixaím bridge at Km 65.

Getting Around

From the airport, bus 24 (R$3.10) runs from outside the Las Velas Hotel – turn left as you leave the airport and walk 100m to Av Getúlio Vargas. A taxi costs around R$35. Buses back to the airport depart from Praça Ipiranga and the corner of Avs Coronel Duarte and Getulio Vargas.

From inside the bus terminal, you can get a Centro bus to Praça Alencastro (R$3.10). More frequent buses marked 'Centro' leave from outside the bus station and drop you along Av Isaac Póvoas; get off in front of the CAT office. A taxi from inside the bus station costs around R$30. Bus 7 runs between the airport and the bus station.

BUSES FROM CUIABÁ

DESTINATION	COST (R$)	TIME (HR)	FREQUENCY	BUS COMPANY
Alta Floresta	197	14	6 daily	Verde Transportes (www.viagemverde.com.br)
Brasília	178-196	23	7 daily	Viação São Luiz (www.viacaosaoluiz.com.br), Eucatur (www.eucatur.com.br)
Bom Jardim	41	5	daily at 2pm	TUT Transportes
Cáceres	42-53	3¾	6 daily	Verde Transportes (www.viagemverde.com.br), Eucatur (www.eucatur.com.br)
Campo Grande	93-116	12	17 daily	Motta (www.motta.com.br), Eucatur (www.eucatur.com.br)
Chapada dos Guimarães	28	1¼	9 daily	Expresso Rubi
Goiânia	115-149	18	8 daily	Viação São Luiz (www.viacaosaoluiz.com.br), Eucatur (www.eucatur.com.br)
Poconé	12	2½	6 daily	TUT Transportes
Porto Velho	156-185	23-26	10 daily	Eucatur (www.eucatur.com.br), Gontijo (www.gontijo.com.br)

Around Cuiabá

Parque Nacional Da Chapada Dos Guimarães

This high plateau 60km northeast of Cuiabá is a beautiful region reminiscent of the American Southwest. Its three exceptional sights are the 60m falls **Cachoeira Véu de Noiva** (Bridal Veil; ⏲9am-4pm; last entry at noon) FREE, the **Mirante de Geodésia** lookout (South America's geographical center) and the colorful rocky outcrops known as **Cidade de Pedra** (Stone City; from R$180 per person; ⏲9am-4pm), providing Guimarães' most transcendent moment. Véu de Noiva is the only part of the park you can visit independently. Otherwise, a certified guide is required. Access is split among three day-trip circuits: **Circuito das Cachoeiras** (Waterfall Circuit; from per person R$160), which takes in six waterfalls; **Circuito Vale de Rio Claro** (Rio Claro Valley Circuit; from per person R$180) and its lush valley views and forest-pool snorkeling; and the **Roteiro da Caverna Aroe Jari e Lagoa Azul** (Aroe Jari Cave Circuit; from per person R$230), which includes Brazil's largest sandstone cave. All trips begin by 9am and return by 6pm and should be reserved in advance, especially in July, August and September. **Chapada Explorer** (☎3301-1290; www.chapadaexplorer.com.br; Praça Dom Wunibaldo 57; ⏲8-11am Mon-Sat) is a great agency to get you into the park.

Expresso Rubi (☎3621-2188) buses leave Cuiabá's bus station for Chapada town (R$18, 1¼ hours, nine daily, 6:30am to 7pm). The miraculous views are out the right-side window from Cuiabá. In the other direction, the first bus leaves Chapada town at 5:30am and the last at 7pm. Chapada's bus station is two blocks from the main plaza (Praça Dom Wunibaldo).

Poconé

The dusty frontier town of Poconé, 100km southwest of Cuiabá, is the sleepy gateway to the Transpantaneira, so sleepy that, as one local put it, 'In Poconé, even the restaurants close for lunch!' Poconé is unlikely to detain you for longer than a meal stop, though those driving themselves along the Transpantaneira might consider overnighting here to get an early start and catch the wildlife in action on the way.

Pousada Pantaneira (☎3345-3357; www.pousadapantaneira.com.br; Rodovia Transpantaneira Km 0; rodizio R$35;) is a justifiably popular *churrascaria* that sits at the top of the Transpantaneira.

Banco do Brasil (Campos Sales) has a Visa/MasterCard ATM but don't bet your life on it working.

TUT Transportes (☎065-3317-2200) has buses from Cuiabá to Poconé (R$12, 2½ hours, six daily) from 6am to 7pm, and six in the opposite direction from 6am to 7:30pm. In Poconé they stop at the bus station about 10 blocks from the center of town, then continue on to Praça da Matriz.

From here, the 'highway' becomes little more than a pockmarked dirt track as it heads 145km south into the Pantanal, terminating at Porto Jofre.

Campo Grande

☎0XX67 / POP 766,500

Mato Grosso do Sul's lively capital is the most sophisticated city in the region and a major jumping-off point for the Pantanal.

Sleeping

Inexpensive hotels surround the old bus station, at the western end of Alfonso Pena. Nightlife is concentrated further east along the same avenue.

Hauzz Hostel HOSTEL $
(☎8118-7270; www.hauzzhostel.com; Piratininga 1527; s/d R$70/140;) A quiet, secure hostel with snug, fan-cooled rooms that share several bathrooms, run by delightful hostess Christina who does her best to help in spite of the language barrier. A three-block walk to Shopping Campo Grande and handy for visiting Parque das Nações.

Oka Hostel HOSTEL $
(☎3026-7070; www.okabrasilhostel.com.br; Jeriba 454; dm/d R$65/150;) Several blocks south of Shopping Campo Grande, this lively backpacker hangout in a converted mansion scores points for its helpful English-speaking staff and common areas that encourage camaraderie between guests. The downside includes cramped dorms, air-con that struggles during the hottest time of year, the ratio of guests per bathroom and a location somewhat removed from the action.

Hotel Nacional HOTEL $
(☎3383-2461; Dom Aquino 610; s/d with air-con R$70/140, without air-con R$65/80;) A

basic budget choice hugely popular with international backpackers and Brazilian student groups. Choose between simple digs with shared facilties and plusher ones with air-con, bathrooms and TV.

Turis Hotel HOTEL **$$**
(☎3382-2461; www.turishotel.com.br; Allan Kardec 200; s/d/tr R$151/226/275; ❄📶) Modern and minimalist, this excellent option is entirely too trendy for its location and is very good value. Great breakfast, and the staff go out of their way to be helpful in spite of limited English.

Eating

Restaurante da Gaucha SELF-SERVE **$**
(Allan Kardec 238; buffet R$13; ⏰11.30am-11pm) Handy cheapie right near several central hotels, and a backpacker favorite due to its rock-bottom prices and all-you-can-gobble, delicious buffet dishes.

Cantina Romana ITALIAN **$$**
(☎3324-9777; www.cantinaromana.com.br; Rua da Paz 237; mains for two R$38-60; ⏰11am-2pm & 6-11pm) Shock-value old school Italian cantina and pizzeria, going strong since 1978. Attentive service, mega portions and authentic surroundings to indulge yourself in. We're big fans of their *gnocchi alla siciliana*. If you graze at their weekday lunchtime buffet, you won't need dinner.

Varandas do Pantanal PANTANEIRO **$$**
(Av Bom Pastor 306; mains R$13-45; ⏰6pm midnight Tue-Sat) At this very local spot, homesick Corumbá transplants gather for true *pantaneiro* cuisine. Standout dishes include *sarrabulho* (a hearty stew made with hearts, kidneys and liver) and *arroz pantaneiro* (rice cooked with sun-dried beef and sausage typical of the region), accompanied by fried banana. Wash it down with strong *caipirinhas* to the accompaniment of live music (Thursday to Saturday; cover R$6).

Information

There are small tourist kiosks at the **bus station** (☎3314-4448; Rodoviária; ⏰6am-10pm), **airport** (☎3363-3116; ⏰6:15am-midnight) and the **Feira Central** (☎3314-3872; Feira Central; ⏰6-10pm Wed-Sun).

Banco do Brasil (Av Afonso Pena 2202; ⏰11am-4pm Mon-Fri) Visa/MasterCard ATM and money exchange.

Bradesco (Av Afonso Pena 1828; ⏰11am-4pm Mon-Fri) Visa/MasterCard ATM.

CAT Morada dos Bais (☎3314-9968; Av Afonso Pena; ⏰8am-6pm Tue-Sat, 9am-noon Sun) This helpful tourist office offers an excellent city map and an extensive database with information about the state, and staff organise city tours. They won't recommend Pantanal tour companies though!

Getting There & Away

Aeroporto Internacional de Campo Grande (☎3368-6050; Av Duque de Caixas) is 7km from town; to get there, take the Expreso Mato Grosso (R$9, hourly) from the bus station. A taxi costs around R$30.

Campo Grande's bus station is 5km south of Centro on Costa e Silva.

The fastest way to Bonito is **Vanzella** (☎3255-3005; www.vanzellatransportes.com.br), a door-to-door van service, departing at 9:30am, 2:30pm, 6pm and 11pm daily (R$100, four to five hours). Return services are at 7:30am, 10am, 12:30pm and 6:30pm.

BUSES FROM CAMPO GRANDE

DESTINATION	COST (R$)	DURATION (HR)	COMPANY
Bonito	55	6½	Cruzeiro do Sul (www.cruzeirodosulms.com.br)
Brasília	238-261	23½-24½	Motta (www.motta.com.br), Viação São Luiz (www.viacaosaoluiz.com.br)
Corumbá	105-125	6	Andorinha (www.andorinha.com)
Cuiabá	92-123	10-13	Andorinha (www.andorinha.com), Eucatur (www.eucatur.com.br)
Iguaçu Falls	150	18	Nova Integração (www.novaintegracao.com.br)
Ponta Porã	80	6	Expresso Queiroz (www.expressoqueiroz.com.br), Cruzeiro do Sul (www.cruzeirodosulms.com.br)
Rio de Janeiro	303-317	24	Andorinha (www.andorinha.com)
São Paulo	207-223	15½	Andorinha (www.andorinha.com), Motta (www.motta.com.br)

Getting Around

Local buses 61 and 87 (R$3) connect the long-distance bus station to the city center. There's also the hourly Expreso Mato Grosso (R$9) door-to-door service. To use city buses you need to buy an an **Assetur** (☎0800-647-0060; www.assetur.com.br; Visconde de Taunay 345) *passe de ônibus* (bus pass) from newsstands, pharmacies or bus-stop kiosks. They come as one-time use *(unitario)* or rechargable *(recarregável)*. A taxi to the center will cost around R$30.

Bonito

☎0XX67 / POP 19,500

Amid spectacular natural wonders, Bonito is both the model and epicenter of Brazil's ecotourism boom, luring visitors with unique crystal-clear rivers and opportunities for rappelling, rafting, horse riding and bird-watching. It's no backpacker haven, but everything is top quality and truly unforgettable.

Sights & Activities

Most local attractions require a guide arranged through one of the authorized travel agencies along Bonito's main street. Prices are controlled, so shop around no further than the nearest agency. Trip prices generally include wetsuits, snorkel gear and sometimes an optional lunch, but never transport. Rappelling at the Abismo de Anhumas involves completing a course the day before at their **Rappelling Training Center** (General Osório; ⏰9am-6pm). No sunscreen or repellent is allowed in water activities.

★Abismo de Anhumas ADVENTURE TOUR
(www.abismoanhumas.com.br; rappelling R$633, scuba diving R$891) You rappel into a gigantic, beautiful cave that culminates in an underground lake. Nothing stands between you and the 72m drop apart from your safety harness and the rope you're clipped to. After you make it down, it's time for a spin around the lake to admire the beautiful rock formations. Then you dive or snorkel in the frigid underwater world (visibility is 30m), with phallic pinnacles rising from the depths, before climbing the rope back out. A heart-stopping experience.

The whole thing is otherworldly – Bonito's most unforgettable attraction by a landslide, limited to 18 visitors per day.

★Rio da Prata SNORKELING
(www.riodaprata.com.br; 5hr trip incl lunch R$218; ⏰6:30am-2pm) The marvelous Rio da Prata, 56km south of Bonito, includes a trek through rainforest and some great snorkeling. The latter involves a 3km float downstream along the Rio Olha d'Agua, amazingly crystal clear and full of fish; and Rio da Prata, a little foggier but still fantastic for viewing massive pacú and big, scary dourado.

Buraco das Araras BIRD-WATCHING
(www.buracodasararas.com.br; admission R$55) A sunset visit to Buraco das Araras, the world's largest sinkhole, is usually tagged on to a day out at Rio da Prata and Laguna Misteriosa. It's a 1km walk, complete with two viewpoints, that allows you to watch dozens of scarlet macaws flying home to roost, their metallic cries piercing the air. An impressive spectacle.

Balneário Municipal SWIMMING
(admission R$25; ⏰8am-6pm) One of the few natural attractions that doesn't need a guide is the Balneário Municipal, a natural swimming pool on the Rio Formoso with clear water, nice beach and lots of fish, 7km southeast of town. You can spend the whole day here and have lunch at the kiosks. Get there

BONITO TRANSPORT

Many of Bonito's attractions are a fair hike from town, and there's no public transport. Some guesthouses lend their guests bicycles, or you can rent a decent mountain bike along the main street for around R$30 per day. Hotels often provide transport, but not always. If you find yourself looking for transport, try the local shuttle service, Vanzella (p352), which will take you to any excursion provided there is a minimum of four people.

If you are part of a group, it might end up being more economical to hire a taxi for the full day (R$80 to R$180 depending on the distance) from any Ponto de Táxi. If you are on your own take your friendly neighborhood moto-taxi: to the Rio Sucuri (38km round-trip, R$56), Gruta do Lago Azul (38km round-trip, R$56), Abismo Anhumas (41km round-trip, R$60), Rio da Prata (100km round-trip, R$120) and Boca da Onça (120km round-trip, R$140). The drivers can either wait around or come back for you.

BUSES FROM BONITO

DESTINATION	COST (R$)	TIME (HR)	FREQUENCY
Campo Grande (bus)	55	6	noon & 6pm
Campo Grande (minibus)	100	5	7:30am, 10am, 12:30pm & 6:30pm
Corumbá (bus)	81	6	12:30pm
Corumbá (minibus)	120	5	2-3 weekly
Estrada Parque (minibus)	100	3½	1 daily
Iguaçu Falls (minibus)	200	12	2 weekly
Ponta Porã (bus)	64	7½	noon

by cycling or else moto-taxi (around R$10 one way).

Sleeping & Eating

Papaya Hostel HOSTEL $
(3255-4690; www.papayahostelbonito.com; Vicente Jacques 1868; dm/d R$50/150;) This papaya-colored hostel, handily located near the bus station, is the kind of place where backpackers find themselves delaying their departure, seduced by the poolside chillout area, communal barbecues, fellow travelers to chat with while cooking and a plethora of tours organised by the helpful, English-speaking owner.

Bonito HI Hostel HOSTEL $
(8180-7231; www.bonitohostel.com.br; Lúcio Borralho 716; dm R$48, d with/without air-con R$135/115;) One of Brazil's top HI hostels, this well-oiled backpacker haunt is a bit far from the action, but perks include hammocks, pool, large lockers, kitchen, laundry, bikes for hire and multilingual staff. Dorms come with private bathrooms, and the private rooms with a/c (a must in summer!) are hotel standard. The owner is unlikely to win any congeniality prizes.

Pousada Muito Bonito POUSADA $$
(3255-1645; www.hotelmuitobonito.com.br; Coronel Pilad Rebuá 1444; s/d/tr R$180/250/230;) You will struggle to find better value than at this excellent budget pousada in the center. Administered by the second generation of the pioneering Doblack family, it offers revamped, well-appointed budget rooms around a small courtyard. These guys also run one of the most popular tour agencies in town and are happy to provide plenty of information on the area.

Vicio da Gula Café BURGERS $
(3255-2041; Coronel Pilad Rebuá 1852; burgers R$13-24; noon-2am) Popular corner spot for great burgers, fries and *açaí na tigela* (a berrylike fruit, in a bowl). The cake display may delay your exit.

O Casarão SELF-SERVE $$
(3255-1970; Coronel Pilad Rebuá 1835; buffet R$35; 11.30am-2.30pm & 6.30-10.30pm Mon-Sat, 11.30am-3pm Sun) Bouncing buffet joint on the main drag. Hugely popular with locals on Sundays, when most other places are closed.

★ **A Casa do João** SEAFOOD $$$
(3255-1212; www.casadojoao.com.br; Nelson Felicio 664a; mains R$28-54; 11:30am-2:30pm & 6-11:30pm) Top spot in town for fish dishes, especially famous for its *traíra* (a predatory fish) which comes in a range of sizes and styles: soup, grilled and served with passionfruit sauce. All the furniture here is made from reclaimed wood from fallen trees in the area.

Drinking

Taboa Bar BAR
(3255-1862; www.taboa.com.br; Coronel Pilad Rebuá 1837; 5pm-late) A graffiti-clad institution on the main drag where locals and travelers converge over the house special: *pinga (cachaça)* with honey, cinnamon and guaraná. The food ain't bad, either.

Information

Bonito is tiny. Everything you need is along its freshly renovated main drag, Pilad Rebuá.

Bradesco (Colonel Pilad Rebuá 1942) Handy for cash withdrawals.

Getting There & Away

There are two weekly flights with **Azul** (www.voeazul.com.br) between Bonito and São Paulo (Campinas) airport on Sunday and Wednesday (1½ hours); more during high season.

Corumbá

'Corumbaly' (old Corumbá) is a gracefully aging port city close to the Bolivian border. Known as Cidade Branca (White City), it is 403km northwest of Campo Grande by road. The city sits atop a steep hill overlooking the Rio Paraguai; on the far side of the river, a huge expanse of the Pantanal stretches out to the horizon.

During a long weekend in mid-February, one of Brazil's biggest and best Carnavals really makes this hot, sleepy backwater come to life. Otherwise the town attracts a contingent of wealthy Brazilian fishermen who head out into the Pantanal on hotel-boats, as well as Bolivia-bound travelers.

If you end up sleeping here, try the central **Hotel Laura Vicuña** (☎3231-5874; www.hotellauravicuna.com.br; Av Cuiabá 775; s/d/tr R$90/130/168; ❄📶) or **Hostel Pantanal** (☎9641-5524; Joaquin Murtino 359; dm/d R$40/130; 📶) near the bus station. The best eats are found on the 400 and 500 blocks of Frei Mariano.

From the **long-distance bus station** (☎3231-2033; Porto Carreiro), regular buses run to Campo Grande (from R$81, six hours) but it pays to buy your ticket in advance. **Vanzella** (☎3255-3005; www.vanzellatransportes.com.br) can get you to Bonito. **Corumbá International Airport** (☎3231-3322; Santos Dumont) is currently only served by Azul to São Paulo (Campinas) three days a week.

THE NORTHEAST

Year-round warm climate, physical beauty and sensual culture rich in folkloric traditions all make Brazil's Northeast a true tropical paradise. More than 2000km of fertile coastline is studded with idyllic white-sand beaches, pockets of lush rainforest, sand dunes and coral reefs. A spectrum of natural environments creates the perfect backdrop for a wide variety of outdoor activities.

These parts of the country also breathe colonial history. The picturesque urban centers of Salvador, Olinda and São Luís are packed with beautifully restored and satisfyingly decaying architecture. Add to this the lively festivals, myriad music and dance styles, and exotic cuisine loaded with seafood, and you will find Brazil's most culturally diverse region.

Salvador

☎0XX71 / POP 2.7 MILLION

Salvador da Bahia is among Brazil's brightest gems. It's the African soul of the country, where the descendants of slaves preserved their African culture more than anywhere else in the New World, creating thriving culinary, religious, musical, dance and martial-arts traditions. Underlying much of Salvador's culture is the Afro-Brazilian religion Candomblé, in which Catholic and animistic traditions blend to form rituals that involve direct communication with the spirit world.

Salvador sits on a peninsula on the Baía de Todos os Santos. The center is bayside

GETTING TO BOLIVIA

The Fronteira bus (R$3, 15 minutes) goes from Corumbá's Praça Independência to the Bolivian border every 25 minutes from 6am to 7pm. A taxi from the center to the border is around R$40. Groups of two or less traveling light are better off using a moto-taxi (R$24).

All Brazilian exit formalities must be completed with the **Polícia Federal** (☎3234-7822; www.dpf.gov.br; ⏰8-11am & 2-5pm Mon-Fri, 9am-1pm Sat & Sun) at the border. Both countries work limited matching office hours, so be prepared to overnight in Corumbá if you are crossing outside these hours. To enter Bolivia, most countries do not need a visa, but US citizens must obtain a visa (US$135) from abroad or at the Bolivian Consulate (p413) in Corumbá.

In Bolivia *colectivos* (B$5) and taxis (around B$30) run the 3km between the border and Quijarro train station for onward travel to Santa Cruz. There are two options: the faster and more comfortable *Ferrobus* which departs at 6pm on Tuesday, Thursday and Saturday (13 hours, B$235), arriving at 7am, and the cheaper *Expreso Oriental* that leaves at 1pm on Tuesday, Thursday and Sunday (16¾ hours; B$70), arriving at 5:40am. Buy tickets in advance if you can.

and divided by a steep bluff into two parts: the Cidade Baixa (Lower City), containing the commercial center and port, and Cidade Alta (Upper City), containing the Pelourinho (Pelô). The Pelô is the center of Salvador's history, tourism and nightlife. Cidade Baixa and the stretch between Praça da Sé and Praça Campo Grande are noisy by day and deserted by night. South, at the tip of the peninsula, is affluent beachside Barra. Residential neighborhoods stretch northeast along the Atlantic coast, with Rio Vermelho and Itapuã the most interesting.

Northeast Brazil

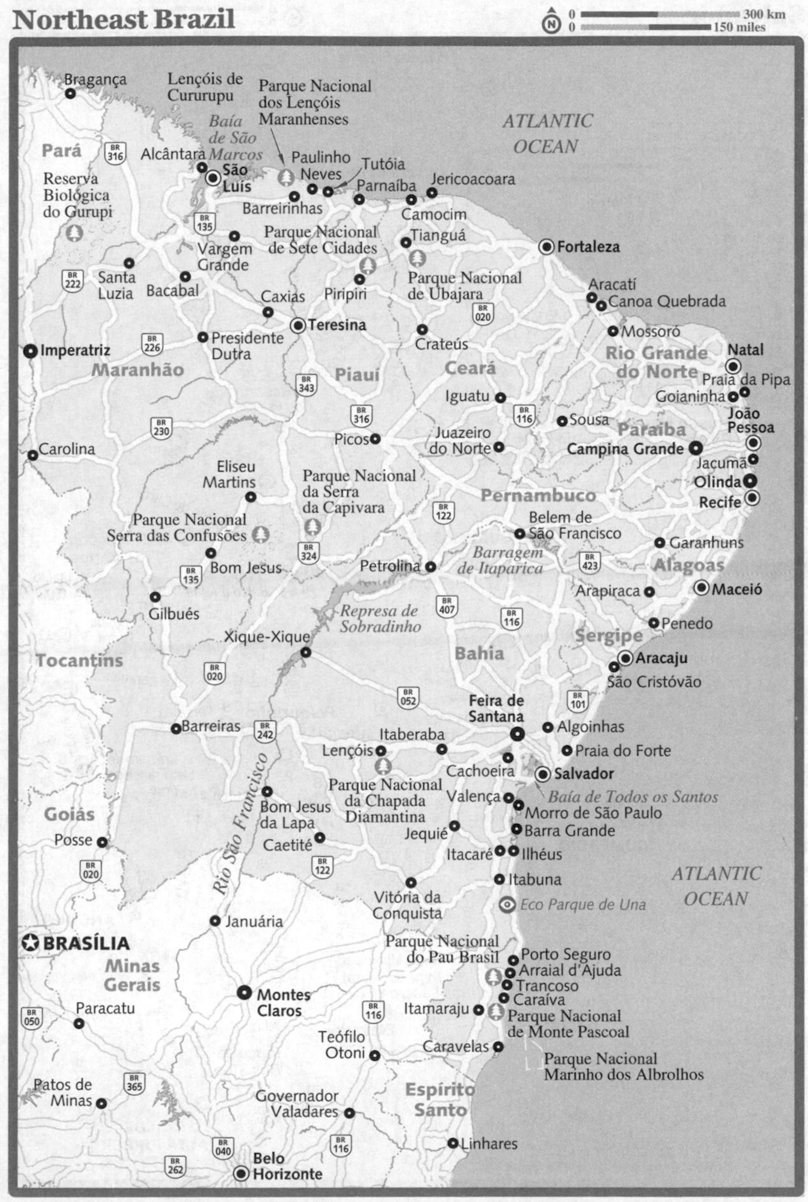

Sights

Cidade Alta

The Pelourinho neighborhood is filled with atmospheric and historic public spaces: the triangular **Largo do Pelourinho** (Pelourinho), named for the whipping post that once stood here during slavery days; the **Praça da Sé**, Salvador's former cathedral square; and **Terreiro de Jesus** (Praça 15 de Novembro), traditionally a site for religious celebrations, now alive with street vendors, musicians and capoeiristas. Other Upper

Salvador

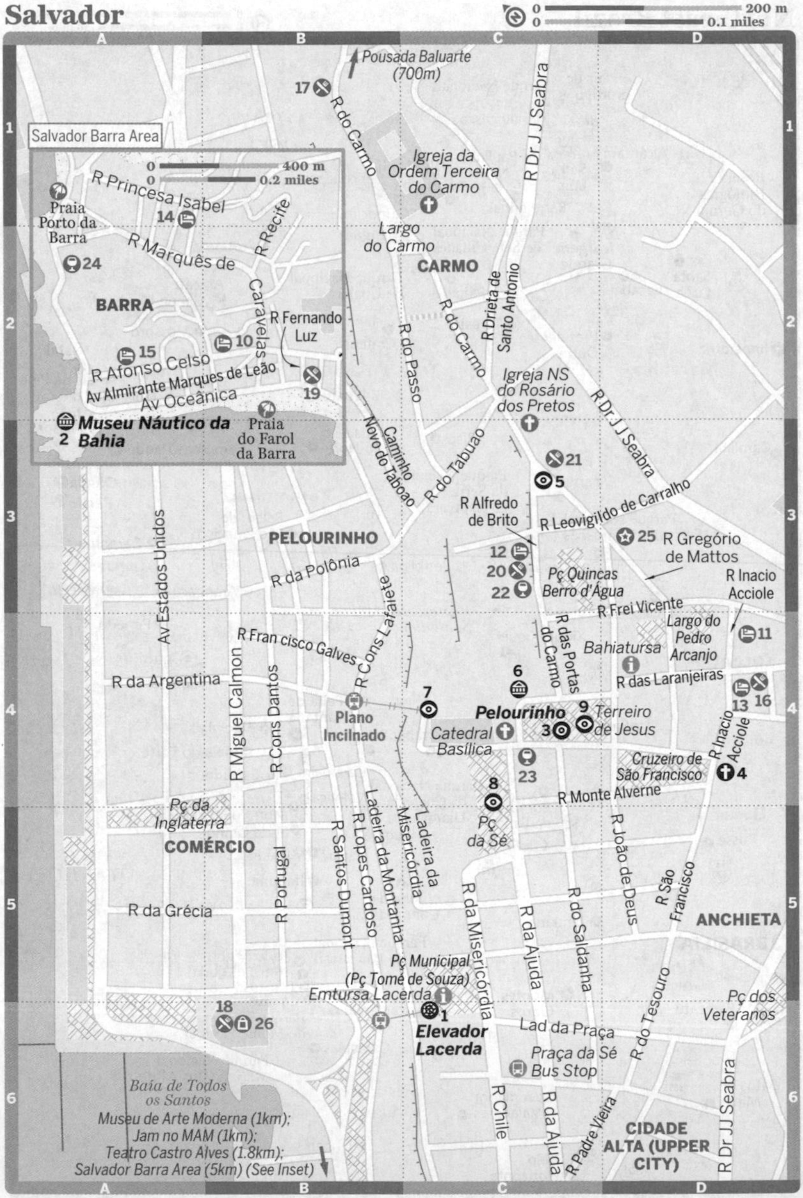

0 200 m
0 0.1 miles
Pousada Baluarte (700m)
17
R do Carmo
R Dr J J Seabra
Igreja da Ordem Terceira do Carmo
Largo do Carmo
CARMO
R do Passo
R do Carmo
R Drieta de Santo Antonio
Igreja NS do Rosário dos Pretos
R Dr J J Seabra
Carminho Novo do Taboao
R do Tabuao
21
5
R Alfredo de Brito
R Leovigildo de Carralho
25
R Gregório de Mattos
PELOURINHO
12
20
22
Pç Quincas Berro d'Água
R Inacio Acciole
R da Polônia
R Frei Vicente
Largo do Pedro Arcanjo
11
Av Estados Unidos
R Fran cisco Galves
R Cons Lafaiete
R das Portas do Carmo
Bahiatursa
R da Argentina
6
R das Laranjeiras
13
16
R Miguel Calmon
R Cons Dantos
Plano Incilnado
7
Pelourinho
9
Terreiro de Jesus
3
Catedral Basílica
R Inacio Acciole
Cruzeiro de São Francisco
4
23
8
R Monte Alverne
Pç da Inglaterra
COMÉRCIO
Pç da Sé
R Portugal
R Santos Dumont
R Lopes Cardoso
Ladeira da Montanha
Ladeira da Misericórdia
R da Misericórdia
R da Ajuda
R do Saldanha
R João de Deus
R São Francisco
ANCHIETA
R da Grécia
Pç Municipal (Pç Tomé de Souza)
Emtursa Lacerda
1
Elevador Lacerda
R do Tesouro
Pç dos Veteranos
18
26
Lad da Praça
Praça da Sé Bus Stop
Baía de Todos os Santos
Museu de Arte Moderna (1km); Jam no MAM (1km); Teatro Castro Alves (1.8km); Salvador Barra Area (5km) (See Inset)
R Chile
R da Ajuda
R Padre Vieira
CIDADE ALTA (UPPER CITY)
R Dr JJ Seabra

Salvador Barra Area
0 400 m
0 0.2 miles
R Princesa Isabel
Praia Porto da Barra
14
R Recife
R Marquês de Caravelas
24
BARRA
R Fernando Luz
15
10
R Afonso Celso
Av Almirante Marques de Leão
19
Av Oceânica
Museu Náutico da Bahia 2
Praia do Farol da Barra

City neighborhoods include Carmo and Santo Antônio.

★Pelourinho NEIGHBORHOOD

The centerpiece of the Cidade Alta is the Pelourinho, a Unesco-declared World Heritage Site of colorful colonial buildings and magnificent churches. As you wander the cobblestone streets, gazing up at the city's oldest architecture, you'll realize that the Pelô is not just for tourists. Cultural centers and schools of music, dance and capoeira pack these pastel-colored 17th- and 18th-century buildings.

★Elevador Lacerda HISTORIC BUILDING

(☎3322-7049; fare R$0.25; ⌚7am-11pm) The beautifully restored, art deco Elevador Lacerda connects the Cidade Alta with Comércio via four elevators traveling 72m in 30 seconds. The Jesuits installed the first manual rope-and-pulley elevator around 1610 to transport goods and passengers from the port to the settlement. In 1868 an iron structure with clanking steam elevators was inaugurated, replaced by an electric system in 1928.

Igreja e Convento São Francisco CHURCH

(Cruzeiro de São Francisco; admission R$3) One of Brazil's most magnificent churches, the baroque Igreja e Convento São Francisco is filled with displays of wealth and splendor. An 80kg silver chandelier dangles over ornate wood carvings smothered in gold leaf, and the convent courtyard is paneled with hand-painted *azulejos* (Portuguese tiles). The complex was finished in 1723.

Museu Afro-Brasileiro MUSEUM

(☎3283-5540; www.mafro.ceao.ufba.br; Terreiro de Jesus; adult/child R$6/3; ⌚9am-5:30pm Mon-Fri, 10am-5pm Sat) Holding one of Bahia's most important collections, the Museu Afro-Brasileiro exhibits wood carvings, baskets, pottery and other artwork and crafts linking Brazilian and African artistic traditions. The highlight of the museum is a room lined with 27 huge, breathtaking carved wooden panels by Argentine-born Carybé, who is perhaps Salvador's most renowned 20th-century fine artist.

Cidade Baixa, Barra & the Coast

On the Barra waterfront, view the sunset at Bahia's oldest fort, **Santo Antônio** (1598). Nearby **Praia do Porto** is a small, usually packed beach with calm waters. For less crowded beaches and cleaner water, head north to **Piatã** (25km), **Itapuã** (27km) or **Praia do Forte** (80km).

★Museu Náutico da Bahia MUSEUM

(Nautical Museum of Bahia; ☎3264-3296; www.museunauticodabahia.org.br; Largo do Farol da Barra s/n, Forte de Santo Antônio da Barra; adult/student R$15/7.50; ⌚9am-6pm Tue-Sun, daily Jan & Jul) In addition to having superb views, the Forte de Santo Antônio da Barra contains the excellent nautical museum, with relics

Salvador

Top Sights
1 Elevador Lacerda C6
2 Museu Náutico da Bahia A3
3 Pelourinho C4

Sights
4 Igreja e Convento São Francisco D4
5 Largo do Pelourinho C3
6 Museu Afro-Brasileiro C4
7 Plano Inclinado Gonçalves C4
8 Praça da Sé C4
9 Terreiro de Jesus C4

Sleeping
10 Âmbar Pousada B2
11 Hostel Galeria 13 D4
12 Hostel Solar dos Romanos C3
13 Laranjeiras Hostel D4
14 Open House Barra A1
15 Pousada Estrela do Mar A2

Eating
16 Bar Zulu D4
17 Cafélier B1
18 Camafeu de Oxossi B6
19 Caranguejo de Sergipe B2
20 Pelô Bistrô C3
21 Restaurante do Senac C3

Drinking & Nightlife
22 Casa do Amarelindo Bar C3
23 O Cravinho C4
24 Pereira A2

Entertainment
25 Balé Folclórico da Bahia D3

Shopping
26 Mercado Modelo B6

CARNAVAL SAFETY TIPS

During Carnaval, which takes place in the week leading up to Ash Wednesday, the greatest threat posed is from crowds clearing to escape a fight, so be aware of your surroundings. Police are a noticeable presence. Hands will be all over you, searching your pockets and groping your person. Costumes aren't common – shorts and tennis shoes are usual. A few tips:

- Form small groups and avoid deserted areas.
- Women shouldn't walk alone or wear skirts.
- Carry little money, stashed in your shoe.
- Leave *all* jewelry, watches and nice-looking sunglasses behind.
- Don't challenge pickpockets – the ensuing fight isn't worthwhile.
- Carry a photocopy of your passport.

and displays from the days of Portuguese seafaring, plus fascinating exhibits on the slave trade. All information is offered in both Portuguese and English – a rarity in Bahia. If you only have time for one museum in Salvador, this is the one.

Itapagipe Peninsula

★Igreja NS do Bonfim CHURCH
(3316-2196; Praça Senhor do Bonfim; 6:30am-noon & 2-6pm Tue-Thu & Sat, 5:30am-noon & 2:30-6pm Fri & Sun) This famous 18th-century church, located a few kilometers north of Comércio on the Itapagipe Peninsula, is the source of the *fitas* (colored ribbons) you see everywhere in Salvador, a souvenir of the church and a symbol of Bahia itself. Bonfim's fame derives from its power to effect miraculous cures, making it a popular shrine.

Courses

Classes in capoeira, African dance and percussion are easily arranged through hostels and *pousadas* in the Pelourinho. Course prices vary depending on season, availability, and the number of people in your party.

Festivals & Events

★Carnaval CULTURAL
Salvador's Carnaval (February or March) is Brazil's second largest and, for many, the best. It's characterized by parades of *axé* and *pagode* bands atop creeping *trios-electricos* (long trucks loaded with huge speakers). A *trio* or drum corps, together with its followers grouped in a roped-off area around it, form a *bloco*. People pay hundreds of reales for the *abadá* (outfit) for their favorite band, mostly for prestige and the safety of those ropes. Choosing to *fazer pipoca* (be popcorn) in the street is still a fine way to spend Carnaval. There are three main areas: the beachside Barra to Rio Vermelho circuit (most touristy), the narrow Campo Grande to Praça Castro Alves circuit and the Pelourinho (no trios here, mostly concerts and drum corps). Check www.carnaval.salvador.ba.gov.br.

Lavagem do Bonfim RELIGIOUS
Salvador's biggest festival outside of Carnaval honors the saint with Bahia's largest following – Senhor do Bonfim, associated with Candomblé. A procession of *baianas* (women dressed as Bahian 'aunts') in ritual dress carrying buckets of flowers walks 6km from Cidade Baixa to Igreja NS do Bonfim. Held on the second Thursday in January.

Festa de Iemanjá RELIGIOUS
Perhaps Candomblé's most important festival, the event pays homage to the *orixá* Iemanjá, goddess of the sea and fertility. Devotees descend on Praia Rio Vermelho in the morning, where ceremonies are held to bless offerings of flowers, cakes, effigies and bottles of perfume. The ensuing street festival is packed with people and some of Salvador's best bands and lasts into the night. February 2.

Sleeping

Staying in the Pelô (packed with hostels) means being in the heart of the action, but it can be noisy and draining. Mellower, beachside Barra has easy transport to the Pelô and the conveniences of a residential neighborhood. Reservations are essential for Carnaval.

Cidade Alta

★Hostel Galeria 13 HOSTEL $
(3266-5609; www.hostelgaleria13.com; Acciole 23; dm/d from R$35/140;) Located in an old colonial house complete with a swimming pool and a Moroccan-style lounge –

rarities at any hostel, but especially in one at such a great location in the middle of the historic center – Galeria 13 is a huge hit with backpackers. Breakfast is served till noon, and non-guests are welcome to hang out. It's affiliated with the excellent Bar Zulu, just around the corner.

Hostel Solar dos Romanos HOSTEL **$**
(3321-6812; www.hostelsolardosromanos.com; Portas do Carmo 14; dm R$35-50, d R$100-120;) This clean and affordable hostel boasts an unusual combination: both a location in the heart of the Pelourinho and a terrace with bay views. Doubles are simple; perks include 24-hour kitchen access.

Laranjeiras Hostel HOSTEL **$**
(3321-1366; www.laranjeirashostel.com.br; Rua da Ordem Terceira 13; dm R$40-48, s from R$65, d R$96-115, tr from R$150; @) This cheerful yellow colonial mansion-turned-hostel is one of the best budget options in the Pelô. High-ceilinged rooms range from dorms to comfortable suites – save cash by choosing a room with a fan instead of air conditioning. Perks include kitchen access, laundry facilities, and an onsite creperie.

Pousada Baluarte POUSADA **$**
(3327-0367; www.pousadabaluarte.com; Ladeira do Baluarte 13; d R$130-190, tr R$250;) Run by a friendly French-Brazilian couple, Baluarte feels like a B&B, with a welcoming, homelike ambience and just five rooms with hardwood floors and beautiful block prints by a local artist. A delicious breakfast is served on the veranda; the Pelourinho is a 10-minute walk away.

Cidade Baixa, Barra & the Coast

★**Open House Barra** POUSADA **$**
(3264-0337; www.openhousebarra.com; Bernardo Catarino 137, Barra; dm R$44, d with/without bathroom R$132/110;) This fantastically colorful and homey place is run by professional artists with deep connections with the local music, dance and film community. Musicians and capoeira demonstrations periodically take place at the hostel, especially during Carnaval, when the guesthouse offers one of Salvador's most memorable party experiences.

Âmbar Pousada POUSADA **$**
(3264-6956; www.ambarpousada.com.br; Afonso Celso 485; dm/s/d R$50/120/135; @) A favorite among budget-minded travelers, this easygoing hostel and guesthouse has a welcoming atmosphere. Dorms are quiet, and doubles are small – note that some of the private bathrooms are only separated by a partition, not a door – but there's ample public space, and it's a two-minute walk to the beach.

Pousada Estrela do Mar POUSADA **$$**
(3264-4882; www.estreladomarsalvador.com; Afonso Celso 119, Barra; d R$190-225;) This white stucco house with dark-blue shutters – very Portugal-meets-the-tropics – is surrounded by greenery, while inside plain white walls set off bright Bahian paintings and vibrant blue tilework. The location is close to the beach on a mellow, tree-shaded street.

Eating

Salvador is well known for its African-influenced Bahian cuisine. A street-food staple is *acarajé* (Bahian fritters made of brown beans and dried shrimp). For cheap seafood snacks, join the locals at the stalls on the ground floor of Mercado Modelo (p359).

Cidade Alta

★**Bar Zulu** INTERNATIONAL **$**
(Laranjeiras 15; mains R$14-30; 1pm-1am Wed-Mon, closed Tue;) This laid-back corner bar and eatery has outdoor tables and serves a wide range of Spanish tapas, Bahian classics and international dishes, plus Argentine wine by the glass and cocktails like the colorful 'Galeria 13', made with lemon, watermelon and *cachaça* (sugarcane alcohol). Try the house burger, Thai curry, or one of the rice-based dishes – like a lighter take on *moqueca* (fish stew).

★**Cafélier** CAFE **$**
(3241-5095; www.cafelier.com.br; Rua do Carmo 50; snacks & light meals R$8-25; 2:30-9:30pm Mon-Tue & Thu-Sat, 2:30-8pm Sun, closed Wed) This quaint hideaway café, located inside an antique house that's positioned dramatically on a cliff top over the ocean, is one of a kind. Come for the views, plus beautifully prepared cappuccino, rich chocolate cake, savory snacks and wines by the glass.

★**Restaurante do Senac** BUFFET **$$**
(www.ba.senac.br; Largo do Pelourinho 13; buffet a quilo per kg R$35, buffet típico R$48 ; buffet a quilo 11:30am-3:30pm Mon-Fri, buffet típico 11:30am-3:30pm daily;) The best Bahian

buffet in town. The cooking school Senac spreads a tempting array of regional dishes, including several varieties of seafood, *moqueca,* and traditional desserts. The impressive buffet *tipico* is on the top floor, not to be confused with the street-level buffet *a quilo,* which is also good for a quick lunch.

Cidade Baixa, Barra & the Coast

The coastal neighborhoods of Barra and Rio Vermelho are full of restaurants, particularly the two parallel streets back from the Praia do Farol beach in Barra, and Rua Feira de Santana in Rio Vermelho.

Camafeu de Oxossi BAHIAN **$**
(3242-9751; Mercado Modelo, Praça Cayru; mains R$18-45; 9am-6pm Mon-Sat, to 2pm Sun) A standard Bahian menu is available at this casual spot on the upper terrace of the Mercado Modelo. Though it's touristy and the food isn't particularly notable, many shoppers or travelers waiting to take the ferry to Morro stop here for coffee, juice, snacks, *moqueca* or cold beer with lovely views over the bay.

★ **Caranguejo de Sergipe** SEAFOOD **$$**
(3248-3331; Av Oceânica & Fernando Luz, Barra; mains R$22-40; 11am-2am Tue-Sun, from 4pm Mon) A local favorite, this always-packed eatery is known for fresh crabs and platters of grilled seafood and vegetables. Don't miss the expertly prepared *maracujá caipirinha* (passion fruit cocktail) – perhaps the most delicious drink on the beach.

Drinking & Nightlife

Cidade Alta

Plazas and cobbled streets fill with revelers sharing beer at plastic tables or dancing behind roaming bands of drummers. Tuesday is the big night.

O Cravinho BAR
(www.ocravinho.com.br; Terreiro de Jesus 3; 11am-11:30pm) This friendly neighborhood bar specializes in flavored shots of *cachaça,* including its trademark clove-infused variety. Decorated with barrels and packed with a vibrant mix of locals and tourists and featuring live music many evenings of the week, it's an atmospheric place to stop in for a quick drink while sightseeing in the Pelourinho.

Casa do Amarelindo Bar COCKTAIL BAR
(3266-8550; www.casadoamarelindo.com; Hotel Casa do Amarelindo, Portas do Carmo 6; noon-late) The chic tropical-style bar at the lovely **Pelô Bistrô** (www.casadoamarelindo.com; Hotel Casa do Amarelindo, Portas do Carmo 6; mains R$45-70; 11:30am-10:30pm;) at Casa do Amarelindo is the ideal spot for a nightcap; better still is the panoramic terrace where a skilled bartender shows up after dark to mix classic cocktails.

Cidade Baixa, Barra & the Coast

Barra's nightlife centers around Jardim Brasil, with cool open-air bars attracting a hip, mostly affluent crowd. Largo de Santana and Largo da Mariquita in bohemian Rio Vermelho pack with people drinking beer and eating *acarajé.* Hip bars surround these squares.

★ **Pereira** BAR
(3264-6464; www.pereirarestaurante.com.br; Sete de Setembro 3959, Barra; noon-4pm & 5pm-1am Tue-Sun) Up a staircase from the seaside road that curves around the tip of Barra, Pereira is a stylish restaurant and wine bar. Excellent *chope* is on tap and the sunset views over the ocean are beautiful.

Entertainment

Salvador is the pulsing center of an incredible music scene. During high season there are almost nightly concerts in the inner courtyards of the Pelourinho, with cover charges ranging from free to R$30. Venues include Largo de Tereza Batista, Largo do Pedro Arcanjo, Praça Quincas Berro d'Água and Terreiro de Jesus. Traditional Afro drum corps also regularly hold *ensaios* (rehearsals), walking through the Pelourinho, blocking traffic and gathering a following as they go.

Groups to be on the lookout for include Filhos de Gandhy, Salvador's most legendary *afoxé* (group tied to Candomblé traditions); Ilê Aiyê, the first exclusively black Carnaval group; the all-female Dida; world-famous Olodum, a Tuesday-night Pelourinho institution; Timbalada, brainchild of master composer and musician Carlinhos Brown; the queens of Salvador pop music – Margareth Menezes, Ivete Sangalo and Daniela Mercury; and others such as Muzenza, Male Debalê and Araketu.

For listings, see www.agendacultural.ba.gov.br and www.aldeianago.com.br.

★**Jam no MAM** LIVE MUSIC
(www.jamnomam.com.br; adult/child R$7/3.50; ⏲6-9pm Sat) Saturday-evening jazz and bossa nova at **MAM** (Museu de Arte Moderna; (☎3117-6139; www.mam.ba.gov.br; Contorno s/n; adult/child R$6/3; ⏲1-7pm Tue-Fri & Sun, to 9pm Sat) is a must for music lovers. Go early to see the museum first and catch the views at sunset. Though the venue is located within walking distance of the Pelourinho, muggings are common along the quiet stretch; taking a taxi is recommended.

★**Balé Folclórico da Bahia** PERFORMING ARTS
(☎3322-1962; www.balefolcloricodabahia.com.br; R Gregório de Mattos 49, Teatro Miguel Santana; admission R$40; ⏲shows 8pm Mon-Sat) The most astounding professional show is put on by this world-renowned folkloric ballet company.

Teatro Castro Alves LIVE MUSIC
(www.tca.ba.gov.br; Praça 2 de Julho, Campo Grande) For the biggest acts, keep your eye on Salvador's finest venue, the Teatro Castro Alves. Its Concha Acústica (amphitheater) has weekly concerts throughout summer.

Shopping

Mercado Modelo HANDICRAFTS
(www.mercadomodelobahia.com.br; Praça Cayru, Cidade Baixa; ⏲9am-7pm Mon-Sat, to 2pm Sun) This two-story market – once the site where slaves were held – has dozens of tourist-oriented stalls selling local handicrafts, plus food stands frequented by locals.

Information

Most pousadas and many restaurants offer wi-fi. ATMs exist throughout the center as well as at the bus station, airport and shopping centers. Use ATMs inside banks instead of freestanding machines that are more susceptible to hackers.

Bahiatursa (☎3321-2463; www.bahiatursa.ba.gov.br; Rua Francisco Muniz Barreto 12, Pelourinho ; ⏲8:30am-9pm Mon-Thu, to 10pm Fri-Sun) The tourism authority is friendly if not terribly organized. The Pelourinho office, which has maps and listings of what's happening around town, is your best bet. There are also desks at the bus station and the airport, and a city tourist office (Emtursa Lacerda; ☎3321-3127; www.emtursa.salvador.ba.gov.br; Elevador Lacerda, Cidade Alta). Also see www.bahia.com.br.

Delegacia do Turista (Tourist Police; ☎3116-6817; Cruzeiro de São Francisco 14, Pelourinho) Any crime involving a tourist must be handled by the city's tourist police. A few speak English or French.

DANGERS & ANNOYANCES

If you're going to be pickpocketed or mugged in Brazil, Salvador is likely to be the place. This shouldn't prevent you from visiting but play it safe, especially at night. Avoid empty areas, and watch your pockets when moving through densely packed crowds. Travelers report 'feeling like a protected species' in the Pelô, but wandering off the beaten path there has proven to be unsafe. The stretch from the Largo do Pelourinho north to Santo Antônio has a reputation for nighttime muggings – take a taxi.

Getting There & Away

AIR

Several domestic and international airlines serve Salvador's Luis Eduardo Magalhães International Airport (SSA). TAP, American Airlines and Aerolineas Argentinas fly directly to Lisbon, Miami and Buenos Aires respectively. Flights to other international destinations generally go via São Paulo or Rio.

BUS

Most travel agencies in town don't sell bus tickets, and Salvador's bus station is a long haul from the center, so it's best to plan ahead and buy tickets when you're passing through. A few bus lines are starting to accept foreign credit cards for online reservations; try your luck with websites such as www.clickbus.com.br or www.busbud.com.

For longer journeys, in addition to the bus fares, you'll often be required to buy an *interestadual* (interstate) card (R$4.50); swipe it at the departure gates for access to the bus platforms.

Sample travel times and fares from Salvador include the following:

DESTINATION	DURATION (HR)	COST (R$)
Belo Horizonte	23	259
Ilhéus	8	76-156
Lençóis	8	65-78
Maceió	11	117-145
Natal	25	212
Porto Seguro	11	176
Recife	16	161
Rio	30	299
São Paulo	32	372

Getting Around

To reach Barra or Cidade Alta from the airport (30km east of the center), catch a local 'Praça da Sé' bus (R$3, one to 1½ hours) or the new First Class executive bus (www.firstclassbus.com.br, R$30).

From Salvador's long-distance bus station (8km east of the center), cross the footbridge to Shopping Bahia and catch any bus marked 'Praça da Sé' (R$3, 30 to 45 minutes).

Regular city buses ($3, 20 to 30 minutes) connect Praça da Sé and Barra.

Linking the lower and upper cities in the center are the fabulous art-deco Elevador Lacerda (p355), and the recently restored **Plano Inclinado Gonçalves** (Praça da Sé & Guindaste dos Padres, Comércio; R$0.15; ⏲7am-7pm Mon-Fri, 7am-1pm Sat) funicular railway.

Lençóis

☎0XX75 / POP 10,000

Lençóis is the prettiest of the old diamond-mining towns in the Chapada Diamantina, a mountainous wooded oasis in the dusty *sertão* (dry interior). The surrounding area – bursting with caves, waterfalls and plateaus promising panoramic views – is a hiking hot spot and a nature lover's dream.

Sights & Activities

Walking & Swimming

Two walks near town are easily taken without a guide. The first heads southwest past the bus stop and follows the Rio Lençois 3km upstream into Parque Municipal da Muritiba. You'll pass a series of rapids known as **Cachoeira Serrano**, the **Salão de Areias Coloridas** (Room of Colored Sands, where artisans gather material for bottled sand paintings), the **Poço Halley** swimming hole, and the **Cachoeirinha** and **Cachoeira da Primavera** waterfalls. The second walk follows Rua São Benedito 4km southeast out of town to **Ribeirão do Meio**, a series of swimming holes with a natural waterslide.

Hiking

Southwest of Lençóis, **Parque Nacional da Chapada Diamantina** comprises 1520 sq km of breathtaking scenery, waterfalls, rivers, monkeys and striking geology. Standout sights near Lençóis include **Poço Encantado**, a cave filled with stunningly beautiful blue water, **Lapa Doce**, another cave with impressive formations, **Cachoeira da Fumaça**, Brazil's highest waterfall (420m), and **Morro do Pai Inácio**, a mesa-style peak affording an awesome view over a plateau-filled valley.

The park has little infrastructure (trails are unmarked) and bus services are infrequent; your best bet is to go with an organized tour or a certified guide.

Tours

Lençóis agencies (there's one on every corner) organize a rotating schedule of half- and full-day car trips (R$140 to R$180 per person depending on group size and destination) and hikes with certified guides, ranging from a couple of hours to a week or longer. Agencies pool customers and rent out necessary gear. Multiday hikes usually involve a combination of camping or staying in local homes and *pousadas*.

H2O Travel Adventures OUTDOORS
(☎3334-1229; www.h2otraveladventures.com; Pousada dos Duendes, Rua do Pires s/n; ⏲10am-9pm) Both day trips and treks are offered; the website offers detailed descriptions of each excursion's attractions and level of difficulty.

Sleeping

Reserve for major holidays, particularly for São João, the town's major festival in late June.

★**Pousada Lua de Cristal** POUSADA $
(☎3334-1658; www.pousadaluadecristal.com.br; Patriotas 27; s/d/tr R$120/150/200; 📶) Run by an exceptionally kind owner, this charming new guesthouse offers sweet, simple rooms with antique stained-glass windows, many opening to views over the town. Outdoor breakfast tables are an added bonus.

Pousada dos Duendes HOSTEL $
(☎3334-1229; www.pousadadosduendes.com.br; Rua do Pires s/n; dm R$50-70, d R$150-260; @📶) 🍃 With a relaxed atmosphere, open-air lounge space, a garden with hammocks, and a vegetarian-friendly eatery on site, Duendes is a backpacker institution. You can arrange everything here – park tours, excursions on horseback, kayak trips – and the kitchen will even pack your lunch on request. It's a five-minute walk outside of town.

Pousada Safira POUSADA $
(☎3334-1443; www.pousadasafira.com; Miguel Calmon 124; d with/without bathroom R$110/90; 📶) This down-to-earth guesthouse is run by

Dona Eulina, something of a local legend for her motherly warmth and hospitality. Basic but cozy, it's a travelers' favorite.

Eating & Drinking

★Cafeteria São Benedito CAFE $

(Rua da Baderna 29; mains R$12-25; ⏲5-11pm Wed-Mon, closed Tue; ☎) This modern coffee shop is a welcome newcomer to Lençóis, serving good coffee, gourmet sandwiches, soups and wraps, and homemade desserts that hit the spot after a day of hiking. The original location is inside Pousada Canto das Águas, but this central café is easier for most travelers to access.

★O Bode BUFFET $

(☎9913-0722; Beco do Rio; per kg R$24; ⏲noon-5pm, to 10pm during peak tourist times) On an open-sided terrace over the river, this pleasant, well-liked per-kilo restaurant spreads a small but enticing buffet that includes meats, pasta and salads. By night, it's an inviting pizzeria.

★Lampião BRAZILIAN $$

(☎3334-1157; Baderna 51; mains R$28-40; ⏲noon-11pm) This popular eatery specializes in cuisine from Brazil's Northwest – think grilled meats, fishes and chicken, served at cute alfresco tables for two – and offers a good-value set lunch.

Information

The online portal of Guia Lençóis (www.guia-lencois.com.br) is a great resource for tourist information. **Banco do Brasil** (Praça Horácio de Mattos 56) has ATMs on the main square.

Associação dos Condutores de Visitantes de Lençóis (☎3334-1425; cnr Baderna & 7 de Setembro ; ⏲8am-noon & 2-8pm) Information about tour guides. Guides may also be hired through the town's various outfitters and travel agencies.

Getting There & Away

AIR

Lençóis' Horacio de Mattos Airport (LEC), 22km east of town, has twice-weekly service to Salvador and Belo Horizonte on Azul Airlines.

BUS

Real Expresso (☎3334-1112; www.realexpresso.com.br) runs four to five daily buses from Salvador (R$65 to R$78, seven to eight hours). Bring a sweater: these buses are notorious for blasting the air-conditioning.

Morro de São Paulo

☎0XX75

Trendy, isolated Morro, across the bay from Salvador and reached by boat, is known for never-say-die nightlife but still has a tranquil charm along its pedestrianized main street running between three jungle-topped hills. The beaches, with their shallow, warm water, disappear with the tides, liberating you for a hike to the waterfall, a round-the-island boat trip, a visit to the quieter neighboring island of **Boipeba** or sunset-watching from the fort. A short climb from the boat dock brings you to Morro's main square. From here, follow Caminho da Praia down to the beaches, which are named in numerical order; most of the action is around Segunda (Second) and Terceira (Third) Praias, a 10- to 15-minute walk from the Praça.

Sleeping

Reservations are required for holiday periods, especially Carnaval and *ressaca* (five days of post-Carnaval hangover). Prices drop considerably in low season.

Che Lagarto Hostel HOSTEL $

(☎3652-1018; www.chelagarto.com; Fonte Grande 11; dm without/with breakfast from R$40/R$65, d without/with breakfast from R$112/R$125; ❄📶) Convenient to the ferry dock and local nightlife, yet with a middle-of-the-jungle feel thanks to its forest-shrouded wooden sundeck, this chain hostel is geared to those looking for a youthful party vibe.

Pousada Natal POUSADA $

(☎3652-1059; Caminho da Praia s/n; d from R$120; ❄📶) This laid-back main-street budget spot has basic rooms and friendly staff; it's well positioned between the harbor and the beaches. To get here, just follow the crowds heading to the beaches from the port – it's about midway between the plaza and Primeira Praia.

★Pousada Porto de Cima POUSADA $$

(☎3652-1562; www.pousadaportodecima.com.br; Porto de Cima 56; d/tr/q from R$209/280/355; ❄📶) Shabby-chic cabins set in a lush jungle-like garden over the sea, along the path to Porto de Cima Beach. Watching electric-blue hummingbirds and the occasional monkey from the vantage point of your porch hammock is about as relaxing as it gets around here, and the breakfast is downright picturesque.

Eating & Drinking

There's a wide choice. The party scene focuses around Segunda Praia.

★ **Pedra Sobre Pedras** CAFE $
(Segunda Praia; mains R$8-15; ⏲24hr) This little cafe is on a wooden deck perched high over Segunda Praia, just off the pedestrian walkway. Pull up a stool and enjoy crepes, well-mixed *caipirinhas* (cocktails) and gorgeous views over the beach action.

Tia Lita BAHIAN $
(www.pousadatialita.com.br; Terceira Praia; mains R$15-35; ⏲11am-10pm) This casual and popular down-home restaurant serves grilled fish, chicken or beef with rice and salad, plus sandwiches and *moqueca* (fish stew). It's located down a narrow lane off Terceira Praia.

★ **Portaló Bar & Restaurante** COCKTAIL BAR
(www.hotelportalo.com; Hotel Portaló; ⏲noon-10pm) This hotel's terrace is the place to be at sunset for glorious views over the harbor, a DJ-spun soundtrack and festive drinks served with the flourish of tropical flowers. There's a full dinner menu, too, if you want to make an evening of it. Look for it when you're stepping off the boat upon arrival on the island.

Information

There are a few ATMs on the island, but it's wise to bring funds from the mainland, especially during high season, when tourists deplete cash supplies. Many establishments also accept credit cards. Internet cafes are plentiful (R$4 to R$7 per hour).

CIT Tur (☎3652-1083; www.morrosp.com.br; Praça Aureliano Lima; ⏲8am-10pm) At the top of the hill up from the dock, Centro de Informações ao Turista sells boat and domestic airline tickets, organizes excursions and distributes maps.

Getting There & Away

Catamarans and small ferries (R$75 to R$80, two hours) cross to Morro five to seven times daily from Salvador's Terminal Marítimo Turístico. Make reservations through travel agencies on the island or directly with **Biotur** (☎3641-3327; www.biotur.com.br), **Farol do Morro** (☎3652-1083; www.faroldomorrotour.com), **IlhaBela** (☎in Salvador 9195-6744; www.ilhabelatm.com.br) or **Lancha Lulalu** (☎9917-1975). The ride can be rough; come with an empty stomach, or Dramamine if you're prone to seasickness. Note that passengers commonly get wet on smaller boats. From the south, or for a cheaper option from Salvador, go to Valença from where regular launches (R$10, 1½ hours) head to Morro. **Cassi Turismo** (☎4101-9760; www.cassiturismo.com.br) also offers boat-plus-bus transfers to Salvador's airport (R$90, three hours).

Itacaré

☎0XX73 / POP 24,000

Itacaré offers postcard-pretty surf beaches backed by wide stretches of Biosphere Reserve Atlantic rainforest. The laid-back surfer vibe makes it a great place to kick back, especially outside peak season. Itacaré has grown considerably from its humble origins as a river-mouth fishing town; recently improved road access now brings in a steady influx of weekend vacationers from Salvador.

There are several internet cafes and an ATM around the main plaza. Visit www.itacare.com.br for an overview.

Activities

Surf lessons and rental are widely available from outfits such as **Brazil Trip Tour** (☎9996-3331; www.braziltriptour.com; R Pedro Longo 235) and **Easy Drop** (☎3251-3065; www.easydrop.com; R João Coutinho 140; 1-day class R$210, 1-week package from R$1795). The pretty town beaches are river-mouth **Praia de Concha** and three tiny surf beaches – **Resende**, **Tiririca**, and **Ribeira** – lined up like manicured fingernails in coves separated by rainforest-covered hills. A trail from Ribeira leads to the thumb, idyllic **Prainha**, but don't walk it alone. Remoter paradises lie beyond; head out to **Engenhoca**, **Havaizinho** and **Itacarezinho**, 12km south of town, or embark on a day-long adventure to the Peninsula de Maraú (R$75), with stops for excellent snorkeling and swimming at **Lagoa Azul** and **Praia Taipús de Fora**.

Sleeping

Numerous budget *pousadas* line the main drag; midrange ones back Praia da Concha. Book ahead between Christmas and Carnaval; prices halve the rest of the year.

★ **Pousada Ilha Verde** POUSADA $
(☎3251-2056; www.ilhaverde.com.br; Ataíde Setúbal 234; s/d from R$100/140, chalet for 4 R$360;) In a lush setting, Ilha Verde has uniquely decorated rooms in-

spired by the owners' world travels. Features include private patios, an inviting swimming pool, abundant outdoor lounge space for luxuriating in the greenery, and a fair-trade shop with handicrafts made from Brazilian straw and shells.

Casarão Verde Hostel HOSTEL $
(☎3251-2037; www.casaraoverdehostel.com; Castro Alves s/n; dm R$30, d without bathroom from R$70; ❄📶) Budget travelers rave about the friendly reception and pristine, spacious rooms at this lovely colonial house – painted pale green, as the name suggests – that's been smartly converted into a hostel.

Albergue O Pharol HOSTEL $
(☎3251-2527; www.alberguoepharol.com.br; Praça Santos Dumont 7; dm/d from R$32/85, apt for 4 from R$190; ❄@📶) A favorite among backpackers, this centrally located and low-key hostel has tidy rooms, some with private balconies. There's a shared kitchen and a guest laundry area; the only downside is that there's no breakfast.

Eating & Drinking

Tio Gu Café Creperia CREPES $
(www.tiogu.com; Pedro Longo 488; mains R$15-30; ⏲5pm-midnight Tue-Sat, to 11pm Sun; 📶🖉) This eco-conscious surfers' hangout has a loyal local following thanks to its perfectly prepared crepes (including delicious dessert options like chocolate and kiwi) and healthy fruit and vegetable infusions.

Alamaim MIDDLE EASTERN $
(www.restaurantealamaim.com.br; R Pedro Longo 204; mains R$15-35; ⏲2:30-10pm Mon-Sat; 🖉) Get your hummus fix here: this cool but casual eatery specializes in vegetarian Arabic food, from falafel to couscous, and has relaxing lounge space where you can kick back after a day of surfing or swimming.

Mar e Mel BAR
(☎3251-2358; www.maremel.com.br; Rua D, Praia da Concha; mains R$20-38; ⏲5pm-midnight) This is the place to hear (and dance to) live *forró* three nights a week (Tuesday, Thursday and Saturday at 9pm). There's a spacious wooden deck and abundant seafood and drink choices.

Getting There & Around

Rota (☎3251-2181) operates buses hourly to Ilhéus (R$14, 1¾ hours) and once daily to Porto Seguro (R$74, eight hours). For northbound travelers, **Cidade do Sol** (www.viacaocidadesol.com.br) offers six daily buses to Bom Despacho (R$42, five hours), from where ferries (R$4, 45 minutes) continue across to Salvador.

Ilhéus

☎0XX73 / POP 184,000

Bright turn-of-the-century architecture and oddly angled streets make Ilhéus' compact center a satisfying wander. The city's fame derives from cocoa and from being the hometown of illustrious novelist Jorge Amado. The best local beaches, such as **Praia dos Milionários**, are to the south.

ATMs and internet places abound in the center. A **tourist information kiosk** (☎3634-1977; www.brasilheus.com.br; Praça Dom Eduardo; ⏲9am-5pm Mon-Sat) lies between the cathedral and the water.

Sights

Casa de Jorge Amado MUSEUM
(☎3634-8986; Amado 20; admission R$2; ⏲9am-noon & 2-6pm Mon-Fri, 9am-1pm Sat) The Casa de Jorge Amado, where the eponymous writer lived with his parents while working on his first novel, has been restored and turned into a lovely and informative museum honoring Amado's life. Not many writers can boast this sort of recognition while still alive, but he became a national treasure well before his death in 2001.

Sleeping & Eating

Ilhéus Praia Hotel HOTEL $$
(☎2101-2533; www.ilheuspraia.com.br; Praça Dom Eduardo, Centro; s/d from R$132/165; ❄📶🏊) This high-rise hotel is fraying around the edges, but many rooms have fine views of the cathedral across the plaza. The relatively high prices don't seem in line with these average rooms, but it's extremely convenient for an overnight stay if you're hoping to sightsee in the historic center.

Berimbau CAFE $
(cnr Paranaguá & Valadares; mains R$12-28; ⏲10am-5pm Mon-Fri) Berimbau is stuck in the past, in the best sense of the phrase: the classic corner diner looks like the setting for a '60s-era Brazilian film. By morning, the café serves up coffee, sandwiches and pastries to the downtown business crowd, and there's a busy buffet at lunchtime. It's the place to soak up a little local culture in Ilhéus.

★**Bataclan** BRAZILIAN **$$**
(☎3634-0088; www.bataclan.com.br; Av 2 de Julho 77; mains R$28-65; ⏲10am-5pm Mon-Sat, event times vary) Once a cabaret frequented by cocoa tycoons (and one of the settings for Amado's *Gabriela*), this colonial building was restored to its original brilliance in 2004. Now it serves as a restaurant and cultural center staging concerts and art exhibitions. There's a lunch buffet from 11:30am to 2:30pm on weekdays.

Getting There & Away

From the *rodoviária*, 4km east of the center, **Rota** (www.rotatransportes.com.br) operates buses to Itacaré (R$14, 1½ hours, roughly hourly) and Porto Seguro (R$54 to R$73, six hours, four daily). **Águia Branca** (www.aguiabranca.com.br) runs north to Salvador (R$76 to R$156, eight hours, five daily).

Porto Seguro

☎0XX73 / POP 127,000

Porto Seguro is a popular Brazilian vacation destination with picturesque beaches and an active nightlife. It's also a gateway to the smaller seaside hideaways of Arraial and Trancoso. Porto is famous as the official first Portuguese landfall in Brazil, and for the lambada dance, so sensual it was once forbidden.

PORTO PARTYING

Porto Seguro is famous for nightly parties (increasingly popular with Brazilian teenagers newly freed from the parental leash) featuring lambada, capoeira, live *axé* (a contemporary Afro-Brazilian pop style, incorporating samba, rock, soul and other influences), *forró* (popular music of the Northeast) and samba. Parties are hosted by local beach clubs, including **Tôa-Tôa** (☎3679-1555; www.portaltoatoa.com.br; Av Beira Mar, km 5, Praia de Taperapuã), **Barramares** (☎3679-2980; www.barramares.com.br; Av Beira Mar, Km 6, Praia de Taperapuã), and **Ilha dos Aquários** (☎3268-2828; www.ilhadosaquarios.com.br; Ilha Pacuio; office in Porto Seguro, Av Conselheiro Luiz Viana Filho 278; adult/child under 10 R$65/free; ⏲8pm-late Fri; box office 8pm-5am Tue-Sun). Admission ranges from R$25 to R$75 (best prices are from vendors around town beforehand). Things start at about 10pm.

Sights

Cidade Histórica HISTORIC SITE
Motivation is required to climb the stairs to Porto Seguro's old town. Rewards include colorful historic buildings and sweeping views over the coastline. Warning: the area is beautifully illuminated at night, and definitely worth a look, but the steps are not safe after dark. Take a taxi.

Beaches
North of town is the Orla Norte (north coast), a long and tranquil bay whose white, fluffy sands are backed by green vegetation and dotted with *barracas* and big beach clubs. Beaches here include **Praia Curuípe** (3km from town), **Praia Itacimirim** (4km), **Praia Mundaí** (6km), **Praia de Taperapua** (7km) and **Praia do Mutá** (10km).

Festivals & Events

Carnaporto CULTURAL
(www.carnaporto-axemoi.com.br) Porto Seguro's Carnaval (February or March), Bahia's most famous after Salvador's, is relatively small and safe, consisting of a few *trios elétricos* cruising the main drag blasting *axé* music. These days, just as many tourists come for the parties across the way in Arraial d'Ajuda.

Sleeping & Eating

There are plenty of budget and midrange *pousadas* just north of the port, but Arraial d'Ajuda (across the water) makes a nicer base. Most dining and drinking options are found around the Passarela do Álcool (Alcohol Walkway) near the port. At night, street performers and live music spill onto the surrounding plazas. Look for fresh-fruit cocktail stands making *capeta* (guaraná, cocoa powder, cinnamon, sweetened condensed milk and vodka) – just the thing to kick off the evening. *Barracas* (food stalls) and beach clubs provide eating options along the length of the beach.

Hotel Estalagem BOUTIQUE HOTEL **$**
(☎3288-2095; www.hotelestalagem.com.br; Marechal Deodoro 66; r R$110-165; ❄📶🏊) One of the more stylish options in Porto Seguro, this affordable boutique hotel is housed inside a colonial building dating from 1801 – check out the antique stones, sourced from the coral reef and originally joined together

with whale oil, in the entryway. Today, renovated guest rooms are understated and comfortable, with private balconies overlooking the swimming pool below.

Tia Nenzinha BAHIAN **$$**
(Av Portugal 170; mains for 2 R$35-70) A classic in Porto since 1976, no-frills Tia Nenzinha serves an assortment of Bahian dishes.

Getting There & Around

Porto Seguro's airport (BPS), served by several domestic carriers, is 1.5km west of the bus station and 3km northwest of the port.

From the bus station, 500m west of the Cidade Histórica, **Rota** (www.rotatransportes.com.br) runs four daily buses to Ilhéus (R$54 to R$73, six hours) and one to Itacaré (R$74, eight hours). **Águia Branca** (www.aguiabranca.com.br) offers overnight service to Salvador (R$176, 11 hours) and Rio de Janeiro (R$207, 22 hours, via Vitória).

Arraial d'Ajuda

0XX73 / POP 13,000

Perched on a bluff above long sandy beaches, Arraial has a curious blend of upmarket tourism and chilled backpackers. Squat buildings painted bright colors surround a traditional plaza; roads lined with pousadas, bars and restaurants slope down to the beaches. Arraial caters to both party animals and those looking to unwind in the tropics.

The closest beach to town is crowded **Praia Mucugê**, but a short walk south brings you to dreamy **Praia de Pitinga** and other gorgeous beaches beyond. Several ATMs and internet places cluster around the center.

Sleeping & Eating

Prices halve outside high season. There are cheap eats on central Praça São Bras and Praia Mucugê.

Arraial d'Ajuda Hostel HOSTEL **$**
(3575-1192; www.arraialdajudahostel.com.br; Campo 94; dm/d from R$48/145;) This colorful HI hostel offers well-equipped private rooms as well as dorm-style accommodations in a funky Greco Bahian–style building with a courtyard swimming pool. Travelers like the communal outdoor kitchen and the location near the beach.

Art Hotel Aos Sinos Dos Anjos POUSADA **$**
(3575-1176; www.aossinosdosanjos.com; Ipê 71; s/d from R$110/140;) A unique gem in Arraial d'Ajuda, this guesthouse is entirely decorated with the works of local artists and filled with colorful mosaics, healing crystals, seashells and sculptures. Two levels of suites, each with its own patio and hammock, face the pretty swimming pool. It's tucked away on a side street that runs parallel to Rua Mucugê.

★Portinha BUFFET **$**
(www.portinha.com.br; Mucugê s/n; per kg R$36; noon-5:30pm Tue-Sun;) Just by looking, you'd never guess this good-looking eatery is a self-service spot: with elegant outdoor tables and a style-conscious crowd, it looks like any of Arraial's upscale restaurants. Like its sister locations in Porto Seguro and Trancoso, Portinha serves an impressive spread of seafood, salads, stews and grilled meats – all kept hot over a wood fire.

Beco das Cores BRAZILIAN **$**
(cnr Mucugê & Beco das Cores; mains R$15-45; 5pm-late) This lively galleria is a big draw for its atmosphere and variety: you'll find good sushi, crepes, pizza and more gourmet fare; there's live music on summer weekend nights, and it's a cozy spot for cocktails on balmy evenings.

Drinking & Entertainment

Downtown Arraial's nightlife scene centers around Rua Mucugê and the adjacent Beco das Cores, a passageway with multiple drinking spots and live music on weekends. In summer, Arraial's beach clubs host huge parties (cover R$25 to R$50).

Morocha Club CLUB
(www.morochaclub.com; Mucugê 260; cover generally free; 6pm-late, event times vary) In town, Morocha is ground zero for nightlife, particularly in summer and around Carnaval. A popular local hangout and restaurant, it's relaxed and lounge-like earlier in the evening, then busy with concerts, dancing, DJs and theme parties late at night.

Getting There & Away

Passenger and car ferries run almost constantly between Porto Seguro and Arraial (R$3.50 to Arraial, free return, 10 to 15 minutes) during the day, and hourly on the hour after midnight. From Arraial's dock, jump on a bus or kombi to the center (R$2.70, 10 minutes).

Trancoso

☎ 0XX73 / POP 10,000

Perched atop a tall bluff overlooking the ocean, this small tropical paradise centers on the utterly picturesque **Quadrado**, a long grassy expanse with a white church flanked by low colorful houses, rooted in the town's history as a Jesuit mission. At night everyone turns out to lounge at outdoor restaurants surrounding the twinkling square. The beaches south of Trancoso are gorgeous, especially **Praia do Espelho** (20km south), off the road to Caraíva.

ATMs and internet cafes are readily available.

Sleeping & Eating

Most accommodations are pricey. Reserve ahead during holidays.

Café Esmeralda Albergue Pousada POUSADA **$**
(☎ 3668-1527; www.trancosonatural.com; Praça São João 272; d from $90; ❄ 📶) The cheapest overnight on the Quadrado is a friendly multilingual guesthouse with basic, fan-cooled rooms – you'll pay slightly more for one of the air-conditioned 'superior' rooms (double from R$120). It's behind the café of the same name, which is convenient, as breakfast isn't included in the room rate.

★ **Pousada Jacarandá** POUSADA **$$**
(☎ 3668-1155; www.pousadajacaranda.com.br; Vieira 91; bungalows for 2 from R$220; ❄ 📶 🏊) This eco-friendly guesthouse features six freestanding bungalows built with natural, locally sourced materials, plus a lovely swimming pool and art-filled interiors. It's a short walk from both the Quadrado and the beach, but the quiet location is a benefit if you're looking to relax.

★ **Rabanete** BUFFET **$**
(www.portinha.com.br; Praça São João s/n; per kg R$44; ⏲ noon-8pm, to 10pm Jan & Feb) This Trancoso classic, which was known as Portinha until a recent change in ownership, woos diners with a sumptuous buffet (don't miss the dessert spread) and atmospheric seating at tree-shaded picnic tables on the Quadrado. It's one of only a few places open for lunch.

Uxua Praia Bar BRAZILIAN **$$**
(www.uxua.com; Praia dos Nativos; mains R$35-50; ⏲ 11:30am-dusk) Even if you're not lucky enough to be staying in Trancoso's top-of-the-line Uxua Casa Hotel & Spa, you can pay a visit to the hotel's stylish but relaxed beach bar. During the day, it's the hippest spot on the sand for cocktails and seafood plates. Just look for the big wooden fisherman's boat, cleverly converted into a bar.

OFF THE BEATEN TRACK

CARAÍVA: END-OF-THE-LINE BEACHSIDE BLISS

For end-of-the-road isolation, head south from Trancoso to remote, magical Caraíva, a sandy hamlet tucked between a mangrove-lined river and a long churning surf beach, made all the more tranquil by the absence of cars. In low season, Caraíva all but shuts down. There are no ATMs – bring cash.

Boat trips upriver, to the spectacular beaches north of town or south to **Parque Nacional de Monte Pascoal**, are easily organized through local pousadas, as are horse rides or walks to **Barra Velha**, an indigenous Pataxó village 6km from Caraíva. A 14km walk, boat trip or bus ride north brings you to celebrated **Praia do Espelho**, widely regarded as one of Brazil's top 10 beaches.

To fully appreciate Caraíva's magic, stay overnight. Accommodations range from simple campsites to midrange beachfront getaways such as **Pousada Cores do Mar** (☎ 3668-5090; www.pousadacoresdomarcaraiva.com.br; Rua da Praia 850 ; cottages for 2/4 people from R$250/350; ❄ 📶). Mosquito nets are essential. For delicious *moquecas* (Bahian seafood stews) with dreamy river views, try **Boteco do Pará** (www.botecodoparacaraiva.com.br; mains for 2 R$45-80; ⏲ 11am-6pm Tue-Sun, closed Jun).

Two daily buses run between Caraíva and the ferry dock in Arraial d'Ajuda (R$20, two hours), stopping en route in Trancoso. From Caraíva's bus stop, canoes (day/night R$4/5, five minutes) ferry you into town, where wheelbarrow-pushers (R$20 per load) can help with your luggage.

Getting There & Away

Hourly buses (R$10) and kombi vans connect Trancoso with Arraial d'Ajuda (50 minutes) and its ferry dock (one hour); some continue to Porto Seguro. At low tide, the 13km walk along the beach from Arraial makes a scenic alternative.

Maceió

☎0XX82 / POP 933,000

Maceió, capital of Alagoas state, offers reef-sheltered swimming in a vivid blue-green sea along its lengthy waterfront. The swaying palms of the city beaches are seductive, but the real beach jewels are out of town, just an hour away.

Sights & Activities

Picturesque *jangadas* (traditional wooden fishing boats of northeastern Brazil) sail 2km out from Praia de Pajuçara, offering opportunities to snorkel in natural pools formed by the reef. **Praia de Ponta Verde** and **Jatiúca** are good city beaches with calm water. Pretty **Praia do Francês** (24km), lined with beach bars, is Maceió's major weekend destination and has lots of *pousadas*. Further south, **Praia do Gunga** sits across a river from Barra de São Miguel (34km). Less crowded beaches north of town include **Garça Torta** (12km), **Riacho Doce** (14km) and **Ipioca** (23km). Another worthwhile excursion is to **Pontal da Barra** (8km south of Maceió), a popular spot to purchase traditional Alagoan *filê* (crochetwork) and embark on scenic four-hour lagoon cruises.

Pedala Maceió BICYCLE RENTAL
(☎9183-9882; www.pedalamaceio.com.br; cnr Dr Antonio Gouveia & JP Filho; per hr R$14; ⏲6am-11pm) Grab a bicycle or a three-wheeler to explore Maceió's 20km-long waterfront bike path. This outfit operates four rental locations along the beaches.

Sleeping & Eating

Accommodations are pricey in Maceió. The beachside *bairros* of Pajuçara and Ponta Verde are much more pleasant than the center. *Barracas* along the beachfront sell cheap treats including *tapiocas recheadas* (tapioca pancakes with savory or sweet fillings) and *caldo de polvo* (octopus stew).

Gogó da Ema POUSADA $
(☎3327-0329; www.hotelgogodaema.com.br; Francisco Laranjeiras 97, Ponta Verde; s/d/tr from R$100/120/150; ❄📶) On a quiet street near two lovely beaches, reliable budget pick Gogó da Ema (named for a famous old palm tree that fell in the city in 1955 and has come to symbolize Maceió itself) is a five-story guesthouse with a tropical theme. The 24-hour front desk is particularly helpful if you're arriving late or catching an early plane.

Maceió Hostel e Pousada HOSTEL $
(☎3231-7762; www.maceiohostel.com.br; Jangadeiros Alagoanos 1528; dm/d from R$50/120; ❄📶) A budget option a few blocks from the beach, this HI hostel is small – shared quads don't leave much room for your backpack – but are friendly and efficiently run. Doubles are basic and spotless, with good showers and large lockers.

Sueca Comedoria SELF-SERVE $
(☎3327-0359; www.suecacomedoria.com.br; Dr Antônio Gouveia 1103, Pajuçara; per kg R$35; ⏲11:30am-4pm Mon-Fri) Despite the name, this sleek eatery across from the beach doesn't serve Swedish food – it's a family-run self-serve spot offering fresh seafood and regional cuisine, ideal for a quick lunch when you need a break from the sun.

★**Divina Gula** BRAZILIAN $$
(www.divinagula.com.br; Nogueira 85, Jatiúca; mains R$29-58; ⏲noon-late, closed Mon; 🍸👪) A Maceió institution, Divina Gula specializes in the hearty cuisine of Minas Gerais and the Northeast. The *picanha* (steak) is excellent as is the *carne de sol* (grilled salted meat) with plantains, corn and zucchini. It has a children's menu, vegetarian options and a full cocktail list.

Entertainment

★**Lopana** BAR
(www.lopana.com.br; Viana 27; ⏲11am-late) Maceió's best beachfront bar is always buzzing: when an acoustic guitarist is playing and a good-looking crowd is drinking beer and *caipirinhas* under the sky-high palm trees, the place looks straight out of a movie.

Information

ATMs can be found in commercial areas along the beach. Internet is readily available at most accommodations.

Getting There & Away

Maceió's Zumbi dos Palmares International Airport (MCZ), 25km north of the center, has domestic connections. The long-distance bus station is 4km north of the center. **Real Alagoas** (www.realalagoas.com.br) offers service to Recife (R$38 to R$68, five hours, 11 daily); **Rota** (www.rotatransportes.com.br) goes to Salvador (R$117 to R$145, 9¾ to 11½ hours, four daily).

City buses (from R$2.50) run to all northern and southern beaches.

Recife

0XX81 / POP 1.54 MILLION

Recife, one of the Northeast's major ports and cities, is renowned throughout Brazil for its dance and musical heritage. The bustling, somewhat gritty commerical center, with water on all sides, is busy during the day but deserted at night and on Sunday. Quieter Recife Antigo, on Ilha do Recife, has picturesque colonial buildings. Most travelers stay in Boa Viagem – an affluent suburb south of the center backing a long golden beach – or in Recife's more peaceful sister city, Olinda.

Sights & Activities

The old city has many restored noble buildings with explanatory panels in English. Strolling through Recife Antigo, you can admire the colorful houses and historic synagogue on **Rua Bom Jesus** and the customs-building-turned-shopping-mall **Paço Alfândega** (www.pacoalfandega.com.br; Rua da Alfândega 35; 10am-10pm Mon-Sat, noon-7pm Sun). A key old city landmark is **Marco Zero** (Praça Rio Branco), a small 'Km 0' marker near the waterfront, designating the place where the Portuguese founded Recife in 1537. Across in Centro, **Pátio de São Pedro** is a pretty cobbled square lined with characterful buildings under the gaze of a handsome baroque church.

Recife

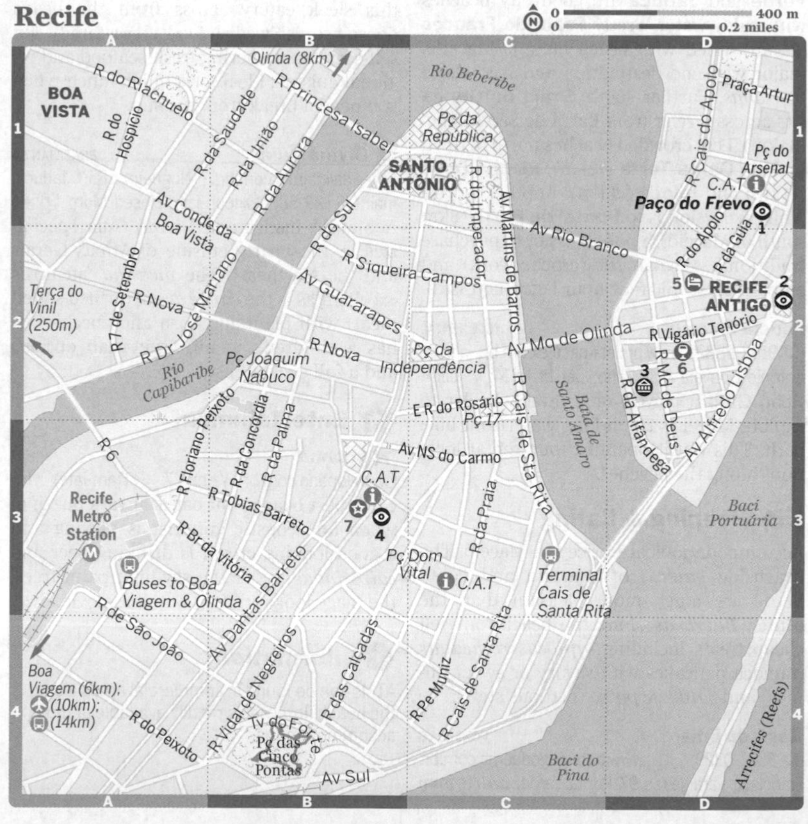

★Paço do Frevo ARTS CENTER
(www.pacodofrevo.org.br; Praça do Arsenal; admission R$6; ⏲9am-6pm Tue, Wed & Fri, to 7pm Thu, noon-7pm Sat & Sun) This new, strikingly red museum is a small and modern house of worship for *frevo*, the quintessential dance of the Recife Carnaval. It hosts exhibits, performances and classes of *frevo*, and highlights include a permanent top-floor exhibit that features giant Carnival insignias from Recife's famous *blocos* (drumming and dancing processions), encased in glass on the floor. Signage is bilingual.

★Oficina Cerâmica Francisco Brennand MUSEUM
(☎3271-2466; www.brennand.com.br; Várzea; admission R$10; ⏲8am-5pm Mon-Thu, to 4pm Fri, 10am-4pm Sat & Sun) Francisco Brennand, born in 1927 into an Irish immigrant family and now considered Brazil's greatest ceramicist, revitalized his family's abandoned tile factory to create his own line of decorative ceramic tiles. The expansive indoor and outdoor space in Várzea, 11km west of central Recife, is now mostly dedicated to his enormous and fascinating oeuvre, which ranges across painting, tile work and hundreds of highly original sculptures. It's best reached by taxi from Boa Viagem (R$200 or so) in combination with **Instituto Ricardo Brennand** (☎2121-0352; www.institutoricardobrennand.org.br; Alameda Antônio Brennand, Várzea; admission adult/child R$20/10; ⏲1-5pm Tue-Sun).

Festivals & Events

Carnaval CARNAVAL
(www.carnavalrecife.com) Recife holds one of Brazil's most colorful and folkloric Carnavals. Groups and spectators deck themselves out in elaborate costumes such as *maracatu* (headpieced warrior), harlequin, bull and *frevo* (crop tops with ruffled sleeves for both genders and a tiny umbrella) and shimmy for days to frenetic *frevo* and African-influenced *maracatu* beats.

Recife

Top Sights
1 Paço do Frevo D1

Sights
2 Marco Zero D2
3 Paço Alfândega D2
4 Pátio de São Pedro B3

Sleeping
5 Azul Fusca Hostel D2

Drinking & Nightlife
6 Burburinho D2

Entertainment
7 Terça Negra B3

Sleeping

Decent budget hotels are in short supply, but thankfully a new crop of hostels has moved in to fill the void.

Azul Fusca Hostel HOSTEL $
(☎3023-5007; www.azulfuscahostel.com; Mariz e Barros 328, Recife Antigo; dm weekend/weekday R$50/45; ❄@📶) The 'Blue Beetle' (as in Volkswagen Beetle) is an intriguing new hostel mere steps from Marco Zero. All spartan chic and minimalist steel, it offers two sparse 12-bed dorms and a design-forward common area full of Mid-Century Modern furniture and top-end kitchen appliances. If you have just one day to take in Recife Antigo's cultural attractions, stay here.

Albergue Piratas da Praia HOSTEL $
(☎3326-1281; www.piratasdapraia.com; Av Conselheiro Aguiar 2034, Boa Viagem; dm with air-con R$53-59, r R$149; ❄@📶) You'd never know it was here, but this friendly, highly colorful hostel occupies the 3rd floor of a building named Edificio Barão de Camaçari (and is entered from Rua Osias Ribeiro). It's a bit like staying in a friend's apartment, as it has a good clean kitchen and wonderfully colorful common areas. The lone private room nets a hammock as well.

Pousada Casuarinas POUSADA $$
(☎3325-4708; www.pousadacasuarinas.com.br; Antônio Pedro Figueiredo 151, Boa Viagem; s/d/tr R$140/160/190, with veranda R$150/170/200; ❄@📶🏊) A tranquil former family home run by two sisters (who speak English, Italian and German), Casuarinas is a marvelous retreat from the heat and bustle outside. Spotless rooms are set around a shady courtyard, where regional folk art and knickknacks spice up the decor. Recife's best-value stay, bar none!

Eating

Bercy Village CREPERIE $
(www.bercyvillage.com.br; Rui Batista 120, Boa Viagem; crepes R$19-29; ⏲6pm-midnight Mon-Thu, to 12:30am Fri & Sat, 5:30-11:30pm Sun; 📶🖋) Atmospheric Bercy Village serves up good-value savory and sweet crepes, and fab

salads and sandwiches in a cool, semi-outdoor ambience that's pretty classy for a creperie. Perpignan (with filet mignon, Gorgonzola and raisins) and Champagne (with shrimp and Gruyère cheese) are big hits.

Mooo BURGERS $
(Av Domingoes Ferreira 4236, Loja B, Boa Viagem; burgers R$26-29; 6pm-midnight;) Brazil's gourmet burger revolution has spread countrywide and this is Recife's trendy entry into the fray. The burgers are great – try the Sertão option with *carne de sol* (a tasty, salted meat) and *coalho* cheese if you want to go local – but the onion rings may just outshine them. There are several options of fries (including poutine) and decent imported beers, too.

★**Camarada Camarão** SEAFOOD $$
(3325-1786; www.ocamarada.com.br; Baltazar Pereira 130, Boa Viagem; mains for 2 people R$73-180; noon-11pm Mon-Thu, to midnight Fri & Sat, to 10pm Sun;) Airy, bustling Camarada does shrimp in endlessly creative ways – think shimp fondue, salads, marinated in beer and served in *moquecas* (stews) – but it's also wildly popular for happy hour, when patrons flood the front deck with ice-cold draft beers in hand. The shrimp and lobster *moqueca* and *bobó de camarão* (shrimp in manioc sauce) are extraordinary.

Drinking & Entertainment

Recife is justly proud of its nightlife and the variety of music that can be found in the city. Many venues are in Boa Viagem, but the streets behind Recife Antigo's Paço Alfândega also have lively bars. Recife has the largest gay scene in the Northeast.

In the Centro, the Patio de São Pedro is a popular hangout, especially on **Terça Negra** (Black Tuesday; www.facebook.com/tercanegrarecife; Pátio de São Pedro; 8pm-1am Tue), a free night of Afro-Brazilian rhythms. Also popular is **Terça do Vinil** (Largo do Santa Cruz, Boa Vista; 7pm-midnight), another free open-air Tuesday concert in Largo do Santa Cruz where DJs spin MPB on vinyl. Watch for *clones* (two-for-one drink specials), which are common throughout Recife.

Burburinho BOTECO
(www.facebook.com/barburburinho; Tomazina 106, Recife Antigo; 11:30am-midnight Mon & Wed, to 6pm Tue, to 1am Thu, to 3am Fri, 6pm-4am Sat) Frequented by students, journalists and a generally bohemian crowd, Burburinho is nicer inside than it appears and usually has live music at least three times weekly – recently,

WORTH A TRIP

PARQUE NACIONAL MARINHO DE FERNANDO DE NORONHA

A one-hour flight from Recife or Natal is Brazil's greenest destination, **Parque Nacional Marinho de Fernando de Noronha** (Fernando de Noronha National Marine Park; www.parnanoronha.com.br; admission Brazilian/foreigner R$89/178) , on the idyllic 21-island archipelago of the same name. Noronha is home to Brazil's most postcard-perfect beaches and staunchly protected marine life; it's a sea-turtle sanctuary, and also the world's best place to see spinner dolphins. With only 270 to 400 plane seats available per day to Noronha, tourism doesn't overwhelm the islands. Throw in Brazil's best surfing and diving and you're rewarded with an unforgettable paradise.

Noronha only opened for tourism in 1988 (it was formerly a military installation and prison). Since then, no new construction has been allowed on its beaches, giving floury patches of sand such as Baía de Sancho and Praia do Leão a dreamlike quality. There are restrictions on vehicles, boats and people as well – Brazilians aren't even allowed to live here unless they were born here (all others get hard-to-secure temporary residence permits). No condos, no chain hotels, no beach vendors, no *people*. In short, it's an environmental success story and a true treat to visit.

But paradise comes at a price. Round-trip flights from Recife (with Azul and Gol airlines) or Natal (with Azul) cost between R$700 and R$1200, and all visitors must pay a daily island tax of R$51.40 plus a one-time national-park entrance fee of R$178/89 for foreigners/Brazilians. Contact **Your Way** (99949-1087; www.yourway.com.br) for English assistance with accommodations and activities on the island.

blues/jazz and soul sessions on Thursdays and rock on Fridays and Saturdays. DJs spin eclectic vinyl on Monday nights.

Companhia do Chope BOTECO
(www.chopperiacompanhia.com.br; Av Conselheiro Aguiar 2775; bar food R$33.50-84.50, chope R$5.35-9.30; 5pm-midnight Mon-Thu, 10am-12:30am Fri & Sat, 10am-midnight Sun;) Swarming with interesting people since 1984, this rambunctious *boteco* fills a breezy open-air shopping plaza in Boa Viagem. Some of Recife's best shared bar food (just try to resist those *coxinhas* and *empadas*) and coldest draft beer is delivered by nimble waiters as the easy-on-the-eyes crowd flirts its way through the evening.

Information

CAT (Centro de Atendimento ao Turista; 3182-8299; www.turismonorecife.com.br; Guararapes International Airport, Arrivals Hall; 24hr); Bus Station (3182-8298; Rodoviária; 7am-7pm); Patio de São Pedro (3355-3311; Patio de São Pedro, Santo Antônio; 9am-6pm Mon-Fri); Praça do Arsenal (3355-3402; Rua da Guia s/n; 8am-8pm); Praça da Boa Viagem (3182-8297; Praça de Boa Viagem; 8am-8pm); Mercado de São José (3355-3022; Mercado de São José; 6am-5pm Mon-Fri, to noon Sun) Do not confuse the airport CAT location with the smaller Jaboatão dos Guararapes, a separate municipality, whose tourist information booth is likely the first you'll see in the arrivals hall.

Delegacia do Turista (Tourist Police; 3322-4867; www.policiacivil.pe.gov.br; Guararapes International Airport, Arrivals Hall; 24hr) Recife's tourist police is (perhaps unhelpfully) located in the airport only, down a hallway to the left of Luck Receptivo.

Getting There & Away

AIR

Several domestic airlines serve Recife's **Guararapes International Airport** (REC; 3322-4353), 10km south of the center and 2km inland from Boa Viagem's south end. International destinations served include Buenos Aires, Lisbon, Frankfurt and Miami.

BUS

Recife's bus station, the **Terminal Integrado de Passageiros** (TIP; 3452-1088), is 17km southwest of the center, connected by metro to the central Recife stop (R$1.60, 25 minutes). Destinations include Natal (R$50, 4½ hours), Maceió (R$38, four hours) and Salvador (R$167, 18 hours, three daily). Long-distance bus tickets can be purchased from **Disk Rodoviária** (3452-1211, Whatsapp 98867-7454; www.diskrodoviaria.com.br), a ticket-delivery service.

Getting Around

Route and schedule information for Recife's buses (R$2.45, R$1.20 on Sunday) is available online at www.granderecife.pe.gov.br (click Serviços, then Atendimento ao Usuário, then Itinerário). Recife also has a two-line metro (R$1.60) that is handy for the bus station and airport.

The 032 'Setúbal/Conde da Boa Vista' bus connects Boa Viagem with Recife Antigo. From Recife's central metro station to Boa Viagem, catch the 'Setubal (Príncipe)' bus.

TO & FROM THE AIRPORT

From a signposted stop outside the airport arrivals hall, air-conditoned bus 042 (R$3) goes to Boa Viagem (20 minutes) and the center (45 minutes) via a slow and convoluted route. A faster, cheaper option for downtown Recife is the metro (R$1.60, 15 minutes), directly across the busy road in front of the airport.

Coopseta prepaid taxis from the airport cost between R$20 and R$33 to Boa Viagem, and R$73 to Olinda or the bus station. During high traffic times, these offer better value then metered taxis; otherwise you'll save money with their metered rivals, Coopstar. Both booths are located near each other inside baggage claim.

Olinda

0XX81 / POP 378,000

If Recife feels like a blue-collar worker scrabbling hard to make ends meet, Olinda is the sibling who dropped out of the rat race to get in touch with its inner artist. This picturesque, bohemian colonial town is packed with painters' studios, impromptu musical events and *cachaça*-fueled parties. Its gorgeous pastel-colored houses flank a stunning ensemble of baroque churches on the historic center's hillside, overlooking the sea.

Sights & Activities

The historic center is easy to navigate and delightful to wander. Climb to **Alto da Sé**, the cathedral square at the top of town, for great views of Olinda's churches backed by the ocean and Recife's distant skyscrapers. The hilltop also hosts a lively street-food scene.

Worthwhile churches include the newly restored **Igreja NS do Carmo** (Praça do Carmo; suggested donation R$2; ⊙9am-noon & 2-5pm Tue-Sun) in the town center; baroque **Mosteiro de São Bento** (Rua São Bento; ⊙8-11:30am & 2:15-5:30pm Mon-Sat, 8-9:30am & 2:30-5pm Sun), with an elaborate gilt altarpiece and a 14th-century Italian painting of St Sebastian; and **Convento de São Francisco** (Rua de São Francisco 280; admission R$3; ⊙9am-12:30pm & 2-5:30pm Mon-Sat), with a memorable tiled cloister.

Festivals & Events

Carnaval CARNAVAL
(www.carnaval.olinda.pe.gov.br) Traditional, colorful and with an intimacy and security not found in big-city Carnavals. Fast and frenetic *frevo* music sets the pace, balanced by the heavy drumbeats of *maracatu*. Costumed *blocos* and spectators dance through the streets in this highly inclusive, playful and lewd festival.

Sleeping

Book well ahead for Carnaval; it can sometimes be cheaper to rent a room or house.

★Cama e Cafe Olinda B&B $
(☎98822-9083; www.camaecafeolinda.com; Rua da Bertioga 93; r R$165; ❄@📶) Austrian Sebastian and his Brazilian wife, Yolanda, are the hospitality gatekeepers at this signless B&B with just two rooms. It's chock-full of local art, lazy-day hammocks and views of both the sea and Recife. You'll encounter extraordinary care and character here; breakfast on the terrace (fruits and juices plucked straight from the property) is just one of many highlights.

Albergue de Olinda HOSTEL $
(☎3429-1592; www.alberguedeolinda.com.br; Rua do Sol 233; dm/s/d/tr R$50/120/130/180; ❄📶🏊) Olinda's excellent HI hostel isn't on a colorful street, but offers modern amenities; spotless no-frills rooms; sex-seperate

Olinda

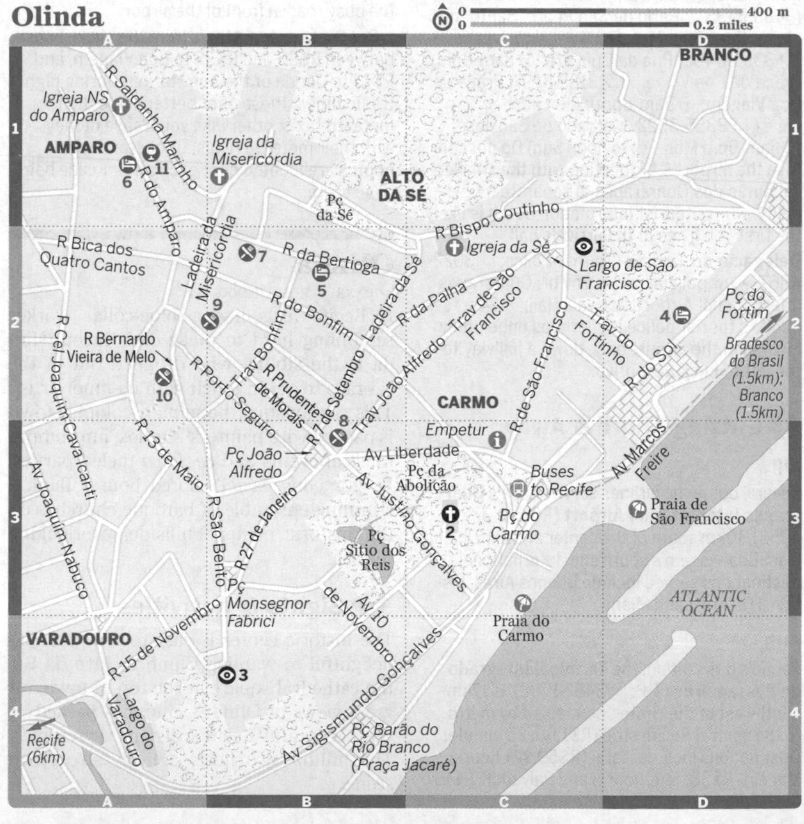

dorms; and a sizable garden with a lovely pool, loungers, outdoor kitchen, barbecue and plenty of hammocks.

Pousada do Carmo POUSADA $
(☎99501-7956; www.pousadadocarmoolinda.com.br; Rua do Amparo 215; d/tr R$130/165;) Having changed from German to Brazilian hands at the time of research (and with its website still in the pipeline), the jury is out on the former Pousada Bela Vista, a long-standing budget staple. However, its large colorful lobby-lounge that leads through to three lower floors with 12 rooms and a pool, a breakfast area and terraces with views all the way to Recife remain.

Eating

For a no-frills snack, hit Alto da Sé, where stalls serve *tapioca* with various fillings, along with ice-cold coconuts and mixed drinks.

Creperia CREPERIE $
(www.facebook.com/creperiaolinda; Praça João Alfredo 168; crepes R$8.50-37, pizzas R$25-39; 11am-11pm;) A nice spot for crepes, pizza and salads, which you can enjoy on a pleasant outdoor patio under tall bamboo trees.

Casa de Noca BRAZILIAN $
(www.casadenoca.com; Rua da Bertioga 243; meals for 2/3/5 people R$60/80/100; 11am-11pm) For simple Northeastern food at its best, you can't beat this backyard restaurant that offers just one dish: large chunks of grilled *queijo coalho* (a salty white cheese that's grillable) and slabs of surprisingly tender *carne de sol* atop a mountain of steamed *macaxeira*.

★Patuá BRAZILIAN $$
(☎3055-0833; www.restaurantepatua.com.br; Rua da Ribeira 79; mains R$35-85, seafood for 2 people R$89-171; 11am-3pm Tue, 11am-3pm & 6-10pm Wed-Sat, 11am-4pm Sun;) Humble, local and a kitchen magician, Chef Alcindo Queiroz serves regional *moquecas* and seafood that are an unexpected joy at this Olinda sleeper. Start with the Taperoá appetizer – flambéed shrimp over a fried banana drizzled with a pink peppercorn and star-anise sauce – then savor an excellent Pernambucana-style seafood stew. Douse it all in the vinegary house-made pepper sauce!

Drinking & Entertainment

On Friday and Saturday evenings there's free bossa nova and *chorinho* (an informal, instrumental genre of music that developed in Rio in the late 19th century) at **Estação Café** (Prudente de Morais 440; items R$3.50-35; 11:30am-8:30pm Tue-Thu, 12:30-11pm Fri & Sat, noon-8:30pm Sun;). You'll usually find these and other Brazilian rhythms elsewhere in Olinda Wednesday to Saturday nights and Sunday afternoons – tourist offices have information. On Friday nights from 9pm strolling musicians make a circuit through town, joined in song by onlookers, in what's known as the *serenata* or *seresta*.

★Bodega de Véio BAR
(www.facebook.com/bodegadoveio; Rua do Amparo 212; 10am-11:30pm Mon-Sat) Also a small and very eclectic general store, this wonderful little bar serves ice-cold bottled beer, shots of *cachaça* (potent sugarcane liquor) and great charcuterie plates (R$8 per 100g), while doing its best to manage the crowds of locals and tourists congregating on the street and small terrace at the side.

Information

The only ATM in the historical center is a Banco 24 Horas inside **Padaria Largo do Amparo** (Rua do Amparo 395; 8am-9pm). Alternatively, bring cash from Recife or take the 10-minute bus ride northeast from Praça do Carmo to Av Getúlio Vargas, where you'll find Banco do Brasil and Bradesco ATMs.

Ciatur (Companhia de Apoio ao Turista; ☎3181-3703; www.ciaturpmpe.blogspot.com.br; Av Justino Gonçalves; 24hr) Rua da Ribeira (www.ciaturpmpe.blogspot.com.br; Rua do Ribeiro s/n) Very helpful and present around

Olinda

Sights
1 Convento de São Francisco C2
2 Igreja NS do Carmo C3
3 Mosteiro de São Bento B4

Sleeping
4 Albergue de Olinda D2
5 Cama e Cafe Olinda B2
6 Pousada do Carmo A1

Eating
7 Casa de Noca B2
8 Creperia B3
9 Estação Café B2
10 Patuá A2

Drinking & Nightlife
11 Bodega de Véio A1

town, though English is only spoken at the airport tourist police.

Empetur (Empresa de Turismo de Pernambuco; ☎3182-8294; www.pe.gov.br/orgaos/empetur-empresa-de-turismo-de-pernambuco; Av da Liberdade s/n; 8am-6pm) The state tourist info office has lovely English-speaking staff.

DANGERS & ANNOYANCES

Crime (mostly petty) exists, especially during Carnaval. Don't walk alone along deserted streets at night.

Getting There & Around

Bus 910 'Piedade/Rio Doce' runs about every half-hour from Boa Viagem to Olinda and back. The 1983 'Rio Doce/Princesa Isabel' and 1992 'Pau Amarelo' buses run from Terminal Cais de Santa Rita in central Recife to Olinda and back. All cost R$3.35. Olinda's main bus stop is on Praça do Carmo.

Taxis to Olinda cost around R$45 from Boa Viagem, R$65 from Recife bus station and R$73 from the airport.

Praia da Pipa

☎0XX84 / POP 3000

Pristine sands backed by handsome cliffs, with dolphins frisking close to shore, make Pipa one of Brazil's premier beach destinations. While the once-peaceful main street has long since become heavily commercialized, Pipa remains a tranquil place outside high season, and the quality of accommodations and food make it easy to lose a week here.

The long main drag has traveler-friendly installations such as internet, ATMs, laundries, bars and restaurants. Local businesses distribute a useful free Pipa map-guide.

Sights & Activities

Guiana dolphins rest and frolic in Baía dos Golfinhos, accessible via Pipa's main beach at low tide only. Let them choose whether to approach you or not; don't chase or feed them.

Several other worthwhile beaches are easily accessed by walking or van, including surfer favorite **Praia do Amor** just south of town; rental boards and lessons are readily available. Another popular destination is **Lagoa de Guarairas**, 8km north of town; **Bicho do Mangue** (☎99928-1087; www.bichodomangue.blogspot.com.br; per person R$30) offers three-hour kayak excursions around the lagoon, and the dockside **Creperia Marinas** (www.hotelmarinas.com.br; Av Governador Aluizio Alves 301; crepes R$16-40; 11am-8pm) is a brilliant sunset-viewing spot.

Santuário Ecológico de Pipa NATURE RESERVE
(☎99982-8044; www.ecopipa.com.br; admission R$10; 7am-5pm) This small, privately owned reserve, 2km west along the main road from the town center, does a valuable job of protecting at least some of the Pipa coast from development. Well-marked trails lead through secondary forest to impressive lookouts over Baía dos Golfinhos and Praia do Madeiro, from which you can often see large green turtles at high tide.

Sleeping

Competition keeps accommodations prices reasonable in Pipa. Reservations are recommended for all major holidays. There are campsites at both ends of town.

★**Pousada Xamã** POUSADA $
(☎3246-2267; www.pousadaxama.com.br; Cajueiro 12; s/d/tr R$90/150/180;) Hidden up a side street near Pipa's southeastern edge is one of the Northeast's best budget *pousadas*. Ultra-hospitable owner Neuza presides over great-value, pleasantly decorated rooms, most of which open onto a leafy, flower-fringed pool and garden area, with hammocks and hummingbirds. The breakfast is good, and the *pousada* offers Natal airport pickups for R$180 to R$200 (up to four people).

Hostel do Céu HOSTEL $
(☎3246-2235; www.hosteldoceu.jimdo.com; Rua do Céu 153; dm/d with fan R$50/150;) It's no party hostel, but this Argentine family-run spot offers the best budget infrastructure in Pipa, with top-notch separate and mixed dorms and, if you can manage to snag it, the best-value private room in town: a colorful top-floor space complete with large, breeze-blown windows, and both sea *and* sunset views!

Media Veronica Hostel HOSTEL $
(☎3246-2607; mediaveronicahostel.com.br; Albacora 267; dm R$45, r R$120, all excl breakfast;) In new, bigger digs just 100m from its old location, this hostel is a labor of love for Argentine Juan Pablo, who impresses with reasonable prices and an emphasis on cleanliness, security and information for guests. Dorms come in four-, six- and 10-bed configurations (the latter is cramped) and a few privates have sea and floral garden views.

Eating & Drinking

There's a wide choice of cuisine in Pipa, much of it pricey. Nightlife is focused along the main drag and at a couple of beachside *barracas*.

Dona Branca BUFFET $

(Av Baia dos Golfinhos; meals from R$15; ⏲11am-9pm) Places like this are a dying breed in popular beach towns like Pipa. Take your pick of any two meat items from the grill, then fill your plate with rice, beans, salad and other goodies from the buffet. It's R$2 extra with fish or shrimp, and there's a R$3 fine if you don't finish your plate!

Oba JAPANESE $

(www.facebook.com/obayakisoba; cnr Albacora & Rua da Arara; mains R$22-33; ⏲6-11pm, closed Wed) It's not often you'll find genuine Japazilian yakisoba from São Paulo at these prices, but this place is the real deal. Heaped plates of noodles with veggies, shrimp, chicken, steak etc are the highlight, and the lychee sakerinhas (using sake instead of *cachaça*) ratchet up the fun.

★**Cruzeiro do Pescador** SEAFOOD $$

(☎3246-2026; www.cruzeirodopescador.com.br; cnr Av Baía dos Golfinhos & Concris; mains R$55-65, for 2 people R$105-150; ⏲1-4pm & 7-10:30pm; 📶) On the southeast edge of town, about 1.5km from the center, what looks like a typical mess of a house hides a don't-miss culinary experience. Chef Daniel does everything with homemade and home-grown finesse, from the poetically hand-written menus and the romantic candlelit setting to the products from his own garden. The flavors of his cooking – some pinched from India and Bahia – are delicious.

Information

For general info on Pipa, see www.pipa.com.br or www.mapaguiapipa.com.br. Cash is king in Pipa – many places do not accept credit cards, and the few ATMs accepting foreign cards are frequently out of money or on the fritz.

Getting There & Away

Oceano (☎3311-3333; www.expresso-oceano.com.br) operates 12 daily buses (six on Sunday) from Natal's Rodoviária Nova to Pipa (R$13.50, 1½ hours). **Alternativo Vans** (☎99973-0353) runs thrice-daily microbuses along this same route (R$12, 2½ hours). A taxi between Natal's airport and Pipa should cost R$170 to R$200.

Coming from Recife and points south, get off at Goianinha and catch a minibus (nicknamed 'Dolphin van') to Pipa (R$3.75, 50 minutes) from behind the faded pale-blue church, 200m off the main highway.

Natal

☎0XX84 / POP 804,000

Sun and sand draw people to Natal, the relaxed capital of Rio Grande do Norte state, near Brazil's northeast corner. Occupying a long sandy peninsula, Natal's kilometers of beaches and dunes are regularly kissed by sunshine; the tourist board talks the town up as 'Sun City' thanks to 10 months of tanning time per year. Fourteen kilometers south of the center, the beach suburb of Ponta Negra is the most rewarding traveler hangout, with numerous places to stay and eat.

Sights & Activities

Forte dos Reis Magos FORT

(admission R$3; ⏲8am-4pm) The fort that got Natal started in 1598 still stands in its original five-pointed star shape on the reef at the tip of the peninsula at the north end of town. The views of the city, the Ponte Nova and the dunes across the Rio Potengi are fantastic.

Praia Ponta Negra BEACH

Of Natal's city beaches, Praia Ponta Negra (14km south of the center) is urbanized but the nicest. **Morro de Careca** – a steep, monstrous dune that drops into the sea – towers over its southern end. Bus 56 runs from here along the other city beaches, so just hop off wherever the water looks good.

Dunas de Genipabu ADVENTURE TOUR

Try a popular and exciting outing to the spectacularly high and steep dunes about 10km north of the city near Genipabu, where you can be driven up and down the sand mountains for an hour or so in a beach buggy. A number of operators are recommended: **Natal Vans** (☎3642-1883; www.natalvans.com.br; Duna Barcane Mall, Av Engenheiro Roberto Freire 3112, Ponta Negra; ⏲7am-10pm Mon-Fri, to 9pm Sun) and **Marazul** (☎3219-6480; www.marazulreceptivo.com.br; Rua Vereador Manoel Sátiro 75, Ponta Negra; ⏲8am-10pm) offer several fairly standardized out-of-town trips, easily booked through your accommodation.

Festivals & Events

Carnatal PARADE, MUSIC

(www.carnatal.com.br) Natal's out-of-season Carnaval, Carnatal, takes to the streets of the Lagoa Nova district over four days in early December, with Salvador-style *trios elétricos* (bands playing atop huge trucks) and *blocos* sporting names such as Burro Elétrico (Electric Donkey) and Cerveja & Coco (Beer & Coconut). It's the wildest out-of-season Carnaval in Brazil.

Sleeping & Eating

Ponta Negra is more welcoming than downtown.

Republika Hostel HOSTEL $

(3236-2782; www.republikahostel.com.br; Porto das Oficinas 8944, Ponta Negra; dm R$45, s/d with fan R$80/100, with air-con R$100/120;) Republika's low-lit bar, comfy hammock and TV areas, and big, clean kitchen and eating area create a cozy atmosphere for mingling with fellow travelers. It's housed in a converted family home that evokes Santorini and is run by local hipster chef Anderson, who lived many years in England and Portugal. It's well located near some of Ponta Negra's best eats.

Albergue da Costa HOSTEL $

(3219-0095; www.alberguedacosta.com.br; Av Praia de Ponta Negra 8932, Ponta Negra; dm/d R$55/110;) This superfriendly HI hostel has comfortable dorms, good breakfasts, ample common spaces and laid-back management. Other attractions include free use of skateboards, bike and surfboard rental, and regular social activities such as live music and barbecues . English, Italian and Spanish are spoken.

Casa de Taipa BRAZILIAN $

(www.facebook.com/casadetaipatapiocariaecuscuzeria; Av Praia de Ponte Negra 8868, Ponta Negra; dishes R$12-36; 5pm-midnight;) What is probably Brazil's most famous *tapiocaria* flips the script on a traditionally R$4 street food and turns it into a gourmet treat fit for foodies. Droves of visitors and locals alike swarm this colorful and festive place for lightly pan-grilled tapioca 'pancakes' stuffed with sweet and savory goodies (vegetables, cheeses, grilled salted meats, prawns – even a *moqueca* version).

★**Camarões Potiguar** SEAFOOD $$

(www.camaroes.com.br; Pedro da Fonseca Filho 8887, Ponta Negra; mains for 2 people R$66-119; 11:30am-3:30pm & 6:30pm-midnight, to 11pm Sun) This bright, stylish and creative homage to the shrimp is arguably Natal's best dining experience, and it's permanently packed. Start with a tradtional shrimp and Catupiry *pastel* (thin square of dough stuffed with shrimp and cheese then fried), then follow up with anything from shrimp in a pumpkin to our fav: the Bonfim (sauteed with cashews, *coalho* cheese and fragrant *biquinho* peppers with *vatapá* risotto).

Cipó Brasil PIZZA $$

(www.cipobrasil.com.br; Aristides Porpino Filho 3111, Alto de Ponta Negra; pizzas R$21.50-83.50; 6pm-midnight;) A unanimous favorite, this fun jungle-themed place is great for sesame-crusted pizza (more than 30 types, from shrimp and four cheese to banana and chocolate) and both savory and sweet crepes. It's a starting point for evenings out. Get there early to avoid waiting.

Drinking & Nightlife

The Alto de Ponta Negra neighborhood in the upper part of Ponta Negra, around Rua MA Bezerra de Araújo and Rua Aristides Porpino Filho, is dense with a variety of bars and packed from Wednesday to Saturday nights. Sex tourism is an unfortunate part of this scene. Petrópolis, in the city center, is the best neighborhood for hip local bars and *botecos* away from tourists.

Information

ATMs line Ponta Negra's beachfront. There are intermittently staffed tourist-information desks in the bus station and at the **Centro de Turismo** (3211-6149; www.turismo.natal.rn.gov.br; Aderbal Figueiredo 980, Petrópolis; 8am-7pm).

Getting There & Away

AIR

Natal's new **Aeroporto de Natal** (Aeroporto Internacional Governador Aluízio Alves; 3343-6060; www.natal.aero; Av Ruy Pereira dos Santos 3100 , São Gonçalo do Amarante), 35km west of Ponta Negra in São Gonçalo do Amarante, has scheduled flights from Lisbon, Buenos Aires, Milan and Cabo Verde in addition to many Brazilian cities.

BUS

Long-distance buses leave the **Rodoviária Nova** (☎3205-2931; Av Capitão Mor Gouveia 1237), 6km south of the center, for Fortaleza (R$85, eight hours), Recife (R$50, 4½ hours), João Pessoa (R$34, three hours) and Salvador (R$212, 21 hours).

Getting Around

Natal's new airport is quite a haul, 35km west of Ponta Negra. Local bus service takes more than two hours and is hardly worth the hassle. Most travelers opt for the far more convenient **Natal Transfer** (☎3343-6272; www.nataltransfer.com.br; R$35) and **Van Service** (☎4141-2848; www.vanservice.com.br; R$40), which run shared vans to Natal and Pipa (R$95) leaving after each flight. A taxi from the airport costs about R$100 to R$120 to Ponta Negra and R$228 or so to Praia da Pipa.

From the bus station to Ponta Negra, catch bus 66 (R$2.65) from the stop opposite the Petrobras gas station; a taxi costs R$30 to R$50 depending on time of day and location in Ponta Negra.

Canoa Quebrada

☎0XX88 / POP 2800

Easily reached from Fortaleza, this fishing village turned hippie hangout has become upmarket, but still represents a relaxing seaside spot for a few days of downtime. Hard-packed beaches backed by rust-colored cliffs are pleasant, and outdoor adventures abound, including beach-buggy tours to **Ponta Grossa** and nearby dunes (R$300 to R$350 for up to four people) or **tandem paragliding** jaunts (R$100) with **Vôo Duplo Jerônimo** (☎98806-6570; 10-20min flight R$100). The kitesurfing season runs from July to December; lessons are available.

For a cheap sleep, check out **Hostel Pousada Ibiza** (☎3421-7262; www.hostelpousadaibiza.com; Dragão do Mar 360; dm R$48-55, d R$140-160;), whose smallish en suite dorms and doubles are complemented by a balcony lounge-bar overlooking the action in the heart of town. Numerous midrange *pousadas* (very affordable off-season) offer considerably more comfort, such as the excellent British-Dutch **Pousada California** (☎3421-7039; www.californiacanoa.com; Nascer do Sol 135; r R$200-300;), one block toward the beach from Canoa's main street.

At lunchtime, don't miss the BBQ fish – simply but perfectly garnished with salt, lime and chimichurri – at Argentine-run **Lazy Days** (www.facebook.com/barraca.days; Praia; mains R$28-40; 9am-5pm), the best of the beach *barracas* that rub up against Canoa's picturesque red cliffs. Nightlife revolves around **Regart Bar** (Dragão do Mar s/n; cover R$3; 3pm-3am) and similar venues along 'Broadway', Canoa Quebrada's main street. In high season, **Freedom Bar** (6pm-midnight Fri & Sun) hosts weekend reggae parties on the beach.

Banco do Brasil and Bradesco both have ATMs in a shopping plaza on Rua Dragão do Mar.

São Benedito (www.gruposaobenedito.com.br) runs five daily buses (R$24.50, 3¼ hours) between Canoa and Fortaleza. Alternatively, **Oceanview Turismo** (☎3219-1300; www.oceanviewturismo.com.br; R$45) offers faster door-to-door van service (R$45, 2½ hours) from hotels on Fortaleza's Meireles strip.

If arriving by bus from Natal or other points south, disembark at Aracati, 13km southwest of Canoa, then hop aboard São Benedito's Fortaleza–Canoa bus (R$1.10), a half-hourly *topique* minibus (R$2.50) or a taxi (R$25 to R$30) for the quick Aracati–Canoa run.

Commercial flights were approved in 2015 for the new airport at Aracati, but at time of writing its runways remained unused.

Fortaleza

☎0XX85 / POP 2.45 MILLION

Fortaleza's sprawling capital city of Ceará is a popular beach destination but offers little to the backpacker besides a couple of days on the sand and facilities to get you sorted before setting out again. Glitzy, gritty or tacky depending on where you find yourself, Fortaleza is best appreciated in its coastal neighborhoods, which have impressive nightlife and numerous restaurants. **Fortal** (www.fortal.com.br) is a Salvador-style, out-of-season Carnaval in the second half of July.

Sights & Activities

Centro Dragão do Mar de Arte e Cultura ARTS CENTER

(☎3488-8600; www.dragaodomar.org.br; Dragão do Mar 81; 8am-10pm Mon-Thu, to 11pm Sat & Sun) This excellent, extensive complex includes cinemas, performance spaces, a good cafe, a planetarium and two good museums: the **Museu de Arte Contemporânea** (MAC;

Fortaleza

www.dragaodomar.org.br; Dragão do Mar 81, Centro Cultural Dragão do Mar; 9am-7pm Tue-Fri, 2-9pm Sat & Sun) FREE, and the **Memorial da Cultura Cearense** (MCC; www.dragaodomar.org.br; Dragão do Mar 81, Centro Cultural Dragão do Mar; 9am-7pm Tue-Fri, 2-9pm Sat & Sun) FREE, which shows exhibits on Ceará's traditional way of life and culture. Elevated walkways join blocks on different streets and it all blends well with the surrounding older buildings, many of which have been restored to house bars, restaurants and artisans' workshops. It's a successful social focus for the city, and is very popular with locals.

Beaches

Praia do Meireles has an attractive waterfront promenade with homey beer *barracas* on the sand side and smart air-con restaurants alternating with hotels across the street. The fish market and evening craft fair are other draws. Further east, **Praia do Futuro** is the cleanest and most popular of the city beaches. Just northwest, tranquil **Praia do Cumbuco** has dunes and *jangada* (traditional sailboat) trips. Local agencies also offer longer-distance 4WD or beach-buggy tours along Ceará's glorious coastline, as far afield as Jericoacoara.

Sleeping

Competition between the many hotels means there are some excellent deals, including some midrange hotels at budget prices.

★ Refugio Hostel Fortaleza HOSTEL $
(3393-4349; www.refugiohostelfortaleza.com; Deputado João Lopes 31, Centro; dm with/without bathroom from R$50/40, r with fan R$120;) This is easily Fortaleza's best hostel. German owner Karl has whipped an old mansion into shape, following an eco-ethos with breezy natural ventilation and solar-heated showers. The bathrooms and kitchen are astonishing for a hostel, while other design-forward common spaces of note include a sunny patio/BBQ area and various terraces. Dorms feature colorful lockers and original tiling and hardwood floors.

Albergaria Hostel HOSTEL $
(3032-9005; www.albergariahostel.com.br; Antônio Augo 111, Praia de Iracema; dm with fan/air-con R$40/45, d/tr R$128/148;) This cheerful, well-located, well-run hostel has very good facilities, including a restaurant-bar (with a trained chef) and a backyard with a pool, plus a sociable atmosphere helped along by the friendly English-speaking

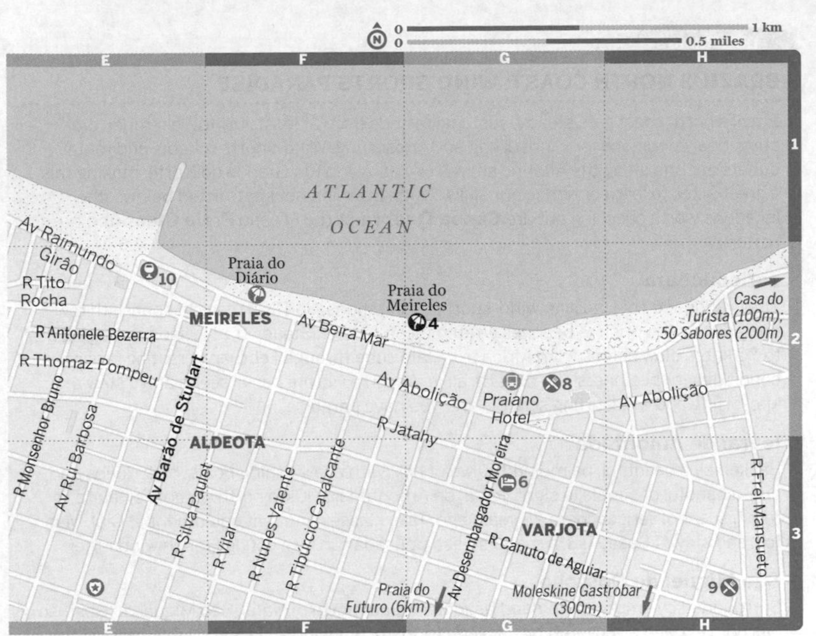

Fortaleza

Sights
1 Centro Dragão do Mar de Arte e Cultura B1
2 Memorial da Cultura Cearense B2
3 Museu de Arte Contemporânea B2
4 Praia do Meireles G2

Sleeping
5 Albergaria Hostel D1
6 Hotel La Maison G3
7 Refugio Hostel Fortaleza B2

Eating
8 50 Sabores G2
9 Colher de Pau H3
Santa Clara Café Orgânico .... (see 13)

Drinking & Nightlife
10 Boteco Praia E2
11 Órbita C1

Shopping
12 Ceart D3
13 Ceart B1

owner. There are separate-sex and mixed four-bed dorms (with privacy curtains and lockers with electrical outlets) and four good private rooms with bathroom. Breakfast is plentiful. Reservations only.

Hotel La Maison HOTEL $
(☎3048-4200; www.hotellamaison.com.br; Av Desembargador Moreira 201, Meireles; r R$150; ❄@📶) This excellent-value place in Meireles is just a couple of blocks from the beach, and has 25 spotless rooms (those upstairs are generally brighter than downstairs) and bright, colorful common areas. The French owner knows the city very well, speaks English, and can point you in the right direction – whatever your needs. The fruit-heavy breakfast is substantial, but where's the Brie?

Eating

Budget eateries abound in Iracema, while smarter restaurants line the Meireles strip. Centro Cultural Dragão do Mar is also good for dinner.

★50 Sabores ICE CREAM $
(☎3023-0050; www.50sabores.com.br; Av Beira Mar 2982, Meirelles; 1/2 scoops R$11/15; ⏲10am-11:45pm; 👪) One of Brazil's most famous ice cream shops, though with a terribly misleading name: there are actually 150

DON'T MISS

BRAZIL'S NORTH COAST: WIND SPORTS PARADISE

Brazil's north coast gets steady, sustained winds from at least July to December, creating ideal conditions for windsurfing and kitesurfing. Wind-sports schools and rental outlets abound along the Atlantic shores of Ceará and Rio Grande do Norte, making this a great place to learn or hone your skills. Aside from the hot spots listed below, other locations worth checking out are **Canoa Quebrada** (p377) and **Praia Cumbuco** near Fortaleza.

Jericoacoara

The granddaddy of Brazilian wind-sports destinations, 'Jeri' is a magical spot, with towering dunes and pristine beaches stretching on forever. Steady trade winds averaging 23 to 30 knots blow across from Africa from late June through February, creating dreamy conditions for beginners and experts alike. Add in a vibrant social scene and a slew of kitesurfing and windsurfing schools and you have paradise.

Icaraí de Amontada

Backed by a beautiful, palm-lined curve of bay, with a few fishing boats, high dunes and only a handful of people in sight, Icaraí de Amontada, 200km northwest of Fortaleza, is reminiscent of Jericoacoara 25 years ago. Take classes and rent equipment at Club Ventos, and stay at Casa Zulu, a rustic-stylish pousada run by a young French windsurfer.

São Miguel do Gostoso

Surrounded by empty white-sand beaches 110km north of Natal, São Miguel do Gostoso has not yet been discovered by package tourism, but windsurfers and kitesurfers in the know head for windswept Ponta de Santo Cristo, where **Clube Kauli Seadi** (99197-1297; www.clubekauliseadi.com; Praia do Cardeiro; 9am-5:20pm) offers lessons and rents equipment.

flavors here, including *caipirinha* (made with *cachaça* sugarcane liquor – you must be 18 to purchase!) and beer, among loads of Brazilian fruits and more classic options. Don't let anyone tell you one scoop of tapioca, one scoop *açaí* isn't the perfect combination! There's a branch in **Mucuripe** (www.50sabores.com.br; Av Beira Mar 3958, Mucuripe; 7am-midnight).

Santa Clara Café Orgânico CAFE **$**
(Centro Dragão do Mar, Praia de Iracema; items R$5-16; 3-10pm Tue-Sun;) Santa Clara is one of the city's hot *pontos de encontros,* which loosely translated means where hot people go to mingle (and cool down in the icy air-con). It's a wonderful little cafe on an upper level of Dragão do Mar, and serves organic coffee, sandwiches, crepes, omelets, waffles, tapiocas and a plethora of fancier coffee drinks.

★**Colher de Pau** BRAZILIAN **$$**
(3267-6680; www.colherdepaufortaleza.com.br; Ana Bilhar 1178, Varjota; mains for 2 people R$30-153; 11am-midnight, closed Mon;) The large, mostly open-air 'Wooden Spoon' is one of the best places in a neighborhood thronged with popular midrange restaurants. It's great for seafood, including a superb chunky *peixada* (fish, vegetables and herbs in coconut sauce) and is consistently voted among the best in town for regional Northeastern cuisine. It's also got atmosphere; there's live *sertanejo* (northeastern country pop), samba and *forró* (northeastern country dance music) from 5pm Wednesday to Sunday.

Drinking & Entertainment

Iracema's legendary nightlife revolves around the bars and clubs surrounding Centro Cultural Dragão do Mar.

Boteco Praia BAR
(3248-4773; www.botecofortaleza.com.br; Av Beira Mar 1680, Meireles; 5pm-3am Mon-Fri, noon-3am Sat & Sun;) The number-one spot for evening drinks and conversation, Boteco Praia attracts all ages to its long, arcaded hall and its terrace facing the seafront promenade. You do pay for the privilege, though – R$7 per *chope*, and R$9 to R$54 for tempt-

ing portions such as *picanha* steak, grilled octopus and spicy sausage offered by the attentive waiters.

Órbita BAR
(www.orbitabar.com.br; Dragão do Mar 207, Praia de Iracema; admission R$30; 9pm-4am Thu-Sun;) Reminiscent of a college-town rock club (but with way better-looking people than your college most likely, or ours), this large, black-and-purple Dragão do Mar bar hosts live rock, surf and pop amid snooker tables and a legion of flirtatious upper-class clientele.

Mucuripe Music CLUB
(www.mucuripe.com.br; cnr Santo Dumont & Engenheiro Santana Júnior, Papicu; cover around R$25; 10pm-5am Fri) In addition to being the best and most stylish disco in the Northeast, Mucuripe Music's new space is a huge, modern, local venue holding 1500 people and featuring VIP suites near the stage, which skirts between DJs and live *forró*, *sertaneja*, *axé*, rock and more. If you lose a friend in here, they'll see you tomorrow.

Shopping

Ceará state has a strong craft tradition (Brazil's best hammocks!).

Ceart HANDICRAFTS
(www.fortaleza.ce.gov.br/turismo/produtos-artesanais; Centro Dragão do Mar; 9am-9pm Tue-Fri, 3-9pm Sat & Sun) This beautiful state-run craft store sells lace, ceramics, wood carvings, baskets and bags of sisal and *carnaúba* palm, and textiles. There's a branch in **Aldeota** (www.fortaleza.ce.gov.br/turismo/produtos-artesanais; Av Santos Dumont 1589, Aldeota; 9am-9pm Mon-Sat, 2:30-8:30pm Sun).

Information

Internet is widely available. There are ATMs at the airport, bus station, Mercado Central and along the Meireles strip, particularly around Av Abolição and the Club Náutico.

Casa do Turista (SETFOR; 3105-2670; www.fortaleza.ce.gov.br/turismo; Av Beira Mar, Mucuripe; 9am-9pm) The city tourism department operates this information booth on Meireles beach; staff may or may not speak English. You'll find good English map-guides and there are additional branches around the city, including Centro (3105-1444; Praça da Ferreira, Centro; 9am-5pm Mon-Fri, 8am-noon Sat) and Mercado Central (3105-1475; Basement level, Mercado Central, Av Nepomuceno 199; 9am-5pm Mon-Fri, 9am-noon Sat).

Deprotur (Delegacia de Proteção ao Turista; 3101-2488; www.policiacivil.ce.gov.br; Costa Barros 1971, Aldeota; 8am-6pm Mon-Fri) Tourist police in Fortaleza. Note the tourist police section is closed on weekends, but this is a 24-hour police station as well.

DANGERS & ANNOYANCES

Beware of pickpocketing and petty theft on beaches, buses, in the city center and along Beira-Mar.

Getting There & Around

Several airlines operate domestically from Fortaleza's **Aeroporto Pinto Martins** (3392-1200; Av Carlos Jereissati 3000); there are also international flights to Buenos Aires, Frankfurt, Lisbon, Miami and Milan. A fixed-rate taxi from the airport to Meireles or Praia de Iracema costs R$42.

Long-distance buses include Nordeste's service to Natal (R$86, nine hours), and Guanabara's services to São Luís (R$132, 19 hours) and Recife (R$92, 14 hours).

Local buses cost R$2.40 (R$1.80 on Sundays and holidays). Bus 013 'Aguanambi I', outside the bus station, runs north up Av Dom Manoel to the Centro Dragão do Mar, while route 078 'Siqueira/Mucuripe' connects the bus station to the beaches at Iracema and Meireles. Route 404 'Aeroporto Benfica Rodoviária' links the airport with the bus station.

Jericoacoara

0XX88 / POP 2000

A truly special place, Jericoacoara (pronounced 'je-ri-kwah-*kwah*-ra,' or just Jeri) offers nightlife, endless beaches and an idyllic remote setting. The sand-street village faces a broad gray beach, shouldered by a huge yellow sand dune and rolling green hills. The relaxed vibe keeps hip Brazilians and travelers staying longer than planned. It's one of South America's best destinations for wind sports and there's a longboarding wave great for learning to surf.

Jeri consists of six parallel *ruas* running westward toward the beach. Starting from the big sand dune and proceeding north, they are: Nova Jeri, Dunas, São Francisco, Principal, Forró and Igreja.

Despite steady growth, Jeri has retained much of its dreamy 'end-of-the-road' feeling. Hopefully the new Jericoacoara airport, which has been under construction 30km away in Cruz municipality on-and-off over the past few years, will not shatter Jeri's otherwordly allure when it finally opens.

Avoid *bichos de pé* (burrowing foot parasites) by not walking barefoot. Note that Jeri has no international-friendly ATM; the closest place to stock up with cash is an hour away at **Banco do Brasil** (Av Manoel Teixeira 139, Jijoca; branch 9am-2pm Mon-Fri, ATMs 7am-6pm daily) in Jijoca. Many places accept credit cards.

Sights & Activities

Whatever you do, don't miss the nightly pilgrimage to watch the sunset atop **Duna Pôr do Sol** (Sunset Dune), a towering mountain of sand at Jeri's western edge. Other popular activities include **buggy trips** to surrounding dunes and lakes, the 3km walk east of town to the rock arch **Pedra Furada**, and the traditional twilight **capoeira** circle on Jeri's main beach. Several outfits, including **MH Kiteschool** (3669-2268; www.mhkiteschool.com; Pousada Bella Jeri, Travessa da Rua do Forró), **Rancho do Kite** (3669-2080; www.ranchodokite.com.br; Principal, Preá; shop 10am-1pm & 3:30-11pm) and **Kiteiscool** (99670-2330; www.kiteiscool.com; Praça Principal; 8:30am-noon & 4:30-11pm) offer **wind-sport lessons** and rental gear.

Sleeping

With dozens of *pousadas* in town, you won't be short of a bed. During the wet season (March to June) prices drop dramatically and midrange places are a real bargain.

Jericoacoara Hostel HOSTEL $
(99747-8070; www.jericoacoarahostel.com.br; São Francisco 202; camping per person R$25, dm with fan/air-con R$50/60, d with fan/air-con R$160/195;) You won't be Instagramming its rather basic dorms and privates, but this hostel wins huge points for its welcoming atmosphere. The large patio and hammock space with well-stocked 'honor fridge' promote easy socializing, and trilingual manager Gaúcho is constantly assisting guests with travel advice, well-organized information boards and reasonably priced laundry service – and keeps on a watchful, anti-shenanigan patrol.

Villa Chic HOSTEL $$
(4062-9624; www.villachicjeri.com; Principal; dm R$65, r R$220;) If you've outgrown the hostel party scene, the excellent dorms here are Jeri's best, but exist within the environment of a boutique *pousada*. Each eight-bed dorm (one mixed, one male, one female) boasts one-and-a-half bathrooms

WORTH A TRIP

FROM JERICOACOARA TO THE LENÇÓIS MARANHENSES

The trip west from Jericoacoara to Parque Nacional dos Lençóis Maranhenses is one of South America's epic journeys. Depending on how you do it, the route can take anywhere from nine to 24 hours; in its most adventurous incarnation, it involves substantial stretches rattling along a rugged track between sand dunes, along deserted beaches, past isolated communities and gorgeous scenery.

The fastest and most costly option is a straight one-day transfer from Jericoacoara to the Lençóis Maranhenses. **Jeri Off Road** (p384) can get you there in about nine hours for around R$1300 (up to four people). The trip heads to Paulino Neves by car (6½ hours), then on to Caburé along the coast by 4WD (40 minutes), then to Barreirinhas by a scenic boat ride (must be reserved in advance), with optional sightseeing en route in the Delta do Parnaíba.

The best combination of speed and economy is on public transport and can be organized by **Global Connection** (p384) in Jericoacoara. You'll catch a late afternoon D-20 passenger truck to Jijoca (R$15, 40 minutes), then transfer to a 7pm bus (5pm on Sunday) operated by **2M** (3322-8596) to Paulino Neves (R$58, 6½ hours), arriving around 2am. Once here, you can either sleep overnight in Paulino Neves or continue with a 4am or 6am Toyota *jardineira* truck to Barreirinhas (R$30, two hours).

If you're not hell-bent on speed, a slower but more scenic alternative is to take a regular bus from Jijoca to Camocim, or a 4WD truck down the beach from Jericoacoara to Camocim, followed by a bus or minibus from Camocim to Parnaíba, where you can make onward connections to Paulino Neves and Barreirinhas.

Heading eastbound from the Lençóis to Jeri, public transportation schedules along the coast are less convenient, so a direct 4WD transfer is well worth considering.

(the 'half' has no shower), which are some of the most fashionable you'll come across at these prices.

Bella Jeri POUSADA **$$**
(☎3669-2268; www.bellajeri.com.br; Travessa da Rua do Forró; s/d R$200/250; ❄📶🏊) Bella Jeri has seven cute, tasteful rooms with brick walls, solid wood furniture and hammocks, plus a pleasant garden, pool and breezy roof terrace with views to the dune and the ocean. Breakfast is great, and the English-speaking owners also run Jeri Off Road (p384) and MH Kiteschool (p382), which makes it a one-stop shop for all you desire in Jeri.

Pousada Surfing Jeri POUSADA **$$**
(☎3669-2260; www.surfingjeri.com.br; São Francisco 150; d R$300-330; ❄📶🏊) Twenty-five solidly constructed rooms and apartments, with wood floors and ceilings, are set along a green, shady garden with a pool. It all adds up to a solidly sensible choice.

Eating

Several simple places around town offer *prato feito* (plate of the day) for less than R$20.

Club Ventos BUFFET **$**
(☎3669-2288; www.clubventos.com; Praia de Jericoacoara; per kg R$60; ⏲noon-5pm; 📶) Soak up the spectacular views from the cashew-tree-shaded oceanfront terrace at Jericoacoara's best *por kilo* eatery, then settle into a lounge chair and catch some rays for the rest of the afternoon. An excellent selection of salads and vegetable options compensate for the limited – but tasty – array of main dishes.

Jeri Jú BRAZILIAN **$**
(Forró; meals R$15-26; ⏲7:30-11:30am & 12:30-8pm) This neat, family-run lunch spot is the best of the local economical eats specializing in *pratos feitos* (daily meal specials).

Gelato & Grano ICE CREAM **$**
(Praça Principal 1; 1/2/3 scoops R$8/10/14; ⏲noon-midnight) If there's one thing you'll eventually pine for in this heat, it's ice cream. This wildly popular, farmhouse-chic gelato shop on the main square serves up 20 flavors and is constantly swarmed by sweet-toothed vacationers and locals alike. Brownie, Belgian chocolate and pistachio are the most popular, but Brazilian staples such as *açaí* and tapioca are here as well.

★**Peixe Brasileiro** SEAFOOD **$$**
(cnr São Francisco & Beco do Guaxêlo; fish/shrimp/lobster per kg R$45/90/130; ⏲7-11:30pm) Just a few tables in the sand alley where local fisherman grill fresh catch nightly. Pick your dinner by size from the family's *peixaria* next door: *pargo* (red snapper), *garoupa* (grouper), *robalo* (sea bass), shrimp and/or *langosta*. Weigh it, sit back and wait while they fire it up on the barbecue, garnished with nothing but lime and salt.

Drinking & Entertainment

Beachfront carts at the foot of Rua Principal sell inexpensive *caipirinhas* and other mixed drinks (R$7 to R$16) to crowds of revelers from early evening onward. Jeri has loads of nightspots with live music, including the legendary *forró* nights at **Restaurante Dona Amélia** (www.facebook.com/donaamelia.restaurante; Forró; ⏲11pm-3am Wed & Sat) and **Maloca** (Igreja), and Friday-night samba at **Pousada Solar de Malhada** (www.solardamalhada.com; Rua da Matriz). New venues pop up regularly, so ask around.

Samba Rock Cafe BAR
(www.sambarockcafe.com; Principal; cocktails R$10-20; ⏲9:45am-1:30am) Sitting on prime corner real estate across from the main square, this is easily Jeri's most atmospheric drinking spot. Rustic wood furniture seating is arranged under a massive, illuminated acacia tree. DJs spin electronica during happy hour from Thursday to Sunday (6pm to 8pm), and there's live MPB (Monday, Wednesday and Saturday), samba (Tuesday and Friday), reggae (Thursday) and Latin (Sunday).

Cachaçaria Gourmet BAR
(www.facebook.com/cachacariagourmetjeri; Travessa Ismael; cachaça R$8-20; ⏲6pm-midnight) If you'd like a stiff drink without a soundtrack, this cute and tiny bar specializes in Brazil's national firewater, *cachaça*. There are 90 or so labels, many of which come from Minas Gerais (as does the owner); around 30 labels are available at any given time, and the liquor is even mixed into frozen *caipirinhas* (a rarity, despite the obviousness of the idea!).

Getting There & Away

Fretcar (☎99700-7373; www.fretcar.com.br; São Francisco; ⏲6-6:15am, 8-11am, noon-5pm & 6-10:30pm) runs up to five daily buses from Fortaleza's bus station to Jericoacoara (from R$55, six to seven hours). Some of Fretcar's afternoon runs also pick up passengers at Fortaleza's airport and at the Praiano Hotel on Meireles beach before proceeding four hours west to Jijoca. The final leg of the journey (included in the ticket price) is a one-hour ride in a *jardineira* (open-sided 4WD truck) along sandy tracks through the dunes from Jijoca to Jericoacoara. Buy Fretcar tickets (a day ahead if possible) at **Beach Point** (☎3086-7055; www.beachpointceara.tur.br; cnr Av Beira Mar & Oswaldo Cruz, No 1 Beira-Mar Trade Center; ⌚9am-noon & 1-8pm) in Fortaleza or **Global Connection** (☎99900-2109; Forró; ⌚9am-10pm) in Jericoacoara.

Numerous companies, such as **Enseada** (☎3091-2762; www.enseada.tur.br; Av Monsenhor Tabosa 1001, Loja 10) and **Victorino** (☎3047-1047; www.vitorinotur.com.br; Av Monsenhor Tabosa 1067), also offer direct door-to-door van transfers from Fortaleza to Jeri (R$75, six hours).

The most exciting way of reaching Jericoacoara from Fortaleza is by 4WD along the coast – an option offered by agencies such as **Jeri Off Road** (☎3669-2268; www.jeri.tur.br; Pousada Bella Jeri, Travessa da Rua do Forró), which charges R$750 for up to four people.

São Luís

☎0XX98 / POP 1.1 MILLION

With its gorgeous colonial center offering just the right blend of crumbling elegance and unobtrusive renovation, São Luís is a real jewel in the Northeast's crown. The cobbled streets are lined with colorfully painted and appealingly tiled mansions, which have also earned a spot on Unesco's World Heritage list. São Luís has a rich folkloric tradition embodied by its colorful festivals and has become Brazil's reggae capital.

São Luís is divided into two peninsulas by the Rio Anil. On the southernmost, the Centro sits on a hill above the historic core of Praia Grande. On the northern peninsula lie affluent suburbs (São Francisco) and city beaches (Calhau).

Sights & Activities

The center of São Luís is the best-preserved colonial neighborhood in the Northeast, full of 18th- and 19th-century mansions covered in colorful European *azulejos* (decorative tiles). Since the late 1980s, Projeto Reviver (Project Revival) has made piecemeal progress in restoring life to the center after decades of neglect and decay. Many of the restored buildings now house government offices, cultural centers, museums, galleries, craft shops, pousadas, bars and restaurants.

On weekends, locals pack **Praia do Calhau**, a broad, attractive beach 9km from the center.

Casa de Nhôzinho MUSEUM
(Portugal 185; ⌚9am-6pm Tue-Sun) FREE At the eclectic and fascinating Casa do Nhôzinho, you can see a collection of ingenious fish traps, rooms of Maranhão indigenous artisanry, and hosts of colorful, delicate Bumba Meu Boi figurines made by the 20th-century master artisan Mestre Nhôzinho.

Casa das Tulhas MARKET
(Largo do Comércio; ⌚7am-8pm) This 19th-century market building now trades in an interesting variety of typical Maranhão crafts and foods, from dried prawns and Brazil nuts to an artificially colored purple cassava liquor called *tiquira* and regional soda Guaraná Jesus. It also has a couple of bars that get animated in late afternoon.

Festivals & Events

São Luís has one of Brazil's richest folklore traditions, evident in its many festivals, including Carnaval. For two to three weeks between early May and early June the city celebrates the **Festa do Divino Espírito Santo**, which has a uniquely strong Afro-Brazilian influence. São Luís' famous festival **Bumba Meu Boi** lasts through the second half of June. In July, the **Tambor de Mina** festivals are important events for followers of the Afro-Brazilian religions.

Sleeping

★ **Casa Frankie** POUSADA $
(☎3222-8198; www.casafrankie.com; Rua do Giz 394; s/d/tr R$80/100/120; ❄@🛜🏊) The historic center's best deal is overseen by a low-key Dane, who has restored this colonial mansion – a former brothel – into simple but superb budget sleeps. Rooms are huge but it

São Luís

Sights
1 Casa das Tulhas....B3
2 Casa de Nhôzinho....B3

Sleeping
3 Casa Frankie....B4
4 Pousada Colonial....C4
5 Solar das Pedras....C3

Eating
6 Dom Francisco....B3
7 Restaurante Senac....C3

Entertainment
8 Bar do Nelson....A2
9 Cafofinho da Tia Dica....B3

is the common spaces, including a breezy veranda with stunning original shutters, a lovely pool and a patio that wraps around a very giving mango tree, that set it apart.

Pousada Colonial POUSADA **$**
(☎3232-2834; www.hotelpousadacolonial.com.br; Afonso Pena 112; s/d/tr R$126/156/186; ❄@📶) A certain colonial charm pervades this refurbished old-town mansion, which featuresa an interior patio and unique raised *azulejos* inside and out. The rooms don't quite live up to the ambience, some having no natural light, but offer new mattresses with crisp sheets, split-system air-con and, in a few cases, views over the old town rooftops.

Solar das Pedras HOSTEL **$**
(☎3232-6694; www.ajsolardaspedras.com.br; Rua da Palma 127; dm/d R$40/90; 📶) This HI hostel in a restored 19th-century home has acceptable and clean facilities, including a sizable sitting area, though the rooms are rather dark and poorly ventilated, and the kitchen is small. Overall, it's the best backpacker option, but the architecture is the best thing it's got going for it. Discounts for HI members.

Eating

★**Restaurante Senac** BUFFET **$$**
(Rua de Nazaré 242; lunch buffet R$38, dinner mains for 2 people R$40-83; ⏲noon-3pm Mon-Sat, 7-11pm Fri; 📶) Showpiece for the São Luis branch of Brazil's best-known cooking school, this place gets packed at lunchtimes for its superb all-you-can-eat buffet, which includes a big salad bar and eight or 10 hot meat and seafood dishes, plus rice, vegetables, yummy desserts – and a piano man. Dinner is Friday nights only; there's a good regional à la carte menu.

L'Apero FRENCH, BRAZILIAN **$$**
(☎3727-8121; Av Litoranêa, Modulo 4A; mains R$35-44; ⏲11am-1am Tue-Sat, 10am-10pm Sun; 📶) This French-run hyperkiosk on São

São Luís

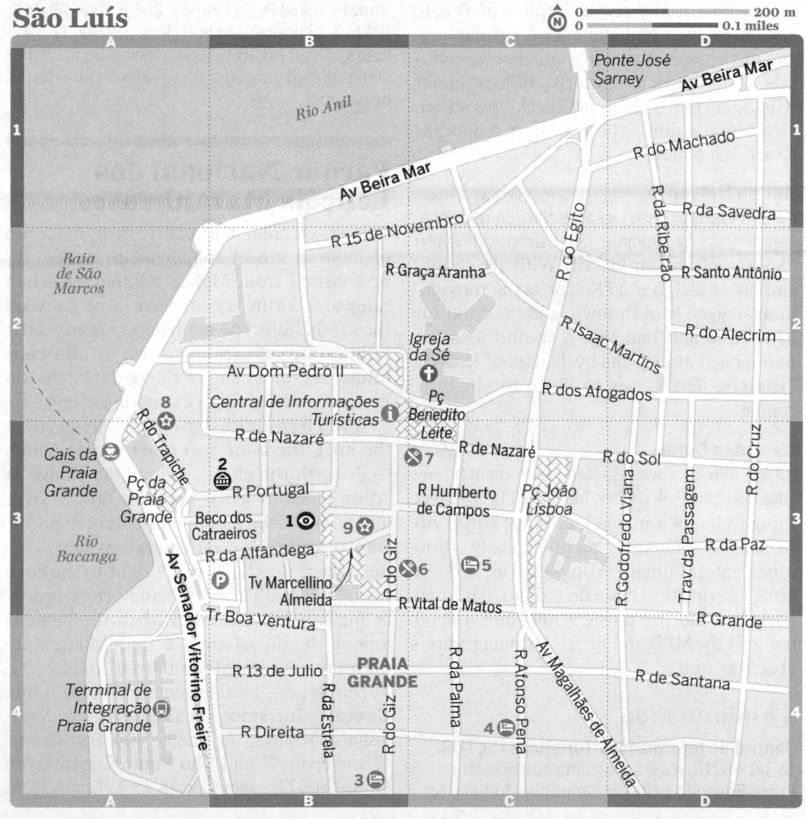

Marcos' sands is a great bet for good food, good music and good times, especially on Sundays, when everyone in São Luís knows it's the only gig in town! There's live music or DJs most nights of the week.

Dom Francisco BRAZILIAN **$$**
(Rua do Giz 155; lunch per kg R$34.90, mains R$25-35; ⏲11am-3:30pm & 6-11pm Mon-Sat) An excellent buffet that doesn't try to do every dish ever known to Maranhão, but rather a select repertoire of meals that are all wonderful. It's open at night for à la carte dining.

Drinking & Entertainment

The *barracas* along Ponta d'Areia, São Marcos and Calhau beaches are popular drinking spots, with the added attraction of a sea breeze and, in the evenings, live music.

In the Centro Historíco, things get lively in the evenings around Largo do Comércio, especially in front of **Cafofinho da Tia Dica** (Beco da Alfândega; ⏲11am-midnight), and along Rua da Trapiche near the water.

São Luís is the reggae capital of Brazil, and many bars and clubs have regular reggae nights, sometimes live, other times with DJs. Ask locals and tourist offices about what's currently hot, or check www.kamaleao.com/saoluis. There is also a vibrant GLBT scene here.

Bar do Nelson LIVE MUSIC
(☎98840-3196; www.facebook.com/bardonelson-reggaeroots; Av Litorânea 135, Calhau; admission R$5-20; ⏲9pm-3am Thu-Sat) With its shanty clubhouse feel, Bar do Nelson is the most famous reggae spot in town, and it's good for live music and dancing. A second location has opened among the lively bars of **Rua da Trapiche** (Rua da Trapiche 39) in the historic center.

Casa das Dunas LIVE MUSIC
(☎3227-8695; www.casadasdunasma.com.br; Av Litorânea s/n; ⏲4pm-2am Tue-Sun) The biggest thing to happen in São Luís since sliced *picanha:* this massive, architecturally stunning entertainment complex opened in 2015. Overlooking Praia do Calhau, it's equal parts bar and live-music venue, and a good bet for DJs, MPB and *forró*. Attracts national acts as well.

Information

Central de Informações Turísticas (SETUR; ☎3212-6210; www.saoluis.ma.gov.br/setur; Praça Benedito Leite; ⏲8am-6pm Mon-Fri, to noon Sat & Sun) The main information office of Setur, the city tourism department, and also the most helpful; English and French were spoken when we visited.

DETUR (Delegacia Especial de Turismo; ☎3214-8682; Rua da Estrela 427; ⏲8am-6pm Mon-Fri) São Luís' tourist police station for reporting crime and obtaining police reports. Unbelievably, English is not spoken.

Getting There & Around

São Luís's **Aeroporto Internacional de São Luís – Marechal Cunha Machado** (☎3217-6100; Av dos Libaneses, Tirirical), 12km southeast of town, is served by all major domestic airlines. A taxi into town costs R$48. Alternatively, bus 901 'São Cristóvão Aeroporto' (R$2.60) runs between the airport and Praça Deodoro, about 1km east of the Centro Histórico, but this is not a safe option at night.

São Luís's long-distance **bus station** (☎3243-1305; www.rodoviariasaoluis.com.br; Av dos Franceses 300, Santo Antônio), 8km southeast of the center, is reached by taxi (R$30 to R$37) or by the Vila Sarney/Africanos bus (R$2.60) from Terminal Praia Grande. Buses run to Belém (R$143, 13 hours) and Fortaleza (R$132, 17 hours). Night buses to Belém have a history of being robbed; consider flying, which can often be cheaper.

Parque Nacional dos Lençóis Maranhenses

This spectacular national park is made up of 1500 sq km of rolling white dunes. It's best visited from May to September, when rainwater forms crystal-clear lakes between the sandy hills. The main access point is the rather unprepossessing town of **Barreirinhas**, set on a bend of the picturesque Rio Preguiças near the park's southeast corner.

If you have at least two nights to spend in the area, there are two other access points well worth the effort. The remote village of **Atins** is sandwiched between dunes, river and ocean at the mouth of the Rio Preguiças. **Santo Amaro** is on the park's western border, where the dunes come right to the edge of the village. There are sandy river beaches for bathing here even when the lagoons among the dunes are dry. Both villages are far more charming than Barreirinhas.

Numerous local agencies – including **Caetés Turismo** (☎3349-0528; www.caetesturismo.com.br; Av Brasilía 40B, Barreirinhas; ⏲8am-6pm) and **São Paulo Ecoturismo** (☎3349-0079; www.saopauloecoturismo.com.br;

Av Brasília 108, Barreirinhas; 7am-8pm) – offer trips into the park. A common excursion from Barreirinhas is a half-day 4WD truck tour to **Lagoa Azul** (R$60) and **Lagoa Bonita** (R$70), two of the park's biggest lagoons. There is also a wonderful seven-hour boat tour (R$70, 8:30am daily) to the mouth of the Rio Preguiças, stopping to hike the dunes at Vassouras, climb the lighthouse at Mandacaru and eat at the day-trippers' beach of Caburé.

If you want to venture further into the park, you can organize memorable multi-day hikes with outfits such as **Terra Nordeste** (3221-1188; www.terra-nordeste.com; Rua do Giz 380; 9am-6pm Mon-Fri) and **Sandwalkers** (98864-0526; sandwalkers.ma@gmail.com; Atins).

Good budget lodging options include **Casa do Professor Hostel** (98808-2546; www.casadoprofessorhostel.com; Projectada 305, Barreirinhas; camp site/hammock/dm R$15/25/35;) in Barreirinhas, **Pousada Irmão Atins** (98864-4288; www.pousadairmaoatins.blogspot.com.br; Rua Principal, Atins; s/d with fan R$80/160, with air-con R$130/190;) in Atins and **Ciamat Camp** (99604-5824; www.ciamatcamp.com; Santo Amaro; s/d R$220/235) in Santo Amaro. For grilled fish, wood-fired pizza and live music nightly, head for **A Canoa** (Av Beira Rio 300, Barreirinhas; mains R$22-39; 11:30am-11:30pm;) on the riverside in Barreirinhas.

Cisne Branco (3243-2847; www.cisnebrancoturismo.com.br; Anacleto de Carvalho 623, Barreirinhas) runs four buses daily between São Luís and Barreirinhas (R$46.50, 4½ hours). Alternatively, vans (R$60) operated by **BRTur** (98896-6610; www.brtur.net.br; R$60) offer more efficient door-to-door service.

The easiest way to get to Atins is by hopping aboard a Toyota 4WD (R$25, two hours) from Barreirinhas, or taking the daily cruise down the Rio Preguiças and disembarking at the river mouth. Getting to Santo Amaro is more complicated; ask locally for details.

Barreirinhas can also be a jumping-off point for Jericoacoara.

RIVER TRAVEL

Riverboat travel is a unique Amazonian experience. Be warned that boats are always slow and crowded, often wet and smelly, sometimes dull and never comfortable. Do you like *forró* music? You won't after this trip! Luckily, Brazilians are friendly and river culture is interesting.

- Downstream travel is considerably faster than upstream, but boats heading upriver travel closer to the shore, which is more scenic.
- Boats often moor in port a few days before departing – check boat quality before committing.
- Fares vary little between boats. Tickets are best bought onboard or at official booths inside port buildings. Street vendors may offer cheaper prices but you run the risk of being cheated.
- *Camarotes* (cabins) are usually available and afford additional privacy and security. Ensure that yours has a fan or air-con. *Camarotes* are usually the same price as flying.
- Put up your hammock (available at any market from R$20; don't forget rope!) several hours before departure. There are usually two decks for hammocks; try for a spot on the upper one (the engine's below), away from the smelly toilets. Others are likely to sling their hammocks above and/or below yours. Porters may offer to help you tie yours for a small tip: well worth it if knots aren't the ace in your pack.
- Bring a rain jacket or poncho, sheet or light blanket, toilet paper and diarrhea medication.
- Meals (included) are mainly rice, beans and meat, with water or juice to drink. It's advisable to bring a few liters of bottled water, fruit and snacks. There is usually a snack bar on the top deck.
- Watch your gear carefully, especially just before docking and while at port. Lock zippers and wrap your backpack in a plastic bag. Keep valuables with you. Get friendly with people around you, as they can keep an eye on your stuff.

North Brazil

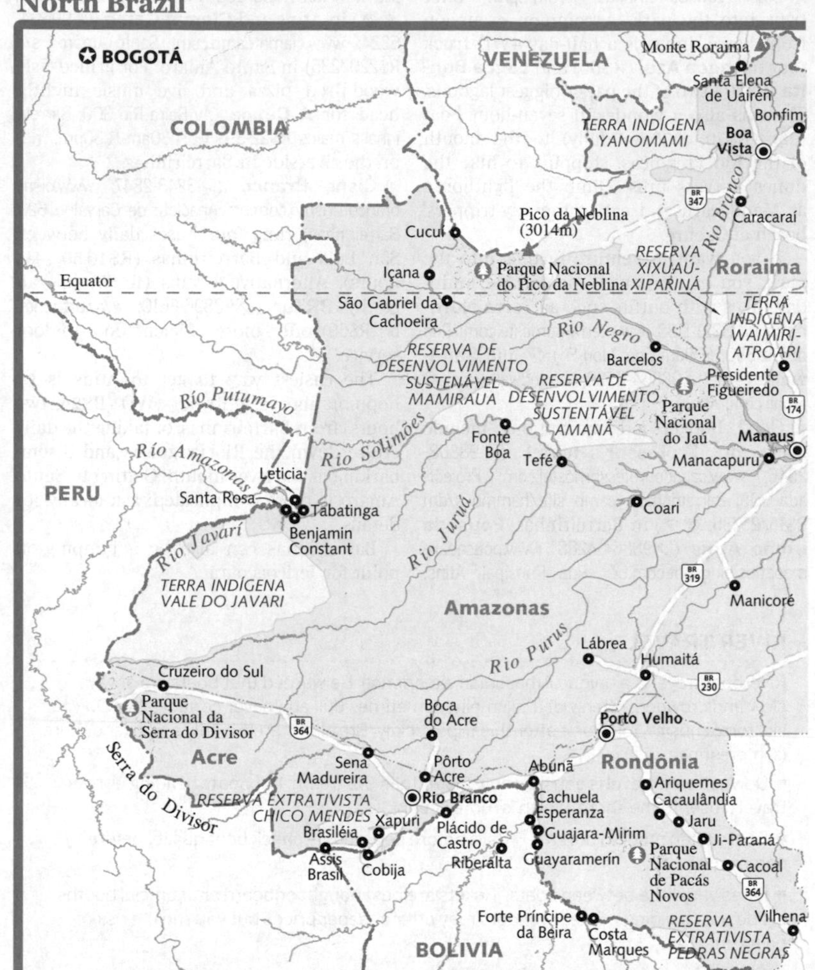

THE NORTH

The Amazon conjures a romantic, near-mythical image in our minds, but nowadays also an urgently real one. The future of this immense expanse of rivers and jungle, a vital lung for the world, is of huge importance.

The numbers alone are mind-boggling: the Amazon Basin contains six-million sq km of river and jungle, and just over half is in Brazil. It contains 17% of the world's fresh water and the main river-flow at its mouth is 12 billion liters per minute.

While you can still have amazing wildlife experiences in the vastness of the forest here, it's important to realize that pouncing jaguars and bulging anacondas are rare sightings. Nevertheless, a trip into the jungle ecosystem is deeply rewarding, both for wildlife-watching and the chance to appreciate how local communities have adapted to this water world. Manaus is a popular base for river trips, but there are other good possibilities. The main city, Belém, is an appealing launchpad to the region, while the tranquil white sands of Alter do Chão make a peaceful stopover on your way upriver.

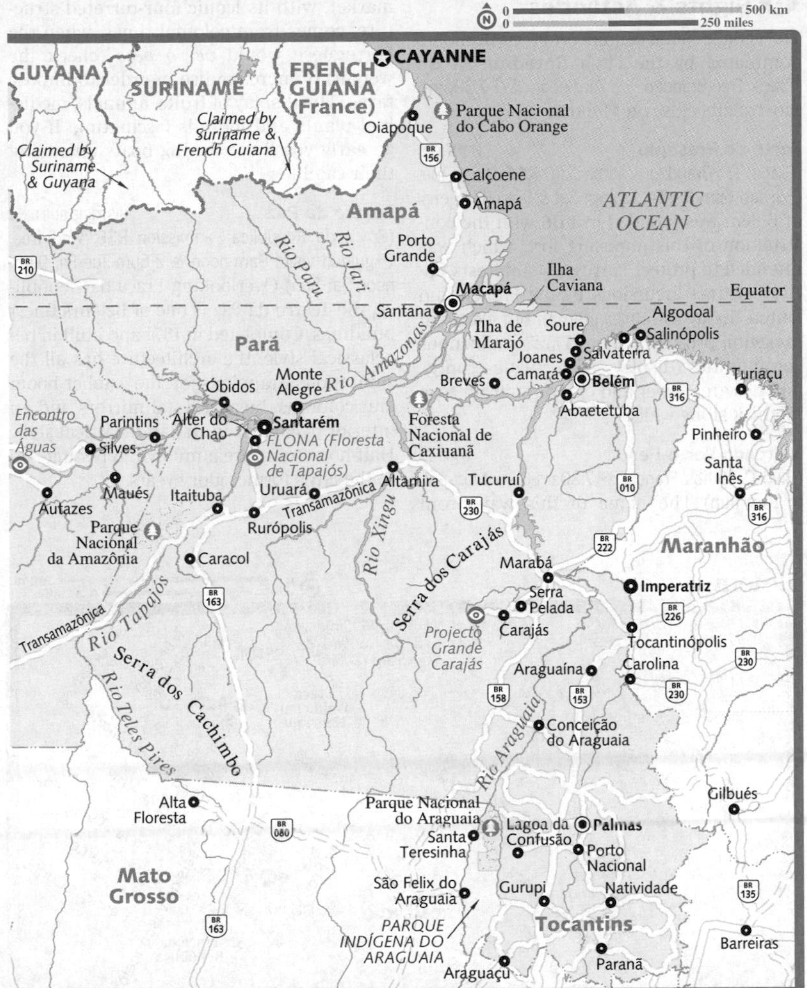

Getting There & Around

Bus travel is limited to a few routes in the North, so rivers serve as highways. Competing airlines occasionally offer fares cheaper than hammock-boat prices; check for specials.

Belém

0XX91 / POP 1.4 MILLION

Prosperous Belém has a cultural sophistication unexpected from a city so isolated. Its wealth comes from its position at the gateway to the Amazon; everything from timber to soybeans passes through here before going to market. Belém has recently invested in tourism, with impressive results. If you take some time to wander the mango-tree-lined boulevards, indulge in its parks and museums, and savor its prime perspective on the Amazon River, this attractive city will reward like few others in Brazil.

The compact Comércio business district, roughly between Av Presidente Vargas and Av Portugal, is noisy by day and deserted by night. The quieter Cidade Velha (Old City) contains Belém's historical buildings. East of the center, prosperous Nazaré has some chic shops and restaurants.

Sights & Activities

The Cidade Velha centers on Praça Brandão, dominated by the city's **Catedral da Sé** (Praça Frei Brandão; ⏲7am-noon & 2-7:30pm). Most sights close on Monday.

Forte do Presépio FORTRESS

(Praça Fr Brandão; admission R$4, free Tue; ⏲10am-6pm Tue-Fri, to 2pm Sat & Sun) The city of Belém was founded in 1616 with the construction of this imposing fort, which was intended to protect Portuguese interests upriver against incursions by the French and Dutch. Today it houses a small but excellent museum, primarily about Pará's indigenous communities (displays in Portuguese only), and has great river and city views from atop its thick stone walls.

Mercado Ver-o-Peso MARKET

(Blvd Castilhos França; ⏲7:30am-6pm Mon-Sat, to 1pm Sun) The name of this waterfront market, with its iconic four-turreted structure, comes from colonial times, when the Portuguese would *ver o peso* (check the weight) of merchandise in order to impose taxes. The display of fruits, animals, medicinal plants and more is fascinating. If you go early you'll see fishing boats unloading their catch.

Teatro da Paz HISTORIC BUILDING

(Praça da República; admission R$6, Wed free; ⏲guided visits 9am-noon & 2-6pm Tue-Fri, 9am-noon Sat-Sun) Overlooking Praça da República, the Teatro da Paz is one of Belém's finest buildings. Completed in 1874 and built in neoclassical style, the architecture has all the sumptuous trappings of the rubber-boom era: columns, busts, crystal mirrors and an interior decorated in Italian theatrical style. Half-hour tours are a mildly interesting trip to the city's former glory years.

Belém

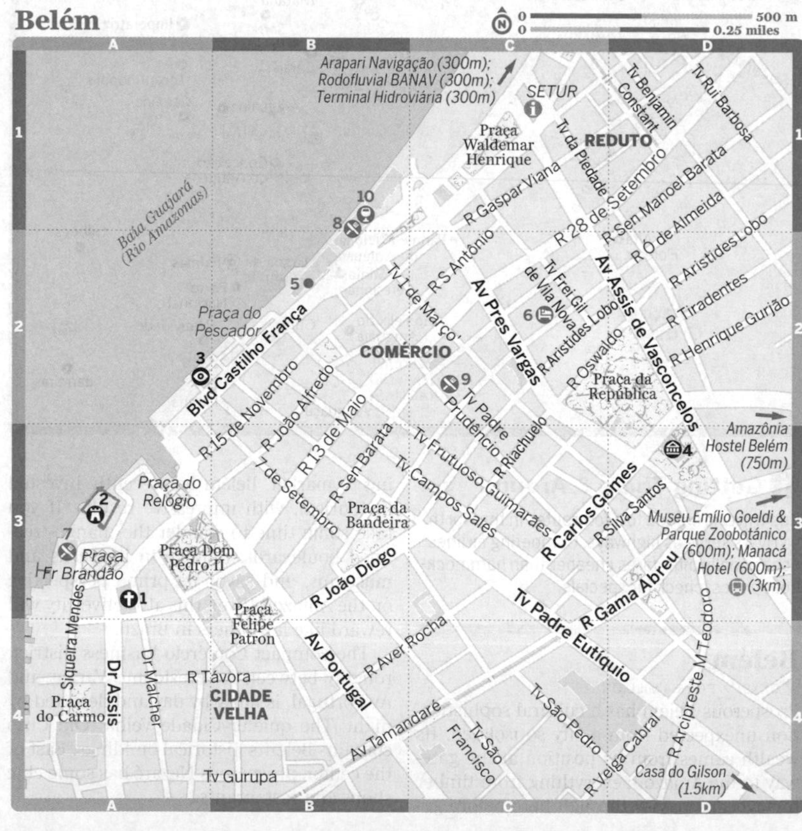

Museu Emílio Goeldi & Parque Zoobotánico ZOO
(☎3219-3300; www.museu-goeldi.br; Av Governador Magalhães Barata 376; park, aquarium & permanent exhibit each R$2; ⏰9am-5pm Tue-Sun) This excellent museum and zoo contains many Amazonian animal species, from manatees and anacondas to jaguars and giant otters, plus an aviary, aquarium and excellent permanent exhibit of artifacts from ancient Amazonian peoples. It's popular with families on Sundays.

Valeverde BOAT TOUR
(☎3213-3388; www.valeverdeturismo.com.br; Estação das Docas) Offers a variety of short tours on the river (per person R$45 to R$160), including sunrise bird-watching tours and pleasant evening cruises. Valeverde has an office and daily schedule at the pier at Estação das Docas; in most cases you can simply show up.

Festivals & Events

Círio de Nazaré RELIGION
During the Círio de Nazaré, which happens on the second Sunday in October, a million people accompany the image of the Virgin of Nazaré from the cathedral to the Basílica de NS de Nazaré. Two weeks of serious partying follow.

Sleeping

Hotel Unidos HOTEL $
(☎3221-0660; www.hotelunidos.com.br; Ó de Almeida 545; s/d/tr R$100/120/150; ❄@📶) Unidos has large spotless rooms and competent, welcoming staff. The decor is admittedly plain with only small windows, but the rates are lower than comparably equipped alternatives, and there's an additional 15% discount for paying in cash. Easy walking distance to many restaurants and sights, and close to the bus stops for everything else.

Amazônia Hostel Belém HOSTEL $
(☎3278-4355; www.amazoniahostel.com.br; Av Governador José Malcher 592; dm R$54, s/d R$81/111, without bathroom R$71/103; ❄@📶) A century-old rubber-baron mansion in a safe area is the perfect home for Belém's longest-running youth hostel. Smallish dorms have solid bunks and large lockers, plus 4m ceilings and gorgeous wood floors. Internet, kitchen and laundry are welcome features. Prices are high for a hostel, and management is oddly stingy with breakfast and linens, but it's still a nice spot.

★Manacá Hotel HOTEL $$
(☎3222-9224; www.manacahotel.com.br; Travessa Quintino Bocaiúva 1645; s/d/tr R$155/180/210; ❄📶🏊) Rooms in this boutique hotel are cozy and up to date (though a bit dark), while the common areas have beautiful wood and stone floors, and creative artwork on the walls. The neighborhood is equally appealing, with stylish shops and restaurants. Small swimming pool.

Eating

Belém is known for *pato no tucupí* (duck in manioc juice and tongue-tingling jambu leaf sauce), Tacacá (a gummy soup made from manioc root, dried shrimp and jambu leaves) and *maniçoba* (black beans, pork and manioc leaves). Classic budget eateries include the Tacacá stands near Basílica de NS de Nazaré, and the vendors selling cheap juices, *salgados* (snacks) and *pratos feitos* in Mercado Ver-o-Peso.

Govinda Belem INDIAN $
(☎3222-2272; www.restaurantegovindabelem.blogspot.com.br; Travessa Padre Prudencio 166; R$20; ⏰11:30am-3pm Mon-Fri, noon-2:30pm Sat; 🌱) Dishes here are Indian-ish (samosas, dahl, etc) with tell-tale signs you're still in Brazil (farofa, jambu) but still perfectly tasty and fully vegetarian – a welcome change from typical Brazilian fare and drawing a diverse clientele. Select three or four dishes from a menu divided by the day; Saturdays are the most inventive. Warmly decorated with fast friendly service.

Belém

★ **Estação das Docas** RESTAURANTS $$
(www.estacaodasdocas.com.br; Blvd Castilho França; ⏲10am-midnight Sun-Wed, to 3am Thu-Sat) One of the best places in Belém to eat no matter what you're hungry for. The bustling complex has almost a dozen restaurants, most with indoor and outdoor seating and open for lunch, dinner and late-night feasting. Favorites include Lá em Casa, serving pricey but outstanding regional food, and Amazon Beer, with tasty pub grub to accompany its artisanal beer.

Boteco das Onze BRAZILIAN $$
(Praça Frei Brandão; mains R$21-63; ⏲noon-midnight Tue-Sun, 5pm-midnight Mon) Part of Casa das Onze Janelas gallery, this is one of the city's best restaurant-bars. It has an indoor dining room with modern art on the walls and a breezy back patio overlooking the river. Meals include *moqueca de filhote*, a tasty stew prepared with catfish, shrimp and lobster. Live music most nights.

Drinking & Entertainment

Amazon Beer BEER HALL
(www.amazonbeer.com.br; Av Marechal Hermes, Estação das Docas; ⏲5pm-1am) As much as Brazilians love beer, it can be surprisingly tough to find anything heftier than a pilsner. This award-winning brewery is an exception, with an amber ale, a Dutch *witbier* (wheat beer), an IPA, even a unique *açaí* stout, all brewed on-site. Indoor and outdoor seating, a full menu, even souvenir beer glasses for sale. Often very busy.

Casa do Gilson LIVE MUSIC
(☎3272-7306; Travessa Padre Eutíquio 3172; ⏲8pm-3am Fri, noon-3am Sat & Sun) Come here for Belém's best live music. Opened in 1987, Gilson's draws intellectuals and hipsters alike with first-rate samba, *choro* (improvised samba-like music) and other music, and terrific food and atmosphere to boot. It's between ruas Nova and Tambés.

Information

Estação das Docas (Blvd Castilhos França) Numerous ATMs in a secure setting.

SETUR (☎3212-0575; www.paraturismo.pa.gov.br; Praça Waldemar Henrique; ⏲8am-2pm Mon-Fri) A reasonably helpful branch office of the state tourism department.

Tourist Police (CIPTUR) (☎3212-0948; Praça Waldemar Henrique s/n, Paratur Office)

DANGERS & ANNOYANCES

Comércio has a reputation for muggings when fairly empty (at night and on Sunday). Take a taxi at night. Pickpocketing is common at Mercado Ver-o-Peso.

Getting There & Away

AIR

Abundant domestic connections as well as flights north to Suriname leave from Belém's **Aeroporto Internacional Val-de-Cans** (☎3210-6000), 8km north of the center. Buses 634 'E Marex–Arsenal' and 638 'Pratinha–P Vargas' run between the traffic circle outside the airport and downtown Belém (R$2.50, 40 minutes). Taxis cost R$50.

BOAT

Boats use Belém's handsomely renovated **Terminal Hidroviária** (Av Marechal Hermes). Tickets are sold at booths inside. Boats to Santarém (hammock/cabin R$230/800, three to four days) and Manaus (hammock/cabin R$370/1200, five to six days) depart on Wednesday and Friday, plus every other Tuesday.

BUS

The bus station is on Av Almirante Barroso, 3km east of the center. To get downtown, catch the 316 'Guamá–P Vargas' bus from across the road. Going to the bus station, take the same bus from Av Presidente Vargas. Taxis to points along Av Presidente Vargas cost between R$20 and R$22.

Sample travel times and fares from Belém include the following:

DESTINATION	DURATION (HR)	COST (R$)
São Luís	10	131
Fortaleza	24	266
Salvador	33	360
Rio de Janeiro	50-53	425-550

Algodoal

☎0XX91

Accessible only by boat, Algodoal is a simple village in an idyllic situation. Its sand streets, lack of cars, cheap accommodations and white beaches make it a relaxing place to kick back.

The village consists of three long parallel streets. At the far end you can cross a small river (wade at low tide, canoe at high) to lovely Praia do Farol, which turns a corner and becomes 8km-long Praia da Princesa.

There are other small hamlets on this island, cut by channels into three main parts. Make your way around on foot, horse and cart, or canoe.

Every second home is nominally a *pousada*, most of which offer very basic rooms, hammocks and maybe a place to camp; bring a mosquito net. Competition keeps prices low, and many places offer wi-fi. Good options include **Hotel Bela Mar** (☎3854-1128; http://belamarhotel.blogspot.com.br; Magalhães Barata; s/d with fan R$60/80, with air-con & minibar R$70/100; ❄), the first hotel you reach from the boat drop-off, and **Pousada Ponta do Boiador** (☎99215-9939; www.boiador.com; Bertoldo Costa; d standard/suite R$150/180; ❄📶), offering direct beach access and a large waterfront deck with meal service, cold beers and occasional live music.

Most hotels serve meals. Family-run **Restaurante La Izla** (Bertolda Costa; mains R$15-30; ⏲11am-11pm) has tables on a sunny patio and a menu of Brazilan basics (fried fish, meat, rice and beans) painted on the wall of the owners' clapboard home.

There are no ATMs, and not all hotels accept credit cards – bring cash from Belém.

Access is via mainland Marudá. **Rápido Excelsior** (☎3249-6365) runs buses (R$21.50, four hours, four daily) from Belém's bus station to Marudá's port, where boats for Algodoal (R$7, 40 minutes) leave five times daily. **Sinprovan** (☎3226-5879) operates quicker air-conditioned minibuses (R$31, 3½ hours) from Belém to Marudá, but these drop you five long blocks from the port. At Algodoal, donkey-cart drivers greet arriving boats, vying for the chance to take you to your hotel (per person R$10); alternatively, it's only a 10-minute stroll into the village.

Ilha de Marajó

☎0XX91 / POP 250,000

Lying at the mouth of the Amazon, this verdant island is larger than 70 of the world's countries but much of its interior is swampy and inaccessible. Though the main settlement, Breves, is in the island's southwest, three southeastern villages – Soure, Salvaterra and Joanes – are easily reached from Belém and make for a relaxing visit. The island is notable for its hospitable people and *carimbó*, a colorful folkloric dance. Buffalo are another trademark and their meat appears on most restaurant menus. Do as the locals do and hire a bike to get around.

Joanes

Closest to Camará, where the boat comes in, Joanes is a sleepy hamlet with the fragments of a 17th-century Jesuit church and a good sandy beach. Livestock wander grassy streets lined with a few shops and sandwich stands. Attractive **Pousada Ventania do Rio-Mar** (☎3646-2067; www.pousadaventania.com; Quarta Rua; s/d R$125/155) sits atop a breezy headland overlooking the shore. The beach is just steps away, and the staff can arrange a variety of excursions, including canoeing and fishing with local guides. Cash only.

Salvaterra

About 18km north of Joanes, Salvaterra has more of a town feel and the island's best and longest beach, Praia Grande.

On an oceanfront lot shaded by mango trees, **Pousada Bosque dos Aruãs** (☎3765-1115; Segunda Rua; s/d R$85/100, suite s/d R$155/175; ❄📶) offers good, simple wooden cabins on stilts overlooking the water. It's somewhat shabby, but very peaceful, with a great restaurant. Praia Grande is a 10-minute walk away.

Soure

Soure, the biggest town on this side of the island, has a spread-out grid of streets that peter out into buffalo paths. **Banco do Brasil** (Rua 3 btwn Travessas 17 & 18; ⏲10am-3pm Mon-Fri) and **Bradesco** (Rua 2 btwn Travessas15 & 16; ⏲10am-3pm Mon-Fri) have ATMs. **Bimba** (Rua 4 btwn Travessas 18 & 19; per hour/day R$2/15) rents bicycles and **Cyber Gigabyte** (Travessa 15 at Rua 2; per hr R$2.50; ⏲8:30am-noon & 3:30-7:30pm Mon-Sat) offers internet.

In town, visit **Cerâmica Mbara-yo** (Travessa 20 btwn Ruas 3 & 4), the workshop of award-winning ceramicist Carlos Amaral, whose work combines Aruã and Marajoara ceramic traditions. A 3km bike ride north of Soure leads to **Praia Barra Velha**, where shacks sell drinks and seafood. Beyond lies **Praia de Araruna**, a long, starkly beautiful and practically deserted beach. There's an intervening river, which requires a boat at high tide. Alternatively, follow Rua 4 inland to **Praia do Pesqueiro** (11km), another popular weekend beach.

Three nearby *fazendas* (ranches) make for interesting half-day trips. **Fazenda Bom Jesus**, **Fazenda São Jerônimo** and **Fazenda Araruna** offer the same basic activities, including riding water buffalo, visiting mangroves and beaches, and spotting birds, monkeys and other animals.

Next to the tall Cosampa water towers, **Hotel Araruna** (8793-2481; nelsonmarajo@hotmail.com; Travessa 14 btwn Ruas 7 & 8; s/d R$75/99) offers large simple budget rooms; for spiffier accommodations with wi-fi, try **Pousada O Canto do Francês** (3741-1298; http://ocantodofrances.blogspot.com.br; cnr Rua 6 & Travessa 8; s/d R$120/150). **Pousada Restaurante Ilha Bela** (Rua 1 at Travessa 13; R$20-30; 7am-3pm & 6-11:30pm, closed Tue) serves fresh typical *marajoara* fare, including fried fish and buffalo steak, with live music on Friday evenings.

Getting There & Around

Arapari Navigação (3241-4977) and **Rodofluvial BANAV** (3269-4494, 8047-2440) run boats from Belém's Terminal Hidroviário to Camará (deck/air-con VIP lounge R$20/35, three hours) Monday through Saturday at 6:30am and 2:30pm, and Sunday at 10am, returning at 6:30am and 3pm (Sunday at 3pm only). Waiting buses and air-con minivans whisk passengers from Camará's dock to Joanes (R$7), Salvaterra (R$7) and Soure (R$10 to R$15).

The centers of Salvaterra and Soure are linked by a boat (R$2, 15 minutes) that leaves when full (this can take a while). A few kilometers west of Salvaterra, an hourly vehicle ferry (free, five minutes) crosses a much narrower channel to Soure. *Mototaxis*, taxis and infrequent vans move people around the island.

Santarém

0XX93 / POP 295,000

Most travelers rush between Belém and Manaus, skipping over the very thing they are desperate to see: the Amazon. A stop in riverfront Santarém not only breaks up a long boat trip, but also provides a chance to investigate the jungle and communities seen from your hammock. Santarém itself is rather bland, but the lovely river beaches and beautiful rainforest preserves nearby may entice you to prolong your stay.

Sights

Santarém's waterfront provides a nice perspective on the meeting of the waters between the tea-colored Rio Tapajós and the *café-au-lait* Rio Amazonas. The two flow side by side for a few kilometers without mingling.

Museu Dica Frazão MUSEUM
(Peixoto 281; admission by donation; 8am-6pm Mon-Sat) Dona Dica Frazão has spent three-quarters of a century making clothing and fabrics from natural fibers, including grasses and wood pulp. Approaching 100 years old and lately confined to a wheelchair, she's still at it, making artwork and guiding guests through the display room of her creations, including a dress made for a Belgian queen, a tablecloth for a Pope and costumes for the Boi-Bumbá festival.

Sleeping & Eating

Hotel Encontro das Águas HOTEL $
(3522-1287; encontrodasaguashotel@hotmail.com; 24 de Octubro 808; s R$95, d R$115-130;) Large clean rooms have OK beds, fairly modern bathrooms and an affordable price, making them popular with tourists, families and traveling business people alike. Friendly attentive service, and a convenient location just west of the market. Some rooms have large windows with river views and nice natural light.

★**Restaurante Piracema** BRAZILIAN $
(3522-7461; www.restaurantepiracema.com.br; Av Mendonca Furtado 73; R$20-45; 11am-11:30pm Tues-Sat, until 3pm Sun) Considered by many to be the best restaurant in town, Piracema uses regional ingredients and flavors but serves dishes you'll find nowhere else. The signature dish is the *peixe á Piracema*, a spherical construction of layered smoked pirarucú (a freshwater fish), banana and cheese – strange but delicious, and large enough for two.

Getting There & Around

AIR

Azul, Gol, MAP and TAM fly to Manaus and/or Belém from Santarém's **Eduardo Gomes Airport** (STM), 14km west of the center. A taxi into town costs R$60. The 'Aeroporto' bus (R$2.25, 30 minutes) runs irregularly from early morning until about 6pm, with reduced service on weekends. Be careful not to catch the 'Aeroporto Velho' bus, which goes to where the airport used to be.

BOAT

Boats to Manaus (hammock/double cabin R$150/600, 40 to 48 hours, noon Monday to

Saturday) and Belém (hammock/double cabin R$180/800, 48 hours, 11am Friday to Monday) leave from Docas do Pará, 2.5km west of the center.

The 'Orla Fluvial' minibus (R$2.25) connects the downtown waterfront with both ports every 20 to 30 minutes until 7pm. Taxis and *mototaxis* to Docas do Pará cost R$15 and R$4, respectively.

BUS

Buses to Alter do Chão (R$2.50, 60 minutes, roughly hourly) or the airport can be caught along Av Rui Barbosa.

Long-distance buses leave Santarém's bus station (2.5km west of town) for Cuiabá (36 hours) when road conditions permit, but service is extremely unreliable in the rainy season.

Around Santarém

Floresta Nacional (Flona) Do Tapajós

Behemoth *samaúma* trees, with trunks too big for even 20 people to stretch their arms around, are a highlight of this 5440-sq-km reserve on the east side of the Rio Tapajós. Within the reserve, numerous small communities live primarily by rubber tapping, fishing and gathering Brazil nuts. Several also have modest ecotourism initiatives, and a trip here is a unique way to experience not just the forest, but also village life within it.

The riverside villages of **Maguarí** and **Jamaraquá** have been hosting travelers the longest, and have the most established accommodations, tours and other services. A third village, **São Domingo**, is at the entrance to the reserve and has modest tourist options as well.

ICMBio (☎3522-0564; www.icmbio.gov.br/flonatapajos; Av Tapajós 2267, Santarém) oversees the reserve and has a base station in São Domingo. Boats and buses entering the reserve stop to allow tourists to register, but there is no longer an entrance fee.

Buses from Santarém to Maguarí and Jamaraquá (R$9, two to three hours) depart at 11am Monday to Saturday, and 6:30am Sunday. Return buses depart Jamaraquá at 4:30am and 6am Monday to Saturday, and at 4:30pm Sunday. The Sunday bus is air-conditioned.

You can also get to Flona by boat from Alter do Chão. Freelance boatmen do day trips for around R$100 per person, but it's a tiring three hours each way in a small motorized canoe, and does not include guide service. The tour agencies charge R$180 to R$200 per person, including a local guide and using faster and more comfortable motorboats. The agencies also do overnight trips to Flona, sleeping on board a river boat.

Alter do Chão

☎0XX93 / POP 7000

Bank on spending longer than you planned at this wonderfully relaxed riverside haven. With its white-sand river beaches and tropical ambience, Alter do Chão is one of Amazonia's most beautiful places to unwind. Beaches are best from June to December (they're more covered in water at other times) but Alter is worth a visit at any time of year.

Opposite the town square, the **Ilha do Amor** is an idyllic sand island in the Rio Tapajós featured on numerous postcards. Nearby, the large **Lago Verde** lagoon is great to explore by boat or canoe. Surrounding attractions include the Flona do Tapajós rainforest and the **Rio Arapiunes**, with blinding white beaches and clear waters.

On the square there's free wi-fi and a **Banco do Brasil ATM** (inside Mini-Center Mingote, Praça 7 de Setembro; ⏲6:30am-8:30pm Mon-Sat, to 7:30pm Sun); some businesses accept credit cards.

Activities

Paddle across to the Ilha do Amor (watch for stingrays), or, when the water's higher, take a rowboat (R$8 return). Kayak rentals are available on the island.

Mãe Natureza ECOTOUR
(☎99131-9870, 3527-1264; www.maenaturezaecoturismo.com.br; Praça 7 de Setembro; ⏲8:30am-1pm & 4-11pm) A reliable and experienced agency run by genial Argentinean expats. Be sure to ask about week-long adventure tours to remote indigenous areas and the Brinco das Moças waterfall, deep in RESEX Tapajós-Arapiuns. Day trips including tree-climbing, kite-surfing, or stand-up paddling can also be arranged.

Festivals & Events

Marked with dancing and processions, the **Festa do Çairé** in the second week of September is the major folkloric event in western Pará.

Sleeping & Eating

There are many low-key and backpacker-friendly accommodations.

★**Pousada do Tapajós Hostel** HOSTEL, INN $
(99210-2166; pousadatapajos.com.br; Rua Lauro Sodré 100; dm R$50, d/tr/q R$140/165/195;) Five blocks west of the center, dorms here are clean and comfortable, though a bit cramped, with sturdy bunks and large lockers. Private rooms are sparkling, modern and well-removed from the dorms. Ample breakfast, open kitchen, large backyard with hammocks. Guests (and even some non-guests) often get together over breakfast to book excursions. Spotty wi-fi.

Albergue da Floresta HOSTEL, POUSADA $$
(99209-5656; www.alberguedafloresta-alterdochao.blogspot.com; Travessa Antônio Pedrosa s/n; hammock R$30, dm $50, cabin s R$120, d R$170-200) This relaxed backpacker favorite has a spacious hammock area, dorms and colorful wood cabins with fans and private bathrooms; breakfast available for R$20 and there's an outdoor kitchen. It's nestled in the trees east of the center; follow the signs past Espaço Alter do Chão up a leafy dirt road. Angolan capoeira classes, bike and kayak rental.

Tribal BRAZILIAN $
(Travessa Antônio Lobato; dishes R$10-36; 11am-11pm) Churrasco plates come with a spear of steak, sausage, chicken and tongue, while well-prepared fish dishes serve two easily, with potato salad to spare. This spacious two-floor open-air dining area is located a block and a half up from the plaza, on the opposite side of Rua Dom Macedo.

Siria VEGETARIAN $
(Travessa Agostinho Lobato S/N; R$20; lunch-dinner;) The lovely chef-owner prepares just one vegan entree per sitting, served as a *prato feito* (plate of the day) and announced on a sandwich board in front. From chickpea omelets to vegetable tarts, count on it being outstanding, served with brown rice, fresh salad and creative drinks, like hibiscus and *maracujá* (passion fruit) iced tea, plus dessert. Colorful outdoor dining area, occasional live music and movies.

Entertainment

★**Epaço Alter do Chão** LIVE MUSIC
(9122-9643; www.espacoalter.com.br; End of PA-457; cover from R$14; 8am-1am Tue-Sat;) There's always something worth seeing at this cool music-culture-restaurant space at the east end of the waterfront promenade. There's live *carimbó* most Saturday nights, and guest bands play rock, *forró*, samba, reggae and more; check Facebook or the chalk board out front for the latest. Meals and drinks are tasty, too, though service can be slow. Free wi-fi.

Shopping

★**Araribá Cultura Indígena** HANDICRAFTS
(3527-1324; www.araribah.com.br; Travessa Antônio Lobato; 9am-9pm) Arguably the best indigenous art store in the Amazon, with items ranging from inexpensive necklaces to museum-quality masks and ceremonial costumes, and representing communities throughout the Amazon basin. Shipping available; credit cards accepted.

Getting There & Away

Hourly buses run to Santarém (R$2.50, one hour) from the corner of Rua Dom Macedo Costa and Travessa Antônio A Lobato (one block up from Praça 7 de Setembro). Coming from Santarém's airport, take the hourly bus to the Alter do Chão intersection and wait there for the Santarém-Alter do Chão bus. A taxi from the airport costs R$90.

Manaus

0XX92 / POP 1.8 MILLION

The mystique of Manaus, the city in the heart of the Amazon jungle and a major port 1500km from the sea, wears off fairly fast – it's a sprawling, largely unromantic spot that doesn't make the most of its riverside position. This is changing little by little, with restoration of noble buildings from the rubber-boom days. Manaus is a friendly place, the transport hub of the Amazon region and the most popular place to organize a jungle trip. Once you're back from a few days in the wild, luxuries such as air-conditioning will make you feel friendlier toward the place.

Teatro Amazonas is the heart of downtown. Adjacent Praça São Sebastião has colorfully restored buildings, terrace cafes, and live music or cultural displays most nights from 7pm. The U-shaped area defined by Av Epaminondas, Av Floriano Peixoto and Av Getúlio Vargas is a busy, noisy commercial district by day, but gets deserted nights and Sundays. The Praça da Matriz and Zona Franca are also seedy at night.

Sights

★**Teatro Amazonas** THEATER
(3232-1768; Praça São Sebastião; guided tour R$20; 9:15am-5pm, tours every 30 mins until

4pm) This gorgeous theater was built at the height of the rubber boom, using European designers, decorators and even raw materials. The original driveway was Brazilian, though, made of Amazonian rubber to soften the clatter of late-arriving carriages. The theater's performance schedule includes an excellent opera festival in April and May. Guided tours offer an up-close look at the theater's opulent construction.

★Jardim Botânico Adolpho Ducke PARK
(☎3582-3188; http://jardimbotanicodemanaus.org; Av Margarita S/N; admission R$8-10, free Tue; with tower R$24-30, R$16 Tue; ⏰9am-5pm Tue-Sun, last entry 4pm) FREE Spanning over 100 sq km, this 'garden' is actually the world's largest urban forest. There's a network of five short trails (guides and closed shoes required, two to three hours, free with admission) and an open-air museum (MUSA; Museu da Amazônia) which includes rotating exhibits on Amazonian flora and fauna and a spectacular 42m observation tower. Busier on weekends. Comfortable shuttles (☎99286-9888, R$30 round trip, 45 minutes) leave from outside the tourist office (CAT) at 9am and 4pm. Otherwise, catch Bus 676 (R$2.50, one hour) from Praça da Matriz.

Centro Cultural Usina Chaminé MUSEUM
(☎3633-3026; Av Beira Rio at José Paranaguá; ⏰10am-4pm Tue-Fri, 5-8pm Sun) FREE Also known as the Museu dos Cinco Sentidos (Museum of the Five Senses), this innovative museum uses the five senses to evoke and illustrate indigenous and Caboclos life and culture. You can hear recordings of native languages, smell Amazonian spices, admire indigenous folk art, and more, as you pass from room to room.

Centro Cultural dos Povos da Amazônia MUSEUM
(☎2123-5301; www.povosdamazonia.am.gov.br; Praça Francisco Pereira da Silva s/n; ⏰9am-4pm Mon-Fri) FREE At the heart of this massive cultural complex is the excellent Museu do Homem do Norte (Museum of Northern Man), which contains an incredible array of artifacts and multimedia exhibits on Amazonian indigenous groups. From the center, buses 625, 711 and 705 all pass by, or ask a taxi to take you to the 'Bola da Suframa'.

Encontro das Águas RIVER
Just beyond Manaus, the warm dark Rio Negro pours into the cool creamy Rio Solimões, but because of differences in temperature, speed and density, their waters don't mix, instead flowing side by side for several kilometers. The bi-color phenomenon occurs throughout the Amazon, but nowhere as dramatically as here. Day trips always include a stop here, and many tour operators at least pass by en route to their lodges.

Sleeping

Location-wise, the area around Teatro Amazonas is ideal, though penny-pinchers can find plenty of cheap *pousadas* near the port.

★Hostel Manaus HOSTEL $
(☎3233-4545; www.hostelmanaus.com; Cavalcante 231; dm with fan/air-con R$45/50, s without bathroom R$80, d with/without bathroom R$140/125; ❄@🛜) Manaus' first hostel is still its best, though competition is getting stiff. Spacious warmly decorated common areas and a rooftop dining area set it apart, and there's a highly recommended tour operator on site. On the downside, it's several long blocks from the center. Large basic dorms and tidy private rooms are adequate. Kitchen access, self-service laundry, friendly staff.

Local Hostel HOSTEL $
(☎3213-6079; localhostel.com.br; Rua Marçal 72; dm R$45-49, d R$130-143, tr R$183; ❄) A great hostel in almost every way: a block from the Opera House, friendly youthful staff and clientele, and clean comfortable dorms with privacy curtains, reading lights and individual power outlets. Spiffy private rooms are a worthwhile splurge. The main drawback is the limited common space, which makes meeting fellow travelers (or just relaxing with a book) somewhat tougher.

Hotel Manaós HOTEL $$
(☎3633-5744; www.hotelmanaos.com.br; Av Eduardo Ribeiro 881; s/d R$139/159; ❄🛜) One of Manaus' oldest hotels, though you'd never know from large modern rooms and updated amenities. Newer bedding, bathrooms, air-cond and TVs lend creature comforts, while the creaky old elevator and the '70s-style lobby are lingering reminders of the hotel's former self. The location is ideal: kitty-corner from Praça Sebastião, with many rooms overlooking the Opera House. Ample breakfast.

Eating

Av Getúlio Vargas and Praça São Sebastião are good places to find food at night.

★Casa do Pensador PIZZERIA, BRAZILIAN $
(Praça São Sebastião; mains R$13-28; ⏰4-11pm) Simple wood tables set up on the plaza facing Teatro Amazonas make this an easy

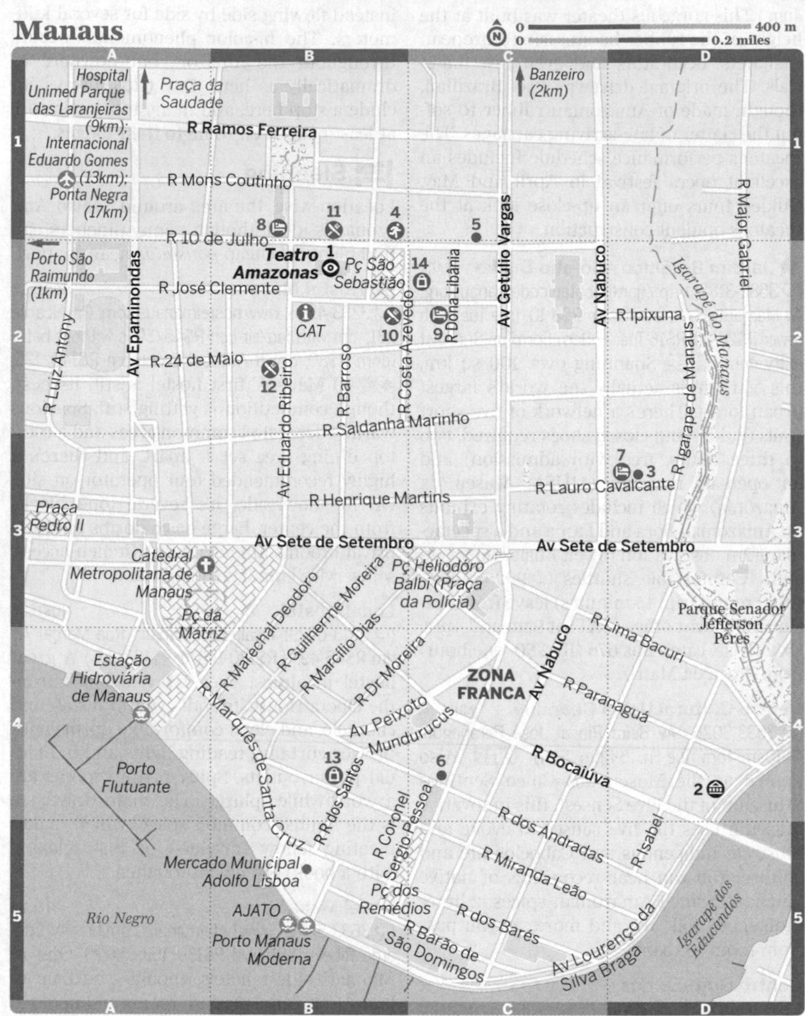

low-key place for dinner and a beer. The menu is equally low-key, mostly pizza (including a couple of veggie options) and standard rice-beans-meat dishes.

Skina dos Sucos JUICE BAR $

(cnr Av Eduardo Ribeiro & Rua 24 de Maio; juices R$4-8, snacks R$4-12; ⏲7am-8pm Mon-Sat) Stake out some counter space at this busy eatery, where you can order filling snacks and sandwiches to go along with large *sucos* (fresh juices) made from Amazonian fruits, including guaraná (a tropical berry thought to have numerous medicinal properties), *cupuaçú* (sweet cousin of the cacao fruit) and *graviola* (custard apple).

Delícias Caseiras BRAZILIAN, SELF-SERVICE $

(Rua 10 de Julho; lunch per kg R$30, mains R$20-45; ⏲11am-3pm) The tables are crammed together and the fans are blowing full blast to accommodate the scads of loyal clients at this great hole-in-the-wall eatery just off Praça São Sebastião. Lunch self-serve is outstanding, especially for the price, but it's also open for dinner, serving home-style classics.

Manaus

Drinking & Entertainment

The area surrounding Teatro Amazonas is the center's best place to hang out. Outside the center, Ponta Negra (13km from the center) is the main nightlife zone, with a river beach, promenade, bars and restaurants. Popular nightspots sit on the Estrada de Ponta Negra just before this area.

★**Porão do Alemão** LIVE MUSIC
(www.poraodoalemao.com.br; Estrada da Ponta Negra 1986; R$25; ⊙10:30pm-late Wed-Sat) Located on Estrada de Ponta Negra, this longtime bar-club features Brazilian and international rock and pop, and has a safe, lively scene popular with tourists and locals alike. VIP area upstairs (R$40).

Shopping

Comercial São Bento OUTDOOR GEAR
(Miranda Leão 133; ⊙8am-5:30pm Mon-Fri, to 4pm Sat) One of several *casas de redes* (hammock shops) clustered around this corner; this one has a monster selection and friendly service. For riverboat trips, suitable cloth hammocks start at R$30, while larger, prettier, more durable ones go for R$60 to R$190. If you'll be sleeping in the jungle, consider getting a mosquito net (R$14 to R$30) as well.

Galeria Amazônica HANDICRAFTS
(☎3233-4521; www.galeriamazonica.org.br; Costa Azevedo 272; ⊙8am-8pm Mon-Sat) Right on Praça São Sebastião, this is Manaus' top shop for genuine-article Amazonian handiwork, including gorgeous basketwork, pottery and folk art. Prices are on the high side, but so is the quality.

Information

CAT (☎3182-6250; www.visitamazonas.am.gov.br; Av Eduardo Ribeiro 666 ; ⊙8am-5pm Mon-Fri, 8am-noon Sat & Sun) Friendly and helpful branch of the state tourism agency, located on the southwest corner of Praça São Sebastião.

Fundação de Medicina Tropical (Tropical Medicine Foundation; ☎2127-3555; Av Pedro Teixeira 25) Also known as Hospital de Doenças Tropicais, this well-regarded hospital specializes in tropical diseases. Free yellow fever vaccines available.

GETTING TO VENEZUELA & GUYANA

The capital of Roraima state, **Boa Vista** is a spot without great traveler thrills, but it's a useful gateway to both Venezuela and Guyana. It's linked to Manaus by five daily buses (R$119, 10 to 12 hours). From Boa Vista, there are four daily buses to little Bonfim (R$18, 1½ hours) on the Guyanese border, and one to Pacaraíma (R$21, 3½ hours) on the Venezuelan border. Collective taxis also make the run to Pacaraíma (R$35, 2½ hours).

Before boarding a bus to Venezuela, verify with the consulate in Manaus or Boa Vista whether you require a Venezuelan tourist card. Buses stop at a Brazilian Polícia Federal border post for exit stamps before entering Venezuela.

Get cash in Brazil before crossing into Venezuela; this will save you from getting hit with the (unfavorable) official exchange rate at Venezuelan ATMs.

For Guyana, get an exit stamp from the Polícia Federal near the river, which forms the international border. Some of the Boa Vista–Bonfim buses stop here and then continue to the riverfront. If yours doesn't, catch a taxi from Bonfim's bus station to the Polícia Federal and walk the short remaining distance to the river. Motorized canoes cross to the Guyana side. Lethem is 5km beyond the river crossing and has better accommodations than Bonfim. Avoid arriving after dark.

GETTING TO PERU & COLOMBIA

Before leaving Brazil, get an exit stamp from the **Polícia Federal** (3412-2180; Av da Amizade 26; 8am-6pm) in Tabatinga.

If you're heading upriver to Iquitos, Peru, catch one of the early-morning fast boats from Tabatinga's Porto da Feira (US$70, 10 hours) operated by **Transtur** (3412-2945, in Iquitos 51-65-29-1324; http://www.transtursa.com; Rua Marechal Mallet 248) or **Transportes Golfinho** (3412-3186, in Iquitos 51-65-225-118; www.transportegolfinho.com; Rua Marechal Mallet 306, Tabatinga). You'll complete Peruvian border formalities en route at Santa Rosa. Between 6am and 6pm, frequent motorboats also connect Tabatinga with Santa Rosa (R$3, five minutes).

To reach Leticia, Colombia, take any northbound taxi, *mototaxi* or kombi along Tabatinga's Av da Amizade (aka Av Principal), or walk 2km north from Tabatinga's port and the Colombian Consulate (p414) to the border.

Tourist Police (3231-1998; Av Eduardo Ribeiro) At Centro de Atendimento ao Turista.

DANGERS & ANNOYANCES

At the airport, avoid the vultures touting jungle trips or city accommodations. After 11pm steer clear of the port area and the Praça da Matriz. If arriving late by boat, take a taxi to a hotel – muggings are common.

Getting There & Away

AIR

Several airlines operate domestic flights from Manaus's **Aeroporto Internacional Eduardo Gomes** (3652-1210; Av Santos Dumont 1350), 13km north of the center. Direct international flights include American Airlines and TAM to Miami, and Copa to Panama City. Smaller airlines use Terminal 2 (Eduardinho), 600m east of Terminal 1.

BOAT

Large passenger boats plying the Rio Solimões use Manaus' main passenger port, **Estação Hidroviária de Manaus** (www.portodemanaus.com.br; Porto Flutuante). Boats going downstream to Belém usually stop at Itacoatiara, Parintins, Santarém and Monte Alegre. Headed up the Rio Solimões, boats call at Tefé, Benjamin Constant and Tabatinga. Boats up the Rio Madeira to Porto Velho stop at Manicoré and Humaitá.

The main port's **ticket office** (3233-7061, 3088-5764; Marquês de Santa Cruz; 6:15am-5:45pm) sells passage for most long-distance riverboats. Avoid the hawkers on the sidewalk out front; their tickets may be cheaper, but if something goes wrong you'll be on your own.

Ajato (3622-6047; www.terminalajato.com.br; Porto Manaus Moderna; 8am-5pm Mon-Fri, 8am-noon Sat) runs comfortable speedboats upriver to Tefé (R$240, 13 hours) and Tabatinga (R$550, 36 hours) from the smaller **Porto Manaus Moderna** (behind Mercado Municipal Adolfo Lisboa), 500m east of the main port.

DESTINATION	COST (R$) HAMMOCK/ DOUBLE CABIN	DURATION
Belém	325/1200	4 days
Porto Velho	200/600	4 days
Santarém	160/750	36hr
Tabatinga	350/1500	7 days
Tefe	150/590	36hr

BUS

Eucatur (3301-5800; www.eucatur.com.br) runs five daily buses to Boa Vista (R$120, 11 to 12 hours). If continuing north to Venezuela, take the 6pm departure from Manaus for the best chance of catching the lone bus to the border, which leaves Boa Vista at 7am.

Getting Around

Bus 306 (R$2.50, 30 minutes) and air-con bus 813 (R$5) run roughly every half hour between the airport and the center. The most convenient downtown stops are Praça da Matriz and Av Getúlio Vargas near Rua José Clemente. These same two buses also stop near the long-distance bus station. Leaving the station, cross the footbridge over Rua Recife, turn left along the busy street on the far side of the gas station, and walk 100m to the bus stop.

Taxis at the airport charge a fixed R$75 for the 20-minute ride into town, while the return trip costs around R$65. In either case, be sure to agree on a price before setting off. A taxi between the bus station and the center costs R$35 to R$40.

Amazon Jungle

Many visitors to Amazonia expect to stare down a growling jaguar or trade beads with spear-toting indigenous people just outside Manaus. This isn't going to happen. Manaus is a big city and the numbers of tourists are high. Even so, on a typical trip you are likely to glimpse pink and gray river dolphins, caymans, monkeys, tarantulas and plenty of birds. Sloths are relatively common. Manatees, anacondas, tapirs and jaguars are extremely hard to spot. The more remote, unpopulated and pristine the area, the better the chances of spotting wildlife.

Planning a Jungle Trip

While anything is possible, the typical jungle trip is two to four days. Most agencies offer a similar program, which usually includes piranha fishing, nighttime caiman-spotting, a jungle walk focusing on traditional medicinal and food plants, one night forest camping, a visit to a local home and a sunrise boat trip to see macaws or dolphins. Canoeing through *igarapés* and *igapós* – which have more flora and fauna than channels and rivers – is a priority. This is one reason the high-water period (roughly March to July) is the best time to visit.

'White' rivers, such as the Lago Mamorí region, tend to have a higher density of wildlife than 'black' ones, like the Rio Negro. But they also have more mosquitoes and somewhat thicker vegetation, which inhibits wildlife-viewing.

You'll need sturdy shoes or boots, long pants, a long-sleeved shirt, a raincoat, insect repellent, a flashlight and a water bottle. High-powered binoculars improve the experience. Ask how much water is on-site and how much you'll need. Bring your passport.

Dangers & Annoyances

You name it, it's happened on a jungle trip outside Manaus. Consider that you are placing your personal safety in another's hands in an unknown, isolated natural environment. It's best to use agencies or guides registered with the Amazonas state tourist office (don't believe the certificates; check online at www.visitamazonastour.com). Using a registered agency or guide means a better chance of being refunded should something go wrong. Women should consider being part of a group of three or more to avoid being alone in a remote location with a guide.

Manaus is full of scammers. Never pay for a tour anywhere other than the registered office of a tour agency. As the industry has become more competitive, scammers have gone so far as to create false IDs and receipts, fake confirmation phone calls to agencies, and falsely represent or impersonate guides and agencies listed in guidebooks. These scammers are most often found at the airport but also work on the street and at hotel receptions. The battle is also waged online, where reputable agencies are criticized on travel websites by 'dissatisfied tourists' who are actually rival agencies.

Tours

Manaus has scores of agencies. Our recommended options offer a reasonably genuine and adventurous experience. Most have a small lodge or jungle camp where guests stay, from where activities such as canoeing, hiking and fishing are launched. Many (but not all) have amenities such as electricity and flush toilets. Prices usually include meals, lodging, transport, activities and guides, and range between R$150 to R$350 per person per day. Prices vary primarily by the type of accommodations: hammocks with shared toilets are the cheapest option, followed by dorms and private rooms, then riverboats and specialized tours.

Amazon Antonio Jungle Tours ECOTOUR
(☎3234-1294, 9961-8314; www.antonio-jungletours.com; Hostel Manaus, Rua Lauro Cavalcante 231) On the scenic (and mosquito-free) Rio Urubú, Amazon Antonio's lodge has dorms, private rooms, chalets, even a two-bedroom cabin, all

TRIPLE FRONTIER

On the Amazon's northeast bank – about 1100km west of Manaus – Tabatinga (Brazil) and Leticia (Colombia) are separated by an invisible international border. The opposite bank of the river and the islands in the middle of it are part of Peru. Santa Rosa, Peru's border settlement, is on an island. This 'triple frontier' has travel routes linking all three countries and is a good base for jungle trips. Leticia is the largest and most pleasant of the three border towns and has the best services.

Tabatinga is linked by air with Manaus. Slow boats to Manaus (hammock R$350, seven days) leave from Tabatinga's Porto Fluvial every Wednesday and Saturday, plus some Tuesdays, between 8am and 2pm. Arrive early to stake out good hammock space, as boats can be quite crowded. Speedboats operated by **Ajato** (☎3412-2227, in Manaus 092-3622-6047; 8am-5pm Mon-Fri, 8am-noon Sat) leave Tabatinga for Manaus (R$550, 35 hours) on Tuesday, Thursday, Saturday and Sunday mornings.

impeccably maintained, warmly decorated, and eco-oriented. Overnight hikes journey deep into primary forest, and you're free to stay after your package is over, relaxing, canoeing and soaking up views from the observation tower. Slightly pricier, but worth it.

Amazon Eco Adventures ECOTOUR (http://amazonecoadventures.com; Rua 10 de Julho at Rua Tapajós; ⏲8am-6pm) This newer floating lodge has five rooms, each with bathroom and fan, and a large patio with hammocks for relaxing and swimming. It's parked on a huge lake where the black water (ie mosquito-free) Rio Urubú meets the white water (ie animal-rich) Amazon – the best of both worlds. Tours ply the floodplains alongside the Amazon, loaded with birds and monkeys.

Amazon Gero Tours ECOTOUR (☎99198-0111, 99983-6273; www.amazongero.com; Rua 10 de Julho 695) Gero Mesquita, an effusive and all-round good guy, runs a popular lodge in the Juma-Mamori area with comfortable dorms and private rooms, and a cadre of skilled guides (several former guides have opened agencies of their own). Besides standard tours, Gero arranges multiday treks into untouched forest and offers 'social sustainability' programs where travelers work on needed community projects.

Amazonas Indian Turismo ECOTOUR (☎99240-5888; amazonasindian@hotmail.com; Andradas 311) This longtime budget agency has a rustic camp on the Rio Urubú, with latrine toilets and no electricity. You won't spend much time there, though, as the operator specializes in multiday hikes through the forest, sleeping in makeshift camps, hammocks slung between two trees. Notable for being indigenous owned and operated; most guides are Wapixano, and all speak English.

Lo Peix ECOTOUR (☎98182-4793; www.lopeix.com; per person R$435-1680, 3-12 days) The Spanish-Brazilian owners spent years exploring the Amazon in a riverboat before starting a tour company offering the same thing. Tours hit places like Anavilhanas archipelago, Jaú National Park, prehistoric sites near Airão Velho and more, with frequent stops for canoeing, hiking, snorkeling and visiting local communities. The custom-built boat has small comfortable berths, solar power, and up-to-date safety equipment.

★**Tropical Tree Climbing** ECOTOUR (www.tropicaltreeclimbing.com; BR-178 Km 144, Presidente Figueiredo) Tours with this warm French-Venezuelan outfit include garden fresh meals, hiking through verdant forest and, of course, climbing a tree (or two) – usually a huge *angelim* or *samaúma*. The owner-guide (photographer Leo Principe) is patient and knowledgeable, and uses a unique rope system that makes the 50m climb reasonably easy. Overnight in comfy new guestrooms or even up in a tree!

Porto Velho

☎0XX69 / POP 429,000

Capital of Rondônia state, Porto Velho is a vital link in Brazil's agricultural economy, as soybeans are shipped on barges from here up the Rio Madeira and onto trans-Atlantic ocean liners. Travelers passing through en route from the Pantanal to Manaus and the Amazon will find a few bright spots, but the city mostly serves as a transfer point.

Well-positioned sleeping options include **Vitória Palace Hotel** (☎3221-9232; Duque de Caxias 745; s/d R$50/60; ❄📶), with aging but tidy, high-ceilinged rooms. For cheap eats, check out the buffet at **Caffé Restaurante** (☎3224-3176; Av Carlos Gomes 1097; per kg R$32-35; ⏲11am-3pm Mon-Sat), and for nightlife, hit the cluster of boisterous bars near Av Pinheiro Machado and Av Presidente Dutra.

Domestic flights leave from Porto Velho's Jorge Teixeira de Oliveira International Airport (PVH), 7km north of the center. A taxi into town costs R$40, or catch a local bus (to your right when exiting the terminal).

Boats to Manaus (hammock R$250, double cabin with fan/air-con R$700/900, 2½ days) leave three times weekly from the river port in the center. Buy tickets from authorized brokers such as **Agência Monte Sinai** (☎99346-7101, 3223-1987; transportesmontesinai@hotmail.com; ⏲8am-6pm Mon-Sat).

Buses (R$63, six hours, seven daily) and collective taxis (R$100, four hours) run to Guajará-Mirim. Buses also serve Rio Branco (R$75, eight to 10 hours, nine daily) and Cuiabá (R$170 to R$270, 24 to 25 hours, seven daily). From the bus station to the center (3km), take a local bus or a cab (R$15).

Guajará-Mirim

☎0XX69 / POP 42,000

In this pleasant backwater of a border town just opposite Guayaramerín (Bolivia), bushy trees shade red-earth-stained sidewalks from the relentless sun.

GETTING TO BOLIVIA FROM GUAJARÁ-MIRIM

Motorboats (R$7, 10 minutes) to Guayaramerín, Bolivia depart 24 hours a day from the port at the end of the main street 15 de Novembro. Get your Brazilian exit stamp at the **Policía Federal** (3541-0200; cnr Avs Presidente Dutra & Bocaiúva; 7am-9pm). Bolivian entry visas (US$160, required for US citizens only) can normally be issued the same day at the Bolivian Consulate (p414) near the riverfront.

The family-run **Hotel Mine-Estrela** (3541-1206; Av 15 de Novembro 460; s/d R$50/80;) offers aging but adequate rooms on the main street between the bus station and the port. Nearby restaurants include **Oásis** (3541-1621; Av 15 de Novembro 460; per kg R$34; 11am-3pm, closed Tue), whose worthwhile lunch buffet features freshly grilled meats.

Bradesco (Av Costa Marques 430) has ATMs. Change bolivianos and reales with the money changers at Guayaramerín's port.

Buses (R$63, six to seven hours, seven daily) and *colectivos* (R$100, four hours) run from the bus station, 2km east of the port, to Porto Velho. Taxis between the station and the center cost R$20 to R$30; *mototaxis* R$12.

Rio Branco

0XX68 / POP 336,000

Remote Acre state is famous as one of the key battlegrounds fought over by the Brazilian environmental and logging lobbies. For travelers, it's a zone for off-the-beaten-track Amazon exploration and a gateway to the jungly north of Bolivia,. Rio Branco, the state's very laid-back riverfront capital, makes a great stop for a day or two.

Beige-green **Palacio Rio Branco** (Praça Povos da Floresta; 8am-6pm Tue-Fri, 4-6pm Sat & Sun) FREE is a restored art-deco masterpiece holding a historical exhibition. Just below here is the not-very-helpful **Centro de Atendimento ao Turista** (Praça Povos da Floresta; 8am-9pm Mon-Sat, 9am-noon Sun). Banks with ATMs are alongside.

Closed for renovation in 2015 but worth a look when open, the **Museu da Borracha** (Rubber Museum; Av Ceará 1441; 8am-6pm Tue-Fri) FREE is housed in a restored mansion, with exhibits on the history of rubber-tapping, and the life and work of Chico Mendes.

The most atmospheric place to stay is in the center, with its riverbank dotted by picturesque bridges and cutely colorful houses. **AFA Hotel** (3224-1396; www.afabistro.com.br; Ribeiro 109; s/d R$92/138;) has spacious, recently renovated rooms, a good lunch buffet and a welcoming attitude. Nearby, the beautifully renovated **Mercado Velho** (Praça Bandeira; dishes from R$6; 7am-10pm) – a historic port building – hosts cultural and musical events, plus a food court with reasonably priced *pratos feitos*.

Rio Branco's small airport, 22km northwest of the center, has daily flights to Porto Velho and Brasília. Bus 304, signed as 'Custódio Freire' (R$2.90, 45 minutes), runs roughly hourly to the center of town.

The sleek **Rodoviária Internacional de Rio Branco** (3221-3693; www.rodoviariainternacional.com; Km 125, Hwy 364) is 8km southwest of town. Buses run to Porto Velho (R$80, eight to 10 hours, four daily), Xapurí (R$30, 3½ hours, 6am and 1:45pm) and Brasiléia (R$36, four hours, three daily). From the bus terminal to the center, catch a 'Norte-Sul', 'Parque Industrial' or 'Jacarandá' bus (R$2.90, 20 to 30 minutes).

Xapuri

0XX68 / POP 16,000

Xapuri, whose sweet houses, thriving trees and red-dirt roads make it a charming stop, was home to rubber-tapper and world-famous environmental martyr Chico Mendes, murdered in 1988 after years of successful campaigning against the destruction of forests by loggers and ranchers. The **Casa Chico Mendes** (www.chicomendes.org.br; Batista de Moraes 494; 8:30am-4:30pm Tue-Fri, 9am-1pm Sat) FREE, a block from the bus station, is the simple wood house where Mendes lived with his family until he was gunned down on the back steps in 1988. Tours include a graphic description of the shooting, illustrated by bloodstains still on the walls. Across the street, the Chico Mendes Foundation center has poster-sized photos of Mendes and a collection of personal items and international awards. The activist's death sparked outrage that has led to extensive forest protection in the state.

A short walk from the bus terminal is **Pousada das Chapurys** (3542-2253; pousada_chapurys@hotmail.com; Sadala Koury 1385; s/d/tr R$70/100/130;), an old standby whose friendly owners were close friends

GETTING TO BOLIVIA & PERU

West of Xapuri, the town of **Brasiléia** sits across the Rio Acre from considerably more hectic Cobija, Bolivia. Brasiléia has ATMs, money changers and a Bolivian consulate. **Pousada Las Palmeras** (☎3546-3284; Rua Odilon Pratagi 125 at Geny Assis; s/d R$60/80; ❄📶) is an appealing sleeping option with an excellent breakfast. Buses run to Rio Branco (R$30, four hours) and Xapuri (R$12, two hours). Collective taxis do the same trips for double the money and half the time.

You can freely cross the bridge between Brasiléia and Cobija, but if you're heading further into Bolivia, get an exit stamp from the **Polícia Federal** (☎3546-3204; ⊙8am-7pm) in Brasiléia's neighboring town, Epitaciolândia. Buses from Rio Branco or Xapuri will drop you there. Cobija has places to stay, an airport and arduous bus connections.

For Peru, get an exit stamp in Epitaciolândia, catch a bus to Assis (R$12, two hours) and cross the Rio Acre to Iñapari (Peru). Assis has better accommodations than Iñapari if you need to spend the night. Buses from Rio Branco to Assis theoretically stop at the Polícia Federal en route – check beforehand. There's a Peruvian consulate in Rio Branco.

of Chico Mendes. A park near the plaza on Rua Brandão has laid-back spots to sit outdoors with a pizza or beer. To experience the natural setting where Mendes first tapped rubber trees and collected Brazil nuts, head 32km outside Xapuri to **Pousada Ecológica Seringal Cachoeira** (☎9947-8399; dm R$60, d R$130, all incl breakfast; ❄), a cozy ecolodge with dorms, chalets, meals (lunch and dinner R$30), guided hikes and activities.

Buses run to Rio Branco (R$30, 3½ hours, 6am and 3:20pm) and Brasiléia (R$10, two hours, 10am).

UNDERSTAND BRAZIL

Brazil Today

Brazil has always been touted as 'The Country of the Future,' based on the longstanding belief that with all its vast resources and wealth, the country would eventually work out. The time-honored punchline among the population, however, always went: 'But the future never arrives.' And once again, it seems they were right.

Things were going along swimmingly. The country weathered the 2008 ongoing global recession better than nearly everyone. Widespread economic growth fattened the pockets for a blossoming middle class while the rest of the world buckled under crisis. Brazil even briefly overtook the UK as the 6th-largest economy in the world in 2012. By 2015, however, Brazilians got a gravity lesson: what goes up, must come down. And come down hard it did.

Despite making headway against its biggest nemesis, the economic disparity between rich and poor (some 20% of the population jumped classes during the much ballyhooed Brazil Boom), Brazil was confronting economic doom by 2015: its biggest recession since the Great Depression. The country's first female president in its 200-year history, Dilma Rousseff, spent much of her second term laying low as her administration became quickly embroiled in what could turn out to be the largest corruption scandal in Brazil's history. *'Operação Lava-Jato'* ('Operation Car Wash'), as the ongoing federal investigation is known, alleges a billion-dollar money-laundering scheme surrounding oil giant Petrobras (and construction monolith Odebrecht, among others) whose vastness still remains to be seen. Amid tremendous accusations of bribes and overbilling, numerous company executives and government officials in Rouseff's administration and political party, the Workers Party (PT), have been investigated and jailed, stopping just short – so far, anyway – of the president herself. Along the way, Petrobras' oil production stagnated on its way to becoming the world's most indebted company. Rousseff's approval rating sank to a record-low 8%.

Meanwhile, Brazil's credit rating was reduced to junk by Standard & Poor's after the government introduced a $17-billion austerity package in late 2015, freezing public hiring, cutting about 1000 jobs, and eliminating 10 government ministries. The country's currency, the Real, considered the world's most overvalued just three short years ago, lost nearly 40% of its value against the dollar in the last year and remains shaky. Unemployment was approaching double-digits by year's end. Brazil Boom had turned to Brazil Gloom.

And just when you thought things couldn't get any worse, the 2015 Bento Rodrigues dam catastrophe, which sent some 60 million cubic meters of toxic mining waste into Minas Gerais' Doce River (and 17 days later into the Atlantic Ocean), has been called the worst environmental disaster in Brazil's history. Rousseff's slow response to the tragedy was widely criticized and, at time of writing, impeachment proceedings were approved by Rousseff's political rival, the lower-house speaker Eduardo Cunha (he himself under investigation for allegedly taking millions in bribe money in the Petrobras kickback scheme). Regardless of how it all shakes out, Brazil closed 2015 about as stable as a Jenga tower in a tornado.

Political, economic and environmental turmoil aside, the excitement (and tension) were building as the world spotlight was turning its critical eye on Rio de Janeiro as the host of the 2016 Olympic Games. After proving the naysayers wrong in 2014 by pulling off a wonderful FIFA World Cup (as hosts, not as footballers, mind you), Brazil could definitely use another celebratory distraction, if only for two short weeks.

History

The Tribal People

Little is known of Brazil's first inhabitants, but from the few fragments left behind (mostly pottery, trash mounds and skeletons), archaeologists estimate that the first humans may have arrived 50,000 years ago, predating any other estimates in the whole American continent.

The population at the time of the Portuguese landing in 1500 is also a mystery, and estimates range from two to six million. There were likely more than 1000 tribes living as nomadic hunter-gatherers or in more settled, agricultural societies. Life was punctuated by frequent tribal warfare and at times, captured enemies were ceremonially killed and eaten after battle.

When the Portuguese first arrived, they had little interest in the natives, who were viewed as a Stone Age people; and the heavily forested land offered nothing for the European market. All that changed when Portuguese merchants expressed interest in the red dye from brazilwood (which later gave the colony its name), and slowly colonists arrived to harvest the land.

The natural choice for the work, of course, was the indigenous people. Initially the natives welcomed the strange, smelly foreigners and offered them their labor, their food and their women in exchange for the awe-inspiring metal tools and the fascinating Portuguese liquor. But soon the newcomers abused their customs, took their best land and ultimately enslaved them.

When colonists discovered that sugarcane grew well in the colony, the natives' labor was more valuable than ever and soon the sale of local slaves became Brazil's second-largest commercial enterprise. It was an industry dominated by *bandeirantes,* brutal men who hunted the indigenous people in the interior and captured or killed them. Their exploits, more than any treaty, secured the huge interior of South America for Portuguese Brazil.

Jesuit priests went to great lengths to protect the indigenous community. But they lacked the resources to stymie the attacks (and the Jesuits were later expelled from Brazil in 1759). Natives who didn't die at the hands of the colonists often died from introduced European diseases.

The Africans

During the 17th century African slaves replaced indigenous prisoners on the plantations. From 1550 until 1888 about 3.5 million slaves were shipped to Brazil – almost 40% of the total that came to the New World. The Africans were considered better workers and were less vulnerable to European diseases, but they resisted slavery strongly. *Quilombos,* communities of runaway slaves, formed throughout the colonial period. They ranged from *mocambos,* small groups hidden in the forests, to the great republic of Palmares, which survived much of the 17th century. Led by the African king Zumbí, it's thought Palmares had between 11,000 and 20,000 residents at its height (scholars debate the population).

According to Comissão Pró-Índio in São Paulo, an estimated 2000 to 3000 villages that formed as *quilombos* remain in Brazil today, their growth only stopped by abolition itself (1888).

Survivors on the plantations sought solace in their African religion and culture through song and dance. The slaves were given perfunctory instruction in Catholicism and a syncretic religion rapidly emerged. Spiritual elements from many African tribes, such as the Yorubá, were preserved and made palatable to slave masters by adopting a facade of Catholic saints. Such were the roots of modern Candomblé (Afro-Brazilian religion of Bahia) and Macumba (religon of African origin), prohibited by law until recently.

Life on the plantations was miserable, but an even worse fate awaited many slaves. In the 1690s, gold was discovered in present-day Minas Gerais, and soon the rush was on. Wild boom towns such as Vila Rica de Ouro Preto (Rich Town of Black Gold) sprang up in the mountain valleys. Immigrants flooded the territory, and countless slaves were brought from Africa to dig and die in Minas.

The Portuguese

For years, the ruling powers of Portugal viewed the colony of Brazil as little more than a money-making enterprise. That attitude changed, however, when Napoleon marched on Lisbon in 1807. The prince regent (later known as Dom João VI) immediately transferred his court to Brazil. He stayed on even after Napoleon's Waterloo in 1815, and when he became king in 1816 he declared Rio de Janeiro the capital of a united kingdom of Brazil and Portugal, making Brazil the only New World colony to serve as the seat of a European monarch. In 1821, Dom João finally returned to Portugal, leaving his son Pedro in Brazil as regent.

The following year the Portuguese parliament attempted to return Brazil to colonial status. According to legend, Pedro responded by pulling out his sword and shouting out '*Independência ou morte!*' (Independence or death!), crowning himself Emperor Dom Pedro I. Portugal was too weak to fight its favorite colony, so Brazil won independence without bloodshed.

Dom Pedro I ruled for nine years. He scandalized the country by siring a string of illegitimate children, and was finally forced to abdicate in favor of his five-year-old son, Dom Pedro II. Until the future emperor reached adolescence, Brazil suffered a period of civil war. In 1840 Dom Pedro II ascended the throne with overwhelming public support. During his 50-year reign he nurtured an increasingly powerful parliamentary system, went to war with Paraguay, meddled in Argentine and Uruguayan affairs, encouraged mass immigration, abolished slavery and ultimately forged a state that would do away with the monarchy forever.

The Brazilians

During the 19th century, coffee replaced sugar as Brazil's primary export, at one time supplying three-quarters of world demand. With mechanization and the building of Brazil's first railroads, profits soared and the coffee barons gained enormous influence.

In 1889 a coffee-backed military coup toppled the antiquated empire, sending the emperor into exile. The new Brazilian Republic adopted a constitution modeled on the US, and for nearly 40 years Brazil was governed by a series of military and civilian presidents through which the armed forces effectively ruled the country.

Coffee remained king until the market collapsed during the global economic crisis of 1929. The weakened planters of São Paulo, who controlled the government, formed an opposition alliance with the support of nationalist military officers. When their presidential candidate, Getúlio Vargas, lost the 1930 elections, the military seized power and handed him the reins.

Vargas proved a gifted maneuverer, and dominated the political scene for 20 years. At times his regime was inspired by the Italian and Portuguese fascist states of Mussolini and Salazar: he banned political parties, imprisoned opponents and censored the press. He remained in and out of the political scene until 1954, when the military called for him to step down. Vargas responded by writing a letter to the people of Brazil, then shooting himself in the heart.

Juscelino Kubitschek, the first of Brazil's big spenders, was elected president in 1956. His motto was '50 years' progress in five.' His critics responded with '40 years of inflation in four.' The critics were closer to the mark, owing to the huge debt Kubitschek incurred during the construction of Brasília. By the early 1960s, inflation gripped the Brazilian economy, and Castro's victory in Cuba had spread fears of communism. Brazil's fragile democracy was crushed in 1964 when the military overthrew the government.

Brazil stayed under the repressive military regime for almost 20 years. Throughout much of this time the economy grew substantially, at times borrowing heavily from international banks. But it exacted a heavy toll on the country. Ignored social problems grew dire. Millions came to the cities, and *favelas* (informal communities) spread at exponential rates.

Recent Decades

The last few decades have been very good to Brazil. After Fernando Collor de Mello, its first democratically elected president in 30 years, was removed from office on charges of corruption in 1992, widespread economic growth stabilized and blessed the South American workhorse.

Collor's replacement, Itamar Franco, introduced Brazil's present currency, the real. This sparked an economic boom that continues to this day, though it was his successor, former finance minister Fernando Henrique Cardoso, who presided through the mid-1990s over a growing economy and record foreign investment. He is most credited with laying the groundwork that put Brazil's hyperinflation to bed, though often at the neglect of social problems.

In 2002, socialist Luiz Inácio Lula da Silva won the presidency under a promise of social reform. From a humble working-class background, Lula rose to become a trade unionist and a strike leader in the early 1980s. He later founded the Workers Party (PT), a magnet for his many followers seeking social reform. Lula ran one of the most financially prudent two-term administrations in years while still addressing Brazil's egregious social problems. Unfortunately, Lula's administration had some setbacks, most notably the wide-reaching *Mensalão* corruption scandal that broke in 2005, causing a number of his PT party members to resign in disgrace, and ended in 2012 in a sensational Supreme Court trial that captivated the country.

Lula's successor and fellow party member, Dilma Rousseff, was elected Brazil's first ever female president in 2011. A former Marxist guerrilla who was allegedly tortured by the former military regime (who also imprisoned her for several years), her past radicalism proved an appropriate resume for her administration's hard line on corruption. But ill-fated economic policies amid a billion-dollar corruption scandal surrounding Brazilian oil giant Petrobras aligned to ensure Brazil's eyebrow-lifting economic growth did an about-face. By 2015, midway through Rouseff's second term, the country was mired in recession and corruption and weathering its worst environmental disaster in history, leaving doubt as to if she would even make it to the end of her second term, be it by impeachment or resignation.

One thing is certain: the stakes couldn't be higher for Brazil's next general election in 2018.

Culture

Brazilian culture has been shaped by the Portuguese, who gave the country its language and religion, and also by the indigenous population, immigrants and Africans. The influence of the latter is particularly strong, especially in the Northeast where African religion, music and cuisine have all profoundly influenced Brazilian identity.

Population

In Brazil the diversity of the landscape matches that of the people inhabiting it. Of the respondents in IBGE's 2010 census, 47.5% of the population are white, 43.4% mixed, 7.5% black, 1.1% Asian and 0.43% indigenous, but the numbers little represent the many shades and types of Brazil's rich melting pot. Indigenous people, Portuguese, Africans (brought to Brazil as slaves) and their mixed-blood offspring made up the population until the late 19th century. Since then there have been waves of immigration by Italians, Spaniards, Germans, Japanese, Russians, Lebanese and others.

Lifestyle

Although Brazil has the world's sixth-largest economy, with abundant resources and developed infrastructure, the living standard varies wildly. Brazil has one of the world's widest income gaps between rich and poor.

Since the mass urban migration in the mid-19th century, the poorest have lived in *favelas* that surround every city. Many dwellings consist of little more than a few boards pounded together, and access to clean water, sewage and healthcare are luxuries few *favelas* enjoy. Drug lords rule the streets and crime is rampant.

The rich often live just a stone's throw away, sometimes separated by nothing more than a highway. Many live in modern fortresses, with security walls and armed guards, enjoying a lifestyle similar to upper classes in Europe and America.

But the beauty of Brazil is when these crowds come together – at a samba club, a football match, a Carnaval parade or on the beach – and meld together seamlessly in celebration. Brazilians love a party, and revelries commence year-round. But it isn't all samba and *sakerinhas* (cocktails) in the land of the tropics. Brazilians suffer from *saudade*, a nostalgic, often deeply melancholic longing for something. The idea appears in many works by Jobim, Moraes and other great songwriters, and it manifests itself in many forms – from the dull ache of homesickness to the deep regret over past mistakes.

When Brazilians aren't dancing the samba or drowning in sorrow, they're often helping each other out. Kindness is both commonplace and expected, and even a casual introduction can lead to deeper friendships. This altruism comes in handy in a country noted for its bureaucracy and long lines. There's the official way of doing things, then there's the *jeitinho*, or the little way around it, and a little kindness – and a few friends – can go a long way.

Religion

Brazil is the world's largest Catholic country, but it embraces diversity and syncretism. Without much difficulty you can find churchgoing Catholics who attend spiritualist gatherings or appeal for help at a *terreiro* (the house of an Afro-Brazilian religious group).

Brazil's principal religious roots comprise the animism of the indigenous people, Catholicism and African religions introduced by slaves. The latest arrival is evangelical Christianity, which is spreading all over Brazil, especially in poorer areas.

The Afro-Brazilian religions emerged when the colonists prohibited slaves from practicing their native religions. Not so easily deterred, the slaves simply gave Catholic names to their African gods and continued to worship them. The most orthodox of the religions is Candomblé. Rituals take place in the Yoruba language in a *casa de santo* or *terreiro,* directed by a *pai de santo* or *mãe de santo* (literally, 'a saint's father or mother' – the Candomblé priests).

Candomblé gods are known as *orixás* and each person is believed to be protected by one of them. In Bahia and Rio, followers of Afro-Brazilian cults turn out in huge numbers to attend festivals at the year's end – especially those held during the night of December 31 and on New Year's Day. Millions of Brazilians go to the beach at this time to pay homage to Iemanjá, the sea goddess, whose alter ego is the Virgin Mary.

Arts

Architecture

Brazil's most impressive colonial architecture dazzles visitors in cities like Salvador, Olinda, São Luís, Ouro Prêto and Tiradentes. Over the centuries, the names of two architects stand out: Aleijadinho, the genius of 18th-century baroque in Minas Gerais mining towns and the late Oscar Niemeyer, the 20th-century modernist-functionalist who was chief architect for the new capital, Brasília, in the 1950s and designed many other striking buildings around the country. Niemeyer passed away in 2012 at the age of 104.

Cinema

Brazil's large film industry has produced a number of good films over the years. One of the most recent hits is 2007's *Tropa do Elite* (Elite Squad), a gritty look at Rio's crime and corruption from the viewpoint of its most elite police force, BOPE (Special Police Operations Battalion); and its sequel, the 2010 *Tropa de Elite 2: O Inimigo Agora É Outro* (Elite Squad 2: The Enemy Within), the highest grossing film in Brazilian history.

The same director, José Padilha, initially garnered Brazilian cinema attention with the 2002 *Ônibus 174* (Bus 174), a shocking look at both the ineptness of the Brazilian police and the brutal reality of the country's socioeconomic disparities. It tells the story of a lone gunman who hijacked a Rio bus in

2000 and held passengers hostage for hours live on national TV. His latest critically hailed project, Netflix's *Narcos*, dramatically portrays the Colombian drug cartels in their '80s heyday. It features another Brazilian, Walter Moura, starring as Colombian drug lord Pablo Escobar.

One of Brazil's top directors, Fernando Meirelles, earned his credibility and an Oscar nomination with the 2002 *Cidade de Deus* (City of God), which showed the brutality of a Rio *favela*. Meirelles followed the success of *Cidade de Deus* with three Hollywood films, the most critically acclaimed of which is *The Constant Gardener* (2004), an intriguing conspiracy film shot in Africa that won the Oscar for Best Supporting Actor for Rachel Weisz.

Walter Salles, one of Brazil's best-known directors, won much acclaim (and an Oscar) for *Central do Brasil* (Central Station; 1998), the story of a lonely woman accompanying a young homeless boy in search of his father.

For a taste of the dictatorship days see Bruno Barreto's *O Que É Isso Companheiro* (released as *Four Days in September* in the US, 1998), based on the 1969 kidnapping of the US ambassador to Brazil by leftist guerrillas.

Another milestone in Brazilian cinema is the visceral film *Pixote* (1981), which shows life through the eyes of a street kid in Rio. When it was released, it became a damning indictment of Brazilian society.

Literature

Joaquim Maria Machado de Assis (1839–1908), the son of a freed slave, is one of Brazil's early great writers. Assis had a great sense of humor and an insightful – though cynical – take on human affairs. His major novels were *Quincas borba, The Posthumous Memoirs of Bras Cubas* and *Dom Casmurro*.

Jorge Amado (1912–2001), Brazil's most celebrated contemporary writer, wrote clever portraits of the people and places of Bahia, notably *Gabriela, Clove and Cinnamon* and *Dona Flor and her Two Husbands*.

Paulo Coelho is Latin America's second-most-read novelist (after Gabriel García Márquez). His new-age fables *The Alchemist* and *The Pilgrimage* launched his career in the mid-1990s.

Music

Samba, a Brazilian institution, has strong African influences and is intimately linked to Carnaval. The most popular form of samba today is *pagode*, a relaxed, informal genre whose leading exponents include singers Beth Carvalho, Jorge Aragão and Zeca Pagodinho.

Bossa nova, another Brazilian trademark, arose in the 1950s, and gained the world's attention in the classic song *The Girl from Ipanema*, composed by Antônio Carlos Jobim and Vinícius de Moraes. Bossa nova's founding father, guitarist João Gilberto, still performs, as does his daughter Bebel Gilberto, who has sparked renewed interest in the genre, combining smooth bossa sounds with electronic grooves.

Tropicalismo, which burst onto the scene in the late 1960s, mixed varied Brazilian musical styles with North American rock and pop. Leading figures such as Gilberto Gil and Caetano Veloso are still very much around. Gil, in fact, was Brazil's Minister of Culture from 2003 to 2008.

The list of emerging talent gets longer each day, topped by actor/musician Seu Jorge, who starred in *Cidade de Deus*. Jorge earned accolades in 2005 for the release of *Cru*, an inventive hip-hop album with politically charged beats, as well as the 2010 *Seu Jorge & Almaz*, a critically acclaimed soul, samba and rock collaboration with drummer Pupillo and guitarist Lucio Maia, both members of the legendary rock/hip-hop hybrid Nação Zumbi, and award-winning film-score composer Antonio Pinto (*Centro do Brasil, Cidade de Deus*) on bass. Jorge performed at the 2012 Summer Olympics closing ceremony in London. His latest, *Músicas Para Churrasco, Vol 2* surfaced in 2015.

Brazilian rock (pronounced 'hock-ey') is also popular. Groups and artists such as Zeca Baleiro, Kid Abelha, Jota Quest, Ed Motta and the punk-driven Legião Urbana are worth a listen.

Wherever you go in Brazil you'll also hear regional musical styles. The most widely known is *forró* (foh-hoh), a lively, syncopated Northeastern music, which mixes *zabumba* (an African drum) beats with accordion sounds. *Axé* is a label for the samba-pop-rock-reggae-funk-Caribbean fusion music that emerged from Salvador in the 1990s, popularized especially by the flamboyant Daniela Mercury and now worshipped stadiums over by Ivete Sangalo. In the Amazon, you'll encounter the rhythms of *carimbo*, and the sensual dance that accompanies it.

Sertanejo, Brazilian country music, catapulted to international fame in 2011 when Michel Teló unleashed the inexplicable phenomenon that was *Ai Se Eu Te Pego* – perhaps the most famous Brazilian song since *The Girl from Ipanema*.

Cuisine

Brazilian restaurants serve huge portions, and many plates are designed for two – not great for single travelers, as the bill can cost 60% to 70% of the price for two when a portion for one is ordered (though often portions for two can feed three – trios beat Brazil at its own illogical math game). The basic Brazilian diet revolves around *arroz* (white rice), *feijão* (black beans) and *farofa/farinha* (flour from the root of manioc or corn). The typical Brazilian meal, called *prato feito* (set meal, often abbreviated 'pf') or *refeição*, consists of these ingredients plus either meat, chicken or fish and costs R$8 to R$14 in most eateries.

Another good option are *por kilo* (per kilogram) lunch buffets. Here you serve yourself and pay by the weight: typically between R$35 and R$60 per kilogram, with a big plateful weighing around half a kilo. Per-kilo places are good for vegetarians too. The fixed-price *rodízio* is another deal, and most *churrascarias* (meat BBQ restaurants) offer *rodízio* dining, where they bring endless skewers of different meat to your table. Overcharging and shortchanging are almost standard procedure. Check your bill carefully.

Regional variations include *comida baiana* from Bahia's northeastern coast, which has a distinct African flavor, using peppers, spices and the potent oil of the *dendê* palm tree. Both the Pantanal and the Amazon region have some tasty varieties of fish. Rio Grande do Sul's *comida gaúcha* is meat-focused. Minas Gerais is legendary for its hearty, vein-clogging fare, often involving chicken and pork (Brazilians also say any dish in Brazil tastes better in Minas); while São Paulo, home to large populations of Italians, Japanese and Arab immigrants, is Brazil's foodie mecca.

The incredible variety of Brazilian fruits makes for some divine *sucos* (juices). Every town has plenty of juice bars, offering 30 or 40 different varieties at around R$8 to R$12 for a good-sized glass.

Cafezinho puro (coffee), as typically drunk in Brazil, is strong, hot and often sickly presweetened in rural or less sophisticated locales, usually served without milk (*leite*). *Refrigerantes* (soft drinks) are found everywhere. *Guaraná*, made from the fruit of an Amazonian plant, is as popular as Coke.

The two key alcoholic drinks in Brazil are *cachaça* (also called *pinga*), a high-proof sugarcane spirit, and *cerveja* (beer). *Cachaça* ranges from excrementally raw to exquisite and smooth, and is the basis of that celebrated Brazilian cocktail, the *caipirinha*. Of the common beer brands, Colorado, Bohemia, Original and Serramalte are generally the best, but the craft-beer scene has exploded since 2013, especially in São Paulo, Paraná, Rio Grande do Sul and Minas Gerais. Invicta, Seasons, Wähls, BodeBrown and Way produce some of Brazil's best craft beers.

BRAZILIAN BREWHAHA!

Chope (shoh-pee) is draft beer and stands pretty much at the pinnacle of Brazilian civilization. The head can take up half the glass – it's believed to be an indicator of quality. You can order it without (*'sim colarinho'*) but some bars refuse to serve a smaller head than the width of two fingers.

Sports

Brazil may be the world's largest Catholic country, but *futebol* (soccer) is its religion. And Brazilians are such a devout bunch for good reason. Most people acknowledge that Brazilians play the world's most creative, artistic and thrilling style of football (Brazil is the only country to have won five World Cups – 1958, 1962, 1970, 1994 and 2002), but the national team has bailed out on the early side of recent World Cups and Olympic Games.

The national team's excruciating 7-1 pounding at the hands of Germany in the 2014 FIFA World Cup semifinal on home soil goes down as the most humiliating sporting moment in the country's history. Germany's relentless offensive blitzkrieg – four goals in six minutes! – not only scarred the population for life, but was Brazil's worst-ever defeat at home. It broke their 62-match streak in competitive home matches going back to 1975. The mortifying loss meant the host team was without a World Cup trophy for the second time in its hosting history (in 1950, the first time Brazil hosted the cup, the national team lost in heartbreaking fashion to Uruguay at Maracanã in Rio). Brazil went on to lose to the Netherlands 3-0 in the third-place match, embarrassingly crashing out of their own World Cup in fourth place. Not a soul was caught dead in a national team jersey for the rest of the year.

Since the heartbreaking summer of 2014, things haven't exactly been looking up for the *Seleção* (Selection), despite being led by Neymar, one of the most dynamic young superstars in the game. Dunga, who played for 1994 world champion national team, returned as manager after the post-World Cup resignation of Luiz Felipe Scolari, and quickly won some impressive friendly games. But a knockout defeat at the hands of Paraguay in the 2015 Copa América proved the team's woes wouldn't be so easily solved. The defeat prevented Brazil from qualifying for the 2017 FIFA Confederations Cup for the first time in almost 20 years.

However, hope for redemption remains right around the corner as the Summer Olympics make their first foray into South America in Rio de Janeiro in 2016. Of course, in order to silence critics and win back the hearts of Brazilian fans, nothing short of an Olympic championship on legendary Maracanã home soil – a trophy Brazil has never managed to win – will do. A loss, however? *Nossa senhora!*

Environment

The Land

The world's fifth-largest country after Russia, Canada, China and the US, Brazil borders every other South American country except Chile and Ecuador. Its 8.5-million-sq-km area covers almost half the continent.

Brazil has four primary geographic regions: the coastal band, the Planalto Brasileiro, the Amazon Basin and the Paraná-Paraguai Basin.

The narrow, 7400km-long coastal band lies between the Atlantic Ocean and the coastal mountain ranges. From the border with Uruguay to Bahia state, steep mountains often come right down to the coast. North of Bahia, the coastal lands are flatter.

The Planalto Brasileiro (Brazilian Plateau) extends over most of Brazil's interior south of the Amazon Basin. It's sliced by several large rivers and punctuated by mountain ranges reaching no more than 3000m.

The thinly populated Amazon Basin, composing 42% of Brazil, is fed by waters from the Planalto Brasileiro to its south, the Andes to the west and the Guyana shield to the north. In the west the basin is 1300km wide; in the east, between the Guyana shield and the Planalto, it narrows to 100km. More than half the 6275km of the Rio Amazonas lies not in Brazil but in Peru, where the river's source is also found. The Amazon and its 1100 tributaries contain an estimated 20% of the world's freshwater. Pico da Neblina (3014m) on the Venezuelan border is the highest peak in Brazil.

The Paraná-Paraguai Basin, in the south of Brazil, extends into neighboring Paraguay and Argentina, and includes the large wetland area known as the Pantanal.

Wildlife

Brazil is the most biodiverse country on Earth. It has more known species of plants (56,215), freshwater fish (3000) and mammals (578) than any other country in the world; and isn't far behind in birds (1721) and reptiles (651). Many species live in the Amazon rainforest, which occupies 3.6 million sq km in Brazil and 2.4 million sq km in neighboring countries. It's the world's largest tropical forest and most biologically diverse ecosystem, with 20% of the world's bird and plant species and 10% of its mammals.

Other Brazilian species are widely distributed around the country. For example the biggest Brazilian cat, the jaguar, is found in Amazon and Atlantic rainforests, the cerrado (savanna) and the Pantanal.

Many other Brazilian mammals are found over a broad range of habitats, including five other big cats (puma, ocelot, margay, oncilla and jaguarundi); the giant anteater; 77 primate species, including several types of howler and capuchin monkey, the squirrel monkey (Amazonia's most common primate) and around 20 small species of marmosets and tamarin; the furry, long-nosed coati (a type of raccoon); the giant river otter; the maned wolf; the tapir; peccaries (such as wild boar); marsh and pampas deer; the capybara (the world's largest rodent at 1m long); the pink dolphin, often glimpsed in the Amazon and its tributaries; and the Amazon manatee, an even larger river dweller.

Birds form a major proportion of the wildlife you'll see. The biggest is the flightless, 1.4m-high rhea, found in the cerrado and the Pantanal. The brilliantly colored parrots, macaws, toucans and trogons come in dozens of species. In Amazonia or the Pantanal you may see scarlet macaws and, if you're lucky, blue-and-yellow ones.

In Amazonia or the Pantanal you can't miss the alligators. One of Brazil's five species, the black caiman, grows up to 6m long. Other aquatic life in the Amazon includes the pirarucu, which grows 3m long – its red and silvery-brown scale patterns are reminiscent of Chinese paintings. The infamous piranha comes in about 50 species, found in the river basins of the Amazon, Orinoco, Paraguai and São Francisco, and the rivers of the Guianas.

National Parks

Brazil is home to 69 national parks, managed by ICMbio (www.icmbio.gov.br), 26 of which are open to the public.

Parque Nacional da Chapada Diamantina (p360) is in a mountainous region in the Northeast. There's excellent trekking with rivers, waterfalls, caves and swimming holes.

Parque Nacional da Chapada dos Guimarães (p348) is a canyon park with breathtaking views and impressive rock formations on a rocky plateau northeast of Cuiabá.

Parque Nacional da Chapada dos Veadeiros (☎3455-1116; www.chapadadosveadeirosoficial.com.br; ⏲8am-6pm Tue-Sun, entry until noon only) FREE, 200km north of Brasília, is a hilly national park set among waterfalls and natural swimming holes, and featuring an array of rare flora and fauna.

Parque Nacional da Serra dos Órgãos is set in the mountainous terrain of the Southeast; this park is a mecca for rock climbers and mountaineers.

Parque Nacional de Aparados da Serra (p333) in the Southeast is famous for its narrow canyon with 700m escarpments. It features hiking trails with excellent overlooks.

Parque Nacional dos Lençóis Maranhenses (p386) in the Northeast has spectacular beaches, mangroves, dunes and lagoons.

Parque Nacional Marinho de Fernando de Noronha (p370) is Brazil's island Eden with pristine beaches, cerulean waters, world-class diving and snorkeling. It's one of the world's best spots to view spinner dolphins.

Environmental Issues

At last count more than one-fifth of the Brazilian Amazon rainforest had been completely destroyed, though deforestation has tapered off somewhat in recent years. The government continues development projects in the Amazon, although the protests have become more vocal in recent years. The longest ongoing controversy surrounds the hydroelectric Belo Monte Dam on the Rio Xingu in Pará (the world's third largest behind China's Three Gorges and Brazil-Paraguay's Itaipu), though, by late 2015, the impending closure of the Rio Xingu – and subsequent initiation of the dam's first turbine – had yet to begin. However, the 2015 Bento Rodrigues dam catastrophe, an epic environmental disaster of as-yet-untold proportions, has quite unfortunately stolen the headlines away from Belo Monte.

On November 5, 2015, two dams under the supervision of Samarco, a joint venture between Anglo-Australian mining giants BHP Billiton and Brazil's Vale, gave way, sending a 60-million-cu-meter toxic sea of sludge barreling down into the Santarém river valley in Minas Gerais. It killed at least 13 people, wiping out the village of Bento Rodrigues. Eventually the sludge made its way to the Atlantic Ocean via the contaminated Doce River 17 days later, destroying everything in its path. The disaster is being compared with the 2010 BP oil spill in the Gulf of Mexico in scope and damage, and is being touted as the worst environmental catastrophe in Brazil's history. Investigations are pending, but initial reports put the blame on lax safety regulations and negligence. There was heavy criticism of the responses of the company and the government: it took President Dilma Rouseff a week to visit the disaster zone, further fueling cries by her critics that she is unfit to run the country. At time of writing, the Brazilian government announced it would sue Samarco for $5.2 billion to pay for environmental recovery and victim compensation, though the grim reality is that no amount of money could ever undo the damage.

SURVIVAL GUIDE

Directory A–Z

ACCOMMODATIONS

Brazilian accommodations are simple yet usually clean and reasonably safe, and nearly all come with some form of *café da manha* (breakfast).

Youth hostels are traditionally called *albergues da juventude*, but carry a somewhat negative connotation in Portuguese. A true hostel scene using the more internationally recognized word is now emerging in Brazil with many excellent choices. A dormitory bed costs between R$45 and R$75 per person.

Brazil hotels are among South America's priciest; a far more charming and local option is a *pousada*, which typically means a small family-owned inn, though some hotels call themselves *pousadas* to improve their charm quotient. *Pousadas* can cost as little as R$140 for a rustic double up to more than R$1000 for the country's most lavish.

ACTIVITIES

Popular activities for adrenaline-fueled adventure include canyoning, paragliding, kitesurfing, wakeboarding, rafting, surfing, trekking, diving and mountain climbing.

Hiking and climbing activities are best during the cooler months, from April to October. Outstanding hiking areas include the national parks of Chapada Diamantina in Bahia, Serra dos Órgãos in Rio de Janeiro state, Chapada dos Veadeiros in Goiás and the Serra de São José near Tiradentes in Minas Gerais.

The best surfing is in Fernando de Noronha between December and March. Also good are the beaches in the South and Southeast: Saquarema, Ilha de Santa Catarina, São Francisco do Sul, Ilha do Mel, Búzios and Rio de Janeiro. In the Northeast, head to Itacaré and Praia da Pipa. The waves are best in the Brazilian winter (June to August).

SLEEPING PRICE RANGES

The following price indicators apply (for high-season double with bathroom):

$ less than R$160

$$ R$160 to R$350

$$$ more than R$350

The price range for Rio, São Paulo and Brasília is higher:

$ less than R$200

$$ R$200 to R$500

$$$ more than R$500

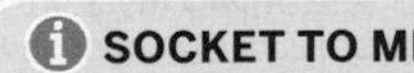

SOCKET TO ME

In 2010, Brazil finally decided to enforce the standardization of its electrical outlets. The new three-prong plug (thus far unique to Brazil and South Africa, though eventually expected to be adopted across Europe), is required for all new electrical appliances. The transition will take years, and the old two-prong/US-style hybrid is still prevalent. If you happen to sleep in a newly constructed hotel or one that has been upgraded, you will need to purchase an adapter (R$6).

Búzios in Rio state has good windsurfing and kitesurfing conditions, and access to rental equipment. But Brazil's hardcore windsurfing hot spot is the Ceará coast northwest of Fortaleza, from July to December. Here, Jericoacoara and Canoa Quebrada are the most popular spots.

ELECTRICITY

Electrical current is not standardized in Brazil and can be almost anywhere between 110V and 220V. Carry a converter and use a surge protector with non-dual electrical equipment.

EMBASSIES & CONSULATES

The embassies are all in Brasília, but many countries have consulates in Rio and São Paulo, and often other cities as well. For addresses in Brasília, SES stands for Setor de Embaixadas Sul.

Argentine Embassy (☎0xx61-3212-7600; www.cpabl.mrecic.gov.ar; SES Quadra 803, Lote 12, Brasília); Iguaçu Falls consulate (☎0xx45-3574-2969; www.cpabl.mrecic.gov.ar; Travessia Bianchi 26; ⏰10am-3pm Mon-Fri); Porto Alegre consulate (☎0xx51-3321-1360; Rua Coronel Bordini 1033); Rio consulate (☎0xx21-2553-1646; Praia de Botafogo 228, Room 201, Botafogo); São Paulo consulate (☎0xx11-3897-9522; www.cpabl.mrecic.gov.ar; Av Paulista 2313, Bela Vista)

Australian Embassy (☎0xx61-3226-3111; www.brazil.embassy.gov.au; Av das Nações, SES, Q 801, Conj K, Lota 7, Brasília); Rio consulate (☎3824-4624; http://brazil.embassy.gov.au; 23rd fl, Av Presidente Wilson 231, Centro)

Bolivian Consulate (☎0xx61-3366-3136; www.embolivia.org.br; SES Av das Nações 06, Quadra 809, Lote 34); Brasiléia consulate (☎0xx68-3546-5760; Julio Matiolli Nro. 84, Centro Municipio de Epitaciolandia Acre, Brasil; ⏰8am-noon & 2-4pm Mon-Fri); Corumbá consulate (☎3231-5605; consuladoboliviacorumba@gmail.com; cnr Porto Carrero & Firmo de Matos; ⏰8am-12:30pm & 2-5:30pm Mon-

Fri); Guajará-Mirim consulate (☎0xx69-3541-8622; Rua 15 de Novembro 255; ⊙8am-noon & 2-6pm Mon-Fri); Rio consulate (☎0xx21-2552-5490; www.consuladodeboliviaenrio.org.br; No 101, Av Rui Barbosa 664)

Canadian Embassy (☎0xx61-3424 5400; www.brazil.gc.ca; Av das Nações, SES, Q 803, Lote 16, Brasília); Rio consulate (☎0xx21-2543-3004; www.brasil.gc.ca; 13th fl, Av Atlântica 1130, Copacabana); São Paulo consulate (☎0xx11-5509-4321; www.canadainternational.gc.ca; 16th Fl, Torre Norte, Av das Nações Unidas 12901)

Colombian Embassy (☎0xx61-3214-8900; brasil.embajada.gov.co; Av das Nações, SES, Q 803, Lote 10, Brasília); Tabatinga consulate (☎3412-2104; http://tabatinga.consulado.gov.co; Sampaio 623)

Dutch Embassy (☎0xx61-3961-3200; http://brazilie.nlambassade.org; Av das Nações, SES, Quadra 801, Lote 05, Brasília); Rio consulate (☎0xx21-2157-5400; riodejaneiro.nlconsulado.org; 6th fl, Ataulfo de Paiva)

French Embassy (☎0xx61-3222-3999; www.ambafrance-br.org; Av das Nações, SES, Q 801, Lote 04, Brasília); Rio consulate (☎0xx21-3974-6699; http://riodejaneiro.ambafrance-br.org; Av Presidente Antônio Carlos 58, Centro)

German Embassy (☎0xx61-3442-7000; www.brasilia.diplo.de; Av das Nações, SES, Q 807, Lote 25, Brasília); Rio consulate (☎0xx21-2554-0004; www.rio-de-janeiro.diplo.de; Carlos de Campos 417)

Guyanese Embassy (☎0xx61-3248-0874; Casa 24, SHIS Quadra 5, Conj 19, Brasília)

Irish Embassy (☎0xx61-3248-8800; SHIS QL 12 Conjunto 5, Casa 9, Brasília)

Israeli Embassy (☎0xx61-2105-0500; embassies.gov.il; Av das Nações, SES, Q 809, Lote 38, Brasília)

New Zealand Embassy (☎0xx-3248-9900; www.nzembassy.com/brazil; SHIS Q1 09, Conjunto 16, Casa 1, Brasília); São Paulo consulate (☎0xx11-3898-7400; www.nzembassy.com/brazil; Paulista 2421, 12th Fl, Bela Vista, São Paulo)

Paraguayan Embassy (☎0xx-61-3242-3968; embaparaguai.org.br; Av das Nações, SES, Quadra 811, Lote 42, Brasília); Iguaçu Falls consulate (☎0xx45-3523-2898; fozconsulpar@mre.gov.py; R Marechal Deodoro da Fonseca 901; ⊙9am-1pm Mon-Fri)

Peruvian Embassy (☎0xx61-3242-9933; www.embperu.org.br; Av das Nações, SES, Quadra 811, Lote 43, Brasília); Rio consulate (☎0xx21-2551-9596; www.consuladoperurio.com.br; 2nd fl, Av Rui Barbosa 314, Flamengo)

UK Embassy (☎0xx61-3329-2300; www.reinounido.org.br; Av das Nações, SES, Quadra 801, Conj K, Lote 08, Brasília); Rio consulate (☎0xx21-2555-9600; www.reinounido.org.br; 2nd fl, Praia do Flamengo 284, Flamengo); São Paulo consulate (☎0xx11-3094-2700; www.ukinbrazil.fco.gov.uk; Fereira de Araujа 741, 2nd fl, Pinheiros, São Paulo)

Uruguayan Embassy (☎0xx61-3322-6534; www.emburuguai.org.br; Av das Nações, SES, Quadra 803, Lote 14, Brasília); Porto Alegre consulate (☎0xx51-3325-6200; Av 24 de Outubro 850); Rio consulate (☎0xx21-2553-6030; www.emburuguai.org.br; 6th fl, Praia de Botafogo 210)

US Embassy (☎0xx61-3312-7000; brazil.usembassy.gov; Av das Nações, SES, Quadra 801, Lote 3, Brasília); Rio consulate (☎0xx21-3823-2000; brazil.usembassy.gov; Av Presidente Wilson 147, Centro); Salvador consulate (☎0xx71-3113-2090; Room 1401, Salvador Trade Center, Torre Sul, Av Tancredo Neves 1632); São Paulo consulate (☎0xx11-3250-5000; http://saopaulo.usconsulate.gov; Henri Dunant 500, Chácara Santo Antônio)

Venezuelan Embassy (☎0xx61-2101-1010; http://brasil.embajada.gob.ve; Av das Nações, SES, Quadra 803, Lote 13, Brasília); Boa Vista consulate (☎0xx95-3623-6612; Av Benjamin Constant 968; ⊙8am-noon Mon-Fri); Manaus consulate (☎0xx92-3584-3813; Río Jamary 10, Conj Vieiralves, Nossa Senhora das Graças); Rio consulate (☎0xx21-2554-5955; 14th fl, Av Presidente Vargas 463, Centro, Rio de Janeiro)

GAY & LESBIAN TRAVELERS

Machismo dominates in Brazil and being out is still a challenge. Rio, São Paulo and Florianópolis have the best gay scenes, though you'll find good gay bars in Salvador and elsewhere. These are all-welcome affairs attended by GLS *(Gays, Lesbians e Simpatizantes)* crowds of straights and gays. Useful websites for gay and lesbian travelers include www.riogayguide.com and www.riog.com.br.

HEALTH

➡ Malaria is a concern in certain areas of the Amazon and Northwest Brazil. Travelers should weigh the risks of an appropriate malaria preventative (Chloroquine is not effective here), and cover up as much as possible to prevent mosquito bites. Brazil has become the epicenter of mosquito-borne dengue fever in

EATING PRICE RANGES

The following price indicators refer to a standard main course (including tax but excluding 10% service charge):

$ less than R$30

$$ R$30 to R$75

$$$ more than R$75

Latin America, especially in and around Rio and Bahía. If you are in an area where mosquitoes are biting during the day, you are at risk and should consider repellent.

- Tap water is safe but not very tasty in most urban areas. In remote areas, filter your own or stick to bottled water.
- The sun is powerful here and travelers should be mindful of heatstroke, dehydration and sunburn. Drink plenty of water, wear a strong sunscreen and allow your body time to acclimatize to high temperatures before attempting strenuous activities. A good drink when dehydrated is *agua de coco* (coconut water), which contains electrolytes.
- A yellow fever immunization certificate is no longer compulsory to enter Brazil, but highly recommended. At most Brazilian borders and major airports there are vaccination posts where you can have the jab (free for foreigners) and get the certificate immediately. But it's wise to do this in advance.

ZIKA VIRUS: WARNING FOR PREGNANT TRAVELERS

Brazil has experienced an outbreak of Zika virus infections since 2015. Transmitted by mosquitoes, Zika rarely causes illness (only one in five infected people will experience the flu-like symptoms). The virus, however, has been linked to microcephaly (abnormally small head size with possible brain damage) in babies born to women who were infected while pregnant. The CDC has recommended pregnant women to consider postponing travel to Brazil (and other countries where virus transmission is ongoing).

INTERNET ACCESS

Wi-fi is widespread throughout Brazil and generally free at most lodgings.

LANGUAGE

Portuguese is generally considered the world's sixth most spoken language. Brazilian Portuguese has many differences from European Portuguese, but speakers can understand one another in most cases. This is not the case with Spanish – if you can speak Spanish, you'll be able to read some Portuguese but comprehending others is difficult. Some Brazilians also find it a tad offensive when foreigners arrive speaking Spanish and expect to be understood. Pick up a copy of Lonely Planet's *Brazilian Portuguese* phrasebook to get you talking.

It's exceedingly popular to arrange Portuguese classes in Brazil. Try **IBEU** (Instituto Brasil Estados Unidos; www.ibeu.org.br) in Rio, or **Polyglot** (www.polyglot.com.br) or **Universidade Presbiteriana Mackenzie** (www.mackenzie.br) in São Paulo. Nationally, try **Wizard** (www.wizard.com.br). **Celpe-Bras** (http://portal.inep.gov.br/celpebras) offers the only certificate of proficiency in Portuguese as a Second Language recognized by the Brazilian Ministry of Education.

LEGAL MATTERS

Be wary but respectful of Brazilian police – you can be arrested in Brazil for shouting, cursing or otherwise losing your temper while interacting with any person of authority or public official.

Stiff penalties are in force for use and possession of drugs; the police don't share most Brazilians' tolerant attitude toward marijuana. Police checkpoints along the highways stop cars at random. Don't even think about drinking and driving – Brazil introduced a zero-tolerance law in 2008 and roadblocks (called '*blitz*') are common in major cities, especially Rio and São Paulo.

A large amount of cocaine is smuggled out of Bolivia and Peru through Brazil. If you're entering Brazil from one of the Andean countries and have been chewing coca leaves, be careful to clean out your pack first.

MAPS

Quatro Rodas produces a good country-wide road atlas, *Rodoviário* (R$25), available at finer bookstores. Good topographical maps are published by the IBGE (www.ibge.gov.br), the government geographical service, and the DSG (www.dsg.eb.mil.br), the army geographical service. Availability is erratic, but IBGE offices in most state capitals sell IBGE maps.

MONEY

Brazil's currency is the real (pronounced 'hay-*ow*,' often written R$); the plural is reais (pronounced 'hay-*ice*'). One real is made up of 100 centavos. Banknotes come in denominations of 2, 5, 10, 20, 50 and 100.

ATMs

ATMs are widely available, but are often finicky with foreign cards. Do yourself a favor and bring a few options, then find a bank that works with one of your cards and stick with it. Four-digit PINs are standard. In general, Citibank, Banco de Brasil, Bradesco and Banco24Horas (a conglomeration of Brazilian banks) are the best ATMs to try. Banco do Brasil and Bradesco are feeless. Transaction limits vary widely (normally between R$300 and R$800), but with a foreign card you can usually pull multiple times up to your own bank's daily limit. Bradesco is the friendliest in this regard.

FRAUD WARNING!

Credit-card and ATM fraud is widespread in Brazil, especially in the Northeast. Card-cloning (*Clonagem* in Portuguese) is the preferred method – an entrepreneurial opportunist sticks a false card reader into an ATM that copies your card and steals the PIN when you come along and withdraw money. Shazam! A few hours later, $1500 disappears from your account in Recife while you and your card are safe and sound sipping *caipirinhas* on the beach in Rio.

To combat fraud, restaurants will bring the credit-card machine to your table or ask you to accompany them to the cashier to run a credit-card transaction. Never let someone walk off with your card.

- Use high-traffic ATMs inside banks during banking hours only.
- Always cover the ATM keypad when entering personal codes.
- Avoid self-standing ATMs if possible and never use an ATM that looks tampered with.

Credit Cards

You can use credit cards to pay for many purchases in Brazil and to make cash withdrawals from ATMs. Visa is the most commonly accepted card, followed by MasterCard. American Express and Diners Club are far less accepted outside major metropolitan areas.

OPENING HOURS

Banks 10am to 4pm Monday to Friday.

Bars 7pm to 2am, to 4am on weekends.

Restaurants 8am to 10:30am (breakfast), noon to 3pm (lunch), and 7pm to 11pm (dinner).

Shops & government services (including post offices) 9am to 5pm Monday to Friday, to 1pm Saturday.

POST

The government-run Brazilian postal service is decked out in can't-miss yellow and blue, and is called *Correios* (www.correios.com.br). Branches are ubiquitous.

PUBLIC HOLIDAYS

Ano Novo (New Year's Day) January 1

Carnaval (Friday to Tuesday preceding Ash Wednesday) February/March. Celebrations usually start well before the official holiday.

Paixão & Páscoa (Good Friday and Easter Sunday) March/April

Tiradentes (Tiradentes Day) April 21

Dia do Trabalho (May Day/Labor Day) May 1

Corpus Christi (60 days after Easter) Sunday May/June

Dia da Independência (Independence Day) September 7

Dia da Nossa Senhora de Aparecida (Day of Our Lady of Aparecida) October 12

Finados (All Souls' Day) November 2

Proclamação da República (Proclamation of the Republic Day) November 15

Natal (Christmas Day) December 25

RESPONSIBLE TRAVEL

We all have an obligation to protect Brazil's fragile environment. You can do your bit by using environmentally friendly tourism services wherever possible and avoiding those that aren't proactively taking steps to avoid ecological damage (this includes Pantanal operators who encourage touching animals).

Using the services of local community groups will ensure that your money goes directly to those who are helping you, as does buying crafts and other products directly from the artisans or their trusted representatives.

SAFE TRAVEL

Brazil receives a lot of bad press about its violence and high crime rate. Use common sense and take general precautions applicable throughout South America.

- Carry only the minimum cash needed plus a fat-looking wad of singles to hand over to would-be thieves.
- Dress down, leave the jewelry at home and don't walk around flashing iPhones, iPads and other expensive electronics.
- Be alert and walk purposefully. Criminals hone in on dopey, hesitant, disoriented-looking individuals.
- Use ATMs inside buildings. Before doing so, be very aware of your surroundings. Thieves case ATMs and exchange houses.
- Check windows and doors of your room for security, and don't leave anything valuable lying around.
- Don't take anything unnecessary to city beaches (bathing suit, towel, small amount of cash – nothing else!).
- After dark, don't ever walk along empty streets, deserted parks or urban beaches.
- Don't wander into *favelas* unaccompanied.

TELEPHONE

Domestic Calls

You can make domestic calls from normal card-pay telephones on the street (called *orelhões*). The cards are sold in units from 20 to 100, and range in price between R$5 and R$20 from vendors, newsstands and anywhere else advertising *cartões telefônicos*.

To make a local collect call, dial ☎9090, then the number.

For calls to other cities, dial 0, then the code of your selected long-distance carrier, then the two digits representing the city, followed by the local number. You need to choose a long-distance carrier that covers both the place you are calling from and the place you're calling to. Carriers advertise their codes in areas where they're prominent, but you can usually use Embratel (code 21) nationwide.

To make an intercity collect call, dial 9 before the 0xx. A recorded message in Portuguese will ask you to say your name and where you're calling from, after the tone.

International Calls

Brazil's country code is 55. When calling internationally to Brazil, omit the initial 0xx of the area code.

International landline-to-landline calls from Brazil using Embratel start from 78¢ a minute to the US, R$1.66 to Europe and R$1.51 to Australia.

Orelhões are of little use for international calls unless you have an international calling card or are calling collect. Most pay phones are restricted to domestic calls, and even if they aren't, a 30-unit Brazilian phone card may last less than a minute internationally.

Without an international calling card, your best option is Skype.

For international *a cobrar* (collect) calls, secure a Brazilian international operator by dialing ☎0800-703-2111 (Embratel).

Cell Phones

Brazil uses the GSM 850/900/1800/1900 network, which is compatible with North America, Europe and Australia. However, the country's 4G LTE network runs on 2500/2690, which is compatible with many but not all imported smartphones. For example, only the following iPhone 6 and iPhone 6 Plus models will work: www.apple.com/iphone/LTE (other models will work but are relegated to 3G). Most *celular* (cell) phones have nine-digit numbers (still eight in some states) starting with a 6, 7, 8 or 9. Calls to mobiles are more expensive than calls to landlines. Mobiles have city codes like landlines, and if you're calling from another city, you have to use them.

Tim (www.tim.com.br), **Claro** (www.claro.com.br), **Oi** (www.oi.com.br) and **Vivo** (www.vivo.com.br) are the major operators. Foreigners can supposedly purchase a local SIM with a passport instead of needing a Brazilian CPF (tax ID number), though most cellular providers seem oblivious to this – prepare for a battle.

TOILETS

Public toilets are available at every bus station and airport; there's usually a small entrance fee of R$1 or so, depending on what you need to do!

TOURIST INFORMATION

Tourist offices in Brazil are nearly all run by individual states or municipalities and are usually given the acronyms CIT (*Centro de Informações Turísticas*), CAT (*Centro de Atendimento ao Turista*) or PIT (*Pontos de Informação Turística*); Setur (*Secretaria de Turismo*), Semtur (*Secretaria Municipal de Turismo*) and Sedtur (*Secretaria de Estado de Desenvolvimento do Turismo*) are also common.

VISAS

Citizens of the USA and Australia need a visa; citizens from the UK, France, Germany and New Zealand do not. At the time of writing, Canadians still needed a visa, though that was likely to change due to the Canadian government's announcement that Brazilians would no longer need a visa to visit Canada from March 2016.

Tourist visas are valid for arrival in Brazil within 90 days of issue and then for a 90-day stay. The fee and length depends on your nationality; it's usually between US$20 and US$65, though US citizens are hit with a whopping US$160 reciprocal bill. Processing times vary from five to 10 business days, sometimes less depending on nationality and consulate efficiency, but consular appointments can be booked as much as three months out – book this *before* you make travel arrangements. Brazilian consulates will never entertain expedited visa services under any circumstance, so plan ahead. You'll generally need to present one passport photograph, proof of onward travel and a valid passport.

People under 18 years of age who wish to travel to Brazil without a parent or legal guardian must present a notarized Visa Consent Form from the nontraveling parent/guardian or from a court. Check with a Brazilian consulate well in advance about this.

For up-to-date information on visas check www.lonelyplanet.com/brazil/visas.

Entry/Exit Card

On entering Brazil, all tourists must fill out a *cartão de entrada/saida* (entry/exit card); immigration officials keep half, you keep the other. Don't lose this card! When you leave Brazil, the second half of the entry/exit card will be taken by immigration officials.

Most visitors can stay for 90 days, but if for some reason you receive fewer days, this will be written in the stamp in your passport.

Visa Extensions

Brazil's Polícia Federal, who have offices in the state capitals and border towns, handle visa extensions for those nationalities allowed to extend (Schengen region passport holders, for example, must leave for 90 days before re-entering for a second 90-days – extending is not an option.

The convoluted visa extension process is as follows:

➡ Fill out and print the form '*Requerimento de Prorrogação de Prazo*' found in the '*Estrangeiros*' section under subheading '*Prorrogar Prazo de Estada de Turista e Viajante a Negócios (Temporário II)*' from the Polícia Federal website (www.dpf.gov.br).

➡ Generate a government tax collection form called a 'GRU (*Guia de Recolhimento da União*),' found by clicking through the link from the same subheading, then '*Pessoas e Entidades Estrangeiras*.' In that form, fill out your personal info; enter code '140090,' under '*Código da Receita STN*;' choose the Polícia Federal office nearest you under the drop-down menu '*Unidade Arrecadadora*;' and enter R$110.44 under '*Valor Total R$*.' Then click '*Gerar Guia*' to generate the bar-coded form.

➡ Take it to any bank, post office or lottery point and pay the R$110.44 fee; then head to the nearest Polícia Federal office with all in hand as well as your passport and original entry card. When you go, dress nicely! Some Fed stations don't take kindly to people in shorts. The extension is at the discretion of the officer and you may be asked to provide a ticket out of the country and proof of sufficient funds. If you get the maximum 90-day extension and then leave the country before the end of that period, you cannot return until the full 90 days have elapsed.

VOLUNTEERING

Rio-based **Iko Poran** (☎ 0xx21-2252-8214; www.ikoporan.org; Pintora Djanira 58, Santa Teresa) links the diverse talents of volunteers with needy organizations. Previous volunteers in Brazil have worked as dance, music, art and language instructors among other things. Iko Poran also provides housing for volunteers. The UK-based **Task Brasil** (www.taskbrasil.org.uk) is another laudable organization that places volunteers in Rio.

WOMEN TRAVELERS

In the cities of the Southeast and South, foreign women without traveling companions will scarcely be given a sideways glance. In the more traditional rural areas of the Northeast, blonde-haired and light-skinned women, especially those without male escorts, will certainly arouse curiosity.

Machismo is less overt in Brazil than in Spanish-speaking Latin America. Flirtation is a common form of communication, but it's generally regarded as innocent banter; no sense of insult, exploitation or serious intent should be assumed.

It's advisable to adapt what you wear to local norms. The brevity of Rio beach attire generally is not suitable for the streets of interior cities, for instance.

Most pharmacies in Brazil stock the morning-after pill *(a pílula do dia seguinte)*, which costs about R$17. Tampons and other sanitary items are widely available in most pharmacies.

WORK

Brazil has high unemployment and tourists are not supposed to take jobs. However, it's not unusual for foreigners to find language-teaching work in the bigger cities, either in language schools or through private tutoring. The pay is not great but if you can work for three or four days a week you can just about not starve.

ℹ Getting There & Away

Brazil has several gateway airports and shares a border with every country in South America except Chile and Ecuador.

Flights, cars and tours can be booked online at lonelyplanet.com/bookings.

AIR

The busiest international airports are Aeroporto Galeão (formally known as Aeroporto Internacional António Carlos Jobim; www.riogaleao.com) in Rio de Janeiro and São Paulo–Guarulhos (GRU Airport; www.gru.com.br). Salvador and Recife also receive a few direct scheduled flights from Europe and North America.

LATAM (formerly Tam; www.latam.com) is Brazil's main international carrier, with flights to New York (USA), Miami (USA), Paris (France), London (UK), Lisbon (Portugal) and seven South American cities.

BUS

Argentina

The main border point used by travelers is Puerto Iguazú–Iguaçu Falls, a 20-hour bus ride from Buenos Aires. Further south, you can cross from Paso de los Libres (Argentina) to Uruguaiana (Brazil), which is also served by buses from Buenos Aires.

Direct buses run between Buenos Aires and Porto Alegre (R$250, 18 hours) and Rio de Janeiro (R$450, 42 hours). Other destinations include Florianópolis (R$315, 25 hours), Curitiba

(R$370, 34 hours) and São Paulo (R$375, 36 hours).

Bolivia

Brazil's longest border runs through remote wetlands and forests, and is much used by smugglers. The main crossings are at Corumbá, Cáceres, Guajará-Mirim and Brasiléia.

The busiest crossing is between Quijarro (Bolivia) and Corumbá (Brazil), which is a good access point for the Pantanal. Quijarro has a daily train link with Santa Cruz (Bolivia). Corumbá has bus connections with Bonito, Campo Grande, São Paulo, Rio de Janeiro and southern Brazil.

Cáceres, in Mato Grosso (Brazil), has a daily bus link with Santa Cruz (Bolivia) via the Bolivian border town of San Matías.

Guajará-Mirim (Brazil) is a short river crossing from Guayaramerín (Bolivia). Both towns have onward bus links into their respective countries (Guayaramerín also has flights), but from late December to late February heavy rains can make the northern Bolivian roads a very difficult proposition.

Brasiléia (Brazil), a 4½-hour bus ride from Rio Branco, stands opposite Cobija (Bolivia), which has bus and plane connections into Bolivia. Bolivian buses confront the same wet-season difficulties.

Chile

Although there is no border with Chile, direct buses run via Argentina between Santiago and Brazilian cities such as Porto Alegre (R$415, 36 hours), São Paulo (R$446, 54 hours) and Rio de Janeiro (R$486, 62 hours).

Colombia

Leticia, on the Rio Amazonas in far southeast Colombia, is contiguous with Tabatinga (Brazil). You can cross the border on foot or by Kombi van or taxi. From within Colombia, Leticia is only really accessible by air. Tabatinga is a quick flight (or a several-day Amazon boat ride) from Manaus or Tefé.

French Guiana

The Brazilian town of Oiapoque, a rugged 560km bus ride from Macapá (R$120, 12 to 15 hours), stands across the Rio Oiapoque from St Georges (French Guiana). A road connects St Georges to the French Guiana capital, Cayenne, with minibuses shuttling between the two. (Get there early in the morning to catch one.)

Guyana & Suriname

From Boa Vista, there are daily buses to Bonfim, Roraima (R$26, 1½ hours), on the Guyanese border, a short motorized-canoe ride from Lethem (R$4; southwest Guyana).

Overland travel between Suriname and Brazil involves first passing through either French Guiana or Guyana.

Paraguay

The two major border crossings are Ciudad del Este (Paraguay)–Iguaçu Falls (Brazil) and Pedro Juan Caballero (Paraguay)–Ponta Porã (Brazil). Direct buses run between Asunción and Brazilian cities such as Florianópolis (R$320, 20 hours), Curitiba (R$240, 14 hours), São Paulo (R$205, 20 hours) and Iguaçu Falls (R$80, five hours).

Peru

There is at least one daily bus connecting Rio Branco (Brazil) to Puerto Maldonado (Peru) via the border at Assis (Brazil)–Iñapari (Peru) on the new US$2.75 billion Interoceanic Hwy. You can also reach Assis on daily buses from Epitáciolândia (R$18, two hours) and cross the Rio Acre to Iñapari.

Uruguay

The crossing most used by travelers is at Chuy (Uruguay)–Chuí (Brazil). Other crossings are Río Branco–Jaguarão, Isidoro Noblia–Aceguá, Rivera–Santana do Livramento, Artigas–Quaraí and Bella Unión–Barra do Quaraí. Buses run between Montevideo and Brazilian cities such as Porto Alegre (R$205.50, 12 hours), Florianópolis (R$275, 18 hours) and São Paulo (R$390, 32 hours).

Venezuela

From Manaus, five daily buses run to Boa Vista (R$120, 12 hours), from where you can connect to Puerto La Cruz (Venezuela; R$240, 20 hours) for access to Caracas or Isla Margarita.

RIVER

Fast passenger boats make the 400km trip (around US$100, eight to 10 hours) along the Amazon River between Iquitos (Peru) and Tabatinga (Brazil). From Tabatinga you can continue 3000km down the river to its mouth.

From Trinidad in Bolivia you can reach Brazil by a boat trip of about five days down the Río Mamoré to Guayaramerín, opposite the Brazilian town of Guajará-Mirim.

HITCHHIKING

Hitchhiking in Brazil, with the possible exceptions of the Pantanal and Fernando de Noronha, is difficult and likely unsafe. The Portuguese for 'lift' is *carona*.

MAJOR DOMESTIC AIRLINES

Avianca	www.avianca.com.br	0300-789-8160
Azul	www.voeazul.com.br	0800-887-1118
Gol	www.voegol.com.br	0300-115-2121
LATAM	www.latam.com	0800-570-5700

Getting Around

AIR

Domestic Air Services

Brazil's biggest domestic carriers are Gol and LATAM (new name announced in 2015 after the merger of Chile's LAN and Brazil's Tam), along with Avianca and Azul, the latter operating out of Campinas, 100km northwest of São Paulo. A free shuttle to Campinas' Viracopas airport runs from Aeroporto Congonhas, Barra Funda metro station and Shopping El Dorado in São Paulo.

Some major domestic airlines now accept major foreign credit cards through their websites, though it often doesn't work – you'll have to pay at an airline office or travel agent if your card is declined.

Air Passes

The Gol South America air pass is valid for travel on Gol's network, including extensive domestic routes in Brazil as well as routes between Brazil and Chile, Argentina, Paraguay, Uruguay, Peru and Bolivia. Fares are US$629 plus tax for four flights, US$822 for five flights; each additional flight is US$140. LATAM's South American Airpass and the Visit South America air pass from **Oneworld Alliance** (www.oneworld.com) offer similar products.

These passes must be purchased before you go to Brazil, and you have to book your air-pass itinerary at the time you buy it – or possibly pay penalties for changing reservations. Many travel agents sell the air pass – your best bet is the Brazilian travel specialist **Brol** (www.brol.com).

If for any reason you do not fly on an air-pass flight you have reserved, you should reconfirm all your other flights. Travelers have sometimes found that all their air-pass reservations had been scrubbed from the computer after they missed, or were bumped from, one flight.

BOAT

The Rios Negro, Solomões and Madeira are the highways of Amazonia. You can travel thousands of kilometers along these waterways (which combine to form the mighty Rio Amazonas), exploring the vast Amazon Basin traveling to or from Peru or Bolivia.

BUS

Bus services in Brazil are generally excellent. **Itapemirim** (www.itapemirim.com.br) and **Cometa** (www.viacaocometa.com.br) are two of the best and biggest companies. The easiest resource to search national bus routes is **Busca Ônibus** (www.buscaonibus.com.br) and **Click-Bus** (www.clickbus.com.br), the latter accepting international cards and PayPal for purchases.

There are three main classes of long-distance buses. The cheapest, *convencional*, is fairly comfortable with reclining seats and usually a toilet and sometimes air-con. The *executivo* provides roomier seats, costs about 25% more and makes fewer stops. The more luxurious *leitos* can cost twice as much as *convencional* and have spacious, fully reclining seats with pillows, air-conditioning and sometimes an attendant serving sandwiches and drinks. Overnight buses, regardless of the class, often make fewer stops.

Bus travel throughout Brazil can be expensive; *convencional* fares average around R$12 to R$15 per hour.

Most cities have one central bus terminal (*rodoviária*, pronounced 'hoe-doe-vee-ah-rhee-ya'). It's wise to book ahead on weekends and holidays (particularly from December to February).

CAR

Brazilian roads can be dangerous, especially busy highways such as the Rio to São Paulo corridor. There are tens of thousands of motor-vehicle fatalities every year. Driving at night is particularly hazardous because other drivers are more likely to be drunk and road hazards are less visible.

That said, driving can be a convenient (if expensive) way to get around Brazil. A small four-seat rental car costs around R$100 to R$120 a day with unlimited kilometers (R$140 to R$160 with air-con) and basic insurance. Ordinary gasoline costs around R$2.80 to R$4 per liter. Ethanol (known as *álcool* and produced from sugarcane) is about 50% less but goes around 30% quicker (most cars take both, known as Flex).

Driver's License

The legal driving age in Brazil is 18. Most foreign licenses are legally valid in Brazil but we recommend obtaining an International Driving Permit, as the police you are likely to encounter as a foreign driver don't always know the law.

LOCAL TRANSPORTATION

Bus

Local bus services are frequent and cheap, with extensive routes. Many buses list their destinations in bold letters on the front, making it easier to identify the one you need. Drivers don't usually stop unless someone flags them.

Typically, you enter the bus at the front and exit from the rear. The price is displayed near the money collector, who sits at a turnstile and provides change for the fare (usually between R$2.90 and R$3.50). Avoid riding the bus after 11pm and at peak (read packed) times: noon to 2pm and 4pm to 6pm in most areas.

Taxi

City taxis aren't cheap. In Rio, meters start at R$5.20 and rise by R$2.05 per kilometer; in São Paulo, meters start at R$4.50 and rise by R$2.75 per kilometer (prices increase at night and on Sunday); other cities go down from there. Make sure the driver turns on the meter when you get in. In some small towns, prices are fixed and meters nonexistent. The handy **Tarifa de Taxi** (www.tarifadetaxi.com) plots point-to-point fares in major Brazilian cities.

TOURS

Both the Amazon and the Pantanal are the two most popular areas for organized tours in Brazil. You will certainly enrich your experience with the services of a trained guide as well as gain the transport upper-hand for reaching difficult-to-access spots for the best wildlife viewing. In many of Brazil's national parks, such as Lençóis Maranhenses, Chapada dos Guimarães and Chapada Diamantina, guides are a necessity, if not required by regulation.

TRAIN

There are very few passenger trains in service. One remaining line well worth riding runs from Curitiba to Morretes, descending the coastal mountain range.

Chile

Includes ➡

Best Places to Stay

➡ El Tesoro de Elqui (p457)
➡ Ecobox Andino (p479)
➡ Palafito Cucao Hostel (p506)
➡ Destino No Turistico (p513)
➡ Ilaia Hotel (p517)

Best Places to Eat

➡ Peumayen (p435)
➡ Cocina Mapuche Mapu Lyagl (p489)
➡ Mercadito (p505)
➡ Mamma Gaucha (p511)
➡ Afrigonia (p521)

Why Go?

Preposterously thin and unreasonably long, Chile stretches from the belly of South America to its foot, reaching from the driest desert on earth to vast southern glacial fields. Diverse landscapes unfurl over a 4300km stretch: parched dunes, fertile valleys, volcanoes, ancient forests, massive glaciers and fjords. There's wonder in every detail and nature on a symphonic scale. For the traveler, it's boggling how so much has stayed intact for so long. Adventure travelers will find themselves wholly in their element.

In Chile, close borders foster backyard intimacy. Bookended by the Andes and the Pacific, the country averages just 175km in width. No wonder you start greeting the same faces. The easy, relaxing ritual, so integral to the fabric of everyday life in this far corner of the world, proves addictive. Pause long enough and Chile may feel like home.

When to Go

Santiago

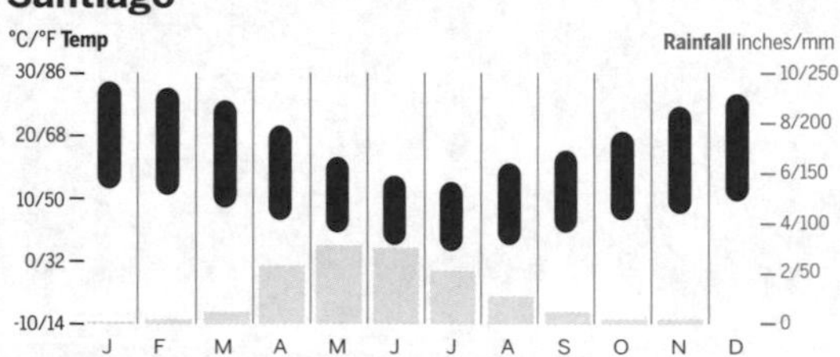

Nov–Feb Patagonia is best (and most expensive) but beaches are often crowded.

Mar–May, Sep & Oct Grape harvests in wine regions; pleasant Santiago temperatures.

Jun–Aug Fine weather in the north; Chileans go on winter vacation in July.

Connections

Chile's northern border touches Peru and Bolivia, while its vast eastern boundary hugs Argentina, with numerous border crossings over the Andes. Note that many passes close in winter.

The gamut of international buses depart from the Terminal de Buses in Santiago. Popular Argentine crossings include Santiago to Mendoza and Buenos Aires, Calama to Jujuy and Salta, La Serena to San Juan, Temuco to San Martín de los Andes, and the bus-ferry combination between Puerto Varas and Bariloche. Other international crossings include Arica to Tacna, Peru (served by train and *colectivo* as well as by buses), and Iquique to Colchane, Bolivia.

Some entering Argentina must register and pay a reciprocity fee online (Australian/Canadian/Mexican US$117/132/23) before entering: see www.migraciones.gov.ar/pdf_varios/reciprocidad/Online_payment_instructions.pdf.

ITINERARIES

One Week

Spend a day exploring the museums and cafes of Santiago, then escape to the picturesque port of Valparaíso. From central Chile, you'll have to decide whether to venture north – to San Pedro de Atacama and its mystical desertscapes, adventure sports and starry skies – or to the glaciers and trekking paradise of Torres del Paine and Patagonia in the south.

Two Weeks

In the second week, choose your own adventure: taste wine in the Colchagua Valley, hike the Andes or go skiing at a resort like Portillo, seek out a surf break in Pichilemu, venture to the end of the earth in Tierra del Fuego, or tour the *pisco* distilleries outside La Serena.

Essential Food & Drink

- **Pisco** The grape brandy is mixed with fresh lemon juice and sugar to make the famous *pisco sour* cocktail.
- **Seafood** Chile's long coastline means a bounty of fabulously fresh *pescados* (fish) and *mariscos* (shellfish) used in soups, stews and *ceviches* (marinated raw seafood).
- **Pasteles** Find these hearty baked casseroles, a traditional specialty made with *choclo* (corn), *carne* (meat), *jaiva* (crab) or *papas* (potatoes), in small towns and at family tables.
- **Wine** Chile's wine regions are rightfully world-famous. One varietal to try is Carmenere, a rich red that originated in Bordeaux but is now produced only here.

AT A GLANCE

- **Currency** Chilean peso (CH$)
- **Language** Spanish
- **Money** ATMs widespread; credit cards widely accepted
- **Visas** Generally not required for stays of up to 90 days
- **Time** GMT minus three hours

Fast Facts

- **Area** 748,800 sq km
- **Population** 17.6 million
- **Capital** Santiago
- **Emergency** ☎133
- **Country code** ☎56

Exchange Rates

Australia	A$1	CH$516
Canada	C$1	CH$535
Euro zone	€1	CH$755
New Zealand	NZ$1	CH$467
UK	UK£1	CH$1075
USA	US$1	CH$712

Set Your Budget

- **Hostel bed** CH$8000–CH$12,000
- **Evening meal** CH$4000–CH$10,000
- **Santiago–Valparaíso bus ticket** CH$5000

Resources

- **Sernatur** (http://chile.travel)
- **Go Chile** (www.gochile.cl)

Chile Highlights

1 Hike to the rugged spires of Chile's finest national park, **Torres del Paine** (p522).

2 Swirl, sniff and sip your way through Chile's best vineyards in the **Colchagua Valley** (p475).

3 Wander steep passageways lined with urban art in the hills of bohemian **Valparaíso** (p441).

4 Drink in the wild starscape above the **Atacama Desert** (462), the driest desert in the world.

5 Encounter penguins, misty seascapes and mythical lore on the otherworldly archipelago of **Chiloé** (p502).

6 Go trekking, camping, kayaking and horse riding in **Patagonia** (p507), a wildly beautiful landscape.

7 Gaze up at the enigmatic *moai* (statues) of **Easter Island** (p526).

8 Catch a wave in the surf capitals of **Iquique** (p467) and **Arica** (p471) on the north coast.

9 Escape to **Tierra del Fuego** (p524), the quiet end of the earth.

SANTIAGO

☎02 / POP 6,034,000

Surprising, cosmopolitan, energetic, sophisticated and worldly, Santiago is a city of syncopated cultural currents, madhouse parties, expansive museums and top-flight restaurants. No wonder 40% of Chileans call the leafy capital city home. With a growing economy, renovated arts scene and plenty of eccentricity to spare, Santiago is an old-guard city on the cusp of a modern-day renaissance.

History

Santiago was founded by Pedro de Valdivia in 1541, and its site was chosen for its moderate climate and strategic location for defense. It remained a small town until the nitrate boom in the 1880s; Gustave Eiffel designed its central station. In 1985 an earthquake shook down some of downtown's classic architecture; thanks to smart design and strict building codes, the February 2010 quake caused comparatively minimal damages to Chile's capital city.

Sights

The wedge-shaped Centro is the oldest part of Santiago, and the busiest, bounded by the Río Mapocho and Parque Forestal in the north, the Vía Norte Sur in the west, and Av General O'Higgins (the Alameda) in the south. North and east of the center is Barrio Bellavista, with Cerro San Cristóbal (Parque Metropolitano). To the west is Barrio Brasil, the bohemian enclave of the city. At the tip of this triangle and extending east are the wealthy *comunas* (sectors) of Providencia and Las Condes, accessed via the Alameda. Nuñoa is a residential neighborhood south of Providencia.

Centro

★Museo Chileno de Arte Precolombino MUSEUM

(Chilean Museum of Pre-Columbian Art; ☎02-928-1500; www.precolombino.cl; Bandera 361; admission CH$3500; ⏲10am-6pm Tue-Sun; Ⓜ Plaza de Armas) Exquisite pottery from most major pre-Columbian cultures is the backbone of Santiago's best museum, the Museo Chileno de Arte Precolombino. As well as dozens of intricately molded anthropomorphic vessels, star exhibits include hefty Maya stone stele and a fascinating Andean textile display.

Plaza de Armas PLAZA

(cnr Monjitas & 21 de Mayo; Ⓜ Plaza de Armas) Since the city's founding in 1541, the Plaza de Armas has been its symbolic heart. In colonial times a gallows was the square's grisly centerpiece; today it's a fountain celebrating *libertador* (liberator) Simón Bolívar, shaded by more than a hundred Chilean palm trees.

Catedral Metropolitana CHURCH

(Plaza de Armas; ⌚9am-7pm Mon-Sat, 9am-noon Sun; Ⓜ Plaza de Armas) Overlooking the Plaza de Armas is the neoclassical Catedral Metropolitana, built between 1748 and 1800. Bishops celebrating mass on the lavish main altar may feel uneasy: beneath them is the crypt where their predecessors are buried. The church's exterior was undergoing renovations as of press time. They expect to pull back the curtains in June 2015.

Barrio París-Londres NEIGHBORHOOD

(cnr París & Londres; Ⓜ Universidad de Chile) This pocket-sized neighborhood developed on the grounds of the Franciscan convent of Iglesia de San Francisco and is made up of two intersecting cobble-stone streets, París and Londres, which are lined by graceful European-style townhouses built in the 1920s. Look for the memorial at Londres 38 (p427), a building that served as a torture center during Pinochet's government.

Estación Mapocho CULTURAL CENTER

(Mapocho Station; www.estacionmapocho.cl; ⌚event times vary, check website; Ⓜ Puente Cal y Canto) Rail services north once left from Estación Mapocho. Earthquake damage and the decay of the rail system led to its closure, but it's been reincarnated as a cultural center which hosts art exhibitions, major concerts and trade expos.

Palacio de la Moneda HISTORIC BUILDING

(Morandé 130; ⌚10am-6pm Mon-Fri; Ⓜ La Moneda) FREE Chile's presidential offices are in the Palacio de la Moneda. The ornate neoclassical building was designed by Italian architect Joaquín Toesca in the late 18th century and was originally the official mint. The inner courtyards are generally open to the public; schedule a guided tour with a week's notice by emailing visitas@presidencia.cl.

Centro Cultural Palacio La Moneda ARTS CENTER

(☎02-355-6500; www.ccplm.cl; Plaza de la Ciudadanía 26; exhibitions from CH$5000; ⌚9am-9pm, exhibitions to 7:30pm; 👪; Ⓜ La Moneda) Underground art takes on a new meaning in one of Santiago's newer cultural spaces: the Centro Cultural Palacio La Moneda beneath Plaza de la Ciudadanía. A glass-slab roof floods the vaultlike space with natural light, and ramps wind down through the central atrium past the Cineteca Nacional, a state-run art-house movie theater, to two large temporary exhibition spaces.

Barrios Lastarria & Bellas Artes

Home to three of the city's best museums and center of Santiago cafe culture, these postcard-pretty neighborhoods are Santiago's twin hubs of hip.

SANTIAGO IN...

Two Days

Start at the bustling **Plaza de Armas**. Peer into the old train-station-turned-cultural-center **Estación Mapocho**, or have a coffee and check out contemporary art and fair-trade crafts at the **Centro Cultural Palacio La Moneda**. Have a seafood lunch at the **Mercado Central**, then hike up **Cerro Santa Lucía** to see the city from above. Head to Bellavista for a classic Chilean dinner at **Galindo**. On your second day, tour Pablo Neruda's house, **La Chascona**, then ride the funicular to the top of **Cerro San Cristóbal**. After an excellent seafood lunch at quirky **Peluquería Francesa**, check out the cultural calendar and bookstore at **Centro Gabriela Mistral**. Later, have a *rica rica sour* (*pisco sour* with desert herbs) at **Catedral** .

Four Days

On your third day, go hiking in the **Cajón del Maipo** or taste-test local varietals at a winery. Spend your fourth day admiring street art in **Barrio Brasil**, stopping for steaks at **Las Vacas Gordas**. Toast your stay in Santiago with dinner and drinks at Providencia's **Liguria**.

Santiago

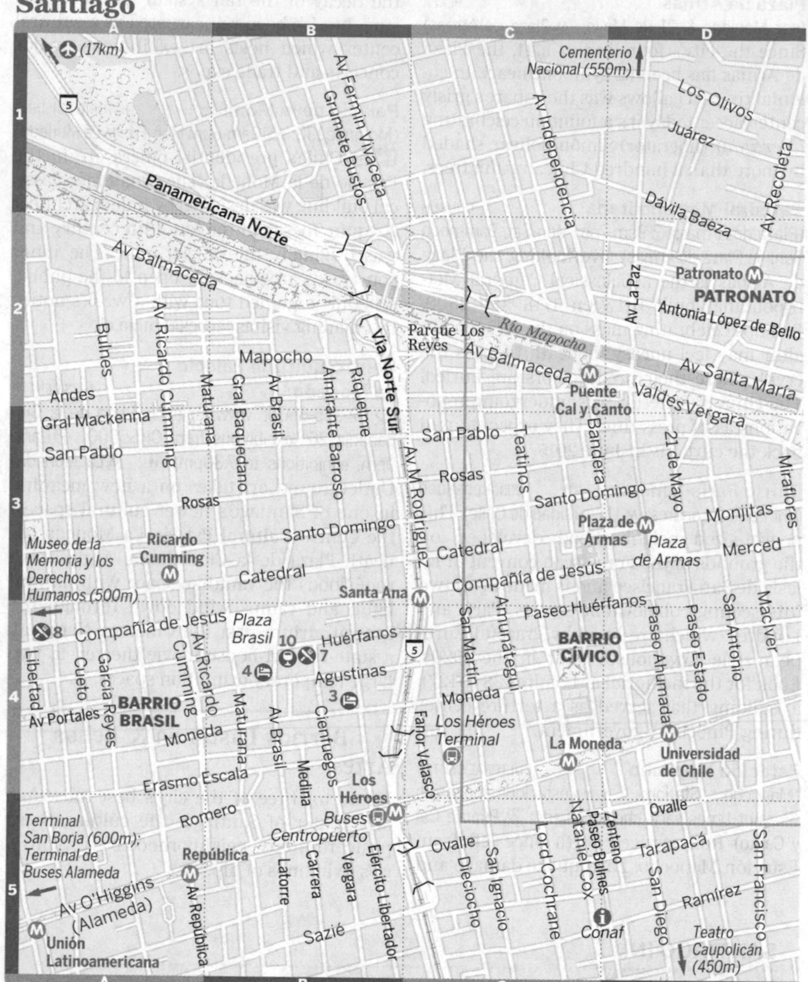

★Centro Gabriela Mistral ARTS CENTER
(GAM; ☎02-566-5500; www.gam.cl; Av O'Higgins 227; ⊙plazas 8am-midnight, exhibition spaces 10am-8pm Tue-Sat, from 11am Sun; M Universidad Católica) FREE This striking cultural and performing arts center – named for Chilean poet Gabriela Mistral, the first Latin American woman to win the Nobel Prize in Literature – is an exciting addition to Santiago's art scene. There are concerts and performances most days.

Cerro Santa Lucía PARK
(entrances cnr O'Higgins & Santa Lucía, cnr Santa Lucía & Subercaseaux; ⊙9am-6pm Mar-Sep, to 8pm Oct-Feb; M Santa Lucía) FREE Take a break from the chaos of the Centro with an afternoon stroll through this lovingly manicured park. It was just a rocky hill until 19th-century mayor Benjamín Vicuña Mackenna had it transformed into one of the city's most memorable parks.

Museo Nacional de Bellas Artes MUSEUM
(National Museum of Fine Art; www.mnba.cl; Parque Forestal s/n; adult/child CH$600/free; M Bellas Ar-

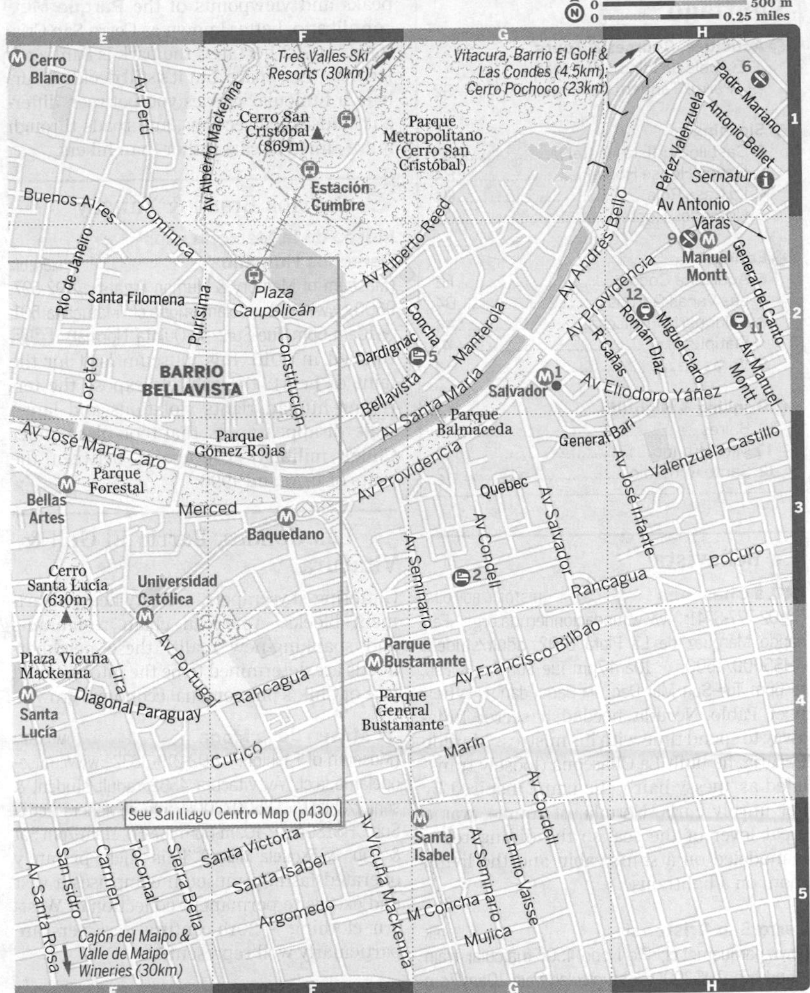

tes) This fine art museum is housed in the stately neoclassical Palacio de Bellas Artes, built as part of Chile's centenary celebrations in 1910. The museum features an excellent permanent collection of Chilean art. There are free guided tours Saturday and Sunday starting at 10:30am.

Museo de Artes Visuales MUSEUM

(MAVI, Visual Arts Museum; ☎02-664-9337; www.mavi.cl; Lastarria 307, Plaza Mulato Gil de Castro; CH$1000, Sun free; ⏲10:30am-6:30pm Tue-Sun; Ⓜ Bellas Artes) Exposed concrete, stripped wood and glass are the materials local architect Cristián Undurraga chose for the stunningly simple Museo de Artes Visuales. The contents of the four open-plan galleries are as winsome as the building: top-notch modern engravings, sculptures, paintings and photography form the regularly changing temporary exhibitions.

Londres 38 HISTORIC SITE

(www.londres38.cl; Londres 38; ⏲10am-1pm & 3-6pm Tue-Fri, 10am-2pm Sat; Ⓜ Universidad de Chile) FREE Explore the dark history of the early days of the Pinochet regime at this former detention center. There are both guided and unguided tours.

Santiago

Activities, Courses & Tours

1 Escuela de Idiomas Violeta Parra/Tandem Santiago ... G2

Sleeping

2 Castillo Surfista Hostel ... G3
3 Happy House Hostel ... B4
4 La Casa Roja ... B4
5 Nomades Hostel ... G2

Eating

6 Aquí Está Coco ... H1
7 Las Vacas Gordas ... B4
8 Peluquería Francesa ... A4
Platipus ... (see 4)
9 Voraz Pizza ... H2

Drinking & Nightlife

10 Baires ... B4
11 Mito Urbano ... H2
12 Santo Remedio ... H2

Bellavista

★La Chascona HISTORIC BUILDING
(02-777-8741; www.fundacionneruda.org; Fernando Márquez de La Plata 0192; adult/student CH$5000/1500; 10am-7pm Tue-Sun Jan & Feb, to 6pm Tue-Sun Mar-Dec; M Baquedano) When poet Pablo Neruda needed a secret hideaway to spend time with his mistress Matilde Urrutia, he built La Chascona (loosely translated as 'messy hair'), the name inspired by her unruly curls. Neruda, of course, was a great lover of the sea, so the dining room is modeled on a ship's cabin and the living room on a lighthouse.

Cerro San Cristóbal PARK
(www.parquemet.cl; Pio Nono 450; funicular train round trip CH$2000; funicular train 10am-7pm Tue-Sun, 2-7pm Mon; ; M Baquedano) The best sweeping views over Santiago are from the peaks and viewpoints of the **Parque Metropolitano**, better known as Cerro San Cristóbal. At 722 hectares, the park is Santiago's largest green space, but it's still decidedly urban: a funicular carries you between different landscaped sections, and roads through it are aimed at cars rather than hikers.

Barrios Brasil & Yungay

Museo de la Memoria y los Derechos Humanos MUSEUM
(Museum of Memory & Human Rights; 02-597-9600; www.museodelamemoria.cl; Matucana 501; 10am-6pm Tue-Sun; M Quinta Normal) FREE Opened in 2010, this museum isn't for the faint of heart: the exhibits expose the terrifying human rights violations and large-scale 'disappearances' that took place under Chile's military government between the years of 1973 and 1990.

Las Condes, Barrio El Golf & Vitacura

Glittering skyscrapers, security-heavy apartment blocks, American chain restaurants and spanking-new malls: these neighborhoods are determined to be the international face of Chile's phenomenal economic growth.

★Museo de la Moda MUSEUM
(Museum of Fashion; 02-219-3632; www.museodelamoda.cl; Av Vitacura 4562; adult/student & senior/child CH$3500/2000/free, all visitors Wed & Sun CH$1800; 10am-6pm Tue-Fri, 11am-7pm Sat & Sun; M Escuela Militar) This slick, privately operated fashion museum comprises a vast and exquisite permanent collection of Western clothing – 20th-century designers are particularly well represented.

Costanera Center BUILDING
(www.costaneracenter.cl; Andrés Bello 2461; M Tobalaba) Financial woes have halted construc-

PARQUE POR LA PAZ

During Chile's last dictatorship, some 4500 political prisoners were tortured and 266 were executed at Villa Grimaldi by the now-disbanded DINA (National Intelligence Directorate). The compound was razed to conceal evidence but since the return of democracy it has been turned into a powerful memorial park known as **Parque por la Paz** (02-292-5229; www.villagrimaldi.cl; Av Jose Arrieta 8401, Peñalolén; 10am-6pm) FREE. Each element of the park symbolizes one aspect of the atrocities that went on here. Visits are fascinating but harrowing – be sensitive about taking pictures as other visitors may be former detainees or family members. Check the website ahead of time to arrange a guided tour. Take Transantiago bus D09 (you need a Bip! card) from outside the Av Vespucio exit of Plaza Egaña metro station; it drops you opposite.

tion several times on this ambitious ongoing project that should be fully operational by the time you read this. The four skyscrapers that make up the Costanera Center include **Gran Torre Santiago**, the tallest building in South America (300m). The towers contain luxury apartments, a high-end hotel, a shopping mall and a food court with panoramic views.

Barrio Recoleta

Bustling Korean eateries, a happening marketplace overflowing with ripe fruit, a colorful jumble of street vendors – this burgeoning *barrio* is just a slight detour off the beaten path.

Cementerio General CEMETERY
(www.cementeriogeneral.cl; Av Profesor Alberto Zañartu 951; 8:30am-6pm; M Cementerios) FREE More than just a graveyard, Santiago's Cementerio General is a veritable city of tombs, many adorned with works by famous local sculptors. The names above the crypts read like a who's who of Chilean history: its most tumultuous moments are attested to by Salvador Allende's tomb and the **Memorial del Detenido Desaparecido y del Ejecutado Político**, a memorial to the 'disappeared' of Pinochet's dictatorship.

Patronato NEIGHBORHOOD
(bordered by Recoleta, Loreto, Bellavista & Dominica; M Patronato) This *barrio* within a *barrio*, roughly bordered by Recoleta, Loreto, Bellavista and Dominica streets, is the heart of Santiago's immigrant communities, particularly Koreans, Chinese and Arabs. The colorful, slightly run-down blocks are lined with antique buildings and illuminated by neon signs; a soundtrack of cumbia always seems to keep the beat in the background.

La Vega Central MARKET
(www.lavega.cl; cnr Nueva Rengifo & López de Bello; 6am-6pm Mon-Sat, to 3pm Sun; M Patronato) Raspberries, quinces, figs, peaches, persimmons, custard apples…if it grows in Chile you'll find it at La Vega Central, which is bordered by Dávila Baeza, Nueva Rengifo, López de Bello and Salas. Go early to see the hollering vendors in full swing.

Activities

Outdoor access is Santiago's strong suit. For a quick hiking fix, hoof it up Cerro San Cristóbal.

Santiago is flat and compact with a small network of *ciclovias* (bike lanes).

CHILENISMOS 101

Chilean Spanish fell off the wagon: it is slurred, singsong and peppered with expressions unintelligible to the rest of the Spanish-speaking world. *¿Cachay?* (You get it?) often punctuates a sentence, as does the ubiquitous *pues*, said as '*po*.' *Sípo*, all clattered together, actually means, 'well, yes.' Country lingo is firmly seeded in this former agrarian society who refer to guys as *cabros* (goats), complain '*es un cacho*' ('it's a horn,' meaning a sticking point) and go to the *carrete* to *carretear* ('wagon,' meaning party/to party). Lovers of lingo should check out John Brennan's *How to Survive in the Chilean Jungle*, available in Santiago's English-language bookstores. *¿Cachay?*

You can rent bikes and helmets from tour operator La Bicicleta Verde (p432). Check out the interactive map of bike paths and cyclist-friendly facilties at **Recicleta** (www.recicleta.cl/mapa-de-santiago-en-bicicleta), a group that promotes urban biking.

Excellent skiing is just a stone's throw from Santiago – the closest resort is **Farellones & El Colorado** (02 880 0210). Rafting enthusiasts head to Cascada de las Animas (p441) from October to March for Class III descents of the Río Maipo; they also organize hiking and horse-trekking trips at reasonable rates.

Courses

Escuela de Idiomas Violeta Parra/Tandem Santiago LANGUAGE COURSE
(02-236-4241; www.tandemsantiago.cl; Triana 863, Providencia; enrollment fee US$55, hour-long course US$22, 20-hour course US$180; M Salvador) Combines an outstanding academic record with a friendly vibe and cultural activities. Accommodations (optional) are in shared or private apartments. Check the website for special courses like 'Spanish for Lawyers' or 'Medical Spanish.'

Natalislang LANGUAGE COURSE
(02-222-8685; www.natalislang.com; Arturo Bürhle 047, Centro; intensive 3-day traveler crash course from CH$135,000; M Baquedano) Great for quick, intense courses. The website has an extensive list of options.

Santiago Centro

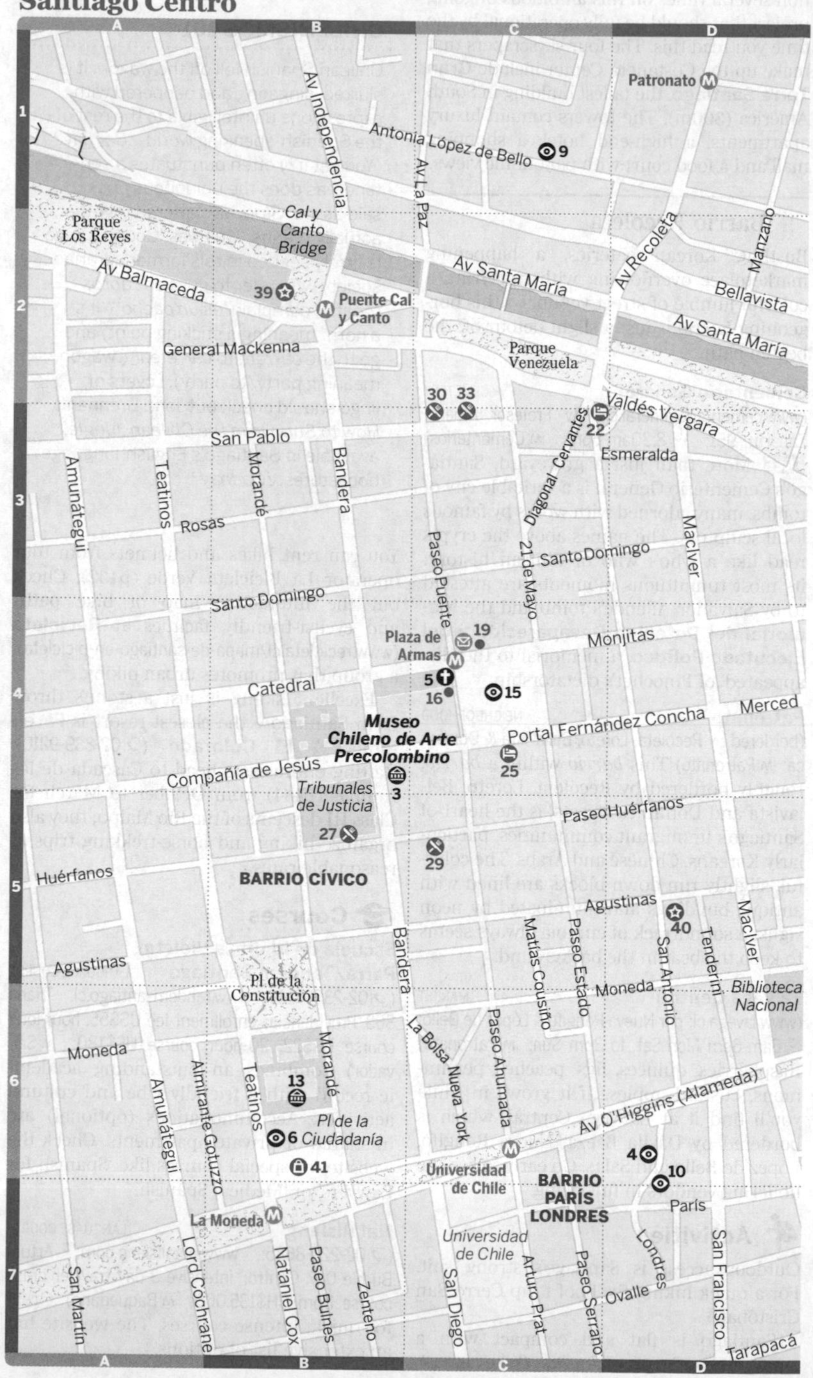

0 500 m
0 0.25 miles
Santa Filomena
Río de Janeiro
Purísima
Av Alberto Reed
Constitución
La Chascona
Patronato
Antonia López de Bello
Bombero Núñez
BARRIO BELLAVISTA
Ernesto Pinto Lagarrigue
Pío Nono
Mallinkrodt
Dardignac
Loreto
Río Mapocho
Bellavista
Facultad de Derecho de la Universidad de Chile
Av Santa María
Av José María Caro
Santo Domingo
Bellas Artes
Parque Forestal
Av Andrés Bello
Pl Italia
Merced
Baquedano
Mosqueto
Coronel Santiago Bueras
Parque General Bustamante
Subercaseaux
Santa Lucía
Rosal
Villavicencio
Lastarria
Carabineros de Chile
Av Vicuña Mackenna
Arturo Burhle
Huérfanos
Edificio Diego Portales
BARRIO LASTARRIA
Centro Gabriela Mistral
Jardín Japonés
Sánchez
Universidad Católica
Miraflores
Av O'Higgins (Alameda)
Av Portugal
Plaza Vicuña Mackenna
Lira
Rancagua
Santa Lucía
Marcoleta
Viollier
Diagonal Paraguay
Curicó
San Isidro
Carmen
San Camilo
Blas Cañas
General Jofré
Granados
Av Santa Rosa
Marín
CHILE SANTIAGO

Santiago Centro

Tours

★ La Bicicleta Verde GUIDED TOUR
(☎02-570-9338; www.labicicletaverde.cl; Loreto 6; bike tours from CH$18,000, rentals hr/full day CH$2000/15,000; Ⓜ Bellas Artes) You can rent bikes and helmets here or choose from highly recommended guided tours like Bike at Night (CH$30,000).

Free Tour Santiago WALKING TOUR
(☎cell 9236-8789; www.freetoursantiago.cl; Catedral Metropolitana, Plaza de Armas; ⏲departs 10am & 3pm; Ⓜ Plaza de Armas) A free four-hour walking tour of downtown Santiago: guides work for tips only, so be prepared to offer gratuity. No booking necessary, just look for the guides wearing red shirts in front of Catedral Metropolitana (p425).

Turistik BUS TOUR
(☎02-820-1000; www.viajesturistik.com; Plaza de Armas s/n, Municipal Tourist Office; day pass from CH$20,000; ⏲9:30am-6pm; Ⓜ Plaza de Armas) Hop-on, hop-off double-decker bus tours run to 12 stops between the Centro district and Parque Arauco mall. Check the online map for further information.

Festivals & Events

Santiago a Mil THEATER
(www.fundacionteatroamil.cl/santiago-a-mil) This major theater festival draws experimental companies from all over the world to the stages of Santiago each January.

Lollapalooza Chile MUSIC
(www.lollapaloozacl.com) The famous music festival now has a Chilean edition; national and international acts roll into Santiago, generally sometime in the month of March.

Fiesta del Vino WINE
(www.fiestadelvinodepirque.cl) This early-April wine festival in Pirque, one of many taking place around Santiago during harvest time, also features traditional cuisine and folkloric music.

Sleeping

Centro

Hostel Plaza de Armas HOSTEL $
(☎02-671-4436; www.plazadearmashostel.com; Compañía de Jesus 960, Apt 607, Plaza de Armas;

dm CH$6000-10,000, d CH$24,000, d without bathroom CH$20,000; @ 📶; Ⓜ Plaza de Armas) You'll think you're in the wrong place when you show up to this busy apartment building on Santiago's main square. Take the elevator to the 6th floor to reach the suprisingly cheery hostel that sports tiny dorms, a well-equipped communal kitchen, and great balconies with views over the Plaza de Armas. All in all, it's a solid budgeteers' buy.

Ecohostel HOSTEL $
(📞 02-222-6833; www.ecohostel.cl; General Jofré 349B, Barrio Estación Central; dm/s/d without bathroom CH$8000/15,000/21,000; @ 📶; Ⓜ Universidad Católica) Backpackers and families looking to chill love this hostel's personalized service, cozy couches and sunny patio (complete with hammock). Six- and eight-bed dorms in the converted old house can be dark, but bunks and lockers are both big and there are plenty of well-divided bathrooms. There's a women's-only dorm.

★ **CasAltura Boutique Hostel** HOSTEL $
(📞 02-633-5076; www.casaltura.com; San Antonio 811; dm/d CH$10,000/24,000, s/d without bathroom CH$18,000/28,000; @ 📶; Ⓜ Puente Cal y Canto) This sophisticated 'boutique hostel' is a travelers' favorite thanks to kitchen access, fine linens, a terrace overlooking Parque Forestal, and a location near Mercado Central.

Barrios Lastarria & Bellas Artes

Andes Hostel & Apartments HOSTEL $
(📞 02-632-9990; www.andeshostel.com; Monjitas 506; dm CH$15,100-16,400, d with/without bathroom CH$55,700/39,000, apt CH$72,200; @ 📶 🏊; Ⓜ Bellas Artes) Pistachio-colored walls, a zebra-print rug, mismatched retro sofas and a mosaic-tiled bar are some of the pop-art charms of this centrally located hostel. The four- and six-bed dorms can get a bit hot on summer nights. It's worth splashing out more for an Andes apartment on the next block if you've got a group.

Hostal Forestal HOSTEL $
(📞 02-638-1347; www.hostalforestal.cl; Coronel Santiago Bueras 120; dm CH$6500-8000, s without bathroom CH$18,000, d with/without bathroom CH$27,000/22,000; @ 📶; Ⓜ Baquedano) This hostel wins big on location, but feels just a little worn, with dorms that are dark and slightly run down. You do get a shared kitchen, a pool table and a great central locale.

Bellavista

La Chimba HOSTEL $
(📞 02-735-8978; www.lachimba.com; Ernesto Pinto Lagarrigue 262; dm CH$11,000, s/d CH$24,000/36,000, without bathroom CH$18,000/30,000; @ 📶; Ⓜ Baquedano) A massive mural announces your arrival at this Bellavista party hostel. There's a cool '50s-style throwback lounge perfectly mismatched with a glowing chandelier and other odds and ends that span the decades. The rooms feel punk-rock beat – it's a bit grungy, but quite flavorful. And you'll love swapping stories at the rambling back plaza.

Nomades Hostel HOSTEL $
(📞 02-789-7600; Bellavista 0318; dm/s CH$10,000/18,000, d with/without bathroom CH$36,000/27,000; Ⓜ Baquedano) Mod-deco design meets old-time architectural elegance in this Bellavista hostel. There's excellent art throughout, a cool outside patio and a gorgeous shared kitchen that plays center stage. The dorms sleep five.

Bellavista Hostel HOSTEL $
(📞 02-899-7145; www.bellavistahostel.com; Dardignac 0184; dm CH$12,000, s/d without bathroom CH$18,000/30,000; @ 📶; Ⓜ Baquedano) This highly social hostel is a Bellavista classic. Brightly painted walls crammed with colorful paintings and graffiti announce the relaxed, arty vibe. There's a super cool terrace and two kitchens. We only wish it was a bit cleaner. The city's best bars and clubs are on your doorstep and so, sometimes, are their clients.

Barrios Brasil & Yungay

Happy House Hostel HOSTEL $
(📞 02-688-4849; www.happyhousehostel.com; Moneda 1829; dm/s/d without bathroom CH$10,000/23,000/30,000, s/d CH$36,000/40,000; @ 📶 🏊; Ⓜ Los Héroes) The best hostel in Barrio Brasil is happy news for weary travelers. This 1910 mansion has a fabulous molded ceiling, funky modern touches and unexpected art-deco stylings. There's a pool, bar and patio out back, a few stories of dorm rooms and definitely worthwhile privates.

La Casa Roja HOSTEL $
(📞 02-696-4241; www.lacasaroja.cl; Agustinas 2113; dm CH$8000-10,000, d with/without bathroom CH$32,000/28,000; @ 📶 🏊; Ⓜ Ricardo Cumming) With its swimming pool, airy

patios, outdoor bar, garden and a huge, well-designed kitchen, it's easy to see why this Aussie-owned outfit is backpacker central. Serious socializing isn't the only appeal: the sweeping staircases and sky-high molded ceilings of this lovingly restored 19th-century mansion ooze character.

Especially great value are the doubles, fitted with stylish retro furniture and bijoux bathrooms.

Providencia

Castillo Surfista Hostel HOSTEL $

(☎02-893-3350; www.castillosurfista.com; Maria Luisa Santander 0329; dm CH$8500, d without bathroom CH$21,400-25,400; @; Ⓜ Baquedano) Off the beaten path and run by a California surfer, this renovated house features homey dorms and doubles, tidy communal areas and laid-back hosts who can help you access the surf scene – the owner even runs daylong surf trips to lesser-known breaks and arranges Wicked camper rentals if you want to venture to the beaches alone.

Intiwasi Hotel BOUTIQUE HOTEL $$

(☎02-985-5285; www.intiwasihotel.com; Josue Smith Solar 380, Providencia; r US$85-90; @; Ⓜ Los Leones) This cozy, centrally located hotel is more like a boutique hostel for grown-ups. The proud owners are eager to help you plan your travels, and the look is native Chilean – Intiwasi means 'House of the Sun' in Quechua – with indigenous textiles, dark wood and bright hues of red and orange throughout. Rooms have LCD televisions.

Eating

Cheap lunches abound in the center; *barrios* Bellavista, Lastarria and Providencia are better suited for dinner.

Centro

★**Mercado Central** SEAFOOD $

(Central Market; www.mercadocentral.cl; cnr 21 de Mayo & San Pablo; food stands & restaurants 9am-5pm Mon-Fri, 7am-3:30pm Sat & Sun; Ⓜ Puente Cal y Canto) Santiago's wrought-iron fish market is a classic for seafood lunches (and hangover-curing fish stews like the tomato- and potato-based *caldillo de congrio,* Pablo Neruda's favorite). Skip the touristy restaurants in the middle and head for one of the tiny low-key stalls around the market's periphery.

Bar Nacional CHILEAN $

(Huérfanos 1151; mains CH$3400-5500; 9am-11pm Mon-Sat; Ⓜ Plaza de Armas) From the chrome counter to the waitstaff of old-timers, this *fuente de soda* (soda fountain) is as vintage as they come. It has been churning out Chilean specialties like *lomo a lo pobre* (steak and fries topped with fried egg) for years. To save a buck (or a few hundred pesos) ask for the sandwich menu.

Empanadas Zunino BAKERY $

(www.empanadaszunino.cl; Puente 801; empanadas CH$650-800; 9am-5pm Mon-Sun; Ⓜ Puente Cal y Canto) Founded in the 1930s, this classic bakery makes fantastic empanadas – Chilean food journalists recently awarded them second place in a contest for the best empanadas in Santiago.

El Naturista VEGETARIAN $

(www.elnaturista.cl; Huérfanos 1046; meals CH$3400-5000; 9am-10pm Mon-Sat; Ⓜ Plaza de Armas) A downtown vegetarian classic, El Naturista does simple but filling soups, sandwiches, salads, tarts and fresh-squeezed juices, plus light breakfasts and fruit-infused ice cream. There's another location nearby at Moneda 846.

Barrios Lastarria & Bellas Artes

Café Bistro de la Barra CAFE $

(JM de la Barra 455; sandwiches CH$3500-7000; 9am-9:30pm Mon-Fri, 10am-9:30pm Sat & Sun; Ⓜ Bellas Artes) Worn old floor tiles, a velvet sofa, 1940s swing and light fittings made from cups and teapots make a quirky-but-pretty backdrop for some of the best brunches and *onces* (afternoon tea) in town. The rich sandwiches include salmon-filled croissants or Parma ham and arugula on flaky green-olive bread, but make sure you save room for the berry-drenched cheesecake.

Tambo PERUVIAN $

(www.tambochile.cl; Lastarria 65; mains CH$5500-7700; noon-11pm Mon-Sat; Ⓜ Universidad Católica) Occupying a prime spot along one of Lastarria's most scenic passages, this contemporary Peruvian eatery offers spicy twists on dishes and drinks that Chileans have since adopted – go ahead, taste-test the fantastic *ceviche*. Kick off your sampling from the other side of the border with a delicious *maracuyá* (passion fruit) *pisco sour*.

Emporio La Rosa ICE CREAM $
(www.emporiolarosa.com; Merced 291; ice cream CH$900-1800, salads & sandwiches CH$2500-3900; 9am-11pm Mon-Sat; ; Bellas Artes) Choco-chili, rose petal and strawberry and black pepper are some of the fabulous flavors of this extra-creamy handmade ice cream, which has been known to cause addiction. Flaky *pains au chocolat* and squishy focaccia sandwiches are two more reasons to plonk yourself at the chrome tables.

Bellavista

Galindo CHILEAN $
(www.galindo.cl; Dardignac 098; mains CH$2800-5800; noon-11pm Mon-Sat; Baquedano) Retro neon signs adorn the wood-backed bar at this long-running local favorite, usually packed with noisy but appreciative crowds. It's easy to see why: unlike the precious restaurants around it, Galindo's all about sizzling *parrilladas* (mixed grills) and hearty Chilean staples like *chorrillana* (french fries topped with grilled onions and meat).

★**Peumayen** CHILEAN $$
(www.peumayenchile.cl; Constitución 136; tasting menu CH$10,500; 7-11pm Tue-Sat, 1-3pm Sun; Baquedano) Without a doubt one of the most unique culinary experiences in Chile, this Bellavista upstart is innovating Chilean cuisine by looking back to the culinary roots of the Mapuche, Easter Islanders and Quechua.

Barrio Brasil

★**Peluquería Francesa** FRENCH $
(Boulevard Lavaud; 02-682-5243; www.boulevardlavaud.cl; Compañía de Jesús 2789; mains CH$3300-7000; noon-11pm Mon-Sat; Ricardo Cumming) This is one of Santiago's more innovative dining experiences. The name means 'French barbershop,' and that's exactly what this elegant corner building, dating from 1868, originally was. Decorated with quirky antiques (all available for purchase), it still has turn-of-the-century charm; it gets crowded on weekend evenings with hip *santiaguinos* who come for the excellent French-inflected seafood dishes.

Platipus ASIAN $
(www.platipus.cl; Agustinas 2099; sushi CH$2900-5900; dinner Mon-Sat; ; Ricardo Cumming) Candles cast a warm glow on the exposed-brick walls of this laid-back sushi spot. Don't come here in a hurry, but both the sushi and the *tablas* (boards of finger food) are worth the wait. Vegetarians will find plenty to dine on here too.

Las Vacas Gordas STEAK $
(Cienfuegos 280; mains CH$4000-7000; noon-11pm Mon-Sat; Ricardo Cumming) Steak, pork, chicken and vegetables sizzle on the giant grill at the front of the clattering main dining area, then dead-pan old-school waiters cart it over to your table. This popular steakhouse is often packed, so reserve or get there early.

Providencia

El Huerto CAFE $
(www.elhuerto.cl; Orrego Luco 054; mains CH$5700-6100; noon-midnight Mon-Sat; ; Pedro de Valdivia) This earthy restaurant's healthy, vegetarian-focused fare is a big hit with both hip young things and ladies who lunch. Come for egg-white omelets, strawberry smoothies, quinoa salads and wonderfully rich desserts with café au lait.

Voraz Pizza PIZZA $
(www.vorazpizza.cl; Av Providencia 1321; CH$3300-4000; noon-11pm Mon-Sat; ; Manuel Montt) This hole-in-the-wall spot serves great-value thin-crust pizzas and craft beers at sidewalk tables; it will happily deliver too. An added bonus for non-meat eaters: the pizzeria has a few tasty vegetarian options and will also cater to vegans.

Liguria MEDITERRANEAN $$
(02-334-4346; www.liguria.cl; Av Pedro de Valdivia 47; mains CH$5300-9800; noon-11pm Mon-Sat; Pedro de Valdivia) A mainstay on the Santiago restaurant circuit, Liguria mixes equal measures of bar and bistro perfectly. Stewed rabbit and other specials are chalked up on a blackboard, then dapper old-school waiters place them on the red-checked tablecloths with aplomb.

Aquí Está Coco CHILEAN $$
(02-410-6200; www.aquiestacoco.cl; La Concepción 236; mains CH$9100-13,000; noon-11pm Mon-Sat; ; Pedro de Valdivia) This beautifully restored mini-mansion – reconstructed with sustainable building materials – houses one of Providencia's hippest dining venues. The name, translating to 'Here's Coco,' refers to the imaginative owner who uses the space to showcase art and artifacts from his world travels (not to mention his considerable culinary talent and zeal for fine wine).

Las Condes, Barrio El Golf & Vitacura

Café Melba CAFE $

(Don Carlos 2898; sandwiches CH$2900, mains CH$4000-7500; 7am-3pm; ; M Tobalaba) Eggs and bacon, muffins, bagels and gigantic cups of coffee are some of the all-day breakfast offerings at this cozy cafe run by a New Zealand expat. Well-stuffed sandwiches and heartier dishes like green fish curry or pork medallions are popular with lunching local finance workers, but the specialty here is leisurely brunch.

Drinking & Nightlife

Catedral COCKTAIL BAR

(www.operacatedral.cl; cnr JM de la Barra & Merced; M Bellas Artes) Classy Catedral has a menu that goes way beyond bar snacks – anyone for a glass of champagne with violet crème brûlée? A poised crew of professionals in their 20s and 30s love this cocktail bar's minimal two-tone couches, smooth wood paneling and mellow music.

Santo Remedio COCKTAIL BAR

(www.santoremedio.cl; Román Díaz 152; 1-3:30pm & 6:30pm-4am Mon-Fri, 1-3:30pm & 8:30pm-4am Sat & Sun; M Manuel Montt) Strictly speaking, this low-lit, high-ceilinged old house is a restaurant, and an aphrodisiacal one at that. But it's the bar action people really come for: powerful, well-mixed cocktails and regular live DJs keep the 20- and 30-something crowds happy.

Baires BAR

(Brasil 255; M Ricardo Cumming) Technically it's a 'sushi club,' but the nightlife at Baires is what brings in the crowds. The terrace tables fill up quickly, even on weeknights; there's an encyclopedia-sized drink list; and DJs get going upstairs on weekends.

Boca Naríz WINE BAR

(02-638-9893; www.bocanariz.cl; Lastarria 276; mains CH$5000-9000; noon-midnight Mon-Sat, 7-11pm Sun; M Bellas Artes) You might get better *ceviche* in the market, but you won't get a better wine list nearly anywhere in Chile. We love the intimate atmosphere, wine flights and oeno-tastic energy. Reservations recommended.

Entertainment

Note that Santiago's excellent cultural centers – especially Centro Gabriela Mistral (p426), Centro Cultural Palacio La Moneda (p425) and Estación Mapocho (p425) – are some of the city's best venues to catch live music, performing arts and entertainment. Admission to cultural events is often free: check the centers' websites or www.estoy.cl for listings.

Live Music

Bar Constitución LIVE MUSIC

(Constitución 62, Bellavista; 8pm-4am; M Baquedano) Bellavista's coolest nightspot hosts live bands and DJs nightly – the bar's eclectic (but infallible) tastes include electroclash, garage, nu-folk, house and more, so check the website to see if the night's program suits.

Teatro Caupolicán LIVE MUSIC

(02-699-1556; www.teatrocaupolican.cl; San Diego 850; 8pm-1am; M Parque O'Higgins) Latin American rockers who've played this stage include far-out Mexicans Café Tacuba, Argentinian electro-tango band Bajofondo and Oscar-winning Uruguayan Jorge Drexler; international acts like Garbage and Snow Patrol also play concert dates at Teatro Caupolicán.

La Batuta LIVE MUSIC

(www.batuta.cl; Jorge Washington 52, Ñuñoa; M Plaza Egaña) Enthusiastic crowds jump to ska, *patchanka* (think: Manu Chao) and *cumbia chilombiana;* rockabilly and surf; tribute bands and Goth rock…at Batuta, just about anything alternative goes.

Nightclubs

Don't even think of showing up to clubs before midnight. In summer many close their doors and follow the crowds to the beach.

Mito Urbano CLUB

(www.mitourbano.cl; Manuel Montt 350; cover CH$4000-6000; M Manuel Montt) At this fun-loving nightclub, disco balls cast lights on good-looking 20-, 30- and 40-somethings dancing to vintage hits and Chilean pop. Check the schedule for salsa classes, karaoke, live jazz and other promotions that aim to bring people in before midnight.

Performing Arts

Teatro Municipal THEATER

(02-463-1000; www.municipal.cl; Agustinas 794, Centro; tickets from CH$3000; box office 10am-7pm Mon-Fri, to 2pm Sat & Sun; M Santa Lucía) This exquisite neoclassical building is the most prestigious performing-arts venue in the city. It's home to the Ballet de Santiago, and also hosts world-class opera, tango and classical-music performances.

Centro Cultural Matucana 100 ARTS CENTER
(☎02-946-9240; www.m100.cl; Matucana 100; ticket prices vary; ⏰11am-1pm & 2-9pm; Ⓜ Quinta Normal) FREE One of Santiago's hippest alternative arts venues, the huge red-brick Centro Cultural Matucana 100 gets its gritty industrial look from its previous incarnation as government warehouses. Renovated as part of Chile's bicentennial project, it now contains a hangar-like gallery and a theater for art-house film cycles, concerts and fringe productions.

Sports

Estadio Nacional FOOTBALL
(National Stadium; ☎02-238-8102; Av Grecia 2001, Ñuñoa; Ⓜ Irarrázaval) On the whole, Chileans are a pretty calm lot – until they step foot in a soccer stadium. The most dramatic matches are against local rivals like Peru or Argentina, when 'Chi-Chi-Chi-Lay-Lay-Lay' reverberates through the Estadio Nacional.

Shopping

For clothes, shoes and department-store goods, hit downtown's pedestrian streets like Ahumada; for even cheaper goods, cross the river to Patronato.

Santiago's posh supermalls, a long haul from the center and often more popular with locals than visitors, include **Parque Arauco** (www.parquearauco.cl; Av Kennedy 5413; ⏰10am-9pm; Ⓜ Manquehue) and **Alto Las Condes** (www.altolascondes.cl; Av Kennedy 9001, Las Condes; ⏰10am-10pm).

★ **Artesanías de Chile** ARTS & CRAFTS
(☎02-235-2014; www.artesaniasdechile.cl; Plaza de la Ciudadanía 26; ⏰10am-6pm Mon-Sat; Ⓜ La Moneda) Not only do this foundation's jewelry, carvings, ceramics and woolen goods sell at reasonable prices, most of what you pay goes to the artisan that made them. Look for other locations in Santiago and throughout Chile.

Galería Drugstore FASHION
(www.drugstore.cl; Av Providencia 2124, Providencia; ⏰10:30am-8pm Mon-Sat; Ⓜ Los Leones) Head to this cool four-story independent shopping center for clothes no one back home will have – it's home to the tiny boutiques of several up-and-coming designers, arty bookstores and cafes.

Centro de Exposición de Arte Indígena CRAFTS
(O'Higgins 499, Centro; ⏰10am-6pm Mon-Sat; Ⓜ Santa Lucia) Indigenous craftspeople sell a small selection of wares at these stalls next to the Terraza Neptuno entrance to Cerro Santa Lucía; goods include silver jewelry, postcards, instruments and Mapuche dictionaries.

Centro Artesanal Santa Lucía CRAFTS
(cnr Carmen & Diagonal Paraguay, Centro; ⏰10am-7pm; Ⓜ Santa Lucía) It's a stretch to call this market's mass-produced weavings and leather goods 'crafts,' but it's certainly a good place to go for cheap souvenirs. Pan pipes, silver jewelry and Andean-style sweaters are some of the been-there-bought-that products available.

Flea Market MARKET
(Franklin Market; ⏰9am-7pm Sat & Sun; Ⓜ Franklin) Antiques, collectibles and fascinating old junk fill the cluttered stalls at this famous flea market between Bío Bío and Franklin. Sifting through the jumble of vintage sunglasses, antique brandy snifters, cowboy spurs, old-fashioned swimsuits and discarded books is an experience.

Information

DANGERS & ANNOYANCES

Santiago is relatively safe, but petty crime exists. Be on your guard around the Plaza de Armas, Mercado Central, Cerro Santa Lucía and Cerro San Cristóbal in particular. Organized groups of pickpockets sometimes target drinkers along Pío Nono in Bellavista, and Barrio Brasil's smaller streets can be dodgy after dark.

EMERGENCY

Ambulance (☎131)
Fire Department (Bomberos; ☎132)
Police (Carabineros; ☎133)
Prefectura de Carabineros (Main police station; ☎02-922-3660; O'Higgins 280, Centro)

INTERNET ACCESS

Cybercafes are a dying breed. Many cafes and most hotels now have free wi-fi for their clients.

MEDICAL SERVICES

Clínica Alemana (☎02-2210-1111; http://portal.alemana.cl; Av Vitacura 5951, Santiago)
Hospital de Urgencia Asistencia Pública (☎02-568-1100; www.huap.cl; Av Portugal 125; ⏰24hr; Ⓜ Universidad Católica) Santiago's main emergency room.

MONEY

ATMs (Redbanc) are found throughout the city.

Cambios Afex (☎02-636-9090; www.afex.cl; Agustinas 1050, Centro; ⏰9am-6pm Mon-Fri, 10am-2pm Sat; Ⓜ Universidad de Chile) Reliable exchange office with branches around town.

POST

Post office (☎800-267-736; www.correos.cl; Catedral 987, Plaza de Armas; ⏰8am-10pm Mon-Fri, to 6pm Sat; Ⓜ Plaza de Armas) With offices around town.

TOURIST INFORMATION

Sernatur (☎02-731-8336; www.chile.travel; Av Providencia 1550; ⏰9am-8pm Mon-Fri,to 2pm Sat; 📶; Ⓜ Manuel Montt) Gives out maps, brochures and advice, and can help reserve winery visits.

TRAVEL AGENCIES

Navimag (☎02-442-3120; www.navimag.cl; Av El Bosque Norte 0440, Piso 11; ⏰9am-6:30pm Mon-Fri; Ⓜ Tobalaba) Book ahead for ferry tickets in Chilean Patagonia.

ℹ Getting There & Away

AIR

Aeropuerto Internacional Arturo Merino Benítez (p538) is in Pudahuel, 20km northwest of downtown Santiago. Domestic carries are **LAN** (☎600-526-2000; www.lan.com), with the most destination coverage, and **Sky** (☎02-353-3100; Huérfanos 815, Centro; Ⓜ Plaza de Armas), usually with cheaper fares. Airfares can vary widely but are always cheaper when purchased in country.

BUS

A bewildering number of bus companies connect Santiago to the rest of Chile, Argentina and Peru. Services leave from several different terminals; make sure you know where you're going.

Santiago has four main bus terminals, from which buses leave for northern, central and southern destinations. The largest and most reputable bus companies are Tur Bus and Pullman Bus.

Terminal San Borja (O'Higgins 3250, San Borja 184; Ⓜ Estación Central) is at the end of the shopping mall alongside the main railway station. The ticket booths are divided by region, with destinations prominently displayed. Destinations are from Arica down to the *cordillera* (mountain range) around Santiago.

Terminal de Buses Alameda (cnr O'Higgins & Jotabeche; Ⓜ Universidad de Santiago) is home to **Tur Bus** (☎600-660-6600; www.turbus.cl) and **Pullman Bus** (☎600-320-3200; www.pullman.cl); both serve a wide variety of destinations north, south and on the coast.

Terminal de Buses Sur (O'Higgins 3850; Ⓜ Universidad de Santiago) has the most services to the central coast, international and southern destinations (the Lakes District and Chiloé).

Terminal Los Héroes (☎02-420-0099; Tucapel Jiménez 21; Ⓜ Los Héroes), near the Alameda in the Centro, is much more convenient and less chaotic. Buses mainly head north along the Carretera Panamericana (Pan-American Hwy), but a few go to Argentina and south to Temuco.

Fares between important destinations are listed in the bus-fares table, with approximate journey times and one-way fares for *clásico* (basic) or *semi-cama* (partly reclining seats). Fares can vary dramatically and spike during holidays.

DESTINATION	COST (CH$)	DURATION (HR)
Antofagasta	30,000	19
Arica	45,900	30
Buenos Aires (Argentina)	81,000	22
Chillán	7900	5
Concepción	8,000	6½
Copiapó	20,000	12
Iquique	37,400	25
La Serena	10,000	7
Mendoza (Argentina)	25,400	8
Osorno	21,800	12
Pucón	16,800	11
Puerto Montt	21,800	12
San Pedro de Atacama	40,600	23
Talca	5000	3½
Temuco	14,900	9½
Valdivia	16,900	10-11
Valparaíso	1900	2
Viña del Mar	1900	2¼

TRAIN

Chile's slick intercity train system, **Trenes Metropolitanos** (☎600-585-5000; www.tmsa.cl), operates out of **Estación Central** (O'Higgins 3170; Ⓜ Estación Central). Train travel is generally slightly slower and more expensive than going by bus, but wagons are well maintained and services are generally punctual.

The TerraSur rail service connects Santiago three to five times daily with Rancagua (CH$5600, one hour), Curicó (from CH$5600, 2¼ hours), Talca (from CH$8000, three hours) and Chillán (CH$8000, 5½ hours). There's a 10% discount when booking online.

GETTING INTO TOWN

Two cheap, efficient bus services connect the airport with the city center: **TurBus Aeropuerto** (☎600-660-6600; www.turbus.cl; CH$1550) runs every 15 minutes between 6am and midnight, stopping at the Universidad de Santiago metro station. **Buses Centropuerto** (☎02-601-9883; www.centropuerto.cl; Manuel Rodríguez 846; 1 way/round trip CH$1500/2900; ⏰5:55am-11:30pm, every 10-15min) provides a similar service to and from the Los Héroes and Estación Central metro stations. Both buses leave from right outside the arrivals hall; they also stop at the Pajaritos metro station. The trip takes about 40 minutes.

Use caution with taxis: although the ride to the city center should cost CH$16,000, drivers are famous for ripping tourists off. A safer bet for door-to-door transfers is **Transvip** (☎02-677-3000; www.transvip.cl), with shared minibus shuttles (from CH$6400) or taxis (CH$18,000). Pay with cash or credit card at the airport desk inside the arrivals hall.

ℹ Getting Around

BUS

Transantiago (☎800-730-073; www.transantiago.cl) buses are a cheap and convenient way of getting around town, especially when the metro shuts down at night. Green-and-white buses operate in central Santiago or connect two areas of town. Each suburb has color-coded local buses and an identifying letter that precedes route numbers (for example, routes in Las Condes and Vitacura start with a C and use orange vehicles).

Buses generally follow major roads and stops are spaced far apart, often coinciding with metro stations. You can only pay for bus rides using a Bip! (a contact-free card you wave over sensors); the card costs CH$2700 and one-way fares range from CH$640 to CH$720, depending on what time of day you're traveling. Bip! cards are available for purchase in almost all metro stations, but cannot be purchased on buses. A full list of locations selling Bip! cards is on the Transantiago website.

On Sundays and holidays, take advantage of the new **Circuito Cultural Santiago** (www.transantiago.cl; ⏰10am-6:30pm Sun & holidays), a bus loop tour that passes by the city's main attractions (museums, cultural centers) starting at Estación Central. Use your Bip! card to pay for one regular bus fare, and the driver will give you a bracelet that allows you to board the circuit's buses as many times as you like. The buses are clearly marked 'Circuito Cultural.'

CAR

Renting a car to drive around Santiago is stressful – if you must have your own set of wheels, the major agencies have offices at the airport. For more detailed information on driving and parking in Santiago, check out the helpful English-language section at **Car Rental in Chile** (www.mietwagen-in-chile.de); they'll also rent you a vehicle.

METRO

The city's ever-expanding **metro** (www.metrosantiago.cl; ⏰6:30am-11pm Mon-Sat, 8am-11pm Sun) is an efficient way to get around. The website has downloadable route maps and a point-to-point journey planner. You can use a Bip! card or buy a one-way ticket.

TAXI

Santiago has abundant metered taxis, all black with yellow roofs. Flag-fall costs CH$250, then it's CH$120 per 200m (or minute of waiting time). It's generally safe to hail cabs in the street.

AROUND SANTIAGO

National parks, sleepy villages, snowy slopes (in winter) and high-altitude hiking trails (in summer) all make easy escapes from the city.

Valle de Maipo

Just south of the center of Santiago lies Valle de Maipo, a major wine region specializing in big-bodied reds. You can go it alone: the wineries described here are within 1½ hours of the city center on public transportation. But if you'd rather hit the wine circuit with a knowledgeable guide, try the specialized tours at **Uncorked Wine Tours** (☎02-981-6242; www.uncorked.cl; half-/full-day tour US$135/195): an English-speaking guide will take you to three wineries, and a lovely lunch is included. Also recommended is the winery bike tour with La Bicicleta Verde (p432), which takes you pedaling around the countryside to wineries within 10km of Santiago.

Worthwhile wineries include **Viña Cousiño Macul** (☎02-351-4100; www.cousinomacul.com; Av Quilín 7100, Peñalolen; tours CH$9000-18,000; ⏲tours 11am, noon, 3pm & 4pm Mon-Fri in English, 11am & noon Sat; Ⓜ Quinlín), where tours take in the production process as well as the underground *bodega* (a storage area for wine), which was built in 1872. It is a 2.25km walk or a quick taxi ride from the metro.

Set at the foot of the Andes is the lovely **Viña Aquitania** (☎02-791-4500; www.aquitania.cl; Av Consistorial 5090; tour & tasting CH$8000-15,000; ⏲by appointment only 9am-5pm Mon-Fri). From Grecia metro station (line 4), take bus D07 south from bus stop 6 and get off at the intersection of Av Los Presidentes and Consistorial (you need a Bip! card). Aquitania is 150m south.

At the boutique vineyard of **Viña Almaviva** (☎02-270-4200; www.almavivawinery.com;

SKI RESORTS AROUND SANTIAGO

Chilean ski and snowboard resorts are open from June to October, with lower rates available early and late in the season. Most ski areas are above 3300m and treeless; the runs are long, the season is long and the snow is deep and dry. Three major resorts are barely an hour from the capital, while the fourth is about two hours away on the Argentine border.

Santiago's four most popular ski centers – El Colorado/Farellones, La Parva and Valle Nevado – are clustered in three valleys in the Mapocho river canyon, hence their collective name, **Tres Valles**. They're only 30km to 40km northeast of Santiago, and the traffic-clogged road up can be slow going. All prices given here are for weekends and high season (usually early July to mid-August). Outside that time, there are hefty midweek discounts on both ski passes and hotels. The predominance of drag lifts means that lines get long during the winter holidays, but otherwise crowds here are bearable. Ask about combination tickets if you're planning on skiing at multiple resorts.

El Colorado and **Farellones**, located approximately 45km east of the capital, are close enough together to be considered one destination, with 18 lifts and 22 runs from 2430m to 3330m in elevation. The eating and after-ski scenes are scanty here, so locals tend just to come up for the day. **Centro de Ski El Colorado** (www.elcolorado.cl; Nevería 4680, Las Condes) has the latest information on snow and slope conditions.

Only 4km from the Farellones ski resort, exclusive **La Parva** is oriented toward posh Chilean families and features 30 runs from 2662m to 3630m. For the latest information, contact **La Parva** (☎02-964-2100; www.laparva.cl; office Av El Bosque Norte 0177, 2nd fl, Las Condes, Santiago; day pass adult/child CH$40,000/27,500).

Another 14km beyond Farellones, the vast **Valle Nevado** (☎02-477-7700; www.vallenevado.com; Av Vitacura 5250, Oficina 304, Santiago; day pass adult/child CH$43,000/31,000) boasts about 28 sq km of skiable domain – the largest in South America. It's also the best maintained of Santiago's resorts and has the most challenging runs, ranging from 2805m to 3670m, and some up to 3km in length.

In a class of its own, the ultrasteep **Portillo**, 145km northeast of the capital on the Argentine border, is one of Chile's favorite ski resorts. The US, Austrian and Italian national teams use it as a base for summer training and the 200km/h speed barrier was first broken here. Portillo has 14 lifts and 35 runs, from 2590m to 3310m; the longest run measures 2.4km. The on-site **Inca Lodge** (☎02-263-0606; www.skiportillo.com; r per person per week full board US$990; 📶🏊) accommodates young travelers in dorms. Tickets are included in the price and low season offers some deals. Contact **Portillo** (☎02-263-0606; www.skiportillo.cl; daily ski pass adult/child CH$39,000/26,000) for the latest details.

Shuttles to the resorts abound. **KL Adventure** (☎02-217-9101; www.kladventure.com; Augusto Mira Fernández 14248, Las Condes, Santiago; round trip to Tres Valles CH$26,500, with hotel pickup CH$37,000) goes to Tres Valles at 8am and returns at 5pm. They also rent equipment and run transportation to Portillo (CH$26,500). **SkiTotal** (☎02-246-0156; www.skitotal.cl; Av Apoquindo 4900, Local 39-42, Las Condes, Santiago; 1 way CH$13,000-15,000) rents equipment and arranges cheaper transportation to the resorts, with 8am departures and 5pm returns.

Av Santa Rosa 821, Paradero 45, Puente Alto; tours incl 1 pour US$80; ⏲by appointment only 9am-5pm Mon-Fri), high-end tastings are available by reservation only. Bus 207 from Estación Mapocho runs past the entrance, about 1km from the winery building.

It's the more sophisticated sister of **Viña Concha y Toro** (☎02-476-5269; www.conchaytoro.com; Virginia Subercaseaux 210, Pirque; standard tour & tasting CH$8000; ⏲10am-5pm) in Pirque, where you can see winemaking on a vast scale on one of the winery's mass-market tours. To get to Pirque, take the Santiago metro to Plaza de Puente Alto, the end of line 4. Then catch a blue minibus (labeled 'Pirque' in the window) and tell the driver you want to go to Plaza Pirque or Concha y Toro.

Cajón del Maipo

Rich greenery lines the steep, rocky walls of this stunning gorge, which the Río Maipo flows through. Starting only 25km southeast of Santiago, it's popular on weekends with *santiaguinos*. November through March is rafting season, ski bums and bunnies flock here June through September, and horseback riding is popular year-round.

The river itself is made up of a series of mostly Class III rapids with very few calm areas – indeed, rafters are often tossed into the water. Try a rafting trip from the private nature reserve and working horse ranch **Cascada de las Animas** (☎02-861-1303; www.cascada.net; Camino al Volcan 31087, Casilla 57, San Alfonso; rafting trips CH$21,000). Led by experienced guides, the route travels some lovely gorges, ending up in San Jose de Maipo. Promotions and packages often include lunch and use of the inviting swimming pool; you can also use the shaded picnic facilities or have a meal at the treehouse-like restaurant perched high on a bluff over the river. You can arrange any number of hiking, riding and rafting options here too.

Many opt to spend the night at the rustic-chic **Cascada Lodge** (campsite per person CH$10,000, d with/without bathroom CH$40,000/25,000, cabins for 3/6/8 people CH$60,000/95,000/120,000), which features gorgeous bungalow suites, wood cabins and a shady campsite.

Only 93km from Santiago, 30-sq-km **Monumento Natural El Morado** (www.conaf.cl/parques/monumento-natural-el-morado; adult/child CH$2000/1000; ⏲8:30am-2:30pm Oct-Apr) rewards hikers with views of 4490m Cerro El Morado at Laguna El Morado, a two-hour hike from the humble hot springs of Baños Morales. There are free campsites around the lake.

Refugio Lo Valdés (☎cell 9230-5930; www.refugiolovaldes.com; Refugio Alemán, Ruta G-25 Km 77; dm CH$15,000, d from CH$48,000), a mountain chalet with simple, wood-clad rooms and a stunning view over the Cajón, is a popular weekend destination. The on-site restaurant is renowned for its hearty meals and *onces*. About 11km on, **Termas Valle de Colina** (☎02-985-2609; www.termasvalledecolina.com; entrance incl camping adult/child CH$8000/4000, d without bathroom CH$30,000; ⏲Oct-Feb) features terraced hot springs overlooking the valley.

To get to San Alfonso from Santiago, take metro line 4 to the Las Mercedes terminal, then hop onto bus 72 (CH$550) – or any bus that says 'San Alfonso' on the window. Some lines continue to Baños Morales from January to March. If you're going to Cascada de las Animas, the ride takes about 1½ hours; ask the driver to drop you off at the entrance to the reserve. Cascada de las Animas also runs private van transportation to and from Santiago (one to two people round trip CH$70,000).

Valparaíso

☎032 / POP 263,500

Poets, painters and would-be philosophers have long been drawn to this frenetic port city. Along with the ever-shifting population of sailors, dockworkers and prostitutes, they've endowed gritty and gloriously spontaneous Valparaíso with an edgy air of 'anything goes.' Add to this the spectacular faded beauty of its chaotic *cerros* (hills), some of the best street art in Latin America, a maze of steep, sinuous streets, alleys and *escaleras* (stairways) piled high with crumbling mansions, and it's clear why some visitors are spending more time here than in Santiago.

History

The leading merchant port along the Cape Horn and Pacific Ocean routes, Valparaíso was the stopover for foreign vessels, including whalers, and the export point of Chilean wheat destined for the California gold rush. Foreign merchants and capital made it Chile's financial powerhouse. Its decline began with the 1906 earthquake and the opening of the Panama Canal in 1914. Today 'Valpo' is back on the nautical charts as a cruise-ship stop-off, and Chile's growing fruit exports have also boosted the port. More significantly, the city has been Chile's legislative capital since 1990 and was voted the cultural capital in 2003. Unesco sealed the deal by giving it World Heritage status, prompting tourism to soar.

Valparaíso

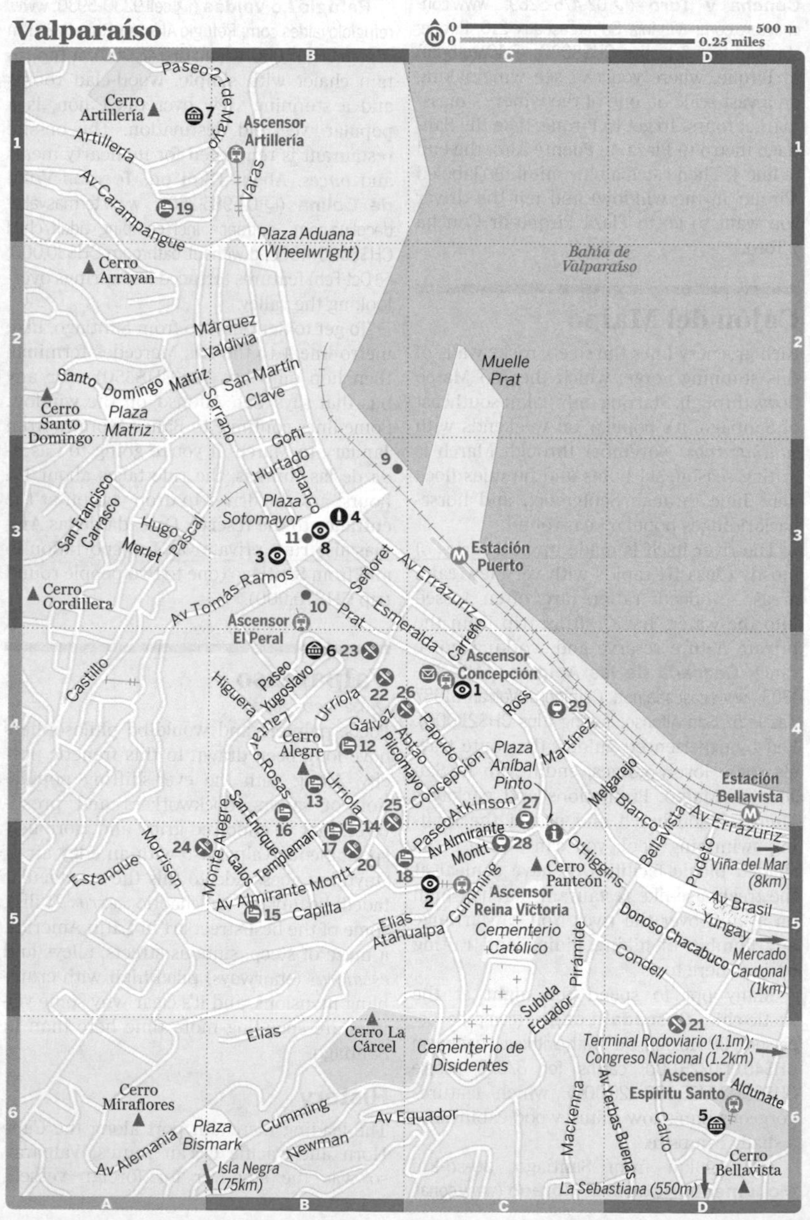

Sights & Activities

Don't take it from us, take it from Unesco: the whole of Valparaíso is a sight worth seeing. The best thing to do here is just walk the city streets and ride some of the 15 rattling *ascensores* (funiculars) built between 1883 and 1916; they crank you up into the hills and meandering back alleys. Wherever you wander, have your camera at the ready: Valpo brings out the photographer in most people.

El Plan & El Puerto

Valparaíso's flat commercial zone, El Plan, isn't as atmospheric as the hills that rise above it, but it contains a few monuments.

Plaza Sotomayor PLAZA
The Plaza Sotomayor is dominated by the impressive blue-colored palatial **Edificio de la Comandancia Naval** (Naval Command Building). In the middle of the square lies the **Monumento a los Héroes de Iquique**, a subterranean mausoleum paying tribute to Chile's naval martyrs.

Congreso Nacional HISTORIC BUILDING
(cnr Av Pedro Montt & Rawson) One of Valpo's only modern landmarks is the controversial Congreso Nacional, located in the east section of El Plan. Its roots lie in Pinochet's presidency both literally and legislatively: it was built on one of his boyhood homes and mandated by his 1980 constitution (which moved the legislature away from Santiago).

Cerros Concepción & Alegre

Ascensor Reina Victoria HISTORIC SITE
(admission CH$250; ⏲7am-11pm) Connects Av Elias to Paseo Dimalow.

Ascensor Concepción HISTORIC SITE
(admission CH$300; ⏲7am-10pm) The city's oldest elevator, Ascensor Concepción takes you from Prat in El Plan to Paseo Gervasoni, at the lower end of Cerro Concepción. Built in 1883, it originally ran on steam power.

Museo de Bellas Artes MUSEUM
(Paseo Yugoslavo 166; admission CH$2000) The rambling art nouveau building at the western end of Cerro Alegre is called Palacio Baburizza; it houses the Museo de Bellas Artes (Fine Arts Museum), which has a decent permanent collection plus plenty of details on the original palace owners.

Cerro Bellavista

Artists and writers have long favored this quiet residential hill; today a steady stream of hotels and eateries are opening here.

★ **La Sebastiana** HISTORIC BUILDING
(☎032-225-6606; www.fundacionneruda.org; Ferrari 692; adult/child & senior CH$5000/1500; ⏲10:30am-6:50pm Tue-Sun Jan & Feb, 10:10am-6pm Tue-Sun Mar-Dec) Bellavista's most famous resident artist was Pablo Neruda, who made a point of watching Valparaíso's annual New Year's fireworks from his house at the top of the hill, La Sebastiana. Because it's

Valparaíso

Sights
1 Ascensor Concepción ... C4
2 Ascensor Reina Victoria ... C5
3 Edificio de la Comandancia Naval ... B3
4 Monumento a los Héroes de Iquique ... B3
5 Museo a Cielo Abierto ... D6
6 Museo de Bellas Artes ... B4
7 Museo Naval y Marítimo ... A1
8 Plaza Sotomayor ... B3

Activities, Courses & Tours
9 Harbor Boat Tours ... B3
10 Natalis Language Center ... B3
11 Tours 4 Tips ... B3

Sleeping
12 Casa Aventura ... B4
13 Hostal Cerro Alegre ... B4
14 Hostal Jacaranda ... B5
15 La Nona ... B5
16 Mm 450 ... B4
17 Pata Pata Hostel ... B5
18 Vía Vía Hotel Art Deco ... B5
19 Yellow House ... A1

Eating
20 Café Vinilo ... B5
21 Casino Social J Cruz ... D6
22 Delicatessen Emporio ... B4
23 Delicias Express ... B4
24 La Cocó ... A5
25 Norma's ... B4
26 Puerto Escondido ... B4

Drinking & Nightlife
27 Cinzano ... C4
28 Fauna ... C5
29 La Piedra Feliz ... C4
Viá Viá Café ... (see 18)

first-come, first-served, it's recommended that you get here in the morning.

Getting here involves a hefty uphill hike, and the climbing continues inside the house – but you're rewarded on each floor with ever more heart-stopping views over the harbor. Unlike Neruda's other houses, you can wander around La Sebastiana at will, lingering over the chaotic collection of ships' figureheads, glass, 1950s furniture and artworks by his famous friends.

Alongside the house, the Fundación Neruda has built the Centro Cultural La Sebastiana, containing a small exhibition space, cafe and souvenir shop. To get here, walk 800m uphill along Héctor Calvo from Ascensor Espíritu Santo. Alternatively, take green bus O on Serrano near Plaza Sotomayor in El Plan, or from the plaza at the top of Templeman on Cerro Alegre and get off at the 6900 block of Av Alemania.

Museo a Cielo Abierto MUSEUM
(Open-Air Museum; cnr Rudolph & Ramos; 24hr) FREE Twenty classic, colorful murals are dotted through this *cerro's* lower streets, forming the Museo a Cielo Abierto, created between 1969 and 1973 by students from the Universidad Católica's Instituto de Arte. The **Ascensor Espíritu Santo** takes you from behind Plaza Victoria to the heart of this art.

Cerro Artillería

Clear views out over the sea made this southwestern hill a strategic defense spot.

DON'T MISS

VALPARAÍSO'S MURALS

Wandering up and down the winding hills of Valparaíso, you'll see colorful public art everywhere, from dreamlike wall paintings of glamorous women to political graffiti-style murals splashed across garage doors. As you cruise the streets keep an eye out for Chilean artist Inti. His large-scale mural, painted across the surface of several neighboring buildings and visible from Cerro Concepción, was unveiled in early 2012. The vibrant sideways image shows a mysterious, partially fragmented figure draped with exotic jewelry.

Museo Naval y Marítimo MUSEUM
(Naval & Maritime Museum; 032-243-7651; www.museonaval.cl; Paseo 21 de Mayo 45, Cerro Artillería; adult/child CH$1000/300; 10am-6pm Tue-Sun) Cannons still stand ready outside this naval museum. Much space is devoted to Chile's victory in the 19th-century War of the Pacific. Other exhibits include historical paintings, uniforms, ships' furniture, swords, navigating instruments and medals, all neatly displayed in exhibition rooms along one side of a large courtyard. Rattling **Ascensor Artillería** (closed for restoration) brings you here from Plaza Aduana.

Courses

Chilean Cuisine COOKING COURSE
(cell 6621-4626; www.cookingclasseschile.cl; location varies; course per person from CH$37,000) An energetic chef takes you to shop for ingredients at the local market, then teaches you to make *pisco sours,* taste local wines, and cook – then eat – a menu of Chilean classics.

Natalis Language Center LANGUAGE COURSE
(032-225-4849; www.natalislang.com; Plaza Justicia 45, 6th fl, Oficina 602, El Plan; courses per week from CH$90,000, 3-day crash courses CH$135,000) Has a good reputation for quick results.

Tours

★ **Tours 4 Tips** WALKING TOUR
(www.tours4tips.com; Plaza Sotomayor, El Plan; 10am & 3pm) Just show up at Plaza Sotomayor, look for the guides with the red-and-white shirts in the middle of the plaza, and head off for a friendly introduction to the city that focuses on street art, cultural history and politics. You only tip if you like the tour. We think CH$5000 to CH$10,000 is a good tip if you enjoy yourself.

Harbor Boat Tours BOAT TOUR
(Muelle Prat; 30min tour CH$3000; 9:30am-6:30pm) Pass alongside giant cruise vessels or naval battleships, or spot sea lions frolicking in the harbor. Several companies operate boats – ask around for the best price and group up for savings.

Festivals & Events

Año Nuevo NEW YEAR
Fantastic fireworks displays over the harbor draw hundreds of thousands of spectators to the city each December 31. Book accommodations well in advance.

Sleeping

La Nona B&B $
(cell 6618-6186; www.bblanona.com; Galos 660, Cerro Alegre; s/d/tr CH$25,000/36,000/46,000;) The English-speaking owners of this B&B are mad about Valpo, and love sharing insider tips with their guests. The rooms are simple but highly passable. Stained glass and skylights add an open air, and the central location on Cerro Alegre is also a serious selling point. Ask for a room with a view.

Yellow House B&B $
(032-233-9435; www.theyellowhouse.cl; Capitán Muñoz Gamero 91, Cerro Artillería; r with/without bathroom CH$38,000/25,000;) Oh-my-god views over the old port set this quiet B&B apart, as does the friendly care lavished on guests by the Chilean owner. The cozy, pastel-painted rooms come with thick white comforters. The Oceano by far has the best views. The only drawback: you're quite removed from the action, dining and nightlife of the more popular *cerros*.

Use caution arriving late at night.

Hostal Jacaranda HOSTEL $
(032-327-7567; www.hostaljacaranda.blogspot.com; Urriola 636, Cerro Alegre; dm/d from CH$7000/20,000;) Small but very welcoming (and perfectly located in a lively section of Cerro Alegre), this cheerful, sustainably run hostel (note the recycling efforts) features a terrace that's romantically illuminated at night. The owners are a wealth of knowledge; if you ask nicely, they might even show you how to make Chilean specialties like *pisco sours* and empanadas.

Pata Pata Hostel HOSTEL $
(032-317-3153; www.patapatahostel.com; Templeman 657, Cerro Alegre; dm CH$7500-10,000, d without bathroom CH$28,000;) The most youth-forward of Valparaíso's hostels, this spot up a picturesque flower-dotted stairway has a positive energy, plenty of hangout places and pumped-in music. It's a bit unkempt (but so is the city) and the dorm mattresses are blandish.

Mm 450 HOSTEL $
(032-222-9919; www.mm450.cl; Lautaro Rosas 450, Cerro Alegre; dm CH$14,080-17,850, r with/without bathroom $71,400/53,500;) This 'boutique hostel' has a streamlined modern look, and super-comfy dorm rooms with new mattresses and gleaming white comforters. It's attached to a hip restaurant and lounge, so there's always somebody around, but despite a gorgeous interior patio, it doesn't seem like there's much of a traveler's scene...at least not yet. There's no shared kitchen.

Hostal Cerro Alegre B&B $
(032-327-0374; www.hostalcerroalegre.cl; Urriola 562, Cerro Alegre; dm CH$12,000, r with/without bathroom CH$39,000/25,000;) Funky antiques, original oil paintings by the former owner and an eclectic mix of colors, styles and design sensibilities make this a good bet for the boho crowd. There's a shared kitchen and smallish living area, and the dorm sleeps just three.

Casa Aventura HOSTEL $
(032-275-5963; www.casaventura.cl; Pasaje Gálvez 11, Cerro Concepción; dm/s/d without bathroom CH$9000/17,000/25,000;) One of Valpo's oldest hostels, this ramshackle old house has airy, pastel-painted dorms, while doubles feature sky-high ceilings and original wooden floors. There's a shared kitchen, but it's missing a cool terrace or large common areas.

Vía Vía Hotel Art Deco BOUTIQUE HOTEL $$
(032-319-2134; www.viaviacafe.cl; Almirante Montt 217, Cerro Alegre; r CH$39,000-58,000;) Run by a friendly Ecuadorian-Belgian couple, this round-walled art-deco boutique is a favorite for the arts-poetry-and-chunky-glasses set. With just five rooms, it's a cozy affair. The rooms are sparse but quite airy, and the bathrooms have solar showers and

TOP FIVE VALPO VIEWS

- Paseo 21 de Mayo on Cerro Artillería to survey the cranes and containers of the port.
- Plaza Bismark on Cerro Carcel for a panoramic take of the bay.
- Mirador Diego Portales on Cerro Baron for a sweeping perspective of Valpo's colorful house-cluttered central views.
- The viewpoint at the end of Calle Merlet on Cerro Cordillera to see the rusting roofs of Barrio El Puerto and the civic buildings of Plaza Sotomayor from above.
- Paseo Atkinson on Cerro Concepción for views of typical Valpo houses during the day, and a twinkling sea of lights on the hills at night.

elegant stone accents. There is an outrageously fun cafe on the main floor, making this a good spot for midnight-candle burners.

Eating

★Café Vinilo CHILEAN $
(Almirante Montt 448, Cerro Alegre; mains CH$5800-8500) Vying for Valparaíso's top spot, this eclectic resto-bar is studied, quirky, esoteric and sublime. The dinner plates feature fresh salmon, albacore and other local catches with inventive presentations and delicious flavor combinations.

Delicatessen Emporio CHILEAN $
(Urriola 383, Cerro Alegre; set lunch CH$3900-5900; 11am-3pm Mon-Thu, to 11pm Fri & Sat;) This small dining room has a high-quality fixed-menu lunch with your choice of soup or salad, main plates like fresh-caught salmon or homemade gnocchi in Tuscan sauce, followed by a sumptious desert. There's a semi-open kitchen – so you know it's clean!

La Cocó SANDWICHES $
(www.lacoco-sangucheriaartesanal.blogspot.com; Monte Alegre 546, Cerro Alegre; sandwiches CH$3800-5000; closed Mon & Tue, lunch only Sun;) Popular with hip *porteños* (people from Valparaíso) and savvy travelers, this *sanguchería artesanal* (artisan sandwich maker) is a true delight. The gourmet sandwiches come piled high with fresh seafood (smoked salmon with spicy chorizo is a current hit) or vegetarian-friendly toppings. A lineup of live-music performances and poetry readings enliven the space in the evening.

Puerto Escondido CHILEAN $
(www.puertoescondido.cl; Papudo 424; mains CH$3500-6200) Situated in one of Valparaíso's quaint antique houses, this family-run eatery offers a short menu of well-made Chilean classics like *pastel de papas* (a potato casserole similar to shepherd's pie) and other homey dishes you won't find in contemporary restaurants. Come for the down-to-earth ambience as well as the food.

Norma's CHILEAN $
(Almirante Montt 391, Cerro Alegre; set lunch $4900-6900; closed Mon) Don't let the name (or the nondescript entryway) throw you off: just climb the tall stairway into this cheerful, casually elegant restaurant for a surprisingly well-prepared set lunch that's friendlier on your wallet than most others in the area. The restored house still has the grand dimensions, polished wood and charming antique window frames of the original structure.

Mercado Cardonal MARKET $
(Mercado Cardonal, 2nd fl, El Plan; mains CH$3500-5000; 9am-10pm) There's a good selection of seafood stands at Valparaíso's main food market.

Casino Social J Cruz CHILEAN $
(Condell 1466, El Plan; mains CH$4500-6000) Liquid-paper graffiti covers the tabletops and windows at this tiny cafe, tucked away down a narrow passageway in El Plan. Forget about menus, there's one essential dish to try: it's said that *chorrillana* (a mountain of french fries under a blanket of fried pork, onions and egg) was invented here. Folk singers serenade you into the wee hours.

Delicias Express CHILEAN $
(Urriola 358, Cerro Alegre; empanadas CH$1000-1300; 8am-6pm) Boasting 60 varieties of empanadas, friendly service and a crispy crust you'll love, this is one of the best empanada joints on the coast.

Drinking & Nightlife

★Viá Viá Café CAFE
(032-319-2134; www.viaviacafe.cl; Almirante Montt 217, Cerro Alegre; noon-2am;) Set below a precipitous stairway and looming three-story mural, this garden cafe brims with creativity and serendipitous energy. There's occasional live music, simple dining options, and a good mix of Belgian beers and Chilean wines on tap. It's a must-stop on any mural crawl or pub crawl.

Cinzano BAR
(www.barcinzano.cl; Plaza Aníbal Pinto 1182, El Plan; closed Sun) Drinkers, sailors and crooners have been propping themselves up on the cluttered bar here since 1896. It's now a favorite with tourists too, who come to see tuneful old-timers knocking out tangos and boleros like there's no tomorrow.

Fauna BAR
(www.faunahotel.cl; Pasaje Dimalow 166, Cerro Alegre; 1-11pm) One of the best decks in town is found at this hip lounge and resto-bar (with a sophisticated attached hotel). It is a top spot for locals to suck down craft beers, cocktails and wine.

La Piedra Feliz BAR, CLUB
(www.lapiedrafeliz.cl; Av Errázuriz 1054, El Plan; admission from CH$3000; from 9pm Tue-Sun)

Jazz, blues, tango, son, salsa, rock, drinking, dining, cinema: is there anything this massive house along the waterfront doesn't do? In the basement, DJs spin till 4am at the nightclub **La Sala**.

Information

DANGERS & ANNOYANCES

The area around the Mercado Central and La Iglesia Matriz has a reputation for petty street crime and muggings. If you go, go early, avoid alleyways and leave valuables at the hostel. At night stick to familiar areas and avoid sketchy *escaleras* (stair passageways).

INTERNET ACCESS

Many lodgings and restaurants have free internet or wi-fi .

MEDIA

El Mercurio de Valparaíso (www.mercuriovalpo.cl) is the city's main newspaper.

MEDICAL SERVICES

Hospital Carlos Van Buren (☎032-220-4000; Av Colón 2454, El Plan) Public hospital.

POST

Post office (Prat 856, El Plan; ⏰9am-6pm Mon-Fri, 10am-1pm Sat)

TOURIST INFORMATION

Tourist Information Kiosks (☎032-293-9262; www.ciudaddevalparaiso.cl; ⏰10am-2pm & 3-6pm Mon-Sat) At these small information stands on Muelle Prat (opposite Plaza Sotomayor, El Plan) and Plaza Aníbal Pinto (cnr O'Higgins & Plaza Aníbal Pinto, El Plan), you can pick up maps and battle with other tourists for a chance to talk to the experts.

USEFUL WEBSITES

Valparaíso Map (www.valparaisomap.cl) Best map of Valparaíso.

Getting There & Away

All major intercity services arrive at and depart from the **Terminal Rodoviario** (Av Pedro Montt 2800, El Plan), across from the Congreso Nacional, about 20 blocks east of the town center. Be aware, especially if you're arriving at night, that taxis often aren't waiting around the terminal; if you need a ride to your hotel or hostel, you might have to call one or arrange a pick-up ahead of time. If you're walking between the bus station and the center, play it safe by sticking to a major thoroughfare like Pedro Montt.

Tur Bus (☎600-660-6600; www.turbus.cl) runs frequently between Santiago and Valparaíso every day (CH$2100 to CH$5000, two hours); from Santiago, it's easy to connect to Chilean destinations north, south and east.

You can reach Mendoza (CH$29,800, eight hours) in Argentina with Tur Bus or **Cata Internacional** (☎800-122-2282; www.catainternacional.com).

The city transportation network, **Transporte Metropolitano Valparaíso** (TMV; www.tmv.cl), has services to Viña del Mar and the northern beach towns. For Reñaca, take the orange 607, 601 or 605; the 605 continues to Concón. All run along Condell then Yungay. You'll see other bus lines to the same destinations running along Av Errázuriz.

Getting Around

Walking is the best way to get about central Valparaíso and explore its *cerros* – you can cheat on the way up by taking an *ascensor* or a *taxi colectivo* (CH$500). *Micros* (minibuses; CH$310 to CH$600) run to and from Viña and all over the city. Avoid the traffic by hopping on **Metro**

DON'T MISS

ISLA NEGRA

The spectacular setting on a windswept ocean headland makes it easy to understand why **Isla Negra** (Pablo Neruda's House; ☎035-461-284; www.fundacionneruda.org; Poeta Neruda s/n; admission by guided tour only CH$5000; ⏰10am-6pm Tue-Sun, to 8pm Sat & Sun Jan-Feb) was Pablo Neruda's favorite house. Built by the poet when he became rich in the 1950s, it was stormed by soldiers just days after the 1973 military coup when Neruda was dying of cancer. The house includes extraordinary collections of bowsprits, ships in bottles, nautical instruments and wood carvings. Neruda's tomb is also here, alongside that of his third wife, Matilde. Reservations are essential in high season. (Note that despite the name, Isla Negra is not an island.)

Isla Negra is an easy half-day trip from Valparaíso: **Pullman Bus Lago Peñuelas** (☎032-222-4025) leaves from Valparaíso's bus terminal (CH$3200, 1½ hours) every 30 minutes. From Santiago, **Pullman Bus** (☎600-320-3200; www.pullman.cl) comes here direct from Terminal de Buses Alameda (CH$7500, 1½ hours, half-hourly).

Regional de Valparaíso (Merval; ☎032-252-7633; www.merval.cl), a commuter train that leaves from **Estación Puerto** (cnr Errázuriz & Urriola) and **Estación Bellavista** (cnr Errázuriz & Bellavista) to Viña del Mar.

Viña del Mar

☎032 / POP 287,000

Clean, orderly Viña del Mar is a sharp contrast to the charming jumble of neighboring Valparaíso. Manicured boulevards lined with palm trees and beautiful expansive parks have earned it the nickname of Ciudad Jardin (the Garden City). Viña remains a popular weekend and summer destination for well-to-do *santiaguinos*, despite the fact that its beaches get seriously packed and the Humboldt Current means that waters are chilly enough to put off most would-be swimmers.

Sights

Museo de Arqueología e Historia Francisco Fonck MUSEUM

(☎032-268-6753; www.museofonck.cl; 4 Norte 784; adult/child CH$2500/500; ⏲10am-2pm & 3-6pm Mon, 10am-6pm Tue-Sat, 10am-2pm Sun) The original *moai* (Easter Island statues) standing guard outside the Museo de Arqueología e Historia Francisco Fonck are just a teaser of the beautifully displayed archaeological finds from Easter Island within, along with Mapuche silverwork and anthropomorphic Moche ceramics. Upstairs are old-school insect cases and a lively explanation of how head shrinking works (finished examples are included).

Parque Quinta Vergara PARK

(Errázuriz 563; ⏲7am-6pm) Nowhere is Viña's nickname of the Garden City better justified than at the magnificently landscaped Parque Quinta Vergara, which you enter from Errázuriz at the south end of Libertad. It once belonged to one of the city's most illustrious families, the Alvares-Vergaras.

Sleeping

Delirio Hostel HOSTEL $

(☎032-262-5759; www.deliriohostel.com; Portales 131; dm CH$6000-10,000; @) The huge long garden in front of Viña's best hostel means you don't have to limit your open-air lounging to the beach. The right-on vibe stops at the door. While there's a shared kitchen, you'll miss a big indoor hang-out area. The good news is that the young owners help organize activities from tours to pub crawls.

Vista Hermosa 26 HOTEL $

(☎032-266-0309; www.vistahermosa26.cl; Vista Hermosa 26; s/d/tr CH$24,000/38,000/42,000;) Polished wooden floors and a big fireplace lend stately charm to the lounge of this quiet but friendly hotel on the edge of Cerro Castillo (a must-see *cerro* with some of the city's prettiest architecture). You get plenty of space in the simple rooms, making this a solid bet for midrange comfort.

Kalagen Hostel HOSTEL $

(☎032-299-1669; www.kalagenhostel.com; Av Valparaíso 618; dm CH$7500-11,200, d with/without bathroom incl breakfast CH$37,000/24,900;) This fun urban hostel contains stylish dorms and doubles with colorful linens, hardwood floors and Asian-style paper lanterns. It's a bit dirty, but the central location is great and there's a communal kitchen, a girls-only dorm and a chill-out room with TV set. The private rooms are actually pretty passable.

Casa Olga B&B $$

(☎032-318-2972; www.casa-olga.com; 18 de Sepiembre 31; d/apt CH$55,000/65,000;) This gorgeous boutique-style B&B, outfitted with breezy all-white decor, brand-new LCD TVs and cozy doubles with renovated private bathrooms, is practically right on the beach. It's just outside of Viña – an advantage or disadvantage depending on your travel plans.

Eating & Drinking

The pedestrian area around Av Valparaíso offers a string of beer-and-sandwich joints and other cheap dining options. Paseo Cousiño is home to convivial pubs, some featuring live music.

Panzoni ITALIAN $

(Paseo Cousiño 12-B; mains CH$3000-4800) One of the best-value eateries in central Viña, Panzoni's well-prepared Italian pastas and friendly service reel in the lunchtime diners. The location is slightly hidden on an out-of-the-way passageway.

Samoiedo SANDWICHES $

(☎032-268-1382; Valparaíso 637; sandwiches CH$2500-4500, set lunch CH$5000-7000) For half a century the old boys have been meeting at this traditional *confitería* (tearoom) for lunchtime feasts of steak and fries or well-stuffed sandwiches. The outdoor seating is greatly preferable to the interior, which is open to a busy shopping mall.

Mercado del Mar CHILEAN $$
(Av Perú s/n; CH$5500-9500; 📶) A sunset drink here should be on everyone's Viña to-do list – there are panoramic views of the Pacific from its glassed-in terrace above the mouth of the Marga Marga.

La Flor de Chile BAR
(www.laflordechile.cl; 8 Norte 601; mains CH$3000-6500) For nearly a century, *viñamarinos* young and old have downed their *schops* (draft beer) over the closely packed tables of this gloriously old-school bar.

Café Journal CLUB
(cnr Agua Santa & Alvares; cover free-CH$3000; ⏲10pm-late Wed-Sat) Electronic music is the order of the evening at this boomingly popular club, which has three heaving dance floors

Scratch CLUB
(www.scratch.cl; Quillota 898; cover CH$2000-5000) This superclub is immensely popular with the university set and 20-something locals who dance to reggaeton and DJ-spun tunes until 5am.

Information

Several banks have ATMs on Plaza Vergara, the main square.

Conaf (☎032-232-0210; www.conaf.cl; 3 Norte 541; ⏲8:30am-5:30pm Mon-Fri) Provides information on nearby parks, including Parque Nacional La Campana.

Hospital Gustavo Fricke (☎032-265-2200; Alvares 1532) Viña's main public hospital, located east of downtown.

Municipal tourist office (☎275-2000; www.visitevinadelmar.cl; Av Valparaíso 1055; ⏲9am-6pm) Distributes an adequate city map and a monthly events calendar.

Post office (Plaza Vergara s/n; ⏲9am-7pm Mon-Fri, 10am-1pm Sat)

Getting There & Away

All long-distance services operate from the **Rodoviario Viña del Mar** (☎032-275-2000; www.rodoviario.cl; Valparaíso 1055), four long blocks east of Plaza Vergara. Nearly all long-distance buses to and from Valparaíso stop here.

Local buses go to Reñaca, Concón and other northern beach towns. To catch one, go to Plaza Vergara and the area around Viña's metro station; expect to pay between CH$1200 and CH$2200 one way, depending on your final destination.

Budget (☎032-268-3420; www.budget.cl; Marina 15) is your best bet for car rental.

A commuter train run by **Metro Regional de Valparaíso** (Merval; ☎032-252-7633; www.merval.cl) connects Viña del Mar and Valparaíso.

Getting Around

Micros (minibuses; CH$400 to CH$600) go around the city and to Valparaíso.

Around Viña del Mar

North of Viña del Mar, a beautiful road snakes along the coast, passing through a string of beach towns that hum with holidaying Chileans from December to February. Towering condos overlook some, while others are scattered with rustic cottages and the huge summer houses of Chile's rich and famous.

Come to **Reñaca**, just north of Viña, for a sunset hike with incredible views on **Roca Oceanica**, a rocky hill looking out over the Pacific. Continue to **Concón**, 15km from Viña, for its unpretentious seafood restaurants. **Las Deliciosas** (Av Borgoño 25370; empanadas CH$900) does exquisite empanadas; the classic is cheese and crab.

Further north, **Horcón** was Chile's first hippie haven. Brightly painted, ramshackle buildings clutter the steep main road down to its small, rocky beach where fishing boats come and go. These days there's still a hint of peace, love and communal living – note the happy-go-lucky folks gathering on the beach at sunset with dogs, guitars and bottles of liquor in paper bags.

About 21km north of Horcón, the long, sandy beaches of **Maitencillo** stretch for several kilometers along the coast. **Escuela de Surf Maitencillo** (☎cell 9238-4682; www.escueladesurfmaitencillo.cl; Av del Mar 1250; group class per person CH$16,000) is a relaxed place to learn how to surf. A favorite restaurant and bar is **La Canasta** (www.hermansen.cl; Av del Mar 592; mains CH$5900-8800, cabin CH$77,000) for wood-baked pizzas and – of course – fresh fish.

The small, laid-back town of **Cachagua**, 13km north of Maitencillo, sits on the northern tip of a long crescent beach. Just across the water is a rocky outcrop that's home to more than 2000 Humboldt penguins, as well as a colony of sea lions.

Continue north 35km to reach **Zapallar**, the most exclusive of Chile's coastal resorts, with still-unspoiled beaches flanked by densely wooded hillsides. Book ahead. Superb seafood is yours at **El Chiringuito** (Caleta de Pescadores; mains CH$8200-12,400), with crushed shells underfoot and a wall of windows that peers to the sea.

Several bus companies visit Zapallar direct from Santiago, including Tur Bus (p438) and Pullman (p438). **Sol del Pacífico** (☎032-275-2030; www.soldelpacifico.cl) comes up the coast from Viña.

NORTHERN CHILE

Traveling inland, the balmy coast of sunbathers and surfers shifts to cactus scrub plains and dry mountains streaked in reddish tones. Mines scar these ore-rich mammoths whose primary reserve, copper, fuels Chile's economic engine. But there's life here as well, in the fertile valleys producing *pisco* grapes, papayas and avocados. Clear skies mean exceptional celestial observation – it's no wonder many international telescopic, optical and radio projects are based here. The driest desert in the world, the Atacama is a refuge of flamingos on salt lagoons, sculpted moonscapes and geysers ringed by snow-tipped volcanoes.

The Norte Chico, or 'region of 10,000 mines,' is a semiarid transition zone from the Valle Central to the Atacama. Ancient South American cultures left enormous geoglyphs on barren hillsides. Aymara peoples still farm the *precordillera* (the foothills of the Andes) and pasture llamas and alpacas in the highlands. You can diverge from the desert scenery to explore the working mine of Chuquicamata or brave the frisky surf of arid coastal cities.

Take precautions against altitude sickness in the mountains and avoid drinking tap water in the desert reaches.

La Serena

☎051 / POP 198,200

Blessed with neocolonial architecture, shady streets and golden shores, peaceful La Serena turns trendy beach resort come summer. Founded in 1544, Chile's second-oldest city is a short jaunt from character-laden villages, sun-soaked pisco vineyards and international observatories for stargazing. Nearby **Coquimbo** is more rough-and-tumble, but lives and breathes a hearty nightlife.

Sights & Activities

Excursions in the Serena region range from national-park visits to nighttime astronomical trips and *pisco*-tasting tours. Agencies in town offer full-day trips through the Valle del Elqui, Parque Nacional Fray Jorge and Parque Nacional Pingüino de Humboldt; try **Elqui Valley Tour** (☎051-221-4846; www.goelqui.com; Prat 567; ⏲9am-6pm Mon-Sat).

La Serena has a whopping 29 churches: on the Plaza de Armas is the 1844 **Iglesia Catedral** (Plaza de Armas; ⏲10am-1pm & 4-8pm), and two blocks west is the mid-18th-century **Iglesia Santo Domingo** (cnr Cordovez & Muñoz). The stone colonial-era **Iglesia San Francisco** (Balmaceda 640) dates from the early 1600s.

Observatorio Turístico Collowara OBSERVATORY

(☎051-243-1419; www.collowara.cl; 599 Urmeneta St; adult/5-12yr CH$4500/3500; ⏲tours 9pm, 10:30pm & midnight) This shiny new observatory is built for tourists; no serious interstellar research is conducted here, but the facility boasts a 40cm telescope for stargazing. Book at the ticket office in nearby

WORTH A TRIP

CLOUD FORESTS & HOT SPRINGS

An ecological island of lush Valdivian cloud forest in semidesert surroundings, **Parque Nacional Fray Jorge** (adult/child CH$2500/1000; ⏲9am-5:30pm) is 82km west of Ovalle. This Unesco World Biosphere Reserve protects 400 hectares of truly unique vegetation nourished by moist fog. There's no public transportation, but agencies in La Serena and Ovalle offer tours.

Stop in at **Termas de Socos**, a tiny spring hidden 1.5km off the Panamericana at Km 370. Private tubs cost CH$4500 for a half-hour soak in steamy baths; access to the cool public swimming pool also costs CH$4500 for nonguests. Stay at the delightful on-site **Hotel Termas Socos** (☎053-198-2505; www.termasocos.cl; s/d CH$45,000/78,000; 🏊), with lush surroundings and private thermal baths. Nearby **Camping Termas de Socos** (☎053-263-1490; www.campingtermassocos.cl; campsites per person CH$6000; 🏊) also offers its own springs and bike rentals.

Northern Chile (Norte Chico)

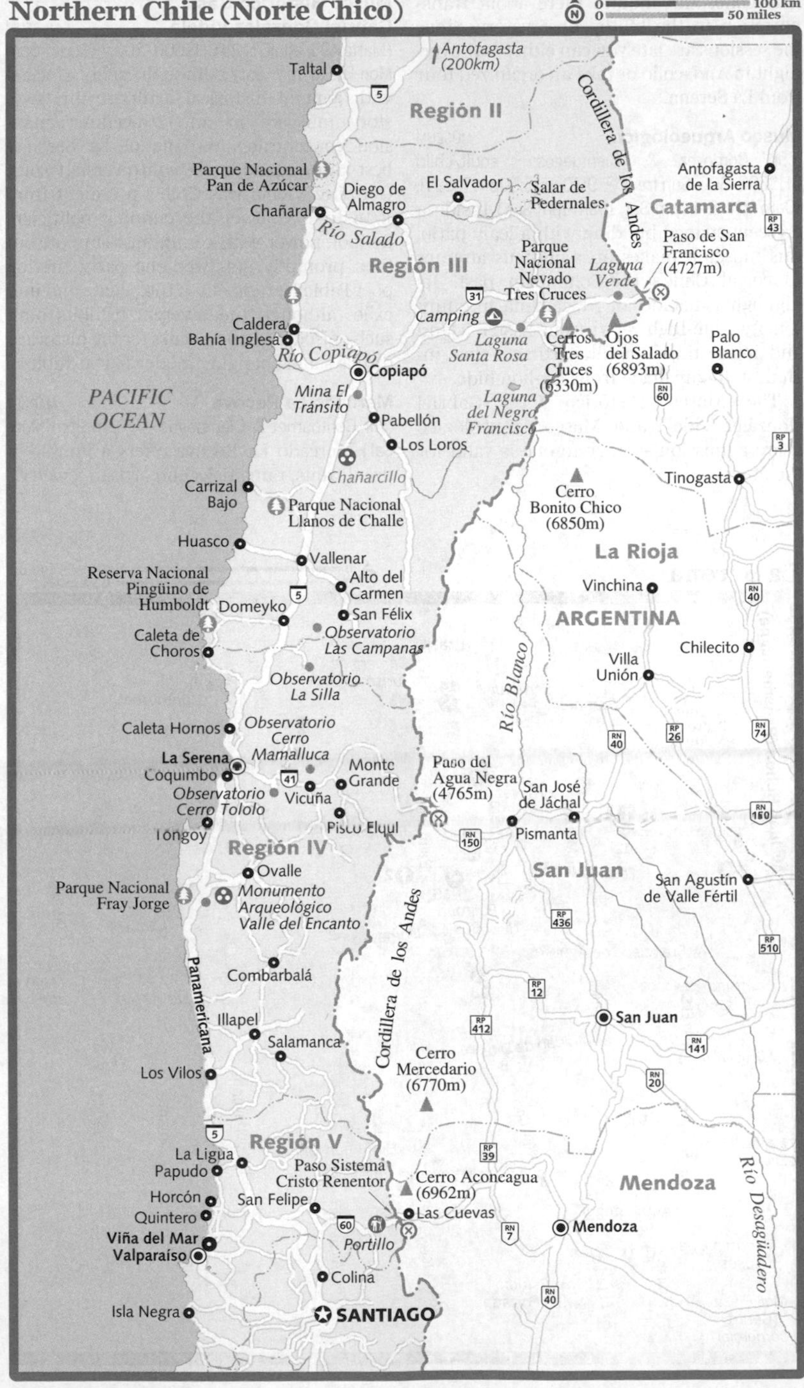

Andacollo, and inquire there about transportation to the hilltop observatory. Since the sessions are late you can either stay overnight in Andacollo or take an organized tour from La Serena.

Museo Arqueológico MUSEUM
(cnr Cordovez & Cienfuegos; adult/child CH$600/300, Sun free; ⏲9:30am-5:50pm Tue-Fri, 10am-1pm & 4-7pm Sat, 10am-1pm Sun) Inside a crescent-shaped building with a leafy patio, this museum makes an ambitious attempt to corral Chile's pre-Columbian past. Its highlights include an Atacameña mummy, a hefty 2.5m-high *moai* from Easter Island and interesting Diaguita artifacts that include a dinghy made from sea-lion hide.

The Museo Histórico Casa Gabriel González Videla and Museo Arqueológico share admission – entry to one is valid for the other.

Museo Histórico Casa Gabriel González Videla MUSEUM
(Matta 495; adult/child CH$600/300; ⏲10am-6pm Mon-Fri, to 1pm Sat) Although richly stocked with general historical artifacts, this two-story museum in an 18th-century mansion concentrates on one of La Serena's best-known (and most controversial) sons. González Videla was Chile's president from 1946 to 1952. Ever the cunning politician, he took power with communist support but then promptly outlawed the party, driving poet Pablo Neruda out of the Senate and into exile (although the reverent exhibits omit such episodes). Pop upstairs for the historical displays and changing modern-art exhibits.

Mercado La Recova MARKET
(cnr Cantournet & Cienfuegos; ⏲9am-9pm Mon-Sat) Mercado La Recova offers a jumble of dried fruits, rain sticks and artisan jewelry.

La Serena

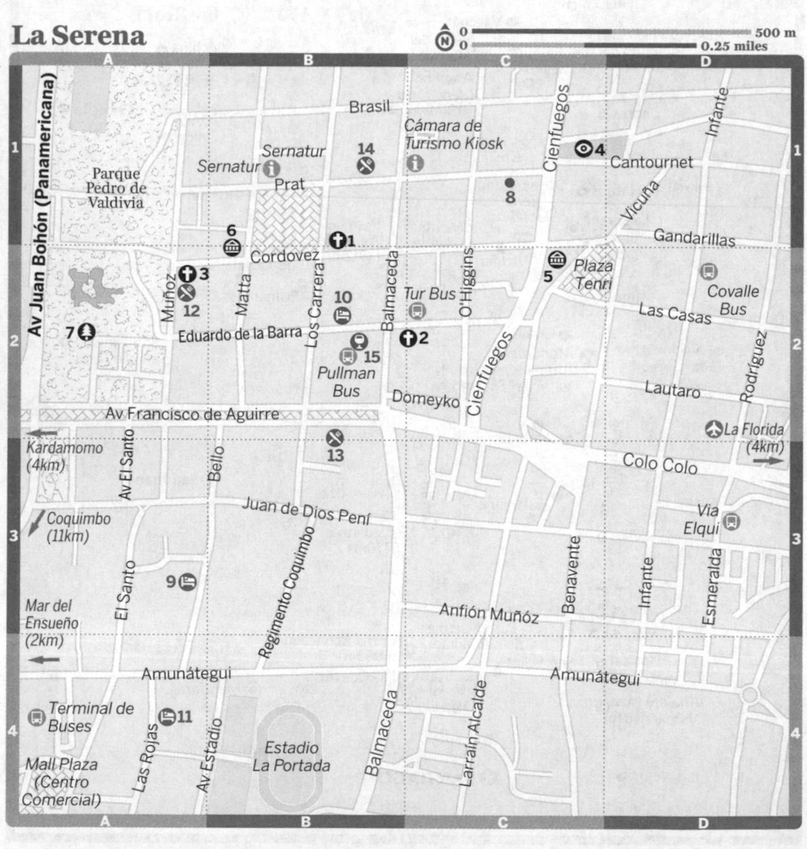

Parque Japones Kokoro No Niwa PARK
(Parque Pedro de Valdivia; adult/5-12yr CH$1000/300; ⏲10am-8pm summer, to 6pm rest of year) With its trickling brooks, drifting swans and neatly manicured rock gardens, this Japanese garden makes a good escape from the city bustle.

Beaches

A swath of wide sandy beaches stretches from La Serena's nonfunctional lighthouse right to Coquimbo: there are so many that you could visit a different beach every day for a two-week vacation. Unfortunately, strong rip currents make some unsuitable for swimming – but good for surfing. Safe swimming beaches generally start south of Cuatro Esquinas.

Sleeping

★Hostal El Punto HOSTEL $
(☎051-222-8474; www.hostalelpunto.cl; Bello 979; dm/s/d without bathroom CH$8500/17,000/18,000, s CH$24,000-26,000, d CH$26,000-30,000; @📶) This is La Serena's best hostel, with a wide range of rooms, a bunch of sunny terraces, bright mosaics and tree-trunk tables. The staff speak German and English, and provide travel tips, tours, bike rental, nice cakes, laundry, book exchange…you name it. You'll want to book months ahead, especially in high season.

Hostal Tierra Diaguita HOSTEL $
(☎051-221-6608; www.fogoncasatamaya.cl; Eduardo de la Barra 440; s/d CH$34,000/40,000, without bathroom CH$28,000/32,000; 📶) Inside a colonial house, this friendly place has well-kept rooms in the main building and add-ons in the back reached through the verdant garden. Guests can use the shared kitchen and the lovely patio. Free perks include breakfast and luggage storage. The sign out front says 'Casa Tamaya.'

Maria's Casa GUESTHOUSE $
(☎051-222-9282; www.hostalmariacasa.cl; Las Rojas 18; dm/s/d without bathroom CH$9000/15,000/18,000; 📶) The cottage-style rooms at this family-run spot are simple and cozy. There's a garden in the back, where you can camp (CH$3500 per person). Other backpacker-friendly amenities include well-scrubbed shared bathrooms, a quaint country kitchen with free tea and coffee, laundry service and bike rental.

Eating

Ayawasi VEGETARIAN $
(Pedro Pablo Muñoz 566; mains CH$4000-6000; ⏲9am-8pm Mon-Sat; 🖉) A short walk from the plaza, this little vegetarian oasis serves some fantastic set lunches, delicious fresh juices and innovative sandwiches and salads in a shady garden setting or laid-back dining room.

★Kardamomo SEAFOOD $$
(Av del Mar 4000; mains CH$7000-11,000; ⏲noon-11pm Mon-Sat, to 4pm Sun; 📶) An excellent beachfront location, art-covered walls and a smooth soundtrack are the foundations for this laid-back but elegant seafood restaurant. Good-value set lunches, a wide menu and carefully prepared sushi platters round out the picture.

Casona del 900 PARRILLA $$
(Av Francisco de Aguirre 431-443; mains CH$4500-9500; ⏲noon-3pm & 7pm-midnight Mon-Sat) Inside an old beer factory, this high-ceilinged steakhouse with a glassed-in garden oozes ambience and packs in meat-loving locals for its good-value barbecues (CH$18,900 for two, with wine).

Rapsodia INTERNATIONAL $$
(Prat 470; mains CH$6000-9500; ⏲9am-9pm Mon-Wed, to 11pm Thu & Fri, to 6pm Sat) With

La Serena

Sights

1 Iglesia Catedral ... B1
2 Iglesia San Francisco ... C2
3 Iglesia Santo Domingo ... A2
4 Mercado La Recova ... C1
5 Museo Arqueológico ... C2
6 Museo Histórico Casa Gabriel González Videla ... B2
7 Parque Japones Kokoro No Niwa ... A2

Activities, Courses & Tours

8 Elqui Valley Tour ... C1

Sleeping

9 Hostal El Punto ... A3
10 Hostal Tierra Diaguita ... B2
11 Maria's Casa ... A4

Eating

12 Ayawasi ... A2
13 Casona del 900 ... B2
14 Rapsodia ... B1

Drinking & Nightlife

15 Cafe W ... B2

several side rooms looking onto the inner courtyard with a giant palm tree, this old *casona* serves up good-value meat and seafood dishes, a range of healthy sandwiches and live music on some nights.

 Drinking & Nightlife

Look for lively student bars around the intersection of O'Higgins and Av Francisco de Aguirre. Nightclubs lining the seafront to Coquimbo go full-on in the summer season.

Cafe W CAFE, BAR
(Eduardo de la Barra 435; sandwiches CH$3000-6000; ⏲9am-11pm Mon-Thu, to 1am Fri & Sat) With a large wooden deck overlooking a relatively quiet street, this is a great stop for coffee and to recharge the batteries. There are some yummy cakes on offer too, and a good range of sandwiches. Turns into a lively bar later at night.

 Information

Banks with 24-hour ATMs line the plaza.

Hospital Juan de Diós (☎051-223-3312; Balmaceda 916; ⏲24hr) The emergency entrance is at the corner of Larraín Alcalde and Anfión Muñóz.

Sernatur (☎051-222-5199; www.turismoregiondecoquimbo.cl; Matta 461; ⏲9am-8pm summer, 9am-6pm Mon-Fri, 10am-2pm Sat winter) Excellent tourist info shelled out from this office by the Plaza de Armas. During the summer, the municipal tourist office runs an information kiosk by Iglesia La Merced and another in the lighthouse by the beach.

Getting There & Away

AIR

La Serena's **Aeropuerto La Florida** (☎051-227-1870; www.aeropuertolaserena.com) is 5km east of downtown. **LAN** (☎600-526-2000; Balmaceda 406; ⏲9am-2pm & 3-6pm Mon-Fri, 10:30am-1:30pm Sat) flies daily to Santiago (CH$124,000, 50 minutes) and Antofagasta (CH$143,000, 1¼ hours).

BUS

La Serena's **Terminal de Buses** (☎051-222-4573; cnr Amunátegui & Av El Santo) has dozens of carriers plying the Carretera Panamericana from Santiago north to Arica, including **Tur Bus** (☎051-221-9828; www.turbus.cl; Balmaceda 437) and **Pullman Bus** (☎051-221-8879; www.pullman.cl; Eduardo de la Barra 435).

Covalle Bus (☎051-221-3127; Infante 538) For Argentine destinations, Covalle Bus travels to Mendoza (CH$34,000, 12 hours) and San Juan (CH$34,000, 18 hours) via the Libertadores pass every Sunday, leaving at 11pm.

Via Elqui (☎051-231-2422; cnr Juan de Dios Pení & Esmeralda) To get to Vicuña (CH$2500, 1½ hours), Ovalle (CH$2500, two hours), Montegrande (CH$3800, two hours) or Pisco Elqui (CH$3800, 2½ hours), try **Via Elqui**.

DESTINATION	COST (CH$)	DURATION (HR)
Antofagasta	31,200	12
Arica	37,600	23
Calama	31,900	14
Copiapó	9000	5
Iquique	32,900	19
Santiago	10,800	6

Getting Around

Women traveling alone should be wary of taxi drivers in La Serena; sexual assaults have been reported. Only take company cabs.

For car hire, try **Avis** (☎051-254-5300; Av Francisco de Aguirre 063; ⏲8:30am-6:30pm Mon-Fri, to 2pm Sat) or **Econorent** (☎051-222-0113; Av Francisco de Aguirre 0135; ⏲8:30am-6pm Mon-Fri, 9am-2pm Sat).

Valle del Elqui

The heart of Chilean pisco production, the Elqui Valley is famous for its futuristic observatories, seekers of cosmic energies, frequent UFO sightings, poet Gabriela Mistral and quaint villages. This is a truly enchanting – and enchanted – area, and one of the must-visit places in Norte Chico.

Vicuña

☎051 / POP 25,100

The spirit of Gabriela Mistral's somnambulist poetry seeps from every pore of snoozy little Vicuña. Just 62km east of La Serena, the town, with its low-key plaza, lyrical air and compact dwellings, is worth a visit for a day or two before you head out into the countryside to indulge in fresh avocados and papayas – not to mention the famous grapes that are distilled into *pisco*.

Sights & Activities

Observatorio Cerro Mamalluca OBSERVATORY
(☎051-267-0330; adult/child CH$4500/2000) Star of the stargazing show, the purpose-built Observatorio Cerro Mamalluca, 9km

northeast of Vicuña, is Elqui Valley's biggest attraction. So big, in fact, that you're likely to share the tour with hordes of other tourists, all looking for their chance to goggle at distant galaxies, star clusters and nebulae through a 30cm telescope.

Museo Gabriela Mistral MUSEUM
(Av Gabriela Mistral 759; adult/child & senior CH$600/300; ⏲10:00am-5:45pm Tue-Fri, 10:30am-6pm Sat, 10am-1pm Sun) The town's landmark Museo Gabriela Mistral, between Riquelme and Baquedano, is a tangible eulogy to one of Chile's most famous literary figures. Gabriela Mistral was born Lucila Godoy Alcayaga in 1889 in Vicuña. The museum charts her life (in Spanish only), from a replica of her adobe birthplace to her Nobel Prize, and has a clutch of busts making her seem a particularly strict schoolmarm.

Planta Pisco Capel PISQUERA
(admission CH$1500; ⏲10am-7:30pm Jan & Feb, to 6pm Mar-Dec) A 20-minute walk from town, here you can take a 45-minute bilingual tour of the facilities, which includes an on-site museum and a few skimpy samples (CH$10,000 gets you the premium tour, with top-shelf tastings). Capel distills pisco at this facility and has its only bottling plant here. To get here, head southeast of town and across the bridge, then turn left.

Inti Runa OBSERVATORY
(☎cell 9968-8577; www.observatorios.cl; Chacabuco 240; tours CH$8000; ⏲closed Jun-Aug) The German owner of this sun observatory claims he has two of the world's biggest solar telescopes. He keeps them in his lovely *casona*, and offers one-hour 'tours.' Basically, he talks while you look at the sun through the telescope.

Elki Magic ADVENTURE SPORTS
(☎cell 7459-8357; www.elkimagic.com; Av Gabriela Mistral 472) Run by an enthusiastic Chilean-French couple, this agency offers guided downhill bike jaunts (from CH$15,000), half-/one-day van tours to valley highlights (from CH$15,000/25,000, with lunch in the solar kitchens) and trips to the lagoons near Argentina. They also rent bikes (CH$7000 per day) and can supply you with a map of the 16km trail around the surrounding villages.

Sleeping

Alfa Aldea GUESTHOUSE $
(☎051-241-2441; www.alfaaldea.cl; La Vinita; s/d/5-person cabin CH$15,000/25,000/60,000) It's worth the CH$2000 taxi ride (or 15-minute walk) to the outskirts of town to stay in this fabulously low-key family-run *hostal*. Nestled in the vineyards and with priceless valley and mountain views, the rooms here are simple but extremely comfortable. The stars (sorry) of the show, however, are the excellent **astronomical tours** (☎051-241-2441; www.alfaaldea.cl; La Vinita; adult/child CH$10,000/5000) held on-site.

Hostal Valle Hermoso GUESTHOUSE $
(☎051-241-1206; www.hostalvallehermoso.com; Av Gabriela Mistral 706; s/d CH$19,000/30,000; 📶) Great lodging choice with eight airy and immaculately clean rooms around a sun-drenched patio inside an old adobe *casona* with Oregon-pine beams and walnut floors. Staff is warm and friendly and the ambience is laid-back – as if staying with old friends.

WORTH A TRIP

EXPLORING THE ELQUI VALLEY

Drive a car or rent a bicycle to explore the charming villages around Pisco Elqui. Highlights include tasting *pisco* (grape brandy) and touring the artisanal *pisquera* **Fundo Los Nichos** (☎051-245-1085; www.fundolosnichos.cl; tours CH$3000; ⏲10am-6pm), established in 1868. It's 3km south of Pisco Elqui.

Moving on from here you'll reach **Horcón Artisanal Market** (☎051-245-1015; ⏲noon-7:30pm summer, 1-6:30pm Tue-Sun rest of year), in the valley of its namesake village. Browse the gorgeous handmade arts and crafts, and local natural food and cosmetic products, all sold out of bamboo stalls.

Fans of Nobel Prize–winning poet Gabriela Mistral shouldn't miss a quick visit to **Monte Grande**, her onetime home, and the **Casa de la Cultura Gabriela Mistral** (admission free, guided tour CH$1000; ⏲9am-1pm & 2-7pm Mon-Fri), a cultural center and women's cooperative that conducts textile and art workshops with underemployed women from the area. Buses between Vicuña and Pisco Elqui stop here.

DON'T MISS

BAHÍA INGLESA

With rocky outcrops jutting out of turquoise waters and a long white-sand beach, this sweet seaside resort offers ideal beachside frolicking. The name originates from the British pirates who anchored here in the 17th century. Today, it's one of the north's most popular vacation spots, hectic in summer and mellow (and much cheaper) in the off-season. There's a cool Mediterranean feel and a lovely beachfront promenade. Locally harvested scallops, oysters and seaweed sweeten the culinary offerings.

Set sail with **Nautica La Rada** (☎cell 6846-4032; www.morroballena.cl), or kayak the crystal waters with **Morro Ballena** (☎cell 9886-3673; www.morroballena.cl; ⊙9am-6pm summer, hours vary rest of year). Even if you can't afford to stay at the swanky Coral de Bahia, it's worth dining on its delectable seafood while enjoying the beachfront views. The **Oficina de Turismo** (⊙10am-9pm Mon-Fri, 11am-9pm Sat & Sun summer, 10am-6pm daily rest of year) has the lowdown on local camping, virgin beaches and day tours.

From Copiapó, bus first to Caldera (CH$3500, one hour). From Caldera's bus terminal and main square, fast *colectivos* run to Bahía Inglesa (CH$1000, 10 minutes).

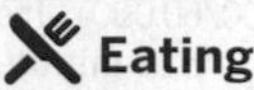

Eating

★Chaski CHILEAN $

(O'Higgins 159; mains CH$6500-8000; ⊙noon-10pm Mon-Thu, to 11pm Sat, to 8pm Sun) This tiny restaurant run by a Diaguita couple offers up Elqui Valley's most innovative dining. Local ingredients, like quinoa, goat and amaranth, are prepared with a twist, and doused in fragrant Andean herbs.

Frida CAFE $

(cnr Baquedano & Mistral; sandwiches around CH$7000; ⊙9am-11pm) Vicuña's coolest cafe is whimsically decorated with Mexican knick-knacks (the owners lived there for a while) and serves up super-strong espresso, good sandwiches and hosts taco night on Fridays.

Information

Oficina de Información Turística (☎051-267-0308; www.munivicuna.cl; San Martín 275; ⊙8:30am-8pm Jan & Feb, 8:30am-5:30pm Mon-Fri, 9am-6pm Sat, 9am-2pm Sun Mar-Dec) Gather a bit of info on the town's past and present at the municipal tourist office.

Getting There & Around

A block south of the plaza, the **bus terminal** (cnr Prat & O'Higgins) has frequent buses to La Serena (CH$2000, one hour), Pisco Elqui (CH$1500, 50 minutes) and Monte Grande (CH$1800, 40 minutes). Expresso Norte has a twice-daily service to Santiago (CH$12,000 to CH$17,000, seven hours). There's a wider choice of destinations in La Serena.

Pisco Elqui

Renamed to publicize the area's most famous product, the former village of La Unión is a laid-back hideaway.

Sights & Activities

Distileria Pisco Mistral PISQUERA

(☎051-245-1358; www.destileriapiscomistral.cl; O'Higgins 746; tours from CH$6000; ⊙noon-7pm Jan & Feb, 10:30am-6pm Tue-Sun Mar-Dec) The star attraction is the Distileria Pisco Mistral, which produces the premium Mistral brand of *pisco*. The hour-long 'museum' tour gives you glimpses of the distillation process and includes a free tasting of two *piscos* and a drink at the adjacent restaurant, which hosts occasional live music.

Turismo Migrantes OUTDOORS

(☎051-245-1917; www.turismomigrantes.cl; O'Higgins s/n; ⊙10am-2pm & 3-7pm) Offers tours.

Sleeping

Refugio del Angel CAMPGROUND $

(☎051-245-1292; refugiodelangel@gmail.com; campsites per person CH$6000, day use CH$3000) This idyllic spot by the river comes complete with swimming holes, bathrooms and a little shop. The turnoff is 200m south of the plaza on Manuel Rodríguez.

Hostal Triskel HOSTEL $

(☎cell 9419-8680; www.hostaltriskel.cl; Baquedano s/n; r without bathroom per person CH$15,000; 🛜) Up the hill from town, this lovely adobe and wood house has seven stylish and clean rooms with four shared bathrooms and a shared kitchen. A giant fig tree provides shade for the patio and there's a fruit orchard with lots of nooks, crannies and hammocks, plus bikes for rent and laundry services.

★El Tesoro de Elqui HOTEL $$
(☎051-245-1069; www.tesoro-elqui.cl; Prat s/n; dm CH$13,000, d CH$32,000-50,000; 📶🏊) Up the hill from the center plaza, this tranquil oasis dotted with lemon trees, lush gardens and flowering vines has 10 wooden bungalows with terraces. There's a restaurant that serves great coffee and cake and you can even get a massage or have your aura cleaned in the cabin by the swimming pool's 'beach.'

Eating & Drinking

El Rumor RESTAURANT, BAR $
(O'Higgins s/n; mains around CH$5000; ⊙noon-late) This jazzy resto-bar on the main road into town serves up great lunches (CH$5000) and giant sandwiches (CH$4000 to CH$5000) and, come night, 15 varieties of pisco cocktails. There's a Moroccan vibe to this tiny colorful spot that buzzes late into the night to a loungey soundtrack and occasional strumming of guitars in the lovely garden with a firepit.

Getting There & Away

Via Elqui (p454) buses run between Pisco Elqui and Vicuña (CH$1500, 50 minutes) throughout the day; catch one at the plaza.

Copiapó

☎052 / POP 154,900

Welcoming Copiapó has little to hold travelers, but it does offer a handy base for the remote mountains bordering Argentina, especially the breathtaking Parque Nacional Nevado Tres Cruces, Laguna Verde and Ojos del Salado, the highest active volcano in the world. The discovery of silver at nearby Chañarcillo in 1832 provided Copiapó with several firsts: South America's first railroad and Chile's first telegraph and telephone lines.

Sleeping & Eating

Hotel El Sol HOTEL $
(☎052-221-5672; Rodríguez 550; s/d CH$22,000/28,000; 📶) A cheerful yellow-painted hotel with a string of simple but clean rooms at a good price, just a short walk from the plaza.

Café Colombia CAFE $
(Colipí 484; snacks CH$1800; ⊙9am-9pm) Right on the main plaza by Mall Plaza Real, this is a good choice for real coffee and snacks. Great people-watching from the sidewalk tables.

Six Fusion FUSION $$
(Atacama 181; mains CH$7000-10,000; ⊙noon-3pm & 8pm-1am; 📶) Specializing in homemade pasta and doing a great sideline in sushi, this laidback restaurant is one of Copiapó's new wave of innovative, stylish

WORTH A TRIP

PARQUE NACIONAL NEVADO TRES CRUCES

Hard-to-reach **Parque Nacional Nevado Tres Cruces** (adult/6-12yr CH$5000/1500; ⊙8:30am-6pm) has all the rugged beauty and a fraction of the tourists of more famous high-altitude parks further north. Quite apart from pristine peaks and first-rate climbing challenges, the park shields some wonderful wildlife: flamingos in summer, large herds of vicuñas and guanacos, giant and horned coots and even the occasional condor and puma. Located just outside the park boundaries, 6893m **Ojos del Salado** is Chile's highest peak, a mere 69m short of Aconcagua, and the world's highest active volcano.

It's easy to get lost on your way to the national park, and there is no public transportation; consider taking a tour from Copiapó. **Puna de Atacama** (☎cell 9051-3202; www.punadeatacama.com; O'Higgins 21; ⊙9am-1pm & 3-6pm Mon-Fri, 9am-1pm Sat) comes recommended for tailored 4WD trips in the region. For rustic overnight accommodations at **Refugio Laguna del Negro Francisico** (per person per night CH$12,500), check with **Conaf** (☎052-221-3404; Juan Martínez 55; ⊙8:30am-5:30pm Mon-Thu, to 4:30pm Fri) in Copiapó.

restaurants. The shady backyard is the place to be on a sunny day.

Information

Numerous ATMs are located at banks around the plaza.

Sernatur (☎052-221-2838; Los Carrera 691; ⏰8:30am-7:30pm Mon-Fri, 9am-3pm Sat & Sun summer, 9am-7pm Mon-Fri, 9am-3pm Sat rest of year) The well-run tourist office on the main plaza gives out a wealth of materials and information in English.

Getting There & Away

Aeropuerto Desierto de Atacama is 50km northwest of Copiapó. **LAN** (☎600-526-2000; Colipí 484, Mall Plaza Real, Local A-102; ⏰9am-2pm & 3pm-6pm Mon-Fri, 10:30am-1:30pm Sat) flies daily to Santiago (CH$178,800, 1½ hours); **Sky** (☎600-600-2828; www.skyairline.cl; O'Higgins 460) offers cheaper fares.

Pullman Bus (☎052-221-2629; Colibrí 109) has a large terminal and a central **ticket office** (cnr Chacabuco & Chañarcillo). **Tur Bus** (☎052-223-8612; Chañarcillo 650) also has a terminal and a **ticket office** (Colipí 510) downtown (tip: save time waiting in line by getting your bus tickets here). Other companies include **Expreso Norte** (☎052-223-1176; Chañarcillo 655), **Buses Libac** (☎052-221-2237; Chañarcillo 655) and **Flota Barrios** (☎052-221-3645; Chañarcillo 631), all located in a common terminal on Chañarcillo. Many buses to northern desert destinations leave at night.

Colectivos go to Caldera/Bahía Inglesa (CH$3500, one hour) from the terminal on Chacabuco.

DESTINATION	COST (CH$)	DURATION (HR)
Antofagasta	10,800	8
Arica	21,900	16
Calama	12,900	10
Iquique	21,100	15
La Serena	10,000	5
Santiago	26,900	11

Parque Nacional Pan de Azúcar

The cold Humboldt Current flows up the desert coastline, bringing with it its peppy namesake penguin and abundant marine life. The worthwhile 440-sq-km **Pan de Azúcar** (www.conaf.cl; admission CH$5000) includes white-sand beaches, sheltered coves, stony headlands and cacti-covered hills.

Hired boats cruise around **Isla Pan de Azúcar** to view its 2000 Humboldt penguins, as well as cormorants, gulls, otters and sea lions. Pay from CH$5000 per person

LOS 33

For 121 years, the San José mine 45km north of Copiapó went about its business of gold and copper extraction deep in the Atacama Desert. Then, on the afternoon of August 5, 2010, a major cave-in trapped 33 of its workers 700m underground. 'Los 33,' as the buried miners became known, became unlikely superstars of one of the most televised rescue efforts in human history.

Under immense pressure, the government took over the rescue from the mine owners. The venture, at an estimated cost of US$20 million, involved international drilling-rig teams and experts from NASA. On October 13, 2010, in a televised 24-hour finale that drew an estimated viewing audience of one billion from around the world, the last of the 33 men was hoisted up to freedom through a narrow shaft.

While they were trapped, the ordeal of Los 33 became a round-the-clock soap opera. At one point, a man had both wife and lover waiting for him above. After 69 days in the pitch-dark depths of the earth, the 33 men resurfaced to find themselves in the spotlight. Afterwards, they were showered with gifts and money and all-expenses-paid trips to Disneyland. Yet the psychological aftermath has been difficult for the survivors.

The incident led to some long-overdue mining reforms, with the adoption of the International Labour Organization's (ILO's) convention on mining safety a year after the incident.

A big-budget film about their ordeal, *The 33*, starring Antonio Banderas, was released in 2015. For a fascinating account of the incident, read Héctor Tobar's 2014 book *Deep Down Dark*.

(with a 10-person minimum). In low season, you could end up forking out as much as CH$50,000 for the whole boat. Round trips take 1½ hours, and run from 10am to 6pm in summer, and to 4pm in winter.

Hike the 2.5km **El Mirador** trail to see sea cacti, guanacos and chilla foxes. Next up is **Las Lomitas**, an easy 4km path.

Camping is available at Playas Piqueros and Soldado, from CH$2000 per person, with toilets, water, cold showers and tables. Lovely adobe cabins at the eco-minded **Pan de Azúcar Lodge** (cell 9444-5416; www.pandeazucarlodge.cl; campsite per person CH$7000, cabins for 2/6/8 people CH$60,000/80,000/100,000) are fully equipped.

Pan de Azúcar is 30km north of Chañaral via a well-maintained paved road. Most people reach it by tour or transfer from Caldera/Bahía Inglesa or Copiapó.

Antofagasta

055 / POP 338,000

Chile's second-largest city, a rough-and-ready jumble of one-way streets, modern mall culture and work-wearied urbanites, is low on travelers' lists. Founded in 1870, the city earned its importance by offering the easiest route to the interior.

Sights

Nitrate-mining heydays left their mark with Victorian and Georgian buildings in the **Barrio Histórico** between the plaza and old port. The British-influenced **Plaza Colón** features Big Ben replica **Torre Reloj**. Sea lions circle Antofagasta's busy fish market **Terminal Pesquero.**

The oft-photographed national icon **La Portada** is a gorgeous natural arch located offshore, 20km north of Antofagasta.

Sleeping & Eating

Sleeping options are few and reduced by the numbers of miners occupying hotels.

Hotel San Marcos HOTEL $
(055-222-6303; www.hotelsanmarcos.cl; Latorre 2946; s/d CH$25,000/33,000;) A reasonable budget hotel on the edge of the city center, offering decent value for the price and very friendly service. The big breakfast takes a bit of the sting out of the inflated room price.

Bongo DINER $
(Baquedano 743; set menu from CH$3000, mains CH$2900-5100; 9am-11pm Mon-Sat) Buzzy eatery with thick-cushioned booths, a tidy mezzanine above and a good-and-greasy menu for those times when only a draft beer and burger will do. Place your order at the counter and pay before you sit down.

★ **Cafe del Sol** CHILEAN $$
(www.cafedelsolchile.com; Esmeralda 2013; set lunch CH$3500, mains CH$7000-8000; closed Sun) On Friday and Saturday nights, this ramshackle corner resto-bar comes alive with live Andean music and dancing (CH$3000 cover after 11pm). Other nights, it serves a good range of mains in the cozy wooden interior with dim lighting. Plus it does a good set lunch for CH$3500.

Information

Hospital Regional (055-265-6729; Av Argentina 1962) Medical services.

Sernatur (055-245-1818; Arturo Prat 384; 8:30am-7pm Mon-Fri, 10am-2pm Sat Jan-Mar, 8:30am-5:30pm Mon-Fri Apr-Dec) The city tourist office, conveniently located by the plaza, gives out a generous amount of brochures.

Getting There & Away

AIR

Antofagasta's Aeropuerto Cerro Moreno is located 25km north of town. **LAN** (600-526-2000; www.lanchile.com; Arturo Prat 445; 9am-6:30pm Mon-Fri, 10am-1pm Sat) and **Sky** (600-600-2828; www.skyairline.cl; General Velasquez 890, Local 3) have daily nonstop flights to Santiago (CH$90,000, two hours) and Iquique (CH$19,000, 45 minutes).

BUS

Terminal de Buses Cardenal Carlos Oviedo (055-248-4502; Av Pedro Aguirre Cerda 5750) serves most intercity destinations. Popular companies include **Condor/Flota Barrios** (055-226-2899; www.flotabarrios.cl; Av Pedro Aguirre Cerda 5750) and **Tur Bus** (055-222-0240; www.turbus.cl; Bolívar 468).

DESTINATION	COST (CH$)	DURATION (HR)
Arica	10,900	9
Calama	4000	3
Copiapó	7100	9
Iquique	7000	6
La Serena	11,200	12
Santiago	22,000	18

Calama

☎055 / POP 138,600

Gritty Calama is a powerhouse pumping truckloads of copper money into the Chilean economy each year. Its existence is inextricably tied to the colossal Chuquicamata mine. For travelers, this murky city makes a quick stopover before San Pedro de Atacama. With inflated service prices and *schops con piernas* (like *cafés con piernas* – 'cafes with legs', named for the scantily clad women who serve the coffee – but with beer) it clearly caters to miners.

Sleeping & Eating

Hostal Abaroa HOTEL $

(☎057-294-1025; Abaroa 2128; s/d CH$28,000/36,000, without bathroom CH$15,000/20,000;) The best buy in its category, this friendly new hostel a couple of blocks from the plaza has bright clean rooms along a back patio, and a convenient location for bus departures. Meals are available.

Boccado INTERNATIONAL $

(cnr Ramírez & Abaroa; mains CH$4500-8000; ⌚8am-10pm;) Right on the plaza, this is a great catch-all place, serving good set meals, healthy salads and excellent coffee. There's a fine selection of ice cream to top it all off.

Mercado Central MARKET $

(Latorre; set meals CH$2200-2500) For quick filling eats, take advantage of the *cocinerías* (greasy spoons) in this busy little market between Ramírez and Vargas.

Information

Hospital Carlos Cisternas (☎055-265-5700; Carlos Cisternas s/n) Five blocks north of Plaza 23 de Marzo.

Oficina Municipal de Información Turística (☎055-253-1707; www.calamacultural.cl; Latorre 1689; ⌚8:30am-1pm & 2-6pm Mon-Fri) The tourist office has cordial, helpful staff and can sign you up for a Chuqui tour.

Getting There & Away

AIR

LAN (☎600-526-2000; www.lanchile.com; Latorre 1726; ⌚9am-1pm & 3-6:45pm Mon-Fri, 9:15am-1:15pm Sat.) flies daily to Santiago (CH$90,000) from Aeropuerto El Loa; **Sky** (☎600-600-2828; www.skyairline.cl; Latorre 1499) often has cheaper fares.

BUS

For frequent buses to Antofagasta or overnights to Iquique, Arica or Santiago, try **Condor Bus/Flota Barrios** (☎055-234-5883; www.condorbus.cl; Av Balmaceda 1852) or **Tur Bus** (☎055-268-8812; www.turbus.cl; Ramírez 1852) – note that the Tur Bus terminal is a short taxi ride (CH$3000) outside of the center.

For San Pedro de Atacama (CH$3000, one hour) head to **Buses Frontera** (☎055-282-4269; Antofagasta 2046), **Buses Atacama 2000** (☎055-231-6664; Abaroa 2106) or Tur Bus.

International buses are invariably full, so reserve as far in advance as possible. To get to Uyuni, Bolivia (CH$12,000, nine hours), ask at Frontera and Buses Atacama 2000; buses only go a few times per week. Service to Salta and Jujuy, Argentina is provided by **Pullman Bus** (☎055-234-1282; www.pullmanbus.cl; Balmaceda 4155) and **Géminis** (☎055-289-2050; www.geminis.cl; Antofagasta 2239) several times weekly.

DESTINATION	COST (CH$)	DURATION (HR)
Antofagasta	5600	3
Arica	8900	6
Iquique	17,700	6½
La Serena	22,800	14
Santiago	27,600	22

Chuquicamata

Slag heaps as big as mountains, a chasm deeper than the deepest lake in the USA, and trucks the size of houses: these are some of the mind-boggling dimensions that bring visitors to gawk into the mine of Chuquicamata (or 'Chuqui'). This awesome abyss, gouged from the desert earth 16km north of Calama, is one of the world's largest open-pit copper mines.

First run by the US Anaconda Copper Mining Company, starting in 1915, Chuqui is now operated by state-owned Corporación del Cobre de Chile (Codelco). The mine, which employs 20,000 workers, spews up a perpetual plume of dust visible for many miles in the cloudless desert. The elliptical pit measures an incredible 8 sq km and has a depth of up to 1250m.

Most of the 'tour' offered by **Codelco** (☎055-232-2122; visitas@codelco.cl; cnr Avs Granaderos & Central Sur, Calama; tour by donation; ⌚bookings 9am-5pm Mon-Fri) is spent simply gazing into its depths and clambering around an enormous mining truck with tires more than 3m high. Arrange visits by

Northern Chile (Norte Grande)

0 100 km
0 50 miles

Arequipa (230km)
Toquepala
Calacoto
Cochabamba
Tacna
Charaña
Paso Chungará
La Paz
Obrajes
Totora
Capachos
PERU
Termas Jurasi
Parque Nacional Sajama
Curahuara de Carangas
Oruro
Tacna
Boca del Rio
Putre
Turco
Toledo
Aeropuerto Internacional Chacalluta
Arica
Parque Nacional Lauca
Parinacota
Corque
Llallagua
Poconchile
BOLIVIA
Monumento Natural Salar de Surire
Reserva Nacional Las Vicuñas
Escara
Lago Poopó
Cha'llapata
Cuya
Oruro
Laguna Coipasa
Quillacas
Condo
Región I
Tonavi
Parque Nacional Volcán Isluga
Salar de Coipasa
Sevaruyo
Pisagua
Cariquima
Reserva Nacional Pampa del Tamarugal
Volcán Tunupa (5400m)
Río Mulatos
El Gigante de Atacama
Tarapacá
Mamiña
Tomave
Humberstone
Salar de Uyuni
Iquique
Pozo Almonte
Salar de Empexa
La Tirana
Colchani
Santa Laura
Salar de Pintados
Uyuni
Aeropuerto Diego Aracena
Pica
Reserva Nacional Pampa del Tamarugal
Cerro Pintados
CHILE
San Juan
Pampa del Amarugal
Panamericana
Atocha
Comunidad Amor
Potosí
Río Seco
Salar de Llamara
Avaroa
Ollagüe
Volcán Ollagüe (5865m)
Alota
San Vicente
PACIFIC OCEAN
Río Loa
San Pablo de Lípez
Cordillera de la Costa
Quillagua
Laguna Colorada
Tocopilla
El Tatio Geysers
Quetena Grande
Chuquicamata
Reserva Nacional de Fauna Andina Eduardo Avaroa
Gatico
Calama
Cobija
Pedro de Valdivia
Termas de Puritama
Volcán Licancábur (5960m)
Jujuy
Sierra Gorda
Valle de la Luna
San Pedro de Atacama
Reserva Nacional Los Flamencos
Mejillones
Región II
Salar de Atacama
Toconao
Aeropuerto Cerro Moreno
Baquedano
Laguna Chaxa
Monumento Natural La Portada
Reserva Nacional La Chimba
Tropic of Capricorn
Antofagasta
Socaire
Reserva Nacional Los Flamencos
Salar de Olaroz
Atacama Desert
Volcán Socompa (6051m)
Mano del Desierto
Panamericana
San Antonio de los Cobres
Paso Socompa
Observatorio Cerro Paranal
Salar Punta Negra
Salta
Reserva Nacional Paposo
Salar de Arizaro
La Poma
Volcán Llullaillaco (6720m)
Payogasta
ARGENTINA
Cachi
Taltal
Catamarca
Molinos
Cerro Galán (6600m)
Cifuncho
Angastaco
Antofagasta de la Sierra
Copiapó (240km)

CHUQUI THROUGH THE EYES OF CHE

Chuqui was already a mine of monstrous proportions when visited by a youthful Ernesto 'Che' Guevara more than 50 years ago. The future revolutionary and his traveling buddy Alberto Granado were midway through their iconic trip across South America, immortalized in Che's *Motorcycle Diaries*. An encounter with a communist during his journey to Chuqui is generally acknowledged as a turning point in Che's emergent politics, so it's especially interesting to read his memories of the mine itself (then in gringo hands).

phone or email. Tours in English and Spanish run weekdays. Report to the Oficina on the corner of Avs Granaderos and Central Sur; bring identification, closed footwear and long pants. Donations are voluntary. Demand is high in January and February, so book at least a week ahead.

San Pedro de Atacama

☎055 / POP 3900

Northern Chile's number-one tourist draw, the adobe oasis of San Pedro de Atacama (elevation 2438m) occupies the heart of some of northern Chile's most spectacular scenery. Nearby attractions include the country's largest salt flat, volcanoes like the conical Licancábur (5960m), fields of steaming geysers, and a host of otherworldly rock formations and cool layercake landscapes.

San Pedro itself, 106km southeast of Calama, seems hardly big enough to absorb the hordes of travelers that arrive; it's little more than a handful of picturesque streets clustering around a pretty tree-lined plaza and postcard-perfect church. A proliferation of guesthouses, eateries and tour agencies are wedged alongside its dusty streets, molding it into a kind of adobe Disneyland.

There are all the cons of fast development – steep prices, lackadaisical tour operators – and yet there is incredible quiet, an addictively relaxed atmosphere, psychedelic landscapes, courtyard bonfires under star-scattered heavens and hammock-strewn hostels. If you can manage to set your hours contrary to the rest of the sightseers, this is a magical destination.

Sights

★Museo Gustavo Le Paige MUSEUM
(Le Paige 380; adult/student CH$2500/1000; ⌚9am-6pm Mon-Fri, 10am-6pm Sat & Sun) Even if museums aren't your thing, make an exception for San Pedro's superb Museo Gustavo Le Paige. The Atacama is nirvana for archaeologists because of its nearly rainless environment, which preserves artifacts for millennia. And so this octagonal museum is packed with such fascinating finds as well-preserved ceramics and textiles, and an extraordinary collection of shamanic paraphernalia for preparing, ingesting and smoking hallucinogenic plants.

Iglesia San Pedro CHURCH
(Le Paige s/n) FREE The sugar white Iglesia San Pedro is a delightful little colonial church built with indigenous or artisanal materials – chunky adobe walls and roof, a ceiling made from *cardón* (cactus wood) resembling shriveled tire tracks and, in lieu of nails, hefty leather straps. The church dates from the 17th century, though its present walls were built in 1745, and the bell tower was added in 1890.

Activities

A bewildering array of activities, from relaxing to the extreme, are on offer. Quality varies (some operators cancel abruptly or run unsafe vehicles) so stick to recommended agencies or ask other travelers before booking.

Vulcano Expediciones ADVENTURE SPORTS
(☎cell 5363-6648; www.vulcanochile.com; Caracoles 317) Runs treks to volcanoes and mountains, including day climbs to Sairecabur (5971m; CH$110,000), Lascar (5592m; CH$100,000) and Tocco (5604m; CH$70,000). Longer climbs take in Licancábur and Llullaillaco. It also runs downhill bike rides (CH$20,000 to CH$35,000) and can hook you up with motorbike tours offered by **On Safari** (www.onsafariatacama.com).

Rancho La Herradura HORSE RIDING
(☎055-285-1956; www.atacamahorseadventure.com; Tocopilla 406) Sightseeing from the saddle is available from several places, including Rancho La Herradura. Tours vary from two hours for CH$15,000 to epic 10-day treks with camping. English-, German- and French-speaking guides are available.

Atacama Inca Tour ADVENTURE SPORTS
(☎055-285-1062; www.sandboardsanpedro.com; Toconao 421-A) While several agencies offer

sand-boarding, many actually sell tours by Atacama Inca Tour, our top pick for its pro boards and experienced instructors. Standard trips, for CH$10,000, depart either at 9am, returning at noon, or 3pm, returning at 7pm. They involve a 20-minute class, plus you get a DVD with a video clip of your escapade.

Tours

Dozens of agencies operate conventional tours. The most reputable include **Cosmo-Andino Expediciones** (055-285-1069; www.cosmoandino.cl; Caracoles 259), known for higher-end tours; **Desert Adventure** (055-285-1067; www.desertadventure.cl; cnr Caracoles & Tocopilla; 9am-1pm & 3-7pm Mon-Sat, 9am-1pm Sun), with bilingual guides; and **Terra Extreme** (055-285-1274; www.terraextreme.cl; Toconao s/n; 9am-1pm & 3-6pm), offering standard tours operated with their own vehicles.

El Tatio Geysers GUIDED TOUR
(tour CH$18,000-20,000, entrance fee CH$5000) This hugely popular tour leaves San Pedro at 4am in order to see the surreal sight of the geysers at sunrise, returning between noon and 1pm. Most tours include thermal baths and breakfast.

Valle de la Luna GUIDED TOUR
(tour CH$8000-10,000, entrance fee CH$2000) Leaves San Pedro mid-afternoon to catch the sunset over the valley, returning early evening. Includes visits to Valle de la Luna, Valle de la Muerte and Tres Marías.

Tulor & Pukará de Quitor GUIDED TOUR
(tour around CH$15,000, entrance fee CH$10,000) Half-day archaeological tours take in this pair of pre-Columbian ruins (departures between 8am and 9am, returning between 1pm and 3pm).

Altiplano Lakes GUIDED TOUR
(tour CH$15,000-30,000, entrance fee CH$5000) Leaves San Pedro between 7am and 8am to see flamingos at Laguna Chaxa in the Salar de Atacama, then moves on to the town of Socaire, Lagunas Miñiques and Miscanti, Toconao and the Quebrada de Jere, returning between 4pm and 7pm.

Sleeping

Water is scarce (and not potable) in San Pedro, so buy your own drinking water and limit your shower time. Note that prices are high here, even outside high season.

Hostal Sonchek HOSTEL $
(055-285-1112; www.hostalsonchek.cl; cnr Paige & Calama; dm CH$8500, d CH$36,000, s/d without bathroom CH$12,000/20,000;) Thatched roofs and adobe walls characterize the carpeted rooms at this lovely hostel. It's centered on a small courtyard, and there's a shared kitchen, luggage storage and a small garden out back with table tennis and a few hammocks. The common bathrooms with solar-heated showers are some of the cleanest in town. English and French spoken.

WORTH A TRIP

4WD TO UYUNI, BOLIVIA

Colorful *altiplano* lakes, weird rock playgrounds worthy of Salvador Dalí, flamingos, volcanoes and, most famously of all, the blindingly white salt flat of Uyuni: these are the rewards of an adventurous excursion into Bolivia, northeast of San Pedro de Atacama. However, be warned that this is no cozy ride through the countryside, and for every five travelers that gush about Uyuni being the highlight of their trip, there is another declaring it a waking nightmare.

The standard trips take three days, crossing the Bolivian border at Hito Cajón, passing Laguna Colorada and continuing to the Salar de Uyuni before ending in the town of Uyuni. The going rate of CH$98,000 includes transportation in crowded 4WD jeeps, basic and often teeth-chatteringly cold accommodations, plus food; approximately CH$23,000 extra will get you back to San Pedro on the fourth day (some tour operators drive through the third night).

Bring drinks and snacks, warm clothes and a sleeping bag. Travelers clear Chilean immigration at San Pedro and Bolivian immigration on arrival at Uyuni. Note that entrance fees to Bolivian parks are usually not included in trip package prices for most operators. These amount to approximately CH$17,000. None of the agencies offering this trip get consistently glowing reports. **Cordillera Traveler** (055-285-1291; www.cordilleratraveller.com; Toconao 447-B & Tocopilla 429-B) gets the best feedback from travelers.

San Pedro de Atacama

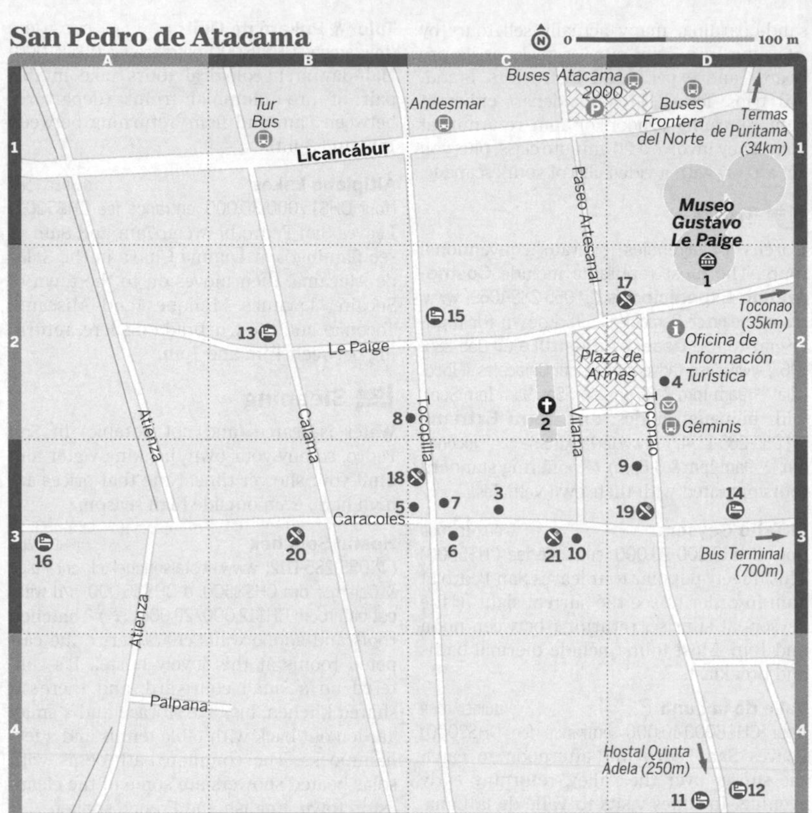

Hostal Edén Atacameño HOSTEL $

(055-285-1154; hostaleden@gmail.com; Toconao 592; s/d CH$25,000/40,000, without bathroom CH$12,000/20,000;) This is a laid-back hostel with rooms around a couple of sociable, hammock-strung patios with plentiful seating. Guests can use the kitchen, and there's laundry service and luggage storage. The shared bathrooms are clean; breakfast is included for rooms with private bathrooms.

Residencial Vilacoyo GUESTHOUSE $

(055-285-1006; vilacoyo@sanpedroatacama.com; Tocopilla 387; r per person CH$10,000) A no-frills but friendly *residencial* with a snug gravel patio hung with hammocks, a kitchen and luggage storage. The shared showers only have hot water between 7am and 10pm.

Hostelling International HOSTEL $

(055-256-4683; hostelsanpedro@hotmail.com; Caracoles 360; dm/s/d CH$7000/33,000/36,000, s/d without bathroom CH$20,000/23,000;) This convivial spot offers dorms – with some bunks nearly 3m up – and a few doubles around a small patio. Services include a shared kitchen, lockers and tour bookings. HI members get a CH$2000 discount.

★ **Hostal Quinta Adela** B&B $$

(055-285-1272; www.quintaadela.wix.com/quinta-adela; Toconao 624; r from CH$70,000;) This friendly family-run place, just a quick walk from town, has seven character-filled rooms (each with its own individual style) and a shady terrace and is situated alongside a sprawling orchard with hammocks. There's luggage storage and they're flexible with check-in and checkout.

Hostal La Ruca HOSTEL $$

(055-285-1568; www.larucahostal.cl; Toconao 513; s/d CH$37,000/50,000;) A nice touch of rustic style – think colorful Andean bedspreads and tapestries – graces the rooms

San Pedro de Atacama

Top Sights
1 Museo Gustavo Le Paige D2

Sights
2 Iglesia San Pedro C2

Activities, Courses & Tours
3 Ahlarkapin C3
4 Atacama Inca Tour D2
5 Cordillera Traveler C3
6 CosmoAndino Expediciones C3
7 Desert Adventure C3
8 Rancho La Herradura C2
9 Terra Extreme D3
10 Vulcano Expediciones C3

Sleeping
11 Hostal Edén Atacameño D4
12 Hostal La Ruca D4
13 Hostal Sonchek B2
14 Hostelling International D3
15 Residencial Vilacoyo C2
16 Takha Takha Hotel & Camping A3

Eating
17 Cafe Peregrino D2
18 El Churruá C3
19 El Toconar D3
20 La Casona B3
21 Salon de Te O2 .... C3

of this sweet hostel with tiny but clean bathrooms, a sunny patio with hammocks and a shared kitchen, all presided over by friendly staff who speak English and some German.

Takha Takha Hotel & Camping HOTEL, CAMPGROUND $$
(☎055-285-1038; www.takhatakha.cl; Caracoles 101-A; campsite per person CH$10,000, s/d CH$38,400/50,000, without bathroom CH$14,400/30,000;) A popular catch-all outfit with decent campsites, plain budget rooms and spotless midrange accommodations set around a sprawling flowery garden with a swimming pool.

Eating & Drinking

Establishments only selling alcohol are outlawed, so nightlife centers around restaurants' open-air bonfires, open until 1am.

Salon de Te O2 CAFE $
(Caracoles 295; breakfast from CH$2500, mains around CH$5000; 7am-9pm;) The early-morning breakfasts (from 7am), great quiches, juicy meat sandwiches and lovely tarts are the highlights of this colorful cafe run by a French-Chilean couple. You can while away the afternoon on the shady back patio.

Cafe Peregrino CAFETERIA $
(Gustavo Le Paige 348; breakfast from CH$3000, sandwiches around CH$4000; 9am-8pm;) The loveliest cafe in town, overlooking the plaza with a few benches strategically placed for people-watching. Inside are only four tables. Foodwise, you'll find pizzas, salads, sandwiches and nice cakes and pastries. And, yes, real espressos and cappuccinos!

El Toconar INTERNATIONAL $
(cnr Toconao & Caracoles; mains CH$4000-9000; noon-1am) The best garden setup in town (complete with bonfires for those chilly desert nights) is at this place. Also on offer is a wide menu, a superb selection of cocktails (including pisco sours infused with desert herbs), cheap beers and a happy hour.

El Churruá PIZZERIA $
(Tocopillo 442; mains CH$5000-8000; 12:30-11pm) The best thin-crust pizzas in town are at this unassuming little place just off the main drag. There's only a few tables, but it's worth the wait. There's no alcohol on the menu, but staff are happy to run to the store for you.

★**La Casona** CHILEAN $$
(www.lacasonadeatacama.cl; Caracoles 195; set lunch CH$6000-7000, mains CH$8000-10,000; noon-1am;) A high-ceilinged dining room with dark wood paneling and an adobe fireplace in the middle, the classic La Casona

ATACAMA DESERT ADVENTURES

A few off-the-beaten-track tours around Atacama are becoming increasingly popular, such as jaunts to **Laguna Cejar** and **Ojos de Salar** (you can swim in both, and in Cejar you can float just like in the Dead Sea), **Valle del Arcoiris**, with its rainbowlike multicolored rock formations, and **Salar de Tara**. The last is one of the most spectacular, if back-breaking. Trips from San Pedro, involving a round-trip journey of 200km, reach an altitude of 4300m.

serves up sizzling *parrilladas* and Chilean staples such as *pastel de choclo* (maize casserole). There's a long list of Chilean wines and a small patio for alfresco lunches.

Information

It's wise to bring plenty of pesos to San Pedro de Atacama, as the three ATMs here (two on Caracoles and another opposite the museum) often run out of money. Currency exchanges offering poor rates dot Caracoles. There's free wi-fi on the main plaza.

Oficina de Información Turística (☎055-285-1420; cnr Toconao & Le Paige; ⏲9am-9pm) Helpful tourist office offering advice and doling out town maps and brochures. Check out the annual book of comments for up-to-date traveler feedback on tour agencies, hostels, restaurants, transportation providers and more.

Post office (Tocanao s/n) The location changes almost yearly, so ask locals if you can't find it here.

Posta Médica (☎055-285-1010; Toconao s/n) The local clinic, on the plaza.

Getting There & Away

Buses Atacama 2000 (Licancábur s/n; ⏲8am-7pm) has regular departures to Calama (CH$2800), where you can connect to its Uyuni bus. **Buses Frontera del Norte** (Licancábur s/n) goes to Calama as well as Arica (CH$16,100) and Iquique (CH$15,000). **Tur Bus** (☎055-851-549; Licancábur 294) has hourly buses to Calama (CH$3000), from where you can connect to all major destinations in Chile. **Andesmar** (☎055-259-2692; www.andesmar.com; Licancábur s/n) serves Salta and Jujuy, Argentina, several times a week (from CH$30,000, 16 hours with border time). **Géminis** (☎055-892-049; Toconao 428) also goes to Salta.

Several agencies in town offer transfer services to Calama airport; expect to pay around CH$16,500 per person.

Buses stop right near the plaza and the whole town can be explored on foot.

Around San Pedro de Atacama

There's always more to see around San Pedro de Atacama. It's worthwhile visiting some tour agencies and asking other travelers about their experiences. The most popular attractions are listed here.

The crumbly 12th-century ruins of fortress **Pukará de Quitor** (admission CH$3000; ⏲9am-7:30pm Jun-Aug, to 6pm Sep-May), 3km northwest of town and accessible by rental bike, afford great views of town and the oasis expanse. Another 3km on the right, **Quebrada del Diablo** (Devil's Gorge) offers a serpentine single track that mountain bikers dream of.

Ninety-five kilometres north of town and 4300m above sea level, the famous **El Tatio** (admission CH$5000) is the world's highest geyser field. Visiting the geysers at dawn is like walking through a gigantic steam bath, ringed by volcanoes and fed by 64 gurgling geysers and a hundred gassy fumaroles striking against the azure clarity of the

DESERT STARGAZING

The flats of Chajnantor plateau, 5000m high and 40km east of San Pedro de Atacama, host the most ambitious radio telescope that the world has ever seen. The **Atacama Large Millimeter/submillimeter Array** (ALMA; meaning 'soul' in Spanish) consists of 66 enormous antennae, most with a diameter of around 12m. This field of interstellar 'ears' simulates a telescope an astonishing 16km in diameter, making it possible to pick up objects in space as much as 100 times fainter than those previously detected. Contact the **ALMA Visitor Center** (☎in Santiago 02-467-6416; www.almaobservatory.org; Hwy 23, Km 121; free with online registration) to visit. It's free but guest numbers are limited; register online.

ALMA is just the latest of northern Chile's cutting-edge astronomical facilities. Climatic conditions in the Atacama Desert make it an ideal location for stargazing. This is not only thanks to cloudless desert nights, but also the predictable winds that blow steadily in from the Pacific Ocean, causing minimal turbulence – a crucial requirement for observatories to achieve optimal image quality.

Ahlarkapin (☎099-579-7816; www.ahlarkapin.cl; Caracoles 151) offers personalized observation tours (12 people maximum) with a focus on Andean cosmology. The two-hour tours (in Spanish and English) run nightly at 9:30pm in summer (earlier in winter) and cost CH$15,000/10,000 per adult/child.

altiplano. Swirling columns of steam envelop onlookers in a Dantesque vision, and the soundtrack of bubbling, spurting and hissing sounds like a field of merrily boiling kettles. As dawn wears on, shafts of sunlight crown the surrounding volcanoes and illuminate the writhing steam. Dress in layers: it's toe-numbingly cold at dawn.

Watching the sun set from the exquisite **Valle de la Luna** (admission adult/child CH$3000/2000; ⏲daylight hours) is an unforgettable experience. As you sit atop a giant sand dune, panting from exertion, a beautiful transformation occurs: the distant ring of volcanoes, rippling Cordillera de la Sal and surreal lunar landscapes of the valley are suddenly suffused with intense purples, pinks and golds. The **Valley of the Moon** is named after its lunarlike landforms, eroded by eons of flood and wind. It's 15km west of San Pedro at the northern end of the Cordillera de la Sal.

The jagged crust of the **Salar de Atacama** looks for all the world like god went crazy with a stippling brush. But in the midst of these rough lifeless crystals is an oasis of activity: the pungent **Laguna Chaxa** (admission CH$5000), 67km south of town and home to three species of flamingo (James, Chilean and Andean), as well as plovers, coots and ducks.

The volcanic hot springs of **Termas de Puritama** (admission adult/child CH$15,000/7000; ⏲9:15am-5:30pm), 30km north of town, are accessible by taxi or tour. The temperature of the springs is about 33°C, and there are several falls and pools.

Iquique

☎057 / POP 180,600

Jutting into the sea and backed by the tawny coastal range, Iquique sits like a stage. And, in fact, the city is no stranger to drama. It first lived off guano reserves, grew lavish with 19th-century nitrate riches, since lost momentum, and now stakes its future on commerce and tourism, manifested in the duty-free megazone, the sparkly glitz of the casino and ubiquitous beach resort development. The real gems of this coastal city are the remainders of lovely Georgian-style architecture, Baquedano's fanciful wooden sidewalks, thermal winds and a ripping good surf.

Sights & Activities

Iquique's most popular beach, **Playa Cavancha** is worth visiting for swimming and body-boarding. Further south, rip currents and crashing waves make the scenic **Playa Brava** better for sunbathing; take a *colectivo* from downtown or walk.

Surfing and body-boarding are best in winter, when swells come from the north, but are possible year-round. There's less competition for early-morning breaks at the north end of Playa Cavancha.

Playa Huaiquique, on the southern outskirts of town, is also an exhilarating choice, but the sea is warmer further north near Arica.

Museo Corbeta Esmeralda MUSEUM
(www.museoesmeralda.cl; Paseo Almirante Lynch; admission CH$3000; ⏲10am-1pm & 2-6pm Tue-Sun) This replica of sunken *Esmeralda*, a plucky little Chilean corvette that challenged ironclad Peruvian warships in the War of the Pacific, is Iquique's new pride and glory. The original ship was captained by Arturo Prat (1848–79), whose name now graces a hundred street maps, plazas and institutions. Guided tours (reserve ahead for a tour in English) take you inside the staff quarters, past the orange-lit engine and onto the ship's deck.

Plaza Prat PLAZA
The city's 19th-century swagger is hard to miss on Iquique's central square. Pride of place goes to the **Torre Reloj** (1877) clock tower, seemingly baked and sugar-frosted rather than built. Jumping fountains line the walkway south to the marble-stepped **Teatro Municipal**, a neoclassical building that has been hosting opera and theater since 1890. A handsomely restored **tram** sits outside and occasionally jerks its way down Av Baquedano in the high season.

Centro Cultural Palacio Astoreca HISTORIC BUILDING
(O'Higgins 350; ⏲10am-6pm Tue-Sat, 11am-2pm Sun) FREE Originally built for a nitrate tycoon, this 1904 Georgian-style mansion is now a cultural center, which exhibits contemporary work produced by local artists. It has a fantastic interior of opulent rooms with elaborate woodwork and high ceilings, massive chandeliers, a gigantic billiard table and balconies.

Iquique

Iquique

Sights

1 Centro Cultural Palacio Astoreca B3
2 Museo Corbeta Esmeralda B1
3 Plaza Prat B2
4 Torre Reloj B2

Activities, Courses & Tours

5 Magical Tour Chile B3
6 OC Travel B2
7 Vertical B5

Sleeping

8 Casa Baquedano B4
9 Hotel de La Plaza B3
10 Hotel Velero C2
11 La Casona 1920 .... C5

Eating

12 Cioccolata B2
13 Club Croata B2
14 El Tercer Ojito B4
15 El Wagón A2
16 M.Koo C3

Drinking & Nightlife

17 Lobby Resto Bar B2
18 Mi Otra Casa B4

Altazor ADVENTURE SPORTS
(☎057-238-0110; www.altazor.cl; Vía 6, Manzana A, Sitio 3, Flight Park, Bajo Molle) Located 500m south of Universidad del Mar (south of Iquique's center), Altazor offers paragliding courses (CH$42,500 per day, including equipment and transportation). An introductory tandem flight costs CH$40,000; two-week courses are also available, as is accommodations at its cozy hostel. Experienced paragliders can rent equipment or have their own repaired. Owners Philip and Marlene speak German, English, Portuguese and French.

Vertical SURFING
(☎057-237-6031; www.verticalst.cl; Av Arturo Prat 580) This is Iquique's surfer central, which sells and rents equipment. Wetsuit and board will set you back CH$12,000 for two hours; one or the other only costs CH$7500. Private lessons start at CH$24,000 for 1½ hours, and it runs surf trips outside the city and **sand-boarding** trips to Cerro Dragón, which cost CH$25,000 for three hours.

Tours

Public transportation to many surrounding attractions is tricky, so tours are worth considering. In summer, agencies set up streetside tables on Prat and along Baquedano. Popular options include a day trip to the oasis towns of **Pica**, **La Tirana** and **Matilla**, taking in the nitrate ruins at **Humberstone** and **Santa Laura** en route (CH$25,000). Another fun excursion takes you for a dip in the thermal waters of **Mamiña** (CH$27,000).

OC Travel GUIDED TOUR
(☎057-257-3260; www.octravel.cl; Luis Uribe 445, Oficina 2H) Offers most of the major tours, including the popular day trip to Pica, which takes in Humberstone and Santa Laura. Also offers diving excursions (CH$38,000) at Playa Blanca and biking jaunts that take in the city and the beaches ($38,000 for six hours).

Magical Tour Chile GUIDED TOUR
(☎057-221-7290; www.magicaltour.cl; Baquedano 1035; per person Ruta del Sol CH$25,000, Aventura Isluga CH$50,000; ⏲10:30am to 8pm Mon-Sat) Sometimes runs creepy nocturnal tours of the *salitreras* (nitrate mines), departing at 8pm and getting you back into town at around 2:30am. There's a 10-person minimum.

Llamatrekking CULTURAL TOUR
(☎cell 7898-6504; www.llamatrekking.cl) Soft treks to surrounding attractions focused on Aymara traditions of the *altiplano*, ranging from day trips to nearby villages to seven-day llama caravans.

Sleeping

Taxi drivers earn commission from some hotels; be firm or consider walking. Wild camping is free on the beaches north of Iquique near Pisagua and Cuya.

La Casona 1920 HOSTEL $
(☎057-241-3000; www.casonahostel.com; Barros Arana 1585; dm CH$9000, s/d without bathroom CH$14,000/22,000; @📶) Iquique's place to be, this cool and colorful hostel inside an old *casona* has four- to nine-bed dorms and a few doubles, some with balconies over the street, others overlooking the back patio. There's a shared kitchen, a pool table, lockers, multilingual staff, weekly sushi parties with live DJs, poker nights, salsa classes and movie nights.

Hotel Velero HOTEL $
(☎057-234-8067; www.hotelvelero.cl; Latorre 596; s/d CH$20,000/30,000, without bathroom CH$14,000/22,000) A very good looking hotel a short walk from the plaza. It doesn't quite live up to its 'boutique' claim, but rooms are spacious with modern fittings and there's a tranquil atmosphere throughout. Book ahead.

Hotel de La Plaza HOTEL $
(☎057-241-9339; Baquedano 1025; s/d CH$20,000/33,000; 📶) One of the best deals in its category, this Georgian style building fronts onto the pedestrian strip. There is a welcoming lobby with a big skylight and comfortable, medium-sized rooms arranged around a patio.

★**Casa Baquedano** HOTEL $$
(☎057-234-7577; Baquedano 1470; s/d CH$35,000/40,000; 📶) Right at the foot of the pedestrian mall, this older building has fantastically spacious rooms featuring king-sized beds, minifridges and modern bathrooms. Those on the ground floor also feature way-high ceilings. A leafy rear patio rounds out the picture.

Eating

Club Croata CHILEAN $
(Plaza Prat 310; set lunch CH$4500; ⏲10am-6pm Mon-Sat; 📶) Plaza-side restaurant with arched windows, Croatian coats of arms and a clutch of tables outside. It has the best fixed-price lunch on the square – you get three courses plus a drink.

Cioccolata CAFE $

(Pinto 487; snacks CH$2000-4500; ⏲8am-10pm Mon-Sat; 📶) Proof positive that Chileans do enjoy a decent espresso, this classy coffee shop is usually crammed with people. It offers filling breakfasts and lunches, plus sandwiches, scrumptious cakes and waffles.

M.Koo SWEETS $

(Latorre 600; snacks from CH$700; ⏲8am-8pm Mon-Sat) Colorful corner shop famous for its crumbly *chumbeques* (sweet regional biscuits), the recipe for which is guarded zealously. It also sells snacks such as *humitas* (corn tamales) and empanadas.

★**El Wagón** CHILEAN $$

(Thompson 85; mains CH$8500-10,000; ⏲noon-3pm & 7pm-midnight Mon-Sat) Almost single-handedly taking on the task of preserving the region's culinary traditions, this rustically decked-out dining hall serves up a fantastic collection of seafood plates, with inspiration for recipes coming from everywhere from grandma's classics to port workers' and miners' staples. Pricey, but worth it.

El Tercer Ojito INTERNATIONAL $$

(www.eltercerojito.cl; Lynch 1420; set weekday lunch CH$4500, mains CH$7500-9000; ⏲noon-3pm Tue-Sun, 7-11:30pm Tue-Sat; 📶🌿) Recognizable by the huge lump of quartz outside, this laid-back restaurant serves great vegetarian and carnivore-friendly dishes. Its globally inspired repertoire includes Peruvian dishes, Thai curries and occasional sushi. A pleasant bamboo-covered patio sports cacti and murals.

Drinking & Nightlife

Iquique has a fun-filled nightlife, with a few laid-back resto-bars in the center and clubs and pubs lining the seafront south of town.

Lobby Resto Bar BAR

(Gorostiaga 142; ⏲from 8pm Tue-Sat) Sweet resto-bar with a boho vibe, Lobby has four small rooms and a loungey back patio. Come for great cocktails (try the *raspirinha*, with raspberry vodka and berries), the sushi bar, DJ-spun tunes on weekends, great-for-sharing *tablas* and happy hour nightly.

Mi Otra Casa BAR

(Baquedano 1334; ⏲3pm-2am Tue-Sat) Laid-back artsy bar at the far end of Baquedano, with an interior full of mismatched objects and a range of different events, from poetry readings to live music.

Information

There are many ATMs downtown; several *cambios* exchange foreign currency and traveler's checks.

Hospital Regional Dr Juan Noé (☎057-239-5555; Av Héroes de la Concepción 502) Ten blocks east of Plaza Condell.

Post office (Bolívar 458)

Sernatur (☎057-241-9241; www.sernatur.cl; Pinto 436; ⏲9am-8pm Mon-Sat, 10am-2pm Sun in summer, 9am-6pm Mon-Fri rest of year) This office has tourist information, free city maps and brochures.

Getting There & Away

AIR

The local airport, **Aeropuerto Diego Aracena** (☎057-242-6530; www.aeropuertodiego aracena.cl), is 41km south of downtown via Ruta 1.

LAN (☎600-526-2000; www.lan.cl; Pinto 699; ⏲8:45am-2pm & 4-6;30pm Mon-Fri, 9:30am-1pm Sat) has daily flights to Arica (CH$35,700, 50 minutes), Antofagasta (CH$19,500, 50 minutes) and Santiago (CH$120,500 to CH$200,000, 2½ hours). **Sky** (☎600-600-2828; www.skyairline.cl; Tarapacá 530), with slightly cheaper fares, also serves Arica, Antofagasta and Santiago as well as further south in Chile.

BUS

Most buses leave from the **Terminal Rodoviario** (☎057-242-7100; Lynch); most companies also have ticket offices clustered around Mercado Centenario. Several bus companies, including **Expreso Norte** (☎057-257-3693; www.expreso-norte.cl; Barros Arana 881), **Pullman** (☎057-242-9852; www.pullman.cl), **Ramos Cholele** (☎057-247-1628; www.ramoscholele.cl; Barros Arana 851) and **Tur Bus** (☎057-242-0634; www.turbus.cl; Mercado Centenario), visit northern Chile and Santiago.

To get to La Paz, Bolivia (CH$7000, 12 hours), try **Lujan** (☎057-326-955; Esmeralda 999), with departures twice daily on weekdays. For Peru, connect with international departures via Arica (CH$7000).

DESTINATION	COST (CH$)	DURATION (HR)
Antofagasta	16,000	6
Arica	7000	4
Calama	10,000	6
Copiapó	30,000	14
La Serena	35,000	18
Santiago	45,000	24

East of Iquique

Ghost towns punctuate the desert as you travel inland from Iquique; they're eerie remnants of once-flourishing mining colonies that gathered the Atacama's white gold – nitrate. Along the way, pre-Hispanic geoglyphs recall the presence of humans centuries before. Further inland the barren landscape yields up several picturesque hot-spring villages.

If you only see one attraction outside Iquique, make it **Humberstone** (www.museodelsalitre.cl; adult/child CH$2000/500; ⏲9am-7pm), 45km northeast of the city. With the spark of the nitrate boom long gone, the ghost town remains a creepy shell. Built in 1872, the town's opulence reached its height in the 1940s: the theater drew Santiago-based performers, workers lounged about the massive cast-iron pool molded from a scavenged shipwreck, and amenities still foreign to most small towns abounded. The development of synthetic nitrates forced the closure of the *oficina* by 1960. Today some buildings are restored, but others are unstable; explore them carefully. A Unesco World Heritage Site, it makes their list of endangered sites for the fragility of the existing constructions. The skeletal remains of **Oficina Santa Laura** are a half-hour walk southwest. To get to Humberstone, catch a *colectivo* for Pozo Almonte from the eastern side of Iquique's Mercado Centenario. To return, stand at the bus stop outside the entrance of Humberstone and flag down any bus marked 'Iquique' (CH$2000).

The whopping pre-Columbian geoglyph **El Gigante de Atacama** (Giant of the Atacama), 14km east of Huara on the slopes of Cerro Unita is, at 86m, the world's largest archaeological representation of a human figure. Representing a powerful shaman, its blocky head emanates rays and its thin limbs clutch an arrow and medicine bag. Experts date it to around AD 900. The best views are from several hundred meters back at the base of the hill. To visit, go in a taxi or on a tour.

Amid Atacama's desolate pampas you'll find straggly groves of resilient tamarugo *(Prosopis tamarugo)* lining the Panamericana south of Pozo Almonte. The forest once covered thousands of square kilometers until clear-cutting for the mines nearly destroyed it. The trees are protected within the **Reserva Nacional Pampa del Tamarugal**, which also features 420 restored geoglyphs of humans, llamas and geometric shapes blanketing the hillside at **Pintados** (adult/child CH$2000/free; ⏲10am-4pm). A derelict nitrate rail yard of ruined buildings and rusting rolling stock, the site lies 4.5km west of the Panamericana via a gravel road, nearly opposite the eastward turnoff to Pica.

The oasis of **Pica** is a chartreuse patch on a dusty canvas, 113km southeast of Iquique. Its fame hails from its pica limes, the key ingredient of the tart and tasty *pisco sour*. Day-trippers can enjoy splashing around the freshwater pool, **Cocha Resbaladero** (admission CH$2000; ⏲9am-8pm), fresh fruit drink in hand.

Mamiña, 125km east of Iquique (not on the same road to Pica) is a quizzical terraced town with thermal baths, a 17th-century church and a pre-Columbian fortress, **Pukará del Cerro Inca**. The village huddles into upper and lower sectors, the former clustered around the rocky outcrop where the 1632 **Iglesia de San Marcos** stands, while the latter lies low in the valley, near the hot springs.

Arica

☎058 / POP 210,200

Arica is warm and sunny year-round, with a delightful easy pace. Come sunset, there's a cool pedestrian mall to flip-flop around and decent brown-sugar beaches are just a short walk from the center. Top this off with some kick-ass surf breaks and a cool cliff-top War of the Pacific battlefield at El Morro, and you may just stay another day before heading to glorious Parque Nacional Lauca.

Sights & Activities

A pedestrian mall is on 21 de Mayo.

★Museo de Sitio Colón 10 MUSEUM

(Colón 10; adult/child CH$2000/1000; ⏲10am-7pm Tue-Sun Jan-Feb, to 6pm Tue-Sun Mar-Dec) See the 32 excavated Chinchorro mummies in situ at this tiny museum below El Morro. They were discovered when an architect bought this former private home with the intention of converting it into a hotel. You can gape at the glass-protected bodies as they were found, in the sand below the floors, in different positions, complete with their funerary bundles, skins and feathers of marine fowl.

El Morro de Arica LOOKOUT
This imposing coffee-colored shoulder of rock looms 110m over the city. It makes a great place to get your bearings, with vulture-eye views of the city, port and Pacific Ocean. This lofty headland was the site of a crucial battle in 1880, a year into the War of the Pacific, when the Chilean army assaulted and took El Morro from Peruvian forces in under an hour.

Catedral de San Marcos CHURCH
(San Marcos 260, Plaza Colón; ⌚8:30am-9pm Mon-Fri, 11am-1pm Sat, 9am-1pm & 7:30-9pm Sun) This Gothic-style church has a threefold claim to fame. First, it was designed by celebrated Parisian engineer Alexandre Gustave Eiffel, before his success with the Eiffel Tower. Second, it was prefabricated in Eiffel's Paris shop in the 1870s (at the order of the Peruvian president) then shipped right around the world to be assembled on site. Still more curious is the construction itself: the entire church is made of stamped and molded cast iron, coated with paint.

Beaches
Along Av Comandante San Martín, the best beaches south of downtown for swimming and lounging around are **Playa El Laucho**, just past the Club de Yates, followed by the comely, sheltered **Playa La Lisera**, with changing rooms and showers.

The beaches north of downtown are rougher but cleaner than those in the south. **Playa Chinchorro**, 2km away, features pricey eateries and jet-ski rentals. **Playa Las Machas**, a few kilometers north, is a surfers' haunt. Take bus 12 or 14 from 18 de Septiembre; get off on the corner of Av Antarctica and Av España.

Tours

Raíces Andinas GUIDED TOUR
(☎058-223-3305; www.ecotourexpediciones.cl; Héroes del Morro 632; ⌚9am-noon & 3-6pm Mon-Sat) A well-run outfit recommended for encouraging better understanding of the local people. It specializes in trips of two or more days, and offers expeditions to Sajama in Bolivia via Lauca as well as adventures into Salar de Uyuni. It has a few bikes for rent (CH$8000 per day).

Chinchorro Expediciones BOAT TOUR
(☎058-223-3404; chinchorroexpediciones@gmail.com; Muelle Pesquero; ⌚8am-4pm) This specialist in marine expeditions offers three-hour sea safaris (with a picnic, swimming and kayaking) from the fishing jetty plus a two-day camping trip to Caleta de Camarones by 4WD, with hikes to virgin beaches, forgotten fishing hamlets and hidden archaeological sites.

Sleeping

Arica Surfhouse HOSTEL $
(☎058-231-2213; www.aricasurfhouse.cl; O'Higgins 661; dm CH$12,000, s/d CH$25,000/36,000, without bathroom CH$20,000/30,000; @ 📶) Doubling as Arica's surfer central, this is one of Arica's top hostels, with a variety of clean rooms, a great open-air communal area, 24-hour hot water and laundry service. There's a shuttle service to the beaches in winter months and they'll hook you up with surf classes and equipment rental.

Hostal Jardín del Sol HOTEL $
(☎058-223-2795; www.hostaljardindelsol.cl; Sotomayor 848; s/d CH$15,000/$29,000; @ 📶) It's been here for ages but still lives up to its reputation as one of Arica's best budget hotels, with small but spotless rooms, fans included. Guests mingle on the leafy patio, the upstairs terrace, in the shared kitchen and the lounge room. There's a book exchange and lots of tourist info.

El Buey Hostal HOSTEL $$
(☎058-232-5530; www.elbueyhostal.com; Punta del Este 605, La Lisera; dm/s/d CH$14,000/20,000/45,000; @ 📶) The coolest beachside option, this whitewashed Med-style house sits on the residential hillside above La Lisera beach. It's for surfers with style, with hardwood floors, gorgeous terraces, sparkling kitchens, ocean views, and a communal rooftop terrace with hammocks. You can rent a whole floor (sleeps eight) for CH$131,000.

Eating & Drinking

Look for traditional seafood lunches on **Muelle Pesquero**, the fishing jetty. Tap water here is laden with chemicals; buy your own bottles. Many of the hippest bars and discos are strung along Playa Chinchorro.

Mata-Rangi SEAFOOD $
(Muelle Pesquero; set menu CH$4000-5000, mains CH$5000-6500; ⌚noon-4pm Mon-Sat) Superb seafood is served at this adorable spot hanging over the harbor by the fishing jetty. A wooden shack-style place packed with wind

chimes, it has a breezy dining room and a small terrace above the ocean. Get here early to grab a seat or be prepared to wait.

Cafe del Mar CAFETERIA **$**
(21 de Mayo 260; mains CH$3000-5000; ⊙9am-10pm Mon-Sat;) A good range of burgers, sandwiches and salads paired with some of the best coffee in town. Pop next door for some of Arica's finest ice cream.

★**Los Aleros de 21** CHILEAN **$$**
(21 de Mayo 736; mains CH$7000-12,000; ⊙noon-3:30pm & 7-11:30pm Mon-Sat;) One of Arica's more highly esteemed restaurants, serving up a good selection of meats and seafood dishes, with a few pasta and chicken dishes rounding out the picture. Good wine list, too.

Así Sea Club BAR
(San Marcos 251; ⊙from 9pm Wed-Sat) This swank hideaway inside a rambling historic town house has a set of sleek rooms featuring original detail, and a back patio. It serves a menu of *tablas* (CH$4200 to CH$9000), cocktails and all-Chilean wines, paired with loungey tunes.

Information

There are numerous 24-hour ATMs and *cambios* along the pedestrian mall (21 de Mayo).

While Arica is a very safe city, it has a reputation for pickpockets. Be especially cautious at bus terminals and beaches.

Hospital Dr Juan Noé (☎058-223-2242; 18 de Sepiembre 1000) A short distance east of downtown.

Post office (Prat 305) On a walkway between Pedro Montt and Prat.

Sernatur (☎058-225-2054; infoarica@sernatur.cl; San Marcos 101; ⊙9am-8pm Mon-Fri, 10am-2pm Sat Jan-Feb, 9am-6pm Mar-Dec) Friendly service with some brochures on Tarapacá and other Chilean regions.

Getting There & Away

AIR

Chacalluta Airport is 18km to the north. **LAN** (☎600-526-2000; www.lan.com; Arturo Prat 391) has several daily flights to Santiago (CH$225,000, 2½ hours). **Sky** (☎600-600-2828; www.skyairline.cl; 21 de Mayo 356) has cheaper but less frequent domestic flights and also flies to La Paz, Bolivia.

BUS

Arica has two main bus terminals. **Terminal Rodoviario de Arica** (Terminal de Buses; ☎058-222-5202; Diego Portales 948) houses most companies traveling south to destinations in Chile. Next door, **Terminal Internacional de Buses** (☎058-224-8709; Diego Portales 1002) handles international and some regional destinations. To reach the terminals, take *colectivo* 8 from Maipú or San Marcos; a taxi costs around CH$3000.

Various companies with destinations south to Santiago have offices in Terminal Rodoviario de Arica. Some major ones are Pullman, Flota Barrios, Ramos Cholele and Tur Bus.

For Putre, **La Paloma** (☎058-222-2710; Riesco 2071) has a direct bus at 7am (CH$3500, 1½ hours). To get to Tacna, Peru, **Adsubliata** (☎058-226-2495) buses leave the international terminal every half-hour (CH$2000). To get to La Paz, Bolivia, the comfiest and fastest service is with **Chile Bus** (☎058-226-0505), but cheaper buses are available with **Trans Salvador** (☎058-224-6064) in the international bus terminal. Buses on this route will drop passengers in Parque Nacional Lauca, but expect to pay full fare to La Paz. **Buses Géminis** (☎058-351-465), in the main terminal, goes to Salta and Jujuy in Argentina (CH$42,000) a few times a week.

GETTING TO PERU & BOLIVIA

Travelers cross from Arica, Chile, into Tacna, Peru, by train, bus or *colectivo* (shared taxi). The border crossing at Tacna is open daily from 8am to midnight and 24 hours from Friday to Sunday. Buses with international routes simply cross; long-distance routes are best booked in Tacna, where you'll find lower prices. Train passengers will go through immigration and customs in the train stations. Have your passport and tourist card on hand and eat any stowaway fruits or vegetables before crossing. Peruvian time is one hour behind Chilean time.

The most popular route to cross into Bolivia is via Parque Nacional Lauca, crossing from the Chilean town of Chungara to Tambo Quemado. Most international buses have morning departures. Immigration is open from 8am to 9pm. You can also reach the border at Chungara via taxi from Putre: cross the border on foot and find local transportation in Tambo Quemado.

For details on making this crossing in the opposite direction, see p828.

DESTINATION	COST (CH$)	DURATION (HR)
Antofagasta	18,000	10
Calama	15,000	9
Copiapó	24,000	18
Iquique	7000	4
La Paz, Bolivia	8000	9
La Serena	25,000	23
Santiago	30,000	27

TRAIN

Estación Ferrocarril Arica-Tacna (☎097-633-2896; Av Máximo Lira 791) Trains to Tacna (CH$1200, 1½ hours) depart from Estación Ferrocarril Arica-Tacna at 9am and 7pm, Monday to Saturday.

Ruta 11 & Putre

The barren slopes of the Lluta Valley host hillside geoglyphs, **Poconchile** and its quake-ridden 17th-century church, candelabra cacti (consider yourself blessed if you see it in bloom, which happens one 24-hour period per year), and the chasm-side ruins of the 12th-century fortress **Pukará de Copaquilla**.

Detour in Poconchile to **Eco-Truly** (☎096-875-0732; www.ecotrulyarica.cl; Sector Linderos, Km 29; campsites per person CH$3000, r CH$8000), a slightly surreal Hare Krishna 'ecotown' and yoga school, for an abundant vegetarian sampler lunch (CH$4000).

Aymara village **Putre** (population 1980; altitude 3530m) is 150km northeast of Arica and an appealing stop for visitors to acclimatize. There's a post office and call center in town, but only one bank – bring cash from Arica. Baquedano is the main strip.

Take advantage of the excellent hikes among ancient stone-faced terraces of alfalfa and oregano and tranquil village ambience. Colonial architecture includes the restored adobe **Iglesia de Putre** (1670). During the frivolously fun **Carnaval** in February, exploding flour balloons and live music rule the day.

Flavio of **Terrace Lodge & Tours** (☎058-258-4275; www.terracelodge.com; Circunvalación 25) runs a range of wonderful guided tours to some hidden spots, both in the immediate area around Putre as well as further up north. The stylish and ecofriendly **Terrace Lodge & Cafe** (☎058-258-4275; www.terracelodge.com; Circunvalación 25; s/d CH$29,000/CH$34,000; @📶) is a lovely place to spend a few nights as well. Budget lodgings are found at **Residencial La Paloma** (☎058-222-2710; lapalomaputre@hotmail.com; O'Higgins 353; r per person with/without bathroom CH$10,000/8000; P), with hot showers but noisy rooms.

On the main plaza, **Cantaverdi** (Arturo Perez Canto 339; set lunch CH$4500, mains CH$4500-6500; ⏲noon-10pm) is a casual eatery featuring *humitas* and home cooking, a roaring fireplace and wi-fi. **Kuchu Marka** (Baquedano 351; set lunch CH$4000, mains from CH$6000; ⏲noon-10:30pm) offers upscale *altiplano* cuisine (think quinoa and alpaca steaks) and good coffee.

Note that things seriously wind down in Putre from mid-December through February, the rainy season.

Buses La Paloma (☎058-222-2710; Germán Riesco 2071) serves Putre daily; buses depart Arica at 7am and return at 2pm (CH$3500). Note that some international buses between Arica and La Paz, Bolivia, stop near Putre; to make the connection into Bolivia, you'll have to coordinate with the ticketing offices in Arica's bus terminal.

Parque Nacional Lauca

At woozy heights with snow-dusted volcanoes, remote hot springs and glimmering lakes, Lauca, 160km northeast of Arica, is an absolute treasure. Herds of vicuña, viscachas and bird species including flamingos, giant coots and Andean gulls inhabit the park (1380 sq km; altitude 3000m to 6300m) alongside impressive cultural and archaeological landmarks.

Lauca's crown jewel, the glittering **Lago Chungará** (4517m above sea level), is a shallow body of water formed by lava flows damming the snowmelt stream from **Volcán Parinacota** (6350m), a beautiful snowcapped cone that rises immediately to the north. **Laguna Cotacotani** has been partially drained by the national electricity company but you will still see diverse birdlife along its shores and scattered groves of queñoa, one of the world's highest-elevation trees. You can wander around beautiful **Parinacota**, a tiny Aymara village of whitewashed adobe and stone streets. If you're lucky, the guide will procure the key for the town's undisputed gem, its 17th-century colonial church, reconstructed in 1789.

At the park's western entrance, **Las Cuevas** has a viewing point marked by a sculpture resembling *zampoña* (panpipes) balanced on a garish staircase. Some tours include a quick dip in **Termas Jurasi** (adult/child CH$2000/1000; ⌚daylight hours), a pretty cluster of thermal and mud baths huddled amid rocky scenery, 11km northeast of Putre.

Many tour agencies offer one-day blitzes from sea-level Arica – a surefire method to get *soroche* (altitude sickness). These tours leave around 7:30am and return about 8:30pm. It is common to become very sick when ascending to high altitudes without proper acclimatization. Avoid overeating, smoking and alcohol consumption the day before and while on tour. Tours that include at least a night in Putre are a wiser option, allowing more time to acclimatize. If you are renting a car, or have your own, carry extra fuel and antifreeze.

MIDDLE CHILE

Chile's heartland, covered with orchards and vineyards, is often skipped by travelers scrambling further afield. But if this region existed anywhere else in the world, it would be getting some serious attention. The harvests of the fertile central valley fill produce bins from Anchorage to Tokyo. Come for wine tasting, unspoiled national parks and excellent skiing and surfing.

The region was at the epicenter of the February 2010 earthquake. Towns and cities like Concepción, Talca and Curicó were the hardest hit. The region has mostly bounced back, though you'll still come across lingering damage.

Colchagua Valley

With around 20 wineries open to the public, the Colchagua Valley is Chile's biggest and best-established wine region. Its deep loamy soils, abundant water, dry air, bright sunshine and cool nights nurture some of the country's best reds. Many travelers who come here to taste wine book hotel rooms in Santa Cruz.

Santa Cruz

☎072

Ground zero of Chile's winemaking and wine-touring scene is a fairly sleepy place with a picturesque main square. The place perks up during the lively **Fiesta de la Vendimia**, the grape-harvest festival held in the plaza at the beginning of March.

While in town, check out the vast **Museo de Colchagua** (☎072-821-050; www.museocolchagua.cl; Errázuriz 145; adult/child CH$7000/3000; ⌚10am-7pm); the collection features pre-Columbian anthropomorphic ceramics from all over Latin America, weapons, religious artifacts, Mapuche silver, and *huasos* (cowboy) gear. Of particular interest is the exhibit *El Gran Rescate* (The Great Rescue), related to the October 2010 rescue of the 33 miners trapped 700m underground in San José.

An extremely helpful resource on the main square is **Ruta del Vino** (☎032-823-199; www.rutadelvino.cl; Plaza de Armas 298; ⌚9am-6pm Mon-Fri, 10am-6pm Sat & Sun). In addition to providing information about the region's wineries, it offers tasting tours (from CH$26,900; reservations required 48 hours before tour). However, transportation to the wineries isn't included in the basic price (for a full tour with lunch and transportation, you'll be paying upwards of CH$89,000). If you're fine sticking with the wineries closer to town, you can pay for taxi rides. Car rental isn't available in Santa Cruz; one option is renting a car in Santiago and driving yourself around the wine country – even if you're planning on joining a guided tour.

The **bus terminal** (Rafael Casanova 478) sits four blocks west of the town plaza. Twice every hour, **Buses Nilahué** (www.busesnilahue.cl) goes to Pichilemu (CH$4000, 3½ hours) and Santiago (CH$7000, four hours).

Colchagua Valley Wineries

Visit top wineries on a guided tour with Ruta del Vino or via reservations with the wineries ahead of time. Visits to **Viu Manent** (☎02-840-3181; www.viumanent.cl; Carretera del Vino, Km 37; tasting CH$10,000; ⌚tours 10:30am, noon, 3pm & 4:30pm), near Santa Cruz, involve a carriage ride through vinyards. Biodynamic growing techniques are explained at **Emiliana** (☎cell 9225-5679; www.emiliana.cl; Camino Lo Moscoso s/n, Placilla; biodynamic tours incl 4 pours CH$10,000; ⌚tours 10:30am, 11:30am, 12:30pm, 2:30pm & 4:30pm). **Lapostolle** (☎072-295-5330; www.lapostolle.com; Apalta Valley; tour CH$20,000, prixe-fixe lunch CH$40,000-60000, r US$1500; ⌚10:30am-5:30pm) has an excellent tasting tour at its six-story complex set on a hill above the Apalta Valley.

Middle Chile

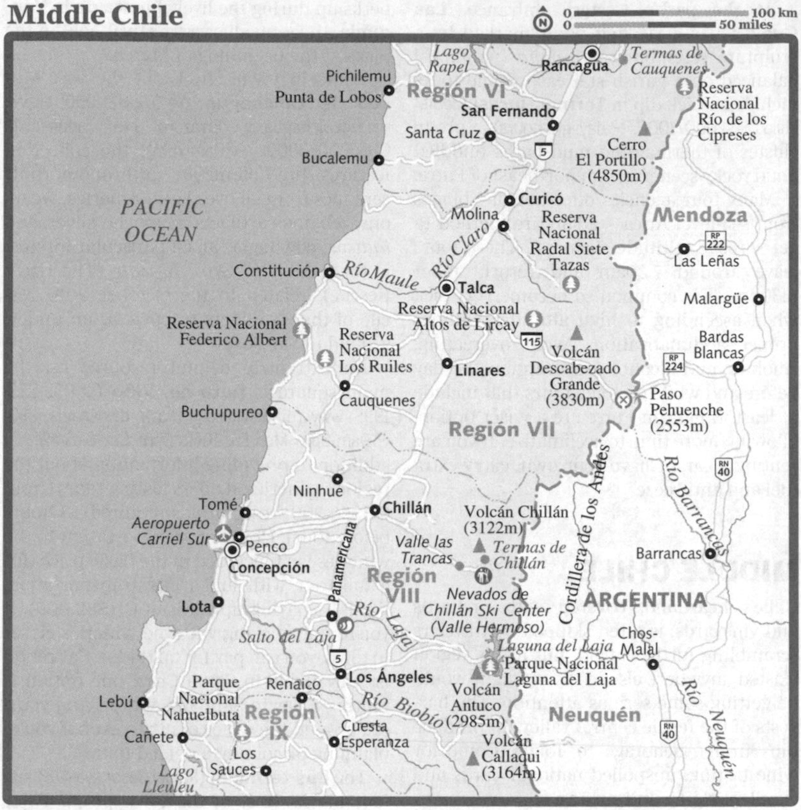

Pichilemu

072 / POP 12,500

Wave gods and goddesses brave the icy waters of Chile's unofficial surf capital year-round, while mere beach-going mortals fill its long black sands December through March. Pichilemu's laid-back vibe and great waves make it easy to see why it's so popular with visiting board-riders.

The westernmost part of 'Pichi' juts out into the sea, forming **La Puntilla**, the closest surfing spot to town. **Escuela de Surf Manzana 54** (cell 9574-5984; www.manzana54.cl; Av Costanera s/n; full day board & gear hire CH$7000-8000, 2hr classes CH$10,000) offers surf rentals and classes here. Fronting the town center to the northeast is calm Playa Principal (Main Beach), while south is the longer and rougher **Infiernillo**, known for its more dangerous waves and fast tow. The best surfing in the area is at **Punta de Lobos**, 6km south of Pichi proper, which you need to drive or hitchhike to.

In town, **Hotel Chile España** (072-841-270; www.chileespana.cl; Av Ortúzar 255; s/d/tr CH$20,000/35,000/50,000;) is a pretty budget hotel that now caters largely to older travelers. Across the street is the rambling cliff-top **Cabañas Guzmán Lyon** (072-284-1068; www.cabanasguzmanlyon.cl; San Antonio 48; d/tr/q CH$40,000/45,000/55,000;), where cute cottages offer private patios with beautiful views over the ocean and lake. Cheap *residenciales* (budget accommodations) pop up around town in summertime too.

Down by the surf breaks, several hostels compete for business, including **Pichilemu Surf Hostal** (cell 9270-9555; www.surfhostal.com; Eugenio Diaz Lira 167; dm/s/d incl breakfast CH$13,000/30,000/45,000;). Also on-site, **El Puente Holandés** (cell 9270-0955; Eugenio Díaz Lira 167; mains CH$3500-6900; 9am-11pm, closed Jun-Aug) is great for seafood ravioli and grilled sea bass – the terrace is spot-on for a beer.

Back in town, pizzeria **Pulpo** (Ortúzar 275; mains CH$6900-7900, set lunch CH$2000-4000; noon-1am Tue-Sun;) serves up crispy thin pizzas. **La Casa de las Empanadas** (Aníbal Pinto 268; empanadas CH$1200-1900) is a cheerful takeaway counter serving up huge gourmet empanadas like *machas y queso* (razor clams and cheese).

From the **Terminal de Buses** (072-841-709; cnr Av Millaco & Los Alerces) on Pichilemu's outskirts, buses run frequently to Santiago (CH$5500, four hours), Santa Cruz (CH$3000, three hours) and San Fernando (CH$4000, 3½ hours), where there are connections north and south.

Curicó

075 / POP 244,100

Drawing visitors interested in local vineyards and the exquisite Reserva Nacional Radal Siete Tazas, Curicó is a laid-back city, best known for its postcard-perfect **Plaza de Armas**, complete with palms and monkey-puzzle trees, a striking early-20th-century wrought-iron bandstand, and a wooden statue of the Mapuche chief Toqui Lautaro. Sadly, up to 90% of the older buildings in Curicó's historic center fell in the February 2010 earthquake.

Curicó bursts into life for the **Festival de la Vendimia** (Wine Harvest Festival) in early fall. **Ruta del Vino Curíco** (075-232-8977; www.rutadelvinocurico.cl; Carmen 727, Hotel Raíces) arranges tours to area vineyards.

Rambling **Hotel Prat** (075-231-1069; www.hotelpratcurico.cl; Peña 427; s/d CH$25,000/35,000, with shared bathroom CH$15,000/25,000;) is an economical sleeping option near the square. To upgrade, try the wine-themed **Hostal Viñedos** (075-326-785; www.hostalvinedos.cl; Chacabuco 645; s/d/tr CH$30,000/40,000/45,000;) with its bright rooms and bouncy beds; it's in the countryside outside town.

The **Terminal de Buses** (cnr Prat & Maipú) and the **train station** (Maipú 657) are four blocks west of Plaza de Armas. There are seven trains a day to Santiago (from CH$5600, 2¼ hours) and Chillán (from CH$8000, 2½ hours). Buses to Santiago (CH$3900, 2½ hours) leave about every half-hour; try **Tur Bus** (600-660-6600; www.turbus.cl; Av Manso de Velasco 0106).

To get to Reserva Nacional Radal Siete Tazas, catch a bus to Molina (CH$500, 35 minutes, every five minutes) with **Buses Aquelarre** (075-314-307) from Terminal de Buses Rurales, opposite the main bus terminal. From Molina there are frequent services to the park in January and February.

Maule Valley

The Maule Valley is responsible for much of the country's export wine; the specialty here is full-bodied cabernet sauvignon. The area was at the epicenter of the February 2010 earthquake – one winery reported losing its 80,000-bottle collection, countless vineyard workers were left homeless and the nearby city of Talca lost its historic marketplace, hospital and museum.

Happily, the wine industry has largely recovered, thanks in part to some inspired community efforts. Many visitors use Talca as a base for exploring the wineries and the nearby Reserva Nacional Altos de Lircay.

Talca

071 / POP 189,500

Founded in 1690, Talca is steeped in history; Chile's 1818 declaration of independence was signed here. These days, it's mainly known as a convenient base for exploring the gorgeous Reserva Nacional Altos de Lircay and the Maule Valley wine country. You'll find a decent range of traveler's services, including dining and lodging options, plus lovely views of the Andes when you're strolling down the sunbaked pedestrian thoroughfare at noon.

Four blocks from the Plaza de Armas, **Cabañas Stella Bordestero** (071-235-545; www.turismostella.cl; 4 Poniente 1 Norte 1183; s/d/cabin CH$22,000/30,000/48,000, s/d without bathroom CH$16,000/24,000;) offers cozy, well-equipped clapboard cabins in a leafy garden. In the countryside outside of town, the lovely **Hostal Casa Chueca** (071-197-0096; www.trekkingchile.com/casachueca; Viña Andrea s/n, Sector Alto Lircay; dm CH$12,500, d CH$44,000-75,000;) is a destination in its own right; the knowledgeable owners can help you plan trekking and horse riding in Altos de Lircay. Contact ahead for pick-up information.

Central **La Buena Carne** (cnr 6 Oriente & 1 Norte; mains CH$3000-5500) is a contemporary steakhouse with friendly service, wines by the glass and classic Chilean platters.

For travel information, consult helpful **Sernatur** (www.chile.travel; 1 Oriente 1150; ⌚8:30am-5:30pm Mon-Fri) on the main square.

North–south buses stop at Talca's main **bus station** (2 Sur 1920, cnr 12 Oriente), 11 blocks east of the plaza, or the nearby **Tur Bus terminal** (☎600-660-6600; www.turbus.cl; 3 Sur 1960). Destinations include Chillán (CH$4800, two hours), Puerto Montt (CH$14,000, 11 hours) and Santiago (CH$4500, three hours). To connect to Pichilemu, take the bus to Curicó (CH$1800). Buses Vilches has several daily services to Vilches Alto (CH$1400, 1¼ hours), the gateway to the Reserva Nacional Altos de Lircay. From the **EFE train station** (11 Oriente 1000), there are eight trains a day north to Santiago (from CH$8000, 2¾ hours) and south to Chillán (CH$8000, two hours).

Maule Valley Wineries

You can visit many of the vineyards independently or through one of the tours run by **Ruta del Vino** (☎08-157-9951; www.valledelmaule.cl; Av Circunvalación Oriente 1055, Casino Talca Hotel Lobby, Talca; ⌚9am-6:30pm Mon-Fri). One of Chile's first certifiably sustainable wineries, **Via Wines** (☎02-2355-9900; www.viawines.com; Fundo Las Chilcas s/n; tour incl 3 pours CH$10,000; ⌚9am-5pm Mon-Sat, reservations required) turns out delicious sauvignon blanc and syrah. No reservations are required at **Viña Balduzzi** (☎073-232-2138; www.balduzziwines.cl; Av Balmaceda 1189, San Javier; tour incl 4 pours from CH$3600; ⌚9am-6pm Mon-Sat), a fourth-generation winery surrounded by spacious gardens.

Chillán

☎042 / POP 180,200

Earthquakes have battered Chillán throughout its turbulent history; the 2010 earthquake was yet another hit. While this perpetually rebuilding city isn't especially interesting, it is a gateway to amazing skiing and summer trekking in the nearby mountains.

In response to the devastation caused by a 1939 quake, the Mexican government donated the **Escuela México** (Av O'Higgins 250; donations welcome; ⌚10am-1:30pm & 2-6pm Mon-Fri, 10am-6pm Sat & Sun) to the city. At Pablo Neruda's request, Mexican muralists David Alfaro Siqueiros and Xavier Guerrero painted tributes to indigenous and post-Columbian figures in history; today it's a working school, and visitor donations are encouraged.

Mercado de Chillán (set lunches CH$1500-3200; ⌚9am-6pm), among Chile's best markets, is also an excellent locale for a budget lunch; *longaniza* (pork sausage) is a local delicacy.

Sleeping & Eating

Hostal Canadá GUESTHOUSE $
(☎042-234-515; Av Libertad 269; s/d CH$8000/16,000; 📶) Spending a night in this no-nonsense mother-and-daughter setup is like staying in their apartment – fraying floral sheets, worn carpets, lumpy pillows and all. Get a room in the back to avoid the street noise.

Hotel Bavaria GUESTHOUSE $
(☎042-221-7235; www.hotelbavaria.cl; 18 de Sepiembre 648; s/d CH$30,000/35,000; 📶) Exit the concrete jungle of Chillán and find yourself in an incongruous Bavarian countryside villa. It's a quiet setting and the rooms are cozy though dated.

Arcoiris Vegetariano VEGETARIAN $
(El Roble 525; buffet CH$5900, mains CH$4000; ⌚9am-6:30pm Mon-Sat; 📶🌶) A good vegetarian restaurant in provincial Chile? We'll take it. Filling lentil-and-bulgur-style buffet lunches are served at the back, while a cafe up front does sandwiches and cakes, all to the tune of wind-chime and whale music.

Information

ATMs abound. There's free wi-fi on the pedestrian walkways downtown.

Hospital Herminda Martín (☎042-208-221; Francisco Ramírez 10) Public hospital on the corner of Av Argentina.

Sernatur (www.chile.travel; 18 de Sepiembre 455; ⌚8:30am-1:30pm & 3-6pm Mon-Fri) Friendly staff provide city maps and information on accommodations and transport.

Getting There & Away

The old **Terminal de Buses Interregional** (Constitución 01), five blocks west of Plaza de Armas, houses **Tur Bus** (☎600-660-6600; www.turbus.cl), going to Talca (CH$4000, two hours), Santiago (CH$7000, six hours), Valparaíso (CH$9000, eight hours) and Temuco (CH$9000, five hours). **Línea Azul** (www.buseslineaazul.cl) has the fastest service to Concepción (CH$2200, 1½ hours).

Other long-distance buses use **Terminal María Teresa** (O'Higgins 010), just north of Av Ecuador.

Local and regional buses use **Terminal de Buses Rurales** (Maipó 890), south of Maipó.

WORTH A TRIP

RESERVA NACIONAL RADAL SIETE TAZAS & RESERVA NACIONAL ALTOS DE LIRCAY

Clear water ladles into seven basalt pools in the lush **Reserva Nacional Radal Siete Tazas** (071-222-4461; www.conaf.cl; adult/child CH$4000/600; 8:30am-8pm Dec-Feb, to 5:30pm Mar-Nov), with the spectacle ending at a 50m waterfall. Two well-marked hiking trails loop from **Camping Los Robles** (075-228-029; 6-person campsites CH$8000): the 1km **Sendero el Coigüe** and 7km **Sendero Los Chiquillanes**, which has great views of the Valle del Indio (plan on about four hours in total). Conaf runs two cold-water **campsites** (075-228-029; campsites per person CH$1500) at Parque Inglés. The park is 65km from Curicó. During January and February Buses Hernández goes frequently from Molina to Parque Inglés (CH$1800, 2½ hours).

In the Andean foothills, 65km east of Talca, **Reserva Nacional Altos de Lircay** (www.conaf.cl/parques/reserva-nacional-altos-de-lircay; adult/child CH$4000/600; 8am-1pm & 2-5:30pm) offers fabulous trekking under a chattery flutter of tricahues and other native parrots. A helpful team of Conaf rangers who run the park give detailed advice about hiking and camping within it. Arguably the best hike in the whole of Middle Chile, the full-day **Sendero Enladrillado** takes you to the top of a unique 2300m basaltic plateau with stunning views. Alternatively, the shorter **Sendero Laguna** leads uphill to the gorgeous Laguna del Alto, a mountain-ringed lake 2000m above sea level. Hostal Casa Chueca (p477) outside Talca offers excellent guided day hikes.

Conaf runs the excellent **Camping Antahuara** (campsites CH$10,000) about 500m beyond the *administración* (headquarters), next to Río Lircay. From Talca, Buses Vilches goes several times daily to Vilches Alto, 5km from the *administración*. It takes about 1½ hours to drive to the reserve from Talca.

Nevados de Chillán & Valle Las Trancas

The southern slopes of the 3122m Volcán Chillán are the stunning setting of the **Nevados de Chillán Ski Center** (042-220-6100; www.nevadosdechillan.com; day ski pass adult/child CH$35,000/23,000). There are 32 runs (up to 2500m long), maxing out at 1100m of vertical. Hikers come out on summer weekends, but it's quiet on a weekday in the off-season – bring your own picnic and don't count on hotels being open. Bring cash from Chillán.

Soak in the thermal springs at **Valle Hermoso** (www.nevadosdechillan.com; adult/child CH$8000/6000, campsite per tent CH$21,000; thermal springs 9am-5pm). Ski-lodge-style **Chil'in Hosteria** (042-224-7075; www.chil-in.com; Ruta 55, Camino Termas de Chillán, Km 72; dm/d without bathroom CH$9000/22,000;) is both hostel and pizzeria. The stunning shipping containers of **Ecobox Andino** (042-242-3134; www.ecoboxandino.cl; Camino a Shangri-Lá, Km 0.2; cabins 2-5 people from CH$120,000, d CH$65,000;) offer an upscale option, while the après-ski scene is happening at **Snow Pub** (Camino Termas de Chillán, Ruta 55 Km 71; mains CH$3200-5000; 1pm-late).

From Chillán's Terminal de Buses Rurales, **Rembus** (042-222-9377; www.busesrembus.cl) has buses to Valle Las Trancas (CH$2000, 1¼ hours) five to seven times a day, with some services continuing to Valle Hermoso (CH$3000, 1½ hours).

Concepción

041 / POP 229,000

Concepción is an important and hard-working port city known for its universities and music scene (many of Chile's best rock acts got their start here). There's an energetic, youthful and left-leaning arts, music and culture scene. 'Conce' was yet another city terribly damaged in the February 2010 earthquake but because of its economic importance it is being quickly rebuilt.

Sights

La Casa del Arte MUSEUM

(041-224-2567; cnr Chacabuco & Paicaví, Barrio Universitario; 10am-6pm Tue-Fri, to 5pm Sat, to 2pm Sun) FREE The massive, fiercely political mural *La Presencia de América Latina* is the highlight of the university art museum La Casa del Arte. It's by Mexican artist Jorge González Camarena, a protégé of the legendary muralist José Clemente Orozco, and celebrates Latin America's indigenous peoples and independence from colonial and imperial powers.

Sleeping & Eating

Catering more to businesses than backpackers, lodging can be slim pickings.

Hotel Alborada BOUTIQUE HOTEL **$**
(041-291-1121; www.hotelalborada.cl; Barros Arana 457; d from CH$37,000;) A surprisingly stylish addition to Concepción's hotel scene is this centrally located, coolly minimalist hotel. The public spaces – outfitted with all-white furnishings, glass and mirrors – are sleeker than the guest rooms themselves, which are spacious and comfortable, but standard.

Hostal Bianca HOSTEL **$**
(041-225-2103; www.hostalbianca.cl; Salas 643-C; s/d CH$22,500/29,900, without bathroom CH$15,900/26,500;) Conce's best-value bargain-basement hotel has bright, newly renovated – if rather small – rooms with firm beds and cable TV.

★ **Deli House** CHILEAN **$**
(www.delihouse.cl; Av Diagonal Pedro Aguirre Cerda 12-34; mains CH$3500-4800;) These leafy sidewalk tables are a relaxed place to kick back for coffee, sandwiches, gourmet pizza or happy hour while watching the bohemian university set pass by.

Information

ATMs abound downtown.

Conaf (041-262-4000; www.conaf.cl; Barros Arana 215; 8:30am-1pm & 2:30-5:30pm Mon-Fri) Limited information on nearby national parks and reserves.

Hospital Regional (041-220-8500; cnr San Martín & Av Roosevelt) Public hospital.

Sernatur (041-741-4145; www.chile.travel; Pinto 460; 8:30am-8pm Jan & Feb, 8:30am-1pm & 3-6pm Mon-Fri Mar-Dec) Provides brochures, but little else.

Getting There & Away

Long-distance buses go to **Terminal de Buses Collao** (Tegualda 860), 3km east of central Concepción. The separate **Terminal Chillancito** (Camilo Henríquez 2565) is northeast along the extension of Bulnes.

There are dozens of daily services to Santiago (CH$7000) with companies including **Eme Bus** (041-232-0094; www.emebus.cl), **Pullman Bus** (600-320-3200; www.pullmanbus.cl) and **Tur Bus** (600-660-6600; www.turbus.cl; Tucapel 530), which also goes to Valparaíso and south to Temuco (CH$7100), Valdivia (CH$8000) and Puerto Montt (CH$9000). **Línea Azul** (042-203-800; www.buseslineaazul.cl) runs frequently to Chillán (CH$2500).

WORTH A TRIP

PN LAGUNA DEL LAJA & PN NAHUELBUTA

The sparkling centerpiece of **Parque Nacional Laguna del Laja** (043-232-1086; http://www.conaf.cl/parques/parque-nacional-laguna-del-laja; adult/child CH$1200/600; 8:30am-8pm Dec-Apr, to 6:30pm May-Nov) is the towering snow cone of Volcán Antuco (2985m). A fantastic trek, **Sendero Sierra Velluda**, circles its skirt, taking three days, or you can go for a day hike to get a taste of the action. Stay at a campsite or cabin at **Lagunillas** (043-232-1086; campsites CH$10,000, 6-person cabins CH$30,000) and eat at the small restaurant at **Club de Esqui de los Ángeles** (043-232-2651; www.skiantuco.cl; lift ticket CH$20,000). Departing from Los Ángeles' Terminal de Buses Rurales, local buses (CH$1600, 1½ hours, seven daily) go to the village of El Abanico, 11km from the park entrance. The last bus back to Los Ángeles leaves Abanico at 5:30pm (Monday to Saturday) and at 7:15pm on Sunday.

Amazing araucaria (monkey-puzzle trees) grow up to 50m tall and 2m in diameter on the green slopes of **Parque Nacional Nahuelbuta** (www.parquenahuelbuta.cl; adult/child CH$4000/2000; 8:30am-8pm), a fine destination for hiking and mountain biking. You can pitch your tent at **Camping Pehuenco** (www.parquenahuelbuta.cl; 6-person campsites CH$12,000). From Angol, 35km to the east, the Terminal de Buses Rurales has buses to Vegas Blancas (CH$1700, 1½ hours). Some lines go on Monday, Wednesday and Friday, others on alternate days. Buses generally return from Vegas Blancas at 6pm – confirm these times so you don't get stranded.

Los Ángeles

☎043 / POP 170,000

A useful base for visiting Parque Nacional Laguna del Laja, Los Ángeles is an otherwise unprepossessing agricultural and industrial service center 110km south of Chillán.

A string of *residenciales* line Caupolicán west of the Plaza de Armas. Despite appearances, they're not particularly cheap and mostly function as men's boarding houses, so women travelers might not feel comfortable there. Recently renovated **Hotel del Centro** (☎043-236-961; www.hoteldelcentro.cl; Lautaro 539; s/d CH$31,500/40,000) is a better option. In the center there are plenty of casual cafes.

Long-distance buses leave from the **Terminal Santa María** (Av Sor Vicenta 2051), on the northeast outskirts of town. The terminal for **Tur Bus** (☎600-660-6600; www.turbus.cl) is nearby. For service to the village of El Abanico, 11km from the entrance of Parque Nacional Laguna del Laja, go to the **Terminal de Buses Rurales** (Terminal Santa Rita; Villagrán 501).

THE LAKES DISTRICT

The further south you go, the greener it gets, until you find snow-clad volcanoes rising over verdant hills and lakes. This bucolic region makes a great escape to a slower pace. The Araucanía, named for the monkey-puzzle tree, is the geographical center of Mapuche culture. Further south, the Lakes District was colonized by Germans in the 1850s and still retains some Teutonic touches.

Outside the shingled homes, many adventures wait: from rafting to climbing, from hiking to hot-springs hopping, from taking *onces* in colonial towns to sipping maté with rural settlers. Hospitality is the strong suit of *sureños* (southerners); take time to enjoy it. Though they love the malls, most city dwellers (about half the population) are still marked by rural roots, and split wood and make homemade jam as part of their daily routine. Seek out the green spaces bursting beyond the city limits.

The recent eruptions of Volcán Villarrica and Volcán Calbuco may have affected some of the activities on offer around Pucón and Ensenada.

Temuco

☎045 / POP 262,500

With its leafy, palm-filled plaza, pleasant Mercado Municipal and intrinsic link to Mapuche culture, Temuco is the most palatable of all Sur Chico's blue-collar cities to visit. It's also the regional transit hub, with steady transportation to Santiago and connections to everywhere in Sur Chico and beyond.

Sights

Museo Regional de La Araucanía MUSEUM
(www.museoregionalaraucania.cl; Av Alemania 084; adult/child CH$600/300; 9:30am-5:30pm Tue-Fri, 11am-5pm Sat, 11am-2pm Sun) Housed in a handsome frontier-style building dating from 1924, this small but vibrant regional museum has permanent exhibits recounting the history of the Araucanían peoples before, during and since the Spanish invasion in its newly renovated basement collection, including an impressive Mapuche dugout canoe.

Monumento Natural Cerro Ñielol HISTORIC SITE
(Calle Prat; adult/child CH$1200/600; 8am-7pm) Cerro Ñielol is a hill that sits among some 90 hectares of native forest – a little forested oasis in the city. Chile's national flower, the *copihue (Lapageria rosea)*, grows here in abundance, flowering from March to July. Cerro Ñielol is also of historical importance, since it was here in 1881, at the tree-shaded site known as La Patagua, that Mapuche leaders ceded land to the colonists to found Temuco.

Sleeping & Eating

Cheap digs around the train station and Feria Pinto can be sketchy, especially for women; the neighborhood between the plaza and university is preferable.

Hospedaje Tribu Piren GUESTHOUSE $
(☎045-298-5711; www.tribupiren.cl; Prat 69; r per person without bathroom CH$15,000; @ wi-fi) The young English-speaking owner at this traveler's *hospedaje* (budget accommodations) makes this a great choice for foreigners. Everything is clean and polished, and rooms, some of which open out onto a small terrace, offer cable TV and central heating. Alvaro, the owner, also guides snow-sport tours in the winter.

The Lakes District

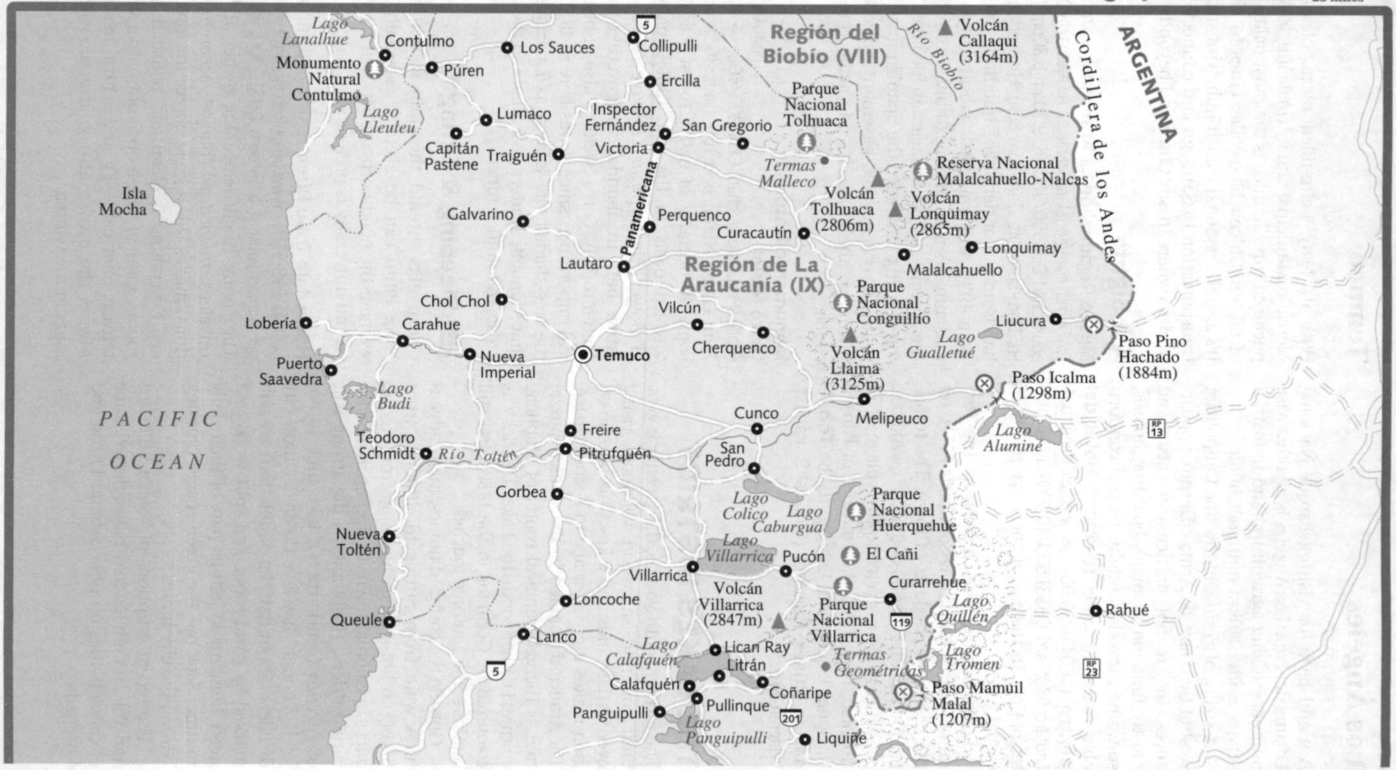

0 — 50 km
0 — 25 miles

ARGENTINA
Cordillera de los Andes
Región del Biobío (VIII)
Región de La Araucanía (IX)
Río Biobío
Volcán Callaqui (3164m)
Parque Nacional Tolhuaca
Termas Malleco
Reserva Nacional Malalcahuello-Nalcas
Volcán Tolhuaca (2806m)
Volcán Lonquimay (2865m)
Lonquimay
Malalcahuello
Curacautín
Parque Nacional Conguillío
Volcán Llaima (3125m)
Lago Gualletué
Liucura
Paso Pino Hachado (1884m)
Paso Icalma (1298m)
Melipeuco
Lago Aluminé
RP 13
Lago Lanalhue
Contulmo
Monumento Natural Contulmo
Los Sauces
Púren
Collipulli
5
Ercilla
Lago Lleuleu
Lumaco
Capitán Pastene
Traiguén
Inspector Fernández
Victoria
San Gregorio
Panamericana
Isla Mocha
Galvarino
Perquenco
Lautaro
Chol Chol
Vilcún
Cherquenco
Lobería
Carahue
Nueva Imperial
Temuco
Puerto Saavedra
Lago Budi
PACIFIC OCEAN
Teodoro Schmidt
Río Toltén
Freire
Pitrufquén
Cunco
San Pedro
Gorbea
Lago Colico
Lago Caburgua
Parque Nacional Huerquehue
Nueva Toltén
Lago Villarrica
Villarrica
Pucón
El Cañi
Curarrehue
Loncoche
Volcán Villarrica (2847m)
Parque Nacional Villarrica
Lago Quillén
Rahué
119
Queule
Lanco
Lago Calafquén
Lican Ray
Litrán
Termas Geométricas
Lago Tromen
RP 23
Calafquén
Coñaripe
Paso Mamuil Malal (1207m)
Pullinque
Panguipulli
201
Lago Panguipulli
Liquiñe

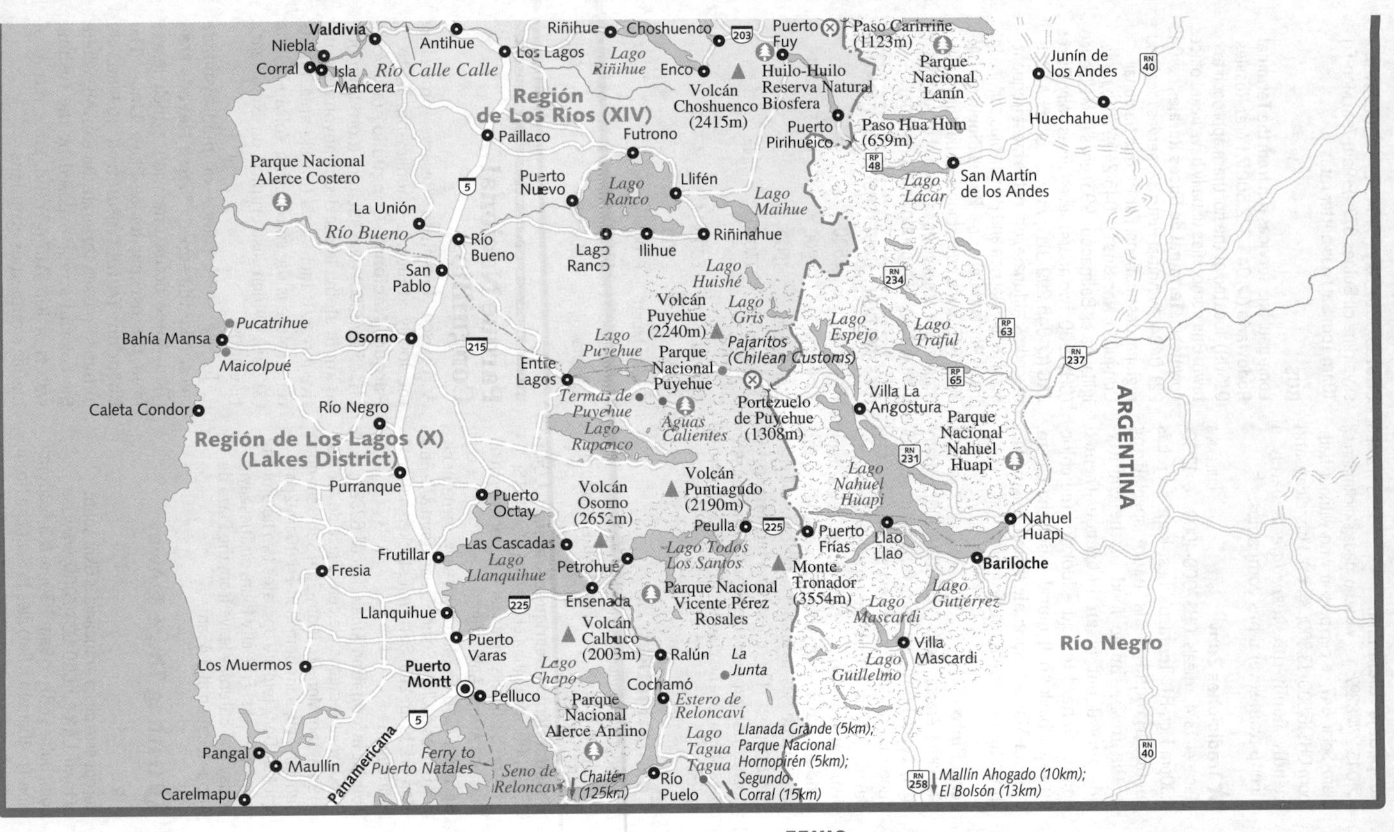

Valdivia
Niebla
Corral
Isla Mancera
Antihue
Río Calle Calle
Los Lagos
Riñihue
Choshuenco
Lago Riñihue
Enco
203
Puerto Fuy
Paso Carirriñe (1123m)
Huilo-Huilo Reserva Natural Biosfera
Volcán Choshuenco (2415m)
Parque Nacional Lanín
Junín de los Andes
RN 40
Huechahue
Región de Los Ríos (XIV)
Paillaco
Futrono
Puerto Pirihueico
Paso Hua Hum (659m)
RP 48
San Martín de los Andes
Lago Lácar
Parque Nacional Alerce Costero
5
Puerto Nuevo
Lago Ranco
Llifén
Lago Maihue
La Unión
Río Bueno
Río Bueno
Lago Ranco
Ilihue
Riñinahue
San Pablo
Lago Huishé
RN 234
Volcán Puyehue (2240m)
Lago Gris
Lago Espejo
Lago Traful
RP 63
Pucatrihue
Bahía Mansa
Maicolpué
Osorno
215
Lago Puyehue
Entre Lagos
Parque Nacional Puyehue
Pajaritos (Chilean Customs)
RN 237
RP 65
Termas de Puyehue
Aguas Calientes
Portezuelo de Puyehue (1308m)
Villa La Angostura
Parque Nacional Nahuel Huapi
ARGENTINA
Caleta Condor
Río Negro
Lago Rupanco
RN 231
Región de Los Lagos (X) (Lakes District)
Purranque
Puerto Octay
Volcán Osorno (2652m)
Volcán Puntiagudo (2190m)
Lago Nahuel Huapi
Peulla
225
Puerto Frías
Llao Llao
Nahuel Huapi
Las Cascadas
Lago Llanquihue
Frutillar
Petrohué
Lago Todos Los Santos
Monte Tronador (3554m)
Bariloche
Fresia
Ensenada
Parque Nacional Vicente Pérez Rosales
Lago Mascardi
Lago Gutiérrez
Llanquihue
225
Volcán Calbuco (2003m)
Puerto Varas
Ralún
La Junta
Villa Mascardi
Río Negro
Los Muermos
Puerto Montt
Lago Chapo
Lago Guillelmo
Pelluco
Cochamó
Estero de Reloncaví
5
Parque Nacional Alerce Andino
Lago Tagua Tagua
Llanada Grande (5km); Parque Nacional Hornopirén (5km); Segundo Corral (15km)
RN 40
Pangal
Maullín
Panamericana
Ferry to Puerto Natales
Seno de Reloncaví
Chaitén (125km)
Río Puelo
RN 258
Mallín Ahogado (10km); El Bolsón (13km)
Carelmapu

Hospedaje Klickmann GUESTHOUSE **$**
(☎045-274-8297; www.hospedajeklickmann.cl; Claro Solar 647; r per person with/without bathroom CH$16,500/13,800; @) This clean and friendly family-run *hospedaje* is barely a hiccup from several bus companies.

★ **Tradiciones Zuny** CHILEAN **$**
(Tucapel 1374; meals CH$2000-4000; ⏲12:30-4:30pm Mon-Fri) Temuco's best-kept secret is an underground locals' haunt specializing in the fresh, simple food of the countryside served out of an indigenous-themed home. It's hard to find – look for the colorful duck/basketball mural – but the cheap, Chilean-Mapuche organic fusion cuisine is a showstopper. You're welcome.

Feria Pinto MARKET **$**
(Av Barros Arana; meals CH$2000-3000; ⏲8am-7pm) Feria Libre is a colorful Mapuche produce market taking up several blocks along Barros Arana. Along the streets more practical wares are sold, while in the Feria itself vendors hawk everything from apples and artisan cheeses to honey and bags of *merquén* pepper. There is also a fair amount of vibrant hot peppers, though it's unclear who buys them, as the cuisine in Chile is far from spicy.

Information

CorreosChile (www.correos.cl; cnr Diego Portales & Prat; ⏲9am-7pm Mon-Fri, to 1pm Sat) Postal services.

Hospital Hernán Henríquez Aravena (☎045-255-9000; www.hhha.cl; Manuel Montt 115; ⏲24hr) Six blocks west and one block north of Plaza de Armas Aníbal Pinto.

Sernatur (☎045-240-6200; www.sernatur.cl; cnr Bulnes & Claro Solar; ⏲9am-2pm & 3-6pm Mon-Fri, 10am-2pm Sat) Well-stocked national tourist info.

Tourist Information Kiosk (☎cell 6238-0660; www.temucochile.com; Plaza de Armas; ⏲9am-6pm Mon-Fri, 10am-2pm Sat, 9am-noon Sun Jan-Feb, 9am-6pm Mon-Fri, 10am-2pm Sat Mar-Dec) Temuco operates two helpful city tourism kiosks. Free city tours on Tuesday, Friday and Saturday leave from the Plaza de Armas location at 9:45am.

Getting There & Away

AIR

Aeropuerto de La Araucanía is 6km south of town. **LAN** (☎600-526-2000; www.lan.com; Bulnes 687; ⏲9am-1:30pm & 3-6:30pm Mon-Fri, 10am-1pm Sat) flies to Santiago (from CH$155,000); **Sky** (☎045-275-7300; www.skyairline.cl; Bulnes 677; ⏲9am-7pm Mon-Fri, 10am-1pm Sat) has better rates.

BUS

Long-haul bus services run from the **Terminal Rodoviario** (☎045-222-5005; Pérez Rosales 01609), located at the northern approach to town. Bus companies usually have ticket offices downtown. **Terminal de Buses Rurales** (☎045-221-0494; Av Aníbal Pinto 32) serves local and regional destinations. For Parque Nacional Conguillío, **Nar-Bus** (☎045-240-7700; www.igillaima.cl; Balmaceda 995) goes to Melipeuco (CH$1900, two hours) seven times daily. **Buses JAC** (☎045-299-3117; www.jac.cl; cnr Av Balmaceda & Aldunate) offers the most frequent service to Villarrica and Pucón, plus service to Lican Ray and Coñaripe. **Buses Biobío** (☎045-265-7876; www.busesbiobio.cl; Lautaro 854) runs frequent services to Angol, Los Ángeles, Concepción, Curacautín and Lonquimay.

DESTINATION	COST (CH$)	DURATION (HR)
Chillán	8500	4
Concepción	7900	4½
Curacautín	1500	2
Neuquén, Argentina	17,000	12
Osorno	5300	4
Pucón	2900	2
Puerto Montt	6700	5
Santiago	12,000	9
Valdivia	4000	3

Parque Nacional Conguillío

A Unesco Biosphere Reserve protecting the lovely araucaria (monkey-puzzle tree), **Parque Nacional Conguillío** (adult/child CH$4500/2500) also shelters more than 600 sq km of alpine lakes, deep canyons and native forest. It includes a tiny ski area, but its centerpiece is the smoldering Volcán Llaima (3125m), which last erupted on New Year's Day 2008.

To see solid stands of monkey-puzzle trees, hike the superb **Sierra Nevada trail** (7km, three hours one way), which leaves from the parking lot at Playa Linda. The **Cañadon Truful-Truful trail** (0.8km, 30 minutes) passes through the canyon, where the colorful strata, exposed by the rushing waters of Río Truful-Truful, are a record of Llaima's numerous eruptions.

In **Laguna Conguillío**, Conaf's **Centro de Información Ambiental** (www.geachile.sernageomin.cl; Laguna Conguillío; ⏲8:30am-9:30pm Dec 16-Mar, 8:30am-1pm & 2:30-6pm Apr-Dec 15) sells trail maps.

Sleeping

Sendas Conguillío CAMPING, CABAÑAS $
(www.parquenacionalconguillio.cl; camping per site CH$5000-40,000, cabañas from CH$90,000) Sendas Conguillío runs five campgrounds inside the park around the south shore of Lago Conguillío and the northwest shore of Laguna Captrén on a concession from Conaf. Accommodations include a special camping sector set aside for backpackers (campsites CH$5000). There are more comfortable cabins as well.

★ **La Baita** BOUTIQUE LODGE $$
(☎045-258-1073; www.labaitaconguillio.cl; s/d CH$48,000/61,000, cabañas 4/6 people CH$58,000/70,000) Spaced amid pristine forest, this is an ecotourism project just outside the park's southern boundary. It's home to eight attractive cabins with slow-burning furnaces, solar-powered electricity and hot water; an extremely cozy, incense-scented lodge and restaurant with six rooms complete with granite showers and design-forward sinks; and a pleasant massage room, outdoor hot tub and sauna.

Getting There & Away

To reach Sector Los Paraguas, Vogabus, at Temuco's Terminal de Buses Rurales, runs hourly Monday through Saturday to Cherquenco (CH$1400, 1½ hours), from where it's a 17km walk or hitchhike to the ski lodge at Los Paraguas.

For the northern entrance at Laguna Captrén, **Buses Curacautín Express** (☎045-225-8125) has four departures from Curacautín on Monday and Friday only (CH$800, one hour, 6am, 9am, 2pm and 6pm); and two departures on Tuesday, Wednesday and Thursday (6am and 6pm). The bus stops at the park border at Guardería Captrén, a 12km walk to the park entrance.

For the southern entrance at Truful-Truful, **Nar-Bus** (☎045-211-611; www.narbus.cl) in Temuco runs eight buses daily to Melipeuco (CH$1900, two hours).

Villarrica

☎045 / POP 49,200

Villarrica is a real living, breathing Chilean town. While not as charming as the Pucón resort, it's more down to earth, lacks the bedlam associated with package-tour caravans and has more reasonable prices than its neighbor. The *costanera* (lakeshore road), rebuilt after the 2010 earthquake, makes for a nice walk. The annual **Muestra Cultural Mapuche**, in January and February, has exhibits of local artisans, indigenous music and ritual dance.

Activities

★ **Aurora Austral Patagonia Husky** DOG SLEDDING
(☎cell 8901-4518; www.auroraaustral.com; Camino Villarrica–Panguipulli Km 19.5) Located about 19km from Villarrica on the road to Lican Ray is this German-run husky farm, where you'll find over 50 of the cutest Siberian and Alaskan huskies you ever did see, ready to take you on the ride of your life. In winter there are day trips (CH$65,000) and a seriously epic seven-day Andean crossing (CH$2,100,000 all-inclusive).

In summer there are 6km rides including a barbecue (CH$33,000) and husky trekking on Volcán Villarrica (CH$48,000). True dog lovers can sleep out here as well in three extremely nice cabins (CH$40,000 to CH$60,000). Four- to 12-week volunteers are also accepted.

Sleeping

More than half a dozen campgrounds can be found along the road between Villarrica and Pucón.

La Torre Suiza HOSTEL $
(☎045-241-1213; www.torresuiza.com; Bilbao 969; dm CH$10,000, s/d from CH$18,000/22,000; 📶) Under new ownership and management, the continued cultivation of a hostel vibe at this once traveller classic has proved a challenge, but this wooden chalet with a fully equipped kitchen remains the best bet for the traveller camaraderie you are seeking.

Voices carry, and there are some missing conveniences (water for sale, late breakfast, bathroom hand soap), but the old-school crunchiness of the place has its charms and the friendly new owners are (hopefully) working on it.

Hostal Don Juan INN $
(☎045-241-1833; www.hostaldonjuan.cl; General Körner 770; s/d CH$28,000/35,000, without bathroom CH$20,000/27,000; @📶) Don Juan wins travelers over around a large *fogón* (outdoor

oven), which was designed by the friendly owner, and offers fabulous volcano views from some rooms on the 2nd floor.

Eating & Drinking

★The Travellers RESTO-BAR $
(www.thetravellers.cl; Valentin Letelier 753; mains CH$4250-8500; ⏲9am-4am Mon-Sat; 📶) Chinese, Mexican, Thai, Indian, Italian – it's a passport for your palate at this resto-bar that is ground zero for foreigners. A makeover marries classic album covers and postcards from amigos the world over with a modern motif and a new expansive terrace.

German and English traveler advice is available, and so are discounted cocktails (stunning raspberry mojitos!) during the lengthy happy hour (6pm to 10pm).

El Sabio PIZZA $
(www.elsabio.cl; Zegers 393; pizzas CH$5700-6900; ⏲12:30-4pm & 6:30-10pm Mon-Sat; 📶) A friendly Argentine couple runs the show here, creating fantastic, uncut oblong pizzas served on small cutting boards. Forget everything you thought you knew about pizza in Chile.

Huerto Azul DESSERTS $
(www.huertoazul.cl; Henríquez 341; desserts CH$800-4990; ⏲9:30am-9:30pm) Blindingly blue, this fabulous gourmet store/ice-cream parlor dares you to walk in without stumbling out in a sugar coma.

Information

Hospital Villarrica (San Martín 460; ⏲24hr) Small hospital in town.
Oficina de Turismo (☎045-220-6619; www.visitvillarrica.cl; Av Pedro de Valdivia 1070; ⏲8:30am-1pm & 2:30-6pm Mon-Fri, 10am-4pm Sat & Sun) Municipal office that has helpful staff and provides many brochures.

Getting There & Away

Villarrica has a main **bus terminal** (Av Pedro de Valdivia 621), though a few companies have separate offices nearby.

Buses JAC (☎045-246-7775; www.jac.cl; Bilbao 610) goes to Pucón (CH$800, 45 minutes) and Temuco (CH$1800, one hour) every 20 minutes. **Buses Coñaripe** (☎cell 7125-8183) has departures throughout the day to Lican Ray (CH$800, 40 minutes) and Coñaripe (CH$1100, one hour). Several other lines make the journeys from the main terminal.

For Argentine destinations, **Igi Llaima** (☎045-241-2753; www.igillaima.cl), in the main terminal, leaves every morning for San Martín de los Andes (CH$12,000, five hours), where you can make connections north or south.

Pucón

☎045 / POP 22,100

Pucón is firmly positioned on the global map as a mecca for adventure sports, set on beautiful Lago Villarrica under the smoldering eye of the volcano of the same name. Once a summer playground for the rich, Pucón is now a year-round adventure machine, especially in February (a time to avoid, if possible), when it is absolutely overrun. The town receives alternating floods of package tourists, Santiago holidaymakers, adventure-seeking backpackers, new age spiritualists and eco-pioneers.

Volcán Villarrica had several eruptions in 2015; as a result, future adventure offerings depend on its status. The town is walkable, with most tour operators and services on the commercial main strip of Av O'Higgins. Restaurants and shops dot Fresia, which leads to the plaza. Slightly beyond the plaza is the beach.

Activities

Hiking & Climbing

Summiting **Volcán Villarrica** has long been a big attraction, yet with the volcano closed due to recent activity, agencies promote hiking nearby Volcán Quetrupillán, a six-hour ascent.

Mountain Biking

Mountain bikes can be rented all over town. The most popular route is the **Ojos de Caburgua Loop**. Take the turnoff to the airfield, about 4km east of town and across Río Trancura.

Rafting & Kayaking

Pucón is known for both its river sports and the quality of the rafting and kayaking infrastructure. The rivers near Pucón and their corresponding rapids classifications are: Lower Trancura (III), Upper Trancura (IV), Liucura (II–III), the Puesco Run (V) and Maichín (IV–V).

Tours

★Aguaventura OUTDOORS
(☎045-244-4246; www.aguaventura.com; Palguín 336; ⏲8:30am-10pm Dec-Mar, to 8:30pm Apr-Nov) This friendly French-owned agency is your one-stop shop, offering highly skilled volcano guides (beer after!) and also specializing in snow sports and kayaking, but can book

it all. It also rents everything for the mountain, water and snow (including GoPro); and books flights and ferries too. Ask co-owner Vincent about Japanese-style capsule dorms at his new hostel, French Andes.

Bike Pucón MOUNTAIN BIKING

(☎cell 9579-4818; www.bikepucon.com) Offers thrilling 17km to 20km downhill rides spread amongst six trails of very slippery volcanic terrain, single-track and old fire roads. It's not for novices – you can make it on limited experience, but expect to kiss some ash at one point or another.

Politur RAFTING

(☎045-244-1373; www.politur.cl; Av O'Higgins 635; ⏰8:30am-8:30pm) Has made bad volcano decisions in the past, but is the go-to agency for rafting.

Kayak Pucón KAYAKING

(☎cell 9716-2347; www.kayakpucon.com; Av O'Higgins 211; ⏰9am-9pm Nov–mid-Mar) This well-regarded kayak operator offers three-day kayak courses (CH$180,000) as well as multiday expeditions for more experienced boaters. Half-day ducky (one-person inflatable boats) tours on Class III rapids are a good option for those with less kayak experience (CH$20,000) and there's rafting for kids as well.

Sleeping

★ iécole! HOSTEL $

(☎045-244-1675; www.ecole.cl; Urrutia 592; dm with/without bedding CH$10,000/8000, d/tr CH$30,000/36,000, s/d/tr without bathroom CH$18,000/20,000/30,000; @🛜) The eco-conscious iécole! is a travel experience in

Pucón

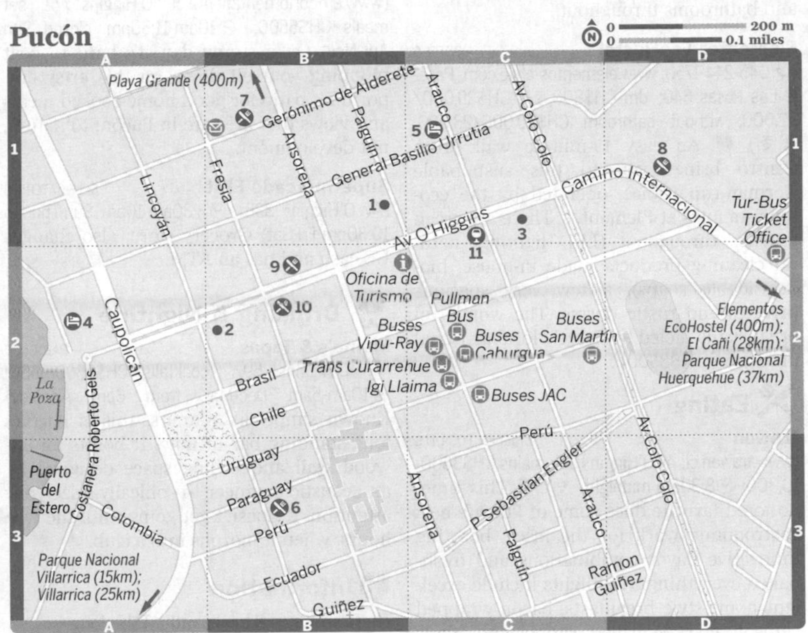

Pucón

Activities, Courses & Tours

1 Aguaventura ... B1
2 Kayak Pucón ... B2
3 Politur ... C1

Sleeping

4 Chili Kiwi ... A2
5 iécole! ... C1

Eating

6 La Picada ... B3
7 Latitude 39° ... B1
8 Menta Negra ... D1
9 Supermercado Eltit ... B2
10 Trawen ... B2

Drinking & Nightlife

11 Mama's & Tapas ... C1

itself. It's a meeting point for conscientious travelers and a tranquil and artsy hangout that has long been Pucón's most interesting place to stay. Rooms are small, clean and comfortable, but walls are thin and voices carry within the leafy grounds, so it's not a wild party hostel.

Chili Kiwi HOSTEL **$**
(045-244-9540; www.chilikiwihostel.com; Roberto Geis 355; dm from CH$9000, r without bathroom from CH$24,000;) Sitting on prime lakeside real estate, this is Pucón's most sociable hostel, run by an enthusiastic Kiwi-Dutch partnership with years of globetrotting experience from which to draw their traveler-centric ideas. There are various dorms and private options (converted vans, tree houses, cabins), the best of which are in the main house, and an overload of kitchens and bathrooms throughout.

Elementos EcoHostel HOSTEL **$**
(045-244-1750; www.elementos-chile.com; Pasaje Las Rosas 640; dm CH$800, s/d CH$29,000/32,000, without bathroom CH$20,000/23,000;) An easy 15-minute walk from Centro brings you to this sustainable German-run choice, operated by the ecotourism folks at Elementos. There are green touches throughout (LED lighting, natural cleaning products made in-house, biodegradable soaps), a few very spacious privates and rustic dorms. The wonderful breakfast is fueled by fiercely local artisanal products (CH$3500).

Eating

Trawen CHILEAN, FUSION **$**
(www.trawen.cl; Av O'Higgins 311; mains CH$3600-10,300; 8:30am-midnight;) This time-honored favorite does some of Pucón's best gastronomic work for the price, boasting innovative flavor combinations and fresh-baked everything. Highlights include excellent home-style breakfasts, bacon-wrapped venison, *merkén*-grilled octopus and salads from its own certified-organic gardens, the first in southern Chile. Creative types tend to congregate here, along with hopheads – it boasts the town's best craft beer selection.

La Picada CHILEAN **$**
(Paraguay 215; set lunch CH$3500; noon-3:30pm, closed Sun Mar-Nov) This local's secret is out: an underground eatery in someone's living room serving fuss-free set lunches, such as salads, *pastel de choclo*, *cazuelas*, and pasta. No sign. Knock to gain entrance.

Latitude 39° AMERICAN **$**
(www.latitude39.cl; Gerónimo de Alderete 324; burgers CH$4600-6100; 11am-11pm;) California transplant owners fill a clearly appreciated gringo niche at this newly expanded homesick remedy of a restaurant. Juicy American-style burgers are a huge hit: try the Grand Prix (caramelized onions, bacon, peanut butter) or the Buddha (Sriracha mayo, Asian slaw, popcorn shrimp), but there are also fat breakfast burritos, fish tacos, BLTs and everything else you might be missing. It has also evolved into the foreigner happy-hour hot spot for beer and camaraderie.

Menta Negra CAFE **$**
(www.emporiomentanegra.cl; O'Higgins 772; set meals CH$5500; 10am-11:30pm, closed Sun Apr-Nov) On a sunny day, it's hard to beat plopping yourself down on this artsy emporium's patio for good home-cooked meals and views that are rare in Pucón: to nature, not development.

Supermercado Eltit SELF-CATERING
(Av O'Higgins 336; 8:30am-10pm Sun-Thu, to 10:30pm Fri-Sat) Grocery store; also changes US cash and has an ATM.

Drinking & Nightlife

Mama's & Tapas BAR, CLUB
(Av O'Higgins 597; cocktails CH$3500-5500; 10am-5am Dec-Mar, from 6pm Apr-Nov) Known simply as 'Mama's,' this is Pucón's long-standing bar of note. It boasts an all-wood wall and ceiling space designed by an acoustic engineer to sonically seize your attention. It doesn't get going until the wee hours, when it morphs into a club.

Information

There are several banks with ATMs along Av O'Higgins. Note that petty theft is on the rise in Pucón, especially in the areas around the beach.

CorreosChile (www.correos.cl; Fresia 183; 9am-1pm & 2:30-6pm Mon-Fri, 9am-noon Sat) Postal services.

Hospital San Francisco (www.hospitalpucon.cl; Uruguay 325; 24hr) Medical services.

Oficina de Turismo (045-229-3001; www.municipalidadpucon.cl; cnr Av O'Higgins & Palguín; 8:30am-7pm) Has stacks of brochures and usually an English speaker on staff.

Getting There & Away

Frequent buses go to/from Santiago (CH$15,000 to CH$31,000, 9½ hours). **Tur Bus** (045-244-3328; www.turbus.com; Av O'Higgins 910; 9am-7pm), east of town, and **Pullman Bus** (045-244-3331; www.pullman.cl; Palguín 555), in the center, are your best bets, with many Chilean destinations.

Buses JAC (045-299-3183; www.jac.cl; cnr Uruguay & Palguín) goes to Puerto Montt (CH$9500, five hours), Valdivia (CH$4500, three hours), and every 20 minutes to Temuco (CH$2900, one hour). From the same station, **Minibuses Vipu-Ray** (cell 6835-5798; Palguín 550) and **Trans Curarrehue** (045-262-5168; Palguín 550) have continuous services to Villarrica (CH$800, 30 minutes). Buses JAC and **Buses Caburgua** (cell 9838-9047; Palguín 555) go to Parque Nacional Huerquehue (CH$2000, 45 minutes). For San Martín de los Andes, Argentina, **Buses San Martín** (045-244-2798; Av Colo Colo 612) departs twice weekly (CH$12,000, five hours), stopping in Junín. **Igi Llaima** (045-244-4762; cnr Palguín & Uruguay) also makes the trip.

Getting Around

Pucón is very walkable. A number of travel agencies rent cars and prices can be competitive.

Around Pucón

Río Liucura Valley

East of Pucón, the Camino Pucón–Huife cuts through a lush valley hosting a myriad of hot springs, a nature sanctuary and views of the silver ribbon Río Liucura.

Formed by citizens to nip logging interests in this spectacular swath of native forest, the nature sanctuary **Santuario El Cañi** (www.santuariocani.cl; Km 21; admission with/without guide CH$15,000/4000) protects some 400 hectares of ancient araucaria forest. A three-hour, 9km hiking trail ascends steeply to gorgeous views. Camp in the park at **La Loma Pucón** (cell 8882-9845; www.lalomapucon.cl; Santuario El Cañi; camping per person CH$3000, dm/d CH$4000/20,000). You can also make arrangements to visit El Cañi at iécole! (p487) in Pucón.

Curarrehue

Heading toward the Argentine border at Mamuil Malal, this route provides off-piste pleasures. Immerse yourself in Mapuche culture in quiet and colorful **Curarrehue**. Before town, the Mapuche family farm Kila Leufu welcomes guests warmly. The small but interesting museum **Aldea Intercultural Trawupeyüm** (Héroes de la Concepción 21; CH$500; 9am-8pm Mon-Fri, from 11am Sat & Sun Jan-Feb, 9am-6pm Tue-Sun Mar-Dec) explores Mapuche culture. Curarrehue's real attraction is **Cocina Mapuche Mapu Lyagl** (cell 8788-7188; anita.epulef@gmail.com; Camino al Curarrehue; menu CH$5600; 1-6pm Dec-Feb, by reservation only Apr-Nov;), where a Mapuche chef turns seasonal ingredients into adventurous vegetarian tasting menus. Indigenous delicacies include *mullokiñ* (bean puree rolled in quinoa). The **Tourism Office** (www.curarrehue.cl; O'Higgins s/n; 9am-7pm mid-Dec–mid-Mar, 9am-5:20pm Mon-Thu, to 4:20pm Fri mid-Mar–mid-Dec) opens in summer only.

Parque Nacional Huerquehue

Rushing rivers, waterfalls, monkey-puzzle trees and alpine lakes adorn the 125-sq-km **Parque Nacional Huerquehue** (adult/child CH$4500/2500), only 35km from Pucón.

The **Los Lagos trail** (7km, four hours round trip) switchbacks through dense lenga forests to monkey-puzzle trees surrounding a cluster of pristine lakes. **Cerro San Sebastián** (16km, seven hours roundtrip) is considered the best trek in all of La Araucanía. From the park entrance, climb from 700m to 2000m. From the top, on a clear day, you can see eight volcanoes and 14 lagoons.

Conaf offers camping at **Lago Tinquilco** (campsites CH$15,000) or **Renahue** (campsites CH$15,000). The excellent **Refugio Tinquilco** (cell 9539-2728; www.tinquilco.cl; camping CH$15,000, dm CH$14,000, d with/without bathroom CH$35,900/28,900, cabin CH$50,000; closed Jun-Aug) is a luxurious lodge with amenities like French-press coffee and a forest sauna. It's at the base of the Lago Verde trailhead. Meals are available (CH$8500), or you can cook for yourself.

Stop at Conaf's **Centro de Informaciones Ambientales** (cell 6157-4809; p.huequehue@gmail.com; 10:30am-2:30pm & 4:30-7:30pm) for maps and information at the entrance.

Buses Caburgua (098-038-9047; Uruguay 540, Pucón) serves Pucón three times daily (CH$2000, one hour). Many agencies offer organized excursions, too. Buses Jac also travels between the park and Pucón.

Parque Nacional Villarrica

This glorious spread of volcanoes and lakes is one of Chile's most popular parks. The highlights of the 630-sq-km park are the three volcanoes: 2847m Villarrica, 2360m Quetrupillán and, along the Argentine border, a section of 3747m Lanín. Due to 2015 volcanic activity, skiing and hiking on Volcán Villarrica has been closed; check with the tourism office in Pucón for updates.

Lago Calafquén

Black-sand beaches and gardens draw tourists to this island-studded lake, to fashionable **Lican Ray** (30km south of Villarrica), and the more down-to-earth **Coñaripe** (22km east of Lican Ray). Out of season, it's dead. Lican Ray is tiny, with campgrounds surrounding town. In Coñaripe, look for a friendly tourist kiosk on the main square. The road heading north of Coñaripe leads to a number of rustic hot springs. Buses JAC (p489) has several buses daily from Villarrica to Coñaripe (CH$1100, one hour) via Lican Ray (CH$800, 30 minutes).

Valdivia

063 / POP 154,400

Valdivia was crowned the capital of Chile's newest region, Región de los Ríos (XIV) in 2007, after years of defection talk surrounding its inclusion in the Lakes District despite its geographical, historical and cultural differences. It's the most important university town in southern Chile and, as such, offers a strong emphasis on the arts, student prices at many hostels, restaurants and bars, and a refreshing dose of youthful energy.

Sights & Activities

Av Costanera Arturo Prat is a major focus of activity, but the most important public buildings are on Plaza de la República.

★Cervecería Kunstmann BREWERY
(063-229-2969; www.lacerveceria.cl; Ruta T-350 950; noon-midnight) On Isla Teja at Km5 on the road to Niebla, you'll find the south's best large-scale brewery. Tours leave hourly from noon to 11pm (CH$10,000; November to March) and include a takeaway glass mug and a 300ml sampling of the Torobayo unfiltered, available only here, straight from the tank. Pitchers are CH$7650 to CH$8250, mains CH$2700 to CH$ 9950.

Feria Fluvial MARKET
(Av Prat s/n; 7am-4pm) A lively riverside market south of the Valdivia bridge, where vendors sell fresh fish, meat and produce. Waterfront sea lions have discovered the Promised Land here – a place where they can float around all day and let tourists and fishmongers throw them scraps from the daily catch.

Museo Histórico y Antropológico MUSEUM
(Los Laureles 47; admission CH$1500; 10am-8pm Jan-5 Feb, 10am-1pm & 2-6pm Mar-Jan 4) Housed in a fine riverfront mansion on Isla Teja, this museum is one of Chile's finest. It features a large, well-labeled collection from pre-Columbian times to the present, with particularly fine displays of Mapuche Indian artifacts and household items from early German settlements.

Boat Cruises

Boat cruises (6½ hours) leave Puerto Fluvial and float the river confluence smattered with 17th-century Spanish forts. Save some bucks by taking a *colectivo* (corner of Chacabuco and Yungay) to Niebla. From Niebla, ferries visit Isla Teja, Corral, Isla Mancera and Isla del Rey every half-hour from 8am to 8pm.

Reina Sofia CRUISE
(063-220-7120; cruises CH$16,000-18,000) A recommended (albeit a bit pushy) outfitter for Valdivia's boat cruises. It departs from Puerto Fluvial at the base of Arauco at 1:30pm daily.

Festivals & Events

Noche de Valdivia CULTURAL
The largest happening is Noche de Valdivia, on the third Saturday in February, which features decorated riverboats and fireworks.

Sleeping

During the school year the university crowd monopolizes the cheap sleeps; summer has better options.

★Airesbuenos Hostel & Permacultura HOSTEL $
(063-222-2202; www.airesbuenos.cl; Garcia Reyes 550; dm/r CH$10,000/28,000; @) Valdivia's best hostel is run by a friendly

northern Californian who has turned this long-standing traveler mainstay into Sur Chico's most ecofriendly place to sleep. Solar heated showers, rainwater catchment, permaculture, vertical gardens, compost, Egyptian bamboo towels – it's all here. Besides the sustainability, you'll find comfy, colorful dorm rooms and simple, well-done private rooms that are a little on the small side.

Hostel Bosque Nativo HOSTEL **$**
(☎063-243-3782; www.hostelnativo.cl; Pasaje Fresia 290; dm CH$10,000, s/d CH$19,000/26,000, without bathroom CH$17,000/22,000; @📶) This hostel, run by a sustainable forestry management NGO, is a wooden den of comfort hidden away down a gravel residential lane a short walk from the bus station.

Hostal Totem GUESTHOUSE **$**
(☎063-229-2849; www.turismototem.cl; Carlos Anwandter 425; s/d/tr CH$25,000/30,000/39,000; @📶) Of the ample choices along residential thoroughfare Carlos Anwandter, this 11-room guesthouse is the best bang for the peso. Clean rooms, a friendly French- and English-speaking upstart owner and a sunny breakfast room make up for the lack of antiquated character, though the hardwood floors in this old house squeak with the best of 'em.

Eating & Drinking

Isla Teja, across the river from the city, is the latest ubertrendy neighborhood for restaurants. The main concentration of nightlife is on Esmeralda – take your pick.

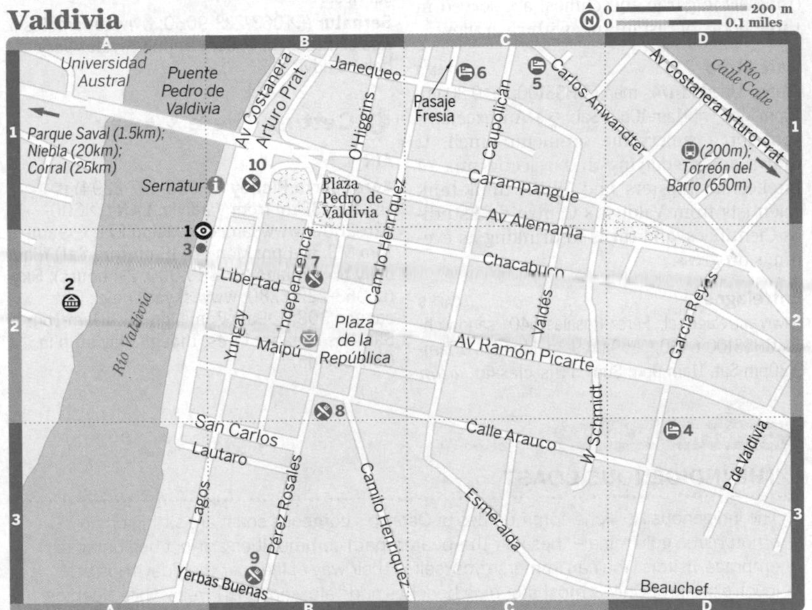

Valdivia

Sights
1 Feria Fluvial ... A2
2 Museo Histórico y Antropológico ... A2

Activities, Courses & Tours
3 Reina Sofia ... A2

Sleeping
4 Airesbuenos Hostel & Permacultura ... D3
5 Hostal Totem ... C1
6 Hostel Bosque Nativo ... C1

Eating
7 Café Moro ... B2
8 Entrelagos ... B2
9 La Última Frontera ... B3
10 Mercado Municipal ... B1

★**La Última Frontera** RESTO-BAR $
(Pérez Rosales 787; sandwiches CH$2800-4400; ⏲10am-2am Mon-Sat; 📶🍴) You'll find one-stop traveler nirvana at this bohemian resto-bar with a vibe unmatched in the whole of Sur Chico. Hidden quietly away in a restored mansion, you'll find a load of outside-the-box sandwiches, fresh juices and local craft beer – 12 or so on draft (start with Cuello Negro Stout) and a few more stragglers in bottles.

At night, it morphs into the best bar for miles and miles courtesy of the town's hip artistic front. Lose yourself in one of the art-saturated rooms or knock back a cold one on the new patio and deck. Don't miss it.

Mercado Municipal CHILEAN $
(Prat s/n; mains CH$2500-4000; ⏲9am-9pm) Fat plates of fish and chips or *choritos al ajillo* (mussels in garlic and chilies) are served in three floors of restaurants with river views.

Café Moro CHILEAN $
(Paseo Libertad 174; menu CH$3100; ⏲9:30am-10pm Mon-Fri, 11am-10pm Sat; 📶) An excellent spot for a supervalue set-menu lunch. It draws an age-defying and eclectic mix of intellectual hipsters and WWF think-tank scientists from Valdivia's Centro de Estudios Científicos, and turns to drinking as evenings progress.

Entrelagos CAFE $
(www.entrelagos.cl; Pérez Rosales 640; sandwiches CH$3100-6400; ⏲9am-9pm Mon-Fri, 10am-9:30pm Sat, 11am-9pm Sun) This classic *salón de té* (teahouse) is where Valdivians talk about you behind your back over delicious *café cortados* (espresso with milk), cakes, sandwiches and crepes. Hearty set menus and toasted sandwiches draw those looking for something more filling (or perhaps just escapists – the Parisian-style seating couldn't be more un-Chilean). On Sunday, there's little else.

ℹ Information

Downtown ATMs are abundant, as are internet cafes. There's a tourist kiosk at the Terminal de Buses.

Clínica Alemana (www.alemanavaldivia.cl; Beauchef 765; ⏲24hr) Better, faster and closer than the public hospital.

CorreosChile (www.correos.cl; O'Higgins 575; ⏲9am-7pm Mon-Fri, 9:30am-1pm Sat) Postal services.

Sernatur (☎063-223-9060; www.turismolosrios.cl; Prat s/n; ⏲9am-9pm) Provides very helpful advice.

ℹ Getting There & Away

AIR

Aeropuerto Pichoy (☎063-227-2294) is situated 32km from Valdivia. **LAN** (☎600-526-2000; www.lan.com; Maipú 271; ⏲9am-1pm & 3:30-6pm Mon-Fri, 10am-1pm Sat) flies daily to Santiago (CH$80,000, 2¼ hours); **Sky** (☎063-222-6280; www.skyairline.cl; Chacabuco 308; ⏲9am-7pm Mon-Fri, 10am-1pm Sat) has cheaper fares, though may stop in Concepción.

OFF THE BEATEN TRACK

THE INDIGENOUS COAST

The indigenous Huilliche communities of Osorno's gorgeous coast are sitting on an *etnoturismo* gold mine – these off-the-beaten-path communities are just beginning to embrace visitors. You can immerse yourself in their way of life over multiday trips that involve some of Chile's most stunning beaches and Valdivian forest treks while sleeping in rural homes around **San Juan de la Costa** and **Territorío Mapa Lahual** (www.mapulahual.cl), an indigenous protected zone including **Caleta Condor**, which stretches south into Río Negro province as well. Tour operator **Mawidan Tour Chile** (☎cell 7771-7275; www.mawidan.com; Camino Cheuquemo Km 1, Rio Negro) 🍃 has good relationships with the local communities.

In San Juan de la Costa, a series of five magnificent *caletas* (bays) are accessible by car and can be visited as day trips from around Osorno for those short on time. **Bahía Mansa**, **Pucatrihue** and **Maicolpué** are villages where dolphins and sea lions practically swim to shore and women scramble about wild and rugged beaches collecting *luga* and *cochayuyo*, two types of seaweed that help fuel the local economy. On either side are the two best *caletas*, **Manzano**, 20km north of Bahía Mansa, and **Tril-Tril**, 7km south of Bahía Mansa.

BUS

Valdivia's **Terminal de Buses** (☎ 063-222-0498; www.terminalvaldivia.cl; Anfión Muñoz 360) has frequent service to destinations between Puerto Montt and Santiago. **Tur Bus** (☎ 063-221-2430; www.turbus.cl) and **Pullman Bus** (☎ 063-220-4660; www.pullman.cl) are just a few of the bus companies to choose from. **Buses JAC** (☎ 063-221-3754; www.busjac.cl) accesses Villarrica, Pucón and Temuco. **Andesmar** (☎ 063-222-4665; www.andesmar.com) travels to Bariloche, Argentina.

DESTINATION	COST (CH$)	DURATION (HR)
Bariloche, Argentina	21,000	7
Castro	9500	7
Neuquén, Argentina	41,900	12
Osorno	5000	2
Panguipulli	2900	2¼
Pucón	4500	3
Puerto Montt	5000	3½
San Martín de los Andes, Argentina	13,000	8
Santiago	34,000	12
Temuco	4200	3½

Osorno

☎ 064 / POP 151,900

Osorno is a bustling place and the commercial engine for the surrounding agricultural zone. Though it's an important transportation hub, most visitors spend little time here.

Sleeping & Eating

Hostel Vermont HOSTEL $

(☎ 064-224-7030; www.hostelvermont.cl; Toribio Medina 2020; dm CH$12,000, s/d without bathroom CH$20,000/30,000, cabins s/d/q CH$25,000/35,000/50,000; @ 📶) Osorno's first decent hostel is run by a bilingual snowboarder who named the hostel after her stint near Burlington, Vermont. It's everything you want in a hostel: friendly, clean and well-equipped (as well as some things you don't want: creaky old floors mixed with rowdiness means it gets sleep-depriving loud).

From the bus station, walk two blocks south to Juan MacKenna, five blocks east to Buenos Aires and one and a half blocks south to Toribio Medina.

Hotel Villa Eduviges HOTEL $$

(☎ 064-223-5023; www.hoteleduviges.cl; Eduviges 856; s/d/tr from CH$25,000/40,000/55,000; 📶) Midrange and comfortable, Eduviges wins props for being in the minority in Región X, allowing singles to sleep in a double bed without paying for a double. The relaxed setting in a residential area south of the bus terminal bodes well, with spacious, somewhat old-fashioned rooms, private bathrooms and kind management.

Café Central CAFE $

(O'Higgins 610; mains CH$2500-8000; ⏰8am-midnight) This bi-level spot on the plaza gets crowded for its coffee, Kunstmann draft, colossal burgers and breakfast. There's also a counter for solo travelers.

Mercado Municipal CHILEAN $

(cnr Prat & Errázuriz; ⏰11am-3pm) Mercado Municipal has an array of lunch stalls serving good and inexpensive food.

Getting There & Away

Long-distance and Argentine-bound buses use the main **Terminal de Buses** (☎ 064-221-1120; Errázuriz 1400), five blocks from Plaza de Armas. Companies include **Pullman Bus** (☎ 064-231-8529; www.pullman.cl) and **Tur Bus** (☎ 064-220-1526; www.turbus.cl), among many others. Most services going north on the Panamericana start in Puerto Montt, departing hourly, with mainly overnight services to Santiago.

Try **Queilen Bus** (☎ 064-226-0025; www.queilenbus.cl) for Coyhaique or Punta Arenas. **Bus Norte** (☎ 064-223-2778; www.busnorte-chile.cl), **Andesmar** (☎ 064-223-3050; www.andesmar.com) and **Via Bariloche** (☎ 064-226-0025; www.viabariloche.com.ar) have daily service to Bariloche and other Argentine destinations.

Other local and regional buses use the **Terminal Mercado Municipal** (Errázuriz btwn Arturo Prat & Cristóbal Colón), two blocks west of the main terminal. **Expreso Lago Puyehue** (☎ 064-224-3919; www.expresolagopuyehue.wix.com/buses-expreso) goes hourly to Termas Puyehue/Aguas Calientes (CH$2200, 1¼ hours). **Buses Río Negro** (☎ 064-223-6748) goes to Caleta Condor (CH$1200, 45 minutes).

To get to the Huilliche communities of San Juan de la Costa (Bahía Mansa, Pucatrihue and Maicolpué), minibuses (CH$1800, 1¾ hours) depart every hour from the **Feria Libre Ráhue** (cnr Chillán & Temuco). Catch bus 1, 6 or 10 from the northeast corner of Errázuriz and Cristóbal Colón (CH$400).

DESTINATION	COST (CH$)	DURATION (HR)
Ancud	6200	4
Bariloche, Argentina	16,000	5
Concepción	12,300	9
Coyhaique	40,000	20
Pucón	8400	4
Puerto Montt	2200	1¾
Punta Arenas	42,000	28
Santiago	20,000	12
Temuco	5800	3½
Valdivia	5800	1¾

Parque Nacional Puyehue

Volcán Puyehue (2240m) blew its top the day after the 1960 earthquake, turning its dense, humid evergreen forest into a stark landscape of sand dunes and lava rivers. In 2011 nearby Cordon Caulle erupted, sending ash as far as Buenos Aires. Today, **Parque Nacional Puyehue** (www.parquepuyehue.cl) FREE protects 1070 sq km of this cool, contrasting environment. **Termas Aguas Calientes** (www.termasaguascalientes.cl; day use without/with meals CH$12,500/28,000) is an unpretentious hot-springs resort. Or access the free Pocitos Termas 80m across the Colgante bridge from the Conaf parking lot.

Small ski resort **Centro de Esqui Antillanca** (064-224-2010; www.skiantillanca.cl; office at O'Higgins 1073, Osorno; lift tickets CH$27,000, rentals CH$26,000-29,000) is 18km beyond Aguas Calientes on the flanks of 1990m-high Volcán Casablanca. In summer a trail leads to a crater outlook with views of the mountain range.

Trails abound at **Anticura**, 17km northwest of the Aguas Calientes turnoff. Pleasant, short walks lead to a lookout and Salto del Indio waterfall. The private **El Caulle**, 2km west of Anticura, accesses the southern entrance for the **Puyehue Traverse**, an iconic three- to four-day hike. **Patagonia Expeditions** (cell 9104-8061; www.anticurachile.cl) runs guided treks and operates **Camping Catrué** (cell 9104-8061; www.anticurachile.cl; camping CH$3500, dm CH$8000, cabañas for 2/4/6 CH$35,000/42,000/52,000), with 18 campsites and fully equipped cabins.

Frutillar

065 / POP 16,300

The mystique of Frutillar is its Germanness, a 19th-century immigrant heritage that the village preserved. To come here is to savor this idea of simpler times, float in the lake, eat home-baked pies and sleep in rooms shaded by lace curtains. For many it is simply too still to linger; for others, it remains a serene alternative to staying in more chaotic Puerto Varas.

The town has two sectors: Frutillar Alto is a no-frills working town; Bajo fronts the lakes and has all of the tourist attractions. Don't miss **Teatro del Lago** (065-242-2900; www.teatrodellago.cl; Av Philippi 1000), a world-class performing-arts center built on stilts over the water, hosting excellent live music. **Museo Colonial Alemán** (www.museosaustral.cl; cnr Pérez Rosales & Prat; admission CH$2500; 9am-7:30pm) features reconstructions of a mill, smithy and mansion set among manicured gardens.

Many visit as a day trip from Puerto Varas; budget sleeping options are scarce. On a lavender farm just outside town, **Lavanda Casa de Te** (cell 9269-1684; www.lavandacasadete.cl; Km 1.5 a Quebrada Honda; menu CH$13,000; 1-8pm Jan-Feb, closed Mon Apr-Dec) is a favorite for tea, gourmet lavender products and farm-fresh lunches. Barbecue restaurant **Meli** (065-242-0766; www.emporiomeli.com; Camino Punta Larga Km 1 ; menu CH$8900-10,900; 12:30-4pm & 7-11pm Mon-Sat, 10am-6pm Sun;) focuses on Patagonian cooking, with salads and fire-roasted lamb.

Minibuses to Puerto Varas (CH$900, 30 minutes), Puerto Montt (CH$1800, one hour) and Osorno (CH$900, 40 minutes) leave from a small parking lot on Pedro Montt near Av Philippi.

Puerto Varas

065 / POP 37,900

Two snowcapped volcanoes stand sentinel over picturesque Puerto Varas like soldiers of adventure. Just 23km from Puerto Montt but worlds apart in charm, scenery and options for the traveler, Puerto Varas has been touted as the 'next Pucón.' There's great access to water sports here – rafting and sea kayaking in particular – as well as climbing, fishing, hiking and even skiing, making it a top choice for an extended stay. Note that while it gets packed in summer, it is quiet in winter.

Sights & Activities

Visitors can stroll around town to take in the 19th-century German architecture. In summer, stand-up paddleboards and kayaks are rented on the lake. Grab a city map at the tourist information office, which highlights the **Paseo Patrimonial**, a suggested walking tour of 10 different houses classified as national monuments.

Tours

★ Secret Patagonia OUTDOORS

(☎065-223-2921; www.secretpatagonia.com; San Pedro 311; ⏰8am-8pm Oct-Apr, 9am-7pm May-Sep) This eco-sensitive collective marries four smaller outfitters – La Comarca, Ko'Kayak, Birds Chile and OpenTravel – which specialize in dramatic and custom-tailored adventure trips to less explored areas of the Río Puelo Valley, Cochamó Valley and beyond.

Highlights include hiking in Cochamó Valley, extensive mountain-bike trips (including an epic 12-day singletrack ride from Bariloche to Puerto Varas), remote French retreats on Isla Las Bandurrias in Lago Las Rocas, multiday horse-riding/cultural farmstay trips between Argentina and Chile, and trips to Parque Tagua Tagua. The newest opus: drinking and biking (not in that order, mind you!). The Bike & Beer tour is a good-fun 30km bike ride along the lake, culminating in a craft brew tasting at Chester Beer. Groups are never more than 12 strong and everyone here is dedicated to giving travelers a unique off-the-beaten-path experience while keeping their carbon footprint at bay. Also rents full-suspension mountain bikes.

Ko'Kayak RAFTING, CANYONING

(☎065-223-3004; www.kokayak.cl; San Pedro 311; ⏰8am-8pm Oct-Apr, 9am-7pm May-Sep) A long-standing favorite for rafting, offering half-day rafting trips for CH$35,000 with two departures daily, full-day/two-day sea kayaking for CH$70,000/160,000 and half-day canyoning (CH$40,000).

TurisTour OUTDOORS, GUIDED TOUR

(☎065-243-7127; www.turistour.cl; Del Salvador 72; ⏰7:30am-7pm Mon-Fri, 7am-2pm & 5-7pm Sat & Sun) Runs the Cruce de Lagos, a bus-and-boat combo transport trip through the majestic lakes and mountains of the Pérez Rosales Pass to Bariloche, Argentina, and vice versa. The total fare is US$280, although there are seasonal discounts and a 50% discount for children. There are daily departures throughout the year, but the 12-hour trip requires a mandatory overnight in Peulla in winter (May to August).

Sleeping

Casa Margouya HOSTEL $

(☎065-223-7640; www.margouya.com; Santa Rosa 318; dm CH$10,000, s/d without bathroom CH$18,000/24,000; @📶) This French-owned, excellently located hostel is smaller than average and fosters a friendly communal vibe between its guests (it's vaguely hippie...and loud).

Hostel Melmac Patagonia HOSTEL $

(☎065-223-0863; www.melmacpatagonia.com; Santa Rosa 608 Interior; dm CH$13,000, s/d from CH$35,000/39,500; @📶) This intimate hostel in perfectly located new digs above downtown is decked out with all the modern fixins – right down to the artisanal

WORTH A TRIP

COCHAMÓ & RÍO PUELO VALLEYS

Emerald rivers and deep, pristine valleys are just some of wonders of this stunning remote region, now threatened by several dam proposals. But something this good should be shared and (we hope) preserved. Rugged and rustic, these valleys get few visitors.

Puerto Varas' excellent **Campo Aventura** (☎cell 9289-4318; www.campoaventura.cl) leads popular horseback-riding excursions, traversing the valley from its riverside lodge, with as much emphasis on a cultural experience as nature. In the hamlet of Río Puelo, **Domo Camp** (☎cell 6802-4275; www.andespatagonia.cl; Puelo Alto; d/tr/q CH$50,000/60,000/70,000, cabaña CH$50,000; @📶) offers a unique sleep in cool domes, connected by planks through native forest and outfitted with fireplaces and sleeping bags. The attached restaurant, open to the public, offers an excellent set lunch. Small-outfitter collective Secret Patagonia brings adventurers to both the Cochamó and Puelo Valleys via kayak, mountain bike and hiking trails.

homebrew beer, which goes down nicely on the front porch (first beer free!), and Wall-E, the Roomba cleaning robot.

Margouya Patagonia HOSTEL $
(☎065-223-7695; www.mapatagonia.com; Purisima 681; dm CH$9000, s/d without bathroom CH$18,000/25,000; @📶) This spacious and historic 1932 home is on the town's list of patrimonial heritage sites. It's the nicest hostel in town, offering quieter and much larger rooms and bathrooms for better prices than most spots and a whole lot of French-Chilean hospitality. Big, bright dorms hold nine beds only.

It also has its own in-house Spanish school and tour agency for activities in the area and good-value bike rentals. No breakfast.

Puerto Varas

Puerto Varas

Activities, Courses & Tours
Ko'Kayak (see 1)
1 Secret Patagonia C3
2 TurisTour D4

Sleeping
3 Casa Margouya D3
4 Compass del Sur B1
5 Galpon Aíre Puro B1
6 Hostel Melmac Patagonia C4
7 Margouya Patagonia A4

Eating
8 Donde El Gordito B4
9 The Office D4

Drinking & Nightlife
10 Caffé El Barrista D3
11 Garage D3

Casa Azul HOSTEL $$
(☎065-223-2904; www.casaazul.net; Manzanal 66; dm CH$10,000, d CH$34,000, s/d without bathroom CH$18,000/26,000; @📶) It's hard to find fault with this impeccably kept German-Chilean operation set in a quieter residential neighborhood just outside downtown. The superbly tranquil garden and koi pond (with bonsai trees) immediately calm your nerves, in any case. Rooms are spacious, in excellent condition and there's an expansive guest kitchen and common area with cool furniture fashioned from tree branches.

Compass del Sur B&B $$
(☎065-233-2044; www.compassdelsur.cl; Klenner 467; camping CH$9000, dm CH$12,000, s/d CH$32,000/42,000, without bathroom CH$27,000/30,000; @📶) This charming colonial house with Scandinavian touches and very friendly staff sits above the main area of town, accessed by a staired walking street. It has comfortable beds and some new rain-style showers that please the flashpacker crowd who dominate the scene here.

Galpon Aíre Puro GUESTHOUSE $$
(☎cell 9979-8009; www.galponairepuro.com; cnr Decher & Independencia; s/d/ste CH$34,000/48,000/60,000; P@📶) American expat Vicki Johnson – chef, chocolatier and purveyor of life's finer things – has transformed this massive 1920s potato storage barn into her very own den of good taste, expanding and moving her artisan chocolate shop and cafe here and offering eight spacious guest rooms for more independently minded travelers above a hip commercial office space.

Eating

★La Gringa AMERICAN $
(www.lagringa.cl; Imperial 605; mains CH$3500-7900; ⏲8am-8pm Mon-Fri, from 10am Sat; 📶) Evoking the rainy-day cafes of the American Pacific Northwest, this charming spot run by an adorable Seattleite dishes up scrumptious muffins and baked goods, creative sandwiches (pulled pork with coffee glaze) and beautiful CH$6500 lunch menus (1pm to 4pm). Browse excellent wines and gourmet artisanal fare for great picnic options as well.

Donde El Gordito CHILEAN, SEAFOOD $
(San Bernardo 560; mains CH$3900-8000; ⏲noon-4:30pm & 6:30-10pm, closed Jun) This down-to-earth local's favorite is an intimate seafooder in the Mercado Municipal. It does wonderful things with crab sauce. It's rich but excellent.

The Office CAFE $
(San Juan 425, 2nd fl; sandwiches CH$1990-5390; ⏲8:30am-8:30pm Mon-Fri, to 10pm Sat; 📶) Overlooking the plaza, this artsy cafe does messy gourmet sandwiches big enough to share, along with organic coffee and good-value steaks, in a stylish, multiroom environment.

Drinking & Nightlife

Caffé El Barrista CAFE
(www.elbarista.cl; Martínez 211; coffee CH$1400-2800, sandwiches CH$3500-6800; ⏲8am-1am; 📶) This Italian-style coffeehouse serves the best brew in Sur Chico bar none, and draws a healthy lunch crowd for its excellent CH$6800 menus and a selection of tasty sandwiches. As night falls, it morphs into the most consistent bar in town, drawing heavily from the gaggles of guides and expats in town.

Garage BAR
(Martínez 220; ⏲hours vary) Attached to the Copec gas station, Garage caters to an artsy, alternative crowd, staying up later than it should and hosting everything from impromptu jazz sessions to all-out Colombian cumbia shakedowns...when it's open (complaints about erratic hours by its devout local following are not unfounded).

Information

There are numerous ATMs downtown.

Clínica Alemana (www.alemanapv.cl; Otto Bader 810; ⏲24hr) Near Del Salvador's southwest exit from town.

Parque Pumalín Office (☎065-225-1910; www.pumalinpark.org; Klenner 299; ⏲9am-6pm Mon-Fri) Though the park is found in Northern Patagonia, this is the official tourism office for Parque Pumalín.

Tourist office (☎065-236-1146; www.ptovaras.cl; Del Salvador 320; ⏲8:30am-9:30pm Aug-May, to 7:30pm Apr-Jul) Helpful, with brochures and free maps of the area.

Getting There & Away

Most long-distance buses originate in Puerto Montt. Buses leave from two terminals. **Cruz del Sur** (☎065-223-6969; www.busescruzdelsur.cl; San Francisco 1317; ⏲office 7am-9:30pm) is best for Chiloé and Punta Arenas, and also serves Bariloche, Argentina, with **Bus Norte** (☎065-223-4298; www.busnortechile.cl;

Andrés Bello 304, 2nd fl, office). **Terminal Tur Bus** (☎065-223-3787; www.turbus.cl; Del Salvador 1093; ⊙office 7am-11:10pm Mon-Fri, 7am-1:50pm & 4:30-11:10pm Sat & Sun) also houses JAC and Condor bus lines, with many departures north, including to Santiago.

Minibuses to and from Ensenada (CH$1200, one hour), Petrohué (CH$2500, 1½ hours), Puerto Montt (CH$800, 15 minutes), Cochamó (CH$2500, 1½ hours) and Río Puelo (CH$4000, three hours) all leave from the corner of Walker Martínez and San Bernardo. For Frutillar (CH$900, 30 minutes), buses depart from Av Gramado near San Bernardo.

DESTINATION	COST (CH$)	DURATION (HR)
Ancud	5000	2½
Bariloche, Argentina	15,000	6
Castro	6500	4½
Osorno	2000	1¼
Pucón	9300	5½
Punta Arenas	40,000	18
Santiago	25,000	12
Temuco	6500	6
Valdivia	4500	3½

Ensenada

Rustic Ensenada, 45km along a picturesque shore-hugging road from Puerto Varas, is really nothing more than a few restaurants, *hospedajes* and adventure outfitters, but for those looking for more outdoors and fewer hardwood floors, it's a nice natural setting in full view of Volcán Osorno and Volcán Calbuco. A great base is the cozy **Hamilton's Place** (☎cell 8466-4146; hamiltonsplaceensenada@gmail.com; Camino a Ensenada Km 42; s/d CH$40,000/49,000, without bathroom CH$22,000/35,000; 📶), run by a welcoming Brazilian-Canadian family who also offer delicious dinners. If you plan to climb or ski Osorno, you can gain an hour of sleep by overnighting here.

The eruption of Volcán Calbuco in April 2014 altered its profile and covered the area in ash and cinder, though tourist operations are back up and running.

Parque Nacional Vicente Pérez Rosales

In this park of celestial lakes and soaring volcanoes, Lago Todos Los Santos and Volcán Osorno may be the standouts, but they're actually just part of a crowd. One lake leads to the next and volcanoes dominate the skyline on all sides of this storied pass through the Andes range.

Parque Nacional Vicente Pérez Rosales protects 2510 sq km, including snow-tipped volcanoes Osorno (2652m), Puntiagudo (2190m) and Monte Tronador (3554m). Ruta 225 ends in Petrohué, 50km east of Puerto Varas, where there's park access. Minibuses from Puerto Varas are frequent in summer, but limited to twice daily the rest of the year.

Waterfalls boom over basalt rock at **Saltos del Petrohué** (admission CH$1500; ⊙8:30am-8pm), 6km before the village. **Petrohué** has beaches, trailheads and the dock for Cruce de Lagos departures to Peulla. Try the woodsy **Conaf campground** (☎cell 5791-4351; www.conaf.cl; campsites 1-5 persons CH$10,000). From there, a dirt track leads to **Playa Larga**, a long black-sand beach, from where **Sendero Los Alerces** heads west to meet up with **Sendero La Picada**. The sandy track climbs to Volcán Osorno's Paso Desolación, with scintillating panoramas of the lake and volcanoes. There is no road around the lake, making the interior trails only accessible by boat.

Access to climb or ski **Volcán Osorno** is near Ensenada. **Centro de Ski y Montaña Volcán Osorno** (☎065-566-624; www.volcanosorno.com; half-/full-day lift tickets CH$19,000/24,000) has two lifts for skiing and sightseeing, plus ski and snowboard rentals. Off-season, ride the ski lift (CH$14,000) up for impossibly scenic views, or take a hike.

Downhill from the ski slopes, the spruced-up **Refugio Teski** (☎065-256-6622; www.teski.cl; dm with bedding/sleeping bag CH$15,000/12,000, r without/with bathroom CH$35,000/47,000; 📶) offers unparalleled access to the mountain. With 24 hours' notice, rent out a mountainside hot tub (CH$40,000 for three hours, including a *pisco sour* and finger food), take advantage of two-for-one happy-hour drinks at sunset and make a night of it.

There is no public transportation to or from the slopes outside of package tours. To reach the ski area and *refugio* if driving, take the Ensenada–Puerto Octay road to a signpost about 3km from Ensenada and continue 10km up the lateral.

Puerto Montt

065 / POP 218,900

The capital of the Lakes District, Puerto Montt is also the region's traffic-choked, fast-growing commercial and transportation hub, with its most redeeming quality its plethora of exit points. Via plane, ferry, bus or rental car, you can get whisked away to a near-endless inventory of memorable locales. Otherwise, travelers have occasionally become endeared of the unpolished working-class Chilean atmosphere here.

Sights

Av Angelmó Street Stalls MARKET

(Av Angelmó) Along busy, diesel-fume-laden Av Angelmó is a dizzying mix of streetside stalls (selling artifacts, smoked mussels, *cochayuyo* – edible sea plant – and mysterious trinkets), crafts markets and touristy seafood restaurants with croaking waiters beckoning you to a table. Enjoy the frenzy, but keep on going...

The best quality crafts and food are found at the end of the road at the picturesque fishing port of Angelmó, 3km west of downtown. It's easily reached by frequent local buses and *colectivos*.

Casa del Arte Diego Rivera GALLERY

(www.culturapuertomontt.cl; Quillota 116; 9am-1pm & 3-6:30pm Mon-Fri) FREE A joint Mexican-Chilean project finished in 1964, the upstairs Sala Hardy Wistuba specializes in works by local artists, sculptors and photographers. Also houses a small cafe and an excellent boutique.

Iglesia Catedral CHURCH

(Urmeneta s/n) Built entirely of *alerce* in 1856, this church, located on the Plaza de Armas, is the town's oldest building and one of its few attractive ones.

Sleeping

Casa Perla GUESTHOUSE $

(065-226-2104; www.casaperla.com; Trigal 312; camping per person CH$6000, dm CH$10,000, r per person without bathroom CH$12,000; @) This welcoming family home's matriarch, Perla, will have you feeling like a sibling. English and German are spoken. All bathrooms are shared and guests can use the kitchen, where Perla makes jam and homemade bread on the wood-burning stove. It's the coziest, knick-knack-filled choice in this neighborhood.

Hospedaje Vista al Mar GUESTHOUSE $

(065-225-5625; www.hospedajevistaalmar.cl; Vivar 1337; s/d CH$25,000/35,000, without bathroom CH$15,000/28,000; @) This family-run favorite is one of nicest of the residential guesthouses, decked out in great-condition hardwoods with spick-and-span bathrooms, rooms with cable TV and wonderful bay views. Eliana fosters a family-friendly atmosphere – helpful to the nth degree – and breakfast goes a step beyond for Chile: yogurt, whole-wheat breads, cakes, muffins and (sometimes) real coffee.

House Rocco Backpacker GUESTHOUSE $

(065-227-2897; www.hospedajerocco.cl; Pudeto 233; dm/s/d CH$12,000/25,000/30,000;) This Chilean-American traveler's mainstay five blocks from the Navimag has a large sunny kitchen, warm wooden walls and floors and feather comforters. Home-cooked breakfasts of sweet crepes with *manjar* (ducle de leche, a caramel sauce) and real coffee are pluses, but it's a little rougher around the edges than the competition. Veronica, the good-hearted owner, is selling if you're interested in shining it up.

Eating & Drinking

Sanito CHILEAN $

(www.sanito.cl; Copiapó 66; menu CH$4000; 9am-8pm Mon-Fri;) Puerto Montt's best bet for healthy and homey food, served up fresh daily in an artistic atmosphere. Each day, there's a soup, salad or main menu (includes juice and coffee/tea) and à la carte salads and sandwiches (CH$2800 to CH$3500), all served up with a funky soundtrack that bounces from Arcade Fire to '70s soul.

Puerto Fritos SEAFOOD $

(Presidente Ibañez 716, Mercado Municipal Presidente Ibañez; mains CH$2800-6700; 9:30am-5:30pm Mon-Sat, 10am-6pm Sun;) Forget touristy Angelmó! All of Puerto Montt is laid out before you at this cute and unassuming local's secret with the best views in town. It's well worth the CH$3000 taxi ride for excellent *caldillo de mariscos* (seafood soup; CH$4200 to CH$4900) and *ceviches* (CH$4700 to CH$6500), all of which are served fresh directly from the colorful market downstairs.

★ **Chile Picante** CHILEAN $$

(cell 8454-8923; www.chilepicanterestoran.cl; Vicente Pérez Rosales 567; menu CH$8500; 11:30am-3:30pm & 7:30-10:30pm Mon-Sat;) Chef Francisco Sánchez Luengo is on

Puerto Montt

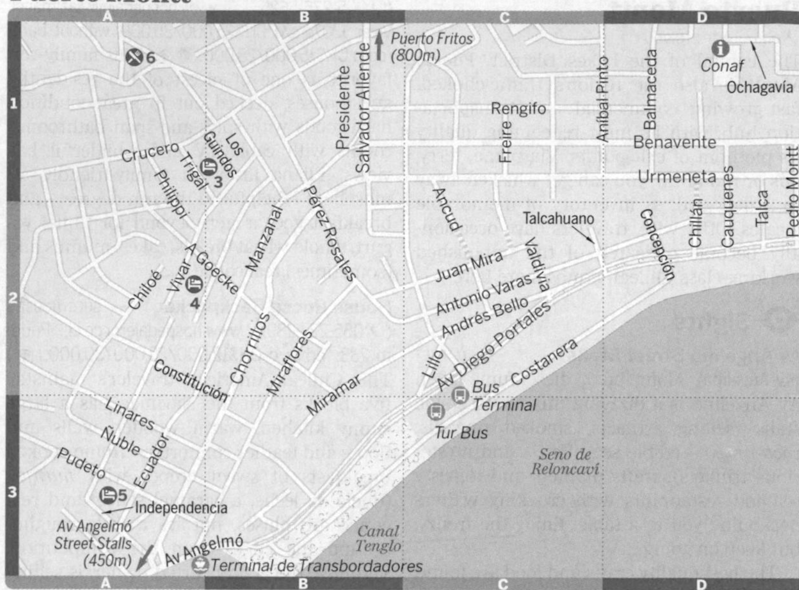

to something at this intimate and playful gourmet hot spot that's ambitious (uphill) walking distance from most of the budget sleeps. With expansive city and sea views as the backdrop, Luengo offers just a few choices in his daily-changing, three-course menu, all delicately presented yet bursting with the flavors of the market that day.

Boule Bar BAR
(Benavente 435; 6pm-3am Mon-Fri, 8pm-4am Sat) Old *Rolling Stone* covers and other musical propaganda dot this classic, multi-roomed bar lit with candles and featuring several tables and a bar rack made from tree bark. It's a good spot to carry on late into the evening with a crowd that appreciates a smart soundtrack. A long list of cocktails is 50% off until 11pm nightly.

Information

Internet cafes and ATMs abound. At night the area around the bus terminal harbors petty crime; take precautions and don't walk alone here or along the waterfront.

Clinica Los Andes (www.clinandes.cl; Av Bellavista 123; 24hr) Best private medical services in town.

Conaf (065-248-6102; Ochagaviá 458; 9am-12:45pm & 2:30-5:30pm Mon-Thu, to 4:30pm Fri) Can provide details on nearby national parks.

Sernatur (065-222-3016; www.sernatur.cl; San Martín 80; 8:30am-5:30pm Mon-Fri, 9am-3pm Sat) On the west side extension of Plaza de Armas and at arrivals in the airport (9am-6pm Mon-Fri). Stocks a wealth of brochures, but little English spoken.

Getting There & Away

AIR

LAN (600-526-2000; O'Higgins 167, Local 1-B; 9am-1:30pm & 3-6:30pm Mon-Fri, 9:30am-1:30pm Sat) flies several times daily to Punta Arenas (from CH$145,000, 2¼ hours), Balmaceda/Coyhaique (from CH$112,000, one hour) and many times daily to Santiago (from CH$185,000, 1½ hours). **Sky Airlines** (600-600-2828; www.skyairline.cl; cnr San Martín & Benavente; 9am-7pm Mon-Fri, 10am-1pm Sat) flies to Punta Arenas and Santiago with slightly cheaper fares.

BOAT

Puerto Montt is the main departure port for Patagonia. At the **Terminal de Transbordadores** (Av Angelmó 2187), you can find ticket offices and waiting lounges for both Navimag and Naviera Austral, housed inside the same building. The most popular trip is Navimag's ferry *Evangelistas*, which sails on Friday from Puerto Montt to Puerto Natales and back on Friday (boarding Thursday

Puerto Montt

Sights
1 Casa del Arte Diego Rivera E1
2 Iglesia Catedral E1

Sleeping
3 Casa Perla B1
4 Hospedaje Vista al Mar A2
5 House Rocco Backpacker A3

Eating
6 Chile Picante A1
7 Sanito F2

Drinking & Nightlife
8 Boule Bar E1

evening). It's a popular three-night journey through Chile's fjords; book passage at Navimag offices in Santiago, Puerto Montt, Puerto Natales or via the website (www.navimag.com).

High season is from November to March and low season is April to October. Prices for the trip include full board (vegetarian meals can be requested). Per-person fares vary according to the view and whether it is a private or shared bathroom; in high season single berths start at around CH$680,000, doubles from CH$359,000 per person. Cars are extra; bicycles and motorcycles can also be carried along for an additional cost. The southern route includes passage by the glacier Pio XI, the largest in South America (it's as big as Santiago), and there are more beautiful and photogenic glaciers along the way.

BUS

Puerto Montt's renovated waterfront **bus terminal** (☎065-228-3000; www.terminalpm.cl; cnr Av Diego Portales & Lillo) is the main transportation hub. Summer trips to Punta Arenas and Bariloche (Argentina) sell out, so book in advance.

Minibuses go to Puerto Varas (CH$800, 25 minutes) and Frutillar (CH$1500, one hour). Buses also go to Cochamó (CH$2500, 2½ hours) four times daily, and all carry on to Río Puelo (CH$4000).

Cruz del Sur (☎065-248-3144; www.busescruzdelsur.cl) has frequent buses to Chiloé. **Tur Bus** (☎249-3401) has daily buses to Valparaíso/Viña del Mar. Both of these, plus **Igi Llaima** (☎065-225-9320; www.igillaima.cl) and **Pullman Bus** (☎065-251-6561; www.pullman.cl), go to Santiago, stopping at various cities along the way.

For Bariloche and Cruz del Sur, **Via Bariloche** (☎065-223-3633; www.viabariloche.com.ar) and **Andesmar** (☎065-228-0999; www.andesmar.com) go daily.

DESTINATION	COST (CH$)	DURATION (HR)
Ancud	4500	2½
Bariloche, Argentina	18,000	6
Castro	6200	4
Concepción	15,000	10
Coyhaique	36,000	24
Osorno	2500	1½
Pucón	9500	5½
Punta Arenas	45,000	30
Quellón	8000	6
Santiago	27,000	12-14
Temuco	6700	5
Valdivia	5000	3½
Valparaíso/Viña del Mar	23,000	15

Getting Around

Andrés Tour (☎065-225-6611; www.andres-tur.com) shuttles go hourly to **Aeropuerto El Tepual** (☎065-229-4161; www.aeropuertoeltepual.cl), 16km west of town, from the bus terminal (CH$3000). Car-rental agency **Europcar** (☎065-236-8216; Antonia Varas 162; 8am-7pm Mon-Fri, to 1:30pm Sat) can help get the permission certificate to take rental vehicles into Argentina with two days' notice.

CHILOÉ

Emerald green and shrouded in fog, the mysteriously appealing Isla Grande de Chiloé is the continent's second-largest island and is home to a fiercely independent, seafaring people who developed culturally and politically out of step with the mainland. Their historic position as Spanish loyalists was largely due to the great Jesuit influence.

On the surface you will see changes in architecture and cuisine: *tejuelas* (the famous Chilote wood shingles), *palafitos* (houses mounted on stilts along the water's edge), more than 150 iconic wooden churches (14 of which are Unesco World Heritage Sites) and *curanto* (the renowned meat, potato and seafood stew). A closer look reveals a rich spiritual culture that is based on a distinctive mythology of witchcraft, ghost ships and forest creatures.

Chiloé

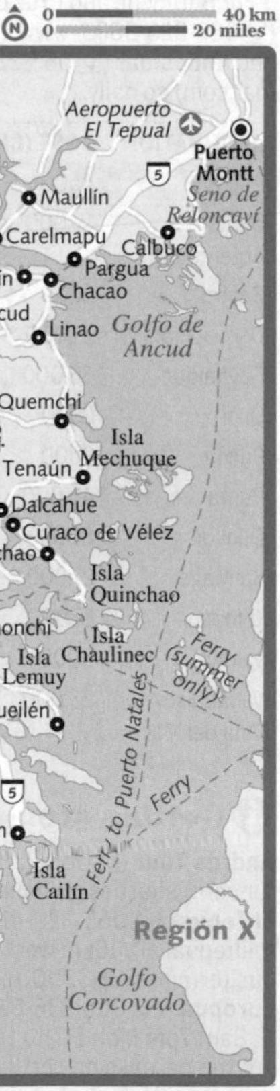

0 — 40 km
0 — 20 miles

The undulating hills, remote national parks, and dense forests of this windswept landscape give Chiloé a flavor that's unique in South America. In an archipelago of more than 40 minor islands, the main island is a lush quilt of hilly pastureland, 180km long but just 50km wide. Towns and farms tilt toward the eastern side; the western shores are a nearly roadless network of thick forests lapping the wild Pacific.

Ancud

☎065 / POP 40,800

Bustling and weathered, urban Ancud offers an earthy base to explore the penguin colonies and walk or sea kayak the blustery, dazzling north coast.

Sights

★Centro de Visitantes Inmaculada Concepción MUSEUM

(www.iglesiasdechiloe.cl; Errázuriz 227; suggested donation CH$500; 10am-7pm Dec-Feb, to 6pm Mar-Nov) Don't even think about visiting Chiloé's Unesco churches without first stopping in at this excellent museum housed in the former Convento Inmaculada Concepción de Ancud (1875). It's home to wooden scale models of all 16 churches, which show the workings of the intricate interior woodwork of each.

★Museo Regional de Ancud MUSEUM

(Museo Chilote; www.museoancud.cl; Libertad 370; adult/child CH$600/300; 10am-7:30pm Jan & Feb, 10am-5:30pm Tue-Fri, 10am-2pm Sat & Sun Mar-Dec) The excellent Museo Regional Aurelio Bórquez Canobra, casually referred to as Museo Chilote, offers fantastic displays tracking the history of the island, including a full-sized replica of the *Ancud,* which sailed the treacherous fjords of the Strait of Magellan to claim Chile's southernmost territories.

Fuerte San Antonio FORTRESS

(cnr Lord Cochrane & Baquedano; 8:30am-9pm Mon-Fri, 9am-8pm Sat & Sun) FREE During the wars of independence, Fuerte San Antonio was Spain's last Chilean outpost. At the northwest corner of town, late-colonial cannon emplacements look down on the harbor from the early-19th-century remains of the fortress. There's a somewhat secluded beach, Playa Gruesa, behind the north wall.

Tours

Many agencies around town run minibus tours to see the penguins at Monumento Natural Islotes de Puñihuil for around CH$17,000.

Austral Adventures OUTDOORS
(065-262-5977; www.austral-adventures.com; Av Costanera 904) This is the go-to agency for English-speaking tours from Ancud, including extended nature-centric jaunts to see the penguins and whales, kayaking on the bay and bird-watching – always with a fierce eco-slant and more elaborate than the cookie-cutter tours. American owner Britt Lewis is impossibly nice and knowledgeable.

Sleeping

★13 Lunas Hostel HOSTEL $
(065-262-2106; www.13lunas.cl; Los Carrera 855; dm from CH$10,500, s/d 19,000/33,000;) The best option for migrating backpackers, this helpful hostel can't be missed, situated directly across from the Cruz del Sur bus terminal: its bright-green-and-yellow motif screams artsy Chiloé. Owner Claudio is young, enthusiastic and speaks English. The lovely hostel oozes coziness with bright hardwoods, beacons of natural light, hotel-level bathrooms, a grassy lawn and a wonderful terrace with views.

Chiloé Turismo Rural HOMESTAY $
(www.chiloeturismorural.cl) Chiloé's agrotourism association organizes excursions to farming and fishing communities, as well as private homes that offer meals and lodging in several small towns and rural outposts. Pick up a catalog at Sernatur.

Camping Arena Gruesa CAMPGROUND $
(065-262-3428; www.hotelarenagruesa.cl; Av Costanera Norte 290; campsites per person CH$5000, s/d incl breakfast from CH$20,080/36,000;) Located atop a bluff on the north side of town, city campsites don't get much better views than this. The area is grassy and decently maintained with electricity, hot water at night, tiny *refugios* for rainy days and bright, surprisingly clean bathrooms. It's also a minute's walk to the beach.

Hostal Mundo Nuevo HOSTEL $$
(065-262-8383; www.hostalmundonuevo.com; Costanera 748; dm CH$13,000, s/d/q CH$32,000/43,000/54,000, s/d without bathroom CH$24,000/34,000;) This Swiss-owned midrange place masquerading as a hostel is just a hop, skip and a jump from Cruz del Sur's bus station. It boasts postcard-perfect sunset views over the Bay of Ancud from a big, comfortable bench on its naturally lit front porch as well as the 12 privates and a six-bed dorm.

The new outdoor hot tub (from CH$12,000 for up to eight guests) is well worth reserving a few hours in advance.

Eating & Drinking

Mercado Gastronómico MARKET $
(Dieciocho) Tucked away off Dieciocho is a series of down-home market stalls doing *cazuela* (meat and vegetable stew), *chupe* (fish casserole) and set lunch menus for around CH$2000 to CH$5000.

Retro's Pub RESTO-BAR $
(Ramírez 317; mains CH$4300-9000, pizza CH$9000-12,500; noon-2am Mon-Fri, 8pm-4am Sat;) Inside this cozy home, Ancud's most timeless bar spreads itself among several rooms. The menu is chock-full of Tex-Mex, as well as killer burgers the size of Kansas (fork required) on sourdough-reminiscent buns, stone-cooked pizza, sandwiches and pasta – everything made from scratch, everything a great homesickness remedy.

Q'ilú RESTO BAR $
(www.qilurestobar.blogspot.com; Ramírez 278; mains CH$3600-8000; 10am-1am Mon-Thu, to 2am Fri-Sat;) This stylish resto-bar does a well-executed and tasty *menú del día* (inexpensive set meal; CH$3500; until 1pm) in a hardwood-heavy atmosphere that doubles – as is usually the case in Ancud – as a great place for a drink as well.

Club Social Mehadier BAR
(Baquedano 469; beers CH$2500; noon-2am, closed Sun) A Temuco nightlife veteran has opened Ancud's most interesting and classiest new bar, housed in a restored shingled Chilote house that once hosted a social club of the same name in the '60s and '70s. There's craft beer on draft – Cuello Negro and Kross – and Victorian-like sofas and decor to lounge on. Pizza and pasta served.

Information

Conaf (065-262-7520; Errázuriz 317; 9am-12:50pm & 2:30-5:30pm Mon & Wed, 9am-12:50pm & 2:30-4:30pm Fri) National park info.

Hospital de Ancud (www.hospitalancud.gov.cl; Almirante Latorre 301; ⌚24hr) Located at the corner of Pedro Montt.

Sernatur (☎065-262-2800; www.sernatur.cl; Libertad 665; ⌚8:30am-7pm Mon-Fri, 9:30am-7pm Sat & Sun Dec-Feb, to 6pm Mon-Thu, 8:30am-5pm Fri Mar-Nov; wi-fi) This is the only formal national tourist office on the island; very helpful staff, brochures, town maps, lists of accommodations and wi-fi.

Getting There & Away

Cruz del Sur (☎065-262-2265; www.busescruzdelsur.cl; ⌚6:30am-10pm Mon-Sat, 7am-10pm Sun) owns and operates the main **Terminal de Buses** (cnr Los Carreras & Cavada), which offers nearly hourly departures to Chiloé's more southerly towns, and to cities on the Panamericana to the north, including three daily departures to Santiago (CH$17,000, 17 hours). It's a five-minute walk from the waterfront and downtown.

Chiloé's more rural destinations to the east are serviced by buses that leave from the small inter-rural bus station on Colo Colo above the Bigger supermarket (buy tickets on the bus.)

Castro

☎065 / POP 41,600

Castro is the attractive, idiosyncratic capital of Chiloé. With the last decade's salmon boom, this working-class town transformed its homespun island offerings with modern mega-supermarkets and boutique hotels. At times loud and boisterous, the capital of the archipelago somehow retains its local Chilote character side by side with a comfortable tourism infrastructure. Located in the dead center of the island, Castro is a perfect base for exploring attractions further afield.

Sights

Don't miss the distinctive *palafitos* houses, which testify to Castro's heritage of humble beginnings in 1567. From the street, they resemble any other houses in town, but their backsides jut over the water and, at high tide, serve as piers with boats tethered to the stilts. They're mostly along Costanera Pedro Montt, north of town.

★Iglesia San Francisco de Castro CHURCH
(San Martín; ⌚9:30am-10pm Jan & Feb, 9:30am-12:30pm & 3:30-8:30pm Mar-Dec) Italian Eduardo Provasoli chose a marriage of neo-Gothic and classical architecture in his design for the elaborate Iglesia San Francisco, one of Chiloé's Unesco gems and finished in 1912 to replace an earlier church that burned down (which had replaced an even earlier church that had burned down).

Museo Regional de Castro MUSEUM
(Esmeralda 255; ⌚9:30am-7pm Mon-Fri, 9:30am-6:30pm Sat, 10:30am-1pm Sun Jan & Feb, 9:30am-1pm & 3-6:30pm Mon-Fri, 9:30am-1pm Sat Mar-Dec) FREE This museum, half a block from Plaza de Armas, houses a well-organized collection of Huilliche relics, musical instruments, traditional farm implements and Chilota wooden boat models, and exhibits on the evolution of Chiloé's towns. Its black-and-white photographs of the 1960 earthquake help you to understand the impact of the tragic event.

Tours

★Chiloétnico CULTURAL, ADVENTURE TOUR
(☎065-630-951; www.chiloetnico.cl; Ernesto Riquelme 1228) This highly recommended trilingual (fluent English and German) agency is doing the right things in the right places. Jata runs great mountain-biking and hiking trips to Parque Nacional Chiloé, Parque Tantauco and nearby islands; and cultural trips out to some of Chiloé's more obscure Unesco churches on the less-trampled secondary islands where tourism is still a novelty.

Also rents camping gear and bikes.

Chiloé Natural KAYAKING
(☎cell 6319-7388; www.chiloenatural.com; Pedro Montt 210) This extremely friendly, environmentally conscious agency specializes in kayaking, both as rentals (CH$5000 per hour) as well as half-/multiday trips around Castro and further afield (from CH$3500 per person).

Sleeping

Hostal Cordillera GUESTHOUSE $
(☎065-253-2247; www.hostalcordillera.cl; Barros Arana 175; s/d CH$18,000/35,000, r per person without bathroom CH$15,000; @wi-fi) Weather dragging you down? The firecracker owner at this traveler's hub will smother you with motherly love and put a big smile on your face. You'll get some sea views, large bathrooms (the two newly renovated ones are upstairs), comfy beds, electric heaters and cable TV.

Palafito Hostel HOSTEL $$
(☎065-253-1008; www.palafitohostel.com; Ernesto Riquelme 1210; dm/s/d CH$15,000/

30,000/42,000; @📶) This flashpackers hostel sitting on Palafitos Gamboa with spiritual views over the Fiordo de Castro revolutionized Castro when it opened in 2008 and was the catalyst for turning the city into a hip destination. You pay more for a dorm here, but the quality (and lockers) outweighs the difference, with great breakfasts, dreamy views and a cabin-cool feel throughout.

Palafito 1326 BOUTIQUE HOTEL **$$**
(☎065-253-0053; www.palafito1326.cl; Ernesto Riquelme 1326; s/d from CH$52,000/62,000; @📶) Following a Chilote design aesthetic carved entirely from tepú and cypress woods, this *palofito* design hotel has 12 smallish rooms with high-style touches like wool throws from Dalcahue. The fjord-view rooms make you feel like you're sleeping over wetlands.

Eating & Drinking

★Hostalomera CHILEAN **$**
(www.hostalomera.com; Balmaceda 241; menu CH$2800; ⏲1-5pm Mon-Sat & 7-10pm Tue-Sat; 📶) You can't eat this well in this cool kind of atmosphere for this price anywhere else. How it can be done without bleeding money is an extraordinary question, but this art-fueled lunch hot spot offers five exceptional home-cooked choices per day, including an appetizer and juice for a wallet-friendly CH$2800.

Café del Puente CAFE, BREAKFAST **$**
(Ernesto Riquelme 1180b; mains CH$1200-5200; ⏲9am-9pm Tue-Sun; 📶) Cure the breakfast blues (and more)! This atmospheric baby-blue cafe-teahouse over the water does everything you're missing: eggs, bacon, French toast, muesli, whole-wheat bread... and does it well. Afternoon tea and classy sandwiches throughout the day.

★Mercadito CONTEMPORARY CHILEAN **$$**
(www.elmercaditodechiloe.cl; Pedro Montt 210; mains CH$6400-8200; ⏲1-4pm & 8-11pm Mon-Wed; 📶) This wonderfully whimsical spot is the place in Castro proper for foodies. Creative takes calling on the wares of local farmers produce outstanding dishes that present painstaking choices: crab phyllo-dough wraps doused in vermouth, tempura hake over mashed fava beans, stuffed shells with surf clams in pil-pil sauce. Dishes tend toward the rich side, but are worth it.

Almud Bar BAR
(Serrano 325; craft beer CH$2500-4000; ⏲6:30pm-2am Mon-Thu, 7:30pm-3:30am Fri, from 8:30pm Sat) The best proper bar in Castro – named after Chiloé's unit of measurement for potatoes – offers a wide range of cocktails, craft beers, sparking wines and some bar grub for it all to be chased by.

Information

ATMs are found around the plaza.

Conaf (☎065-253-2501; Gamboa 424; ⏲9am-1pm & 2-6pm Mon-Thu, to 5pm Fri) The official Chilean parks department has a limited amount of information in Spanish and English on Parque Nacional Chiloé.

CorreosChile (www.correos.cl; O'Higgins 388; ⏲9am-1:30pm & 3-6pm Mon-Fri, 9:30am-12:30pm Sat) On the west side of Plaza de Armas.

Hospital de Castro (www.hospitalcastro.gov.cl; Freire 852)

Parque Tantauco Office (☎065-263-3805; www.parquetantauco.cl; Panamericana Sur 1826; ⏲9am-6pm Jan & Feb, 9am-6pm Mon-Fri Mar-Dec) The official office of Parque Tantauco.

Tourist Information (☎065-254-7706; www.visitchiloe.cl; Plaza de Armas; ⏲10am-9pm Jan & Feb, to 7pm Mar-Dec) A large kiosk stocking some helpful brochures and maps.

Getting There & Away

AIR

Newish **Aerodrómo Mocopulli**, located 20km north of town, offers commercial flights. **LAN** (☎065-263-2866; www.lan.com; O'Higgins 412; ⏲9am-1pm & 3-6:15pm Mon-Fri, 9:30am-1:15pm Sat) flies from Santiago via Puerto Montt.

BOAT

Naveira Austral (☎065-263-5254; www.navieraustral.cl; Latorre 238) Summer ferries to/from Chaitén depart Sunday at midnight in January and February. Fares range from CH$12,000 (seat) to CH$25,700 (berth with window). Vehicles cost CH$82,000.

BUS

Centrally located Castro is the bus hub for Chiloé. **Terminal de Buses Municipal** (San Martín) has the most services to smaller destinations around the island and some long-distance services. Buses to Mocopulli (CH$600), Dalcahue (CH$800), Chonchi (CH$800), Isla Quinchao (CH$1400) and Tenaún (CH$1500) all leave from here. The **Cruz del Sur terminal** (☎065-263-5152; www.busescruzdelsur.cl; San Martín 486) focuses on transportation to Quellón and Ancud, and has more long-distance services. Fares include Ancud (CH$1500,1½ hours), Puerto Montt (CH$6200, four hours) and Temuco (CH$12,000, 10 hours).

Dalcahue & Isla Quinchao

Dalcahue, 20km northeast of Castro, has a 19th-century Unesco church, **Nuestra Señora de Los Dolores**, and a famous **crafts fair** (9am-6pm Dec-Feb, 9am-5pm Sun Mar-Nov) where you can buy the island's most authentic arts and crafts: sweaters, socks and hats woven from *oveja* (wool) and dyed with natural pigments made from roots, leaves and iron-rich mud. It's open daily but best on Sundays. **Hostal Encanto Patagon** (065-264-1651; www.hostalencantopatagon.blogspot.com; Perdro Montt 148; dm CH$8000, r without bathroom per person CH$10,000;) offers rooms in an enchanting, century-old Chilote home, with home cooking.

Midway between Dalcahue and Achao, **Curaco de Vélez** dates from 1660 and has a treasure of Chilote architecture, plus an outstanding open-air oyster bar at the beach. Buses between Achao and Dalcahue stop in Curaco.

Isla Quinchao, southeast of Dalcahue, is one of the most accessible islands, and worth a day trip. Isla Quinchao's largest town, **Achao**, features Chiloé's oldest church. Wooden pegs, instead of nails, hold together **Iglesia Santa María de Loreto**. Stay at **Hospedaje Plaza** (065-266-1283; Amunátegui 20; s/d CH$8000/16,000, without bathroom CH$7000/14,000), a friendly family home. Overlooking the pier, **Mar y Velas** (Serrano 2; mains CH$4500-8000; 9am-1am) serves up mussels, clams and cold beer. The **bus terminal** (cnr Miraflores & Zañartu) is a block south of the church. Buses run daily to Dalcahue (CH$1200) and Castro (CH$1600) every 15 to 30 minutes.

Parque Nacional Chiloé

Gorgeous evergreen forests meet taupe stretches of sand and the boundless, thrashing Pacific in this 430-sq-km **national park** (065-297-0724; adult/child CH$1500/750; 9am-8:30pm Dec-Mar 15, to 6:30pm Mar 16-Nov), 54km west of Castro. The park protects diverse birds, Chilote foxes and the reclusive *pudú* (the world's smallest deer.) Visitors are at the mercy of Pacific storms, so expect lots of rain.

Access the park through Cucao, a minute village with growing amenities, and park sector Chanquín, where Conaf runs a **visitor center** (9am-8:30pm Dec-Mar 15, to 6:30pm Mar 16-Nov) with information. **Sendero Interpretivo El Tepual** winds 1km along fallen tree trunks through thick forest. The 2km **Sendero Dunas de Cucao** leads to a series of dunes behind a long, white-sand beach. The most popular route is the 25km **Sendero Chanquín–Cole Cole**, which follows the coast past Lago Huelde to Río Cole Cole. The hike continues 8km north to Río Anay, passing through groves of red myrtles.

Sleeping & Eating

Most accommodations and restaurants are past the bridge from Cucao.

Cucao Home GUESTHOUSE $
(cell 5400-5944; cucaohome@gmail.com; Laura Vera, Cucao; dm CH$7000, s/d without bathroom CH$15,000/30,000;) A young upstart from Puerto Natalas has rented this traditional budget option in Cucao (formerly Hospedaje Paraiso) and given it a backpacker-friendly makeover. There's a small cafe and it has the cheapest dorm beds in town. It's inside a faded pink house a few hundred meters before the bridge and offers a fantastic river view.

Camping Chanquín CAMPGROUND $
(cell 9507-2559; contacto@parquechiloe.cl; campsite per person CH$5000, cabañas CH$60,000) In the park, 200m beyond the visitors center. Good amenities and a covered rain area. Cabins are spacious and recently renovated.

★**Palafito Cucao Hostel** HOTEL $$
(065-297-1164; www.hostelpalafitocucao.cl; Sector Chanquín; dm CH$15,000, s/d/tr CH$40,000/50,000/70,000;) This equally chic sister hotel of Palafito 1326 and Palafito Hostel in Castro offers by far the best and most comfortable bed in Cucao, whether you lay your head in the stylish private rooms or equally fashionable six-bed dorm.

It's a beautiful hotel on the Lago Cucao, with a cozy common area and kitchen, and a lovely wraparound terrace with outstanding views and an outdoor hot tub.

Getting There & Away

There is regular bus transportation between Castro and Cucao. Schedules vary, but there are usually numerous buses daily (CH$1800, one hour).

Quellón

065 / POP 24,000

Those imagining a pot of gold and rainbows at the end of the Carretera Panamericana will be surprised by this dumpy port – most travelers only head this way to make ferry connections to Chaitén. Waterfront lodging **Hotel El Chico Leo** (065-268-1567; ligorina@hotmail.com; Costanera Pedro Montt 325; r per person CH$15,000-28,000, without bathroom CH$9000;) offers the best value, with clean, bright rooms, attentive staff and quality beds. Eat seafood lunches there or gourmet sandwiches at **Isla Sandwich** (Juan Ladrilleros 190; sandwiches CH$3500-6500; 10:30am-9pm Mon-Fri, noon-8pm Sat;).

Cruz del Sur and Transchiloé buses leave from the **bus terminal** (065-268-1284; cnr Pedro Aguirre Cerda & Miramar) for Castro frequently (CH$2000, two hours). **Naviera Austral** (065-268-2207; www.navieraustral.cl; Pedro Montt 457; 9am-1pm & 3-7pm Mon-Fri, 10am-1pm & 4-10pm Sat) sails to Chaitén (from CH$15,500) on Thursday at 3am throughout the year.

NORTHERN PATAGONIA

A web of rivers, peaks and sprawling glaciers long ago provided a natural boundary between northern Patagonia and the rest of the world. Pinochet's **Carretera Austral** (Hwy 7) was the first road to effectively link these remote regions in the 1980s. Isolation has kept the local character fiercely self-sufficient and tied to nature's clock. '*Quien se apura en la Patagonia pierde el tiempo,*' locals say ('Those who hurry in Patagonia lose time'). Weather decides all in this nowhere land beyond the Lakes District. So don't rush. Missed flights, delayed ferries and floods are routine to existence; take the wait as locals would – another opportunity to heat the kettle and strike up a slow talk over maté.

Starting south of Puerto Montt, the Carretera Austral links widely separated towns and hamlets all the way to Villa O'Higgins, a total of just over 1200km. High season (from mid-December through February) offers considerably more travel options and availability. Combination bus and ferry circuits afford visitors a panoramic vision of the region. As well as Parque Pumalín to Lago General Carrera, there's plenty more to see in this region. Don't hesitate to tread off the beaten track: the little villages along the road and its furthest hamlets of Cochrane, Caleta Tortel and Villa O'Higgins are fully worth exploring.

Parque Pumalín

Verdant and pristine, this 2889-sq-km park encompasses vast extensions of temperate rainforest, clear rivers, seascapes and farmland. A remarkable forest-conservation effort, **Parque Pumalín** (www.pumalinpark.org) FREE attracts international visitors keen to explore these tracts of forest stretching from near Hornopirén to Chaitén. Founded by American Doug Tompkins, it is Chile's largest private park and one of the largest private parks in the world. Visit the excellent website for more information.

The 2008 eruption of Volcán Chaitén kept the park closed for a few years; it reopened in 2011. The most popular route – for a good reason – is the **Volcán Chaitén Crater Trail**. The five-hour round trip ascends the blast path to view the puffing crater. **Sendero Cascadas** (three hours round trip) is an undulating climb through dense forest that ends at a large waterfall. Ko'Kayak (p495) does kayak trips through Pumalín's fjords. Information centers and the park website detail available campgrounds, including **Camping Rio Gonzalo** (Caleta Gonzalo; campsites per person CH$2500), north of Chaitén on the shores of Reñihué Fjord, and the lovely, expansive **Sector Amarillo** (campsites per person CH$2500), south of Chaitén.

Information

Centros de Visitantes (www.parquepumalin.cl; Caleta Gonzalo & El Amarillo; 9am-7pm Mon-Sat, 10am-4pm Sun) has park brochures, photographs and environmental information as well as regional artisan goods for sale. If it's locked, ask someone at the café to open it for you. The website has updated information.

Getting There & Away

Naviera Austral (065-270-431; www.taustral.cl; passenger/car CH$10,000/64,000)

Carretera Austral

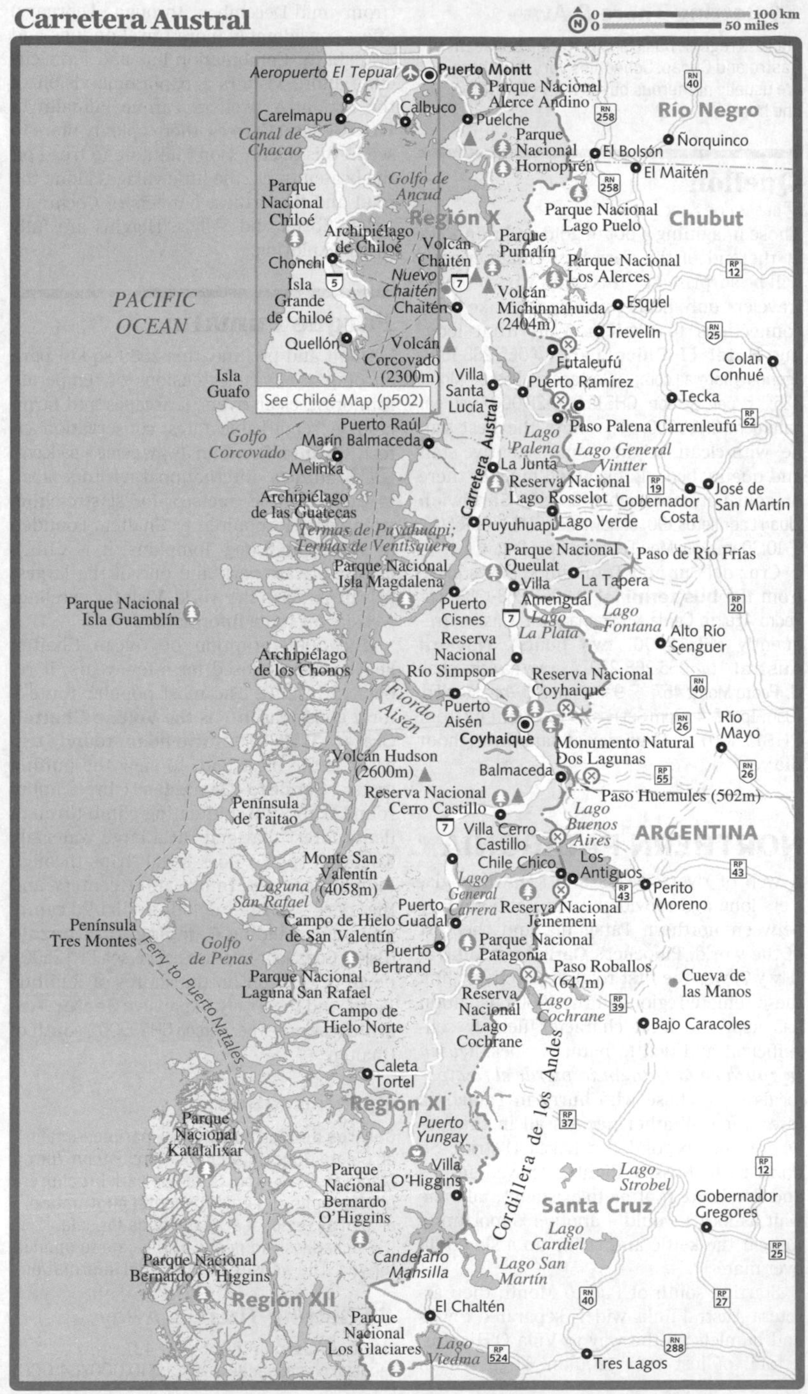

ferries sail daily from Caleta Gonzalo to Hornopirén (five to six hours) twice daily in high season. Bus-boat combos from Puerto Montt can drop visitors in the park on the way to Chaitén. See the website for details.

Futaleufú

065 / POP 1800

The Futaleufú's wild, frosty-mint waters have made this modest mountain town famous. A small 20-block grid of pastel-painted houses 155km southeast of Chaitén, it's not just a mecca for kayaking and rafting, it also boasts fly-fishing, hiking and horse riding. Improved roads and growing numbers of package-tour visitors mean it isn't off the map anymore – just note the ratio of Teva sandals to woolen *mantas* (shawls). That said, it's still a fun place to be.

Tours

The Futa or 'Fu,' as it's known, is a demanding river, with some sections only appropriate for experienced rafters. Depending on the outfitter you choose and the services included, rafting the Futaleufú starts at CH$40,000 per person for a half-day section known as Bridge to Bridge.

Ideal for families, rafting trips on the Class III Río Espolón cost around CH$15,000 for the five-hour trip. Novice kayakers can try this river or head to Lago Espolón for a float trip.

Bio Bio Expeditions OUTDOORS
(022-196-4258, US toll free 1-800-246-7238; www.bbxrafting.com) A pioneer in the region, this ecologically minded group offers river descents, horse treks and more. It is well established but may take walk-ins.

Expediciones Chile OUTDOORS
(065-562-639; www.exchile.com; Mistral 296) A secure rafting operator with loads of experience. Specializes in weeklong packages but offers kayaking, mountain biking and horse riding as well.

Sleeping & Eating

Las Natalias HOSTEL $
(cell 9631-1330; www.hostallasnatalias.info; dm/d/tr CH$10,000/24,000/30,000, d without bathroom CH$20,000) Named for four generations of Natalias, this welcoming spot is a great deal for backpackers, with tips on outdoor options. There are plenty of shared bathrooms, a large communal area, mountain views and a guest kitchen. It's a 10-minute walk from the center. Follow Cerda and signs for the northwest outskirts of town; it's on the right after the hill climb.

Camping Puerto Espolón CAMPGROUND $
(cell 7721-9239; http://lagoespolon.cl; campsite per person CH$5000, cabins from CH$35,000; Jan & Feb;) A gorgeous setting on a sandy riverbank flanked by mountains, just before the entrance to town. Campers have hot showers. Hosts Anibal and Elma also offer *asados* (barbecues; CH$10,000 per person), meals and discounts for longer stays.

Rincón de Mama CHILEAN $
(065-272-1208; O'Higgins 465 alley; mains CH$6000; 11:30am-2:30pm & 6:30-10pm Mon-Sat) This homespun restaurant with citrus colors and plastic tablecloths is one of the better deals in town for home-cooked meals and friendly service. It's on the 2nd floor of a rambling alleyway house.

VOLCÁN CHAITÉN WAKES UP

No one had even considered it a volcano, but that was to change quickly. On May 2, 2008, Volcán Chaitén, 10km northeast of its namesake town, began a monthlong eruption with a 20km-high column of ash. The rampage caused flooding and severe damage to homes, roads and bridges, decimated thousands of livestock and spewed ash as far as Buenos Aires. Chaitén's 4000 inhabitants were evacuated.

Located in Parque Pumalín, the volcano is viewed from the main park road. For stunning views of the smoking crater, hike the **Volcán Chaitén Crater Trail**. Go early or late in the day during summer, as there's little shade. You will see forests on the volcano's northeastern flank calcified by pyroclastic flows. The crater has yawned open to 3km in diameter, hosting within it a new complex of quickly formed rhyolitic domes.

The park reopened in 2011, thanks to park rangers who worked tirelessly on its recovery. Volcán Chaitén remains under constant monitoring by Sernageomin (www.sernageomin.cl), the government agency for geology and mining.

Information

Bring all the money you'll need; **BancoEstado** (cnr O'Higgins & Manuel Rodríguez) has the only ATM, and it only takes Mastercard. The helpful **tourist office** (O'Higgins 536; 9am-9pm) has information on local treks.

Getting There & Away

Buses Becker (065-272-1360; www.buses-becker.com; cnr Balmaceda & Pratt; 9am-1pm & 3-7pm) goes to Coyhaique (CH$24,000, 10 hours) every Friday via Villa Santa Lucía (two hours), La Junta and Puyuhuapi. Cumbres Nevadas goes north to Chaitén (CH$3000, 3½ hours) at 11am and 2pm from Monday to Saturday. Frontera Sur travels to Palena (CH$1200, two hours) three times per week.

TransAustral (065-721-360; cnr Balmaceda & Pratt) travels to Puerto Montt at 8am on Wednesday and Sunday (CH$25,000, 12 hours, via Argentina). The same office also sells air and ferry tickets originating from Chaitén to Puerto Montt, worth buying in advance.

International buses (065-272-1458; Cerda 436, Telefonica office) to the Argentine border (CH$2500) leave at 9am on Monday and Friday. The Futaleufú border post is far quicker and more efficient than the crossing at Palena, opposite the Argentine border town of Carrenleufú.

Puyuhuapi

In 1935 four German immigrants settled this remote rainforest outpost, inspired by explorer Hans Steffen's adventures. The agricultural colony grew with Chilote textile workers, whose skills fed the success of the 1947 German **Fábrica de Alfombras** (www.puyuhuapi.com; Aysen s/n; tours per group CH$5000), still weaving carpets today. Located 6km south of Puyuhuapi, **Termas del Ventisquero** (067-231-4686; www.termasventisqueropuyuhuapi.cl; admission CH$17,000; 9am-11pm Dec-Feb, reduced winter hours) is a peaceful hot-springs complex. Contact **Experiencia Austral** (cell 7766-1524, cell 8258-5799; www.experienciaaustral.com; Otto Uebel 36) to kayak the fjord, rent bikes or take a guided hike in Parque Nacional Queulat.

The best bargain accommodations option is **Hostal Comuyhuapi** (cell 7766-1984; www.comuy-huapi.cl; Llautureo 143; dm/d CH$10,000/30,000;). The historic **Casa Ludwig** (067-232-5220; www.casaludwig.cl; Uebel 202; s/d CH$25,000/48,000, without bathroom from CH$18,000/30,000; Oct-Mar) is elegant and snug – a real treat with a roaring fire and big breakfasts at the large communal table. **El Muelle** (cell 7654-3598; Otto Ubel s/n; mains CH$5000-8000; noon-10pm Tue-Sun) does big lunches of fresh seafood.

For information, stop by the helpful **tourist office** (www.puertopuyuhuapi.cl; Otto Uebel s/n; 10am-1:30pm & 3-8pm Fri-Wed). Buses that run between Coyhaique and Chaitén will drop passengers in Puyuhuapi. Buy your return ticket as far ahead as possible. **Buses Becker** (067-232-167) goes to Chaitén and Futaleufu a few days per week. **Terra Austral** (Nido de Puyes supermarket) and **Aguilas Patagonicas** (in Coyhaique 067-221-1288; http://aguilaspatagonicas.cl) leave at 6am daily for Coyhaique.

Parque Nacional Queulat

The 1540-sq-km **Parque Nacional Queulat** (admission CH$4000; 8:30am-5:30pm) is a wild realm of rivers winding through forests thick with ferns and southern beech. Its steep-sided fjords are flanked by creeping glaciers. From Conaf's **Centro de Información Ambiental** (8:30am-5:30pm) there is a 3km hike to a lookout with views of **Ventisquero Colgante**, a chalk blue hanging glacier.

Just north of the southern entrance at Pudú (Km 170), a damp trail climbs the valley of the **Río de las Cascadas** through a dense forest to a granite bowl where half a dozen waterfalls spring from hanging glaciers.

Coyhaique

067 / POP 59,000

The cow town that kept growing, Coyhaique is the regional hub of rural Aisén, urbane enough to house the latest techie trends, mall fashions and discos. All this is plopped in the middle of an undulating mountain range, with rocky humpback peaks and snowy summits in the backdrop. For the visitor, it's the launch pad for far-flung adventures, be it fly-fishing, trekking the ice cap or rambling the Carretera Austral to its end. For those fresh from the rainforest wilderness of northern Aisén, it can be a jarring relapse into the world of semi trucks and subdivisions. Rural workers come to join the timber or salmon industries and add to the growing urban mass.

Sights & Activities

Lago Elizalde LAKE

One of many serene mountain lakes surrounding Coyhaique and great for trout fishing, kayaking or simply time at the beach. It's just 33km from Coyhaique. Buses depart from the bus terminal.

Reserva Nacional Coyhaique PARK

(admission CH$2000) Draped in lenga, ñire and coigue, the 21.5-sq-km Reserva Nacional Coyhaique has small lakes and Cerro Cinchao (1361m). The park is 5km from Coyhaique (about 1½ hours on foot), with views of town and Cerro Macay's enormous basalt columns in the distance. Take Baquedano north, across the bridge, then go right at the gravel road, a steep climb best accessed by 4WD.

Tours

Casa del Turismo Rural CULTURAL TOUR

(cell 7954-4794; www.casaturismorural.cl; Plaza de Armas; 10:30am-7:30pm Mon-Fri, 2-6pm Sat) This organization networks visitors to rural homestays and local guide services for a grassroots approach to trekking, fishing and horse riding. Also offers city tours and *asados* (barbecues).

Sleeping

Patagonia Hostel HOSTEL $

(cell 6240-6974; www.patagonia-hostel.com; Lautaro 667; dm/d CH$14,000/34,000;) A welcoming German-run hostel. The rooms are stylish and minimal, but splurge with 2m-long beds and huge pillows. Tea is always available and breakfast includes fruit, cheese, salami and jam. Also offers tour services and bike rentals (CH$15,000/day).

Residencial Mónica GUESTHOUSE $

(067-223-4302; Lillo 664; r per person CH$12,000) Well-attended and warm, this prim '60s-style home is always full.

Camping La Alborada CAMPGROUND $

(067-223-8868; Km 1 Coyhaique-Puerto Aysén; campsite per person CH$4000) Only 1km from the city, this campground has exceptionally clean and sheltered sites (with roofs), lots of bathrooms and individual sinks, hot showers, fire pits and electricity.

Patagonia Live GUESTHOUSE $$

(067-223-0892, cell 9886-7982; www.hostalpatagonialive.cl; Lillo 826; s/d/tw CH$28,000/39,000/45,000;) Victor warmly welcomes guests into his immaculate suburban home with a guest breakfast nook. Rooms are comfortable and modern. With discounts for carbon offsets and a list of local artists who welcome visits.

Eating

★Mamma Gaucha PIZZA $

(067-221-0721; www.mammagaucha.cl; Paseo Horn 47; mains CH$5000-9000; 10am-1:30am Mon-Sat) Fusing Patagonian lore with a sophisticated palette and reasonable prices, Mamma Gaucha could please the fussiest road warrior. Cane ceilings and whitewashed barn-board walls create a down-home setting. Start with fresh-mint lemonade, organic wine or a pint of La Tropera. The mainstay are clay-oven pizzas, but the homemade pastas and salad bowls filled with local produce are just as worthy.

Cafe de Mayo CAFE $

(cell 9709-8632; 21 de Mayo 543; mains CH$3000-6000; 9am-10pm;) A meeting spot specializing in espresso drinks, farm egg breakfasts or filling staples like *pastel de choclo*. There are also sandwiches, cheese boards and homemade cakes. With shady outdoor tables or a cozy indoors with hanging teapots and fireplace.

Café Confluencia INTERNATIONAL $

(067-224-5080; 21 de Mayo 544; mains CH$4000-7000; closed Sun;) A chic eatery serving lovely oversized salads, healthy mains and the occasional stir-fry or taco. Mint *pisco sours* are the standout, but tea and fresh juices are good daytime fixes.

Café Holzer CAFE $

(www.holzer.cl; Dussen 317; cakes CH$2000; 9:30am-9pm Tue-Fri, 10am-9pm Sat & Sun;) This tiny cafe with a grassy front patio is a local favorite for sweets and caffeine. Cakes and tarts are flown in from a reputable Santiago bakery. Real coffee is served and you can also sample a gourd of maté to see what all the buzz is about.

Casino de Bomberos CHILEAN $

(067-223-1437; Parra 365; mains CH$5000; noon-3:30pm) Call it a cultural experience – this classic but windowless eatery gets packed with locals downing seafood plates or steak and eggs.

Carnes Queulat PARRILLA $$

(067-225-0507; www.carnesqueulat.cl; Ramón Freire 327; mains CH$5000-8000; 1-3:30pm &

DON'T MISS

PATAGONIA NATIONAL PARK

Valle Chacabuco (Parque Nacional Patagonia) FREE, 18km north of Cochrane, is a reformed *estancia* (grazing ranch) home to flamingo, guanaco, *huemul* (endangered Andean deer), puma, viscacha and fox. Conservacion Patagonica, the NGO behind the Patagonia National Park project, began this initiative in 2004. Now dubbed the Serengeti of the Southern Cone, the 690-sq-km Valle Chacabuco features Patagonian steppe, forests, mountains, lakes and lagoons. The park stretches from the Río Baker to the Argentine border. In a private vehicle, it's possible to cross here at Paso Roballos.

7:30-11pm) Tucked away down a gravel alleyway, this friendly plain-Jane place happens to serve the best steaks in the region. *Carne a las brasas* – meat attentively grilled over wood fire – is the worthy house specialty, best matched with some piping-hot homemade empanadas and the secret-recipe *pisco sour.*

Drinking

Cerveceria Arisca BREWPUB
(Baquedano 400; 12:30-3pm & 7:30-11:30pm Tue-Sat) Artisan beer in a cheerful, modern space. Wash it down with *ceviche* or homemade shredded lamb sandwiches (CH$5000) with mint chimichurri.

Bajo Marquesina SPORTS BAR
(067-221-0720; bajo.marquesina@gmail.com; 21 de Mayo 306; 5pm-midnight Tue-Fri, 1:30-10pm Sat & Sun) Lovers of football, unite! With vintage photos of Patagonian cowboys playing football and jerseys from clubs all over Chile, this sports pub and dedicated football (soccer) museum has wonderful relics of bygone eras, best enjoyed if you can get the friendly owner chatting.

Information

Banks with ATMs and internet cafes line Condell. Get cash here; it is one of the few stops on the Carretera Austral with Visa ATM access.

Conaf (067-221-2109; Av Ogaña 1060; 9am-8pm Mon-Sat, 10am-6pm Sun) Provides information on area parks and reserves.

Hospital Regional (067-221-9100; Ibar 68; 24hr) Emergency is open 24 hours.

Post office (Lord Cochrane 202) Near Plaza de Armas.

Sernatur (067-223-3949; www.recorreaysen.cl; Bulnes 35; 9am-9pm Mon-Fri, 10am-9pm Sat & Sun summer) A helpful office with lists of activity, lodging and transportation options and costs. Regional information is also available.

Getting There & Away

AIR

Lan (600-526-2000; Parra 402) has several daily flights (most leaving in the morning) to Puerto Montt (CH$100,000) and Santiago (CH$214,000) from the Balmaceda airport; note that rates can be deeply discounted if purchased in-country.

Flights with **Sky Airline** (067-240-827; www.skyairline.cl; Arturo Prat 203) from Santiago stop at Balmaceda airport on the way to Punta Arenas.

BUS

Buses operate from the **bus terminal** (067-225-8203; cnr Lautaro & Magallanes) and separate offices. Schedules change continuously; check with Sernatur for the latest information. The following leave from the terminal.

For northern destinations, companies include **Aguilas Patagonicas** (067-221-1288; www.aguilaspatagonicas.cl), **Transaustral** (067-223-2067), **Buses Becker** (067-223-2167; www.busesbecker.com; General Parra 335), **Transportes Terra Austral** (067-225-4355) and **Queilen Bus** (067-224-0760). For southern destinations, try **Acuario 13/Buses Sao Paulo** (067-252-2143, cell 9874-8022) or **Buses Don Carlos** (067-223-1981; Cruz 63).

DESTINATION	COST (CH$)	DURATION (HR)
Chaitén	24,000	9-11
Chile Chico	6000	3½ with ferry
Cochrane	13,000	7-10
Futaleufú	20,000	8-9
Puerto Montt	30,000	23
Puyuhuapi	8000	5

Lago General Carrera

Shared with Argentina (where it's called Lago Buenos Aires), this massive 2240-sq-km lake is a wind-stirred green-blue sea in the middle of sculpted Patagonian steppe. Its rough and twisty roads dwarf the traveler: you'll feel like you're crawling through the landscape. An excellent journey follows the Carretera Austral south from Coyhaique, around the lake's western border.

Just before reaching Balmaceda from Coyhaique, a right-hand turnoff (the sign points to Cochrane) heads toward **Reserva Nacional Cerro Castillo**. The spires of glacier-bound Cerro Castillo tower over some 1800 sq km of southern-beech forest, an excellent trekking destination. In nearby Villa Cerro Castillo, **Senderos Patagonia** (☎cell 62-244-725; www.aysensenderospatagonia.com; dm CH$11,000) has great bilingual guide services and a new hostel.

Along the western shore, **Puerto Río Tranquilo** is the launch point for more budget-minded tours to the stunning Glaciar San Rafael with **Emtrex** (☎cell 8259-4017; www.exploradores-sanrafael.cl; per person day trip/overnight CH$140,000/220,000) or **Destino Patagonia** (☎cell 9158-6044; www.destinopatagonia.cl; per person full day CH$140,000). Boat tours visit the gorgeous caves of **Capilla de Mármol** (Marble Chapel) when the water's calm. North of town a glacier-lined road to **Parque Nacional Laguna San Rafael** bumps toward the coast. Adventure base camp **El Puesto** (☎cell 6207-3794; www.elpuesto.cl; Pedro Lagos 258; s/d/tr US$131/184/210; wifi) is a lovely B&B owned by a professional adventure guide. **Camping Pudu** (☎cell 8920-5085; www.puduexcursiones.cl; campsites per person CH$6000; ⊙Dec-Mar) offers excellent waterfront sites.

About 13km east of Cruce El Maitén, **Puerto Guadal** has gas and provisions. With rave reviews, ecocamp and hostel **Destino No Turistico** (☎cell 8756-7545; www.destino-noturistico.com; Camino Laguna La Manga, Km 1; campsites per person CH$5500, dm/d CH$12,000/28,000) provides a lovely countryside getaway.

Chile Chico

☎067 / POP 4600

Gold and silver mines dot the roller-coaster road from Puerto Guadal, ending in Chile Chico, a sunny oasis of wind-pummeled poplars and orchards. From here, buses connect to Los Antiguos and Ruta 40 leading to southern Argentine Patagonia. **Reserva Nacional Jeinimen** (admission CH$2000), 60km away, is a treasure of flamingos and turquoise mountain lagoons. Aside from a few tours, there's little transportation; try **Expeditions Patagonia** (☎cell 8464-1067;

ARGENTINA VIA THE BACK DOOR

Gonzo travelers can skirt the southern ice field to get from Villa O'Higgins to Argentina's Parque Nacional Los Glaciares and El Chaltén. The one- to three-day trip can be completed between November and April. Bring all of your provisions, plus your passport and rain gear. Travel delays due to bad weather or boat problems do happen. Travel with extra food and extra pesos. The trip goes as follows:

➡ Catch the 8am bus from Villa O'Higgins to Puerto Bahamondez (CH$2500).

➡ Take catamaran *La Quetru* (CH$44,000, four hours) from Villa O'Higgins to Candelario Mansilla on the south edge of Lago O'Higgins. It goes one to three times a week, mostly on Saturdays with some Monday or Wednesday departures. Candelario Mansilla has basic lodgings, guided treks and pack-horse rental. Pass through Chilean customs and immigration here.

➡ Trek or ride to Laguna Redonda (two hours). Camping is not allowed.

➡ Trek or ride to Laguna Larga (1½ hours). Camping is not allowed.

➡ Trek or ride to the north shore of Lago del Desierto (1½ hours). Pass through Argentine customs and immigration here. Camping is allowed only at the border post.

➡ Take the ferry from the north to the south shores of Lago del Desierto (AR$480, 2¼ hours). Another option is to hike the coast (15km, five hours). Camping is allowed. Check current ferry schedules with Argentine customs.

➡ Grab the shuttle bus to El Chaltén, 37km away (AR$350, one hour).

For more information, consult El Mosco (p515) in Villa O'Higgins or Rancho Grande Hostel (p163) on the Argentine side.

www.expeditionspatagonia.com; O'Higgins 333, Galeria Municipal; ⌚9am-1pm & 2:30-8pm).

Stay at **Ñandu Camp** (☎cell 6779-3390; www.nanducamp.com; O'Higgins 750; dm CH$12,000; 📶), with helpful trekking information, or Belgian farmhouse **Hostería de la Patagonia** (☎067-241-1337, cell 8159-2146; hdelapatagonia@gmail.com; Camino Internacional s/n; camping per person CH$4000, s/d/tr CH$35,000/50,000/61,000, cabin CH$50,000, per person without bathroom CH$15,000; 📶), with charming rooms among the gardens.

There is a helpful **Oficina de Informacion Turistica** (☎067-241-1338; www.chilechico.cl; cnr O'Higgins & Blest Ghana; ⌚8am-1pm & 2-5pm Mon-Fri) and a **BancoEstado** (González 112; ⌚9am-2pm Mon-Fri) for money exchange; the ATM only takes Mastercard.

Getting There & Away

An almost-daily ferry run by **Naviera Sotramin** (☎067-223-7958; www.sotramin.cl; Muelle Chile Chico; passenger/automobile CH$2000/17,700) crosses Lago General Carrera to Puerto Ingeniero Ibáñez, a big shortcut to Coyhaique.

A number of shuttle buses leave from O'Higgins 420 and cross the border to Los Antiguos, Argentina (CH$2000, 20 minutes), just 9km east. Los Antiguos has connections to El Chaltén.

Bus providers and schedules vary from year to year. To Puerto Guadal (CH$7000, 2½ hours), **Seguel** (☎067-243-1214; O'Higgins 394) and **Buses Eca** (☎067-243-1224) go Monday to Friday at 4pm or 5pm. To Puerto Río Tranquilo (CH$14,000, four hours), **Costa Carrera** has service on Tuesday and Friday at 11am.

Buses Acuña (☎067-225-1579; Rodríguez 143) and **Buses Carolina** (☎067-241-1490; ferry office) go to Coyhaique (CH$5000, 3½ hours) with a ferry-bus combination; reserve ahead. You will first take the Naviera Sotramin ferry to Puerto Ibáñez.

South to Villa O'Higgins

An old ranching outpost, languorous **Cochrane** is the southern hub of the Carretera Austral. Though oblivious to tourism, Cochrane is the gateway to the new Parque Nacional Patagonia. To check out nearby Calluco Glacier, contact **Lord Patagonia** (☎cell 8267-8115; www.lordpatagonia.cl; Lago Brown 388; full-day trip CH$50,000) for guide services. Stay at **Residencial Cero a Cero** (☎067-252-2158, cell 7607-8155; ceroacero@gmail.com; Lago Brown 464; d CH$30,000, r per person without bathroom CH$10,000; 📶), a log home that has ample space. **Cafe Tamango** (☎cell 9158-4521; Esmeralda 464; mains CH$5000; ⌚9am-7:30pm Mon-Sat; 🌿) prepares good sandwiches, hearty vegetarian fare like lentil burgers, and homemade chestnut ice cream. The **tourist kiosk** (www.cochranepatagonia.cl; Plaza de Armas; ⌚9am-1pm & 2-9pm Jan-Mar) on the plaza has bus schedules, if little else.

From Cochrane, buses go daily to Coyhaique (CH$14,000, 10 hours) at 8am. Chile Chico is served three days per week, with stops in Puerto Guadal. There are several buses daily between Caleta Tortel (CH$7000, three hours) and Cochrane.

You could spend a whole day exploring the network of creaky boardwalks of fabled **Caleta Tortel**, perched over the milky waters of the glacier-fed sound. Dedicated as a national monument, this fishing village cobbled around a steep escarpment is seated between two ice fields at the mouth of Río Baker. The road stops at the edge of town at the helpful **tourism kiosk** (www.municipalidaddetortel.cl; ⌚9am-11pm Tue-Sun), with maps, lodging and bus information. **Brisas del Sur** (☎cell 5688-2723; valerialanderos@hotmail.com; Playa Ancha sector; d CH$35,000, r per person without bathroom CH$12,000; 📶) offers snug rooms, but if you can splurge, go for the stylish lodge **Entre Hielos** (☎cell 9579-3779; www.entrehielostortel.cl; s/d US$118/150; 📶), which also arranges private boat trips to the glaciers. Cheaper boat taxis do tours of the bay (CH$10,000) from the Rincon sector.

Though Caleta Tortel is only four hours from Villa O'Higgins via a road and ferry crossing, there was no bus service at the time of research.

Villa O'Higgins

Wild stretches of rushing rivers and virgin forest flank the curvy road south of Caleta Tortel. At **Puerto Yungay** a free government ferry (www.barcazas.cl) hauls passengers and cars across the Mitchell fjord to the final 100km stretch of the Carretera Austral. This famed road ends at the remote village of Villa O'Higgins, stopped by the massive glacial barrier of the Southern Ice Field. That doesn't stop hardy adventurers from tackling the ferry-trek-ferry combination to El Chaltén, Argentina. Guided horseback riding, trekking trips and bike rental are available with advance bookings through **Villa O'Higgins Expediciones** (☎067-243-1821, cell 8210-3191; www.villaohiggins.com). Just before Villa O'Higgins, friendly **Ecocamp Tsonek** (☎cell 7892-9695; www.tsonek.cl; Carretera Austral s/n; campsites per person/cyclist CH$4000/3000; 📶) offers camping in an enchanted wood. In town, **El Mosco** (☎067-243-1819; www.patagoniaelmosco.blogspot.com; Carretera Austral Km 1240; campsites per person CH$5000, dm CH$9000, d CH$45,000, s/d without bathroom CH$18,000/30,000) offers friendly lodgings and the lowdown on local hikes. There's no ATM here so bring all the cash you'll need.

Buses Catalina goes to Cochrane (CH$8000, six hours) on Friday and Monday at 8am. Frequency changes in low season.

SOUTHERN PATAGONIA

The wind is whipping, the mountains are jagged and waters trickle clear. This desolate area first attracted missionaries and fortune seekers from Scotland, England and Croatia. Writer Francisco Coloane described these early adventurers as 'courageous men whose hearts were no more than another closed fist.' The formation of *estancias* (extensive grazing establishments for cattle or sheep, with a dominant owner/manager and dependent resident labor force), and the wool boom that followed, created reverberating effects: great wealth for a few gained at the cost of indigenous populations, who were nearly exterminated by disease and warfare. Later the region struggled as wool values plummeted and the Panama Canal diverted shipping routes.

Patagonia's worth may have been hard-won and nearly lost but it is now under reconsideration. While wealth once meant minerals and livestock, now it is in the very landscape. For visitors, the thrill lies in Patagonia's isolated, spectral beauty. Parque Nacional Torres del Paine is the region's star attraction. Among the finest parks on the continent, it attracts hundreds of thousands of visitors every year.

Punta Arenas

☎061 / POP 130,100

If these streets could talk: this wind-wracked former penitentiary has hosted tattered sailors, miners, seal hunters, starving pioneers and wealthy dandies of the wool boom. Exploitation of one of the world's largest reserves of hydrocarbon started in the 1980s and has developed into a thriving petrochemical industry. Today's Punta Arenas is a confluence of the ruddy and the grand, geared toward tourism and industry.

Sights

Plaza Muñoz Gamero PLAZA

A central plaza of magnificent conifers surrounded by opulent mansions. Facing the plaza's north side, **Casa Braun-Menéndez** (☎061-224-1489; admission CH$1000; ⏰10:30am-1pm & 5-8:30pm Tue-Fri, 10:30am-1pm & 8-10pm Sat, 11am-2pm Sun) houses the private Club de la Unión, which also uses the tavern downstairs (open to the public). The nearby **monument** commemorating the 400th anniversary of Magellan's voyage was donated by wool baron José Menéndez in 1920. Just east is the former **Sociedad Menéndez Behety**, which now houses Turismo Comapa. The **cathedral** sits west.

Museo Regional de Magallanes MUSEUM

(Museo Regional Braun-Menéndez; ☎061-224-4216; www.museodemagallanes.cl; Magallanes 949; admission CH$1000; ⏰10:30am-5pm Wed-Mon, to 2pm May-Dec) This opulent mansion testifies to the wealth and power of pioneer sheep farmers in the late 19th century. The well-maintained interior houses a regional historical museum (ask for booklets in English) and original exquisite French-nouveau family furnishings, from intricate wooden inlaid floors to Chinese vases. In former servants' quarters, a downstairs cafe is perfect for a *pisco sour* while soaking up the grandeur.

★**Cementerio Municipal** CEMETERY

(main entrance at Av Bulnes 949; ⏰7:30am-8pm) FREE Among South America's most fascinating cemeteries, with both humble immigrant graves and flashy tombs, like that of wool baron José Menéndez, a scale replica of Rome's Vittorio Emanuele monument, according to author Bruce Chatwin. See the map inside the main entrance gate.

It's an easy 15-minute stroll northeast of the plaza, or catch any *taxi colectivo* in front of the Museo Regional de Magallanes on Magallanes.

Punta Arenas

Punta Arenas

Top Sights

1 Cementerio Municipal ... D1

Sights

2 Casa Braun-Menéndez ... B4
3 Cathedral ... B4
4 Museo Regional de Magallanes ... C4
5 Plaza Muñoz Gamero ... B4

Activities, Courses & Tours

6 Turismo Aonikenk ... C3

Sleeping

7 Hospedaje Magallanes ... D2
8 Hostal Fitz Roy ... C4
9 Hostal Independencia ... A4
10 Hostal La Estancia ... D3
11 Ilaia Hotel ... B2

Eating

12 Café Almacen Tapiz ... C4
13 Kiosco Roca ... C4
14 La Marmita ... C3
15 La Mesita Grande ... C4
16 Mercado Municipal ... B5

Drinking & Nightlife

17 Jekus ... C4

Tours

Worthwhile day trips include tours to the town's first settlements at Fuerte Bulnes and Puerto Hambre. If you have the time, visit the thriving Magellanic penguin colonies of Monumento Natural Los Pingüinos.

Turismo Aonikenk TOUR
(061-222-8616; www.aonikenk.com; Magallanes 570) Recommended English-, German- and French-speaking guides. Offers Cabo Froward treks, visits to the king-penguin colony in Tierra del Fuego, and cheaper open expeditions geared at experienced participants. Also has information on Estancia Yendegaia.

Turismo Pali Aike TOUR
(061-261-5750; www.turismopaliaike.com) Recommended tour company.

Sleeping

Hospedaje Magallanes B&B $
(061-222-8616; www.aonikenk.com; Magallanes 570; dm/d without bathroom CH$18,000/40,000; @) A great inexpensive option run by a German-Chilean couple who are also Torres del Paine guides with an on-site travel agency. With just a few quiet rooms, there are often communal dinners or backyard barbecues by the climbing wall. Breakfast includes brown bread and strong coffee.

Hostal Fitz Roy GUESTHOUSE $
(061-224-0430; www.hostalfitzroy.com; Navarro 850; dm CH$10,000, d with/without bathroom CH$30,000/25,000, 5-person cabin CH$35,000; @) This country house in the city offers rambling, good-value rooms and an inviting, old-fashioned living room to pore over books or sea charts. Rooms have phones and TVs.

Hostal Independencia GUESTHOUSE $
(061-222-7572; www.hostalindependencia.cl; Av Independencia 374; campsite per person CH$2000, dm CH$7000; @) One of the last diehard backpacker haunts with cheap prices and bonhomie to match. Despite the chaos, rooms are reasonably clean and there are kitchen privileges, camping and bike rentals.

Hostal La Estancia GUESTHOUSE $
(061-224-9130; www.estancia.cl; O'Higgins 765; d CH$48,000, dm/s/d without bathroom CH$12,500/20,000/38,000; @) An old downtown house with big rooms, vaulted ceilings and tidy shared bathrooms. Longtime owners Alex and Carmen are eager to help with travel plans. There's a book exchange, kitchen use, laundry and storage.

★**Ilaia Hotel** BOUTIQUE HOTEL $$$
(061-272-3100; www.ilaia.cl; Carrera Pinto 351; s/d/tr from US$105/140/195;) Playful and modern, this high-concept boutique hotel is run with family warmth. Sly messages are written to be read in mirrors, rooms are simple and chic and an incredible glass study gazes out on the Strait. Offers a shuttle to yoga class and healthy breakfasts with chapati bread, homemade jam, avocados, yogurt and more. But you won't find a television.

Eating

Local seafood is an exquisite treat: go for *centolla* (king crab) or *erizos* (sea urchins).

Café Almacen Tapiz CAFE $
(cell 8730-3481; www.cafetapiz.cl; Roca 912; mains CH$5000; 9am-9:30pm;) Cloaked in *alerce* shingles, this lively cafe makes for an ambient coffee break. In addition to gorgeous layer cakes, there are salads and pita sandwiches with goat cheese, meats or roasted veggies.

Mercado Municipal MARKET $
(21 de Mayo 1465; 8am-3pm) Fish and vegetable market with cheap second-floor *cocinerías* (eateries), a great place for inexpensive seafood dishes.

La Mesita Grande PIZZA $
(061-224-4312; O'Higgins 1001; mains CH$3000-6000; noon-11:30pm) If you're homesick for Brooklyn, La Mesita Grande might do the trick. This mod exposed-brick pizzeria serves them up thin and crisp, with organic toppings and pints of local brew. Save room for the homemade ice cream. The original outlet is in Puerto Natales.

Kiosco Roca SANDWICHES $
(Roca 875; snacks CH$500; 7am-7pm Mon-Fri, 8am-1pm Sat) An irresistible stop, with locals patiently waiting for counter stools, and U of Chile paraphernalia plastering the walls. It only turns out bite-sized sandwiches with chorizo or cheese or both, best paired with a banana milkshake.

★**La Marmita** CHILEAN $$
(061-222-2056; www.marmitamaga.cl; Plaza Sampaio 678; mains CH$6000-12,000; 12:30-3pm & 6:30-11:30pm Mon-Sat;) This classic bistro enjoys wild popularity for its lovely, casual ambience and tasty fare. Besides fresh salads and hot bread, hearty dishes such as casseroles or seafood hark back to

grandma's cooking, Chilean-style. With good vegetarian options and take-out service.

Drinking & Nightlife

Jekus PUB

(O'Higgins 1021; ⏲6pm-3am) A restaurant that serves as a popular meeting spot for drinks, with happy hours, karaoke and soccer on the tube.

Shopping

Zona Franca DUTY FREE

(Zofri; Km3.5 Norte Zona Franca Punta Arenas; ⏲Mon-Sat) The duty-free zone is a large, polished conglomeration of shops that is worth checking out if you're looking for electronics, outdoor gear, computer accessories or camera equipment. *Colectivos* shuttle back and forth from downtown along Av Bulnes throughout the day.

Information

Internet access is widely available and ATMs are common.

Conaf (☎061-223-0681; Bulnes 0309; ⏲9am-5pm Mon-Fri) Has details on the nearby parks.

Hospital Regional (☎061-220-5000; cnr Arauco & Angamos)

Information kiosk (☎061-220-0610; Plaza Muñoz Gamero; ⏲8am-7pm Mon-Sat, 9am-7pm Sun Dec-Feb) South side of the plaza.

Post office (Bories 911) Located one block north of Plaza Muñoz Gamero.

Sernatur (☎061-224-1330; www.sernatur.cl; Navarro 999; ⏲8:30am-8pm Mon-Fri, 10am-6pm Sat & Sun) With friendly, well-informed, multilingual staff and lists of accommodations and transportation. Reduced hours in low season.

Getting There & Away

The tourist offices distribute a useful brochure that details all forms of transportation available.

AIR

Aeropuerto Presidente Carlos Ibáñez del Campo is 20km north of town.

Aerovías DAP (☎061-261-6100; www.aeroviasdap.cl; O'Higgins 891) From November to March, flies to Porvenir (CH$55,000 round trip) Monday through Saturday several times daily, and to Puerto Williams (CH$143,000 round trip) Monday through Saturday at 10am. Luggage is limited to 10kg per person.

LanChile (☎061-224-1100; www.lan.com; Bories 884) Flies several times daily to Santiago (CH$162,000 round trip) with a stop in Puerto Montt (CH$153,000), and on Saturday to the Falkland Islands (round trip CH$530,000).

Sky Airline (☎061-271-0645; www.skyairline.cl; Roca 935) Flies daily between Santiago and Punta Arenas, with a stop either in Puerto Montt or Concepción.

BOAT

Transbordador Austral Broom (☎061-258-0089; www.tabsa.cl) Operates three ferries to Tierra del Fuego from the Tres Puentes ferry launch. The car-and-passenger ferry to/from Porvenir (CH$6200/39,800 per person/vehicle, 2½ to four hours) usually leaves at 9am but has some afternoon departures; check the current online schedule. From Punta Arenas, it's faster to do the Primera Angostura crossing (CH$1700/15,000 per person/vehicle, 20 minutes), northeast of Punta Arenas, which sails every 90 minutes between 8:30am and 11:45pm.

Broom sets sail for Isla Navarino's Puerto Williams (reclining seat/bunk CH$103,000/143,000 including meals, 30 hours) three or four times per month on Thursday only, returning Saturday.

BUS

Buses depart from company offices, most within a block or two of Av Colón. Buy tickets several hours (if not days) in advance. The **Central de Pasajeros** (☎061-224-5811; cnr Magallanes & Av Colón) is the closest thing to a central booking office.

Bus Sur (☎061-261-4224; www.bus-sur.cl; Av Colón 842) Puerto Natales.

Buses Fernández/Buses Pingüino (☎061-224-2313; www.busesfernandez.com; Sanhueza 745) Puerto Natales and Río Gallegos.

Buses Pacheco (☎061-224-2174; www.busespacheco.com; Av Colón 900) Puerto Natales, Río Gallegos and Ushuaia.

Cruz del Sur (☎061-222-7970; www.busescruzdelsur.cl; Sanhueza 745) Puerto Montt, Osorno and Chiloé.

DESTINATION	COST (CH$)	DURATION (HR)
Osorno	30,000	30
Puerto Natales	6000	3
Río Gallegos	12,000	5-8
Río Grande	25,000	7
Ushuaia	30,000	10

Getting Around

Buses depart directly from the airport to Puerto Natales. Punta Arenas has Chilean Patagonia's most economical car-rental rates; try **Adel Rent a Car/Localiza** (☎061-222-4819; www.adelrentacar.cl; Pedro Montt 962). Cars are a good option for exploring Torres del Paine, but renting one in Chile to cross the border into Argentina gets expensive due to international insurance requirements.

Puerto Natales

☎061 / POP 18,000

A pastel wash of corrugated-tin houses shoulder to shoulder, this once-dull fishing port on Seno Última Esperanza has become the hub of Gore-Tex-clad travelers headed to the continent's number-one national park. While not a destination in itself, the village is pleasant, the austral light is divine and visitor services are getting ever more savvy.

Sights & Activities

Museo Histórico MUSEUM
(☎061-241-1263; Bulnes 28; admission CH$1000; ⊗8am-7pm Mon-Fri, 10am-1pm & 3-7pm Sat & Sun) A crash course in local history, with archaeological artifacts, a Yaghan canoe, Tehuelche bolas and historical photos.

Mirador Dorotea HIKING
(admission CH$5000) A day hike through a lenga forest on private land to splendid views of Puerto Natales and the glacial valley. Less than 10km from Natales. Dorotea is the large rocky outcrop just off Ruta 9.

Tours

Antares/Big Foot Patagonia ADVENTURE TOUR
(☎061-241-4611; www.antarespatagonia.com; Ave Pedro Montt/Costanera 161) Specializing in Torres del Paine, Antares can facilitate climbing permits and made-to-order trips. It also has the park concession for Lago Grey activities including Glacier Grey ice trekking and kayak trips.

Baqueano Zamora HORSE RIDING
(☎061-261-3530; www.baqueanozamora.cl; Baquedano 534) Runs recommended horse-riding trips and wild horse viewing in Torres del Paine.

Erratic Rock ADVENTURE TOUR
(☎061-241-4317; www.erraticrock.com; Baquedano 719) Guides bare-bones Torres del Paine trips plus alternative options and rents gear. Alternative treks include Cabo Froward, Isla Navarino and lesser-known destinations.

Sleeping

Hostels often rent equipment and help arrange park transportation.

Singing Lamb HOSTEL $
(☎061-241-0958; www.thesinginglamb.com; Arauco 779; dm US$22-30, d US$80; @ 📶) A clean and green hostel with compost, recycling, rainwater collection and linen shopping bags. Dorm rooms are priced by the number of beds (maximum nine) and shared spaces are ample. Nice touches include central heating and homemade breakfasts. To get here, follow Raimírez one block past Plaza O'Higgins.

Lili Patagonico's Hostal HOSTEL $
(☎061-241-4063; www.lilipatagonicos.com; Arturo Prat 479; dm CH$10,000, d with/without bathroom CH$32,000/24,000; @ 📶) A sprawling house with a climbing wall, a variety of dorms and colorful doubles with newer bathrooms and down comforters.

Hostal Dos Lagunas GUESTHOUSE $
(☎cell 8162-7755; hostaldoslagunas@gmail.com; cnr Barros Arana & Bories; dm/d CH$12,000/$30,000; 📶) Natales natives Alejandro and Andrea are attentive hosts, spoiling guests with filling breakfasts, steady water pressure and travel tips. Among the town's most long-standing lodgings, the place is spotless.

Hostal Nancy GUESTHOUSE $
(☎061-241-0022, dorm 061-241-4325; www.nataleslodge.cl; Raimírez 540; dm CH$9000, s/d/tr CH$15,000/32,000/36,000; 📶) Praised for its adoptable hostess Nancy, this family guesthouse recently remodeled, adding TVs and bathrooms in all rooms. There are still kitchen privileges in the annex across the street. It's a family environment with twin or double beds available.

★ **We Are Patagonia** B&B $$
(☎cell 7389-4802; www.wearepatagonia.com; Galvarino 745; r with/without bathroom US$70/60; 📶) A lovely art hotel with minimalist Nordic charm, central heating and homespun charms. Mantras stenciled on the walls provide some not-so-subliminal positive messaging. The breakfast of champions includes real coffee, fruit, oatmeal and whole-wheat bread. It's located in a small house.

Amerindia B&B $$
(☎061-241-1945; www.hostelamerindia.com; Barros Arana 135; d with/without bathroom CH$45,000/35,000, 6-person apt CH$80,000; ⊗Aug-Jun; @ 📶) An earthy, tranquil retreat with a wood stove, beautiful weavings and raw wood beams. Guests wake up to cake,

eggs and oatmeal in a cozy cafe open to the public, also selling organic chocolate, teas and gluten-free options. Also rents cars.

Eating & Drinking

La Mesita Grande PIZZA $

(☎cell 6141-1571; www.mesitagrande.cl; Arturo Prat 196; pizza CH$5000-7000; ⊙12:30-3pm & 7-11:30pm Mon-Sat, 1-3pm & 7-11:30pm Sun) Happy diners share one long, worn table for outstanding thin-crust pizza, quality pasta and organic salads.

Cafe Kaiken CHILEAN $

(☎cell 8295-2036; Baquedano 699; mains CH$5000-7000; ⊙1-3:30pm & 6:30-11pm Mon-Sat) With just five tables and one couple cooking, serving and chatting up customers, this is as intimate as it gets. The owners moved here to get out of the Santiago fast lane, so you'd best follow their lead. Dishes like slow-roasted lamb or homemade smoked-salmon stuffed ravioli are well worth the wait. Arrive early to claim a spot.

El Bote CHILEAN $

(☎061-241-0045; Bulnes 380; set menu CH$3500; ⊙noon-11:30pm Mon-Sat) A haven for Chilean comfort food, this unpretentious restaurant dishes out roast chicken, seafood casseroles and homemade soups in addition to more expensive game dishes featuring guanaco and venison. For dessert, go with the classic chestnuts in cream.

El Living CAFE $

(www.el-living.com; Arturo Prat 156; mains CH$4000-6000; ⊙11am-10pm Mon-Sat Nov–mid-April; ✎) Indulge in the London lounge feel of this chill cafe, one of Natales' first. There's fresh vegetarian fare (plus vegan, gluten-free), stacks of European glossies and a hidden backyard with outdoor tables.

Puerto Natales

Cangrejo Rojo CAFE $$
(☎061-241-2436; Santiago Bueras 782; mains CH$6000-8500; ⊙1:30-3pm & 5:30-10pm Tue-Sun) Unfathomably friendly and reasonable, this cute corrugated-tin cafe serves pies, ice cream, sandwiches and hot clay-pot dishes like seafood casserole or lamb chops. To get here, follow Baquedano four blocks south of Plaza O'Higgins to Bueras.

Afrigonia FUSION $$
(☎061-241-2877; Eberhard 343; mains CH$10,000-14,000; ⊙12:20-3pm & 6:30-11pm) Outstanding and wholly original, Afrigonia has Afro-Chilean cuisine you won't find on any NYC menu. This romantic gem was dreamed up by a hardworking Zambian-Chilean couple. Fragrant rice, fresh ceviche and mint roasted lamb are prepared *with* succulent precision. Make reservations.

Baguales MICROBREWERY
(www.cervezabaguales.cl; Bories 430; ⊙6pm-2:30am; 📶) Climber friends started this microbrewery as a noble quest for quality suds and the beer (crafted on-site) does not disappoint. A 2nd-floor addition seeks to meet the heavy demand. The gringo-style bar food is just so-so.

ℹ Information

Most banks in town are equipped with ATMs. The best bilingual portal for the region is www.torresdelpaine.cl.

Conaf (☎061-241-1438; Baquedano 847; ⊙8:30am-12:45pm & 2:30-5:30pm Mon-Fri) National parks service administrative office.

Municipal tourist office (☎061-261-4808; Plaza de Armas; ⊙8:30am-12:30pm & 2:30-6pm Tue-Sun) In the Museo Histórico and the Rodoviario (Bus Terminal), with regionwide lodgings listings.

Post office (Eberhard 429)

Sernatur (☎061-241-2125; infonatales@sernatur.cl; Ave Pedro Montt/Costanera 19; ⊙9am-7pm Mon-Fri, 9:30am-6pm Sat & Sun) With useful city and regional maps and a second plaza location in high season.

ℹ Getting There & Away

BOAT

Navimag Ferry (☎061-241-1421, Rodoviario 061-241-1642; www.navimag.com; Ave Pedro Montt/Costanera 308, 2nd office in the Rodoviario; ⊙9am-1pm & 2:30-6:30pm Mon-Fri) For many travelers, a journey through Chile's spectacular fjords aboard the Navimag Ferry becomes a highlight of their trip. This four-day and three-night northbound voyage has become so popular it should be booked well in advance. To confirm when the ferry is due, contact Turismo Comapa or Navimag a couple of days before your estimated arrival date.

BUS

Buses arrive at the **Rodoviario** (Bus Terminal; Av España 1455), a bus terminal on the town outskirts, though companies also sell tickets at their downtown offices. Book at least a day ahead, especially for early-morning departures. Services are greatly reduced in the low season.

Buses leave for Torres del Paine two to three times daily at around 7am, 8am and 2:30pm. Companies include **Buses Gomez** (☎061-241-5700; www.busesgomez.com; Arturo Prat 234), **Buses Pacheco** (☎061-241-4800, www.buses pacheco.com; Ramírez 224) and **Buses JBA** (☎061-241-0242; Arturo Prat 258). For Mountain Lodge Paine Grande in low season, take the morning bus to meet the catamaran. Tickets are valid for transfers within the park. Schedules change, so double-check them.

Bus Sur (☎061-261-4220; www.bus-sur.cl; Baquedano 668) and Buses Pacheco go to Punta Arenas; the latter also goes to Ushuaia. **Turismo**

Puerto Natales

Sights
1 Museo Histórico B2

Activities, Courses & Tours
2 Antares/Big Foot Patagonia A1
3 Baqueano Zamora D3
4 Erratic Rock D3
5 Turismo 21 de Mayo C2

Sleeping
6 Amerindia B2
7 Hostal Dos Lagunas B2
8 Hostal Nancy D2
9 Lili Patagonico's Hostal C3
10 Singing Lamb D4
11 We Are Patagonia D3

Eating
12 Afrigonia B2
13 Cafe Kaiken D3
14 Cangrejo Rojo D4
15 El Bote B2
16 El Living C1
17 La Mesita Grande C2

Drinking & Nightlife
18 Baguales B1

Zaahj (☎ 061-241-2260; www.turismozaahj.co.cl; Arturo Prat 236/270) and **Cootra** (☎ 061-241-2785; Baquedano 244) serve El Calafate.

DESTINATION	COST (CH$)	DURATION (HR)
El Calafate	15,000	5
Punta Arenas	6000	3
Torres del Paine	8000	2
Ushuaia	36,000	13

Getting Around

Many hostels rent bikes. Car rental is expensive and availability is limited; you'll get better rates in Punta Arenas or Argentina.

Parque Nacional Torres del Paine

Soaring almost vertically more than 2000m above the Patagonian steppe, the granite pillars of Torres del Paine (Towers of Paine) dominate the landscape of what may be South America's finest national park. A Unesco Biosphere Reserve since 1978, the park covers 1810 sq km. Most visitors come for the park's greatest hit but, once here, realize that other (less crowded) attractions offer equal wow power: azure lakes, trails that meander through emerald forests, roaring rivers to cross on rickety bridges and one big, radiant blue glacier.

The park is home to flocks of ostrich-like rhea (known locally as the *ñandú*), Andean condor, flamingo and many other bird species. Its star success in conservation is undoubtedly the guanaco, which grazes the open steppes where pumas cannot approach undetected. After more than a decade of effective protection from poachers, these large and growing herds don't even flinch when humans or vehicles approach.

When the weather is clear, panoramas are everywhere. However, unpredictable weather systems can sheath the peaks in clouds for hours or days. Some say you get four seasons in a day here, with sudden rainstorms and knock-down gusts part of the hearty initiation. Bring high-quality foul-weather gear, a synthetic sleeping bag and, if you're camping, a good tent. If you want to sleep in hotels or *refugios*, you must make reservations in advance. Plan a minimum of three to seven days to enjoy the hiking and other activities.

At the end of 2011, a raging fire burned over 160 sq km, destroying old forest, killing animals and burning several park structures. An international visitor was charged with accidentally setting the fire while trying to start an illegal campfire. The affected area, mostly between Pehoé and Refugio Grey, is essentially the western leg of the 'W' trek. The panoramic views remain, but it may take centuries for the forest to recover. Be conscientious and tread lightly – you are among hundreds of thousands of annual guests.

Activities

Hiking

Torres del Paine's 2800m granite peaks inspire a mass pilgrimmage of hikers from around the world. Most go for the Circuit or the 'W' to soak in these classic panoramas, leaving other incredible routes deserted. The Circuit (the 'W' plus the backside of the peaks) requires seven to nine days, while the 'W' (named for the rough approximation to the letter that it traces out on the map) takes four to five. Add another day or two for transportation connections.

Tour operators in Puerto Natales offer guided treks, which include all meals and accommodations at *refugios* or hotels. For a day hike, walk from Guardería Pudeto, on the main park highway, to **Salto Grande**, a powerful waterfall between Lago Nordenskjöld and Lago Pehoé. Another easy hour's walk leads to **Mirador Nordenskjöld**, an overlook with superb views of the lake and mountains.

The 'W' HIKING

The park highlights of **Mirador Las Torres**, **Valle Francés** and **Lago Grey** are included in this iconic multiday trek. To start the 'W' from the west, catch the catamaran across Lago Pehoe to Mountain Lodge Paine Grande and do the first 'W' leg to Lago Grey before doubling back east. From this direction, the hike is roughly 71km in total.

The Circuit HIKING

For solitude, stellar views and bragging rights over your compadres doing the 'W,' this longer 112km trek is the way to go. This loop takes in the 'W,' plus the backside between Refugio Grey and Refugio Las Torres via challenging Paso John Gardner (1214m, closed seasonally). The landscape is desolate yet beautiful.

Kayaking

A great way to get up close to glaciers. **Indomita Big Foot** (☎061-241-4525; www.indomitapatagonia.com) leads three-hour tours of the iceberg-strewn Lago Grey in summer.

Horse Riding

Baqueano Zamora (p519) runs excursions to Lagos Pingo, Paine and Azul, and Laguna Amarga; to ride the Torres area, contact the activities desk at **Hotel Las Torres** (☎061-271-0050; www.lastorres.com).

Ice Trekking

A fun walk through a sculpted landscape of ice, and you don't need experience to go. Antares/Big Foot Patagonia (p519) is the sole company with a park concession for ice hikes (CH$90,000) on Glacier Grey, using the Conaf house (former Refugio Grey) as a starting point. The five-hour excursion is available from October to May, in high season at 8:30am and 2:30pm.

Parque Nacional Torres del Paine

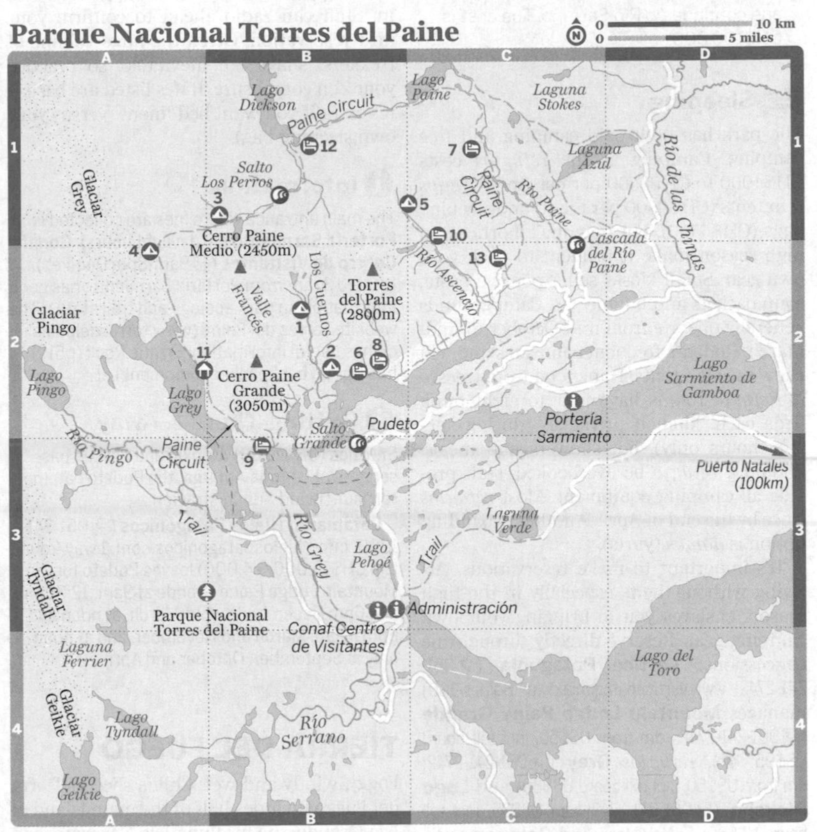

Parque Nacional Torres del Paine

Sleeping

1 Campamento Británico B2
2 Campamento Italiano B2
3 Campamento Los Perros B1
4 Campamento Paso A2
5 Campamento Torres C1
6 Domos El Francés B2
7 Domos El Serón C1
8 Domos Los Cuernos B2
9 Mountain Lodge Paine Grande B3
10 Refugio Chileno C1
11 Refugio Grey A2
12 Refugio Lago Dickson B1
13 Refugio Las Torres C2

WORTH A TRIP

PARQUE NACIONAL BERNARDO O'HIGGINS

Virtually inaccessible, O'Higgins remains an elusive cache of glaciers. As it can be entered only by boat, full-day excursions with **Turismo 21 de Mayo** (☎614420; www.turismo21demayo.com; Eberhard 560, Puerto Natales) run to the base of Glaciar Serrano. Passengers stop for lunch at Estancia Balmaceda and continue up Río Serrano. The cost is CH$100,000.

Sleeping

The park has both paid camping and free camping. Camping at the *refugios* costs CH$4000 to CH$8500 per person. *Refugios* rent tents (CH$9500 per night) and sleeping bags (CH$5500), but potential shortages in high season make it prudent to pack your own gear. Small kiosks sell expensive pasta, soup packets and butane gas. Campgrounds generally operate from mid-October to mid-March. Rodents frequent campsites and will chew through tents. Hang food from trees.

Refugio rooms have four to eight bunk beds each, kitchen privileges (during specific hours only), hot showers and meals. Should a *refugio* be overbooked, staff provide all camping equipment. Most *refugios* close by the end of April. Another expanding option is *domos* (yurts).

It's important to make reservations. Arriving without them, especially in the high season, enslaves you to bringing your own camping gear. Reserve directly through the concessions: **Vertice Patagonia** (☎061-241-2742; www.verticepatagonia.com; Bulnes 100) manages **Mountain Lodge Paine Grande** (☎061-241-2742; dm from US$50, incl full board US$95; @), *refugios* **Grey** (☎061-241-2742; dm from US$50, incl full board US$80) and **Lago Dickson** (☎061-241-2742; dm US$35, incl full board US$80; ⊙Nov-Mar), and **Campamento Los Perros**. **Fantástico Sur** (☎061-261-4184; www.fantasticosur.com; Esmeralda 661; ⊙9am-1pm & 3-6pm Mon-Fri) owns *refugios* **Las Torres** (☎061-261-4184; dm US$86, incl full board US$145; ⊙Sep-Apr; @), **Chileno** (☎061-261-4184; dm US$55, incl full board US$114; ⊙Oct-Mar) and **Domos El Francés** (☎061-261-4184; dm US$73, incl full board US$132; ⊙Oct-Mar, varies), as well as **Domos Los Cuernos** (☎061-261-4184; www.fantasticosur.com; dm US$66, incl full board US$125; ⊙Sep-Mar, varies), and **Domos El Serón** (☎061-261-4184; dm US$38, incl full board US$118) and their associated campgrounds.

Campsites on the trekking routes administered by Conaf are free but very basic; they do not rent equipment or offer showers. These include Campamento Británico, Campamento Italiano, Campamento Paso, Campamento Torres and Camping Guardas.

Bring your passport or a copy for check-in. Staff can radio ahead to confirm your next reservation. Given the huge volume of trekkers, snags are inevitable, so practice your Zen composure. Rates listed are basic – it's extra if you want bed linens (versus your own sleeping bag).

Information

The main entrance where fees are collected is **Portería Sarmiento** (⊙daylight hours). **Conaf Centro de Visitantes** (⊙9am-8pm Dec-Feb), located 37km from Portería Sarmiento, has good information on park ecology and trail status. The website Torres del Paine (www.torresdelpaine.cl) has useful information; Erratic Rock (p519) has a good backpacker equipment list.

Getting There & Away

Shuttles (CH$2500) drop off and pick up passengers at Laguna Amarga, the Pudeto catamaran launch and Administración.

Catamaran Hielos Patagónicos (☎061-241-1380; info@hielospatagonicos.com; 1 way/round trip CH$15,000/24,000) leaves Pudeto for Mountain Lodge Paine Grande at 9am, 12:30pm and 6pm December to mid-March, at noon and 6pm in late March and November, and at noon only in September, October and April.

TIERRA DEL FUEGO

Foggy, windy and wet, Chile's slice of Tierra del Fuego includes half of the main island of Isla Grande, the far-flung Isla Navarino, and a group of smaller islands, many of them uninhabited. Only home to 7000 people, this is the least populated region in Chile. Porvenir is considered the main city, though even that status could be considered an overstatement. These parts can't help but exude a rough and rugged charm, and those willing to venture this far can relish its end-of-the-world emptiness.

Isla Navarino

Forget Ushuaia – the end of the world starts here. With more than 150km of trails, Isla Navarino is a rugged backpackers' paradise, with remote slate-colored lakes, mossy *lenga* forests and the ragged spires of the **Dientes de Navarino**. The only town, **Puerto Williams** (population 2500), is a naval settlement and the official port of entry for vessels en route to Cape Horn and Antarctica.

Sights & Activities

Museo Martín Gusinde MUSEUM
(cnr Araguay & Gusinde; donation requested; 9am-1pm & 3-6:30pm Tue-Fri, 3-6:30pm Sat & Sun, reduced hours off-season) An attractive museum honoring the German priest and ethnographer who worked among the Yaghans from 1918 to 1923. Focuses on ethnography and natural history. Public wi-fi is available in the library.

★**Dientes de Navarino** HIKING
This trekking circuit offers impossibly raw and windswept vistas under Navarino's toothy spires. Beginning at the Virgin altar just outside of town, the five-day, 53.5km route winds through a spectacular wilderness of exposed rock and secluded lakes. Fit hikers can knock it out in four days in the (relatively) dry summer months. Markings are minimal: GPS, used in conjunction with marked maps, is a handy navigational tool.

Cerro Bandera HIKING
With expansive views of the Beagle Channel, this four-hour round trip covers the first approach of the Navarino Circuit. The trail ascends steeply through lenga to blustery stone-littered hillside planted with a Chilean flag.

Sleeping & Eating

Lodgings often offer meals and can arrange tours of the island or airport transfers; expensive provisions are available at a few supermarkets in town.

Residencial Pusaki GUESTHOUSE $
(cell 9833-3248; pattypusaki@yahoo.es; Piloto Pardo 222; s/d CH$12,500/27,000) With legendary warmth, Patty welcomes travelers into this cozy home with comfortable, carpeted rooms with private bathrooms. Patty also organizes group dinners, which are also available to nonguests.

Refugio El Padrino HOSTEL $
(061-262-1136, cell 8438-0843; Costanera 276; camping per person CH$6000, dm CH$12,000) Friendly and conducive to meeting others, this clean self-service hostel doubles as a social hub hosted by the effervescent Cecilia. The small dorm rooms are located right on the channel.

Puerto Luisa Cafe CAFE $
(cell 9934-0849; Costanera 317; snacks $3000; 10am-8pm Mon-Fri, 7am-8pm Sat Nov-Mar) Next to the dock, this welcoming haven offers espresso drinks, chocolates and pies in a cozy setting of oversized chairs with great sea views.

Information

Municipal tourist information (cell 8383-2080; www.ptowilliams.cl/Turismo.html; cnr Piloto Pardo & Arturo Prat; 8am-1pm & 2-5pm Mon-Fri) Offers city and day-trek maps, as well as weather and route conditions for Lago Windhond and Dientes de Navarino treks. Located in a small kiosk.

Turismo Shila (cell 7897-2005; www.turismoshila.cl; O'Higgins 220) Very helpful stop for trekkers. Offers local guides, camping rentals, bicycle rentals (CH$5000 per day), snowshoes, fishing gear and GPS maps. Also sells boat tickets and can arrange charter flights to Ushuaia.

Getting There & Away

Puerto Williams is accessible by plane or boat.
Aerovias DAP (061-262-1051; www.aeroviasdap.cl; Plaza de Ancla s/n; one-way CH$75,000) flies from Punta Arenas (1¼ hours) at 11:30am Monday to Saturday from November to March, with fewer flights in winter.

Transbordador Austral Broom (061-272-8100; www.tabsa.cl) sails from the Tres Puentes sector of Punta Arenas to Puerto Williams three or four times a month.

Porvenir

For a slice of home-baked Fuegian life, this is it. Spending a night in this rusted village of metal-clad Victorians affords you an opportunity to explore the nearby bays and countryside and absorb the laid-back local life. The king-penguin colony is usually accessed as a day tour from Punta Arenas. Stay at the wonderful **Hostería Yendegaia** (061-258-1919; www.hosteriayendegaia.com; Croacia 702; s/d/tr CH$25,000/40,000/55,000;) in a historic Magellanic home. Expect an abundant breakfast, views of the strait and spacious rooms with thick down comforters.

RAPA NUI (EASTER ISLAND)

Easter Island (Rapa Nui to its indigenous Polynesian inhabitants) is like nowhere else on earth. Historically intriguing, culturally compelling and scenically magical, this tiny speck of land looks like it's fallen off another planet. In this blissfully isolated, unpolished gem it's hard to feel connected even to Chile, over 3700km to the east, let alone the wider world. It's just you, the indigo depths and the strikingly enigmatic *moai* (giant statues) scattered amid an eerie landscape.

Dutch admiral Roddeveen landed here on Easter Sunday, 1722, creating the name. Designated Chilean territory in 1888, the island was run as a sheep *estancia*, confining indigenous Rapa Nui to Hanga Roa until 1953. Finally, in the 1960s they regained access. Today's islanders speak Spanish and Rapa Nui, an eastern Polynesian dialect. Essential expressions include *iorana* (hello), *maururu* (thank you), *pehe koe?* (how are you?) and *riva riva* (fine, good).

Each February island culture is celebrated in the elaborate and colorful **Tapati Rapa Nui festival**. Peak tourist season coincides with the hottest months from January to March; off-season is comparatively quiet. Allow at least three days to see the major sites. Rapa Nui is two hours behind mainland Chile, six hours behind GMT (five in summer).

Getting There & Away

LAN (032-210-0279; www.lan.com; Av Atamu Tekena s/n; 9am-4.30pm Mon-Fri, to 12.30pm Sat) is the only airline serving Rapa Nui. There are daily flights to/from Santiago (US$600 to $900) and twice weekly flights to/from Lima, Peru and Papeete (Tahiti).

Getting Around

Rent a Car Insular (032-210-0480; www.rentainsular.cl; Av Atamu Tekena s/n; 9am-8pm) rents scooters and motorcycles (per day from CH$20,000).

Hanga Roa

032 / POP 6700

Hanga Roa is the island's sole town, home to nearly all the island's hotels, restaurants, shops and services.

Sights

Museo Antropológico Sebastián Englert MUSEUM
(032-255-1020; www.museorapanui.cl; Tahai s/n; 9.30am-5.30pm Tue-Fri, to 12.30pm Sat & Sun)

Rapa Nui (Easter Island)

0 — 5 km
0 — 2.5 miles

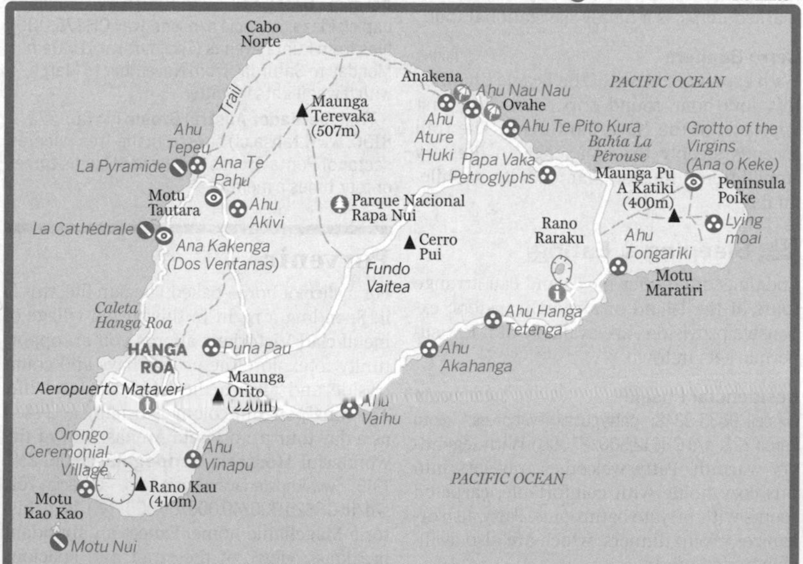

Cabo Norte
Trail
Maunga Terevaka (507m)
Anakena
Ahu Nau Nau
Ovahe
Ahu Ature Huki
Ahu Te Pito Kura
PACIFIC OCEAN
Ahu Tepeu
La Pyramide
Ana Te Pahu
Motu Tautara
Ahu Akivi
Parque Nacional Rapa Nui
Papa Vaka Petroglyphs
Bahía La Pérouse
Grotto of the Virgins (Ana o Keke)
Maunga Pu A Katiki (400m)
Península Poike
Lying moai
La Cathédrale
Ana Kakenga (Dos Ventanas)
Cerro Pui
Rano Raraku
Ahu Tongariki
Motu Maratiri
Fundo Vaitea
Caleta Hanga Roa
Ahu Hanga Tetenga
HANGA ROA
Puna Pau
Ahu Akahanga
Aeropuerto Mataveri
Maunga Orito (220m)
Ahu Vaihu
Orongo Ceremonial Village
Ahu Vinapu
Rano Kau (410m)
Motu Kao Kao
Motu Nui
PACIFIC OCEAN

FREE This well-organized museum makes a perfect introduction to the island's history and culture. It displays basalt fishhooks, obsidian spearheads and other weapons, circular beehive-shaped huts, the ceremonial houses at Orongo and a *moai* head with reconstructed fragments of its eyes. It also features replica Rongo-Rongo tablets, covered in tiny rows of tiny symbols resembling hieroglyphs.

Caleta Hanga Roa & Ahu Tautira ARCHAEOLOGICAL SITE

Your first encounter with the *moai* will probably take place at **Ahu Tautira** (Av Te Pito o Te Henua), which overlooks Caleta Hanga Roa, the fishing port in Hanga Roa at the foot of Av Te Pito o Te Henua. Here you'll find a platform with two superb *moai*.

Activities

Opportunities abound for hiking, sailing, and cycling. There's also excellent **diving** on Easter Island, with gin-clear visibility and a dramatic seascape. Try **Mike Rapu Diving Center** (032-255-1055; www.mikerapu.cl; Caleta Hanga Roa s/n; 8am-6:30pm Mon-Sat); all operators also offer snorkeling trips to Motu Nui.

A network of trails leading to some of the most beautiful sites can be explored on horseback – expect to pay about CH$30,000 for a half-day tour. One reliable operator is **Pantu** (032-210-0577; www.pikerauri.com; Sector Tahai s/n; half-/full-day tour CH$35,000/75,000; daily by reservation).

Tours

Plenty of operators do tours of the major sites, typically charging CH$42,000 for a full day and CH$25,000 for a half day. Reputable agenices include **Aku Aku Turismo** (032-210-0770; www.akuakuturismo.cl; Av Tu'u Koihu s/n; 8:30am-5pm) and **Kia Koe Tour** (032-210-0852; www.kiakoetour.cl; Av Atamu Tekena s/n; 9am-1pm & 3-6pm).

Sleeping

Book well ahead for high season. Lodgings usually provide transportation from the airport.

Camping Mihinoa CAMPGROUND $

(032-255-1593; www.camping-mihinoa.com; Av Pont s/n; campsites per person CH$5000, dm CH$10,000, d CH$20,000-30,000; wi-fi) You have options here: a clutch of well-scrubbed rooms (the dearer ones offer more privacy), several two- to six-bed dorms, some with their own bathroom, or a campsite on a grassy plot (no shade). The ablution block has hot showers (mornings and evenings). Perks include tent hire, wi-fi access (CH$5000 flat fee), a well-equipped communal kitchen and laundry service.

Hostal Tojika GUESTHOUSE $$

(7125-2210; www.rapanuiweb.com/hostaltojika/hostal.htm; Av Apina s/n; d/tr/q CH$45,000/55,000/65,000; wi-fi) A good bet for budgeteers, Hostal Tojika has several rooms that are all different, a five-bed dorm and a communal kitchen in a single building overlooking the sea. Some rooms lack natural light but the dorm is an excellent bargain. No breakfast is served but there's a small eatery at the entrance of the property.

★**Cabañas Christophe** BUNGALOW $$

(032-210-0826; www.cabanaschristophe.com; Av Policarpo Toro s/n; d CH$60,000-90,000; wi-fi) Hands down the best-value option in Hanga Roa, this charming venue seduces those seeking character and comfort, with three handsomely designed bungalows that blend hardwoods and volcanic stones. They're spacious, well appointed – think king-size beds, kitchen facilities and a private terrace – and inundated with natural light. It's at the start of the Orongo trail, about 1.5km from the centre. Reserve well in advance.

Eating & Drinking

For self-caterers, there are a couple of supermarkets on Av Atamu Tekena.

★**Mikafé** CAFETERIA, SANDWICHES $

(Caleta Hanga Roa s/n; ice cream CH$1800-3200, sandwiches & cakes CH$3500-6000; 9am-8:30pm Mon-Sat) Mmm, the *helados artesanales* (homemade ice creams)! Oh, the damn addictive banana cake! Other treats include panini, sandwiches, muffins and brownies. Also serves breakfast (from CH$3500).

★**Te Moana** CHILEAN $$$

(032-255-1578; Av Policarpo Toro s/n; mains CH$10,000-21,000; 12:30-11pm Tue-Sun) One of the most reliable options in Hanga Roa, this buzzy restaurant boasts a spiffing location, with an atmospheric veranda opening onto the ocean. It's renowned for its tasty meat and fishes dishes. The Polynesian decor is another clincher, with wood carvings and traditional artefacts adorning the walls.

Information

Banco Santander (Av Policarpo Toro; 8am-1pm Mon-Fri) Currency exchange (until 11am), and has two ATMs that accept Visa and Master Card. Credit-card holders can also get cash advances at the counter during opening hours (bring your passport).

Hospital Hanga Roa (032-210-0215; Av Simon Paoa s/n) Recently modernized.

Post office (Av Te Pito o Te Henua s/n; 8:30am-12:30pm & 2-4pm Mon-Fri, 9am-noon Sat)

Sernatur (032-210-0255; www.chile.travel/en.html; Av Policarpo Toro s/n; 9am-6pm Mon-Fri, 10am-1pm Sat) Has various brochures, maps and lists of accommodations. Some staff speak good English.

Parque Nacional Rapa Nui

Teeming with caves, *ahu* (stone platforms), fallen *moai* and petroglyphs, this **national park** (www.conaf.cl; adult/child CH$30,000/15,000; 9am-4pm) encompasses much of Rapa Nui and all the archaeological sites. The admission fee is charged in Orongo and Rano Raraku. Respect the sites: walking on the *ahu* and removing or relocating rocks of archaeological structures are strictly taboo. Handle the land gently and the *moai* will smile upon you.

Near Hanga Roa, **Ahu Tahai** is a short hike north of town, lovely at sunset, with three restored *ahu*. About 4km north of Tahai, **Ahu Tepeu** has several fallen *moai* and a village site. On the nearby coast, **Ana Kakenga** has two windows open to the ocean. **Ahu Akivi** is the site of seven *moai,* unique because they face the sea, though like all *moai* they overlook the site of a village. At the equinoxes their gaze meets the setting sun.

With white sands, clear water and leggy palms, Anakena beach is a stunning destination that abuts two major archaeological sites: **Ahu Nau Nau** and **Ahu Ature Huki**, the latter re-erected by Thor Heyerdahl and a dozen islanders.

Dazzling in scale, **Ahu Tongariki** has 15 *moai* along the largest *ahu* built against the crashing surf. A 1960 tsunami demolished several *moai* and scattered topknots, but the Japanese company Tadano re-erected *moai* in the early 1990s.

An ethereal setting of half-carved and buried *moai,* **Rano Raraku** is known as 'the nursery,' where *moai* were quarried from the slopes of this extinct volcano. It's worth a wander through the rocky jigsaw patterns of unfinished *moai*. There are 600, with the largest 21m tall. The crater holds a reedy lake under an amphitheater of handsome heads.

Visitors shouldn't miss **Rano Kau** and its crater lake, a cauldron of *tortora* reeds. Along a sea cliff 400m above, the fragile **Orongo Ceremonial Village** (adult/child CH$30,000/15,000; 9am-4pm) is where bird-cult rituals were performed. A cluster of boulders with petroglyphs depict Tangata Manu (the birdman) and Make Make (their god). Walking (7km) or biking is possible; take water.

UNDERSTAND CHILE

Chile Today

In Chile, the ground is shifting, yet for once it's not another earthquake. Former President Michelle Bachelet is back at the helm, and she has made addressing inequality the mandate of her administration. At the same time, Chile's steady growth spurt is showing signs of fatigue. With the price of number-one export copper falling, many wonder if the country will see through massive reforms. One thing is certain for this small engine that could: the status quo is no longer enough.

On the Rebound

The highest building on the continent, the 64-story Gran Torre Santiago was completed in 2013, an irrefutable symbol of the country's newfound eminence. At around the same time, Chile became the first South American country to earn membership in the Organisation for Economic Cooperation and Development (OECD). Yet, there is room for improvement. Of all OECD members, Chile has the greatest levels of inequality.

Half the country's wealth is held by 1% of the population. The number of millionaires here doubled in the early 2000s, but those living in poverty represent 14.4% of the population. Although poverty has declined by a third in the past decade, critics argue that much more can be done. The plan is to invest in public education and health care, two areas where the public has been clamoring for improvement.

Urban, poor, liberal, conservative; all of Chile is reaching for an upgrade. While its citizens negotiate the terms with some frustration, it helps to remember that Chile has been through so much in recent years. In February 2010, an 8.8-magnitude earthquake hit off the central coast with the power of 10,000 Hiroshima bombs. With the ensuing tsunamis, there were hundreds of deaths and US$30 billion in damage. Yet two months later, students returned to school, and the affected roads, ports and airports were back up and running. In large part the recovery depended on citizens who helped each other with no formal emergency response in place.

Only months later, national solidarity strengthened as the country cheered on 33 miners trapped in the San José mine, who emerged after spending 69 days underground. In 2015 another earthquake, 8.3 in magnitude, struck off the central coast near the port of Coquimbo, killing five and triggering a tsunami and the evacuations of millions.

Too bad there is no award for the most dogged country, because Chile would be a serious candidate.

History

Early History

The discovery of a single 12,500-year-old footprint in Monte Verde, near Puerto Montt, marks Chile's earliest tangible roots. In the north, Aymara and Atacameño farmers and herders predated the Inca. Other early peoples include the El Molle and the Tiwanaku, who left their mark with geoglyphs; Chango fisherfolk on the northern coast; and Diaguita who inhabited inland river valleys.

The Mapuche, shifting cultivators from the southern forests, were the only indigenous group to successfully hold off Inca domination. Meanwhile, the Cunco fished and farmed Chiloé and the mainland. In the south, groups such as Selk'nam and Yaghan long avoided contact with Europeans, who would eventually bring them to the brink of extinction.

Colonial Times

Conquistador Pedro de Valdivia and his men crossed the harsh Atacama Desert to found Santiago in the fertile Mapocho Valley in 1541. They set up the famous *encomiendas:* forced labor systems exploiting the north's relatively large, sedentary population. In the south there was no such assimilation – the Mapuche fought European colonization for over three centuries. When the *encomiendas* lost value, agricultural haciendas or *fundos* (farms), run by South American-born Spanish, took their place. These *latifundios* (estates) became the dominant force in Chilean society, with many remaining intact into the 1960s.

Revolutionary Wars & the Early Republic

Spain's trade control over the Viceroy of Peru provoked discontent among the colonies. Independence movements swept South America, with Argentine José de San Martín liberating Santiago in 1818. Under San Martín's tutelage, Chilean Bernardo O'Higgins, the illegitimate son of an Irishman, became 'supreme director' of the Chilean republic.

O'Higgins dominated politics for five years after independence, decreeing political, social, religious and educational reforms, but landowners' objections to these egalitarian measures forced his resignation. Businessman Diego Portales, spokesman for the landowners, became de facto dictator until his execution in 1837. His custom-drawn constitution centralized power in Santiago and established Catholicism as the state religion.

Expansion & Development

Chile's expansion began with its triumph over Peru and Bolivia in the War of the Pacific (1879–83), which added the nitrate-rich Atacama Desert, and treaties with the Mapuche, which added the southern Lakes District. In 1888 Chile annexed remote Rapa Nui (Easter Island).

British, North American and German capital turned the Atacama into a bonanza; nitrate prosperity also funded the government. The nitrate ports of Antofagasta and Iquique boomed until the Panama Canal (1914) reduced traffic around Cape Horn and the development of petroleum-based fertilizers made mineral nitrates obsolete.

Mining also created a new working class and nouveau riche, both of whom challenged the landowners. Elected in 1886, President José Manuel Balmaceda tackled the dilemma of unequally distributed wealth and power, igniting congressional rebellion in 1890 and a civil war that resulted in 10,000 deaths, including his own suicide.

The Struggle to Form & Reform

As late as the 1920s, up to 75% of Chile's rural population still depended on haciendas, which controlled 80% of prime agricultural land. As industry expanded and public works advanced, urban workers' welfare improved, but that of rural workers declined, forcing day laborers to the cities. The period from 1930 to 1970 saw a multifaceted struggle for agrarian reform.

During this period, the copper mines, a future cornerstone of Chile's economy, were North American–run. Elected in 1964, reformist president Eduardo Frei advocated the 'Chileanization' of the industry, giving the government 50% ownership of US-controlled mines.

Too reformist for the right and too conservative for the left, Frei's Christian Democratic administration faced many challenges, including from violent groups like the MIR (the Leftist Revolutionary Movement), which found support among coal miners and urban laborers. Activism also caught on with peasants who agitated for land reform. As the 1970 election grew near, the Christian Democratic Party, unable to satisfy society's expectations for reform, grew weaker.

Allende Comes to Power

Socialist candidate Salvador Allende's Unidad Popular (UP; Popular Unity) coalition offered a radical program advocating the nationalization of industry and the expropriation of *latifundios*. Elected in 1970 by a small margin, Allende instituted state control of many private enterprises, creating massive income redistribution. Frustrated with slow reforms, peasants seized land and the country became increasingly unstable. Declining harvests, nationalization and the courting of Cuba provoked US hostility and meddling. By 1972 Chile was paralyzed by strikes supported by the Christian Democrats and the National Party.

After a failed military coup in June 1973, the opposition gathered force and a *golpe de estado* (coup d'état) by relative unknown General Augusto Pinochet took place on September 11, 1973. The coup resulted in the death of Allende (an apparent suicide) and thousands of his supporters. Thousands of leftists, suspected leftists and sympathizers were apprehended. In Santiago's National Stadium, many detainees suffered beatings, torture and execution. Hundreds of thousands went into exile.

The Pinochet Dictatorship

From 1973 to 1989, General Pinochet headed a durable junta that dissolved congress, prohibited nearly all political activity and ruled by decree. In 1980 voters supported a new constitution that ratified Pinochet's presidency until 1989. Progress came in the form of a stabilized and prosperous economy. Nonetheless, voters rejected Pinochet's 1988 bid to extend his presidency until 1997. In 1989, 17 parties formed the coalition Concertación para la Democracia (Consensus for Democracy), whose candidate Patricio Aylwin easily won. Aylwin's presidency suffered the constraints of the new constitution, but it did see the publication of the Rettig report, which documented thousands of deaths and disappearances during the Pinochet dictatorship.

In September 1998 General Pinochet was put under house arrest in London following investigation of the deaths and disappearances of Spanish citizens in the 1973 coup aftermath. Despite international uproar, both the Court of Appeals (in 2000) and the Supreme Court (2002) ruled him unfit to stand trial. Pinochet returned to Chile, where he died in 2006. His legacy remains extremely controversial among Chileans.

Resetting the Compass

The 21st-century governments across South America became increasingly left-leaning. In Chile the trend resulted in the 2000 election of moderate leftist Ricardo Lagos, followed by his 2005 successor, Michelle Bachelet. A watershed event, it marked Chile's first woman president, a single mother who had been detained and tortured under the Pinochet regime. Suddenly, conservative Chile looked a lot more progressive.

The first Bachelet presidency was plagued by divisions within her coalition (La Concertación Democrática), which made pushing through reforms difficult. Emerging crises like the chaotic institution of a new transportation system in Santiago, corruption scandals and massive student protests made her tenure a difficult one.

After nearly 20 years of rule by the liberal Concertacíon, Chile elected as president the conservative billionaire businessman Sebastián Piñera from the center-right Alianza por Chile. Though Piñera enjoyed early popularity for his successful handling of the operation to rescue 33 trapped miners near Copiapó (see p458), his approval rating dipped sharply after the student-led educational protests (the 'Chilean Winter') in 2011. At one point, a 26% approval rating was the lowest of any postdictatorship administration.

A Seismic Shift

In the early hours of February 27, 2010, one of the largest quakes ever recorded in history hit off the coast of central Chile. The 8.8-magnitude earthquake caused massive destruction, triggering tsunamis on the coast and Archipiélago Juan Fernández and claiming 525 lives. Many homes and highways were destroyed and insurance companies estimated billions of dollars' worth of damages. After some initial looting in affected areas, order returned quickly. Chile's Teletón, an annual charity fundraising event, raised an unprecedented US$39 million for the cause. Overall, the government was praised for its swift action in initial reparations, and the outpouring of solidarity demonstrated by the Chilean people was a boost to national pride.

Brave New World

In the first decade of the millennium Chile rose as an economic star, boosted by record prices for its key export, copper. When the world economic crisis hit, Chile remained in good standing. It was the first Latin country to enter into a free trade agreement with the US, though China is now its main trading partner. As hard as Chile tries to diversify, copper still accounts for a whopping 60% of exports. Yet, with diminishing demand for copper in China, the once-bulletproof Chilean peso is finally slipping in value.

Chile closed out 2013 by electing Michelle Bachelet once again to the presidency. Voter turnout was notably low for the first presidential election in Chile in which voting was no longer mandatory. The elections also brought young reform candidates to congress, such as Camila Vallejo and Giorgio Jackson, the former undergraduate leaders of the student protests.

Finding its way through financial highs and domestic snags, Chile may have to reset its compass to navigate its mounting social, ecological and economic issues; such complications are inevitable on the path to progress.

Culture

Centuries with little outside exposure, accompanied by an especially influential Roman Catholic Church, fostered a high degree of cultural conformity and conservatism in Chile. The Pinochet years of repression and censorship compounded this isolation. But the national psyche is now at its most fluid, as Chile undergoes radical social change.

The Catholic Church itself has gotten more progressive. Society is opening up, introducing liberal laws and challenging conservative values. Nowhere is this trend more evident than with the urban youth, with Generations Y and Z – the first to grow up without the censorship, curfew or restrictions of dictatorship – far more questioning and less discouraged by theoretical consequences. Authorities may perceive it as a threat, but Chile's youth is taking a stand.

The momentum has also influenced the provinces, namely Magallanes and Aisén, to protest higher costs and general neglect by the central government.

Population

While the vast majority of the population is of Spanish ancestry mixed with indigenous groups, several moderate waves of immigrants have also settled here – particularly British, Irish, French, Italians, Croatians and Palestinians. Germans also began immigrating in 1848 and left their stamp on the Lakes District. The northern Andes is home to around 69,000 indigenous Aymara and Atacameño peoples. Almost 10 times that amount (around 620,000 people) are Mapuche. About 3800 Rapa Nui, of Polynesian ancestry, live on Easter Island. Over a third of the country's estimated 17.6 million people reside in the capital and its suburbs.

Lifestyle

Travelers crossing over from Peru or Bolivia may wonder where the stereotypical 'South America' went. Chilean lifestyle superficially resembles its European counterparts. A yawning gulf separates the highest and lowest incomes in Chile, resulting in a dramatic gap of living standards and an exaggerated class consciousness. Lifestyles are lavish for Santiago's *cuicos* (upper class), with swish apartment blocks and a couple of maids, while at the other end of the scale people live in precarious homes without running water.

Chileans have a strong work ethic, but are always eager for a good *carrete* (party). Young people usually remain dependent on their parents through university years and live at home through their 20s.

Generally, the famous Latin American machismo (masculine pride) is subtle in Chile and there's a great deal of respect for women. For gays and lesbians, Chile is still quite a conservative culture with little public support for alternate lifestyles.

Religion

About 55% of Chileans are Catholic, 13% are Evangelical Protestants, 7% belong to other religions and 25% are without any religious affiliation.

Arts

Literature

This land of poets earned its repute with Nobel Prize winners Gabriela Mistral and Pablo Neruda. Vicente Huidobro is considered one of the founders of modern Spanish-language poetry and Nicanor Parra continues the tradition.

Chile's best known export, contemporary writer Isabel Allende, bases much of her fiction in her native country. Other key literary figures include José Donoso, whose novel *Curfew* narrates life under dictatorship through the eyes of a returned exile, and Antonio Skármeta, who wrote the novel *Burning Patience,* upon which the award-winning Italian film *Il Postino* (The Postman) is based. Luis Sepúlveda (1949–) has made outstanding contributions such as *Patagonia Express* and the novella *The Old Man Who Read Love Stories.*

Marcela Serrano (1951–) is praised as the best of current Latina authors. Pedro Lemebel (1955–) writes of homosexuality, transgender issues and other controversial subjects with top-notch shock value. Worldwide, Roberto Bolaño (1953–2003) is acclaimed as one of Latin America's best. The posthumous publication of his encyclopedic *2666* sealed his cult-hero status.

Cinema

Chilean cinema has proved dynamic and diverse in recent years. Addressing class stratification, Sebastián Silva's *La nana* (The Maid) won two Sundance awards in 2009. Twentysomething director Nicolás López used dark humor and comic-book culture to the delight of youth audiences with *Promedio rojo* (2005). *Mi mejor enemigo* (My Best Enemy; 2004) tells of not-so-distant enemies in a 1978 territorial dispute with Argentina in Tierra del Fuego. Andrés Wood's hit *Machuca* (2004) chronicles coming-of-age during class-conscious and volatile 1973. Acclaimed documentarian Patricio Guzmán explores the social impact of the dictatorship; his credits include the fascinating *Obstinate Memory* (1997).

The documentary-style film *180° South* (2010) uses a surfer's quest to explore Patagonia to highlight environmental issues. In 2012 two Chilean films won notable Sundance awards: *Violeta se fue a los cielos*, another Andrés Wood film, about the life of folk artist Violeta Parra, and *Joven y alocada*, a provocative coming-of-age story that was the cinematic debut of director Marialy Rivas.

Crystal Fairy & the Magical Cactus (2013) brought comedic actor Michael Cera to Chile to play an arrogant tourist on a quest to trip on San Pedro cactus. The 2015 film *The 33* tells the story of 'Los 33' – the trapped Chilean miners (see p458) – courtesy of producer Michael Medavoy of *Black Swan* fame.

Cuisine

Food

Chilean cuisine is built around fantastic raw materials: in the market you can get anything from goat cheese to avocados, fresh herbs and a fantastic variety of seafood. Though breakfast is meager – instant coffee or tea, rolls and jam – food and drink options get more appealing as the day progresses. At lunch, fuel up with a hearty *menú del día* (inexpensive set meal), with soup and a main dish of fish or meat with rice or vegetables. Central markets are an ideal place for these cheap and traditional meals; even the most basic eateries offer plenty of fresh lemon wedges and spicy sauces you can use to doctor up your plate.

Favorite sandwiches include the prolific *completo* (hot dog with mayo, avocado and tomato) and *churrasco* (steak sandwich with avocado and tomato). Empanadas are everywhere, from the classic *pino* (beef) to the gourmet seafood-stuffed varieties in coastal towns. Indeed, some of Chile's most delicious specialties are found at the beach, from *machas a la parmesana* (razor clams baked in parmesan cheese and white wine) to aromatic seafood stews like *paila marina* and *caldillo de congrio* – the latter was famously Pablo Neruda's favorite. *Chupe de mariscos* is shellfish baked in a medley of butter, bread crumbs and cheese.

Everywhere in Chile, you'll find hearty classics like *lomo a lo pobre* (steak topped with fried eggs and french fries), *pastel de choclo* (baked corn casserole) and the heart-stopping *chorrillana* (a mountain-high platter featuring fries topped with onions, fried eggs and beef).

Drink

Chile and Peru both claim authorship of pisco, a potent grape brandy, and the famous *pisco sour* cocktail, in which *pisco* is mixed with fresh lemon juice and sugar. Many Chileans indulge in the citrusy aperitif at the start of a leisurely lunch or dinner. Young Chilenos drink *piscolas* (pisco and Coca-Cola) at parties.

With ample sunshine and moderate temperatures, Chile also has the ideal terroir for growing and producing wine. While cabernet sauvignon still reigns supreme, many foreigners fall in love with another red: Carmenere, originally produced in France and now unique to Chile. Check out www.winesofchile.org to learn more about Chilean wine regions and labels.

Kunstmann and Cólonos are Chile's best beers. A draft beer is called *schop*. *Bebidas* (soft drinks) are universally adored. Street vendors sell *mote con huesillo*, a refreshing peach nectar made with barley and peaches – it's a unique liquid snack you should try at least once.

Instant Nescafé is a national plague, though more cafes are starting to offer *cafe en grano* ('real' coffee).

Sports

Fútbol (soccer) is the most rabidly popular spectator sport. Most recently, the Chilean national team made an excellent showing at the 2014 World Cup. Tennis has gained ground, thanks to Nicolás Massú and Fernando González being awarded Olympic gold medals in 2004, and González' silver medal in 2008. Most young Chileans who can afford it go big on individual sports like surfing, skiing and mountain biking. Chilean rodeos proliferate in the summer, when flamboyantly dressed *huasos* (cowboys) compete in half-moon stadiums.

Environment

The Land

Continental Chile stretches 4300km from Peru to the Strait of Magellan. Less than 200km wide on average, the land rises from sea level to above 6000m in some areas, pocked with volcanoes and with a narrow depression running through the middle.

Mainland Chile, dry-topped and glacial heavy, has distinct temperate and geographic zones, with the length of the Andes running alongside. Norte Grande runs from the Peruvian border to Chañaral, dominated by the Atacama Desert and the *altiplano* (Andean high plain). Norte Chico stretches from Chañaral to Río Aconcagua, with scrubland and denser forest enjoying increased rainfall. Here, mining gives way to agriculture in the major river valleys.

Middle Chile's wide river valleys span from Río Aconcagua to Concepción and the Río Biobío. This is the main agricultural and wine-growing region. The Araucanía and Lakes District go south of the Biobío to Palena, featuring extensive native forests and lakes. Chiloé is the country's largest island, with dense forests and a patchwork of pasturelands. Patagonia has indeterminate borders: for some it begins with the Carretera Austral, for others it starts in rugged Aisén, running south to the Campos de Hielo (the continental ice fields), and ending in Magallanes and Tierra del Fuego.

Flora & Fauna

Bounded by ocean, desert and mountain, Chile is home to a unique environment that developed much on its own, creating a number of endemic species.

In the desert north, candelabra cacti grow by absorbing water from the fog *(camanchaca)*. Animals include guanaco (a large camelid), vicuña (found at high altitudes), and their domestic relatives llama and alpaca. The gangly ostrich-like rhea (called *ñandú* in Spanish) and the plump, scraggly-tailed viscacha (a wild relative of the chinchilla) are other unusual creatures. Birdlife is diverse, from Andean gulls and giant coots to three species of flamingo.

Southern forests are famed for the monkey-puzzle tree *(pehuén)* and *alerce*, the world's second-oldest tree. Abundant plant life in Valdivian temperate rainforest includes the nalca, the world's largest herbaceous plant. Puma roam the Andes, along with a dwindling population of *huemul (Andean deer) in the south. The diminutive pudú* deer inhabits thick forests, *bandurrias* (buff-necked ibis) frequent southern pastures and *chucao* tweet trailside. A colony of Humboldt and Magellanic penguins seasonally inhabit the northwestern coast of Chiloé.

From the Lakes District to Magallanes, you'll find verdant upland forests of the widespread genus *Nothofagus* (southern beech). Decreased rainfall on the eastern plains of Magallanes and Tierra del Fuego creates extensive grasslands. Protected guanaco have made a comeback within Torres del Paine, and Punta Arenas hosts colonies of Magellanic penguins and cormorants. Chile's long coastline features diverse marine mammals, including sea lions, otters, fur seals and whales.

National Parks

Parklands comprise 19% of Chile, a nice number until you realize that some of these 'protected' areas allow logging and dams. Though tenuous and fragile, these wild places are some of the most stunning and diverse landscapes on the continent. In terms of visitors, Chilean parks are considerably underutilized, with the notable exception of Torres del Paine. Parks and reserves are administered by the underfunded Corporación Nacional Forestal, with an emphasis on forestry and land management, not tourism. Visit **Conaf** (Corporación Nacional Forestal; ☎02-663-0000; www.conaf.cl; Bulnes 285, Centro; ⏰9:30am-5:30pm Mon-Thu, to 4:30pm Fri; Ⓜ Toesca) in Santiago for inexpensive maps and brochures.

Chile has around 133 private reserves, covering almost 4000 sq km. Highlights include Parque Pumalín in northern Patagonia and El Cañi, near Pucón (the country's first). Big projects in the works include Parque Tantauco on Chiloé and Valle Chacabuco (Patagonia National Park), near Cochrane.

Here are some popular and accessible national parks and reserves:

Alerce Andino Preserves stands of *alerce* trees near Puerto Montt.

Altos del Lircay A reserve with views of the Andean divide and a loop trek to Radal Siete Tazas.

Chiloé (p506) Features broad sandy beaches, lagoons and myth-bound forests.

Conguillío (p484) Mixed forests of araucaria, cypress and southern beech surrounding the active, snowcapped Volcán Llaima.

Huerquehue (p489) Near Pucón, hiking trails through araucaria forests, with outstanding views of Volcán Villarrica.

Lauca (p474) East of Arica, with active and dormant volcanoes, clear blue lakes, abundant birdlife, *altiplano* villages and extensive steppes.

Los Flamencos In and around San Pedro de Atacama, a reserve protecting salt lakes and high-altitude lagoons, flamingos, eerie desert landforms and hot springs.

Nahuelbuta (p480) In the high coastal range, preserves the area's largest remaining araucaria forests.

Nevado Tres Cruces (p457) East of Copiapó, with a 6330m-high namesake peak and 6893m-high Ojos del Salado.

Puyehue (p494) Near Osorno, with fancy hot springs and a family ski resort. Has a popular hike through volcanic desert, up the crater, to thermals and geyser fields.

Queulat (p510) Wild evergreen forest, mountains and glaciers stretch across 70km of the Carretera Austral.

Torres del Paine (p522) Chile's showpiece near Puerto Natales, with an excellent trail network around the country's most revered vistas.

Vicente Pérez Rosales (p498) Chile's second-oldest national park includes spectacular Lago Todos los Santos and Volcán Osorno.

Villarrica (p490) Villarrica's smoking symmetrical cone attracts trekkers, snowboarders and skiers.

Environmental Issues

With so much recent growth in industry, Chile is facing a spate of environmental issues. Santiago is among the Americas' most polluted cities. Further afield, Chile's forests continue to lose ground to plantations of fast-growing exotics, such as eucalyptus and Monterey pine. Caught in a tug-of-war between their economic and ecological value, native tree species have also declined precipitously due to logging. In the south of Chile, an area considered ideal for dams due to its many rivers and heavy rains, there's an ongoing battle between construction companies and environmental groups, with the government in the middle. Nearby, the continued expansion of southern Chile's salmon farms is polluting water, devastating underwater ecology and depleting other fish stocks. In Torres del Paine, the notorious 2011 fire (allegedly ignited accidentally by a camper) brought to public attention the lack of funding for professional firefighting.

SURVIVAL GUIDE

Directory A–Z

ACCOMMODATIONS

Chile has accommodations to suit every budget. Listings are organized in order of our preference considering value for cost. All prices listed are high-season rates for rooms that include breakfast and a private bathroom, unless otherwise specified. Room rates may be the same for single or double occupancy. Yet there may be a price difference between a double with two beds and one matrimonial bed (often with the shared bed more expensive). Wi-fi is common.

In tourist destinations, prices may double during the height of high season (late December to mid-March), and extra-high rates are charged at Christmas, New Year and Easter week. If you want to ask about discounts or cheaper rooms, do so at the reservation phase. Bargaining for better accommodation rates once you have arrived is not common and frowned upon.

At many midrange and top-end hotels, payment in US dollars (either cash or credit) legally sidesteps the crippling 19% IVA (*impuesto de valor agregado;* value-added tax). If there is any question as to whether IVA is included in the rates, clarify before paying. A hotel might not omit the tax from your bill without your prodding. In theory, the discount is strictly for those paying in dollars or with a credit card.

If trying to reserve a room, note that small lodgings in Chile are not always responsive to emails. Call them instead to make bookings more quickly.

> **SLEEPING PRICE RANGES**
>
> The following price indicators apply for a double room in high season. Prices include breakfast and private bathroom unless otherwise indicated.
>
> **$** less than CH$40,000
>
> **$$** CH$40,000 to CH$75,000
>
> **$$$** more than CH$75,000

ACTIVITIES

Climbers intending to scale border peaks like the Pallachatas or Ojos del Salado must have permission from Chile's **Dirección de Fronteras y Límites** (Difrol; 02-671-4110; www.difrol.cl; Bandera 52, 4th fl, Santiago). It's possible to request permission prior to arriving in Chile on the agency's website.

EMBASSIES & CONSULATES

Argentine Embassy (02-2582-2606; http://csigo.cancilleria.gov.ar/; Vicuña Mackenna 41, Santiago)

Australian Embassy (02-2550-3500; www.chile.embassy.gov.au; Goyonochea 3621, 12th fl, Las Condes, Santiago) Australian Embassy in Santiago handles services for Chile, Colombia, Ecuador and Venezuela.

Bolivian Embassy (02-2232-8180; cgbolivia@manquehue.net; Av Santa María 2796, Santiago)

Brazilian Embassy (02-2698-2486; santiago.itamaraty.gov.br; Ovalle 1665, Santiago)

Canadian Embassy (02-2362-9660; enqserv@dfait-maeci.gc.ca; Tajamar 481, 12th fl, Santiago)

French Embassy (02-2470-8000; www.ambafrance-cl.org; Av Condell 65, Santiago)

German Embassy (02-2463-2500; www.santiago.diplo.de; Las Hualtatas 5677, Vitacura, Santiago)

Irish Embassy (02-245-6616; Goyenechea 3162, Oficina 801, Las Condes, Santiago)

Israeli Embassy (02-750-0500; http://embassies.gov.il; San Sebastián 2812, 5th fl, Las Condes, Santiago)

New Zealand Embassy (02-616-3000; http://www.nzembassy.com/chile; Goyenechea 3000, 12th fl, Las Condes, Santiago)

Peruvian Embassy (☎02-2235-4600; conpersantiago@adsl.tie.cl; Padre Mariano 10, Oficina 309, Providencia, Santiago)

UK Embassy (☎02-2370-4100; www.gov.uk/government/world/chile; Av El Bosque Norte 0125, 3rd fl, Las Condes, Santiago)

US Embassy (☎02-2330-3000; chile.usembassy.gov; Av Andrés Bello 2800, Las Condes, Santiago)

GAY & LESBIAN TRAVELERS

Chile is a very conservative, Catholic-minded country, yet strides in tolerance are being made. In 2015, Chile legalized same-sex civil unions. Santiago has an active gay scene, concentrated in Barrio Bellavista. **Movil H** (Movement for the Integration and Liberation of Homosexuals; www.movilh.cl) advocates for gay rights. **Guia Gay Chile** (www.guiagay.cl) lists gay nightlife throughout Chile.

HEALTH

Medical care in Santiago and other cities is generally good, but it may be difficult to find assistance in remote areas. Public hospitals in Chile are reasonable but private *clínicas* are your best option. Outside of the Atacama Desert, tap water is safe to drink. Altitude sickness and dehydration are the most common concerns in the north, and sunburn in the ozone-depleted south – apply sunscreen and wear sunglasses. Chile does not require vaccinations.

INSURANCE

Signing up for a travel-insurance policy is a good idea. For Chile, a basic theft/loss and medical policy is recommended – note that some companies exclude adventure sports from coverage.

Worldwide travel insurance is available at www.lonelyplanet.com/travel-insurance. You can buy, extend and claim online anytime – even if you're already on the road.

INTERNET ACCESS

Most regions have excellent internet connections, wi-fi access and reasonable prices. Wi-fi may be slow in rural areas.

LEGAL MATTERS

Chile's *carabineros* (police) have a reputation for being professional and polite. Don't *ever* make the error of attempting to bribe the police, whose reputation for institutional integrity is high. Penalties for common offenses are similar to those given in much of Europe and North America. However, the possession, use or trafficking of drugs – including soft drugs such as cannabis – is treated very seriously and results in severe fines and imprisonment. Police can demand identification at any time, so carry your passport. Throughout the country, the toll-free emergency telephone number for the police is ☎133.

EATING PRICE RANGES

The following price ranges refer to a standard main course.

$ less than CH$8000

$$ CH$8000 to CH$14,000

$$$ more than CH$14,000

MAPS

In Santiago, the **Instituto Geográfico Militar** (☎02-2460-6800; www.igm.cl; Dieciocho 369, Centro; ⊙8:30am-1pm, 2-5pm Mon-Fri) near Toesca metro station sells 1:50,000 regional topo maps; you can also buy them online. These are the best maps for hikers, though some are outdated. Conaf in Santiago allows photocopying of national-park maps. JLM Mapas publishes regional and trekking maps at scales ranging from 1:50,000 to 1:500,000. While helpful, they don't claim 100% accuracy.

Santiago maps are available on **Map City** (www.mapcity.cl). If driving, pick up a Copec driving guide with detailed highway maps and excellent plans of Chilean cities, towns and many villages.

MONEY

The Chilean unit of currency is the peso (CH$). Bank notes come in denominations of 500, 1000, 2000, 5000, 10,000 and 20,000 pesos. It can be difficult to change bills larger than CH$5000 in rural areas. Solicit change with an apologetic face and the words *'¿Tiene suelto?'* (Do you have change?).

Santiago has the best exchange rates and a ready market for European currencies. Chile's currency has been stable in recent years, with the value of the US dollar lower during peak tourist season. It's best to pay all transactions in pesos.

ATMs

Chile's many ATM machines, known as Redbanc, are the easiest and most convenient way to access funds. Your bank will likely charge a small fee for each transaction. Most ATMs have instructions in Spanish and English: choose 'foreign card' *(tarjeta extranjera)* when starting the transaction. You *cannot* rely on ATMs in San Pedro de Atacama, Pisco Elqui, Bahía Inglesa or in small Patagonian towns.

Cash

A few banks will exchange cash (usually US dollars only); *casas de cambio* (exchange houses) in Santiago and more tourist-oriented destinations will also exchange cash.

Credit Cards

Most established businesses welcome credit cards, although it's best not to depend on it. Consumers may be charged the 6% surcharge businesses must pay. Credit cards can also be useful to show 'sufficient funds' before entering another country.

Tipping

It's customary to tip 10% of the bill in restaurants. Taxi drivers do not require tips, although you may round off the fare for convenience.

OPENING HOURS

High season hours are given in listings. In many provincial cities and towns, restaurants and services are closed on Sunday and tourist offices close in low season.

Banks 9am to 2pm weekdays; sometimes 10am to 1pm Saturday

Government offices & businesses 9am to 6pm weekdays

Museums Often closed Monday

Shops 10am to 8pm; some close between 1pm and 3pm

POST

Correos de Chile (☎800-267-736; www.correos.cl), Chile's national postal service, has reasonably dependable but sometimes rather slow postal services. Sending parcels is straightforward, although a customs official may have to inspect your package before a postal clerk will accept it.

PUBLIC HOLIDAYS

Following are Chile's national holidays, when government offices and businesses are closed:

Año Nuevo (New Year) January 1

Semana Santa (Easter Week) March or April

Día del Trabajo (Labor Day) May 1

Glorias Navales Commemorating the naval Battle of Iquique; May 21

Corpus Christi May/June; dates vary

Día de San Pedro y San Pablo (St Peter and St Paul's Day) June 29

Asunción de la Virgen (Assumption) August 15

Día de Unidad Nacional (Day of National Unity) First Monday of September

Día de la Independencia Nacional (National Independence Day) September 18

Día del Ejército (Armed Forces Day) September 19

Día de la Raza (Columbus Day) October 12

Todo los Santos (All Saints' Day) November 1

Inmaculada Concepción (Immaculate Conception) December 8

Navidad (Christmas Day) December 25

SAFE TRAVEL

Compared with other South American countries, Chile is remarkably safe. Petty thievery is a problem in larger cities, bus terminals and at beach resorts in summertime, so always keep a close eye on all belongings. Photographing military installations is strictly prohibited.

TELEPHONE

Call centers with private cabins are rapidly being replaced by internet cafes with Skype.

Chile's country code is ☎56; most landline numbers have six or seven digits. Remote tour operators and lodges have satellite phones with a Santiago prefix.

Cell-phone numbers have eight digits, plus the two-digit prefix ☎09. The prefix must be used when calling from a landline or Skype-type calling service. Drop the prefix when calling cell-to-cell. If calling cell-to-landline, add the landline's area code. Cell phones sell for as little as CH$12,000 and can be charged up with prepaid phone cards.

Do your homework if you want to bring your own cell phone: you'll need a SIM unlocked GSM-compatible phone that operates on a frequency of 850MHz or 1900MHz (commonly used in the US). If you have such a phone you can buy a new SIM card from a Chilean operator such as Entel or Movistar, then purchase phone credit in kiosks.

TIME

Chile is three hours behind GMT.

TOILETS

Used toilet paper should be discarded in trash bins. Public toilets rarely provide toilet paper, so carry your own wherever you go.

TOURIST INFORMATION

The national tourist service, **Sernatur** (www.sernatur.cl), has offices in Santiago and most cities. Many towns have municipal tourist offices, usually on the main plaza or at the bus terminal.

VISAS

Nationals of the US, Canada, Australia and the EU do not need a visa to visit Chile. Passports are obligatory and are essential for cashing traveler's checks and checking into hotels.

The Chilean government collects a US$117/132/23 'reciprocity' fee from arriving Australian/Canadian/Mexican citizens, in response to their governments imposing a similar fee on Chilean citizens applying for visas. The payment applies only to tourists arriving by air in Santiago and is valid for the life of the passport.

On arrival, you'll be handed a 90-day tourist card. Don't lose it! You will be asked for it upon leaving the country.

VOLUNTEERING

Experiment Chile (www.experiment.cl) organizes 14-week language-learning and volunteer programs. Language schools can often place students in volunteer work as well. The non-profit organization **Un Techo Para Chile** (www.untechoparachile.cl) builds homes for low-income families throughout the country.

Getting There & Away

ENTERING THE COUNTRY

Most short-term travelers touch down in Santiago, while those on a South American odyssey come via bus from Peru, bus or boat from Argentina, or 4WD trip from Bolivia. Entry is generally straightforward as long as your passport is valid for at least six months beyond your arrival date.

Chile's northern border touches Peru and Bolivia, while its vast eastern boundary hugs Argentina. Of the numerous border crossings with Argentina, only a few are served by public transportation. Most international buses depart from Terminal de Buses in Santiago.

Crossing the border into Argentina is the easiest option. Buses with international routes simply cross – no changing, no fees. Border outposts are open daylight hours, although a few long-haul buses cross at night.

Flights, cars and tours can be booked online at lonelyplanet.com/bookings.

AIR

Chile has direct connections with North America, the UK, Europe, Australia and New Zealand, in addition to neighboring countries. International flights within South America tend to be fairly expensive, but there are bargain round-trip fares between Santiago and Buenos Aires and Lima.

Santiago's **Aeropuerto Internacional Arturo Merino Benítez** (www.aeropuertosantiago.cl) is the main port of entry. Some regional airports have international services to neighboring countries. Only LAN flies to Rapa Nui (Easter Island). DAP Airlines flies between Patagonia and Tierra del Fuego.

BUS

Argentina

There are 19 crossings between Chile and Argentina. Popular crossings include the following:

- Calama to Jujuy and Salta
- La Serena to San Juan
- Santiago or Valparaíso to Mendoza and Buenos Aires
- Temuco to San Martín de los Andes
- Osorno to Bariloche via Paso Cardenal Samoré
- Puerto Ramírez to Esquel
- Puerto Natales to Río Turbio and El Calafate

Bolivia

Road connections between Bolivia and Chile have improved, with a paved highway running from Arica to La Paz. The route from Iquique to Colchane is also paved – although the road beyond to Oruro is not. There are buses on both routes, but more on the former.

Brazil

Long-haul buses leave from Santiago. The São Paulo–Santiago trip takes a punishing 55 hours.

Peru

Tacna to Arica is the only overland crossing, with a choice of bus, *colectivo*, taxi or train.

CAR & MOTORCYCLE

In order to drive into Argentina, special insurance is required (try any insurance agency; the cost is about CH$20,000 for seven days). There can be additional charges and confusing paperwork if you're taking a rental car out of Chile; ask the rental agency to talk you through it.

Getting Around

AIR

Time-saving flights have become more affordable in Chile and are sometimes cheaper than a comfortable long-distance bus. **LAN** (☎ 600-526-2000; www.lan.com) and **Sky** (☎ 600-600-2828; www.skyairline.cl) are the two principal domestic carriers; the latter often offers cheaper fares.

BICYCLE

To pedal your way through Chile, a *todo terreno* (mountain bike) is essential – find them for rental in more touristy towns and cities. For cyclists, the climate can be a real challenge. Chilean motorists are usually courteous, but on narrow two-lane highways without shoulders cars passing can be a hazard. Most towns outside the Carretera Austral have bike-repair shops.

BOAT

Passenger/car ferries and catamarans connect Puerto Montt with points along the Carretera Austral, including Caleta Gonzalo (Chaitén) and Coyhaique. Ferries and catamarans also connect Quellón and Castro, Chiloé to Chaitén.

A highlight is the trip from Puerto Montt to Puerto Natales on board Navimag ferries. Book with **Navimag** (☎ 065-243-2361; www.navimag.com; Angelmó 1735; ⏲ 9am-1pm & 2:30-6pm Mon-Fri, 11am-1pm Sat) far in advance. Note that this is a cargo vessel outfitted for tourism, not a cruise ship.

Known as the Cruce de Lagos, a 12-hour scenic boat/bus combination travels between Petrohué, Chile, and Bariloche, Argentina.

BUS

The Chilean bus system is fabulous. Tons of companies vie for customers with *ofertas* (seasonal promotions), discounts and added luxuries like movies. Long-distance buses are comfortable, fast and punctual with safe luggage holds and toilets.

Chile's biggest bus company is the punctual Tur Bus (p438), with an all-embracing network of services around the country. Its primary competitor is Pullman Bus (p438), with extensive services around Chile.

Specifically aimed at backpackers, **Pachamama by Bus** (☎ 02-2688-8018; www.pachamamabybus.com; Agustinas 2113, Barrio Brasil, Santiago) is a hop-on, hop-off service with two long routes exploring the north and south, respectively. It's not cheap, but it takes you straight to many out-of-the-way national parks and other attractions not accessible by public transportation.

CAR & MOTORCYCLE

Having wheels gets you to remote national parks and most places off the beaten track. This is especially true in the Atacama Desert, Carretera Austral and Rapa Nui (Easter Island). Security problems are minor, but always lock your vehicle and remove valuables.

Driver's License

Bring along an International Driving Permit (IDP) as well as the license from your home country. Some rental-car agencies don't require an IDP.

LOCAL TRANSPORTATION

Towns and cities have taxis, which are metered or have set fees for destinations. *Colectivos* are taxis with fixed routes marked on signs. Rates are about CH$400 per ride. *Micros* are city buses, clearly numbered and marked with their destination. Santiago's quick and easy-to-use metro system connects the most visited neighborhoods.

TOURS

Adventure-tour operators have mushroomed throughout Chile; most have offices in Santiago and seasonal offices in the location of their trips. **Chilean Travel Service** (CTS; ☎ 02-251-0400; www.ctsturismo.cl; Antonio Bellet 77, Providencia) has well-informed multilingual staff and can organize accommodations and tours all over Chile through your local travel agency.

TRAIN

Empresa de los Ferrocarriles del Estado (www.efe.cl) runs a southbound passenger service from Santiago to Chillán, with many intermediate stops. Check the website for updates and information.

Colombia

Includes ➡

Best Adventures

- ➡ Trekking to Ciudad Perdida (p572)
- ➡ Caving in Río Claro (p595)
- ➡ Exploring the Paso del Conejo circuit in PNN El Cocuy (p558)
- ➡ Rafting Río Suárez (p559)
- ➡ Journeying to Punta Gallinas (p574)

Best Festivals

- ➡ Carnaval de Barranquilla (p575)
- ➡ Festival de Música del Pacífico Petronio Álvarez (p605)
- ➡ Carnaval de Negros y Blancos (p615)
- ➡ Desfile de Yipao (p601)
- ➡ Feria de las Flores (p591)

Why Go?

Colombia is an exhilarating cocktail of condensed South America with a shot of Caribbean thrown in. Boasting colorful traditions, striking landscapes and extremely hospitable locals, Colombia has an incredible variety of experiences to keep those magic travel moments coming thick and fast.

In one day it's possible to travel from glacier-covered Andean peaks to crystalline Caribbean beaches, or from immense sand dunes to lush tropical rainforest. Beyond the cinematic panoramas, Colombia is also a fascinating mix of the old and new, with impressive pre-Hispanic ruins and enchanting colonial towns vying for your attention alongside progressive cities with chic dining and vibrant nightlife.

Add in a rich mix of indigenous, Afro-descendant and European cultures and you'll discover why so many visitors rework their travel plans to return. Check your preconceptions at the door and uncover more than a few surprises in this accessible and utterly thrilling destination.

When to Go

Bogotá

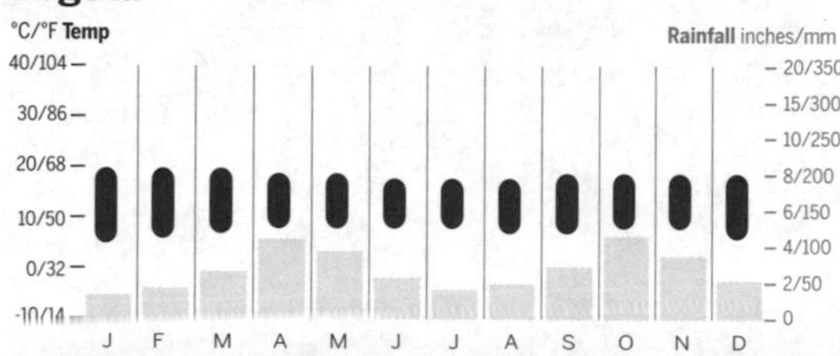

Feb Sunny skies throughout the Andean and Caribbean regions are perfect for outdoor activities.

Aug & Sep The cultural scene blossoms, with festivals including Medellín's Feria de las Flores.

Oct & Nov Heavy rains send the crowds packing and prices drop; best trekking in the Amazon.

Connections

Sitting proudly at the top of the continent, Colombia is a strategic gateway between South and Central America. While there is no land crossing with Panama, it is possible to cross via ship or private yacht from Cartagena or by small boat from the idyllic Caribbean town of Capurganá.

Major land crossings include the borders with Venezuela at Maicao, in the arid Guajira, and Cúcuta, on the far side of the soaring peaks of the Cordillera Oriental. The main crossing point to Ecuador is at Ipiales in the southern mountainous region of Nariño.

Heading further south, there are adventurous river crossings into Brazil and Peru from Leticia in the Amazon.

ITINERARIES

One Week

Begin your whirlwind Colombian tour by walking the romantic streets of colonial Cartagena before heading along the Caribbean coast to cool off beneath the majestic Sierra Nevada at the jungle-clad beaches of Parque Nacional Natural Tayrona. Then head south for a day of high-adrenaline outdoor adventure in San Gil. Finish your trip in Bogotá, visiting the capital's fascinating museums and atmospheric nightspots.

Two Weeks

After completing the above, head south to San Agustín for horse riding among the impressive pre-Columbian statues scattered around rolling hills. Continue on to Salento to stroll through coffee plantations and learn to prepare the perfect cup. Crane your neck to admire towering wax palms in nearby Valle de Cocora before continuing onto Medellín to party with the *paisas* (people from northwest Colombia), Colombia's most outgoing residents.

Essential Food & Drink

- **Bandeja paisa** Artery-clogging tray of sausage, beans, ground beef, pork rind, avocado, egg, plantains and rice.
- **Ajiaco** Andean chicken soup with corn, many kinds of potatoes and a local herb known as *guasca*.
- **Aguardiente** Alcoholic spirit flavored with anise that produces wild nights and shocking hangovers.
- **Tamale** Chopped pork with rice and vegetables folded in a maize dough, steamed in banana leaves with many different regional varieties.
- **Chocolate santafereño** A cup of hot chocolate served with a chunk of cheese and bread.
- **Lulada** Refreshing iced drink from Valle de Cauca made from crushed *lulo* fruit and lemons.
- **Hormigas culonas** Large fried ants, unique to Santander.

AT A GLANCE

- **Currency** Peso (COP$)
- **Language** Spanish
- **Money** ATMs in most towns; credit cards widely accepted
- **Visas** Not required for citizens of most Western countries
- **Time** GMT minus five hours

Fast Facts

- **Area** 1.14 million sq km
- **Population** 47 million
- **Capital** Bogotá
- **Emergency** ☎123
- **Country Code** ☎57

Exchange Rates

Australia	A$1	COP$2164
Canada	C$1	COP$2283
Euro zone	€1	COP$3423
New Zealand	NZ$1	COP$1917
UK	UK£1	COP$4668
USA	US$1	COP$3026

Set Your Budget

- **Dorm bed** US$8
- **Set lunch** US$3
- **Beer in a bar** US$1.50-2
- **Local bus ride** US0.60

Resources

- **ProExport** (www.colombia.travel)
- **El Tiempo** (www.eltiempo.com)
- **Colombia Reports** (www.colombiareports.com)

Colombia Highlights

1. Wander the enchanting, perfectly preserved streets of colonial **Cartagena** (p575).
2. Visit excellent museums, cozy bars and vibrant discos in **Bogotá** (p544).
3. Soak up the sun on the spectacular jungle-lined beaches of **Parque Nacional Natural Tayrona** (p570).
4. Hike through the dense jungle of the Sierra Nevada to the mysterious ruins of **Ciudad Perdida** (p572).
5. Try your hand picking fresh coffee beans on a working farm in the **Zona Cafetera** (p588).
6. Paddle through flooded forests and spot pink dolphins in the **Amazon** (p620).

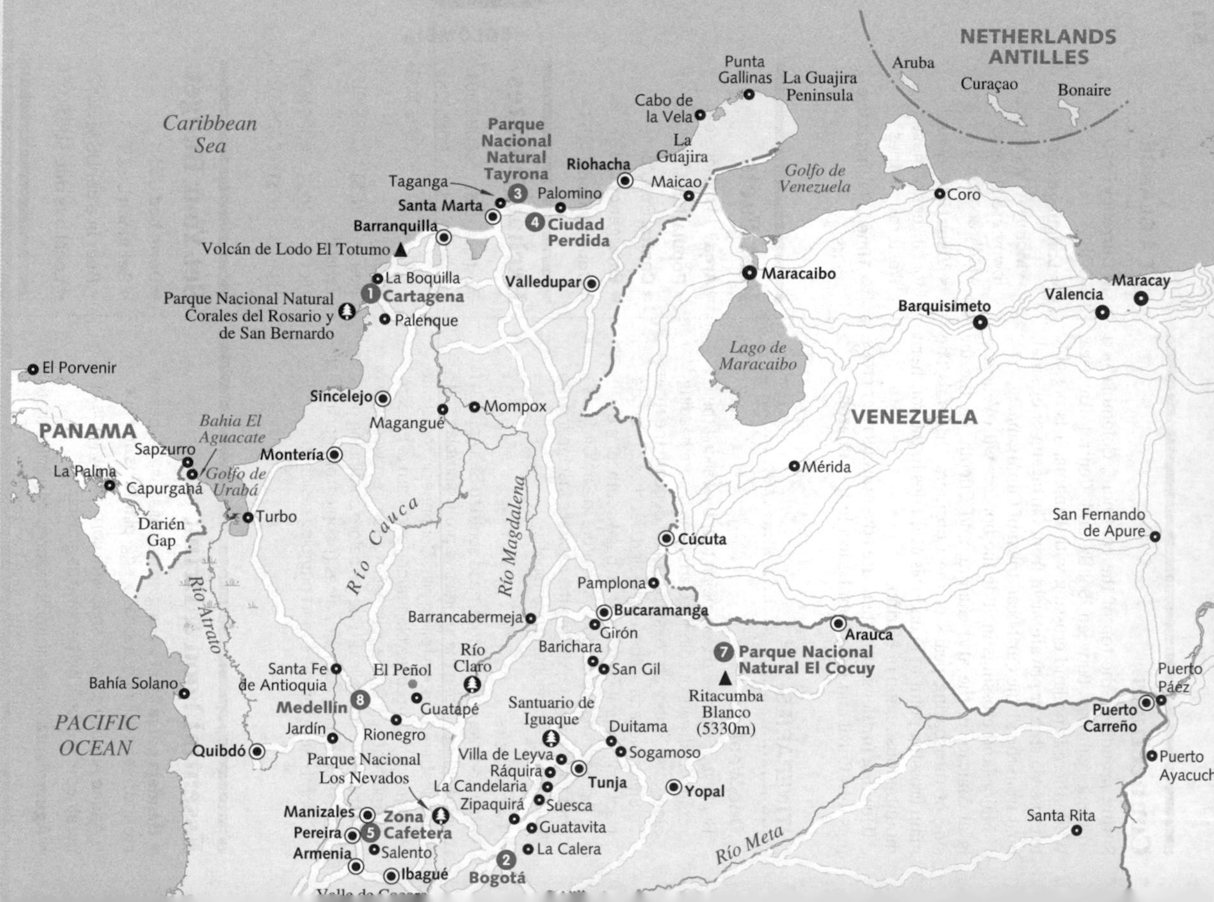

7 Trek among the glaciers of **Parque Nacional Natural El Cocuy** (p558).

8 Soar high above **Medellín** (p588) in a cable car before sampling its many bars and restaurants.

9 Gallop around the glorious countryside peppered with ancient sites and statues in **San Agustín** (p612).

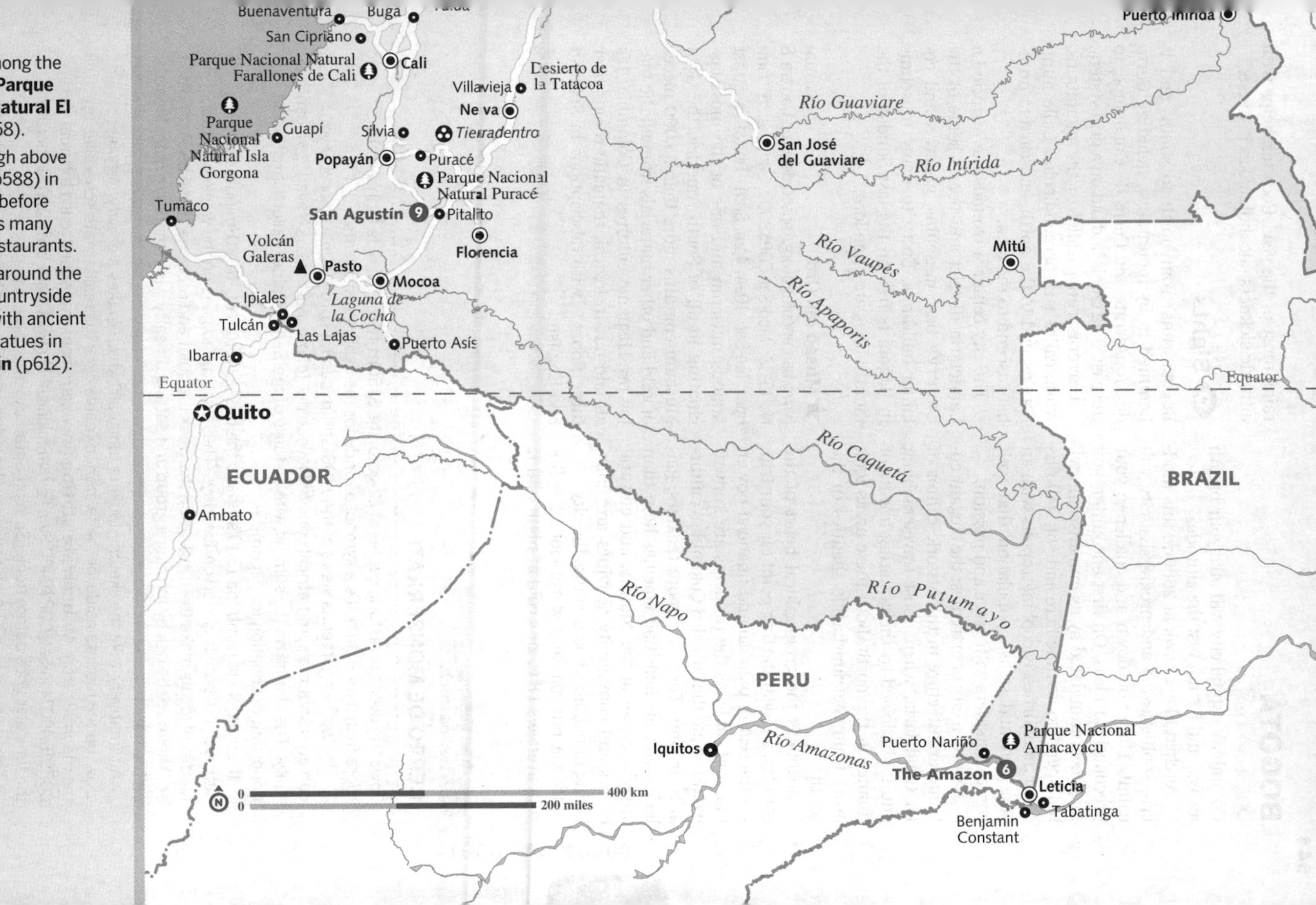

BOGOTÁ

☎1 / POP 7.4 MILLION

Colombia's capital city will take your breath away – and it's not just the altitude.

Perched like a hawk at 2600m, this modern, sophisticated and progressive city will calmly stare you down and challenge your preconceived ideas. On first encounter, you may feel intimidated by its immense sprawl, but spend some time here and you will discover an effortlessly cool metropolis with an educated and stylish population that welcomes outsiders with grace and passion.

It's also a city of extremes: the elegant colonial architecture in the historic center of La Candelaria, where most travelers hang out, is shadowed by the glittering towers of finance in the north. Both these areas look away from the ramshackle shanties of the south.

Bogotá is the geographical heart of the country, an ideal starting point for your trip. It's the seat of political and financial power, too, and *rolos* (as the residents are known) would argue that it's also Colombia's cultural heartland. There are more theaters, galleries, concert halls and cinemas here than anywhere else in the country, and cultural events and community activities are flourishing in neighborhoods across the city.

Pack a raincoat and warm clothes – Bogotá averages 14°C, gets cold at night and it rains most of the year. Coca tea helps with altitude sickness; alcohol makes it worse.

Sights

Bogotá runs from north to south, and is hemmed in by mountains, including Cerro de Monserrate and Cerro de Guadalupe, to the east. The city is laid out on a grid system.

Carreras run parallel to the mountains, while calles run perpendicular. Calle numbers ascend to the north, and carrera numbers ascend to the west.

The city center surrounds the historic La Candelaria district and boasts some of the country's best museums, galleries and colonial buildings. Entry to many museums in Bogotá is free on the last Sunday of the month; lines are often long.

★Museo del Oro MUSEUM

(www.banrepcultural.org/museo-del-oro; Carrera 6 No 15-88; Mon-Sat COP$3000, Sun free; 9am-6pm Tue-Sat, 10am-4pm Sun) Bogotá's most famous museum and one of the most fascinating in all of South America, the Gold Museum contains more than 55,000 pieces of gold and other materials from all the major pre-Hispanic cultures in Colombia. It's all laid out in logical, thematic rooms over three floors – with descriptions in Spanish and English.

DON'T MISS

CERRO DE MONSERRATE

Towering over the historic center of Bogotá, the 3150m-high Cerro de Monserrate is more than a mountain, it's a symbol of pride for the capital's residents.

The top has gorgeous views of the 1700-sq-km capital sprawl. On a clear day you can even spot the symmetrical cone of Nevado del Tolima, part of Los Nevados volcanic range. The church on the summit with a statue of the Señor Caído (Fallen Christ) is an important destination for pilgrims.

It's possible to climb the 1500 steps to the top – a tough 60-to-90-minute walk – although the path is closed on Tuesdays. The best time to go is on the weekend, when hordes of locals make the trip. During the week it's quiet and robberies have been reported. Minimize the risk by forming a group and setting off early when there are more locals on the trail.

Alternatively, take the sketchy-looking funicular, which makes a gravity-defying crawl up the mountainside, or the *teleférico* (cable car); these alternate schedules up the mountain from **Monserrate station** (www.cerromonserrate.com; round trip from COP$16,400 Mon-Sat, COP$9400 Sun; 7am-midnight Mon-Sat, 6am-6pm Sun). Generally the funicular goes before noon (3pm on Saturday), the cable car after.

The funicular is a 20-minute walk up from the Iglesia de las Aguas at the northeast edge of La Candelaria. The stretch between Quinta de Bolívar and Monserrate station has a reputation for muggings – band together or take a taxi.

★Museo Botero MUSEUM
(www.banrepcultural.org/museo-botero; Calle 11 No 4-41; ⌚9am-7pm Mon & Wed-Sat, 10am-5pm Sun) FREE The highlight of Banco de la República's massive museum complex is several halls spread over two floors dedicated to all things chubby: hands, oranges, women, mustached men, children, birds, Fuerzas Armadas Revolucionarias de Colombia (FARC; Revolutionary Armed Forces of Colombia) leaders. All of these are, of course, the robust paintings and sculptures of Colombia's most famous artist, Fernando Botero (Botero himself donated these works).

★Iglesia Museo de Santa Clara CHURCH
(www.museoiglesiasantaclara.gov.co; Carrera 8 No 8-91; adult/child COP$3000/500; ⌚9am-5pm Tue-Fri, 10am-4pm Sat & Sun) One of Bogotá's most richly decorated churches and also it's oldest (along with Iglesia de San Francisco). It's now run by the government as a museum. Considering all the other churches from the same era that can be seen for free, many visitors pass on this one, but it is a stunner.

★Iglesia de San Francisco CHURCH
(www.templodesanfrancisco.com; cnr Av Jiménez & Carrera 7; ⌚6:30am-10:30pm Mon-Fri, 6:30am-12:30pm & 4-6:30pm Sat, 7:30am-1:30pm & 4:30-7:30pm Sun) Built between 1557 and 1621, the Church of San Francisco, just west of the Museo del Oro, is Bogotá's oldest surviving church. Of particular interest is the extraordinary 17th-century gilded main altarpiece, which is Bogotá's largest and most elaborate piece of art of its kind.

Plaza de Bolívar PLAZA
(Plaza de Bolívar, btwn Calle 10 & 11) The usual place to start discovering Bogotá is Plaza de Bolívar, the heart of the original town. In the middle of the square is a bronze statue of Simón Bolívar (cast in 1846), the work of an Italian artist, Pietro Tenerani. This was the first public monument erected in the city. In the center, beside the statue, are flocks of pigeons that dive-bomb anyone within 50m of the square – a hat is a good idea.

Museo Nacional MUSEUM
(National Museum; www.museonacional.gov.co; Carrera 7 No 28-66; ⌚10am-6pm Tue-Sat, to 5pm Sun) FREE This museum is housed in the expansive, Greek-cross-shaped building called El Panóptico (designed as a prison by English architect Thomas Reed in 1874). Walking through the (more or less) chronological display of Colombia's past, you pass iron-bar doors into white-walled halls. Signage is in Spanish only, but each floor offers handy English placards that you can take along with you for the highlights.

Quinta de Bolívar MUSEUM
(www.quintadebolivar.gov.co; Calle 20 No 2-91 Este; adult/child COP$3000/1000, free Sun; ⌚9am-5pm Tue-Fri, 11am-4pm Sat & Sun) About 250m downhill to the west from Monserrate station, this lovely historic-home museum is set in a garden at the foot of the Cerro de Monserrate. The mansion was built in 1800 and donated to Simón Bolívar in 1820 in gratitude for his liberating services. Bolívar spent 423 days here over nine years. Its rooms are filled with period pieces, including Bolívar's sword. Less is said about its later days as a mental institution.

Mirador Torre Colpatria VIEWPOINT
(Carrera 7 No 24-89; admission COP$4500; ⌚6-9pm Fri, 2-8pm Sat, 11am-5pm Sun) From the 48th-floor outside deck of the Colpatria Tower you can catch a superb view of the decommissioned bullring, backed by office buildings and the mountains – there are also fine 360-degree vistas across the city. The 162m-high skyscraper – Colombia's tallest – was finished in 1979.

Museo Histórico Policía MUSEUM
(Museum of Police History; www.policia.gov.co; Calle 9 No 9-27; ⌚8am-5pm Tue-Sun) FREE This surprisingly worthwhile museum not only gets you inside the lovely ex-HQ (built in 1923) of Bogotá's police force, but gives you 45 minutes or so of contact time with English-speaking, 18-year-old local guides who are serving a one-year compulsory service with the police (interesting tales to be heard).

Activities

Gran Pared ROCK CLIMBING
(☎285-0903; www.granpared.com; Carrera 7 No 50-02; full day COP$25,000; ⌚10am-9:45pm Mon-Fri, 8am-7:45pm Sat, 10am-5:45pm Sun) Bogotá rock climbers head off to nearby Suesca, but if you want to hone your skills in town, this towering climbing wall is challenging and well organized.

Sal Si Puedes HIKING
(☎283-3765; www.salsipuedes.org; Carrera 7 No 17-01, Oficina 640; ⌚8am-5pm Mon-Thu, to 2pm Fri) This is an association of outdoor-minded people which organizes weekend walks in the countryside (COP$45,000 per person, including transportation and

Bogota

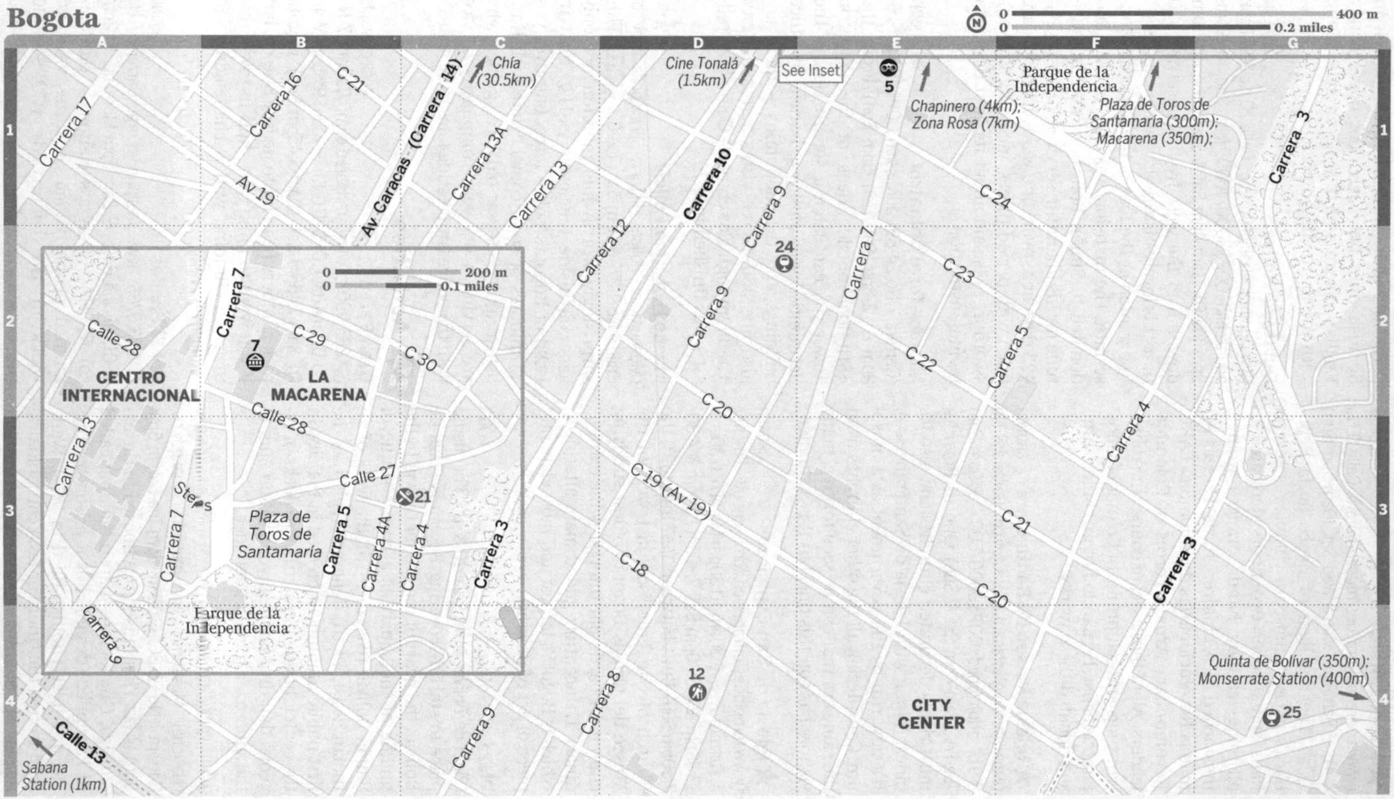

0 400 m
0 0.2 miles

A B C D E F G
1 2 3 4

Chía (30.5km)
Cine Tonalá (1.5km)
See Inset
5
Chapinero (4km); Zona Rosa (7km)
Parque de la Independencia
Plaza de Toros de Santamaría (300m); Macarena (350m);
Carrera 17
Carrera 16
C 21
Av 19
Av Caracas (Carrera 14)
Carrera 13A
Carrera 13
Carrera 12
Carrera 10
Carrera 9
24
Carrera 7
C 24
C 23
C 22
Carrera 5
Carrera 4
Carrera 3
C 20
C 19 (Av 19)
C 21
C 18
C 20
Carrera 3
Carrera 8
12
Carrera 9
CITY CENTER
Quinta de Bolívar (350m); Monserrate Station (400m)
25
Calle 13
Sabana Station (1km)

0 200 m
0 0.1 miles
Carrera 7
Calle 28
7
C 29
C 30
CENTRO INTERNACIONAL
LA MACARENA
Calle 28
Carrera 13
Calle 27
21
Steps
Plaza de Toros de Santamaría
Carrera 7
Carrera 5
Carrera 4A
Carrera 4
Carrera 3
Parque de la Independencia
Carrera 9

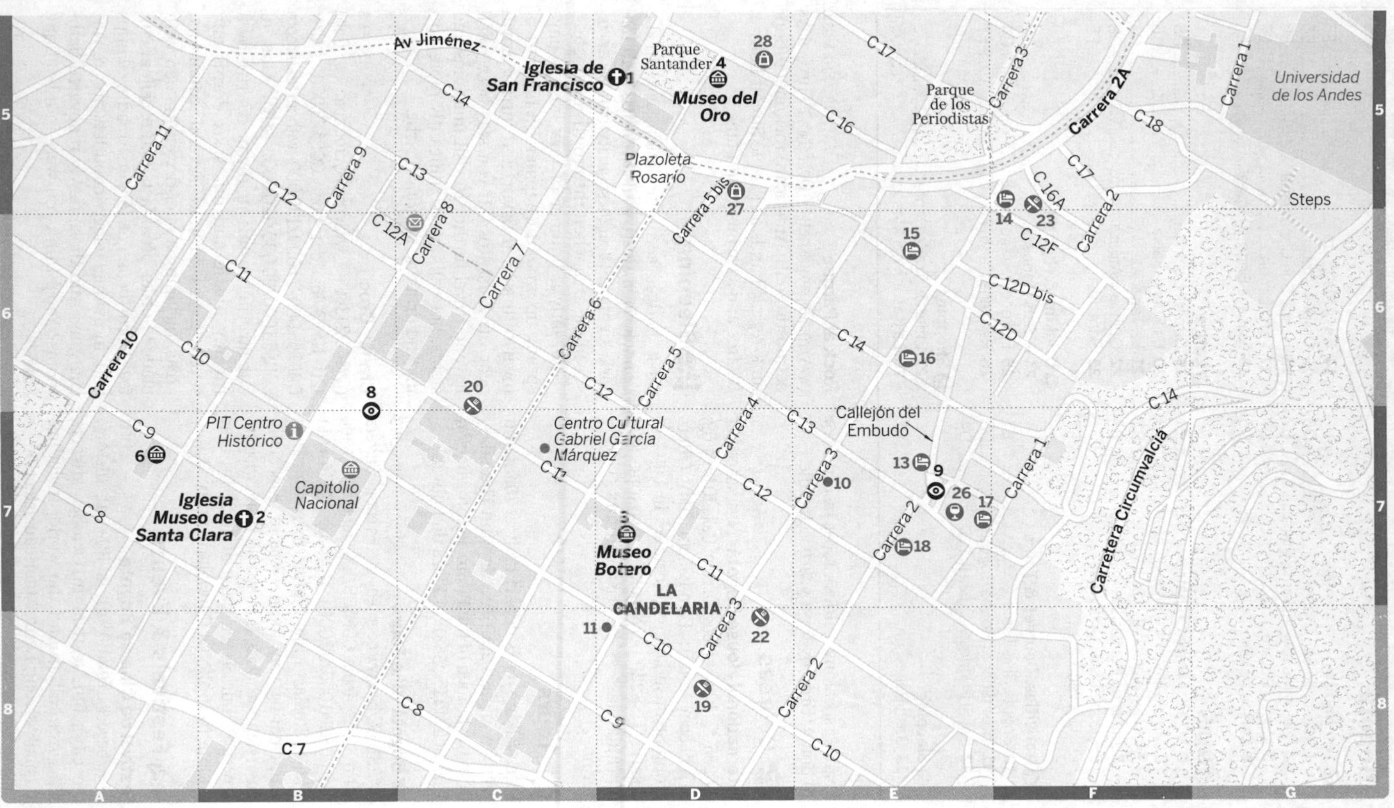

Av Jiménez
Iglesia de San Francisco
1
Parque Santander
4
Museo del Oro
28
C 17
Parque de los Periodistas
Carrera 3
Carrera 2A
C 18
Carrera 1
Universidad de los Andes
C 14
C 16
Carrera 11
Carrera 9
C 13
C 12
Plazoleta Rosario
Carrera 5 bis
27
C 17
C 16A
14
23
Carrera 2
Steps
C 12A
Carrera 8
15
C 12F
C 11
Carrera 7
C 12D bis
C 12D
Carrera 6
C 14
16
Carrera 10
C 10
Carrera 5
C 12
20
8
Carrera 4
C 13
Callejón del Embudo
C 14
PIT Centro Histórico
Centro Cultural Gabriel García Márquez
C 9
6
C 11
13
9
Carrera 3
10
C 12
26
17
Carrera 1
Carretera Circumvalcia
Capitolio Nacional
Iglesia Museo de Santa Clara
2
C 8
5
Museo Botero
Carrera 2
18
C 11
LA CANDELARIA
Carrera 3
22
11
C 10
19
Carrera 2
C 8
C 9
C 7
C 10
A
B
C
D
E
F
G
5
6
7
8

Bogotá

Spanish-speaking guides). Most last nine or 10 hours. Drop by for a yearly schedule.

Courses

International House Bogotá LANGUAGE COURSE
(336-4747; www.ihbogota.com; Calle 10 No 4-09; 7am-8pm Mon-Fri, 8am-1:30pm Sun) Offers group Spanish-language courses in La Candelaria (US$220 per week for five four-hour morning classes) or private tutors (US$30 per hour).

Tours

Free walking tours depart daily at 10am and 2pm (in English 2pm Tuesday and Thursday) from the branch of the Punto de Información Turística (PIT; p553) on Plaza de Bolívar.

★**Bogotá Bike Tours** CYCLING
(281-9924; www.bogotabiketours.com; Carrera 3 No 12-72; tours COP$35,000, rentals half/full day COP$20,000/35,000) Run by California bike-enthusiast Mike Caesar, these tours are a fascinating way to see Bogotá, especially the neighborhoods that would otherwise be a no-go. Tours leave daily at 10:30am and 1:30pm from the La Candelaria office.

Festivals & Events

Festival de Cine de Bogotá FILM
(www.bogocine.com) With a 30-year history, the city's film festival in October attracts films from all around the world, including a usually strong Latin American selection.

Rock al Parque MUSIC
(www.rockalparque.net; Oct & Nov) Three days of (mostly South American) rock/metal/pop/funk/reggae bands at Parque Simón Bolívar. It's free and swarming with fans.

Sleeping

Most budget accommodations are in La Candelaria, a short walk from Bogotá's historic sights, although security can be an issue in the area when the crowds dissipate.

Recently a number of new hostels have sprung up around Chapinero, a hip part of town with a local flavor, and further north near the Zona Rosa. If you stay here you'll have to travel further to visit museums and sights, but will have significantly more dining and drinking options nearby.

Cranky Croc HOSTEL $
(342-2438; www.crankycroc.com; Calle 12D No 3-46; dm from COP$23,000, s/d/tr COP$56,000/74,000/105,000, without bathroom COP$66,000/90,000/120,000; @) One of our favorite hostels in town. It's run by a friendly Aussie and offers six dorms and seven rooms around several communal areas, including a chef-driven kitchen with made-to-order breakfasts and excellent coffee. Dorm beds get lockers, reading lamps and individual electric outlets for device charging. And those newly renovated bathrooms? You'd think you were in a boutique hotel.

Lima Limon HOSTEL $

(☎281-1260; www.limalimonhostel.com.co; Carrera 1 No 12B-15; dm from COP$22,000, s/d without bathroom COP$40,000/60,000, all incl breakfast; @📶) Set around a colorful internal courtyard, this cozy hostel has tons of character. Its small size and chilled, artistic vibe make it feel more like a houseshare than a big-city hostel and there is an excellent kitchen for preparing communal meals. Bonus: 24-hour reception and hot water all day.

Hostal Sue Candelaria HOSTEL $

(☎344-2647; www.suecandelaria.com; Carrera 3 No 12C-18; dm COP$23,000, s/d without bathroom COP$45,000/60,000, r COP$70,000, all incl breakfast; @📶) The friendly and bright Sue Candelaria wins Candelaria's most festive bedspreads competition in a fine string of rooms (albeit the privates are tiny) in a smaller, colonial-style layout around a bright courtyard.

Casa Bellavista HOSTEL $

(☎334-1230; www.bellavistahostelbogota.com; Carrera 2 No 12B-31; dm from COP$18,000, s/d COP$60,000/70,000, all incl breakfast; @📶) You'll find good value and loads of antiquated character at this small, family-run choice in a historic house steps from Plazoleta del Chorro de Quevedo. Creaky hardwood floors lead to colorful dorms that have their own bathrooms, and the two spacious private rooms are chock-full of detail such as original tile flooring.

★**Masaya Bogota Hostel** HOSTEL $$

(☎747-1848; www.masaya-experience.com; Carrera 2 No 12-48; dm from COP$20,000 r with/without bathroom from COP$100,000/70,000; @📶) Taking flashpacker luxury to a new level, this large French-owned hostel has notably comfortable dorms, with privacy curtains, bean bags, and fluffy pillows and duvets, while the private hotel-quality rooms are very spacious and boast first-rate wardrobes and flat-screen TVs. You'll also find great common areas, piping-hot high-presure showers and a wealth of cultural activities.

★**La Pinta** HOSTEL $$

(☎211-9526; www.lapinta.com.co; Calle 65 No 5-67; dm from COP$26,000, s/d COP$90,000/120,000, without bathroom COP$70,000/96,000; @📶) In an unmarked residential home in a great Chapinero location just steps from La Séptima (Carrera 7), this spotless little secret offers a fantastic back garden; big, modern bathrooms; and colorful down comforters in hardwood-floored rooms that approach boutique-hotel levels. There's a large, communal kitchen; a cozy new bar; and a whacky, lovable dog.

Casa Platypus GUESTHOUSE $$

(☎281-1801; www.casaplatypus.com; Carrera 3 No 12F-28; dm/s/d/tr COP$44,000/144,000/166,000/188,000; @📶) This upscale guesthouse is the flashpacker choice. Simple rooms have masculine hardwoods and private bathrooms, a narrow terrace perfect for watching the 5pm weekday university fashion show in the street below, and a wonderful rooftop terrace with Montserrat views.

12:12 Hostel HOSTEL $$

(☎467-2656; www.1212hostels.com; Calle 67 No 4-16; dm COP$26,000-40,000, r COP$116,000;

BOGOTÁ: A CYCLIST'S PARADISE

One of the best ways to get around Bogotá and avoid its gnarly traffic is on two wheels. Bogotá has around 375km of dedicated cycle lanes, making it one of the most bike-friendly cities in South America.

Not being a city to rest on its infrastructure laurels, there is also the **Ciclovía** (www.idrd.gov.co): from 7am to 2pm every Sunday, 120km of Bogotá's main highways are closed to traffic and cyclists rule the roads. Fruit-juice stands, street-food vendors and performers lining the routes give the event a festive vibe. It's another example of how this progressive city puts many of its developed-world counterparts to shame.

For more social two-wheeled fun, check out the **Ciclopaseo**, a nocturnal cruise through the city accompanied by throngs of like-minded strangers. The Ciclopaseo takes a new route every week and visits interesting parts of the city that you may not otherwise see. It takes place every Wednesday with riders meeting at 7pm at **Plaza CPM** (Carrera 10 at Calle 96).

To join the action, either rent a bike from your hostel or hire a deluxe model from Bogotá Bike Tours.

(@ 🛜) 🍃 This artsy new hostel epitomizes the cutting-edge Chapinero Alto scene: recycled materials such as discarded bikes, which climb the walls like funhouse art installations, and tossed-aside books, which pepper the walls instead of wallpaper, are the backbone of this design-forward choice.

Chapinorte Bogotá HOSTEL **$$**
(☎ 317-640-6716; www.chapinortehostelbogota.com; Calle 79 No 14-59, Apt 402; s/d/tr COP$85,000/100,000/145,000, without bathroom COP$60,000/80,000/120,000; @ 🛜) In a nondescript residential building just beyond the northern edges of the Chapinero, this eight-room guesthouse on two floors is a great anti-Candelaria choice. Run by a friendly Spaniard, some of the hostel's stylish rooms have enormous bathrooms and cable TVs, and surround a cute island kitchen in the living room. No breakfast.

Eating

You can fill yourself to bursting with an *almuerzo corriente* (set lunch) at one of a thousand spots around Bogotá. The historic center is light on for dining options in the evening but the Macarena area just to the north has numerous hip places for a bite. Many of Bogotás upmarket restaurants are located in the Zona G while nearby Chapinero has some of the city's most creative cuisine. There are also many options around the Zona Rosa to get a meal before hitting the bars.

Quinua y Amaranto VEGETARIAN **$**
(www.blog.colombio.co/quinua-y-amaranto.html; Calle 11 No 2-95; set lunch COP$14,000; ⏲ 8am-4pm Sat & Mon, to 7pm Tue-Fri; 🖉) This sweet spot – run by ladies in the open-front kitchen – goes all vegetarian during the week (there's often chicken soup on weekends), with tasty set lunches and empanadas, salads and coffee. A small section of coco leaves, baked goods and tempting chunks of artisanal cheese (on Saturdays) round out the homey offerings.

La Puerta Falsa FAST FOOD **$**
(Calle 11 No 6-50; candies COP$1500-2000, snacks COP$3500-6300; ⏲ 7am-9pm Mon-Sat, 8am-7pm Sun) This is Bogotá's most famous snack shop. Displays of multicolored candies beckon you into this tiny spot that's been in business since 1816. Some complain it's nothing but foreigners with their Lonely Planet guides these days, but don't buy it – there were no other gringos on our visit.

Arbol de Pan BAKERY **$**
(Calle 66 No 4A-35; items COP$1500-6500; ⏲ 8am-8pm Mon-Sat; 🛜) Forget about breakfast at your hotel or hostel, this all-natural bakery and pastry shop pumps out a long list of daily just-baked breads (multigrain, dates and oats, etc) and a slew of delectable pastries. There's also heartier breakfast fare, such as croissants stuffed with poached egg, ham and spinach (COP$12,500).

La Areparia Venzolana FAST FOOD **$**
(Calle 85 No 13-36; arepas COP$11,00-13,500; ⏲ 9am-10pm Mon-Thu, to 4am Fri & Sat; 🛜) Firmly rooted late-night hot spot for drunken munchies right off Zona Rosa. Venezuelan-style *arepas* (corn cakes; better than Colombian) are stuffed with all manner of fillings.

★ **Sant Just** FRENCH **$$**
(Calle 16A No 2-73; mains COP$14,000-32,000; ⏲ noon-4pm Mon-Sat; 🛜) 🍃 This wonderful French-owned cafe serves a daily changing menu of Colombian-leaning French fare presented tableside via chalkboard. Whatever the kitchen churns out that day – fresh juices, sustainably caught seafood, wonderful lamb served alongside previously out-of-favor veggies such as *cubio* (an Andean root) – it nails, both in the presentation and the comfort-food-goodness quotient. Expect a wait. Cash only.

★ **Central Cevicheria** SEAFOOD **$$**
(☎ 644-7766; www.centralcevicheria.com; Carrera 13 No 85-14; ceviche COP$17,800-19,800; ⏲ noon-11pm Mon-Wed, to midnight Thu-Sat, to 10pm Sun; 🛜) This good-time, high-concept *cevichería* is the real deal: Bogotá's high and mighty ogle over the superb *ceviches* (marinated raw seafood), split into spicy and nonspicy categories, of which there are a dozen inventive offerings. Reservations are recommended.

Capital Cocina COLOMBIAN **$$**
(Calle 10 No 2-99; mains COP$15,500-25,000; ⏲ noon-3:30pm & 6:30-10pm Mon-Sat) Prepare to fight for tables at this quaint cafe serving a few takes on simple Colombian comfort food – fish of the day, pork chop, steak, *pollo suprema* – that are in fact anything but simple. The daily menu (COP$16,500) is a three-course steal considering the quality of Chef Juan Pablo's food; and there are artisanal beers, decent wines and single-origin coffee.

For dinner in La Candelaria, it's tough to beat.

La Tapería TAPAS $$

(www.lataperia.co; Carrera 4A No 26D-12; tapas COP$9900-27,000; ⊙noon-3pm & 6pm-late Mon-Fri, 1-11pm Sat, to 4pm Sun;) To the delight of nearly everyone in the know, delectable tapas such as cherry tomatoes wrapped in blue cheese and bacon with a balsamic reduction (our fave!) are churned out under the guidance of a Dutch music fiend in this cool, loft-aesthetic Macarena lounge. There's live flamenco (Thursdays and Saturdays) and Friday's neighborhood-curated Musica del Barrio playlist draws the young and restless.

Drinking & Nightlife

Bogotá's most atmospheric cafes and drinking holes are around La Candelaria, where drinks are served in old colonial houses with fireplaces. Begin your evening with a spot of street drinking among the bohemian crowd in the weed-scented **Plazoleta del Chorro de Quevedo** (cnr Carrera 2 & Calle 12B).

Most late-night action is located in the north of the city in the Zona Rosa between Carreras 11 and 15, and Calles 81 and 84. Dress up or you'll feel out of place. There are several more low-key alternatives around Chapinero.

Pequeña Santa Fe BAR

(Carrera 2 No 12B-14; canelazo COP$6500-7000; ⊙noon-1am) A cozy, historic two-story home with a fireplace by the bar and a softly lit loft upstairs sits next to the evocative Plazoleta del Chorro de Quevedo. It's one of a few great spots where you can sample a hot mug of '*canelazo* Santa Fe' (a yerba-buena tea with *aguardiente*), or a beer.

Mi Tierra BAR

(Calle 63 No 11-47; ⊙6pm-late) Find a space among the busted typewriters, sombreros, moose heads, musical instruments and TVs at this friendly Chapinero bar that resembles a licensed flea market. It's popular with a chilled crowd so you don't need to be overly concerned about the collection of old machetes; and the music is particularly well curated.

Taller de Té TEAHOUSE

(www.tallerdete.com; Calle 60A No 3A-38; tea COP$3000-9000; ⊙10am-8pm Mon-Sat;) This adorable cafe is unique in Bogotá for serious tea. Owner Laura sources more than 50 teas and infusions from plantations around the world and blends with Colombian teas; and there are organic, vegetarian and vegan light bites from trusted culinary artisans around Colombia to pair along with them.

Amor Perfecto CAFE

(www.amorperfectocafe.net; Carrera 4 No 66-46; coffee COP$3500-11,000; ⊙8am-9pm Mon-Sat;) This seriously hip Chapinero Alto coffeehouse is for serious coffee lovers. Pick your single-origin regional Colombian specialty bean; select your method of preparation (Chemex, Siphon, AeroPress or French press); and let the highly knowledgeable baristas do the rest. You can also pop in for a tasting and a course. Hardwood floors and sexy red booths complement the evolution of Bogotá's caffeine scene.

DON'T MISS

PARTY IN A PIÑATA

Legendary bar-restaurant **Andrés Carne de Res** (☎863-7880; www.andrescarnederes.com; Calle 3 No 11A-56, Chía; mains COP$16,700-75,500, cover Fri & Sat COP$10,000-15,000; ⊙11am-3am Thu-Sat, to midnight Sun) is not your average Latin dining experience. It's a sprawling, gloriously theatrical complex that's a cross between a Cirque du Soleil show, the best steakhouse you've ever visited and a liquor-drenched Colombian knees-up. More than 250,000 people eat 10 tons of meat a year here, before partying till 5am in a series of interlinked rooms and dance floors bedecked with magic-realist bric-a-brac. By midnight it's a total madhouse, with hundreds of crazed-but-friendly locals dancing on the tables to *vallenato* (Colombian accordion music), disco or cumbia, and pouring rum into any passing mouth.

The catch is that it's in Chía – a COP$70,000 cab ride from downtown. Hostal Sue Candelaria (p549) runs a party bus here on weekends. It costs COP$60,000 and includes round-trip transportation, entry and booze on the bus. Alternatively, save a bit of money getting there by catching a Chía-bound bus from inside the TransMilenio's Portal del Norte station from the Buses Intermuncipales platform; buses leave every two minutes until midnight (COP$2300, 30 minutes).

El Titicó BAR

(Calle 64 No 13-35; cover COP$10,000) Inspired by the classic *salsatecas* (salsa clubs) in the south of the country, this sexy hidden bar in Chapinero is like a piece of Cali in the capital with its plush red booths and a big octagonal dance floor. Get your salsa on.

Azahar Cafe CAFE

(www.azaharcoffee.com; Carrera 14 No 93A-48; coffee COP$3000-5000; ⏲8am-9pm Mon-Sat, noon-9pm Sun; 📶) Extreme exportation means coffee snobs have more than a little bit of trouble finding a passable cup of Joe in Colombia, but this dead-serious java joint serves single origin, micro-lot coffee prepared in all the ways only considered routine by serious caffeine fiends: AeroPress, Chemex and the like.

El Goce Pagano CLUB

(www.elgocepagano.co; Carrera 1 No 20-04; ⏲7pm-3am Fri & Sat) Pushing 40, this divey salsa and reggae bar near Universidad de Los Andes is a smoky place with DJs and sweat-soaked bodies from all over Colombia, moving to ethnic rhythms.

A Seis Manos BAR

(Calle 22 No 8-60; cocktails COP$8000-14,000; ⏲8am-11pm; 📶) This cool, contemporary cultural space and bar lures the artistically inclined, who mingle at communal tables in the industrial, warehouse-like space. People eat, drink, work, read, flirt and unwind with good mojitos and standard bar fare.

Theatron CLUB

(www.theatron.co; Calle 58 No 10-32; ⏲9pm-late Thu-Sat) On a small road between Carreras 9 and 13 in the heart of Chapinero, the classic Theatron is carved from a huge converted film house. It draws gays and straights – some 3000 on weekends – among its eight different environments. Some areas are men-only.

Armando Records CLUB

(www.armandorecords.org; Calle 85 No 14-46; cover Thu-Sat COP$15,000-20,000; ⏲8pm-2:30am Tue-Sat) Still all the rage in Bogotá after several years, this multilevel hot spot features the 2nd-floor Armando's All Stars, which skews younger for crossover tunes and includes a back garden packed in with the young and the restless; and the 4th-floor retro rooftop, where the tunes guide your evening – think LCD Soundsystem and Empire of the Sun.

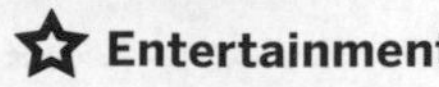

Entertainment

Bogotá has far more cultural activities than any other city in Colombia. For listings check out **Vive.In** (www.vive.in). For cultural events and commentary in English, pick up the free monthly *City Paper*.

Cinema

★Cine Tonalá CINEMA, CLUB

(www.cinetonala.com; Carrera 6A No 35-27; films COP$7000-9000; ⏲noon-3am Tue-Sun; 📶) Bogotá's only independent cinema champions Latin and Colombian films and international cult classics, but this Mexico City import refuses to be categorized. The multifaceted cultural center, in a renovated 1930s La Merced mansion, is the city's newest shelter for artistic refugees, who retreat here for a very hip bar scene, excellent Mexican food and rousing club nights Thursday to Saturday.

Sports

Big local soccer rivals are **Millonarios** (www.millonarios.com.co) in blue and white and **Santa Fe** (www.independientesantafe.co) in red and white.

Estadio El Campín STADIUM

(☎315-8726; Carrera 30 No 57-60) The principal venue for soccer is the Estadio El Campín. Games are played on Wednesday nights and Sunday afternoons. Tickets can be bought at the stadium before the matches.

Shopping

La Casona del Museo HANDICRAFTS

(www.lacasonadelmuseo.com; Calle 16 No 5-24; ⏲9am-7pm Mon-Sat, 10am-5pm Sun) This old building near Museo del Oro houses a convenient, cheerful collection of souvenir stands and two nice cafes (the upper level one, La Fuente, does good coffee by a trickling fountain).

Information

DANGERS & ANNOYANCES

Like any major urban center, Bogotá requires common sense and moderate vigilance. The center of town including the Candelaria is generally safe during working hours but once crowds dissipate things take a turn for the worse and muggings are far too common. Walk in groups and stick to major roads. Taxis are cheap, secure, metered and plentiful – use them if you're nervous. Overcrowding has seen a significant increase in crime on public transportation – always be on guard to avoid pickpocketing while riding the buses.

EMERGENCY

For ambulance service dial ☎125. For police and fire call ☎123.

Tourist Police (☎280-9900) Bilingual staff.

MEDICAL SERVICES

Fundación Santa Fe (☎603-0303; www.fsfb.org.co; Calle 119 No 7-75) Very professional private hospital.

MONEY

There are two exchange houses in the **Emerald Trade Center** (Av Jiménez No 5-43; ⊙7:30am-7pm Mon-Fri, 8am-5pm Sat).

Bancolombia (Carrera 8 No 12B-17) Changes traveler's checks.

Western Union (www.westernunion.com; Calle 28 No 13-22, local 28; ⊙9am-5pm Mon-Fri, to 1pm Sat) Can wire money.

POST

Post Office (4-72; Carrera 8 No 12A-03, La Candelaria; ⊙8am-5:30pm Mon-Fri, 9am-1pm Sat)

TOURIST INFORMATION

The **Instituto Distrital de Turismo** (☎800-012-7400; www.bogotaturismo.gov.co) runs Puntos de Información Turística (PITs) throughout the city, at the bus terminal and at the airport.

PIT Centro Histórico (☎283-7115; cnr Carrera 8 & Calle 10; ⊙7am-6pm) Inside the Casa de Comuneros facing Plaza de Bolívar, this tourist office has walking tours in English at 2pm Tuesdays and Thursdays.

VISA INFORMATION

Migración Colombia (☎511-1150; www.migracioncolombia.gov.co; Calle 100 No 11B-27; ⊙8am-4pm Mon-Fri) Handles visa extensions for foreigners.

ℹ Getting There & Away

AIR

Bogotá's airport, **Aeropuerto Internacional El Dorado** (www.elnuevodorado.com; Av El Dorado), is 13km northwest of the city center. All international and most domestic flights arrive and depart from the massive new Terminal 1, although some flights with Avianca to smaller domestic destinations are based at the Puente Aéreo or Terminal 2, 1km west of the main building. Check your ticket details to be sure.

BUS

Bogotá's main bus terminal, **La Terminal** (☎423-3630; www.terminaldetransporte.gov.co; Diagonal 23 No 69-11), is around 5km west of the city center in the neighborhood of La Salitre. It's large, functional and extremely well organized. It has a tourist office, restaurants, cafeterias, showers and left-luggage rooms. The website has a full schedule of departures.

Buses travel to the following destinations among others:

DESTINATION	COST (COP$)	DURATION (HR)
Bucaramanga	40,000	9
Cali	59,000	9
Cartagena	140,000	22
Cúcuta	100,000	15
Ipiales	120,000	22
Medellín	55,000	9
Popayán	80,000	12
San Agustín	64,000	12
San Gil	35,000	7
Santa Marta	100,000	18
Villa de Leyva	23,000	4

ℹ GETTING INTO TOWN

Both El Dorado Airport and the Puente Aéreo are connected with the TransMilenio via a free shuttle bus to the nearby Portal El Dorado station. There is also one line that runs from the airport to the north of the city without the need to change buses, but the service doesn't accept cash, so if you don't have a TransMilenio pass you will still need to take the shuttle to Portal El Dorado to pick up a ticket before continuing on your journey.

Taxis from either facility to the center cost around COP$25,000 to COP$30,000 including the airport surcharge, while to the north expect to pay up to COP$37,000.

If arriving at the bus terminal, there are no bus services directly to the center. To get a bus, take a right as you leave zone 5 and walk 50m to the intersection where you'll take a left and walk three blocks until you reach Av Esperanza near the Salitre Plaza mall. To get to La Candelaria, take west-to-east-bound service 583 or 236 with the destination 'Germania.' Alternatively, if you only have light bags, the El Tiempo TransMilenio station is around a 1km walk from the terminal.

There is a taxi booth at the bus terminal inside zone 5 where you will be given a receipt for travel in an authorized vehicle. A taxi to La Candelaria will cost around COP$12,500.

Getting Around

BUS & BUSETA

TransMilenio (www.transmilenio.gov.co) has revolutionized Bogotá's public transportation. Huge articulated buses charge through the main thoroughfares on their own dedicated roads. The service is made up of 12 lines covering 112km and calls at 144 dedicated stations. TransMilenio is cheap (COP$1700 peak, COP$1400 off-peak), frequent and fast, and runs from 5am to around 12:15am on most lines. Buses get very crowded at rush hour. Watch your pockets.

Tickets are bought at the stations. A variety of frequent-rider cards are available in order to bypass the lines. The most useful for visitors is the *Tarjeta Cliente Frecuente* (COP$2000), which can be loaded with up to 50 rides. It takes some practice to work out how the system works. Plan your journey online at www.surumbo.com.

Aside from TransMilenio, Bogotá's public transportation is operated by buses and *busetas* (small buses) that travel all over the city at full speed. There are few bus stops – you just wave down the vehicle. The flat fare (around COP$1500, depending on the class of the vehicle) is posted by the door or on the windscreen.

TAXI

Bogotá's efficient, bright-yellow taxis are metered; the meter registers 'units,' which are then converted to a price at the end of the trip. When you get in, the meter should read '25.' The minimum fare is 50 units, or COP$3600. There is normally a price chart hanging from the back of the passenger seat. There is a COP$1700 surcharge after dark or on weekends.

For security reasons, it's best to avoid hailing cabs on the street. Call a radio taxi such as **Taxis Libres** (☎311-1111; www.taxislibres.com.co) or **Taxi Express** (☎411-1111; www.4111111.co), or if you have a smartphone download the Tappsi app.

AROUND BOGOTÁ

Zipaquirá

☎1 / POP 101,000

One of Colombia's most fascinating attractions is the hauntingly beautiful underground **salt cathedral** (☎594-5959; www.catedraldesal.gov.co; adult/child COP$20,000/10,000; ⏰9am-5:30pm) near the pretty town of Zipaquirá, 50km north of Bogotá. The cathedral was born from an old salt mine, dug straight into a mountain outside the town. The mines date back to the Muisca period and have been intensively exploited, but they still contain vast reserves that will last another 500 years.

Opened to the public in 1995, the cathedral is 75m long and 18m high and can accommodate 8400 people. Buses from Bogotá to Zipaquirá (COP$4300, one hour) run every 10 minutes from the northern terminus of TransMilenio (known as Portal del Norte). TransMilenio from Bogotá's center will take you to Portal del Norte in 40 minutes. The mines are a 15-minute walk uphill from Zipaquirá's center. The alternative is to take the **Turistren** (☎375-0557; www.turistren.com.co; round trip adult/child COP$43,000/27,000), a steam locomotive, which runs from Bogotá to Zipaquirá on weekends and holidays. The train departs **Sabana station** (Calle 13 No 18-24) at 8:30am, stops briefly at Usaquen station at 9:20am and reaches Zipaquirá at 11:30am.

Suesca

☎1 / POP 14,000

Suesca is an adventure-sports center near Bogotá, with rock climbing, mountain biking and white-water rafting. Visit at weekends, when local outfitters are open. The main attractions here are the 4km-long Guadalupe rock formations along the Río Bogotá, which rise to 370m and feature around 400 distinct climbs.

Veteran climber and mountaineer Rodrigo Arias of Colombia Trek (p559) is a great guide in the area and arranges multiday rock-climbing, mountain-biking and hiking adventures. Climbing school **DeAlturas** (☎301-642-6809; www.dealturas.com) offers a five-day course for COP$500,000 and day climbs for COP$120,000 as well as accommodations for COP$20,000 per visitor.

On a local farm, **El Vivac Hostal** (☎311-480-5034; www.elvivachostal.com; camp sites per person COP$15,000, dm COP$25,000, d COP$70,000) is run by a local ecologist and climbing pioneer. It arrange climbs and bike rental.

To get to Suesca, take the TransMilenio to its northern terminus at Portal del Norte, and catch a frequent direct bus (COP$5100, one hour).

NORTH OF BOGOTÁ

This is Colombia's heartland. The region of deep gorges, fast-flowing rivers and soaring peaks was the first to be settled by the conquistadores, and a number of their colonial towns stand today. It's also the revolutionary heart of the country: it was here that Simón

WORTH A TRIP

TUNJA

Tunja, the chilly capital of Boyacá, sits at 2820m and has fine colonial architecture and elegant mansions adorned with some of South America's most unique artwork. Many travelers rush through on their way to Villa de Leyva, but fans of colonial history and ornate churches may enjoy a day or two here.

The town's churches are noted for their *mudéjar* art, an Islamic-influenced style that developed in Christian Spain between the 12th and 16th centuries. It is particularly visible in the ornamented, coffered vaults.

Iglesia y Convento de Santa Clara La Real (320-856-3658; Carrera 7 No 19-58; admission COP$3000; 8am-noon & 2-6pm) is thought to be the first convent in Nueva Granada. It has been converted into a museum. The single-naved church interior shelters a wealth of colonial artwork on its walls. Other churches worth a visit include **Iglesia de Santo Domingo** (Carrera 11 No 19-55) – note the exuberant Capilla del Rosario, to the left as you enter the church – and **Templo Santa Barbara**.

If you want to spend the night, **Hotel Casa Real** (743-1764; www.hotelcasarealtunja.com; Calle 19 No 7-65; s/d COP$62,000/86,000;) is the most charismatic option in town, with smartly furnished rooms surrounding a pleasant courtyard.

The bus terminal is on Av Oriental, a short walk southeast of Plaza de Bolívar. Buses to Bogotá (COP$19,000, three hours) depart every 10 to 15 minutes. Buses to Bucaramanga (COP$35,000, seven hours) run hourly and pass through San Gil (COP$25,000, 4½ hours). Minibuses to Villa de Leyva (COP$6000, 45 minutes) depart regularly until around 6:30pm.

Bolívar took on Spain in the decisive fight for Colombia's independence.

The departments (regions) of Boyacá, Santander and Norte de Santander are tourist friendly: they're within easy reach of Bogotá on a good network of roads with bus services, and there's loads to see and do, including 450-year-old colonial towns, craft markets, heart-pumping adventure sports and spectacular national parks.

Villa de Leyva

8 / POP 9600

Enchanting Villa de Leyva, declared a national monument in 1954, is a beautiful colonial settlement that has been preserved in its entirety; virtually no modern architecture exists here. If you are only going to visit one colonial town on your trip, this is the place.

The town, founded in 1572, is much more than just a walk-through museum. It enjoys a healthy, dry and mild climate, far warmer than Tunja (a mere 39km away) and is close to some wonderful landscapes. There are great bird-watching opportunities, ancient stone monuments, impressive waterfalls, good food and excellent hiking; nature-lovers could easily spend a week here.

Villa de Leyva is a place to relax and escape the chilly heights of Bogotá, and as such, it's a popular getaway for *bogotanos* (residents of Bogota), who fill the town's many hotels, craft shops and tourist-oriented restaurants at weekends. Come early in the week for better-value hotel deals.

Sights

The splendid **Plaza Mayor** is one of the largest town squares in the Americas. It is paved with large cobblestones and surrounded by magnificent whitewashed colonial houses and a charming **parish church** (Plaza Mayor; mass 6pm Mon, Wed, Thu & Fri, noon & 7pm Sat, 7am, 10am, noon & 7pm Sun).

Check out **Casa de Juan de Castellanos** (Carrera 9 No 13-15), **Casa Quintero** (cnr Carrera 9 & Calle 12) and **Casona La Guaca** (Carrera 9 No 13-57), three meticulously restored colonial mansions on Carrera 9 (just off the plaza) that now house cafes, craft shops and restaurants.

There's a colorful **market** held on Saturday on the square three blocks southeast of Plaza Mayor – it's best and busiest early in the morning.

★**Museo del Carmen** MUSEUM

(Plazuela del Carmen; admission COP$3000; 10:30am-1pm & 2:30-5pm Sat & Sun) One of the best museums of religious art in the country, Museo del Carmen is housed in the convent of the same name. It contains valuable paintings, carvings, altarpieces and other religious objects dating from the 16th century onward.

Casa Museo de Luis Alberto Acuña MUSEUM
(www.museoacuna.com.co; Plaza Mayor; admission adult/child COP$4000/2000; ⌚9am-6pm) Featuring works by one of Colombia's most influential painters, sculptors, writers and historians, who was inspired by sources ranging from Muisca mythology to contemporary art. This museum has been set up in the mansion where Acuña (1904–93) lived for the last 15 years of his life and is Colombia's most comprehensive collection of his work.

Activities

The area surrounding Villa de Leyva is pleasant for **hiking**. There are several routes taking in some of the many attractions around the town, or you can climb the path beside Renacer Guesthouse to reach a natural lookout point with great views.

Other ways to explore the area include **cycling** and **horse riding** organized through tour agencies around town. Bikes cost around COP$15,000/25,000 per half/full day; horses are COP$30,000 per hour with a guide.

Tours

Villa de Leyva's small fleet of taxis offer trips to the attractions surrounding the town. The classic route takes in El Fósil, the Estación Astronómica Muisca and Convento del Santo Ecce Homo and costs around COP$75,000 for up to four passengers.

Colombian Highlands ECOTOURS
(☎310-552-9079, 732-1201; www.colombianhighlands.com; Av Carrera 10 No 21-Finca Renacer) Run by biologist and Renacer Guesthouse owner Oscar Gilède, this agency has a variety of off-beat tours including ecotours,

Villa de Leyva

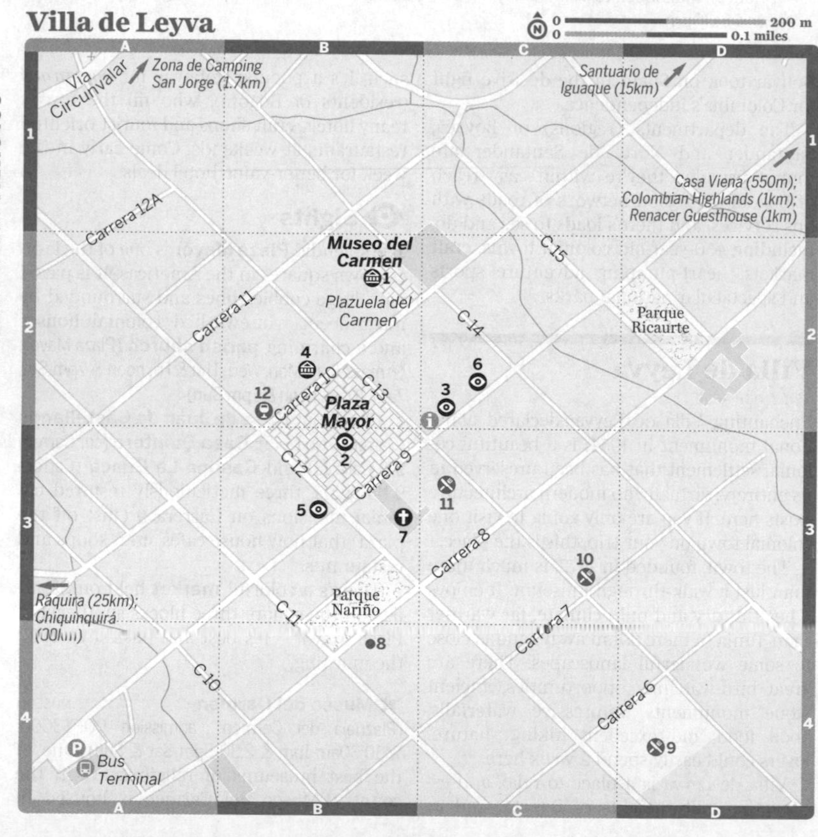

mountain trips, nocturnal hikes, birdwatching, rappelling/abseiling, canyoning, caving and hiking, and rents bikes and horses. English spoken.

Ciclotrip CYCLING TOURS
(☎320-899-4442; www.ciclotrip.com; Carrera 8 No 11-32; ⏰9am-5pm Mon-Fri, 8am-8pm Sat & Sun) This highly recommended bike outfitter/tour agency gets you out on two wheels to all the usual suspects, but also to more obscure waterfalls and points of interests, including a winery. The owner, Francisco, is a good guy and trained in first aid and mountain rescue. Day trips run COP$21,000 to COP$50,000. Also rents bikes.

Sleeping

Prices in town rocket and rooms become scarce during holidays and long weekends. We've listed weekday rates here.

★Renacer Guesthouse HOSTEL $
(☎732-1201, 311-308-3739; www.colombianhighlands.com; Av Carrera 10 No 21-Finca Renacer; campsite per person with/without tent rental COP$20,000/14,000, dm COP$22,000-24,000, s/d from COP$60,000/70,000; @🛜🏊) Located about 1.2km northeast of Plaza Mayor, this delightful 'boutique hostel' is the creation of biologist and tour guide extraordinaire Oscar Gilède of Colombian Highlands. Everything about this place feels like home – hammocks surrounding an immaculate garden, a communal, open-air kitchen with brick oven, and spotless dorms and rooms.

Zona de Camping San Jorge CAMPGROUND $
(☎732-0328; campingsanjorge@gmail.com; Vereda Roble; campsite per person high/low season COP$17,000/15,000; 🛜) Located approximately 2km northeast of town, this huge grassy field has space for 120 tents with lovely views of the surrounding mountains. Amenities include a small restaurant and shop, and spotless bathrooms with hot water.

It's a 25-minute walk from the plaza: walk north on Carrera 9, passing Museo Paleontológico. At the T-intersection, turn right, then make an immediate left down the well-signed gravel road to the campground.

Casa Viena HOSTEL $
(☎314-370-4776; www.casaviena.com; Carrera 10 No 19-114; dm COP$15,000, s/d without bathroom COP$28,000/38,000, r COP$45,000; @🛜) Hans and family of Cartagena's Casa Viena fame fled the Caribbean heat and opened this small guesthouse just outside the village. They spend a lot of time on their nearby farm, though, so the vibe has suffered, but the four simple rooms are still a good-value bed down, especially for long-term stays.

Eating & Drinking

Not all restaurants are open on weekdays.

Restaurante Estar de la Villa COLOMBIAN $
(Calle 13 No 8-75; set meals COP$10,000; ⏰9am-5pm Mon-Fri, 8:30-8pm Sat & Sun) Honest to goodness, clean-cut cheapie serving up wholesome daily set meals with just the right amount of motherly love. There's a menu but why bother – just go for the set meal, especially if it's serving *sopa de colí* (green banana soup). It's tucked away inside the Luna Lunera Centro Comercial.

Don Salvador COLOMBIAN $
(market; meals from COP$7000; ⏰6am-3pm Sat) Dig into regional *boyacense* cuisine at Villa's bustling Saturday market. Look for this stall, where don Salvador does the best *mute* (puffed corn soup, served with a side of cow's feet or chicken thigh) and *carne asada* (grilled steak) at the market.

Restaurante Casa Blanca COLOMBIAN $$
(Calle 13 No 7-16; set meals COP$9500, mains COP$15,000-25,500; ⏰8am-9pm) One of the better cheap restaurants in town. Prepare to wait.

Villa de Leyva

Top Sights
1 Museo del Carmen B2
2 Plaza Mayor B3

Sights
3 Casa de Juan de Castellanos C2
4 Casa Museo de Luis Alberto Acuña B2
5 Casa Quintero B3
6 Casona La Guaca C2
7 Iglesia Parroquial B3

Activities, Courses & Tours
8 Ciclotrip B4

Eating
9 Don Salvador D4
10 Restaurante Casa Blanca C3
11 Restaurante Estar de la Villa C3

Drinking & Nightlife
12 La Cava de Don Fernando B2

La Cava de Don Fernando BAR
(Carrera 10 No 12-03; ⏲2pm-1am Sun-Thu, to 2am Fri & Sat; 📶) A cozy bar on the corner of Plaza Mayor with excellent tunes, atmospheric candles and one of the better beer selections in town.

ℹ Information

There are several ATMs around the plaza.

Tourist Office (Oficina de Turismo; ☎732-0232; Carrera 9 No 13-11; ⏲8am-12:30pm & 2-6pm Mon-Fri, 8am-6pm Sat, 9am-5pm Sun) Provides free maps, brochures and information in Spanish.

ℹ Getting There & Away

The bus terminal is three blocks southwest of Plaza Mayor, on the road to Tunja. Minibuses run between Tunja and Villa de Leyva every 15 minutes from 5am to 7:45pm (COP$6500, 45 minutes). There are more than a dozen direct buses to Bogotá (COP$22,000, four hours) between 4:30am and 5pm. For San Gil, there are better connections in Tunja than in Arcabuco.

Around Villa de Leyva

Here you'll find archaeological relics, colonial monuments, petroglyphs, caves, lakes, waterfalls and fossils. You can walk to some of the nearest sights, or go by bicycle or on horseback.

El Fósil (www.museoelfosil.com; admission adult/child COP$6000/4000; ⏲8am-6pm) is an impressive 120-million-year-old baby kronosaurus fossil. It's the world's most complete specimen of this prehistoric marine reptile. The fossil is 7m long; the creature was about 12m in size but the tail did not survive. It is located off the road to Santa Sofía, 6km west of Villa de Leyva. It's a little more than an hour walking, or take the Santa Sofía bus, which will drop you off 80m from the fossil.

The **Estación Astronómica Muisca** (El Infiernito; admission adult/child COP$6000/5000; ⏲9am-noon & 2-5pm Tue-Sun) dates from the early centuries AD and was used by indigenous people to determine the seasons. It was named 'Little Hell' by Catholics who wanted to put the fear of (a Christian) God into the locals, and encourage them to associate it with the devil. It is made up of large, cylindrical stone monoliths sunk into the ground in two parallel lines. By measuring the length of shadows, the *indígenas* were able to identify the planting seasons. You can walk here from El Fósil in 25 minutes.

Around 16km out of town, but well worth the journey is **Convento del Santo Ecce Homo** (admission COP$5000; ⏲9am-5pm Tue-Sun), a large stone-and-adobe convent founded in 1620 that features a lovely courtyard.

Santuario de Iguaque

Covering the mist-covered upper slopes of an imposing mountain range to the northeast of Villa de Leyva, Iguaque is a 67.5-sq-km **nature reserve** (Colombians/foreigners COP$14,500/38,000; ⏲8am-5pm) in an area of pristine wilderness held sacred by the indigenous Muiscas.

The **visitors center** (dm per person COP$38,000, campsite per person COP$10,000; ⏲8am-5pm) is at an altitude of 2950m, 3km off the Villa de Leyva–Arcabuco road. It offers meals, dorm beds, and collects the entrance fee. Take warm clothing.

From Villa de Leyva take a bus to Arcabuco (COP$4000), get off after 12km at Casa de Peidra (also known as Los Naranjos) and walk to the visitors center (3km). The walk from the visitors center uphill to the Laguna de Iguaque takes two to three hours.

Parque Nacional Natural El Cocuy

With snowcapped peaks, scintillating alpine lakes and glorious green valleys, **Parque Nacional Natural (PNN) El Cocuy** ranks as one of Colombia's most spectacular protected areas. Located in the highest part of the Cordillera Oriental, it tops out at Ritacumba Blanco, a 5330m peak.

The mountain chain is relatively compact and not difficult to reach – the gateway towns are Güicán and El Cocuy in northern Boyacá. It's an ideal place for trekking, although the routes are more suited to experienced walkers. There are no facilities in the park so you'll need to bring all your food and equipment including sleeping bags, warm clothing and a tent. If you don't have gear, the only way to explore the mountains is in a series of day hikes.

The classic Cocuy circuit has been closed by park authorities citing environmental damage, but there are still many breathtaking treks on offer including the spectacular Paso del Conejo circuit, which crosses from Valle de Lagunillas to Laguna Grande de la Sierra. All visitors to the park must report to Parques Nacionales offices in either **Güicán** (☎789-7280; cocuy@parquenacionales.gov.co; Transversal 3 No 9-17; Colombians/foreigners COP$25,000/50,000; ⏲7am-11:45am & 1-4:45pm) or **El Cocuy** (☎789-0359; cocuy@parquesnacionales.gov.co; Calle 5A No 4-22; Colombians/foreigners COP$25,000/50,000; ⏲7-11:45am & 1-4:45pm), register their itineraries and pay the park admission fee. You will need to show proof of insurance for coverage above 4000m or buy the park's version of insurance.

Guides are not mandatory, but are highly recommended. Hire guides at any of the cabañas (cabins) near the park boundary or at **Ecoturismo Comunitario Sisuma** (☎321-345-7076; www.elcocuyboyaca.com) in El Cocuy. Expect to pay about COP$80,000 a day for a campesino (who can merely show you the way) for up to eight people; or COP$100,000 to COP$150,000 for an actual accredited trekking guide for up to six people. Pack animals are now prohibited above 4000m, but porters are available for COP$60,000 to COP$80,000.

Veteran climber Rodrigo Arias of **Colombia Trek** (☎320-339-3839; www.colombiatrek.com) is an experienced, highly recommended guide who can organize all kinds of treks and mountaineering expeditions in the park.

San Gil

☎7 / POP 44,600

There are few small cities that are able to demand as many days on your itinerary as San Gil, the beating heart of Colombia's burgeoning adventure-sports industries. And with the mighty Río Suárez boasting some of the best class 4+ rapids in South America, your heart might just stop beating.

San Gil is a center for rafting, rappelling, *torrentismo* (rappelling down a waterfall), horse riding, paragliding, hydrospeeding, caving and mountain biking, but there are also enough calmer activities to please nature-lovers who want the view without the adrenaline. There are fantastic swimming holes, waterfalls, beautiful rivers and easy, wonderful hikes within 30 minutes of the town.

However, San Gil offers more than just top natural attractions; it's also a pleasant and authentic small Colombian city, an unpretentious place that goes about its business quietly, where tourism is important but not all consuming. It's where locals like to meet for evening drinks under the huge old ceiba trees in the main square and where the local market is full of wonderful fresh fruit and vegetables, not souvenirs. It all pulls together into a highly entertaining destination that many travelers wish they had discovered earlier.

Sights

In Town

Parque El Gallineral PARK

(☎724-4372; cnr Malecón & Calle 6; admission adult/child COP$5000/3000; ⏲8am-5:30pm) San Gil's showpiece is the mystical Parque El Gallineral, a 4-hectare park set on a triangle-shaped island between two arms of the Quebrada Curití and Río Fonce. Nearly all of the 1876 trees are covered with long silvery tendrils of moss called *barbas de viejo* (old man's beard), hanging from branches to form translucent curtains of foliage and filtered sunlight. It's like a scene set in JRR Tolkien's Middle Earth.

Out of Town

Cascadas de Juan Curi WATERFALL

(entrance COP$7000-10,000) Take a day trip to this spectacular 180m-high waterfall where you can swim in the natural pool at its base or relax on the rocks. Adventure junkies can rappel the sheer face of the falls; book this activity with one of the tour companies. Juan Curi is 22km from San Gil on the road to Charalá. Charalá buses depart twice hourly from the local bus terminal.

Pescaderito OUTDOORS

FREE This free group of five swimming holes is a great little place to relax the day away. Skip the first one, they get better the further up you go (the fifth is the best, no diving from the third!). To reach here, catch a bus from the local bus terminal to Curití's main square (COP$2400, every 15 minutes), walk four blocks past the church and take the road leading out of town about 40 minutes upriver.

It's also a nice camping spot.

Activities

There are loads of adventure-tour agencies in San Gil. The most popular activity is white-water rafting. A standard 10km run on Río Fonce (classes 1 to 3) costs COP$30,000 per person and takes 1½ hours. The perilous and thrilling Río Suárez is a world-class run that even experienced rafters say still scares them. It's a full day's trip and costs COP$125,000.

There are several great caves to explore around San Gil, the best of which is the water-filled Cueva Vaca. Most operators also offer horse riding, paragliding, rappelling, rock climbing and ecological walks. Many firms act as intermediaries between the few companies that have the right to operate in each location.

★Colombian Bike Junkies MOUNTAIN BIKING
(☎316-327-6101; www.colombianbikejunkies.com; incl breakfast & lunch COP$175,000) Modeled after Gravity in Bolivia, this Colombian/Ecuadorean-owned extreme mountain-bike company offers a 50km downhill adrenaline overdose on two wheels through the Cañon del Río Suárez, with catering by Gringo Mike's. It's an high-adrenaline, all-day affair that takes in absolutely epic countryside. If you don't own padded cycling shorts, consider stuffing your pants with household sponges!

Colombia Rafting Expeditions RAFTING
(☎724-5800; www.colombiarafting.com; Carrera 10 No 7-83; ⏲8am-6pm) The rafting specialist for the Río Suárez; also offers hydrospeeding and kayaking. The more centrally located satellite **office** (☎724 5800; www.colombiarafting.com; Calle 12 No 8-32; ⏲8-11am & 4-9pm Mon-Sat) is open late.

Macondo Adventures ADVENTURE SPORTS
(☎724 8001; www.macondohostel.com; Carrera 8 No 10-35) Organizes all the usual suspects, plus a great regional foodie tour that takes in local specialties such as *cabra* (goat) and *carne oreada* (sun-dried beef).

Sleeping

Macondo Guesthouse HOSTEL $
(☎724-8001; www.macondohostel.com; Carrera 8 No 10-35; dm COP$20,000-25,000, s COP$55,000-65,000, d COP$65,000-75,000, s/d without bathroom COP$45,000/55,000; @📶) This San Gil classic remains a laid-back but secure (CCTV) hostel that's a bit like crashing at a friend's place. The space offers a wonderful leafy courtyard with a 10-person Jacuzzi, and there's a variety of dorm and room options, including three upgraded privates that outpunch their hostel weight class. Not the flashiest choice, but nails the San Gil vibe.

Hostal de la Nueva Baeza GUESTHOUSE $
(☎724-2606; hostaldelanuevabaeza@hotmail.com; Calle 9 No 8-49; r with/without air-con COP$40,000/35,000; ❄📶) Early risers looking for a very comfortable room in a quiet colonial house without all the fuss should consider this 10-room guesthouse. Attention is limited, but rooms feature vaulted bamboo ceilings, new flat-screen TVs and very nice bathrooms. It's a step up despite the price, but you'll hear those church bells a ringin'. Prices spike in high season.

La Posada Familiar GUESTHOUSE $
(☎724-8136; laposadafamiliar@hotmail.com; Carrera 10 No 8-55; r per person COP$35,000; @📶) Señora Esperanza dotes over guests at this most Colombian of choices, a lovely six-room guesthouse wrapped around a plant-jammed courtyard with a gurgling fountain. Well-maintained rooms are unembellished, but offer modern bathrooms and hot water and there's a small but nice guest kitchen with a hardwood sink.

Hostal Le Papillon HOSTEL $
(☎723-6350; hostallepapillon@hotmail.com; Calle 7 No 8-28; campsite per person COP$10,000, dm COP$17,000, s/d without bathroom COP$25,000/40,000; @📶) This quiet hostel on a quieter street than most is a good choice for peso-pinchers. It's run by a nice Colombian-Swiss couple and has good dorms, a few privates with shared bathrooms and a grassy area out back for camping and hammocks. Two cute cats and a dog have the run of the place. English and French spoken.

Sam's VIP HOSTEL $$
(☎724-2746; www.samshostel.com; Carrera 10 No 12-33; dm COP$22,000, s/d COP$60,000/80,000, without bathroom COP$40,000/60,000; @📶🏊) San Gil's shiniest hostel is right on the plaza and wins accolades for approaching boutique levels with its furnishings and decor. The staff is very friendly – invite them into the small pool with wonderful mountain views, or for a drink on the expansive terrace overlooking the plaza. There is also a superb, straight-out-of-suburban-USA kitchen for guests.

Eating

★Gringo Mike's AMERICAN $
(www.gringomikes.net; Calle 12 No 8-35; burgers COP$11,000-18,000; ⏲8am-noon & 5-10pm Sun-Thu, to 11pm Fri & Sat; 📶) What *isn't* good? In a moody, candlelit courtyard, you'll find this

US-UK operation thrilling homesick travelers with a surplus of American-portioned gourmet burgers, bacon-heavy sandwiches, breakfast burritos and French Press coffee! Highlights are deep and long: the spicy jalapeño burger; the mango, peanut and blue cheese salad with prawns; the Mexican bacon burrito. Great cocktails and veggie choices, too.

★El Maná COLOMBIAN $
(Calle 10 No 9-42; set meals COP$11,500; ⏲11am-3:30pm & 6-8:30pm Mon-Sat, to 3:30pm Sun) This popular, word-of-mouth favorite is the best Colombian restaurant in town. You can taste the extra love in the fantastic set meals – seven or so to choose from daily – featuring traditional dishes like chicken in plum sauce, *estofado de pollo* (chicken stew) and grilled mountain trout. The bummer is it closes early if you're out all day.

Plaza de Mercado MARKET $
(Carrera 11; arepas COP$1500-1800; ⏲6am-3pm Mon-Wed, to 2pm Thu & Sun, to 4pm Fri & Sat) For a true locals' experience, head to this bustling covered market where you can grab plenty of *comidas corrientes,* tamales and fresh-squeezed juices. Don't miss the stuffed *arepas* that a few kiosks do in the middle aisle nearest the Calle 13 side entrance – one of the tastiest breakfasts in town

Drinking & Nightlife

Most of the action in the early evening revolves around beers in the central plaza.

La Habana BAR
(Carrera 9 No 11-68, Local 212; ⏲6pm-midnight Mon-Thu, to 2am Fri & Sat) Located on the 2nd floor of Centro Comercial Camino Real, this hot nightspot is a hidden local gem. Besides being the best bar, its high-reaching walls are decorated in canvas artwork by local artists.

La Isla BARS
(Vía San Gil-Bogotá, Km1) This glorified gas pump on the way out of town is the hottest after-hours ticket in town. There's One Shot (loud and hip bar), Caña Brava (karaoke lounge) and Rodeo (Latin crossover disco). There is also a great food court for late munchies, full of locals sitting around drinking. Go early and grab a bite at the proper Mexican restaurant.

HORMIGAS CULONAS: A SULTRY SNACK

While traveling in Santander, make sure to keep a look-out for the peculiar local delicacy, the *hormiga culona,* or big-assed ant. The giant dark-brown leafcutter ants are fried or roasted and eaten whole in a tradition inherited from the indigenous Guane. Only the voluptuous fertile princess ants are eaten – the humble workers simply don't have the curves. They are sold at small shops throughout the region, especially in Bucaramanga, San Gil and Barichara.

Information

There are several ATMs around the plaza. The official tourism website is www.sangil.com.co.

4-72 (Carrera 10 No 10-50; ⏲8am-noon & 1-6pm Mon-Fri, 9am-noon Sat) Post office.

Tourist Police (☎350-304-5600; Carrera 11 at Calle 7) Police.

Getting There & Away

The main, intercity bus terminal is 3km west of the town center on the road to Bogotá. Urban buses shuttle regularly between the terminal and the center, or you can take a taxi (COP$3600). Frequent buses run to Bogotá (COP$35,000, seven hours) and Bucaramanga (COP$15,000, three hours). Copetran has a direct(ish) service to Santa Marta (COP$60,000, 14 hours) and will also sell you a ticket through to Medellín (COP$85,000, 12 hours), although you'll need to change buses in Bucaramanga.

Minibuses to Bucaramanga (COP$15,000, three hours) via Parque Nacional del Chicamocha leave every 20 minutes from the **Cotrasangil office** (☎724 3434; www.cootrasangil.co; cnr Carrera 11 & Calle 8) on the *malecón* (waterfront) until 8pm.

Buses to Barichara (COP$4200, 40 minutes) leave every 30 minutes from 5am to 6:30pm from the **local bus terminal** (☎724-2155; www.cotrasangil.com; cnr Calle 15 & Carrera 11) in the center. Buses to Guane, Charalá and Curití also leave from here.

Barichara

☎7 / POP 7400

Tiny Barichara is like a film set, boasting immaculately renovated 300-year-old white-washed buildings and atmospheric stone streets. Visit on the weekend and you'll have hordes of visitors from Bogotá for company;

during the week you'll have the place to yourself, although many bars and restaurants may be closed.

The 18th-century sandstone **Catedral de la Inmaculada Concepción**, on the main plaza, is the largest and most elaborate building in town. The **Casa de la Cultura** (Calle 5 No 6-29; admission COP$1000; ⏲8am-noon & 2-6pm Wed-Mon) features a small fossil collection and pottery by the local Guane indigenous people.

The nearby village of **Guane**, 10km to the northwest, is the land that time forgot. It has a fine rural church and a museum with a collection of fossils and Guane artifacts.

Sleeping & Eating

★Tinto Hostel HOSTEL $
(☎726-7725; www.hostaltintobarichara.com; Carrera 4 No 5-39; dm from COP$20,000, s/d from COP$40,000/60,000; @📶🏊) Barichara's best hostel occupies a great multilevel home. There are three dorms and three privates with rustic bathrooms, vaulted ceilings and hot water. The common areas – guest kitchen with artsy ceramic pottery, lounge, hammock space and terrace – are all wonderful, and the last has expansive town views. Artistic touches throughout. Tuck in and stay awhile.

Color de Hormiga Hostel HOSTEL $
(☎726-7156; www.colordehormiga.com; Calle 6 No 5-35; dm/s/d COP$20,000/50,000/60,000; 📶) This charming hostel is one of Barichara's best. Small, green-accented rooms surround a leafy courtyard and offer little design touches like wall-hung chairs for bedside tables and modern bathrooms. The only pity is the dreaded cold, one-spigot showers.

★Color de Hormiga Posada Campestre GUESTHOUSE $$
(☎315-297-1621; www.colordehormiga.com; Vereda San José; r per person incl breakfast COP$70,000; 📶) After operating Santander's most popular restaurant of the same name for years, Chef 'Jorge Hormiga' hung up his apron, then turned his attention to his countryside *finca* (farm), a wonderful four room guest house. Set on a 29-hectare nature reserve where he grows thousands of the region's famous *hormigas culonas* (fat-bottom ants), the rustic rooms here feature boutique beds, memorable outdoor bathrooms and rain-style showers.

Shambalá VEGETARIAN $
(Carrera 7 No 6-20; mains COP$11,000-20,000; ⏲12:30-4pm & 6-9:30pm Thu-Tue; 📶🖉) Tiny and extremely popular cafe doing tasty made-to-order, mostly vegetarian dishes. Pick from wraps, rices and pasta in Mediterranean, Indian or Thai styles (you can add chicken or shrimp) and chase it with excellent juices, teas and the like.

El Compa COLOMBIAN $
(Calle 5 No 4-48; meals COP$8000-18,000; ⏲8am-6pm) The best local restaurant – unpretentious, not touristy, not particularly service oriented, it does 15 or so workhouse Colombian meals. Tasty *cabrito* (baby goat) as well as *sobre barriga* (flank steak), trout, chicken, *carne oreada* (sun-dried beef) etc are all served piled with a host of sides such as salad, yuca, *pepitoria* (goat innards, blood, seasoned rice – we passed on that!) and potatoes.

7 Tigres PIZZA $$
(Calle 6 No 10-24; pizza COP$14,000-16,000; ⏲6-9:30pm Mon-Thu, noon-4pm & 6-10pm Fri-Sun) A good traveler staple for thin-crust pizzas. The Mediterranea, with eggplant, olives, tomatoes, oregano and pesto, is best in show.

Getting There & Away

Buses shuttle between Barichara and San Gil every 45 minutes (COP$4200, 40 minutes). They depart from the **Cotrasangil bus office** (☎726-7132; www.cotrasangil.com; Carrera 6 No 5-70) on the plaza.

There are also regular buses to Guane (COP$1800, 15 minutes) from 5:30am to 5:45pm. You can also hike there on the ancient, fossil-encrusted Camino Real, which starts at the north end of Calle 4. It's not strenuous, but take a hat and water.

Parque Nacional del Chicamocha

This so-called **national park** (www.parquenacionaldelchicamocha.com; Km54 Via Bucaramanga-San Gil; adult/child COP$17,000/11,000; ⏲10am-6pm Wed-Fri, 9am-6pm Sat & Sun; 👪) is not really a park at all (in Colombia real national parks are called Parque Nacional Natural), but rather a glorified rest stop in a spectacular location overlooking the Cañon del Chicamocha. Nicknamed 'Panachi,' it is on the main highway between San Gil and Bucaramanga, a scenic mountain-hugging road that winds through glorious barren landscapes.

Most of the tourist activities here are a waste of both time and money; the real reason to come here is the **canyon**. There is a 360-degree lookout point, though some of the best shots are obstructed by the park's 'attractions.' For the best views, take a ride in the **teleférico** (return cable-car ticket incl park entrance COP$42,000; ⏲9-11am & 1-5:30pm Wed & Thu, 9am-4:30pm Fri-Sun; 👪), which first swoops you down into the depths and then raises you back up on the other side of the canyon. If you want more action, there are also ziplines (COP$22,000).

Any bus between San Gil and Bucaramanga will drop you here. Book your round-trip ticket at the small Cotransangil ticket office inside the main entrance. It is also possible to travel by bus from Bucaramanga to less developed Mesa de Los Santos on the other side of the canyon and buy a one-way ticket across on the *teleférico* (cable car).

Bucaramanga

☎7 / POP 524,000

The capital of Santander is a modern, busy commercial and industrial center with a mild climate. Dubbed 'The City of Parks,' there are indeed several lovely green spaces here, however, in general the city is not particularly noteworthy. Most travelers only stop here to break up an overland journey to the coast, although Buca's friendly locals and throbbing4 nightlife means those that like to party may end up staying a little longer than planned.

Sights

Museo Casa de Bolívar MUSEUM

(Calle 37 No 12-15; admission COP$2000; ⏲8am-noon & 2-6pm Mon-Fri, 8am-noon Sat) Housed in a colonial mansion where Bolívar stayed for two months in 1828, this museum displays various historic and archaeological exhibits, including weapons, documents, paintings, and mummies and artifacts of the Guane people who inhabited the region before the Spaniards arrived.

Catedral de la Sagrada Familia CHURCH

(Calle 36 No 19-56) Facing Parque Santander is Buca's most substantial piece of religious architecture. Constructed over nearly a century (1770–1865), it's a massive, eclectic edifice with fine stained-glass windows and a ceramic cupola brought from Mexico.

Activities

With spectacular surrounding countryside and consistent thermal winds, Bucaramanga has become a popular paragliding destination.

Colombia Paragliding PARAGLIDING

(☎312-432-6266; www.colombiaparagliding.com; Km2 Via Mesa Ruitoque) Bucaramanga's most popular sport is paragliding. The hub for this high-flying activity is atop the Ruitoque mesa. Colombia Paragliding offers 10-/20-/30-minute tandem rides for COP$50,000/80,000/100,000, or go all-out and become an internationally licensed paragliding pilot; 12-day courses including lodging begin at COP$2.8 million. Owner/instructor Richi speaks English and is a well-known Buca character.

Sleeping

Kasa Guane Bucaramanga HOSTEL **$$**

(☎657-6960; www.kasaguane.com; Calle 49 No 28-21; dm from COP$23,000, s/d COP$65,000/85,000, without bathroom COP$40,000/65,000; @📶) Two helpful English lads manage this Buca staple, better known as KGB, located in one of the nicest neighborhoods in town. It offers dorms and private rooms, hot-water bathrooms (no, really), kitchen and laundry facilities, hammocks, a satellite TV room and pool-table terrace – there's even nice-smelling soap!

Nest HOSTEL **$$**

(☎678-2722; www.thenesthostel.com; Km2 Via Mesa Ruitoque; dm/s/d per person COP$35,000/70,000/95,000; @📶🏊) This fly-site hostel is located next to Colombia Paragliding's launch pad, 20 minutes' drive from downtown and perched on a hilltop with amazing views of the city. The majority of guests are paragliding students, but it's also a good choice for anyone seeking peace and quiet. Rates include breakfast and laundry services, and there's a wonderful kitchen for guests plus a small pool.

Eating & Drinking

Cure Cuisine LEBANESE **$**

(Carrera 37 No 41-08; mains COP$1500-6500, combos COP$12,000-22,000; ⏲11am-10pm) Lebanese-descended Colombians do a commendable job at this clean-cut Middle Eastern that's just a step above fast food. Falafel, shawarma, kibe, tabbouleh, baklava – it's all here and accompanied nicely with excellent

GETTING TO VENEZUELA

If you are heading to Venezuela from the interior, the most direct route is via Cúcuta in Norte de Santander. The border between Colombia and Venezuela at Cúcuta was closed by the Venezuelan government at the time of research. While the border is likely to reopen – cross-border trade is too important for both countries – tensions are likely to remain and it's worth checking on the latest before heading out.

To reach San Antonio del Táchira in Venezuela take one of the frequent buses or *colectivos* (shared taxis; COP$1400) departing between 5am and 6:30pm from Cúcuta's bus terminal. A private taxi costs around COP$12,000. Get your exit stamp at **Migración Colombia** (573-5210; www.migracioncolombia.gov.co; CENAF - Simón Bolívar) on the left just before the bridge. From there walk across or grab a *mototaxi* (motorcycle rickshaw).

Once in Venezuela, head into the immigration building for entrance formalities at the SAIME office in central San Antonio del Táchira (not the SAIME office right at the bridge). It's best to have the moto-boys take you all the way there.

Move your watch forward 30 minutes when crossing from Colombia into Venezuela. Take as much US currency as possible into Venezuela to change into Bolívares in order to avoid poor rates from local ATMs.

From San Antonio buses leave regularly for San Cristóbal (BsF40, one hour) from where there are connecting services to Caracas. For details on making this crossing in the opposite direction, see p997.

toasted almond rice. The cheese and onion *fatayers* (small fried pastry pies) are especially tasty.

★Mercagán STEAK $$

(www.mercaganparrilla.com; Carrera 33 No 42-12; steaks COP$18,500-39,000; 11:30am-11pm Tue, Wed & Fri, to 3pm Mon & Thu, to 4pm Sun) Often touted as the best steak in the whole of Colombia, this traditional *parrilla* (grillhouse) run in four locations by four brothers *is* all it's cracked up to be: perfect slabs of meat from their own farm come in 200g, 300g or 400g sizes (good luck!), served on sizzling iron plates.

Coffeehouse San Fernando CAFE

(Carrera 29 No 41-40; coffee COP$2000-10,000; 10am-8pm;) Rainforest Alliance–certified coffee from Mesa de Los Santos. Good espresso.

La Birrería 1516 BAR

(Carrera 36 No 43-46; beers COP$4500-22,000; 10am-midnight Mon-Thu, to 1:30am Fri & Sat) Kick back with a good selection of imported standards and domestic craft brews (Bogotá's Tres Marías is the house draft) on the breezy outdoor patio at this sophisticated pub-restaurant. The food is distinctly average.

Information

There are many ATMs near Parque Santander and in Sotomayor on Carrera 29.

Tourism Police (634-5507; www.imct.gov.co; Parque de Los Niños; 8am-noon & 2-7pm) At the Biblioteca Pública Gabriel Turbay, the tourism police pull double-duty here, surprisingly well. There are maps, brochures, a little English and lots of willingness to help. There are also Puntos de Información Turística (PIT) locations at the airport and bus terminal.

Getting There & Away

Bucaramanga's **Terminal TB** (637-1000; www.terminalbucaramanga.com; Transversal Central Metropolitana) is southwest of the center, midway to Girón; frequent city buses marked 'Terminal' go there from Carrera 15 (COP$1850). Taxis are around COP$8000. Buses depart from here regularly for Bogotá (COP$70,000, 10 hours), Cartagena (COP$90,000, 12 hours), Cúcuta (COP$40,000, six hours) and Santa Marta (COP$70,000, 10 hours).

Palonegro airport is on a plateau high above the city 30km west in Lebrija. *Colectivos* charge COP$10,000 and leave from near Parque Santander on Carrera 20. A private taxi from the center costs COP$32,000.

THE CARIBBEAN COAST

Colombia's Caribbean coast is a sun- and rum-drenched playground that stretches 1760km from the jungles of the Darién in the west to the striking barren landscapes of La Guajira in the wild, wild east.

With the lures of pristine beaches, coral reefs and virgin rainforest in Parque Nacional Natural Tayrona, or the renowned jungle trek to the ancient Ciudad Perdida (Lost City), your main problem will be packing it all in. The budget diving at Taganga and the intoxicating colonial city of Cartagena – one of the continent's most beautiful and historically important destinations – suck many travelers in for months.

For more low-key times, check out Mompox, a living museum that's straight out of a Gabriel García Márquez novel, or laid-back Sapzurro and Capurganá, where time gently vanishes into the sunset of each day. Then snap out of your hammock-swinging reverie with Colombia's most giddying party, the Carnaval of Barranquilla, a week-long Mardi Gras riot of dancing, booze and music.

The Caribbean coast region also happens to be Colombia's main tourist destination for the locals, which means that most people you meet will be in holiday mode and ready to rumba, or to just kick back and idle the time away.

Santa Marta

☎5 / POP 426,000

Santa Marta is where Colombians go when they want sun on their backs, sand under their feet and rum in their glasses. It has a famous colonial past as one of the continent's oldest cities, and is where Simón Bolívar died after a heroic attempt to make Latin America one united republic.

Its grace as a colonial city has faded somewhat because of newer concrete buildings, but it's still a pleasant enough seaside town, and ongoing restoration work is bringing back some of the downtown area's lost charm.

Most travelers whiz through and base themselves in Taganga, or head directly to Parque Nacional Natural Tayrona, leaving downtown Santa Marta with a local, untouristy feel. Spend some time here and you'll find fine restaurants, pleasant plazas and good nightlife. It's also the place to organize a trip to Ciudad Perdida, the great pre-Hispanic city of the Tayrona.

Sights

Catedral CHURCH

(cnr Carrera 4 & Calle 17) This massive whitewashed cathedral claims to be Colombia's oldest church, but work wasn't actually completed until the end of the 18th century, and thus reflects the influences of various architectural styles. It holds the ashes of the town's founder, Rodrigo de Bastidas (just to the left as you enter the church). Simón Bolívar was buried here in 1830, but in 1842 his remains were taken to Caracas, his birthplace.

Museo del Oro MUSEUM

(Calle 14 No 1-37; ⌚11am-6pm) FREE The Gold Museum is in the fine colonial mansion known as the Casa de la Aduana (Customs House) and was fully renovated in 2014. It has an interesting collection of Tayrona objects, mainly pottery and gold, as well as artifacts of the indigenous Kogi and Arhuaco. Don't miss the impressive model of Ciudad Perdida, especially if you plan on visiting the real thing.

Quinta de San Pedro Alejandrino MUSEUM

(☎433-1021; www.museobolivariano.org.co; Av Libertador; adult/child COP$12,000/10,000; ⌚9:30am-4:30pm) This hacienda on the outskirts of town is where Simón Bolívar spent his last days and died. At the time the hacienda was owned by a Spanish supporter of Colombia's independence cause. He invited Bolívar to stay and take a rest at his home before his intended journey to Europe. Several monuments have been built on the grounds in remembrance of Bolívar, the most imposing of which is a massive central structure called the **Altar de la Patria**.

Sleeping

Dreamer HOSTEL $

(☎433-3264; www.thedreamerhostel.com; Diagonal 32, Los Trupillos, Mamatoco; dm from COP$20,000, d from COP$70,000; ❄📶🏊) A very high-end, self-contained and intelligently designed hostel with rooms clustered around one of Santa Marta's best swimming pools. Even the dorms get air-con, a clean shared bathroom and good beds. It's hugely popular with discerning travelers. The Italian owners oversee the kitchen, so the food is fantastic, too.

Aluna HOSTEL $

(☎432-4916; www.alunahotel.com; Calle 21 No 5-72; dm COP$25,000, s/d COP$70,000/90,000, without air-con COP$50,000/70,000; ❄📶) A lovely hotel with nicely proportioned dorms, cosy private rooms and spacious, breezy communal areas. The well-equipped kitchen has lockers, and the best book exchange on the coast speaks of an intelligent, widely read crowd. Ask owner Patrick about his place up in nearby Paso del Mango, a bird-watcher's paradise. Breakfast can be had in the ground-floor cafe, but isn't included.

★**Hostel Masaya Santa Marta** BOUTIQUE HOSTEL **$$**
(☎423-1770; www.masaya-experience.com; Carrera 14 No 4-80; dm COP$22,000-33,000, r incl breakfast COP$110,000-140,000; ❄@🛜🏊) This fabulous addition to the hostel scene takes some beating. It's a clever and stylish multilevel conversion of an old mansion in the center of town, and has a bunch of superb-value dorms and gorgeous private rooms for those on a more generous budget. There's a busy rooftop bar, three plunge pools, a large outdoor kitchen and activities galore. Breakfast on the roof is an extra COP$7500 for those staying in dorms. The staff is kind and knowledgeable and the vibe superb.

La Brisa Loca HOSTEL **$$**
(☎431-6121; www.labrisaloca.com; Calle 14 No 3-58; dm with/without air-con from COP$35,000/20,000, r with/without bathroom COP$100,000/80,000; ❄@🛜🏊) The 'crazy breeze' is the choice for a young, festive crowd who crowd into the 100 or so beds here. Dorms run from four to 10 beds, and there's an array of private rooms too, all with firm beds, high ceilings, ancient tilework, and in-room lockers that

Santa Marta

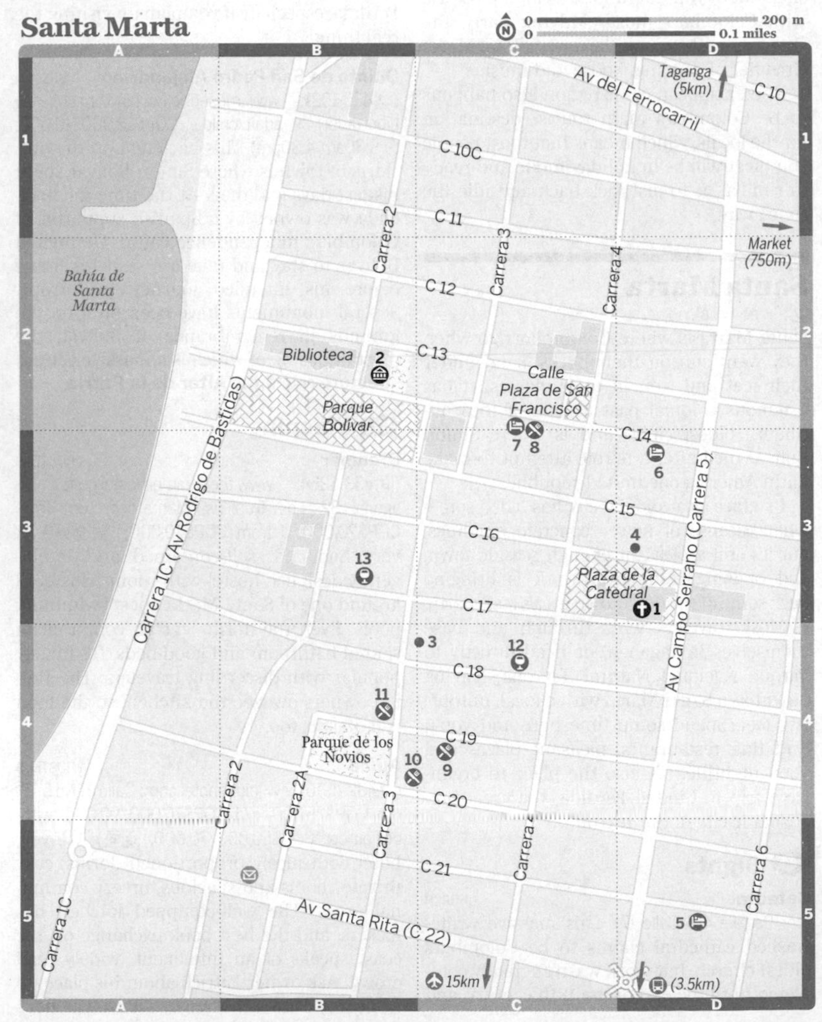

COLOMBIA SANTA MARTA

GETTING TO VENEZUELA

Half-hourly buses depart Santa Marta for Maicao (COP$25,000, four hours), where you change for a *colectivo* to Maracaibo (Venezuela). *Colectivos* depart regularly from about 5am to 3pm and go as far as Maracaibo's bus terminal. Maicao is an edgy, gritty town, so be alert.

Venezuelan entry formalities are done in Paraguachón, on the Venezuelan side of the border. Make sure your driver is prepared to wait while you get your stamp, as locals don't need to go through the same process. Wind your watch 30 minutes forward when crossing from Colombia into Venezuela.

This border had been closed by the Venezuelan government at the time of research. The closure is likely to be temporary but check the latest before making plans.

even allow you to charge you phone securely while you're out.

Eating

There are a lot of cheap restaurants around the budget hotels, particularly on Calles 11 and 12 near the waterfront.

★Ouzo MEDITERRANEAN **$$**
(☎423-0658; Carrera 3 No 19-29, Parque de los Novios; mains COP$17,000-38,000; ⏰6-11pm Mon-Sat; 📶) Ouzo offers a stripped-back, classic Greek and Italian menu that includes superb pizza from a wood-fired oven and a good wine list. The octopus is slow-cooked for two hours in a garlicky broth, then slammed on the coals to sear and seal in the flavor. Great service, and a superbly designed interior means the heat stays in the kitchen.

Santa Marta

Sights
1 Catedral D3
2 Museo del Oro B2

Activities, Courses & Tours
3 Expotur C4
4 Magic Tours D3

Sleeping
5 Aluna D5
6 Hostel Masaya Santa Marta D3
7 La Brisa Loca C2

Eating
8 Agave Azul C3
9 El Bistró C4
10 Ouzo B4
11 Radio Burger B4

Drinking & Nightlife
12 Crabs C4
13 La Puerta B3

El Bistró INTERNATIONAL **$$**
(Calle 19 No 3-68; mains COP$18,000-30,000; ⏰11am-11pm; 📶) A charming new venue just off Parque de los Novios, El Bistró has a fully translated menu that includes classics such as steak tatare, lamb shank, filet mignon and a delicious array of fish and seafood. The portions are big and there's great people-watching from the sidewalk tables.

Agave Azul MEXICAN **$$**
(☎431-6121; Calle 14 No 3-58; mains COP$18,000-25,000; ⏰dinner Mon-Sat; 📶) OK, so you're not in Mexico. But bite into a perfect tostada that totters with toppings including the town's most tender meat; the sweetest, most buttery avocados; and a tart, crispy salad; and you might be forgiven for thinking you are. Presentation is superbly delicate. Steaks are amazing, too.

Radio Burger BURGERS **$$**
(Parque de los Novios; mains COP$15,000-25,000; ⏰5-11pm; 📶) This curious little restaurant is actually the site of Santa Marta's first ever radio station, and it's now a burger-producing homage to the fact, crammed with antique radios. The burgers are delicious and there's a great outdoor seating area right on the square.

Drinking & Nightlife

Begin your evening in the freshly remodeled Parque de los Novios, either at one of the many small bars or in the plaza itself.

La Puerta CLUB
(Calle 17 No 2-29; ⏰6pm-1am Tue & Wed, to 3am Thu-Sat) Students and gringos eye each other up and get happily trashed in a beautifully benign Colombian style. Soca, salsa, house, hip-hop and reggae warm up the packed

dance floor. The gusting fans surrounding it will make you and other dancers look dramatically windswept and much more attractive – especially after half a bottle of *aguardiente*.

Crabs BAR

(Calle 18 No 3-69; ⏲ 8pm-3am Wed-Sat) A perenially busy bar with pool table, outdoor smoking terrace, decent-priced beers and spirits, and video screens paying homage to some of the more obscure monsters of rock.

Information

4-72 (☎ 421-0180; Calle 22 No 2-08; ⏲ 8am-noon & 2-6pm Mon-Fri, to noon Sat) Post office.

Fondo de Promoción Turística de Santa Marta (☎ 422-7548; www.fonproturssantamarta.com; Calle 10 No 3-10, El Rodadero; ⏲ 8am-noon & 2-6pm Mon-Fri, 8am-noon Sat) Santa Marta's member-based tourist office provides the best information for travelers.

Policía Nacional (☎ 421-4264; Calle 22 No 1C-74)

Getting There & Away

AIR

The airport is 16km south of the city on the Bogotá road. City buses marked 'El Rodadero Aeropuerto' will take you there in 45 minutes.

BUS

The bus terminal is on the southeastern outskirts of the city. Local buses run into town, but it's far faster in a taxi (COP$6000).

Half-a-dozen buses run daily to Bogotá (COP$80,000, 18 hours) and there are less frequent services to Bucaramanga (COP$80,000, nine hours). Buses to Barranquilla (COP$12,000, two hours) depart every 15 to 30 minutes. Some of them continue on to Cartagena (COP$25,000, four hours), but if not, there are immediate connections in Barranquilla.

Taganga

☎ 5 / POP 5000

Taganga is a tiny fishing village that doesn't quite know what's hit it. Set around an iridescently turquoise horseshoe-shaped bay near Santa Marta, with beautiful coral reefs nearby, its location and pace of life have attracted backpackers in their thousands. It has a reputation for cheap scuba diving and lodgings, easy camaraderie and a youthful, hedonistic atmosphere. It's a popular base from which to explore nearby Parque Nacional Natural Tayrona or Ciudad Perdida.

However, popularity brings pitfalls, and Taganga has its share. The town's infrastructure is not built for the massive influx of visitors and litter is a serious problem.

CHOOSING A DIVE SCHOOL

When choosing a dive school, consider the following factors:

- Is the dive center authorized by PADI or NAUI?
- Does the dive center look organized and professional?
- Is the dive equipment well maintained?
- Is all paperwork in order?
- Will you have a certified instructor with you underwater?
- Will this same instructor sign your scuba diving forms and certification?
- Does the price include a study book and a certification for every course you take?
- When was the last hydrostatic test carried out on the tanks? It should be every five years.
- Ask to test the tank's air. It should be smell- and taste-free.
- What is the instructor-to-student ratio?
- How is the theory component of your course taught?
- Do the firm's boats have two engines?
- Is there oxygen on board?
- Are the staff certified oxygen providers?
- Do boats have adequate and sufficient lifejackets and a radio?

WORTH A TRIP

MINCA

If you need to escape the heat of the coast, head to this small village with great coffee and good bird-watching opportunities 600m up into the Sierra Nevada above Santa Marta. It's very quiet and slow-paced but is also a popular destination for adventure sports including mountain biking, tubing and canyoning.

For outdoor adventures, visit **Jungle Joe Minca Adventures** (317-308-5270; www.junglejoeminca.com), which offers all kinds of activities in the surrounding mountains.

High in the mountains, **Casa Elemento** (313-587-7677, 311-655-9207; www.casaelemento.com; above Minca; dm COP$25,000, d from COP$70,000;) is a social place with enviable views that is the perfect place to unwind. It's a 30-minute, COP$15,000 ride by *mototaxi*. Closer to town, but also with fine vistas, is **Casa Loma** (313-808-6134; www.casalomaminca.com; hammock COP$15,000, r without bathroom from COP$65,000), a fine budget lodge with a relaxed vibe.

Minca is reached by *colectivo* (COP$7000, 45 minutes) from the 'estación Minca' on the corner of Calle 11 and Carrera 12 in Santa Marta. The battered old vehicles only leave when full, so if you're in a hurry pay for all four seats.

Many still-impoverished locals feel crowded out by the foreign newcomers. Add to this a small but aggravating local petty crime spree (especially on beaches and from hotel rooms) and you have to question the impact of unregulated development on small communities.

Taganga's beach is dirty, overcrowded and not particularly attractive. Better, but still far from top class, is **Playa Grande**, a short boat ride away.

Activities

Taganga is one of the world's cheapest places to get PADI (Professional Association of Diving Instructors) or NAUI (National Association of Underwater Instructors) certified. A four-day open-water course including six dives costs COP$600,000 to COP$750,000. A two-tank dive for trained divers with lunch and all gear costs around COP$150,000. It's often possible to find even cheaper deals on offer around town, but don't be lured by low prices alone. Be sure to choose a good-quality and safe dive school.

Aquarius Diving Club DIVING
(422-2263; www.aquariusdivingclub.com; Calle 13 No 2-06) A five-star PADI diving center right in the heart of the town. Charges COP$150,000 for a two-tank dive and COP$650,000 all-inclusive for an open-water course.

Poseidon Dive Center DIVING
(421-9224; www.poseidondivecenter.com; Calle 18 No 1-69) Well-equipped and experienced dive school; open-water courses cost COP$720,000.

Sleeping

Casa de Felipe HOSTEL $
(316-318-9158, 421-9120; www.lacasadefelipe.com; Carrera 5A No 19-13; dm COP$20,000-23,000, s/d from COP$50,000/60,000, apt COP$100,000;) This French-run hostel is the best budget option in town. It's also very secure, though be sure to take a taxi here after dark. It's in a beautiful house on lush grounds above the bay, and boasts great staff, pleasant rooms, a good bar, a kitchen, cable TV, numerous hammocks, an excellent breakfast and friendly folk from around the world.

Divanga GUESTHOUSE $$
(421-9092; www.divanga.com; Calle 12 No 4-07; dm COP$32,000-44,000, s/d per person incl breakfast from COP$74,000/94,000;) Another French-run place not short on atmosphere – colorful local artworks don the walls and doors of the rooms, most of which surround a swimming pool. There's a rooftop deck and bar that catches a lovely sea breeze. It's more tranquil than Casa de Felipe, so opt to stay here if that's a priority.

Eating

Fishermen sell small tuna, jackfish, barracuda and snapper at decent prices at the far end of the beach.

★**Babaganoush** INTERNATIONAL $$
(Carrera 1C No 18-22; mains COP$15,000-25,000; noon-11pm Wed-Mon;) This cosy rooftop restaurant has great bay views and an eclectic menu that keeps the crowds returning

again and again. Try the excellent pumpkin soup, the perfectly cooked filet mignon or the sublime Thai green curry. It's up the hillside on the road towards Santa Marta.

Pachamama FRENCH **$$**
(☎ 421-9486; Calle 16 No 1C-18; mains COP$15,000-30,000; ⊙ 6-11pm Mon-Sat; 📶) You'll find Pachamama down a quiet backstreet in a small walled compound. With Tiki stylings and a laid-back vibe, it's like an indoor beach bar – but casual as it may be, the French chef has produced one of the most creative menus on the coast. The langoustines in bacon and tarragon are sensational, and the tuna carpaccio is perfect.

ℹ Information

The path to Playa Grande is a hot spot for robberies. Don't take anything you can't afford to lose. Taganga's sole Bancolombia ATM is often out of service, so bring plenty of funds.

ℹ Getting There & Away

Taxis between Santa Marta and Taganga cost COP$10,000. Buses (COP$1500, 20 minutes) run every 10 minutes. Pick them up anywhere along Carrera 5 in Santa Marta.

There is a boat service from Taganga to Cabo San Juan de la Guía in Parque Nacional Natural Tayrona (COP$45,000, one hour) at 10am daily, returning at 4pm. Park officials will meet your boat on arrival to charge the entrance fee.

Parque Nacional Natural Tayrona

One of Colombia's most popular national parks, **Parque Nacional Natural Tayrona** (adult/under 26yr & student COP$38,000/7500) is set in a supernaturally beautiful region. Its palm-fringed beaches are scattered with huge boulders that were once worshipped by the local indigenous people, after whom the park is named. It has become an essential stop-off for travelers and has plenty of places to stay. Beware: many of the beaches here are tormented by treacherous currents that have killed hundreds of foolhardy daredevils.

The region was once the territory of the Tayrona indigenous people and some remnants have been found in the park, the most important being the ruins of the pre-Hispanic town of Pueblito.

Food inside the park is expensive and pretty poor, so self-catering is essential for longer visits. Leave all your bulky items in a garbage bag at your hostel and fill your backpack with food and bags of water. It is prohibited to bring alcohol into the park; rangers will search your bags on arrival.

👁 Sights & Activities

The park is covered in dense jungle full of birds, squirrels and monkeys, and is perfect for exploring on foot. Set out early, before it gets too hot, and take plenty of water.

The park's main entrance is in **El Zaíno**, on the Santa Marta–Riohacha coastal road, where you pay the entrance fee. From El Zaíno, a paved road runs for 6km past the turtle-nesting area of **Castilletes** to **Cañaveral**. Here you'll find the park's administrative center, a campground, ludicrously overpriced so-called 'ecohabs' (in reality these are just thatched cottages) and a restaurant.

Parque Nacional Natural Tayrona

From Cañaveral, most visitors take a 45-minute walk west to **Arrecifes**, where there are budget lodgings and eating facilities; the coast around here is spectacular, dotted with massive boulders. If you have plenty of gear, consider hiring a horse (COP$20,000).

From Arrecifes, a 20-minute walk northwest along the beach will bring you to **La Aranilla**, a sandy beach surrounded by huge boulders in a tiny bay, where the water dances with light and is flecked with sparkling golden mineral flakes. Snacks are available here.

Next along is **La Piscina**, a deep bay partly cut off from the open sea by an underground rocky chain. Another 20-minute walk will take you to **Cabo San Juan de la Guía**, a beautiful cape with fantastic beaches and views.

From the Cabo, a scenic path goes inland uphill to **Pueblito**, a 1½-hour walk away, providing some splendid tropical forest scenery. While not much of Pueblito settlement remains, it's still well worth a visit, especially for those not planning to hike to Ciudad Perdida. Take a flashlight, spare batteries and watch out for snakes after dark.

Other entrances to the park include Palangana, from where its possible to access **Bahía Neguanje** via a rough road if you have your own transportation. From Neguanje launches leave for the **Playa Cristal**, a gorgeous palm-fringed stretch of sand with several restaurants where you can enjoy a cold beer and fresh fish after a refreshing swim.

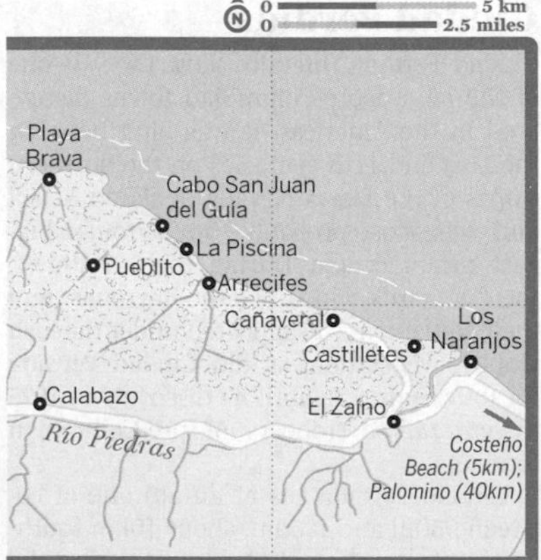

Sleeping & Eating

The best budget accommodations are in the area around Arrecifes. While the beach here is not apt for swimming, you are a short walk away from several calm bays. The other popular budget option is at Cabo San Juan de la Guía, which has fantastic beaches, but is noisy and overcrowded.

Camping Castilletes CAMPGROUND $
(313-653-1830; www.campingcastilletespnntayrona.blogspot.com; campsite/tent per person COP$15,000/25,000) This campground sits on 1.5km of beach that is also the park's most popular spot for sea-turtle nesting. The beach is swimmable in September and October (other months are only safe for advanced swimmers). It's a good choice if you want to dump your bags and crash out.

Camping Don Pedro CAMPGROUND $$
(317-253-3021, 315-320-8001; campingdonpedro@hotmail.com; hammocks COP$12,000, campsite per person with/without tent hire COP$14,000/12,000, cabañas incl breakfast COP$100,000) Of the three places to stay and eat in Arrecifes, this is the best. It's reached via a 300m split off the main trail just before Arrecifes. The spacious grounds are well maintained and have an abundance of fruit trees. Cooking facilities are available to guests, while excellent meals, including superb fresh fish, cost an average COP$12,000. The welcome is warm.

Camping Cabo San Juan del Guía CAMPGROUND $$
(314-385-2546, 312-604-2941; www.cecabosanjuandelguia.com.co; campsite COP$15,000, hammocks with/without view COP$25,000/20,000, r COP$150,000) Most backpackers end up at this campground, which has the air of a music festival in high season. There are two gorgeous swimming beaches here as well as a restaurant. For COP$25,000, you can sleep in the hammocks high atop the *mirador* (lookout) on the rocks above the beach, giving fantastic views of the sea, beaches and mountains.

Getting There & Away

You can get to El Zaíno (COP$5000, one hour) by Palomino buses that depart regularly from Santa Marta's market. From El Zaíno, catch the jeep that shuttles between the entrance and Cañaveral (COP$2000, 10 minutes) or walk for 45 minutes.

Palomino

☎5 / POP 4000

While technically in La Guajira department, this lovely Caribbean beach, a short bus ride east of Parque Nacional Natural Tayrona, is geographically and culturally tied to the Sierra Nevada. It's framed by two majestic rivers and accessed from the nondescript town of Palomino, which is little more than a truck stop on the highway.

If the beaches of Taganga seem scruffy and rowdy, and Parque Nacional Natural Tayrona feels like a ganja-scented social club, a trip here will reinvigorate your faith in the simple pleasures of wandering along an empty beach, buying a fish from a local, cooking it on a fire and eating it as the sun sets.

Be aware that the dangerous currents mean that swimming in the sea off Palomino is a risky affair and is often off limits – exercise extreme caution. However, if you want to cool down, the shallow rivers flanking the town are fed by fresh mountain waters and are a great place for a paddle. The town is also a great base from which to explore less visited areas of the majestic Sierra Nevada mountain range.

Sleeping & Eating

La Casa de Rosa CAMPGROUND $

(☎315-445-9531; campsite with/without tent hire COP$8000/6000, hammocks COP$8000) This is the simplest campsite on the coast, with bucket showers drawn from a well. The two twinkly eyed sisters, Milena and Paolina, are sweeter than *panela* (raw sugarcane juice) and will make you supper if you order in the morning. If Milena *really* likes you, she might kill you a cockerel.

Jaguar Azul HOSTEL $

(☎313-800-9925313-800-9925; www.jaguarazulpalomino.com; dm COP$20,000, s/d COP$50,000/60,000;) It's a rather different approach to tourism that you'll find here. This place is not on the beach, but on the other side of the main road, in a barrio of Palomino known as La Sierrita. Here you'll find simple fan-cooled accommodations, a shared kitchen and a big garden that's full of fruit trees and backed by the mountains.

★Dreamer HOSTEL $$

(www.thedreamerhostel.com; dm COP$25,000, d from COP$110,000;) This excellent new hostel on the beach is run by the same team running the original Dreamer in Santa Marta. Centered on a large garden with a fantastic pool, the tile-floored rooms here are spacious and have thatched roofs. There's a really social vibe, plenty of activities to keep you occupied, a busy bar and a superb restaurant that's busy all day.

Finca Escondida HOSTEL $$

(☎310-456-3159, 315-610-9561; www.chillandsurfcolombia.com; hammocks COP$15,000, dm COP$25,000, r from COP$80,000;) Run by a friendly international crowd, this large beachfront complex includes a number of rooms in various shapes and sizes, the better of which are huge and enjoy large balconies. The feel is rustic, with wooden buildings set in grounds full of fruit trees. A host of activities from surfing to pilates is offered, making it a firm backpacker favorite.

Suá COLOMBIAN $$

(mains COP$12,000-28,000; ⏲noon-9pm Wed-Sun) On the main road through town, Suá is one of the few restaurants in Palomino not associated with a hotel. The fare is inventive, with a fully translated English menu that includes specialties such as lion fish in a coconut, orange and ginger sauce; prawns marinated in garlic, sea salt and butter; and beef loin in a red wine and spice sauce.

It's poorly signed, but you'll find it across the road from the Ayatawacoop gas station.

Getting There & Away

Buses to Palomino (COP$7000, 2½ hours) leave regularly from the market in Santa Marta. Jump off at the gas station and walk 20 minutes down to the beach or take a *mototaxi* (COP$2000).

Ciudad Perdida

Ciudad Perdida (literally, 'Lost City') is one of the largest pre-Columbian towns discovered in the Americas. It was built between the 11th and 14th centuries on the northern slopes of the Sierra Nevada de Santa Marta and was most probably the Tayronas' biggest urban center. During their conquest, the Spaniards wiped out the Tayronas, and their settlements disappeared under the lush tropical vegetation, as did Ciudad Perdida for four centuries, until its discovery in 1975 by *guaqueros* (robbers of pre-Columbian tombs).

Ciudad Perdida sits at an altitude of between 950m and 1300m, about 40km southeast of Santa Marta. The central part of the city is set on a ridge, from which various stone paths descend. There are about 150 stone terraces that once served as foundations for the houses. Originally the urban center was completely cleared of trees, before being reclaimed by the jungle.

While the ruins are a fascinating place, this trip is really all about the journey and the breathtaking scenery along the way. The round trip is a stiff four- to six-day hike, challenging but not overly difficult. The trail begins in El Mamey and goes up along the Río Buritaca. The section between Santa Marta and El Mamey is done by vehicle.

Access to Ciudad Perdida is by tour only. Tours begin and end in Santa Marta and there are four operators all offering a similar product; sometimes the companies pool together to form groups when demand is low. The official price for the tour is COP$700,000 – pay any less and the money will be taken from your guide's fees, health insurance or life insurance.

The price includes transportation, food, accommodations (normally mattresses with mosquito nets, though some agencies still use hammocks on one night), porters for your food, non-English-speaking guides and all necessary permits. The price does not go down if you complete the walk in fewer days. Most groups tend to do the trek in four days, but less fit walkers and those who want to take their time often do it in five. Six-day trips are the maximum; we recommend the four-day version.

The walk normally takes 1½ days uphill to Ciudad Perdida, with a half-day at the site on the morning of the third day, then one full day's walking back downhill that is split over two days. The round trip covers 40km and there are several rivers to cross on the way.

Groups number four to 15 people, and tours depart year-round as soon as a group is assembled. Expect departures every day during high season. You carry your own personal belongings. Take a flashlight, a water container, diarrhea medicine, plus masses of insect repellent (this cannot be stressed strongly enough).

Among the tour operators, **Expotur** (☎420-7739; www.expotur-eco.com; Carrera 3 No 17-27, Santa Marta) stands out for its professional approach and top customer service and is also the only company to send translators with groups. **Magic Tour** (☎421-5820; Calle 16 No 4-41, Santa Marta) is another professionally run outfit with knowledgeable guides.

La Guajira Peninsula

Say 'La Guajira' to Colombians and most people's expressions will sharpen. This remote peninsula is seen as the wild, wild east, a place beyond the back of beyond, but it rewards the intrepid with solitude and landscapes unlike any others on the continent: scenes of epic, inhospitable beauty softened by the glow of the brilliant Caribbean Sea.

Riohacha (population 170,000), the capital of La Guajira, is 175km northeast of Santa Marta and was traditionally the furthest east most travelers reached unless they were heading for the Venezuelan border. However, there isn't much here for travelers and these days most pass right through on their way to the surreal landscapes of the Alta Guajira around Cabo de La Vela and Punta Gallinas.

The local indigenous people of the peninsula, the Wayuu, have a fierce reputation going back to the revolutionary days of Simón Bolívar, when they supported 'El Libertador' and were the only indigenous people in Colombia who knew how to ride horses and use firearms. They have never been ruled by the Spanish, and 20,000 of them fought the colonists with arms smuggled by the Dutch and English, contributing to Colombia's independence.

That said, today the Wayuu are not running off visitors but rather welcoming them into their homes, as tourism on the peninsula, still in its infancy, begins to take hold.

Cabo de la Vela

☎5 / POP 1500

Cabo de la Vela isn't for everybody. Really. Getting here by public transportation involves a bone-shaking ride in the back of a truck, possibly driven at lunatic speed by a man with no apparent fear of death or injury. He may spend much of the journey draining beer cans in a single slug. With luck, his assistant will be reasonably sober and will manage not to fall out of the truck. Fingers crossed.

The landscape is brutal scrub, and the local dish is *viche,* goat cooked in its own fat and served with its innards. Thankfully, lobster is cheap, fresh, plentiful and exquisite, and the harsh landscape is offset by the brilliantly blue Caribbean Sea that hugs a coastline of small cliffs and deserted sandy beaches. There are also fantastic sunsets viewed from the lighthouse.

Sights

If you're not into kitesurfing, there's absolutely nothing to do in Cabo except swim in the sea and take a walk to **El Faro** (the lighthouse) to watch the sunset. It's a 45-minute walk from town, or you can wrangle a ride with a local for COP$30,000 or so for a round trip. Take plenty of water, insect repellent and a hat.

Just beyond El Faro is **Ojo del Agua**, a nicely sized crescent-shaped dark-sand beach bound by 5m-high cliffs. The beach gets its name from a small freshwater pool that was discovered here, a deeply sacred site for the Wayuu.

But the jewel of the area is **Playa del Pilón**, far and away the most beautiful beach in Cabo. Here you'll find a startling rust-orange collection of sand backed by craggy cliffs that glow a spectacular shade of greenish-blue, especially at sunrise and sunset. **Pilón de Azucar**, a 100m hillside, looms over the beach and provides the area's most picturesque viewpoint, the whole of Alta Guajira displayed before you with the Serranía del Carpintero mountain range in the distance.

Sleeping & Eating

You can stay with almost any Wayuu family in Cabo, under the government's *posadas turísticas* (tourist guesthouse) scheme. You'll be sleeping in simple rooms, hammocks or more comfortable *chinchorros* (locally made woolen hammocks). Nearly all the *posadas* have restaurants serving pretty much the same thing: fish or goat for around COP$10,000 to COP$15,000, and lobster at market price.

Posada Pujuru GUESTHOUSE **$**
(☎300-279-5048, 310-659-4189; posadapujuru@gmail.com; hammocks/chinchorros COP$10,000/15,000, s/d COP$25,000/50,000) This *posada ecoturística* offers 10 well-constructed huts for private rooms, and luggage lockers for those in hammocks. The generators run from 6pm to 10pm and the restaurant (mains COP$10,000 to COP$15,000) serves up a tasty *pargo rojo* (red snapper), though the shrimp and rice is greasy and best avoided. You'll find it on the seafront.

Hostería Jarrinapi GUESTHOUSE **$**
(☎311-683-4281; hammocks COP$15,000, r per person COP$35,000, mains COP$15,000-40,000) One of the more central options in Cabo, this place has very nicely maintained public areas and spotless rooms with tiled floors (a big deal in these parts!). A front desk and running water make you feel almost like you're in an actual hotel. The generators pump all night – meaning your fan whirs and you can sleep.

Getting There & Away

From Riohacha, catch a *colectivo* at **Cootrauri** (☎728-0000; Calle 15 No 5-39) to Uribia (COP$12,000, one hour); they depart when full from 5am to 6pm daily. Leave Riohacha before 1pm in order to make the Uribia–Cabo connection. The driver will know you are going to Cabo and will bundle you from the bus onto an ongoing 4WD service to Cabo (COP$12,000 to COP$15,000, two hours). You may have to wait while your vehicle is packed to bursting point with other passengers, boxes and goats.

Punta Gallinas

Literally the end of the road for travelers, Punta Gallinas is the northernmost point in South America and is surrounded by some of the most spectacular landscapes on the continent. Immense sand dunes roll down to the Caribbean Sea, while impossibly iridescent bays lined with green mangroves contrast against the brilliant yellow and red sands.

Punta Gallinas is also one of the harshest environments in Colombia and not an easy place for budget travelers. It's home to just eight Wayuu families, some of which run simple guesthouses a fair way from each other. The best are **Hospedaje Alexandra** (☎318-500-6942, 315-538-2718; hospedajealexandra@hotmail.com; hammocks/chinchorros/cabañas per person COP$15,000/20,000/30,000), which has a great location right on Bahía Hondita, and **Hospedaje Luzmila** (☎312-626-8121, 312-647-9881; luzmilita10@gmail.com; hammocks/chinchorros per person COP$15,000/20,000, r per person COP$30,000), which has great views.

To really get a feel for the immense variety of landscapes you have to get out and explore either on foot, by bicycle or on a tour. Don't miss **Playa Taroa**, a magical beach accessed by sliding down a giant sand dune all the way to the water. The sense of isolation here is entrancing.

Getting to Punta Gallinas is difficult to organize independently and can be costly. If there is sufficient demand and road conditions are good, guesthouses may be able to pick you up in Cabo de la Vela by 4WD vehicle. The other option is vehicle transportation to Puerto Bolívar followed by a two-hour boat trip across the open ocean. Either way, the larger the group the less costly the transfer.

If you are on a tight schedule, **Kai Ecotravel** (☎311-436-2830; www.kaiecotravel.com; Hotel Castillo del Mar, Calle 9A No 15-352) organizes all-inclusive trips with private transportation, including visits to many sites along the way.

Barranquilla

☎5 / POP 1.9 MILLION

Barranquilla seems like one long, intensely hot traffic jam hemmed in by heavy industry and Caribbean swamps. Colombia's fourth-biggest city is focused on trade and shipping, and other than its four-day Carnaval there's little to detain the traveler here.

The city's pre-Lenten Mardi Gras Carnaval is a one-way trip into bedlam, with revelers from all over the country descending on the town to drink it dry, while flinging flour and water bombs at each other – you'd be mad to miss it if you're nearby. Watch for pickpockets in the crowd, buy a disposable camera and don't dress to impress. Book accomodations way in advance.

If you end up in Barranquilla and are looking for a cheap bed, the **Meeting Point** (☎320-502-4459, 318-2599; ciampani@gmail.com; Carrera 61 No 68-100; dm/r from COP$15,000/40,000; ❄📶) is a friendly hostel with a family atmosphere and air-con dorms.

Cartagena

☎5 / POP 945,000

A fairy-tale city of romance, legends and sheer beauty, Cartagena de Indias is the most beautiful city in Colombia, with cobbled alleys, enormous balconies shrouded in bougainvillea and massive churches casting their shadows across leafy plazas.

Founded in 1533, Cartagena swiftly blossomed into the main Spanish port on the Caribbean coast and the gateway to the north of the continent. Treasure plundered from the indigenous people was stored here until the galleons were able to ship it back to Spain. It attracted pirates and in the 16th century alone suffered five sieges, the best known of which was led by Francis Drake in 1586.

In response, the Spaniards made Cartagena an impregnable port and constructed elaborate walls encircling the town, and a chain of forts. These fortifications helped save Cartagena from subsequent sieges.

Modern Cartagena has expanded dramatically and is surrounded by vast suburbs. It is Colombia's largest port and an important industrial center. Nevertheless, the old walled town has changed very little.

Cartagena has also become a fashionable seaside resort. A modern tourist district has sprung up on Bocagrande and El Laguito, south of the old town. Most backpackers, however, stay in the historic part of town.

Sights

Cartagena's old town is its principal attraction, particularly the inner walled town consisting of the historical districts of El Centro and San Diego, with many beautiful squares and flower-bedecked balconies. Almost every street is a postcard-worthy scene of 16th- and 17th-century architecture.

Getsemaní, the outer walled town, is not so well preserved but there is more street life here, a few good drinking holes and one lovely square, Plaza Trinidad.

The old town is surrounded by **Las Murallas**, the thick walls built to protect it. Construction was begun toward the end of the 16th century after the attack by pirate Francis Drake; until that time Cartagena was almost completely unprotected.

Many churches have entrance fees, but if you are on a tight budget, it is possible to visit for free during mass; there are usually services around 5pm to 6pm. Many museums are free on the last Sunday of the month.

★Castillo de San Felipe de Barajas FORTRESS

(Av Arévalo; adult/child COP$17,000/8000; ⏲8am-6pm) The castillo is the greatest fortress ever built by the Spaniards in any of their colonies. It still dominates an entire section of Cartagena's cityscape today, and should definitely be your first choice of fortresses to visit. The original fort was commissioned in 1630 and was quite small. Construction began in 1657 on top of the 40m-high San Lázaro hill. In 1762 an extensive enlargement was undertaken, which resulted in the entire hill being covered over with this powerful bastion.

★Palacio de la Inquisición MUSEUM

(Plaza de Bolívar; adult/child COP$16,000/13,000; ⏲9am-6pm) The Palace of the Inquisition may today be one of the finest buildings in

Cartagena Old Town

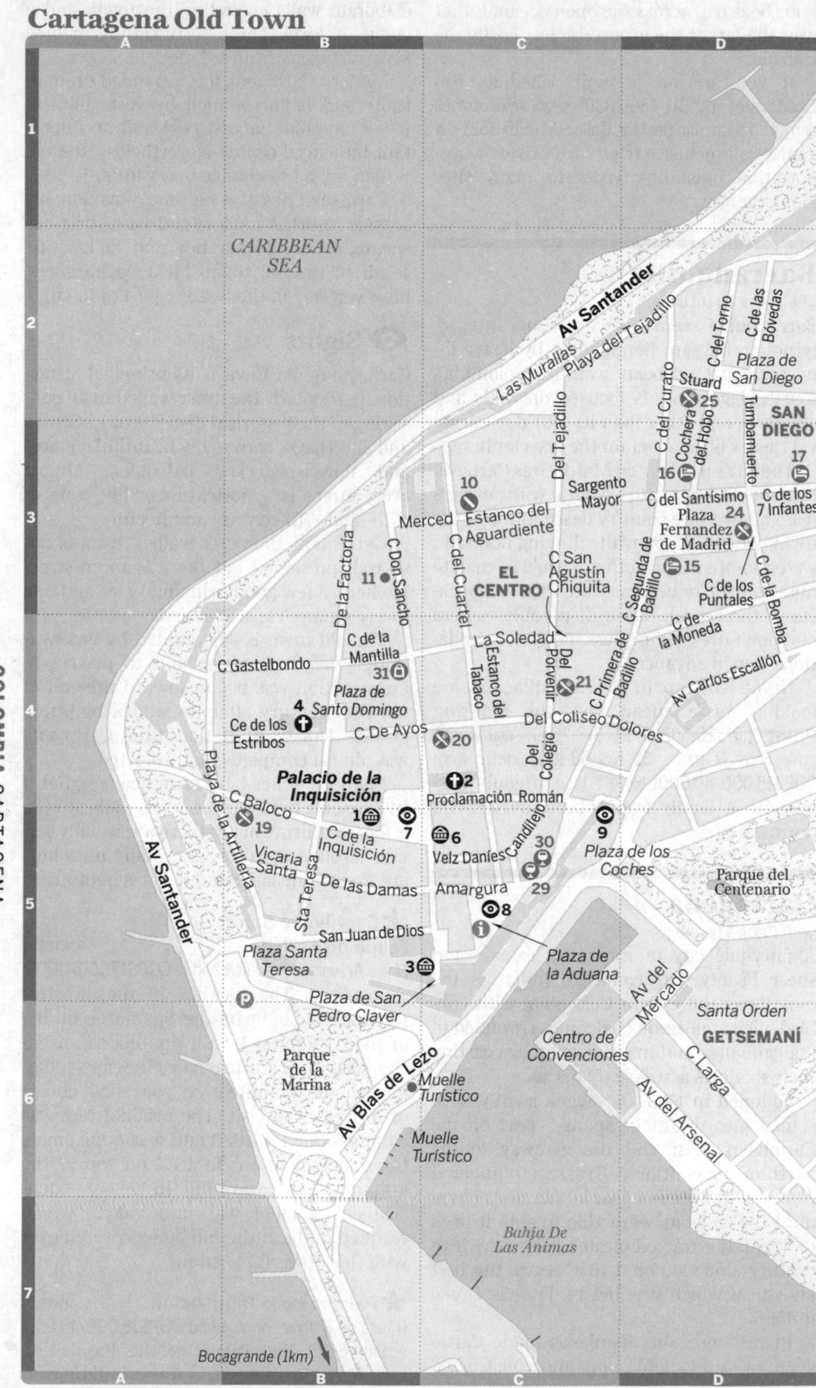

COLOMBIA CARTAGENA

the city, but in the past it housed the notoriously grizzly Inquisition, whose bloody task it was to stamp out heresy in colonial Cartagena. The palace is today a museum, displaying the Inquisitors' gnarly instruments of torture, some of which are quite horrific. The museum also houses pre-Columbian pottery and historical objects dating from both colonial and independence times, including arms, paintings, furniture and church bells.

Convento & Iglesia de San Pedro Claver MUSEUM

(☎664-4991; Plaza de San Pedro Claver; adult/child COP$9000/6000; ⊙9:30am-noon & 3-5pm Mon-Fri) This convent was founded by Jesuits in the first half of the 17th century, originally as San Ignacio de Loyola. The name was later changed in honor of Spanish-born monk Pedro Claver (1580–1654), who lived and died in the convent. Called the 'Apostle of the Blacks' or the 'Slave of the Slaves,' the monk spent all his life ministering to the enslaved people brought from Africa. He was the first person to be canonized in the New World (in 1888).

Plaza de Bolívar PLAZA

Formerly the Plaza de Inquisición, this leafy and shaded plaza is surrounded by some of the city's most elegant balconied colonial buildings. It's one of Cartagena's most alluring plazas and offers wonderful respite from the Caribbean heat. A statue of the eponymous Simón Bolívar stands in the middle of the plaza.

Convento de la Popa CHURCH

(adult/child COP$8000/6000; ⊙8am-6pm) On a 150m-high hill, the highest point in Cartagena, stands this convent. A beautiful image of La Virgen de la Candelaria, the patroness of the city, is in the convent's chapel, and there's a charming flower-filled patio. There is also a chilling statue of a speared Padre Alonso García de Paredes, a priest who was murdered along with five Spanish soldiers for trying to spread Christianity. The views from here are outstanding and stretch all over the city.

Take a cab and expect to pay up to COP$40,000 including waiting time. Haggle politely but insistently and you might get it for less than that.

Iglesia de Santo Domingo CHURCH

(Plaza de Santo Domingo; adult/child COP$12,000/8000; ⊙9am-7pm Tue-Sat, noon-8pm

Cartagena Old Town

Top Sights
1 Palacio de la Inquisición B5

Sights
2 Catedral C4
3 Convento & Iglesia de San Pedro Claver C5
4 Iglesia de Santo Domingo B4
5 Las Bóvedas E1
6 Museo del Oro Zenú C5
7 Plaza de Bolívar B5
8 Plaza de la Aduana C5
9 Puerta del Reloj C5

Activities, Courses & Tours
10 Diving Planet C3
11 Vélo Tours B3

Sleeping
12 Casa Marco Polo E3
13 Casa Viena E5
14 Casa Villa Colonial F5
15 Chill House D3
16 El Genovés Hostal D3
17 El Viajero Cartagena D3
18 Media Luna Hostel E5

Eating
19 Crepe Xpress B5
20 El Bistro C4
21 Espíritu Santo C4
22 Gastrolab Sur F5
23 Gato Negro E5
24 Girasoles D3
I Balconi ..... (see 28)
25 La Cevicheria D2
26 Restaurante Coroncoro E5

Drinking & Nightlife
27 Bazurto Social Club E5
28 Café Havana E5
29 Donde Fidel C5
30 Tu Candela C5

Shopping
31 Ábaco B4

Sun) Santo Domingo is reputedly the oldest church in the city. It was originally built in 1539 in Plaza de los Coches, but the original building succumbed to fire and was rebuilt in its present location in 1552. Builders gave it a particularly wide central nave and covered it with a heavy roof, but it seems they were not too good at their calculations as the vault began to crack afterwards.

Puerta del Reloj GATE
Originally called the Boca del Puente, this was the main gateway to the inner walled town and was linked to Getsemaní by a drawbridge over the moat. The side arches of the gate, which are now open as walkways, were previously used as a chapel and armory. The republican-style tower, complete with a four-sided clock, was added in 1888.

Catedral CHURCH
(Calle de los Santos de Piedra; adult/child incl audio tour COP$12,000/800; 10:30am-7pm; P) Work on Cartagena's cathedral began in 1575, but in 1586, while still under construction, it was partially destroyed by the cannons of Francis Drake, and was not completed until 1612. Alterations were made between 1912 and 1923 by the first archbishop of Cartagena, who covered the church with stucco and painted it to look like marble. He also commissioned the dome on the tower.

Plaza de la Aduana PLAZA
This is the largest and oldest square in the old town and was used as a parade ground. In colonial times, all the important governmental and administrative buildings were here. The old Royal Customs House was restored and is now the City Hall. A statue of Christopher Columbus stands in the center of the square.

Museo del Oro Zenú MUSEUM
(Plaza de Bolívar; 9am-5pm Tue-Sat, 10am-3pm Sun) FREE This is like a miniature version of Bogotá's world-class gold museum, Museum del Oro. Though small, it offers a fascinating collection of the gold and pottery of the Zenú (also known as Sinú) people, who inhabited the region of the present-day departments of Bolívar, Córdoba, Sucre and northern Antioquia before the Spanish Conquest. Some pieces are exquisitely detailed.

Mercado Bazurto MARKET
(Av Pedro de Heredia; 24hr) For adventurous souls only, Cartagena's labyrinthine central market is both dirty and enthralling, an all-out assault on your senses. If it's marketable, it's for sale here: there are endless stalls of fruits and vegetables, meat and fish, and plenty of options to grab a quick bite or juice up on a chilled beverage. Don't wear flashy jewelry and pay close attention to your camera and wallet. Grab a taxi (COP$7000 from the old town) and explore away.

Las Bóvedas HISTORIC BUILDING

(Playa del Tejadillo) These are 23 dungeons, built between 1792 and 1796, hidden within the 15m-thick city walls. These dungeons were the last major construction carried out in colonial times and were destined for military purposes. The vaults were used by the Spaniards as storerooms for munitions and provisions. Later, during the republican era, they were turned into a jail. Today they house rather touristy craft and souvenir shops.

Activities

Cartagena has grown into an important scuba-diving center. However, prices are far lower in Taganga.

Diving Planet DIVING

(☎300-815-7169, 320-230-1515; www.divingplanet.org; Calle Estanco del Aguardiente No 5-09) This five-star PADI diving school offers two-tank dives in the Islas del Rosario including transportation, equipment, lunch and instructors for COP$300,000. Discounts are available if you book online.

Vélo Tours CYCLING TOURS

(☎300-276-5036, 664-9714; Calle don Sancho; tours per person COP$80,000-100,000) This innovative bike-tour agency offers tours of the city, nocturnal tours and tours of the fortifications and the nearby coastline, all by bike, as well as renting out bikes (COP$80,000 per 24 hours) for individual use.

Festivals & Events

Concurso Nacional de Belleza BEAUTY PAGEANT

(www.srtacolombia.org) On November 11 the national beauty pageant celebrates Cartagena's independence day. Miss Colombia, the beauty queen, is elected as the high point of the event. The fiesta, which includes street dancing, music and fancy-dress parades, strikes up several days before the pageant and the city goes wild. Also known as the Carnaval de Cartagena or Fiestas del 11 de Noviembre, it's the city's most important annual bash.

Sleeping

Most backpackers stay in Getsemaní. It was once a red-light district, but things have changed dramatically with the influx of travelers. Hostels, hip bars and restaurants now far outnumber flophouses and brothels and the streets are for the most part safe to explore. There are also a number of budget accommodations in the inner walled town.

Casa Viena HOSTEL $

(☎668-5048; www.casaviena.com; Calle San Andrés No 30-53, Getsemaní; dm COP$20,000, s/d COP$40,000/70,000, s/d without bathroom COP$35,000/50,000; ❄@📶) An old-school Austrian-run joint on a rowdy street in Getsemaní – earplugs are your friend. The busy dorm is cramped and needs a lick of paint, but you get free internet and coffee. It's sociable and there's a kitchen to use, and you won't find better conditions at other hostels at this price elsewhere in town.

Chill House HOSTEL $

(☎660-2386; www.chillhousebackpackers.hostel.com; Calle de la Tablada, Parque Fernandez de Madrid, No 7-12, San Diego; dm from COP$21,000, r with/without air-con COP$90,000/70,000; ❄📶) You won't find a cheaper dorm room in the heart of the old town, and even though it's rather cramped here, there's a sociable vibe (and, weirdly enough, a weight machine in the lobby). The hostel is on a beautiful square near some good, cheap places to eat, which is good as there's no food provided on-site.

★**Casa Marco Polo** BOUTIQUE HOTEL $$

(☎316-874-9478; casamarcopolo@hotmail.com; Calle de los 7 Infantes No 9-89; s/d/tr incl breakfast COP$150,000/160,000/200,000; ❄📶) A superb deal in the old town, this beautiful private home is a gorgeously renovated and remodeled colonial house with just three individually designed guest rooms. Each is en suite, wonderfully decorated with traditional arts and crafts and offers access to a great roof terrace. There's also both hot water and one of Colombia's best breakfasts to greet you in the morning.

Casa Villa Colonial HOTEL $$

(☎664-5421; www.casavillacolonial.com; Calle de la Media Luna No 10-89, Getsemaní; s/d COP$100,000/150,000; ❄📶) A complete bargain for the price – you'll get four-star personal service, beautiful communal areas with comfortable sofas, and silent air-con. The best rooms have small balconies onto the courtyard, and there's a small kitchen for guest use and endless great coffee.

El Genovés Hostal HOSTEL $$

(☎646-0972; www.elgenoveshostal.com; Calle Cochera del Hobo No 38-27, San Diego; dm COP$30,000-35,000, r from COP$171,000, all incl breakfast;) A welcome addition to the hostels in San Diego, this charming, colorful place has a 12-bed and a four-bed dorm as well as a number of private double and triple rooms with private bathrooms. The hostel surrounds a welcome plunge pool and is topped off with a small roof terrace. There's also a full communal kitchen.

Media Luna Hostel HOSTEL **$$**
(664-3423; www.medialunahostel.com; Calle de la Media Luna No 10-46, Getsemaní; dm with/without air-con COP$35,000/30,000, r COP$120,000;) This boutique hostel is undoubtedly the hub of the backpacking scene in Getsemaní. It is centered on its big courtyard and roof terrace, which is also home to the biggest single party in Cartagena each Wednesday night. Rooms are clean and well kept, with crisp linens and good mattresses. Look no further if you want to party.

El Viajero Cartagena HOSTEL **$$**
(660-2598; www.hostelcartagena.com; Calle de los 7 Infantes No 9-45; dm from COP$36,000, d COP$170,000, s/d without bathroom COP$81,000/162,000, all incl breakfast;) This massive backpacker blockbuster is both the most centrally located and one of the most social hostels in the city. All rooms have air-con – an absolute dream in this heat and at this price. The beds are firm, the kitchen is well organized and spotless, and there's a very friendly, social vibe in the lovely open courtyard.

Eating

Cartagena is a good place to eat, especially at the top end, but cheap places are also plentiful and interesting street food is just around every corner. Among the fried local specialties is *arepas de huevo* (fried maize dough with an egg inside). There are also numerous small *ceviche* stands serving the local version of this classic and also the less appealing *coctel,* which is smothered in mayonnaise and ketchup.

Dozens of spots around town serve *almuerzos* for COP$8000 to COP$10,000. Among the best is **Restaurante Coroncoro** (664-2648; Calle Tripita y Media No 31-28, Getsemaní; mains COP$7000-13,000; 7:30am-10pm). For veggie meals, try **Girasoles** (664-5239; Calle de los Puntales No 37-01, San Diego; set meals COP$7000; 7:30am-6pm Mon-Fri, 8am-4pm Sat;). Small stalls in Plaza Trinidad serve up cheap street food in the evenings.

★**Gastrolab Sur** CARIBBEAN, MEDITERRANEAN **$**
(Calle del Espiritu Santo No 29-140; mains COP$8000-16,000; 5-11pm) This gem of a place is easy to miss if you don't know it's there. In the beautifully lit pebbly back garden of the Ciudad Móvil cultural center, the humming heart of the revivified Getsemaní community, it serves up delicious *aranchinas* (rice balls) with various flavors (try the *tríptico,* a combination of all three), *bruschettas costeñas* and pizzas.

The staff is super friendly and it's also a great place to come for drinks.

★**Crepe Xpress** CREPERIE **$**
(Calle Baloco No 220; crepes COP$6000-12,000; 4-10pm) This charmimg little place serves up crepes that are the perfect combination of crispy outside and moist in the middle. You're free to design your own, though we're not sure you can actually top the spinach, cheese and caramelized onion. Don't even bother looking for better crepes in Cartagena, as you won't find them.

Espíritu Santo COLOMBIAN **$**
(Calle del Porvenir No 35-60; mains COP$10,000-14,000; 11:30am-3:30pm) There's no telling from the outside, but this fiercely popular Centro lunch spot stretches back cavernously, and usually it feels as if half the city is in here for simple and damn tasty *comida corriente* each lunchtime. Staples include fish fillet in coconut milk, fried beef and some excellent salads. Portions are big and the value is terrific.

Gato Negro CAFE **$**
(660-0958; Calle San Andrés No 30-39, Getsemaní; mains COP$6000-9000; 7am-2pm Mon-Sat;) A favorite Getsemaní option that concentrates on a plain and simple breakfast menu – omelets, crepes, muesli and continental breakfasts are all available – but does it well. There's a set lunch, too, and it's all served up in a colonial house with contemporary art on the walls.

★**La Cevicheria** SEAFOOD **$$**
(664-5255; Calle Stuart No 7-14, San Diego; mains COP$20,000-60,000; noon-11pm Wed-Mon;) This place is tiny and hidden, but its *ceviche* is the best this side of heaven, and its chili sauce would scare Lucifer. Each dish is prepared with panache and elegance: the octopus in peanut sauce is incredible, as is the black squid ink rice and Peruvian fish and shrimp *ceviche.*

I Balconi PIZZA $$

(☎660-9880; Calle del Guerrero No 29-146, 2nd fl, Getsemaní; pizzas COP$12,500-26,000; ⏲4pm-midnight Tue-Sun) Perched above Havana bar, this is where you'll find the best pizza in Cartagena. The Italian owner is so fanatical about quality ingredients that he has commissioned a local cheesemaker and schooled him in the ways of gorgonzola and parmesan. The results are great. Service is impeccable and the room is breezy with cool art on the walls.

El Bistro EUROPEAN $$

(☎664-1799; Calle de Ayos No 4-46, El Centro; sandwiches from COP$10,000, mains COP$18,000-47,000; ⏲9am-11pm Mon-Sat) An ecclectic and popular place filled with curios, this charmer sells fresh bread and offers a full menu. Daily lunch specials include a soup to start as well as a filling main course. Do not miss the particularly good *limonada de coco* (coconut lemonade).

Drinking & Nightlife

★**Café Havana** CLUB

(cnr Calles del Guerrero & de la Media Luna, Getsemaní; cover COP$10,000; ⏲8pm-4am Thu-Sat, 5pm-2am Sun) Café Havana has it all: live salsa from horn-blowing Cubans, strong drinks, a gorgeous horseshoe bar surrounded by brilliant eccentrics, wood paneled walls and a ceiling full of whirring fans. This was where Hillary Clinton chose to take the party during the Summit of the Americas in 2012, and rightly so: it's still the best bar in town.

★**Bazurto Social Club** CLUB

(www.bazurtosocialclub.com; Av del Centenario No 30-42; cover COP$5000; ⏲7pm-3:30am Wed-Sat) Join the crowds at this wonderfully lively spot where locals dance in unison under an enormous glowing red fish to live *champeta* music; sip knock-out cocktails; and catch up on the local Getsemaní gossip. The music is great, and even if you don't feel like dancing, after a few drinks you'll find yourself being dragged in.

Tu Candela CLUB

(☎664-8787; El Portal de los Dulces No 32-25, El Centro; ⏲8pm-4am) Wall-to-wall reggaeton, vallenato, merengue and some decent salsa. Tu Candela is always cramped – but the atmosphere is cool and anything goes. This is the place that Barack Obama's errant Secret Service detail famously began their cocaine and prostitute exploits, and it's easy to see why: this place is off the hook.

Convert the cover charge to cocktails at the bar.

Donde Fidel BAR

(☎664-3127; El Portal de los Dulces No 32-09, El Centro; ⏲11am-2am) The sound system here, when it kicks, has been known to reduce grown men to tears – as does the extraordinary salsa collection of don Fidel himself. This is music of love, loss and lament. A Cartagena institution, it hosts smooching couples dancing in alcoves under portraits of the owner and various gurning megastars. The vast seated terrace is perfect for people-watching.

Shopping

Ábaco BOOKS

(☎664-8338; cnr Calles de la Iglesia & de la Mantilla; ⏲9am-9pm Mon-Sat, 3-9pm Sun) A good selection of books on Cartagena and a few English-language choices, including everything ever written by a certain Gabriel García Márquez. There's also Italian beer, Spanish wine and strong espresso.

Information

There is a real lack of ATMs in the old town but there is a proliferation on Av Venezuela. Avoid the street 'money changers' fluttering around the city offering fantastic deals; they are all, without exception, expert swindlers.

4-72 (Calle 8B, Edificio Villa Anamaria, Local 1, Bocagrande; ⏲8am-5pm Mon-Fri, to noon Sat) Post office.

Hospital Naval de Cartagena (☎655-4306; Carrera 2 No 14-210, Bocagrande; ⏲24hr) Hospital with hyperbaric chamber.

Ministerio de Relaciones Exteriores (☎666-0172; Carrera 20B No 29-18, Pie de la Popa; ⏲8am-noon & 2-5pm) Immigration and visa extensions office, located about 1km east of the old town. Plan on a half-day minimum to get it sorted.

Tourist Office (Turismo Cartagena de Indias; ☎660-1583; www.turismocartagenadeindias.com; Plaza de la Aduana; ⏲9am-noon & 1-6pm Mon-Sat, 9am-5pm Sun) The main tourist office has a friendly and helpful English-speaking staff. There are also small booths in Plaza de San Pedro Claver and Plaza de los Coches as well as the administrative offices at Muelle Turístico.

Getting There & Away

AIR

All major Colombian carriers operate flights to and from Cartagena. The airport is in the suburb of Crespo, 3km northeast of the old city, and is serviced by frequent local buses. *Colectivos* (COP$1500) and nicer air-con shuttles called Metrocar (COP$2000) depart from Monumento a la India Catalina. A private cab is COP$9000 to COP$12,000 from the center; from the airport into town it's a flat COP$10,000.

BOAT

Sailboat is a popular way to get to Panama. Various boats leave from Cartagena to Panama via the San Blas Archipelago and vice versa, but there is no set schedule. The trip normally takes five days and includes three days in San Blas for snorkeling and island-hopping. Trips tend to come in at around US$450 to US$650 all-inclusive per person; this varies as there are many factors involved.

Most boats arrive in the Panamanian ports of Portobelo or Porvenir. A few go to Colón, which is a tough town and a place where you should take taxis everywhere. It's easy to connect to Panama City from all three ports.

The industry has been transformed in recent years by **Blue Sailing** (☎321-687-5333, 310-704-0425; www.bluesailing.net; Calle San Andrés No 30-47), a Colombian-American run agency that has sought to legalize what has always been an unregulated business. Currently Blue Sailing represents 22 boats, and ensures all have proper safety equipment for open sea navigation. It also monitors boat locations 24 hours a day and uses only licensed captains. It is therefore highly recommended to find a boat for the trip through Blue Sailing to ensure a safe and legal crossing. There is normally a daily departure, even in low season; simply email Blue Sailing with your preferred departure dates and staff will try to hook you up with a boat.

Other agencies in Cartagena offer boat crossings, but do ask to see evidence of their safety equipment and the captain's license. Ideally also ask around and check online for any reviews of the boat and crew before committing to a crossing.

For those travelers with less than five days to spare, **Ferry Xpress** (☎368-0000; www.ferryxpress.com) offers a regular 1000-person passenger ferry service (seat/cabin one way US$99/155, 18 hours) between Cartagena and Colón. Ferries depart Cartagena Tuesday and Thursday, and return from Colón Monday and Wednesday. It's possible to take cars on the ferry.

BUS

If heading to Barranquilla or Santa Marta, the easiest option is to leave from the **Berlinastur Terminal** (www.berlinastur.com; off Calle 47 & Carrera 3), a short taxi ride from the old town. Air-conditioned minibuses depart from here every 20 minutes from 5am to 8pm, stopping first in Barranquilla (COP$18,000, two hours) and then in Santa Marta (COP$36,000, four hours).

An even better, but pricier, option for this route is a bus with **MarSol** (☎656-0302; www.transportesmarsol.net) between Cartagena and Santa Marta (COP$42,000, three hours). It picks you up from any hotel or hostel, skips Barranquilla entirely and then drops you at any hotel or hostel in Santa Marta. There are two buses a day; simply call at least a day ahead to reserve your seat.

For other destinations, the main bus terminal is on the eastern outskirts of the city; it can take up to an hour to get there from the old town. Large green-and-red-signed air-conditioned Metrocar buses make the trip every 15 to 30 minutes (COP$2500, 40 minutes). In the center, you can catch them on Av Santander. A taxi will run around COP$15,000.

Half-a-dozen buses go daily to Bogotá (COP$120,000, 18 hours) and another half-a-dozen to Medellín (COP$85,000, 13 hours). **Caribe Express** (☎371-5132) has one bus to Mompox at 7am (COP$50,000, eight hours).

For Turbo, take one of the frequent departures to Montería (COP$55,000, 4½ hours) and change. Leave before 11am to make sure of the connection.

Around Cartagena

Islas del Rosario

This archipelago, about 35km southwest of Cartagena, consists of 27 small coral islands, including some tiny islets only big enough for a single house. The whole area has been protected as **Parque Nacional Corales del Rosario y de San Bernardo**. Unfortunately the reef system has been damaged by warm water currents and diving in the area is not fantastic.

Cruises through the islands are well established. Tours depart year-round from the Muelle Turístico (Turismo Cartagena de Indias) in Cartagena. Boats leave between 8am and 9am daily and visit a number of islands and Playa Blanca, before returning around 4pm to 6pm. The cruise office at the *muelle* (dock) sells tours in big boats for around

COP$70,000, although you may find cheaper deals at some of the budget hotels around town – COP$40,000 is common. Avoid the freelance salesmen who will try to sell you the same tour for double the price.

Tours normally include lunch, but not the entrance fee to the park, the aquarium on one of the islands or the port tax. Check the details with your operator before heading out.

Playa Blanca

5

This is one of the most beautiful beaches around Cartagena. It's about 20km southwest of the city, on Isla de Barú, and is a usual stop for the boat tours to the Islas del Rosario. The place is also good for snorkeling, as a coral reef begins just off the beach. You can hire snorkeling gear for around COP$5000.

The beach has some rustic places to stay. The best option is the friendly **La Estrella** (312-602-9987; hammock COP$10,000, d from COP$50,000), which has tents under a thatched roof, hammocks with nets and rustic huts. A few restaurants serve up fresh fish and rice for COP$20,000.

Direct boat services (COP$25,000, one hour) leave from the Mercado Bazurto in Cartagena to Playa Blanca every morning except Sunday between 7:30am and 9:30am. Coming back, it's usually possible to jump on one of the Islas del Rosario tour boats for around COP$10,000.

The cheapest way to reach the beach is to take a bus from Mercado Bazurto to Pasocaballos (COP$1500), take a boat across the river (COP$1500) and hire a *colectivo* or *mototaxi* to Playa Blanca (COP$15,000). Plan about three hours for the trip.

Volcán de Lodo El Totumo

About 50km northeast of Cartagena, on the bank of the shallow Ciénaga del Totumo, is a 15m mound that looks like a miniature volcano, but instead of lava it spews mud forced out by the pressure of gases emitted by decaying organic matter underground.

You can climb to the top by specially built stairs, then go down into the crater and have a lukewarm mud bath (entry COP$5000). The mud contains minerals acclaimed for their therapeutic properties. Once you've finished your session, go down and wash the mud off in the *ciénaga* (lagoon).

A tour is by far the most convenient and fastest way of visiting El Totumo, and no more expensive than doing it on your own. Several tour operators in Cartagena organize minibus trips to the volcano (COP$30,000 to COP$40,000, depending on whether lunch is included). Tours can easily be purchased through almost any hotel.

Mompox

5 / POP 42,600

Stranded on an island in the eastern backwaters of the muddy Río Magdalena, Mompox is a town lost in space and time. Founded in 1537, 230km southeast of Cartagena, Mompox became an important port – all merchandise from Cartagena passed to the interior of the colony through here, and several imposing churches and many luxurious mansions were built.

Toward the end of the 19th century shipping was diverted to the other branch of the Magdalena as the river silted up, ending the town's prosperity. Mompox has been left in isolation and little has changed since. It's now a Unesco World Heritage Site.

Mompox is a place to take a wander. Most of the central streets are lined with fine whitewashed colonial houses with characteristic metal-grill windows, imposing doorways and lovely hidden patios. Six colonial churches complete the scene; all are interesting, though rarely open. Don't miss the **Iglesia de Santa Bárbara** (Carrera 1 & Calle 14), with its Moorish-style tower, unique in Colombian religious architecture. Also worth a visit is the **Museo de Arte Religioso** (Carrera 2 No 17-07; admission COP$4000; 8-11:45am & 2-4pm Tue-Sat).

There are numerous ATMs in the town center.

Sleeping & Eating

Hostal La Casa del Viajero HOSTEL $
(684-0657; www.hotelenmompos.besaba.com; Carrera 2 No 13-54; dm with/without air-con COP$20,000/25,000, r COP$35,000;) This spacious and friendly traveler hangout has all you need for a cheap stay in Mompox: a shared kitchen, a patio strewn with hammocks, a central location and roomy dorms – one with a great walk-out balcony. There's even a karaoke machine for those long Momposina nights.

★La Casa Amarilla BOUTIQUE HOTEL $$
(☎310-606-4632, 685-6326; www.lacasaamarillamompos.com; Carrera 1 No 13-59; dm/s/d/tr/q/ste incl breakfast COP$25,000/90,000/145,000/175,000/200,000/185,000; ❄📶) This beautiful hotel was created by a British journalist and his Momposina wife inside a restored 17th-century mansion overlooking the river. It has several wonderfully atmospheric rooms, as well as a couple of roomy upstairs suites that are perfect for romantic stays.

Comedor Costeño COLOMBIAN $
(Carrera 1 No 18-45; mains COP$7000; ⏱7am-5pm) This rustic riverfront restaurant in the market area serves wonderful set meals, including *bocachico* fish numerous ways. The delicious, wholesome food includes various meat and fish dishes doused in housemade *ají picante* (hot pepper sauce). Lunch plates also come with an excellent soup, salad and the usual three starches.

ℹ Getting There & Away

Mompox is well off the main routes, but can be reached by road and river from the coast or by road from Bogotá. Cartagena is the usual departure point. Caribe Express has one direct bus leaving Cartagena at 7am daily (COP$50,000, eight hours). Otherwise take one of the regular buses to Magangué (COP$40,000, four hours), change for a boat to Bodega (COP$7000, 20 minutes, frequent departures until about 3pm) and continue by *colectivo* to Mompox (COP$12,000, 40 minutes).

From Medellín, Copetran runs a direct service to Mompox via Magangué (COP$120,000, 10 hours).

Departing from Bogotá, take an overnight bus to El Banco, Magdalena (COP$100,000, 14 hours) and continue to Mompox by jeep (COP$35,000, two hours).

DON'T MISS

WHAT AN ASS!

Colombia has plenty of entertaining festivals, but few are as bizarre as the **Festival del Burro** (Donkey Festival), a colorful five-day event in the small town of San Antero, Córdoba. Held during Semana Santa (Holy Week), the festival includes concerts, dance and traditional foods, but the undeniable highlights are the *desfile de burros disfrazados*, where donkeys are dressed as celebrities and paraded through town, and the coronation of the king and queen donkeys. Keep your eyes peeled for the equine Shakira or you may even spot Burrock Obama! Charge your camera batteries, you're guaranteed to get some classic 'only-in-Colombia' shots.

Golfo de Urabá

The pristine Golfo de Urabá is home to charming small towns nestled between the dense jungle-covered mountains of the Darién and brilliant Caribbean Sea. Most of the region is undeveloped and security remains an issue with the exception of the ultra-chilled getaway spots of Capurganá and Sapzurro right by the Panamanian border. The gateway to the area is the scruffy port of Turbo.

Turbo

☎4 / POP 139,000

Turbo is a gritty port town and maritime gateway to Capurganá and Sapzurro. Unless you are coming on the night bus from Medellín, you will have to spend the night here before taking the morning boat.

🛏 Sleeping & Eating

There are a number of small and largely indistinguishable cafes along the waterfront by the docks where you can eat from around 5am until dusk.

Hotel El Velero HOTEL $$
(☎312-618-5768, 827-4173; Carrera 12 No 100-10; r from COP$80,000; ❄📶) A moment's walk from the dock where the boats leave for Capurganá, this modern place is definitely the best place to stay in Turbo. Its rooms are small but very comfortable, with crisp linen bedding and well-stocked minibars. It can feel like a little slice of heaven after the long journey to Turbo.

ℹ Getting There & Away

From Cartagena, take a bus to Montería (COP$55,000, 4½ hours) and change for Turbo (COP$41,000, four hours). Leave Cartagena before 11am to make it to Turbo the same day. Buses to and from Medellín run almost hourly from 5am to 10pm (COP$62,000, eight hours).

Boats to Capurganá/Sapzurro (COP$55,000 to COP$60,000, 2½ hours) leave daily from the port at 7am. Boats fill up quickly, so arrive one

GETTING TO PANAMA

The lack of a highway through the impenetrable Darién Gap has wrecked many overland dreams, forcing travelers to take long boat trips or expensive flights from Colombia to Panama. However, there is another – almost overland – route via the Golfo de Urabá that offers plenty of adventure.

The basic route is Turbo–Capurganá by boat, Capurganá–Puerto Obaldia (Panama) by boat, and Puerto Obaldia–Panama City by plane. It's slow, but it's a safe, cheap way to pass from South to Central America.

➡ Ensure your yellow-fever vaccination is up to date. Panama demands it.

➡ Get your Colombian exit stamp at the Migración Colombia office (p586) in Capurganá the day before heading to Puerto Obaldia. Spend the night in Capurganá; it's lovely.

➡ Catch a motorboat from Capurganá's harbor to the first town in Panama, Puerto Obaldia (COP$25,000, 45 minutes). These leave at 7:30am but you want to be on the dock by 7am.

➡ Get a Panama entry stamp at Panamanian immigration when you arrive. From here, you can fly onward to Panama City with **Air Panama** (☎ in Panama +507-316-9000; www.flyairpanama.com). Puerto Obaldia is a particularly unpleasant place – make sure you have a confirmed flight reservation before leaving Colombia or you'll be scurrying back. Panama's currency is the US dollar.

hour early to buy your ticket or, if possible, buy it the day before. The tickets are numbered and the first arrivals get to choose the best seats. It can be a horrifically bumpy journey. Sit near the back of the boat and buy a trash bag at the dock (COP$1000) to keep your luggage dry. You'll laugh about this journey one day – if you don't bite your tongue off and smash all your teeth en route.

Capurganá

☎4 / POP 2000

Capurganá is everything Taganga once was: a Caribbean backwater where you drop your gear the second you arrive. With its painted wooden houses, lack of cars, and extremely laid-back atmosphere, it has a distinct island vibe. Children fish from the pier in the afternoon, the taxi service is a horse and cart, and locals are in no rush to do anything.

Tourism here is dominated by all-inclusive hotels focused on the domestic market, though this is changing, and there are a number of backpacker-friendly accommodations.

There are fantastic nature-watching opportunities nearby, and you can spot hundreds of varieties of birds and howler-monkey troops. Fishing in the bay is said to be excellent, with huge fish landed often.

Note that no addresses are given, because none exist. The town is *tiny*.

Activities

The diving here beats Taganga on a few important points: you can dive without a wetsuit and the coral is better preserved and closer to land. Though prices are higher, groups are smaller, and attention is more personalized. Two-tank dives cost COP$170,000 to COP$190,000.

Dive & Green DIVING
(☎311-578-4021, 316-781-6255; www.diveandgreen.com) This popular PADI diving center is right by the arrival jetty in Capurganá. It offers a full range of courses and certification, as well as cheap rooms for divers (COP$25,000 per person).

San Blas Tours TOURS
(☎321-505-5008; www.sanblasadventures.com) Offers tours to the Kuna Yala in Panama, departing from Sapzurro, or border crossings if you're headed that way. You'll need to get your exit stamp in Capurganá.

Walking

Sapzurro is a short and fairly easy hike through the teeming jungle just outside Capurganá. It's well signposted and you don't need a guide. **El Cielo** is another popular jungle route, with natural *piscinas* (swimming pools) to cool down in. **Aguacate** is also a pleasant one-hour walk. Wear walking shoes or trainers for all of these, as it gets muddy.

Sleeping & Eating

★Posada del Gecko GUESTHOUSE $
(☎313-651-6435, 314-525-6037; www.posadadelgecko.com; s/d/tr/q COP$25,000/70,000/95,000/120,000; 📶) A friendly guesthouse with simple wooden rooms that are great value; smarter options include rooms with air-con and private bathrooms, too. The owner organizes three-day trips to the San Blas Islands for US$185. The attached bar-restaurant serves authentic pizza and pastas and is a fine place for a drink; it has an impressively indie playlist.

Hostal Capurganá HOSTEL $
(☎316-482-3665; www.hostalcapurgana.net; Calle de Comercio; dm COP$18,000, r incl breakfast per person COP$35,000) On the main street, just back from the dock, this excellent option has six rooms, each with fan, private bathroom and access to a charming courtyard garden. This is the only place in town that takes credit cards, should you have failed to bring enough cash. Its clued-up staff is good at helping with onward travel bookings as well.

Luz de Oriente HOTEL $$
(☎310-371-4902; www.luzdeoriente.com; Playa Blanca; r per person incl half board COP$72,000; 📶) Right on the harbor, Luz de Oriente's fan-cooled rooms are clean and tidy, and all have sea views. They do a mean mojito in the bar, and you feel right in the center of things, just seconds to the beach.

★Josefina's SEAFOOD $$
(mains COP$20,000-40,000; ⏰noon-9:30pm) Scour the entire coast and you won't find better seafood – or a more wonderful welcome – than at Josefina's. Her crab in spicy coconut-cream sauce, served in impossibly crispy, wafer-thin plantain cups, is superb, as is the *crema de camerón* (cream of shrimp soup) and her take on *langostinos* (crayfish). You'll find Josefina in an unremarkable hut on the main beach in Capurganá.

Information

Bring enough funds with you – the closest ATM is in Turbo.

Capurganá Tours (☎824-3173) A friendly English-speaking agency that can book flights in Panama as well as excursions in the area. This agency can do cash advances on credit cards – handy given there are no banks in Capurganá – and can arrange transportation from Turbo throughout Colombia.

Migración Colombia (☎311-746-6234; www.migracioncolombia.gov.co; ⏰8am-5pm Mon-Fri, 9am-4pm Sat) Immigration and visa extensions; about 1km east of the old town.

Getting There & Away

There are only two ways to reach Capurganá and Sapzurro. Cheapest is to catch a boat from Turbo.

Searca (www.searca.com.co) and **TAC** (www.taccolombia.com) operate flights from Medellín (COP$400,000 one way) on Monday and Friday in low season, and up to three flights daily in high season.

Sapzurro

☎4 / POP 1000

Sapzurro is an archetypal small Caribbean town, with children strolling the narrow streets carrying fresh fish, elderly ladies with hair curlers selling coconut ice cream and men wandering about at a snail's pace. The beaches are pristine and the surrounding forest is a riot of wildlife. There are no cars and it's blissful. Beware: it's often plagued by mosquitoes and sandflies once night falls.

La Miel is one of the area's loveliest beaches, and lies over the hill from Sapzurro, just inside Panama. Bring your passport for the checkpoint. You don't need to get entry or exit stamps.

Sleeping & Eating

There is a lack of budget restaurants in Sapzurro, although some hotels offer plans with meals. If you're on a tight budget, bring food to cook or eat fresh *patacones* (fried green plantains) smothered with cheese by the dock.

Campamento Wittenberg HOTEL $
(☎311-436-6215; hammocks COP$10,000, r per person COP$20,000) A friendly French-owned joint right on the border of Panama, where you can find a basic room or two, cheap, healthy breakfasts, fishing trips and sailing courses. The owner has been in Colombia for years and is friendly, professional and very helpful.

Zingara GUESTHOUSE $
(☎320-687-4678; www.hospedajesapzurrozingara.com; r per person COP$25,000-45,000; 📶) Owner Clemencia will make you feel instantly welcome in this rustic wooden guesthouse. The two rooms here are on the mountain-side and have private bathrooms, mosquito

nets and balconies surrounded by fruit trees. The top room is the best: it sleeps five and has a huge balcony with gorgeous views. Find the guesthouse on the pathway that leads to the climb up to the Panamanian border.

La Gata Negra GUESTHOUSE $
(☎320-610-5571; www.lagatanegra.net; Sapzurro; r per person without bathroom COP$20,000-45,000) This Italian-run guesthouse is in a gorgeous timber chalet set back a short distance from the town beach. The three rooms share bathrooms and are fan cooled. Prices vary according to season and how many are sharing; the cabaña sleeps four in a double bed and two bunks. The Italian home cooking, courtesy of owner Giovanni, is another draw.

Restaurante Doña Triny COLOMBIAN $
(set meals COP$17,000; ⊙noon-9pm) Facing you as you get off the launch from Capurganá, this local fish restaurant is demonstrably popular, with locals and visitors alike crowding in. The set meal includes a soup, a fish or seafood main course and some kind of dessert.

SAN ANDRÉS & PROVIDENCIA

The islands of San Andrés and Providencia offer a tranquil and idyllic taste of Caribbean life, with gorgeous beaches lapped by turquoise seas rammed with pristine coral – the second-largest barrier reef in the northern hemisphere is here. For reggae, rum, sun and sand, a splurge here is well worth considering.

These Colombian territories lie 220km off Nicaragua's Miskito coast, and 800km northwest of Colombia. Both islands have a strong British influence, in food, language and architecture, and are popular snorkeling and scuba centers. The rainy season is September to December and average temperatures are 26°C to 29°C, with high humidity.

The islands were originally claimed by the Spanish but were pretty much ignored until the British invaded in 1631. The new colonizers immediately began to bring in African slaves to work on the plantations. The descendants of these slaves would go on to be known as the Raizal, the Afro-Caribbean indigenous inhabitants of the islands.

Getting There & Away

Buy a tourist card (COP$44,000) on the mainland before checking in for your San Andrés–bound flight. The airport is in San Andrés Town, a 10-minute walk northwest of the center or COP$10,000/5000 by taxi/*mototaxi*. **Avianca** (☎512-3349; Av Colón, Edificio Onaissi, San Andrés Town; ⊙8am-noon & 2-6pm Mon-Fri, 8am-1pm Sat), **Copa** (☎512-7619; www.copaair.com; Sucursal Centro Comercial San Andrés, San Andrés Town; ⊙8am-noon & 2-6pm Mon-Fri, 9am-1pm Sat) and budget carrier **VivaColombia** (www.vivacolombia.co) have flights from many major Colombian cities.

Satena (☎512-3139; www.satena.com; Gustavo Rojas Pinilla International Airport) operates two flights per day between San Andrés and Providencia in low season (round trip from COP$400,000) and up to six when it's busy.

A cheaper option is to cross the sea by boat on the **Catamaran Sensation** (☎318-347-2336, 310-223-5403; Bay Point Bldg, Suite 6, Av Newball; ticket one way COP$65,000). It generally operates Monday, Wednesday, Friday and Sunday leaving San Andrés at 7:30am and returning from Providencia at 3:30pm. If you get seasick take a flight though, as the boat is often rough.

San Andrés

☎8 / POP 68,000

The larger of the two islands, at 12.5km long and 3km wide, San Andrés has the most developed tourist infrastructure. Its isolated beaches are postcard-perfect, though the island's commercial center is far from pretty. All the amenities are in San Andrés Town: there's a **tourist office** (Secretaría de Turismo; ☎513-0801; Av Newball, San Andrés Town; ⊙8am-noon & 2-6pm Mon-Fri) and several ATMs.

The other two small towns, La Loma in the central hills and San Luis on the eastern coast, are far less tourist-oriented and still boast the occasional fine English-Caribbean wooden architecture. The **Johnny Cay Natural Regional Park** is a protected coral islet 1.5km north of San Andrés Town, covered with coconut groves and surrounded by a lovely, white-sand beach.

Due to the beautiful coral reefs all around, San Andrés has become an important diving center, with more than 35 dive spots. **Banda Dive Shop** (☎513-1080; www.bandadiveshop.com; Hotel Lord Pierre, Av Colombia, San Andrés Town) is a friendly dive center offering two-tank dives for COP$180,000 and PADI open-water certification for COP$800,000.

Lodge with Raizal locals at **Cli's Place** (☎512-0591; luciamhj@hotmail.com; Av 20 de Julio

No 3-47; s/d/tr COP$70,000/130,000/180,000; ❄📶) or **Posada Henry** (☎512-6150; libiadehenry@hotmail.com; Av 20 de Julio No 1-36; s/d COP$40,000/80,000). The spacious rooms at **Apartahotel Tres Casitas** (☎512-5813; www.apartahoteltrescasitas.com; Av Colombia No 1-60; r per person incl half board COP$120,000; ❄📶🏊) are also a fine deal, especially if you can snag one with a balcony over the water. If you're looking for a dorm bed, check out **El Viajero** (☎512-7497; www.elviajerohostels.com; Av 20 de Julio 3A-12; dm/r incl breakfast COP$35,000/140,000; ❄📶). In San Luis, **Posada Nativa Green Sea** (☎512-6313, 317-751-4314; Harmony Hall Hill; r per person COP$40,000; ❄) has peaceful, simple cottages with kitchens.

The open-air **Fisherman Place** (☎512-2774; Av Colombia; mains COP$15,000-50,000; ⏲noon-4pm) has great lobster. Across from the Club Náutico is **Miss Celia O'Neill Taste** (Av Colombia; mains COP$20,000-40,000; ⏲lunch & dinner), with local specialties such as rondon (steamed seafood with starchy vegetables in coconut sauce), stewed crab and fish. For nightspots in San Andrés Town, head along the eastern end of Av Colombia.

Providencia

☎8 / POP 5000

Lying 90km north of San Andrés, Providencia is 7km long and 4km wide, and is less commercialized than the larger island, with dozens of small villages of multicolored wooden houses. Santa Isabel is the main town and is where you'll find the **tourist office** (☎514-8054; Santa Isabel; ⏲9am-noon & 2-5pm Mon-Fri) and an ATM at **Banco de Bogotá** (⏲8-11:30am & 2-4pm Mon-Thu, 8-11:30am & 2-4:30pm Fri).

Diving trips and courses can be arranged with **Felipe Diving Shop** (☎514-8775; www.felipediving.com; Aguadulce), run by a native Raizal. Don't miss **El Pico Natural Regional Park** for outstanding 360-degree views of the Caribbean. The most popular trail begins in Casabaja, where you can find a guide, or seek directions. Take water and sunscreen.

For accommodations, **Mr Mac** (☎316-567-6526, 316-695-9540; posadamistermack@hotmail.com; Aguadulce; r per person with kitchen & fan/air-con COP$50,000/70,000) is one of the cheapest places around and offers large rooms right by the water in the Aguadulce area. In Santa Isabel, **Hotel Flaming Trees** (☎514-8049; Santa Isabel; s/d COP$60,000/120,000; ❄) has spacious rooms with fridge, TV and local art.

Blue Coral Pizza (☎514-8224; Aguadulce; mains COP$15,000-40,000; ⏲5-10pm Wed-Mon) serves sandwiches, pizza and island staples, while **Caribbean Place** (☎311-287-7238; Aguadulce; mains COP$30,000-75,000; ⏲12:30-4pm & 7-10pm Mon-Sat) is worth a splurge, with specialties including mountainous black crab, unique to the archipelago. **Roland Roots Bar** (☎514-8417; Bahía Manzanillo; ⏲10am-midnight, until 2am Fri & Sat) is an atmospheric, archetypal bamboo beach bar with booming reggae and strong booze.

NORTHWEST COLOMBIA

The northwest of Colombia is mountainous with a mild climate, fertile volcanic soil that blooms with millions of flowers, verdant coffee farms, ethereal cloud forests and small, busy university towns full of hard-working *paisas,* as locals are known here.

The department of Antioquia is the biggest, richest and most populous in the region, with Medellín, a gleamingly modern and forward-looking metropolis in its center. Its inhabitants are renowned nationally for their independent and entrepreneurial spirit.

To the south of Antioquia, spread over parts of the Cordillera Occidental and the Cordillera Central mountain ranges is the Zona Cafetera, Colombia's major coffee-growing area and the exporter of many sleepless nights. Coffee is the world's second-most traded commodity after oil, and Colombia is the world's third-biggest exporter.

Medellín

☎4 / POP 3 MILLION

Medellín, the city of Colombia's proudest residents, the *paisas,* is back with a vengeance. Once the world's most murderous city, you'd never know it today. With a perfect, perpetual spring-like climate, chic shopping malls, fine restaurants and vibrant nightlife, the city seduces the senses and will make you feel instantly at home.

Medellín has always dwelt in the shadows of Cartagena and Bogotá, but many visitors find this city, which also has pleasant green spaces and striking public art, more relaxing than the former and more welcoming

Central Medellín

than the latter. It's got culture, class and the friendliest locals in Colombia; no wonder tourism is flourishing.

In the '90s, Medellín was the center of the worldwide cocaine trade, with motorbike-riding *sicarios* (hitmen) carrying out gangland hits for the city's most notorious son, drug lord Pablo Escobar (who remains popular here with some for his generosity to the poor). Escobar was so rich he once offered to pay off Colombia's foreign debt, and paid his hitmen US$1000 for every cop they killed. The city was a no-go zone for foreigners until the kingpin was gunned down on a Medellín rooftop by security forces in 1993.

The economic engines of the city today are cut flowers, coffee and textiles, and *paisas* are known for their industriousness and shrewd business acumen. This has been coupled in recent years with intelligent planning and investment in innovative urban

Central Medellín

infrastructure. The result is a sleek, modern city that boasts Colombia's only metro system – a clean, graffiti-free, safe and affordable public transportation system that shuttles you around comfortably and quickly. The cable cars that swoop over some of the poorer barrios have fostered peace, and are well worth the ride.

The city's character of proud self-reliance stems from its history: the town was founded in 1616 by European immigrants who worked hard, farming the land themselves to achieve their successes. The city is surrounded by lush, mountainous terrain and spills north and south down a narrow valley, with soaring buildings blooming like geometric sunflowers.

But beware: they play as hard as they work here – if you're heading for a night out with a group of *paisas* you likely won't get home before dawn.

Sights

Apart from a few old churches, the city's colonial architecture has virtually disappeared.

For a spectacular bird's-eye look at the city, ride one of the two Metrocable lines running up the mountainsides. The San Javier line offers the most spectacular views, but complete a full loop and don't hop out during the route, as it passes over some of Medellín's roughest barrios.

★Plazoleta de las Esculturas PLAZA

(Plaza Botero; Map p589) This public space in front of the Museo de Antioquia is home to 23 large bronze sculptures by renowned local artist Fernando Botero. For more Botero, check out the iconic **La Gorda**, in front of the Banco de la República in Parque Berrío. There are three more Botero sculptures in Parque San Antonio, including the **Pájaro de Paz** (Bird of Peace), which sits alongside its earlier incarnation that was destroyed in a terrorist bomb attack.

★Cerro Nutibara VIEWPOINT

On top of this 80m-tall hill, 2km southwest of the city center, sits the kitschy **Pueblito Paisa**, a miniature version of a typical Antioquian township. Views across the city from the adjacent platform are stunning. Next to the lookout you'll find the **Museo de la Ciudad** (admission COP$1000; ⏲10am-6pm), a small museum dedicated to the history of Medellín and mainly showcasing old photographs of the city.

Museo de Antioquia MUSEUM

(Map p589; ☎251-3636; www.museodeantioquia.org.co; Carrera 52 No 52-43; admission COP$10,000; ⏲10am-5:30pm Mon-Sat, to 4:30pm Sun) In the grand art deco Palacio Municipal, Colombia's second-oldest museum (Museo Nacional in Bogotá is the oldest) is also one of its finest. The collection includes pre-Columbian, colonial and modern art collections, as well as many works donated by native son Fernando Botero.

Parque Arví PARK

(www.parquearvi.org; Veredas Mazo & Piedras Blancas, Santa Elena) Accessible by the fantastic new Cable Arví Metrocable (Linea L) from the Santo Domingo interchange (COP$4600 one way, 15 minutes), Parque Arví is a big chunk of mountain wilderness in Santa Elena that makes a great escape from the city. Inside the boundaries of the 17.61-sq-km reserve are hiking trails, canopy lines, lakes and a *mariposario* (butterfly enclosure).

Free guided walks leave every hour from 10am to 3pm from the tourist information point. The cable car is closed for maintenance on Mondays.

Biblioteca España BUILDING

(☎385-6717; Carrera 33B No 107A-100; ⏲8am-7pm Mon-Fri, 11am-5pm Sun) Constructed high on the mountainside in a marginalized neighborhood, this huge library is one of Medellín's most recognized landmarks and an emblem of the city's revival. At the time of research the entire structure was cloaked in a protective net after serious structural issues were identified, but it's still worth a trip up here to see another side of the city and take in the views from the adjacent park. It's next to the Santo Domingo Metrocable interchange.

Jardín Botánico GARDENS

(www.botanicomedellin.org; Calle 73 No 51D-14; ⏲9am-5pm) FREE One of Medellín nicest green spaces, the botanic gardens covers 14 hectares, showcases 600 species of trees and plants, and includes a lake, a herbarium and a butterfly enclosure. A couple of hours here offers a fine respite from the bustle of the city. The gardens are easily accessed from the nearby metro stop Universidad.

Basílica de la Candelaria CHURCH

(Map p589; cnr Carrera 50 & Calle 51) Medellín's most important church stands guard over Parque Berrío, and was constructed in the

1770s on the site of an earlier wooden structure. It features a German-made pipe organ brought to the city by boat up the Río Magdalena and then on horseback.

Activities

Zona de Vuelo PARAGLIDING
(☎388-1556, 312-832-5891; www.zonadevuelo.com; Km5.6 Via San Pedro de los Milagros) This experienced operator offers tandem flights (from COP$85,000 to COP$105,000) and 15-day courses (COP$1.5 million).

Courses

Universidad EAFIT LANGUAGE COURSE
(☎261-9399; www.eafit.edu.co; Carrera 49 No 7 Sur-50) Private university offering intensive and semi-intensive Spanish study in a group setting. Individual tuition is also available.

Tours

Paisa Road GUIDED TOURS
(☎317-489-2629; www.paisaroad.com) Runs the original Pablo Escobar–themed tour (COP$40,000) as well as sociable football tours (COP$50,000) on weekends where you'll sit among the most passionate supporters at a national league match.

Real City Tours GUIDED TOURS
(☎319-262-2008; www.realcitytours.com) Run by enthusiastic young locals, this company offers a free walking tour through the city center with detailed explanations in English of the stories behind the main points of interest. Tips for the guides are encouraged. It also runs a paid fruit-themed tour to Medellín's largest market. You need to reserve online to secure your spot.

Festivals & Events

Feria de las Flores CULTURAL
(www.feriadelasfloresmedellin.gov.co) This week-long festival in August is Medellín's most spectacular event. The highlight is the Desfile de Silleteros, when up to 400 *campesinos* (peasants) come from the mountains to parade along the streets with flowers on their backs.

Alumbrado Navideño RELIGIOUS
A colorful Christmas illumination of the city, with thousands of lights strung across streets and alongside the Río Medellín.

Sleeping

The El Poblado barrio, with its shopping malls, office blocks and *zona rosa* (nightlife zone) filled with neon-lit bars, clubs and restaurants has hoovered up most of the new gringos, and its environs are now considered a new central district. The area around 'La 70' in Laureles is another popular upmarket area. The rough-and-tumble center provides easy access to the sights but is desolate once the crowds dissipate.

Casa Kiwi HOSTEL $
(Map p592; ☎268-2668; www.casakiwi.net; Carrera 36 No 7-10; dm COP$20,000-24,000, s/d COP$60,000/80,000, without bathroom COP$40,000/60,000; @📶) With an enviable location on the edge of the *zona rosa* in El Poblado, Casa Kiwi is a popular choice among those keen to sample Medellín's famous nightlife. There are a variety of elegant private rooms alongside more standard dorms. The appealing common areas include a spacious hammock terrace, a cinema-like TV room, a rooftop dipping pool, a vibrant bar and a fantastic deck overlooking the street.

Black Sheep HOSTEL $
(Map p592; ☎311-1589, 317-518-1369; www.blacksheepmedellin.com; Transversal 5A No 45-133; dm COP$22,000-25,000, s/d COP$60,000/80,000, without bathroom COP$50,000/65,000; @📶) Conveniently located close to the Poblado metro, this well run hostel has a pleasant social vibe without being rowdy. There are a variety of common areas, including a lovely new terrace, and a good selection of comfortable, modern, private rooms. The knowledgeable staff is particularly helpful in arranging activities and onward travel plans. The on-site Spanish lessons get top reviews.

Wandering Paisa HOSTEL $
(☎436-6759; www.wanderingpaisahostel.com; Calle 44A No 68A-76; dm COP$21,000-25,000, s/d COP$55,000/60,000; @📶) Right by the bars and restaurants of La 70, this dynamic hostel is a great choice for those wanting to find a middle ground between the bright lights of El Poblado and the chaos of downtown. There is a small bar and the enthusiastic management is constantly arranging social events and group outings. Bikes are available to explore the neighborhood.

61 Prado GUESTHOUSE $
(☎254-9743; www.61prado.com; Calle 61 No 50A-60; s/d/ste COP$55,000/75,000/85,000; @📶) This elegant place in the historic Prado neighborhood is a great base from which to explore the sights around the center. Carefully renovated rooms are spacious with high ceilings and touches of art throughout. The candlelit dining room is a fine place to enjoy a meal from the on-site restaurant. Guests can use the well-equipped kitchen.

Palm Tree Hostal HOSTEL $
(☎444-7256; www.palmtreemedellin.com; Carrera 67 No 48D-63; dm COP$$25,000, r without bathroom COP$66,000; @📶) In a middle-class neighborhood close to the metro and plenty of cheap eateries, Medellín's original backpacker hostel has simple but comfortable rooms and friendly staff.

Happy Buddha HOSTEL $$
(Map p592; ☎311-7744; www.thehappybuddha.co; Carrera 35 No 7-108; dm/r/tw incl breakfast COP$30,000/110,000/120,000; 📶) Boasting top-notch facilities and a sleek, modern design, this new hostel on the edge of the *zona rosa* in El Poblado has quickly become a popular choice for those looking for both nightlife and comfort. The common areas include a pleasant terrace and a lounge with sofas, Ping Pong and a pool table. Added extras include a free weekly BBQ and dance classes.

Eating

The center is flooded with affordable restaurants. Restaurants in El Poblado are pricier. Self-caterers should check out **Plaza Minorista** (cnr Carrera 57 & Calle 55) – a large covered market full of fresh fruit and vegetables.

★**Itaca** COLOMBIAN $
(Carrera 42 No 54-60; set lunch COP$8500, mains COP$10,000-25,000; ⏰noon-3pm & 6-10pm Mon-Sat, noon-5pm Sun) It doesn't look like much but this tiny hole-in-the-wall restaurant on the outskirts of downtown prepares fantastic gourmet plates bursting with flavor at bargain prices. There is no menu; just tell friendly chef Juan Carlos what you like and he will whip up a modern Colombian classic from his collection of market-fresh ingredients. There's no sign – look for the blue door.

Cafe Zorba INTERNATIONAL $
(Map p592; Calle 8 No 42-33; pizza COP$11,500-18,500; ⏰5-11:45pm; 📶) Nestled on the edge of Parque La Presidenta, this fashionable open-air cafe serves up excellent pizzas, salads and dips as well as delicious desserts. It's

El Poblado

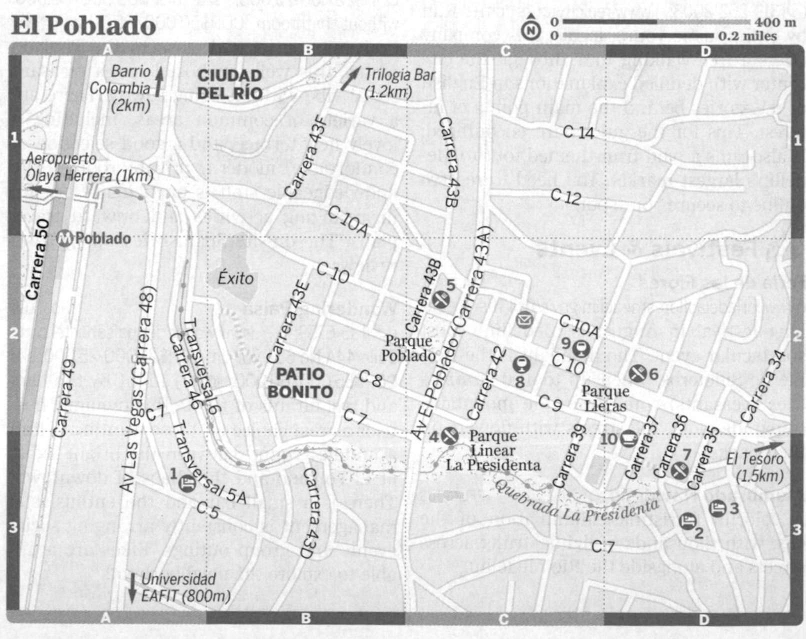

also a great place to enjoy an after-dinner drink.

El Taxista COLOMBIAN $

(Map p592; Carrera 43B No 10-22; meals COP$6500; ⏲7am-4pm) Tradespeople sit shoulder-to-shoulder with sharp-suited business folk at this no-nonsense diner near Parque Poblado. It serves cheap and cheerful *paisa* favorites from a tiny kitchen full of frantically frying women.

Salón Versalles COLOMBIAN $

(Map p589; www.versallesmedellin.com; Pasaje Junín 53-39; meals COP$13,900; ⏲7am-9pm Mon-Sat, 8am-6pm Sun) Famous for its scrumptious Argentine-style empanadas, this Medellín institution also serves up a good set meal and is a great place to take a rest from the bustle of the center. It is frequented by everyone from hard-up pensioners to young entrepreneurs and is worth checking out just to observe the crowd.

Verdeo VEGETARIAN $$

(Map p592; www.ricoverdeo.com; Carrera 35 No 8A-3; mains COP$14,500-21,800; ⏲noon-10pm Tue-Sun, to 4pm Mon;) You don't have to be vegetarian to enjoy the creative dishes on offer at this groovy Poblado restaurant. Take your pick from delicious vegetarian shawarma, burgers, ravioli and salads. The attached grocer is a great place to pick up organic veggies, tofu and other products not found in local supermarkets.

Mondongos COLOMBIAN $$

(Map p592; www.mondongos.com.co; Calle 10 No 38-38; mains COP$21,000-28,000; ⏲11:30am-9:30pm Mon-Sat, to 8pm Sun) Medellín families flock to this unremarkable-looking eatery to fill up on *sopa de mondongo* (tripe soup). It is served with avocado, banana, lemon and *arepas* (corn cakes), which are added or dunked in the bowl according to each diner's personal ritual. For the full experience, come for Sunday lunch. There is another branch on La 70.

Drinking & Nightlife

El Poblado is rammed with bars and discos, full of foreigners and Colombians looking for a good time. Parque Periodista in the center is grittier. Many clubs and discos are located in the former industrial district of Barrio Colombia and on the Autopista Sur.

Pergamino CAFE

(Map p592; www.pergamino.co; Carrera 37 No 8A-37; ⏲8am-9pm Mon-Fri, 9am-9pm Sat) It's worth the effort to wait in line for a drink at this popular cafe, which serves up the best coffee in Medellín. There is a full range of hot and cold beverages, all made with top-quality beans sourced from small farms around the country. You can also buy coffee in bags to take home.

Son Havana CLUB

(Carrera 73 No 44-56; ⏲8:30pm-3am Wed-Sat) The bar of choice for serious salsa fans, this popular place just off La 70 has a great tropical vibe. The small dance floor fills up fast, so most patrons end up dancing around the tables. It's pretty dark so you don't need to worry too much if you lack the moves. It gets packed on Thursdays and Saturdays for its live band performances.

Berlín PUB

(Map p592; ☎266-2905; Calle 10 No 41-65; ⏲6pm-2am) The only real pub in El Poblado, Berlín comes complete with dingy lighting, pool tables and rock classics. It's a welcome respite from the neon-clone bars that dominate the area.

Eslabon Prendido CLUB

(Papayera; Map p589; Calle 53 No 42-55; ⏲9pm-3am) Hugely popular with backpackers and Medellín's expat community, this unpretentious salsa bar attracts a crowd on Tuesdays and Thursdays for its live band. The vibe is very sociable; you don't need to bring a dance partner.

Calle 9 + 1 BAR

(Map p592; Carrera 40 No 10-25; ⏲9pm-late) Set around a spacious covered courtyard, this hip alternative hangout has DJs spinning independent electronic music to an

El Poblado

Sleeping
1 Black Sheep A3
2 Casa Kiwi D3
3 Happy Buddha D3

Eating
4 Cafe Zorba C3
5 El Taxista C2
6 Mondongos D2
7 Verdeo D3

Drinking & Nightlife
8 Berlín C2
9 Calle 9 + 1 .... C2
10 Pergamino D3

arty crowd, and a different vibe to most of the mainstream bars in the Parque Lleras area.

Trilogia Bar CLUB
(www.trilogiabar.com; Carrera 43G No 24-08; ⏲8:30pm-3:30am) For a dynamic night out, head to this friendly club in Barrio Colombia where bands perform Colombian crossover music from a revolving stage while tipsy locals sing along. Come with a group, and make reservations on the website to avoid missing out.

☆ Entertainment

Greater Medellín is well represented in top-flight Colombian football. Traditional rivals **Atlético Nacional** (www.atlnacional.com.co) and **Independiente Medellín** (DIM; www.dimoficial.com) both play at the **Estadio Atanasio Giradot**, while **Envigado Fútbol Club** (www.envigadofutbolclub.net) play in the southern municipality of Envigado.

Teatro Lido CINEMA, THEATER
(Map p589; ☎251-5334; www.medellincultura.gov.co; Carrera 48 No 54-20) On Parque de Bolívar, this refurbished theater has regular free screenings of documentaries and alternative films as well as concerts and other events.

Shopping

Centro Artesanal Mi Viejo Pueblo HANDICRAFTS
(Map p589; Carrera 49 No 53-20; ⏲9am-7:30pm Mon-Thu, to 8pm Fri & Sat, 10am-6pm Sun) This tourist-oriented handicraft market has a wide selection of souvenirs, including hammocks, bags and traditional clothing.

ℹ Information

There are numerous ATMs throughout the city including at Parque Berrío in the center, along Av El Poblado and around Parque Lleras.

Medellín makes it easy to get tourist information through a network of Puntos de Información Turística (PITs), operated by courteous and knowledgeable bilingual staff. In addition to those we list here, there are also branches in Pueblito Paisa and in each of the airports and bus terminals.

4-72 (Map p592; Calle 10A No 41-11; ⏲8am-noon & 1-6pm Mon-Fri, 9am-noon Sat) Post office in El Poblado.

Clínica Las Vegas (☎315-9000; www.clinicalasvegas.com; Calle 2 Sur No 46-55) Professional private medical facility. Staff speaks some English.

Migración Colombia (☎345-5500; www.migracioncolombia.gov.co; Calle 19 No 80A-40, Barrio Belén; ⏲8am-4pm Mon-Fri) For visa extensions. From El Poblado take the Circular Sur 302/303 bus heading south along Av Las Vegas.

PIT Plaza Botero (Map p589; www.medellin.travel; cnr Carrera 51 & Calle 53; ⏲8am-5pm Mon-Sat) Tourist office just outside the Plazoleta de las Esculturas.

PIT Plaza Mayor (☎261-7277; www.medellin.travel; Calle 41 No 55-80; ⏲8am-6pm Mon-Fri) The main tourist office in the Palacio de Exposiciones.

ℹ Getting There & Away

AIR

Medellín's main airport, **Aeropuerto Internacional José María Córdoba** (www.aeropuertojosemariacordova.com; Rionegro, Medellín), 35km southeast of the city, takes all international and most domestic flights. Frequent minibuses (COP$9000, one hour) shuttle between the city center and the airport (leaving from behind the Hotel Nutibara). Regular taxis charge COP$60,000.

Some regional flights to destinations within Antioquia and adjacent departments use the smaller **Aeropuerto Olaya Herrera** next to to the Terminal Sur, a short taxi ride from El Poblado.

BUS

Medellín has two bus terminals. The **Terminal del Norte**, 2km north of the city center, handles buses to the north, east and southeast, including Santa Fe de Antioquia (COP$14,000, two hours), Bogotá (COP$60,000, nine hours), Cartagena (COP$120,000, 13 hours) and Santa Marta (COP$130,000, 16 hours). It's easily accessed by metro (alight at Estación Caribe).

The **Terminal del Sur**, 4km southwest of the center, handles all traffic to the west and south including Manizales (COP$35,000, five hours), Armenia (COP$40,000, six hours), Pereira (COP$35,000, five hours) and Cali (COP$50,000, nine hours). From El Poblado, take a cab (COP$6000).

For more destinations and departure details check out www.terminalesmedellin.com.

ℹ Getting Around

BICYCLE

Medellín has a fledgling free public bicycle system called **Encicla** (www.encicla.gov.co). Visitors are able to take out bicycles for short trips using their passport. A network of new bicycle

DON'T MISS

RÍO CLARO

Three hours east of Medellín lies the **Reserva Natural Cañón de Río Claro** (☎313-671-4459, 4-268-8855; www.rioclaroelrefugio.com; Km152, Autopista Medellín-Bogotá; admission COP$10,000, campsite per person COP$15,000, r per person incl 3 meals COP$80,000-140,000), a tranquil river with a marble bed running through a spectacular jungle-lined canyon. Here you can visit a wonderful cave, go white-water rafting, canopying, or just swim and hike along its banks, which have great bird-watching. Maniacs leap into the water from some of the 15m-high banks of the canyon – emulate them at your peril.

Make sure to visit the **Caverna de los Guácharos** (guided tour COP$20,000), an impressive cave complex filled with guacharos, a missing link in bat–bird evolution. You'll be given a life vest and expected to swim part of the way.

There are a number of accommodation options available within the reserve with open walls facing the jungle. The best places to stay are the cabins set on a hillside a 15-minute walk upstream from the reception area, where the jungle thrum will lull you to sleep and wake you with a start. You can arrive unannounced midweek, but the owners advise early reservations, especially at weekends and holidays.

If you are on a tight budget, consider visiting the reserve as a day trip and basing yourself in the nearby town of Doradal, which has several cheap hotels.

Many Medellín–Bogotá buses, with the exception of some of the bigger express services, will drop you at the reserve's entrance. From any other direction, look for transportation to Doradal, from where you can pick up a bus to the main gate (COP$5000, 20 minutes).

paths is planned for the second phase of the project. Check the website for station locations.

BUS

Apart from the metro, urban transportation is serviced by buses and *busetas*. The majority of routes originate on Av Oriental and Parque Berrío, from where you can get to almost anywhere within the metropolitan area.

METRO

Medellín's **Metro** (www.metrodemedellin.gov.co; single ticket COP$1900; ⊙4:30am-11pm Mon-Sat, 5am-10pm Sun) consists of a 26km north–south line and a 6km western leg, with 27 stations. Three Metrocable cable-car systems connect the service to low-income barrios in the hills and up to Parque Arví in Santa Elena.

TAXI

Taxis are plentiful in Medellín and all are equipped with meters. The minimum charge is COP$4700. A taxi from the center to El Poblado will cost around COP$10,000.

Santa Fe de Antioquia

☎4 / POP 23,700

Santa Fe de Antioquia is a wonderfully preserved colonial town that makes a great day trip from Medellín. Founded in 1541, it is the oldest town in the region. It was a prosperous center during Spanish rule and the capital of Antioquia until 1826. When the capital moved to Medellín, it lost commercial importance and as a result escaped the wrecking ball of progress, leaving its narrow cobblestone streets, lovely plazas and whitewashed houses intact. These days its warm climate makes it a popular getaway for Medellín urbanites.

Sights

The town is famous for its carved wooden doorways and flower-filled patios.

Puente de Occidente BRIDGE

This unusual 291m bridge over the Río Cauca is 5km east of town. When completed in 1895, it was one of the first suspension bridges in the Americas. José María Villa, its designer, was also involved in the creation of the Brooklyn Bridge in New York. It's a boring and hot 45-minute walk downhill. You're best to take a tuk-tuk (round trip COP$15,000). The driver will wait while you walk across.

Iglesia de Santa Bárbara CHURCH

(cnr Calle 11 & Carrera 8; ⊙5-6:30pm & Mass Sun morning) Built by Jesuits in the mid-18th century, Santa Fe's most interesting church has a fine, baroque facade. The interior has an interesting, if time-worn, retable over the high altar.

Museo Juan del Corral MUSEUM
(☎853-4605; Calle 11 No 9-77; ⊙9am-noon & 2-5:30pm, closed Wed) FREE Visit this interesting museum dedicated to the history of the region in order to check out the perfectly preserved colonial mansion it is set in.

Festivals & Events

Fiesta de los Diablitos CULTURAL
The town's most popular festival is held annually over the last four days of the year. It includes music, dance, parades and – like almost every party in the country – a beauty contest.

Sleeping & Eating

Prices increase by 25% on weekends.

Hotel Plaza HOTEL $
(☎853-2851; Plaza Mayor; r per person COP$35,000;) Set in an old colonial building on the main square, this budget hotel is good value considering the location. The recently renovated rooms are generally cool but many don't have windows and the toilets are literally in the shower.

Restaurante Portón del Parque COLOMBIAN $$
(☎853-3207; Calle 10 No 11-03; mains COP$22,000-28,000; ⊙noon-8pm) Occupying an elegant colonial house with high ceilings and a flowery courtyard, this restaurant is widely considered the best in town. The walls are covered with some pretty shoddy artwork but the kitchen prepares quality traditional food and international favorites.

Getting There & Away

There are buses/minivans (COP$10,000 to COP$14,000, two hours) every half-hour between Santa Fe and Medellín's Terminal del Norte.

Guatapé

☎4 / POP 4200

The tiny town of Guatapé is a popular weekend getaway for *paisas* who want to wander its pretty streets and take trips out onto the artificial lake, El Embalse del Peñol. Looming over the lake on the road into town is Piedra del Peñol, a vast granite monolith you can climb.

Part of Guatapé was flooded in 1970 in order to create the lake that now generates much of the region's power. Today the town is noted for its cute streets; many houses are decorated with *zocalos* (colorful concrete bas-relief scenes). They were originally designed to prevent chickens pecking at the walls, and to stop children chipping away at the buildings with ball games. Visit during the week for low prices and peace,

WORTH A TRIP

JARDÍN

The self-proclaimed most beautiful town in Antioquia, Jardín is an enchanting rural settlement boasting brightly painted two-story houses surrounded by small coffee farms that cling impossibly to the slopes of majestic green mountains.

At the center of town life is the breezy cobblestone plaza, dominated by the immense neo-Gothic church and chock-full of colorful wooden tables and chairs where fruit sellers hawk delicious cocktails and old-timers converse between measured sips of coffee.

The mountains surrounding the town shelter many attractions including **Cerro Cristo Rey**, a panoramic lookout point accessed by a modern cable car, and **Cueva del Esplendor** (admission COP$6000), a spectacular cave with a 10m waterfall gushing through the roof.

Condor de Los Andes (☎310-379-6069; condordelosandes@colombia.com; Carrera 6 No 1-100) is a dynamic adventure company that organizes fantastic activities throughout the region and also runs a great hostel at the entrance to town. Another good accommodation option is **Balcones del Parque** (☎845-6844; www.balconesdelparque.com; Calle 9 No 2-75; r per person incl meals COP$60,000-80,000;), which offers good-value rooms with high wood ceilings right on the plaza.

Around a dozen buses (COP$18,000, three hours) head daily to Jardín from Medellín's southern bus terminal. If you are continuing south to the Zona Cafetera, **Rapido Ochoa** (☎845-5051; Calle 8 No 5-24) has a direct service to Manizales (COP$37,000, five hours) at 6:25am.

or at weekends for a hard-drinking *paisa* jamboree.

Sights

A block south from the main square is **Calle de los Recuerdos**, a cobblestone street that angles uphill and showcases the best example of the local frescoes.

Piedra del Peñol VIEWPOINT
(El Peñon de Guatapé; per climb COP$10,000; 8am-5:40pm) A 200m-high granite monolith set near the edge of the Embalse Guatapé. A brick-and-mortar staircase of 659 steps rises up through a broad fissure in the side of the rock. From the top there are magnificent views of the region, the fingers of the lake sprawling amid a vast expanse of green mountain.

Casa del Arriero NOTABLE BUILDING
(Carrera 28) The oldest and biggest house in Guatapé is still occupied by descendants of the original owners. They usually leave their front door open so visitors can wander into the central courtyard. Take note of the ornate, painted folding doors as you enter. Very typical of Guatapé.

Activities

Boat trips out to the islands in the center of the lake are the main activity here. The large boats (per person COP$10,000) are slow but have a bar and dance floor; they are a great chance to get to know the phenomenon that is partying *paisas*. The smaller boats (up to six passengers, COP$90,000) are more flexible if you want to visit specific destinations.

Sleeping & Eating

Guatapé makes a great day trip from Medellín but there are plenty of accommodations around town if you want to stay longer.

Guatatur HOTEL $$
(861-1212; www.hotelguatatur.com; s/d from COP$50,000/100,000, ste COP$224,000;) This modestly priced resort near the plaza specializes in weekend package deals for visitors from Medellín; during the week you can snag great deals. Several of the rooms have views of the lake, and the suites have Jacuzzis and even lovelier views.

Donde Sam INDIAN, INTERNATIONAL $$
(Calle 32 No 31-57; set lunch COP$8000, mains COP$18,000-22,000; 9am-9pm) This spacious 2nd-floor restaurant has great views of the lake and even better food. Choose from a variety of authentic, freshly prepared Indian and Thai classics as well as some Italian, Chinese and Mexican dishes. Vegetarians are well catered for and prices are very reasonable for the quality.

La Fogata COLOMBIAN $$
(mains COP$13,000-20,000; 7am-9pm) Right opposite the lake with an elevated, open-air dining area, this popular place does quality *paisa* food, including filling breakfasts (COP$9000). Go for the *trucha* (trout), or if you're really hungry, a *bandeja paisa*.

Getting There & Away

Buses to and from Medellín run on the hour all day (COP$12,000, two hours) from the northern bus terminal. Purchase your return ticket on arrival in Guatápe to be sure of getting a seat.

It makes sense to visit Piedra del Peñol on your way to Guatapé to avoid doubling back. Don't get off the bus in the town of Peñol – ask the driver to let you off at 'La Piedra,' which is another 10 minutes down the road. Take the road that curves up past the gas station (1km) to reach the parking lot at the base of the rock. Taxi drivers and horse owners will try to convince you that it's a long, exhausting climb but while it's steep, it's not far.

Manizales

6 / POP 388,500

This prosperous mountain city is home to numerous universities and although it is not classically pretty its modern houses and steep, tidy streets offer a curious contrast to many other Colombian destinations. Manizales has a fresh, chilly climate and an air of scholarly seriousness that gives way as the sun drops and the students kick back. It was founded in 1849 but was later leveled by earthquakes. From here, you can visit coffee farms and gaze in awe at the glacier-covered peak of the active volcano, Nevado del Ruiz, one of Colombia's most majestic mountains.

Sights

The tribute to El Libertador in **Plaza de Bolívar** is curious: Rodrigo Arenas Betancur has cast his subject here as a condor atop a horse.

★**Monumento a Los Colonizadores** MONUMENT
(Av 12 de Octubre, Chipre) Located atop a hill in the neighborhood of Chipre, this massive

monument to the city's founders was crafted from 50 tonnes of bronze. It's an impressive work, but the real attraction here is the spectacular views over town and to Parque Nacional Natural (PNN) Los Nevados.

Catedral de Manizales CHURCH
(tower access adult/child COP$10,000/7000; ⏲9am-8pm) Plaza de Bolívar's south side is dominated by the odd but impressive Catedral de Manizales. Begun in 1929 and built of reinforced concrete, it is among the first churches of its kind in Latin America. Its main tower is 106m high, making it the highest church tower in the country. You can climb to the top for great views of the city.

Los Yarumos PARK
(☎875-3110; Calle 61B No 15A-01; ⏲8:30am-5:30pm Tue-Sun) This 53-hectare municipal park offers panaoramic views of the city, forest trails and canopy lines. Adventure activities include a guided hike to four small waterfalls (two hours, COP$8000) and abseiling (four hours, COP$15,000). It's also a great place to just come and chill on a clear afternoon, when you can see the peaks of PNN Los Nevados.

Tours

Kumanday Adventures ADVENTURE TOURS
(☎315-590-7294, 887-2682; www.kumanday.com; Calle 66 No 23B-40) This full-service adventure company in the hostel of the same name runs treks in PNN Los Nevados and mountaineering trips nationwide. It also offers scenic mountain-bike tours through nearby coffee farms, a high-adrenaline downhill run from the edge of Nevado del Ruiz (4050m) back to Manizales, and three-day cycling trips through the Andes. Mountaineering gear and tent rental is available.

RETRO RIDES: COLOMBIA'S CHIVAS

Part-truck, part-bus, with a custom-built wooden body and bright paintwork, *chivas* are more than a means of transportation – they are part of Colombia's cultural identity. Fast to load and unload, these open-sided workhorses with rows of hard bench seats were once the principal means of road transportation around the country. These days, their work in cities is mainly restricted to *chivas rumberas* (a kind of party bus) but they are still in dignified employment in some rural regions, particularly in mountainous areas.

Sleeping

The best places to stay are near the *zona rosa*, off Cable Plaza. (Check out the old cable-car tower, which used to haul goods across the ridgetops.)

Mountain Hostels HOSTEL $
(☎887-0871, 887-4736; www.manizaleshostel.com; Calle 66 No 23B-91; dm COP$20,000-23,000, s/d/t COP$60,000/65,000/90,000; 📶) A short walk from the *zona rosa,* this fine choice spread over two buildings is one of the few hostels where backpackers and Colombian travelers mix. There are a variety of social areas including rear patios with hammocks, and the staff is helpful in organizing activities around town. The rooms in the reception building are the most comfortable.

Kumanday Hostal HOSTEL $
(☎315-590-7294, 887-2682; www.kumanday.com; Calle 66 No 23B-40; dm incl breakfast COP$25,000, s/d incl breakfast COP$50,000/70,000; 📶) Friendly, compact hostel near the *zona rosa* with simple but clean and comfortable rooms.

Eating & Drinking

La Suiza BAKERY $
(Carrera 23 No 26-57; mains COP$8500-17,500; ⏲9am-8:30pm Mon-Sat, 10am-7:30pm Sun) This scrumptious bakery does great pastries and even homemade chocolate. It also does tasty breakfasts, plus light lunches, such as mushroom crepes and chicken sandwiches. There's another branch near Cable Plaza.

Rushi VEGETARIAN $
(Carrera 23C No 62-73; meals COP$7000-9000; ⏲8am-9pm Mon-Sat; 🌿) Hip vegetarian restaurant serving up great juices and interesting meat-free dishes prepared before your eyes in the open kitchen. The changing lunch menu is top value.

Bar La Plaza BAR
(Carrera 23B No 64-80; ⏲11am-11pm Mon-Wed, to 2am Thu-Sat) Delicatessen by day, bar by night; this is the place to start your evening. Fills up fast and by 9pm you'll have to wait for a table. The music isn't too loud, so you can converse. There's a young, student vibe, and it offers gourmet sandwiches (COP$5900 to COP$14,800) and snack plat-

ters of quality salami and cheese to help line your stomach. Does good cocktails.

Information

The area around the central market just north of the city is a favored hangout for thieves and is best avoided.

There are several ATMs inside Cable Plaza.

4-72 (Carrera 23, No 60-36; ⌚8am-noon & 1-6pm Mon-Fri, 9am-noon Sat)

Tourist Office (☎873-3901; www.ctm.gov.co; cnr Carrera 22 & Calle 31; ⌚7am-7pm) Tourist office with enthusiastic staff and plenty of maps and brochures.

Getting There & Away

AIR

Aeropuerto La Nubia (☎874-5451) is 8km southeast of the city center, off the Bogotá road. Take a city bus to La Enea, from where it's a five-minute walk to the terminal, or take a taxi (COP$10,000). The airport is often closed because of the weather, so don't book tight connections from here.

BUS

Manizales' bright and modern **bus terminal** (☎878-7858; www.terminaldemanizales.com; Carrera 43 No 65-100) is connected to the center of town by a cable car (COP$1500), which offers panoramic views over the city. If you are staying near the *zona rosa* it is cheaper and faster to take a taxi (COP$6500) direct to your accommodations.

Buses depart regularly to Bogotá (COP$50,000, eight hours), Medellín (COP$35,000, five hours) and Cali (COP$38,000, five hours). There are many minibuses to Pereira (COP$9,000, 1¼ hours) and Armenia (COP$17,000, 2¼ hours).

Around Manizales

Recinto del Pensamiento NATURE RESERVE
(☎889-7073; www.recintodelpensamiento.com; Km11, Vía al Magdalena; admission with/without telesilla COP$17,400/13,000; ⌚9am-4pm Tue-Sun) Set in the cloud forest 11km from Manizales, this nature park has a fine *mariposario*, several short walks through an impressive orchid-populated forest, and a medicinal herb garden. You'll also see plantations of *guadua* and *chusqué* (two kinds of Colombian bamboo). There's even a *telesilla* – a kind of chair lift to take you up the mountain slope on which the park sits.

Hacienda Venecia FARM
(☎320-636-5719; www.haciendavenecia.com; Vereda el Rosario, San Peregrino; main house r with/without bathroom COP$250,000/340,000, hostel dm COP$30,000, r with/without bathroom COP$95,000/80,000;) This hacienda has won numerous awards for its coffee. It offers a coffee tour (COP$45,000) in English that includes an informative presentation about Colombian coffee, an introduction to coffee cupping, a class in coffee preparation and a walking tour through the plantation. You can use the pool afterwards, and a typical lunch is available for COP$12,000. The tour price includes transport to/from your hotel in Manizales.

Hacienda Guayabal FARM
(☎314-772-4900; www.haciendaguayabal.com; Km3, Vía Peaje Tarapacá, Chinchiná) This slow-paced working coffee farm near Chinchiná, is a great place to come and unwind surrounded by *cafetero* culture. It runs a coffee tour (Spanish/English COP$30,000/35,000) that follows the coffee process from the plant to the cup. It is a bit more personal than those offered by some of the larger outfits and the guides are very keen to share their knowledge. Bags of the coffee are available to purchase as souvenirs.

Termales Tierra Viva THERMAL BATHS
(☎874-3089; www.termalestierraviva.com; Km2, Vía Enea-Gallinazo; admission COP$12,000-14,000; ⌚9am-11:30pm) Located next to the Río Chinchiná just outside town, this thermal baths complex has two pools made of rocks set among a pretty garden that attracts hummingbirds and butterflies. There is an excellent elevated, open-air restaurant and a small spa offering massages. The baths are quiet during the week, but on the weekends it can feel a little overcrowded.

Parque Nacional Natural Los Nevados

Following a spine of snow-covered volcanic peaks, this 583-sq-km **national park** (www.parquesnacionales.gov.co; Colombian/foreigner COP$14,000/37,500) provides access to some of the most stunning stretches of the Colombian Andes. Its varied altitude range encompasses everything from humid cloud forests and *páramo* (high mountain plains) to glaciers on the highest peaks. The main peaks, from north to south, are El Ruiz (5325m), El Cisne

(4750m), Santa Isabel (4965m), El Quindío (4750m) and El Tolima (5215m).

At the time of research, most of the northern section of the park around Nevado del Ruiz remained off-limits because of volcanic activity. The restrictions are liable to change; check on the situation in Manizales before heading out.

Fortunately for nature lovers, the southern part of the park remains open and offers a variety of breathtaking day trips and multiday treks. The main access points are from Potosi near Santa Rosa de Cabal; the Refugio La Pastora in the Parque Ucumarí, from where a 12km trail goes uphill to the magnificent Laguna del Otún; and Valle de Cocora near Salento, where a path heads uphill to the *páramo* around Paramillo del Quindío (4750m).

Public transportation to most entry points of the park is nonexistent. While it's possible to hike into the park from either Parque Ucumarí or Valle de Cocora, it's often more convenient to organize a package including guides and transportation in Manizales or Salento.

Both **Ecosistemas** (☎312-705-7007, 880-8300; www.ecosistemastravel.com.co; Carrera 21 No 20-45) and Kumanday Adventures (p598) in Manizales offer day trips to Nevado de Santa Isabel, as well as multiday hikes through the park and ascents of the various other peaks. In Salento, **Paramo Trek** (☎311-745-3761; paramotrek@gmail.com) offers a variety of hikes in the park entering through Valle de Cocora.

Pereira

☎6 / POP 457,100

You don't come to Pereira for the architecture, the food, or to hang out. Neither do Colombians – they come to make money and do business in this city, the largest of the coffee region. The streets are hectic with commercial activity, and there is really nowhere to escape the bedlam. Although if you are looking for a friendly, authentic city off the traveler trail in which to immerse yourself in Colombian culture, Pereira certainly fits the bill.

The curious centerpiece of the town, **Bolívar Desnudo** (Plaza Bolívar), is a huge bronze sculpture of El Libertador riding his horse Nevado bareback – and fully naked.

DON'T MISS

HOT SPRINGS OF RISARALDA

The **Termales de Santa Rosa** (☎320-680-3615, 364-5500; www.termales.com.co; admission adult/child Fri-Sun COP$42,000/21,000, Mon-Thu COP$30,000/15,000; ⊙9am-10pm) are 9km east of Santa Rosa de Cabal, a town on the Pereira–Manizales road. A tourist complex including thermal pools, a hotel, restaurant and bar has been built near the springs at the foot of a 170m-high waterfall. You can stay on-site, but it's overpriced.

Around 800m down the hill, and under the same management, are the more low-key thermal pools **Balneario de Santa Rosa** (☎314-701-9361; www.termales.com.co; admission adult/child COP$32,000/16,000; ⊙9am-10pm), which are surrounded by fantastic gardens and constructed under a splendid waterfall that divides into half-a-dozen different streams. If you want to stay nearby, try **Cabaña El Portal** (☎320-623-5315; r per person COP$30,000), a couple of blocks further downhill from the baths.

Urban buses to the pools (COP$1300, 45 minutes) leave from the main plaza in Santa Rosa de Cabal every two hours from 6am to 6pm, returning an hour later from the Hotel Termales.

Set in a spectacular misty valley at the foot of PNN Los Nevados 18km from Santa Rosa de Cabal, the **Termales San Vicente** (www.sanvicente.com.co; admission adult/child COP$30,000/12,000, r per person incl breakfast COP$74,000-198,000; ⊙8am-midnight) are the most relaxing option for all water babies. Here you will find several concrete pools, natural saunas and a canopy line, but the clear highlight are the *pozos de amor* – natural pools formed in a fast-flowing river surrounded by lush vegetation. You can stay here in a variety of pricey-but-worth-it accommodations or sign up at the **Termales San Vicente booking office** (☎333-6157; Av Circunvalar No 15-62; ⊙8am-5pm Mon-Fri, to 3pm Sat) in Pereira for the excellent-value day trip (COP$60,000), which includes round-trip transportation, admission, lunch and a refreshment.

He seems to be flying furiously toward the town's grand cathedral across the plaza.

If you plan to spend the night, **Kolibri Hostel** (☎331-3955; www.kolibrihostel.com; Calle 4 No 16-35; dm COP$22,000, r with/without bathroom COP$65,000/50,000; 📶) has a fantatic location just off the *zona rosa* and is easily the best budget option in town. **Grajales Autoservicios** (Carrera 8 No 21-60; mains COP$10,000; ⏲24hr) is a self-service restaurant that has basic fodder and good breakfast choices.

Aeropuerto Matecaña (☎314-8151) is 5km west of the city center, 20 minutes by urban bus, or COP$12,000 by taxi. The **bus terminal** (☎321-5834; Calle 17 No 23-157) is about 1.5km south of the city center.

Armenia

☎6 / POP 272,500

Like Manizales and Pereira, this departmental capital offers few sights for the visitor but is the gateway to a number of interesting attractions and some enchanting small towns in Quindío department.

If you need to kill time, check out the **Museo del Oro Quimbaya** (☎749-8169; museoquimbaya@banrep.gov.co; Av Bolívar 40N-80; ⏲10am-5pm Tue-Sun) FREE, a small but interesting gold museum located 5km northeast of the center, on the road to Pereira. And if you are lucky enough to be around in October, don't miss the **Desfile de Yipao** (⏲Oct), when the department's classic Willys jeeps are driven down from the mountains and paraded fully loaded through the city's streets – on two wheels!

Casa Quimbaya (☎732-3086; www.casaquimbaya.com; Calle 16N No 14-92; dm COP$23,000, s/d COP$50,000/70,000; @📶) is a comfortable hostel run by friendly young locals. The **bus terminal** (www.terminaldearmenia.com; Calle 35 No 20-68) is around 1.5km southwest of the center. **Aeropuerto Internacional El Edén** (www.aeropuertoeleden.com) is 18km southwest of Armenia, near the town of La Tebaida.

Salento

☎6 / POP 7200

After the jarring concrete horrors of Manizales, Pereira and Armenia, Salento comes as a relief to the senses. Despite being a very popular destination, for Colombian and international visitors alike, Salento still retains much of its small-town charm. The gentle rolling hills are carpeted in thick forest that embrace the undulations of the land like a mother with her newborn, while the town's architecture is a chocolate-box colonial fantasy. The peaceful streets are lined with many shops selling handicrafts and there are many relaxing bars, cafes and billiard halls.

Its proximity to the fabulously beautiful Valle de Cocora makes Salento a required stop on any Colombian itinerary, however tight. During the week it's serene, but on weekends hordes of day-trippers descend on the town and the main square is full of families laughing, singing and dancing.

Sights & Activities

Charismatic coffee grower don Elías offers tours of his **organic farm** (near Vereda Palestina; tour COP$5000). The farm is about a 45-minute walk from town – from the central park walk north for a block, then west across the yellow bridge. Keep going straight, it is about 200m after the turnoff to El Ocaso.

For hikes through tropical Andean cloud forest, head to **Kasaguadua** (☎313-889-8273; www.kasaguaduanaturalreserve.org), a 14-hectare private nature reserve about 2km from town on the road to El Ocaso.

Horse riding is a popular activity in Salento; however, there have been some accidents involving tourists riding here. Go with an experienced guide, and if your travel insurance doesn't cover horse riding, make sure your guide has a policy.

Sleeping

Tralala HOSTEL $
(☎314-850-5543; www.hosteltralalasalento.com; Carrera 7 No 6-45; dm COP$20,000-22,000, s/d COP$50,000/65,000, without bathroom COP$40,000/50,000; 📶) In a brightly renovated colonial house, this small, well-run hostel was clearly created by someone who knows exactly what travelers want. Facilities include comfortable mattresses, piping-hot showers, two kitchens, an extensive DVD library, fast wi-fi and there is even rubber-boot rental for muddy treks.

La Floresta Hostel HOSTEL $
(☎759-3397; www.laflorestahostel.com; Carrera 5 No 10-11; dm COP$18,000-20,000; s/d COP$44,000/54,000, without bathroom COP$34,000/44,000; 📶) In a new building

just across the yellow bridge from the center of Salento, this friendly locally owned hostel is excellent value. Rooms are well equipped and comfortable, and the ample garden, where you're able to pitch a tent, has hammocks and mountain views. La Floresta also rents decent bicycles for exploring the area.

★Ciudad de Segorbe HOTEL $$
(☎759-3794; www.hostalciudaddesegorbe.com; Calle 5 No 4-06; s/d incl breakfast COP$70,000/95,000; P ☎) While the elegant rooms with wooden floors and tiny balconies overlooking the mountains in this two-story house are an excellent deal, it is the wonderfully warm Spanish-Colombian hosts that make this small and peaceful hotel really stand out from the pack. An excellent breakfast is served in the interior courtyard.

La Serrana HOSTEL $$
(☎316-296-1890; www.laserrana.com.co; Km1.5 Via Palestina; dm COP$23,000-25,000; s/d COP$80,000/85,000, without bathroom COP$70,000/75,000; P ☎) On a peaceful hilltop dairy farm with stunning views across the valley, this hostel has top-notch facilities and a fantastic atmosphere. The restaurant prepares good budget meals and there is a lovely yard in which to pitch a tent. There are also luxurious permanent tents (single/double/triple COP$65,000/70,000/80,000). It's well worth the 20-minute walk from town. If you've heavy bags, hire a jeep (COP$6000).

Eating

In the main plaza many stands and kiosks sell excellent-value local dishes, including cracker-thin *patacones* loaded with tasty *hogao* (warm tomato chutney), shredded chicken and guacamole, and delicious local trout.

Rincón del Lucy COLOMBIAN $
(Carrera 6 No 4-02; meals COP$6000) Sit on great tree-trunk slabs of tables to eat the best-value meal in town: fish, beef or chicken served with rice, beans, plantain and soup.

La Eliana INTERNATIONAL $
(Carrera 2 No 6-65; mains COP$10,000-14,000; ⊙noon-9pm) Prepares quality breakfasts as well as gourmet pizzas, sandwiches and, if you're in the mood for something different, real Indian curries. The portions are generous and prices are very reasonable for the quality involved. Try the delicious orange brownies.

Drinking & Nightlife

The main plaza is lined with bars that kick out the jams at the weekends. Take your pick – they're all great.

Billar Danubio Hall BAR
(Carrera 6 No 4-30; ⊙8am-midnight Mon-Fri, to 2am Sat & Sun) This is every Latin small-town fantasy rolled into one. Old men in nonironic ponchos and cowboy hats sip *aguardiente* (anise-flavored liquor) as they play dominos. The clientele breaks into ragged harmony whenever an anthem of heartbreaking personal relevance is played. It's a bastion of unreconstructed male behavior, so women may be treated as a curiosity, but these are total gentlemen.

Café Jesús Martín CAFE
(www.cafejesusmartin.com; Carrera 6A No 6-14; ⊙8am-8pm) This groovy cafe serves top-quality espresso coffee roasted and prepared in the owner's factory. It's got a distinctly upper-crust feel to it; don't expect to see too many local farmers drinking here. Also serves wine, beer and light meals. Ask about the high-end coffee-tasting tours.

Getting There & Away

Buses to Salento from Armenia (COP$3800, 50 minutes) run every 20 to 30 minutes until 8pm.

There are four buses a day between Pereira and Salento (COP$6000, 1¼ hours) during the week. On weekends, buses ply this route frequently. Alternatively, take any Armenia-bound bus to Los Flores, cross the road and flag down an Armenia–Salento service.

Valle de Cocora

East of Salento, the stunning Valle de Cocora is like a lush, tropical version of Switzerland, with a broad, green valley floor framed by rugged peaks. However, you'll remember you're a few degrees from the equator when, a short walk past Cocora, you suddenly encounter hills covered with the *palma de cera* (wax palm). The trees tower above the cloud forests in which they thrive. It is an almost hallucinatorily beautiful sight.

The most spectacular part of the valley is east of Cocora. Take the rough road heading downhill to the bridge over the Río Quindío (just a five-minute walk from the restaurants) and you will see the strange

60m-high palms. After an hour or more of walking you'll come to a signpost, with **Reserva Natural Acaime** (admission incl refreshment COP$5000) to the right. Here you'll find a wonderful hummingbird reserve; at least six varieties are always present, with dozens of birds zipping past at once. Admission includes a piping hot cup of coffee or *aguapanela* (sugar cane and water drink). You can also stay here in basic dormitories (COP$15,000).

Head back to the signpost, and either double back the way you came or take the harder road uphill toward La Montaña for some of Colombia's most mind-blowing landscapes.

Six jeeps (COP$3400, 35 minutes, 6:10am, 7:30am, 9:30am, 11:30am, 2pm and 4pm) depart daily from Salento's plaza to Cocora. Arrive 15 minutes before the departure time to ensure you get a spot.

SOUTHWEST COLOMBIA

Southwest Colombia will spin your head with its blend of ancient and modern culture. Cali, its largest city, throbs with tropical energy and attitude; the remarkable archaeological sites of San Agustín and Tierradentro, nestled deep in majestic mountain landscapes, are benign and fascinating, while the Desierto de la Tatacoa is an arid anomaly.

The colonial city of Popayán, the other major tourist draw, is a living museum of Spanish rule, with many ornate churches and a smart, relaxed atmosphere.

Approaching the border with Ecuador at Ipiales, the landscape gets vertiginous and the scene gets Andean; here you'll feel more like you're in Ecuador than Colombia. The beautiful Laguna de la Cocha, in Pasto, and the Santuario de las Lajas, a neo-Gothic church in Ipiales that spans a wide gorge, are the main attractions here.

Cali

☎2 / POP 2.5 MILLION

Cali is Colombia right in your face. The attitude, the heat, the traffic, the music and the food all combine in a delightful, dizzying haze. Compared with Popayán's genteel politeness, Medellín's confident strut and Bogotá's refined reserve, Cali is all front – but just behind that front is a passionate, rebellious Colombian city that will love you if you love it.

It's not a city without attractions: the arty colonial neighborhood of San Antonio with its bohemian park is a great place for a wander and there are several classy dining districts, but without a doubt Cali's biggest attribute is its proud residents, a multiethnic mix rich in Afro-Colombian heritage, for whom there is no greater blessing than being born *caleño.*

If salsa is the soul music of Latin America then it's no surprise that Cali, a tough, working town that has seen its fair share of trouble, is obsessed with it. Salsa is not entertainment here, it's a way of life. If you've never heard the explosive, insurrectionary power of a salsa orchestra live, this is your chance – don't miss it.

Cali doesn't cater to tourists with the same eagerness as other destinations, but this somehow contributes to its charm. Cali needs you less than you need it. It's a busy, tough and at times grimy and unsafe town, but when evening comes and the temperature drops on the streets, the locals seize the night with the ferocity of people who've worked hard and who want, no, *need,* to party. You're welcome along for the ride.

Sights

Museo Arqucológico la Merced MUSEUM
(☎885-4665; Carrera 4 No 6-59; admission adult/child COP$4000/2000; ⏲9am-1pm & 2-6pm Mon-Sat) In the former La Merced convent, Cali's oldest building, this interesting museum contains a collection of pre-Columbian pottery left behind by the major cultures from central and southern Colombia.

Iglesia de la Merced CHURCH
(cnr Carrera 4 & Calle 7; ⏲6:30-10am & 4-7pm) Begun around 1545, this is the city's oldest church. It's a lovely whitewashed building in the Spanish colonial style, with a long, narrow nave, and humble wood and stucco construction. Inside, a heavily gilded baroque high altar is topped by the Virgen de las Mercedes, the patron saint of the city.

Museo de Arte Moderno La Tertulia GALLERY
(☎893-2939; www.museolatertulia.com; Av Colombia 5 Oeste-105; admission COP$4000; ⏲10am-6pm Tue-Sat, 2-6pm Sun) Presents exhibitions of contemporary painting, sculpture and photography. It's a 15-minute walk from the city center along the Río Cali.

Cali

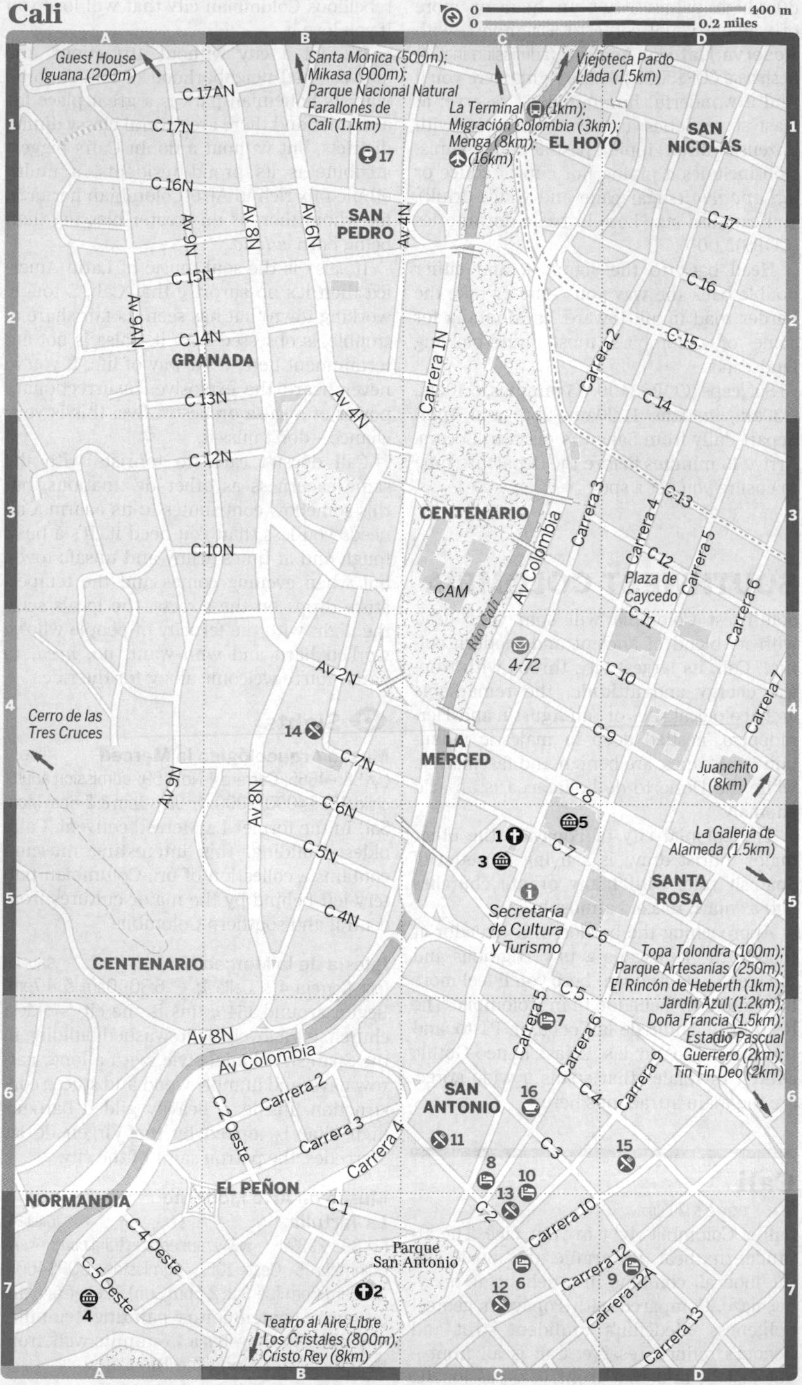

0 400 m
0 0.2 miles
A B C D
1 2 3 4 5 6 7
Guest House Iguana (200m)
Santa Monica (500m); Mikasa (900m); Parque Nacional Natural Farallones de Cali (1.1km)
Viejoteca Pardo Llada (1.5km)
La Terminal (1km); Migración Colombia (3km); Menga (8km); (16km)
EL HOYO
SAN NICOLÁS
SAN PEDRO
GRANADA
CENTENARIO
CAM
LA MERCED
SANTA ROSA
CENTENARIO
SAN ANTONIO
EL PEÑON
NORMANDIA
Plaza de Caycedo
Parque San Antonio
Río Cali
Cerro de las Tres Cruces
Juanchito (8km)
La Galeria de Alameda (1.5km)
Secretaría de Cultura y Turismo
Topa Tolondra (100m); Parque Artesanías (250m); El Rincón de Heberth (1km); Jardín Azul (1.2km); Doña Francia (1.5km); Estadio Pascual Guerrero (2km); Tin Tin Deo (2km)
Teatro al Aire Libre Los Cristales (800m); Cristo Rey (8km)
C 17AN
C 17N
C 16N
C 15N
C 14N
C 13N
C 12N
C 10N
C 7N
C 6N
C 5N
C 4N
Av 9N
Av 8N
Av 6N
Av 4N
Av 9AN
Av 2N
Carrera 1N
Av Colombia
Av 8N
C 2 Oeste
C 4 Oeste
C 5 Oeste
C 1
C 2
C 3
C 4
C 5
C 6
C 7
C 8
C 9
C 10
C 11
C 12
C 13
C 14
C 15
C 16
C 17
Carrera 2
Carrera 3
Carrera 4
Carrera 5
Carrera 6
Carrera 7
Carrera 9
Carrera 10
Carrera 12
Carrera 12A
Carrera 13
4-72
1 2 3 4 5 6 7 8 9 10 11 12 13 14 15 16 17

Iglesia de San Antonio CHURCH

Constructed in 1747, this small church is set atop a hill, the Colina de San Antonio, west of the old center. It shelters valuable *tallas quiteñas,* 17th-century carved-wood statues of the saints, representing the style known as the Quito School. The park surrounding the church offers great views of the city.

Cristo Rey MONUMENT

Resembling a scaled-down version of Río's famous monument, this towering Christ statue atop Cerro las Cristales affords panoramic views of the city. A round-trip taxi up here should cost around COP$50,000. Walking here is not recommended.

Museo del Oro MUSEUM

(Calle 7 No 4-69; 10am-5pm Tue-Sat) FREE One block east from Iglesia de la Merced, this museum has a small but fine collection of gold and pottery of the Calima culture.

Activities

Colombia Walking Tours GUIDED TOUR

(310-398-5513; www.colombiawalkingtours.com) FREE This group of enthusiastic young guides offers a free walking tour around the city center on Monday and Friday at 4pm beginning from outside the Iglesia de la Merced. They also offer a number of other on-demand tours around Cali.

Courses

Manicero DANCE

(314-658-7457; Calle 5 No 39-71) Dance school offering cheap group salsa classes.

Festivals & Events

★Festival de Música del Pacífico Petronio Álvarez MUSIC

(www.festivalpetronioalvarez.com;) A festival of Pacific music, heavily influenced by the African rhythms brought by the many slaves that originally populated the Pacific coast. *Caleños* turn up en masse for nonstop dancing and copious amounts of *arrechón* (a sweet artisanal alcohol). Held in August.

Festival Mundial de Salsa DANCE

(www.mundialdesalsa.com) Amazing dancers from Cali and beyond take to the stage in colorful costumes during this competitive salsa event held in September.

Sleeping

For a chilled Cali experience, choose San Antonio; for nightlife, go for Granada.

Guest House Iguana HOSTEL $

(382-5364; www.iguana.com.co; Av 9N No 22N-46; dm COP$19,000-21,000, s/d with bathroom COP$50,000/60,000, without bathroom COP$40,000/50,000; @ wi-fi) This laid-back hostel has a variety of comfortable accommodations spread over two adjoining houses. There is a pleasant garden area, helpful management and free salsa classes several times a week. It's north of the center, within walking distance of the restaurants in Granada and Chipichape.

La Maison Violette HOSTEL $

(371-9837; www.maisonviolettehostel.com; Carrera 12A No 2A-117; dm COP$23,000, s/d COP$65,000/75,000, ste COP$85,000; wi-fi) A new arrival in San Antonio, this hostel has tastefully decorated rooms, spacious suites and a rooftop terrace with panoramic views of the city.

Café Tostaky HOSTEL $

(893-0651; www.tostakycali.com; Carrera 10 No 1-76; dm COP$20,000, s/d without bathroom COP$35,000/50,000; @ wi-fi) Right in the heart of San Antonio, this popular hostel has basic but functional rooms, good hot water and a kitchen you can use. Downstairs it runs

Cali

Sights

1	Iglesia de la Merced	C5
2	Iglesia de San Antonio	D7
3	Museo Arqueológico la Merced	C5
4	Museo de Arte Moderno La Tertulia	A7
5	Museo del Oro	C5

Sleeping

6	Café Tostaky	C7
7	El Viajero	C6
8	La Casa Café	C6
9	La Maison Violette	D7
10	Ruta Sur	C6

Eating

11	El Buen Alimento	C6
12	El Zaguán de San Antonio	C7
13	Lulodka	C7
14	Platillos Voladores	B4
15	Zahavi	D6

Drinking & Nightlife

16	Macondo	C6
17	Zaperoco	B1

Entertainment

	Cinemateca La Tertulia	(see 4)

COLOMBIA CALI

DON'T MISS

SAN CIPRIANO

Surrounded by thick jungle, **San Cipriano** is a tiny Afro-Colombian town that is a fantastic budget destination for nature lovers. A crystal-clear river flows through the center of the community. Walk upstream and float back down on an inner tube or cool off in one of the many swimming holes.

The town is as famous for its mode of arrival as for its natural wonders. Situated on the little-used Cali–Buenaventura railroad and 15km from the nearest road, residents have come up with ingenious homemade rail trolleys powered by motorcycles that fly through the jungle at breakneck speed. Hold on tight and wear shoes so you can jump off in an emergency.

It's possible to visit on a day trip from Cali but why rush? There are a number of extremely basic budget hotels here all charging COP$15,000 to COP$25,000 per person.

From Cali, any Buenaventura-bound bus will drop you at Córdoba (COP$18,000, three hours), from where it's a 15-minute ride by moto-trolley (COP$5000).

a chilled cafe that serves crepes, sandwiches and good coffee. Worth visiting even if you're not staying here.

La Casa Café HOSTEL $
(☎893-7011; lacasacafecali@gmail.com; Carrera 6 No 2-13; dm COP$18,000, s/d without bathroom COP$25,000/40,000; @📶) For an old-school, no-frills backpacking experience head to this groovy cafe-bar which rents good-value dorm beds and private rooms on the 2nd floor of its colonial building.

El Viajero HOSTEL $$
(☎893-8342; Carrera 5 No 4-56; dm COP$23,000-25,000, s/d with bathroom COP$75,000/100,000, without bathroom COP$47,000/88,000; 📶🏊) In a renovated colonial house, El Viajero is a popular choice among young travelers looking for a social vibe. The private rooms are a little on the small side, but the large pool in the rear courtyard provides respite from the heat and the adjacent bar area is lively in the evenings. There are regular free dance classes.

Jardín Azul GUESTHOUSE $$
(☎556-8380; www.jardinazul.com; Carrera 24A No 2A-59; r COP$115,000-165,000; 📶🏊) Set in a converted house on a hill near the colonial sector east of the center, this spotless small hotel has spacious, bright rooms with big beds and imported cotton sheets. Some rooms have private balconies and views of the city. There is a small pool set in an appealing garden that attracts plenty of birds.

Ruta Sur HOSTEL $$
(☎893-6946; hostalrutasur@gmail.com; Carrera 9 No 2-41; s/d COP$75,000/95,000) This homey, welcoming hostel in San Antonio is popular with travelers looking for a quiet base in a central location. Rooms are tastefully decorated but the bathrooms are tiny.

Eating

The best cheap eats in town are at Alameda's colorful local food market, **La Galeria de Alameda** (cnr Calle 8 & Carrera 26), which has plenty of small lunch counters serving seafood and *comidas tipicas* (typical food).

El Buen Alimento VEGETARIAN $
(☎375-5738; Calle 2 No 4-53; set meal COP$10,000, mains COP$12,500-15,500; ⏲11:30am-10pm Mon-Sat, to 5pm Sun; 🌿) This hip vegetarian restaurant serves excellent meat-free versions of Colombian classics, as well as creative fusion dishes such as Mexican lasagna and great fresh juices.

Doña Francia ICE CREAM $
(Carrera 27 No 3-100; snacks COP$2000-5000; ⏲8am-7pm) Sit on benches outside this Cali institution and enjoy sensational juices, sorbets and possibly the best *salpicón* (fruit salad) in all of Colombia. It's one block east from Parque del Perro.

Zahavi BAKERY $
(Carrera 10 No 3-81; pastries COP$2000-6000; ⏲11am-8pm Mon-Fri, 8am-7:30pm Sat & Sun) This posh bakery in San Antonio serves excellent coffee, rich gooey brownies and delicious gourmet sandwiches.

★**Lulodka** FUSION $$
(Calle 2 No 6-17; set meals COP$15,000, mains COP$14,000-28,000; ⏲10am-3:30pm & 6-11pm Mon-Sat) You won't find better value for your peso than at this groovy fusion restaurant in a lovely colonial house. The gourmet set

lunches include soup, salad, main course, fresh juice and dessert. Everything is cooked to perfection with delicately balanced flavors and textures. Try the signature 'Lulodka' – a *lulo*-based beverage mixed with vodka.

El Zaguán de San Antonio COLOMBIAN **$$**
(Carrera 12 No 1-29; mains COP$25,000; noon-midnight) This San Antonio institution serves big portions of traditional *vallecaucana* food and excellent fresh juices. The food is delicious but the real reason to come here is for the amazing view from the rooftop, which is also a great place for a drink.

★ **Platillos Voladores** FUSION **$$$**
(668-7750; www.platillosvoladores.com.co; Av 3N No 7-19; mains COP$27,000-45,000; noon-3pm & 7-11pm Mon-Fri, 1-4pm Sat) Cali's best fine dining experience, Platillos Voladores offers an interesting and varied menu of beautifully presented gourmet dishes combining Asian, European and local influences, served in either the outdoor garden area or one of several air-conditioned dining rooms. Wash your meal down with an offering from the impressive wine list. Reservations are essential.

Drinking & Nightlife

Grassy Parque San Antonio offers great views of the city lights and is a popular place for some early evening beers. There are dozens of small bars in the area around Parque del Perro.

Cali's dance floors are not for the faint-hearted or stiff-hipped – the salsa style here is faster and more complex than elsewhere, with fancier footwork. The most exclusive clubs are in the north. Calle 5 south of the river is less dressy.

★ **Zaperoco** SALSA CLUB
(www.zaperocobar.com; Av 5N No 16-46; 9pm-late Thu-Sat) If you only visit one salsa bar in Cali, make sure it's Zaperoco. Here the veteran DJ spins pure *salsa con golpe* (salsa with punch) from old vinyl while rows of industrial fans try in vain to keep the place cool. Somewhere under the mass of moving limbs there is a dance floor – but we've never worked out exactly where it is.

It's a high-energy place – a night out here will burn more calories than a half marathon in the tropics.

Tin Tin Deo SALSA CLUB
(www.tintindeocali.com; Calle 5 No 38-71; 8pm-late Thu-Sat) This iconic, unpretentious 2nd-floor salsa joint features a large dance area overseen by posters of famous salsa singers. While it sometimes feels like an expat hangout (especially on Thursdays), it's an excellent place for novice dancers to get on the floor. There is no need to bring a dance partner, you'll find plenty of volunteers among the friendly regulars.

El Rincón de Heberth BAR
(Carrera 24 No 5-32; Thu-Sat 8pm-3am) In a shop front in a strip mall, this humble salsa bar is an unlikely hit but it packs a crowd who come for the great music and laid-back vibe. Most sit outside and drink in the street where it's fresher until a particular song inspires them to take to the steamy dance floor.

Macondo CAFE
(Carrera 6 No 3-03; 11am-11pm, from 4pm Sun) This San Antonio institution does great coffee and a wide range of desserts. It also serves beer and wine till late. Try one of the scrumptious cocktails.

Topa Tolondra BAR
(Calle 5 No 13-27; 6pm-late Thu-Mon) Humble small salsa bar with a fun ambience near Loma de la Cruz. The tables are all pushed right up against the walls leaving the concrete floor free to get your boogie on.

Mikasa BAR
(Calle 26N No 5AN-51; 9pm-3am Thu-Sat) An alternative for those who don't breathe salsa, this hip bar has skilled DJs spinning all kinds of music, an outdoor dance area with retractable roof and an open-air terrace upstairs. Don't be put off by the commando security team – inside it's actually quite chilled.

Entertainment

Cali has two *fútbol* (soccer) teams: **Deportivo Cali** (www.deportivocali.co), based near the airport in Palmira, compete in the top flight, while **América de Cali** (www.america.com.co), who play in the more convenient **Estadio Pascual Guerrero** (cnr Calle 5 & Carrera 34), languishes in the lower divisions.

Cinemateca La Tertulia CINEMA
(893-2939; www.museolatertulia.com; Av Colombia No 5 Oeste-105; admission COP$5000) Check out the art-house cinema program at this gallery. It generally has two shows daily from Tuesday to Sunday.

WORTH A TRIP

PACIFIC COAST

Colombia's Pacific coast hasn't traditionally offered much love to the budget traveler. The infrastructure is poor, and traveling is improvised and expensive – mainly by ship, speedboat and light plane, since only one road links it with the interior of the country (the Cali–Buenaventura road).

However, things are changing. Security has improved dramatically and now the only stretches that remain off-limits are the departments of Cauca and Nariño south of Buenaventura and the extreme northern Chocó near the border with Panama. And while most accommodations in these parts are still targeted at wealthy domestic tourists, the first backpacker hostel in the region has opened near **El Valle**, and several places around **Ladrilleros** in Valle de Cauca now offer budget whale-watching tours.

Community-based tourism is taking off too. In villages throughout the Chocó there are cooperatives of guides that take visitors on cheap trips in the jungle, along rivers or in the mangroves, while to the south of El Valle volunteers are able to contribute to an important turtle conservation program.

If you do choose to visit the Pacific Coast, a copy of Lonely Planet's *Colombia* is highly recommended.

Shopping

Parque Artesanías MARKET
(⏰10am-8pm) On Loma de la Cruz, this is one of Colombia's best *artesanía* (handicrafts) markets. You'll find authentic, handmade goods from the Amazon, Pacific coast, southern Andes and even Los Llanos.

Information

Cali has an edge, especially south of the river: avoid walking alone east of Calle 5. Taxis are the safest way to travel.

4-72 (Carrera 3 No 10-49; ⏰8am-noon & 2-6pm Mon-Fri, 9am-noon Sat) Post office.

Banco de Occidente (Av Colombia 2-72) Most secure ATM close to San Antonio. Avoid banks in the center at night.

Migración Colombia (☎397-3510; www.migracioncolombia.gov.co; Av 3N 50N-20, La Flora; ⏰8am-noon & 2-5pm Mon-Fri) For visa extensions.

Secretaría de Cultura y Turismo (☎885-6173; www.cali.gov.co/turista; cnr Calle 6 & Carrera 4; ⏰8am-noon & 2-5pm Mon-Fri, 10am-2pm Sat) City tourist information office.

Getting There & Away

AIR

The Palmaseca airport is 16km northeast of the city. Minibuses between the airport and the bus terminal run every 10 minutes until about 8pm (COP$5000, 30 minutes), or take a taxi (COP$50,000).

BUS

The bus terminal, **La Terminal** (www.terminalcali.com; Calle 30N No 2AN-29), is 2km north of the center. It's a sweaty walk in Cali's heat; take the Mio or a taxi (COP$8000).

Buses run regularly to Bogotá (COP$65,000, 10 hours), Medellín (COP$50,000, nine hours) and Pasto (COP$40,000, nine hours). Pasto buses will drop you off in Popayán (COP$15,000, three hours) or you can take the hourly minibuses (COP$16,000, 2½ hours). There are also regular departures to Armenia (COP$21,000, four hours), Pereira (COP$24,000, four hours) and Manizales (COP$38,000, five hours).

Getting Around

You can cover the new and old centers on foot. Taxis in Cali are all metered; make sure the driver turns it on when you hop in. The meter records 'units,' which represent distance covered. The minimum fare is COP$4200.

Cali's air-conditioned integrated bus system, the **Mio** (www.mio.com.co), is similar to the TransMilenio in Bogotá. The most useful route for visitors runs from north of the bus terminal along the river, through the center, and down the length of Av 5 to the Universidad del Valle. Single journeys cost COP$1600.

Popayán

☎2 / POP 266,000

Popayán is an enigma. It's a delightful, elegantly preserved town, second only to Cartagena as Colombia's most impressive colonial settlement, with excellent cheap eats and a lively young population. It should be a booming budget travel hot spot but receives surprisingly few visitors.

However, Popayán's lack of tourist game is a windfall for those who make the effort to know it. It's an immaculate example of Spanish colonial architecture, with chalk-white houses, magnificent museums set in old mansions, splendid churches and a central plaza where locals fan themselves against the noon heat in the shade of palm trees and tropical conifers. The town also boasts one of Colombia's best universities and is famed for its flavorful culinary traditions.

Founded in 1537, Popayán quickly became an important political, cultural and religious center, and was a key stopping point on the route between Quito and Cartagena as the Spanish plunderers looted the continent of much of its gold. The town's mild climate attracted wealthy Spanish settlers from the sugarcane farms near Cali. Several imposing churches and monasteries were built in the 17th and 18th centuries, when the city was flourishing.

In just 18 seconds, all this was unceremoniously torn down when a powerful earthquake ripped through the town on March 1, 1983, before the Maundy Thursday religious procession. The rebuilding work took more than 20 years, but all of its churches have now been restored.

Today, the town is best known for its eerie Easter Week celebrations, when huge, neo-kitsch floats depicting the Passion of Christ are carried through town by bearers in medieval costume amid a fog of incense.

Sights

Popayán has some of Colombia's finest museums, most of which are set in old colonial mansions.

Walk north up Carrera 6 to the river to see two unusual old bridges. The small one, **Puente de la Custodia**, was constructed in 1713 to allow the priests to cross the river to bring the holy orders to the sick of the poor northern suburb. About 160 years later the 178m-long 12-arch **Puente del Humilladero** was built alongside the old bridge and is still in use.

Iglesia de San Francisco CHURCH
(cnr Carrera 9 & Calle 4; guided tour COP$2000) The city's largest colonial church is also its most beautiful. Inside are a fine high altar and a collection of seven unique side altars. The 1983 earthquake cracked open the ossuary, revealing six unidentified mummies. Two are left, and when guides are available, it is possible to visit them on a one-hour guided tour of the church. Ask in the office to the left of the entrance.

El Morro de Tulcán HILL
Behind the university, this hill is said to be the sight of a pre-Columbian pyramid and offers great views over the city.

Casa Museo Mosquera MUSEUM
(Calle 3 No 5-38; admission COP$2000; 9am-noon & 3-5pm) This interesting museum is housed in an 18th-century mansion that was once home to General Tomás Cipriano de Mosquera, who was Colombia's president on four occasions between 1845 and 1867. The original French crystal chandelier in the dining room was transported from the Caribbean to Popayán by mule. Note the urn in the wall; it contains Mosquera's heart.

Iglesia La Ermita CHURCH
(cnr Calle 5 & Carrera 2) Constructed in 1546, Popayán's oldest church is worth seeing for its fine main retable and the fragments of old frescoes, which were only discovered after the earthquake.

Activities

Popayan Tours ADVENTURE TOURS
(831 7871; www.popayantours.com) Offers a variety of adventurous tours in the countryside around Popayán including a downhill mountain-bike run from the Coconuco thermal springs.

Festivals & Events

Semana Santa RELIGIOUS
(Holy Week) Popayán's Easter celebrations are world-famous, especially the nighttime processions on Maundy Thursday and Good Friday. Thousands of the faithful and tourists from all over come to take part in this religious ceremony and the accompanying festival of religious music. Hotel prices soar at this time; book well in advance.

Sleeping

Prices in many places increase dramatically during Semana Santa.

Hosteltrail HOSTEL $
(831-7871; www.hosteltrail.com; Carrera 11 No 4-16; dm COP$20,000, s/d with bathroom COP$45,000/65,000, without bathroom COP$35,000/50,000;) Popayán's most

Popayán

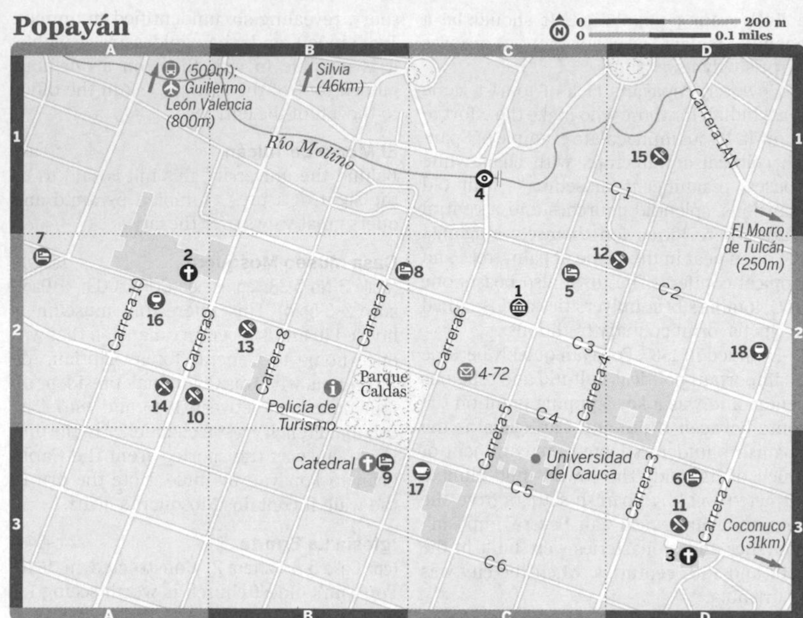

popular budget choice, Hosteltrail is a friendly, modern place on the edge of the colonial center with everything weary travelers need. There is fast internet, express laundry, a fully equipped kitchen and eager staff with a wealth of local know-how.

Parklife Hostel HOSTEL $
(☎300-249-6240; www.parklifehostel.com; Calle 5 No 6-19; dm COP$20,000, s/d with bathroom COP$45,000/55,000, without bathroom from COP$35,000/48,000; @📶) You'd be hard pressed to find a hostel with a better location than Parklife – it's attached to the cathedral wall. The house has plenty of its original style; there are wood floors, chandeliers and antique furniture. It's an atmospheric place – you can hear the church choir from the communal lounge. The front rooms have superb views over Parque Caldas.

Hostel Caracol HOSTEL $
(☎820-7335; www.hostelcaracol.com; Calle 4 No 2-21; dm COP$20,000, s/d without bathroom COP$35,000/50,000; @📶) In a renovated colonial house, this homey hostel is popular with laid-back independent travelers. It has smallish but comfortable rooms set around a pleasant courtyard common area and plenty of information about attractions and entertainment in town.

Casa Familiar Turística HOSTEL $
(☎824-4853; casafamiliarturistica@hotmail.com; Carrera 5 No 2-07; dm COP$15,000, s/d COP$30,000/35,000; 📶) Popayán's original budget digs are a good option for those looking to immerse themselves in local culture – you are basically sharing the house with a Colombian family. Rooms are basic but spacious and you can use the kitchen.

★**Hotel Los Balcones** HOTEL $$
(☎824-2030; www.hotellosbalconespopayan.com; Carrera 7 No 2-75; s/d/apt COP$73,700/137,500/171,000; @📶) Climb 200-year-old stone stairs to your room in this regal 18th-century abode. The place has an almost medieval feel with old wooden furniture, stuffed eagles and a maze of corridors. In the lobby, MC Escher sketches hang next to a case of ancient pottery and plush leather furniture. The rooms on the top floor are quieter.

Eating

Plenty of places in the center offer set lunches for as little as COP$4000.

Mora Castilla CAFE $
(Calle 2 No 4-44; snacks COP$2500-4000; ⏲9am-7pm) This tiny cafe prepares excellent traditional snacks and drinks including *salpicón*

Popayán

Sights

1 Casa Museo Mosquera C2
2 Iglesia de San Francisco A2
3 Iglesia La Ermita D3
4 Puente del Humilladero C1

Sleeping

5 Casa Familiar Turística C2
6 Hostel Caracol D3
7 Hosteltrail A2
8 Hotel Los Balcones B2
9 Parklife Hostel B3

Eating

10 La Fresa A2
11 La Semilla Escondida D3
12 Mora Castilla D2
13 Restaurante Italiano B2
14 Tequila's A2
15 Tienda Regional del Macizo D1

Drinking & Nightlife

16 Bar La Iguana A2
17 Capriccio Café C3
18 Wipala D2

payanese, champus, tamales and *carantantas*. If you're still hungry, pop next door to sample some of doña Chepa's famous *aplanchados* (flat pastries).

Tienda Regional del Macizo COLOMBIAN $
(Carrera 4 No 0-42; meals COP$3500; ⌚8am-4pm) This small cafe is part of an organization that works to develop markets for farmers in the Macizo Colombiano. Needless to say the absurdly cheap lunches are made with the freshest ingredients and are bursting with flavor.

Tequila's MEXICAN $
(Calle 5 No 9-25; set lunch $6500, mains COP$10,000-20,000; ⌚noon-10pm) Run by a Mexican expat and his local wife, this small restaurant in the center prepares up good-value Mexican favorites.

La Fresa CAFE $
(Calle 5 No 8-89; snacks COP$200-2000; ⌚7am-7pm) A grimy corner store with a couple of plastic tables, La Fresa is famed throughout Popayán for its delicious *empanadas de pipián*. Most locals wash them down with a *malta* (a malt-based soda).

Restaurante Italiano ITALIAN $$
(Calle 4 No 8-83; mains COP$15,000-26,000; ⌚noon-10pm) Swing open the saloon doors of this Swiss-owned Italian joint and you'll find great pizza and pasta as well as authentic fondue for those cool mountain nights. The set meal (COP$7500) is one of the best of its kind in Colombia.

La Semilla Escondida FRENCH $$
(Calle 5 No 2-26; mains COP$10,000-25,000; ⌚noon-3pm Mon, noon-3pm & 6-10pm Tue-Sat) This bright bistro in one of Popayán's oldest streets prepares great savory and sweet crepes as well as pasta dishes. The gourmet set lunch (COP$7700) is fantastic value.

Drinking & Entertainment

Wipala BAR
(Carrera 2 No 2-38; ⌚2:30-9:30pm Mon-Thu, to 11:30pm Fri & Sat; 📶) Groovy cafe-bar with a small garden that serves organic local coffee, *hervidos* (fruit infusions) and its own energy drink made with coca tea, ginger and ginseng. It also serves a good veggie burger. Come for the entertainment, which could be anything from belly dancing to rock.

Capriccio Café CAFE
(Calle 5 No 5-63; ⌚9:30am-12:30pm & 2-8pm Mon-Sat) Popular cafe that roasts coffee from rural Cauca and prepares great iced drinks.

Bar La Iguana BAR
(Calle 4 No 9-67; ⌚noon-late) The place to go in the center to show off your salsa moves. Sometimes has live bands.

Information

There are many ATMs around the plaza.

4-72 (Calle 4 No 5-74; ⌚9am-5pm) Post office.

Migración Colombia (☎823-1027; Calle 4N No 10B-66; ⌚9am-noon & 2-5pm) Visa extensions.

Policía de Turismo (☎822-0916; Carrera 7 No 4-36) Tourist office on main plaza.

Getting There & Away

AIR

The airport is just behind the bus terminal, a 15-minute walk or COP$5000 taxi north of the city center. Avianca has three flights daily to and from Bogotá.

BUS

The bus terminal is 1km north of the city center. There are frequent services to Cali (COP$16,000, three hours). Direct buses to Bogotá (COP$85,000, 12 hours) and Medellín (COP$70,000, 11 hours) depart in the evenings.

There are regular minibuses to San Agustín (COP$30,000, five hours), although avoid traveling this route at night. Buses to Tierradentro (COP$22,000, five hours) leave at 5am, 8am, 10:30am, 1pm and 3pm. The 10:30am service takes you all the way to the Museo Arqueológico entrance.

There are hourly buses to Pasto (COP$32,000, six hours) and Ipiales (COP$40,000, eight hours). Security on the road from Popayán to the Ecuadorean border has improved and robberies are no longer common, although night buses are still required to travel in convoy for part of the journey as a precaution. It's best to travel during the day if possible.

Around Popayán

Silvia

2 / POP 31,500

Of Colombia's 68 indigenous groups, the Guambino are the most immediately recognizable, and have survived colonialism, repression and modernization with their language, dress and customs intact. On Tuesday, they descend from their *resguardo* (reserve), which lies an hour further east, and hit Silvia for market day, to sell their produce, to buy tools and clothes, and to hang out in the main square of this small and otherwise unremarkable town.

The men and women dress in flowing, shin-length blue woolen skirts, edged with pink or turquoise, with a thin, dark woolen poncho laid over the shoulders – this is 2800m above sea level, and their reserve lies higher still. Scarves are ubiquitous, and both men and women wear a kind of felt bowler hat, some choosing to fold in the top of it so it resembles a trilby. It's a rakish look however it's worn.

Most of the older women wear many strings of small beads clustered about their necks, and carry a wooden needle that they use to spin yarn from a ball of sheep fleece stored in their net sacks.

Keep your camera in your pocket unless you enjoy needless aggravation. True, it can be frustrating not to record such a colorful and 'foreign' scene, but you'll quickly make yourself a spectacle and cause offense, period.

The main square, and the market southwest of it, are where the action's at. Don't expect some kind of theme-park show for your entertainment, though. This is a working town, and people are here to do business. There are few arts and crafts on sale, and you're more likely to see an indigenous elder haggling over the price of boots and saucepans (or chatting on his cell phone) than offering wisdom for coins.

The best entertainment is provided by traveling performers, snake-oil salesmen, bogus telepathists and assorted magicians and mentalists who perform in the square on market day. Stand and watch some tricksters putting on a show as the raucous church bell clangs through the cool mountain air, surrounded by the smiling, impossibly ancient faces of the Guambino and dozens of laughing Colombians, and divisions soon dissolve.

There are hourly buses to Silvia from Popayán's terminal (COP$7000, 1½ hours). Leave by 8am to catch the market in full swing.

San Agustín

8 / POP 11,000

Long before Europeans came to the Americas, the rolling hills around San Agustín were ruled by a mysterious group of people who buried their dead and honored them with magnificent statues carved from volcanic rock. The legacy that they left behind is now one of the continent's most important archaeological sites. Hundreds of freestanding monumental statues were left next to the tombs of elders of a now disappeared tribe. Pottery and gold objects were also left behind, although much of it was stolen over the centuries.

San Agustín culture flourished between the 6th and 14th centuries AD. The best statuary was made only in the last phase of the development, and the culture had presumably vanished before the Spaniards came. The statues were not discovered until the middle of the 18th century.

So far more than 500 statues have been found and excavated. A great number are anthropomorphic figures – resembling masked monsters. Others are zoomorphic, depicting sacred animals including the eagle, the jaguar and the frog. The statues vary both in size, from about 20cm to 7m, and in their degree of detail.

Today, San Agustín captivates travelers thanks to its history and tranquility, along with the significantly reduced security risks for foreigners in the area. The countryside is beautiful, prices are low and the air and light is crystalline. It's a perfect place to decompress.

San Agustín

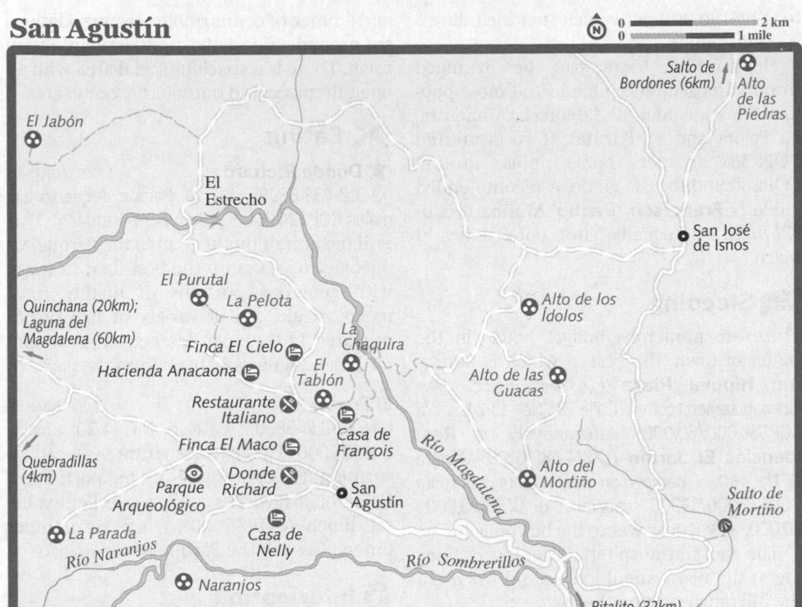

Sights & Activities

The statues and tombs are scattered over a wide area on both sides of the gorge formed by the upper Río Magdalena. Upon paying your admission at either the Parque Arqueológico or Alto de Los Ídolos you will be given a 'passport,' which is valid for entrance to both sites for two consecutive days.

More than a dozen other archaeological sites are scattered over the area including El Tablón, La Chaquira, La Pelota and El Purutal, four sites close enough to each other that you can see them in one trip. The waterfalls Salto de Bordones and Salto del Mortiño are impressive, as is El Estrecho, where the Río Magdalena, that runs from here to the Caribbean, gushes dramatically through a 2m narrows.

★Parque Arqueológico ARCHAEOLOGICAL SITE
(www.icanh.gov.co; admission adult/student/child COP$20,000/10,000/5000; ⏲8am-4pm) The 78-hectare archaeological park is 2.5km west of the town of San Agustín. There are in total about 130 statues in the park, either found in situ or collected from other areas, including some of the best examples of San Agustín statuary. Plan on spending around three hours in the park. Reputable guides congregate around the museum.

Alto de los Ídolos ARCHAEOLOGICAL SITE
(admission adult/student/child COP$20,000/10,000/5000; ⏲8am-4pm) Located across the Río Magdalena 4km southwest of San José de Isnos (a clutch of houses 26km northeast of the town of San Agustín), this is the second-most important archaeological park in the region. It's home to the largest statue in the San Agustín area, which is 7m tall but with only 4m visible above ground.

Magdalena Rafting RAFTING
(☎311-271-5333; www.magdalenarafting.com; Calle 5 No 16-04) The Río Magdalena offers challenging white-water rafting through some phenomenal landscapes. Magdalena Rafting offers 1½-hour tours (COP$50,000 per person) with Classes II to III rapids for novices, and full-day, Class V tours (COP$120,000) for experienced pros. Minimum four people per group. It also offers kayaking classes.

Tours

The usual way of visiting San Agustín's sights (apart from the Parque Arqueológico) is by jeep tour and horse-riding excursion. The standard jeep tour includes El Estrecho, Alto de los Ídolos, Alto de las Piedras, Salto de Bordones and Salto del Mortiño. It takes seven to eight hours and costs COP$150,000 to COP$180,000 per vehicle, not including a specialist guide.

Horse-riding tours can be arranged through most hotels. One of the most popular trips includes El Tablón, La Chaquira, La Pelota and El Purutal. It costs around COP$30,000 per horse, plus around COP$60,000 for the guide. A recommended guide is **Francisco 'Pacho' Muñoz** (☎311-827-7972), who usually hangs out at Finca El Maco.

Sleeping

There are numerous budget hotels in the center of town, the best of which is family-run **Hipona Plaza** (☎314-454-8497; www.hiponaplazahotel.com; Calle 3 No 13-24; s/d COP$30,000/60,000). Alternatively try **Residencias El Jardín** (☎314-488-6220; Carrera 11 No 4-10; r per person with/without bathroom COP$22,000/17,000, cabaña s/d COP$30,000/50,000; P☎), near where the bus pulls in.

The most atmospheric sleeping options are at the many small lodges and *fincas* in the hills surrounding the town.

Finca El Maco HOSTEL $
(☎320-375-5982, 837-3847; www.elmaco.ch; campsite per person COP$10,000, dm COP$18,000, s/d from COP$44,000/63,000; P@☎) This tranquil hostel has a variety of cabins set amid a pretty garden. The restaurant serves homemade organic yogurt and an excellent curry. The owner can organize trips throughout the region. Take the road to the Parque Arqueológico and turn right at the Hotel Yalconia. From here it's a 400m walk uphill. Take a taxi (COP$7000) if you have luggage.

Casa de François HOSTEL $
(☎837-3847; www.lacasadefrancois.com; campsite per person COP$10,000, dm COP$19,000, r with/without bathroom COP$50,000/40,000, cabaña COP$80,000; ☎) Set in a garden just above town overlooking the hills, this creative, ecological hostel is constructed of glass bottles embedded in rammed-mud walls. The breezy, elevated dormitory has fantastic views and there is a spacious shared kitchen. The small restaurant serves up a variety of quality meals and snacks.

Casa de Nelly HOSTEL $
(☎310-215-9067; www.hotelcasadenelly.co; Vereda La Estrella; dm COP$18,000, s/d with bathroom COP$35,000/70,000, without bathroom COP$25,000/50,000; P☎) The original San Agustín hostel has friendly management and a range of comfortable accommodations set around one of the prettiest gardens in town. There is a spacious social area with an open fireplace and outdoor barbecue area.

Eating

★**Donde Richard** COLOMBIAN $$
(☎312-432-6399; Vía al Parque Arqueológico; mains COP$24,000; ⊙8am-6pm Wed-Mon) This grill restaurant on the road to the Parque Arqueológico serves up the best food in town, with generous portions of quality roast meats, steaks and a variety of fish dishes prepared in the open kitchen. A great spot for lunch on the way back from the park.

El Fogón COLOMBIAN $$
(☎320-834-5860; Calle 5 No 14-30; mains COP$18,000-20,000; ⊙7am-9pm) A local institution, El Fogón serves up big portions of Colombian favorites and an excellent-value set lunch (COP$6000). There is another branch close to the Parque Arqueológico.

Information

Banco de Bogotá (Calle 3 No 10-61) Reliable ATM.

Oficina de Turismo (☎320-486-3896; Carrera 11 No 3-61; ⊙8am-noon & 2-5pm Mon-Fri) Tourist office inside the Casa de Cultura.

Getting There & Away

Bus-company offices are on the corner of Calle 3 and Carrera 11 (known as Cuatro Vientos). There are regular minibuses to Neiva (COP$28,000, four hours), Popayán (COP$30,000, five hours) and Cali (COP$40,000, eight hours). There are several buses in the early morning and evening to Bogotá (COP$50,000, 11 hours).

If you prefer a bit more comfort, **Colombia on the Road** (☎837-3437; www.colombiaontheroad.com) offers a door-to-door van service to Popayán (COP$40,000) and Cali (COP$70,000).

The road to Popayán passes through the spectacular *páramo* landscapes of Parque nacional Natural Puracé. Do not travel on this route at night as robberies have been reported.

For Tierradentro, go to Pitalito (COP$6000, 45 minutes) and change for La Plata (COP$25,000, 2½ hours), where you can get a bus or *colectivo* to San Andrés (COP$10,000, 2½ hours).

Getting Around

Taxis have set prices depending on the zone with a full list posted inside the vehicle. Buses run every 15 minutes between town and the Parque Arqueológico (COP$1200).

GETTING TO ECUADOR

The road to Ecuador takes in Pasto and Ipiales, neither of which will detain travelers much. Pasto is really only worth a stay during the crazy festival, **Carnaval de Negros y Blancos** (Black and White Festival), held January 4 and 5, when the entire city throws paint, flour, soot and chalk at each other in commemoration of a colonial-era festival, when slaves and owners switched face color for a day.

The only must-see is nearby **Laguna de la Cocha**, one of Colombia's most beautiful lakes. It's surrounded by ramshackle wooden houses painted in bright colors, many of them budget hotels and restaurants serving fresh trout. You can rent a motorboat (per hour COP$25,000), seating up to eight people, and buzz across the lake to visit **Isla Corota** (corota@parquesnacionales.gov.co; admission COP$1000) in its center. *Colectivos* (COP$4000, 30 minutes, 25km) to the lake depart from the Plaza de Carnaval in central Pasto and from behind the Hospital Departamental (corner Calle 22 and Carrera 7).

Pasto's only backpacker hostel is the **Koala Inn** (2-722-1101; hotelkoalainn@hotmail.com; Calle 18 No 22-37; s/d with bathroom COP$30,000/45,000, without bathroom COP$20,000/40,000;); it offers spacious rooms and is cheap, friendly and centrally located. **Hotel Sello Dorado** (2-721-3688; hotelsellodorado@hotmail.com; Calle 13 No14-19; s/d COP$30,000/40,000;) doesn't have the most romantic location – it's surrounded by car-parts outlets – but is a short walk from the center and its comfortable private rooms are fantastic value.

Ipiales, a major crossing point to Ecuador, is 1½ hours further down the Panamericana. It's a functional border town saved by its famous neo-Gothic **Santuario de las Lajas**. You don't need to stay overnight to visit the church. Drop your bags in the bus terminal's left luggage and take a *colectivo* (COP$2000, 20 minutes) to see the church, which spans a gorge and contains the cliff face where a local man said he saw an image of the Virgin appear in 1754. Pilgrims nationwide flock here and attribute thousands of miracles to the Virgin.

If you need to stay the night in Ipiales, try the simple rooms at the family-run **Hotel Belmonte** (2-773-2771; Carrera 4 No 12-111; s/d COP$16,000/26,000;). For a bit more comfort, check out **Gran Hotel** (2-773-2131; granhotel_ipiales@hotmail.com; Carrera 5 No 21-100; s/d/tr COP$35,000/50,000/90,000;).

Ipiales has a large bus terminal about 1km northeast of the center. It's linked to the center by buses (COP$1000) and taxis (COP$3000). Avoid walking between here and your hotel. There are regular buses to Bogotá (COP$100,000, 22 hours) and Cali (COP$45,000, 11 hours). All these will drop you in Popayán in eight hours.

Regular *colectivos* travel the 2.5km to the border at Rumichaca (COP$1600), leaving from the bus terminal and the market area near the corner of Calle 14 and Carrera 10. After crossing the border on foot, take another *colectivo* to Tulcán (6km). On both routes, Colombian and Ecuadorean currency is accepted.

For details on making this crossing in the opposite direction, see p667.

Tierradentro

2 / POP 600

Travelers who brave the rough ride along the mountain roads that lead to Tierradentro will find tranquility, friendly locals, and one of the continent's most important and awe-inspiring archaeological sites.

Buried under the lush green fields above the tiny *pueblo* (town) of San Andrés de Pisimbalá are dozens of intricately designed and decorated sacred burial sites. These were hewn out of the volcanic rock, and left behind by a disappeared tribe of indigenous Colombians, who archaeologists say lived around the 7th and 9th centuries AD. The Páez people who live here today say they are not connected to the tomb-diggers, and so the sites' origins remain uncertain.

Around 100 tombs have been excavated so far and several dozen statues similar to those found at San Agustín are also found here.

Tierradentro used to have a bad reputation as a guerrilla stronghold and although there is still occasional guerilla activity in the area, travelers are unlikely to have any problems here. Check the latest situation in Popayán or San Agustín before heading out. As a result of the negative publicity, if you visit the sites soon you'll likely be alone, staring at the tombs with unanswered questions in your head and ripe guavas in your pocket, taken from the trees that line the paths.

Sights

The **Parque Arqueológico** (Archaeological Park; 311-3900-324; www.icanh.gov.co; adult/student/child COP$20,000/10,000/5000; 8am-4pm) is made up of four main archaeological sites and two museums. Tickets are valid for two consecutive days and include access to all the tomb sites and two museums.

It's worth visiting the museums before heading out to the tombs. The **Museo Arqueológico** contains pottery urns that were found in the tombs; the **Museo Etnográfico** has utensils and artifacts of the Páez.

You'll need at least half a day to see a good selection of tombs here, so arrive before noon. Some of the tombs have electric lights, but it's also worth bringing a flashlight.

A 20-minute walk up the hill north of the museums will bring you to **Segovia**, the most important burial site. There are 28 tombs here, some with well-preserved decoration.

Other burial sites include **El Duende** (four tombs without preserved decoration) and **Alto de San Andrés** (six tombs, two of which have their original paintings). High on a mountain ridge, **El Aguacate** is the most remote site and has a few dozen tombs, although most have been destroyed by *guaqueros* (grave robbers). Statues have been gathered together at **El Tablón**.

The tiny village of **San Andrés de Pisimbalá**, a 25-minute walk west of the Tierradentro museums, is home to a beautiful, thatched **adobe church** (San Andres de Pisimbalá); it had been torched by arsonists at the time of research but restoration work is on the agenda.

Sleeping & Eating

Whether it's the result of walking all day or the crystalline mountain air, every single thing you eat and drink here is delicious.

There are several cheap *hospedajes* (lodgings) clustered around the entrance to the museums. They are fine for a short visit, but if you plan to stick around longer you might prefer to stay in San Andrés de Pisimbalá.

In addition to the following, also worth a look are **Mi Casita** (312-764-1333; Tierradentro; r per person COP$12,000), **Residencias y Restaurante Pisimbalá** (311-605-4835, 321-263-2334; Tierradentro; r per person with/without bathroom COP$15,000/10,000), **Residencia El Viajero** (321-349-4944; Calle 6 No 4-09, San Andrés de Pisimbalá; r per person COP$12,000) and **Residencias Lucerna** (Tierradentro; r per person COP$10,000).

★La Portada GUESTHOUSE $
(311-601-7884; laportadahotel.com; San Andrés de Pisimbalá; s/d COP$30,000/35,000, without bathroom COP$15,000/20,000) Right by where the bus stops in town, this wooden lodge has large, clean rooms with hot-water bathrooms downstairs and cheaper rooms with shared cold-water bathrooms upstairs. It also serves the best food in town in its breezy restaurant – try the homemade ice cream.

Hospedaje Tierradentro GUESTHOUSE $
(313-651-3713; alorqui@hotmail.com; Tierradentro; r per person COP$15,000) Offers the most privacy of the budget choices, with spotless, freshly painted rooms located in a new building in the garden of the main house.

Hotel El Refugio HOTEL $
(321-811-2395; hotelalbergueelrefugio@gmail.com; Tierradentro; s/d/tr COP$45,000/63,000/80,000;) The most luxurious option in the area, this community-run hotel has comfortable, if a little generic, rooms with mountain views, cable TV and a big pool.

Getting There & Away

Arriving at Tierradentro, most buses will drop you at El Crucero de San Andrés, from where it's a 20-minute walk uphill to the Tierradentro museums and another 20 minutes to San Andrés. Very irregular *colectivos* (COP$1000) make the trip. Otherwise a *mototaxi* costs COP$3000.

A direct bus to Popayán (COP$22,000, four hours) leaves San Andrés de Pisimbalá at 6am and passes in front of the museums. There are other buses to Popayán (9am, 11am, 1pm and 4pm) from El Crucero de San Andrés.

Buses and pickups leave San Andrés de Pisimbalá at 6:30am, 8am, noon and 4pm for La Plata (COP$10,000, two hours), where you can pick up connections to Bogotá, Neiva for the Desierto de la Tatacoa, and Pitalito for San Agustín.

Desierto de la Tatacoa

The 330-sq-km Tatacoa desert is a curiosity, as it's surrounded on all sides by greenery. The mountain peaks around Nevado de Huila grab most of the incoming precipitation, leaving Tatacoa a parched spot where temperatures reach up to 50°C. It features a variety of landscapes ranging from eroded gray-sand ridges to other-planet-like labyrinths carved out of bright red rock, and is made up of several distinct ecosystems where skipping goats, inquisitive foxes and scampering armadillos dodge between the cacti.

Apart from the magnificent panoramas, the main attraction here is the **Observatorio Astronómico de la Tatacoa** (☎312-411-8166; www.tatacoa-astronomia.com; El Cusco; viewings COP$10,000; ⊙visitors center 10am-9pm). The lack of light pollution and the thin air facilitate spectacular stargazing. Between 7pm and 9pm, local astronomer **Javier Fernando Rua Restrepo** (☎310-465-6765) shows visitors around the sky using two tripod telescopes. Call ahead to check on conditions.

Despite being conveniently located midway between Bogotá and San Agustín, Tatacoa remains off the gringo trail and has little in the way of tourist facilities. It's accessed by the sleepy town of Villavieja, where the locals have a fantastic, sing-song way of speaking. There are a number of small hotels in the town, the best of which is **Villa Paraiso** (☎879-7727; hotelvillaparaiso-villavieja@gmail.com; Calle 4 No 7-69, Villavieja; s/d COP$20,000/50,000).

For the full Tatacoa experience, stay at one of the many simple *posadas* (guesthouses) in the desert with local residents. About 400m past the observatory, **Estadero Doña Lilia** (☎313-311-8828; Observatorio, 400m E, Tatacoa; r per person COP$25,000) has comfortable rooms with impressive views and serves delicious meals. Behind the observatory is a large **campground** (☎312-411-8166; Cusco, Tatacoa; campsite per person COP$7000), with room for 40 tents. You can also rent a hammock for COP$10,000 and string it up outside on the Greek pillars on the front porch.

The classiest place to stay is the safari-style **El Peñon de Constantino** (☎317-698-8850, 310-255-5020; elpenonconstantino@hotmail.com; Observatorio, 2km E, Tatacoa; campsite/hut per person COP$10,000/25,000, luxury tent d/tr COP$80,000/100,000; 🏊), 2km past the observatory, which has bamboo huts, canvas perma-tents and a rock-walled pool fed by a natural spring.

There are a handful of *mototaxis* in Villavieja that charge COP$20,000 to take up to three passengers to the observatory. Several guesthouses around Tatacoa rent horses for COP$10,000 to COP$15,000 per hour.

ℹ Getting There & Away

Vans hop the 37km between Neiva and Villavieja (COP$6000, one hour) from 5am to 7pm. There are regular buses from Neiva to Bogotá (COP$55,000, six hours) and San Agustín (COP$30,000, four hours).

AMAZON BASIN

Colombia's Amazon makes up a third of the national territory, as large as California but with hardly a trace of infrastructure. It's mostly rainforest, woven loosely together by rivers and sparsely populated by isolated indigenous communities, many of whom shun the modern world.

Nothing can prepare visitors for their first glimpse of the Amazon rainforest; neither a guidebook, nor a film. Its total size is staggering beyond any conception; 5.5 million sq km. Looking at its seemingly infinite forests from an airplane window is like visiting a new planet; it seems to mock human attempts to comprehend its size. Paddling through it in a canoe is exhilarating and life-affirming.

While massive in scale, the ecosystem is fragile so it is important to minimize the impact that your presence inevitably makes here. Use small boats where possible, travel in groups, travel by public transportation, and use operators that support indigenous communities.

Much of the Amazon territory is held by guerrilla groups and coca producers and is not somewhere that fosters independent travel. However, the town of Leticia, which boasts easy access to Peru and Brazil, and the surrounding border region along the Amazon river, is safe and relatively easy to explore.

Leticia

☎8 / POP 39,700

Leticia could be considered the end of the road in Colombia, that is if it wasn't located more than 800km from the nearest national highway. Lying in splendid isolation in the far south of the country, it's an outpost of cold beer and grilled fish, paved roads and internet cafes, tooting mopeds, ATMs, nightclubs, comfortable beds and air-con. But just a few hours away from this curious city lie thrilling rainforest excursions, fascinating indigenous communities, and flora and fauna in abundance.

Many travelers use Leticia as a transit point for onward travel – there are boat connections to Iquitos (Peru) and Manaus (Brazil), but a trip here in its own right is definitely worth making.

Leticia lies right on the Colombia–Brazil border. Just south across the frontier is Tabatinga, a Brazilian town of similar size. The towns are virtually merging together, and there are no border checkpoints between the two. On an island in the Amazon opposite Leticia–Tabatinga is Santa Rosa, a Peruvian village.

July and August are the only relatively dry months. The wettest period is from February to April. The Amazon River's highest level is from May to June, while the lowest is from August to October. The difference between low and high water can be as great as 15m.

Sights & Activities

Have a look around the **market** and stroll along the waterfront. Visit the **Parque Santander** before sunset for an impressive spectacle, when thousands of screeching parrots (locally called *pericos*) arrive for their nightly rest in the park's trees.

Leticia

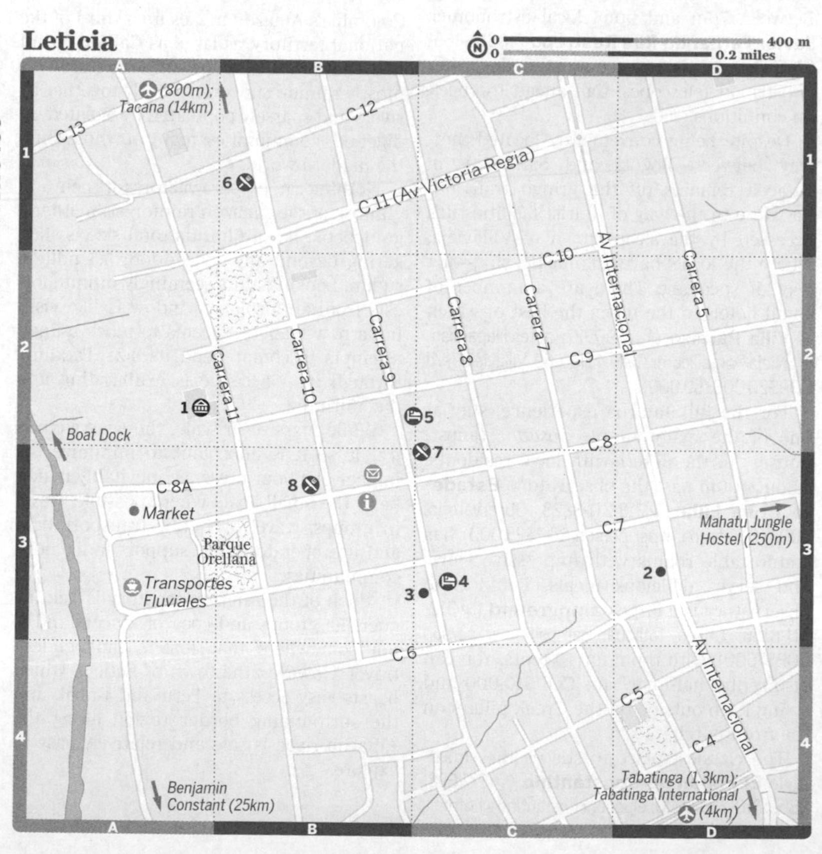

Around 14km from Leticia along the region's only road, **Río Tacana** is a jungle-clad river that is a popular bathing spot for locals. It's also a good place for a short nature hike.

★Mundo Amazónico GARDENS
(☎592-6087, 321-472-4346; www.mundoamazonico.com; Km7.7, Via Tarapacá; tours COP$10,000; ⏲8am-3pm) This 29-hectare reserve was designed to preserve endangered flora and fauna of the Amazon, and functions as a center for environmental education. The extensive botanical gardens boast some 700 species of flora that can be visited on four differently themed tours (the botanical garden, sustainable processes, cultural scenarios and the aquarium), each lasting between 30 and 45 minutes.

Museo Etnográfico Amazónico MUSEUM
(☎592 7729; Carrera 11 No 9-43; ⏲8:30-11:30am & 1:30-5pm Mon-Fri, 9am-1pm Sat) This small museum located inside the dolphin-pink-colored Biblioteca del Banco de la República building has a small collection of indigenous artifacts including musical instruments, textiles, tools, pottery and weapons, and lots of ceremonial masks. It's all signed in English, and makes a good introduction to the indigenous cultures of the region.

Tours

Authentic jungle experiences are generally not found along the Amazon proper but rather upstream in its many tributaries. The deeper you go, the better the chances of seeing wildlife in pristine habitats. This doesn't come cheap.

For a real low-cost jungle fix, it's better to arrange short trips with the locals from the smaller town of Puerto Nariño. Bring plenty of sunscreen and mosquito repellent.

Leticia

Sights

1 Museo Etnográfico Amazónico..........A2

Activities, Courses & Tours

2 Amazon Jungle Trips..........D3
3 Selvaventura..........C3

Sleeping

4 La Casa del Kurupira..........C3
5 La Jangada..........B2

Eating

6 El Santo Angel..........B1
7 La Cava Tropical..........C3
8 Viejo Tolima..........B3

Jungle Guides

Tourism here is not geared toward independent travel, as there is little public transportation and remote accommodations are not prepared for drop-in visitors.

The closest thing to an independent experience is hiring a guide and creating your own trip. The following recommended companies can tailor excursions by land or river. Expect to pay around COP$250,000 to COP$400,000 per day for tours deep in the jungle, including crocodile-spotting, piranha-fishing, dolphin-watching, jungle walks and river trips, with transportation, food and accommodation included.

Amazon Jungle Trips TOURS
(☎592-7377, 321-426-7757; www.amazonjungletrips.com.co; Av Internacional No 6-25) With more than 25 years of experience catering to backpackers, Amazon Jungle is one of the oldest and most reliable tour companies in Leticia. Owner Antonio Cruz Pérez speaks fluent English and can arrange individually tailored tours, including trips to the two very different reserves the company runs: Reserva Natural Zacambú and Tupana Arü Ü.

Selvaventura TOURS
(☎592-3977, 311-287-1307; www.selvaventura.org; Carrera 9 No 6-85) Owner Felipe Ulloa speaks English, Spanish and Portuguese and can arrange a variety of trips into the jungle to both high-forest and *igapó* (flooded) ecosystems, as well as selling tickets for various river trips into Peru and Brazil. The agency makes use of the Maloka jungle camp and the less remote Agape (at Km 10).

Sleeping

Leticia

La Casa del Kurupira HOSTEL $
(☎592-6160, 311-287-1307; www.casadelkurupira.com; Carrera 9 No 6-85; dm COP$25,000, d COP$75,000, d without bathroom COP$40,000-60,000;) Operated by the owners of Selvaventura across the street (whose offices also function as bar and social area for the hostel), this new hostel is very clean, bright and modern, with ceiling fans cooling the rooms and a large shared kitchen and roof terrace strewn with hammocks to chill out in. Laundry costs COP$10,000 and breakfast COP$7000.

Mahatu Jungle Hostel HOSTEL $
(☎311-539-1265; www.mahatu.org; Calle 7 No 1-40; dm COP$25,000, s/d COP$60,000/70,000;)

You can begin your jungle exploration in Leticia at this beautiful hostel, which sits on 5 hectares, complete with duck- and geese-filled ponds, throngs of *pericos* and loads of exotic fruit trees – cashew, *asaí, canangucha* and *copasú* among them. Rooms are very simple and fan cooled with shared bathroom, but you're paying for the lush environs.

La Jangada GUESTHOUSE $
(☎312-361-6506, 311-498-5447; lajangadaleticia@gmail.com; Carrera 9 No 8-106; dm COP$25,000, s/d COP$50,000/70,000, without bathroom COP$35,000/50,000; @) An excellent guesthouse run by a young Swiss-Colombian couple; the Swiss half has traversed 45,000km of Amazon rivers in his ecologically sound bicycle-powered boat, on which you can now do day tours (from COP$60,000). There's a five-bed dorm with a breezy balcony and hammock and a few private rooms with fan.

Omshanty LODGE $
(☎311 489 8985; www.omshanty.com; Km11 Via Tarapaca; dm/s/d/tr/q COP$15,000/40,000/60,000/80,000/95,000) In a thick jungle setting and not strictly in Leticia itself, Omshanty is nevertheless an option to consider if you'd rather spend all your time in the Amazon in the jungle. The cabins sleep up to four and each has its own kitchen for self-caterers. Friendly English-speaking owner Kike organizes jungle excursions.

Tabatinga

Novo Hotel HOTEL $
(☎3412-3846; novohoteltbt@hotmail.com; Rua Pedro Texeira 9; s/d/tr R$50/70/90;) Conveniently located just three blocks from Porta da Feira, this friendly, clean option is perfect if you're catching an early boat.

Eating

Local fish *gamitana* and *pirarúcu* – which can grow to 300kg – are delicious. The best cheap eats in town are at the barbecue stands that set up on the corner of Av Internacional and Calle 7 in the evenings.

La Cava Tropical COLOMBIAN $
(Carrera 9 No 8-22; set meals COP$7000; ⏱10am-6pm;) This open-air restaurant is the locals' lunchtime favorite. The set meals include a soup (often a tasty *sancocho*), small salad, a meat dish with a side of beans or veggies, and bottomless fresh juice at a very reasonable price. It can get quite crowded during the weekday lunch rush and there's an air-con section!

Viejo Tolima COLOMBIAN $
(Calle 8 No 10-20; mains COP$2500-15,000; ⏱8am-8pm Mon-Sat) This friendly, clean and atmospheric spot is a great place to come for an excellent breakfast (yummy *caldos* – soups) as well as fresh fruit juices and other local bites at any other time.

★**El Santo Angel** INTERNATIONAL $$
(Carrera 10 No 11-119; mains COP$10,000-25,000; ⏱5pm-midnight Tue-Sat, noon-midnight Sun) This newcomer easily has the most varied and interesting menu in town; it includes wraps, nachos, salads, grills, panini, burgers and pizza. With inventive touches to the cooking and pleasant outside dining (avoid the sterile interior if possible), this may well be Leticia's best eating option.

PINK DOLPHINS OF THE AMAZON

Playful, intelligent and mysterious, the Amazonian pink dolphin, known locally as a *bufeo* (thanks to the sound they make when surfacing), is a fascinating creature, seen as a good omen.

Nobody quite knows how or when they ended up living in freshwater – they may have entered the Amazon from the Pacific Ocean approximately 15 million years ago, or from the Atlantic Ocean between 1.8 million and five million years ago.

Their brains are 40% bigger than humans', and among other highly specialized evolutionary traits, their neck bone is not fused with their spine, giving their heads great mobility to allow them to hunt for fish in the flooded rainforest. According to local myths the dolphins shift shape and leave the water at night to impregnate girls while in human form.

Responsible tour guides should never use large boats to go and watch the dolphins. Some operators use 200HP engines, whose sound distresses the dolphins. A 10.5HP *peque peque* engine is all you need. Insist your guide does not approach the dolphins, and never interact with them physically.

GETTING TO BRAZIL & PERU

Leticia may be in the middle of nowhere, but it's a popular route to Brazil and Peru. The quickest way out is by air from Tabatinga to Manaus in Brazil. Although slower, the more enjoyable route is by boat to Manaus, or Iquitos in Peru. Iquitos is as isolated as Leticia, if not more so.

To Manaus, three boats a week leave from Porto Fluvial de Tabatinga, at noon on Tuesday, Wednesday and Saturday, although customs and embarkation procedures begin from 9am. The boats stop downriver at Benjamin Constant. The trip to Manaus takes three days and four nights and costs R$200 in your own hammock, or R$800 to R$1000 for two passengers in a double cabin. Food is included. Bring snacks and bottled water and watch your bags. Rápida Puma runs a fast boat service (R$430, 30 hours) that leaves from Porto Bras in Tabatinga at 9am on Friday and Sunday. Embarkation begins at 6:30am. Travel agencies around Leticia sell tickets for both services.

Golfinho and Transtur run modern, high-speed passenger boats between Santa Rosa and Iquitos. There are departures at 5am daily except Monday. The trip costs US$70 (or COP$150,000) and takes around 10 hours. Buy your tickets at the offices in Tabatinga or Selvaventura (p619) in Leticia and complete your immigration formalities the day before the trip. From Iquitos into Peru, you have to fly or continue by river to Pucallpa (five to seven days), from where you can go overland to Lima and elsewhere.

For details on making this crossing in the opposite direction, see p899.

Information

EMERGENCY

Police (☎592-5060; Carrera 11 No 12-32) Between Calles 12 and 13.

MEDICAL SERVICES

San Rafael de Leticia Hospital (☎592 7826; Carrera 10 No 13-78) The only hospital in town.

MONEY

Change all the money of the country you're leaving in Leticia–Tabatinga. There are exchange offices on Calle 8 between Carrera 11 and the market.

Banco de Bogotá (cnr Carrera 10 & Calle 7) ATM.

POST

4-72 (Calle 8 No 9-56; ⌚8am-noon & 2-5pm Mon-Fri) Post office.

TOURIST INFORMATION

Tourist Office (Secretaría de Turismo y Fronteras; ☎592-7569; Calle 8 No 9-75; ⌚7am-noon & 2-5pm Mon-Sat, 7am-noon Sun) Friendly, English-speaking. There is also a small booth at the airport during scheduled flights.

VISA INFORMATION

Locals and foreigners are allowed to come and go between Leticia, Tabatinga and Benjamin Constant in Brazil, and Santa Rosa in Peru without visas or passport control. If you plan on traveling further, get your exit stamp at the Migración Colombia office at Leticia's airport.

Complete your entry formalities in Brazil at Policía Federal, near the hospital in Tabatinga. If you're heading to Peru, get your stamp at the immigration office in Santa Rosa.

Citizens of many countries need a visa to enter Brazil. It is highly recommended to obtain it before traveling to the Amazon, but if you still need one, bring your passport and yellow-fever certificate to the **Brazilian consulate** (☎8-592-7530; Calle 9 No 9-73) – the visa can take up to three days.

Getting There & Away

AIR

Tourists arriving at Leticia's airport are charged a compulsory COP$20,000 tax.

LAN (www.lan.com; Alfredo Vásquez Cobo Airport) and **Avianca** (☎592-6021; www.avianca.com; Alfredo Vásquez Cobo Airport; ⌚8am-1.30pm Mon-Sat & 3-6pm Mon-Fri) fly from Leticia to Bogotá daily. **Trip** (www.voetrip.com.br) and **TAM** (www.tam.com.br) fly from Tabatinga International Airport to Manaus.

BOAT

Leticia connects downstream to Manaus (Brazil) or upriver to Iquitos (Peru).

To get to Puerto Nariño and Parque Nacional Amacayacu, buy tickets for the fast boat from **Transportes Fluviales** (☎592-5999, 592-6711), near the market in Leticia. Boats leave at 8am, 10am and 2pm, take 2½ hours and cost COP$29,000.

Getting Around

The *mototaxi* is king in Leticia; a short ride in the center costs COP$2000 at night. Flag down any

OFF THE BEATEN TRACK

SAN MARTÍN DE AMACAYACU

Getting truly off the beaten path in the Colombian Amazon can be tricky, especially if you want to combine being in nature with experiencing the daily lives of the indigenous peoples of the region. One solution is a visit to the wonderful **Casa Gregorio** (☎310-279-8147, 311-201-8222; casagregorio@outlook.com; San Martin de Amacayacu; full board per person from COP$170,000), a small family-run hotel in the Tikuna indigenous community of San Martín de Amacayacu, surrounded by majestic rivers and impressive rainforest.

Rates include full board, rubber boots, rain gear, drinking water and various nature activities, workshops and river trips. Prices range between COP$170,000 and COP$250,000 per person per day, depending on the activities and number of travelers (maximum four per group).

You have to book ahead to stay here as you need to be picked up on arrival. To reach Casa Gregorio from Leticia, take one of the three daily boats heading to Puerto Nariño and request the Bocana Amacayacu stop, from where you will be picked up by the Casa Gregorio staff (COP$30,000 per person).

of the dudes riding round with a spare helmet in their hands. There is also a small fleet of tuk-tuks that charge roughly double the motorbike price. Regular taxis here are more expensive than elsewhere in Colombia; the short trip from the airport to town costs COP$8000.

There is a regular bus service during daylight hours from Parque Orellana to the Km 11 mark on Leticia's only highway, the Via Tarapacá.

Minibuses (COP$2000) run between Leticia and Tabatinga, departing from morning until early evening. Boat taxis to Santa Rosa (COP$3000, 10 minutes) congregate near the market.

Parque Nacional Amacayacu

Parque Nacional Amacayacu takes in 2935 sq km of jungle on the northern side of the Amazon, about 55km upstream from Leticia. It offers a wide range of wildlife-viewing opportunities.

A luxury hotel chain has been given the concession to run the facilities and offers a sanitized version of the rainforest experience at sky-high prices to visitors who don't want to get their shoes dirty. The combined cost of the park entry fee (adult/student under 26 COP$38,000/7000) and accommodations (simple dorm beds cost COP$112,000 to COP$210,000 depending on the season) rules this out for most budget travelers.

Boats from Leticia to Puerto Nariño will drop you off at the park's visitors center. Getting back to Leticia is trickier – your best bet is to call Transportes Fluviales (p621) in Leticia to reserve a seat otherwise you'll be out on the dock trying to flag down passing vessels.

Puerto Nariño

☎8 / POP 2000

Puerto Nariño, a charming small town 60km up the Amazon from Leticia, is an appealing oddity. It's the second-biggest settlement in the Colombian Amazon but there are no motor vehicles, and all rainwater is recycled – as is all garbage. Its narrow 'streets' are kept incredibly clean, thanks to daily sweeping patrols by proud women and girls, known as *escobitas*.

Sights & Activities

On a hill in the center of town, the shaky **Mirador Naipata** (Calle 4; high/low season COP$7000/5000; ⏲6am-5pm) affords spectacular views over the town and surrounding forest. On the riverfront, the **Centro de Interpretación Natütama** (admission COP$5000; ⏲9am-5pm Wed-Mon) has a fascinating museum with nearly 100 life-sized wood carvings of Amazonian flora and fauna. Also on the riverfront, **Fundacíon Omacha** (www.omacha.org) FREE works to protect river dolphins and manatees, and staff here arrange wildlife-spotting activities.

About 10km west of Puerto Nariño is **Lago Tarapoto**, a tranquil lake accessible only by river, where you can see pink dolphins playing. A half-day trip to the lake in a small boat can be informally organized with locals from Puerto Nariño (per boat for up to four people around COP$50,000).

Sleeping & Eating

Malokas Napü GUESTHOUSE $
(☎314-235-3782; www.maiocanapo.com; Calle 4 No 5-72; r per person with/without balcony COP$30,000/25,000; @) Our favorite hotel has the look and feel of a treehouse fort, surrounded as it is by a thickly forested garden. The rooms are simple but comfortable, with basic furnishings, fans and shared bathrooms with super-refreshing rain-style showers, and everyone who works here is above and beyond friendly.

Cabañas del Friar CABAÑAS $
(☎311-502-8592; altodelaguila@hotmail.com; r per person COP$20,000) About 15 minutes west of town, famous friar Hector José Rivera and his crazy monkeys run this hilltop jungle oasis overlooking the Amazon. The complex includes several extremely simple huts, shared facilities and a lookout tower. The true joy of staying here is the playful interaction between the monkeys, dogs and macaws, and the utter isolation.

★**Las Margaritas** COLOMBIAN $$
(Calle 6 No 6-80; set meals COP$15,000; ⏰8am-9pm) Hidden behind a picket fence under a huge *palapa* (thatched roof) just beyond the football pitch, Las Margaritas is the best restaurant in town. Excellent home-cooked meals are served buffet-style from traditional clay cookware, there's always a delicious variety of local specialties and it's all shockingly tasty. The place can get swamped when large tours come through town, though.

Information

There are no banks or ATMs in Puerto Nariño, so bring enough cash from Leticia.

Tourist Office (☎313-235-3687; cnr Carrera 7 & Calle 5; ⏰9am-noon & 2-5pm Mon-Sat) Located inside the *alcaldía* (town hall building), but there's a kiosk just outside on the riverfront.

Getting There & Away

Fast boats leave Puerto Nariño for Leticia (COP$29,000, 2½ hours) at 7:30am, 11am and 4pm. Buy your ticket in advance at the office by the dock.

UNDERSTAND COLOMBIA

Colombia Today

In every corner of Colombia, the one topic that dominates conversation is the ongoing peace process between the government and the Fuerzas Armadas Revolucionarias de Colombia (FARC).

After around half a century of conflict, both sides began meeting in Havana in 2012 to discuss an end to hostilities. President Juan Manuel Santos, who has endured consistently low approval ratings, has bet his legacy on the process and managed to win reelection in 2014 by framing a vote for his party as 'a vote for peace.'

But even while the two parties talk, violence continues around the country, albeit with far less intensity than during the height of the conflict.

By 2015 significant progress had been made in the peace process, with President Santos flying to Havana for a symbolic handshake with FARC leader Timochenko, the first meeting between the men. The two parties announced a deal on transitional justice – the most controversial point on the talks agenda – and a final date for a binding peace accord of no later than March 2016. Whether this deadline is met remains to be seen at the time of research, but many observers believe that the talks have passed the point of no return and a formal end to South America's longest insurgency is imminent.

History

Pre-Columbian Times

Colombia's original inhabitants have left behind three main prehistoric sites: San Agustín, Tierradentro and Ciudad Perdida, along with the continent's finest gold work. They were highly skilled goldworkers and metalsmiths. Their efforts can be seen throughout Colombia in *museos del oro* (gold museums). Bogotá's is the best.

Scattered throughout the Andean region and along the Pacific and Caribbean coasts, the pre-Columbian cultures of Colombia developed independently. The most notable were the Calima, Muisca, Nariño, Quimbaya, San Agustín, Sinú, Tayrona, Tierradentro, Tolima and Tumaco.

The Conquistadores Arrive

In 1499 Alonso de Ojeda was the first conquistador to set foot on Colombian soil and to see its people using gold objects. Several short-lived settlements were founded, but it was not until 1525 that Rodrigo de Bastidas laid the first stones of Santa Marta, the earliest surviving town. In 1533, Pedro de Heredia founded Cartagena, which soon became the principal center of trade.

In 1536 a general advance toward the interior began independently from both the north and south. Jiménez de Quesada set off from Santa Marta and founded Santa Fe de Bogotá two years later. On the way he conquered the Muisca, a blow that would foretell the ultimate ruin of civilizations throughout the New World.

Meanwhile, Sebastián de Benalcázar deserted from Francisco Pizarro's army, which was conquering the Inca empire, and mounted an expedition from Ecuador. He subdued the southern part of Colombia, founding Popayán and Cali along the way, before reaching Bogotá in 1539.

Independence Wars

As the 18th century closed, disillusionment with Spanish domination matured into open protests and rebellions. When Napoleon Bonaparte invaded Spain and placed his own brother on the throne in 1808, the colonies refused to recognize the new monarch. One by one Colombian towns declared their independence.

In 1812 Simón Bolívar, who was to become the hero of the independence struggle, arrived in Cartagena to attack the Spanish. In a brilliant campaign to seize Venezuela, he won six battles, but was unable to hold Caracas and had to withdraw to Cartagena. By then Napoleon had been defeated at Waterloo, and Spain set about reconquering its colonies. Colonial rule was reestablished in 1817.

Bolívar doggedly took up arms again. After assembling an army of horsemen from the Venezuelan Llanos, strengthened by a British legion, he marched over the Andes into Colombia. Independence was won at Boyacá on August 7, 1819.

Independence & Civil War

Two years after declaring independence, revolutionaries sat down in Villa del Rosario (near Cúcuta) to hash out a plan for their new country. It was there that the two opposing tendencies, centralist and federalist, came to the fore. Bolívar, who supported a centralized republic, succeeded in imposing his will. The Gran Colombia (which included modern-day Ecuador, Colombia, Venezuela and Panama) came into being and Bolívar was elected president.

From its inception, the state started to disintegrate. It soon became apparent that a central regime was incapable of governing such a vast and diverse territory. The Gran Colombia split into three separate countries in 1830.

The centralist and federalist political currents were both formalized in 1849 when two political parties were established: the Conservatives (with centralist tendencies) and the Liberals (with federalist leanings). Colombia became the scene of fierce rivalries between the two forces; chaos ensued. During the 19th century the country experienced no less than eight civil wars. Between 1863 and 1885 there were more than 50 anti-government insurrections.

In 1899 a Liberal revolt turned into a full-blown civil war – the so-called War of a Thousand Days. That carnage resulted in a Conservative victory and left 100,000 dead. In 1903 the US took advantage of the country's internal strife and fomented a secessionist movement in Panama (at that time a Colombian province). By creating a new republic, the US was able to build a canal across the Central American isthmus.

La Violencia

After a period of relative peace, the struggle between Liberals and Conservatives broke out again in 1948 with La Violencia, the most destructive of Colombia's many civil wars, which left a death toll of some 300,000. Urban riots broke out on April 9, 1948 in Bogotá following the assassination of Jorge Eliécer Gaitán, a charismatic populist Liberal leader. Liberals soon took up arms throughout the country.

By 1953 some groups of Liberal supporters had begun to demonstrate a dangerous degree of independence. As it became evident that the partisan conflict was taking on revolutionary overtones, the leaders of both the Liberal and Conservative parties decided to support a military coup as the best means of retaining power and pacifying the countryside. The 1953 coup of General

Gustavo Rojas Pinilla was the only military intervention the country experienced in the 20th century.

The dictatorship of General Rojas was not to last. In 1957 the leaders of the two parties signed a pact to share power. The party leaders, however, repressed all political activity that remained outside the scope of their parties, thus sowing the seeds for the appearance of guerrilla groups.

Birth of FARC & the Paramilitaries

During the late 1950s and early 1960s Colombia witnessed the founding of many guerrilla groups, each with its own ideology and its own political and military strategies. The most significant – and deadly – movements included FARC, Ejército de Liberación Nacional (ELN; National Liberation Army) and Movimiento 19 de Abril (M-19; April 19 Movement).

Until 1982 the guerrillas were treated as a problem of public order and persecuted by the army. President Belisario Betancur (1982–86) was the first to open direct negotiations with the guerrillas in a bid to reincorporate them into the nation's political life. Yet the talks ended in failure, and the M-19 guerrillas stormed the capital's Palacio de Justicia in November 1985, leaving more than 100 dead.

The Liberal government of President Virgilio Barco (1986–90), succeeded in getting M-19 to lay down their arms and incorporated them into the political process.

Another group emerging in the 1980s was the Autodefensas Unidas de Colombia (AUC; United Self-Defense Forces of Colombia). The AUC, paramilitary groups formed by rich Colombians looking to protect their lands, was responsible for dozens of massacres. This group supposedly disbanded in Uribe's second term, but many observers including Human Rights Watch say the disarmament was a sham.

All sides have committed and continue to commit atrocities, and the UN High Commissioner for Refugees says Colombia has more than five million internally displaced people (around 10% of the population), with the rural poor caught in the crossfire between the guerrillas, the neoparamilitaries and the army.

White Gold

The cocaine mafia started in a small way in the early 1970s but, within a short time, the drug trade developed into a powerful industry with its own plantations, laboratories, transportation services and protection.

The boom years began in the early 1980s. The Medellín Cartel, led by Pablo Escobar, became the principal mafia and its bosses lived in freedom and luxury. They even founded their own political party and two newspapers, and in 1982 Escobar was elected to congress.

In 1983 the government launched a campaign against the drug trade, which gradually turned into an all-out war. The war became even bloodier in August 1989 when Luis Carlos Galán, the leading Liberal contender for the 1990 presidential election, was assassinated.

The election of the Liberal President César Gaviria (1990–94) brought a brief period of hope. Following lengthy negotiations, which included a constitutional amendment to ban extradition of Colombians, Escobar and the remaining cartel bosses surrendered and the narcoterrorism subsided. However, Escobar escaped from his palatial prison following the government's bumbling attempts to move him to a more secure site. An elite 1500-man special unit hunted Escobar for 499 days, until it tracked him down in Medellín and killed him in December 1993.

Despite this, the drug trade continued unaffected. The Cali Cartel, led by the Rodríguez Orejuela brothers, swiftly moved into the shattered Medellín Cartel's markets and became Colombia's largest trafficker. Although the cartel's top bosses were captured in 1995, the drug trade continued to flourish, with other regional drug cartels, paramilitaries and the guerrillas filling the gap left by the two original mafias.

In 1999 then-President Andrés Pastrana launched Plan Colombia with US backing. The plan called for the total eradication of the coca plant from Colombia by spraying fields with herbicide. While the program achieved some initial success on paper (in the early stages cultivated land was cut by around half), it has also generated dire environmental effects, as impoverished growers moved their crops into national parks, where the spraying is banned.

The job of eradicating cocaine from Colombia appears Sisyphean. Despite US aid of around US$8 billion, latest figures show that cocaine production has soared once again and Colombia is still the world's largest producer.

President Álvaro Uribe

Right-wing hard-liner Álvaro Uribe was elected president in 2002. He inherited a country on the brink of collapse, a pariah state plagued by security problems, with many highways in the country roadblocked and controlled by the rebels. Uribe promised decisive military action against the guerrillas – and he delivered. Suddenly, the country's roads were open, swamped with military, and safe.

Hugely popular, Uribe took a second term in 2006 after a constitutional amendment allowed him to run for power again. Uribe was viewed as a national hero but his presidency was ultimately tainted by scandal. By 2008, 60 congressmen had been arrested or questioned for alleged 'parapolitics' (links with paramilitaries).

The biggest scandal broke in October 2008, when journalists discovered that the army was killing civilians, dressing them in rebel uniforms and claiming them as combat kills in order to gain promotions or days off. It is estimated that during Uribe's presidency the Colombian army killed 3000 young, uneducated, so-called 'false positive' *campesinos* (peasant farmers), in a strategy described by UN Special Rapporteur on extrajudicial, summary or arbitrary executions, Philip Alston, as 'systemic.' When the scandal hit, Uribe launched a purge of the army, but prosecutions remain rare.

Yet more embarrassment for the Uribe regime came in early 2009, when the magazine *Semana* reported that the country's secret police, the Departamento Administrativo de Seguridad (DAS), had been tapping the phones of judges, opposition politicians, journalists and human-rights workers.

FARC on the Defensive

The last decade has been a disastrous period for FARC. The armed group has lost as many as half of its fighters and several key leaders through a combination of combat deaths and demobilizations.

In 2008 the rebels' chief bargaining pawn, French-Colombian presidential candidate Ingrid Betancourt, kidnapped six years earlier, was snatched in an audacious and legally questionable jungle raid by army forces.

But the biggest blow to the organization was delivered in November 2011 when army troops shot dead FARC leader and chief ideologist Alfonso Cano in rural Cauca. Within days of the death of Cano, new leader Rodrigo Londoño Echeverry, alias Timochenko, took control of the organization, announcing that FARC would continue to battle on all fronts, but behind the scenes the seriously weakened FARC entered preliminary talks with the government and within a year were sitting at the table in formal peace negotiations.

Culture

Every traveler you meet who comes to Colombia with an open mind says the same thing: the people are genuinely friendly and helpful.

Colombia is the third-most populous country in Latin America. Its diverse population is an amalgam of three main groups – indigenous, Spanish and African. While 58% of the country claims mestizo (mixed indigenous and Spanish) heritage, other ethnicities include: 20% white, 14% mixed white and black, 4% black, 3% mixed black and indigenous, and 1% indigenous. Colombia's indigenous population speaks about 65 languages and nearly 300 dialects belonging to several linguistic families.

The divide between rich and poor in Colombia remains enormous. The wealthiest 10% of the country controls 65% of the country's wealth, while the poorest 10% control less than 1%, making Colombia one of the most inequitable countries on the continent. While the nation's rapidly growing economy has seen some reduction in poverty, almost one in three Colombians still live below the poverty line.

Colombian families are tight-knit and supportive and, as with most Latin Americans, children are adored. Most couples that live together are married, though this is beginning to change.

The majority of Colombians are Roman Catholic. However, over the past decade there has been a proliferation of various Protestant congregations, which have succeeded in converting millions of Colombians, especially in rural areas.

Arts

Literature

During the independence period and up to WWII, Colombia produced few internationally acclaimed writers other than José Asunción Silva (1865–96), perhaps the country's best poet, and considered the precursor of modernism in Latin America.

A postwar literary boom thrust many great Latin American authors into the international sphere, including Colombian Gabriel García Márquez (1927–2014). Gabo's novel *Cien años de soledad* (One Hundred Years of Solitude), published in 1967, immediately became a worldwide best seller. It mixed myths, dreams and reality, and amazed readers with a new form of expression that critics dubbed *realismo mágico* (magic realism). In 1982 García Márquez won the Nobel Prize in Literature.

There are several contemporaries who deserve recognition, including poet, novelist and painter Héctor Rojas Herazo, and Álvaro Mutis, who was a close friend of Gabo.

Music

Colombians love music and it is ever present in any journey through the country. From first thing in the morning sound systems are turned up to full to play a variety of music as diverse as the country itself.

The Caribbean coast is the birthplace of *vallenato,* based (some might say excessively) on the European accordion. This is the most popular Colombian musical genre today and is played nonstop at earsplitting volume on long-distance buses. The region also vibrates with African-inspired rhythms including cumbia, Colombia's most famous musical export, *mapalé* and *champeta,* an Afro-electronic fusion.

The music of the Pacific coast, such as *currulao,* is even more influenced by African elements and features a strong drum pulse with melody supplied by the *marimba de chonta,* also known as the 'piano of the jungle.'

Salsa is adored by everyone here, and nowhere is it more popular than in Cali, which has adopted the genre as its own and produced more than its share of great *salseros.*

Colombian Andean music has been strongly influenced by Spanish rhythms and instruments, and differs notably from its Peruvian and Bolivian counterparts.

Visual Arts

The colonial period in Colombia was dominated by Spanish religious art. The most renowned colonial artist was Bogotá-born Gregorio Vásquez de Arce y Ceballos, who painted more than 500 works that are now distributed among churches and museums across the country.

Among the most distinguished modern painters and sculptors are Pedro Nel Gómez (known for his murals, oils and sculptures), Luis Alberto Acuña (a painter and sculptor who used motifs from pre-Columbian art), Alejandro Obregón (a painter tending to abstract forms), Rodrigo Arenas Betancourt (Colombia's most famous monument creator) and Fernando Botero (the most internationally renowned Colombian artist). Spot a fat statue or portrait in Colombia and it's likely Botero's.

Cuisine

While you probably didn't come to Colombia for the food, it's fairly easy to eat well, especially if you seek out some of the varied regional specialties.

Variety does not, unfortunately, apply to the *comida corriente* (basic set meal). It is a two-course meal with *sopa* (soup) and *bandeja* (main plate). A *seco* (literally 'dry') is just the main course without soup. At lunchtime (from noon to 2pm) it is called *almuerzo;* at dinnertime (after 6pm) it becomes *comida,* but it is identical to lunch. *Almuerzos* and *comidas* are the cheapest way to fill yourself up, usually costing between COP$7000 and COP$10,000. Breakfasts are dull and repetitive, normally *arepa* (grilled cornmeal patty) and eggs.

Typical food along the Caribbean coast tends to involve fish, plantains and rice with coconut, while in the interior, meat, potatoes and beans are the norm.

Colombian food generally doesn't involve too many vegetables. However, many towns have dedicated vegetarian restaurants, and local markets are full of great fresh produce, including amazing fruits, some of which you won't find anywhere else. Try *guanábana* (soursop), *lulo, curuba, zapote, mamoncillo* (Spanish lime), *uchuva, granadilla, maracuyá* (passion fruit), *tomate de árbol, borojó* (tamarillo), *mamey* and *tamarindo* (tamarind).

Coffee is the number-one drink – though the quality in most establishments will not impress aficionados. *Tinto,* a small cup of (weak) black coffee, is served everywhere. Other coffee drinks are *perico* or *pintado,* a small milk coffee, and *café con leche,* which is larger and uses more milk.

Beer is popular, cheap and generally not bad. Colombian wine is vile. In rural areas, try homemade *chicha* and *guarapo* (alcoholic fermented maize or sugarcane drinks).

Sports

Soccer *(fútbol)* and cycling are Colombia's most popular spectator sports. Colombia regularly takes part in international events in these two fields, such as the World Cup and the Tour de France, and has recorded some successes. The national soccer league has matches most of the year. Baseball is limited to the Caribbean coast.

Tejo is a truly Colombian sport that involves throwing large metal discs at paper bags filled with gun powder that let off a loud bang when you hit the target. It is usually accompanied by copious amounts of beer drinking.

Environment

Colombia covers about the same size as France, Spain and Portugal combined. It occupies the northwestern part of the continent and is the only South American country with coasts on both the Pacific (1448km long) and the Caribbean (1760km). Colombia is bordered by Panama, Venezuela, Brazil, Peru and Ecuador.

The physical geography of Colombia is extremely diverse. Most of the population live in the western part, which is mountainous with three Andean chains – the Cordillera Occidental, Cordillera Central and Cordillera Oriental – running roughly parallel north–south. More than half of the territory lies east of the Andes and is a vast lowland, which is divided into two regions: the savanna-like Los Llanos in the north and the rainforest-covered Amazon in the south.

There are more plant and animal species per unit area in Colombia than any other country in the world. This abundance reflects Colombia's numerous climatic zones and microclimates, which have created many different habitats and biological islands in which wildlife has evolved independently.

Colombia is home to the jaguar, ocelot, peccary, tapir, deer, armadillo, spectacled bear and numerous species of monkey, to mention just a few of the 350-odd species of mammals. There are 1889 recorded species of birds (nearly a quarter of the world's total), ranging from the huge Andean condor to the tiny hummingbird. Colombia's flora is equally impressive and includes some 3000 species of orchid alone. The national herbariums have classified more than 130,000 plants.

SURVIVAL GUIDE

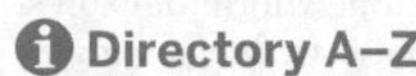

Directory A–Z

ACCOMMODATIONS

Colombia's backpacker market is growing daily, and with it comes the huge growth in facilities familiar to the continent. Even smaller, less-visited cities now have hostels with dormitories, internet, wi-fi, laundry services and travel advice. See www.colombianhostels.com for some of the most popular hostels in each city.

While dormitories are usually the cheapest option for budget travelers, private rooms in hostels in Colombia are often fancier and more expensive than local-oriented budget options. It's usually possible to find cheaper rooms, albeit with less facilities at your disposal, at local *hospedajes, residencias* and *posadas*.

A hotel generally suggests a place of a higher standard, and almost always has private bathroom, while *residencias, hospedajes* and *posadas* often have shared facilities.

Motels rent rooms by the hour. They're found on the outskirts of the city and usually have garish signs. Many Colombians live at home until marriage, so couples check in here for a few hours of passion and privacy.

Camping is gaining in popularity as the country's safety improves. Note that army-style kit is forbidden for private use.

SLEEPING PRICE RANGES

The following price ranges refer to a double room with bathroom.

$ less than COP$75,000

$$ COP$75,000 to COP$175,000

$$$ more than COP$175,000

ACTIVITIES

Hikers planning to visit remote national parks, including PNN El Cocuy, need to register their itineraries with the local **Parques Nacionales** (www.parquesnacionales.gov.co) office beforehand.

ELECTRICITY

Colombia uses two-pronged US-type plugs that run at 110V, 60Hz.

EMBASSIES & CONSULATES

Brazilian Embassy (☎1 218 0800; www.bogota.itamaraty.gov.br; Calle 93 No 14-20, piso 8, Bogotá) Also in Leticia (p621).

Canadian Embassy (☎1 657 9800; www.colombia.gc.ca; Carrera 7 No 114-33, Bogotá)

Ecuadorian Consulate (☎1 212 6512; www.colombia.embajada.gob.ec; Calle 89 No 13-07, Bogotá) Also in Ipiales (☎2 773 2292; Carrera 7 No 14-10).

French Embassy (☎1 638 1400; www.ambafrance-co.org; Carrera 11 No 93-12, Bogotá) Also in Bucaramanga (☎7 645 9393; www.bucaramanga.alianzafrancesa.org.co; Calle 42 No 37-19).

German Embassy (☎1 423 2600; www.bogota.diplo.de; Calle 110 No 9-25, 11th fl, Edificio Torre Empresarial Pacífic, Bogotá)

Panamanian Embassy (☎1 257 5067; www.panamaenelexterior.gob.pa/bogota; Calle 92 No 7A-40, Bogotá) Also in Barranquilla (☎5 360 1870; Carrera 57 No 72-25, Edificio Fincar 207-208); Cali (☎2 486 1116; Av 6 No 25-58, Piso 3); Cartagena (☎5 655 1055; Carrera 1 No 10-10, Bocagrande); Medellín (☎4 312 4590; Calle 10 No 42-45, oficina 266).

Peruvian Embassy (☎1 746 2360; www.embajadadelperu.org.co; Calle 80A No 6-50, Bogotá) Also in Leticia (☎8 592 7755; Calle 11 No 5-32).

UK Embassy (☎1 326 8300; www.ukincolombia.fco.gov.uk; Carrera 9 No 76-49, 8th fl, Bogotá)

US Embassy (☎1 275 2000; http://bogota.usembassy.gov; Calle 24 Bis No 48-50, Bogotá)

Venezuelan Embassy (☎1 644 5555; www.colombia.embajada.gob.ve; Carrera 11 No 87-51, 5th fl, Edificio Horizonte, Bogotá) Also in Barranquilla (☎5 360 6285; Carrera 52 No 69-96); Cartagena (☎5 665 0382; Edificio Centro Executivo, Carrera 3 No 8-129, Piso 14); Cúcuta (☎7 579 1951; http://cucuta.consulado.gob.ve; Av Camilo Daza at Calle 17, Cucutá); Medellín (☎4 444 0359; www.consulvenemedellin.org; Calle 32B No 69-59).

GAY & LESBIAN TRAVELERS

Compared with other Latin American nations, homosexuality is well tolerated in Colombia. Bogotá has the largest gay and lesbian community and the most open gay life; head to the Chapinero district for bars and clubs. Visit www.gaycolombia.com, which lists bars, discos, events, activities, publications and other related matters.

EATING PRICE RANGES

The following price ranges refer to a standard main course.

$ less than COP$15,000

$$ COP$15,000 to COP$30,000

$$$ more than COP$30,000

HEALTH

Colombia has some of the best medical facilities in South America, but they are not cheap. Many private clinics will not begin treatment (other than emergency stabilization) until your insurance has cleared or a deposit is made. Keep your travel-insurance details handy. Public hospitals are generally overcrowded and should be considered only as a last resort.

Tap water in the large cities is safe to drink, but in rural areas water should be boiled or disinfected with tablets.

Yellow-fever vaccinations are required for those visiting several national parks and may be required by your next destination after a visit to Colombia.

INTERNET ACCESS

Except for La Guajira, every place we have reviewed has public net access, and nearly every backpacker hostel has wi-fi. Internet connections are fastest in the major urban centers, while they can be pretty slow in some remote places. Access normally costs around COP$1500 to COP$2000 per hour. Many public spaces, including all town plazas in Antioquia, have free wi-fi.

LANGUAGE COURSES

Colombia can be a good place to study Spanish. The Spanish spoken in Colombia is clear and easy to understand and there are language schools in the big cities.

The most intense option is to enroll in a specialist language course at one of Colombia's major universities. They are able to organize long-term visas. Private language centers are often more costly but require less of a commitment.

LEGAL MATTERS

If arrested, you have the right to an attorney. If you don't have one, an attorney will be appointed to you (and paid for by the government). There is a presumption of innocence.

The most common situation that many travelers find themselves in involves drugs. It is illegal to buy or sell drugs in any quantity. The possession of small quantities of marijuana (22g) and cocaine (1g) for personalized use has been decriminalized by the Santos government and police are no longer authorized to detain civilians in these situations. However some officials may still attempt to shake down naive visitors.

If you do have to deal with the police, maintain a respectful attitude and ask to speak with a member of the Tourist Police, who are usually far less uptight than their bullet-dodging colleagues.

MAPS

The widest selection of maps of Colombia is produced and sold by the **Instituto Geográfico Agustín Codazzi** (IGAC; ☎ 369 4000; www.igac.gov.co; Carrera 30 No 48-51, Bogotá), the government mapping body. Folded national road maps are sold at the entrances of toll roads. They're really useful for off-the-beaten-track journey planning.

MONEY

Colombia's official currency is the peso. There are 50-, 100-, 200-, 500- and 1000-peso coins, and paper notes of 1000, 2000, 5000, 10,000, 20,000 and 50,000 pesos. No one ever has change, so try to avoid the biggest bills. Forged 50,000-peso notes are easy to spot for a local, not so for a visitor. While it's possible to change dollars, euros and other currencies in all cities, most travelers find it easy to rely on Colombia's extensive ATM network. Consider bringing a small stash of foreign currency (either US dollars or euros) for an emergency.

Bargaining is limited to informal trade and services such as markets, street stalls and unmetered taxis.

ATMs

Most towns have ATMs linked to Cirrus (Mastercard) and Plus (Visa) but they don't always work with all foreign cards. ATH machines are the most reliable.

Credit Cards

Credit cards are widely accepted in urban areas, and most banks offer peso advances. Visa is the best card for Colombia, followed by MasterCard.

Money Changers

Most major banks change cash and traveler's checks (principally Amex), though these are uncommon. The most useful bank is Bancolombia.

Currencies other than US dollars are best changed in major cities. Always take your passport original – not a copy.

You can also change cash at *casas de cambio* (authorized money-exchange offices), found in virtually all major cities and border towns. They are secure, efficient and offer similar rates to banks.

The only street money markets worth considering are those at border crossings, where there may be simply no alternative.

OPENING HOURS

The working day is usually eight hours long, from 8am to noon and 2pm to 6pm Monday to Friday. Many offices in bigger cities have adopted the *jornada continua,* a working day without a lunch break, which finishes two hours earlier.

Banks 9am to 4pm Monday to Friday (to 5pm in Bogotá), 9am to noon on Saturday, although varies by city and rural area.

Entertainment Bars from 6pm until around 2am; nightclubs from 9pm or 10pm until late from Thursday to Saturday.

Post Generally 9am to 5pm Monday to Friday (some Saturday morning) in Bogotá, varies widely elsewhere.

Restaurants 8am (for breakfast) or noon (for lunch) until 9pm (smaller cities) or 10pm (larger cities).

Shops 9am to 5pm Monday to Friday, 9am to noon or 5pm Saturday; large stores and supermarkets usually stay open till 8pm or 9pm Monday to Friday; some also open Sunday.

POST

The official Colombian postal service is operated by **4-72** (www.4-72.com.co). Postal charges in Colombia are exorbitant – a letter to the US costs around COP$10,000. Identification is required to ship packages or letters from Colombia, so head to the post office with your passport.

PUBLIC HOLIDAYS

The following holidays and special events are observed as public holidays in Colombia. When the dates marked with an asterisk do not fall on a Monday, the holiday is moved to the following Monday to make a three-day-long weekend, referred to as a *puente* (bridge).

There are three local high seasons, when Colombians rush to travel: late December to mid-January, the Easter Week, and mid-June to mid-July, when buses and planes get more crowded, fares rise and hotels fill up faster.

Año Nuevo (New Year's Day) January 1

Los Reyes Magos (Epiphany) January 6*

San José (St Joseph) March 19

Jueves Santo (Maundy Thursday) March/April, date varies

Viernes Santo (Good Friday) March/April, date varies

Día del Trabajador (Labor Day) May 1

La Ascensión del Señor (Ascension) May, date varies

Corpus Cristi (Corpus Christi) May/June*, date varies

Sagrado Corazón de Jesús (Sacred Heart) June*

San Pedro y San Pablo (St Peter & St Paul) June 29*

Día de la Independencia (Independence Day) July 20

Batalla de Boyacá (Battle of Boyacá) August 7

La Asunción de Nuestra Señora (Assumption) August 15*

Día de la Raza (Discovery of America) October 12*

Todos los Santos (All Saints' Day) November 1*

Independencia de Cartagena (Independence of Cartagena) November 11*

Inmaculada Concepción (Immaculate Conception) December 8

Navidad (Christmas Day) December 25

RESPONSIBLE TRAVEL

When visiting national parks, hire guides from the closest local community; not only are you creating jobs, you'll learn a whole lot more about the area than with a tour from the city.

Respect indigenous culture and beliefs – ask permission before taking pictures and only enter communities if you have been explicitly invited. Support local artisans by purchasing crafts direct at the source, but avoid those made from coral, turtles or fossils.

Colombians rarely talk politics with anyone but friends and you should follow their lead. The country is polarized by the conflict and many Colombians have first-hand experience of the violence. You never really know who you are talking to, or who is listening to your conversation, and it can be quite easy to offend someone if you start ranting about the government or guerrillas.

SAFE TRAVEL

If you use common sense, you'll find that Colombia is far safer for travelers than Venezuela, Ecuador and Brazil. Kidnapping of foreigners is almost unheard of these days, and urban attacks by FARC have been cut back to irrelevance.

Drugs

Consuming illegal drugs in Colombia directly funds the armed conflict that has killed hundreds of thousands of Colombians and displaced millions more around the country. Cocaine is widely available and you will likely be offered it at some point on your journey. If you do decide to take it, be aware that it is far stronger than in the US and UK. Paranoid delusions, tachycardia, stroke or overdose can and do occur. If somebody you are with overdoses, call an ambulance immediately, and tell the paramedics exactly what happened.

Burundanga is a legitimate concern. The usual method of administration is a spiked drink or cigarette. It is tasteless and odorless and renders victims senseless, only to wake up with no recollection of the previous few hours, minus their wallets and valuables. The drug is obtained from a nightshade species widespread in Colombia. Don't accept a drink, snack or cigarette from a stranger, especially when traveling alone, and especially on buses.

Guerrillas

The threat of guerrilla activity to travelers has decreased to such a point that traveling in the most visited areas of Colombia no longer requires any special planning.

Throughout the country cases of kidnapping for ransom have decreased significantly and, in 2012, shortly before the announcement of peace talks with the government, FARC publicly declared an end to the kidnapping of civilians. The smaller ELN guerrilla group has yet to sign up.

At the time of research, the principal areas of conflict were in rural Cauca, Chocó, Putumayo, southwest Nariño, the jungle region east of the Andes (excluding Leticia) and areas bordering Venezuela in Norte de Santander and Arauca.

TELEPHONE

Landline numbers are seven digits long. Area codes are single digits. If you are calling a landline from a cell phone you need to add '03' before the area code. Cell phone numbers are 10 digits and have no area codes.

Cell-phone networks are operated by Movistar, Claro and Tigo. Claro leads the pack for network coverage. You can buy a SIM card for around COP$5000.

If you need to make a call within Colombia, look for the fluorescent signs advertising '*minutos*' in small shops or the roaming vendors with various cell phones chained to their shirts. Calls cost from COP$150 to COP$300 per minute.

Colombia's country code is ☎57. Many internet places have a couple of booths for cheap international calls.

TOILETS

Public toilets are rare in Colombia and where they do exist, you'll almost always pay a fee to use them. The attendant will give you a miserly amount of toilet paper (it always pays to carry a spare roll). Most big shopping centers and museums have free toilets.

TOURIST INFORMATION

Municipal tourist information offices in departmental capitals and other popular destinations administer tourist information. In some locations, the tourist police also run an office. Colombia's main tourist information portal is the excellent www.colombia.travel.

VISAS

Nationals of many countries, including most of Western Europe, the Americas, Japan, Australia and New Zealand, don't need a visa to enter Colombia. It's a good idea for you to check this before your planned trip, as visa regulations change frequently.

All visitors get an entry stamp in their passport from Migración Colombia upon arrival at any international airport or land border crossing. Make sure your passport is stamped immediately. The stamp indicates how many days you can stay in the country; 90 days is most common. An onward ticket is legally required and you may be asked to show one. Upon departure, immigration officials put an exit stamp in your passport. Again, check it to avoid future problems.

Visa Extensions

Visitors are entitled to extend their stay into Colombia in 30-day increments up to a total of six months in a year by visiting Migración Colombia in any departmental capital.

To apply for an extension, known as a 'Prórroga de Permanencia,' you'll be asked to submit your passport, two photocopies of your passport (picture page and arrival stamp) and two passport-sized photos. You may also be asked for an air ticket out of the country.

VOLUNTEERING

Foreign volunteering is in its infancy in Colombia, but there are a number of organizations that accept travelers.

Tiempo de Juego (www.tiempodejuego.org) Welcomes volunteers to take part in sports-based programs for underprivileged children around Colombia.

Techo para mi País (www.techo.org) Accepts volunteers to work on its housing and social development projects in impoverished urban communities around Cali and Medellín.

Misíon Gaia (www.misiongaia.org) An environmental education project in the Sierra Nevada that is often looking for volunteers.

WOMEN TRAVELERS

Women traveling in Colombia's cities and rural areas are unlikely to get major hassle. Culturally, you'll have to deal with a little more machismo than at home: you'll definitely receive more overtly flirtatious attention from males simply for being foreign.

If you want to fend off unwelcome advances, dress conservatively. A cheap wedding band is also worth a shot.

WORK

It's illegal to work in Colombia on a tourist visa and you are potentially at risk of deportation, although in practice this is unlikely.

DEPARTURE TAX

The airport tax on international flights out of Colombia is US$37. It's usually included in your ticket, but check with your airline. A further exit tax of US$38 is payable if you have been in the country longer than two months. It is usually paid at the airport in US dollars or pesos but may also be included in your ticket.

You may be able to find some informal work teaching English, but your pay will probably barely cover your costs. Professionally run language institutes will arrange working visas for their teachers.

Some hostel and bar owners offer work to backpackers, however, think twice about accepting such an offer as it takes jobs away from a sector of Colombian society where they are desperately needed.

Getting There & Away

Flights, cars and tours can be booked online at lonelyplanet.com/bookings.

AIR

Sitting on the northwestern edge of the continent, Colombia is a convenient and reasonably cheap gateway to South America from the US and even from Europe. Despite their proximity, flights between Central America and Colombia are generally fairly expensive.

Bogotá has Colombia's major international airport, but some other cities including Cartagena, Medellín and Cali also handle international flights.

The country is serviced by many major international airlines, including Air Canada, Air France, Iberia, United and American Airlines, and several regional carriers. Budget carriers Spirit and JetBlue fly to Colombia from the US, while local low-cost operator VivaColombia flies to Panama, Quito and Lima.

LAND

Almost all travelers crossing between Ecuador and Colombia use the Carretera Panamericana border crossing through Ipiales and Tulcán.

There are several crossings between Colombia and Venezuela although recent political tensions have seen the borders closed on occasion – check the latest before setting out.

The most popular crossing with travelers is the route via Cúcuta and San Antonio del Táchira, on the main Bogotá–Caracas road. Another major border crossing is at Paraguachón, on the Maicao–Maracaibo road. There are shared taxis between Maicao and Maracaibo, and direct buses between Cartagena and Caracas.

There is no overland route between Colombia and Panama, but it is possible to deliver a car between the two countries on a cargo ship. The pick-up and drop-off points are Colón and Cartagena.

RIVER & SEA

Regular riverboat services connect Leticia in the Colombian Amazon with Iquitos, Peru and Manaus, Brazil.

There is one passenger ship and many private sailboats running between Colón in Panama and Cartagena in Colombia. It's also possible to cross from Colombia to the San Blas region in Panama via small boat from Capurganá/Sapzurro.

ℹ Getting Around

AIR

Colombia has a well-developed airline system and a solid network of domestic flights. The most commonly used passenger airlines include **Avianca** (☎1 401 3434; www.avianca.com), **Copa** (☎1 320 9090; www.copaair.com) and **LAN** (☎1 800 094 9490; www.lan.com), all of which also have international flights. **Satena** (☎1 800 091 2034; www.satena.com) services more remote domestic destinations.

Budget airline **VivaColombia** (☎4 444 9489; www.vivacolombia.co) serves a growing number of cities around the country.

BUS

Buses are the main means of getting around Colombia. The bus system is well developed and extensive, reaching even the smallest villages. Buses range from ordinary bangers to modern-day luxury liners.

The best buses have plenty of leg room, reclining seats, large luggage compartments and toilets. Carry warm clothes, as drivers usually set the air-con to full blast.

On the main routes buses run frequently, so there is little point in booking a seat in advance. In some places off the main routes, where there are only a few buses daily, it's better to buy a ticket some time before departure. The only time you really need to book is during the Christmas and Easter periods, when hordes of Colombians are on holiday.

Colectivos are a cross between a bus and a taxi. They are usually large cars (sometimes jeeps or minibuses) that cover fixed routes, mainly over short and medium distances. They leave when full, not according to a schedule, and are a reasonable option if there is a long wait for the next bus or if you are in a hurry.

Bus travel is reasonably cheap in Colombia. As a rule of a thumb, the *climatizado* (air-conditioned) bus costs roughly COP$8000 for every hour of travel. When demand is low, it's often possible to arrange a discount from the list price.

CAR & MOTORCYCLE

Traveling around with your own vehicle is getting easier in Colombia. There are still security concerns in some remote parts of the country, but your main danger nowadays is haphazard Colombian drivers and the shocking condition of some of the highways.

Hiring vehicles is expensive in Colombia and with cheap taxis in the cities and comfortable intercity buses it makes little sense to do so.

Driver's License

If you plan on driving in Colombia your foreign driver's license is technically sufficient, but avoid debates with traffic cops by obtaining an International Driving Permit.

Ecuador

Includes ➡

Best Adventures

- ➡ Climbing Cotopaxi (p667)
- ➡ Whitewater rafting near Tena (p689)
- ➡ Mountain biking down Chimborazo (p674)
- ➡ Trekking to Ingapirca (p683)
- ➡ Wildlife-watching on the Galápagos Islands (p710)

Best Places to Stay

- ➡ Secret Garden Cotopaxi (p668)
- ➡ La Luna (p664)
- ➡ Pululahua Hostel (p660)
- ➡ Black Sheep Inn (p669)
- ➡ Cuyabeno Lodge (p688)

Why Go?

Amazonian rainforest, snow-covered mountains, premontane cloud forests and the Galápagos Islands set the stage for incredible adventures in this small Andean nation. You can spend one day whitewater rafting and the next gazing up to the summit of a 6000m-high volcano. You can take dramatic treks through the *páramo* (high-altitude grassland), surf excellent breaks off the west coast, and hike, mountain bike or simply unwind amid dramatic scenery.

Wildlife-watching is another way to enjoy Ecuador, with dozens of animal and plant species found nowhere else on earth. Even on a short adventure, it's possible to photograph monkeys from jungle canopy towers, swim with sea lions in the Pacific and see some of 1600 bird species in misty forests.

Ecuador harbors a rich cultural heritage, from gorgeous Spanish colonial centers to traditional highland towns, where buzzing Kichwa markets and baroque 16th-century churches are all part of the dramatically varied landscape.

When to Go

Quito

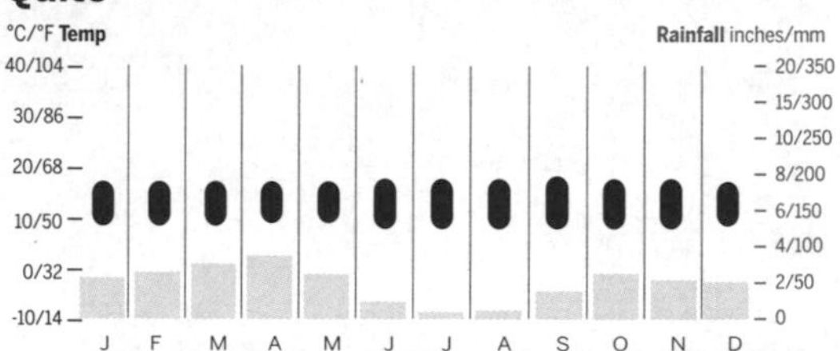

Jun–Sep Best weather for visiting the highlands with less rain and warmer, clearer days.

Oct & Nov Best time to visit the Amazon (Oriente): rivers are passable, and it's not too wet.

Dec–May Rainy season on the coast, but sunny and lush between downpours – good beach days.

Connections

Major border crossings into Peru are at busy Tumbes–Aguas Verdes (near the coast), Macará and La Balsa (a few hours south of Vilcabamba); hardy travelers with heaps of time can also go by river via Nuevo Rocafuerte. To Colombia, the safest crossing (and the only one we recommend) is at Tulcán–Ipiales, a few hours northwest of Ibarra.

ITINERARIES

Three Weeks

Begin your trip in Quito. Spend two days soaking up the architectural gems of the Old Town, then head northwest to the lush cloud forests of Mindo, continuing east to Otavalo for its famous Saturday markets and hikes around alpine lakes. Next go to Coca, gateway to the Amazon. Spend a few nights at a jungle lodge on the lower Río Napo. On your way back to Quito, stop in Tena, for a whitewater rafting trip, and Baños, for thermal baths, waterfalls and great scenery. End the tour amid spectacular Andean scenery near Cotopaxi or Quilotoa.

Six Weeks

From Quito head west, spending a week exploring the coast: beach days in Canoa, whale-watching in Puerto López and surf culture in Montañita. Continue onto Guayaquil and fly out to the Galápagos Islands for a week of wildlife-watching and island-hopping. Back in Guayaquil, head east to lovely Cuenca. Visit nearby Parque Nacional Cajas, and the Inca ruins of Ingapirca. Continue south to Loja and the stunning cloud forests of Parque Nacional Podocarpus, and then onto peaceful Vilcabamba, a scenic base for outdoor adventures.

Essential Food & Drink

- **Llapingachos** Fried potato-and-cheese pancakes, often served with fried eggs and roast meat.
- **Seco de chivo** Goat stew.
- **Locro de papa** Creamy potato soup served with avocado and cheese.
- **Churrasco** Fried beef, eggs and potatoes, a few veggies, slices of avocado and tomato, and rice.
- **Arroz con pollo** Rice with small pieces of chicken mixed in.
- **Cuy** Roasted guinea pig.
- **Ceviche** Marinated raw seafood.
- **Encocado** Shrimp or fish cooked in a rich coconut sauce.
- **Encebollado** Seafood and onion soup over *yuca* (cassava) and served with *chifles* (fried banana chips) and popcorn.
- **Sopa marinera** Soup loaded with fish, shellfish, shrimp and sometimes crab.

AT A GLANCE

- **Currency** US dollar
- **Language** Spanish
- **Money** ATMs in cities and larger towns; credit cards accepted only at high-end places
- **Visas** not required for most nationalities
- **Time** GMT minus five hours

Fast Facts

- **Area** 283,560 sq km
- **Population** 16 million
- **Capital** Quito
- **Emergency** ☎131 (ambulance)
- **Country code** ☎593

Exchange Rates

Australia	A$1	US$0.73
Canada	C$1	US$0.76
Euro zone	€1	US$1.10
Japan	¥100	US$0.83
New Zealand	NZ$1	US$0.68
UK	UK£1	US$1.53

Set Your Budget

- **Hostel bed** US$7-10
- **Two-course evening meal** US$10
- **Almuerzo (fixed-price set lunch)** US$2.75
- **Six-hour bus ride** US$6

Resources

- **Lonely Planet** (lonelyplanet.com/ecuador)
- **Hip Ecuador** (www.hipecuador.com)
- **Ministry of Tourism Ecuador** (http://ecuador.travel)

Ecuador Highlights

1. Delve into Quito's picturesque **Old Town** (p638), its cobblestones streets crisscrossing one of Latin America's finest colonial centers.
2. Experience the **Amazon** (p687) by staying in a jungle lodge, taking wildlife-watching excursions and visiting indigenous villages.
3. Snorkel with sea lions, spot penguins, and come face to face with gigantic tortoises on the spectacular **Galápagos Islands** (p710).
4. Haggle over handmade treasures in **Otavalo** (p663), home to one of South America's biggest open-air markets.
5. Hike in cloud forests, cool off in waterfalls and go zip-lining over the canopy in pretty **Mindo** (p661).
6. Trek past topaz lakes and peaceful villages high up in the Andes on the **Quilotoa Loop** (p669).
7. Chill out on the beach in the surf-loving town of **Montañita** (p701).

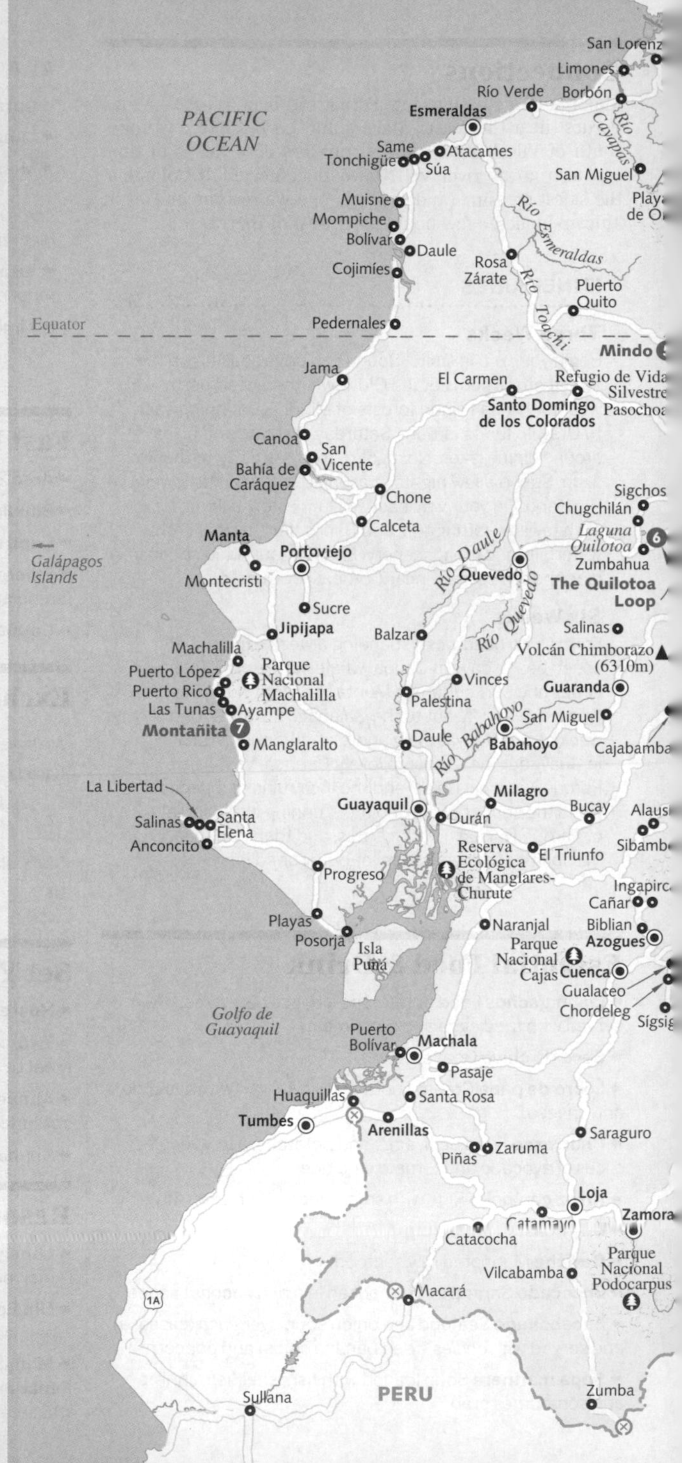

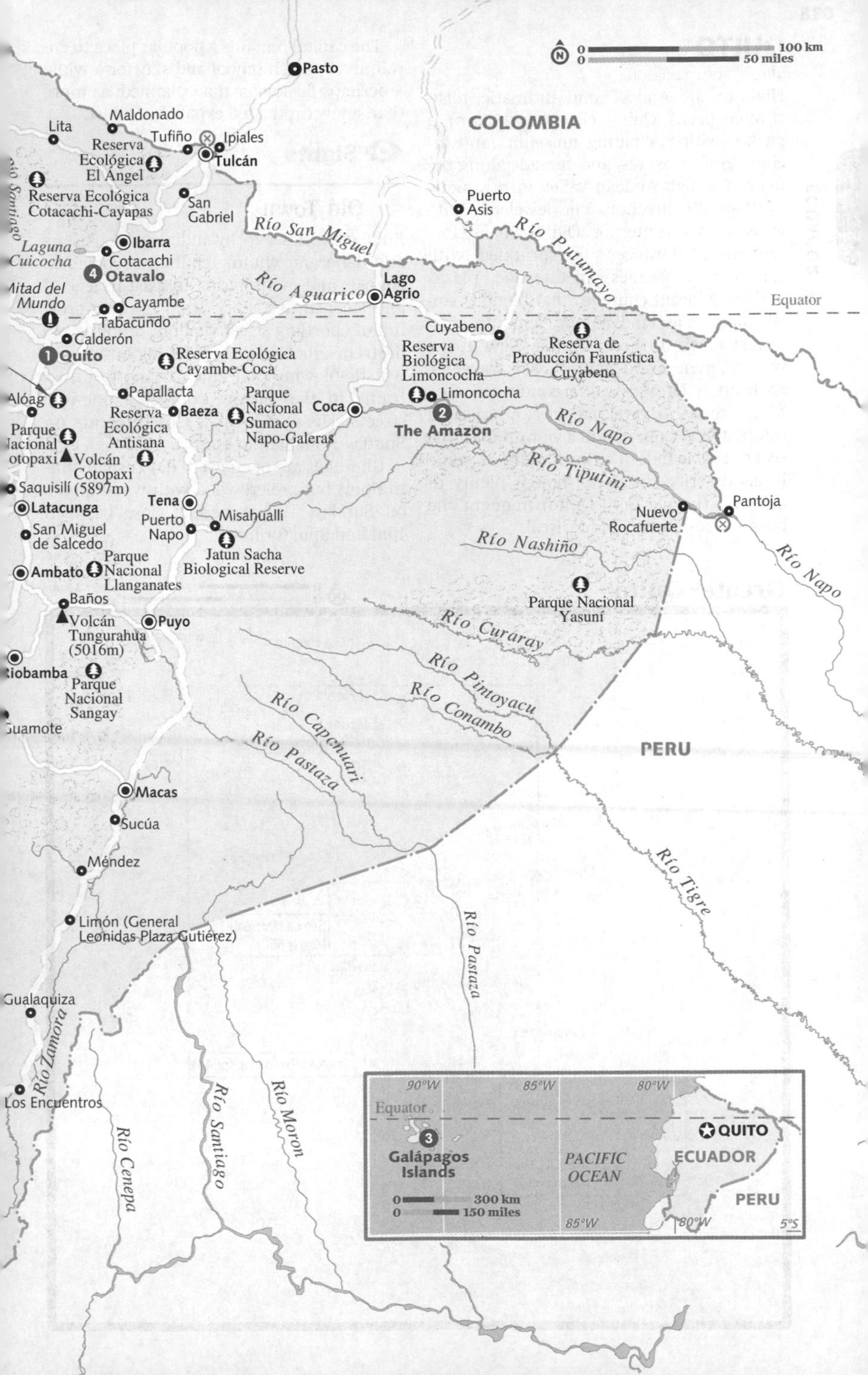

0 100 km
0 50 miles
Pasto
COLOMBIA
Maldonado
Lita
Tufiño
Ipiales
Reserva
Ecológica
El Ángel
Tulcán
Reserva Ecológica
Cotacachi-Cayapas
San
Gabriel
Puerto
Asis
Río San Miguel
Río Putumayo
Laguna
Cuicocha
Ibarra
Cotacachi
4 Otavalo
Río Aguarico
Lago
Agrio
Mitad del
Mundo
Cayambe
Tabacundo
Equator
Calderón
1 Quito
Reserva Ecológica
Cayambe-Coca
Cuyabeno
Reserva
Biológica
Limoncocha
Reserva de
Producción Faunística
Cuyabeno
Alóag
Papallacta
Parque
Nacional
Sumaco
Napo-Galeras
Limoncocha
Reserva
Ecológica
Antisana
Baeza
Coca
2
The Amazon
Río Napo
Parque
Nacional
Cotopaxi
Volcán
Cotopaxi
(5897m)
Río Tiputini
Saquisilí
Latacunga
Tena
Puerto
Napo
Misahuallí
Nuevo
Rocafuerte
Pantoja
San Miguel
de Salcedo
Río Nashiño
Parque
Nacional
Llanganates
Jatun Sacha
Biological Reserve
Río Napo
Ambato
Baños
Volcán
Tungurahua
(5016m)
Puyo
Parque Nacional
Yasuní
Río Curaray
Riobamba
Parque
Nacional
Sangay
Río Pintoyacu
Río Conambo
Guamote
Río Capahuari
Río Pastaza
PERU
Macas
Sucúa
Méndez
Río Tigre
Limón (General
Leonidas Plaza Gutiérez)
Río Pastaza
Gualaquiza
Río Zamora
Los Encuentros
Río Santiago
Río Moron
Río Cenepa
90°W
85°W
80°W
Equator
3
Galápagos
Islands
QUITO
PACIFIC
OCEAN
ECUADOR
PERU
0 300 km
0 150 miles
85°W
80°W
5°S

QUITO

02 / POP 1.7 MILLION

High in the Andes amid dramatic mist-covered peaks, Quito (elevation 2850m) is packed with fascinating museums and architectural treasures, and spreads along the floor of a high Andean valley in a roughly north–south direction. The jewel of Quito is its historic center, or 'Old Town,' a Unesco World Heritage site, sprinkled with 17th-century facades, picturesque plazas and magnificent churches that blend Spanish, Moorish and indigenous elements.

Just north of there, Quito's 'New Town' is a different world entirely. For travelers, its heart is La Mariscal, a condensed area of guesthouses, travel agencies, ethnic and international eateries and a vibrant nightlife scene. This is indeed 'gringolandia' as some locals describe the area, though plenty of *quiteños* (people from Quito) frequent the bars and restaurants of Mariscal.

The capital remains a popular place to enroll in a Spanish school and stay for a while – perhaps far longer than planned, as more than a few captivated expats can attest.

Sights

Old Town

Built centuries ago by indigenous artisans and laborers, Quito's churches, convents, chapels and monasteries are cast in legend and steeped in history. It's a bustling area, full of chortling street vendors, ambling pedestrians, tooting taxis, belching buses, and whistle-blowing policemen trying to direct traffic in the narrow, congested one-way streets. The Old Town is closed to cars on Sunday from 8am to 4pm.

Churches are open every day (usually until 6pm) but are crowded with worshippers on Sunday. They generally close between 1pm and 3pm for lunch.

Greater Quito

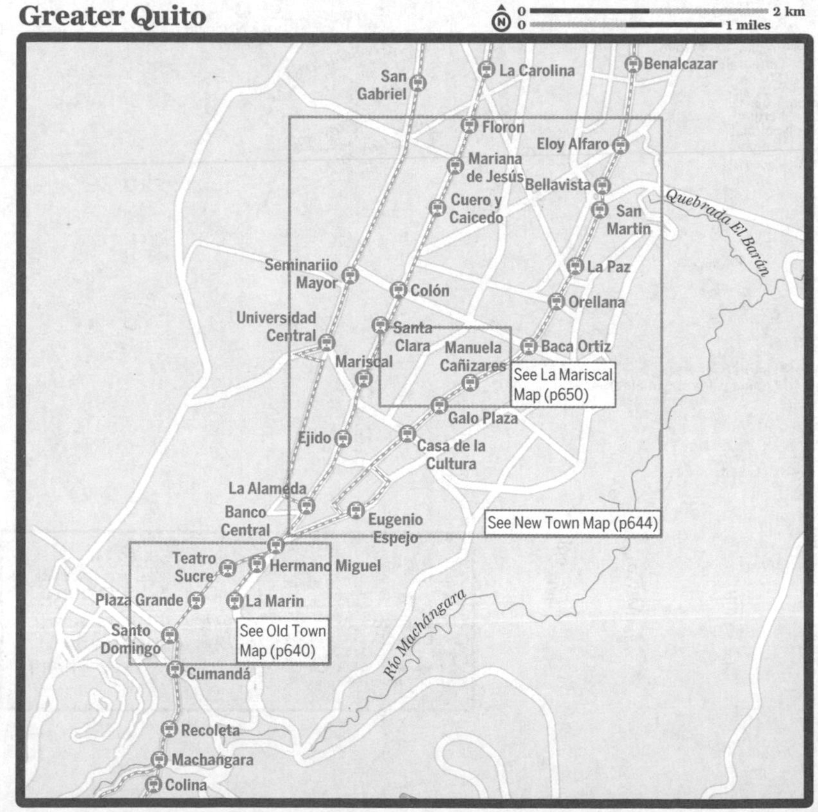

Plaza Grande PLAZA

(Plaza de la Independencia; Map p640) While wandering around colonial Quito, you'll probably pass through the Plaza Grande (formally known as Plaza de la Independencia) several times. Its benches are great for soaking up the Andean morning sun and watching the bustle all around.

Palacio del Gobierno NOTABLE BUILDING

(Presidential Palace; Map p640; Moreno; ⏲guided tours 10am, 11:30am, 1pm, 2:30pm & 4pm) FREE The white building on the plaza's northwest side is the seat of the Ecuadorian presidency. Visitors can enter by guided tours (in Spanish and sometimes English), which offer a glimpse of the brilliantly hued mosaic depicting Francisco de Orellana's descent of the Amazon and a few of the staterooms. The president carries out business in this building, so sightseeing is limited to rooms not currently in use. On Monday, the changing of the guards takes place on the plaza at 11am.

Cathedral CHURCH

(Catedral Primaria; Map p640; Plaza Grande; admission $1.50; ⏲9am-5:15pm Mon-Sat) On Plaza Grande's southwest side stands Quito's cathedral. Although not the most ornate of the Old Town's churches, it has some fascinating religious works from artists of the Quito School. You'll also see the ornate tomb of Mariscal Sucre, the leading figure of Quito's independence. And behind the main altar is a plaque marking where President Gabriel García Moreno died on August 6, 1875; after being slashed with a machete outside the Palacio del Gobierno, he was carried, dying, to the cathedral.

Palacio Arzobispal NOTABLE BUILDING

(Archbishop's Palace; Map p640; Chile) On the northeast side of the plaza, this former archbishop's palace is now a colonnaded row of small shops and restaurants, located between García Moreno and Venezuela. Concerts are often held on the covered patio on weekends.

Centro Cultural Metropolitano ARTS CENTER

(Map p640; cnr Moreno & Espejo; ⏲9am-5pm Tue-Sun, patio to 7:30pm) FREE Just off Plaza Grande, this beautifully restored building houses the municipal library and lecture rooms and hosts temporary art exhibitions. The location is rich in history: supposedly the pre-Hispanic site of one of Atahualpa's palaces; a Jesuit school from 1597 to 1767; an army barracks after the expulsion of the Jesuits in the late 1700s; and in 1809 the site at which royalist forces held a group of revolutionaries, before murdering them a year later.

★**Iglesia de la Compañía de Jesús** CHURCH

(Map p640; www.fundacioniglesiadelacompania.org.ec; García Moreno & Sucre; adult/student $4/2; ⏲9:30am-6:30pm Mon-Fri, to 4pm Sat, 12:30-4pm Sun) Capped by green-and-gold domes, La Compañía de Jesús is Quito's most ornate church and a standout among the baroque splendors of the Old Town. Free guided tours in English or Spanish highlight the church's unique features, including its Moorish elements, perfect symmetry (right down to the *trompe l'oeil* staircase at the rear), symbolic elements (bright-red walls are a reminder of Christ's blood) and its syncretism (Ecuadorian plants and indigenous faces hidden along the pillars).

Iglesia y Monasterio de San Francisco CHURCH, MONASTERY

(Map p640; Cuenca near Sucre; ⏲7-11am daily, 3-6pm Mon-Thu) FREE Construction of the monastery, the city's largest colonial structure, began only a few weeks after the founding of Quito in 1534, but wasn't finished for another 70 years. Although much of the church has been rebuilt because of earthquake damage, some is original. The **chapel of Señor Jesús del Gran Poder**, to the right of the main altar, has original tile work. The **main altar** itself is a spectacular example of baroque carving, while much of the roof shows Moorish influences.

El Museo Francisco MUSEUM

(Museo Fray Pedro Gocial; Map p640; Cuenca 477 & Sucre; admission $2; ⏲9am-5:30pm Mon-Sat, to 1pm Sun) To the right of the Iglesia de San Francisco's main entrance, and within the Convent of St Francis, this museum contains some of the church's finest artwork including paintings, sculpture and 16th-century furniture, some of which is fantastically wrought and inlaid with thousands of pieces of mother-of-pearl. The admission fee includes a guided tour in English or Spanish.

Casa del Alabado MUSEUM

(Map p640; ☎02-228-0940; www.alabado.org; Cuenca N1-41; admission $4; ⏲9:30am-5:30pm) Housed in a stolid-looking colonial-era home, this privately owned museum with

Old Town

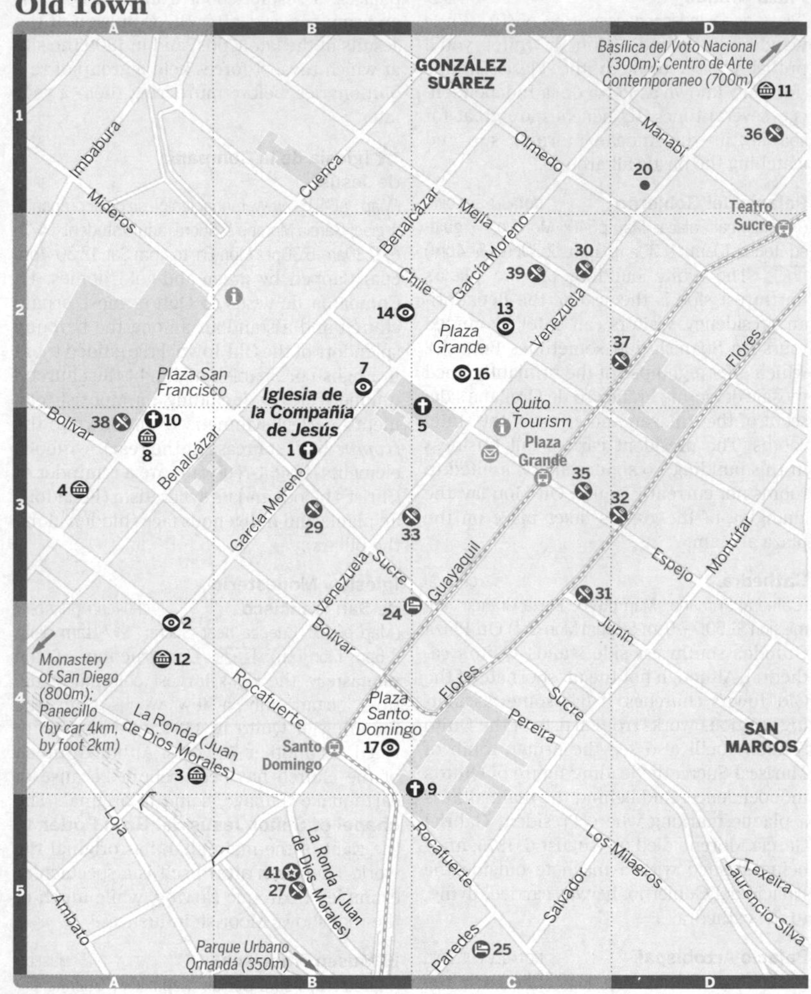

contemporary-style displays showcases an impressive collection of pre-Columbian artifacts. Thematically organized around subjects such as shamans and the afterlife, explanations in English and Spanish (audio guides are available) explore the indigenous beliefs represented by the finely crafted ceramic pieces and jewelery.

Museo de la Ciudad MUSEUM

(Map p640; ☎02-295-3643; www.museociudadquito.gob.ec; García Moreno near Rocafuerte; admission $3; ⏱9:30am-4:30pm Tue-Sun) Just past the 18th-century arch, **Arco de la Reina** (cnr García Moreno & Rocafuerte), built to give shelter to churchgoers, this first-rate museum depicts Quito's daily life through the centuries, with displays including dioramas, model indigenous homes and colonial kitchens. The 1563 building itself (a former hospital) is a work of art. Admission includes a free guided tour in Spanish. Guides are also available in English and French (for an extra $4).

Plaza Santo Domingo PLAZA

(Map p640) Plaza Santo Domingo, near the southwest end of Calle Guayaquil, is a reg-

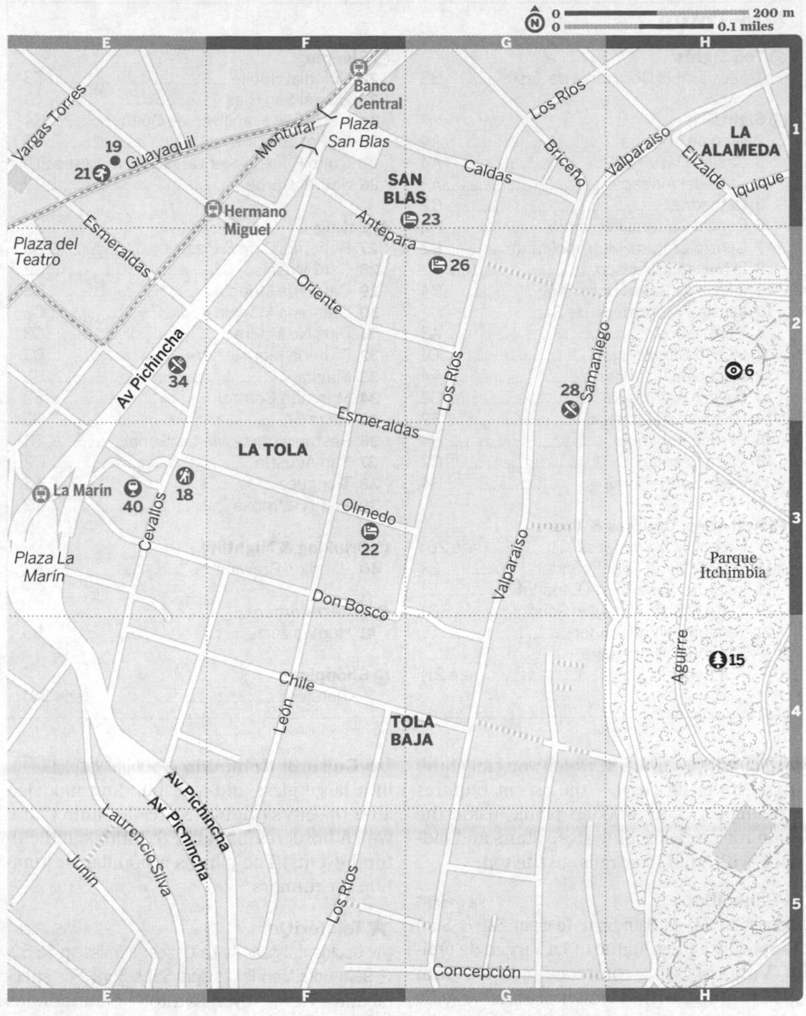

ular haunt for street performers. Crowds of neighborhood *quiteños* fill the plaza to watch pouting clowns and half-cocked magicians do their stuff. The plaza is beautiful in the evening, when the domes of the 17th-century **Iglesia de Santo Domingo** (cnr Flores & Rocafuerte; 7am-1pm & 5-7pm) FREE, on the southeast side of the plaza, are floodlit.

Museo Camilo Egas MUSEUM
(Map p640; Venezuela 1302 & Esmeraldas; 8am-5pm Tue-Sat, 10am-4pm Sat & Sun) FREE Inside a restored colonial home, there is a small but iconic collection of work by painter Camilo Egas (1899–1962), Ecuador's first *indigenista* (indigenous movement) painter. One of the galleries showcases temporary exhibitions by contemporary painters.

Basílica del Voto Nacional CHURCH
(cnr Venezuela & Carchi; admission church/tower $1/2; 9am-4:30pm) High on a hill in the northeastern part of the Old Town looms this massive Gothic church, built over several decades beginning in 1926. Rather than gargoyles, however, turtles and iguanas protrude from the church's side. The highlight

Old Town

is the basilica's **towers**, which you can climb if you have the nerve – the ascent requires crossing a rickety wooden plank inside the main roof and climbing steep stairs and ladders (with solid handrails) to the top.

El Panecillo VIEWPOINT

(admission $1; 9am-6pm, to 5pm Sat & Sun) Topped by a huge statue of La Virgen de Quito (Virgin of Quito; construction lasted from 1955 to 1975), with a crown of stars, angelic wings and a chained dragon atop the world, the hill to the south of Old Town called El Panecillo (the Little Bread Loaf) is a major Quito landmark. *Quiteños* proudly claim she is the only Madonna in the world depicted with wings. From the summit, there are marvelous views of the sprawling city and the surrounding volcanoes.

Parque Itchimbia PARK, VIEWPOINT

(Map p640) High on a hill of the Old Town, this grassy park boasts magnificent views of the city. It's the perfect spot to spread out a picnic lunch, soak up the sun and take in the views. The park's centerpiece is the **Centro Cultural Itchimbia** (hours vary) FREE, in a large glass-and-iron building modeled after the city's original Mercado Santa Clara, which hosts regular art exhibitions and cultural events. The park is a popular destination for runners.

★TeleferiQo VIEWPOINT

(Av Occidental near Av La Gasca; admission $8.50; 9am-6pm Mon-Fri, to 8pm Sat & Sun) For spectacular views over Quito's mountainous landscape, hop aboard this sky tram that takes passengers on a 2.5km ride (10 minutes) up the flanks of Volcán Pichincha to the top of Cruz Loma. Once you're at the top (a mere 4100m), you can hike to the summit of Rucu Pichincha (4680m), about a three-hour hike for fit walkers – some scrambling is required and you should ask about the safety situation before attempting.

New Town

★Museo Nacional MUSEUM

(Map p644; cnr Av Patria & Av 12 de Octubre; 8:30am-4:30pm Tue-Fri, 10am-4pm Sat & Sun)

FREE Located in the circular, glass-plated, landmark building of Casa de la Cultura Ecuatoriana is one of the country's largest collections of Ecuadorian art, with magnificent works of pre-Hispanic and colonial religious art. The Sala de Arqueología showcases more than 1000 ceramic pieces dating from 12,000 BC to AD 1534; displays in the Sala de Oro (Gold Room) include a magnificent radiating, golden sun mask; and the Sala de Arte Colonial (Colonial Art Room) showcases masterful works from the Quito School.

Quito Observatory MUSEUM

(Map p644; Parque la Alameda; admission $2; 10am-5pm Tue-Sun) Opened by President García Moreno in 1864, this four-sided observatory is the oldest on the continent. It houses a museum of 19th-century pendulums, sextants, chronometers and other historic instruments, and opens for stargazing on Thursday and Friday nights (with sessions at 6pm and 7:30pm, admission $3) – but only go if the sky is clear. It sits inside the small Parque La Alameda.

Centro de Arte Contemporáneo MUSEUM

(www.centrodeartecontemporaneo.gob.ec; Dávila & Venezuela; 9am-5:30pm Tue-Sun) FREE Inside a beautifully restored former military hospital, this excellent museum showcases cutting-edge multimedia exhibits as well as top modern-art shows that travel to the city. There's a cafe on-site.

Parque La Carolina PARK

(Map p644) North of the Mariscal lies the giant Parque La Carolina, which fills with families on weekends who come out for paddleboats, soccer and volleyball games, and exercise along the bike paths.

Jardín Botánico GARDENS

(Map p644; www.jardinbotanicoquito.com; adult/child $3.50/2; 9am-5pm) Parque Carolina's most popular attraction is this peacefully set botanical garden with native habitats covering *páramo* (high-altitude Andean grasslands), cloud forest, wetlands and other areas, plus an *orquideario* (orchid greenhouse), ethnobotanical garden (exploring the plants used by indigenous groups) and Amazonian greenhouse. There's also a kids' play/discovery area.

★ **Museo Guayasamín** MUSEUM

(www.guayasamin.org; Calvache E18-94 & Chávez, Bellavista; adult/senior & student/child $6/3/free, incl Capilla del Hombre; 10am-5pm Tue-Sun) In the former home of the legendary painter Oswaldo Guayasamín (1919–99), this wonderful museum houses the most complete collection of his work. Guayasamín was also an avid collector, and the museum displays his outstanding collection of pre-Columbian ceramic, bone and metal pieces.

Capilla del Hombre ART MUSEUM

(Chapel of Man; www.guayasamin.org; Calvache E18-94 & Chávez, Bellavista; adult/senior & student/child $6/3/free, incl Museo Guayasamín; 10am-5pm Tue-Sun) A few blocks away from the Museo Guayasamín stands one of the most important works of art in South America, Guayasamín's **Capilla del Hombre**. The fruit of Guayasamín's greatest vision, this giant monument-cum-museum is a tribute to humankind, to the suffering of Latin America's indigenous poor and to the undying hope for something better. It's a moving place and the tours (in English, French and Spanish, included in the price) are highly recommended. They usually leave upon request during opening hours.

Mindalae – Museo Etnográfico de Artesanía de Ecuador MUSEUM

(Map p644; Reina Victoria N26-166 & La Niña; admission $3; 9am-6pm Mon-Sat) Just north of the Mariscal, this small but worthwhile museum exhibits the artwork, clothing and utensils of Ecuador's indigenous people, with special emphasis on the peoples of the Oriente. It's run by the outstanding Fundación Sinchi Sacha, and there's a nice outdoor cafe on-site (open 7am to midnight).

Santuario de Guápulo CHURCH

(El Calvario N27-138; admission $1.50; 8am-5:30m, sometimes closed for lunch) At the bottom of the hill above Guápulo stands the neighborhood's centerpiece, the 17th-century Santuario de Guápalo. It has an excellent collection of Quito School art and sculpture, and a stunning 18th-century pulpit carved by master wood-carver Juan Bautista Menacho.

Activities

Quito is one of the best places to hire guides and organize both single- and multiday excursions.

Those seeking local adventure can spend the day rock climbing, hiking and cycling – all within city limits. The Old Town's old bus terminal has been converted into **Parque Urbano Qmandá** (02-257-3645; 24 de Mayo),

New Town

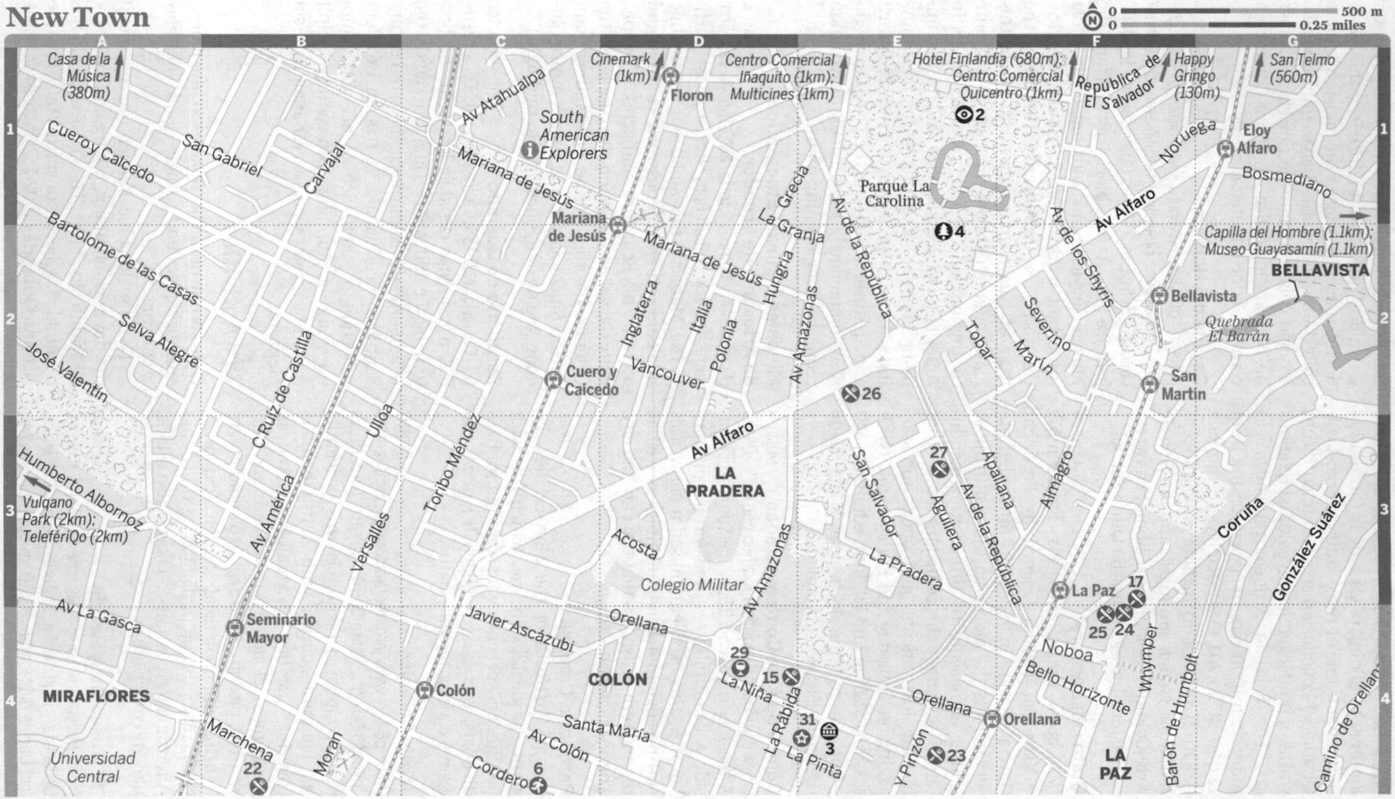

0 500 m
0 0.25 miles

Casa de la Música (380m)
Cinemark (1km)
Floron
Centro Comercial Iñaquito (1km); Multicines (1km)
Hotel Finlandia (680m); Centro Comercial Quicentro (1km)
República de El Salvador
Happy Gringo (130m)
San Telmo (560m)
Av Atahualpa
South American Explorers
2
Cueroy Calcedo
San Gabriel
Carvajal
Mariana de Jesús
Parque La Carolina
Noruega
Eloy Alfaro
Bosmediano
Mariana de Jesús
Grecia
La Granja
Av de la República
4
Av Alfaro
Av de los Shyris
Capilla del Hombre (1.1km); Museo Guayasamín (1.1km)
BELLAVISTA
Bartolome de las Casas
Hungria
Bellavista
Selva Alegre
Inglaterra
Italia
Polonia
Av Amazonas
Tobar
Severino
Marín
Quebrada El Barán
José Valentín
C Ruiz de Castilla
Cuero y Caicedo
Vancouver
26
San Martín
Ulloa
Toribo Méndez
Av Alfaro
27
Apallana
Almagro
Humberto Albornoz
Vulqano Park (2km); TeleféríQo (2km)
Av América
LA PRADERA
San Salvador
Aguilera
Av de la República
Coruña
González Suárez
Versalles
Acosta
Av Amazonas
La Pradera
Colegio Militar
La Paz
17
Av La Gasca
Seminario Mayor
Javier Ascázubi
Orellana
25
24
Noboa
29
Whymper
MIRAFLORES
Colón
COLÓN
15
La Niña
Bello Horizonte
Orellana
Orellana
Barón de Humbolt
Camino de Orellana
Marchena
Santa María
La Rábida
31
3
Moran
Av Colón
La Pinta
Y Pinzón
23
LA PAZ
Universidad Central
22
Cordero
6

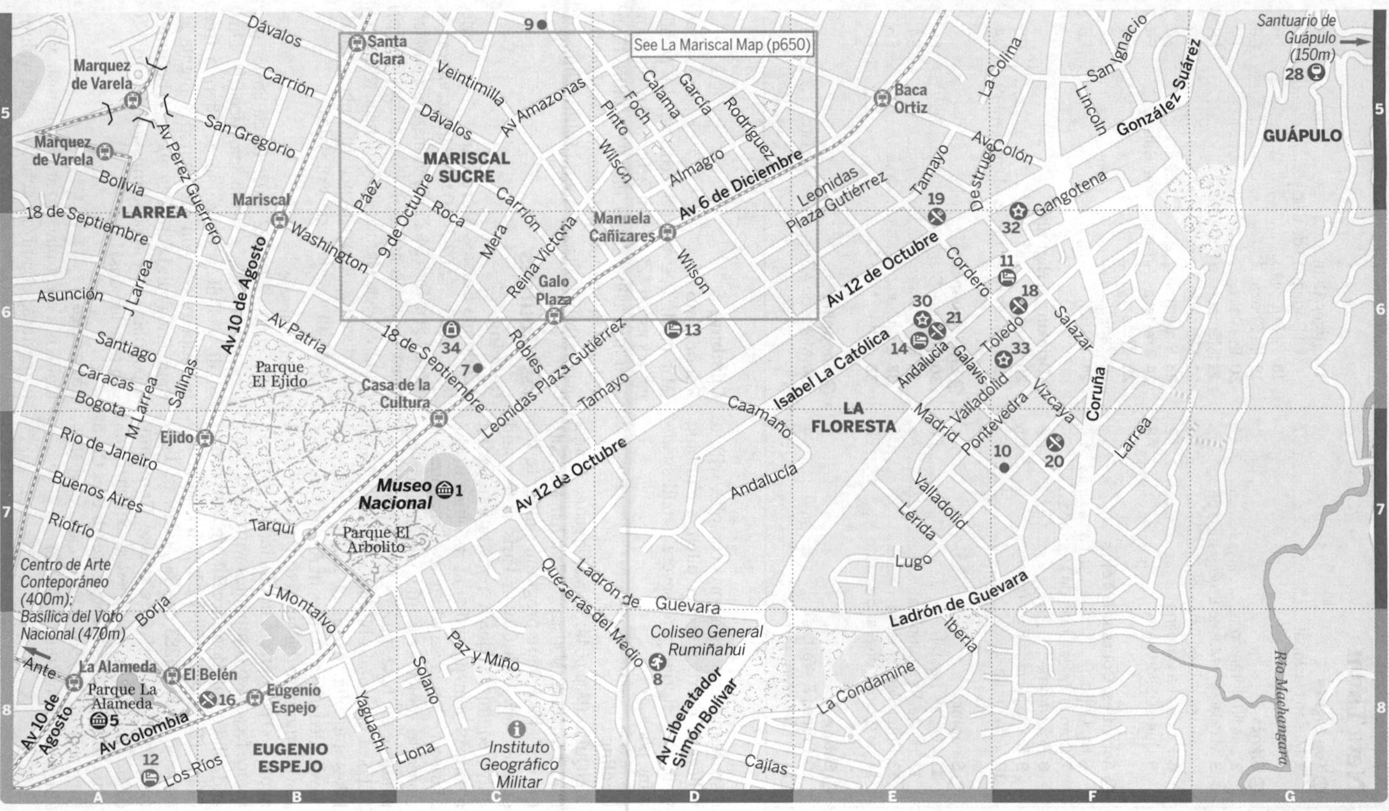

See La Mariscal Map (p650)
Santuario de Guápulo (150m)
28
GUÁPULO
González Suárez
San Ignacio
Lincoln
La Colina
Av Colón
Destruge
Baca Ortiz
Gangotena
32
Tamayo
19
Leonidas Plaza Gutiérrez
Av 6 de Diciembre
Rodríguez
García
Calama
Foch
Pinto
Almagro
Wilson
Manuela Cañizares
Av 12 de Octubre
Cordero
11
18
30
21
Toledo
33
14
Andalucía
Galavis
Salazar
Coruña
Vizcaya
Valladolid
Pontevedra
Madrid
10
20
Larrea
Isabel La Católica
LA FLORESTA
Caamaño
Andalucía
Valladolid
Lérida
Lugo
Ladrón de Guevara
Iberia
La Condamine
Cajías
Av Liberatador Simón Bolívar
Coliseo General Rumiñahui
8
Ladrón de Guevara
Queseras del Medio
Paz y Miño
Solano
Yaguachi
Llona
Instituto Geográfico Militar
Río Machangara
9
Santa Clara
Veintimilla
Av Amazonas
Dávalos
MARISCAL SUCRE
Carrión
Páez
9 de Octubre
Roca
Mera
Reina Victoria
Galo Plaza
13
Wilson
34
7
18 de Septiembre
Robles
Leonidas Plaza Gutiérrez
Tamayo
Casa de la Cultura
Av Patria
Parque El Ejido
Museo Nacional 1
Parque El Arbolito
Av 12 de Octubre
Tarqui
J Montalvo
Dávalos
Carrión
Marquez de Varela
San Gregorio
Av Perez Guerrero
Bolivia
LARREA
18 de Septiembre
Mariscal
Washington
Av 10 de Agosto
Asunción
J Larrea
Santiago
Caracas
Bogota
M Larrea
Salinas
Ejido
Rio de Janeiro
Buenos Aires
Riofrío
Centro de Arte Conteporáneo (400m); Basílica del Voto Nacional (470m)
Borja
Ante
La Alameda
El Belén
Parque La Alameda
5
16
Eugenio Espejo
EUGENIO ESPEJO
Av 10 de Agosto
Av Colombia
12
Los Ríos
A
B
C
D
E
F
G
5
6
7
8

New Town

Top Sights

1 Museo Nacional C7

Sights

2 Jardín Botánico E1
3 Mindalae – Museo Etnográfico de Artesanía de Ecuador E4
4 Parque La Carolina E2
5 Quito Observatory A8

Activities, Courses & Tours

6 BiciQuito C4
7 Compañía de Guías de Montaña C6
8 Rocódromo D8
9 Sierra Nevada Expeditions C5
10 Vida Verde F7

Sleeping

11 Aleida's Hostal F6
12 Hostel Revolution A8
13 Hotel Sierra Madre D6
14 La Casona de Mario E6

Eating

15 Crepes & Waffles D4
16 Frutería Monserrate B8
17 Jürgen Cafe F3
La Bodeguita de Cuba .... (see 31)
18 La Briciola F6
19 La Choza E6
20 La Cleta F7
21 Mercado La Floresta E6
22 Mercado Santa Clara B4
23 Supermaxi E4
24 Traviesas Artesanos del Cafe F4
25 Z(inc) F4
26 Zao E2
27 Zazu E3

Drinking & Nightlife

28 Ananké G5
29 Turtle's Head Pub & Microbrewery D4

Entertainment

30 El Pobre Diablo E6
31 El Veradero E4
32 La Juliana F6
33 Ocho y Medio F6

Shopping

34 Mercado Artesanal La Mariscal C6

a sparkling, covered sports complex with a volleyball court, a soccer pitch, a climbing wall, yoga studios and several small swimming pools.

Cycling

BiciQuito (Map p644; www.biciq.gob.ec; Cordero 1221 & Joaquin, Mariscal; 7am-7pm Mon-Sat), the city's bike-share program, similar to the ones in New York City or Paris, is free and only requires a quick registration (bring a copy of your passport) at its office in the Mariscal. Sundays, when Av Amazonas is closed to vehicular traffic, you can register at any of the bike stations around town.

Local mountain-biking companies rent bikes and offer excellent single- and two-day guided off-road rides in Andean settings you'd otherwise never see. Day trips cost about $50 per person, not including park entrance fees. Two companies with good bikes and solid reputations are **Biking Dutchman** (Map p650; 02-256-8323; www.bikingdutchman.com; Foch E4-283 near Av Amazonas; 1-day tours from $50) and **Arie's Bike Company** (02-238-0802; www.ariesbikecompany.com). You can hire bikes through **Retro Bici Club** (Map p650; 099-502-9088; Av Amazonas N23-78 near Wilson; half/full day $8/12).

Climbing

Rocódromo ROCK CLIMBING
(Map p644; Queseras del Medio s/n, La Vicentina; admission $2; 8am-7:30pm) An outdoor 25m-high climbing facility with more than a dozen routes on the main walls. Located across from Coliseo General Rumiñahui.

Courses

Dancing

Academia Salsa & Merengue DANCE
(Map p650; 02-222-0427; tropicaldancing@hotmail.com; Foch E4-256 & Av Amazonas; private/group lessons per hr $10/6; 10am-8pm Mon-Fri) Run by Sylvia Garcia, a pro dancer with several decades of experience, this place offers lessons in a wide variety of styles.

Ritmo Salvaje DANCE
(Map p650; 02-222-4603; García E5-45; private lessons $10; 10am-8pm Mon-Fri) This small, well-liked dance space offers a free introductory lesson on Thursday nights at 8pm. Friday and Saturday nights, it becomes a popular salsa spot (admission $3; free if you take lessons).

Language

Quito is a great place to study Spanish, with homestays, organized activities and volunteer opportunities on offer. Group/private lessons start at $8/10 per hour.

Ecole Idiomas LANGUAGE COURSE

(Map p650; ☎02-601-4757; www.ecoleidiomas.com; García E6-15 near Mera) Conversation-based group ($7 per hour) and private ($10 per hour) Spanish classes held in a beautiful, old building with wood floors, a garden in front and a great lounge space in back on a busy Mariscal street. Salsa classes every Wednesday and a sign-up board with other activities on offer.

Quito Antiguo Spanish School LANGUAGE COURSE

(Map p640; ☎02-228-8454; www.quitoantiguospanish.com; Venezuela 1129) Housed in a run-down and somewhat dismal building in the center of the Centro Histórico, Quito Antiguo offers a wide range of study options (including courses for older learners), a variety of excursions, inexpensive apartment rentals and homestays.

Yanapuma Language School LANGUAGE COURSE

(Map p640; ☎02-254-6709; www.yanapuma.org; Guayaquil N9-59 & Oriente) This excellent foundation-run school is located in the heart of the Centro Histórico in an old building with a light-filled courtyard. A $25 registration fee goes to the foundation, which supports sustainable development in indigenous communities, as do profits from the conversation-focused lessons. Salsa lessons every Tuesday and Ecuadorian snacks on Wednesday.

Vida Verde LANGUAGE COURSE

(Map p644; ☎02-252-4333; www.vidaverde.com; Madrid E13-137 near Lugo, La Floresta) A recommended Ecuadorian-owned school in an airy and bright converted home with a kitchen, lounge and small lending library in a university neighborhood. Feels out of the way if staying in the Mariscal. Can also arrange for travel and study in the rainforest (near Tena or Coca) and on the coast (at Puerto López and at Rio Muchacho Organic Farm near Canoa). Ten percent of profits go to environmental and social projects in Ecuador.

Tours

Quito is one of the easiest places in Ecuador to arrange a guided tour, be it a Galápagos cruise, climbing trip or jungle tour. Be sure to stop by on weekdays; many offices close on weekends.

CarpeDM Adventures GUIDED TOUR

(Map p640; ☎02-295-4713; www.carpedm.ca; Antepara E4-70) CarpeDM earns high marks for its affordable prices and wide range of tours, though it's the excellent service that makes this agency, run by the friendly, reliable and knowledgeable Paul Parreno, stand out from many others. Day trips to Cotopaxi, Otavalo and Mindo for those short on time. Free walking tours of the Old Town Monday through Friday. The office is in the Secret Garden Hostel in the San Blas part of the Old Town.

Compañía de Guías de Montaña ROCK CLIMBING

(Map p644; ☎02-290-1551; www.companiadeguias.com; Av 6 de Diciembre N20-50 & Washington) Top-notch mountain-climbing operator, with guides who are all Asociación Ecuatoriana de Guías de Montaña (ASEGUIM; Ecuadorian Association of Mountain Guides) instructors and who speak several languages.

Condor Trek ADVENTURE TOUR

(Map p650; ☎02-222-6004; Reina Victoria N24-295) Reputable climbing operator offers guided climbs up most of Ecuador's peaks.

Eos Ecuador GUIDED TOUR

(Map p650; ☎02-601-3560; www.eosecuador.travel; Av Amazonas N24-66 & Pinto) Eos offers a full range of climbing, trekking, Galápagos and Amazon trips, as well as stays in community-oriented tourism initiatives.

Gulliver GUIDED TOUR

(Map p650; ☎02-252-9297; www.gulliver.com.ec; Mera 24-156 near Calama) Well-regarded operator offering hiking, climbing, mountain-biking and horse-riding trips in the Andes. Excellent prices, daily departures.

Happy Gringo GUIDED TOUR

(☎02-512-3486; www.happygringo.com; Aldaz N34-155 near Portugal, Edificio Catalina Plaza, 2nd fl) A British- and Dutch-owned company catering to a midrange market, Happy Gringo can organize week- to month-long customized itineraries throughout the country, from the Galápagos to the Amazon. Professionally run with English-speaking guides and private drivers available, it's one of the best all-around tour companies in the city.

Safari Tours GUIDED TOUR
(Map p650; ☎02-255-2505; www.safari.com.ec; Reina Victoria N25-33, 10th fl, near Av Colon) Excellent reputation and long in the business. Offers all range of tours and trips, from volcano climbs and jungle trips to local jeep tours and personalized off-the-beaten-track expeditions. Located in the Mariscal.

Sierra Nevada Expeditions ADVENTURE TOUR
(Map p644; ☎02-255-3658; www.sierranevadatrek.com; Pinto 4E-152 near Cordero) Long in the business, Sierra Nevada offers climbing and river-rafting trips. Owner Freddy Ramirez is well established and a very reputable mountain guide.

Tropic GUIDED TOUR
(☎888-207-8615; www.tropiceco.com; Pasaje Sanchez Melo near Av Galo Plaza Laso) Long-standing agency offering numerous three- to six-day tours to the Oriente, the Andes and cloud forests.

Yacu Amu Rafting ADVENTURE TOUR
(Map p650; ☎02-290-4054; www.raftingecuador.com; Foch 746 near Mera) Excellent river-rafting operator with daily departures to the Río Toachi and Río Blanco and several other Class III to IV options.

Free Walking Tour Ecuador WALKING TOUR
(Map p640; www.freewalkingtourecuador.com; Cevallos N6-78) Local Ecuadorean guides give daily (except Sunday) tours beginning at 10:30am from the Community Hostel in the Old Town. Free, but tips expected.

Festivals & Events

The city's biggest party celebrates the founding of Quito in the first week of December, when bullfights are held daily at Plaza de Toros. On New Year's Eve, life-size puppets (often of politicians) are burned in the streets at midnight. **Carnaval** is celebrated with intense water fights – no one is spared. Colorful religious processions are held during Easter week.

Sleeping

Most travelers stay in the Mariscal neighborhood so they can be near the many bars, cafes and restaurants. Street noise can be an issue at many places but is especially bad in the Mariscal.

While lacking in Thai restaurants and expat bars, the Old Town has much better colonial ambience, and you won't feel like you're bunking in gringolandia.

Adjacent to the Mariscal, the hip La Floresta neighborhood has a few inviting places to stay.

Old Town

★ **La Posada Colonial** GUESTHOUSE $
(Map p640; ☎02-228-2859; www.laposadacolonial.com; Paredes S1-49 & Rocafuerte; r per person $11; @ 📶) A no-brainer for those looking for low-key, low-budget non-hostel accommodations in the Old Town. It's even within stumbling distance of La Ronda. The rooms have high ceilings and wood floors, and most have several beds, making it good value for groups. Bathrooms, however, are compact. It has a small, unfinished rooftop with good views and a kitchen for guests' use.

Quito Backpacker Guesthouse GUESTHOUSE $
(Map p640; ☎02-257-0459; www.quitobackpackerguesthouse.com; cnr Oriente E3-108 & Léon, San Blas; dm $7, r $20, without bathrom $9; 📶) A great choice for those seeking hostel prices with a family-run guesthouse vibe. Newly opened at the time of our visit, this large converted colonial home in the San Blas neighborhood has several floors of spacious, high-ceilinged, wood-floor rooms; kitchens on every floor; and a rooftop terrace with views of the Old Town.

Secret Garden HOSTEL $
(Map p640; ☎02-295-6704; www.secretgardenquito.com; Antepara E4-60, San Blas; dm $11, d $39, without bathroom $32; @ 📶) This perennially popular hostel has an undeniably social vibe, and wallflowers or those seeking privacy will want to head elsewhere. Long-term travelers getting by on bartending jobs in Quito and others on the South America circuit swap stories over a beer on the rooftop terrace with magical views over the Old Town. You'll also find simple but clean wood-floor rooms.

Colonial House HOSTEL $
(Map p640; ☎02-316-3350; www.colonialhousequito.com; Olmedo E-432 & Los Ríos; dm $10, r $25, without bathroom $20; @ 📶) The facade might be colonial but there's nothing stately, historic or elegant about this haphazardly designed guesthouse. In fact, it's fairly messy, especially the neglected backyard garden where you can camp or work out with weights (these might be centuries old). The 16 guest rooms are variously shaped as well as variously appealing, though all have (sloping) wood floors.

Hostal San Blas HOTEL $
(Map p640; ☎02-228-9480; www.hostalsanblas.com.ec; Caldas E1-38, Plaza San Blas; s/d $15/24, without bathroom $13/20) Because of its location on an attractive plaza and convenience to public transportation, San Blas is an acceptable option for those who don't mind, small, dim windowless rooms (despite the cheesy yellow walls). Discounts to use the small gym next door.

Hostel Revolution GUESTHOUSE $
(Map p644; ☎02-254-6458; www.hostelrevolutionquito.com; Los Ríos N13-11 near Castro; dm/s/d/tr $10/15/27/33; @📶) For an escape from the Mariscal circus, this colonial is an excellent, laid-back option with comfy rooms, shared kitchen, terrace with views and colorful bar-lounge where you can meet other travelers. Just a block uphill from Parque La Alameda.

★**Hotel San Francisco de Quito** HOTEL $$
(Map p640; ☎02-228-7758; www.sanfranciscodequito.com.ec; Sucre Oe3-17; s/d $32/51; @📶) No exaggerating, stepping through the medieval-looking doorway into the bright, plant-filled inner courtyard of this historic hotel is like being transported to another century. Specifically, to 1698 when the bones of this house were originally built. There's a variety of differently configured and sized rooms, though all are wood floored and have cozy furnishings.

La Mariscal

Blue House GUESTHOUSE $
(Map p650; ☎02-222-3480; www.bluehousequito.com; Pinto E8-24; dm $8, d $30, without bathroom $24; @📶) This friendly guesthouse has eight pleasant rooms (four dorm rooms, with six to eight beds, and four private rooms) with wood floors in a converted house on a quiet street. It has a front concrete 'garden' space for occasional barbecues, a comfy lounge with fireplace, and a kitchen for guest use.

Magic Bean GUESTHOUSE $
(Map p650; ☎02-256-6181; www.magicbeanquito.com; Foch E5-08 & Mera; dm/s/d $14/28/36; 📶) Better known for its lively restaurant, the Magic Bean has just four rooms – all very tidy and nicely designed. Light sleepers beware: it can get noisy on the weekends.

Casa Helbling GUESTHOUSE $
(Map p650; ☎02-222-6013; www.casahelbling.de; Veintimilla E8-152 near Av 6 de Diciembre; s/d $32/44, without bathroom $21/32; @📶) In a homey, colonial-style house in the Mariscal, Casa Helbling is clean, relaxed and friendly; and it has a guest kitchen, laundry facilities and relaxing common areas.

El Cafecito HOSTEL $
(Map p650; ☎02-223-4862; www.cafecito.net; Cordero 1124; dm $8, r per person $25, without bathroom $15; 📶) Inside a yellow colonial house with graffitti scrawled on the outside wall, this is a popular budget choice, mostly for its mellow vibe and charming cafe-restaurant. The wood-floored dorm rooms are fine, if small and well worn. The claustrophobic private rooms are best avoided.

Vibes HOSTEL $
(Map p650; ☎02-255-5154; www.vibesquito.com; Pinto near Av 6 de Diciembre; dm $9; 📶) This messy, seven-room hostel with fourth-hand furniture in a converted colonial is good for those looking to party in the Mariscal with other travelers. Sunday mornings, it has the look and feel of a frat house recovering from a blowout the night before. The owner is friendly and laid-back, and there's a bar and pool table.

★**Hostal El Arupo** GUESTHOUSE $$
(Map p650; ☎02-255-7543; www.hostalelarupo.com; Rodríguez E7-22; s/d/tw incl breakfast $30/45/48; @📶) A cozy and homey refuge from nearby Plaza Foch's madness, El Arupo is a spotless and warmly decorated converted house with a small, lovely front patio. The rooms have dark wood floors and firm beds. It also offers an immaculate communal kitchen where breakfast is served and a small lounge. Its sister hotel, **El Arupo Bed & Breakfast** (Map p650; ☎02-252-3528; www.hostalelarupo.com; García E5-45; s/d $25/42; P📶), has smaller wood-floored rooms and is on a noisier block.

Hotel Sierra Madre GUESTHOUSE $$
(Map p644; ☎02-250-5687; www.hotelsierramadre.com; Veintimilla 464; s/d $66/79; @📶) In a handsomely restored colonial building, the Sierra Madre has 21 rooms of varying size. Most have wood floors, excellent beds and a warm color scheme, while the best quarters have vaulted ceilings and verandas. There's a restaurant below.

★**Café Cultura** GUESTHOUSE $$$
(Map p650; ☎02-222-4271; www.cafecultura.com; Robles 513; s/d $100/122; @📶) This atmospheric old mansion-turned-guesthouse

La Mariscal

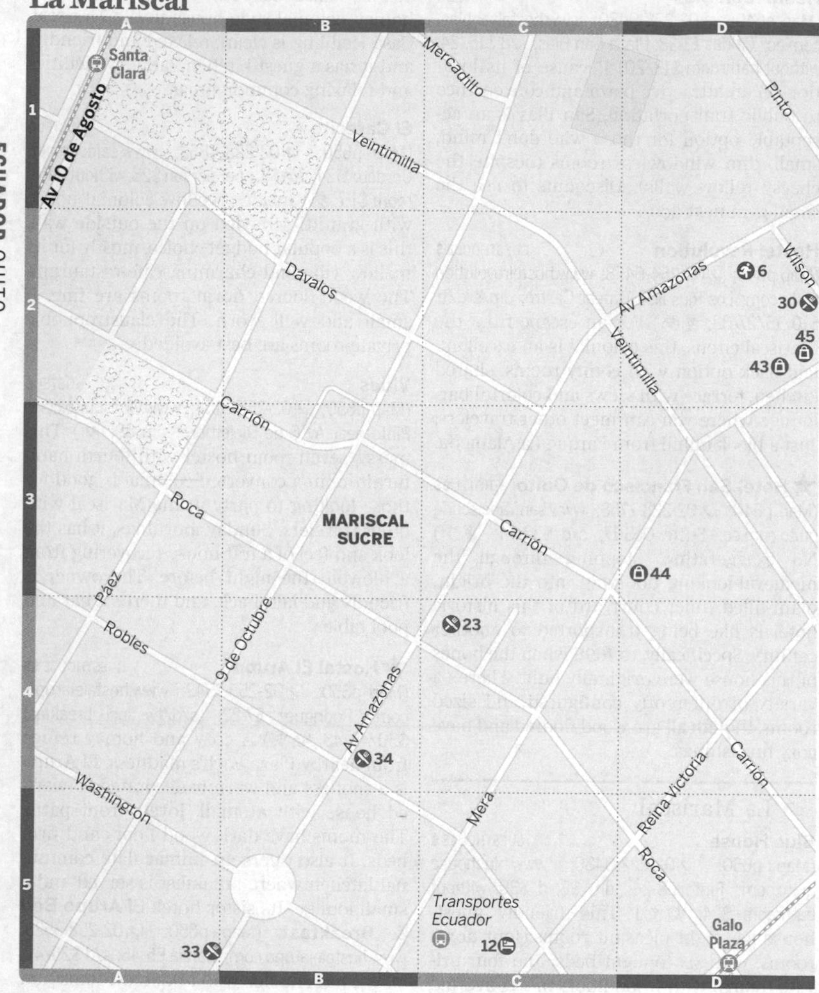

has a garden, crackling fireplaces, a first-rate cafe-restaurant and handsome mural-filled bedrooms.

La Floresta & Around

La Casona de Mario GUESTHOUSE $
(Map p644; ☎02-254-4036; www.casonade-mario.com; Andalucía N24-115; r per person without bathroom $12;) In a lovely old house, La Casona de Mario is outstanding value, with homey rooms, shared bathrooms, a flower-filled garden, TV lounge and guest kitchen.

Aleida's Hostal GUESTHOUSE $$
(Map p644; ☎02-223-4570; www.aleidashostal.com.ec; Andalucía 559; s/d $28/45, without bathroom $19/34; @) This friendly, family-run guesthouse in La Floresta has comfortably furnished rooms with wood floors. The best (like No 15) have fine views; others are dark with internal windows.

Eating

Quito has a rich and varied restaurant scene, with all budgets and tastes catered for. You'll find everything from sleek sushi bars to

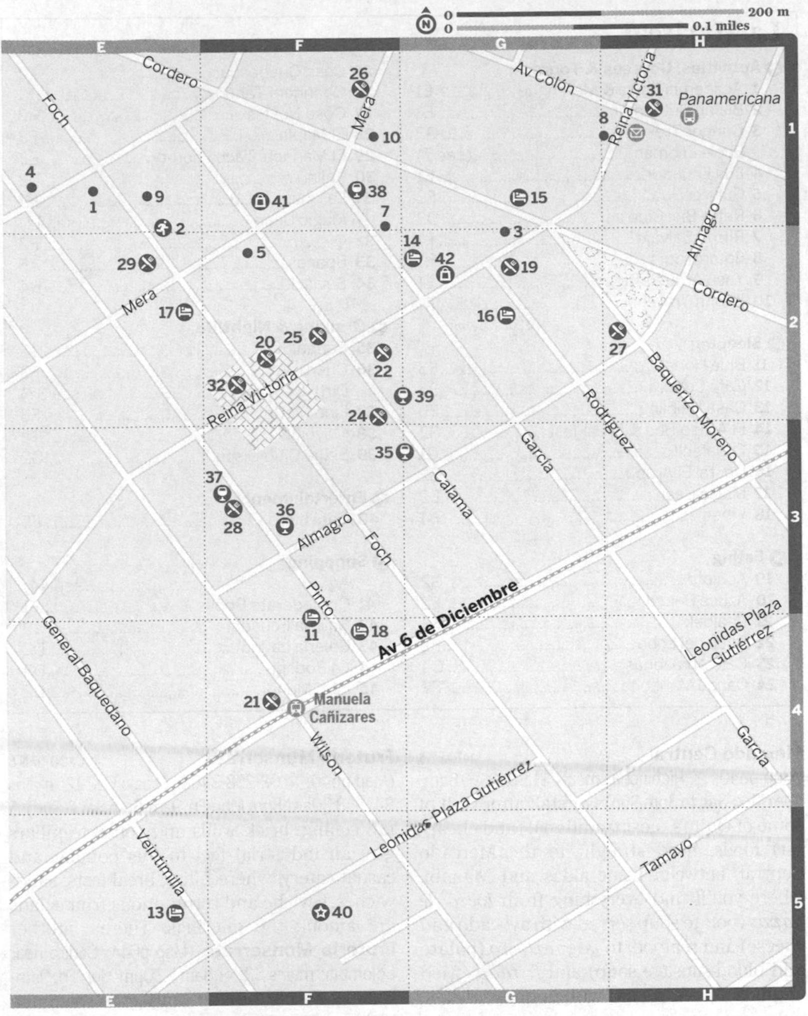

old-fashioned dining rooms serving up Andean classics.

The Mariscal has the densest concentration of restaurants, with local and international eateries. For more high-end dining, look to La Floresta, La Pradera and neighboring areas: these are home to the city's best restaurants.

If you're low on funds, stick to good-value *almuerzos* or *meriendas* (fixed-price set lunches and dinners). Many restaurants close on Sunday.

Old Town

★Bohemia Cafe & Pizza PIZZA $

(Map p640; La Ronda; medium pizza $12) Feel like a *Quiteño* at this tiny spot on happening (on weekend nights) La Ronda where the wonderfully energetic owner will greet you like family on repeat visits. The menu, though limited, has excellent pizza and layered nachos made with homemade corn chips. And you can't beat $4 for a giant *micheladas*, a mix of beer, lime, salt and various salsas.

La Mariscal

Activities, Courses & Tours
1 Academia Salsa & Merengue E1
2 Biking Dutchman E1
3 Condor Trek G2
Ecole Idiomas .... (see 7)
4 Eos Ecuador E1
5 Gulliver F2
6 Retro Bici Club D2
7 Ritmo Salvaje F1
8 Safari Tours H1
9 Yacu Amu Rafting E1
10 Zenith Travel F1

Sleeping
11 Blue House F3
12 Café Cultura C5
13 Casa Helbling E5
14 El Arupo Bed & Breakfast G2
15 El Cafecito G1
16 Hostal El Arupo G2
17 Magic Bean E2
18 Vibes F4

Eating
19 Achiote G2
20 Azuca Beach F2
21 Baalbek F4
22 Boca del Lobo F2
23 Café Amazonas C4
24 Canoa Manabita F2
25 Casa Quebecua F2
26 Chandani Tandoori F1
27 Cosa Nostra H2
28 El Maple F3
29 El Mariachi Taco Factory E2
30 Kallari D2
31 La Union H1
Magic Bean .... (see 17)
32 Q F2
33 Spanes A5
34 Suvlaki B4

Drinking & Nightlife
35 Bungalow 6 .... G3
36 Cherusker F3
Dirty Sanchez .... (see 37)
37 Finn McCool's F3
38 Mayo 68 .... F1
39 Selfie Club Disco G2

Entertainment
40 Café Libro F5

Shopping
Ag .... (see 44)
41 Confederate Books F1
42 Galería Ecuador G2
43 Galería Latina D2
44 La Bodega D3
45 Libri Mundi D2

Mercado Central MARKET **$**
(Map p640; Av Pichincha; meals $1.50-4; 8am-4pm Mon-Sat, to 3pm Sun) For stall after stall of some of Quito's most traditional (and cheapest) foods, head straight to the Mercado Central, between Esmeraldas and Manabí, where you'll find everything from *locro de papas* (potato soup served with avocado and cheese) and seafood, to *yaguarlocro* (potato and blood-sausage soup) and *fritada* (fried chunks of pork, served with hominy).

Cafetería Modelo ECUADORIAN **$**
(Map p640; cnr Sucre & García Moreno; mains $2-5; 8am-8pm Mon-Sat, to 6pm Sun) Opened in 1950, Modelo is one of the city's oldest cafes and a great spot to try traditional snacks such as *empanadas de verde* (empanadas made with plantain dough), *quimbolitos* (sweet, cakelike corn dumplings) and tamales. **Cafetería Modelo II** (Map p640; Venezuela N6-19; mains $2-5; 8am-8pm Mon-Sat, to 6pm Sun) offers the same old-world trappings (plus live music some weekend nights) on Venezuela.

Frutería Monserrate ECUADORIAN **$**
(Map p640; 02-258-3408; Espejo Oe2-12; mains $4; 8:30am-8pm Mon-Fri, 9am-6pm Sat & Sun) A tall ceiling, brick walls and concrete pillars give an industrial feel to this popular and casual eatery, where filling breakfasts, sandwiches, ceviche and scrumptious fruit salads are among the offerings. There's another **Frutería Monserrate** (Map p644; Sodiro near Colombia; mains $2; 8am-7:30pm Mon-Fri, 9am-5pm Sat & Sun) on the border between the Old and New Town just north of Parque La Alameda.

Restaurante Govindas Gopal VEGETARIAN **$**
(Map p640; Esmeraldas 853; mains $1.50; 9am-3pm Mon-Sat;) Proudly serving 100% vegetarian cuisine, the Krishna devotees here whip up tasty, fresh lunch plates from a changing menu, plus yogurt and granola, juices and sweets.

Magda SUPERMARKET **$**
(Map p640; Venezuela N3-62; 8:30am-7pm Mon-Sat, 9am-5pm Sun) A conveniently located and well-stocked supermarket.

★Dios No Muere STEAKHOUSE, INTERNATIONAL $$
(Map p640; cnr Junin & Flores; mains $5.50-17.50; ⊙8am-10pm Mon-Sat) The Louisiana native who owns this eccentrically designed restaurant attached to a 17th-century monastery rightfully takes pride in the quality of the Ecuadorian and imported meats cooked up in the kitchen squeezed into a corner on the ground floor. Space fills up fast, as there are only two tables on each of the next two tiny floors, plus a few alleyway tables.

San Agustín ECUADORIAN $$
(Map p640; Guayaquil N5-59; mains $6-9; ⊙9:30am-6pm Mon-Fri, 10:30am-4pm Sat & Sun; 📶) Kitschy religous icons and old-fashioned radios decorate this old-school classic serving Ecuadorian fare to bustling workaday crowds. Opt for first-rate *seco de chivo*, (goat stew), *corvina* (sea bass) or *arroz marinero* (seafood rice), followed by old-fashioned *helados de paila* (ice cream handmade in big copper bowls).

Vista Hermosa INTERNATIONAL $$
(Map p640; ☎02-295-1401; Mejía 453, 5th fl; mains $10-13; ⊙1pm-midnight Mon-Sat, to 9pm Sun) A much-loved spot in El Centro, Vista Hermosa (Beautiful View) delivers the goods with a magnificent 360-degree panorama over the Old Town from its open rooftop terrace. Live music on Thursday to Saturday (from 8pm onwards) adds to the magic. Arrive early to beat the crowds.

Café Mosaico CAFE $$
(Map p640; ☎02-254-2871; Samaniego N8-95; mains $9-16; ⊙4-11pm Mon-Wed, 1-11pm Thu-Sun) Serving up a mix of Ecuadorian and Greek fare near Parque Itchimbia, vine-covered Mosaico is famed for its magnificent views. The open-sided terrace is great for a sundowner.

Tianguez ECUADORIAN $$
(Map p640; Plaza San Francisco; mains $6-14; ⊙9am-7pm Sun-Thu, to 8am-11pm Fri & Sat; 📶) Tucked into the stone arches beneath the Monastery of San Francisco, this cafe-crafts shop prepares tasty appetizers (tamales, soups, messy BBQ wings) as well as heartier mains. The tables on the plaza are perfect for people-watching with an evening *canelazo* (*aguardiente* with hot cider and cinnamon) or an afternoon *té de coca* (coca-leaf tea).

Pizza SA PIZZA $$
(Map p640; Espejo Oe2-46; pizzas $8-16; ⊙noon-9pm Mon-Sat, to 8pm Sun) On a pedestrian lane dotted with restaurants facing the Teatro Bolívar, this casual spot with sidewalk seating bakes up satisfying medium-crust pizzas. You can also enjoy sandwiches, salads and calzones.

La Mariscal

★La Union BAKERY $
(Map p650; cnr Reina Victoria & Colón; mains $2-3; ⊙6am-10pm) Bustling La Union always packs a crowd, with its glass displays of croissants, berry tarts and ice cream, plus filling sandwiches.

Suvlaki GREEK $
(Map p650; Av Amazonas N21-108; mains $4; ⊙8:30am-7pm Mon-Fri, to 4pm Sat) The go-to spot for skewers of tasty grilled meat (the eponymous souvlaki), this casual spot has a growing following for its speedy service, cheery interior (complete with photos of Greek icons) and outdoor seating.

Casa Quebecua QUEBECOIS $
(Map p650; Calama near Reina Victoria; mains $5; ⊙noon-midnight Mon-Thu, to 2am Fri & Sat) Homesick for his motherland's cholesterol-laden signature dish and perhaps for the wintry feel of a north country log cabin, the Quebecois owner serves up satisfying poutine, a pile of fries, cheese curds and gravy, cooked up with a variety of extras like chicken and steak. Burgers and hot dogs make it a popular spot for those on a Mariscal pub crawl.

Chandani Tandoori INDIAN $
(Map p650; Mera 1333; mains $3.50-8; ⊙noon-10pm Mon-Sat, to 4pm Sun; 🖉) Bouncy Bollywood hits and sizzling platters of tikka masala make up the soundtrack to this good, inexpensive and unadorned Indian restaurant. Choose from two-dozen preparations of meat and vegetable dishes.

El Maple VEGETARIAN $
(Map p650; Pinto E7-68 near Almagro; mains $5-8; ⊙noon-9pm Mon & Tue, to 10:30pm Wed-Sat, to 6pm Sun; 🖉) This well-loved restaurant serves good vegetarian food with global influences (Tex-Mex burritos, Asian noodle dishes, creamy pastas). The four-course set lunches are good value, and the juices are tops.

Canoa Manabita SEAFOOD $

(Map p650; Calama 247; mains $6-8; ⏲10am-7pm Tue-Sun) This casual and unassuming place with picnic-table seating is popular with locals for its tasty ceviche, *cazeulas* (seafood stews), *encebollado* (soup with fish, *yuca* and onion) and other seafood dishes.

Spanes COLOMBIAN $

(Map p650; Av Amazonas N20-51; mains $5-9; ⏲8am-8pm Mon-Sat, to 5pm Sun; 📶) Fast food Colombian-style, including *arepas* and *ajiaco*, a Bogata specialty of three types of potatoes with chicken and corn. Plus, cheap and filling *almuerzos* (set lunches).

Kallari CAFE $

(Map p650; www.kallari.com; Wilson E4-266 & Mera; mains $3-5; ⏲10am-6pm Mon-Fri; 📶) Owned by the Kichwa community of Napo, this co-op serves up satisfying breakfasts and lunches, and stocks its famous chocolate bars.

Mercado Santa Clara MARKET $

(Map p644; cnr Dávalos & Versalles; ⏲8am-5pm) This is the main produce market in the new town. Besides an outstanding produce selection, it has cheap food stalls.

Supermaxi SUPERMARKET $

(Map p644; cnr La Niña & Pinzón) Biggest and best supermarket near the Mariscal.

★**Crepes & Waffles** INTERNATIONAL, DESSERTS $$

(Map p644; ☎02-250-0658; cnr Orellana & La Rabida; mains $9-15; ⏲noon-10pm Mon-Sat, 9am-9pm Sun; 📶 👪) Mouthwatering and stomach-enlarging sundaes, as well as more than two-dozen varieties of sweet and savory crepes, waffles, salads and more conventional vegetarian, meat and seafood dishes are on the menu at this outpost of a South American chain with several other locations in Quito. It has an upscale feel with very warm and welcoming service.

★**Cosa Nostra** ITALIAN $$

(Map p650; ☎02-252-7145; cnr Baquerizo Moreno & Almagro; mains $9-16; ⏲12:30-3pm & 6:30-10:30pm Tue-Sun; 📶) Italian-owned Cosa Nostra has a pleasant front patio, cozy dining room and nearly three-dozen varieties of pizza piled with generous toppings and fired up in a brick oven – we consider it the best in town. Good gnocchi and other pastas and tiramisu for dessert.

Q INTERNATIONAL $$

(Map p650; Plaza Foch; mains $5-15; ⏲6am-midnight Mon-Thu, to 2am Fri & Sat; 📶) Fashion types and TV personalities gather at this hip restaurant midweek, where a real live hummingbird ('Q' stands for *quinde*, Spanish for hummingbird) has made a nest in the ceiling decorated to resemble Amazonian vegetation. Live music most nights, including jazz and blues Wednesdays. A DJ plays lounge-style beats on Saturdays.

Boca del Lobo INTERNATIONAL $$

(Map p650; Calama 284; mains $8-14; ⏲5pm-1am) Beneath the soundtrack of ambient grooves, a mix of stylish Ecuadorians and neatly dressed foreigners mingle over raclette, crepes, open-face sandwiches, baked desserts and sugary cocktails. The ambience is pure kitsch, with colored-glass globes, empty birdcages and psychedelic paintings.

Azuca Beach SEAFOOD $$

(Map p650; Foch near Reina Victoria; mains $10-14; ⏲closed Sun; 📶) Everyone from students to professionals head to this cool and sophisticated place overlooking buzzing Plaza Foch. Dishes from coastal regions throughout South America, including various ceviches, are among the hits. Tropical cocktails

DON'T MISS

LA RONDA

One of the biggest Old Town success stories of recent years is the restoration of 'La Ronda.' This narrow lane is lined with colorful colonial buildings, with placards along the walls describing (in Spanish) some of the street's history and the artists, writers and political figures who once resided here. Today, it is home to a jumble of restaurants, cafes, shops and galleries – such as the excellent **Casa de las Artes** (Map p640; Casa 989, La Ronda; ⏲10am-7pm Tue-Thu, to 10pm Fri & Sat, 11am-3pm Sun) FREE – though La Ronda remains a delightfully local and unpretentious affair. The street is at its liveliest on Friday and Saturday nights, when *canelazo* (*aguardiente* – sugarcane alcohol – with hot cider and cinnamon) vendors keep everyone warm and cozy and live music spills out of restaurant windows.

(try the friut-flavored mojitos and caipirinhas), a bamboo-trimmed bar and potted palms add to the loungelike space, which becomes a popular drinking spot at night.

Baalbek MIDDLE EASTERN $$
(Map p650; Av 6 de Diciembre & Wilson; mains $6-15; noon-5pm Sun-Tue, to 10:30pm Wed-Sat) Authentic Lebanese fare served up quickly in a comfortable and contemporary dining room with a Middle Eastern soundtrack and aesthetic. Most of the menu items can be ordered as a half or full plate, which makes family-style sharing the way to to go.

La Bodeguita de Cuba CUBAN $$
(Map p644; Reina Victoria 1721; mains $8; noon-11pm Mon & Tue, to 1am Wed-Thu, to 2am Fri & Sat) With its warmly lit interior, graffiti-covered walls and outdoor seating, this is a great place for Cuban food and fun. Live bands perform here on Wednesday and Thursday nights (check out attached El Veradero for salsa weekend nights).

Magic Bean INTERNATIONAL $$
(Map p650; Foch E5-08; mains $6-12; 8am-11pm;) Magic Bean nearly always packs a crowd with its ample American-style breakfasts and lunches, plus frothy juices, coffees and desserts, best enjoyed on the covered front terrace.

El Mariachi Taco Factory MEXICAN $$
(Map p650, Foch near Mera; mains $7-9) Colorfully woven tablecloths, Mexican mariachi posters and adobe-esque walls conjure a faint impression of Old Mexico in this rather sedate Mariscal eatery. Sizzling plates of fajitas go nicely with frozen margaritas.

Café Amazonas ECUADORIAN $$
(Map p650; cnr Av Amazonas & Roca; mains $5-9; 7am-9pm Mon-Sat, to 7pm Sun;) A loyal contingent of regulars come for *seco de chivo* (goat stew), *locro de papas* (potato soup) and other comfort fare, as well as good people-watching at the outdoor tables. Soccer is always on one of the small TVs.

Achiote ECUADORIAN $$$
(Map p650; cnr Rodriguez & Reina Victoria; mains $9-30; noon-10pm) Ecuadorian dishes with an upscale twist in a warmly lit contemporary setting. Empanadas, ceviches, rich seafood stews and *llapingachos* (fried pancakes of mashed potatoes with cheese) are all first-rate. Live music Thursday to Sunday nights (from 7pm).

La Floresta & Around

Traviesas Artesanos del Cafe CAFE $
(Map p644; La Coruña N30-123 near Whymper; mains $5; 8am-8pm Mon-Fri, 10am-8pm Sat & Sun;) Discerning coffee drinkers and aspiring baristas should make their way to this friendly upscale cafe. Choose your method – pour over, filter, chemex, french press or aeropress – and chow down on a sandwich, salad or delicious cheesecake while you wait.

Mercado La Floresta MARKET $
(Map p644; cnr Galavis & Andalucía; 9am-4pm Fri) A small but delightful fruit market set in the peaceful Floresta neighborhood.

★ Jürgen Cafe DUTCH $$
(Map p644; Coruña N30-123 & Whymper, La Floresta; mains $6.50-10; 7am-8pm Mon-Sat, to 2pm Sun) Owned and operated by Jürgen Spelier, a fourth-generation baker from Holland, this casually sophisticated restaurant is Scandanavian through and through – from its clean lines and blond-wood decor to its *pannekoek*, the Dutch version of pancakes.

★ La Choza ECUADORIAN $$
(Map p644; 02-223-0839; www.lachozaec.com; Av 12 de Octubre N24-551 near Cordero; mains $7-12; noon-4pm & 6:30-10pm Mon-Fri, noon-4pm Sat & Sun) One of Quito's best restaurants for traditional Ecuadorian cuisine, La Choza serves up hearty plates of *llapingachos* (fried pancakes of mashed potatoes with cheese), grilled *corvina* (sea bass) and steak with all the fixings in an airy setting with colorfully woven tablecloths and Andean music.

La Briciola ITALIAN $$
(Map p644; 02-254-5157; Toledo 1255; mains $10-13; 12:30-3pm & 7:30-11pm Mon-Sat) This longtime favorite has an outstanding and varied menu. The portions are large, and the wine is fairly priced. Reservations recommended.

La Cleta CAFE $$
(Map p644; Lugo N24-250; pizzas $4-12; 3-11pm Mon-Sat;) Bicycle-lovers shouldn't miss this small, cleverly designed cafe-restaurant, where everything (chairs, bar stools, tables, hanging lamps) is fabricated from bicycle parts. The staff cooks up tasty pizzas and lasagnas, and there's coffee, wine and other drinks.

Z(inc) LOUNGE $$
(Map p644; Rivet near Coruña; mains $10-16; ⊙noon-4pm & 7pm-midnight Mon-Sat) Equal parts restaurant and bar, Z(inc) has a multi-level industrial-chic interior of untreated timber, dark metals, exposed brick and flame-lit walls. Sip a lychee-infused cocktail on the front patio before heading inside for brick-oven flatbread pizza, mini sirloin burgers, tempura prawns and other dishes ideal for sharing.

La Pradera & La Carolina

Zao ASIAN $$
(Map p644; ☎02-252-3496; Av Alfaro N10-16 near San Salvador; mains $8-10; ⊙12:30-3:30pm Mon-Sun, 7-11:30pm Mon-Sat) Adorned with carved wooden screens, statues resembling samurai and glowing paper lanterns, Zao is a buzzing spot serving up samosas, rich noodle dishes, vegetable stir-fries, sushi and other flavors from Asia. A DJ on weekend nights adds to the festive vibe.

★**Zazu** FUSION $$$
(Map p644; ☎02-254-3559; www.zazuquito.com; Aguilera 331; mains $18-33; ⊙12:30pm-midnight Mon-Fri, 7pm-midnight Sat) One of Quito's best restaurants, Zazu serves beautifully prepared seafood dishes, grilled meats and ceviches in a stylish setting of light brick, ambient electronica and an inviting, backlit bar. The Peruvian chef seamlessly blends east with west, with dishes such as pistachio-crusted tuna, Wagyu tartar with gorgonzola mousse and seafood bouillabaisse.

Drinking & Nightlife

Much of the *farra* (nightlife) in Quito is concentrated in and around the Mariscal, where things get raucous most nights (and very crowded on weekends). A weekend night wandering up and down **La Ronda**, a narrow cobblestone lane in the Old Town lined with bars and restaurants, should not be missed. For generally more relaxed, low-key affairs, head to one of the sophisticated spots in La Floresta or Guápulo.

Definitely carry ID when going out at night in case you're carded.

Cherusker BAR
(Map p650; cnr Pinto & Diego de Almagro; ⊙1pm-1am Mon-Thu, to 3am Fri & Sat) In a red, two-story colonial house, Cherusker has earned a loyal following for its tasty artisanal microbrews, warm bohemian ambience and buzzing front patio. Occasional live bands play on weekends.

Finn McCool's PUB
(Map p650; Diego de Almagro near Pinto; ⊙5pm-2am) Proudly flying the orange and green, this Irish-owned bar gathers a mix of locals and expats who come for games of pool, table football, pub grub and theme nights (pub quiz on Tuesdays, live bands or open-mic Thursdays, game nights whenever there's football on). Not much elbow room on weekend nights.

Dirty Sanchez LOUNGE
(Map p650; Pinto E7-38 near Reina Victoria) The cheekily named Dirty Sanchez is a small art-filled lounge with a bohemian vibe. Decent cocktails (and coffee), better music and a more laid-back crowd make this expat-owned place a standout.

Bandido Brewing BREWPUB
(Map p640; Olmedo E1-136 near Cevallos, San Blas; ⊙4-11pm Mon-Sat) These guys from Oregon are producing their own IPAs, including one brew, the Macuipucuna Cloud Forest Coffee Porter, that uses locally grown coffee. The Old Town neighborhood where Bandido is located can feel sketchy at night.

Bungalow 6 CLUB
(Map p650; cnr Calama & Diego de Almagro; ⊙7pm-3am Wed-Sat) A popular nightspot among foreigners and locals alike, Bungalow 6 often features long lines on weekends and Wednesday ladies' night (gals drink for free to 10pm). It plays a good mix of beats, with a small but lively dance floor and a warren of colorfully decorated rooms (with table football, pool table and small outdoor terrace) upstairs.

Ananké LOUNGE
(Map p644; Orellana 781, Guápulo) Well worth the trip out here, Ananké is a stylish and warmly lit bar-pizzeria with small colorfully decorated rooms spread out among an old two-story house. It has a small terrace (complete with fireplace) and several good nooks for hiding away with a cocktail and a few friends. When the fog clears, the views over Guápulo are superb.

Selfie Club Disco CLUB
(formerly El Aguijón; Map p650; Calama E7-35; admission $5-10; ⊙9pm-3am Tue-Sat) It's mostly locals bumping and grinding at this open,

somewhat industrial space, with video art playing on a large screen above the dance floor. DJs spin a little of everything on the weekends.

Mayo 68 CLUB
(Map p650; García 662) This popular salsa club is small and conveniently located in the Mariscal and has a local following.

Turtle's Head Pub & Microbrewery BAR
(Map p644; La Niña E4-451) Scottish-owned pub serving decent microbrews and pub grub; table football, pool table, and occasional bands.

☆ Entertainment

★El Pobre Diablo LIVE MUSIC
(Map p644; 02-223-5194; www.elpobrediablo.com; Isabel La Católica E12-06; noon-3pm & 7pm-2am Mon-Sat) Locals and expats rate El Pobre Diablo one of Quito's best places to hear live music. It's a friendly, laid-back place with a well-curated selection of talent (jazz, blues, world music, experimental sounds) performing most nights. It's also a great place to dine, with delectable fusion fare, a solid cocktail menu and a great vibe.

La Juliana LIVE MUSIC
(Map p644; Av 12 de Octubre near Coruña; admission $10-20; 10pm-2am Thu-Sat) In an old converted house, La Juliana is a colorfully decorated space with a good mix of bands (rock, salsa, merengue) lighting up the dance floor most weekend nights.

El Veradero LIVE MUSIC
(Map p644; cnr Reina Victoria & La Pinta) This space, attached to the restaurant El Bodeguita de Cuba, comes alive on weekend nights when it's transformed into a lively salsateca. It's worth the price of admission when the owner, a talented Cuban woman, performs.

Café Libro LIVE MUSIC
(Map p650; 02-250-3214; www.cafelibro.com; Leonidas Plaza Gutiérrez N23-56; admission $3-20; noon-2pm Mon-Fri, 5pm-midnight Tue-Thu, 6pm-2am Fri & Sat) Live music, poetry readings, contemporary dance, tango, jazz and other performances draw an arts-loving crowd to this long-running venue. Jazz, salsa and tango classes ($10) are offered, and you can always pull up a table for a game of chess or go.

Humanizarte DANCE
(Map p640; 02-257-3486; fundacion_humanizarte@hotamil.com; Casa 707, La Ronda; admission $5; from 9pm Fri & Sat) This excellent theater and dance group, currently in La Ronda on weekend nights, presents Andean dance performances. You can also enquire about taking Andean folk-dancing classes.

Ocho y Medio CINEMA
(Map p644; www.ochoymedio.net; Valladolid N24-353 & Vizcaya; cafe 11am-10:30pm) This Floresta film house shows great art films (often in English) and has occasional dance, theater and live music. There's a cafe attached.

Shopping

Stores in the Mariscal sell traditional indigenous crafts. Quality is often high, but so are the prices.

On Saturday and Sunday, the northern end of Parque El Ejido turns into Quito's biggest crafts market and sidewalk art show. Two blocks north, **Mercado Artesanal La Mariscal** (Map p644; Washington btwn Mera & Reina Victoria; 9am-7pm) is an entire block filled with craft stalls.

Apart from Tianguez, which is in the Old Town, all other listings following are in the New Town.

★Galería Ecuador HANDICRAFTS, BOOKS
(Map p650; www.galeriaecuador.com; Victoria N24 263 near García) This sparkling two-story complex is just off Plaza Foch and offers top-quality Ecuadorian-made productsthat range from handicrafts, jewelry, clothing, CDs and coffee-table books to chocolates, wine and liqueurs (including a smooth chocolate elixir). There's an excellent on-site café. The store can provide tourism information, including maps.

Galería Latina HANDICRAFTS
(Map p650; Mera N23-69) One of the finest handicraft and clothing shops in the city, Galería Latina has a huge selection of beautifully made pieces: tagua carvings, colorful Andean weavings, textiles, jewelry, sweaters and handmade items from across Latin America. Prices are higher, but so is the craftsmanship.

Tianguez HANDICRAFTS
(Map p640; Plaza San Francisco) Attached to the eponymous cafe, Tianguez is a member

of the Fair Trade Organization and sells outstanding crafts from throughout Ecuador.

La Bodega HANDICRAFTS
(Map p650; Mera N22-24) In business for 30-odd years, La Bodega stocks a wide and wonderful range of high-quality crafts, both old and new.

Ag JEWELRY
(Map p650; ☎02-255-0276; Mera 614) Ag's selection of rare, handmade silver jewelry from throughout South America is outstanding. You'll also find antiques.

Confederate Books BOOKS
(Map p650; cnr Calama & Mera) Large selection of secondhand books in English and several other languages.

Libri Mundi BOOKS
(Map p650; Mera 851; ⏲9am-7pm Mon-Fri, 9am-2pm & 3-6pm Sat) One of Quito's best bookstores, with a good selection of titles in English, German, French and Spanish.

ℹ Information

DANGERS & ANNOYANCES

Quito has a bad reputation for robberies and petty crime, and you should take precautions to avoid becoming a target. Despite the animated streets of the Mariscal area, it remains a dangerous neighborhood after dark; a police presence keeps Plaza Foch safe, but a few dark streets away, muggings still occur. Take a taxi after dark – even if you have only a few blocks to walk. Sundays, when no one else is around, is a dodgy time to wander around.

With the restoration of the Old Town and increased police presence there, the historic center is safe until 10pm or so. Don't climb up El Panecillo hill; take a taxi instead (there are plenty up top for the return trip). The buses are prime hunting ground for thieves; keep a close watch on your belongings – backpacks and handbags are routinely and adroitly slashed and pilfered without the owner even realizing it. If you are robbed, obtain a police report within 48 hours from the police station either in the **New Town** (☎02-254-3932; Reina Victoria N 21-208 near Roca; ⏲24hr) or the **Old Town** (Map p640; ☎02-251-0896; Chile btwn Moreno & Venezuela, Plaza Grande; ⏲10am-6pm).

If you are arriving from sea level, Quito's 2850m elevation might make you somewhat breathless and give you headaches or cotton mouth. These symptoms of *soroche* (altitude sickness) usually disappear after a day or two. To minimize symptoms, take it easy upon arrival, drink plenty of water and lay off the smokes and alcohol.

EMERGENCY

Emergency (☎911)
Fire (☎102)
Police (☎101)
Red Cross Ambulance (☎131, ☎258-0598)

INTERNET ACCESS

Many guesthouses, cafes, restaurants and even public parks offer free wi-fi.

MEDICAL SERVICES

Hospital Metropolitano (☎02-399-8000; www.hospitalmetropolitano.org; Mariana de Jesús near Arteta) The best hospital in town. Located west of Parque la Carolina in the district of San Gabriel.

Hospital Voz Andes (☎02-226-2142; www.hospitalvozandes.org; cnr Villalengua Oe2-37 & Av 10 de Agosto) American-run hospital with an outpatient department and emergency room near the Iñaquito trolley stop northwest of Parque La Carolina.

MONEY

There are several banks and *casas de cambio* (currency exchange bureaus) in the New Town along Av Amazonas between Av Patria and Orellana, and dozens of banks throughout town.

Banco de Guayaquil (Av Amazonas N22-147 at Veintimilla) ATM and changes traveler's checks.

Banco de Guayaquil (Colón at Reina Victoria) ATM and changes traveler's checks.

Banco del Pacífico (cnr 12 de Octubre & Cordero) ATM and changes traveler's checks.

Banco del Pacífico (cnr Guayaquil & Chile) ATM and changes traveler's checks.

Banco del Pichincha (Guayaquil btwn Olmedo & Manabí) ATM and changes traveler's checks.

Producambios (Av Amazonas 350, La Mariscal) ATM and changes traveler's checks.

Western Union (Av de la República) Money transfers from abroad, ATM and changes traveler's checks.

Western Union (Av Colón 1333) Money transfers from abroad, ATM and changes traveler's checks.

POST

Central Post Office (Map p640; Reina Victoria & Colón; ⏲8am-7pm Mon-Fri, to noon Sat & Sun) The Mariscal location is most convenient.

La Mariscal Post Office (Map p650; cnr Av Colón & Reina Victoria)

TOURIST INFORMATION

Quito Tourism (Corporación Metropolitana de Turismo; Map p640; ☎02-257-2445; www.quito.com.ec; Venezuela near Chile; ⏲9am-6pm Mon-Fri, to 8pm Sat, 10am-5pm Sun; 📶) The Old Town branch is well located and helpful for general questions, directions and maps; a handicrafts store called Tienda el Qunde occupies half of the space. It also runs guided walking tours of Old Town.

South American Explorers (SAE; Map p644; ☎02-222-7235; www.saexplorers.org; Mariana de Jesus Oe3-32 & Ulloa, Mariana de Jesus;) The clubhouse of this member-supported nonprofit organization (other locations in Quito, Lima and Cuzco in Peru, Buenos Aires and a head office in Ithaca, New York) is an information hub for travelers, adventurers and researchers etc, with binders full of advice and information about Latin America. A 10-minute walk west of Parque La Carolina.

Getting There & Away

AIR

Quito's **Aeropuerto Mariscal Sucre** (☎02-395-4200; www.aeropuertoquito.aero) is 37km east of the city. There are regular flights connecting Quito with Coca, Cuenca, Esmeraldas, the Galápagos, Guayaquil, Lago Agrio, Loja, Macas, Machala, Manta and Tulcán. All mainland flights last under one hour and cost around $70 to $100 one way. Galápagos flights cost significantly more (from $500 round-trip) and take 3¼ hours from Quito (including a layover in Guayaquil) and 1½ hours from Guayaquil.

BUS

Quito has two bus terminals and they are both a long way from the center (allow at least an hour by public transit, 30 minutes or more by taxi).

Terminal Quitumbe (☎02-398-8200; Cóndor Ñan & Sucre), located 10km southwest of the Old Town, handles the Central and Southern Andes, the coast and the Oriente (ie Baños, Cuenca, Guayaquil, Coca and – aside from Otavalo – most destinations of interest to travelers). It can be reached by Trole bus (C4); get off at the last stop. A taxi to/from here costs about $12 to $15.

Terminal Terrestre Carcelén (☎02-396-1600; Eloy Alfaro), in the north, services Otavalo, Ibarra, Santo Domingo, Tulcán and other northern destinations. To get here, you can take the Trole bus north to La Y Terminal and transfer to a 'Carapungo'-bound bus; tell the driver where you're headed as this bus passes about a block from the terminal, where you can continue on foot. A taxi runs $10 to $12.

For comfortable buses to Guayaquil from the New Town, travel with **Panamericana** (Map p650; ☎02-255-7134; Av Colón btwn Reina Victoria & Almagro) or **Transportes Ecuador** (Map p650; ☎02-222-5315; Mera N21-44). Panamericana also has long-distance buses to other towns, including Machala, Loja, Cuenca, Manta and Esmeraldas.

A few buses leave from other places for some destinations in the Pichincha province. **Cooperativa Flor de Valle/Cayambe** (www.flordelvalle.com.ec) goes daily to Mindo ($2.50, 2½ hours) from Quito's northern Ofelia station, reachable by taking the Metrobus line to the last stop.

Approximate one-way fares and journey times are shown in the following table. More expensive luxury services are available for long trips.

DESTINATION	COST ($)	DURATION (HR)
Ambato	2.50	2½
Atacames	9	7
Bahía de Caráquez	10	8
Baños	3.50	3
Coca	10	9 (via Loreto)
Cuenca	10-12	10-12
Esmeraldas	9	5-6
Guayaquil	7-10	8
Huaquillas	10	12
Ibarra	3	2½
Lago Agrio	8	7-8
Latacunga	1.50	2
Loja	14-17	14-15
Machala	10	10
Manta	10	8-9
Otavalo	2	2¼
Portoviejo	9	9
Puerto López	12	12
Puyo	6	5½
Riobamba	4	4
San Lorenzo	7	6½
Santo Domingo	3	3
Tena	6	5-6
Tulcán	5	5

TRAIN

After massive investment, the country's newly revitalized train network is once again ferrying passengers on slow-motion journeys through breathtaking high-altitude scenery. **Tren Ecuador** (www.trenecuador.com) has four routes (Thursday through Sunday) leaving from Quito's beautifully renovated train station, **Estación de Ferrocarril Chimbacalle**, located 2km south of the Old Town. Trains go to Machachi (round-trip $15); the foot of Cotopaxi (round-trip $20); Latacunga (round-trip $10); and along the flagship route called **Tren Crucero**, which takes four days and three nights for the 450km to coastal Guayaquil ($1270).

Getting Around

BUS

The local buses ($0.25) are fairly convenient, but keep a close watch on your belongings. Buses have destination placards in their windows (not route numbers), and drivers will usually tell you which bus to take if you flag the wrong one.

TAXI

Cabs are yellow and have taxi-number stickers in the window. Drivers may or may not use a *taxímetro* (meter); to be safe, it's best to agree on a price before entering a taxi. The going rate between the Mariscal and Old Town is about $2, though you'll have to pay more at night and on Sundays.

TROLE, ECOVÍA & METROBUS

Quito has three electrically powered bus routes: the Trole, the Ecovía and the Metrobus. Each runs north–south along one of Quito's three main thoroughfares. Each line has designated stations and car-free lanes, making them speedy and efficient; however, as the fastest form of public transportation, they are usually crowded and notorious for pickpockets. They run about every 10 minutes from 6am to 12:30am (more often in rush hours), and the fare is $0.25.

The Trole runs along Maldonado and Av 10 de Agosto. In the Old Town, southbound trolleys take the west route (along Guayaquil), while northbound trolleys take the east route (along Montúfar and Pichincha). The Ecovía runs along Av 6 de Diciembre, and the Metrobus runs along Av América.

GETTING INTO TOWN

Airport taxi prices into the city from Quito's Aeropuerto Mariscal Sucre are fixed and cost between $24 and $26 for Mariscal or the Old Town. The trip takes between 50 and 90 minutes.

There are also express shuttle buses operated by **Aeroservicios** (http://aeroservicios.com.ec; $8) departing every 30 minutes, which connect the new airport with the old airport (8km north of La Mariscal). From there, you can take a taxi to La Mariscal or the Old Town for around $8 to $12.

The least expensive and least convenient option is to take a public bus ($2) to or from the Rio Coca bus terminal north of the Mariscal. To get to Rio Coca station, take the north-bound Ecovia ($0.25), which runs along Av 6 de Diciembre and has a stop near the Mariscal. It's about a 30-minute trip from the Mariscal to Rio Coca.

AROUND QUITO

Mitad del Mundo & Around

☎02

Ecuador's biggest claim to fame is its location on the equator. **Mitad del Mundo** (Middle of the World City; www.mitaddelmundo.com; admission $2, monument admission $3; ⌚9am-6pm Mon-Fri, to 7pm Sat & Sun), 22km north of Quito, is the place where Charles-Marie de la Condamine made the measurements in 1736, proving that this was the equatorial line. Although the monument constructed there isn't actually on the equator (GPS readings indicate true 0°00' latitude lies about 300m north), it remains a popular, if touristy, destination. On Sunday afternoons live salsa bands play in the central plaza area. The ethnographic museum (and its viewing platform up top), a scale model of Quito's Old Town and other attractions cost extra. **Calima Tours** (☎02-239-4796; www.mitaddelmundotour.com; hike per person $8), located inside the complex, offers trips to Pululahua hourly. The 10am trip includes a hike around the rim. At 3pm Calima runs a tour to **Rumicucho**, a small pre-Inca site under excavation, 3.5km north of Mitad del Mundo; the tour includes a visit to a shaman's house.

A few hundred meters north is **Museo Solar Inti Ñan** (adult/child $4/2; ⌚9:30am-5pm), offering a fun-house atmosphere of water and energy demonstrations. You'll have to decide for yourself if the 'scientific' experiments are hoaxes.

On the way to Calacalí, about 5km north of Mitad del Mundo, is the ancient volcanic crater and geobotanical reserve of **Pululahua**. The views (in the morning) are great from the rim, or you can hike down to the tiny village on the crater floor. You can overnight inside the crater at **Pululahua Hostel** (☎099-946-6636; www.pululahuahostal.com; cabana s/d from $30/40, without bathroom $20/30) 🌿, an ecofriendly guesthouse with simple, comfortable rooms. Tasty meals (lunch or dinner $10) feature ingredients from the organic farm. Guests can hire bikes ($5 per hour) or horses ($10 per hour). Near the rim of Pululahua is the castle-like **Templo del Sol** (admission $3; ⏲10am-5pm Tue-Sun), a re-creation of an Incan temple, complete with pre-Columbian relics and stone carvings. The guided tour (in Spanish) is a bit gimmicky, led by a heavily decorated 'Incan prince' who touches on presumed ancient beliefs and rituals.

To get to Mitad del Mundo from Quito, take the Metrobus ($0.25) north to the last stop, Ofelia station. From there, transfer to the Mitad del Mundo bus (an additional $0.25); the entire trip takes one hour to 1½ hours. The bus drops you off right in front of the entrance.

Buses continue past the complex and will drop you off at the entrance road to Pululahua – ask for the Mirador de Ventanillas (the lookout point where the trail into the crater begins).

Termas de Papallacta

☎02

Home to Ecuador's most luxurious and most scenic thermal baths, the Termas de Papallacta are pure medicine for long days of travel. **Balneario** (admission $8; ⏲6am-10:30pm, last entry 9pm) boasts more than 25 blue pools of varying temperatures surrounded by plush grass and red-orange blossoms. Towels and lockers are available. There's little reason to spend the extra $11 to visit the spa pools.

About 67km (two hours) from Quito, the complex, part of the posh **Hotel Termas de Papallacta** (☎in Papallacta 06-232-0042, in Quito 02-256-8989, 06-289-5060; www.papallacta.com.ec; r 1-3 person from $150-200, 6-person cabins $225; P@) , makes for an excellent jaunt from Quito. Cheaper hotels are available outside the complex in the village of Papallacta itself, though it's easy enough to head back to Quito. It's best to go during the week to avoid the huge weekend crowds.

Any of the buses from Quito heading toward Baeza, Tena or Lago Agrio can drop you off in Papallacta. To visit the Termas de Papallacta complex, ask the driver to let you off on the road to the baths, 1.5km before the village. Then catch an awaiting *camioneta* (small truck) for the $2 ride up the bumpy road.

NORTHERN HIGHLANDS

The steep green hills, dust-blown villages, bustling provincial capitals and cultural riches of the northern highlands lie a few hours' drive northeast of Quito. Those traveling to or from Colombia are bound to pass through the region, and there's plenty worth stopping for: the famous Otavalo market, which dates back to pre-Inca times, is the largest crafts market in South America, and several small towns are known for their handicrafts, including wood carvings and leatherwork.

Northwest of Quito lie the misty cloud forests hugging the western slopes of the Andes. The big draw here is Mindo, a tranquil village transformed into an ecotourist hot spot, with bird-watching, hiking and river tubing the orders of the day.

Mindo

☎02

With its breathtaking setting surrounded on all sides by steep mountainsides of cloud forest, tiny Mindo has become a magnet for backpackers and now lives and breathes tourism. Located just off the main road from Quito to Esmeraldas, Mindo is entered by a dramatically steep and curvy hillside descent that takes you down past dozens of hotels and lodges to a sleepy town center. Bird-watchers, hikers and weekenders from Quito and beyond all flock here and friendly locals have created an impressive infrastructure for actively enjoying the cloud forest, including butterfly farms, ziplines over the treetops, mountain biking, tubing and orchid collections.

Sights & Activities

Tarabita CABLE CAR

(road to Cascada de Nambillo; admission $5; ⏲8:30am-4pm Tue-Sun) This unique hand-powered cable car takes you soaring across a lush river basin over thick cloud forest to the Bosque Protector Mindo-Nambillo, where you can hike to a number of waterfalls. Certainly not for the acrophobic, the wire basket on steel cables glides 152m above the ground. Your ticket includes a map with routes shown on it; while the Cascada Nambillo is the closest (15 minutes' walk), it's the series of five waterfalls (one hour's walk) that's really worth the effort. It's a $2 taxi or pleasant uphill walk 7km from town.

Mariposas de Mindo BUTTERFLY FARM
(☎02-224-2712; www.mariposasdemindo.com; admission $5; ⊙9am-4pm) Mindo has several butterfly farms, but this is the best of them. Visit in the warmest part of the day, around 11am, when butterflies are most active. It also has a restaurant and lodging.

Tubing

Tour operators along Av Quito offer low-tech thrill rides (per person with four-person minimum $6) along the churning Río Mindo. You and a group of three others will jostle down white water on a raft of thick inner tubes lashed together. The price should include transportation, a helmet, life vest and a guide, as tubing the rapids on the Río Mindo can be dangerous.

Ziplining

Halfway up the road to the *tarabita* (cable car), two dueling zipline companies compete for adrenaline seekers. Fly over the canopy in a harness attached to a cable strung above the trees, an activity that gets faster in the rain. **Mindo Canopy Adventure** (☎09-453-0624; www.mindocanopy.com; 2½hr circuit per person $20), the original company, has 13 different cables ranging from 20m to 400m in length.

Bird-Watching

With more than 400 species of birds recorded, Mindo has become a major center for bird-watchers. The going rate for a competent, professional guide runs from $80 to $220 per day. Recommended English-speaking guides include **Irman Arias** (☎099-170-8720; www.mindobirdguide.com), **Danny Jumbo** (☎099-328-0769) and **Julia Patiño** (☎088-616-2816, 02-390-0419; juliaguideofbird@yahoo.com).

Sleeping & Eating

Caskaffesu GUESTHOUSE $
(☎099-386-7154, 02-217-0100; www.caskaffesu.com; Sixto Duran Ballen near Av Quito; r per person $20;) Run by a kind and friendly American-Ecuadorian couple, Caskafessu is a lovely low-key refuge just off the main road in the center of town. The two stories of brightly painted adobe rooms have a vaguely Mediterranean feel and surround a small, leafy courtyard.

La Casa de Cecilia HOSTEL $
(☎099-334-5393, 02-217-0243; www.lacasadececilia.com; Av 9 de Octubre; r per person $7-10;) The bucolic outdoor patio – even if it is concrete – and riverside location add an out-of-the-way feel and a place to relax for those staying in the maze of bunk beds. Several good-value private rooms are in the two-story buildings next door. You'll find an outdoor fireplace on the hammock deck and an open-air kitchen on the river.

★**Beehive** CAFE $
(www.thebeehivemindo.com; sandwiches $5; ⊙8am-8pm Mon-Thu & Sun, to 10pm Fri & Sat;) Run by Ingo and Genny, a German-Ecuadorian couple (and their two lumbering Great Danes), the Beehive is a cool hangout with a Scandinavian design perched over a river in back. The smorgasbord plate of falafel, hummus, cheese, meatballs, sausages, salad and refrigerator leftovers is the house specialty, but brownies, cakes and coffee drinks are equally good.

Columpios JUICES, VEGETARIAN $
(mains $3) Known around town appropriately enough as 'Swings Place' for the swings that function as seats, this tiny outdoor juice bar does *batidos*, salads and veggie burgers. It's a few blocks away from the parque central on the road to the *tarabita*.

El Quetzal ECUADORIAN $$
(www.elquetzaldemindo.com; Av 9 de Octubre; mains $6-15; ⊙8am-11pm;) This wonderful, laid-back coffee shop and restaurant, easily the largest in town, does it all right: there's excellent coffee as well as locally grown beans and chocolate for sale, a great selection of breakfasts and sandwiches, and a daily changing array of Ecuadorian main courses. The American owner's proud specialty is the locally famous brownie.

Information

There's an ATM near Parque Central, but it doesn't always work, so get cash before arriving.

Centro Municipal de Información Turistica (Avs Quito & 9 de Octubre) A helpful, tourist office (Spanish-speaking only) across from the Plaza Grande that gives out maps and advice on hiking, tours and lodging.

Getting There & Away

There are several daily buses to Quito ($3, 2½ hours) and seven daily buses to Santo Domingo ($3, three hours), which has onward connections to the coast. Other buses to Quito or the coast can be picked up at the top of the hill, where the road to Mindo intersects the main highway.

Otavalo

☎06 / POP 52,700

The friendly and prosperous town of Otavalo (2550m) is famous for its giant Saturday market, where traditionally dressed indigenous people sell handicrafts to hordes of foreigners who pour in every Saturday to get in on the deals. Despite the market's popularity, the *otavaleños* themselves remain self-determined and culturally uncompromised. The setting is fabulous, and the entire experience remains enchanting.

Sights

Crafts Market MARKET

(Plaza de Ponchos;) Plaza de Ponchos, the nucleus of the crafts market, is filled every day with vendors selling woolen goods, such as rugs, tapestries, blankets, ponchos, sweaters, scarves, gloves and hats – as well as embroidered blouses, hammocks, carvings, beads, paintings, woven mats and jewelry made from tagua nut (also known as vegetable ivory). But it metastasizes on Saturday, official market day, swelling into adjacent roads and around half of the town center.

Animal Market MARKET

(Panamericana; 6am-1pm Sat) You might have little use for screaming piglets, bags of guinea pigs or a lethargic cow, but it's worth visiting this weekly market for the atmosphere and general chaos. Cross the bridge at the end of Colón and follow the crowds across the Panamericana.

Activities

There's great hiking around Otavalo, especially in the Lagunas de Mojanda area.

★Runa Tupari Native Travel CULTURAL, OUTDOOR ADVENTURES

(☎292-2320; www.runatupari.com; Calle Sucre 14-15 y Quiroga) Deservedly renowned and respected, Runa Tupari has partnered with indigenous, mestizo and Afro-Ecuadorian rural communities to offer sightseeing, hiking, horseback-riding and biking trips. Rural homestays are $25 per night, while various volunteering options cost $15 per day and include room and board.

Courses

Otavalo is a good place to learn Spanish. Recommended language schools, with homestay and volunteer options, include **Mundo Andino** (☎06-292-1864; www.mandinospanishschool.com; Salinas 404 near Bolívar; individual/group lessons per hr $6/4.50) and **Instituto Superior de Español** (Map p640; ☎06-292-7354; www.instituto-superior.net; Guayaquil N9-77 y Oriente St; courses per week from $129).

Festivals & Events

Inti Raymi RELIGIOUS

Millennia-old indigenous celebration of the summer equinox celebrated throughout the northern highlands, especially in Otavalo, where it's also combined with feasts of **St John the Baptist** (June 24) and **Sts Peter and Paul** (June 29). Held from June 21 to 29.

Fiesta del Yamor CULTURAL

Otavalo's best-known celebration occurs during the first two weeks of September in honor of the fall harvest. An elected queen oversees processions, live music and dancing, fireworks displays and cockfights. Revelers consume copious amounts of *chicha de yamor* – seven varieties of corn are slowly simmered together to produce this unusual nonalcoholic drink (longer-fermented versions are alcoholic).

Sleeping

Guesthouses fill on Friday, so arrive early for the best choice of accommodations.

★Hotel Riviera-Sucre GUESTHOUSE $

(☎06-292-0241; www.rivierasucre.com; cnr García Moreno 380 & Roca; r per person $18; @) Offering the best value in town, the charming wood-floored, high-ceilinged rooms here surround a delightful inner courtyard with a regal-looking centerpiece fountain and swinging hammocks. Prepare a meal or a coffee in the communal kitchen then enjoy it in the flowering garden that extends out back. Weekend reservations are a necessity.

Hotel Santa Fé 2 HOTEL $

(☎06-292-0161; www.hotelsantafeotavalo.com; Colón 507 & Sucre; r per person $13; P) If you love wooden interiors you will find this Southwestern-style place very much to your liking, even if the polished, faux-wood decor shines like plastic flowers. The original, older **Hotel Santa Fé 1** (☎06-292-3640; Roca 7-34 & Moreno; r per person $13) has smaller rooms, with the bathrooms an especially tight squeeze for the wider-girthed among us.

Cabañas El Rocío GUESTHOUSE **$**

(☎06-292-4606; rocioe@hotmail.com; Barrio San Juan; r per person $11; P 📶) Don't be put off by the faded sign and the roadside location: this charming place belies its uninviting exterior and has a range of vaguely alpine rooms and cabins just a short walk from the center of Otavalo.

Hostal Valle del Amanecer GUESTHOUSE **$**

(☎06-292-0990; www.hostalvalledelamanecer.com; cnr Roca & Quiroga; r per person incl breakfast $16, without bathroom $13; 📶) Very small rooms – couples seeking privacy might want to avoid – surround a welcoming, pebbled courtyard filled with hammocks. There's an on-site restaurant. Bicycle rentals cost $8 per day.

★**Hostal Doña Esther** GUESTHOUSE **$$**

(☎06-292-0739; www.otavalohotel.com; Montalvo 4-44; s/d/tr $34/49/61; @📶) This small, Dutch-owned colonial-style hotel is cozy, with attractive rooms surrounding a courtyard ornamented with ceramics and ferns. The service is personable; there's a popular book exchange and a recommended restaurant.

★**La Luna** GUESTHOUSE **$$**

(☎099-829-4913; www.lalunaecuador.com; camping $8, dm $12, s/d $30/45, without bathroom from $22/36; 📶) Located 4.5km south of Otavalo on the long uphill to Lagunas de Mojanda, La Luna has million-dollar views for budget-minded travelers. Guests dine in the cozy main house, where the fireplace is the nexus of evening activity. Showers are hot and four of the doubles have a private bathroom and fireplace. Lunchboxes can be arranged for hikes.

Rose Cottage CABIN **$$**

(☎099-772-8115; www.rosecottageecuador.com; dm $14, r from $40, s/d without bathroom $16/35; 📶) If you're looking to combine budget

Otavalo

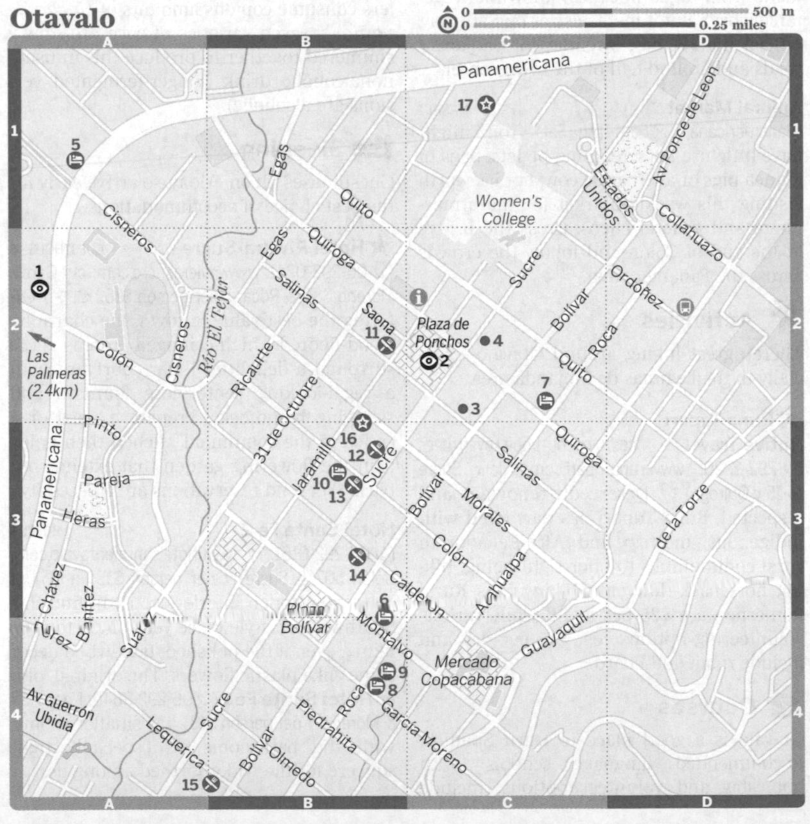

accommodation with spectacular scenery, Rose Cottage is a great choice. Located 3km from Otavalo up a steep hill, this place packs in awesome views and offers a wide range of accommodation options that allow you to enjoy the Andean scenery while still being within easy reach of Otavalo.

Eating

★Cosecha Coffee Shop CAFE, SANDWICHES $
(Jaramillo near Salinas; sandwiches $5-7; ⏰8am-9pm, closed Mon; 📶) Owned by a young American expat, this contemporary cafe with Santa Fe–like adobe walls and minimalistic design wouldn't look out of place in a cool outer borough NYC neighborhood (it even serves bagels!). Sandwiches on homemade focaccia bread are made with local ingredients, and the cappuccinos are the best in town.

Taco Bello MEXICAN $
(Mejia 5-23; mains $2.50-4; ⏰noon-10pm) Puns aside, the tacos, burritos, enchiladas and fajitas are most definitely more beautiful than those of this small, simple restaurant's titular namesake (which it comes by honestly, as the owner once managed a Taco Bell in the US). Decor is a unique mix of headshots of American actresses, sombreros and religious iconography.

Oraibi VEGETARIAN $
(cnr Sucre & Colón; mains $3-10; ⏰11am-7pm Wed-Sat; 🌱) Right in the heart of town you'll find this charming vegetarian oasis in an old hacienda. The menu consists of pizza, sandwiches, salads and tortillas, while the decor is rustic-chic. Outside there's a spacious garden complete with white tablecloths, plenty of shade and live Andean music from 1pm to 4pm daily.

SISA INTERNATIONAL $$
(☎06-292-5624; Calderón 4-9 near Sucre; mains $5-12; 📶) An attractive three-story complex: the ground-floor Daily Grind is good for coffee and desserts, the 2nd floor for sandwiches and the top floor for standard international fare, plus up-to-date Hollywood flicks and art-house films are shown on a large drop-down screen on Saturdays and Sundays.

Mi Otavalito ECUADORIAN $$
(Sucre 11-19; mains $6.50-11; ⏰11:30am-9pm) Catering to groups of Ecuadorian and foreign tourists alike, this Otavalo-themed place has sweet rustic decor. Its fresh ingredients shine in grilled meats, trout and hearty soups.

Entertainment

Otavalo slumbers midweek but draws revelers – mostly very young *otavaleños* – on the weekends.

Peña La Jampa LIVE MUSIC
(cnr Av 31 de Octubre & Panamericana; ⏰7pm-3am Fri & Sat) A long-running favorite with locals. Head to this club for a mix of salsa, merengue, *rock en español* and *folklórica* (folk music); usually doesn't get started until after 11pm.

Amauta LIVE MUSIC
(Morales 5-11 & Jaramillo; ⏰8pm-4am Fri & Sat) Live Andean music, generally after 10pm, is performed at this basement space in the center of town.

Information

Tourist Office (iTur; ☎06-292-7230; www.visitotavalo.com; cnr Quiroga & Jaramillo; ⏰8am-6pm Mon-Sat) Helpful staff here speak some English and can recommend tours, hotels

Otavalo

Sights
1 Animal Market ... A2
2 Crafts Market ... C2

Activities, Courses & Tours
3 Mundo Andino ... C2
4 Runa Tupari Native Travel ... C2

Sleeping
5 Cabañas El Rocío ... A1
6 Hostal Doña Esther ... B3
7 Hostal Valle del Amanecer ... C2
8 Hotel Riviera-Sucre ... B4
9 Hotel Santa Fé 1 ... B4
10 Hotel Santa Fé 2 ... B3

Eating
11 Cosecha Coffee Shop ... B2
12 Mi Otavalito ... B3
13 Oraibi ... B3
14 SISA ... B3
15 Taco Bello ... B4

Entertainment
16 Amauta ... B3
17 Peña La Jampa ... C1

and other activities. The building also houses art, photography and history exhibitions and has computers available to the public on the 2nd floor. Might be open on Sundays in future.

Getting There & Around

The **bus terminal** (cnr Atahualpa & Ordoñez) is two blocks north of Av Quito. Transportes Otavalo/Los Lagos is the only company from Quito ($2, 2½ hours) that enters the terminal. Other companies drop passengers on the Panamericana (a 10-minute walk from town) on their way north or south. Frequent buses depart from the terminal to Ibarra ($0.50, 35 minutes).

Around Otavalo

06

Scattered with lakes, hiking trails and traditional indigenous villages, the enchanting region beyond Otavalo is well worth exploring. Tour agencies in Otavalo can provide information or organize hikes, or you can explore on your own.

The beautiful **Lagunas de Mojanda**, in the high *páramo* some 17km south of Otavalo, make for unforgettable hiking. Taxis from Otavalo charge about $20 each way. You could also organize a trip through Rose Cottage (p664). Runa Tupari (p663) offers guided hikes that include transportation.

Strung along the eastern side of the Panamericana, a few kilometers north of Otavalo, are the mostly indigenous villages of **Peguche**, **Ilumán** and **Agato**. You can walk or take local buses to all three. In Peguche, **Hostal Aya Huma** (06-269-0333; www.ayahuma.com; Los Corazos, Peguche; s/d/tr/q $22/35/46/57, dm $7, camping per person $4) is a beautifully set, mellow *hostal* that serves good, cheap homemade meals (veggie options too). You can also hike to a pretty **waterfall** 2km south of Peguche.

Laguna de San Pablo can be reached on foot from Otavalo by heading roughly 3km southeast on any of the paths heading over the hill behind the railway station. You can then walk the paved road that goes all the way around the lake.

The village of **Cotacachi**, some 15km north of Otavalo, is famous for its leatherwork, which is sold in stores all along the main street. There are hourly buses from Otavalo and a few hotels in Cotacachi.

About 12km west of Cotacachi, the spectacular crater lake **Laguna Cuicocha** lies within an extinct, eroded volcano. The lake is part of **Reserva Ecológica Cotacachi-Cayapas** (lake $1, entire park $2), established to protect the large area of western Andean forest that extends from **Volcán Cotacachi** (4939m) to the Río Cayapas in the coastal lowlands. A walk around the lake takes from 3½ to five hours. You can also take a short boat trip on the lake ($15 per 25-minute trip split by up to six people). You can stay and eat by the lake at **Hostería Cuicocha** (06-301-7219; www.cuicocha.org; per person incl breakfast & dinner $55, mains $4-9; wi-fi). To get there, take a taxi (about $6, one way) from Cotacachi.

Ibarra

06 / POP 140,000

Though growth has diminished the allure of this small Andean town (elevation 2225m), Ibarra's colonial architecture, leafy plazas and cobbled streets make it a handsome city – at least on weekends when the streets aren't so choked with traffic. For a look at archaeological relics as well as masks and costumes from local festivals, visit **Centro Cultural** (cnr Sucre & Oviedo; 9am-5pm Mon-Fri, 10am-4pm Sat & Sun) FREE.

Ibarra's old architecture and shady plazas sit north of the center. The latest tourist attraction is Ibarra's restored rail line, which departs Ibarra **train station** (295-0390; Espejo; round trip US$20) at 10:30am Wednesday to Sunday and makes a 90-minute journey to Salinas (returning at 4:30pm).

Sleeping

Hotel Barcelona HOTEL $

(06-260-0871; suarezmagdalena@yahoo.es; Flores 8-51 near Sánchez y Cifuentes; r per person $10, without bathroom $8; wi-fi) Ignore the inauspicious-looking lobby of this whitewashed three-story hotel overlooking Parque La Merced. You'll likely be pleasantly surprised by the large, wood-floored rooms with high-ceilings; park-facing ones get lots of light, plus early-morning noise. Expect some quirks like the bathroom light switch in the shower.

Eating

La Hacienda ECUADORIAN, INTERNATIONAL $

(cnr Oviedo & Sucre; mains $4-8; 8am-10:30pm Mon-Sat) Pull up a hay-stuffed bench at this friendly, barn-themed deli. Baguette sandwiches are the specialty, but if you've got

GETTING TO COLOMBIA

The Rumichaca border crossing, 6.5km north of Tulcán, is the principal gateway to Colombia and currently the only recommended crossing. Formalities are straightforward at the border, which is open 6am to 10pm daily. Crossing is free. Minibuses ($0.80) and taxis ($5) run regularly between the border and Tulcán's Parque Ayora, about five blocks north of the central plaza. Once across the border, there is frequent taxi transportation to Ipiales ($1), the first town in Colombia, 2km away.

If you need to break your journey at Tulcán, there are many basic but adequate guesthouses such as **Hotel Lumar** (06-298-7137; hotel_lumar@hotmail.com; Sucre near Pichincha; r per person $16.50;). Direct buses from Ibarra ($3, 2½ hours) and Quito ($5, five hours) go to Tulcán. The **bus terminal** (cnr Bolívar & Arellano) is 2.5km southwest of the town center on the road to Ibarra; to get to downtown Tulcán, take a city bus ($0.25) or taxi (about $1).

For information on making this crossing in the opposite direction, see p615.

dining companions, try the multiperson tapas plates ($15) for two to three people. It also offers decent coffee (scarce in Ibarra) and a full breakfast menu.

Entertainment

Café Arte LIVE MUSIC, FILM

(Salinas 5-43; 5pm-3am Fri & Sat) Surprisingly, one of the better live-music venues in Ecuador is here in Ibarra. It hosts bands from as far away as Cuba and Spain. The music ranges from jazz and flamenco to rock. Shows start Fridays and Saturdays around 10pm. Films, dance lessons and art shows are also on the program.

Information

Tourist Office (iTur; 098-123-2789, 06-260-8489; www.touribarra.gob.ec; cnr Oviedo & Sucre; 3-5pm Mon & Tue, 9:30am-12:30pm Wed-Fri) Extremely helpful staff can organize community-tourism activities, mountaineering and hiking. English speakers should ask for the knowledgeable Iriña Gomez.

Getting There & Away

BUS

Ibarra's bus terminal is located on Av Teodoro Gómez near Espejo. A taxi to or from the center costs $1. There are regular departures to Quito ($3, 2½ hours), Guayaquil ($10, 10 hours), Tulcán ($3, 2½ hours) and Otavalo ($0.50, 35 minutes).

CENTRAL HIGHLANDS

South of Quito, the Panamericana winds past eight of the country's 10 highest peaks, including the picture-perfect snowcapped cone of Volcán Cotopaxi and the glaciated behemoth Volcán Chimborazo. For trekkers and climbers, the central highlands are a paradise, and even inexperienced climbers can have a go at summiting some of the country's highest peaks. You can also hike between remote Andean villages near the Quilotoa Loop, gorge yourself on homemade cheeses and chocolate in Guaranda and Salinas, barrel downhill to the Oriente on a rented mountain bike from Baños, hike or trek in spectacular national parks or ride the scenic train down the famous Nariz del Diablo. The central highlands are home to scores of tiny indigenous villages and many of the country's most traditional markets.

Parque Nacional Cotopaxi

03

The centerpiece of Ecuador's most popular **national park** (Mon-Fri 02-204-1520, Sat & Sun 099-498-0121; admission US$10) is the snowcapped and downright astonishing **Volcán Cotopaxi** (5897m), Ecuador's second-highest peak. The park is almost deserted midweek, when nature freaks can have the breathtaking scenery nearly to themselves.

The park has a small museum, an information center, a *refugio* (climbers' refuge) and some camping and picnicking areas. The park's main entrance is via a turnoff from the Panamericana, roughly 30km north of Latacunga. From the turnoff, it's 6km to **Control Caspi**, the entrance station. Any Quito–Latacunga bus will let you off at the turnoff. Follow the main unpaved roads (also signed) to the entrance. It's another 9km or so to the museum. About 4km beyond the museum is **Laguna de Limpiopungo**, a shallow Andean lake 3830m above sea level; a trail circles the lake and takes about half an hour to walk. The *refugio* is about 12km past (and 1000m above) the lake.

Continuing beyond the *refugio* requires snow- and ice-climbing gear and expertise. Quito and Latacunga outfitters offer guided summit trips and downhill mountain-biking tours of Cotopaxi. A two-day summit trip costs about $210 per person from Quito, or $180 from Latacunga.

One of the best-value accommodations in the area is the **Secret Garden Cotopaxi** (☎099-357-2714; www.secretgardencotopaxi.com; dm/d incl 3 meals from US$38/76). This lovely but rustic property on the way to the northern entrance has superb views (when the clouds clear) and loads of activities: hiking, horse riding, mountain biking or simply relaxing in a hammock, sitting fireside or soaking in the Jacuzzi. Transfers from Quito are available through the sister hostel Secret Garden (p648). At the base to the summit, climbers also bunk in the refuge; there are cooking facilities, or you can order meals in the restaurant.

Latacunga

☎03 / POP 87,400

Many travelers end up passing through Latacunga, either to access the Quilotoa Loop, the Thursday-morning market in Saquisilí or Parque Nacional Cotopaxi. But for those who stick around, Latacunga also offers a quiet and congenial historic center.

Activities

Several tour operators offer day trips and two- to three-day climbing trips to Cotopaxi. Day trips run about $50 per person, depending on the size of your group. Two-day climbing trips to Cotopaxi cost about $180 per person – make sure your guide is qualified and motivated if you're attempting the summit.

Tovar Expeditions ADVENTURE TOUR
(☎03-281-1333; www.tovarexpeditions.com; Vivero 1-31, Hostal Tiana) This friendly long-standing operator is based at Hostal Tiana. Licensed by Ecuador's department of tourism.

Sleeping

Hotels fill up fast on Wednesday afternoon for the Thursday-morning indigenous market at Saquisilí.

Hostal Tiana HOSTEL $
(☎03-281-0147; www.hostaltiana.com; Vivero 1-31; dm $10, r per person $15, without bathroom $12; @📶) This good-vibes hostel has everything a good hostel should: cool common area to swap tales, kitchen, free internet, book exchange, clean rooms and bathrooms, free luggage storage, good information and a free breakfast. The old colonial atmosphere lends an air of cool, while the old pipes will leave you wanting come hot-shower time.

Hotel Rosim HOTEL $
(☎03-280-0956; www.rodelu.com.ec; Quito 16-49; s/d $15/28; 📶) With lots of emphasis on cleanliness, this budget alternative has high ceilings and original floors. All the beds are firm and extra long. Cable TV and wi-fi are included in the price – plus you have access to the lobby of the connected Rodelu hotel – making this a top budget bet for the non-hostel crowd.

Eating

Latacunga's traditional dish is the *chugchucara,* a tasty plate of *fritada* (pieces of fried pork), *mote* (hominy) and various sides.

Chugchucaras La Mamá Negra ECUADORIAN $
(Quijano y Ordoñez 1-67; chugchucaras $6; ⏲10am-7pm Tue-Sun) There are several *chugchucara* restaurants on Quijano y Ordoñez, a few blocks south of downtown – they're all family friendly. La Mamá Negra is one of the best.

Guadalajara Grill MEXICAN $
(Quijano y Ordoñez 5-110; mains $4-9; ⏲11am-9pm; 📶) The only Mexican joint in town, this small, well-conceived spot has a wide variety of Mexican standards including flautas, nachos and fajitas. The service is snail-paced, but we love the silver dragonflys climbing the wall, and it's a welcome break from double-fried pork!

Pizzería Buona PIZZA $
(Orellana 1408; pizza $5-7, mains $5-10; ⏲1-11pm) This warm and inviting pizzeria serves up savory pizza pies, slightly overcooked pasta dishes and fresh salads. The split-level dining room features crooked pictures of the

leaning tower of Pisa, muted red walls and a rather fascinating antique hoe.

Information

Banco de Guayaquil (Maldonado 7-20) Bank with ATM.

Getting There & Away

Buses from Quito ($1.50, two hours) will drop you off at the **bus terminal** (Panamericana) if Latacunga is their final destination. If you're taking a bus that's continuing to Ambato or Riobamba, it will drop you off at the corner of 5 de Junio and Cotopaxi, about five blocks west of the Panamericana.

Buses to Ambato ($1, 45 minutes) and Quito leave from the bus terminal. If you're heading south to Riobamba, it's easiest to catch a passing bus from the corner of 5 de Junio and Cotopaxi.

The Quilotoa Loop

☎03

Bumping along the spectacular dirt roads of the Quilotoa Loop and hiking between the area's Andean villages is one of Ecuador's most exhilarating adventures. Transportation is tricky but the rewards are abundant: highland markets, the breathtaking crater lake of Laguna Quilotoa, splendid hikes and traditional highland villages. Allow yourself *at least* three days for the loop and bring warm clothes (it gets painfully cold up here), water and snacks. If you're planning a multiday hike through the area, do yourself a favor and leave your heavy backpack in a guesthouse in Latacunga (carrying only the essentials).

Latacunga to Zumbahua

Heading west of Latacunga, the road winds into the upper reaches of the *páramo*, passing the speck-like village of Tigua around 45km on the Latacunga–Zumbahua road. Tigua is known for the bright paintings of Andean life made on sheepskin canvases. Cozy lodging is available at **Posada de Tigua** (☎03-281-4870; posadadetigua@yahoo.com; vía Latacunga-Zumbahua Km 49; dm/r per person incl breakfast & dinner $25/35), a working dairy ranch. Horse riding is also available.

Some 15km west of Tigua, the tiny village of Zumbahua has a small but fascinating Saturday market and is surrounded by green patchwork peaks, a setting that makes for spectacular walking.

Accommodations and food in Zumbahua are basic. The town's few lodgings fill up fast on Friday, so get there early; the best of them is **Hotel Quilotoa** (Market Plaza; r $8), on the main plaza.

Zumbahua to Saquisilí

From Zumbahua buses and hired trucks trundle up the 14km of unpaved road leading north to one of Ecuador's most staggering sights – **Laguna Quilotoa**, a stunning volcanic crater lake. Near the crater rim are several extremely basic, inexpensive accommodations owned by friendly indigenous folks. Bring a warm sleeping bag. If you want to stay near the lake, **Hostería Alpaca Quilotoa** (☎099-212-5962; www.alpacaquilotoa.com; r per person $25; @) is the best option.

About 14km north of the lake is the wee village of **Chugchilán**, which is an excellent base for hiking and has several traveler-friendly hotels. Rates include dinner and breakfast. **Hostal Mama Hilda** (☎03-270-8005; www.mamahilda.com; s/d incl breakfast & dinner from $30/60; wi-fi) is friendly and popular with backpackers. Delightful **Hostal Cloud Forest** (☎03-270-8181; josecloudforest@gmail.com; dm/s/d incl breakfast & dinner $12/15/30; @ wi-fi) is the cheapest and simplest. A pricier, but highly rated option is the ecofriendly **Black Sheep Inn** (☎03 270-8077; www.blacksheepinn.com; dm $35, r per person incl 3 meals $60-80; wi-fi) .

Some 14km northeast of Chugchilán and just off the Quilotoa Loop, the beautiful village of **Isinliví** makes a good hike from either Chugchilán or Sigchos. Locals can direct you to nearby *pucarás* (pre-Inca hill fortresses). **Llullu Llama** (☎03-281-4790; www.llullullama.com; dm/r/cabin per person incl breakfast & dinner from $18/21/30) is an enchanting old farmhouse with comfortable rooms and a wood-burning stove. A delicious dinner and breakfast is included in the price.

About 23km north of Chugchilán is the village of **Sigchos**, which has a couple of basic lodgings. From here, it's about 52km east to Saquisilí, home of one of the most important indigenous markets in the country. It happens on Thursday mornings. Accommodations are available in several cold-water cheapies.

Getting There & Around

No buses go all the way around the loop. From Latacunga they only travel as far as Chugchilán ($4, four hours), and they either go clockwise (via Zumbahua and Quilotoa) or counterclockwise (via Saquisilí and Sigchos). The bus via Zumbahua departs Latacunga's bus terminal daily at 9:30am and 11:30am, passing Zumbahua around 11am and 1pm, Laguna Quilotoa 30 minutes later, arriving in Chugchilán another 30 minutes later. The bus via Sigchos departs daily at 10:30am, 11:30am and 1pm.

From Chugchilán, buses returning to Latacunga via Zumbahua leave Chugchilán Monday through Friday at 4am (good morning!), passing Quilotoa at around 5am, Zumbahua at around 5:30am, arriving in Latacunga at around 7:30am. On Saturday this bus leaves Chugchilán at 3am, and on Sunday at 6am and 9am. Buses via Sigchos leave Monday through Saturday at 3am, passing Sigchos at around 4am, Saquisilí at around 7am, arriving in Latacunga at around 7:30am. On Sunday this bus departs at 4am and noon, but you must switch buses in Sigchos.

A morning milk truck ($1) leaves Chugchilán for Sigchos around 8am and will take passengers, allowing you to skip the predawn wake-up. In Zumbahua, trucks can be hired to Laguna Quilotoa or anywhere on the loop.

Be sure to confirm bus times at your guesthouse.

Baños

03 / POP 14,700

Hemmed in by luxuriant green peaks, blessed with steaming thermal baths and adorned by a beautiful waterfall, Baños (elevation 1800m) is one of Ecuador's most enticing and popular tourist destinations. Ecuadorians and foreigners alike flock here to hike, soak in the baths, ride mountain bikes, zip around on rented quad-runners, volcano-watch, party, and break their molars on the town's famous *melcocha* (chewy taffy). Touristy as it is, it's a wonderful place to hang out for a few days.

Baños is also the gateway town into the jungle via Puyo. East of Baños, the road drops spectacularly toward the upper Amazon Basin and the views are best taken in over the handlebars of a mountain bike, which you can rent in town.

Baños' annual fiesta is held on December 16 and preceding days.

Activities

A small town in a fabulous setting, Baños offers an excellent range of outdoor adventures, plus hot baths for a refreshing soak when the day is done.

Thermal Baths

A soak in a thermal bath is an essential Baños experience. Go on weekdays to beat the crowds. Towels are generally available for rent, though sometimes they run out.

Las Piscinas de La Virgen SWIMMING
(Montalvo; adult/child $2/1; 5am-5pm & 6-9:30pm) These are the only hot pools in the town proper. Built as a community project in 1928, they are named for the Virgin Mary, who is said to have come here to dip her own feet. One bath is cold, another warm and a third reaches an intense 42°C (118°F).

Piscina El Salado SWIMMING
(admission day/night $3/4; 5am-5pm & 6-10pm) The best hot springs around, El Salado is 2.5km from town in a cozy canyon. It consists of hot, medium and cool pools with an icy river close by.

Hiking

Baños has some great hiking. The tourist office (p673) provides a crude but useful map showing some of the trails around town.

From the bus terminal, a short trail leads to Puente San Francisco (San Francisco

Baños

Activities, Courses & Tours
1 Baños Spanish Center C1
2 Expediciones Amazónicas A3
3 Geotours A3
4 Las Piscinas de La Virgen D3

Sleeping
5 Hostal Chimenea D3
6 Hostal Huillacuna C4
7 Hostal Plantas y Blanco C3
8 La Floresta Hotel A4
9 La Petite Auberge B4
10 Posada del Arte D4

Eating
11 Café Good B3
12 Café Mariane B4
13 Casa Hood B3
14 Mercado Central B3
15 Posada del Arte D4
16 Super Bodega B3
17 Tasca de Baños C3

Drinking & Nightlife
18 Leprechaun B2
19 Stray Dog A3

Bridge), across Río Pastaza. Continue up the other side as far as you want.

At the southern end of Maldonado a footpath leads to **Bellavista** (the white-cross lookout high over Baños) and then to the settlement of **Runtún**, about two hours away. You can then loop around and back down to Baños, ending up at the southern end of Mera. This takes you past the statue of **La Virgen del Agua Santa** about a half hour from town. The whole walk takes four to five hours.

Mountain Biking

Numerous companies rent bikes for $6 to $10 per day. You can find several outfitters along the streets south of Parque de la Basílica. Check the equipment carefully. The best paved ride is the dramatic descent to Puyo, about 60km away by road. Be sure to stop at the spectacular **Pailón del Diablo** (admission $1.50), a waterfall about 18km from Baños. There is a passport control near the town of Shell so carry your documents. From Puyo (or anywhere along the way) take a bus back to Baños with the bike on the roof.

Courses

One-on-one language classes start at around $7 per hour (slightly less for small-group instruction). Schools offerings homestays include **Baños Spanish Center** (☎098-704-5072; www.spanishcenter.banios.com; Oriente & Cañar) and **Raíces Spanish School** (☎03-274-1921; www.spanishlessons.org; Calle 16 de Diciembre & Pablo Suarez).

Tours

For rafting, jungle treks, trips to the neighboring national parks, rafting, volcano climbs, canyoneering, puenteing (like bungee jumping) and more, check out **Geotours** (☎03-274-1344; www.geotoursbanios.com; cnr Ambato & Halflants) and **Expediciones**

Baños

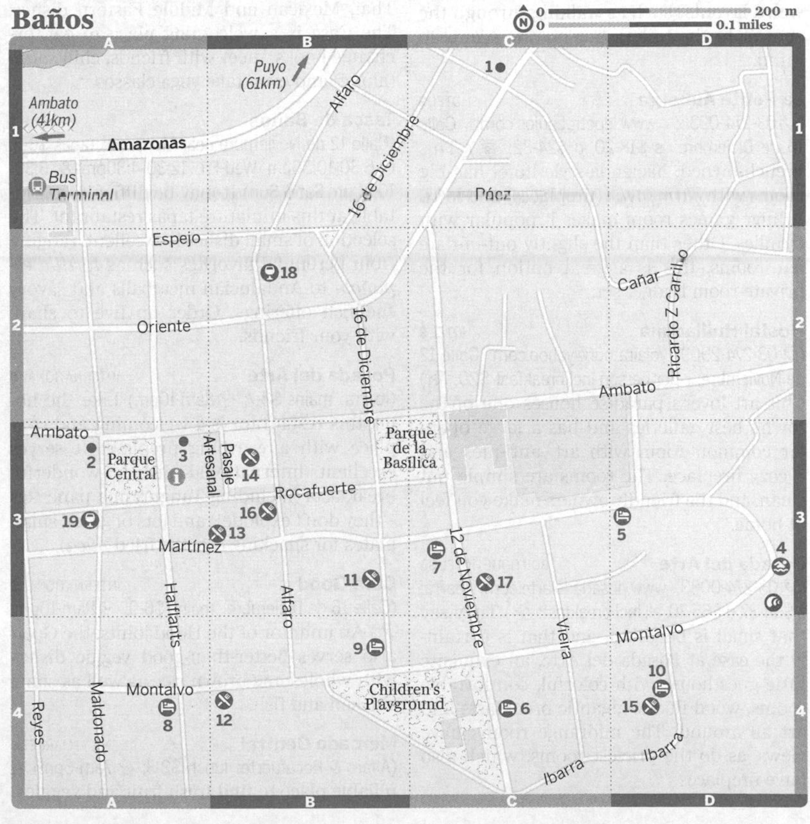

Amazónicas (098-513-8651; amazonicas 2002@hotmail.com; Maldonado).

Sleeping

Hostal Chimenea HOSTEL $
(03-274-2725; www.hostalchimenea.com; Martínez near Vieira; dm/s/d from $7.50/12/19;) From the rather dark reception area, you wouldn't know that this reader-recommended hostel is the best budget offering in town. The bright and clean rooms and dorms come with rainbow-colored blankets, and the upstairs terrace has great views of the waterfall.

Hostal Plantas y Blanco HOSTEL $
(03-274-0044; www.plantasyblanco.com; Martínez near Calle 12 de Noviembre; dm $6-9, s $15, d $20-24;) A bit disco in the common areas, the hyperclean and eternally popular 'Plants and White' (you figure it out) scores big points for its rooftop terrace, outstanding breakfasts, on-site steam bath and overall value. Some rooms have weird layouts (such as walking through the shower to the toilet), but no one seems to mind.

La Petite Auberge HOTEL $
(03-274-0936; www.lepetit.banios.com; Calle 16 de Diciembre; s $18-20, d $24-32;) This French-owned, hacienda-style hotel has big rooms with *chimeneas* (fireplaces) and lofts. A huge games room makes it popular with families. Other than the slightly out-of-date bathrooms, this is a great option for the private-room budget set.

Hostal Huillacuna HOTEL $
(03-274-2909; yojairatour@yahoo.com; Calle 12 de Noviembre; r per person incl breakfast $20;) This art lover's paradise houses one of the town's best galleries and has a large open-air common room with art, antiques and a cozy fireplace. The rooms are simple but clean, and the friendly owners make you feel at home.

Posada del Arte BOUTIQUE HOTEL $$
(03-274-0083; www.posadadelarte.com; Ibarra; s $34-37, d $65-70, all incl breakfast;) They say that small is beautiful, and that is certainly the case at Posada del Arte, an exquisite little guesthouse with colorful, comfortable rooms, wood floors, gigantic breakfasts and art all around. The midrange rooms have views, as do the priciest rooms, which also have fireplaces.

La Floresta Hotel HOTEL $$
(03-274-1824; www.laflorestahotel.com; cnr Montalvo & Halflants; s/d/tr incl breakfast $40/60/85;) This comfortable inn situated around a pretty interior garden with plenty of hang-out areas offers a quiet retreat. The staff here are friendly, and the spacious, tile-floor rooms have big windows, modern bathrooms and comfortable beds – though we wish they were a little brighter.

Eating

Baños is famous for its *melcocha*; makers pull it from wooden pegs in doorways around town. For a pick-me-up, try a glass of fresh *jugo de caña* (sugarcane juice), sold at stalls behind the bus station.

Casa Hood INTERNATIONAL $
(Martínez near Halflants; mains $4-7; 8am-10:15pm;) Named for owner Ray Hood, a long-standing gringo-in-residence, this excellent cafe has nourishing breakfasts, a cheap *almuerzo* (set lunch) and a menu of Thai, Mexican and Middle Eastern dishes. The Casa is a welcoming place to eat, exchange books, meet with friends, chill *solito* (alone) and even take yoga classes.

Tasca de Baños SPANISH $
(Calle 12 de Noviembre near Montalvo; tapas $3-5; 6:30-10:30pm Wed-Fri, 12:30-4:30pm & 6:30-10:30pm Sat & Sun) It may be difficult to get a table at this miniature tapas restaurant. The selection of small dishes is excellent, ranging from perennial favorites such as *tortilla española* to Andalucian meatballs and savory shellfish offerings. Order up five to share with your friends.

Posada del Arte INTERNATIONAL $
(Ibarra; mains $3-7; 8am-10pm) Like the hotel, this restaurant is a welcoming and cozy place with a warming fireplace. It serves excellent international dishes, wonderful breakfasts (including Tungurahua pancakes – they don't explode!) and lots of great, small plates for snacking (try the fried *yuca*).

Café Good INTERNATIONAL $
(Calle 16 de Diciembre; mains $6-9; 8am-10pm;) An imitator of the Hood joints, the Good also serves better-than-good veggie dishes with wholesome brown rice as well as some chicken and fish.

Mercado Central MARKET $
(Alfaro & Rocafuerte; lunch $2-3; 7am-6pm) A reliable place to find fresh fruit and veggies.

Super Bodega SUPERMARKET $
(Alfaro near Rocafuerte; ⌚8:30am-8pm) This centrally located market is the best place to stock up.

Café Mariane FRENCH $$
(Montalvo; mains $7-11; ⌚11am-11pm) Mariane's French-Mediterranean cuisine is a real standout in Baños. The cheese-and-meat fondues are a lot – even for two people – and the pasta and meat dishes are quite elegant. It's a popular spot, so you'll need to be patient when it comes to service.

Drinking & Entertainment

Nightlife in Baños means dancing in local *peñas* (folk-music clubs) and hanging out in bars. The best place to bar-hop is the two-block strip along Alfaro, north of Ambato.

Leprechaun CLUB
(Alfaro btwn Oriente & Espejo; ⌚8pm-2am) One of the hottest spots in town, this large complex has a bonfire in the back patio, dancing in the middle and a roaring salsa dance party at the Salsateca next door Wednesday through Saturday.

Stray Dog BREWPUB
(cnr Rocafuerte & Maldonado; ⌚3-11pm Tue-Sun) The only brewpub in Baños features surprisingly good artisanal offerings like light Llamas' Breath Belgian and bold Stray Dog Stout.

Information

Banco del Pichincha (cnr Ambato & Halflants) Bank with ATM; changes traveler's checks.
Tourist Office (☎03-274-0483; mun_banos@andinanet.net; Halflants near Rocafuerte; ⌚8am-12:30pm & 2-5:30pm Mon-Fri) Lots of info, free maps and emergency-evacuation information.

Getting There & Away

From many towns it may be quicker to change buses in Ambato, where there are frequent buses to Baños ($1, one hour).

From the **terminal** (Amazonas) in Baños many buses leave for Quito ($3.50, 3½ hours), Puyo ($2.50, two hours), Tena ($4, five hours) and Coca ($10, 10 hours).

Guaranda

☎03 / POP 31,000

Half the fun of Guaranda is getting there. The 99km 'highway' & Ambato reaches an altitude over 4000m and passes within 5km of the glacier on Volcán Chimborazo (6310m).

The capital of Bolívar province, Guaranda is small and uneventful, though it is famous for its Carnaval celebrations. It's also the departure point for the delightful village of Salinas.

Sleeping & Eating

Hostal Bolívar HOTEL $$
(☎03-298-0547; www.hotelbolivar.wordpress.com; Sucre 7-04; s/d $20/35; P 📶) A good option for discerning travelers, the rooms here are welcoming and clean – though slightly dated save for the flat-screens – and there's a pleasant courtyard. The attached restaurant has good *almuerzos* (set lunches; $2 to $3). It's two blocks south of Parque Simón Bolívar.

Los 7 Santos CAFE $
(Convención de 1884; mains $1-3; ⌚10am-11pm Mon-Sat) A half a block downhill from Parque Simón Bolívar, Los 7 Santos offers all that you would expect from an artsy cafe in Quito. There's breakfast in the morning and small sandwiches and *bocaditos* (snacks) all day.

Getting There & Away

The bus terminal is 1km east of downtown, just off Av de Carvajal. Buses run to Ambato ($2.10, two hours), Quito ($5, five hours), Riobamba ($2, two hours) and Guayaquil ($4, five hours).

Salinas

☎03 / POP 1000

Set in wild, beautiful countryside and famous for its excellent cheeses, salamis, divine chocolate and rough-spun sweaters, the tiny mountain village of Salinas, 35km north of Guaranda, makes for an interesting jaunt off the beaten track. The elevation is a whopping 3550m. Facing the main plaza, the tourist office will organize visits to Salinas' unique cooperatives.

Two blocks above the plaza, **El Refugio** (☎03-221-0044; www.salinerito.com; r per person $14; 📶) is a nice travelers' lodge with wood details, views of town, and a roaring fireplace in the lobby. It is owned and operated by the community of Salinas.

Facing the main plaza, **La Minga Café** (main plaza; mains $4.50-10; ⌚7:30am-10pm) has good set meals and serves tourists and locals throughout the day.

Buses to Salinas ($0.25, one hour) leave Plaza Roja in Guaranda at 6am and 7am daily and hourly from 10am to 4pm Monday through Friday. Buses for Guaranda ($0.25, one hour) depart at 11am, 1pm and 3pm daily. Collective taxis also run frequently ($1, 45 minutes).

Riobamba

03 / POP 156,000

Deemed 'the Sultan of the Andes,' Riobamba (elevation 2750m) is an old-fashioned, traditional city that both bores and delights travelers. It's sedate yet handsome, with wide avenues and random mismatched shops tucked into imposing 18th- and 19th-century stone buildings. It's also a good place to hire mountain guides.

Sights

Mercado MARKET

On market day (Saturday), Riobamba's streets become a hive of activity, especially along the streets northeast of Parque de la Concepción.

Activities

Thanks to the proximity of Volcán Chimborazo, Riobamba is one of Ecuador's most important climbing towns. Two-day summit trips start around $260 per person for Chimborazo and include guides, climbing gear, transportation and meals.

Mountain biking is also popular, and one-day trips start at $45 per person depending on the route. Downhill descents from the refuge on Chimborazo are an exhilarating way to take in the views.

Riobamba

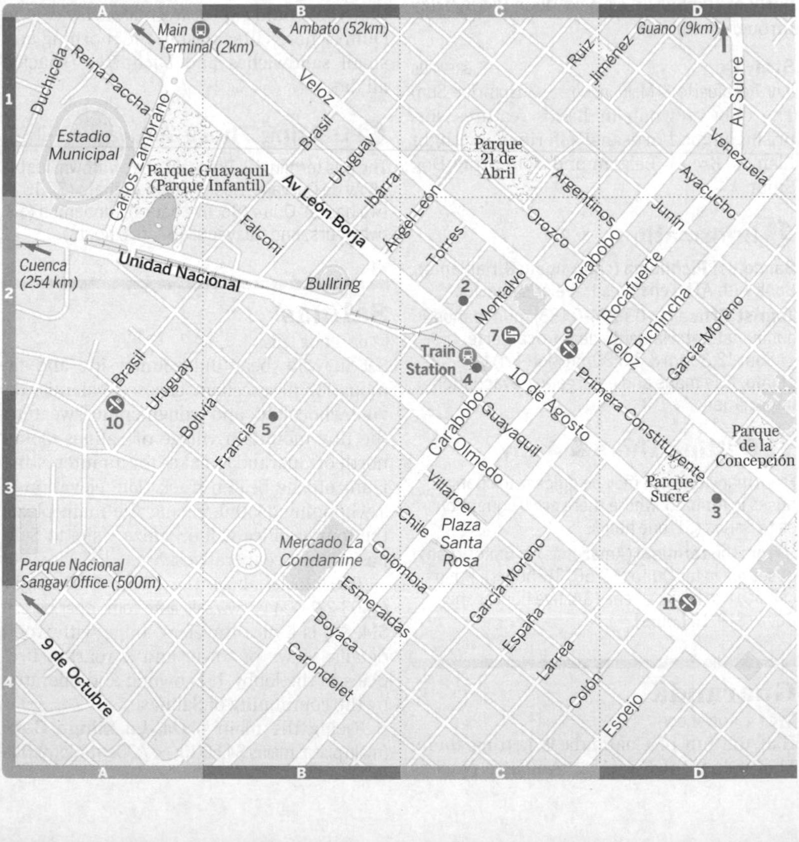

Veloz Coronado Mountain Guides ADVENTURE TOUR
(☎03-296-0916; www.velozexpeditions.com; Chile 33-21 & Francia) A pioneer in Ecuadorian mountaineering, and owner of this excellent guide shop, Enrique Veloz is practically a historical personage in Ecuador, having climbed Chimborazo more than 500 times. Guides have high standards for safety, climb most of the peaks in the central sierra, and also offer mountain-climbing courses.

Julio Verne Tour Operator ADVENTURE TOUR
(☎03-296-3436; www.julioverne-travel.com; Espectador 22-25) A respected Ecuadorian-Dutch full-service operator offering affordable, two-day summit trips to Chimborazo and other peaks, as well as to the Oriente and Galápagos. The company also offers downhill mountain biking on Chimborazo.

Pro Bici ADVENTURE TOUR
(☎03-295-1759; www.probici.com; Primera Constituyente & Larrea) Located on the 2nd floor through the fabric store, this is one of the country's best mountain-bike operators, with many years of experience and excellent trip reports from clients. It offers mountain-bike rentals (per day $15 to $25, depending on the bike), excellent maps, good safety practices and fascinating day tours ($40 to $60) to Chimborazo, Atillo and Colta. The friendly owners speak English.

Sleeping

★Hostal Oasis GUESTHOUSE $
(☎03-296-1210; www.oasishostelriobamba.com; Veloz 15-32; s/d $13/24; P @) When it comes to friendliness, value and down-home cutesiness, this guesthouse is hard to beat. Rooms and apartments are grouped around a garden, complete with a shared kitchen. It has a book exchange and free calls to the US and Canada. We only wish it were a little closer to the downtown action.

Hotel Tren Dorado HOTEL $
(☎03-296-4890; www.hoteltrendorado.com; Carabobo 22-35; r per person $15; P) Not surprisingly, the 'Golden Train' is close to the train station. Get past the dark reception to reach the spotless, comfortable rooms, an airy terrace and sweet lion bed covers (grrrr). A self-serve breakfast will cost you $3 extra. The hot water seems infallible and the TVs are big.

Riobamba

Sights
1 Mercado ... E2

Activities, Courses & Tours
2 Julio Verne Tour Operator ... C2
3 Pro Bici ... D3
4 Tren del Hielo I ... C2
5 Veloz Coronado Mountain Guides ... B3

Sleeping
6 Hostal Oasis ... F4
7 Hotel Tren Dorado ... C2

Eating
8 Colibrí ... F4
9 El Delirio Restaurante ... C2
10 La Abuela Rosa ... A3
11 Mercado La Merced ... D4

Eating & Drinking

Colibrí ECUADORIAN $
(Veloz 15-25; breakfast $1.75, set meals $2-3; 7am-8pm) Made with the international backpacker crowd in mind, this adorable little cafe is the best value in town. The wholesome breakfasts include whole-grain bread and can easily last you through the morning. The set lunches and dinner are simple and savory, with meat, pasta, soups and dessert.

La Abuela Rosa ECUADORIAN $
(Brasil & Esmeraldas; mains $1-3; 4-9pm Mon-Sat) Drop by Grandma Rosa's for *comida típica* (traditional Ecuadorian food) and tasty snacks, including sandwiches, chocolate and cheese. Friendly, cozy and popular with locals.

Mercado La Merced MARKET $
(Mercado M Borja; Guayaquil btwn Espejo & Colón; mains $3; 7am-6pm) The ladies hawking *hornado* (whole roast pig) put on a pretty hard sell, yelling out for your attention and offering samples. If you can stand the pressure and you're up for dining with flayed Wilburs on every side, then the market is fun and interesting. The pork is superfresh. Saturdays are busiest.

El Delirio Restaurante ECUADORIAN $$
(Primera Constituyente 28-16; mains $7-10; noon-10pm Tue-Sun) Named for a poem by the great liberator, Simón Bolívar, this historic monument turned restaurant serves *comida típica* in a candlelit, antique atmosphere. Service is slow, but the patio is simply amazing.

Information

Banco de Guayaquil (Primera Constituyente) Bank with ATM.

Parque Nacional Sangay Office (03-295-3041; parquesangay@andinanet.net; Av 9 de Octubre; 8am-1pm & 2-5pm Mon-Fri) West of downtown, near Duchicela; get information and pay entry fees to Parque Nacional Sangay here.

Getting There & Away

BUS

The **main bus terminal** (Av León Borja at Av de la Prensa) is 2km northwest of the center. Buses run frequently to Quito ($4, four hours), Guayaquil ($5, five hours) and Alausí ($2, two hours), and less frequently to Cuenca ($6, six hours). There's at least one morning bus to Machala ($6.40, seven hours). Local buses run along Av León Borja, connecting the terminal with downtown.

Buses to Baños ($2, two hours) and the Oriente leave from the **Oriente bus terminal** (cnr Espejo & Luz Elisa Borja) just northeast of the center.

Volcán Chimborazo

Not only is the extinct Volcán Chimborazo the highest mountain in Ecuador, but its peak (6310m), due to the earth's equatorial bulge, is also the furthest point from the center of the earth – tell that to your K2-climbing buddies. The mountain is part of **Reserva de Producción de Fauna Chimborazo**, which also encompasses **Volcán Carihuairazo** (5020m). Incidentally, it is called a 'fauna-production reserve' because it is home to hundreds of *vicuña* (a wild relative of the llama). You're sure to see them if you explore the park.

Two small lodges on the lower slopes of Chimborazo are interesting places to see the countryside and learn about local culture. **La Casa del Cóndor** (099-8575-5031; Pulinguí San Pablo; dm $12, incl 3 meals $30) in the small

RIDING THE ANDEAN RAILS

Ecuador's train service has received a massive makeover in recent years, and Riobamba currently runs two different tourist trains from its restored **train station** (1-800-873-637; www.trenecuador.com; Calle 10 de Agosto near Carabobo; fare $12).

The **Tren del Hielo** (return $14) goes from Riobamba to Urbina and back, departing at 8am on Thursdays to Sundays. On clear days, you'll have fine views of Chimborazo. In Urbina, you can visit a small museum exploring the history of the *hieleros* (men who harvested ice from the glaciers). Visitors arrive back in Riobamba around noon.

The **Sendero de los Ancestros** (return $17) train goes 25km from Riobamba to Colta, where you can take a scenic boat ride on Lago Colta and visit the 16th-century Balbanera church. The train departs Riobamba at noon Thursdays to Sundays and returns around 4pm.

indigenous community of **Pulinguí San Pablo** (3900m) on the Riobamba–Guaranda road offers simple accommodations; locals provide basic guiding services, mountain bikes are available, and there are fascinating interpretation trails in the area.

The two high **climbers' refuges** (dm $10), at 4800m and 5000m, on the other hand, are pretty much places to eat some grub and catch a few winks before heading out on an all-night climb.

Climbing beyond the refuge requires snow- and ice-climbing gear and mountaineering experience, as does the ascent of Carihuairazo. Avoid inexperienced guides; a climb at this altitude is not to be taken lightly.

There are also excellent trekking opportunities between the two mountains. Topographical maps of the region are available at the Instituto Geográfico Militar (p727) in Quito. June through September is the dry season in this region, and the nights are very cold year-round.

Alausí

☎03 / POP 8100

The busy little railroad town of Alausí (elevation 3323m) draws visitors who come for a look at the famous **Nariz del Diablo** on one of Ecuador's most dramatic train rides.

The touristic train ride (return $30) includes a guide who provides commentary about the line in both Spanish and English; there's also a small interpretation center in Sibambe that provides more details on the line's construction. Unless you're a train buff, you might find the 12km journey poor value. Current departure times from Alausí are 8am, 11am and 2pm Thursdays to Sundays.

Sundays are the best time to come to town, as you can check out the lively market, which takes over many of the town's streets. Many hotels are found along Alausí's main street (Av 5 de Junio). The pleasant **Hotel Europa** (☎03-293-0200; www.hoteleuropa.com.ec; Av 5 de Junio 175 at Orozco; r per person $18, without bathroom $10; P) is a good central option. Some 3km outside of town, **Hostería Pircapamba** (☎03-293-0180; www.pircapamba.com; r per person incl breakfast $20) has a more charming setting with great views.

Buses run hourly to and from Riobamba ($2, two hours) and several buses a day also go to Cuenca ($5, four hours).

SOUTHERN HIGHLANDS

As you roll down the Panamericana into the southern highlands, the giant snowcapped peaks of the central highlands fade from view. The climate gets a bit warmer, distances between towns become greater, and the frozen-in-time settlements drift slowly past. Cuenca – arguably Ecuador's most beautiful city – and handsome little Loja are the region's only sizable towns.

Other attractions here include the lake-studded Parque Nacional Cajas, which offers excellent hiking. In Parque Nacional Podocarpus you can explore cloud forest, tropical humid forest and *páramo* within the same park. There's also the laid-back gringo hangout of Vilcabamba, where you can spend days walking or horse riding through captivating mountain country, returning each evening to hot tubs and delicious food.

Cuenca

☎07 / POP 332,000

Captivating Cuenca (elevation 2530m) has narrow cobblestone streets, whitewashed red-tiled buildings, handsome plazas and domed churches, and its setting above the grassy banks of the Río Tomebamba is supremely impressive. Though firmly anchored in its colonial past, Ecuador's third-largest city also has a modern edge, with international restaurants, art galleries, cool cafes and welcoming bars tucked into its architectural gems.

Sights

For a scenic stroll, head down to 3 de Noviembre, a lane lined with colonial buildings, which follows the northern bank of the **Río Tomebamba**.

Clustered around the Plazoleta de la Cruz del Vado are a few interesting sites, including the **Prohibido Museo de Arte Extremo** (La Condamine 12-102; noon-late), a goth-lovers' gallery, bar and cafe, and **Laura's Antiguidades y Curiosidades** (La Condamine 12-112; 9am-1pm & 3-6pm Mon-Fri), which showcases a hodgepodge of curios and objets d'art in a 19th-century house.

★**Museo del Banco Central 'Pumapungo'** MUSEUM
(www.pumapungo.org; Larga btwn Arriaga & Huayna Capac; 8am-5:30pm Tue-Sat) FREE It's worth the walk east along Calle Larga to one of

Ecuador's most significant museums. While there's some great modern art downstairs, the highlight is on the 2nd floor. Here begins a comprehensive voyage through Ecuador's diverse indigenous cultures, with colorfully animated dioramas and reconstructions of typical houses, including Afro-Ecuadorians from Esmeraldas province, the cowboy-like *montubios* (coastal farmers) of the western lowlands, several rainforest groups and all major highland groups.

Cuenca

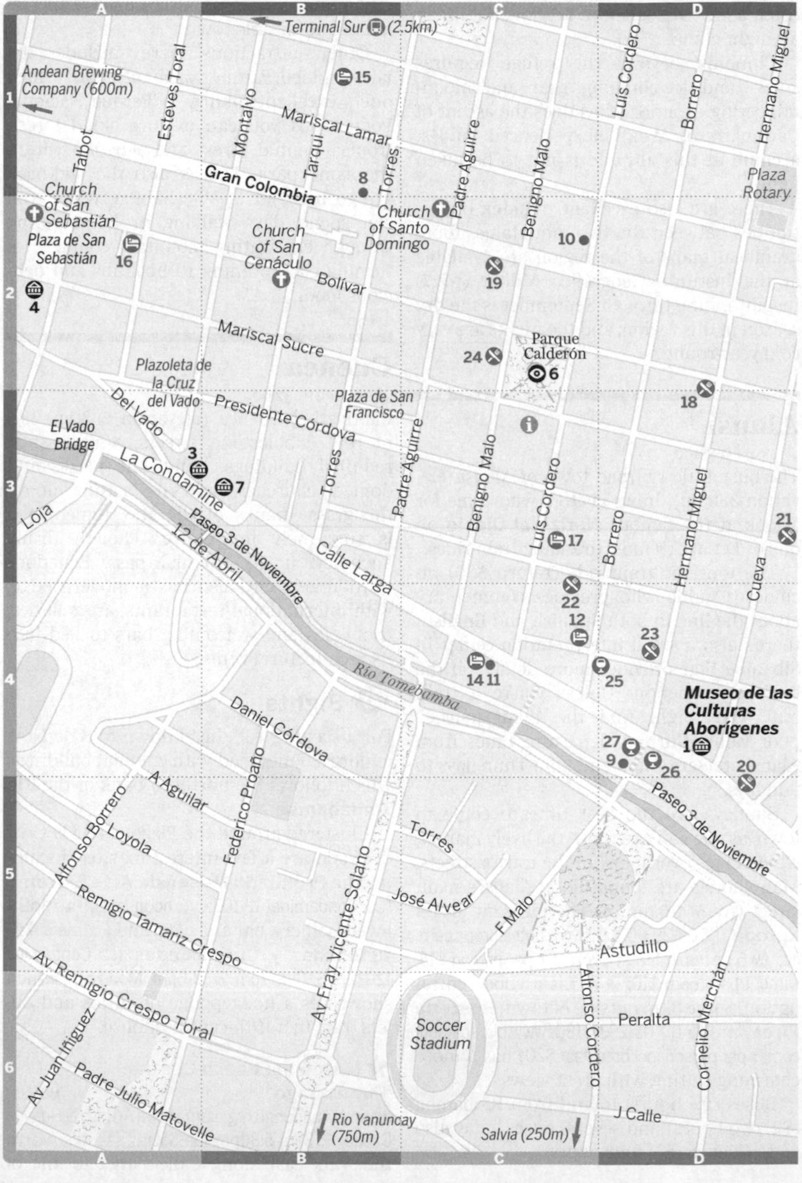

Museo Manuel Agustín Landivar MUSEUM

(cnr Larga 2-23 & Vega; ⏲9am-1pm & 3-6pm Mon-Fri) FREE At the east end of Calle Larga, this museum has archaeological exhibits and tours of the **Ruinas de Todos Santos**, which reveal Cañari, Inca and Spanish ruins, layered one over the other. If you don't want a guide, you can also look at them from below on Avenida de Todos Santos.

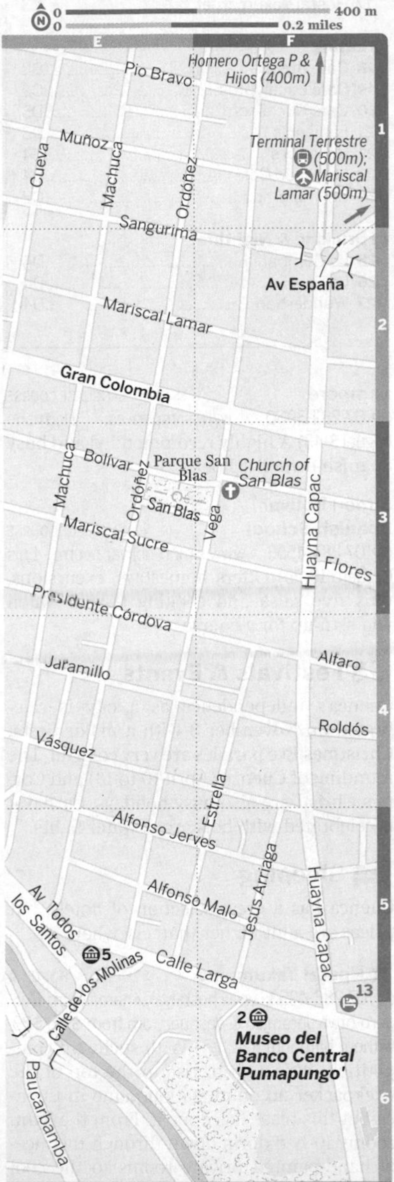

Parque Calderón PLAZA

On one side of this park/plaza stands the whitewashed 'old cathedral,' also known as **El Sagrario**. Construction began in 1557, the year Cuenca was founded, and in 1739 La Condamine's expedition used its towers as a triangulation point to measure the shape of the earth. It is now deconsecrated and serves as a religious museum and recital hall.

Museo de Arte Moderno MUSEUM

(cnr Mariscal Sucre & Talbot; admission by donation; ⏲9am-5pm Mon-Fri, to 1pm Sat & Sun) On the south side of Plaza de San Sebastián, this fun museum was once a home for the insane. It now houses a highly regarded collection of Ecuadorian and Latin American art.

★**Museo de las Culturas Aborígenes** MUSEUM

(museoarq@etapaonline.net.ec; Larga 5-24; admission $2; ⏲9am-6pm Mon-Fri, to 1pm Sat) This indigenous culture museum has more than 5000 archaeological pieces representing more than 20 pre-Hispanic Ecuadorian cultures going back some 15,000 years. But what makes this such a gem of a museum is the informative guided tour – touching upon such unexpected items as combs and obsidian mirrors and rather sophisticated cooking equipment, as well as explaining the striking designs.

Activities

Cuenca is an ideal base for exploring nearby attractions such as Parque Nacional Cajas, the Inca ruins of Ingapirca and indigenous villages. Day trips cost about $45 per person. You can also arrange horse riding, biking, canyoning and other adventures.

Expediciones Apullacta ADVENTURE TOUR

(☎07-283-7815; www.apullacta.com; Gran Colombia 11-02, 2nd fl) A big operation that organizes day tours to Ingapirca ($50), Parque Nacional Cajas ($55) and the Gualaceo area ($63), among other sites. They offer a 3-day/2-night Inca Trail trek package too ($280), besides multi-day trips to different parts of Ecuador.

Cuenca

Top Sights

1 Museo de las Culturas Aborígenes D4
2 Museo del Banco Central 'Pumapungo' F6

Sights

3 Laura's Antiguidades y Curiosidades A3
4 Museo de Arte Moderno A2
5 Museo Manuel Agustín Landivar E5
6 Parque Calderón C2
7 Prohibido Museo de Arte Extremo B3

Activities, Courses & Tours

8 Centers for Interamerican Studies B1
Expediciones Apullacta .... (see 8)
9 Sampere D4
10 Simón Bolívar Spanish School C2
11 Terra Diversa Travel Center C4

Sleeping

12 El Cafecito C4
13 Hostal Alternative F6
14 Hostal Casa de Barranco C4
15 Hostal Macondo B1
16 Hostal Posada del Angel A2
17 Hostal Yakumama C3

Eating

18 Café Austria D2
19 Café Eucalyptus C2
20 Café Nucallacta D5
21 Fabiano's D3
22 Govinda's C4
23 Moliendo Café D4
24 Raymipampa C2

Drinking & Nightlife

25 La Compañía D4
26 La Parola D4
27 Wunderbar D4

Terra Diversa Travel Center TOUR
(☎999-204-832, 07-282-3782; www.terradiversa.com; Larga near Cordero) Specializes in biking and horseback-riding day trips – as well as overnight horseback-riding trips that include staying at haciendas or camping along the Inca Trail north of Ingapirca. They also have Parque Nacional Cajas and Amazon tours. Three-hour Cuenca city tours cost $25.

Kushiwaira ECOTOUR
(☎07-244-0411, 099-747-6337; kushiwaira@gmail.com; per person $40) This is one of the Cuenca region's best-run community tourism projects, running on demand to the nearby community of Tarqui. One-of-a-kind day-long programs include visiting a *cuy* (guinea pig) breeding center, demonstrations of typical Inca rituals, picnics with the locals and the like. Trips leave from the Carolina Bookstore (inquire here when the next trip is leaving).

Courses

Cuenca is an excellent setting to study Spanish. One-on-one classes cost around $10 per hour.

Centers for Interamerican Studies LANGUAGE COURSE
(CEDEI; ☎07-283-9003; www.cedei.org; cnr Gran Colombia 11-02 & General Torres) A nonprofit school offering drop-in and/or long-term courses in Spanish, Kichwa and Portuguese.

Sampere LANGUAGE COURSE
(☎07-282-3960; www.sampere.es; Hermano Miguel 3-43) A highly recommended and busy Spanish-owned school.

Simón Bolívar Spanish School LANGUAGE COURSE
(☎07-284-4555; www.simon-bolivar2.com; Luís Cordero 10-25) Offers homestays, excursions, plus free salsa and cooking lessons when you sign up for a course.

Festivals & Events

Cuenca's independence as a city is celebrated on November 3 with a major fiesta. Christmas Eve parades are very colorful. The founding of Cuenca (April 10 to 13) and Corpus Christi are also busy holidays. Carnaval is celebrated with boisterous water fights.

Sleeping

Cuenca has a great selection of hotels, but prices are a bit higher than elsewhere.

★ **Hostal Yakumama** HOSTEL $
(☎07-283-4353; www.hostalyakumama.com; Cordero btwn Jaramillo & Vásquez; dm from $7, d $29, without bathoom $20; 📶) With such stiff competition, it's tough to rise to the top of the backpacker accommodation game in Cuenca but this place has done it. From the light, roomy 10-bed dorm down through the nicely hand-painted private rooms to the cool common areas (a courtyard full of murals

and plants and table football in a room off to the side), the owners clearly know what a great hostel needs.

Hostal Alternative HOSTEL $

(07-408-4101; www.alternativehostal.com; cnr Huayna Capac & Cacique Duma; dm $9, d without bathroom $20;) Although it's a bit removed from the action, this sparkly new hostel (with a scary logo, cleaner-than-Clorox rooms, shared kitchen, TV room and excellent terrace) has a ton of potential. The modern octagon-shaped building offers small- and medium-size dorm rooms with good mattresses and plenty of space.

El Cafecito HOSTEL $

(07-283-2337; www.cafecito.net; Vásquez 7-36; dm $7.50, r $26, without bathroom $16;) Not much has changed at long-term backpacker fave El Cafecito since our last visit. This is both good (why change a good thing – this probably remains ground zero for meeting other travelers) and bad (rooms look a tad battered and other hostels in town have overtaken the place in quality). The courtyard cafe-bar is still charming and atmospheric – but rooms nearby stay noisy until the wee hours.

Hostal Casa de Barranco GUESTHOUSE $$

(283-9763; www.casadelbarranco.com; Larga btwn Benigno Malo & Cordero; s/d/tr $29/44/58) This astounding colonial abode drips over the high cliffs of El Barranco. The rooms are of a high standard (well, some low on light) with creaking wooden floors and reading lamps (four have river-facing terraces). The cafeteria, all bare stone walls, haughty furniture and more river views from its terrace, makes a good breakfast spot.

Hostal Posada del Angel B&B $$

(07-284-0695; www.hostalposadadelangel.com; Bolívar 14-11; s/d/tr incl breakfast $42/68/75;) This yellow-and-blue B&B in a – you guessed it! – colonial-era house has comfortable rooms with cable TV and big beds. Those off the interior balconies have high ceilings, and several others reached by a narrow wooden staircase are tucked away in the quiet reaches (actually our favourites). Breakfasts in the sunlit lobby are watched over by the eponymous angel.

Hostal Macondo HOTEL $$

(07-282-1700; http://hostalmacondo.com; Tarqui 11-64; s/d incl breakfast $35/50;) The colonial-style Hostal Macondo has spotless palatial rooms in the front, older section, and small but cozy rooms situated around a big, sunny garden out back, making this one of the best lower-end deals in town. Longer-staying guests will enjoy access to the well-equipped and spotless kitchen, and everyone likes the continental breakfasts with bottomless cups of coffee.

Eating

★Moliendo Café COLOMBIAN $

(Vásquez 6-24; mains $3-6; noon-9pm Mon-Sat;) This is one of the best little eateries you'll find in Ecuador – and that's why Moliendo Café is always rammed. The hearty *arepas* (maize pancakes) herald from Ecuador's northern neighbors but are a specialty here. Topped with anything from beans and cheese to slow-cooked pork, they go well with a cold beer or a strong Juan Valdez coffee.

Café Nucallacta CAFE $

(http://cafenucallacta.com; Larga 6-42 between Borrero & Hermano Miguel; light meals $2-5; 8am-6pm Mon-Sat, 9am-1pm Sun;) The best cafe in Cuenca. Artisan Ecuadorian coffee is roasted and the resulting brews are the main reason to stop by – along with gleaning an insight into Ecuador's coffee industry from the knowledgable owner. But they also do nice breakfasts and cakes and the tables fill up fast in the mornings.

Govinda's INTERNATIONAL $

(Jaramillo 7-27; set lunches $2.50, mains $4; 8:30am-3pm Mon-Sat, 6-10pm Wed-Sat;) Pizzas, lentil burgers and a little good karma to wash it down.

★Salvia EUROPEAN $$

(093-951-3820; www.salviacuenca.com; cnr Roberto Crespo Toral & Mora; mains $10-13; noon-3pm & 6-9pm Wed-Sat, noon-3pm Sun;) The 'O!' is firmly placed in the local gastropub scene (indeed, Salvia *is* the scene in its entirety). This new British-owned restaurant is now making some of the city's best food out of a beautifully refurbished house on the up-and-coming 'south side' of Cuenca.

Raymipampa ECUADORIAN $$

(Benigno Malo 8-59; mains $5-11; 8:30am-10:30pm Mon-Fri, from 9.30am Sat & Sun;) This Cuenca institution is overwhelmingly popular with locals and travelers and stays open late. The food hangs somewhere between Ecuadorian comfort food and diner fare. Get a pew on the upstairs deck for a view of what Ecuadorian meals are all about.

Café Eucalyptus INTERNATIONAL **$$**
(www.facebook.com/pages/Cafe-Eucalyptus/122414164525146; Gran Colombia 9-41; mains $6-23; ⌚noon-10pm Mon-Thu, until 2am Fri & Sat, 5-10pm Sun; 📶) The irreverent Eucalyptus menu proudly declares that it doesn't serve 'customs officials, crazy bus drivers, or airline executives.' For the rest of us, dozens of Asian, seafood and other reliably delicious international dishes are served at tables near roaring fireplaces, and an extensive variety of wines and beers flows from the gorgeous bar.

Café Austria EUROPEAN **$$**
(cnr Hermano Miguel & Bolívar; mains $6-9; ⌚9am-10.30pm; 📶) Does exactly what it says on the label. Austrian-esque comfort food such as goulash, strudel and decent espresso taste particularly divine after days/weeks on the road, and the new location is as traveler friendly as the old. But they could improve on the sacher torte.

Fabiano's PIZZERIA **$$**
(cnr Presidente Córdova & Cueva; pizzas $6-17; 📶) Amiable, family-friendly Fabiano's is a tried, tested gringo hangout but garners a following among Ecuadorians too. Pizzas are generous and tasty – try the stodge fest that is lasagna pizza, and, should it prove too much, these guys'll willingly wrap it up for you to take home.

Drinking & Entertainment

Outside of Thursday to Saturday nights, Cuenca is pretty sedate. You'll find the densest collection of bars along Calle Larga and nearby Vásquez and Hermano Miguel.

La Compañía BREWERY
(cnr Borrero & Vásquez) Cuenca's first microbrewery is still the best (but only by a beer-mat's breadth) – it caters to a young rocker crowd and offers up decent hand-crafted stouts, Irish reds and golden brews.

Wunderbar BAR
(Escalinata 3-43; ⌚11am-midnight Mon-Thu, until 2am Fri & Sat) This Austrian-owned place is *voon*derful if you want a classic bar with big wooden tables to sit around with friends. Food is served, and there's a happy 'hour' from 11am to 6pm. They have an American pool table and big-screen sports.

La Parola LIVE MUSIC
(cnr Larga & Hermano Miguel; ⌚4:30pm-2am Tue-Sat) Food and cocktails complement a great variety of live music at this hangout high on the cliffs of Barranco. It's right above the La Escalinata staircase.

Information

Banco de Guayaquil (Mariscal Sucre near Borrero) Bank with ATM.

Banco del Pichincha (cnr Solano & 12 de Abril) Bank with ATM.

Clínica Hospital Monte Sinaí (☎07-288-5595; www.hospitalmontesinai.org; cnr Av Solano & Miguel Cordero) An excellent clinic with some English-speaking staff.

Tourist Office (iTur; ☎07-282-1035; Mariscal Sucre at Luís Cordero; ⌚8am-8pm Mon-Fri, 8:30am-1:30pm Sat) Friendly and helpful; English spoken.

Getting There & Away

AIR

Cuenca's **Aeropuerto Mariscal Lamar** (Av España) is 2km from downtown. **TAME** (☎07-288-9581/9097; www.tame.com.ec; Astudillo 2-22; ⌚8:30am-1pm & 2-6:30pm Mon-Fri, 9:30am-12:30pm Sat) flies daily to Quito and Guayaquil; prices for both cities range from $80 to $120.

BUS

Cuenca has two major bus stations. The majority of buses leave from **Terminal Terrestre** (Av España), 1.5km northeast of the center. Buses to Guayaquil ($8) either via Parque Nacional Cajas (3½ hours) or Cañar (5½ hours). There are regular departures to Quito ($10, 10 to 12 hours). Several buses go to Machala ($5.50, four hours); a few continue on to Huaquillas ($7, seven hours). Buses go regularly to Alausí ($6, four hours). Several buses a day head to Loja ($7.50, 5½ hours), Macas ($8.50) and other Oriente towns. Buses for Gualaceo ($0.80, one hour) leave every 30 minutes.

Some buses (including those to Parque Nacional Cajas) leave from Terminal Sur, 2.5km west of the center.

Getting Around

Cuenca is very walkable. A taxi to or from the bus terminal or airport costs about $2. Buses depart regularly to downtown ($0.25) from the front of the Terminal Terrestre bus station.

Around Cuenca

07

From small indigenous villages to hot springs and hiking, there's ample opportunity for excursions from Cuenca.

Ingapirca

The most important Inca site in Ecuador, Ingapirca was built toward the end of the 15th century during the Inca expansion into present-day Ecuador. The **site** (admission with/without guided tour $6; 8am-6pm), 50km north of Cuenca, was built with the same mortarless, polished-stone technique used by the Inca in Peru. Although less impressive than sites in Peru, it's definitely worth a visit. A guided tour (English available) explains the design and significance of the various ruins.

For an economical visit, catch a direct Transportes Cañar bus ($2.50, two hours) from Cuenca's bus terminal at 9am or 12:20pm. Buses return to Cuenca at 1pm and 3:45pm. More frequent buses from Cuenca depart half-hourly to El Tambo, where you can catch an onward bus or taxi ($5) to Ingapirca, 8km further.

Gualaceo, Chordeleg & Sígsig

Seeing these three villages (famous for their Sunday markets) together makes a great day trip from Cuenca. If you start early, you can be back in Cuenca by the afternoon. Gualaceo has the biggest market, with fruit and vegetables, animals and various household goods. Chordeleg's market, 5km away, is smaller and more touristy. Sígsig's market is 25km from Gualaceo and is an excellent place to see the art of panama hat making.

From Cuenca's bus terminal, buses leave every 30 minutes to Gualaceo ($0.80, one hour), Chordeleg ($1, one hour) and Sígsig ($1.25, 1½ hours). You can walk the 5km from Gualaceo to Chordeleg if you don't want to wait for the bus.

Parque Nacional Cajas

The stunning, chilly, moorlike *páramo* of **Parque Nacional Cajas** (Cajas National Park; 8am-4:30pm) FREE is famous for its many lakes, great trout fishing and rugged camping and hiking. It's a good day trip from Cuenca (only 30km away). Camping (per person $4) is allowed, and a small *refugio* has eight cots and a kitchen; the *refugio* fills up fast. Hiking solo in Cajas can be dangerous – the abundance of lakes and fog is disorienting. It's best to be finished by 4pm when the fog gets thick. Shorter trails are well marked. Glossy, topographical trail maps are free with admission.

Transporte Occidental buses ($1.25, one hour) leave from Terminal Sur in Cuenca (2.5km west of the historic center) at 6:15am, 7am, 8am, 10am, noon and in the afternoon. To return to Cuenca, you can flag any passing Cuenca-bound bus. Cuenca tour agencies run day trips for about $50 per person.

DON'T MISS

THE INCA TRAIL TO INGAPIRCA

Though it sees only a fraction of the traffic that the Inca Trail to Machu Picchu gets, the three-day hike to Ingapirca is a memorable trek. Parts of the approximately 40km hike follow the original royal road that linked Cuzco with Quito and Tomebamba (at present-day Cuenca).

The starting point for the hike is the village of **Achupallas**, 23km southeast of Alausí. The route is faint in places and sometimes even nonexistent, so travel with a compass and three 1:50,000 topographical maps – Alausí, Juncal and Cañar – available at **Instituto Geográfico Militar** (p727) in Quito.

To get to Achupallas, take one of the daily trucks from Alausí or, more reliably, hire a taxi-pickup for about $10 to $15 one way. Alternatively, south-bound Panamericana buses from Alausí can drop you off at La Moya (also known as Guasuntos), where you can wait for passing trucks headed to Achupallas, 12km up a slim mountain road. You can hire guides in Achupallas for about $30 to $40 per day. Among other operators, **Julio Verne** (p675) in Riobamba runs trips for about $320 per person. If you want to go on your own, check out a hiking guide, such as *Ecuador: Climbing and Hiking Guide* by Rob Rachowiecki and Mark Thurber.

Saraguro

07

Quaint little Saraguro, 165km south of Cuenca, is home to the indigenous Saraguro, the most prosperous indigenous group in the southern highlands. The group originally lived in the Lake Titicaca region of Peru but were forcibly relocated through the Inca empire's system of colonization.

Today, the Saraguro are readily identifiable by their traditional dress. Both men and women wear striking, flat, white, felt hats with wide brims that are often spotted on the underside.

The best day to be in Saraguro is Sunday, when the local market draws Saraguros from the surrounding countryside. Sleep at the pretty **Hostal Achik Wasi** (07-220-0058; Intiñan, Barrio La Luz; r per person incl breakfast $20), 10 minutes out of town. For memorable homestays in nearby villages, contact **Operadora de Turismo Comunitario Saraurku** (07-220-0331; www.turismosaraguro.com; cnr 18 de Noviembre & Loja; 8:30am-6pm Mon-Fri). You'll find tasty meals at indigenous-run **Mamá Cuchara** (Parque Central; mains $3; 7am-7pm Sun-Fri).

Any Loja-bound bus from Cuenca ($5, 3½ hours) will drop you off a block from the main plaza. Buses to Loja ($2.50, 1½ hours) leave hourly during the day.

Loja

07 / POP 181,000

Thanks to its proximity to the Oriente, Loja (elevation 2100m) is blessed with a delightfully temperate climate. The city is famous for its musicians (a result of Loja's important conservatory) and its parks. The town itself is noisy and bustling, though its historic center makes for a fine day of exploring. Loja is a good base for visiting nearby Parque Nacional Podocarpus and the main stop before heading south to Vilcabamba and Peru.

Good views can be had from the **Virgen de Loja Statue** (La Salle). The annual fiesta of the Virgen del Cisne (August 20) is celebrated with huge parades and a produce fair.

Sleeping

Hotel Londres HOSTEL $

(07-256-1936; Sucre 07-51; r without bathroom per person $6;) With creaky wooden floors and saggy beds, Hotel Londres is as basic as they come, but it's a tried-and-true travelers' favorite, with spotless shared bathrooms and friendly young owners.

★**Hosteria Quinta Montaña** CABINS $$

(07-257-8895; Barrio Colinas del Norte; s/d $25/45;) City address; countrified experience – 2km north of the bus terminal, serene Hosteria Quinta Montaña's well-kept cabins skitter down a steep hillside. Grounds include a nice restaurant, a great pool and even a sauna. Swinging on a hammock might be commonplace in the jungle but in Loja, doing so with such a lush view is the preserve of guests staying here.

Eating & Drinking

El Tamal Lojano ECUADORIAN $

(18 de Noviembre 05-12; light items $1-4, set lunches $2; 8am-8pm Mon-Sat) The *almuerzos* are good, but the real reason to come is for the delicious *quimbolitos, humitas, empanadas de verde* and *tamales lojanos*. All the Loja region's foodie classics, in short.

★**Zarza Brewing Company** MICROBREWERY

(cnr Puerto Bolívar & Esmeraldas; evenings Mon-Sat) In the El Valle neighborhood, Zarzas is a brand-new brewpub that seems as popular with locals as with Loja expats. The owner is Texan and clearly knows a thing or two about the microbrewing business. They do a mean Irish stout and possibly Ecuador's hottest barbecued ribs. There's often live music. A taxi here costs $1.

Information

Banco de Guayaquil (Eguiguren, near Valdivieso) Bank with ATM.

Clinica San Augustin (07-258-7339; www.hospitalclinicasanagustin.com; cnr 18 de Noviembre & Azuay) Recommended hospital for foreigners.

Ministerio del Medio Ambiente (07-257-9595/258-5927; Sucre 4-35, 3rd fl) Responsible for administering Parque Nacional Podocarpus; provides information and simple maps.

Tourist Office (iTur; 07-258-1251/257-0485; cnr Bolívar & Eguiguren; 8am-6pm Mon-Fri, 9am-6pm Sat) Helpful, with some maps available.

Getting There & Away

Loja is served by La Toma airport in Catamayo, 30km west of town. **TAME** (07-257-0248; www.tame.com.ec; Av Ortega near 24 de Mayo;

⏲8:30am-1pm & 2:30-6pm Mon-Fri, 9am-1pm Sat) flies to Quito Monday to Saturday and to Guayaquil on Monday to Friday for around $80 one way.

Loja's bus terminal is 2km north of town. Several buses a day run to Quito ($15 to $17, 15 hours), Macará ($6, six hours), Guayaquil ($10, nine hours), Machala ($6, five hours), Zamora ($2.50, two hours) and Cuenca ($7.50, five hours), as well as other destinations.

Vilcabambaturis has fast minibuses to Vilcabamba ($1.30, one hour). There are also speedier *taxis colectivos* (shared taxis; $2, 45 minutes), which leave from the Ruta 11 de Mayo taxi stop (at the corner of Av Universitaria), 10 blocks south of Alonso de Mercadillo; ask a local taxi driver to take you.

GETTING TO PERU

The crossing into Peru via Macará is much quieter than at Huaquillas and busier than Zumba. Macará is 3km from the actual border crossing, or *puente internacional* (international bridge). Most people buy tickets direct to Piura, Peru, from Loja aboard **Loja Internacional** (☎257-0505, 257-9014). Several buses depart daily from Loja, stop at the border for passengers to take care of exits and entries, and then continue on to Piura. The entire ride takes nine hours and costs $10. There are no border crossing fees.

If you're coming from Macará, take Transportes Loja Internacional (Lázaro Vaca at Juvenal Jaramilla) or Unión Cariamanga (corner Loja and Manuel E Rengel) to Piura ($3, three hours).

For information on making this crossing in the opposite direction, see p877.

Zamora

☎07 / POP 13,400

Perspiring peacefully on the tropical banks of the Río Zamora, this easygoing jungle town (elevation 970m) is the best launching pad for exploring the verdant lowlands of Parque Nacional Podocarpus. Although it's geographically part of the Oriente, Zamora is closer to Loja by bus (two hours) than to other jungle towns, most of which are quite a long way north. Decent budget hotels in town include **Hotel Chonta Dorada** (☎07-260-6384; Jaramillo near Amazonas; s/d $13/22; P) and **Hotel Betania** (☎07-260-7030; Francisco de Orellana; r per person $15; P 📶). Outside town, bird-watchers should book a cabin in the lovely private reserve of **Copalinga** (☎099-347-7013; www.copalinga.com; Vía al Podocarpus Km 3; cabins per person s/d from $55/84, without bathroom $28/50, all incl breakfast) 🍃. Meals are also available.

Continuing north through the Oriente by bus, you will find a few basic hotels in the small towns of **Gualaquiza** (five hours), **Limón** (about nine hours), **Méndez** and **Sucúa**. **Macas** is approximately 13 to 15 hours away.

Parque Nacional Podocarpus

One of the most biologically rich areas in the country and a wonderful park to explore, **Parque Nacional Podocarpus** (admission free, refugios $3) protects habitats at altitudes ranging from 3600m in the *páramo* near Loja to 1000m in the steamy rainforests near Zamora. The topography is wonderfully rugged and complex, and the park is simply bursting with plant and animal life. Parque Nacional Podocarpus' namesake, *Podocarpus*, is Ecuador's only native conifer.

The main entrance to the highland sector of the park is **Cajanuma**, about 10km south of Loja. From here, a track leads 8.5km up to the ranger station and trailheads. The best bet for a day trip is to ride all the way up in a taxi from Loja (about $10), hike for several hours and walk the 8.5km back to the main road where you can flag a passing bus.

To visit the tropical, lowland sector, head to Zamora and get a taxi ($4 one way) or walk the 6km dirt road to the **Bombuscaro entrance**, where there is a ranger station, trails, swimming, waterfalls, a free camping area and a small **refugio** (cabin per person $3) without mattresses. Access from Vilcabamba is possible by horseback.

Vilcabamba

☎07 / POP 4800

Deemed the valley of longevity, Vilcabamba (elevation 1500m) is famous for its long-lived inhabitants. Although few residents celebrate a 100th birthday anymore, most agree that their simple, stress-free lives amid lovely Andean scenery and fresh air are conducive to a long life. Backpackers stop here to get in on the mellowness and to hike, ride horses, enjoy the food, get massages and chill out in Vilcabamba's inexpensive guesthouses. It's also the perfect stopping point en route to or from Peru via Zumba.

Activities

There's great hiking in the area. The most popular hike is up **Cerro Mandango** (but there have been robberies, so enquire about safety and leave behind valuables before setting out). Most naturalists and horse guides charge about $35 per day.

The Rumi-Wilco Ecolodge has signed trails ranging from one to three hours in length ($2 for a three-day pass).

Caballos Gavilán HORSE RIDING
(07-264-0256; gavilanhorse@yahoo.com; Sucre 10-30) Highly recommended, Gavin is a New Zealander who has lived here for years. He guides two-hour to three-day horse-riding trips with overnight stays in his refuge near the park.

El Chino BICYCLE RENTAL
(cnr Sucre & Agua de Hierro) Rents bikes/motorbikes for $10/50 per day. For a little more, they'll offer tours on both sets of wheels too. Check the shop next door: wondrous sculptures made out of bicycle parts!

Sleeping

★Hosteria Margarita HOSTERIA $
(cnr Jaramillo & Sucre; s/d incl breakfast $15/30; P) Margarita's high white walls secrete clean rooms reminiscent of a trim English B&B and a fantastic breakfast room overlooking the pool, wrapped in a lush garden. It's not quite the backpacker hangout that other addresses in the center are, but it's better value than the lot of them.

Hostal Jardín Escondido HOSTEL $
(07-264-0281; www.jardin.ec; Sucre & Agua de Hierro; dm/r per person incl breakfast $12.50/20;) Built around a tranquil interior garden filled with songbirds, this is a good budget bet. All rooms have high ceilings and big bathrooms, and breakfast comes with homemade bread and good coffee. A great spot to meet other travelers.

Rumi-Wilco Ecolodge LODGE $
(www.rumiwilco.com; campsite per person $4, 2-person adobe houses/cabins per person $7/14) A 10-minute walk from the bus station up a track over the river, Rumi-Wilco has a series of remote houses, cabins and camping space within the evergreen confines of the 40-hectare Rumi-Wilco Nature Reserve.

★Hostería y Restaurante Izhcayluma RESORT $$
(07-302-5162; www.izhcayluma.com; dm $8.50, s/d/tr $25/32/39, without bathroom $19/25/35, cabins d $59; P) Located 2km south of town, German-owned Izhcayluma is an excellent value, refined hilltop retreat. The outdoor dining area serves German-Ecuadorian cuisine and has sweeping panoramic views. An 'holistic wellness room' offers massages and other treatments, and there is a bar and swimming pool. As for the cabins and rooms, all are quiet and spacious.

Eating & Drinking

Midas Touch BREAKFAST $
(Sucre 11-35; breakfasts/lunches $3-5; 8am-5pm Mon, Wed & Thu, 8am-late Fri-Sun) While it's open all day, this newly done-up place is mostly about the great breakfasts – the

GETTING TO PERU

About 125km south of Vilcabamba lies the wonderfully remote border crossing known as La Balsa, near the outpost of Zumba. From Vilcabamba (or Loja), it's an all-day journey to San Ignacio, Peru, the best place to spend the night before continuing the journey. **Transportes Nambija** (07-257-9018; Loja) and Sur Oriente buses depart several times daily from Loja for Zumba, all stopping in Vilcabamba.

From Zumba, several daily *rancheras* (open-sided trucks) go to the border at La Balsa ($2.75, 1½ hours to 2½ hours), where you get your exit stamp; there are no border crossing fees. Enquire about conditions on the road between Zumba and La Balsa before setting out.

On the other side of the 'international bridge' in Peru there are *taxis colectivos* (shared taxis) to San Ignacio ($3, 1½ hours), where you can spend the night before heading to Jaén (three hours), on to Bagua Grande (another hour) and then to Chachapoyas (three more hours), the first sizable town. From Jaén you can also travel to Chiclayo, on the Peruvian coast.

banana and cinnamon hotcakes and the 'pumpkin eggs' are particularly addictive. A real hanging-out spot.

★ **Shanta's Bar** PIZZA $$
(Diego Vaca de la Vega; mains $6-10; ⏱1-9pm Tue-Sun) We love Shanta's – and have done for years. It serves pizza and big plates of frog's legs in an innovative rustic setting with saddle seats at the bar and a bartender with a handlebar mustache. Ask about the *licor de serpiente* (snake liquor).

Jardín Escondido INTERNATIONAL $$
(www.jardin.ec; Sucre & Agua de Hierro; mains $5-10; ⏱8am-8:30pm;) You can't go wrong with the tasty international fare – which include great vegetarian options – at the Jardín's atmospheric open-air restaurant. Big breakfasts include homemade bread, too.

ℹ Getting There & Away

Vilcabambaturis minibuses leave every hour to Loja ($1.30, one hour). Shared taxis leave from the bus terminal and take five passengers to Loja ($2, 45 minutes). Buses leave daily to Zumba ($6.50, five hours), near the Peruvian border.

THE ORIENTE

Ecuador's slice of the Amazon Basin – aka El Oriente – is one of the country's most thrilling travel destinations. Here you can paddle canoes up to caimans lurking in blackwater lagoons, spot two-toed sloths and howler monkeys, fish for piranhas and hike through some of the wildest plantlife you'll ever lay eyes upon. At night, after quelling your fear of the things outside, you'll be lulled to sleep by a psychedelic symphony of insects and frogs.

This section describes the Oriente from north to south (Zamora and the region's southernmost towns). The northern Oriente sees more travelers, while the region south of Río Pastaza has a real sense of remoteness. Buses from Quito frequently go to Puyo, Tena, Coca and Lago Agrio. Buses from Cuenca go through Limón to Macas. Buses from the southern highlands town of Loja go via Zamora to Limón and on to Macas. From Macas, a road leads to Puyo and the northern Oriente. It's possible, although arduous, to travel down the Río Napo to Peru and the Amazon.

Lago Agrio

☎06 / POP 58,000

Unless you like edgy frontier towns, Lago's main tourist draw is its status as the jumping-off point for the nearby Cuyabeno wildlife reserve. Booking a tour to Cuyabeno from Lago can be difficult: most people arrive from Quito with a tour already booked, guides show up, and everyone's gone the next morning.

The indigenous Cofan people offer excellent ecotourism expeditions. Contact **Noa'ike** (☎06-2364287; noaike@hotmail.com; Via Quito Km 3.5, Barrio la Libertad) for details.

If stuck in town, try **Hotel D'Mario** (☎06-283-0172; www.hoteldmario.com; Av Quito 263; s/d from $15/30;) on the main drag, where you'll find just about everything else. The hotel has a popular pizzeria.

ℹ Information

The nearby activity of Colombian guerrillas, antirebel paramilitaries and drug smugglers make Lago Agrio an unsafe place. Bars can be sketchy and side streets unsafe, so stick to the main drag. Take a taxi at night.

ℹ Getting There & Away

The airport is 3km east of town; taxi fare is $3. **TAME** (☎06-283-0113; Orellana near 9 de Octubre) has daily flights to Quito; it's best to book in advance.

The bus terminal is about 2km northwest of the center. Buses head to Quito regularly ($8, eight hours). There are one or two daily departures, mainly overnight, to Tena ($7, eight hours), Cuenca, Guayaquil ($14, 14 hours) and Machala.

Reserva de Producción Faunística Cuyabeno

This beautiful, 6034-sq-km **reserve** (www.reservacuyabeno.org) protects the rainforest home of the Siona, Secoya, Cofan, Quichua and Shuar people. It also conserves the Río Cuyabeno watershed, whose rainforest lakes and swamps harbor fascinating aquatic species such as freshwater dolphins, manatees, caimans and anaconda. Monkeys abound, and tapirs, peccaries, agoutis and several cat species have been recorded. The birdlife is abundant. Though there have been numerous oil spills, huge parts of the reserve remain pristine and worth a visit. Most visitors to the reserve arrive via Cuyabeno Lodge. The nearest town is Lago Agrio.

Sleeping

Cuyabeno Lodge LODGE $$$
(per person 4 days & 3 nights $260-440) This highly recommended place is run by Quito-based **Neotropic Turis** (☎02-292-6153; www.neotropicturis.com; Los Shyris N36-188 near Naciones Unidas), in close cooperation with the local Siona people. Thatched huts spread over a hillside offer some privacy, most with private bathroom and hot water, although cheapest rooms are four-berth dorms with shared facilities.

Coca

☎06 / POP 45,000

The starting point for many jungle tours, Coca is a rather charmless oil-industry town – though things are improving. A pretty *malecón* (waterfront) extends along the riverfront, and a new archaeology museum, the **MACCO** (cnr Malecón & 9 de Octubre), showcases treasures from the Orellana region. Meanwhile, an attractive, new suspension bridge spans the Napo, and a new park has added green space to Coca's concrete-filled center.

Sleeping

Hotel San Fermin HOTEL $
(☎06-288-0802; cnr Quito & Bolívar; s/d from $15/25, without bathroom $8/16, ste $32; P ❄ @ ᯤ) This friendly and well-run place is an excellent deal: following a recent revamp, rooms are spacious, decked out in timbers and featuring TV, desks, and either fans or air-con ($7 extra). Grab a room on the highest floor if possible – these get the most light and are the most spacious.

Hotel Santa María HOTEL $
(☎06-288-0287; Rocafuerte btwn Quito & Napo; r per person $13, d with air-con $25) Here you'll find the cheapest acceptable bed in town. Don't hit your head on the low ceiling in the stairwell on the way to the cramped rooms.

Hostería La Misión HOTEL $$
(☎06-288-0260; hlamision@hotmail.com; Camilo de Torrano; s/d $34/50; P ❄ ᯤ ≋) This long-time Coca staple makes the most of its location right by the Yasuni departure dock. Some of the clean but stuffy rooms have Río Napo views. All come with cable TV, fridges and modern bathrooms. Multiple swimming pools are invariably teeming with screaming children, but you can't get a more convenient location for embarking on a Yasuni trip. Views from the riverside La Misión restaurant-bar can't be bettered in town.

Eating & Drinking

La Casa del Maito FISH $
(Espejo; mains $4-6; ⏲7am-6pm) Locals flock in to lunch on delectable fish (mostly tilapia and piranha) cooked in palm leaves on the grill outside. The friendly owner, Luis Duarte, also offers guiding services.

Papadan's BAR
(cnr Chimborazo & Napo; ⏲6pm-late Mon-Sat) Coca's first decent-looking bar is a brand-new *palapas*-style place with prime river views and good cocktails.

Information

Banco del Pichincha (cnr Bolívar & Quito) Has ATMs – and queues for them.

Tourist Information Office (☎06-288-0532; www.orellanaturistica.gob.ec; Transportes Fluviales Orellana Bldg, Chimborazo; ⏲7:30am-noon & 2-4:30pm Mon-Sat) The new and helpful tourist office offers travelers free internet access, advice on transport to Río Napo lodges, and lectures about the indigenous peoples and rare animals living in Yasuní National Park. No English is spoken, though staff are very friendly.

Getting There & Away

AIR

The airport is 2km north of town. **TAME** (☎06-288-1078; cnr Castillo & Quito; ⏲9am-1pm & 2-6pm Mon-Fri, 2-6pm Sat, 9am-1pm Sun) flies daily to Quito (one way around $110).

BOAT

Around 7am on Sunday, Wednesday, Thursday and Friday, **Coop de Transportes Fluviales Orellana** (☎06-288-2582/0231; Chimborazo at docks) offers passenger service to Nuevo Rocafuerte ($15, 10 hours) on the Peruvian border. Another boat returns upriver to Coca (12 to 14 hours) on the same days, departing Nuevo Rocafuerte at 5am. Although there's usually a stop for lunch, you should bring some food and water for the trip. Travelers arriving and departing by river must register their passport at the *capitanía* (harbormaster's office) by the landing dock. If you're on an organized tour, your guide will usually take care of this.

BUS

Coca has a new bus terminal, 3km north of town. A taxi here costs $2. Several buses a day go to Quito ($10, 10 hours), Tena ($7, four hours) and Lago Agrio ($3, two hours). Open-sided trucks called *rancheras* or *chivas* leave from the market on Alejandro Labaka two blocks back from the river, heading for various destinations between Coca and Lago Agrio, and to Río Tiputini to the south.

Nuevo Rocafuerte

☎06

A distant dot on the map for most, Nuevo Rocafuerte lies five hours' downstream from Pañacocha (eight to 10 hours from Coca), completing a seriously arduous journey to the Peruvian border. There are several lodging options, the best of which is **Hotel Chimborazo** (☎06-233-2109; r per person $7) with clean, wood-paneled rooms.

If you are continuing to Peru, first enquire at the Coop de Transportes Fluviales Orellana in Coca, when you buy your ticket downstream, for phone numbers of cargo boats which may be connecting to Pantoja/Iquitos.

You'll also need patience and a high tolerance for squalor while traveling by cargo boat. Bring adequate supplies of water-purification tablets, insect repellent, food and Peruvian soles. For less hassle, some operators in Coca offer jungle tours that end in Iquitos, Peru.

Parque Nacional Yasuní

Ecuador's largest mainland **park** (www.mdtf.undp.org/yasuni; admission $2, parrot clay lick $20) is a massive 9620-sq-km swath of wetlands, marshes, swamps, lakes, rivers and tropical rainforest. It contains a variety of rainforest habitats, wildlife and a few Huaorani communities. Unfortunately, poaching and (increasingly) oil exploration are damaging the park.

Visiting the park independently is difficult, but operators in Coca and Quito offer tours. Napo Wildlife Center (p691) is located in the park.

Tena

☎06 / POP 34,000

Ecuador's de facto whitewater-rafting capital (elevation 518m) sits at the confluence of two lovely rivers, Río Tena and Río Pano, and draws paddlers from all over the world. It's an attractive, relaxed town where kayaks lie around hotel-room entrances and boaters hang out in pizza joints, rapping about their day on the rapids. Rafting tours, which offer an adrenaline rush amid stunning jungle and cloud-forest scenery, are easily arranged. Depending on difficulty, day trips

GETTING TO PERU

While backpackers may bubble with excitement at the idea of floating along the Río Napo all the way to Peru and the Amazon River, only the most intrepid travelers (with plenty of time to kill) should rise to the occasion. Nuevo Rocafuerte is on the Peruvian border, eight to 10 hours from Coca along the Río Napo. This is a legal border crossing with Peru, although regular passenger-boat transport is lacking and accommodations are basic.

First enquire at the Coop de Transportes Fluviales Orellana in Coca, when you buy your ticket downstream, for phone numbers of cargo boats that may be connecting to Pantoja/Iquitos. But nothing guarantees timing; there's a good chance you'll get stuck in Pantoja, so be prepared. Bring adequate supplies of water-purification tablets, insect repellent and food. Also, consider getting Peruvian currency in Quito before you arrive.

Exit and entry formalities in Ecuador are handled in Nuevo Rocafuerte; in Peru, try your best to settle them in Pantoja, with Iquitos as backup. Boats from Nuevo Rocafuerte charge $70 per boat to Pantoja. Cargo boats travel from Pantoja to Iquitos (a three- to five-day trip) when they have enough cargo to justify the trip. Boats vary in quality, but if you've been waiting a long time for one to arrive, you may not want to be picky. Pantoja has a hotel, restaurant and disco.

For less hassle, some tour operators in Coca offer jungle tours that end in Iquitos, Peru.

EXPERIENCING THE AMAZON

Organized tours and jungle lodges help you get close to an incredible array of wildlife. Some outfits are also run by the indigenous, and include visits to local communities.

Quito is generally the best place to arrange a jungle trip.

Tours

Amazon Wildlife Tours (☎06-288-0802; www.amazonwildlife.ec; Hotel San Fermin, cnr Quito & Bolívar; per person per day $100) This is the best reason to book a jungle jaunt within Coca: an experienced agency with an array of nature-watching tours, including a specialty jaguar expedition in Yasuní National Park, tours to see Amazon dolphins and general wildlife-watching in the Limoncocha Reserve.

Jorge Carriel (☎093-971-2597; loresalavarria84@hotmail.com; cnr Alejandro Labaka & Camilo de Torrano; per person per day $120) Jorge specializes in six- to eight-day adventure trips deep into the jungle (you pay a little more because of corresponding diesel costs) – down to the Nuevo Rocafuerte area near the Peruvian border – on blackwater tributaries where there are higher chances of seeing more exciting wildlife. Sleeping will be in basic jungle shelters.

Otobo's Amazon Safari (www.rainforestcamping.com; per person per night $200) Operated by indigenous Huaorani Otobo and his family, this remote site on the Río Cononaco has platform tents and a thatched-roofed lodge. Visitors hike in the Parque Nacional Yasuní with a native English-speaking guide, and visit lagoons and a local village.

run $50 to $85 per person. Several operators offer interesting jungle trips.

Sights & Activities

Parque Amazónico ZOO

(btwn Ríos Pano & Tena; admission $2; ⊙8am-5pm) Take that snazzy new footbridge partway across the river to this 27-hectare island. There's a self-guided trail whisking you past labeled local plants and animal enclosures, including those of tapirs and monkeys. It's no substitute for the real thing, though! It's worth the clamber up to the park's lofty *mirador* to see Tena's rather stunning surrounding terrain.

★River People RAFTING

(☎06-288 7887/8384; http://riverpeopleecuador.com; cnr Calles 15 de Noviembre & 9 de Octubre) Run by the Dent family from England, River People is a top-notch outfitter that consistently gets rave reviews. River People has been pioneering rafting on previously untried rivers throughout the region, including the remote Río Hollín, where groups of experienced rafters camp overnight in pristine rainforest.

One popular tour is the challenging two-day expedition to the nearby Río Quijos, site of the 2005 world rafting championships.

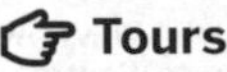

Tours

Juan Garces JUNGLE TOURS

(☎06-306-2907, 098-461-4199; joseluisgarces2002@yahoo.com) Enterprising Juan Garces speaks fluent English, French and Kichwa and, more critically, knows the jungle hereabouts like the back of his hand. Kayaking, chocolate-making and jungle hikes are all available. He can also guide you on a multiday adventure downriver towards the Peruvian frontier. Prices start around $50 per person per day – more, naturally, if you stay at Juan's recently constructed Sacha Sisa Lodge out past Misahuallí.

Sleeping

★La Casa del Abuelo GUESTHOUSE $

(☎06-288-8926; www.tomas-lodge.com; Calle Mera 628; s/d/tr $22/33/49.50; P ❄ @ ☜) This attractively refurbished colonial-style home, tucked away on a quiet street, easily keeps its place in the city's elite digs after seven or so years in the game. Public areas are full of local arts and crafts; rooms themselves are akin to those at a jungle lodge in style – high ceilings give them a spacious feel. Free coffee, too. Ask the owners about their rural guesthouse on the river, 5km away.

Luis Duarte (☎06-288-2285; cocaselva@hotmail.com) Organizes customized tours, including river passage to Peru or stays with Huaorani families. Find him at La Casa del Maito.

Sleeping

Napo Wildlife Center (NWC; www.napowildlifecenter.com; s/d full board 3 nights $1379/1838; @ 📶) As the lodge most ensconced within Parque Nacional Yasuní, the sumptuous Napo Wildlife Center enjoys a pristine setting with rarely paralleled access to wildlife. This ecotourism project is 100% owned by Añangu's Kichwa community; they comprise almost the entire lodge staff.

Yarina Lodge (www.yarinalodge.com; per person 2/3/4 nights $370/460/550) The Río Manduro meets the Napo an hour downstream from Coca, and a further 10 minutes down this blackwater stream you'll find Yarina Lodge, a hillside camp of 26 bamboo, thatched-roofed *cabañas*. Yarina is geared toward budget travelers and doesn't feel as remote as those camps further downstream, but it provides good services and has enthusiastic and professional English-speaking guides.

Sani Lodge (per person 3-night & 4-day tent/s/d $664/1092/1560; 📶) Owned by the local Sani community, Sani Lodge is one of the lower-priced options around, but unlike other economy lodges it's located very deep in the rainforest and enjoys one of the most beautiful locations of any lodge in Ecuador.

★Hostal Pakay — HOSTEL $

(☎06-284-7449; above Av Perimetral; dm/s/d incl breakfast $12/24/32; P 📶) Surrounded by woodland, a stay at German-Ecuadorian owned Hostal Pakay is more like a jungle lodge experience than a town hostel experience. Wooden rooms are so new they still smell of varnish, kayakers and backpackers love the chill-out terrace and the on-site tour agency is increasingly renowned. Much of the breakfast fruit is grown in the lush grounds.

It's a steep 20-minute hike up from the bus station so get a taxi here.

La Casa Blanca — HOSTEL $

(☎06-264-8579; www.casablancatena.com; cnr Churiyuyo & Ishpingo; dm/s/d $12/25/40) Situated 1.5km northwest of the center, laid-back, spick-and-span Casa Blanca aims to provide weary backpackers with everything they wanted to find in a hostel elsewhere, but couldn't. The wonderfully equipped kitchen, the spacious rooms hung with Otavalo tapestries, the 'honesty system' for chilled beers, the special boot-wash area, the in-house tour agency...they do seem to have it nailed.

Brisa del Río — GUESTHOUSE $

(☎06-288-6444; Orellana; r per person $15, without bathroom $9; P ❄ 📶 🏊) Rarely are backpacker places in the jungle so clean and well located. This is. Right on the riverfront, there is also a kitchen and a miniscule plunge pool. Shared bathrooms are very clean, while rooms with private bathrooms also have air-con.

Eating & Drinking

For the adventurous, grills by the pedestrian bridge cook up sausages, chicken and *guanta* (a jungle rodent). There's also cold beer and riverside seating.

★Café Tortuga — INTERNATIONAL $

(Orellana; snacks $1.50-5; ⏲7:30am-7pm Mon-Sat, to 1pm Sun; 📶) Everyone in town seems to drop by this super-popular Swiss-run riverfront joint, whether it's for its wide choice of breakfasts, its delicious *batidos* (fruit shakes) or its range of salads, sandwiches and cakes. Tortuga is especially popular with backpackers, and is a great place to meet other travelers. There is a good book exchange.

La Araña Bar Coctelería — BAR

(Main Plaza; ⏲5pm-midnight Mon-Thu, to 2am Fri & Sat) The most popular place for drinking and carousing is the raucous 'spider,' across the river at the end of the footbridge. It's busy nightly, but rammed with locals and travelers on the weekend. Expect a hangover.

Information

Banco del Austro (15 de Noviembre) Changes traveler's checks in the mornings only. Has an ATM.

Police Station (☎288-6101; main plaza)

Tourism Office (☎06-288-8046; Rueda; ⏲7:30am-5pm Mon-Fri) The friendly staff here will do their best to help you with whatever you need. Some staff members speak English.

Getting There & Away

The bus terminal is less than 1km south of the main plaza. Several buses a day head for Quito ($6, five hours), Lago Agrio ($7, six hours), Coca ($7, four hours), Baños ($4, five hours) and Puyo ($3, 2½ hours). Buses for Misahuallí ($1, one hour) depart hourly from in front of the terminal.

Misahuallí

☎06

One of the Oriente's sleepiest jungle towns, Misahuallí sits swathed in greenery at the junction of two major rivers. The town has popular sandy beaches and a famous cadre of monkeys adept at swiping sunglasses and cameras from visitors. While wildlife-watching isn't the draw here, there are lovely walks to be had, and a variety of jungle birds, tropical flowers, army ants, dazzling butterflies and other insects can be seen. There's no bank, so get cash before arriving.

Activities

The dirt roads around Misahuallí make for relaxing walks to outlying villages. You can also visit the nearby **Las Latas waterfall** for swimming and picnics. To get there, take a Misahuallí–Puerto Napo bus and ask the driver to drop you off at Río Latas, about 20 minutes from Misahuallí; ask for *el camino a las cascadas* (the trail to the falls). Follow the river upstream to the falls, about 30 minutes' walk.

Tours

If you're hoping to see any of the wildlife, make sure you're venturing well away from Misahuallí, and be sure to hire an experienced and licensed guide (not the touts in the main plaza). Tours range from one day to 10 days and prices usually include the guide, food, water, accommodations (which range from jungle camping to rustic cabins) and rubber boots. Rates run from $45 to $100 per person per day.

★Teorumi ECOTOUR
(☎06-289-0213; www.teorumi.com; tours per day $65) Working with local indigenous communities, Teorumi is a great choice for anyone interested in native culture as well as wildlife. Tours can be tailored to fit your interests, though most feature bird-watching, fishing, medicinal plant demonstrations and jungle hikes. Other activities include panning for gold and horse-riding. English and French are spoken. The office is on the main square.

Selva Verde ECOTOUR
(☎098-590-4101, 06-289-0165; www.selvaverde-misahualli.com; tours per day $60-95) Luís Zapata, an English-speaking guide with years of experience in the region, runs this recommended tour agency that has an office on the main square. He specializes in river trips and visits to indigenous villages.

Sleeping & Eating

Don't miss *maitos* (whole tilapia or chicken wrapped in a leaf and char-grilled), which are fired up by the plaza around lunchtime from Friday to Sunday.

Hostal Shaw HOSTEL $
(☎06-289-0163; r per person $10) This friendly *hostal* on the plaza has simple rooms with fans, mosquito nets and private bathrooms with hot water. You'll find espresso and a good book exchange at the downstairs cafe, which is Misahualli's premier hang-out spot, as well as morning pancakes and vegetarian dishes.

Shiripuno Lodge JUNGLE LODGE $
(☎06-289-0203; r per person $15, without bathroom $10) A couple of kilometres downriver from town is this lodge, run by Teorumi tour agency and focussing on community tourism. Visitors usually come as part of a tour but it's fine to stay anyway. Cabins are in secondary jungle and right on-site is a huge rock believed to be a crashed meteorite, central to Kichwa mythology. A canoe ride here from town is $5.

Hotel El Paisano GUESTHOUSE $$
(☎06-289-0027; hotelelpaisano@yahoo.com; cnr Riva deneyra & Tandalia; r per person incl breakfast $18; P@☎) This popular traveler haunt is one of the more charming places in town, with bright rooms, wooden floors, mosquito nets, laundry service, good coffee served at breakfast and a book exchange.

France-Amazonia GUESTHOUSE $$
(☎06-289-0009; www.france-amazonia.com; Av Principal; r per person incl breakfast $18-24, d $50; P 📶 🏊) Located just outside of town on the lip of the river, shady thatched huts surround a sparkling pool and sandy fire pit. Beds are small but rooms are sizeable and pleasantly rustic. The garden offers plenty of nooks for enjoying the pleasant climate and sound of the river – the river itself can be accessed via a small trail.

El Jardín ECUADORIAN $$
(mains $10-15; ⏲10am-4pm, 6-10pm; P 📶) Over the bridge up on the road to La Punta, El Jardín is a beautiful addition to the local eating scene. In a flower-festooned garden, you can eat very well on the huge platters of meat, *tilapia* (river fish) and seafood.

Getting There & Away

Buses to Tena ($1, one hour) leave hourly from the plaza.

Jatun Sacha Biological Reserve

On the southern bank of the Río Napo, about 7km east of Misahuallí, **Jatun Sacha Biological Reserve** (☎099-490-8265, 02-243-2240/331-8156; www.jatunsacha.org; Psje Eugenio de Santillan N.34 248, Quito; admission $6) is a biological station and rainforest reserve with hiking trails and a narrow 30m tower affording views over the rainforest. Lodging is mostly for volunteers, though if space is available, you can stay in one of the rustic **cabins** (per person incl 3 meals US$30).

To get there, take an Ahuano or Santa Rosa bus from Tena and ask the driver to drop you off at the entrance. It's about 27km east of Tena.

Puyo

☎03 / POP 36,500

A lazy river slinks through this concrete outpost, which is part mellow jungle town and part commercial, government hub. The streets are filled with missionaries, vendors pushing street carts and indigenous people from far-flung corners of the Amazon. Dense green jungle flourishes around the town's edges while jagged snowcapped mountains rise in the distance. It's a good starting point for reaching indigenous villages.

Marín and Atahualpa are the principal downtown streets with the most services.

Sights & Activities

Parque Omaere PARK
(www.fundacionomaere.org; child/adult $1.50/3; ⏲9am-5pm Tue-Sun) Less than 1km north of the city center, this ethno-botanical park offers one- to two-hour guided tours (free with admission) of rainforest plants and indigenous dwellings, by mostly indigenous guides. The park is run by Shuar plant expert Teresa Shiki and her biologist husband, Chris Canaday, a font of knowledge about everything from jungle plants to ecological dry toilets. Teresa helped found and plant the park and prepares natural medicine.

Jardín Botáncio las Orquídeas GARDENS
(☎03-253-0305; admission $5; ⏲8am-6pm) Visitors rave about this privately run botanical garden, located 15 minutes south from Puyo on the road to Macas. Enthusiastic owner Omar Taeyu guides visitors through hills of lush foliage and fish ponds to see gorgeous plants and countless rare orchids. Call ahead to let them know you're coming.

Tours

Papangu Tours TOUR
(☎ 9955 04983; info@papangutours.com.ec; cnr Calle 27 de Febrero & Sucre; 3-day/2-night tours per person from $45) An indigenous-run agency with a focus on community tourism. Trips go to Sarayaku (Kichwa communities) and Cueva de los Tayos (Shuar). Guides are indigenous and speak Spanish and Kichwa, and some of the fees go to participating communities. Highly recommended by readers.

Sleeping

Hostal Las Palmas GUESTHOUSE $
(☎03-288-4832; cnr 20 de Julio & 4 de Enero; s/d incl breakfast $25/40; @) This big yellow colonial place is aimed at an upmarket backpacking crowd. It features attractive gardens, chattering parrots and uncannily lifelike models of rainforest animals. Rooms here are neat and bright. A cute cafe serves wine, coffee and snacks. Take advantage of the hammocks and outdoor fire pit.

Hotel Libertad HOTEL $
(☎03-288-3282; cnr Orellana & Manzano; r per person $8) Rooms are cramped but the place is spotless, plus there's hot water and TV. At this price, it's a great deal.

El Jardín HOTEL **$$**

(☎03-288-7770; http://eljardinrelax.com.ec; Paseo Turístico, Barrio Obrero; r per person incl breakfast $45; P@📶) This gorgeous spot is just across the footbridge by the entrance to the Parque Omaere, 1km from the center of town. It feels more like a jungle lodge than a city hotel, with the 10 rooms housed in a wooden building on two floors and decorated with local arts and crafts.

Eating

Escobar ECUADORIAN **$**

(cnr Atahualpa & Marín; mains $4-8; ⏲9am-late) Only time will tell if Escobar is too much, too soon for Puyo. With panache to punch its weight in the coolest neighborhoods of Quito, Escobar makes *palapas* (rustic, palm-thatched dwellings) seem chic. Sample the Ecuadorian microbrews, cocktails and a menu of *patacones* (fried bananas), *yuca* (cassava) or salads served with meat within the 2nd-floor open-sided bar-restaurant.

★**El Jardín** ECUADORIAN **$$**

(☎03-288-7770; Paseo Turístico, Barrio Obrero; mains $8-16; ⏲noon-4pm & 6-10pm Mon-Sat; 📶) The best food in the Oriente may be at this ambient house by the river inside the charming hotel of the same name, 1km north of town. The award-winning chef-owner Sofia prepares fragrant *pollo ishpingo* (cinnamon chicken – *ishpingo* is a type of cinnamon native to the Oriente); its decadent, delicate flavors awake the palate.

Information

Banco Pichincha (10 de Agosto btwn Atahualpa & Orellana) The only reliable bank from which to withdraw money.

Huaorani Community Office (Juan de Velasco & Tungurahua) Useful information source on the region's Huaorani; ask here about visits to communities.

Getting There & Away

The bus terminal is 3km out of town (a taxi should cost $1). Buses run regularly to Baños ($2.50, 1½ hours), Quito ($5.50, 5½ hours), Macas ($5, four hours) and Tena ($3, 2½ hours).

Macas

☎07 / POP 19,000

Macas' slow and steady pace and approachable locals make it a welcoming stop. It's also an excellent launch pad for adventures further afield. Macas is situated above the banks of the wild Río Upano, and there are great views of the river and the Río Upano valley from behind the town's cathedral. On a clear day you can glimpse the often smoking Volcán Sangay, some 40km to the northwest.

Tours

Be aware that the Shuar don't want unguided visitors in their villages. Multiday trips cost $50 to $80 per day.

Tsuirim Viajes TOUR

(☎07-270-1681; leosalgado18@gmail.com; cnr Don Bosco & Sucre; tours per person per day $50-70) Offers a range of jungle tours, including Shuar community visits, shamanic rituals, canyoning, rafting, tubing and jungle trekking. Owner Leo Salgado grew up in a Shuar community and so knows the area well.

Sleeping & Eating

The *comedores* (cheap restaurants) on Comín near Soasti sell tasty *ayampacos*, a jungle specialty of meat, chicken or fish grilled in *bijao* leaves.

Hostal Casa Blanca HOTEL **$**

(☎07-270-0195; Soasti; r incl breakfast $15-35; ❄📶🏊) The most pleasant rooms surround the small pool in the garden out back, even though they're the oldest rooms. Cheaper rooms don't have air-con. The best option in the city center.

La Maravilla ECUADORIAN **$**

(Soasti near Sucre; mains $3-6; ⏲4pm-midnight Mon-Sat) Easily the most charming place in town, this blue *casita* is all ambience, from the twinkling porch lights to the stuffed red-leather armchairs. Come to chill with *tablas* (cutting-boards) of meat and cheese and *yuca* (cassava) fries. There's live Andean music here at weekends, making it the town's best entertainment option, too.

Getting There & Away

TAME (☎07-270-4940; Edmundo Carvajal Airport terminal) flies daily to Quito. The bus terminal has several daily departures for Cuenca ($8.50, eight hours), Guayaquil ($10, 10 hours) and Riobamba ($5, five hours). Buses to Puyo ($6, three hours) leave 10 times daily; some continue to Tena.

PACIFIC COAST & LOWLANDS

Ecuador, land of lively Andean markets, Amazon adventures and…palm-fringed beaches? While not a high priority for most travelers, Ecuador's coast offers a mix of surf towns, sleepy fishing villages, whale-watching in the south and Afro-Ecuadorian culture in the north. Keep in mind the weather: December to May is the rainy season, but also the sunniest; the sun blazes both before and after the afternoon downpour. June through November has mild days (and chilly nights), but it's often overcast.

Getting There & Away

Most places along the coast can be reached from Quito in a day's travel. Key gateways are Esmeraldas in the north (six hours from Quito) and Puerto Lopez (10 hours from Quito or 4½ hours from Guayaquil) in the south. Once on the coast, it's fairly easy to make your way in either direction. For speedier access, catch a flight to Manta.

Esmeraldas

06 / POP 161,000

Lively, noisy and notoriously dodgy, Esmeraldas is an important port and home to a major oil refinery. For travelers, it's little more than a necessary stop to make bus connections. If you need to spend the night, **Hotel Central** (06-272-2502; Sucre 9-03; r per person $17;) on the plaza is a decent option.

The airport is 25km up the road to San Lorenzo; taxi fare is around $7. **TAME** (06-272-6863; www.tame.com.ec; Calle 9 de Octubre near Bolívar; 8am-12:45pm & 3-5:30pm Mon-Fri), near the plaza, has daily flights to Quito ($75) and less frequent services to Guayaquil ($100).

Buses leave from a terminal 4km from the city center in the direction of Atacames. Regular departures go to Atacames ($1, one hour), Quito ($7.25, six hours), Mompiche ($3.15, 2½ hours) and Guayaquil ($9.20, nine hours).

Atacames

06 / POP 16,800

The raucous beach town of Atacames has a packed beach, bustling guesthouses and a jumble of thatched-roof bars blaring salsa and reggaeton at all hours of the day. Most travelers avoid this place.

The beach is unsafe at night, when assaults and rapes have been reported. Robberies have also occurred on isolated sections of the beach between Atacames and Súa.

Buses drop passengers off in the center of town, on the main road from Esmeraldas (get off at the motorized-tricycle stand). The center is on the inland side of the highway, and the beach is reached by a small footbridge over the Río Atacames or by tricycle 'eco-taxi' ($1). Most of the hotels and bars are along the *malecón*.

Sleeping & Eating

You'll find *ceviche* (marinated raw seafood) stands along the beach and in a couple of central spots along the *malecón*.

Hotel Jennifer HOTEL $

(06-273-1055; near malecón; s/d with hot water $12/25, without hot water $10/18) This simple, straightforward place has clean, spartan rooms that get a decent amount of light (windows in every room). Kind staff.

Pizzeria D'Chris PIZZERIA $$

(malecón; pizzas $7-11) On the 2nd floor and with a bird's-eye view to the drunk-and-disorderlies down on the *malecón*, this pizzeria is bathed in a gauzy, yellow light with low-slung tables, rope swings, and the best service and thin-crusted pizza in town.

2016 EARTHQUAKE

On 16 April 2016 a devastating 7.8-magnitude earthquake struck Ecuador's north coast. It was the worst earthquake the country had experienced since 1979, with some 650 deaths and over 16,000 injuries reported. With an epicenter less than 30km from the towns of Pedernales and Muisne, the quake caused widespread damage across the provinces of Manabí, Esmeraldas and Guayas. The city of Manta was among the hardest hit, with the bustling district of Tarqui completely destroyed; the town of Pedernales was also badly damaged as was Canoa, Bahía de Caráquez, Muisne and Portoviejo. Some city blocks were so devastated they resembled war zones. The destruction even reached Guayaquil and Quito. Rebuilding costs are estimated to be around US$3 billion.

Getting There & Away

There are regular buses to Esmeraldas ($1, one hour), as well as south to Súa ($0.30, 10 minutes), Same ($0.30, 15 minutes) and Muisne ($1.50, 1½ hours). Transportes Occidentales and Aerotaxi, whose offices are near the highway, both go to Quito daily ($8, seven hours).

Súa

06

This friendly fishing village, 6km west of Atacames, is far more tranquil than its party-town neighbor. The mellow bay is a fine spot for a swim, although early in the morning it's busy with trawlers.

There are fewer lodgings here than in Atacames, but they're also quieter and often better value if you aren't looking for nightlife. All have cold-water bathrooms. **Hotel Chagra Ramos** (06-247-3106; hotelchagra ramos@hotmail.com; north side of malecón; r per person $13-16;) is a friendly, wind-battered classic.

Same & Tonchigüe

06

Same (*sah*-may) boasts the prettiest beach in the area, a 3km-long stretch of palm-fringed coast only lightly touched by development. The village itself, which lies 7km southwest of Súa, is small with only a sprinkling of (pricier) guesthouses and restaurants. At the turnoff where Same's main 'street' leaves the coastal road, **Azuca** (08-882-9581; azuca2@hotmail.com; Same; r per person $10;) has good-value wooden rooms and a decent restaurant (mains $4 to $6). One kilometer south of Same, **El Acantilado** (06-302-7620; www.elacantilado.ec; s/d $55/75;) has lovely sea views from its clifftop cabins. Don't miss a seafood feast at **Seaflower Lateneus** (06-247-0369; Same; mains $10-25; 8am-midnight), probably the best restaurant on Ecuador's Pacific Coast.

About 3km past Same, Tonchigüe is a tiny fishing village whose beach is a continuation of the Same beach. **Playa Escondida** (06-302-7496; www.playaescondida.com.ec; Corredor Turistico Km 10; cabin per person $25, day use $5;) is 3km west of Tonchigüe and 10km down the road to Punta Galeras. It's an isolated, beautiful spot with tours on offer, a restaurant and a scenic beach cove.

Mompiche

05

Mompiche is a tiny fishing village with a pretty beach, whose wide, hard-packed sands stretch for 7km. The surfing here can be excellent. The town itself is just a few sandy lanes, dotted with simple guesthouses and laid-back eateries that cater to a mostly surf and backpacker crowd. A high-end resort (the Decameron) was completed in 2012 and more construction dots the village, but for the moment, Mompiche retains its peaceful, end-of-the-road vibe.

The most popular place to bunk for the night is the seafront **Hostería Gabeal** (09-969-6543; mompiche_gabeal@hotmail.com; r/camping per person $15/5;), which is a large complex of bamboo rooms with cold-water bathrooms. You can also camp on the lawn. Decent meals and a beachside bar add to the appeal. About 10 minutes north, up the beach, small German-run **Casa Yarumo** (098-867-2924; muska.saygili@gmail.com; 1km north of Mompiche on the beach; cabin per person $15) is a pleasant getaway with several large, nicely designed cabin-style rooms. If you really want to escape the crowds, head to **Iruña** (099-947-2458; teremompiche@yahoo.com; d $40, f from $50), which has spacious wooden cabins surrounding a palm-fringed restaurant and social area. It's 2.3km north on the beach.

La Chillangua (10m north of T-Junction; mains $5-8; 7am-7pm) is a thatch-roof eatery with water views and tasty seafood. One street back from the beach, **La Facha** (100m north of T-Junction; mains $5-8; noon-10pm) serves up mouthwatering burgers, salads and sandwiches.

Buses go to and from Esmeraldas several times per day ($4, 3½ hours), passing Same and Atacames on the way.

Canoa

05 / POP 6800

Surfers, fishers and sunseekers share this attractive strip of beach – and the village continues to grow. In addition to surfing and beach walks, you can arrange boat trips, go biking in the countryside and visit the **Río Muchacho Organic Farm** (05-258-8184; www.riomuchacho.com; via Canoa Jama Km 10) , which offers sustainable-farming classes and accepts volunteers. Surfboard rental (about $10 per day) is available at many guesthouses, as well as along the beach.

Sleeping

Coco Loco HOSTEL $
(☎09-924-63508; www.hostalcocoloco.com; dm $7-9, d $26, without bathroom $24; 📶) This backpacker favorite right on the beach has clean rooms with softish mattresses and bamboo furnishings, and a sand- and palm-filled yard in the front. There's a laid-back happy hour, barbecue nights (Thursday to Sunday) and lots of activities on offer.

Casa Shangri-La GUESTHOUSE $
(☎099-146-8470; 100m north of town on main road; r per person $10; 📶🏊) This fantastic place is owned by a friendly Dutch guy who has created a chilled-out surfer spot with a big garden, plunge pool, very nice rooms and a super-relaxed vibe. It's a short walk from town, which also means you won't hear the reggaeton from the beachfront bars all night.

★**Hotel Bambu** CABIN $$
(☎05-258-8017; www.hotelbambuecuador.com; north end of malecón; dm/s/d $10/30/40; 📶) The nicest hotel in town has a great sand-floored restaurant and bar area, cabins with exposed cane roofs, wood-panel windows and mosquito nets – plus delicious hot-water showers. There are just a few with ocean views, but most catch a breeze and stay cool.

Eating

Surf Shack INTERNATIONAL $
(Malecón; mains $5-10; ⏰8am-midnight; 📶) Surf Shack serves up pizzas, burgers, filling breakfasts and plenty of rum cocktails to a fun-seeking foreign crowd. Its California-dreamin' surf vibe is studied and perfected.

Amalur SPANISH $$
(www.amalurcanoa.com; soccer field; mains $6.50-10; ⏰8am-10pm) Owned by a Spanish chef ('Amalur' means 'Mother Earth' in Basque), this trim, minimalist restaurant is a great place to dine and is a major step up from your average Ecuadorian small-town restaurant. It's two blocks back from the beach overlooking the soccer field.

Getting There & Away

Buses between Bahía de Caráquez and Esmeraldas will all stop in Canoa.

Bahía de Caráquez

Chalk-colored high-rises, red tile roofs, manicured yards and swept sidewalks give this self-proclaimed 'eco-city' a tidy impression. Today, the town market recycles its waste, organic shrimp farms flourish, and reforestation projects dot the hillside. There are several interesting eco and cultural tours worth checking out, as well as a small beach. Bird-watchers shouldn't miss a visit to **Isla Corazon** (☎302-9316; www.islacorazon.com; admission incl 2hr guided tour from $10), where you can take guided tours through mangroves in search of frigate birds, herons, egrets and other species. It's 7km east of San Vicente, reachable by bus ($0.50) or taxi ($5).

Banco de Guayaquil (cnr Bolívar & Riofrío) has an ATM.

Tours

Tours in Bahía have an ecotourism focus: you can learn about local environmental projects, or take a day trip to Islas Fragatas in the Chone estuary.

Bahía Dolphin Tours TOUR
(☎05-269-0257; www.bahiadolphintours.com; Virgílio Ratti 606, Casa Grande) This company owns the Chirije archaeological site, and offers day visits or overnight tours to the site. The staff can arrange packages with overnight stays at Chirije and in Bahía, combined with visits to panama-hat workshops, an organic shrimp farm, frigate-bird islands and other local points of interest. Guides speak English, French and German.

Sleeping

Centro Vacacional Life CABIN $
(☎05-269-0496; cnr Octavio Vitteri & Muñoz Dávila; r per person $20; ❄📶) Ideal for families, these institutional-feeling cabins have kitchens, two bedrooms, and sleep up to five people. There's a grassy playground, pool table and ping-pong.

Hotel La Herradura HOTEL $$
(☎05-269-0265; www.laherradurahotel.com; Bolívar 202; s/d from $30/40; P❄📶) This old Spanish home brims with antiques and artwork and has been lovingly furnished. The rooms are pretty beat up – you'll definitely miss the toilet seats. But there's tons of character and a cool porch.

Eating

D'Camaron SEAFOOD $
(Bolívar; mains $3-7; ⏰9am-6pm) As the name implies, shrimp is the specialty at this casual open-air spot near the water. Order them

grilled, with a cocktail, and enjoy the ocean breezes.

Arena Bar PIZZA $$
(Marañón; mains $4-8; ⏲5pm-midnight) Chow down to international rhythms and casual surf decor at this friendly place. The pizzas are good, but there are plenty of other choices, including excellent salads and tasty sandwiches.

Puerto Amistad INTERNATIONAL $$
(Malecón Santos; mains $6-12; ⏲noon-11pm Mon-Sat) Puerto Amistad is an expat favorite for its delicious fare, strong cocktails and the attractive and airy deck over the water. Salads, savory crepes, quesadillas, seafood dishes and steaks are all excellent, and service is friendly and professional. This slightly upscale restaurant also functions as Bahía's yacht club and is the place to bump into other visiting yachties.

Getting There & Away

A bridge from San Vicente across the Río Chone links Bahía with the north coast, making it an easy stop when coming from Canoa.

The bus terminal is 4km east of the centre. From there, you'll find regular services to Manta ($3, three hours, three daily), Quito ($8 to $10, eight hours, four daily), Guayaquil ($7, six hours, seven daily) and Canoa ($1, 45 minutes).

Manta

☎05 / POP 221,000

The largest city in the province, Manta is a bustling and prosperous port town, graced with high-rises and a few urban beaches that draw mostly national tourists. As an important center for the fishing and tuna industries, Manta is not a huge draw for foreign travelers. It does have a lively nightlife scene, and you may pass through if you're visiting the handicraft town of Montecristi.

A fetid inlet divides the town into Manta (west side) and Tarqui (east side); the two sides are joined by a vehicle bridge. Manta has the main offices, shopping areas and bus terminal, while Tarqui has cheaper hotels.

Sights

Playa Murciélago BEACH
This beach is less protected than most beaches in the area and has bigger waves (although they're not very big, there's a powerful undertow). It's a couple of kilometers northwest of downtown and is the town's most popular beach, backed by snack bars, restaurants and umbrella-rental spots.

Tarqui Beach BEACH
The east end of this stretch of sand is a hive of activity early in the mornings, as vendors sell row upon row of shark, tuna, swordfish, dorado and other fish (whose sizes decrease with each passing year). You'll also find the so-called Parque del Marisco here: lots of stalls serving up fresh fish and seafood in a variety of different styles right on the beach, including what locals will swear to you is the best *ceviche* in the country.

Museo del Banco Central MUSEUM
(Malecón de Manta near Calle 20; admission $1; ⏲9am-5pm Tue-Sat, 11am-3pm Sun) The fully modernized city museum showcases valuable artifacts from pre-Columbian Manta culture, a selection of Ecuadorian paintings and quirky fishing paraphernalia.

Sleeping

The best eating and nightlife options are out near Playa Murciélago. Avoid staying in Tarqui, which is not very safe.

Leo Hotel HOTEL $
(☎05-262-3159; Av 24 de Mayo; s/d $15/25; ❄) Across from the bus terminal, Leo offers small, clean rooms, some of which lack windows. Convenient if you're just passing through.

Manakin GUESTHOUSE $$
(☎05-262-0413; hostalmanakin@hotmail.com; Calle 17 & Av 21; s/d incl breakfast $48/61; ❄📶) Near the heart of all the nightlife, Manakin is a converted one-story house with a pleasant laid-back vibe. Narrow, well-ordered and highly perfumed rooms are nicely furnished, and the house offers fine places to unwind – including the front patio.

Eating & Drinking

The epicenter of Manta's nightlife is the intersection of Av Flavio Reyes and Calle 20, uphill from Playa Murciélago.

Trovador Café CAFE $
(Av 3 & Calle 10; mains $2-5; ⏲8am-8pm Mon-Sat) On a pleasant pedestrian lane set back just a short distance from the *malecón,* this place offers frothy cappuccinos, sandwiches and inexpensive lunch plates, with outdoor seating.

Beachcomber STEAK $$
(cnr Calle 20 & Flavio Reyes; mains $4-10; ⏲6pm-midnight) Near the heart of the night-

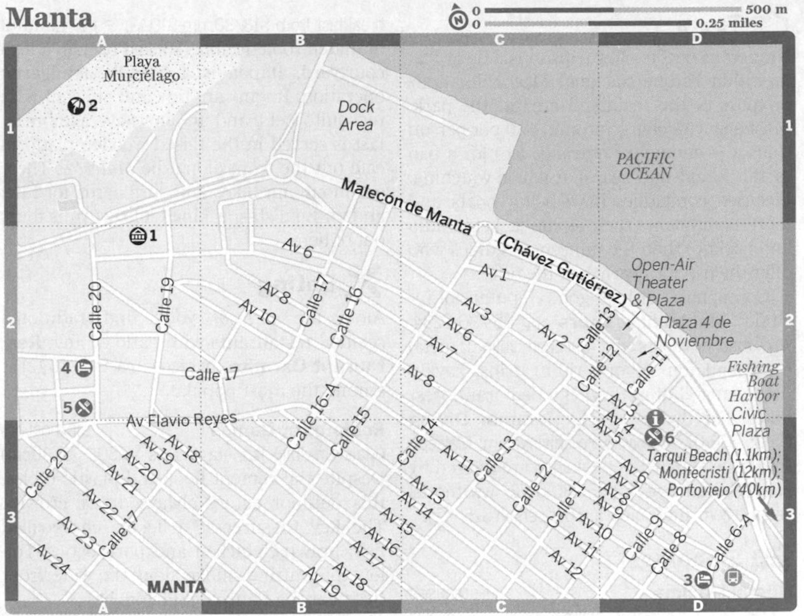

Manta

Sights

1 Museo del Banco Central....A2
2 Playa Murciélago....A1

Sleeping

3 Leo Hotel....D3
4 Manakin....A2

Eating

5 Beachcomber....A2
6 Trovador Café....D3

life, the popular Beachcomber is a favorite for its grilled meats. Dine in the lush backyard garden or on the open-sided front porch.

Information

Municipal Tourist Office (05-262-2944; Av 3 N10-34; 8am-12:30pm & 2:30-5pm Mon-Fri) Friendly and helpful.

Getting There & Away

The airport is some 3km east of Tarqui; a taxi costs about $2. **TAME** (05-262-2006; Malecón de Manta) flies daily to Quito (around $90).

Frequent buses depart from the terminal, conveniently located in Manta, one block off the *malecón*, to Montecristi ($0.50, 30 minutes), Guayaquil ($5, four hours), Quito ($10, nine hours), Bahía de Caráquez ($3, 2½ hours), Puerto López ($3, 2½ hours) and Montañita ($5.50, 3½ hours).

Montecristi

05

Montecristi is known throughout the world for producing the finest straw hat on the planet – the mistakenly labeled panama hat. In Ecuador they're called *sombreros de paja toquilla* (*toquilla* straw is a fine fibrous straw endemic to the region). Countless places in town sell hats, but for a proper *super-fino* (the finest, most tightly woven hat of all), you'll need to visit the shop and home of **José Chávez Franco** (Rocafuerte 386; 7am-7pm), behind the church. You can pick up a beauty for less than $100, cheaper than just about anywhere else in the world. Montecristi is 30 minutes by bus from Manta ($0.50). Cuenca is another great place to buy these hats.

Puerto López

05 / POP 16,000

Chipped blue fishing boats bob on a beautiful fishhook bay, and cheerful hotels, a smattering of expats, slow smiles, happy cafes and a dirt-road pace of life make it tough to leave. With its unbeatable location near Parque Nacional Machalilla, Puerto López is an obligatory stop on any coastal jaunt.

On the waterfront, **Banco del Pichincha** (Malecón Julio Izurieta) has an ATM.

Tours

Numerous outfits offer trips to Isla de la Plata within Parque Nacional Machalilla, and/or tours of the mainland area of the park. Most agencies charge around $50 per person (plus a $1 municipal entrance fee) for a trip to the island and seasonal whale-watching. Licensed companies have better boats and more equipment (such as life jackets, radio and backup) than the unlicensed guides who offer the trip for nearly half the price.

Companies with a good reputation include **Machalilla Tours** (05-230-0234; www.machalillatours.org; Malecón Julio Izurieta) for island tours, horse-riding trips, kayaking, hang-gliding and guided rainforest hikes. For diving, try **Exploramar Diving** (05-230-0123; www.exploradiving.com; Malecón Julio Izurieta). Surfing packages are offered by **Hostal Yemayá** (05-230-0122; www.hostalyemaya.com; Gral Córdova; r per person $15;).

Sleeping

Hostal Maxima GUESTHOUSE **$**
(05-230-0310; www.hotelmaxima.org; Gonzales Suarez near Machalilla; r per person $10, without bathroom $7;) This good-value hotel has clean, pleasant rooms and a friendly English-speaking owner. The grassy courtyard is strung with hammocks, and faces an open-sided kitchen where you can whip up a meal. You can also pitch a tent here (per person $4).

Hostal Monte Libano GUESTHOUSE **$**
(05-230-0231; hostalmontelibano@yahoo.com; Malecón Julio Izurieta; d $30-40, dm/d without bathroom from $10/20;) At the south end of the beach (near the pier), Monte Libano has simple, clean rooms and a friendly, familial ambience. There's a guest kitchen and a small deck with hammocks on the upper floor. One much-requested room is perched atop a tree. Maria, the owner, also offers cooking classes.

★ **Hostería Mandála** CABINS **$$**
(05-230-0181; www.hosteriamandala.info; s/d from $41/58; @) Easily the nicest place to stay in town, Mandála boasts a beachfront location north of the *malecón*. Cabins are scattered throughout a thick and lush flower garden, and the rooms are subdued, rustic and sophisticated: wood, bamboo and colorful textiles combine to make charming, cozy hideaways.

Hostería Itapoá HOSTEL **$$**
(05-230-0071; www.hosteriaitapoa.com; Malecón Julio Izurieta near Calle Abdon Calderon; s/d incl breakfast from $18/30, dm $10-13;) A handful of thatch-roofed cabins tucked back in a lush courtyard, Itapoá is a friendly, family-run operation. Rooms are tidy and efficient with mosquito nets, and an above-average breakfast is served in the raised wooden platform cafe out the front along the *malecón*. There are mountain bikes and surfboards for hire, and an English-speaking biologist runs tours out of here.

Eating

Along the *malecón* you'll find traditional seafood restaurants with patio dining. **Restaurant Carmita** (malecón; mains US$6-12) is among the most popular.

Restaurant Danica ECUADORIAN **$**
(Malecón Julio Izurieta; mains $3.50; 7-10pm) Despite the cement floor and plastic tables, this outdoor eatery always draws crowds. The key to success: delicious char-grilled fish, prawns, chicken and pork chops. Follow the wafting smoke along the waterfront (it's near the Banco del Pichincha).

Patacon Pisa'o COLOMBIAN **$**
(Gral Córdova; mains $5-8; noon-9:30pm;) This friendly eatery, nothing more than a few outdoor tables, serves delicious Colombian specialties such as *arepas* (maize pancakes) and its namesake dish: large, thin, crisply fried plantains with your choice of meat topping. Good also for brewed coffee. Opens for breakfast in high season.

Etnias Café CAFE **$**
(Gral Córdova; mains $3-5; 8am-3pm Mon-Sat;) A cozy place, this French-owned spot does good crepes, waffles, desserts and frozen coffee drinks.

Bellitalia ITALIAN **$$**
(099-617-5183; Juan Montalvo; mains $9-12; 6-10pm Mon-Sat) This delightful spot serves high-quality Italian cooking in a romantic, garden-like setting. It's one block inland from the beach (around the corner from Hostería Itapoá). Reserve ahead, especially on weekends.

Whale Cafe INTERNATIONAL **$$**
(Café Bellena; Malecón Julio Izurieta; mains $8-11; 5-9pm Tue-Sat;) For Thai-style stir-fries, veggie wraps, taco salads, spaghetti bolognese and hummus and garlic toast, grab a table on the balcony at this charming American-owned spot just above street level. It's toward the southern end of the *malecón*.

Getting There & Away

The bus station is 2.5km north of town (on the road to Agua Blanca); a *mototaxi* (motorbike rickshaw) costs $0.50 per person. There are several daily buses to Quito ($12, 11 hours). Buses to Jipijapa can drop you off at the national park entrance and at other coastal points. Hourly buses head south to Santa Elena and can drop you off at points along the way.

Parque Nacional Machalilla

05

Preserving isolated beaches, coral formations, two offshore islands, tropical dry forest, coastal cloud forest, archaeological sites and 200 sq km of ocean, Ecuador's only coastal **national park** FREE is a marvelous and unique destination. The tropical dry forest seen here used to stretch along much of the Pacific Coast of Central and South America, but it has been whacked nearly into extinction. Plants in the park include cacti, various figs and the giant kapok tree. Howler monkeys, anteaters and some 200 bird species inhabit the forest interior, while the coastal edges are home to frigate birds, pelicans and boobies, some of which nest in colonies on the offshore islands.

The turnoff to the lovely beach of **Los Frailes** is about 10km north of Puerto López, just before the town of Machalilla. Framed by dramatic headlands, the picturesque beach is one of Ecuador's loveliest. Buses stop near the ranger station, from where a 3km road and a 4km trail lead to the beach. Seabirds are plentiful and camping is allowed.

The barren, sun-charred **Isla de la Plata**, an island 40km northwest of Puerto López, is a highlight of the park, especially from mid-June to September when humpback whales mate offshore and sightings from tour boats (arranged in Puerto López) are practically guaranteed. The island itself hosts nesting seabird colonies, and a guided hike is usually included in the tour. Fast boats make the trip in about an hour.

From the mainland park entrance, 6km north of Puerto López, a dirt road goes 5km to **Agua Blanca** (admission $5), a small indigenous village. Admission includes a visit to the small intriguing **archaeological museum** (8am-6pm), followed by a walk through the community to a sulfur pool where you can take a dip and cover yourself with therapeutic mud if so inclined. You can also arrange longer hiking and horse treks, including overnight trips.

South of Puerto López

04

This stretch of the south coast is dotted with tiny fishing villages and wide beaches. Some 14km south of Puerto López (right after the village of Puerto Rico) on the inland side of the road, you'll come to the thatched-roof bungalows of **Azuluna Eco-Lodge** (05-234-7093; www.azuluna-ecuador.com; r from $70;), a peaceful place to recharge.

The next village south is **Las Tunas**. The beach here is long, wide and empty. Along the shore is **Hosteria Tsafiki** (098-334-8759; www.tsafiki.com; r per person incl breakfast $25;), a complex of attractive two-story *cabañas*, made of white adobe-style walls with blue trim.

At **Ayampe**, where the Río Ayampe empties into the ocean (the strong undertow here makes swimming difficult), the luxuriant green hills close in on the beach. Run by an Ecuadorian-American couple, **La Buena Vida** (099-486-3985; www.suflabuenavida.com; dm/s/d incl breakfast $23/35/60;) has colorful rooms, all with ocean views. Another tranquil option is the lovely **Finca Punta Ayampe** (099-189-0982; www.fincapuntaayampe.com; r $55-65;). On the beach, **Cabañas La Tortuga** (05-258-9363; www.latortuga.com.ec; cabaña $20-30;) has worn thatched-roof cabins and an open-sided restaurant facing the surf.

About 22km south of Ayampe (and just 4km north of Montañita) is the coastal village of **Olón**. A fine base for taking in the scene is the Italian-run **La Mariposa** (04-278-8120; http://lamariposahostal.com; Calle 13 de Deciembre near Rosa Mística; r $30-35;), a simple but welcoming place one block from the beach.

Montañita

04

Blessed with the country's best surf – and more budget hotels than you can shake your board at – Montañita means bare feet, baggy shorts, surf and scene. Some dig it, others despise it. Despite its rapid growth, it's as mellow and friendly as ever. Banco de Guayaquil has an ATM and there are several cybercafes in town.

Activities

You can arrange horse riding, rainforest walks and biking tours at **Machalilla Tours** (☎099-169-4213) on the main street. Several shops in town rent boards.

Overlooking town, **Montañita Spanish School** (☎206-0116; www.montanitaspanishschool.com; per person per 20hr incl registration fee $240) is a great place to take classes.

Sleeping

Book a room in advance (and bring earplugs) during the December-to-April high season. Expect lower prices and fewer crowds out of season.

Hotel Hurvínek HOSTERÍA $
(☎04-206-0068; www.actiweb.es/hurvinek; Calle 10 de Agosto; r per person incl breakfast $20; 📶) The spacious, fan-cooled rooms at this bright and sunny guesthouse are beautifully crafted, from the polished-wood floors and rustic wood furniture to the charmingly tiled bathrooms. A buffet breakfast is served in the ground-floor lounge area. To find the Hurvínek, make your first left after turning into town from the highway; it's located halfway down on the right.

Hostal Mohica Sumpa GUESTHOUSE $
(☎098-289-6109; hostalmohicasumpa@hotmail.com; Calle Principal; r $20-30; 📶) The two two-story thatch-roofed buildings here occupy prime real estate overlooking the ocean at the end of Calle Principal. All rooms are small, basic wood and bamboo affairs, but those with views are worth the extra bucks.

Tiki Limbo HOSTEL $
(☎04-206-0019; www.tikilimbo.com; r per person from $15; 📶) Tiki Limbo outdoes its cheapie competitors in terms of style: the pastel-colored rooms have four-poster beds made of bamboo, and zebra-print bedspreads add a dash of style. You can relax in a hammock or lounge chair on the 2nd-floor lounge, or sign up for surf lessons.

Hostal Mama Cucha GUESTHOUSE $
(☎04-206-0080; r per person from $10; 📶) Adorned with murals and color-saturated walls, this good-value cheapie has simple rooms surrounding a small garden courtyard. It's a friendly family-run place, and you can arrange bike tours and surf lessons here.

Hostal Las Palmeras HOTEL $
(☎06-969-2134; Av 15 de Mayo; r per person from $12) Although it needs some upkeep, Las Palmeras is a good-value choice for Montañita. In the whitewashed adobe building in back, rooms are spacious with mosquito nets, rustic light fixtures and modern bathrooms (which lacked hot water when we passed through). There's a small courtyard with loungers where you can hear the crashing waves

Hostal Kundalini HOSTEL $$
(☎095-950-5007; www.hostalkundalini.com.ec; r $40-50; 📶) Sitting directly in front of a surf break, Kundalini is nothing more than a thatch-roofed building set out on a lawn with beachfront access. There are four small rooms here, each with bamboo walls and furniture, and private hammocks.

Nativa Bambu CABIN $$$
(☎04-206-0097; www.nativabambu.com; cabin incl breakfast from $70; ❄📶) These peacefully set all-wood cabins with thatch roofs and small front decks have lovely views overlooking Montañita and the ocean beyond. Nativa Bambu is also known for its friendly, professional service and high-end fittings (good beds, coffee makers, Direct TV in some cabins). Look for the signed entrance off the highway near Calle Principal.

Eating & Drinking

Carts near the beach whip up inexpensive fruit-filled cocktails. One block over, **Lost Beach Club** (www.lostbeachclub.com; malecón; ⏰10pm-late) throws big dance parties. Hola Ola is another big bar with live music and dancing.

Kaffeina INTERNATIONAL $
(mains $4-8; ⏰11am-9pm Thu-Mon, from 4pm Sat; 🌿) This tiny Danish-Ecuadorian-run cafe serves a range of healthy and delicious dishes made from scratch, including veggie burgers, stir-fries, crepes and salads. It's located just past the church.

Papillon FRENCH $
(crepes $3-10; ⏰8am-10pm; 📶) You'll find an excellent variety of sweet and savory crepes at this place, which is on the street lined with cocktail vendors (not far from Tiki Limbo).

Tiki Limbo INTERNATIONAL $$
(mains $7-14; ⏰8.30am-midnight; 📶🌿) In the epicenter of town, Montañita's best restaurant has an eclectic menu of global dishes (fajitas, falafels, burgers, sesame-crusted shrimp, seafood platters) and a charming

setting of bamboo furniture (including a few lounge beds-cum-tables).

Hola Ola INTERNATIONAL **$$**
(mains $7-14; 8am-midnight) Israeli-owned Hola Ola is a laid-back spot that's good any time of day for a meal or drink. The wide-ranging menu features omelets, fish-and-chips, barbecue chicken, *shawerma* and falafel wraps and pizzas, plus good coffees (real espresso) and desserts.

Getting There & Away

Three CLP buses pass Montañita each day on their way south to Guayaquil ($5.50, 3½ hours). Buses south to Santa Elena ($2, two hours) and La Libertad, or north to Puerto López ($2.50, one hour) pass every 15 minutes.

Guayaquil

04 / POP 2.4 MILLION

Although it's hot, noisy and chaotic, Guayaquil has come a long way from its dismal days as the crime-ridden port of yesteryear. The transformed *malecón* overlooking the Río Guayas has helped redefine the city. The historical neighborhood of Las Peñas, as well as Guayaquil's principal downtown thoroughfare, 9 de Octubre, have also been restored. There's much to explore in these areas, although if you're not enamored of big cities, you probably won't like this one either.

Most travelers stay in the center of town, which is organized in a gridlike fashion on the west bank of Río Guayas. The main east-west street is 9 de Octubre. The riverfront Malecón 2000 stretches along the bank of the Río Guayas, from the Mercado Sur at its southern tip, to Barrio Las Peñas and the hill of Cerro Santa Ana to the north. The suburb of Urdesa, which is frequently visited for its restaurants and nightlife, is about 4km northwest and 1.5km west of the airport.

All flights to the Galápagos either stop or originate in Guayaquil. Subsequently, it's the next best place (after Quito) to set up a trip to the islands.

Sights & Activities

Malecón 2000

If you've just arrived, head down to the **waterfront promenade** (7am-midnight) and take a stroll beside the Río Guayas. Known as Malecón 2000, the waterfront is Guayaquil's flagship redevelopment project, stretching 2.5km along the river, with playgrounds, tropical gardens, restaurants and an IMAX movie theater. The area is well policed and generally safe, even at night.

Bustling 9 de Octubre is Guayaquil's main commercial street; it intersects the *malecón* at the impressive **La Rotonda** monument.

★Museo Antropológico y de Arte Contemporáneo MUSEUM
(MAAC; 04-230-9383; cnr Malecón Simón Bolívar & Loja; 9am-4:30pm Tue-Fri, 10am-4pm Sat & Sun) FREE Marking the end of the riverfront is the modern MAAC, a museum of anthropology and archaeology that hosts a superb permanent collection of pre-Colombian pieces and videos showing artistic techniques of early peoples. Changing exhibitions showcase works by contemporary Ecuadorian artists. MAAC also has a modern 350-seat **theater** (230-9400; www.maaccine.com; admission $2) for plays, concerts and films.

Las Peñas & Cerro Santa Ana

At the northern end of the *malecón*, these two historic neighborhoods have been refurbished into an idealized version of a quaint South American hillside village – brightly painted homes, cobblestone alleyways and all. The stairway winding up Cerro Santa Ana past the brightly painted buildings is lined with informal restaurants and neighborhood bars. The views from the hilltop fort, called **Fortín del Cerro** (Fort of the Hill), and the **lighthouse** (10am-10pm) FREE are spectacular.

To the right of the stairs, the historic cobbled street of **Numa Pompillo Llona** winds past elegantly decaying wooden colonial houses, some of which house art galleries.

Downtown Area

The main thoroughfare, 9 de Octubre, is definitely worth a stroll to experience Guayaquil's commercial vibrancy.

SAFETY IN GUAYAQUIL

The downtown area is fine during the day, but sketchy after dark. Watch your belongings in the bus terminal. There is a persistent problem with post-ATM-withdrawal robberies, so be extra aware for at least a few blocks after leaving the bank.

Guayaquil – City Center

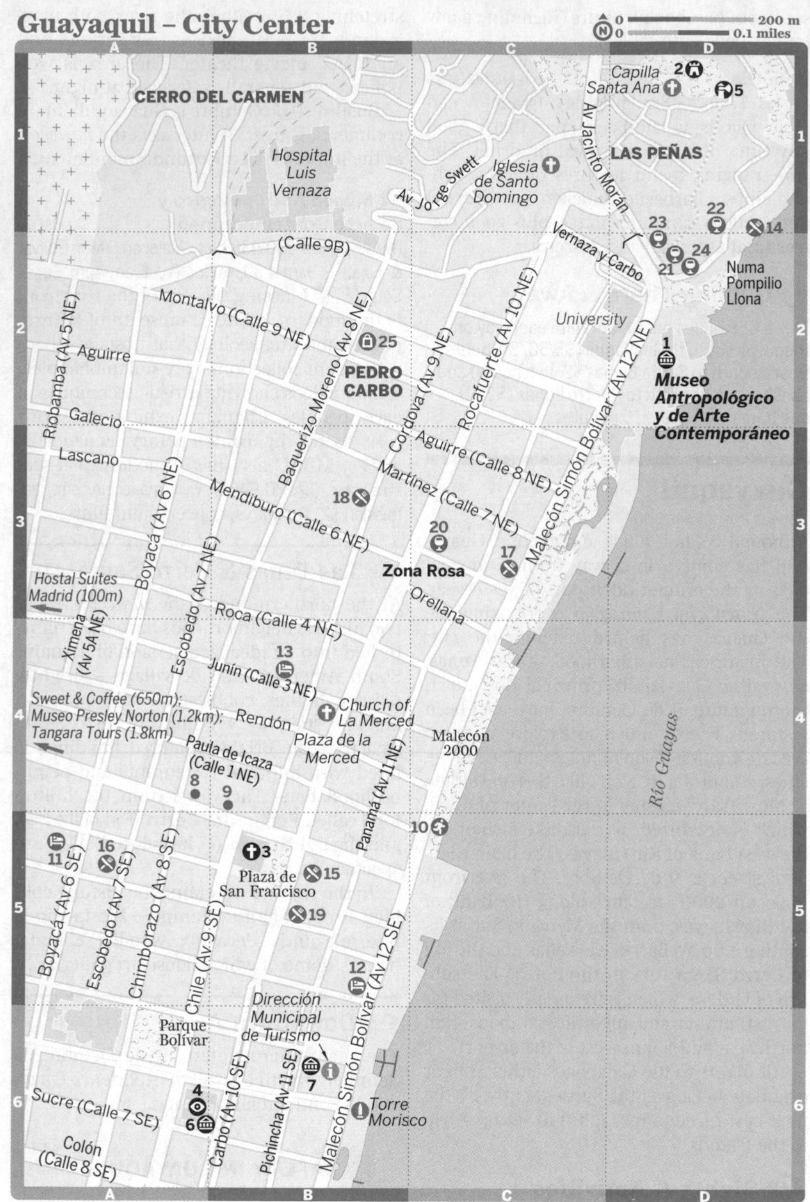

Museo Municipal MUSEUM

(☎04-252-4100; Sucre; ⏱9am-5:30pm Tue-Sat) **FREE** A block south of Parque Bolívar, you'll find this museum and the municipal **library**. The archaeology room on the ground floor has mainly Inca and pre-Inca ceramics, and several figurines from the oldest culture in Ecuador, the Valdivia (c 3200 BC). Also on the ground floor is a colonial room with mainly religious paintings and a few period household items. Upstairs, there's a jumble of modern art and ethnography rooms.

Guayaquil – City Center

Top Sights
1 Museo Antropológico y de Arte Contemporáneo D2

Sights
2 Fortín del Cerro D1
3 Iglesia de San Francisco B5
4 Library A6
5 Lighthouse D1
6 Museo Municipal A6
7 Museo Nahim Isaias B6

Activities, Courses & Tours
8 Centro Viajero A4
9 Galasam Tours B4
10 Vintage Train Car C5

Sleeping
11 Casa de Romero A5
12 Manso Boutique Hotel B5
13 Re Bed & Breakfast B4

Eating
14 Artur's Café D1
15 Cocolon B5
16 Dulceria La Palma A5
17 Frutabar C3
Manso Mix .... (see 12)
18 Picanteria La Culata B3
19 Sweet & Coffee B5

Drinking & Nightlife
20 Bar El Colonial C3
21 Diva Nicotina D2
22 La Paleta D1
23 La Taberna D2
24 Rayuela D2

Entertainment
MAAC Theater .... (see 1)

Shopping
25 El Mercado Artesanal Loja B2

Museo Nahim Isaias MUSEUM
(cnr Pichincha & Ballén; ⏰8:30am-4pm Tue-Fri, from 10am Sat & Sun) FREE Nahim Isaias, located in the Plaza de Administración building, exhibits an excellent collection of sculptures, paintings and artifacts from the colonial period.

Iglesia de San Francisco CHURCH
(9 de Octubre near Chile) The city's most impressive church is the Iglesia de San Francisco, which has been reconstructed and beautifully restored since the devastating 1896 fire.

Parque Bolívar Area

Guayaquil may be the only city in the world that has **land iguanas**, some over 1m in length, living downtown. These prehistoric-looking animals (a different species from those found in the Galápagos) are a startling sight in one of Guayaquil's most famous plazas, **Parque Bolívar**, which is also known as Parque Seminario. Around its small ornamental gardens are several of Guayaquil's top-end hotels.

Malecón El Salado & Around

Smaller than the more famous development on the Río Guayas, the Malecón El Salado is a waterfront promenade dotted with eateries and cafes. **Rowboats** (per 30min $3.50) are available for a short paddle along the mangrove-lined estuary.

Museo Presley Norton MUSEUM
(☎04-229-3423; Av 9 de Octubre; ⏰9am-5pm Tue-Fri, 10am-5pm Sat & Sun) FREE This museum, featuring an impressive collection of archaeological artifacts, including pottery and figurines made by the original settlers of Ecuador, is housed in a beautifully restored mansion. It occasionally stages concerts and screens films.

Tours

The following recommended companies can organize tours both to the Galápagos and within the local area.

Centro Viajero TOUR
(☎04-256-4034; www.centroviajero.com; Baquerizo Moreno 1119 near Av 9 de Octubre, Office 805, 8th fl) Organizes Galápagos packages. Spanish, English and French is spoken; ask for the manager, Douglas Chang.

Dreamkapture Travel TOUR
(☎04-224-2909; www.dreamkapture.com; Alborada 12A etapa, Manzana 2, Villa 21, Juan Sixto Bernal) Good deals on Galápagos cruises and other trips. French, Spanish and English are spoken.

Galasam Tours TOUR
(☎04-230-4488; www.galasam.com.ec; Av 9 de Octubre 424, Grand Pasaje Bldg, ground fl, Office 9A) Known for economical Galápagos cruises; however, go in with your eyes open.

SANTAY ISLAND

Long off the radar for most visitors to Guayaquil, the mangrove-covered Santay Island is an emerging destination, thanks to its new status as a protected reserve. Part of the government's plans to add more green space to the city, Santay is front and center in the recently inaugurated ecotourism project 'Guayaquil Ecológico.' A new vehicle-free bridge gives pedestrian and bicycle access to the island.

The allure of this lush 22-sq-km island in the Río Guayas is that it makes a peaceful refuge from bustling downtown Guayaquil; it's also a good bird-watching spot with more than 128 species. You can also spy caimans in the muddy waters. Wooden walkways lead through a small fishing community of 230 residents (with simple eating options on the island). A newly completed second pedestrian bridge also connects the island to the canton of Durán.

The 840m-long Santay Island bridge is located a few kilometers south of the *malecón*. By bus, take the Metrovia to the Barrio Centenario stop, which is two blocks from the bridge.

Tangara Tours TOUR
(☎04-228-2828; www.tangara-ecuador.com; Ciudadela Bolivariana, cnr Manuela Sáenz & O'Leary, Block F, Casa 1) Run out of the guesthouse of the same name, and highly recommended for local day tours including trips to the Reserva Ecológica Manglares Churute.

Tren Ecuador TRAIN TOUR
(☎1800-873-637; www.trenecuador.com; round trip $22; ⏱tours 8am Thu-Sun) This all-day train excursion takes you from Durán to Yaguachi and on to Bucay, 88km east of Guayaquil. Once in Bucay, you'll have about four hours of free time, which you can spend on a range of outdoor activities – including horse riding, mountain biking and visiting waterfalls (you can even rappel down them) – all of which costs extra. Tour operators meet the train in Bucay.

The return journey happens by bus, and you'll arrive back in Guayaquil around 5:30pm. It's a bit touristy (a dance troupe puts on a show at Bucay station), but still an enjoyable outing that's popular with Ecuadorian travelers. A taxi to the start of the trip in Durán should cost around $7 from the city center. Tickets are sold from the **vintage train car** (⏱10am-6pm Mon-Fri, to 3:30pm Sat & Sun) on the *malecón*.

Trips & Dreams TOUR
(☎099-235-1335; www.tripsanddreams.com; Quísquis 305 near Rumichaca) This especially recommended agency shares space and management with Hostal Suites Madrid. Ask for Christopher Jimenez, the extremely knowledgeable and affable manager. Can arrange all manner of trips, especially discounted trips to the Galápagos.

Festivals & Events

The whole city parties during the last week of July, celebrating Simón Bolívar's birthday (July 24) and Guayaquil Foundation Day (July 25). Hotels fill up and services are disrupted. Celebrations are huge during Guayaquil's Independence Day (October 9) and Día de la Raza (October 12). New Year's Eve is celebrated with bonfires.

Sleeping

Hostal Suites Madrid HOTEL $
(☎04-230-7804; www.hostalsuitesmadrid.com; Quísquis 305 near Rumichaca; r incl fan/air-con from $25/30; P ❄ @ ☎) One of the few hotels in the city geared toward foreign travelers, Madrid offers a super-clean and secure refuge within 10 minutes' walk of the *malecón*. It has high ceilings, a bright and cheerful color scheme and a rooftop terrace with computers for guests' use. Staff are extremely helpful and friendly.

NucaPacha HOSTEL $
(☎04-261-0553; www.nucapacha.com; Bálsamos Sur 308; dm $11, s/d $22/33, without bathroom $17/27; @ ☎ ≋) On a peaceful street in Urdesa, NucaPacha has an appealing pool and patio, rimmed by tropical foliage (including mango and papaya trees). The rooms are quite basic (bare walls, a neon light bulb, noisy fan) and the beds aren't very comfortable, but the staff is friendly and the price is right. There's also a shared kitchen and tours on offer.

Manso Boutique Hotel HOTEL $$
(☎04-252-6644; www.manso.ec; cnr Malecón Simón Bolívar & Aguirre; dm $17, r $41-82; ❄@📶) The unrivalled location aside – boasting a *malecón* address – Manso is at least as much hostel as boutique hotel. Rooms vary in comfort and style, with the best being bright and airy, and livened up with a splash of color on the walls and framed artwork. There's a bohemian vibe to the place, with yoga classes, bike hire and an appealing cafe serving up organic fare.

Re Bed & Breakfast GUESTHOUSE $$
(☎04-231-0111; www.rebandb.com; Junín 428 near Córdova, 3rd fl, apt D; dm/s/d incl breakfast $17/37/64; ❄📶) Tucked away in an apartment building, this small five-room guesthouse has simple rooms decorated with stencils, pop art and colorful curtains. There's a kitchen for guests, a small living room with lots of natural light and a friendly bohemian vibe that makes everyone feel at home.

Casa de Romero B&B $$
(☎04-603-6244; www.hostelromero.com; cnr Vélez 501 & Boyacá, 7th fl; s/d incl breakfast $28/45; ❄@📶) For a taste of downtown *guayaquileño* living, try this friendly place, located in a high-rise apartment building. It has good-sized rooms (all but one with private bathroom), including several with balconies. There's also an attractive lounge area and a kitchen (and laundry) for guests.

Eating

Downtown Guayaquil has an abundance of inexpensive restaurants, including informal *parrillas* (grill restaurants) near Parque del Centenario and fast-food restaurants along the Malecón 2000. For high-end dining, head to the northwestern suburb of Urdesa.

Frutabar JUICE BAR $
(Malecón Simón Bolívar; mains $5-7; ⏲9am-midnight) This surfer-themed eating and drinking spot serves up gourmet sandwiches, snacks and tasty tropical-fruit juices and cocktails. It's a fun spot for a drink, with a soundtrack of reggae and loungey beats.

Sweet & Coffee CAFE $
(cnr Carbo & Luque; snacks $2-3.50; ⏲7:30am-8:30pm Mon-Fri, from 9am Sat, noon-6pm Sun; 📶) A popular dark-wood cafe with excellent cakes and quiches (the *torta de jamón y queso* is quite good); there's another **branch** (cnr 9 de Octubre & José de Antepara; snacks $2-3.50; ⏲7:30am-8:30pm Mon-Fri, from 9am Sat, noon-6pm Sun) near Oro de Verde on Av 9 de Octubre.

Dulceria La Palma CAFE $
(Escobedo, btwn Vélez & Luque; ⏲7:45am-7pm Mon-Sat, 8am-5pm Sun) One of the most atmospheric places downtown is this old-school cafe with swirling overhead fans and black-and-white photos of Guayaquil. Stop in for breakfast or snacks like *cachitos* (crispy mini-croissants; $0.11) or varied pastries (all $0.27 each).

Mercado El Norte ECUADORIAN $
(cnr Baquerizo Moreno & Martínez; ⏲9am-7pm Mon-Sat, 10am-4pm Sun) For fresh fruits and vegetables, plus inexpensive set lunches, hit this bustling market near the Mercado Artesanal Loja.

Picanteria La Culata SEAFOOD $$
(Córdova btwn Mendiburo & Martínez; mains $4-9; ⏲8am-midnight Mon-Thu, to 2am Fri & Sat) Bringing a taste of the coast to the big city, La Culata serves excellent *ceviches*, *encocados* (shrimp or fish cooked in a rich, spiced coconut sauce) and seafood rices. It's a laid-back, open-sided joint (with beachy, *cabaña*-style murals on the walls) that draws crowds at all hours of day and night.

Cocolon ECUADORIAN $$
(Av Carbo; mains $8-12; ⏲noon-9pm Mon-Sat, to 5pm Sun) Directly across from the plaza for the Church of San Francisco, Cocolon has a modern but festive interior and is well-known for its Ecuadorian dishes. *La ultima cena* (grilled loin with rice, beans and all the fixings) is a classic. Adventurous palates: try *guatita* (a tripe and potato stew in a seasoned, peanut-based sauce).

Manso Mix FUSION $$
(cnr Malecón Simón Bolívar & Aguirre; mains $7-9; ⏲8am-10pm; 📶🌱) Inside the Manso Boutique Hotel, this colorful cafe serves up tasty healthy fare (including quinoa tortillas, fish in coconut sauce and bean burgers).

Artur's Café INTERNATIONAL $$
(☎04-231-2230; Numa Pompilio Llona 127, Las Peñas; mains $6-9; ⏲6pm-midnight Sun-Thu, to 2am Fri & Sat) A longstanding hideaway perched over the Río Guayas, Artur's serves ordinary Ecuadorian fare, but it's a lively starting point for a nighttime libation before exploring Las Peñas. There's live music most weekends.

Drinking & Entertainment

The *farra* (nightlife) in Guayaquil is spread around town, but some of the most atmospheric bars are found in Las Peñas.

Rayuela BAR

(Numa Pompilio Llona; ⏲9am-late Tue-Sun) This hip new spot has a candlelit, lounge-like vibe that's just the right setting for a few drinks among friends. Well-mixed cocktails ($7 to $9) and good snacks are on hand (quesadillas, tapas, fondues), plus low-key bands on Thursday nights. Minimum consumption of $15 per person. It's also open for brunch and daytime drinking (with two-for-one drink specials until 8pm)!

La Paleta BAR

(Numa Pompilio Llona 174; ⏲9pm-2am Tue-Sat) La Paleta is a great little lounge to while away an evening, with cave-like nooks, a hipster crowd and good ambient grooves. Serves beers and high-end cocktails, as well as tapas.

Diva Nicotina BAR

(Cerro Santa Ana; ⏲7pm-midnight Mon-Thu, to 2am Fri & Sat) At the foot of the hill, atmospheric Diva Nicotina draws a festive young crowd who pack the house when there's live music.

La Taberna BAR

(Cerro Santa Ana) Walking up the steps in Las Peñas, take the first lane off to the left to reach this lively, bohemian drinking den. It has salsa beats, a fun crowd, and plenty of love for Guayaquil's Barcelona Sporting Club with its hanging jerseys and old football mementos.

Bar El Colonial BAR

(Rocafuerte 623; ⏲4pm-midnight Mon-Thu, to 2am Fri & Sat) One of the Zona Rosa's longest-surviving hot spots with live music on weekend nights.

Shopping

El Mercado Artesanal Loja MARKET

(Baquerizo Moreno; ⏲9am-7pm Mon-Sat, 10am-5pm Sun) This large artisans' market has a huge variety of crafts from all over Ecuador, including Otavalo-style sweaters, panama hats, carved chessboards and mass-produced paintings. Bargaining is expected.

Information

EMERGENCY

Cruz Roja (Red Cross) ☎131

Police ☎101

MEDICAL SERVICES

Clínica Kennedy (☎04-228-9666; Av del Periodista) One of the better hospitals in Guayaquil, by the Policentro shopping center in the suburb of Kennedy. Av del Periodista is also known as San Jorge.

MONEY

There are ATMs all over downtown, especially around Plaza de la Merced.

TOURIST INFORMATION

Dirección Municipal de Turismo (☎04-232-4182; www.thisisecuador.com; cnr Pichincha & Ballén, Museo Nahim Isaias; ⏲9am-5pm Tue-Sat) This small office for city and regional tourist info often has only one staff member on hand. Friendly, but usually Spanish-speaking only.

GETTING TO PERU

The Ecuadorian immigration office and the Peruvian immigration office are right next to one another, 4km outside Huaquillas and 1km off the highway. All entrance and exit formalities are carried out here; there are no fees. If you're coming by bus, it's easier to disembark in Huaquillas and hire a taxi to take you out to the immigration offices. Taxis ask around $3 to $5 each way. After you take care of formalities, head back to Huaquillas and make the border crossing on foot over the short international bridge.

The Peruvian side of the border is notorious for scams. Keep your wits about you. Try to change some dollars into soles before arriving to avoid having to deal with the money changers.

In Aguas Verdes, Peru, there are *colectivos* and *mototaxis* (motorbike rickshaws; per person S5) running to Tumbes, which has plenty of hotels, as well as transportation to take you further south.

For information on making this crossing in the opposite direction, see p878.

Getting There & Away

AIR

TAME (☎04-256-0728; www.tame.com.ec; Av 9 de Octubre 424, Gran Pasaje) and **LAN** (www.lan.com) have daily flights to Quito (from $80, one hour). TAME also flies to Cuenca ($92, 30 minutes) and Loja ($75, 45 minutes). LAN and TAME fly to Isla Baltra and San Cristóbal in the Galápagos (from $400 round-trip, 1½ hours).

BUS

The bus terminal is 2km beyond the airport. There are services to most major towns in the country. Many buses go daily to Quito ($10, seven to 10 hours), Manta ($7.50, four hours) and Cuenca ($9, 3½ hours).

Several companies at the terminal go to Machala ($5, three hours) and Huaquillas ($6, four hours) on the Peruvian border. The easiest way to Peru, however, is with one of the international lines. Most highly recommended is **Cruz del Sur** (www.cruzdelsur.com.pe), which charges $85 to $100 all the way to Lima (26 hours, 2pm Tuesday, Wednesday, Friday and Sunday). Next is **Expreso Internacional Ormeño** (☎04-214-0847; www.grupo-ormeno.com.pe/ormeno.php; Centro de Negocios El Terminal, Bahia Norte, Office 34, Bloque C), then **Rutas de America** (☎223-8673; www.rutasenbus.com; Los Rios 3012 near Letamendi), and finally **Ormeño** (☎213-0379; www.cifainternacional.com), which has daily departures for Lima ($90, 11:30am). Ormeño's office and terminal is on Av de las Américas, just north of tho main buc terminal.

These services are convenient because you don't have to get off the bus to take care of border formalities.

Getting Around

TO/FROM THE AIRPORT

The airport is about 5km north of the center on Av de las Américas. The bus terminal is 2km north of the airport. A taxi to the center should cost about $5 from either location.

For a bus, cross the street in front of the airport to take a Metrovia ($0.25). The 'Plaza del Centenario' stop on Av Machala is the most convenient downtown stop. Heading back out to the airport, catch the Metrovia one block south on Av Quito.

BUS

By bus from the city center to the bus terminal, there are two convenient Metrovia lines that go to Terminal Rio Daule, across from the bus station. Handy stops include Av Quito (near Parque del Centenario) and Rocafuerte, one block north of 9 de Octubre.

TAXI

A taxi within downtown shouldn't cost more than $1.50. To Urdesa, count on $3 to $4. Agree on fares before entering a taxi.

Machala

☎07 / POP 231,000

The self-proclaimed 'banana capital of the world,' Machala is a chaotic, workaday city. Most travelers going to and from Peru pass through here, but few stay more than a night. Páez is a pedestrian-only zone between Rocafuerte and 9 de Octubre.

Sleeping & Eating

For a fresh seafood feast, consider heading over to Puerto Bolívar, 7km to the west (take bus 1 or 13 along Sucre, or a taxi for $3).

Hostal Saloah HOTEL $
(☎07-293-4344; Colón 1818; s/d from $20/24; ❄@🛜) Steps away from several bus companies, the good-value rooms at the Saloah are quiet, if rather dark (owing to tiny windows and dim lighting). Each of the four floors has a larger, brighter street-facing suite that's worth the few extra dollars. There's also a rooftop deck.

Hotel Bolívar Internacional HOTEL $
(☎07-293-0727; cnr Bolívar & Colón; s/d $20/30; ❄🛜) Clean and friendly and only a short walk from several bus companies. Some of the tiled rooms have windows overlooking a small park.

Information

The **tourism office** (cnr Calle 9 de Mayo & Av 25th de Junio; ⏲8am-1pm & 2:30-5pm Mon-Sat) has city and area maps. A few major banks with ATMs are located around the central plaza.

Getting There & Away

The airport is 1km southwest of town; a taxi costs about $1. Weekday morning flights to Quito ($125) are with TAME.

There is no central bus terminal. Buses with **CIFA** (cnr Guayas & Bolívar) run regularly to Huaquillas ($1.50, 1½ hours) at the Peruvian border, and to Guayaquil ($5, three hours) from 9 de Octubre near Tarqui. **Rutas Orenses** (Rocafuerte near Tarqui) also serves Guayaquil.

Panamericana (Colón near Bolívar) offers several buses a day to Quito ($11, 10 hours). **Transportes Cooperativa Loja** (Tarqui near Bolívar) goes to Loja ($4.50, five hours).

Huaquillas

☎07 / POP 30,000

Called Aguas Verdes on the Peruvian side, Huaquillas is the main border town with Peru and lies 80km south of Machala. There's little reason to stop. Almost everything happens on the long main street. Ecuadorian banks don't change money (though they have ATMs). The briefcase-toting money changers do change money, but numerous rip-offs have been reported.

If you need to spend the night, **Hotel Vanessa** (☎07-299-6263; www.hotelvanessa-ec.com; Calle 1 de Mayo & Hualtaco; s/d from $10/20; ❄📶) is a safe bet.

CIFA buses run frequently to Machala ($2, 1½ hours) and five times daily to Guayaquil ($7, four hours) from the main street, two blocks from the border crossing. Panamericana runs 10 buses daily to Quito ($12, 11 hours). Azuay Internacional, on Teniente Cordovez, has four departures daily to Cuenca ($7, five hours).

GALÁPAGOS ISLANDS

☎05 / POP 30,000

Inspiration to Charles Darwin (who came here in 1535), the Galápagos Islands may make you think differently about the world. A trip to this extraordinary region is like visiting an alternate universe, some strange utopian colony organized by sea lions – the golden retrievers of the Galápagos – and arranged on principles of mutual cooperation. What's so extraordinary for visitors is the fearlessness of the islands' famous inhabitants. Blue-footed boobies, sea lions, prehistoric land iguanas – all act as if humans are nothing more than slightly annoying paparazzi. Nowhere else can you engage in a staring contest with wild animals and lose!

Visiting the islands is expensive, however, and the only way to truly experience their marvels is by taking a cruise. It's possible to visit four of the islands independently, but you will not see the wildlife or the many smaller islands that you will aboard a cruise.

The most important island is Isla Santa Cruz. On the southern side of the island is Puerto Ayora, the largest town in the Galápagos and where most of the budget tours are based. It has many hotels and restaurants. North of Santa Cruz, separated by a narrow strait, is Isla Baltra, home of the islands' main airport. A public bus and a ferry connect the Baltra airport with Puerto Ayora.

Isla San Cristóbal, the most easterly island, is home to the provincial capital, Puerto Baquerizo Moreno, which also has hotels and an airport. The other inhabited islands are Isabela and Floreana. Note that most of the islands have two or even three names.

Environment

The Galápagos Islands were declared a national park in 1959. Organized tourism began in the 1960s and by the 1990s some 60,000 people visited annually. Today, around 150,000 people visit each year, which continues to place added stress on the islands' delicate ecology.

Other problems facing the Galápagos include oil spills, the poaching of sea lions for bait, overfishing, illegal fishing for shark, lobster and other marine life, and the introduction of non-native animals. Despite conservation efforts by organizations such as the **Galapagos Conservancy** (www.galapagos.org), the future of the islands remains unclear.

Practicalities

Fees Before boarding a flight to the islands, foreign visitors must pay $10 at the airport in either Guayquail or Quito. Upon arrival in the Galápagos, visitors must pay another $100 (cash only) to the national park.

High Season The high season is from December to January, around Easter, and from June to August; during these periods, budget tours may be difficult to arrange.

Time Galápagos time is one hour behind mainland Ecuador.

Goings-on For the latest news on the islands, check out the **Charles Darwin Foundation** (www.darwinfoundation.org) news site.

Costs

Plan on spending more money than you want to. The least expensive boat tours (economy class) cost around $200 per day, not including airfare and the $110 park entrance fee. Prices fall by about 20% between September and November, when the seas are rough and business is slower. You can save money by taking day trips, basing

The Galápagos Islands

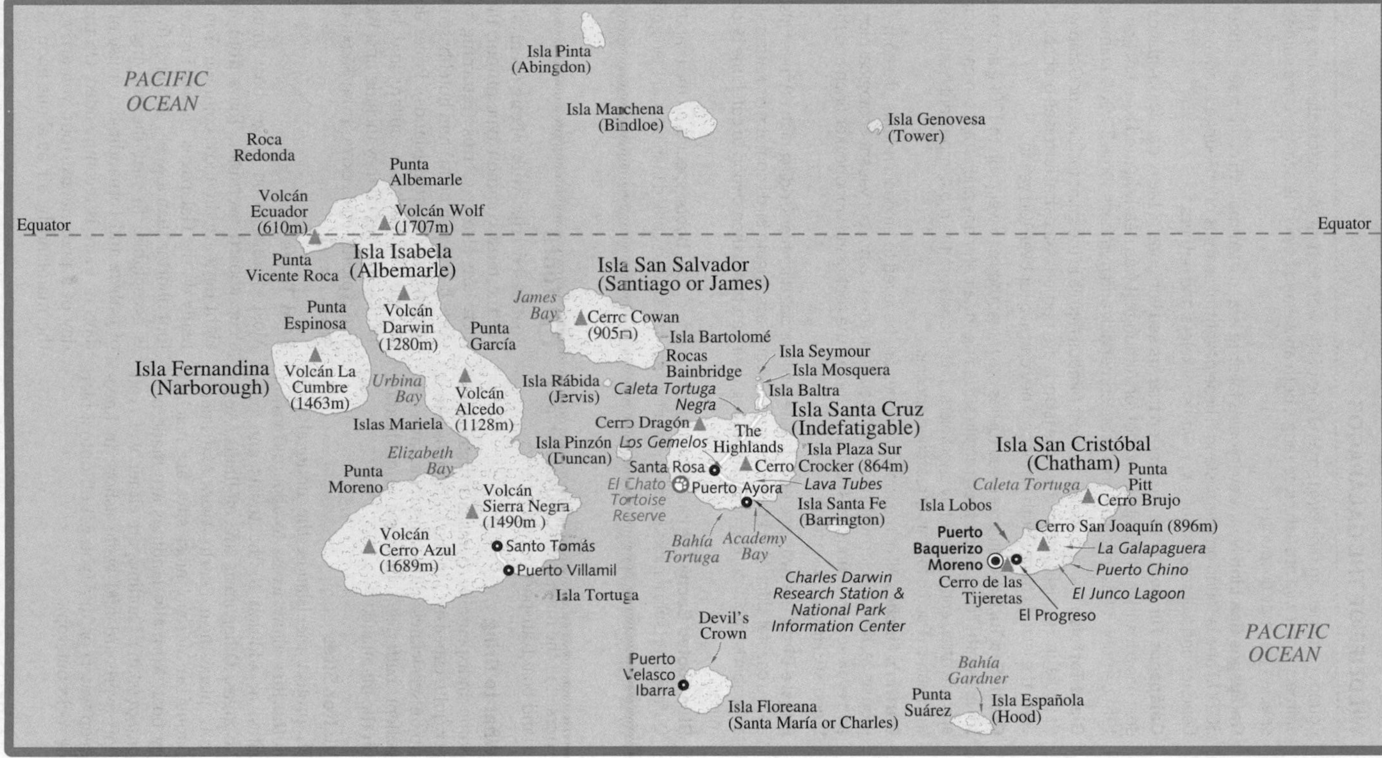

WILDLIFE OF THE GALÁPAGOS

Ecuador's famed archipelago remains one of the world's best places for interacting with animals in the wild at such close range, both above and below the sea. Here are some of the species you may encounter:

Galápagos Sea Lion Nearly everyone's favorite island mammal, which numbers about 50,000 and is found on every island. These delightful animals often lounge about on sandy beaches and will sometimes swim with snorkelers and bathers.

Galápagos Fur Seal More introverted than its sea lion cousin, the endemic Galápagos fur seal has a luxuriant, insulating layer of fur. Although it was nearly hunted to extinction in the 19th century, it has made a remarkable comeback and numbers some 30,000 animals.

Giant Tortoise The archipelago's most famous reptile is the giant tortoise, or Galápagos ('saddle' in Spanish), after which the islands are named. Ancestral tortoises probably drifted to the islands from South America. They can live for over 100 years.

Green Sea Turtle Adult green sea turtles are huge: they can weigh up to 150kg and reach 1m in length. They can be seen readily surfacing for air at many anchorages in calm water and are often encountered by snorkelers. The islands are the most important nesting site in the eastern Pacific for this threatened species.

Darwin's Finches All of the islands' finches are believed to be descendants of a common ancestor. Upon arrival in the archipelago, it found a host of vacant ecological niches and evolved into 13 unusual species, including the tool-using woodpecker finch and the blood-sucking vampire finch.

Frigate Birds The two species of frigate bird are dazzling fliers, riding high on thermals above coastal cliffs. Also known as man-o'-war birds, frigate birds sometimes harass smaller seabirds into dropping or regurgitating their catch and then swoop to catch the booty in midair.

Blue-Footed Booby The blue-footed booby is one of four booby species on the islands. During courtship it picks up its bright-blue feet in a slow, dignified fashion and then grows

yourself in the main towns and taking inter-island boat transport between them.

What to Bring

Some indispensable items are unavailable (or quite expensive) in the Galápagos. Stock up on seasickness pills, sunscreen, insect repellent, batteries, toiletries and medication on the mainland.

Visitor Sites

To protect the islands, the national park authorities allow access to about 50 visitor sites, in addition to the towns and public areas. Other areas are off-limits. Apart from places near Puerto Ayora and Puerto Baquerizo Moreno, most sites are reached by boat. Normally, landings are made in a *panga* (skiff). Landings are either 'wet' (you hop overboard and wade ashore in knee-deep water) or 'dry' (you get off onto a pier or rocky outcrop).

Tours

Boat-based trips with nights spent aboard are the most common type of tour, though there are also day trips (returning to the same hotel each night) and hotel-based trips (staying on different islands). Prices do not include the park fee, airfare and bottled drinks. Neither do they include tips. Wetsuit hire typically costs extra (from $5 per day to $10 per week).

Boat Tours

Most visitors go on longer boat tours and sleep aboard overnight. Tours from five to eight days are the most common. You can't really do the Galápagos Islands justice on a tour shorter than a week, although five days is acceptable. To visit the outlying islands of Isabela and Fernandina, a cruise of eight days or more is recommended. On the first day of a prearranged tour, you arrive from the mainland by air at about noon, so this more animated, bowing, wing-spreading and sky-pointing in an enchanting, if rather clownish, display. They are also magnificent fishers, diving like arrows into the sea.

Flightless Cormorant Apart from penguins, the flightless cormorant is the only flightless seabird in the world, and it is endemic to the Galápagos. When an ancestral population colonized this predator-free archipelago, the birds eventually lost the need for flight. About 700 pairs remain.

Galápagos Penguin Long ago, a population of penguins followed the cool Humboldt Current up from Antarctica and settled in the Galápagos. Today, it is the most northerly penguin in the world and the only species that lives in the tropics.

Waved Albatross The waved albatross is helpless in calm weather, relying utterly on southeast trade winds to transport it to feeding areas. The archipelago's largest bird (weighing 5kg, with a 2.4m wingspan) is the only albatross species that breeds at the equator.

Galápagos Flamingo Pretty in pink, these striking and unmistakable birds are part of the largest of the world's five species.

Marine Iguana The remarkable marine iguana is the world's only seagoing lizard, and is common on the rocky shores of all the Galápagos Islands. Its size and coloration vary between islands, with the largest specimens growing up to 1.5m.

Galápagos Land Iguana Despite their large size and fearsome appearance, land iguanas are harmless vegetarians that thrive on succulent opuntias (pear cactuses). Mature males weigh up to 13kg and grow to 1m; they are territorial, engaging in head-butting contests to defend their terrain.

Lava Lizards Tortoises and iguanas may be more famous, but the most commonly seen reptiles on the islands are the various species of lava lizard, which are frequently seen scurrying across rocks or even perched on the backs of iguanas.

Sally Lightfoot Crab This abundant marine animal is blessed with spectacular coloration. Sally Lightfoot crabs (named by English seafarers) adorn the rocks on every island and are extremely agile.

leaves only half a day in the Galápagos; on the last day, you have to be at the airport in the morning. Thus a 'five-day' tour gives only three full days in the islands.

Tour boats range from small yachts to large cruise ships. The most common type of boat is a motor sailer carrying up to 20 passengers. The four categories and price per day are roughly as follows: economy class (up to $200), tourist class ($200 to $300), 1st class ($300 to $400) and luxury (from $400).

Seven-night/eight-day economy tours are generally aboard small boats with six to 12 bunks in double, triple and quad cabins. Bedding is provided and the accommodations are clean, but damp and cramped, with little privacy. Plenty of simple but fresh food and juice is served at all meals, and an English-speaking guide accompanies the boat.

There are toilets, and fresh water is available for drinking. Bathroom facilities may be saltwater deck hoses or freshwater showers on some boats. The preset itineraries allow you to visit most of the central islands and provide enough time to see the wildlife.

There are some common pitfalls with Galápagos boat tours. It's sometimes the case that the cheaper the trip, the more likely you are to experience problems. That's not to say that costlier boasts are glitch-free, but the companies are often more attentive and quick to respond to complaints.

Occasionally, things go wrong, and when they do, a refund is difficult to obtain. Recurring complaints include last-minute changes of boat (which the contractual small print allows), poor crew, a lack of bottled drinks, changes to the agreed itinerary, mechanical breakdowns, poor-quality snorkeling gear, bad smells, bug infestations and overbooking. Passengers have to share cabins and are not guaranteed that their cabin mates will be of the same gender; if you are uncomfortable sharing a cabin with a stranger of the opposite sex, make sure you are guaranteed in writing that you won't have to do this. Generally speaking, the cheaper the tour, the less comfortable the boat and the less knowledgeable the guide.

Arranging Tours in Advance

Most travelers arrange tours in Quito or Guayaquil. Check various agencies to compare prices and get a departure date that works for you. Sometimes you can get on a great boat for a budget price, particularly when business is slow – agencies will drop their prices at the last minute rather than leave berths empty.

Recommended operators include Trips & Dreams (p706), an excellent Guayaquil-based outfit that often has good last-minute deals, along with the following:

Columbus Travel CRUISE
(☎02-222-6612, in the US 877-436-7512; www.columbusecuador.com) Excellent customer service; can book a range of boats depending on budget and dates of travel.

Ecoventura CRUISE
(☎02-283-9390, in the US 800-633-7972; www.ecoventura.com) One of the pioneers in conservation and sustainable tourism. All of its four boats, including its diving live-aboards, are highly recommended.

Ecuador Adventure ADVENTURE TOUR
(☎02-604-6800, in the US 800-217-9414; www.ecuadoradventure.ec) Specializes in hotel-based and multisport tours including hiking, mountain biking and kayaking.

Happy Gringo Travel CRUISE
(☎02-512-3486; www.happygringo.com) Excellent agency that books a wide range of boats, plus offers last-minute deals.

Sangay Touring CRUISE
(☎02-222-1336; www.sangay.com) An experienced outfit that books over 60 boats.

Getting There & Away

Flights from the mainland arrive at two airports: Isla Baltra, just north of Santa Cruz, and Isla San Cristóbal. The airlines flying to the Galápagos Islands are **TAME** (www.tame.com.ec), **Avianca** (www.avianca.com) and **LAN** (www.lan.com). All except Avianca operate morning flights daily from Quito via Guayaquil to the Isla Baltra airport (just over an hour away from Puerto Ayora by public transportation), as well as several flights weekly to San Cristóbal airport. All return flights are in the early afternoon of the same day. Unlike the other airlines, Avianca offers direct flights from Quito to Baltra (as well as indirect flights via Guayaquil). Its San Cristóbal flights, however, all go via Guayaquil.

Round-trip flights start at $360 from Guayaquil and $440 from Quito. The latter generally takes 3½ hours, due to the layover in Guayaquil (Avianca being the exception, with two-hour direct flights). It's also possible to fly from Quito and return to Guayaquil or vice versa; it's often more convenient to fly into Baltra and out of San Cristóbal or vice versa. A transit control fee of $10 must be paid at the Instituto Nacional Galápagos (Ingala) office next to the ticket counter at either Quito or Guayaquil airport; the charge may be included in some prearranged boat tours.

Flights to the Galápagos are sometimes booked solid, so make sure you arrange your trip well in advance.

Getting Around

Most people get around the islands by organized boat tour, but it's easy to visit some of the islands independently. Santa Cruz, San Cristóbal, Isabela and Floreana all have accommodations and are reachable by affordable inter-island boat rides or more expensive flights. Keep in mind, however, that you'll only scratch the surface of the archipelago's natural wonders if traveling independently.

AIR

The small airlines **Emetebe** (☎05-252-4978; Av Darwin near Tomás de Berlanga) and **Air Zab** (☎05-252-7261; Indefatigable near Av Charles Darwin) fly small passenger aircrafts between Baltra and Puerto Villamil (Isla Isabela), Baltra and Puerto Baquerizo Moreno (Isla San Cristóbal), and Puerto Baquerizo Moreno and Puerto Villamil. Fares start at around $150 one way, and you'll pay extra if you're over the 11kg baggage limit per person.

BOAT

Private speedboats known as *lanchas* or fibras (short for 'fiberglass boats') offer daily passenger ferry services between Santa Cruz and San Cristóbal; Santa Cruz and Isabela; and Santa Cruz and Floreana (there are no direct trips between San Cristóbal and Isabela). Fares are $30 on any passage and are purchased either on the day before or the day of departure. Ask around in Puerto Ayora, Puerto Baquerizo Moreno and Puerto Villamil.

Isla Santa Cruz

Most visitors don't spend much time exploring Isla Santa Cruz (Indefatigable) outside of Puerto Ayora. Yet despite being the archipelago's most populous island, Santa Cruz is a destination in and of itself, with easily accessible beaches and remote highlands that offer adventurous activities far from the tourist trail.

Puerto Ayora

Clean, prosperous Puerto Ayora is the Galápagos' main population center and the heart of the tourist industry. It's a friendly place to linger for a few days and the best place in the islands to set up a cruise.

Sights

Aside from Tortuga Bay, the following sites are popular with visiting groups, but you can easily go on your own. Arrive early in the day to beat the crowds.

Charles Darwin Research Station WILDLIFE RESERVE

(05-252-6146; www.darwinfoundation.org; 6am-6pm) Just northeast of town is this iconic national park site, where more than 200 scientists and volunteers are involved with research and conservation efforts, the most well known of which involves a captive breeding program for giant tortoises. Paths leading through arid-zone vegetation take you past tortoise enclosures, where you can get a good look at these Galápagos giants. There's also a **baby-tortoise house** with incubators (when the tortoises weigh about 1.5kg or are about four years old, they're repatriated to their home islands).

Tortuga Bay & Around BEACH

In terms of sheer white-sand beauty, this beach is the rival of any in South America. You'll find it at the end of a 2.5km paved trail southwest of Puerto Ayora. In addition to swimming (a spit of land provides protection from the strong and dangerous currents on the exposed side), surfing or just sunbathing, you can see sharks, marine iguanas, pelicans and the occasional flamingo. There's no drinking water or other facilities. It's about a half-hour walk from the start of the path – often used by local runners – where you must sign in between 6am and 6pm.

If you walk the length of Tortuga Bay, on the backside you'll reach Playa Mansa, a picturesque lagoon lined with mangroves. Here you can spot marine iguanas, brown pelicans and blue herons, among other species. On the nearby dunes, sea turtles lay their eggs. The placid, shallow water is a great swimming spot for kids. Kayaks are available for hire.

At the foot of the hill before the start of the path to Tortuga Bay is the Centro Comunitaria de Educación Ambiental Miguel Cifuente Arias, where you can learn about conservation efforts and issues in the waters around the archipelago. To get here you have to take the road out of Puerto Ayora about 500m, before reaching the paved path that begins at the top of a hill and runs the rest of the way to Tortuga Bay. Right before this paved path on the hill is the center. Nearby stands a new museum on Galápagos ecology.

Las Grietas LAKE

For nice swimming and snorkeling, head to this water-filled crevice in the rocks. Talented and fearless locals climb the nearly vertical walls to plunge into the water below. Take a water taxi (per person $0.60 from 6am to 7pm) to the dock for the Angermeyer Point restaurant, then walk past the Finch Bay Hotel, then past an interesting salt mine, and finally up and around a lava-rock-strewn path to the water. It's about a 700m walk from the dock.

Laguna de las Ninfas LAGOON

FREE This peaceful lagoon has a short boardwalk path, where you can stop to take in the mangroves while looking for sting rays, baby sharks, sea turtles and other creatures sometimes spotted here.

Rancho Primicias WILDLIFE RESERVE

(admission $3; 8am-5pm) Next to El Chato is this private ranch, owned by the Devine family. There are dozens of giant tortoises, and you can wander around at will. The entrance is beyond Santa Rosa, off the main road – ask locals for directions. Remember to close any gates that you go through. There is a cafe selling cold drinks and hot tea, which is welcome if the highland mist has soaked you.

Lava Tunnels UNDERGROUND TUNNELS

(admission $3; 8am-5pm) These impressive underground tunnels southeast of the village of Santa Rosa are more than 1km in length and were formed when the outside skin of a molten-lava flow solidified. When the lava flow ceased, the molten lava inside the flow kept going, emptying out of the solidified skin and thus leaving tunnels. Because they are on private property, the tunnels can be visited without an official guide. The tunnels have electrical lighting (you can also hire flashlights/torches). Tours to the lava tunnels are offered in Puerto Ayora.

Activities

The best dive center in town is **Scuba Iguana** (☎05-252-6497; www.scubaiguana.com; Av Darwin), near the cemetery. The standard rate for two boat dives is about $180. Full PADI-certification courses are available.

Tours

You can arrange a wide range of day trips to snorkeling sites as well as wildlife-watching in the interior.

Albatros Tours TOUR
(☎05-252-6948; albatrostours@gpsinter.net; Av Charles Darwin) Santa Cruz day tours, snorkel-gear rental and dive trips.

Joybe Tours TOUR
(☎05-252-4385; Av Baltra near Av Opuntia) Last-minute overnight boat deals and day tours.

Moonrise Travel TOUR
(☎05-252-6402; www.galapagosmoonrise.com; Av Darwin) Run by a family of Galápagos experts and guides, who can arrange camping at their private highlands ranch, plus boat- and hotel-based tours and diving trips.

Sleeping

Most hotels are within a few blocks of Av Charles Darwin (the meandering main road closest to the waterfront).

Hostal Los Amigos HOSTEL $
(☎05-252-6265; hostal.losamigos@gmail.com; Av Charles Darwin; s/d/q without bathroom $15/30/60; 📶) Possibly the best-value cheapie in town. The lack of private bathrooms (aside from one room for four) is excused by the absolutely central location and gleaming wood-floored, though admittedly small, rooms. A kitchen and a lounge with TV is available for guests.

Galapagos Native GUESTHOUSE $$
(☎05-252-4730; www.galapagosnative.com.ec; Tomas de Berlanga near Av 12 de Febrero; s/d from $25/30) This new place offers decent value for its clean rooms with white adobe-like walls. Three rooms (the best) are bright and airy with balconies.

Hotel Gardner HOTEL $$
(☎05-252-6979; Tomás de Berlanga; s/d from $20/35; ❄📶) The budget-minded Gardner has simple rooms and a covered rooftop patio with lounge chairs and hammocks.

Hotel Sir Francis Drake HOTEL $$
(☎05-252-6221; www.sirfrancisdrakegalapagos.com; Av Baltra; s/d from $25/30; ❄📶) Hidden behind a small department store, the Sir Francis Drake is one of the better values in town. Ask for one of the ground-floor rooms all the way in the back – these have large windows that let in lots of natural light. Common space is limited to an inner patio with no seating and a single balcony. It's located just a short walk from the pier.

Eating

A handful of popular kiosks whip up *encocado* (seafood stew with coconut milk), lobster and grilled meat along Charles Binford, just east of Av Padre Julio Herrera. There's a festive atmosphere at the outdoor tables on the street.

El Atardecer del Nene SEAFOOD $$
(Av Darwin; mains $7-9; ⏲5-8pm Mon-Sat) Next to the fish market. The handful of plastic tables in the open air draws a mostly local crowd, who come for incredibly fresh fish and lobster (seasonally). It's a festive spot, with salsa tunes and cool sea breezes.

Galápagos Deli DELI, PIZZERIA $$
(Tomás de Berlanga; mains $5-9; ⏲7am-10pm Tue-Sun; 📶) Tired of standard *almuerzos* (set lunches)? Head to this sleek and modern place for brick-oven pizza (small $5) and high-quality deli sandwiches, as well as fish and chips, espresso and delicious gelato. Because it's on a block with few pedestrians, it feels like a secret.

Casa del Lago Café Cultural CAFE $$
(cnr Moisés Brito & Montalvo; mains $7-9; ⏲7am-7pm Mon-Sat; 📶✎) This boho cafe with a few indoor and outdoor patio tables serves excellent breakfasts, sandwiches, empanadas and salads, as well as homemade cakes, fruit drinks and brewed coffee.

Information

Banco del Pacífico (Av Darwin near Los Colonos; ⏲8am-3:30pm Mon-Fri, 9:30am-12:30pm Sat) Has an ATM and changes traveler's checks. There are two other ATMs near the pier and in front of Proinsular Supermarket.

Cámara de Turismo (Tourist Information Office; Av Darwin near Av 12 de Febrero; ⏲8am-12:30pm & 2:30-6pm) Has hotel information and maps; some staff speak English. Report any complaints here about boats, tours, guides or crew.

Getting There & Away

Reconfirming your flight departures with Avianca, **LAN** (05-269-2850; Av Charles Darwin; 8am-6pm Mon-Sat, 10am-1pm Sun) or **TAME** (05-252-6527; cnr Av Charles Darwin & Av 12 de Febrero; 8am-noon & 2-5pm Mon-Fri, 8am-1pm Sat) offices is recommended.

If you are traveling independently, take the public bus signed 'Muelle' from the airport on Isla Baltra to the dock (a free 10-minute ride) for the ferry to Isla Santa Cruz. A 10-minute ferry ride ($1) will take you across to Santa Cruz, where you will be met by a Citteg bus to take you to the Puerto Ayora bus station, about one hour away ($2). The bus station is a further 2km from the dock (and town center); a taxi costs $1. Taxis from town to the dock at the end of Santa Cruz (where you catch onward transportation to the airport via ferry and airport bus) cost $18.

Arriving air passengers on prebooked tours will be met by a boat representative for the bus-boat-bus journey to Puerto Ayora.

Private speedboats head twice daily to both Isabela and San Cristóbal at 7am and 2pm ($30, two hours). There's also one boat daily to Floreana at 8am ($30, two hours). Buy tickets from travel agencies or the small kiosk near the water-taxi pier.

Around Puerto Ayora

You can arrange day trips with tour operators in Puerto Ayora.

A footpath north from Bellavista leads toward the highlands, including **Cerro Crocker** and other hills and extinct volcanoes. This is a good chance to see local vegetation and birds. It is about 6km from Bellavista to the crescent-shaped hill of Media Luna and another 3km to the base of Cerro Crocker. This is a national park, so a guide is required.

The twin craters called **Los Gemelos** are 5km beyond Santa Rosa. They are sinkholes, rather than volcanic craters, and are surrounded by Scalesia forest. Vermilion flycatchers are often seen and short-eared owls are spotted on occasion. Although less than 100m from the road, the craters are hidden by vegetation, so ask your driver to stop at the trailhead.

Near Santa Rosa, **El Chato Tortoise Reserve** (admission $3; 8am-5pm) protects giant tortoises roaming in the wild. You can also visit this area by horseback.

Isla San Cristóbal

Locals call San Cristóbal the capital of paradise, and since Puerto Baquerizo Moreno is the capital of Galápagos province, it technically is. The island has several easily accessible visitor sites, incredible surf and the lovely, laid-back capital itself.

Puerto Baquerizo Moreno

Often just called Cristóbal, Puerto Baquerizo Moreno is a relaxed little town, busy with tourists during the high season and sleepy the rest of the year. It's possible to arrange tours here, though it's a great spot just to unwind. Three world-class surf breaks are nearby.

The intriguing exhibits at the modern **Interpretation Center** (05-252-0358; 8am-5pm) FREE on the north side of the bay explain the history and significance of the Galápagos better than anywhere else in the islands. There are also some great walks here to tranquil beaches where you can see plenty of marine iguanas.

Air passengers arriving in Puerto Baquerizo Moreno can walk into town in about 10 minutes.

Sights & Activities

La Lobería BEACH

Southwest of town, a road leads 2.5km (about a 30-minute walk) to La Lobería, a rocky beach with a lazy sea-lion colony. It's good for year-round surfing, and there are lots of iguanas along the trail leading past the beach. Bring water and sun protection. Taxis charge about $3 to take you out here and you can walk back. Once there, a cliff-side path takes you past marine iguanas, lava lizards and soaring frigate birds. To get here on foot, take Av Alsacio Northia toward the airport, turn left after the stadium (look for the murals) and then take the first right.

Sharksky Tours SNORKELING, DIVING

(05-252-1188; www.sharksky.com; Av Darwin) This company has snorkeling day trips ($80), overnight hotel-based tours, kayaking tours, and scuba diving (two boat dives $160).

Sleeping & Eating

Inexpensive restaurants abound and *almuerzos* are good value. Be sure to have a *batido* (fruit shake) at **Cabaña Mi Grande** (Villamil; mains around $3; 6am-3pm & 6-10pm).

★Casa de Laura Hostal HOSTEL $
(☎05-252-0173; hostalcasadelaura@hotmail.com; Av de la Armada; r per person $20; ❄@📶) This friendly, family-owned hideaway is one of the best-value places in town. Located in a two-story adobe building with modern hot-water rooms, there's a nicely landscaped courtyard, and hammocks in the tiny cacti garden in front. It's just off the western end of Av Charles Darwin.

Hostal San Francisco GUESTHOUSE $
(☎05-252-0304; Av Darwin; s/d $15/30; 📶) The best of several cheapies on the waterfront, Hostal San Francisco has simple but clean rooms with hot-water bathrooms and friendly owners who also run the shop below.

Casa Blanca HOTEL $$
(☎05-252-0392; www.casablancagalapagos.com; Av Darwin; s/d incl breakfast from $50/70; ❄📶) There's no better place to base yourself in town: not only does this whitewashed adobe building have charmingly decorated rooms and tile floors, but it sits on the *malecón* directly across from the passenger pier, meaning rooms with sea-facing balconies have great views. There's even a top-floor cupola suite, with its own private balcony.

Around Puerto Baquerizo Moreno

Apart from Isla Lobos, you can visit the following sites without a guide. About 1.7km northeast of Puerto Baquerizo Moreno, **Cerro de las Tijeretas** (Frigate-Bird Hill) provides good views and can be reached on a trail. You'll pass a national park information office en route, and there's excellent snorkeling on the ocean side.

For about $20 round trip, taxis in Puerto Baquerizo Moreno will go to the farming center of **El Progreso**, about 8km east at the base of the Cerro San Joaquín (896m), the highest point on San Cristóbal. From El Progreso, you can catch one of the occasional buses (or hire a jeep or walk the 10km) to **El Junco Lagoon**, a freshwater lake about 700m above sea level with superb views. The road continues beyond the lagoon and branches to the isolated beach of **Puerto Chino**, where you can camp with permission from the Galápagos **national park office** (☎252-0138; www.galapagospark.org) in Puerto Baquerizo Moreno. The other branch goes to **La Galapaguera**, where giant tortoises can be seen.

About an hour north of Puerto Baquerizo Moreno by boat is tiny, rocky **Isla Lobos**, the main sea lion and blue-footed booby colony open to visitors (a guide is required) to Isla San Cristóbal. The island has a 300m trail and you can see lava lizards here.

Isla Isabela

Isabela is the largest island in the archipelago and boasts dramatic landscapes sprinkled with active volcanoes.

Puerto Villamil is the main town on seldom-visited Isla Isabela. Backed by a lagoon where flamingos and marine iguanas live and situated on a beautiful white-sand beach, it's a sleepy little village of sandy roads and small homes. All of the town's and island's fresh water is shipped by boat from Santa Cruz.

Behind and to the west of the village is the **Villamil Lagoon** (⏲trail 6am-6pm), which is known for its marine iguanas and migrant birds, especially waders – more than 20 species have been reported here. A 1km-long trail begins just past the Iguana Crossing Hotel as a wooden boardwalk over the lagoon passing through mangroves and dense vegetation, eventually ending in the **Centro de Crianza de Tortugas** (Giant Tortoise Breeding Center). Volunteers here can explain the work being done to help restore the population of this species on Isabela.

About 4km west of town is the **Muro de las Lágrimas** (Wall of Tears), a 100m-long wall of lava rocks built by convicts under harsh and abusive conditions. The penal colony closed in 1959 but the wall stands as a monument to an infamous chapter in the island's history. Accommodations on the island run a wide range of tours on and around the island.

With its beachfront bar, hammocks, bonfires, live music and sea-facing deck, **Caleta Iguana Hotel & Surf Camp** (☎05-252-9405; www.iguanacove.com; Av Antonio Gil; dm $23, d with/without bathroom from $90/68, r with view $124-140) is the place to go for a lively, laid-back social scene. It's on the beach at the western edge of town. A good-value budget guesthouse is **La Brisa del Mar** (☎05-301-6800; r per person with fan/air-con $15/20), located a few blocks from the Central Plaza (you'll pass it on the way in from the dock).

There are a half-dozen restaurants located on the central square on Av Antonio Gill, between Las Fragatas and 16 de Marzo.

Floreana

Also known as Isla Santa María, this island has fewer than 100 inhabitants, most spread near **Puerto Velasco Ibarra**, the island's only settlement. There you will find **Hostal Wittmer** (☎05-253-5033; erikagarciawittmer@hotmail.com; s/d from $30/60), which has beachfront rooms with private balconies. It's run by the family of late Margaret Wittmer, who is famous for being one of the islands' first settlers. Other simple but pleasant options are **Casa de Huespedes Hildita** (☎05-253-5079; s/d $20/40) and **Hostal Santa Maria** (☎05-253-5022; malourdes.soria@hotmail.com; s/d incl breakfast $35/70; 📶). Hands down the best place for a meal on Floreana is **Conchalagua** (mains $8-12; ⏰Tue-Sun), run by the charming Señora Cruz who has loads of great stories about growing up on the island.

Note that many operators in Santa Cruz offer day trips to Floreana. Don't do it! You'll spend over four hours of your day on a bumpy boat ride and miss out on the best part of the experience, which is soaking up the beauty of this enchanting island at your leisure. There are plenty of guesthouses, so there's no reason not to stay.

UNDERSTAND ECUADOR

Ecuador Today

Until recently, Ecuador was an economic basket case, a prototypical 'banana republic,' plagued by widespread poverty, economic inequality and political turmoil – with more than 80 changes of government since the republic's founding in 1830. But over the last decade, Ecuador has seen momentous development, with huge investments in education, healthcare and infrastructure. For many Ecuadorians, it's one of the most hopeful and empowering times in the nation's history.

Much of the credit for this dramatic turn of events is given to Rafael Correa, Ecuador's popular young president. The 'Citizens' Revolution' is how President Correa describes the big changes that have swept across Ecuador, and despite the hyperbole, it's hard to deny the enormous gains many citizens have made during Correa's administration. Since he first took office in 2007, the poverty rate has fallen dramatically (from 45% in 2006 to 25% by 2014), as has unemployment (to below 5%), while wages have risen and inflation has been tamed. Annual growth in GDP has churned along at a steady 4%. Correa's administration has nearly doubled government spending on public investment (from 21% in 2006 to over 40% by 2014), pouring money into healthcare and education. The result: infant mortality rates are down, and with the building of new schools and universities, more students have access to schools than ever before.

Big infrastructure projects have sprung up across the nation, including new hydroelectric dams, brand-new highways and bridges, and Quito's new airport. Other projects are in the works, including a 23km metro system underway in the capital (at a cost of around $1.6 billion) and a new airport for Guayaquil. One of the country's most ambitious projects is the creation of Yachay, a sprawling university and research campus under construction in the northern province of Imbabura. Described as 'a city of knowledge' (*yachay* means 'knowledge' in Kichwa), this site is about the size of Atlantic City and is intended to be a major hub for science, technology and innovation – perhaps the next Silicon Valley if things pan out as planned.

Given all this, it's not surprising that Correa enjoys widespread popularity. With an approval rating fluctuating between 60% and 80%, he's one of the most popular leaders in Latin America, and probably the most popular president in the nation's history.

History

The land of fire and ice has certainly had a tumultuous history. Since becoming an independent nation in 1830, Ecuador has gone through countless changes in government and 20 constitutions – the most recent drafted in 2008. Fueling the Andean nation's volatility are rivalries both internal (conservative, church-backed Quito versus liberal, secular Guayaquil) and external (border disputes with Peru and Colombia).

Early Cultures

The oldest tools found in Ecuador date back to 9000 BC, meaning people were mucking about the region in the Stone Age. The most important early societies developed along the coast, which was a more habitable landscape than the frigid highlands. Ecuador's first permanent settled culture was the Valdivia, which emerged along the Santa Elena Peninsula nearly 6000 years ago.

By the 11th century AD, Ecuador had two dominant cultures: the expansionist Cara along the coast and the peaceful Quitu in the highlands. These cultures merged and became known as the Quitu-Caras, or the Shyris. They were the dominant force in the highlands until the 1300s, when the Puruhá of the central highlands became increasingly powerful. The third important group was the Cañari, further south. These were the cultures the Inca encountered when they began their expansion north from present-day Peru.

Land of the Four Quarters

Until the early 15th century, the Inca empire was concentrated around Cuzco, Peru. That changed dramatically during the rule of Inca Pachacutec, whose expansionist policies set into motion the creation of the vast Inca empire, Tahuantinsuyo, meaning 'Land of the Four Quarters' in Quichua (called Quechua elsewhere in South America). By the time the Inca reached Ecuador they were under the rule of Túpac Yupanqui, Pachacutec's successor, and they met with fierce resistance, both from the Cañari and the Quitu-Caras. In one battle the Inca massacred thousands of Caras and dumped them in a lake near Otavalo, which supposedly turned the waters red and gave the lake its name, Laguna Yaguarcocha (Lake of Blood).

The subjugation of the north took many years, during which the Inca Túpac fathered a son with a Cañari princess. The son, Huayna Capác, grew up in present-day Ecuador and succeeded his father to the Inca throne. Huayna Capác had two sons: Atahualpa, who grew up in Quito, and Huáscar, who was raised in Cuzco.

When Huayna Capác died in 1527, he left his empire not to one son, as was traditional, but to two. Rivalry developed between the sons, which eventually boiled into civil war. After several years of fighting, Atahualpa defeated Huáscar near Ambato in central Ecuador. Atahualpa was thus ruling a weakened and still divided Inca empire when Francisco Pizarro landed in Peru in 1532.

The Spanish Power Play

Pizarro's advance was rapid and dramatic. He successfully exploited divisions within the Inca empire and enlisted many non-Inca ethnic groups that had been recently and reluctantly subjugated by the Inca. Most importantly, Inca warriors on foot were no match for the fully armored conquistadors on horseback who slaughtered them by the thousands. Within three years, and after betraying Inca rulers on several occasions, the Spanish controlled the former Inca empire.

Settling In

From 1535 onward, the colonial era proceeded with no major uprisings by indigenous Ecuadorians. Francisco Pizarro made his brother Gonzalo the governor of Quito in 1540. Hoping to find more gold, Gonzalo sent his lieutenant, Francisco de Orellana, to explore the Amazon. The lieutenant and his force ended up floating all the way to the Atlantic, becoming the first party to descend the Amazon and cross the continent. This feat took almost a year and is still commemorated in Ecuador.

During the first centuries of colonial rule, Lima (Peru) was the seat of Ecuador's political administration. Ecuador, originally a *gobernación* (province), became known as the Audiencia de Quito in 1563, a more important political division. In 1739 the Audiencia de Quito was transferred from the viceroyalty of Peru, of which it was a part, to the viceroyalty of Colombia (then known as Nueva Grenada).

Ecuador remained a peaceful colony during these centuries, and agriculture and the arts flourished. Churches and monasteries were constructed atop every sacred indigenous site and were decorated with unique carvings and paintings, the result of a blend of Spanish and indigenous artistic influences. This so-called Escuela Quiteña (Quito school of art), still admired by visitors today, has left an indelible stamp on both the colonial buildings of the time and Ecuador's unique art history.

Life was comfortable for the ruling colonialists, but the indigenous people – and later, the *mestizos* (people of mixed Spanish and indigenous descent) – were treated abysmally under their rule. A system of forced labor was not only tolerated but encouraged, and by the 18th century there were several indigenous uprisings against the Spanish ruling classes. Social unrest, as well as the introduction of cocoa and sugar plantations in the northwest, prompted landowners to import African slave laborers. Much of the rich Afro-Ecuadorian culture found in Esmeraldas province today is a legacy of this period.

Adiós, España

The first serious attempt at independence from Spain was made on August 10, 1809, by a partisan group led by Juan Pío Montúfar. The group took Quito and installed a government, but royalist troops regained control in only 24 days.

A decade later, Simón Bolívar, the Venezuelan liberator, freed Colombia in his march southward from Caracas. Bolívar then supported the people of Guayaquil when they claimed independence on October 9, 1820. It took another two years for Ecuador to be entirely liberated from Spanish rule. The decisive battle was fought on May 24, 1822, when Mariscal (Field Marshall) Sucre, one of Bolívar's best generals, defeated the royalists at Pichincha and took Quito.

Bolívar's idealistic dream was to form a united South America. He began by amalgamating Venezuela, Colombia and Ecuador into the independent state of Gran Colombia. This lasted only eight years, with Ecuador becoming fully independent in 1830. That same year a treaty was signed with Peru, establishing a boundary between the two nations.

Liberals Versus Conservatives

Following independence from Spain, Ecuador's history unfolded with the typically Latin American political warfare between liberals and conservatives. Quito emerged as the main center for the church-backed conservatives, while Guayaquil has traditionally been considered liberal and socialist. The rivalry between these groups has frequently escalated to extreme violence: conservative President García Moreno was shot and killed in 1875, and liberal President Eloy Alfaro was killed and burned by a mob in Quito in 1912. The rivalry between the two cities continues on a social level today. Over time, the military began assuming control, and the 20th century saw more periods of military than civilian rule.

War with Peru

In 1941 war broke out with Peru over border disputes. The boundary was finally redrawn by a conference of foreign-government ministers in the 1942 Protocol of Rio de Janeiro. Ecuador never recognized this border, and minor skirmishes with Peru have occurred because of it – the most serious was the short war in early 1995, when several dozen soldiers on both sides were killed. Finally, after more fighting in 1998, Peru and Ecuador negotiated a settlement in which Peru retained a majority of the land in question.

Recent Political Developments

Ecuador's most recent period of democracy began in 1979, when President Jaime Roldos Aguilera was elected. Over the next two decades, control flip-flopped democratically between liberals and conservatives.

In the 1998 elections, Jamil Mahuad, former mayor of Quito, emerged victorious and was immediately put to the test. The devastating effects of El Niño and the sagging oil market of 1997–98 sent the economy into a tailspin in 1999. The sucre, Ecuador's former currency, depreciated from about 7000 per US dollar to about 25,000 by January 2000.

When Mahuad declared his plan to dump the national currency in exchange for the US dollar, the country erupted in protest. On January 21, 2000, marches shut down the capital and protesters took over the Ecuadorian congress building, forcing Mahuad to resign. The protesters were led by Antonio Vargas, Coronel Lucio Gutiérrez and former supreme court president Carlos Solórzano, who immediately turned the presidency over to former vice president, Gustavo Noboa. Noboa went ahead with 'dollarization,' and in September 2000, the US dollar became Ecuador's official currency.

Presidential Comings & Goings

President Noboa was succeeded in 2002 by former coup leader Lucio Gutiérrez, whose populist agenda led to his election. But shortly after taking office, Gutiérrez began backing down on his promises of radical reform and implemented IMF-encouraged austerity measures to finance the country's massive debt. In 2004 he also tossed out most of the supreme court, which allowed him to expel his rivals from the court and change the constitution in order to drop corruption charges against his former ally, the popularly despised ex-president, Antonio Bucaram.

As a consequence, protests erupted in the capital, and in April 2005 the congress finally voted Gutiérrez out, replacing him with vice president Alfredo Palacios. Ousted and exiled, Gutiérrez made a surprise return to Ecuador in 2005, claiming he was the country's rightful leader. He was immediately jailed, but upon his release began campaigning for the presidency once again. However, his political days were over, and in 2006 Rafael Correa, a US-educated economist and former finance minister (under Palacios) was elected president.

Culture

Population

Ecuador has the highest population density of any South American country – about 53 people per sq km. Despite this, the country still feels incredibly wild, mainly because over 30% of the population is crammed into the cities of Quito and Guayaquil, and another 30% resides in Ecuador's other urban areas. Nearly half of the country's people live on the coast (including the Galápagos), while about 45% live in the highlands. The remainder live in the Oriente, where colonization is slowly increasing.

About 65% of the Ecuadorian people are *mestizos,* 25% are indigenous, 7% are Spanish and 3% are black. Other ethnicities account for less than 1%. The majority of the indigenous people speak Quichua and live in the highlands. A few small groups live in the lowlands.

Lifestyle

How an Ecuadorian lives is a matter of geography, ethnicity and class. A poor *campesino* (peasant) family that cultivates the thin volcanic soil of a steep highland plot lives very differently from a coastal fishing family residing in the mangroves of Esmeraldas province, or a family staying in the slums of Guayaquil. An indigenous Saraguro family that tends communally owned cattle in the southern highlands has a dramatically different life to that of an upper-class *quiteño* family, which might have several maids, all the latest electronic gadgets and an expensive car in the garage.

An estimated 40% of Ecuadorians live below the poverty line, and paying for cooking fuel and putting food in the belly is a constant concern for most people. But, as most first-time visitors are astounded to experience, even the poorest Ecuadorians exude an openness, generosity and happiness all too rare in developed countries. Fiestas are celebrated with fervor by everyone, and you'll sometimes roll around in bed, kept awake until dawn by the noise of a nearby birthday bash.

Religion

The predominant religion (over 80% of the population) is Roman Catholicism, with a small minority of other churches. Indigenous people tend to blend Catholicism with their own traditional beliefs.

Arts

Music

Música folklórica (traditional Andean music) has a distinctive, haunting sound that has been popularized in Western culture by songs such as Paul Simon's version of 'El cóndor pasa' ('If I Could'). Its otherworldly quality results from the use of a pentatonic (five-note) scale and pre-Colombian wind and percussion instruments that conjure the windswept quality of *páramo* life. It is best heard at a *peña* (folk-music club or performance).

Northwest Ecuador, particularly Esmeraldas province, is famous for its marimba music, historically the sound of the Afro-Ecuadorian population. Today, it's becoming increasingly difficult to hear live because many Afro-Ecuadorians have swapped it for salsa and other musical forms.

If there's one music you won't escape, it's *cumbia*, whose rhythm resembles that of a trotting three-legged horse. Originally from Colombia, Ecuadorian *cumbia* has a more raw (almost amateur), melancholic sound and is dominated by the electronic keyboard. Bus drivers love the stuff, perhaps because it so strangely complements those back-road journeys through the Andes.

Although most people associate Ecuador with *folklórica,* the country's most popular national music is the *pasillo,* which is rooted in the waltz. The origins of *pasillo* date back to the 19th century when Ecuador was part of Gran Colombia. These poignant songs with their melancholic melodies often touch on themes of disillusionment, lost love and unquenchable longing for the past. *Pasillo*'s most famous voice was that of Julio Jaramillo (1935–78), who popularized the genre throughout Latin America.

When it comes to youth culture, Caribbean-born reggaeton (a blend of Puerto Rican *bomba,* dance hall and hip-hop) is the anthem among urban club-goers. Ecuador also has its share of Latin pop artists, with singers such as teen-idol Fausto Miño filling the airwaves.

Architecture

Many of Quito's churches were built during the colonial period, and the architects were influenced by the Escuela Quiteña (Quito school of art). In addition, churches often show Moorish influences, particularly in the decorative details of interiors. Known as *mudéjar,* this reflects an architectural style that developed in Spain beginning in the 12th century. The overall architecture of colonial churches is overpoweringly ornamental and almost cloyingly rich – in short, baroque.

Many colonial houses have two storys, with the upper floors bearing ornate balconies. The walls are whitewashed and the roofs are red tile. Quito's Old Town and Cuenca are Unesco World Heritage sites and both abound with beautifully preserved colonial architecture.

Visual Arts

The colonial religious art found in many churches and museums – especially in Quito – was produced by indigenous artists trained by the Spanish conquistadors. The artists portrayed Spanish religious concepts, yet infused their own indigenous beliefs, giving birth to a unique religious art known as the Escuela Quiteña. The Quito school died out with independence.

The 19th century is referred to as the Republican period, and its art is characterized by formalism. Favorite subjects included heroes of the revolution, important members of the new republic's high society and florid landscapes.

The 20th century saw the rise of the indigenist school, whose unifying theme is the oppression of Ecuador's indigenous inhabitants. Important *indigenista* artists include Camilo Egas (1889–1962), Oswaldo Guayasamín (1919–99), Eduardo Kingman (1913–97) and Gonzalo Endara Crow (1936–96). You can (and should!) see the works of these artists in Quito's galleries and museums. The former home of Guayasamín, also in Quito, houses a stunning showcase of his work.

Cuisine

Food

Lunch is the main meal of the day for many Ecuadorians. A cheap restaurant will serve a decent *almuerzo* (lunch of the day) for as little as $2.50. An *almuerzo* consists of a *sopa* (soup) and a *segundo* (second dish), which is usually a stew with plenty of rice. Sometimes the *segundo* is *pescado* (fish), *lentejas* (lentils) or *menestras* (generally, bean stew). Some places serve salad, juice and *postre* (dessert), as well as the two main courses.

The *merienda* (evening meal) is a set meal, usually similar to lunch. If you don't want the *almuerzo* or *merienda,* you can choose from the menu, but this is always more expensive.

Parrillas (or *parrilladas*) are grillhouses. Steaks, pork chops, chicken breasts, blood sausage, liver and tripe are all served (together or individually, depending on the establishment).

Chifas (Chinese restaurants) are generally inexpensive. Among other standards, they serve *chaulafan* (rice dishes) and *tallarines* (noodle dishes). Vegetarians will find that *chifas* are reliable spots for a meatless dish.

Seafood can be delicious, particularly in Esmeraldas and Manabí provinces. The most common types of fish are *corvina* (technically white sea bass, but usually just a white fish) and *trucha* (trout). Popular throughout Ecuador, *ceviche* is uncooked seafood marinated in lemon and served with popcorn and sliced onions. *Ceviche* comes as *pescado* (fish), *camarones* (shrimp), *concha* (shellfish) or *mixto* (mixed). Unfortunately, improperly prepared *ceviche* is a source of cholera, so avoid it if in any doubt.

It's impossible to consider food from the highlands without discussing the once highly revered crop, *maìz* (corn). In its numerous varieties, corn has been the staple of the Andean diet for a millennium, and today it forms the basis of countless highland specialties. Kernels are toasted into *tostada* (toasted corn), popped into *cangil* (popcorn), boiled and treated to make *mote* (hominy) and milled into cornmeal.

Potatoes, of course, originated in the Andes, and are another essential food.

Drink

Purify all tap water or buy bottled water. Some pharmacies, cafes and a growing number of guesthouses allow travelers to refill their water bottles from their purified source – a good option for those concerned about all the empty bottles that end up in landfills. *Agua con gas* is carbonated; *agua sin gas* is not carbonated.

Bottled drinks are cheap and all the usual soft drinks are available. Ask for your drink *helada* if you want it out of the refrigerator, *al clima* if you don't. Remember to say *sin hielo* (without ice) unless you really trust the water supply.

Jugos (juices) are available everywhere. Make sure you get *jugo puro* (pure) and not *con agua* (with water). The most common kinds are *mora* (blackberry), *tomate de árbol* (a strangely addictive local fruit), *naranja* (orange), *toronja* (grapefruit), *maracuyá* (passion fruit), *piña* (pineapple), *sandía* (watermelon), *naranjilla* (a local fruit that tastes like bitter orange) and papaya.

Coffee is widely available but often disappointing. Instant coffee, served *en leche* (with milk) or *en agua* (with water), is the most common. Espresso is found in better restaurants.

Té (tea) is served black with lemon and sugar. *Té de hierbas* (herb tea) and hot chocolate are also popular.

For alcoholic drinks, local *cervezas* (beers) are palatable and inexpensive. Pilsener is available in 650mL bottles, while Club comes in 330mL bottles. Imports are tough to find.

Ron (rum) is cheap and can be decent. The local firewater, *aguardiente,* is sugarcane alcohol, and is an acquired taste. A favorite Quito drink is *canelazo,* which is similar to a hot spiced rum. It's made with *aguardiente,* cinnamon and citrus juice, and is the perfect antidote to chilly highland nights.

Environment

Land

Despite its diminutive size, Ecuador has some of the world's most varied geography. The country can be divided into three regions: the Andes form the backbone of Ecuador; the coastal lowlands lie west of the mountains; and the Oriente, to the east, comprises the jungles of the upper Amazon Basin. In only 200km as the condor flies, you can climb from the coast to snowcaps, over 6km above sea level, and then descend to the jungle on the country's eastern side. The Galápagos Islands lie on the equator, 1000km west of Ecuador's coast, and constitute one of the country's 21 provinces.

Wildlife

Ecuador is one of the most species-rich countries on the globe, deemed a 'megadiversity hot spot' by ecologists. The country has more than 20,000 plant species, with new ones discovered every year. In comparison, there are only 17,000 plant species on the entire North American continent. The tropics, in general, harbor many more species than temperate regions do, but another reason for Ecuador's biodiversity is simply that the country holds a great number of habitat types. Obviously, the Andes will support very different species than the tropical rainforests, and when intermediate biomes and the coastal areas are included, the result is a wealth of different ecosystems, a riot of life that draws nature lovers from the world over.

Bird-watchers flock to Ecuador for the great number of bird species recorded here – some 1600, or about twice the number found in any one of the continents of North America, Europe or Australia. But Ecuador isn't just for the birds: some 300 mammal species have been recorded, from monkeys in the Amazon to the rare Andean spectacled bears in the highlands.

National Parks

Ecuador has over 30 government-protected parks and reserves (of which nine carry the title of 'national park'), as well as numerous privately administered nature reserves. Eighteen percent of the country lies within protected areas. Ecuador's first *parque na-*

cional (national park) was the Galápagos, formed in 1959. Scattered across mainland Ecuador are eight other national parks, including the most visited (from north to south):

Parque Nacional Cotopaxi (p667) The towering ice-capped cone of Volcán Cotopaxi makes for spectacular year-round hiking and mountaineering.

Parque Nacional Yasuní (p689) Amazon rainforest, big rivers and caiman-filled lagoons, plus monkeys, birds, sloths and more, mean year-round forest fun.

Parque Nacional Machalilla (p701) Coastal dry forest, beaches and islands are home to whales, seabirds, monkeys and reptiles. Hiking opportunities and beaches are superb.

Parque Nacional Sangay (p676) Volcanoes, *páramo* and cloud forest harbor spectacled bears, tapirs, pumas and ocelots, and offer hiking, climbing and wildlife-watching year-round.

Parque Nacional Cajas (p683) Shimmering lakes and moorlike *parámo* make this highland park an excellent adventure from Cuenca.

Parque Nacional Podocarpus (p685) From cloud forest to rainforest, this epic southern park is best explored from Loja, Zamora or Vilcabamba.

Many parks are inhabited by native peoples who were living in the area long before it achieved park status. In the case of the Oriente parks, indigenous hunting practices (which have a greater impact as outside interests diminish their original territories and resources) have met with concern from those seeking to protect the park. The issue of how to protect these areas from interests such as oil, timber and mining industries, while recognizing the rights of indigenous people, continues to be extremely tricky.

All national parks – apart from the Galápagos (which costs $110 to enter) – are free.

Environmental Issues

Ecuador has one of South America's highest deforestation rates. In the highlands, almost all of the natural forest cover has disappeared, and only a few pockets remain, mainly in privately administered nature reserves. Along the coast, once plentiful mangrove forests have all but vanished to make way for artificial shrimp ponds.

About 95% of the forests of the western slopes and lowlands have become agricultural land, mostly banana plantations. Although much of the rainforest in the Ecuadorian Amazon remains standing, it is being seriously threatened by fragmentation. Since the discovery of oil, roads have been laid, colonists have followed and the destruction of the forest has increased exponentially. The main drives behind the destruction are logging, cattle ranching, and oil and mineral extraction.

The rainforest's indigenous inhabitants – who depend on the rivers for drinking water and food – are also dramatically affected. Oil residues, oil treatment chemicals, erosion and fertilizers all contaminate the rivers, killing fish and rendering formerly potable water toxic. The documentary *Crude,* which premiered in 2009, provides a disturbing portrait of the heavy toll exacted on local inhabitants.

SURVIVAL GUIDE

Directory A–Z

ACCOMMODATIONS

There is no shortage of places to stay in Ecuador, but during major fiestas or the night before market day, accommodations can be tight, so plan ahead. Most hotels have single-room rates, although during high season some beach towns charge for the number of beds in the room, regardless of the number of people checking in. In popular resort areas, high-season prices (running from June to August and mid-December to January) are about 30% higher than the rest of the year.

Ecuador has a growing number of youth hostels, as well as inexpensive *pensiones* (short-term budget accommodations in a family home). Staying with families is an option in remote villages.

SLEEPING PRICE RANGES

The following price ranges refer to a double room in high season. Room prices include bathroom. Exceptions are noted in specific listings.

$ less than $30

$$ $30 to $80

$$$ more than $80

ACTIVITIES

Where to begin? There are so many exciting activities in Ecuador that any list will certainly miss something. For climbers, the volcanic, snow-capped peaks of Ecuador's central highlands – including Chimborazo (a doozy at 6310m) and Cotopaxi (5897m) – attract mountaineers from around the world. Quito, Riobamba, Baños and Latacunga are the best towns to hire guides and gear.

How about hiking? The moorlike landscape of Parque Nacional Cajas; the cloud forests of Parque Nacional Podocarpus or Mindo; the windswept *páramo* of Lagunas de Mojanda near Otavalo; the spectacular high-Andean Quilotoa Loop area; and the coastal dry forests of Parque Nacional Machalilla are just a few of Ecuador's hiking possibilities.

Ecuador is also one of the world's top bird-watching destinations, with over 1600 species on record. Mindo, the lower Río Napo region of the Amazon and the Galápagos are extraordinary places for bird-watching.

Tena in the Oriente is Ecuador's kayaking and river-rafting capital, where it's easy to set up day runs down the nearby Río Napo (class III) or Río Misahuallí (class IV+).

The surfing is excellent at Montañita and on Isla San Cristóbal in the Galápagos. Playas has some decent nearby breaks, but you'll have to make friends with the locals (try the Playas Club Surf) to find them. The Galápagos are also famous for scuba diving and snorkeling (think hammerhead sharks and giant manta rays).

Mountain biking is growing in popularity, with a handful of outfitters in Quito and Riobamba offering memorable trips over challenging terrain (like Volcán Chimborazo). You can also head off on your own on trips like the dramatic descent from Baños to Puyo. You can rent bikes for about $7 to $10 per day in places such as Baños, Vilcabamba and Riobamba, or go for the extreme downhill day trips offered by outfitters in those towns, as well as in Quito and Cuenca.

BOOKS

Lonely Planet's *Ecuador & the Galápagos Islands* has more detailed travel information on the country.

For a look at Ecuadorian lifestyles along the north coast, read *Living Poor,* by Moritz Thomsen. Joe Kane's *Savages* illustrates the oil industry's impacts on the Ecuadorian Amazon.

The Panama Hat Trail, by Tom Miller, is a fascinating book about the author's search for that most quintessential and misnamed of Ecuadorian products, the panama hat. For a more literary (and surreal) impression of Ecuador, read Henri Michaux' *Ecuador: A Travel Journal,* or Kurt Vonnegut's absurd *Galápagos,* which takes place in a futuristic Guayaquil as well as on the islands.

ELECTRICITY

Ecuador uses 110V, 60 cycles, AC (the same as in North America). Plugs have two flat prongs, as in North America.

EMBASSIES & CONSULATES

Embassies and consulates are best visited in the morning. New Zealand has no consular representation in Ecuador.

Australian Embassy (☎04-601-7529; ausconsulate@unidas.com.ec; Rocafuerte 520, 2nd fl, Quito)

Canadian Embassy (☎02-245-5499; www.canadainternational.gc.ca/ecuador-equateur; Av Amazonas 4153 & Unión de Periodistas, Quito)

Canadian Consulate (☎04-263-1109; Av Francisco de Orellana 234, 6th fl, Guayaquil)

Colombian Embassy (☎02-333-0268; http://quito.consulado.gov.co; Catalina Aldaz N34-131 near Portugal, 2nd fl, Quito)

Colombian Consulate (☎04-263-0674; http://guayaquil.consulado.gov.co; Francisco de Orellana 111, World Trade Center, Tower B, 11th fl, Guayaquil)

Colombian Consulate (☎06-283-2114; http://nuevaloja.consulado.gov.co; Av Quito near Colombia, Edificio Moncada, 4th fl, Lago Agrio)

Colombian Consulate (☎06-298-0559; http://tulcan.consulado.gov.co; Calle Bolívar btwn Junín & Ayacucho, Tulcán; ⏲8am-1pm & 2:30-3:30pm Mon-Fri)

French Embassy (☎02-294-3800; www.ambafrance-ec.org; cnr Leonidas Plaza 127 & Av Patria, Quito)

French Consulate (☎04-232-8442; cnr José Mascote 909 & Hurtado, Guayaquil)

German Embassy (☎02-297-0820; Naciones Unidas E10-44 at República de El Salvador, Edificio Citiplaza, 12th fl, Quito)

German Consulate (☎04-220-6867/8; www.quito.diplo.de; cnr Avs Las Monjas 10 & CJ Arosemena, Km 2.5, Edificio Berlín, Guayaquil)

Irish Honorary Consul (☎02-380-1345; Calle del Establo 50, tower III, office 104, Urb Santa Lucia Alta, Cumbaya, Quito)

Peruvian Embassy (☎02-225-2582; www.embajadadelperu.org.ec; Av República de El Salvador 495 & Irlanda, Quito)

Peruvian Consulate (☎04-263-4014; www.consuladoperuguayaquil.com; Av Francisco de Orellana 501, 14th fl, Guayaquil)

Peruvian Consulate (☎07-257-9068; Av Zoilo Rodriguez 03-05, Ciudadela Zamora, Loja)

Peruvian Consulate (☎07-293-7040; Urbanización Unioro Manzana 14, villa 11, Machala)

UK Embassy (☎02-297-0800; http://ukinecuador.fco.gov.uk/en; cnr Naciones Unidas & República de El Salvador, Edificio Citiplaza, 14th

FOOD PRICE RANGES

The following price ranges refer to a main course. Unless otherwise stated, service charges and taxes are included in the price.

$ less than $7

$$ $7 to $14

$$$ more than $14

fl, Quito) The UK Embassy is conveniently located by the electric bus line, just north of the New Town. For help with visas and passports, consular support and travel advice, this is your spot. It has a brilliant website (in English) – log on before you line up!

UK Consulate (☎04-256-0400; cnr Córdova 623 & Padre Solano, Guayaquil)

USA Embassy (☎02-398-5000; http://ecuador.usembassy.gov; cnr Av Avigiras E12-170 & Eloy Alfaro, Quito)

USA Consulate (☎04-371-7000; http://guayaquil.usconsulate.gov; Santa Ana near Av José Rodriguez Bonin, Guayaquil)

GAY & LESBIAN TRAVELERS

Ecuador is probably not the best place to be outwardly affectionate with a partner of the same sex. Homosexuality was illegal until 1997. Quito and Guayaquil have underground social scenes, but outside the occasional dance club, they're hard to find. **Zenith Travel** (Map p650; ☎02-252-9993; www.zenithecuador.com; Mera N24-264 & Cordero) specializes in gay and lesbian tours.

HEALTH

Medical care is available in major cities, but may be difficult to find in rural areas. Most doctors and hospitals will expect payment in cash, regardless of whether you have travel health insurance. Pharmacies in Ecuador are known as *farmacias*.

The main health hazards to be aware of are altitude sickness, malaria, typhoid and yellow fever.

INTERNET ACCESS

All but the smallest of towns have internet cafes. Prices hover around $1 per hour, though they get higher in small towns and on the Galápagos.

LANGUAGE

Ecuador is one of the best places to study Spanish on the continent. Quito and Cuenca, and to a lesser extent Otavalo and Baños, all have schools where you can have one-on-one classes and stay with a host family. Private classes (one-on-one) range from $7 to $10 per hour; group classes are marginally cheaper (about $5 to $6 per hour).

LEGAL MATTERS

Drug penalties in Ecuador for possession of even small amounts of illegal drugs (which include marijuana and cocaine) are severe. Defendants often spend months in jail before they are brought to trial, and if convicted (as is usually the case), they can expect several years in jail.

Treat plainclothes 'policemen' with suspicion. If you're asked for ID by a uniformed official in broad daylight, show your passport.

In the event of a car accident, unless extremely minor, the vehicles should stay where they are until the police arrive and make a report. If you hit a pedestrian, you are legally responsible for the pedestrian's injuries and can be jailed unless you pay, even if the accident was not your fault. Drive defensively.

MAPS

Ecuadorian bookstores carry a limited selection of Ecuadorian maps. The best selection is available from the **Instituto Geográfico Militar** (IGM; Map p644; ☎02-397-5129, 02-397-5100; www.igm.gob.ec; Seniergues E4-676, near Gral Telmo Paz y Miño; ⏲map sales room 8am-4pm Mon-Thu, 7am-12:30pm Fri) in Quito.

MONEY

Ecuador's currency was the sucre until it was switched to the US dollar in 2000, a process called 'dollarization.'

ATMs

ATMs are the easiest way of getting cash. They're found in most cities and even in smaller towns, although they are sometimes out of order. Make sure you have a four-digit PIN. Banco del Pacífico and Banco del Pichincha have Mastercard/Cirrus ATMs. Banco de Guayaquil has Visa/Plus ATMs.

Bargaining

Bargaining is expected at food and crafts markets. Sometimes you can bargain on hotels during low season.

Cash

Bills are the same as those used in the US. Coins are identical in shape, size and material to their US counterparts, but instead of US presidents, they feature the faces and symbols of Ecuador. US coins are also used interchangeably.

Change is often quite difficult to come by. Trying to purchase inexpensive items with a $20 bill (or even a $10 bill) generally results in either you or the proprietor running from shop to shop until someone produces some change. If no one does, you're out of luck. Change bills whenever you can. To ask for change, make a deeply worried face and ask *'¿Tiene suelto?'* (Do you have change?).

Credit Cards

Credit cards are a fine backup, but not widely accepted. Merchants accepting credit cards will often add from 4% to 10% to the bill. Paying cash is often better value. Visa and Mastercard are the most widely accepted cards.

Exchanging Money

Foreign currencies can be exchanged into US dollars easily in Quito, Guayaquil and Cuenca, where rates are also the best. You can also change money at most of the major border crossings. In some places, however, notably the Oriente, it is quite difficult to exchange money. Exchange houses, called *casas de cambio*, are normally the best places; banks will also exchange money but are usually much slower. Generally, exchange rates are within 2% of one another in any given city.

Traveler's Checks

Very few banks, hotels or retailers will cash traveler's checks, making them a poor option in Ecuador. Those that do typically tack on a rate of 2% to 4%. It's much more useful to have a supply of US cash and an ATM card (plus a backup ATM card just in case).

OPENING HOURS

Opening hours are provided when they differ from the following standard hours.

Banks 8am to 2pm or 8am to 4pm Monday to Friday

Bars 6pm to midnight Monday to Thursday, to 2am Friday and Saturday, closed Sunday

Post offices 8am to 6pm Monday to Friday, 8am to 1pm Saturday

Restaurants 10:30am to 11pm Monday to Saturday

Shops 9am to 7pm Monday to Friday, 9am to noon Saturday

Telephone call centers 8am to 10pm daily

PUBLIC HOLIDAYS

On major holidays, banks, offices and other services close. Transportation gets crowded, so buy bus tickets in advance. Major holidays are sometimes celebrated for several days around the actual date. If an official public holiday falls on a weekend, offices may be closed on the nearest Friday or Monday.

New Year's Day January 1

Epiphany January 6

Semana Santa (Easter Week) March/April

Labor Day May 1

Battle of Pichincha May 24; this honors the decisive battle of independence from Spain in 1822

Simón Bolívar's Birthday July 24

Quito Independence Day August 10

Guayaquil Independence Day October 9; this combines with the October 12 national holiday and is an important festival in Guayaquil

Columbus Day/Día de la Raza October 12

All Saints' Day November 1

Day of the Dead (All Souls' Day) November 2; celebrated by flower-laying ceremonies in cemeteries

Cuenca Independence Day November 3; combines with the national holidays of November 1 and 2 to give Cuenca its most important fiesta of the year

Christmas Eve December 24

Christmas Day December 25

SAFE TRAVEL

Ecuador has a growing crime problem, and you'll need to travel smart to avoid becoming a victim. Armed robbery targeting tourists occurs in Quito and Guayaquil. Despite a police presence, Quito's Mariscal neighborhood is particularly bad. Always take a taxi after dark in Quito, even if your guesthouse is only a few blocks away.

Buses – both local and long-distance – are prime targets for thieves. Keeping your bag under your seat or on your back is a bad idea, as adroit thieves can slash-and-steal before you even realize anything is amiss. Every year or so, a few long-distance night buses are robbed on the way to/from the coast. Avoid taking night buses through the provinces of Guayas or Manabí unless you have to.

Bandits have begun targetting tourists heading to jungle lodges in the Oriente, and there are also occasional flare-ups of guerrilla activity in some areas near the Colombian border. Before you go to this area, do some research.

As elsewhere in South America, take the normal precautions: ie, pickpocketing occurs in crowded places, such as markets and terminals. If you are robbed, get a *denuncia* (police report) from the local police station within 48 hours – they won't process a report after that.

TELEPHONE

Travelers who aren't sporting a smartphone or wi-fi-enabled laptop can make international calls through internet cafes, most of which have terminals equipped with Skype.

Public street phones are also common. Some use phone cards, which are sold in convenient places such as newsagents. Others only accept coins. All but the most basic hotels will allow you to make local city calls.

Hotels that provide international phone connections very often surcharge extremely heavily.

All telephone numbers in Ecuador have seven digits, and the first digit – except for cellular phone numbers – is always a '2.' If someone gives you a six-digit number (which sometimes happens), simply put a '2' in front of it.

From a private phone within Ecuador, dial ☎116 for an international operator.

Two-digit area codes (indicated after town headings) change by province. Drop the area code if you're calling within a province. If calling from abroad, drop the 0 from the code. Ecuador's country code is ☎593.

Cell Phones

- Cellular telephone numbers in Ecuador are always preceded by ☎09.
- If bringing your own phone, GSM cell phones operating at 850MHz (GSM 850) will work on Claro and Movistar networks. Alegro uses the 1900MHz (GSM 1900).
- The cheapest way of staying connected is to purchase a SIM card (called a 'chip,' and costing around $5 to $7) from one of the above networks. Add credit by purchasing a *tarjeta pregago* (phone card) with your chosen carrier, which are available at many convenience stores, supermarkets and pharmacies.

TOILETS

Ecuadorian plumbing has very low pressure. Putting toilet paper into the bowl may clog the system, so use the waste basket. This may seem unsanitary, but it's much better than clogged bowls and water overflowing onto the floor. Expensive hotels have adequate plumbing.

Public toilets are limited mainly to bus terminals, airports and restaurants. Toilets are called *servicios higiénicos* and are usually marked 'SS. HH.' People needing to use the toilet often ask to use the *baño* in a restaurant; toilet paper is rarely available – carry a personal supply.

TOURIST INFORMATION

The government-run **Ministerio de Turismo** (http://ecuador.travel) is responsible for tourist information at the national level. It is slowly opening tourist information offices – known as iTur offices – in important towns throughout Ecuador.

South American Explorers (p659) has a clubhouse in Quito.

TRAVELERS WITH DISABILITIES

Unfortunately, Ecuador's infrastructure for travelers with disabilities is virtually nonexistent.

VISAS

Most travelers entering Ecuador as tourists, including citizens of Australasian countries, Japan, the EU, Canada and the USA, do not require visas. Upon entry, they will be issued a T-3 tourist card valid for 90 days. Sixty-day stamps are rarely given, but double-check if you're going to be in the country for a while. Residents of most Central American and some Asian countries require visas.

All travelers entering as diplomats, refugees, students, laborers, religious workers, businesspeople, volunteers and cultural-exchange visitors require nonimmigrant visas. Various immigrant visas are also available. Visas must be obtained from an Ecuadorian embassy and cannot be arranged within Ecuador.

Officially, to enter the country you must have a ticket out of Ecuador and sufficient funds for your stay, but border authorities rarely ask for proof of this. International vaccination certificates are not required by law, but some vaccinations, particularly against yellow fever, are advisable.

Visa Extensions

Strict regulations mean it's a real headache getting visa extensions. Unless you're from an Andean pact country, tourist visas are not extendable. If you wish to stay longer than 90 days, you'll need to apply for a 12-IX Visa; you can also do this in the country, though it's more time-consuming. Pick up the necessary paperwork for the 12-IX Visa, and pay the $230 fee at the **Ministerio de Relaciones Exteriores** (☎02-299-3200; http://cancilleria.gob.ec; Carrión E1-76 & Av 10 de Agosto, Quito) in Quito.

No matter what, don't wait until your visa has expired to sort out your paperwork, as the fine for overstaying can be hefty – $200 to $2000.

VOLUNTEERING

Numerous organizations look for the services of volunteers; however, many require at least a minimal grasp of Spanish, a minimum commitment of several weeks or months, as well as fees (anywhere from $300 to $600 per month) to cover the costs of room and board. Volunteers can work in conservation programs, help street kids, teach, build nature trails, construct websites, or do medical or agricultural work – the possibilities are endless. Many jungle lodges also accept volunteers for long-term stays. To keep your volunteer costs down, your best bet is to look for a position when you get to Ecuador. Plenty of places need volunteers who only have their hard work to offer.

South American Explorers (p659) in Quito has a volunteer section where current offerings are posted. The classifieds section of the **Ecuador Explorer** website (www.ecuadorexplorer.com) has a list of organizations seeking volunteers.

AmaZOOnico (www.amazoonicorescuecenter.com) Work in the animal rehabilitation sector.

Andean Bear Conservation Project (www.andeanbear.org) Trains volunteers as bear trackers.

Bosque Nublado Santa Lucia (www.santaluciaecuador.com) Involved in reforestation, trail maintenance, construction, teaching English.

FEVI (www.fevi.org) The Fund for Intercultural Education & Community Volunteer Service works with children, the elderly, women's groups and indigenous communities.

Junto con los Niños (www.juconi.org.ec) Work with street kids in the slum areas of Guayaquil.

Merazonia (www.merazonia.org) A refuge for injured animals.

New Era Galápagos Foundation (www.neweragalapagos.org) Sustainable tourism in the Galápagos. Volunteers live and work on Isla San Cristóbal.

Rainforest Concern (www.rainforestconcern.org) British nonprofit.

Reserva Biológica Los Cedros (www.reservaloscedros.org) In the cloud forests of the western Andean slopes.

Río Muchacho Organic Farm (www.riomuchacho.com) Volunteer opportunities in organic agriculture.

Yanapuma Foundation (Map p640; ☎02-228-7084; www.yanapuma.org; Guayaquil E9-59 near Oriente, Quito) Teaching English, reforestation, building houses, coastal clean-ups.

WOMEN TRAVELERS

Women travelers will generally find Ecuador safe and pleasant, although machismo is alive and well. Ecuadorian men often make flirtatious comments and whistle at single women. Women who firmly ignore unwanted verbal advances are often treated with respect.

On the coast, you'll find that come-ons are more predatory, and solo female travelers should take precautions such as staying away from bars and discos where they will likely get hit on, opting for taxis over walking etc. Racy conversation with a guy, while it may be ironic or humorous, is not common here, and a man will probably assume you're after one thing.

We have received warnings from women who were molested while on organized tours. If you're traveling solo, it's essential to do some investigating before committing to a tour: find out who's leading the tour, what other tourists will be on the outing and so on. Women-only travel groups or guides are available in a few situations.

WORK

Officially, you need a work visa to get a job in Ecuador. English-teaching positions occasionally pop up in Quito or Cuenca. The pay is low but enough to live on. Tourist services (jungle lodges, tour operators etc) are good places to look for work.

ℹ Getting There & Away

ENTERING THE COUNTRY

Entering the country is straightforward, and border officials, especially at the airports, efficiently whisk you through. At land borders, officers may take a little more time examining your passport, if only to kill a little time. Officially, you need proof of onward travel and evidence of sufficient funds for your stay, but this is rarely requested. Proof of $20 per day or a credit card is usually evidence of sufficient funds. However, international airlines flying to Quito may require a round-trip or onward ticket or a residence visa before they let you on the plane; you should be prepared for this possibility, though it's unlikely. Though not law, you may be required to show proof of vaccination against yellow fever if you are entering Ecuador from an infected area.

AIR

Airports & Airlines

Ecuador has two international airports.

Quito's new **Aeropuerto Internacional de Quito** (www.aeropuertoquito.aero) is located about 38km east of the center. Guayaquil's **Aeropuerto José Joaquín de Olmedo** (GYE; ☎04-216-9000; www.tagsa.aero; Av de las Américas s/n) is just a few kilometers from downtown.

TAME (☎ in Quito 02-396-6300; www.tame.com.ec) is Ecuador's main airline, and it has had a good safety record in recent years, with a modern fleet of Boeing, Airbus and Embraer aircraft as well as several turboprop ATRs.

Tickets

Ticket prices are highest during tourist high seasons: mid-June through early September, and December through mid-January. Working with a travel agent that deals specifically in Latin American travel is always an advantage.

BUS

International bus tickets sold in Quito often require a change of bus at the border. It's usually cheaper and just as convenient to buy a ticket to the border and another ticket in the next country. The exceptions are the international buses from Loja to Piura, Peru (via Macará), and from Guayaquil to Peru (via Huaquillas); on these, you don't have to change buses, and the immigration officials usually board the bus to take care of your paperwork. These are the primary routes between Ecuador and Peru. Zumba, south of Vilcabamba, is an alternative route to/from Peru in a scenic and less used location. The main bus route between Colombia and Ecuador is via

Tulcán. Other border crossings between Colombia and Ecuador are not recommended owing to safety concerns.

RIVER

It is possible but not easy to travel down the Río Napo from Ecuador to Peru, joining the Amazon near Iquitos. The border facilities are minimal, and the boats doing the journey are infrequent. It is also geographically possible to travel down Río Putumayo into Colombia and Peru, but this is a dangerous region because of drug smuggling and terrorism, and is not recommended.

Getting Around

You can usually get anywhere quickly and easily. Bus is the most common mode of transportation, followed by plane. Buses can take you from the Colombian border to Peru's border in 18 hours. Boats are used in the northern coastal mangroves and in the Oriente.

Whatever form of transportation you choose, always carry your passport with you, both to board planes and to proffer during document checks on the road. People without documents may be arrested. If your passport is in order, these procedures are cursory. If you're traveling anywhere near the borders or in the Oriente, expect more frequent passport checks.

AIR

With the exception of flying to the Galápagos, most internal flights are relatively cheap. One-way flights average $70 to $100. Almost all flights originate or terminate in Quito or Guayaquil. Some domestic flights have marvelous views of the snowcapped Andes – when flying from Quito to Guayaquil, sit on the left.

The main carriers in Ecuador are as follows:

Avianca (www.avianca.com) Flies from Quito to Isla Baltra and Isla San Cristóbal in the Galápagos. Avianca also flies between Quito and Coca.

Emetebe (☎ in Guayaquil 04-230-9209; www.emetebe.com.ec) Galápagos-based airline that flies between Isla Baltra, Isla San Cristóbal and Isla Isabela.

LAN (☎ in Quito 1-800-842-526; www.lan.com) Flies from Quito to Cuenca, Guayaquil and the Galápagos (San Cristóbal and Isla Baltra, both via Guayaquil).

TAME (www.tame.com.ec) Serves Coca, Cuenca, Esmeraldas, Isla Baltra (Galápagos), Isla San Cristóbal (Galápagos), Guayaquil, Lago Agrio, Loja, Macas, Manta, Portoviejo, Quito and Tulcán, plus Cali (Colombia) and Manaos (Brazil).

BOAT

Motorized dugout canoes are the only transportation available in some roadless areas. Regularly scheduled boats are affordable, although not as cheap as a bus for a similar distance. Hiring your own boat and skipper is possible but extremely expensive. The lower Río Napo from Coca to Peru are the places you'll most likely travel to by boat (if you get out that far).

DEPARTURE TAX

In Ecuador the international departure tax is $25, but this is always included in ticket prices rather than payable at the airport.

BUS

Buses are the lifeblood of Ecuador and the easiest way to get around. Most towns have a *terminal terrestre* (central bus terminal) for long-distance buses, although in some towns buses leave from various places. To get your choice of seat, buy tickets in advance from the terminal. During holiday weekends, buses can be booked up for several days in advance.

If you're traveling lightly, keep your luggage with you inside the bus. Otherwise, heave it onto the roof or stuff it into the luggage compartment and try to keep an eye on it.

Long-distance buses rarely have toilets, but they usually stop for 20-minute meal and bladder-relief breaks at fairly appropriate times. If not, drivers will stop to let you fertilize the roadside.

Local buses are usually slow and crowded, but cheap. You can get around most towns for about $0.25. Local buses also often go out to nearby villages (a great way to explore an area).

CAR & MOTORCYCLE

Few people rent cars in Ecuador, mainly because public transportation makes getting around so easy. Ecuador's automobile association is **Aneta** (☎1-800-556-677; www.aneta.org.ec), which offers 24-hour roadside assistance to its members. It offers some services to members of foreign automobile clubs, including Canadian and US AAA members.

HITCHHIKING

Hitchhiking is possible, but not very practical in Ecuador. Public transportation is relatively cheap and trucks are used as public transportation in remote areas, so trying to hitch a free ride isn't easy. If the driver is stopping to drop off and pick up other passengers, assume that payment will be expected. If you're the only passenger, the driver may have picked you up just to talk to a foreigner. Remember that getting into a car or truck with strangers carries a potential risk, however small.

TAXI

Taxis are relatively cheap. Bargain the fare beforehand though, or you're likely to be overcharged. A long ride in a large city (Quito or Guayaquil) shouldn't go over $5, and short hops in small towns usually cost about $1 to $2. Meters are sometimes used during the day in Quito (where the minimal fare is $1) but rarely seen elsewhere. On weekends and at night, fares are always about 25% to 50% higher. Full-day taxi hire should cost around $50.

TOURS

Much of the Galápagos archipelago is accessible to visitors only by guided tour (ie a cruise). Many travelers also opt to visit the Amazon on organized tours, as these are efficient, educational and often the only way to get deep into the rainforest.

TRAIN

Much to the delight of train enthusiasts, Ecuador's rail system has finally been restored. Unfortunately, it's not useful for travel, as the routes run as day trips designed exclusively for tourists. The trains run along short routes, typically on weekends, sometimes with return service by bus. The most famous line is the dramatic descent from Alausí along La Nariz del Diablo (The Devil's Nose), a spectacular section of train track that was one of the world's greatest feats of railroad engineering. The second is the weekend train excursion between Quito and the Area Nacional de Recreación El Boliche, near Cotopaxi.

Other routes run from Durán (near Guayaquil), Ibarra, Ambato, Riobamba and El Tambo (near Ingapirca).

For departure times, ticket prices and itinerary information, visit **Tren Ecuador** (www.trenecuador.com).

TRUCK

In remote areas, *camiones* (trucks) and *camionetas* (pickup trucks) often double as buses. If the weather is OK, you get fabulous views; if not, you have to crouch underneath a dark tarpaulin and suck dust. Pickups can be hired to get to remote places such as climbers' refuges.

French Guiana

Includes ➡

Best Places to Eat

- Central Market (p736)
- Les Palmistes (p738)
- Cacao's Sunday market (p741)
- Chez Félicia (p745)
- Auberge des Îles du Salut (p743)

Best Walks

- Îles du Salut (p742)
- Downtown Cayenne (p736)
- Sentier Molokoï de Cacao (p741)
- Trésor (p741)

Why Go?

French Guiana is a tiny country of cleaned-up colonial architecture, eerie prison-camp history and some of the world's most diverse plant and animal life. It's a strange mix of French law and rainforest humidity where only a few destinations along the coast are easily accessed and travel can be frustratingly difficult as well as expensive. As a department of France, it's one of South America's wealthiest corners, with funds pouring in to ensure a stable base for the satellite launcher. But not even a European superpower can tame this vast, pristine jungle: you'll find potholes in newly paved roads, and ferns sprouting between bricks, while Amerindians, Maroons and Hmong refugees live traditional lifestyles so far from *la vie Metropole* that it's hard to believe they're connected at all.

When to Go

Cayenne

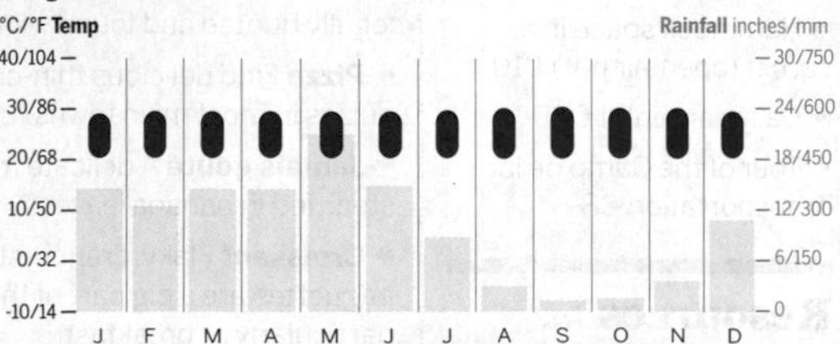

Jan–Jun Expect sogginess during these months, with the heaviest rains in May.

Late Jan–Mar Dates vary but you can expect Cayenne to throw a wild and exciting Carnaval.

Jul–Sep It rains less during the dry season although it's hot and humid year round.

AT A GLANCE

- **Currency** Euro (€)
- **Languages** French, Creole
- **Money** ATMs in bigger towns; *cambios* only in Cayenne; credit cards widely accepted
- **Visas** Not needed for 90 days for most nationalities
- **Time** GMT minus three hours

Fast Facts

- **Area** 91,000 sq km
- **Population** 250,400
- **Capital** Cayenne
- **Emergency** ☎17
- **Country code** ☎594

Exchange Rates

Australia	A$1	€0.64
Canada	C$1	€0.68
New Zealand	NZ$1	€0.60
UK	UK£1	€1.36
USA	US$1	€0.88

Set Your Budget

- Pho at the Cayenne Central Market €5
- Hammock space in a *carbet* (open-air hut) €10
- Daily car rental €45
- Tour of the Camp de la Transportation €8

Resources

- **French Guiana Tourism Committee** (www.guyane-amazonie.fr)
- **Guyane 1ère** (http://guyane.la1ere.fr)
- **Guyane.fr** (www.guyane.fr)

Connections

French Guiana has a border crossing at St Georges, where the Oyapock River marks the frontier with Brazil, and at St Laurent, where the Maroni River is the border with Suriname. Both border crossings are made by boat, although a bridge, which may open in the lifetime of this book, has been built to Brazil.

ITINERARIES

One Week

Start in Cayenne, making sure to visit the market, stroll the streets and to eat out often. Drive to Cacao on a Sunday for the Laotian market. If there's a shuttle launch in Kourou, call or write to the Centre Spatial Guyanais to secure an invitation to see it, then try to work in an overnight visit to the Îles du Salut that won't conflict with the launch (the islands close before and after launches). Spend a final day or two exploring the prison camps in St Laurent du Maroni.

Two Weeks

Follow the above itinerary, extending your stay to two or more nights on the Îles du Salut. Take an overnight tour of Kaw, where you'll stay on a floating lodge, and look for scarlet ibis, black caiman and a huge array of other bird species. Before heading to St Laurent du Maroni, detour to Mana and Awala-Yalimopo to watch nesting turtles if the season is right or otherwise to enjoy the gorgeous beach.

Essential Food & Drink

- **Pho** Vietnamese soup made with beef broth, rice noodles, many fragrant herbs and meat.
- **Mie/nasi goreng** Javanese-style fried noodles/rice.
- **Gibier** Bush meat like capybara, wild boar and agouti is legally hunted and found widely on restaurant menus.
- **Pizza** Find delicious thin-crust, French-style, wood-fired pizzas in most main towns.
- **Jamais goûté** A delicate freshwater fish that's best steamed in banana leaves.
- **Croissant** Flaky, French-style pastries as well as simple baguettes are a big part of the French Guianan diet, particularly at breakfast.
- **Ti'punch** Literally a 'small punch' made with local rum, lime juice and sugarcane syrup – a Caribbean favorite.
- **Fricassee** Rice, beans and sautéed meat stewed in gravy – unlike French fricassee, the Caribbean style has a brown or red sauce with a kick of cayenne pepper.

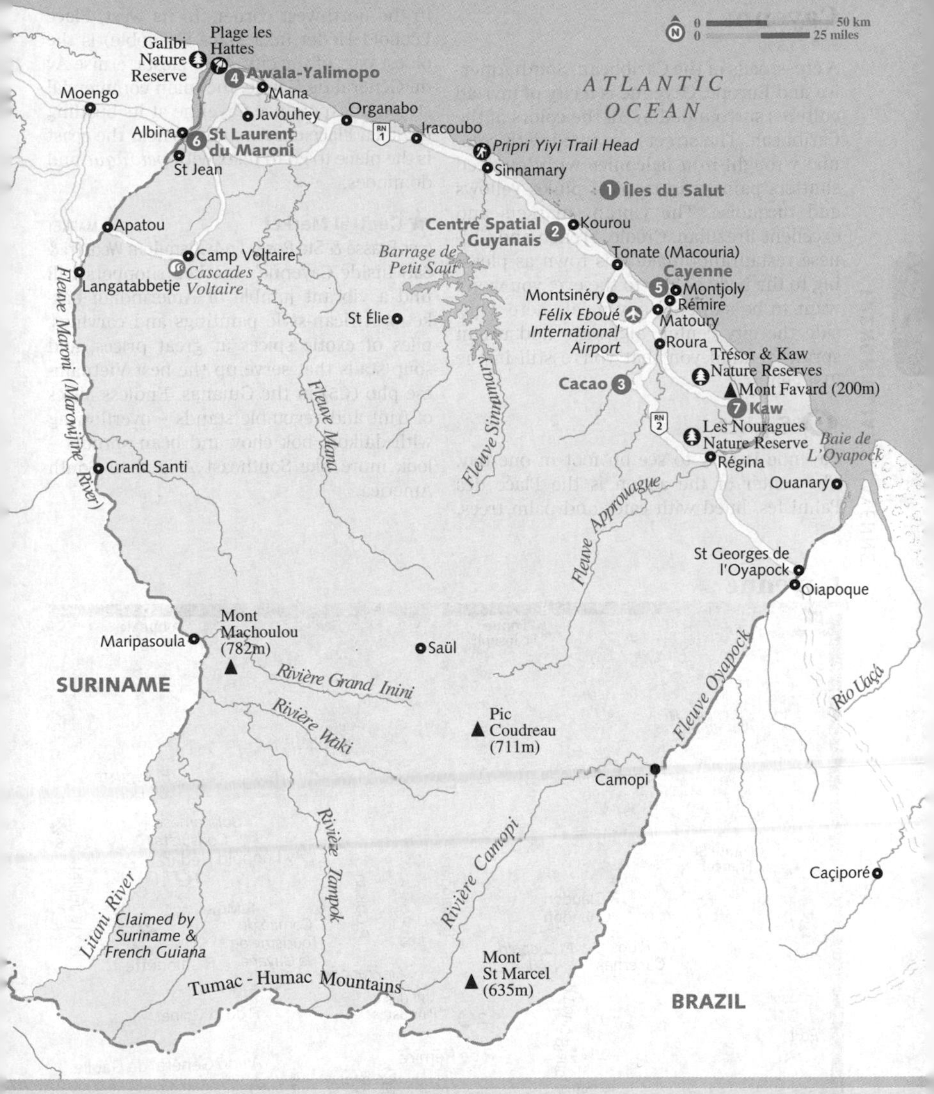

French Guiana Highlights

1. Cast away to **Îles du Salut** (p742) for sand, palms and a creepy, defunct penal colony.
2. See one of the world's busiest satellite launchers at the **Centre Spatial Guyanais** (p741) and, with luck, watch a launch.
3. Gorge on Laotian treats and admire ornate embroidery in the Hmong community of **Cacao** (p741).
4. Watch the peaceful ritual of dinosaur-like leatherback turtles laying their eggs in the moonlit sand of **Awala-Yalimopo** (p746).
5. Sip a cold beer and people watch at Cayenne's quintessential cafe, **Les Palmistes** (p738).
6. Get an eerie tour of the **Camp de la Transportation** (p743) in prisoner-haunted St Laurent du Maroni.
7. Spend the night in a floating lodge surrounded by jungle and flourishing birdlife at **Kaw** (p741).

Cayenne

POP 64,300

A crossroads of the Caribbean, South America and Europe, Cayenne is a city of myriad cultures surrounded by all the colors of the Caribbean. The streets are lined with colonial wrought-iron balconies with louvered shutters painted in tropical pinks, yellows and turquoise. The vibrant markets and excellent Brazilian, Creole, French and Chinese restaurants make this town as pleasing to the belly as it is to the eye; you won't want to be skipping any meals here. Outside the city center, highways and urban sprawl remind you that you're still in the 21st century.

Sights

Cayenne is easy to see on foot in one day. The center of the action is the Place des Palmistes, lined with cafes and palm trees, in the northwest corner. To its west, Place Léopold Héder (aka Place Grenoble) is the oldest part of the city. After siesta, cruise Av du Général de Gaulle, the main commercial street, to experience Cayenne at its bustling peak. La Place des Amandiers near the coast is the place to go to relax with *pétanque* and dominoes.

★Central Market MARKET

(cnr Brassé & Ste Rose; ⌚4:30am-1pm Wed, Fri & Sat) Inside Cayenne's market, shoppers will find a vibrant jumble of Amerindian basketry, African-style paintings and carvings, piles of exotic spices at great prices, and soup stalls that serve up the best Vietnamese pho (€5) in the Guianas. Endless aisles of fruit and vegetable stands – overflowing with daikon, bok choy and bean sprouts – look more like Southeast Asia than South America.

Cayenne

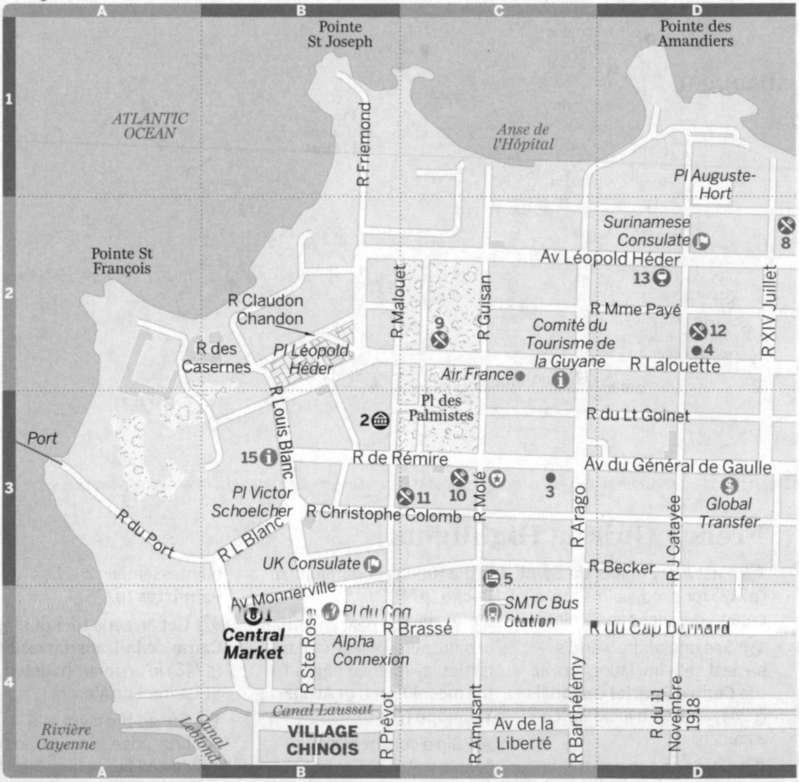

Musée Départemental MUSEUM

(1 Rue de Rémire; adult/child & student €3/free; ⏲10am-2pm & 3-6pm Mon, 8am-2pm & 3-6pm Wed-Fri, 9am-1:30pm Sat) The centrally located Musée Départemental features a frighteningly large stuffed black caiman, as well as other preserved local critters, an ethno-botanical display and an air-conditioned 'butterfly room.' The upstairs area recaptures life in the old penal colony and displays some Amerindian handicrafts.

Botanical Gardens GARDENS

(Blvd de la République) The sizable Botanical Gardens, built in 1879 and renovated in 2009, today flourish with tropical Guianese flora, including many species of palms.

Tours

French Guiana's pristine jungles are impenetrable and dangerous without a knowledgeable guide. Licensed Cayenne-based agencies run tours, often hiring out guides throughout the country (and taking a commission on their services). The better companies include the following.

GETTING INTO TOWN

Félix Eboué International Airport is about 16km southwest of Cayenne. From the airport, consider sharing a taxi (€35 to €40, 20 minutes). To the airport, it's cheaper to take a *taxi collectif* (minibus) to Matoury (€2, 10km, 15 minutes), then a taxi for the remaining 6km.

JAL Voyages TOUR

(☎31-6820; www.jal-voyages.com; 26 Av du Général de Gaulle; ⏲8:30am-noon & 3-6pm Mon-Fri, 9:30am-noon Sat) Offers half-day trips to Gabriel Creek from €30, a popular overnight jaunt on a floating *carbet* in Kaw (from €148) and four-day trips down the Maroni River (€598) – and much more.

Takari Tour TOUR

(☎28-9555; www.takaritour.com; 17-19 Lalouette; ⏲8:30am-5:30pm Mon-Fri, 9am-1pm Sat) The oldest and most respected operator runs a handful of day trips, including a boat journey to the jungle-clad Islet La Mer (from €45), 12km off the coast. There are also longer trips on offer, from two-week forest jaunts (€2405) to weekend camping excursions to Saül (from €395).

Festivals & Events

Carnaval CARNIVAL

Carnaval is a gigantic, colorful occasion, with festivities from Epiphany to several solid days of partying before Ash Wednesday. Dates vary; it can be January, February or March.

Sleeping

Central Hôtel HOTEL $

(☎25-6565; www.centralhotel-cayenne.fr; cnr Molé & Becker; s/d €70/80; ❄📶) The utilitarian Central isn't interesting in any particular way, but the big, comfortable, clean rooms, tip-top location and great service make it the best deal in town.

Oyasamaïd PENSION $

(☎31-5684; www.oyasamaid.com; studio/d incl breakfast from €60/70; ❄📶🏊) A French family pension *à la Guianese,* this four-room place is friendly, bright and impeccably clean. All the spacious rooms have Jacuzzi bathtubs, and a swimming pool seals the deal. It's a short drive from the town center so you'll need a car. You'll see signs for it on the Route de la Madeleine; they're near the roundabout and Geant supermarket.

Mo Ti Koté B&B $
(☎386-598; www.motikote.com; 42 Schoelcher; d €75-120; ❄📶) Suites in this beautifully renovated Creole home – some with kitchens, two bedrooms or even a private garden – are a steal. Central location and a great choice for families (€10 extra per night per child).

Hotel Ket Tai HOTEL $
(☎28-9777; 72 Blvd Jubelin; s/d/tr €46/56/65; ❄📶) Rooms are bland, small and institutional feeling but the Ket Tai is cheap, relatively well located and there are often rooms available when everything else is full.

Eating

For the best bang for your buck, you can slurp noodles at Cayenne's daytime market or browse the nighttime **food stalls** (Place des Palmistes) for burgers (about €3). Small Chinese takeout joints and grocery shops make self-catering a breeze. The sit-down options in Cayenne can be outstanding.

★Couleurs et Saveurs de Jo le Glacier ICE CREAM $
(cnr 14 Juillet & Schoelcher; 1 scoop €2; ⏲3-8pm Mon-Fri, noon-8pm Sat; ❄👪) Choose from a huge assortment of delicious ice cream flavors such as *patawa* (a palm fruit), citronella, moka and passion fruit. The menu changes seasonally. Take it away (which is cheaper) or enjoy at cozy tables in the air-conditioned shop.

Nath Cafe CAFE $
(33 Catayée; ⏲7am-7pm; ❄📶) Air-con bliss with espresso drinks, chai, teas, bubble teas, smoothies and decadent pastries. Soft music and a coffeehouse ambience that could be at home in a much more cosmopolitan city.

★Les Palmistes FRENCH $$
(12 Av du Général de Gaulle; pizzas from €12, mains around €20; ⏲6:30am-1am Mon-Sat, 10am-11pm Sun; 📶) The best place to people-watch on the palm-tree-lined Place des Palmistes also serves up perfect Caribbean-French ambience. Sit on the wooden terrace with its wrought-iron balustrade to dine on fantastic salads, crepes, pizzas and full meals while sipping a cold beer. Bliss.

La Kaz Kréòl CREOLE $$
(☎39-0697; 35 Av d'Estrées; mains €14-20; ⏲noon-2pm & 6:30-10:30pm Tue-Sun) The best sit-down Creole restaurant in Cayenne serves outstanding stuffed cassava, meat stews and seafood in a homey setting. Try the Creole breakfasts on Saturdays and Sundays.

Les Pyramides MIDDLE EASTERN $$
(cnr Colomb & Malouet; mains €20; ⏲noon-3pm & 7-11pm Tue-Sun) This superb Middle Eastern restaurant makes hearty, heaping platters of couscous to rave reviews.

Drinking & Entertainment

Live music, wine and rum punch flow freely in bars and clubs throughout Cayenne and

Cayenne

Top Sights
1 Central Market ... B4

Sights
2 Musée Départemental ... B3

Activities, Courses & Tours
3 JAL Voyages ... C3
4 Takari Tour ... D2

Sleeping
5 Central Hôtel ... C3
6 Hotel Ket Tai ... E4
7 Mo Ti Koté ... F2

Eating
8 Couleurs et Saveurs de Jo le Glacier ... D2
9 Food Stalls ... C2
10 Les Palmistes ... C3
11 Les Pyramides ... C3
12 Nath Cafe ... D2

Drinking & Nightlife
13 Cafe de la Gare ... D2
14 Le Cosmopolitan ... E3

Information
15 Office du Tourisme ... B3

there are many, many more than those we've listed – ask around.

Reggae music rocks small clubs in Village Chinois, and a few Brazilian and Dominican bars dot Av de la Liberté.

Cafe de la Gare BAR

(42 Av Léopold Héder; ⌚7:30pm-1am Tue-Sat) A fun spot with live music and early-evening, local-style dance lessons Tuesday through Friday.

Le Cosmopolitan BAR

(☎35-8566; 118 Av du Général de Gaulle; ⌚5pm-1am Mon-Sat) Trendy nightspot with a young, mixed clientele getting down to electronica and Caribbean music.

Information

DANGERS & ANNOYANCES

Petty and violent crime is rife, mostly as a result of increasing drug problems. At night, walk in groups or take a taxi. The Village Chinois (aka Chicago) area, south of the market, should be reached by taxi.

EMERGENCY

Fire (☎18)
Police (☎17)

INTERNET ACCESS

Most hotels and many French-oriented cafes and restaurants have free wi-fi.

MEDICAL SERVICES

Centre Hospitalier Cayenne (☎39-5050; 3 Av Flamboyants)

MONEY

Banks and ATMs are all over the city, but traveler's checks and foreign currency can only be cashed at *cambios* (currency-exchange offices).

Global Transfer (64 Av du Général de Gaulle; ⌚7:30-11am & 3-6pm Mon-Fri, 7:30-11am Sat) Central location.

POST

Bureau de Poste (Rte de Baduel; ⌚8am-1pm & 3-5pm Mon-Fri) The most central post office in Cayenne is near the Botanical Gardens.

TELEPHONE

Digicel has SIM cards for €20, which includes €5 of talk credit. The most convenient place to buy one in Cayenne is **Alpha Connexion** (☎25-0212; 2 Place du Coq). Top ups are available at shops and restaurants all around town.

TOURIST INFORMATION

Comité du Tourisme de la Guyane (☎29-6500; www.tourisme-guyane.com; 12 Lalouette; ⌚8am-1pm & 3-6pm Mon-Fri, 8am-noon Sat) Filled with pamphlets, maps and information, this tourist office, geared toward all of French Guiana rather than Cayenne specifically, is always staffed with someone to answer questions. An information desk at the airport stays open late for arriving flights.

Office du Tourisme (www.ville-cayenne-fr; 1 Rue de Rémire; ⌚8:30am-noon & 2-5pm Mon-Fri, 8:30am-1pm Sat) A helpful tourist office with information specific to Cayenne.

Getting There & Away

All international and domestic flights leave from **Félix Eboué International Airport** (Rochambeau; ☎29 9700).

Getting Around

At the time of writing there were no public buses serving destinations within the Cayenne area.

TO/FROM THE AIRPORT

Félix Eboué International Airport is about 16km southwest of Cayenne. The main way to/from the airport is by taxi (€35 to €40, 20 minutes).

BUSES FROM CAYENNE

Minibuses leave from the **SMTC bus station** (☎for schedule 25-4929; cnr Rue du Cap Bernard & Molé) when full, Monday to Friday, with fewer services on the weekend. For more information go to www.cg973.fr/Lignes-de-transport-prevues (although the timetables are only approximations and some buses, particularly those on Sundays, may never leave at all).

DESTINATION	COST (€)	DURATION (HR)	FREQUENCY (DAILY)
Kourou	15	1¼	4
Regina	20	1½	8
Sinnamary	15	2½	5
St Georges	30	5	8
St Laurent	30	4	1

GETTING TO BRAZIL

Getting to the Border

Minibuses leave when full from Cayenne to St Georges (€30, five hours), located on the border with Brazil. You may need to transfer buses in Regina. This is the only public-transport option to the border.

At the Border

St Georges serves as a departure point for visits to Amerindian villages and the ruins of Silver Mountain Penal Colony on the Oyapock River, but not much else. Accessing the villages requires permission from local authorities and an experienced guide, so it's best to contact a Cayenne-based tour company. If you get stuck in St Georges for a night (and many travelers do), try the popular **Chez Modestine** (37-0013; modestine@wanadoo.fr; Place du Village, Rue Elie-Elfort; s/d from €39/45;) or the quieter **Caz-Calé** (37-0054; Rue Elie-Elfort; s/d from €50/55;). Stamp out at the Douane (open 8am to 12pm and 2pm to 6pm) on the riverside in St Georges. A gigantic bridge was slated to open in spring of 2013 but at the time of research it was still not in operation due to political problems. Dugouts make the crossing to Oiapoque in Brazil for €4 (15 minutes).

There are no fees at the border; many nationalities will need a Brazilian visa to enter Brazil.

Moving On

Once in Oiapoque, it's a 10-minute walk away from the river to the Police Federal, where you stamp into Brazil. Daily buses (R$156, 11 to 14 hours, morning and afternoon) and planes leave Oiapoque for Macapá.

CAR

Renting a car can be cheaper than public transport if two or more people are traveling together. Some companies have offices in Kourou, St Laurent du Maroni and at the airport (some have airport-pickup surcharges of up to €25). Expect to pay from €35 per day for a compact with unlimited mileage. Cars are not allowed over the border.

Avis (30-2522; www.avis.fr; 58 Blvd Jubelin) Also has an office at the airport.

Budget (35-1020; www.budget-guyane.com; Zone Galmot) Zone Galmot is on the Cayenne outskirts, just off Av Galmot; also has an office at the airport.

TAXI

Taxis charge a hiring fee of €2, plus €0.85 per kilometer; the per-kilometer charge increases to €1 from 7pm to 6am and on Sundays and holidays. There's a taxi stand on the southeast corner of Place des Palmistes.

Rémire-Montjoly

POP 20,700

Though technically two separate towns, Rémire-Montjoly, only 8km from Cayenne, functions as a single village. Its sweeping beaches are some of the country's best waterfront.

Sights & Activities

Plage Montjoly BEACH

The best beach in the area gets busy on weekends and holidays but is otherwise empty. The water is shallow and murky but there are a few deeper areas OK for a dip. Bring repellent for biting sand flies.

Fort Diamant RUIN

(35-4110; admission with/without guided tour €5/3) The renovated historical ruins at Fort Diamant, an old coastal battery dating from the early 19th century, are along the main beach road.

Salines Trail WALKING

The easy 2.5km Salines Trail, at the end of Rue St Domenica, offers excellent views of the coastal marshland and the ocean.

Rorota Trail WALKING

An easy but beautiful 4km loop through forest and past lakes, with some views of the coast. Look for morpho butterflies and monkeys.

Sleeping

Motel du Lac HOTEL $

(38-0800; moteldulac@orange.fr; Chemin Poupon, Rte de Montjoly; d €70;) Motel du

Lac is a well-run place with a great pool near Montjoly beach and a lakeside ecological reserve.

Cacao

POP 950

A tidy slice of Laos in the hills of Guiana, Cacao, about 75km southwest of Cayenne, is a village of clear rivers, vegetable plantations and wooden houses on stilts. The Hmong refugees who left Laos in the 1970s keep their town a safe, peaceful haven, and it's now a favorite weekend day trip among locals from Cayenne. Sunday, **market** day, is the best time for a visit if you want to shop for Hmong embroidery and weaving, and feast on a smorgasbord of Laotian treats. Don't miss the museum **Le Planeur Bleu** (27-0034; cleplaneurbleu@wanadoo.fr; adult/child under 12 €4/free; 9am-1pm & 2-4pm Sun, by appointment other times) to see butterflies and arachnids, both dead and alive, or hold live tarantulas.

For a wildlife- and insect-spotting adventure, embark on the 18km hike along the **Sentier Molokoï** (Cacao Molokoï Nature Trail), one of the few deep-forest jaunts that can be accomplished independently. The track links the rustic-chic **Auberge des Orpailleurs** (27-0622; www.aubergedesorpailleurs.com; PK62, RN 2; r per person from €42, hammock spaces per person €36, all incl full board), on the road to St Georges, with the more basic, activity-oriented **Quimbe Kio** (27-0122; www.quimbekio.com; Le Bourg de Cacao; d €75, hammock spaces €40, with hammock €45, all incl half board;) in Cacao. These two *gîtes* (guesthouses) are also great places to arrange other ecotourism excursions within this region; both also have good restaurants. Bring plenty of water, insect repellent and rain gear. A small refuge hut midway is the best place to overnight (€5 per person). Make reservations and get maps and advice at either *gîte*.

At the time of research there was no public bus to Cacao.

Trésor & Kaw Nature Reserves

The Trésor Nature Reserve is one of French Guiana's most accessible primary rainforests, and the bordering swamps of the Kaw Nature Reserve are excellent for observing caimans (best at night) and spectacular waterfowl like the scarlet ibis. Getting to Trésor is easy enough if you have a car: drive 17km from Roura on the D6 to Trésor's 1.75km **botanical trail** (admission free) with its rich diversity, plenty of deep forest atmosphere and protected wildlife.

However, Kaw, which is partially reached by another 18km along the D6 from Trésor, is nearly impossible to get to unless you're on a tour; reaching the village requires boat transport. JAL Voyages (p737) is a good tour choice. Lodging is on tour operator's floating *carbets* included in the price.

Kourou

POP 24,000

On a small peninsula overlooking the Atlantic Ocean and Kourou River, this small city of modern apartment blocks once existed solely to serve the mainland and offshore penal colonies. Now it seems to exist solely to serve the Centre Spatial Guyanais (Guyanese Space Center), a satellite-construction facility and launchpad that employs thousands of people. A few beaches suitable for sunbathing line the easternmost part of town, but Kourou is mostly a way station for visiting the Space Center and catching a boat to the Îles du Salut. If you must hang out, head to Le Vieux Bourg (Old Town), a great strip for eating and drinking.

Sights

Centre Spatial Guyanais SPACE CENTER

(CSG; 32-6123; www.cnes-csg.fr; tours 7:45am & 12:45pm Mon-Thu, 7:45am Fri) FREE

In 1964 Kourou was chosen to be the site of the Centre Spatial Guyanais because it's close to the equator, is away from tropical storm tracks and earthquake zones, and has a low population density. The center is run by Centre National d'Études Spatiales (CNES; www.cnes.fr) in collaboration with the European Space Agency (ESA; www.esa.int) and Arianespace (www.arianespace.com). Three launchers are now in service, increasing the number of liftoffs to over a dozen per year; this frequency makes it that much easier to coordinate your visit with a launch.

The launch site is the only one in the world this close to the equator (within five degrees), where the earth's spin is significantly faster than further north or south;

this means that the site benefits from the 'slingshot effect,' which boosts propulsion and makes launches up to 17% more energy-efficient than those at sites further away from the equator. Since 1980 two-thirds of the world's commercial satellites have been launched from French Guiana.

Visit the ESA website to find out the launch schedule and reserve a space at one of the observation points within the space center. Email csg-accueil@cnes.fr well ahead of time, providing your full name, address, phone number and age. It's free, but children under 16 are not permitted at sites within 6km of the launchpad and those under eight are not permitted within 12km. You can watch it, reservation-free, with locals at Kourou's beaches or at the Carapa Observation Site, 15km west of the city center.

Space junkies will love the free three-hour tours at the space center, which include a visit to the massive launchpad; phone ahead for reservations and bring your passport. Tour guides sometimes speak English or German; ask when you book.

Musée de l'Espace MUSEUM
(Space Museum; adult/child €5/3, with tour €7/4; 8am-6pm Mon-Fri, 2-6pm Sat) Don't miss the excellent Musée de l'Espace within the space-center complex, with informative displays in English and French. Note that the space center is closed on days after a launch.

Sleeping & Eating

Kourou has pitifully few inexpensive options. Both of the budget places have reception hours from noon to 2pm and 6pm to 8pm every day. Unexciting eating options are scattered around town – expect lots of Chinese food and pizza.

Hotel Ballahou GUESTHOUSE $
(22-0022; http://pagesperso-orange.fr/ballahou; 1-3 Martial; d/apt €60/65;) The best beds are at the welcoming Hotel Ballahou, within short walking distance of the beaches. It can be tricky to find, but the owners will pick you up in town. Reserve well in advance.

Le Gros Bec GUESTHOUSE $
(32-9191; hotel-legrosbec@wanadoo.fr; 56 Rue du De Floch; s/d/tr from €75.50/83.50/92;) Right next to Le Vieux Bourg, it has spacious split-level studios with kitchenettes.

Information

Point Information Tourisme (32-9833; Ponton Balourous; 7:30-9am & 4.30-6pm) Where the boats leave for the Îles du Salut.

Getting There & Away

Buses run four times per day between Kourou and Cayenne (€15, 1¼ hours) and five times to St Laurent (€30, three hours). **Budget** (32-4861; ZI Paracaibo) car rental services both Cayenne and Kourou to enable one-way jaunts, but these include a hefty fee.

Îles du Salut

Known in English as the Salvation Islands, these were anything but that for prisoners sent here from the French mainland by Emperor Napoleon III and subsequent French governments. The three tiny islands (Île du Diable, Île Royale and Île St Joseph), 15km north of Kourou over choppy, shark-infested waters, were considered escape-proof and particularly appropriate for political prisoners, including Alfred Dreyfus. From 1852 to 1947, some 80,000 prisoners died from disease, inhumane conditions and the guillotine on these sad isles.

PAPILLON: ESCAPE ARTIST OR CON MAN?

Of all the prisoners who did hard time on Île du Diable (Devil's Island), only Alfred Dreyfus, the Frenchman wrongly convicted of treason in 1894, achieved anything near the fame of Henry Charrière, who became known – or notorious – for his epic tale of nine remarkable escapes from French Guiana's infamous prison camps. Nicknamed Papillon (Butterfly) for a tattoo on his chest, Charrière claims in his autobiography that after being wrongly convicted of murder he escaped from Îles du Salut by floating toward the mainland on a sack full of coconuts and braved harsh malarial jungles to flee eastward. Fashioning himself into an international man of mystery living among native villagers, he eventually became a Venezuelan citizen and was portrayed by Steve McQueen in a Hollywood version of his life. His published story is widely believed to be a compilation of his own adventures and stories he heard about other convicts' escapades while he was in prison.

Since then, the islands have become a relaxing delight – a place to escape *to*. **Île Royale**, once the administrative headquarters of the penal settlement, has several restored prison buildings, including a restaurant-auberge, while the smaller **Île St Joseph**, with its eerie solitary-confinement cells and guards' cemetery, is overgrown with coconut palms.

The old **director's house** (admission free; 2-4pm Tue-Sun) has an interesting English-language history display; free, two-hour guided tours of Île Royale (usually in French) begin here. Surprisingly abundant wildlife includes green-winged Ara macaws, agoutis, capuchin monkeys and sea turtles. Carry a swimsuit and towel to take advantage of the white-sand beach and shallow swimming holes on St Joseph. The Centre Spatial Guyanais has a huge infrared camera on Île Royale, and the islands are evacuated when there's an eastward launch from the space center.

Sleeping & Eating

It's possible to camp for free along some of the paradisaical areas along the shore of Île Royale (but bring mosquito repellent, nets and rain gear).

★Auberge des Îles du Salut INN **$$**
(33-4530, 32-1100; hammock spaces €10, 'guard rooms' from €60, director's house s/d €165/235) The welcome hasn't improved much since the days of arriving convicts, but the rooms, in the artfully renovated director's house, are something out of a breezy Bogart film. If you want a more Papillon-like experience, you can stay in simpler rooms in old guards' quarters (some with terraces) or sling a hammock in the cleaned-up prison dormitories.

Don't leave without having at least one meal (set menu €26) at the restaurant, which serves the best fish soup (€10) this side of Provence. There are no cooking facilities, but bringing picnic supplies (and plenty of water – it's not potable on the islands) can keep your costs to a minimum.

Getting There & Away

Comfortable, fume-free catamarans and sailboats, including the **Îles du Salut** (32-3381; return trip €48), run by the auberge, and **Tropic Alizés** (25-1010; www.ilesdesalute-guyane.com; return trip €48), take about 1½ to two hours to reach the islands. Most boats to the islands depart around 8am from Kourou's *ponton des pêcheurs* (fishermen's dock, at the end of Av Général de Gaulle) and return between 4pm and 6pm. Usual itineraries stay on Île Royale through lunchtime, then visit Île Saint Joseph in the afternoon before returning to Kourou. Call to reserve 48 to 72 hours in advance, or book with tour operators in Cayenne or Kourou.

St Laurent du Maroni

POP 40,600

St Laurent is an intriguing place with some of the country's finest colonial architecture and, even 60 years after the penitentiary's closure, it's dominated by penal buildings and the ghosts of its prisoners. Along the banks of the Fleuve Maroni (Marowijne River), bordering Suriname, St Laurent is also a place to take a river trip to Maroon and Amerindian settlements. It's set up better for tourism than any other town in the country including Cayenne and, if you've been getting frustrated by the difficulty of travel in French Guiana, you'll find it refreshingly easy to organize activities here.

Sights & Activities

Stop by the tourist office for excellent and free maps for self-guided walking tours as well as information on the full range of activities available in the area.

You can get combination tickets at the tourist office for the Camp de la Transportation and Le Camp de la Relégation prison camps for €10.

★Camp de la Transportation HISTORIC SITE
(tours per person €8; tours 9:30am, 11am, 3pm & 4:30pm Tue-Sat, 9:30am & 11am Sun) The eerie Camp de la Transportation, where prisoners arrived for processing, was the largest prison in French Guiana. Convicts arrived by boatfuls and it took 20 days to cross the Atlantic. The tourist office offers 1½-hour tours; most guides speak minimal English. One cell has Papillon's name engraved, but whether this was really his cell is up for debate.

Fleuve de Maroni RIVER
(half-day tours around €45) Explore the Amerindian and Maroon cultures that inhabit the shores of this great river. You'll usually also visit the island of an old leper colony (mentioned in *Papillon*) and take a jungle stroll. The tourist office will know which of the several local river-tour companies have

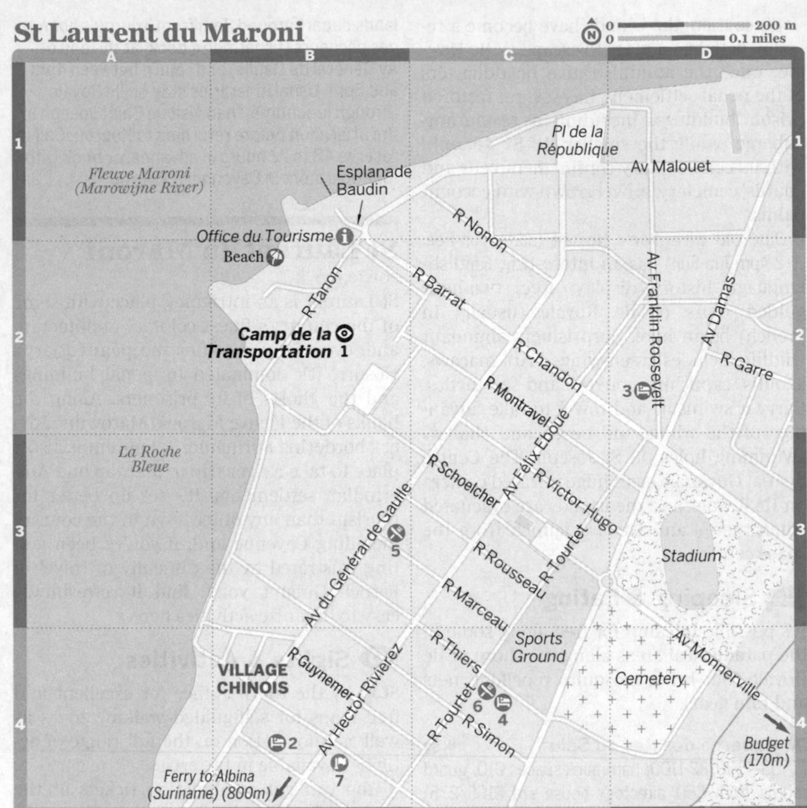

St Laurent du Maroni

Top Sights

Sleeping

Eating

Information

scheduled trips and can direct you to guides who speak English. Agami is a great choice for accommodations.

Longer multi-jaunts usually involve more exploration, a night or more in a hammock in a traditional Amerindian hut and a taste of the local cuisine.

Le Camp de la Relégation HISTORIC SITE
(St Jean; per person €6; ⏲tours 3:30pm Sat & Sun) Le Camp de la Relégation, aka St Jean and 17km from St Laurent, is another abandoned prison camp. It's accessed via two-hour tours offered by the tourist office. These buildings once were home to 'the claws' – light offenders who were given more freedom. As such, the atmosphere here isn't as creepy as French Guiana's other prison-day relics. There may be weekday tours available again in the future.

Sleeping & Eating

Several small grocery stores and a midsize market provide self-catering options. Stalls at the lovely **food and craft market** (⏲5am-1pm Wed & Sat) offer filling *bami goreng* (fried noodles), pho (noodle soup) and French-style quiche, all for around €5.

★Hôtel La Tentiaire HOTEL $
(☎34-2600; tentiaire@wanadoo.fr; 12 Av Franklin Roosevelt; r from €63; ❄📶🏊) The best in the center, Tentiaire has classy rooms with wood accents in a renovated administrative penitentiary building. Some rooms have balconies looking over the little adjacent park and two levels that comfortably sleep a family of four.

Agami LODGE $
(☎34-7403; PK10; hammock spaces with/without hammock €15/10) Dominican Carmen and her husband have traditional Amerindian huts for hammocks in their gardens of grapefruits and bananas. The restaurant serves the best set meal (€20) of traditional Amerindian food found in the Guianas. Reasonably priced, low-key and very non-touristy-feeling canoe tours are also available. Agami is on the road to St Jean, 10km from St Laurent's town center.

Amazonie Accueil LODGE $
(☎41-2350, 34-3612; am.ac@orange.fr; 3 Barrat; hammock space €10, hammock rental €5; 📶) A central and friendly place to hang a hammock (or rent one if you don't have your own). The hammock lodge has a gravel floor and room for five. There's a breakfast area and shared bathrooms.

Hôtel Star HOTEL $
(☎34-1084; 26 Thiers; r from €68; ❄📶🏊) Given Hôtel Star's public-high-school decor and mildewy rooms, only stay here if the Tentiaire is full.

Chez Félicia CREOLE $
(23 Av du Général de Gaulle; mains €12-16; ⏲lunch & dinner, closed Sun nights) This local favorite has tasty Creole cuisine (including bush meat) enjoyed in a homey, checkered-tablecloth setting with friendly staff and happy regulars. Portions are huge and sharing is encouraged.

Tipic Kreol CREOLE $$
(cnr Thiers & Tourtet; mains €13-22; ⏲dinner Mon-Sat, lunch Tue-Sun) Busy and central with a choice of sidewalk seating for people-watching or more intimate inside tables in a plant-filled, polished-wood restaurant area. The food, including bush meat, fish, steaks and salads, is copious and tasty.

ℹ Information

INTERNET ACCESS

Wi-fi is widely available.

MONEY

Banks and ATMs are scattered throughout town but none of them exchange foreign currency or traveler's checks. You'll have to wait to get to Cayenne if you need to exchange money.

TOURIST INFORMATION

Office du Tourisme (☎34-2398; www.ot-saintlaurentdumaroni.fr; Esplanade Baudin; ⏲8am-12:30pm & 2-6pm) Everything there is to do and see in St Laurent can be arranged from here. Plus the staff speak English and give out free maps.

ℹ GETTING TO SURINAME

Getting to the Border

The international quay is about 2km south of central St Laurent, down Av Eboué, and you can walk or take a taxi from town (€4). Be sure to stamp out at customs and immigration at the quay. Note that you can now get Suriname Tourist Cards and visas from Saint-Laurent's efficient **Surinamese Consulate** (26 Catayée; ⏲8am-12.30pm & 2-6pm Mon-Fri), as well as at the one in Cayenne.

At the Border

Private *pirogues* (dugout canoes; €4, 10 minutes) are the easiest option and leave the quay on demand all day, dropping passengers at the Albina ferry dock in Suriname. Otherwise, the car ferry **Bac La Gabrielle** (passenger/car & driver €10/40) crosses the river several times per day in 30 minutes.

Moving On

Share taxis (SR$75, two hours), minibuses (SR$30 to SR$40, 2½ hours) and public buses (SR$8.50, three hours) to Paramaribo meet the boats in Albina.

For information on making this crossing in the opposite direction, see p924.

Getting There & Around

A bus for Cayenne (€30, 250km, four hours) leaves once daily (except Sundays) from the *gare routière* (bus station) at the stadium. Contact the tourist office for times.

Budget (☎34-0294; www.budget-guyane.com; 328 Av Gaston Monnerville; per day from €45) tacks on a €100 fee for one-way rentals to Cayenne.

St Laurent's wide, colonial streets are perfect for wandering around.

Mana & Awala-Yalimopo

About 50km northeast of St Laurent lies the rustic village of Mana (population 600), which boasts a particularly scenic waterfront on the Mana River, considered one of the loveliest and least spoiled rivers in northern South America.

In Mana, stay at the excellent value, riverside **Le Samana Hotel** (☎27-8667; hotelsamana@orange.fr; 18 Aubert; d/studio €60/70; P❄🛜) – which is near the roundabout when you drive into town – and don't miss a chance to dine on French cuisine with a Guianese twist at **Le Buffalo** (☎34-4280; 36 Javouhey; mains €15-25; ⏰9:30am-3pm & 7pm-close Tue-Sun).

There's an ATM at the **post office** (Rue Bastille) in Mana, and the last gas station heading east is at the roundabout at the Mana entrance. There's no other way to get to this area than by car.

Amerindian settlements populate Awala-Yalimopo (population 1200; 22km northwest of Mana) and **Plage Les Hattes**. The latter is one of the world's most spectacular nesting sites for giant leatherback turtles, which can grow up to 600kg; nesting occurs from April to July, and their eggs hatch between July and September. The number of turtles that come ashore is so high that one biologist has likened the scene to a tank battle.

Maison de la Reserve Natural l'Amana (☎34-8404; adult/child €2/free; ⏰8am-noon & 2-6pm Mon, Wed, Fri & Sat, 2-6pm Tue & Thu) has a little museum, information about turtle biology and two nature trails leading from its premises.

Awala-Yalimopo lodging (reserve in advance) includes the simple and clean **L'Auberge de Jeunesse Simili** (☎34-1625; ajs.simili@orange.fr; dm €15, hammock spaces with/without hammock €15/7). Try to reserve a French-Amerindian lunch or dinner at **Yalimalé** (☎34-3432; meals €23; ⏰closed Sun dinner & Mon), although it's rarely open outside of turtle season.

UNDERSTAND FRENCH GUIANA

French Guiana Today

Developments at the Centre Spatial Guyanais (Guyanese Space Center) in Kourou dominate the news in French Guiana. Meanwhile, more and more countries are using Kourou as their spaceport.

In 2010 the population voted against increased autonomy from France, so it seems the country will remain an overseas department with European funds flooding in for some time.

With gold prices increasing, gold mining has become more prevalent around the country, particularly along the eastern Brazilian border. The government has been battling a massive illegal gold-mining industry – which involves the dumping of tons of polluting mercury into French Guiana's once pristine rivers – with some success, but the logistics of managing so much jungle and the long, lonely borders of Suriname and Brazil make it an extremely challenging task.

History

The earliest French settlement was in Cayenne in 1643, but tropical diseases and hostile local Amerindians limited plantation development. After various conflicts with the Dutch and British and an eight-year occupation by Brazil and Portugal, the French resumed control only to see slavery abolished (1848), and the few plantations almost collapsed.

About the same time, France decided that penal settlements in Guiana would reduce the cost of French prisons and contribute to colony development. Napoleon III sent the first convicts in 1852; those who survived their sentences had to remain there as exiles for an equal period of time. With 90% of them dying of malaria or yellow fever, this policy did little to increase the population or develop the colony. French Guiana became notorious for the brutality and corruption of its penal system, which lasted until 1953.

Guiana became an overseas department of France in 1946, and in 1964 work began on the Centre Spatial Guyanais, which has brought an influx of scientists, engineers, technicians and service people from Europe and elsewhere, turning the city of Kourou into a sizable, modern town responsible for 15% of all economic activity. The first Hmong refugees from Laos arrived in 1975 and settled primarily in the towns of Cacao and Javouhey. They now make up about 1.5% of the population and have become vital agricultural producers, growing about 80% of the department's produce.

Successive French governments have provided state employment and billions of euros in subsidies, resulting in a near-European standard of living in urban areas. Rural villages are much poorer, and in the hinterland many Amerindians and Maroons still lead a subsistence lifestyle.

Culture

French Guiana is a tantalizing mélange of visible history, fabulous cuisine and the sultry French language with the vastness and ethnic diversity of Amazonia. Though Cayenne and Kourou enjoy somewhat continental economies, the majority of the populace struggles financially and lives a modest lifestyle.

Guianese people take pride in their multicultural universe borne of multiregional influences. Around 38% of the population claims a mixed African (or Creole) heritage, 8% are French, 8% Haitian, 6% Surinamese, 5% are from the French Antilles, 5% are Chinese and 5% are Brazilian. The remainder is a smattering of Amerindian, Hmong and other South American ethnicities.

The country is predominantly Catholic, but Maroons and Amerindians follow their own religious traditions. The Hmong also tend to be Roman Catholic due to the influence of Sister Anne-Marie Javouhey, who brought them to French Guiana.

Environment

French Guiana borders Brazil to the east and south, while the Maroni and Litani Rivers form the border with Suriname.

The majority of Guianese people live in the Atlantic coastal zone, which has most of French Guiana's limited road network. The coast is mostly mangrove swamp with only a few sandy beaches. The densely forested interior, the terrain of which rises gradually toward the Tumac-Humac Mountains on the Brazilian frontier, is largely unpopulated.

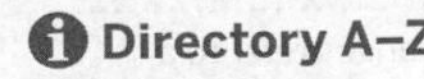

SURVIVAL GUIDE

Directory A–Z

ACCOMMODATIONS

Hotels in French Guiana are generally charmless but comfortable. Most hotels have some English-speaking staff.

The most economical options include long-stay *gîtes* (guesthouses; inquire at tourist offices) in Cayenne, Kourou and St Laurent, and rustic *carbets* (open-air huts) for hammocks.

ACTIVITIES

Bird-watching, hiking and canoeing are popular in French Guiana. Water sports – windsurfing, kitesurfing and sailing – are a major pastime on beaches at Montjoly and Kourou, but renting gear is practically impossible.

BUSINESS HOURS

Many businesses close up shop in the heat of the day; generally hours are 8am to noon and 2pm to 6pm, while restaurants tend to serve from noon to 2pm and again from 7pm to 10pm or later. The country stops on Sunday and sometimes Monday, just about everywhere. Nightclubs and bars open at around 10pm.

ELECTRICITY

Plugs are three-pronged European. Currents are 220/127V, 50 Hz.

EMBASSIES & CONSULATES

Brazilian Embassy (29-0010; 444 Chemin St Antoine, Cayenne) Off Rue de Baduel.

Dutch Honorary Consulate (23-7756; consulat-pays-bas@wanadoo.fr; 9 Lotissement les Nénuphares, Montjoly) Off the main highway toward the airport.

Surinamese Consulate (28-2160; cg.sme.cay@wanadoo.fr; 3 Av Léopold Héder, Cayenne; 8:30am-5:30pm Mon-Fri) Often busy, but if you're lucky you can get a tourist card issued within a few minutes. There's a smaller consulate in St Laurent du Maroni (p745) that's less busy and offers the same services.

SLEEPING PRICE RANGES

The following price ranges refer to a double room with bathroom outside of Carnaval (which runs from January to February or March). Unless otherwise stated, all taxes are included.

$ less than €85

$$ €85 to €150

$$$ more than €150

FOOD PRICE RANGES

The following price ranges refer to a standard main course, including service.

$ less than €12

$$ €12 to €20

$$$ more than €20

UK Consulate (☎31-1034; 16 Av Monnerville, Cayenne)

HEALTH

Chloroquine-resistant malaria is present in the interior, and French Guiana is considered a yellow-fever-infected area. If you need a vaccination while here, contact the **Centre de Prévention et de Vaccination** (☎30-2585; Rue des Pommes Rosas, Cayenne; ⏰8:30am-noon Mon & Thu). Excellent medical care is available, but few doctors speak English. Water is fine in bigger towns; drink bottled or boiled water elsewhere.

LANGUAGE

The official language is French and most people speak it fluently. Creole is spoken casually by the Creole population, while French Guianese is a mixture of Creole and other languages. Otherwise, the Hmong population speak Hmong, there are several Amerindian dialects spoken by the indigenous population, and along the Suriname border many Maroons speak Sranan Tongo (the language of Suriname).

MONEY

French Guiana is one of the most expensive regions in South America, in part because it uses the euro and imports many goods from France. The only *cambios* for currency exchange are in Cayenne, but *guichets automatiques* (ATMs) are found in most midsized to large towns.

Credit cards are widely accepted, and you can get Visa or MasterCard cash advances at *guichets automatiques*, which are on the Plus and Cirrus networks. Eurocard and Carte Bleu are also widely accepted.

POST

The postal service is very reliable, although all mail is routed through France. To receive mail in French Guiana, it's best to have the letters addressed to France but using the French Guianese postal code.

PUBLIC HOLIDAYS

New Year's Day January 1

Ash Wednesday February/March

Good Friday/Easter Monday March/April

Labor Day May 1

Bastille Day July 14

All Saints' Day November 1

All Souls' Day November 2

Armistice (Veterans' Day) November 11

Christmas Day December 25

SAFE TRAVEL

Larger towns warrant caution at night. Crime and drug trafficking have increased throughout the country in recent years, and you'll often find customs roadblocks on coastal routes. Both locals and foreigners may be searched.

Locals hitchhike around Cayenne and west toward St Laurent, but it's riskier for travelers, who may be seen as money-laden targets. Never hitchhike at night or on the road between Régina and St Georges, which is more dangerous and remote.

TELEPHONE

Digicel SIM cards are available in Cayenne, Kourou and St Laurent for €20 including €5 of credit. There are no area codes in French Guiana.

VISAS

Passports are obligatory for all visitors, except those from France. Visitors should also have a yellow-fever vaccination certificate. Australian, New Zealand, Japanese, EU and US nationals, among others, do not need a visa for stays up to 90 days.

Those who need visas should apply with two passport photos at a French embassy and be prepared to show an onward or return ticket. Officially, all visitors, even French citizens, should have either onward or return tickets.

Getting There & Away

AIR

All international passengers must fly through Cayenne's Félix Eboué International Airport (p739).

Air Caraïbes (☎29-3636; www.aircaraibes.com; Centre de Katoury, Rte Rocade) Flights to Paris. Rte Rocade is off the D18 on the way into Cayenne.

Air France (☎29-8700; www.airfrance.gf; 17 Lalouette, Cayenne) Flies to Paris, Fort-de-France, Pointe-à-Pitre and Miami.

Air Guyane (☎29-3630; www.airguyane.com; Félix Eboué International Airport) Flies to Saül and other destinations within French Guiana as well as Paramaribo.

Suriname Airways (www.flyslm.com; airport) Flights to Belem and Paramaribo.

BOAT

From St Laurent du Maroni (in the west), boats and a car ferry head to Suriname, and there are boats (and a nonfunctioning bridge that may

DEPARTURE TAX

For flights to any international destination (besides Paris, which is considered a domestic flight), the departure tax (US$20) is included in the ticket price.

open eventually) from St Georges de l'Oyapock (in the east) to Brazil.

Getting Around

Getting around French Guiana without your own wheels is much more difficult and costly than in mainland France, where public transport and hitchhiking are more common. Even though renting a car might blow your budget, it's probably the most cost-efficient way to cruise the country.

AIR

From Cayenne, small planes operated by Air Guyane fly to Saül.

BOAT

Tours often use river transport, but individuals can try to catch a boat at Kaw and St Laurent. Catamarans sail to the Îles du Salut.

CAR

Although most roads are in exceptional condition, some secondary and tertiary roads can be bad in the rainy season – have a spare tire, spare gas and spare time. If you are traveling in a group, renting a car (from €35 per day) may actually save money. An International Driving Permit is recommended but not legally required. You must be at least 21 years old to rent.

Guyana

Includes ➡

Best Adventures

➡ Dadanawa Ranch (p763)
➡ Kaieteur Falls (p759)
➡ Saddle Mountain (p763)
➡ Bushmasters (p762)

Best Wildlife Encounters

➡ Caiman House (p761)
➡ Shell Beach turtles (p759)
➡ Rewa Eco-Lodge (p761)
➡ Karanambu Ranch (p761)

Why Go?

Few places on the planet offer raw adventure as authentic as densely forested Guyana. Although the country has a troubled history of political instability and inter-ethnic tension, underneath the headlines of corruption and economic mismanagement is a joyful and motivated mix of people who are turning the country into the continent's best-kept ecotourism destination secret.

Georgetown, the country's crumbling colonial capital, is distinctly Caribbean with a rocking nightlife, great places to eat and an edgy market. The interior of the country is more Amazonian with its Amerindian communities and unparalleled wildlife-viewing opportunities tucked quietly away from the capital's hoopla. From sea turtle nesting grounds along the country's north coast to riding with *vaqueros* (cowboys) at a ranch in the south, Guyana is well worth the mud, bumps and sweat.

When to Go

Georgetown

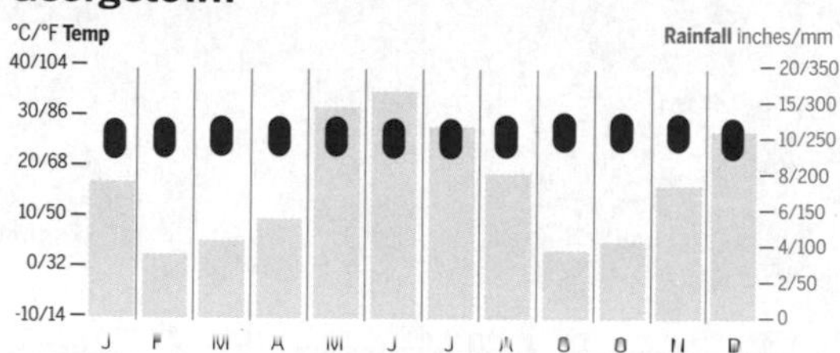

Mid-Nov–Mid-Jan Coastal rainy season and the height of tourism for expat Guyanese.

May–Aug Interior and a second coastal rainy season. Road travel becomes difficult.

Late Dec 'Cashew rains' in the interior – light showers often provide a welcome temperature drop.

Connections

Guyana's only legal border crossings are at Nieuw Nickerie (Suriname) and Bonfim (Brazil); both can be reached by minibus. Venezuela shares much of the country's west coast, but crossing anywhere is illegal and not recommended. Flights from Georgetown, Guyana, go to destinations including Paramaribo, the Caribbean islands and Miami.

ITINERARIES

One Week

Stay in Georgetown for a night then take a day trip by plane to outrageous Kaieteur Falls. Next, fly or travel overland into the interior to stay in the Amerindian village of Surama for two nights. From here take road and river to either Caiman House to help with caiman research or Lethem to explore the nearby Kanuku Mountains, waterfalls and villages.

Two Weeks

Follow the above itinerary but begin your adventure with a night at Iwokrama's Canopy Walkway before going to Surama. After Caiman House spend your last nights at either Rewa Eco-Lodge to search for arapaima (the world's largest scaled fish) or put on your cowboy hat to live with the *vaqueros* at Dadanawa Ranch or Saddle Mountain in South Rupununi.

Essential Food & Drink

- **Pepper pot** A savory Amerindian game-and-cassava stew.
- **Cook-up rice** Beans and rice mixed with whatever else happens to be on hand.
- **Farine** Tasty cassava meal served as an accompaniment like rice.
- **Bake and saltfish** Fried bread and salted cod.
- **El Dorado rum** The 15-year-old drop is considered one of the world's best rums, but most people settle for the less expensive, but undeniably good five-year-old variety.
- **Roti** Soft Indian flatbread, usually wrapped around a curry concoction of meat or vegetables.
- **Ox heel soup** A very popular savory Caribbean soup made with split peas, vegetables, dumplings and ox heels.
- **Banks beer** Brewed in Georgetown; comes in both regular and premium versions, both of which are delicious.

AT A GLANCE

- **Currency** Guyanese Dollar (G$), US Dollars (US$) widely accepted
- **Language** English
- **Money** Not all ATMs accept foreign cards; credit cards rarely accepted
- **Visas** 90 days on arrival for most countries
- **Time** GMT minus four hours

Fast Facts

- **Area** 215,000 sq km
- **Population** 799,613
- **Capital** Georgetown
- **Emergency** ☎ 911
- **Country Code** ☎ 592

Exchange Rates

Australia	A$1	G$150
Canada	C$1	G$156
Euro Zone	€1	G$231
New Zealand	NZ$1	G$136
UK	UK£1	G$312
USA	US$1	G$203

Set Your Budget

- **Budget hotel room** US$35
- **Minibus Georgetown to Annai** US$50
- **Three meals at an eco-lodge** US$22
- **Banks beer** US$2

Resources

- **Guyana Tourism** (www.guyana-tourism.com)
- **Stabroek News** (www.stabroeknews.com)
- **Explore Guyana** (www.exploreguyana.org)

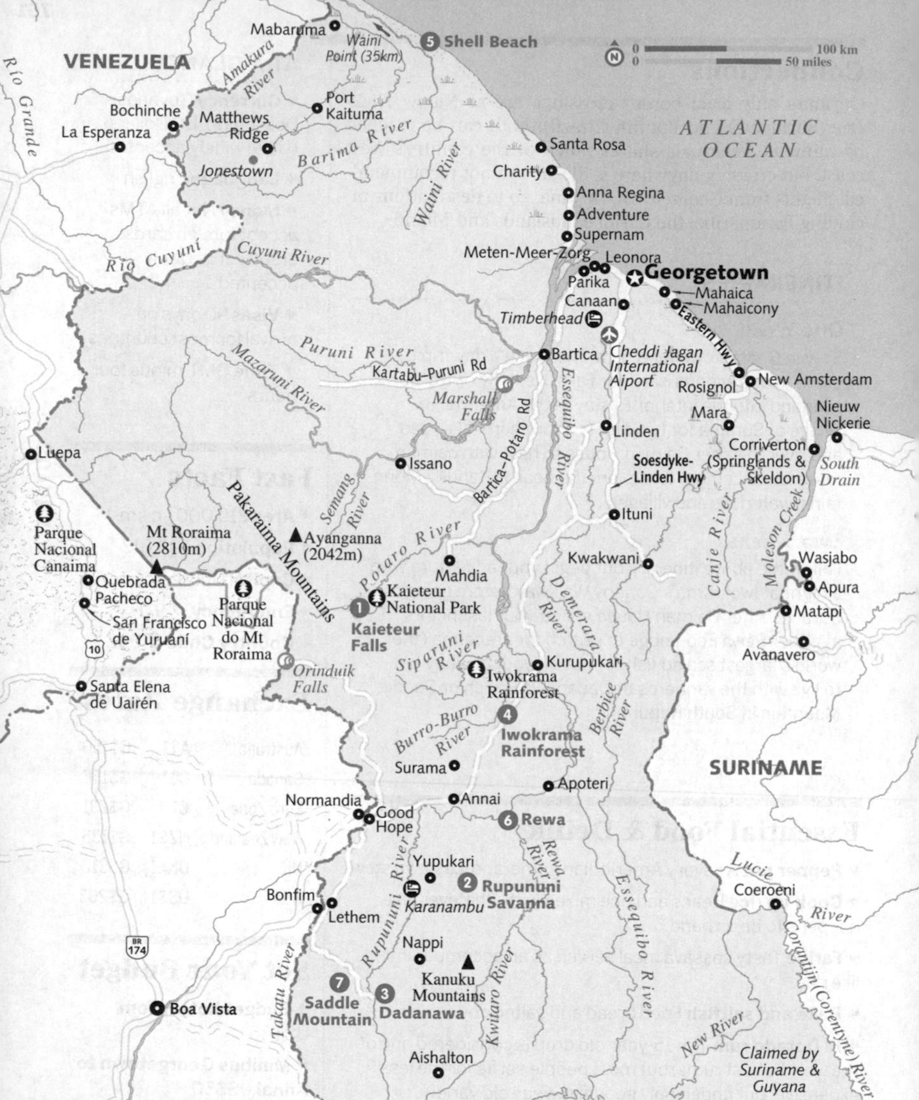

Guyana Highlights

1. Stand on the ledge of the world's highest single-drop fall, **Kaieteur Falls** (p759).

2. Paddle though thriving populations of giant river otters and black caimans in the **Rupununi Savanna** (p761).

3. Go on a cattle drive with local *vaqueros* at **Dadanawa Ranch** (p763).

4. Eco-tour the deep forests of **Iwokrama** (p760).

5. Pass through rice-farming villages and cross rivers teeming with wildlife en route to **Shell Beach** (p759).

6. Catch a glimpse of Nessie-sized arapaima, the planet's biggest freshwater scaled fish, near **Rewa Eco-Lodge** (p761).

7. Horse ride and search for giant anteaters at beautiful **Saddle Mountain** (p763).

Georgetown

POP 239,227

Although the glory days may be over, Georgetown's easy-to-navigate streets, dilapidated architecture and unkempt parks offer a laid-back feel amid real-life chaos. Seeking out the city's riches – historic monuments, a thriving intellectual scene and fabulous restaurants – behind its hard-boiled exterior is part of the adventure.

Sights

Georgetown sits on the east bank of the Demerara River, where the river empties into the Atlantic. A long seawall prevents flooding, and a Dutch canal system drains the town, which is actually 7ft below sea level.

The city is divided into several small districts: Kingston (in the northwest); Cummingsburg, Alberttown, Queenstown and Newtown (in the center); Robbstown, Lacytown, Stabroek and Bourda (south of Church St); Werk-en-Rust, Wortmanville, Charlestown and Le Repentir (further south); Thomas Lands (east); and Kitty (further east).

The best 19th-century buildings are along Main St and especially along Ave of the Republic, just east of the Demerara River.

St George's Cathedral CHURCH

(North Rd) The most impressive building in town is the Anglican, Gothic-style St George's Cathedral, said to be the world's tallest wooden building. It was completed in 1892 and was built with a native hardwood called greenheart.

Stabroek Market MARKET

(Water St) One of the city's most prominent landmarks is Stabroek Market, a cast-iron building with a corrugated-iron clock tower. The frenetic and colorful market dates back to the late 1700s, although the current structure was built in 1880. Visiting here is a must but don't bring any valuables and keep a grip on your bag.

Botanical Gardens GARDENS

(Regent Rd) Many bird-watching groups visit Georgetown's botanical gardens as an introduction to Guyana's birdlife. The gardens' **zoo** (www.guyanazoo.org.gy; cnr Regent & Vlissengen Rds; adult/child G$200/100; 7:30am-5:30pm) has a diminishing collection of creatures kept in troublingly small and neglected cages.

Demerara Distillers DISTILLERY

(256-5019; www.theeldoradorum.com; Plantation Diamaon, East Bank Demerara; tours G$3000; tours 9am & 1pm Wed & Thu, or by appointment) One-hour tours take you through the distillery – where you'll see the last operating wooden Coffey still in the world – warehouse, heritage center and gift shop.

Castellani House MUSEUM

(cnr Vlissengen Rd & Homestretch Ave; 10am-5pm Mon-Fri, 2-6pm Sat) FREE This gorgeous wooden building erected in 1877 is home to the National Art Gallery and rotating art exhibits, many by local artists.

Promenade Garden GARDENS

(cnr Middle & Carmichael Sts) During daylight hours, the Promenade Garden in Cummingsburg is a quiet place to relax, read and enjoy the flowers. It's peaceful now but was used in the 19th century slave uprising as a public execution area.

City Hall ARCHITECTURE

(cnr Regent Rd & Ave of the Republic) The distinctive neo-Gothic City Hall (1868) has a 75ft tower where colonial-period wives apparently watched for their husbands' ships to come into port. It's one of Georgetown's more striking buildings.

National Library LIBRARY

(cnr Ave of the Republic & Church St; 8:30am-5:30pm Mon-Fri, 9am-1pm Sat) Andrew Carnegie built the National Library in 1909. Go inside to find a collection of old books.

National Museum MUSEUM

(Museum of Guyana; cnr North Rd & Hincks St; 9am-5pm Mon-Fri, to noon Sat) FREE An old-fashioned institution documenting the nation's cultural, social and political history via some odd artifacts and very old stuffed critters.

Walter Roth Museum of Anthropology MUSEUM

(61 Main St; 8am-4:30pm Mon-Fri) FREE A small museum in a breezy old building with lots of Amerindian items from Guyana's nine tribes.

Tours

Although it's possible (and adventurous) to visit the interior of Guyana independently, most visitors go with a tour. Tours can make your life a lot easier and save you lots of time but they will also cost much more money.

Wilderness Explorers ADVENTURE TOUR
(☎227-7698; www.wilderness-explorers.com; 141 4th St) A long-running, reliable company with tons of itinerary choices all around the country, including specialty tours such as fishing and remote trekking.

Evergreen Adventures Inc ADVENTURE TOUR
(☎222-8053, 222-8050; www.evergreenadventuresgy.com; Ogle Aerodrome, Ogle, ECD) Puts together superb customized trips, and is run by the same company that owns Trans Guyana Airways, so it's a reliable choice for

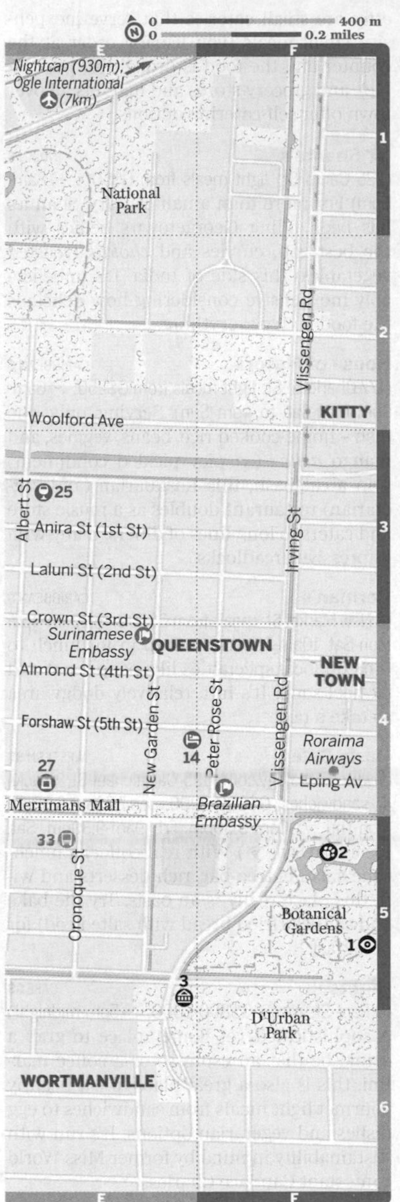

booking flights with lodges all around the country.

Rainforest Tours ADVENTURE TOUR
(☎231-5661; www.rftours.com; Lot 5, Ave of the Republic) Frank Singh's Rainforest Tours arranges an adventurous five-day overland journey to Kaieteur Falls (G$176,000).

Georgetown

Sights
1 Botanical Gardens F5
2 Botanical Gardens Zoo F5
3 Castellani House E5
4 City Hall B5
5 National Library B4
6 National Museum A4
7 Promenade Garden B3
8 St George's Cathedral B4
9 Stabroek Market A5
10 Walter Roth Museum of Anthropology B3

Activities, Courses & Tours
11 Rainforest Tours B5
12 Wilderness Explorers D4

Sleeping
13 Cara Lodge D4
14 Rainforest B&B E4
15 Rima Guest House B3
16 Sleepin Guesthouse D4
17 Sleepin International Hotel B6
18 Tropicana Hotel C4

Eating
19 Brasil Churrascaria & Pizzaria C5
20 German's A3
21 House of Flavors C5
22 New Thriving A4
23 Oasis Café B4
24 Shanta's C3

Drinking & Nightlife
25 704 Sports Bar E3
26 Palm Court A3

Shopping
27 Austin's Book Services E4

Information
28 DHL D4
29 Iwokrama Centre for Rainforest Conservation and Development Office B2
30 Ministry of Home Affairs B6
31 UPS C3

Transport
32 Caribbean Airlines B5
33 Carly's E5
34 Suriname Airlines B2

Sleeping

Unless otherwise noted, all the following charge a 5% service fee when accepting credit cards.

Rima Guest House GUESTHOUSE $
(225-7401; rima@networksgy.com; 92 Middle St; s/d/tr G$5500/6500/9000;) This backpackers' favorite is a family-run place with giant rooms and shared bathrooms in a large colonial house. The owners are friendly and helpful. Cash only.

Sleepin International Hotel HOTEL $
(227-3446; www.sleepininternationalhotel.com; 24 Brickdam St; r with fann G$8300, air-con G$12,500-20,700;) Sleepin has two locations in town; this is the flashier choice with a pool and big restaurant. Rooms are clean, modern and bright and service is professional.

Sleepin Guesthouse GUESTHOUSE $
(231-7667; www.sleepinguesthouse.com; 151 Church St; r with fan G$7300, air-con G$9300-15,500) Centrally located with clean, modern, great-value rooms with hot water and TVs.

Tropicana Hotel GUESTHOUSE $
(592 Hub; 226-4760, 226-4444; www.the592hub.com; 177 Waterloo St; d without/with bathroom from G$7200/8200;) Better known as Jerries and under new ownership in 2015, this Wild West–feeling hotel/restaurant/bar was getting a makeover at the time of research, including better sound-proofing in the rooms and more professional management – but it still promised its old boisterous ways.

★ **Rainforest B&B** B&B $$
(227-7800; www.rainforestbbguy.com; 272 Forshaw St; s/d/t G$14,500/18,600/22,800;) Somewhere between an art gallery and a botanical garden, this grand home with four guestrooms is an oasis from Georgetown's chaos, and yet it's also conveniently located just a few minutes' walk from it all. Charming hosts Saeyeda and Jerry are dedicated to animal welfare, the arts and making sure their guests are fed a delicious breakfast.

Cara Lodge HOTEL $$$
(225-5301; www.carahotels.com; 294 Quamina St; d from G$23,000;) Something about the gingerbread details and art-adorned corridors make this feel like a hideaway for glamorous film stars – even though the rooms are small and plain. There's an old-fashioned ballroom, a patio bar around a 100-year-old mango tree, and a classy, rich-and-famous-worthy restaurant downstairs.

Eating

Some of the best food in the Guianas can be had for a few coins in Georgetown. *Snackettes* are small eateries that serve inexpensive small meals (you usually order at the counter and the food is brought to your table), and grocery stores and markets all over town offer self-catering options.

★ **Shanta's** INDIAN $
(225 Camp St; light meals from G$500; 8am-6pm) For more than a half century, Shanta's has been filling Georgetown's bellies with the best roti, curries and *chokas* (roasted vegetables) this side of India. It's unbelievably inexpensive considering how delicious the food is. Try everything.

House of Flavors CARIBBEAN $
(177 Charlotte St; light meals from G$250; 6am-9pm Mon-Sat, to 4pm Sun) Serving only one dish – home-cooked rice, beans, veggies, and mango *achar* (a spicy pickled condiment) – in a calabash, this Rastafarian (and vegetarian) restaurant doubles as a music store and caters to long lines of diners, many with impressive dreadlocks.

German's CARIBBEAN $
(8 New Market St; meals from G$500; 10am-4pm Mon-Sat, 10am-3pm Sun) Stop in for lunch to dine on local specialties like pepper pot and ox heel soup. It's in a relatively dodgy area so take a taxi.

Oasis Café WESTERN $$
(www.oasiscafegy.com; 125 Carmichael St; snacks & sandwiches G$600-2000; 7:30am-6:30pm Mon-Thu, 7:30am-8:30pm Fri, 9am-9:30pm Sat, 10am-6pm Sun;) With real coffee, a lunchtime salad/entrée bar, rich desserts and wi-fi, this place really is an oasis. Try the bake and saltfish (fried bread with salted cod) for breakfast.

Nightcap CAFE $$
(8 Pere St; meals G$800-3000; 5pm-midnight) A sophisticated yet homey place to grab a drink, be that an espresso or a coffee martini, this is also a great place to eat healthy gourmet light meals from sandwiches to egg dishes and vegetarian options. It's run with sustainability in mind by former Miss World contestant Candace Charles.

New Thriving CHINESE $$
(cnr Main & Hope Sts; mains G$1100-2500; 10:30am-9:30pm) Extremely popular, central and with more upscale decor than most Georgetown favorites, we found the mediocre Chinese food here overpriced but locals never cease to recommend it.

Brasil Churrascaria & Pizzaria BRAZILIAN $$$
(208 Alexander St; per kilo G$4000, all-you-can-eat G$3500; ⌚11am-9pm Mon-Sat) If you're a big meat eater, head here. Start with the salad and buffet bar, then servers carve perfectly grilled meats onto your plate as they come off the grill. Great pizzas too.

Drinking & Entertainment

East of Newtown, Sheriff St is a raucous parade of bars, discos and nightclubs with an equally raucous clientele plying the streets; it might be the action you're looking for, but it's not Georgetown's safest strip. A recent law stops the fun at 2am, which many locals are not very happy about.

704 Sports Bar BAR
(1 Lamaha St; ⌚noon-2am) Named for the lucky gold mining claim that funded it to life, this new hot spot has a sports bar on the 1st floor and a very popular nightclub upstairs.

Palm Court BAR
(Main St; ⌚nightly to 2am) At over 70 years old, one of Georgetown's oldest bars still pulls an impressive crowd. It's a good place to start the night and grab a bite to eat. There's a varying cover charge on DJ nights.

Shopping

You can find local handicrafts at the kiosks in Hibiscus Craft Plaza, in front of the post office.

Austin's Book Services BOOKS
(190 Church St; ⌚8am-4pm Mon-Fri, to 1pm Sat) Offers the widest selection of books and maps.

Information

DANGERS & ANNOYANCES

Although Georgetown has more crime than other cities in the Guianas, you can safely explore the city by using a good dose of precaution: be aware of your surroundings, don't wear jewelry or expensive-looking clothes or carry more cash than you need when walking. Also, you should avoid deserted streets, especially on the weekends, and use taxis, which are inexpensive, to get around at night.

INTERNET ACCESS

Wi-fi is widely available and generally free. Internet cafes can be found around Georgetown with rates of around G$200 to G$400 per hour.

MEDICAL SERVICES

St Joseph's Mercy Hospital (☎227-2072; 130-132 Parade St) This private clinic and hospital has a 24-hour emergency room and pharmacy.

MONEY

Scotiabank (104 Carmichael St; ⌚8am-6pm Mon-Fri) The most reliable bank; accepts international ATM cards and processes credit-card advances. There are other branches, including at the Pegasus Hotel (least busy), and an ATM on the corner of Robb St and Ave of the Republic.

POST

Post Office (☎225-7071; Robb St) This central postal hub can be hectic.

TELEPHONE

A SIM card with **Digicel** (☎toll free 100; www.digicelguyana.com; cnr Fort & Barrack Sts) or **GT&T Cellink** (☎225-1513; www.cellinkgy.com; 79 Brickdam St), Guyana's two mobile carriers, costs G$1000, and minutes cost from G$10. Technically you need proof of residency to get a SIM card, but a friendly clerk may let that pass. Bring your passport.

TOURIST INFORMATION

Tourism & Hospitality Association of Guyana (THAG; ☎225-0807; 157 Waterloo St; ⌚8am-5pm Mon-Fri) Publishes the useful *Explore Guyana* guide and has maps and pamphlets.

Getting There & Away

AIR

Several international flights arrive and depart from Cheddi Jagan International Airport, 41km south of Georgetown. Domestic and many regional international flights run out of Ogle International Airport closer to town.

Air Services Limited (☎222-4357; www.aslgy.com; Ogle Aerodrome) Regular flights to Lethem (G$46,600), Kaieteur (G$30,000) and several other destinations in the interior.

Caribbean Airlines (☎1800 744 2225; www.caribbean-airlines.com; 91-92 Ave of the Republic, Georgetown; ⌚8am-3:30pm Mon-

GETTING INTO TOWN

The Timeri bus (G$500, one hour) services Cheddi Jagan International Airport to/from the Timeri Bus Park behind the Parliament Building in central Georgetown; the bus is safe enough, but at night a taxi (G$5000) is a much wiser choice. For early morning flights from Cheddi Jagan International Airport, make taxi arrangements the day before.

GETTING TO SURINAME

Getting to the Border

For minibus service from Georgetown to the border or all the way to Paramaribo (G$8000, nine to 12 hours), call **Champ** (☎629-6735), who picks up at around 5am.

At the Border

The Canawaima ferry to Suriname (one-way/round-trip per person G$3200/4200, 25 minutes, 10am and noon daily) leaves from Moleson Creek and crosses the Corentyne River to the Suriname border at South Drain, 45 minutes south of Nieuw Nickerie. Get to the ferry no later than one hour before departure to stamp passports and go through customs control. There are no border-crossing fees and immigration remains open to coincide with boat arrivals and departures.

Most nationalities will need a Suriname Tourist Card or visa from a Surinamese consulate or embassy to enter Suriname.

Moving On

Minibuses to Nieuw Nickerie and Paramaribo meet the ferry on the Suriname side. It's best to change your Guyanese currency before leaving Guyana in case no one's buying across the river. Make sure you know your rates before you make the exchange.

Suriname is an hour ahead of Guyana; remember to set your watch *ahead* one hour. For information on making this crossing in the opposite direction, see p923.

Fri, 8:30am-noon Sat) Flights to Trinidad with connecting flights to many more destinations.

Roraima Airways (☎225-9648; www.roraimaairways.com; R8 Eping Ave, Bel Air Park) Charter flights mainly to the interior.

Suriname Airlines (☎225-4249, Cheddi Jagan airport office 261-2292; www.flyslm.com; cnr Duke & Barrack sts) Flights to Paramaribo, Orlando and Miami.

Trans Guyana Airways (TGA; ☎222-2525; http://transguyana.net; Ogle Aerodrome) Services the most flights to the most destinations within the country (around 35), as well as daily code-share flights with Gum Air to Paramaribo in Suriname (G$46,620, one hour). Has the best safety reputation.

BUS & MINIBUS

Economical, cramped minibuses to destinations along the coast depart from Stabroek Market and have no fixed schedules (they leave when full). Fares around Georgetown cost G$80 to G$300.

Getting Around

CAR

Dolly's Auto Rental (☎225-7126; www.dollysautorental.com; 272 Bissessar Ave) and **Sleepin Guesthouse** (p756) rent cars (G$7000 per day), but with bad roads full of farm animals and crazy drivers, you may as well leave the driving to others.

TAXI

For simplicity and safety, taxis are *the* way to get around central Georgetown; trips around the center cost G$300 to G$500 or so, even at night. Have your hotel call a reliable cab company. If you need to flag down a taxi, use only registered ones painted yellow (all registered taxi license plates start with a 'H') and try to find ones with a company logo on the side.

Berbice

The Eastern Hwy follows the coastal plain from Georgetown to the Suriname border. The road travels through town after unremarkable town, passing potholes, suicidal dogs, unfenced livestock and the resultant roadkill. At **Rosignol**, about two hours' drive from Georgetown, you cross the Berbice River to **New Amsterdam** via a floating bridge.

The whole coastal region stretching from Rosignol to Corriverton is collectively known as Berbice, and Corriverton is actually the two small towns of **Springlands** and **Skeldon** on the west bank of the Corentyne River, bordering Suriname.

Corriverton's main street, Public Rd, is a lively strip with mosques, churches, a Hindu temple, cheap hotels, eateries and bars. Brahman cattle roam around the market like the sacred cows of India. If you need to stay the night, try the **Ritz** (☎335-3605; 171 Springlands; r G$4600-8000; ❄📶), which is clean and easy to find.

The little towns have hidden (although run-down) colonial buildings. The quintessential Berbice activity, however, is taking a ride in a Tapir, the only car ever to be manufactured in Guyana. Named after one of the most awkward and lethargic animals in the wild, these boxy cars are proudly decorated by their owners and used as taxis to ferry passengers through and between the towns.

Buses and Tapirs run from Public Rd in Corriverton to New Amsterdam and, the other way, to the Suriname ferry at Moleson Creek. Be sure to depart Corriverton before 10am to reach the noon ferry.

Northwest Coast

Boats travel from **Parika** on the coastal highway southward to the lively mining town of **Bartica** (population 11,100). Near Bartica, the Essequibo meets the Mazaruni River and Marshall Falls, a series of rapids and a jungle waterfall reached by a short hike. **Arrowpoint Nature Resort** (☎225-9650; www.roraimaairways.com; per person incl full board & activities from G$40,000; 📶) is pricey but has tons of activities and is in a gorgeous location; from here you can easily access the Amerindian village of **Santa Mission**, a favorite destination for Guyanese who want to appreciate Carib and Arawak customs, such as making cassava bread. Tour operators offer day trips to all of the above places from Georgetown.

The west bank of the Essequibo River can be reached by boat (G$1000, 45 minutes, leaves when full from dawn to dusk) from Parika to **Supernam**. Heading west from the Essequibo, a coastal road passes quaint rice-mill and farming villages to the town of **Charity**, about 50km away. From here you'll need a boat to go further – through bird-filled rivers, mangrove swamps and savannas – to **Shell Beach**, which extends for about 140km along the coast toward the Venezuelan border and is a nesting site for four of Guyana's eight sea turtle species. This is one of the least developed areas of the entire South American coastline; the only human alterations are in the form of temporary fishing huts and small Amerindian settlements. **Waini Point** near the beautiful town of **Mabaruma** (population 700) is the most spectacular sighting area for the scarlet ibis. Georgetown agencies can help you set up a tour through the area or arrange a flight or boat directly to Mabaruma.

Kaieteur National Park

This area is home to one of the world's most impressive waterfalls, a tiny population of Amerindians and the endless biodiversity of the Guiana shield, a massive geological formation covered in rainforest and savanna. It has, however, been subject to the strategies of government and mining interests to limit its boundaries since it first became a park in 1929; after several expansions and contractions, it now encompasses 627 sq km and is actively protected by the government – largely because the park's tourism potential depends on it being intact.

Sights

★Kaieteur Falls WATERFALL

(www.kaieteurpark.gov.gy) You may have been to Salto Ángel or Iguazú Falls, seen Niagara or not even be that interested in waterfalls, but it doesn't matter: go to Kaieteur Falls. Watching 30,000 gallons of water shooting over a 250m cliff (allegedly making this the world's highest single-drop falls) in the middle of an ancient jungle with few tourists in sight is a once-in-a-lifetime experience.

Depending on the season, the falls are from 76m (250ft) to 122m (400ft) wide. The trail approaching the falls is home to scarlet Guiana cock-of-the-rock birds, and miniscule golden frogs (best seen in the rainy season and/or in the morning) that produce a potentially fatal poison.

Sleeping

Lodge LODGE

(per person G$3600) It's possible to stay in a rustic lodge at Kaieteur Falls, bookable through the **National Parks Commission** (☎226-8082, 226-7974). You'll have to bring your own food and may have to pay extra freight charges on your flight if you're carrying over 10kg total.

Getting There & Away

Several Georgetown tour operators offer day trips with small planes; make early inquiries and be flexible. The cheapest option to Kaieteur only is to book directly with **Air Services Limited** (p757), which usually runs two flights per day that allow you to spend two hours, with a guide, at the falls. Return flights cost G$30,000. Most tour companies also offer charter tours where you can choose to add in Orinduik Falls (with massive falls cascading over several levels where you can bathe) or a stop at Baganara

Resort (on an island with white-sand beaches in the Essequibo River), for an additional cost.

More adventurous options include a five-day overland journey to Kaieteur (from G$176,000) through **Rainforest Tours** (p755).

Iwokrama Rainforest

The **Iwokrama Centre for Rainforest Conservation and Development**, established in 1996, is a unique living laboratory for tropical forest management and socioeconomic development for Amerindians. Amid 3710 sq km of virgin rainforest, this exceptional region is home to the world's highest recorded number of fish and bat species, South America's largest cat (jaguar), the world's largest freshwater scaled fish (arapaima), and the world's largest otters, river turtles, anteaters, snakes, rodents, eagles and caimans – but the wildlife can be difficult to spot.

Iwokrama's Georgetown **office** (☎225-1504; www.iwokrama.org; 77 High St) arranges transportation and accommodations; stay in riverside cabins or a more economical hammock camp at the **field station** (Iwokrama base camp; cabins s/d G$24,000/30,000, hammocks G$5000). Full board is an additional G$10,000 per day. Mix and match tours can include visits to Amerindian villages, forest walks and nighttime caiman-spotting, with each activity costing between G$2000 and G$20,000.

Only 60km south of the field station, Iwokrama's **Canopy Walkway** (www.iwokramacanopywalkway.com; day pass G$5000), a series of suspension bridges hoisted 30m above the forest floor, offers bird's-eye views of native greenheart trees, high-dwelling red howler monkeys and lots of birds. Part of the walkway closed recently after being knocked

TRANSPORTATION IN THE INTERIOR

Air

Flights to/from Georgetown leave daily stopping at Annai, Lethem and sometimes Karanambu. Charter flights are available to a few other destinations including the Iwokrama field station. Air Guyana, Air Services Limited and TGA each ply the Georgetown–Annai–Lethem–Georgetown route twice a day – only the TGA service will stop at Karanambu on the morning flight and only on demand. One way to any destination costs G$25,000.

Boat & 4WD

If you book your trip on a tour or directly through lodges, they will shuttle you around in their high-cost overland 4WDs and boats. The lodges aren't trying to pillage you – it's the cost of fuel in the Rupununi that makes these options so expensive, and yet most people choose to travel this way for convenience. Sample one-way fares for a 4WD for up to four people are: Annai to Lethem G$56,000; Annai to Karanambu G$90,000; and Lethem to Dadanawa G$50,000. Travel times are highly variable, depending on the season. Traveling in groups can ease the expense.

Motorbike

If you're not in a group, getting around by motorbike is a much cheaper option. This entails finding a local willing to take you (lodges will help with this), having small enough luggage to strap on the back of a motorbike or wear on your back, and having a very sturdy rear end (expect *very* bumpy rides). Sample costs per person are: Lethem to Dadanawa G$12,000; and Caiman House to Karanambu G$8000.

Minibus

Georgetown–Lethem–Georgetown minibuses (daily, may be cancelled during the wet season) leave Georgetown – we suggest **Carly's** (☎616-5984; cnr Robb & Oronoque Sts; one-way Georgetown–Lethem G$10,000) – and Lethem at 6pm and take around 16 hours. The long, bumpy, dusty voyage involves stopping to sleep at a hammock camp for a few hours (hammock rental available for G$500), a 6am ferry at Kurukupari Crossing, and several police checkpoints; bring warm clothes, your passport and patience. The buses stop along the main road on demand and pick up also as long as they have empty seats (which they often do not – ask your lodging to call and reserve a spot ahead of time for any stop besides Lethem and Georgetown).

down by a tree, but will hopefully be repaired by the time you read this book; the rest of the walkway remains open. To be ready for the early morning canopy action, sleep at **Atta Rainforest Camp** (www.iwokramacanopywalkway.com; s/d per person G$44,000/36,500), which offers comfortable brick cabins about 500m from the canopy walkway. Full board is an additional G$12,000 per day.

North Rupununi

The Rupununi Savannas are Africa-like plains scattered with Amerindian villages, small 'islands' of jungle and an exceptional diversity of wildlife. Rivers full of huge caimans and the world's largest water lilies *(Victoria amazonica)* cut through plains of golden grasses and termite mounds, and a mind-boggling array of birds fly across the sky. On a human level, the Rupununi feels like a tight-knit, safe, small town spread over 104,400 sq km.

The heart of the north Rupununi is at **Annai** (population 300), a crossroads of Amerindian peoples with a police station and an airstrip at Rock View Lodge.

Sleeping

A phone tower in Annai means great phone reception. There is also internet and wi-fi at many of the lodges, so reservations can be made through their websites (but it still may take days to hear back from them).

Michelle's Island LODGE $

(639-5716; per person G$3000) A beautiful, private jungle island right on the Essequibo River. Rustic but clean huts have decent mattresses, mosquito nets, iffy electricity and some running water. Lots of activities are offered (from G$7000), including jungle walks, village visits, fishing and caiman-spotting tours, and delicious local and East Indian meals are G$1000 each. Michelle is a delight. No internet – contact by phone only.

Rewa Eco-Lodge LODGE $

(www.rewaguyana.com; hammock/s/d from G$3000/4200/6000;) Deep in the jungle 80km up the Rupununi River, this lovely lodge sits beside a river and is a short walk from the beautiful, tiny, thatched village of Rewa. The specialty here is catch-and-release fishing and arapaima spotting, but there are also hikes and cultural village visits. Full board is an additional G$8400 per person per day.

Pakaraima Mountain Inn LODGE $

(658-6523, 662-7235; sebastian.m.defreitas@hotmail.com; Annai; hammock/bed G$3000/7500;) Beautiful, simple lodge just off the main road 20 minutes west of Annai. Offers rooms, hammock space and meals (G$1500 to G$2000), all with beautiful views over the savanna.

Surama LODGE $$

(www.suramaecolodge.com; huts per person incl full board & activities from G$37,500;) The Amerindian village of Surama will impress you with its dignified approach to tourism. Local guides lead visitors through the village to learn about daily life, including cassava processing and medicinal plant usage. There are plenty of hiking and dugout canoe trips on offer too. Digs are in a simple yet beautiful lodge about 1km from the village.

Caiman House LODGE $$

(www.rupununilearners.com; r per person incl full board G$20,000;) This lovely lodge with spacious, ranch-style rooms is in the heart of the lively Amerindian village of Yupikari. The lodge was started as a caiman research center and now tourism is the key to financing the ongoing study. Take part in nighttime (dry season only) 'caimaning,' where you help catch caiman to tag. Walks and river trips are also available.

Rock View Lodge LODGE $$$

(226-5412; www.rockviewlodge.com; Annai; s/d incl full board G$37,300/62,100;) Hummingbirds may flit through the windows of your room at this elegant hacienda-style retreat at the scenic Annai airstrip. Find cheaper, equally plush bungalows, basic hammock spaces and cheap meals (G$700 to G$1200) at nearby Oasis (p762), which is under the same management (although its roadside setting isn't nearly as nice). Both places arrange walks, village visits and horse riding.

Karanambu Ranch LODGE $$$

(www.karanambutrustandlodge.com; bungalow per person incl meals & activities G$41,500;) About 60km south by road and boat from Annai, extremely welcoming Salvador and Andrea continue the work of the legendary Diane McTurk, who devoted her life to saving giant river otters. Accommodations are in spacious ranch-meets-Amerindian-style huts, and activities range from bird-watching to giant anteater tracking.

South Rupununi

The biggest settlement in the Rupununi is at **Lethem**, a dusty *vaquero* town on the Brazilian border. In past years it experienced growth thanks to Brazilian shoppers who crossed the bridge for cheap groceries, but with the currency exchange becoming less favorable for Brazilians, the flood of shoppers is slowing down. Other than bargain hunters, the region attracts gold miners and a collection of eccentric characters fanatical about wildlife and conservation. Every Easter, the Rupununi Rodeo in Lethem attracts hundreds of visitors to see the rodeo spectacles with a distinctly Rupununi/Amerindian touch. Local waterfalls, several ranches and a cooperative cashew-processing plant are interesting year-round attractions.

At the time of writing, the nearest ATM that accepted foreign cards was in Bonfim, Brazil.

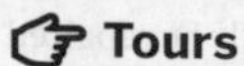

Tours

Bushmasters ADVENTURE TOUR
(☎682-4175; www.bushmasters.co.uk; Lethem) One- and two-week jungle survival courses, as well as cowboy holidays, horse-riding tours and safaris, mostly through the Rupununi.

Sleeping & Eating

The lodges far from Lethem get poor phone reception and no internet, so it can take a while to hear back if you want to make a booking. Plan ahead.

Lethem has a few basic eating options. Your best hunting grounds are around the airstrip.

Takutu Hotel HOTEL $
(☎772-2094; takutuhotel@gmail.com; Takutu Dr, Lethem; d from G$5200; ❄@📶) The best all-rounder in Lethem, Takutu Hotel is popular with traveling Rupununi locals. It has everything from cheap and clean air-con doubles to fancier suites and a *benab*

RUPUNUNI BACKPACKER'S TRAIL

As more options open close to the main public transport arteries, it's becoming easier to see this amazing area on the cheap. This route, all done via the Georgetown–Lethem–Georgetown minibus, can also be done in reverse. Book lodging in advance for best results.

Georgetown–Kurukupari Crossing

After a long night on the minibus, you have two options at this ferry crossing: Michelle's Island (p761), the best budget choice, is right on the Essequibo River complete with swimming hole. Otherwise, the Iwokrama field station (p760) is a quick jump across the river and offers a higher level of comfort and prices.

Kurukupari Crossing–Annai

Only 50km from the Kurukupari Crossing, Annai also has two options. **Oasis** (☎226-5412; www.rockviewlodge.com; bungalow/hammock space G$10,500/1000; 📶) is basically a truck stop but offers cheap hammock lodging, affordable meals and a good, friendly base from which to explore the surrounding area. You may be able to rent motorbikes here. A newer and more scenic option is Pakaraima Mountain Inn (p761), 20 minutes west of Annai with beds or hammock space in a lovely, family-run atmosphere.

Annai–Lethem

Lethem, the biggest settlement in the Rupununi, is 120km down the road on the Brazilian border. Here you can choose to either sling a hammock or stay in pricier rooms at the popular Takutu Hotel, or try out the new but very basic **Rupununi Backpacker Hostel** (☎604-3231; s/d with breakfast G$2000/3000; 📶) right across from the airport.

Around Lethem

There's plenty to do around this dusty and otherwise not-very-appealing *vaquero* town. Options include camping/trekking trips in the nearby Kanuku Mountains (from G$12,500 per person) and day or overnight Amerindian village trips, staying at lesser-visited, small, community-run lodges. Check in at **Visit Rupununi Tourist Information** (☎772-2227; Conservation International (CI) Office; ⏰9:30am-4:30pm Mon-Fri, 9:30am-12:30pm Sat) or **Shirley & Son's Shop** (☎772-2085; ⏰8am-11pm) to find out what's available and to book.

GETTING TO BRAZIL

Crossing the Border

A Brazilian-built bridge – with a cool lane-crossing system that switches from Guyana's left-hand driving to Brazil's right-hand driving – straddles the Takutu River from Lethem on Guyana's side to Bonfim, Brazil, on the other. Stamp out of customs and immigration at the bridge on the Guyana side and stamp into the corresponding office at the Brazil end. There are no fees at the border and the immigration office hours are 7am to 5pm.

Note that American, Canadian and Australian nationals need visas (available in Georgetown – count on a week for processing), and all nationalities need to present their yellow fever certificate. Money changers abound – you can't miss 'em.

Moving On

There are five buses to Boa Vista (R$19, 1¼ hours) between 7am and 2pm daily. The 'Federales' customs officials on the Brazilian side of the bridge are very friendly and can update you on the schedule. From Boa Vista, planes and buses connect to further destinations.

(palm-thatched hut), where you can sling a hammock for G$1000. There's an on-site restaurant and a bar, which can get loud – especially on Wednesday karaoke nights.

Saddle Mountain LODGE $$

(☎604-5600; a.kenyon47@yahoo.com; per person incl meals & activities G$25,000; 📶) This small ranch lodge 80km from Lethem has the most beautiful location in the Rupununi, up on a ridge overlooking the savannas, rivers and mountains. The main activity is horse riding – expect wild rides at a full gallop. Owners Tommy and Joan and their daughters cook up great food and better conversation. Wildlife is everywhere.

Dadanawa Ranch RANCH $$

(www.dadanawaranchguyana.com; hammock/dorm G$5000/12,000, r per person including meals & activities G$33,000) The DuFrietas' remote ranch at the base of the Kanuku Mountains is straight out of *National Geographic*. Extreme treks – tracking harpy eagles, jaguars and the recently rediscovered red siskin finch – complement days partaking in ranch work or even riding on a cattle drive to Lethem. Rooms in the guesthouses are basic with mosquito nets, but have an undeniable cowboy charm to them.

Meals with the hammock/dorm option cost G$1000 for breakfast and G$2000 for dinner – a really great deal.

Manari Ranch LODGE $$

(☎668-2006; manariranch@gmail.com; per person incl meals G$21,000; 📶) This historic family ranch renovated by dynamic, charming Lisa Melville is about 15 minutes from Lethem. It's a comfortable, homey hacienda-style place that's more modern than the other ranches, plus there's a great swimming hole and a supremely laid-back vibe. Tons of activities are on offer, from horse riding to canoe trips.

UNDERSTAND GUYANA

Guyana Today

Guyana is a part of Caricom (Caribbean Community) and has strong relations with Caribbean nations, particularly Trinidad and Tobago and Barbados. Disputes with Venezuela over a maritime area near the border between the two countries is ongoing, however, so relations between the two countries are strained and there's no official border crossing. In 2015 an Exxon oil discovery in this region was estimated to be worth 12 times the current Guyanese economy.

The election of David A Granger to the presidency in 2015, with his anti-money-laundering, constitutional reform and crime fighting agenda, has left many people hopeful for a better future for the country.

Gold and bauxite mining and logging have greatly benefited the top tier of Guyana residents in recent years, although the wealth hasn't trickled down to the masses. Roads are still waiting to be paved and areas of extreme poverty are put in greater perspective by massive housing developments for the nouveau riche. Guyana has been feeling pressures from overseas investors, particularly China, to 'develop resources' – this is often at odds with the country's long-standing dedication to preserving its forests.

History

Both Carib and Arawak tribes inhabited the land that is now Guyana before the Dutch arrived in the late 16th century. Running a plantation economy dependent on African slaves, the Dutch faced a widespread rebellion, known as the Berbice Slave Revolt, in 1763. The rebel leader, Kofi, remains a national hero despite the ultimate failure of the slaves to gain their freedom.

The British took control in 1796, and in 1831 the three colonial settlements of Essequibo, Demerara and Berbice merged to become British Guiana. After the abolition of slavery in 1834, Africans refused to work on the plantations for wages, and many established their own villages in the bush and became known as Maroons. Plantations closed or consolidated because of the labor shortage, but the sugar industry was resurrected with the help of imported, indentured labor from Portugal, India, China and other countries, drastically transforming the nation's demographic.

British Guiana was run very much as a colony until 1953, when a new constitution provided for home rule and an elected government. In 1966 the country became an independent member of the British Commonwealth with the new name, Guyana, and in 1970 it became a republic with an elected president.

For decades after independence, most of the important posts had been occupied by Afro-Guyanese, but more recently Indo-Guyanese have been appointed to influential positions, fueling racial tensions between groups of African and East Indian descent. Cheddi Jagan, Guyana's first elected president, died in office in 1997 and was replaced by his US-born wife Janet, resulting in continued political tension. In 1999 Janet Jagan retired from the presidency on health grounds and named Bharrat Jagdeo her successor.

Delayed elections in 2001 resulted in entire blocks of Georgetown being set ablaze by opposition supporters. The police and protesters clashed in the capital for weeks. Fortunately, violence on this scale has not returned to Georgetown since, but racial tensions continue to be a part of Guyanese politics. However, efforts at tolerance education have made a positive impact on Guyanese youth, and many people acknowledge that more cooperation to end racial conflict is needed.

Guyana's economy relies on commodities exports, especially bauxite but also gold, sugar, rice, timber and shrimp. Indo-Guyanese control most of the small business, while the Afro-Guyanese dominated the government sector until the late '90s, and the current president is Afro-Guyanese.

TRAGEDY AT JONESTOWN

On November 18, 1978, 913 people (including over 270 children) were killed in a mass suicide-murder in a remote corner of Guyana's northwestern rainforest. Since then, Guyana has been sadly associated with this horrific event that became known as the Jonestown Massacre.

In the 1950s, Jim Jones, a charismatic American leader, started a religious congregation in Indiana called the Peoples Temple. With utopian ideas of an egalitarian agricultural community, Jones attracted hundreds of followers, but by the 1960s, after moving his church to San Francisco, he became increasingly paranoid and the Peoples Temple started to resemble a cult. Jones' next move took the congregation to the Guyanese bush, and by 1977 word leaked from escaped members that Jones was running the settlement in questionable ways.

California congressperson Leo Ryan, along with journalists and worried family members, visited Jonestown, where they encountered several frightened Temple members who wanted to leave. Not realizing how dangerous Jones really was, Ryan tried to take several residents with him, only to meet gunfire from Jones' followers on the Jonestown airstrip. Ryan and four others were killed. That night Jones ordered his followers to drink cyanide-laced punch; while many 'drank the Kool-Aid,' others were found shot or with slit throats. Jones either shot himself or ordered someone to do it.

Director Stanley Nelson has provided a modern perspective on this mysterious tragedy in his excellent 2006 documentary *Jonestown: The Life and Death of Peoples Temple*.

Culture

Guyana's culture is a reflection of its colonialist plantation past. African slaves lived under severe conditions that destroyed much – but not all – of their culture. East Indian laborers arrived under better circumstances and managed to keep much of their heritage intact. The main groups of Amerindians, who reside in scattered interior settlements – Arawak, Carib, Makushi and Wapishana – still live significantly off the land. Ethnic tension and distrust come out during election times and there's increasing distrust of Brazilians, who are perceived to want access to Guyana's natural resources. Today, about 44% of the population is East Indian, 30% African, 17% mixed heritage and 9% Amerindian.

Some 500,000 Guyanese live abroad, mostly in Canada, the UK, USA, and Trinidad and Tobago. Some Guyanese are concerned, and probably justifiably so, about 'brain drain,' as the country loses skilled workers overseas.

Most Afro-Guyanese are Christian, usually Anglican; a handful are Muslim. The Indo-Guyanese population is mostly Hindu, with a sizable Muslim minority, but Hindu-Muslim friction is uncommon. Since independence, efforts have been made to recognize all relevant religions in national holidays.

Environment

Guyana is swarming with rivers, including its three principal waterways (listed east to west): the Berbice, Demerara and Essequibo. The narrow strip of coastal lowland (with almost no sandy beaches) is 460km long and comprises 4% of the total land area but is home to 90% of the population. The Dutch, using a system of drainage canals and seawalls, reclaimed much of the marshy coastal land from the Atlantic and made it available for agriculture.

Tropical rainforest covers most of the interior, though southwestern Guyana features extensive savannas between the Rupununi River and the Brazil border.

Guyana is home to over 2000 animal species and the likelihood of seeing some of the bigger and more famous ones – such as the black caiman, giant anteater, howler monkey, peccary, capybara, giant river otter and tapir – are high. You'll probably see a slew of monkeys and, if you're lucky, spot a jaguar or harpy eagle.

SURVIVAL GUIDE

ℹ Directory A–Z

ACCOMMODATIONS

In Georgetown, the cheapest hotels often double as 'love inns,' which locals use by the hour – so be careful of questionably low rates. There are a few good, clean guesthouses around town, however, with rooms that include shared bathrooms from around G$6000. Rainforest lodges and savanna ranches may seem expensive but note that food and activities are often included – although this still doesn't make them cheap. In the interior, the most budget-friendly accommodation is in a hammock, either your own or one provided by your hosts (for an extra G$1000); space in a hut costs around G$1000 to G$2000 per night.

ACTIVITIES

The interior and coastal areas offer countless outdoors adventure possibilities, from river rafting, trekking and bird-watching to wildlife-viewing and fishing. Community tourism is growing, particularly in the Rupununi. Most folks arrange adventures through Georgetown's tour agencies, but independent travel is possible.

BOOKS

Tracing the country's history with a modern-day voyage, *The Wild Coast* by John Gimlette is a must for any visitor to the region. It also includes shorter chapters on Suriname and French Guiana.

Ninety-Two Days by Evelyn Waugh describes a rugged trip from Georgetown across the Rupununi Savanna.

Journey to Nowhere: A New World Tragedy by Shiva Naipaul is a moving account of the Jonestown tragedy, published in the UK as *Black and White*.

BUSINESS HOURS

Commerce awakens around 8:30am and tends to last until 4pm or so. Saturdays are half days, if shops open at all, and Georgetown becomes a ghost town on Sundays. Restaurants generally serve lunch from about 11:30am to 3pm and dinner from around 6:30pm to 10pm.

SLEEPING PRICE RANGES

The following price ranges refer to a double room and include a private bathroom unless otherwise indicated:

$ less than G$12,000

$$ G$12,000 to G$30,000

$$$ more than G$30,000

FOOD PRICE RANGES

The following price ranges refer to a standard main course:

$ less than G$800

$$ G$800 to G$2000

$$$ more than G$2000

ELECTRICITY

Guyana uses American two-square pronged plugs. Currents are 127V, 60Hz.

EMBASSIES & CONSULATES

Most countries' embassies and consulates are in Georgetown.

Brazilian Embassy (☎225-7970; bragetown@solutions2000.net; 308-309 Church St) Visa processing takes three to seven days.

British High Commission (☎226-5881; http://ukinguyana.fco.gov.uk/en; 44 Main St)

Surinamese Embassy (☎226-9844; surnmemb@gol.net.gy; 54 New Garden St) Visa services are open from 9am to 11:30am Monday, Wednesday and Friday only; Tourist Card applications can be dropped off from 8:30am to 10:30am Monday to Friday, with pick-up the same day from 1pm to 3pm. Visa processing takes one to five days, depending on nationality. No flip-flops or tank tops allowed, so dress appropriately to be let in.

US Embassy (☎225-4902; http://georgetown.usembassy.gov; 100 Young St)

HEALTH

Adequate medical care is available in Georgetown, at least at private hospitals, but facilities are few elsewhere. Chloroquine-resistant malaria is endemic, and dengue fever is also a danger, particularly in the interior and even in Georgetown – protect yourself against mosquitoes and take a malaria prophylaxis. Typhoid, hepatitis A, diphtheria/tetanus and polio inoculations are recommended. Guyana is regarded as a yellow-fever-infected area, and your next destination may require a vaccination certificate, as does Guyana when you arrive. Tap water is suspect, especially in Georgetown. Cholera outbreaks have occurred in areas with unsanitary conditions, but precautions are recommended everywhere.

INTERNET ACCESS

Georgetown's internet cafes charge about G$600 per hour and free wi-fi is widely available.

LANGUAGE

English is the official language, but it's distinctly Guyanese with plenty of musical lilts and colorful idioms that can make it nearly impossible to understand at first. Creole is a language spoken by most of the African community, mixing several languages, but can be relatively easy to understand once you develop an ear for it. More difficult are the many Amerindian dialects and the East Indian languages of Hindi and Urdu.

MONEY

The Guyanese dollar (G$) is stable and pegged to the US dollar, which is widely accepted. You also may be able to spend your euros or even British pounds. Credit cards are accepted at Georgetown's better hotels and restaurants (usually for a 5% service charge), although not at gas stations or most anywhere else. Scotiabank is the easiest place to get cash advances, and its ATMs are the only ones that accept foreign cards.

Cash can be exchanged at banks, but *cambios* (foreign-exchange offices) offer better rates and less red tape. Sometimes hotels change cash for a small commission.

POST

Postal services are iffy. For important shipments, try these international shippers with offices in Georgetown businesses: **UPS** (Mercury Couriers; ☎227-1853; 210 Camp St) and **DHL** (USA Global Export; ☎225-7772; 50 E 5th St, Queenstown).

PUBLIC HOLIDAYS

Republic Day celebrations in February are the most important national cultural events of the year, though Hindu and Muslim religious festivals are also significant. Amerindian Heritage Month (September) features cultural events, such as handicraft exhibits and traditional dances. An annual Rupununi Rodeo at Easter is held in Lethem.

New Year's Day January 1

Republic Day (marking the slave rebellion of 1763) February 23

Phagwah/Holi (Hindu New Year) March/April

Good Friday/Easter Monday March/April

Labor Day May 1

Emancipation Day August 1

USING US DOLLARS

If you aren't planning on traveling far off the tourist trail, you can get by using US dollars at most hotels, rainforest lodges, restaurants and taxis to the airports. The going user rate is G$200 for US$1, which is close to the bank rate. However, do plan on having a small stash of Guyanese dollars for short taxi rides and snacks.

Diwali (Hindu Festival of Lights) October/November

Christmas Day December 25

Boxing Day December 26

Eid ul-Fitr end of Ramadan; dates vary

TELEPHONE

SIM cards are available with local mobile companies. Hotels and restaurants generally allow free local phone calls. There are no area codes in Guyana.

VISAS

Travelers from the USA, Canada, EU countries, Australia, New Zealand, Japan, the UK and most Caribbean countries do not need a visa; confirm with the nearest embassy or consulate. A 90-day stay is granted on arrival in Guyana with an onward ticket. If you do need a visa, file your application at least six weeks before you leave your home country.

As well as a passport, carry an international yellow-fever vaccination certificate with you (although you probably won't be asked for this), and keep other immunizations up to date.

To stay longer than 90 days, appeal to the **Ministry of Home Affairs** (☎226-2445; 6 Brickdam Rd, Georgetown; ⏰8-11:30am & 1-3pm Mon-Fri).

WOMEN TRAVELERS

Guyana's not-so-safe reputation should put women travelers on particular alert. Never go out alone at night and stick to well-peopled areas if walking alone during the day in Georgetown. In the interior, traveling alone should pose few problems.

Getting There & Away

Travelers flying to Guyana arrive at **Cheddi Jagan International Airport** (www.cjairport-gy.com; East Coast Demerara), south of the capital, or **Ogle International Airport** (☎222-4132; East Coast Demerara) closer to town, which services smaller regional flights.

In the far south of Guyana, via Lethem, a bridge connects Guyana with Boa Vista, Brazil. In the northeast, a ferry connects Corriverton (Springlands) via Moleson Creek to Suriname. The only crossing between Venezuela and Guyana is the remote, difficult and dangerous road between Bochinche and Mabaruma, but there are no immigration officials; you're better off going through Brazil.

DEPARTURE TAX

Outbound passengers pay a departure tax of US$20 or G$4000. This fee is not included in airfares and needs to be paid by each person at the airport.

Getting Around

AIR

Charter air services to interior destinations such as Annai, Kaieteur and Iwokrama are available from the Ogle International Airport in Georgetown.

BOAT

Regular ferry services cross the Essequibo River between Charity and Bartica, with a stop at Parika (reached by paved highway from Georgetown). More frequent speedboats (river taxis) carry passengers from Parika to Bartica.

CAR

Rental cars are available in Georgetown, though not from the airport at the time of writing. A Driving Permit (available for free at the Cheddi Jagan International Airport arrivals terminal) is required for car rental (an International Driving Permit won't suffice).

MINIBUS

Cheap local buses speed between points all over Georgetown. Minibuses from Georgetown to destinations along the coast cost up to G$1100. From Georgetown to Lethem one way is G$10,000.

TAXI

Many taxi companies travel between Georgetown and coastal destinations, although they cost significantly more than buses and minibuses. They can be good value for a group. A taxi from Georgetown to the Cheddi Jagan International Airport costs G$5000.

Paraguay

Includes ➡

Best Places to Eat

- Paulista Grill (p775)
- Ciervo Blanco (p775)
- Milord (p782)
- Hiroshima (p782)
- Meshin (p790)

Best Places to Stay

- Casa de la Y B&B (p781)
- Mbaracayú Eco-lodge (p786)
- Santa María Hotel (p783)
- Hotel Tirol (p783)
- Para La Tierra Biological Station (p787)

Why Go?

Little-visited, little-known Paraguay is a country much misunderstood. Despite its location at the heart of the continent, it is all too often passed over by travelers who wrongly assume that a lack of mega-attractions means there's nothing to see. But it's ideal for those keen to get off the gringo trail for a truly authentic South American experience.

Paraguay is a country of remarkable contrasts: it's rustic and sophisticated; it's extremely poor and obscenely wealthy; it boasts exotic natural reserves and massive human-made dams; it is a place where horses and carts pull up alongside Mercedes-Benz vehicles, artisans' workshops abut glitzy shopping centers, and Jesuit ruins in rural villages lie just a few kilometers from sophisticated colonial towns. The steamy subtropical Atlantic Forest of the east is a stark contrast to the dry, spiny wilderness of the Chaco, the location of the isolated Mennonite colonies.

When to Go

Asunciona

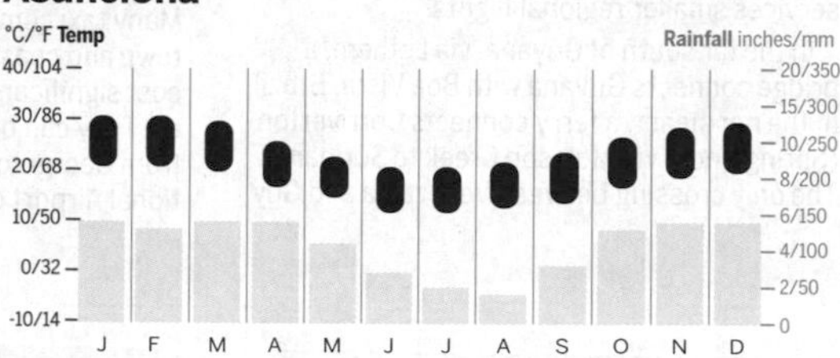

Feb Let loose during Carnaval season in Encarnación.

Jul–Aug Pleasant winter climate makes it the best time to visit the Chaco.

Dec Follow the pilgrims to the Caacupé basilica on the Día de la Virgen (8 December).

Connections

Despite its location at the heart of the continent, Paraguay is often circumvented by travelers. A country almost surrounded by major rivers, many of its land border points involve a bridge crossing with customs offices at either end. The main border crossings are Foz do Iguaçu (Brazil) to Ciudad del Este; Posadas (Argentina) to Encarnación; or via the Ruta Trans-Chaco from Bolivia.

As a member of Mercosur, a trade bloc of southern states, Paraguayans don't need to complete customs formalities to cross to Brazil and Argentina. Foreigners do!

ITINERARIES

Two Weeks

Start with a historic tour of Asunción, take day trips to Itauguá, Yaguarón, Caacupé and San Bernardino. From here head east to Laguna Blanca, where you could volunteer with Para la Tierra Biological Station, before moving on to Ciudad del Este to visit the awe-inspiring Itaipú Dam. A night in the forest at Hotel Tirol will prepare you for a few days' bird-watching in the real wilderness at Parque Nacional San Rafael. Return to civilization at Encarnación, a great base for visiting the Jesuit Missions before crossing the international bridge to Posadas, Argentina.

Three Weeks

Complete the two-week itinerary but return to Asunción via Santa María de la Fe and head north to colonial Concepción. Take a boat up the Río Paraguay to Bahia Negra and visit the Paraguayan Pantanal, before experiencing the landscape contrast in the dry Chaco at the Mennonite colonies of Loma Plata and Filadelfia. Visit one of the Chaco national parks before continuing along the Ruta Trans-Chaco and crossing into Bolivia.

Essential Food & Drink

- **Asado** Grilled slabs of beef and pork: the focal point of every social event.
- **Chipa** Cheese bread made with manioc flour.
- **Chipa guasú** Hot maize pudding with cheese and onion.
- **Empanadas** Pasties stuffed with chicken, cheese and ham, beef or other fillings.
- **Locro** Maize stew.
- **Mbeyú** A grilled cheese and manioc pancake.
- **Queso Paraguay** The unusual local cheese.
- **Sooyo** Thick soup of ground meat, often with a floating poached egg.
- **Tereré** Iced yerba maté tea drank ubiquitously and constantly.

AT A GLANCE

- **Currency** Guaraní (G)
- **Official languages** Spanish, Guaraní
- **Money** ATMs widespread, plastic rarely used
- **Time** GMT minus four hours

Fast Facts

- **Area** 406,752 sq km
- **Population** 6.9 million
- **Capital** Asunción
- **Emergency** ☎ 911
- **Country Code** ☎ 595

Exchange Rates

Australia	A$1	3750G
Canada	C$1	4050G
Euro zone	€1	6000G
New Zealand	NZ$1	3375G
UK	UK£1	8250G
USA	US$1	5350G

Set Your Budget

- **Hostel bed** US$15
- **Evening meal** US$7.50
- **Bus ticket** US$15

Resources

- **FAUNA Paraguay** (www.faunaparaguay.com) Animals and wildlife.
- **Senatur** (www.senatur.gov.py) Tourist ministry portal.
- **Discovering Paraguay** (http://discoveringparaguay.com) Paraguayan life and culture.

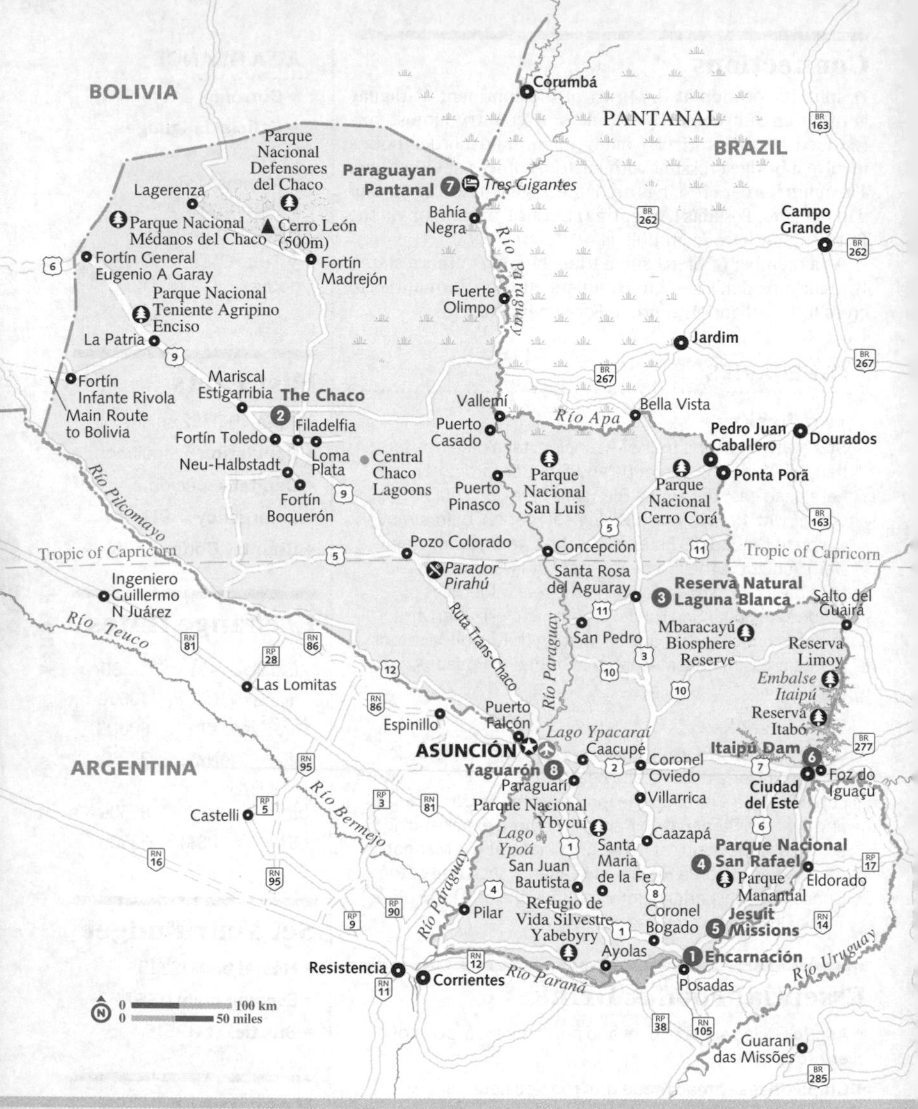

Paraguay Highlights

1 Party until well after dawn during Encarnación's original take on **Carnaval** (p781).

2 Watch a jaguar laze in the scrub, sleep under billions of stars and experience the absence of humanity in the **Chaco** (p789).

3 Be a conservation volunteer or relax on the beach at tranquil **Laguna Blanca** (p787).

4 Wild out in the endangered Atlantic Forest in **Parque Nacional San Rafael** (p784), Paraguay's most biodiverse reserve.

5 Explore the picturesque remnants of the **Jesuit Missions** (p783).

6 Gaze in awe at **Itaipú Dam** (p786), now only the second biggest in the world, but still damned big.

7 Ogle the animals in Paraguay's little corner of the **Pantanal** (p788).

8 Admire the ornate interior of the Franciscan church at **Yaguarón** (p777).

ASUNCIÓN

021 / POP 2.54 MILLION

It's hard to get your head around Asunción. At heart the city is beautiful and simple, with a sprinkling of original colonial and beaux arts buildings, international cuisine, shady plazas and friendly people. Probe a little deeper, however, and you'll see another side: smart suburbs, ritzy shopping malls and fashionable nightclubs. Despite the heavy traffic and diesel fumes in the historic center, this is one of South America's greener and more likable capitals, and it doesn't take long to learn your way around.

Asunción claims to have 2.5 million people, yet seems to hold many more – its sprawling suburbs swallow up neighboring towns.

Sights

City Center

Panteón de los Héroes HISTORIC BUILDING
(Plaza de los Héroes; 6am-6:30pm Mon-Sat, to noon Sun) FREE Center of life in Asunción is Plaza de los Héroes, where a military guard protects the remains of Mariscal Francisco Solano López and other key figures from Paraguay's catastrophic wars in the Panteón de los Héroes, the city's most instantly recognizable building.

Casa de la Independencia MUSEUM
(www.casadelaindependencia.org.py; 14 de Mayo; 7am-6:30pm Mon-Fri, 8am-noon Sat) FREE The Casa de la Independencia dates from 1772 and is where Paraguay became the first country on the continent to declare its independence in 1811.

Palacio López PALACE
(Paraguayo Independiente) The grand Palacio López is the seat of government. During the early years of independence you could be shot for merely looking at the exterior!

Manzana de la Rivera MUSEUM
(Ayolas 129; 7am-9pm) FREE Just across the street from Palacio López is the Manzana de la Rivera, a complex of nine colorful and restored houses. The oldest is Casa Viola (1750), where the **Museo Memoria de la Ciudad** houses a history of Asunción's urban development.

Cabildo MUSEUM
(www.cabildoccr.gov.py; Plaza de Armas; 9am-7pm Tue-Fri, 10am-5pm Sat & Sun) FREE North of the Plaza de los Héroes near the waterfront is the pink *cabildo* (colonial town council), which was once the center of government. This influential cultural center is a meeting place for bohemian thinkers, hosting regular cultural events and exhibitions by local artists, historians and academics.

Estación Ferrocarril MUSEUM
(Plaza Uruguaya; 7am-5pm Mon-Fri) FREE The Asunción–Encarnación railway line was the first in South America. One of the first trains to run the route is on display at the old Estación Ferrocarril (railway station), along with other items from the period.

Museum aside, these days the station is used more for concerts and recitals than anything else.

Suburbs

Museo del Barro MUSEUM
(www.museodelbarro.org; Grabadores del Cabichui s/n; 3:30-8pm Wed-Thu, 9am-noon & 3:30-8pm Fri & Sat) FREE Everyone's favorite, Museo del Barro displays everything from modern paintings to pre-Columbian and indigenous crafts to political caricatures of prominent Paraguayans. Take bus 30 from Oliva and get off at Shopping del Sol. It's three blocks from there off Callejón Cañada.

Stay on the bus and you'll pass **Parque Ñu Guazú**, a pleasant place to pass an afternoon, with lakes and walking trails.

Jardín Botánico GARDENS
(admission 5000G for museums; 7am-7pm; museums 9am-6pm Tue-Fri, to 4pm Sat & Sun)

POMBERO

Guaraní folklore has many colorful mythological figures, but none is so widely believed to be true as **Pombero**. A mischievous little imp, said to be short, muscular and hairy, he emerges at night when he should only be referred to as Karai Pyhare (Lord of the Night). His presence is used to explain anything from strange sounds and missing items to unfortunate minor accidents. Pombero's penchant for young women, accompanied or otherwise, can only be overcome by diverting his attentions with a glass of *caña* (rum) or cigarettes, left as a gift. Place them on the roadside and hightail it out of there!

From the center, Av Artigas runs approximately 6km to the Jardín Botánico. The former estate of the ruling López dynasty, it now houses the city **zoo**, a small **nature reserve** and a couple of odd museums: a small **natural history museum** in Carlos Antonio's humble colonial house and the **Museo Indigenista** in his son Francisco's former mansion.

Take bus 24 or 35 from Cerro Corá.

Supermercado Ykua Bolaños MEMORIAL
(Av Artigas) FREE En route to the Jardín Botánico, you'll pass the charred remains of the Supermercado Ykua Bolaños, which hit the world headlines in 2006. Almost 1000 people burnt to death inside when the owner elected to 'lock-down' after a small fire broke out in the kitchen. A moving **shrine** to the deceased is worthy of reflection.

Cementerio de la Recoleta CEMETERY
FREE The Cementerio de la Recoleta, 3km east of the center along Av Mariscal López, is a maze of incredible mausoleums as Asunción's wealthy try to do outdo each other in the grandeur of their resting places. Eliza Lynch, hated mistress of Mariscal López, is buried here.

Asunción

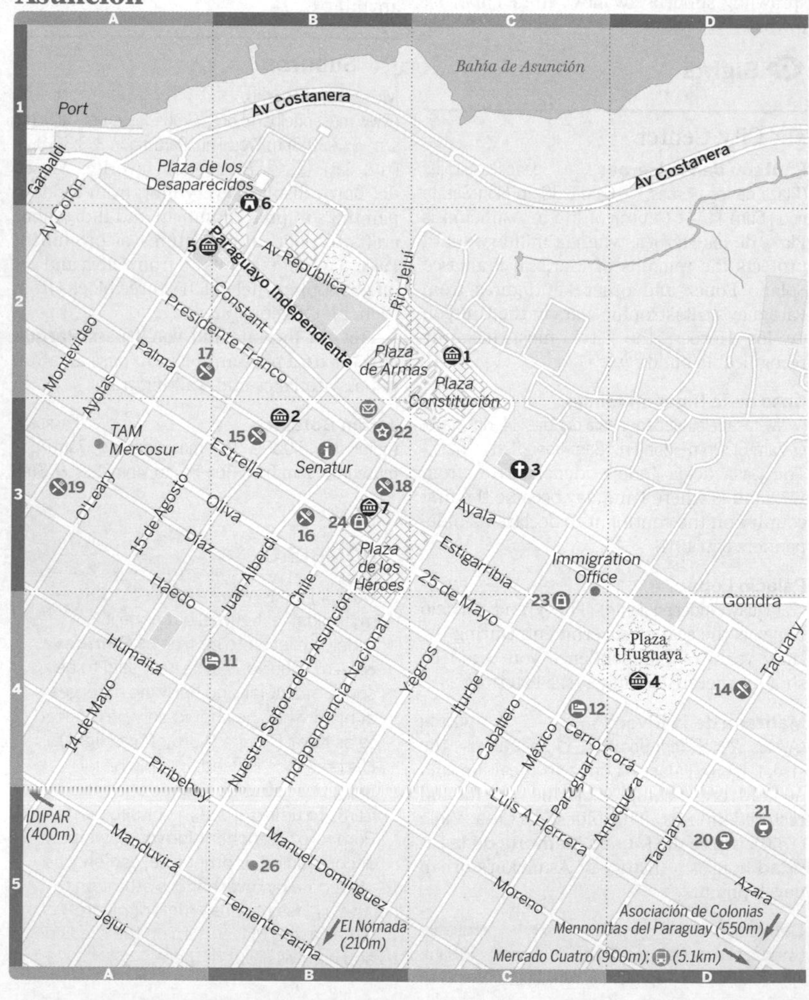

Sleeping

Accommodation is more expensive in Asunción than in the rest of the country, but it's unlikely to bust your budget.

City Centre

Hotel Miami HOTEL **$**
(☎44-4950; México 449; s/d 80,000/120,000G; ❄) A very bland hospital-type hallway, but it's clean, central and is an acceptable budget option.

El Nómada HOSTEL **$$**
(☎cell 0992-272946; www.hostel-asuncion-paraguay.com; Iturbe 1156; dm 50,000-65,000G, s/d incl breakfast 95,000/180,000G; ❄🛜🏊) Colorful and cute, this place is getting rave reviews at the budget end of the spectrum because of its impeccable service and great central location.

El Viajero Hostel & Suites HOSTEL **$$**
(☎44-4563; www.elviajerohostels.com; Juan Alberdi 73; incl breakfast dm 50,000-60,000G, d 130,000-170,000G; ❄@🛜🏊) Part of a successful chain of South American hostels

Asunción

Sights
1 Cabildo ... C2
2 Casa de la Independencia ... B3
3 Catedral Metropolitana ... C3
4 Estación Ferrocarril ... D4
5 Manzana de la Rivera ... A2
6 Palacio López ... B1
7 Panteón de los Héroes ... B3

Activities, Courses & Tours
8 Alianza Francesa ... E5
9 Centro Cultural Paraguayo-Americano ... F4
10 Instituto Cultural Paraguayo Alemán ... F4

Sleeping
11 El Viajero Hostel & Suites ... B4
12 Hotel Miami ... C4
13 Palmas del Sol ... E4

Eating
14 Bar San Roque ... D4
15 Bellini ... B3
16 Confitería Bolsi ... B3
17 La Vida Verde ... A2
18 Lido Bar ... B3
19 Taberna Española ... A3

Drinking & Nightlife
20 904 ... D5
21 Britannia Pub ... D5

Entertainment
22 Teatro Municipal ... B3

Shopping
23 Folklore ... C4
24 Open-Air Market ... B3

Information
25 Touring y Automóvil Club Paraguayo ... E5

Transport
26 American Airlines ... B5

with air-conditioned dorms, a spacious garden and a refreshing splash pool in an old colonial mansion. Cheaper rooms are with shared bathroom.

Palmas del Sol HOTEL **$$**
(☎ 44-9485; www.hotelpalmasdelsol.com; Av España 202; s/d 170,000/231,000G; ❄@☜🏊) Despite its location on a noisy central road, this place is a real oasis with a quiet courtyard and tastefully functional rooms. The included breakfast is a treat. Relaxing on a poolside sun lounger, you'll feel a million miles from the traffic fumes outside.

Gran Hotel del Paraguay HOTEL **$$$**
(☎ 20-0051; www.granhoteldelparaguay.com.py; cnr De la Residenta & Pucheu; s/d 350,000/430,000G; ❄@☜🏊) Dripping with the kind of colonial-era luxury that you will either love or hate, this historic hotel is said to be the place where the national anthem was heard for the first time in July 1860.

Suburbs

Portal del Sol HOTEL **$$**
(☎ 60-9395; www.portaldelsol.com; Roa 1455; s/d 210,000/265,000G; ❄@☜🏊) Beautiful rooms, mammoth breakfast, a pleasant splash pool, good restaurant and airport pick-up. Out by the Shopping del Sol in a plush residential area, this is one of the most popular hotels with tour groups, so book ahead.

La Misión Hotel Boutique BOUTIQUE HOTEL **$$$**
(☎ 62-1800; www.lamision.com.py; Eulogio Estigarribia 4990, Villa Morra; per room 1,100,000G; ❄@☜🏊) A charismatic Jesuit-style boutique hotel close to the Shopping Mariscal López. Individually decorated rooms range from minimalist to classy and cozy, and extend to the oddly floral octagon rooms. Rooms are 25% cheaper on weekends.

Posada del Cielo HOTEL **$$$**
(☎ 66-4882; www.hotelposadasdelcielo.com.py; Del Maestro 1446, Villa Morra; s/d 250,000/300,000G; ❄@☜🏊) Colorful Posada del Cielo makes you feel like you are staying in somebody's house, while packing a number of individually decorated rooms into the illusion. Some rooms are a little pokey though, so ask to see a selection.

Eating

Asunción's eating options reflect its cultural diversity: sophisticated local, Asian and international foods abound and even vegetarians are catered for. Meat lovers, however, will find the ubiquitous all-you-can-eat grill restaurants hard to resist. Though there are some good pit-stops in the center, Asunción's most refined restaurants are in the eastern suburbs, especially Villa Morra.

City Center

For typical Paraguayan food, try out the million and one options south of the center along Avenida Figueroa, known locally as La Quinta Avenida, or sample the *asadito* (mini-meat kebabs with mandioca; 3000G) from stands on street corners.

Lido Bar DELI **$**
(cnr Chile & Palma; mains 7000-35,000G) Asunción's historic diner is famous for its sidewalk tables opposite the Panteón de los Héroes, making it the city's most popular meeting place. Though it serves a variety of Paraguayan specialties in generous portions, the location is better than the food.

Confitería Bolsi INTERNATIONAL **$$**
(www.bolsi.com.py; Estrella 399; mains 25,000-85,000G) More than a *confitería* (cafe/snack bar), this traditional place has been going since 1960 and serves everything from sandwiches to curried rabbit and garlic pizza. Try the *surubí casa nostra* (a delicious fish dish). Open 24 hours.

Bellini ITALIAN **$$**
(Palma near 15 de Agosto; 28,000-32,000G) Join the queue to pick your ingredients and watch while the chefs cook up a delicious plate of fresh pasta before your eyes. Hugely popular and deservedly so.

La Vida Verde VEGETARIAN **$$**
(Palma near 15 de Agosto; per kg 35,000G; ✎) Assess your mood with one of the 32 quirky sculptured emotional 'faces' on the wall – 'satisfied' is how you'll feel after this eating experience. A delicious daily buffet of Chinese vegetarian delights (although they bend the rules a bit!).

Bar San Roque INTERNATIONAL **$$**
(cnr Tacuary & Ayala; mains 20,000-75,000G) An Asunción landmark, with a warm turn-of-the-20th-century atmosphere. The counter displays fresh goods from the family farm and the wine list is as impressive as the menu of fish and meat dishes. As many locals will attest, it's a culinary must, with service to match.

Taberna Española SPANISH $$$
(☎44-1743; Ayolas 631; mains 33,000-195,000G) A slice of Spain in Paraguay. The energetic ambience of this 'food museum', with dangling bottles, cooking implements and bells, is only the backdrop for good-value tapas and paella.

Suburbs

On Sundays it's best to head to one of the large shopping centers such as Mariscal López (p776) or Shopping del Sol (p776), both with large food courts.

Ala Turk TURKISH $$
(meals 20,000-35,000G) Family-owned Turkish food truck with outdoor seating, serving cracking kebabs and fantastic falafel and offering a puff on nargile sisha. Cheap and cheerful, it's just around the corner from the Mariscal López.

★**Paulista Grill** BRAZILIAN $$$
(cnr San Martín & Mariscal López, Villa Morra; buffet 75,000G) One of the city's most famous all-you-can-eat restaurants. There are more than 15 different cuts of mouthwatering meats, salad, pasta and sushi bars to peruse, as well as exotic desserts. Attentive table service.

★**Ciervo Blanco** BARBECUE $$$
(cnr Flores & Radio Operadores del Chaco, Barrio Pinozá; meals 45,000-75,000G) If you're looking for a traditional Paraguayan experience, this place just southeast of the center has it. Juicy *asado*, traditional music and bottle dancers will keep you entertained.

Le Sommelier FRENCH $$$
(cnr Roa & Irala; mains 55,000-90,000G) Not as pretentious as you might expect from the name (wine recommendations for each dish apart), this is a cozy little restaurant with an inventive menu.

Hacienda Las Palomas MEXICAN $$$
(Guido Spano 1481, Villa Morra; mains 55,000-80,000G) Hacienda Las Palomas manages to capture the vibrant colors of Mexico in the decor as much as it captures the country's vibrant flavors on the plate. With friendly waitstaff and generous portions, it's a refined yet casual dining experience.

Drinking & Nightlife

Some bars and all discos charge admission for men (women usually get in free) if you arrive after 10pm. Options are limited in the center and most of the flashy clubs are a short cab ride east of downtown. For a more upmarket (and pricier) scene, head to Paseo Carmelitas off Av España.

Britannia Pub PUB
(Cerro Corá 851; ⌚Tue-Sun) Casually hip with an air-conditioned international ambience and outdoor patio, the Brit Pub is a favorite among foreigners and locals alike for its pub grub. It even has its own beer!

904 BAR
(Cerro Corá; admission 10,000G) Down-to-earth disco-pub with live music most nights, big-screen soccer matches and pool tables.

Seven CLUB
(República Argentina 222, near Mariscal López; admission 20,000G) The disco-bar of the moment, where the young and the restless party to techno and house tunes until the sun comes up.

Coyote CLUB
(Sucre 1655; admission 40,000-80,000G) Starts late, ends late – this bouncing disco is for young, wealthy, beautiful people who like to dance till they drop.

Entertainment

Asunción's main shopping malls have multiscreen cinemas. Films are often in English with Spanish subtitles. Tickets start from around 25,000G, and may be more at weekends. See www.cines.com.py for schedules.

Asunción has several venues for live music and theater; the season is March to October.

Teatro Municipal PERFORMING ARTS
(cnr Alberdi & Presidente Franco) Check the listing outside for show times.

Shopping

Asunción offers Paraguay's best souvenir shopping. The typical Paraguayan souvenir is a *matero, bombilla* and *termos* (cup, straw and flask) for *tereré* (herbal tea) consumption, and these are ubiquitous – though quality varies. The ground floor of the Senatur office (p776) has examples of local *artesanías* (craft work) from around the country, ranging from intricate Luque silver to fine *ñandutí* (lace).

Folklore HANDICRAFTS
(cnr Caballero & Estigarribia) A good bet for quality Paraguayan handicrafts, though not cheap.

Open-Air Market MARKET
(Plaza de los Héroes) Stocked with *ao po'i* or *lienzo* (loose-weave cotton) garments and other indigenous crafts, it expands considerably on weekends.

Mercado Cuatro MARKET
Mercado Cuatro is a lively trading lot occupying the wedge formed by the intersection of Avs Francia and Pettirossi and stretching over several blocks. It sells everything from produce to Chinese imports.

Shopping del Sol MALL
(cnr Aviadores del Chaco & González) Shopping del Sol is Asunciónś biggest and glitziest mall.

Shopping Mariscal López MALL
(cnr Quesada & Charles de Gaulle) A trendy mall and city landmark.

Information

DANGERS & ANNOYANCES

Asunción is a comparatively safe city but, as with anywhere else, keep your eye on your belongings, particularly at the bus station. Plaza Uruguaya and the streets around Palma are frequented by prostitutes after dark – males shouldn't be surprised if they are solicited. On Sundays the city center is a ghost town.

EMERGENCY

Medical emergency (20-4800)
Police (911)

MEDICAL SERVICES

Hospital Bautista (60-0171; Av República Argentina) Recommended private hospital.

MONEY

All the major banks have ATMs, though most have a daily withdrawal limit of 1,500,000G, and some charge a usage fee of 25,000G. Along Palma and its side streets it is hardly possible to walk a block without money changers shouting *'cambio'* at you, but rates are better in the numerous *casas de cambio* (currency exchanges) and banks that line this road. There are ATMs and money changers at the bus station and airport.

POST, INTERNET & TELEPHONE

Numerous *locutorios* (telephone offices) offer call booths and internet access for around 4000G per hour. There is a handy one in the bus terminal. Wi-fi is widespread.

Directory Inquiries (112)

Main Post Office (cnr Alberdi & Paraguayo Independiente; 7am-7pm Mon-Fri) In a historic colonial mansion. Send your mail *certificado* (registered) if you want it to have a hope of arriving.

TOURIST INFORMATION

For online city information, see www.quickguide.com.py. It periodically publishes an excellent magazine packed with maps and current events.

Senatur (0800-11-3030; www.senatur.gov.py; Palma 468; 7am-7pm) City info and plenty of locally produced arts and crafts also on sale here.

Getting There & Away

AIR

Asunción's tiny airport receives regional international flights from Buenos Aires, Santiago de Chile, São Paulo and Santa Cruz, as well as destinations further afield such as Miami and Madrid.

Aeropuerto Internacional Silvio Pettirossi (64-5600) In the suburb of Luque, 20km east of Asunción.

BUS

Bus Terminal (55-1740; www.mca.gov.py/toa.htm; Av República Argentina) Asunción's bus terminal is several kilometers southeast of downtown – the website provides full details of

BUSES FROM ASUNCIÓN

DESTINATION	COST (G)	DURATION (HR)
Buenos Aires (Argentina)	140,000-290,000	18-21
Ciudad del Este	40,000-75,000	4½-6
Concepción	55,000-70,000	4½-6
Encarnación	50,000-90,000	5-6
Filadelfia	70,000	8
Pilar	50,000-55,000	5-6
Rio de Janeiro (Brazil)	450,000	30
Santa Cruz (Bolivia)	200,000-300,000	20-24
São Paulo (Brazil)	230,000-400,000	18-20

schedules and costs. Purchase long-distance tickets at the company offices on the 2nd floor. City buses 8 and 31 run along Oliva to the terminal, while buses 14, 18.2 and 38 run along Haedo.

Don't be put off by the touts shouting destinations at you – take your time to choose the company you want. The ground floor is the departure lounge and the basement *(subsuelo)* is for departures to the Circuito Central.

Getting Around

TO/FROM THE AIRPORT

Buses displaying *'Aeropuerto'* signs head out along Av Aviadores del Chaco between the airport and the center. Airport taxis are expensive (from 100,000G to the center), but if you flag one down on the road outside it's half the price.

BUS

Noisy, bone-rattling kamikaze-like city buses (2300G) go almost everywhere, but few run after 10pm. Nearly all city buses start their route at the western end of Oliva and post their destinations in the front window.

TAXI

Taxis are metered and reasonable but tack on a surcharge late at night and on Sunday. A taxi from the center to the bus terminal costs about 50,000G.

AROUND ASUNCIÓN

Circuito Central

Prepare yourself for a taste of rural and historical Paraguay in the lazy villages that surround the capital. Plugged by the tourist industry as the Circuito Central, this series of humble communities is dominated by colonial buildings and observes long siestas, disturbed only by occasional ox- or horse-drawn carts clacking up cobbled streets.

All towns can be visited in a day trip from Asunción on frequent local buses that leave from the *subsuelo* (lower floor) of the bus terminal (platforms 30 and 35; 5000G to 7000G).

Sights

★Yaguarón Church CHURCH

FREE The 18th-century Franciscan church at Yaguarón, 48km southeast of Asunción, is a landmark of colonial architecture that is not to be missed. The simple design of the exterior with its separate wooden bell tower belies the extraordinary beauty of the painted and carved interior, a masterpiece of religious art and one of the most ornate churches in South America.

San Buenaventura buses depart hourly to Yaguarón from platform 30 in the Asunción terminal *subsuelo*.

Basilica de Caacupé CHURCH

Paraguay's answer to the Vatican City, the enormous Basilica de Caacupé looks quite out of place in this otherwise quiet provincial town. Caacupé really comes alive on El Día de la Virgen (8 December) when crowds of worshipers undertake pilgrimages from all corners of the country to worship and ask the Virgin for favors.

As many as 300,000 of the faithful may crowd onto the plaza during the festival and participate in a spectacular candlelit procession.

Caacupé is 54km east of Asunción and Empresa Villa Serrana departs every 10 minutes from platform 35 on the ground floor of the Asunción terminal.

Itauguá VILLAGE

Itauguá's women are famous for their unique weaving of multicolored *ñandutí* (spiderweb lace). These exquisite pieces range in size from doilies to bedspreads. Smaller ones cost a few dollars but larger ones are upward of 250,000G. In July the town celebrates its annual Festival de Ñandutí.

La Itaugueña buses leave approximately hourly from just outside the bus terminal in Asunción, a distance of 32km.

Areguá VILLAGE

Areguá is renowned for its ceramics, displayed en masse along the main street. The historic cobbled lanes are lined with exquisite colonial homes, and the village atmosphere is completed with a church perched

> **GETTING TO ARGENTINA**
>
> The San Ignacio de Ayolas bridge links Puerto Falcón with Clorinda in Argentina, and customs offices are found at either end. A local bus marked Falcón leaves hourly from Mercado Cuatro and passes the stop at Av República Argentina outside the Asunción bus terminal. The ferry crossing to Clorinda is not recommended for tourists.

on the hill and an enviable position overlooking Lago Yparacaí.

La Aregueña buses run the 27km every half hour from Av República Argentina just outside the Asunción bus terminal.

A ferry from San Bernardino operates to Areguá in the high season.

Piribebuy VILLAGE

Piribebuy is a rural town that was briefly the capital of the nation during the War of the Triple Alliance (1865–70). With Asunción captured, it became the site of a famous siege in 1869, when an army of children led by the local schoolteacher bravely held off the invading Brazilians. The remarkable events are recounted in the small museum.

Empresa Piribebuy runs 75km south from Asunción every 45 minutes from platform 35 in the *subsuelo.*

San Bernardino

☎0512

Renowned as the elite escape for the privileged of Asunción, tranquil 'San Ber' is a trendy place to relax or party: pubs, discos, upmarket hotels and restaurants line the

Southern & Eastern Paraguay

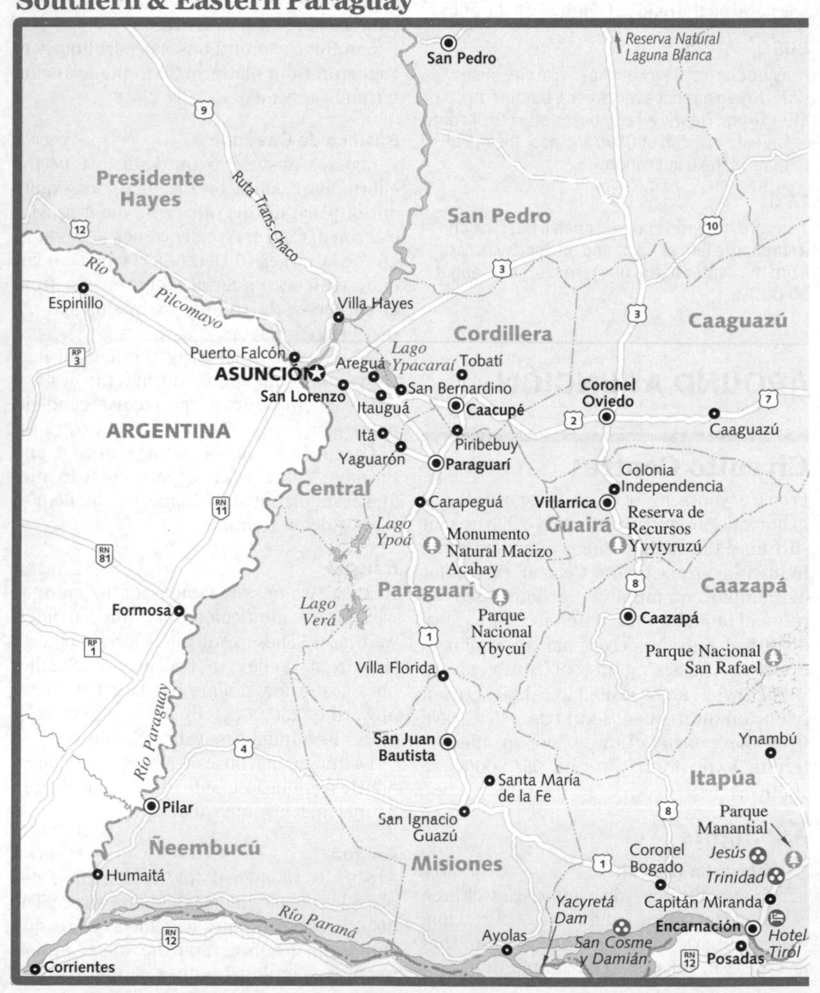

shady cobbled streets of Lago Ypacaraí's eastern shore. Despite its reputation, there's plenty for budget travelers as well. In high season a pleasure boat takes passengers for short cruises on the lake. Unfortunately, you won't want to swim in the lake – it's filthy.

Sleeping

Hostal Brisas del Mediterraneo HOSTEL **$$**
(☎23-2459; Ruta Kennedy; camping 60,000G, d 300,000G;) Travelers rave about this place, which is perched on the edge of the lake and offers excellent facilities with prices that include breakfast. Follow the cobbled Ruta Kennedy for 2km around the lake from outside the Copaco office.

Hotel del Lago HOTEL **$$$**
(☎23-2201; Teniente Weiler 411; s/d 240,000/310,000G;) On the lakeside of the plaza, this hotel is worn and romantically Victorian, full of antique furniture. Each room is different.

Getting There & Away

From Asunción Cordillera de los Altos buses run hourly from platform 35 (1½ hours).

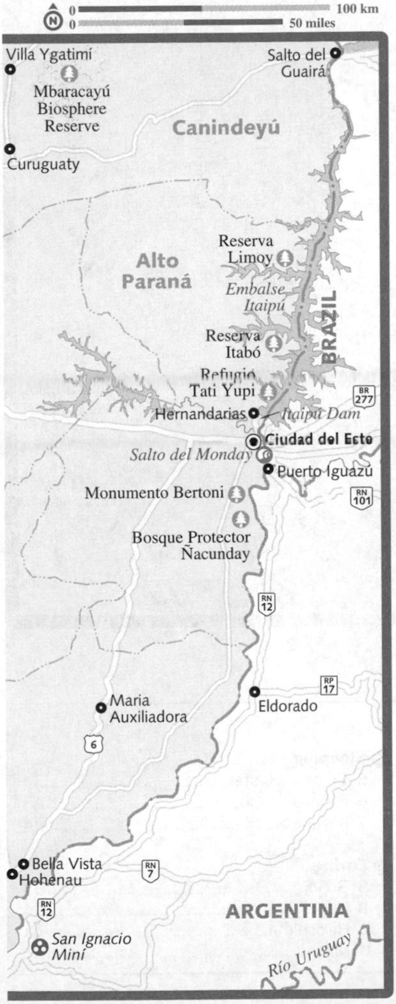

SOUTHERN PARAGUAY

Paraguay's southernmost region, east of the Río Paraguay, is home to some of the country's most important historical sites. The Jesuit ruins, national parks and the *locura* (madness) of Carnaval make it an eclectic and fascinating area to visit.

On the way from Asunción to Encarnación you'll pass through the town of **Coronel Bogado**. Known as the 'Capital de Chipa' – *chipa* is a bread made of manioc flour, eggs and cheese – Coronel Bogado is the best place to sample this national obsession. There's no need to get off the bus; the vendors will come to you and it's as cheap as *chipa* (2000G).

Encarnación

☎071 / POP 150,000

Encarnación, 'La Perla del Sur', is Paraguay's most attractive city. It's also known as the 'Capital de Carnaval' and, following the completion of the new *costanera* (riverside promenade) with its fabulous river beach, is sometimes referred to – rather ambitiously – as the new Rio de Janeiro. It has very quickly metamorphosed into the place to be seen in Paraguay during the stifling summer months.

It is rather less proud to be the birthplace of dictator Alfredo Stroessner. His **former house** (cnr Memmel & Carlos Antonio Lopez) is now a private university just behind the bus terminal.

Sights & Activities

The city center is a pleasant enough place for a stroll, but there isn't much in the way of sights, so you might as well head for the river.

Encarnación

Encarnación

Top Sights

1 Costanera & Beach....A3

Sights

2 Former House of Stroessner....C5

3 Sambadromo Carnaval....A1

Activities, Courses & Tours

4 Karumbés....C4

Sleeping

5 Colonial Hostel....B4

6 Hotel de la Costa....A3

7 Kerana....B4

Eating

8 Gosh....C2

9 Habib´s....D4

10 Hiroshima....C1

11 Milord....A2

CARNAVAL!

Paraguayan-style Carnaval might not be on the same scale or as famous as Rio's, but if you are young and looking for a wild party, then you may find it more fun. More bare flesh, louder music and obligatory crowd involvement all make for a mad night out. Don't forget your *lanzanieves* (spray snow) and a pair of sunglasses (you don't want that stuff in your eyes!), pick your place in the stands and get ready to party hard with the locals – it's surprisingly infectious!

Carnaval now spans every weekend in late January and February, from Saturday to Sunday night. The **Sambadromo** (carnival parade ground) is along Av Costanera, which is Encarnación's main strip for nightlife. Tickets (from 60,000G) can be bought in advance around the city or from touts on the night at a slightly higher price. Gates open around 9pm, but the action starts around 10pm. It's all over by 2am, when everybody piles into the local discos.

★Costanera & Beach BEACH
(Av Costanera) Slap on your flip-flops and jostle for a place on Encarnación's new river beach, located on the flash coastal promenade, a hive of activity during the summer months. If you prefer to avoid the crowds there is another quieter beach at Quiteria, a 30,000G taxi ride away.

Karumbés TOUR
(Cabañas; per person 10,000G) Look out for *karumbés*, yellow horse-drawn carriages that once served as city taxis. Rides are free on weekends. Pick one up at the bus terminal.

Sleeping

There are plenty of clean, reasonably priced places to choose from in Encarnación. Most of the cheaper places also have rooms with air-conditioning for about twice the price. You won't regret splashing out. Book ahead during Carnaval when prices rise considerably.

★Casa de la Y Bed & Breakfast B&B $
(☎0985-77-8198; casadelay@gmail.com http://casadelay.wix.com/casa-de-la-y; Carmen de Lara Castro 422; dm 70,000G, d/t 180,000/250,000G; ❄@☜) A tiny homestay with a warm welcome from hostess Doña Yolanda and a delicious home-cooked menu of *comida típica* (25,000G). There are only two rooms: a tasteful, spacious double/triple with gigantic bathroom and a traditionally adorned, expansive six-bed dorm/family room. The wonderfully floral garden is a cute place to sip *tereré* in the sunshine. Reservation by email essential. A kitchen is available for guest use and it's perfect for small groups and families. Same price during Carnaval, but book ahead!

Kerana HOSTEL $$
(☎0975-13-9593; www.keranahostel.com; Mallorquín 950; dm 90,000G, s/d 150,000/200,000G) A nice, clean hostel conveniently located close to the bus terminal, with regular price offers during the low season. Staff are enthusiastic, but the private rooms are a little small. A kitchen is available for guests.

Colonial Hostel HOSTEL $$
(☎20-1500; Artigas 762; dm 65,000G, s/d 120,000/240,000G, without bathroom 90,000/180,000G) A good budget option with a range of basic but nicely decorated rooms in a colonial house. Camping permitted in the garden.

Hotel de la Costa HOTEL $$$
(☎20-0590; cnr Av Francia & Cerro Corá; s/d 178,000/312,000G, ste 476,000G; ❄@☜≋) A mega hotel on the *costanera* with a welcoming pool and a plum location near the beach. The suite, with Jacuzzi and champagne breakfast, is good value but some rooms are small.

Eating

Encarnación has some of the best eats in Paraguay outside of Asunción, as well as an astounding number of fast-food joints. You shouldn't leave without trying a *lomito Arabe* – a Paraguayan-style kebab invented by the expat Arab community.

Gosh SANDWICHES $
(Mariscal Estigarribia; 15,000G) Choose your own fillings to knock up gigantic subs or three-tier sandwiches. A great way to eat well for less.

GETTING TO ARGENTINA

International buses (5000G) cross to Posadas in Argentina via the Puente San Roque leaving from outside the bus terminal in Encarnación. You must get off at the immigration offices at both ends of the international bridge for exit and entry stamps. Buses don't always wait – take your luggage and keep your ticket to catch the next one.

A new air-conditioned train service (7000G) that departs from Av Von Winkel near the international bridge is the quickest way to cross. Alternatively, picturesque ferries (5000G) cross the Río Paraná between the eastern end of the *costanera* in Encarnación to/from the *costanera* of Posadas.

If you are in a group, a taxi to the Paraguayan customs post will cost around 30,000G, but the price rises exponentially to take it across the bridge.

Habib´s FAST FOOD **$**

(Av Irrazabal; lomito Arabe 15,000G) Habib's is the best bet for local specialty *lomito Arabe*.

Heladería Mako ICE CREAM **$**

(cnr Av Caballero & Lomas Valentinas; ice cream per kg 40,000G) Delicious pastry delights, artisanal ice cream, great coffee and magazines make this well worth the trek.

★Hiroshima JAPANESE **$$**

(cnr 25 de Mayo & Lomas Valentinas; mains 20,000-80,000G) This place has top-notch Japanese food and is a deserved local favorite with unbelievable udon, super sushi and tempting tofu dishes. Food fit for a Japanese crown prince.

La Piccola Italia ITALIAN **$$**

(cnr Ruta 1 & Av Francia; mains 12,000-40,000G) Great-value pizza and pasta in huge portions served in distinctly Mediterranean surroundings. This is probably your best bet if you want to eat well on a tight budget.

★Milord EUROPEAN **$$$**

(www.milord.com.py; cnr Av Francia & 25 de Mayo; mains 40,000-100,000G) With a chef who studied in Paris, formal waiters and a more refined atmosphere than other city restaurants, Milord is widely regarded as the place to be seen by fine diners. The menu is varied and inventive and, despite the slightly more elevated price tag, you won't feel that you've overspent.

Churrasquería Novo Rodeio BRAZILIAN **$$$**

(Galeria San Roque, Ruta Internacional; per person 65,000G) All you can eat meats, salads and pastas at the most established Brazilian buffet in the city. Attentive service and music at weekends. A great feed, but discipline is required to avoid overdoing it! Located in a small shopping center on the road to Argentina.

Information

INTERNET ACCESS

Ciberkfe (Mcal Estigarribia near Constitución; per hr 4,000G)

MONEY

Most banks are on or near the plaza and all have ATMs. Money changers congregate around the bus station and at the border, but check rates before handing over any money.

Cambios Chaco (Av Irrazábal; ⊙8am-9pm Mon-Sat) A reliable option for exchanging money, next to Super 6 supermarket.

TELEPHONE

Telephone cabins are scattered around town, especially in the area around the bus terminal.

TOURIST INFORMATION

Senatur (☎20-4800; cnr Ruta 1 & Padre Bolik; ⊙8am-6pm Mon-Fri, to noon Sat & Sun) In a large new building at the western end of the *costanera* near the entrance to town.

Getting There & Away

The **bus terminal** (☎20-2412; Cabañas) is a few blocks north of the *costanera*. Frequent buses run from Encarnación to Asunción (50,000 to 90,000G, 5½ hours) with La Encarnacena and Nuestra Señora de la Asunción providing the best service. The latter also runs an executive minibus service for the same cost. Buses run east almost hourly to Ciudad del Este (60,000G to 80,000G, six hours), though they stop frequently and the route is painfully slow.

Around Encarnación

Encarnación is a great base for exploring the south of the country. Though the Jesuit Missions are the headline grabbers, there are plenty of other activities to keep you busy in the surroundings.

Activities

Bella Vista Yerba Factories TOUR

FREE A few days in Paraguay are all you need to grasp the importance of yerba maté in the local culture. For a full immersion, take one of the factory tours, which incorporate plantations, production, packaging and, of course, the practice of drinking the tea.

Visits to the Selecta and Pajarito factories are arranged through the tourist office on the main road in the yerba maté capital, Bella Vista, 40km or so east of Encarnación. With the giant *matero* and *bombilla* in front you can't miss it! Selecta also includes a visit to its small nature reserve in its tour.

Parque Manantial RESORT

(0755-23-2250; entry 10,000G, camping 20,000G, pool per day 15,000G;) A forested oasis for travelers who like to get away from it all, Parque Manantial is located on Ruta 6, 35km outside of Encarnación near the town of Hohenau. There is a pleasant new hotel here, but for much of the year you'll likely have the 200 hectares with swimming pools and walking trails to yourself.

Horseback riding and a zipline are available; there's also a river for paddling.

Sleeping

Hotel Tirol HOTEL $$

(071-20-2388; www.hoteltirol.com.py; Ruta VI at Capitán Miranda; s/d 210,000/260,000G;) A favorite with the king of Spain, the timeless red-stone Hotel Tirol is set in 20 hectares of humid forest and makes for a great day trip from Encarnación. Over 300 species of bird have been observed here and four inviting swimming pools (10,000G for nonguests) are a great way to cool off after walking the *senderos* (trails).

Should you wish to stay, you'll need to book ahead in the high season (October to December), though it's often empty at other times of year. To get here take local bus 1y2 (marked Capitán Miranda) from along Av Artigas in Encarnación. The end of the line is the entrance to the hotel. Any bus headed for Trinidad or Ciudad del Este also passes in front.

The Jesuit Missions

Set atop a lush green hill 28km northeast of Encarnación, **Trinidad** is Paraguay's best-preserved Jesuit *reducción* (settlement). You can hire a Spanish-speaking guide near the gate (tip generously) or hang around until dark for the atmospheric light show, which projects a history of the site onto the walls of the ruins.

Jesús, 12km north, is a nearly complete reconstruction of the Jesuit mission that was interrupted by the Jesuits' expulsion in 1767.

WORTH A TRIP

SANTA MARÍA DE LA FE

A must-see for those interested in Jesuit history is the **museum of Jesuit art** in the village of Santa María de la Fe, which houses the finest examples of religious carving. The indigenous carvers were taught their trade by a Jesuit master who carved a miniature template, which was then copied in full size by the students. The museum holds examples of both, glorious in their imperfections. To get into the museum, ask at the Santa María Hotel.

Santa María was also home to **Aimé Bonpland**, a famous French botanist, and a small monument in his honor stands on the plaza. Look out for howler monkeys in the trees, which are surprisingly tame!

It can be a bit of a challenge to get to Santa María on public transport; the easiest way is to take any bus between Asunción and Encarnación and get off at San Ignacio, and taxi it from there. Alternatively, there is a single direct Mariscal López bus from Asunción at 11:45am.

Santa María Hotel (0781-28-3311; www.santamariahotel.org; r per person 140,000G, meals 35,000G) is a lovely little Jesuit-themed hotel on the main plaza. Atmospheric rooms contain replica Jesuit carvings and the owners are knowledgeable local guides who can show you around the museum. The hotel is involved in a number of superb community projects with a strong women's empowerment theme. They will be more than happy to tell you more.

WORTH A TRIP

PILAR

Squirreled away in the far southwest corner of Paraguay in the tongue-twister department of Ñeembucú (pronounced *Nyeembookoo*), the dusty streets of Pilar give a charming insight into traditional Paraguay. Though the town is the textile capital of Paraguay and its threads are much sought after nationwide, visitors may be more interested in the statues of native animals located around the town (pick up a guidebook and do the statue tour).

More difficult to access but well worth the effort is **San Cosme y Damián**, 27km south of the main road to Asunción at Km 308 (about 57km west of Encarnacion), which was the location of the astronomical observatory.

Getting There & Away

From Encarnación, frequent buses go to Trinidad (5000G) between 6am and 7pm, but any bus headed east along Ruta 6 to Ciudad del Este or Hohenau will drop you off nearby – get off when you see the power station on your right. The entry ticket to any one *reducción* (35,000G) includes entry to all the others.

Getting to Jesús from Encarnación without your own transport is difficult, but there are sometimes taxis hanging around (15,000G per person). Alternatively walk 100m along the *ruta* to the crossroads – you'll see the sign to Jesús – and wait for the Jesús–Obligado bus, which supposedly passes hourly (3000G).

If you want to visit San Cosme and get back to Encarnación on the same day, you need to take the 9:30am San Cosmeña bus. Later services will leave you short of time. FAUNA Paraguay (p800) runs guided day tours in English from Encarnación that include brief visits to all three ruins.

Parque Nacional San Rafael

Southern Paraguay's last great tract of Atlantic Forest, gorgeous San Rafael is a lush wilderness and a bird-watcher's paradise with more than 430 species recorded. Endangered species abound in this exotic but easily accessible wilderness.

Sleeping & Eating

Pro Cosara LODGE **$**

(☎0768-29-5046; http://procosara.org/es; r per person with meals 150,000G, without meals 70,000G;) The Hostettler family will give you a warm welcome at this charming jungle lodge on the southern tip of the park. As the HQ of local conservation group Pro Cosara, it's a wonderful source of information about the reserve. Accommodation is in comfortable wooden cabins and the surroundings are beautiful, with forest trails and a tantalizing lake for swimming.

Guyra Reta LODGE **$$**

(☎021-22-9097; www.guyra.org.py; r per person 100,000G, meals by arrangement per person 80,000G) To get deeper into the park, you'll need your own 4WD or a guide. The dorm rooms in the grasslands at Guyra Reta lodge are the only other place to stay, but you must contact Guyra Paraguay in Asunción well in advance to arrange your visit, especially if you want to be fed.

Getting There & Away

Ricketty Pastoreo buses run from Encarnación to Ynambú, 12km outside the reserve, every morning at 8am and 11:30am (25,000G, three hours), but if you are not part of a tour you will have to arrange a pick up from there in advance. FAUNA Paraguay (p800) runs recommended all-inclusive three- to four-day bird-watching trips to the park from Encarnación, which include visits to both Pro Cosara and Guyra Reta.

EASTERN PARAGUAY

Corresponding to the region known as Alto Paraná, this area was once the domain of ancient impenetrable forests teeming with wildlife. The building of the second-largest dam in the world changed all that, flooding huge areas of pristine forest and swallowing up a set of waterfalls comparable to those at Iguazú. The dam brought development to this primeval region, leading to the founding of a city once named after a hated dictator and an influx of farmers bent on turning what was left of the ancient forests into soy fields.

Ciudad del Este

☎061 / POP 550,000

Originally named Puerto Presidente Stroessner after the former dictator, the 'City of the East' is a renowned center for contraband goods, earning it the nickname 'the Supermarket of South America.' The part near the busy Brazilian border is chaotic and it can be a massive shock to the system if it's your first experience of Paraguay, but rest assured there is nowhere else quite like this. Give it a chance and you'll find the rest of the city is surprisingly pleasant, with some interesting attractions nearby. Of course, if you're here to shop, then dive headfirst into the chaos and you will be in your element.

Sleeping

Most accommodations in Ciudad del Este are aimed at business travelers using expense accounts. Midrange places, however, are worth the extra couple of bucks, especially once you sample the megavalue breakfast buffets, which are included in the price.

Hotel Tía Nancy HOTEL $
(☎50-2974; cnr Garcete & Cruz del Chaco; r with fan 80,000G, with air-con 100,000G; ❄) Near the bus terminal, this friendly place has dark rooms but is perfectly adequate for a tranquil transit stop. It's better value if you are a couple, as the prices are per room.

Hotel Austria HOTEL $$
(☎50-0883; www.hotelrestauranteaustria.com; Fernández 165; s/d 220,000/245,000G; ❄@📶) Super-clean European number with spacious rooms, big bathrooms and even bigger breakfasts. Great restaurant, too, with German and Austrian specialties.

Hotel Munich HOTEL $$
(☎50-0347; Fernández 71; s/d 200,000/240,000G; ❄@📶) Solid midrange bet a stone's throw from the border, with comfortable and spacious rooms including cable TV.

Eating

The cheapest options are the stalls along Capitán Miranda and Av Monseñor Rodriguez. Av del Lago is lined with Brazilian-style *rodízio* restaurants, where slabs of meat are brought to your table and you eat until you (almost) explode.

Gugu's CHINESE $$
(cnr Boquerón & Jára; mains 27,000-55,000G; ⏲Mon-Sat) If you haven't had a decent Chinese for a while you may go gaga over Gugu's. It's great value and pretty tasty; portions serve two.

SAX BISTRO $$
(Av San Blás; pizzas from 60,000G, bistro from 25,000G) This unusual eatery features a triple menu (pizza, sushi and bistro) served above the trendy SAX department store.

Information

MONEY

Street money changers lounge around the Pioneros del Este rotunda near the border. Banks line Av Adrián Jara and all have ATMs.

POST

Post Office (cnr Alejo Garcia & Centro Democrático; ⏲8am-5pm Mon-Fri, to noon Sat)

TOURIST INFORMATION

Senatur Office (☎50-8810; cnr Adrián Jara & Mcal Estigarribia; ⏲7am-7pm daily) There is a smaller office at the international bridge.

Getting There & Away

AIR

The minor Aeropuerto Guaraní is 30km west of town on Ruta 2. Flights pass through here en route between Asunción and Brazil whenever there is enough demand.

BUS

The **bus terminal** (☎51-0421; Chaco Boreal) is about 2km south of the center. City buses (3000G) shuttle frequently between here and the center, continuing on to the border. There

GETTING TO BRAZIL OR ARGENTINA

The border with Brazil (Foz do Iguaçu) is at the Puente de la Amistad (Friendship Bridge). Immigration is at both ends of the bridge. Buses to Ciudad del Este run from the local terminal in Foz do Iguaçu (R$3, every 10 minutes) from 6am to 7:30pm. Locals don't need to stop at immigration, but you do, so make sure you tell the driver you want to get off.

Locals use a direct car ferry service between Ciudad del Este and Puerto Iguazú (Argentina), but it can be sometimes difficult to get your entry/exit stamps if you do this. Alternatively, you need to cross to Brazil first and take the land border there – which means two sets of customs. No visa is necessary unless you are staying in Brazil.

are frequent buses to Asunción (60,000G to 120,000G, 4½ to six hours) and Encarnación (60,000G to 80,000G, 5½ hours). Daily buses with Pluma and Sol del Paraguay run to São Paulo, Brazil (240,000G, 17 hours).

TAXI

Taxis are fairly expensive, costing around 30,000 to 40,000G to downtown.

Around Ciudad del Este

With the exception of shopping, most of Ciudad del Este's tourist attractions are just outside the city.

Sights & Activities

Itaipú Dam TOUR

Paraguay's publicity machine is awash with facts and figures about the Itaipú hydroelectric project – the world's second-largest dam (only China's Three Gorges Dam is bigger). Itaipú's generators supply nearly 80% of Paraguay's electricity and 25% of Brazil's entire demand. While project propaganda gushes about this human accomplishment, it omits the US$25 billion price tag and avoids the mention of environmental consequences.

The 1350-sq-km, 220m-deep reservoir drowned Sete Quedas, a set of waterfalls that was more impressive than Iguazú. Free tours leave from the visitors center, north of Ciudad del Este, near the town of Hernandarias; passports are required. Any bus marked 'Hernandarias' (3000G, every 15 minutes) passes in front of the dam and Flora and Fauna Itaipú Binacional. A taxi will charge around 45,000G one way or 70,000G return, including waiting time.

Salto del Monday WATERFALL

(admission 5000G) Pronounced 'Mon-Da-OO,' this impressive 80m-high waterfall 10km outside of Ciudad del Este suffers from its close proximity to Iguazú Falls on the other side of the border. It's well worth the visit, especially as dusk falls and clouds of swifts gather in the air before zipping in to their precarious roosts on the slippery rocks behind the cascades.

A return taxi ride will cost around 75,000G, including waiting time.

Monumento Bertoni MONUMENT

A family of Swiss immigrants led by father Moisés, the Bertonis had the idea of breeding a community of scientists deep in the Paraguayan jungle. With each of his children given a branch of the sciences to study, they made a significant impact on the (admittedly limited) Paraguayan scientific community of the early 20th century.

Perhaps the most famous of his offspring was his son Winkelried, a world-renowned biologist who published tirelessly until his early 30s, when he decided that science wasn't really his calling and moved to Asunción to work in a bank. The monument is the family home, and contains a museum documenting the family's not inconsiderable achievements. Ask at Senatur (p785) for information on how to visit.

Mbaracayú Biosphere Reserve

Singled out by the WWF as one of the 100 most important sites for biodiversity on the planet, the 70,000-hectare Mbaracayú Biosphere Reserve is one of Paraguay's natural treasures. Consisting of pristine Atlantic Forest and *cerrado* (savanna) in approximately equal quantities, it is home to more than 400 bird species and a range of large mammals. Bird-watchers will be in search of the bare-throated bellbird (Paraguay's national bird), the rare helmeted woodpecker and the endangered black-fronted piping-guan. There is also a resident Aché indigenous tribe here who are allowed to hunt using traditional methods.

This model reserve is run by the Fundación Moisés Bertoni (p798). You'll need a 4WD if you want to drive here yourself, or else take the 11:30am or 11:30pm Perla del Sur bus from Asunción to Villa Ygatimi (65,000G, eight hours) and arrange pick up from there in advance.

Sleeping

★Mbaracayú Eco-lodge LODGE $$

(0985-26-1080; Jejui-Mi; reserve admission 10,000G, s/d 150,000/220,000G, meals 40,000G;) The best eco-lodge in Paraguay, this is part of an innovative tourism project combining education, conservation, female empowerment and tourism. The lodge is run by the local female students at the on-site eco-school, who handle reception, cook, wait and clean, on their way to earning a valuable diploma in hostelery.

DON'T MISS

RESERVA NATURAL LAGUNA BLANCA

A pristine, crystal-clear lake, Laguna Blanca is named for its breathaking sandy beach and lake bed – it looks pure white when viewed from the air. The surrounding *cerrado* habitat is home to rare birds and mammals such as the maned wolf and the endangered white-winged nightjar, this being one of only three places in the world where the latter species breeds.

To get to Laguna Blanca, take any one of the frequent buses from Asunción to San Pedro or Concepción and get off at Santa Rosa del Aguaray (50,000G, five hours) where volunteers will be met. If you are not volunteering, infrequent local buses to Santa Barbara pass the entrance to the property, from where it is a 3km walk to the accommodation. Santa Barbara buses leave at 10am, 2:30pm and occasionally 5pm (10,000G, one hour), so you'll need to leave Asunción before 8am to avoid getting stranded in Santa Rosa.

Para La Tierra Biological Station (☎0985-26-0074; www.paralatierra.org; Reserva Natural Laguna Blanca; incl meals 125,000G, reductions for longer stays) If lounging around on the beach isn't your cup of tea, there are volunteering opportunities with scientific research, outreach and environmental education projects at the Para La Tierra Biological Station, which also offers accommodation.

NORTHERN PARAGUAY

Northern Paraguay is off the radar for most travelers, but the colonial city of Concepción is the best place to catch a boat heading north along the Río Paraguay. Natural wonders abound in this remote area, and the road east from Pozo Colorado to Concepción is famed for its abundance of wildlife.

Concepción

☎0331 / POP 90,000

'La Perla del Norte' is an easygoing city on the Río Paraguay with poetic early-20th-century buildings and a laid-back ambience. Action around here means a trotting horse hauling a cart of watermelons or a boatload of people and their cargo arriving at the port. Indeed, river cruises are the main reason travelers come to Concepción, whether it's for an adventurous odyssey north to Brazil or just a short weekend jaunt upriver with the locals to nearby sandy beaches.

Sights & Activities

Several stunning **mansions**, now municipal buildings, stand out along Estigarribia.

Maria Auxiliadora MONUMENT
(Agustín Pinedo) The city's most eye-catching monument is the enormous statue of Maria Auxiliadora (Virgin Mary), which towers over the northern end of the main avenue.

Museo del Cuartel de la Villa Real MUSEUM
(cnr Marie López & Cerro Cordillera; ⏲7am-noon Mon-Sat) FREE If you don't catch the town's sleepy syndrome, the museum in the beautifully restored barracks exhibits historical and war paraphernalia.

Museo de Arqueología Industrial MUSEUM
(Agustín Pinedo) FREE If machines rev you up, this open-air museum features an assortment of antique industrial and agricultural mechanisms.

Sleeping & Eating

It's not cheap to stay in Concepción and you may be a little disappointed at what you get for your money. For food you are best eating at one of the hotels, unless you happen to be addicted to rotisserie chicken – in which case Franco is lined with places ready to sell you a fix.

Hotel Frances HOTEL $$
(☎24-2383; cnr Franco & CA López; s/d 130,000/190,000G; ❄@≋) Whet your appetite in every respect at this pleasant place – lovely gardens, buffet breakfast (and restaurant) and unique handmade lamps in every room.

Concepción Palace HOTEL $$$
(☎24-1858; www.concepcionpalace.com.py; Mcal López 399; s/d 330,000/390,000G; ❄@☜≋) Far and away the most upmarket hotel in the city, the stylish wood-and-leather rooms

have pretensions that look beyond the dusty streets outside. An impressive pool and the best restaurant in town complete the effect.

Getting There & Away

BUS

The **bus terminal** (☎24-2744; cnr Koff & Asunción) is eight blocks north of the centre.

For Asunción (80,000G, 4½ to six hours), La Santaniana and La Concepciónera offer the best service. Several services head to Pedro Juan Caballero (35,000G, five hours) and Filadelfia (90,000G, six hours). There are daily departures with NASA at 12:30pm and 8pm to Ciudad del Este (100,000G, nine hours).

Bahía Negra & the Paraguayan Pantanal

The Paraguayan Pantanal (Pantanal Paraguayo) is remote and rarely visited, but if you are willing to make the effort and spend more than you would in Brazil, then it is a fantastic, adventurous, off-the-beaten track destination for those with an interest in wildlife. There is little in the way of tourist infrastructure up here though, so this is very much a DIY experience, and there are no local wildlife guides to show you around.

The main access town is Bahía Negra, and while there isn't much there except a military base, a visit is a necessary evil to organize your river trips along the Río Negro. Wildlife abounds in this area, with raptors and waterbirds flushing from the riverside, marsh deer grazing in reed beds and caiman and capybara sunning themselves on exposed banks.

Sleeping & Eating

Accommodation is poor and overpriced in Bahía Negra town, a result of its remoteness. The ramshackle places along the main road charge around 50,000G per person. Food is also hard to come by, so bring it with you if you want anything other then the absolute basics.

Tres Gigantes LODGE **$$**

(☎021-22-9097; per person 100,000G, meals extra) The only place to stay in the Pantanal itself, this is an attractive wooden lodge with ceiling fans overlooking the Río Negro, an hour or so west of Bahía Negra by boat. You should reserve your visit in advance with Guyra Paraguay (p798) in Asunción to organize a boat transfer. Electricity is by generator only; it costs extra and is expensive.

Ask them about providing food; if it isn't possible you will have to bring your own, but there is at least a kitchen you can use.

Getting There & Away

From Asunción, **Stel Turismo** (☎021-551-647; cnr Avs República Argentina & Fernando de la Mora, Asunción) runs an uncomfortable weekly bus to Bahía Negra (200,000G, 18 hours) leaving at 7pm on Thursdays and returning on Saturdays, weather permitting. Access from Bahía Negra to the best wildlife areas is by motorboat only but options are limited and expensive, as fuel costs in this remote area are high. Expect to pay around 350,000G per day, plus fuel if you want to hire your own boatman.

UP THE RÍO PARAGUAY TO THE PANTANAL

North of Concepción, the Río Paraguay wends its way slowly to the Paraguayan Pantanal. Unlike in the Brazilian Pantanal, you are unlikely to see another tourist here, and except for your boat mates your main companions will be the wildlife. Bring a hammock and a mosquito net for the boat trip, prepare yourself for unusual bedfellows and claim your territory early – it gets crowded with locals. Some boats have basic cabins (around 30,000G per night) but they need to be booked well in advance. Bring your own food.

Typical routes leave Concepción for Vallemí, then Fuerte Olimpo (last place to obtain an exit stamp, though it's safer to get one before leaving Asunción) with some continuing on to tiny Bahía Negra, near the frontiers with Bolivia and Brazil. The exit stamp is only required if you're considering carrying on north into Brazil or Bolivia; if staying in Paraguay it's not needed.

Boats heading upriver from Concepción to Vallemí (65,000G, 30 hours) or as far as Bahía Negra (120,000G, 2½ to three days) include the *Aquidabán* (departs Tuesdays at 11am, returns on Fridays) and the erratic *Guaraní*, which leaves fortnightly on Monday afternoons but goes only as far as Fuerte Olimpo via Vallemí, and returns on Thursdays. Check **schedules** (☎0331-24-2435) and boats in advance; they change frequently.

GETTING TO BOLIVIA

The Ruta Trans-Chaco was once fully paved on the Paraguayan side, but after the town of Mariscal Estigarribia (the customs point at Km 510), the surface has deteriorated horribly. Despite this, several bus companies run the route from Asunción to Santa Cruz (Bolivia) daily, all leaving in the early evening. The journey supposedly takes 24 hours (200,000-300,000G) but often takes longer.

All buses stop at the customs building in Mariscal Estagarribia in the wee hours of the morning, where you must get your exit stamp, before crossing a few hours later into Bolivia at Fortín Infante Rivola (this is a border post only – no stamps!). The Bolivian customs post is a further 60km away at Ibibobo. Quality of service provided by Bolivia-bound bus companies varies considerably. Unfortunately they operate a passenger-share policy, so the company you buy your ticket with isn't necessarily the one that you travel on.

Bolivia-bound buses do not pass through the Mennonite colonies (though you can buy tickets there) and you will need to head to Mariscal Estigarribia on the morning NASA bus from Filadelfia and hang around until the early hours of the following morning to make your connection. Alternatively plan your trip so that heading back to Asunción is not too much of a hassle.

If you have time on your hands and prefer river travel, the dawdling *Aquidabán* departs from Concepción on Tuesdays at 11am for Bahía Negra (120,000G, 2½ to three days) and returns on Fridays.

THE CHACO

Large-scale deforestation in the Gran Chaco has made its way into the international headlines in recent times, and although the situation continues, for the time being the Chaco remains a great place to see wildlife. This vast plain – roughly divided into the flooded palm savannas of the Humid Chaco (the first 350km west of Asunción) and the spiny forests of the Dry Chaco (the rest) – encompasses the entire western half of Paraguay and stretches into Argentina and Bolivia.

Bisected by the **Ruta Trans-Chaco**, it's an animal-lover's paradise, with flocks of waterbirds and birds of prey abounding, easily spotted along the roadside. Although the Chaco accounts for more than 60% of Paraguayan territory, less than 3% of the population actually lives here. Historically it was a refuge for indigenous hunter-gatherers; today the most obvious settlements are the Mennonite communities of the Central Chaco.

The Mennonite Colonies

Of the three Mennonite Colonies in the Central Chaco, only two are easily accessible on public transport – Filadelfia and Loma Plata. Many people are surprised by just how small these towns are. Although there's not much to do here except take in the unique atmosphere, they make for an interesting short break and are good bases for exploring the surrounding area.

Getting There & Away

Bus companies have offices along and near Av Hindenburg in Filadelfia. NASA has a daily service to Asunción (70,000G, eight hours), and a daily bus runs to Concepción (90,000G, eight hours). Buses to/from Filadelfia pass through Loma Plata en route.

As most locals have their own transport, getting between the colonies by bus is tricky. Local transport is infrequent, usually leaving in the early morning and late evening.

Filadelfia

0491 / POP 8000 (COLONY)

This neat Mennonite community, administrative center of Fernheim colony, resembles a suburb of Munich plonked in the middle of a sandy desert. Though dusty Av Hindenburg is the main street, the town lacks a real center; its soul is the giant dairy cooperative.

Sights

Jakob Unger Museum MUSEUM

(Av Hindenburg; 7-11:30am Mon-Fri) FREE The flash new natural history museum, named after the famous Mennonite naturalist, is stuffed with taxidermied animals.

Colonist's Museum MUSEUM
(Av Hindenburg; ⏲7-11.30am Mon-Fri) FREE The creaky wooden building that houses the museum is the original colony headquarters. It's filled with a bit of everything, from information about Mennonite history to handmade flamethrowers for combating locusts and colorful Nivaclé headdresses.

Sleeping & Eating

Hotel Florida HOTEL $$
(☎43-2151; www.hotelfloridachaco.com; Hindenburg 984; s 200,000-250,000G, d 240,000-320,000G; ❄📶🏊) As orderly as a German train schedule and by far Filadelfia's nicest accommodation. Variations in room prices refer to the difference between 'new' and 'old' rooms. The newer rooms are nicer and a little larger.

Girasol BRAZILIAN $$
(Unruh; buffet 60,000G) Girasol is a good option that serves delicious all-you-can-eat Brazilian *asados*.

Shopping

Cooperativa Mennonita SUPERMARKET
(Unruh cnr Hindenburg) It's worth a trip to the gigantic, well-stocked Cooperativa Mennonita supermarket. It's amazing how much you can fit under one roof, but you may find yourself the only person paying; the Mennonites deal in credit more than hard currencies.

Information

Tourist Information (Av Hindenburg, Filadelfia; ⏲7-11:30am Mon-Fri) Information in English, German and Spanish.

Loma Plata

☎0492 / POP 12,500 (COLONY)

The Menno colony's administrative center is the oldest and most traditional of the Mennonite settlements. The rambling Cooperativa Supermarket is worth a visit for an insight into Mennonite life.

Sights

Museum of Mennonite History MUSEUM
(Loma Plata; ⏲8am-noon Mon-Fri) FREE An excellent little museum and tourist information center, in a complex of pioneer houses, with an interesting display of original photographs and documents chronicling the colony's history. It's next to the town's Cooperativa.

Sleeping & Eating

Loma Plata Inn HOTEL $$
(☎25-3235; Eligio Ayala; s/d 200,000/250,000G, buffet 78,000G; ❄@📶) Comfortable and professionally run. It's the best place to stay in town and has a pricey but excellent *rodízio* restaurant, Chaco Grill.

Hotel Mora HOTEL $$
(☎25-2255; Sandstrasse 803; s/d 110,000G/200,000G; ❄@📶) Appealing, spotless rooms around a grassy setting.

★**Meshin** CHINESE $$
(Loma Plata; buffet per kilo 40,000G) A real treat and a bit of a surprise considering the location. Out near the airstrip, the Meshin serves probably the best Chinese buffet in the country.

MENNONITE COMMUNITIES IN THE CHACO

Some 15,000 Mennonites inhabit the Chaco. According to their history, Canadian Mennonites were invited to Paraguay to settle what they believed to be lush, productive territory in return for their rights – religious freedom, pacifism, independent administration of their communities, permission to speak German and practice their religious beliefs. The reality of the harsh, arid Chaco came as a shock, and a large percentage of the original settlers succumbed to disease, hunger and thirst as they struggled to gain a foothold.

There are other Mennonite communities elsewhere in Paraguay, but those in the Chaco are renowned for both their perseverance in the 'Green Hell' and subsequent commercial success; their cooperatives provide much of the country's dairy products, among other things.

Today there are three main colonies in the Chaco. The oldest colony, **Menno**, was founded by the original settlers in 1927, and is centered around Loma Plata. **Fernheim** (capital Filadelfia), was founded in 1930 by refugees from the Soviet Union, followed by **Neuland** (capital Neu-Halbstadt), founded by Ukrainian Germans in 1947.

Around the Mennonite Colonies

Unless you have your own transport or can arrange something locally, it can be difficult to explore the area around the Mennonite towns. But if you make the effort, there are some fantastic natural attractions that will make it worth your while.

Sights & Activities

Laguna Capitán WILDLIFE WATCHING
A series of ephemeral saline lakes that form in the area to the east of Loma Plata are a key habitat for migrating birds. Though individual lagoons may be dry for several years before filling after a good rainstorm, the birds somehow find them. Laguna Capitán is one of the most accessible.

It is best from May to September when flocks of exotic ducks and flamingos obscure the water. From October to December and March to April they are used by waders on passage. Accommodation is available in **dorm rooms** (0983-34-4463; r per person 50,000G) with advance booking, and there is a kitchen available for use (50,000G per day).

Fortín Boquerón MUSEUM
(admission 5000G; 8am-6pm Tue-Sat) Fortín Boquerón is the site of one of the decisive battles of the Chaco War (1932–35). There is an excellent museum as well as a graveyard of the fallen and a gigantic monument constructed from the original defenses and trenches. The site is 65km south of a turnoff at Cruce Los Pioneros on the Ruta Trans-Chaco.

Look for the hollowed-out palo borracho tree used as a sniper's nest. From the front it looks like a woodpecker hole but, despite being gutted more than 70 years ago, the tree is still alive.

Fortín Toledo WILDLIFE WATCHING
(www.cccipy.org; admission 20,000G) Fortín Toledo also preserves Chaco War trenches but is perhaps more interesting for the **Proyecto Taguá** breeding project. The Chacoan peccary (or taguá) is a pig-like creature that was known only from subfossil remains until its remarkable rediscovery in the 1970s. The project, initiated by San Diego Zoo, acts as a reintroduction program for this painfully shy and critically endangered species.

DON'T MISS

THE TRANSCHACO RALLY

The **Transchaco Rally** (http://rally.com.py) is a three-day world motorsports competition, held in September and said to be one of the toughest on the planet. Book accommodation in advance if visiting at this time.

Herds of friendly collared peccaries and nasty white-lipped peccaries are also kept here, giving you a unique opportunity to compare all three species and their differing characters. Also look out for the rare black-bodied woodpecker.

Fortín Toledo is accessed via a turnoff from the Ruta Trans-Chaco at Km 475. Follow the peccary signs for 5km or so. There is self-catering **accommodation** (0985-10-7200; per person 80,000G) in a spic-and-span house here, but you'll need to book in advance and take your own food and drink.

Northwestern National Parks

Once the realm of nomadic Ayoreo foragers, **Parque Nacional Defensores del Chaco** is a wooded alluvial plain; isolated **Cerro León** (500m) is its greatest landmark. The dense thorn forest harbors large cats such as jaguars and pumas, as well as tapirs and herds of peccary. The free accommodation is dreadful, and you'll need to bring all your own food, drink and fuel for the generator. 'Defensores' is a long 830km from Asunción, over roads impassable to ordinary vehicles, and there's no regular public transport. It's not a good idea to attempt to visit without a guide, and don't bother if you don't have a 4WD vehicle.

A more accessible option is **Parque Nacional Teniente Agripino Enciso**, which boasts a better infrastructure including an interpretation center and a visitors' house with kitchen and some air-conditioned rooms. Again, bring all your own food and water.

A short hop further north is **Parque Nacional Médanos del Chaco**. There are no accommodations here and it should not be attempted without a guide. The habitat is more open than at Enciso and birdwatchers should keep their eyes peeled for local species such as the quebracho crested-tinamou and spot-winged falconet.

NASA runs a single weekly minibus on Wednesday at 5am from Mariscal Estigarribia to Enciso (60,000G, six hours) that returns at 3pm the same afternoon. Your best bet for coordinating with it is to take one of the Santa Cruz–bound buses from Asunción on Monday evening and get off at Mariscal (70,000G, eight hours) when everybody else does their customs formalities. There is a half-decent **hotel** (☎cell 0975-513371; opposite the military base; s/d 120,000/180,000G) in Mariscal Estigarribia with a wildly charismatic (or perhaps slightly unhinged) owner, Dardo. He alone is worth the cost of a room. Otherwise be prepared to sit around for a few hours before the sun comes up.

UNDERSTAND PARAGUAY

Paraguay Today

Paraguay is currently somewhat of a pariah in South America, following a series of events in 2012 that led to the impeachment of the elected president Fernando Lugo. Vice president Federico Franco took the reins following a political struggle in which Lugo was tried and found guilty of failing to perform his presidential duties by the senate, with regards to his handling of land-rights disputes. The brevity of the trial process, which was completed in less than 24 hours, raised eyebrows internationally and resulted in accusations of an anti-democratic abuse of process from neighboring countries.

The events were officially declared a coup d'état by the trade bloc Mercosur, of which Paraguay is a member; Argentina, Brazil and Uruguay all refused to recognize the legitimacy of the Franco government. Mercosur suspended Paraguay from the bloc until free elections were held in April 2013, and this position was later followed unanimously by Unasur (Union de Naciones Suramericanas; every country in South America is a member). Following the suspension of Paraguay from Mercosur, Venezuela was admitted as a full member. Paraguay had previously vetoed Venezuela's inclusion.

Defenders of the process claim that Paraguay was exercising its democratic and sovereign rights to govern as permitted in the national constitution, and called the disapproval of its neighbors a modern-day attack by the Triple Alliance.

When elections were finally held in April 2013, the Colorado Party found itself back in power under the leadership of tobacco magnate Horacio Cartes. Cartes promised a 'new direction' for Paraguay by improving infrastructure, and he continued the economic upswing by inviting foreign investment. However, he raised suspicions about his intentions when he publicly invited multinationals to 'use and abuse' Paraguay. With frequent corruption scandals linking prominent politicians with the drug trade (coined *narcopoliticos* by the press), the accelerating deforestation of the Chaco and the abandonment of many of the social policies introduced by Lugo, the Cartes government hasn't yet delivered on the promises it made when taking office.

History

Pedro de Mendoza's expedition founded Asunción in 1537, and the city became the most significant Spanish settlement east of the Andes for nearly 50 years until Buenos Aires was fully established. It declined in importance once it became clear that the hostile Chaco impeded the passage towards the fabled 'City of Gold' in modern-day Peru.

In the early 17th century, Jesuit missionaries created *reducciónes* (settlements) where the indigenous Guaraní were introduced to European high culture, new crafts, new crops and new methods of cultivation. By the time of their expulsion in 1767 (because of Madrid's concern that their power had become too great), the Jesuit influence had spread to what is today Bolivia, Brazil and Argentina.

The bloodless revolution of May 1811 gave Paraguay the distinction of being the first South American country to declare its independence from Spain. Since independence, however, Paraguayan history has been dominated by a cast of dictators who have influenced the direction of the country.

Dr José Gaspar Rodríguez de Francia was the first leader of independent Paraguay. Chosen as the strongest member of the Próceres de Mayo (founding fathers), the 'El Supremo' was initially reluctant to take charge, insisting he would accept the role only until somebody better equipped was found. That somebody never was found, and he ruled until his death in 1840. Francia sealed the country's borders to promote self-sufficiency, expropriated the properties of landholders, merchants and even the church, and established the state as the only political and economic power. Though controversial, under his rule Paraguay became the dominant power on the continent.

By the early 1860s, Francia's successor, Carlos Antonio López, had ended Paraguay's isolation by building railroads, a telegraph system, a shipyard and a formidable army. Paraguay was in a strong position at the time of his death, when power passed to his son, Francisco Solano López. Seduced by his European education, Mariscal López longed to be seen as the Napolean of the Americas. At his side was the Irish courtesan Eliza Lynch who had her own fantasies about French high society. Her dream of making Asunción the 'Paris of the Americas' turned her into an unpopular Marie Antoinette figure, and the country rapidly deteriorated under their combined rule.

When Brazil invaded Uruguay in 1865, López jumped at the opportunity to prove his military genius and save the smaller nation from its fate. In order to send his army to the rescue, permission was required to cross Argentine territory. Argentina's refusal led him to declare war on them too. With Uruguay quickly overwhelmed by the Brazilians, Paraguay suddenly found itself at war with three of its neighbors simultaneously. The disastrous War of the Triple Alliance had begun and the course of Paraguayan history would be changed forever. Allied forces outnumbered Paraguayans 10 to one, and by the end of the campaign boys as young as 12 years old were fighting on the front lines armed only with farm implements. Paraguay eventually lost half of its prewar population and 26% of its national territory.

The next war wasn't too far away. In the early 1900s and with Paraguay in political turmoil, the Bolivians began to slowly advance into the Chaco, resulting in the eruption of full-scale hostilities in 1932. The exact reasons for the Chaco War are debated, but Bolivia's desire for a sea port (via the Río Paraguay) and rumors of petroleum deposits in the area are often cited as factors.

In the punishingly hot, arid Chaco, access to water was key to military success and the war hinged around the capture and protection of water sources. Paraguay further benefited from a British-built railway line, which allowed them to bring supplies to troops from Asunción. The British had earlier warned the Bolivians not to touch their railway line or risk adding another more formidable enemy to their list. As a result the Paraguayan troops were able to overcome Bolivia's numerically stronger forces and even advance as far as the southern Bolivian town of Villamontes. With the futility of the war becoming ever more obvious, a 1935 cease-fire left no clear victor but more than 80,000 dead.

RECOMMENDED READS: PARAGUAY

At the Tomb of the Inflatable Pig (John Gimlette) Interweaves humorous travel accounts with social commentary.

Chronicle of the Guayaki Indians (Pierre Clastres) For an anthropological slant.

Historical Dictionary of Paraguay (Andrew Nickson) For history buffs.

I, the Supreme (Agusto Roa Bastos) This thoughtful novel about the dictator Dr Francia is widely considered Roa Bastos' best work.

Land Without Evil (Matthew Pallamary) Fantasy novel about the birth of modern Guaraní culture and its struggle for survival.

The Liberation of Little Heaven and Other Stories (Mark Jacobs) Collection of fictional Paraguayan short stories.

The News from Paraguay (Lily Tuck) Historical fiction focusing on Mariscal López and his relationship with Eliza Lynch, and the consequences for the nation.

Rebirth of the Paraguayan Republic (Harris Gaylord Warren) For more about Paraguay's notorious wars.

Son of Man (Augusto Roa Bastos) Paraguay's most famous author explores the country's conflict-strewn history.

The Stroessner Era (Carlos Miranda) For a look at Paraguay's infamous dictator.

Paraguay subsequently entered into a decade of disorder before a brief civil war brought the Colorado Party to power in 1949. A 1954 coup installed General Alfredo Stroessner as president. His brutal 35-year, military-dominated rule was characterized by repression and terror and is the longest dictatorship in South American history. Perceived political opponents were persecuted, tortured and 'disappeared,' elections were fraudulent and corruption became a national industry. By the time Stroessner was overthrown in yet another coup, 75% of Paraguayans had known no other leader.

Stroessner was eventually driven into exile on 3 February 1989 and Paraguay's first democratic elections were held the same year. They were won by the Colorado candidate Andrés Rodríguez, who had masterminded the coup. The Colorados then went on to win every successive election until their grip was finally broken during the historic events of April 2008, which saw Archbishop Fernando Lugo, a man with no prior political experience, elected president of the republic. Campaigning on social reform, an end to corruption and equal opportunities for all, Lugo's power base stemmed from the numerically superior lower classes – his campaign slogan 'Paraguay Para Todos' (Paraguay for everybody) struck the right note with voters. With the Colorado Party in turmoil, there was at last a sense that corruption and social injustice really could be consigned to the dustbin of history.

President Lugo's government viewed social and economic progress as one and the same and actively sought closer trade links with neighboring countries. His relationship with Evo Morales and the late Hugo Chávez brought criticism from his opponents, but marked improvements at the domestic level kept his critics at bay. In 2010 Paraguay had the third-fastest-growing economy in the world, a positive renegotiation of the greatly unfavorable Itaipú Dam contracts had been completed – ensuring that Brazil would pay Paraguay a fair rate for its electricity usage – and at last the country was beginning to move away from the bottom of the international corruption tables.

There were obstacles, however, and Lugo's election had come at a price. In order to form a government he was required to broker an uneasy alliance with several political parties, the largest of which, the Liberals, provided his vice president Federico Franco. From the outset the relationship with the Liberals and Franco in particular was a tense one, as they demanded ever increasing influence in government. To complicate matters the Colorado Party retained a majority in the senate (which must approve new government policy) and used this power to pressure for their own demands.

Following a breakdown in relations in 2012, the Liberal party withdrew its support for Lugo and joined forces with its traditional rivals the Colorados to impeach the president. The official reasons given included a breakdown of security and a failure to address the problems associated with land rights. Over 80% of the land in Paraguay is owned by just 1% of the population, and Lugo had promised to address the decades-long social imbalance by providing land for landless *campesinos*. This had infuriated the land-owning classes, who accused him of failing to protect their interests, while a lack of progress had also led to the mobilization of the *campesino* groups, pressurizing for their own rights to be respected.

With his future in the hands of a senate dominated by the same parties that sought to oust him, Lugo was declared guilty on 22 June 2012 after a shotgun trial. Vice president Franco was sworn in the same day.

Culture

Some 95% of Paraguayans are considered *mestizos* (of mixed indigenous and Spanish descent). Spanish is the language of business and most prevalent in the cities, while in the *campaña* (countryside) Guaraní is more common. Jopará (a mixture of the two) is used in some parts of the media. The remaining 5% of the population are descendants of European immigrants (mainly Ukrainians and Germans), Mennonite farmers and indigenous tribes. Small but notable Asian, Arab and Brazilian communities are found, particularly in the south and east of the country.

More than 95% of the population lives in eastern Paraguay, only half in urban areas. Unicef reports a literacy rate of 94%, an infant mortality rate of 2% and an average life expectancy of 72 years. The annual population growth rate is 1.5%.

Statistically, Paraguay is the second-poorest South American country, though walking around the countrýs cities you might find it hard to believe. Lines of souped-up Mercedes Benz' whiz around, classy restaurants are full to bursting and there are houses the size of palaces. Contrast this with the lives of the rural poor, where landless *campesinos* live hand to mouth and are exploited by wealthy landowners who employ long discredited *latifundi* (large landholding) models. They continue to represent the country's biggest social problem.

Paraguayan towns are frequently nicknamed 'Capital of…' after their most notable features or products. Encarnación for example is 'Capital de Carnaval,' Coronel Bogado 'Capital de Chipa' and Itauguá 'Capital de Ñandutí.'

Paraguayans are famously laid-back and rightly renowned for their warmth and hospitality. Sipping *tereré* in the 40 degrees C shade while shooting the breeze takes the better part of a day. Siesta is obligatory and in some communities extends from noon to sunset, making the early morning and dusk the busiest times of day.

Though things have improved, corruption remains a part of daily life. For visitors, corruption is most likely to manifest itself in the form of police soliciting bribes or higher prices for gringos.

Ninety percent of the population claims to be Roman Catholic, but folk variants are common and evangelical Christianity is on the rise. Most indigenous peoples have retained their core religious beliefs, or modified them only slightly, despite nominal allegiance to Catholicism or evangelical Protestantism.

Arts

As many intellectuals and artists will tell you, the government gives little funding to the arts. Many artists, musicians and painters have left the country to perform or work elsewhere. Nevertheless, the country boasts some well-known figures.

Paraguay's major literary figures are poet-critic and writer Josefina Plá and poet-novelist Augusto Roa Bastos, winner of the 1990 Cervantes Prize (he died in 2005 aged 87). Despite many years in exile, Bastos focused on Paraguayan themes and history drawing from personal experience. Contemporary writers include Nila López, poet Jacobo A Rauskin, Luis María Martínez, Ramón Silva Ruque Vallejos, Delfina Acosta and Susy Delgado.

Paraguayan music is entirely European in origin. The most popular instruments are the guitar and the harp, while traditional dances include the lively *polkas galopadas* and the *danza de la botella*, where dancers balance bottles on their heads. A trip to the theater or the opera is something of a status symbol for Asunción's moneyed classes, but is less prevalent elsewhere.

Cuisine

Beef is succulent, abundant and easily rivals that of Argentina. The best cuts are *tapa de cuadril* (rump steak) and *corte americano* (T-bone), though the most common (and cheapest) are fatty *vacio* (flank) and chewy but flavorsome *costillas* (ribs).

Grains, particularly maize, are common ingredients in traditional foods, while *mandioca* (manioc) is the standard accompaniment for every meal. *Chipa* (a type of bread made with manioc flour, eggs and cheese) is sold everywhere but is best in the southern town of Coronel Bogado. Empanadas are great wherever you buy them.

Paraguayans consume massive quantities of yerba maté (a type of tea), most commonly as refreshing ice-cold *tereré* (iced maté) and generously spiked with *yuyos* (medicinal herbs). Roadside stands offer *mosto* (sugarcane juice), while *caña* (cane alcohol) is the fiery alcoholic alternative. Local beers, especially Baviera and Pilsen, are excellent.

Sports

Paraguayans are *fútbol*-mad. It's not uncommon to see large groups of men in bars supping Pilsen and watching the Copa Libertadores on a communal TV. The most popular soccer teams, Olímpia and Cerro Porteño, have a fierce rivalry and the national team defied the odds to reach the quarterfinals of the 2010 World Cup and finished runner-up in the 2011 Copa America. Tennis, basketball, volleyball, hunting and fishing are also popular. The headquarters of **Conmebol** (☎021-65-0993; www.conmebol.com; Av Sudamericana Km 12, Asunción), the South American football confederation, is in Luque, on the road to the airport. It houses an impressive museum depicting the history of the sport on the continent.

Environment

The country is divided into two distinct regions, east and west of the Río Paraguay. Eastern Paraguay historically was a mosaic of Atlantic Forest and *cerrado* savanna, with the unique Mesopotamian flooded grasslands in the extreme south of the country. Much of the original habitat has now been converted to agriculture, especially in Departamentos Itapúa and Alto Paraná, but substantial tracts of these pristine but globally endangered habitats still remain. To the west is the Gran Chaco, a lush palm savanna in its lower reaches (Humid Chaco), and a dense, arid, thorny forest (Dry Chaco) further north and west. The northeastern Chaco represents the southern extent of the great Pantanal wetland.

Wildlife

Wildlife is diverse, but the expanding rural population is putting increasing pressure on eastern Paraguay's fauna. Mammals are most abundant and easy to see in the largely unpopulated Chaco. Anteaters, armadillos, maned wolves, giant otters, lowland tapirs, jaguars, pumas, peccaries and brocket deer are all still relatively numerous here. In the mid-1970s the Chacoan peccary, a species previously known only from subfossilized remains, was found alive and well in the Paraguayan Chaco, where it had evaded discovery for centuries.

Birdlife is abundant, and Paraguay is home to 713 bird species. The national bird is the bare-throated bellbird, named for its remarkable call, but serious bird-watchers will be in search of endangered, limited-range species, such as the white-winged nightjar, saffron-cowled blackbird, lesser nothura, helmeted woodpecker and black-fronted piping-guan. Reptiles, including caiman and anaconda, are widespread. The amphibian that will most likely catch your eye is the enormous rococo toad, which is attracted to lights, even in urban areas.

National Parks

Paraguay's national parks are largely remote and typically inadequately protected. Most have no visitor facilities, but those we have covered have some kind of infrastructure set up for visitors. If you want to visit you should take all your food and drink with you. There is also a series of excellent and well-run private reserves across the country.

SEAM TOURIST INFORMATION
(☎021-61-5805; www.seam.gov.py; Av Madame Lynch 3500, Asunción; ⏰7am-1pm Mon-Fri) Responsible for the maintenance of national parks.

Red de Conservación de Tierras Privadas TOURIST INFORMATION
(☎021-67-4989; www.conservacionprivadapy.org; cnr Viñuales & Mariscal López, Fernando de la Mora) Coordinates the private reserve network.

Environmental Issues

The disappearance of the eastern Atlantic Forest has been alarming; much of the rainforest has been logged for agriculture, especially soybean and wheat crops, and mostly for the benefit of large-scale, wealthy farmers. The construction of the Itaipú hydroelectric plant was not without controversy, and a second dam at Yacyretá, near Ayolas, has permanently altered the country's southern border (made up of riverbanks).

The country's most pressing environmental worry, however, now concerns the rapid deforestation of the previously pristine Chaco. With the Paraguayan economy healthy and new technological advances making it easier than ever to raise cattle in this harsh environment, wealthy ranchers are taking advantage of the low land prices in the western region to establish new *estancias* (ranches). The resulting deforestation has been rapid and has made international headlines.

Furthermore, experiments in the development of soybean strains that can withstand the harsh Chaco climate potentially pose a serious threat to the remaining natural habitats. Such a prospect would introduce highly profitable monocultures into this delicate ecosystem, threatening to tip the ecological balance permanently.

SURVIVAL GUIDE

Directory A–Z

ACCOMMODATIONS

City hotels and hostels are generally good value with air-conditioning, private bathrooms and wifi access. *Residenciales* (guesthouses), though worn and of a distant era, are usually basic but

SLEEPING PRICE RANGES

The following price ranges refer to a double room with bathroom in high season. Unless otherwise stated, breakfast is included in the price.

$ less than 150,000G

$$ 150,000G to 300,000G

$$$ more than 300,000G

clean. *Hospedajes* are at the lowest end of the scale and can attract suspect clientele. Camping facilities are rare. Most land is privately owned, so you can't pitch a tent without permission. In the Chaco, outside of the main towns, you will need your own food, drink and bed sheets.

ACTIVITIES

Extraordinary biodiversity makes Paraguay a notable destination for ecotourism, in particular bird-watching.

BUSINESS HOURS

Banks 8am to 1pm Monday to Saturday; *casas de cambio* (exchange houses) keep longer hours.

Government offices 7am to 1pm or 2pm Monday to Friday.

Restaurants noon to 3pm & 6pm to 11pm. Many close on Mondays.

Shops 8am to noon & 2pm to 7pm Monday to Friday & Saturday mornings.

ELECTRICITY

Use plugs with two round or flat pins and no grounding pin – 220V, 50Hz.

EMBASSIES & CONSULATES

A full, updated list of diplomatic offices in Paraguay is available at www.mre.gov.py/v2/Contenido/334/representaciones-diplomaticas-extranjeras-en-paraguay. All of the embassies listed here are in Asunción.

Argentinian Embassy (021-21-2320; cnr España & Perú)

Bolivian Embassy (021-21-1430; Israel 309)

Brazilian Embassy (021-24-8400; cnr Irrazábal & Eligio Ayala, Asunción; 7am-noon Mon-Fri) Consulates in Encarnación and Ciudad del Este (061-50-0984; Pampliega 205; 7am-noon Mon-Fri).

French Embassy (021-21-3840; Av España 893)

German Embassy (021-21-4009; Av Venezuela 241)

UK Embassy (021-328-5507; Av Marsical López 3794 near Cruz del Chaco, Edificio Citicenter, 5th fl)

US Embassy (021-21-3715; Av Mariscal López 1776)

GAY & LESBIAN TRAVELERS

Paraguay is an old-fashioned country, with conservative views. Despite a growing LGBT movement in the country, high-ranking government officials, including the president, have expressed views that suggest that reviewing equality laws is not high on their agenda. Public displays of affection between same-sex couples are unknown. Gay bars are appearing in Asunción, but on the whole homosexuality is not yet widely accepted.

HEALTH

Paraguay presents relatively few health problems for travelers. Private hospitals are better than public hospitals, and those in Asunción, Ciudad del Este and Encarnación are the best.

- There are occasional minor outbreaks of dengue fever, but no malaria.
- Water is drinkable in the cities, but avoid it in the countryside. In the Chaco it is positively salty.
- Carry sunscreen, a hat and plenty of bottled water to avoid becoming dehydrated.
- Avoid cheap condom brands.

INTERNET ACCESS

Internet is widely available in cities, but limited in smaller towns. An hour of use costs around 3000G to 6000G. Wi-fi is common in the cities, and all hotels and most bars have it, though it is usually password protected.

LANGUAGE COURSES

Alianza Francesa (021-21-0503; Estigarribia 1039, Asunción)

Centro Cultural Paraguayo-Americano (021-22-4831; www.ccpa.edu.py; Av España 352, Asunción)

IDIPAR (021-44-7896; www.idipar.net; Manduvirá 963, Asunción) Spanish and Guaraní courses with homestay options.

Instituto Cultural Paraguayo Alemán (021-20-9060; Juan de Salazar 310, Asunción)

MAPS

Instituto Geográfico Militar (021-20-6344; Artigas 920, Asunción; 7am-5:30pm Mon-Fri) For more detailed maps of the interior, the

EATING PRICE RANGES

The following price ranges refer to a standard main course.

$ less than 15,000G

$$ 15,000G to 55,000G

$$$ more than 55,000G

Instituto Geográfico Militar sells topographical maps that cover most of the country.

Touring y Automóvil Club Paraguayo (☎021-21-0550; www.tacpy.com.py; cnr 25 de Mayo & Brasil) Produces a series of road and town maps for tourists that are often available in gas stations.

MONEY

On the back of the soy boom, Paraguay continued to enjoy a healthy economy, even while the rest of the world plunged into economic crisis. The guaraní currency remains strong and the cost of living in dollars has risen exponentially over the last decade. Though it is still a reasonably cheap country to visit, first-time visitors often find costs to be higher than they had expected.

Banknote values are 2000G, 5000G, 10,000G, 20,000G, 50,000G and 100,000G; increasingly useless coins come in denominations of 50G, 100G, 500G and 1000G. Keep plenty of change and small notes as you go along – it comes in handy.

ATMs & Credit Cards

- ATMs in major cities and towns are connected to Visa, MasterCard and Cirrus networks but sometimes incur usage charges.
- Outside of the Mennonite Colonies there are no ATMs in the Chaco.
- Plastic is rarely accepted outside the major cities, and sometimes comes with a surcharge.

Exchanging Money

- *Casas de cambio* are abundant in major cities, but shop around for best rates.
- Street money changers give slightly better rates for cash and can be lifesavers at weekends, but do your calculations in advance!
- Rates for changing pounds sterling are poor outside of Asunción.
- Change all your unwanted guaraníes before you leave Paraguay or risk being stuck with them!

POST

- The Paraguayan *correo* claims to be the best on the continent, but in reality things are regularly lost en route.
- Essential mail should be sent *certificado* (registered) for a small additional fee (4000G).
- Take packages to the post office unsealed so that the contents can be verified, and close them up with your own materials after inspection.

PUBLIC HOLIDAYS

Government offices and businesses in Paraguay are closed for the following official holidays.

Año Nuevo (New Year's Day) 1 January

Cerro Corá (Heroes Day) 1 March

Semana Santa (Easter) March/April, dates vary

Día de los Trabajadores (Labor Day) 1 May

Independencia Patria (Independence Day) 15 May

Paz del Chaco (End of Chaco War) 12 June

Fundación de Asunción (Founding of Asunción) 15 August

Victoria de Boquerón (Battle of Boquerón) 29 September

Día de la Virgen (Immaculate Conception Day) 8 December

Navidad (Christmas Day) 25 December

RESPONSIBLE TRAVEL

- Avoid buying crafts made from native woods (such as *lapacho* and *palo santo*) or wild animals.
- Visitors interested in natural history and conservation should contact Para la Tierra (p787), the **Fundación Moisés Bertoni** (☎021-60-8740; www.mbertoni.org.py; Argüello 208, Villa Morra, Asunción) or **Guyra Paraguay** (☎021-22-9097; Gaetano Martino 215, Asunción).

SAFE TRAVEL

- Despite what you may hear from people who have never been, Paraguay is one of the continent's safest countries for travelers. With the exception of Ciudad del Este and certain parts of Asunción, cities are quite safe to walk around, even at night.
- The Chaco environment is hostile and desolate with limited infrastructure – it is highly recommended that you go with a guide.
- Beware of strong currents when swimming in rivers.

TELEPHONE

- With the cell phone revolution near complete, private *locutorios* (phone offices) are less common than before, though most have internet service as well.
- International calls cost more than US$1 per minute, even with lower nighttime rates.
- Local cell phone rates are low and some companies offer free SIM cards, or SIM cards with *saldo* (credit) already charged to them for a small fee. Though they are much cheaper than using roaming, they do not allow you to make (only to receive) international calls.
- The best cell phone companies are Tigo, Personal and Claro; their *tarjetas* (cards) for charging credit to your phone are sold at every newsagent.
- Claro SIM cards can be formatted to work in both Brazil and Argentina.
- International operator: (☎0010)
- International direct dial: (☎002)

TOILETS

➡ Public toilets are thin on the ground. Most bus terminals have one – for 1500G you get a smelly loo and an (often insufficient) wad of paper.

➡ Go when you can in restaurants or hotels.

➡ Carry your own toilet paper and don't flush it.

➡ Most buses have an on-board toilet (liquid only please!) but cheaper services and those in more remote areas do not.

TOURIST INFORMATION

The government tourist ministry Senatur (p776) has picked up its game in the last few years and there are good tourist offices in Asunción and the other major cities.

Asociación de Colonias Mennonitas del Paraguay (☎021-22-6059; www.acomepa.org; Colombia cnr Estados Unidos, Asunción) Has brochures about Mennonite communities and runs informative offices in Loma Plata and Filadelfia.

VISAS

Visitors from Canada, New Zealand and the US need visas that must be solicited in the Paraguayan embassy of the respective countries prior to travel or in a Paraguayan consulate in a bordering country. It is theoretically possible to get visas at the border only if arriving by air, but complications sometimes arise and you can save the stress with a bit of planning.

Visas may be requested and obtained on the same day at most consulates but requirements and cost depend where you are applying. Typically you will need two passport photos and two copies of each of the following: your passport, proof of onward travel and proof of sufficient funds. Other nationalities need only a valid passport for entry.

Visa requirements change frequently. Check www.lonelyplanet.com for the latest information.

Immigration Office (☎021-44-6673; cnr Ayala & Caballero, Asunción; ⌚7am-1pm Mon-Fri) For information about immigration points, entrance or exit stamps, or visa paperwork.

VOLUNTEERING

Volunteering is a comparatively new concept in Paraguay, but the idea is starting to take root. Para la Tierra (p787), based at Laguna Blanca, are pioneers of the idea, offering an award-winning volunteer and intern program for socially aware, eco-minded visitors.

Apatur (☎021-49-7028; www.turismorural.org.py) A rural tourism association that can help make placements on *estancias* (ranches) with a little advance warning.

WOMEN TRAVELERS

Paraguay is a reasonably safe country for women, but solo travelers should take care. Young unaccompanied women are likely to be hit on by Paraguayan men, especially if they are drinking alcohol. Generally it is harmless; be firm but polite. Modest dress is recommended, Paraguayan women tend not to show much skin, and flaunting that custom risks misinterpretation.

ℹ Getting There & Away

AIR

Paraguay's **Silvio Pettirossi International Airport** (☎021-64-5600) is in Luque, a satellite town of Asunción. The airport in Ciudad del Este connects Asunción and major Brazilian destinations. Airline offices are at the airport unless otherwise stated.

Airlines

Air Europa (www.aireuropa.com) Two weekly flights between Asunción and Madrid.

American Airlines (www.aa.com; Independencia Nacional 557, Asunción) Flies to Miami.

Avianca (☎021-60-5708; www.avianca.com; cnr Recalde & Dra Dávalos, Asunción) Direct daily flight to Lima (Peru) on weekends.

Copa Airlines (☎021-61-4300; www.copaair.com; Av Boggiani, Edificio Boggiani, Asunción) Flies to Panama City.

Gol (☎021-64-5553; www.voegol.com.br) Flies to Brazilian destinations via Ciudad del Este.

LAN Chile (☎021-23-3487; www.lan.com; cnr Juan de Salazar 791 & Washington, Asunción) Flies to Santiago.

TAM Mercosur (☎021 45 1535; www.tam.com.br; Oliva 761, Asunción) Has the most daily flights from/to Buenos Aires (Argentina), São Paulo (Brazil), Santa Cruz (Bolivia) and Santiago de Chile (Chile), as well as to Ciudad del Este.

RIVER

Ferries cross into Ciudad del Este and Encarnación from Argentina. With patience, stamina, some negotiation and likely a fair amount of expense, unofficial river travel from Bahía Negra into Brazil or Bolivia is possible.

DEPARTURE TAX

There is a US$40 airport tax on all departing flights. It is usually included in the ticket, but if it isn't then pay at the desk adjacent to the entrance to the departure lounge and get a sticker on your ticket to prove it.

LAND

Negotiating Paraguayan borders can be harrowing; on the bus, off the bus, on the bus... Pay special attention when crossing from Brazil or Argentina. Ask the driver to stop at immigration (locals don't always need to) and be sure your papers are in order. Get your passport stamped on entering the country or face a fine upon leaving.

Getting Around

Buses dominate transportation, offering reasonable fares and usually efficient service. Journeys between Paraguayan cities typically take less than eight hours, depending on the start and end destinations.

AIR

Flights save time, but are not cheap. Flights link Asunción with Ciudad del Este en route to/from Brazilian destinations, and there are now charter flights between the capital and Bahía Negra for the Pantanal. A new airport at Encarnación recently began receiving infrequent charter flights, but is inconveniently located some distance outside of the city.

BOAT

You can travel by boat up the Río Paraguay. You will need a boat if you plan on exploring the Pantanal region.

BUS

Bus quality varies from luxury services with TV, air-conditioning and comfortable reclining seats to bumpy sardine cans with windows that don't open and aisles crammed with people picked up along the way. Typically you get what you pay for.

Larger towns have central terminals. Elsewhere, companies are within easy walking distance of each other.

CAR & MOTORCYCLE

It is not cheap to rent (or buy!) a car in Paraguay, but it can be worth it if there's a few of you. Flexibility is your main advantage, although buses go most places accessible to an ordinary car. Anywhere away from the main *rutas* and you'll need a 4WD (around US$150 per day). Companies often charge extra mileage for distances above 100km and gas costs about 50% more than in neighboring countries. Better deals are available for longer rentals.

Driver's License

Most rental agencies accept a home driver's license, but it's wise to back it up with an International Driver's License – the lack of one is a favorite scam for soliciting bribes.

TAXI

In Asunción taxi fares are metered; don't get in the taxi if it's not. In other cities they often are not, but no trip within city limits should cost more than 35,000G in Ciudad del Este and 25,000G elsewhere (usually less). Drivers in Asunción legally levy a 30% *recargo* (surcharge) between 10pm and 5am, and on Sundays and holidays.

TOURS

DTP (☎021-22-1816; www.dtp.com.py; Gral Brúguez 353) Tour operator/travel agent that can organize trips.

FAUNA Paraguay (☎0985-74-6866; faunaparaguay@gmail.com; www.faunaparaguay.com) Best for ecotourism, natural parks and animal-watching excursions with professional biologist guides. Reservations by email.

Peru

Includes ➡

Best Places to Eat

- ➡ Central (p815)
- ➡ Taita (p883)
- ➡ La Patarashca (p891)
- ➡ Al Frio y al Fuego (p898)

Best Places to Stay

- ➡ Niños Hotel (p849)
- ➡ Loki del Mar (p878)
- ➡ Pachamama (p837)
- ➡ Ecopackers (p849)
- ➡ Backpacker's Family House (p811)

Why Go?

Welcome to a land of extreme and intrigue. Peru's terrain ranges from glaciated Andean peaks and sprawling coastal deserts to the steamy rainforests of the Amazon Basin. Excavate the past – with temples entangled in jungle vines, windswept desert tombs and shamanic rituals still used today – to find your own lost-world adventure.

You can take the standard route chasing perfect waves off a sunny Pacific beach and ending at the cloud-topping Inca citadel of Machu Picchu. Or step off the beaten path and groove to Afro-Peruvian beats, explore remote ruins in the north or ride a slow boat down the Amazon. Wildlife, from soaring Andean condor to tapir marauding through the tropical forest, provides one more connection to the elemental.

Wherever your journey takes you, you'll find that the complex Peruvian culture holds a deep lust for life. Small wonder, then, that the land of the Incas is one of the continent's top picks for adventurous travelers.

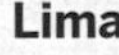

When to Go

Lima

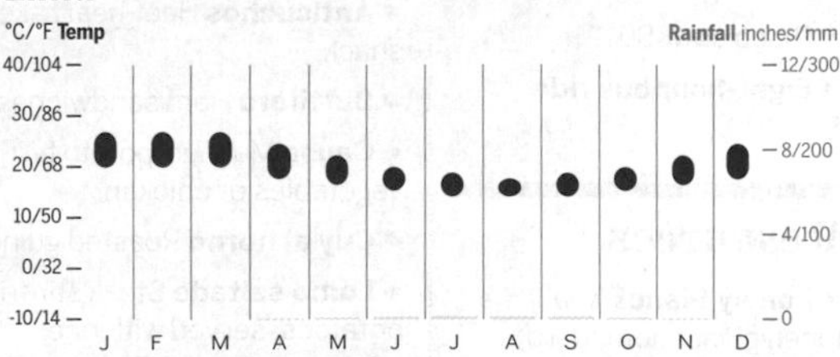

Dec–Mar The hottest, blue-sky months ideal for surf and sun on the coast.

Jun–Aug Dry season ideal for hiking the Andean highlands and eastern rainforest.

Sep–Nov & Mar–May Decent travel weather and fewer tourists.

AT A GLANCE

- **Currency** nuevo sol (S)
- **Languages** Spanish, Quechua, Aymara
- **Money** ATMs widely available, except in small villages
- **Visas** Generally not required for tourism
- **Time** GMT minus five hours

Fast Facts

- **Area** 1,285,220 sq km
- **Population** 31.1 million
- **Capital** Lima
- **Emergency** ☎105 (police)
- **Country Code** ☎51

Exchange Rates

Australia	A$1	S2.26
Canada	C$1	S2.41
Euro Zone	€1	S3.59
New Zealand	NZ$1	S2.04
UK	UK£1	S4.86
USA	US$1	S3.20

Set Your Budget

- **Budget hotel room** S85
- **Set lunch** S15
- **Pisco sour** S9
- **Eight-hour bus ride** S35-100

Resources

- **Lonely Planet** (www.lonelyplanet.com/peru)
- **Peru Official Tourism Website** (www.peru.info)
- **Living in Peru** (www.livinginperu.com)
- **Peru Links** (www.perulinks.com)

Connections

Border crossings include Arica (Chile) via Tacna; Huaquillas, Guayaquil and Macará (all in Ecuador), reached from the northern coast and highlands at Tumbes, La Tina or Jaén; Copacabana and Desaguadero (Bolivia) along Lake Titicaca; and multiple Brazilian and Bolivian towns and river ports in the Amazon.

ITINERARIES

Two Weeks

Start by exploring Lima's great food scene, nightlife and museums. Journey south by boat to the wildlife-rich Islas Ballestas. Then it's on to the sandboarding oasis of Huacachina. Fly over the mysterious Nazca Lines, then turn inland to Arequipa to trek the incredible canyons of Cañón del Colca or Cañón del Cotahuasi. Climb to Puno. From here you can boat to Lake Titicaca's floating-reed and traditional islands. Go on to Cuzco, with history, ruins and the colorful markets of the Sacred Valley. Finish by trekking to Machu Picchu via an adventurous alternative route.

Four Weeks

Follow the two-week itinerary. From Cuzco, brave the 10-hour bus ride to Puerto Maldonado to kick back at a riverside Amazon Basin wildlife lodge. Alternatively, overland tours from Cuzco visit the Manu area; with animals from the kinkajou to caiman, it's one of the planet's most biodiverse regions. Back in Lima, head to Huaraz and trek around the precipitous peaks of the Cordillera Blanca. Then bus up the coast to historic Trujillo and hit the ruins of the largest pre-Columbian city in the Americas, Chan Chan, and Huacas del Sol y de la Luna. Wrap up with a seaside break at the bustling surf town of Máncora.

Essential Food & Drink

- **Aji de gallina** Shredded-chicken and walnut stew.
- **Anticuchos** Beef-heart skewers, usually grilled as a street snack.
- **Buttifara** Ham sandwiches served on French bread.
- **Causa** Mashed-potato terrines stuffed with seafood, vegetables or chicken.
- **Cuy al horno** Roasted guinea pig.
- **Lomo saltado** Steak stir-fried with onions, tomatoes and potatoes, served with rice.
- **Novoandina** Sculptural haute cuisine devised with traditional Andean ingredients.
- **Rocoto relleno** Pepper stuffed with spicy ground meat.
- **Pisco sour** Peru's national drink is a tart grape brandy mixed with lime, sugar, egg white and bitters.

LIMA

☎01 / POP 7,606,000

With fog rolling over its colonial facades and high-rises, Lima creates a gritty first impression. Peru's fast-moving metropolis is home to almost a quarter of the country's population, a fact made most obvious by the deafening blare of car horns. After Cairo, this sprawling city is the second-driest world capital, rising above a long coastline of crumbling cliffs. Blow off the dust, though, and – like most who stay a while – you'll find that this modern city has plenty to explore, including a hip arts scene and world-class cuisine.

Once considered a dangerous place, Lima has vastly improved in security terms over the years. Miraflores and colonial Barranco are ideal for strolling, with a string of landscaped gardens with sea views. While *limeños* may prefer their chic malls, there are also crumbling pre-Inca pyramids, the waning splendor of Spanish-colonial architecture and many of the country's best museums. Escape the hubbub by dining on seafood on the waterfront, paragliding off the cliffs of Miraflores or grooving until sunrise in bohemian Barranco's bars and clubs.

History

Lima was christened the 'City of Kings' when Francisco Pizarro founded it on the Catholic feast day of Epiphany in 1535. During early Spanish-colonial times it became the continent's richest, most important town, though this all changed in 1746 when a disastrous earthquake wiped out most of the city. However, rebuilding was rapid, and most of the old colonial buildings still to be seen here date from after the earthquake.

Argentinean general José de San Martín proclaimed Peruvian independence from Spain here on July 28, 1821. Three decades later the city took a crucial step over other

Metropolitan Lima

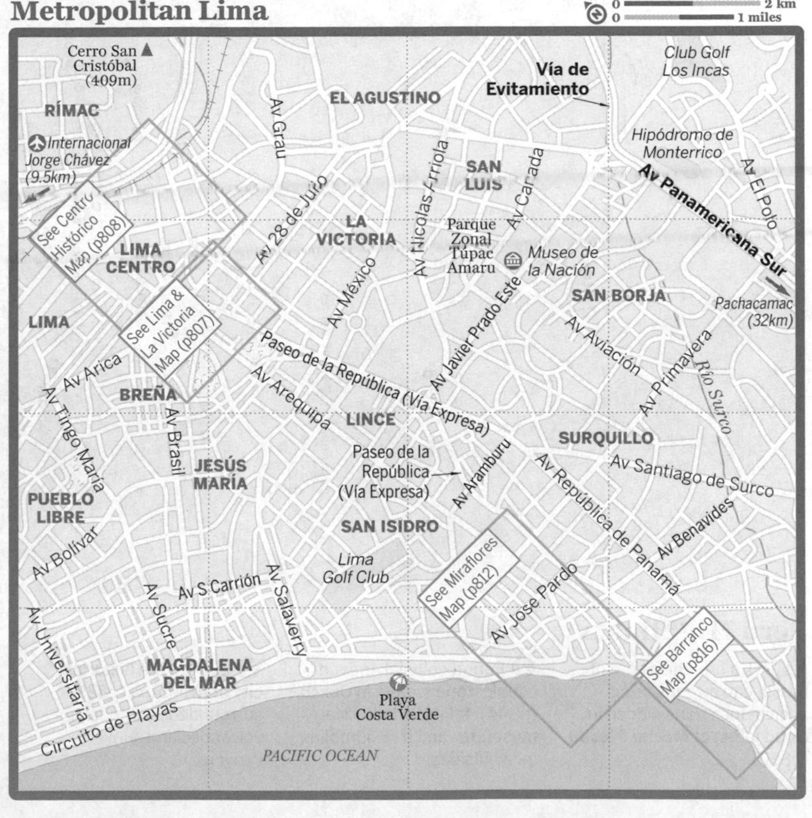

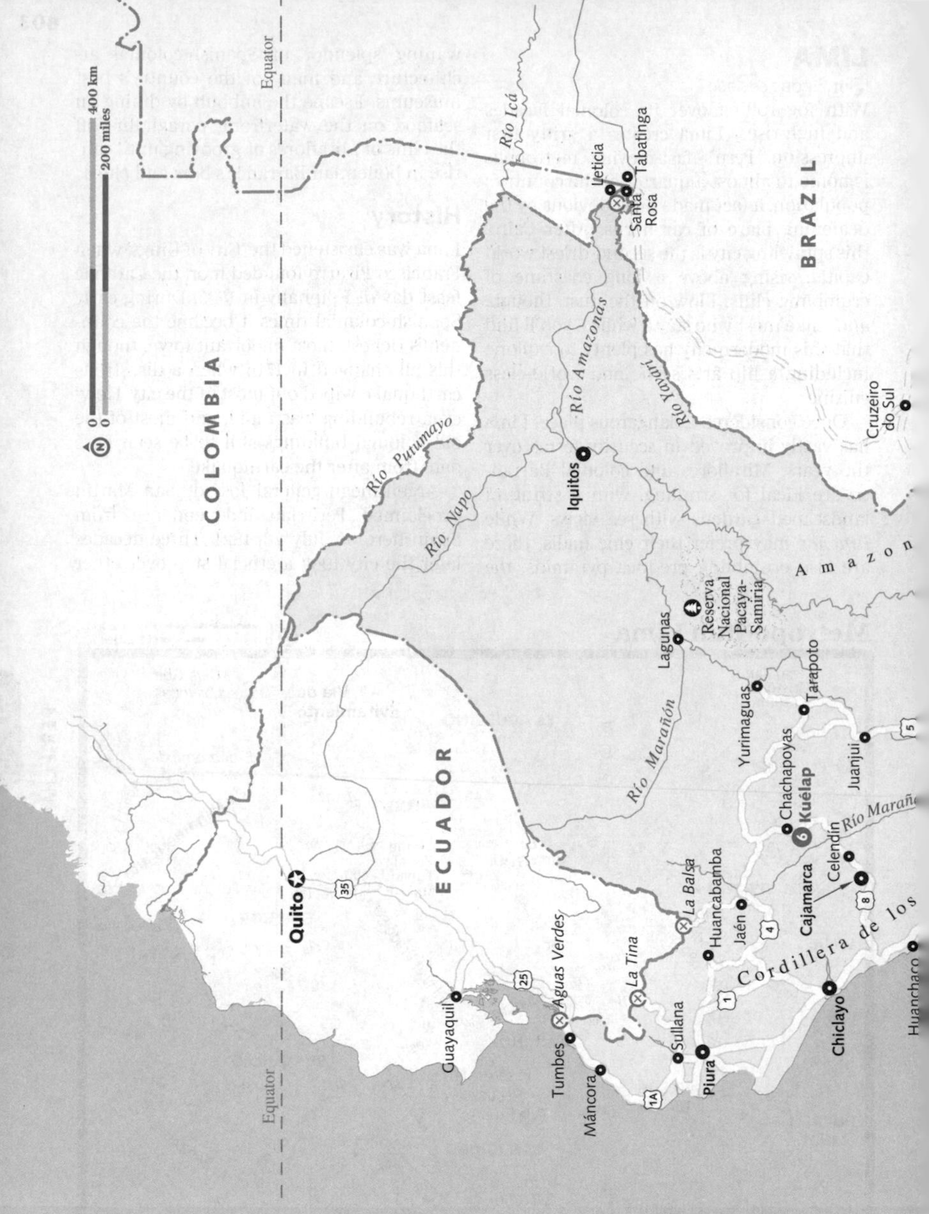

Peru Highlights

1. Trek a breathless rite of passage to awe-inspiring ancient Inca ruins hidden in cloud forest at **Machu Picchu** (p860).

2. Pound colonial Andean cobblestone streets in **Cuzco** (p844), taking in historical museums, and trek humbling Inca hillsides.

3. Explore the historical city of **Arequipa** (p829) surrounded by imposing volcanoes and sunken canyons.

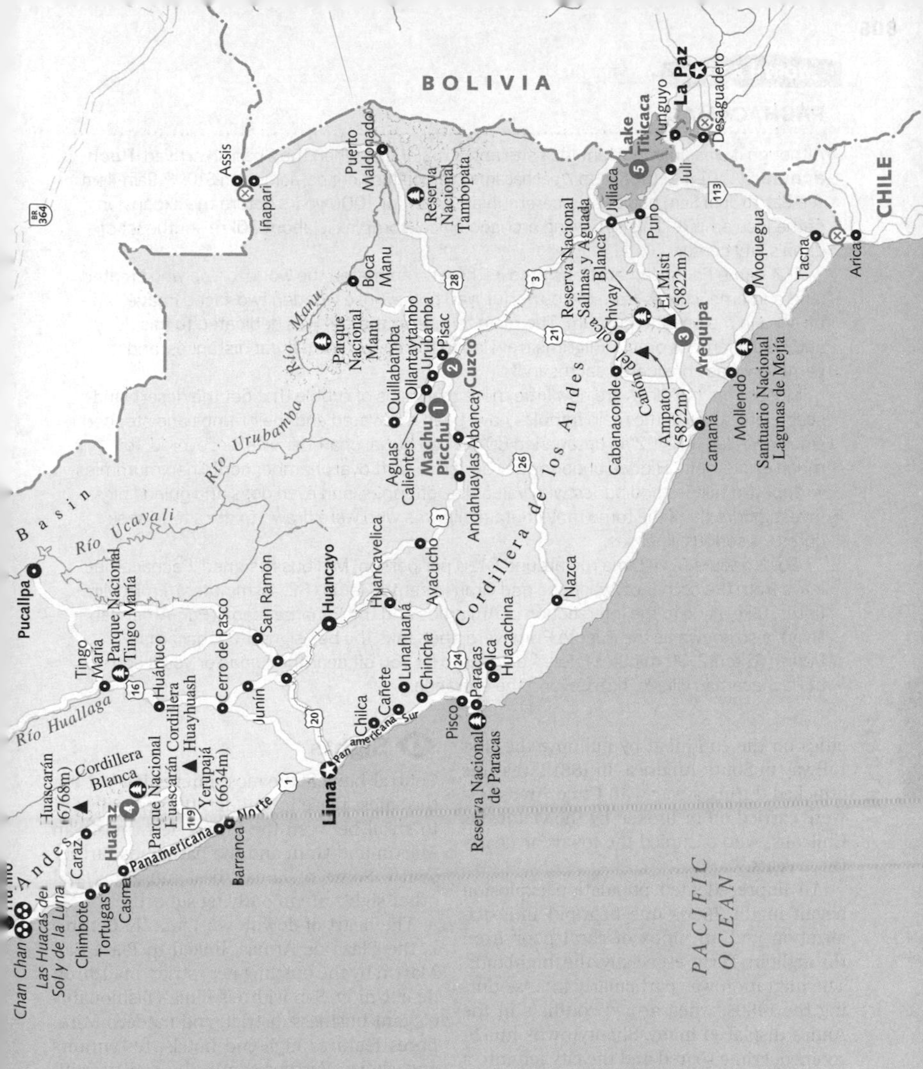

4 Tackle **Huaraz** (p880) and the **Cordillera Blanca** (p885), one of South America's most spectacular mountain ranges.

5 Visit storybook isles on **Lake Titicaca** (p837), considered the world's largest high-altitude lake, straddling the Peru–Bolivia border.

6 Scramble through **Kuélap** (p890), an immense citadel shrouded in misty cloud forest off the beaten track.

WORTH A TRIP

PACHACAMAC

Although it was an important Inca site and a major city when the Spanish arrived, **Pachacamac** (☎01-430-0168; http://pachacamac.perucultural.org.pe; admission S10; ⏲9am-4pm Tue-Sat, to 3pm Sun) had been a ceremonial center for 1000 years before the expansion of the Inca empire. This sprawling archaeological complex is about 30km southeast of Lima's city center.

The name Pachacamac, translated as 'he who animated the world' or 'he who created land and time,' comes from the powerful Wari god, whose wooden two-faced image can be seen in the on-site museum. The main temple at the site was dedicated to this deity and held a famous oracle. Pilgrims traveled to the center from great distances, and its cemetery was considered sacrosanct.

Most of the buildings are now little more than piles of rubble that dot the desert landscape, but some of the main temples have been excavated and their ramps and stepped sides revealed. In 2012 an untouched 80-person burial chamber was discovered, to much excitement. Hidden under newer burials, a 60ft oval chamber contained mummies wrapped in textiles and buried with valuables, offerings, and even dogs and guinea pigs. Investigators think the tomb may contain pilgrims who were drawn to the site to seek cures for serious illnesses.

Guided tours from Lima run around S120 per person. Minibuses signed 'Pachacamac' leave from the corner of Ayacucho and Grau in central Lima (S2, 45 minutes). From Miraflores, take a taxi to the intersection of Angamos and the Panamericana (Pan-American Hwy), also known as the Puente Primavera, then take the bus signed 'Pachacamac/Lurín' (S1 to S2, 30 minutes). Tell the driver to let you off near the *ruinas* or you'll end up at Pachacamac village, 1km beyond the entrance.

cities on the continent by building the first railway in South America. In 1881 Lima was attacked during a war with Chile. Treasures were carried off or broken by the victorious Chileans, who occupied the town for nearly three years.

An unprecedented population explosion began in the 1920s due to rapid industrialization and an influx of rural poor from throughout Peru, especially the highlands. The migration was particularly intense during the 1980s, when armed conflicts in the Andes displaced many. Shantytowns mushroomed, crime soared and the city fell into a period of steep decay.

President Fujimori took power in 1990, implementing an austere economic plan that drove up the price of gasoline by 3000%, but ultimately these extreme measures, known as 'Fujishock,' reduced inflation and stabilized the economy. Unfortunately, however, it cost the average Peruvian dearly.

Today's Lima has been rebuilt to an astonishing degree. A robust economy and a vast array of municipal improvement efforts have repaved the streets, refurbished parks and created safer public areas to bring back a thriving cultural and culinary life.

Sights

Central Lima is the most interesting but not the safest place to wander. It's generally OK to stroll between the Plazas de Armas, San Martín and Grau and the parklands further south. Some of Lima's best museums and other sights are in outlying suburbs.

The heart of downtown Lima (El Centro) is the Plaza de Armas, linked to Plaza San Martín by the bustling pedestrian mall Jirón de la Unión. San Isidro is Lima's fashionably elegant business district, and modern Miraflores features high-end hotels, restaurants and shops. Further south, the artistic clifftop community of Barranco has the hottest nightlife in town.

Museo de la Nación MUSEUM

(Museum of the Nation; ☎01-476-9878; Av Javier Prado Este 2466, San Borja) At the time of research, this museum was closed but may reopen soon, check iPerú (p810) for updates. In a brutalist concrete tower, it provides a cursory overview of Peru's civilizations, from Chavín stone carvings and the knotted-rope *quipus* (used for record-keeping) of the Incas to colonial artifacts. One must-see is the permanent exhibit **Yuyanapaq**. Quechua for 'to remember,' it's a moving photographic tribute to the Internal Conflict (1980–2000) created by Peru's Truth & Reconciliation Commission in 2003.

★ **Museo Larco** MUSEUM
(☎ 01-461-1312; www.museolarco.org; Bolívar 1515, Pueblo Libre; adult/child under 15 S30/15; ⏱ 9am-10pm) In an 18th-century viceroy's mansion, this museum offers one of the largest, best-presented displays of ceramics in Lima. Founded by pre-Columbian collector Rafael Larco Hoyle in 1926, the collection includes over 50,000 pots, with ceramic works from the Cupisnique, Chimú, Chancay, Nazca and Inca cultures. Highlights include the sublime Moche portrait vessels, presented in simple, dramatically lit cases, and a Wari weaving in one of the rear galleries that contains 398 threads to the linear inch – a record.

★ **Museo de Arte de Lima** MUSEUM
(Map p807; ☎ 01-204-0000; www.mali.pe; Paseo Colón 125; adult/child S12/4; ⏱ 10am-8pm Tue, Thu & Fri, to 5pm Sat & Sun) Known locally as MALI, Lima's principal fine-art museum is housed in a striking beaux-arts building that was recently renovated. Subjects span from pre-Columbian to contemporary art, and there's also guided visits to special exhibits. On Sunday, entry is just S1. A satellite museum is under construction in Barranco.

Museo de la Cultura Peruana MUSEUM
(Museum of Peruvian Culture; Map p808; ☎ 01-423-5892; www.limacultura.pe/directorio-cultural/museo-nacional-de-la-cultura-peruana; Alfonso Ugarte 650; admission S5; ⏱ 10am-5pm Tue-Sat) About half-a-dozen blocks west of the Plaza San Martín, on a traffic-choked thoroughfare, resides the Museo de la Cultura Peruana, a repository of Peruvian folk art. The

Lima & La Victoria

Top Sights
1 Museo de Arte de Lima B1

Sleeping
2 1900 Backpackers B1
3 Hostal Iquique A1

Eating
4 Cevichería la Choza Nautica A1

Entertainment
5 Estadio Nacional C3
6 Las Brisas del Titicaca A2

Centro Histórico

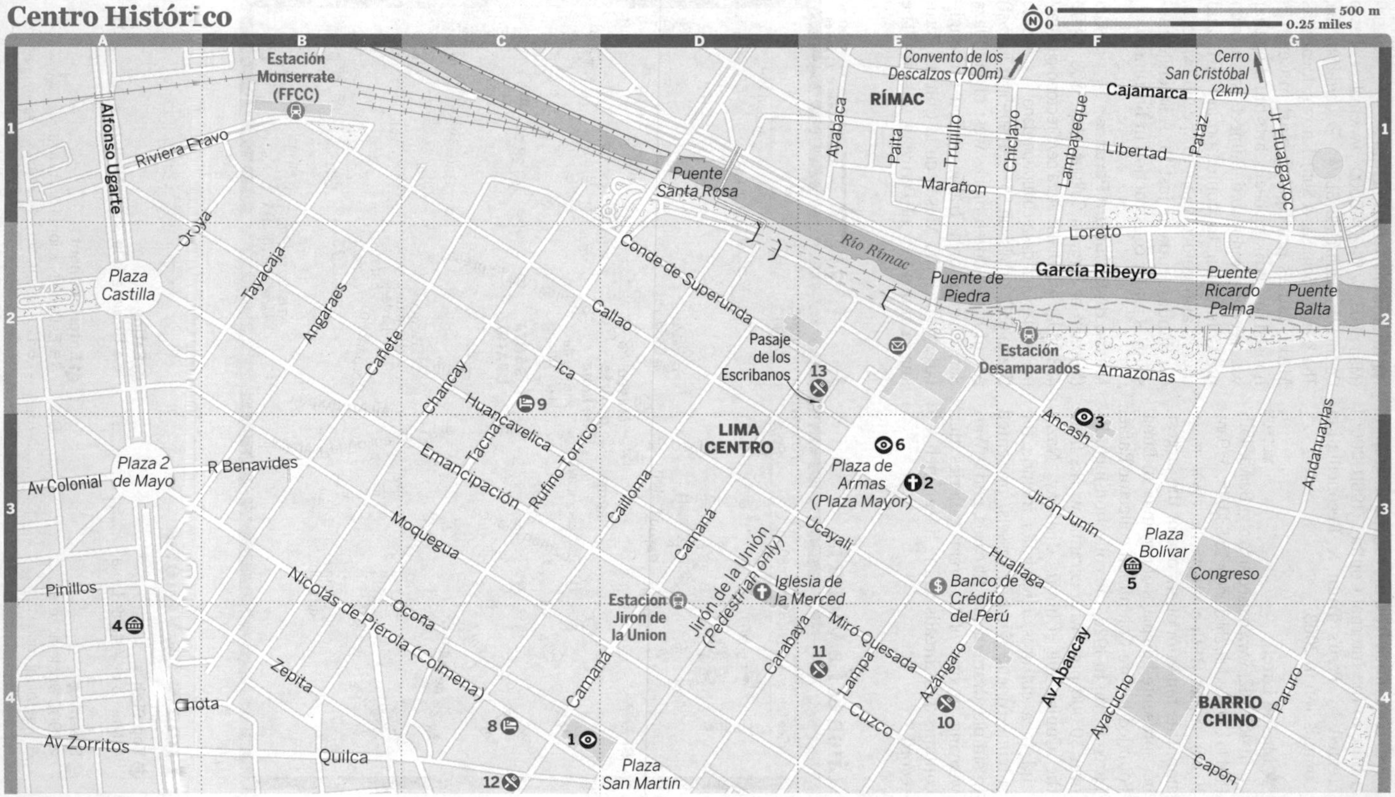

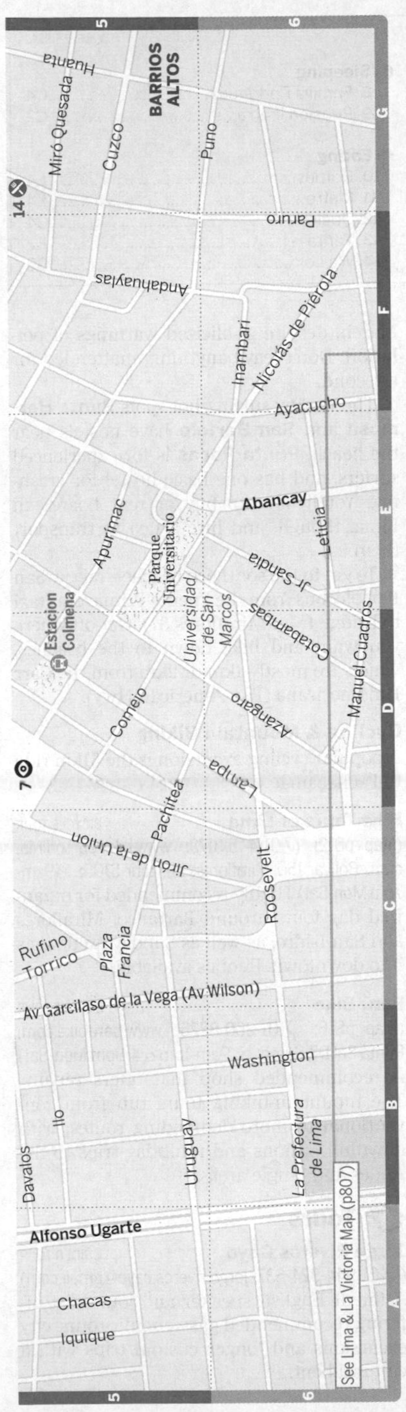

collection, consisting of elaborate *retablos* (religious dioramas) from Ayacucho, historic pottery from Puno and works in feathers from the Amazon, is displayed in a building whose exterior facade is inspired by pre-Columbian architecture.

Museo de la Inquisición MUSEUM

(Map p808; ☎01-311-7777, ext 5160; www.congreso.gob.pe/museo.htm; Jirón Junín 548; ⏰9am-5pm) FREE A graceful neoclassical structure facing the Plaza Bolívar houses this diminutive museum where the Spanish Inquisition once plied its trade. In the 1800s, the building was expanded and rebuilt into the Peruvian senate. Today, guests can tour the basement, where morbidly hilarious wax figures are stretched on racks and flogged – to the delight of visiting eight-year-olds. The old 1st-floor library retains a remarkable baroque wooden ceiling. After an obilgatory half-hour tour (in Spanish or English), guests can wander.

La Catedral de Lima CHURCH

(Map p808; ☎01-427-9647; museum S10; ⏰9am-5pm Mon-Fri, 10am-1pm Sat) Next to the Palacio Arzobispal, the cathedral resides on the plot of land that Pizarro designated for the city's first church in 1535. Though it retains a baroque facade, the building has been built and rebuilt numerous times: in 1551, in 1622 and after the earthquakes of 1687 and 1746. The last major restoration was in 1940.

Monasterio de San Francisco MONASTERY

(Map p808; ☎01-426-7377; www.museocatacumbas.com; cnr Lampa & Ancash; adult/child under 15 S7/1; ⏰9:30am-5:30pm) This bright yellow Franciscan monastery and church is most famous for its bone-lined **catacombs** (containing an estimated 70,000 remains) and its remarkable **library** housing 25,000 antique texts, some of which predate the Conquest. Admission includes a 30-minute guided tour in English or in Spanish. Tours leave as groups gather.

Huaca Huallamarca RUINS

(☎01-222-4124; Nicolás de Rivera 201, San Isidro; adult/child S10/5; ⏰9am-5pm Tue-Sun) Nestled among condominium towers and sprawling high-end homes, the simple Huaca Huallamarca is a highly restored adobe pyramid, produced by the Lima culture, that dates to somewhere between AD 200 and 500. A small on-site **museum**, complete with mummy, details its excavation.

Centro Histórico

Sights
1 Gran Hotel Bolívar C4
2 La Catedral de Lima E3
3 Monasterio de San Francisco F3
4 Museo de la Cultura Peruana A4
5 Museo de la Inquisición F3
6 Plaza de Armas E3
7 Plaza San Martín D5

Sleeping
8 Familia Rodríguez C4
9 Pensión Ibarra C2

Eating
10 Domus E4
11 Metro E4
12 Queirolo C4
13 Tanta E2
14 Wa Lok G5

Huaca Pucllana RUINS
(Map p812; ☎01-617-7138; cnr Borgoño & Taracpacá; adult/student S12/5; ⏰9am-4:30pm) Located near the Óvalo Gutiérrez, this *huaca* is a restored adobe ceremonial center from the Lima culture that dates back to AD 400. In 2010, an important discovery was made of four Wari mummies, untouched by looting. Though vigorous excavations continue, the site is accessible by regular guided tours in Spanish (for a tip). In addition to a tiny on-site **museum**, there's a celebrated **restaurant** that offers incredible views of the illuminated ruins at night.

Plaza de Armas PLAZA
(Map p808) Lima's 140-sq-meter Plaza de Armas, also called the Plaza Mayor, was not only the heart of the 16th-century settlement established by Francisco Pizarro, it was a center of the Spaniards' continent-wide empire. Though not one original building remains, at the center of the plaza is an impressive bronze fountain erected in 1650.

Plaza San Martín PLAZA
(Map p808) Built in the early 20th century, Plaza San Martín has come to life in recent years as the city has set about restoring its park and giving the surrounding beaux-arts architecture a much-needed scrubbing. It is especially lovely in the evenings, when illuminated. The plaza is named for the liberator of Peru, **José de San Martín**, who sits astride a horse at the center of the plaza.

Activities

Peru Fly PARAGLIDING
(Map p812; ☎01-959-524-940; www.perufly.com) A paragliding school that also offers tandem flights in Miraflores.

Swimming & Surfing

Limeños hit the beaches in droves during the coastal summer months of January to March, despite publicized warnings of pollution. Don't leave anything unattended for a second.

The nearby surfing hot spots **Punta Hermosa** and **San Bartolo** have hostels near the beach. **Punta Rocas** is for experienced surfers, and has one basic hostel for crashing. You'll have to buy or rent boards in Lima, though, and hire a taxi to transport them.

To get to the southern beaches, take a 'San Bartolo' bus from the Puente Primavera (taxi to bridge from Miraflores S7). Get off where you want and hike down to the beaches, which are mostly 1km or 2km from the Carr Panamericana (Pan-American Hwy).

Cycling & Mountain Biking

A popular cycling excursion is the 31km ride to Pachacamac.

Bike Tours of Lima BICYCLE TOUR
(Map p812; ☎01-445-3172; www.biketoursoflima.com; Bolívar 150, Miraflores; 3hr tour S105; ⏰9am-7pm Mon-Sat) Highly recommended for organized day tours around Barranco, Miraflores and San Isidro, as well as Sunday excursions into downtown. Rentals available.

Perú Bike BICYCLE TOUR
(Map p816; ☎01-260-8225; www.perubike.com; Punta Sal D7, Surco; ⏰9am-1pm & 4-8pm Mon-Sat) A recommended shop that offers repairs. The mountain-biking tours run from conventional to more demanding routes, with downhill options and multiday trips to the Andes and jungle areas.

Tours

Jorge Riveros Cayo GUIDED TOUR
(☎01-944-324-637; jorge.riveros.cayo@gmail.com) A fluent English speaker and journalist offering recommended gastronomic tours, city excursions and longer custom trips with a cultural bent.

Festivals & Events

Festival of Lima CULTURAL
Celebrates the anniversary of Lima's founding on January 18.

Feria de Santa Rosa de Lima RELIGIOUS
Held on August 30, this feast honors Santa Rosa, the venerated patron saint of Lima and the Americas. Believers visit the Santuario de Santa Rosa de Lima in the Centro Historico. From here a procession goes to the saint's hometown Santa Rosa de Quives near Lima.

Sleeping

The *cheapest* guesthouses are generally in central Lima; the best and most popular ones are in the more upmarket and safer neighborhoods of Miraflores and Barranco.

Central Lima

★1900 Backpackers HOSTEL $
(Map p807; ☎01-424-3358; www.1900hostel.com; Av Garcilaso de la Vega 1588; dm S25-37, s/d/tr incl breakfast 62/87/130; @📶) A downtown hot spot, this old mansion designed by Gustavo Eiffel is revamped with modern design touches, though it maintains the marble floors and other turn-of-the-century flourishes. For a hostel it's downright gorgeous. Rooms are smart and simple, with bunks shoulder-to-shoulder.

There's a tiny kitchen and cool common spaces, including a pool room with bar and red chandelier.

Familia Rodríguez HOMESTAY $
(Map p808; ☎01-423-6465; jotajot@terra.com.pe; Nicolás de Piérola 730, No 201, apt 201; d incl breakfast S70; @📶) An early-20th-century building west of the Plaza San Martín houses a sprawling old apartment with parquet floors and spotless bathrooms in this tranquil, well-recommended family homestay. All bathrooms are shared.

Pensión Ibarra GUESTHOUSE $
(Map p808; ☎01-427-8603; pensionibarra@gmail.com; Tacna 359, No 152, 14th fl; s/d without bathroom from S25/35; 📶) Inside a scruffy concrete apartment block, the helpful Ibarra sisters keep seven basic guest rooms that are clean and stocked with firm beds. There is a shared kitchen and laundry service. A small balcony has views of the noisy city.

Hostal Iquique HOTEL $
(Map p807; ☎01-433-4724; www.hostaliquique.com; Iquique 758; s/d without bathroom S54/90, s/d/tr incl breakfast S75/96/132; @) Recommended Iquique is basic but clean and safe, with small, dark, concrete rooms sporting remodeled bathrooms with hot showers. The rooftop terrace features a pool table, and guests get to use shared kitchen facilities. Credit cards are accepted.

Miraflores

The area around Parque Kennedy is gringo ground zero.

Backpacker's Family House HOSTEL $
(Map p812; ☎01-447-4572; www.backpackersfamilyhouse.com; Juan Moore 304; dm/d incl breakfast S47/126; @📶) A small brick home with parquet floors, graffiti murals and games like foosball and ping-pong. It's uncluttered but a little rundown, and we wish the beds had some backbone. Be warned, the top floor rooms have bathrooms one flight down.

Ekeko Hostel HOSTEL $
(Map p812; ☎01-635-5031; Garcia Calderon 274; dm/s/d without bathroom S31/50/93, d incl breakfast S99; @📶) Tucked into a comfortable middle-class neighborhood, this spacious home features a huge kitchen and oversized breakfast table, plus nonstandard amenities, such as hairdryers. Guests will enjoy the nice backyard and good service.

Hitchhikers HOSTEL $
(Map p812; ☎01-242-3008; www.hhikersperu.com; Bolognesi 400; dm/s/d without bathroom S28/65/70, s/d incl breakfast S70/84; @📶) Occupying an enormous century-old *casona*, this longtime hostel has a wide array of rooms. Secure and sleeper-friendly, it includes a lounge with cable TV and a DVD library, while a bare outdoor patio has barbecue facilities and ping-pong. Also parks campers (S18). Overall, a good choice.

Flying Dog HOSTEL $
(Map p812; ☎01-444-5753; www.flyingdogperu.com; Lima 457; dm S35, d with/without bathroom S115/135; @📶) Of Flying Dog's four Lima hostels, this is the best, featuring a lovely outdoor garden bar and 3rd-floor lounge area with expansive views over Parque Kennedy. Two kitchens make for a shorter cooking queue, and the included breakfast is taken at the terrace restaurant across the

Miraflores

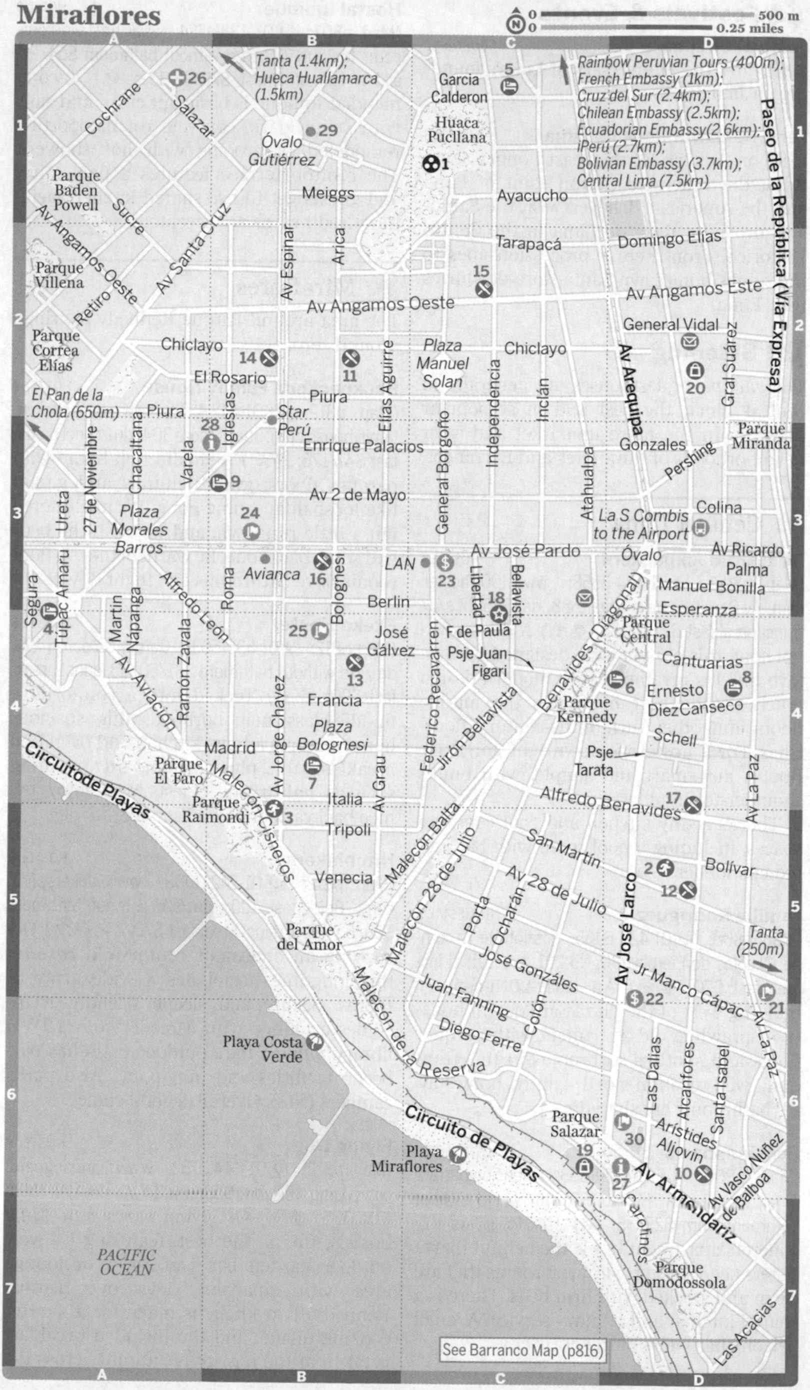

0 500 m
0 0.25 miles

Tanta (1.4km); Hueca Huallamarca (1.5km)
Rainbow Peruvian Tours (400m); French Embassy (1km); Cruz del Sur (2.4km); Chilean Embassy (2.5km); Ecuadorian Embassy(2.6km); iPerú (2.7km); Bolivian Embassy (3.7km); Central Lima (7.5km)
El Pan de la Chola (650m)
Tanta (250m)

26
Cochrane
Salazar
Óvalo Gutiérrez
29
Garcia Calderon
5
Huaca Pucllana
1
Paseo de la República (Vía Expresa)
Parque Baden Powell
Sucre
Av Santa Cruz
Meiggs
Ayacucho
Av Angamos Oeste
Parque Villena
Retiro
Av Espinar
Arica
Tarapacá
Domingo Elías
15
Av Angamos Este
Parque Correa Elías
Chiclayo
14
11
Plaza Manuel Solan
Chiclayo
General Vidal
Av Arequipa
20
Gral Suárez
El Rosario
Piura
Piura
28
Iglesias
Star Perú
Elías Aguirre
Independencia
Inclán
Parque Miranda
Gonzales
Pershing
Enrique Palacios
27 de Noviembre
Chacaltana
Varela
9
Av 2 de Mayo
General Borgoño
Atahualpa
Colina
Ureta
Plaza Morales Barros
24
La S Combis to the Airport
Av José Pardo
Óvalo
Av Ricardo Palma
Avianca
16
Bolognesi
LAN
23
Libertad
Bellavista
Manuel Bonilla
Segura
Túpac Amaru
4
Martin Nápanga
Alfredo León
Roma
Berlin
18
Esperanza
Benavides (Diagonal)
Parque Central
25
José Gálvez
Federico Recavarren
F de Paula
Psje Juan Figari
Cantuarias
Av Aviación
Ramón Zavala
13
6
Ernesto Diez Canseco
8
Av Jorge Chavez
Francia
Jirón Bellavista
Parque Kennedy
Plaza Bolognesi
Schell
Madrid
Circuito de Playas
Parque El Faro
Malecón Cisneros
7
Av Grau
Psje Tarata
Av La Paz
Parque Raimondi
3
Italia
Alfredo Benavides
17
Tripoli
Malecón Balta
San Martín
Malecón 28 de Julio
Av 28 de Julio
2
Bolívar
Venecia
Av José Larco
12
Parque del Amor
Porta
Ocharán
José Gonzáles
Jr Manco Cápac
Juan Fanning
Malecón de la Reserva
Colón
22
21
Diego Ferre
Av La Paz
Playa Costa Verde
Las Dalias
Alcanfores
Santa Isabel
Circuito de Playas
Parque Salazar
30
Arístides Aljovin
Av Vasco Núñez de Balboa
Playa Miraflores
19
27
Av Armendariz
10
Carolinos
PACIFIC OCEAN
Parque Domodossola
Las Acacias
PERU

See Barranco Map (p816)

park. The biggest outlet, across the park, is rather dusty and rundown.

Hostal El Patio GUESTHOUSE **$$**
(Map p812; 01-444-2107; www.hostalelpatio.net; Ernesto Diez Canseco 341A; s/d incl breakfast S126/156, s/d superior S156/186; @) On a quiet side street just steps from the Parque Kennedy, this gem of a guesthouse is named for its plant-filled courtyard with a trickling fountain. With a cheery English- and French-speaking owner, it features small, spotless rooms with cast-iron beds and colonial-style art. A few are equipped with small kitchenettes and minifridges. Check the website for special offers.

Inka Frog HOTEL **$$**
(Map p812; 01-445-8979; www.inkafrog.com; Iglesias 271; s/d/tr incl breakfast S170/201/263; @) As lodgings go, this is among Lima's best values, targeted at mature hostel-goers wanting private rooms. Subdued and friendly, it features ample and spotless modern rooms with fans and flat-screen TVs, those on a cute roof patio feature air-conditioning at no extra cost. Enjoy the complimentary coffee hour on plush sofas. Staff is helpful and the street is refreshingly quiet.

Barranco

Backpackers Inn HOSTEL **$**
(Map p816; 01-247-1326; www.barrancobackpackersperu.com; Mariscal Castilla 260; dm/tw incl breakfast S37/109) A British-run backpacker hang-out housed in a weathered but essentially clean mansion on a quiet street with 24-hour security. Dorms are ample, some with ocean views. There's a kitchen, eight rooms, help with trips and tours, a TV lounge and convenient access to Bajada de Baños, leading to the beach.

Hostal Kaminu B&B **$**
(Map p816; 01-252-8680; www.kaminu.com; Bajada de Baños 342; dm S30-35, d incl breakfast with/without bathroom S100/68; @) Tiny and rambling, this sardine-can hostel sits in the thick of Barranco nightlife – for better or worse. Highlights include an ambient rooftop deck.

★3B Barranco B&B B&B **$$**
(Map p816; 01-247-6915, 01-719-3868; www.3bhostal.com; Centenario 130; s/d incl breakfast S230/250; @) Cool, clean and modern, this service-oriented lodging is poised to be a traveler favorite. A common area charged with Warholesque pastiche art leads to 16 minimalist rooms with plush burlap-colored bed covers, granite vanities and windows opening on lightboxes of tended greenery. Good value.

Hostal Gémina HOTEL **$$**
(Map p816; 01-477-0712; http://hostalgemina.com; Av Grau 620; s/d/tr incl breakfast S105/150/195; @) Tucked into a small shopping gallery, this welcoming surprise offers 31

Miraflores

Sights
1 Huaca Pucllana ... C1

Activities, Courses & Tours
2 Bike Tours of Lima ... D5
3 Peru Fly ... B5

Sleeping
4 Backpacker's Family House ... A4
5 Ekeko Hostel ... C1
6 Flying Dog ... D4
7 Hitchhikers ... B4
8 Hostal El Patio ... D4
9 Inka Frog ... B3

Eating
10 Central ... D6
11 El Enano ... B2
12 El Punto Azul ... D5
13 El Rincón del Bigote ... B4
14 La Pascana de Madre Natura ... B2
15 Quattro D ... C2
16 Vivanda ... B3
17 Vivanda ... D4

Entertainment
18 Cocodrilo Verde ... C3

Shopping
19 LarcoMar ... C6
20 Mercado Indio ... D2

Information
21 Australian Embassy ... D5
22 Banco de Crédito del Perú ... D5
23 Banco de Crédito del Perú ... C3
24 Brazilian Embassy ... B3
25 Canadian Embassy ... B4
26 Clínica Anglo-Americana ... A1
iPerú ... (see 19)
27 Peru Rail ... D6
28 South American Explorers Club ... B3
29 Teleticket ... B1
30 UK Embassy ... D6

spacious units with 1970s style. Think shipshape, accidental-retro. There's an ample living room, and clean rooms feature TVs and folksy textiles. Credit cards accepted.

Eating

Lima's dining scene is among the best on the continent. Miraflores houses most of the gourmand haunts. *Ceviche* (raw seafood marinated in lime juice, onions and spices) is sublime here.

Central Lima

Cheap lunch *menús* (set meals) are offered in local restaurants. Barrio Chino (Chinatown), southeast of the Plaza de Armas, is blessed with Asian eateries.

For self-catering, there's **Metro** (Map p808; Cuzco 255; ⏲9am-10pm).

Domus PERUVIAN **$**

(Map p808; ☎01-427-0525; Miró Quesada 410; 3-course menús S20; ⏲7am-5pm Mon-Fri) A restored 19th-century mansion houses this modern-yet-intimate two-room restaurant that caters to journalists from the nearby offices of *El Comercio*. There is no à la carte dining, just a rotating daily list of well-executed Peruvian–Italian specialties that always includes a vegetarian option in the mix. Freshly squeezed juices accompany this well-tended feast. Excellent value; highly recommended.

Queirolo PERUVIAN **$**

(Map p808; ☎01-425-0421; Camaná 900; mains S12-38; ⏲9:30am-1am Mon-Sat) Lined with wine bottles, Queirolo is popular with office workers for cheap *menús* featuring staples such as *papa rellena* (stuffed potatoes). It is also popular for evening gatherings, when locals pop in for *chilcano de pisco* (*pisco* with ginger ale and lime juice) and chit-chat. Dinner offerings are sparse.

Cevichería la Choza Nautica CEVICHE **$$**

(Map p807; ☎01-423-8087; www.chozanautica.com; Breña 204; ceviches S20-42, mains S19-45; ⏲8am-11pm Mon-Sat, to 9pm Sun) A surprisingly bright spot in a slightly dingy area, this popular *cevichería,* tended to by bow-tied waiters, offers more than a dozen types of *ceviches* and *tiraditos* (Japanese-style *ceviche,* without onions). There is also a long list of soups, seafood and rice dishes. Live music plays on busy nights.

Wa Lok CHINESE **$$**

(Map p808; ☎01-447-1329, 01-427-2750; Paruro 878; mains S15-80; ⏲9am-11pm Mon-Sat, to 10pm Sun) Serving seafood, fried rice as light and fresh as it gets, and sizzling meats that come on steaming platters, Wa Lok is among the best *chifas* (Chinese restaurants) in Chinatown. The 16-page Cantonese menu includes dumplings, noodles, stir-fries and a good selection of vegetarian options (try the braised tofu casserole). Portions are enormous; don't over-order.

Tanta CAFE **$$**

(Map p808; ☎01-428-3115; Pasaje de los Escribanos 142, Lima Centro; mains S21-46; ⏲9am-10pm Mon-Sat, to 6pm Sun) One of several informal bistros in the Gastón Acurio brand, Tanta serves Peruvian dishes, fusion pastas, heaping salads and sandwiches. It's a good bet in the city center where pickings are slim. The food is generally good but desserts shine: try the heavenly passion-fruit cheesecake mousse. There are other branches in **Miraflores** (☎01-447-8377; Av 28 de Julio 888) and **San Isidro** (☎01-421-9708; Pancho Fierro 115).

Miraflores

By far the most varied neighborhood for eating, with open-air cafes and pizzerias around Parque Kennedy. For self-caterers, there's **Vivanda** (Map p812; http://www.vivanda.com.pe; Benavides 487; ⏲24hr); another **branch** (Map p812) is located on Av José Pardo.

El Enano SANDWICHES **$**

(Map p812; Chiclayo 699; sandwiches S8-12; ⏲6am-1am Sun-Thu, to 3am Fri & Sat) Grab a stool at the open-air counter and watch the masters at work. Fresh-roasted chicken, ham, turkey and *chicharrón* sandwiches on French bread are dressed with marinated onions and chilies. After one too many *piscos*, this is the cure. Exotic fresh juices are served in glass jars.

El Pan de la Chola CAFE **$**

(Av La Mar 918; mains S8-18; ⏲8am-10pm Mon-Sat) In South America, finding real, crusty whole-grain bread is rarer than striking gold. Enter this small brick cafe baking four scrumptious varieties, with organic coffee from the Peruvian Amazon, Greek yogurt and sweets. There's European-style seating at big wooden tables; grab a sandwich or share the tasting plate with bread, olives, hummus and fresh cheese.

Quattro D ICE CREAM $
(Map p812; ☎01-445-4228; Av Angamos Oeste 408; mains S18-32, ice cream from S10; ⏲6:30am-11:45pm Mon-Thu, to 12:30am Fri & Sat, 7-11am Sun) A bustling cafe that serves hot pressed sandwiches, pasta and other dishes, in addition to a diabetes-inducing assortment of sweets and gelato (including a few sugar-free flavors).

La Pascana de Madre Natura CAFE $
(Map p812; Chiclayo 815; ✎) A natural-food store and bakery.

Las Mesitas PERUVIAN $
(Map p816; ☎01-477-4199; Av Grau 341; mains S8-30; ⏲noon-2am) A vintage spot with little ambience beyond the terracotta-tile floors. Diners come for the cheap Peruvian classics, their *ahi de gallina* (chicken stew) is renowned. Or just stop in for a traditional dessert, like their wonderful *suspiro limeño* (a caramel-meringue sweet).

El Punto Azul CEVICHE $$
(Map p812; ☎01-445-8078; San Martín 595; mains S22-40; ⏲noon-5pm) Awash in Caribbean blues, this pleasant family eatery dishes up fresh *ceviches, tiraditos* and family-sized rice dishes. Try their risotto with parmesan, shrimp and *ají amarillo* (yellow chili) – and don't miss the line-up of beautiful desserts. It gets packed, so show up before 1pm if you want a table. Excellent value.

El Rincón del Bigote CEVICHE $$
(Map p812; José Galvez 529; mains S32-36; ⏲noon-4pm Tue-Sun) Go early. On weekends, locals and tourists line up for seating in this bare-bones *ceviche* house. The specialty is *almejas in su concha:* pair these marinated clams with a side of crisp *yuca* fries and a bottle of cold pilsner and you're in heaven.

Barranco

A charming little district for a bite to eat, especially along the passageway below the Puente de los Suspiros.

Burrito Bar MEXICAN $
(Map p816; ☎987-352-120; Av Grau 113; mains S12-18; ⏲1-11pm Tue-Sat, noon-5pm Sun) Londoner Stew created this Mexican fast, fresh food sensation after studying tortilla making on YouTube. The experiment was a smash hit, from Baja-style fish tacos to fresh salsas and thirst-quenching mint limeade. Also serves Sierra Andina microbrews. For dessert, the chocolate tamal is a no-brainer.

Cafe Bisetti CAFE $
(Map p816; ☎01-713-9565; Av Pedro de Osma 116; coffee S8-16; ⏲8am-9pm Mon-Fri, 10am-11pm Sat, 3-9pm Sun) Locals park their designer dogs out front of this roasting house with some of the finest lattes in town, well matched with fresh pastries or bitter chocolate pie. Check out the courses on roasting and tasting.

La Canta Rana CEVICHE $$
(Map p816; ☎01-247-7274; Génova 101; mains S28-45; ⏲8am-11pm Tue-Sat) Around for decades, this unpretentious spot draped in flags and plastered in photos packs in the locals with its offering of more than 17 different types of *ceviche*.

DON'T MISS

ANDEAN CUISINE INNOVATION

Central (Map p812; ☎01-242-8515; centralrestaurante.com.pe; Santa Isabel 376; mains S52-88; ⏲12:45-3:15pm & 7:45-11:15pm Mon-Fri) Part restaurant, part laboratory, Central reinvents Andean cuisine and rescues age-old Peruvian edibles you'd find nowhere else. Dining here is an experience, evidenced by the tender native potatoes served in edible clay. Chef Virgilio Martinez wants you to taste the Andes. He paid his dues in Europe and Asia's top kitchens, but it's his work here that dazzles.

Seafood – like the charred octopus starter – is a star, but classics like suckling pig deliver, served with pickled vegetables and spiced squash. A menu supplied by sustainable fish and a rooftop herb garden enhance the ultra-fresh appeal.

Drinking

Lima overflows with bars, from San Isidro's pricey havens for the urbane elite to Barranco's cheap, cheerful watering holes. Plaza de Armas downtown and Miraflores have several street-front cafes. The latter is also home to the low-rent pedestrianized San

Ramón (aka Calle Pizza), where touristy pizzerias and Latin-themed clubs fight for real estate – this is your best bet for a cheap pub crawl (trendier options abound around the corner on Francisco de Paula Camino). In Barranco, bounce among the tight-knit nightclubs near Parque Municipal and the pedestrianized Calle Carrión all night long.

In Central Lima, drop in at the **Gran Hotel Bolívar** (Map p808) to quaff Peru's national cocktail, the *pisco sour*, in a traditional setting. Barranco throngs with revelers on Friday and Saturday nights.

Barranco

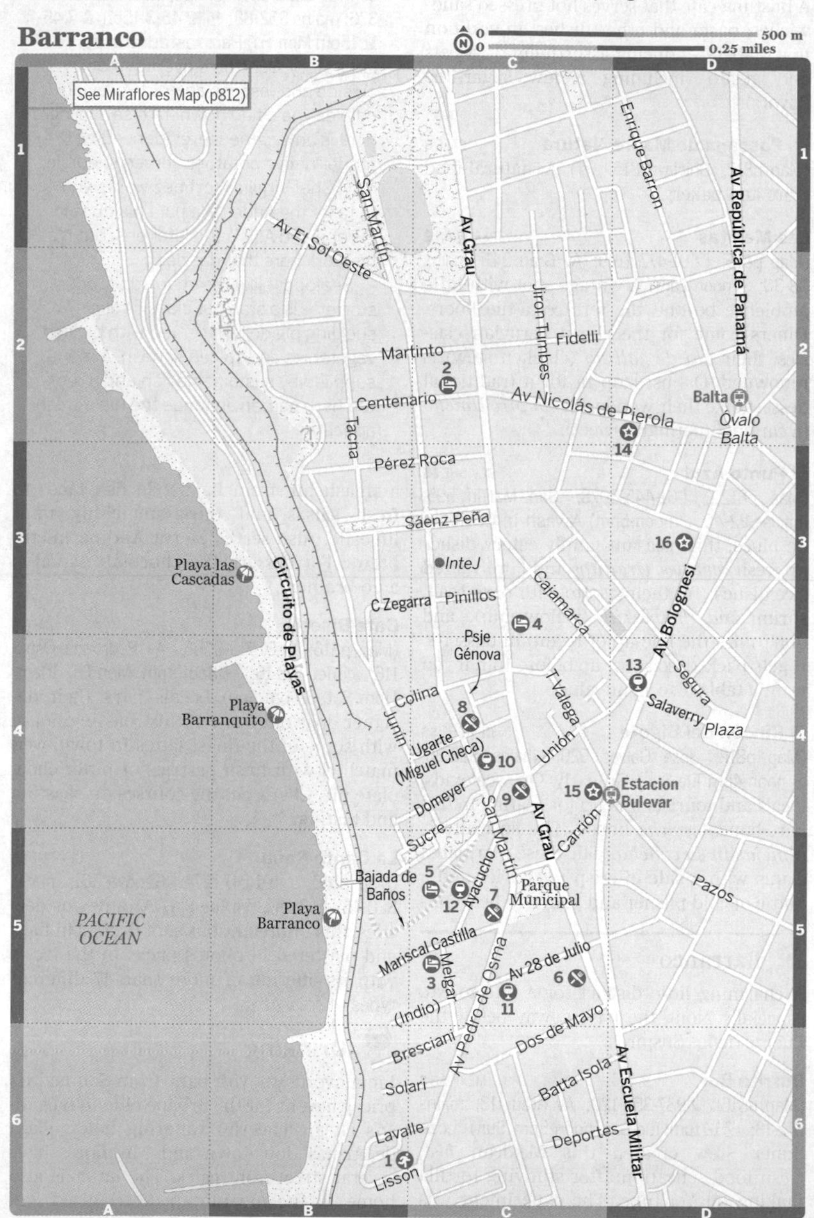

★Ayahuasca COCKTAIL BAR
(Map p816; ☎01-247-6751; http://ayahuascaresto bar.com; San Martín 130, Barranco; ⏲8pm-close Mon-Sat) Lounge in a stunning restored *casona* full of Moorish architectural flourishes. Few actually admire the architecture, most guests are busy checking out everyone else. The hyper-real decor includes a dangling mobile made with costumes used in Ayacucho folk dances. There's a long list of contemporary *pisco* cocktails, like the tasty *Ayahuasca* sour made with jungle fruit *tambo* and coca leaves.

Santos LOUNGE
(Map p816; ☎01-247-4609; Jirón Zapita 203, Barranco; ⏲5pm-1am Mon-Thu, to 3am Fri & Sat; 📶) In a creaky old mansion, this funky and congenial bar has multiple rooms and a balcony with sea views (also perfect for people-watching). Local 20- and 30-somethings start their night out here with tapas and the daily two-for-one that goes until 9pm.

Wahio's BAR
(Map p816; ☎01-477-4110; Plaza Espinosa, Barranco; ⏲Thu-Sat) A large and lively bar with a fair share of dreadlocks and a classic soundtrack of reggae, ska and dub attracting a young crowd.

Bar Piselli BAR
(Map p816; ☎01-252-6750; Av 28 de Julio 297, Barranco; ⏲10am-11pm Mon-Thu, to 3am Fri & Sat) This neighborhood bar reminiscent of old Buenos Aires beats all for ambience. There's live music on Thursdays provoking boisterous sing-alongs of Peruvian classics.

✩ Entertainment

Many top-end hotels downtown and in San Isidro and Miraflores have slot-machine casinos.

La Noche LIVE MUSIC
(Map p816; ☎01-247-1012; www.lanoche.com.pe; Av Bolognesi 307, Barranco) This well-known tri-level bar is *the* spot to see rock, punk and Latin music acts in Lima, though drinks could be better.

Cocodrilo Verde LIVE MUSIC
(Map p812; ☎01-242-7583; www.cocodriloverde.com; Francisco de Paola 226; minimum tab S25; ⏲6:30pm-close Mon-Sat) With great bands that range from popular music to jazz and bossa nova, this hip lounge is good for a night out.

Sargento Pimienta CLUB
(Map p816; ☎01-247-3265; www.sargentopimienta.com.pe; Av Bolognesi 755, Barranco; admission from S15) A reliable spot in Barranco whose name means 'Sergeant Pepper.' The barnlike club hosts various theme nights and occasional live bands.

Las Brisas del Titicaca TRADITIONAL MUSIC
(Map p807; ☎01-715-6960; www.brisasdeltiticaca.com; Wakuski 168, Lima Centro; admission from S30) A lauded *folklórica* show near Plaza Bolognesi downtown, in an enormous venue.

El Dragón LIVE MUSIC
(Map p816; ☎01-715-5043; www.eldragon.com.pe; Av Nicolas de Pierola 168, Barranco; cover up to S20; ⏲Thu-Sat) With live music or DJs, this popular venue draws a diverse crowd for Latin rock, *tropicalismo,* soul and funk.

Estadio Nacional STADIUM
(Map p807; Lima Centro) *Fútbol* is the national obsession, and Peru's Estadio Nacional, off *cuadras* 7 to 9 of Paseo de la República, is the venue for the most important matches and other events. **Teleticket** (Map p812;

Barranco

Activities, Courses & Tours
1 Perú Bike B6

Sleeping
2 3B Barranco B&B C2
3 Backpackers Inn C5
4 Hostal Gémina C3
5 Hostal Kaminu C5

Eating
6 Burrito Bar C5
7 Cafe Bisetti C5
8 La Canta Rana C4
9 Las Mesitas C4

Drinking & Nightlife
10 Ayahuasca C4
11 Bar Piselli C5
12 Santos C5
13 Wahio's D4

Entertainment
14 El Dragón D2
15 La Noche C4
16 Sargento Pimienta D3

☎01-613-8888; www.teleticket.com.pe) has listings and sales.

Shopping

Shopping malls include the underground **LarcoMar** (Map p812; Malecón de la Reserva 610), with a spectacular location built right into the oceanfront cliffs, selling high-end artisan crafts, electronics, photographic supplies, outdoor gear, books and music.

Mercado Indio MARKET
(Map p812; Av Petit Thouars 5245, Miraflores) The best place to find everything from pre-Columbian-style clay pottery to alpaca rugs to knock-offs of Cuzco School canvases. Prices vary; shop around.

Feria Artesanal MARKET
(Av de la Marina, Pueblo Libre) Slightly cheaper than Mercado Indio is this crafts market in Pueblo Libre.

Information

DANGERS & ANNOYANCES

Like any large Latin American city, Lima is a land of haves and have-nots, something that has made stories about crime here the stuff of legend. To some degree, the city's dangers have been overblown. The most common offense is theft and readers have reported regular muggings. You are unlikely to be physically hurt, but it is nonetheless best to keep a streetwise attitude.

> **GETTING INTO TOWN**
>
> From **Aeropuerto Internacional Jorge Chávez** (☎01-517-3500, schedules 01-511-6055; www.lap.com.pe) take a taxi (S45 to S60, 30 minutes to one hour for rush hour – faster for downtown Lima) to Miraflores, Barranco or San Isidro. Many flights arrive in the wee hours, so be sure to have a hotel booked ahead. Otherwise the *combi* (minibus) company **La S** (Map p812; per person from S2.50) – with a giant 'S' pasted to the windshield – runs various routes to Miraflores and beyond. From the airport, these can be found heading south along Av Elmer Faucett. For the return trip, La S *combis* can be found traveling north along Av Petit Thouars and east along Av Angamos in Miraflores.

Take extra care on the beaches, where violent attacks have happened. Bus terminals are in disadvantaged neighborhoods and notorious for theft, so buy your tickets in advance and take a taxi. It's much safer and quicker to take a taxi from the airport.

EMERGENCY

Policía de Turismo (Tourist Police, Poltur; ☎01-225-8698; Av Javier Prado Este 2465, 5th fl, San Borja; ⏰24hr) Main division of the Policía Nacional (National Police) at Museo de la Nación. English-speaking officers who can provide theft reports for insurance claims or traveler's-check refunds. In heavily touristed areas, it is easy to identify members of Poltur by their white shirts.

MEDICAL SERVICES

The following clinics offer emergency services and some have English-speaking staff.

Clínica Anglo-Americana (Map p812; ☎616-8900; Salazar 350, San Isidro) Stocks yellow-fever and tetanus vaccines.

Clínica San Borja (☎01-475-4000; www.clinicasanborja.com.pe; Av Guardia Civil 337, San Borja) Another reputable clinic, with cardiology services.

MONEY

You'll find 24-hour ATMs throughout Lima. Other *casas de cambio* (foreign-exchange offices) are scattered about Camaná in central Lima and along Larco in Miraflores. Green- and blue-vested official money changers *(cambistas)* are all over Lima's streets and safe to use, but get their official stamp on your bills to protect yourself against counterfeits.

Banco de Crédito del Perú (BCP; Map p812; www.viabcp.com; cnr Av José Larco & José Gonzales; ⏰9am-6:30pm Mon-Fri, 9:30am-1pm Sat) Has 24-hour Visa and Plus ATMs; also gives cash advances on Visa, and changes Amex, Citicorp and Visa traveler's checks. The Central Lima (Map p808; ☎427-5600; cnr Lampa & Ucayali) branch has incredible stained-glass ceilings. There's another branch at José Pardo (Map p812; ☎445-1259; Av José Pardo 491).

POST

Federal Express (FedEx; Map p812; ☎01-242-2280; www.fedex.com.pe; Pasaje Olaya 260, BSC Miraflores, Miraflores; ⏰9am-7pm Mon-Fri, 10am-3pm Sat)

Main Post Office (Map p808; ☎01-511-5000; www.serpost.com.pe; Pasaje Piura, Central Lima; ⏰8am-9pm Mon-Sat) Poste restante mail can be collected here, though it's not 100% reliable. Bring ID.

Serpost (Map p812; Av Petit Thouars 5201; ⌚8am-8:45pm Mon-Sat, 9am-1:30pm Sat, 9am-2pm Sun)

TOURIST INFORMATION

iPerú (☎01-574-8000; Aeropuerto Internacional Jorge Chávez) The government's reputable tourist bureau dispenses maps, offers good advice and can help handle complaints. The Miraflores office (Map p812; ☎01-445-9400; LarcoMar; ⌚11am-2pm & 3-8pm) is tiny but is highly useful on weekends. There's another branch in San Isidro (☎01-421-1627; Jorge Basadre 610; ⌚9am-6pm Mon-Fri).

Peru Rail (Map p812; ☎084-58-1414; www.perurail.com; LarcoMar; ⌚11am-10pm) Get information and make bookings for Cuzco–Machu Picchu and Cuzco–Puno trains.

South American Explorers Club (SAE; Map p812; ☎447-7731; www.saexplorers.org; Enrique Palacios 956, Miraflores; ⌚9:30am-4:30pm Mon-Fri, to 1pm Sat) Now more than three decades old, the venerable South American Explorers Club is an indispensable resource for long-term travelers, journalists and scientists spending long periods in Peru, Ecuador, Bolivia and Argentina.

Getting There & Away

AIR

Lima's **Aeropuerto Internacional Jorge Chávez** (p818) is in Callao. International airport taxes (payable in US dollars or nuevos soles, cash only) are US$31 but are now usually included in ticket prices; domestic flight taxes are always included.

Student airfares can be booked through the official ISIC office **IntcJ** (Map p816; ☎01-247-3230; www.intej.org; San Martín 240, Barranco; ⌚9:30am-12:45pm & 2-5:45pm Mon-Fri, 9:30am-12:45pm Sat).

Many international airlines have offices in Lima. Airlines offering domestic flights include the following:

LAN (Map p812; ☎01-213-8200; www.lan.com; Av José Pardo 513, Miraflores) LAN goes to Arequipa, Chiclayo, Cuzco, Iquitos, Juliaca, Piura, Puerto Maldonado, Tacna, Tarapoto and Trujillo. Additionally it offers link services between Arequipa and Cuzco, Arequipa and Juliaca, Arequipa and Tacna, Cuzco and Juliaca, and Cuzco and Puerto Maldonado.

LC Peru (☎01-204-1313; www.lcperu.pe; Av Pablo Carriquirry 857, San Isidro) Flies from Lima to Andahuaylas, Ayacucho, Cajamarca, Huánuco, Huaraz, Iquitos and Huancayo (Jauja) on smaller turbo-prop aircraft.

Star Perú (Map p812; ☎01-705-9000; www.starperu.com; Av Espinar 331, Miraflores) Flies to Ayacucho, Cuzco, Huanuco, Iquitos, Pucallpa, Puerto Maldonado and Tarapoto.

BUS

Lima has no central bus terminal. Each company runs its own office and station, many of which cluster around Av Javier Prado Este in La Victoria. Others are found in central Lima several blocks east of Plaza Grau, just north of Av Grau and south of Av 28 de Julio, on both sides of Paseo de la República. Make sure you verify which station your bus departs from when buying tickets. There are countless companies, so examine the quality of the buses before deciding.

Major companies include the following:

Civa (Map p807; ☎01-418-1111; www.civa.com.pe; cnr Av 28 de Julio & Paso de la Republica 569) For Arequipa, Cajamarca, Chachapoyas, Chiclayo, Cuzco, Ilo, Máncora, Nazca, Piura, Puno, Tacna, Tarapoto, Trujillo and Tumbes. The company also runs a more luxurious sleeper line to various coastal destinations called **Excluciva** (www.excluciva.com).

Cruz del Sur (www.cruzdelsur.com.pe; Av Javier Prado Este 1109) One of the biggest companies, serving the coast – as well as inland cities such as Arequipa, Cuzco, Huancayo and Huaraz – with three different classes of service: the cheaper Ideal, and the more luxurious Imperial and Cruzero.

Móvil Tours (Map p807; ☎01-716-8000; www.moviltours.com.pe; Paseo de la República 749) For Chachapoyas, Chiclayo, Huancayo, Huaraz and Tarapoto.

Soyuz (☎01-205-2370; www.soyuz.com.pe; Av México 333, La Victoria) Frequent buses to Cañete, Chincha, Ica and Nazca.

Approximate Fares

This table indicates approximate fares and durations for one-way travel from Lima with the top companies. Prices are general estimates for normal/luxury buses.

DESTINATION	COST (S)	DURATION (HR)
Arequipa	80-170	16-18
Ayacucho	70-160	9-11
Cajamarca	90-150	16
Chiclayo	60-125	12-14
Cuzco	110-210	22-23
Huancayo	35-80	7-8
Huaraz	60-160	8
Ica	30-80	4½
Nazca	80-160	6-8
Piura	80-184	16
Puno	140-170	22
Tacna	115-190	18-22
Trujillo	40-125	9-10
Tumbes	80-200	20

TRAIN

Highland rail services to Huancayo leave from Lima's **Estación Desamparados** (☎ 01-263-1515; Ancash 203).

ℹ Getting Around

TO/FROM THE AIRPORT

The **airport** (p818) is in the port city of Callao, 12km west of downtown.

Official taxis directly outside the terminal exit charge from S45 to S60 to the city center and Miraflores. Taxis in the lot charge S10 or so less, but it's notably less secure. Most hostels also offer airport pickup for slightly less. Alternatively, turn left outside the terminal, walk 100m to the pedestrian gate, turn right and walk 100m to the road outside the airport, where you can get an unofficial taxi for less, or a *combi* to Miraflores. Look for the 'Callao-Ate' minibus (spy the red 'S' or ask for it by its nickname, 'La S,' pronounced 'la e-se') for S2 to S3 (more for bulky luggage).

A safe and secure option is **Taxi Green** (☎ 01-484-4001; www.taxigreen.com.pe). Maddening traffic and road construction often lead to lengthy delays, so allow at least an hour for the ride to/from the airport.

Unfortunately, there is no central bus terminal in Lima. Each bus company runs its own offices and terminals, mostly in shady neighborhoods east of the city center – take a taxi.

BUS

El Metropolitano, a modern trans-Lima electric express bus system, is the fastest and most efficient way to get into the city center. Routes are few, though there are intentions to expand coverage to the northern part of the city. Ruta Troncal (S1.50) goes through Barranco, Miraflores and San Isidro to Plaza Grau in the center of Lima. Users must purchase a *tarjeta intelligente* card (S4.50), which can be credited for use.

Otherwise, minivans are organized by destination placards taped to the windshield. *Combis* are generally slow and crowded, but they're startlingly cheap: fares run from S1 to S3, depending on the length of your journey.

The most useful routes link central Lima with Miraflores along Av Arequipa or Paseo de la República. Minibuses along Garcilaso de la Vega (also called Av Wilson) and Av Arequipa are labeled 'Todo Arequipa' or 'Larco/Schell/Miraflores' when heading to Miraflores and, likewise, 'Todo Arequipa' and 'Wilson/Tacna' when leaving Miraflores for central Lima. Catch these buses along Av José Larco or Av Arequipa in Miraflores.

To get to Barranco, look for buses along Av Arequipa labeled 'Chorrillos/Huaylas/Metro' (some will also have signs that say 'Barranco'). You can also find these on the Diagonal, just west of Parque Kennedy, in Miraflores.

TAXI

Taxis don't have meters, so make sure you negotiate a price before getting in. As a (very) rough guide, a trip within Miraflores costs around S5 to S10. From Miraflores to central Lima is S15 to S20, to Barranco from S5 to S10, and to San Isidro from S7 to S14. You can haggle fares, though it's harder during rush hour. If there are two or more passengers, ask whether the fare is per person or for the car.

SOUTH COAST

Inspect the barren, foggy, bone-dry desert of Peru's southern coastline for the first time and you will inevitably wonder: how does anyone live here? Yet people don't just live here, they positively thrive – check out Ica's wine industry or Chincha's Afro-Peruvian culture if you want proof. What's more, they've been thriving for millennia. The perplexing Nazca Lines, a weird collection of giant geoglyphs etched into the desert, date from 400 to 650 AD, while intricate cloths unearthed on the Paracas peninsula were woven 1000 years before Pachacuti led the Incas out of Cuzco.

Though Machu Picchu hogs most of the limelight in southern Peru, the south coast is pierced by a lesser 'gringo trail' whose obligatory stops include wildlife-obsessed Paracas, Nazca and the desert oasis of Huacachina.

Pisco

☎ 056 / POP 54,000

Crushed by a 2007 earthquake that destroyed its infrastructure but not its spirit, Pisco is a town on the rebound. Irrespective of the substantial damage, the town remains open for business, promoting itself along with nearby beach resort El Chaco (Paracas) as a base for forays to the Paracas Reserve and Islas Ballestas.

Located 235km south of Lima, Pisco is generally the base from which to see the abundant wildlife of the Islas Ballestas and Península de Paracas, but the area is also of historical and archaeological interest, having hosted one of the most highly developed pre-Inca civilizations – the Paracas culture – from 900 BC until AD 200.

Sights & Activities

Post-earthquake, Pisco's main **Plaza de Armas** is a mishmash of the vanquished and the saved. The equestrian **statue of José de San Martín**, sword bravely raised in defiance, falls into the latter category. The **cemetery** has a few hidden secrets: buried here is suspected 19th-century English vampire Sarah Ellen Roberts, who claimed that she would arise again after 100 years. In 1993, much to everyone's disappointment, she didn't. The cemetery is now a memorial to the more than 500 victims of the 2007 earthquake.

Islas Ballestas

Nicknamed 'the poor man's Galápagos,' these offshore islands make for a worthwhile laid-back excursion. The outward boat journey takes about 1½ hours. En route you'll see the famous three-pronged **Candelabra**, a giant figure etched into the sandy hills. An hour is spent cruising around the islands' arches and caves, watching noisy sea lions sprawl on the rocks. You may also spot Humboldt penguins, Chilean flamingos and dolphins. The most common guano-producing birds are cormorants, boobies and pelicans, present in thousands-strong colonies.

Tours

Boat tours to the Islas Ballestas leave daily at 7am (S45 plus S1 dock tax). Minibuses go from Pisco to the port at Paracas, where there is a nice seafront full of sidewalk restaurants and vendors (look out for Viviana's *chocotejas,* addictive pecans doused in caramel and covered in chocolate, a specialty of Ica). There are no cabins on the boats, so dress for wind, spray and sun. Wear a hat, as it's not unusual to receive direct guano hits. You can continue on a less interesting afternoon tour of the Península de Paracas (S25 with Islas Ballestas), which briefly stops at the visitors center and museum (entry fees not included) and whizzes by coastal geological formations.

Aproturpisco TOURS

(☎056-50-7156; aproturpisco@hotmail.com; San Francisco 112) This laid-back but business-like travel company organizes trips to all the local sights, including Islas Ballestras (S70) and even the Nazca Lines (US$140). Guides speak six languages, including Hebrew.

Sleeping

Many hotels will pick you up from the San Clemente turnoff on Carr Panamericana Sur.

Posada Hispana Hotel HOTEL **$**

(☎056-53-6363; www.posadahispana.com; Bolognesi 236; s/d S50/70; P) This is as good as it gets. Rooms feature local textiles and hardwood accents. There's a rooftop terrace for kicking back. The restaurant is one of the best in town, with a S10 lunchtime *menú* (set meal) served in a two-level bamboo dining room.

Hostal La Casona HOTEL **$**

(☎056-53-2703; www.hostallacasona.com; San Juan de Dios 252; s S60-70 d S70-90; P) A massive wooden door serves as a slightly deceiving portal to this hotel half a block from the main square, which, though clean, isn't anywhere near as grand as its entryway suggests. The rooms can be a bit stale, but air out quickly.

Hostal Villa Manuelita HOTEL **$$**

(☎056-53-5218; www.villamanuelitahotel.com; San Francisco 227; s/d/tr incl breakfast S110/150/190; P) While it had to be heavily renovated post-earthquake, this hotel still retains the grandeur of its colonial foundations. Plus, it's very conveniently located only half a block from the plaza.

Eating & Drinking

La Concha de Tus Mares PERUVIAN **$$**

(Calle Muelle 992; mains S15-25) Old pictures of what Pisco used to look like pre-2007 adorn the walls of this nostalgic place next to the Colegio Alexander Von Humboldt about 1km south of the center. The fish comes in big portions and is lauded by the locals.

★ **As de Oro's** PERUVIAN **$$$**

(www.asdeoros.com.pe; San Martín 472; mains S30-50; ⊙noon-midnight Tue-Sun) Talk about phoenix from the flames; the plush As de Oro serves up spicy mashed potato with octopus, plaice with butter and capers, and grilled prawns with fried *yuca* and tartare sauce overlooking a small swimming pool, as the rest of the town struggles back to its feet.

Taberna de Don Jaime BAR

(☎056-53-5023; San Martín 203; ⊙4pm-2am) This clamorous tavern is a favorite with locals and tourists alike. It is also a showcase for artisanal wines and *piscos*. On weekends, the crowds show up to dance to live Latin and rock tunes into the small hours.

Information

Internet cafes and banks with 24-hour ATMs surround the main plaza.

DANGERS & ANNOYANCES

On its knees post-earthquake, Pisco acquired a reputation for crime, but the curtain continues to lift. The commerce-packed streets are fine during the daytime (there's a notable police presence in the city center). Nonetheless, it is best to take a taxi after dark, particularly around the bus station and market areas. If you arrive late, get the ticket agent at your bus-company office to hail you a reputable cab.

Getting There & Around

Pisco is 6km west of Carr Panamericana Sur, and only buses with Pisco as the final destination actually go there. **Ormeño** (☎056-53-2764; San Francisco), **Flores** (☎056-79-6643; San Martín) and **Soyuz** (www.soyuz.com.pe; Av Ernesto R Diez Canseco 4) offer daily departures north to Lima and south to Ica, Nazca and Arequipa. If you're not on a direct bus, ask to be left at the San Clemente turnoff, where fast and frequent *colectivos* (shared taxis) wait to shuttle passengers to central Pisco's Plaza de Armas (S3, 10 minutes) or Paracas (S10, 20 minutes).

Transportation from Pisco to Paracas is possible via *combi* (S1.50, 30 minutes) or *colectivo* (S2.50, 20 minutes), which leave frequently from near Pisco's central market.

DESTINATION	COST (S)	DURATION (HR)
Arequipa	60-144	12-15
Ica	4-15	1½-2
Lima	28-76	4½
Nazca	17-35	4

Ica

☎056 / POP 220,000

There are worse places to be stuck than Ica, the capital of the department of the same name. The bustling city boasts a thriving wine and *pisco* industry, raucous festivals and an excellent museum. The leafy plaza ain't bad either. Still, most travelers opt to bed down in nearby Huacachina. Remnants of damaged buildings from the 2007 earthquake remain, but Ica is more or less business as usual.

Sights & Activities

Peruvian wines and *piscos* can be sampled at **bodegas** outside town. Dozens of smaller, family-owned artisanal wineries lie further afield.

Museo Regional de Ica MUSEUM
(Ayabaca cuadra 8; admission S10; 8am-7pm Mon-Fri, 9am-6pm Sat & Sun) In the suburban neighborhood of San Isidro, Ica pulls out its trump card: a museum befitting a city three times the size. While it might not be the Smithsonian in terms of layout and design, this understated gem catalogs the two key pre-Inca civilizations on Peru's southern coast, namely the Paracas and Nazca cultures, the former famed for its intricate textiles and the latter for its instantly recognizable ceramics.

Bodega Tacama WINE TASTING
(☎056-58-1030; www.tacama.com; Camino Real s/n, Tinguiña; 9:30am-4:30pm Tue-Sun) FREE Possibly the most professional and lauded of Ica's wineries, Tacama is run out of a sprawling pink hacienda backed by striped fields lined by vines. Eschewing Peru's penchant for sickly sweet wines, Tacama produces some rather good chardonnays and malbecs that might one day give the Chileans a run for their money.

Bodega Vista Alegre WINE TASTING
(www.vistaalegre.com.pe; Camino a La Tinguina, Km 2.5; admission S5; 8am-noon & 1:45-4:45pm Mon-Fri, 7am-1pm Sat) About 3km northeast of Ica in the La Tinguiña district, this is the easiest of the large commercial wineries to visit (taxi one way S5). It's best to go in the morning, as the winery occasionally closes in the afternoon.

Festivals & Events

Fiesta de la Vendimia HARVEST
Held early to mid Match, this famous grape-harvest festival includes all manner of processions, beauty contests, cockfights and horse shows, music and dancing, and of course, free-flowing *pisco* and wine.

El Señor de Luren RELIGION
This religious pilgrimage in late October culminates in fireworks and a traditional procession of the faithful that keeps going all night.

Tourist Week MUSIC, FOOD

Tourist Week brings food, festivals, dancing and more in mid-September.

Sleeping

Most travelers stay in nearby Huacachina, where there are more popular backpacker crash pads. If you end up in Ica overnight, dozens of depressing budget hotels line the streets east of the bus terminals and north of the plaza, especially along Tacna.

Hostal Soyuz HOTEL $

(056-22-4138; Manzanilla 130; s/d/tr S40/50/70;) Sitting directly over the Soyuz bus terminal, this handy option for late arrivals or early departures has carpeted rooms with air-con and cable TV, but is only for heavy sleepers on account of the rumpus below. Check-in is at the bus ticket desk.

Hotel Sol de Ica HOTEL $$

(056-23-6168; www.hotelsoldeica.com; Lima 265; s/d/tr incl buffet breakfast S145/180/230;) This three-story central hotel is hidden down a long dark passage behind reception that delivers more than it initially promises. Remarkably small rooms have natural wood touches, but don't sparkle (perhaps because of the mustard yellow sheets). The hotel has a large garden and swimming pool.

Eating

Several shops east of the main plaza sell *tejas* (caramel-wrapped candies flavored with fruit and nuts).

El Otro Peñoncito PERUVIAN, INTERNATIONAL $

(Bolívar 225; mains S9-26; 8am-midnight Mon-Fri;) Ica's most historic and characterful restaurant serves a varied menu of Peruvian and international fare that includes plenty of options for vegetarians. The formal bartenders here shake a mean *pisco sour*.

Plaza 125 PERUVIAN $

(Lima 125; mains S10-16, menú S14) Your quick stop on the main square backs up homespun *lomo saltado* (strips of beef stir-fried with onions, tomatoes, potatoes and chili) with more internationally flavored chicken fillets. It's riotously popular with locals in a hurry, and the set lunch is a good deal.

Anita BAKERY $$

(Libertad 135; mains S15-36, menús from S12; 8am-midnight) True, the bow-tied waiters are a bit over the top (this ain't the Ritz), but Anita does a mean stuffed avocado and the bakery counter knocks out some hard-to-resist cakes. Best restaurant in the main square by far.

Information

Around the plaza, internet cafes stay open until late.

BCP (Plaza de Armas) Has a Visa/MasterCard ATM and changes US dollars.

Hospital Regional de Ica (056-23-4798; www.hrica.gob.pe; Prolongación Ayabaca s/n; 24hr) For emergency services.

Police (056-23-5421; JJ Elias, 5th block; 24hr) At the city center's edge.

Serpost (San Martín 521) Southwest of the Plaza de Armas.

DANGERS & ANNOYANCES

Take the normal precautions against petty theft, particularly around the bus terminals and market areas.

Getting There & Away

Bus companies cluster on Lambayeque at the west end of Salaverry and along Manzanilla west of Lambayeque. For Lima, **Soyuz/PerúBus** (056-22-4138; www.soyuzonline.com.pe; Manzanilla 130) has departures every 10 to 15 minutes, while less-frequent luxury services **Cruz del Sur** (0-801-11111; www.cruzdelsur.com.pe; Lambayeque 140) and **Ormeño** (056-21-5600; www.grupo-ormeno.com.pe; Lambayeque s/n) go to Pisco; Ormeño has direct buses, while other bus companies drop passengers at the San Clemente turnoff on the Panamericana. Most companies have direct daytime buses to Nazca. Services to Arequipa and Cuzco are mostly overnight. Tacna (S80, 15 hours), near the Chilean border, is serviced by Ormeño.

DESTINATION	COST (S)	DURATION (HR)
Arequipa	50-144	12
Chincha	7-10	2
Lima	22-76	4½
Nazca	7-35	2½
Pisco	4-15	1½-2

Huacachina

056 / POP 200

Surrounded by mountainous sand dunes that roll into town over the picturesque lagoon featured on the back of Peru's S50 note, there's no denying Huacachina's majestic setting. Just 5km west of Ica, this tranquil oasis boasts graceful palm trees, exotic flowers and attractive antique buildings – all testament to the bygone glamour of this resort town built for the Peruvian elite. These days, it's a sandy gringo playground where backpackers tend to lose themselves for days.

Activities

You can rent sandboards for S5 an hour to slide, surf and somersault your way down the irresistible dunes. Thrilling rollercoaster-esque dune-buggy/sandboarding tours cost S45 (plus S3.60 'sand tax'). Go at sunset, when the scenery is at its most miraculous, rather than in the morning. All the *hostales* organize tours.

Sleeping & Eating

Camping is possible in the dunes around the lagoon – just bring a sleeping bag. For entertainment, follow the music.

Casa de Arena HOSTEL **$**
(056-21-5274; www.casadearena.net; Balneario de Huacachina; dm S25, s/d S40/120, without bathroom S35/100;) Cast with a rowdy reputation, the Arena knows how to party. The rooms come with or without baths, allowing scrimpers to....well...scrimp. The boisterous Friday night disco can get wild. If you want peace, go elsewhere. If you want to party, this is the place.

★ **Banana's Adventure** HOSTEL **$$**
(056-23-7129; bananasadventure@hotmail.com; Perotti s/n; r per person incl breakfast and excursion S75-110;) This peaced-out crash pad on the north side of the lagoon only offers packaged stays. They include a room for the night – choose between four-bed dorms with super firm mattresses or elegant deluxe rooms with glass on all sides and modern fixings – plus a dune-buggy and sandboarding excursion the next day.

We don't love that you are roped into the package tour, but with huge windows, a fun bar, and little dip pool, this is the best budget spot in town.

El Huacachinero Hotel HOTEL **$$**
(056-21-7435; www.elhuacachinero.com; Perotti; s/d/tr incl breakfast S176/202/265;) Recently upgraded, the Huacachinero logs the finest restaurant in the oasis (by a stretch), a relaxing pool area (no blaring music), and immediate dune access via the back gate if you're up for a 45-degree one-step-forward-two-steps-back climb to the sunset of your dreams. Agreeably rustic rooms have super-comfortable beds and cane accents.

Hostal Curasi HOTEL **$$**
(056-21-6989; www.huacachinacurasi.com; Balneario de Huacachina; s/d incl breakfast S105/150;) This quiet oasis has a garden and pool in the middle to cool off on those hot south-coast days. The rooms have ocean-evoking bedspreads and a few über-kitsch oil paintings.

Desert Nights INTERNATIONAL **$**
(Blvd de Huacachina; mains S15-25;) The menu might have been ripped off from anywhere else on the banana-pancake trail, but this international hostel with a decent and very popular cafe out front is somewhere you're guaranteed to meet other travelers. The excellent shade-grown Peruvian coffee is backed up by peanut butter and jam sandwiches, burgers, pizza and brownies.

Information

There's a global ATM at El Huacanicero.

DANGERS & ANNOYANCES

Though safer than Ica, Huacachina is not a place to be lax about your personal safety or to forget to look after your property. Some guesthouses have reputations for ripping off travelers and also harassing young women with sexual advances. Check out all of your options carefully before accepting a room.

Getting There & Away

A taxi between Ica and Huacachina costs S6 to S12.

Nazca

056 / POP 22,000

Bone dry and baking hot, Nazca was a desert-scorched dead town until a flyby by American scientist Paul Kosok revealed one of Peru's most enigmatic and mysterious achievements – the world-famous Nazca Lines. In 1939, a routine ancient-irrigation research flight across the barren region unearthed the puzzling scratches in the sand, engraved on the desert floor like the graffiti of giants armed with sticks the size of redwoods. Now a Unesco World Heritage Site, the lines draw floods of travelers to this otherwise unremarkable small town.

Sights

Nazca Lines RUINS

Spread over 500 sq km (310 sq miles) of arid, rock-strewn plain in the Pampa Colorada (Red Plain), the Nazca Lines are one of the world's great archaeological mysteries. Comprising over 800 straight lines, 300 geometric figures (geoglyphs) and 70 animal and plant drawings (biomorphs), the lines are almost imperceptible on the ground. From above, they form a striking network of stylized figures and channels, many of which radiate from a central axis.

Museo Didáctico Antonini MUSEUM

(056-52-3444; Av de la Cultura 600; admission S20, plus camera S5; 9am-7pm) On the east side of town, this excellent archaeological museum has an aqueduct running through the back garden, as well as interesting reproductions of burial tombs, a valuable collection of ceramic pan flutes and a scale model of the Lines.

Outlying Sites

It's safest to visit the outlying archaeological sites with an organized tour and guide, as robberies and assaults on tourists have been reported.

At the **Cantallo aqueducts**, just outside town, you can descend into the ancient stonework by means of spiraling *ventanas* (windows) – a wet, claustrophobic experience.

The popular **Cemetery of Chauchilla** (admission S7.50; 8am-2pm), 30km south of Nazca, will satisfy any macabre urges you have to see bones, skulls and mummies.

A dirt road travels 25km west to **Cahuachi**, an important Nazca center still being excavated.

Activities

Cerro Blanco ADVENTURE TOUR

Stand down all other pretenders. Cerro Blanco, 14km east of Nazca, is the highest sand dune in the world: 2078m above sea level and – more importantly – 1176m from base to summit, that's higher than the tallest mountain in England and numerous other countries. If Huacachina's sand didn't irrevocably ruin your underwear, this could be your bag.

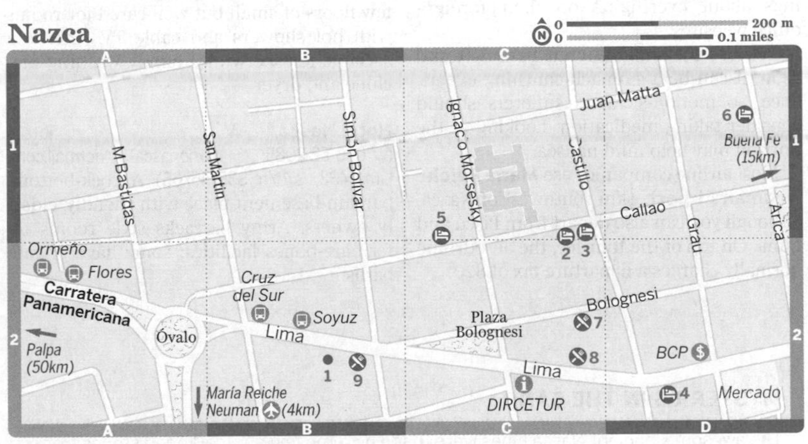

Nazca

Activities, Courses & Tours

- Alas Peruanas .... (see 1)
- 1 Alegría Tours B2

Sleeping

- 2 Hospedaje Yemayá C1
- 3 Hotel La Encantada C1
- 4 Hotel Nasca D2
- 5 Hotel Oro Viejo C1
- 6 Kunan Wasi Hotel D1

Eating

- 7 La Encantada Cafe C2
- 8 La Taberna C2
- 9 Rico Pollo B2

Tours

Overflights of the Nazca Lines are tinged with controversy. In 2010, two small aircraft carrying tourists on *sobrevuelos* (overflights) crashed within eight months of each other, resulting in a total of 13 fatalities. The crashes followed a 2008 accident that killed five French tourists, and a 2009 incident when a plane was forced to make an emergency landing on the Carr Panamericana Sur.

In reaction to these incidents some changes were made: all planes now fly with two pilots, and prices rose to ensure that companies don't cut corners with poorly maintained aircraft or overfilled flights.

Nonetheless, it pays to put safety before price when choosing your overflight company. Avoid anyone who offers less than US$80 for the standard 30-minute excursion and don't be afraid to probe companies on their safety records and flight policies. **Aeroparacas** (☎01-641-7000; www.aeroparacas.com) is one of the better companies. Other longstanding operators include **Aerodiana** (☎01-447-6824; www.aerodiana.com.pe) and **Alas Peruanas** (☎056-52-2444; www.alasperuanas.com). Some countries, including the UK and USA, still place warnings about overflights on their foreign-office websites.

Because the small aircraft bank left and right, it can be a stomach-churning experience, so motion-sickness sufferers should consider taking medication. Looking at the horizon may help mild nausea.

Most airline companies use **María Reiche Neuman Airport**, 4km southwest of Nazca, although you can also depart from Pisco and Lima. On top of the tour fee, the aerodrome normally charges a departure tax of S20.

Alegría Tours ADVENTURE TOUR
(☎056-52-3775; www.alegriatoursperu.com; Hotel Alegría, Lima 168) Behemoth agency offers all the usual local tours, plus off-the-beaten-track and sandboarding options. The tours are expensive for one person, so ask to join up with other travelers to receive a group discount. Alegría can arrange guides in Spanish, English, French and German in some cases.

Sleeping

Kunan Wasi Hotel HOTEL $
(☎056-52-4069; www.kunanwasihotel.com; Arica 419; s/d/tr S70/90/120; @) Very clean and very bright with each room conforming to a different color scheme. Kunan Wasi is run by English-speaking Yesenia. It's super friendly, immaculately clean, and travelers will love the top-floor terrace. Welcome to a perfectly packaged Nazca bargain.

Hospedaje Yemayá HOTEL $
(☎056-52-3146; www.hospedajeyemaya.com; Callao 578; s/d S45/60, without bathroom S30/45; @) An indefatigably hospitable family deftly deals with all of the backpackers that stream through their doorway. They offer a few floors of small but well cared for rooms with hot showers and cable TV. There's a sociable terrace with a handy washing machine and dryer.

Hotel Nasca HOTEL $
(☎056-52-2085; marionasca13@hotmail.com; Lima 438; s/d/tr S35/45/65) A rock-bottom, bargain-basement place with friendly, elderly owners. Army barracks–style rooms offer bare-bones facilities; some have private baths.

MYSTERIES IN THE SAND

The awesome, ancient Nazca Lines were made by removing sun-darkened stones from the desert surface to expose the lighter soil below. But who constructed the gigantic lines and for what reason? And why bother when they can only be properly appreciated from the air? Maria Reiche, a German mathematician and longtime researcher of the lines, theorized that they were made by the Paracas and Nazca cultures from 900 BC to AD 600, with additions by the Wari in the 7th century. She believed the lines were an astronomical calendar mapped out by sophisticated mathematics (and a long rope). Others theorize that the lines were ritual walkways connected to a water or fertility cult, giant running tracks, extraterrestrial landing sites or representations of shamans' dreams brought on by hallucinogenic drugs. Take your pick – no one really knows!

★Hotel Oro Viejo HOTEL $$

(☎056-52-2284; www.hoteloroviejo.net; Callao 483; s/d/tr/ste incl buffet breakfast S150/200/240/450; P❄@🛜🏊) There's a decidedly oriental feel to this excellent midrange hotel with it's open gardens and glistening swimming pool. Occasional farming artifacts grace the common areas and lounge, while the well-fragranced rooms deliver comfort, quiet and relaxation. Ask for a new room out back.

Hotel La Encantada HOTEL $$

(☎056-52-2930; www.hotellaencantada.com.pe; Callao 592; s/d/tr S105/140/160; @🛜) While the rooms lack some tidiness (just below cleanliness and godliness in our books), this modernish hotel offers bright, freshly painted rooms and a pleasant terrace out front.

Eating & Drinking

West of the Plaza de Armas, Bolognesi is lined with backpacker pizzerias, restaurants and bars.

La Taberna PERUVIAN $

(Lima 321; mains from S15, menú S6; ⏲lunch & dinner; 🌿) It's a hole-in-the-wall place, and the scribbles covering every inch of wall are a testament to its popularity. Try the spicy fish topped with sauce and mixed shellfish challengingly named *Pescado a lo Macho* (no that doesn't mean Macho-man fish), or chose from a list of vegetarian options.

Rico Pollo PERUVIAN $

(Lima 190; mains from S12) A local lunchtime phenomenon, this very cheap, very crowded chicken joint offers some of the best barbecued meat cuts on the south coast. For S12 you get a filling meal of chicken breast with fries and vegetables. Cakes and salads provide an excellent supporting act.

La Encantada Cafe INTERNATIONAL $$

(www.hotellaencantada.com.pe; Bolognesi 282; mains S20-40) A top spot on the 'Boulevard' (Bolognesi), La Encantada sparkles in Nazca's dusty center with well-placed wine displays, great coffee and courteous and friendly wait staff. The extensive menu mixes Europhile flavors (pasta etc) with Peruvian favorites.

Information

BCP (Lima 495) Has a Visa/MasterCard ATM and changes US dollars.

DIRCETUR (Parque Bolognesi, 3rd fl) This government-sponsored tourist information office; can recommend local tour operators. There's an information booth in the park itself.

Getting There & Around

Bus companies cluster at the western end of Calle Lima, near the *óvalo*. Buses to Arequipa generally originate in Lima; to get a seat you have to pay the Lima fare.

Most long-distance services start in the late afternoon. Located on Av Los Incas, **Cruz del Sur** (☎0801-11111; www.cruzdelsur.com.pe; Av Los Incas) and **Ormeño** (☎056-52-2058; www.grupo-ormeno.com.pe; Av Los Incas) have luxury buses daily to Lima. Intermediate points like Ica and Pisco are faster served by smaller, *económico* (cheap) bus companies, such as Flores and **Soyuz** (☎056-52-1464), which run buses to Ica every half-hour from Av Los Incas.

To Cuzco, several companies take the paved road east via Abancay. This high-altitude route gets very cold, so bring warm clothes and your sleeping bag (if you have one) onboard. There are also direct buses to Cuzco via Arequipa.

For Ica, fast *colectivos* (S15, two hours) and slower minibuses leave when full from near the gas station on the *óvalo*.

A taxi from central Nazca to the aerodrome, 4km away, costs about S4.

DESTINATION	COST (S)	DURATION (HR)
Arequipa	59-140	10-12
Cuzco	80-140	14
Ica	30-65	2½
Lima	55-145	8
Pisco	30-65	1½-2
Tacna	70-165	15

Tacna

☎052 / POP 242,500

It's a long and dusty trail to Tacna, Peru's most heroic city, sitting staunchly at the tail end of the Carr Panamericana, nearly 1300km southeast of Lima. In fact, this well-developed border outpost was occupied by Chile after the War of the Pacific in 1880, but townsfolk staged a border-shuffle coup in 1929 and voted to return to Peru's welcoming arms. You'll also find that there is added civility in this part of the country. For travelers, it's mostly a transit stop on the way to Chile.

The countryside around Tacna is known for its olive groves, orchards and *bodegas* (wineries). Catch a bus or *micro* along Bolognesi (S0.50, 10 minutes) to visit the *bodegas* and restaurants in suburban Pocollay.

Sleeping

Hotel rooms are overpriced and fill up very fast, especially on weekends.

Hostal Le Prince HOTEL $
(052-42-1252; Zela 728; s/d S70/80;) This is an economical and modern spot that's hard to resist if you aren't willing to cough up the extra cash to stay in one of the fancier digs in town.

Dorado Hotel HOTEL $$
(052-41-5741; www.doradohoteltacna.com; Av Arias Aragüez 145; s/d/tr incl breakfast S129/179/209;) Posing as Tacna's grandest hotel, the Dorado is the sort of place where the curtains are heavy, the lobby sports shiny balustrades, and a bellboy will carry your bags to your room. While it can't emulate the classy exclusivity of a European city hotel, it makes a good job of trying.

Eating & Drinking

Pocollay is popular for its rural restaurants, which often have live music on weekends. The small pedestrian streets of Libertad and Vigil are ground zero for Tacna's limited nightlife.

★**Café Da Vinci** EUROPEAN $$
(Calle Arias Aragüez 122; mains S23-40; 11am-11pm) There's a Euro-feel to the food and decor in this wood-paneled domain where well-dressed wait staff give out Mona Lisa smiles along with menus that highlight fabulous baguettes, pizzas, generous glasses of dry red wine, and decent Peruvian staples. Pride of place goes to the real Italian espresso machine.

Uros Restaurante FUSION $$
(www.restauranteuros.com; Av San Martín 608; mains S22-35) Tacna's stab at *novoandina* (Peruvian nouvelle cuisine) avoids too many pretensions, if you can get past the (admittedly photogenic) photos of the food on the menu.

Information

Chilean pesos, nuevos soles and US dollars can be easily exchanged.

BCP (San Martín 574) Has a Visa/MasterCard ATM and gives cash advances on Visa cards.

iPerú (052-42-5514; San Martín 491; 8:30am-7:30pm Mon-Fri, to 2:30pm Sat) National tourist office, provides free information and brochures.

Getting There & Around

AIR

Tacna's **airport** (TCQ) is 5km west of town. **LAN** (052-42-8346; www.lan.com; Apurímac 101; 8:30am-7pm Mon-Fri, 9am-2pm Sat) and **Peruvian Airlines** (www.peruvian.pe; Av Bolognesi 670) both offer daily passenger services to Lima, and some seasonal services to Arequipa and Cuzco.

BUS

Most long-distance departures are from the Terminal Terrestre (departure tax S1), a taxi ride from the center (S3). Most Lima-bound buses

GETTING TO CHILE

Border-crossing formalities are relatively straightforward. There are three main transport options: train, public bus or *colectivo*, with the latter proving to be the most efficient. The five-passenger taxis are run by professional companies with desks inside Tacna's international bus terminal. They charge approximately S18 to take you the 65km to Arica in Chile with stops at both border posts. It's fast and efficient – most of the paperwork is done before you get in the car. The public bus is cheaper (S10), but slower, as you have to wait for all the passengers to disembark and clear customs.

The Chilean border post is open 8am to midnight from Sunday to Thursday, and 24 hours on Friday and Saturday. Nationals of the USA, Canada, Australia, the EU and UK do not need a visa to enter Chile for stays of up to 90 days. Of these, only Australians must pay an admin fee (US$95) on arrival in cash or by card. In 2014, Chile ended its US$160 fee for citizens of the USA.

Note that Chile is an hour ahead of Peru (two hours during daylight-saving time from the last Sunday in October to the first Sunday in April). From Arica, you can continue south (by air or bus) into Chile or northeast into Bolivia.

For information on making this crossing in the opposite direction, see p473.

will drop you off at other coastal towns, including Nazca and Ica. Comfortable overnight buses with **Julsa** (☎24-7132) reach Puno via Desaguadero. For Cuzco, switch in Arequipa or Puno.

Frequent buses (S10) to Arica, Chile, leave between 6am and 10pm from the international terminal across the street from the Terminal Terrestre.

DESTINATION	COST (S)	DURATION (HR)
Arequipa	15-35	7
Cuzco	60-125	17
Lima	50-144	18-22
Puno	25-45	10

TRAIN

Trains between Tacna's **train station** (Av 2 de Mayo) and Arica, Chile (S10/CH$2000, 1½ hours) are the cheapest and most charming but also the slowest way to cross the border. An entry stamp is made upon arrival. Service can be erratic and inconveniently timed: visit the station for up-to-date schedules.

AREQUIPA & CANYON COUNTRY

Colonial Arequipa, with its sophisticated museums, architecture and nightlife, is surrounded by some of the wildest terrain in Peru. This is a land of active volcanoes, thermal springs, high-altitude deserts and the world's deepest canyons. Traveling overland, it's a must-stop en route to Lake Titicaca and Cuzco.

Arequipa

☎054 / POP 969,300

Bombarded by volcanic eruptions and earthquakes nearly every century since the Spanish arrived in 1540, Arequipa doesn't lack for drama. The perfect cone-shaped volcano of El Misti (5822m) rises behind the cathedral on the Plaza de Armas, flanked to the left by ragged Chachani (6075m) and to the right by Pichu Pichu (5571m). Set against this majestic backdrop are Arequipa's grand colonial buildings, whitewashed in volcanic stone called *sillar* that dazzles in the sun and on camera. Yes, you're still in the Andes, but with the cosmopolitan flair of cobblestones, gourmet restaurants and raucous nightlife – after all, this is Peru's second-largest city.

Sights

Arequipa is known as 'the white city' for the distinctive stonework that graces the stately Plaza de Armas and its enormous *sillar* **cathedral**, as well as many other exquisite colonial churches, convents and mansions. Don't miss **La Casa de Moral** and **Casa Ricketts**, which are well-preserved examples of the latter.

Monasterio de Santa Catalina MONASTERY

(☎054-22-1213; www.santacatalina.org.pe; Santa Catalina 301; admission S40; ⏲8am-5pm, to 8pm Tue & Thu, last entry 1hr before closing) Even if you're overdosed on colonial edifices, this convent shouldn't be missed. Occupying a whole block and guarded by imposing high walls, it is one of the most fascinating religious buildings in Peru. Nor is it just a religious building – the 20,000-sq-meter complex is almost a citadel within the city. It was founded in 1580 by a rich widow, Doña María de Guzmán. Enter from the southeast corner.

Museo Santuarios Andinos MUSEUM

(☎054-20-0345; www.ucsm.edu.pe/santury; La Merced 110; admission S20; ⏲9am-6pm Mon-Sat, to 3pm Sun) There's an escalating drama to this theatrically presented museum, dedicated to the preserved body of a frozen 'mummy,' and its compulsory guided tour (free, but a tip is expected at the end). Spoiler: the climax is the vaguely macabre sight of poor Juanita, the 12-year-old Inca girl sacrificed to the gods in the 1450s and now eerily preserved in a glass refrigerator. Tours take about an hour and are conducted in Spanish, English and French.

Iglesia de La Compañía CHURCH

(⏲9am-12:30pm & 3-6pm Sun-Fri, 11:30am-12:30pm & 3-6pm Sat) FREE If Arequipa's cathedral seems *too* big, an interesting antidote – proving that small can be beautiful – is this diminutive Jesuit church on the southeast corner of the Plaza de Armas. The facade is an intricately carved masterpiece of the *churrigueresque* style (think baroque and then some – a style hatched in Spain in the 1660s). The equally detailed altar, completely covered in gold leaf, takes the style further and will be eerily familiar to anyone who has visited Seville cathedral in Spain.

Monasterio de la Recoleta MONASTERY

(La Recoleta 117; admission S10; ⏲9am-noon & 3-5pm daily, to 8pm Wed & Fri) Bibliophiles will delight in this musty monastery's huge library, which contains more than 20,000 dusty books and maps; the oldest volume dates to 1494. Scholarship was an integral part of the Franciscans' order; the library is open for supervised visits, just ask at the entrance.

There is also a well-known museum of Amazonian artifacts (including preserved jungle animals) collected by the missionaries, and an extensive collection of pre-Conquest artifacts and religious art of the *escuela cuzqueña* (Cuzco School).

Activities

Santa Catalina and Jerusalén have dozens of fly-by-night travel agencies that offer overly lengthy bus tours around Arequipa, disappointingly rushed tours of the Cañón del Colca and also trekking, mountaineering and rafting trips. There are many folks muscling in on the action, so shop carefully.

Arequipa

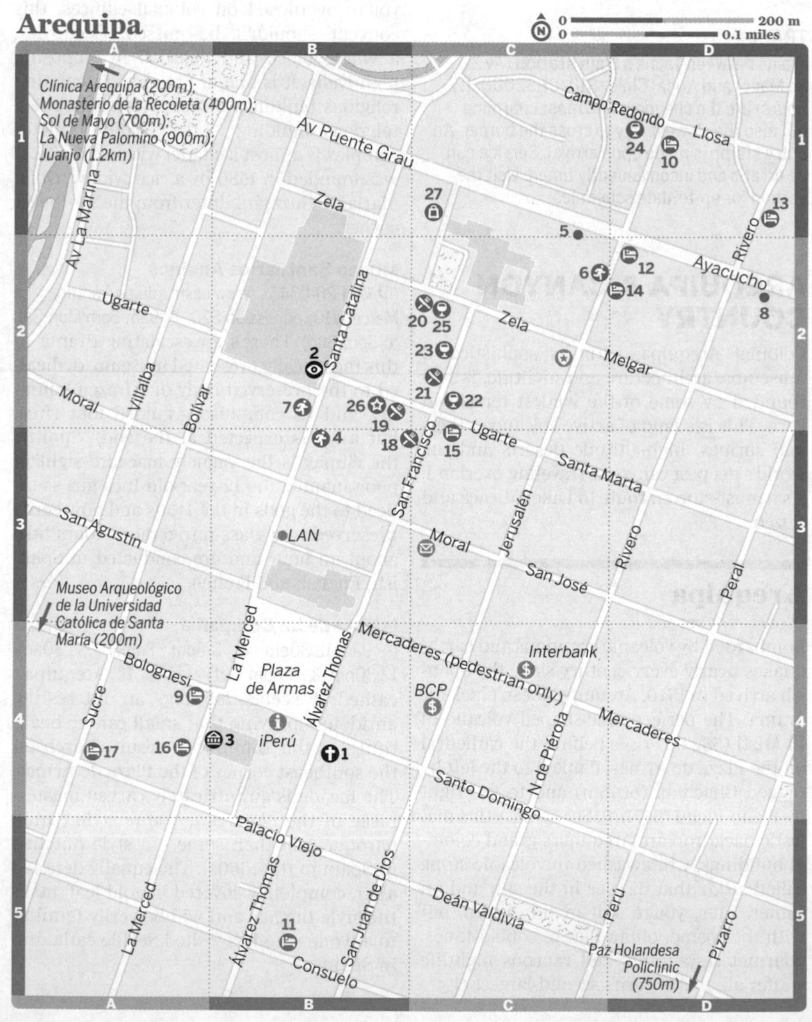

PERU AREQUIPA

Carlos Zárate Adventures ADVENTURE SPORTS
(☎054-20-2461; www.zarateadventures.com; Santa Catalina 204, Oficina 3) This highly professional company was founded in 1954 by Carlos Zárate, the great-grandfather of climbing in Arequipa. One of Zárate's sons, Miguel, was responsible, along with archaeologists, for unearthing Juanita 'the Ice Maiden' (p829) atop Mt Ampato in 1995. Now run by another son, experienced guide Carlos Zárate Flores, it offers various treks, and climbs all the local peaks.

Colca Trek ADVENTURE SPORTS
(☎054-20-6217; www.colcatrek.com.pe; Jerusalén 401B) Colca Trek is an ecoconscious adventure-tour agency and shop run by the knowledgeable, English-speaking Vlado Soto. In addition to trekking tours, it organizes mountaineering, mountain-biking and river-running trips; and is one of the few shops selling decent topographical maps of the area. It is a venerable source of information for those hoping to explore the area on their own.

Naturaleza Activa ADVENTURE SPORTS
(☎96-896-9544; naturactiva@yahoo.com; Santa Catalina 211) A favorite of those seeking adventure tours, and offering a full range of trekking, climbing and mountain-biking options. A major advantage over going to an agency is that the people you speak to at Naturaleza Activa are actually the qualified guides, not salespeople, so can answer your questions with genuine knowledge. Guides speak English, French and German.

Mountaineering

Superb mountains surround Arequipa. Though many area climbs aren't technically difficult, they should never be undertaken lightly. Hazards include extreme weather, altitude and lack of water (carry 4L per person per day). The Association of Mountain Guides of Peru warns that many guides are uncertified and untrained, so climbers are advised to go well informed about medical and wilderness-survival issues and carry first aid.

Looming above Arequipa, **El Misti** (5822m) is the most popular local climb. It can be tackled solo, but going with a guide helps protect against robberies, which have happened on the Apurímac route. One popular route is from Chiguata, an eight-hour hard uphill slog on rough trails to base camp (4500m). From there to the summit and back takes eight hours. The return from base camp to Chiguata takes three hours or less. **Chachani** (6075m) is one of the easiest 6000m peaks in the world, but you'll still need crampons, an ice ax and a good guide.

Trekking

Agencies offer off-the-beaten-track tours in Arequipa's canyon country, but it's better to DIY if you're just visiting the Cañón del Colca. Optimal hiking season is from May to November. Cañón del Colca has a smattering of campgrounds, but it's forbidden to camp by Cruz del Cóndor. For indispensable trekking maps and excellent guided trips into Cañón del Cotahuasi, contact Colca Trek.

Arequipa

Sights
1 Iglesia de La Compañía B4
2 Monasterio de Santa Catalina B2
3 Museo Santuarios Andinos B4

Activities, Courses & Tours
4 Carlos Zárate Adventures B3
5 CEPESMA C1
6 Colca Trek C2
7 Naturaleza Activa B2
8 ROCIO D2

Sleeping
9 Casablanca Hostal A4
10 Hostal Núñez D1
11 Hotel Casona Solar B5
12 Hotel Real Arequipa D2
13 La Casa de Sillar D1
14 La Posada del Cacique D2
15 Le Foyer C3
16 Los Andes Bed & Breakfast A4
17 Point Hostel A4

Eating
18 Café Fez-Istanbul B3
19 Hatunpa B2
20 Zig Zag C2
21 Zingaro C2

Drinking & Nightlife
22 Brujas Bar C2
23 Casona Forum C2
24 Chelawasi Public House D1
25 Split C2

Entertainment
26 Café Art Montréal B2

Shopping
27 Fundo El Fierro C1

Rafting

The **Río Chili** is the most frequently run local river, with a half-day beginners' trip leaving daily from March to November. Further afield, the **Río Majes** passes grade II and III rapids.

Casa de Mauro (☎98-383-9729; lacasademauromajes@hotmail.com; Ongoro, Km 5; sites per person S15, dm S30) is a convenient base for rafting the Majes. Take a Transportes del Carpio bus from Arequipa's Terminal Terrestre to Aplao (S12, three hours, hourly) and then a *combi* (S1.50) or a taxi (S15) to the village of Ongoro, 190km by road west of Arequipa.

Courses

Many schools offer Spanish classes (about S15 to S30 per hour).

CEPESMA LANGUAGE
(☎054-95-996-1638; www.cepesmaidiomasceci.com; Av Puente Grau 108) You can take Spanish language courses of between two (US$16) and eight hours (US$64) per day. Cooking, dancing and volunteer opportunities are also available.

Juanjo LANGUAGE
(www.spanishlanguageperu.com; Los Arces 257A, Distrito Cayma) Recommended by travelers, Juanjo provides one-on-one Spanish classes from S350 per week, which include one free salsa lesson or cooking class. Homestays and volunteer work can also be arranged.

ROCIO LANGUAGE
(☎054-22-4568; www.spanish-peru.com; Ayacucho 208) Charges S18 per hour for an individual Spanish class, while small group lessons cost S290 per 20-hour week. Ring bell number 21 at the communal entrance.

Festivals & Events

Arequipeños are a proud people, and their fiery celebration of the city's founding on August 15 renews their sense of difference from coastal Lima.

Sleeping

Many more budget guesthouses lie along Puente Grau, west of Jerusalén.

La Casa de Sillar HOTEL $
(☎054-28-4249; www.lacasadesillar.com; Rivero 504; with/without bathroom s S45/35, d S70/60; @📶) Another of those thick-walled colonial mansions made – as the name implies – out of *sillar* rock hewn from El Misti, this one doesn't pretend to be boutique, but it does offer a fine bargain, especially if you're prepared to share a bathroom. Huge maps and an equally huge TV adorn a communal lounge.

La Posada del Cacique HOTEL $
(☎054-20-2170; Jerusalén 404; s/d/tr S30/50/60; @📶) This 2nd-floor hostel has spacious, sunny rooms, a well-equipped shared kitchen, reliable hot water, and a tranquil rooftop sitting area. The father-son owners are great resources for local info and make guests feel right at home.

Hotel Real Arequipa HOTEL $
(☎054-79-9248; hotelrealarequipa@hotmail.com; Jerusalén 412; r with/without bathroom S70/40; 📶) The rooms are basic and dark but there is a tidy kitchen and it is perfectly fine if you are counting your soles but don't want to stray far from the plaza.

Le Foyer HOSTEL $
(☎054-28-6473; www.hlefoyer.com; Ugarte 114; s/d/tr with bathroom 75/95/115, dm/d/tr without bathroom 25/60/85, all incl breakfast; @📶) There's a distinct New Orleans look to this cheap hostel-like hotel with its wraparound upstairs veranda where you can enjoy a standard bread and jam breakfast overlooking busy Calle Jerusalén. Rooms are nothing to brag about but the proximity to plenty of restaurants and nightlife (there's an alluring Mexican place downstairs) means you don't need GPS to find the action.

Hostal Núñez HOSTEL $
(☎054-21-8648; www.hotel-nunez.de; Jerusalén 528; s/d with bathroom S100/120, without bathroom S50/80, all incl breakfast; 📶) On a street full of not-so-great guesthouses, this secure, friendly hostel is always stuffed with gringos. The colorful rooms sport frilly decor and cable TV, though the singles are a bit of a squeeze.

Los Andes Bed & Breakfast HOTEL, B&B $
(☎054-33-0015; www.losandesarequipa.com; La Merced 123; s/d without bathroom S31/50, with bathroom S48/72; @📶) There's a bit of a hospital feel to this hotel's giant rooms and ample communal kitchen, popular with climbing groups and long-term stays. But the pricing is good and it's a font of information for the surrounding area.

Point Hostel HOSTEL $
(☎054-28-6920; www.thepointhostels.com; Palacio Viejo 325; dm/d incl breakfast S21/70; @📶) One of five Point backpackers hostels in Peru, this one is two blocks from the main square. It has a popular billiards table and bar; but beware, this is a place for people who like to socialize and don't necessarily need to be tucked up in bed quietly by 10pm.

★ **Hotel Casona Solar** HOTEL $$
(☎054-22-8991; www.casonasolar.com; Consuelo 116; s/d/ste S158/240/354; 📶) Live like a colonial *caballero* (gentleman) in this gorgeous 'secret garden' situated – incredibly, given its tranquility – only three blocks from the main square. Grand 18th-century rooms are crafted from huge *sillar* stones, some with mezzanine bedrooms. The service (same-day laundry, bus reservations, free airline check-in) is equally dazzling. Best value in the city – maybe even Peru.

Casablanca Hostal HOTEL $$
(☎054-22-1327; www.casablancahostal.com; Puente Bolognesi 104; s/d/tr incl breakfast S95/145/200; @) The *New York Times'* 'Frugal Traveler' wasn't the only budget-seeker to marvel at what he was getting for his money in this place. It has a prime corner location on the main plaza, beautiful exposed *sillar* brickwork and rooms large enough to keep a horse (or two) in. Service is discreet and breakfast is taken in a lovely sun-filled cafe.

Eating

Trendy upscale restaurants are on San Francisco, while a few outdoor cafes line Pasaje Catedral. Good-value *picanterías* (informal local restaurants) abound in the city centre and Yanahuara district, serving a set lunch of traditional Arequipan dishes that are a must-try for the local atmosphere alone.

Café Fez-Istanbul MIDDLE EASTERN $
(San Francisco 229; mains S9-14; ⏲9am-midnight) The name suggests two cities, but the food is distinctly Middle Eastern rather than Moroccan. Falafels are the main draw – in a crepe or in a sandwich – served in a rather trendy resto-bar with a people-watching mezzanine floor. Other favorites include hummus, fresh cut fries and various sandwiches. Portions are snack fodder mainly, but in a cool environment.

Hatunpa PERUVIAN $
(Ugarte 208; dishes S11-15; ⏲12:30-9:30pm Mon-Sat) With just four tables and the common garden spud as its star ingredient, Hatunpa probably doesn't sound promising, but it has a fervent and fast-growing following. The trick? Potatoes originate in Peru and the *arequipeños* know how to embellish them with imaginative sauces and toppings such as alpaca, chorizo or veg. Even better, they're cheap (and filling) too.

★ **Zingaro** PERUVIAN $$
(www.zingaro-restaurante.com; San Francisco 309; mains S30-49; ⏲noon-11pm Mon-Sat) In an old *sillar* building with wooden balconies, stained glass and a resident pianist, culinary legends are made. Zingaro is a leading font of gastronomic innovation, meaning it's an ideal place to try out *nouveau* renditions of Peruvian standards including alpaca ribs, *ceviche*, or perhaps your first *cuy* (guinea pig).

Zig Zag PERUVIAN $$
(☎054-20-6020; www.zigzagrestaurant.com; Zela 210; mains S33-45; ⏲noon-midnight) Upscale but not ridiculously pricey, Zig Zag is a Peruvian restaurant with European inflections. It inhabits a two-story colonial house with an iron stairway designed by Gustave Eiffel (blimey, that bloke must have been busy). The menu classic is a meat selection served on a unique volcano-stone grill with various sauces. The fondues are also good.

La Nueva Palomino PERUVIAN $$
(Leoncio Prado 122; mains S14-29; ⏲noon-6pm) Definitely the local favorite, the atmosphere at this *picantería* is informal and can turn boisterous even during the week when groups of families and friends file in to eat local specialties and drink copious amounts of *chicha de jora* (fermented corn beer). The restaurant is in the Yanahuara district (2km northwest of the city center), east of the *mirador* (lookout).

Drinking

A slew of great bars and clubs are concentrated just north of the plaza at the corner of San Francisco and Ugarte.

Split PUB
(Zela 207; ⏲5pm-1am Mon-Wed, 6pm-2am Thu-Sat) Two bars split into upstairs and downstairs (with no ground level). Both are dark,

narrow and popular with locals who like to kick-start the night with a strong drink such as Misti Colodo, a *pisco* piña colada; or drinks labelled 'Tóxicos' for a pot-luck concoction of alcohol. There are pizzas, crepes and pasta to tempt you to stay.

Chelawasi Public House MICROBREWERY
(Campo Redondo 102; beer S12; ⏱4pm-midnight Thu-Sat, to 10pm Sun) New to craft beer? The friendly Canadian-Peruvian owners will step you through the best beers from Peru's microbreweries, with bonus local travel advice. Arequipa's first craft-beer bar is a modern but unpretentious pub in the village-like San Lázaro area. You can even order pizza from nearby to eat at the handmade tables.

Brujas Bar BAR
(San Francisco 300; ⏱5pm-late) Nordic-style pub with Union Jack flags, happy-hour cocktails and plenty of locals and expats having a chin-wag.

Casona Forum CLUB
(www.casonaforum.com; San Francisco 317) A five-in-one excuse for a good night out in a *sillar* building incorporating a pub (Retro), pool club (Zero), sofa bar (Chill Out), nightclub (Forum) and restaurant (Terrasse).

Entertainment

Café Art Montréal LIVE MUSIC
(Ugarte 210; ⏱5pm-1am) This smoky, intimate little bar with live bands playing on a stage at the back would be equally at home as a bohemian student hangout on Paris' Left Bank.

Shopping

Artisan and antique shops abound, especially around Monasterio Santa Catalina.

Fundo El Fierro CRAFT MARKET
(San Francisco 200; ⏱9am-8pm Mon-Sat, to 2pm Sun) The city's primary craft market occupies a beautiful colonial *sillar* courtyard next to the San Francisco church. Garments, paintings, handmade crafts and jewelry predominate, but you can also procure rare alpaca carpets from Cotahuasi. There's an artisanal fair with special stalls held here in August.

Information

DANGERS & ANNOYANCES

Petty theft is often reported in Arequipa, so travelers are urged to hide their valuables. Be wary of wandering outside of touristy zones at night. Take great care in Parque Selva Alegre, north of the city center, as muggings have been reported. Instead of hailing a cab on the street, ask your hostel or tour operator to call you an official one; it's worth it for the added safety.

EMERGENCY

Policía de Turismo (Tourist Police; ☎054-20-1258; Jerusalén 315-317; ⏱24hr) May be helpful if you need an official theft report for insurance claims.

MEDICAL SERVICES

Clínica Arequipa (☎054-25-3424, 054-25-3416; Bolognesi, near Puente Grau; ⏱8am-8pm Mon-Fri, to 12:30pm Sat) Arequipa's best and most expensive medical clinic.

Paz Holandesa Policlinic (☎054-43-2281; www.pazholandesa.com; Av Chávez 527; ⏱8am-8pm Mon-Sat) This appointment-only travel clinic provides vaccinations. Doctors

WORTH A TRIP

YANAHUARA

The peaceful neighborhood of Yanahuara makes for a diverting excursion from downtown Arequipa. It's within walking distance: go west on Av Puente Grau over the Puente Grau (Grau Bridge) and continue on Av Ejército for half a dozen blocks. Turn right on Av Lima and walk five blocks to a small plaza and *mirador* (lookout), which has excellent views of Arequipa and El Misti.

Head back along Av Jerusalén, parallel to Av Lima. Just before reaching Av Ejército you'll see the well-known restaurant **Sol de Mayo** (☎054-25-4148; Jerusalén 207, Yanahuara; mains S28-50), where you can stop for a tasty lunch of typical *arequipeño* food. The walk is two hours round-trip. Otherwise, *combis* (minibuses) to Yanahuara leave from along Av Puente Grau (and return from Yanahuara's plaza to the city) every few minutes (S1, 10 minutes).

here speak English and Dutch. Profits go toward providing free medical services for underprivileged Peruvian children.

MONEY

Money changers are found east of the Plaza de Armas. There are also global ATMs inside the Terminal Terrestre.

BCP (San Juan de Dios 125) Has a Visa ATM and changes US dollars.

Interbank (Mercaderes 217) Has a global ATM.

POST

Serpost (Moral 118; 8am-8pm Mon-Sat, 9am-1pm Sun)

TOURIST INFORMATION

iPerú (☎054-22-3265; iperuarequipa@promperu.gob.pe; Portal de la Municipalidad 110, Plaza de Armas; 9am-6pm Mon-Sat, to 1pm Sun) Government-supported source for objective information on local and regional attractions. There is also an office at the airport (☎054-44-4564; 1st fl, Main Hall, Aeropuerto Rodríguez Ballón; 10am-7:30pm).

Getting There & Away

AIR

The airport is 8km northwest of the center. **LAN** (☎054-20-1100; Santa Catalina 118C) serves Lima and Cuzco daily. A taxi to Centro runs S25. There are no airport buses or shared taxis. It is possible to take a *combi* marked 'Río Seco' or 'Zamacola' from Av Puente Grau and Ejército that will let you off in a sketchy neighborhood about 700m from the airport entrance.

BUS

Most companies leave from the Terminal Terrestre or the smaller Terrapuerto bus station next door. Both are 3km south of the center (departure tax S2).

For Lima, **Cruz del Sur** (☎054-42-7375; www.cruzdelsur.com.pe), **Ormeño** (☎054-42-3855) and other companies operate several daily buses, mostly afternoon departures. Many buses stop en route at Nazca and Ica. Many companies also have overnight buses to Cuzco.

Buses to Puno leave frequently; since this route is notorious for accidents, day buses are best. Ormeño continues on to Desaguadero on the Bolivian border and La Paz (Bolivia). Cruz del Sur has the most comfortable buses to Tacna via Moquegua.

For Cañón del Colca, there are a few daily buses for Chivay, continuing to Cabanaconde. Recommended companies include **Andalucía** (☎054-44-5089).

DESTINATION	COST (S)	DURATION (HR)
Cabanaconde	20	6
Chivay	15	3½
Cuzco	70-135	6-11
Ica	45-120	11-15
Lima	80-160	14-17
Moquegua	18	4
Nazca	59-154	10-12
Pisco	40-144	15
Puno	20-90	6
Tacna	20-57	6

Getting Around

Combis and minibuses go south along Bolívar to the Terminal Terrestre (S0.80, 25 minutes), next door to the Terrapuerto bus terminal, but it's a slow trip via the market area. Always use officially licensed taxi companies like **Turismo Arequipa** (☎054-45-8888) and **Taxitel** (☎054-45-2020), which cost about S8 to Terminal Terrestre.

Cañón del Colca

One of the world's deepest canyons at 3191m, Colca ranks second only to neighboring Cañón del Cotahuasi, which is 163m deeper. Trekking is by far the best way to experience village life, although the roads are dusty. As you pass through the villages, look out for the local women's traditional embroidered clothing and hats. On an environmental note, do not dispose of trash at the bins in the canyon as they overflow and locals simply dump them in the river. Take your own trash out.

The road from Arequipa climbs north through **Reserva Nacional Salinas y Aguada Blanca**, where *vicuñas* – the endangered wild cousins of llamas and alpacas – are often sighted. The road continues through bleak *altiplano* (high Andean plateau) over the highest point of 4800m, before dropping spectacularly into Chivay.

Chivay

☎054 / POP 7700

The provincial capital at the head of the canyon is a small, dusty transit hub. Bring plenty of Peruvian cash, as only a few stores exchange US dollars or euros.

Sights & Activities

Astronomical Observatory OBSERVATORY
(Planetario; 054-53-1020; Huayna Cápac; admission S25; ⏲Apr-Dec) No light pollution equals excellent Milky Way vistas. The Casa Andina hotel has a tiny observatory which holds nightly sky shows in Spanish and English. The price includes a 30-minute explanation and chance to peer into the telescope. It is closed between January and March as it is hard to catch a night with clear skies.

La Calera Hot Springs THERMAL BATHS
(admission S15; ⏲4:30am-7pm) If you've just bussed or driven in from Arequipa, a good way to acclimatize is to stroll 3km to La Calera Hot Springs and examine the canyon's (surprisingly shallow) slopes alfresco while lying in the naturally heated pools. The setting is idyllic and you'll be entertained by the whooping zipliners as they sail overhead. *Colectivos* from Chivay cost S1 to S2.

Sleeping

Though it's a tiny town, Chivay has plenty of *hostales* to choose from.

Hostal La Pascana HOTEL $
(☎054-53-1001; Siglo XX 106; s/d/tr incl breakfast S50/70/100; 📶) La Pascana is a good old-fashioned crash pad that will probably seem like luxury after a few days of hiking in the canyon. Simple rooms have blankets (thank heavens!), the staff is gracious and there's a small but decent restaurant. It's several notches above the other more modest guesthouses and lies adjacent to the plaza.

BOLETO TURÍSTICO

To access the sites in the Colca canyon you will need to purchase a *boleto turístico* (tourist ticket; S70) from a booth on the Arequipa road just outside Chivay. If you are taking an organized tour, the cost of the tour usually does not include this additional fee. If you are traveling alone, tickets can be purchased on most public buses entering or leaving Chivay, or in the town of Cabanaconde. Half of the proceeds from this ticket go to Arequipa for general maintenance and conservation of local tourist attractions, while the other half goes to the national agency of tourism.

Hostal Estrella de David PENSION $
(☎054-53-1233; Siglo XX 209; s/d/tr S30/40/60) A simple, clean *hospedaje* (small, family-owned inn) with bathrooms and some rooms with cable TV. It's a couple blocks from the plaza in the direction of the bus terminal. For budgeters, single rooms with shabby shared bathrooms are S20.

Colca Inn HOTEL $$
(☎53-1111; www.hotelcolcainn.com; Salaverry 307; s/d incl breakfast S75/101) The most comfortable, well-run midrange option in town, for those seeking added creature comforts such as heaters and hotel-level service.

★**Hotel Pozo del Cielo** HOTEL $$$
(☎054-34-6547; www.pozodelcielo.com.pe; Calle Huascar s/n; d/ste S310/637; 📶) Looking a bit like something Gaudí might have crafted, 'Heaven's Well,' as the name translates, is all low doorways, weirdly shaped rooms and winding paths. One half expects the seven dwarfs to come marching out. But, surrealism aside, this place works – a functional yet comfortable abode with an almost boutique-like feel to its individually crafted rooms and fine *'mirador'* restaurant.

Casa Andina BOUTIQUE HOTEL $$$
(☎054-53-1020, 054-53-1022; www.casa-andina.com; Huayna Cápac; s/d incl breakfast from S250; 📶) The purposefully rustic rooms here inhabit thatched-roof stone cottages in neatly sculpted grounds. The best features are the unusual extras such as an observatory, oxygen (should you be feeling lightheaded for a lack of it) and nightly culture shows where local musicians and artisans mingle, and a shaman tells fortunes with coca leaves.

Eating

Innkas Café PERUVIAN $
(Plaza de Armas 705; mains S12-20; ⏲7am-10pm) An old building with cozy window nooks warmed by modern gas heaters (and boy do you need 'em). Maybe it's the altitude, but the *lomo saltado* tastes Gastón Acurio–good here. The sweet service is backed up by even sweeter cakes and coffee.

Cusi Alina PERUVIAN $$
(Plaza de Armas 201; buffet S27; 🌿) One of a couple of restaurants in Chivay that offers an all-you-can-eat lunchtime buffet. The food represents a good Peruvian smorgasbord with plenty of vegetarian options. It's

popular with tour buses, so get in before 1pm to enjoy more elbow room.

Getting There & Away

The bus terminal is a 15-minute walk from the plaza. There are nine buses daily to Arequipa (S15, three hours) and four to Cabanaconde (S5, 2½ hours) via Cruz del Cóndor.

Chivay to Cabanaconde

The main road follows the south bank of the upper Cañón del Colca and leads past several picturesque villages and some of the most extensive pre-Inca terracing in Peru. One of these villages, the more culturally intact **Yanque**, has an attractive 18th-century church at the plaza. A 30-minute walk to the river leads to some hot springs (admission S3). There are simple guesthouses and hotels scattered around town.

Eventually the road reaches **Cruz del Cóndor** (entry with *boleto turístico*). Andean condors that nest by the rocky outcrop can occasionally be seen gliding on thermal air currents. Early morning or late afternoon are the best viewing times, but you'll need luck.

If traveling independently with plans to stop in Cruz del Cóndor before continuing on to Cabanaconde, it's best to leave Arequipa on the unfortunately timed 1am bus. You will be in Cruz del Cóndor at daybreak with enough time to enjoy it and still catch a bus on to Cabanaconde from Arequipa. Later in the afternoon, those buses are few and far between, and you could be stuck in Cruz del Cóndor for several hours.

Cabanaconde

☎054 / POP 2400

Cabanaconde is an excellent base for some spectacular hikes into the canyon, including the popular two-hour trek down to Sangalle (the Oasis) at the bottom, where there are natural pools for swimming (S5), simple bungalows and campsites. The return trek is thirsty work; allow three to four hours.

Local guides can also be hired by consulting with your hostel or the *municipalidad* in Cabanaconde. The going rate for guides is S30 to S60 per day. They can also suggest a wealth of other treks, to waterfalls, geysers, remote villages and archaeological sites.

Pachamama (☎054-25-3879, 95-931-6322; www.pachamamahome.com; San Pedro 209; incl breakfast dm S25, d without/with bathroom S50/70; @) is an ubercozy place offering simple dorms and rooms as a complement to the canyon's best hang-out spot: a candlelit pizzeria and bar run by a hip, guitar-wielding brother team from Ayacucho, who provide the singalong soundtrack to cavorting travelers. You can rent bikes, chill in the hammocks or just soak up the global vibe. This is travel.

The basic **La Posada del Conde** (☎054-40-0408, 054-83-0033; www.posadadelconde.com; San Pedro s/n; s/d incl breakfast S95/128; wi-fi) has well-cared-for doubles.

Several daily buses bound for Chivay (S5, 2½ hours) and Arequipa (S17, six hours) via Cruz del Cóndor leave from the plaza.

LAKE TITICACA

Covering 8400 sq km and sitting at 3808m, Lake Titicaca is considered the world's largest high-altitude lake. At this altitude the air is crisp and sunlight suffuses the *altiplano* and sparkles on the deep waters. Swaths of blue sky are marked with ancient funerary towers and crumbling colonial churches. The port of Puno is a good base for visiting the far-flung islands dotted across Lake Titicaca – from fascinating artificial ones constructed of reeds to remote, rural isles where villagers live much as they have for centuries.

Juliaca

☎051 / POP 220,000

This is a brash, unfinished eyesore on an otherwise beautiful big-sky landscape. Principally a market town, it has the department's only commercial airport, though most tourists hightail it out of baggage claim for its more attractive lakeside neighbor, Puno. The city bustles with the commerce (and contraband) due to its handy location near the border. Daytime muggings and drunks on the street are not uncommon.

If you are in a pinch, the towering **Royal Inn Hotel** (☎051-32-1561; www.royalinnhoteles.com; San Román 158; s/d/tr incl breakfast S315/330/420) boasts newly revamped modern rooms with hot showers, heating and cable TV, plus one of Juliaca's best restaurants (mains from S20).

The **airport** (JUL; ☎051-32-4248) is 2km west of town. **LAN** (☎051-32-2228; San Roman

Arequipa's Canyon Country & Lake Titicaca

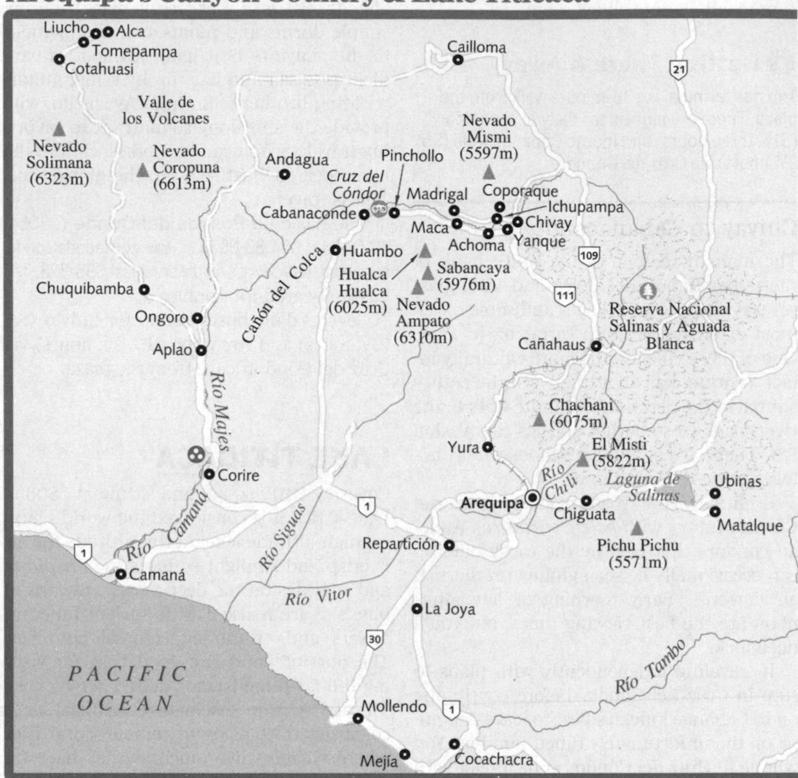

125) has daily flights to/from Lima, Arequipa and Cuzco. To the airport, take a taxi (S10). Direct minibuses to Puno (S15, 45 minutes) usually await incoming flights. Cheaper minibuses depart from the intersection of Piérola and 8 de Noviembre, northeast of the plaza (S3.50, 45 minutes).

Puno

051 / POP 141,100

With a regal plaza, concrete-block buildings and crumbling bricks that blend into the hills, Puno has its share of both grit and cheer. Few colonial buildings remain, and local women garbed in multilayered dresses and bowler hats bustle on the streets. You'll want to multilayer too – Puno nights are bitterly cold, especially in winter, when temperatures reel below freezing.

Sights & Activities

Yavari HISTORIC SITE

(051-36-9329; www.yavari.org; admission by donation; 8am-1pm & 3-5:30pm) The oldest steamship on Lake Titicaca, the famed *Yavari* has turned from British gunship to a museum and recommended bed and breakfast, with bunk-bed lodging and attentive service under the stewardship of its captain. And no, you don't have to be a navy buff reflecting on Titicaca. The Yavari is moored behind the Sonesta Posada Hotel del Inca, about 5km from the center of Puno. It's probably the most tranquil spot in Puno.

Museo Carlos Dreyer MUSEUM

(Conde de Lemos 289; admission with English-speaking guide S15; 9am-7pm Mon-Fri, to 1pm Sat) This museum houses a fascinating collection of Puno-related archaeological artifacts and art. Upstairs there are three

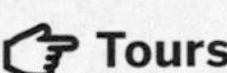

mummies and a full-scale fiberglass *chullpa* (funerary tower).

It's around the corner from **Casa del Corregidor** (051-35-1921; www.casadelcorregidor.pe; Deustua 576; 9am-8pm Mon-Sat, 10am-7pm Sun) FREE.

Coca Museum MUSEUM
(051-36-5087; Deza 301; admission S5; 9am-1pm & 3-8pm) Tiny and quirky, this museum offers lots of interesting information – historical, medicinal, cultural – about the coca plant and its many uses. Presentation isn't that interesting, though: reams of text (in English only) are stuck to the wall and interspersed with photographs and old Coca-Cola ads. The display of traditional costumes is what makes a visit here worthwhile.

Though the relation between traditional dress and coca is unfathomable, it's a boon for making sense of the costumes worn in street parades.

Tours

Some travelers find the island-hopping tours disappointing, even exploitative; others report great fun. Ask around at your guesthouse for a local guide, preferably someone with ties to the islands, then go to the docks in the early morning and get on the next boat; or choose your tour company wisely.

All Ways Travel CULTURAL TOUR
(051-35-3979; www.titicacaperu.com; 2nd fl, Deustua 576) Offers both classic and 'nontourist' tours.

Edgar Adventures CULTURAL TOUR
(051-35-3444; www.edgaradventures.com; Lima 328) Longtime agency with positive community involvement.

Festivals & Events

La Virgen de la Candelaria RELIGION
(Candlemas; Feb 2-18) The region's most spectacular festival spreads out for several days around the actual date (Candlemas), depending upon which day of the week Candlemas falls. If it falls between Sunday and Tuesday, things get under way the previous Saturday; if Candlemas occurs between Wednesday and Friday, celebrations will get going the following Saturday.

Puno Week CULTURAL
A huge celebration marking the legendary birth of Manco Cápac, the first Inca. Events are held the first week of November, centered on Puno Day (November 5).

Epiphany RELIGION
Held on January 6 and also known as El Día de Los Reyes, this celebrates the day that the three wise men visited baby Jesus. Outside of every church, and in the Plaza de Armas, you will find women in traditional dress selling dolls for children to lay on church altars at Mass.

Sleeping

Inka's Rest HOSTEL $
(051-36-8720; www.inkasresthostel.com; Pasaje San Carlos 158; dm/d incl breakfast S23/70; @) Tucked into a small alley, this hostel earns high marks for service. Very clean, it features bunks with down duvets, attractive old tile and parquet floors. There's a cute breakfast area as well as a guest kitchen and room with a huge flat-screen TV. Private rooms are

Puno

Sights
- 1 Casa del Corregidor B4
- 2 Coca Museum B2
- 3 Museo Carlos Dreyer B4

Activities, Courses & Tours
- All Ways Travel .... (see 1)
- 4 Edgar Adventures B3

Sleeping
- 5 Hostal Uros C2
- 6 Hotel Italia C2
- 7 Inka's Rest C3
- 8 Posada Luna Azul C4

Eating
- 9 Loving Hut D3
- 10 Machu Pizza B3
- 11 Mojsa B4
- 12 Ukuku's B3

Drinking & Nightlife
- 13 Kamizaraky Rock Pub B3

less attractive. There is intercom entry but take a taxi if arriving at night.

Duque Inn HOTEL **$**
(☎051-20-5014; www.duqueinn.com; Ayaviri 152; s/d with bathroom S25/45, without bathroom S20/35) Cordial but kooky, this budget lodging is spruced up with satin bedspreads and chandeliers. Archaeologist owner Ricardo Conde is eccentric gold, offering free tours. It's a steal for budget travelers and serious trekkers. To find it, take Ilave for three blocks beyond Huancané, then turn right

into Ayaviri. When you see the endless hill, you may want to splurge on taxis.

Hostal Uros HOTEL $

(051-35-2141; Valcárcel 135; s/d/tr S30/50/75;) Serene but close to the action, this friendly, good-value hostel has its best rooms on the upper floors. The roomy light-filled patio can store bicycles or motorbikes. Ask for a room with a window. Heaters are S10 extra. If you're counting pennies, those with grubby shared bathroom are S5 cheaper per person.

★Casa Panq'arani B&B $$

(951-677-005, 051-36-4892; www.casapanqarani.com; Jr Arequipa 1086; s/tw/d incl breakfast S80/135/145;) This delightful traditional Puno home has a flower-filled courtyard and inviting rooms lining a 2nd-floor balcony. But the real draw is the sincere hospitality of owners Edgar and Consuelo. Rooms are ample, with comfortable beds with crocheted bedspreads and fresh flowers. There are ample sunny spots for lounging. Don't miss Consuelo's gourmet *altiplano* cooking (meals S35 with advance request).

Posada Luna Azul HOTEL $$

(95-159-0835; www.posadalunaazul.com; Cajamarca 242; s/d incl breakfast S60/90;) The 'blue moon' name might conjure images of a cozy, tranquil night's rest. And this small hotel is tucked far enough away from the noise that it's true. The petite, clean, carpeted rooms have flat-screen TV and good heaters, making them impressively warm all night, and the showers are strong and hot. Warmth at last in Puno.

Hotel Italia HOTEL $$

(051-36-7706; www.hotelitaliaperu.com; Valcárcel 122; s/d/tr S110/150/190;) Snug rooms have parquet floors, cable TV, hot showers and heating but vary in quality at this large, well-established spot. There are old-world touches with antique telephones and long-serving staff who are cordial and well groomed. The delicious buffet breakfast includes salty black olives and Puno's own triangular anise bread. Credit cards are accepted.

Eating & Drinking

Many restaurants don't advertise their *menús*, which are cheaper than ordering à la carte. Locals eat *pollo a la brasa* (roast chicken) and economical *menús* on Jirón Tacna between Deustua and Libertad.

For a cheap snack, try *api* (hot, sweet corn juice) – a serious comfort food found in several places on Oquendo between Parque Pino and the *supermercado*. Order it with a paper-thin, wickedly delicious envelope of deep-fried dough.

Loving Hut VEGETARIAN $

(www.lovinghut.com; Choque Huanca 188; mains S15-18, menú S12; 9am-6pm Mon-Sat;) Filling vegetarian lunches with salad, gluten, soy-meat and brown-rice options in Asian and Peruvian styles. Try the quinoa burger or *anticuchos veganos* (vegan beef skewers). The warm unsweetened soy milk or *mate* (tea) on tap makes the *menú* worth it alone.

Machu Pizza PIZZA $

(95-139-0652; Arequipa 409; mains S8-18; 5:30-11pm Mon-Sat, to 10pm Sun;) It might not be Colosseum authentic, but the *ají* (chili) aioli that you are given to spread over the thin-crust pizzas is a delicious Peruvian twist. The dim lighting, cozy mezzanine and back room, plus personal-sized pizzas make it a good place to dine alone or with your favorite person.

★Mojsa PERUVIAN $$

(051-36-3182; Jr. Lima 635; mains S22-30; noon-9.30pm) The go-to place for locals and travelers alike, Mojsa lives up to its name, Aymara for 'delicious.' It has a thoughtful range of Peruvian and international food, including innovative trout dishes and a design-your-own salad option. All meals start with fresh bread and a bowl of local olives. In the evening, crisp brick-oven pizzas are on offer.

Ukuku's PERUVIAN $$

(Grau 172, 2nd fl; mains S20-27, dinner menú S25; noon-10pm;) Crowds of travelers and locals thaw out in this toasty restaurant, which dishes up good local and Andean food (try alpaca steak with baked apples, or the quinoa omelet), as well as pizza, pasta, Asian-style vegetarian fare and espresso drinks. The good-value dinner set menu includes a *pisco*.

Kamizaraky Rock Pub PUB

(Grau 158) With a classic-rock soundtrack, grungy cool bartenders and liquor-infused coffee drinks essential for staying warm during Puno's bone-chilling nights, it may be a hard place to leave.

Information

Bolivianos can be exchanged in town or at the border.

Interbank (Lima 444) Global ATM; changes traveler's checks.

iPerú (051-36-5088; Plaza de Armas, cnr Lima & Deustua; 9am-6pm Mon-Sat, to 1pm Sun) Puno's helpful and well-informed multilingual tourist office; also runs Indecopi, the tourist-protection agency, which registers complaints about travel agencies and hotels.

Medicentro Tourist's Health Clinic (051-36-5909, 951-62-0937; Moquegua 191; 24hr) English and French spoken; they will also come to your hotel.

Policía de Turismo (Tourist Police; 051-35-3988; Deustua 558; 24hr) There is a police officer on duty in the *Terminal Terrestre* (24 hours) – ask around if you need assistance.

Scotiabank (Jirón Lima 458) ATM.

Serpost (Moquegua 267; 8am-8pm Mon-Sat)

Getting There & Around

AIR

The nearest airport is in Juliaca. Airlines with offices in Puno include **LAN** (051-36-7227; Tacna 299) and **Star Perú** (Jirón Lima 154).

BUS

The **Terminal Terrestre** (051-36-4737; Primero de Mayo 703), three blocks down Ricardo Palma from Av El Sol, houses Puno's long-distance bus companies. Direct services go to Lima, Arequipa and Cuzco via Juliaca. *Económico* buses go to Tacna via Moquegua six times daily.

Inka Express (051-36-5654; www.inkaexpress.com; Tacna 346) runs luxury tour buses to Cuzco (S159) every morning. Fares include beverages and an English-speaking guide who explains sites that are briefly visited en route, including Pucará, Raqchi and Andahuaylillas.

Minibuses to Juliaca, lakeshore towns and the Bolivian border leave from Terminal Zonal on Simón Bolívar, a few blocks north of the Terminal Terrestre.

Prices given here are general estimates for normal/luxury buses.

GETTING TO BOLIVIA

There are two overland routes from Puno to La Paz, Bolivia. The Yunguyo route, which is safer and easier, allows you to take a break at the lakeshore resort of Copacabana. The Desaguadero route, which is slightly faster and cheaper, can be combined with a visit to the ruins at Tiwanaku. Beware of immigration officials trying to charge an illegal 'entry tax' or search your belongings for 'fake dollars' to confiscate.

US citizens require a visa to enter Bolivia (US$135 plus two passport-sized photos at border posts). Most other nationalities don't require visas for stays of 30 days or less, including passport holders from Canada, Australia, Japan, Mexico and the EU. There are no border fees if your nationality does not require a visa.

For information on making this crossing in the opposite direction, see p213.

Via Yunguyo

The most convenient way to reach Bolivia is with a cross-border company like **Tour Peru** (051-20-6088; www.tourperu.com.pe; Tacna 285); purchase tickets a day ahead. Buses depart at 7:30am, stopping at Peruvian and Bolivian border posts, then Copacabana (S25, three to four hours), where you board another bus to La Paz (S30, 3½ hours).

Alternatively, frequent minibuses depart Puno's Terminal Zonal for Yunguyo (S6.50, 2½ hours), where you can grab a taxi for the final leg to the border (S4). In Bolivia, which is an hour ahead of Peru, the border post is open from 8:30am to 7pm daily. From the border, it's another 10km to Copacabana (*combis* B$3).

Via Desaguadero

Combis leave Puno's *terminal zonal* for Desaguadero (S8, 2½ hours) throughout the day. Avoid spending the night here. Border hours are 8:30am to 8:30pm, but because Bolivia is an hour ahead of Peru, plan to cross before 7pm Peruvian time. Many buses go from Desaguadero to La Paz (B$30, three hours) during daylights hours, passing the turnoff for Tiwanaku. There are no ATMs in Desaguadero, so bring cash from Puno if your nationality requires a tourist visa.

DESTINATION	COST (S)	DURATION (HR)
Arequipa	25/75	5
Copacabana, Bolivia	25	3-4
Cuzco	30/80	6-7
Juliaca	3.50/15	1
La Paz, Bolivia	50	6
Lima	140/170	18-21

TAXI

A short taxi ride around town costs S4.50. *Mototaxis* (motorbike rickshaws) are S2.50, and *triciclos*, cheapest of all, are S2 – but make sure the negotiated fare is per ride, not per person.

TRAIN

Cuzco-bound trains depart from Puno's **train station** (☎051-36-9179; www.perurail.com; Av La Torre 224; ⏰7am-noon & 3-6pm Mon-Fri, 7am-3pm Sat) at 8am, arriving at 6pm. Services run on Monday, Wednesday and Saturday from November to March, with an extra departure on Friday from April to October. Tickets can be purchased online.

Around Puno

Sillustani

Sitting on rolling hills in the Lago Umayo peninsula, these ruined **towers** (admission S10) stand out for miles against the unforgiving landscape. The ancient Colla people were a warlike, Aymara-speaking tribe that buried their nobility in these impressive *chullpas* (funerary towers), made from massive coursed blocks and reaching heights of up to 12m. There are also 20 or so local *altiplano* homes in the area that welcome visitors.

Puno travel agencies run 3½-hour tours (S35 including entrance fee) that leave around 2:30pm daily. To DIY, catch any bus to Juliaca and get off where the road splits to Sillustani. From there, occasional *combis* (S3, 20 minutes) go to the ruins.

Titicaca Islands

The only way to see Lake Titicaca is to spend a few days visiting its fairy-tale islands. That said, negative impacts from tourism are being felt in many communities. You could also hop over the Bolivian border to visit the more chilled Isla del Sol from Copacabana.

Islas Uros

The unique **floating islands** (admission S8) of the Uros people – around 50 reed islands in all – have become quite commercial, though there is still nothing quite like them anywhere else. The islands are built using layers of the buoyant *totora* reeds that grow abundantly in the shallows of Lake Titicaca.

Intermarriage with Aymara-speaking indigenous peoples has seen the demise of the pure-blooded Uros. Always a small tribe, they began their floating existence centuries ago in an effort to isolate themselves from the aggressive Collas and the Incas. Today several hundred people still live on the islands.

Indeed, the lives of the Uros are completely interwoven with the reeds, which are used to make their homes, boats and crafts. The islands' reeds are constantly replenished from the top as they rot away, so the ground is always soft and springy – mind your step!

Those seeking homestays on **Isla Khantati** meet with boundless personality **Cristina Suaña** (☎951-69-5121, 951-47-2355; uroskhantati@hotmail.com; per person full board S180), an Uros native whose entrepreneurship has earned her international accolades.

Ferries leave from the port for Uros (return trip S10) at least once an hour from 6am to 4pm. The community-owned ferry service visits two islands, on a rotation basis. Ferries to Taquile and Amantaní can also drop you off in the Uros.

Isla Taquile

Inhabited for many thousands of years, this 7-sq-km island often feels like its own little world. The Quechua-speaking islanders maintain lives minimally changed by mainland modernities and have a long tradition of weaving. Look for the menfolk's tightly woven woolen hats, resembling floppy nightcaps, which denote social status. Women wear multilayered skirts and delicately embroidered blouses.

Several hills have pre-Inca terracing and small ruins set against the backdrop of Bolivia's snowcapped Cordillera Real. Visitors are free to wander around, but you can't do that on a day trip without missing lunch or the boat back, so stay overnight if you can. Travelers will be met by islanders next to the arch atop the steep stairway up from the dock. Homestays can be arranged here (per person S20), though tourism has altered the landscape somewhat and travelers looking for a less tainted experience should sleep on nearby Amantaní, which is still in its tourism infancy and offers a more authentic sleepover. If you do sleep on Taquile, beds are basic but clean, and facilities are minimal. You'll be given blankets, but bring a sleeping bag and flashlight.

Most island shops and restaurants close by mid-afternoon, when all the tour groups leave, so arrange dinner with your host family in advance. Gifts of fresh fruit from Puno's markets are appreciated. You can buy bottled drinks at the shops, though it's worth bringing purifying tablets or a water filter. Also bring small bills (change is limited) and extra money for souvenirs.

Boats leave Puno's dock for the incredibly slow 34km trip to Taquile daily at 6:45am (S30 round-trip, three hours; S8 admission to island); some stop at Islas Uros. The return boat leaves in the early afternoon, arriving in Puno around nightfall. Remember to bring sunscreen and mosquito repellent.

Puno travel agencies organize two-day guided tours for S50 and up (some with much faster boats charge upwards of S180).

CUZCO & THE SACRED VALLEY

As the heart of the once mighty Inca empire, the magnetic city of Cuzco heads the list of many traveler itineraries. Each year it draws hundreds of thousands of visitors to its lofty elevations, lured by the colonial splendor built on hefty stone foundations of the Incas. And lying within easy hopping distance of the city is the country's biggest drawcard: the 'lost' city of the Incas, Machu Picchu, perched high on a remote mountaintop. The department of Cuzco also has superb trekking routes and a long list of flamboyant fiestas and carnivals in which Peru's pagan past colorfully collides with Catholic rituals and modern Latin American mayhem.

Cuzco

084 / POP 427,000

The high-flying city of Cuzco (Qosq'o in the Quechua language) sits at a 3300m crossroads of centuries-old Andean tradition and modern Peruvian life. As the continent's oldest continuously inhabited city, it was once the Inca empire's foremost stronghold, and is now both the undisputed archaeological capital of the Americas as well as one of the continent's most staunchly preserved colonial living museums. Massive Inca-built walls line steep, narrow cobblestone streets and plazas thronged with the descendants of the mighty Incas and Spanish conquistadors – who hobble about in colorful traditional wares among the hustle and bustle of contemporary *cuzqueños* making a living from the town's present-day lifeblood: tourism. And lots of it.

Though Cuzco is at the tipping point of being completely overrun with international tourism, its historical charms and breathtaking setting cannot be denied.

History

Cuzco is so steeped in history, tradition and myth that it can be difficult to know where fact ends and story begins. Legends tell that in the 12th century the first Inca, Manco Capác, was charged by the ancestral sun god Inti to find the *qosq'o* (the navel of the earth). When at last Manco discovered such a point, he founded the city there.

The ninth Inca Pachacutec wasn't only a warmonger; he also proved himself to be a sophisticated urban developer, devising Cuzco's famous puma shape and diverting rivers to cross the city. Pachacutec also built the famous Qorikancha temple and the palace fronting what is now the Plaza de Armas.

After murdering the 12th Inca Atahualpa, the Spanish conquistador Francisco Pizarro marched on Cuzco in 1533 and appointed Manco Inca as puppet ruler of the Incas. After a few years, Manco rebelled and laid siege to Spanish-occupied Cuzco. Only a desperate battle at Saqsaywamán saved the Spanish from annihilation. Manco was forced to retreat to Ollantaytambo and eventually into the jungle at Vilcabamba. Once the city had been safely recaptured, looted and settled, the seafaring Spaniards turned their attentions to coastal Lima, making Cuzco just another quiet colonial backwater.

Earthquakes rocked Cuzco in 1650 and 1950, and a failed indigenous uprising was led by Túpac Amaru II in 1780. But the rediscovery of Machu Picchu in 1911 has affected the city more than any event since the arrival of the Spanish.

Sights

Students usually pay half-price admission. To visit most sites, you will need Cuzco's official *boleto turístico* (tourist ticket; adult/student under 26 with ISIC card S130/70), valid for 10 days. Among the 17 sites included are: Saqsaywamán, Q'enqo, Pukapukara, Tambomachay, Pisac, Ollantaytambo, Chinchero and Moray, as well as an evening performance of Andean dances and live music at the Centro Qosqo de Arte Nativo. While some inclusions are duds, you can't visit any of them without the ticket. It's also possible to buy partial one-day *boletos* costing S70. A similar scheme for religious sites, the Circuito Religioso, costs S50 and is valid for a month. Purchase *boletos turísticos* from **Dircetur/Cosituc** (084-261-465; www.boletoturisticocusco.com; La Municipalidad, office 102, Av El Sol 103; 8am-6pm Mon-Fri) or at participating sites outside the city.

The city centers on the Plaza de Armas, while traffic-choked Av El Sol is the main business thoroughfare. The alley off the northwest side of the plaza is Procuradores (Tax Collectors), nicknamed 'Gringo Alley.' Beside the cathedral, Triunfo climbs to San Blas, Cuzco's artistic *barrio* (neighborhood).

Plaza de Armas PLAZA

In Inca times the plaza, called Huacaypata or Aucaypata, was the heart of the capital. Today it's the nerve center of the modern city. Two flags are usually flying here – the red-and-white Peruvian flag and the rainbow-colored flag of Tahuantinsuyo. Easily mistaken for an international gay-pride banner, it represents the four quarters of the Inca empire.

Qorikancha RUIN

(Plazoleta Santo Domingo; admission S10; 8:30am-5:30pm Mon-Sat, 2-5pm Sun) If you visit only one site in Cuzco, make it these Inca ruins, which form the base of the colonial church and convent of Santo Domingo. Qorikancha was once the richest temple in the Inca empire; all that remains today is the masterful stonework.

Museo de Arte Precolombino MUSEUM

(084-23-3210; http://map.perucultural.org.pe; Plazoleta Nazarenas 231; admission S20; 9am-10pm) Housed inside a Spanish colonial mansion with an Inca ceremonial courtyard, this dramatically curated pre-Columbian art museum showcases a stunningly varied, if selectively small, collection of archaeological artifacts previously buried in the vast storerooms of Lima's Museo Larco. Dating from between 1250 BC and AD 1532, the artifacts show off the artistic and cultural achievements of many of Peru's ancient cultures, with exhibits labeled in Spanish, English and French.

OVER THE RAINBOW

A common sight in Cuzco's Plaza de Armas is the city's much-loved flag representing the *arco iris* (rainbow) sacred to the Incas. Don't take it for the international gay-pride banner, though it's remarkably similar!

Museo Inka MUSEUM

(084-23-7380; Tucumán near Ataúd; admission S10; 8am-6pm Mon-Fri, 9am-4pm Sat) The charmingly modest Museo Inka, a steep block northeast of the Plaza de Armas, is the best museum in town for those interested in the Incas. The restored interior is jam-packed with a fine collection of metal- and gold-work, jewelry, pottery, textiles, mummies, models and the world's largest collection of *queros* (ceremonial Inca wooden drinking vessels). There's excellent interpretive information in Spanish and English-speaking guides are usually available for a small fee.

Choco Museo MUSEUM

(084-24-4765; www.chocomuseo.com; Garcilaso 210; 10:30am-6:30pm;) FREE The wafting aromas of bubbling chocolate will mesmerize you from the start. While the museum is frankly lite, the best part of this French-owned enterprise is the organic chocolate-making workshops (S70 per person). You can also come for fondue or a fresh cup of fair-trade hot cocoa. It organizes chocolate farm tours close to Santa María. It's multilingual and kid-friendly.

Iglesia de San Blas CHURCH

(Plaza San Blas; admission S10; 10am-6pm Mon-Sat, 2-6pm Sun) This simple adobe church is comparatively small, but you can't help but be awed by the baroque, gold-leaf principal altar. The exquisitely carved pulpit, made from a single tree trunk, has been called the finest example of colonial wood carving in the Americas.

Museo Quijote MUSEUM
(www.museoelquijote.com; Galería Banco la Nacion, Calle Almagro s/n; ⏲9am-6pm Mom-Fri, 9am-1pm Sun) FREE In a new location housed inside a bank, this privately owned museum of contemporary art houses a diverse, thoughtful collection of painting and sculpture ranging from the folksy to the macabre. There's good interpretive information about 20th-century Peruvian art history, some of it translated into English.

Activities

Scores of outdoor outfitters in Cuzco offer trekking, rafting and mountain-biking adventures, as well as mountaineering, horse-riding and paragliding trips. With the wide choice of places lining Plateros and Santa Ana, there is great variety in quality and reliability, so do your research carefully.

Trekking

The Inca Trail is on most hikers' minds, but a dizzying array of other treks surround Cuzco. Many agencies organize trips to remote

Cuzco

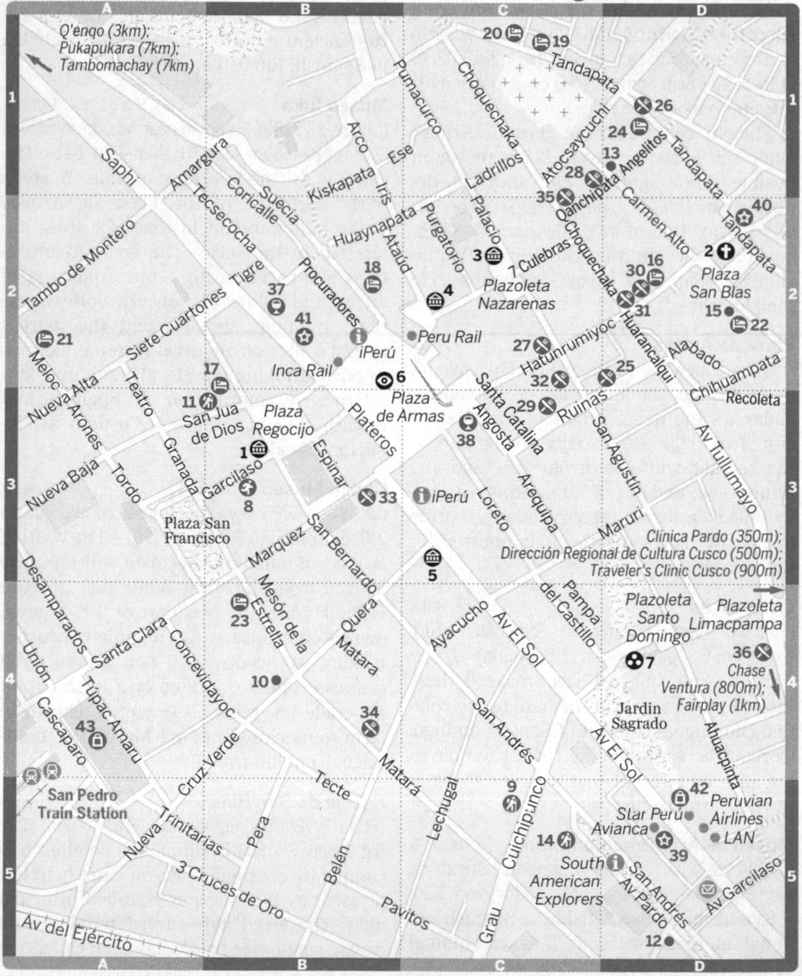

0 — 200 m
0 — 0.1 miles

Inca ruins, such as Choquequirau and Vilcabamba and around Ausangate. Prices are *not* fixed. Shop around and ask questions (eg How many people per tent? How many porters are coming? What are the arrangements for special diets?). Inspect all rental gear carefully. South American Explorers (p852) sells topo maps and is an excellent source of independent info.

Travelers flock to the following agencies:

★Apu's Peru HIKING
(☎084-23-3691; www.apus-peru.com; Cuichipunco 366) A recommended outfitter for the Inca Trail also offering conventional tours. Responsible and popular with travelers.

★Journey Experience ADVENTURE TOUR
(JOEX; ☎084-24-5642; www.joextravel.com; Av Tupac Amaru V-2-A, Progreso) A recommended outfitter for hiking and cultural activities.

Llama Path HIKING
(☎084-24-0822; www.llamapath.com; San Juan de Dios 250) Friendly, small trekking company that has received good reports from some travelers.

> **THINK AHEAD: MACHU PICCHU TICKETS**
>
> Since Machu Picchu tickets can no longer be purchased online, get this business done early with an authorized agent listed at www.machupicchu.gob.pe or in person at Cuzco's **Dirección Regional de Cultura** (p852). To add entry to the coveted Huayna Picchu hike, purchase even earlier.

Peru Treks HIKING
(☎084-22-2722; www.perutreks.com; Av Pardo 540) Offers hiking tours to Machu Picchu.

River Running & Mountain Biking

Popular whitewater-rafting trips visit **Río Urubamba**. It's not very wild but offers some spectacular scenery and a chance to visit some of the best Inca ruins near Cuzco. Rivers here are unregulated. For more remote rivers, book with a top-quality outfit using experienced rafting guides who know first aid, because you will be days away from help in the event of illness or accident. The same goes for mountain-biking trips.

Cuzco

Sights

1 Choco Museo ... B3
2 Iglesia de San Blas ... D2
3 Museo de Arte Precolombino ... C2
4 Museo Inka ... C2
5 Museo Quijote ... C3
6 Plaza de Armas ... B2
7 Qorikancha ... D4

Activities, Courses & Tours

8 Apumayo ... B3
9 Apu's Peru ... C5
10 Excel Language Center ... B4
11 Llama Path ... B3
12 Milla Turismo ... D5
13 Party Bike ... D1
14 Peru Treks ... C5
15 San Blas Spanish School ... D2

Sleeping

16 Amaru Hostal ... D2
17 Ecopackers ... B2
18 Hostal Suecia I ... B2
19 Kuntur Wasi Cusco ... C1
20 La Encantada ... C1
21 Niños Hotel ... A2
22 Pantastico ... D2
23 Pariwana ... B4
24 Tika Wasi ... D1

Eating

25 Aldea Yanapay ... D2
26 Cafeteria 7&7 ... D1
27 Cicciolina ... C2
28 El Hada ... C1
29 Gato's Market ... C3
30 Granja Heidi ... D2
31 Jack's Café ... D2
32 La Bodega 138 ... C2
33 Market ... B3
34 Mega ... B4
35 Prasada ... C1
36 Trujillo Restaurant ... D4

Drinking & Nightlife

37 Memoria ... B2
38 Norton Rats ... C3

Entertainment

39 Centro Qosqo de Arte Nativo ... D5
40 Km 0 ... D2
41 Ukuku's ... B2

Shopping

42 Center for Traditional Textiles of Cuzco ... D5
43 Mercado San Pedro ... A4

The **Río Apurímac** has challenging rapids through deep gorges and protected rainforest but can only be run from May to November. A wilder trip is the technically demanding **Río Tambopata**, run from June to October. Trips start north of Lake Titicaca and reach Reserva Nacional Tambopata in the Amazon.

If you're experienced, there are awesome mountain-biking possibilities around the Sacred Valley and downhill trips from Cuzco to the Amazon jungle. Always inspect rental bikes carefully. Make sure you get a helmet, puncture-repair kit, pump and tool kit.

Some reputable companies for rafting and biking trips:

Amazonas Explorer ADVENTURE TOUR
(084-25-2846; www.amazonas-explorer.com; Av Collasuyu 910, Miravalle) Offers excellent two- to 10-day mountain-biking adventures; great for families, with kids' bikes available.

Apumayo RAFTING
(084-24-6018; www.apumayo.com; Jirón Ricardo Palma Ñ-11, Urb Santa Monica) A professional outfitter that takes advance international bookings for Río Tambopata trips. Also equipped to take travelers with disabilities.

Party Bike ADVENTURE TOUR
(084-24-0399; www.partybiketravel.com; Carmen Alto 246) Traveler recommended, with downhills, and tours to the valley and through Cuzco.

Courses

Excel Language Center LANGUAGE COURSE
(084-23-5298; www.excel-spanishlanguageprograms-peru.org; Cruz Verde 336) Highly recommended for its professionalism.

Fairplay LANGUAGE COURSE
(984-78-9252; www.fairplay-peru.org; Pasaje Zavaleta C-5) A unique nonprofit NGO, Fairplay trains Peruvian single mothers to provide Spanish lessons and homestays. Students pay two-thirds of their class fees directly to their teachers. Individual classes only, priced according to the teacher's level of experience.

San Blas Spanish School LANGUAGE COURSE
(24-7898; www.spanishschoolperu.com; Carmen Bajo 224) Students enjoy the informal teaching here, in tune with the school's location in the heart of bohemian San Blas.

Tours

There are hundreds of registered travel agencies in Cuzco, but none can ever be 100% recommended. Ask around.

Cuzco is an excellent place to organize trips to the jungle, especially to Parque Nacional Manu. None are cheap, though. Try the following:

Chaski Ventura CULTURAL TOUR
(084-23-3952; www.chaskiventura.com; Manco Cápac 517) Pioneer of alternative and community tourism, with quality itineraries and guides, also involved in community development. Offers package trips to the jungle, and overnights in Sacred Valley communities and Machu Picchu. French, English and Spanish are spoken.

Milla Turismo TOUR
(084-23-1710; www.millaturismo.com; Av Pardo 800) Reputable conventional tour operator with travel agency services and recommended private tours with knowledgeable drivers.

Festivals & Events

El Señor de los Temblores CULTURAL
(The Lord of the Earthquakes) This procession on the Monday before Easter dates to the earthquake of 1650.

Q'oyoriti CULTURAL
Less well-known than June's spectacular Inti Raymi are the more traditional Andean rites of this festival, which is held at the foot of Ausangate the Tuesday before Corpus Christi, in late May or early June.

Corpus Christi RELIGION
Held on the ninth Thursday after Easter, Corpus Christi usually occurs in early June and features fantastic religious processions and celebrations in the cathedral.

Inti Raymi CULTURAL
Cuzco's most important festival, the 'Festival of the Sun' is held on June 24. It attracts tourists from all over Peru and the world, and the whole city celebrates in the streets. The festival culminates in a re-enactment of the Inca winter-solstice festival at Sacsaywamán. Despite its commercialization, it's still worth seeing it for the street dances and parades, as well as the pageantry at Sacsaywamán.

Sleeping

Side streets northwest of the Plaza de Armas (especially Tigre, Tecsecocha and Suecia) are bursting with dime-a-dozen *hostales*. Budget guesthouses also surround the Plaza San Blas, though you'll have to huff and puff to get up there.

★Ecopackers HOSTEL **$**
(☎084-23-1800; www.ecopackersperu.com; Santa Teresa 375; dm S35-52, d/ste S120/165; @📶) Thought has been put into this big backpacker haven that's a stone's throw from Plaza Regocijo. One of the all-inclusives (with bar, pool room and sunbathing), it ups the ante by being clean, friendly and service-minded. There's lovely wicker lounges in the courtyard and the sturdy beds are extra long. There's also 24-hour security.

Kuntur Wasi Cusco GUESTHOUSE **$**
(☎084-22-7570; www.hospedajekunturwasi.com; Tandapata 352; r per person incl breakfast S50) Quiet and economical, this simple hotel features ship-shape rooms, attentive service and free buffet breakfast. Interior rooms lack natural light, but feature pleasant decor and cozy down duvets. It's a hard bargain to beat.

Pariwana HOSTEL **$**
(☎084-23-3751; www.pariwana-hostel.com; Av Mesón de la Estrella 136; dm S22-42, d/tr S150/195; @📶) Resembling spring break, this notably clean, newer hostel is among the better ones, filled with uni-types lounging on poufs and playing ping-pong in the courtyard of a huge colonial. Wi-fi connection comes in the common areas. Beds in newish dorms are well spaced and the penthouse suite is well worth the splurge. The chic bar is invite only. With an on-site travel agency.

Pantastico GUESTHOUSE **$**
(☎084-954-387; www.pan-tastico.com; Carmen Bajo 226; dm S35, s/d S75/105, s/d/tr without bathroom S50/90/120, all incl breakfast; @📶) French-run with a friendly, bohemian air, this bed-and-bakery has good water pressure but beds that are a little bit saggy. Highlights include piping-hot bread at 5am and the residual warmth coming from the big oven. Offers cooking classes and travel agency services. The one double with a view fetches S20 extra.

Hospedaje Turismo Caith GUESTHOUSE **$**
(☎084-23-3595; www.caith.org; Pasaje Sto Toribio N4, Urb Ucchullo Alto; s/d/tr incl breakfast S80/150/190; 📶) This rambling farmhouse-style hostel also runs an onsite girls foundation. Huge picture windows and various balconies and patios look toward the Plaza de Armas, a 20-minute walk or a five-minute taxi ride away. It's great for families – big rooms and cots are available, and the rambling, grassy garden is a perfect place for kids to run around.

Hostal Suecia I HOTEL **$**
(☎084-23-3282; www.hostalsuecia1.com; Suecia 332; s/d/tr incl breakfast S90/120/150; 📶) Most rooms in this pint-sized guesthouse are very basic, but location and staff are fabulous and there's a sociable, stony, indoor courtyard. The two newer doubles on the top floor (311 and 312) are good value.

★Niños Hotel HOTEL **$$**
(☎084-23-1424; www.ninoshotel.com; Meloc 442; s without bathroom S77, d with/without bathroom S170/155, tr S244; @📶) Long beloved and highly recommended, this hotel is run by a Dutch-founded nonprofit foundation that serves underprivileged children in Cuzco. It is a rambling colonial with sunny courtyard. Refurbished rooms are bordered with bright trim and feature plaid throws and portable heaters. In the coldest months there's hot water bottles to tuck in bed. A second branch is located at Fierro 476.

The public cafeteria features homemade cakes and breads as well as box lunches. Breakfast is not included.

La Encantada BOUTIQUE HOTEL **$$**
(☎084-24-2206; www.encantadaperu.com; Tandapata 354; s/d incl breakfast S278/340; @📶) Bright and cheerful, this modern boutique hotel features terraced gardens and immense views from iron-rail balconies. A circular staircase leads to small, tasteful rooms with soft linens and king-sized beds. The on-site spa helps hikers work out the aches and kinks. Be aware that check-out is at 9am.

Tika Wasi BOUTIQUE HOTEL **$$**
(☎084-23-1609; www.tikawasi.com; Tandapata 491; s/d/tr incl breakfast from S163/195/226; 📶) Behind a tall wall, this modern inn offers a personable option with bright, imaginatively themed rooms, with family photos and colonial accents. Rooms overlook small, sunny

decks to hang out on. Breakfast is buffet. Non-nationals should be sure to get the tax subtracted from the room price.

Amaru Hostal HOTEL $$
(☎084-22-5933; www.amaruhostal.com; Cuesta San Blas 541; s/d/tr incl breakfast S150/180/240; @) In a characterful old building in a prime location, Amaru is deservedly popular. Flowerpots sit outside well-kept rooms with styles that are a little dated. Some feature rocking chairs from which to admire the rooftop view. Rooms in the outer courtyard are noisy, and those at the back are newest.

Eating

Budget eateries abound on Plateros and Gringo Alley, where you can walk away for under S10. For *chicharrón* (deep-fried pork rinds), head to 'pork street,' Pampa del Castillo.

Grocery shops include **Gato's Market** (Santa Catalina Ancha 377; 9am-11pm) and the original **market** (Mantas 119; 8am-11pm), however, both are overpriced. For a more serious stock-up, head to supermarket **Mega** (cnr Matará & Ayacucho; 10am-8pm Mon-Sat, to 6pm Sun).

Aldea Yanapay CAFE $
(☎084-25-5134; Ruinas 415, 2nd fl; lunch buffet S10, mains from S22; 9am-11:30pm;) The stuffed animals, board games and decor perfectly evoke the circus you dreamed of running away with as a child. Aldea Yanapay is pitched at families but will appeal to anyone with a taste for the quixotic. Food includes burritos, falafel and tasty little fried things to pick at, and a great-value vegetarian lunch buffet.

Profits go to projects helping abandoned children. Highly recommended.

Jack's Café CAFE $
(☎084-25-4606; Choquechaca 509; mains S12-26; 7:30am-11:30pm) A line often snakes out the door at this consistently good Western-style eatery with Aussie roots. With fresh juices blended with mint or ginger, strong coffee and eggs heaped with smoked salmon or roasted tomatoes, it's easy to get out of bed. Also has nice cafe food, soups and good service.

Prasada VEGETARIAN $
(☎084-25-3644; Qanchipata 269; mains S9-12; 10am-9pm Mon-Fri, 10am-4pm Sat & Sun;) The best bang for your pesos, serving tacos, tortilla soup and lentil burgers with fresh toppings and generous servings. Pair with a jar of fresh-squeezed juice or kombucha and you're ready for the hike up to Sacsaywamán.

Cafeteria 7&7 CAFE $
(Tandapata s/n; mains S7-9; 10am-2pm & 4-10pm Mon-Sat, to 2pm Sun;) A wonderful addition to the neighborhood, this sleek 3rd-story cafe bursts with city views. Yet the off-street location means it's quiet and conducive to chilling out. With white leather booths and a nice selection of homemade German cakes, light food like quinoa salads and espresso drinks. Also serves ice-cream sundaes.

El Hada ICE CREAM $
(Qanchipata 596; ice cream from S10; 8am-7pm) Served in fresh-made cones with a hint of vanilla or lemon peel, these exotic ice creams are ecstasy. Flavors like Indonesian cinnamon, bitter chocolate or roasted apples do not disappoint. Cap it off with an *espress* – Café Bisetti, Peru's best roaster, is offered.

★ **Cicciolina** INTERNATIONAL $$
(☎084-23-9510; Triunfo 393, 2nd fl; mains S35-55; 8am-late) On the 2nd floor of a lofty colonial courtyard mansion, Cicciolina has long been among Cuzco's best restaurant. The eclectic, sophisticated food is divine, starting with house-marinated olives, continuing with crisp polenta squares with cured rabbit, huge green salads, charred octopus and satisfying mains like squid-ink pasta, beet ravioli and tender lamb. With impeccable service and warmly lit seating.

★ **La Bodega 138** PIZZA $$
(☎084-26-0272; Herrajes 138; mains S23-35; 6:30-11pm Mon-Sat) Sometimes you are homesick for good atmosphere, uncomplicated menus and craft beer. In comes La Bodega, a fantastic laid-back enterprise run by a family in what used to be their home. Thin-crust pizzas are fired up in the adobe oven, organic salads are fresh and abundant and the prices are reasonable. A true find. Cash only.

Trujillo Restaurant PERUVIAN $$
(☎084-233-465; Av Tullumayo 542, near Plaza Limacpampa; mains S17-37; 9am-8pm Mon-Sat, to 5pm Sun) Run by a northern Peruvian family, this simple, spotless dining hall by Qorikan-

cha nails northern classics such as *seco de cabrito* (goat stewed in beer and cilantro) and a variety of ceviches served with jars of *chicha morada* (a nonalcoholic purple maize drink). The *aji de gallina* (a creamy chicken stew served with rice and potatoes) is the best in all of Cuzco.

Granja Heidi CAFE $$
(☎084-23-8383; Cuesta San Blas 525, 2nd fl; mains S10-46; ⊙11:30am-9:30pm Mon-Sat) A cozy alpine cafe serving healthy fare that's consistently good, some of it provided from the small farm of the German owner. In addition to wonderful Peruvian fare (*rocoto relleno* is served vegetarian, with stuffed chili and peanuts), there are crepes and huge bowls of soups and salads. Save room for dessert.

Drinking

In popular backpacker bars, especially around the Plaza de Armas, both sexes should beware of drinks being spiked – don't let go of your glass, and think twice about using free-drink coupons. Happy hour kicks off as early as 1pm.

Memoria BAR
(☎084-24-4111; Plateros 354; ⊙8pm-late) A wonderful, elegant bar with attentive bartenders and drinks that merit seconds. Check their Facebook site for events like live jazz, acoustic and techno music.

Norton Rats PUB
(cnr Santa Catalina Angosta & Plaza de Armas, 2nd fl; ⊙7am-late) Run by a motorcycle enthusiast, this unassuming expat-style bar overlooks the Plaza de Armas. It's a boon for people-watching, if you can get a balcony seat. Though known for delicious 200g burgers, it's also got TVs, darts and billiards to help you work up a thirst. Avoid the burritos. Happy hour is 7pm to 9pm.

☆ Entertainment

Several restaurants have evening *folklórica* music and dance shows; expect to pay S50 to S60 including buffet. Most live-music venues don't charge admission.

★Ukuku's LIVE MUSIC
(☎084-24-2951; Plateros 316; ⊙8pm-late) The most consistently popular nightspot in town, Ukuku's plays a winning combination of crowd pleasers – Latin and Western rock, reggae and *reggaetón* (a blend of Puerto Rican *bomba,* dancehall and hip-hop), salsa, hip-hop etc – and often hosts live bands. Usually full to bursting after midnight with as many Peruvians as foreign tourists, it's good, sweaty, dance-a-thon fun. Happy hour is 8pm to 10:30pm.

Centro Qosqo de Arte Nativo PERFORMING ARTS
(☎084-22-7901; www.boletoturisticocusco.net/arte-nativo.html; Av El Sol 604; adult/student under 26 with ISIC card S130/70) Has live nightly performances of Andean music and dance at 6:45pm. Admission is with the *boleto turístico* tourist card only, which is valid for 10 days and covers 16 other sights and venues.

Km 0 LIVE MUSIC
(☎084-23-6009; Tandapata 100; ⊙11am-late Tue-Sat, 5pm-late Sun & Mon) This convivial bar just off Plaza San Blas has a bit of everything. It serves good Thai food in the evening, and there's live music late every night – local musicians come here to jam after their regular gigs. Happy hour is 9pm to midnight.

Shopping

Cuzco offers a cornucopia of artisan workshops and stores selling knitted woolens, woven textiles, colorful ceramics, silver jewelry and more, as well as contemporary art galleries. Book exchanges abound.

Mercado San Pedro MARKET
(Plazoleta San Pedro) Cuzco's central market is a must-see. Pig heads for *caldo* (soup), frogs (to enhance sexual performance), vats of fruit juice, roast *lechón* (suckling pig) and tamales are just a few of the foods on offer. Around the edges are typical clothes, spells, incense and other random products to keep you entertained for hours.

Center for Traditional Textiles of Cuzco HANDICRAFTS
(Av El Sol 603A; ⊙7:30am-8:30pm) This nonprofit organization, founded in 1996, promotes the survival of traditional weaving. You may be able to catch a shop-floor demonstration illustrating different weaving techniques in all their finger-twisting complexity. Products for sale are high end.

ℹ Information

DANGERS & ANNOYANCES

Train stations, festivals and markets are prime areas for pickpockets. Use only official taxis (look for the company's telephone number on the roof), lock your doors and never allow additional passengers. Late-night revelers returning from bars or trekkers setting off before sunrise are most vulnerable to 'choke and grab' muggings. Drug dealers and police are known to work together, especially on Procuradores, where locals warn you can make a drug deal and get busted, all within a couple of minutes.

Beware of altitude sickness if you're flying in from sea level – it's no joke.

EMERGENCY

Policía de Turismo (PolTur, Tourist Police; ☎084-23-5123; Plaza Túpac Amaru s/n; ⏲24hr) If you have something stolen, you'll need to see these guys to get an official police report for insurance claims.

MEDICAL SERVICES

Medical facilities are limited: go to Lima for serious procedures.

Clinica Pardo (☎084-24-0997; Av de la Cultura 710; ⏲24hr) Well equipped and expensive – perfect if you're covered by travel insurance.

Traveler's Clinic Cusco (☎084-22-1213; Puputi 148; ⏲24hr) A private clinic with swift bilingual service and on-call doctor, deals mostly with altitude-sickness patients and travelers' illnesses. It's a 10-minute walk from San Blas.

MONEY

Many banks on Av El Sol and shops around the Plaza de Armas have ATMs. The main bus terminal has a global ATM.

POST

Serpost (Av El Sol 800; ⏲8am-8pm Mon-Sat) General delivery (poste restante) mail is held here at the main post office; bring proof of identity.

TOURIST INFORMATION

Dirección Regional de Cultura Cusco (☎084-58-2030; www.drc-cusco.gob.pe; Av de La Cultura 238; ⏲7:15am-6:30pm Mon-Sat) The organizing body for tourism in Cuzco.

iPerú (☎084-25-2974; www.peru.travel; Portal de Harinas 177, Plaza de Armas; ⏲9am-7pm Mon-Fri, to 1pm Sat & Sun) Efficient and helpful. Excellent source for tourist information for both the region and entire country. There's an adjoining section of guarded ATMs. Also has a branch at the airport (☎084-23-7364; ⏲6am-5pm).

South American Explorers (SAE; ☎084-24-5484; www.saexplorers.org; Av Pardo 847; ⏲9:30am-5pm Mon-Fri, to 1pm Sat; 📶) SAE's Cuzco clubhouse has good-quality maps, books and brochures for sale, a huge stock of travel information and recommendations, wi-fi access, a book exchange and rooms for rent. Weekly events and limited volunteer information are available to nonmembers.

ℹ Getting There & Away

AIR

Most flights from Cuzco's **airport** (CUZ; ☎084-22-2611), 2km southeast of the center, are in the morning.

Avianca (☎0800-18-2222; www.avianca.com; Av El Sol 602; ⏲8:30am-7pm Mon-Fri, 9am-2pm Sat) Service to/from Lima Monday to Saturday.

LAN (☎084-25-5555; www.lan.com; Av El Sol 627B; ⏲8:30am-7pm Mon-Sat, to 1pm Sun) Direct flights to Lima, Arequipa, Juliaca and Puerto Maldonado.

Peruvian Airlines (☎084-25-4890; www.peruvianairlines.pe; Av El Sol 627-A; ⏲9am-7pm Mon-Sat, 9am-noon Sun)

Star Perú (☎01-705-9000; www.starperu.com; Av El Sol 679; ⏲9am-1pm & 3-6:30pm Mon-Sat, 9am-12:30pm Sun)

BUS

International

All international services depart from the **Terminal Terrestre** (☎084-22-4471; Vía de Evitamiento 429), about 2km out of town toward the airport. Take a taxi (S14) or walk via Av El Sol. Straight after the tower and statue of Pachacutec, turn right, following the railway lines into a side street, which reaches the terminal in five minutes.

For Bolivia, catch a **Transporte Salvador** (☎084-23-3680), **Littoral** (☎24-8989), **Real Turismo** (☎24-3540) or **San Luis** (☎22-3647) service to La Paz via Copacabana; all depart at 10pm. **Tour Peru** (☎084-23-6463; www.tourperu.com.pe) offers the best-value service to Copacabana, departing at 8am daily. **CIAL** (☎in Lima 01-330-4225) departs at 10:30pm for La Paz via Desaguadero (S80, 12 hours). This is the quickest way to La Paz.

Ormeño (☎084-24-1426) travels to most South American capitals.

Long-Distance

Buses to major cities leave from the Terminal Terrestre. Buses for more unusual destinations leave from elsewhere, so check carefully in advance.

Ormeño and **Cruz del Sur** (☎084-74-0444; www.cruzdelsur.com.pe) have the safest and most comfortable buses across the board. Of the cheaper companies, **Wari** (☎084-22-2694) and Tour Peru have good buses.

There are hourly departures to Juliaca and Puno. Cheap, slow options include **Power**

(☎22-7777) and **Libertad** (☎084-22-4571); use them to access towns along the route. Midrange-priced **Littoral** (☎23-1155) and **CIAL** (☎965-401-414) are faster and more comfortable.

The most enjoyable way to get to Puno is via **Inka Express** (☎084-24-7887; www.inkaexpress.com; Av 28 de Julio 211) or **Turismo Mer** (☎084-24-5171; www.turismomer.com; El Óvalo, Av La Paz A3), which run luxury buses every morning.

Departures to Arequipa cluster around 6am to 7am and 7pm to 9:30pm. Ormeño offers a deluxe service at 9am.

Cruz del Sur, **CIVA** (☎084-24-9961; www.civa.com.pe) and **Celtur** (☎23-6075) offer relatively painless services to Lima. Wari is the best of the cheaper options. Most buses to Lima stop in Nazca (12 hours) and Ica (14 hours). These buses go via Abancay and can suffer holdups in rainy season. Between January and April, it may be worth going via Arequipa (25 to 27 hours) instead.

If you're going to Ayacucho by bus, wear all of your warm clothes; if you have a sleeping bag, bring it onboard.

San Martín (☎984-61-2520) and **Expreso Sagitário** (☎22-9757) offer direct buses to Tacna (S70, 17 hours). Expreso Sagitário also goes to Arequipa, Lima and Puno.

Various companies depart for Puerto Maldonado between 3pm and 4:30pm; CIVA is probably the best option.

Buses to Quillabamba via Santa María (change here for Santa Teresa) leave from the Santiago terminal, a brisk 20-minute walk from the center. Departures leave at 8am, 10am, 1pm and 8pm.

Transportes Gallito de las Rocas (☎22-6895; Diagonal Angamos) buses depart to Pilcopata (S20, 10 to 12 hours) Monday, Wednesday and Friday at 5am. The office is on the first block off Av de la Cultura.

Prices following are general estimates for normal/luxury buses.

DESTINATION	COST (S)	DURATION (HR)
Arequipa	25/126	9-11
Ayacucho	65/95	14-16
Copacabana, Bolivia	60/80	10-15
Ica	100/190	14-16
Juliaca	30/40	5-6
La Paz, Bolivia	80/120	12
Lima	100/190	18-22
Nazca	100/140	13
Puerto Maldonado	50/70	10
Puno	20/70	6-7
Tacna	70/100	15

TRAIN

Cuzco has two train stations. **Estación Huanchac** (☎084-58-1414; ⏲7am-5pm Mon-Fri, to midnight Sat & Sun), near the end of Av El Sol, serves Puno. Estación Poroy, east of town, serves Ollantaytambo and Machu Picchu.

You can take a taxi to Estación Poroy (S30) or the station in Ollantaytambo (S80) from Cuzco. Return trips are slightly more expensive.

To Ollantaytambo & Machu Picchu

The only way to reach Aguas Calientes (and access Machu Picchu) is via train. It takes about three hours. Two companies currently offer the service; Inca Rail only runs from Ollantaytambo.

Fares may vary according to departure hours: more desirable times are usually more expensive. It's common for trains to sell out, especially at peak hours, so buy your ticket as far ahead as possible.

The quickest 'cheaper' way to get from Cuzco to Aguas Calientes is to take a *combi* to Ollantaytambo and catch the train from there.

Inca Rail (☎084-25-2974; www.incarail.com; Portal de Panes 105, Plaza de Armas; ⏲8am-9pm Mon-Fri, 9am-7pm Sat, to 2pm Sun) Has three departures daily from Ollantaytambo and four levels of service. Children get a significant discount. Environmentally sustainable business practice.

Peru Rail (www.perurail.com; Estación Poroy; ⏲7am-5pm Mon-Fri, to noon Sat) The flagship service to Aguas Calientes, with multiple departures daily from Estación Poroy, 20 minutes outside of Cuzco. There are three service categories: Expedition (from S223 one way), Vistadome (from S261 one way) and the luxurious Hiriam Bingham (from S1153 one way). The Hiram Bingham includes brunch, afternoon tea, entrance to Machu Picchu and a guided tour. It runs daily except Sunday.

To Puno

Peru Rail The Andean Explorer (tickets S505) is a luxury train with a glass-walled observation car. Trains depart from Estación Huanchac at 8am, arriving at Puno around 6pm, on Monday, Wednesday and Saturday from November to March, with an extra departure on Friday from April to October. Lunch is included.

ℹ Getting Around

TO/FROM THE AIRPORT

Frequent *colectivos* run along Ayacucho to just outside the airport (S0.70). An official taxi to/from the city center costs S20 to S25. Be wary of rogue taxis working outside the terminal building – robberies are not uncommon. Many guesthouses offer free airport pickups.

BUS & COLECTIVO

In 2014 the government began the process of restricting the use of old *colectivos*; some of these services continue to change as they are cut or reduced.

Minibuses to Pisac (S4, one hour) leave frequently both from the terminal at Av Tullumayo 207 and the terminal in Puputi, just north of Av de la Cultura.

Minibuses to Urubamba (S8, 1½ hours) and Ollantaytambo (S12, two hours) via Chinchero (S4, one hour) leave from near the Puente Grau. Just around the corner in Pavitos, faster *colectivos* leave when full for Urubamba (S7, one hour) and Ollantaytambo (S12, two hours) via Chinchero.

TAXI

Trips around town cost S5. Official taxis (identifiable by a lit company telephone number on the roof) are much safer than 'pirate' taxis (with only a taxi sticker in the window). A reliable company is **AloCusco** (084-22-2222).

Around Cuzco

The archaeological ruins closest to Cuzco are Saqsaywamán, Q'enqo, Pukapukara and Tambomachay – admission is with a *boleto turístico*. Take a Pisac-bound bus and get off at Tambomachay, the ruin furthest away from Cuzco (and, at 3700m, the highest). It's an 8km walk back to Cuzco. Be aware that violent attacks against tourists have occurred along this route, even during daylight hours. Go in a group, and return before nightfall.

Saqsaywamán

The name means 'satisfied falcon,' though most travelers remember it by the mnemonic 'sexy woman.' The sprawling site is 2km

Around Cuzco

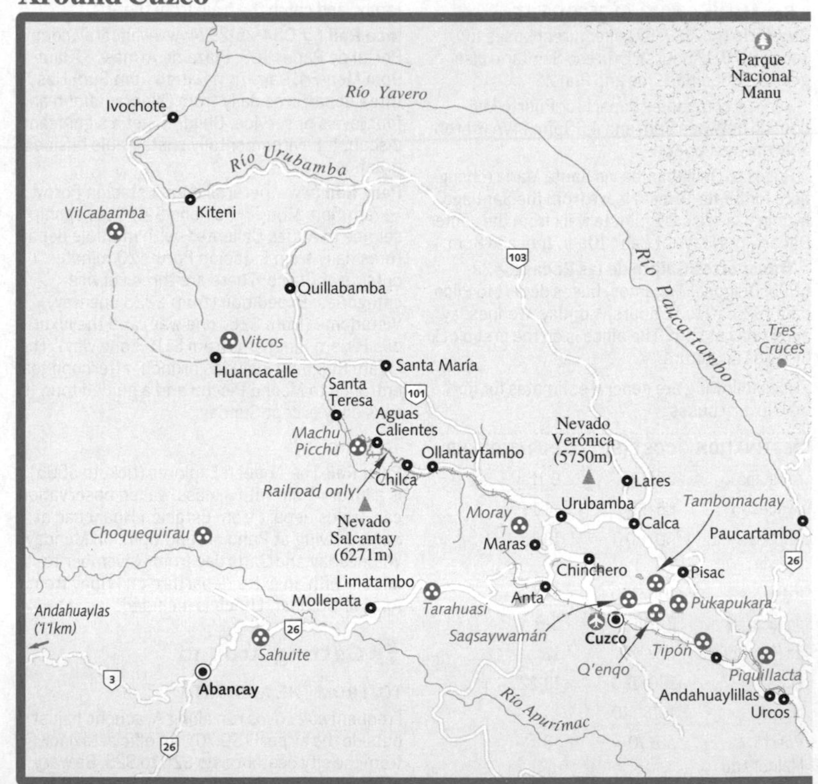

from Cuzco. Climb steep Resbalosa, turn right past the **Iglesia de San Cristóbal** and continue to a hairpin bend in the road. On the left is a stone staircase, an Inca stone road leading to the top.

Although Saqsaywamán seems huge, what today's visitor sees is only about 20% of the original structure. Soon after the Conquest, the Spaniards tore down walls and used the blocks to build their own houses in Cuzco.

In 1536 the fort saw one of the fiercest battles between the Spanish and Manco Inca, who used Saqsaywamán to lay siege to the conquistadors. Thousands of dead littered the site after the Inca defeat, which attracted swarms of Andean condors. The tragedy was memorialized by the inclusion of eight condors in Cuzco's coat of arms.

Most striking are the magnificent three-tiered fortifications. Inca Pachachutec envisioned Cuzco in the shape of a puma, with Saqsaywamán as the head, and these 22 zigzag walls form the teeth. The parade ground is used for Inti Raymi celebrations.

Admission is through the *boleto turístico.*

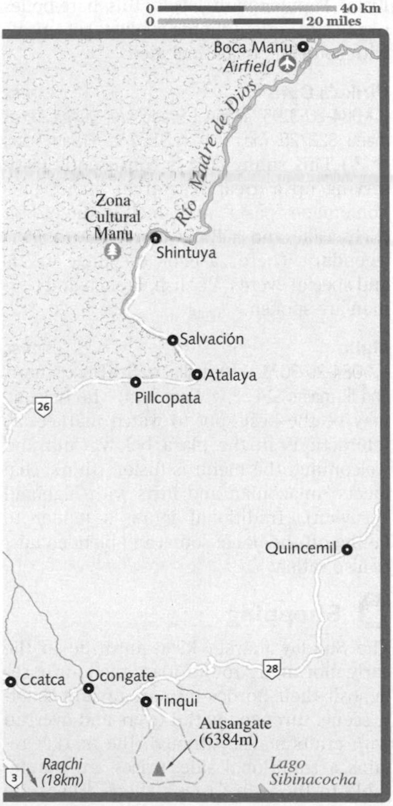

Q'enqo

The name of this fascinating small ruin means 'zigzag.' It's a large limestone rock riddled with niches, steps and extraordinary symbolic carvings, including channels that may have been used for ritual sacrifices of *chicha* (corn beer), or perhaps blood. Scrambling up to the top of the boulder you'll find a flat surface used for ceremonies and laboriously etched representations of animals. Back below, explore the mysterious subterranean cave with altars hewn into the rock.

The site is 2km from Saqsaywamán, on the left as you descend from Tambomachay.

Tambomachay & Pukapukara

About 300m from the main road, **Tambomachay** (dawn-dusk) is a beautifully wrought ceremonial bath, still channeling clear spring water that earns it the title El Baño del Inca (Inca Bath). On the opposite side of the road is the commanding ruin of **Pukapukara**. Its name means 'red fort,' though it was more likely a hunting lodge, guard post or stopping point for travelers. The upper esplanade has panoramic views.

The Sacred Valley

The Valle Sagrado (Sacred Valley) of the Río Urubamba is about 15km north of Cuzco as the condor flies. Its star attractions are the lofty Inca citadels of Pisac and Ollantaytambo, but the valley is also packed with more peaceful Inca sites, as well as frenzied markets and high-altitude Andean villages. Investigate the idyllic countryside with Peter Frost's in-depth *Exploring Cusco.*

Pisac

084 / POP 900

It's not hard to succumb to the charms of sunny Pisac (elevation 2715m), a bustling colonial village just 33km northeast of Cuzco at the base of a spectacular Inca fortress perched on a mountain spur. Its pull is universal; recent years have seen an influx of expats and new age followers in search of an Andean Shangri-La.

Sights & Activities

Pisac Ruins RUINS

(boleto turístico adult/student under 26 with ISIC card S130/70; dawn-dusk) A truly awesome site with relatively few tourists, this hilltop Inca citadel lies high above the village on a triangular plateau with a plunging gorge on either side. Allow several hours to explore. To walk from town, a steep but spectacular 4km trail starts above the west side of the church. It's a two-hour climb and 1½ hour return. Worthwhile but grueling, it's good training for the Inca Trail! Taking a taxi up and walking back is a good option.

Sleeping

Hotel Pisac Quishu GUESTHOUSE $

(084-43-6921; www.pisacinca.com; Vigil 242; s/d S50/100, without bathroom S40/70, all incl breakfast;) A small, cheerful family-run lodging run by friendly host Tatiana. There's a handful of colorful rooms around a tiny courtyard. Offers kitchen use. A larger, recently built sister guesthouse is a 10-minute walk away.

Hospedaje Beho GUESTHOUSE $

(084-20-3001, 984-848-538; hospedajebehopisac@gmail.com; Intihuatana 113; s/d S40/80, without bathroom S30/70;) On the path to the ruins, this family-run lodging beyond a handicrafts shop offers no-frills lodging with warm showers. The raggedy, rambling garden is a tranquil haven from the madness of the market streets just outside. Also offers airport transfers and car rentals.

Kinsa Ccocha Inn HOTEL $

(084-20-3101; kinsaccocha_inn@hotmail.com; Arequipa 307A; s/d S60/80, tr/q without bathroom S75/100;) With a fertile fig tree in its stony patio, this simple lodging has a nice vibe and thoughtful touches, such as plenty of power plugs, good towels and strong, hot showers. Breakfast is not offered, but there's an adjoining cafe.

★ **Pisac Inn** INN $$

(084-20-3062; www.pisacinn.com; Plaza de Armas; s/d/tr incl breakfast S185/230/295;) Location, location, location! This lovely plaza hotel features an inviting courtyard and romantic rooms with down bedding, dark blue walls and Andean decor. Rooms with king-sized beds are a slight upgrade. Unlike others, it's open year-round, with good off-season discounts. The location means some rooms get noisy early when merchants are setting up outside. German, English and French are spoken.

La Casa del Conde GUESTHOUSE $$

(084-78-7818; www.cuzcovalle.com; s/d/ste incl breakfast S185/247/309;) Guests rave about this lovely country house, nestled into the foothills with blooming flower patches. Family-run and brimming with personality, its lovely rooms feature down duvets, heat and cable TV. There's no car access. It's a 10-minute walk uphill from the plaza, but a *mototaxi* (three-wheeled motorcycle rickshaw taxi) can leave you at the chapel that's five minutes away.

Eating

Massive clay-oven bakeries on Mariscal Castilla vend piping-hot flatbreads and empanadas.

Restaurante Yoly PERUVIAN $

(084-20-3114; Amazonas s/n; menú S5; 6am-10pm) Popular with locals, this bare-bones restaurant offers home-cooked set meals with soup and drink included.

Ulrike's Café CAFE $$

(084-20-3195; Manuel Prado s/s; veggie/meat menú S22/25, mains from S15-33; 9am-9pm;) This sunny cafe is consistently tasty, serving up a great vegetarian *menú*, plus homemade pasta and melt-in-the-mouth cheesecake and a fluffy carrot cake that is legendary. There's a book exchange, DVDs and special events. English, French and German are spoken.

Mullu FUSION $$

(084-20-3073; www.mullu.pe; San Francisco s/n, 2nd fl; mains S14-32; 9am-9pm) The balcony may be the best spot to watch market-day interactions in the plaza below. Chill and welcoming, the menu is fusion (think Thai meets Amazonian and flirts with highland Peruvian). Traditional lamb is tender to falling-off-the-bone; soups and blended juices also satisfy.

Shopping

The Sunday market kicks into life in the early morning. Around 10am the tour buses deposit their hordes into an already chaotic scene, thronged with buyers and overrun with crafts stalls. Although the market retains a traditional side, prices are comparable to those in Cuzco's shops. There are smaller markets on Tuesday and Thursday and an excellent daily artisan market in the plaza.

Getting There & Away

Buses to Urubamba (S3, one hour) and Cuzco (S5, one hour) leave from near the bridge at Plazoleta Leguiz and Av Amazonas.

Urubamba

084 / POP 17,500

There is precious little to see in Urubamba (elevation 2870m), at the junction of the valley thoroughfare with the road back to Cuzco via Chinchero, but for those traipsing through the Sacred Valley, it's a necessary transit hub. There's a global ATM at the *grifo* (gas station) on the main road, about 1km east of the bus terminal.

Sights & Activities

Many outdoor activities that are organized from Cuzco take place at Urubamba, including horse riding, mountain biking, paragliding and hot-air balloon trips. Trips often take in the nearby amphitheater-like terraces of **Moray** (admission via boleto parcial S70; dawn to dusk) and **Salinas** (admission S5), where thousands of salt pans have been harvested since Inca times.

Sleeping & Eating

Los Jardines HOTEL $

(084-20-1331; www.losjardines.weebly.com; Jr Convención 459; s/d/tr S60/80/90) Noted for its accommodating service, this reader-recommended family hotel occupies a walled compound with a large adobe home and flowering gardens that make it feel like the city isn't even there. Rooms are basic but clean, some feature large picture windows. The buffet breakfast served in the garden is extra (S12). It's within walking distance of the plaza.

Hostal los Perales GUESTHOUSE $

(084-20-1151; http://ecolodgeurubamba.com; Pasaje Arenales 102; r per person S35) Tucked down a hidden country lane, this welcoming family-run guesthouse offers good-value, basic rooms around lovely overgrown gardens. Its elderly owners are sweet, serving banana pancakes and tomato jam from their own tree for breakfast. It's easy to get lost, so take a *mototaxi* ((three-wheeled motorcycle rickshaw taxi; S1) from the terminal.

★ **Huacatay** PERUVIAN $$

(084-20-1790; Arica 620; mains S32-50; 1-9:30pm Mon-Sat) In a little house tucked down a narrow side street, Huacatay makes a lovely night out. Though not every dish is a hit, the tender alpaca steak, served in a port reduction sauce with creamy quinoa risotto and topped with a spiral potato chip, is the very stuff memories are made of. Staff aim to please and there's warm ambience.

Getting There & Away

Buses going to Cuzco (S4, two hours) via Pisac (S4, one hour) or Chinchero (S3, 50 minutes) and *colectivos* to Ollantaytambo (S2.50, 25 minutes) all leave frequently from the bus terminal.

Ollantaytambo

084 / POP 700

Tiny Ollantaytambo (elevation 2800m) is the best surviving example of Inca city planning and the most atmospheric of Sacred Valley destinations – its massive fortress stands sentinel over the cobblestoned village like a guardian against the heavens. Apart from the advent of the internet, nothing much has changed here in 700 years.

Sights

Ollantaytambo Ruins RUINS

(7am-5pm) Both fortress and temple, these spectacular Inca ruins rise above Ollantaytambo, making a splendid half-day trip. (Admission is via the *boleto turístico* tourist card, valid for 10 days and for 16 other sites across the region.)

Sleeping

Casa de Wow HOSTEL $

(084-20-4010; www.casadewow.com; Patacalle s/n; dm S62, s S124, d with/without bathroom S155/185; @) A cozy little home away from home run by Wow, a local artist. Bunks are snug and couples have a shot at the fantastic handmade Inca royalty bed (though unlike the original, these raw beams are held together with rope, not llama innards). Sign the world's biggest guestbook before leaving.

Chaska Wasi HOSTEL $

(084-20-4045; www.hostalchaskawasi.com; Plaza de Armas s/n; dm/d incl breakfast S20/60; @) Backpackers enjoy the company of the lovely, helpful Katy and her tribe of cats. Cheerful but quite basic rooms with electric showers are good value.

Hospedaje las Portadas GUESTHOUSE $
(084-20-4008; las.portadas@yahoo.com; Principal s/n; dm S15, s/d S30/50, without bathroom S20/35) Although all of the tourist and local buses pass by outside, this friendly, family-run place still manages to achieve tranquility. It has a flowery courtyard, a grassy lawn and a rooftop terrace made for star-gazing. Rooms are dated, with tired pillows, but it's still a steal.

★ Apu Lodge INN $$
(084-79-7162; www.apulodge.com; Lari s/n; s/d/q incl breakfast S170/190/280; @ wi-fi) Backed against the ruins, this modern lodge with a sprawling lawn is a real retreat, thanks to the welcoming staff and the helpful attention of its Scottish owner. Ample, cozy rooms feature powerful hot showers that melt your muscle aches. Wi-fi is available in the common area. Breakfast includes yogurt, cereal, fresh fruit and eggs.

Eating & Drinking

Hearts Café CAFE $$
(084-20-4078; cnr Ventiderio & Av Ferrocarril; mains S10-28; 7am-9pm;) Serving healthy and hearty food, beer and wine and fabulous coffee, Hearts is a longtime local presence, with some organic produce and box lunches for excursions. Breakfasts like *huevos rancheros* (fried eggs with beans served on a tortilla) target the gringo palate perfectly, and the corner spot with outdoor tables was made for people-watching.

Ganso BAR
(984-30-8499; Waqta s/n; 2pm-late) Treehouse meets circus meets *Batman!* The hallucinatory decor in tiny, friendly Ganso is enough to drive anyone to drink. A firemen's pole and swing seats are the icing on the cake.

Getting There & Away

Frequent *colectivos* for Urubamba's bus terminal (S2.60, 25 minutes) depart just southeast of the plaza next to the market from 6am to 5pm. *Colectivos* (S15, 1½ hours) and taxis (S110) for Cuzco mill about the train station only when trains arrive. Alternatively, head to Urubamba and transfer there.

Trains to Aguas Calientes are much cheaper from here than from Cuzco.

Aguas Calientes

084 / POP 1000

Also known as Machu Picchu Pueblo, this town lies in a deep gorge below the ruins. A virtual island, it's cut off from all roads and enclosed by stone cliffs, towering cloud forest and two rushing rivers. Despite its gorgeous location, Aguas Calientes has always been a bit of a no-man's land, with a large itinerant population, slack services that count on one-time customers and an architectural tradition of rebar and unfinished cement. With merchants pushing the hard sell, it's hard not to feel overwhelmed. Your best bet is to go without expectations.

Yet spending the night offers one distinct advantage: early access to Machu Picchu, which turns out to be a pretty good reason to stay.

Sights & Activities

Museo de Sitio Manuel Chávez Ballón MUSEUM
(admission S22; 9am-5pm) This museum has superb information in Spanish and English on the archaeological excavations of Machu Picchu and Inca building methods. Stop here before or after the ruins to get a sense of context (and to enjoy the air-conditioning and soothing music if you're walking back from the ruins after hours in the sun).

Las Termas HOT SPRINGS
(admission S10; 5am-8:30pm) Weary trekkers soak away their aches and pains in the town's hot springs, 10 minutes' walk up Pachacutec from the train tracks. These tiny, natural thermal springs, from which Aguas Calientes derives its name, are nice enough but far from the best in the area, and get scummy by late morning.

Sleeping

Everything is grossly overpriced, but the off season offers discounts. Early checkout times are the norm.

Hospedaje los Caminantes GUESTHOUSE $
(084 21 1007; los caminantes@hotmail.com; Av Imperio de los Incas 140; per person with/without bathroom S35/20; wi-fi) Great value, this big, multistory guesthouse has dated but clean rooms with laminate floors. Features include reliable hot water and a few balconies. The train whistle at 7am is an unmistakable wake-up call. Breakfast isn't included. but is

available (S8 to S10) at the strangely upscale in-house cafe.

Supertramp Hostel HOSTEL $
(☎084-43-5830; www.supertramp.com; Chaskatika s/n; dm S30-34, d with shared bathroom S90, all incl breakfast; 📶) Cloaked in psychedelic murals, this recommended but sometimes cramped hostel has good, helpful staff and a small adjoining cafe that whips up salads and gourmet burgers. Early starters can get egg breakfasts with coffee, toast and jam at 4:30am. Train station pickup available.

Municipal Campground CAMPGROUND $
(sites per tent S15) This small, charming campground has toilets, showers and kitchen facilities for rent. It's a 20-minute walk downhill from the center of town on the road to Machu Picchu, before the bridge.

Hostal Muyurina HOTEL $$
(☎084-21-1339; www.hostalmuyurina.com; Lloque Yupanqui s/n; s/d/tr incl breakfast S120/150/270; 📶) Sparkling new and keen to please, Mayurina is a friendly option. Rooms have phones and TV.

Eating & Drinking

Tourist restaurants (all practically identical) cluster alongside the railway tracks and Pachacutec toward the hot springs. You'll find backpacker bars with extra-long happy hours up Pachacutec, but you don't need to hear it from us – every one of them will try to lure you in.

La Boulangerie de Paris BAKERY $
(☎084-79-7798; Jr Sinchi Roca s/n; snacks S3-10; ⏰5am-9pm; 📶) We don't know how these Frenchmen got here, we're just thankful. This small cafe sells *pain au chocolat*, fresh croissants, espresso drinks and desserts, with a few gluten-free items. You can also order boxed lunches.

★ Indio Feliz FRENCH $$
(☎084-21-1090; Lloque Yupanqui 4; mains S34-48; ⏰11am-10pm) Hospitality is the strong suit of French cook Patrik at this multi-award-winning restaurant, but the food

Aguas Calientes

Sleeping
1 Hospedaje los Caminantes A1
2 Hostal Muyurina C1
3 Supertramp Hostel D3

Eating
4 Indio Feliz C1
5 La Boulangerie de Paris C2

Aguas Calientes

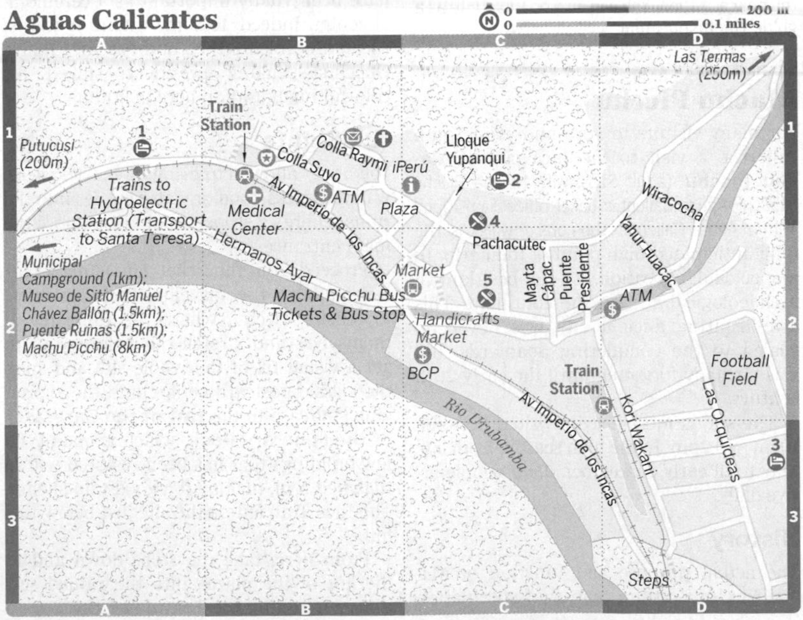

0 — 200 m
0 — 0.1 miles
Las Termas (250m)
Putucusi (200m)
Train Station
Colla Raymi
Colla Suyo
iPerú
Lloque Yupanqui
Trains to Hydroelectric Station (Transport to Santa Teresa)
Medical Center
ATM
Av Imperio de los Incas
Plaza
Wiracocha
Yahur Huacac
Municipal Campground (1km); Museo de Sitio Manuel Chávez Ballón (1.5km); Puente Ruinas (1.5km); Machu Picchu (8km)
Hermanos Ayar
Pachacutec
Market
Mayta Cápac
Puente
Presidente
ATM
Machu Picchu Bus Tickets & Bus Stop
Handicrafts Market
BCP
Train Station
Football Field
Río Urubamba
Av Imperio de los Incas
Kori Wakani
Las Orquideas
Steps

PERU AGUAS CALIENTES

does not disappoint. Start with *sopa criolla* (a potent and flavorful broth, served with hot bread, homemade butter and optional chilis). There are also nods to traditional French cooking – like Provençal tomatoes, crispy-perfect garlic potatoes and a melt-in-your-mouth apple tart.

Information

There's a helpful branch of **iPerú** (☎084-21-1104; cuadra 1, Pachacutec; ⏰9am-1pm & 2-6pm Mon-Sat, to 1pm Sun) near the Machu Picchu ticket office. If the ATM at **BCP** (Av Imperio de los Incas s/n) runs out of money, there are four others, including one on Av Imperio de los Incas. Currency and traveler's checks can be exchanged in various places at highly unfavorable rates. Pay phones and cybercafes are scattered around the town, and there's a small **post office** (Colla Raymi s/n). There's a **medical center** (☎084-21-1005; Av Imperio de los Incas s/n; ⏰emergencies 24hr) by the train tracks.

Getting There & Around

Aguas Calientes is the final train stop for Machu Picchu.

To Santa Teresa (45 minutes), Peru Rail travels at 8:53am, 2:55pm and 9:50pm daily. Tickets (S88) can only be bought from Aguas Calientes train station on the day of departure, but trains actually leave from the west end of town, outside the police station. You can also do this route as a guided multisport tour.

Machu Picchu

For many visitors to Peru and even South America, a visit to the Inca city of **Machu Picchu** (adult S128, with Huiana Picchu S152; ⏰Aguas Calientes ticket office 5am-10pm; 🚂from Aguas Calientes, then bus or walk) is the long-anticipated high point of their trip. In a spectacular location, it's the best-known archaeological site on the continent. This awe-inspiring ancient city was never revealed to the conquering Spaniards and was virtually forgotten until the early 20th century.

The site is most heavily visited between 10am and 2pm. In the high season, from late May until early September, 2500 people arrive daily.

History

The actual purpose and function of Machu Picchu is still a matter of speculation and educated guesswork. The citadel was never mentioned in the chronicles kept by the colonizing Spaniards, which served as a written archive of thitherto unrecorded Inca history.

Apart from the indigenous Quechuas, nobody knew of Machu Picchu's existence until American historian Hiram Bingham came upon the thickly overgrown ruins in 1911 while being guided by a local boy. Bingham's search was actually for the lost city of Vilcabamba, the last stronghold of the Incas, and he thought he had found it at Machu Picchu. His book *Inca Land: Explorations in the Highlands of Peru* was first published in 1922. It's downloadable for free from Project Gutenberg (www.gutenberg.org).

Despite more recent studies of the 'lost' city of the Incas, knowledge of Machu Picchu remains sketchy. Some believe the citadel was founded in the waning years of the last Incas as an attempt to preserve Inca culture or rekindle Inca predominance, while others think it may have already become a forgotten city at the time of the Conquest. Another theory suggests that the site was a royal retreat abandoned upon the Spanish invasion.

Whatever the case, the exceptionally high quality of the stonework and ornamentation tell that Machu Picchu must once have been vitally important as a ceremonial center. Indeed, to some extent, it still is: Alejandro Toledo, the country's first native Quechua-speaking president, staged his colorful inauguration here in 2001.

Sights

You aren't allowed to bring large backpacks, walking sticks, food or water bottles into the ruins. There's a storage room just before the main entrance.

Proceed from the ticket gate along a narrow path to the mazelike main entrance to Machu Picchu, where the ruins reveal themselves and stretch out before you. To get a visual fix of the whole site and snap the classic postcard shot, climb the zigzagging staircase to the **Hut of the Caretaker of the Funerary Rock**, which is one of the few buildings that has been restored with a thatched roof, making it a good rain shelter. The Inca Trail enters the site just below this hut.

From here, take the steps down and to the left of the plazas into the ruined sections containing the **Temple of the Sun**, a

Machu Picchu

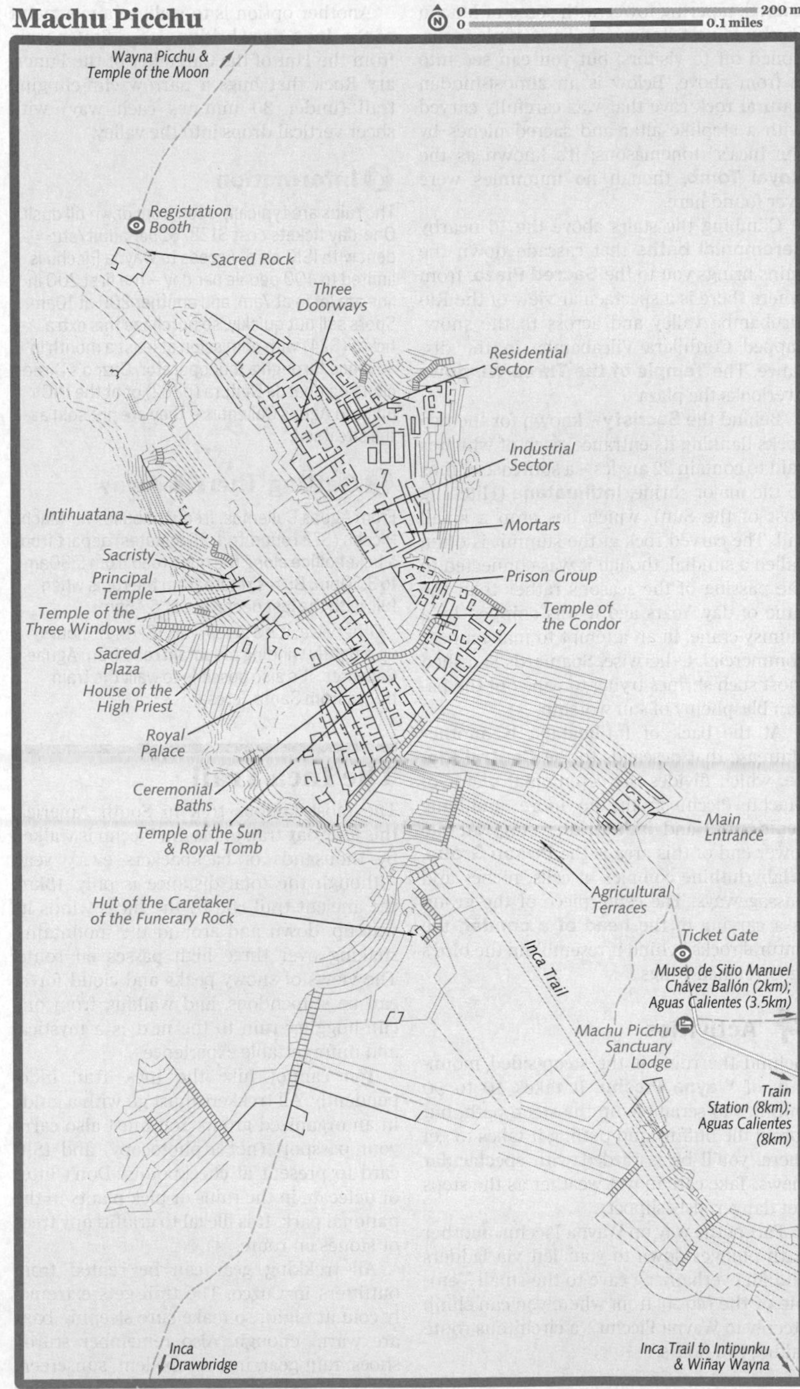

curved, tapering tower with some of Machu Picchu's finest stonework. The temple is cordoned off to visitors, but you can see into it from above. Below is an almost-hidden natural rock cave that was carefully carved with a steplike altar and sacred niches by the Inca's stonemasons; it's known as the **Royal Tomb**, though no mummies were ever found here.

Climbing the stairs above the 16 nearby **ceremonial baths** that cascade down the ruins brings you to the **Sacred Plaza**, from where there is a spectacular view of the Río Urubamba valley and across to the snow-capped Cordillera Vilcabamba in the distance. The **Temple of the Three Windows** overlooks the plaza.

Behind the **Sacristy** – known for the two rocks flanking its entrance, each of which is said to contain 32 angles – a staircase climbs to the major shrine, **Intihuatana** (Hitching Post of the Sun), which lies atop a small hill. The carved rock at the summit is often called a sundial, though it was connected to the passing of the seasons rather than the time of day. Years ago it was chipped by a clumsy crane, in an attempt to make a beer commercial. Otherwise, Spaniards smashed most such shrines trying to wipe out the pagan blasphemy of sun worship.

At the back of Intihuatana is another staircase that descends to the **Central Plaza**, which divides the ceremonial sector of Machu Picchu from the more mundane **residential** and **industrial** sectors. At the lower end of this area is the **Prison Group**, a labyrinthine complex of cells, niches and passageways. The centerpiece of the group is a carving of the **head of a condor**, the natural rocks behind it resembling the bird's outstretched wings.

Activities

Behind the ruins is the steep-sided mountain of **Wayna Picchu**. It takes 40 to 90 minutes to scramble up the steep path, but for all the huffing and puffing it takes to get there, you'll be rewarded with spectacular views. Take care in wet weather as the steps get dangerously slippery.

Part of the way up Wayna Picchu, another path plunges down to your left via ladders and an overhanging cave to the small **Temple of the Moon**, from where you can climb steeply to Wayna Picchu – a circuitous route taking two hours.

Another option is to walk to a viewpoint of the **Inca drawbridge**. It's a flatter walk from the Hut of the Caretaker of the Funerary Rock that hugs a narrow cliff-clinging trail (under 30 minutes each way) with sheer vertical drops into the valley.

Information

The ruins are typically open from dawn till dusk. One-day tickets cost S128/61 per adult/student with ISIC card. Access to Wayna Picchu is limited to 400 people per day – the first 200 in line are let in at 7am, and another 200 at 10am. Spots sell out quickly, so purchase this extra ticket (S24) with admission at least a month in advance through a tour operator, Cuzco's Dirección Regional de Cultura (p852) or at the INC office in Aguas Calientes – they are not sold at the site itself.

Getting There & Away

From Aguas Calientes, frequent buses for Machu Picchu (S72 round-trip, 25 minutes) depart from a ticket office along the main road from 5:30am to 3:30pm. Buses return from the ruins when full, with the last departure at 5:45pm.

Otherwise, it's a steep walk (8km, 1½ hours) up a tightly winding mountain road from Aguas Calientes. It's also possible to walk the train tracks from Santa Teresa.

The Inca Trail

The most famous trek in South America, this four-day trail to Machu Picchu is walked by thousands of backpackers every year. Although the total distance is only 43km, the ancient trail laid by the Incas winds its way up, down and around the mountains, snaking over three high passes en route. The views of snowy peaks and cloud forest can be stupendous, and walking from one cliff-hugging ruin to the next is a mystical and unforgettable experience.

You cannot hike the Inca Trail independently. All trekkers must go with a guide in an organized group. You must also carry your passport (not a photocopy) and ISIC card to present at checkpoints. Don't litter or defecate in the ruins or pick plants in the national park. It is illegal to graffiti any trees or stones en route.

All trekking gear can be rented from outfitters in Cuzco. The trail gets extremely cold at night, so make sure sleeping bags are warm enough. Also remember sturdy shoes, rain gear, insect repellent, sunscreen, a flashlight (with fresh batteries), water-purification tablets, high-calorie snacks and a basic first-aid kit. Take a stash of small Peruvian currency for buying bottled water and snacks along the way, as well as for tipping the guide, cook and porters (around S100 in total, or S130 in total if you also hire a personal porter). You will not regret picking up a walking stick from vendors in Ollantaytambo on the first morning, either.

Tours

Guided tours depart year-round, except during February when the trail is closed for maintenance. However, in the wettest months (December to March), trails can be slippery, campsites muddy and views obscured behind a thick bank of clouds. The dry season from June to August is the most popular and crowded time to go. To skip the crowds, consider going before or after the rainy season: from April to May (best vegetation, orchids and birdlife) or September to November.

Tour prices range from S1650 to S2020 and above, plus tips for guides, porters and cooks. Only 500 people each day (including guides and porters) are allowed to start the trail. Permits are issued to operators on a first-come, first-served basis.

Take some time to research your options – you won't regret it. It's best to screen agencies for a good fit before committing. Also make sure you have international travel insurance that covers adventure activities.

If price is your bottom line, keep in mind that cheapest agencies may cut corners by paying their guides and porters lower wages. Other issues are substandard gear (ie leaky tents) and dull or lackadaisical guiding. Yet paying more may not mean getting more, especially since international operators take their cut and hire local Peruvian agencies. Talk with a few agencies to get a sense of their quality of service. You might ask if the guide speaks English (fluently or just a little), request a list of what is included,

THE INCA TRAIL: THE GOOD, THE BAD & THE UGLY

The Inca Trail is a rite of passage for many (some say too many), but what's it really like? Here's the lowdown:

The Good

Besides the spectacular scenery – jaw-dropping mountain vistas, Inca ruins bathed in eerie morning mists, moss-draped cloud forests and lush lower jungle – there are some unexpected treats along the way. The food is shockingly good considering the circumstances – there are trout, lamb, beef, pork and plenty of veggie options, to name just a few of the borderline gourmet meals served en route. Kudos to the chefs. The camping equipment is in good condition and not of the cheap variety. There is even 'tent service' on some days, where the guides deliver your morning pick-me-up of choice (coca tea, coffee) along with your wake-up call. And let us not forget the porters, who are clearly not of this earth! Hiring one will incalculably enhance your enjoyment of this adventure; not hiring one could easily ruin it.

The Bad

Regardless of season, you are almost guaranteed cold weather at night, bone-chillingly so on some nights, even in summer. With bathrooms almost always a considerable hike away, this makes for some excruciating nights battling the dilemma: to go or not to go? Despite the very nice tents and sleeping bags, the mats are a little skimpy, and you won't forget that you're sleeping on the ground. Although there are well-built bathroom facilities along the way, showers are not part of the equation before the third day. Bring deodorant.

The Ugly

It's difficult to find fault with this trek in all aspects except one: the bathrooms. Though much nicer than expected from a facility standpoint, their daily maintenance is atrocious. The experience hovers somewhere between European rock festival, day two, and Bangkok nightclub, 5am. A bucket of cleaner and a hose could go a long way here.

and inquire about group size and the kind of transport used. Ensure that your tour includes a tent, food, a cook, one-day admission to the ruins and the return train fare.

It is important to book your trip at least six months in advance for dates between May and August. Outside these months, you may get a permit with a few weeks' notice, but it's very hard to predict.

The Hike

This is not an easy trek. Altitude and seemingly endless climbs, especially on day two, combine to make for a very challenging walk in the mountains. Though altitude sickness does not discriminate between the fit and the unfit, the long, steep climbs, generally thin air and knee-seizing steps along the way do pose a challenge for those in less than stellar physical condition. By all means go, but don't expect a breezy Sunday stroll.

Most agencies run minibuses to the start of the trail past the village of Chilca at Piscakucho (Km 82). After you cross the Río Urubamba (and take care of trail fees and registration formalities), you'll follow the gently sloping trail alongside the river to the first archaeological site of **Llactapata** before heading south down a side valley of the Río Cusichaca. The trail south leads 7km to the hamlet of **Wayllabamba** (3100m), where you can take a breather to appreciate the views of snowy Nevado Verónica (5750m).

You'll cross the Río Llullucha, then climb steeply up along the river. This area is known as **Tres Piedras** (Three Stones), and from here it is a long, very steep 3km climb. The trail eventually emerges on the high, bare mountainside of **Llulluchupampa**, where the flats are dotted with campsites.

From Llulluchupampa, a good path up the left-hand side of the valley climbs for

Inca Trail

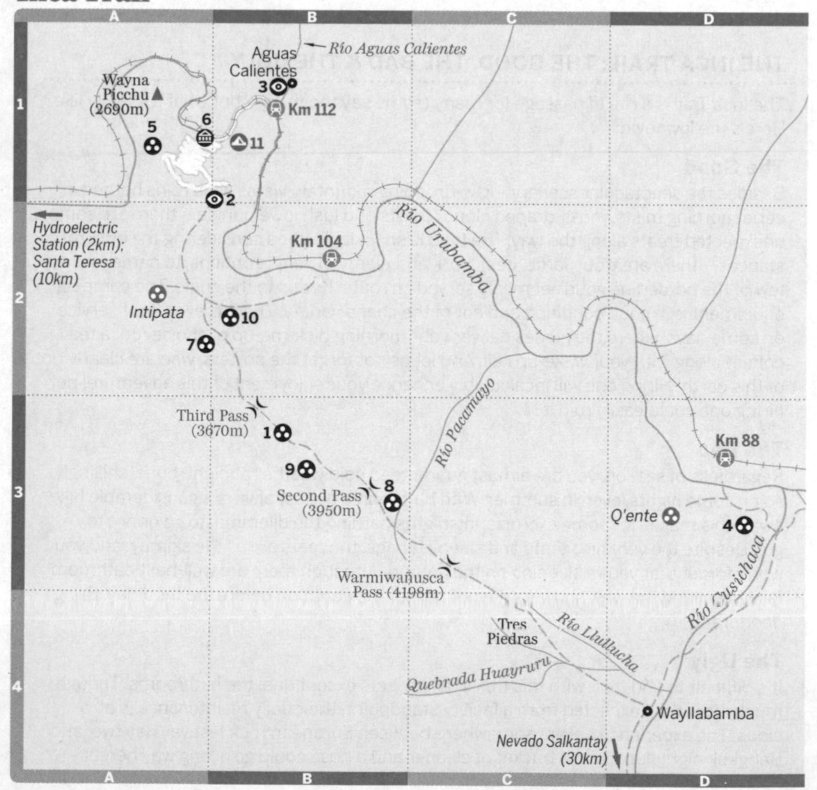

the two-hour ascent to **Warmiwañusca** (4198m), colorfully known as 'Dead Woman's Pass.' This is the highest and most difficult point of the trek, which leaves many a trekker gasping. From Warmiwañusca, the trail continues down a long and knee-jarringly steep descent to the river, where there are large camp sites at **Paq'amayo** (3500m). The trail crosses the river over a small footbridge and climbs right toward **Runkurakay** (Egg-Shaped Building), a round ruin with superb views about an hour's walk above the river.

Above Runkurakay, the trail climbs to a false summit before continuing past two small lakes to the top of the second pass at 3950m, which has views of the snowcapped Cordillera Vilcabamba. The trail descends to the ruin of **Sayaqmarka** (Dominant Town), a tightly constructed complex perched on a small mountain spur with incredible views, then continues downward, crossing a tributary of the Río Aobamba.

The trail leads on across an Inca causeway and up again through cloud forest and an **Inca tunnel** carved into the rock to the third pass at 3670m. Soon afterward, you'll reach the beautiful, well-restored ruin of **Phuyupatamarka** (City Above the Clouds; 3600m above sea level). The site contains a beautiful series of ceremonial baths with water running through them.

From Phuyupatamarka, the trail takes a dizzying dive into the cloud forest below, following an incredibly well-engineered flight of many hundreds of Inca steps, affectionately known as the Gringo Killer. After passing through a tunnel, the trail eventually zigzags its way down to **Wiñay Wayna** (Huiñay Huayna).

From the **Wiñay Wayna guard post**, the trail contours around through cliff-hanging cloud forest for about 1½ hours to reach **Intipunku** (Sun Gate; checkpoint closes around 3pm) – where you may get lucky enough to catch your first glimpse of majestic Machu Picchu as you wait for the sun to rise over the mountaintops.

The final triumphant descent takes 30 minutes. Backpacks are not allowed into the ruins, and guards will pounce upon you to check your pack and to stamp your trail permit. Trekkers generally arrive before the morning trainloads of tourists, so you can enjoy the exhilarated exhaustion of reaching your goal without having to push through as many crushing crowds.

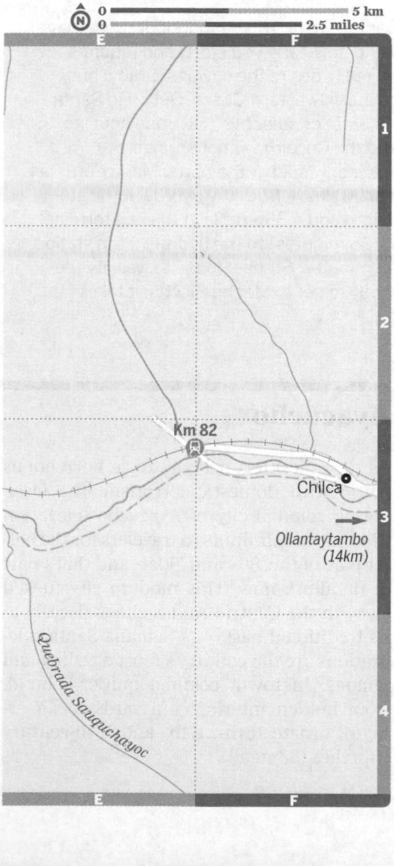

0 5 km
0 2.5 miles
E F
1
2
Km 82
Chilca
3
Ollantaytambo (14km)
Quebrada Sauquchayoc
4
E F

Inca Trail

Sights

1 Inca Tunnel ... B3
2 Intipunku ... B1
3 Las Termas ... B1
4 Llactapata ... D3
5 Machu Picchu ... A1
6 Museo de Sitio Manuel Chávez Ballón ... A1
7 Phuyupatamarka ... A2
8 Runkurakay ... B3
9 Sayaqmarka ... B3
10 Wiñay Wayna ... B2

Sleeping

11 Municipal Campground ... B1

ALTERNATIVE ROUTES TO MACHU PICCHU

Gaining in popularity, these alternative routes to reach Machu Picchu also cover Inca ground. Tours are usually cheaper than the standard Inca Trail, and can be booked much closer to your departure date.

Trekking

Valle Lares Trek Spend three days or more walking between rural Andean villages in the Sacred Valley, past hot springs, archaeological sites, lush lagoons and gorges. Trekkers finish by taking the train to Aguas Calientes from Ollantaytambo. This is more of a cultural trek, not a technical one, though the highest mountain pass (4450m) is nothing to sneeze at. The average price is S1580.

Salkantay Trek This demanding four- to seven-day trek offers two possible routes, both around 55km. The Mollepata–Huayllabamba route, with views of snowbound Salkantay, tops out at 4880m and can link up with the Inca Trail (but you'll need a permit), while the Mollepata–Santa Teresa route heads through La Playa and dumps you in Aguas Calientes. The average price is S1010.

Inca Jungle Trail With hiking, biking and rafting options, this guided multisport route stages to Machu Picchu via Santa Teresa. Booked with Cuzco outfitters, a three-day, two-night trip costs around S975, and usually includes a guided tour of Machu Picchu and a return train ticket to Ollantaytambo.

Bus/Train from Santa Teresa

Lots of people are going to Machu Picchu via Santa Teresa. This roundabout route may take two days (depending on ticket availability and how early you start) and requires some harrowing driving, so think carefully if you really desire the savings. Grab a bus headed for Quillabamba from the Santiago terminal in western Cuzco. Get off in Santa María (S25 to S35, 4½ hours) and catch a local *combi* or *colectivo* (S10, one hour) to Santa Teresa, where there are basic lodgings and the Cocalmayo hot springs.

For Machu Picchu, train tickets on this route are only sold at the Santa María Peru Rail ticket office. Daily trains (one way/return US$18/30) leave from the hydroelectric station, about 8km from Santa Teresa, at 7:54am, 3pm and 4:35pm. Be at the bus terminal an hour prior to your train to catch a *combi* (S3, 25 minutes) to the hydroelectric station. The 13km train ride to Aguas Calientes takes 45 minutes. Some choose to walk by the railway tracks instead, an outstandingly cheap way to get to Machu Picchu; it takes around four very dusty and sweaty hours.

CENTRAL HIGHLANDS

Far off the gringo trail, the central Peruvian Andes are ripe for exploration. Traditions linger longer here, with delightful colonial towns among the least spoiled in the entire Andean chain. A combination of geographical isolation, harsh mountain terrain and terrorist unrest (Maoist group the Sendero Luminoso was born in Ayacucho) made travel difficult for decades. Over the past decade a more stable political situation and improved transportation infrastructure have made travelers' lives easier. But visiting the region is still challenging enough, with ear-popping passes and wearisome bus journeys.

Ayacucho

☎066 / POP 181,000

As the epicenter of Peru's once horrendous battle with domestic terrorism, the fascinating colonial city of Ayacucho (elevation 2750m) was off-limits to travelers for the better part of the '80s and '90s – and that's part of its allure now. This modern city tucked away in the Central Andes clings fiercely to its traditional past – its Semana Santa celebrations are the country's most dazzling and famous. In town, colonial quirks abound, from hidden interior courtyards to an array of ornate 16th-, 17th- and 18th-century churches (33 in all).

Sights

The town center has a 17th-century **cathedral**, along with a dozen other elaborate **churches** from the past 300 years, and several old **mansions** near the main plaza.

★Cathedral
CHURCH

(Portal Municipal) This spectacular 17th-century cathedral on the Plaza de Armas has a religious-art museum. The moody facade doesn't quite prepare you for the intricacy of the interior, with its elaborate gold-leaf altar being one of the best examples of the Baroque-Churrigueresque style (in which cornices and other intricate, Spanish-influenced workmanship mingled with Andean influences, often evinced by the wildlife depicted).

★Museo de Arte Popular
MUSEUM

(Portal Independencia 72; ⌚8am-1pm & 2-4:30pm Mon-Fri) FREE The popular art here covers the *ayacucheño* (natives of Ayacucho) spectrum – silverwork, rug- and tapestry-weaving, stone and woodcarvings, ceramics (model churches are especially popular) and the famous *retablos* (ornamental religious dioramas). These are colorful wooden boxes varying in size and containing intricate papier-mâché models: Peruvian rural scenes or the nativity are favourites, but interesting ones with political or social commentary can be seen here. Photographs show how Ayacucho changed during the 20th century. Opening hours here change frequently.

★Museo de la Memoria
MUSEUM

(Prolongación Libertad 1229; admission S2; ⌚9am-1pm & 3-5pm) In an unlikely location 1.5km northwest of the center is Ayacucho's most haunting museum, remembering the impact the Sendero Luminoso (Shining Path) had on Peru in the city that was most deeply affected by the conflict. Its simple displays (in Spanish) are nonetheless moving: there are eyewitness accounts of the horrors that went on and a particularly poignant montage of photos of mothers who had children killed in the fighting.

Wari Ruins
RUINS

(Huari; admission S3; ⌚8am-5:30pm) Sprawling for several kilometers along a cactus-forested roadside are the extensive ruins of Wari, the capital of the Wari empire, which predated the Incas by five centuries.

Festivals & Events

Semana Santa
RELIGION

Held the week before Easter, this is Peru's finest religious festival and attracts visitors from all over the country. Rooms in most hotels fill well in advances so book well ahead. The tourist office has lists of local families who provide accommodations for the overflow.

Sleeping

Prices skyrocket during Semana Santa.

Hostal Tres Máscaras
GUESTHOUSE $

(☎066-31-2921; hoteltresmascaras@yahoo.com; Tres Máscaras 194; s/d without bathroom S30/50, with bathroom S53/70) The pleasing walled garden and friendly staff make this an enjoyable place to stay, and garden-facing rooms are of a generous size. Hot water is on in the morning and later on request. A room with TV is S5 extra. Continental and American breakfast is available for S7 and S8 respectively.

Via Via
HOTEL $

(☎066-31-7040; Bolognesi 720; s/d S95/125; P) This lovely, unsignposted colonial building is about 700m from the center, with recently changed ownership to the city center's famous Via Via company. While it is in a quiet location, the walk back at night involves passing through some dark neighborhoods. The rooms have beautiful furniture, and there is a grassy garden.

Hostal Florida
GUESTHOUSE $

(☎066-31-2565; Cuzco 310; s/d S35/50) This traveler-friendly *hostal* (guesthouse) has a relaxing courtyard garden and clean rooms (those on the upper level are better) with bathrooms and TV, hot water in the morning and later on request. There is a basic cafeteria too.

Hotel La Crillonesa
HOTEL $

(☎066-31-2350; www.hotelcrillonesa.com; Nazareno 165; s/d from S40/60) A popular and helpful hotel, it offers a rooftop terrace with photogenic views, a TV room, tour information and 24-hour hot water. Its rather small, clean rooms have comfy beds and generally functioning cable TV. The best rooms are right at the top.

★Via Via
HOTEL $$

(☎066-31-2834; www.viaviacafe.com/en/ayacucho; Portal Constitucion 4; s/d S115/150; 📶) One of the more imaginative sleeping options in central Ayacucho is Via Via, with an enviable plaza location and cool, vibrantly decorated rooms themed around different continents. Travelers will feel like they've landed in a veritable oasis, all centered on a plant-filled courtyard. English and Dutch are spoken, and their popular restaurant hang-out is alongside.

Hotel Sevilla HOTEL **$$**

(☎066-31-4388; www.hotelsevillaperu.com; Libertad 635; s incl breakfast S75, d incl breakfast 100-120; 📶) The Sevilla is one of the nicest, brightest, best-value hotels in Ayacucho, and more backpacker-friendly than most. Ample, cozy rooms get desks, minibars and microwaves. Accommodations are set back across a courtyard from the street. There is a downstairs restaurant, and breakfast is enjoyed from the top-floor cafe commanding great views across the city.

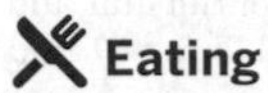

Eating

Regional specialties include *puca picante*, a curry-like potato stew in peppery peanut sauce, served with rice and a side of *chicharrones* (fried pork cutlets). The colonial courtyard inside **Centro Turístico Cultural San Cristóbal** (Jirón 28 de Julio 178) is full of travel-friendly bars and cafes. Further down, Plaza Moré offers eateries that are positively gourmet.

Café Miel CAFE **$**

(Portal Constitución 4; snacks from S2; ⏲10am-10pm) Breakfast is the best time to visit this reader-recommended place with its chirpy atmosphere strangely reminiscent of an English tearoom – we're talking great fruit salads and some of Ayacucho's best (freshly brewed) coffee. It serves hearty lunches and phenomenal chocolate cake too.

El Niño PARRILLA **$**

(9 de Diciembre 205; mains around S15; ⏲11am-2pm & 5-11pm) In a colonial mansion with a sheltered patio containing tables overlooking a garden, El Niño specializes in grills yet dishes up a variety of Peruvian food. The individual *parrillada* (grilled-meat platter) is good, although in practice sufficient for two modest eaters. This is one of the city's better restaurants.

La Casona PERUVIAN **$**

(Bellido 463; mains S12-35; ⏲7am-10:30pm) This popular, ambient courtyard restaurant has been recommended by several travelers for its big portions. It focuses on Peruvian food such as the excellent *lomo saltado* (strips of beef stir-fried with onions, tomatoes, potatoes and chili) and often has regional specialties.

Guilles SANDWICHES **$**

(Bellido, btwn Garcilaso de la Vega & 9 de Diciembre; sandwich & juice S10-15; ⏲8am-1pm & 4-9pm) Show up here for the best sandwiches and smoothies in Ayacucho – if not in the entire central highlands.

★Via Via INTERNATIONAL **$$**

(☎066-31-2834; Portal Constitucion 4; mains S17-28; ⏲10am-10pm Mon-Thu, to midnight Fri & Sat; 📶✍) 🌿 With its upstairs plaza-facing balcony, Via Via has the best views with which to accompany your meal in Ayacucho. It's ethically sourced, organic food – but this is Peruvian-European fusion cuisine, so you'll find something to sate you – like *quinnoto* (a risotto with quinoa) or *salteado de alpaca* (strips of alpaca meat stir-fried with onions, tomatoes, potatoes and chili), and crisp South American wine to wash it down.

Drinking & Nightlife

Taberna Magía Negra BAR

(Jirón 9 de Diciembre 293; ⏲4pm-midnight Mon-Sat) It's been around longer than most and the youth of today prefer the newer venues but this bar-gallery has local art, beer, pizza and great music.

Rock CLUB

(Cáceres 1035; ⏲10pm-2am Wed-Sat) The liveliest local disco, known locally as Maxxo, where gringos, as well as locals, go to strut their stuff. There is another disco on the same block playing mostly salsa.

Shopping

Ayacucho is famous for folk crafts. The **craft market** (Independencia & Quinua) is a good place to start.

Information

BBVA Banco Continental (Portal Unión 20) Visa ATM.

Clínica de la Esperanza (☎066-31-2180; www.hospitalregionalayacucho.gob.pe; Independencia 355; ⏲8am-8pm) English is spoken.

iPerú (☎066-31-8305; cnr Cusco & Asamblea; ⏲9am-6pm Mon-Sat, to 1pm Sun) One of Peru's best tourist offices. Helpful advice; English spoken.

Policía de Turismo (☎066-31-7846; 2 de Mayo 100) Handles emergencies.

Serpost (Asamblea 293) It's 150m from the Plaza de Armas.

Wari Tours (☎066-31-1415; Lima 138) Runs experience-rich multilingual tours to regional destinations. Half-day tours cost around S50.

Getting There & Away

The airport is 4km from the town center (taxis cost S10). Daily flights to Lima are with **LC Peru** (☎066-31-2151; Jirón 9 de Diciembre 139) at 6:45am.

Most buses (to long-distance north- and south-bound destinations) arrive and depart from the the grandiosely named **Terrapuerto Libertadores de America** (Terminal Terrestre; end of Perez de Cuellar) bus terminal to the north of the city center. For Lima (S40 to S90, nine hours), there are **Empresa Molina** (☎066-31-9989; 9 de Diciembre 473) and **Cruz del Sur** (☎066-31-2813; www.cruzdelsur.com.pe; Cáceres, btwn Libertad & Calle de la Vega) buses, the latter with its own terminal.

Heading north to Huancayo (S30 to 40, seven hours), there is now a paved road, although there are still vertiginous drops with precious little protection. Change in Huancayo for onward services to Huánuco, Tingo María, Pucallpa and Satipo.

Heading southeast, the road to Andahuaylas (S30, six hours) and on to Cuzco (S50 to 60, 14 to 15 hours) is fully paved, but few companies thus far have the licenses to run the route, meaning limited choices. Both of these trips boast fantastic scenery, and are worth doing in daylight.

NORTH COAST

The unruly northern coast is a haven of sun and surf, but in its distant past it was a thriving center of pre-Inca peoples, going back to the continent's oldest civilization. Come north to explore its animated colonial towns, laze away days at seaside resorts and watch world-class surfers take on the gnarled breaks. If you're heading to Ecuador, the further north you go, the better the weather gets.

Trujillo

☎044 / POP 709,500

Francisco Pizarro's Trujillo marks a notable change from other northern Peruvian cities. Here colonization *has* left an indelible mark, from the immense and beautiful Plaza de Armas to the little architectural hallmarks that pepper many of the city's colorful colonial constructions. Founded by Pizarro in 1534 and named after his hometown in Spain, Trujillo quickly grew into northern Peru's biggest city, though it had been ground zero for several civilizations prior to the Spanish. Nearby, 1500-year-old Moche pyramids, Las Huacas del Sol y de la Luna, and the ancient Chimú adobe metropolis of Chan Chan loom over the desertscape as testament to once great empires turned to sand and mud.

If you want to take in the ancient culture but not the bustling city, base yourself in the nearby surfing hamlet of Huanchaco, once a tranquil fishing village, now a full-on sea-and-sun affair.

Sights

An 18th-century **cathedral** with a famous basilica fronts the Plaza de Armas.

Many other elegant colonial churches and mansions have wrought-iron grillwork and pastel coloring that typify Trujillo. **Casa de la Emancipación** (Pizarro 610), **Palacio Iturregui** (Pizarro 688; ⊙9am-5pm daily) and **Casa Ganoza Chopitea** (Independencia 630), with its art gallery and two lions standing guard out front, all deserve a look.

Museo Cassinelli MUSEUM
(N de Piérola 607; admission S7; ⊙9am-1pm & 3-6pm Mon-Sat) This private archaeological collection housed in the basement of a Repsol gas station (the one on the west side of the intersection, not the east side) is fascinating, with some 2000 ceramic pieces on display (curated from a collection owned by Italian immigrants) that certainly don't belong under a gritty gas dispensary.

Museo de Arqueología MUSEUM
(Junín 682; admission S5; ⊙9am-5pm Mon-Sat, to 1pm Sun) This well-curated museum features a rundown of Peruvian history from 12,000 BC to the present day, with an emphasis on Moche, Chimu and Inca civilizations as well as the lesser-known Cupisnique and Salinar cultures. But it's also worth popping in for the house itself, a restored 17th-century mansion known as La Casa Risco, which features striking cedar pillars and gorgeous painted courtyard walls.

Tours

Chan Chan Tours CULTURAL TOUR
(☎044-24-3016; chanchantourstrujillo@hotmail.com; Independencia 431; ⊙8am-1pm & 3-8pm)

Trujillo

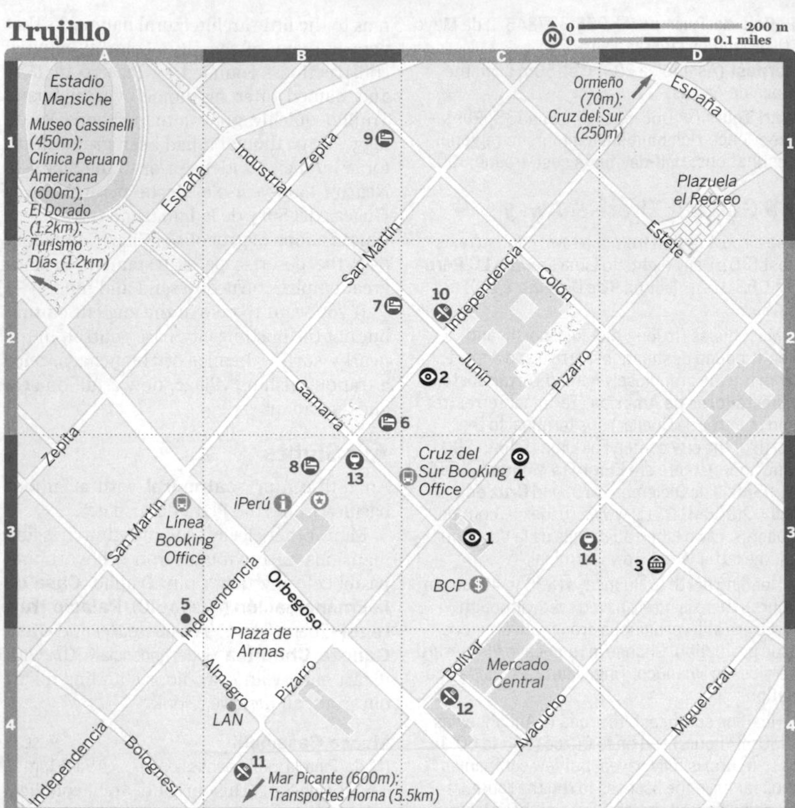

Right on Plaza de Armas, this established agency organizes trips to Chan Chan and Moche Huacas Sol y de la Luna, as well as trips further afield. The guides speak some English.

Festivals & Events

The *marinera* dance and *caballos de paso* (horseback dressage displays) are highlights of many festivals.

La Fiesta de la Marinera DANCE

This is the national *marinera* contest; held in the last week in January.

Sleeping

Many travelers prefer the beach vibe in nearby Huanchaco.

Hostal Colonial HISTORIC HOTEL $

(044-25-8261; www.hostalcolonial.com.pe; Independencia 618; dm/s/d/tr S35/90/110/140;) This tastefully renovated, rose-colored colonial mansion has a great location just a block from the Plaza de Armas. It's a top contender in both the midrange and budget categories. It's an HI affiliate, with two- to five-bedroom dorms, and plenty of private rooms spread out over three levels.

Munay Wasi Hostel GUESTHOUSE $

(044-23-1462; munaywasi@hotmail.com; Colón 250; dm S35, s/d/tr without bathroom incl breakfast S50/70/90; @) A pleasant, family-run budget option that woos travelers with a nice courtyard, eight rooms with hot water (as well as a small communal lounge, a guest kitchen and a wholly different atmosphere than most spots in Trujillo). The shared bathrooms have been newly remodeled.

House-Lodge el Conde de Arce GUESTHOUSE $

(044-29-5117; nathalyarrascue@hotmail.com; Independencia 577; dm S20, s/d S45/60;) With a giant, cluttered patio, this is a simple, safe

Trujillo

Sights

Activities, Courses & Tours

Sleeping

Eating

Drinking & Nightlife

budget lodging right in the center of town. It's one hot, disorganized mess, but the rooms are spacious and empty out onto a bright cement courtyard. It's all overseen by young, friendly and English-speaking Nathaly, the daughter of the longtime owner.

Hostal el Ensueño GUESTHOUSE **$**
(☎99-441-1131; www.elensuenohostal.com; Junín 336; s S50/60; 📶) This hot-as-Hades guesthouse has its own personal Jesus poster at the entrance. The rooms are as clean as St Peter's Pearly Gates, with tiled floors and dated furniture. Make sure to get a room with a fan.

Eating

Jugería San Augustín JUICE, SNACKS **$**
(Bolívar 526; juice S2-5, sandwiches S6-8; ⊙8:30am-1pm & 4-8pm Mon-Sat, 9am-1pm Sun) You can spot this place by the near-constant lines snaking around the corner in summer as locals queue for the drool-inducing juices. But don't leave it at that. The chicken and *lechón* (suckling pig) sandwiches, slathered with all the fixings, are what you'll be telling friends back home about on a postcard.

Café Bar Museo CAFE **$**
(cnr Junín & Independencia; mains S6-15, cocktails S18-22; ⊙closed Sun) This locals' favorite shouldn't be a secret. The tall, wood-paneled walls covered in artsy posters and the classic marble-top bar feels like a cross between an English pub and a Left Bank cafe.

Chifa Heng Lung CHINESE **$**
(☎044-24-3351; Pizarro 352; mains S10.50-42.50, menús S7-9.50; ⊙to 11:30pm) Owned by a Chinese family of veteran chefs, this vaguely upscale, tasty option packs a wallop of flavorful infusion for Peruvinized palettes. The menu is a predictable list of Cantonese dishes, but very long on options and flavors.

Mar Picante PERUVIAN **$$**
(www.marpicante.com; Húsares de Junín 412; mains S18-30; ⊙10am-5pm) If you come to Trujillo without sampling this bamboo-lined seafood palace's *ceviche mixto* ordered with a side of something spicy, you haven't lived life on the edge. You'll get raw fish, crab, scallops and onions, marinated as usual in lime juice, piled on top of *yuca* and sweet potato with a side of toasted corn *(canchas)* and corn on the cob.

Drinking

★**El Celler de Cler** PERUVIAN
(cnr Gamarra & Independencia; mains S24-48; ⊙6pm-1am) This atmospheric spot is the only place in Trujillo to enjoy dinner (coupled with an amazing cocktail) on a 2nd-floor balcony; the wrap-around number dates to the early 1800s. The food is upscale, featuring pasta and grills, and delicious. Antiques fuel the decor, from a '50s-era American cash register to an extraordinary Industrial Revolution pulley lamp from the UK.

Picasso Lounge BAR
(Bolivar 762) This shotgun-style cafe and bar approaches Trujillo's trendiness tipping point and is a great place to check out some contemporary local art. Exhibitions change every two months. When the bartender is on (Thursday to Saturday from 8pm), there's a well-rounded cocktail list with some creative *pisco* concoctions.

Information

BCP (Gamarra 562) Bank with ATM.

Clínica Peruano Americana (☎044-24-2400; Mansiche 802) The best general medical care in town, with English-speaking doctors. It charges according to your means, so let the clinic know if you don't have medical insurance.

iPerú (044-29-4561; www.peru.travel; Independencia 467, oficina 106; 9am-6pm Mon-Sat, to 2pm Sun) Provides tourist information and a list of certified guides and travel agencies.

Policía de Turismo (044-29-1770; Independencia 572) Shockingly helpful. Tourist police wear white shirts around town and some deputies speak English, Italian and/or French.

Getting There & Away

AIR

The airport is 10km northwest of town. Take a taxi (S15 to S18) or a bus bound for Huanchaco and walk 1km. **LAN** (044-22-1469; www.lan.com; Pizarro 340) has three daily flights to/from Lima. **Avianca** (0-800-1-8222; www.avianca.com; Real Plaza, César Vallejo Oeste 1345) flies the same route twice per day for as low as S150.

BUS

Buses are often full, so purchase seats in advance and double-check where your bus leaves from.

DESTINATION	COST (S)	DURATION (HR)
Cajamarca	16-135	6-7
Chachapoyas	65-85	15
Guayaquil (Ecuador)	138-201	18
Huaraz	45-65	5-9
Lima	30-110	8-9
Máncora	30-70	8-9
Piura	25-45	6
Tarapoto	95-115	18
Tumbes	39-100	9-12

Cruz del Sur (0-801-11111; www.cruzdelsur.com.pe; Amazonas 437) One of the biggest and priciest bus companies in Peru. It goes to Lima five times a day and Guayaquil at 11:45pm on Sunday, Wednesday and Friday. They also have a booking office (Gamarra 439; 9am-9pm Mon-Sat) in the centre.

El Dorado (044-29-1778; Nicolás de Piérola 1070) Has rudimentary buses to Piura five times daily (12:30pm, 8pm, 8:30pm, 10:20pm, 11pm) and four to Máncora and Tumbes (12:30pm, 8pm, 8:30pm, 9pm).

Línea (044-29-7000; www.linea.pe) The company's booking office (044-24-5181; cnr San Martín & Obregoso; 8am-9pm Mon-Sat) is conveniently located in the historical center, although all buses leave from the terminal (044-29-9666; Panamerica Sur 2855), a S5 taxi ride away.

Móvil Tours (01-716-8000; www.moviltours.com.pe; Panamerica Sur 3955) Specializes in very comfortable long-haul tourist services. It has a 10pm service to Lima; 10am, 9:40pm and 10:20pm departures to Huaraz, the former two continuing on to Caraz; a bus at 4:45pm to Chachapoyas; and a 3pm bus to Tarapoto. A taxi to the station is S5 or catch a red-signed A *combi* (California/Esperanza) on Av España and hop off at Ovalo Larco.

Ormeño (044-25-9782; Ejército 233) Has two night buses to Lima leaving at 7pm and 10pm, as well as one night bus (9pm) to Máncora and Tumbes, continuing on to Guayaquil, on the Ecuadorean coast. Additionally, they have a Monday and Friday departure (10pm) to Quito, continuing on to Bogotá in Colombia.

Getting Around

White-yellow-and-orange B *combis* to La Huaca Esmeralda, Chan Chan and Huanchaco run along España past the corners of Ejército and Industrial every few minutes. Buses for La Esperanza go northwest along the Panamericana to La Huaca Arco Iris. Fares run S1.50 to S2.

A taxi to the airport from the city center costs S15.

Around Trujillo

The Moche and the Chimú are the two cultures that have left the greatest mark on the Trujillo area, but they are by no means the only ones – more new sites are being excavated each year.

A combined ticket (adult/student S11/6), valid for two days, has to be purchased for Chan Chan and its museum; this ticket also allows entry to Huaca Esmeralda and Huaca Arco Iris, two smaller temples in the area. All sites are open 9am to 4pm daily.

Chan Chan

Built around AD 1300, Chan Chan is the largest pre-Columbian city in the Americas, and the largest adobe city in the world. As you approach along the Panamericana, it's impossible not to be impressed by the vast area of crumbling mud walls stretching away into the distance.

At the height of the Chimú empire, Chan Chan housed an estimated 60,000 inhabitants in thousands of structures, from royal palaces lined with precious metals to huge burial mounds. Although the Incas conquered the Chimú around 1460, the city was not looted until the gold-hungry Spanish arrived, and *guaqueros* (robbers of pre-Columbian tombs) finished their work.

The Chimú capital contained nine subcities, or royal compounds. The restored **Tschudi complex** is near the entrance area by the **site museum** on the main road about 500m before the Chan Chan turnoff. Tschudi's walls once stood over 10m high with impressive friezes of fish, waves and sea life. A king was once buried in the mausoleum with a treasure trove of ceremonial objects for the afterlife – and plenty of sacrificial companions.

Combis to Chan Chan (S1.50) leave Trujillo every few minutes, passing the corners of España and Ejército, and España and Industrial. A taxi from Trujillo costs S10.

Las Huacas del Sol y de la Luna

These **Moche temples** (www.huacasdemoche.pe; site admission S10, museum S5; ⊙9am-4pm), 10km southeast of Trujillo, are 700 years older than Chan Chan, and are attributed to the Moche period.

The **Huaca del Sol** is Peru's largest pre-Columbian structure; 140 million adobe bricks were used to build it. Originally the pyramid had several levels, connected by steep stairs, huge ramps and walls sloping at 77 degrees to the horizon. Now it resembles a giant sand pile, but its sheer size makes it an awesome sight nonetheless.

The smaller **Huaca de la Luna** is riddled with rooms containing ceramics, precious metals and the beautiful polychrome friezes for which the Moche were famous. Their custom of 'burying' old temples under new ones has facilitated preservation, and archaeologists are still peeling away the layers. The **Museo Huacas de Moche** here is a long-time-coming permanent home for numerous objects excavated from Huacas del Sol y de la Luna.

WARNING!

It is dangerous to walk along Buenos Aires beach between Chan Chan and Huanchaco. Travelers have also been attacked while visiting archaeological sites. Go in a group, stay on the main paths and don't visit late in the day.

Keep an eye out for Peruvian hairless dogs that hang out here. The body temperature of these dogs is higher than that of normal dogs, and they've traditionally been used as body-warmers for people with arthritis!

Combis for the Huacas del Sol y de la Luna pass Ovalo Grau in Trujillo every 15 minutes or so. It's also possible to take a taxi (S15).

Huanchaco

☎044 / POP 41,800

Once upon a time, the quaint fishing village of Huanchaco, 12km northwest of Trujillo, must have been quite a scene, what with all those high-ended, cigar-shaped *totora* boats called *caballitos* (little horses) on which fishermen paddled beyond the breakers and all. Today a few remain on what is a distinctly average beach, but surfers and other bohemians have taken over Huanchaco and turned it into a less nocturnally oriented Máncora.

For those seeking more sun and sand between their archaeological visits in the Trujillo area, Huanchaco offers a laid-back vibe that's only disrupted by armies of bleached-blond surfers (December to April) and packs of wild Peruvian holidaymakers (weekends).

Activities

You can rent surfing gear (S30 per day for a wetsuit and surfboard) or take lessons (about S50 for a 90- to 120-minute session) from several places along the main drag.

Muchik Surf School SURFING
(☎044-63-3487; www.escueladetablamuchik.com; Av Victor Larco 650) Huanchaco's longest-running surf school is said to be the most reliable.

Sleeping

You'll find budget lodgings all over town. If there's a particular restaurant or hangout whose vibe you're digging, chances are it has rooms, too.

★**Naylamp** GUESTHOUSE $
(☎044-46-1022; www.hostalnaylamp.com; Larco 1420; camping S15-18, dm/s/d S20/40/60; @📶) At the northern end of Huanchaco, and top of the pops in the budget stakes, Naylamp has one building on the waterfront and a second, larger building behind the hotel. Great budget rooms share a spacious

sea-view patio, and the lush camping area has perfect sunset views. Kitchen, laundry service, hammocking zone and a cafe are all thrown in.

Hospedaje Oceano GUESTHOUSE $
(044-46-1653; www.hospedajeoceano1.com; Los Cerezes 105; r per person S15;) Ideally located between one of the town's most lush and pleasant *plazoletas* and the ocean, this superbly welcoming family-run spot will have you feeling like kin within minutes of arrival. From the outside, it's indistinguishable from any number of dismissible Peruvian guesthouses, but the great Mediterranean-inspired rooms offer a pleasant surprise upon popping your bags down.

La Casa Suiza HOSTEL $
(044-63-9713; www.lacasasuiza.com; Los Pinos 308; dm/s/d S25/35/85;) The Swiss House's spacious and sparkling rooms have Peru-themed, airbrushed murals. The little cafe downstairs prepares crunchy-crust pizzas, and the patio upstairs hosts a nice view and the occasional barbecue. It's less of a surfer hangout than the other budget spots in town, but retains a cool vibe nevertheless.

Surf Hostal Meri HOSTEL $
(044-53-8675; www.surfhostelmeri.com; La Rivera 720; dm/s/d S20/30/50;) Full of tattered antique furniture, this rustic place across the street from the beach is vaguely hippie-esque with a good communal hostel surf-til-you-turn-gray vibe. This doubles as a surf school, and there are ample public hang spaces, including a couple of great hammocks and sun-drenched sea-view decks. The restaurant serves a broad mix of international favorites.

Eating

Huanchaco has oodles of seafood restaurants on the beach – the food is generally good, however, the weak-stomached should be wary of anything not well cooked.

Otra Cosa VEGETARIAN $
(Larco 921; dishes S6-13; from 8am;) This Dutch-Peruvian beachside pad is Huanchaco's requisite travelers' hub, serving up yummy vegetarian victuals like falafel, crepes, Spanish tortillas, Dutch apple pie and tasty curry-laced burritos (one of which is *almost* a breakfast burrito). Coffee is organic as well. The restaurant has a great record for giving back to the community.

Restaurante Mococho PERUVIAN, SEAFOOD $$
(www.facebook.com/RestauranteMococho; Bolognesi 535; menú S45; 1-3pm, closed Mon) This tiny place sits secluded in a walled garden where the legend of chef Don Victor is carried on by his widow and son, Wen. It's not cheap, but it's fresh and excellent, despite the Halls served as an after-meal mint.

El Caribe PERUVIAN $$
(Athualpa 150; mains S20-25; 10am-5pm) This is a local favorite for the reasonably priced seafood and *comida criolla* (local cuisine). *Ceviche* here is half the price of the expensive options and double the price of the cheapies, but do you really want to eat raw fish for under S10? Their grouper (*mero*) *ceviche* was featured in *Saveur* magazine.

Getting There & Away

Combis will take you from España (near Industrial) in Trujillo to Huanchaco's beachfront (S1.50). A taxi costs S12.

Chiclayo

074 / POP 553,200

Lively Chiclayo saw its share of Spanish missionaries in the 16th century, though never its share of *conquistadors*, but what it lacks in colonial beauty it more than makes up for in thrilling archaeological sites. The Moche, the Sícan and the Chimú all thrived in the area, making this well-rounded city an excellent base for exploring their ancient pyramids, tombs and artifacts.

Tours

Moche Tours SIGHTSEEING TOURS
(074-23-2184; www.mochetourschiclayo.com.pe; Calle 7 de Enero 638; 8am-8pm Mon-Sat, to noon Sun) Highly recommended for cheap daily tours with Spanish- or English-speaking guides.

Sleeping

Hostal Sicán HOTEL $
(074-20-8741; hsican@hotmail.com; Izaga 356; s/d/tr incl breakfast S40/55/75;) This appealing pick has lots of polished wood and wrought iron creating an illusion of grandeur. The rooms are small, comfortable and cool. All feature wood paneling, as well as tasteful bits of art and a TV. A great choice, it sits on one of Chiclayo's most charming brick-lined streets.

Hospedaje San Lucas GUESTHOUSE $
(☎074-20-6888; www.chiclayohostel.com; Aguirre 412; s/d S20/35; @📶) Elementary but trim and tidy, this shoestringer steps up successfully to its 'Welcome Backpackers' motto. There's a nice city view from the top floor, electric hot showers and some locally made laurel wood furniture to give it some flair.

Hotel Paraíso HOTEL $$
(☎074-22-8161; www.hotelesparaiso.com.pe; Ruiz 1064; s/d incl breakfast S100/110, air-con S30 extra; ❄@📶) Brighter and cheerier than its immediate neighbors, the value equation falls in Hotel Paraíso's favor, boasting all the mod cons of far fancier hotels for a fraction of the price. Spotless cell-like rooms boast decent furniture, hot showers and cable TV. The staff could take some lessons from Ms Manners.

Eating & Drinking

El Pescador SEAFOOD, PERUVIAN $
(San José 1236; mains S10-20; ⏲11am-6pm) This little local's secret packs in the droves for outstanding seafood and regional dishes at laughable prices. The *ceviches* here are every bit as good as places charging double or even triple the price; and weekend specials like *cabrito con frijoles* (goat with beans; Saturday) and *arroz con pato* (duck with rice; Sunday) are steals.

Mi Tia BURGERS $
(Aguirre 662; burgers S1-6) Lines run very deep at this no-frills Peruvian haunt, whose burger stand draws legions of *céntimo* pushers for burgers (loaded with fries) that are practically free if you take them away (S1 to S4). Inside, they're pricier (S2 to S6), along with a long list of country staples served by smiling staff.

Restaurant Romana PERUVIAN $$
(Balta 512; mains S13-25; ⏲7am-1am; 📶) This popular place serves a bunch of different dishes, all of them local favorites. If you're feeling brave, try the *chirimpico* for breakfast: it's stewed goat tripe and organs and is guaranteed to either cure a hangover or give you one.

Tribal Lounge BAR
(Lapoint 682; cocktails S12-22; ⏲closed Mon) An actual living, breathing bar in Chiclayo, this rock-themed spot is run by a local who returned from San Francisco after a decade. Good cocktails as well as live music (acoustic on Thursday, rock on Friday and Saturday from midnight). A great spot for a tipple.

Information

Internet cafes abound. Several banks are on the 600 block of Balta.

BCP (Balta 630) Has a 24-hour Visa and MasterCard ATM.

Clínica del Pacífico (☎074-22-8585; www.clinicadelpacifico.com.pe; Ortiz 420) The best medical assistance in town.

iPerú (Saenz Peña 838; ⏲7am-4:30pm Mon-Fri) The best spot for tourist info in town; with other spots at the Municipalidad de Chiclayo building at 823 Calle San José, and at the Museo de Tumbas Reales in Lambayeque. If they're closed, hit up the tour agencies.

Policía de Turismo (☎074-49-0892; Saenz Peña 830) Useful for reporting problems.

Getting There & Around

AIR

The airport is 2km southeast of town (taxi S5). **LAN** (☎074-27-4875; www.lan.com; Izaga 770) and (the more economical) **Avianca** (☎0-800-1-8222; www.avianca.com; Cáceres 222, C.C. Real Plaza) offer twice-daily flights to Lima. Prices for the latter can be as low as S97.

BUS & COLECTIVO

Many bus companies are along Bolognesi, including **Cruz del Sur** (☎0-801-1111; www.cruzdelsur.com.pe; Bolognesi 888), **Línea** (☎074-23-2951; Bolognesi 638) and **Móvil Tours** (☎01-716-8000; www.moviltours.com.pe; Bolognesi 199). A sample of long-distance destinations:

DESTINATION	COST (S)	DURATION (HR)
Cajamarca	16-40	6
Chachapoyas	30-50	10
Jaén	20-25	6
Lima	40-125	12-14
Máncora	30-35	6
Piura	15-21	3
Tarapoto	45-120	14
Tumbes	25-50	8

The minibus terminal at the intersection of San José and Lora y Lora has regular *combis* to Lambayeque (S1.50, 20 minutes). Buses for Ferreñafe (S2, 30 minutes) and Sipán (S3.50, 15 minutes) leave from the **Terminal de Microbuses Epsel** (Nicolás de Píerola, at Oriente). *Colectivos* depart from Prado near Sáenz Peña.

For Túcume, buses leave from the 13th block of Leguia near Óvalo del Pescador (S2.50, one hour).

Around Chiclayo

Tours to the archaeological sites cost between S45 and S60. **Reserva Ecológica Chaparrí** tours are much more extensive and offer guided hikes (S130 to S140) through the reserve, visiting animal rescue centers. Prices include transport but not admission fees.

Lambayeque

The pride of northern Peru, the impressive **Museo Tumbas Reales de Sipán** (www.museotumbasrealessipan.pe; admission S10; ⏲9am-5pm Tue-Sun) is a world-class facility (save the Spanish-only signage), showcasing the dazzling finds of the Royal Tombs of Sipán, including that of the Lord of Sipán himself. Also in Lambayeque is the older **Bruning Museum** (www.museobruning.com; admission S8; ⏲9am-5pm), which houses artifacts from the Chimú, Moche, Chavín and Vicus cultures.

Sipán

The story of this **site** (Huaca Rayada; ☎074-80-0048; admission S10; ⏲9am-5pm), 30km southeast of Chiclayo, is an exciting one of buried treasure, *guaqueros,* the black market, police, archaeologists and at least one murder. Hundreds of exquisite and priceless artifacts have been recovered, and a gold-smothered royal Moche burial site – of the Lord of Sipán – was discovered in 1987. A small but well-done museum opened here in 2009, showcasing finds from the 2007 opening of the chamber of the warrior priest.

Ferreñafe

About 18km northeast of Chiclayo, the excellent **Museo Nacional Sicán** (admission S8; ⏲9am-5pm Tue-Sun) displays replicas of some of the largest tombs ever found in South America. Interestingly, the Lord of Sicán was buried upside down, in a fetal position with his head chopped off, along with a sophisticated security system to ward off *guaqueros* – a red dust that's toxic when inhaled.

Túcume

This little-known **site** (www.tucume.com; admission S8; ⏲8am-4:30pm Tue-Sun) can be seen from a spectacular clifftop *mirador* about 30km north of Lambayeque on the Panamericana. It's worth the climb to see the vast complex of crumbling walls, plazas and more than two dozen pyramids.

Piura

☎073 / POP 387,200

Sun-scorched Piura presents itself out of the dusty tumbleweeds of the Desierto de Sechura as a mere regional transportation hub. There's little to do here, but it works just fine as a speed bump in your journey north or south – some cobblestone streets boasting character-filled houses and northern Peru's best crafts market in nearby Catacaos add to the appeal.

Sights & Activities

Catacaos VILLAGE

A bustling small town 12km southwest of Piura, Catacaos is the self-proclaimed capital of *artesanía* (handicrafts) in the region. And justifiably so: its **arts market** (⏲10am-4pm) is the best in northern Peru. Sprawling for several blocks near the Plaza de Armas, here you will find excellent weavings, gold and silver filigree jewelry, wood carvings, ceramics (including lots of pieces from Chulucanas), leather goods and more. The weekends are the best and busiest times to visit.

Combis and *colectivos* leave frequently for Catacaos from Av Tacna in Piura (S1.50 to S2, 15 minutes).

Sleeping & Eating

Hospedaje Frente del Mar HOTEL $

(☎96-966-914; just north of T-Junction; s S35, d 70-100) The best budget spot in town. The rooms are hot and the beds are spongy. But it's friendly and clean, and there's a laid-back porch looking onto the beach. The new top-floor rooms are the best.

★Capuccino CAFE $$

(www.facebook.com/CapuccinoGourmet; Tacna 786; mains S22-45; ⏲closed Sun; 📶) The real deal. This modern cafe offers gourmet sandwiches and salads that are great for lunch (though it's shockingly empty). There's more

GETTING TO ECUADOR

The border post of La Tina lacks hotels, but the Ecuadorean town of Macará (3km from the border) has adequate facilities. La Tina can be reached by *colectivo* (S12, 2½ hours) from Sullana, 40km north of Piura, throughout the day. A better option is **Transportes Loja** (073-30-5446; Sánchez Cerro, Km 1, Piura), with three daily buses from Piura (9:30am, 1pm and 9pm) that conveniently go straight through here and on to Loja in Ecuador (S28, eight hours).

The border is the international bridge over the Río Calvas and is open 24 hours. Formalities are relaxed as long as your documents are in order. There are no banks; you'll find money changers at the border or in Macará. A new bridge and completely revamped immigration facilities, with both Peruvian and Ecuadorean immigration offices sharing the same building on the bridge, make the crossing easy peasy.

Citizens of the USA, Canada, EU and Australia do not require a visa for stays of up to 90 days, and are not required to pay any kind of border-crossing fee. Most nationalities are simply given a T3 tourist card, which must be surrendered when leaving.

Travelers entering Ecuador will find taxis (US$1) and *colectivos* (US$0.50) to take them to Macará. There is a Peruvian **consulate** (07-269-4030; www.consuladoperu macara.com; Bolivar 134) in Macará.

For information on making this crossing in the opposite direction, see p685.

sophisticated fare for a fine night out with a bottle of wine at dinner.

Getting There & Away

AIR

The airport is 2km southeast of the city center. **LAN** (073-30-2145; www.lan.com; Grau 140), **Taca** (0-800-1-8222; www.avianca.com; Sánchez Cerro 234, CC Real Plaza) and **Peruvian Airlines** (011-716-6000; www.peruvian.pe; Libertad 777) have daily flights to/from Lima.

BUS

Buses go to Lima (S59 to S135, 12 to 16 hours) with **Cruz del Sur** (0-801-11111; www.cruz delsur.com.pe; cnr Bolognesi & Lima), **Tepsa** (01-617-9000; www.tepsa.com.pe; Loreto 1198), Línea, Ittsa and Transportes Chiclayo. For other destinations try the companies listed following.

For Cajamarca and the northern Andes, it's best to connect in Chiclayo.

Combis for Catacaos (S1.50 to S2, 15 minutes) leave east of the San Miguel pedestrian bridge. Buses to Huancabamba depart from **Terminal Terrestre Castilla** (Panamericana s/n), a 1km and S3.50 *mototaxi* ride east of town.

El Dorado (073-32-5875; www.transportes eldorado.com.pe; Cerro 1119) Has 14 buses for Tumbes between 6:30am and 12:30am that stop in Máncora.

Ittsa (044-33-3982; www.ittsabus.com; Cerro 1142) Has buses to Trujillo (9am, 1:30pm, 11:15pm), Chimbote (11pm), and a *bus-cama* to Lima at 6pm.

Linea (073-30-3894; www.linea.pe; Cerro 1215) Hourly buses to Chiclayo between 5am and 8pm, and a 1:30pm and 11pm bus to Trujillo.

Transportes Chiclayo (074-50-3548; www. transporteschiclayo.com; Cerro 1121) Hourly buses to Chiclayo.

Máncora

073 / POP 9700

Despite being Peru's principal beach resort and home to one of northwestern South America's best beaches, Máncora itself is little more than a glorified surfing village of shockingly rustic proportions (the fancy stuff combs its outskirts). Year-round sunshine and waves pushing 3m draw in swaths of surfers, who rub sunburnt shoulders with locals on weekends throughout the year. From December to March the scene gets deliriously rowdy and prices skyrocket.

Activities

You can go **surfing** year-round, but the best waves hit from November to February. Rent surfboards at the beach's southern end (per hour S10, per day S20). The best breaks in the area are on **Máncora Beach** in town and **Lobitos**, a 64km trek south. Haggle a taxi (S20 to S50).

Winds can reach 30 knots during kitesurfing season (from April to November).

Laguna Surf Camp SURFING

(☎99-401-5628; www.vivamancora.com/lagunacamp; Veraniego s/n) The friendly Pilar at Laguna Camp does surf lessons for S60 for 90 minutes of instruction (including board rental).

Iguana Tours ADVENTURE TOUR

(☎073-63-2762; www.iguanastrips.com; Piura 245) Iguana's organizes full-day trips to the Los Pilares dry forest, which include wading through sparkling waterfalls, swimming, horseback riding, a soak in the mud baths and lunch for S180 per person, along with other standard tours.

Sleeping

Cheap sleeps are mostly found in the center and at the beach's southern end.

★Loki del Mar HOSTEL $

(☎073-25-8484; www.lokihostel.com; Av Piura 262; dm S28-39, r S96, all incl breakfast;) Social butterflies flock to this mother of all beach hostels, which is really a self-contained resort masquerading as a backpackers' hangout. Tucked away in the whitewashed building are spacious dorm rooms with extra wide beds, and minimalist privates for those seeking a hostel vibe without the communal snoring.

GETTING TO ECUADOR

Shady practices at the border crossing between Ecuador and Peru at Aguas Verdes have earned it the dubious title of 'the worst border crossing in South America.' We can't prove it, but it pays to be wary. If you need to change money, avoid doing so at the border as scams and counterfeit bills are rampant here.

The Peruvian border town of Aguas Verdes is linked by an international bridge across the Río Zarumilla with the Ecuadorian border town of Huaquillas. A new **CEBAF** (Centro Binacional de Atención de Frontera; 24hr) office in Huaquillas means you now get off your bus at the immigration control, present your Peruvian tourist card to immigration authorities, then step a few feet over to have your passport stamped for Ecuador.

The last major hub north on the Peru side is **Tumbes**, 107km north of Máncora, not a bad little spot to shack up for a night and explore the surrounding mangroves and ecological reserves. **Preference Tours** (☎072-52-5518; turismomundial@hotmail.com; Grau 427; 9am-7:30pm Mon-Sat, to 11am Sun) can get you out and about. On the plaza, **Sí Señor** (Bolívar 115; mains S15-35) does the usual array of cheap Peruvian staples, and **Hotel Roma** (☎072-52-4137; hotelromatumbes@hotmail.com; Bolognesi 425; s/d S45/70;) offers wi-fi, cable TV, high-powered fans and hot showers. Beware of vicious mosquitoes in the area, and book ahead – the busy border means rooms go quickly.

Frequent *combis* for Tumbes (S10, two hours) drive along Máncora's main drag. From Lima, **Cruz del Sur** (☎0-801-11111; www.cruzdelsur.com.pe; Tumbes 319) offers the most comfortable services to Tumbes (S60 to S175).

To avoid scams, it is smart to take a direct bus across the border with a major bus company from Tumbes like Cruz del Sur, Civa, Ormeño or **Cifa** (☎072-52-5120; www.cifainternacional.com; Tumbes 958); options include to Machala (S12, three hours) or Guayaquil (S25 to S118, six hours) in Ecuador, departing every two hours. From Tumbes to the border, the cheap way is *colectivo* taxis (S3.50, 25 minutes) and minibuses (S2, 40 minutes) leaving from various spots, including from the corner of Puell and Tumbes or Castilla and Feijoo, the latter near the market.

The **immigration office** (☎072-56-1178; El Complejo; 24hr) in Aguas Verdes is 3km from the border. On public transportation, make sure you stop there for border formalities. *Mototaxis* will then whisk you to the border (S3).

About 3km to the north of the bridge, Ecuadorian immigration is also open 24 hours. There are no entry fees into Ecuador, so be polite but insistent with any border guards trying their luck. Take a taxi from the bridge (US$2.50). There are basic hotels in Huaquillas, but most people catch an onward bus to Machala.

For information on making this crossing in the opposite direction, see p709.

Laguna Surf Camp BUNGALOW $
(☎99-401-5628; www.vivamancora.com/laguna camp; Veraniego s/n; dm/s/d S30/90/120, bungalows S80-120; 📶🌊) This laid-back pad is a hidden gem, one block back from the beach in its own rustic oasis. Older Indonesian-style bamboo bungalows sit around a pleasant sandy garden right near the water and lots of swinging, shady hammocks will provide days of entertainment. New five-bed dorms are a boon for budgeteers.

Kokopelli HOSTEL $
(☎073-25-8091; www.hostelkokopelli.com; Piura 209; dm S32-40, r S100, all incl breakfast; ❄@📶🌊) Part of a successful chain of Peruvian hostels, this is the most intimate hostel in town. It doesn't have beach access, but there's a small pool, cool bar area, colorful dorm rooms boasting loads of exposed brick and three private rooms with in-room safes, a rarity in Peruvian hostels. It's a great alternative if your first choice is booked.

Marcilia Beach Bungalows BUNGALOW $$
(☎073-69-2902; www.marciliadevichayito.com; Antigua Panamericana Km 1212; r per person with/without sea-view S100/80, all incl breakfast; @📶) A friendly trilingual Peruvian couple started these rustic bungalows on Vichayito Beach after years working the cruise-ship circuit. Each bungalow has electric hot water and very nice bathrooms, but the real coup here is the one that sits seaside: book it and you'll feel like the entire stretch of beach is your own private paradise.

Eating & Drinking

Seafood rules here, but the gringo onslaught has inspired everything from breakfast burritos to Greek salads. Breakfast is well spoken for, but forget about lunch before 1pm.

Angela's Place BREAKFAST $
(Piura 396; breakfasts S6.50-14, mains S5-12; ⏲from 8am; 🖉) Angela the Austrian bread wizard started selling her delicious sweet potato, *yuca* and wheat breads from her bicycle years ago. Now you can get them at her cheery cafe on the main drag, along with creative and substantial vegetarian (and vegan) dishes, energizing breakfast combos and sweet pastries.

Green Eggs & Ham BREAKFAST $
(Grau 503; meals S15-18; ⏲7:30am-4:30pm) There's nothing silly about this *Dr Seuss*-inspired breakfast spot, which counts a battalion of gringo fans for its homesick-remedy breakfasts (pancakes, French toast, hash browns). Yes, you'll like them Sam I Am, but the real coup is the 2nd-floor patio – a straight shot through a thatch of tall palms to the crashing waves.

★**La Sirena d'Juan** PERUVIAN $$
(☎073-25-8173; Piura 316; mains S30-35; ⏲closed Tue; 📶) Local boy done good, Juan has turned his intimate little main-drag seafooder into northern Peru's best restaurant. Yellowfin tuna fresh from Máncora's waters is the showstopper here, whether it's prepared as a *tiradito* (a sort of Peruvian sashimi) in yellow curry or grilled with a mango-*rocoto*-red pepper chutney.

Information

Av Piura is lined with internet cafes, ATMs and *lavanderías* (laundries). Exchange US dollars at **Banco de la Nación** (Piura 625). Tread warily on the beach at night, as thieves pose as joggers and run away with your phone! The website www.vivamancora.com has useful tourist information.

Getting There & Away

Most southbound coastal buses headed for Lima originate in Tumbes. Frequent *combis* for Tumbes (S10, two hours) drive along Máncora's main drag. **El Dorado** (☎073-25-8161; www.transporteseldorado.com.pe; Grau 213) offers the most frequent services to more southerly towns of interest, like Piura (S20 to S95), Chiclayo (S39 to S100) and Trujillo (S30 to S87).

HUARAZ & THE CORDILLERAS

All around Huaraz, the mountainous region of the Cordilleras Blanca and Huayhuash, boasts calm topaz lakes huddled below peaks teetering on avalanche – some 22 ostentatious summits over 6000m make this the highest mountain range in the world outside the Himalayas.

Both Peru's highest point, the 6768m Huascarán, and the picture-perfect 5999m Artesonraju (rumored to be the mountain in Paramount Pictures' live-action logo), loom here over Andean villages as well as the pleasant city of Huaraz, the nerve center of one of South America's premier trekking, mountain-biking and climbing areas. Superlatives crash and burn in a brazen attempt to capture the awesome natural beauty of it all.

Huaraz

043 / POP 64,110

The restless Andean adventure capital of Huaraz came into its own based on a blessed location amidst some of the prettiest mountains in the world. Though nearly wiped out by the earthquake of 1970, Huaraz rebounded to become Peru's high-adrenaline showpiece, with trekking and mountaineering leading the heart-thumping charge. It buzzes with adventure seekers of all ilks in high season (May to September) and slows to little more than a crawl the rest of the year, when many folks shut up shop and head for the beaches.

Sights

Museo Regional de Ancash MUSEUM

(Plaza de Armas; adult/child S5/1; 8:30am-5:15pm Tue-Sat, 9am-2pm Sun) The Museo Regional de Ancash houses one of the most significant collections of ancient stone sculptures in South America. Small but interesting, it has a few mummies, some trepanned skulls and a garden of stone monoliths from the Recuay culture (400 BC–AD 600) and the Wari culture (AD 600–1100).

Huaraz

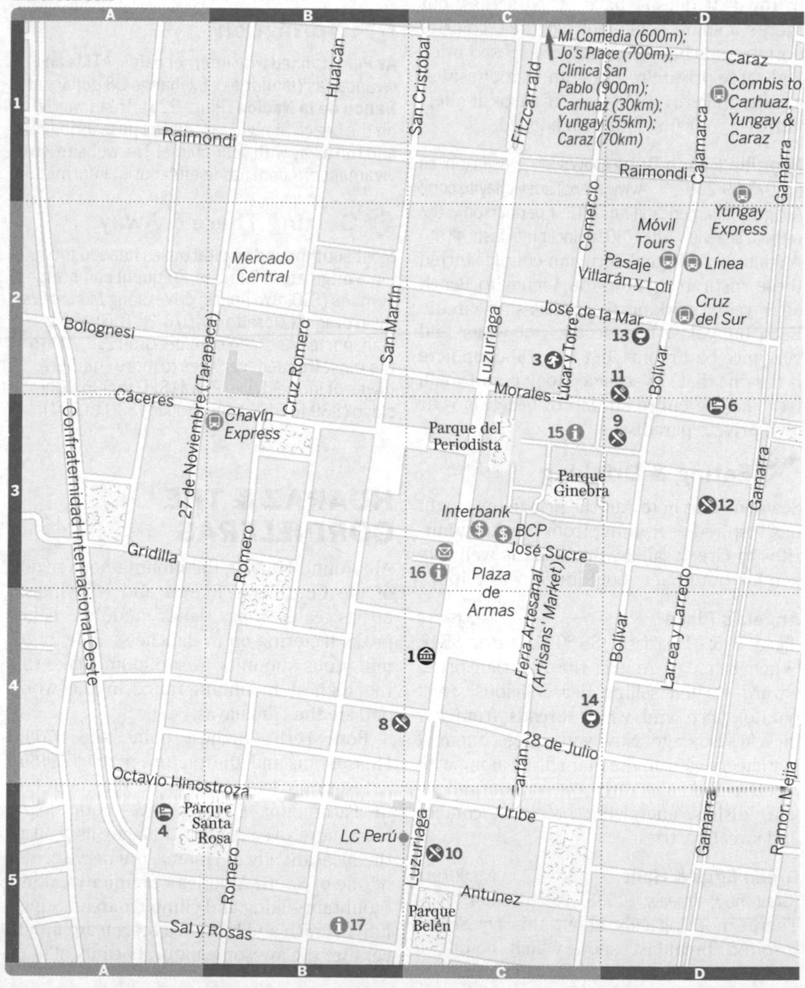

Monumento Nacional Wilkahuaín RUIN
(adult/student S5/2; ⏲9am-5pm Tue-Sun) This small Wari ruin about 8km north of Huaraz is remarkably well preserved, dating from about AD 600 to 900. It's an imitation of the temple at Chavín done in the Tiwanaku style. Wilkahuaín means 'grandson's house' in Quechua. The three-story temple has seven rooms on each floor, each originally filled with bundles of mummies. The bodies were kept dry using a sophisticated system of ventilation ducts. Another smaller set of ruins, **Wilkahuaín Pequeno**, can be seen nearby.

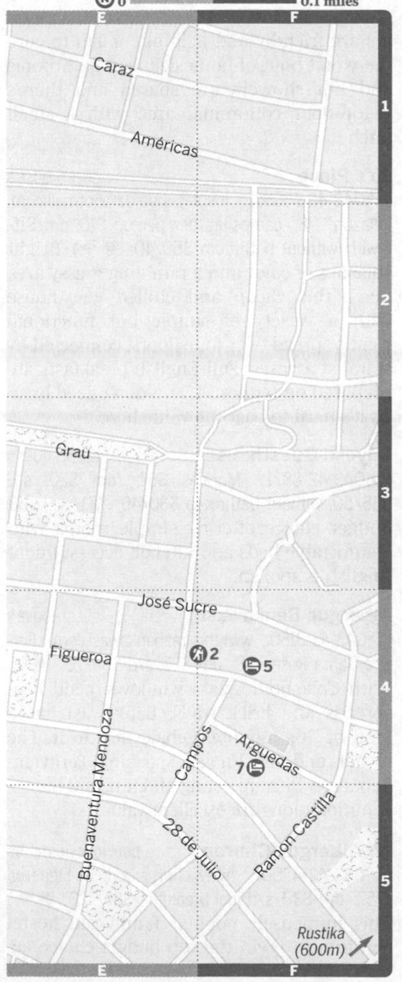

Activities

Trekking & Mountaineering

The best treks are in the **Cordillera Blanca** inside Parque Nacional Huascarán and in the **Cordillera Huayhuash**. All the equipment and help you need can be hired or bought, including trail maps, guidebooks, pack animals, *arrieros* (drivers) and local guides. Expect to pay around S120 to S150 per person per day for an all-inclusive trek or climbing expedition. Always inspect rental gear carefully.

Check certified guides and register before heading out at Casa de Guías (p884).

Skyline Adventures TREKKING, MOUNTAINEERING
(☎043-42-7097; www.skyline-adventures.com; Pasaje Industrial 137) Based just outside Huaraz, this high-end operator comes highly recommended and provides guides for treks and mountain climbs. Leads six- and 12-day mountaineering courses.

Eco Ice Peru TREKKING
(www.ecoice-peru.com; Figueroa 1185; ⏲8am-6pm) Run by a gregarious and passionate young guide, this new agency gets top reviews from travelers for its customer service. Treks often end with a dinner at the owner's pad in Huaraz.

Rock Climbing

You'll find great bolted sports climbs in the Cordillera Blanca, particularly at Chancos (near Marcará), Monterrey and Recuay. For big-wall action to keep you chalked up for days, head to the famous **Torre de Parón** (aka the Sphinx) at Laguna Parón, 32km east of Caraz. Many trekking agencies offer rock-climbing trips and rent gear. **Galaxia Expeditions** (www.galaxia-expeditions.com) has an indoor climbing wall, too.

Mountain Biking

Mountain Bike Adventures MOUNTAIN BIKING
(☎043-2-4259; www.chakinaniperu.com; Lúcar y Torre 530, 2nd fl; ⏲9am-1pm & 3-8pm) Mountain Bike Adventures has been in business for more than a decade and receives repeated visits by mountain bikers for its decent selection of bikes, knowledgeable and friendly service, and good safety record. It offers guided tours, ranging from an easy five-hour cruise to 12-day circuits around the Cordillera Blanca. Rates start at around S160 for a day circuit.

Huaraz

Sights
1 Museo Regional de Ancash C4

Activities, Courses & Tours
2 Eco Ice Peru F4
3 Mountain Bike Adventures C2

Sleeping
4 Albergue Benkawasi A5
5 Albergue Churup F4
6 Cayesh Guesthouse D3
Familia Meza Lodging .... (see 3)
7 Olaza's Bed & Breakfast F4

Eating
Café Andino .... (see 3)
8 California Café B4
9 Chili Heaven D3
10 La Brasa Roja C5
11 Rinconcito Mineiro D2
12 Taita D3

Drinking & Nightlife
13 El Tambo D2
Los 13 Buhos .... (see 9)
14 Tio Enrique C4

Information
15 Casa de Guías C3
16 iPerú C3
17 Parque Nacional Huascarán Office B5
Policía de Turismo .... (see 16)

Tours

One bus tour visits the ruins at Chavín de Huántar; another goes through Yungay to the beautiful Lagunas Llanganuco, where there are spectacular views of Huascarán; a third takes you through Caraz to scenic Laguna Parón; and a fourth goes to see the extraordinary giant *Puya raimondii* plant (which can take 100 years to grow to its full height – often 10m!) and the glacier at Nevado Pastoruri. Full-day tours cost S30 to S45, excluding entry fees. Services are geared towards Peruvians – do not count on English.

Festivals & Events

El Señor de la Soledad CULTURAL
Huaraz pays homage to its patron (the Christ of Solitude) beginning May 3. This weeklong festival involves fireworks, music, dancing, elaborately costumed processions and lots of drinking.

Festival de Andinismo MOUNTAINEERING
Held annually in June, it attracts mountaineers from several countries, and competitions and exhibitions are held.

Sleeping

Locals meet buses to offer rooms in their houses, and *hostales* do the same. Don't pay until you've seen the room.

Familia Meza Lodging GUESTHOUSE $
(☎94-369-5908; Lúcar y Torre 538; r per person S25;) In the same building as Café Andino, this charming family guesthouse has cheery rooms and is decorated throughout with homey touches. What's more, the owners are friendly and helpful enough to cure the worst bout of homesickness. Bathrooms and hot showers are shared and there's a top-floor communal area with a small kitchen.

Jo's Place GUESTHOUSE $
(☎043-42-5505; josplacehuaraz@hotmail.com; Villazón 278; campsites per person S10, dm S15, r with/without bathroom S50/40; @) Bright splashes of color and a rambling grassy area mark this cheap and chilled guesthouse with a variety of simple but functional rooms spread over four floors, connected by spiral staircases. Full English breakfasts are prepared on request. If you don't need luxury, it's hard to beat the value here.

Cayesh Guesthouse GUESTHOUSE $
(☎043-42-8821; Morales 867; dm S20, s/d S35/50, without bathroom S30/40;) A solid budget choice offering simple rooms with comfortable beds and kitchen access; fluent English is spoken.

Albergue Benkawasi GUESTHOUSE $
(☎043-43-3150; www.huarazbenkawasi.com; Parque Santa Rosa 928; dm S25, s/d S50/70; @) With Coke-bottle glass windows, plaid bedspreads and brick walls, Benkawasi has a kind of '70s mountain chalet feel to it. The owner and his English-speaking Peruvian-Lebanese wife are young and fun, and the accommodations are excellent value.

★ **Albergue Churup** BOUTIQUE HOSTEL $$
(☎043-42-4200; www.churup.com; Figueroa 1257; dm S30, s/d incl breakfast S85/120; @) This immensely popular family-run hostel continues to win the top budget-choice ac-

colade. Immaculate and comfortable rooms share comfortable, colorful lounging areas on every floor. The building is topped by a massive, fireplace-warmed lounge space with magnificent 180-degree views of the Cordillera.

Olaza's Bed & Breakfast GUESTHOUSE **$$**
(☎043-42-2529; www.olazas.com; Arguedas 1242; s/d/tr incl breakfast S80/100/150; @) This smart little hotel has spacious bathrooms and comfortable beds, but the best part is the big lounge area upstairs and massive panoramic terrace. The owner is an established figure in the Huaraz trekking and tourism scene; he can provide advice no matter where you want to go (as long as he's around). Bus-station pickup is included.

Eating

Café Andino CAFE **$**
(www.cafeandino.com; Lúcar y Torre 530, 3rd fl; breakfast S8-24, mains S18-25;) This modern top-floor cafe has space and light in spades, comfy lounges, art, photos, crackling fireplace, books and groovy tunes – it's the ultimate South American traveler hangout and meeting spot. You can get breakfast any time (Belgian waffles, *huevos rancheros*), and snacks you miss (nachos). It's the best place in town for information about trekking in the area.

Rustika PERUVIAN **$**
(Ricardo Palma 200; mains S12-25; 9:30am-11:30pm) For a full-on local experience, trek up the hill to this atmospheric restaurant constructed from logs and colored glass. It serves tasty typical dishes including *ceviche* and barbecue *cuy* (guinea pig). Tables are tucked into various nooks and crannies, but the best place to eat is out on the terrace – it offers great mountain views with a Peruvian pop-music soundtrack.

Taita PERUVIAN **$**
(Larrea y Laredo 633, 2nd fl; mains S5.50-18; 11am-3pm) This atmospheric local's haunt is an excellent spot to try *chocho,* the alpine answer to *ceviche,* with the fish replaced with *lupine* (an Andean legume). It also does *ceviche, leche de tigre* (*ceviche* juice) and *chicharrónes* (deep-fried pork rinds). It's a top spot.

Rinconcito Mineiro PERUVIAN **$**
(Morales 757; menu S8-16, mains S12-35; 7am-11pm;) This popular place is *the* spot to tuck into homey and cheap Peruvian daily *menús* (set meals). The daily blackboard of 10 or so options includes an excellent *lomo saltado* (strips of beef stir-fried with onions, tomatoes, potatoes and chili), plus grilled trout, *tacu-tacu* (a Peruvian fusion dish of rice, beans and a protein) and the like.

California Café BREAKFAST, CAFE **$**
(www.huaylas.com; Jiron 28 de Julio 562; breakfast S13-25; 7:30am-6:30pm, to 2pm Sun;) Managed by an American from California, this hip traveler magnet does breakfasts at any time, plus light lunches and salads – it's a funky, chilled space to while away many hours. You can spend the day listening to the sublime world-music collection or reading one of the hundreds of books available for exchange.

La Brasa Roja PERUVIAN **$**
(Luzuriaga 915; mains S11.50-27; noon-11pm) This upscale *pollería* (restaurant specializing in roast chicken) is the ultimate budget refueling stop. Not only is the chicken perfect, but you get five sauces – count 'em, five! – instead of the usual three (black olive and mustard make a surprise appearance). The other mains are hit and miss but if you're lucky you'll get a live violinist. No lie.

★**Mi Comedia** ITALIAN **$$**
(Centenario 351; mains S25-32; 5-11pm Mon-Sat) Pizzerias are ubiquitous in Huaraz but once you've eaten in this friendly place you won't go anywhere else. The pizzas are prepared right in the dining room and all feature a delicious crust and farm-fresh tomato sauce. There is also a small selection of excellent pasta dishes. Reservations are advisable.

Chili Heaven INDIAN, THAI **$$**
(Parque Ginebra; mains S17-35; noon-11pm) Whether you send your appetite to India or Thailand, the fiery curries at this hot spot will seize your taste buds upon arrival, mercilessly shake them up and then spit them back out the other side as if you've died and gone to chili heaven (hence the name). They also bottle their own hot sauces. A critical Peruvian food antidote.

Drinking

★**Los 13 Buhos** BAR
(Parque Ginebra; 11am-late) A supremely cool cafe-bar in newly upgraded Parque Ginebra digs. The owner, Lucho, was the first

craft-beer brewer in Huaraz and offers five tasty choices, including red and black ales. It also prepares top Thai curries and fantastic set menu meals. It's the best bar in town for kicking back over cold homebrews and liquid-courage-inspired conversation.

El Tambo BAR, CLUB

(José de la Mar 776; ⌚9pm to 4am) If you're hankering to shake your groove-thang, this is the most popular disco in town, complete with dance-floor trees and loads of nooks and crannies so you can hide yourself away. Fashionable with both *extranjeros* (foreigners) and Peruvians, the music swings from techno-*cumbia* to Top 20, salsa and reggae, and most things in between.

Tio Enrique BAR

(Bolivar 572; ⌚5-11pm) If you like beer, you'll like this cozy Swiss-themed drinking hole with a long bar and communal pine tables. Popular with hardcore climbers, it serves around three dozen varieties of imported beers from the UK, Belgium and Germany as well as tasty sausages grilled at the door by the charismatic apron-toting owner.

ℹ Information

DANGERS & ANNOYANCES

Huaraz is a safe city that experiences little crime; unfortunately, robberies of trekkers and tourists do happen, especially in the area of the Mirador de Retaqeñua and the Wilkahuaín (sometimes also spelled Wilcawain) ruins, and to groggy backpackers arriving early in the morning on overnight buses. In these cases, stay alert and walk with a group or hire a taxi to avoid problems.

EMERGENCY

Casa de Guías (☎043-42-1811; www.casadeguias.com.pe; Parque Ginebra 28G; ⌚9am-1pm & 4-8pm Mon-Fri, 8am-noon Sat) Runs mountain safety and rescue courses and maintains a list of internationally certified guides. Also mounts rescue operations to assist climbers in emergencies. If you are heading out on a risky ascent, it's worth consulting with these guys first.

Policía de Turismo (☎043-42-1341; Luzuriaga 724; ⌚24hr) On the west side of the Plaza de Armas.

MONEY

BCP (Luzuriaga 691)

Interbank (José Sucre 687)

POST

Serpost (Luzuriaga 702; ⌚8:30am-8pm Mon-Fri, to 5:30pm Sat) Postal services.

TOURIST INFORMATION

iPerú (☎043-42-8812; iperuhuaraz@promperu.gob.pe; Pasaje Atusparia, Oficina 1, Plaza de Armas; ⌚9am-6pm Mon-Sat, to 1pm Sun) Has general tourist information but little in the way of trekking info.

Parque Nacional Huascarán Office (☎043-42-2086; www.sernanp.gob.pe; Sal y Rosas 555; ⌚8:30am-1pm & 2:30-6pm Mon-Fri, to noon Sat) Staff have limited information about visiting the park.

ℹ Getting There & Away

The Huaraz airport is actually at Anta, 23km north of town. A taxi will cost about S40. **LC Perú** (☎043-42-4734; www.lcperu.pe; Luzuriaga 904) operates daily flights from Lima at 5:30am.

Expect midmorning or late-evening departures for Lima. **Cruz del Sur** (☎043-42-8726; Bolívar 491) has nonstop luxury bus services. **Móvil Tours** (☎043-42-2555; www.moviltours.com.pe; Confraternidad Internacional Oeste 451) is also comfortable and has a **ticket office** (Bolívar 452) in town.

Línea (☎043-42-6666; Bolívar 450) and Móvil Tours go direct to Chimbote, continuing to Trujillo. Spectacular though rough rides via the amazing Cañón del Pato (that will have you scavenging for Xanax) or 4225m-high Punta Callán to Chimbote are worth seeing with **Yungay Express** (☎043-42-4377; Raimondi 930).

Chavín Express (☎42-8069; Cáceres 330) goes to Chavín de Huántar, continuing to Huari.

Daytime **minibuses** for Caraz and Yungay depart frequently from near the Quilcay bridge on Fitzcarrald.

Sample travel times and costs from Huaraz are as follows (prices fluctuate with the quality of the bus/classes):

DESTINATION	COST (S)	DURATION (HR)
Caraz	6	1½
Chavín	12	2½
Chimbote	20-60	5-9
Huari	15	5
Lima	35-100	8
Trujillo	35-60	7
Yungay	5	1

Parque Nacional Huascarán

Encompassing almost the entire area of the Cordillera Blanca above 4000m, this 3400-sq-km national park is bursting with picturesque emerald lakes, brightly colored alpine wildflowers and red *quenua* trees.

The most popular backpacking circuit, the **Santa Cruz** trek, takes four days and rises to the Punta Unión pass (4760m), which arguably has the best Andean views in Peru. The trail, which passes by icy waterfalls and lakes, mossy meadows and verdant valleys, is well marked. *Colectivo* taxis frequently leave from Caraz for the main trailhead at Cashapampa (S10, 1½ hours).

While Santa Cruz attracts the lion's share of visitors, dozens of other trekking possibilities in the Cordillera Blanca supply scenery and vistas just as jaw-dropping (minus the crowds). Trails range from day hikes to ambitious two-week treks. Many routes aren't clearly marked, however, so go with a guide or take along top-notch topographic maps. If you are short on cash or time, the day-long trek to **Laguna 69** is stunning, dripping with marvelous mountain and waterfall views, and culminating in the Photoshop-blue lake that gives the trek its name – a perfect peek into the awesome scenery in this area.

Register with your passport at the national park office in Huaraz and pay the park entrance fee. You can also register and pay at control stations, but operating hours vary. Don't dodge or begrudge paying the fee: the Cordillera Blanca is one of the most amazing places on the planet. Some trailhead communities, such as Cashapampa, charge a fee (around S10 per person).

Though arbitrarily enforced, law requires a licensed guide to accompany all trekkers, unless you are a card-carrying member of a

Huaraz & the Cordilleras

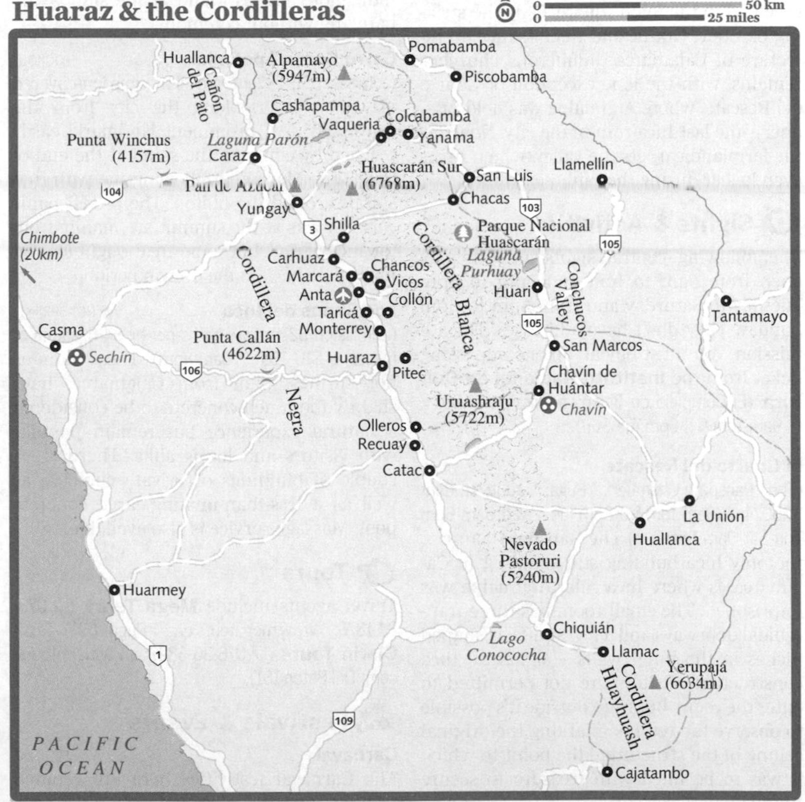

UIAA-approved mountaineering club. This is especially enforced for any mountaineering activity.

NORTHERN HIGHLANDS

Vast tracts of unexplored jungle and mountain ranges shrouded in mist guard the secrets of Peru's northern highlands, where Andean peaks and cloud forests stretch all the way from the coast to the deepest Amazon jungle. These outposts are interspersed with the relics of ancient warriors and Inca kings, their connections by better routes just emerging.

Cajamarca

076 / POP 246,536

The cobblestone colonial streets of Cajamarca mark the last stand for the powerful Inca empire – Atahualpa, the last Inca, was defeated here by Francisco Pizarro and later executed in the main square. Only the striking baroque, Gothic and Renaissance architecture of Cajamarca's numerous churches remains, with the lone exception of Cuarto del Rescate, where Atahualpa was held prisoner – the last Inca ruin in the city. Now fertile farmland carpets the valley, which turns even lusher during the rainy season.

Sights & Activities

The following central sights are officially open from 9am to 1pm and 3pm to 6pm Tuesday to Saturday and from 3pm to 6pm Sunday. They don't have addresses. For admission, you must buy an all-encompassing ticket from the **Instituto Nacional de Cultura** (El Complejo de Belén; admission S7.50/4; 9am-1pm & 3-6pm Tue-Sun).

El Cuarto del Rescate RUIN

(The Ransom Chamber; Puga; adult/student S7.50/4; 9am-1pm & 3-8pm Tue & Wed, 9am-8pm Thu-Sat, 9am-1pm Sun) The Ransom Chamber, the only Inca building still standing in Cajamarca, is where Inca ruler Atahualpa was imprisoned. The small room has three trapezoidal doorways and a few similarly shaped niches in the inner walls – signature Inca construction. Visitors are not permitted to enter the room, but from outside it's possible to observe the red line marking the original ceiling of the structure – the point to which it was to be filled with treasure to secure Atahualpa's release.

Museo de Arqueológico & Etnografía MUSEUM

(cnr Belén y Commercio; admission S5; 9am-1pm & 3-6pm Tue-Sat, 9am-1pm Sun) This small but interesting museum housed inside the Antigua Hospital de Mujeres, just a few meters from El Complejo de Belén, has exhibits of pre-Columbian pottery and stone statues, as well as displays on local costumes and clothing, domestic and agricultural implements, musical instruments and crafts made from wood, bone, leather and stone.

Iglesia de San Francisco CHURCH, MUSEUM

(Calle 2 de Mayo; admission S5; 10am-noon & 4-6pm Mon-Fri, 10am-noon Sat) Inside Iglesia de San Francisco you'll find elaborate stone carvings and decadent altars. Visit the church's **Museo de Arte Religioso** (Religious Art Museum) to see 17th-century religious paintings by indigenous artists. It also has the creepy **catacombs** – in one room you'll see the orderly tombs of monks, and in another are the skeletons recovered from indigenous graves found at the site, laying bare and without ceremony.

Cerro Santa Apolonia LOOKOUT

(admission S1; 7am-7pm) This garden-covered viewpoint, overlooking the city from the southwest, is a prominent landmark, easily reached by climbing the stairs at the end of Calle 2 de Mayo and following the path that spirals around the hilltop. The pre-Hispanic carved rocks at the summit are mainly from the Inca period, but some are thought to originally date back to the Chavín period.

Los Baños del Inca HOT SPRINGS

(admission S2, private baths per hr S4-6, sauna or massage S10-20; 5am-8pm) These famous hot springs, 6km from Cajamarca, have slightly too much concrete to be considered a natural experience but remain popular with visitors and locals alike. There are a couple of buildings of private cubicles, as well as a less-than-inviting large concrete pool. Massage service is also available.

Tours

Travel agents include **Mega Tours** (076-34-1876; www.megatours.org; Puga 691) and **Clarín Tours** (076-36-6829; www.clarintours.com; Del Batán 161).

Festivals & Events

Carnaval FESTIVAL

The Carnaval festivities here are reputed to be among the most popular and rowdy events in the country. They're held in the last few days before Lent.

Sleeping

★Hospedaje Los Jazmines HOTEL $

(076-36-1812; www.hospedajelosjazmines.com.pe; Amazonas 775; s/d/t with bathroom S50/80/110; without bathroom S40/60/80; @ 📶) 🍃 In a land of ubiquitous colonial courtyards, this friendly inn is a value standout for its lush version and even more extensive back gardens. With comfy rooms, piping hot water and a great central location it is a top choice, even more so considering the profits help sustain an orphanage for special-needs children in Baños de Inca.

Hostal Plaza HOTEL $

(076-36-2058; Puga 669; s/d/tr S30/50/70; 📶) Set right on the plaza, this budget traveler's favorite is located in a rambling old colonial mansion that has two interior courtyards. The 10 good-value private rooms are fairly basic, although they have been colorfully decorated with kitschy objects. The rooms have cable TV as well as 24-hour hot water.

Casa Mirita HOMESTAY $

(076-36-9361; www.casa-mirita.blogspot.com; Cáceres 1337; s without bathroom S20, r S30; @ 📶) This simple homestay is a *mototaxi* (three-wheeled motorcycle rickshaw taxi) ride (S3)

Cajamarca

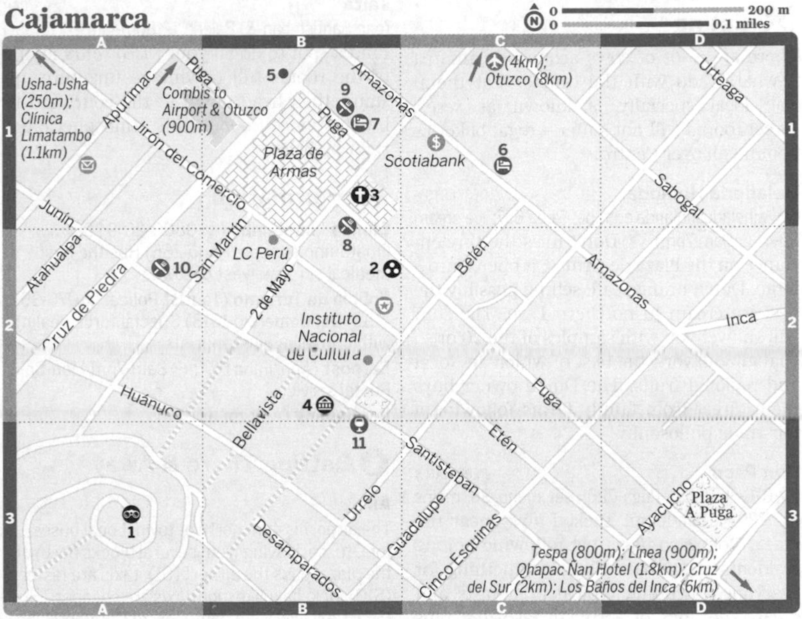

0 200 m
0 0.1 miles

A B C D
1 2 3
Usha-Usha (250m); Clínica Limatambo (1.1km)
Combis to Airport & Otuzco (900m)
✈(4km); Otuzco (8km)
Apurimac
Puga
Amazonas
Urteaga
Jirón del Comercio
Plaza de Armas
Scotiabank
Sabogal
Junín
Atahualpa
San Martin
LC Perú
Belén
Amazonas
Cruz de Piedra
2 de Mayo
Instituto Nacional de Cultura
Inca
Huánuco
Bellavista
Puga
Etén
Santisteban
Urrelo
Guadalupe
Desamparados
Cinco Esquinas
Ayacucho
Plaza A Puga
Tespa (800m); Linea (900m); Qhapac Ñan Hotel (1.8km); Cruz del Sur (2km); Los Baños del Inca (6km)

Cajamarca

Sights

1 Cerro Santa Apolonia A3
2 El Cuarto del Rescate B2
3 Iglesia de San Francisco B1
4 Museo de Arqueológico & Etnografía B2

Activities, Courses & Tours

5 Clarín Tours B1
Mega Tours .... (see 7)

Sleeping

6 Hospedaje Los Jazmines C1
7 Hostal Plaza B1

Eating

8 Don Paco B1
9 Heladería Holanda B1
10 Sanguchon.com A2

Drinking & Nightlife

11 Taita B3

to a residential neighborhood southeast of the center. It's an interesting choice for long-term stayers or those looking to be off the gringo grid. Two sisters, Mirita, the cook, and Vicki, a tourism official, run the show. Rooms are rustic and there's a kitchen, or meals cost S10.

Qhapac Ñan Hotel HOTEL **$$**
(☎956-037-357; www.qhapacnanhotel.com; Nogales, Villa Universitaria; s/d S120/170) Convenient to the bus offices, this new hotel in a residential neighborhood offers very comfortable modern rooms with firm beds, well-equipped bathrooms and fast internet. Service is very efficient and there is an on-site restaurant.

Eating

There are a lot of cows around Cajamarca – what to do with the brains? Eat them! The local specialty is known as *sesos*. Sweet tooths will not suffer – regal bakeries abound all over Centro.

Heladería Holanda DESSERTS **$**
(www.heladosholanda.com.pe; Puga 657; ice cream S2-4; ⏲9am-7pm) Don't miss the tiny entrance on the Plaza de Armas; it opens into a large, Dutch-orange cafe selling possibly the best ice cream in northern Peru. The staff will shower you with samples of the 20 or so changing flavors, the best of which are local and regional fruits. The Dutch owner buys them direct from family farms following a fair-trade philosophy.

Don Paco PERUVIAN **$**
(☎076-36-2655; Puga 726; set menu S8, mains S12-22; ⏲11am-10pm) Tucked away near the plaza, Don Paco has a big following among residents and expats. There's something for everyone, including typical breakfasts and great renditions of Peruvian favorites, plus more sophisticated *novocajamarquino* (new Cajamarcan) fare such as chicken cordon bleu with Andean ham and local cheese in a pomegranate sauce, and the recommended duck breast with *sauco* (elderberry) sauce.

Sanguchon.com FAST FOOD **$**
(www.sanguchon.com.pe; Junín 1137; sandwiches from S8.50-12; ⏲6pm-midnight; 📶) This wildly popular, hipster hamburger and sandwich joint features an extensive menu of hand-held drunken eats. It has 16 varieties of burgers and another half-dozen sauces – the combinations are staggering. The tasty food is very convenient, as it's a rowdy bar as well.

Drinking & Entertainment

The best bars congregate around the corner of Puga and Gálvez.

★**Usha-Usha** BAR
(Puga 142; admission S5; ⏲9pm-late) For an intimate local experience, head to this hole-in-the-wall dive bar run by an eccentric local musician Jaime Valera, who has managed to cultivate a heap of charisma in such a small space. He sings his heart out with his musician friends and you walk out with an unforgettable travel memory.

Taita BAR
(cnr Santisteban & Belén; ⏲8pm-late Fri & Sat) Find a spot to down your *pisco sours* in one of the rooms full of vintage furniture upstairs, then head down to the courtyard to hit the dance floor in this atmospheric bar right by Belén.

Information

Clínica Limatambo (☎0800-20-900; www.limatambo.com.pe; Puno 265) Has the best medical service; west of town.

Policía de Turismo (Tourist Police; ☎076-36-4515; Del Comercio 1013) Special force dealing with crimes against tourists.

Serpost (Apurimac 624; ⏲8am-7pm Mon-Sat) Postal service.

Scotiabank (Amazonas 750)

Getting There & Away

AIR

The airport is 4km north of town. Local buses for Otuzco, leaving from several blocks north of the plaza, pass the airport (S1); taxis are faster (S10), rickshaw-like *mototaxis* are cheaper (S3). **LAN** (www.lan.com; Centro Commercial El Quinde) and **LC Perú** (☎076-36-3115; www.lcperu.pe; Jirón del Comercio 1024) serve Lima daily.

BUS

Most terminals are between the 2nd and 3rd blocks of Atahualpa, 1.5km southeast of town on the road to Los Baños del Inca.

Many companies have buses to Chiclayo (S20 to S45, six hours), Trujillo (S20 to S40, six hours) and Lima (S80 to S136, 15 hours). **Línea** (☎076-34-0753; Atahualpa 316) and **Tepsa** (☎076-36-3306; Sucre 422) have comfortable Lima-bound buses. Luxury *bus-camas* to Lima go with **Cruz del Sur** (☎076-36-2024; Atahualpa 884).

Línea also has buses to Piura (S45, nine hours) via Chiclayo, where you can continue on to Ecuador.

A few companies go to Celendín (S10, 3½ hours). It's easier to reach Chachapoyas from Chiclayo.

Chachapoyas

041 / POP 28,730

Colonial Chachapoyas seems wildly out of place, both as the unlikely capital of the Amazonas department, and in its location: surrounded by more mountainous terrain than jungle. But 'Chacas' is a bustling market town and an ideal place from which to explore Kuélap – the awesome ruins left behind by the fierce cloud-forest-dwelling civilization that ruled here from AD 800 until the Incas came in the 1470s – and the surrounding waterfalls and trekking routes.

Activities

The dry season (May to September) is best for hiking, including the five-day **Gran Vilaya** trek to the Valle de Belén or a three-day trip to **Laguna de los Cóndores** on foot and horseback.

Tours

Day tours from Chacas focus on Kuélap. Travel agencies hover around the plaza.

Turismo Explorer GUIDED TOUR
(041-47-8162; www.turismoexplorerperu.com; Grau 549) This company has a great reputation among travelers and offers short trips and multiday treks. It has professional guides who speak excellent English.

Sleeping

★**Chachapoyas Backpackers** HOSTEL $
(041-47-8879; www.chachapoyasbackpackers.com; Calle 2 de Mayo 639; d/tr S60/90, dm/s/d with shared bathroom S18/30/42; @) Offering cheap, clean rooms with kitchen access in a central location, this new hostel run by an amiable local couple is already a favorite with budget travelers. Owner and former guide José is extremely helpful and knowledgeable about the region. He can organize tours through his agency or provide detailed explanations if you want to go it alone.

Hostal Las Orquídeas GUESTHOUSE $$
(041-47-8271; www.hostallasorquideas.com; Ayacucho 1231; s/d/t incl breakfast S80/110/120; @) This upscale guesthouse offers tile-floor rooms that are bright and open and the public area is decorated with cheerful colors and some wood and artsy accents. Some rooms are more appealing than others; the renovated rooms at the front of the building offer carpeted walls and granite-slab bathrooms, although the TVs are still old-school.

Eating & Drinking

Look for *juanes* (*bijao*-leaf-steamed fish, beef or chicken with olives), made locally with *yuca* (manioc tuber) instead of rice.

El Tejado PERUVIAN $
(Santo Domingo 426; mains S15-25; noon-4pm) This charming little spot doesn't look much from the outside, but a lovely interior courtyard and dining room awaits. It's a great lunch spot, with *menús* (set meals) for S8 Monday to Friday. The specialty is *tacu-tacu* (a Peruvian fusion dish of rice, beans and a protein), seen here in nine varieties.

Café Fusiones CAFE, BREAKFAST $
(www.cafefusiones.com; Ayacucho, Plaza de Armas; breakfast S8-11, light meals S4-15; 7am-1pm & 2-9:30pm;) The traveler congregation gathers at this artsy cafe on the plaza that serves organic coffee and espresso, good breakfasts (including regional choices such as *juanes*), lentil burgers and other light meals. There is also a book exchange, travel agency and fair-trade shop selling regional products.

Terra Mia Café BREAKFAST, PERUVIAN $
(Chincha Alta 557; breakfast S12.50-13.50; 7am-10:30pm;) A chic spot with the fanciest espresso machine in town. Its wonderful menu has regional and international breakfasts (ahem...waffles!), plus sandwiches and salads all served up in a cozy and clean atmosphere with colonial archways and indigenous-motif seat cushions. Service could be a lot better though.

Dulcería Santa Elena DESSERTS $
(Amazonas 800-804; cakes S2-5; 8am-9pm) The crotchety old man here serves the town's best pastries and cakes; if he likes you, though, he might throw something in for free.

★**La Reina** BAR
(Ayacucho 520; 9am-1pm & 3pm-1am Mon-Sat, 7pm-midnight Sun) An artsy spot to lubricate your mind very cheaply on exotic fruit and

Amazonian liqueurs by the shot (S1.50) or the jar (from S18). There are 11 flavors to choose from, including *mora* (blackberry), the most popular; *maracuyá* (passion fruit), the best; and seven *raíces* and *chuchuhuasi,* two notorious Amazonian aphrodisiacs.

ℹ Information

Most of the following are on the Plaza de Armas, plus internet cafes and several shops changing dollars.

BCP (Plaza Burgos) Changes US dollars and has an ATM.

iPerú (☎041-47-7292; iperuchachapoyas@promperu.gob.pe; Ortiz Arrieta 582; ⏲9am-6pm Mon-Sat, to 1pm Sun) has excellent maps, transportation information and recommendations.

Serpost (Salamanca 940; ⏲8am-1pm & 2-7pm Mon-Fri, 8am-1pm Sat) Postal services; in the market district.

ℹ Getting There & Away

Buses to Chiclayo (S30 to S55, nine hours) and on to Lima (S80 to S135, 22 hours) take a route that is paved beyond Pedro Ruíz. Companies include **Civa** (☎041-47-8048; cnr Ortiz Arrieta y Salamanca) and comfortable **Móvil Tours** (☎041-47-8545; Libertad 464).

Getting directly to Kuélap independently is a bit of a pain and requires an early rise. **Transportes Roller** (☎94-174-6658; Terminal Terrestre) has one 4am bus that goes to Tingo Viejo, María and on to La Marca, where you'll find the ticket booth and parking lot for Kuélep, returning at 6am. It's a 15-minute walk along a stone sidewalk to the ruins from there. Otherwise, frequent minibuses and *colectivo* taxis for Tingo Viejo and María depart from the 300 block of Grau, from where you'll need to leg an additional two hours (from María) or five to six hours (from Tingo Viejo).

There are frequent *colectivos* for Tingo Viejo (S8, 45 minutes), which may continue to María (S15, 2½ hours). *Colectivos* also go to Pedro Ruíz (S5, 45 minutes), where eastbound buses to Tarapoto stop.

A taxi for the day to Kuélap or to sites around Chachapoyas and Leimebamba costs S150.

Kuélap

Matched in grandeur only by the ruins of Machu Picchu, this fabulous, ruined **citadel city** (adult/child S15/2; ⏲8am-5pm) in the mountains southwest of Chachapoyas is the best preserved and most dramatic of the district's extraordinary archaeological sites. This monumental stone-fortified citadel crowns a craggy limestone mountain and affords exceptional panoramas of a land once inhabited by the Chachapoya. The site receives remarkably few visitors, although that might change with the construction of a proposed cable car. Those who make it here get to witness one of the most significant and impressive pre-Columbian ruins in all of South America.

🛏 Sleeping

Kuélap itself has limited sleeping options, although there are a couple of basic *hospedajes* in family homes down an often muddy trail from the ruins. Ask for Doña Teodula or Doña Juana – both hosts offer basic rooms with cold showers, and budget meals can be arranged. Bringing your own sleeping bag is recommended.

The next closest sleeping choices and a step up in quality are in the hamlet of María, a two-hour walk from Kuélap and connected to Chachapoyas by daily minibuses. Here you will find a cottage industry of half a dozen charming and near-identical *hospedajes* (rooms per person S15) – they all go to the same sign-maker for their signs. All offer clean, modest rooms with electric hot water and some will cook hearty meals for guests for about S10.

Tarapoto

☎042 / POP 73,015

A muggy and lethargic rainforest metropolis, Tarapoto balances precariously between the tropical Amazon Basin and weathered Andean foothills. If it weren't for the lengthy umbilical cord that is the long, paved road back to the rest of Peru, it would sit as isolated – and nearly as manic – as Iquitos. From here you can take the plunge deeper into the Amazon, or just enjoy the easily accessible jungle lite.

Tours

Martín Zamora Tours GUIDED TOURS

(☎042-52-5148; www.martinzamoratarapoto.com; Grau 233; ⏲8am-1pm & 4-7:30pm) Tarapoto's go-to operator for day tours, cultural trips, and longer excursions to local lakes and waterfalls.

Sleeping

El Mirador GUESTHOUSE $
(042-52-2177; www.elmiradortarapoto.com; San Pablo de la Cruz 517; s/d incl breakfast S60/80, with air-con S100/150;) Travelers swoon over this budget spot, probably because of the welcoming family vibe; or perhaps it's the excellent breakfast served on the terrace with hammocks and jungle views? Rooms in the main house are nothing beyond basic, with fans, hot showers and cable TV; whereas those in the new annex are more spacious with air-con and bright yellow bathrooms.

La Posada Inn GUESTHOUSE $
(042-52-2234; laposada_inn@latinmail.com; San Martín 146; s/d incl breakfast S60/80, with air-con S75/100;) This quaint hotel has beamed ceilings and an inviting wooden staircase. The rooms are a mixed bag: some have balconies, some have air-con. Even though it's right in the town center, La Posada manages to remain quiet.

La Patarashca GUESTHOUSE $$
(042-52-7554; www.lapatarashca.com; De la Cruz 362; s/d incl breakfast S90/140, with air-con S100/190;) This popular guesthouse is tucked away on sprawling grounds flush with jungle-like fauna. It has a good-sized swimming pool, spacious common areas, and two floors of comfortable rooms adorned with nice furniture and crafty lamps that feel homey and welcoming. A few ornery macaws drive home a sense of place, as does the best regional restaurant in town, attached by a walkway.

Eating & Drinking

★ **La Patarashca** PERUVIAN $$
(www.lapatarashca.com; Lamas 261; mains S19-38; noon-11pm;) Outstanding regional Amazon cuisine is on tap at this casual 2nd-floor place. Don't miss the salad of *chonta,* thin strips of local hearts of palm, with avocados doused in vinaigrette; or the namesake *patarashcas,* heaping platters of giant shrimp served in a warm bath of tomatoes, sweet peppers, onions, garlic and *sacha culantro* (cilantro) wrapped in a *bijao* leaf.

Café d' Mundo ITALIAN $$
(Calle de Morey 157; mains S24-35, pizza S16-18; 6pm-midnight) This dark, sexy restaurant-bar is illuminated nightly by moody candlelight. It has outdoor seating and snug indoor lounges. Good pizzas are the mainstay (try the caprese with avocado), but interesting regional lasagnas and pastas adorn the small menu. The full bar will help you pass the rest of the evening. Service plays second fiddle to food and atmosphere.

★ **La Alternativa** BAR
(Grau 401; 9am-1am) Like drinking in a medieval pharmacy or maybe a Tarantino film, a night out here hearkens to a time when alcohol was literally medicine (like, for ailments, not for your emotional problems); and your local apothecary was the place to get sauced on God-knows-what elixir that happened to be inside the bottle.

Stonewasi Taberna BAR
(Lamas 218; noon-3am) Pretenders come and go, but this local institution is still the place to see and be seen in Tarapoto. Recycled sewing tables street side are chock-full of punters, *mototaxi* drivers and the town's bold and beautiful thronging to a theme of international rock and house music.

Information

BCP (Maynas 130) Has several ATMs.

Clínica San Martín (San Martín 274; 24hr) The best medical care in town.

Tourist Information Office (042-52-6188; Hurtado s/n; 7:30am-11pm) The municipal tourist office on Plaza Mayor. Local police keep it open when tourism officials go home.

Getting There & Around

The **airport** (TPP; 042-53-1165) is 3km southwest of the center. **LAN** (042-52-9318; www.lan.com; Hurtado 183) has daily flights to/from Lima. **Star Perú** (042-52-8765; San Pablo de la Cruz 100; 9am-7pm Mon-Fri, to 5pm Sat, to noon Sun) flies daily to Lima.

All of the following companies can be found along the same block of Salaverry in the Morales district, a S2 *mototaxi* ride from the town center. If you're heading to Chachapoyas, you'll need to change in Pedro Ruíz.

A short *mototaxi* ride around town costs S2; to the bus terminal/airport costs S3/5.

DESTINATION	COST (S)	DURATION (HR)
Chiclayo	50-80	14
Lima	90-165	26-30
Pedro Ruíz	40-45	7
Piura	60	16-17
Pucallpa	100	16-18
Tingo María	80	13
Trujillo	65-150	15-18
Yurimaguas	15-20	2½

Civa (☎042-52-2269; www.civa.com.pe; Salaverry 840) Has a comfortable 3:10pm bus to Lima, stopping at Chiclayo and Trujillo.

Movil Tours (☎042-52-9193; www.moviltours.com.pe; Salaverry 880) Top-end express buses to Lima leave at 8am and 1pm, with a 3pm departure to Trujillo and a 4pm bus to Chiclayo.

Transmar Express (☎042-53-2392; Amoraca 117) Departs at 10am on Monday, Wednesday and Friday for the ride to Pucallpa via Juanjuí, Tocache Nuevo and Tingo María. Also has cheap buses to Lima.

AMAZON BASIN

Thick with primary and secondary jungle, Peru's Amazon Basin is dense and dizzying, an exotic and isolated frontier zone that spills out from all sides with exhilarating jungle-adventure opportunities. Iquitos, the area's largest city, is the gateway to once-in-a-lifetime excursions down the Amazon River but also holds interest for its solitary, end-of-the-road atmosphere (even though the road ended in Yurimaguas). Pucallpa and Yurimaguas offer slow boats that ply the waterways to Iquitos, accessible otherwise only by air. The country's largest reserve, the bigger-than-New-Jersey Reserva Nacional Pacaya-Samiria, is also here, home to pink dolphins and 449 bird species.

Further south, the Unesco-declared Parque Nacional Manu is considered one of the world's most pristinely preserved thatches of Tarzan terrain and one of South America's best spots to see tropical wildlife. Around Puerto Maldonado, jungle lodges beckon along the Madre de Dios and Tambopata rivers (the latter is in the Reserva Nacional Tambopata) – two more of Peru's most unspoiled settings for wildlife and jungle adventure.

Puerto Maldonado

☎082 / POP 56,000

Diesel-fumed Puerto Maldonado, capital of the Madre de Dios region, is the ramshackle epicenter of Peru's southern Amazon. Were it not the gateway to one of South America's finest jungles, it might be forgotten. The completion of the controversial Interoceánica Hwy, which now links the Atlantic and Pacific, reroutes massive commerce through here (and foretells the expedited extraction of natural resources). For most travelers, the city is a launching pad to a wild and exotic Amazon adventure.

Tours

If you haven't prearranged a river and jungle tour, there are several local guides, some quite reputable and experienced, others just interested in making quick money. Shop around, never pay for a tour beforehand and, when you agree on a price, make sure it includes the return trip! Officially licensed guides charge around S75 to S175 per person per day (excluding park fees), depending on the destination and number of people. Boat rides, which are usually needed to get out of Puerto Maldonado, are notoriously expensive.

Rainforest Expeditions TOURS
(☎082-57-2575; www.perunature.com; Av Aeropuerto, Km 6, CPM La Joya) Coordinates various area lodges and has reputable rainforest tours and budget-oriented Tambopata homestays (from US$24).

Sleeping

Watch out for overcharging. Outside town are some jungle lodges.

★**Tambopata Hostel** HOSTEL $
(☎082-57-4201; www.tambopatahostel.com; Av 26 de Diciembre 234; dm S30, s with/without bathroom S50/40, d with/without bathroom S80/70; P) Puerto Maldonado finally has the backpacker accommodations it desperately needed. This clean, relaxing hostel has a mix of dorm and private rooms abutting a garden courtyard with hammocks, and a nice breakfast is included in the price. You can even brush up on your Peruvian street talk courtesy of the board in the common room.

Hospedaje Royal Inn GUESTHOUSE $
(☎082-57-3464; Av 2 de Mayo 333; s/d with fan S35/50, d with air-con S80;) A good choice for travelers, sporting lots of large, clean rooms with fans. The courtyard has seen better days, but still, get a room here as street-facing digs are noisy. Cable TV comes with each room.

★**Anaconda Lodge** LODGE $$
(☎082-79-2726; www.anacondajunglelodge.com; Av Aeropuerto Km 6; s with/without bathroom S100/S50, d with/without bathroom S160/S80, tr S220; P) The most original airport hotel in South America? Cocooned in its own tropical garden on the edge of town,

this lodge has a more remote feel than its location would suggest. There are eight double-room bungalows with shared bathroom and four luxury bungalows with private facilities; all are mosquito netted.

Eating

Regional specialties include *chilcano* (fish-chunk soup flavored with cilantro) and *parrillada de la selva* (marinated-meat barbecue in an *ají* – chili – and Brazil-nut sauce).

Los Gustitos del Cura DESSERTS $
(Loreto 258; snacks S3-8; ⏲8am-10pm) For a sweet treat or the best ice cream in town, drop in to this French-owned patisserie with a pleasant courtyard at the rear. Sandwiches, cakes and drinks are dished up, and local objets d'art are on sale.

★**Burgos's Restaurante** PERUVIAN $$
(cnr Av 26 de Diciembre & Loreto; mains S15-25; ⏲11am-4pm, 5pm-midnight) This has quickly developed into Puerto Maldonado's standout restaurant. It calls itself an exponent of Novo Amazonica cuisine – that's like Novo Andino, only making those bold culinary adaptations to jungle dishes – but this is still more about dependable Peruvian Amazon staples, cooked to perfection rather than with particular innovation.

El Catamaran CEVICHE $$
(Jirón 26 de Deciembre 241; mains S20-30; ⏲7:30am-3pm) Gravitate to this quiet place to feast on great freshwater *ceviche* (raw seafood marinated in lime juice), along with the contingent of local dignitaries: there's a nice decked seating area out back with river views.

Drinking & Nightlife

The best-known nightclub is **Discoteca Witite** (Velarde 151; ⏲9pm-late Fri & Sat). **Tsaica** (Loreto 329) is a lively watering hole.

Puerto Maldonado

Sleeping
1 Hospedaje Royal Inn B2
2 Tambopata Hostel C2

Eating
3 Burgos's Restaurante D2
4 El Catamaran C2
5 Los Gustitos del Cura C2

Drinking & Nightlife
6 Discoteca Witite C1
7 Tsaica C1

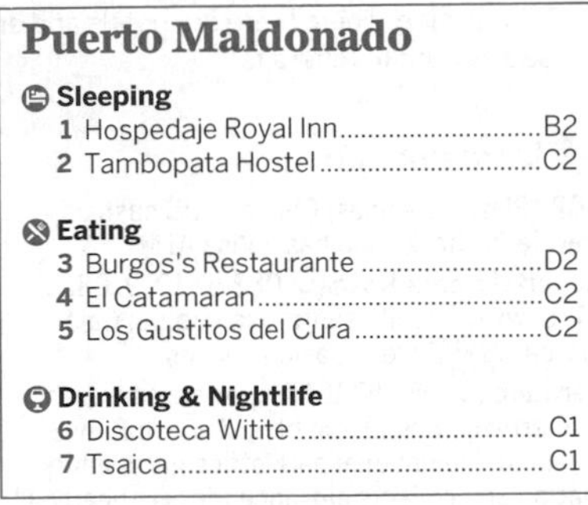

Puerto Maldonado

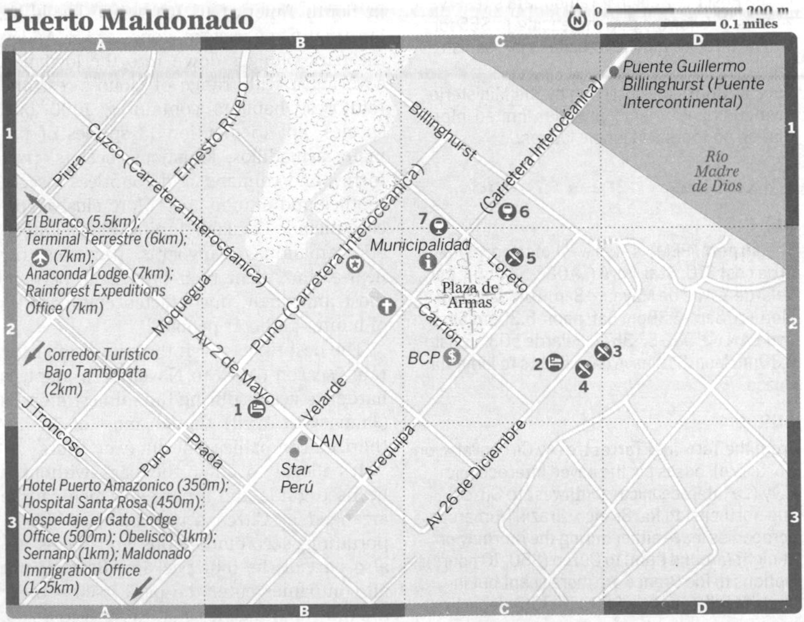

GETTING TO BRAZIL & BOLIVIA

The paved Interoceánica goes from Puerto Maldonado to Iñapari on the Brazilian border. *Colectivos* to Iñapari (S30, three hours) leave when they have four passengers. Iberia, 170km north of Puerto Maldonado, and Iñapari, 70km beyond Iberia, have a couple of basic hotels. At Iñapari, where Peruvian exit formalities are conducted, cross the bridge to Assis, Brazil, which has better hotels and a paved road via Brasiléia to Rio Branco. US, Australian and Canadian citizens need to get a Brazilian visa in advance.

From Puerto Maldonado, boats can be hired for the half-day trip to the Bolivian border at Puerto Pardo for about S340. Cheaper passages are available on infrequent cargo boats. Make sure to get exit stamps before leaving Peru at Puerto Maldonado's **immigration office** (082-57-1069; Av 15 de Agosto 658; 8am-1pm & 2:30-4pm Mon-Fri). From Puerto Heath, a few minutes away from Puerto Pardo by boat, it takes several days (even weeks) to arrange a boat (expensive) to Riberalta, which has road and air connections. Travel in a group to share costs, and avoid months when the water is too low. Another option is to go to Brasiléia and cross the Río Acre by ferry or bridge to Cobija, on the Bolivian side, where there are hotels and erratic flights. There's also a dry-season gravel road onward to Riberalta.

Information

BCP (Plaza de Armas) Changes US cash or traveler's checks and has a Visa ATM.

Hospital Santa Rosa (082-57-1019, 082-57-1046; www.hospitalsantarosa.gob.pe; Cajamarca 171) Provides basic services.

Sernanp (082-57-1247; www.sernanp.gob.pe/sernanp; Cajamarca btwn Ancash & Av 28 de Julio) The national park office gives information and collects entrance fees (in nearly all cases, guides sort this out); standard entrance to the Reserva Nacional Tambopata's reserve zone is S30 for the day, increasing to S65 for two or three days. The website is in Spanish only.

Tourist Booth (airport) Run by the Ministerio de Industria y Turismo; provides limited information on tours and jungle lodges.

Getting There & Around

AIR

The **airport** (PEM) is 7km west of town; *mototaxis* cost S10. **Star Perú** (082-57-3564; cnr Velarde & Av 2 de Mayo; 8am-1pm & 4-8pm Mon-Fri, 8am-6:30pm Sat, noon-6:30pm Sun) and **LAN** (082-57-3677; Velarde 503; 8am-6:30pm Mon-Sat) have daily flights to Lima via Cuzco.

BUS

From the **Terminal Terrestre** (Av Circunvalación Norte s/n), buses ply the paved Interoceanic Hwy (La Interoceánica) southwest to Cuzco and northeast to Rio Branco, Brazil. Numerous companies leave either during the morning or at night (around 8pm) to Cuzco (S50, 10 hours). Options to Rio Branco are more scant but include **Móvil Tours** (989-176-306) departing Tuesday and Friday at 12:30pm. It's advisable to buy your ticket as much in advance of travel as possible.

Parque Nacional Manu

Covering almost 20,000 sq km, **Parque Nacional Manu** (entry S150) is widely regarded as the most pristine and best-preserved thatch of jungle in the world. This Unesco Natural Heritage Site is one of the best spots in South America to see tropical wildlife. Starting in the eastern slopes of the Andes, the park plunges down into the lowlands, covering a wide range of cloud-forest and rainforest habitats containing 1000 bird species, not to mention 13 species of primate, armadillos, kinkajous, ocelots, river turtles and caimans, and countless insects, reptiles and amphibians. More elusive species include jaguars, tapirs, giant anteaters, tamanduas, capybaras, peccaries, the near-extinct giant river otter, and, perhaps most amazingly, uncontacted communities of hunter-gatherer peoples!

The best time to visit the park is after the rainy season (April to November). Manu is harder to access during the rainiest months (January to April), though most of the authorized companies still run (wet) tours.

It's illegal to enter the park without a licensed guide and a permit, which can be arranged at Cuzco travel agencies. Transportation, accommodations and meals are also part of the tour package. Beware: not all companies enter the park itself – there are only eight agencies authorized to do so.

Others offer cheaper 'Manu tours' that cover areas outside the park, but these still boast good wildlife-watching.

Costs depend on whether you arrive and depart overland or by air, but they range from S340 to S1010 per day for four- to nine-day itineraries, ranging from overland trips to all-inclusive with flights. Book well in advance, but be flexible with your travel plans, as tours can often return a day late. Camping is only permitted in the multiuse zone (not the reserve).

It is possible for independent travelers to reach the reserve's environs without taking a tour, but it is time-consuming and somewhat dangerous. If you're determined to go solo, buses leave from Cuzco via Pilcopata to Shintuya (three hours past Pilcolpata). From Pilcolpata on, it's possible to switch to sporadic river transport. On the road, breakdowns, extreme overcrowding and delays are common, and during the rainy season (even during the dry) vehicles slide off the road. It's safer, more comfortable and more reliable to take the costlier tourist buses offered by Cuzco tour operators.

The boat journey down the Alto Madre de Dios to the Río Manu takes almost a day. A few minutes from the village of Boca Manu is an airstrip, often the starting or exit point for commercial trips into the park, where entry is paid.

Despite its preservation and world-class setting, the park sees few visitors per year, and is under a threefold threat from narcotraffickers, illegal timber exploitation and illegal gold panning.

Pucallpa

061 / POP 205,000

A trip to tumbledown Pucallpa, capital of the Ucayali department, is like a visit with the in-laws: it ain't fun, but you gotta do it. However, it is pleasant to land in the tropics after the long bus ride down from the chilly Andes, and the view of the torrential Río Ucayali tearing through town from the relatively nice *malecón* (waterfront) is an impressive sight. Travelers come here in search of the riverboats combing the first navigable Amazon tributary to Iquitos or to visit indigenous communities near Yarinacocha.

Activities

Most activities revolve around the lovely oxbow lake of **Yarinacocha**, 10km northwest of Pucallpa. You can go canoeing, watch wildlife, and visit matriarchal Shipibo communities and local shamans. Most boat tours can be arranged at the waterfront itself. *Peki-peki* boats with drivers cost about S20 per hour.

Sleeping

Hospedaje Komby GUESTHOUSE **$$**
(061-59-2074, 061-57-1562; www.elkombypucallpa.com; Ucayali 360; s S65-80, d S85-130;) In a quandary about whether to aim for budget or luxury? Komby has rooms that veer between the two brackets. Accommodations overall are clean but basic, brightened by the small pool. Higher tariffs are for rooms with air-con.

Getting There & Away

AIR

Pucallpa's airport is 5km northwest of town. Taxis/*mototaxis* charge S15/7 for the trip. Currently scheduled flights are to Lima with **LAN** (Tarapacá 805) and **Star Perú** (061-59-0585; 7 de Junio 865). The latter flies direct to Iquitos as well.

BOAT

During high water (January to April), boats depart from next to Parque San Martín. As water levels drop, the port creeps northeast to several places along the banks, including **Puerto Henry** (Manco Capác s/n) and beyond, eventually ending up 3km northeast of Centro.

Crowded boats to Iquitos (S80 to S100) take three to five days. Passengers can sleep aboard in hammocks, which are sold in the market on 9 de Diciembre, or in prison-like cabins, and basic meals are provided. In the past, travelers have used Tingo María as a breaking point on this journey, but think twice: it's well regarded around Peru as a jungle no-man's land, and readers have reported armed robberies and even rape. Single travelers must spring for cabins to ensure the safety of their belongings. Bring a lock.

It's worth noting that this trip is easier and more organized from Iquitos to Pucallpa than the reverse.

BUS

Several companies go to Lima (S70 to S90, 18 to 20 hours) via Tingo María, Huánuco, Cerro de Pasco and Junín, though armed robberies have happened on this route. **León de Huánuco** (061-57-5049; Tacna 765) serves Lima at 8:30am, 1pm *(bus-cama)* and 5:30pm. Another good company is **Turismo Central** (061-60-

0122), which has one morning departure and two afternoon departures.

Getting Around

Mototaxis to the airport or Yarinacocha are about S7; taxis are S10.

Iquitos

065 / POP 472,000

Linked to the outside world by air and by river, Iquitos is the world's largest city that cannot be reached by road. It's a prosperous, vibrant place teeming with the usual, inexplicably addictive Amazonian anomalies. The city is well known for many things one might expect from a jungle metropolis, not least of which are its steamy humidity, sexy population and gaggle of expat characters with entertaining – if not questionable – back stories.

Iquitos is your launching pad for trips along the famed Amazon River, but don't discount a few days in town, taking in the vibe in this manic jungle Sodom.

Sights & Activities

Casa de Fierro HISTORIC BUILDING
(Iron House; cnr Putumayo & Raymondi) Every guidebook mentions the 'majestic' Casa de

Iquitos

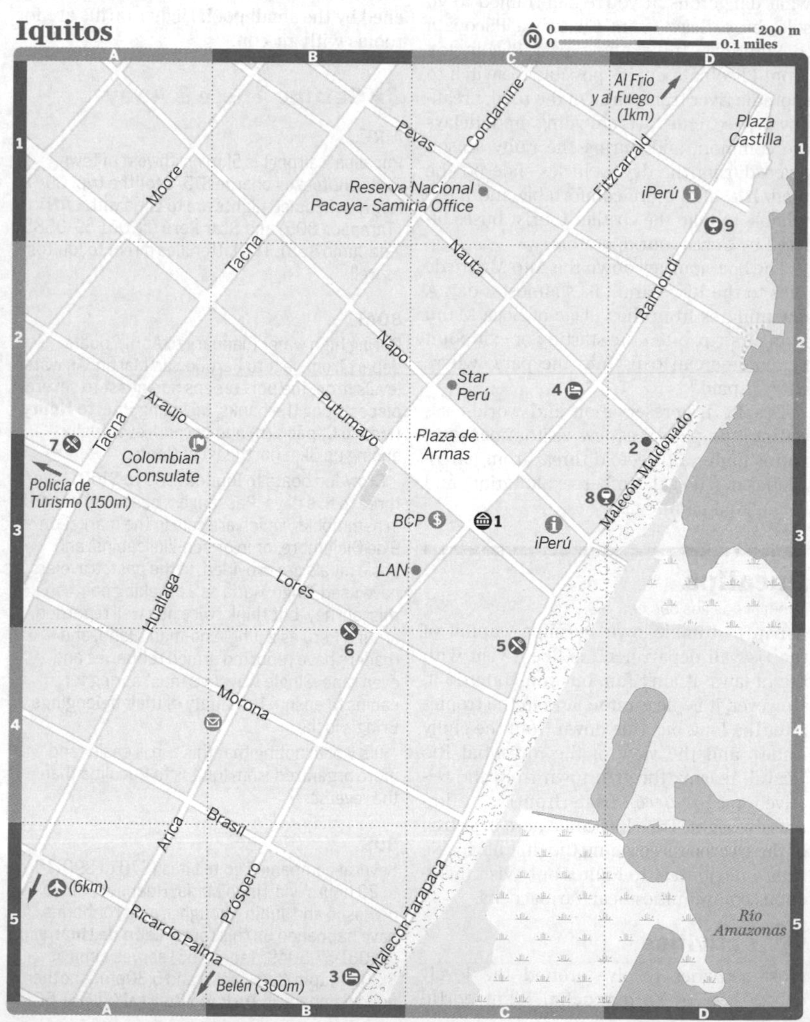

Fierro (Iron House), designed by Gustave Eiffel (of Eiffel Tower fame). It was made in Paris in 1860 and imported piece by piece into Iquitos around 1890, during the opulent rubber-boom days, to beautify the city. It's the only survivor of three different iron houses originally imported here. It resembles a bunch of scrap-metal sheets bolted together, was once the location of the Iquitos Club and is now, in humbler times, a general store.

★Belén NEIGHBOURHOOD

At the southeast end of town is the floating shantytown of Belén, consisting of scores of huts built on rafts, which rise and fall with the river. During the low-water months, these rafts sit on the river mud and are dirty and unhealthy, but for most of the year they float on the river – a colorful and exotic sight. Seven thousand people live here, and canoes float from hut to hut selling and trading jungle produce.

Pilpintuwasi Butterfly Farm WILDLIFE RESERVE

(☎065-23-2665; www.amazonanimalorphanage.org; Padre Cocha; adult/student S15/9; ⏱9am-4pm Tue-Sun) A visit to the fascinating Pilpintuwasi Butterfly Farm is highly recommended. Ostensibly this is a conservation and breeding center for Amazonian butterflies. Butterflies aplenty there certainly are, including the striking blue morpho *(Morpho menelaus)* and the fearsome-looking owl butterfly *(Caligo eurilochus)*. But it's the farm's exotic animals that steal the show. Raised as orphans and protected within the property are several mischievous monkeys, a tapir, an anteater and Pedro Bello, a majestic jaguar.

Amazon Golf Club GOLF

(☎065-22-3730; www.amazongolfcourse.com; Quistacocha; per day incl golf-club rental S75; ⏱6am-6pm) Amazing as it may seem, you can play a round or two on the nine holes of the only course in the entire Amazon. Founded in 2004 by a bunch of nostalgic expats, the 2140m course was built on bush land around 15km outside Iquitos and boasts, apart from its nine greens, a wooden clubhouse with a bar. Hole 4 is a beauty: you tee onto an island surrounded by piranha-infested waters. Don't go fishing for lost balls!

Tours

★Dawn on the Amazon Tours & Cruises CRUISE

(☎065-22-3730; www.dawnontheamazon.com; Malecón Maldonado 185; per person day trips incl lunch US$79, multiday cruises per day from US$150) This small outfit offers the best deal for independent travelers. The *Amazon I* is a beautiful 11m wooden craft with modern furnishings, available for either day trips or longer river cruises up to two weeks. Included are a bilingual guide, all meals and transfers. You can travel with host Bill Grimes and his experienced crew along the Amazon, or along its quieter tributaries (larger cruise ships will necessarily stick to the main waterways).

Sleeping

Mosquitoes are rarely a serious problem, so netting isn't provided. All rooms have fans unless otherwise noted.

Flying Dog Hostel HOSTEL $

(☎in Lima 01-445-6745; www.flyingdogperu.com; Malecón Tarapaca, btwn Brasil & Ricardo Palma; dm/s/d/tr incl breakfast S26/75/90/99; @📶) The Flying Dog, part of the same hostel chain you'll find in Lima and Cuzco, is leader of the pack for traditional backpacker digs: clean, bright rooms, hot water and kitchen facilities. The doubles are a tad pricey for what you get but some have private bathrooms.

La Casa Del Francés GUESTHOUSE $

(☎065-23-1447; http://en.lacasadelfrances.com; Raimondi 183; dm/s/d S20/45/60) A secure,

Iquitos

Sights
1 Casa de Fierro C3

Activities, Courses & Tours
2 Dawn on the Amazon Tours & Cruises D3

Sleeping
3 Flying Dog Hostel B5
4 La Casa Del Francés C2

Eating
5 Amazon Bistro C4
Dawn on the Amazon Café .... (see 2)
6 Ivalú B4
7 Mercado Central A3

Drinking & Nightlife
8 Arandú Bar C3
9 Musmuqui D1

hammock-strung courtyard leads back to this decent budget choice. The colonial rooms show the wear and tear of generations of budget-minded backpackers, but they're alright.

Eating

★Belén Mercado MARKET $

(cnr Prospero & Jirón 9 de Diciembre; menús from S5) There are great eats at Iquitos' markets, particularly the Belén *mercado* where a *menú*, including *jugo especial* (jungle juice) costs S5. Look out for specialties including meaty Amazon worms, *ishpa* (simmered sabalo fish intestines and fat) and *sikisapa* (fried leafcutter ants; abdomens are supposedly tastiest) and watch your valuables. Another good market for cheap eats is **Mercado Central** (Lores cuadra 5).

Ivalú PERUVIAN $

(Lores 215; snacks from S3; ⊙8am-early afternoon) One of the most popular local spots for juice and cake and tamales (corn cakes filled with chicken or fish and wrapped in jungle leaves). As for the opening: go earlier, before they sell out!

★Al Frio y al Fuego FUSION $$

(☎965-607-474; www.alfrioyalfuego.com; Embarcadero Av La Marina 138; mains S20-40; ⊙noon-4pm & 7-11pm Tue-Sat, noon-5pm Sun) Take a boat out to this floating foodie paradise in the middle of the mouth of the Río Itaya to sample some of the city's best food. The emphasis is on river fish (such as the delectable *doncella*), but the *parrillas* (grills) are inviting too. The address given is the boat embarkation point.

★Amazon Bistro INTERNATIONAL $$

(Malecón Tarapaca 268; breakfasts S12, mains S20-40; ⊙6am-midnight; 📶) This is laid out with TLC by the Belgian owner with a New York–style breakfast bar (OK, Amazon version thereof) and upper-level mezzanine seating looking down on the main eating area. The cuisine refuses to be pigeon-holed: there's Argentine steaks not to mention the Belgian influence, which creeps across in the crepes, and with the L'escargot and the range of Belgian beers.

Dawn on the Amazon Café INTERNATIONAL $$

(Malecón Maldonado 185; mains S18-32; ⊙7:30am-10pm; 📶) This traveler magnet on the *malecón*, with its tempting row of street-front tables, sports a menu divided up into North American, Peruvian, Spanish and (logically) Chinese. Travel wherever your taste buds desire but bear in mind that the steamed fresh fish is very good. Ingredients are all non-MSG and those on gluten-free diets are catered for.

Drinking

Arandú Bar BAR

(Malecón Maldonado 113; ⊙till late) The liveliest of several thumping *malecón* bars, great for people-watching and always churning out loud rock-and-roll classics.

Musmuqui BAR

(Raimondi 382; ⊙to midnight Sun-Thu, to 3am Fri & Sat) Locally popular lively bar with two floors and an extensive range of aphrodisiac cocktails concocted from wondrous Amazon plants.

Information

DANGERS & ANNOYANCES

Aggressive street touts and many self-styled jungle guides are irritatingly insistent and dishonest. They are working for commissions, and usually for bog-standard establishments. There have been reports of these guides robbing tourists. It is best to make your own decisions by contacting hotels, lodges and tour companies directly. Exercise particular caution around Belén, which is very poor and where petty thieving is quite common. That said, violent crime is almost unknown in Iquitos.

EMERGENCY

Clínica Ana Stahl (☎065-25-2535; www.facebook.com/caas.iquitos; La Marina 285; ⊙24hr) Private clinic 2km north of the center.

Policía de Turismo (☎965-935-932, 065-24-2081; Lores 834)

MONEY

Many banks change traveler's checks, give credit-card advances and have ATMs. Changing Brazilian or Colombian currency is best done at the borders.

BCP (Próspero & Putamayo) Has a secure ATM.

POST

Serpost (Arica 402; ⊙8am-6pm Mon-Fri, to 5pm Sat)

TOURIST INFORMATION

iPerú (☎065-23-6144; Napo 161; ⊙9am-6pm Mon-Sat, to 1pm Sun) There's also a branch at the airport (☎065-26-0251; Main Hall, Francisco Secada Vignetta Airport; ⊙whenever flights are arriving/departing).

Reserva Nacional Pacaya-Samiria Office (☎065-60-7299; Pevas 339; ⏲7am-3pm Mon-Fri)

Getting There & Away

AIR

Iquitos' airport is 6km south of town. Lima is served daily with **LAN** (☎065-23-2421; Próspero 232), and Lima and Pucallpa with **Star Perú** (☎065-23-6208; Napo 260). The latter also flies to Tarapoto. For Panama City, **Copa Airlines** (☎in Panama 1-800-359-2672; www.copaair.com) operates twice-weekly flights.

BOAT

Most cargo boats leave from **Puerto Masusa** (Los Rosales), 2.5km north of the town center. Dry-erase boards at the office (look for 'AquíRadio Masusa' on the left side of Los Rosales just before the port entrance) tell you which boats are leaving when (though departures often change overnight, and boats tend to leave hours or days late). Boats (hammock/cabin S100/180) go to Yurimaguas (upriver, three to six days) and Pucallpa (upriver, four to seven days). Tickets are sold on the boats. Be sure to pop into the port and inspect the boats before committing. *Eduardo 1-6* are considered the most comfortable to Yurimaguas.

The Henry Boats ply the Iquitos–Pucallpa route and have their own more organized **port** (☎965-678-622; Av La Marina s/n; ⏲7am-7pm) on Av La Marina, closer to the center.

If you are traveling these waterways alone, a cabin is almost essential in order to secure your valuables. Without a companion to watch over them, they will be stolen. Bring a lock. Note that these boats are blatantly unfriendly to the fragile Amazon ecosystem: they dump their trash and waste straight into the river, even at port.

Getting Around

Taxis from the airport cost S15, *mototaxis* S8. Buses and trucks for nearby destinations, including the airport, leave from Arica at 9 de Diciembre. *Motocarro* (motorbike rickshaw) rides around town cost S1.50 to S3.

GETTING TO COLOMBIA & BRAZIL

Colombia, Brazil and Peru share a three-way border. Even in the middle of the Amazon, border formalities must be adhered to and officials will refuse passage if your passport, tourist card and visas are not in order. Regulations change, but the riverboat captains know where to go. You can travel between the three countries without formalities, as long as you stay in the tri-border area. However, if you're leaving Peru, get an exit stamp at the Peruvian immigration post in Santa Rosa, on the south side of the river, just before the border (boats stop for this – ask the captain).

From Iquitos, boats to the Peruvian border with Brazil and Colombia leave from **Puerto Masusa**. A few weekly departures make the two day journey (per person S65 to S80). Boats will stop at Pevas (hammock space S40, about 15 hours) and other ports en route. Boats may dock closer to the center if the water is very high (from May to July).

Speedboats to the tri-border leave from tiny Puerto Embarcadero in Iquitos, departing at 6am daily except Monday. Purchase your ticket in advance from speedboat offices on Raimondi near the Plaza Castilla. Standard fares are S170 to Pevas or S200 for the 10- to 12-hour trip to Santa Rosa, on the Peruvian side, including meals.

The biggest town is Leticia (Colombia), which has hotels, restaurants and a hospital. Get your passport stamped at the **immigration office** (⏲8am-noon, 2-5pm) here for official entry into Colombia. Ferries from Santa Rosa (S8) reach Leticia in about 15 minutes. From Leticia there are daily flights to Bogotá. Otherwise, infrequent boats go to Puerto Asis on the Río Putumayo, a trip of up to 12 days. From Puerto Asis, buses go further into Colombia.

Leticia is linked with Tabatinga (Brazil) by road (a short walk or taxi ride). Get your official entry stamp for Brazil from Tabatinga's police station. Tabatinga has an airport with flights to Manaus, Brazil. Boats to Manaus, about four days away, leave from downriver twice weekly. Speedboats leave from Porto Brass, a three-day trip.

For Brazil, nationals of the US, Canada and Australia need to get a Brazilian visa in advance. The visa lasts for 10 years, except for Australians, for whom it's valid for 90 days. For Colombia, a visa is not required for nationals of the US, Canada, Australia, EU or UK for stays of up to 90 days.

For information on making this crossing in the opposite direction, see p621.

Reserva Nacional Pacaya-Samiria

Boats from Yurimaguas to Iquitos usually stop in the remote village of **Lagunas**, which has no money-changing facilities and limited food, but it's a launching pad for visiting the wildlife-rich **Reserva Nacional Pacaya-Samiria** (3-day pass S60), home to Amazon manatees, caimans, river dolphins, turtles, monkeys and abundant birdlife. Avoid visiting during the February to May rainy season. Your experience will largely depend on your guide – try to meet this person beforehand. A highly regarded guide association is **Estypel** (☎065-40-1080; www.estypel.com.pe; Jr Padre Lucero 1345, Lagunas). Tours cost approximately S150 per person per day, including accommodations, food and transportation, but not park entrance fees. Boats from Yurimaguas take 10 to 12 hours and arrive in Lagunas most days. Both towns have basic lodging options.

In Lagunas, make sure you double-check the departure times for your boat at the port and be on alert. If you depend on others to ensure that you're ready to go when the boat departs, you could very well be left behind.

UNDERSTAND PERU

Peru Today

Between the violence of the Conquest, the chaos of the early republic and the succession of dictatorships that swallowed up much of the 20th century, stability has been a rare commodity in Peru. But the first decade of the new millennium has offered uncharacteristic grace. Peru's economy has grown every year since 2003. Foreign investment is up and exports – in agriculture, mining and manufacturing – have been strong. Tourism is also big: the number of foreign travelers doubled between 2003 and 2010.

In 2011 former army officer Ollanta Humala was elected to the presidency. He is the son of a Quechua labor lawyer from Ayacucho, and social inclusion is a theme of his presidency. For starters, he made it a legal requirement for native peoples to be consulted on mining or other extractive activities in their territories.

The good times have resulted in a surge of cultural productivity – much of it revolving around food. Local celebrity chefs and gastronomic festivals highlight one of the most exciting cuisines on the planet. Inspiration has rippled to the arts, with music fusing folk with electronica and a booming contemporary arts scene.

Yet serious challenges remain. Though the poverty rate has plummeted a staggering 23% since 2002, rural poverty remains nearly double the national average.

In addition, Sendero Luminoso (Shining Path), the Maoist guerilla group that took the country to the brink of civil war in the 1980s, has seen a comeback with help from narcotrafficking, occasionally launching attacks on police and high-profile industrial projects in the central Andes.

In mid-2012 the city of Cajamarca was wracked by civil unrest over proposed gold mining in the region, with locals protesting its possible effect on the water supply. And, of course, there is the Amazon, now bisected by the Interoceánica Hwy connecting Peru and Brazil. There is ongoing concern about the impact this engineering marvel is having on one of the world's last great wilderness areas.

History

Early Cultures

The Inca civilization is merely the tip of Peru's archaeological iceberg.

The country's first inhabitants were loose-knit bands of nomadic hunters, fishers and gatherers, living in caves and killing fearsome (now extinct) animals like giant sloths, saber-toothed tigers and mastodons. Domestication of the llama, alpaca and guinea pig began between 7000 and 4000 BC. Various forms of the faithful potato (Peru boasts almost 4000 varieties!) were domesticated around 3000 BC.

Roughly from 1000 to 300 BC, the Early Horizon or Chavín Period evidenced at Chavín de Huántar near Huaraz saw widespread settled communities, plus the interchange of ideas, enhanced skills and cultural complexity, although the Chavín horizon inexplicably disappeared around 300 BC. The next 500 years saw the rise and fall of the Paracas culture south of Lima, which produced some of the most exquisite textiles in the Americas.

Between AD 100 and 700, pottery, metalwork and textiles reached new heights, and the Moche built their massive pyramids near Trujillo and at Sipán near Chiclayo. Around this time, the Nazca sculpted their enigmatic lines in the desert.

From about 600 to 1000 the first Andean expansionist empire emerged, and the influence of the Wari (Huari), from north of Ayacucho, can still be seen throughout most of Peru.

During the next four centuries several states thrived, including the Chimú, who built the city of Chan Chan near Trujillo, and the Chachapoyas, who erected the stone fortress of Kuélap. Several smaller, warlike highland groups lived near Lake Titicaca and left impressive circular funerary towers, including those at Sillustani and Cutimbo.

Inca Empire & Spanish Conquest

For all its glory, Inca pre-eminence only lasted around 100 years. The reign of the first eight Incas spanned the period from the 12th century to the early 15th century, but it was the ninth Inca, Pachacutec, who gave the empire its first bloody taste of conquest. A growing thirst for expansion had led the neighboring highland tribe, the Chankas, to Cuzco's doorstep around 1438, and Viracocha Inca fled in the belief that his small empire was lost. However, his son Pachacutec rallied the Inca army and, in a desperate battle, he famously routed the Chankas.

Buoyed by victory, Pachacutec embarked upon the first wave of Inca expansion, promptly bagging much of the central Andes. Over the next 25 years, the Inca empire grew until it stretched from the present-day border of Ecuador and Colombia to the deserts of northern Chile. During this time scores of fabulous mountaintop citadels were built, including Machu Picchu.

When Europeans came to the New World, epidemics including smallpox swept down from Central America and the Caribbean. In 1527 the 11th Inca, Huayna Capác, died in one such epidemic. He had divided his empire between his two sons – Atahualpa, born of a *quiteña* mother, who took the north, and the pure-blooded native Cuzqueñan Huáscar, who took Cuzco and the south. Civil war eventually ensued, precipitating the slow downfall of the Inca empire.

By 1526, Francisco Pizarro had started heading south from Panama and soon discovered the rich coastal settlements of the Inca empire. After going back to Spain to court money and men for the conquest, he sailed to Ecuador and marched overland toward Peru and the heart of the Inca empire, reaching Cajamarca in 1532, by which time Atahualpa had defeated his half-brother Huáscar.

This meeting was to change the course of South American history. Atahualpa was ambushed by a few dozen armed conquistadors who killed thousands of unarmed indigenous tribespeople in his capture. For his freedom, the Inca offered a ransom of gold and silver from Cuzco, including that stripped from the walls of Qorikancha.

But after imprisoning Atahualpa for months and adding ransom requests, Pizarro had him killed anyway, and marched on Cuzco. Wearing armor and carrying steel swords, the Spanish cavalry was virtually unstoppable. Despite sporadic rebellions, the Inca empire was forced to retreat into the mountains and jungle, and never recovered its glorious prestige or extent.

Colonial Peru

In 1535 Pizarro founded the capital of Lima. Decades of turmoil ensued, with Peruvians resisting their conquerors, who were fighting among themselves for control of the rich colony. Pizarro was assassinated in 1541 by the son of conquistador Diego de Almagro, whom Pizarro had put to death in 1538. Manco Inca nearly regained control of the highlands in 1536 but by 1539 had retreated to his rainforest hideout at Vilcabamba, where he was killed in 1544. Inca Túpac Amaru also attempted to overthrow the Spaniards in 1572 but was defeated and executed.

For the next two centuries Lima was the major political, social and commercial center of Andean nations, while Cuzco became a backwater. The *encomienda* system, whereby settlers were granted land and native slaves, exploited natives. This system eventually spurred the 1780 uprising under the self-proclaimed ruler Inca Túpac Amaru II. The rebellion was crushed and its leaders cruelly executed.

Independence

By the early 1800s, rebellion was stirring. Colonists resisted high taxes imposed by

Spain, and hoped to take control of the country's rich mineral deposits, beginning with prime guano (seabird droppings) used for fertilizer.

Change came from two directions. After liberating Argentina and Chile from Spain, José de San Martín entered Lima and formally proclaimed Peru's independence in 1821. Meanwhile Simón Bolívar had freed Venezuela, Colombia and Ecuador. San Martín and Bolívar met in Ecuador and Bolívar continued into Peru. Two decisive battles were fought at Junín and Ayacucho in 1824, and the Spanish finally surrendered in 1826.

Peru also won a brief war with Spain in 1866 and lost a longer war with Chile (1879–83) over the nitrate-rich northern Atacama Desert. Chile annexed much of coastal southern Peru but returned some areas in 1929. A little over a decade later, Peru went to war with Ecuador over another border dispute. A 1942 treaty gave Peru the area north of the Río Marañón, but Ecuador disputed this and skirmishes occurred every few years. It wasn't until 1998 that a peace treaty finally put an end to the hostilities.

Modern Times

Despite periods of civilian rule, coups and military dictatorships characterized Peru's government during most of the 20th century.

In the late 1980s the country experienced severe social unrest. Demonstrations protesting the disastrous handling of the economy by President Alan García Pérez were an everyday occurrence – at one point, inflation reached 10,000%! His first term was shadowed by the disruptive activities of Maoist terrorist organization Sendero Luminoso, which waged a guerrilla war resulting in the death or disappearance of at least 40,000 people, mostly in the central Andes.

In 1990 Alberto Fujimori, the son of Japanese immigrants, was elected president. Strong, semidictatorial actions led to unprecedented improvements in the economy. Popular support propelled Fujimori to a second term in 1995 (after he amended the constitution expressly so he could run again), but that support was dwindling by 1998. In September 2000 a video was released showing Fujimori's head of intelligence bribing a congressman, causing Fujimori's 10-year presidency to spiral out of control. Amid the scandal and human-rights abuse accusations, Fujimori resigned during a state trip to Asia and hid in Japan, which refused Peru's repeated extradition requests. In 2005 he was arrested while on a trip to Chile, and extradited to Peru in 2007, when he was initially tried and convicted for ordering an illegal search and sentenced to six years in prison. In 2009 Fujimori was sentenced to an additional 25 years for crimes against humanity. He was found guilty of murder, bodily harm and two incidences of kidnapping.

Despite the blemish on the family record, Fujimori's daughter Keiko was elected to the Peruvian Congress in a landslide in 2006 and ran for president in 2011, losing in a tight run-off election to former army officer Ollanta Humala.

Humala was initially thought to be a populist in the Hugo Chávez vein (the Lima stock exchange plunged when he was first elected), but his administration turned out to be quite friendly to business. Though the economy functioned well under his governance, a botched raid on a Sendero Luminoso encampment in the highlands sent his approval rating into a tailspin by the middle of 2012. Extraordinarily Humala's approval rebounded in August 2015, his final year in power, despite (or due to) declaring martial law on the south coast in reaction to violent conflict between local farmers and the forces of the Tía María copper mine.

Culture

With a geography that encompasses desert, highland and jungle, Peru is relentlessly touted as a land of contrasts. This also applies to the lives of its people: the country is a mix of rich and poor, modern and ancient, agricultural and urban, indigenous and white. Day-to-day existence can be difficult – but it can also be profoundly rich. For centuries, this has been the story of life in Peru.

Population

Peru is essentially a bicultural society: the part that is indigenous, and the part that is European influenced. Peruvians who speak Spanish and adhere to *criollo* tradition (Peru-born Spaniards during the colony) are a racial mix of those who are white (15% of the population) and those who are *mestizo*, people of mixed indigenous and European heritage (another 37%).

About 45% of Peru's population is pure *indígena* (people of indigenous descent), making it one of three countries in Latin America to have such high indigenous representation. A disproportionate share of *indígenas* inhabit rural areas in the Andes and work in agriculture. Most *indígenas* speak Quechua and live in the Andean highlands, while a smaller percentage speak Aymara and inhabit the Lake Titicaca region. In the vast Amazon, various indigenous ethnicities speak a plethora of other languages.

About 3% of Peruvians are of African or Asian descent. Afro-Peruvians are descended from slaves brought by the Spanish conquistadors.

Lifestyle

Though the recent economic boom has been good to the country, there is still a yawning disparity between rich and poor. The minimum monthly wage stands at less than US$200. And, according to a UN report from 2010, almost a third of the population lives below the poverty line, while one in 10 survive on less than US$1 a day. Though the official national unemployment rate is only 7.9%, underemployment is rampant, especially in cities. In Lima, underemployment is estimated to affect 42.5% of the population.

In rural areas, the poor survive largely from subsistence agriculture, living in traditional adobe or tin houses that often lack electricity and indoor plumbing. In cities, the extreme poor live in shantytowns, while the lower and middle classes live in concrete, apartment-style housing or small stand-alone homes. More affluent urban homes consist of large stand-alone houses, often bordered by high walls.

Across the board, homes are generally shared by more than one generation.

Religion

More than 81% of Peruvians identify as Roman Catholics, and Catholicism is the official religion. However, while some *indígenas* are outwardly Catholic, they often combine elements of traditional beliefs into church festivals and sacred ceremonies. Evangelicals and other Protestants are now around 13% of the population.

Cuisine

Peru has long been a place where the concept of 'fusion' was a part of everyday cooking. Over the course of the last 400 years, Andean stews mingled with Asian stir-fry techniques, and Spanish rice dishes absorbed flavors from the Amazon, producing the country's famed *criollo* (creole) cooking. In the past decade, a generation of experimental young innovators has pushed this local fare to gastronomic heights. This *novoandina* approach interprets Peruvian cooking through the lens of haute cuisine.

Food tends toward the spicy, but *ají* (chili condiment) is served separately. Conventional eaters can find refuge in a *chifa* (Chinese restaurant) or *pollería* (rotisserie restaurant). Vegetarian options are expanding, and Peru's many innovative potato dishes are worth trying. Restaurants commonly offer a *menú del día* (set meal, usually lunch), consisting of soup, main course and possibly dessert for S8 to S22. Dried corn called *canchita* is an ubiquitous table snack.

Incluye impuesto (IGV) means a service charge has been included in the price. Better restaurants add 18% in taxes and 10% in tips to the bill.

Drinks

ALCOHOLIC DRINKS

Beers come light or sweet and dark (called *malta* or *cerveza negra*). Cuzco and Arequipa are fiercely proud of their beers, Cusqueña and Arequipeña.

Dating back to pre-Columbian times, traditional highland *chicha* (corn beer) is stored in earthenware pots and served in huge glasses in small Andean villages and markets, but is not usually commercially available. This home brew is an acquired taste – the fermentation process begins with someone chewing the corn.

WARNING

Avoid food prepared from once or currently endangered animals. Sometimes *chanco marino* (dolphin) may be served up or, in the jungle areas, *huevos de charapa* (tortoise eggs), *paiche* (the largest scaled freshwater fish), caiman, *motelo* (turtle) or even *mono* (monkey).

Peruvian wines are decent but not up to the standard of Chilean or Argentine tipples. A white-grape brandy called *pisco* is the national drink, usually served in a *pisco sour,* a cocktail made from *pisco,* egg white, lemon juice, syrup, crushed ice and bitters. The firewater of choice in the jungle is *aguardiente* (sugarcane spirits flavored with anise).

NONALCOHOLIC DRINKS

Agua mineral (mineral water) is sold *con gas* (with carbonation) or *sin gas* (without carbonation). Don't leave without trying Peru's top-selling, fizzy-bubblegum-flavored Inca Kola at least once. *Jugos* (fruit juices) are widely available, and in reputable spots made with filtered water. You can also get yours with *leche* (milk). *Chicha morada* is a sweet, refreshing, noncarbonated drink made from purple corn. *Maté de coca* (coca-leaf tea) does wonders for warding off the effects of altitude. Though the country exports coffee to the world, many Peruvians drink it instant. In touristy areas, cafes serving espresso and cappuccino have proliferated.

Sports

Fútbol (soccer) inspires fanaticism in Peru, even though its national squad hasn't qualified for the World Cup since 1982. The big-boy teams mostly hail from Lima: the traditional *clásico* (classic match) pitches Alianza Lima against rivals Universitario (La U). The season is late March to November.

Bullfighting is also part of the national culture. Lima's Plaza de Acho attracts international talent. In remote Andean festivals, condors are tied to the back of the bull – representative of indigenous struggle against Spanish conquistadors.

Arts

The country that has been home to empires both indigenous and European has a wealth of cultural and artistic tradition. Perhaps the most outstanding achievements are in the areas of music (both indigenous and otherwise), painting and literature – the latter of which received plenty of attention in 2010 when Peruvian novelist Mario Vargas Llosa won the Nobel Prize for Literature.

Music

Like its people, Peru's music is an intercontinental fusion of elements. Pre-Columbian cultures contributed bamboo flutes, the Spaniards brought stringed instruments and the Africans gave it a backbone of fluid, percussive rhythm. By and large, music tends to be a regional affair: African-influenced *landós* with their thumbing bass beats are predominant on the coast; high-pitched indigenous *huaynos,* heavy on bamboo wind instruments, are heard in the Andes; and *criollo* waltzes are a must at any dance party on the coast.

Over the last several decades, the *huayno* has blended with surf guitars and Colombian *cumbia* (a type of Afro-Caribbean dance music) to produce *chicha* – a danceable sound closely identified with the Amazon region. (Well-known *chicha* bands include Los Shapis and Los Mirlos.) *Cumbia* is also popular. Grupo 5, which hails from Chiclayo, is currently a favorite in the genre.

On the coast, guitar-inflected *música criolla* (*criollo* music) has its roots in both Spain and Africa. The most famous *criollo* style is the *vals peruano* (Peruvian waltz), a three-quarter-time waltz that is fast moving and full of complex guitar melodies. The most legendary singers in this genre include singer and composer Chabuca Granda (1920–83), Lucha Reyes (1936–73) and Arturo 'Zambo' Cavero (1940–2009). Cavero in particular was revered for his gravelly vocals and soulful interpretations. *Landó* is closely connected to this style of music but features the added elements of call-and-response. Standout performers in this vein include singers Susana Baca (b 1944) and Eva Ayllón (b 1956).

Visual Arts

The country's most famous art movement dates to the 17th and 18th centuries, when the native and *mestizo* artists of the Cuzco School produced thousands of religious paintings, the vast majority of which remain unattributed. *Cuzqueña* canvases are proudly displayed in many highland churches.

Traditional Crafts

Peru has a long tradition of producing extraordinarily rendered crafts and folk art. Here's what to look for:

Textiles You'll see intricate weavings with elaborate anthropomorphic and geometric designs all over Peru. Some of the finest can be found around Cuzco.

Pottery The most stunning pieces of pottery are those made in the tradition of the pre-Columbian Moche people of the north coast. But also worthwhile is Chancay-style pottery: rotund figures made from sand-colored clay. Find these at craft markets in Lima.

Religious crafts These abound in all regions, but the *retablos* (three-dimensional dioramas) from Ayacucho are the most spectacular.

Literature

Peru's most famous novelist is the Nobel Prize–winning Mario Vargas Llosa (b 1936), who ran unsuccessfully for president in 1990. His complex novels including *The Time of the Hero* delve into Peruvian society, politics and culture.

Considered Peru's greatest poet, César Vallejo (1892–1938) wrote *Trilce,* a book of 77 avant-garde, existentialist poems. Vallejo was known for pushing the Spanish language to its limits, inventing words when real ones no longer served him.

Two writers noted for their portrayals of indigenous communities are José María Arguedas (1911–69) and Ciro Alegría (1909–67). Rising literary star Daniel Alarcón (b 1977) is a Peruvian-American whose 2007 debut novel *Lost City Radio* achieved wide acclaim.

Environment

Few countries have topographies as rugged, as forbidding and as wildly diverse as Peru. The third-largest country in South America – at 1,285,220 sq km – it is five times larger than the UK, almost twice the size of Texas and one-sixth the size of Australia. It lies in the tropics, south of the equator, straddling three strikingly different geographic zones: the arid Pacific coast, the craggy Andes mountain range and a good portion of the Amazon Basin.

The Land

The coastal strip is mainly desert, punctuated by cities and rivers down from the Andes forming agricultural oases. The country's best road, the Carr Panamericana, slices through coastal Peru from border to border.

The Andes rise rapidly from the coast to spectacular heights over 6000m just 100km inland. Most mountains are between 3000m and 4000m, with jagged ranges separated by deep, vertiginous canyons. Huascarán (6768m) is Peru's highest peak.

The eastern Andes get more rainfall than the dry western slopes, and so they're covered in cloud forest, merging with the rainforest of the Amazon Basin.

Wildlife

With mammoth deserts, glaciated mountain ranges, tropical rainforests and almost every imaginable habitat in between, Peru hosts a menagerie of wildlife.

Bird and marine life is abundant along the coast, with colonies of sea lions, Humboldt penguins, Chilean flamingos, Peruvian pelicans, Inca terns and the brown booby endemic to the region. Remarkable highland birds include majestic Andean condors, puna ibis and a variety of hummingbirds. The highlands are also home to

TOP WILDLIFE-WATCHING SPOTS

- Remote jungle in **Parque Nacional Manu** (p894); your best chance to see jaguars, tapirs and monkeys
- The coastal reserve of **Islas Ballestas** (p821), with penguins, flamingos and sea lions
- Canopy walkways, jungle lodges and river cruises in **Iquitos** (p896)
- Andean condors and *vicuñas* in **Parque Nacional Huascarán** (p885)
- Capybaras and macaws near **Puerto Maldonado** (p892)
- **Cañón del Colca** (p835)– the easiest place to spot Andean condors
- Oxbow lake **Yarinacocha** (p895), home to pink dolphins, huge iguanas and myriad bird species
- Pristine rainforest reserve **Reserva Nacional Pacaya-Samiria** (p900), explored by dugout canoe
- More than 400 species of rare and endemic birds around **Machu Picchu** (p860)

camelids such as llamas, alpacas, guanacos and *vicuñas,* while cloud forests are the haunts of jaguars, tapirs and endangered spectacled bears.

Swoop down toward the Amazon and with luck you'll spot all the iconic tropical birds – parrots, macaws, toucans and many more. The Amazon is home to over a dozen species of monkey, plus river dolphins, frogs, reptiles, fish and insects galore. Snakes? Don't panic. Many species live here, but they're mostly shy of humans.

National Parks

Peru's wealth of wildlife is protected by a system of national parks and reserves, with 60 areas covering almost 15% of the country. Yet these areas seriously lack infrastructure and are subject to illegal hunting, fishing, logging and mining.

Some highlights include Parque Nacional Huascarán, a prime spot for trekking in the Cordillera Blanca, and Parque Nacional Manu, among the world's most biodiverse rainforests, located northwest of Cuzco. Many reserves or *reservas nacionales* and protected areas – such as Cañon del Colca and Lake Titicaca – are just as worthy of a visit.

After decades in waiting, in August 2015 Sierra del Divisor Reserve Zone was set to finally become Peru's latest national park. This offers protection for its 1.5 million hectares of rainforest on the Brazilian border, including unique flora, fauna and indigenous communities.

Environmental Issues

Peru faces major challenges in the stewardship of its natural resources, with problems compounded by a lack of law enforcement and its impenetrable geography. Deforestation and erosion are major issues, as is industrial pollution, urban sprawl and the continuing attempted eradication of coca plantations on some Andean slopes. In addition, the Interoceánica Hwy through the heart of the Amazon may imperil thousands of square kilometers of rainforest.

DEFORESTATION & WATER PROBLEMS

At the ground level, clear-cutting of the highlands for firewood, of the rainforests for valuable hardwoods, and of both to clear land for agriculture, oil drilling and mining has led to severe erosion. In the highlands, where deforestation and overgrazing of Andean woodlands and *puna* grass is severe, soil quality is rapidly deteriorating. In the Amazon rainforest, deforestation has led to erosion and a decline in bellwether species such as frogs. Erosion has also led to decreased water quality in this area, where silt-laden water is unable to support micro-organisms at the base of the food chain.

Other water-related problems include pollution from mining in the highlands. Sewage contamination along the coast has led to many beaches around some coastal cities being declared unfit for swimming. In the south, pollution and overfishing have led to the continued decline of the Humboldt penguin (its numbers have declined by more than a third since the 1980s).

PROTECTIVE STEPS

In late 2014, Peru signed an agreement with Norway and Germany to reduce its forest-related emissions in an effort to become carbon-neutral by 2021. Norway pledged to pay up to US$300 million for verified results.

Some positive measures are being taken to help protect the country's environment. For example, the Peruvian government and private interests within the tourism industry have come together to develop sustainable travel projects in the Amazon.

SURVIVAL GUIDE

Directory A–Z

ACCOMMODATIONS

Lima and the tourist mecca of Cuzco are the most expensive places to stay in Peru. During high season (June through August), major holidays and festivals, accommodations are likely to be full and rates can triple. At other times, the high-season rates we quote taper off. Foreign tourists normally aren't charged the 10% sales tax on accommodations. *Incluye impuesto* (IGV) means a service charge has been included in the price. At better hotels, taxes and service charges combined may total 28%. Budget hotels usually have hot (or, more likely, tepid) showers some of the time. Dormitory beds come with shared bathrooms, while single and double rooms (including those in *hostales*, which are guesthouses and not the same as backpacker hostels) have private bathrooms unless otherwise noted.

ACTIVITIES

Most activities are available year-round, but certain times of year are better than others. Peak season for most outdoor activities is during the winter dry season (June to August). Trekking in the highlands is a muddy proposition during the wet season, especially December to March, when the heaviest rains fall. However, those hotter summer months are best for swimming and surfing along the Pacific Coast.

For your safety, avoid the cheapest, cut-rate tour agencies and outdoor outfitters. For specialized activities, bring high-quality gear from home.

If bird-watching gets you in a flap, head for the Amazon Basin, Islas Ballestas and Cañón del Colca for starters.

When it comes to mountain climbing, Huascarán (6768m), Peru's highest mountain, is experts-only, but easier peaks abound near Huaraz and Arequipa. Rock and ice climbing are popular around Huaraz .

Horse rentals can be easily arranged. For a real splurge, take a ride on a graceful Peruvian *paso* horse near Urubamba.

Gearing up for some downhill adventures? Easy or demanding single-track trails await mountain bikers outside Huaraz, Cuzco and Arequipa.

Paragliding is especially popular in Lima.

Whitewater-rafting (river-running) agencies in Cuzco and Arequipa offer a multitude of day runs and longer hauls (grade III to IV+ rapids). Travelers have died on these rivers, so be especially cautious about which rafting company to trust with your life. The best place for beginners is Lunahuaná.

Surfing has a big fan base in Peru. There are some radical waves up north, famously at Huanchaco, Máncora and just south of Lima. For something completely different, sandboard down humongous dunes in the coastal desert near Huacachina and Nazca.

Trekkers, pack your boots – the variety of trails in Peru is staggering. The Cordillera Blanca can't be beaten for peaks, while the nearby Cordillera Huayhuash is similarly stunning. But if you've heard of *any* trek in Peru, you'll have heard of the world-famous Inca Trail to Machu Picchu – and everyone else has, too, so consider taking an alternative route. The spectacular six-day Ausangate circuit and ancient ruins hidden in cloud forests outside Chachapoyas are a couple of other possibilities. Alternatively, get down into the world's deepest canyons – the Cañón del Cotahuasi and Cañón del Colca.

SLEEPING PRICE RANGES

The following price ranges refer to a double room with bathroom in high season, unless otherwise stated.

$ less than S85 (includes dorm rooms)

$$ S85 to S250

$$$ more than S250

BUSINESS HOURS

Shops open at 9am or 10am and close from 6pm to 8pm. A two-hour lunch break is common. Shops may stay open through lunch in big cities, and there are 24-hour supermarkets in Lima. Banks are generally open 9am to 6pm Monday to Friday, to 1pm Saturday. Post offices and *casas de cambio* (money-exchange offices) keep highly variable hours. Almost everything closes on Sunday.

ELECTRICITY

Peru runs on a 220V, 60Hz AC electricity supply. Even though two-pronged outlets accept both flat (North American) and round (European) plugs, electronics built for lower voltage and cycles (eg 110V to 120V North American appliances) will function poorly or not at all, and plugging them in without using a converter can damage them.

EMBASSIES & CONSULATES

Argentinian Embassy (☎01-433-3381; Av 28 de Julio 828, Lima 1)

Australian Embassy (Map p812; ☎01-630-0500; www.peru.embassy.gov.au; Av La Paz 1049, piso 10, Miraflores, Lima; ⊙9am-5pm Mon-Fri) For Australian citizens, the embassy is located in the heart of the Miraflores district. For all your visa inquiries and travel advice, come on down and get in the queue!

Bolivian Embassy (☎01-440-2095; www.boliviaenperu.com; Los Castaños 235, San Isidro, Lima) There's a consulate in Puno (☎051-35-1251; fax 051-35-1251; Arequipa 136, 3rd fl; ⊙8am-4pm Mon-Fri).

Brazilian Embassy (Map p812; ☎01-512-0830; www.embajadabrasil.org.pe; Av José Pardo 850, Miraflores, Lima 18)

Canadian Embassy (Map p812; ☎01-319-3200; www.canadainternational.gc.ca/peru-perou; Bolognesi 228, Miraflores, Lima; ⊙8am-12:30pm & 1:15-5pm Mon-Thu, 8am-12:30pm Fri) With a helpful website.

Chilean Embassy (☎01-710-2211; http://chileabroad.gov.cl/peru; Javier Prado Oeste 790, San Isidro, Lima 27)

Colombian Embassy (☎01-462-0294; http://peru.embajada.gov.co; Calle Clemente X, 335, San Isidro, Lima) There's a consulate in Iquitos (☎065-23-1461; Calvo de Araujo 431).

FOOD PRICE RANGES

Restaurant listings are organized according to author preference, considering value for cost. Midrange to high-end restaurants charge a 10% service fee and a 19% tax. The following price ranges refer to a main course.

$ less than S20

$$ S20 to S60

$$$ more than S60

Ecuadorian Embassy (☎01-212-4027; http://peru.embajada.gob.ec; Las Palmeras 356, San Isidro, Lima 27) There's a consulate in Tumbes (☎072-52-5949; Bolívar 129, 3rd fl, Plaza de Armas).

French Embassy (☎01-215-8400; www.ambafrance-pe.org; Av Arequipa 3415, San Isidro)

German Embassy (☎01-203-5940; www.lima.diplo.de; Av Dionisio Derteano 144, 7th & 8th fl, San Isidro, Lima)

UK Embassy (Map p812; ☎01-617-3000; www.ukinperu.fco.gov.uk; Av José Larco 1301, Edificio Parquemar, 22nd fl, Miraflores, Lima 18)

US Embassy (☎01-618-2000; http://lima.usembassy.gov; Av Encalada, cuadra 17, Surco, Lima) This place is a fortress – call before showing up in person.

GAY & LESBIAN TRAVELERS

Peru is a strongly conservative, Catholic country. Gays and lesbians tend to keep a low profile. Homosexual rights in a political or legal context don't even exist as an issue for most Peruvians. (Note that the rainbow flag seen around Cuzco is *not* a gay-pride flag – it's the flag of the Inca empire.) When the issue does arise in public, hostility is most often the official response.

Kissing on the mouth is rarely seen in public, by either heterosexual or homosexual couples. Peruvians are physically demonstrative with their friends, though, so kissing on the cheek in greeting or an *abrazo* (backslapping hug exchanged between men) are innocuous, everyday behaviors. When in doubt, do as locals do.

Lima is the most accepting of gay people, while Cuzco, Arequipa and Trujillo are more tolerant than the norm. Lima has Peru's most openly gay scene. **Gayperu.com** (www.gayperu.pe), a Spanish-language guide, lists bars to bathhouses. **Rainbow Peruvian Tours** (☎01-215-6000; www.perurainbow.com; Río de Janeiro 216, Miraflores, Lima) is a gay-owned tour agency with a multilingual website.

INTERNET ACCESS

Internet cafes *(locutorios)* are found on every other street corner in Peru. Even small towns will have at least one *cabina* tucked away somewhere. Access is fast and inexpensive (around S1.50 per hour) in cities, but pricier and painfully unreliable in rural areas. Often internet cafes have 'net-to-phone' and 'net-to-net' capabilities (such as Skype).

LANGUAGE

Peru has language schools in Lima, Cuzco, Arequipa, Huaraz, Puerto Maldonado and Huancayo.

LEGAL MATTERS

There are *policía de turismo* (tourist police) stations in over a dozen major cities, and they usually have someone on hand who speaks at least a little English. Although bribery is illegal, some police officers (including tourist police) may be corrupt. As most travelers won't have to deal with traffic police, the most likely place you'll be expected to pay officials a little extra is at overland border crossings. This too is illegal, and if you have the time and fortitude to stick to your guns, you will eventually be allowed in.

MAPS

The best road map of Peru, *Mapa Vial* (1:2,000,000), published by Lima 2000, is sold in bookstores. Topographic maps are easily available from outdoor outfitters in major cities and tourist destinations.

MONEY

The currency is the nuevo sol (S), divided into 100 *céntimos*.

ATMs

Most cities and some small towns have 24-hour ATMs on the Plus (Visa) and Cirrus (Maestro/MasterCard) systems. American Express and other networks are less widespread. Bigger airports and bus stations, as well as Interbank and BCP branches, have global ATMs that accept almost all foreign cards. ATMs in Peru will only accept your debit, bank or traveler's-check card if you have a four-digit PIN. Both US dollars and Peruvian currency are dispensed.

Cash

The following bills are commonly in circulation: S10, S20, S50, S100. When changing money, always ask for plenty of small bills. Coins of S0.05, S0.10, S0.20, S0.50, S1, S2 and S5 are also in use. US dollars are accepted at many tourist-oriented establishments, but you'll need nuevos soles to pay for transportation, cheap meals and guesthouses etc. Counterfeiting is a major problem in Peru.

Credit Cards

Better hotels, restaurants and shops accept *tarjetas de crédito* (credit cards) but usually tack on a fee of 7% or more for paying with plastic. Your own credit card may add an international-use fee (around 3%).

Exchanging Money

Currencies other than US dollars can be exchanged only in major cities and at a high commission. Worn, torn or damaged bills are not accepted. *Casas de cambio* are open longer than banks and are much faster. Official money-changers *(cambistas)* are useful for exchange outside banking hours or at borders where there are no banks, but beware of 'fixed' calculators, counterfeit notes and short-changing.

POST

Serpost is the privatized postal system. It's relatively efficient, but expensive. Airmail postcards and letters cost about S5 to S6.50 each to most foreign destinations, arriving in about two weeks from Lima, longer from provincial cities.

Lista de correos (poste restante/general delivery) can be sent to any major post office. South American Explorers will hold mail and packages for members at its clubhouses in Lima and Cuzco.

PUBLIC HOLIDAYS

On major holidays, banks, offices and other services are closed, fully booked hotels double or triple their rates, and transportation becomes overcrowded. Fiestas Patrias is the biggest national holiday, when the entire nation seems to be on the move.

Año Nuevo (New Year's Day) January 1
Good Friday March/April
Día del Trabajador (Labor Day) May 1
Inti Raymi June 24
Fiestas de San Pedro y San Pablo (Feast of St Peter and St Paul) June 29
Fiestas Patrias (National Independence Days) July 28 and 29
Fiesta de Santa Rosa de Lima August 30
Battle of Angamos Day October 8
Todos Santos (All Saints Day) November 1
Fiesta de la Purísima Concepción (Feast of the Immaculate Conception) December 8
Navidad (Christmas Day) December 25

RESPONSIBLE TRAVEL

Archaeologists are fighting a losing battle with *guaqueros* (grave robbers), particularly along the coast. Refrain from buying original pre-Columbian artifacts, and do not contribute to wildlife destruction by eating endangered animals or purchasing souvenirs made from skins, feathers, horns or turtle shells. Some indigenous communities make their living from tourism. Visiting these communities may financially support their initiatives but also weaken traditional cultures. If you go on an organized tour, make sure the company is locally owned and ask if any of the proceeds benefit the places you'll be visiting.

SAFE TRAVEL

Peru has its fair share of traveler hassles, which may often be avoided by exercising common sense.

The most common problem is theft, either stealth or snatch – theft by violent mugging is rare, though it's not to be ruled out. Watch out for 'choke and grab' attacks, especially at archaeological sites. Robberies and fatal attacks have occurred even on popular trekking trails, notably around Huaraz.

Avoid unlicensed 'pirate' taxis, as some drivers have been known to be complicit in 'express' kidnappings. Take good-quality day buses instead of cheap, overnight services to lower the risk of having an accident or possibly being hijacked.

Do *not* get involved with drugs. Gringos who have done so are being repaid with long-term incarceration in harsh Peruvian prisons. Any suspect in a crime (which includes vehicle accidents, whether or not you're the driver at fault) is considered guilty until proven innocent.

While terrorism lingers in Peru, narcotrafficking is serious business. Areas to avoid are the Río Huallaga valley between Tingo María and Juanjul, and the Río Apurímac valley near Ayacucho, where the majority of Peru's illegal drug-growing takes place. Currently, it is inadvisable to visit Vilcabamba, Ivochote, Kiteni and beyond, but the situation is subject to change.

Not all unexploded ordinance (UXO) along the Ecuadorian border has been cleaned up. Use only official border crossings and don't stray off the beaten path in border zones.

Soroche (altitude sickness) can be fatal.

TELEPHONE

Public payphones are available in even the tiniest towns. Most work with phone cards, and many with coins. Dial ☎109 for a Peruvian operator, ☎108 for an international operator and ☎103 for information. Internet cafes are often much cheaper for making local, long-distance and international phone calls than **Telefónica-Perú** (www.telefonica.com.pe) offices.

Cell Phones

It's possible to use a tri-band GSM world phone in Peru (GSM 1900). Other systems in use are CDMA and TDMA. This is a fast-changing field, so check the current situation before you travel. In larger cities, you can buy cell phones in stands at the supermarket that use SIM cards for about S50, then pop in a SIM card that costs from S15. Claro has a popular pay-as-you-go plan. Cell-phone rentals may be available in major cities and tourist centers. Cell-phone reception may be poor in the mountains or jungle.

Phone Cards

Called *tarjetas telefónicas*, phone cards are widely available from street vendors or kiosks. Some have an electronic chip, but most make you dial a code to obtain access. Dial a three-digit connection and enter the code on the back of your card; a message in Spanish conveys your balance, then you dial the number and your call connects. Ask around for which companies' cards offer the best deals.

Phone Codes

Peru's country code is ☎51. To call a foreign country, dial ☎00, the country code, area code and local number.

Each region of Peru (called a department) has its own area code, which begins with 0 (☎01 in Lima, 0 plus two digits elsewhere). To call long distance within Peru, include the 0 in the area code. If calling from abroad, dial your international access code, the country code (☎51), the area code without the 0, then the local number.

TOILETS

Peruvian plumbing leaves something to be desired. Even a small amount of toilet paper in the bowl can muck up the entire system – that's why a small plastic bin is routinely provided for disposing of it. Except at museums, restaurants, hotels and bus stations, public toilets are rare in Peru. Always carry toilet paper with you.

TOURIST INFORMATION

PromPerú's official tourism website (www.peru.info) offers information in Spanish, Portuguese, English, French, German and Italian. PromPerú also runs **iPerú** (☎24hr hotline 01-574-8000; www.peru.travel/iperu.aspx) information offices in Lima, Arequipa, Ayacucho, Chiclayo, Cuzco, Huaraz, Iquitos, Piura, Puno, Tacna and Trujillo. Municipal tourist offices are found in other cities we cover. South American Explorers' clubhouses in Lima and Cuzco are good sources of information for travelers, but you'll get more help as a paying member.

TRAVELERS WITH DISABILITIES

Peru offers few conveniences for travelers with disabilities. Peru's official tourism organization PromPerú has a link to Accessible Tourism from the 'Special Interests' section of its website (www.peru.info) for reports on wheelchair-accessible hotels, restaurants and attractions in Lima, Cuzco, Aguas Calientes, Iquitos and Trujillo.

VISAS

With few exceptions (for citizens of a handful of Asian, African and communist countries), visas are not required for tourism. Passports should be valid for at least six months from your departure date. Travelers are permitted a 90-day initial stay, stamped into their passports and onto an Andean Immigration Card that you must keep and return when leaving Peru.

If you lose your card, visit an *oficina de migraciónes* (immigration office; www.migraciones.gob.pe) for a replacement. Extensions can be obtained at immigration offices in Lima, Arequipa, Cuzco, Iquitos, Puerto Maldonado, Puno and Trujillo, as well as near the Chilean and Ecuadorian borders. Forms and information in English can be found online. For extensions, click on 'Foreigners' and 'Extension of Stay'. The cost is S12.25 for a right of paperwork and an additional US$20 for the 30-day extension. Two extensions are allowed per year.

While traveling around Peru, carry your passport and immigration card with you at all times, as you can be arrested if you don't have proper ID.

See lonelyplanet.com and its links for up-to-date visa information.

VOLUNTEERING

Most volunteer programs charge you for program fees, room and board. Watch out for fake charities and illegitimate programs that are scams. Spanish-language schools usually know of casual volunteer opportunities. South American Explorers' clubhouses have firsthand reports from foreign volunteers in Lima and Cuzco. **ProWorld Service Corps** (ProPeru; ☎in UK 0-18-6559-6289, in USA 877-429-6753; www.proworldsc.org) organizes two- to 26-week cultural, service and academic placements in the Sacred Valley and is affiliated with NGOs throughout Peru.

WOMEN TRAVELERS

Most women encounter no serious problems in Peru, though they should come mentally prepared for being a conspicuous center of attention. Machismo is alive and well in Peruvian towns and cities, where curious staring, whistling, hissing and *piropos* (cheeky, flirtatious or vulgar remarks) are an everyday occurrence. Ignoring provocation is generally the best response. Most men don't follow up their idle chatter with something more threatening unless they feel you've insulted their manhood.

If you appeal to locals for help, you'll find most Peruvians act protectively toward women traveling alone, expressing surprise and concern when you tell them you're traveling without your husband or family. If a stranger approaches you on the street to ask a question, *don't* stop walking, which would allow attackers to quickly surround you. Never go alone to a bar, and stay alert at archaeological sites, even during daylight hours. Take only authorized taxis and avoid overnight buses.

Abortions are illegal in Peru, except when they can save the life of the mother. Planned Parenthood–affiliated **Instituto Peruano de Paternidad Responsable** (Inppares; ☎ 01-583-9012; www.inppares.org.pe) runs a dozen sexual- and reproductive-health clinics for both sexes around the country.

WORK

Officially you need a work visa in Peru, though language centers in Lima or Cuzco sometimes hire native speakers to teach English. This is illegal, and such jobs are increasingly difficult to get without a proper work visa.

Getting There & Away

AIR

Lima's **Aeropuerto Internacional Jorge Chávez** (p818) is the main hub for flights to Andean countries and Latin America, North America and Europe.

BOAT

Boats ply the Amazon from Iquitos to Leticia, Colombia, and Tabatinga, Brazil. It's difficult to reach Bolivia by river from Puerto Maldonado. It's possible, but time-consuming, to travel along the Río Napo from Iquitos to Coca, Ecuador.

BUS, CAR & MOTORCYCLE

The major border crossings: Tacna to Chile; Tumbes, La Tina or Jaén to Ecuador; and Copacabana or Desaguadero at Lake Titicaca to Bolivia. Brazil is reached (but not easily) via Iñapari or multiple towns and river ports in the Amazon.

TRAIN

There are inexpensive, twice-daily trains between Tacna and Arica, Chile.

Getting Around

On the road keep your passport and Andean Immigration Card with you, not packed in your luggage, as overland transport goes through police checkpoints.

AIR

Most airlines fly from Lima to regional capitals, but service between provincial cities is limited. The domestic airlines listed following are the most established and reliable.

Morning departures are most likely to be on time. Show up at least one hour early for all domestic flights (90 minutes in Lima, two hours in Cuzco). Flights are often fully booked during holidays.

Avianca (Map p812; ☎ 511-8222; www.avianca.com) Service between Lima and Cuzco.

Peruvian Airlines (www.peruvianairlines.pe) Flies to Lima, Arequipa, Cuzco, Piura, Iquitos and Tacna.

BOAT

Small, slow motorboats depart daily from Puno for Lake Titicaca's islands.

In Peru's eastern lowlands, *peki-pekis* (dugout canoes, usually powered by an outboard engine) act as water buses on the smaller rivers. Where the rivers widen, larger cargo boats are normally available. This is the classic way to travel down the Amazon – swinging in your hammock aboard a banana boat piloted by a grizzled old captain. You can travel from Pucallpa or Yurimaguas to Iquitos, and on into Brazil, Colombia or Ecuador this way. These boats aren't big, but they have two or more decks: the lower deck is for cargo, the upper for passengers and crew. Bring a hammock. Basic food is provided, but you may want to bring your own. To get aboard, just go down to the docks and ask for a boat to your destination. Arrange passage with the captain (nobody else). Departure time normally depends on filling up the hold. Sometimes you can sleep on the boat while awaiting departure to save costs.

BUS

Peru's notoriously dangerous buses are cheap and go just about everywhere.

Less traveled routes are served by ramshackle old chicken buses, but more popular destinations are served by fast luxury services (called *imperial* or something similar), charging up to 10 times more than *económico* (economy) buses. It's worth paying more for long-distance bus trips, if only for safety's sake. Some overnight routes offer *bus-camas* (bed-buses) with seats that fully recline. For safety, security and comfort, there is Cruz del Sur at the top and pretty much all goes downhill from there. Peruvians swear by **Oltursa** (☎ 01-708-5000; www.oltursa.com.pe).

Many cities now have central bus terminals, while others have bus companies clustered around a few blocks or scattered all over town.

DEPARTURE TAX

International airport taxes are now almost always included in your ticket price. Lima's international tax is US$31, payable in US dollars or nuevos soles (cash only). Domestic airport taxes are included in ticket prices.

Travel agencies are convenient for buying tickets but will overcharge you. Instead, buy them directly from the bus company at least a day in advance. Schedules and fares change frequently. Prices skyrocket around major holidays, when tickets may be sold out several days ahead of time. Coastal buses are packed all summer long, especially on Sunday.

Buses rarely leave or arrive on time and can be greatly delayed during the rainy season due to landslides and treacherous road conditions. Try not to take overnight buses, which are more vulnerable to fatal accidents, hijackings and luggage theft. It can get freezing cold on highland buses, so dress warmly. Long-distance buses generally stop for meals, though toilets are highly unpredictable. Some companies have their own restaurants in the middle of nowhere, practically forcing you to eat there. But you can also buy snacks from onboard vendors or bring your own food and drinks.

CAR & MOTORCYCLE

With the exception of the Carr Panamericana and new roads leading inland from the coast, road conditions are generally poor, distances are great and renting a car is an expensive, often dangerous hassle. Keep in mind that road signage is deficient and most major roads are also toll roads. Renting a private taxi for long-distance trips costs little more than renting a car, and avoids most of these pitfalls. Motorcycle rental is an option mainly in jungle towns, and there are a few outfitters in Cuzco.

Driver's License

A driver's license from your home country is sufficient for renting a car. An International Driving Permit (IDP) is only required if you'll be driving in Peru for more than 30 days.

LOCAL TRANSPORTATION

Taxis are unmetered, so ask locals about the going rate, then haggle; drivers often double or triple the standard rate for unsuspecting foreigners. A short run in most cities costs S3 to S5 (in Lima S5 to S8). Be aware that street hawkers sell fluorescent taxi stickers throughout Peru, and anybody can just stick one on their windscreen. Some drivers of these unlicensed 'pirate' taxis have been known to be complicit in violent crimes against passengers, especially in Arequipa. It's safer, if more expensive, to take officially regulated taxis, requested by telephone.

Mototaxis (motorized rickshaws) are common in some of the smaller towns. *Colectivos* (shared minivans, minibuses or taxis) and trucks (in the Amazon) run between local and not-so-local destinations.

TOURS

Some protected areas such as the Inca Trail and Parque Nacional Manu can only be entered with a guided tour. Other outdoor activities, such as trekking in the Andes or wildlife watching in the Amazon, may be more rewarding with an experienced guide.

TRAIN

Two rail companies link Cuzco and the Sacred Valley with Aguas Calientes, the town near Machu Picchu. **Peru Rail** (www.perurail.com) offers a scenic thrice-weekly service that travels between Cuzco and Lake Titicaca.

Other railways connect Lima and the Andean highland towns of Huancayo and Huancavelica.

Suriname

Includes ➡

Best Places to Stay

➡ Kabalebo (p924)
➡ Greenheart Hotel (p919)
➡ Awarradam (p923)
➡ Tei Wei (p922)
➡ GuestHouse TwenTy4 (p918)

Best Tour Destinations

➡ Raleighvallen (p923)
➡ Palumeu (p922) & Awarradam (p923)
➡ Brownsberg Nature Reserve (p922)
➡ Commewijne River (p921)

Why Go?

Suriname is a warm, dense convergence of rivers that thumps with the lively rhythm of ethnic diversity. From Paramaribo, the country's effervescent Dutch-colonial capital, to the fathomless jungles of the interior, you'll get a genuine welcome to this tiny country – whether from the descendants of escaped African slaves, Dutch and British colonialists, Indian, Indonesian and Chinese indentured laborers or indigenous Amerindians.

Paramaribo is loaded with interesting shopping venues, party-hard night spots and exceptional restaurants, while the untamed jungle, just a few hours away by road or boat, is utterly away from modern development. It's relatively easy to get around this river-heavy, forest-dense country. The mix of languages can make communications interesting, but there is almost always someone around who speaks some English. Don't forget that a meeting of culinary traditions means the food here is as spicy and rich as the country itself.

When to Go

Paramaribo

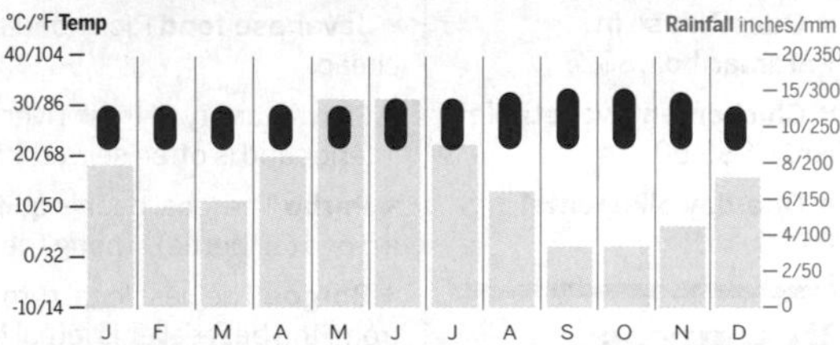

Feb–Apr The first dry season is slightly cooler than the second, and is the best time to visit.

Aug–Nov The second dry season is busier and hotter than the first.

Dec–Jan Paramaribo is known for its explosive New Year's Eve celebrations.

AT A GLANCE

- **Currency** Suriname Dollar (SR$)
- **Languages** Dutch, Sranan Tongo (Surinaams/Taki Taki)
- **Money** Republic Bank ATMs accept most foreign cards; credit cards rarely accepted
- **Visas** 90-day tourist cards need to be obtained at Suriname embassies before arrival
- **Time** GMT minus three hours

Fast Facts

- **Area** 163,800 sq km
- **Population** 581,444
- **Capital** Paramaribo
- **Emergency** ☎112
- **Country Code** ☎597

Exchange Rates

Australia	A$1	SR$2.38
Canada	C$1	SR$2.53
Euro Zone	€1	SR$3.70
UK	UK£1	SR$5.03
USA	US$1	SR$3.25

Set Your Budget

- **Guesthouse in Paramaribo** US$25
- **Chicken-and-vegetable roti** US$3.50
- **One-day bike rental** US$5

Resources

- **Suriname Tourism Foundation** (www.suriname-tourism.org)
- **Suriname Online Tourist Guide** (www.surinametourism.com)

Connections

Suriname's border crossings are at Corriverton (Guyana) and St Laurent du Maroni (French Guiana). Both of these crossings are made by boat across massive rivers that flow into the Caribbean. While Brazil borders the country to the south, there are no roads through the impenetrable jungle into Suriname and thus you can't cross the border here.

ITINERARIES

One Week

Spend three days exploring Paramaribo and the plantations of the Commewijne River by bike or on foot. On one afternoon be sure to take a sunset dolphin-viewing tour and, if you've still got energy, get out on the town for a night of dancing, Suriname style. Next head to the interior – either Raleighvallen, the Upper Suriname River or Brownsberg Nature Reserve – for your remaining days to look for Amazonian critters and meet the locals.

Two Weeks

Follow the above itinerary but take the trip further. You could make brief visits to Raleighvallen, the Upper Suriname River and Brownsberg Nature Reserve or visit several places on the Upper Suriname, 'island-hopping' along the river to different resorts. Taking the route south, you may be able to fly back to Paramaribo so you don't have to backtrack. If it's turtle season (April through August), consider substituting your time at either Raleighvallen or Brownsberg with a trip to the Galibi Nature Reserve.

Essential Food & Drink

- **Pom** Creole creation using grated *tayer* root, shredded chicken, onion and spices baked into a yummy casserole.
- **Roti** Indian flatbread stuffed with all sorts of curries, from potato-heavy vegetarian to chunks of beef.
- **Javanese food** Rice noodle and soup dishes are tasty and cheap.
- **Fish** A variety of fresh river fish is the staple in most of the interior and is often served fried or in soup.
- **Parbo** The local beer is quite good; it's customary to share a *djogo* (1L bottle) among friends.
- **Borgoe** The best local rum, with many types to choose from; the best seller is lethal Mariënburg White, which is 90% alcohol and flavorless in cocktails.
- **Pastei** A Creole-style chicken pot pie with peas and carrots.
- **Moksi-alesi** Mixed boiled rice with salted meat or fish and vegetables – the best include coconut cream.
- **Hagelslag** Dutch-style chocolate sprinkles to go on toast for breakfast.

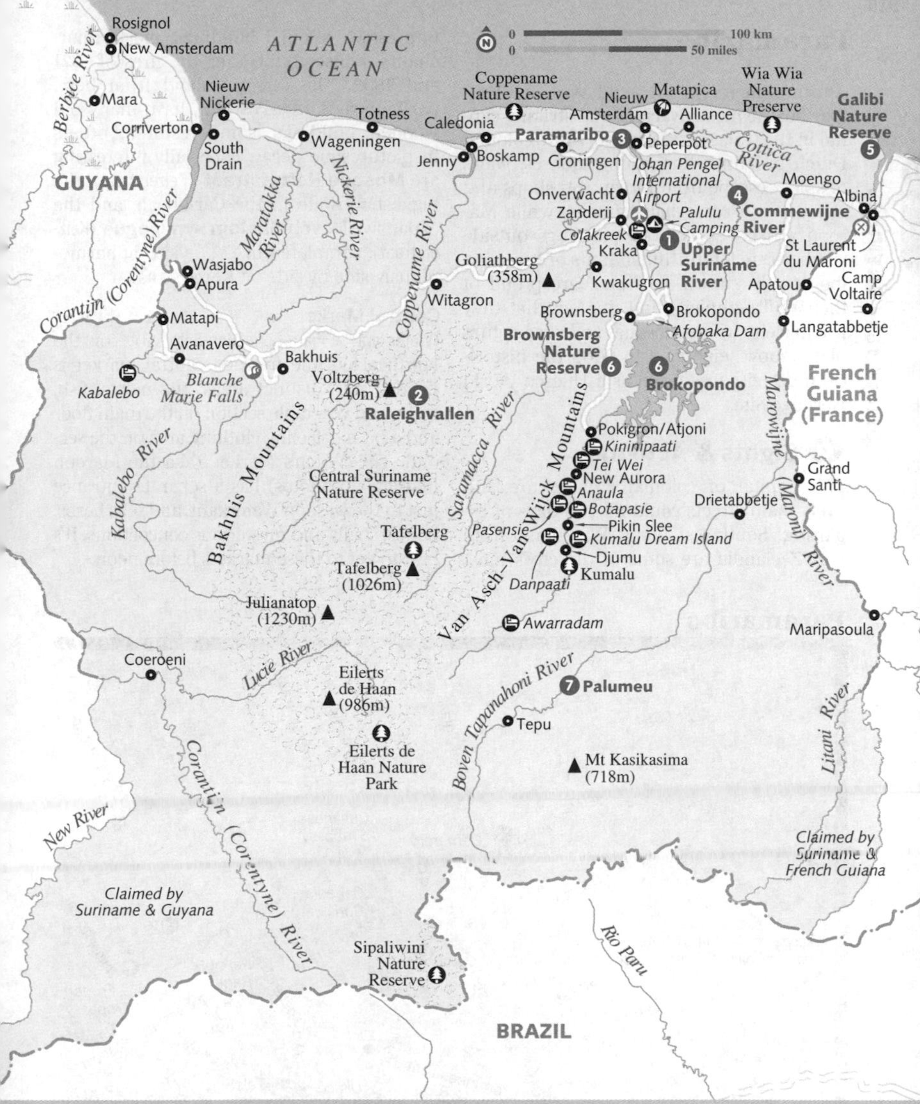

Suriname Highlights

1 Explore Maroon culture, swim in jungle rivers and relax along the **Upper Suriname River** (p922).

2 Drive 190km through jungle and savanna, then canoe past Maroon villages to **Raleighvallen** (p924), gateway to the Central Suriname Nature Reserve.

3 Stroll along **Paramaribo** (p916)'s Unesco-listed historic waterfront lined with stately colonial architecture.

4 Discover the **Commewijne River** (p921) via bicycle or boat tour, and possibly spot pink river dolphins.

5 Tread the beaches at **Galibi Nature Reserve** (p925), where giant leatherback turtles lay eggs in the sand.

6 Marvel at primate-filled forests around an eerie artificial lake at **Brownsberg** (p922) and **Brokopondo** (p922).

7 Listen to the unsurpassed jungle knowledge of Amerindian elders in tranquil **Palumeu** (p922).

Paramaribo

POP 250,000

Amsterdam meets the Wild West in Paramaribo, the most vivacious and striking capital in the Guianas. Black-and-white colonial Dutch buildings line grassy squares, wafts of spices escape from Indian roti shops and mingle with car exhaust fumes, while Maroon artists sell colorful paintings outside somber Dutch forts. Inhabitants of Paramaribo, locally known as 'Parbo,' are proud of their multi-ethnicity and the fact that they live in a city where mosques and synagogues play happy neighbors. In 2002 the historical inner city was listed as a Unesco World Heritage Site.

Sights & Activities

This capital of colonial architecture and lively main streets could fill two days of exploring. Southwest along Waterkant from Fort Zeelandia are some of the city's most impressive colonial buildings, mostly merchants' houses built after the fires of 1821 and 1832. The streets inland from here, particularly Lim-a-Postraat, have many old wooden buildings, some restored, others in picturesque decay. Especially interesting are **Mosque Keizerstraat** (Keizerstraat), the biggest mosque in the Caribbean, and the expansive **Neveh Shalom synagogue** (Keizerstraat), completed in 1723 – sitting harmoniously side by side on Keizerstraat.

Central Market MARKET
(Waterkant; 5am-5pm Mon-Sat) Not for the fainthearted, the frenzied central market is divided into distinct areas: the meats, fish, fruits and vegetable section on the main floor and a bazaar-feeling clothing area on the second. The 'Witch's Market' (aka the Maroon Market; no photos) has a separate entrance just to the west on Waterkant, and sells herbs, bones, shells and mysterious concoctions. It's best to get to these markets before noon.

Paramaribo

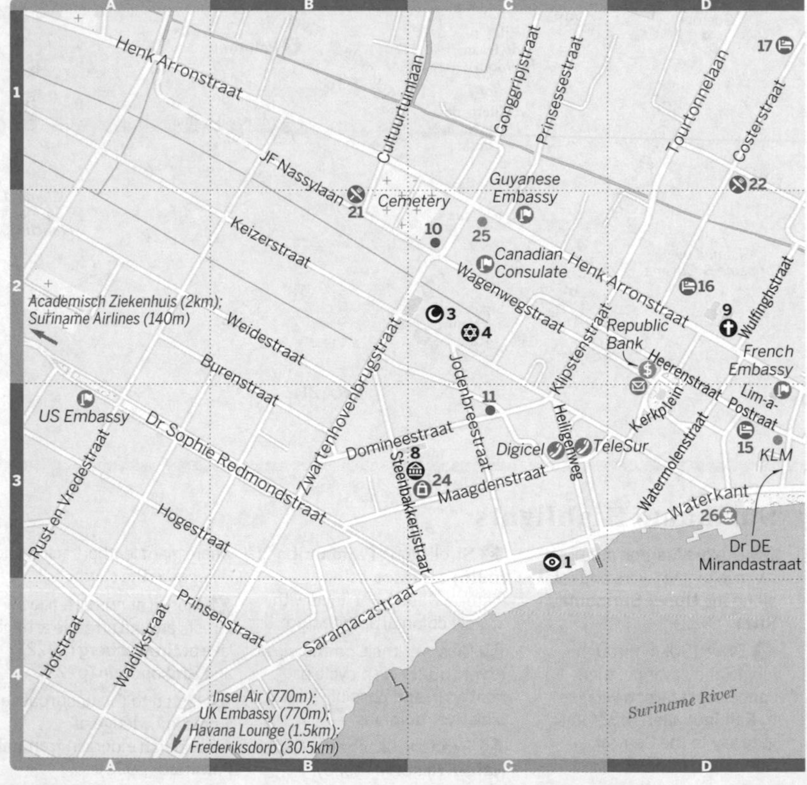

Saint Peter & Paul Cathedral-Basilica CHURCH
(Henk Arronstraat; ⌚6am-1.30pm Mon-Fri, 8am-1pm Sat, 8:30am-noon Sun) Commonly called 'the Cathedral,' this gorgeously restored building was designated a Minor Basilica by Pope Francis in 2014. It's said to be the largest wooden structure in the Western Hemisphere and is worth a peek inside for the masterful woodwork and carvings. Mass is held daily and English tours are available on demand.

Fort Zeelandia MUSEUM
(⌚9am-5pm Tue-Sun, tours in Dutch 11am & 12:30pm Sun) Inside well-restored Fort Zeelandia, a star-shaped, 18th-century fort built on the site where the first colonists alighted, is the worthwhile **Stichting Surinaams Museum** (☎42-5871; admission SR$5; ⌚9am-2pm Tue-Sat, 10am-2pm Sun), featuring colonial-era relics, period rooms and temporary exhibitions.

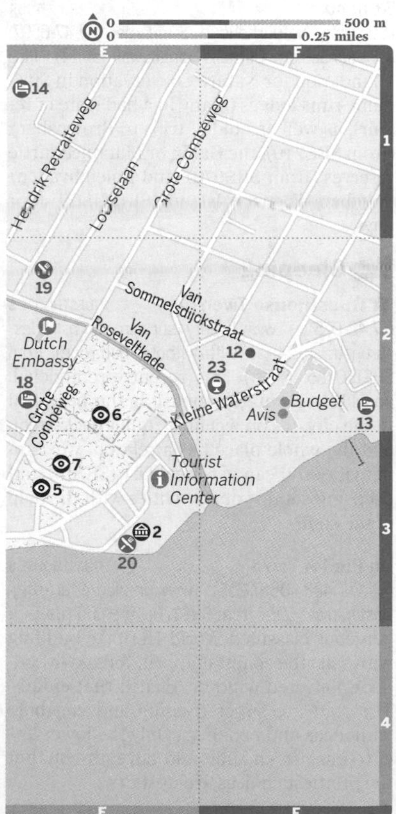

ReadyTex Art Gallery GALLERY
(Steenbakkerijstraat; ⌚8am-4:30pm Mon-Fri, 8:30am-1:30pm Sat) FREE Five glorious floors of colorful, local sculpture and paintings. Also check out the **ReadyTex craft and souvenir shop** (44-48 Maagdenstraat; ⌚8am-4.30pm Mon-Fri, 8:30am-1pm Sat) just around the corner.

Onafhankelijkheidsplein SQUARE
Surrounding the centrally located Onafhankelijkheidsplein (Independence Square) are the contrasting stately 18th-century **Presidential Palace** (Henk Arronstraat) – open to the public November 25 only – and aging

Paramaribo

Sights
1 Central Market C3
2 Fort Zeelandia E3
3 Mosque Keizerstraat C2
4 Neveh Shalom Synagogue C2
5 Onafhankelijkheidsplein E3
6 Palmentuin E2
7 Presidential Palace E3
8 ReadyTex Art Gallery C3
9 Saint Peter & Paul Cathedral-Basilica D2
Stichting Surinaams Museum .... (see 2)

Activities, Courses & Tours
Fietsen in Suriname .... (see 18)
10 METS C2
11 Orange Suriname C3
12 Orange Suriname F2

Sleeping
13 Eco-Resort F2
14 Greenheart Hotel E1
15 Guesthouse Albergo Alberga D3
16 Guesthouse TwenTy4 .... D2
17 Un Pied A Terre D1
18 Zus & Zo E2

Eating
19 Carili Roti E2
20 De Gadri E3
21 Restaurant Dumpling #1 .... B2
22 Souposo D1
Zus & Zo .... (see 18)

Drinking & Nightlife
23 Café-Bar 't Vat F2

Shopping
24 ReadyTex Craft & Souvenir Shop C3

Information
25 Vreemdelingenpolitie C2

Transport
26 Water Taxis D3

PAY WITH EUROS & US DOLLARS

Most Paramaribo businesses take euros and US dollars, and most tours and guesthouses quote prices in euros. Know your exchange rates, although most businesses give an honest exchange.

colonial government buildings. Behind the palace is the **Palmentuin** (Van Roseveltkade), a shady haven of tall royal palms.

Het Surinaamsch Rumhuis DISTILLERY
(473-3344; www.rumhuis.sr; 18 Cornelis Jongbawstraat; 1½-/2hr tours SR$55/65; 2hr tours 9.30am Tue, other times by request) Tours here begin with a 'happy shot,' then it's through the distillery, rum museum and tasting room, where you will learn to sample each variety like a pro. Finish with cocktails on the patio. The shorter tours skip the distillery.

Tours

Suriname's exemplary national parks, reserves and cultural offerings are most easily accessed via tours with Paramaribo-based operators. You should shop around, but not too much: prices are competitive, and most of the agencies work together to assemble the minimum number of participants for trips. All charge 5% extra for credit card payments.

METS ECOTOUR
(Movement for Eco-Tourism in Suriname; 47-7088; www.mets.sr; JF Nassylaan 2) Organized and easily the most professional and eco-minded agency, METS donates proceeds to conservation and conducts a wide range of trips. It specializes in jungle expeditions to the deep interior, including Palumeu or the Gran Rio River (both from SR$2200, five days).

Orange Suriname TOUR
(42-6409; www.orangesuriname.com; Van Sommelsdijckstraat; 9am-6pm) A comprehensive and professional company with extremely knowledgeable and helpful staff. There's another **office** (www.orangesuriname.com; Domineestraat 39; 8:30am-4:40pm Mon-Fri, 9am-1pm Sat) at Domineestraat.

Waterproof Suriname BOAT TOUR, ECOTOUR
(96-2927; www.waterproofsuriname.com) Runs laid-back boat cruises (SR$100) to see river dolphins (sometimes combined with walks around the Commewijne River plantations), as well as day trips to watch sea turtles at Galibi and in French Guiana (SR$650). The company will pick you up; it doesn't have an office.

Cardy Adventures CYCLING
(42-2518; www.cardyadventures.com; Cornelis Jongbawstraat 31; bike rental per day SR$17-35; 8am-7pm Mon-Sat) Has bike tours to the nearby Commewijne plantations, as well as longer tours of up to 10 days to the interior.

Fietsen in Suriname CYCLING
(52-0781; www.fietseninsuriname.com; Zus & Zo, Grote Combéweg 13A; bike rental per day SR$20-50) A slick bike tour and rental agency at Zus & Zo guesthouse. Self-guided bike maps are SR$15 and day tours start at SR$95.

Stinasu TOUR
(Stichting Natuurbehoud Suriname; 47-6597; www.stinasu.sr; Cornelis Jongbawstraat 14) The Foundation for Nature Conservation in Suriname runs lodges (many in a bad state of repair), as well as guided trips to Brownsberg (from SR$240), the Galibi or Matapica turtle reserves (from SR$670), and Raleighvallen/Voltzberg/Foengoe Island (SRD$1800, four days).

Sleeping

★**Guesthouse TwenTy4** GUESTHOUSE $
(42-0751; www.twenty4suriname.com; Jesurunstraat 24; r with/without bathroom from SR$130/85;) This recently remodeled, sparkling clean guesthouse is the best deal in the city. It's on a central, quiet backstreet, and the whole place has a relaxed, welcoming vibe. You can get breakfast (SR$18) and beer, and set up your activities with the help of the staff.

Un Pied A Terre GUESTHOUSE $
(47-0488, 0867-2551; www.un-pied-a-terre.org; Costerstraat 59; r from SR$120;) This is a gorgeous classified World Heritage building with all the paint-chipped, creaky-wood-floor, louvered-window charm that entails. The staff are super friendly and can help with ideas and bookings. Only the lower level rooms are en suite and have air-con, but the prettiest choices are upstairs.

Zus & Zo GUESTHOUSE $

(☎52-0905; www.zusenzosuriname.com; Grote Combéweg 13A; s/d/t/q SR$55/90/150/185; ❄📶) A backpacker's hostel, the bright and inviting Zus & Zo (say it 10 times fast!) has rooms with a shared hot-water bathroom on the top floor of a classic Paramaribo colonial-style house. There's also an excellent ground-floor cafe. The staff can help you arrange almost any excursion in Suriname. Some fan and air-con rooms are equal in price.

Guesthouse Albergo Alberga GUESTHOUSE $

(☎52-0050; www.guesthousealbergoalberga.com; Lim-a-Postraat 13; s/d SR$80/100, d with air-con SR$140; ❄📶🏊) This long-running favorite is situated on a quintessentially colonial Parbo street in an endearing yet palpably aging World Heritage–listed building. Some rooms are quite spacious. The little pool out back is great for a dunk after a long day exploring Parbo.

★**Greenheart Hotel** HOTEL $$

(☎52-1360; www.greenheart-hotel.com; Costerstraat 68; s/d/t/f incl breakfast SR$210/300/390/480; 📶🏊) A lovely hotel in a converted colonial mansion of polished hardwoods. Many rooms have loft spaces, perfect for families, and there are lots of inviting communal spaces. Breakfast and dinner (on request) are served in the open-air dining area out back. The pool is reminiscent of a Balinese resort. There's no air-con, but this is a fantastic bargain.

Eco-Resort HOTEL $$

(☎42-5522; www.ecoresortinn.com; Cornelis Jongbawstraat 16; r incl breakfast from SR$300; ❄@📶🏊) What makes this modern and professional hotel 'eco' is not clear, but the price includes a buffet breakfast, free airport transfer with a two-night stay and use of the swanky facilities at the Hotel Torarica. The more expensive 'river view' rooms don't really have river views, but they are set closer to the water than the standards.

Eating

Tourists frequent 'the strip' across from Hotel Torarica, which has restaurants to fit all budgets – take your pick of Dutch pancake shops, Indonesian, Creole and others. The cheapest city-center options are at the frenetic Central Market and Indonesian stalls along Waterkant. **Eating in Suriname** (www.eteninsuriname.com) is a useful website with information on restaurants in Paramaribo.

Family-run Javanese eateries (open for dinner only) line Blaugrond, a laid-back residential street about 10 minutes by taxi from downtown Paramaribo. Rena, Mirioso, Pawiro and Saoto are some of the better-known spots, but any of them will serve cheap and delicious noodle, rice and soup dishes. It's worth making this trip for the ambience alone.

De Gadri CREOLE $

(Zeelandiaweg 1; mains SR$15-32; ⏰8am-10pm Mon-Fri, 11am-10pm Sat) This quiet, outdoor eatery overlooking the river has Parbo's best Creole food along with exceptionally friendly service. Try the delicious soup of the day – peanut, cassava or banana accompanied by roast chicken and *pom,* a kind of casserole.

JUNGLE AIRPORT ACCOMMODATIONS

The area around Suriname's Zanderij International Airport is beautiful savanna forest with white-sand earth, wildlife-filled jungle and cold, clean streams blackened to a cola color by fallen leaves. This is a great area to look for sloths, tamarins, saki monkeys, giant anteaters and an impressive variety of birds. Taxis cost SR$150 to/from Paramaribo. Alternatively, you could hop on an airport shuttle or minibus (from the Maagdenstraat station in Paramaribo) to the tiny town of Zanderij and take a taxi from there.

They certainly don't advertise themselves as such, but gorgeous and welcoming **Palulu Camping** (☎864-5223; www.surinamecamping.com; per person SR$80) 🍃 and the more upscale **Colakreek** (☎47-2621; www.mets.sr; hammock lodge/tent SR$50/95, cabins SR$295) could uniquely be considered airport jungle lodges. Early flight out or late flight in? Instead of driving into Paramaribo, go straight into the jungle – and maybe stay a few days. It's SR$50 and a 10-minute drive to both of these places from the airport.

Restaurant Dumpling #1 CHINESE $
(JF Nassylaan 12; mains SR$13-35; ⏲7am-2pm & 5-11pm Tue-Sun) The name says it all. Don't miss the succulent dumplings and other Chinese classics, like steamed spare ribs and tofu soup pot.

Carili Roti INDIAN $
(Julianastraat 6; roti around SR$12; ⏲6:15am-2.30pm Mon-Fri, 6:45am-1.30pm Sat) Small roti shop that beats the chains in town for both taste and price.

★**Souposo** FUSION $$
(Costerstraat 20A; mains SR$25-60; ⏲10am-11pm Tue-Sat) The food here – delicious daily soups and mains from duck leg confit in masala to an amazing pesto pasta topped with home-smoked *bang bang* (freshwater fish) and sundried tomatoes – would stand out anywhere in the world. Brunch includes omelets, fresh juices and salads. The heritage home garden setting makes the experience even more lovely.

Zus & Zo INTERNATIONAL $$
(Grote Combéweg 13A; meals from SR$30; ⏲9am-11pm; wi-fi) This restaurant and bar serves up some of the best food and cocktails in town. Dishes range from Surinamese soups to French cheese pies, burgers and salads. Live music is held here on occasion. There's also a good guesthouse upstairs.

Drinking & Nightlife

Casinos are everywhere in Paramaribo and are extremely popular with locals and Dutch tourists. Duck inside a few to see a different side of the city. This is also a town that loves to party with hopping nightlife from Wednesday through Saturday. For cheap drinks with locals, head to the outdoor stalls near Platte Brug on Waterkant.

TWEETY FEST

On Sunday mornings, people – mostly men – engage in peaceful yet secretly cutthroat birdsong competitions on the Onafhankelijkheidsplein. Everyone brings their favorite *twatwa* (song bird), usually a seed finch purchased from Amerindian people in the interior. The *twatwa* that can best belt it out wins. Something of a national obsession, this competition is well worth observing, though its popularity is petering out.

Café-Bar 't Vat BAR
(Kleine Waterstraat 1; ⏲8am-1am Mon-Thu, 8am-3am Fri, 9am-3am Sat, 9am-1am Sun) The night begins at Café-Bar 't Vat, an outdoor bar-cafe with occasional live music.

Havana Lounge CLUB
(☎40-2258; Hogerhuystraat 13) FREE The club of the moment is at its best on Thursdays when salsa plays till 1am then switches from reggae to hip-hop. Expect a meat market.

Information

DANGERS & ANNOYANCES

Avoid quiet streets and secluded areas after dark; the Palmentuin and Watermolenstraat in particular are known for drug dealing and robberies at night (Watermolenstraat is central and leads from Waterkant through the Unesco area). Watch for pickpockets around the market area, even in daylight hours.

INTERNET ACCESS

Most hotels and guesthouses have free wi-fi, which is also available at many more upscale restaurants and cafes around town.

MEDICAL SERVICES

Academisch Ziekenhuis (AZ; ☎44-2222; Flustraat; ⏲6-10pm Mon-Fri, 9am-10pm Sat & Sun) Has general practitioners who provide excellent care and speak English. Only hospital with an emergency room.

MONEY

You can change money or traveler's checks or get credit-card advances at most major banks.

Republic Bank (Kerkplein 1) Has ATMs that most reliably accept international cards. There are several other branches around town.

POST

Post Office (Korte Kerkstraat 1) Opposite the Dutch Reformed Church.

TELEPHONE

SIM cards are available at **TeleSur** (p927) and **Digicel** (p927) for SR$20, which includes SR$5 worth of credit; calls are around SR$0.75 per minute. Digicel's offices are more efficient than TeleSur's.

TOURIST INFORMATION

Tourist Information Center (☎47-9200; Waterkant 1; ⏲9am-3:30pm Mon-Fri) The friendly folks here can welcome you in several languages, provide a walking-tour map and guide you in the right direction for most activities in Suriname.

Getting There & Away

AIR

There are two airports in Paramaribo: nearby Zorg-en-Hoop (for domestic and Guyana flights) and the larger **Johan Pengel International Airport** (www.japi-airport.com; usually referred to as Zanderij and used for all other international flights), 45km south of Parbo.

BUS & MINIBUS

Minibuses to Brownsberg and Atjoni (SR$50 to SR$70, three hours) leave from the corner of Prinsenstraat and Saramacastraat. Public buses to Nieuw Nickerie (SR$20 to SR$40, four hours) and other western destinations leave throughout the day from the corner of Dr Sophie Redmondstraat and Hofstraat; for a private minibus, ask your hotel for a list of prices and companies that will pick you up. To Albina, public buses (SR$8.50, 140km, three hours) leave hourly and private buses (SR$30, 3½ hours) leave when full from Waterkant at the foot of Heiligenweg. There are connecting boats to Albina and Nieuw Nickerie.

CAR

Both **Avis** (☎ 42-1567; www.avis.com) and **Budget** (☎ 42-4631; www.budgetsuriname.com) have offices at the Hotel Torarica and the airport. Compact cars rent from SR$85 per day, and 4WDs are available.

TAXI

Taxis are fast and many work on a share system. Most share taxis are minivans that hold up to eight people and if you leave in the morning they fill quickly. Expect to pay SR$70 per person to Albina and SR$100 per person to Nieuw Nickerie. Ask your hotel for a list of drivers and/or to call them for you.

Getting Around

BICYCLE

In good Dutch fashion, many people see Parbo and its environs, including the old plantations across the Suriname River, on bicycles. Helmets are rarely worn and are hard to rent. Road and mountain bikes are available for rent from SR$17 per day.

BUS

Most of Parbo's buses leave from Heiligenweg. Ask about schedules at points of departure or your guesthouse.

TAXI

Taxis are usually reasonably priced but unmetered and negotiable (a short trip will cost around SR$10).

GETTING INTO TOWN

From Johan Pengel International Airport (aka Zanderij), 45km south of Parbo, you can grab a taxi into town (SR$150, one hour). Airport shuttles organized through your hotel are SR$75. Still cheaper, minibuses go to and from Zanderij (SR$7) and the Zorg-en-Hoop airfield (SR$5) from Heiligenweg in daytime hours only. A taxi from Zorg-en-Hoop is about SR$25.

WATER TAXI

Fast and frequent **water taxis** (short trips SR$15) leave from Platte Brug dock on Waterkant just south of Keizerstraat.

Commewijne River

Opposite Paramaribo, the banks of the Commewijne River are lined with old plantation properties divided by canals and strewn with the remains of coffee, cacao and cane-processing buildings.

Many visitors rent a bike to spend a full day touring the well-defined routes past the plantations. The most popular route crosses the Suriname and Commewijne rivers using water taxis to reach **Frederiksdorp** (☎ 45-3083; www.frederiksdorp.com; r per person incl full board SR$190), a plantation complex that has been lovingly restored and turned into a hotel and restaurant. **Fort Nieuw Amsterdam** is the place to go to see artifacts of the slave trade and an impressive Dutch-engineered system of locks holding back the river. Beautiful **Peperpot Nature Park**, about 10km from Parbo, stands in eerie dilapidation across the Meerzorg bridge and is a favorite bird-watchers' locale. Cardy Adventures (p918), Fietsen in Suriname (p918) and Paramaribo's tourist information center can provide maps and information about the routes.

Tours

Popular boat tours are available to the same sites you can get to by bike. These can save you from the heat, but they are expensive and – without the thrill of exploration – are much less exciting.

North of Fort Nieuw Amsterdam, **Matapica** is a tranquil and almost mosquito-free beach where sea turtles come ashore

OFF THE BEATEN TRACK

AMERINDIAN EXPERIENCE

Palumeu (☎47-7088; www.mets.sr; 4-5 day packages from SR$2580) This very remote lodge is located in the Amerindian village of Palumeu on the stunning banks of the Boven Tapanahoni River off the Upper Suriname. It's managed by METS in collaboration with the locals. Stay in comfortable thatched huts and enjoy guided tours of the village and jungle walks (it's forbidden to go off anywhere on your own). Minimum three-night stay.

April to August. Tours generally reach it by boating through the plantation canals and a swamp rich in birdlife. Stinasu (p918) runs a small camp here.

Spotting friendly-faced river dolphins along the Commewijne is also popular, especially at sunset, and most plantation boat tours will attempt to point them out to passengers when passing through the dolphins' feeding grounds. One-day boat excursions dedicated to dolphin-viewing are available year-round.

Brownsberg Nature Reserve & Brokopondo

Brownsberg's park headquarters are located on a high plateau overlooking Brokopondo, about 100km from Paramaribo along a red-dirt highway. Monkeys seem to be everywhere, whether they're red howlers growling in the canopy, or precious black-bearded sakis checking you out from a tree limb. Stinasu (p918) has rustic lodges (from SR$120) for groups, and camping (SR$50) and hammock sites (SR$30) at the headquarters.

Brokopondo is really a man-made reservoir, created in 1964 when the government dammed the Suriname River to produce hydroelectric power for processing bauxite. Views of storm clouds moving in over the 1550-sq-km lake are breathtaking, but a closer look reveals a rainforest graveyard, in which dead trees stick up over the water's surface from what was once the forest floor. The park has interesting displays explaining how the dam project required relocating thousands of mostly Maroon and Amerindian people as well as hundreds of thousands of animals.

It's relatively easy to visit Brownsberg on your own: take an Atjoni-bound bus from the Saramacastraat bus station near the central market in Paramaribo and ask to be let off at the village of Brownsberg (SR$60, three hours). From here, arrange in advance for Stinasu to pick you up and drive you to the park (SR$70, 30 minutes); several Parbo-based tour agencies also do Brownsberg as a (very) long day trip.

Upper Suriname River

Stay in river lodges on stunning white-sand beaches amid the jungle and get a glimpse into the neighboring Saamaca villages. Swimming and village visits are the main activities, and the more established places put on dance or live music performances at night. Don't expect to see too much wildlife since the locals source much of their meat from the bush. A visit to the interesting and well-managed **Maroon Museum** (Marronmuseum Saamaka; Kumalu; admission SR$20; ⏲10am-3pm) in Pikin Slee is a must for understanding the culture.

Stichting Lodeholders Boven Suriname (Association of Saramacaan Lodge Holders; www.upper-suriname.com) maintains an online map of villages and lodges, although it's not always up to date.

Sleeping & Eating

★Tei Wei LODGE $

(☎85-6142, 859-1946; bertajaiso@gmail.com; Gunsi, near New Aurora; per person incl meals SR$85) Run by the tiny (population 55), very traditional and welcoming village of Gunsi, this is the best place to immerse yourself into Saamaca culture. Huts with beds and mosquito nets are basic but clean with fantastic, hammock-strewn terraces overlooking the river. Bathrooms are shared. Activities range from village visits (SR$50) to overnight jungle treks (SR$500 per group).

Botopasie LODGE $$

(☎865 0702; www.botopasie.com; Botopasi; hammock/room/cabin per person incl meals SR$115/160/180; 📶) Dutch and Surinamese-run, this exceptionally clean and comfortable small lodge sits just across the river from the lively Saamaca town of Botopasi. Bungalows have en-suite bathrooms, meals are taken on a beautiful terrace with river views and there's even hot water!

Pasensie LODGE **$$**
(☎868-5572; pasensie.slee@gmail.com; Pikin Slee; per person incl meals SR$135; 📶) Ideally located just outside of Pikin Slee, this tidy riverside lodge is walking distance to the Maroon Museum and a few other villages, so visitors can really delve into the Saamaca culture. Bathrooms are shared. Museum trips (SR$20) and half/full-day jungle tours (SR$50/100 per group) are two of the activities on offer.

Kumalu Dream Island LODGE **$$**
(☎886-7059; www.kumaludreamisland.com; Djumu; per person incl meals SR$125) One of the longest-running lodges in the region, this island-bound, solar-powered place is in a stunning riverside setting. Cabins are large and en suite. Activities include hikes up the aptly named Ananas Mountain, which has wild pineapples growing on it and outrageous views over the jungle from the top.

★ **Awarradam** LODGE **$$$**
(☎47-7088; www.mets.sr; near Kajana; 4-day, 3-night package per person incl meals and activities SR$2500) This very remote METS-run lodge is a great place for those who want to get deep into the jungle while experiencing Saamaca culture. Digs are very comfortable and there's even a spa. Minimum stay is three nights.

Anaula LODGE **$$$**
(www.anoulanatureresort.com; near New Aurora; 3-day/2-night package per person incl transport SR$900; 📶🏊) Spacious, manicured grounds, comfortable en-suite cabins and even a swimming pool sit next to scenic rapids on a jungle island in the river. It's popular yet tranquil. Stay here to relax and get away from it all rather than experience Saamaca culture.

ℹ Getting There & Away

Plenty of tours go to the lodges in private buses but it's easy and much cheaper to take public transport. The lodges near New Aurora are the easiest to reach and are about one to two hours upriver from Atjoni, depending on the season. Add another hour to get to lodges near Pikin Slee and Botopasi and two more hours to Djumu. Getting to Kajana can require an overnight in Djumu.

From Paramaribo, take an early morning minibus to Atjoni (SR$20 to SR$50, 3½ hours; buses leave when full) from the Saramacastraat bus station. Most likely your lodge will have given you the name of a boat person, but if not, ask at the information desk and they will help find you a boat. Count on paying SR$50 to New Aurora, SR$75 to Pikin Slee and more beyond. If you don't want to backtrack, several airstrips along the way offer regular connections to Paramaribo, and some tour-agency charters might be able to offer you a seat as well. Bring plenty of cash as no one down here will take credit cards.

Central Suriname Nature Reserve

One of the biggest swaths of Suriname's protected regions, covering 12% of Suriname's land area, this nature reserve covers 16,000 sq km and was established in 1998 with a US$1 million donation from Conservation International. Around 40% of Central

ℹ GETTING TO GUYANA

Getting to the Border

Minibuses from Paramaribo to Georgetown (nine to 12 hours), via South Drain and Moleson Creek, leave around 5am and cost around SR$120 (not including the boat crossing). The Canawaima ferry (one-way/round-trip SR$48/65, 25 minutes, 10am and noon daily) from South Drain crosses the Corantijn River to Moleson Creek, Guyana. You'll have to wait in line to stamp out of Suriname before getting on the boat. Money changers abound and tend to offer good rates. There are no fees at the border and immigration is always open to coincide with boat departures and arrivals.

Moving On

After waiting in line again to get stamped in and passing a customs check in Guyana, you'll find the minibuses to Georgetown.

Guyana is an hour behind Suriname; remember to set your watch *back* one hour.

For information on making this crossing in the opposite direction, see p758.

Suriname Nature Reserve's plants and animals are found only in the Guianas.

Raleighvallen (Raleigh Falls) is a low, long staircase of cascading water on the upper Coppename River, about two hours upriver from the nearest Maroon (Kwinti people) village. Resident wildlife includes spider monkeys, electric eels and Guiana cock-of-the-rock, a spectacular blood-orange bird. Stinasu (p918) has well-run tourist lodges – accessible by a flight or a five-hour drive and two-hour boat ride (via tour only) – on **Foengoe Island** next to the falls. **Voltzberg** is a 240m granite dome accessible by a 2½-hour jungle trail and then a steep ascent – the 360-degree views of the jungle from the top are simply astounding.

Kabalebo River

★ **Kabalebo** LODGE **$$$**
(☎42-6532; www.kabalebo.com; 3-night standard packages per person all-incl from SR$1300 ; ❄) Way out west near the Guyana border, remote Kabalebo is in the middle of pristine jungle. Accommodations here range from an economical 'jungle camp' to some of the most private and luxurious retreats in the country. Tons of activities are on offer, from fishing and wildlife-spotting to hiking and kayaking.

Nieuw Nickerie

POP 13,842

This bustling border town of wide streets was once a major balata collecting center, although now it's mostly a banana and rice production hub with a large port. It's also the last stop before Guyana and the departure point for exploring **Bigi Pan**, a swampy reservoir known for caimans, scarlet ibis and more than 100 other birds. Tours are easily organized from Paramaribo.

To stay overnight, the **Concord Hotel** (☎23-2345; Wilhelminastraat 3; d SR$105; ❄) is a good, small and clean motel-style place.

All buses and minibuses arrive at and leave from the market. Government buses travel to Paramaribo (SR$15, four hours) at 6am and 1pm daily, and a private bus (SR$22) leaves when full after the first government bus leaves. Taxis to Paramaribo (SR$100 per person) take three to four hours. Minibuses to South Drain (SR$15) for the ferry to Guyana leave at 8am, and it's best to reserve with the driver the day before; your hotel can help with this.

GETTING TO FRENCH GUIANA

Getting to the Border

Destroyed during the Maroon rebellion of the 1980s and still recovering, Albina (population 5000) is the last stop before crossing the Marowijne River to St Laurent du Maroni, French Guiana. Some travelers pass through here on tours to the Galibi Reserve to see turtles, but the town is notorious for crime and there's little reason to stay.

Share taxis (SR$75, two hours), minibuses (SR$30 to SR$40, 2½ hours) and public buses (SR$8.50, three hours) leave from Paramaribo to central Albina.

At the Border

During daylight hours, motorboats leave on demand from the Albina ferry dock for the crossing (SR$20, 10 minutes) and are the way most people without cars cross the river. For those with cars, a French **car ferry** (per passenger SR$20, car & driver SR$160; ⏲8am & 5pm Mon-Fri, 8:30am & 9:30am Sat, 3pm & 4pm Sun) crosses the Marowijne River in 30 minutes a couple of times per day. From the St Laurent du Maroni dock, you'll probably have to walk into town (about half a mile) unless you've organized a pickup in advance. Be sure to get your exit and entrance stamps at immigration at the ferry docks on both sides of the river. There are no border fees.

Note there is no place to change money in St Laurent du Maroni but there is an ATM. There are plenty of money changers in Albina who will approach you before you cross – know your rates in advance.

Moving On

Irregular buses from the station in St Laurent go to Cayenne. Because the public transport in French Guiana is unreliable and inconvenient, most people rent a car.

For information on making this crossing in the opposite direction, see p745.

Galibi & Coppename Nature Reserves

Galibi's turtle-nesting area hosts hordes of sea turtles, including the giant leatherback, during egg-laying season (April through August). You can get there from Albina with permission from members of the local Carib community and a hired canoe, or more easily from Paramaribo with the tour operator Stinasu (p918).

The Coppename Nature Reserve, at the mouth of the Coppename River, is home to the endangered manatee and is a haven for bird-watchers. Stinasu organizes trips by request.

UNDERSTAND SURINAME

Suriname Today

Suriname's president since 2010 is Desiré Bouterse, a former coup leader who, in the 1980s civil war period, was the country's military-backed dictator. In 2012 the Suriname parliament passed an amnesty law protecting Bouterse from the trial for 1982's 'December Murders'. Despite this history, the Surinamese love their multi-ethnic president, particularly the younger generations who weren't alive during the civil war.

The Netherlands ended its security aid to Suriname with the election of Bouterse, who was convicted in 1999 of smuggling over 1000lb of cocaine into the Netherlands. If he should alight on Dutch soil, he will be arrested.

Suriname relies on bauxite for 70% of its foreign exchange. Agriculture, particularly irrigated rice cultivation and bananas, is a major industry for the republic, and the fishing industry is growing. The country is also making a conscious effort to develop ecotourism in the interior.

History

Suriname was the last outpost of what was once a substantial Dutch presence in South America. During the 19th century, Indians and Indonesians (locally referred to as 'Javanese') arrived as indentured plantation workers.

Despite limited autonomy, Suriname remained a colony until 1954, when the area became a self-governing state; it gained full independence in 1975. A coup in 1980, led by Sergeant Major (later Lieutenant Colonel) Desiré Bouterse, brought a military regime to power. Bouterse was later brought to trial for ordering the execution of 15 prominent opponents in Fort Zeelandia – an event now called the 'December Murders' – in 1982. In 1986 the government carried out a campaign to suppress Maroon rebellion, led by Ronnie Brunswijk and his Jungle Commando (the Maroon military). Many of those loyal to Brunswijk fled to French Guiana as their villages were destroyed.

In 1987 a civilian government was elected, but it was deposed by a bloodless coup in 1990. Another civilian government led by Ronald Venetiaan was elected in 1991 and signed a peace treaty with the Jungle Commando and other armed bands in 1992.

Venetiaan was re-elected in May 2000 and held office until 2010. This period was marked by economic difficulty and unrest: flooding in 2006 caused a national disaster and left up to 20,000 people homeless; and in 2009 government troops were sent to gold mining areas near Albina to quell anti-Chinese and anti-Brazilian protests.

Culture

Suriname is a cultural free-for-all of incredibly friendly and generous people. Paramaribo's level of acceptance and unity is primarily undisturbed by religious and racial tension, which is remarkable given the intimacy of so many groups living in such a small corner of the world; however, Maroons and Amerindians in the interior live with high poverty levels and fewer educational opportunities.

Many Surinamese live or have lived in the Netherlands, either to enjoy its greater economic opportunities or to escape military repression, and are consequently knowledgeable of European trends.

About 40% of the country's well-integrated population are nominally Christian, but some also adhere to traditional African beliefs. Hindus compose 26% of the population (most of the East Indian community), while 19% are Muslim (ethnic Indonesians plus a minority of East Indian origin). A small number are Buddhists, Jews and followers of Amerindian religions. In terms of ethnicities, 37% of the population are Indian, 31% are Creole, 15% are Indonesian, 10% are Maroons, 2% are Amerindian, 2% are Chinese and 1% are Dutch (the remaining 2% percent are 'other').

Some cultural forms – such as gamelan music, often heard at special events – derive from the Indonesian immigrant populations. Other art forms that visitors enjoy include intricate Amerindian basketry and wood carvings by Maroons, who are widely regarded as the best carvers in tropical America.

Environment

Suriname is divided into a coastal region and dense tropical forest and savannas. To its west, the Corantijn (Corentyne in Guyana) River forms the border, disputed in its most southerly reaches with Guyana; the Marowijne (Maroni in French Guiana) and Litani Rivers form the border with French Guiana.

The majority of Surinamese inhabit the Atlantic coastal plain, where most of the country's few roads are located. The nearby Afobaka Dam created one of the world's largest (1550 sq km) reservoirs, Brokopondo, on the Upper Suriname River.

Being mostly rainforest, Suriname has diverse wildlife, from the flashy jaguar and black caiman to humble agouti and squirrel monkeys. Birders flock to see a wide range of bird species including the red ibis and harpy eagle.

SURVIVAL GUIDE

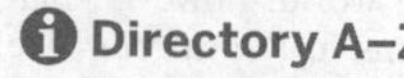

Directory A–Z

ACCOMMODATIONS

Fairly affordable hotels and guesthouses are readily found in Paramaribo starting at SR$80, while sleeping in the interior can involve more rustic accommodations to luxurious eco-lodges.

> **SLEEPING PRICE RANGES**
>
> The following price ranges refer to a double room with bathroom in high season.
>
> **$** less than SR$150
>
> **$$** SR$150 to SR$400
>
> **$$$** more than SR$400

ACTIVITIES

Suriname's best activity is experiencing nature and culture in the interior. Bird-watching and other wildlife-spotting adventures are once-in-a-lifetime experiences, as many of the critters are endemic or more prolific in this big, healthy swath of jungle, and boating and trekking opportunities are abundant. The accessible Maroon cultures are something unique to the country. People explore by bike, but only in areas around the coastal cities.

BOOKS

The most popular book on Suriname is Mark Plotkin's *Tales of a Shaman's Apprentice*, which also includes information on Brazil, Venezuela and the other Guianas.

Willoughbyland: England's Lost Colony by Matthew Parker covers the country's European history via the rise and fall of the British in Suriname.

How Dear Was the Sugar? by Cynthia McLeod, perhaps Suriname's most important historical novelist, explores the sugarcane industry of the 18th century.

BUSINESS HOURS

General business hours are 7:30am to 3pm weekdays, with perhaps a few hours on Saturday. Most restaurants serve lunch from around 11am to 2:30pm, and dinner from about 6pm to 10pm. A small number of places open for breakfast at 8am.

ELECTRICITY

Plugs are European standard two round prong. Currents are 110/220V, 60Hz.

EMBASSIES & CONSULATES

Most embassies and consulates are in Paramaribo.

Brazilian Embassy (☎40-0200; www.brazil-embassy.net/suriname-paramaribo.html; Maratakkastraat 2, Zorg-en-Hoop)

Canadian Consulate (☎47-1222; Wagenwegstraat 50)

Dutch Embassy (☎47-7211; http://suriname.nlambassade.org; Van Roseveltkade 5)

French Embassy (☎47-6455; www.ambafrance-sr.org; Henk Arronstraat 5-7, 2nd fl)

Guyanese Embassy (☎47-7895; guyembassy@sr.net; Henk Arronstraat 82)

UK Embassy (☎40-2870; Van't Hogerhuysstraat 9-11, VSH United Bldg)

US Embassy (☎47-2900; http://suriname.usembassy.gov; Dr Sophie Redmondstraat 129) Also responsible for US citizens in French Guiana.

FOOD PRICE RANGES

The following price ranges refer to a standard main course. Most restaurants charge 10% for service; if it's not on the bill, leave between 10% and 15%.

$ less than SR$25

$$ SR$25 to SR$50

$$$ more than SR$50

HEALTH

A yellow fever vaccination certificate is technically required for travelers arriving from infected areas, although you probably won't be asked for one. Typhoid and chloroquine-resistant malaria are present in the interior. Tap water is safe to drink in Paramaribo but not elsewhere.

INTERNET ACCESS

Most guesthouses, hotels and some cafes offer free wi-fi.

LANGUAGE

Dutch is the official national language, but many people speak Sranan Tongo (similar to Creole and also called Taki Taki), which can be understood fairly well by English speakers once you develop an ear for it. Other languages include Hindi, Urdu, Javanese, Mandarin, Cantonese and several dialects of both Maroon and Amerindian languages. English is also widely spoken.

MONEY

Although the official unit of currency is the Surinamese dollar (SR$), some businesses quote prices in euros or US dollars. Most banks will accept major foreign currencies, but you may run into difficulty trying to change Guyanese dollars and Brazilian reals.

Republic Bank ATMs are the most reliable at accepting foreign cards.You can exchange traveler's checks and get credit card advances at RBC banks and some hotels. Major hotels and travel agencies – but hardly anywhere else – accept credit cards (usually for a fee).

PUBLIC HOLIDAYS

New Year's Day January 1; the biggest celebration of the year

Day of the Revolution February 25

Phagwah/Holi (Hindu New Year) March/April

Good Friday/Easter Monday March/April

Labor Day May 1

National Union Day/Abolition of Slavery Day July 1

Independence Day November 25

Christmas Day December 25

Boxing Day December 26

Eid ul-Fitr (Lebaran or Bodo in Indonesian) end of Ramadan; dates vary

TELEPHONE

The national telephone company is **TeleSur** (Telecommunicatiebedrijf Suriname; Heiligenweg 1), which sells SIM cards, although service is considerably better at **Digicel** (cnr Maagdenstraat & Heiligenweg; ⏲8am-4:30pm Mon-Fri, 8am-1:30pm Sat) and the cost is the same (SR$20). There are no area codes in Suriname.

VISAS

Visitors from the US, UK, Australia, Canada, New Zealand and Western Europe need to apply for a tourist card (US$25) valid for 90 days and available at any Surinamese Embassy. Longer stays or multiple entries will require a visa – US passport holders must pay US$100 for a five-year multiple-entry visa, while all other nationalities requiring a visa have to pay from US$30 to US$175, depending on the length of stay and number of entries. For up-to-date info and embassy locations check www.surinameembassy.org.

Allow approximately four weeks for a postal visa or tourist card application. The Surinamese consulates in Georgetown (Guyana) and Cayenne (French Guiana) can issue tourist cards within a couple of hours, but visas can take up to five working days. Bring a passport-size photo and your ticket out of South America.

Visitors planning to stay in Suriname for more than 30 days should register at the **Vreemdelingenpolitie** (Immigration Service; ☎40-3609; Henk Arronstraat 1; ⏲7am-2pm Mon-Fri) in Paramaribo within eight days of their arrival.

WOMEN TRAVELERS

Female travelers, especially if traveling alone, may encounter harassment from local males, but they are rarely physically threatening. Constant 'hissing' and 'sucking' noises can be annoying, if not truly disconcerting – ignore them if you can.

ℹ Getting There & Away

AIR

Long-haul international flights arrive at Suriname's outdated Johan Pengl International Airport (more often called Zanderij), while domestic and regional international flights arrive mostly at Zorg-en-Hoop. The following airlines fly from Paramaribo.

DEPARTURE TAX

Suriname's departure tax is US$66 and is usually included in ticket prices.

Blue Wings (☎43-0370; www.bluewingairlines.com; Zorg-en-Hoop) Scheduled and charter services to many domestic destinations.

Caribbean Airlines (☎43-2700; Dr Sophie Redmondstraat 219)

Insel Air (☎40-3866; www.fly-inselair.com; Van't Hogerhuysstraat 9-11) Service to Curaçao with connections to other Caribbean Islands, the USA and northern South American countries.

KLM (☎47-2421; www.klm.com; Dr DE Mirandastraat 9) Services Amsterdam.

Suriname Airlines (☎43-2700; www.slm.firm.sr; Dr Sophie Redmondstraat 219) Flies to many destinations including Georgetown (Guyana), Cayenne (French Guiana), Trinidad, Curaçao, Belem (Brazil), Panama City, Miami and Amsterdam.

BOAT

From Albina (in the east of Suriname) and Nieuw Nickerie via South Drain (in the west of Suriname), ferries traverse the river borders with French Guiana and Guyana, respectively.

ℹ Getting Around

AIR

Small planes shuttle people between Paramaribo and remote destinations, including some nature reserves.

BOAT

Rivers offer scenic routes to parts of the interior that are otherwise inaccessible. Scheduled services are few, and prices are negotiable. Ferries and launches cross some major rivers, such as the Suriname and the Coppename.

BUS & MINIBUS

In order from cheapest to priciest, you can choose from scheduled government buses, private minibuses that leave when full from designated points, and minibuses that pick you up from your hotel. Trips to the interior cost significantly more than those on coastal routes.

CAR

Suriname's roads are limited and difficult to navigate. Passenger cars can handle the roads along the coast and to Brownsberg, but tracks into the interior are for 4WDs only. Driving is on the left. An International Driving Permit is required.

TAXI

Shared taxis cover routes along the coast. They can be several times more expensive than minibuses but are markedly faster. Local cab fares are negotiable and reasonable; set a price before getting in.

Uruguay

Includes ➡

Best Places to Eat

- ➡ Mercado del Puerto (p937)
- ➡ Café Picasso (p949)
- ➡ Don Joaquín (p941)
- ➡ Resto-Pub 70 (p955)
- ➡ Candy Bar (p937)

Best Places to Stay

- ➡ El Galope Horse Farm & Hostel (p941)
- ➡ Estancia Panagea (p947)
- ➡ Ukelele Hostel (p936)
- ➡ Tas D'Viaje (p951)
- ➡ El Diablo Tranquilo (p954)
- ➡ Ah'Lo Hostel Boutique (p943)

Why Go?

Now more than ever, Uruguay is a country that moves to its own grooves. While its neighbors lurch from one crisis to the next, Uruguay as a nation moves forward much like her citizens – calm and self-assured. Social reforms are moving along nicely and, while there will always be complaints, much of the population seems pretty happy.

Traveling in Uruguay has never been easier. The excellent hostel scene, extensive bus network, good restaurants and abundant campsites make it a backpacker's dream. Even world-class destinations such as Colonia del Sacramento and Punta del Este offer abundant cheap sleeps in all but the absolute peak periods.

People come for celeb-spotting at Punta, the history-soaked smugglers' port of Colonia, the Atlantic coast's wild, surf-pounded beaches and the wide-open skies of Uruguay's interior. They stay for the people – warm, open and sincere folk who have constructed one of South America's most progressive societies.

When to Go

Montevideo

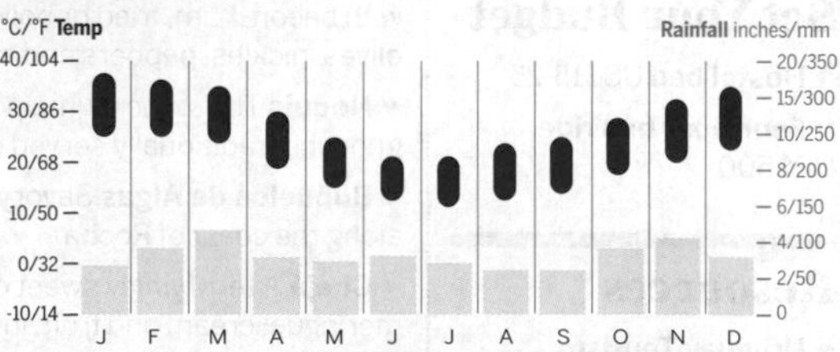

Jan & Feb Street theater and *candombe* drumming consume Montevideo during Carnaval.

Mar Tacuarembó's *gaucho* festival, plus smaller crowds and lower prices on the sunny Atlantic.

Nov Enjoy a springtime soak in Salto's thermal baths or experience Uruguay's *estancias*.

AT A GLANCE

- **Currency** Uruguayan peso (UR$)
- **Language** Spanish
- **Money** ATMs widespread; credit card widely accepted
- **Visas** Not required for many nationals of Western Europe, Australia, USA, Canada or New Zealand
- **Time** GMT minus three hours

Fast Facts

- **Area** 176,215 sq km
- **Population** 3.3 million
- **Capital** Montevideo
- **Emergency** ☎911
- **Country Code** ☎598

Exchange Rates

Australia	A$1	UR$21.2
Canada	C$1	UR$21.4
Euro zone	€1	UR$32.2
New Zealand	NZ$1	UR$19.9
UK	UK£1	UR$44.4
USA	US$1	UR$29.8

Set Your Budget

- **Hostel bed** US$15-25
- **Four-hour bus ride** UR$500

Resources

- **Uruguay Tourism Ministry** (www.turismo.gub.uy)
- **Guru'Guay** (http://guruguay.com)
- **Uruguay surf info** (www.olasyvientos.com)

Connections

Coming from Argentina, most people arrive by boat, departing either from Buenos Aires (for Montevideo and Colonia del Sacramento) or Tigre (for Carmelo). Land crossings are also possible from the Argentine towns of Colón, Gualeguaychú and Concordia. The most common point of entry from Brazil is at Chuí/Chuy.

ITINERARIES

One Week

With a week up your sleeve you won't see it all, but if you keep on the move you can see some of the best of what Uruguay has to offer. Start in the easygoing, picturesque historical river port of Colonia and head for the urban attractions of Montevideo, both an easy ferry ride from Buenos Aires. From Montevideo, continue north along the Atlantic coast and sample a few of Uruguay's best beaches: the 1930s vintage resort of Piriápolis, glitzy Punta del Este, isolated Cabo Polonio, surfer-friendly La Paloma or the relaxed beach-party town of Punta del Diablo. Alternatively, follow the Río Uruguay upstream toward Iguazú Falls via the quirky industrial museum at Fray Bentos and the wonderful hot springs of Salto.

Two Weeks

Adding another week will allow you to do the above at a more leisurely pace, plus get out and explore Uruguay's scenic and little-visited interior, where the *gaucho* tradition lives on.

Essential Food & Drink

- **Asado** Uruguay's national gastronomic obsession, a mixed grill cooked over a wood fire, featuring various cuts of beef and pork, chorizo, *morcilla* (blood sausage) and more.
- **Chivito** A cholesterol bomb of a steak sandwich piled high with bacon, ham, fried or boiled egg, cheese, lettuce, tomato, olives, pickles, peppers and mayonnaise.
- **Ñoquis** The same plump potato dumplings the Italians call gnocchi, traditionally served on the 29th of the month.
- **Buñuelos de Algas** Savory seaweed fritters, a specialty along the coast of Rocha.
- **Chajá** A terrifyingly sweet concoction of sponge cake, meringue, cream and fruit, invented in Paysandú.
- **Medio y medio** A refreshing blend of half white wine, half sparkling wine, with ties to Montevideo's historic Café Roldós.
- **Grappamiel** Strong Italian-style grappa (grape brandy), sweetened and mellowed with honey.

Uruguay Highlights

❶ Get snap-happy on the picturesque cobbled streets of **Colonia del Sacramento** (p940).

❷ Catch a wave or a beachside bonfire in **Punta del Diablo** (p954), way up near the Brazilian border.

❸ Get those hips moving to the *candombe* rhythm at Montevideo's **Carnaval** (p933) party.

❹ Soak those weary traveling bones in the **hot springs around Salto** (p946).

❺ Mingle with sea lions, penguins and whales in the secluded hippie beach town of **Cabo Polonio** (p953).

❻ Herd cattle on horseback at an estancia near **Tacuarembó** (p947), riding through beautiful countryside few travelers ever see.

❼ Ferry across the beautiful Paraná Delta to the laid-back riverside town of **Carmelo** (p943).

MONTEVIDEO

POP 1.3 MILLION

Uruguay's capital and largest city, Montevideo is a favorite for many travelers: small enough to walk or cycle around, but big enough to have some great museums and nightlife, plus an impressive string of beaches along the Río de la Plata. Young *montevideanos* (people from Montevideo) take genuine pride in their city, and the arts and artisan scene is particularly strong.

Sights

Montevideo's most interesting buildings and museums are in the Ciudad Vieja (Old Town), west of **Plaza Independencia**, the city's largest square. Here, remnants of the colonial past such as **Puerta de la Ciudadela**, a vestigial stone gateway from Montevideo's 18th-century citadel, rub shoulders with grand 19th-century legacies of the beef boom, including the beautifully restored, neoclassical **Teatro Solís** (2950-3323; www.teatrosolis.org.uy; Buenos Aires 678; tours 4pm Tue-Sun, plus 11am & noon Wed, Fri, Sat & Sun).

Museo del Carnaval MUSEUM

(2916-5493; www.museodelcarnaval.org; Rambla 25 de Agosto 218; admission UR$90; 11am-5pm Wed-Sun Apr-Nov, daily Dec-Mar) This museum houses a wonderful collection of costumes, drums, masks, recordings and photos documenting the 100-plus-year history of Montevideo's Carnaval. Behind the museum is a cafe and a courtyard where spectators can view performances during the summer months. Touch-screen displays added in 2014 offer limited English-language commentary.

Museo de los Andes MUSEUM

(2916-9461; www.mandes.uy; 619 Rincón; admission UR$200; 10am-5pm Mon-Fri, 10am-3pm Sat) Opened in 2013, this unique museum documents the 1972 Andean plane crash (made famous in the book *Alive!*) that cost 29 Uruguayans their lives and profoundly impacted Uruguay's national psyche. Using original objects and photos from the crash site, it tells the story of the 16 survivors, who battled harrowing conditions for 72 days before returning alive to a stunned nation. The museum is a labor of love for director Jörg Thomsen, a personal friend of many of the families affected.

Casa Rivera MUSEUM

(2915-1051; Rincón 437; 11am-4:45pm Wed-Sun) FREE Former home of Fructuoso Rivera (Uruguay's first president and Colorado Party founder), this neoclassical 1802 building is the centerpiece of Montevideo's National Historical Museum, with a collection of paintings, documents, furniture and artifacts that trace the history of Uruguay's 19th-century path to independence. Several other historic Ciudad Vieja homes nearby, officially part of the museum, are rarely open to visitors.

Museo del Gaucho MUSEUM

(2900-8764; Av 18 de Julio 998; 10am-4pm Mon-Fri) FREE Housed in the ornate Palacio Heber, this museum eloquently conveys the deep attachments between the gauchos, their animals and the land. Its superb collection of historical artifacts includes horse gear, silver work, and *mates* and *bombillas* (metal straws with filters, used for drink-

LOCAL KNOWLEDGE

WHAT'S THE BUZZ? URUGUAY'S NEW MARIJUANA LAW

In December 2013 Uruguay became the first country in the world to fully legalize cannabis. Uruguayan citizens are now allowed to grow up to six marijuana plants for personal use each year, and will be able to purchase up to 40g per month at local pharmacies once the government fully implements its national distribution system.

Meanwhile, smoking pot in public is already legal – for anyone, foreigners included – in the same places where cigarette smoking is permitted. Paradoxically, however, non-Uruguayans are not allowed to purchase weed.

What's a cannabis-loving gringo to do? One obvious answer is to make Uruguayan friends at local hostels; alternatively, those with deeper pockets can indulge in a marijuana tour led by **MVD High** (099-707302; mvdhigh.com; tour per person US$200-250). Their psychedelic sightseeing itinerary lets you 'sample the goods' at various spots around Montevideo – including on the steps of the national assembly where Uruguay's pot legislation was originally passed.

CARNAVAL IN MONTEVIDEO

If you thought Brazil was South America's only Carnaval capital, think again! *Montevideanos* cut loose in a big way every February, with music and dance filling the air for a solid month.

Not to be missed is the early February Desfile de las Llamadas, a two-night parade of *comparsas* (neighborhood Carnaval societies) through the streets of Palermo and Barrio Sur districts, just southeast of the Centro. *Comparsas* are made up of *negros* (persons of African descent) and *lubolos* (whites who paint their faces black for Carnaval, a long-standing Uruguayan tradition). Neighborhood rivalries play themselves out as wave after wave of dancers whirl to the electrifying rhythms of traditional Afro-Uruguayan *candombe* drumming, beaten on drums of three different pitches: the *chico* (soprano), *repique* (contralto) and *piano* (tenor). The heart of the parade route is Isla de Flores, between Salto and Gaboto. Spectators can pay for a chair on the sidewalk or try to snag a spot on one of the balconies overlooking the street.

Another key element of Montevideo's Carnaval are the *murgas*, organized groups of 15 to 17 gaudily dressed performers, including three percussionists, who perform original pieces of musical theater, often satirical and based on political themes. During the dictatorship in Uruguay, *murgas* were famous for their subversive commentary. All *murgas* use the same three instruments: the *bombo* (bass drum), *redoblante* (snare drum) and *platillos* (cymbals). *Murgas* play all over the city, and also compete throughout February in Parque Rodó at the Teatro de Verano. The competition has three rounds, with judges determining who advances and who gets eliminated.

The fascinating history of Montevideo's Carnaval is well documented in the city's Museo del Carnaval. Another great way to experience Carnaval out of season is by attending one of the informal *candombe* practice sessions that erupt in neighborhood streets throughout the year. Two good places to find these are at the corner of Isla de Flores and Gaboto in Palermo, and in Parque Rodó, where the all-female group La Melaza gathers at the corner of Blanes and Gonzalo Ramírez and continues down San Salvador. Drumming at both locations usually starts around 7pm on Sunday nights.

ing maté; a bitter ritual tea) in whimsical designs.

Museo Nacional de Artes Visuales MUSEUM
(MNAV; ☎2711-6124; www.mnav.gub.uy; Giribaldi 2283, Parque Rodó; ⏲9am-4pm Tue, Wed & Fri, 2-4pm Thu) FREE Uruguay's largest collection of paintings is housed here in Parque Rodó. The spacious rooms are graced with works by Blanes, Cúneo, Figari, Gurvich, Torres García and other famous Uruguayans. For a closer look at some of these same artists, visit the **Museo Torres García** (☎2916-2663; www.torresgarcia.org.uy; Sarandí 683; admission UR$100; ⏲10am-6pm Mon-Sat), **Museo Figari** (☎2915-7065; www.museofigari.gub.uy; Juan Carlos Gómez 1427; ⏲1-6pm Tue-Fri, 10am-2pm Sat) FREE and **Museo Gurvich** (☎2915-7826; www.museogurvich.org; Sarandí 524; admission UR$100; ⏲10am-6pm Mon-Fri, 11am-3pm Sat) in Ciudad Vieja, or the **Museo Blanes** (☎2336-2248; blanes.montevideo.gub.uy; Av Millán 4015; ⏲1-7pm Tue-Sun) FREE in the Prado neighborhood north of Centro.

Museo del Fútbol MUSEUM
(☎2480-1259; www.estadiocentenario.com.uy/site/footballMuseum; Estadio Centenario, Av Ricaldoni s/n, Parque José Batlle y Ordóñez; admission UR$150; ⏲10am-5pm Mon-Fri) A must-see for any *fútbol* (soccer) fan, this museum displays memorabilia from Uruguay's 1930 and 1950 World Cup wins. Visitors can also tour the stands.

Activities

Hire a bicycle from **Orange Bike** (☎2908-8286; www.facebook.com/orange.bike.7; Pérez Castellano 1417bis; bike rental per 4/24hr US$15/20) and go cruising along the riverfront Rambla, a 20km walking-jogging-cycling track that leads past Parque Rodó, one of Montevideo's most popular parks, then follows the shoreline to the city's eastern beaches: Punta Carretas, Pocitos, Buceo, Malvin and Carrasco.

Montevideo

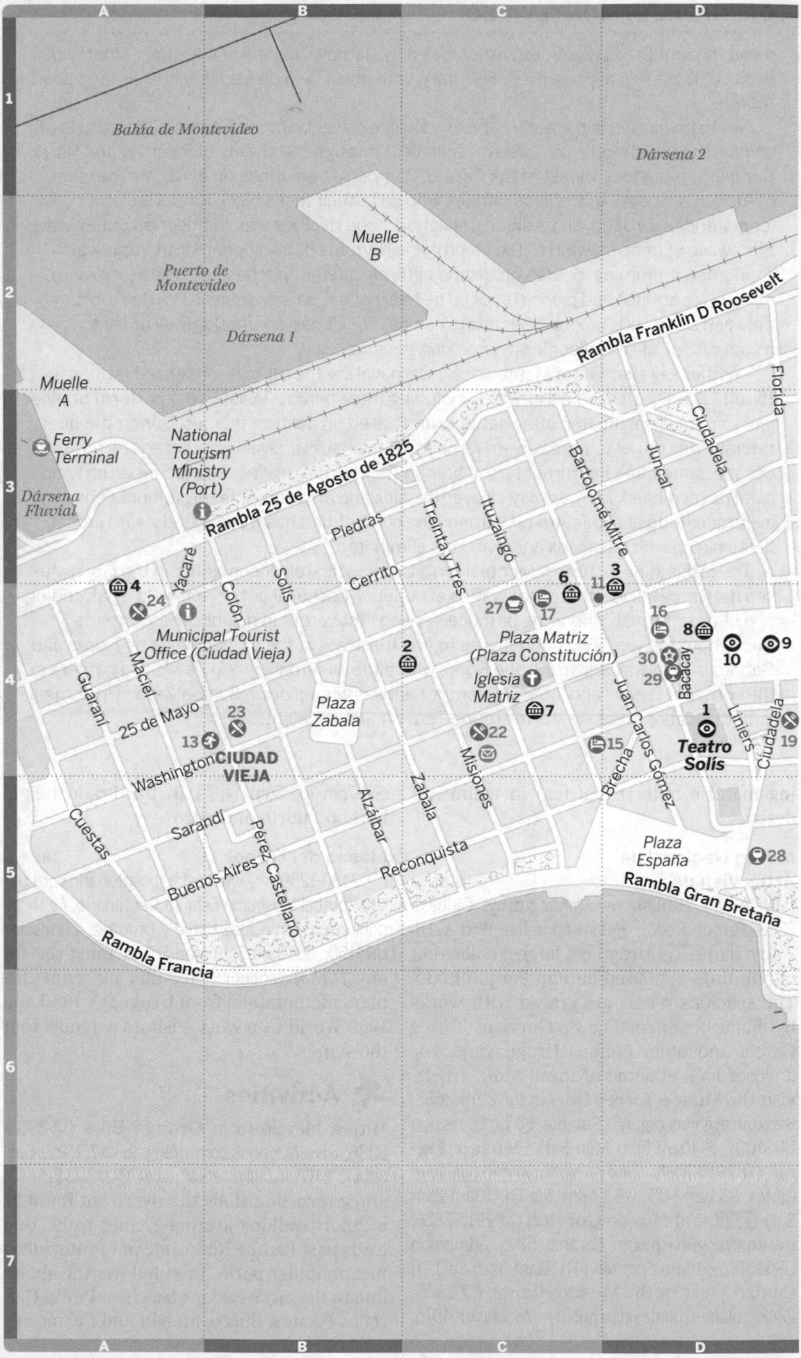

A
B
C
D
1
2
3
4
5
6
7
Bahía de Montevideo
Dársena 2
Muelle B
Puerto de Montevideo
Dársena 1
Rambla Franklin D Roosevelt
Muelle A
Ferry Terminal
Dársena Fluvial
National Tourism Ministry (Port)
Rambla 25 de Agosto de 1825
Florida
Ciudadela
Juncal
Bartolomé Mitre
Itusaingó
Treinta y Tres
Piedras
Cerrito
Solís
Colón
Yacaré
Maciel
Guaraní
25 de Mayo
Washington
CIUDAD VIEJA
Municipal Tourist Office (Ciudad Vieja)
Plaza Zabala
Plaza Matriz (Plaza Constitución)
Iglesia Matriz
Bacacay
Juan Carlos Gómez
Brecha
Misiones
Zabala
Alzáibar
Pérez Castellano
Sarandí
Buenos Aires
Cuestas
Reconquista
Liniers
Teatro Solís
Plaza España
Rambla Gran Bretaña
Rambla Francia
1
2
3
4
6
7
8
9
10
11
13
15
16
17
19
22
23
24
27
28
29
30

0 500 m
0 0.25 miles
E
F
G
H
Nueva York
Chopería Mastra (1.3km)
Rambla Sudamérica
Old Train Station
Valparaiso
Yí
Yaguarón
La Paz
Paraguay
Terminal Suburbana
Galicia
Av Libertador General Lavalleja
Cerro Largo
Río Branco
Río Negro
Rondeau
Cuareím
Paysandú
Paysandú
Av Uruguay
Feria de Tristán Narvaja (650m)
CENTRO
Mercedes
Colonia
Municipal Tourist Office (Centro)
Plaza del Entrevero
Seacat
Plaza Cagancha
Av 18 de Julio
Terminal Tres Cruces (2.5km)
Av 18 de Julio
21
5
32
San José
12
26
Florida
Andes
Convención
WF Aldunete
Julio Herrera y Obes
Río Negro
Paraguay
14
25
Soriano
31
Santiago de Chile
Canelones
BARRIO SUR
Gutiérrez Ruiz
18
Zelmar Michelini
Carlos Quijano
Aquiles Lanza
Ejido
Maldonado
Durazno
20
Isla de Flores
Carlos Gardel
Av Gonzalo Ramírez
Cementerio Central
Rambla República Argentina
La Cumparsita
Río de la Plata
1
2
3
4
5
6
7

Montevideo

Top Sights
1 Teatro Solís D4

Sights
2 Casa Rivera C4
3 Museo de los Andes D4
4 Museo del Carnaval A4
5 Museo del Gaucho F4
6 Museo Figari C4
7 Museo Gurvich C4
8 Museo Torres García D4
9 Plaza Independencia D4
10 Puerta de la Ciudadela D4

Activities, Courses & Tours
11 Academia Uruguay C4
12 Joventango H4
13 Orange Bike B4

Sleeping
14 Caballo Loco Hostel G4
15 Casa Sarandi Guesthouse C4
16 Hotel Palacio D4
17 Punto Berro Hostel Ciudad Vieja C4
18 Ukelele Hostel G5

Eating
19 Bar Tasende D4
20 Candy Bar H5
21 Comi.K E4
22 Estrecho C4
23 La Fonda B4
24 Mercado del Puerto A4
25 Shawarma Ashot G4

Drinking & Nightlife
26 Barón: la Barbería que Esconde un Secreto H4
27 Café Brasilero C4
28 La Ronda D5
29 Shannon Irish Pub D4

Entertainment
30 El Pony Pisador D4
31 Fun Fun E4
32 Sala Zitarrosa F4
Teatro Solís .... (see 1)

Courses

Academia Uruguay LANGUAGE COURSE
(☎2915-2496; www.academiauruguay.com; Juan Carlos Gómez 1408; group classes per week US$245, individual classes per hr US$30) One-on-one and group Spanish classes with a strong cultural focus. Also arranges homestays, private apartments and volunteer work.

Joventango DANCE COURSE
(☎2901-5561; www.joventango.org; Aquiles Lanza 1290) Tango classes for all levels, from beginner to expert.

Festivals & Events

Much livelier and longer-lasting than its Buenos Aires counterpart, Montevideo's multi-week **Carnaval** is the cultural highlight of the year. Festivities begin as early as January and end as late as March, depending on the year.

At Parque Prado, north of downtown, Semana Criolla festivities during **Semana Santa** (Holy Week) include displays of *gaucho* skills, *asados* (barbecues) and other such events.

In the last weekend of September or first weekend of October, Montevideo's museums, churches, and historic homes all open their doors free to the public during the **Días del Patrimonio** (National Heritage Days).

Sleeping

★ **Ukelele Hostel** HOSTEL $
(☎2902-7844; www.ukelelehostel.com; Maldonado 1183; dm US$16-22.50, tw US$48-52, d US$50-60; @ 📶 🏊) This attractive 1920s family home, lovingly renovated into a hostel, features high ceilings, beautiful wood floors, vintage architectural details, an on-site bar, a cozy music room and a grassy pool and patio area out back for lounging. Top it off with friendly staff and a good mix of dorms and private rooms and you've got the perfect midtown budget option.

★ **Hotel Palacio** HOTEL $
(☎2916-3612; www.hotelpalacio.com.uy; Bartolomé Mitre 1364; r without/with balcony US$45/50; ❄ 📶) If you can snag one of the two 6th-floor rooms at this ancient family-run hotel one block off Plaza Matriz, do it! Both feature air-conditioning and balconies with superb views of Ciudad Vieja's rooftops. The rest of the hotel also offers great value, with wood floors, antique furniture, a vintage elevator and old-school service reminiscent of a European pensión. No breakfast.

Caballo Loco Hostel HOSTEL $
(☎2902-6494; www.caballolocohostel.com; Gutierrez Ruiz 1287; dm US$18-22; ❄ 📶) This newer hostel in a remodeled historic building enjoys an unbeatable downtown location,

only steps from leafy Plaza Cagancha and the bus stops for Montevideo's bus station and beaches. Six spic-and-span four- to 10-bed dorms surround a welcoming, high-ceilinged common area with guest kitchen, pool table and TV lounge. Other pluses include friendly owners and on-site bike rentals.

Punto Berro Hostel HOSTEL $

(☎2707-7090; puntoberrohostel.com; Berro 1320, Pocitos; dm US$18-22, s US$32-45, d US$50-65, tw US$54-65;) Only two blocks from the beach in the upscale neighborhood of Pocitos, this hostel has clean, bright rooms and homey touches including comfy couches, a well-equipped guest kitchen and an affectionate geriatric cat. The same management offers a more urban experience at its sister **hostel** (☎2914-8600; puntoberrohostel.com; Ituzaingó 1436; dm US$16-22, d US$50-60;) in the heart of Ciudad Vieja, a stone's throw from lively Plaza Matriz.

★Casa Sarandi Guesthouse GUESTHOUSE $$

(☎2400-6460; www.casasarandi.com; Buenos Aires 558, 3rd fl; r without breakfast US$75;) One block south of Plaza Matriz, three attractive guest rooms in a vintage apartment share a guest kitchen and comfortable living room adorned with local artwork and parquet wood floors. Reserve ahead to set a time to meet the Welsh-Argentine owners, who live off-site but provide a key and oodles of up-to-the-minute tips on eating, entertainment and transport.

Eating

★Candy Bar TAPAS, BURGERS $

(☎2904-3179; www.facebook.com/CandyBarPalermo; Durazno 1402; tapas UR$100, mains UR$240-260; noon-3pm & 7pm-1am Tue-Fri, noon-4pm & 8pm-3am Sat, noon-6pm Sun) At this stellar street corner eatery, colorful folding chairs fill the sidewalk beneath a spreading sycamore tree, while the chefs inside mix drinks, whip up meals and juggle fresh-baked bread behind a countertop overhung with artsy lampshades. Reasonably priced tapas and burgers (carnivorous and vegetarian) rule the menu, complemented by artisan beers and mixed drinks. Sunday brunch is especially popular.

Shawarma Ashot MIDDLE EASTERN $

(www.facebook.com/ShawarmaAshot; Zelmar Michelini 1295; sandwiches UR$130-220; 11am-5pm Mon-Fri, noon-4pm Sat) Superbly prepared Middle Eastern classics such as falafel and shawarma draw loyal lunchtime crowds at this unpretentious hole-in-the-wall. For a special treat, don't miss the Saturday special: Uruguayan lamb with rice pilaf!

Bar Tasende PIZZA $

(cnr Ciudadela & San José; pizza slices UR$90; 10am-1am Sun-Thu, to 2am Fri & Sat) This classic high-ceilinged corner bar has been wooing patrons since 1931 with its trademark *muzzarella al tacho,* simple but tasty pizza slices laden with mozzarella, a perfect snack to accompany a beer any time of day.

★La Fonda VEGAN, HEALTH FOOD $$

(☎097-300222; www.facebook.com/lafondamori; Pérez Castellano 1422; mains UR$300-370; noon-4pm Tue-Sun, plus 8-11pm Thu-Sat) Grab a table on the pedestrianized street, or enter the high-ceilinged, brick-walled interior to watch the cheerfully bantering, wild-haired chefs at work: bopping to cool jazz as they roll out homemade pasta, carefully lay asparagus spears atop risotto or grab ingredients from the boxes of organic produce adorning their open kitchen. The ever-changing chalkboard menu always includes one vegan option.

Estrecho INTERNATIONAL $$

(Sarandí 460; mains UR$270-390; noon-4pm Mon-Fri) Grab a seat at the long stove-side counter and watch the chefs whip up delicious daily specials at this cozy Ciudad Vieja lunch spot. French owner Bénédicte Buffard's international menu includes baguette sandwiches with steak or smoked salmon, a variety of salads, fresh fish of the day and divine desserts.

Comi.K BRAZILIAN $$

(☎2902-4344; www.facebook.com/COMIKRestaurante; Av 18 de Julio 994, 2nd fl; specials incl drink & dessert UR$320; 9am-9pm Mon-Fri, 9am-4pm Sat) Inside the Brazilian cultural center, reasonably priced meals – including *feijoada* (Brazil's classic meat-and-black-bean stew) – are served in an elegant 2nd-floor salon with high ceilings and stained glass. There's live Brazilian music most Friday evenings.

★Mercado del Puerto PARRILLA $$$

(www.mercadodelpuerto.com; Pérez Castellano; mains UR$260-700; noon-5pm daily year-round, to 11pm Tue-Fri Nov-Feb) This converted market on Ciudad Vieja's waterfront remains a

Montevideo classic, even if the steady influx of cruise ships into the adjacent port has made it increasingly pricey. Take your pick of the densely packed *parrillas* and pull up a stool. Weekends are ideal for savoring the market's vibrant energy.

Drinking

Ciudad Vieja's favorite bar precinct is along Mitre, between Buenos Aires and Sarandí. Classics here include the **Pony Pisador** (2915-7470; www.facebook.com/pony.pisador.1; Bartolomé Mitre 1324; 5pm-late Mon-Fri, 8pm-late Sat & Sun) and **Shannon Irish Pub** (www.theshannon.com.uy; Bartolomé Mitre 1318; 7pm-late), which both have reasonably priced drinks, DJs and occasional live music. East of Centro in the Parque Rodó neighborhood, Calle Jackson is another up-and-coming drinking hotspot.

★Café Brasilero CAFE

(www.cafebrasilero.com.uy; Ituzaingó 1447; 9am-8pm Mon-Fri, 10am-6pm Sat) This vintage 1877 cafe with dark wood paneling and historic photos gracing the walls makes a delightful spot for morning coffee or afternoon tea. It's also an excellent lunch stop, with good-value *menus ejecutivos* (all-inclusive daily specials) for UR$400.

La Ronda BAR

(Ciudadela 1182; noon-late Mon-Sat, 7pm-late Sun) At this often jam-packed bar, youthful patrons straddle the windowsills between the dark interior plastered with vintage album covers and the sidewalk tables cooled by breezes off the Rambla.

Barón: la Barbería que Esconde un Secreto COCKTAIL BAR

(www.facebook.com/LaBarberiaQueEscondeUnSecreto; Santiago de Chile 1270; 6pm-2am Tue-Sat) Like a trip back to America's Prohibition days, 'the barbershop that hides a secret' is a clandestine cocktail bar tucked behind an unassuming-looking storefront. Walk past the vintage barber chairs and open the secret doorway into one of Montevideo's coolest new nightspots. (And yes, you can still get your hair cut too!)

Chopería Mastra MICROBREWERY

(mastra.com.uy; Mercado Agrícola de Montevideo, Local 17; 11am-11pm) This convivial pub in Montevideo's agricultural market is the flagship outlet for Uruguay's beloved Mastra microbrewery. Pints go for UR$130, but with a dozen varieties to choose from you may prefer to opt for the *tabla degustación* (a four-beer sampler for UR$260, available weekdays only). Mastra has recently opened several other pubs around town, including near the beach in **Pocitos** (mastra.com.uy; Benito Blanco 1017, Pocitos; 8pm-3am Mon-Sat).

Entertainment

★Fun Fun LIVE MUSIC

(2904-4859; www.barfunfun.com; Soriano 922, Centro; 8:30pm-late Tue-Sat) Since 1895 this intimate, informal venue has been serving its famous *uvita* (a sweet wine drink) while hosting tango and other live music on a tiny stage. Temporarily moved to Calle Soriano in 2014, it's due to return four blocks west to its traditional location in the Mercado Central once renovation work is finished (most likely in 2017).

Sala Zitarrosa PERFORMING ARTS

(2901-7303; www.salazitarrosa.com.uy; Av 18 de Julio 1012, Centro) Montevideo's best informal auditorium venue for big-name music and dance performances, including tango, rock, flamenco, reggae and *zarzuela* (traditional Spanish musical theater).

Teatro Solís PERFORMING ARTS

(1950-3323; www.teatrosolis.org.uy; Buenos Aires 678, Ciudad Vieja; admission from UR$75) The city's top performing-arts venue is home to the Montevideo Philharmonic Orchestra and hosts formal concerts of classical, jazz,

GETTING INTO TOWN

From Montevideo's Carrasco airport, Copsa buses 700, 710 and 711 and Cutcsa buses C1 and C5 (UR$51, 40 minutes) offer the cheapest transport into town, arriving at **Terminal Suburbana** (1975; cnr Río Branco & Galicia). Alternatively take COT's direct service between the airport and Tres Cruces bus terminal (UR$159, 30 minutes). A taxi from the airport into Montevideo costs UR$1050 to UR$1420 depending on neighborhood.

From the bus terminal, local bus CA1 (UR$19) serves destinations in the Centro and Ciudad Vieja. Buses to other neighborhoods cost UR$26. For a clickable route map, see www.montevideobus.com.uy (in Spanish).

GETTING TO ARGENTINA

Ferries offer the most popular and convenient way to cross between Uruguay and Argentina – routes include Montevideo to Buenos Aires, Colonia del Sacramento to Buenos Aires and Carmelo to the Buenos Aires suburb of Tigre. Immigration is carried out at the port, so try to arrive an hour ahead of your departure time.

Further north, local buses run across the Río Uruguay from Fray Bentos, Paysandú and Salto (Uruguay) to their Argentine counterparts, Gualeguaychú, Colón and Concordia. Immigration procedures are often handled on the bus, and borders are generally open 24 hours.

tango and other music, plus music festivals, theater, ballet and opera.

Shopping

Plaza Constitución hosts an enjoyable flea market on Saturday.

Feria de Tristán Narvaja MARKET
(Tristán Narvaja, Cordón; 9am-4pm Sun) This colorful Sunday-morning outdoor market is a decades-long tradition begun by Italian immigrants. It sprawls from Av 18 de Julio northwards along Calle Tristán Narvaja, spilling over onto several side streets. You can find used books, music, clothing, jewelry, live animals, antiques and souvenirs in its many makeshift stalls.

Information

EMERGENCIES

Ambulance (105)

Police (911)

MEDICAL SERVICES

Hospital Británico (2487-1020; www.hospitalbritanico.com.uy; cnr Av Italia & Avelino Miranda) Highly recommended private hospital with English-speaking doctors; 2.5km east of downtown.

MONEY

Most downtown banks have ATMs; 18 de Julio is lined with *casas de cambio* (exchange houses).

TOURIST INFORMATION

Municipal Tourist Office (www.descubrimontevideo.uy) Centro (1950-1830; cnr Av 18 de Julio & Ejido; 10am-4pm); Ciudad Vieja (2916-8434; cnr Piedras & Pérez Castellanos; 9am-5pm Mon-Fri) City maps and general Montevideo information. Downloadable visitor's guide to the city in English, Spanish and Portuguese.

National Tourism Ministry (2188-5100; www.turismo.gub.uy) Carrasco Airport (2604-0386; 8am-8pm); Port (2188-5111; Rambla 25 de Agosto & Yacaré; 9am-5pm Mon-Fri); Tres Cruces Bus Terminal (2409-7399; cnr Bulevar Artigas & Av Italia; 8am-8pm) Info about Montevideo and destinations throughout Uruguay.

Getting There & Away

AIR

Montevideo's **Carrasco international airport** (2604-0272; www.aeropuertodecarrasco.com.uy) is 20km east of downtown.

BOAT

Buquebus (130; www.buquebus.com.uy) runs high-speed ferries directly to Buenos Aires from Montevideo (UR$3320, 2¼ hours). **Seacat** (2915-0202; www.seacatcolonia.com.uy; Río Negro 1400; 9am-7pm Mon-Fri, 9am-noon Sat) and **Colonia Express** (2401-6666; www.coloniaexpress.com; Tres Cruces Bus Terminal, ticket counter 31A; 5:30am-10:30pm) offer slower but more economical bus-ferry combinations to Buenos Aires, via Colonia del Sacramento (UR$998 to UR$1398, 4¼ hours).

Cacciola (2407-9657; www.cacciolaviajes.com; Tres Cruces Bus Terminal, ticket counter 25B; 8:30am-11:30pm), at Terminal Tres Cruces, runs a bus-launch service to Buenos Aires (UR$850, eight hours) via Carmelo and the Argentine Delta suburb of Tigre.

BUS

Montevideo's **Terminal Tres Cruces** (2401-8998; www.trescruces.com.uy; cnr Bulevar Artigas & Av Italia) has restaurants, clean toilets, a left-luggage facility, a *casa de cambio* (money exchange office) and ATMs.

There are daily departures to various destinations in Argentina, including Buenos Aires (UR$1345, 10 hours) and Córdoba (UR$2535, 15 hours).

EGA (2402-5164; www.ega.com.uy) serves Porto Alegre (UR$2285, 12 hours), Florianópolis (UR$3475, 18 hours) and São Paulo, Brazil (UR$4895, 28 hours), Asunción, Paraguay (UR$3730, 21 hours) and Santiago, Chile (UR$4590, 28 hours).

Bus Fares

DESTINATION	COST (UR$)	DURATION (HR)
Cabo Polonio	530	4½
Carmelo	424	3¼
Chuy	600	5
Colonia	318	2¾
La Paloma	424	3½
La Pedrera	442	4
Mercedes	494	4
Paysandú	671	4½
Piriápolis	177	1½
Punta del Diablo	530	5
Punta del Este	256	2¼
Salto	883	6½
Tacuarembó	689	4½

WESTERN URUGUAY

The land west of Montevideo is in many ways the 'real' Uruguay – little river towns separated by large expanses of pampas and wheat fields. It's far off the tourist trail, mostly, except for the region's superstar, Colonia del Sacramento, whose charms attract visitors from all over the world.

Colonia del Sacramento

POP 23,100

Take some cobbled streets and picturesque plazas, add an intriguing history and put them on a gorgeous point overlooking the Río de la Plata. What do you get? A major tourist attraction. Colonia's compact historic center, packed with atmospheric eateries and enshrined as a Unesco World Heritage site, is a major draw for Argentines, who visit in droves every weekend.

The Portuguese founded Colonia in 1680 to smuggle goods across the Río de la Plata into Buenos Aires. The Spanish captured it in 1762 and held it until 1777, when tax reforms finally permitted foreign goods to proceed directly to Buenos Aires.

Sights

The Barrio Histórico begins at the restored **Portón de Campo** (Manuel Lobo), built in 1745, where a thick fortified wall runs to the river. Inside the walls, picturesque spots to wander include the cobbled **Calle de los Suspiros** and **Paseo de San Gabriel**, and the historic center's two main squares: **Plaza Mayor 25 de Mayo** and **Plaza de Armas**. For another nice perspective on the river, head to the grassy grounds behind **Teatro Bastión del Carmen** (Rivadavia 223; ⊙noon-8pm) FREE.

A single UR$50 ticket grants admission to Colonia's eight **historical museums** (☎4523-1237; www.museoscolonia.com.uy; ⊙11:15am-4:45pm), including the two listed here; note that all museums maintain identical hours but closing days vary, as indicated on the website.

Museo Portugués MUSEUM
(Plaza Mayor 25 de Mayo 180; 8-museum admission UR$50; ⊙11:15am-4:45pm, closed Wed & Fri) In this beautiful old house you'll find Portuguese relics including porcelain, furniture, maps, Manuel Lobo's family tree and the old stone shield that once adorned the Portón de Campo.

Museo Municipal MUSEUM
(☎4522-7031; Plaza Mayor 25 de Mayo 77; 8-museum admission UR$50; ⊙11:15am-4:45pm Wed-Mon) Houses an eclectic collection of treasures including a whale skeleton, an enormous rudder from a shipwreck, historical timelines and a scale model of Colonia (c 1762).

Faro LIGHTHOUSE
(admission UR$25; ⊙11am-sunset) One of the town's most prominent landmarks, Colonia's 19th-century lighthouse provides an excellent view of the old town and the Río de la Plata. It stands within the ruins of the 17th-century **Convento de San Francisco** (Plaza Mayor 25 de Mayo), just off the southwest corner of Plaza Mayor 25 de Mayo.

Sleeping

Colonia is short on budget hotels, but hostels offer some decent-value private rooms.

★**El Viajero Hostel** HOSTEL $
(☎4522-2683; www.elviajerohostels.com/hostel-colonia; Washington Barbot 164; dm US$17-19, s/d US$40/65; ❄@📶) With bike rental, a bar for guests and air-con in all rooms, this hostel is brighter, fancier and somewhat cozier than the competition, and the location two blocks east of Plaza de Armas couldn't be better.

Remus-Art Hostel B&B $
(☎9206-6985; www.facebook.com/remusarthostel; 18 de Julio 369; r UR$60-65) This new B&B in the home of German visual artist Christiane Brockmeier has three comfortable, colorful rooms with shared bath and a spacious roof terrace where you can sunbathe, reach out and touch the overhanging sycamore leaves, or enjoy home-cooked candlelight dinners (specialties include raclette and fondue from Switzerland, where Christiane lived for 20 years).

Hostel del Río HOSTEL $
(☎4523-2870; www.hosteldelrio.com; Rivadavia 288; dm US$15-20, d US$61-108) Well-placed at the edge of the historic center, this new hostel offers squeaky-clean four- to six-bed dorms and private rooms, along with a guest kitchen and back patio. The atmosphere is rather sterile, but the bright white rooms come with thoughtful features like individual bedside reading lights on the bunk beds.

Eating & Drinking

★**Don Joaquín** PIZZA $
(☎4522-4388; www.facebook.com/donjoaquinartesanalpizza; 18 de Julio 267; pizzas UR$120-190; ⊙8pm-midnight Tue-Sun, noon-3pm Sat & Sun) After 13 years in Europe, Colonia natives Yancí and Pierina returned home with a genuine Neapolitan pizza oven in tow. The result is this cheerful, high-ceilinged eatery where diners can watch the *pizzaiolo* (pizza chef) creating thin-crusted beauties with superb homemade sauce. Don't miss the carbonara with cheese, egg and delicately crunchy bacon, or the *pescatore* with mussels and shrimp.

La Bodeguita INTERNATIONAL $$
(www.labodeguita.net; Comercio 167; mini pizzas UR$140, dishes UR$270-440; ⊙8pm-midnight Tue-Sun, 12:30-4pm Sat & Sun) Nab a table out back on the sunny two-level deck and soak up the sweeping river views while drinking sangria (UR$260 per liter) or munching on La Bodeguita's trademark mini pizzas, served on a cutting board. The wide-ranging menu also includes pasta, salads, steaks and *chivitos*.

Buen Suspiro SNACKS $$
(☎4522-6160; www.buensuspiro.com; Calle de los Suspiros 90; picadas for 2 UR$255-830; ⊙11am-midnight) Duck under the wood beams into this cozy spot specializing in *picadas* (little snacks eaten with a toothpick). Sample local wines by the bottle or glass, accompanied by spinach and leek tarts, ricotta-and-walnut 'truffles,' local cheese, sausage, soups and salads. Reserve ahead for a fireside table in winter, or while away a summer afternoon on the intimate back patio.

Papá Ramón BAR
(Misiones de los Tapes 49; ⊙11am-1am Wed-Mon) Opened in 2015, this friendly retro corner bar has a compact tiled interior and sidewalk tables perfect for gazing down the cobbled street toward the river at sunset. It prides itself on reasonably priced (by Colonia standards) cold beer, sandwiches, empanadas and *platos del día* (daily specials under UR$300).

Barbot MICROBREWERY
(☎4522-7268; www.facebook.com/barbotcerveceria; Washington Barbot 160; ⊙6pm-2am Mon-Thu, noon-4am Fri-Sun) This sleek brewpub (Colonia's first, opened in 2013) is well worth a visit for its ever-evolving collection of 15 home

WORTH A TRIP

ESTANCIA LIVING ON A BUDGET

El Galope Horse Farm & Hostel
(☎099-105985; www.elgalope.com.uy; Colonia Suiza; dm US$25, d with/without bathroom US$80/70;) What do you get when you cross a tourist *estancia* and a hostel? Find out at this unique country retreat 115km west of Montevideo and 60km east of Colonia. Experienced world travelers Mónica and Miguel offer guests a chance to 'get away from it all' and settle into the relaxing rhythms of rural life for a few days.

Horseback jaunts for riders of all levels (US$40 for beginners within the farm property, US$80 for longer rides for experienced riders) are expertly led by Miguel himself, and there's a sauna (US$8) and small swimming pool to soothe those aching muscles at the end of the day. Breakfast is included; other meals, from lunches to fondue to full-fledged *asados* (barbecues) are available for US$9 to US$15. Taxi pickup from the bus stop in nearby Colonia Valdense is available upon request (US$10).

Colonia del Sacramento

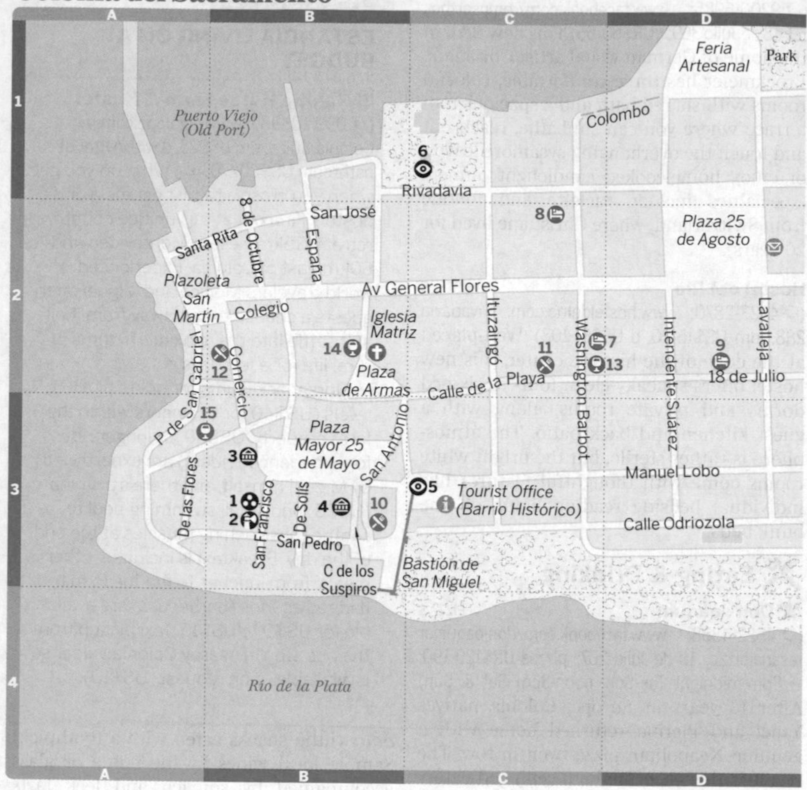

Colonia del Sacramento

Sights

1 Convento de San Francisco B3
2 Faro B3
3 Museo Municipal B3
4 Museo Portugués B3
5 Portón de Campo C3
6 Teatro Bastión del Carmen C1

Sleeping

7 El Viajero Hostel C2
8 Hostel del Río C2
9 Remus-Art Hostel D2

Eating

10 Buen Suspiro B3
11 Don Joaquín C2
12 La Bodeguita B2

Drinking & Nightlife

13 Barbot C2
14 El Drugstore B2
15 Papá Ramón A3

brews on tap, although the bar snacks (pizza, *picadas* and Mexican fare) are best avoided.

El Drugstore COCKTAIL BAR
(Portugal 174; ⏲noon-midnight) Touristy but fun, this funky corner place has polka-dot tablecloths, a vividly colored interior, outdoor seating with perfect views of Plaza de Armas, and two vintage cars on the cobblestones doubling as romantic dining nooks. Half of the 24-page menu is devoted to drinks; the other half to so-so tapas and international fare (mains UR$180 to UR$500). There's frequent live guitar music.

Information

Banks are clustered along Av General Flores.

BIT Welcome Center (☎4522-1072; www.bitcolonia.com; Odriozola 434; ⏲9am-6pm) In a sparkling glass-walled building opposite the port, this modern welcome center, operated

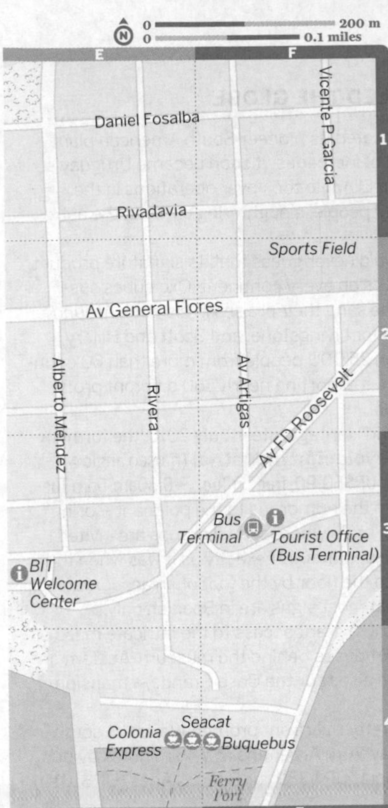

by Uruguay's national tourism ministry, has tourist information, touch-screen displays, a handicrafts shop and an overpriced (UR$50) 'Welcome to Uruguay' video presentation.

Tourist Office (☎4522-8506; www.colonia turismo.com) Barrio Histórico (Manuel Lobo 224; ⊙9am-6pm); Bus Terminal (cnr Manuel Lobo & Av FD Roosevelt; ⊙9am-6pm)

Getting There & Away

BOAT

Buquebus (☎130; www.buquebus.com.uy; ⊙9am-10pm) runs two slow boats (UR$750, 3¼ hours) plus at least three fast boats (UR$1580, 1¼ hours) daily to Buenos Aires. **Colonia Express** (☎4522-9676; www.colonia-express.com.uy; Ferry Terminal; ⊙9am-10pm) and **Seacat** (☎4522-2919; www.seacatcolonia.com.uy; Ferry Terminal; ⊙7:30am-7pm) also offer one-hour crossings, at slightly better rates (UR$798 to UR$1198). Advance bookings qualify for huge discounts; see company websites for details. Immigration is located at the port.

BUS

Colonia's **terminal** (cnr Manuel Lobo & Av FD Roosevelt) is near the port.

Bus Fares

DESTINATION	COST (UR$)	DURATION (HR)
Carmelo	141	1¼
Mercedes	318	3½
Montevideo	318	2¾
Paysandú	583	6
Salto	795	8

Getting Around

Walking is enjoyable in compact Colonia, but motor scooters, bicycles and gas-powered buggies are popular alternatives. Rental agencies include **Thrifty** (☎4522-2939; www.thrifty.com.uy; Av General Flores 172; bicycle/scooter/golf cart per hr US$6/12/17, per 24hr US$24/40/66), **Multicar** (☎4522-4893; www.multicar.com.uy; Manuel Lobo 505) and **Motorent** (☎4522-9665; www.motorent.com.uy; Manuel Lobo 505).

Local COTUC buses (UR$19) run along Av General Flores, serving the beaches north of town.

Carmelo

POP 17,800

This super mellow river town is reached by the most interesting (and cheapest) of the Argentine ferry crossings – a 2½-hour ride through the delta from the Buenos Aires suburb of Tigre.

The town centers on Plaza Independencia, seven blocks north of the ferry docks. A large park on the opposite side of the *arroyo* (creek) offers camping, swimming and a monstrous casino. The surrounding area is home to several well-regarded wineries.

Sleeping & Eating

★ Ah'Lo Hostel Boutique HOSTEL $
(☎4542-0757; ahlo.com.uy; Treinta y Tres 270; dm US$18-23, d US$61-87, d without bathroom US$46-55, ste US$59-99; ❄📶) Hands down Carmelo's best downtown option, this brand-new hostel delivers on its 'boutique' moniker, offering super-comfortable dorms with plush comforters, immaculate shared bathrooms and well-priced private rooms, all in an attractively restored colonial building seven

WORTH A TRIP

THE LITTLE BEEF CUBE THAT CIRCLED THE GLOBE

In 1865 the Liebig Extract of Meat Company located its pioneer South American plant near the river town of Fray Bentos, 35km west of Mercedes. It soon became Uruguay's most important industrial complex. British-run El Anglo took over operations in the 1920s and by WWII the factory employed 4000 people, slaughtering cattle at the astronomical rate of 2000 a day.

Looking at the abandoned factory today, you'd never guess that its signature product, the Oxo beef cube, once touched millions of lives on every continent. Oxo cubes sustained WWI soldiers in the trenches, Jules Verne sang their praises in his book *Around the Moon*, Stanley brought them on his search for Livingstone, and Scott and Hillary took them to Antarctica and Everest. More than 25,000 people from more than 60 countries worked here, and at its peak the factory was exporting nearly 150 different products, using every part of the cow except its moo.

Enshrined as Uruguay's newest Unesco World Heritage site in July 2015, the former factory is now a museum: the **Museo de la Revolución Industrial** (museo.anglo@rionegro.gub.uy; admission UR$40, incl guided tour UR$50-90, free on Tue; 9:30am-5pm Tue-Sun). Dozens of colorful displays – ranging from the humorous to the poignant – bring the factory's history vividly to life: a giant cattle scale where school groups are invited to weigh themselves, or the old company office upstairs, left exactly as it was when the factory closed in 1979, with grooves rubbed into the floor by the foot of an accountant who sat at the same desk for decades. Note that most signs are in Spanish only.

One- to two-hour guided tours (schedule varies) grant access to the intricate maze of passageways, corrals and abandoned slaughterhouses behind the museum. At 11am on Thursdays, Saturdays and Sundays visitors can also tour the Casa Grande, a mansion that once housed the factory's manager.

The adjacent town of Fray Bentos, with its pretty riverfront promenade, is the southernmost overland crossing over the Río Uruguay from Argentina. It's 45 minutes by bus from Mercedes (UR$53), four hours from Colonia (UR$389) or Buenos Aires (UR$1010), and 4½ hours from Montevideo (UR$547).

blocks from the ferry terminal and two blocks from the main square. Bike rentals (per day US$10) and cycling tours to local wineries are available.

Camping Náutico Carmelo CAMPGROUND $
(4542-2058; dnhcarmelo@adinet.com.uy; Arroyo de las Vacas s/n; per tent site UR$322, shower per 7min UR$49) South of the arroyo, this pleasant tree-shaded campground with hot showers caters to yachties but accepts walk-ins too. Sites accommodate up to four people.

Piccolino URUGUAYAN $
(4542-4850; cnr 19 de Abril & Roosevelt; dishes UR$175-300; 9am-midnight Wed-Mon) This corner place has decent *chivitos* and views of Carmelo's central square.

Information

Banks are concentrated near central Plaza Independencia.

Casa de la Cultura (4542-2001; carmeloturismo.com.uy; 19 de Abril 246; 9am-6pm Mar-Nov, to 7pm Dec-Feb) Three blocks south of the main square and eight blocks northeast of the launch docks.

Getting There & Away

Berrutti (4542-2504; www.berruttiturismo.com/horarios.htm; Uruguay 337) is on Uruguay, with most departures for Colonia (UR$141, 1½ hours).

Cacciola (4542-4282; www.cacciolaviajes.com; Wilson Ferreyra s/n; Carmelo-Tigre one way UR$770; ticket office 3:30-4:30am & 8:30am-8pm) has launches to the Buenos Aires suburb of Tigre (UR$770, 2½ hours).

Chadre/Sabelin (4542-2987; www.agenciacentral.com.uy; 18 de Julio 411) on Plaza Independencia goes to Montevideo (UR$424, 3½ hours), Paysandú (UR$424, five hours) and Salto (UR$636, seven hours).

Mercedes

POP 44,820

Capital of the department of Soriano, Mercedes is a livestock center with cobblestone streets and a small pedestrian zone around the 18th-century cathedral on central Plaza Independencia. The town's most appealing feature is its leafy waterfront along the south bank of the Río Negro.

Sleeping & Eating

Camping Isla del Puerto CAMPGROUND $

(☎9401-6049; Isla del Puerto; sites per person/tent UR$24/78) Mercedes' spacious campground, one of the region's best, occupies half the Isla del Puerto in the Río Negro. Connected to the mainland by a bridge, it has swimming, fishing and sanitary facilities.

★**Estancia La Sirena** ESTANCIA $$$

(☎4530-2271, 9953-2698; www.lasirena.com.uy/hosteria.html; Ruta 14, Km 4.5; per person incl horseback rides & other activitieswith half/full board US$110/135) Surrounded by rolling open country 15km upriver from Mercedes, this *estancia* is one of Uruguay's oldest and most welcoming. The spacious 1830 ranch house, with its cozy parlor and fireplaces and end-of-the-road setting, makes a perfect base for relaxation, late-afternoon conversation under the eucalyptus trees, stargazing and horseback excursions to the nearby Río Negro. Homemade meals are delicious.

Martiniano Parrilla Gourmet PARRILLA $$

(☎4532-2649; Rambla Costanera s/n; dishes UR$190-390; ⊙noon-3pm & 7:30pm-midnight Tue-Sun) Prime riverfront setting at the foot of 18 de Julio is complemented by a varied menu featuring homemade pasta, grilled meat and fish.

Information

Banks are all concentrated near Plaza Independencia.

Municipal Tourist Office (☎4532-2201 ext 2501; turismo@soriano.gub.uy; Plaza El Rosedal, Av Asencio btwn Colón & Artigas; ⊙8am-6:30pm) In a crumbling white building opposite the bridge to the campground.

Getting There & Away

Mercedes' modern, air-conditioned **bus terminal** (Plaza General Artigas) has departures to Colonia (UR$318, three hours), Montevideo (UR$494, four hours), Salto (UR$491, four hours) and Buenos Aires (UR$1010, five hours). Plaza Independencia is 10 blocks north of the bus terminal. Walk straight up Colón with Plaza Artigas on your right or catch any local bus.

Paysandú

POP 78,900

On the east bank of the Río Uruguay, connected to Colón, Argentina, by the Puente Internacional General Artigas, Uruguay's third-largest city is mainly of interest as a stepping stone for travelers en route to or from Argentina. To see the city's wilder side, visit during Easter Week for the annual **beer festival** (www.facebook.com/SemanadelaCervezaPaysandu), when there's plenty of live music, open-air cinema and a ready supply of a certain carbonated alcoholic beverage.

Sights

Museo Histórico MUSEUM

(☎4722-6220 ext 247; Av Zorrilla de San Martín 874; ⊙9am-2pm Tue-Sat, to 3pm Sun) FREE This historical museum displays evocative images from the multiple 19th-century sieges of Paysandú, including of the bullet-riddled shell of the cathedral and women in exile watching the city's bombardment from an island offshore.

Sleeping & Eating

The tourist office keeps a list of *casas de familia* (family homes) offering simple accommodations.

Hotel Rafaela HOTEL $

(☎4722-4216; 18 de Julio 1181; s/d with fan & without bathroom UR$650/850, with air-con & bathroom UR$900/1150; ❄📶) A decent budget option just west of the main square. Rafaela's rooms are dark but large, and some have their own small patios.

Pan Z URUGUAYAN $$

(☎4722-9551; cnr 18 de Julio & Setembrino Pereda; dishes UR$195-495; ⊙noon-3pm & 7pm-1am) Popular 'Panceta' serves steaks, pizza, *chivitos* stacked high with every ingredient imaginable, and tasty desserts such as strawberry cake and tiramisu.

El Bar PIZZA, URUGUAYAN **$$**
(☎4723-7809; es-es.facebook.com/ElBarPaysandu; cnr 18 de Julio & Herrera; mains UR$140-420; ⌚6:30am-late) Smack in the heart of town (one block west of Plaza Constitución), this corner resto-bar is open all day long for pizza, burgers and standard Uruguayan fare. After dark it shifts smoothly into bar mode, getting especially packed on Fridays when there's live music.

Information

Banks with ATMs are concentrated along 18 de Julio downtown.

Tourist Office Centro (☎4722-6220 ext 184; turismo@paysandu.gub.uy; 18 de Julio 1226; ⌚9am-7pm); Riverfront (☎4722-9235; plandelacosta@paysandu.gub.uy; Av de Los Iracundos; ⌚9am-5pm); Bus Terminal (cnr Artigas & Av Zorrilla de San Martin; ⌚7am-1pm Dec-Apr, noon-6pm May-Nov) The Centro office is on Plaza Constitución; the riverfront office is next to the Museo de la Tradición.

Getting There & Away

Paysandú's **bus terminal** (☎4722-3225; cnr Artigas & Av Zorrilla de San Martín) has buses to Colón, Argentina (UR$109, 45 minutes), Buenos Aires (UR$750, five hours) and several other international destinations. Domestic departures include Montevideo (UR$679, 4½ hours) and Salto (UR$217, two hours). To reach the center from the bus terminal, walk seven blocks north on Zorilla de San Martín or take any local Copay bus (UR$20).

Salto

POP 108,200

Uruguay's second-largest city and the most northerly crossing point to Argentina, Salto is a relaxed place with some 19th-century architecture and a pleasant riverfront. People come here for the nearby hot springs and the recreation area above the enormous Salto Grande hydroelectric dam.

Sights & Activities

Museo del Hombre y la Tecnología MUSEUM
(cnr Av Brasil & Zorrilla; ⌚1-7pm Mon-Fri, 2-7pm Sat Feb-Dec) FREE Housed in an historic market building, this museum features excellent displays on local cultural development and history upstairs, and a small archaeological section downstairs.

DON'T MISS

SALTO'S HOT SPRINGS

A whole slew of hot springs bubbles up around Salto.

Termas San Nicanor (☎4730-2209; www.sannicanor.com.uy; Ruta 3, Km 475; campsite per person UR$200-250, dm US$25-40, d US$100-150, 4-person cabin US$180-230; 📶🏊) Surrounded by a pastoral landscape of cows, fields and water vaguely reminiscent of a Flemish painting, this is the most tranquil of Salto's hot-springs resorts. It has two gigantic outdoor thermal pools, a restaurant, and accommodations for every budget, including campsites, no-frills dorms, four-person cabins and private rooms in a high-ceilinged *estancia* house with large fireplaces and peacocks strolling the grounds.

Day use of the springs (8am to 10pm, available Friday to Sunday only) costs UR$150 (UR$100 in low season).

The 12km unpaved access road leaves Ruta 3 10km south of Salto. Occasional **shuttles** (☎driver Martín Lombardo 099-732368; one way UR$400) to San Nicanor depart from Salto (corner of Larrañaga and Artigas) and Termas de Daymán. Schedules vary; phone ahead to confirm schedules.

Termas de Daymán (☎4736-0711; www.termasdedayman.com; admission UR$100; ⌚9am-9pm) About 8km south of Salto, Daymán is a heavily developed Disneyland of thermal baths complete with kids' water park. It's popular with Uruguayan and Argentine tourists who roam the town's block-long main street in bathrobes. For comfortable accommodations adjacent to the springs, try **La Posta del Daymán** (☎camping 4736-9094, hotel 4736-9801; www.lapostadeldayman.com; campsite per person UR$150, r per person incl breakfast UR$1100-1550; 📶🏊).

Sleeping & Eating

Accommodations at nearby hot springs offer an alternative to sleeping in town.

Hostal del Jardín HOTEL $
(☎4732-4274; www.hostaldeljardin.com.uy; Colón 47; s/d UR$800/1000; ❄📶) Convenient to the port, this place has simple, clean rooms (the cheapest in town) lined up motel-style along a small, grassy side yard.

La Caldera PARRILLA $
(Uruguay 221; dishes UR$130-300; ⏱11am-3pm & 8pm-midnight Tue-Sun) With fresh breezes blowing in off the river and sunny outdoor seating, this *parrilla* makes a great lunch stop; at dinnertime, the cozy interior dining room, with its view of the blazing fire, is equally atmospheric.

La Trattoria URUGUAYAN $$
(Uruguay 754; dishes UR$180-415; ⏱noon-2am) Locals flock to this high-ceilinged downtown eatery for fish, meat and pasta. Sit in the wood-paneled dining room or people-watch from a sidewalk table on busy Calle Uruguay.

Information

Casas de cambio and banks are concentrated downtown near the corner of Uruguay and Lavalleja.

Tourist Office (☎4733-4096; turismo@salto.gub.uy) Bus Terminal (Salto Shopping Center, cnr Ruta 3 & Av Bastille; ⏱8am-10pm); Centro (Uruguay 1052; ⏱8am-7pm Mon-Sat)

Getting There & Around

Chadre/Agencia Central buses go to Buenos Aires (UR$1005, seven hours) and Concordia, Argentina (UR$121, one hour) Monday to Saturday. Domestic buses go to Montevideo (UR$883, 6½ hours) and Paysandú (UR$217, two hours). Local bus 1 connects the bus terminal with the center of town.

From the port at the foot of Av Brasil, Transporte Fluvial San Cristobal runs **launches** (☎4733-2461) across the river to Concordia (UR$160, 15 minutes) Monday to Saturday.

Tacuarembó & Around

POP 55,000

This is *gaucho* country. Not your 'we pose for pesos' types, but your real-deal 'we tuck our baggy pants into our boots and slap on a beret just to go to the local store' crew.

It's also the alleged birthplace of tango legend Carlos Gardel. **Valle Edén**, a lush valley 24km southwest of Tacuarembó, is home to the **Museo Carlos Gardel** (☎099-107303; admission UR$25; ⏱9:30am-5:30pm Tue-Sun), which documents various facets of the singer's life, including the birth certificate which Uruguayans hold as proof of his local provenance – a claim vigorously contested by Argentina and France!

Sights

Museo del Indio y del Gaucho MUSEUM
(cnr Flores & Artigas; ⏱10am-5pm Tue-Sat) FREE Paying romantic tribute to Uruguay's *gauchos* and indigenous peoples, this museum's collection includes stools made from leather and cow bones, elegantly worked silver spurs and other accessories of rural life.

Festivals & Events

Fiesta de la Patria Gaucha CULTURAL
(www.patriagaucha.com.uy) This colorful, authentically home-grown five-day festival in early March attracts visitors from around the country to exhibitions of traditional *gaucho* skills, music and other activities. It takes place in Parque 25 de Agosto, north of town.

Sleeping & Eating

Inexpensive but bland accommodation is available downtown at places like **Hospedaje Márfer** (☎4632-3324; Ituzaingó 211; s/d with bathroom UR$650/1150, without bathroom from UR$390/780, all without breakfast). Nearby estancias offer a more meaningful and memorable taste of Tacuarembó's *gaucho* culture.

★**Estancia Panagea** ESTANCIA $$
(☎4630-2670, 9983-6149; panagea-uruguay.blogspot.com.uy; Ruta 31, Km 189; dm per person incl full board, farm activities, horseback riding & transport US$60) For a spectacular introduction to life on the Uruguayan land, head to this 970-hectare working *estancia* 40km northwest of Tacuarembó. Juan Manuel, who was born and raised here, his Swiss wife Susana and *gaucho* Bilingue invite guests to get fully immersed in farm activities from the mundane (tagging and vaccinating animals) to the classic (herding cattle on horseback).

Guests sleep dorm-style in simple rooms, eat three home-cooked meals a day (including self-serve bacon and eggs cooked on the

WORTH A TRIP

VALLE DE LUNAREJO

This gorgeous valley, 95km north of Tacuarembó, is a place of marvelous peace and isolation, with birds and rushing water providing the only soundtrack.

Visitors can spend the night at enchanting **Posada Lunarejo** (☎4650-6400; www.posadalunarejo.com; Ruta 30, Km 238; r per person incl full board UR$1700 Mon-Thu, UR$2000 Fri-Sun), a restored 1880 building 2km off Ruta 30, 3km from the river and a few steps from a bird colony teeming with *garzas* (cranes) and *espátulas rosadas* (roseate spoonbills). The posada organizes nearby hikes (UR$200, three hours) and horseback rides (UR$200, one hour).

The most convenient schedule is with **CUT** (www.cutcorporacion.com.uy), which goes to Valle del Lunarejo on its daily Montevideo–Tacuarembó–Artigas bus (leaving Montevideo at noon, UR$830, six hours; leaving Tacuarembó at 4:50pm, UR$141, 1½ hours). Posada Lunarejo can meet your bus if you call ahead.

woodstove), hit the basketball and volleyball courts at sunset and congregate around the fireplace at night. Call ahead to coordinate dates and arrange transportation from Tacuarembó's bus station.

★Yvytu Itaty ESTANCIA **$$**
(☎4630-8421, 099-837555; www.viviturismorural.com.uy; s incl full board, farm activities & horseback riding UR$2200, per person 2 or more people UR$2000) Pedro and Nahir Clariget's unpretentious ranch-style home, 50km southwest of Tacuarembó, offers a first-hand look at real *gaucho* life. Guests are invited to accompany Pedro and his friendly cattle dogs around the 636-hectare working *estancia* on horseback, participate in daily *estancia* routines and sip maté on the patio at sunset in anticipation of Nahir's tasty home cooking.

Call in advance for driving directions or to arrange pickup at Tacuarembó's bus station (UR$1500 roundtrip for a group of any size).

La Rueda PARRILLA **$**
(W Beltrán 251; mains UR$140-300; ⌚noon-3pm & 7pm-midnight Mon-Sat, noon-4pm Sun) With its thatched roof and walls covered with *gaucho* paraphernalia, this neighborhood *parrilla* is a perennial local favorite.

Cabesas Bier PUB FOOD **$**
(cabesasbier.uy/#brewpub; Sarandí 349; pub food from UR$200; ⌚8pm-late Thu-Sat) One of Tacuarembó's unexpected pleasures is this great little microbrewery, serving eight varieties of craft beer on tap, accompanied by pizza, *picadas* and other pub food.

ℹ Information

Banks are clustered downtown near Plaza Colón.
Tourist Office (☎4632-7144; tacuarembo.gub.uy; ⌚8am-7pm Mon-Fri, 8am-noon Sat & Sun) Just outside the bus terminal.

ℹ Getting There & Away

The **bus terminal** (☎4632-4441; cnr Ruta 5 & Av Victorino Pereira) is 1km northeast of town. Fares include Montevideo (UR$689, 4½ hours), and Salto (UR$512, four hours). A taxi to the center costs about UR$70.

EASTERN URUGUAY

This is Uruguay's playground (and, to an extent, Argentina's, Brazil's, Chile's and Spain's) – a long stretch of beaches all the way from Montevideo to the Brazilian border offering something for everyone: surfers, party animals, nature lovers and family groups.

Conflicts between Spain and Portugal, and then between Argentina and Brazil, left eastern Uruguay with historical monuments such as the imposing fortress of Santa Teresa. Just inland lies a varied landscape of palm savannas, lagoons and marshes rich in birdlife.

In midsummer, prices skyrocket and these beach towns seriously pack out. During the rest of the year you might have them to yourself.

Piriápolis

POP 8600

In the 1930s entrepreneur Francisco Piria built the landmark Hotel Argentino and an eccentric residence known as Piria's castle, and ferried tourists directly from Argentina. Nowadays it's a budget alternative to beach resorts further east, mostly attracting families from Montevideo on short breaks.

The problem with this town is obvious – a four-lane highway separates it from the beach. Still, if you don't mind doing the chicken run a couple of times a day, the water's clean and there are plenty of places to lay your towel.

For spectacular views over town, take the **chairlift** (Aerosilla; adult/child UR$160/140; ⏲10am-sunset) to the top of Cerro San Antonio.

Sleeping & Eating

Hostel de los Colores HOSTEL **$**
(☎4432-6188; www.hosteldeloscolores.com.uy; Simón del Pino, btwn Barrios & Reconquista; dm US$15-27, d from US$47; @📶) Directly opposite Piriápolis' more institutional 240-bed HI hostel, this newcomer two blocks from the beach offers clean, colorful four- and six-bed dorms, plus a lone double. Bikes (per day UR$400) and a kayak (per day UR$500) are available for rent.

Bungalows Margariteñas BUNGALOW **$**
(☎4432-2245, 099-890038; www.margaritenias.com; cnr Zufriategui & Piedras; d/tr/q US$60/65/70; @📶) Near the bus terminal, this place has well-equipped, individually decorated bungalows that sleep two to four. Affable owner Corina speaks English and meets guests at the bus station upon request.

★ **Café Picasso** SEAFOOD **$$**
(☎4432-2597; cnr Rojas & Caseros; dishes UR$240-480; ⏲noon-3:30pm & 8-11:30pm daily Dec-Apr, noon-3:30pm daily & 8-11:30pm Fri & Sat May-Nov) Hidden down a residential backstreet several blocks from the beach, septuagenarian chef-owner Carlos has converted his carport and front room into an informal, colorfully decorated restaurant with open-air grill. Locals chat astride plastic chairs and listen to tango recordings while Carlos cooks up some of the best fish anywhere on Uruguay's Atlantic coast, along with paella (UR$560) on Sundays.

Information

Banco de la República (Rambla de los Argentinos, btwn Sierra & Sanabria) has an ATM opposite the waterfront.

Tourist Office (☎4432-5055; www.destinopiriapolis.com; Rambla de los Argentinos; ⏲10am-6pm Apr-Nov, 9am-8pm Dec & Mar, to midnight Jan & Feb) Helpful staff and public toilets, on the waterfront near Argentino Hotel.

Getting There & Away

The **bus terminal** (☎4432-4526; cnr Misiones & Niza) is three blocks from the beach. Destinations include Montevideo (UR$177, 1½ hours) and Punta del Este (UR$116, 50 minutes).

Around Piriápolis

Pan de Azúcar & Sierra de la Ánimas

Six kilometers north of Piriápolis there's a trail to the top of **Cerro Pan de Azúcar** (389m), Uruguay's fourth-highest point, crowned by a 35m-high cross and a conspicuous TV aerial. Just below is the small **Reserva de Fauna Autóctona** (Ruta 37, Km 5; ⏲7am-8:30pm) FREE, with native species such as capybaras and gray foxes. Across the highway you can tour **Castillo de Piria** (☎4432-3268; Ruta 37, Km4; ⏲8am-3:30pm Tue-Sun Apr-Nov, to 6pm Dec-Mar) FREE, Francisco Piria's outlandishly opulent former residence.

Back on the Interbalnearia (coastal highway), 25km toward Montevideo from Piriápolis, the private nature reserve **Sierra de las Ánimas** (📱SMS only 094-419891; www.sierradelasanimas.com; Ruta 9, Km 86; admission UR$80; ⏲9am-sunset Sat & Sun, plus Carnaval & Easter weeks) 🌿 has two good hiking trails, one leading to the 501m summit (Uruguay's second highest), the other to the **Cañadón de los Espejos**, a series of waterfalls and natural swimming holes. Coming from Montevideo by bus, get off at Parador Los Cardos restaurant and cross the highway. In cold or rainy weather, send an SMS in advance to verify they're open.

Punta del Este

POP 6800

OK, here's the plan: tan it, wax it, buff it at the gym and then plonk it on the beach at 'Punta.' Once you're done there, go out and shake it at one of the town's famous clubs.

Punta's an international beach resort, packed with celebrities and swarming with Brazilian and Argentine tourists from Christmas through Carnaval. Out of season it's a bit of a ghost town, although the surrounding beaches are still nice.

Sights & Activities

Surf shops such as **Sunvalleysurf** (☎4248-1388; www.sunvalleysurf.com; Parada 3, Playa Brava; ⏰11am-7pm) rent surfboards and wetsuits. During summer, parasailing, waterskiing and jet skiing are possible on Playa Mansa.

Town Beaches BEACH

Beaches are the big daytime draw in sunny Punta. On the peninsula's western (Río de la Plata) side, Rambla Gral Artigas snakes past calm **Playa Mansa**, then passes the busy **yacht harbor**, overflowing with boats, restaurants and nightclubs, before circling east to meet the open Atlantic Ocean. On the peninsula's eastern side, waves and currents are rougher, as reflected in the name **Playa Brava** (Fierce Beach) and in the surfers flocking to **Playa de los Ingleses** and **Playa El Emir**.

Isla de Lobos ISLAND

About 10km offshore, this small island is home to the world's second-largest southern sea-lion colony (200,000 at last count), along with colonies of southern fur seals and South America's tallest lighthouse. The island is protected and can only be visited on an organized tour.

Punta del Este

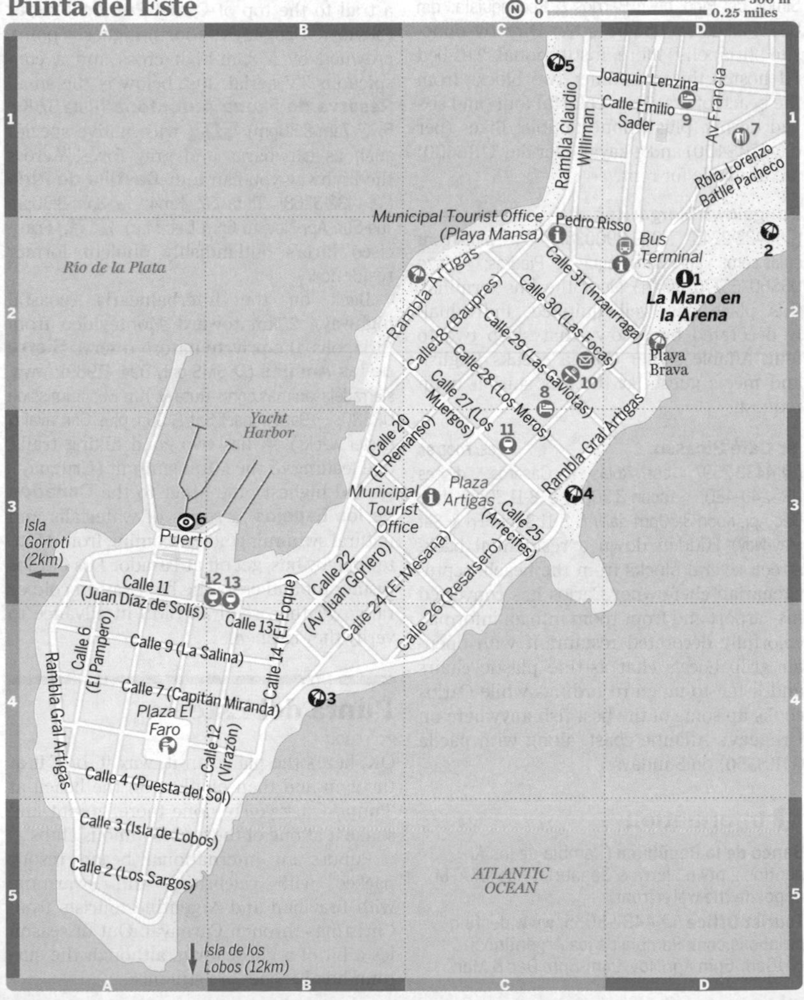

Isla Gorriti ISLAND

Boats leave every half-hour or so (daily in season, weekends in off-season) from Punta del Este's yacht harbor for the 15-minute trip to this nearby island, which has excellent sandy beaches, a couple of restaurants and the ruins of Baterías de Santa Ana, an 18th-century fortification.

★Casapueblo GALLERY

(☎4257-8041; carlospaezvilaro.com.uy/nuevo/museo-taller; admission UR$220; ⏰10am-sunset) Gleaming white in the sun and cascading nine stories down a cliffside, Uruguayan artist Carlos Páez Vilaró's exuberantly whimsical villa and art gallery sits atop Punta Ballena, a jutting headland 15km west of Punta del Este. Visitors can tour five rooms, view a film on the artist's life and travels, and eat up the spectacular views at the upstairs cafeteria-bar. There's a hotel and restaurant, too. It's a 2km walk from the junction where Codesa's Línea 8 bus drops you.

Sleeping

Many of Punta's accommodations close off-season; those that remain open slash prices dramatically.

★Tas D'Viaje Hostel HOSTEL $

(☎4244-8789; www.tasdviaje.com; Calle 24 btwn 28 & 29; dm US$15-35, d US$50-100; ❄@📶) Just one block from Playa El Emir, Punta's best-located hostel offers everything from low-cost fan-cooled dorms to brand-new air-conditioned suites with private bathrooms, nice wood floors and flat-screen cable TV. There's a sea-facing breakfast deck, an inviting living room with fireplace, an attractive guest kitchen and a hammock-strung back patio. On-site bike and surfboard rentals cost US$10 each per day.

Trip Hostel HOSTEL $

(☎4248-8181; www.thetriphostel.com; Sader btwn Artigas & Francia; dm US$12-30, d US$50-80; @📶) Founded by three Uruguayan friends, this small hostel has plenty of *onda* (good vibes), with its cozy lounge, on-site bar selling local microbrews, and rooftop terrace sporting six homegrown cannabis plants (Uruguay's new legal maximum). It's on a residential street within a five-minute walk of the bus station and beaches. Avoid the lone private room, which is windowless and claustrophobic.

La Lomita del Chingolo GUESTHOUSE $

(☎099-758897, 4248-6980; www.lalomitadelchingolo.com; Las Acacias btwn Los Eucaliptus & Le Mans; dm/d Dec & Mar US$20/40, Jan & Feb US$50/100, Apr-Nov US$17/30; @📶) With one six-person dorm and five private rooms, this relaxed place is in a residential neighborhood about 4km north of the center. Hospitable owners Rodrigo and Alejandra welcome guests with kitchen facilities, tasty breakfasts, impromptu backyard barbecues and plenty of information about the local area.

DON'T MISS

HAND IN THE SAND

La Mano en la Arena (The Hand in the Sand; Playa Brava) Punta's most famous landmark is this monster-sized sculpted hand protruding from the sands of Playa Brava. Constructed in iron and cement by Chilean artist Mario Irarrázabal, it won first prize in a monumental art contest in 1982 and has been a Punta fixture ever since. The hand exerts a magnetic attraction over thousands of visitors every year, who climb and jump off its digits and pose for photos with it. Look for it just southeast of the bus station.

Punta del Este

Top Sights

1 La Mano en la Arena D2

Sights

2 Playa Brava D2
3 Playa de los Ingleses B4
4 Playa El Emir C3
5 Playa Mansa C1
6 Yacht Harbor A3

Activities, Courses & Tours

7 Sunvalleysurf D1

Sleeping

8 Tas D'Viaje Hostel C2
9 Trip Hostel D1

Eating

10 Rustic C2

Drinking & Nightlife

11 Capi Bar C3
12 Moby Dick B3
13 Soho B3

Eating & Drinking

In summer Punta is famed for its club scene, which extends 10km east along the beaches all the way to La Barra. Outside of the peak Christmas-to-Carnaval period, you can still stomp the sand until the sun comes up at **Ocean Club** (www.facebook.com/OceanClubPunta; Rambla Batllé Parada 12; ⏲1-7am), one of the few beachfront dance spots operating year-round. In town, the most happening nightspots are down by the port. Places like **Soho** (www.facebook.com/SohoPuntaUy; Calle 13, btwn Calles 10 & 12; ⏲midnight-6am) and **Moby Dick** (www.mobydick.com.uy; Calle 13, btwn Calles 10 & 12; ⏲6pm-5am Mon-Thu, noon-5am Fri-Sun) stay open year-round as long as there's a crowd; they sometimes have live music on weekends.

Rustic INTERNATIONAL **$**
(☎092-007457; www.facebook.com/Rusticbarpuntadeleste; Calle 29, btwn Gorlero & Calle 24; mains UR$150-350; ⏲11am-4pm Wed-Mon, plus 8pm-3am Fri & Sat) Rustic wood tables, exposed brick walls, retro decor, and tasty food at affordable prices make this one of the peninsula's most attractive lunch spots. Friendly young owners Luciana and Sebastian offer service with a smile, bustling from table to table with *chivitos*, *milanesas*, quesadillas, salads and fish of the day. There's a UR$150 lunch special daily (UR$130 for takeaway).

OFF THE BEATEN TRACK

HORSING AROUND IN THE HILLS

About halfway between Punta del Este and the Brazilian border, the Sierra de Rocha is a lovely landscape of grey rocky crags interspersed with rolling rangeland. **Caballos de Luz** (☎099-400446; www.caballosdeluz.com; horseback rides from US$45, s/d US$40/50, incl full board US$95/170), run by the multilingual Austrian-Uruguayan couple Lucie and Santiago, offers hill-country horse treks lasting from two hours to a week, complete with three delicious vegetarian meals daily and overnight accommodation in a pair of comfortable thatched guest houses. They offer pickup at the bus station in Rocha (US$20), or you can drive there yourself (it's about 30 minutes off Hwy 9).

Capi Bar PUB
(www.facebook.com/capipde; Calle 27, btwn Gorlero & Calle 24; ⏲noon-late) Launched in 2015, Punta del Este's first artisanal brewpub serves up its own Capitán home brew along with craft beers from all over Uruguay. The classy, low-lit interior also makes a nice place to linger over reasonably priced fish and chips, *rabas* (fried squid) and other bar snacks.

Orientation

Punta sits on a narrow peninsula that divides the Río de la Plata from the Atlantic Ocean. The town has two separate grids: north of the yacht harbor is the high-rise hotel zone; the southern area is largely residential. Streets bear both names and numbers. Av Juan Gorlero (Calle 22) is the main commercial street.

East and west of town, locations along the *ramblas* (waterfront boulevards) are identified by *paradas* (numbered signposts).

Information

Banks and *casas de cambio* are concentrated along Av Juan Gorlero.

Municipal Tourist Office (☎4244-6510; www.maldonado.gub.uy; Plaza Artigas; ⏲8am-11pm mid-Dec–Feb, 11am-5pm rest of year) A full-service office with hotel-booking desk attached. Additional branches at the port, the bus terminal (☎4249-4042; ⏲8am-10pm mid-Dec–Feb, 11am-5pm rest of year) and Playa Mansa (☎4244-6519; cnr Calles 18 & 31; ⏲9am-10pm mid-Dec–Mar, 11am-5pm rest of year).

Getting There & Away

AIR

Aeropuerto Internacional de Punta del Este is at Laguna del Sauce, 20km west of Punta del Este. Direct international flights include Aerolíneas Argentinas to Buenos Aires' Aeroparque (AEP) and TAM to São Paulo, Brazil (GRU).

BUS

From Punta's **bus terminal** (☎4249-4042; cnr Calle 32 & Bulevar Artigas), **COT** (www.cot.com.uy) and **Copsa** (www.copsa.com.uy) run dozens of daily buses along the coastal route to Montevideo (UR$266, 2¼ hours). COT also runs two daily buses northeast up the coast to the Brazilian border, with intermediate stops at Rocha (UR$187, 1½ hours, transfer point for La Paloma, La Pedrera and Cabo Polonio) and Punta del Diablo (UR$363, 3 hours).

TTL (www.ttl.com.br) serves Brazilian destinations including Porto Alegre (UR$2340 to UR$3000, 10 hours), São Paulo (UR$5010,

28 hours) and Florianópolis (summer only, UR$3555, 16 hours).

Getting Around

Door-to-door **minivan transfers** (099-903433, 4223-0011; btwn airport & bus terminal or port UR$220, btwn airport & hotel UR$320) are the most convenient way to reach Punta del Este's airport. Alternatively, any Montevideo-bound bus can drop you at the airport entrance on the main highway (UR$81), 250m from the terminal building.

Cabo Polonio

POP 150

Cabo Polonio, one of Uruguay's wildest areas and home to its second-biggest sea-lion colony, occupies a pristine location. Imagine a tiny fishing village on a windswept point, nestled in sand dunes and crowned by a lonely lighthouse and you've got a good idea of what awaits. In 2009 the region was declared a national park, under the protective jurisdiction of Uruguay's SNAP program. Despite a growing influx of tourists (and an incongruously spiffy entrance portal erected in 2012), Cabo Polonio remains one of Uruguay's most rustic coastal villages. There are no banking services, and the town's limited electricity is derived from generators, solar and wind power.

The turnoff is northeast of La Paloma at Km 264.5 on Ruta 10.

Activities

★Cabalgatas Valiceras HORSEBACK RIDING
(099-574685; cabalgatasvaliceras.com.uy; Barra de Valizas) Based in nearby Barra de Valizas, this excellent operator offers horseback excursions into the national park, through the dunes and along the beaches north of Cabo Polonio, including monthly full-moon rides.

Wildlife Watching

Wildlife viewing in Cabo Polonio is excellent year-round. Below the lighthouse, southern sea lions *(Otaria flavescens)* and South American fur seals *(Arctocephalus australis)* frolic on the rocks. You can also spot southern right whales from August to October, penguins on the beach between May and August, and the odd southern elephant seal *(Mirounga leonina)* between January and March on nearby Isla de la Raza.

Sleeping & Eating

Viejo Lobo Hostel HOSTEL $
(091-413013; www.viejolobohostel.com; Dec-Feb dm/d US$25/60, Mar-Nov US$12.50/34;) On the sandy plaza where buses turn around, this newer hostel has three dorms sleeping four to seven people, plus a couple of basic doubles. Electricity is generated with solar panels and a windmill, and wi-fi is available one hour per night (to quote the friendly English-speaking manager Vicky: enough to stay connected, but not enough to turn people into zombies!)

Cabo Polonio Hostel HOSTEL $
(099-445943; www.cabopoloniohostel.com; mid-Dec–Feb dm/d US$33/100, US$16/50 other times; Oct-Apr) Recently expanded to include a larger, brighter kitchen and a brand-new ocean-view dorm, this rustic beachfront hostel is a Polonio classic, with a hammock-strewn patio and a woodstove for stormy nights. The abandoned TV in the dunes out front and the custom-designed NoFi logo epitomize owner Alfredo's low-tech philosophy: if you're in Polonio, it's time to slow down and unplug!

Pancho Hostal del Cabo HOSTEL $
(095-412633; dm Jan & Feb US$30, Mar-Dec US$11) Providing bare-bones dorms on two levels, Pancho's popular hostel is impossible to miss, look for the yellow corrugated roof, labeled with giant red letters, toward the beach from the bus stop. Nice features include a spacious new kitchen, a beachfront lounging area and the 2nd-floor dorm under the A-frame roof, with its small terrace looking straight out at the ocean.

El Club PARRILLA, INTERNATIONAL $$
(mains UR$200-400; 11am-late mid-Dec–Easter) Decked out in mosaics and colorfully painted furniture, Cabo Polonio's newest eatery combines the creative efforts of Colombian artist Camila, her Uruguayan partner Fernando and revered local chef Martín. Specialties include grilled fish, artisanal beer, wood-fired pizza and fondue cooked atop recycled tin cans. It doubles as a social club where people gather to play chess and enjoy live music.

Getting There & Away

Rutas del Sol runs two to five buses daily from Montevideo to the Cabo Polonio entrance portal on Ruta 10 (UR$530, 4½ hours). Here you'll pile

WORTH A TRIP

LA PALOMA & LA PEDRERA

Some 225km east of Montevideo, in the pretty rural department of Rocha, the coastal towns of La Paloma and La Pedrera offer some of Uruguay's best surfing. La Paloma owes its remarkably dependable waves to its tip-of-the-peninsula location: if there's no swell on the left, it'll be coming in on the right. La Pedrera, set atop a bluff with magnificent beach views, is also famous for its lively Carnaval festivities. Both towns fill up with young Uruguayans in summertime but get downright sleepy in the off-season.

Friendly **Peteco Surf Shop** (www.facebook.com/peteco.surf; Av Nicolás Solari, btwn Av El Sirio & Av del Navío; ⏲10am-8pm Thu-Mon, to 6pm Tue & Wed) in La Paloma rents all the necessary equipment (shortboards, longboards, bodyboards, sandboards, wetsuits and kayaks) and can hook you up with good local instructors. The best surfing beaches are Los Botes, Solari, Anaconda, La Aguada and La Pedrera.

Both towns have an active summer hostel scene. In La Paloma, surfer-friendly **La Balconada Hostel** (☎4479-6273; www.labalconadahostel.com.uy; Centauro s/n; dm US$18-35, d with bathroom US$60-80, d without bathroom US$50-60; 📶) has an enviable location a stone's throw from the beach. In La Pedrera, **El Viajero Hostel** (☎4479-2252; www.elviajerolapedrera.com; Venteveo, btwn Pirincho & Zorzal; dm US$18-38, d US$60-120; ⏲mid-Dec–early Mar; @📶) is 200m from the bus stop and 500m from the waterfront.

COT, Cynsa and Rutas del Sol all run frequently from Montevideo to La Paloma (UR$424, four hours) and La Pedrera (UR$442, 4¼ hours). Additional buses run between the two towns (UR$53, 15 minutes) and northeast to the Cabo Polonio turnoff (UR$88 to UR$106, 30 to 45 minutes).

onto a 4WD truck for the lurching, bumpy ride across the dunes into town (UR$170 round trip, 30 minutes each way).

Punta del Diablo

POP 750

Up near the Brazilian border, this once-sleepy fishing village has become a prime summer getaway for Uruguayans and Argentines, and the epicenter of Uruguay's backpacker beach scene. With its low-key wooden cabins and winding dirt streets, it's like an anti-Punta del Este and attracts a corresponding crowd – more nature-oriented and far less glamorous. Waves of uncontrolled development have pushed further inland and along the coast in recent years, but the stunning shoreline and laid-back lifestyle still exude a timeless appeal.

In the winter months it's like a ghost town, but when summer rolls around the population swells dramatically. To avoid the crowds, come outside the Christmas-to-February peak season; in particular, avoid the first half of January, when as many as 30,000 visitors inundate the town.

From the town's traditional center, a sandy 'plaza' 200m inland from the ocean, small dirt streets fan out in all directions.

Sights & Activities

During the day you can rent surfboards or horses along the town's main beach, or trek an hour north to Parque Nacional Santa Teresa. In the evening there are sunsets to watch, spontaneous bonfires and drum sessions to drop in on…you get the idea.

Sleeping & Eating

There are a multitude of private *cabañas* (cabins) for rent in the village; ask locally or check online at www.portaldeldiablo.com.uy. For cheap eats, don't miss the Acosta sisters' empanada stands down near the port, open daily in summer, and on weekends in low season.

★**El Diablo Tranquilo** HOSTEL $
(☎4477-2519; www.eldiablotranquilo.com; Av Central; dm US$12-25, d with bathroom US$50-90, d without bathroom US$38-70; @📶) Follow the devilish red glow into one of South America's most seductive hostels, whose endless perks include inviting chill-out areas, bike and surfboard rentals, yoga and language classes, horseback excursions and PayPal cash advances. At the beachside Playa Suites annex, upstairs rooms have full-on ocean views, while the raucous bar-restaurant of-

fers meals, beach service and a late-night party scene.

Hostel de la Viuda HOSTEL $
(☎4477-2690; www.hosteldelaviuda.com; cnr San Luis & Nueva Granada; dm US$18-29, d US$54-58; @☎≋) Friendly, family-run La Viuda sits on a forlorn, remote back street 2km southwest of the town center, but compensates with super-clean dorms and doubles, free bus-station pickup, a backyard pool, a spacious kitchen and a lounge that's perfect for movie-watching by the fireplace on chilly nights. It's five long blocks inland from Playa La Viuda, Punta del Diablo's southern beach.

La Casa de las Boyas HOSTEL $
(☎4477-2074; www.lacasadelasboyas.com.uy; Playa del Rivero; Christmas-Feb dm US$18-55, d US$100-150, rest of year dm/d/tr/q from US$15/50/60/70; @☎≋) A stone's throw from the beach and a 10-minute walk north of the bus stop, this hostel offers a pool, a guest kitchen and 13 dorms of varying sizes. Outside of peak season, the better rooms – equipped with en-suite bathrooms, kitchenettes and satellite TV – are rented out as private apartments.

★**Resto-Pub 70** ITALIAN $
(mains UR$200-280; ⏲12:30-4pm & 7:30-11pm Nov-Easter) Run by an Italian family from the Veneto, this portside eatery serves divine, reasonably priced homemade pasta such as *lasagne alle cipolle* (veggie lasagna with walnuts and caramelized onions), accompanied by UR$50 glasses of house wine. Afterwards, don't miss the *cantucci con vino dolce* (almond biscotti dipped in sweet wine) and *limoncino* (an artisanal liqueur made with fragrant Uruguayan lemons).

Cero Stress INTERNATIONAL $$
(Av de los Pescadores; mains UR$290-450; ⏲noon-5pm & 7:30pm-midnight; ☎✎) By far the greatest asset at this laid-back eatery is its outdoor deck, which offers amazing ocean views. It's the perfect place to sip a *caipirinha* (Brazilian cocktail with sugarcane alcohol) at sunset while contemplating your evening plans. There's also occasional live music.

ℹ Getting There & Away

Rutas del Sol, COT and Cynsa all offer service to Punta del Diablo's dreary new bus terminal, 2.5km west of town. Between Christmas and Carnaval, all buses terminate here, leaving you with a five- to 10-minute shuttle (UR$25) or taxi (UR$100) into town. In low season, some buses continue from the terminal to the town plaza near the waterfront.

Several direct buses run daily to Montevideo (UR$530, five hours) and Chuy on the Brazilian border (UR$88, one hour); for other coastal destinations, you'll usually need to change buses in Castillos (UR$70, one hour) or Rocha (UR$177, 1½ hours).

Parque Nacional Santa Teresa

More a historical than a natural attraction, this coastal **park** (☎4477-2101; sepae.webnode.es; Ruta 9, Km 302; ⏲8am-8pm Dec-Mar, to 6pm Apr-Nov) FREE 35km south of Chuy is popular for its uncrowded beaches and its im-

ℹ GETTING TO BRAZIL

The rather dreary border town of Chuy (population 11,300, called Chuí on the Brazilian side) is the main gateway from Uruguay into Brazil. Av Brasil/Uruguay, a wide avenue lined with moneychangers and vendors of pirated CDs, forms the international border. There's no reason to linger, but if you find yourself stuck here, **Etnico Hostel** (☎4474-2281; etnicohostelchuy@gmail.com; Liber Seregni 299; dm UR$400, s/d UR$800/1200; ❄@☎) is your best bet for an overnight stay.

The Uruguayan and Brazilan customs offices are a couple of kilometers apart, on opposite sides of the border. Long-distance buses operated by TTL (www.ttl.com.br) and EGA (www.ega.com.uy) stop at both offices on their international runs up the Atlantic coast from Montevideo and Punta del Este to Porto Alegre, Florianópolis and São Paulo.

COT and Cynsa buses for Punta del Diablo (UR$88, one hour) and Montevideo (UR$600, five hours) leave from near the corner of Brasil and Oliviera. Two blocks west, at the corner of Brasil and Mauro Silva, Tureste buses head inland to Treinta y Tres (UR$283, three hours), where you can make onward connections to Tacuarembó (via Melo).

pressive hilltop fortress, **Fortaleza de Santa Teresa** (admission UR$30; ⊙10am-7pm daily Dec-Mar, 10am-5pm Wed-Sun Apr-Nov), begun by the Portuguese in 1762, then captured and finished by the Spaniards. The park offers decentralized forest **camping** (UR$170 to UR$220) with basic facilities, along with four- to six-person **cabañas** (UR$1400 to UR$4800). Services at park headquarters include a post office, supermarket and restaurant.

The park gets crowded during Carnaval, but otherwise absorbs visitors well. Buses from Punta del Diablo (UR$47, 15 minutes) will drop you off at Km 302 on Hwy 9 (1km from park headquarters via a flat road) or at Km 306 (1km below the fortress).

UNDERSTAND URUGUAY

Uruguay Today

Recent years have seen remarkable developments in Uruguayan culture and politics. After nearly two centuries of back-and-forth rule between the two traditional parties, Blancos and Colorados, Uruguayans elected the leftist Frente Amplio (Broad Front) to power in 2004 and again in 2009 and 2014. Over that span, the Frente Amplio government has presided over numerous social changes, including the legalization of marijuana, abortion and same-sex marriage.

Many of these changes occurred during the five-year term of José Mujica (2010–15), a former guerrilla who famously survived 13 years of imprisonment and torture during Uruguay's period of military rule. As president, Mujica (affectionately nicknamed 'Pepe') was best known for his grandfatherly style and humility, famously donating the majority of his salary to charities and refusing to live in the presidential palace. Mujica's tenure saw substantial decreases in poverty and income inequality and increases in per capita income, and he left office with a 65% approval rating.

Uruguay's October 2014 elections returned the Frente Amplio to power, with former president Tabaré Vázquez reassuming the position he had held from 2005 to 2010. Under Vazquez's leadership, Uruguay has continued to buck the status quo, opting out of the massive TISA international trade agreement in late 2015 and making bold strides in the development of renewable energy; Uruguay already expects to have the world's highest percentage of wind power by the end of 2016 and aims to achieve total carbon neutrality by 2030.

History

Uruguay's aboriginal inhabitants were the Charrúa along the coast and the Guaraní north of the Río Negro. The hunting-and-gathering Charrúa put a halt to early European settlement by killing Spanish explorer Juan de Solís and most of his party in 1516. In any event there was little to attract the Spanish, who valued these lowlands along the Río de la Plata mainly as an access route to gold and other quick riches further inland.

The first Europeans to settle on the Banda Oriental (Eastern Shore) were Jesuit missionaries near present-day Soriano, on the Río Uruguay. Next came the Portuguese, who established present-day Colonia in 1680 as a beachhead for smuggling goods into Buenos Aires. Spain responded by building its own citadel at Montevideo in 1726. The following century saw an ongoing struggle between Spain and Portugal for control of these lands along the eastern bank of the Río de la Plata.

Napoleon's invasion of the Iberian peninsula in the early 19th century precipitated a weakening of Spanish and Portuguese power and the emergence of strong independence movements throughout the region. Uruguay's homegrown national hero, José Gervasio Artigas, originally sought to form an alliance with several states in present-day Argentina and southern Brazil against the European powers, but he was ultimately forced to flee to Paraguay. There he regrouped and organized the famous '33 Orientales,' a feisty band of Uruguayan patriots under General Juan Lavalleja who, with Argentine support, crossed the Río Uruguay on April 19, 1825, and launched a campaign to liberate modern-day Uruguay from Brazilian control. In 1828, after three years' struggle, a British-mediated treaty established Uruguay as a small independent buffer between the emerging continental powers.

For several decades, Uruguay's independence remained fragile. There was civil war between Uruguay's two nascent political parties, the Colorados and the Blancos (named, respectively, for the red and white bands they wore); Argentina besieged Montevideo from 1838 to 1851; and Brazil was an ever-present threat. Things finally settled down in the second half of the 19th century, with region-wide recognition of Uruguay's independence and the emergence of a strong national economy based on beef and wool production.

In the early 20th century, visionary president José Batlle y Ordóñez introduced such innovations as pensions, farm credits, unemployment compensation and the eight-hour work day. State intervention led to the nationalization of many industries, the creation of others, and a new era of general prosperity. However, Batlle's reforms were largely financed through taxing the livestock sector, and when exports faltered mid-century, the welfare state crumbled. A period of military dictatorship began in the early 1970s, during which torture became routine, and more than 60,000 citizens were arbitrarily detained before the 1980s brought a return to democratic traditions.

Culture

The one thing Uruguayans will tell you that they're *not* is anything like their *porteño* cousins across the water. Where Argentines can be brassy and sometimes arrogant, Uruguayans tend to be more humble and relaxed. Where the former have always been a regional superpower, the latter have always lived in the shadow of one. Those jokes about Punta del Este being a suburb of Buenos Aires don't go down so well on this side of the border. There are plenty of similarities, though: the near-universal appreciation for the arts, the Italian influence and the *gaucho* heritage.

Uruguayans like to take it easy and pride themselves on being the opposite of the hotheaded Latino type. Sunday's the day for family and friends, to throw half a cow on the *parrilla* (grill), sit back and sip some maté. The population is well educated, and the gap between rich and poor is much less pronounced than in most other Latin American countries.

Population

With 3.3 million people, Uruguay is South America's smallest Spanish-speaking country. The population is predominately white (88%); 8% are *mestizo* (people with mixed Spanish and indigenous blood) and 4% are black. Indigenous peoples are practically nonexistent. The average life expectancy (77 years) is one of Latin America's highest. The literacy rate is also high, at 98.5%, while population growth is a slow 0.27%. Population density is roughly 19 people per sq km.

Religion

Uruguay has more self-professed atheists per capita than any other Latin American country. According to a 2014 American Religious Identification Survey, only slightly more than half of Uruguayans consider themselves religious. Forty-two percent identify themseles as Roman Catholic, with 15% claiming affiliation with other Christian denominations. There's a small Jewish minority (less than 1% of the population).

Sports

Uruguayans, like just about all Latin Americans, are crazy about *fútbol* (soccer). Uruguay has won the World Cup twice, including the first tournament, played in Montevideo in 1930. The national team (known commonly as La Celeste) has continued to excel periodically at the international level, winning the 2011 Copa America and appearing in the 2014 World Cup in Brazil.

The country's two most venerable teams are Montevideo-based Nacional and Peñarol. **Fanáticos Fútbol Tours** (☎099-862325; www.futboltours.com.uy) in Montevideo offers customized soccer-themed tours and organized trips to see matches.

Arts

Despite its small population, Uruguay has an impressive literary and artistic tradition. The country's most famous writers include Juan Carlos Onetti and José Enrique Rodó – the latter is best known for his classic 1900 essay *Ariel*, which contrasts North American and Latin American civilizations.

Most Uruguayans also have a soft spot for journalist Eduardo Galeano (1940–2015), author of *Las venas abiertas de América Latina*.

Other major contemporary writers include journalist Hugo Burel, postmodernist Enrique Estrázulas, rising star Ignacio Alcuri and the late poet, essayist and novelist Mario Benedetti.

Uruguay's most renowned painters are the late Juan Manuel Blanes, Pedro Figari and Joaquín Torres García, each of whom has a museum dedicated to his work in Montevideo. Sculptors include José Belloni, whose life-size bronzes can be seen in Montevideo's parks.

The Uruguayan film industry is developing nicely; successes include *Whisky* (2004), a witty black comedy set in Montevideo and Piriápolis that won a couple of awards at Cannes and was selected as Uruguay's best film by the national critics' association in 2015. Theater is also popular and playwrights like Mauricio Rosencof are prominent.

Tango is big in Montevideo – Uruguayans claim tango legend Carlos Gardel as a native son, and one of the best-known tangos, 'La Cumparsita,' was composed by Uruguayan Gerardo Matos Rodríguez. During Carnaval, Montevideo's streets reverberate to the energetic drumbeats of *candombe,* an African-derived rhythm brought to Uruguay by slaves from 1750 onwards. Other deeply rooted Carnaval traditions include the *murgas,* satirical musical theater groups who perform throughout the city. On the contemporary scene, several Uruguayan rock bands have won a following on both sides of the Río de la Plata, including Buitres, La Vela Puerca and No Te Va Gustar.

Cuisine

Uruguayan cuisine revolves around grilled meat. *Parrillas* (restaurants with big racks of meat roasting over a wood fire) are everywhere, and weekend *asados* (barbecues) are a national tradition. *Chivitos* (steak sandwiches piled high with an absurd quantity of toppings) are hugely popular, as are *chivitos al plato* (the same ingredients served with fried potatoes instead of bread).

Vegetarians often have to content themselves with the ubiquitous pizza and pasta, although there are a few veggie restaurants lurking about. Seafood is excellent on the coast. Desserts are heavy on meringue, *dulce de leche* (milk caramel), burnt sugar and custard.

Tap water is OK to drink in most places. Uruguayan wines (especially tannats) are excellent, and local beers (Patricia, Pilsen and Zillertal) are reasonably good. *Grappamiel* (honey-infused grape brandy) is another Uruguayan classic.

Uruguayans consume even more maté (a bitter tea-like beverage indigenous to South America) than Argentines. If you get the chance, try to acquire the taste – there's nothing like whiling away an afternoon with new-found friends passing around the maté.

In major tourist destinations such as Punta del Este and Colonia, restaurants charge *cubiertos* – small 'cover' charges that theoretically pay for the basket of bread offered before your meal.

Environment

Though one of South America's smallest countries, Uruguay is not so small by European standards. Its area of 176,215 sq km is greater than England and Wales combined, or slightly bigger than the US state of Florida.

Uruguay's two main ranges of rolling interior hills are the Cuchilla de Haedo, west of Tacuarembó, and the Cuchilla Grande, south of Melo; neither exceeds 500m in height. West of Montevideo the terrain is more level. The Río Negro flowing through the center of the country forms a natural dividing line between north and south. The Atlantic coast has impressive beaches, dunes, headlands and lagoons. Uruguay's grasslands and forests resemble those of Argentina's pampas or southern Brazil, and patches of palm savanna persist in the east, along the Brazilian border.

The country is rich in birdlife, especially in the coastal lagoons of Rocha department. Most large land animals have disappeared, but the occasional *ñandú* (rhea) still races across northwestern Uruguay's grasslands. Whales, fur seals and sea lions are common along the coast.

SURVIVAL GUIDE

Directory A–Z

ACCOMMODATIONS

Uruguay has an excellent network of hostels and campgrounds, especially along the Atlantic coast. Other low-end options include *hospedajes* (family homes) and *residenciales* (budget hotels).

Posadas (inns) are available in all price ranges and tend to be homier than hotels. Hotels are ranked from one to five stars, according to amenities.

Country *estancias turísticas* (marked with blue National Tourism Ministry signs) provide lodging on farms.

ACTIVITIES

Punta del Diablo, La Paloma, La Pedrera and Punta del Este all get excellent surfing waves, while Cabo Polonio and the coastal lagoons of Rocha department are great for whale and bird watching, respectively. Punta del Este's beach scene is more upmarket, with activities such as parasailing, windsurfing and Jet Skiing.

Horseback riding is very popular in the interior and can be arranged on most tourist *estancias*.

ELECTRICITY

Uruguay runs on 220V, 50Hz (same as Argentina). There are various types of plugs in use, the most common being the two round pins with no earth/ground pin.

EMBASSIES & CONSULATES

Argentine Embassy (☎2902-8166; eurug cancilleria.gov.ar; Cuareim 1470); Consulate (☎2902-8623; cmdeo.mrecic.gov.ar; WF Aldunate 1281)

Brazilian Embassy (☎2707-2119; montevideu.itamaraty.gov.br; Artigas 1394); Consulate (☎2901-2024; cgmontevideu.itamaraty.gov.br; Convención 1343, 6th fl)

Canadian Embassy (☎2902-2030; uruguay.gc.ca; Plaza Independencia 749, Oficina 102)

SLEEPING PRICE RANGES

The following price ranges refer to a double room with bathroom in high season. Note that prices at most accommodations are quoted in US dollars rather than Uruguayan pesos.

$ less than US$75

$$ US$75 to $US150

$$$ more than US$150

EATING PRICE RANGES

The following price indicators apply to the cost of a main course.

$ less than UR$300

$$ UR$300 to UR$450

$$$ more than UR$450

French Embassy (☎1705-0000; www.ambafranceuruguay.org; Av Uruguay 853)

German Embassy (☎2902-5222; www.montevideo.diplo.de; La Cumparsita 1435)

UK Embassy (☎2622-3630; ukinuruguay.fco.gov.uk; Marco Bruto 1073)

US Embassy (☎1770-2000; uruguay.usembassy.gov; Lauro Muller 1776)

GAY & LESBIAN TRAVELERS

Uruguay is generally GLBT friendly. In 2008 Uruguay became the first Latin American country to recognize same-sex civil unions, and in 2013 same-sex marriage was legalized. In Montevideo, look for the pocket-sized **Friendly Map** (www.friendlymap.com.uy) listing GLBT-friendly businesses throughout the country.

INSURANCE

Worldwide travel insurance is available at www.lonelyplanet.com/travel-insurance. You can buy, extend and claim online anytime – even if you're already on the road.

INTERNET ACCESS

Wi-fi zones and internet cafes are commonplace in cities and larger towns. Antel (state telephone company) offices sell SIM cards with reasonably priced data plans for unlocked phones.

LEGAL MATTERS

Uruguay has some of Latin America's most lenient drug laws. Possession of small amounts of marijuana or other drugs for personal use has been decriminalized, although their sale remains illegal.

MONEY

The unit of currency is the Uruguayan peso (UR$). Banknote values are 20, 50, 100, 200, 500, 1000 and 2000. There are coins of one, two, five, 10 and 50 pesos.

ATMs

In all but the smallest interior towns, getting cash with your ATM card is easy. Machines marked with the green Banred or blue Redbrou logo serve all major international banking networks. ATMs dispense bills in multiples of 100 pesos. Many also dispense US dollars, designated as U$S, but only in multiples of US$100.

Credit Cards

Most upmarket hotels, restaurants and shops accept credit cards.

Moneychangers

There are *casas de cambio* in Montevideo, Colonia, the Atlantic beach resorts and border towns such as Chuy. They typically keep longer hours than banks but may offer slightly lower rates. There's no black market for currency exchange.

Tipping

- In restaurants, leave 10% of the bill.
- In taxis, round up the fare a few pesos.

OPENING HOURS

Banks 1-6pm Mon-Fri

Bars 6pm-late

Clubs Midnight-late

Restaurants noon-3pm & 8pm-midnight; some open at 8am for breakfast

Shops 9am-1pm & 3-7pm Mon-Sat; extended hours in larger cities

PUBLIC HOLID7AYS

Año Nuevo (New Year's Day) January 1

Día de Reyes (Epiphany) January 6

Semana de Turismo/Semana Santa (Holy Week) March/April

Desembarco de los 33 (Return of the 33 Exiles) April 19

Día del Trabajador (Labor Day) May 1

Batalla de Las Piedras (Battle of Las Piedras) May 18

Natalicio de Artigas (Artigas' Birthday) June 19

Jura de la Constitución (Constitution Day) July 18

Día de la Independencia (Independence Day) August 25

Día de la Raza (Columbus Day) October 12

Día de los Muertos (All Souls' Day) November 2

Navidad (Christmas Day) December 25

TELEPHONE

Uruguay's country code is ☎598. **Antel** (www.antel.com.uy) is the state telephone company, with offices in every town.

All Uruguayan landline numbers are eight digits long, beginning with ☎2 for Montevideo or ☎4 for elsewhere in the country. Cell (mobile) phone numbers consist of a three-digit prefix (most commonly ☎099) followed by a six-digit number. If dialing internationally, drop the leading zero.

Cell Phones

Three companies – **Antel** (www.antel.com.uy), **Claro** (www.claro.com.uy) and **Movistar** (www.movistar.com.uy) – provide cell-phone service in Uruguay. Rather than use expensive roaming plans, many travelers bring an unlocked cell phone (or buy a cheap one here) and insert a local pay-as-you-go SIM card. SIMs can readily be purchased at Antel offices and recharged at service stations, shopping malls and streetside kiosks throughout Uruguay.

TIME

Uruguay Standard Time is three hours behind GMT, same as in Argentina. Daylight-saving time was abolished in 2015.

TOURIST INFORMATION

The **National Tourism Ministry** (Ministerio de Turismo y Deporte; www.turismo.gub.uy), with 10 offices around the country, distributes excellent free maps for each of Uruguay's 19 departments, along with specialized information on *estancia* tourism, Carnaval, surfing and other subjects of interest to travelers. Most towns also have a municipal tourist office on the plaza and/or at the bus terminal.

TRAVELERS WITH DISABILITIES

Uruguay is slowly beginning to plan for travelers with special needs. In Montevideo, you'll find newly constructed ramps and dedicated bathrooms in high-profile destinations such as Plaza Independencia and Teatro Solis, disabled access (*accesibilidad universal*) on some bus lines and a growing number of ATM machines for the visually impaired. However, there's still a long way to go. Spanish-language websites providing useful resources for the disabled include pronadis.mides.gub.uy, www.accesibilidad.gub.uy and www.discapacidaduruguay.org.

VISAS

Nationals of Western Europe, Australia, the USA, Canada and New Zealand automatically receive a 90-day tourist card, renewable for another 90 days. Other nationals may require visas. For an official list of current visa requirements by nationality, see migracion.minterior.gub.uy.

VOLUNTEERING

Basic Spanish proficiency is generally a prerequisite for volunteer work in Uruguay.

Karumbé (www.karumbe.org) Sea turtle conservation in Parque Nacional Santa Teresa.

WOMEN TRAVELERS

Women are generally treated with respect, and travelling alone is safer here than in many other Latin American countries.

Getting There & Away

AIR

- Airlines flying directly from North America and Europe to Montevideo's **Carrasco**

international airport (☎2604-0272; www.aeropuertodecarrasco.com.uy) include American (from Miami), plus Iberia and Air Europa (from Madrid). Most others connect through Buenos Aires or São Paulo.

➡ A few direct flights from Argentina and Brazil also serve **Punta del Este international airport** (Aeropuerto de Punta del Este; ☎4255-9777; www.puntadeleste.aero).

➡ Uruguayan departure tax is automatically included in all ticket prices.

BOAT

Most visitors enter Uruguay by ferry from Buenos Aires, arriving in Colonia, Montevideo or Carmelo.

BUS

➡ Direct buses run from Montevideo to Buenos Aires via the Fray Bentos-Gualeguaychú bridge, but these are slower than bus/ferry combinations across the Río de la Plata. Two other bridges connect Uruguay with Argentina, over the Río Uruguay from Paysandú to Colón and Salto to Concordia.

➡ There are multiple crossings to Brazil – the most popular is the Atlantic coast route from Chuy to Chuí, with northbound connections to Porto Alegre, Florianópolis and São Paulo.

➡ Buses generally continue through the border and passport formalities are conducted on the bus.

ℹ Getting Around

BUS

➡ Uruguay is perfect for bus travel. Buses are comfortable, roads are well-maintained, the government-regulated fares are reasonable, service is frequent on main routes (especially along the Atlantic coast and the Río Uruguay) and distances are short – due to Uruguay's small size, the longest ride you're likely to take is six hours. Many companies offer free wi-fi on board, and most bus terminals have a reasonably priced left-luggage facility.

➡ Reservations are unnecessary outside of holiday periods (although you'll have a better choice of seats with advance purchase). On peak travel dates a single company may run multiple departures at the same hour, in which case they'll mark a bus number on your ticket; check with the driver to make sure you're boarding the right bus, or you may find yourself in the 'right' seat on the wrong bus!

CAR & MOTORCYCLE

➡ Having your own transport can be convenient, especially in Uruguay's interior where bus service is less frequent. Visitors to Uruguay who are staying less than 90 days need only bring a valid driver's license from their home country. Uruguayan drivers are extremely considerate, and even bustling Montevideo is quite sedate compared with Buenos Aires.

➡ Due to government regulation, all service stations, including the ubiquitous state-owned Ancap, charge the same price for fuel. Unleaded gasoline cost UR$42.50 a liter at the time of research.

LOCAL TRANSPORTATION

Taxis, *remises* (radio-dispatched taxis) and local buses are similar to those in Argentina. Taxis are metered; fares are 20% higher between 10pm and 6am, and on Sundays and holidays. City bus service is excellent in Montevideo and other urban areas, while *micros* (minibuses) form the backbone of the local transit network in smaller coastal towns.

Venezuela

Includes ➡

Best Places to Eat

➡ Granja Natalia (p982)
➡ Come a Casa (p975)
➡ Madera Fina (p987)
➡ El Canto de la Ballena (p984)
➡ La Casa Bistro (p975)

Best Places to Stay

➡ Posada Casa Sol (p993)
➡ Tepuy Lodge (p1010)
➡ La Casa del Mono (p988)
➡ Posada La Casita (p1006)
➡ Alquimia Paria (p999)

Why Go?

Spectacular Venezuela, home to some of South America's most incredible landscapes, rightly has a terrible image problem at the moment. Hyperinflation has led to a dramatic drop in living standards and issues with the supply of basic goods, while personal safety, particularly in Caracas, is worse than anywhere else on the continent. And yet, visiting Venezuela is both possible and remarkably cheap, with dollars instantly making even backpackers feel wealthy. Safety is a serious concern, of course, but sensibly managed it should be no deterrent to a trip.

The rewards if you do go are, frankly, immense. Few countries in the world have this degree of natural beauty: Andean peaks, Caribbean coastline, idyllic islands, grasslands teeming with wildlife, the steamy Orinoco Delta and the world's highest waterfall, Angel Falls. This is true trip-of-a-lifetime stuff, and right now you'll have it pretty much all to yourself.

When to Go

Caracas

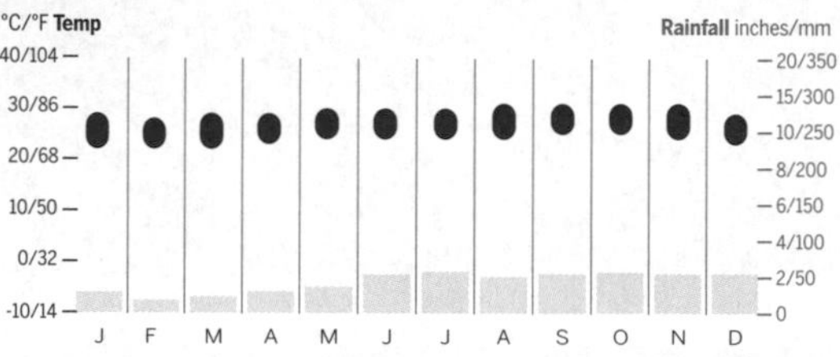

May–Nov Salto Ángel and the Gran Sabana waterfalls gush, swollen with rainy-season flow.

Oct–Nov Low-season travel means empty beaches before the Christmas holidays.

Feb/Mar The whole country vacations during Carnaval, with special festivals in some cities.

Connections

Caracas is Venezuela's main transportation hub, with buses and flights radiating out to much of the country. There are four border crossings to Colombia, with the coastal Maracaibo to Maicao route being the most heavily used by foreign travelers, followed by the Andean route between San Antonio del Táchira and Cúcuta. Only one main road connects Brazil and Venezuela; it leads from Manaus through Boa Vista in Brazil, to the border crossing at Santa Elena de Uairén and continues to Ciudad Guayana. Brazil can also be accessed via remote southern Amazonas and onward to Manaus along the Río Negro. There is no border crossing between Venezuela and Guyana, you have to transit through Brazil.

ITINERARIES

One Week

One week will barely scratch the surface, but you can get a taste. Make your way to the colonial city of Ciudad Bolívar and explore the historical district along the mighty Río Orinoco. From there, fly to the lagoon-side village of Canaima, skirting the iconic tabletop *tepui* mountains. Take a boat tour to the base of Salto Ángel (Angel Falls), and spend the night in the jungle. Then head to the beach either at Puerto Colombia or Los Roques.

One Month

Take in the Andes and some extreme sports in Mérida, then make your way east across Los Llanos on a wildlife tour. Fly to Canaima and visit Salto Ángel from Ciudad Bolívar and follow up with an outdoor adventure to the Orinoco Delta or a weeklong trek to Roraima. Then get some sand in your shoes as you sunbathe and snorkel in the islands of Los Roques, or along the virgin beaches of the Península de Paria.

Essential Food & Drink

- **Arepa** A grilled corn pancake stuffed with cheese, beef or other fillings. Ubiquitous fast food, often eaten for breakfast.
- **Pabellón criollo** The Venezuelan national dish of shredded beef, black beans, rice and plantains.
- **Polar beer** If there were a national beverage, it would be these icy minibottles of brew.
- **Coffee** Aromatic espresso shots of homegrown liquid heaven, served in little plastic cups at the *panadería* (bakery).
- **Chocolate** Not widely exported, Venezuelan chocolate is some of the best in the world.

AT A GLANCE

- **Currency** Bolívar Fuerte (BsF)
- **Languages** Spanish; dozens of indigenous languages
- **Money** Use the black market to change money. Never use ATMs or official exchange offices.
- **Visas** US and Israeli citizens need visas, which must be obtained in advance.
- **Time** GMT minus 4½ hours

Fast Facts

- **Area** 912,050 sq km
- **Population** 30.4 million
- **Capital** Caracas
- **Emergency** ☎171
- **Country Code** ☎58

Official Exchange Rates

Australia	A$1	BsF4.50
Canada	C$1	BsF4.80
Euro	€1	BsF7.18
New Zealand	NZ$1	BsF4.06
UK	UK£1	BsF9.86
USA	US$1	BsF6.35

Set Your Budget

- **Budget lodging** US$5
- **Dinner mains** US$2
- **Salto Ángel three-day tour** US$200

Venezuela Highlights

1. Marveling at **Salto Ángel (Angel Falls)** (p1008), the world's highest waterfall, dropping over 300 stories in Parque Nacional Canaima.
2. Feeling the adrenaline rush while playing outside in the adventure-sports capital of **Mérida** (p990).
3. Hiking to the lost world of the **Roraima** (p1011) table mountain for moonscape scenery and unique plant life.
4. Stretching out on white-sand beaches or snorkeling and diving the day away at the tiny, undeveloped islands of **Archipiélago Los Roques** (p982).
5. Being on the lookout for capybaras, anacondas, caimans and other wildlife in **Los Llanos** (p996), the grassy flatlands of Venezuela's cowboy country.
6. Encountering dolphins, howler monkeys and parrots in the wildlife-rich **Delta del Orinoco** (p1007).
7. Kicking back and watching the world-famous lightning show over Lake Maracaibo in **Catatumbo** (p991).
8. Getting truly off the grid and exploring the pristine beaches of **Península de Paria** (p999).

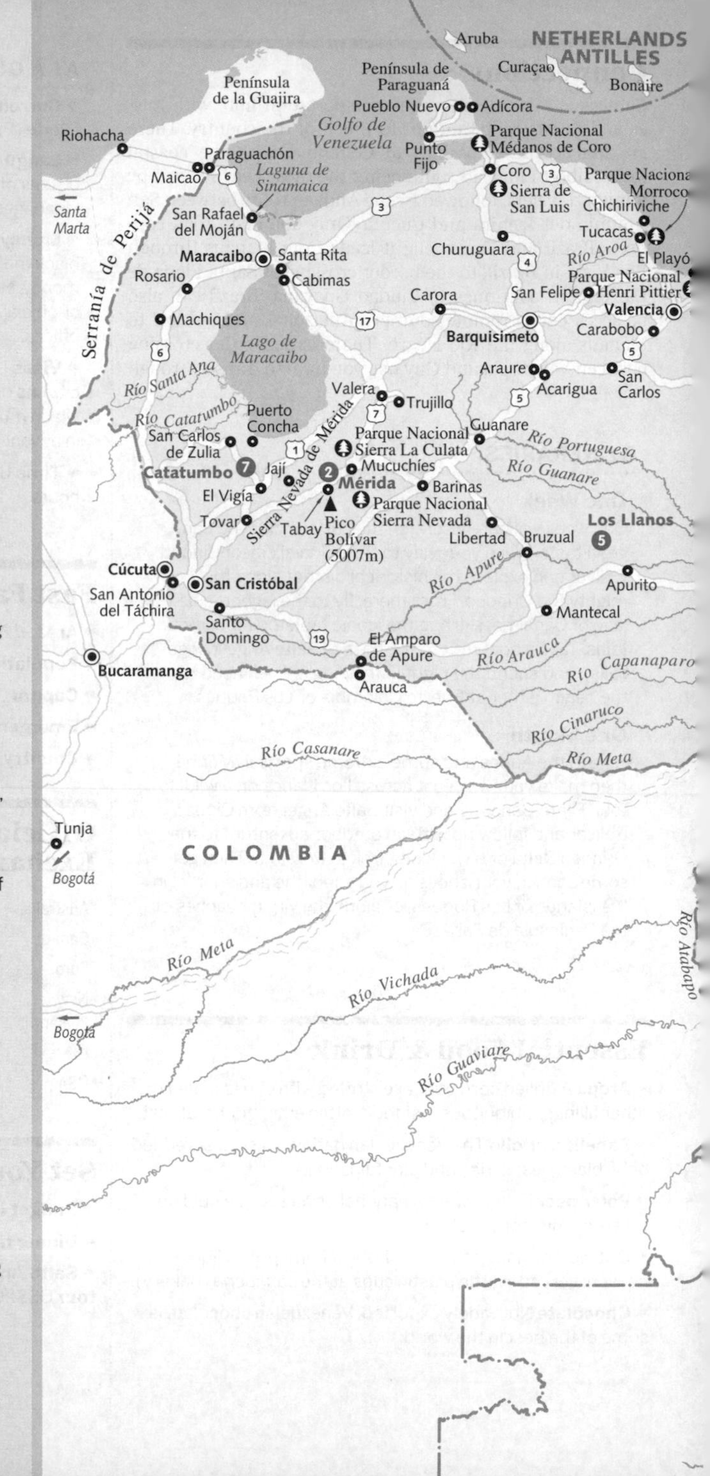

Caribbean Sea
ST VINCENT & THE GRENADINES
GRENADA
Parque Nacional Archipiélago Los Roques
4
Archipiélago Los Roques
Isla La Blanquilla
Islas de Aves
Isla La Orchila
200 km
100 miles
Isla La Tortuga
Isla de Margarita
La Asunción
Porlamar
Tobago
TRINIDAD & TOBAGO
Catia La Mar
Puerto Colombia
Chuao
Maiquetía
Parque Nacional El Avila
CARACAS
Maracay
Lago de Valencia
Isla Cubagua
Carúpano
Río Caribe
Península de Araya
Cumaná
Puerto La Cruz
Barcelona
Parque Nacional Mochima
Parque Nacional Península de Paria
8
Península de Paria
Güiria
PORT OF SPAIN
Trinidad
Caripe
Parque Nacional El Guácharo
Maturín
ATLANTIC OCEAN
Cúa
El Guapo
Valle del Tuy
San Francisco de Yare
Píritu
El Sombrero
Anaco
Zaraza
Valle de la Pascua
Tucupita
El Tigre
Calabozo
Barrancas
6
Delta del Orinoco
Piacoa
Río Manapire
Ciudad Bolívar
Ciudad Guayana
Upata
Río Orinoco
San Fernando de Apure
Caicara del Orinoco
Maripa
Ciudad Piar
Embalse de Guri
Bochinche
El Callao
Tumeremo
Río Caura
La Paragua
El Dorado
El Playón
Río Paragua
Canaima
Puerto Páez
El Burro
Puerto Carreño
Sierra de Maigualida
Río Caroní
1
Salto Ángel (Angel Falls)
GUYANA
Puerto Ayacucho
Casuarito
Amazonas
Parque Nacional Canaima
Roraima
3
Samariapo
Morganito
Río Ventuari
Gran Sabana
Cerro Autana (1248m)
Santa Elena de Uairén
El Paují
Icabarú
Pacaraima
San Fernando de Atabapo
Río Orinoco
Río Uracicoera
Yavita
Río Guainía
Maroa
Boa Vista
San Carlos de Río Negro
Brazo Casiquiare
BRAZIL
Caracaraí
San Simón de Cocuy
Parque Nacional Serranía la Neblina
Río Negro
Río Branco
São Gabriel da Cachoeira (70km)
Manaus

BEFORE YOU TRAVEL – IMPORTANT VENEZUELA INFORMATION

Venezuela is a tricky place to travel at present and showing up on a whim is a bad idea. That said, with a bit of forward planning and lots of common sense, a trip is well worth the effort. The following information is essential to read before embarking on a trip here, however.

Money & the Black Market

Venezuela is in the process of a slow economic meltdown, mainly due to the government keeping the Bolívar Fuerte (BsF) pegged at a totally unrealistic rate of six to the US dollar. This has created hyperinflation and a thriving black market, which all travelers need to use to be able to afford travel here. The black market gives a realistic value of between BsF500 and 700 to the dollar, which makes the country an incredible bargain. Traveling in Venezuela is simply not possible without using this system, and so it's important to either bring cash US dollars with you to change on arrival (ask at any hotel or any travel agency and they'll be able to point you in the direction of a money changer) or by sending money electronically to a trusted travel agency or *posada* (hotel or guesthouse), who will then provide you with cash on arrival. It's important therefore to be met when you arrive in the country, as even paying for a taxi or bus fare without the black market will be prohibitively expensive. Never use ATMs or credit cards in Venezuela, as these will give you the terrible official rates as well.

Safety

Venezuela is without doubt one of the most dangerous destinations in South America and it's important to know that there are always risks in coming here, mainly of mugging. That said, by being sensible, planning carefully and taking some extra precautions, there's absolutely no reason to avoid the country entirely. Some easy ways to minimize your exposure include avoiding Caracas altogether, always taking taxis after dark, avoiding public buses, not using your phone or camera on the streets, not wearing expensive jewellery or watches and arranging for transfers from airports and bus stations in advance with your hotel or travel agency. Do not use unofficial taxis, change money with strangers or stay in hotels you don't know to be safe. Take local advice seriously and carry a copy of your passport and entry stamp with you at all times rather than carrying your actual passport with you. Finally, be discreet about the often enormous piles of cash you're forced to carry due to the bolivar being so weak and the highest note being worth the equivalent of US$0.20.

Getting Around

We recommend using a travel agency in Venezuela, however independent and experienced a traveler you may be. Travel agencies know the most up-to-date information, can book internal flights and buses for you (both impossible from abroad), and can assist with changing money and organizing transfers. Internal flights should be reserved several weeks in advance due to overbooking and enormous demand as domestic routes shrink, and you should check in at least two hours in advance, preferably three, to ensure you can board. Long-distance buses are generally safe, but tickets are not always available at short notice. Many travelers go between cities using taxis as fuel prices are so low and the powerful dollar makes this affordable. It's also the safest method to get around over land. You should avoid using buses to get around Caracas, though the metro is fine.

Visas

US and Israeli citizens require visas to visit Venezuela. These must be obtained in advance and in person from a Venezuelan consulate abroad, and are a headache. While they only cost US$30, they can take several weeks to issue, so plan well in advance. Citizens of most other countries can travel visa-free.

CARACAS

0212 / POP 5.2 MILLION

A sprawling metropolis choked with traffic, Caracas incites no instant love affairs. The political and cultural capital of Venezuela is densely overpopulated and hectic, with a solid dose of crime and pollution. Few sections of the city are pedestrian-friendly, most are downright dangerous and after dark, it's strictly taxis only.

That said, it's a shame to miss Caracas entirely, as many travelers choose. The city has a spectacular setting, with the jungle-clad mountains of the Parque Nacional El Ávila towering over it as well as some good museums and Venezuela's best eating options. Evocative fog descends from the lush mountains, keeping the city comfortable year-round, and chirping *sapitos* (little frogs) and crickets form a lovely evening chorus.

Safety, the single factor that prevents many from visiting, is a big concern, but if you keep your wits about you, ask locals before heading anywhere you're not sure about and take taxis after dark, you should be fine. Caracas is a tough but fascinating place that won't be for everyone, but which almost always impresses the few who make it here these days.

Sights

Sprawling for 20km along a narrow coastal valley, Caracas is bordered to the north by the dramatic peaks of the Parque Nacional El Ávila and to the south by a mix of modern suburbs and *barrios* (shantytowns) stacked along the steep hillsides. Downtown Caracas stretches for 8km from the neighborhood of El Silencio to Los Palos Grandes. Museums are clustered around Parque Central on the eastern edge of the historic center, while increasingly the 'safe' areas around Altamira and Los Palos Grandes are where most travelers find themselves, full as they are with decent eating and sleeping options.

The Center & Around

The historic sector is the heart of the original Caracas. It still retains glimpses of its colonial past but is peppered with newer buildings and a lot of questionable architecture from the last century. It's a lively area and worth visiting for its historical sites, particularly those pertaining to Simón Bolívar. Despite being the center of the city it's unsafe when it empties out after 6pm, and can be dangerous even during the day. Proceed with caution.

Plaza Bolívar PLAZA

(Map p972; M Capitolio, El Silencio) This leafy square is the nucleus of the old town. It's always alive with huddled groups of *caraqueños* engaged in conversation and children feeding freshly popped corn to the black squirrels in the trees. Vendors hawk lemonade and *cepilladas* (shaved ices) on the sidelines, and the whole scene is shaded by African tulip trees and jacarandas. Golden cherubs gather round the fountains at each corner of the square.

In the center is the obligatory monument to Bolívar – the equestrian statue was cast in Munich, shipped in pieces, and eventually unveiled in 1874 after the ship carrying it foundered on the Archipiélago los Roques. The plaza is a favorite stage for political visionaries and religious messiahs, who deliver their passionate speeches to a casual audience. In recent years it's been a focus for supporters of Venezuela's left-wing government, with stalls selling videos, paintings and photos of the late Hugo Chávez alongside saints and musical legends.

Catedral CHURCH

(Map p972; 862-4963; Plaza Bolívar; 8-11:30am & 4-6pm Mon-Fri, 9am-noon & 4:30-6pm Sat & Sun; M Capitolio, El Silencio) FREE Set on the eastern side of Plaza Bolívar, Caracas' cathedral started its life in the mid-16th century as a mere mud-walled chapel. A church later replaced it, only to be flattened by the 1641 earthquake. Built from 1665 to 1713, the 'new' cathedral is packed with dazzling gilded altars and elaborate side chapels; the most famous is that of the Bolívar family,

CORNER TO CORNER

A curiosity of Caracas is the center's street-address system. It's not the streets that bear names here, but the *esquinas* (street corners); therefore, addresses are given 'corner to corner.' So if an address is 'Piñango a Conde,' the place is between these two street corners. If a place is situated on a corner, just the corner will be named (eg Esq Conde). As a result, you won't normally find street numbers with addresses either, it's more a case of finding where the two streets intersect and looking around!

Greater Caracas

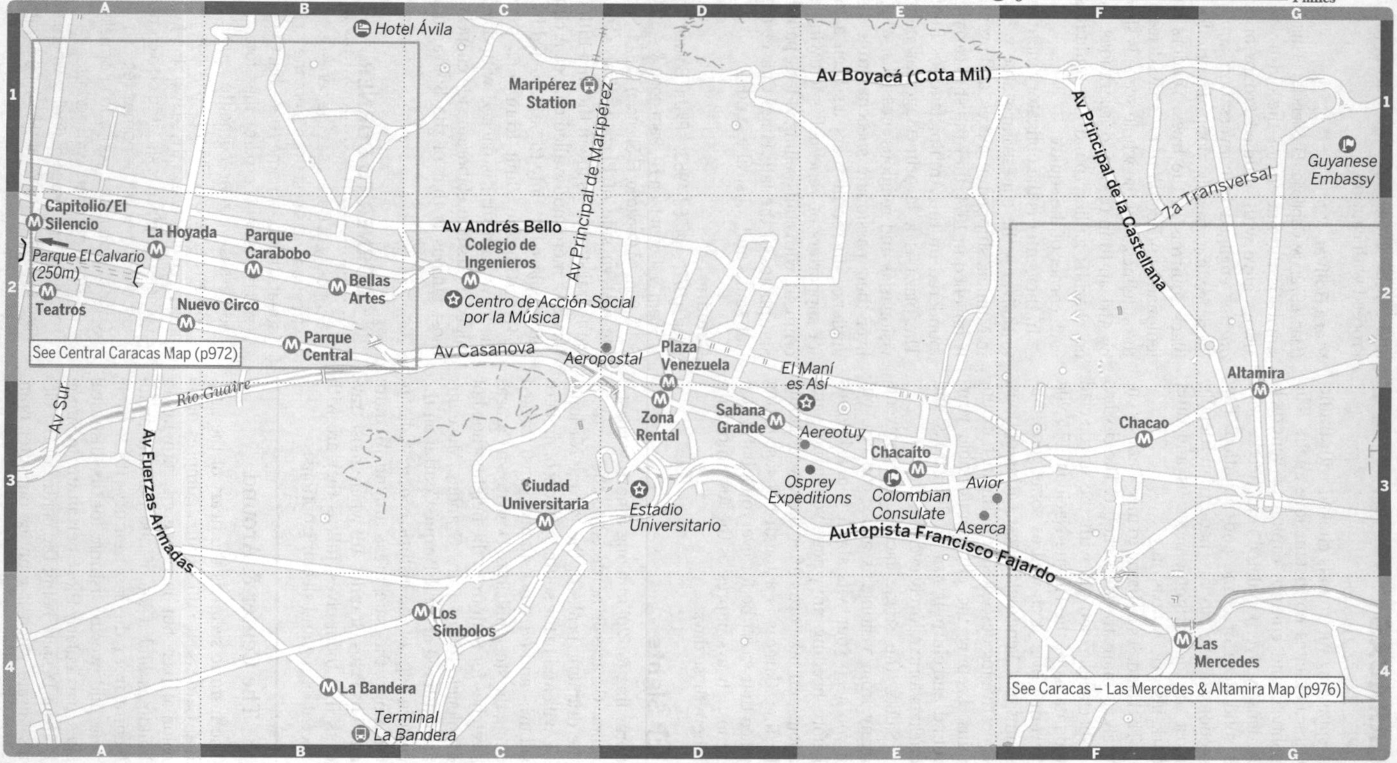

0 2 km
0 1 miles

Hotel Ávila
Maripérez Station
Av Boyacá (Cota Mil)
Av Principal de la Castellana
7a Transversal
Guyanese Embassy
Av Principal de Maripérez
Capitolio/El Silencio
La Hoyada
Parque Carabobo
Av Andrés Bello
Colegio de Ingenieros
Parque El Calvario (250m)
Bellas Artes
Teatros
Nuevo Circo
Centro de Acción Social por la Música
Parque Central
See Central Caracas Map (p972)
Av Casanova
Aeropostal
Plaza Venezuela
El Maní es Así
Altamira
Río Guaire
Av Sur
Zona Rental
Sabana Grande
Aereotuy
Chacao
Chacaíto
Av Fuerzas Armadas
Ciudad Universitaria
Estadio Universitario
Osprey Expeditions
Colombian Consulate
Avior
Aserca
Autopista Francisco Fajardo
Los Símbolos
Las Mercedes
La Bandera
Terminal La Bandera
See Caracas – Las Mercedes & Altamira Map (p976)

which can be easily recognized by a modern sculpture of The Liberator mourning his parents and bride.

Bolívar was baptized here, but the baptismal font now stands in the Casa Natal de Bolívar. Also take a look at the fine colonial altarpiece at the back of the chapel. The wide, five-nave interior, supported on 32 columns, was largely remodeled in the late 19th century.

Simón Bolívar Mausoleum MAUSOLEUM
(Map p972; Av Norte 1 near Av Oeste 13; ⏲9am-4pm Tue-Sun; Ⓜ La Hoyada) FREE After a 2010 exhumation to confirm cause of Bolívar's death, Chávez built his hero this grand new mausoleum, which opened in 2013. The US$140 million price tag and bold architecture – a gleaming white wave that mirrors the Ávila range or a gnarly 17-story skate ramp, depending on your opinion – set tongues wagging even before Chávez' death, with some cheeky pundits opining that he had plans to join Bolívar here in perpetuity.

To go inside, visitors must wear smart clothing, which in Venezuela means skirts for women, long pants and a shirt with a collar for men.

Casa Natal de Bolívar MUSEUM
(Bolívar's birthplace; Map p972; ☎541-2563; San Jacinto a Traposos; ⏲9am-4:30pm Mon-Fri, 10am-3pm Sat & Sun; Ⓜ La Hoyada) FREE Bolívar's funeral took place just two blocks from the house where, on July 24, 1783, he was born. The interior of Bolívar's birthplace has been enthusiastically reconstructed. The walls are splashed with a score of huge paintings by Tito Salas depicting Bolívar's heroic battles and scenes from his life. All *caraqueños* take cheesy photos – notebooks in hand – under the backyard tree beneath which Simon Rodriguez was said to have taught Bolívar to read and write.

Museo Sacro de Caracas MUSEUM
(Map p972; ☎861-6562; Plaza Bolívar; admission adult/student BsF30/20; ⏲9am-4pm Mon-Sat; Ⓜ Capitolio, El Silencio) Set in a meticulously restored colonial building that stands upon the site of the old cathedral cemetery, this museum displays a modest but carefully selected collection of religious art. Duck through the low doorway into the dark, old ecclesiastical prison, where remains of early church leaders still lie in sealed niches. The Museo Sacro also stages concerts and recitals. There is a delightful cafe at the back, inside a former chapel of the adjacent cathedral.

Asamblea Nacional HISTORIC BUILDING
(Capitolio Nacional; Map p972; ☎483-8240; off Plaza Bolívar; ⏲8am-noon Sat & Sun; Ⓜ Capitolio, El Silencio) FREE As part of his mad dash toward modernization in the 1870s, Guzmán Blanco commissioned an ambitious, neoclassical seat of congress, the National Assembly, to occupy the entire block just southwest of Plaza Bolívar. It was formerly known as the Capitolio Nacional. The two-building complex was erected on the site of a convent; its occupants were promptly expelled by the dictator and their convent razed. It's open to the public on the weekend.

Museo Bolivariano MUSEUM
(Map p972; ☎545-3396; San Jacinto a Traposos; ⏲9am-4:30pm Mon-Fri, 10am-4pm Sat & Sun; Ⓜ La Hoyada) FREE This museum has successfully preserved its colonial style and displays a variety of independence memorabilia, from muskets to medals and shaving sets to swords. It also has some fascinating documents and letters written by Bolívar himself, as well as numerous portraits. More on the morbid side are the coffin in which the remains of Bolívar were brought from Santa Marta in Colombia and the *arca cineraria* (funeral ark) that conveyed his ashes to the Panteón Nacional.

Parque Central & Around

Not a park at all, but a series of cement high-rises, the Parque Central area is Caracas' art and culture hub, boasting half-a-dozen museums, the major performing-arts center, two art cinemas and one of the best theaters in town. This is a dangerous area of the city, however, with muggings common even during daylight. Proceed with extreme caution, and consider using taxis to get around.

★Museo de Arte Contemporáneo de Caracas MUSEUM
(Map p972; ☎573-8289; www.fmn.gob.ve; Parque Central; ⏲9am-5pm Tue-Fri, 10am-5pm Sat & Sun; Ⓜ Parque Central or Belles Artes) FREE Occupying the eastern end of the Parque Central complex, the Museum of Contemporary Art is by far the best in the country, though it can be a little tricky to find amid the concrete jungle. In a dozen halls on five levels, you'll find works by many prominent Venezuelan artists, such as Jesús Soto, famous for his kinetic pieces, plus multiple paintings by international stars such as Picasso, Chagall, Mondrian and Léger.

Galería de Arte Nacional MUSEUM

(Map p972; ☎578-8707; www.fmn.gob.ve; Av México s/n; ⊙9am-5pm Mon-Fri, 10am-5pm Sat & Sun; Ⓜ Bellas Artes) FREE Venezuela's largest museum began construction in 1989 but was abandoned in the mid-'90s. Architect Carlos Gómez persevered though and construction resumed in 2006, with the gallery finally opened to the public in 2009. Its galleries house a selection of the 7000-piece collection that embraces five centuries of Venezuelan artistic expression. Venezuela's most important artists are well represented, including in the museum's most important work, Arturo Michelena's portrayal of Francisco Miranda, *Miranda en La Carraca* (1896).

Museo de Bellas Artes MUSEUM

(Map p972; ☎578-0275; www.fmn.gob.ve; Parque Central; ⊙9am-4pm Mon-Fri, 10am-5pm Sat & Sun; Ⓜ Bellas Artes) FREE The Museum of Fine Arts is a beautiful museum with lots of breathing room housed in two buildings: a functional modern six-story building and a graceful building radiating from a neoclassical-style courtyard with a pond and weeping willow – both were designed by Venezuelan architect Carlos Raúl Villanueva. The museum features permanent exhibitions from Egypt and China, and on Cubism, as well as mostly temporary exhibitions in 18 galleries. It includes a little shop selling contemporary art and crafts.

Sabana Grande & Around

Sabana Grande, 2km east of Parque Central, is an energetic district packed with love motels, restaurants and shops. Locals come en masse to stroll along its teeming market street, **Blvd de Sabana Grande**, which stretches between Plaza Venezuela and Plaza Chacaíto. It used to be the closest Caracas got to a backpacker neighborhood, but security has deteriorated in recent years and we currently suggest avoiding walking here entirely. If you plan to visit somewhere here, do so by taxi, day or night.

Altamira & Los Palos Grandes

East of Sabana Grande lie some of Caracas' more fashionable areas, especially in **La Castellana**, **Las Mercedes**, **Los Palos Grandes** and **Altamira**. These areas have no sights as such, but plenty of eating, drinking and sleeping options. More importantly, they are by far the safest neighborhoods in Caracas, and some of the few where it's alright to wander the streets after dark, as long as you're careful and stick to the busier streets. Be aware that as you travel further east, you quickly descend the social ladder, eventually reaching some of the city's most downtrodden *barrios*.

El Hatillo

El Hatillo was once its own village, but has now been absorbed into Caracas. It's a popular getaway for folks who live in the more congested urban core, with narrow central streets and plazas stacked with brightly painted colonial buildings that house restaurants, art galleries and craft shops. Located 15km southeast of the city center, this area overflows with people on the weekend. There's always a tranquil atmosphere in the afternoon and early evening, when diners and cafe-goers can sit back and relax to the sounds of crickets and *sapitos*. Take a taxi here.

Tours

Leo Lameda Tours WALKING TOUR

(☎0412-998-1998; leo.lameda@gmail.com; full-day tour US$60) For a less conventional view of Caracas, these walking tours hit some of the city's less-visited pockets, such as the central university and cemetery, while offering plenty of illuminating historical insights along the way.

Zam Hernandez GUIDE

(☎0414-201-7077; zamhernandez@gmail.com; full-day city tour from US$45) Zam is a tourism professional and speaks superb English. He leads folks through the city and provides tours with humor, plus superb knowledge of Caracas and its historical sites.

Sociedad Conservacionista Audubón de Venezuela BIRD-WATCHING

(SCAV; Map p976; ☎272-8708; www.audubonvenezuela.org) The conservationist society organizes expert-led bird-watching tours as well as guided walks in and around Caracas, Parque Nacional Henri Pittier and other national parks.

Festivals & Events

The biggest celebrations are Christmas, Carnaval and Easter. All offices close, as do most shops, and transportation is very busy.

CARACAS SAFETY GUIDE

Caracas is a poor and often dangerous city with a terrible reputation for muggings, kidnappings and holdups. It's never a good idea to venture to parts of the city you don't know are relatively safe; *barrios* (shantytowns) are completely out of bounds at any time of day, and many areas of the city that aren't *barrios* are nevertheless dangerous to walk about even in daylight. Outside the relatively safe oasis between Altamira and Los Palos Grandes, it's never a good idea to get your phone or camera out in public, to wear expensive jewellery or watches, or backpacks and shorts (two things that will instantly mark you as a wealthy tourist). Take taxis after nightfall.

Despite the city's terrible reputation, its excellent metro system is generally safe, though you should always be on the look out for pickpockets and avoid using the system at night. Do not assume that an area is safe just because public transport goes there: new cable cars to the *barrios* are definitely not there for travelers to satisfy their curiosity, and city buses are frequently held up by gunman, so avoid these.

A further worry is so-called 'express kidnapping', where individuals are abducted by gunmen on the street, put into a car and their relatives contacted for a ransom. The ransoms are not generally very big, and the ordeal is normally over quickly, but it's an extremely frightening and unpleasant scenario, so avoid walking alone at night, especially on empty streets.

Semana Santa (Holy Week, culminating in Easter) is also a major celebration, with festivities focused in Chacao. Traditional outlying areas celebrate holy days with more vigor than the central districts. El Hatillo boasts local feasts on several occasions during the year (including May 3, July 16 and September 4).

Sleeping

For years Caracas has had the reputation of being one of the least backpacker-friendly destinations in South America, specifically as almost no safe budget option existed. However, the instant wealth now offered to anyone changing dollars on the black market, means that suddenly three- and even four-star hotels are often affordable. It's worth staying in a midrange place in a safer neighborhood such as Altamira or Los Palos Grandes so you can walk around at night and breathe easier. Reserving ahead is always a good idea, as Caracas is not the sort of place you want to wander about looking for a cheap room.

Central Caracas

Central Caracas is bustling during the day, but the area mostly shuts down and empties by 6pm, and it's dangerous at night. One of the city's few backpacker-oriented lodgings is here, but due to Venezuela's current peculiar economic situation, it's no less expensive than many smarter hotels in the far safer east of the city.

Dal Bo Hostal HOSTEL **$**
(Map p972; ☎0424-215-0799; dalbohostel@gmail.com; Pajaritos a San Francisco; dm/d incl breakfast US$13/40; wi-fi; Ⓜ Capitolio, El Silencio) A modest and windowless apartment near the Plaza Bolívar, this improvised hostel has two dorms with bunks (a two-bed and six-bed), a gleaming shared bathroom and a small kitchen. English-speaking Gustavo equips all guests with cell phones, there's a huge movie collection and welcome beers on the house. Reserve ahead. Airport pickups cost US$4 per car.

Hotel Ávila HOTEL **$$$**
(☎555-3000; www.hotel-avila.com.ve; Av Jorge Washington s/n, San Bernadino; s/d incl breakfast US$23/26; wi-fi) Opened by Norman Rockefeller as a venue for Caracas' jet set to stay in the 1940s, this old-world hotel high above the city in hilly San Bernadino may have seen better days, but remains secure, friendly and full of character. Rooms all have a safe and TV, while the public areas include an oval pool and beautifully maintained gardens.

You'll need to take a taxi to get downtown, but these are cheap and plentiful and wait right outside the hotel.

Central Caracas

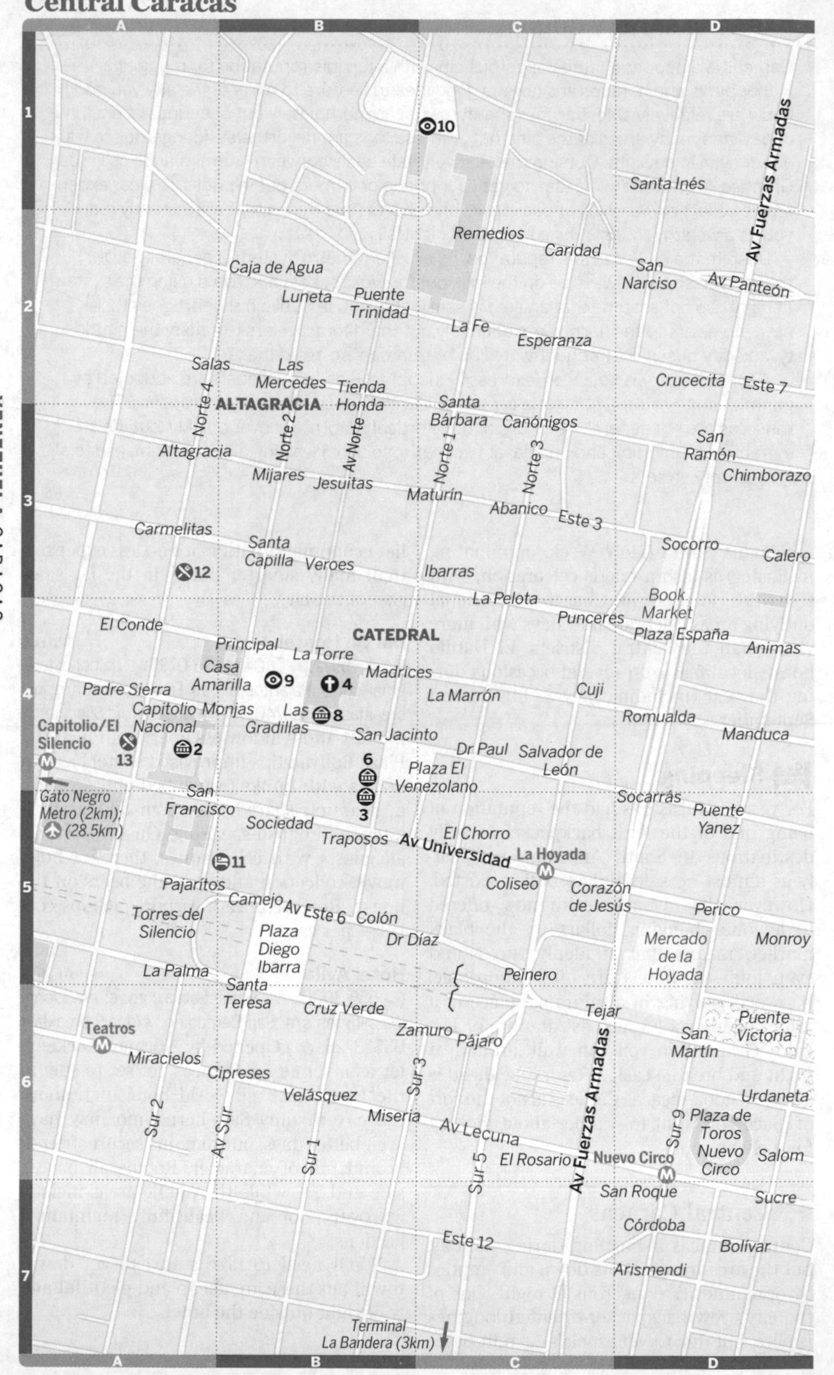

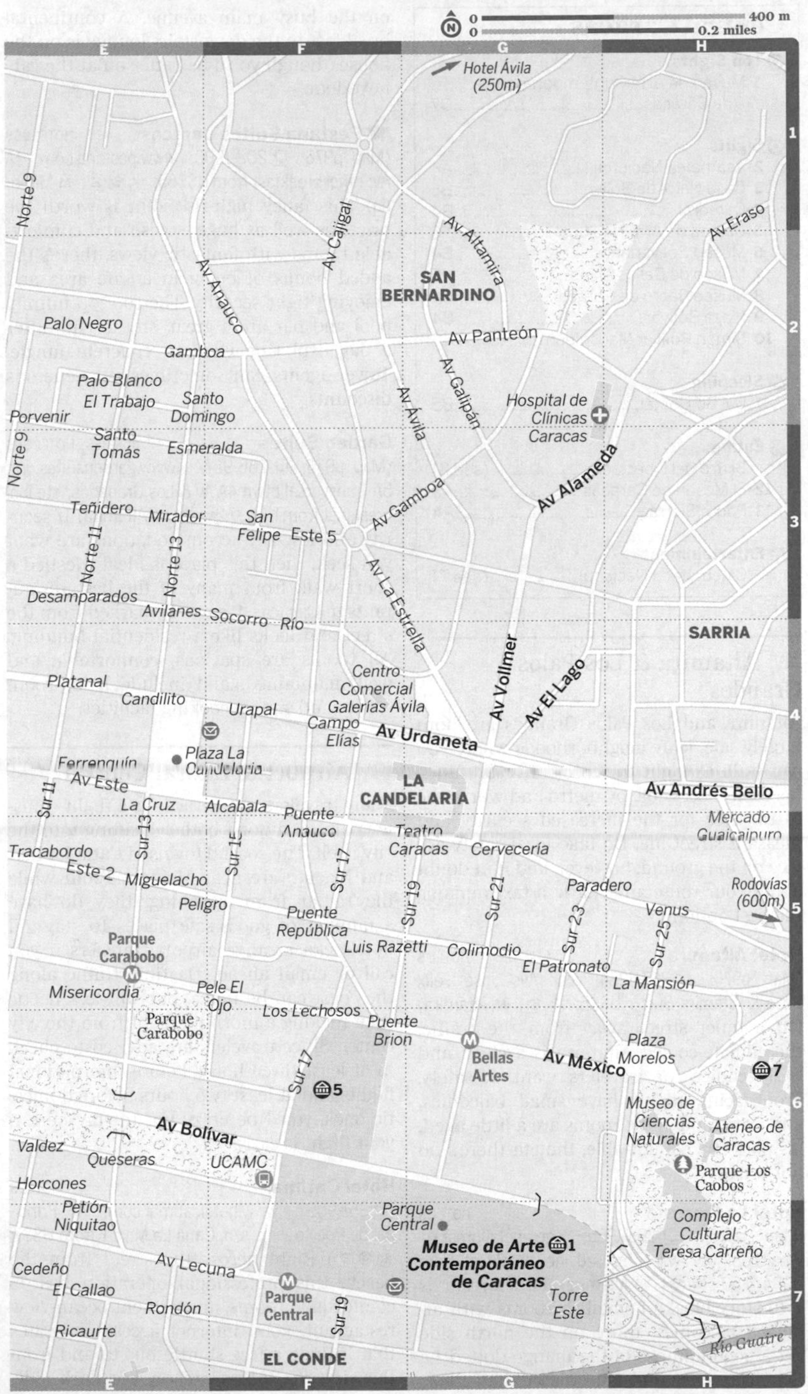
0 400 m
0 0.2 miles
Hotel Ávila (250m)
SAN BERNARDINO
SARRIA
LA CANDELARIA
EL CONDE
Av Cajigal
Av Anauco
Av Altamira
Av Eraso
Av Panteón
Av Galipán
Av Ávila
Av Gamboa
Av La Estrella
Av Alameda
Av Vollmer
Av El Lago
Av Urdaneta
Av Andrés Bello
Av Este 2
Av México
Av Bolívar
Av Lecuna
Norte 9
Norte 11
Norte 13
Sur 11
Sur 13
Sur 15
Sur 17
Sur 19
Sur 21
Sur 23
Sur 25
Este 5
Este 2
Palo Negro
Gamboa
Palo Blanco
El Trabajo
Santo Domingo
Porvenir
Santo Tomás
Esmeralda
Teñidero
Mirador
San Felipe
Desamparados
Avilanes
Socorro
Río
Platanal
Candilito
Urapal
Centro Comercial Galerías Ávila
Campo Elías
Plaza La Candelaria
Ferrenquín
La Cruz
Alcabala
Puente Anauco
Teatro Caracas
Cervecería
Tracabordo
Miguelacho
Peligro
Puente República
Luis Razetti
Colimodio
Paradero
Venus
Rodovías (600m)
El Patronato
La Mansión
Mercado Guaicaipuro
Hospital de Clínicas Caracas
Parque Carabobo
Misericordia
Pele El Ojo
Los Lechosos
Puente Brion
Bellas Artes
Plaza Morelos
Museo de Ciencias Naturales
Ateneo de Caracas
Parque Los Caobos
Complejo Cultural Teresa Carreño
5
7
Valdez
Queseras
UCAMC
Horcones
Petión
Niquitao
Parque Central
Museo de Arte Contemporáneo de Caracas
1
Torre Este
Cedeño
El Callao
Rondón
Ricaurte
Río Guaire
E
F
G
H
1
2
3
4
5
6
7

Central Caracas

Altamira & Los Palos Grandes

Altamira and Los Palos Grandes are both largely safe, leafy neighborhoods where you can walk at night to scores of restaurants. It's easily accessible by metro and worth the extra price for the increased security and pleasant street life. Do take local safety advice on the ground, however, and if in doubt about your route after dark, a taxi remains the best option.

Hotel Altamira HOTEL $
(Map p976; 267-4284; cnr Avs José Félix Sosa & Altamira Sur; r US$5; ; M Altamira) On a quiet street away from the traffic, the climate-cooled Altamira is a clean and basic choice for travelers wanting safety. Front-facing rooms have small balconies, and even though the rooms are a little aged, it's perfectly comfortable, though there's no hot water.

Hotel La Floresta HOTEL $
(Map p976; 263-1955; gerenciafloresta@gmail.com; Av Ávila s/n; s/d incl breakfast from US$4/4.50; ; M Altamira) La Floresta is a 10-story block of smallish rooms with attached balconies; those on the north side get a good glimpse of the mango-dotted La Estancia estate and are quieter than those on the busy main avenue. A continental breakfast in the downstairs lounge is on the house, though you'd be better off at the cafe next door.

★ **Pestana Suites Caracas** HOTEL $$$
(Map p976; 208-1900; www.pestana.com; 1A Av; r incl breakfast from US$65; ; M Miranda) This fancy high-rise joint is worth the price: as well as huge, stylish and comfortable rooms with fantastic views, there's the added bonus of being in a safe area and enjoying tight security. The rooftop infinity pool and bar are a great way to chill after a day exploring Caracas' concrete jungle. Travel agents can sometimes get generous discounts.

Garden Suites BUSINESS HOTEL $$$
(Map p976; 266-9844; www.gardensuites.org; 5A Transversal btwn 4A Av & Los Granados; ste incl breakfast from US$37; ; M Altamira) If security and low-key accommodations are what you seek, then this place is ideal. Nestled a short walk from many of the best restaurants in Caracas, it's barely marked from the street and looks like a residential building. All rooms are spacious, comfortable and well maintained, and include living-room spaces and simple cooking facilities.

Airport & Litoral Central

Many travelers use Caracas as a flight transfer point and don't bother heading into the city itself. The coastal towns of Catia La Mar and Macuto are near Maiquetía and while they're far from charming, they do have a number of good, safe places to stay. All hotels can arrange airport transfers if you call or email ahead. Daytime traffic along the coast can be fierce, but still less hectic than making a morning flight from the city center. Since travelers are advised to check in at least three hours before international flights and at least two hours before domestic ones, you'd be crazy not to stay here if your flight is early.

Hotel Catimar HOTEL $
(351-9097; www.hotelcatimar.com; Av Principal de Puerto Viejo s/n, Catia La Mar; r from US$7;) Right across the street from the beach, this professional operation has 75 comfortable rooms, an excellent ocean-view restaurant, good internet access and rates that include a free shuttle bus to and from the airport. Rooms are on the dark side,

but are clean and feature towels made into swans.

Hostal Tanausu HOTEL $
(☎352-1704; hoteltanausu1@yahoo.es; Av Atlántida s/n, Catia La Mar; r from US$7; ❄📶) This busy motel-style option on a busy junction has kitschy exterior decor – check out the whimsical patchwork tiling in the hallways – but firm new beds. Some of the windowless rooms off the upstairs corridor are worth avoiding, but there's a *tasca* (Spanish-style bar-restaurant) sprouting tree columns that serves all meals.

Hotel Playa Grande Caribe HOTEL $$
(☎350-2500; www.hotelplayagrandecaribe.com; Av Principal de Puerto Viejo s/n, Catia La Mar; r from US$15; ❄📶🏊) As its name suggests, this hotel is right on the Caribbean, while also being a 10-minute drive from the airport. Its public areas have definitely seen better days, but its rooms are enormous suite-like creations, all in white with crisp linens and sea views.

Eating

Downtown Caracas is packed with cheap restaurants, and sidewalk vendors who sell *cachapas* (small corn pancakes) and *arepas,* which are handy if you're sightseeing. Come evening, Altamira and Los Palos Grandes are the best places to eat, both for reasons of local safety and good quality.

Central Caracas

Padre Sierra VENEZUELAN $
(Map p972; Esq Padre Sierra; mains US$1-3; ⏰8am-10pm; Ⓜ Capitolio/El Silencio) Usefully located in front of the Asamblea Nacional building, this somewhat somber lunch option is nevertheless popular with a boisterous crowd of locals who come here for the large servings of good-value Venezuelan dishes, as well as pizzas.

El Méson de Caracas VENEZUELAN $
(Map p972; El Conde a Carmelitas; mains US$1-5; ⏰noon-11pm Mon-Sat; Ⓜ Capitolio/El Silencio) A dash of formality marks this all-but-hidden place as an oasis of old-world calm amid the chaos of downtown. Tuxedo-sporting waiters and a classic rectangular wooden bar add to the sense of the surviving spirit of old Caracas. Seafood, fish and *ceviche* (marinated raw seafood) are the house specialties, but there's also a fast-food menu and plenty of meat on offer.

Bistro del Libertador CAFE $
(Map p972; Esq Las Gradillas; mains US$1-2; ⏰8am-8pm; 📶; Ⓜ Capitolio/El Silencio) Sparkling air-conditioned premises with a chessboard floor and lots of light set this new cafe apart from the crowd. Given its central location around many of the city's main sights, it's a good place for a light lunch or afternoon coffee and cake. The menu includes sandwiches and salads.

Altamira & Los Palos Grandes

Arábica Coffee Bar CAFE $
(Map p976; ☎286-3636; Av Andrés Bello s/n, Los Palos Grandes; mains US$1-3; ⏰7am-11pm Mon-Wed, to midnight Thu-Sun; 📶; Ⓜ Altamira) 🌿 The incredible range of house-roasted beans at this friendly and immensely popular cafe is discernible up and down the block. The Moorish-accented interior and shady terrace are a delightful place to sample made-to-order empanadas, excellent pastries or a full meal. Products served here are all sourced locally and the coffee is perhaps the best in the city.

Delicatesses Rey David DELI $
(Map p976; Transversal 4, Los Palos Grandes; mains US$2-6; ⏰7am-11pm; 📶; Ⓜ Altamira) This deli has an amazing array of products, luxury goods, chocolates and much more on sale to anyone who can afford the prices, which are high by local standards. There's also a busy restaurant on site where you can have anything from smoked salmon and eggs in a croissant for breakfast, to kosher hot dogs.

★**Come a Casa** ITALIAN $
(Map p976; Av 1 & Transversal 1; mains US$2-4; ⏰noon-2.30pm Tue, noon-7pm Wed & Thu, noon-10pm Fri & Sat, 1.30-4.30pm Sun; 📶; Ⓜ Altamira) An instantly likable Sicilian restaurant in the heart of Los Palos Grandes, Come a Casa serves up daily specials, stellar salads, interesting appetizers and a full pasta and risotto list. There's even excellent Venezuelan craft beer on sale, which should seal the deal for anyone sick of Polar Light.

★**La Casa Bistro** INTERNATIONAL $
(Map p976; Av 3 & Transversal 4, Los Palos Grandes; mains US$2-5; ⏰8am-5pm; 📶; Ⓜ Altamira) Few places stand out in rundown Caracas as much as this gleaming temple of sophistication, where you may have to wait for a table at breakfast or lunch due to its fearsome neighborhood popularity. The

Caracas – Las Mercedes & Altamira

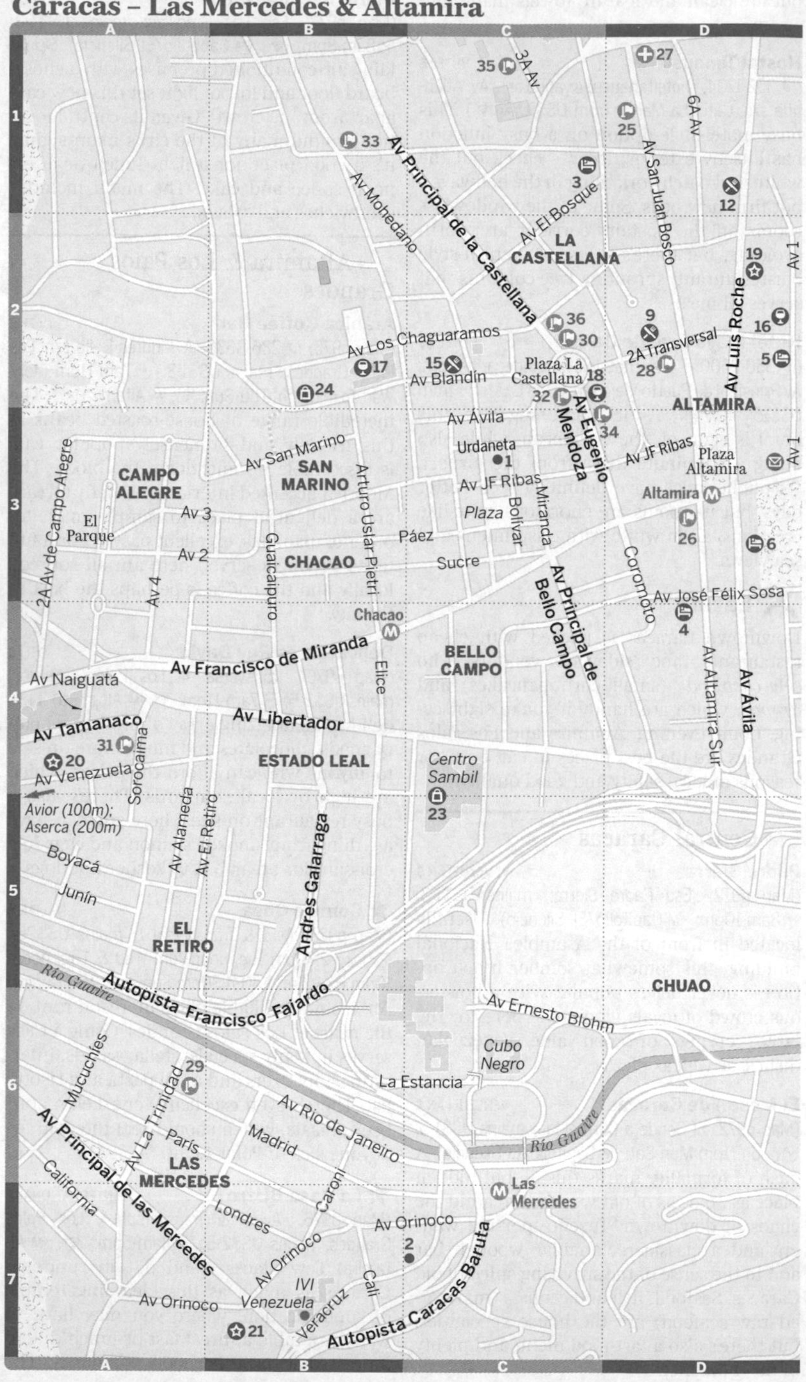

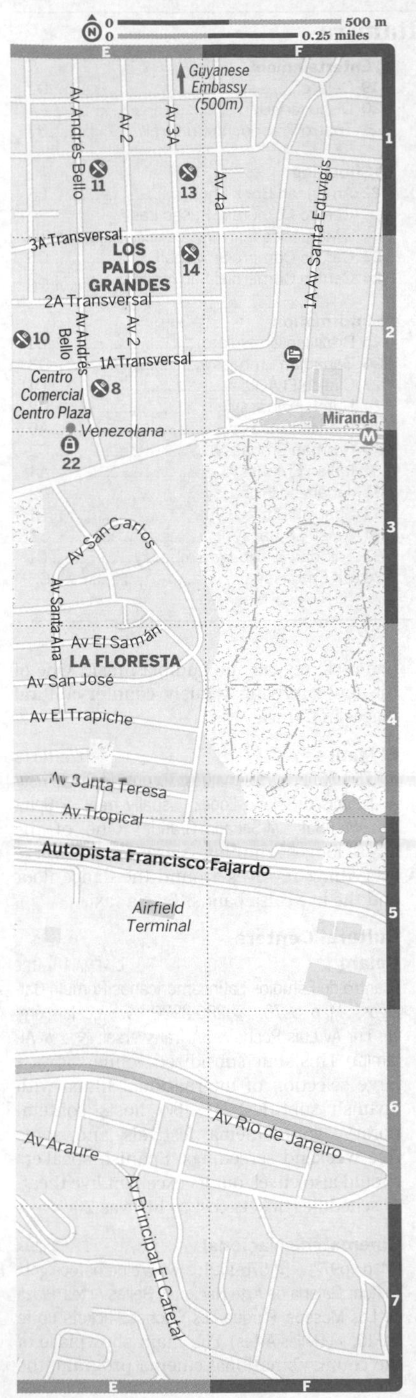

international menu includes excellent salads, big burgers, grilled meats and a delicious pastrami sandwich, while the service is friendly, professional and fast.

El Barquero SEAFOOD **$$**
(Map p976; 261-4645; Av Luis Roche s/n; US$3-8; Altamira) Well known for its excellent seafood, this old-world Caracas restaurant is actually best used for its animated bar, which attracts a louche and fascinating crowd of characters that would look at home in a David Lynch movie.

Café Il Botticello ITALIAN **$**
(Map p976; 266-1618; 2A Transversal s/n; meals US$1-2; noon-3pm & 6-10pm Mon-Sat; ; Altamira) Look for the dusty, off-yellow tasseled awning between Farmarebajas and Pirelli, and then ring the bell to enter this tiny dining room serving pastas and excellent pizzas. It's otherwise unmarked, but is a real local find.

Pollo en Brasas El Coyuco FAST FOOD **$**
(Map p976; 285-9354; cnr Av 3 & 3A Transversal, Los Palos Grandes; half-/full-roast chicken US$1-3; noon-3pm & 6-10pm; Altamira) This classic *pollería* in a popular restaurant corridor is often packed with locals chowing down on lusciously seasoned roasted chicken and yucca within a rustic, log-cabin setting.

Restaurant Gran Horizonte VENEZUELAN **$**
(Map p976; Av Blandín s/n; arepas & cachapas US$1-2, mains US$2-3; 24hr; Chacao) Tuck into your favorite *arepa* (stuffed corn pancake) combo, a perfect sweet-corn *cachapa* or a filling plateful of BBQ meats at this cow-themed all-hours *arepera* (snack bar) near the Centro Comercial San Ignacio.

Drinking & Nightlife

Nightlife in Caracas has suffered enormously in recent years, with its once carefree decadence replaced by mundane concerns about street safety. Even locals often prefer to start early and make it home before midnight, so this has been reflected in the range of options available.

360° Roof Bar BAR
(Map p976; 284-1874; 1A Av btwn 1A & 2A Transversal, Hotel Altamira Suites, Los Palos Grandes; 5pm-late; Altamira) This incredible open-air lounge atop the Altamira Suites attracts member of Caracas' glitzy crowd, who come to chill out on hammocks and sofas in the 19th-floor restaurant and sip cocktails over

Caracas – Las Mercedes & Altamira

Activities, Courses & Tours
1 Akanan Travel & Adventure C3
2 Sociedad Conservacionista Audubón de Venezuela C7

Sleeping
3 Garden Suites C1
4 Hotel Altamira D4
5 Hotel Altamira Suites D2
6 Hotel La Floresta D3
7 Pestana Suites Caracas F2

Eating
8 Arábica Coffee Bar E2
9 Café Il Botticello D2
10 Come a Casa E2
11 Delicatesses Rey David E1
12 El Barquero D1
13 La Casa Bistro E1
14 Pollo en Brasas El Coyuco E2
15 Restaurant Gran Horizonte C2

Drinking & Nightlife
16 360° Roof Bar D2
17 Centro Comercial San Ignacio B2
18 El León C2

Entertainment
19 Celarg D2
20 Discovery Bar A4
21 Teatro Trasnocho Cultural B7

Shopping
22 American Book Shop E3
Centro Comercial Paseo Las Mercedes .... (see 21)
23 Centro Comercial Sambil C5
24 Centro Comercial San Ignacio B2

Information
25 Brazilian Consulate D1
26 Canadian Embassy D3
27 Clínica El Ávila D1
28 Dutch Embassy D2
29 French Embassy A6
30 German Embassy C2
31 Italian Embassy A4
32 Japanese Embassy C2
33 Spanish Embassy B1
34 Swiss Embassy C3
35 Trinidad & Tobago Embassy C1
36 UK Embassy C2

startling panoramic views of the city. Access is through the hotel's rear entrance on 1A Av – you'll be subjected to a coolness size-up. Go on a clear night.

El León BEER HALL, PIZZERIA
(Map p976; 263-6014; Plaza La Castellana, La Castellana; M Altamira) Sit on a lofty concrete terrace and knock back cheap beers and pizza in this well-known Caracas spot.

Centro Comercial San Ignacio BAR
(Map p976; www.centrosanignacio.com; cnr Blandín & Arturo Uslar Pietri; M Altamira) With more than a dozen nightclubs and bars, this mall comes alive at night. Dress to impress.

Entertainment

The arts and entertainment section of the daily newspaper *El Universal* (www.eluniversal.com/arte-y-entretenimiento) gives descriptions of selected upcoming events.

Live Music

★Discovery Bar LIVE MUSIC
(Map p976; www.discoverybar.com.ve; Av Tamanaco s/n, Planta Baja; cover charge free-US$1.50; 9pm-late Tue-Sat; M Chacaito) A down-to-earth, genuine alt-rock dive, catering to an alternative crowd who come for the alternative rock, reggae and cumbia music. One of the few surviving vaguely counter-cultural places in Caracas.

El Maní es Así LIVE MUSIC
(763-6671; www.elmaniesasi.com; El Cristo near Av Francisco Solano López; usually free; 9pm-late Wed-Sat; M Sabana Grande) One of the city's longest-running salsa spots, where everything revolves around the dance floor and the live salsa bands. Take a taxi.

Cultural Centers

Celarg CINEMA, THEATRE
(Centro de Estudios Latinoamericanos Rómulo Gallegos; Map p976; 285-2990; www.celarg.org.ve; cnr Av Luis Roche & 3A Transversal; ; M Altamira) This state-subsidized venue shows a large selection of international films (with Spanish subtitles). It also hosts contemporary world-cinema festivals and some free weekend screenings. Spanish speakers should also check out its excellent live theater schedule (tickets cost as little as 20c).

Cinemateca Nacional CINEMA
(Map p972; 576-1491; www.cinemateca.gob.ve/fcn; Galería de Arte Nacional, Bellas Artes, Plaza de Los Museos, Parque Los Caobos; tickets up to BsF10; M Bellas Artes) The main showplace of the country's national cinema program, the

Cinemateca Nacional screens a wide range of domestic and international films (subtitled in Spanish).

Centro de Acción Social por la Música CLASSICAL MUSIC
(Center for Social Action Through Music; ☎597-0511; www.fundamusical.org.ve; Blvd Amador Bendayán s/n, Quebrada Honda; Ⓜ Colegio de Ingenieros) FREE Hear top-notch classical recitals for free at the Sala Simón Bolívar, one of the venues for El Sistema, Venezuela's world-renowned youth orchestra program.

Teatro Trasnocho Cultural ARTS CENTER
(Map p976; ☎0212-993-1910; www.trasnochocultural.com; Av Principal de Las Mercedes s/n, Las Mercedes, Centro Comercial Paseo Las Mercedes; Ⓜ Las Mercedes) This buzzing contemporary-arts center buried in a mall sub-basement contains a theater, cinema, cafes, a yoga studio and a gay-friendly hipster bar.

Sports

Estadio Universitario BASEBALL
(University Stadium; ☎0500-226-7366; tickets US$0.20-0.75; ⓂCiudad Universitaria) *Béisbol* (baseball) is the local sporting obsession. Professional-league games are played from October to February at this 18,500-seat stadium, home to the Leones de Caracas (Caracas Lions). Tickets can be purchased until game time, usually 7:30pm Tuesday to Friday nights, 6pm Saturday and 4:30pm Sunday.

Shopping

Shopping is one of the city's greatest pastimes and malls are an important part of middle-class *caraqueño* life.

Centro Comercial Sambil MALL
(Map p976; ☎263-9323; www.sambilmall.com; Av Libertador s/n; ⏲10am-9pm Mon-Sat, noon-8pm Sun; ⓂChacao) Touted as South America's largest shopping mall, there's an enormous range of shopping on offer here.

Centro Comercial Paseo Las Mercedes MALL
(Map p976; Av Principal de las Mercedes s/n; Ⓜ Las Mercedes) An upscale shopping destination with restaurants, a movie theater and an excellent cultural center.

Centro Comercial San Ignacio MALL
(Map p976; www.centrosanignacio.com; Av Blandín s/n, La Castellana; Ⓜ Altamira) This shopping mall is also one of the city's best centers for nightlife.

American Book Shop BOOKS
(Map p976; ☎285-8779; Centro Comercial Centro Plaza, Jardín level, Los Palos Grandes; Ⓜ Altamira) A decent selection of English titles and used books.

Information

DANGERS & ANNOYANCES

Caracas has a justifiably bad reputation for petty crime, robbery and armed assaults. Sabana Grande and the city center are the riskiest neighborhoods, although they are generally safe during the day (watch for pickpockets in dense crowds). Altamira and Las Mercedes are considerably safer. Travelers should always stick to well-lit main streets or use taxis after dark. Be alert about your surroundings, but don't succumb to paranoia.

Perhaps more than street crime, traffic in Caracas is the greatest danger, particularly for pedestrians. Cars, but especially motorcycles, routinely ignore traffic signals and often speed up to show dominance over life forms with legs. Never assume you have right of way in any crossing, and try to cross with others.

The Caracas airport, especially the international arrivals area, is awash with official-looking touts trying to arrange your transportation or change your cash. In the past, travelers using unofficial airport transportation have been robbed or 'express kidnapped,' where they are held and forced to withdraw money from ATMs. If you haven't arranged an airport pickup, only use the official airport taxis (black Ford Explorers with yellow shields on the doors), or the airport buses. Black-market money changers at the airport (and other locations) may rip you off if you aren't aware of the current exchange rate or appearance of the currency.

Always carry your passport, or a copy of it that includes the entrance stamp, as police have been known to harass foreigners not carrying documents.

EMERGENCY

Call ☎171 for the police, fire department and ambulance. If your Spanish is not up to scratch, try to get a local to call on your behalf. Operators rarely speak English.

INTERNET ACCESS

Internet cafes can be found in some parts of Caracas, though wi-fi is ubiquitous in hotels and restaurants. Maiquetía's airport terminals have free wi-fi (post-security), though don't expect it to be reliable. It's easy to buy a SIM card with internet data; simply bring your passport to an outlet of one of the major cell-phone operators.

MEDICAL SERVICES

Most minor health problems can be solved in a *farmacia* (pharmacy). There's always at least one open in every neighborhood and you can easily recognize them by the neon sign that says 'Turno.' Some dependable *farmacia* chains found throughout the city include Farmatodo and FarmAhorro.

Clínica El Ávila (Map p976; ☎276-1111; www.clinicaelavila.com; cnr Av San Juan Bosco & 6A Transversal, Altamira; Ⓜ Altamira) This is one of the best located and reputable medical facilities in Caracas. In the Altamira district, it offers inpatient and outpatient services and has some English-speaking doctors.

Hospital de Clínicas Caracas (Map p972; ☎508-6111; www.clinicaracas.com; cnr Avs Panteón & Alameda, San Bernardino) Reputable medical facilities.

MONEY

International banks and ATMs blanket the city and the airport terminals, but you should not use them save in an emergency, as the exchange rate means you'll get nothing for the money you withdraw. Arrange to change money on the black market via a travel agency or hotel.

POST

FedEx (☎205-3333; www.fedex.com/ve) International courier company operating in Caracas.

Ipostel (Map p976; Av Francisco de Miranda s/n, Altamira; ⏲8am-noon & 1-4:30pm Mon-Fri) Also branches at La Candelaria (Map p972; www.ipostel.gob.ve; Plaza La Candelaria) and Parque Central (Map p972; Av Lecuna, Edif Mohedano).

TOURIST INFORMATION

Inatur (☎355-2104, 355-1442; www.inatur.gob.ve; Maiquetía Airport International Terminal; ⏲6am-10pm) Has free city and country maps, and can arrange lodging. Sometimes has English or French speakers. Has another office in the domestic terminal (⏲7am-8pm).

TRAVEL AGENCIES

Akanan Travel & Adventure (Map p976; ☎0212-264-2769; www.akanan.com; Bolívar, Edif Grano de Oro, ground fl; Ⓜ Chacao) This major operator in Caracas doesn't have the most budget prices, but has reliable quality trips, including treks to Auyantepui and Roraima, and bicycle trips from La Paragua to Canaima.

Global Exchange (www.globalexchange.org/tours) A US-based social justice organization, its 'reality tours' meet with community activists and cultural workers.

GETTING TO & FROM CARACAS

Caracas' main airport is at Maiquetía, 26km northwest of the city center. It's linked to the city by a freeway that cuts through the coastal mountain range with a variety of tunnels and bridges. The journey takes approximately 45 minutes without traffic, but can take up to two hours if you're unlucky. Almost all hotels and travel outfitters can arrange for transfers from the airport, which is recommended if you've just arrived in Venezuela. The airport is fine during daytime, but do not hang around outside the terminals at night.

Bus

Comfortable and safe government-run airport buses (US$0.50) run every half-hour, departing from the domestic terminal to the Hotel Alba Caracas (next to Parque Central) from 7am to 10:30pm and from outside the hotel to the airport from 5.30am to 7pm. At the airport, buy tickets inside at either the international or domestic terminals. In town, purchase tickets from the office inside the hotel's shopping arcade.

UCAMC (Map p972; ☎0212-576-9851; Sur 17, btwn Mexico & Av Lecuna; US$0.20) airport–city buses depart from the domestic terminal approximately every half-hour between 7am and 10:30pm. In the city, buses depart between 5am and 5pm from beside Parque Central (at Sur 17, directly underneath Av Bolívar). With traffic, the fastest option from the airport is to take this bus to the Gato Negro metro station and hop on the metro, though this is not recommended after dark. Other city drop-off points include Plaza Miranda and Parque Central (the final stop). The Parque Central location is under a busy overpass, and rather noisy and dark.

Taxi

In both terminals, official airport-taxi kiosks print out tickets listing the posted price of your destination (US$4 to US$7 to central Caracas, depending on area and time of day; cash only); pay the driver upon arrival. Do not travel with unofficial taxis or allow a tout to find you a cab in the arrivals area: robberies and kidnappings are common.

IVI Venezuela (Map p976; ☎992-3739; www.ivivenezuela.com; Av Principal de las Mercedes s/n, Residencia La Hacienda; ⏰8am-6pm Mon-Fri) Airfares for students, teachers and people under 26 years of age; issues ISIC, ITIC cards and Hostelling International cards.

Osprey Expeditions (☎0414-310-4491; www.ospreyexpeditions.com; Av Casanova near 2A Av de Bello Monte, Edificio La Paz, office 51, Sabana Grande, Caracas; Ⓜ Sabana Grande) This excellent Venezuelan-owned agency specializes in helping independent budget travelers negotiate the country. It offers invaluable services such as domestic flight bookings, transfers, tours and activities across Venezuela. English is spoken.

Getting There & Away

AIR

The **Aeropuerto Internacional Simón Bolívar** (www.aeropuerto-maiquetia.com.ve;) is in Maiquetía, near the port of La Guaira on the Caribbean coast, 26km from central Caracas. It's generally referred to as 'Maiquetía.' There are three terminals: the **international terminal** (☎303-1526), the **domestic terminal** (☎303-1408) and a small auxiliary terminal used by some smaller charter airlines. The two main terminals are separated by an easy walk of 400m, and it's about the same distance to the auxiliary terminal. There's no shuttle service between them.

The terminals have most conveniences, including tourist offices, car-rental desks, *casas de cambio* (authorized foreign currency-exchange houses), banks, ATMs, post and telephone offices, restaurants and a bunch of travel agencies, but no left-luggage office.

Arrive at least three hours before international flights, as security screenings can be lengthy.

BUS

Caracas has two modern intercity bus terminals and a central terminal for shorter regional journeys. The **Terminal La Bandera** (Av Nueva Granada; Ⓜ La Bandera), 3km south of the center, handles long-distance buses to anywhere in the country's west and southwest. It has good facilities, including computerized ticket booths, telephones, a left-luggage office, an information desk and lots of food outlets. The terminal is 300m from La Bandera metro station, but day and night it's safer to take a taxi; after dark it's essential. If you do take the metro, then take the Granada/Zuloaga exit, cross the avenue and turn left.

The city's other main bus terminal, the **Terminal de Oriente** (☎243-3253; Autopista Caracas-Guarenas), is on the eastern outskirts of Caracas, on the highway to Barcelona, 5km beyond Petare (about 18km from the center). It's accessible by many local buses from the city center or via a 15-minute minibus ride from the Petare metro stop. It handles much of the traffic to the east and southeast of the country. It also houses government-run **SITSSA** (☎0800-748-7720; www.sitssa.gob.ve) buses serving the entire country, which cost about half as much but require queuing before the ticket windows open at 6am. A taxi here from the center of Caracas will be about US$2.

Buses from Terminal de Oriente

DESTINATION	COST (US$)	DURATION (HR)
Cartagena, Colombia	12	23
Ciudad Bolívar	2.50	9
Ciudad Guayana	2.50	10
Cumaná	1.50	6½
Río Caribe	2	9
Puerto La Cruz	1.25	5
Santa Elena	7	20
Santa Marta, Colombia	10	18

Buses from Terminal La Bandera

DESTINATION	COST (US$)	DURATION (HR)
Barinas	2	8½
Coro	1.50	7
Maracaibo	2.50	10½
Maracay	1.25	1½
Mérida	3.25	13
San Cristóbal	3.50	13

Getting Around

BUS

An extensive bus network covers all suburbs within the metropolitan area of Caracas, as well as major neighboring localities. Privately run *carritos* (small buses) are the main type of vehicle operating city routes, but they are frequently targeted by armed gangs, and not recommended for travelers. The city-run **metrobus** (p982) system is considered to be far safer. Buses run frequently, but move only as fast as traffic allows. However, they go to many destinations inaccessible by metro and are the same price. Do not use buses after dark.

CAR & MOTORCYCLE

Caracas is a big and intimidating city with terribly clogged streets and long journeys at rush hour. But with a GPS and some nerve, it's possible to drive here. Car-rental agencies have offices downtown and at the airport, though cars tend to be hard to obtain and in bad condition.

METRO

A godsend to this chaotic city, the **metro** (www.metrodecaracas.com.ve; ⏲5:30am-11pm) is safe, fast, easy, well organized, clean and affordable – and it serves most major city attractions and tourist facilities. A single ticket for a ride of any distance is BsF4 (less than US$0.01). A 10-trip *multiabono* costs BsF36 (US$0.07) and is well worth it to avoid the ticket lines.

While the metro is generally safe, some opportunistic pickpockets exist, and it is best avoided late at night, when taxis are really the only safe option.

TAXI

Identifiable by the 'Taxi' or 'Libre' sign, taxis are a very cheap means of getting around the city and the only option at night. None have meters, so always fix the fare before boarding – don't be afraid to bargain. It is recommended that you use only white cars with yellow plates and preferably those from taxi ranks, of which there are plenty, especially outside shopping malls. Alternatively, many hotels and restaurants will call a reliable driver upon request. Expect to pay US$0.50 for a trip around town, shorter distances can be even less.

AROUND CARACAS

Want a break from the chaos of Caracas? There are a number of exciting places to visit nearby, including the Caribbean islands of Los Roques for which Caracas is the main jumping-off point.

Parque Nacional El Ávila

One of the great attractions of the Caracas area, this national park encompasses some 90km of the coastal mountain range north of the city. The highest peak in the range is Pico Naiguatá (2765m), while the most visited is Pico El Ávila (2105m), which is accessed by the *teleférico* (cable car). The southern slope of the range, overlooking Caracas, is uninhabited but crisscrossed with about 200km of walking trails. Most of the trails are well signposted and there are a number of campgrounds.

A dozen entrances lead into the park from Caracas; all originate from Av Boyacá, commonly known as Cota Mil (closed to traffic on Sunday between 6am and 1pm, it's a popular place for riding bikes and jogging) because it runs at an altitude of 1000m. Because of safety concerns, solo hiking is not recommended; check with park staff about camping.

There are plenty of options for a half- or full-day hike. One recommended way is to catch a bus from the east side of Plaza de Francia in Altamira (by the Hotel Caracas Palace) to the Sabas Nieves entrance, from where it's a 300m hike up to the ranger post. From there, you can pick up an easy-to-handle nature trail along the southern slope that passes a series of streams, waterfalls and caves. Another trail from Sabas Nieves climbs the mountain, one of four main ascents to the park's highest points, Pico Oriental (2640m) and Pico Naiguatá. One of the most scenic routes is along the Fila Maestra, following the crest of the Ávila range from Pico de Ávila to Pico Naiguatá and rewarding hikers with splendid views toward both the valley of Caracas and the Caribbean Sea.

If hiking isn't your bag, then one option is taking a 4WD jeep taxi (US$6 per person return) from outside the Hotel Ávila (p971) to the mountain hamlet of Galipan. The almost vertical 30-minute drive takes you over the top of the mountains and deposits you in Galipan, which has incredible views over the coast and where there are several restaurants catering to day-trippers. Picks of the bunch are **Granja Natalia** (☎0414-272-3005, 0416-308-2800; http://granjanatalia.blogspot.de; Galipan; mains US$5-8; ⏲noon-10pm) and **Recoveco** (☎0426-131-9786, 0424-144-6572; www.recoveco.com.ve; Galipan; mains US$5-10; ⏲noon-10pm Wed-Sun), both of which have some of the best food in the country. Reserving a table in advance is essential.

Archipiélago Los Roques

☎0237 / POP 1800

Island-hopping is the primary activity on Los Roques, a group of nearly 300 shimmering, sandy islands that lie in aquamarine waters some 160km due north of Caracas. It's far pricier than the mainland because everything is imported, but for those who love undeveloped beaches, snorkeling and diving, the trip is worth every bolívar. There is just one settlement on the main island of Gran Roque, and even that is limited to a few sandy and car-free streets, a charming contrast to the relentless traffic and overcrowding of most other towns in the country. The whole archipelago, complete with the surrounding waters (2211 sq km), was made a national park in 1972.

Almost all the islands are uninhabited and can be visited on day trips from Gran Roque. Indeed, while Gran Roque has a

DON'T MISS

TELEFÉRICO WARAIRAREPANO

Rising high above the city to the peak of El Ávila (2105m), the **Teleférico Warairarepano** (Warairarepano Cable Car; ☎792-7050; www.ventel.gob.ve; adult/child US$0.50/0.20; ⏱9:30am-8pm Tue-Thu, to 10pm Fri & Sat, to 8pm Sun, closed Mon Jul 22–Sep 15, noon-8pm Tue, 10:30am-8pm Wed-Sun Sep 16–Jul 21) runs 4km from Maripérez station (980m), next to Av Boyacá in Caracas, to Pico El Ávila. It's a phenomenal gondola ascent with some nail-biting heights, counting views of thick forest canopy, secret falls and the whole of Caracas.

The summit also offers breathtaking views of Caracas and the Valle del Tuy beyond; toward the north is a stunning panorama of the coastline and the Caribbean Sea stretching away to the horizon. The area around the *teleférico* station has been developed as a sort of fun park with a playground, 3D cinema and an ice-skating rink, as well as several restaurants and numerous stands along the main path selling coffee, hot chocolate and snacks. To get here, take a taxi (US$1) from anywhere in central Caracas.

wonderful stretch of beach itself, it's taken up by fishing boats and other vessels along its whole length, meaning that visitors have little choice but to go on day trips to other islands in order to enjoy the alternatives. The surrounding waters are known for their sea life, which attracts divers and snorkelers, while also meaning that there's excellent fresh seafood on most menus.

For sunset views at Gran Roque, climb the hill to the remains of the **Faro Holandés**, an 1870s lighthouse. Do bring a flashlight to Los Roques in case of power outages. All visitors to Los Roques must pay a US$0.75 national-park entry fee upon arrival.

Activities

Diving & Watersports

With the third largest reef in the world, Los Roques is Venezuela's top destination for snorkeling and diving. Among the best places are Boca de Cote, Crasquí and Noronquises (here you can swim with the sea turtles), but there are other excellent reef sites closer to Gran Roque. The most popular snorkeling spot is the so-called *piscina* (literally 'swimming pool') on Francisquí de Arriba. You can get snorkeling gear at many shops and most *posadas*, while scuba-diving outfits all charge US$95 for a two-dive excursion including equipment and transfers. Los Roques is also a top-notch spot for windsurfing and kitesurfing.

Aquatics Diving Center DIVING
(☎0416-626-2326, 0412-626-2320; www.adclosroques.com; Plaza Bolívar) Offers two daily diving trips as well as night dives.

Arrecife DIVING
(☎0414-335-9355, 0412-249-5119; www.divevenezuela.com) Next to Inparques. Offers three dives per day as well as guided snorkeling and courses.

Ecobuzos DIVING
(☎0414-395-4208; www.ecobuzos.com) Near the lagoon. Offers PADI certification and has years of experience. Good English is spoken.

Play Los Roques WATER SPORTS
(☎0414-905-5557; www.playlosroques.com) Next to Inparques, with stand-up paddleboarding rentals (US$5/10 for half/full day) and excursions.

Sleeping

Accommodations are not as cheap in Los Roques as elsewhere in the country, but it's still possible to find affordable places. See www.los-roques.com/posadas.htm for photos and more information about *posadas* and private campgrounds.

Camping

Free camping is permitted on all the islands within the recreation zone, including Gran Roque. After arrival, go to **Inparques** (☎0416-614-2297; www.infoinparques.com.ve; ⏱8am-noon & 2-5pm Mon-Fri, longer hours in high season) at the far end of the village for a free permit and information (note that fires and hanging hammocks are prohibited). They will often safeguard passports and valuables if asked. Oscar Shop (p985) rents tents and Roquelusa charges US$0.50 daily for bathroom use for Gran Roque campers, though shower access is limited in high season.

Posadas

There are more than 60 *posadas* providing some 500 beds on Gran Roque; almost all offer meals, many include at least half-board in the price. Rates, which are some of the highest in the country, tend to be similar year round, though prices jump during Venezuelan holidays (Christmas, Carnaval, Semana Santa and August through mid-September), and it's best to avoid traveling at these times. On weekdays during low season you can show up and bargain, especially for longer stays. Conserve water – it's a very precious resource here.

Posada Acquamarina GUESTHOUSE **$$$**
(☎0412-310-1962; www.posada-acquamarina.com; r per person incl full board US$36; ❄📶) This charming midrange option has mottled walls, gorgeous public areas, tiled bathrooms and conveniences such as safes, TVs and a communal roof terrace.

El Botuto GUESTHOUSE **$$$**
(☎0416-622-0061; www.posadaelbotuto.com; r per person incl breakfast/half-board US$16/23; 📶) Known for its fantastic service and sociable dining area, beachside El Botuto has six colorful, airy rooms with small private patios and outdoor showers.

Ranchito Power GUESTHOUSE **$$$**
(☎0414-291-9020; www.posadaranchitopower.com; r per person incl breakfast US$65; ❄📶) Tiny and simple, this great five-room, Italian-run option offers clean rooms with both fan and air-conditioning, along with a nice rooftop area. There's a charming breakfast nook, and pancakes are on the menu.

Posada La Laguna GUESTHOUSE **$$$**
(☎0424-262-7913; www.lalaguna.it; r per person incl breakfast US$70; ❄) Blue cement floors and sparkling white walls give this homey Italian-run place a Mediterranean feel. Excellent multicourse dinners upon request.

Doña Carmen GUESTHOUSE **$$$**
(☎0414-318-4926, 221-1004; richardlosroques@hotmail.com; Plaza Bolívar; r per person incl half-board US$25; ❄📶) Right on the beach, the longest-running *posada* on the island has rather dark, concrete rooms, but you won't be spending much time in them. The tasteful public areas and upstairs terrace surveying the sea are a far better draw.

Posada Karlin GUESTHOUSE **$$$**
(☎0414-288-1054, posadakarlin@gmail.com; per person incl half-board US$14; ❄📶) It may be rather charmless, but the rooms are cheap given that they include two meals a day. Lodgings come complete with the family's children, who give the place plenty of atmosphere, although also potentially less peace and quiet.

Eating & Drinking

Most visitors eat at their *posadas*, but self-catering or eating out at a less expensive restaurant will cut costs. Some *posadas* permit kitchen use, but it's not the norm.

For self-caterers there's a decent **grocery store** near the Inparques office (p983); a **bakery** by the school sells sandwich meat and fresh bread.

Kiosko La Sirena FAST FOOD **$**
(empanadas US$0.30, mains US$0.50; ⏰6-10am, noon-2pm & 6pm-midnight) If you're on a strict budget, settle in at this food shack by the lagoon. Breakfast is empanadas, and hamburgers and meat grills are available in the evening.

Las Guaras BARBECUE **$**
(half/whole chicken US$1.50/3, parilla US$1.50; ⏰dinner Tue-Sat) On the beach behind the Guardia Nacional, this driftwood-signed eatery does two things and does them well – chicken and *parilla* (grilled meat).

La Chuchera PIZZERIA **$$**
(☎221-1417; Plaza Bolívar; mains US$3-5; ⏰noon-10pm Tue-Sun; 📶🖉) Stick around long enough and La Chuchera is where you'll meet most people on the island at some point. The food may not be cheap, but it's cheap for Los Roques. The beloved pizzas are served after 4pm each day, but there's a full and inventive menu to enjoy if you're not at the beach for lunch: try the tuna tartar.

★ **El Canto de la Ballena** SEAFOOD **$$$**
(☎221-1160; www.cantodelaballena.com; dinner US$14; ⏰6-10pm) Right on the beach in the heart of the village, the 'whale song' is an excellent place for an evening meal. You'll get a varied and innovative selection of local dishes ranging from octopus carpaccio to an almost cake-like savory corn bread and wonderful fresh fish. Reserve ahead.

Aquarena Cafe INTERNATIONAL **$$$**
(☎0414-131-1282; mains US$5-10; ⏰9am-midnight Tue-Sun, food served from 1pm) This beachside cafe amid billowing palms serves sushi, cooked fish, hamburgers, pizza and salads. It's rather overpriced, but with gorgeous views like this, you might as well just put up with it and enjoy.

Information

There's a simple medical clinic next to the school in Gran Roque, though for any serious illness, you must return to Caracas.

Oscar Shop (☎0414-291-9160; oscarshop@hotmail.com) This small shop and informal tourist office near the airport organizes boat transportation to the islands and full-day boat tours. Also rents snorkeling equipment, surfboards, beach chairs and tents (per night US$10).

Getting There & Away

AIR

Flights from Caracas to Los Roques take about 30 minutes and tend to be full. It is easiest to book flights through a Venezuelan travel agency, as the small airlines that fly here don't have online booking systems. Normally only 10kg of free luggage is permitted on flights to Los Roques; you'll need to pay extra if you have more.

Caracas-based **Aereotuy** (p1031) and **Chapi Air** (☎0212-355-1965; reservacioneschapiair@gmail.com; Maiquetía domestic terminal) fly daily to Los Roques.

BOAT

There are no passenger boats to Los Roques from mainland Venezuela.

Getting Around

Boat operators in Gran Roque will take you to the island of your choice and pick you up at a prearranged time. The main pier right next to the airport on the beach is where most boats depart, and the best place to ask about transfers – or ask at your *posada*. Round-trip fares per person run from US$1 per person for a return transfer to Fransisqui up to US$25 per person for a multi-island day trip.

THE NORTHWEST

Easily reached from Caracas, the country's northwest is stocked with beaches, rainforests, deserts, caves, waterfalls, a dozen national parks and South America's largest lake. Parque Nacional Morrocoy attracts visitors with its colorful reefs, beaches and Sahara-like desert near the colonial town of Coro. Puerto Colombia is a favorite stop for backpackers and locals to hang out, soak up the sun and enjoy a few drinks or break out the binoculars and spot rare birds.

Parque Nacional Henri Pittier

☎0243

Venezuela's oldest national park, Henri Pittier rolls over 1078 sq km of rugged coastal mountain range and then plunges down to epic Caribbean beaches. There's something for everyone to love here: a glistening coastline, 600 species of birds, twisting hiking trails through verdant mountains, and quaint colonial towns with tasty food and comfortable *posadas*.

The national park is also home to various towns and villages, and these are usually reached these days by *por puestos* (shared taxi; literally 'by the seat') or private taxis via the only two paved roads crossing the park from north to south. One of the biggest and most popular towns is Puerto Colombia, at the end of the eastern road. It's the park's main tourist destination and offers the widest choice of services. El Playón, toward the end of the western road, is a bit rougher and less popular with foreign tourists. When traveling to either, expect crowds and traffic on holidays and weekends, and potential carsickness from the narrow winding curves.

Puerto Colombia

In this laid-back colonial village, packed with *posadas* and restaurants, most folks spend their days on the beach and evenings sipping *guarapita* (cane alcohol mixed with passion-fruit juice and lots of sugar) down on the waterfront, where drumming circles rev up on weekends. Note that Venezuelans refer collectively to the whole area, including Puerto Colombia, as Choroní, the name of the town just before Puerto Colombia proper.

The most popular beach is **Playa Grande**, a five- to 10-minute walk by road east of town. It's a real stunner, half a kilometer long and shaded by coconut palms, but you'll need to walk a long way down to find a quiet spot and even that can be impossible on weekends. The water is often rough, however, so don't swim if nobody else is. There are several simple food shacks at the entrance to the beach, and while you can theoretically camp on the beach or sling your hammock between the palms, we don't recommend it for safety reasons.

Far more enjoyable (as much as for the journey as for the peace and quiet you'll find on arrival) can be taking a boat up the coast (there is no road) to visit the other beaches in the area. These include Playa Aroa (US$1, 15 minutes), Playa Uricao (US$1.20, 20 minutes), Playa Aroa (US$1, 15 minutes), Playa Valle Seco (US$1.25, 20 minutes – for good snorkeling), Playa Chuao (US$1.50, 30 minutes) and Playa Cepe (US$2, 45 minutes). Prices are per person return. All beaches are far less crowded tha. Playa Grande, and most have some basic facilities such as restaurants and bars. Chuao is perhaps the most interesting. As well as enjoying the gorgeous 1km-long beach, you can take a trip to the village (take the shuttle bus from the harbor) where you can buy the famous local chocolate.

Sleeping

Casa Nova GUESTHOUSE $
(☎951-5318; www.jungletrip.de; Parcellamiento San Antonio 7A; r/apt from US$7/11; ❄@📶🏊) Tucked away down a series of rough roads off the main drag, this modern guesthouse offers eight simple but clean and comfortable rooms and a family apartment in a hacienda-style building. There's a small pool, a communal kitchen and a warm welcome from Claudia, the German owner who has made this village her home and can offer great local advice.

Nova Colonial GUESTHOUSE $
(☎431-8757; www.choroni.net; Morillo 37; r/apt from US$3.50/9; ❄@📶🏊) Housed in a converted colonial house, this friendly and central *posada* offers comfortable, fan-cooled rooms and a couple of spacious air-con apartments. A new swimming pool was being completed at the back on our last visit, while the hammock-strewn public areas and spacious communal kitchen are further draws.

Posada Casa Riqui Riqui GUESTHOUSE $
(☎0416-709-6366, 991-1061; www.posadacasariquiriqui.com; Morillo 56; d/tr/q/apt from US$6/7/8/12; ❄📶🏊) Near the Guardia Nacional post, this comfortable *posada* is set on lovely planted grounds with a bit of a hacienda feel. The tasteful 2nd-floor rooms offer the most character and style, though at the sacrifice of space. Hammocks and a small pool offer relaxation, and there's a wonderful barbecue area. There's no breakfast, but it has a new communal kitchen.

IguanAcción CAMPGROUND $
(☎0424-741-6035; iguanaccion@hotmail.com; Parcellamiento San Antonio s/n; hammock & tent per person US$1, r per person US$2) Along the river, camp in an artsy and ramshackle wonder-world of zip lines and mosaic-tiled archways. There's a basic kitchen and lockers (bring a lock), and reservations aren't necessary. A few rooms are available in the main building, but they're pretty dumpy and mostly used for luggage storage.

★**Posada La Bokaina** GUESTHOUSE $$
(☎0414-453-9220, 991-1291; www.labokaina.com; Hacienda El Portete, Sector La Bokaina 4; r per person incl breakfast US$18; ❄📶🏊) Located far enough away from the busy (and often loud) village center, this magical converted 17th-century mansion is ideal for an idyllic stay. Set in extensive gardens, the 10 rooms arch around the pool and include comforts such as hot water, fridges and TV. Don't miss walking to what is effectively a nearby private beach, also a perfect sunset spot.

Hostal Casagrande BOUTIQUE HOTEL $$
(☎991-1251; www.hostalcasagrande.com.ve; Calle Morillo 33; d/tr/q incl breakfast US$13/15.50/17; ❄@📶🏊) This character-heavy place inside a converted colonial house in the center of the town is stuffed full of tasteful art, local crafts and antiques. The centerpiece is a pool in the courtyard, while the rooms are cool and spartan, with the odd heirloom placed for individuality. There's a modern wing too, popular with Venezuelan families – go colonial.

Eating & Drinking

For late-night cheap eats, look for the half-dozen fast-food shacks across the road from the *malecón* (waterfront promenade).

CHOCOLATE COAST

The production of Venezuela's world-famous cocoa is most heavily concentrated around Chuao and along the coast of Parque Nacional Henri Pittier, home to the most rare and sought after variety, *criollo*. Chocolatiers the world over seek out its virtually bitter-free, delicate taste, and you'll find broad swaths of red-scorched cocoa drying in the sun at plantations in the area. Representing only 5% to 10% of the world's cocoa production, *criollo* is considered a delicacy among cocoa varieties. You can seek it out on a day trip to Chuao, where locals peddle everything from hot chocolate and chocolate ice cream to chocolate liqueurs – a real sweet treat.

In Puerto Colombia, look for **Coco Café Cacao** (José Maitín; ⏲9am-10pm), a small family-run shop on the corner of Plaza Bolívar selling milk chocolates wrapped in colorful recycled government pamphlets, chocolate ice cream, hot chocolate and brownies.

A small supermarket, **Abasto Colonial**, sits on Morillo right before the beach. It's inside a courtyard and looks nothing like a supermarket from the outside.

Oasis VENEZUELAN, SEAFOOD $
(Trino Rangel s/n; mains US$0.50-1; ⏲lunch & dinner) Housed under a tin roof, this economical restaurant serves pastas, fresh fish and *pollo al gusto* (chicken made to order).

Paco's Pizza PIZZA $
(Trino Rangel s/n; mains US$1.50-2.50; ⏲breakfast, lunch & dinner;) A popular Italian restaurant with tasty thin-crust pizzas and homemade pastas. Excellent ravioli.

Araguaneyes VENEZUELAN, SEAFOOD $
(Los Cocos 8; mains US$1-4, breakfast US$0.50-1; ⏲8.30am-9pm) Sit on the airy upstairs terrace and enjoy international and *criollo* fare, including a good selection of fresh fish.

★**Madera Fina** INTERNATIONAL $$
(☎991-1043; mains US$2-5; ⏲1pm-9.30pm) Outside the village, this place appears to be something of a brightly lit vision emerging from the foliage. And what a vision it is! The impressive indoor-outdoor premises include a wonderful viewpoint that overlooks the sea and is perfect for a sundown aperitif. But the food is the main draw: the *ceviche* is wonderful, as are the accompanying salads. Reservations recommended.

Paco's Fish SEAFOOD $$
(☎991 1474; Los Cocos s/n; mains US$4-6; ⏲1-11pm Thu-Sun) This brand new *cevichería*, fish and seafood restaurant is perhaps the smartest in town. Try one of various *ceviches* to start, followed by dishes such as barbecued catch of the day with Thai prawns or marlin risotto. The place itself is thoroughly charming, with local art on the walls, friendly staff and much-needed air-conditioning cooling the proceedings.

Getting There & Away

Most travelers coming from Caracas take private transfers directly to Puerto Colombia (around five hours). From Maracay's Interurbano terminal, buses depart every one or two hours (US$0.40, 2¼ hours). The last bus back to Maracay departs Puerto Colombia at around 6pm (later on weekends). *Por puestos* (shared taxis; US$1 during the day, US$1.25 at night and weekends, 1¾ hours) are faster and more frequent. Avoid traveling on the weekend, when traffic is heavy and slow on the winding road here.

Parque Nacional Morrocoy

☎0259

One of the most spectacular coastal environments in Venezuela comprises a strip of park on the mainland, and extends offshore to scores of islands, islets and cays. Some islands are fringed by white-sand beaches and surrounded by coral reefs. The most popular of the islands is Cayo Sombrero, which has fine (though increasingly damaged) coral reefs and some of the best shaded beaches. Other snorkeling spots include Cayo Borracho, Playuela and Playuelita.

The park gets rather crowded on weekends, but is considerably less full during the week. Holidays are complete bumper-to-bumper madness. Morrocoy lies between the towns of Tucacas and Chichiriviche, which are its main gateways. Neither is a particularly pleasant place, though if you need to stay at one of them, Chichiriviche has the edge over Tucacas.

Getting Around

Boats to the islands from both Tucacas and Chichiriviche take up to eight people and charge round-trip by the boat, though you can also do combinations. Bargain hard if the boat's not full.

Coro

☎0268 / POP 260,000

Caressed by pleasant sea breezes, Coro is one of the prettier colonial cities in Venezuela and the entry point to the magnificent sand dunes of the Parque Nacional Médanos de Coro. The cobblestone **Zamora**, where most of the historic mansions are located, rivals any other colonial architecture in the country, and the city has been on Unesco's World Heritage list since 1993. Though it's important to remember that Venezuela is not as blessed with colonial towns as its neighbours Brazil and Colombia, and much of Coro is a hectic, modern city like any other in Venezuela. Coro is best employed as an excellent base for exploring the region, especially the Península de Paraguaná and the mountainous Sierra de San Luis. It boasts a large student population and excellent budget accommodations.

Sights

Parque Nacional Médanos de Coro NATIONAL PARK
Mesmerizing zebra stripes of sand shimmer in the breeze at the Parque Nacional

Médanos de Coro, a spectacular desert landscape with sand dunes of 30m in height. Late afternoon is the best time to visit, when the sun is not so fierce. To get here, take the Carabobo bus from Calle 35 Falcón and get off 300m past the large *Monumento a la Federación*. From here it's a 10-minute walk north along a wide avenue to the dunes. Far easier is to take a tour that includes equipment and transport, and which can be arranged by any *posada* in town for around US$10.

La Vela de Coro BEACH
This colonial port town to the northeast has a sandy beach punctuated by orange rock columns and a view of a half-sunk shipwreck. It's easy to reach by public transit – *por puestos* (US$0.10, 20 minutes) leave from the corner of Avs Manuare and Rómulo Gallegos.

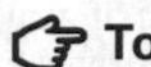

Tours

Full-day tours (US$20 per person for up to four people) to the windy desert of Península de Paraguaná or the cooler pine forest, caves and evocative sinkholes of the Sierra de San Luis can be organized by **Araguato Expeditions** (0426-560-0924; www.araguato.org; Calle Zamora No 92) and **Eco Latino Adventures** (0416-469-2240, 251-1590; www.ecolatinoadventures.com; Federacion 16B), or Posada El Gallo, La Casa de los Pájaros and other guesthouses. Boards and transportation for sandboarding are also offered (US$7 per person per half day).

Sleeping

Coro has some excellent accommodations including several delightful colonial *posadas*.

La Casa de los Pájaros GUESTHOUSE $
(0416-668-1566, 252-8215; www.casadelospajaros.com.ve; Monzón near Ampies; s/d/tr/q US$5/5/6.50/8;) Built by architect owners, this gorgeous six-room house has high ceilings, good lighting and artisan mosaic bathrooms. Breakfast in the courtyard is delightful. English-speaking Roberto also leads tours in the region, including walking tours of the sand dunes, trips to Península de Paraguaná and tours of the remains of Taima Taima, a 14,000-year-old civilization 20km east of Coro.

Posada El Gallo GUESTHOUSE $
(252-9481; posadagallo@gmail.com; Federación 26; per person with fan & shared bathroom/with air-con & private bathroom US$5/7;) In a restored colonial building with bright colors, wood beams and a lovely terrace, this guesthouse offers regional tours including excellent sandboarding excursions on boards they custom-make. The owner also has his folk-art studio in the front of the house, in case you're in the market for a satirical wood-carved statue of Mother Theresa.

Hotel Santa Ana HOTEL $
(250-0111; www.hotelsantaana.com.ve; Urdaneta near Manaure; s/d from US$8/10;) If you're not in the mood for an old fashioned *posada*, try this gleaming new 50-room hotel, popular with Venezuelan weekenders. Rooms are clean and modern, if a little pokey, while public areas are stylish and smart, with bits of folk art livening up the lobby. There's a small gym.

★**La Casa del Mono** GUESTHOUSE $$
(0146-469-2240, 251-1590; adrijana.mandl@gmail.com; Federación 16B; s/d US$10/15;) One of Coro's loveliest *posadas*, this place can be found in the heart of the old town and is looked after by enthusiastic Slovene Adrijana and her collection of animal rescues. Crack open a beer from the honor

DON'T MISS

SURFING THE SANDS OF CORO

The climb, calf-deep in sand, seems interminable. You reach the top of the dune, breathless. Wax the board, strap both feet in and zoom – you've zipped down 100m in seconds flat. Despite the difficulty – or maybe because of it – sandboarding the finger of land known as Los Médanos is both exhilarating and addictive.

Only the basics are required: a board, some sunblock and a little *joie de vivre*. It's hands-down the best way to see the sunset over Coro. A background in snowboarding is helpful but by no means required. Should you lose your balance, just lean back and let the bottomless *arena* (sand) cushion the blow.

All the *posadas* and travel agents in town can arrange equipment and transfers to the dunes, though it's also possible to go yourself by bus or taxi.

bar, make your own dinner in the communal kitchen or swing in a hammock in the garden courtyard, and you'll quickly feel at home.

Eating

Most *posadas* in Coro offer meals if you order in advance, though there are several decent dining options elsewhere. It's generally quite safe to wander the streets at night here, but the usual precautions apply.

★ **Pizzería La Barra del Jacal** PIZZA $
(cnr 29 Unión & Manaure; meals US$1.25-4; noon-midnight;) This attractive open-air restaurant offers more than just pizzas, and is a refreshing spot to sit with a beer, especially in the evening when a gentle breeze dissipates the heat of the day. Service is professional and there's a child's play area.

Jengibre & Albahaca INTERNATIONAL $
(cnr Avs Josefa Camejo & Manaure; mains US$1-2; 11:30am-11pm Sat-Thu, 6:30pm-midnight Fri;) Despite being by far Coro's most sophisticated dining spot, Ginger & Basil is also surprisingly great value. The menu is streets ahead of most in Venezuela, with organic burgers, Caprese salad and seafood pasta on offer, and you can choose between the air-conditioned dining room and the breezy terrace. Expect live music at weekends.

Panaderia La Gran Costa Nova BAKERY $
(Av Manaure near Zamora; sandwiches US$0.50, pastries US$0.25; 6am-9:30pm) This mammoth bakery packs them in at all times of the day, and no wonder – they crank out yummy breakfasts, lunches and snacks. It also has good pastries and coffee.

Restaurante Shangri La VEGETARIAN $
(Av Josefa Camejo s/n; per portion US$0.50; breakfast & lunch Mon-Sat;) A few blocks east of the strangely central airport, Lee Tzu serves up veggie breakfasts and lunches in this small joint, as well as a variety of herbal teas to cure what ails you. The offerings change daily.

Getting There & Away

AIR

The **Aeropuerto Internacional José Leonardo Chirinos** (251-5290; Av Josefa Camejo) is located in the center of the city just a five-minute walk north of the old town. **Conviasa** (p1031) flies to and from Caracas three times weekly, but flights are usually booked up weeks in advance.

BUS

The **Terminal de Pasajeros** (Av Los Médanos) is 2km east of the city center and accessible by frequent city transport or a taxi (US$0.20). Most of the direct buses to Caracas (US$2, seven hours) depart in the evening. The one direct bus to Mérida (US$4, 13 hours) goes the long route via Maracaibo.

You can make it to Santa Marta, Colombia, in one (long) day by taking an early morning *por puesto* to Maracaibo (US$1.50, three hours) and continuing from there.

Adícora

0269

On the eastern coast of the Península de Paraguaná, the small blustery town of Adícora is one of the country's windsurfing and kitesurfing capitals. Pros and beginners come from all over the world to ride the local winds. It is the most popular destination on the peninsula and offers a reasonable choice of accommodations and restaurants. Windsurfing lessons run from US$6 per hour, and an eight-hour (two-day) kitesurfing course costs US$150. Tourist numbers have dropped enormously in recent years, but you can still find very comfortable accommodations at **Posada La Casa Rosada** (988-8004; www.posadalacasarosada.com; Malecón; r US$5;), a beautifully restored colonial building with a lovely garden courtyard.

Adícora is linked to Coro (US$0.10, one hour) by eight buses a day, the last departing at around 5pm. *Por puestos* charge double. A taxi transfer is around US$10.

THE ANDES

Hot-blooded Venezuela is not usually associated with snow-encrusted mountains and windswept peaks. However, Venezuela is, in fact, home to the 400km-long northern end of the Andes range, crowned by the country's tallest mountain, called (what else?) Pico Bolívar, which towers at 5007m. For those who aren't hard-core mountaineers, the region offers lush valleys of cloud forest, cascading creeks and waterfalls, and charming mountain villages accessible by narrow winding roads.

Mérida state is in the heart of the Venezuelan Andes and has the highest mountains and the best-developed facilities for travelers. The city of Mérida is one of the continent's top adventure-sports destinations, and is also the gateway to Los Llanos grasslands,

Venezuela's most famous wildlife-watching destinations. Mérida is one of the few places in Venezuela that has maintained a steady flow of visitors despite the economic situation. The two other Andean states, Trujillo and Táchira, are less visited, but have many trekking opportunities for intrepid travelers.

Mérida

0274 / POP 244,000 / ELEV 1600M

The adventure-sports capital of Venezuela, progressive Mérida is an affluent Andean city with a youthful energy and a spectacular mountain position. It has an unhurried, friendly and cultured atmosphere derived from the massive university, its outdoor-sports presence and its wonderful climate, which attracts lowlanders for its bright but breezy days and cool nights. Active visitors will be spoiled for choice, with myriad options for hiking, canyoning, rafting, mountain biking and Mérida's specialty: paragliding. The city is also the major jumping-off point for wildlife-viewing trips to Los Llanos and lightning-viewing trips in Catatumbo.

Affordable and relatively safe, Mérida has a high standard of accommodations and numerous good places to eat. While not a place to indulge in colonial architecture, it has some of Venezuela's best nightlife, and is a major stop for backpackers.

Sights

Teleférico CABLE CAR

(Parque Las Heroínas) Mérida's famed *teleférico,* the world's highest and longest cable-car system, has been being rebuilt for years, with the government promising a series of ever-pushed back reopening dates. When in service, the *teleférico* runs 12.5km from the bottom station of Barinitas (1577m) in Mérida to the top of Pico Espejo (4765m), covering the ascent in four stages and giving staggering mountain views.

Parque Las Heroínas PARK

This recently remodeled plaza, in front of the cable-car station in the heart of Mérida, is a popular local place to hang out in the shade of the trees and in front of the impressive fountains. It really comes to life at night when it's full of young revelers, musical performers and busy bars.

Catedral de Mérida CHURCH

(cnr Av 4 Simón Bolívar & 22 Uzcategui) Work on this monumental cathedral began in 1800, based on the plans of the 17th-century cathedral of Toledo in Spain, but it wasn't completed until 1958, and probably only then because things were sped up to meet the 400th anniversary of the city's founding. Check out the gargoyle detailing visible from 22 Uzcategui.

Activities

There's nowhere in South America with cheaper activities and extreme sports than in Mérida, meaning that the city still attracts a steady stream of hard-core thrill seekers. And it's not only a question of price: adventurers love this region for the excellent range of sports and activities on offer, including rock climbing, canyoning, ziplining, bird-watching, horse riding, hiking, mountaineering and rafting.

Paragliding

Paragliding (*parapente*) is Mérida's most iconic adventure sport. There are even pictures of paragliders on the side of the city's garbage trucks.

Most visitors fly on tandem gliders with a skilled pilot, so no previous experience is necessary. The usual starting point for flights is Tierra Negra, an hour-long jeep ride from Mérida, from where you glide for 20 to 30 minutes down 850 vertical meters to the landing spot at Las González. The cost (around US$25) includes jeep transportation, all equipment and the pilot.

If you're serious about the sport, you can take a paragliding course (about US$1200) that takes 10 days, covering theory (available in English) and practice (including solo flights).

Gravity Tours ADVENTURE SPORTS

(0424-760-8327, 251-1279; www.gravity-tours.com; Calle 24, btwn Avs 7 & 8) This well-established agency has young and experienced guides, and fluent English-speaking owner Gustavo Viloria is a keen and expert wildlife spotter who specializes in Los Llanos trips. On offer are paragliding, rafting, ziplining and canyoning, as well as tours to Los Llanos, Roraima and Catatumbo.

Xtreme Adventours ADVENTURE SPORTS

(0424-702-3464, 252-7241; www.xatours.co.ve; 24 Rangel btwn Av 8 Paredes & Parque Las Heroínas) The main place in town for paragliding, this young, adventurous Venezuelan-owned agency offers hiking, mountain biking, ATV and bridge-jumping as well as a full array of hotel, tour and flight booking.

Rafting & Canyoning

Rafting is organized on some rivers at the southern slopes of the Andes. It can be included in a tour to Los Llanos or done as a two-day rafting tour (US$50 to US$60 per person) during the rainy season between May and November. The rapids range from class II to IV.

Canyoning (climbing, rappelling and hiking down a river canyon and its waterfalls) is another popular activity. Full-day, all-inclusive canyoning tours go for around US$25 to US$30.

Mountain Biking

Several tour companies in Mérida organize bike trips. Shop around, as bicycle quality and rental prices (US$5 to US$10 per day) may differ substantially between the companies. A full-day bike tour with a guide is usually US$20 to US$25 per person, including the hire of a bike. One of the popular bike tours is the loop around the remote mountain villages south of Mérida known as Pueblos del Sur. For a more challenging ride, try a trip up and back to El Refugio in Parque Nacional Sierra la Culata. The downhill through the high grasslands really gets the adrenaline pumping.

Courses

Venezuela was once a big center for Spanish language courses, but ongoing economic problems have led to many schools closing in recent years. There are plenty of students and tutors offering private language lessons – check *posada* bulletin boards.

★Jakera LANGUAGE COURSE
(☎0426-475-3178, 252-9577; www.jakera.com; 24 Rangel 8-205; 20hr of group classes per week incl lodging, breakfast & dinner US$325) Jakera is a popular Spanish language school with a 'traveling classroom' program that incorporates Spanish classes on the shady terrace with great Andes views, volunteering and countrywide adventure travel. It's based in the homey *posada* of the same name.

Tours

There are plenty of agencies in town, many of which nestle near Parque Las Heroínas and along 24 Rangel. Shop around, talk to other travelers and check things thoroughly before deciding. Mountain trips are popular and include treks to Pico Bolívar, Pico Humboldt and Pico Pan de Azucar.

An excellent excursion out of Mérida is a wildlife safari to Los Llanos, and most

DON'T MISS

CATATUMBO'S INCREDIBLE LIGHTNING

Centered on the mouth of the Río Catatumbo, where it runs into the vast Lago de Maracaibo, the Relámpago de Catatumbo (Catatumbo Lightning) is an amazing phenomenon that consists of frequent flashes of lightning with little or no accompanying thunder. The eerie, silent electrical storm can be so strong and constant that you will often be able to read this book at night.

The phenomenon can be observed at night all over the region, weather permitting, from as far away as Maracaibo and San Cristóbal. You'll get a glimpse of it traveling by night on the Maracaibo–San Cristóbal or San Cristóbal–Valera roads but, the closer you get, the more impressive the spectacle becomes. Tours organized from Mérida are the easiest way to see the Catatumbo lightning close up, and normally involve an enjoyable boat journey from Puerto Concha down the Río Catatumbo (look out for the incredible birdlife, caimens and howler monkeys), before spending the night in hammocks in a simple over-water *posada* on Lago de Maracaibo.

Various hypotheses have been put forth to explain the lightning, but so far none have been proven. The theory that stands out is based on the topography of the region, characterized by the proximity of 5000m-high mountains (the Andes) and a vast sea-level lake (Lago de Maracaibo) – a dramatic configuration found nowhere else in the world. The clash of the cold winds descending from the freezing highlands with the hot, humid air evaporating from the lake is thought to produce the ionization of air particles responsible for the lightning.

Sightings are best from September through November, when there can be 150 to 200 flashes per minute. All Mérida travel agencies can arrange the tours, which normally include staying at one of two *posadas* with similar facilities.

companies offer this trip as a four-day tour costing around US$70 to US$80 per person (depending on the number of people and the quality of transportation, guide and accommodations). Two-day, one-night trips to see Relámpago de Catatumbo (Catatumbo Lightning) run around US$50 per person including all meals, accommodations and transportation. Remember that you usually get what you pay for. If you're pressed for time and cash, reserve in advance to ensure a spot in a group.

Most agencies can also book airline tickets.

Mérida

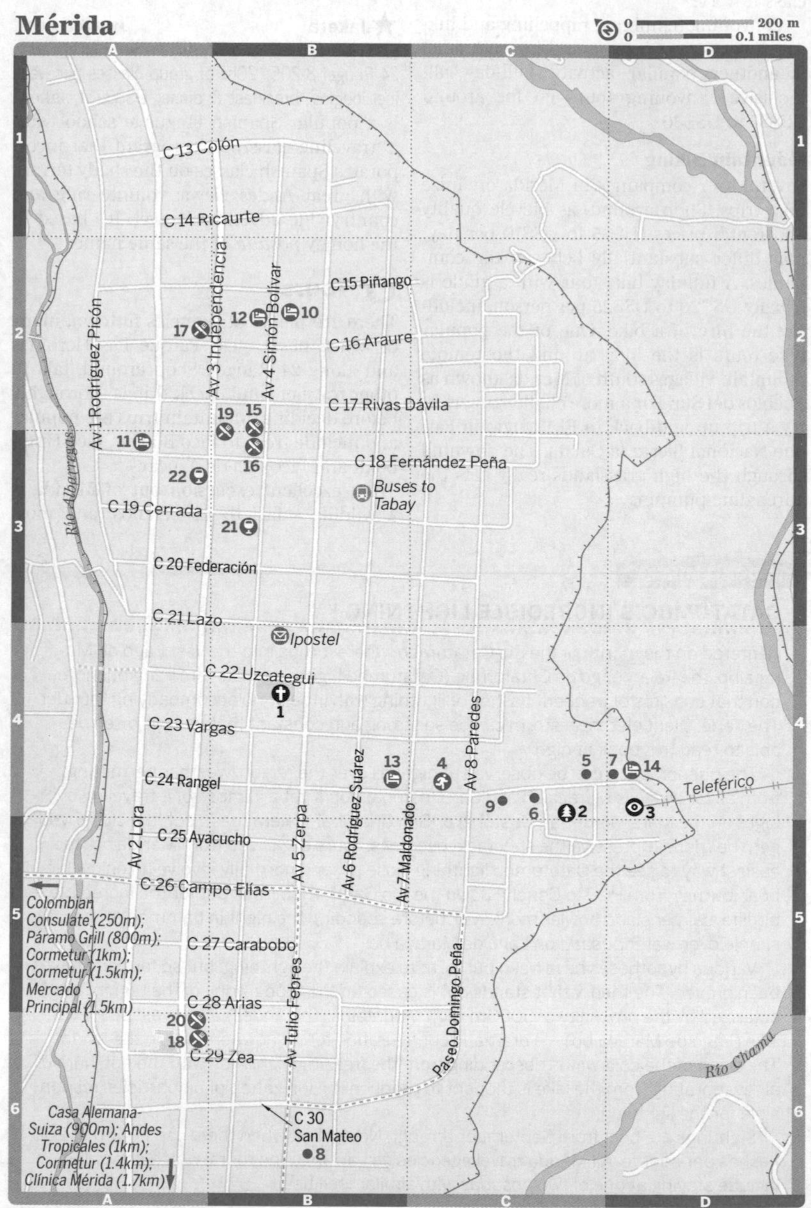

★ **Andes Tropicales** TOUR
(☎263-8633; www.andestropicales.org; cnr Av 2 Lora & Calle 41) A nonprofit foundation that helps organize hiking itineraries to rural mountain homes known as *mucuposadas* (*mucu* means 'place of' in the local dialect).

★ **Catatumbo Tour** TOUR
(☎0414-756-2575; www.catatumbotour.com) Respected naturalist Alan Highton specializes in Catatumbo tours, which he runs all year round, hosting travelers at his unique *posada* that stands on stilts in Lake Maracaibo opposite the settlement of Ologa and among amazing wildlife. During the dry season (December to April), Alan also leads Los Llanos tours with passion and great expertise.

★ **Natoura Travel & Adventure Tours** TOUR
(☎0416-674-8442, 252-4075; www.natoura.com; 31 Junín near Av Tulio Febres) Run by English-speaking José Luis Troconis, this experienced and highly regarded local operator is well known for mountain trekking and climbing, and organizes small group tours with quality camping and mountaineering equipment. Other destinations include Los Llanos, Gran Sabana and Saltó Angel, meaning Natoura can arrange you entire trip through Venezuela.

Guaguanco Tours TOUR
(☎252-3709; www.aguaguanco.com.ve; 24 Rangel s/n) An experienced operator with a large variety of tours, including Los Llanos, paragliding, Catatumbo, coffee plantations and local hot springs.

Guamanchi Expeditions TOUR
(☎252-2080; www.guamanchi.com; 24 Rangel s/n) A long-running, well-equipped and experienced operator, Guamanchi is particularly strong on mountain-related activities, but also has a whole range of multiday Los Llanos trips, and kayaking, bird-watching and bike tours.

Mérida

Sights

1	Catedral de Mérida	B4
2	Parque Las Heroínas	C4
3	Teleférico	D4

Activities, Courses & Tours

4	Gravity Tours	C4
5	Guaguanco Tours	C4
6	Guamanchi Expeditions	C4
7	Jakera	D4
8	Natoura Travel & Adventure Tours	B6
9	Xtreme Adventours	C4

Sleeping

10	La Casona de Margot	B2
11	Posada Alemania	A3
12	Posada Casa Sol	B2
	Posada Guamanchi	(see 6)
13	Posada La Montaña	B4
14	Posada Patty	D4

Eating

15	Burger Bar	B2
16	El Vegetariano	B3
17	Guacamole	A2
18	Heladería Coromoto	A6
19	La Abadía	B3
20	La Sazón del Llano	A6

Drinking & Nightlife

21	El Hoyo del Queque	B3
22	Gurten Café Poco Loco	A3

Sleeping

There's plenty of choice in Mérida, and one outstanding and affordable *posada* that never disappoints: Posada Casa Sol. Prices rise for traditional Venezuelan high season.

★ **Posada Casa Sol** BOUTIQUE HOTEL $
(☎252-4164; www.posadacasasol.com; Av 4 btwn 15 Piñango & 16 Araure; r incl breakfast US$10; @) Adorned with colorful folk art and gorgeous public areas, this exquisite and luxurious boutique hotel inhabits a colonial mansion with paint-textured walls, rainforest showers and a lovely garden with a mature avocado tree, under which breakfast is served. German owner Renate and her local team will ensure that you feel properly taken care of here.

Posada Guamanchi GUESTHOUSE $
(☎252-2080; www.guamanchi.com; 24 Rangel No 8-86; dm US$2.50, r with/without bathroom US$4/3, q with/without bathroom US$6/5;) Popular with its tour clients, this rambling *posada* in the center of town has two kitchens and is a good place to meet like-minded travelers. Back rooms have killer mountain views and there's hot water in the bathrooms.

Posada Alemania GUESTHOUSE $
(☎252-4067; www.posadaalemania.com; Av 2 Lora No 17-76; dm US$1.20, s/d without bathroom US$1.75/2.50, d with bathroom US$4; @) This popular Venezuelan-run *posada* is a simple and wonderfully cheap place that has a large range of rooms including dorms and private

rooms, both of which share a large kitchen at the back. Rooms surround a central garden courtyard, and there's a popular in-house tour agency that can help you do anything from Los Llanos tours to mountain climbing.

Posada La Montaña GUESTHOUSE $
(☎252-5977; www.posadalamontana.com; 24 Rangel btwn Avs 6 & 7; s/d US$3/4; 📶) A gorgeous colonial house, with comfortable rooms featuring decorative mosaic bedside tables, fridges, safety boxes and daily room cleaning. There's a restaurant downstairs serving all meals and the public areas are plant-strewn and generally very well maintained.

Casa Alemana-Suiza GUESTHOUSE $
(☎263-6503; www.casa-alemana.com; cnr Av 2 & Calle 38; s/d/tr/q US$3/4.50/6/8; @📶) A spacious and stylish building away from the more touristy center, with ample and quiet retro-style rooms, a mountain-view roof deck, pool table and breakfast upon request.

La Casona de Margot GUESTHOUSE $
(☎252-3312; www.lacasonademargot.com; Av 4 Simón Bolívar s/n; r from US$5; 📶) Built around two cute courtyards, some of the updated rooms have tall loft ceilings and house up to eight. There's hot water, but no breakfast.

Posada Patty GUESTHOUSE $
(☎251-1052; claferlis_diana_24@hotmail.com; 24 Rangel s/n; dm US$1.50, r without bathroom US$2) A friendly and familiar basic backpacker place with a kitchen and shared meals, and an inexpensive laundry.

Eating

★Burger Bar BURGERS $
(☎0414-175-9183; Av 4 Simon Bolívar btwn 17 Rivas Dávila & 18 Fernández Peña; burgers US$1-2; ⏱11:30am-11:30pm; 📶) This recently opened gourmet burger joint serves up a very welcome range of high-quality medium-rare burgers in numerous different styles, has craft beers on tap and also does crispy chicken and paninis. The whole place is streets ahead of the other local eating options, and there are often art shows and musical performances to boot.

Guacamole MEXICAN $
(Av 3 Independencia btwn Calle 15 & 16; mains US$1.50-4; ⏱6:30-11pm Mon-Sat, 5:30-10:30pm Sun) A friendly and rather charming place with a full Tex-Mex menu stretching from burritos to quesadillas, Guacamole is a colorful multiroom affair that provides a much needed change of culinary pace for those who've been in Venezuela for a while.

La Abadía INTERNATIONAL $
(Av 3 Independencia s/n; mains US$1-4; ⏱3-10pm Tue-Sun; 📶🍴) This atmospheric colonial mansion serves quality salads, meats and pastas. It has a cocktail bar in a basement catacomb, plus several intimate indoor and alfresco dining nooks.

Páramo Grill STEAK $
(☎244-9295; Av Cardenal Quintero s/n; mains US$3-5; ⏱noon-11pm; 📶) A large and relatively formal place by local standards, this locally famous steakhouse features waiters in tuxedos and a bullfighting theme on the walls. Meat can be a little overcooked, so if you like it medium-rare, try ordering it rare. It's in the new town, a US$0.50 taxi ride from the town center.

La Sazón del Llano VENEZUELAN, BAKERY $
(Av 3 Independencia s/n; menú US$1; ⏱cafeteria 7-11am & 11:30am-9pm Mon-Sat, bakery 6:30am-9pm Mon-Sat, 7am-2:30pm Sun) A side-by-side bakery and cafeteria always abuzz with happy diners. You could bust a gut polishing off the four-dish *criollo* and international *menú,* and the bakery is a good bet when everything's closed tight on Sunday.

Heladería Coromoto ICE CREAM $
(Av 3 Independencia s/n; ice cream US$0.25; ⏱2:15-9pm Tue-Sun) An ice-cream shop in the *Guinness World Records* for the largest number of flavors, it scoops out more than 900 types (not all at the same time!), including Polar beer, salmon and black bean.

Mercado Principal MARKET $
(Av Las Américas s/n; ⏱7am-4pm; 🍴) Some of the city's best traditional food is to be found on the 2nd floor. Try dishes such as *pechuga rellena a la merideña* (chicken breast stuffed with ham and cheese, breaded, deep-fried, and slathered in mushroom sauce).

El Vegetariano VEGETARIAN $
(cnr Av 4 Simón Bolívar & 18 Fernández Peña; menú US$0.50; ⏱10am-11pm Mon-Sat; 🍴) This rather run-down place is nonetheless a good option for vegetarians, as it has a daily changing set menu of Venezuelan food. There are also good cakes.

Drinking & Nightlife

Mérida is a lively place, with a large student population and lots of domestic holidaymakers who come here to party. The hub of the town's nightlife is Parque Las Heroínas. A number of clubs and bars can also be found in the *centros comerciales* (shopping centers) of Viaducto, Mamayeya, Las Tapias and Alto Prado.

★**El Hoyo del Queque** CLUB
(cnr Av 4 Simón Bolívar & 19 Cerrada; admission Thu-Sat US$1; ⊙until 1am) This renowned and endlessly fun venue always fills up, with live bands and DJs playing salsa, reggae and pop.

Gurten Café Poco Loco SPORTS BAR
(Av 3 Independencia, btwn 18 Fernández Peña & 19 Cerrada) This Swiss-owned sports bar packs them in till late with a mixture of rock, reggae and salsa. The owner loves *fútbol* (soccer) and it's on every hour the bar is open.

Information

MEDICAL SERVICES

Clínica Mérida (☎263-6395, 263-0652; Av Urdaneta No 45-145) Clinica Mérida offers medical services.

POST

Ipostel (21 Lazo s/n)

TOURIST INFORMATION

Cormetur (☎263-1603, 800-637-4300; cormeturpromocion@hotmail.com; cnr Av Urdaneta & Calle 45, Main Tourist Office; ⊙7am-7pm) One of the most helpful tourism offices in the country; English spoken at the toll-free number and at the main office. Other branches are at the bus terminal (☎263-3952; Av Las Américas; ⊙7am-6pm) and Mercado Principal (☎263-1570; Av Las Américas; ⊙8am-3pm, to 1:30pm Tue & Sun).

Getting There & Away

AIR

Mérida's **airport** (Av Urdaneta) has been closed since 2008. Flights did briefly resume in 2013, but were again suspended at the time of writing. It's 2km southwest of Plaza Bolívar, next to the tourist office. The closest airport is an hour away in El Vigía, where there are direct flights from Caracas. Another possibility is to use the airport at Barinas, a four-hour drive away.

Transfers Mérida (☎0414-723-4680; www.transfersmerida.com.ve) runs air-conditioned vans (per person US$1.50) from Centro Comercial Glorias Patrias to El Vigía airport. There's a five-person minimum from El Vigía airport to Mérida. Reserve three days in advance. Taxis charge around US$10.

BUS

The bus terminal is on Av Las Américas, 3km southwest of the city center; it's linked by frequent public buses that depart from the corner of 25 Ayacucho and Av 2 Lora. Buses serve El Vigía (US$1) throughout the day. For Ciudad Bolívar, it's fastest to take a bus to Barinas and change there.

WORTH A TRIP

HOT SPRINGS

Tabay Only 12km from Mérida, these *aguas termales* (hot springs) consist of a cement pool a half hour's walk in and a second natural one 30 minutes past it. Frequent *busetas* (small buses) leave from from Av 6 Rodríguez Suárez.

La Musui (www.aguastermaleslamusui.blogspot.com) Take an early-morning *buseta* to Mucuchíes (1¼ hours) and then a taxi (20 minutes) up to the high elevation town of La Musui. From here, it's about an hour-long walk up to a stone-walled natural pool. Last transport back to Mérida from Mucuchíes departs around 4:30pm, though it's worth strolling the charming 400-year-old, 3000-meter-high Andean town, where lots of accommodations are available if you want to stay overnight.

Bus Fares from Mérida

DESTINATION	COST (US$)	DURATION (HR)
Barinas	1.50	4
Caracas	3.25	13
Coro	4	13
Maracaibo	3	9
Maracay	3.50	11
San Cristóbal	1.25	5

Around Mérida

The most popular high-mountain trekking area in the region is the **Parque Nacional Sierra Nevada**, east of Mérida, which has all of Venezuela's highest peaks. Pico Bolívar (5007m), Venezuela's highest point and a mere 12km from Mérida, is one of the most popular peaks to climb. Without a guide you can hike along the trail leading up to Pico Bolívar, which roughly follows the cable-car line, but be careful walking from Loma Redonda to Pico Espejo – the trail is not clear and it's easy to get lost. Five-day, four-night guided climbs of Pico Bolívar cost US$150 per person from agencies in Mérida.

Venezuela's second-highest summit, **Pico Humboldt** (4942m) is also popular with high-mountain trekkers, and can be summited in a four-day climb for US$120 per person.

An easier destination is **Los Nevados**, a charming mountain village nestled at about 2700m. Jeeps to Los Nevados (US$4, four hours) leave from Mérida's Parque Las Heroínas between 7am and 8am, and at noon in high season. Simple accommodations and food are available here, or you can walk an hour to overnight in the *mucuposada* and working farm of **Hacienda El Carrizal** (☎0274-789-5723; dm US$2).

The **Parque Nacional Sierra La Culata**, to the north of Mérida, also offers some amazing hiking territory and is particularly noted for its desertlike highland landscapes. Take a *por puesto* to La Culata (departing from the corner of 19 Cerrada and Av 2 Lora), from where it's a three- to four-hour hike uphill to a primitive shelter known as El Refugio, at about 3700m. Continue the next day for three to four hours to the top of **Pico Pan de Azúcar** (4660m). Consider staying another night to explore local hot springs and swimming holes. The last *por puesto* back to Mérida leaves around 4pm. Some agencies in Mérida offer three-day guided Pan de Azúcar trips for US$90 per person, all inclusive. Other great hikes in the region include **Pico El Águila** (4118m), **Paso del Cóndor** (4007m) and **Pico Mucuñuque** (4672m).

To overnight in the parks independently, you need a permit from **Inparques**. Offices are located in Mérida, Tabay and Los Nevados, and caretakers stationed at park entry points also issue on-the-spot permits.

For hikers, one of the most interesting (and supersafe) off-the-beaten-path experiences is the network of trails to indigenous mountain villages, where you can spend the night in *mucuposadas*. Spaced a day's walk apart, you can traipse through cloud forest, pastureland and glacial landscapes from village to village and end the day with hot showers, cooked meals and a comfy bed. Prices are US$2 per person per day for lodging and US$3 for full board. Guides aren't necessary, but can be hired for about US$10 per day.

In Mérida, the EU-funded foundation Andes Tropicales (p993), which helped develop the network, can organize *mucuposada*, walking, biking or jeep tours, or consult with travelers (for free) on how to arrange independent trips; their **Pueblos del Sur network** (www.destinopueblosdelsur.com), helps culturally curious travelers explore the spectacular Andean villages southwest of Mérida.

One very beautiful route that's easy to organize with public transportation includes stays at **Mucuposada Michicaba** (☎0274-511-8701, 0426-702-9467; Gavidia; dm US$2), **Mucuposada El Carrizal** (☎0273-511-6941; Carrizal; dm US$2), **Mucuposada San José** (☎0273-414-3502; San José; dm US$2) and **Mucuposada Los Samanes** (☎0273-400-1299; Santa María de Canaguá; dm US$2). From Mérida, take a bus 48km east to Mucuchíes (US$0.75, 1½ hours), a 400-year-old town, and then a jeep to Gavidia (one hour). At the end of the route, Mucuposada Los Samanes can organize your transportation or you can hike 20km to the highway and take a *por puesto* to Barinas.

DON'T MISS

LOS LLANOS

One of Venezuela's best destinations is the wildlife-rich Los Llanos, an immense savanna plain south of the Andes that's also the home of Venezuela's cowboys and the twangy harp music of *joropo* (traditional music of Los Llanos). With Venezuela's greatest repository of wildlife found here, you'll be flat-out dazzled by caimans, capybaras, piranhas, anacondas and anteaters, plus an enormous variety of birds. In the rainy season, the land is half-flooded and animals are dispersed but still visible everywhere. The dry months (mid-November to April) are the high season, with a greater concentration of animals clustered near water sources.

Mérida's tour companies provide fascinating excursions for US$200 to US$300, usually as four-day all-inclusive packages; add extra for rafting.

Keep in mind that wildlife-watching should not be stressful for the animals. Guides should not be encouraged to handle or harass animals, including anacondas.

GETTING TO COLOMBIA

San Antonio del Táchira is the busy Venezuelan border town across from Cúcuta, Colombia (12km). Wind your watch back 30 minutes when crossing from Venezuela to Colombia. In late 2015 the border was closed following a diplomatic dispute between the Venezuelan and Colombian governments. Check the latest situation before heading here, although observers on both sides expected the border to reopen again shortly.

From San Antonio, buses and *por puestos* run frequently to the Cúcuta bus terminal in Colombia (12km). You can catch both on Av Venezuela, or save yourself some time by walking across the bridge over the Río Táchira (the actual border), getting your Colombian entry stamp from the Migración Colombia office (on your right), and looking for a shared taxi on the other side. You can pay in Venezuelan bolívares or Colombian pesos.

From Cúcuta, there are frequent buses and flights to all major Colombian destinations.

San Cristóbal

0276 / POP 286,000

Encircled by evocative green hills, San Cristóbal is a thriving commercial center fueled by its proximity to Colombia, just 40km away. This proximity has also raised safety concerns in recent years, with drug and gas smuggling endemic in the area, paramilitary activity and high levels of street crime. You'll pass through San Cristóbal if you are traveling overland to or from anywhere in Colombia except the Caribbean Coast, though some people stop overnight to break the long bus ride. While no traveler destination in itself, the city is a modern and comfortable place with friendly inhabitants. It is worth staying a bit longer in January, when the city goes wild for two weeks celebrating its Feria de San Sebastián.

Sleeping & Eating

If you're coming by bus and just need a budget shelter for the night, check out one of several basic hotels on Calle 4, a short block south of the bus terminal. There are several inexpensive Chinese restaurants on Avs 5 and 7 that stay open until 10pm or 11pm.

MonCricket Hotel HOTEL $

(344-6204; www.moncricketthotel.com.ve; Carr 13 No 11-79, cnr Calle 12; s/d incl breakast US$8/10;) This comfortable and contemporary place has some of the most comfortable accommodations in town, and is centrally located, though rooms can get quite a bit of street noise. Staff are superhelpful and rooms are spacious, colorful and spotless.

Tienda Naturista Gustico VEGETARIAN $

(0416-579-0609; Calle 7 btwn Av 7 Isaias Medina Angarita & Carr 8; mains US$1-2; 8am-6pm Mon-Sat;) This lunchtime veggie place cranks out homemade yogurt, wholemeal bread, wholemeal empanadas and other yummy snacks. Excellent juices too.

Getting There & Away

AIR

The main regional airport, Aeropuerto Base Buenaventura Vivas, is about 1½ hours away in Santo Domingo, with no direct public transportation. A taxi costs US$10.

BUS

From the bus terminal, more than a dozen buses daily go to Caracas (US$2.50, 13 hours). Most depart in the late afternoon or evening for an overnight trip via El Llano highway. Ordinary buses to Barinas (US$1.25, five hours) run hourly between 5am and 6:30pm.

Expresos Unidos buses to Mérida (US$1.25, five hours) go every 1½ hours from 5:30am to 7pm, but depart earlier if full (arrive by 6pm to make the last departure). Frequent buses depart nightly for Maracaibo (US$1.80, eight hours); make sure the route takes the faster Panamerican Hwy.

Minibuses to San Antonio del Táchira (US$0.25, 1¼ hours), on the Colombian border, run every 10 or 15 minutes; it's a spectacular but busy road. If you are in a rush, consider taking a *por puesto* (US$0.50).

THE NORTHEAST

Venezuela's northeast is a little known and little explored mosaic of natural marvels, with Caribbean beaches, coral reefs and spectacular mountains. This region is home to Venezuela's most famous island, Margarita, once a big draw for foreign travelers, but now a rather overdeveloped holiday destination favored far more by local holidaymakers than backpackers. Infinitely more rewarding are the stunning and still largely undeveloped Península de Paria, the Cueva del Guácharo, and the beaches and islands of the Parque Nacional Mochima. This is the only place on the South American mainland where Colombus set foot, and anybody lucky enough to be taking a boat down the coastline of the extraordinary Península de Paria will understand what led the explorer to declare the region 'paradise on earth.'

Parque Nacional Mochima

0293

Straddling the states of Anzoátegui and Sucre, Parque Nacional Mochima comprises a low, dry mountain range that drops down to fine bays and beaches, and continues offshore to a mesmerizing constellation of three dozen arid islands. Dolphins are a common sight in the area's waters. The best beaches are on the islands and accessed by short boat trips from Santa Fe, Mochima or other coastal towns. Coral reefs surround a few of the islands and provide decent snorkeling and scuba diving. Tranquility seekers should visit midweek – at weekends and during summer the park gets lots of visitors from nearby cities. The towns within the park are generally very poor and not particularly safe. Mochima is an exception, though it's lacking appealing *posadas*.

Playa Colorada draws weekend hordes of young Venezuelan partygoers and sunseekers, but it's very quiet during the week. An adventure-sports boot camp, Spanish-language school and an excellent place to meet up with other energetic travelers, **Jakera Lodge** (995-5841; www.jakera.com; hammock/dm incl half-board US$3/5;) offers dorm accommodations with communal meals and scores of scuba, canyoning and kayak outings. Its full-day boat tours to go bouldering at Isla de Mono are very popular. Look for its corrugated-steel gate on the highway.

Santa Fe is a beachside town that was once a common stop for backpackers. These days it's sadly rather unsafe, though it still has a great beach and is a good base for visiting the pristine beaches on the islands of Parque Nacional Mochima by boat. **Le Petit Jardin** (0416-387-5093, 231-0036; www.lepetitjardin-mochima.com; Cochaima; s/d/tr incl breakfast US$15/20/25;), just a block from the beach, is the best place to stay.

At the eastern end of the national park, the wonderfully located town of **Mochima** is found at the end of a winding road that has fantastic sea and mountain views. It's rather scruffy and run down these days and has a dearth of good accommodations, though it's a good place from which to explore the islands. Launches leave from the dock throughout the day, taking small groups to various islands and collecting them later on, or doing tours of several different islands and returning to Mochima. Mochima is home to **Restaurant Puerto Viejo** (mains US$1-3; noon-8pm Wed-Mon), a pleasant spot for a fish lunch served right by the water.

Cueva del Guácharo

Venezuela's longest and most magnificent cave, **Cueva del Guácharo** (admission US$0.20; tours every 20min btwn 8am & 2pm Tue-Sun, daily Jul & Aug), 12km from Caripe toward the coast, has 10km of caverns. An impressive portal and cave system, it's inhabited by the shrieking *guácharo* (oilbird), which lives in total darkness and leaves the cave only at night in search of food. *Guácharos* have a radar-location system (similar to bats) and enormous whiskers that enable them to navigate in the dark. From August to December, the population in the cave is estimated at 10,000 and occasionally up to 15,000. Within its maze of stalactites and stalagmites, the cave also shelters crabs, fish and rodents. If you want to see the birds leaving the cave, arrange a late taxi pickup after closing time. Alternatively, camp for a small fee across from the cave entrance and witness the birds pouring out of the cave mouth at around 6:30pm and returning at about 4am.

All visits to the cave are by guided group tour; full tours take about 1½ hours. The tour visits 1200m of the cave, but high water in August and/or September occasionally limits sightseeing to 500m. Across the road, it's a 20-minute hike to Salto La Paila, where you can swim in a chilly pool at the foot of a ribbon cascade.

The nearby town of Caripe is a real charmer, with a gorgeous mountain setting and friendly locals who seem happy to see visitors. The best place to stay for access to the cave is the **Hotel Samán** (0292-545-1183; www.hotelsaman.com; Av Chaumer 29; r US$5;) and there's also a good restaurant next door.

Getting to Caripe isn't particularly easy by bus, though there are regular connections from Maturín (US$0.50, 2½ hours) and Cumaná (US$0.50, 2½ hours), both of which can drop you at the cave entrance on their way into town. In Caripe, taxis charge US$0.50 to the cave.

Río Caribe

0294 / POP 14,000

The former splendor of the old port town of Río Caribe can be spotted along the wide, tree-shaded Av Bermúdez with its once-magnificent mansions. Once a major cacao exporter, the town, a perfect example of faded grandeur, now serves as a laid-back holiday destination and a springboard for incredible beaches further east. Don't miss the 18th-century church on Plaza Bolívar or the weekend activity at Plaza Sucre, along Av Bermúdez closer to the beach. Do, however, be careful at night, and don't roam off the main avenue. Río Caribe is best used as a base for exploring the fantastic Península de Paria.

Sleeping & Eating

Posada Shalimar GUESTHOUSE $
(0414-762-8700, 646-1135; www.posada-shalimar.com; Av Bermúdez s/n; d/tr/q US$4/5/6;) The Arabic-style courtyard here contains a small lap pool around which are arranged two levels of comfortable and well-appointed rooms. Though it's definitely not looking its best these days (the pool was a murky green due to chlorine shortages), this otherwise charming place makes for an excellent base, with surfboards for rent and numerous local tours available.

Posada de Arlet GUESTHOUSE $
(646-1290; 24 Calle de Julio 22; s/d/tr/q US$4/5/7/8;) This immaculate Swiss-owned *posada* near the Plaza Bolívar has cheerful light-filled upstairs rooms – some with great hill views – along a breezy terrace.

★ **Alquimia Paria** GUESTHOUSE $$
(0414-232-2693, 646-2126; www.alquimiaparia.com; Rivero 46; d/tr incl breakfast US$10/15;) Set just off the charming Plaza Bolívar a five-minute walk from the seafront, this new *posada* is the dazzling conversion of a once-crumbling colonial mansion. Set around a gorgeous plant-filled courtyard, the five rooms are uniquely appointed, though due to constraints in the building layout each has its own private bathroom and toilet outside the room. Tours can be arranged.

La Tasca de Luís VENEZUELAN $
(Av Bermúdez s/n; mains US$1.50-3.50; 11am-9pm;) The mounted head of a bull flanked by two calves is the charmingly shameless centerpiece of this *tasca* restaurant's decor. Dark wood furniture, an old-school bar and unfortunate white strip lighting complete the scene, while the menu of meat and seafood is good and varied. Try the *asado negro* (eye of round roast beef cooked in a red-wine sauce).

Mi Cocina VENEZUELAN $
(Juncal s/n; mains US$1-2; noon-4pm) Down an unlikely side street parallel to Av Bermúdez, this little air-conditioned oasis comes complete with a religious shrine. The dishes on offer form a standard Venezuelan set (fried catch of the day, grilled meats, seafood stew) but the quality is higher here than you'll find elsewhere locally. Look for the sign on the door saying *Tasca Restaurant Aqui*.

Da More ITALIAN $
(646-1622; Av Bermúdez 72; mains US$1-2; noon-9pm Tue-Sun;) This relaxed and airy place cooks up excellent pizzas and tasty pastas, which many locals call ahead to order as wait times can be long on the weekend. You can create your own topping combination or choose from the menu. No alcohol served.

Getting There & Away

There is a daily bus to Caracas (US$2, 10 hours) that leaves from the Plaza Bolívar at 6pm. Local buses and *por puestos* leave from the small bus station at the end of Av Bermudez, by the port, connecting Río Caribe to other towns on the Península de Paria, including Carupano, the main settlement on the peninsula and the transport hub to other areas in the country. As public transport here is slow and unreliable, most travelers arrive by private transfer.

Península de Paria

The Península de Paria – the only place in South America where Columbus actually set foot – has some of the most gorgeous and least-visited spots in the country, all backed by the thick jungle-covered mountains of the peninsula's largely untouched interior. Dozens of white- and gold-sand beaches await travelers on the 50km coastal stretch between Río Caribe and San Juan de Unare, the last seaside village accessible by road. Beyond San Juan de Unare you can only continue by boat, making a trip to futher flung villages such as **Santa Isabel** a real adventure. Bring repellent if you stay overnight, and always check with locals before swimming, as some beaches have treacherous currents.

An easy jaunt from Río Caribe before hitting the beach, chocoholics shouldn't miss **Chocolates Paria** (☎411-8860; www.chocolatesdeparia.com.ve; US$1; ⏲9am-5pm Mon-Sat), where you can tour the small-scale organic shade-grown cacao plantation and nibble on samples of varying concentration. Tours are available in German, English and French. Take a *por puesto* (US$0.05, 15 minutes) to Hacienda Bukare.

Playa Medina

Crescent-shaped Playa Medina is fringed by tall palms and has gentle surf perfect for swimming. There's no camping permitted, and the only beachside lodging is pricey, so it's better as a day trip, which can be done very easily from Río Caribe. In summer it's packed with vacationing locals; food vendors fill the beach and it can feel a long way from paradise.

Playa Pui Puy

Beautiful Playa Pui Puy has free camping plus several simple *posadas* and restaurants. It's an enormous stretch of perfect sand backed by palm trees and mountains.

Sleeping

Posada Rincón de Pui Puy GUESTHOUSE **$**
(☎0414-942-3625; Playa Pui Puy; r per person US$1.50, with full board US$3; ❄) This charming *posada* right on the beach has panoramic bay views from its patio and 20 colorful rooms ranging from tiny to large, the best of which have their own huge balconies.

Playa Querepare

Gorgeous and remote Playa Querepare is best known for the enormous sea turtles that nest here from April to August. A conservation project collects the eggs in a beachside hatchery, and it's possible to arrange trips to see the turtles making their way to the sea at night.

Sleeping

Campamento Querepare LODGE **$**
(☎0212-237-2648, 0245-261-4419; www.naturaraid.com; Playa Querepare; r incl full board US$4) This rustic lodge right on the beach has 13 basic cabanas and rooms with mosquito nets. Arrange in advance for a full-board package through Natura Raid. There is no electricity in turtle-nesting season.

San Juan de Las Galdonas

The seaside village of San Juan de Las Galdonas has especially fine beaches.

Sleeping

Posada Las Tres Carabelas GUESTHOUSE **$**
(☎0294-411-2265; lastrescarabelas3@gmail.com; San Juan de las Galdonas; r per person incl half-board US$5) This rustic *posada* sits spectacularly on top of a cliff high above the beach, providing gorgeous views over the sea. It has 14 good fan-cooled rooms. There's also a restaurant here that serves delicious dishes – try the sublime fish soup.

Getting There & Away

It's easiest to visit beaches by boat from Río Caribe; the road to Playa Medina is bad, it's tortuous to Pui Puy, and does not extend beyond San Juan de Unare. Return fares per boatload (up to 12 people) are US$7 to Playa Medina (25 minutes) and US$12 to Playa Pui Puy (40 minutes), US$20 to San Juan de las Galdonas or US$30 to Santa Isabel (2½ hours).

From the southeastern end of Río Caribe, opposite the gas station, infrequent *por puesto* pickup trucks run Monday to Saturday morning to the villages of Medina (US$0.05), Pui Puy (US$0.10) and San Juan de Las Galdonas (US$0.75, 1½ hours). They don't get as far as the beaches of Medina and Pui Puy; you'll need to walk for a half-hour (about 2.5km) to get the rest of the way, though locals sometimes run *mototaxis*. Río Caribe *posadas* can also arrange drivers or boat tours.

From the town of Güiria, on the far end of Península de Paria, there used to be a regular ferry connection from the Port of Spain in Trinidad and Tobago, but this was not running at the time of research. However, it's likely that determined travelers will eventually find a passage to Trinidad here if they are prepared to wait around in this small and rather desolate town.

ISLA DE MARGARITA

0295 / POP 462,000

While Isla de Margarita itself certainly has some of the country's best beaches and enjoys a dramatic, mountainous interior to boot, its unchecked development, traffic-clogged roads and creeping urban sprawl has made something of a mockery of its tropical paradise image. Still trading on its '80s and '90s reputation as a jet-set destination, the reality is disappointing today, and we advise beach lovers to head to Península de Paria, Los Roques or Puerto Colombia rather than here. That said, direct air connections to Caracas make it easy to get here, hotels are plentiful and cheap, and tourist infrastructure is far more developed than elsewhere in the country.

The urban sprawl around the island's largest town, Porlamar, is the favored haunt of holidaying Venezuelans and is full of glitzy shops, huge hotels and beach bars. By far the best bits of the island are to be found elsewhere – the beach towns of El Yaque and Juangriego, the inland mountains and the largely untouched Península de Macanao are the real highlights of any visit here.

Getting There & Away

AIR

Most travelers arrive by air at **Aeropuerto Internacional del Caribe General Santiago Mariño** (PMV; 400-5057; www.aeropuerto-margarita.gob.ve). Most international flights here have been cancelled due to low demand, but there are still domestic connections to Caracas, Barcelona and Puerto Ordaz. There are no buses servicing the airport. An official taxi stand covers the entire island at fixed prices.

BOAT

Isla de Margarita has links with the mainland cities of Puerto La Cruz and Cumaná from the ferry terminal, Punta de Piedras (29km west of Porlamar). From side-by-side terminals in Puerto La Cruz, government-owned **Conferry** (0501-2663-3779; www.conferry.com; Av Llano Adentro) and **Gran Cacique/Naviarca** (0281-263-0935; www.grancacique.com.ve; Prolongación Paseo Colón; 8am-noon & 2-6pm Mon-Fri, 8am-2pm Sat) run daily departures. Both charge around US$1 per passenger and US$2 per car, and take about 4½ hours. Check websites for exact dates and times.

Small buses regularly shuttle from Punta de Piedras to Porlamar (US$0.10); taxis to El Yaque are US$1.50 and US$3 for Juangriego.

Porlamar

0295 / POP 101,500

Porlamar is Margarita's main city, but it's far more of a place to get through than visit. Despite this, some travelers stop over here on their way through to elsewhere on the island. Tree-shaded Plaza Bolívar is Porlamar's historic center, but the city has expanded eastward, merging with Los Robles and Pampatar to form an ugly scar across this section of the island. Porlamar is unsafe at night; avoid walking the streets after dark.

Sleeping & Eating

Casa Lutecia B&B $

(263-8526; Campos btwn Cedeño & Marcano; d/ste incl breakfast US$4/6;) Your best bet in Porlamar, this Mediterranean-style *posada* has adobe-colored walls, a Spanish tile roof and a courtyard of brilliant bougainvillea. Comfortable rooms sport mosquito nets and some have ceiling fans plus air-con. The rooftop pool is heavenly. French is spoken.

Hotel Jinama HOTEL $

(261-7186; Mariño btwn Maneiro & Zamora; r from US$3;) A simple and cheerful hotel, with in-room fridges and cable TV making up for thinnish mattresses. Also has a pleasant common area overlooking the street.

Restaurant Punto Criollo VENEZUELAN $$

(Igualdad 19 btwn Fraternidad & Fajardo; mains US$1-2; 10:30am-10:30pm;) A large, no-nonsense Venezuelan restaurant with a lengthy bit-of-everything menu, smartly bow-tied waiters and a long drinks list.

Getting There & Around

A **minibus station** (Velásquez btwn Buenaventura & Meneses), four blocks west of Plaza Bolívar, serves western destinations including El Yaque (hourly until 6pm), Punta de Piedras (very frequent) and Macanao (when full), all for tiny amounts.

Minibuses for Pampatar, Juangriego and Playa El Agua depart from stops along the first and second blocks north of Plaza Bolívar.

El Yaque

0295 / POP 1500

Just south of the airport, and with a guarded entrance, El Yaque enjoys tranquil waters and steady winds that are perfect for **windsurfing** and **kitesurfing**.

Isla de Margarita

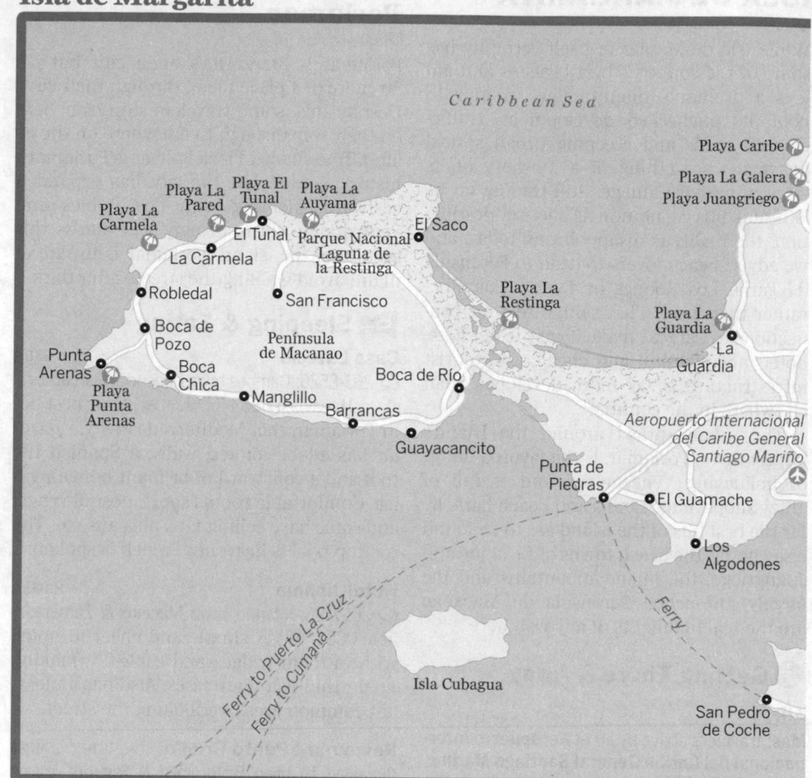

Several professional outfits on the beachfront offer windsurf rental (per hour/day US$0.50/4). Lessons (in a variety of languages) average US$3 per hour, or US$25 for an advanced course of 10 hours. Kitesurfing lessons run about US$5 per hour.

Taxis from the airport cost US$1.50 from Punta de Piedras. Hourly minibuses run from Porlamar (US$0.10).

Sleeping & Eating

Pricier hotels, bars and restaurants are clustered along the beach at the east end of town. Kiosks sell very cheap *arepas* and empanadas.

★Stevie Wonderland BOUTIQUE HOTEL **$$**
(0414-790-5050, 872-6052; www.steviewonderland.com; r incl breakfast from US$9;) This wonderful little German-run place is traveler favorite and is streets ahead of the local competition, despite its groan-worthy name. Its rooms are pristine and stylishly decorated, and the location is great, just a short wander from El Yaque beach. The nine rooms share access to a pool and wonderful garden, and the breakfasts are superb.

Surfhotel Jump'n Jibe GUESTHOUSE **$$$**
(263-8396; www.jumpnjibe.com; Principal s/n; r/tr incl breakfast US$28/38;) Of several hotels fronting onto El Yaque beach, this cool, relaxed choice is one of the best. It has 17 sparkling rooms (including one apartment), a palm-filled garden and terrific sea views (the best have balconies). A small terrace overlooks the beach area.

Juangriego

0295 / POP 34,000

One of the nicest and most low-key beach towns on the island, Juangriego is famous for its burning sunsets. Set on the edge of a

dramatic bay in the north of the island, it's a relaxing place to hang out on the beach, with rustic fishing boats, visiting yachts and pelicans. Nearby beach options are Playa La Galera, within easy walking distance and favored by locals, and the lovely Playa Caribe, 10 minutes away by taxi. When the sun sets over the peaks of Macanao far off on the horizon, the hillside **Fortín de la Galera** (dawn-dusk) FREE is the place to watch the blazing show.

Por puestos only arrive from Porlamar, so take a taxi from Punta de Piedras (US$3) or the airport (US$2).

Sleeping & Eating

Curiously, one of the best places to eat inexpensively is at the bus terminal (a 10-minute walk from the beach), which has a dozen food stalls. Numerous good seafood restaurants can be found along the beach.

Hotel Patrick GUESTHOUSE $
(253-6218; El Fuerte s/n; s/d/tr US$5/7/9;) Not far from the beach, Hotel Patrick is a perennial favorite, run by a friendly and voluble Irishman and his Venezuelan wife. There are nine colorful and attractive rooms (those upstairs have fantastic views toward the sunset from the balcony), plus a good hangout area with tables, sofas, hammocks, a pool table, a plunge pool and a popular bar.

El Caney GUESTHOUSE $
(253-5059; elcaney1@hotmail.com; Guevara 17; s/d/tr/q US$4/5/6/7;) El Caney is a colorful *posada* run by a Peruvian-Canadian couple. There's a shared kitchen, and nice touches include a palm-thatched terrace out front and a plunge pool with waterfall.

Around the Island

Isla de Margarita has some 50 beaches large enough to deserve a name, not to mention a number of other anonymous stretches of sand. Sadly, today nearly all the best beaches are built up with restaurants, bars and other facilities, but even though the island is no longer a virgin paradise, you can still search out a relatively deserted spot if you look hard enough.

At **Playa La Restinga**, breeze by motorboat (half /one-hour tour US$5/10 per five-person boat) through the narrow mangrove tunnels and open lagoons of this national park – watch for the strong currents – and have the driver pick you up later at the beach. The Macanao mountain views are divine. Bird-watching is best in the morning; seafood and beer are available at the dock.

Candy-striped colonial houses front the shaded swimming cove of **Playa Zaragoza**. Stay overnight at the gorgeous **Posada Atlantic** (258-0061; www.posadaatlantic.com; Blvd Pedro González s/n, Playa Zaragoza; r BsF300-350, apt BsF650), a boutique inn awash in colors. It features a good restaurant that serves breakfast and lunch (mains from BsF62).

Playa La Pared is a gorgeous crescent of golden sand with a good swimming beach. A cute thatch-roofed restaurant overlooks the water.

Playa El Agua is Margarita's busiest stretch of sand, though its tall waves are better for surfing than swimming. During holidays, the beach is crammed with visitors. It's generally an upmarket place, but there are some budget options in the backstreets.

Other popular beaches include **Playa Guacuco** and **Playa Manzanillo**. Perhaps Margarita's finest beach is **Playa Puerto Cruz**, which arguably has the island's widest, whitest stretch of sand and isn't yet overdeveloped. **Playa Parguito**, next to Playa El Agua, has strong waves good for surfing, with rentals available. If you want to escape from people, head for **Península de Macanao**, the wildest part of the island, where there are only a few settlements and almost no development.

GUAYANA

The southeastern region of Guayana (not to be confused with the country Guyana) showcases Venezuela at its exotic best. The area is home to the world's highest waterfall, Salto Ángel; the impossibly lush Parque Nacional Canaima; the wildlife-rich Orinoco Delta (Delta del Orinoco) and Río Caura; the Venezuelan Amazon and La Gran Sabana (The Great Savanna) where flat-topped *tepui* mountains lord over rolling grasslands. Visitors often spend an entire trip in this area of the country.

The majority of the country's indigenous groups live in Guayana, including the Warao, the Pemón and the Yanomami, which constitute about 10% of the region's total population.

Ciudad Bolívar

☎0285

The proud capital of Venezuela's largest state, Ciudad Bolívar has an illustrious history as a center of the independence struggle, and wears its status proudly. The Casco Historico (historic center) is one of the country's finest – a gorgeous ensemble of brightly painted colonial buildings, shady squares and the fine Paseo Orinoco – overlooking the country's greatest river. Travelers on their way through to Angel Falls and the Parque Nacional Canaima are usually glad to have made a stopover here, though the town's charm is limited once you stray beyond the old town and the magnificent Paseo Orinoco.

Simón Bolívar came here in 1817, soon after the town had been liberated from Spanish control, and set up base for the military operations that led to the final stage of the War of Independence. The town was made the provisional capital of the yet-to-be-liberated country. The Angostura Congress convened here in 1819 and gave birth to Gran Colombia, a unified republic comprising Venezuela, Colombia and Ecuador.

The historic center clears out after dark and everything is closed on Sunday. Walking alone at night is not recommended.

Sights

The colonial heart of the city is **Plaza Bolívar**. The lively waterfront, **Paseo Orinoco**, is lined with street vendors and old arcaded houses, some of which go back to the days of Simón Bolívar. From the Río Orinoco shoreline or viewpoints in the city, you can see the appropriately named island **Piedra del Medio** (Rock in the Middle).

Airplane of Jimmie Angel LANDMARK

Standing in front of the airport terminal is the restored airplane of gold-seeker Jimmie Angel, who landed atop what was eventually named Salto Ángel (Angel Falls) in 1937, and couldn't take off again. The plane he made his historic journey in was removed from the mountaintop by the Venezuelan military in 1970.

Museo de Arte Moderno Jesús Soto MUSEUM

(☎632-0518; www.jr-soto.com; cnr Avs Germania & Briceño Iragorry; ⏰9:30am-5:30pm Tue-Fri, 10am-5pm Sat & Sun) FREE This excellent museum has an extensive collection of kinetic works by internationally renowned artist Jesús Soto, as well as temporary exhibits. It's in the new town and most easily reached by taxi.

Tours

Ciudad Bolívar is the main departure point for tours to Canaima (for Salto Ángel), as well as for the Río Caura. A three-day all-inclusive tour to Salto Ángel runs about US$200 to US$300. One-day tours to Canaima with a Salto Ángel overflight and tour of the lagoon cost around US$120 (minimum four people).

Almost all operators broker Salto Ángel tours through either Excursiones Kavac or Tiuna Tours, both based in Canaima, so often there is relatively little difference in price and quality between agencies. Nearly all *posadas* in town can arrange tours.

Gekko Tours TOUR

(☎632-3223, 0414-854-5146; www.gekkotours-venezuela.de; airport terminal) Run by Posada

La Casita, Gecko Tours is a responsible full-service agency offering a wide range of tours and flights across the region and the country, specializing in Canaima, Kavac, Roraima and Gran Sabana tours.

Sapito Tours TOUR
(☎0414-854-8234; www.sapitotours.com; airport terminal) Representative of Bernal Tours from Canaima; runs all manner of excursions, treks and tours in Gran Sabana and beyond.

Excursiones Salto Ángel TOUR
(☎632-1904; www.saltoangel.com.ve; Libertad 31) Offers the standard budget-range tours to Salto Ángel and Gran Sabana.

Sleeping

Ciudad Bolívar has a number of lovely *posadas*.

★Posada Don Carlos GUESTHOUSE $
(☎0424-958-8682; www.posada-doncarlos.com; Boyacá 26; hammock or outdoor bed US$2, r with fan/air-con US$4/6; ❄@📶) A wonderfully restored and atmospheric colonial mansion with two ample patios, a kitchen and an antique bar, this *posada* is clean and makes meals on request. Air-con rooms have towering ceilings and enormous wood doors, while owner Martin leads sports-fishing and Río Caura tours, and can organize Salto Ángel trips as well. Safe parking is also available.

Posada Doña Carol GUESTHOUSE $
(☎634-0989, 0426-999-5724; www.hosteltrail.com/posadadonacarol; Libertad 28; r with fan & shared bathroom US$2, with air-con US$4; ❄@📶) This friendly, kitsch-filled establishment in the heart of town has five simple rooms, and use of the kitchen, though Doña Carol's home-cooked meals are amazing (and inexpensive). Downstairs rooms have no exterior windows, but one of the large upstairs rooms has a breezy patio.

Ciudad Bolívar

Activities, Courses & Tours
1 Excursiones Salto Ángel ... C2

Sleeping
2 Posada Amor Patrio ... B2
3 Posada Casa Grande de Angostura ... B2
4 Posada Don Carlos ... B2
5 Posada Doña Carol ... C2

Eating
6 Boulevard ... C2
7 En Casa de Wannia ... B3
8 Tostadas Juancito's ... C2

Ciudad Bolívar

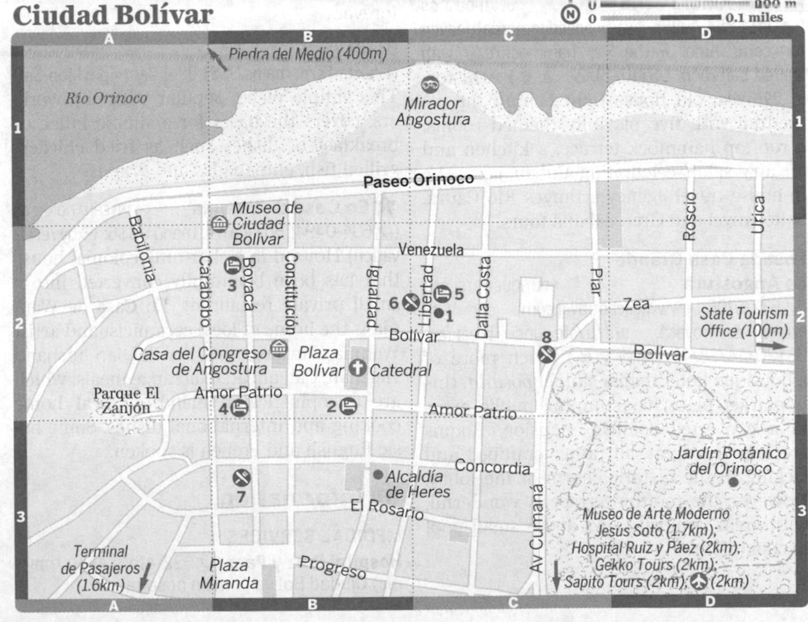

CIUDAD GUYANA: GATEWAY TO LA GRAN SABANA

Officially 'founded' in 1961 to serve as an industrial center for the region, Ciudad Guayana sits on two rivers, the Río Orinoco and Río Caroní, and encompasses the unlikely twin cities of Puerto Ordaz and San Félix. The colonial town of San Félix, on the eastern side of the Caroní, is a working-class city with a historical center, but little tourist infrastructure and a reputation for being unsafe. Puerto Ordaz is a wealthy and modern prefab city, with a large middle-class population. Neither is, frankly, of much interest to visitors, but it's a useful transport hub, being the gateway to Venezuela's spectacular Gran Sabana. Travelers may need to stay overnight here between bus rides south or flights to Caracas. Your best bet for accommodations is **La Casa del Lobo** (961-6286, 0414-871-9339; www.lobo-tours.de; Zambia 2, Manzana 39, Villa Africana; r US$3;), the city's long-established German-run backpacker option. From the city's bus station, there are regular buses to Santa Elena de Uairén (nine to 11 hours, US$7), as well as connections to Ciudad Bolívar (US$0.50, 1½ hours) and Caracas (US$8, 11 hours), although most visitors fly the last route.

Posada La Casita GUESTHOUSE $$
(617-0832, 0414-856-2925; www.posada-la-casita.com; Av Ligia Pulido, Urbanización 24 de Julio; camping & hammock per person US$11 s/d/tr/q US$20/26/30/34;) Lounge by the pool at this relaxing rural self-contained compound just outside the city. There's easy access (free 24-hour pickup from the airport or bus station, and a shuttle to town), a sociable atmosphere and excellent rooms, all with private facilities. Drinks and good meals are available on-site, and Salto Ángel tours can be arranged.

Posada Amor Patrio GUESTHOUSE $$
(0414-854-4925; www.posadaamorpatrioaventura.com; Amor Patrio 30; hammock/d/tr with shared bathroom US$10/19/27;) A historic 275-year-old house right behind the cathedral, with five playfully themed rooms, a rooftop hammock terrace, a kitchen and an airy salon celebrating Cuban jazz. The in-house travel agency arranges Río Caura, Salto Ángel and Gran Sabana tours.

Posada Casa Grande de Angostura BOUTIQUE HOTEL $$$
(632-6706; www.cacaotravel.com; cnr Venezuela & Boyacá; s/d/tr/ste incl breakfast US$20/24/28/40;) Much more of a boutique hotel than a simple *posada*, this upmarket place has stunning public areas in a converted colonial mansion. Rooms are less of a treat, all rather cramped and lacking in the historic charm of the lobby. However, the rooftop terrace is wonderful, with great Orinoco views and a small pool to cool off in.

Eating & Drinking

Ciudad Bolívar has very slim pickings when it comes to eating. Street food can be had along the riverfront throughout the day and early evening, but the old town clears out after dark and you have very little on offer: consider booking evening meals with your *posada*.

Tostadas Juancito's VENEZUELAN $
(cnr Avs Cumaná & Bolívar; arepas US$0.50, menú US$2; 7am-6pm Mon-Sat) Hang out with the locals at this popular *arepera* and snack bar that has occupied this busy street corner forever.

Boulevard VENEZUELAN $
(Libertad s/n; mains US$1-2; 7am-4pm Mon-Sat) This simple place, popular with city workers, covers the bases for a simple lunch or breakfast of dishes such as fried chicken, grilled fish, empanadas and *arepas*.

★ **En Casa de Wannia** INTERNATIONAL $$
(634-0494; Boyacá 40; menú US$6; by reservation) Housed in a charming colonial house that has been beautifully converted into a small private restaurant, En Casa de Wannia is the home of local ceramicist and artist Wannia Chiriboga and her Belgian husband Herman. Call ahead to arrange meals, which are a sophisticated blend of local home cooking and international dishes. Some basic English and French is spoken.

Information

MEDICAL SERVICES

Hospital Ruiz y Páez (632-4146; Av Germania) Ciudad Bolívar's main hospital.

Getting There & Away

AIR

The **airport** (☎0285-632-4978; Av Jesús Soto) is 2km southeast of the riverfront and linked to the city center by local buses. There are normally daily flights to Caracas, but these have been unreliable recently, and many visitors now fly to Puerto Ordaz and take a taxi to Ciudad Bolívar. Most flights from the airport are charters to Canaima, run by various travel agencies.

BUS

The **Terminal de Pasajeros** (cnr Avs República & Sucre) is 2km south of the center. To get there, take the westbound *buseta* marked 'Terminal' from Paseo Orinoco. The Rodovías terminal is also here; its Caracas-bound buses arrive at a convenient downtown terminal instead of the Terminal de Oriente.

Frequent buses go to Caracas (US$2.50, nine hours); most depart in the evening. Direct buses service Valencia (US$3.50, 10½ hours) via the shorter Los Llanos route that bypasses Caracas. Take these to go to Venezuela's northwest or the Andes without connections in Caracas.

Buses depart several times a day to Puerto Ayacucho (US$3.50, 10½ to 12 hours), but only some have air-con. To avoid the longer 12-hour journey, take a *directo* bus. To Puerto Ordaz (US$0.50, 1½ hours), buses depart every 15 to 30 minutes, and a half-dozen daily departures go to Santa Elena de Uairén (US$4, 10 to 12 hours).

TOURING THE ORINOCO DELTA

Roaring howler monkeys welcome the dawn. Piranhas clamp onto anything that bleeds. Screaming clouds of parrots gather at dusk, and weaving bats gobble insects under the blush of a million stars. For wildlife-viewing on the water's edge, it's hard to outshine the Orinoco Delta (Delta del Orinoco).

A deep-green labyrinth of islands, channels and mangrove swamps engulfing nearly 30,000 sq km – the size of Belgium – this is one of the world's great river deltas and a mesmerizing region to explore. Mixed forest blankets most of the land, which includes a variety of palms. Of these, the moriche palm is the most typical and important, as it is the traditional staple food for the delta's inhabitants, the Warao people, and provides material for their crafts, tools, wine and houses.

The best time to see the wildlife in the delta is in the dry season (January to May), when wide, orange, sandy beaches emerge along the shores of the channels. In the rainy months (August and September), when rivers are full, boat travel is easier, but the wildlife disperses and is more difficult to see.

All-inclusive three-day tours average US$150 to US$200. The recommended companies listed here have their own *campamentos* (camps).

Campamento Oridelta (☎0286-961-5526, 0414-868-2121; www.deltaorinoko.com.ve; per person incl full board & transfers US$40) Runs trips in the Río Grande area of the Delta del Orinoco, with a *campamento* in Piacoa. The owner, Roger Ruffenach, is an authority on the wildlife of the delta, speaks English, German and French, and personally guides all the trips, which never have more than 10 guests.

Cooperativa Osibu XIV (☎721-3840; campamentomaraisa@hotmail.com; cnr Mariño & Pativilca; per person incl full board & transfers US$35-45) This longstanding family-owned business conducts tours to San Francisco de Guayo, in the far eastern part of the delta. It's a four-hour boat ride to their *cabaña* camp with beds. Minimum six people.

Orinoco Eco Camp (☎0414-091-4844; www.orinoco-eco-camp.com; per person incl full board & transfers US$30) Within the Reserva Nacional de Fauna Silvestre Gran Morichal; traveler recommended.

Orinoco Queen (☎0414-871-9339, 0286-961-6286; www.lobo-tours.de; per person incl full board & transfers US$35) This German-run camp is a new addition to the Orinoco's river lodges and gets great reviews from travelers.

Viajes & Excursiones Turísticas Delta (☎0416-897-2285, 0287-721-0835; www.aventuraturisticadelta.com; Centurión 62, Tucupita; per person incl full board & transfers US$20) One of the least expensive agencies (almost half as much as the others), with a hammock-only *campamento* in Pedernales.

Salto Ángel (Angel Falls)

Salto Ángel is the world's highest waterfall and Venezuela's number-one tourist attraction. Its total height is 979m, with an uninterrupted drop of 807m – about 16 times the height of Niagara Falls. The cascade pours off the towering Auyantepui, one of the largest of the *tepuis*. Salto Ángel is not named, as one might expect, for a divine creature, but for an American bush pilot, Jimmie Angel, who landed his four-seater airplane atop Auyantepui in 1937 while in search of gold. In the local Pémon language the falls are called Parakupá Vená, or 'waterfall of the highest place.'

The waterfall is in a distant, lush wilderness with no road access. The village of Canaima, about 50km northwest, is the major gateway to the falls. Canaima doesn't have an overland link to the rest of the country either, but is accessed by numerous small planes from Ciudad Bolívar and Puerto Ordaz.

A visit to Salto Ángel is normally undertaken in two stages, with Canaima as the stepping-stone. Most tourists fly into Canaima, from where they take a boat to the falls. Most visitors who visit by boat opt to stay overnight in hammocks at one of the camps near the base of the falls. The trip upriver, the surrounding area and the experience of staying at the camp are as memorable as the waterfall itself. An alternative is to take a six-seat Cessna flight over Auyantepui and the falls, which can be done in around 45 minutes from Canaima airport for around US$60 to US$80 per person. If you have time, do both, as the experiences are both unforgettably spectacular and offer very different perspectives on this most extraordinary chunk of nature.

Salto Ángel, Auyantepui, Canaima and the surrounding area lie within the boundaries of the 30,000-sq-km Parque Nacional Canaima. All visitors need to pay a US$1.50 national-park entrance fee at Canaima airport.

RAIN OR SHINE?

The amount of water going over Salto Ángel (Angel Falls) depends on the season, and the contrast can be dramatic. In the dry months (January to May), it can be pretty faint – just a thin ribbon of water fading into mist before it reaches the bottom. Boat access is impossible in the driest months. In the rainy season, particularly in the wettest months (August and September), the waterfall is a spectacular cascade of plummeting water – but you run the risk of rain and of the view being obscured by clouds.

Canaima

☎0286 / POP 1500

The closest population center to Salto Ángel, Canaima is a remote indigenous village that hosts and dispatches a huge number of tourists. Although it's a base to reach Venezuela's number-one natural attraction, Canaima is truly gorgeous as well. The Laguna de Canaima sits at the heart of everything, a broad blue expanse framed by a palm-tree beach, a dramatic series of seven picture-postcard waterfalls and a backdrop of anvil-like *tepuis*. Most tours to Salto Ángel include a short boat trip and hike that allows you to walk behind some of the falls and get the backstage experience of the hammering curtains of water. The color is a curious pinky orange, caused by the high level of tannin from decomposed plants and trees. Do not miss walking up to the viewpoint overlooking the falls, which is truly spectacular.

When swimming, stay close to the main beach – the current can be fierce and a number of drownings have occurred close to the hydroelectric plant and the falls. Ask for advice from locals if you're unsure.

Tours

Almost everyone arrives in Canaima on an all-inclusive tour, as it's not really worth the hassle or negligible savings to do it independently. Moreover, recent fuel rationing here means that it's not a good idea to simply turn up in Canaima without a tour booked.

Angel-Eco Tours ECOTOUR
(☎0424-156-6162; www.angel-ecotours.com) One of the few operators practicing true sustainable tourism within Canaima National Park, this British-run agency is popular with tourists and has an excellent relationship with the local Pemón people. They can assist with all destinations around Canaima, including Salto Ángel visits, the seven- to 12-day trek up Auyantepui, Kamadak Waterfall and the Kamarata Valley.

Parque Nacional Canaima

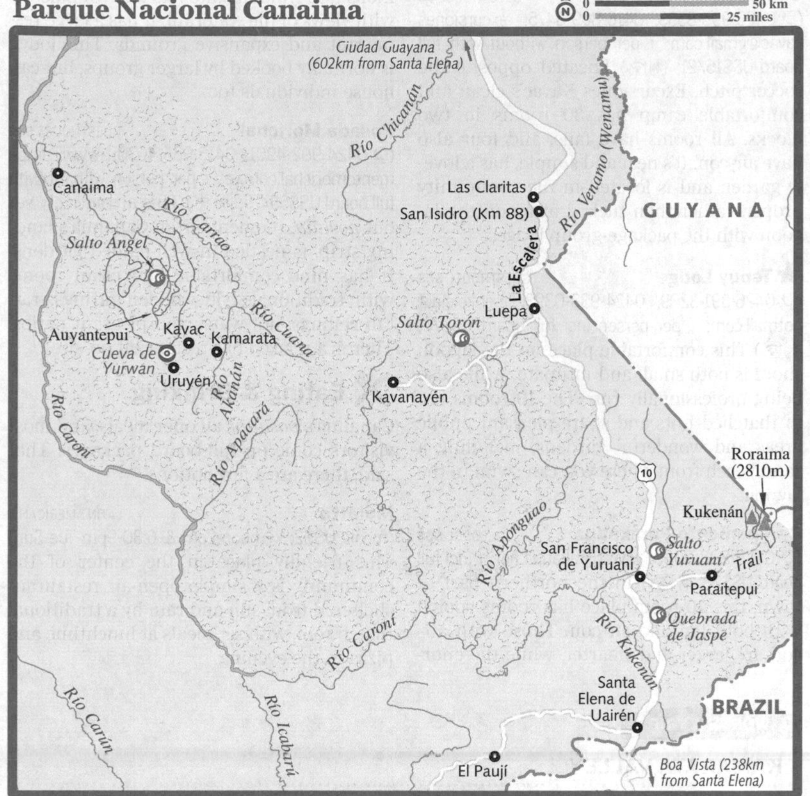

Excursiones Kavac TOUR
(☎0414-385-0165, 0416-285-9919; excursioneskavac@gmail.com) A good agency managed by the indigenous Pemón community, it runs a basic *posada* in Canaima as well as a *campamento* in front of Salto Ángel. It also offers Kamarata Valley tours.

Bernal Tours TOUR
(☎0414-854-8234; www.bernaltours.com) Family-run company based on an island in Laguna de Canaima, where participants stay and eat before and after the tour. Bernal Tours has its *campamento* on Isla Ratoncito, opposite Salto Ángel.

Tiuna Tours TOUR
(☎0286-962-4255, 0416-692-1536; tiunatours@hotmail.com) The cheapest local player, with a large *campamento* in Canaima and another up the Río Carrao at the Río Aonda.

Sleeping

There are a dozen *campamentos* and *posadas* in Canaima. Most are managed by the main tour agencies, all serve meals and will meet you at the airport. Camping on the lagoon is not permitted. Prices given here are very approximate: nearly all people come on multiday packages that include flights, transfers, food, accommodations and the trip to Salto Ángel. Few *posadas* are used to providing simple overnight rates.

Posada Wey Tepuy GUESTHOUSE $
(☎0416-185-7231; r per person with/without meals US$8/15) Wey Tupuy may be rather lacking in charm, with its simple and poorly maintained rooms, but it's nonetheless the cheapest bed in town and provides some of the lowest priced meals for guests. It's opposite the old school in the south part of the village.

Campamento Churúm GUESTHOUSE $$
(☎0426-995-8533, 0416-899-3475; excursiones kavac@gmail.com; r per person without/with full board US$15/21; ❄📶) Located opposite the soccer pitch, Excursiones Kavac's clean and comfortable camp has 30 rooms in two blocks. All rooms have fans, and four also have air-con. It's neat and simple, has a lovely garden and is located in the community proper, rather than tucked away on the lagoon with the package-group lodges.

★**Tepuy Lodge** GUESTHOUSE $$$
(☎0426-391-3209, 0424-938-0393; seriko.c.a@hotmail.com; r per person incl full board US$70; ❄📶) This comfortable place on the lagoon shore is both small and intimate, while also being professionally run. The 10 rooms are in thatched huts and share pleasant public areas and wonderful gardens, including a sand beach from where you can swim in the lagoon.

Campamento Parakaupa LODGE $$$
(☎0289-808-9080; www.parakaupa.net; r incl full board US$65; ❄📶) In the northern part of town, this 20-room place has rooms cooled with both fan and air-con. Those with air-con are larger and smarter, while the enormous honeymoon suite has its own balcony with views of the waterfall. It has a large restaurant and expansive grounds. This lodge is normally booked by larger groups, but can house individuals too.

Posada Morichal GUESTHOUSE $$$
(☎0424-902-4901, 0416-985-4630; www.campamentomorichal.com.ve; r per person without/with full board US$55/75; ❄📶) This attractively set out *posada,* moments from Canaima's landing strip, is nestled in well-tended gardens. It has nine comfortable and clean rooms with traditional-style wooden fittings, rattan ceilings, hot water and pleasant patios. There's a relaxed bar-restaurant on-site.

Eating & Drinking

Canaima's *posadas* all offer meals, and most visitors come on full-board packages. That said, there are a few options.

Mulatto LATIN AMERICAN $
(meals US$2; ⏲noon-2pm & 6:30-9pm Tue-Sun) This friendly place in the center of the community is a simple open-air restaurant sheltered from sun and rain by a traditional thatch roof, with set meals at lunchtime and pizza in the evening.

WORTH A TRIP

KAMARATA VALLEY

The Kamarata Valley, on the other side of massive Auyantepui, is a wonder-world of massive waterfalls, traditional indigenous settlements and virgin rainforest, only accessible by air taxi. Come here to explore the Parque Nacional Canaima without the crowds; it's even possible to hike to Salto Ángel.

Kamarata Kamarata is the chief settlement on the eastern side of Auyantepui, an old Pemón village on the Río Akanán and a growing access point for Salto Ángel. There are a few simple places to stay and eat in town. Most travelers stay at the nearby tourist camp at Kavac, a two-hour walk from here, or a short drive on a dirt road by the town's service jeep.

Kavac Consisting of 20-odd *churuatas* (traditional circular palm-thatched huts) built in the traditional style, Kavac resembles a manicured Pemón settlement. It sits at the bottom of Auyantepui with some fabulous views toward the summit. The area's major attraction is the spectacular **Cueva de Kavac**, not a cave but a deep gorge with a waterfall plunging into it. There's a natural pool at the foot of the waterfall, which you reach by swimming upstream in the narrow canyon.

Uruyén This newer community-owned *campamento* is at the foot of gorgeous Auyantepui, by a small river with a great swimming hole. Uruyén's stellar attraction is the easy hike to the **Cueva de Yurwan**, a breathtaking river gorge that culminates in a spectacular waterfall an hour's walk from the camp.

Angel-Eco Tours (p1008) and Osprey Expeditions (p980) in Caracas, Excursiones Kavac (p1009) in Canaima and Gekko Tours (p1004) in Ciudad Bolívar can help with travel planning and tours of all lengths, including the epic 11-day trek over Auyantepui to Salto Ángel.

Mentanai PUB FOOD $
(mains US$1-2; ⏲6-11:30pm Fri-Sun, longer hours Aug-Sep) This little burger and sandwich grill inside Campamento Churúm in the heart of Canaima's indigenous community has a pool table and a bar serving beer and Cuba Libres.

Bar Morichal BAR
(⏲6-11pm) This is as raucous as Canaima's nightlife gets: a pleasant bar with a spectacular view of the waterfalls on the lagoon where locals and tourists alike gather at sundown to drink cold beers and cocktails.

ℹ Information

There is an internet cafe in the center of Canaima, and most of the *posadas* have some form of wi-fi for guests.

Tienda Canaima (☎0414-884-0940) Near the airport, this expensive shop stocks the biggest inventory of groceries (including ice cream), toiletries, maps and souvenirs. It also changes US dollars and euros at an intermediary rate and has pay phones available.

ℹ Getting There & Away

Several regional carriers fly between Canaima and Ciudad Bolívar on a semi-regular or charter basis, and there are also flights from Puerto Ordaz. However, most of these are sold as part of a package deal, so it's hard to give flight-only prices. Very annoyingly, there is no longer any air connection between Canaima and Santa Elena de Uairén, which means you'll need to backtrack to Puerto Ordaz and head down by road to the Brazilian border if you plan to continue to La Gran Sabana.

GRAN SABANA

A wide open grassland that seems suspended from endless sky, the Gran Sabana invites poetic description. Scores of waterfalls appear at every turn, and *tepuis,* the savanna's trademark table mountains, sweep across the horizon, their mesas both haunting and majestic. More than 100 of these plateaus dot the vast region from the Colombian border in the west to Guyana and Brazil in the east, but most are here in the Gran Sabana. One of the *tepuis,* Roraima, can be climbed and it's an extraordinary natural adventure.

The largest town is isolated little Santa Elena de Uairén, close to the Brazilian border. The rest of the sparsely populated region is inhabited mostly by the 30,000 indigenous Pemón people, who live traditional lifestyles in nearly 300 scattered villages.

ℹ Getting Around

The Ciudad Guayana–Santa Elena de Uairén Hwy provides access to this fascinating land, but public transportation on this road is infrequent, making individual sightseeing inconvenient and time consuming. Tours from Ciudad Bolívar or Santa Elena de Uairén are far more convenient and highly recommended. Fuel rationing in this part of the country also makes driving here challenging – be sure to plan ahead with the help of an agency or local *posada* if you plan to drive.

Passengers taking the bus from Santa Elena de Uairén to Ciudad Guayana and points beyond should note that there's a major security checkpoint along the highway near Upata, about an hour before Ciudad Guayana. Be prepared to claim your luggage for a full baggage search, plus the inconvenience of an extra hour added to your journey.

Roraima

A stately table mountain towering into churning clouds, Roraima (2810m) lures hikers and nature-lovers looking for Venezuela at its natural and rugged best. Unexplored until 1884, and studied extensively by botanists ever since, the stark landscape contains strange rock formations and graceful arches, ribbon waterfalls, glittering quartz deposits and carnivorous plants. The frequent mist only accentuates the otherworldly feel.

Although it's one of the easier *tepuis* to climb and no technical skills are required, the trek is long and demanding. However, anyone who's reasonably fit and determined can reach the top. Be prepared for wet weather, nasty *puri puris* (invisible biting insects) and frigid nights at the summit. In recent years with the decline in international travelers, Roraima has marketed itself more to domestic travelers. Sadly this has led to a noticeable increase in littering and disrespect for the special status of this incredible place. If you come here, do your bit and collect any trash you find, and be sure to emphasize the importance of responsible tourism to anyone else in your group who might not be aware of the subject.

Climbing Roraima

Roraima lies approximately 47km east of the El Dorado–Santa Elena de Uairén Hwy, just east of the town of San Francisco de Yuruaní. The hamlet of Paraitepui, 26km east of San Francisco, is the usual starting point for the trip, and hikers must sign in at the Inparques office there before setting out.

You can organize a compulsory Pemón guide in Santa Elena de Uairén, San Francisco de Yuruaní or Paraitepui. Most people opt to go on an organized tour from Santa Elena de Uairén, where agencies contract guides and porters and arrange for meals, transportation and equipment. Though it costs less to organize a trip from San Francisco de Yuruaní or Paraitepui, remember that in terms of quality, you generally get what you pay for; some travelers have complained about hiring guides there who were careless with safety, unknowledgeable or inebriated.

The trip to the top normally takes two to three days (total net walking time is about 12 hours up and 10 hours down). There are several campsites (with water) on the way. They are Río Tek (four hours from Paraitepui), Río Kukenán (30 minutes further), and at the foot of Roraima at the so-called *campamento base* (base camp), three hours uphill from the Río Kukenán. The steep, tough, four-hour ascent from the base camp to the top is the most spectacular (yet demanding) part of the hike.

Once atop Roraima, you'll camp in one of the dozen or so *hoteles* (hotels) – semi-sheltered camping spots under rock overhangs. The guides coordinate which group sleeps where.

The scenery is a moonscape sculpted by the wind and rain, with gorges, creeks, pink beaches, lookout points and gardens filled with unique flowering plants. An eerie, shifting fog often snakes across the mountaintop. While guides may have seemed superfluous on the clear trails below, they are helpful on the labyrinthine plateau. If you stay for two nights on the top you will have time to hike with your guide to some of the attractions, including **El Foso** (a crystalline pool in a massive sinkhole), the **Punto Triple** (the triborder of Venezuela, Brazil and Guyana), **Bahia de Cristal** (a small valley brimming with quartz) and the stunning viewpoint of **La Ventana** (the Window).

The *tepui* is an ecologically delicate area. Visitors need to pack out all garbage, including human waste, and collecting quartz is strictly forbidden. Inparques searches bags at the end of the hike, and will fine you for collecting souvenirs.

Make sure to pack good rain gear, extra socks, warm clothes, insect repellent, plastic bags (essential for keeping wet and dry clothes separate), flip flops and a camera.

Santa Elena de Uairén

☎0289 / POP 30,000

A bustling low-key border town where dusty 4WD drivers wave at their friends, Santa Elena is the primary transit point for treks to Roraima and the first stop in Venezuela for travelers entering by land from Brazil. This small, friendly town is also a good base for exploring the Gran Sabana, though accommodations, food and tour prices are far higher here than elsewhere in the country, with the local economy calibrated more to neighbouring Brazil than the distant nearest cities of Venezuela.

Though the city is quite safe, it's also a brazen black-market and smuggling hub. Gas prices in Brazil are almost 30 times higher than those in Venezuela, which means that there is serious money to be made. As a result there's a strong police and military presence around the town, but it shouldn't be anything to worry about as a traveler.

Tours

All Santa Elena tour agencies run one-, two- or three-day jeep tours around the Gran Sabana, with visits to the most interesting sights, mostly waterfalls. Budget between US$70 and US$100 per person per day, depending on group size and whether the tour includes just guide and transportation, or food and accommodations as well.

For most visitors, the main attraction is a Roraima tour, generally offered as an all-inclusive six-day package for US$300 to US$400 per person (you get what you pay for). If you have your own gear and food and don't need a porter, most agencies will organize a guide and transportation to Paraitepui, the starting point for the Roraima trek, for US$150. Check on specifics, including group size, hiker-to-guide ratio and equipment quality before signing up for any Roraima tour.

Most agencies also sell Salto Ángel and Orinoco Delta tours.

Backpacker Tours ADVENTURE TOUR
(☎0414-886-7227, 995-1430; www.backpacker-tours.com; Urdaneta s/n) The local powerhouse, it has the most organized, best equipped and most expensive tours of Roraima and the region. Also rents mountain bikes.

Kamadac ADVENTURE TOUR
(☎0414-094-4341, 995-1408; www.kamadac.de; Urdaneta s/n) A German- and Venezuelan-

owned agency, Kamadac offers staples (Gran Sabana, six-day Roraima climbs) as well as some more adventurous tours (Auyantepui, Akopán Tepui).

Ruta Salvaje ADVENTURE SPORTS
(0414-889-4164, 995-1134; www.rutasalvaje.com; Av Mariscal Sucre s/n) Ruta Salvaje offers Roraima and Gran Sabana tours, plus rafting trips, paragliding and day trips to various sights around the region.

Mystic Tours TOUR
(0424-912-3741, 416-1081; www.mystictours.com.ve; Urdaneta s/n) Operating for more than 20 years, Mystic Tours offers some of the least expensive tours to Roraima, as well as other local tours with a New Age bent.

Nativa Tours Khasen TOURS
(0414-853-7903, 995-1861; www.nativatourskhasen.com; Av Perimetral s/n) Family-run agency with a specialization in bird-watching tours, Nativa Tour Khasen offers regular Roraima trips, tours of Gran Sabana and trips to Salto Ángel as well.

Sleeping

Posada Michelle GUESTHOUSE $
(995-2017; hotelmichelle@cantv.net; Urdaneta s/n; s/d/tr US$5/6/7;) The undisputed backpacker headquarters and the best place to find companions to form a tour group. The 23 rooms have private bathrooms, hot water and fans to cool you down. There's also a basic kitchen. Recently returned Roraima hikers can take advantage of half-day rest and shower (US$2 per room) or shower only (US$0.50) rates before taking the night bus out.

Posada Backpacker Tours GUESTHOUSE $
(995-1415; www.backpacker-tours.com; Urdaneta s/n; dm/s/d/tr US$4/6/7/8; @) This simple but friendly 12-room *posada* in the center of Santa Elena has brightly painted rooms with

Santa Elena de Uairén

Activities, Courses & Tours
Backpacker Tours .... (see 4)
1 Mystic Tours B2
2 Nativa Tours Khasen C2
3 Ruta Salvaje C1

Sleeping
4 Posada Backpacker Tours C2
5 Posada Los Pinos B1
Posada Michelle .... (see 4)

Eating
6 Alfredo's Restaurant C2
7 ServeKilo Nova Opção C3
8 Tienda Naturalista Griselda Luna B3
9 Tumá Serö A2

Santa Elena de Uairén

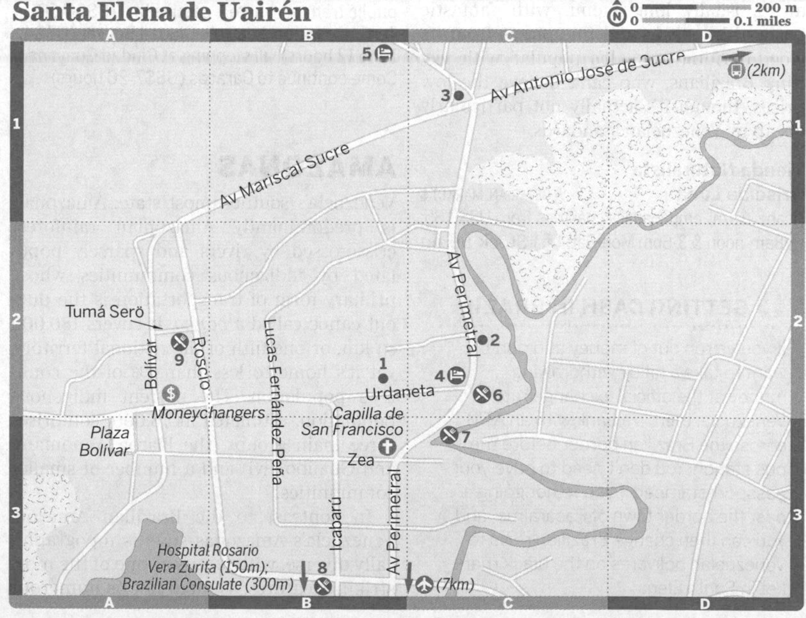

private bathrooms and hot water. It's run by Backpacker Tours, who tend to lodge travelers booked on Roraima treks here.

Posada Los Pinos GUESTHOUSE **$**
(☎0289-995-1524, 0414-886-7227; www.backpacker-tours.com; Los Pinos s/n; s/d/tr US$8/10/12; @🛜🏊) You'll receive a warm welcome at this excellent, super-comfortable option a short walk from the center. Los Pinos has colorful en-suite rooms with fridge and TV, all set in a large garden with a small pool. Mountain bikes can also be hired.

Eating

ServeKilo Nova Opção BRAZILIAN, BUFFET **$**
(Av Perimetral s/n; buffet per kg US$0.50; ⏲11am-3pm; 🖉) For almost two decades, this Brazilian eatery has replenished famished hikers with its scrumptious buffet. Vegetarian options are available.

Tumá Serö VENEZUELAN, INTERNATIONAL **$**
(off Calle Bolívar; menú US$1.50; ⏲7am-8pm) For a cheap meal in a fun atmosphere head to this 'boulevard of food' with dozens of different outlets serving everything from *arepas* to noodles.

Alfredo's Restaurant ITALIAN **$**
(☎995-1628; Av Perimetral s/n; mains US$2-4; ⏲11am-3pm & 6-10pm Tue-Sun; 🖉) Perhaps the best restaurant in town, Alfredo's has an unusually long menu, with fantastic pasta, thick steaks and fine pizzas from its wood-burning oven. It's popular with visiting Brazilians, who can't believe the low prices, though it's actually not particularly cheap by Venezuelan standards.

Tienda Naturalista Griselda Luna VEGETARIAN, MARKET **$**
(Icabarú s/n; empanadas & pastries from US$0.35; ⏲8am-noon & 3-6pm Mon-Sat; 🖉) Stock up on dried fruit and vegetarian protein for the Roraima trek. Awesome wholewheat fruit pastries and natural yogurt are available.

GETTING CASH IN BRAZIL

If you've run out of money and don't want to take a hit by withdrawing money at the official exchange rate in Venezuela, there's a bank with an ATM across the Brazilian border before the bus station. You don't need to have your passport stamped if you're not going past the border town of Pacaraima, and you can then change Brazilian reals to Venezuelan bolívares on the black market in Santa Elena.

Information

Money changers (for US dollars and euros) work the corner of Bolívar and Urdaneta, popularly known as Cuatro Esquinas. Here you'll find some of the best rates in the country – though like anywhere, it's technically illegal. It's safer to ask your *posada* or travel agency to arrange currency exchange.

Hospital Rosario Vera Zurita (☎995-1155; Icabarú) The main hospital in Santa Elena is very basic. If you have a serious complaint, cross the border into Brazil or head for Ciudad Guayana.

Getting There & Away

AIR

Santa Elena's tiny airport is 7km southwest of town, off the road to the Brazilian border. At present there are no scheduled flights here, and even the irregular Cessna service from Canaima, a godsend for travelers not wanting to do the punishingly long overland journey via Ciudad Guyana, is no longer running. Only chartered planes currently land here, so if you're in a group it's worth investigating prices.

BUS & JEEP

The bus terminal is on the Ciudad Guayana Hwy, about 2km east of the town's center. There is no public transport here – catch a taxi (US$0.50). Ten buses depart daily to Ciudad Bolívar (US$4, 10 to 12 hours), all stopping at Ciudad Guayana. Some continue to Caracas (US$7, 20 hours).

AMAZONAS

Venezuela's southernmost state, Amazonas, is predominantly Amazonian rainforest crisscrossed by rivers and sparsely populated by indigenous communities whose primary form of transportation is the dugout canoe called a *bongo*. It covers 180,000 sq km, or one-fifth of the national territory, yet it's home to less than 1% of the country's population. The current indigenous population, estimated at 76,000, comprises three main groups (the Piaroa, Yanomami and Guajibo/Jivi) and a number of smaller communities.

In contrast to the Brazilian Amazon, Venezuela's Amazonas state is topographically diverse, with *tepuis* as one of the most striking features. Though not as numerous

> **GETTING TO BRAZIL**
>
> Both Venezuelan and Brazilian passport formalities are done at the border itself, locally known as La Línea, 15km south of Santa Elena de Uairén. *Por puestos* from Icabarú travel to the bus station in the Brazilian border town of Pacaraima, but you have to commandeer the whole taxi or they won't wait for you while you have your passport stamped at the Venezuelan and Brazilian immigration offices at La Línea. There's no departure tax here. Yellow-fever vaccinations are not required but are recommended.

as those in the Gran Sabana, the *tepuis* give the green carpet of rainforest a distinctive appearance.

At the southernmost part of Amazonas, along the border with Brazil, is the Serranía la Neblina, a scarcely explored mountain range containing the highest South American peaks east of the Andes.

The best time to explore the region is from October to December, when the river level is high enough to navigate but rains have started to ease.

Getting Around

The region has almost no roads, so most transportation is by river or air. Other than a few short hops from Puerto Ayacucho, there's no regular passenger service on the rivers, which makes independent travel difficult, if not impossible. Tour operators in Puerto Ayacucho can take you just about everywhere, however, so this is one place where you pretty much have to put yourself in the hands of an agency.

Puerto Ayacucho

☎0248 / POP 91,000

Walk on the shady side of the street or you'll wilt in the heat of this riverside city. The only significant urban center in Venezuela's Amazon, Puerto Ayacucho is a languid and often rainy place with a slow tempo, frequent power outages and – these days – almost no tourists. Set on a colorful section of the Río Orinoco, just down from the spectacular rapids of Raudales Atures, it's the starting point for adventurous trips into the roadless state of Amazonas.

Sights

For a true sense of the city and its river history, get a bird's-eye view from one of its hills. **Cerro Perico** is a good place to survey the Río Orinoco and the city, and Cerro El Zamoro, commonly known as **El Mirador**, overlooks Orinoco's feisty Raudales Atures rapids.

Museo Etnológico de Amazonas MUSEUM
(Av Río Negro s/n; admission US$0.20; ⌚8:30-11:30am & 2:30-6pm Tue-Fri, 9am-noon & 3:30-6pm Sat) A fascinating display of regional indigenous culture, the Museo Etnológico de Amazonas displays personal items and model-housing replicas from groups including the Piaroa, Guajibo, Ye'kwana and Yanomami.

Mercado Indígena MARKET
(Av Río Negro s/n) Across from the museum, the market sells some indigenous crafts and lots of black-velvet paintings. But the most interesting items are the bottles of *catara* sauce (hot sauce made from ants), and the medicinal barks and herbs for sale.

Tours

Popular shorter tours include three-day trips either up the Río Cuao, or up the Ríos Sipapo and Autana to the foot of Cerro Autana (1248m). Expect to pay from US$80 to US$100 per person per day.

The far southeastern part of Amazonas beyond La Esmeralda, basically all of Parque Nacional Parima-Tapirapeco, where the Yanomami live, is a restricted area. You need special permits that are virtually impossible to get – some agents get around the ban by visiting Yanomami villages on the Río Siapa off Brazo Casiquiare.

Booking in advance is recommended. Puerto Ayacucho gets almost no tourists these days, and most operators fashion individualized trips. Autana trips are more frequent, and one-day area tours can visit the pre-Columbian petroglyphs of Piedra Pintada, Piedra La Tortuga, an enormous boulder that looks like a giant turtle; and the Parque Tobogan de la Selva, a natural waterslide.

Cooperativa Coyote Tour TOUR
(☎521-3750, 0414-486-2500; coyotexpedition@cantv.net; Av Aguerrevere s/n) In business for almost 25 years, its main offerings are three-day Autana and Cuao tours, but it also runs longer trips and can book flights.

Expediciones Selvadentro TOUR
(☎414-7458, 0414-487-3810; www.selvadentro.com; Vía Alto Carinagua s/n) Long, adventurous trips to distant destinations aboard the *Iguana,* its 17m-long comfortable catamaran with toilet and kitchen.

Tadae TOUR
(☎0414-486-5923, 0248 521-4882; www.tadaeaventura.wordpress.com) Apart from the staple Autana and Cuao tours, it offers sport fishing plus rafting on Raudales Atures.

Sleeping

Residencia Internacional GUESTHOUSE $
(☎521-0242; Av Aguerrevere s/n; r with fan/air-con US$2/3; ❄📶) A long-time backpacker favorite, this friendly, family-operated place in a quiet residential area has a rooftop terrace and a rainbow palette of basic rooms with TVs, set around a long patio. Kitchen use is OK.

Hotel Apure HOTEL $
(☎521-4443; fax 521-0049; Av Orinoco 28; r US$3-6; ❄📶) Slightly sterile but spotlessly clean, the Apure has 17 good-sized rooms with air-con and cable TV. Comfy lounges and a dramatic wooden entryway add nice touches, and there's a convenient restaurant downstairs.

Hotel Cosmopolita HOTEL $
(☎521-3037; Av Orinoco s/n; r from US$4; ❄📶) A central if somewhat bland midrange option, it offers three floors of comfortable executive-style rooms with phones, TVs and fridges.

Eating

For cheap evening eats, try a *pepito cubano* from the street-food stands that set up outside the Hotel Cosmopolita from about 4pm until 6am. Big enough to satisfy two, these megasandwiches are crammed with eggs,

Puerto Ayacucho

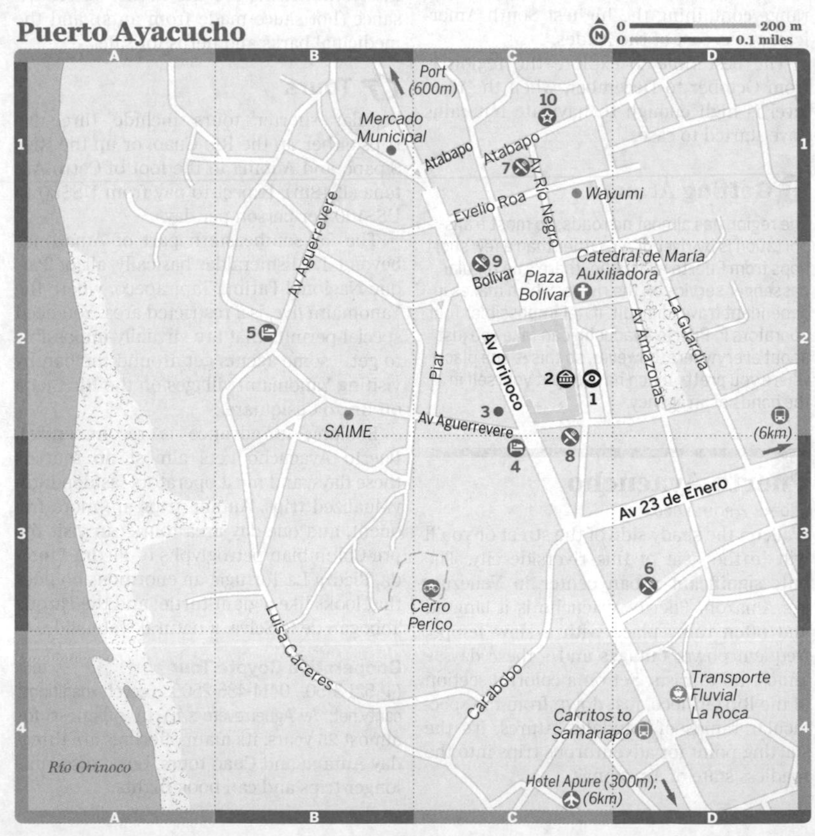

ham, cheese, veggies and potato chips, and drowned in sauce.

Restaurant Cherazad INTERNATIONAL $
(cnr Avs Aguerrevere & Río Negro; mains US$2-3; ⏲lunch & dinner Mon-Sat) One of the best restaurants in town, drape-shrouded Cherazad provides a sizable choice of pasta, steaks and fish, plus Middle Eastern dishes.

Panadería Las Tres Espigas BAKERY $
(Av Río Negro s/n; pastries from US$0.20; ⏲6am-8pm Mon-Sat, to noon Sun; ❄) Four powerful air-conditioners will keep you cool while you recharge on strong coffee and morning pastries.

Restaurant El Amir MIDDLE EASTERN $
(Av Orinoco s/n; mains US$1-2; ⏲lunch & dinner Mon-Sat; ✎) This family-run local favorite has decent falafels and tasty yogurt.

Mercadito MARKET $
(Av Orinoco s/n) For an inexpensive meal or a quick empanada fix, duck into this maze of food stalls, or try one of the basic *criollo* eateries nearby on Av Amazonas.

☆ Entertainment

Sala Cinemateca Puerto Ayacucho CINEMA
(www.cinemateca.gob.ve; Atabapo s/n) This is a government-subsidized art-house cinema. International films with Spanish subtitles.

ℹ Information

SAIME (Av Aguerrevere s/n; ⏲8am noon & 1-4pm Mon-Fri) Have your passport stamped here when leaving or entering Venezuela via Amazonas. No departure tax.

Puerto Ayacucho

Sights
1 Mercado Indígena......C2
2 Museo Etnológico de Amazonas......C2

Activities, Courses & Tours
3 Cooperativa Coyote Tour......C2

Sleeping
4 Hotel Cosmopolita......C3
5 Residencia Internacional......B2

Eating
6 Mercadito......D3
7 Panadería Las Tres Espigas......C1
8 Restaurant Cherazad......C3
9 Restaurant El Amir......C2

Entertainment
10 Sala Cinemateca Puerto Ayacucho......C1

ℹ Getting There & Away

AIR

At the airport, 6km southeast of town, Conviasa flies to Caracas three times per week. One small local carrier, **Wayumi** (☎521-0635; Evelio Roa), operates scheduled and charter flights within Amazonas to a few airstrips in jungle settlements.

BOAT

Transporte Fluvial La Roca (☎809-1595; Av Orinoco, Pasaje Orinoco, Centro Comercial Rapagna) has a daily service to San Fernando de Atabapo (US$2.50, 2½ hours).

BUS

The small bus terminal is 6km east of the center, on the outskirts of town. City buses go there from Av 23 de Enero, but are so infrequent citywide that taxis are the standard form of transportation. *Busetas* to Ciudad Bolívar (US$3.50, 10½ to 12 hours) depart regularly throughout the day. Until 3pm, eight buses depart daily to San Fernando de Apure (US$2, seven hours), from where you can get buses to Caracas, Maracay, Valencia, Barinas and San Cristóbal.

UNDERSTAND VENEZUELA

Venezuela Today

Venezuela's fortunes since the death of former President Hugo Chávez in March 2013 have been decidedly poor, and the country, once a beacon for left-wing causes around the world, is now in a state of near economic collapse. Endemic corruption, poor governance, the world's highest inflation rate, spiraling crime levels and huge lines outside supermarkets and pharmacies at any time of day are the defining features of contemporary life here. Once one of South America's wealthiest and safest countries, it's no exaggeration to call Venezuela today one of the continent's poorest and most dangerous places. Most Venezuelans simply shake their head when the inevitable discussion about politics starts: despair tempered by the trademark Venezuelan dry humor seems to be a common reaction to the topic.

Nicolás Maduro, the current president (and previously Chávez's deputy and anointed successor, who came to the presidency on his predecessor's death in 2013), is continuing most of Chávez's policies, but without any of Hugo's trademark charisma, which was always so vital to his popularity and appeal. Indeed, Maduro has done little to define himself politically, save arresting and imprisoning several of his political enemies and starting a diplomatic spat with Colombia that dramatically backfired in 2015, sparking some in South America to publicly question his fitness for office.

Parliamentary elections in December 2015 saw the opposition gain control of parliament for the first time since Chávez came to power in 1999, although it's yet to be seen if long-term or significant change to the Chavista-dominated political scene can be effected.

Other indicators are not good, particularly the sentence handed down to opposition leader Leopoldo López, who in September 2015 received a 13-year sentence for inciting violence during anti-government protests in 2014, and who is now in solitary confinement in a Venezuelan prison. Considered by Amnesty International to be prisoner of conscience, López is currently Maduro's biggest problem – he is Venezuela's most popular politician, with approval ratings over 50%.

On the ground, life has changed enormously in recent years for the majority of Venezuelans. Many people simply earn money by lining up all day for food and other basic goods such as toilet paper at state stores, which they resell on the black market for huge markups. You will see these so called *bachacos* (ants) in enormous lines all over the country – today the country is divided into those who line up and those who pay others to line up for them. With state salaries now worth barely US$20 a month, corruption or moonlighting often become the only viable ways to earn a living wage.

Sadly, unless political change comes via the ballot box or voluntarily from the Maduro government, it looks like it will sooner or later come from the increasingly angry and restive population, who feel their well-being has been ignored for too long.

History

Pre-Columbian Times

There is evidence of human habitation in northwest Venezuela going back more than 10,000 years. Steady agriculture was established around the first millennium, leading to the first year-round settlements. Formerly nomadic groups began to develop into larger cultures belonging to three main linguistic families: Carib, Arawak and Chibcha. By the end of the 15th century, during the Spanish conquest, some 300,000 to 400,000 indigenous people inhabited the region that is now Venezuela.

The Timote-Cuica tribes, of the Chibcha linguistic family, were the most technologically developed of Venezuela's pre-Hispanic societies. They lived in the Andes and developed complex agricultural techniques including irrigation and terracing. They were also skilled craftspeople, as we can judge by the artifacts they left behind – examples of their fine pottery are shown in museums across the country.

Spanish Conquest

Christopher Columbus was the first European to set foot on Venezuelan soil, which was also the only place where he landed on the South American mainland. On his third trip to the New World in 1498, he anchored at the eastern tip of the Península de Paria, just opposite Trinidad. He originally believed that he was on another island, but the voluminous mouth of the Río Orinoco hinted that he had stumbled onto something slightly larger.

A year later, Spanish explorer Alonso de Ojeda, accompanied by the Italian Amerigo Vespucci, sailed up to the Península de la Guajira, on the western end of present-day Venezuela. On entering Lago de Maracaibo, the Spaniards saw indigenous people living in *palafitos* (thatched homes on stilts above the water). Perhaps as a bit of sarcasm, they called the waterside community 'Venezuela,' meaning 'Little Venice,' and simultaneously gave birth to the country's name. The first Spanish settlement on Venezuelan soil, Nueva Cádiz, was established around 1500 on the small island of Cubagua, just south of Isla de Margarita. The earliest Venezuelan town still in existence, Cumaná (on the mainland directly south of Isla Cubagua) dates from 1521.

Simón Bolívar & Independence

Venezuela lurked in the shadows of the Spanish empire through most of the colonial period. The country took a more primary role at the beginning of the 19th century, when Venezuela gave Latin America one of its greatest heroes, Simón Bolívar. A native of Caracas, Bolívar led the forces that put the nail in the coffin of Spanish rule over South America. He is viewed as being largely responsible for ending colonial rule all the way to the borders of Argentina.

Bolívar assumed leadership of the revolution, which had kicked off in 1806. After unsuccessful initial attempts to defeat the Spaniards at home, he withdrew to Colombia and then to Jamaica to plot his final campaign. In 1817 Bolívar marched over the Andes with 5000 British mercenaries and an army of horsemen from Los Llanos, defeating the Spanish at the battle of Boyacá and bringing independence to Colombia. Four months later in Angostura (present-day Ciudad Bolívar), the Angostura Congress proclaimed Gran Colombia a new state, unifying Colombia (which included present-day Panama), Venezuela and Ecuador – though the last two were still under Spanish rule.

The liberation of Venezuela was completed with Bolívar's victory over Spanish forces at Carabobo in June 1821, though the royalists put up a rather pointless fight from Puerto Cabello for another two years. Gran Colombia existed for only a decade before splitting into three separate countries. Bolívar's dream of a unified republic fell apart before he died in 1830.

Caudillo Country

On his deathbed, Bolívar proclaimed: 'America is ungovernable. The man who serves a revolution plows the sea. This nation will fall inevitably into the hands of the unruly mob and then will pass into the hands of almost indistinguishable petty tyrants.' Unfortunately, he was not too far off the mark. Venezuela followed independence with nearly a century of rule by a series of strongmen known as *caudillos*. It wasn't until 1947 that the first democratic government was elected.

The first of the *caudillos,* General José Antonio Páez, controlled the country for 18 years (1830–48). Despite his tough rule, he established a certain political stability and strengthened the weak economy. The period that followed was an almost uninterrupted chain of civil wars that was only stopped by another long-lived dictator, General Antonio Guzmán Blanco (1870–88). He launched a broad program of reform, including a new constitution, and assured some temporary stability. Nonetheless his despotic rule triggered popular opposition, and when he stepped down, the country fell back into civil war.

20th Century Oil State

The first half of the 20th century was dominated by five successive military rulers from the Andean state of Táchira. The longest lasting and most ruthless was General Juan Vicente Gómez, who seized power in 1908 and didn't relinquish it until his death in 1935. Gómez phased out the parliament and crushed the opposition on his path to monopolizing power.

The discovery of oil in the 1910s helped the Gómez regime to put the national economy on its feet. By the late 1920s, Venezuela was the world's largest exporter of oil, which not only contributed to economic recovery but also enabled the government to pay off the country's entire foreign debt.

As in most petrol states, almost none of the oil wealth made its way to the common citizen. The vast majority continued to live in poverty. Fast oil money led to the neglect of agriculture and development of other types of production. It was easier to just import everything from abroad, which worked temporarily but proved unsustainable.

After a short flirtation with democracy and a new constitution in 1947, the inevitable coup took place and ushered in the era of Colonel Marcos Pérez Jiménez. Once in control, he smashed the opposition and plowed oil money into public works and modernizing Caracas – not making many friends in the process.

Coups & Corruption

Pérez Jiménez was overthrown in 1958 by a coalition of civilians and military officers. The country returned to democratic rule, and Rómulo Betancourt was elected president. He enjoyed popular support and was the first democratically elected president to complete his five-year term in office.

There was a democratic transition of power though the country drifted to the right.

Oil money buoyed the following governments well into the 1970s. Not only did production of oil rise but, more importantly, the price quadrupled following the Arab–Israeli war in 1973. The nation went on a spending spree, building modern skyscrapers in Caracas and Maracaibo, and importing all sorts of luxury goods. But what goes up must come down, and by the late 1970s the bust cycle was already in full swing, and the economy continued to fall apart through the 1980s.

In 1989 the government announced IMF-mandated austerity measures, and a subsequent protest over rising transportation costs sparked the *caracazo,* a series of nationwide riots quelled by military force that killed hundreds – maybe thousands – of citizens. Lingering instability brought two attempted coups d'état in 1992. The first, in February, was led by a little-known paratrooper named Colonel Hugo Chávez Frías. The second attempt, in November, was led by junior air-force officers. The air battle over Caracas, with warplanes flying between skyscrapers, gave the coup a cinematic dimension. Both attempts resulted in many deaths.

Corruption, bank failures and loan defaults plagued the government in the mid-1990s. In 1995, Venezuela was forced to devalue the currency by more than 70%. By the end of 1998, two-thirds of Venezuela's 23 million inhabitants were living below the poverty line.

A Left Turn

Nothing is better in political theater than a dramatic comeback. The 1998 election put Hugo Chávez, the leader of the 1992 failed coup, into the presidency. After being pardoned in 1994, Chávez embarked on an aggressive populist campaign: comparing himself to Bolívar, promising help (and handouts) to the poorest masses and positioning himself in opposition to the US-influenced free-market economy. He vowed to produce a great, if vague, 'peaceful and democratic social revolution.'

However, the Chávez 'social revolution' was anything but peaceful. Shortly after taking office, Chávez set about rewriting the constitution. The document was approved in a referendum in December 1999, granting him new and sweeping powers. The introduction of a package of new decree laws in 2001 was met with angry protests and was followed by a massive and violent strike in April 2002. It culminated in a coup d'état run by military leaders sponsored by a business lobby, in which Chávez was forced to resign. He regained power two days later, but this only intensified the conflict.

While the popular tensions rose, in December 2002 the opposition called a general strike in an attempt to oust the president. The nationwide strike paralyzed the country, including its vital oil industry and a good part of the private sector. After 63 days, the opposition finally called off the strike, which had cost the country 7.6% of its GDP and further devastated the oil-based economy. Chávez again survived and claimed victory.

21st-Century Socialism

National politics continued to be shaky until Chávez survived a 2004 recall referendum and consolidated his power. He won re-election in 2006 by a comfortable margin. After an unsuccessful attempt in 2007 to eliminate presidential term limits, Chávez won a referendum to amend the constitution in 2009, positioning him to run for re-election indefinitely.

Chávez expanded his influence beyond the borders of Venezuela, reaching out to leftist leaders across the continent, oil-producing countries in the Middle East, and China – an increasingly important South American trade partner. He allied himself with Cuba's Fidel Castro and Bolivia's Evo Morales, and stoked a combustible relationship with the US. Bad blood continues to this day between Venezuela and neighboring Colombia over accusations that Venezuela has been supporting the FARC guerrillas (Colombia's main insurgent group, Fuerzas Armadas Revolucionarias de Colombia) and shelters its members within its borders.

Supporters highlighted the country's programs for the poor. Under Chávez, government-sponsored projects called *misiones* (missions) provided adult literacy classes, free medical care and subsidized food. Large land holdings were broken up in land redistribution programs and given to subsistence farmers. Opponents criticized the centralization of power, intolerance of political dissent, a policy of nationalization that scared away international investment and the liberal use of government funds for partisan affairs.

After Chávez

Despite presiding over the slow collapse of the national economy and lurching from crisis to crisis, Chávez's position seemed unassailable after a decade in power, in which it essentially became impossible to rise in politics unless you were a 'Chavista'. Having abolished presidential term limits, Chávez won a third term in power in 2012, albeit by a far smaller majority than in previous elections, and despite having been diagnosed with cancer in 2011, something long rumored but never announced to the electorate before the ballot. Indeed, Chávez had barely been seen in public in the run up to the election, instead spending months in Cuba undergoing treatment and even missing his third inauguration as president.

Chávez died on March 5, 2013. Nicolás Maduro, the vice president (who had been anointed his successor by Chávez shortly before his death), was elected to the presidency in April 2013 by a wafer-thin majority in a special election where fairness was contested by his opponent, Henrique Capriles Radonski. Maduro, a former bus driver and trade union leader, has hardly made a mark on Venezuela's national psyche since coming to power, and Chávez' image and rhetoric continues to dominate the country's political scene.

Culture

Venezuela is an intensely patriotic nation that's proud of its history. The War of Independence and the exploits of Simón Bolívar are still championed throughout the country, and Venezuelans love to see themselves on the world stage. Whether it's the crowning of its most recent Miss Universe or a major league baseball shutout, you can guarantee that the folks at home will be cheering.

However, unlike some neighboring South American nations, there are few defining factors of contemporary Venezuelan culture. Many attribute this to the fact that, as a petrol state, Venezuela has spent much of its existence consuming goods from abroad and not needing or bothering to produce much at home. But just like the oil pumped out of the country, Venezuela does produce raw materials and raw talent, including a prolific supply of beauty queens and baseball players.

Regardless of national ills and social tensions, Venezuelans are full of life and humor. People are open, willing to talk and not shy about striking up conversations with a stranger who becomes an instant *chamo* (pal or friend). The nature of the current moribund political and economic situation is something locals are always willing to discuss (and if you can find a single person with anything good to say about the government, consider yourself to have made a serious anthropological find). Wherever you are, you're unlikely to be alone or feel isolated, especially if you can speak a little Spanish: in Venezuela there's always a rumba brewing somewhere.

Population

Venezuela has a young and mostly urban population, with half its population under 27

DANCING WITH DEVILS

Drums pound while hundreds of dancers clad in red devil costumes and diabolical masks writhe through the streets. This is the festival of the **Diablos Danzantes (Dancing Devils)**, a wild spectacle that takes place in Venezuela one day before Corpus Christi (the 60th day after Easter, a Thursday in May or June) and on the holy day itself.

Why devils on such a holy day in such a Catholic country? It is said that the festival demonstrates the struggle between good and evil. In the end, the costumed devils always submit to the church and demonstrate the eventual triumph of good.

The festival is a blend of Spanish and African traditions. The origins lie in Spain, where devils' images and masks were part of Corpus Christi feasts in medieval Andalucía. When the event was carried over to colonial Venezuela, it resonated with African slaves who had their own tradition of masked festivals. They also added African music and dance to the celebration. The celebrations in San Francisco de Yare and Chuao are best known throughout the country, as are their masks.

There is no direct transportation from Caracas to San Francisco de Yare, and the easiest way to get there is to organize a transfer with a travel agency.

NONVERBAL GESTURES

➡ A subtle and quick nose wrinkling (think rabbit) is the equivalent of 'huh?' or 'what?'

➡ When asking about price or indicating desired items to a salesperson, people will pucker and point their lips toward what they're referring to.

and 90% living in urban areas. Venezuela's population density is a low 32 people per sq km. However, the population is unevenly distributed: more than one-fifth of the country's population lives in Caracas alone, while Los Llanos and Guayana are relatively empty.

About 70% of the population is a blend of European, indigenous and African ancestry, or any two of the three. The rest of the population trace their roots entirely to European (about 20%), African (8%) or indigenous (3%) ancestors. Of that 3%, there are about 24 highly diverse indigenous groups comprising some 725,000 people, scattered throughout the country, the majority of whom still remain apart from mainstream Venezuelan society.

Lifestyle

The country's climate and the restricted space of Venezuelan homes create a more open, public life where many activities take place outside. Don't be surprised to see people getting together for a beer on the street, serenaded by a car stereo at full volume. That said, noise is a constant companion, and locals are undisturbed by blaring music, ear-splitting car horns and screeching street vendors.

Except when driving, Venezuelans seldom seem to be in a rush. People amble at a leisurely pace best suited for the tropics. This tempo also extends to business and consumer interactions, where you may need to wait while someone finishes gabbing with coworkers or watching TV before they acknowledge your presence.

There is a significant divide between rich and poor in Venezuela, with about 30% of the population living below the poverty line, though government programs have increased access to medical care and education for many people. Women make up about a third of Venezuela's workforce, and a large majority of the nation's workers currently earn their living within the untaxed informal economy: mainly buying and reselling consumer goods on the black market.

Religion

Some 95% of Venezuelans are at least nominally Roman Catholic, and respect for the church and its cultural influence can be felt on all levels of what is still a rather conservative country. That said, church attendance is relatively low, and the Catholic Church has had strained relations with the left-wing government for years.

Many indigenous groups adopted Catholicism and only a few isolated tribes still practice their traditional beliefs. Evangelicals compete with Catholics for converts and are gaining ground across the country. There are small populations of Jews and Muslims, particularly in Caracas.

Arts

Literature

The classic work in Latin American colonial literature on the treatment of the indigenous populations by the Spanish – which happens to also document Venezuela's early years – is *Brevísima relación de la destrucción de las Indias Occidentales* (A Short Account of the Destruction of the West Indies), written by Fray Bartolomé de las Casas in 1542.

As for contemporary literature, a groundbreaking experimental novel from the middle of the century is *El falso cuaderno de Narciso Espejo* (The False Notebook of Narciso Espejo, 1950) by Guillermo Meneses (1911–78). Another influential work was Adriano Gonzalez Leon's (1931–2008) powerful magical-realism novel *País portátil* (Portable Country, 1968), which contrasts rural Venezuela with the urban juggernaut of Caracas.

Ednodio Quintero is another contemporary writer to look for. His work *La danza del jaguar* (The Dance of the Jaguar, 1991) is one of several translated into other languages. Other writers worth tracking down include Teresa de la Parra, Antonia Palacios, Carlos Noguera and Orlando Chirinos.

Cinema

Venezuela's film industry is small, but produced some noteworthy films until the economic crisis pretty much ended funding for movies.

The biggest smash in new Venezuelan cinema was 2005's *Secuestro Express* (Kidnap Express) by Jonathan Jakubowicz. The film, which was criticized by the government for its harsh portrayal of the city, takes a cold look at crime, poverty, violence, drugs and class relations in the capital. It broke all box-office records for a national production and was the first Venezuelan film to be distributed by a major Hollywood studio.

Those interested in learning more about Venezuelan film should track down a couple of films. *Oriana* (Fina Torres, 1985) recounts a pivotal childhood summer at a seaside family hacienda; *Huelepega* (Glue Sniffer; Elia Schneider, 1999) is a portrayal of Caracas street children using real street youth; *Amaneció de golpe* (A Coup at Daybreak; Carlos Azpúrua, 1999) is the story of how Chávez burst onto the political scene; and *Manuela Saenz* (Manuela Saenz; Diego Risquez, 2000) depicts the War of Independence through the eyes of Bolívar's mistress.

Also worth seeing is *The Revolution Will Not Be Televised,* a documentary shot by Irish filmmakers who were inside the presidential palace during the coup d'état of 2002.

Music

Music is omnipresent in Venezuela. Though the country hasn't traditionally produced a lot of its own music, by law at least 50% of radio programming must now be by Venezuelan artists, and, of that music, 50% must be 'traditional.' The result has been a boon for Venezuelan musicians. The most common types of popular music are salsa, merengue and reggaeton, *vallenato* from Colombia, and North American and European pop – everything from rock to hip-hop to house. The king of Venezuelan salsa is Oscar D'León (b 1943).

The country's most popular folk rhythm is the *joropo,* also called *música llanera,* which developed in Los Llanos. The *joropo* is usually sung and accompanied by the harp, *cuatro* (a small, four-stringed guitar) and maracas.

Caracas is a center of Latin pop and the *rock en español* movement, which harnesses the rhythm and energy of Latin beats and combines them with international rock and alternative-rock trends. The most famous product of this scene is the Grammy-winning band Los Amigos Invisibles.

Begun in 1975, a nationwide orchestra program for low-income youth (nicknamed *El Sistema* – the System) has popularized classical music and trained thousands of new musicians. The top ensemble is the Orquesta Sinfónica Simón Bolívar, which performs around the world.

Visual Arts

Venezuela has a strong contemporary art movement. The streets and public buildings of Caracas are filled with modern art and the city houses some truly remarkable galleries.

Large-scale public art developed with the internal investment of the Guzmán Blanco regime in the late 19th century. The standout painter of that period – and one of the best in Venezuelan history – was Martín Tovar y Tovar (1827–1902). Some of his greatest works depicting historical events can be seen in Caracas' Asamblea Nacional.

There is a rich visual-arts scene among the current generation. Keep an eye out for the works of Carlos Zerpa (painting), the quirky ideas of José Antonio Hernández-Díez (photo, video, installations) and the emblematic paintings, collages and sculptures of Miguel von Dangel. And you'll see plenty more in the contemporary art museum of Caracas.

Jesús Soto (1923–2005) was Venezuela's number-one internationally renowned contemporary artist. He was a leading representative of kinetic art (art, particularly sculpture that contains moving parts). The largest collection of his work is in the museum dedicated to him in Ciudad Bolívar.

Cuisine

Food

On the whole, dining options in Venezuela are extremely cheap but of very variable quality and low on variety. In many places, a stock list of local meat and fish dishes is all that's available. However, in Caracas, and in several other larger towns and places that attract well-heeled locals and foreigners, such as Los Roques, there's a lot more variety and quality is also generally high.

Due to the dire economic situation in Venezuela, budget travelers will often find that midrange and even top-end eating options are within their budgets, though for even bigger savings, restaurants that offer a *menú del día* or *menú ejecutivo,* a set meal consisting of soup and a main course, remain a good choice. Another budget alternative can be roasted chicken, usually called *pollo en brasa.* Filling local choices also include *pabellón criollo, arepas, cachapas* and empanadas.

If breakfast isn't included where you are staying, the easiest (and most social) option is to visit any of the ubiquitous *panaderías* (bakeries), which sell sandwiches, pastries and yogurt, and delicious espresso.

Venezuela is very much a meat-eating country, though vegetarian restaurants now exist in most cities. That said, good fresh vegetables can be hard to find. Meatless *arepas* or empanadas are a reliable option, and Chinese, Middle Eastern and Italian restaurants often have some nonmeat dishes.

In almost every dining or drinking establishment, a 10% service charge will automatically be added to the bill. It's customary to leave a small tip at fancier places.

By law, all restaurants forbid smoking indoors, and most ban smoking anywhere on the premises.

The following are some typical Venezuelan dishes and a few international foods that have different names in Venezuelan Spanish:

arepa (a·re·pa) – small, grilled corn pancake stuffed with a variety of fillings

cachapa (ka·cha·pa) – larger, flat corn pancake, served with cheese and/or ham

cachito (ka·chee·to) – croissant filled with chopped ham and served hot

cambur (kam·boor) – banana

caraota (ka·ra·o·ta) – black bean

casabe (ka·sa·be) – huge, flat bread made from yucca; a staple in indigenous communities

empanada (em·pa·na·da) – deep-fried cornmeal turnover stuffed with various fillings

hallaca (a·ya·ka) – maize dough with chopped meat and vegetables, wrapped in banana leaves and steamed; like a Mexican tamale

lechosa (le·cho·sa) – papaya

pabellón criollo (pa·be·yon cree·o·yo) – shredded beef, rice, black beans, cheese and fried plantain; Venezuela's national dish

papelón (pa·pe·lon) – crude brown sugar; also drink flavoring

parchita (par·chee·ta) – passion fruit

parrilla (pa·ree·ya) – mixed grill

patilla (pa·tee·ya) – watermelon

quesillo (ke·see·yo) – caramel custard

teta (te·ta) – iced fruit juice in plastic wrap, consumed by sucking

Drinks

Venezuela has good, strong espresso coffee at every turn. Ask for *café negro* if you want it black; *café marrón* if you prefer half coffee, half milk; or *café con leche* if you like milkier coffee.

A staggering variety of fruit juices is available in restaurants, cafes and even in some fruit stores. Juices come as *batidos* (pure or cut with water) or as *merengadas* (made with milk).

The number-one alcoholic drink is *cerveza* (beer), particularly Polar and Solera (also owned by Polar). Beer is normally sold everywhere in cans or tiny bottles at close to freezing temperature, though in late 2015 there was a significant beer shortage, with Polar halting production at two breweries due to a lack of barley and an ongoing conflict with the government. Among spirits, whiskey and then *ron* (rum) lead the pack in popularity.

Sports

Soccer? What soccer? In Venezuela, *béisbol* (baseball) rules supreme. The next most popular sports are *básquetbol* (basketball, also known as *básquet* or *balon-cesto*), followed by *fútbol* (soccer), which has a professional league that plays from August till May. That said, soccer is still the sport of choice among the country's indigenous population, and is increasing in popularity.

Environment

The Land

About twice the size of California, Venezuela claims a multiplicity of landscapes. The traveler can encounter all four primary South American landscapes – the Amazon, the Andes, savannas and beaches – all in a single country.

The country has two mountain ranges: the Cordillera de la Costa, which separates the valley of Caracas from the Caribbean Sea, and the northern extreme of the Andes range, with its highest peaks near Mérida.

The 2150km Río Orinoco is Venezuela's main river, its entire course lying within national boundaries. The land south of the Orinoco, known as Guayana, includes the Río Caura watershed, the largely impenetrable Amazon rainforest, vast areas of sun-baked savanna and hundreds of *tepuis,* the unique table mountains that so define this area of wilderness.

A 2813km-long stretch of coast features a 900,000-sq-km Caribbean marine zone with numerous islands and cays. The largest and most popular of these is Isla de Margarita, followed by the far less developed Archipiélago Los Roques.

Wildlife

Along with the variety of Venezuelan landscape, you will encounter an amazing diversity of wildlife including anacondas, capybaras and caimans. There are 341 species of reptiles, 284 species of amphibians, 1791 species of fish, 351 species of mammals and many butterflies and other invertebrates. More than 1417 species of birds – approximately 20% of the world's known species – reside in the country, and 48 of these species are endemic. The country's geographical setting on a main migratory route makes it a bird-watcher's heaven.

National Parks

Venezuela's national parks offer a diverse landscape of evergreen mountains, beaches, tropical islands, coral reefs, high plateaus and rainforests. The national parks are the number-one destination for tourism within the country. Canaima, Los Roques, Mochima, Henri Pittier, El Ávila and Morrocoy are the most popular parks. Some parks, especially those in coastal and marine zones, are easily accessible and tend to be overcrowded by locals during holiday periods and weekends; others remain unvisited. A few of the parks offer tourism facilities, but these are generally not very extensive.

Some 50% of the country is protected under national law. Many of these areas are considered national parks and natural monuments, though some are designated as wildlife refuges, forests and biosphere reserves.

Environmental Issues

Far and away the most obvious environmental problem in Venezuela is waste management (or lack thereof). There is no recycling policy, and dumping of garbage in cities, along roads and in remote areas is common practice. Untreated sewage is sometimes dumped in the sea and other water bodies. There's a general lack of clear environmental policy and little to no culture of environmental stewardship outside park areas. Many of the waste and pollution issues are a direct result of overpopulation in urban areas, the existence of shanty towns and a lack of civil planning and funds to cope with the rampant development.

Other major environmental issues include the hunting and illegal trade of fauna and flora that takes place in many parts of the country – even in protected areas – and the inevitable pollution from oil refineries and mining. Food security is also a concern. Two-thirds of the country's food supply is imported, and it's rare to see agricultural land use besides cattle pasture.

SURVIVAL GUIDE

Directory A-Z

ACCOMMODATIONS

Given that anyone with dollars to exchange on the black market suddenly finds themselves extremely wealthy indeed, most hotels in Venezuela are now within the budget of backpackers. This may change, of course, but at the time of writing it was possible to get a room for under US$10 almost everywhere.

Even Caracas, which is famously backpacker unfriendly, can be done comfortably for under US$15 per night. Demand from the local tourism market however, is high, particularly in high season (July and August) and on major holidays (Christmas, Carnaval and Semana Santa), when

SLEEPING PRICE RANGES

The following price ranges refer to a double room with bathroom in high season.

$ less than US$10

$$ US$10 to US$20

$$$ more than US$20

beach towns will rarely have vacancies. Campgrounds are rare, and though you can rough it in the countryside, do be extremely cautious and don't leave your tent unattended. Be aware that during the day, urban budget hotels often double as hourly rate love motels, which are a common – though not necessarily sleazy – option in this privacy-starved country. However, even the cheapest places still provide towels and soap.

The most popular accommodations choice is the *posada*, a small, family-run guesthouse. They usually have more character than hotels and offer more personalized attention. Most are budget places but there are some midrange ones and a few top-end *posadas* as well.

Another countryside lodging is the *campamento* (literally 'camp'), which exists even in very remote areas. Not to be confused with campgrounds, this can be anything from a rustic shelter with a few hammocks to a posh country lodge with a swimming pool and its own airstrip. More commonly, it will be a collection of cabanas (cabins) plus a restaurant. *Campamentos* provide accommodations, food and usually tours, sometimes selling these services as all-inclusive packages.

As in most developing countries, prices are not set in stone and can change due to the day of the week or the mood of the person at the front desk. Many *posadas*, especially those run by expatriates, will discreetly accept cash or online money transfers in dollars or euros.

While many accommodations list email addresses or websites, the reality is that management may not respond to queries or reservation requests in a timely manner (if at all). If possible, calling is always a better bet.

BOOKS

German geographer and botanist Alexander von Humboldt describes exploring various regions of Venezuela in *Volume 2 of Personal Narratives of Travels to the Equinoctial Regions of America During the Year 1799–1804* (also abridged into the slim *Jaguars and Electric Eels*). *The Search for El Dorado* by John Hemming offers a fascinating insight into the conquest of Venezuela.

Sir Arthur Conan Doyle's *The Lost World* was inspired by the Roraima *tepui*. *Venezuela: A Century of Change* by Judith Ewell provides a comprehensive 20th-century history and H Micheal Tarver and Julia Frederick's *The History of Venezuela* skims the period from Columbus' first sighting through to the Chávez presidency.

There are dozens of books on Chávez and his 'Bolívarian Revolution,' though most sources take either a fervent pro- or anti-Chávez stance. One recent even-handed exploration is *Comandante: The Life and Legacy of Hugo Chávez* by Rory Carroll.

Serious bird-watchers may want to get *A Guide to the Birds of Venezuela* by Rodolphe Meyer de Schauensee and William H Phelps, Steven Hilty's *Birds of Venezuela* or *Birding in Venezuela* by Mary Lou Goodwin.

CHILDREN

Venezuela's child protection law requires that children not traveling with two parents carry a copy of their birth certificate and a notarized permission letter from the non-traveling parent(s). Single, widowed and same-sex parents should check with their home country to ensure that they bring sufficient documentation.

ELECTRICITY

Venezuela operates on 110V at 60 Hz. The country uses US-type plugs.

EMBASSIES & CONSULATES

Most countries have an embassy in Caracas. Both Brazil and Colombia have consulates in other parts of the country to aide overland travelers who might need visas. A yellow-fever vaccination certificate and two passport photos are required for a Brazilian visa.

Brazilian Consulate Caracas (Map p976; ☎0212-956-7800; http://cgcaracas.itamaraty.gov.br; Av San Juan Bosco btwn 5A & 6A Transversal); Santa Elena de Uairén (☎995-1256; Antonio José de Sucre s/n, Edificio Galeno; 8am-2pm Mon-Fri)

Canadian Embassy (Map p976; ☎0212-600-3000; www.canadainternational.gc.ca/venezuela; cnr Avs Francisco de Miranda & Sur Altamira, Altamira, Caracas; Ⓜ Altamira) Provides consular assistance to Australians as well as Canadians.

Colombian Consulate Caracas (☎0212-951-3631; http://caracas.consulado.gov.co; Guaicaipuro s/n, El Rosal; Ⓜ Chacaito); Puerto Ayacucho (☎521-0789; http://puertoayacucho.consulado.gov.co; Calle Yacapana, Quinta Beatriz 5; 8am-1pm Mon-Fri); Mérida (☎0274-245-9724; http://merida.consulado.gov.co; Av de las Américas s/n)

Dutch Embassy (Map p976; ☎0212-276-9300; http://venezuela.nlembajada.org; cnr 2A Transversal & Av San Juan Bosco, Edif San Juan, 9th fl, Altamira, Caracas; Ⓜ Altamira)

French Embassy (Map p976; ☎0212-909-6500; www.ambafrance-ve.org; cnr Madrid & Av La Trinidad, Edif Embajada de Francia, Las Mercedes, Caracas)

German Embassy (Map p976; ☎0212-219-2500; www.caracas.diplo.de; Av Principal de la Castellana s/n, Torre La Castellana, Caracas; Ⓜ Altamira)

Guyanese Embassy (☎0212-267-7095; 2A Av btwn 9A & 10A Transversal, Quinta Los Tutis, Altamira, Caracas)

Italian Embassy (Map p976; ☎0212-952-7311; www.ambcaracas.esteri.it; Sorocaima s/n, Edificio Atrium, El Rosal, Caracas)

Japanese Embassy (Map p976; ☎0212-262-3435; www.ve.emb-japan.go.jp; Torre Digitel, Plaza La Castellana, La Castellana, Caracas; Ⓜ Altamira)

Spanish Embassy (Map p976; ☎0212-263-2855; www.maec.es/embajadas/caracas; Av Mohedano s/n, Quinta Marmolejo, La Castellana, Caracas; Ⓜ Altamira)

Swiss Embassy (Map p976; ☎0212-267-9585; www.eda.admin.ch/caracas; Av Eugenio Mendoza near San Felipe, Centro Letonia, Torre Ing-Bank, La Castellana, Caracas; Ⓜ Altamira)

Trinidad & Tobago Embassy (Map p976; ☎0212-261-3748; 3A Av btwn 6A & 7A Transversal, Quinta Poshika, Altamira, Caracas; Ⓜ Altamira)

UK Embassy (Map p976; ☎0212-319-5800; www.ukinvenezuela.fco.gov.uk; Av Principal de la Castellana s/n, Torre La Castellana, La Castellana, Caracas; Ⓜ Altamira)

US Embassy (☎0212-975-6411; http://caracas.usembassy.gov; cnr Calles F & Suapure, Urbanización Colinas del Valle Arriba, Caracas)

GAY & LESBIAN TRAVELERS

Homosexuality isn't illegal in Venezuela, but it is largely frowned upon by the overwhelmingly Catholic society. Discretion is always a good idea in smaller towns and rural areas. At the same time, pockets of tolerance do exist. Caracas has the largest gay and lesbian community and the most open gay life, including an annual gay pride festival in June that draws tens of thousands.

When looking for gay-oriented venues, the phrase to watch out for is *en* (or *de*) *ambiente*. However, most contact these days happens online.

HEALTH

Venezuela has a wide array of pharmacies, clinics and hospitals. Good medical care is available in Caracas, but may be difficult to find in rural areas. Public hospitals and clinics are free, but the quality of medical care is better in private facilities. If you need hospital treatment in Venezuela, by far the best facilities are in Caracas. Smaller issues can be dealt with directly in pharmacies, as they are allowed to give injections and administer a wide range of medicines, although in recent years shortages have dogged pharmacies as well, so bring any medication you need with you.

Malaria and dengue fever are present in some tropical areas, and while other insect bites don't necessarily cause illness, they can cause major discomfort. Overall, your biggest dangers are the standard risks of travel: sunburn, food-borne illness and traffic.

Tap water is generally fine for brushing your teeth, but is not recommended for consumption.

EATING PRICE RANGES

The following price ranges refer to a standard main course.

$ less than US$3

$$ US$3 to US$6

$$$ more than US$6

INTERNET ACCESS

Wi-fi is available everywhere but the most remote rainforest lodge. It's free in nearly all hotels and *posadas*, as well as in many restaurants and cafes. If you don't have a smart phone or laptop with you, many *posadas* have computer terminals you can use, and most towns still have a trusty old internet cafe, although you may have to look harder for them these days. Free wi-fi is often provided by the government in public squares, though in our experience it's often not working.

LANGUAGE COURSES

Venezuela has language schools in most big cities, although uptake has undoubtedly suffered in recent years with the safety and economic situation. Mérida remains a popular place to study Spanish, however, as it is an attractive, affordable city with a major university and a young and progressive population.

LEGAL MATTERS

Venezuelan police are to be treated with respect, but also with a healthy dose of caution. Cases of police corruption, abuse of power and use of undue force are unfortunately common. Having your passport or a copy of it with you at all times, including a photocopy of your entry stamp, will fend off the most obvious attempts at bribery. In other cases, remain polite and calm, and call your hotel or travel agency in an attempt to resolve the problem before calling your embassy.

You will be subject to several checks daily if you're traveling around Venezuela, as there are roadblocks at the entrance to most towns. These are rarely a problem, just be sure to have your passport to hand.

Penalties for trafficking, possessing and using illegal drugs are some of the heaviest in all of Latin America. Venezuelan jails are dangerous free-for-alls, and consular officials can do little besides visit you.

MONEY

ATMs

Cajeros automáticos (ATMs) can be found everywhere, and often have lines in front of them. No visitor should use an ATM in the country, however, as it will mean getting the terrible official exchange rate.

Black Market

The black market (*mercado negro* or *dólar paralelo*) is not nearly as sinister as it sounds, and is essential for all visitors to Venezuela, although always check the latest information with your hotel or travel agency. It's best to arrange currency exchange in advance, rather than attempt to do it at the airport, where your chance of getting ripped off is high. Websites such as www.dollar.nu list the current black-market exchange rates. Though changing money in this way is strictly speaking illegal, it's not something the government prosecutes except in the case of career currency traders. That said, be discreet and make the change in your hotel room or in a private office. Beware of counterfeit bills, especially at Maiquetía airport. As the highest banknote (BsF100) is worth just 20c, expect to be given a laundry bag full of money.

Though they don't advertise it, most established *posadas* and tour operators will accept payment (or sometimes give you cash at the black-market rate) through online money transfers to international bank accounts.

Cash

Venezuela's ironically named bolívar fuerte (strong bolívar) is a tiresome currency to use. There are worthless coins and paper notes in denominations of two, five, 10, 20, 50 and 100. Expect to carry around huge wads of cash, as the 100 note is worth just 20c. It's impossible to get Venezuelan currency before you enter the country.

Credit Cards

Never use your credit card in Venezuela, as transactions will always be calculated using the ruinous official exchange rate.

Money Changers

While it is just about possible to change euros, and Brazilian and Colombian money in Venezuela, US dollars will get you the best rate and will be simplest to change. Do not use the *casas de cambio* (authorized money-exchange offices), however, as you will get a terrible rate.

Tipping

- Most restaurants include a 10% service charge and list it clearly on the bill, and when it's not included, they usually tell you about it rather shamelessly!
- A small tip of around 5% to 10% beyond the service charge is standard in a nicer restaurant, but not required.
- Taxi drivers are not usually tipped unless they help carry bags.
- Tipping of hotel employees, dive masters, guides and so on is left to your discretion; it is rarely required but always appreciated, and let's face it, there are a lot of banknotes in your pocket due to the economic situation.

OPENING HOURS

The working day is theoretically eight hours, from 8am to noon and 2pm to 6pm Monday to

ESSENTIAL PRICE WARNING!

Venezuelan government currency controls peg the bolívar fuerte to the US dollar at a totally artificial rate. This has resulted in an absurd situation that forces all visitors to use the black market. At the time of research, the official exchange rate was, as it had been for years, fixed at BsF6.3 per dollar, but a dollar's street value was between BsF500 and BsF700. This means that anyone changing money at a bank, taking money out on a credit card or even paying by credit card will be getting a crippling poor rate. It's therefore essential to use the black market if you want to be able to afford to visit Venezuela. Prices are often quoted in US dollars as the bolívar fuerte is too volatile. However, we convert using a conservative black-market rate of 500BsF to the dollar, not the official rate. Therefore a bed that costs US$5, actually cost BsF2500 on the ground. To pay for the same bed using the official rate would make the bed cost US$397.

Therefore either bring cash US dollars to Venezuela and change them on the black market locally (it's best to ask your *posada* or travel agent about this in advance), or wire US dollars to a trusted travel agency or *posada* and they will bring you cash in bolívares on arrival. If you're coming overland, neither Brazilian nor Colombian currencies are subject to controls; therefore, it's a good strategy to withdraw money from ATMs in those countries and change it on the black market at the border or nearest town.

Venezuela has the highest rate of inflation in the world and prices are extremely vulnerable to change. Prices quoted should be used as a rough guide only.

Friday, but in practice many businesses work shorter hours. Almost everything is closed on Sundays (except museums, *panaderías* and some restaurants).

Banks Monday to Friday, 8:30am to 3:30pm.

Restaurants Monday to Saturday, noon to 9pm or 11pm.

Shops Monday to Friday, 9am to 6pm or 7pm; Saturdays are usually the same, but some shops close at 1pm.

POST

Ipostel, the Venezuelan postal service, has post offices throughout the country. Some are in combined government services offices called Puntos de Gestión Centralizada (Central Administration Offices). The usual opening hours are 8:30am to 11:30am and 1:30pm to 5pm Monday to Friday, with regional variations. Offices in the main cities may open longer hours and on Saturday.

Service is extremely unreliable and slow. Mail can take up to a month to arrive, if it arrives at all. If you are mailing something important or time-sensitive, use a reliable international express mail carrier.

PUBLIC HOLIDAYS

Given the strong Catholic character of Venezuela, many holidays follow the church calendar – Christmas, Carnaval, Easter and Corpus Christi are celebrated all over the country. The religious calendar is dotted with saints' days, and every village and town has its own patron saint and will hold a celebration on that day.

Most Venezuelans take vacations over Christmas, Carnaval (several days prior to Ash Wednesday), Semana Santa (the week before Easter Sunday) and during July and August. In these periods, it can be tricky to find a place to stay in more popular destinations, and prices shoot up. The upside is that they really come alive with holiday merrymakers.

Some official public holidays:

New Year's Day January 1

Carnaval Monday and Tuesday prior to Ash Wednesday, February/March

Easter Maundy Thursday and Good Friday, March/April

Declaration of Independence April 19

Labor Day May 1

Battle of Carabobo June 24

Independence Day July 5

Bolívar's Birthday July 24

Discovery of America October 12

Christmas Day December 25

SAFE TRAVEL

There is no denying it: Venezuela cannot be called a safe country, with muggings, kidnappings and robberies a big risk, especially in larger cities such as Caracas. That said, by using some common sense and taking local advice, you can minimize your exposure to such things and most likely have a safe visit.

- Always be aware of your surroundings and keep displays of wealth to an absolute minimum. This means don't carry big cameras or backpacks, don't wear expensive jewellery or watches or use smart phones in public. Theft is more serious in the larger cities and urban centers than in the countryside, but can happen anywhere.
- Caracas is by far the most dangerous place in the country, and you should take care while strolling around the streets, and always take taxis after dark. Elsewhere ask locally about safety, but when in doubt, take a taxi.
- Remember that police are not necessarily trustworthy (though many are), so do not blindly accept the demands of these authority figures. Travelers have also reported theft by security personnel during airport screenings and border crossings.
- Venezuela is somewhat obsessed with identification, and *cédulas* (Venezuelan ID cards) or passport numbers are often required for the most banal transactions. Always carry your passport (or a copy with the entrance stamp), or you may end up explaining yourself in a police station.
- The border with Colombia is considered generally risky because of cross-border drug-trafficking and the presence of FARC guerrillas. It was closed at the time of reseach during a diplomatic spat, but will most likely be open by the time you read this. If you're passing through this area to or from Colombia, it's wise not to dawdle along the route.

TELEPHONE

Those who plan to stay longer in Venezuela may opt to purchase a local SIM card for their own handset. The malls all have numerous competing cell-phone offices. Movilnet, Movistar and Digitel all have generally excellent coverage, including 3G in most populated areas. As with most transactions in the country, you'll need to show your passport to buy a SIM card. Venezuela has one of the highest cell-phone-per-capita ratios in Latin America, and phone time is dirt cheap.

All phone numbers in the country are seven digits and area codes are a zero plus three digits. Note that all cell phones have an area code that begins with ☎04. The country code for Venezuela is ☎58. To call Venezuela from abroad, dial the international access code of the country you're calling from, Venezuela's code (☎58), the area code (drop the initial 0) and the local phone number. To call internationally from Venezuela, dial the international access code (00), then the country code, area code and local number.

TIME
Venezuela has a unique time zone that's 4½ hours behind Greenwich Mean Time. There's no daylight saving time.

TOILETS
Public toilets are rare in Venezuela, so instead use the toilets of restaurants, hotels, museums, shopping malls and bus terminals. Don't rely on a public bathroom to have toilet paper or soap and remember to always throw the used paper into the wastebasket provided. Many public restrooms charge a small fee, which includes an allotment of paper.

TOURIST INFORMATION
Inatur (www.mintur.gob.ve/mintur/inatur) is the Caracas-based government agency that promotes tourism and provides tourist information; it has offices at Maiquetía airport. Outside the capital, tourist information is handled by regional tourist bodies. Some are better than others, but on the whole they lack city maps and brochures, and the staff members rarely speak English. Tour agencies and *posadas* are always the best source of up-to-date information.

Some useful websites:

Today Venezuela (www.todayvenezuela.com)
El Universal (www.eluniversal.com/english)
Venezuelan Politics & Human Rights (www.venezuelablog.tumblr.com)

VISAS
Nationals of Australia, Canada, the EU, Japan, New Zealand and Switzerland do not need a visa to enter Venezuela, passports are simply stamped upon arrival and bearers may stay for up to 90 days in the country. US and Israeli citizens require visas, and these must be obtained in advance through a Venezuelan embassy abroad. For US citizens, tourist visas currently cost US$30, but obtaining them is a headache that involves traveling to a Venezuelan consulate in person. Once issued they are valid for a year, of which 90 days may be spent in Venezuela. For more details see www.eeuu.embajada.gob.ve.

WOMEN TRAVELERS
Like most of Latin America, Venezuela is very much a man's country. Women will constantly be asked about their marital status and whether they have children, and women travelers will attract curiosity, attention and advances from local men, who are not shy to show their admiration through whistles, endearments and flirtatious comments. The best way to deal with unwanted attention is simply to ignore it. Dressing modestly will make you less conspicuous, as although Venezuelan women wear revealing clothes, they're more aware of the culture and the safety of their surroundings. Given Venezuela's terrible security situation, women are particularly advised to take taxis after dark and not to risk walking alone at night.

Getting There & Away

AIR
Nearly all international visitors arrive at Caracas' **Aeropuerto Internacional Simón Bolívar** (www.aeropuerto-maiquetia.com.ve) in Maiquetía, 26km from Caracas. Venezuela has several other airports that take international flights, but none were regularly scheduled at the time of research.

Set at the northern edge of South America, Venezuela has one of the fastest journey times from North America, making it a convenient northern gateway to the continent. However, air-traffic disputes between the US and the government have trimmed the number of flights to and from the US. Venezuela is also served by flights to several cities in Europe, the Caribbean and South America.

The national carrier is Conviasa.

BOAT
There are no longer scheduled ferries between Venezuela and the Netherlands Antilles or Trinidad and Tobago, though it may well be possible to find passage to each if you're prepared to wait around at nearby ports.

BUS, CAR & MOTORCYCLE
Passengers must disembark for passport control along the borders. There's sometimes a small land departure tax, though it's not collected at the Brazilian border crossing at Santa Elena de Uairén.

Getting Around

AIR
Venezuela has a number of airlines and a reasonable network of air routes, though due to a chronic lack of spare parts grounding more and more aircraft, routes are generally shrinking, and tickets are becoming ever more scarce. Be aware that several once useful airports, including those in Mérida and Santa Elena de Uairén, are currently closed.

Maiquetía, where Caracas' airport is located, is the country's major aviation hub and handles flights to most airports around the country. Cities most frequently serviced from Caracas include Porlamar, Maracaibo and Puerto Ordaz (Ciudad Guayana). The most popular destinations with travelers are El Vigía (for Mérida), Ciudad Bolívar, Canaima, Porlamar and Los Roques.

A number of provincial carriers cover regional and remote routes on a regular or charter basis. Canaima and Los Roques have their own fleets of Cessnas and other smaller planes that fly for a number of smaller airlines. It is best to book these flights through an agent, as they generally aren't bookable from abroad.

Though flights aren't very expensive, they can be unreliable, and delayed flights are unfortunately extremely common. It's risky to schedule a domestic flight to connect with a same-day international flight. Do also be aware that due to frequent overbooking of flights, it's important to check in a minimum of two or even three hours before domestic flights.

Domestic Airlines

Aeropostal (☎0800-284-6637, 0212-708-6220; www.aeropostal.com; Av Paseo Colón, Torre Polar Oeste, ground fl, Plaza Venezuela, Caracas; Ⓜ Plaza Venezuela) Services Maracaibo, Porlamar and Puerto Ordaz.

Aereotuy (LTA; ☎0212-212-3110; www.tuy.com; Blvd de Sabana Grande, Edif Sabana Grande, 5th fl, Caracas; Ⓜ Sabana Grande) Serves the tourism hot spots of Canaima, Los Roques and Porlamar.

Aserca (☎0212-905-5333; www.asercaairlines.com; Guaicaipuro, Edif Taeca, ground fl, Caracas; Ⓜ Chacaíto) Flies to domestic airports including Barcelona, Maracaibo and Porlamar.

Avior (☎213-0600; www.avior.com.ve; Av Venezuela, Torre Clement, ground fl, El Rosal, Caracas; Ⓜ Chacaíto) Destinations include Porlamar and Puerto Ordaz.

Conviasa (☎0500-266-8427, 578-4767; www.conviasa.aero; cnr Avs Sur 25 & México, Hotel Alba Caracas; Ⓜ Parque Central) State-owned airline with destinations including Barinas, El Vigía, Maracaibo, Puerto Ayacucho, Puerto Ordaz and the Caribbean.

Laser (☎0212-202-0106; www.laser.com.ve; Av Francisco de Miranda, Torre Bazar Bolivar, Piso 8, Caracas; Ⓜ La California) Carrier with service between Caracas and Porlamar, El Vigía and Aruba.

Rutaca (☎0212-237-9317, 0800-788-2221; www.rutaca.com.ve; Av Francisco de Miranda, Centro Seguros La Paz, Caracas; Ⓜ Los Cortijos) Serves Canaima, Ciudad Bolívar, Porlamar, Puerto Ordaz and Santo Domingo.

Venezolana (Map p976; ☎0261-730-2907; www.ravsa.com.ve; Centro Comercial Centro Plaza, Mezzanina, Los Palos Grandes, Caracas; Ⓜ Altamira) Flights to Cumaná, Santo Domingo, Porlamar, Maracaibo and Caribbean destinations.

BOAT

Venezuela has a number of islands, but only Isla de Margarita is serviced by regular scheduled ferries.

The Río Orinoco is the country's major inland waterway. The river is navigable from its mouth up to Puerto Ayacucho, with limited scheduled passenger service.

DEPARTURE TAX

Departure taxes are included in all airfares to and from Aeropuerto Internacional Simón Bolívar (but only here), so you no longer need to pay at the airport. Elsewhere you may have to pay a small surcharge at your departing airport, but this is usually a tiny amount in bolívares.

BUS

Buses are the workhorse of Venezuela and are generally reliable and incredibly cheap, though demand is often very high and safety is a growing concern.

Buses range from sputtering pieces of junk to the most recent models. All major companies offer *servicio ejecutivo* (executive class) in comfortable (but seriously icy) air-conditioned buses, which cover all the major long-distance routes and are the dominant means of intercity transportation.

Caracas is the most important transport hub, handling buses to just about every corner of the country. Except for the almost-free SITSSA buses, which sell out right after the ticket windows open, there's usually no need to buy tickets more than a couple of hours in advance for major routes, except around holidays or if you want to get on the one long-distance service per day.

Many short-distance regional routes are served by *por puestos*, a cross between a bus and a taxi. *Por puestos* are usually large old US-made cars (less often minibuses) that ply fixed routes and depart when all seats are filled. They cost about 40% to 80% more than buses, but they're faster and often leave more frequently.

Always travel with your passport handy, warm clothes for any bus with air-con, and earplugs for amped-up radio volume on smaller buses. As a security measure, some long-distance bus companies videotape passengers before departing. Most bus terminals require payment of a tiny departure tax. Get a receipt at the kiosk; the bus or *por puesto* driver will collect them.

CAR & MOTORCYCLE

You can use any type of driver's license to drive a car in Venezuela. The road network is extensive and mostly in acceptable shape. Gas stations are numerous and fuel is just about the cheapest in the world – you can fill up your tank for well under a dollar, though always plan ahead with getting gas, as many areas have controls on who can buy how much, to deter smugglers. Venezuelan driving is another concern. Traffic lights are routinely ignored throughout the country, speed limits are a pipe dream and police are known to pull over motorists for nonexistent infractions in an attempt to collect bribes.

Bringing a car to Venezuela (or to South America in general) is time-consuming, expensive and involves plenty of paperwork, and few people do it. It's cheaper and much more convenient to rent a car locally. Major international rental companies are in all the large cities, though due to the economic situation there are very few rental cars available and their quality is generally terrible. Rental rates aren't necessarily budget-oriented, but at least gas isn't a major expense. If your lodging doesn't have parking, monitored lots are recommended at night.

PRIVATE TRANSFERS

The current economic situation in Venezuela means that it's actually very common for foreign travelers to arrange long-distance private transfers these days, effectively taking taxis between cities. These can be arranged through travel agencies or *posadas*, and tend to be a more expensive, but still affordable, way to get around, especially if you're traveling with others. The advantages are extra safety and reliability, as well as additional speed in getting from A to B.

LOCAL TRANSPORT

Bus & Metro

All cities and many major towns have their own urban transportation systems, which usually include small buses or minibuses. Depending on the region, these are called *busetas, carros, carritos, micros* or *camionetas*, and fares are dirt cheap. In many larger cities you can also find urban *por puestos*, swinging faster than buses through the chaotic traffic. Caracas has a comprehensive subway system, though its buses aren't noted for their good safety record, and armed muggings are a frequent occurrence.

Taxi

Taxis are extremely cheap and worth using as much as possible, particularly for transportation between the bus terminal and city center when you are carrying all your bags. Taxis don't have meters, so always fix the fare with the driver before boarding the cab. It's a good idea to find out the correct fare beforehand from an independent source, such as someone who works in the bus station or a hotel reception desk.

Anyone can slap a neon sticker on their car windshield and declare it a taxi. Unlicensed taxis are known as *piratas*, and they're fine to take in most situations. But at night, it's best to have a hotel or restaurant call a trusted driver or to seek out a *línea* (officially licensed) taxi. Indeed taxis are so cheap in Venezuela, that it's quite common for travelers to use them to get between towns.

TOURS

Independent travelers who have never taken an organized tour in their lives will often find themselves signing up with a group in Venezuela. As vast areas of the country are virtually inaccessible by public transportation (eg the Orinoco Delta or Amazon Basin) or because a solitary visit to scattered sights in a large territory (eg the Gran Sabana) may be inconvenient, time-consuming and expensive, tours are a standard option in Venezuelan travel.

Although under some circumstances it makes sense to prebook tours (eg when stringing together various tours in a short period of time), it is most cost-effective to arrange a tour from the regional center closest to the area you are going to visit.

Even if you don't want to join a group tour, having a travel agency assist you with bookings is normally essential. Companies can arrange transfers, book domestic flights (normally very hard from outside the country), arrange for safe currency exchange and hook you up with other travelers to share long-distance taxis or excursions.

Understand South America

South America Today

There's optimism in the air across South America, with a rising middle class, falling poverty rates and strong economies. As the continent has veered to the left, wage disparities have fallen and social justice seems to be the hot topic of the day. Big challenges remain, however, particularly in the realm of public corruption. The economic good times may also be coming to an end, spurred in part by plummeting oil prices.

Best on Film

Motorcycle Diaries (2004) The road trip that made a revolutionary.

Central do Brasil (Central Station; 1998) Walter Salles' moving tale of a homeless boy and an older woman on a road trip across Brazil.

Fitzcarraldo (1982) Werner Herzog's wild tale of a foreigner obsessed with building an opera house in the jungle.

The Mission (1986) Jesuit missionaries in Guaraní communities of Spanish-controlled colonies.

Cidade de Deus (City of God; 2002) Fernando Meirelles' powerful portrait of life in a Rio favela.

Best in Print

The Lost City of Z (David Grann) Gripping journey into the Amazon to retrace the steps of lost explorer Colonel Fawcett.

In Patagonia (Bruce Chatwin) Evocative writing on Patagonia's history and mystique.

One Hundred Years of Solitude (Gabriel García Márquez) Magic realist masterpiece.

Aunt Julia & the Scriptwriter (Mario Vargas Llosa) A classic unconventional love story.

Gabriela, Clove and Cinnamon (Jorge Amado) Hilarious tale set in Bahia, by Brazil's greatest writer.

A New Dawn

Brighter days have arrived in South America. A little over a generation ago, military dictatorships and repressive regimes ruled much of the continent. Thankfully, the era of bloody coups, guerrilla warfare and runaway inflation is now a thing of the past, and the gloom that seemed to hang over South America has lifted (save in Venezuela, where the economy remains on a perilous downward spiral). In place of right-wing regimes, South America has moved toward peace and prosperity, with more socially responsible leadership that's also mindful of fueling economic growth. Progressives like former Brazilian president Lula helped pave the way, demonstrating that you could both grow an economy and help lift people out of poverty. Income inequality has fallen – not only in Brazil but across South America, where the middle class is growing and fewer people than ever before are living in extreme poverty.

Breaking Down Barriers

Machismo has also taken a blow, with the first female presidents in South America helping to break down barriers. Cristina Kirchner of Argentina, Dilma Rousseff of Brazil and Michelle Bachelet of Chile have all recently served as presidents of some of South America's largest economies. Speaking of historic elections, Evo Morales (now in his third term) also deserves special mention, becoming the first president of Bolivia to hail from an indigenous background. He follows on the heels of Alejandro Toledo, who became Peru's first indigenous president back in 2001.

On other fronts, there have been equally dramatic changes in recent years. Gay marriage has been legalized in Argentina, Brazil and Uruguay, and three other countries (Chile, Colombia and Ecuador) have a form of same-sex civil union. Gay marriage is also legal in French Guiana, which is considered part of France.

Social & Environmental Threats

Meanwhile, it's not all ponies and rainbows in South America. Despite the economic boom, not all have benefited. Rural poverty remains a gripping problem in every country in South America, with many families still struggling with basic needs: adequate nutrition, health care and clean water. And one in seven still live in extreme poverty, subsisting on less than US$2.50 per day.

When it comes to the environment, there's a mix of good and bad news. On the plus side, the frightening rates of rainforest deforestation have fallen in the last two decades. At the same time, oil production will soon begin in Ecuador's Parque Nacional Yasuní, a pristine area of the Amazon that happens to hold one of the country's largest reserves. The building of access roads and pipelines – not to mention the possibility of oil spills – could be devastating for Yasuní. In the Brazilian Amazon, construction is nearly officially complete on the massive Belo Monte Dam. At least 450 sq km of forest will be flooded, forcing the relocation of around 12,000 people. A 100km stretch of the mighty Xingu River will essentially dry up, including the part that runs alongside the Paquiçamba territory, home of the Juruna indigenous group. And experts say draining the river would threaten dozens of fish and other species, including many found nowhere else in the world.

In Peru, coca and cocaine production have not only serious social repercussions, but also affect Peru's environment through deforestation in remote growing areas and chemical contamination that's a by-product of production. The Amazon is also now bisected by the Interoceanic Highway, an overland trade route that links Peru to Brazil. Economics aside, there's great concern about the irrevocable impact this could have on the world's most biologically rich rainforest.

Corruption Scandals

Political corruption remains pervasive in South America. In Brazil, one of the largest scandals in the nation's history came to light in 2014, when an undercover investigation revealed a massive US$3 billion kickback scheme. It's caused nationwide protests, and may even bring down President Dilma Rousseff, who was facing impeachment proceedings in early 2016. In Argentina, former president Cristina Kirchner had to deal with damaging allegations that she and her late husband (who was president before her) enriched themselves at taxpayers' expense. Likewise, Chilean president Michelle Bachelet has also found herself embroiled in a corruption scandal – involving abuse of power by her son – which has led to her plummeting popularity ratings.

POPULATION: **395 MILLION**

AREA: **18 MILLION SQ KM**

GDP PER CAPITA: **US$8720**

UNEMPLOYMENT: **7.5%**

ANNUAL INFLATION: **7.2%**

if South America were 100 people

45 would be White (of European descent)
31 would be Mestizo (of mixed Amerindian and European descent)
17 would be Black or Mulato (of African descent)
7 would be Amerindian (of pure Indigenous descent)

belief systems
(% of population)

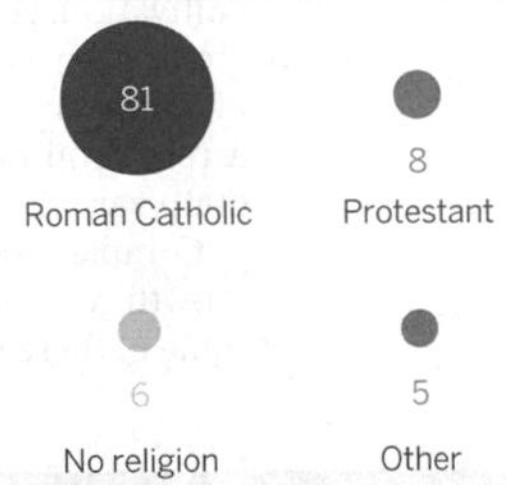

population per sq km

History

South America has a long and tumultuous history. It was the birthplace of one of the great empires, sadly brought to ruin upon the European arrival, and the destination for millions of men, women and children who were enslaved and brought over from Africa. The drive toward independence freed the continent from foreign rule, though it did little to address the yawning divide between rich and poor. Homegrown social justice movements were later crushed in the 20th century when military dictatorships ruled much of the continent.

The Indigenous

Norwegian Thor Heyerdahl explored Easter Island while crossing the Pacific in the 1950s; it became the centerpiece of his theories about the South American origins of Polynesian civilization. For more details, read *Aku-Aku* and *The Kon-Tiki Expedition*.

There are various competing theories about how the first peoples arrived in the Americas. Until recently, it was generally believed that early inhabitants traveled from present-day Siberia to Alaska over a land bridge across the Bering Strait. Some scholars estimate this epic migration occurred around 14,000 years ago. In the last several decades, new evidence of older sites in the southern reaches of South America has challenged the land bridge theory. Early humans may have arrived by combination of foot and on boats following the coastline south as early as 23,000 years ago. In Monte Verde, Chile, scientists have discovered some of the oldest undisputed evidence of human occupation in the Americas. Apparently, early peoples were seafarers (or at least seafood lovers): among the artifacts found were 10 different species of seaweed.

The earliest groups were nomadic hunter-gatherers who lived in small groups. Agriculture likely developed around 5000 BC with the planting of wild tubers such as manioc and sweet potato under systems of shifting cultivation. About the same time, highland people began to farm seed crops, such as beans, and to domesticate animals, such as the llama. One of South America's greatest foodstuffs is the humble but versatile potato, a root crop domesticated in the Andean highlands. Today, more than 6000 varieties of potato are cultivated there.

Complex societies first developed in the valleys of coastal Peru. Their growth was unsustainable, however – it's thought that the population of some of these valleys grew until all the cultivable land was occupied. The

TIMELINE

14,000–23,000 BC

Humans traveling from Asia, probably across the Bering land bridge, reach the Americas in one of the greatest human migration events in history.

1493

Inca Huayna Cápac begins his reign, pushing his vast empire north to Colombia; his untimely death in 1525 – probably from smallpox – leaves the kingdom fatally divided.

1494

Spain and Portugal sign the Treaty of Tordesillas, dividing newly discovered lands in the New World between them. The eastern half of South America will 'belong' to Portugal.

need to expand into neighboring valleys led the inhabitants to organize, innovate and conquer. Not dissimilar from what would happen after the Europeans arrived, conquerors became the rulers and the conquered became their subjects, thus developing the social and economic hierarchies of these early states and beyond.

These embyronic societies ultimately developed into major civilizations, such as the Wari empire of the Peruvian central highlands, the Tiahuanaco culture of highland Bolivia, the Chimú of northern Coastal Peru and the Inca empire of Cuzco.

The Chinchorro culture began mummifying their dead some 2000 years before the Egyptians. The oldest known mummy dates from around 5050 BC.

The Inca Empire

According to legend, the Inca civilization was born when Manco Cápac and his sister Mama Ocllo, children of the sun, emerged from Lake Titicaca to establish a civilization in the Cuzco Valley. Whether Manco Cápac was a historical figure is up for debate, but what is certain is that the Inca civilization was established in the area of Cuzco at some point in the 12th century. The reign of the first several incas (kings) is largely unremarkable, and for a couple of centuries they remained a small, regional state.

Expansion took off in the early 15th century, when the ninth king, Inca Yupanqui, defended Cuzco – against incredible odds – from the invading Chanka people to the north. After the victory, he took on the boastful new name of Pachacutec (Transformer of the Earth) and spent the next 25 years bagging much of the Andes. Under his reign, the Incas grew from a regional fiefdom in the Cuzco Valley into a broad empire of about 10 million people known as Tawantinsuyo (Land of Four Quarters). The kingdom covered most of modern Peru, in addition to pieces of Ecuador, Bolivia and Chile. The empire traversed the Andes with more than 8000km of highways and managed to control peoples from 100 separate cultures and 20 different language groups for about a century. This was made more remarkable by the fact that the Incas, as an ethnicity, never numbered more than about 100,000.

SETTLEMENTS IN THE AMAZON

New discoveries are reshaping the dominant thinking about pre-Columbian societies. The Amazon, once thought to be a wilderness incapable of supporting large populations, is now viewed as home to mound-building societies with some settlements containing as many as 100,000 inhabitants. At least 12% (and probably more) of the non-flooded Amazon forest is of anthropegenic origin (directly or indirectly altered by humans). Evidence of agriculture in the rainforest exists as far back as 4000 years ago, with as many as 140 different crops grown. Anthropologists have even found proof that early peoples used complex farming techniques to enrich the earth with microorganism-rich *terra preta* (black soil).

1548

Wine comes to Chile via missionaries and conquistadores. Jesuit priests cultivated early vineyards of rustic pais grapes; today Chile has more than 120 wineries and international distribution.

1550

Facing a shortage of labor (as *índios* die from introduced European diseases), Portugal turns to the African slave trade; open-air slave markets flourish in the slowly growing colony.

1807

Napoleon invades Portugal; the Portuguese prince regent (later known as Dom João VI) and his entire court of 15,000 flee for Brazil. The royal coffers shower wealth upon Rio.

1819

Simón Bolívar – crossing Los Llanos with an army of Venezuelans and Nueva Granadans from present-day Colombia – defeats the Spanish army at Boyacá; the Republic of Gran Colombia is founded.

Pachacutec allegedly gave Cuzco its layout in the form of a puma and built fabulous stone monuments in honor of Inca victories, including Sacsaywamán, the temple-fortress at Ollantaytambo and possibly Machu Picchu. He also improved the network of roads that connected the empire, further developed terrace agricultural systems and made Quechua the lingua franca.

The Portuguese Arrival

Portuguese explorers were the first Europeans to set foot on the South American continent. In 1500 a fleet of 12 Portuguese ships carrying nearly 1200 men dropped anchor near what is today Porto Seguro. There they erected a cross and held Mass in the land they baptized Terra da Vera Cruz (Land of the True Cross) before taking to the waves once again. Over the next century, the Portuguese set up coastal settlements in present-day Salvador, Rio de Janeiro and other coastal areas. There they harvested the profitable *pau brasil* (brazilwood), which gave the country its name.

Over the following centuries a four-front war was waged on the indigenous way of life. It was a cultural war, as well as a physical, territorial and biological one. Many indigenous peoples fell victim to the *bandeirantes* – groups of roaming adventurers who spent the 17th and 18th centuries exploring Brazil's interior, pillaging native settlements as they went. Those who escaped such a fate were struck down by the illnesses that traveled from Europe, to which they had no natural resistance. Others were worked to death on sugar plantations.

Historical Reads

1491: New Revelations of the Americas before Columbus (Charles C Mann)

Last Days of the Incas (Kim MacQuarrie)

Open Veins of Latin America (Eduardo Galeano)

Prisoner without a Name, Cell without a Number (Jacobo Timerman)

French philosopher Jean-Jacques Rousseau based his optimistic view of human nature (the noble savage) in part on early Portuguese descriptions of natives who were 'innocent, mild and peace-loving.'

Conquest of the Inca

While the Portuguese were battling for control over the eastern half of the continent, the Spaniards set their sights on South America's Pacific coast. Following rumors of golden splendor in the interior, Francisco Pizarro led an exploratory journey to the north coast of Peru. There, near Tumbes, a crew of welcoming natives offered them meat, fruit, fish and corn beer. To their delight, a cursory examination of the city revealed an abundance of silver and gold. The explorers quickly returned to Spain to court royal support for a bigger expedition.

They returned in September 1532, with a shipload of arms, horses and slaves, as well as a battalion of 168 men. Tumbes, the rich town Pizarro had visited just four years earlier, had been devastated by epidemics, as well as the recent Inca civil war. Atahualpa, in the meantime, was in the process of making his way down from Quito to Cuzco to claim his hard-won throne. When the Spanish arrived, he was in the highland settlement of Cajamarca, enjoying the area's mineral baths.

1830

Gran Colombia splits into Colombia (including modern-day Panama), Ecuador and Venezuela. Bolívar sends himself into exile; he dies in Santa Marta.

1834–35

HMS *Beagle* explores South America with Charles Darwin on board; the planned two-year expedition lasts five, giving Darwin fodder for his theory of evolution.

1865–70

Brazil, allied with Uruguay and Argentina, wages the 'War of the Triple Alliance' on Paraguay. South America's bloodiest conflict leaves untold thousands dead, and wipes out half of Paraguay's population.

1879–83

Chile wages war against Peru and Bolivia over nitrate-rich lands in the Atacama Desert; Bolivia loses its coastline and Peru and loses its southernmost region of Tarapacá.

Pizarro quickly deduced that the empire was in a fractious state. He and his men charted a course to Cajamarca and approached Atahualpa with royal greetings and promises of brotherhood. But the well-mannered overtures quickly devolved into a surprise attack that left thousands of Incas dead and Atahualpa a prisoner of war. (Between their horses, their armor and the steel of their blades, the Spanish were practically invincible against fighters armed only with clubs, slings and wicker helmets.)

In an attempt to regain his freedom, Atahualpa offered the Spanish a bounty of gold and silver. Thus began one of the most famous ransoms in history – with the Incas attempting to fill an entire room with the precious stuff in order to placate the unrelenting appetites of the Spanish. But it was never enough. The Spanish held Atahualpa for eight months before executing him with a garrote at the age of 31.

The Inca empire never recovered from this fateful encounter. The arrival of the Spanish brought on a cataclysmic collapse of indigenous society. One scholar estimates that the native population – around 10 million when Pizarro arrived – was reduced to 600,000 within a century.

At the height of its empire, the Inca ruled more than 12 million people across some 1 million sq km.

The Africans

The slave trade practiced by early European traders from the 1500s to 1866 enslaved as many as 12.5 million people – some 10.7 million surviving the grueling journey to the Americas. Only a fraction (around half a million) ended up in North America. The rest were destined for Latin America and the Caribbean with the majority (as many as six million) ending up in Brazil, most of them working on the back-breaking sugarcane plantations. They were torn from a variety of tribes in Angola, Mozambique and Guinea, as well as the Sudan and Congo. Whatever their origins and cultures, their destinations were identical: slave markets such as Salvador's Pelourinho or Belém's Mercado Ver-o-Peso. Elsewhere, smaller numbers of Africans were taken to Peru, Colombia, the Guianas and all along the Caribbean coast.

For those who survived such ordeals, arrival in the New World meant only continued suffering. A slave's existence was one of brutality and humiliation. Kind masters were the exception, not the rule, and labor on the plantations was relentless. Slaves were required to work as many as 17 hours each day, before retiring to the squalid *senzala* (slave quarters), and with as many as 200 slaves packed into each dwelling, hygiene was a concept as remote as the distant coasts of Africa. Dysentery, typhus, yellow fever, malaria, tuberculosis and scurvy were rife; malnutrition a fact of life.

Syphilis also plagued a slave population sexually exploited by its masters. Sexual relations between masters and slaves were so common that a large mixed-race population soon emerged. Off the plantations there

Guns, Germs & Steel, the Pulitzer Prize–winning book by Jared Diamond is a thoughtful, biological examination of why some European societies triumphed over so many others. The battle for Cajamarca and Atahualpa's capture by the Spanish are discussed at length.

1888

Slavery is abolished in Brazil, the last country in the New World to do so. The law is signed by Princesa Isabel, admired by many blacks as their benefactress.

1890s

With slavery abolished, Brazil opens its borders to meet its labor needs. Over the next four decades, millions arrive from Italy, Portugal, Spain, Germany and later Japan and other countries.

1967

Argentine revolutionary Ernesto 'Che' Guevara, having failed to foment a peasant revolt in Bolivia, is executed by a US-backed military squad in the hamlet of La Higuera.

1970

A 7.7-magnitude earthquake in northern Peru kills almost 80,000 people, leaves 140,000 injured and another 500,000 homeless.

was a shortage of white women, so many poorer white settlers lived with black or indigenous women.

Many slaves escaped from their masters to form *quilombos*, communities of runaway slaves that quickly spread across the countryside. The most famous, the Republic of Palmares, which survived through much of the 17th century, was home to some 20,000 people before it was destroyed by federal troops.

Most countries in South America banned slavery between 1816 and 1831, but in Brazil, it wasn't until 1888 that slavery was finally outlawed. Unsurprisingly, this didn't make a huge immediate difference to the welfare of the 800,000 freed slaves, who were largely illiterate and unskilled. Thousands were cast into the streets without any kind of infrastructure to support them. Many died, while others flooded to Brazil's urban centers, adding to the cities' first slums. Even today, blacks overall remain among the poorest and worst-educated groups in the country.

One of Brazil's great folk heroes is Chico Rei, an African king enslaved and brought to work in the mines, but who managed to buy his freedom and later the freedom of his tribe.

Independence

By the early 19th century, *criollos* (creoles, born in the New World to Spanish parents) in many Spanish colonies had grown increasingly dissatisfied with their lack of administrative power and the crown's heavy taxes – leading to revolutions all over the continent. Argentine revolutionary José de San Martín led independence campaigns in Argentina and Chile (1818), before sailing up the coast to take Lima in 1821. From the opposite direction came Simón Bolívar, the Venezuelan revolutionary who had been leading independence fights in Venezuela, Colombia and Ecuador.

The two famous liberators met in Guayaquil, Ecuador, in 1822. At this famous meeting, the apolitical San Martín found himself in conflict with Bolívar, who had strong political ambitions. San Martín considered the installation of a powerful leader, even a monarch, as essential to avoid the disintegration of Peru, while Bolívar insisted on a constitutional republic. In a complicated exchange, which aroused ill-feeling in both camps, Bolívar won the day and San Martín returned to the south. In the long run, both were disappointed. The proliferation of *caudillos* (local warlords) set a deplorable pattern for most of the 19th century.

The first *favela* (slum or shantytown) appeared on Rio's landscape in 1897, but it wasn't until 1994 that the communities (which today number over 600) were included on maps.

Ever in its own world, Brazil followed quite a different path to independence. Unlike other countries in the New World, Brazil had a European monarch living within its borders in the early 1800s. Brazil became a temporary sanctuary to the Portuguese royal family, who fled from the advance of Napoleon in Iberia in 1807. The prince regent – and future king, Dom João VI – fell in love with Rio, naming it the capital of the United Kingdom of Portugal, Brazil and the Algarves. His affection for Brazil was so strong that he didn't want to return to Portugal even after Napoleon's defeat at Waterloo in 1815. He finally returned to Europe six

1970

Chile's Salvador Allende becomes the world's first democratically elected Marxist president. Radical social reform follows; the state takes control of private enterprises alongside massive income redistribution.

1973–89

Following a military coup, General Augusto Pinochet takes charge of Chile. He dissolves Congress, prohibits nearly all political activity and rules by decree.

1976–83

Under the leadership of General Jorge Videla, a military junta takes control of Argentina, launching the country into the Dirty War. In eight years, an estimated 30,000 people 'disappear.'

1992

Thousands of indigenous protesters seeking land reform march in Quito on the 500th anniversary of Columbus' arrival. In ensuing negotiations, they are granted title to 2.5 million acres in Amazonia.

years later, leaving his son Pedro as prince regent. When the Portuguese parliament attempted to restore Brazil to its previous status as subservient colony, Dom Pedro rebelled and declared Brazil independent, declaring himself at the country's head as Emperor Dom Pedro I. Portugal was too weak to fight its favorite son, so without spilling blood, Brazil attained its independence in 1822.

Robert Harvey's extremely readable *Liberators: South America's Struggle for Independence* (2002) tells the epic history of colonial Latin America through larger-than-life heroes and swashbucklers such as O'Higgins, San Martín and Lord Cochrane.

Modern Times

The 20th century was a tumultuous period for South America, with political turmoil and economic crises paving the way for the rise of military dictatorships. The social unrest that followed the Great Depression of 1929 provided justification for the army to intervene in countries across the continent. In Argentina, the pro-fascist general José Félix Uriburu seized control during a military coup in 1930, ushering in the so-called Infamous Decade. Likewise, the 1930s saw military coups and repressive regimes rise in Peru and Chile. In Brazil, it was the era of the autocratic Getulio Vargas, when rival political parties were banned, the press was muzzled and opponents were imprisoned.

Unfortunately, this was just the beginning, with far more horrifying dictatorships on the horizon. The 1960s and 1970s were an even darker period in South America when military dictatorships ruled in Argentina, Bolivia, Brazil, Chile, Paraguay, Peru, Suriname and Uruguay. Student- and worker-led movements crying out for social justice were met with increasing brutality.

In the late 1960s and '70s in Argentina, anti-government feeling was rife and street protests often exploded into all-out riots. Armed guerrilla organizations emerged as radical opponents of the military, the oligarchies and US influence in Latin America. In 1976, the army general Jorge Rafael Videla seized power, ushering in a bloody seven-year period known as the Dirty War. Security forces went about the country arresting, torturing and killing anyone on their hit list of suspected leftists. As many as 30,000 people were 'disappeared' – that is, murdered.

In his magic realism novel *One Hundred Years of Solitude* (1967), Gabriel García Márquez depicts the back-and-forth brutality of Liberal and Conservative rivalries and vendettas in ongoing conflicts from 1885 to 1902 in the fictional village of Macondo.

In Chile, there was hope for a brighter future when socialist candidate Salvador Allende was elected in 1970. This was soon crushed, however, when Augusto Pinochet led a coup in 1973. Ruling until 1989, he would become Latin America's most notorious dictator, with thousands of suspected leftists jailed, tortured and executed, and hundreds of thousands fleeing the country.

Meanwhile in Brazil, military dictators ran the show from 1964 to 1984. Though not as brutal as the Chilean or Argentine regime, it was still a period when dissent was crushed, political parties were banned and the media was muzzled. Things remained grim throughout South America until the early 1990s when democracy at last returned to most of the continent.

1998

Hugo Chavez becomes president of Venezuela. He invests in social programs, while also nationalizing industries, centralizing power and crushing dissent.

2001

Unemployment reaches 18.3% as a vast financial crisis hits Argentina. Interim president Duhalde devalues the peso and defaults on US$140 billion in debt, the biggest default in world history.

2014

Brazil hosts the 2014 FIFA World Cup, spending around US$12 billion in preparation for the event, which was staged at 12 different cities across the country.

2015

Pope Francis visits Bolivia and humbly begs forgiveness for the grave sins committed against indigenous peoples of America in the name of God.

South American People & Culture

There are so many layers to South American culture. Religion is a key component of life on the continent, where Christianity, indigenous beliefs and African religions have all shaped identity. South America is also the birthplace of great music including samba, tango, Andean sounds and countless other regional genres. While religion and music can be great unifiers across the socioeconomic divide, there is still a huge gulf between haves and have-nots in this highly stratified society.

Multiculturalism

Dozens of uncontacted indigenous groups still live in the Amazon. In 2007, 89 Metyktire suddenly emerged in a village in Pará, the first time this particular group (feared dead) had been encountered since 1950.

One of the more unusual Amazonian leaders is the 50-something 'Gringo Chief,' Randy Borman. Born to American missionaries living in the Amazon, he has become one of the Cofán's most influential chiefs. He speaks flawless Cofán and has helped the tribe win major land concessions.

South America boasts astonishing diversity. The continent has been shaped by the original indigenous inhabitants, European colonists and Africans brought over as slaves to toil in the plantations and mines in the New World. The level of intermixing varied greatly from country to country, which has led to the relative diversity or homogeneity of the population.

Immigration has also added to the complex ethnic tapestry of the continent. For decades, the US was a major destination for migrants from South America. These days, there's much more migration happening internally (ie between South American countries), with Brazil, Argentina and Chile attracting the largest numbers of migrants, largely from neighboring countries. There are also complicated dynamics at work in each of the continent's 13 countries. Ecuador for instance, with a population of just 16 million, has an estimated two million emigrants, living in the US, Italy and Spain; in the latter, they make up the largest contingent of Latin Americans. On the flipside, Ecuador has seen an influx of refugees (in the 1980s and 1990s) fleeing from conflicts in neighboring Colombia, and opportunity-seeking migrants from Peru. The situation, however, remains quite fluid. Since 2008, with improved job opportunities at home, a growing number of Ecuadorians are choosing to return home.

In the 19th century, Brazil and Argentina saw mass immigration from Europe: Spaniards, Italians, Germans and Eastern Europeans were the most common immigrants moving to the New World. Brazil also welcomed immigrants from Japan, Portugal and the Middle East. They worked in a wide variety of fields, from coffee plantations and farming to heavy industry in the continent's growing cities. The influx of new arrivals continued well into the 20th century, with tumult in Europe causing the flight of Jews fleeing persecution from the Nazis, followed by Nazis looking to avoid being put on trial for war crimes, in addition to Italians and others escaping their ravaged cities in the postwar period.

Lifestyles

No matter where you go in South America, you'll likely encounter a yawning divide between rich and poor. Modern-day South Americans inherited a highly stratified society from the slave-owning European colonial founders, and this dispiriting chasm persists centuries later between the haves and have-nots of both urban and rural society. At the bottom of the heap are those struggling in low-wage jobs in the city, or scraping out a meager existence in the countryside – many are barely able to put food on the table. Those who live in rural areas are practically invisible to urban middle and upper classes.

The middle and upper class live in comfortable apartments or houses, with all the trappings of the developed world, including good healthcare in private clinics, cars, vacations away and easy access to the latest gadgets and trends (though iPhones and laptops are pricier here). Owing to low wages, maids are common, even among the middle class. Crime is likely to be of high concern, and those who can afford it live in high-security buildings or gated residential complexes.

Domesticas (Maids), the first film by Fernando Meirelles, delves into the lives of five women who work as *domesticas*, creating a compelling portrait of Brazil's often overlooked underclass.

The divide is greatest in struggling countries like Bolivia, where nearly half the population lives below the poverty line. There many live without running water, electricity and heat, and the threat of illness looms high over children – with the majority of childhood deaths associated with malnutrition and poverty.

There is some good news, however. Throughout South America, the poverty rate has fallen over the past decade, from 17% to 7% overall, according to a recent Pew Research Center report. During the same period, South America has also seen a substantial boost to the middle class (growing from 16% to 27% of the population). Income redistribution policies have helped expand the middle class and lessen the gap between rich and poor.

Religion

Christianity

The dominant religion in South America is Roman Catholicism, a legacy from the early Spanish and Portuguese colonizers. The number of followers varies by region, with no small degree of complexity from country to country (in Argentina, for instance, 92% of the population call themselves Catholic, though less than 20% practice regularly). On average though, typically 70% or more of each country's population professes to be Roman Catholic. The ranks are declining from year to year, and many people (particularly in urban areas) merely turn up to church for the basics: baptism, marriage and burial. Nevertheless, the church still has a strong visible presence here. Nearly every city, town or village has a central church or cathedral, and the calendar is loaded with Catholic holidays and celebrations.

It was a Peruvian priest, Gustavo Gutiérrez, who first articulated the principles of liberation theology – the theory that links Christian thought to social justice – in 1971. He now teaches in the United States.

Evangelical Christianity, meanwhile, is booming. All across the continent, especially in poor communities where people are most desperate, stand simple, recently built churches full of worshipers. The religion has done particularly well here with converts from Catholicism often citing a more personal relationship with God, as well as receiving more direct guidance in the realm of health, jobs and living a moral life. The firebrand Pentecostal branch attracts many new followers, with its emphasis on divine healing, speaking in tongues and receiving direct messages from God. With the current growth of the Evangelical church, some predict that the majority of South America will be Protestant by 2050.

Indigenous Beliefs

Among indigenous peoples, allegiance to Catholicism was often a clever veneer adopted to disguise traditional beliefs ostensibly forbidden by the church.

In parts of the interior, the Amazon and the Andes, shamanism and animism still flourish. There is also a strong belief in powerful spirits that inhabit the natural world – the sky, mountains, lightning and the wind. Some groups, like the Andean Aymara, practice a syncretic religion that pays equal homage to both deities and Catholic saints. They may attend Mass, baptisms and saint's day celebrations, while also paying respect to Pachamama (Mother Earth) come harvest time. The old Inca celebration of Inti Raymi (Festival of the Sun) is celebrated with fervor in some parts of the Andes. It happens on the solstice (late June) and commemorates the mythical birth of the Inca.

African Religions

Slaves brought over a handful of West African religions to the New World, which were adapted over the centuries. The best known and most orthodox is Candomblé, which arrived in Brazil via the Nago, Yoruba and Jeje peoples. It later found root in Bahia, where it is still practiced today. Candomblé denotes a dance in honor of the gods, and indeed trance-like dancing is an essential part of the religion. Afro-Brazilian rituals are directed by Candomblé priests, the *pai de santo* or *mãe de santo* (literally 'saint's father' or 'saint's mother'), and practiced in a *casa de santo* or *terreiro* (house of worship).

The religion centers upon the *orixás*. Like the gods in Greek mythology, each *orixá* has a unique personality and history. Although *orixás* are divided into male and female types there are some that can switch from one sex to the other, such as Logunedé, the son of two male gods, or Oxumaré, who is male for six months of the year and female for the other six months. (Candomblé, not surprisingly, is much more accepting of homosexuality and bisexuality than other religions.)

Candomblé followers believe that every person has a particular deity watching over them, and followers give food or other offerings to their respective *orixá*.

Of the infinite varieties of music that exist all over Peru, the Afro-Peruvian tunes from the coast are perhaps the grooviest. For an excellent primer, listen to the David Byrne–produced compilation *Afro-Peruvian Classics: The Soul of Black Peru*.

Music

Tango

Music plays a key part in festivities across the continent, and it also takes center stage when it comes to nightlife in many cities. The tango is deeply linked to Buenos Aires (though the music also has ties to lesser known Montevideo in Uruguay). It emerged from the country's bordellos in the late 19th century, though it didn't become mainstream until Carlos Gardel helped popularize the songs in the 1920s and 1930s. Although Gardel was born in France, he was brought by his destitute single mother to Buenos Aires when he was three years old. In his youth he entertained neighbors with his rapturous singing, then went on to establish a successful performing career. He single-handedly helped bring tango out of the tenement and onto the world stage. He died tragically in a plane crash at the height of his career and was mourned around the world.

Another seminal figure in the tango world was Astor Piazzolla, who moved the genre from the dance halls into the concert halls. Tango nueva, as it was called when it emerged in the 1950s, was given a newfound respect, with its blend of jazz and classical elements and new forms of melodic structures. Piazzolla also paved the way for the tango fusion, which emerged in the 1970s and continues to this day with tango electrónico groups such as Gotan Project Bajofondo Tango Club and Tanghetto.

Samba & Bossa Nova

The birth of modern Brazilian music essentially began with the birth of samba, first heard in the early 20th century in a Rio neighborhood near present-day Praça Onze. Here, Bahian immigrants formed a tightly knit community in which traditional African customs thrived – music, dance and the Candomblé religion. Such an atmosphere nurtured the likes of Pixinguinha, one of samba's founding fathers, as well as Donga, one of the composers of 'Pelo Telefone,' the first recorded samba song (1917) and an enormous success at the then-fledgling Carnaval.

Samba continued to evolve in the homes and *botequims* (neighborhood bars) around Rio. The 1930s are known as the golden age of samba. Sophisticated lyricists such as Dorival Caymmi and Noel Rosa wrote popular songs featuring sentimental lyrics and an emphasis on melody (rather than rhythm), foreshadowing the later advent of cool bossa nova. The 1930s were also the golden age of samba songwriting for Carnaval.

In the 1950s came bossa nova (literally, 'new wave'), sparking a new era of Brazilian music. Bossa nova's founders – songwriter and composer Antônio Carlos (Tom) Jobim and guitarist João Gilberto, in association with the lyricist-poet Vinícius de Moraes – slowed down and altered the basic samba rhythm to create a more intimate, harmonic style. Bossa nova was also associated with the new class of university-educated Brazilians. Its lyrics reflected the optimistic mood of the middle class in the 1950s, and by the following decade it had become a huge international success.

Cumbia villera is a relatively recent musical phenomenon: a fusion of cumbia and gangsta posturing with a punk edge and reggae overtones. Born of Buenos Aires' shantytowns, its aggressive lyrics deal with marginalization, poverty, drugs, sex and the Argentine economic crisis.

Andean Sounds

The breathy, mournful songs played by groups across the western half of the continent (from Chile up to Venezuela) are all part of the legacy of Andean folk music. Its roots date back to pre-Inca times when music was

PROTEST SONGS

South America went through a dark epoch in the 20th century, when military dictatorships controlled vast swaths of the continent. Crying out against the oppression were a handful of brave singers and songwriters who targeted the atrocities being committed, and led the call for social justice. The socially progressive folk music of *nueva canción* (literally, 'new song'), which emerged from Latin America in the 1960s, flourished in Chile during the dictatorship of Pinochet and soon spread to other countries. Singer Víctor Jara, who sang of peace and social justice, paid for his activist views with his life, when he was tortured and murdered by the Chilean military in 1973.

In Argentina, singer Mercedes Sosa was one of the leading figures of the protest movement, and became known as 'the voice of the voiceless' for her courageous performances. Antagonized by Argentina's military rulers, she was banished from the country in 1979, and returned in 1982 shortly before the collapse of the military regime.

In Brazil, one of the seminal figures of protest against the military (in power from 1964 to 1984) was Chico Buarque, considered one of the country's finest songwriters. His poetic lyrics were cleverly worded and used cryptic analogies that were often overlooked by military censors. Songs like 'A Pesar de Você' (In Spite of You) became national songs of protest for social justice.

largely played during religious ceremonies. It was viewed as a sacred art with connections to the divine world, and it paid homage to the spirits that were believed to inhabit the natural world.

Bossa Nova: The Story of the Brazilian Music that Seduced the World, by Ruy Castro, is an excellent book that captures the vibrant music and its backdrop of 1950s Rio.

Musical styles vary from region to region (with four-, five-, six- or seven-note scales), but the instruments are often quite similar. Panpipes are a staple: usually made of bamboo, these instruments consist of a single or double row of hollow tubes, and come in a bewildering variety of sizes. These are often accompanied by a smaller flute-like *quena*, a bass drum and a stringed instrument (an influence adopted from Europe), such as the 10-string *charango*, which is similar to a mandolin.

Prior to the Spaniards, wind and percussion were the dominant sounds – fitting for a region of fiery volcanoes and bone-chilling gales that blow across the highlands.

Survival Guide

Directory A–Z

Accommodations

Costs vary from country to country, with Andean countries (especially Bolivia) being the cheapest (from around US$10 per night) and Brazil, Chile, Argentina and the Guianas the costliest (upwards of US$30).

Camping

Camping is an obvious choice in parks and reserves and is a useful budget option in pricier countries such as Chile. Bring all your own gear. While camping gear is available in large cities and in trekking and activities hubs, it's expensive and choices are usually minimal. Camping gear can be rented in areas with substantial camping and trekking action (eg the Lake District, Mendoza and Huaraz), but quality is sometimes dubious.

An alternative to tent camping is staying in *refugios* (simple structures within parks and reserves), where a basic bunk and kitchen access are usually provided. For climbers, most summit attempts involve staying in a *refugio*.

Hostels

Albergues (hostels) have become increasingly popular throughout South America and, as throughout the world, are great places to socialize with other travelers. You'll rarely find an official *albergue juvenil* (youth hostel); most hostels accept all ages and are not affiliated with Hostelling International (HI).

Hotels

When it comes to hotels, both terminology and criteria vary. The costliest are *hoteles* (hotels) proper. A step down in price are *hostales* (small hotels or guesthouses). The cheapest places are *hospedajes, casas de huéspedes, residenciales, alojamientos* and *pensiones*. A room in these places includes a bed with (hopefully) clean sheets and a blanket, maybe a table and chair and sometimes a fan. Showers and toilets are generally shared; there may not be hot water. Cleanliness varies widely, but many places are remarkably tidy. In some areas, especially southern Chile, the cheapest places may be *casas familiares*, family houses whose hospitality makes them excellent value.

In Brazil, Argentina and some other places, prices often include breakfast, the quality of which is usually directly related to the room price.

Hot-water supplies are often erratic, or may be available only at certain hours of the day. It's something to ask about (and consider paying extra for), especially in the highlands and far south, where it gets cold.

When showering, beware the electric shower head, an innocent looking unit that heats cold water with an electric element. Don't touch the shower head or anything metal when the water is on or you may get shocked – never strong enough to throw you across the room, but hardly pleasant.

Dormitory prices are for rooms with shared bathrooms, while room prices include private bathrooms, unless otherwise noted.

BOOK YOUR STAY ONLINE

For more accommodations reviews by Lonely Planet authors, check out http://lonelyplanet.com/hotels/. You'll find independent reviews, as well as recommendations on the best places to stay. Best of all, you can book online.

Business Hours

Generally, businesses are open from 8am or 9am to 8pm or 9pm Monday through Friday, with a two-hour lunch break around noon. Businesses are often open on Saturday, usually with shorter hours. Banks usually only change money Monday through Friday. On

Sunday, nearly everything is closed. In the Andean countries, businesses tend to close earlier.

Customs Regulations

Customs vary slightly from country to country, but you can generally bring in personal belongings, camera gear, laptops, handheld devices and other travel-related gear. All countries prohibit the export (just as home countries prohibit the import) of archaeological items and goods made from rare or endangered animals. Avoid carrying plants, seeds, fruits and fresh meat products across borders.

Discount Cards

A Hostelling International–American Youth Hostel (HI-USA) membership card can be useful in Brazil and Chile (and to a lesser extent in Argentina and Uruguay) where there are many hostels, and accommodations tend to be, or traditionally have been, costlier. Elsewhere on the continent, cheap hotels and *pensiones* typically cost less than affiliated hostels.

An International Student Identity Card (ISIC) can provide discounted admission to archaeological sites and museums. It may also entitle you to reductions on bus, train and air tickets. In less developed countries, student discounts are rare, although high-ticket items such as the entrance to Machu Picchu (discounted 50% for ISIC holders under 26) may be reduced. In some countries, such as Argentina, almost any form of university identification will suffice where discounts are offered.

Electricity

Electricity is not standard across South America. Voltage ranges from 100 to 240V, with the most common plug types being flat-pronged American style and rounded European style. See individual country directories for details.

Embassies & Consulates

As a visitor in a South American country, it's important to realize what your own embassy – the embassy of the country of which you are a citizen – can and cannot do. Generally speaking, it won't be much help in emergencies where you're even remotely at fault. Remember that you are bound by the laws of the country you are in. Your embassy will not be sympathetic if you end up in jail after committing a crime locally, even if such actions are legal in your own country.

In genuine emergencies you may get some assistance, but only if other channels have been exhausted. For example, if you have all your money and documents stolen, it might assist in getting a new passport, but a loan for onward travel will be out of the question.

For embassy and consulate addresses and phone numbers, see each country's Directory section.

Gay & Lesbian Travelers

Buenos Aires, Rio de Janeiro and São Paulo are the most gay-friendly cities, though gay couples are openly out only in certain neighborhoods. Salvador (Brazil), Bogotá and to a lesser extent Santiago also have lively gay scenes. Elsewhere on the continent, where public displays of affection by same-sex couples may get negative reactions, do as the locals do – be discreet to avoid problems.

Despite a growing number of publications and websites devoted to gay travel, few have specific advice on South America. One exception is **Purple Roofs** (www.purpleroofs.com), an excellent guide to gay-friendly accommodations throughout South America.

Insurance

A travel insurance policy covering theft, loss, accidents and illness is highly recommended. Many policies include a card with toll-free numbers for 24-hour assistance, and it's good practice to carry it with you. Note that some policies compensate travelers for misrouted or lost luggage. Baggage insurance is worth its price in peace of mind. Also check that the coverage includes worst-case scenarios: ambulances, evacuations or an emergency flight home. Some policies specifically exclude 'dangerous activities,' such as scuba diving, motorcycling or even trekking. If such activities are on your agenda, avoid this sort of policy.

There is a wide variety of policies available and your travel agent will be able to make recommendations. The policies handled by student-travel organizations usually offer good value. If a policy offers lower and higher medical-expense options, the low-expenses policy should be OK for South America – medical costs are not nearly as high here as elsewhere in the world.

If you have baggage insurance and need to make a claim, the insurance company may demand a receipt as proof that you bought the stuff in the first place. You must usually inform the insurance company by airmail and report the loss or theft to local police within 24 hours. Make a list of stolen items and their value. At the police station, you complete a *denuncia* (statement), a copy of which is given to you for your insurance claim.

Worldwide travel insurance is available at www.lonelyplanet.com/bookings. You can buy, claim and extend online anytime – even if you're already on the road.

Internet Access

Wi-fi access is widely available, with many hostels, cafes and guesthouses offering free wi-fi. In contrast, internet cafes aren't as prevalent as they once were. Rates generally hover around US$1 to US$2 per hour (upwards of US$6 per hour in Brazil, Argentina and Chile).

Language Courses

Spanish-language courses are available in many South American cities, with Cuzco (Peru), Arequipa (Peru), Quito and Cuenca (Ecuador) and Buenos Aires being some of the best. For Portuguese, Rio de Janeiro is a great place to spend some time studying. For Quechua and Aymara, try Cochabamba (Bolivia) or Cuzco.

Legal Matters

In city police stations, an English-speaking interpreter is a rarity. In most cases you'll either have to speak the local language or provide an interpreter. Some cities have a tourist police service, which can be more helpful.

If you are robbed, photocopies (even better, certified copies) of original passports, visas and air tickets and careful records of credit card numbers and traveler's checks will prove invaluable during replacement procedures. Replacement passport applications are usually referred to the home country, so it helps to leave a copy of your passport details with someone back home.

Maps

International Travel Maps & Books (www.itmb.com) produces a range of excellent maps of Central and South America. For the whole continent, they have a reliable three-sheet map at a 1:4,000,000 scale and a commemorative edition of their classic 1:500,000 map. The maps are huge for road use, but they're helpful for pre-trip planning. More detailed ITMB maps are available for the Amazon Basin, Ecuador, Bolivia and Venezuela. All are available on the ITMB website.

Maps of the South American continent as a whole are widely available; check any well-stocked map or travel bookstore. **South American Explorers** (www.saexplorers.org) has maps, including topographical, regional and city maps.

Money

Prices quoted are given in the locally used currency. Note that US dollars are used in Ecuador and euros in French Guiana. For exchange rates, see www.xe.com.

Fraud

Unfortunately, ATM-card cloning is a big worry in Brazil, and your account can be drained of thousands of dollars before you even realize it. While fool-proof prevention is nearly impossible, the Brazil section lists a few tips that can help minimize the risk.

ATMs

ATMs are available in most cities and large towns, and are almost always the most convenient, reliable and economical way of getting cash. The rate of exchange is usually as good as any bank or legal money changer. Many ATMs are connected to the Cirrus or Plus network, but many countries prefer one over the other. If your ATM card gets swallowed by a machine, generally the only thing you can do is call your bank and cancel the card. Although such events are rare, it's well worth having an extra ATM card (to a different account), should something go wrong.

If possible, sign up with a bank that doesn't charge a fee for out-of-network ATM withdrawals. Also, find a bank that offers a low exchange rate fee (1% to 2%). Before hitting the road, call your bank, informing them of your travel plans – that way the bank won't put a hold on foreign withdrawals while you're on the road.

Many ATMs will accept a personal identification number (PIN) of only four digits; find out whether this applies to the specific countries you're traveling to before heading off.

Bargaining

Bargaining is accepted and expected when contracting long-term accommodations and when shopping for craft goods in markets. Haggling is a near sport in the Andean countries, with patience, humor and respect serving as the ground rules of the game. Bargaining is much less common in the Cono Sur (Southern Cone; a collective term for Argentina, Chile, Uruguay and parts of Brazil and Paraguay). When you head into the bargaining trenches, remember that the point is to have fun while reaching a mutually satisfying end: the merchant should not try to fleece you, but you shouldn't try to get something for nothing either.

Black Market

Nowadays, official exchange rates are generally realistic in most South American countries, so the role of the black market is declining. Most people end up using the *mercado negro* (black market) when crossing isolated borders, where an official exchange facility might be hours away. Some travelers might still want to use street money changers if they need to exchange cash outside business hours, but with the convenience of ATM cards, this necessity is declining. The one notable exception to this is Venezuela, where ATM withdrawals and credit-card transactions cost about twice as much as exchanging cash on the black market.

Street money changers may or may not be legal (but are often tolerated), and the practice of changing money on the street is prone to scams – one such trick consists of money changers handing their client the agreed amount less a few pesos; when the client complains, they will take it back adding the few pesos while making a few larger notes disappear. Money changers may also distract their customers during the transaction alerting them to supposed alarms such as 'police' or any other 'danger,' or use fixed calculators which give an exchange rate favorable only to the money changer, or pass counterfeit, torn, smudged or tattered bills.

Cash

It's convenient to have a small wad of US dollars tucked away (in 20-dollar denominations and less; 100-dollar bills are difficult to exchange). US currency is by far the easiest to exchange throughout South America. Of course, unlike traveler's checks, nobody will give you a refund for lost or stolen cash. When you're about to cross from one country to another, it's handy to change some cash. Trying to exchange worn notes can be a hassle, so procure crisp bills before setting out.

In some countries, especially in rural areas, *cambio* (change) can be particularly hard to come by. Businesses even occasionally refuse to sell you something if they can't or don't want to change your note. So break down those larger bills whenever you have the opportunity, such as at busy restaurants, banks and larger businesses.

Credit Cards

The big-name credit cards are accepted at most large stores, travel agencies and better hotels and restaurants. Credit card purchases sometimes attract an extra *recargo* (surcharge) on the price (from 2% to 10%), but they are usually billed to your account at favorable exchange rates. Some banks issue cash advances on major credit cards. The most widely accepted card is Visa, followed by MasterCard (those with UK Access should insist on its affiliation with MasterCard). American Express and Diners Club are also accepted in some places.

Exchanging Money

Traveler's checks and foreign cash can be changed at *casas de cambio* (currency-exchange offices) or banks. Rates are usually similar, but *casas de cambio* are quicker, less bureaucratic and open longer hours.

It is preferable to bring money in US dollars, although banks and *casas de cambio* in capital cities will change euros, pounds sterling, Japanese yen and other major currencies. Changing these currencies in smaller towns and on the street is next to impossible.

Traveler's Checks

Traveler's checks are not nearly as convenient as ATM cards, and you may have difficulty cashing them – even at banks. High commissions (from 3% to upwards of 10%) also make them an unattractive option. If you do take traveler's checks, American Express is the most widely accepted brand, while Visa, Thomas Cook and Citibank are the next best options. To facilitate replacement in case of theft, keep a record of check numbers and the original bill of sale in a safe place. Even with proper records, replacement can be a tedious, time-intensive process.

Photography

Photographing People

Ask for permission before photographing individuals, particularly indigenous people. Paying folks for their portrait is a personal decision; in most cases, the subject will tell you right off the going rate for a photo.

Restrictions

Some tourist sites charge an additional fee for tourists with cameras. Don't take photos of military installations, military personnel or security-sensitive places such as police stations. Such activities may be illegal and could even endanger your life. In most churches, flash photography (and sometimes any photography) is not allowed.

Post

International postal rates can be quite expensive. Generally, important mail and parcels should be sent by registered or certified service; otherwise, they may go missing. Sending parcels can be awkward: often an *aduana* (customs) officer must inspect the contents before a postal clerk can accept them, so wait to seal your package until after it has been checked. Most post offices have a parcels window, usually signed *encomiendas* (parcels). The place for posting overseas parcels is sometimes different from the main post office.

UPS, FedEx, DHL and other private postal services are available in some countries, but are prohibitively expensive.

Safe Travel

There are potential dangers to traveling in South America, but with sensible precautions, you are unlikely to encounter serious problems. Your greatest threats will likely be reckless drivers, pollution, fiesta fireworks and low-hanging objects (watch your head!).

Confidence Tricks & Scams

Keep your wits about you if nefarious substances (mustard, bird droppings, human excrement) are thrown upon you followed by the appearance of someone who lends a helping hand, while others steal your belongings. Other scams to be aware of involve a quantity of cash being 'found' on the street, whereby the do-gooder tries to return it to you, elaborate hard-luck stories from supposed travelers and 'on-the-spot fines' by bogus police. Be especially wary if one or more 'plainclothes' cops demand to search your luggage or examine your documents, traveler's checks or cash. Insist that you will allow this only at an official police station or in the presence of a uniformed officer, and don't allow anyone to take you anywhere in a taxi or unmarked car. Thieves often work in pairs to distract you while lifting your wallet. Simply stay alert.

Kidnapping

Be careful when taking taxis. 'Express' kidnappings occur in some cities. These incidents involve whisking travelers to far-off neighborhoods and holding them there while their ATM accounts are emptied; sometimes assaults have also occurred. We've noted in individual country chapters the known places that pose this kind of risk to travelers. To be on the safe side, have your guesthouse call you a taxi rather than hailing one on the street, and use official taxis at airports rather than those outside the gates. And never ride in a vehicle that already has a passenger in it.

Drugging

Lonely Planet has received correspondence from travelers who were unwittingly drugged and robbed after accepting food from a stranger.

Be very careful in bars, there are occasional reports of folks being unwittingly drugged then raped or robbed. Always keep a close eye on your drink, and be cautious when meeting new friends.

Drugs

And now a word from your mother: marijuana and cocaine are big business in parts of South America. They are available in many places but illegal everywhere (with the exception of marijuana in Uruguay; see p932). Indulging can either land you in jail or worse. Unless you're willing to take these risks, avoid illegal drugs.

Beware that drugs are sometimes used to set up travelers for blackmail and bribery. Avoid any conversation with someone proffering drugs. If you're in an area where drug trafficking is prevalent, ignore it entirely, with conviction.

In Bolivia and Peru, chewing coca leaves or drinking *maté de coca* (coca leaf-infused tea) may help alleviate some of effects of altitude. Keep in mind, though, that transporting coca leaves over international borders is illegal.

Natural Hazards

The Pacific Rim 'ring of fire' loops through eastern Asia, Alaska and all the way down through the Americas to Tierra del Fuego in a vast circle of earthquake and volcanic activity that includes the whole Pacific side of South America. Volcanoes usually give some notice before blowing and are therefore unlikely to pose any immediate threat to travelers. Earthquakes, however, are not uncommon, occur without warning and can be very serious. The last big one in the region was an 8.3-magnitude quake that hit the north coast of Chile in 2015, causing the evacuation of a million people. Amazingly, only 10 people died. Andean construction rarely meets seismic safety standards; adobe buildings are particularly vulnerable. If you're in an earthquake, take shelter in a doorway or dive under a table; don't go outside.

Police & Military

In some places you may encounter corrupt officials who are not beyond enforcing minor regulations in the hopes of extracting a bribe.

If you are stopped by 'plainclothes policemen,' never get into a vehicle with them. Don't give them any documents or show them

GOVERNMENT TRAVEL ADVICE

The following government websites offer travel advisories and information on current hot spots.

- Australian Department of Foreign Affairs (www.smarttraveller.gov.au)
- British Foreign Office (www.gov.uk/browse/abroad)
- Canadian Department of Foreign Affairs (www.dfait-maeci.gc.ca)
- US State Department (http://travel.state.gov)

any money, and don't take them to your hotel. If the police appear to be the real thing, insist on going to a police station on foot.

The military often maintains considerable influence, even under civilian governments. Avoid approaching military installations, which may display warnings such as 'No stopping or photographs – the sentry will shoot.' In the event of a coup or other emergency, state-of-siege regulations suspend civil rights. Always carry identification and be sure someone knows your whereabouts. Contact your embassy or consulate for advice.

Theft

Theft can be a problem, but remember that fellow travelers can also be accomplished crooks, so where there's a backpacker scene, there may also be thievery. Here are some common-sense suggestions to limit your liability:

- A small padlock is useful for securing your pack zippers and hostel door, if necessary. Twist ties, paper clips or safety pins can be another effective deterrent when used to secure your pack zippers.
- Even if you're just running down the hall, never leave your hotel door unlocked.
- Always conceal your money belt and its contents, preferably beneath your clothing.
- Keep your spending money separate from the big stuff (credit cards, tickets etc).
- Be aware of the risk of bag slashing and the theft of your contents on buses. Keep close watch on your belongings – the bag isn't safe under your seat, above your head or between your legs (it's better on your lap). Be mindful in crowded markets or terminals where thefts are more likely to occur.
- When exploring cities, consider ditching the daypack and carrying what you need in a plastic bag to deter potential thieves.

Trouble Spots

Some countries and areas are more dangerous than others. The more dangerous places warrant extra care, but don't feel you should avoid them altogether. Venezuela, especially Caracas and anywhere near the Colombian border, is particularly volatile. Colombia is much safer than it has been in years, but certain regions are still off-limits. The northern border region of Ecuador, specifically in the Oriente, can be dodgy due to guerrilla activity. Travelers have been assaulted at remote and even well-touristed archaeological sites, primarily in Peru; stay informed. La Paz (Bolivia), Caracas (Venezuela), Rio and São Paulo (Brazil) and Quito (Ecuador) are all notorious for assaults on tourists.

Tours

There are loads of great adrenaline activities on offer, from rafting to mountain biking, but do your research on an agency before joining a tour. Travelers have lost their lives owing to poorly maintained equipment and reckless, ill-prepared guides. It's never wise to choose an operator based on cost alone. In Bolivia, for instance, the mine tours in Potosí, bike trips outside La Paz and the 4WD excursions around Salar de Uyuní have become so hugely popular that some agencies are willing to forgo safety. Talk to other travelers, check out equipment and meet with guides before committing to anything.

Telephone

Skype and other net-to-phone services are the best way to call abroad.

From traditional landlines, the most economical way of calling abroad is by phone cards. You can also try direct-dial lines, accessed via special numbers and billed to an account at home. There are different access numbers for each telephone company in each country – get a list from your phone company before you leave.

Cell Phones

Cell-phone numbers in South America often have different area codes than fixed-line numbers, even if the cell-phone owner resides in the same city. Calling a cell phone number is always more expensive (sometimes exorbitantly so) than calling a fixed line.

If you carry your own cell phone, a GSM tri- or quad-band phone is your best bet. Another option is purchasing a prepaid SIM card (or cards) for the countries where you plan on traveling. You will need a compatible international GSM cell phone that is SIM-unlocked. Or you can simply purchase one when you arrive (a cheap phone costs about US$30).

If you plan to travel with an iPhone or other smartphone, you may want to purchase an international plan to minimize (what could be) enormous costs. Remember it's possible to call internationally for free or very cheaply using Skype or other VoIP (Voice over Internet Protocol) systems.

Phone Cards

Aside from Skype, the cheapest way to make an international call is by using a phone card, the type you purchase at a kiosk or corner store. These allow you to call North America or Europe for as little as US5¢ per minute with a good card. The caveat is that you need a private phone line or a permissive telephone kiosk operator to use them.

Time

South America spans four time zones. Chile and parts of Brazil observe daylight savings time from October to February or March.

Toilets

There are two toilet rules for South America: always carry your own toilet paper and don't ever throw anything into the toilet bowl. Except in the most developed places, South American sewer systems can't handle toilet paper, so all paper products must be discarded in the wastebasket. Another general rule is to use public bathrooms whenever you can, as you never know when your next opportunity will be. Folks posted outside bathrooms proffering swaths of paper require payment.

Tourist Information

Every country in South America has government-run tourist offices, but their quality and breadth of coverage vary. Local tourist offices are mentioned wherever they exist.

South American Explorers (www.saexplorers.org) One of the most helpful organizations for travelers to South America. Founded in 1977, SAE functions as an information center for travelers, adventurers and researchers. It supports scientific fieldwork, mountaineering and other expeditions, wilderness conservation and social development in Latin America. It has traveler clubhouses in Lima, Cuzco, Quito and Central Chile (near Limache). The clubhouses have extensive libraries of books, maps and travelers' reports, plus a great atmosphere. The club itself sells maps, books and other items at its offices and by mail order.

Annual SAE membership is US$60/90 per individual/couple. Members can use services at any club, including internet access, libraries, storage facilities, mail service, trip reports and book exchange, and discounts at numerous hotels and travel services. Clubs also host workshops, Spanish conversation classes, excursions and other events.

Travelers with Disabilities

In general, South America is not well set up for travelers with disabilities, but the more modernized Southern Cone countries are slightly more accommodating – notably Chile, Argentina and the bigger cities of Brazil. Unfortunately, cheap local lodgings probably won't be well equipped to deal with physically challenged travelers; air travel will be more feasible than local buses (although this isn't impossible); and well-developed tourist attractions will be more accessible than off-the-beaten-track destinations. Start your research here:

Access-able Travel Source (www.access-able.com) Offers little information specifically on South America, but provides some good general travel advice.

Emerging Horizons (www.emerginghorizons.com) Features well-written articles and regular columns full of handy advice.

Mobility International (www.miusa.org) This US-based outfit advises travelers with disabilities and runs educational-exchange programs – a good way to visit South America.

Royal Association for Disability and Rehabilitation (www.disabilityrightsuk.org) Good resource for travelers from the UK.

Society for Accessible Travel & Hospitality (www.sath.org) Good, general travel information; based in the USA.

Visas & Arrival Fees

Some travelers – including those from the USA – may require visas to enter several countries. These are best arranged in advance. Some countries like Argentina don't generally require visas but still require a reciprocity fee (typically US$75 to US$160), paid in advance upon arrival. If no visa is required, a tourist card is issued upon arrival. See individual countries for more details.

Carry a handful of passport-sized photos for visa applications. Hold onto any entry-exit cards you are given. There can be serious fines and complications if you lose them!

If you need a visa for a country and arrive at a land border without one, be prepared to backtrack to the nearest town with a consulate to get one. Airlines won't normally let you board a plane for a country to which you don't have the necessary visa. Also, a visa in itself does not guarantee entry: you may still be turned back at the border if you don't have 'sufficient funds' or an onward or return ticket.

Onward or Return Tickets

Some countries require you to have a ticket out of their country before they will admit you at the border, grant you a visa or let you board their national airline. The onward or return ticket requirement can be a major nuisance for travelers who want to fly into one country and travel overland through others. Officially, Peru, Colombia, Ecuador, Venezuela, Bolivia, Brazil, Suriname and French Guiana demand onward tickets, but only sporadically enforce it. Still, if you arrive in one of the countries technically requiring an onward ticket or sufficient funds and a border guard is so inclined, he or she *can* enforce these rules (yet another reason to be courteous and neatly dressed at border crossings).

While proof of onward or return tickets is rarely asked for by South American border officials, airline officials, especially in the US, sometimes refuse boarding passengers with one-way tickets who cannot show proof of onward or return travel or proof of citizenship (or residency) in the destination country. One way around this is to purchase a cheap, fully refundable ticket out of the country and cash it in after your arrival. The downside is that the refund can take up to three months. Before purchasing the ticket, you should also ask specifically where you can get a refund, as some airlines will only refund tickets at the office of purchase or at their head office.

Any ticket out of South America plus sufficient funds are usually an adequate substitute for an onward ticket. Having a major credit card or two may help.

Sufficient Funds

Sufficient funds are often *technically* required but rarely asked for. Immigration officials may ask (verbally or on the application form) about your financial resources. If you lack 'sufficient funds' for your proposed visit, officials may limit the length of your stay, but once you are in the country, you can usually extend your visa by producing a credit card or two.

Volunteering

If you just want to donate your hard work, there are plenty of local organizations that will take you on, though you'll have better luck looking once you're in the country. A good place to start is at a Spanish-language school (Quito, Cuenca or Cuzco are top choices); many schools link volunteers with organizations in need.

If you prefer to set something up before you go, keep in mind that most international volunteer organizations require a weekly or monthly fee (sometimes up to US$1500 for two weeks, not including airfare), which can feel a bit harsh. This is usually to cover the costs of housing you, paying the organization's staff, rent, website fees and all that stuff.

Here are a few places to start the search:

Amerispan (www.amerispan.com/volunteer_intern) Volunteer and internship programs in Argentina, Bolivia, Brazil, Chile, Ecuador and Peru.

Cross Cultural Solutions (www.crossculturalsolutions.org) Volunteer programs with an emphasis on cultural and human interaction in Brazil and Peru.

Go Abroad (www.goabroad.com) Extensive listings of volunteer and study-abroad opportunities.

Idealist.org (www.idealist.org) Action Without Borders' searchable database of thousands of volunteer positions throughout the world. Excellent resource.

Rainforest Concern (www.rainforestconcern.org) British nonprofit offering affordable volunteer positions in forest environments in several South American countries. Volunteers pay a weekly fee.

Transitions Abroad (www.transitionsabroad.com) Useful portal for both paid and volunteer work.

UN Volunteers (www.unv.org) The lofty international organization offers volunteer opportunities for peace and development projects across the globe.

Volunteer Latin America (www.volunteerlatinamerica.com) Worth a peek for its interesting programs throughout Latin America.

Working Abroad (www.workingabroad.com) Online network of grassroots volunteer opportunities with trip reports from the field.

Women Travelers

At one time or another, solo women travelers will find themselves the object of curiosity – sometimes well intentioned, sometimes not. Avoidance is an easy, effective self-defense strategy. In the Andean region, particularly in smaller towns and rural areas, modest dress and conduct are the norm, while in Brazil and the more liberal Southern Cone, standards are more relaxed, especially in beach areas.

Machista (macho) attitudes, stressing masculine pride and virility, are fairly widespread among South American men (although less so in indigenous communities). They are often expressed by boasting and in exaggerated attention toward women. Snappy put-down lines or other caustic comebacks to unwanted advances may make the man feel threatened, and he may respond aggressively. Most women find it easier to invent a husband and leave the guy with his pride intact, especially in front of others.

There have been isolated cases of South American men raping women travelers. Women trekking or taking tours in remote or isolated areas should be especially cautious. Some cases have involved guides assaulting tour group members, so it's worth double-checking the identity and reputation of any guide or tour operator. Also be aware that women (and men) have been drugged, in bars and elsewhere, using drinks, cigarettes or pills. Police may not be very helpful in rape cases – if a local woman is raped, her family usually seeks revenge rather than calling the police. Tourist police may be more sympathetic, but it's possibly better to see a doctor and contact your embassy before reporting a rape to police.

Tampons are generally difficult to find in smaller towns, so stock up in cities or bring a supply from home. Birth-control pills are sometimes tricky to find outside metropolitan areas, so you're best off bringing your own supply from home. If you can't bring enough, carry the original package with you so a pharmacist can match a local pill to yours.

Work

Aside from teaching or tutoring English, opportunities for employment are few, low-paying and usually illegal. Even tutoring, despite good hourly rates, is rarely remunerative because it takes time to build up a clientele. The best opportunities for teaching English are in the larger cities, and, although you won't save much, it will allow you to stick around longer. Other work opportunities may exist for skilled guides or in restaurants and bars catering to travelers. Many people find work at foreign-owned lodges and inns.

There are several excellent online resources, including the following:

Association of American Schools in South America (www.aassa.com) Places accredited teachers in many academic subjects in schools throughout South America.

Dave's ESL Café (www.eslcafe.com) Loads of message boards, job boards, teaching ideas, information, links and more.

EnglishClub.com (www.englishclub.com) Great resource for ESL teachers and students.

TEFL Net (www.tefl.net) This is another rich online resource for teachers from the creators of EnglishClub.com.

Transportation

GETTING THERE & AWAY

Entering South America

Make sure your passport is valid for at least six months beyond the projected end of your trip and has plenty of blank pages for stamp-happy officials. Carrying a photocopy of your passport (so you can leave the original in your hotel) is sometimes enough if you're walking around a town, but *always* have the original if you travel anywhere (never get on a bus leaving town without it).

Land

From North America, you can journey overland only as far south as Panama. There is no road connection onward to Colombia: the Carretera Panamericana (Pan-American Hwy) ends in the vast wilderness of the Darién Province, in southeast Panama. This roadless area between Central and South America is called the Darién Gap. In the past it has been difficult, but possible, to trek across the gap with the help of local guides, but since around 1998 it has been prohibitively dangerous, especially on the Colombian side. The region is effectively controlled by guerrillas and is positively unsafe.

Border Crossings

There are ample border crossings in South America, so you generally never have to travel too far out of your way to get where you eventually want to go. This is particularly true in Argentina and Chile, where a shared 3500km-long frontier provides many opportunities (especially in Patagonia) to slide between countries. Most crossings are by road (or bridge), but there are a few that involve boat travel (such as across the Río de la Plata between Buenos Aires and Uruguay; and several lake crossings between Argentina and Chile, and across Lake Titicaca between Bolivia and Peru).

With the influx of footloose foreigners in the region, border police are used to backpackers turning up at their often isolated corner of the globe. That said, crossing is always easier if you appear at least somewhat kempt, treat the guards with respect and make an attempt at Spanish or Portuguese. If, on the off chance, you encounter an officer who tries to extract a little *dinero* from you before allowing you through (it does happen occasionally), maintain your composure. If the amount is small (and it generally is), it's probably not worth your trouble trying to fight it. Generally, border police are courteous and easygoing.

CLIMATE CHANGE & TRAVEL

Every form of transport that relies on carbon-based fuel generates CO_2, the main cause of human-induced climate change. Modern travel is dependent on airplanes, which might use less fuel per kilometer per person than most cars but travel much greater distances. The altitude at which aircraft emit gases (including CO_2) and particles also contributes to their climate change impact. Many websites offer 'carbon calculators' that allow people to estimate the carbon emissions generated by their journey and, for those who wish to do so, to offset the impact of the greenhouse gases emitted with contributions to portfolios of climate-friendly initiatives throughout the world. Lonely Planet offsets the carbon footprint of all staff and author travel.

Before heading to a border, be sure to get the latest information on visas – whether or not you need one – with a little on-the-ground research.

Bus

The cheapest but most time-consuming way to cross South American borders is to take a local bus to the border, handle immigration formalities and board another bus on the other side. To save a few hours, you might consider boarding an international bus that connects major towns in neighboring countries.

Sea

One of the most popular modes of travel between South and Central America is the foreign sailboats that travel between Cartagena and the San Blás islands, with some boats continuing to Colón (Panama). The typical passage takes four to six days and costs between US$375 and US$600. A good source of information regarding schedules and available berths is at **Casa Viena** (Map p576; ☎05-664-6242; www.casaviena.com; Calle San Andrés 30-53, Getsemaní) in Cartagena and **Captain Jack's** (www.captainjackpanama.com; Hostel Portobelo, Calle Guinea, Portobelo, Colón) in Portobelo, Panama. Do some serious research before joining any tour; there are many unsavory operators out there, and a few boats have even sunk.

A less expensive way to reach Panama from Colombia is via small boat from Capurgana to Puerto Obaldia from where you can take a domestic flight to Panama City or continue up through the San Blás islands.

Officially, both Panama and Colombia require an onward or return ticket as a condition of entry. This may not be enforced in Colombia, but it's wise to get one anyway, or have lots of money and a plausible itinerary. Panama requires a visa or tourist card, an onward ticket and sufficient funds, and has been known to turn back arrivals who don't meet these requirements.

There are occasional reports of pirate attacks off the coast of South America, most of which occur in the Caribbean region.

GETTING AROUND

Whether aboard a rickety *chiva* (open-sided bus) on the Ecuadorian coast, a motorized canoe in the Amazon or a small aircraft humming over the Andes, transport on this continent is a big part of the South American adventure.

Air

There is an extensive network of domestic flights, with refreshingly low price tags, especially in the Andean countries (Bolivia, Ecuador and Peru). After 18-hour bus rides across 350km of mountainous terrain on atrocious roads, you may decide to take the occasional flight.

There are drawbacks to flying, however. Airports are often far from city centers, and public buses don't run all the time, so you may end up spending a bit on taxis (it's usually easier to find a cheap taxi *to* an airport than *from* one). Airport taxes also add to the cost of air travel; they are always higher for international departures. If safety concerns you, check out the 'Fatal Events by Airline' feature at www.airsafe.com.

Avoid scheduling a domestic flight with a close connection for an international flight or vice versa. Reconfirm all flights 48 hours before departure and allow ample extra time at the airport.

Air Passes

Air passes offer a number of flights within a country or region, for a specified period, at a fixed total price. Passes are an economical way to cover long distances in limited time, but they have shortcomings. Some are irritatingly inflexible: once you start using the pass, you're locked into a schedule and can't change it without paying a penalty. The validity period can be restrictive and some passes require that you enter the country on an international flight – you can't travel overland to the country and then start flying around with an air pass. Citizens of some countries are not eligible for certain air passes.

MULTICOUNTRY AIR PASSES

A few South America air passes exist and can save you a bit of money, provided you can deal with a fixed itinerary. These mileage-based passes allow travelers to fly between cities in a limited set of countries. The restrictions vary, but flights must be completed within a period ranging from 30 days to 12 months. You'll pay higher rates (or be ineligible) if you arrive in South America on a carrier other than the one sponsoring the air pass.

South American Pass (www.aerolineas.com.ar) Aerolíneas Argentinas offers this multicountry pass, which includes Argentina, Bolivia, southern Brazil, Chile, Colombia, Paraguay, Peru, Uruguay and Venezuela.

Gol Mercosul Airpass (www.voegol.com.br) Includes Brazil, Argentina, Bolivia, Chile, Paraguay and Uruguay.

One World Alliance Visit South America Airpass (www.oneworld.com) Includes Argentina, Bolivia, southern Brazil, Chile, Colombia, Ecuador, Paraguay, Peru, Uruguay and Venezuela.

LATAM South American Airpass (www.latamapairpass.com) One of the most extensive networks around the continent;

covers destinations in Argentina, Bolivia, Brazil, Chile, Colombia, Ecuador, Paraguay, Peru, Uruguay and Venezuela.

SINGLE-COUNTRY AIR PASSES

Most air passes are only good within one country and are usually purchased in combination with a round-trip ticket to that country. In addition, most air passes must be purchased outside the destination country; check with a travel agent. Argentina, Brazil and Chile all offer domestic air passes.

Bicycle

Cycling South America is a challenging yet highly rewarding alternative to public transport. While better roads in Argentina and Chile make the Cono Sur (Southern Cone; a collective term for Argentina, Chile, Uruguay and parts of Brazil and Paraguay) countries especially attractive, the entire continent is manageable by bike, or – more precisely – by mountain bike. Touring bikes are suitable for paved roads, but only a *todo terreno* (mountain bike) allows you to tackle the spectacular back roads (and often main roads!) of the Andes.

There are no multicountry bike lanes or designated routes. Mountain bikers have cycled the length of the Andes, and a select few have made the transcontinental journey from North to South America. As for road rules, forget it – except for the logical rule of riding with traffic on the right-hand side of the road, there are none. Hunt down good maps that show side roads, as you'll have the enviable ability to get off the beaten track at will.

Bring your own bicycle since locally manufactured ones are less dependable and imported bikes are outrageously expensive. Bicycle mechanics are common even in small towns, but will almost invariably lack the parts you'll need. Before setting out, learn bicycle mechanics and purchase spares for the pieces most likely to fail. A basic road kit will include extra spokes and a spoke wrench, a tire patch kit, a chain punch, inner tubes, spare cables and a cycling-specific multitool. Some folks box up spare tires, leave them with a family member back home and have them shipped to South America when they need them.

Drawbacks to cycling include the weather (fierce rains, blasting winds), high altitude in the Andes, poor roads and reckless drivers – the biggest hazard for riders. Safety equipment such as reflectors, mirrors and a helmet are highly

SAMPLE AIRFARES

Unless noted otherwise, the following chart shows sample mid-season, one-way airfares, quoted directly by airlines for purchase in South America. Sometimes, purchasing an *ida y vuelta* (round trip) ticket is cheaper than buying a one-way ticket; be sure to ask.

ORIGIN	DESTINATION	COST (US$)
Asunción	Buenos Aires	305
Bogotá	Quito	308
Buenos Aires	Santiago	230
Buenos Aires	Ushuaia	240
Guayaquil	Galápagos Islands	375 (round trip)
Guayaquil	Lima	405
Lima	La Paz	315
Punta Arenas	Santiago	415
Quito	Galápagos Islands	440 (round trip)
Rio de Janeiro	Buenos Aires	405
Rio de Janeiro	Manaus	250-500
Rio de Janeiro	Montevideo	325
Rio de Janeiro	Santa Cruz, Bolivia	300
Salvador	Rio de Janeiro	175
Santa Cruz, Bolivia	Florianópolis	340
Santiago	Rapa Nui (Easter Island)	970-1420 (round trip)
Santiago	La Paz	150
Santiago	Lima	470-650

recommended. Security is another issue: always take your panniers with you, lock your bike (or pay someone to watch it) while you sightsee and bring your bike into your hotel room overnight.

Boat

From cruises through the mystical fjords of Chilean Patagonia and riverboat chugs up the Amazon to outboard canoe travel in the coastal mangroves of Ecuador, South America offers ample opportunity to travel by boat. Safety is generally not an issue, especially for the established ferry and cruise operators in Chile and Argentina. There have been a couple of recent problems with tourist boats in the Galápagos (including a few that have sunk over the years), so do some research before committing to a cruise.

Lake Crossings

There are outstanding (but expensive) lake excursions throughout southern Chile, Argentina, Bolivia and Peru. Some of the most popular routes:

- Copacabana (Bolivia) to the Lake Titicaca islands of Isla del Sol and Isla de la Luna
- Lago General Carrera (Chile) to Chile Chico and Puerto Ingeniero Ibáñez (Chile)
- Puerto Montt and Puerto Varas (Chile) to Bariloche (Argentina)
- Puno (Peru) to the Lake Titicaca islands

Riverboat

Long-distance travel on major rivers such as the Orinoco or Amazon is possible, but you'll have a more idyllic time on one of the smaller rivers such as the Mamoré or Beni, where boats hug the shore and you can see and hear the wildlife. On the Amazon, you rarely even see the shore. The river is also densely settled in its lower reaches, and its upper reaches have fewer passenger boats than in the past. River travel in Bolivia is less common than it once was, with more folks opting to take short flights between destinations.

Riverboats vary greatly in size and standards, so check the vessel before buying a ticket and shop around. When you pay the fare, get a ticket with all the details on it. Downriver travel is faster than upriver, but boats going upriver travel closer to the shore and offer more interesting scenery. The time taken between ports is unpredictable, so river travel is best for those with an open schedule.

Food is usually included in ticket prices and means lots of rice and beans and perhaps some meat, but bring bottled water, fruit and snacks as a supplement. The evening meal on the first night of a trip is not usually included. Drinks and extra food are generally sold on board, but at high prices. Bring some spare cash and insect repellent.

Unless you have cabin space, you'll need a hammock and rope to sling it. It can get windy and cool at night, so a sleeping bag is recommended. There are usually two classes of hammock space, with space on the upper deck costing slightly more; it's cooler there and worth the extra money. Be on the boat at least eight hours prior to departure to get a good hammock space away from engine noise and toilet odors.

Overcrowding and theft on boats are common complaints. Don't allow your baggage to be stored in an insecure locker; bring your own padlock. Don't entrust your bag to any boat officials unless you are quite certain about their status – bogus officials have been reported.

Sea Trips

The best-known sea trip, and a glorious one at that, is the **Navimag** (☎022-442-3120; www.navimag.cl; Av El Bosque Norte 0440, Piso 11, Santiago; ⊙9am-6:30pm Mon-Fri) ferry ride down the Chilean coast, from Puerto Montt to Puerto Natales. Short boat rides in some countries take you to islands not far from the mainland, including Ilha Grande and Ilha de Santa Catarina in Brazil, Isla Grande de Chiloé in Chile and Isla Grande de Tierra del Fuego in Argentina. More distant islands are usually reached by air. In parts of coastal Ecuador, outboard canoes act as public transport through the mangroves.

Bus

In general, bus transport is well developed throughout the continent. Note that road conditions, bus quality and driver professionalism, however, vary widely. Much depends on the season: vast deserts of red dust in the dry season become oceans of mud in the rainy season. In Argentina, Uruguay, Ecuador, coastal and southern Brazil, and most of Venezuela, roads are generally better. Chile and much of Argentina have some of the best-maintained roads and most comfortable and reliable bus services in South America.

Most major cities and towns have a *terminal de autobuses* or *terminal de ómnibus* (bus terminal); in Brazil, it's called a *rodoviária*, and in Ecuador it's a *terminal terrestre*. Terminals are often on the outskirts of town, and you'll need a local bus or taxi to reach it. The biggest and best terminals have restaurants, shops, showers and other services, and the surrounding area is often a good (but frequently ugly) place to look for cheap sleeps and eats. Village 'terminals' in rural areas often amount to dirt lots flanked by dilapidated metal hulks called 'buses' and men hawking various destinations to passersby; listen for your town of choice.

Some cities have several terminals, each serving a different route. Sometimes each bus company has its own terminal, which is particularly inconvenient. This is most common in Colombia, Ecuador and Peru, especially in smaller towns.

Classes

Especially in the Andean countries, buses may be stripped nearly bare, tires are often treadless, and rock-hard suspension ensures a less-than-smooth ride, particularly for those at the back of the bus. After all seats are taken, the aisle is packed beyond capacity, and the roof is loaded with cargo to at least half the height of the bus, topped by the occasional goat or pig. You may have serious doubts about ever arriving at your destination, but the buses usually make it. Except for long-distance routes, different classes often don't exist: you ride what's available.

At the other extreme, you'll find luxurious coaches in Argentina, Brazil, Chile, Colombia, Uruguay, Venezuela and even Bolivia along main routes. The most expensive buses usually feature reclining seats, and meal, beverage and movie services. Different classes are called by a variety of names, depending on the country. In Argentina, Chile and Peru, the deluxe sleeper buses, called *coche-cama* or *bus-cama* (literally 'bus-bed') – or *leito* (sleeping berth) in Brazil – are available for most long-distance routes.

Costs

In the Andean countries, bus rides generally add up to about US$1 per hour of travel. When better services (such as 1st class or *coche-cama*) are offered, they can cost double the fare of a regular bus. Still, overnighters obviate the need for a hotel room, thereby saving you money.

Reservations

It's always wise to purchase your ticket in advance if you're traveling during peak holiday seasons (January through March in the Southern Cone; and around Easter week and during holiday weekends everywhere). At best, bus companies will have ticket offices at central terminals and information boards showing routes, departure times and fares. Seats will be numbered and booked in advance. In places where tickets are not sold in advance, showing up an hour or so before your departure will usually guarantee you a seat.

Safety

Anyone who has done their share of traveling in South America can tell you stories of horrifying bus rides at the mercy of crazed drivers. And there are occasionally accidents. Choosing more expensive buses is no guarantee against accidents; high-profile crashes sometimes involve well-established companies. Some roads, particularly those through the Andes, can be frightening to travel. A few well-placed flights can reduce bus anxiety.

Car & Motorcycle

Driving around South America can be mentally taxing and at times risky, but a car allows you to explore out-of-the-way places – especially parks – that are totally inaccessible via public transport. In places like Patagonia and other parts of Chile and Argentina, a short-term rental car can be well worth the expense.

There are some hurdles to driving. First off, it's a good idea to have an International Driving Permit to supplement your license from home. Vehicle security can be a problem anywhere in South America. Avoid leaving valuables in your car, and always lock it.

Bring Your Own Vehicle

Shipping your own car or motorcycle to South America involves a lot of money and planning. Shipping arrangements should be made at least a month in advance. Stealing from vehicles being shipped is big business, so remove everything removable (hubcaps, wipers, mirrors), and take everything visible from the interior. Shipping your vehicle in a container is more secure, but more expensive.

Driver's License

If you're planning to drive anywhere, obtain an International Driving Permit or Inter-American Driving Permit (Uruguay theoretically recognizes only the latter). For about US$10 to US$15, any motoring organization will issue one, provided you have a current driver's license.

Insurance

Home auto insurance policies generally do not cover you while driving abroad. Throughout South America, if you are in an accident that injures or kills another person, you can be jailed until the case is settled, regardless of culpability. Fender benders are generally dealt with on the spot, without involving the police or insurance agents. When you rent, be certain your contract includes *seguro* (insurance).

Purchase

If you're spending several months in South America, purchasing a car is worth considering. It will be cheaper than renting if you can resell it at the end of your stay. On the other hand, any used car can be a financial risk, especially on rugged roads, and the bureaucracy involved in purchasing a car can be horrendous.

The best countries in which to purchase cars are Argentina, Brazil and Chile, but, again, expect exasperating bureaucracies. Be certain of the title; as a foreigner, getting a notarized document authorizing your use of the car is a good idea, since the bureaucracy may take its time transferring the title. Taking a vehicle purchased in South America across international borders may present obstacles.

Officially, you need a *carnet de passage* or a *libreta de pasos por aduana* (customs permit) to cross most land borders in your own vehicle, but you'll probably never have to show these documents. The best source of advice is the national automobile club in the country where you buy the car.

Rental

Major international rental agencies such as Hertz, Avis and Budget have offices in South American capitals, major cities and at major airports. Local agencies, however, often have better rates. To rent a car, you must be at least 25 and have a valid driver's license from home and a credit card. Some agencies rent to those under 25 but charge an added fee. If your itinerary calls for crossing borders, know that some rental agencies restrict or forbid this; ask before renting.

Rates can fluctuate wildly (ranging from US$40 to US$80 per day). It's always worth getting a group together to defray costs. If the vehicle enables you to camp out, the saving in accommodations may offset much of the rental cost, especially in Southern Cone countries.

Road Rules

Except in Guyana and Suriname, South Americans drive on the right-hand side of the road. Road rules are frequently ignored and seldom enforced; conditions can be hazardous; and many drivers, especially in Argentina and Brazil, are reckless and even willfully dangerous. Driving at night is riskier than during the day due to lower visibility and the preponderance of tired and/or intoxicated nighttime drivers sharing the road.

Road signs can be confusing, misleading or nonexistent – a good sense of humor and patience are key attributes. Honking your horn on blind curves is a simple, effective safety measure; the vehicle coming uphill on a one-way road usually has the right of way. If you're cruising along and see a tree branch or rock in the middle of the road, slow down: this means there's a breakdown, rock slide or some other trouble up ahead. Speed bumps can pop up anywhere, most often smack in the center of town, but sometimes inexplicably in the middle of a highway.

Hitchhiking

Hitchhiking is never entirely safe in any country. Travelers who decide to hitch should understand they are taking a potentially serious risk. Hitching is less dangerous if you travel in pairs and let someone know where you are planning to go.

Though it is possible to hitch all over South America, free lifts are the rule only in Argentina, Chile, Uruguay and parts of Brazil. Elsewhere, hitching is virtually a form of public transport (especially where buses are infrequent) and drivers expect payment. There are generally fixed fares over certain routes; ask the other passengers what they're paying. It's usually about equal to the bus fare, marginally less in some places. You get better views from the top of a truck, but if you're hitching on the *altiplano* (Andean high plain of Peru, Bolivia, Chile and Argentina) or *páramo* (humid, high-altitude grassland) take warm clothing. Once the sun goes down or is obscured by clouds, it gets very cold.

There's no need to wait at the roadside for a lift, unless it happens to be convenient. Almost every town has a central truck park, often around the market. Ask around for a truck going your way and how much it will cost; be there about 30 minutes before the departure time given by the driver. It is often worth soliciting a ride at *servicentros* (gas stations) on the outskirts of large cities, where drivers refuel their vehicles.

Local Transportation

Local and city bus systems tend to be thorough and reliable throughout South America. Although in many countries you can flag a bus anywhere on its route, you're best off finding the official bus stop. Still, if you can't find the stop, don't hesitate to throw your arm up to stop a bus you know is going in your direction. Never hesitate to ask a bus driver which is the right bus to take; most of them are very generous in directing you to the right bus.

As in major cities throughout the world, pickpockets are a problem on crowded buses and subways. If you're on a crowded bus or subway, always watch your back. Avoid crowded public transport when you're loaded down with luggage.

Taxis in most big cities (but definitely not all) have meters. When a taxi has a meter, make sure the driver uses it. When it doesn't, always agree on a fare *before* you get in the cab. In most cities, fares are higher on Sundays and after 9pm.

Train

Trains have slowly faded from the South American landscape, but several spectacular routes still operate. Ecuador has invested heavily in rehabilitating its old lines. Uruguay is also revitalizing its old rails, though it's still years from completion.

For great scenery with a touch of old-fashioned railway nostalgia, try the following routes:

Curitiba–Paranaguá (Brazil) Descending steeply to the coastal lowlands, Brazil's best rail journey offers unforgettable views.

Oruro–Uyuni–Tupiza–Villazón (Bolivia) The main line from Oruro continues south from Uyuni to Tupiza (another scenic rail trip through gorge country) and on to Villazón at the Argentine border.

Puno–Juliaca–Cuzco (Peru) From the shores of Lake Titicaca and across a 4600m pass, this train runs for group bookings in high season. Departures are unpredictable, but when it does run, it's open to nongroup passengers.

Riobamba–Sibambe (Ecuador) One of a growing number of short tourist-train jaunts in the country, the Nariz del Diablo (Devil's Nose) is an exhilarating, steep descent via narrow switchbacks.

Salta–La Polvorilla (Argentina) The Tren a las Nubes (Train to the Clouds) negotiates switchbacks, tunnels, spirals and death-defying bridges during its ascent into the Andean *puna* (highlands). Unfortunately, schedules are extremely unreliable.

Uyuni (Bolivia)–Calama (Chile) On Monday at 3am, a train trundles five hours west to Avaroa on the Chilean border, where you cross to Ollagüe and may have to wait a few hours to clear Chilean customs. From here, another train continues to Calama (six hours further). The whole trip can take up to 24 hours but it's a spectacular, if uncomfortable, journey.

There are several types of passenger trains in the Andean countries. The *ferrobus* is a relatively fast, diesel-powered single or double car that caters to passengers going from A to B but not to intermediate stations. Meals are often available on board. These are the most expensive trains and can be great value.

The *tren rápido* is more like an ordinary train, pulled by a diesel or steam engine. It is relatively fast, makes few stops and is generally cheaper than a *ferrobus*. Ordinary passenger trains, sometimes called *expresos*, are slower, cheaper and stop at most intermediate stations. There are generally two classes, with 2nd class being very crowded. Lastly, there are *mixtos*, mixed passenger and freight trains; these take everything and everyone, stop at every station and a lot of other places in between, take forever and are dirt cheap.

The few remaining passenger trains in Chile and Argentina are generally more modern, and the salon and Pullman classes are generally comfortable and still more affordable than flying. The *economía* or *turista* classes are slightly cheaper, while the *cama* (sleeper class) is even more comfortable.

Health

Prevention is the key to staying healthy while in South America. Travelers who receive the recommended vaccines and follow common-sense precautions usually go away with nothing more than a little diarrhea.

BEFORE YOU GO

Bring medications in their original, clearly labeled containers. A signed and dated letter from your physician describing your medical conditions and medications, including generic names, is also a good idea. If carrying syringes or needles, be sure to have a physician's letter documenting their medical necessity.

Insurance

If your health insurance doesn't cover you for medical expenses abroad, consider getting extra insurance. Find out in advance if your insurance plan will make payments directly to providers or reimburse you later for overseas health expenditures. (In many countries, doctors expect payment in cash.)

Recommended Vaccinations

Since most vaccines don't produce immunity until at least two weeks after they're given, visit a physician four to eight weeks before departure. Ask your doctor for an International Certificate of Vaccination (otherwise known as the yellow booklet), which will list all the vaccinations you've received. This is mandatory for countries that require proof of yellow-fever vaccination upon entry, but it's a good idea to carry it wherever you travel.

The only required vaccine is yellow fever, and that's only if you're arriving from a yellow fever–infected country in Africa or the Americas. (The exception is French Guiana, which requires yellow-fever vaccine for all travelers.) However, a number of vaccines are recommended.

Medical Checklist

- acetaminophen (Tylenol) or aspirin
- acetazolamide (Diamox; for altitude sickness)
- adhesive or paper tape
- antibacterial ointment (eg Bactroban; for cuts and abrasions)
- antibiotics for diarrhea (eg Norfloxacin, Ciprofloxacin or Azithromycin)
- antihistamines (for hay fever and allergic reactions)
- anti-inflammatory drugs (eg ibuprofen)
- bandages, gauze, gauze rolls
- diarrhea 'stopper' (eg loperamide)
- insect repellent containing DEET for the skin
- iodine tablets (for water purification)
- oral rehydration salts
- permethrin-containing insect spray for clothing, tents and bed nets
- pocket knife
- scissors, safety pins, tweezers
- steroid cream or cortisone (for poison ivy and other allergic rashes)
- sunblock
- thermometer

Internet Resources

There is a wealth of travel health advice on the internet. The **World Health Organization** (www.who.int/ith) publishes a superb book called *International Travel and Health,* which is revised annually and available online (as a downloadable pdf) for $12. Another resource of general interest is **MD Travel Health** (www.mdtravelhealth.com), which provides complete travel health recommendations for every country in the world; information is updated daily.

It's usually a good idea to consult your government's travel health website before departure, if one is available:

Australia (www.smartraveller.gov.au)

Canada (www.travelhealth.gc.ca)

UK (www.fco.gov.uk)

USA (wwwnc.cdc.gov/travel)

IN SOUTH AMERICA

Availability & Cost of Health Care

Good medical care may be more difficult to find in smaller cities and impossible to locate in rural areas. Many doctors and hospitals expect payment in cash, regardless of whether you have travel health insurance. If you develop a life-threatening medical problem, you'll probably want to be evacuated to a country with state-of-the-art medical care. Since this may cost tens of thousands of dollars, be sure you have insurance to cover this before you depart. You can find a list of medical evacuation and travel insurance companies on the **US State Department website** (http://travel.state.gov).

Infectious Diseases

Dengue

Dengue fever is a viral infection found throughout South America. Dengue is transmitted by Aedes mosquitoes, which bite preferentially during the daytime and are usually found close to human habitations, often indoors. They breed primarily in artificial water containers, such as jars, barrels, cans, cisterns, metal drums, plastic containers and discarded tires. As a result, dengue is especially common in densely populated, urban environments.

Dengue usually causes flu-like symptoms, including fever, muscle aches, joint pains, headaches, nausea and vomiting, often followed by a rash. The body aches may be quite uncomfortable, but most cases resolve uneventfully in a few days.

There is no treatment for dengue fever except to take analgesics such as acetaminophen/paracetamol (Tylenol) and drink plenty of fluids. Severe cases may require hospitalization for intravenous fluids and supportive care. There is no vaccine. The cornerstone of prevention is protection against insects.

Keep an eye out for outbreaks in areas where you plan to visit. A good website on the latest information is the **CDC** (wwwnc.cdc.gov/travel).

Malaria

Malaria occurs in every South American country except Chile, Uruguay and the Falkland Islands. It's transmitted by mosquito bites, usually between dusk and dawn. The main symptom is high spiking

RECOMMENDED VACCINATIONS

VACCINE	RECOMMENDED FOR	DOSAGE	SIDE EFFECTS
chickenpox	Travelers who've never had chickenpox	Two doses one month apart	Fever; mild case of chickenpox
hepatitis A	All travelers	One dose before trip; booster 6-12 months later	Soreness at injection site; headaches; body aches
hepatitis B	Long-term travelers in close contact with the local population	Three doses over six-month period	Soreness at injection site; low-grade fever
measles	Travelers born after 1956 who've had only one measles vaccination	One dose	Fever; rash; joint pains; allergic reactions
rabies	Travelers who may have contact with animals and may not have access to medical care	Three doses over three- to four-week period	Soreness at injection site; headaches; body aches
tetanus-diphtheria	Travelers who haven't had booster within 10 years	One dose lasts 10 years	Soreness at injection site
typhoid	All travelers	Four oral capsules, one taken every other day	Abdominal pain; nausea; rash
yellow fever	Travelers to jungle areas at altitudes below 2300m	One dose lasts 10 years	Headaches; body aches; severe reactions are rare

fevers, which may be accompanied by chills, sweats, headache, body aches, weakness, vomiting or diarrhea. Severe cases may involve the central nervous system and lead to seizures, confusion, coma and death.

There is a choice of three malaria pills, all of which work about equally well. Mefloquine (Lariam) is taken once weekly in a dosage of 250mg, starting one to two weeks before arrival and continuing through the trip and for four weeks after your return. The problem is that a certain percentage of people (the number is disputed) develop neuropsychiatric side effects, which may range from mild to severe. Atovaquone/proguanil (Malarone) is a newly approved combination pill taken once daily with food starting two days before arrival and continuing through the trip and for seven days after departure. Side effects are typically mild. Doxycycline is a third alternative, but may cause an exaggerated sunburn reaction.

Protecting yourself against mosquito bites is just as important as taking malaria pills, since none of the pills are 100% effective.

If you do not have access to medical care while traveling, bring along additional pills for emergency self-treatment, which you should take if you can't reach a doctor and you develop symptoms that suggest malaria, such as high spiking fevers. One option is to take four tablets of Malarone once daily for three days. However, Malarone should not be used for treatment if you're already taking it for prevention. An alternative is to take 650mg quinine three times daily and 100mg doxycycline twice daily for one week. If you start self-medication, see a doctor at the earliest possible opportunity.

If you develop a fever after returning home, see a physician, as malaria symptoms may not occur for months.

Rabies

Rabies is a viral infection of the brain and spinal cord that is almost always fatal. The rabies virus is carried in the saliva of infected animals and is typically transmitted through an animal bite, though contamination of any break in the skin with infected saliva may result in rabies. Rabies occurs in all South American countries.

Rabies vaccine is safe, but a full series requires three injections and is quite expensive. Those at high risk for rabies, such as animal handlers and spelunkers (cave explorers), should certainly get the vaccine. The treatment for a possibly rabid bite consists of the rabies vaccine with rabies-immune globulin. It's effective, but must be given promptly. Most travelers don't need rabies vaccine.

All animal bites and scratches must be promptly and thoroughly cleansed with large amounts of soap and water, and local health authorities should be contacted to determine whether further treatment is necessary.

Typhoid

Typhoid fever is caused by ingestion of food or water contaminated by a species of salmonella known as *Salmonella typhi*. Fever occurs in virtually all cases. Other symptoms may include headache, malaise, muscle aches, dizziness, loss of appetite, nausea and abdominal pain. Either diarrhea or constipation may occur. Possible complications include intestinal perforation, intestinal bleeding, confusion, delirium or (rarely) coma.

Unless you expect to take all your meals in major hotels and restaurants, the typhoid vaccine is a good idea.

The drug of choice for typhoid fever is usually a quinolone antibiotic such as ciprofloxacin (Cipro) or levofloxacin (Levaquin), which many travelers carry for treatment of travelers' diarrhea. However, if you self-treat for typhoid fever, you may also need to self-treat for malaria, since the symptoms of the two diseases may be indistinguishable.

Yellow Fever

Yellow fever is a life-threatening viral infection transmitted by mosquitoes in forested areas. The illness begins with flu-like symptoms, which may include fever, chills, headache, muscle aches, backache, loss of appetite, nausea and vomiting. These symptoms usually subside in a few days, but one person in six enters a second, toxic phase characterized by recurrent fever, vomiting, listlessness, jaundice, kidney failure and hemorrhage, leading to death in up to half of the cases. There is no treatment except for supportive care.

Yellow-fever vaccine can be given only in approved yellow-fever vaccination centers, which provide validated International Certificates of Vaccination (yellow booklets). The vaccine should be given at least 10 days before any potential exposure to yellow fever and remains effective for approximately 10 years. Reactions to the vaccine are generally mild and may include headaches, muscle aches, low-grade fevers, or discomfort at the injection site. Severe, life-threatening reactions have been described but are extremely rare. In general, the risk of becoming ill from the vaccine is far less than the risk of becoming ill from yellow fever, and you're strongly encouraged to get the vaccine.

Taking measures to protect yourself from mosquito bites is an essential part of preventing yellow fever.

Other Infections

CHAGAS DISEASE

Chagas disease is a parasitic infection that is transmitted by triatomine insects (reduviid bugs), which inhabit crevices in the walls and roofs of substandard housing in South and Central America. Chagas disease is extremely rare in travelers. However, if you sleep in a poorly constructed house, especially one made of mud, adobe or thatch, be sure to protect yourself with a bed net and a good insecticide.

GNATHOSTOMIASIS

Gnathostomiasis is an intestinal parasite acquired by eating raw or undercooked freshwater fish, including *ceviche* (marinated, uncooked seafood).

LEISHMANIASIS

Leishmaniasis occurs in the mountains and jungles of all South American countries except for Chile, Uruguay and the Falkland Islands. The infection is transmitted by sand flies, which are about one-third the size of mosquitoes. Leishmaniasis may be limited to the skin, causing slow-growing ulcers over exposed parts of the body or (less commonly) disseminate to the bone marrow, liver and spleen. There is no vaccine. To protect yourself from sand flies, follow the same precautions as for mosquitoes, except that netting must be finer mesh (at least 18 holes to the linear inch).

Environmental Hazards

Altitude Sickness

Altitude sickness may develop in those who ascend rapidly to altitudes greater than 2500m. Being physically fit offers no protection. Those who have experienced altitude sickness in the past are prone to future episodes. The risk increases with faster ascents, higher altitudes and greater exertion. Symptoms may include headaches, nausea, vomiting, dizziness, malaise, insomnia and loss of appetite. Severe cases may be complicated by fluid in the lungs (high-altitude pulmonary edema) or swelling of the brain (high-altitude cerebral edema).

When traveling to high altitudes, it's also important to avoid overexertion, eat light meals and abstain from alcohol.

If your symptoms are more than mild or don't resolve promptly, see a doctor. Altitude sickness should be taken seriously; it can be life-threatening when severe.

Animal Bites

Do not attempt to pet, handle or feed any animal, with the exception of domestic animals known to be free of any infectious disease.

Any bite or scratch by a mammal, including bats, should be promptly and thoroughly cleansed with large amounts of soap and water, followed by application of an antiseptic such as iodine or alcohol. The local health authorities should be contacted immediately for possible post-exposure rabies treatment, whether or not you've been immunized against rabies.

Snakes and leeches are a hazard in some areas of South America. In the event of a bite from a venomous snake, place the victim at rest, keep the bitten area immobilized and move the victim immediately to the nearest medical facility. Avoid tourniquets, which are no longer recommended.

Cold Exposure & Hypothermia

Cold exposure may be a significant problem in the Andes, particularly at night. Be sure to dress warmly, stay dry, keep active, consume plenty of food and water, get enough rest, and avoid alcohol, caffeine and tobacco. Watch out for the 'umbles' – stumbles, mumbles, fumbles and grumbles – which are important signs of impending hypothermia.

Hypothermia occurs when the body loses heat faster than it can produce it and the core temperature of the body falls. If you're trekking at high altitudes or simply taking a long bus trip over mountains, particularly at night, be prepared. In the Andes, you should always be prepared for cold, wet or windy conditions even if it's just for a few hours. It is best to dress in layers, and a hat is also important.

The symptoms of hypothermia include exhaustion, numbness, shivering, slurred speech, irrational or violent behavior, lethargy, stumbling, dizzy spells, muscle cramps and violent bursts of energy. To treat mild hypothermia, first get people out of the wind or rain, remove their clothing if it's wet and give them something warm and dry to wear. Make them drink hot liquids – not alcohol – and some high-calorie, easily digestible food. Do not rub victims – instead allow them to slowly warm themselves.

Heatstroke

To protect yourself from excessive sun exposure, you should stay out of the midday sun, wear sunglasses and a wide-brimmed sun hat, and apply sunscreen with SPF 15 or higher, with both UVA and UVB protection. Travelers should also drink plenty of fluids and avoid strenuous exercise when the temperature is high.

Insect Bites & Stings

To prevent mosquito bites, wear long sleeves, long pants, a hat and shoes (rather than sandals). Bring along a good insect repellent, preferably one containing DEET, which should be applied to exposed skin and clothing, but not to eyes, mouth, cuts, wounds or irritated skin.

Products containing lower concentrations of DEET are as effective, but for shorter periods of time. In general, adults and children over 12 years should use preparations containing 25% to 35% DEET, which usually lasts about six hours. Children between two and 12 years of age should use preparations containing no more than 10% DEET, applied sparingly, which will usually last about three hours. DEET-containing compounds should not be used on children under age two.

Insect repellents that contain certain botanical products, including oil of eucalyptus and soybean oil, are effective but last only 1½ to two hours. DEET-containing repellents are preferable for areas where there is a high risk of malaria or yellow fever. Products based on citronella are not effective.

For additional protection, you can apply permethrin to clothing, shoes, tents and bed nets. Permethrin treatments are safe and remain effective for at least two weeks, even when items are laundered. Permethrin should not be applied directly to skin.

Parasites

Intestinal parasites occur throughout South America. Common pathogens include Cyclospora, amoebae and Isospora. A tapeworm called Taenia solium may lead to a chronic brain infection called cysticercosis. If you exercise discretion in your choice of food and beverages, you'll sharply reduce your chances of becoming infected. Choose restaurants or market stalls that are well attended. If there's a high turnover, it means food hasn't been sitting around that long.

A parasitic infection called schistosomiasis, which primarily affects the blood vessels in the liver, occurs in Brazil, Suriname and parts of north-central Venezuela. The disease is acquired by swimming, wading, bathing or washing in fresh water that contains infected snails. It's therefore best to stay out of bodies of fresh water, such as lakes, ponds, streams and rivers, in places where schistosomiasis might occur.

A liver parasite called Echinococcus (hydatid disease) is found in many countries, especially Peru and Uruguay. It typically affects those in close contact with sheep. A lung parasite called Paragonimus, which is ingested by eating raw infected crustaceans, has been reported from Ecuador, Peru and Venezuela.

Travelers' Diarrhea

To prevent diarrhea, avoid tap water unless it has been boiled, filtered or chemically disinfected (with iodine tablets); only eat fresh fruits or vegetables if cooked or peeled; be wary of dairy products that might contain unpasteurized milk; and be highly selective when eating food from markets and street vendors.

If you develop diarrhea, be sure to drink plenty of fluids, preferably an oral rehydration solution containing salt and sugar. Gastrolyte works well for this. A few loose stools don't require treatment but you may want to take antibiotics if you start having more than three watery bowel movements within 24 hours, and it's accompanied by at least one other symptom – fever, cramps, nausea, vomiting or generally feeling unwell. Effective antibiotics include Norfloxacin, Ciprofloxacin or Azithromycin – all will kill the bacteria quickly. Note that an antidiarrheal agent (such as loperamide) is just a 'stopper' and doesn't get to the cause of the problem. Don't take loperamide if you have a fever or blood in your stools. Seek medical attention quickly if you don't respond to an appropriate antibiotic.

Water

Tap water is generally not safe to drink. Vigorous boiling for one minute is the most effective means of water purification. At altitudes greater than 2000m, boil for three minutes.

Other methods of treating water include using a handheld ultraviolet light purifier (such as a SteriPEN), iodine and water filters.

Language

Latin American Spanish is the language of choice for travelers in all of South America except for Brazil (where Portuguese is the national tongue) and the Guianas (where French, Dutch or English are widely spoken).

PORTUGUESE

A characteristic feature of Brazilian Portuguese is the use of nasal vowels (pronounced as if you're trying to force the sound through the nose). In Portuguese, vowels followed by a nasal consonant (*m* or *n*) or those written with a tilde over them (eg *ã*) are nasal. In our pronunciation guides, the ng after a vowel indicates a nasal sound. The consonant sounds are very similar to those of English. Keep in mind that rr is strongly rolled, zh is pronounced as the 's' in 'pleasure', ly as the 'll' in 'million' and ny as in 'canyon'. If you read our colored pronunciation guides as if they were English, you'll be understood. The stressed syllables are in italics.

Where necessary, both masculine and feminine forms of words are included, separated by a slash and with the masculine form first, eg *obrigado/obrigada* (m/f).

Basics

Hello.	*Olá.*	o·*laa*
Goodbye.	*Tchau.*	tee·*show*
How are you?	*Como vai?*	*ko*·mo vai
Fine, and you?	*Bem, e você?*	beng e vo·*se*
Excuse me.	*Com licença.*	kong lee·*seng*·saa
Sorry.	*Desculpa.*	des·*kool*·paa
Please.	*Por favor.*	por faa·*vorr*
Thank you.	*Obrigado/ Obrigada.* (m/f)	o·bree·*gaa*·do/ o·bree·*gaa*·daa
You're welcome.	*De nada.*	de *naa*·daa
Yes./No.	*Sim./Não.*	seeng/nowng

WANT MORE?

For in-depth language information and handy phrases, check out Lonely Planet's *Latin American Spanish Phrasebook*. You'll find it at **shop.lonelyplanet.com**, or you can buy Lonely Planet's iPhone phrasebooks at the Apple App Store.

What's your name?
Qual é o seu nome? — kwow e o *se*·oo *no*·me

My name is ...
Meu nome é ... — *me*·oo *no*·me e ...

Do you speak English?
Você fala inglês? — vo·*se faa*·laa eeng·*gles*

I don't understand.
Não entendo. — nowng eng·*teng*·do

Accommodations

Do you have a single/double room?
Tem um quarto de solteiro/casal? — teng oom *kwaarr*·to de sol·*tay*·ro/kaa·*zow*

How much is it per night/person?
Quanto custa por noite/pessoa? — *kwang*·to *koos*·taa porr *noy*·te/*pe*·so·aa

Does it include breakfast?
Inclui café da manhã? — eeng·*kloo*·ee kaa·*fe* daa ma·*nyang*

campsite	*local para acampamento*	lo·*kow paa*·raa aa·kang·paa·*meng*·to
guesthouse	*hospedaria*	os·pe·daa·*ree*·a
hotel	*hotel*	o·*tel*
youth hostel	*albergue juventude*	ow·*berr*·ge zhoo·veng·*too*·de
air-con	*ar condicionado*	aarr kong·dee·syo·*naa*·do
bathroom	*banheiro*	ba·*nyay*·ro

bed	*cama*	*ka*·maa
window	*janela*	zhaa·*ne*·laa

Directions

Where's ...?
Onde fica ...? — *ong*·de fee·kaa ...

What's the address?
Qual é o endereço? — kwow e o eng·de·*re*·so

Could you please write it down?
Você poderia escrever num papel, por favor? — vo·se po·de·*ree*·aa es·kre·*verr* noom paa·*pel* porr faa·*vorr*

Can you show me (on the map)?
Você poderia me mostrar (no mapa)? — vo·se po·de·*ree*·aa me mos·*traarr* (no *maa*·paa)

at the corner	*à esquina*	aa es·*kee*·naa
at the traffic lights	*no sinal de trânsito*	no see·*now* de *trang*·zee·to
behind ...	*atrás ...*	aa·*traaz* ...
in front of ...	*na frente de ...*	naa *freng*·te de ...
near ...	*perto ...*	*perr*·to ...
next to ...	*ao lado de ...*	ow *laa*·do de ...
opposite ...	*do lado oposto ...*	do *laa*·do o·*pos*·to ...
right	*à direita*	aa dee·*ray*·taa
straight ahead	*em frente*	eng *freng*·te

Eating & Drinking

I'd like the menu, please.
Eu queria o cardápio, por favor. — e·oo ke·*ree*·aa o kaar·*daa*·pyo porr faa·*vorr*

What would you recommend?
O que você recomenda? — o ke vo·se he·ko·*meng*·daa

Do you have vegetarian food?
Você tem comida vegetariana? — vo·se teng ko·*mee*·daa ve·zhe·taa·ree·*a*·naa

I don't eat (red meat).
Eu não como (carne vermelha). — e·oo nowng *ko*·mo (*kaar*·ne verr·*me*·lyaa)

That was delicious!
Estava delicioso! — es·*taa*·vaa de·lee·see·*o*·zo

Cheers!
Saúde! — sa·*oo*·de

Please bring the bill.
Por favor traga a conta. — porr faa·*vorr* *traa*·gaa aa *kong*·taa

I'd like a table for ...	*Eu gostaria uma mesa para ...*	e·oo gos·taa·*ree*·aa *oo*·maa *me*·zaa *paa*·raa ...
(eight)	*(às oito)*	(aas *oy*·to)

KEY PATTERNS

To get by in Portuguese, mix and match these simple patterns with words of your choice:

When's (the next flight)?
Quando é (o próximo vôo)? — *kwaang*·do e (o *pro*·see·mo *vo*·o)

Where's the (tourist office)?
Onde fica (a secretaria de turismo)? — *ong*·de *fee*·kaa (aa se·kre·taa·*ree*·aa de too·*rees*·mo)

Where can I (buy a ticket)?
Onde posso (comprar passagem)? — *ong*·de *po*·so (kong·*praar* paa·*sa*·zheng)

Do you have (a map)?
Você tem (um mapa)? — vo·se teng (oom *maa*·paa)

Is there (a toilet)?
Tem (banheiro)? — teng (ba·*nyay*·ro)

I'd like (a coffee).
Eu gostaria de (um café). — e·oo gos·taa·*ree*·aa de (oom *kaa*·fe)

I'd like (to hire a car).
Eu gostaria de (alugar um carro). — e·oo gos·taa·*ree*·aa de (aa·loo·*gaarr* oom *kaa*·ho)

Can I (enter)?
Posso (entrar)? — *po*·so (eng·*traarr*)

Could you please (help me)?
Você poderia me (ajudar), por favor? — vo·se po·de·*ree*·aa me (aa·zhoo·*daarr*) por faa·*vorr*

Do I have to (get a visa)?
Necessito (obter visto)? — ne·se·*see*·to (o·bee·*terr* *vees*·to)

o'clock	*horas*	*aw*·raas
(two) people	*(duas) pessoas*	(*doo*·aas) pe·*so*·aas

Key Words

appetisers	*aperitivos*	aa·pe·ree·*tee*·vos
bottle	*garrafa*	gaa·*haa*·faa
bowl	*tigela*	tee·*zhe*·laa
breakfast	*café da manhã*	kaa·*fe* daa ma·*nyang*
children's menu	*cardápio de crianças*	kaar·*da*·pyo de kree·*ang*·saas
(too) cold	*(demais) frio*	(zhee·*mais*) *free*·o
dinner	*jantar*	zhang·*taarr*
food	*comida*	ko·*mee*·daa
fork	*garfo*	*gaar*·fo
glass	*copo*	*ko*·po

hot (warm)	*quente*	*keng*·te
knife	*faca*	*faa*·kaa
lunch	*almoço*	ow·*mo*·so
main courses	*pratos principais*	*praa*·tos preeng·see·*pais*
plate	*prato*	*praa*·to
restaurant	*restaurante*	hes·tow·*rang*·te
spoon	*colher*	ko·*lyer*
with	*com*	kong
without	*sem*	seng

Meat & Fish

beef	*bife*	*bee*·fe
chicken	*frango*	*frang*·go
duck	*pato*	*paa*·to
fish	*peixe*	*pay*·she
lamb	*ovelha*	o·*ve*·lyaa
lobster	*lagosta*	laa·*gos*·taa
pork	*porco*	*porr*·ko
prawn	*camarão*	kaa·maa·*rowng*
tuna	*atum*	aa·*toong*
turkey	*perú*	pe·*roo*
veal	*bezerro*	be·*ze*·ho

Fruit & Vegetables

apple	*maçã*	maa·*sang*
apricot	*damasco*	daa·*maas*·ko
asparagus	*aspargo*	aas·*paarr*·go
avocado	*abacate*	aa·baa·*kaa*·te
banana	*banana*	baa·*na*·naa
bean	*feijão*	fay·*zhowng*
beetroot	*beterraba*	be·te·*haa*·baa
cabbage	*repolho*	he·*po*·lyo
carrot	*cenoura*	se·*no*·raa
cauliflower	*couve flor*	*ko*·ve flor
cherry	*cereja*	se·*re*·zhaa
corn	*milho*	*mee*·lyo
cucumber	*pepino*	pe·*pee*·no
fruit	*frutas*	*froo*·taas
grapes	*uvas*	*oo*·vaas
lemon	*limão*	lee·*mowng*
lentil	*lentilha*	leng·*tee*·lyaa
lettuce	*alface*	ow·*faa*·se
mushroom	*cogumelo*	ko·goo·*me*·lo
nut	*noz*	noz
onion	*cebola*	se·*bo*·laa
orange	*laranja*	laa·*rang*·zhaa
peach	*pêssego*	*pe*·se·go
pea	*ervilha*	err·*vee*·lyaa
pepper (bell)	*pimentão*	pee·meng·*towng*
pineapple	*abacaxi*	aa·baa·kaa·*shee*
plum	*ameixa*	aa·*may*·shaa
potato	*batata*	baa·*taa*·taa
pumpkin	*abóbora*	aa·*bo*·bo·raa
spinach	*espinafre*	es·pee·*naa*·fre
strawberry	*morango*	mo·*rang*·go
tomato	*tomate*	to·*maa*·te
vegetables	*legumes*	le·*goo*·mes
watermelon	*melancia*	me·lang·*see*·aa

Other

bread	*pão*	powng
butter	*manteiga*	mang·*tay*·gaa
cheese	*queijo*	*kay*·zho
eggs	*ovos*	*o*·vos
honey	*mel*	mel
jam	*geléia*	zhe·*le*·yaa
oil	*óleo*	*o*·lyo
pasta	*massas*	*maa*·saas
pepper	*pimenta*	pee·*meng*·taa
rice	*arroz*	aa·*hos*
salt	*sal*	sow
sugar	*açúcar*	aa·*soo*·kaarr
vinegar	*vinagre*	vee·*naa*·gre

Drinks

beer	*cerveja*	serr·*ve*·zhaa
coffee	*café*	kaa·*fe*
(orange) juice	*suco de (laranja)*	*soo*·ko de (laa·*rang*·zhaa)
milk	*leite*	*lay*·te
red wine	*vinho tinto*	*vee*·nyo *teeng*·to
tea	*chá*	shaa
(mineral) water	*água (mineral)*	*aa*·gwaa (mee·ne·*row*)
white wine	*vinho branco*	*vee*·nyo *brang*·ko

Signs – Portuguese

Banheiro	Toilet
Entrada	Entrance
(Não) Tem Vaga	(No) Vacancy
Pronto Socorro	Emergency Department
Saída	Exit

Emergencies

Help! *Socorro!*	so·*ko*·ho
Leave me alone! *Me deixe em paz!*	me *day*·she eng paas
Call the police! *Chame a polícia!*	*sha*·me aa po·*lee*·syaa
Call a doctor! *Chame um médico!*	*sha*·me oom *me*·dee·ko
I'm lost. *Estou perdido/ perdida.* (m/f)	es·*to* perr·*dee*·do/ perr·*dee*·daa
I'm ill. *Estou doente.*	es·*to* do·*eng*·te
I'm allergic to (antibiotics). *Tenho alergia à (antibióticos).*	*te*·nyo aa·lerr·*zhee*·aa aa (ang·tee·bee·*o*·tee·kos)
Where are the toilets? *Onde tem um banheiro?*	*on*·de teng oom ba·*nyay*·ro

Shopping & Services

I'd like to buy ... *Gostaria de comprar ...*	gos·taa·*ree*·aa de kong·*praarr* ...
I'm just looking. *Estou só olhando.*	es·*to* so o·*lyang*·do
Can I look at it? *Posso ver?*	*po*·so verr
Do you have any others? *Você tem outros?*	vo·*se* teng *o*·tros
How much is it? *Quanto custa?*	*kwang*·to *koos*·taa
That's too expensive. *Está muito caro.*	es·*taa* *mweeng*·to *kaa*·ro
Can you lower the price? *Pode baixar o preço?*	*po*·de bai·*shaarr* o *pre*·so
There's a mistake in the bill. *Houve um erro na conta.*	*o*·ve oom *e*·ho naa *kong*·taa

ATM	*caixa automático*	*kai*·shaa ow·to·*maa*·tee·ko
market	*mercado*	merr·*kaa*·do
post office	*correio*	ko·*hay*·o

Question Words – Portuguese

How?	*Como?*	*ko*·mo
What?	*Que?*	ke
When?	*Quando?*	*kwang*·do
Where?	*Onde?*	*ong*·de
Who?	*Quem?*	keng
Why?	*Por que?*	porr ke

tourist office	*secretaria de turismo*	se·kre·taa·*ree*·aa de too·*rees*·mo

Time & Dates

What time is it? *Que horas são?*	ke *aw*·raas sowng
It's (10) o'clock. *São (dez) horas.*	sowng (des) *aw*·raas
Half past (10). *(Dez) e meia.*	(des) e *may*·aa

morning	*manhã*	ma·*nyang*
afternoon	*tarde*	*taar*·de
evening	*noite*	*noy*·te
yesterday	*ontem*	*ong*·teng
today	*hoje*	*o*·zhe
tomorrow	*amanhã*	aa·ma·*nyang*
Monday	*segunda-feira*	se·*goong*·daa·*fay*·raa
Tuesday	*terça-feira*	*terr*·saa·*fay*·raa
Wednesday	*quarta-feira*	*kwaarr*·taa·*fay*·raa
Thursday	*quinta-feira*	*keeng*·taa·*fay*·raa
Friday	*sexta-feira*	*ses*·taa·*fay*·raa
Saturday	*sábado*	*saa*·baa·doo
Sunday	*domingo*	do·*meeng*·go
January	*janeiro*	zha·*nay*·ro
February	*fevereiro*	fe·ve·*ray*·ro
March	*março*	*marr*·so
April	*abril*	aa·*bree*·oo
May	*maio*	*maa*·yo
June	*junho*	*zhoo*·nyo
July	*julho*	*zhoo*·lyo
August	*agosto*	aa·*gos*·to
September	*setembro*	se·*teng*·bro
October	*outubro*	o·*too*·bro
November	*novembro*	no·*veng*·bro
December	*dezembro*	de·*zeng*·bro

Transportation

Public Transportation

boat	*barco*	*baarr*·ko
bus	*ônibus*	*o*·nee·boos
plane	*avião*	aa·vee·*owng*
train	*trem*	treng

Numbers – Portuguese

1	*um*	oom
2	*dois*	doys
3	*três*	tres
4	*quatro*	*kwaa*·tro
5	*cinco*	*seeng*·ko
6	*seis*	says
7	*sete*	*se*·te
8	*oito*	*oy*·to
9	*nove*	*naw*·ve
10	*dez*	dez
20	*vinte*	*veeng*·te
30	*trinta*	*treeng*·taa
40	*quarenta*	kwaa·*reng*·taa
50	*cinquenta*	seen·*kweng*·taa
60	*sessenta*	se·*seng*·taa
70	*setenta*	se·*teng*·taa
80	*oitenta*	oy·*teng*·taa
90	*noventa*	no·*veng*·taa
100	*cem*	seng
1000	*mil*	*mee*·oo

first	*primeiro*	pree·*may*·ro
last	*último*	*ool*·tee·mo
next	*próximo*	*pro*·see·mo
airport	*aeroporto*	aa·e·ro·*porr*·to
aisle seat	*lugar no corredor*	loo·*gaarr* no ko·he·*dorr*
bus stop	*ponto de ônibus*	*pong*·to de *o*·nee·boos
cancelled	*cancelado*	kang·se·*laa*·do
delayed	*atrasado*	aa·traa·*zaa*·do
ticket office	*bilheteria*	bee·lye·te·*ree*·aa
timetable	*horário*	o·*raa*·ryo
train station	*estação de trem*	es·taa·*sowng* de treng
window seat	*lugar na janela*	loo·*gaarr* naa zhaa·*ne*·laa
a ... ticket	*uma passagem de ...*	*oo*·maa paa·*sa*·zheng de ...
1st-class	*primeira classe*	pree·*may*·raa *klaa*·se
2nd-class	*segunda classe*	se·*goom*·daa *klaa*·se
one-way	*ida*	*ee*·daa
return	*ida e volta*	*ee*·daa e *vol*·taa

Does it stop at ...?
Ele para em ...? e·le *paa*·raa eng ...

What station is this?
Que estação é esta? ke es·taa·*sowng* e *es*·taa

What time does it leave/arrive?
A que horas sai/chega? aa ke *aw*·raas sai/*she*·gaa

Please tell me when we get to ...
Por favor me avise quando chegarmos à ... porr faa·*vor* me aa·*vee*·ze *kwang*·do she·*gaarr*·mos aa ...

I'd like to get off here.
Gostaria de saltar aqui. gos·taa·*ree*·aa de sow·*taarr* aa·*kee*

Driving & Cycling

I'd like to hire a/an ...	*Gostaria de alugar ...*	gos·taa·*ree*·aa de aa·loo·*gaarr* ...
4WD	*um carro quatro por quatro*	oom *kaa*·ho *kwaa*·tro porr *kwaa*·tro
bicycle	*uma bicicleta*	*oo*·ma bee·see·*kle*·taa
car	*um carro*	oom *kaa*·ho
motorcycle	*uma motocicleta*	*oo*·ma mo·to·see·*kle*·taa

child seat	*cadeira de criança*	kaa·*day*·raa de kree·*ang*·saa
diesel	*diesel*	*dee*·sel
helmet	*capacete*	kaa·paa·*se*·te
hitchhike	*pegar carona*	pe·*gaarr* kaa·*ro*·naa
mechanic	*mecânico*	me·*ka*·nee·ko
petrol/gas	*gasolina*	gaa·zo·*lee*·naa
service station	*posto de gasolina*	*pos*·to de gaa·zo·*lee*·naa
truck	*caminhão*	kaa·mee·*nyowng*

Is this the road to ...?
Esta é a estrada para ...? es·*taa* e aa es·*traa*·daa *paa*·raa ...

Can I park here?
Posso estacionar aqui? *po*·so es·taa·syo·*naarr* aa·*kee*

The car has broken down.
O carro quebrou. o *kaa*·ho ke·*bro*

I had an accident.
Sofri um acidente. so·*free* oom aa·see·*deng*·te

I've run out of petrol/gas.
Estou sem gasolina. es·*to* seng gaa·zo·*lee*·naa

I have a flat tyre.
Meu pneu furou. *me*·oo pee·*ne*·oo foo·*ro*

SPANISH

Latin American Spanish pronunciation is easy, as most sounds are also found in English. The stressed syllables are indicated with italics in our pronunciation guides.

Note that kh is a throaty sound (like the 'ch' in the Scottish *loch*), v and b are like a soft English 'v' (between a 'v' and a 'b'), and r is strongly rolled. There are some variations in spoken Spanish across Latin America, the most notable being the pronunciation of the letters *ll* and *y*. In our pronunciation guides they are represented with y because they are pronounced as the 'y' in 'yes' in most of Latin America. In some parts of the continent, though, they sound like the 'lli' in 'million', while in Argentina, Uruguay and highland Ecuador they are pronounced like the 's' in 'measure', or the 'sh' in 'shut'.

Where both polite and informal options are given in this section, they are indicated by the abbreviations 'pol' and 'inf'. The masciline and feminine forms are indicated with 'm' and 'f' respectively.

Basics

Hello.	*Hola.*	o·la
Goodbye.	*Adiós.*	a·*dyos*
How are you?	*¿Qué tal?*	ke tal
Fine, thanks.	*Bien, gracias.*	byen *gra*·syas
Excuse me.	*Perdón.*	per·*don*
Sorry.	*Lo siento.*	lo *syen*·to
Please.	*Por favor.*	por fa·*vor*
Thank you.	*Gracias.*	*gra*·syas
You are welcome.	*De nada.*	de *na*·da
Yes.	*Sí.*	see
No.	*No.*	no

My name is ...
Me llamo ... me *ya*·mo ...

What's your name?
¿Cómo se llama Usted? ko·mo se *ya*·ma oo·*ste* (pol)
¿Cómo te llamas? ko·mo te *ya*·mas (inf)

Signs – Spanish

Abierto	Open
Cerrado	Closed
Entrada	Entrance
Hombres/Varones	Men
Mujeres/Damas	Women
Prohibido	Prohibited
Salida	Exit
Servicios/Baños	Toilets

Do you speak English?
¿Habla inglés? a·bla een·*gles* (pol)
¿Hablas inglés? a·blas een·*gles* (inf)

I don't understand.
Yo no entiendo. yo no en·*tyen*·do

Accommodations

I'd like a single/double room.
Quisiera una habitación individual/doble. kee·*sye*·ra *oo*·na a·bee·ta·*syon* een·dee·vee·*dwal*/*do*·ble

How much is it per night/person?
¿Cuánto cuesta por noche/persona? *kwan*·to *kwes*·ta por *no*·che/per·*so*·na

Does it include breakfast?
¿Incluye el desayuno? een·*kloo*·ye el de·sa·*yoo*·no

air-con	*aire acondicionado*	*ai*·re a·kon·dee·syo·*na*·do
bathroom	*baño*	*ba*·nyo
bed	*cama*	*ka*·ma
campsite	*terreno de cámping*	te·*re*·no de *kam*·peeng
guesthouse	*pensión*	pen·*syon*
hotel	*hotel*	o·*tel*
youth hostel	*albergue juvenil*	al·*ber*·ge khoo·ve·*neel*
window	*ventana*	ven·*ta*·na

Directions

Where's ...?
¿Dónde está ...? don·de es·*ta* ...

What's the address?
¿Cuál es la dirección? kwal es la dee·rek·*syon*

Could you please write it down?
¿Puede escribirlo, por favor? *pwe*·de es·kree·*beer*·lo por fa·*vor*

Can you show me (on the map)?
¿Me lo puede indicar (en el mapa)? me lo *pwe*·de een·dee·*kar* (en el *ma*·pa)

at the corner	*en la esquina*	en la es·*kee*·na
at the traffic lights	*en el semáforo*	en el se·*ma*·fo·ro
behind ...	*detrás de ...*	de·*tras* de ...
in front of ...	*enfrente de ...*	en·*fren*·te de ...
left	*izquierda*	ees·*kyer*·da
near	*cerca*	*ser*·ka
next to ...	*al lado de ...*	al *la*·do de ...
opposite ...	*frente a ...*	*fren*·te a ...
right	*derecha*	de·*re*·cha
straight ahead	*todo recto*	to·do *rek*·to

KEY PATTERNS

To get by in Spanish, mix and match these simple patterns with words of your choice:

When's (the next flight)?
¿Cuándo sale (el próximo vuelo)? — *kwan*·do sa·le (el *prok*·see·mo *vwe*·lo)

Where's (the station)?
¿Dónde está (la estación)? — *don*·de es·*ta* (la es·ta·*syon*)

Where can I (buy a ticket)?
¿Dónde puedo (comprar un billete)? — *don*·de *pwe*·do (kom·*prar* oon bee·*ye*·te)

Do you have (a map)?
¿Tiene (un mapa)? — *tye*·ne (oon *ma*·pa)

Is there (a toilet)?
¿Hay (servicios)? — ai (ser·*vee*·syos)

I'd like (a coffee).
Quisiera (un café). — kee·*sye*·ra (oon ka·*fe*)

I'd like (to hire a car).
Quisiera (alquilar un coche). — kee·*sye*·ra (al·kee·*lar* oon *ko*·che)

Can I (enter)?
¿Se puede (entrar)? — se *pwe*·de (en·*trar*)

Could you please (help me)?
¿Puede (ayudarme), por favor? — *pwe*·de (a·yoo·*dar*·me) por fa·*vor*

Do I have to (get a visa)?
¿Necesito (obtener un visado)? — ne·se·*see*·to (ob·te·*ner* oon vee·*sa*·do)

Eating & Drinking

Can I see the menu, please?
¿Puedo ver el menú, por favor? — *pwe*·do ver el me·*noo* por fa·*vor*

What would you recommend?
¿Qué recomienda? — ke re·ko·*myen*·da

Do you have vegetarian food?
¿Tienen comida vegetariana? — *tye*·nen ko·*mee*·da ve·khe·ta·*rya*·na

I don't eat (red meat).
No como (carne roja). — no *ko*·mo (*kar*·ne *ro*·kha)

That was delicious!
¡Estaba buenísimo! — es·*ta*·ba bwe·*nee*·see·mo

Cheers!
¡Salud! — sa·*loo*

The bill, please.
La cuenta, por favor. — la *kwen*·ta por fa·*vor*

I'd like a table for ...	*Quisiera una mesa para ...*	kee·*sye*·ra *oo*·na *me*·sa *pa*·ra ...
(eight) o'clock	*las (ocho)*	las (*o*·cho)
(two) people	*(dos) personas*	(dos) per·*so*·nas

Key Words

appetisers	*aperitivos*	a·pe·ree·*tee*·vos
bottle	*botella*	bo·*te*·ya
bowl	*bol*	bol
breakfast	*desayuno*	de·sa·*yoo*·no
children's menu	*menú infantil*	me·*noo* een·fan·*teel*
(too) cold	*(muy) frío*	(mooy) *free*·o
dinner	*cena*	*se*·na
food	*comida*	ko·*mee*·da
fork	*tenedor*	te·ne·*dor*
glass	*vaso*	*va*·so
hot (warm)	*caliente*	kal·*yen*·te
knife	*cuchillo*	koo·*chee*·yo
lunch	*comida*	ko·*mee*·da
main course	*segundo plato*	se·*goon*·do *pla*·to
plate	*plato*	*pla*·to
restaurant	*restaurante*	res·tow·*ran*·te
spoon	*cuchara*	koo·*cha*·ra
with	*con*	kon
without	*sin*	seen

Meat & Fish

beef	*carne de vaca*	*kar*·ne de *va*·ka
chicken	*pollo*	*po*·yo
duck	*pato*	*pa*·to
fish	*pescado*	pes·*ka*·do
lamb	*cordero*	kor·*de*·ro
lobster	*langosta*	lan·*gos*·ta
pork	*cerdo*	*ser*·do
shrimps	*camarones*	ka·ma·*ro*·nes
tuna	*atún*	a·*toon*
turkey	*pavo*	*pa*·vo
veal	*ternera*	ter·*ne*·ra

Fruit & Vegetables

apple	*manzana*	man·*sa*·na
apricot	*albaricoque*	al·ba·ree·*ko*·ke
artichoke	*alcachofa*	al·ka·*cho*·fa
asparagus	*espárragos*	es·*pa*·ra·gos
banana	*plátano*	*pla*·ta·no
beans	*judías*	khoo·*dee*·as
cabbage	*col*	kol
carrot	*zanahoria*	sa·na·*o*·rya
celery	*apio*	*a*·pyo

cherry	*cereza*	se·*re*·sa
corn	*maíz*	ma·*ees*
cucumber	*pepino*	pe·*pee*·no
fruit	*fruta*	*froo*·ta
grape	*uvas*	*oo*·vas
lemon	*limón*	lee·*mon*
lentils	*lentejas*	len·*te*·khas
lettuce	*lechuga*	le·*choo*·ga
mushroom	*champiñón*	cham·pee·*nyon*
nuts	*nueces*	*nwe*·ses
onion	*cebolla*	se·*bo*·ya
orange	*naranja*	na·*ran*·kha
peach	*melocotón*	me·lo·ko·*ton*
peas	*guisantes*	gee·*san*·tes
pepper (bell)	*pimiento*	pee·*myen*·to
pineapple	*piña*	*pee*·nya
plum	*ciruela*	seer·*we*·la
potato	*patata*	pa·*ta*·ta
pumpkin	*calabaza*	ka·la·*ba*·sa
spinach	*espinacas*	es·pee·*na*·kas
strawberry	*fresa*	*fre*·sa
tomato	*tomate*	to·*ma*·te
vegetable	*verdura*	ver·*doo*·ra
watermelon	*sandía*	san·*dee*·a

Other

bread	*pan*	pan
butter	*mantequilla*	man·te·*kee*·ya
cheese	*queso*	*ke*·so
egg	*huevo*	*we*·vo
honey	*miel*	myel
jam	*mermelada*	mer·me·*la*·da
oil	*aceite*	a·*sey*·te
pasta	*pasta*	*pas*·ta
pepper	*pimienta*	pee·*myen*·ta
rice	*arroz*	a·*ros*
salt	*sal*	sal
sugar	*azúcar*	a·*soo*·kar
vinegar	*vinagre*	vee·*na*·gre

Question Words – Spanish

How?	*¿Cómo?*	*ko*·mo
What?	*¿Qué?*	ke
When?	*¿Cuándo?*	*kwan*·do
Where?	*¿Dónde?*	*don*·de
Who?	*¿Quién?*	kyen
Why?	*¿Por qué?*	por ke

Drinks

beer	*cerveza*	ser·*ve*·sa
coffee	*café*	ka·*fe*
(orange) juice	*zumo (de naranja)*	*soo*·mo (de na·*ran*·kha)
milk	*leche*	*le*·che
red wine	*vino tinto*	*vee*·no *teen*·to
tea	*té*	te
(mineral) water	*agua (mineral)*	*a*·gwa (mee·ne·*ral*)
white wine	*vino blanco*	*vee*·no *blan*·ko

Emergencies

Help!	*¡Socorro!*	so·*ko*·ro
Go away!	*¡Vete!*	*ve*·te
Call ...!	*¡Llame a ...!*	*ya*·me a ...
a doctor	*un médico*	oon *me*·dee·ko
the police	*la policía*	la po·lee·*see*·a

I'm lost.
Estoy perdido/a. es·*toy* per·*dee*·do/a (m/f)

I'm ill.
Estoy enfermo/a. es·*toy* en·*fer*·mo/a (m/f)

I'm allergic to (antibiotics).
Soy alérgico/a a (los antibióticos). soy a·*ler*·khee·ko/a a (los an·tee·*byo*·tee·kos) (m/f)

Where are the toilets?
¿Dónde están los baños? *don*·de es·*tan* los *ba*·nyos

Shopping & Services

I'd like to buy ...
Quisiera comprar ... kee·*sye*·ra kom·*prar* ...

I'm just looking.
Sólo estoy mirando. *so*·lo es·*toy* mee·*ran*·do

Can I look at it?
¿Puedo verlo? *pwe*·do *ver*·lo

I don't like it.
No me gusta. no me *goos*·ta

How much is it?
¿Cuánto cuesta? *kwan*·to *kwes*·ta

That's too expensive.
Es muy caro. es mooy *ka*·ro

Can you lower the price?
¿Podría bajar un poco el precio? po·*dree*·a ba·*khar* oon *po*·ko el *pre*·syo

There's a mistake in the bill.
Hay un error en la cuenta. ai oon e·*ror* en la *kwen*·ta

ATM	*cajero automático*	ka·*khe*·ro ow·to·*ma*·tee·ko

market	*mercado*	mer·*ka*·do
post office	*correos*	ko·*re*·os
tourist office	*oficina de turismo*	o·fee·*see*·na de too·*rees*·mo

Time & Dates

What time is it?
¿Qué hora es? — ke o·ra es

It's (10) o'clock.
Son (las diez). — son (las dyes)

It's half past (one).
Es (la una) y media. — es (la *oo*·na) ee *me*·dya

morning	*mañana*	ma·*nya*·na
afternoon	*tarde*	*tar*·de
evening	*noche*	*no*·che
yesterday	*ayer*	a·*yer*
today	*hoy*	oy
tomorrow	*mañana*	ma·*nya*·na

Monday	*lunes*	*loo*·nes
Tuesday	*martes*	*mar*·tes
Wednesday	*miércoles*	*myer*·ko·les
Thursday	*jueves*	*khwe*·ves
Friday	*viernes*	*vyer*·nes
Saturday	*sábado*	*sa*·ba·do
Sunday	*domingo*	do·*meen*·go

January	*enero*	e·*ne*·ro
February	*febrero*	fe·*bre*·ro
March	*marzo*	*mar*·so
April	*abril*	a·*breel*
May	*mayo*	*ma*·yo
June	*junio*	*khoon*·yo
July	*julio*	*khool*·yo
August	*agosto*	a·*gos*·to
September	*septiembre*	sep·*tyem*·bre
October	*octubre*	ok·*too*·bre
November	*noviembre*	no·*vyem*·bre
December	*diciembre*	dee·*syem*·bre

Transportation

Public Transportation

boat	*barco*	*bar*·ko
bus	*autobús*	ow·to·*boos*
plane	*avión*	a·*vyon*
train	*tren*	tren
first	*primero*	pree·*me*·ro
last	*último*	*ool*·tee·mo
next	*próximo*	*prok*·see·mo

airport	*aeropuerto*	a·e·ro·*pwer*·to
aisle seat	*asiento de pasillo*	a·*syen*·to de pa·*see*·yo
bus stop	*parada de autobuses*	pa·*ra*·da de ow·to·*boo*·ses
cancelled	*cancelado*	kan·se·*la*·do
delayed	*retrasado*	re·tra·*sa*·do
ticket office	*taquilla*	ta·*kee*·ya
timetable	*horario*	o·*ra*·ryo
train station	*estación de trenes*	es·ta·*syon* de *tre*·nes
window seat	*asiento junto a la ventana*	a·*syen*·to *khoon*·to a la ven·*ta*·na

A ... ticket, please. — *Un billete de ..., por favor.* — oon bee·*ye*·te de ... por fa·*vor*

1st-class	*primera clase*	pree·*me*·ra *kla*·se
2nd-class	*segunda clase*	se·*goon*·da *kla*·se
one-way	*ida*	ee·da
return	*ida y vuelta*	ee·da ee *vwel*·ta

Does it stop at ...?
¿Para en ...? — pa·ra en ...

Numbers – Spanish

1	*uno*	*oo*·no
2	*dos*	dos
3	*tres*	tres
4	*cuatro*	*kwa*·tro
5	*cinco*	*seen*·ko
6	*seis*	seys
7	*siete*	*sye*·te
8	*ocho*	*o*·cho
9	*nueve*	*nwe*·ve
10	*diez*	dyes
20	*veinte*	*veyn*·te
30	*treinta*	*treyn*·ta
40	*cuarenta*	kwa·*ren*·ta
50	*cincuenta*	seen·*kwen*·ta
60	*sesenta*	se·*sen*·ta
70	*setenta*	se·*ten*·ta
80	*ochenta*	o·*chen*·ta
90	*noventa*	no·*ven*·ta
100	*cien*	syen
1000	*mil*	meel

What stop is this?
¿Cuál es esta parada? kwal es *es*·ta pa·*ra*·da

What time does it arrive/leave?
¿A qué hora llega/sale? a ke o·ra *ye*·ga/*sa*·le

Please tell me when we get to ...
¿Puede avisarme cuando lleguemos a ...? *pwe*·de a·vee·*sar*·me *kwan*·do ye·*ge*·mos a ...

I want to get off here.
Quiero bajarme aquí. *kye*·ro ba·*khar*·me a·*kee*

Driving & Cycling

I'd like to hire a ...	*Quisiera alquilar ...*	kee·*sye*·ra al·kee·*lar* ...
4WD	*un todo-terreno*	oon to·do·te·*re*·no
bicycle	*una bicicleta*	*oo*·na bee·see·*kle*·ta
car	*un coche*	oon *ko*·che
motorcycle	*una moto*	*oo*·na *mo*·to
child seat	*asiento de seguridad para niños*	a·*syen*·to de se·goo·ree·*da* *pa*·ra *nee*·nyos
diesel	*petróleo*	pet·*ro*·le·o
helmet	*casco*	*kas*·ko
hitchhike	*hacer botella*	a·*ser* bo·*te*·ya
mechanic	*mecánico*	me·*ka*·nee·ko
petrol/gas	*gasolina*	ga·so·*lee*·na
service station	*gasolinera*	ga·so·lee·*ne*·ra
truck	*camion*	ka·*myon*

Is this the road to ...?
¿Se va a ... por esta carretera? se va a ... por es·ta ka·re·*te*·ra

Can I park here?
¿Puedo aparcar aquí? *pwe*·do a·par·*kar* a·*kee*

The car has broken down.
El coche se ha averiado. el *ko*·che se a a·ve·*rya*·do

I had an accident.
He tenido un accidente. e te·*nee*·do oon ak·see·*den*·te

I've run out of petrol/gas.
Me he quedado sin gasolina. me e ke·*da*·do seen ga·so·*lee*·na

I have a flat tyre.
Se me pinchó una rueda. se me peen·*cho* *oo*·na *rwe*·da

AYMARÁ & QUECHUA

The few Aymará and Quechua words and phrases included here will be useful for those traveling in the Andes. Aymará is spoken by the Aymará people, who inhabit the highland regions of Bolivia and Peru and smaller adjoining areas of Chile and Argentina. While the Quechua included here is from the Cuzco dialect, it should prove helpful wherever you travel in the Andes. The exception is Ecuador, where it is known as Quichua – the dialect that's most removed from the Cuzco variety.

In the following lists, Aymará is the second column, Quechua the third. The principles of pronunciation for both languages are similar to those found in Spanish. An apostrophe (') represents a glottal stop, which is the 'nonsound' that occurs in the middle of 'uh-oh.'

Hello.	*Kamisaraki.*	*Napaykullayki.*
Please.	*Mirá.*	*Allichu.*
Thank you.	*Yuspagara.*	*Yusulipayki.*
Yes.	*Jisa.*	*Ari.*
No.	*Mana.*	*Janiwa.*
How do you say ...?	*Cun saña-sauca'ha ...?*	*Imainata nincha chaita ...?*
It's called ...	*Ucan sutipa'h ...*	*Chaipa'g sutin'ha ...*
Please repeat.	*Uastata sita.*	*Ua'manta niway.*
How much?	*K'gauka?*	*Maik'ata'g?*
father	*auqui*	*tayta*
mother	*taica*	*mama*
food	*manka*	*mikíuy*
river	*jawira*	*mayu*
snowy peak	*kollu*	*riti-orko*
water	*uma*	*yacu*
1	*maya*	*u'*
2	*paya*	*iskai*
3	*quimsa*	*quinsa*
4	*pusi*	*tahua*
5	*pesca*	*phiska*
6	*zo'hta*	*so'gta*
7	*pakalko*	*khanchis*
8	*quimsakalko*	*pusa'g*
9	*yatunca*	*iskon*
10	*tunca*	*chunca*

GLOSSARY

Unless otherwise indicated, the terms listed in this glossary refer to Spanish-speaking South America in general, but regional variations in meaning are common. Portuguese phrases, which are only used in Brazil, are indicated with 'Bra.'

aduana – customs
aguardiente – sugarcane alcohol
ají – chili
albergue – hostel
alcaldía – town hall; virtually synonymous with *municipalidad*
almuerzo – fixed-price set lunch
alojamiento – rock-bottom accommodations with shared toilet and bathroom facilities
altiplano – Andean high plain of Peru, Bolivia, Chile and Argentina
apartamento – apartment or flat; in Brazil, a hotel room with private bathroom
artesanía – handicrafts; crafts shop
asado – roasted; in Argentina, a barbecue which is often a family outing
ascensor – elevator
audiencia – colonial administrative subdivision
ayahuasca – hallucinogenic brew made from jungle vines
Aymará – indigenous people of highland Bolivia, Peru and Chile (also called *Kolla*); also their language

balneario – bathing resort or beach
baños – baths
barrio – neighborhood, district or borough; in Venezuela, a shantytown; in Brazil, *bairro*
bloco (Bra) – group of musicians and dancers who perform in street parades during Brazil's Carnaval
bodega – winery or storage area for wine
bus-cama – literally 'bus-bed'; very comfortable bus with fully reclining seats; also called *coche-cama*

cabaña – cabin
cabildo – colonial town council
cachaça (Bra) – sugarcane rum, also called *pinga;* Brazil's national drink
cachoeira (Bra) – waterfall
caipirinha (Bra) – Brazil's national cocktail
calle – street
cambista – street money changer
camino – road, path, way
camión – open-bed truck; popular form of local transport in the Andean countries
camioneta – pickup or other small truck; form of local transport in the Andean countries
campamento – campsite
campesino/a – rural dweller who practices subsistence agriculture; peasant
caña – rum
Candomblé (Bra) – Afro-Brazilian religion of Bahia
capoeira (Bra) – martial art/dance developed by Bahian slaves
Carnaval – all over Latin America, pre-Lenten celebration
casa de cambio – authorized foreign-currency exchange house
casa de familia – modest family accommodations
casa de huésped – literally 'guesthouse'; form of economical lodging where guests may have access to the kitchen, garden and laundry facilities
casona – large house, usually a mansion; term often applied to colonial architecture in particular
catarata – waterfall
caudillo – in 19th-century South American politics, a provincial strongman
cazuela – hearty stew
cena – dinner; often an inexpensive set menu
cerro – hill; also refers to very high Andean peaks
certificado – registered (for mail)
cerveza – beer
ceviche – marinated raw seafood (it can be a source of both cholera and gnathostomiasis)
charango – Andean stringed instrument, traditionally made with an armadillo shell as a soundbox
chicha – in Andean countries, a popular beverage (often alcoholic) made from ingredients such as yucca, sweet potato or maize
chifa – Chinese restaurant (term most commonly used in Peru, Bolivia and Ecuador)
chiva – in Colombia, basic rural bus with wooden bench seats
churrasquería – restaurant featuring barbecued meat; in Brazil, *churrascaria*
cocalero – coca grower
coche-cama – see *bus-cama*
colectivo – depending on the country, either a bus, a minibus or a shared taxi
combi – small bus or minibus; also called *micro*
comedor – basic eatery or dining room in a hotel
comida corriente – in Colombia, basic set meal
confitería – cafe that serves coffee, tea, desserts and simple food orders
cordillera – mountain range
correo – post office; in Brazil, *correio*

costanera – in the Southern Cone, a seaside, riverside or lakeside road
costeño – inhabitant of the coast
criollo/a – Spaniard born in colonial South America; in modern times, a South American of European descent
cumbia – big on horns and percussion, a cousin to salsa, merengue and lambada
curanto – Chilean seafood stew
cuy – roasted guinea pig, a traditional Andean food

denuncia – affidavit or statement, usually in connection with theft or robbery

edificio – building
esquina – corner (abbreviated to 'esq')
estancia – extensive grazing establishment, either for cattle or sheep, with a dominant owner or manager *(estanciero)* and dependent resident labor force

FARC – Fuerzas Armadas Revolucionarias de Colombia (Revolutionary Armed Forces of Colombia); guerrilla movement
farmacia – pharmacy
favela (Bra) – slum or shantytown
fazenda (Bra) – large ranch or farm, similar to *hacienda*
ferrobus – type of passenger train
ferrocarril – railway, railroad
ferroviária (Bra) – railway station
flota – fleet; often a long-distance bus line
fútbol – soccer; in Brazil, *fútebol*

gaucho – in Argentina and Uruguay, a cowboy, herdsman; in Brazil, *gaúcho*
golpe de estado – coup d'état
gringo/a – a foreigner or person with light hair and complexion; not necessarily a derogatory term
guanaco – undomesticated relative of the llama
guaraná – Amazonian shrub with berries believed to have magical and medicinal powers; in Brazil, a popular soft drink
Guaraní – indigenous people of Argentina, Brazil, Bolivia and Paraguay; also their language

hacienda – large rural landholding with a dependent resident labor force under a dominant owner *(hacendado)*
hidroviária – boat terminal
hospedaje – budget accommodations with shared bathroom; usually a family home with an extra guest room
hostal – small hotel or guesthouse
huaso – cowboy
humita – a sweet-corn tamale or dumpling

iglesia – church; in Brazil, *igreja*
Inca – dominant indigenous civilization of the central Andes at the time of the Spanish Conquest; refers both to the people and, individually, to their leader
indígena – native American; indigenous person
isla – island; in Brazil, *ilha*

lago – lake
laguna – lagoon; shallow lake
lanchero – boat driver
latifundio – large landholding, such as a *hacienda* or cattle *estancia*
lavandería – laundry
leito (Bra) – luxury overnight express bus
licuado – fruit shake blended with milk or water
lista de correos – poste restante
locutorio – small telephone office

machismo – exaggerated masculine pride
malecón – shoreline promenade
Mapuche – indigenous people of northern Patagonia
marisquería – seafood restaurant
maté – see *yerba maté*
mate de coca – coca-leaf tea
menú del día – inexpensive set meal
mercado – market
mercado negro – black market
mestizo/a – a person of mixed indigenous and Spanish descent
micro – small bus or minibus; also called *combi*
migración – immigration office
minuta – short-order snack in Argentina, Paraguay and Uruguay
mirador – viewpoint or lookout, usually on a hill but often in a building
moai – enormous stone statues on Easter Island
mototaxi – in Peru, three-wheeled motorcycle rickshaw; also called *motocarro*
mudéjar – a Moorish-influenced architectural style that developed in Spain beginning in the 12th century
mulato/a – person of mixed African and European ancestry
municipalidad – city or town hall
museo – museum; in Brazil, *museu*
música criolla – creole music
música folklórica – traditional Andean music

nevado – snow-covered peak

oferta – promotional fare for plane or bus travel
oficina – office (abbreviated to 'of')
onces – morning or afternoon tea; snack
Pachamama – Mother Earth, deity of the indigenous Andean people
panadería – bakery
panama – traditional lightweight straw hat, actually of Ecuadorian origin
parada/paradero – bus stop
páramo – humid, high-altitude grassland of the northern Andean countries
parque nacional – national park
parrilla/parrillada – barbecued or grilled meat; also used to refer to a steakhouse restaurant or the grill used to cook meat
paseo – avenue, promenade

patio de comidas – food court

peatonal – pedestrian mall

pehuén – the monkey-puzzle tree of southern South America

peña – club/bar that hosts informal folk music gatherings; performance at such a club

pensión – short-term budget accommodations in a family home, which may also have permanent lodgers

piropo – sexist remark, ranging from relatively innocuous to very offensive

pisco – white-grape brandy, Peruvian national drink; most frequently served as a pisco sour cocktail

Planalto – enormous plateau that covers much of southern Brazil

pollería – restaurant serving grilled chicken

por puesto – in Venezuela, shared taxi or minibus

posada – small family-owned guesthouse; term sometimes also used for a hotel; in Brazil, *pousada*

prato feito (Bra) – literally 'made plate' or 'plate of the day'; typically an enormous and very cheap, fixed-price meal

precordillera – foothills of the Andes

pucará – an indigenous Andean fortification

puna – Andean highlands, usually above 3000m

quebrada – ravine, normally dry

Quechua – indigenous language of the Andean highlands; 'Quichua' in Ecuador

quena – simple reed flute

quinoa – native Andean grain, the dietary equivalent of rice in the pre-Columbian era

rancho – rural house

recargo – surcharge; added by many businesses to credit-card transactions

reducción – in colonial Latin America, the concentration of native populations in central settlements, usually to aid political control or religious instruction; also known as *congregación*

refugio – rustic shelter in a national park or remote area

reggaeton – Caribbean-born popular music which combines Latin rhythms with rap

remise – in Argentina, taxi booked over the phone

residencial – budget accommodations, sometimes only seasonal; in general, *residenciales* are in buildings designed expressly for short-stay lodging

río – river; in Brazil, *rio*

rodoferroviária (Bra) – combined bus and train station

rodoviária (Bra) – bus station

ruta – route or highway

s/n – *sin número;* indicating a street address without a number

salar – salt lake or salt pan, usually in the high Andes or Argentine Patagonia

salsoteca – salsa club

salteña – meat and vegetable pasty, generally a spicier version of empanada

Semana Santa – celebrated all over South America, Holy Week, the week before Easter

Sendero Luminoso – Shining Path, Peru's Maoist terrorist group which led a guerrilla war in the late 1980s

serrano – inhabitant of the mountains

siesta – lengthy afternoon break for lunch and, occasionally, a nap

soroche – altitude sickness

Sranan Tongo – creole widely spoken in Suriname; also called Surinaams

suco (Bra) – fruit juice; fruit-juice bar

tasca – Spanish-style bar-restaurant

teleférico – cable car

telenovela – TV soap opera

tenedor libre – in Argentina, 'all-you-can-eat' buffet

tepui – flat-topped mountain; home to unique flora

termas – hot springs

terminal de ómnibus – bus station; also called *terminal terrestre*

tinto – red wine; in Colombia, small cup of black coffee

todo terreno – mountain bike

torrentismo – rappelling down a waterfall

totora – type of reed, used as a building material

vaquero – cowboy; in Brazil, *vaqueiro*

vicuña – wild relative of the domestic llama and alpaca, found only at high altitudes in the south-central Andes

yerba maté – 'Paraguayan tea' *(Ilex paraguariensis);* consumed regularly in Argentina, Paraguay, Uruguay and Brazil

zampoña – pan flute featured in traditional Andean music

zona franca – duty-free zone

Behind the Scenes

SEND US YOUR FEEDBACK

We love to hear from travelers – your comments keep us on our toes and help make our books better. Our well-traveled team reads every word on what you loved or loathed about this book. Although we cannot reply individually to your submissions, we always guarantee that your feedback goes straight to the appropriate authors, in time for the next edition. Each person who sends us information is thanked in the next edition – the most useful submissions are rewarded with a selection of digital PDF chapters.

Visit **lonelyplanet.com/contact** to submit your updates and suggestions or to ask for help. Our award-winning website also features inspirational travel stories, news and discussions.

Note: We may edit, reproduce and incorporate your comments in Lonely Planet products such as guidebooks, websites and digital products, so let us know if you don't want your comments reproduced or your name acknowledged. For a copy of our privacy policy visit lonelyplanet.com/privacy.

OUR READERS

Many thanks to the travelers who used the last edition and wrote to us with helpful hints, useful advice and interesting anecdotes.

Aaron Strathearn, Adeline Jeancler, Alan Maher, Alex Curry, Analisa Areyan, Angie Jones, Antony Reed, Bernard Tarkali, Bob Domhof, Brian Sincock, Cagdas Citirikkaya, Lisbeth Nørholm, Carly Richardson, Caspar Höyng, Charlotte Stichele, Christian Schuhmann, Cortney Cooper, Cristobal Lamarca, Daniel Badenas, Debbie Spicer, Dee McCombie, Don Plimer, Douglas Burton, Elaine Kesten, Elena Morris, Ellen Brookes, Ellis Polin, Emma Sealey, Emma Townsin, Florian Hoefliger, Frank Thomson, Gorgonio Ruiz, Gu Xu, Hannah Small, Helen Rossdale, Helene Wallach, Henry Twinch, Janet Clough, John Hunkler, Jon Wisloff, Josh Hollick-Kenyon, Katja Rantala, Katryn Mercer, Ken Bastiaensen, Kristen Kiely, Lai Fatt, Lars Jensen, Lisbeth Nørholm, Louise Gungaram, Maria Cortese, Mark Candey, Martin Hellwagner, Matt Elliott, Mónica Puma, Nicholas McPhee, Nicola Mitchell, Ofir Magdaci, Omar Medina, Peter Westöö, Rachel Saum, Reinhold Grawe, Ricardo Blasco, Robert Moltmaker, Rory O'Brien, Rosie Fowler, Rosie Leutzinger, Sara Lopes, Stefan Lissinna, Steve Mirro, Teresa Meadows, Thijs Plegt, Tobias van Leijsen, Uwe Lask, Zahyra Ceballos

AUTHOR THANKS

Regis St Louis

I am grateful to the countless locals, expats and friends who helped me along the way. In particular, I'd like to thank Christopher Jimenez in Guayaquil, John and Eva in Quito, Claudio Cruz and Aura on Floreana, Christoph Köhncke for more Floreana insight, Jacqueline Bruns on Isabela and fellow Eden shipmates Ryan, Sarah, Kara, Owian, Amy, Nat, Havard and Mette. As always, big thanks to my partner in crime Cassandra and daughters, Magdalena and Genevieve, who joined me on the road in Brazil.

Sandra Bao

This was the first time I've returned to Buenos Aires without seeing my godmother, Elsa Mallarini, who had passed earlier in the year. I'll miss her welcoming arms and smiles. Many thanks to Graciela and Silvia Guzmán, Lucas Markowiecki, Lisa Power, Sylvia Zapiola, Madi Lang, Jed Rothenburg, Ivan Carrasco and Claudina Galiñarez (and family). *Cariños* to my parents, Fung and David Bao, and brother, Daniel. Finally, lots of love to my husband, Ben Greensfelder.

Celeste Brash

In Guyana thanks to Kayla, Justin and Sebastian DeFreitas, Rustom, Leroy, Vanda, Shirley, Michelle, Lisa, Joan, Fernando, Salvador,

Andrea and Loverboy. In Suriname thanks to Kooksie, Bert, Paul and Joke and Peter and in French Guiana to my bearshapedshere travel buddy Eileen Smith.

Gregor Clark

Muchísimas gracias and *muito obrigado* to the many Brazilians, Uruguayans and resident expatriates who shared their love of country and local knowledge with me, especially Maira, Alex, Gloria, Tino, Miguel, Monica, Karen, Pasca, Alain, Youri, Cecilia, Juan Manuel, Susana, Bilingue, Lucia and Rodney. Back home, *abrazos* to Gaen, Meigan and Chloe, who always make coming home the best part of the trip.

Alex Egerton

In Colombia thanks to the usual suspects: Olga Mosquera, Laura Cahnspeyer, Oscar Gilede, Melissa Montoya, Nicolas Solorzano, Richard, Felipe Goforit, Tyler, Alexa and Oscar Payan – *abrazos para todos*. Also a big shout to Kevin Raub, Tom Masters and MaSovaida for being wonderfully supportive colleagues. And big thanks to Kent '¿Q mas?' and Warren for the write-up pad.

Brian Klupfel

Thanks always to Goyo for friendship and sage advice, and getting me a few gigs along the way; to MaSovaida for putting her faith in me; to my fellow authors Michael and Paul for their input; to Ximena at Casa Fusion for making some connections; to Michael Dirninger of Andes Expeditions for the mountaineering information and the amazing Viennese dessert; to Tjalle Boorsma of Armonia, Ruth of Bird Bolivia, and Rodrigo Mariaca of Chalalan for encouraging my bird obsession; to Derren at Gravity Extreme for info galore; to Jane and Dianne of Lonely Planet for their patience in schooling me on the CMS; to Roscio Ugartche in La Paz for kindness and restaurant advice; to Stacey and Peggy for covering for me in NY; above all to my family and Eli, who encouraged and waited for me back home.

Tom Masters

I'm supremely grateful to Ben Rodríguez and his team at Osprey Expeditions in Caracas, who helped me at every step of the way around Venezuela. Another huge debt of thanks to Paul Stanley of Angel Eco-Tours, who took so much time to read this chapter and suggest changes and additions. Elsewhere in Venezuela, thanks to Claudia and Francisco in Choroní, Gustavo Viloria of Gravity Tours in Catatumbo, Renate and José Luis of Casa del Sol and Alan Highton of Catatumbo Tours in Mérida, José Yepez Vera in Canaima, Carlos Acosta in Caracas, John Carlos for his driving and to the dozens of other *posada* owners, travel agents and travelers I met on the way.

Carolyn McCarthy

Many thanks go to coordinator Regis St Louis and the many who helped me in my research.

Kevin Raub

Thanks to my wife, Adriana Schmidt Raub, who sure does do her best to teach me the Brazilian dance when I run into roadblocks on the road (even though I don't dance!); MaSovaida Morgan; and my partners-in-crime on this book, Regis St Louis and Gregor Clark. On the road, Malu Sabatino, Daniella Barbosa, Helena Costa, Rodrigo Angel, Ion David, Kely Zimath, Thiago Luiz, Marcia Gazola, Edu Passarelli, Vanessa Carvalho, Mario Saraiva, Craig Smith and Lucas Mello.

Paul Smith

Thanks to everybody who was so generous with their information and time while I was on the road researching. Special thanks to Christine Hostettler (Pro Cosara) and Karina Atkinson (Para La Tierra) for their hospitality and great conservation work. Special thanks to Carol and Shawn for making sure that coming home is more fun than being away!

THIS BOOK

This 13th edition of Lonely Planet's *South America on a shoestring* guidebook was researched and written by Regis St Louis, Sandra Bao, Celeste Brash, Gregor Clark, Alex Egerton, Brian Kluepfel, Tom Masters, Carolyn McCarthy, Kevin Raub, Paul Smith, Phillip Tang and Lucas Vidgen.

This guidebook was produced by the following:

Destination Editor MaSovaida Morgan

Product Editor Kate James

Senior Cartographer Mark Griffiths

Book Designer Virginia Moreno

Assisting Cartographers Julie Dodkins, Valentina Kremenchutskaya, James Leversha

Assisting Editors Michelle Bennett, Nigel Chin, Bruce Evans, Kate Evans, Helen Koehne, Kellie Langdon, Charlotte Orr, Christopher Pitts

Cover Researcher Naomi Parker

Thanks to Paul Harding, Indra Kilfoyle, Claire Murphy, Kirsten Rawlings, Dianne Schallmeiner, Angela Tinson, Tony Wheeler, Amanda Williamson

Phillip Tang

Thanks to those who kept near (virtually or literally) while I was far: Lisa N'paisan, Shane, Lee, Vek Lewis, Wendy Risteska, Ben and Waimei Garcia-Lee, Craig Burgess, Jocsan L Alfaro, Anna Glayzer, Geraldine Galvaing and Ernesto A Alanis Cataño.

Lucas Vidgen

Thanks once again to the Argentines for making a country where it's such a joy to travel and work. On the road, to Guillermo Santos for driving way out of his way just to make sure I got there and 'Peluca' Dominguez for the serious schooling on San Marcos history. To América for an amazing year on top of an amazing decade and to Sofía and Teresa for being there, and being there when I got back.

ACKNOWLEDGEMENTS

Climate map data adapted from Peel MC, Finlayson BL & McMahon TA (2007) 'Updated World Map of the Köppen-Geiger Climate Classification', *Hydrology and Earth System Sciences*, 11, 163344.

Cover image: Scarlet Macaw, Parque Nacional Yasuní, Ecuador; Danita Delimont Stock/ AWL ©

Index

ABBREVIATIONS

Arg	Argentina
Bol	Bolivia
Bra	Brazil
Chi	Chile
Col	Colombia
Ecu	Ecuador
FG	French Guiana
Guy	Guyana
Par	Paraguay
Per	Peru
Sur	Suriname
Uru	Uruguay
Ven	Venezuela

A

Map Pages **000**
Photo Pages **000**

Map Pages **000**
Photo Pages **000**

C

Map Pages **000**
Photo Pages **000**

D

E

Map Pages **000**
Photo Pages **000**

Map Pages **000**
Photo Pages **000**

Q

R

Map Pages **000**
Photo Pages **000**

S

T

U

Map Legend

Sights
- Beach
- Bird Sanctuary
- Buddhist
- Castle/Palace
- Christian
- Confucian
- Hindu
- Islamic
- Jain
- Jewish
- Monument
- Museum/Gallery/Historic Building
- Ruin
- Shinto
- Sikh
- Taoist
- Winery/Vineyard
- Zoo/Wildlife Sanctuary
- Other Sight

Activities, Courses & Tours
- Bodysurfing
- Diving
- Canoeing/Kayaking
- Course/Tour
- Sento Hot Baths/Onsen
- Skiing
- Snorkeling
- Surfing
- Swimming/Pool
- Walking
- Windsurfing
- Other Activity

Sleeping
- Sleeping
- Camping

Eating
- Eating

Drinking & Nightlife
- Drinking & Nightlife
- Cafe

Entertainment
- Entertainment

Shopping
- Shopping

Information
- Bank
- Embassy/Consulate
- Hospital/Medical
- Internet
- Police
- Post Office
- Telephone
- Toilet
- Tourist Information
- Other Information

Geographic
- Beach
- Gate
- Hut/Shelter
- Lighthouse
- Lookout
- Mountain/Volcano
- Oasis
- Park
- Pass
- Picnic Area
- Waterfall

Population
- Capital (National)
- Capital (State/Province)
- City/Large Town
- Town/Village

Transport
- Airport
- Border crossing
- Bus
- Cable car/Funicular
- Cycling
- Ferry
- Metro station
- Monorail
- Parking
- Petrol station
- Subway/Subte station
- Taxi
- Train station/Railway
- Tram
- Underground station
- Other Transport

Note: Not all symbols displayed above appear on the maps in this book

Routes
- Tollway
- Freeway
- Primary
- Secondary
- Tertiary
- Lane
- Unsealed road
- Road under construction
- Plaza/Mall
- Steps
- Tunnel
- Pedestrian overpass
- Walking Tour
- Walking Tour detour
- Path/Walking Trail

Boundaries
- International
- State/Province
- Disputed
- Regional/Suburb
- Marine Park
- Cliff
- Wall

Hydrography
- River, Creek
- Intermittent River
- Canal
- Water
- Dry/Salt/Intermittent Lake
- Reef

Areas
- Airport/Runway
- Beach/Desert
- Cemetery (Christian)
- Cemetery (Other)
- Glacier
- Mudflat
- Park/Forest
- Sight (Building)
- Sportsground
- Swamp/Mangrove

Lucas Vidgen

Argentina (Northeast Argentina, Northwest Argentina, Atlantic Coast, Central Argentina, The Lake District) Lucas first visited Argentina in 2001 and was captivated by the country's wide open spaces and cosmopolitan cities. The huge amount of quality beef and wine didn't go unnoticed, either. Lucas has contributed to a variety of Latin American Lonely Planet titles, including various editions of the *Argentina* and *South America* books. He currently divides his time between his hometown of Melbourne, Australia, and his adopted mountain home in Quetzaltenango, Guatemala.

Alex Egerton

Colombia A journalist by trade, Alex has worked in Latin America for more than a decade, regularly wandering the back roads from Mexico to Argentina. He is currently based in southern Colombia where he travels extensively and writes about the country for a variety of media. When not on the road researching guidebooks, you'll find him hiking around the remote landscapes of the upper Amazon, Chocó and southern mountains or working on his *tejo* technique closer to home.

Brian Kluepfel

Bolivia Brian lived in La Paz at the cusp of the 21st century, working for the late, great *Bolivian Times*. He's since returned to interview musicians for a proposed book, *The Charango Road,* and contributed cultural materials to Lonely Planet's 2006 *Bolivia* guide. His favorite tasks this time were being compelled to watch gorgeous birds in the Amazon, being force-fed delicious *sonsos* against his will, walking down the Prado at rush hour and running off the side of a mountain in La Paz (with a paraglider attached).

Tom Masters

Venezuela Tom has traveled widely in Venezuela since first visiting as a backpacker and was one of the authors on the last Lonely Planet *Venezuela* guide in 2010. Returning for *South America on a shoestring* to update the Venezuela content, Tom found the country as friendly, fun and staggeringly beautiful as ever, despite its poor safety record and myriad economic problems. Tom lives in Berlin and can be found online at www.tommasters.net.

Carolyn McCarthy

Argentina (Esqual, Patagonia, Tierra del Fuego), Chile Author Carolyn McCarthy has spent over a decade exploring Patagonia, which amounts to many rounds of maté, cracked windshields and altered plans. She specializes in Latin America and the US West, and has contributed to more than 30 titles for Lonely Planet, including *Chile, Panama, Trekking in the Patagonian Andes, Argentina, Peru, Colorado, The Southwest* and US national parks guides. She has written for *Outside, BBC Magazine, National Geographic* and others. Follow her travels on Instagram @masmerquen and Twitter @RoamingMcC.

Kevin Raub

Brazil (Rio de Janeiro, The Southeast, The South, The Central West) Kevin Raub grew up in Atlanta and started his career as a music journalist in New York, working for *Men's Journal* and *Rolling Stone* magazines. He ditched the rock 'n' roll lifestyle for travel writing and moved to Brazil, where he has now traversed 21 of 26 Brazilian states in pursuit of caipirinha bliss. He was also LP's man on the ground for the 2014 FIFA World Cup in Brazil. This is Kevin's 36th Lonely Planet guide. Follow him on Twitter (@RaubOnTheRoad).

Read more about Kevin at:
http://auth.lonelyplanet.com/profiles/kraub

Paul Smith

Paraguay Paraguay is South America's forgotten corner, and after 12 years living here, working as a biologist/travel writer, Paul has a good case for claiming that he knows the ins and outs of the country better than most. Paul has been working for Lonely Planet since 2006, working on numerous guidebooks, especially in South America, a region that he is fascinated by. He lives in Encarnación with his wife, Carol, and son, Shawn, Paraguay's future Lionel Messi.

Phillip Tang

Peru A degree in Latin America studies brought Phillip Tang to these shores, and over a decade later he still finds himself feeling breathless (only slightly literally) pondering a canyon in Colca or the ocean in Miraflores. He writes about travel on his two loves, Asia and Latin America, and has contributed to Lonely Planet's guides to China, Japan and Mexico, and on Peru elsewhere. Find his Peru Insta-photos from this visit through philliptang.co.uk.

OUR STORY

A beat-up old car, a few dollars in the pocket and a sense of adventure. In 1972 that's all Tony and Maureen Wheeler needed for the trip of a lifetime – across Europe and Asia overland to Australia. It took several months, and at the end – broke but inspired – they sat at their kitchen table writing and stapling together their first travel guide, *Across Asia on the Cheap*. Within a week they'd sold 1500 copies. Lonely Planet was born.

Today, Lonely Planet has offices in Dublin, Franklin, London, Melbourne, Oakland, Beijing and Delhi, with more than 600 staff and writers. We share Tony's belief that 'a great guidebook should do three things: inform, educate and amuse'.

OUR WRITERS

Regis St Louis

Coordinating Author, Ecuador, Plan, Understand, Survival Guide After Regis' first journey to the Andes in 1999, he returned home, sold all his belongings and set off on a classic journey across South America. Since then, he's returned numerous times, traveling dodgy roads by truck, horse and bicycle; scaling Andean peaks (small ones) and flailing away at Spanish and Portuguese. On his most recent trip he enjoyed biking, kayaking and boating around the Galápagos; he made friends with local storytellers on enchanting Floreana; and he developed a newfound admiration for the tropically infused city of Guayaquil. Regis is also the coordinating author of Lonely Planet's *Ecuador* and *Brazil* guidebooks, and he has contributed to more than 50 Lonely Planet titles. When not on the road, he lives in New Orleans.

Sandra Bao

Argentina (Buenos Aires) Sandra is a Chinese-American who was born in Argentina and lived there until she was nine. She's traveled to around 60 countries and now lives in the USA's gorgeous Pacific Northwest. She's proud to be a *porteña* and regularly returns to Argentina to investigate what the wildly fluctuating peso is doing, as well as catch up on her steak-eating quota. Over the last 15 years Sandra has contributed to a few dozen Lonely Planet titles.

Read more about Sandra at:
http://auth.lonelyplanet.com/profiles/sandrabao

Celeste Brash

Guyana, French Guiana, Suriname Celeste Brash has written over 50 Lonely Planet guidebooks. Although she specializes in the South Pacific and Southeast Asia titles, these trail-blazing and utterly adventurous Guianas chapters have become some of her all-time favorites to research. When not on the road she's in Portland, Oregon hiking, foraging, dancing and trying to write a book about her five years on a remote coral atoll. Find more about her writing at www.celestebrash.com.

Gregor Clark

Brazil (The Northeast, The North), Uruguay Over the past 25 years, Gregor has traveled South America from tip to tail, developing a special fondness for Brazil and Uruguay while researching the last three editions of this book. Favorite memories from this trip include spotting wildlife and climbing mountains in Brazil with his two teenage daughters and herding cattle on horseback in Uruguay's vast interior. He has contributed to two dozen other Lonely Planet titles, including *Brazil*, *Argentina*, *France* and *Italy*. He lives in Vermont (USA).

Read more about Gregor at:
http://auth.lonelyplanet.com/profiles/gregorclark

OVER PAGE MORE WRITERS

Published by Lonely Planet Global Limited
CRN 554153
13th edition – Oct 2016
ISBN 978 1 78657 118 2

10 9 8 7 6 5 4 3 2 1
Printed in Singapore